INNER DEVELOPMENT

Published by Yes! Inc.
1035 31st Street, N.W.
Washington, D.C. 20007

Distributed by Random House

INNER DEVELOPMENT

Cris Popenoe

ISBN: 0-394-73544-7

LC: 78-56250

COVER PHOTOGRAPH: from **The Blue Ridge**, William A. Blake. The Viking Press, 1977.

Contents

Introduction

Inner Development is a completely revised edition of **Books for Inner Development**, a work which appeared in 1976, but whose genesis goes back several years further. In 1972 when I started the Yes! Bookshop there were few guides to the literature and the available books were hard to find. I had some idea of the kind of bookshop I wanted to create, but with no experience in the book business, little idea of how to go about it. There were a few fine bookshops in this field for models: Samuel Weiser's in New York City and Watkins in London, to name two. With the exception of Weiser's, from which I got considerable help, I did not visit the other specialized shops until some years later. Nevertheless, I checked the stock of many general bookshops, poured through an endless number of catalogs and bibliographies, and got advice from anyone who came into Yes! who knew more about a subject than I did. Gradually the stock and my knowledge grew. And as my awareness and understanding of the literature deepened, I began to refine the categories in which I placed books and attempt as clear an organization of the stock as possible.

In recent years I have visited most of the leading bookshops specializing in this field in the United States and Great Britain and have followed up every lead I encountered. I have also read many books in each of the fields we cover, more deeply of course in some areas than others. All of the books listed in **Inner Development** are ones that I have actually gone through. Needless to say, I haven't read all of them—if I had I would not have had time to put this book together and write the reviews! When I am working on the floor of the Yes! Bookshop, I try to get customers' feedback on the books we stock so my critique will be as informed as possible.

After a couple of years, we started selling our books by mail. We did this first of all to expand our potential market. But we were, and are, equally interested in rendering a real service by making the literature we are interested in, and believe to be important, as widely available as possible. We issued a few small annotated catalogs and began to get back many mail orders and praise for the catalogs' content and style—even from competing booksellers! As my knowledge and our business expanded, our number of titles grew. We gradually evolved the idea of converting our mail order catalog into a book that could stand on its own merits and provide an authoritative guide to the field. When Random House agreed to distribute the book, the die was cast and **Books for Inner Development: The Yes! Guide** was born.

The result has been most gratifying. Aside from the high praise the reviewers gave **Books for Inner Development**, and the practical appreciation readers showed by buying copies, booksellers have liked it as well. For those booksellers who want to get more deeply into this field, the **Guide** advises them on recommended books for beginners in each category, gives them an introduction to areas they may know little or nothing about, and supplies the names and addresses of all the publishers. Booksellers can therefore profit not only by selling the **Guide** to their customers, but also by consulting it to stock their shelves or to special order books. I frequently get phone calls or letters from booksellers asking about sources for new books reviewed in our regular supplements. I have been told that a number of shops have used our classification system to arrange their own stock.

When I included a couple of order blanks for our mail order service in the first edition, officals at Random House were horrified, feeling that it made the **Guide** seem more like a store catalog, and fearing that book dealers would not want to stock the book because we might be taking away business from them. Well obviously it is our store's catalog as well as what has been widely regarded as the definitive guide to the field. In any event the feared negative reaction from booksellers did not come to pass. In the previous **Guide** and this one we specifically urge readers to try their local bookshop before ordering from us. We want to see these books as widely available as possible.

We're involved in this business because to us it's much more than a business. I strongly feel that we need to get more in touch with our inner beings. I also believe that we can live more conscious lives if we gain perspective by studying how people through the ages have dealt with the basic questions of life. Too many of us simply move through each day, very full of activity—but totally unaware of the real meaning of our actions and their effects on others. We live on a small planet and every aspect of life is interconnected. Our concern at Yes! is making widely available information which we regard as *sacred* (in contrast to the *profane* which daily assails us from our newspapers, radio and TV). We do this three ways. First, we stock the largest selection of books in our field of any bookshop anywhere. Second, we list and describe our stock in **Inner Development** and **Wellness**—our companion guide—so that other stores and libraries can also find out about and stock as many of the books as possible. And third, we supply all of the books by mail to individuals and libraries around the world.

I am very proud of our mail order service. We try to get the books out the day an order comes in—and we usually succeed. Our mail order staff take a personal interest in their customers. We have a file on each customer and we keep copies of all orders so we are usually aware of an individual's particular interests. Many of our customers live in far-flung parts of the world and it's wonderful to be able to supply them with books and information they could not otherwise get. We usually have about eighty-five percent of the books we review in stock at all times, with the out-of-stock titles on order, and due in soon. Our **Yes! Guides** have helped thousands of people learn of new books and new areas of study, and thus helped them in their own inner development. And the discipline of putting together these mammouth guides and the things I've learned while working on them has certainly helped me to focus on the here and now and realize the vast scope of available knowledge.

People often ask why I have included certain fields and excluded others under the rubric of inner development. Why ancient civilizations? Why no books by Freud, or works on general psychology or Western philosophy? I suppose the first answer is that any book of this sort inevitably reflects the interests and idiosyncrasies of its author. Although my own academic studies were primarily in international relations and politics, I always had a deep interest in history and culture and fascination with ancient times and the Orient. I got a Master's Degree in Latin American Studies partly because of my interest in pre-Columbian civilizations. While in college in the late 1960s and early 1970s I became a vegetarian, meditated and did yoga, studied astrology, and took a number of courses in Eastern philosophy. In 1971 I went to work for Yes! Inc., which at that time was a natural foods store with a book section and a vegetarian restaurant. As a life-long bibliophile I was delighted when Yes! bought the building next door and offered me the opportunity to start a full-fledged bookshop. My goal was to create a spiritual shop which would provide literature and a sacred space to individuals concerned with their own growth—whatever their particualr path might be. I decided that, within this goal, I would not sell books simply because they would sell. In many shops the motto is "caveat emptor", but I didn't and don't feel comfortable with this. I won't sell books which I think are either worthless or potentially dangerous. Of course, that's not to say that I feel all the books we sell are equally valuable or worthy, but I do try to weed out the really bad ones. After that, it's up to each reader to sense what's right for him or her. Usually when I read about a new book I order one copy and examine it carefully to see if it fits in with my conception of our stock before deciding whether to reorder. Early on, I decided not to stock magic and witchcraft and many *occult* books. In my opinion, these lead people to look for shortcuts to gaining potentially dangerous powers without the more difficult and longterm development of their own beings which should guide all such power.

In the field of religion, my interest is primarily in the more mystical traditions which involve a direct relation between humans and the universe or God, however defined. Chinese, Buddhist, and Islamic traditions have the most appeal to me personally. In the listings I try to be as complete as possible in covering all the Eastern religions and Islam. In covering the Judeo-Christian tradition, I have limited our scope to the mystical aspects of the religions as well as the teachings of the early Fathers and prophets. I also have made a careful selection of the major texts. There are tens of thousands of books on the theological and popular aspects of the Judeo-Christian tradition, and many thousands of bookshops that specialize in the area. We couldn't begin to duplicate them and have no desire to, but we do carry a number of scholarly books on Christianity and Judaism that religous book stores seldom stock. In dealing with Eastern cultures we focus on the religious and philosophical aspects; not the economic or political. Our listings on literature and art incorporate the classical works and styles, not contemporary works, by and large. Our Islamic books delve into politics, jurisprudence, and like areas more than other sections because all aspects of human life are encompassed in Islamic doctrine and there is little distinction made between that which is God's and that which is Caesar's.

Inner Development is a vastly better and more complete book than its predecesor. Books on holistic health, nutrition, and body work have been eliminated—these are all reviewed in our companion **Yes! Bookshop Guide, Wellness**. Of the areas that remain, about twice as many books have been reviewed in most sections, and I have rewritten or expanded many of the earlier reviews. I have also added a great many new subsections and have carefully researched introductions to each one of these subsections. I've learned a lot that I didn't know when I put together **Books for Inner Development**, so I have changed a lot of the information that was included in my earlier book. All of the major subject introductions are new and each has been carefully chosen. Some, of course, are more informative than others, but in each case I have selected the best essay I could track down from among the in-print books on the subject. Many new subjects have been added, among them Ancient Greece and Rome, African Philosophies, and Renaissance Thought. Other subjects have been greatly expanded. For example, American Indian Religion has gone from one to nine pages. I have also attempted to provide a more holistic treatment of many subjects. Sections on major cultures include general histories, more books on artistic traditions, and, in some cases (such as China and Japan) lengthy literature selections. Many books on language are also included.

With the simultaneous publication by Yes! in the United States (again with distribution by Random House) and Penguin Books, Ltd. in Great Britain, **Inner Development** has become a trans-Atlantic book guide, with both British and American publishers being listed for the first time. We've also revamped the format and added useful aids such as running heads to make it easier to use. It's a less funky book this time, and hopefully a clearer one.

An incredible amount of work has gone into this new edition and I am pleased with it. I hope you will be too. If you have suggestions for ways in which it can be improved, please let me hear from you.

—Cris Popenoe

How to Use This Guide

Books in **Inner Development** are arranged by subject chapters, as listed in the Table of Contents, then alphabetically by author. Within each chapter are subsections containing groups of books about particular individuals, disciplines, or significant concepts. When you start to look at a chapter, skim though it quickly to find what subsections it contains. This will help you to find a particular book you may be looking for.

If you don't find the book you are looking for in the chapter or subsection you expect to find it in and you know the author, turn to the author index at the back of the book. It lists all the pages on which books by that author appear, and you can see where else to try. Our ideas about classification and yours may not agree.

Following the author and title we list the number of pages, US$ price, and a miscellany of bibliographic data. If the price is followed by a "c", it means the book is in cloth (hardcover); if it is followed by a "p", it means the book is a paperback. Sometimes two different paper prices are listed—the less expensive one is generally a smaller mass market edition. Our policy is to list the paper edition wherever one exists. We sometimes list the cloth edition as well when it is markedly superior or there is a substantial demand for it. The prices are the prices at which we sell the book at this writing. Because many books are imported, prices at your local bookstore may be above or below ours from time to time. Also, book prices fluctuate as books are reprinted and new editions come out.

The three-letter code at the end of the bibliographic data refers to the publisher of this particular edition. There is a listing of publishers' names and addresses at the end of the book. Where there are both American and British editions, the British publisher code is listed following the American. Foreign publishers are only listed when there is no American or British edition of the book. However, in all cases the prices listed are in US dollars.

The date we cite is not that of the most recent printing or the paperback edition, but generally represents when the book first came out with this exact text. The idea is to let you know how current the material is.

Quotations within reviews are set in italics; book and magazine titles are in bold. When we are using a portion of a book as an introduction to a section or subsection, we have left the italics out to make the copy easier to read. In this case, the quotation is attributed at the end of the selection.

We have picked out a few books in each section that we particularly recommend. These entries are prefaced with this symbol—■—in front of the author's name for easy identification. These are usually introductory books or books suitable for the general reader.

AFRICAN PHILOSOPHIES

Africans are notoriously religious, and each people has its own religious system with a set of beliefs and practices. Religion permeates into all the departments of life so fully that it is not easy or possible always to isolate it. A study of these religious systems is, therefore, ultimately a study of the peoples themselves in all the complexities of both traditional and modern life. Our written knowledge of traditional religions is comparatively little, though increasing, and comes chiefly from anthropologists and sociologists. Practically nothing has been produced by theologians, describing or interpreting these religions theologically.

We speak of African traditional religions in the plural because there are about one thousand African peoples (tribes), and each has its own religious system. To ignore these traditional beliefs, attitudes and practices can only lead to a lack of understanding African behaviour and problems. Religion is the strongest element in traditional background, and exerts probably the greatest influence upon the thinking and living of the people concerned.

Because traditional religions permeate all the departments of life, there is no formal distinction between the sacred and the secular, between the religious and non-religious, between the spiritual and the material areas of life. Wherever the African is, there is his religion: he carries it to the fields where he is sowing seeds or harvesting a new crop; and if he is educated, he takes religion with him to the examination room at school or in the university. Although many African languages do not have a word for religion as such, it nevertheless accompanies the individual from long before his birth to long after his physical death. Through modern change these traditional religions cannot remain intact, but they are by no means extinct. In times of crisis they often come to the surface, or people revert to them in secret.

Traditional religions are not primarily for the individual, but for the community of which he is a part. Chapters of African religions are written everywhere in the life of the community, and in traditional society there are no irreligious people. To be human is to belong to the whole community, and to do so involves participating in the beliefs, ceremonies, rituals and festivals of that community. A person cannot detach himself from the religion of his group, for to do so is to be severed from his roots, his foundation, his context of security, his kinships and the entire group of those who make him aware of his own existence. To be without one of these corporate elements of life is to be out of the whole picture. Therefore, to be without religion amounts to a self-excommunication from the entire life of society, and African peoples do not know how to exist without religion.

A great number of beliefs and practices are to be found in any African society. These are not, however, formulated into a systematic set of dogmas which a person is expected to accept. People simply assimilate whatever religious ideas and practices are held or observed by their families and communities. These traditions have been handed down from forefathers, and each generation takes them up with modifications suitable to its own historical situation and needs. Individuals hold differences of opinion on various subjects; and the myths, rituals and ceremonies may differ in detail from area to area. But such ideas or views are not considered as either contrary or conforming to any orthodox opinion. In traditional religions there are no creeds to be recited; instead, the creeds are written in the heart of the individual, and each one is himself a living creed of his own religion. Where the individual is, there is his religion, for he is a religious being. It is this that makes Africans so religious: religion is in their whole system of being.

One of the difficulties in studying African religions and philosophy is that there are no sacred scriptures. Religion in African societies is written not on paper but in people's hearts, minds, oral history, rituals and religious personages like the priests, rainmakers, officiating elders and even kings. Everybody is a religious carrier. Therefore we have to study not only the beliefs concerning God and the spirits, but also the religious journey of the indiviudal from before birth to after physical death; and to study also the persons responsible for formal rituals and ceremonies. What people do is motivated by what they believe, and what they believe springs from what they do and experience. So then, belief and action in African traditional society cannot be separated: they belong to a single whole.

—*condensed from* **African Religions and Philosophy**, *by John Mbiti*

AARDEMA, VERNA. **BEHIND THE BACK OF THE MOUNTAIN: BLACK FOLKTALES FROM SOUTHERN AFRICA. Glossary, 6¾"x 9¼", 86pp. Dia73, 5.95c.**
A collection of folk legends of southern Africa retold from the Hottentot, Zulu, Bantu, Bushman, Thonga, and Tshindao languages. The stories are of tricks and counter tricks, captures and escapes, foolish trades, and impossible tasks. Leo and Diane Dillon's striking drawings reflect the fantasy and drama of the African imagination. An ALA Notable Book.

AARDEMA, VERNA. **WHO'S IN RABBIT'S HOUSE? 7.95p.**
See the Children's Books section.
02
AARDEMA, VERNA. **WHY MOSQUITOES BUZZ IN PEOPLE'S EARS. 6.95c/2.50p.**
See the Children's Books section.

A nineteenth century tomb at Ununio, north of Dar es-Salaam—an example of the Islamic influence in African architecture.

9

ABIMBOLA, WANDE, tr. **IFA DIVINATION POETRY. Notes, bibliography, 180pp. NOK77, 3.95p.**
Ifa is an important system of divination found in many cultures of West Africa. In Yorubaland where Ifa is a major divinity, this fascinating system of divination has been closely identified with Yoruba history, mythology, religion and folk-medicine. The Yoruba regard Ifa as the repository of their beliefs and moral values. The Ifa divination system and the extensive poetic chants associated with it are used by the Yoruba to validate important aspects of their culture....In traditional Yoruba society, the authority of Ifa permeated every aspect of life because the Yoruba regard Ifa as the voice of the divinities and the wisdom of the ancestors. This work presents sixty-four poems of Ifa from the sixteen major categories of Ifa literary corpus.—from the preface. Half of the book is devoted to an excellent introduction.

AWOONOR, KOFI. **THE BEAST OF THE EARTH: A SURVEY OF THE HISTORY, CULTURE AND LITERATURE OF AFRICA SOUTH OF THE SAHARA. Notes, bibliography, index, 402pp. Dou75, 3.95p.**
Setting the stage for a full discussion of contemporary African literature, Awoonor weaves together the elements of traditional African society and philosophy with its oral literature, art, music, and languages. The result is a tapestry of ideas and background against which the reader can begin to understand not only the literary, but also the social and cultural forces at work in Africa today.

AWOONOR, KOFI, tr. **GUARDIANS OF THE SACRED WORD: EWE POETRY. 104pp. NOK74, 10.00c.**
The work of three important traditional Ewe poets (Vinoko Akpalu, Amega Dunyo, and Komi Ekpe) collected, translated, and with an introduction by *a child of the soil eager to absorb the sounds, rhythms and rituals that nurtured him.*

BARKER, CAROL. **AN OBA OF BENIN. 7.00c.**
See the Children's Books section.

BASCOM, WILLIAM. **IFA DIVINATION: COMMUNICATION BETWEEN GODS AND MEN IN WEST AFRICA. Illustrations, notes, bibliography, 785pp. IUP69, 35.00c.**
Ifa is a system of divination based on sixteen basic and 256 derivative figures (odi) obtained either by the manipulation of sixteen palm nuts or by the toss of a chain of eight half seed shells. The worship of Ifa as God of Divination entails ceremonies, sacrifices, tabus, paraphernalia, drums, songs, praises, initiations, and other ritual elements.—from the introduction. This is the most complete study imaginable of Ifa divination. Bascom reproduces all of the 256 interpretative verses in both translation and transliteration and includes extensive commentary on each one along with an abundance of introductory and explanatory material.

BASCOM, WILLIAM. **THE YORUBA OF SOUTHWESTERN NIGERIA. Photographs, annotated bibliography, 118pp. HRW69, 6.00c.**
The Yoruba are among the most cultured peoples of sub-Saharan Africa. This book contains a detailed description of the elaborate economic, political, and social structures of the Yoruba. There is also information on their complex religious beliefs and art. This is basically a work of cultural anthropology and reads, at times, like a textbook. Bascom has visited Yorubaland many times and his academic speciality is West African cultural anthropology.

BEIER, ULLI, ed. **YORUBA POETRY. Introduction, notes, 126pp. CUP70, 9.50c.**
An illustrated anthology of traditional Yoruba poems.

BIEBUYCK, DANIEL and KAHOMBO MATEENE, trs. **THE MWINDO EPIC. Index, 220pp. UCa69, 2.45p.**
A translation of the complete text of a Bantu epic which records the feats and deeds of the hero Mwindo. The epic is in prose form with verse songs and proverbs interspersed. This is a classic of African oral literature. The translators provide a lengthy introduction as well as an abundance of textual notes. The original Nyanga text is also included.

BRAVMANN, RENE. **ISLAM AND TRIBAL ART IN WEST AFRICA. Notes, bibliography, index, 202pp. CUP74, 14.95c.**
Most writers have assumed that the spread of the Islamic faith has tended to weaken and undermine the foundations of traditional African society and culture. In this original study, Dr. Bravmann reexamines and refutes the assumption that the aniconic attitudes of Islam, especially the prohibition of representational imagery, have had a detrimental effect on the visual arts in the areas of West Africa in which Islam has had the greatest influence. Eighty-three photographs accompany the text.

BURT, BEN. **THE YORUBA AND THEIR GODS. 16pp. BMP77, 1.30p.**
A fine photographic essay.

COURLANDER, HAROLD. **TALES OF YORUBA GODS AND HEROES. Illustrations, glossary and pronunciation guide, bibliography, 243pp. Crn73, 6.95c.**
A collection of myths, legends, and semi-historical recollections passed down through the ages by the Yorubas. The Yorubas form one of Africa's most advanced and important civilizations, having developed flourishing kingdoms in southwestern Nigeria over two millenia ago.

■ COURLANDER, HAROLD. **A TREASURY OF AFRICAN FOLKLORE. Illustrations, bibliography, index, 636pp. Crn75, 14.95c.**
In his tales, myths, epics and legends, the African bridges back to the morning of his creation, asserts the worth and weaknesses of the human species, ponders on courage, life and death, and reflects the learning of centuries about the character of man. Courlander is a specialist in African and Afro-American life and traditions and here he presents a definitive account of the oral literature, traditions, myths, legends, and epics of Africa. He is a good storyteller too.

COURLANDER, HAROLD and GEORGE HERZOG. **THE COW-TAIL SWITCH AND OTHER WEST AFRICAN TALES. Illustrations, glossary, notes, 6¼"x9½", 143pp. HRW47, 5.95c.**
The stories of West Africa are about men and animals, about kings, warriors, and hunters. They tell about clever people and stupid people, about good ones and bad ones, about how things and animals got to be how they are. Sometimes they are just tall tales. There are stories about Frog, Rabbit, Turtle, Guinea Fowl, and all the other animals that West Africans know. Some of the stories make you think. Some make you laugh. Here are some of the stories of the peoples of the forests, the seacoast, the hills, and the plains. The people of West Africa give them to you.—from the introduction. This is our favorite collection of West African tales.

DAVIDSON, BASIL. **THE AFRICAN GENIUS. Illustrations, notes, bibliography, index, 367pp. LBC69, 2.95p.**
A well written survey of African cultural and social history. As Davidson says, *Here I have attempted three things. First, to offer a summary of what is now known, or what now seems reasonable to think, about the ideas and social systems, religions, moral values, magical beliefs, arts and metaphysics of a range of African peoples, chiefly in tropical Africa. Then to consider the ways in which these cultures have grown and changed from distant times until now. Lastly, to fit these aspects of African civilisation into their modern perspective as the connected parts of a living whole.*

DAVIDSON, BASIL. **AFRICAN KINGDOMS. Chronology, bibliography, index, 8¾"x10¾", 192pp. TLB71, 8.95c.**
A collection of beautifully illustrated pictorial essays. Most of the photographs are in color and the accompanying text is clear and more than adequate. This is an excellent work for those who want to get a feeling for what traditional African society was like and learn a bit of African history. Part of Time-Life's **Great Ages of Man** series.

DAVIDSON, BASIL. **A HISTORY OF WEST AFRICA TO THE NINETEENTH CENTURY. Maps, dating guide, bibliography, index, 358pp. Dou66, 2.50p.**
With the aid of two African scholars, F.K. Buah and J.F. Ade Ajayi, Davidson—one of the foremost specialists on the African past—has prepared a comprehensive history of West African civilization from the days of the empire of ancient Ghana until the beginnings of colonization in the nineteenth century. Two continuing themes form the story: the importance of trade routes in the shifting fortunes of cities and empires, and the religious and political struggles of the local cultures with Islam, which often strengthened (and created) the rivalry between country and town.

DAVIDSON, BASIL. **OLD AFRICA REDISCOVERED. Notes, bibliography, index, 287pp. Glz59, 8.40c.**
This is an important and impressive inquiry into the nature of African civilization in the fifteen hundred or so years before the European conquest. Davidson bases his survey on recent archaeological discoveries and makes his history into a vivid drama. The common conception of Africa as a dark continent of tribal savagery, devoid of kingdoms, literature, art, and culture, is shown to be pure illusion. Many photographs, maps, and line drawings accompany the text.

DAYRELL, ELPHINSTONE. **WHY THE SUN AND MOON LIVE IN THE SKY.** 1.95p.
See the Children's Books section.

DENYER, SUSAN. **AFRICAN TRADITIONAL ARCHITECTURE. Notes, bibliography, index, 7"x9¾", 226pp. HeG78, 10.60p.**
This excellent survey of the rich architectural heritage of Africa is illuminated with 329 photographs and drawings selected from a wide variety of sources to show the exceptional variety of building styles and forms. Ms. Denyer worked and lived in Africa for a number of years and her aim is to classify African building and relate its forms to ecological and historical factors.

EGUDU, ROMANUS, tr. **THE CALABASH OF WISDOM AND OTHER IGBO STORIES. Illustrations, 141pp. NOK73, 3.50p.**
In traditional Igbo homes, storytelling is an art commonly performed and enjoyed by both parents and children. In this volume Dr. Egudu has collected twenty-eight tales and arranged them in the following categories: *Origin Stories, Explanatory Stories, Trick Stories, Contest Stories*, and *Didactic Stories*.

ELLIOT, GERALDINE. **THE LONG GRASS WHISPERS: A BOOK OF AFRICAN FOLK TALES.** 2.95p.
See the Fairy Tales section.

ELLIOT, GERALDINE. **THE SINGING CHAMELEON.** 5.00c.
See the Fairy Tales section.

ELLIOT, GERALDINE. **WHERE THE LEOPARD PASSES.** 2.95p.
See the Fairy Tales section.

ELLIOTT, AUBREY. **THE MAGIC WORLD OF THE XHOSA. Many illustrations, including some color plates, glossary, bibliography, index, 11½"x8½", 144pp. WCS70, 9.25c.**
The world of the Xhosa tribesmen is both strange and mystifying, filled with dark and powerful forces that surround and command their daily life. As a child Elliott came into contact with the Xhosa, who lived in the kraals of his father's farm in South Africa. He learned their language and in time, he earned their trust. Now, after years of research and observation, Elliott gives us a unique account of the rich life of a Bantu tribe. As anthropologist, author, and photographer, he records and analyzes their customs and myths; he converses with their wise men and warriors; and is present with his camera at their most secret ceremonies. The result is a fascinating document which should interest the specialist and general reader alike.

ELLIS, A.B. **THE YORUBA-SPEAKING PEOPLES. Notes, 402pp. Cur74, 10.55c.**
This is an early study of the religion, manners, customs, mythology, language, and laws of the Yorubas by an officer in the British colonial army. The Yoruba form the most important ethnic grouping within their territory, which extends over the southern parts of western Nigeria and eastern Dahomey.

FORDE, DARYLL, ed. **AFRICAN WORLDS. Notes, index, 269pp. Oxf54, 10.50p.**
A collection of nine essays, each describing the world outlook of an African people as expressed in their creation myths and religious beliefs. The studies cover such widely divergent systems of thought as the complex metaphysics of the Dogon of Mali, the magical cults of the Abaluyia of Kenya, the religious practices of the LeLe of Kasai (in which the forest is a major focus), the secret societies of the Mende, and the ancestor cult of the Ashanti. The authors show how concepts of the divine ordering of the universe are closely related to the organization of society and everyday life.

FUJA, ABAYOMI, ed. **FOURTEEN HUNDRED COWRIES AND OTHER AFRICAN TALES. 191pp. S&S71, 1.25p.**
A fine collection of folktales of the Yoruba people, collected from the oral tradition by Fuja, himself a Yoruba. Illustrated with black and white contemporary style drawings.

GABA, CHRISTIAN, tr. **SCRIPTURES OF AN AFRICAN PEOPLE: THE SACRED UTTERANCES OF THE ANLO. 169pp. NOK73, 12.50c.**
The knowledge of the religions of Africa that has come to Europe and America, and to much of Africa itself, has been partial and often misleading....The greatest obstacle to understanding African religion has been the absence of written scriptures. This has meant the lack both of ritual texts and of accounts of spiritual experiences, by the people who hold these beliefs themselves....What is revealed in this splendid collection of over a hundred chapters is a wide range of religious life and thought. The Anlo people, though occupying a small corner of Ghana, are related to other people round about them, and their religion uses the names of deities from even farther away....The religiousness of the Anlo, as Dr. Gaba remarks, covers the whole of life, and shows a feeling of the constant presence of the spiritual world.—from the foreword by Dr. Geoffrey Parrinder. An introduction and detailed notes are included.

GLEASON, JUDITH. **ORISHA: THE GODS OF YORUBALAND. Illustrations, 122pp. Ath71, 5.25c.**
The Orisha are not gods as we generally think of gods. They are the embodiment of certain truths, both human and divine, that people have come to recognize. Many of the Orisha are thought to have been historical personages. Others are in the lightening, the thunder, the flow of water in a river, and in the tricks that the world plays; they are life and creation and love and hate. And yet they are more than all this. Ms. Gleason has collected many of the Orisha myths out of the oral tradition and she retells them here.

HALEY, GAIL. **A STORY, A STORY.** 1.95p.
See the Children's Books section.

IDOWU, E. BOLAJI. **AFRICAN TRADITIONAL RELIGION. Notes, index, 240pp. Orb73, 6.95c.**
Idowu is Professor of Religious Studies in the University of Ibadan, Nigeria. This book is the result of years of teaching, writing, researching, and observing. It is an academic work in which the bulk of attention is devoted to a description of the nature and structure of African traditional religion. Fairly lengthy chapters analyze the nature of religion itself and survey the study of African traditional religion. Idowu is most concerned with what Africans actually know, think, and believe about deities and the supersensible world, and how these beliefs have inspired their world view and moulded their cultures.

ILOGU, EDMUND. **CHRISTIANITY AND IGBO CULTURE. Notes, bibliography, index, 278pp. NOK74, 5.95p.**
This book...is an attempt to provide some concrete theological and sociological suggestions as to how Christianity can be related to some aspects of African culture.... Patterns of Igbo life, values, and therefore culture are brought into the Christian milieu to indicate how such African cultural patterns can be baptised into the Christian Church.—from the preface.

JACKSON, JOHN. **INTRODUCTION TO AFRICAN CIVILIZATION. Notes, bibliography, index, 384pp. Stu70, 4.95p.**
This is a fine survey which incorporates myths, legends, rituals, and religious beliefs. It is based on good scholarship.

■ JAHN, JANHEINZ. **MUNTU: AN OUTLINE OF THE NEW AFRICAN CULTURE. Illustrations, notes, bibliography, indices, 269pp. Grv61, 4.95p.**
This book is must reading for all who are interested in understanding Africa and the African peoples. Muntu is a Bantu word which is usually translated as man—but the concept of muntu embraces the living and dead and even the gods. Jahn portrays the whole range of traditional and contemporary African thought expressed in religion, language, philosophy, literature, art, music, and dance. He tells what happens in the encounter between Christian and African cultures and uses these examples to introduce the underlying principles of African philosophy. Jahn is coeditor of **Black Orpheus**, a publication devoted to African and Afro-American literature and art. He has written extensively on African literature and seems to have come as near as anybody who is not African will get to understanding what makes the African tick.

JOHNSON, SAMUEL. **HISTORY OF THE YORUBAS. Maps, chronology, index, 739pp. RKP21, 31.50c.**
This is the standard work on the history of the Yorubas, from the earliest times to the beginning of the British protectorate. Johnson begins with a discussion of the people, land, language, religion, manners, and customs. The second part traces Yoruba history, beginning with prehistoric, mythological kings.

JORDAN, A.C., tr. **TALES FROM SOUTHERN AFRICA. Illustrations, 300pp. UCa73, 11.00c.**
The late Xhosa novelist and critic, A.C. Jordan, was an enthusiastic observer of the customs and histories of the various Xhosa peoples of South Africa. In this book he constructs written versions of the oral narratives of the Xhosa people. He has done a marvelous job of reforming the texts, while retaining the themes and structures of the originals. Harold Scheub provides an excellent introduction as well as commentaries on the majority of the stories.

LAUDE, JEAN. **THE ARTS OF BLACK AFRICA. 201 plates, bibliography, index, 305pp. UCa71, 3.45p.**
African Arts called this book A marvelous introduction to the traditional sculpture of Black Africa. It is an up-to-date, well informed and reliable synthesis, as well as an aesthetically perceptive book. The text contains much African history—in fact, most tribal history must be traced through art alone, since there are no written records. The book also contains a table of known historical events in Africa with dates when the art was created.

LEUZINGER, ELSY. **THE ART OF BLACK AFRICA. Introduction, 244 illustrations, including twenty-seven color pages, index, 8¼"x8¼", 346pp. Riz77, 29.50c.**
The art of Black Africa is rooted in religion, the author writes. But unlike the ancient Greeks who represented their gods in their own image, or the Arabs, who condemned the painted or carved figure as blasphemous, Africans traditionally regarded the representation of human features both as a way of communicating with the supernatural world and of exorcising malevolent spirits. African chieftains and kings expected their artists to create effigies of ancestors, masks, thrones, drums, decorations, and other symbols of their power, skillfully enough to persuade the divinity to confer magical power on the objects and, by extension, to their owners.

LINDFORS, BERNTH, ed. **FORMS OF FOLKLORE IN AFRICA. Index, 281pp. UTx77, 7.05p.**
All the essays in this volume were published in **Research in African Literatures**, a journal founded in 1970 to encourage serious study of African oral and written literatures.... It affords a selective rather than an exhaustive introduction to a vast field.... Most of the major genres of African folklore and several of the largest ethnic groups (Yoruba, Xhosa, Kongo, Berber) are represented here.... Several essays discuss texts from a wide variety of cultures, while others concentrate on materials collected from a single ethnic group—sometimes that to which the writer belongs.—from the preface.

MCDERMOTT, GERALD. **ANANSI THE SPIDER: A TALE FROM THE ASHANTI. 1.95p.**
See the Children's Books section.

MCDERMOTT, GERALD. **THE MAGIC TREE. 1.95p.**
See the Children's Books section.

MAQUET, JACQUES. **CIVILIZATIONS OF BLACK AFRICA. Photographs, maps, bibliography, index, 226pp. Oxf72, 3.95p.**
Maquet, a distinguished anthropologist, begins with a general survey of African civilization. Next he divides the history of sub-Saharan Africa into six main currents: The Bow, The Clearings, The Granaries, The Spear, The Cities, and Industry. He introduces each by contemplating its characteristic art forms, from the skilled rock paintings of the prehistoric hunters and the songs and poems of the aristocratic East African warriors, to the visual arts, dance, and music of contemporary Africa. These cultural expressions become the framework for a discussion of the economic systems, family and political institutions, myths, rituals, and religious beliefs which evolved.

MATTHIESSEN, PETER and ELIOT PORTER. **THE TREE WHERE MAN WAS BORN: THE AFRICAN EXPERIENCE. Notes, bibliography, index, 7½"x10", 246pp. Avo74/WCS, 6.95p.**
A gifted writer and a superb photographer combine their talents in a revealing look at the human and natural history of East Africa. Porter's color photographs of landscapes, animals, and people are breathtaking; Mathiessen's text conveys a sense of agelessness, innocence, and mystery surrounding the continent—together they have produced a moving portrait.

■ MBITI, JOHN. **AFRICAN RELIGIONS AND PHILOSOPHY. Bibliography, index, 400pp. Dou69, 2.95p.**
Mbiti writes that African man lives in a religious universe. Both that world and practically all his activities in it are seen and experienced through religious understanding and meaning. This comprehensive study includes sections on the concepts which define God throughout Africa; on death, time, and morality; on the religious orientation of various rites and social relationships; on the influence of foreign religions; and on the search for new values.

MBITI, JOHN. **THE PRAYERS OF AFRICAN RELIGION. Introduction, notes, indices, 204pp. Orb75, 6.95c.**
In this volume Professor Mbiti demonstrates that prayer contains the most intense expression of African traditional spirituality. The comprehensive collection of African prayers presented here has been taken from different tribes and different countries. Each chapter contains prayers for specific occasions together with a commentary on the text.

MITCHELL, ROBERT. **AFRICAN PRIMAL RELIGIONS. Glossary, 112pp. Arg77, 2.95p.**
This is an introductory survey of African traditional religion, emphasizing the tribal character of the religions. Mitchell surveys divinities, ancestors and spirits, festivals, rites of passage, divine healers, destiny, natural and cosmic forces, the nature of evil, and much else. Concluding chapters view the place that African primal religions occupy in contemporary Africa. Mitchell writes simply. Many color photographs accompany the text.

MURPHY, E. JEFFERSON. **THE BANTU CIVILIZATION OF SOUTHERN AFRICA. Annotated bibliography, index, 285pp. Cro74, 8.95c.**
For more than 2,000 years, the Bantu civilization flourished in southern Africa. By 1500 it had expanded to cover more than a third of the continent. Yet, despite major achievements, the Bantu-speaking peoples have been virtually ignored by European and American historians because they left no written records. In this illustrated volume, Dr. Murphy has recreated the unwritten history, drawing on the latest scholarship in linguistics, archaeology, and anthropology. The narrative flows well and all aspects of Bantu social, political, cultural, and spiritual life are surveyed.

■ *MURPHY, E. JEFFERSON.* **HISTORY OF AFRICAN CIVILIZA-TION.** Bibliography, index, 454pp. Del72, 3.75p.
This is generally considered the best introductory, comprehensive history of African civilization. Murphy has lived in or traveled through all the major regions of Africa over a period of twenty years. He is an anthropologist and there is much more ethnographic material here than in most histories. The book begins with early man in Africa; the rest is organized around a discussion of major African civilizations, the interconnections between them, and the impact of European and Islamic cultures upon them. Many illustrations and quotations from primary sources are also included.

MUSGROVE, MARGARET. **ASHANTI TO ZULU: AFRICAN TRADI-TIONS.** 8.95c.
See the Children's Books section.

OLIVER, ROLAND, ed. **THE DAWN OF AFRICAN HISTORY. Plates,** index, 106pp. Oxf68, 4.00p.
A series of fourteen short essays by as many scholars, summarizing a number of aspects of early African history. Each is illustrated with maps and is designed to be as simple and straightforward as possible.

OLIVER, ROLAND, ed. **THE MIDDLE AGE OF AFRICAN HISTORY.** Maps, index, 105pp. Oxf70, 4.00p.
Fourteen more essays, each dealing with a somewhat later period than Oliver's first book. Again, the selections are succinct and to the point.

OLIVER, ROLAND and BRIAN FAGAN. **AFRICA IN THE IRON AGE.** Notes, annotated bibliography, index, 239pp. CUP75, 5.95p.
A fine introduction to African history between 500 BC and AD 1400. Oliver is a leading African historian and the author of several standard books on the subject; Fagan is an authority on African Iron Age archaeology. Sixty-four plates accompany the text.

OLIVER, ROLAND and J.D. FAGE. **A SHORT HISTORY OF AFRICA.** Many maps, bibliography, 304pp. Vik75, 3.95p.
An overall survey of African history from the earliest times to the 1960s. The authors have drawn on the whole range of literature about Africa and on evidence from archaeology, oral traditions, social institutions, and material cultures.

PARRINDER, GEOFFREY. **AFRICAN TRADITIONAL RELIGION.** Bibliography, index, 156pp. H&R62, 3.95p.
Parrinder is currently Professor of the Comparative Study of Religions at the University of London. He spent over twenty years teaching in West Africa and studying African religions and he founded the Department of Religious Studies at the University College of Ibadan, Nigeria. This is a good general study of African religious beliefs and practices.

PEARSON, EMIL. **PEOPLE OF THE AURORA.** 168pp. Bet77, 3.95p.
A collection of maxims, tales, myths, and spiritual beliefs of the VaNgangela people, written by a man who lived with them for many years. Reproductions of their sandgraphs, with commentary, are also included.

POST, LAURENS VAN DER. **THE LOST WORLD OF THE KALA-HARI. Photographs,** 279pp. HBJ58/Pen, 3.95p.
Van der Post was born in South Africa and grew up with legends of the Bushmen told to him by his grandfather and two aged Bushmen servants. From boyhood he dreamed of one day finding the last of these nearly exterminated mystical people. The opportunity came in 1957 when he was able to organize an expedition into the Kalahari Desert of what is now Botswana. This is a fascinating account of his grueling journey through a remote, primitive region of Africa. From the narrative the reader can glimpse what remains of *the lost world* and gain some insight into the ways of the Bushmen.

POST, LAURENS VAN DER. **PATTERNS OF RENEWAL.** 32pp. PHP62, .85p.
A Jungian-oriented study of the mythological pattern of renewal. Van der Post bases this essay on his own experience in Africa where, he believes, the earliest known human pattern is still alive and accessible to us today.

RACHEWILTZ, BORIS DE. **INTRODUCTION TO AFRICAN ART.** **Eighty-seven plates, many in color, bibliography, index, 220pp.** **Mur66, 10.40c.**
The African craftsman, or artist, breathed life into a particular form, or limited himself to the repetition of certain traditional themes for reasons which were in no sense artistic. To understand these reasons, and the purpose of the objects produced, it is necessary to place oneself in the psychological context of the civilizations of which they form a part. They must be viewed in the conceptual framework which generated them. To explain that framework is the purpose of this book.—from the introduction. This is an excellent work; the author succeeds admirably in his stated aim.

RADIN, PAUL, ed. **AFRICAN FOLKTALES. Glossary, index, 7½"x10",** **334pp. PUP52, 5.95p.**
A selection of eighty-one folktales from the vast complex of cultures that makes up native Africa south of the Sahara. The narratives—which range from myth to humorous anecdote—are divided into four categories: *The Universe and Its Beginning, The Animal and His World, The Realm of Man,* and *Man and His Fate.* Radin also includes an excellent introduction.

SHAW, THURSTAN. **NIGERIA: ITS ARCHAEOLOGY AND EARLY** **HISTORY. 147 illustrations, bibliography, index, 6½"x10", 216pp.** **T&H78, 16.95c.**
Investigations carried out during the past forty years have shown Nigeria to be the country with the richest archaeological heritage south of the Sahara. This is a fine overview of all that is known about Nigerian archaeology. Part of the **Ancient Peoples and Places** series.

SHORTER, AYLWARD. **PRAYER IN THE RELIGIOUS TRADITIONS** **OF AFRICA. Notes, bibliography, 156pp. Oxf75, 8.95c.**
A comprehensive study of African prayer. Shorter begins with a general introduction on the nature of African prayer. There follow 152 texts from the religious traditions of Africa, the African independent churches, African Christianity, and Islam. Each text has a separate introduction, and all are arranged thematically.

SWEENEY, JAMES. **AFRICAN SCULPTURE. Index, 7½"x10", 201pp.** **PUP64, 5.95p.**
A collection of 187 striking photographs, the majority by Eliot Elisofon and Walker Evans, of native African sculpture. Sweeny contributes an introduction in which he discusses the various forms of native art and their geographic distribution.

THOMPSON, ROBERT. **BLACK GODS AND KINGS. 8¾"x11¼",** **about 200pp. IUP76, 18.50c.**
This striking volume combines dozens of magnificent illustrations, both color and black and white, with a landmark study of the art of the Yoruba people—the creators of one of the most sophisticated artistic traditions in Africa. Originally written as a catalogue of one of the world's outstanding collections of Yoruba art, that of the Museum of Ethnic Art at UCLA, **Black Gods and Kings** transcends the genre of museum catalogues and has established itself as a classic study of African art. There is a great deal more text than in most museum catalogues. Thompson is Professor of African and Afro-American Art History at Yale.

TURNER, VICTOR. **THE FOREST OF SYMBOLS: ASPECTS OF** **NDEMBU RITUAL. Illustrations, notes, bibliography, index, 417pp.** **Cor67, 5.95p.**
A collection of ten of the most brilliant and important essays on ritual yet written.— **American Anthropologist.** The Ndembu are a people from Zambia in Central Africa.

WILLET, FRANK. **AFRICAN ART. 261 plates, sixty-one in color,** **bibliography, index, 288pp. Oxf71, 6.95p.**
Only in recent times have the tribal arts of sub-Saharan Africa been recognized among the great creative achievements of mankind. Willet, who spent several years heading excavations in Nigeria, reviews here the astonishing variety and expressive power of African art and examines its modes, meanings, and complex social, religious, and practical functions.

ALCHEMY

The commonly accepted view of alchemy among contemporary scientists is that though their researchers had the merit of paving the way for the development of modern chemistry, yet they were regrettably steeped in the useless and superstitious quest to make gold. This despite the repeated and insistent statements of the alchemists that *aurum nostrum non est aurum vulgum, our gold is not the common gold*; and that *our* mercury is not the common mercury. Thus, the anonymous author of an alchemical tract entitled *An Open Entrance to the Closed Palace of the King* says: *I have spoken about mercury, sulphur, the vessel, the treatment, etc.—and of course, all these things are to be understood with a grain of salt. You must understand. . .that I have spoken metaphorically; if you take my words literally you will reap no harvest.*

Here, and elsewhere, it is clearly stated that the language of chemistry employed by the alchemists is a metaphor for the inner work, the *opus*, of psychic transformation. The transmutation of *base metals* into *gold* is the transmutation of psychophysical elements within man from an impure, obstructed state to a fine state of responsiveness to high-frequency energy. The precious metals were regarded as the most evolved members of the mineral kingdom; so, by analogy, to *make gold* by *our art* was to make oneself into a more highly evolved member of the human kingdom.

And this was not an exclusive, separative endeavor: when the alchemists say *our gold*, they do not mean ours as opposed to yours, but the gold that is within us, as opposed to the gold of the goldsmiths. There is in the writings of the alchemists an intense, almost poignant ambivalence between their desire to share the valuable knowledge and art they have learned and the knowledge that this sharing is possible only to a very limited degree, because of the possible danger both to the art and to the individual, if premature information came into the wrong hands. *For the matter is so glorious and wonderful that it cannot be fully delivered to any one but by word of mouth.*

The genuine alchemical adepts were aware of course that their teachings were being distorted and abused by charlatans who claimed to be able to make physical gold, and who preyed on the concupiscence of the ignorant. They denounced the *huffers and puffers* who said they could *multiply metals*; and pointed out, quite logically, that if these imposters really were able to make gold, they wouldn't be wandering around boasting of it, and *cheating the credulous out of their money*. Yet their protestations were in vain, and the low reputation, which alchemy acquired as the result of the activities of fraudulent imitators, has prevailed to this day.

In modern times the study of alchemy has received a new infusion of interest due to the work of Carl Jung. In his autobiography, Jung relates how during a period of several years in the middle of his life, he was exposed to a *confrontation with the unconscious*, that is, images, dreams, and fantasies which were both very strange and very powerful rose up uncontrollably into his awareness. He had a dream in which he felt that he was *caught in the seventeenth century*. Soon he began to notice that *analytical psychology coincided in a curious way with alchemy*. The dream symbols and images he encountered had numerous parallels in the alchemical literature. This discovery was extremely important to Jung because it indicated to him that the psychic experiences he was undergoing were not purely personal-subjective, but had collective, historical antecedents.

Jung had no external teacher or companion explorers with whom to verify his experiences, and he found himself in an extremely isolated position without such external confirmation. For this reason, Jung regarded his work in alchemy as that which gave his psychology *its place in reality and established [it] upon its historical fundations*.

Jung made pioneering advances in recognizing the importance of the alchemical tradition and its continued relevance to modern man's quest for self-understanding and individuation, yet he was not able to step outside the role of the scholar. *I worked along philological lines, as if I were trying to solve the riddle of an unknown language.* The actual experimental practice of the art of alchemy eluded him, because, as they themselves repeatedly said, this could only be taught by word of mouth, by a teacher. In this way, despite his sincere and persevering efforts in the realm of scholarship, Jung fell victim to the inherent trap of the intellectual approach: that of assuming that mental knowledge is true understanding. Hence he accuses the alchemists of *incredible naivete*, in projecting their *fantasies* into matter; although the contradiction between this and the great psychological wisdom with which he credits them, seems to escape him. A mere projection of fantasies into matter would not have lasted a thousand years with such profound effects on all areas of European life and culture.

Jung's blind spot regarding the role of the body led him to miss the point that the transmutation of substances took place within the psychophysical organism, even when the alchemists say this explicitly. Thus, when Paracelsus says, *The microcosm in its interior anatomy must be reverberated up to the highest reverberation*, Jung interprets this as, *While the artifex heats the chemical substance in the furnace he himself is morally undergoing the same fiery torment and purification*. Yet Paracelsus is quite literally referring to an actual process of raising the vibratory rate of structures in the *interior anatomy* by means of *fire* (*reverberation is ignition*). It is not just a *projection* of a *moral* purification, or becoming *unconsciously identical* with a process going on in an external furnace, as Jung would have it.

Perhaps this difference of interpretation can best be made clear by relating a personal experience. A short while after having begun to study the Yoga of Fire, which has many points in common with the alchemical work, I interrupted a yoga session in order to brew myself a cup of tea. While waiting for the water to boil, I sat down in the kitchen and continued to work with the *fire*. Shortly I became aware of the sound of the water beginning to heat up. As I was attempting to increase the heat of the inner fire, a linkage was spontaneously set up between the internal and the external heating. When the water reached the boiling point, there was a definite discontinuous energy change internally, experienced subjectively as a kind of release. In other words, the external heating provided a kind of support to the inner work, akin to the role of *mandala* in visual meditation. There was no projection of images, or identification going on here; I was fully aware of both processes and the difference between them.

This experience suggested to me that where the alchemists actually employed physical apparatus in their experiments, which was not necessarily very often, they were perhaps working with this type of procedure. They might have been setting up laboratory analogues of internal transformation processes, and using these analogues as supports for inner work. In the text entitled *The Sophic Hydrolith*, or *Water-Stone of the Wise*, there is a passage which seems to refer to this procedure: *We saw that in our chemical operation the regulation of the fire, and a most patient and careful tempering of its heat, was of the greatest importance . . . we also spoke of the "fire of the Sages" as being one of the chief agents in our chemical process, and said that it was an essential, preternatural and Divine fire, that it lay hid in our substance, and that it was stirred into action by the influence and aid of the outward, material fire.*

Another author makes a careful distinction between the *truly secret furnace, which a vulgar eye never saw*, and the *common furnace, made of potter's earth*. One of the essential requirements of the latter was that *you must be able to keep up in it a fire for ten or twelve hours, without looking to it*; which suggests that it was used as an external support to the inner or *living fire* that burns in *our vessel*.

The alchemists were adepts first and natural scientists second. That is, their goal and purpose and main endeavor was evolutionary transformation of man's total being. Their methods were taught by direct contact between teacher and student. Yet they believed that since man is a microcosm, the processes they observed and studied internally could also be found externally, in Nature, and vice versa. *If, therefore, we wish to exercise the fine Art of Alchemy, we must imitate the method by which Nature does her work in the bowels of the earth.* Alchemical texts are laboratory manuals for the great experiment of Nature, which we carry out in our own nature: self-transformation.

It is impossible at this date to determine to what extent actual physical experimental setups were used by the alchemical adepts. Many were evidently distressed at and disapproving of an increasing trend to use external materials. One author, quoting Nature, writes: *Let me tell you that your artificial fire will never impart my heavenly warmth.* And continues later: *All you want is leisure, and some place where you can be without any fear of interruptions.* Another author emphasizes: *There is but one vessel, one method, and one consummation.* Yet another implores: *Relinquish the multiplicity of methods and substances, for our substance is one.* Clearly, the setting up of laboratory analogues as aids established a tendency for some of the alchemists to concern themselves more and more with the nature and composition of external elements and thus lose track of the original goal. This is essentially the birth of modern chemistry, which, in the course of time, then proliferated into numberless specialized sub-disciplines.

—*condensed from* **Maps of Consciousness**, *by Ralph Metzner*

AGRIPPA, CORNELIUS. **OCCULT PHILOSOPHY OR MAGIC. Illustrations, 288pp. Wei1897, 8.95c.**
Contains the basic works of Agrippa, a fifteenth century German alchemist and philosopher. Influenced by the works of Albertus Magnus, he combines the influence of Magnus with his own investigations into the elements, their divine correspondence, astrological correspondence, occult properties, and astrological symbolism. This edition also contains a critique of Agrippa by Henry Morley. This volume is one of the foundations of Western occultism.

ALBERTUS, FRATER. **THE ALCHEMIST'S HANDBOOK. 124pp. Wei74/RKP, 8.50c.**
Frater Albertus is a member of the Paracelsus Research Society of Salt Lake City, Utah—a group which attempts to present the ancient teachings in a practical, easily understood fashion. This volume gives detailed directions for setting up an inexpensive home alchemical laboratory, and includes photographs of the necessary equipment. This information is followed by step-by-step instructions for the work of the *Lesser Circulation*: the alchemical transformation within the plant kingdom which is a prerequisite for work in the mineral kingdom.

ALBERTUS, FRATER. **THE ALCHEMIST OF THE ROCKY MOUNTAINS. 167pp. PaS76, 9.25c.**
This book, written in the form of a novel, recounts a small group's contact with a living alchemist. The alchemist discusses both mundane

and esoteric matters, and some material from the alchemical lexicon is retold in everyday language. The process of making *materia prima* is given along with related information. The book itself is not very well written and will interest only those who are deeply involved in alchemy. Our assumption is that the four people in the book make up the Paracelsus Research Society, of which Frater Albertus is one.

ALLEN, PAUL, ed. **A CHRISTIAN ROSENKREUTZ ANTHOLOGY. Oversize, 704pp. Mul68, 45.35c.**
This massive 8½"x11" anthology presents an excellent study of the life and work of Christian Rosenkreutz, a legendary figure. Included in this volume is **The Chemical Wedding of Christian Rosenkreutz** and **The Fame and Confession of the Rosy Cross**. These are amplified by writings from some of the most important figures in this field, among them Robert Fludd, Thomas Vaughn, Hinricus Madathanus, Daniel Stolcius, Heinrich Khunrath, and Rudolf Steiner. **The Secret Symbols of the Rosicrucians**, one of the most prized works, is reproduced here in its entirety. For us, the highlight of the text is the incredible selection of illustrations, woodcuts, and emblems. The reproduction is fairly good and most of these cannot be found in any other book in print today. Extensive notes and an annotated bibliography accompany the text. This is an essential work for all seriously interested in the study of alchemy.

ASHMOLE, ELIAS. **THEATRUM CHEMICUM BRITANNICUM. 563pp. JRC67, 28.80c.**
During the latter part of the fourteenth century in Europe a reaction developed among natural philosophers, as scientists were then called, against a dogmatic reliance on Aristotle. This reaction resulted in a new emphasis on Neoplatonic, Pythagorean, and Hermetic philosophies. These philosophies saw in nature mystical interrelationships of the great and small worlds. In England the greatest philosopher in the Hermetic tradition was John Dee. Ashmole perpetuated this tradition by gathering in the **Theatrum** the writings of early seventeenth century English Hermetic philosophers. It was an important collection read by Isaac Newton and Robert Boyle, two of the founders of modern science. This is a facsimile reprint of the 1952 London edition, with a long, good introduction by Allen Debus, professor of the History of Science at the University of Chicago.

The marriage of the king and queen, sun and moon, under the influence of spiritual Mercury.

AYLESWORTH, THOMAS. **THE ALCHEMISTS: MAGIC INTO SCI-
ENCE.** Index, 127pp. AdW73, 5.95c.
A simplified discussion of alchemy geared toward young readers and
illustrated with line drawings and woodcuts. The history of alchemy is
surveyed, followed by a discussion of the philosophical basis of
alchemical thought and short biographies of some of the major
alchemists. As might be expected, the discussion does not reach into
the heart of alchemy—but as an overview for older children, the book
is successful.

BAKER, DOUGLAS. **DIARY OF AN ALCHEMIST, VOLUME I.**
7½"x11½", about 150pp. Bak77, 12.00p.
This book has less to do with alchemy as a philosophical system and a
means for growth and integration than it does with Baker's own
esoteric beliefs. It is a scattered book and will probably be of interest
only to those who follow Baker's work. Many illustrations, some in
color, are included.

BARBAULT, ARMAND. **GOLD OF A THOUSAND MORNINGS.**
147pp. Spe75, 7.00c
Barbault was a practicing French alchemist who died recently. This
volume is a detailed, step-by-step account of his discoveries which have
effected the miraculous cure of disease, and which he felt to be an
alchemical elixir for long life. The preparation is a mixture of a few
drops of potable gold, incinerated ash, powdered gold, and distilled
dew, combined at the right astrological moment. Barbault was known
as a modern day Paracelsus who could condense energies and use them
to create new matter with properties unknown to science. The text
includes clear information about alchemy and many illustrations.

BEST, MICHAEL and FRANK BRIGHTMAN, eds. **BOOK OF SECRETS
OF ALBERTUS MAGNUS.** Index, 148pp. Oxf73, 2.95p.
This book was compiled in Latin toward the end of the thirteenth
century and translated into all major European languages. The first
English translation was published about 1550. It is one of the best
known of all early works. An anthology, it is divided into the following
sections, *herbs, stones, beasts,* and *astrology.* Extensive notes and illustrations accompany the text, and the editors supply a long introduction.

BONELLI, M.L. and WILLIAM SHEA, eds. **REASON, EXPERIMENT,
AND MYSTICISM.** Notes, 320pp. WAP75, 26.90c.
A collection of recent essays which demonstrate that hermeticism and
alchemy contributed positively to the development of the experimental
method by stressing the importance of observation. Included are
selections by Newton, Galileo, Robert Fludd, and other important
seventeenth century figures, along with several essays on alchemy.

■ BURCKHARDT, TITUS. **ALCHEMY.** 206pp. Vik74, 3.25p.
An excellent alchemical survey by a noted Sufi scholar. In these pages,
Burckhardt relates alchemy to some of the world's great psychospirit-
ual teachings. Most important, he discredits the false view of alchemists as primitive chemists who tried to change lead into gold. To the real
alchemist, *man himself is the dull lead that by a refining process can become the Gold
of the Sun.* Every aspect of alchemy is introduced and discussed at length
here, and the text contains reproductions of many alchemical drawings. Highy recommended.

CHKASHIGE, MASUMI. **ORIENTAL ALCHEMY.** 110pp. Wei36,
1.95p.
A brief survey of the alchemical traditions of China and Japan. Special
attention is paid to the composition, properties, and uses of alchemical
elixirs. This is basically a discussion of the outer aspect of alchemy,
with chapters on the making of gold and bronze. Many Chinese words
are interspersed in the text.

COCHRAN, ARCHIBALD. **ALCHEMY REDISCOVERED AND RE-
STORED.** Offset, spiral bound, 158pp. HeR63, 3.00p.
An historical portrait of some of the major alchemists, combined with a
discussion of the inner nature of the alchemical process and its
outward manifestation and practice. Mr. Cochran's language tends to
be a bit flowery; nonetheless, he does present interesting material
including the results of his own practical experiments.

John Dee

John Dee, who lived from 1527 until 1608, was one of the
most celebrated and remarkable men of the Elizabethan age.
Philosopher, mathematician, technologist, antiquarian, teacher and friend of powerful people, Dee was at the center of some
of the major developments of the English Renaissance; in fact,
he inspired several of these developments through his writings
and his teachings. But Dee was also a magician deeply
immersed in the most extreme forms of occultism: he was
Elizabethan England's great magus. As magus, Dee's world
view was thoroughly of the Renaissance. He was one of a line
of philosopher-magicians who lived in a world that was half
magical, half scientific. Astronomy and astrology were not yet
completely separated; chemistry was not fully differentiated
from alchemy and was as much an occult cosmic philosophy as
a form of science. To John Dee everything was a form of
science and everything was worth exploring.
—*condensed from the introduction to* **John Dee**, *by Peter French*

CASAUBON, MERIC. **A TRUE AND FAITHFUL RELATION OF
WHAT PASSED BETWEEN DR. JOHN DEE AND SOME SPIRITS
AND APPARITIONS.** 8½"x13", APL74, 60.00c.
This is a reprint of a 1659 edition of John Dee's diaries of the teachings
he received from spirits. The book also discusses Dee's views on how
the spirits were summoned, the help and advice they gave, and much
else. This is a limited edition, beautifully bound and boxed.

DEE, JOHN. **THE HIEROGLYPHIC MONAD.** 76pp. Wei75, 9.50c.
*This book, written in thirteen days in 1564 by the Elizabethan magus, Dr. John Dee,
explains his discovery of the "monad," or unity underlying the universe, as expressed in
a hieroglyph, or symbol. The monad represents the alchemic process and the goal of the
Magus, who in partaking of the Divine, achieves that gnostic regeneration experience
of becoming God, and thus furthering the redemption and transmutation of worlds.—*
from the introduction. This is a very difficult text by a person
considered by many to be the Einstein of his time. A short but helpful
introduction by Diane di Prima is included.

DEE, JOHN. **THE MATHEMATICAL PREFACE.** About 100pp. WAP75,
12.00c.
This is generally considered one of Dee's most important scientific
works. It was designed as a commentary to a translation of **Euclid.** In
the preface Dee discusses the essential nature of mathematics—and, in
fact, discusses mathematics so well that Dee's work became far better
known than the translation. This is a photographic reprint of the first
edition of 1570 and includes an excellent introduction by Allen Debus
which covers Dee the man, his work, and his times. The reproduction
of the text is more than adequate.

■ FRENCH, PETER. **JOHN DEE: THE WORLD OF AN ELIZABE-
THAN MAGUS.** Sixteen plates, notes, bibliography, index, 254pp.
RKP72, 15.00c.
This is the first adequate biographical study of John Dee. French
devoted about five years to researching the material and he has
produced a biography which is not only an impeccable work of
scholarship, but also a fascinating study of a man and his times.

HALLIWELL, JAMES, ed. **THE PRIVATE DIARY OF DR. JOHN DEE
AND THE CATALOGUE OF HIS LIBRARY OF MANUSCRIPTS.**
Notes, index, 145pp. AMS1842, 18.85c.
The documents reprinted here have been taken from the original
manuscripts in the Ashmolean Museum at Oxford and Trinity College
Library, Cambridge.

——————— **END OF JOHN DEE SUBSECTION** ———————

DOBBS, BETTY. **THE FOUNDATIONS OF NEWTON'S ALCHEMY.** **Index, 315pp. CUP75, 26.50c.**
This is a comprehensive, definitive volume which traces Newton's heretofore little studied alchemical work and integrates it with the English alchemical currents which influenced him deeply. Dr. Dobbs collates the chemical experiments Newton recorded in his notebooks with his alchemical manuscripts, establishing that Newton's chemical research can be interpreted only from an alchemical point of view. Included are Newton's own procedures for the preparation of *philosophical mercury*. Biographical material on Newton and his colleagues is also included along with extensive textual notes. The bibliography is the longest and the best we have ever seen.

DOBERER, KURT. **THE GOLDMAKERS. Bibliography, 301pp. Gre48, 17.15c.**
Subtitled, *10,000 Years of Alchemy,* this is an account of the major figures in alchemy throughout the ages. Each of the biographical sketches is fairly short—however, the main value of this book lies in the comprehensiveness of its coverage. Biographical material of any reputable scholarship (which this seems to be) is very hard to come by on alchemists since their trade was, by nature, secretive. The emphasis is on the facts of their lives rather than on their philosophies.

FABRICIUS, JOHANNES. **ALCHEMY: THE MEDIEVAL ALCHEMISTS AND THEIR ROYAL ART. Leather bound, 14"x10¼", 228pp. R&B76, 49.00c.**
This magnificently produced volume contains more than 400 woodcuts, engravings, water colors, and paintings—all of which have been photographed directly from the original books. The reproductions are uniformly excellent and are worth the price of the book alone. All the plates are explained and analyzed. The text presents the alchemical work *in its uninterrupted sequence from its chaotic beginning to its solar conclusion and apotheosis. The chief source of this reconstruction is the medieval* **Rosarium** *series of the work, followed by the later* **Splendour solis** *series, the* **Crowne of Nature** *(or* **Barchusen***) series, the* **Pandora** *series, the* **Mutus liber** *series, and the* **Twelve Keys of Basil Valentine.** The text integrates both Jungian and Freudian psychological concepts and psychedelic psychology with alchemical thought. This linkage makes many of the more obscure alchemical insights comprehensible. The author goes a bit far with his analogies at times; nonetheless, we found that our understanding of alchemy deepened considerably after reading through this volume. And as we said before, the plates are incomparable.

FRANZ, MARIE-LOUISE VON, ed. **AURORA CONSURGENS. 555pp. RKP66, 31.50c.**
A translation of a rare medieval alchemical treatise—reputed to be the last work of St. Thomas Aquinas—which was discovered by Carl Jung in the course of his researches. It bears out Jung's view that the alchemical tradition, through its symbols, served to express unconscious psychic content. Edited, with a commentary by Marie-Louise von Franz; originally published as part of **Mysterium Coniunctionis** (without the commentary). The medieval Latin text is given.

GERVASO, ROBERTO. **CAGLIOSTRO. Notes, bibliography, index, 272pp. Glz74, 9.60c.**
This biography is written in a lively, popularized style. Gervaso's study includes both the facts and the abundant folklore about the life of this eighteenth century mystery man. Cagliostro, who traveled throughout Europe under many guises, was controversial during his lifetime, and remains controversial to this day. The book seems to be based on solid research.

HALL, MANLY P. **ORDERS OF THE GREAT WORKS: ALCHEMY. 107pp. PRS49, 5.75c.**
A discussion of the origins of alchemy along with a survey of the major alchemical figures. Written in simple language and illustrated with woodcuts.

HITCHCOCK, ETHAN. **ALCHEMY AND THE ALCHEMISTS. 318pp. PRS76, 15.00c.**
General Hitchcock was a military adviser to President Lincoln and the author of several books on Christian mysticism and esoteric philosophy. This is his most important work. He analyzes the findings of several of the major alchemists; his discussion is remarkably similar to some of the psychological insights of Carl Jung. He also surveys the contributions of prominent Rosicrucians and the close relationship between the Bible and alchemical philosophy. Although the book does not have as nice a feeling as many of the alchemical books and is not very well organized, it does offer some important insights. A facsimile of the original 1857 edition.

HOPKINS, ARTHUR. **ALCHEMY, CHILD OF GREEK PHILOSOPHY. Notes, bibliography, 272pp. AMS67, 12.75c.**
This is a detailed academic study of alchemy, beginning with a survey of Greek and Egyptian influences and a study of the early literature and ending with a review of the Muhammadan revival. The information presented here is not readily available in any other volume. The account is historically-oriented, and Hopkins presents complicated information in as clear a fashion as possible.

JOHNSON, OBED. **A STUDY OF CHINESE ALCHEMY. Notes, bibliography, index, 167pp. Arn28, 13.45c.**
This is the most simplified text available on Chinese alchemy. Dr. Johnson writes in a stilted manner and devotes much of his book to a survey of Taoism and Taoist teaching. Nonetheless, there is a fair amount of value for all who are seriously interested in Chinese alchemy.

JUNG, C.G. **ALCHEMICAL STUDIES, VOLUME 13 OF THE COLLECTED WORKS. Many notes, extensive bibliography, index, 444pp. PUP67/RKP, 15.00c.**
Introductory work for Jung's alchemical volumes, this book consists of essays outlining and explaining the development of his basic alchemical constructs. Essays on Paracelsus, *spirit mercurius*, philosophical tree, and much else.

JUNG, C.G. **MYSTERIUM CONIUNCTIONIS, VOLUME 14 OF THE COLLECTED WORKS. Many notes, extensive bibliography, index, 697pp. PUP70/RKP, 16.50c/6.50p.**
One of Jung's last works, it represents his synthesis of alchemical symbolism and modern psychoanalytic thinking. Dealing with the relationship of esoteric development and psychoanalysis, Jung uses the archetypal symbolism found in ancient and modern man as the starting point and structure for the evolution of the whole and complete man.

JUNG, C.G. **PSYCHOLOGY AND ALCHEMY, VOLUME 12 OF THE COLLECTED WORKS. Many notes, extensive bibliography, index, 571pp. PUP68/RKP, 16.50c.**
This work deals with a psychoanalytic interpretation of archetypal symbols that have existed for 1,700 years. These alchemical symbols are analyzed in depth as they appear in the dreams of a patient. The manifestation of these symbols in modern patients is Jung's basis for his hypothesis of the collective unconscious. The book contains 270 illustrations, mostly from old alchemical manuscripts.

LAPIDUS. **IN PURSUIT OF GOLD: ALCHEMY IN THEORY AND PRACTICE. Bibliography, index, 176pp. Wei76, 10.00c.**
This is a unique book by a practicing alchemist which takes a completely practical approach to alchemy and explains the precise chemical and metallurgical equivalents of alchemical terms. Many noted texts are analyzed and quoted either fully or *systematically reduced in length by the elimination of irrelevant and misleading material.* The last chapters provide complete instructions for performing alchemical experiments. Appendices give a listing of all the needed equipment, define the conventional signs and symbols, and provide an abridgment of Paracelsus' questions and answers on alchemy.

MAIER, MICHAEL. **LAWS OF THE FRATERNITY OF THE ROSE CROSSE (THEMIS AUREA). 136+pp. PRS76, 10.00c.**
A.E. Waite refers to Maier (1568-1622) as *the greatest adept of his age.* This book amplifies the rules of the Rosicrucian Fraternity as set forth in the **Fama** issued by the order in 1615. The **Fama** contains an outline of a universal reformation and affirms the existence of a secret body of enlightened mystics dedicated to the general improvement of mankind and the advancements of the practical purposes of alchemy. Maier's small volume sets forth the department advocated by these philosophers, with special emphasis on the obligations of physicians and the higher ethics of medicine. This facsimile reprint of the original English edition of 1656 has an introduction by Manly Hall.

NEEDHAM, JOSEPH. **SCIENCE AND CIVILISATION IN CHINA, VOLUME 5, PART II. Notes, index, 510pp. CUP74, 35.00c.**
One part of what must be the most exhaustive academic study in the West of Chinese alchemy and its relation to the rise of modern science. Dr. Needham traces Chinese alchemy from three roots: the pharmaceutical-botanical search for macrobiotic plants to produce immortality; the metallurgical-chemical practices for making artificial gold; and the medical-mineralogical use of inorganic substances in therapy. The book includes illustrations, photographs, bibliographies of Chinese and Japanese books both before and after 1800, and a bibliography of books and journal articles in Western languages.

NEEDHAM, JOSEPH. **SCIENCE AND CIVILISATION IN CHINA, VOLUME 5, PART III. 42.00c.**
See the Chinese Philosophy section.

Paracelsus

We know little about the life of Paracelsus (1493-1541); he is an enigmatic figure who lies enveloped in an imposing aura of myth. Controversies over the essential value and nature of the man and his work have existed since his time and continue to this day. The list of achievements attributed to him is impressive and he made his mark in the realms of medicine, psychiatry, pharmacology, metaphysics, and alchemy. He waged war against the medical and ecclesiastical authorities of his day, for he had no use for empty theory untested by practical application. Paracelsus is primarily known as an alchemist and as the father of modern medicine. His studies began at an early age and carried him throughout Europe and the Middle East, accumulating medical and esoteric teachings. The core of his teaching was the doctrine of correspondence between the outward and the inward, and the principle of complementary pairs of opposites. The writings attributed to him encompass many large volumes and his influence remains paramount.

HALL, MANLY P. **THE MYSTICAL AND MEDICAL PHILOSOPHY OF PARACELSUS. 78pp. PRS64, 2.50p.**
An excellent introduction to the life, work, and philosophy of Paracelsus. This is a developmental, historical tracing of his life and confrontations with medical men of his time. Deals with theory of disease, metaphysical healing, sympathetic forces, universal energy, and much else.

HARTMANN, FRANZ. **PARACELSUS: LIFE AND PROPHECIES. 220pp. Mul73, 2.75p.**
A reproduction of **The Prophecies of Paracelsus: Occult Symbols, and Magic Figures with Esoteric Explanations,** extensively illustrated. This is one of the rarest of all Paracelsus' writings. It is supplemented by the often cited, very readable and comprehensible survey of his life and teachings by Hartmann. Dr. Hartmann also supplies a long, detailed explanation of the terms used by Paracelsus, and a complete list of his writings.

JACOBI, JOLANDE, ed. **PARACELSUS: SELECTED WRITINGS. Bibliography, index, 362pp. PUP69/RKP, 18.15c.**
A systematic selection of passages from the broad range of Paracelsus' writings. The themes dealt with include the human body, the role of work, ethics, the spirit, human destiny, the cosmos, and God. Dr. Jacobi has also provided an introduction, a biography, and a vocabulary of Paracelsian terms. The volume is illustrated with reproductions of over 150 contemporary woodcuts. This is an excellent book, which we highly recommend to all who have a deep interest in the alchemical art.

PARACELSUS. **ARCHIDOXES OF MAGIC. 168pp. Wei75/AsK, 13.50c.**
This is a verbatim reprinting (in the original style and type) of Robert Turner's 1655 translation. The text itself is a source work on medieval angelic magic which gives complete sets of zodiacal characters, and planetary signs, with full details of their manufacture and consecration. Paracelsus here is primarily concerned with the practical applications of this magic, especially with regard to healing. Other sections

include details of the planetary spirits, the conjunction of the male and female principles, and each step on the *Path to the Tincture.* The text includes many illustrations and is considered one of the most accurate descriptions in the whole Hermetic canon.

PARACELSUS. **THE PROPHECIES OF PARACELSUS. 115pp. Wei74/HPG, 2.50p.**
The prophecies comprise thirty-two allegorical pictures, each accompanied by a prognostication, a preface, and an elucidation. Most of the events predicted are concerned with the church or state and the span of time involved seems to be twenty-four and forty-two, or multiples thereof. With introductory commentary.

WAITE, ARTHUR E., ed. **THE HERMETIC AND ALCHEMICAL WRITINGS OF PARACELSUS. ShP1894, 5.95p/each.**
This is considered the definitive collection of Paracelsus' writings. Waite includes extensive notes, commenting on various aspects of the text. Volume I covers *Hermetic Chemistry;* and Volume II is devoted to *Hermetic Medicine and Hermetic Philosophy.* Each volume is indexed and contains about 400 pages.

————— **END OF PARACELSUS SUBSECTION** —————

PERNETY, ANTOINE-JOSEPH. **AN ALCHEMICAL TREATISE ON THE GREAT ART. 255pp. Wei73, 12.50c.**
Pernety lived in the eighteenth century and spent over twenty-five years researching the material ultimately incorporated in this volume. He carefully compared all the schools of Hermetism, and has here presented a synthesis of their doctrines as well as introductory material and a concise and complete system of *The Great Art.* The editors have preserved all his notes and added notes from several other sources. The volume also includes the *Dictionary of Hermetic Symbols* from Albert Poisson's **Theories et Symboles des Alchimistes.** Following the dictionary is a complete display of alchemical characters.

POWELL, NEIL. **ALCHEMY: THE ANCIENT SCIENCE.** 8"x10½", 144pp. Dou76/ALd, 8.95c.
A profusely illustrated history of alchemy and alchemists, including many color plates and some philosophical discussion. This is designed as an overview, and the author emphasizes the more sensational aspects of the alchemical art.

REGARDIE, ISRAEL. **THE PHILOSOPHER'S STONE.** LlP38, 3.95p.
As Regardie says, *Alchemy is philosophy; it is the philosophy, the seeking out of Sophia in the mind.* This book is an analysis of three alchemical texts— **The Golden Tractate of Hermes, The Six Keys of Eudoxus,** and Basil Valentine's **Triumphant Chariot of Antimony**—interpreted with extensive commentary from the standpoint of psychological and mystical symbolism. A very clear presentation.

REIDY, JOHN, ed. **THOMAS NORTON'S ORDINAL OF ALCHEMY.** Glossary, notes, 200pp. Oxf75, 14.10c.
This is a reprint of a major Middle English alchemical treatise. It is an authoritative work, containing a number of anecdotes and a defense of the alchemical work. A lengthy introduction by Reidy analyzes the text in depth.

■ ROLA, STANISLAS KLOSSOWSKI DE. **ALCHEMY: THE SECRET ART.** 128pp. T&H73, 6.95p.
An 8"x11" book, with 193 illustrations (thirty-three in full color), which presents a picture of what alchemy was and is in the true spiritual sense. Each of the original plates is commented on and de Rola provides a short, excellent introduction. Since alchemy in medieval times often took the form of paintings and drawings, this book is a very good introduction to this esoteric science.

SADOUL, JACQUES. **ALCHEMISTS AND GOLD.** Glossary, 285pp. Spe73, 9.15c.
This book, written by a young French historian, shows that the knowledge gleaned by alchemists over the centuries can still be of real use today. Sadoul traces the history of Hermes Trismegistus, Albertus Magnus, Roger Bacon, Paracelsus, Fulcanelli, and many others. A very full, detailed explanation.

SILBERER, HERBERT. **HIDDEN SYMBOLISM OF ALCHEMY AND THE OCCULT ARTS.** Extensive notes, bibliography, 451pp. Dov17, 4.50p.
A thoughtful study, the first serious attempt (antedating the work of Jung) to correlate the methods of psychoanalysis with the literature of alchemy. Included is a wealth of material taken directly from alchemical and Rosicrucian sources. Passages from the work of Hermes Trismegistus, Flamel, Lacinius, Michael Maier, Paracelsus, and Boehme are cited. This is an unaltered republication of the first English edition originally entitled **Problems of Mysticism and its Symbolism.**

STILLMAN, JOHN MAXSON. **THE STORY OF ALCHEMY AND EARLY CHEMISTRY.** 566pp. Dov60, 4.00p.
The more scientific aspects of alchemy are dealt with in this volume. The author has constructed his text from many original sources and has quoted liberally from writers of all periods.

SWORDER, MARY, tr. **FULCANELLI: MASTER ALCHEMIST.** Many plates, 190pp. Spe71, 8.40c.
Rosicrucian and Masonic legend asserts that Fulcanelli (whose real name, to this day, is unknown) is the only man in the West to have *made the Stone* in this century and that on the eve of completing the *magnum opus* he handed over to his student, Eugene Canseliet what was, in effect, the literary counterpart of his own great work. Then he vanished—never to be seen again. This is his masterpiece, **Le Mystere des Cathedrales** (translated here for the first time). It has long been believed that the Gothic cathedrals of Europe were secret textbooks of a hidden science, that behind the gargoyles and the glyphs, a mighty secret lay—all but openly—displayed. Fulcanelli's work is a masterly exposition of an incredible fact: that the Gothic cathedrals have, for 700 years, offered mankind instruction in the technique of its own evolution. *About one thing there is no possible doubt. Fulcanelli KNEW. There is no speculation.*—from the introduction.

■ TAYLOR, F. SHERWOOD. **THE ALCHEMISTS.** Illustrations, bibliography, index, 191pp. Grn76, 3.95p.
Taylor is the Director of the Science Museum in London and the author of many textbooks on chemistry. He has studied alchemy for many years and in this book attempts to write of its essence. He writes in a popular vein, and does a good job of surveying the history of alchemy, the major alchemists and alchemical movements, and the inner meaning of the alchemical process. This is a fine, sympathetic introduction.

TRISMOSIN, SOLOMON. **SPLENDOR SOLIS.** 10¼"x7", 104pp. YPS nd, 12.50c.
This is a rare alchemical manuscript which is often referred to in alchemical literature. Solomon Trismosin is thought to be Paracelsus' teacher. Trismosin writes allegorically, using veiled language and esoteric symbology. Nonetheless, if deeply studied, this book is one of the finest discussions of the alchemical work and the philosopher's stone available to the noninitiate. A series of twenty-two allegorical pictures reproduced from the original 1582 manuscript are included, with commentary by J.K., the editor and translator. J.K. also provides explanatory notes and translations of Trismosin's autobiographical account of his travels in search of the philosopher's stone and of a summary of his alchemical process called *The Red Lion.*

WAITE, A.E. **THE ALCHEMICAL WRITINGS OF EDWARD KELLY.** 211pp. Wei1893, 9.50c.
Kelly was a very controversial figure in his time. He worked with Dr. John Dee, and some consider his writings to contain keys to understanding the Stone. His knowledge is said to have been acquired from the **Book of St. Dunstan.** This edition contains the full text of his treatises, **The Philosopher's Stone,** and **The Theatre of Terrestrial Astronomy,** along with a long biographical preface by Waite.

WAITE, A.E. **ALCHEMISTS THROUGH THE AGES.** 320pp. Mul70, 2.75p.
A compact presentation of the lives of all the great alchemists. Waite also outlines the principles and aims of alchemy in an introductory essay.

WAITE, A.E. **AZOTH OR THE STAR IN THE EAST.** 239pp. UnB73, 10.00c.
Azoth *was written at a time when Waite was immersed in the mysteries of alchemy and its texts, of which he came to have an unrivaled knowledge. . . . He realized that mysticism consisted of both transcendental science and transcendental religion, and that the alchemy of transformation was both physical and spiritual.*—from the introduction by L. Shepard. In this book he surveys the entire field in great detail.

WAITE, A.E. **THE HERMETIC TRADITION.** Two volumes, illustrations, 679pp. Wei1893, 35.00c/set.
The **Hermetic Museum** was originally published in Latin in 1625. It was designed as a compact, representative edition of the writings of the ancient alchemists. In all, twenty-two texts were included. This translation by Waite contains all of the original material.

WAITE, A.E., tr. **THE TURBA PHILOSOPHORUM.** 215pp. Wei73, 9.50c.
A translation of the most ancient extant Latin treatise on alchemy.

WAITE, A.E. **THE WORKS OF THOMAS VAUGHAN: MYSTIC AND ALCHEMIST.** 498pp. UnB68, 15.00c.
A complete presentation of the writings of perhaps the most authoritative and significant European alchemist. It concludes with a discourse on the nature of man and his state after death. Many explanatory notes accompany the text.

WARE, JAMES, tr. and ed. **ALCHEMY, MEDICINE AND RELIGION IN THE CHINA OF A.D. 320: THE NEI P'IEN OF KO HUNG.** 20.00c.
See the Chinese Philosophy section.

WILSON, FRANK. **ALCHEMY AS A WAY OF LIFE.** 96pp. Dan76, 5.40c.
A general discussion of the principles of alchemy as they appear in nature and in the human mind. Wilson makes virtually no reference to the symbolism of the ancient texts but does offer some insights into alchemical thought.

ZAIN, C.C. **SPIRITUAL ALCHEMY.** 4.75p.
See the Astrology section.

AMERICAN INDIAN RELIGION

The American Indian has already taught us a great deal, whether we remember it or not. In the far north of this continent, life is still dependent in part on the technology of the Eskimo and Indian, who gave us among other things the parka, snowshoe, toboggan, and kayak. Maize, potatoes, sweet potatoes, and manioc, which today make up more than half the world's tonnage of staple foods, were first domesticated in the New World. Most modern cotton, including that grown in the Old World, is the long-staple cotton of the American Indian. Some 220 American Indian drugs have been or still are official in the *Pharmacopeia of the United States of America* or the *National Formulary*. Even in these practical areas, we have sometimes been slow to learn.

Although we have accepted a great deal of technology from the American Indian, we have not yet learned his more difficult lessons, lessons about the mind and spirit. In order to become the Indian's students, we have to recognize that some of what he has to teach transcends cultural or historical boundaries. Paul Radin took precisely this position with respect to American Indian religion, saying that we would never make any progress in our understanding *until scholars rid themselves, once and for all, of the curious notion that everything possesses an evolutionary history; until they realize that certain ideas and certain concepts are ultimate for man.* Mircea Eliade, in his classic study of shamanism, puts the matter this way: *The various types of civilization are, of course, organically connected with certain religious forms; but this in no sense excludes the spontaneity and, in the last analysis, the ahistoricity of religious life.* And the Sioux holy man Lame Deer, fully aware of the diversity of external religious forms among American Indians, says, *I think when it comes right down to it, all the Indian religions are somehow part of the same belief, the same mystery.*

The realm that Radin, Eliade, and Lame Deer all have in mind is open to all men in all places at all times, but it is also universally hard to talk about in ordinary language. Carlos Castaneda has called it *nonordinary* or *separate* reality, as opposed to *ordinary* reality. The Hopis refer to it as *'a' ne himu, Mighty Something.* It is open to what Martin Heidegger calls *contemplative* as opposed to *calculative* thought, or thinking that is oriented toward meaning as opposed to thinking that is oriented toward results. For the American Indian in general, it is a world composed entirely of persons, as opposed to the everyday world of ego and object. For the Hopi, Tewa, Zuni, and Wintu it is the realm of soft, unripe, unmanifest essence, as opposed to hard, ripe manifest forms; its location in space is above and below the horizontal plane of our everyday world, and is reached through a vertical axis that passes through the seeker; it is also encountered at the periphery of the horizontal plane. In these upper, lower, and peripheral regions, linear, historical, irreversible time gives way to a time which is far in the past when viewed objectively, but the very present moment when experienced.

Sometimes the entering of this other world just happens. Black Elk, a Sioux, had his first and greatest vision during a childhood illness. Don Talayesva blundered into a Hopi shrine as a boy and was captured by the being who lived there. Isaac Tens, a Gitksan, was out cutting wood one evening when a loud noise carried him into the other world. More commonly, the experience must be sought. In some ways of seeking, the mind is prepared with drugs.

Whether or not drugs are used, the body and mind must be purified or emptied. A Sioux, for example, must take a sweat bath before his vision quest, and the Peyotist must bathe and put on clean clothes. Both the Sioux and Papago fast from food and water; the Peyotist is purged of whatever is in him by his sacrament, which may cause him to vomit. The mind must be set upon the sacred task itself and emptied of all else; as Black Elk says, the seeker *must be careful lest distracting thoughts come to him.* The Papago on a pilgrimage even ties up his hair so that he will not distract himself or others by having to brush it back from his face in the wind; he must concentrate on the rules of the journey and give no thought to home. In this emptying of the everyday mind, the seeker humbles himself; in the words of Black Elk, he must see himself as *lower than even the smallest ant.* This means that he must let go of the self, which belongs to the calculative world of ego and object. He experiences this letting go as death itself; as Lame Deer puts it, *You go up on that hill to die.*

The death which opens the way to the other world requires a special setting. The Zuni priest, when he seeks contact with the rainmakers of the world-encircling ocean, secludes himself in a windowless room, four rooms removed from any outside door. The Eskimo shaman who seeks to travel to the bottom of the sea puts himself behind a curtain in the sleeping place of a darkened house. Participants in the Ghost Dance of the Plains, seeking visions of their lost relatives, moved in a circle on consecrated ground just outside the camp. The Sioux, seeking the knowledge of the oneness of all things, goes away to a mountaintop and places himself within a sacred circle. The Papago salt pilgrim travels on foot and horseback all the way to the edge of the world and even beyond, walking into the ocean until four waves have broken behind him.

The experience itself is difficult to translate without destroying its nature, for ordinary language belongs to the world of the self and is concerned with the differentiation of the multitude of objects. Black Elk puts the matter this way: *While I stood there I saw more than I can tell and I understood more than I saw; for I was seeing in a sacred manner the shapes of all things in the spirit, and the shape of all shapes as they must live together like one being.* One approach to this problem of inexpressibility is to approximate the experience of oneness by using language in a way that draws the speaker and his subject closer together than they would ordinarily be. The nouns that best express a speaker's nearness to his subject are those of blood relationship. The seeker, as Black Elk says, must *know that all things are our relatives,* and he must use terms of relationship whether he is talking about a coyote, a willow, a lump of salt, the earth, or the sun. The verbs that draw speaker and subject most strongly together are those of being and becoming. An Ojibwa, describing what happened during a boyhood fast, says that when he discovered that his own body was covered with feathers, he realized that he had become an eagle. Black Elk, speaking of a visionary encounter with the Spirit of Earth, says, *I stared at him, for it seemed I knew him somehow; and as I stared, he slowly changed, for he was growing backwards into youth, and when he had become a boy, I knew that he was myself.*

The vision itself may provide the seeker with the voice of its own expression, but this will be in chant or song rather than in the plainspoken word. The songs are not merely ordinary descriptions set to music; instead, the words may give brief, enigmatic sketches which evoke a whole vision. Some of the words may be archaic, or the whole song may seem to be in another language. The syllables of the words may be embedded in other syllables which are meaningless, or the entire song may be in nonsense syllables.

Some visionaries, instead of expressing the enigmatic quality of the other world by using strange language or nonlanguage, take ordinary language and break it in half, separating the words from their meanings and putting them back together again the wrong way around. Then, whatever they may seem to be saying, they mean just the opposite. If they say *Turn to the left*, they mean, *Turn to the right*. This is the way of the sacred clown of the Plains and Southwestern tribes.

Another way of talking about the experience of the other world is to give names to its enigmatic qualities, names which will evoke these qualities when the experiencer speaks them. If a name of this kind is further understood to be that of a person, a blood relative of the other world, then it simultaneously expresses the strangeness of that world and the seeker's own nearness to all things when he is in that world. These are the names of God.

In the other world, everything is numinous, suffused with sacredness, holiness, light in proportion to the seeker's nearness to the ultimate being. The Sioux call this holiness *wakan*, the Ojibwa and other Algonkian peoples call it *manitu*, and the Iroquois call it *orenda*. The vision of this holiness, once ended, is of no value unless something of it can be brought back into the ordinary world and kept alive there. For the Papago pilgrim, it was possible to bring back a token, a strand of seaweed, a shell, or a pebble that he noticed while he was at the edge of the world. The Plains seeker who saw an eagle in his vision might later put an eagle's head in his personal medicine bundle, or paint an eagle on his shield, or his vision might even show him directly the actual design he should paint on his shield, or his drum or, in the case of the Ghost Dance, his shirt. If the use of a particular plant was suggested to him in his vision, he might later include this plant in his medicine bundle.

A person who has these gifts from the other world can use them to help him see as he did there, to recognize manifestations of that world in this one. This ability to see what is going on in the world is the source of good fortune, of sudden strength in times of danger or uncertainty, as when a man hunts or goes to war. A person who has had an especially potent vision may be able to make himself a manifestation of the holiness of the other world, giving him the ability not only to see but to work a change. This is the shaman, the holy man, who uses this power to cure the sick and may even translate his visions into ceremonies that give a whole group of people some access to the cosmos, some understanding, as when Black Elk dramatized his great vision in the Horse Dance. Among the Navajo, it was similarly powerful visions that gave rise to the present-day ceremonies called *sings*, with their long chants and elaborate sand paintings. Throughout North America, there are secret societies in which holy men share the power of their visions with a group of initiates.

But it is not enough to share the visions of others. Over much of North America, young Indians are encouraged and even expected to seek their own visionary encounters with the other world. Indeed, the seeking is a prerequisite for adulthood itself. In some tribes, the first attempt may be made as early as age five, and in most it has to be made before adolescence. Wherever there were secret societies, the initiate had to have visions of his own in order to rise to the highest ranks.

When we reflect about the way Indian religion has been studied, we can see the single vision in action. We have studied it solely with the eyes open and kept it outside. Our museums place once-sacred objects on display, so schoolchildren can examine their outward forms. Groups of hobbyists perform exact replicas of Indian ceremonies, with everything there but the meaning. Many anthropologists can only tell us that meaning lies in historical contexts, or is revealed by logical or mathematical transformations of the outward forms. All of this amounts to a hermetic seal between the Indian and ourselves. When an Indian voice penetrates this seal, whether indirectly through Joseph Epes Brown's **The Sacred Pipe**, or directly through Hyemeyohsts Storm's **Seven Arrows**, the experts do no better than quarrel about the accuracy of details. Vine Deloria, who has a clearer vision, comments on **Seven Arrows** as follows: *Storm in great measure succeeded in stepping outside of a time-dominated interpretation of Indian tribal religion and created a series of parabolic teachings concerning the nature of religion. Few people have understood him—or forgiven him.* The teachings of American Indian religion have always been parabolic; their meaning is discovered by reflection, not through historical exactness. As a Zuni once said to an anthropologist who was carefully transcribing each word of a traditional story, *When I tell these stories, do you see it or do you just write it down?*.

Our road, if we now wish to hear the Indian and learn to think, to see like him, is not an easy one. Even if we succeed in abandoning a purely historical approach, there is a further pitfall. In attempting a straight intellectual experiment with Indian thought, we might assume, for the sake of argument, that *everything is alive*. If we were to do that, we might get a response like the one an old Ojibwa gave the anthropologist who asked, *Are all the stones we see about us here alive?* The answer was, *No! But some are.* This old man had the double vision. He did not live solely in the other world, where indeed all stones are alive, but he had the capacity to recognize that world in the appearance of this one. The way to his understanding is not found with the road maps of the measurable world. One begins by finding the four roads that run side by side and choosing the middle one. The Road, once found, is cut by an impassable ravine that extends to the ends of the world. One must go right through. Then there is an impenetrable thicket. Go right through. Then there are birds making a terrible noise. Just listen. Then there is a place where phlegm rains down. Don't brush it off. Then there is a place where the earth is burning. Pass right through. Then a great cliff face rises up, without a single foothold. Walk straight through.

If you travel as far as this and someone threatens you with death, say, *I have already died.*

—*condensed from* **Teachings from the American Earth**, *by Dennis Tedlock and Barbara Tedlock*

ALEXANDER, HARTLEY. **THE WORLD'S RIM.** Introduction, illustrations, notes, index, 279pp. UNP53, 2.95p.
A philosophical analysis of a number of native American rituals and beliefs which incorporates a great deal of mythology. In rich, vivid, and intensely poetic language, Alexander conveys the life and minds of the native Americans and shows how they expressed their beliefs. Alexander was a specialist in American Indian art and mythology.

ANGULO, JAIME DE. **INDIAN TALES.** Illustrations, 253pp. FSG53, 3.45p/1.75p.
A fascinating collection of native California folklore. The author's firsthand knowledge of the tribes has enabled him to convey more of the authentic flavor than could have been possible in any literal translation. He includes tall tales and jokes, ceremonial rituals, poetic allegories, gambling games, and hunting adventures. The collection should appeal to readers of all ages, even though the author originally wrote the tales for his children.

ASHTON, ROBERT and JOZEFA STUART. **IMAGES OF AMERICAN INDIAN ART.** Bibliography, 9½"x12¾", 72pp. Wal77, 6.95p.
More than 200 photographs, in color and black and white, display the panorama of North American Indian art.

BELLEROPHON. A COLORING BOOK OF AMERICAN INDIANS. 8½"x11", BlB nd, 1.95p.

BIERHORST, JOHN, ed. THE GIRL WHO MARRIED A GHOST AND OTHER TALES FROM THE NORTH AMERICAN INDIANS. Bibliography, 7¾"x9¼", 120pp. FWP78, 9.95c.
The haunting tales in this anthology are drawn from one of the little known masterpieces of American Indian folklore—the great collection of Indian narratives gathered firsthand by photographer-writer-explorer Edward S. Curtis during the early 1900s. Matched with the stories, for the first time, are Curtis' famous photographs of Indian monsters, maidens, and spirit-persons. The tales include a ghost story from the Northwest Coast, a trickster tale from the Plains, a sacred origin myth from the Southwest, and stories from California, Canada, and Alaska. The photographs are well reproduced. The retellings are geared toward older children.

BIERHORST, JOHN, ed. IN THE TRAIL OF THE WIND: AMERICAN INDIAN POEMS AND RITUAL ORATIONS. Introduction, illustrations, glossary, bibliography, 201+pp. FSG71, 4.95p.
An unusual collection of native American poetry, translated from over forty languages, representing all the best known Indian cultures of North and South America. Bierhorst includes omens, battle songs, orations, love lyrics, prayers, dreams, and incantations. Beginning with the origin of the earth and the emergence of man, the sequence proceeds through the rituals of birth, love, war, and death to the foreshadowing of the Conquest, the days of despair, and, finally, the apocalyptic visions of a new life. Detailed notes are supplied for each of the 126 selections.

■ *BIERHORST, JOHN.* THE RED SWAN: MYTHS AND TALES OF THE AMERICAN INDIANS. Glossary, 386pp. FSG76, 7.95p.
This is far and away the best collection we know of. The myths are works of art, blending form and content into an organic whole in which the great themes of human experience are interwoven. Over forty cultures, including the Eskimo, Iroquois, Navajo, Maya, and Bororo are represented by sixty-four carefully selected myths and tales. An excellent long introduction and extensive notes are also included.

BLACKBURN, THOMAS, ed. DECEMBER'S CHILD: A BOOK OF CHUMASH ORAL NARRATIVES. Bibliography, 381pp. UCa75, 12.95c.
An explicit, critical retelling of the folklore of a previously obscure group of California Indians. Blackburn analyzes, in terms of recurrent themes and patterns, a highly diverse corpus of 111 Chumash narratives. Extensive introductory ethnographic material is included.

■ *BOYD, DOUG.* ROLLING THUNDER. 283pp. Del74, 3.95p.
Rolling Thunder is an American Indian medicine man. As a medicine man, or shaman, he is guardian of a wealth of knowledge that has been passed down through countless Indian generations. This knowledge includes the power to cure disease and heal wounds, to find and use medicinal herbs, to make rain, to transport objects through the air, and to communicate telepathically. These powers come out of his special relationship with nature, with what can only be called a *spirit of the earth.* This remarkable book is a record of an attempt to learn something about the sources of the medicine man's powers. With Rolling Thunder's full cooperation, Doug Boyd, on a research field trip for the Menninger Foundation, spent a long time observing him and he reports in detail on his observations here. A fascinating account.

BRODER, PATRICIA. HOPI PAINTING: THE WORLD OF THE HOPIS. 296 illustrations, thirty-two in color, bibliography, index, 8½"x11", 320pp. Dut78, 25.00c.
Hopi art is perhaps the oldest surviving artistic tradition in North America. Better than any other tribe, the Hopi have managed to preserve their culture and adapt to the challenge of the white man. Twentieth century Hopi artists have taken the ancient myths and symbols and synthesized them with the needs and perspectives of the present. In explaining this synthesis, Ms. Broder explores the history, religion, culture, and arts and crafts of the Hopi. She also includes biographical sketches of leading contemporary Hopi artists.

BROWN, JOSEPH EPES, ed. THE SACRED PIPE. Index, 164pp. Vik53, 2.95p.
This is a unique account of the ancient religion of the Sioux Indians. Black Elk was the only qualified priest still alive when he dictated the information in this book to Brown. He tells of the seven rites, which were disclosed to the Sioux through visions, beginning with White Buffalo Cow Woman's first visit to the Sioux to give them the sacred pipe. The reader is led through the sun dance, the purification rite, the *keeping of the soul,* and the other ceremonies, and learns how the Sioux have come to terms with God, nature, and their fellow men.

BROWN, JOSEPH EPES. THE SPIRITUAL LEGACY OF THE AMERICAN INDIAN. Bibliography, 32pp. PHP64, 1.20p.
A beautifully written, succinct discussion of the religious beliefs and practices of the Plains Indians.

BROWN, VINSON. GREAT UPON THE MOUNTAIN. Introduction, glossary, 191pp. McM71, 6.95c.
This is a personal study of Crazy Horse, based on fact and legend. Crazy Horse was driven by visions in which he saw himself leading his braves through a hail of bullets. He had visions of impenetrable darkness and also of a new and better age. He has been an inspiration to all the generations after him. As Brown says, *It is very possible this new spirit is in the world now and beginning to grow...and when the light comes...our spirit will come back again...our people will be in the forefront of the greatest of battles, the battle to unite the great circle of earth and sky and bring justice to all men.* The book reads as well as a novel.

BROWN, VINSON. VOICES OF EARTH AND SKY. Bibliography, 84pp. Nat76, 4.00p.
This is a personal document, relating what Brown himself has discovered about the native American vision. As he says, *The purpose of the vision is not only to find a vision, but also to find in this vision help for yourself to lead a better life and help for other people also.* Brown conveys the sense of spiritual renewal he has derived from the Indian concepts of harmony with the universe and love of nature and all beings. In the process of his narrative he retells many native American visions.

CAPPS, WALTER, ed. SEEING WITH A NATIVE EYE. Notes, bibliography, 140pp. H&R76, 3.95p.
A collection of essays on the nature of native American religion. The selections are fairly academic; nonetheless, they successfully convey the essence of the religious traditions.

CATLIN, GEORGE. LETTERS AND NOTES ON THE MANNERS, CUSTOMS, AND CONDITIONS OF NORTH AMERICAN INDIANS. Dov1844, 4.50p/each.
For eight years (1832-39) Catlin lived with the Plains Indians, capturing in verbal and visual pictures every facet of their lives. The Indians called Catlin *the great white medicine man* because of his painting

ability. This two volume set includes 257 photographs of Catlin's original oil paintings as well as fifty-five of his original book illustrations. This is a vivid text and remains one of the most readable books about the Plains Indians, capturing as it does the tribes when they were still in touch with their most important traditions. Each volume is about 300 pages long.

CATLIN, GEORGE. **O-KEE-PA. Thirteen full page color plates, notes, bibliography, index, 114pp. UNP67, 7.95p.**
In 1832 George Catlin, a renowned painter of American Indian life, observed and recorded the four day O-kee-pa, the major religious ceremony of the Mandan Indians of the Upper Missouri. When his description of it was challenged a quarter of a century later, he prepared a much fuller, illustrated account of the reenactment of the tribal myths and the self tortures that were performed during the O-kee-pa. It is this later version that is reprinted here, along with an insert describing the explicitly sexual aspects of the ceremony. Catlin's account has become an ethnographic and historical classic. A lengthy introduction by the editor, John Ewers, is also included.

COOKE, GRACE. **SUNMEN OF THE AMERICAS. 104pp. WET75, 5.00c.**
A presentation of White Eagle's teaching on the American Indians: *Try to forget all you have read and heard about savage Indians...our ancient Indian bretheren were simple at heart, loving and gentle. They were men of character and strength of purpose, possessing great courage and endurance.... The civilisation of the Indian was one of the most beautiful and ancient civilisations there has ever been on earth.*

COURLANDER, HAROLD. **THE MESA OF FLOWERS. 259pp. Crn77, 8.95c.**
A novel by one of the most eminent American folklorists. Courlander brilliantly evokes an epic test of human endurance and character, chronicling the journey of the Grey Fox clan across the American southwest in search of a prophesied mesa of flowers where the people may live in peace and harmony with the great forces of nature. Guided by shooting stars, visions, and natural signs, they live out an odyssey of unforeseen events, obstacles of all kinds, encounters with strange peoples, and supernatural experiences. Above all, this is a story of people living out their myths.

CRAPANZANO, VINCENT. **THE FIFTH WORLD OF FORSTER BENNETT: PORTRAIT OF A NAVAHO. 252pp. Vik72, 2.25p.**
Today the Navajo inhabit the largest Indian reservation in the United States—some 24,000 square miles of semi-arid land in Utah, New Mexico, and Arizona. This is a moving, anthropologically-oriented study of the reservation as seen through the life of one of the inhabitants, Forster Bennett. Crapanzano lived on the reservation for a summer, and during that time he researched this book. It is an unadorned, vivid, and readable account; a realistic and disturbing portrait of life on reservations today.

CURTIS, EDWARD. **PORTRAITS FROM NORTH AMERICAN INDIAN LIFE. 12"x9", 192pp. A&W72, 8.95p.**
In the early twentieth century Curtis took about 2,500 photographs of North American Indian life. His goal was to document all aspects of Indian cultural life in such a way as to retain the spirit of that culture and keep it alive. This is the only inexpensive edition of his work ever produced. The reproductions are excellent and there is also some introductory material.

DELORIA, VINE. **GOD IS RED. Notes, appendices, index, 376pp. Del73, 3.95p.**
Deloria is generally recognized as today's leading Indian spokesman. Here he offers an alternative to Christianity through a return to Indian beliefs and concepts. He explains that Christianity, an imported religion, has failed the Indian both in terms of its theology and its application to social issues. He urges his fellow Indians to seek God in the North American landscape and think of the land and feel its richness.

EASTMAN, CHARLES. **INDIAN BOYHOOD. 255pp. Dov02, 2.50p.**
Eastman was a fullblooded Indian; this is a first person account of the life he led, until he was fifteen, with the nomadic Sioux. An orphan, he was brought up by his grandmother and taught all the traditional skills. Here he offers observations about Indian character, social customs, and way of life as well as memories of attacks and games of combat.

EATON, EVELYN. **SNOWY EARTH COMES GLIDING. 8½"x10¾", 108pp. DrF74, 10.00p.**
A photographic essay, combined with Ms. Eaton's moving recreation of Indian myths and poems. The author has had a close relationship with a number of Indian communities and her sympathy for their way of life is apparent.

ERDOES, RICHARD. **THE RAIN DANCE PEOPLE. Bibliography, index, 6¾"x9¼", 280pp. RaH76, 7.95c.**
A simply written, illustrated portrait of the Pueblo Indians. The Pueblos are one of the oldest North American tribes. Originally nomads, they finally settled down as farmers and began to weave baskets and make beautiful pottery. They also built giant apartment cities and cliff dwellings. Reconstructing the chain that links the present Southwest Indians to these ancestors, Erdoes presents a powerful and moving picture of a people struggling to preserve its identity and moral values through centuries of oppression.

ERDOES, RICHARD, ed. **THE SOUND OF FLUTES AND OTHER INDIAN LEGENDS. 132pp. RaH76, 5.95c.**
A collection of legends from the Plains Indians which came to Erdoes directly out of the oral tradition. They are beautifully retold and the original magic can still be sensed. Geared toward young readers and illustrated throughout.

ERDOES, RICHARD. **THE SUN DANCE PEOPLE—THE PLAINS INDIANS, THEIR PAST AND PRESENT. Index, 6¾"x9¼", 218pp. RaH72, 5.95c.**
An informative, informal account of the life and traditions of the Plains Indians accompanied by over 100 photographs and drawings.

FARB, PETER. **MAN'S RISE TO CIVILIZATION: THE CULTURAL ASCENT OF THE INDIANS OF NORTH AMERICA. Illustrations, notes, bibliography, index, 336pp. Dut78, 15.00c.**
When first published in 1968 this volume was one of the most widely discussed books of the year and was largely responsible for the subsequent rebirth of popular interest in the cultures of the North American Indians. Since then many new interpretations of native American culture have been offered. Instead of merely updating the volume, Farb has taken the opportunity to revise almost every paragraph. This remains one of the most complete studies of native American prehistory, culture, language, and religion.

FEDER, NORMAN. **AMERICAN INDIAN ART. Bibliography, 13"x 12", 446pp. Abr66, 35.00c.**
This is by far the finest book on native American Indian art we have ever seen. All of the major Indian nations are considered and the text, while concise, fully explores the profundity of their artistic achievement. 302 illustrations, including sixty handtipped color plates, are included.

GORSLINE, MARIE and DOUGLAS. **NORTH AMERICAN INDIANS. .95p.**
See the Children's Books section.

GRINNELL, GEORGE BIRD. **BLACKFOOT LODGE TALES. Introduction, index, 327pp. UNP62, 3.50p.**
A collection of authentic Blackfoot stories, recorded from original sources by Grinnell in the late nineteenth century. The anthology is divided into *Stories of Adventure, Stories of Ancient Times, Stories of Old Man,* and *The Story of the Three Tribes.*

HAMILTON, CHARLES, ed. **CRY OF THE THUNDERBIRD. Notes, bibliography, index, 301pp. UOk72, 4.95p.**
This collection of more than 100 tales by fifty American Indian writers provides an authentic, intimate portrait of the Indian and his vanished way of life. Black Elk describes a Sioux courtship; Chief Plenty Coups reports on the medicine man who cured a dying Crow warrior; Long Lance recalls the rites of the Sun Dance; Geronimo talks of selling his autograph at the World's Fair; and some battles are reviewed. Many color paintings by George Catlin are included.

HEALING SONGS OF THE AMERICAN INDIANS (A RECORD-ING). 8.95p.
This 33 1/3 rpm record was produced from original recordings made in the early 1900s. Very extensive descriptive notes.

HIGHWATER, JAMAKE. **ANPAO, AN AMERICAN INDIAN ODYS-SEY. Illustrations, notes, bibliography, 256pp. Lip77, 8.95c.**
Highwater has woven together a collection of traditional native American tales out of the oral tradition into one story that relates the adventures of a boy growing into manhood. He has done a wonderful job with his material. A Newberry Honor Book.

HIGHWATER, JAMAKE. **MANY SMOKES, MANY MOONS: A CHRONOLOGY OF AMERICAN INDIAN HISTORY THROUGH INDIAN ART. Bibliography, index, 8¼"x10¼", 128pp. Lip78, 8.95c.**
Highwater uses the art and artifacts of various Indian cultures to illustrate events affecting their history from earliest times through 1973. The text is simple and brief, geared to young readers.

HIGHWATER, JAMAKE. **RITUAL OF THE WIND: NORTH AMERI-CAN INDIAN CEREMONIES, MUSIC, AND DANCES. Bibliography, index, 8¾"x11¼", 192pp. Vik77, 18.95c.**
This is a revealing, moving portrait of the sacredness that surrounds American Indian rituals and their relationship to the entire fabric of Indian life. Highwater is of Blackfoot and Cherokee parentage, so he writes as an insider, not as one apart. He says that he has *made no effort to create an exhaustive catalogue of all Indian rituals and dances, but rather I have tried by the elaborate examples of several specific ceremonies of various tribes to provide an exciting experience fairly free of analysis....My sharpest focus is on the way in which the ceremonies and dances perfectly reflect the otherwise obscure principles of Indian sensibility.* The volume is profusely illustrated with rare old photographs and drawings by Asa Battles.

HIGHWATER, JAMAKE. **SONG FROM THE EARTH: AMERICAN INDIAN PAINTING. Chronology, bibliography, index, 8¾"x11¼", 221pp. NYG76, 19.95c.**
In the opening chapters Highwater describes the Indian world view and its *otherness* from that of white people. A look at pre-1900 art forms—rock pictographs, *kiva* murals, rawhide painting, and sand painting—prepares the reader for the book's main theme, twentieth century painting. Highwater covers the main artists and their creations in a fair amount of depth and illustrates his discussion with 162 plates, thirty-two in color.

HUNGRY WOLF, ADOLF. **THE GOOD MEDICINE BOOK. 473pp. War73, 2.50p.**
A compilation of all eight of Hungry Wolf's **Good Medicine Books,** chronicling the legends, lore, and spirituality of the American Indians. Drawn from song fragments and stories, the ways of the *ancient ones* are described. The narrative includes portraits of tribal life and sacred ritual, instructions and patterns for making tipis, moccasins, bead-work, and ceremonial dress. The author also reviews the Indians' cosmology. Many illustrations accompany the text.

KATZ, JANE, ed. **I AM THE FIRE OF TIME: THE VOICES OF NATIVE AMERICAN WOMEN. Photographs, introduction, 220pp. Dut77, 6.95p.**
A collection of writings by native American women, containing ninety examples of their songs, poetry, prose, prayer, narrative, and oral history—describing their everyday environment, the Earth's past beauty and harmony, marriages and children, their roots, and tribal history.

KROEBER, A.L. **YUROK MYTHS. Bibliography, index, 7"x9½", 528pp. UCa76, 18.50c.**
Between 1901 and 1907 Alfred Kroeber, then a young professor, made numerous trips into the country of the Yurok Indians, along the far northern California coast and inland. He collected both material artifacts and Yurok myths. From thirty informants Kroeber obtained over 150 myths and variants and, over the years, worked at editing and annotating them. This is a complete collection, published post-humously. Following Kroeber's plan, the myths told by each Yurok informant are grouped together. Each group is preceded by Kroeber's biographical and psychological study of the informant, and accompanied by explanatory notes.

The Navajo record of Kit Carson's 1863-64 campaign.

KROEBER, THEODORA. **ISHI IN TWO WORLDS. Many photo-graphs, bibliography, 261pp. UCa61, 3.95p.**
A beautifully written biography of Ishi, the last wild Indian in the U.S. Ishi was discovered in 1911, and for the next five years he lived in a museum in California. Visitors watched him chip arrowheads, shape bows, and make fire using age old techniques—until he died. Ms. Kroeber's husband had been Ishi's trusted friend and he helped her to assemble this book. The book begins with the story of a tribe that survived almost unchanged to the time of the California Gold Rush; the author follows with a summary of the tribe's decay and destruction. The second half of the book belongs to Ishi. In sympathetic language, Ms. Kroeber describes Ishi's adjustment to his museum-prison in San Francisco and, as much as possible, illumines Ishi's reactions to modern civilization.

LA BARRE, WESTON. **THE PEYOTE CULT. Illustrations, notes, bibliography, index, 313pp. ScB75, 4.95p.**
A new edition of La Barre's classic study of Mexican and American Indian ritual use of the peyote cactus. La Barre strongly supports what he considers the legitimate use of natural peyote and he discusses the ways peyote has been used both traditionally and in recent times. A number of technical papers are included.

LA FARGE, OLIVER. **LAUGHING BOY. 192pp. NAL29, 1.50p.**
A moving fictional portrayal of a young Navajo and his mate in the early years of the twentieth century. The author reveals their thoughts and feelings and penetrates to the core of the Indian psyche and lifestyle. This Pulitzer Prize winner is often considered the greatest novel ever written about an American Indian.

■ *LAME DEER, JOHN and RICHARD ERDOES.* **LAME DEER—SEEK-ER OF VISIONS. Illustrations, glossary, 288pp. S&S72, 3.95p.**
Lame Deer is a Sioux medicine man who upholds the old religion and ancient ways of his people. This is the story of his life today, his visions, and his problems living in the contemporary world. The reader can get a good idea of what it means to be an Indian from this account.

LAUBIN, REGINALD and GLADYS. **THE INDIAN TIPI: ITS HISTORY, CONSTRUCTION, AND USES. Bibliography, index, 368pp. UOk77, 12.50c.**
When the first edition of this book was published in 1957, the art of making a tipi was almost lost, even among American Indians. Since that time a tremendous resurgence of interest in the Indian way of life has occurred. In this new edition the Laubins have retained all the invaluable aspects of the first edition, and added a tremendous amount of new material on day to day living in the tipi. Over a hundred line drawings and photographs as well as twenty-two color plates amplify the text. We recommend this book to all who are interested in the Indian way of life.

LECHAPELLE, DOLORES and JANET BOURQUE. **EARTH FESTIVALS: SEASONAL CELEBRATIONS FOR EVERYONE YOUNG AND OLD. Notes, bibliography, 8½"x11", 196pp. FHA74, 11.00p.**
This is a beautifully illustrated exploration of traditional ways that the American Indians have celebrated the seasons. The approach is spiritual and the emphasis is on finding ways to unite our energies with those of the Earth as it goes through its natural cycles. The book contains hundreds of exercises along with a scattering of philosophy and many quotations from the sacred literature of the American

Indians and other religious traditions, including the Tibetan. A number of full color mandalas are included.

LOPEZ, BARRY. **GIVING BIRTH TO THUNDER, SLEEPING WITH HIS DAUGHTER: COYOTE BUILDS NORTH AMERICA.** 201pp. SAM77, 8.95c.
This is not a scholarly book; but then, Old Man Coyote is not a scholarly character. He has consistently evaded academic capture and definition and has tricked nearly every commentator into at least one outrageous and laughable generalization. He is blamed and praised by a wide variety of native tribes for originating death, mixing up the stars, fornicating with birds, bringing fire, losing his eyes, freeing the buffalo. . . . The stories are retold in a way that is both faithful to native concepts of Coyote and how his stories should go, and phrased for an audience which reads without listening, for whom literature is studied and reflected upon, for whom Coyote is an imaginary but interesting protagonist.—from the introduction.

MCDERMOTT, GERALD. **ARROW TO THE SUN.** 1.95p.
See the Children's Books section.

■ *MCLUHAN, T.C., ed.* **TOUCH THE EARTH: A SELF-PORTRAIT OF INDIAN EXISTENCE.** Notes, bibliography, 7"x8¼", 185pp. S&S71/SBL, 4.95p.
This is a moving compilation of statements and writings by North American Indians, chosen to illuminate the course of Indian history and the abiding values of Indian life. The selections are accompanied by a beautiful series of photographs taken by Edward Curtis in the early years of this century. We highly recommend this book to all who seek a better understanding of the American Indians and their way of life.

MCNICKLE, D'ARCY. **THEY CAME HERE FIRST: THE EPIC OF THE AMERICAN INDIAN.** Notes, 320pp. H&R75, 2.95p.
In researching the material for this book McNickle realized that, in order to understand the contemporary native American peoples, he had to start way back and answer a number of questions. Where did they come from? When? How? What was it like when they first came to this land? Where did they make their homes? In this volume he compresses answers to these questions and many more, tracing the whole story of the American Indians' 25,000 years of life on this continent. This is a readable account which contains quite a bit of information on the nineteenth and twentieth centuries.

MALLERY, GARRICK. **PICTURE-WRITING OF THE AMERICAN INDIANS.** 846pp. Dov1889, 6.00p/each.
An important early report, based mainly on contemporary examples gathered by ethnologists and explorers. The emphasis is on the meaning of the pictures and the differences between the picture writing styles of the various tribes. This two volume set includes 1,290 pictures and fifty-four plates, all fully discussed.

MARRIOTT, ALICE and CAROL RACHLIN. **AMERICAN EPIC: THE STORY OF THE AMERICAN INDIAN.** Photographs, bibliography, index, 217pp. NAL69, 1.50p.
In **American Epic**, two eminent anthropologists, with over forty-five years of combined research and fieldwork between them, have written an unparalleled account of the different tribes, their varied responses to the alien invasion, the fates they suffered, and the conditions they face today.

MARRIOTT, ALICE and CAROL RACHLIN. **AMERICAN INDIAN MYTHOLOGY.** Bibliography, 252pp. NAL68/NEL, 1.75p.
A representative collection selected from the literature of more than twenty major North American tribes. The authors have done a remarkable job of writing down these myths and tales from the oral tradition.

MARRIOTT, ALICE and CAROL RACHLIN. **PEYOTE.** Bibliography, index, 128pp. NAL71, 1.50p.
An exploration of the sacramental use of peyote and an analysis of the peyote religion which is widely diffused among North American Indian tribes. The authors, anthropologists who have participated in peyote ceremonies, describe the effects of the drug, the rituals that surround its use, and the symbolic significance of the objects used in the rite. They also examine peyote's relationship to other facets of Indian culture.

MARRIOTT, ALICE and CAROL RACHLIN. **PLAINS INDIAN MYTHOLOGY.** Bibliography, 197pp. NAL75, 1.75p.
A fine retelling of both the great myths (stories of creation and of the gods) and the minor ones (tales which teach manners, behavior, and ethics, and explain common phenomena). The book includes stories from the eighteenth century to the present.

MAY, KARL. **WINNETOU.** 763pp. Sea77, 13.95c.
Karl May's most popular novel is the story of a young Apache chief, as told by his white friend and blood brother. The action takes place about one hundred years ago in the American southwest, where the Indian way of life is threatened by the construction of the first transcontinental railroad. Winnetou, the only Indian chief who could have united the various quarreling tribes and reached an equitable settlement with the whites, is murdered by thugs. His tragic death foreshadows the death of his people. May has written a romantic elegy on the destruction of beauty and bravery, a protest against the seemingly inevitable brutality of modern civilization. All the characters represent archetypal figures engaged in eternal struggles for human dignity, love, and peace.

MOMADAY, N. SCOTT. **HOUSE MADE OF DAWN.** 191pp. H&R68/Pen, 1.95p.
A moving novel about a young Indian torn between the world of his ancestral fathers and the harsh realities of the twentieth century. Momaday is a Kiowa Indian who spent his childhood on Indian reservations in the southwest.

MOMADAY, N. SCOTT. **THE NAMES.** Illustrations, glossary, 170pp. H&R76, 4.95p.
In this memoir Momaday writes eloquently of what it means to grow up with a strong spiritual relationship with the American wilderness. Each of the names in this book—of animals, plants, places, and those that Indians give to each other—has a special ritual significance. Momaday's own name was given him by an old storyteller who believed that a man's life proceeds from his name, in the way that a river proceeds from its source.

MOMADAY, N. SCOTT. **THE WAY TO RAINY MOUNTAIN.** 88pp. UNM69, 2.95p.
Momaday retells some of the Kiowa myths that he learned from his grandmother, speculates on the actual history they may symbolize, and describes the Indian way of life he knew as a child. He writes with great dignity and conveys the essence of these time shrouded myths.

MOON, SHEILA. **A MAGIC DWELLS.** Notes, index, 208pp. WUP70/HPG, 4.40p.
A poetic, psychological study of the Navajo emergence myth centering on the relevance of that myth to the psychological and spiritual growth of the individual.

MOREY, SYLVESTER and OLIVIA GILLIAM, eds. **RESPECT FOR LIFE: THE TRADITIONAL UPBRINGING OF AMERICAN INDIAN CHILDREN.** 224pp. WaI74, 3.50p.
A report of a conference on the title theme; present were Indians from the Navajo, Mohawk, Crow, Kiowa, Pueblo, and Arapaho tribes. Though the discussions focus on the rearing of children from birth to adolescence, they include crucial observations on the Indian's dilemma in today's society.

NAYLOR, MARIA, ed. **AUTHENTIC INDIAN DESIGNS.** 6.00p.
See the Sacred Art section.

■ *NEIHARDT, JOHN.* **BLACK ELK SPEAKS.** 238pp. S&S32/SBL, 2.50p.
My friend, I am going to tell you the story of my life. . . . It is the story of all life that is holy and is good to tell, and us two-leggeds sharing in it with the four-leggeds and the wings of the air and all green things; for these are children of one mother and their father is one spirit. This, then, is not the tale of a great hunter or of a great warrior, or of a great traveler. . .it was the story of a mighty vision given to a man too weak to use it; of a holy tree that should have flourished in a people's heart with flowers and singing birds, and now is withered; and of a people's dream that died in the bloody snow. This is universally considered one of the greatest of all books about the life of an American Indian. This edition includes a series of watercolors of Black Elk's visions.

NEIHARDT, JOHN. **WHEN THE TREE FLOWERED. 208pp. S&S51, 1.50p.**
This is a moving account of the life and visions of a warrior and medicine man of the Oglala Sioux, told in the form of a fictional autobiography. The book is based on the tales that the author heard about a vanished way of life when the white men were few and Sioux roamed freely on the vast prairies of the American west.

NEWCOMB, FRANC and GLADYS REICHARD. **SANDPAINTING OF THE NAVAJO SHOOTING CHANT. 9¼"x12", 132pp. Dov37, 6.00p.**
A full color reproduction of the sandpaintings—one of the most important Navajo healing ceremonies—together with a thorough description and explanation of the rites. The Navajo were not allowed to put the paintings down in permanent form, so Mrs. Newcomb learned to memorize them as they were made, then produced exact copies once the ceremony was over. Her drawings capture not only the prescribed details but also the style and form of the originals. The accompanying text by Ms. Reichard describes the role of chant and chanter in Navajo culture, the details of the ceremony, and the many symbolic elements that go into the paintings.

PARSONS, ELSE CREWS, ed. **AMERICAN INDIAN LIFE. Notes, 419pp. UNP22, 4.50p.**
An anthology of twenty-seven tales of Indian life from eight different tribal groups. In the introduction, A.L. Kroeber says, *The fictional form of a presentation... has a definite merit. It allows a freedom in depicting or suggesting the thoughts and feelings of the Indian, such as is impossible in a formal, scientific report.... At the same time customs depicted are never invented. Each author has adhered strictly to the social facts as he knew them. He has merely selected those that seemed most characteristic, and woven them into a plot around an imaginary Indian hero or heroine.*

RADIN, PAUL. **THE ROAD OF LIFE AND DEATH. Notes, 359pp. PUP45, 18.15c.**
A translation of a stirring ritual drama of the Winnebago Indians. One of the participants told the drama directly to Radin and he has translated it as literally as possible. In a long prologue, Radin discusses the medicine rite and the mythology of the Winnebagos.

RADIN, PAUL. **THE TRICKSTER: A STUDY IN AMERICAN INDIAN MYTHOLOGY. 236pp. ScB56, 3.45p.**
The myth of the trickster—ambiguous creator and destroyer, cheater and cheated, subhuman and superhuman—is one of the earliest and most universal expressions of mankind. Nowhere does it survive in more starkly archaic form than in the episodes of the Winnebago Trickster Cycle, recorded here in full. Anthropological and psychological analyses by Radin, Carl Kerenyi, and Carl Jung reveal the trickster as filling a twofold role: on the one hand he is *an archetypal psychic structure* that harks back to *an absolutely undifferentiated human consciousness, corresponding to a psyche that has hardly left the animal level;* and on the other, his myth is a contemporary outlet for the most unabashed and liberating satire on the onerous obligations of social order, religion, and ritual.

RADIN, PAUL. **THE WINNEBAGO TRIBE. Ninety-six plates and drawings, index, 527pp. UNP23, 8.50p.**
The information included in this volume was obtained during the years 1908-13 while employed by the Bureau of American Ethnology and on private expeditions.... It has been the aim of the author to separate as definitely as possible his own comments from the actual data obtained, and for that reason every chapter, with the exception of those on history, archaeology, and material culture, is divided into two parts, a discussion of the data and the data itself.... [The book] does not claim to be a comparative study, but simply as intensive an investigation as the time spent allowed, of an unusually interesting tribe.... Throughout the work, the Indian has been allowed to tell the facts his own way.—from the preface by Radin.

REICHARD, GLADYS. **NAVAJO MEDICINE MAN SANDPAINTINGS. 9¼"x12", 118pp. Dov39, 6.95p.**
This book reproduces sandpaintings of the Navajo bead chant and shooting chant, two of the most important Navajo rites, together with a thorough description and explanation of the rites and the legends associated with them. The shooting chant is one of the most important healing ceremonies, and perhaps the richest in sandpaintings of all Navajo chants. The bead chant is typical of the *evil chasing* phase contained in most chants. The paintings reproduced here were done by a Navajo medicine man, who also narrated the legends and explained

their meaning and symbolism. Ms. Reichard lived and studied with this medicine man. Fifty-nine plates, including twenty-five in color, accompany the text. A detailed explanatory key on the page facing each color illustration discusses the religious symbolism and characters of the painting.

REICHARD, GLADYS. **NAVAHO RELIGION. Illustrations, notes, bibliography, index, 852pp. PUP63, 7.95p.**
In writing Navaho Religion, *Gladys Reichard undertook a stupendous task, at which she was eminently successful. She set out to expound all the manifold elements...that make up a complex and apparently disorderly ceremonial system, to classify and explain the symbolism, and, in her "Concordances," to reduce most of the diverse elements at least tentatively to order....An able writer, aesthetically sensitive, she has the quality that enables some students to penetrate to the full values and beauties of an alien belief and ceremonial, as many anthropologists never do, and to communicate her findings.*—Oliver La Farge.

ROCKWOOD, JOYCE. **TO SPOIL THE SUN. 180pp. HRW76, 6.95c.**
A portrayal of traditional Cherokee Indian life as seen through the eyes of Rain Dove, a young squaw. The story opens when Rain Dove is eleven years old and spans two generations, taking her through two marriages—one of which was to the most spiritually powerful man in the village—and motherhood. The story evokes the now vanished lifestyle and culture of the Cherokees and traces the beginning of the dissolution of the traditional society.

ROSEN, KENNETH, ed. **THE MAN TO SEND RAIN CLOUDS: CONTEMPORARY STORIES BY AMERICAN INDIANS. Illustrations, 192pp. RaH74, 2.95p.**
A collection of nineteen stories that reflect the preoccupations of young native Americans today. From the title story by Leslie Silko, which is a beautiful understated celebration of the death of her beloved Indian grandfather, to *Kaiser and the War*, in which an Indian brave goes to jail rather than serve in the U.S. army, the stories all convey the conflict between the Indian heritage and his inferior status in American society.

ROTHENBERG, JEROME, ed. **SHAKING THE PUMPKIN: TRADITIONAL POETRY OF THE AMERICAN INDIANS. 502pp. Dou72, 4.95p.**
A wonderful, diverse collection of traditional native American poetry. The majority of the translations and renderings have been done especially for this volume and Rothenberg includes commentaries on each one.

SANDOZ, MARIA. **CRAZY HORSE: A BIOGRAPHY OF THE STRANGE MAN OF THE OGLAS. Notes, bibliography, 438pp. UNP42, 3.50p.**
And now my book of Crazy Horse is done. In it I have tried to tell not only the story of the man but something of the life of his people.... To that end I have used the simplest words possible, hoping by idiom and figures and the underlying rhythm pattern to say some of the things of the Indian for which there are no white-man words, suggest something of his innate nature, something of his relationship to the earth and the sky and all that is between. I hope I have not failed too miserably, for they were a great people, these old buffalo-hunting Sioux, and some day their greatness will reach full flowering again in their children as they walk the hard new road of the white man.

SILVERBERG, ROBERT. **THE MOUND BUILDERS. Photographs and line drawings, bibliography, index, 184pp. RaH70, 1.50p.**
Large mounds appear in the area between the southeast and Ohio and the Mississippi Valley, which the American Indians claim predate their culture considerably. No one knows who built the mounds or what their function was. This is a very full exploration of all that is known about the mounds and the research that has been undertaken.

SIMMONS, LEO, ed. **SUN CHIEF. Introduction, index, 480pp. YUP42, 4.95p.**
This is a fascinating autobiography of a twentieth century Indian. Sun Chief was born and reared, until he was ten, as a Hopi Indian. Between the ages of ten and twenty he left the reservation and became immersed in the American way of life. Then he returned to Hopiland and entered into all the rituals of tribal adulthood. Simmons, a white man who was adopted as a clan brother, edited Sun Chief's life story. This is a revealing document which helps the reader see into another world.

SONGS OF THE EARTH, WATER, FIRE, AND SKY: MUSIC OF THE AMERICAN INDIAN, VOLUME I (A RECORDING). 8.60.
A well produced 33 1/3 rpm record containing an excellent selection of music from the following tribes: San Juan Pueblo, Seneca, Northern Arapaho, Northern Plains, Creek, Yurok, Navajo, Cherokee, and Southern Plains. All of the pieces were recorded on location and each is discussed at length in the liner notes.

SPENCE, LEWIS. **MYTHS AND LEGENDS OF THE NORTH AMERICAN INDIANS. Index, 397pp. Mul75, 5.50p.**
This is a recent reprint of an early twentieth century text that is generally considered one of the finest collections of North American Indian mythology ever published. All the important traditions are included and the selections read well.

SPIER, LESLIE. **YUMAN TRIBES OF THE GILA RIVER. Illustrations, notes, index, 451pp. Dov33, 6.00p.**
This work is generally regarded as the best study of a major culture area of the Indians of the U.S. The Yuma are a southwestern tribal group. This is a complete ethnographic account of the Yuma material and social culture and history. A section of folktales is also included.

STEIGER, BRAD. **MEDICINE POWER. 237pp. Dou74, 2.95p.**
A survey of the American Indian's religious heritage, which draws on firsthand research—including extensive interviews with medicine people from many tribes. Steiger explores what past and present Indian mystics and prophets say about man's future. He also demonstrates how American Indian mystical thought has had a strong influence on today's young people. As usual, Steiger writes in a simple, often glib fashion and includes many photographs and quotations.

STEIGER, BRAD. **MEDICINE TALK. 213pp. Dou75, 2.95p.**
Brad Steiger believes that the spirituality of the American Indian medicine man offers the single most effective kind of mystical experience for our hemisphere. It provides a means of transcending an automated and impersonal society through the spiritual heritage bequeathed to this continent by its native people. This volume includes the direct accounts of several medicine men. Twylah Nitsch, a Seneca, shares the account of the seven worlds and the meditative techniques called the *pathway of peace.* Dallas Chief Eagle, chief of the Teton Sioux and a descendent of the spiritual warrior Crazy Horse, translates the legend of the White Buffalo and defines *Indianism.* Sun Bear, a Chippewa medicine man, explains how to survive off the land and prepare for the coming *great purification.* This is an illuminated account which explores the ancient techniques and gives practical instructions for living in today's world.

■ *STORM, HYEMEYOHSTS.* **SEVEN ARROWS. 9½"x8¼", 374pp. RaH72, 15.95c/8.95p.**
This is the first book about the ancient ways of the Plains Indians to be written entirely by an Indian. It is a moving novel about their proud but doomed struggle against the white tide and its *manifest destiny.* We learn about the symbolic meaning of the people's names and shields, of the medicines of the *Four Great Directions* and the *Vision Quest,* and about the brotherhood of all Earth's creatures and the *Great Balancing Harmony of the Total Universe.* Many old photographs and a series of beautiful full color mandalas accompany the narrative.

SUN BEAR, et al. **THE BEAR TRIBE'S SELF RELIANCE BOOK. Illustrations, 143pp. BTP77, 3.50p.**
The Bear Tribe describes itself as *a group of people striving to re-learn the proper relationship with Mother Earth, the Great Spirit, and all our relations in the mineral, plant, animal and human kingdoms. The Bear Tribe is based on the medicine visions of Sun Bear, a Chippewa medicine man. We are a tribe of teachers responsible for sharing with others those lessons of harmony that we have successfully learned.*

SUN BEAR. **BUFFALO HEARTS. Photographs, 124pp. Nat70, 3.50p.**
A short treatise on the beliefs of the American Indians, accompanied by biographies of some of the great Indian chiefs.

TAMARIN, ALFRED and SHIRLEY GLUBOK. **ANCIENT INDIANS OF THE SOUTHWEST. Index, 96pp. Dou75, 5.95c.**
A pictorial essay on the lives of the Anasazi, Mogollon, Hohokam, and Patayan Indians of the southwest—the ancient people who lived on the mesa tops and in cliff dwellings, irrigated the desert, and made it bloom. These native peoples created one of the richest of all Indian

civilizations, one which is still reflected in the lives of descendent tribes.

■ *TEDLOCK, DENNIS and BARBARA, eds.* **TEACHINGS FROM THE AMERICAN EARTH: INDIAN RELIGION AND PHILOSOPHY. Introduction, notes, index, 304pp. Nor75, 5.45p.**
An extremely useful, well edited book. One thing unites all the authors—they are either Indians who have tried to make themselves heard, or white men who have tried to hear Indians and were changed by this experience. The selections illuminate the variety of the American Indian religious experience and philosophical beliefs, largely from the native American point of view. The editors are young anthropologists specializing in the religion of the North American Indian.

THOMPSON, STITH, ed. **TALES OF THE NORTH AMERICAN INDIANS. Introduction, bibliography, 411pp. IUP29, 3.95p.**
This is a good collection of tales from all parts of North America, grouped into the following general categories: mythological tales which explain the origins of all creation; legends of animal-like tricksters who bring incidental benefit to their people in spite of, or because of, particular vices; and stories of ordinary human beings caught up in marvelous or supernatural occurrences. Thompson was a professor of folklore at Indiana University. Eighty-eight pages of comparative notes are included, along with lists of motifs and sources.

TURNER, FREDERICK W. III, ed. **THE PORTABLE NORTH AMERICAN INDIAN READER. Introduction, bibliography, 639pp. Vik74, 4.95p.**
An anthology of literature of and about the American Indians—myths, tales, poetry, oratory, and autobiographical accounts from the Iroquois, Cherokee, Winnebago, Sioux, and many other tribes. Accounts by white men from Bernal Diaz del Castillo to Parkman and contemporary reassessments by such writers as Luther Standing Bear, N. Scott Momaday, Vine Deloria, Thomas Berger, and Gary Snyder are also included.

UNDERHILL, RUTH. **RED MAN'S RELIGION: BELIEFS AND PRACTICES OF THE INDIANS NORTH OF MEXICO. Illustrations, bibliography, index, 311pp. UCh65, 16.80c.**
A well written, nontechnical survey of all aspects of American Indian religion and culture. Many tribal rites are discussed at length and most of the major tribal groupings are covered. The book is intended to be an introductory survey and Ms. Underhill succeeds in her aim of creating a readable, interesting account.

VOGEL, VIRGIL **AMERICAN INDIAN MEDICINE. Illustrations, index, 578pp. UOk70, 17.50c.**
To American Indians the term medicine embraced much more than the cure of disease and the healing of injuries, but the focus here is on these aspects, and particularly those that we have borrowed.—from the introduction. Vogel is a historian rather than a medical doctor and he presents a comprehensive historical account. Every aspect of the subject is thoroughly discussed and extensive notes and a long bibliography are also included.

WATERS, FRANK. **BOOK OF THE HOPI. Glossary, 446pp. Vik63, 3.95p**
This is unquestionably the best book ever published about history, mythology, and rituals of the Hopi Indians of the American southwest. The thirty-two Hopi elders told their legends, the meaning of their religious rituals and annual ceremonies, and their deeply rooted view of the world to Waters for the first time. Waters himself writes beautifully and the result is a deeply moving book which brings to life a culture now almost completely destroyed. The volume includes many drawings by Oswald White Bear Fredericks, who also helped transcribe the source material. There are also a number of photographs.

■ *WATERS, FRANK.* **MASKED GODS. 477pp. RaH50, 2.45p.**
This is a profound exploration of the history, legends, and ceremonialism of the Navajo and Pueblo Indians of the southwest. Waters himself is deeply immersed in these cultures and he brings his material to life.

WATERS, FRANK. **PUMPKIN SEED POINT: BEING WITHIN THE HOPI. Glossary, 175pp. Swa69, 2.50p.**
Waters lived for three years among the Hopi and was drawn into their mythic, timeless reality. This is a beautifully written personal account of Waters' inner and outer experiences during that time.

WELLOYA, WILLIAM and VINSON BROWN. **WARRIORS OF THE RAINBOW. Illustrations, including full color foldouts, index, 96pp. Nat62, 3.50p.**
A collection of prophetic visions, gathered mainly from the American Indians. Each of the visions and dreams is retold in simple language and then commented upon by the authors—one of whom is an Eskimo and the other a man who has devoted his life to studying and interacting with many native tribes.

WELTFISH, GENE. **THE LOST UNIVERSE: PAWNEE LIFE AND CULTURE. Notes, bibliography, index, 526pp. UNP65, 6.95p.**
Dr. Weltfish guides us through a typical Pawnee year. In the process, we learn of the spectacular, the philosophical, and the mundane aspects of Pawnee life. She describes (sometimes using the words of the Pawnee themselves) the planting of corn in the early spring, the mass migration to the buffalo hunting grounds in mid-summer, the harvest after their return from the hunt, the great autumn ceremonials, and the winter hunting expedition. We learn of their world view and the complex cosmic religion of the Pawnee. . . . The Lost Universe is an important book in which scholarship is fused with the literary; and the literary is fused with current problems; and current problems are fused with the permanent problems of our age.—Charles Wagley, Professor of Anthropology, Columbia University.

WHERRY, JOSEPH. **INDIAN MASKS AND MYTHS OF THE WEST. Bibliography, index, 287pp. Cro69, 3.50p.**
The American Indian tribes evolved a remarkable body of mythology to account for creation as well as many daily events. The masks illustrated and explored here were used in a variety of ceremonies and dramas to bring cosmological concepts to life. In addition to discussing the masks and ceremonies, Wherry retells many of the myths.

WITHERSPOON, GARY. **LANGUAGE AND ART IN THE NAVAJO UNIVERSE. Illustrations, including eight color plates, notes, bibliography, index, 233pp. UMP77, 10.70p.**
This is a sensitive, perceptive work which combines excellent scholarship with a true understanding of and appreciation for the nature of Navajo thought. Professor Witherspoon lived and worked with the Navajos; here he offers far more than mere theory. He divides his material into the following general chapters: *Creating the World through Language, Controlling the World through Language, Classifying the World through Language,* and *Beautifying the World through Art.*

WITT, SHIRLEY and STAN STEINER, eds. **THE WAY: AN ANTHOLOGY OF AMERICAN INDIAN LITERATURE. Introduction, 290pp. RaH72, 2.45p.**
The first comprehensive anthology on Indians, this book is like no other. Steiner and Witt have accomplished a major work of compilation of original source documents. It includes material not previously published, with many talented Indian writers and poets making their first appearance on the literary scene. You will be seeing some of these names in the future, as the field of Indian literature develops.—Vine Deloria, Jr.

WOOD, NANCY. **THE MAN WHO GAVE THUNDER TO THE EARTH. 165pp. Dou76, 6.95c.**
In the land of the Taos Pueblo Indians. . . a vast, old religion which once swayed the earth lingers in unbroken practice. In the oldest religion, everything was alive, not supernaturally but naturally alive. There were only deeper and deeper streams of life. . . . So rocks were alive, but a mountain had a deeper, vaster life than a rock. . . . The whole life-effort of man was to get his life into direct contact with the elemental life of the cosmos.—D.H. Lawrence, who lived in New Mexico nearly half a century ago. This narrative presents the Taos way of seeing and understanding and discusses the nature of the cosmos and how man fits into its scheme. Ms. Wood lived among the Indians and shared their lifestyle.

WOOD, NANCY. **MANY WINTERS. 78pp. Dou74, 6.95c.**
A sensitive collection of poems and prose writings which interpret the Pueblo Indian way of life, accompanied by drawings and paintings by Frank Howell.

ANCIENT AMERICAS

When the news of Cortes' exploits in Mexico suddenly burst upon the world in 1519, man in Europe had almost forgotten the very existence of an America. This was understandable. During the years that has passed since its discovery America had provided only false hopes. It had been expected that new foodstuffs would pour out unrestrainedly from the *spiceries* to relieve the monotony of European diet. Broadsides affixed to walls had proclaimed the discovery and books had told of *Joyful Newes out of the Newe Founde Worlde, of rare and singular vertues of divers Herbes, of Trees and Plantes of Oyles and stones.* . . . Even the discoverer of it all, Cristobal Colon, now Admiral of the Ocean Sea, had fed the illusions by talking without stint of gold, rubies, and silver, which were to be found there more abundantly than in King Solomon's mines.

In anticipation of such riches, a convention between Spain and Portugal early in the discovery had, with the Pope's blessing, divided the Americas; the New World was to be shared between them in exclusivity. The King of France, witty Francois I, asked to see . . . *that clause in Adam's will which allowed the kings of Castille and Portugal to divide the earth between them.* . . . But his irony availed him nothing and these two kingdoms soon settled themselves into the New World. Europe had waited with a certain breathlessness, one gathers from reading the contemporary accounts, and people expected the floodgates of plenty to open up. But, at best, the opening was a timorous settling; the Portuguese merely touched Brazil, and the Spanish confined themselves for the first twenty years to a small piece of the Isthmus of Panama and to the islands of the Antilles. Here was found nothing of the riches so highly vaunted by the original discoverers. Europeans dismissed *America* as yet one more instance of Spanish braggadocio—until there arrived in Seville, on December 9, 1519, the first treasure ship from Mexico.

Its arrival caused a tremendous sensation. Cortes had sent four fantastically attired Totonacs from the Mexican coasts to accompany the treasures, and in the golden cache there were bells and jewels, earrings and nose ornaments of exquisite workmanship, and feather ornaments mounted in jewels, and there were even *books such as the Indians use.* But that which stirred most was a golden wheel *seventy-nine inches in diameter; of a thickness of four reales,* an Aztec calendar swarming with strange designs hammered out in *repousse.* From the documents now extant one can still feel the contagious excitement of those who saw these treasures for the first time.

They so impressed Charles V that he took them to Ghent. Albrecht Durer saw them in Brussels and wrote in his diary . . . *I have never seen anything heretofore that has so rejoiced my heart. I have seen the things which were brought to the King from the new golden land . . . a sun entirely of gold a whole fathom broad; likewise a moon entirely of silver, equally large . . . also two chambers full of all sorts of weapons, armour, and other wondrous arms, "all of which is fairer to see than marvels". . . these things are so precious that they are valued at 100,000 gulden. I saw among them amazing artistic objects that I have been astonished at the subtle "ingenia" of these people in these distant lands. Indeed cannot say enough about the things which were before me.*

The Italian humanist Pietro Martire d'Anghiera himself could not say enought about *the two books such as the Indians use.* He remained *wrapped in astonishment* for to him the *books* were a greater index to the quality of this new civilization than the gold. *The Indians of the golden land write in books,* he said in his letters to other humanists as he analyzed the technique of the book and the hieroglyphics . . . *which almost resemble those of the Egyptians . . . among the figures of men and animals are those of kings and great lords . . . so it may be presumed that they made report of each one's deeds.*

Unfortunately, while the learned debated the Aztec civilization, speculating as to its origin, it was already being overwhelmed and destroyed. Thousands more of these golden Aztec objects, brought to the king as his royal fifth, were melted down and minted into coin to pay off his immense debts incurred by European wars. As for other Aztec *books,* and exquisitely made golden ornaments, as well as these other objects of Aztec culture, they perished in the Conquest. In the process of being taken, Tenochtitlan, the Aztec capital was utterly destroyed. *One of the most beautiful cities in the world,* wrote Cortes, his eyes brimming with simulated tears as he walked through the stench of the fires and singed flesh. In the end that which survived of Aztec architecture was torn down to build churches and mansions for the victor, and what was not destroyed by man was overwhelmed by the insults of time.

Six years later, in 1527, the Mayas found themselves on the agenda of conquest: Francisco de Montejo, the would-be conqueror, promised much to Charles V, his liege lord, more gold than he had received as his royal fifth from the rape of Mexico. The Maya conquest went off badly. After conquest and pillage, slavery followed. Those chieftains and priests, *in whom all learning reposed,* who were not killed took refuge either in flight or silence. No intellectual in Europe ever saw a Maya *book,* and since there was little or no gold to act as stimulant, the learned of Europe never had any communication about those marvellously contrived stone cities which the Mayas had built. This was not the fault of the participants in conquest nor the priests nor the administrators who followed. They penned voluminous reports; yet they went unpublished.

New Spanish cities were fashioned out of the rubble of Maya ruins; other unruined temples were torn down to supply building material for Spanish churches, mansions, and administrative centres. Ancient Maya Tiho became Merida, the Yucatan capital *on account of the singularity of its buildings,* the size of which, said a Spaniard in 1550, *fills one with amazement.* As mere building material bishop Landa doubted that *it will never come to be entirely exhausted.* It was *exhausted* in two decades. Those Maya structures which survived man's destruction were slowly over-run by jungle verdure until, in time, all of these magnificent cities had vanished.

Peru, the real Kingdom of Gold, appeared on the horizon just as the Maya civilization was in its death throes. On May 16, 1532, Pizarro set out from the coast of Peru with his 130 foot soldiers and 40 mounted cavaliers, following the Inca royal road to seek the capital. In the varied history of man, was this not the most quixotic of journeys—170 men against three million, 170 men dedicated to conquer what was then one of the largest empires on earth? The sequence is known to every schoolboy, how Pizarro seized by stratagem the person of the Inca in the midst of his thirty thousand armed warriors and within one half hour—certainly among the most famous thirty minutes in history—subdued his whole empire.

On January 9, 1534, the galleon *Santa Maria del Campo* wharfed in Seville. Officials there who believed they had seen almost everything to be seen in these last fabulous years could not take in with their eyes the treasures that lay there: gold and silver lay pile on the dock, ingot upon ingot, all stamped with the royal seal. In a separate inventory to the king was a list of objects so beautiful that not even the most hardened conquistador in Peru could commit them to the crucible—thirty-four jars of gold, a golden stalk simulating maize, two golden platters, an idol of man, life-size, over one hundred silver objects, the largest piece weighing 167 pounds. The total was worth twenty million dollars in bullion, and equal to twenty times that amount in terms of modern purchasing power. Never in history had so much bullion arrived at a single moment in Europe. The effect of that treasure ship on the human imagination never quite wore off; even now in Italy when one speaks of something of fantastic value it is a *Peru*.

At this golden moment Charles V still had greater preoccupations. He was undertaking the conquest of Tunis, so that ships, men, and money were of supreme importance. This time he did not even stop to look at the fabulous golden ornaments. He did that which for instinctive aesthetic reasons even the most debased of his subjects had not done; he ordered the whole of the Incas' treasure to be melted down into ingots. Of the long ton of original golden ornaments from the Inca's ransom not a single example exists in Spain today.

With that conquest, the animus, the soul, of the Peruvian was forever lost. The physical remains of that immense civilization, the buildings and temples of varying forms and functions that spread over two thousand miles along the Andes and the coast went the way of the conquest. Those which were not destroyed then were later toppled by the civil wars fought between the conquistadors over the carcass of the Inca Empire. As with the Aztecs and Mayas, so with the Incas—churches were either built out of the rubble or were set over the temples; Inca buildings were torn down to provide the stone to build manorial dwellings, and administration buildings were set up among the ruins. The lands being depopulated, a road system nearly as fine as that of the Roman Empire went into decay. The *tampu* resthouses which had appeared along the entire length and breadth of the network were reclaimed by the earth, and the suspension bridges which had spanned the awesome canyons along the route rotted and fell. The ingenious *acequias*, which had conducted water for irrigation into the desert, were neglected. The land was reclaimed by sand.

It was the Age of Reason that brought about a renaissance of archaeological interest in the Americas. In 1773 the Maya ruins of Palenque lying in the tangled tropical forests of Chiapis, Mexico, were discovered. Its discovery was brought to the personal attention of Charles III of Spain. He ordered his officials to explore the ruins carefully, to make drawings and preserve all the artifacts found so that they could form the basis for an **Ancient History of America**. Italian scholars were sent from Spain to Mexico to seek out ancient documents in order to prepare such a history. In 1777, a Mexican, Antonio Alzate, found the ruins of Xochicalco, and a few years later, in 1790, while excavations were going on to alter the foundations of the Cathedral of Mexico City, the workmen came across a gigantic monolith—the Aztec calendar stone. Carved out of a single piece of volcanic trachyte, it was eighteen feet in diameter with its centre dominated by the figure of Tonatiuh, the sun god, sculpted in large dimensions; ringed about it were symbols of calendric day-signs. In a previous time the archbishop would have ordered it to be smashed and worked into church masonry; now it was brought intact to the museum.

In Mexico those whose vocation was the antique hopefully believed that the Aztec calendar stone might be another Rosetta stone; such a speculation was still current when Alexander von Humboldt arrived in Mexico City on April 18,

1803. Already well known—his letters to scientific associates in Paris had been published in various journals—Humboldt had, since 1799, travelled and explored in South America with his friend, Aime Bonpland, botanist and physician. The Spanish viceroy, Jose de Iturrigaray, himself welcomed Humboldt and let it be known that since Humboldt carried the King of Spain's rubric whatever he wished to see in Mexico was to be placed at his disposal.

Humboldt has been fully and rightfully extolled for his immense contributions to botany, geography, geology, astronomy, geophysics, meteorology, oceanography, and zoology; yet there is more to him. It was he who brought the buried American cultures into focus. His volume on American archaeology was contained in one large folio and published in Paris in 1810 with the title of **Vues des Cordilleres et Monuments des Peuples Indigenes de L'Amerique**. This gave the world for the first time a panorama of ancient American history, displayed as never before in accurate scale drawings of Inca buildings, calendar stones from Colombia, bas-reliefs of Aztec sculptures, coloured engravings of pages of the Maya **Dresden Codex**; and drawings of the Aztec calendar stone with detailed explanations and numerous illustrations of Aztec, Zapotec and Mixtec manuscripts with learned commentaries. Under this immense authority America was seen as a civilization with its art placed on the high levels of culture. That volume went through four editions in eight years.

In 1840, William H. Prescott began to write the **History of the Conquest of Mexico**. Few then believed that the Aztecs had reared the buildings ascribed to them; few accepted the fact that the American Indian had ever been capable of producing the civilization described by the early Spaniards. So Prescott went to the original unpublished records that lay in Spanish archives. With the appearance of his **Conquest of Mexico** in 1843, the evidence he had amassed was so formidable and the style of his writing so impressive that Prescott in that one book succeeded in giving America back to the Indians. At the same time, his friend John Lloyd Stephens, a New York lawyer who had travelled *for his health* through Egypt, Arabia Petraea, Poland, and Russia, was then exploring Central America and helped to provide factual evidence. Frederick Catherwood, an architect, was his companion. Catherwood had taken part in some of the earliest English expeditions to Egypt and, being thoroughly immersed in the art of the Old World, he was prepared to evaluate what had been discovered in the new. His accurate drawings with the dramatic overtones of Piranesi illustrated wonderfully well the text of Stephens; together they authored publications which were then avidly read and which time has made into classics of archaeology; **Incidents of Travel in Central America** (1841) and **Incidents of Travel in Yucatan** (1843).

It was Alfred Maudslay who, in 1880, began the modern phase of American archaeology. His explorations, excavations, and recording of all that was then known of Maya texts (on monuments and buildings) gave scholars throughout the world a firm basis on which to assault the mystery of the Maya hieroglyphs. He was the spiritual successor of Stephens.

After Maudslay's publications, interest in the Aztec, Maya, and Inca civilizations quickened. Archaeologists of many nations were drawn to these lost civilizations, and each in his own way, peculiar to the intellectual background of his native land, made his contribution. More and yet more lost cities were rediscovered; and the problems which each new discovery posed grew in number and profundity as the literature mounted.

What, after all, is this search for ancient man in the Americas? It is basically a tremendous and fascinating mystery. With the absence of written records such as occur in the Old

World what do we have to go on? We have a profusion of strange-sounding names—Toltec, Mixtec, Chibcha, Cuqisnique. We have a scale—the vastness of the American milieu. We have an enigmatic plot. Who was this mysterious Plumed Serpent god that permeates the whole of Mexico? Why did the Mayas suddenly abandon hundreds of their cities? Why were the Incas and the Mayas unaware of each other's existence? We have sets of clues from which deductions can be made, clues which might well puzzle a Sherlock Holmes. And there is continued novelty: the finding of tombs, such as that of a warrior god in a beautifully wrought underground sanctuary at Palenque, where a tomb was not supposed to be; or the finding of barbarically beautiful murals, such as those at Bonampak in the jungle, unseen by any other human eyes since their abandonment a millennium before. More than a mystery, the quest is also a dream...a dream of every archaeologist that someday in the hushed sanctity of the forest he will find a place, a city, a ruin which no other explorer has ever seen. This is a fundamental human instinct, for life exists for the sake of newness. So archaeology is endowed with suspense; it combines the excitement of treasure hunting with romance. Potsherds and mummies, liths and skeletons are all clues on the road of cultural history.

—condensed from **The Ancient Sun Kingdoms of the Americas**, by Victor Wolfgang von Hagen

ADAMS, RICHARD E.W., ed. **THE ORIGINS OF MAYA CIVILIZATION. Notes, bibliography, index, 481pp. UNM77, 10.10p.**
An in depth scrutiny of the rise of Mayan civilization based on the latest archaeological findings and including selections by many of the leading scholars. Virtually every aspect of early Mayan civilization is covered.

ANDREWS, GEORGE. **MAYA CITIES. Bibliography, index, 10½"x 9½", 486pp. UOk75, 29.95c.**
In this volume an architect, who is also an excellent photographer, turns his trained eye on Mayan cities from the point of view of their physical form and spatial organization. The book is arranged in two parts. The first discusses Maya architecture and settlements in general and shows how small ceremonial centers developed into large cities. Basic building groupings are examined in detail. The second part describes and analyzes twenty settlements from all parts of the Maya area. Emphasis is on physical form and spatial organization, and the basic differences between ceremonial centers and urban centers are clearly set forth. The discussion of each site is supplemented with maps, drawings, and photographs.

AVENI, ANTHONY, ed. **ARCHAEOASTRONOMY IN PRE-COLUMBIAN AMERICA. Illustrations, notes, long bibliography, index, 7¼"x 10¼", 451pp. UTx, 22.15c.**
This volume contains selected papers from a symposium that was part of the first joint scientific meeting of the American Association for the Advancement of Science and the Consejo Nacional de Ciencia y Tecnologia held in Mexico City in 1973. Contributors include anthropologists, astronomers, a geographer, a psychologist, an architect, and a historian. Three broad interlocking topics are discussed: early American rock art in the southwestern United States, astronomical orientations of buildings, and native American calendars. The papers are all carefully written and contain important and often controversial new insights.

AVENI, ANTHONY, ed. **NATIVE AMERICAN ASTRONOMY. Many illustrations, bibliography, index, 7¼"x10½", 303pp. UTx77, 21.45c.**
An edited collection of papers presented at a symposium on the title theme. Fifteen specialists in archaeology, astronomy, architecture, art history, mathematics, solar physics, and anthropology explore the astronomical knowledge and beliefs of the pre-Columbian peoples. North American Indian beliefs are included. A technical work.

BANKES, GEORGE. **PERU BEFORE PIZARRO. 150 plates, sixteen in color, 208pp. Dut77, 7.95p.**
A highly readable account of life in ancient Peru based on the Spanish chronicles, archaeological surveys, and the author's personal observa-

tions as a traveler and archaeologist. The narrative is organized under the following general headings: *Conquest and Rediscovery, Environment, Dating Ancient Peru, Economic Life, The Social System, Religion,* and *Craftsmanship.*

BAUDEZ, CLAUDE. **CENTRAL AMERICA. Chronological chart, notes, detailed bibliography, index, 6½"x9½", 254pp. Nag70, 22.95c.**
This is a fairly dry analysis of important archaeological information about the Central American region—an area that is often considered *peripheral* and is ignored by the specialists who concentrate on Mexico or South America. M. Baudez has based this comprehensive study on documentation assembled throughout Central America and he includes introductory material along with detailed studies of specific sites and analyses of theories, problems, and methods.

BELLEROPHON. **THE INCAS, AZTECS, AND MAYAS COLORING BOOK. 8½"x11". BlB77, 1.95p.**

■ BENSON, ELIZABETH. **THE MAYA WORLD. Bibliography, index, 181pp. Cro77, 4.95p.**
A fully revised edition of Ms. Benson's excellent survey of Maya civilization. The author is director of the Center for Pre-Columbian Studies at Dumbarton Oaks in Washington, D.C. Ms. Benson covers the place and the peole, the cities, agriculture and trade, artisans and artifacts, science, and religion. She writes clearly and concisely and has a wonderful gift for making the civilization come to life. This is the best introduction we know of to the Maya world. Over sixty plates accompany the text.

BERNAL IGNACIO. **MEXICO BEFORE CORTES. 140pp. Dou75, 2.50p.**
A vivid cultural history of the origins and development of the civilizations in Mexico from the eighth century BC to the Spanish conquest. Ignacio Bernal is Director of the National Museum of Anthropology in Mexico City. The narrative is geared toward the general reader and often reads like a novel, and yet the scholarship is impeccable. A chapter is devoted to each of the major civilizations and the text is well illustrated. There is also an extensive glossary with pronunciation keys.

BERNAL, IGNACIO. **THE OLMEC WORLD. Index, 8½"x11", 287pp. UCa69, 7.95p.**
The Olmecs developed the first great civilization in the Western hemisphere between the thirteenth and first century BC. They built ceremonial centers such as La Venta, with monumental pyramids, a spacious courtyard, a basalt columned tomb, and offerings of stones, celts, and mosaics. At La Venta also are four of the twelve colossal carved Olmec heads that have thus far been discovered. The Olmecs were not only artists but engineers and scientists as well. They discovered the value of zero and achieved the most complete system of calculating time conceived in America. In an engrossing reconstruction, Bernal examines Olmec art, society, and religious beliefs. He traces the efflorescence and decline of the Olmecs and insists on the basic unity of all Mesoamerican civilizations. This is the first full length study of the Olmecs in English and is illustrated with 150 maps, photographs, and drawings.

BIERHORST, JOHN, tr. **BLACK RAINBOW: LEGENDS OF THE INCAS AND MYTHS OF ANCIENT PERU. Glossary, bibliography, 131pp. FSG76, 7.95c.**
An anthology of twenty myths and legends gathered from the sixteenth century chronicles of missionaries and conquistadors and from the reports of Andean folklorists. Many of the stories are translated into English for the first time. Bierhorst's introduction provides an historical and cultural background and offers insights into the stories themselves.

BIERHORST, JOHN, ed. **FOUR MASTERWORKS OF AMERICAN INDIAN LITERATURE. Foreword, annotated bibliography, index, 395pp. FSG74, 6.95p.**
Excellent translations of **Quetzalcoatl**, an Aztec hero myth; **The Ritual of Condolence**, an Iroquois ceremonial; **Cuceb**, a Maya prophecy; and **The Night Chant**, a Navajo ceremonial. **Choice** described Bierhorst's notes to each piece as *brilliant, thorough, and an important contribution to the scholarship on these works.*

BOLLES, JOHN. LAS MONJAS: A MAJOR PRE-MEXICAN ARCHI-TECTURAL COMPLEX OF CHICHEN ITZA. Glossary, bibliography, index, 11½"x10", 318pp. UOk77, 35.00c.
One of the most important buildings in Maya culture is Las Monjas (the Nunnery) at Chichen Itza. It is the most impressive complex in the city, with the longest and by far the most continuous period of structural and artistic development. In this volume the massive structure is described in detail by the man who directed the excavation and repair of the complex. Stunning photographs and detailed drawings are included. J. Eric Thompson has contributed a section on the hieroglyphic texts at Las Monjas and explained their bearings on the building. John Jennings has provided an historical introduction.

BRINTON, DANIEL, tr. THE ANNALS OF THE CAKCHIQUELS. Vocabulary, notes, index, 234pp. AMS1885, 10.75c.
An early translation of this important Maya historical document, taken directly from the original text. Sixty-two pages of introductory material on every aspect of the Cakchiquels' life and culture is also included.

BRINTON, DANIEL. MYTHS OF THE AMERICAS. Index, 339pp. Mul1868, 5.50p.
A study of the mythology and symbolism of the North American Indians. *Among the universally interesting questions which I attempt to solve in this book are: What are man's earliest ideas of his own origin and destiny? Why do we find certain myths, such as of a creation, a flood, an after-world; certain symbols, as the bird, the serpent, the cross; certain numbers, as the three, the four, the seven—intimately associated with these ideas by every race?* The myths are topically discussed and many of the early cultures are cited. This remains one of the best books on the subject.

Quetzalcoatl

BRUCE, ROBERT. LACANDON DREAM SYMBOLISM. 6.90p.
See the Dreams section.

BRUHNS, KAREN. A COLORING ALBUM OF ANCIENT MEXICO AND PERU. 11"x14", about 100pp. Stw73, 7.50p.
This exquisitely produced book contains plates too detailed for most young children to color, but we can think of lots of adults who would love to do so! The plates themselves appear authentic and are extremely well reproduced. A descriptive paragraph in Spanish and English accompanies each.

BRUNDAGE, BURR. EMPIRE OF THE INCA. Extensive notes, index, 413pp. UOk63, 10.95c.
This well written history of the Incas begins by tracing the legends and known facts about their initial settlements and goes from there to a discussion of the development of their civilization and empire. There are also sections on Inca religious beliefs and rituals and on their engineering prowess, as evidenced in the still existing Royal Road.

BRUNDAGE, BURR. A RAIN OF DARTS: THE MEXICA AZTECS. Maps, notes, bibliography, index, 372pp. UTx72, 15.45c.
This is the definitive history of the Mexica, historically the most important of the Aztec peoples. The focus of the narrative is on the political state produced by the Mexica during their stormy history. The eleven Mexica reigns that preceded the Spanish conquest are investigated, their triumphs and errors examined, and the lives of their great men illuminated, where the sources allow.

BRUNDAGE, BURR. TWO EARTHS, TWO HEAVENS. Annotated bibliography, index, 138pp. UNM75, 7.75c.
A philosophical essay contrasting the Aztecs and the Incas. Brundage is a pre-Columbian historian who has written extensively about the Aztecs and the Incas. Here he compares their origins, creation myths, religions, ways of life, and warfare. He portrays the Inca Empire as *synonymous with order* and the Aztec Empire as a *byproduct of warfare*.

BRUNHOUSE, ROBERT. IN SEARCH OF THE MAYA. Illustrations, bibliography, index, 243pp. RaH73, 1.95p.
The remains of Maya civilization were first discovered during the eighteenth and nineteenth centuries by amateur archaeologists who came to Mexico, Guatemala, and Honduras to search for ruins. This book tells the story of the rediscovery of the Maya cities by describing the explorations of eight of these pioneering archaeologists. The emphasis is as much on personality as it is on contributions to knowledge and it makes an exciting story, using firsthand accounts to recreate the flavor of the initial discoveries.

BRUNHOUSE, ROBERT. PURSUIT OF THE ANCIENT MAYA. Notes, bibliography, index, 252pp. UNM75, 9.90c.
In this sequel to In Search of the Maya, Brunhouse tells the story of seven later Maya archaeologists, and describes the coming of age of Maya studies. The subjects of this book are a great deal better known than the men in the earlier one. Again, a vivid picture is given of the discoveries and personalities of the individuals.

BURLAND, C.A. PERU UNDER THE INCAS. Bibliography, index, 7¼"x9¾", 144pp. Put67/Hul, 6.95c.
This is a nice account of Inca Peru, entertainingly written and replete with photographs and drawings. Burland is an ethnographer and he has written many books. Here he begins by reviewing the land of the Incas and the characteristics of the people who lived there. The next chapter is devoted to an exposition of their tight governmental adminstration. From there Burland discusses the Incas' religious beliefs, social life, territorial expansion, and artistic achievement.

■ BURLAND, C.A. and WERNER FORMAN. FEATHERED SERPENT AND SMOKING MIRROR: THE GODS AND CULTURES OF MEXICO. Glossary, chronology, bibliography, index, 9"x12", 128pp. Put75/OPL, 12.95c.
This book includes some of the most beautiful color photographs we have seen along with an excellent text. The general reader with little background in the area can get a good feeling for the civilization and the cosmological and mythological beliefs of the people. The story of the two main gods is related in detail. While the early cultures in Mesoamerica are reviewed briefly, the bulk of the text is devoted to the Aztec culture. There is a chapter on each of the main gods, Quetzalcoatl and Tezcatlipoca; one on the daily life of the people; and another one on astrology and the priesthood. A final chapter, *The Earthly Confrontation*, reviews the Conquest and the early omens of its coming.

BUSHNELL, G.H.S. ANCIENT ARTS OF THE AMERICAS. 252 plates, some in color, index, 287pp. T&H74, 5.00p.
A carefully documented survey which traces the history of pre-Columbian art from 2500 BC to the Spanish conquest. Drawing upon more than a decade spent living and working in Latin America, Dr. Bushnell discusses the many phases of the art within their historical framework. He focuses on Mexico and Peru and he also reviews the artistic achievements of the peoples of North America, the West Indies, and Central America.

BUSHNELL, G.H.S. THE FIRST AMERICANS. Bibliography, 144pp. MGH73, 3.95p.
A pictorial essay presenting the history of American civilizations from 5000 BC to the Spanish conquest. Bushnell presents a brief review of each of the civilizations.

CALVANI, VITTORIA. **THE MAYA. 8"x9½", 144pp. Mnr77, 3.98c.**
This is an adequate introduction to Mayan civilization. Calvani's text is concise and to the point; his scholarship is all right; and the material is well organized. The more than 100 black and white and color photographs which amplify the text are the best part of the book.

CARLSON, VADA. **THE GREAT MIGRATION: EMERGENCE OF THE AMERICAS AS INDICATED IN THE READINGS OF EDGAR CAYCE. Bibliography, 58pp. ARE70, 1.50p.**
This pamphlet traces the rise of South and North American Indian cultures from Lemurian and Atlantian migrations.

CASO, ALFONSO. **THE AZTECS. Index, 7½"x10½", 140pp. UOk58, 9.95c.**
Here, translated into English for the first time, is Alfonso Caso's brilliant account of the Aztec people: their art, customs, religion, and magical practices. Caso surveys the gods that appear in the codices and archaeological remains and the purposes they fulfilled with respect to nature and society, supporting his conclusions by reference to the accounts of the Spanish chroniclers. Caso directed the explorations at Monte Alban and is director of archaeology in the National Museum in Mexico City. Miguel Covarrubias, who painted the colorful illustrations, is one of Mexico's best known illustrators. His drawings portray the divinities and objects related to Aztec religious life.

CERAM, C.W. **THE FIRST AMERICAN: A STORY OF NORTH AMERICAN ARCHAEOLOGY. Many illustrations, including some color plates, notes, bibliography, index, 445pp. NAL71, 2.25p.**
A layman's account of the development of the first civilizations in North America, filled with speculation on where the people came from and how they survived. Ceram presents an amazing amount of archaeological information in a highly readable manner.

CHAN, ROMAN PINA. **A GUIDE TO MEXICAN ARCHAEOLOGY. Bibliography, index, 128pp. LiB71, 3.40p.**
A summary of ancient Mexican archaeology covering the pre-classic, classic, and post-classic periods. The author is Chief of the Department of Archaeological Research at the National Institute of Anthropology and History and former curator of the National Museum of Anthropology. Numerous color and black and white plates illustrate the artifacts.

CHARROUX, ROBERT. **THE MYSTERIES OF THE ANDES. 239pp. Avo77, 2.25p.**
Charroux describes his discovery of 11,000 engraved stones at Ica, Peru—stones which he says document the biblical flood, show ancient astronomers peering at comets on a collision course with Earth, depict surgeons performing kidney, heart, and even brain transplants, thousands of years before Christ, and relate the history of intelligent life on this planet fifty million years ago. This book is a provocative analysis of this discovery and countless other *ancient mysteries*. Many illustrations and allegations, but virtually no documentation. Charroux writes well.

COE, MICHAEL. **THE MAYA. Index, 252pp. HRW66/Pen, 9.35p.**
Dr. Coe...has written an excellent survey of the civilization of the ancient Maya, concentrating mainly on the achievements of the classic period. The rise, development, and fall of this amazing culture is explained factually and succinctly. Mayan life and thought are not neglected either. The maps and life figures are so well integrated into the text that a visual understanding of the Maya is also obtained. The plates and a select bibliography of the most important major works enhance the value of this book.— **Library Journal.** The material is organized in chronological order and is succinctly presented. Coe devotes chapters to Mayan life and thought, and each of the eighty-three plates is described. Coe's work is generally considered the finest available from an academic point of view.

COE, MICHAEL. **MEXICO. Index, 245pp. HRW62, 9.35p.**
Coe has produced an excellent volume, synthesizing Mesoamerican cultural history and tracing its development from earliest times in a chronological sequence. Fact and speculation are carefully distinguished and line drawings are well integrated into the text. A series of photographs (all described) follow the main body of the text and there is a chapter-by-chapter bibliography. The style is less dry than in Coe's more detailed books. An admirable general introduction to the archaeology of the area.

COLLIER, JOHN. **INDIANS OF THE AMERICAS. Index, 191pp. NAL75, 1.75p.**
A good general history of the native populations of North and South America from earliest times to the present. The emphasis is on political events. This edition is slightly abridged.

COLLIS, MAURICE. **CORTES AND MONTEZUMA. 251pp. Fab54, 2.50p.**
A novelistic study of the characters of Cortes and Montezuma, along with a detailed retelling of the story of the Conquest.

CRAINE, EUGENE and REGINALD REINDORP. **THE CHRONICLES OF MICHOACAN. Illustrations, index, 276pp. UOk70, 9.95c.**
This document, the primary source for the study of Tarascan prehistory, was written down about 1539 by the Spanish Friar Martin de Jesus de la Coruna from the oral traditions of the Tarascans. The chronicles describe the customs of the Indians, the gods they worshiped, their religious rites, social classes, feasts, administration of justice, and their calendar and the reckoning of time. A number of appendices are also included.

CULBERT, T. PATRICK, ed. **THE CLASSIC MAYA COLLAPSE. Notes, bibliography, index, 569pp. UNM73, 10.10p.**
Of the many mysteries surrounding ancient Maya civilization, none has attracted greater interest than its collapse in the eighth and ninth centuries AD. In this book thirteen leading scholars use new data to revise the image of Classic Maya civilization and create a new model of its collapse—a general model of sociopolitical collapse not limited to the Maya alone.

■ DAVIES, NIGEL. **THE AZTECS. Illustrations, notes, bibliography, index, 380pp. Put74/SBL, 10.00c/7.35p.**
Davies is an Englishman who has lived in Mexico since 1962 and has studied the history and culture of the ancient peoples of the country at length. He holds advanced degrees from the National University and has had books published by the National Institute of Anthropology of Mexico. Most of the books on Mesoamerica give short shift to the Aztecs; if they are discussed in any depth it is the Conquest and the horrors of their bloodthirsty wars that are concentrated on. This is an excellent presentation of the Aztec civilization, from its beginnings to the time of the Conquest. The mythological and religious underpinnings are discussed at some length. An excellent account; the book reads well and the scholarship is excellent.

DAVIES, NIGEL. **THE TOLTECS. Notes, bibliography, index, 561pp. UOk77, 14.95c.**
The Toltecs, a post-classical people of central Mexico, flourished from about 900 to 1179, succeeding the Teotihuacan culture and preceding the Aztec. Drawing upon archaeological records and documentary sources, Davies attempts to compile an accurate history of the Toltecs. As far as possible, he sorts out what is fact, what may be fact, and what is pure legend. He also sets up a chronology of events in Toltec history and reviews the extent of their empire at its zenith (with particular emphasis on their government structure and economic and social organization). The book closes with a detailed discussion of the collapse of the Toltec capital, Tula. Davies writes well.

DEUEL, LEO, ed. **CONQUISTADORS WITHOUT SWORDS—ARCHAEOLOGISTS IN THE AMERICAS. Introduction, illustrations, index, 620pp. ScB67, 3.95p.**
A collection of firsthand reports by forty-two archaeologists, with an interpretation of each selection by Deuel. The anthology covers all parts of the Americas from Andean South America to the Eskimos and Vikings. *A superb selection of significant accounts....The book is the best of its kind.—***The New York Times Book Review.**

DIAZ DEL CASTILLO, BERNAL. **THE CONQUEST OF NEW SPAIN. Introduction, maps, 416pp. Vik63/Pen, 2.95p.**
A fine translation by J.M. Cohen of this important source document.

DIAZ DEL CASTILLO, BERNAL. **THE DISCOVERY AND CONQUEST OF MEXICO. Index, 509pp. FSG56, 4.95p.**
Diaz del Castillo served under Cortes throughout the entire Mexican campaign. This volume was written late in his life from memory and his journal notes, and is considered the basic sourcebook on the Conquest. All the later writers, including W.H. Prescott, have relied

heavily on this account when writing their histories. Diaz is not always the most objective narrator; however, he was definitely in on the action and his is a fascinating account not only of the Conquest, but also of the Mexican civilizations. This edition was edited by Genaro Garcia from an exact copy of the original manuscript and extracts from Garcia's long introduction are printed together with the commentary and notes of the translator, A.P. Maudslay. There is also additional introductory material.

DIGBY, ADRIAN. MAYA JADES. Bibliography, 48pp. BMP72, 2.15p.
A survey of Maya jades, illustrated with many plates and line drawings.

DRAKE, W. RAYMOND. GODS AND SPACEMEN IN THE ANCIENT WEST. 281 item bibliography, 230pp. NAL74/SBL, 1.50p.
Formerly titled, Ancient Secrets of Mysterious America, this is a readable look into America's past, beginning with the origin of man and continuing through the last of the pre-Columbian civilizations.

DURAN, DIEGO. BOOK OF THE GODS AND RITES AND THE ANCIENT CALENDAR. Glossary, bibliography, index, 526pp. UOk71, 8.95p.
This is the first English translation of two classic works about Aztec ritual and calendar which, though written in the late 1500s by Fray Duran, a Dominican missionary, were not published until 1867. Since that time they have been among the most quoted works on ancient Mexico. Duran's stated purpose was to help the missionaries combat the religious beliefs of the Indians. But despite himself he became deeply absorbed in their rich culture. To assure the accuracy of his account, he searched out Indian survivors of pre-Conquest times and Spaniards who had accompanied Cortes to Mexico. He recorded descriptions of the gods and goddesses, the rituals attending their worship, the festivals and ceremonies, the calendrical system, and the Indians' occupations, games, and social life. The translators based their work on the original manuscript, now in the National Library of Madrid. Accompanying the text are reproductions of the excellent illustrations from Ramirez' nineteenth century copy of the manuscript. The drawings vividly portray the Aztec pantheon, the temples and public buildings, and the rites and dress of the people. They were executed at Duran's request by an anonymous fellow missionary (or perhaps a mission-trained Indian) who copied them from ancient Aztec manuscripts.

ENCISO, JORGE. DESIGN MOTIFS OF ANCIENT MEXICO. 2.50p.
See the Sacred Art section.

ENCISO, JORGE. DESIGNS FROM PRE-COLUMBIAN MEXICO. 2.00p.
See the Sacred Art section.

ENGEL, FREDERIC. AN ANCIENT WORLD PRESERVED. Illustrations, index, 7¼"x10¼", 314pp. Crn76, 12.95c.
Dr. Engel has spent many years of study and research in Central and South America and now lives in Lima, Peru, where the Peruvian National University founded a chair for him. An earlier edition of this book won the History Prize of the French Academy. In this edition Dr. Engel summarizes and provides details of twelve years of his excavations in the Andes. He also vividly portrays the social, economic, and political lives of the Andean people over the last ten thousand years.

FAGAN, BRIAN. ELUSIVE TREASURE: THE STORY OF EARLY ARCHAEOLOGISTS IN THE AMERICAS. Annotated bibliography, index, 7½"x9¼", 385pp. Scr77, 17.50c.
Fagan says, This book is an attempt to distill a narrative from the enormous body of literature on the major controversies of American archaeology from the time of the conquistadores to about 1900. It is a well connected, fascinating narrative of exploration and conflict in both North and Central America. Well over 200 unusual photographs and line drawings illuminate the text.

FELL, BARRY. AMERICA B.C.: ANCIENT SETTLERS IN THE NEW WORLD. Photographs, line drawings, notes, bibliography, index, 320pp. S&S76/Wdw, 4.95p.
This is a highly controversial study of North American prehistory. Fell contends that about 3,000 years ago bands of roving Celtic mariners crossed the Atlantic from Portugal and Spain and established settlements in New England and Oklahoma. They were followed by other colonists from Europe and North Africa, speaking Basque, Phoenician, and Libyan. These later settlers established dominion over other parts of the northeastern United States, and some of the settlements lasted until the time of Julius Caesar. Fell backs up his thesis with a fair amount of documentation—all of which has been hotly disputed by many scholars. It makes for an interesting story, in any event, and opens up a whole new arena of possible activity.

FERGUSON, WILLIAM and JOHN ROYCE. MAYA RUINS OF MEXICO IN COLOR. Notes, index, 8¾"x11½", 246pp. UOk77, 25.00c.
Over 200 color photographs reveal the grandeur of the Maya centers in a way never before shown. As Michael Coe says, I doubt that aerial coverage has been used by anyone so effectively. The color views…at low altitudes give one a far better idea of Maya buildings and their relationship to one another and to the landscape than any amount of maps and plans. A brief account of Maya history and culture introduces the reader to nine major sites: Palenque, Labna, Uxmal, Kabah, Sayil, Xlapak, Chichen Itza, Coba, and Tulum. Each photograph is accompanied by descriptive and background information.

FOX, HUGH, ed. FIRST FIRE. Introduction, glossary, notes, 480pp. Dou78, 5.95p.
An excellent collection of verses and tales from Central and South America, recorded by Spanish priests as examples of pagan beliefs and inadvertently spared during the Inquisition. Beginning with passages from the earliest post-Conquest literature, the anthology presents a series of mytho-historical events. Later works focus on specific life events and belief systems of the mythic world; the major mythic heroes; and concepts of sacred time and space. Throughout, the themes of the spirit world as the core of reality and enlightenment as the purpose of life are primary.

■ GALLENKAMP, CHARLES. MAYA. Bibliography, index, 234pp. McK76, 12.95c.
In the sixteen years since the publication of the highly acclaimed first edition of Maya, scientific knowledge about the Mayas has grown rapidly. This completely revised edition incorporates a great deal of new information. Drawing upon the research of numerous scholars, as well as his own exploration, Gallenkamp provides a vivid reconstruction of Mayan art, literature, science, and ritual. In addition, he recounts the exploits of a number of the region's early explorers. This is an extremely readable account. Many photographs and line drawings accompany the text.

GARCILASO DE LA VEGA. ROYAL COMMENTARIES OF THE INCAS AND GENERAL HISTORY OF PERU. Notes, index, 1,574pp. UTx66, 31.50c/set.
An unabridged two volume edition of this classic study, translated and with an introduction by Harold Livermore and a foreword by Arnold Toynbee.

GATES, WILLIAM. OUTLINE DICTIONARY OF MAYA GLYPHS. Introduction, 217pp. Dov78, 3.50p.
A study of the glyphs in the three surviving Maya books—the Dresden, Paris, and Madrid codices. As groundwork for deciphering the codices, Gates has tabulated all character variants, attempted to work out meaning from their counterparts, and interrelated these meanings with Maya culture. In all, about 3,000 symbols—all clearly drawn—are covered. An essay by Gates, Glyph Studies, is appended.

GILLMOR, FRANCES. FLUTE OF THE SMOKING MIRROR—A PORTRAIT OF NEZAHUALCOYOTL, POET-KING OF THE AZTECS. Many line drawings, notes, bibliography, index, 183pp. UAr49, 6.50c.
Nezahualcoyotl lived from 1402 to 1472, more than a generation before the Conquest. His multiple roles as poet-philosopher, engineer, codifier of laws, and builder of civilization were played against the harsh background of Aztec wars and alliances, festivals and sacrifice. Ms. Gillmore has a Doctorate in Letters from the Universidad Nacional de Mexico. Her account is well researched and extremely readable, written in a poetic, singing style.

GOMARA, FRANCISCO LOPEZ DE. CORTES—THE LIFE OF THE CONQUEROR BY HIS SECRETARY. Illustrations, glossary, notes, bibliography, index, 455pp. UCa64, 5.95p.
Lesley Byrd Simpson's excellent and perceptive translation of Gomara's Historia de la Conquista de Mexico is the only English translation of this important work to

appear since a truncated version was published in England in 1578. . . . Gomara's narrative covers the entire span of Cortes' life and the exploration and conquest of outlying areas of New Spain as well as the overthrow of the Aztec Empire. His subject is epic and he conceives and writes of it accordingly with a sense of mission and destiny. His account of the conquest is clear-cut and his portraiture and characterization of Cortes reflect the understanding he developed through his close association with the conqueror. . . .Simpson preserves and projects the spirit, style, and period in his translation.—**The Hispanic American Historical Review.**

GORENSTEIN, SHIRLEY. **NOT FOREVER ON EARTH: PRE-HISTORY OF MEXICO. Bibliography, index, 169pp. Scr75, 7.95c.**
This is a well written general account of the native civilizations in Mexico from their beginnings to the Spanish Conquest. Introductory chapters set the stage and discuss elements common to all the civilizations. This is followed by a chronological discussion of the major cultures, with accompanying photographs and line drawings. The emphasis is on what archaeological findings have revealed about political organization, military systems, hunting and farming practices, social relationships, and religious beliefs and ideology. Ms. Gorenstein is an anthropology professor at Columbia University and she has directed several digs in Mexico. The book is neither technical nor a detailed account of the cultures.

GORENSTEIN, SHIRLEY, et al. **PREHISPANIC AMERICA. Notes, bibliography, index, 165pp. SMP74/T&H, 8.00p.**
Four essays by specialists survey the present state of archaeology in the Paleoamerican period, among the Mesoamericans, and in western and eastern South America. Two others review the transformation to civilization in the area and transoceanic diffusion and nuclear America.

GRIEDER, TERENCE. **THE ART AND ARCHAEOLOGY OF PASHASH. Bibliography, 7¼"x10¾", 272pp. UTx78, 30.25c.**
Only a small fraction of the vast treasures discovered in Peru since its conquest have been excavated scientifically. This volume contains an account of the discovery and excavation of the richest pre-Columbian burial ever scientifically excavated in Peru. The tomb and its offerings provide new perspectives on the cultural meaning of Andean funerary treasure. The site and its contents are thoroughly illustrated with photographs and line drawings.

GUIDONI, ENRICO and ROBERTO MAGNI. **THE ANDES. Maps, glossary, chronology, bibliography, index, 10"x13¼", 189pp. G&D77, 19.95c.**
A magnificent volume, sumptuously illustrated with well over 100 color photographs and containing a lucid text. The authors have organized their material chronologically and according to groupings of cultures. In their discussion of the remaining monuments and artifacts, they interrelate the cultural and political history of the area. Many books on early South American civilization focus almost exclusively on the Inca period, thereby omitting the cultures which flourished earlier. This book is one of the best introductions we know to the Andean cultures.

■ *HAGEN, VICTOR VON.* **THE ANCIENT SUN KINGDOMS OF THE AMERICAS. Bibliography, index, 351pp. Grn73, 4.50p.**
Von Hagen describes the history and culture of the Aztec, Maya, and Inca civilizations, drawing on a lifetime's study. His detailed knowledge of their institutions, economic structures, and religious practices enables him to reconstruct the pattern of their daily living, and to explore their distinctive achievements. A vivid account which is illustrated throughout with photographs, line drawings, and reproductions from original prints. There is also a parallel chronology.

HAGEN, VICTOR VON. **THE AZTEC, MAN AND TRIBE. Bibliography, index, 224pp. NAL61, 1.25p.**
This is one of the best general accounts available of the Aztec people and their civilization. Von Hagen is a scientist who has devoted much of his life to analyzing and writing about the pre-Columbian civilizations. Here he discusses the Aztecs, from the political and social structure of their city state to their method of preparing human beings for religious sacrifice (and the reasons behind this sacrifice). He tells how the Aztec made war and conquest the basic pattern of their daily life; analyzes their advanced forms of art, writing, and sculpture; and describes their temples and palaces, particularly the lavish city of Tenochtitlan, built in the midst of a lake deep in the interior of Mexico.

Every aspect of the Aztec culture is well represented and the text is illustrated with photographs and fifty-five line drawings.

HAGEN, VICTOR VON, ed. **THE INCAS OF PEDRO DE CIEZA DE LEON. Illustrations, bibliography, index, 479pp. UOk59, 15.00c.**
Cieza arrived in Cartagena in 1535, a boy of thirteen, and for the next seventeen years traveled through South America, observing and describing the country and its peoples and preserving for posterity the achievements of the Inca civilization even as it was being destroyed. The *Chronicler of the Indies* was not a scholar making a record of the Conquest, rather he *saw strange and wonderful things that exist in this New World . . .and there came over me a great desire to write certain of them.* And write them he did—so well that his contemporaries plagiarized from him freely and present day scholars regard his histories as *the cornerstone when writing of Inca achievements.* This translation is universally regarded as the finest one. Von Hagen also supplies an excellent introduction and many notes.

■ *HAGEN, VICTOR VON.* **REALM OF THE INCAS. Many line drawings and photographs, chronology, bibliography, index, 223pp. NAL61, 1.50p.**
An archaeological history of the Incas, written in von Hagen's usual flowing style. This is as good a brief introduction to Inca and pre-Inca culture as anything we know of. Von Hagen has traveled widely in the old Inca lands and divides his account into sections on *The Historical and Geographical Background, The People,* and *The Inca and His City.*

HAGEN, VICTOR VON. **THE ROYAL ROAD OF THE INCA. Index, 200pp. Cre76, 29.95c.**
A beautifully produced, boxed, fully illustrated account of von Hagen's discovery of the *golden roads of the royal Inca,* with an account of the history and legends about the roads.

■ *HAGEN, VICTOR VON.* **WORLD OF THE MAYA. Notes, bibliography, index, 224pp. NAL60/NEL, 1.75p.**
A vivid exploration of Maya civilization. Von Hagen, through his personal knowledge of the land, and through archaeology and ancient documents, restores the picture of Maya society as it was at its height. He explores the everyday life of the people (birth, marriage, sex, customs) which was regulated by complicated rituals. He also details the amazing Maya astronomical calculations and their philosophy of time. Another section is devoted to the life of the ruling theocracy and nobles and life in the Mayan cities. Von Hagen is writing for the general reader and his account is comprehensive, a work of good scholarship, and interesting reading as well. Many line drawings and photographs illustrate the text.

HAMMOND, NORMAN, ed. **MESOAMERICAN ARCHAEOLOGY. Notes, bibliography, indices, 6¼"x10", 498pp. Duc74, 49.90c.**
The twenty-five papers in this volume include the most recent work of many of the leading scholars in the field. Among the contributors are Eric Thompson, Gordon Willey, and many younger researchers. The *new approaches* of the title include the movement of research into previously uninvestigated, or under-investigated, regions of Mesoamerica; the application of complex geographic and trade models; and the use of the techniques of archaeoastronomy and ethnohistory.

HAMMOND, NORMAN, ed. **SOCIAL PROCESS IN MAYA PREHISTORY. Many illustrations, notes, bibliographies, 7½"x10", 623pp. AcP77, 73.55c.**
Twenty-five essays by leading scholars currently active in the field of Maya studies, including the results of new and mainly unpublished research work as well as up to date reviews of major areas of concern.

HANSEN, L. TAYLOR. **HE WALKED THE AMERICAS. 255pp. Amh63, 6.95c.**
A unique account of the various legends existing in North and South America telling of a mysterious and powerful saint, imbued with supernormal healing abilities who apparently came from Palestine at the time of Christ. The author researched for over twenty-five years in an attempt to ascertain the identity of this great healing prophet who was in some way associated with Christ and whose message was similar. This edition has many line drawings and its appearance reminds us of a junior high school text. An excellent annotated bibliography.

HATT, CAROLYN. **THE MAYA. Notes, 68pp. ARE72, 1.50p.**
A collection of excerpts from the Edgar Cayce readings tied together
with commentary from many of the most noted works on the ancient
Maya. Ms. Hatt critiques both Cayce's comments and those of the
scholars she cites. The material is topically arranged and there is an
emphasis on Mayan concepts of time, predictions for the future, and
explanations of the past.

HAY, CLARENCE, et al., eds. **THE MAYA AND THEIR NEIGHBORS.
Tables, map, index, 618pp. Dov40, 7.50p.**
A while ago it became obvious to a group of leading American
archaeologists and ethnologists that a familiar problem was emerging
in Middle American studies: hyperspecialization. One solution to the
problem was the present volume, which is also popularly known as the
Tozzer Memorial Volume, since most of the contributing writers
were students of Professor Alfred Tozzer. Thirty-four chapters by the
leading authorities cover virtually every aspect of Middle American
culture and civilization and most of the major authors are represented.
A 102 page bibliography accompanies the text.

HEMMING, JOHN. **THE CONQUEST OF THE INCAS. Photographs,
line drawings, maps, many notes, long bibliography, index, 641pp.
HBJ70/SBL, 4.95p.**
This book has been widely praised as the finest account of the
annihilation of the Incan Empire since W.H. Prescott's **History of the
Conquest of Peru.** Hemming spent six years preparing the volume and
during that time he consulted more than a thousand books and
documents, and traveled to Peru and Spain to investigate sources. It is
an excellent, moving account, distinguished by an extraordinary
empathy. The reader is drawn into the minds of the sixteenth century
Spaniards and Indians and he can sense their response as events move
quickly around them.

HEMMING, JOHN. **REDGOLD: THE CONQUEST OF THE BRAZIL-
IAN INDIANS, 1500-1760. Illustrations, many notes, bibliography,
index, 701pp. HUP78, 18.50c.**
This is an authoritative exploration of the elements of a major
historical tragedy: the defeat and decimation of Brazil's native population. Hemming also fully discusses the discovery, conquest, and
exploration of Brazil. This vital account is fascinating reading from
start to finish.

HEWETT, EDGAR. **ANCIENT ANDEAN LIFE. Many photographs,
index, 333pp. B&T39, 16.80c.**
A comprehensive historical and cultural portrayal. Hewett attempts to
show how the ancient American civilizations fit into the pattern of
world history. In addition, there is a chapter on Andean life today. The
work is based on solid scholarship, although references are not given,
and the writing style is in a popular vein.

HEWETT, EDGAR. **ANCIENT LIFE IN MEXICO AND CENTRAL
AMERICA. Many photographs, index, 373pp. B&T36, 16.80c.**
This study is based on the author's twenty-five years of research, and
incorporates the findings of numerous field trips. Hewett discusses
typical cultural examples from the region and his treatment embraces
both archaeology and cultural anthropology.

HEYDEN, DORIS and PAUL GENDROP. **PRE-COLUMBIAN ARCHI-
TECTURE OF MESOAMERICA. 363 illustrations, including ninety-
five reconstructions, diagrams, groundplans, index, 10"x11", 340pp.
Abr76, 37.50c.**
The awesome temples and cities of the Mayas, Toltecs, and Aztecs, and
all the other higly developed cultures of Mexico and Mesoamerica are
shown in hundreds of unusually fine photographs and discussed by
two leading scholars.

HOMET, MARCEL. **ON THE TRAIL OF THE SUN GODS. Good
bibliography, 272pp. Spe65, 4.70c.**
Professor Homet details further discoveries he made in the Amazon in
his search for the lost cities of the sun worshipers. He has also
attempted to link, by scientific hypotheses, the civilizations of the Old
World with those of the Brazil and Peru. A fascinating personal
narrative, well illustrated with photographs and line drawings.

HOMET, MARCEL. **SONS OF THE SUN. Many photographs and
drawings, thirty page glossary, bibliography, 239pp. Spe63, 7.50c.**
The firsthand account of Homet's perilous scientific journeys into the
Green Hell of the Amazon jungles of Brazil and Peru and the discoveries
made by him. It is an exciting and adventurous narrative.

HUNTER, C. BRUCE. **A GUIDE TO ANCIENT MAYA RUINS. Index,
349pp. UOk74, 5.95p.**
An illustrated guide to the Maya ceremonial areas of Mexico, Guatemala, and Honduras. Following an introduction to the civilization and
history of the Mayas, the author lists and discusses separate archaeological areas. Each is presented in the light of recent excavations and
restorations, and illuminated by photographs and site maps. Appended
are a list of selected readings and suggestions for reaching the
archaeological zones.

HUNTER, C. BRUCE. **A GUIDE TO ANCIENT MEXICAN RUINS.
Index, 280pp. UOk77, 5.95p.**
This guide is arranged by geographical area and Hunter discusses the
development of the ancient civilizations, the manner in which they
functioned, and the importance of their architecture, sculpture, and
arts and crafts. Special attention is given to art styles and their
influence by cross cultural zones. Profusely illustrated with photographs, some in color, maps, site plans, and building plans.

IVANOFF, PIERRE. **MAYA. 9¾"x13", 191pp. G&D74, 19.95c.**
A monumental work, illustrated with over 150 color plates. In simple
narrative and stunning photographs the complete survey of the
Mayan world unfolds: its religious and ceremonial beliefs, agriculture
and commerce, social, political and everyday life, its scientific achievements in astronomy and the development of a calendar, the language,
literature, art, and architecture. Selections from indigenous sacred and
historical writings provide an insight into this civilization as seen by
the Mayans themselves.

JAIRAZBHOY, R.A. **ANCIENT EGYPTIANS AND CHINESE IN
AMERICA. 135pp. GPA74, 16.10c.**
A carefully documented, profusely illustrated work which presents the
author's thesis that America's first civilization, the Olmec, was the

result of two voyages in the second millennium—one across the Atlantic and the other across the Pacific. The book is based almost solely on the author's original research and interpretation.

JOSEPHY, ALVIN M., JR. THE INDIAN HERITAGE OF AMERICA. Illustrations, 404pp. Ban66, 2.25p.
A readable discussion of the history, archaeology, and ethnology—including origins and languages—of all the major Indian cultures from Alaska to Patagonia from the earliest times to the present day.

KATZ, FRIEDRICH. THE ANCIENT AMERICAN CIVILIZATIONS. Glossary, notes, bibliography, index, 398pp. HRW72, 8.00p.
A survey of the early civilizations in the Americas which takes into account archaeological, linguistic, anthropological, geographical, and historical sources. Katz discusses how the cultures developed from village communities to prosperous city states, laying the groundwork for the rise of the Aztec and Inca civilizations. The bulk of the book is devoted to a detailed assessment of the Aztects and Incas; Katz describes their religion, militarism, technological advances, and social change. A final chapter compares the two civilizations. A dry, scholarly account.

KELLEY, DAVID. DECIPHERING THE MAYA SCRIPT. Glossary, extensive bibliography, index, 9¼"x12¼", 351pp. UTx76, 47.00c.
This is the most comprehensive study available. A summary of what is known about Maya writing is presented, accompanied by critical analyses of the work of many scholars, including the author. The discussion of the glyphs is topically organized and very clear line drawings of the glyphs abound.

KUBLER, GEORGE. THE ART AND ARCHITECTURE OF ANCIENT AMERICA. Extensive textual notes, detailed topical bibliography, index, 7½"x10½", 652pp. Vik75/Pen, 36.90c.
This beautifully produced, comprehensive volume surveys the development of the principal art forms in ancient America up to the sixteenth century. It is a definitive study which is organized chronologically and according to geographical regions in three main divisions: Mexico, Central America, and western South America. 404 half tones and line drawings illuminate the text.

LACROIX, JORGE. ITINERARY OF HERNAN CORTES. Bibliography, 173pp. EdE73, 7.80p.
A study of the itinerary followed by Cortes from his departure from Santiago de Cuba to his arrival at Tenochtitlan. Many photographs and woodcuts illustrate the text and both the Spanish and English versions are presented. A beautifully produced book.

LANDA, DIEGO DE. YUCATAN, BEFORE AND AFTER THE CONQUEST. Illustrations, 177pp. Dov37, 3.00p.
Friar Diego de Landa's Relacion de las cosas de Yucatan of 1566 is the basic book in Maya studies. Landa did all he could to wipe out Maya culture and civilization; on one occasion he destroyed 5,000 idols and burned twenty-seven hieroglyphic rolls. And yet, paradoxically, his book, written in Spain to defend himself against charges of despotic mismanagement, is the only significant account of the Yucatan done in early post-Conquest times. As the translator of this edition, William Gates says in his introduction, ninety-nine percent of what we today know of the Mayas, we know as a result either of what Landa has told us in the pages that follow, or have learned in the use and study of what he told. This is a reproduction of the first English translation of Landa's book. Gates also adds a variety of useful appendices.

LAPINER, ALAN. PRE-COLUMBIAN ART OF SOUTH AMERICA. 911 illustrations, 226 in color, maps and charts, chronological tables, visual glossary, index, 10"x13", 460pp. Abr76, 50.00c.
Emphasizes the art and artifacts of Peru. Cultural contexts are provided, and works now in collections all over the world are compared. This is considered the definitive work in the field.

LAS CASAS, BARTOLOME DE. THE DEVASTATION OF THE INDIES: A BRIEF ACCOUNT. Notes, 182pp. Sea74, 3.95p.
Las Casas' story of the exploitation and destruction of the Indians by the Conquistadores, which he witnessed and fought against for forty years, has been a controversial document since its first publication in Sevilla in 1552. His eyewitness account of modern genocide, colonization, and primary capital accumulation provides us with a harrowing picture of the origins of modern civilization in the Americas. Hans Magnus Enzensberger's introduction lays out the historical setting, the circumstances of Las Casas' life, and the history of his book. An appended dossier by Michael van Nieuwstadt details the continued exploitation and extermination of the few remaining Indians in present day Brazil.

LE PLONGEON, AUGUSTUS. QUEEN MOO AND THE EGYPTIAN SPHINX. Illustrations, appendix, index, 384pp. Mul73, 2.95p.
Le Plongeon, a controversial researcher, wrote the book and took the photographs presented here over eighty years ago. His aim was to present to the world the true esoteric, occult, and historical significance of the ancient Mayans. He shows the connection between the Mayan temples and pyramids and the Sphinx and the Great Pyramid in Egypt.

LE PLONGEON, AUGUSTUS. SACRED MYSTERIES AMONG THE MAYAS AND THE QUICHES. Photographs, 153pp. Wiz1886, 7.95c.
In the last century Le Plongeon discovered numerous ruins and ancient relics of the Mayans. His knowledge of esoteric lore enabled him to reconstruct their sacred cosmology. This book communicates the extent of his discoveries.

LEON-PORTILLA, MIGUEL. AZTEC THOUGHT AND CULTURE. Bibliography, index, 260pp. UOk63, 9.95c.
The fundamental concepts of the Aztecs presented and examined in this study have been taken from more than ninety original Aztec documents. They concern the origin of the universe and of life, conjectures on the mystery of God, the possibility of comprehending things beyond the realm of experience, life after death, and the meaning of education, history, and art. The documents were generally written by natives after the Conquest. Adapting the Latin alphabet, which they had been taught by the missionary friars, to their native tongue, they recorded the poems, songs, chronicles, and traditions that they or their fathers had learned by rote before Spanish domination. Leon-Portilla is a widely respected Mexican scholar.

LEON-PORTILLA, MIGUEL, ed. THE BROKEN SPEARS. Bibliography, 200pp. Bea59, 2.95p.
Leon-Portilla presents a coherent view of the Spanish Conquest as witnessed and experienced by the Aztecs themselves, based on post-Conquest chronicles written by the remnants of the Aztec intellectual class. The introduction details the historical and cultural background of the Aztecs as well as the origins and histories of the native texts.

LEON-PORTILLA, MIGUEL. PRE-COLUMBIAN LITERATURES OF MEXICO. Bibliography, index, 199pp. UOk69, 7.95c.
This volume presents a selection of myths and sacred hymns, lyric poetry, rituals, drama, and various forms of prose—together with critical commentary and background information. The selections come from the Aztecs, Mayas, Mixtecs, Zapotecs, Tarascans, Otomis, and others. Many of them are translated into English for the first time.

LEONARD, JONATHAN. ANCIENT AMERICA. Bibliography, index, 10"x11¾", 192pp. TLB67, 7.95c.
This Time-Life book is an excellent introduction to the ancient civilizations of the Americas. Hundreds of color plates accompany a highly readable, informative text. Some black and white photographs are also included.

LOPEZ PORTILLO, JOSE. QUETZALCOATL. 151pp. Sea76/Cla, 8.95c.
Lopez Portillo is currently the President of Mexico. In this volume he retells the Quetzalcoatl legend, synthesizing not only his teachings, but also the legends and teachings of all great religious leaders. Quetzalcoatl is the god of the Anahuac nation and he takes as his symbol the cross. He teaches his people how to develop their rich natural resources; he also teaches them about sin and redemption, but secretly they continue to worship their serpent idol. Finally, when the nation is irretrievably divided, Quetzalcoatl realizes that there is nothing more he can do for his people, and he returns to the sea from whence he originally came. He foretells the arrival of the conquistadores as he sails off with his cross, promising some day to return.

LUCKERT, KARL. OLMEC RELIGION. Bibliography, index, 199pp. UOk76, 10.95c.
This is a revolutionary interpretation of the oldest religion in Middle America. A religious historian proposes that it was a serpent, not the

commonly represented jaguar, that was the religious symbol of the ancient Olmecs. The author's primary objective in this study is an interpretation of Olmec religious symbolism. An engrossing presentation, illustrated with sixty-four photographs and drawings.

MASON, J. ALDEN. **ANCIENT CIVILIZATIONS OF PERU. Many illustrations, forty-three page bibliography, index, 350pp. Vik57, 5.95p.**
This is considered the definitive work on the subject. Topics discussed include environment; physique and language; history of Peruvian culture; Incan history, economic life, public works, social organization, political organization and government, religion; intellectual life; and arts and crafts. The scholarship is excellent and the writing style is not overly ponderous.

MERCER, HENRY. **THE HILL CAVES OF YUCATAN. 227pp. UOk75, 4.50p.**
This book, originally published in 1896, details Mercer's search through twenty-nine caves, thirteen of which he himself excavated. While he did find evidence of occupation, he found no trace of early man. This is a classic account which has been an extremely rare book. The Yucatan landscape, the caves, and the native population come alive. Mercer speculates on the uses of the caves and cites the findings of his exploratory group. J. Eric Thompson has contributed an extensive introduction to this edition and the text is enhanced by forty-four photographs and a number of line drawings.

MERTON, THOMAS. **ISHI MEANS MAN. 71pp. Ucr76, 4.00p.**
A collection of five beautifully written essays on the native peoples of North and Central America. Merton introduces many literary concepts and draws parallels with contemporary times and ways of being.

MERTON, THOMAS, tr. **THE JAGUAR AND THE MOON. 39pp. Ucr71, 4.00p.**
A reprint of Merton's translation of poems from **El Jaguar y la Luna** by Pablo Antonio Cuadra, originally published in **Emblems of a Season of Fury.** The poems speak of the living heritage of the ancient American cultures. The Spanish text is on facing pages and the pamphlet is beautifully produced and illustrated.

METRAUX, ALFRED. **THE HISTORY OF THE INCAS. Chronology, bibliography, 205pp. ScB69, 4.50p.**
This is a readable work of fairly good scholarship, eminently suitable for the general reader. The Inca civilization is discussed in historical, sociological, and religious terms from its earliest stages through the Conquest and up to the twentieth century (although the emphasis is on the Empire as it was at its height). M. Metraux was a French ethnologist who worked in South America for many years. He writes well and illustrates his account with seventy-nine photographs and line drawings.

MEYER, KARL. **TEOTIHUACAN. Index, 9"x11½", 172pp. Nsw73/ReD, 12.95c.**
In the high point of its culture and prestige—around AD 500—Teotihuacan was the most important city in the Americas. For some two and a half centuries the city held sway. Then, for reasons we cannot yet fathom, it was suddenly, totally abandoned. This volume examines the rise and fall of the city, and also the area's other civilizations, notably the Olmec, Toltec, Mixtec, Maya, and Aztec. Supplementing the text are some 140 illustrations, over a third in full color. The pictures range from ritual objects to everyday ware, and from whimsical creations to depiction of historical events by the peoples concerned. A special section, *Ancient Mexico in Literature*, contains accounts of the confrontation between European and Indian culture, as well as reports of explorations and of scholars.

MORALES, DEMETRIO SODI. **THE MAYA WORLD. Bibliography, 144pp. LiB76, 5.00p.**
A simple, brief survey of the major features of Mayan civilization. Line drawings and photographs help bring the narrative to life. This is a fine introduction.

■ MORLEY, SYLVANUS. **THE ANCIENT MAYA. Notes, bibliography, index, 507pp. 6"x9", SUP46, 6.95p.**
The most noted study of every aspect of the ancient Mayas, a delight to read and to look at. This is a revised edition which incorporates the most recent archaeological findings. Illustrated with hundreds of plates and line drawings and extensively documented.

MORLEY, SYLVANUS. **AN INTRODUCTION TO THE STUDY OF THE MAYA HIEROGLYPHS. 312pp. Dov75, 4.00p.**
Morley was one of the leading twentieth century Maya scholars and he devoted much of his attention to deciphering the Maya hieroglyphs. This book, originally published in 1915, remains the best introductory account available. Morley summarizes his researches, and includes an abundnce of illustrative and background material. J. Eric S. Thompson has contributed an introduction to this edition, commenting on Morley's work and life, as well as the present applicability of the book.

NELSON, RALPH, tr. **POPOL VUH. 86pp. HMC76, 3.95p.**
The **Popol Vuh** is the sacred book of the Quiche Maya. As Nelson says in his introduction, it *was probably once a scattering of songs and stories in the oral tradition of Native America; later elaborately fitted into one body, it became an embodiment of the Mayan world-view.* This is a lively new translation which opens up the world of the ancient Maya to all readers interested in mythology and native American culture. A fine introduction explores Mayan culture and places the **Popol Vuh** in context. The book is illustrated with half tone prints of Mayan glyphs.

NUTTALL, ZELIA, ed. **THE CODEX NUTTALL. Excellent long introduction, eighty-eight color plates, 11"x8½", Dov75, 7.50p.**
Originating in what is now the State of Oaxaca, Mexico, the **Codex Nuttall** was painted by Mixtec artists at some time not too long before the Conquest. It is, in effect, a Book of Kings, one of a series of masterworks narrating in picture and hieroglyph the sacred history of the Mixtecs. Centering around the year AD 1000, it shows the births of kings, their marriages, offspring, and major events in their lives. Over a dazzling white background swarm hundreds of figures painted in rich earth colors. Kings in elaborate costumes of textiles and skins, ornamented with feathers, wearing elaborate masks of the gods, carrying ceremonial objects, appear throughout. Warriors in battle dress advance, marriage ceremonies are celebrated, kings and their consorts face one another in solemn rites, a child is born, a naked priest rips the heart out of a victim in a stark temple, rows of figures bear tribute or offer ceramics and decorated aprons, fantastic twin temples rise to the sky. This is a strange world of vision, awe-inspiring for its simple, powerful technique—at times baffling, but a realm of beauty and visual symbol without modern counterpart. This volume is the only pre-Columbian codex that is generally available and it is an essential work for all who seek to understand the culture of the early Americas which the Spaniards so ruthlessly wiped out. The reproductions are excellent.

PADDOCK, JOHN, ed. **ANCIENT OAXACA. Many photographs, including some color plates, drawings, maps, notes, bibliography, index, 7"x10", 431pp. SUP70, 18.50c.**
The Mexican state of Oaxaca lies between the centers of the two most renowned civilizations of ancient Mesoamerica: the great metropolis of Teotihuacan and the jungle cities of the ancient Maya. For over thirty years archaeologists have been gathering evidence of the existence of a third major civilization, centered at Monte Alban in Oaxaca, but until recently we have had only isolated glimpses of a brilliant culture whose larger outlines were generally unknown. New research has filled in this picture. Nine authorities have contributed to this important study of the history and culture of ancient Oaxaca.

PAGDEN, A.R., tr. **THE MAYA: DIEGO DE LANDA'S ACCOUNT OF THE AFFAIRS OF THE YUCUTAN. Introduction, notes, index, 7"x9¼", 224pp. OHa75, 15.00c.**
A well edited, authoritative translation of de Landa's masterwork. The book includes illustrations and a reproduction of the Maya alphabet.

PRESCOTT, WILLIAM. **HISTORY OF THE CONQUEST OF MEXICO AND HISTORY OF THE CONQUEST OF PERU. 1,324pp. RaH nd/Den, 7.95c.**
This is the only edition of these classic works in which the complete texts of both of Prescott's histories are published together in one volume. Prescott's delight in vivid narrative and his striking descriptions of all aspects of the native cultures are evident throughout these pages. Together wtih Bernal Diaz del Castillo's volume on Mexico, Prescott's work is considered the definitive account of the Conquest. And while he did not participate directly in the events he discusses so

compellingly, he lived close enough to their time that many firsthand accounts have been integrated into the narratives. And Prescott was an excellent historian, whose accounts range far beyond a mere military history and delve into the *weltanschauung* of the conquered civilizations.

PROSKOURIAKOFF, TATIANA. **AN ALBUM OF MAYA ARCHITECTURE. Index, 10½"x8", 153pp. UOk63, 8.95p.**
A volume of drawings, geographically arranged, which presents thirty-six sites as they appeared in their prime. Facing each is a documented text of archaeological findings and a line drawing of the existing remains. A variety of other line drawings of artifacts are also included, as well as an excellent introduction.

RANNEY, EDWARD. **STONEWORK OF THE MAYA. Bibliography, index, 10"x8½", 133pp. UNM74, 11.15p.**
The stonework illustrated and discussed in this volume is viewed not as a demonstration of a particular style, but rather as part of the natural setting in which it stands today. The sites chosen include many lesser known ones, and Ranney provides a good cross section of all the sites. Extensive commentary on each selection is included.

RECINOS, ADRIAN and DELIA GOETZ, trs. **THE ANNALS OF THE CAKCHIQUELS AND THE TITLE OF THE LORDS OF TOTONICAPAN. Notes, bibliography, index, 232pp. UOk53, 4.95p.**
Two recent translations of important Mayan native documents. **The Annals** was written at the end of the sixteenth century. The manuscript corroborates the theories of the creation of man advanced in the **Popol Vuh** (the Cakchiquels were originally part of the Quiche nation) and relates many tales of the heroic age, enveloped in the mists of legend. But its principal value is its important contribution to history, from the beginnings of the Indian culture through the Spanish conquest and the first century of colonization. **The Title of the Lords**, written in 1554, contains a brief history of the Quiches from their legendary origins to the reign of their greatest king, Quikab. Signed by the kings and dignitaries of the Quiche court, it completes the source material provided by the **Popol Vuh** for the study of the life and thought of the Quiche Mayas before the coming of the Spaniards.

RECINOS, ADRIAN and DELIA GOETZ, trs. **POPOL VUH, THE SACRED BOOK OF THE ANCIENT QUICHE MAYA. Bibliography, index, 267pp. UOk50, 9.95c.**
This is the finest English version of the **Book of the People** of the Quiche Maya, generally regarded as America's oldest book. The mythology, traditions, cosmogony, and history of the Quiche Maya—including the chronology of their kings down to 1550—are related in simple yet literary style by the Indian chronicler. Adrian Recinos has provided an illuminating eighty page introduction and many detailed notes, as well as the Spanish translation from which this English edition was taken.

REICHEL-DOLMATOFF, GERARDO. **AMAZONIAN COSMOS: THE SEXUAL AND RELIGIOUS SYMBOLISM OF THE TUKANO INDIANS. Bibliography, index, 313pp. UCh71, 5.25p.**
A detailed ethnographic study of an isolated northwest Amazon tribe. The author worked with a single informant over a prolonged period,

and later checked his findings extensively in the field. This is an in depth investigation, written for the specialist but comprehendable by all interested readers. Much of the anthropological detail can be skipped over and the myths and symbols present a fascinating universe, so unlike our modern society. The ideas of man and the universe expressed by these people can help the reader understand some of the motivation and beliefs of the pre-Columbian native cultures.

RIVET, PAUL. **MAYA CITIES. Notes, index, 6¼"x10", 234pp. Ele60, 19.95c.**
This handsome summary of Maya civilization is illustrated with 136 plates and ten foldout color reproductions of portions of the codices. The book is written in a popular style and the material is divided into sections on the Mayan people, history, life and beliefs, cities, arts, and the modern Maya.

ROYS, RALPH, tr. **THE BOOK OF CHILAM BALAM OF CHUMAYEL. Illustrations, bibliography, index, 8½"x12", 247pp. UOk67, 8.95c.**
A translation of one of the **Books of the Prophet Balam**, native Maya documents written after the Conquest which contain much of what the Mayas remembered of their old culture. This volume contains comparatively little of the intrusive European material which predominates in the other **Books**. It is rich in Maya rituals, history, and traditions. Roy also provides extensive notes and there is an introduction by J. Eric Thompson.

ROYS, RALPH. **THE INDIAN BACKGROUND OF COLONIAL YUCATAN. Notes, index, 255pp. UOk72, 9.95c.**
A detailed examination of Yucatan Maya civilization at the time of the Conquest. There is an emphasis on the political history, although the culture is also reviewed.

ROYS, RALPH, tr. **RITUAL OF THE BACABS. Illustrations, notes, index, 222pp. UOk65, 7.95c.**
This is the first English translation of a Maya colonial manuscript, never before published in any language, containing forty-two incantations which add materially to knowledge of the religion of the Mayas and their conception of the cosmos and ideas about the origin of life. The gods themselves are often cited, but rarely, if ever, are they addressed in supplication. The role of the speaker is to give orders. The title comes from the four Bacabs, who hold up the sky, the deities most frequently mentioned. In addition to the translation, the book contains a transcription in the original Maya, a comprehensive introduction, glossaries of Maya terms, and an appendix of intrusive material in the manuscript.

SAHAGUN, FRAY BERNARDINO DE. **A HISTORY OF ANCIENT MEXICO. Index, BlE32, 18.80c.**
Fray Bernardino is without question the premier historian of the Aztec civilization. He came over to Mexico soon after the Conquest and learned the native language almost immediately. He had been trained as a historian and *he gathered about him native informants, first writing down in the original language what these informants narrated. Yet, not content with this procedure, other informants were sought out to listen to these texts and comment upon their accuracy. Further, natives were encouraged to sketch and write in their own symbols, and finally, with all these original materials in hand, the good Father sat himself down to write. His final history was divided into the following four sections, all of which are reproduced here in full in a translation into English from Bustamante's Spanish version: I: The Gods Which Ancient Mexicans Adored; II: Calendar-Festivals; III: The Origin of the Mexican Gods; and IV: Astrology of the Ancient Mexicans.* The text reads very well and its accuracy has never been questioned. A fairly extensive biographical sketch is included along with a detailed study of Sahagun's writing and his work with the native population.

SANDERS, WILLIAM and BARBARA PRICE. **MESOAMERICA: THE EVOLUTION OF A CIVILIZATION. Illustrations, notes, bibliography, index, 283pp. RaH68, 6.65p.**
The enormous amount of archaeological research conducted during the past decade in Mesoamerica—work in which we have participated—has increased the need for an interpretive synthesis of a huge and ever-growing body of data. Just such a synthesis is presented in this volume, which views these data from the perspective of recent developments in general anthropological theory.—from the preface.

SAVOY, GENE. **PROJECT X: THE SEARCH FOR THE SECRETS OF IMMORTALITY. Illustrations, bibliography, index, 287pp. BoM77, 15.00c.**
Savoy is an archaeologist and explorer. In this volume he takes the reader through the jungles of the Amazon and the mountains of Peru in search of clues to the ancient mysteries of the pre-Columbian civilizations. The book consists of his diary entries and many far-out concepts are introduced. Some chapter headings should give an idea of the scope: *The Fountain that Regenerates the Aged, Introduction of Solar Energy into the Brain, Fusion of Heaven and Earth, Cosmic/Solar Energy Intelligence Factors,* and *The Enigma of Man's Origins*. No documentation is offered.

SEJOURNE, LAURETTE. **BURNING WATER: THOUGHT AND RE-LIGION IN ANCIENT MEXICO. Index, 192pp. ShP76, 3.95p.**
This is a vivid reconstruction by a leading contemporary archaeologist. Ms. Sejourne relates the findings of her excavations at Teotihuacan and retells the fundamental myths of the Toltec religion to demonstrate that the doctrine of Quetzalcoatl marked the advent of the soul and spirituality in pre-Columbian life. She presents the Toltecs as unique and magnificent craftsmen and artists who bequeathed their religion to the conquering Aztecs. 104 drawings and photographs bring the ancient culture to life.

SERTIMA, IVAN VAN. **THEY CAME BEFORE COLUMBUS. Illustrations, notes, index, 303pp. RaH76, 15.00c.**
A nontechnical study and documentation of the presence and legacy of Africans in pre-Columbian America. The book often reads like a novel, but is a work of painstaking scholarship. Van Sertima has done an excellent job of presenting his evidence.

SHAO, PAUL. **ASIATIC INFLUENCES IN PRE-COLUMBIAN A-MERICAN ART. Notes, bibliography, 14"x11¼", 202pp. ISU76, 38.30c.**
This is an in depth investigation of the author's theory of cultural contacts between Asia and pre-Columbian America supported by extensive pictorial evidence. The pictures of dated artifacts from East Asia and Mesoamerica are displayed side-by-side, along with information on location and date, as well as explanatory material. There are an impressive number of correlated motifs.

SILVESTER, HANS and JACQUES SOUSTELLE. **THE ROUTE OF THE INCAS. Seventy-four color plates, 10½"x12", 96pp. Vik77, 35.00c.**
Soustelle, an authority on the archaeology and anthropology of Latin America, has contributed a lengthy preface on the Inca civilization to this stunning photographic essay on the Inca way of life today. Silvester has captured the brilliance of the mountain landscapes, and, particularly, their harshness, an element that bred unswerving determination in the Andean Indians which was to endure through invasions, Christianization, and the spread of technology. He has photographed the still-splendid Inca achievements: the temples, the walls, and the elaborate highway system—many parts of which are still in use—that connected the empire. With equal skill he portrays the people.

SMITH, MARY ELIZABETH. **PICTURE WRITINGS FROM AN-CIENT SOUTHERN MEXICO. 164 plates, technical appendices, 9½"x12½", 363pp. UOk70, 25.00c.**
Among the greatest of the pre-Columbian American artists were the Mixtec Indians of Mexico, who recorded much of their history in picture manuscripts. This richly illustrated book presents a comprehensive study of the surviving Mixtec manuscripts and includes an analysis of the methods used to recount history and the relationship of the pictorial signs to the Mixtec language. Ms. Smith discusses the place signs, or pictures which represent the names of places, in great depth.

SOUSTELLE, JACQUES. **THE DAILY LIFE OF THE AZTECS ON THE EVE OF THE SPANISH CONQUEST. Illustrations, notes, bibliography, index, 343pp. SUP61, 3.95p.**
An interesting account which details all aspects of Aztec life and society at the beginning of the sixteenth century.

SOUSTELLE, JACQUES. **MEXICO. Bibliography, index, 6½"x9½", 285pp. Nag67, 26.20c.**
All aspects of pre-Columbian archaeology in Mexico are surveyed and 184 full pages of plates, many in color, illustrate the exposition. The plates are well integrated into the text and the study is as good a work of its type as any we know. The scholarship is excellent and the presentation is lucid.

SPENCE, LEWIS. **THE CIVILIZATION OF ANCIENT MEXICO. Bibliography, index, 127pp. HeR12, 2.50p.**
A comprehensive account derived totally from original sources covering the following topics: the Mexican peoples, their early history, the settlements, mythology and religion, and the calendar system.

SPINDEN, HERBERT. **ANCIENT CIVILIZATIONS OF MEXICO. Bibliography, index, 270pp. B&T28, 11.45c.**
A well written, carefully researched summary of all that is known about the ancient Mexican civilizations, arranged in chronological order and illustrated with eighty-seven line drawings and forty-seven plates. Spinden is a respected scholar.

SPINDEN, HERBERT. **A STUDY OF MAYAN ART. Many plates, index, 8½"x11", 308pp. Dov75, 5.95p.**
This book created a field of art history and interpretation. Before Spinden, Maya studies consisted of a few field reports of excavations, some architectural surveys, and the germs of paleography. It was Spinden's contribution to provide the first cartography of the ranges of Maya art, to offer the first understanding of its subject matter, and to supply the first appreciation of the aesthetics that underlie its manifestations. Every aspect of Maya art is considered in detail: from the basic religious and philosophical ideas to town planning and ceramics. While much work has obviously been done in the sixty odd years since Spinden wrote, much of this simply expands certain areas in Spinden. J. Eric Thompson has supplied an introduction and a long bibliography for this edition.

STEN, MARIA. **THE MEXICAN CODICES AND THEIR EXTRA-ORDINARY HISTORY. Bibliography, 140pp. LiB74, 1.75p.**
An analysis and retelling of the stories in all of the Mexican codices known today. The history of some of the codices is also discussed and many illustrations are reproduced.

STEPHENS, JOHN. **INCIDENTS OF TRAVEL IN CENTRAL AMER-ICA, CHIAPAS, AND YUCATAN. 898pp. Dov1841, 4.50p/each.**
Stephens' two expeditions to Mexico and Central America in 1839 and 1841 yielded the first solid information on the culture of the Maya Indians. In this book and its companion volume, **Incidents of Travel in Yucatan**, he tells the story of his travels to some fifty ruined Maya cities. This two volume set is an unabridged reproduction of the first edition and includes 111 illustrations by Frederick Catherwood—highly exact, realistic drawings which show overall views, ground plans of the cities, elevations of palaces and temples, sculpture, carved hieroglyphics, and much else.

STEPHENS, JOHN. **INCIDENTS OF TRAVEL IN YUCATAN. Two volumes, 127 illustrations and one foldout plate, maps, 671pp. Dov1841, 3.00p/each.**
A companion volume to Stephens' other set.

SWANSON, EARL, WARWICK BRAY and IAN FARRINGTON. **THE NEW WORLD. Glossary, index, 8¾"x11½", 151pp. Pdn75, 5.98c.**
A beautifully illustrated pictorial overview of the archaeology of the pre-Columbian cultures of the Americas. The early chapters are devoted to an individual survey of each area as well as an account of the pioneering explorers and archaeologists who worked and traveled there. The last three chapters present in depth analyses of the pre-Columbian history and archaeology of North America, Mesoamerica, and South America. Many of the lesser known sites are discussed. The illustrations are among the finest we have seen and 140 of the 194 illustrations are in color. The authors are noted archaeologists.

SZEKELY, EDMOND B. **ANCIENT AMERICA: PARADISE LOST. 95pp. Aca74, 4.80p.**
An authentic collection of early sixteenth century native drawings of plants and animals and arts and crafts. The drawings are topically arranged and they impart a flavor of the civilization. Some commentary is also included.

SZEKELY, EDMOND B. **THE SOUL OF ANCIENT MEXICO. 9"x12", 135pp. Aca68, 7.50p.**
A monumental work, presenting a complete philosophical reconstruction of the world picture of the Toltec-Aztec civilizations and the key to understanding the spiritual significance of their rituals—including the Toltec ball game. Large album, illustrated with hundreds of photographs.

THOMPSON, J. ERIC. **MAYA ARCHAEOLOGIST. Glossary, index, 295pp. UOk63, 3.95p.**
Dr. Thompson is one of the world's foremost Maya scholars and is a veteran of many archaeological field expeditions to southern Mexico and Central America. Here Thompson relates his experiences during expeditions to the Maya area at a time when the attitudes and patterns of daily life were very similar to those of the time of the Conquest. Along with an account of the people and the most memorable field studies, the reader also gets some fine descriptions of the early archaeologists.

THOMPSON, J. ERIC. **MAYA HIEROGLYPHIC WRITINGS. 9"x12", 400pp. UOk60, 9.95p.**
The greatest development of Maya civilization was its philosophy of time. So far as it is known, the hieroglyphic texts deal largely with the passage of time and astronomical matters, and the gods and ceremonies associated therewith. In the absense of a Maya equivalent of a Rosetta stone and of an alphabet, progress has been slow in deciphering the glyphs. This is a new, greatly enlarged edition of this definitive work. The text covers the principles of Mayan glyphic writing; the cycle of 260 days; the year of 365 days; methods of recording numbers; the ritualistic and astronomical cycles; the moon; and aids to decipherment. There is a detailed introduction summarizing what is known of Mayan history, as well as a plethora of technical material. Many drawings of glyphs illustrate the text.

THOMPSON, J. ERIC. **MAYA HISTORY AND RELIGION. Bibliography, index, 445pp. UOk70, 12.95c.**
This is a scholarly study of Maya history and religion, from the standpoint of ethnohistory. Here Thompson seeks to correlate data from colonial writings and observations of the modern Indian with archaeological information in order to extend and clarify the panorama of Maya culture.

■ THOMPSON, J. ERIC. **THE RISE AND FALL OF MAYA CIVILIZATION. Illustrations, bibliography, 343pp. UOk66, 12.95c.**
This is an absorbing account of Maya civilization. Dr. Thompson begins with a discussion of the emergence of the culture and goes from there to a description of Maya art and architecture as well as Maya achievements in the fields of astronomy, mathematics, and hieroglyphic writing. One chapter contains sketches of daily life based on careful archaeological and ethnological research. This is a revised version of the highly acclaimed first edition which is enlarged to include recent archaeological discoveries. It contains new and expanded material on the beginnings of Maya culture, political and social organization, settlement patterns, commerce, and their philosophy of time. Thompson writes well and his text is suitable both for the interested layman and the specialist. This is as good a place as we can think of to learn about Maya civilization.

TOMPKINS, PETER. **MYSTERIES OF THE MEXICAN PYRAMIDS. Bibliography, index, 8"x10", 320pp. H&R76, 20.00c.**
This magnificent volume by the author of the highly acclaimed **Secrets of the Great Pyramid** probes the history, origin, and purpose of the pyramids in the Valley of Mexico, Yucatan, and Central America. Tompkins recounts the history of these structures from their first sightings by the Spaniards in the sixteenth century to the present day. He shows what discoveries have been made and what conclusions can be drawn about how and why the Mayan and Mexican pyramids were built, and what links there might have been between their builders and other historic and prehistoric cultures such as the lost continent of Atlantis. Four hundred illustrations illuminate the text.

TOZZER, ALFRED. **A MAYA GRAMMAR. 317pp. Dov21, 4.00p.**
Tozzer, Professor of Anthropology at Harvard, was one of the great authorities on all aspects of Mayan culture. This book remains the only grammar of the Mayan language. He begins with a systematic structural analysis and follows with a discussion of Mayan syntax.

Selected modern texts and excerpts from older works follow, with interlinear word for word analysis and translations. A sixty-six page bibliography is appended along with sections of paradigms and comparative vocabularies.

TRENTO, SALVATORE. **THE SEARCH FOR LOST AMERICA: THE MYSTERIES OF THE STONE RUINS. Bibliography, index, 308pp. Reg78, 9.95c.**
All throughout the northeast United States there are heaps of megalithic stones. This is a thorough, site-by-site analysis of the meaning of these remains. Trento, director of the Middletown Archaeological Research Center in New York, has led many field expeditions in both Spain and the northeastern United States. His controversial account is fully illustrated and thoroughly documented. This is a fascinating account. Appendices list research organizations and all the major stone sites in North America.

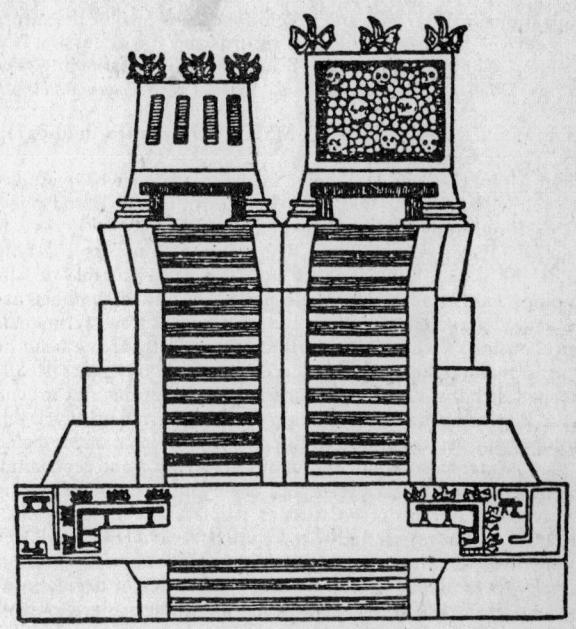

UMLAND, ERIC and CRAIG. **MYSTERY OF THE ANCIENTS. Bibliography, index, 160pp. NAL74/Sou, 1.50p.**
This is an exploration of some of the mysteries of the Maya civilization. The Umlands analyze the latest findings of archaeology, lunar research, and geology of the polar ice caps to paint a picture of the Mayas as the remnants of space explorers whose attempts to colonize our planet went awry more than 40,000 years ago. Many of the most noted aspects of the Maya culture are analyzed in light of this hypothesis and some startling theories are advanced. Interesting food for thought, although the scholarship can by no means be considered careful.

VAILLANT, GEORGE. **AZTECS OF MEXICO. Sixty-four plates, nearly 100 pages of notes, bibliography, index, 427pp. Vik44, 3.95p.**
Vaillant was considered the foremost authority of his day on the early civilization of Mexico and Central America. This monumental study was first published in 1950 and then totally revised and updated by Vaillant's wife Suzannah in 1962. In this definitive work Dr. Vaillant discusses the historical and cultural background of Aztec civilization, the basic beliefs of Aztec society in relation to government, education, and law. At the same time he captures the spirit of the age, and in one fascinating chapter takes the reader on a conducted tour of the capital city of Tenochtitlan at the heyday of its power.

VARNER, JOHN. **EL INCA: THE LIFE AND TIMES OF GARCILASO DE LA VEGA. Notes, index, 437pp. UTx68, 19.50c.**
Garcilaso de la Vega was the son of a conquistador and an Indian princess. He personally witnessed the dying gasps of the Inca Empire and left for posterity one of the earliest accounts of the ancient Incas, a chronicle which remains the definitive account today. His life and times are richly evoked in this narrative.

VAZQUEZ, PEDRO. **THE NATIONAL MUSEUM OF ANTHROPOL-OGY, MEXICO. 285 illustrations, fifty-four in color, indices, 11½"x 13¼", 257pp. Abr68, 30.00c.**
The National Museum in Mexico City has the most extensive collection anywhere of pre-Columbian and later Mexican art and artifacts. This volume is designed to evoke the total experience of the museum. It was planned and written by the men who created the museum itself and the chapters follow the order of the museum's halls, as a visitor would approach them, setting forth in each one all aspects of a particular civilization.

VLAHOS, OLIVIA. **NEW WORLD BEGINNINGS. Maps, bibliography, index, 320pp. Vik70, 10.00c.**
A simply written, illustrated tribe-by-tribe discussion of the Indians who lived in the Americas before the coming of the Europeans. Ms. Vlahos covers tribes from the northern woods of Canada to Tierra del Fuego and she includes information on their social and political organizations, arts, crafts, and religious customs. All of the information is derived from archaeological records and the discussion is very interesting. The tribes are grouped according to the following general headings: *Hunters, Fishermen, Gatherers, Farmers,* and *Empire Builders.*

■ *WATERS, FRANK.* **MEXICO MYSTIQUE. Notes, bibliography, index, 326pp. Swa75, 15.00c.**
Ancient Mesoamerican civilization is an area that we have studied in depth and we have read most of the literature. This is far and away the most exciting study we have seen. Part I, *The History*, gives a brief summary of the primary cultures. The major section, Part II, *The Myths*, extends the limit of this history into the immeasurable depths of mythology expressed in Hermetic myths, religious symbols, astronomical cycles, and mathematical computations of time far beyond our comprehension. Two main exploratory approaches have been made into this realm: one into the Hermetic myth of Quetzalcoatl, so concerned with the meaning of space; and the other the Mayan concept of time. Waters offers interpretation of the present world cycle whose beginning was projected to 311 BC and whose end was predicted by AD 2011. Waters also explores in depth the creation and destruction of the four previous world cycles and their suns and includes a good summary of the myth of Atlantis as it relates to Mesoamerica. An especially fascinating section, *The Voyage of Venus Through Hell*, details one of these creation myths and also explores the relation of Quetzalcoatl to Venus. Further along Waters delves deeply into the images and symbols of this civilization and their esoteric meanings. The final section on time is perhaps the most fascinating of all. The calendric and astrological systems are studied along with astronomical and cosmological ideas and the whole is fitted into an exploration of the present Great Cycle and the coming *Sixth World*—or Age of Aquarius. Most of Waters' examples and references are well documented. His command of both the academic and the esoteric literature relating to his subject is most impressive.

WAUCHOPE, ROBERT. **LOST TRIBES AND SUNKEN CONTINENTS. Illustrations, bibliography, index, 165pp. UCh62, 3.25p.**
An enduring source of speculation for over four centuries, the origin of the American Indian has been the subject of a highly emotional debate involving not only scholars, but organizations and nations. Bitterly opposing the more cautious theories of professional anthropologists, the supporters of various popular beliefs have defended their imaginative and occasionally outlandish alternatives. In this book Wauchope surveys the many theories about American Indian origins and provides portraits of the men and groups who advocated them. He himself is firmly convinced of the validity of the Bering Strait hypothesis, and this tends to color his presentation of the other theories.

WAUCHOPE, ROBERT, ed. **THEY FOUND BURIED CITIES. Photographs, index, 390pp. UCh65, 4.50p.**
A nice selection of first person accounts of the adventures of archaeological explorers in Mexico, Central America, and Peru. The narratives range over a century and a half and they are marked by bizarre events, almost unbelievable hardships, and humor. The character of each writer emerges in a clear perspective.

WEAVER, MURIEL. **THE AZTECS, MAYA, AND THEIR PREDECESSORS. Glossary, notes, bibliography, index, 8½"x11¼", 363pp. HBJ 72, 17.15c.**
An in depth, academic study of Mesoamerican archaeology. The author treats Mesoamerica as a whole, beginning with the earliest inhabitants (c. 38,000 BC) and ending with the arrival of the Spaniards. She begins with a description of the physical setting and then focuses on a chronological discussion of the main settlement areas. All of the major cultures are related, compared, and contrasted. An abundance of photographs, line drawings, and maps accompany the text.

WHITECOTTON, JOSEPH. **THE ZAPOTECS: PRINCES, PRIESTS AND PEASANTS. Many photographs and line drawings, notes, bibliography, index, 352pp. UOk77, 14.95c.**
For more than 3,000 years, the Zapotec speaking peoples have occupied the fertile Valley of Oaxaca of southern Mexico—a region that was one of the earliest fully developed civilizations in the Americas. The Zapotec temple city of Monte Alban was one of the great cultural centers of Mesoamerica. This account draws on archaeology, ethnohistory, social anthropology, and other disciplines and traces the Zapotecs from earliest times to the present.

WHITLOCK, RALPH. **EVERYDAY LIFE OF THE MAYA. Glossary, bibliography, index, 173pp. Put76/Bat, 9.50c.**
A simplified pictorial recreation of the everyday life of the Mayans at the height of their culture. Religion, daily routine, social hierarchy, literature, and science are surveyed. There is also an adequate amount of attention paid to history.

WILKINS, HAROLD. **MYSTERIES OF ANCIENT SOUTH AMERICA. Bibliography, index, 216pp. Stu56, 2.95p.**
This is an interesting account which ranges over all the pre-Columbian civilizations in an informal manner, relating some of the most interesting tales and legends, and discussing the most important theories and explorers. Nothing is analyzed in detail; the reader can get a feeling for the culture without being overwhelmed by information. We would have liked a bit more depth to the narration and a great deal more organization.

WILLEY, GORDON and JEREMY SABLOFF. **A HISTORY OF AMERICAN ARCHAEOLOGY. Index, 252pp. Fre74/T&H, 5.50p.**
This is the first detailed history of American archaeology. Beginning with the awakening of interest at the time of the Conquest, it traces the story to the present day. All the important stages are covered and the innovations are related to the intellectual climate in which they were made. The book also shows the relationship of archaeology to ethnology and anthropology, and how archaeology has drawn on history, biology, natural science, and the physical sciences. A wide range of illustrations complements the text, and ample notes and a comprehensive bibliography are included. The authors are both Harvard professors.

WINNING, HASSO VON. **PRE COLUMBIAN ART OF MEXICO AND CENTRAL AMERICA. 595 plates, 175 in full color, 10¼"x13¾", 388pp. Abr nd, 35.00c.**
This is the definitive study of Mesoamerican art. Introductory texts to each section trace the beginnings and diffusion of the various cultures. There are comments and notes on each of the plates as well as chronological tables, maps, and an excellent bibliography.

WOLF, ERIC. **SONS OF THE SHAKING EARTH. Notes, index, 314pp. UCh59, 2.45p.**
An anthropological study of the people of Mexico and Guatemala: their land, history, and culture. The narrative reads well and the text is illustrated throughout. This is the best book we know of to read to get an idea of the subject.

Subject Index for Ancient Americas

AZTEC
Brundage - A Rain of Darts
Burland and Forman - Feathered Serpent and Smoking Mirror
Caso - The Aztecs
Davies - The Aztecs
Duran - Book of the Gods and Rites and the Ancient Calendar
Gillmor - Flute of the Smoking Mirror
Hagen - The Aztec, Man and Tribe
Leon-Portilla - Aztec Thought and Culture
Leon-Portilla - The Broken Spears
Soustelle - The Daily Life of the Aztecs
Vaillant - Aztecs of Mexico

INCA
Bankes - Peru Before Pizarro
Bierhorst - Black Rainbow
Brundage - Empire of the Inca
Burland - Peru Under the Incas
Engel - An Ancient World Preserved
Garcilaso de la Vega - Royal Commentaries of the Incas
Grieder - The Art and Archaeology of Pashash
Hagen - Realm of the Incas
Hagen - Royal Road of the Inca
Hemming - The Conquest of the Incas
Metraux - The History of the Inca
Silvester and Soustelle - The Route of the Incas
Varner - El Inca

MAYA
Adams - The Origins of Maya Civilization
Andrews - Maya Cities
Benson - The Maya World
Bolles - Las Monjas
Brinton - The Annals of the Cakchiquels

Brunhouse - In Search of the Maya
Brunhouse - Pursuit of the Ancient Maya
Culbert - The Classic Maya Collapse
Ferguson and Royce - Maya Ruins of Mexico in Color
Gallenkamp - Maya
Gates - An Outline Dictionary of Maya Glyphs
Hagen - World of the Maya
Hatt - The Maya
Hay - The Maya and their Neighbors
Hunter - A Guide to Ancient Maya Ruins
Ivanoff - Maya
Kelley - Deciphering the Maya Script
Landa - Yucatan, Before and After the Conquest
Morales - The Maya World
Morley - The Ancient Maya
Nelson - Popol Vuh
Pagden - The Maya: Diego de Landa's Account
Proskouriakoff - An Album of Maya Architecture
Ranney - Stonework of the Maya
Recinos and Goetz - The Annals of the Cakchiquels
Recinos and Goetz - Popol Vuh
Rivet - Maya Cities
Roys - The Book of Chiam Balam of Chumayel
Roys - The Indian Background of Colonial Yucatan
Roys - Ritual of the Bacabs
Spinden - A Study of Mayan Art
Thompson - Maya Archaeologist
Thompson - Maya Hieroglyphic Writings
Thompson - Maya History and Religion
Tozzer - A Maya Grammar
Umland - Mystery of the Ancients
Whitlock - Everyday Life of the Maya

ANCIENT BRITAIN

Britain's ancient past, the time before the arrival of the Romans, is shrouded in mystery. The general picture held by most people is of a land of savages, living degraded lives in caves or rough huts, meeting together every so often to erect a Stonehenge or Silbury Hill at the dictates of the priests. Then the Romans came and civilised them, and the march of progress has continued ever since. It is tacitly assumed that our distant ancestors were ignorant and dull-witted, and that our present attitudes and mode of life must be superior in every way. Undoubtedly there are some people who do not hold these views. Today especially there is a wide interest in prehistory, from both the archaeological and mystical approaches. Archaeologists sieve the soil for the material fragments that remain from earlier civilisations; while mediums tune in to other-dimensional sources of knowledge. Both approaches produce results, and any individual's acceptance of them must depend on his own inclination.

During the period between the end of the last Ice Age and the arrival of the Romans, a period of approximately 4,000 years, a geat number of structures were raised throughout the British Isles. Still remaining are 1,500-2,000 megalithic tombs, 10,000-20,000 round barrows, 200 long barrows, many hundreds of stone circles, several thousand hillforts, and countless thousands of standing stones, with lesser numbers of henges, settlements, and cursuses. How many more have been destroyed by the encroachments of man during the past 2,000 years? There are traditions connected with many ancient sites which might, if carefully interpreted, provide new insights into the nature, abilities, and beliefs of prehistoric man. There are risks, of course, in following such a line of research, one being that we rarely have any means of knowing how old any particular tradition is. But even if a tradition is relatively recent, perhaps only 500 years old, it still indicates the attitude of the originator towards the ancient site to which it relates, and this attitude would itself be based on inherited attitudes. A growing interest in Britain's past has resulted in the development of a number of unconventional, non-academic theories.

The principle behind the theory of leys is deceptively simple. It is that ancient sites of all kinds can be found to align. The minimum number of aligning sites needed before a ley can be tentatively established is disputed, but the greater the number of points there are in a short distance, the smaller is the possibility of ascribing an alignment to coincidence. Our own suggestion is that there should be at least five points within ten miles. Alfred Watkins concluded in print that leys marked ancient tracks, but it has been suggested that even he was not absolutely convinced that this was the true answer, because there are obvious absurdities to be explained if it was so. Leys that lead directly up steep hillsides, cross marshes, and go through ponds and rivers surely do not mark the paths over which prehistoric man travelled.

Some believe that ley lines marked an energy current which flowed through the earth, and that the various mark points along a ley, standing stones, stone circles, etc., were crucial in the build-up, storage, and dispersal of this energy current. This theory is entirely alien to present-day prehistoric knowledge, for it presupposes skills in ancient man which are not only lost today, but which would generally be considered impossible for us to recover. However, if one carries in one's mind the idea that ancient sites were associated with the manipulation and storage of power or energy, one continually comes across traditions which tend to support this. Some people have experienced shocks when touching old stones, which strongly suggests that some stones carry a current of some kind. Not all people can feel them, and they are not always present. This latter feature may suggest an ebb and flow of current, possibly connected with the phases of the moon, or the positions of the planets.

Guy Underwood wrote a book, which has a strong bearing on the subject of earth currents. He called it **The Pattern of the Past**, and in it he set out the results of many years' practical and theoretical research. He was a dowser, and by diligent and imaginative use of his divining rod he discovered far more than underground streams. He found a complex system of water lines and secondary patterns, to all of which he gave identifying names, calling the whole the Geodetic System. He felt strongly that the geodetic lines provided a clue to the religion of prehistory, because his investigations showed that all ancient structures mark significant geodetic features. He also felt that an unknown force was involved, the characteristics of which he outlines in this quotation from his book: *Observations of the influence which affects the water diviner suggests that a principle of nature exists which is unknown to, or unidentified by science. Its main characteristics are that it appears to be generated with the Earth, and to cause wave motion perpendicular to Earth's surface; that it has great penetrative power; that it affects the nerve cells of animals; that it forms spiral patterns; and is controlled by mathematical laws involving principally the numbers three and seven. Until it can be otherwise identified, I shall refer to it as the Earth Force. It could be an unknown principle, but it seems more likely that it is an unrecognized effect of some already established force, such as magnetism or gravity.*

The Earth Force manifests itself in lines of discontinuity, which I call geodetic lines, and which form a network on the surface of the Earth. The lower animals instinctively perceive and use these lines, and their behaviour is considerably affected by them. Man is similarly affected, but less strongly, and cannot usually perceive the lines without artificial assistance.

It has long been believed that prehistoric monuments, especially stone circles, were originally used for rituals of some kind, but any suggestions as to the nature of the rituals have only been speculative. It seems possible that at least part of their function involved energetic dances designed to accumulate power, which was then stored in the stones. T.C. Lethbridge discovered through his long experimentation with the pendulum that *something from the human field can be fixed for long periods in the fields of various inanimate objects, including bits of stone,* and his interpretation of the possible ancient use of stone circles is worth quoting: *Apparently the belief that power could be obtained by stepping up the current in human bodies is very old indeed. The stone circles, which are usually thought to be temples of some kind, are more probably places where violent dancing in a ring took place to engender power, much in the same way as in electricity a moving coil generates power. The stones were probably put there with the idea of containing the power once it had been generated.*

Another approach to the question of the motivation for building stone circles may be found in the works of Thom and Hawkins, whose detailed measurements and mathematics have shown that constructions such as Stonehenge and many stone circles could have been used as astronomical calculators. Their builders (or, more likely, a priesthood) may have calculated the future movements of the planets and stars, and one theory proposes that they would need to do this in order to have a calendar to tell them when to perform the many agricultural tasks vital to their livelihood.

The detailed surveying done by Professor Alexander Thom provides very positive indications that at least one function of stone circles was astronomical, but the precise calculations obtainable from these stone observatories were surely used for some purpose other than a farming calendar. It could be that the scientists of that age, by accurately plotting the positions and relationships in the heavens of the sun, moon, planets, and stars, could calculate the optimum time to capture and store the inflow of cosmic energies and the most favourable time for these energies to be released. If this should be so, then the stone circles had four mutually compatible purposes: 1. Astronomical calculators; 2. Generators of terrestrial energy; 3. Storage batteries for both cosmic and terrestrial energies; 4. Radiating devices to broadcast these energies across the land (possibly through the ley system).

If prehistoric stone structures were used for the purposes listed above, two vital questions are: What was the nature of the energy involved, and for what purpose was it used? The first question is the more difficult to answer, simply because so little is as yet known about the earth currents. At present we can only refer to undefined cosmic or terrestrial energies. For those who are the pioneers of the science of the coming century these energies are no less real, and their effects far more pervasive, than is electro-magnetism to the science of the twentieth century. But just as electric power, radio, and TV transmissions were matters for incredulity or derision in the late nineteenth and early twentieth centuries, so the concepts of radionics, parapsychology, and the electro force-fields of the human body meet with similar resistance from the established scientists of today, who are of the twentieth century and, understandably, cannot make use of the concepts of the twenty-first. Radionics is concerned with the balanced flow of subtle energies through the various levels of being that make man, thereby ensuring perfect health and vitality. This principle must also apply to all other living forms including our planet, which is no less alive than we are. Our evidence suggests that it was the original intention of early men to ensure the correctly balanced flow of life-giving energies throughout the planet and all the life forms upon it.
—*condensed from* **The Secret Country**, *by Janet and Colin Bord*

ALCOCK, LESLIE. **ARTHUR'S BRITAIN. Illustrations, extensive bibliography, 415pp. Vik73, 5.95p.**
This book assembles all that is known or can be deduced about life between the fourth and seventh centuries in Celtic Britain. Alcock is a noted archaeologist who directed the excavations at Cadbury Castle in Somerset, the site originally identified with Camelot.

ALCOCK, LESLIE. **BY SOUTH CADBURY, IS THAT CAMELOT? Many photographs, line drawings, color plates, chronology, notes, index, 7½"x9¾", 224pp. T&H72, 6.50p.**
Ever since the sixteenth century when the king's antiquary, John Leland, first identified South Cadbury with Camelot and King Arthur, archaeologists have speculated about this large hill fort. Some slight excavations took place in the nineteenth century, but it was not until 1965 that major excavations began. Leslie Alcock served as director of the excavations and in this volume he presents his findings and speculations. It is a fairly technical work, recommended only to those who have a strong interest in archaeology.

ASHE, GEOFFREY. **CAMELOT AND THE VISION OF ALBION. Bibliography, index, 233pp. PnB71, 2.00p.**
Drawing on varied researches and on the insight embodied in William

Blake's symbol of the shadowy *Giant Albion* behind Arthur, the author goes into the deep psychological basis that underlies the story of the enchanted king, his city Camelot, his mysterious departure to Avalon, his promised return. The inquiry starts from the facts discovered in the Cadbury/Camelot excavation and moves on to the world of gods and mortals.

ASHE, GEOFFREY. **THE FINGER AND THE MOON. 1.60p.**
See the Occult Fiction section.

■ *ASHE, GEOFFREY.* **KING ARTHUR'S AVALON: THE STORY OF GLASTONBURY. Illustrations, bibliography, index, 315pp. Fon57, 2.80p.**
This is an historical recreation of Glastonbury, including information on its early years as a cultural site and its classical period and connections with Arthur and his court. Ashe devotes a great deal of space to the Grail legend, presenting many of the most common speculations and formulating his own hypothesis. The book reads well and is more historical than archaeological.

ASHE, GEOFFREY, ed. **THE QUEST FOR ARTHUR'S BRITAIN. Many illustrations, index, 238pp. Grn71, 4.50p.**
A collection of essays by noted archaeologists and scholars which examine the historical foundations of the Arthurian tradition and then present the results of excavations at Cadbury, Tintagel, Glastonbury, and less well known sites. This is the most complete account available of western Britain between AD 400 and 600.

BAIN, GEORGE. **CELTIC ART. 4.00p.**
See the Sacred Art section.

BERGSTROM, THEO. **STONEHENGE. 9"x8¾", about 100pp. TCP74, 3.95p.**
A stunning collection of photographs taken in one midsummer day from before dawn to dusk. An essay following the photographs discusses the construction of the three stages of Stonehenge, and the reasons behind the construction. This section is illustrated with line drawings. Next to visiting the site, browsing through this book is the best way to realize the visual impact of Stonehenge.

■ *BORD, JANET and COLIN.* **MYSTERIOUS BRITAIN. Bibliography, 262pp. Grn73, 5.15p.**
A lavishly illustrated account of the archaeological remains in England, Wales, Scotland, and Ireland. The full page photographs and commentary suggest many unsuspected properties in ancient sites. The text is both authoritative and vividly written.

Gargoyles of pagan origin
from All Saints Church, Ashcott.

BORD, JANET and COLIN. **THE SECRET COUNTRY. Bibliography, index, 238pp. Wal76, 5.35p.**
This is a readable guide to the ancient sites of the British Isles—standing stones, stone circles, henges, hill forts, and burial mounds—and the folklore that surrounds these sites. The Bords are professional photographers, writers, and tireless investigators of ancient Britain. Here they present over 650 folktales with the aim of shedding light on the enigmatic prehistoric structures and the character, abilities, and beliefs of their architects. An abundance of photographs and line drawings accompany the text.

BRANSTON, BRIAN. **THE LOST GODS OF ENGLAND. Index, 216pp. Oxf57/T&H, 10.00c.**
The Old English gods, still around each week from Sunday to Friday—Sun, Moon, Tiw, Woden, Thunor, and Frig—are described in this book and illustrated with many fine photographs. The author points out the meaning that the northern deities had for the early Anglo-Saxons; how Christianity did and did not accept the customs associated with these older gods; and how, to a certain degree, these early beliefs affect our outlook today. This is an excellent study.

BROWN, PETER LANCASTER. **MEGALITHS, MYTHS, AND MEN. Notes, index, 324pp. H&R76/BIP, 4.95p.**
A lavishly illustrated introductory survey of astroarchaeology, discussing all the latest developments and thoroughly reviewing the major and minor findings. The structures in Britain are analyzed in the greatest depth. Brown has done an excellent job of organizing and synthesizing many complex theories and astronomical data.

BURL, AUBREY. **THE STONE CIRCLES OF THE BRITISH ISLES. Notes, bibliography, index, 7½"x10", 431pp. YUP76, 20.00c.**
A comprehensive, scholarly study. Burl analyzes and synthesizes all the relevant archaeological data and presents an objective view of the megalithic rings—of which nearly a thousand still survive in the British Isles. Burl first provides a hypothetical chronological framework for the circles and considers their origins and purpose, examining in particular their possible astronomical function. He then discusses each regional grouping of circles, describing their architectural types and the finds from excavations. Special attention is paid to Stonehenge and Avebury, the two best known and most spectacular rings. The book also includes a catalogue providing a corpus of stone circles. Fifty diagrams and thirty-six photographs illustrate the text.

■ *CHADWICK, NORA.* **THE CELTS. Illustrations, maps, index, 301pp. Vik70, 3.50p.**
Ms. Chadwick, a Celtic scholar of international repute, describes the rise and spread of the Celts and their arrival in the British Isles in about the eighth century BC. Her study includes information on their history, religion, art, and literature. **The Celts** is a work of excellent scholarship, incorporating the most modern theories, and geared toward the general reader.

COOKE, GRACE and IVAN. **THE LIGHT IN BRITAIN. 118pp. WET71, 5.00c.**
Describes what was revealed when Grace Cooke, a highly developed clairvoyant, used her faculty to uncover some of the mysteries of such prehistoric centers as Stonehenge, Avebury, and Silbury Hill. The text centers on the spiritual development of the ancient British people.

CRITCHLOW, KEITH and GRAHAM CHALLIFOUR, eds. **EARTH MYSTERIES: A STUDY IN PATTERNS. 8¼"x11¾", 56pp. RLK77, 7.65p.**
An illustrated collection of essays on various aspects of British Earth mysteries published in conjunction with *Earth Mysteries: RILKO Artists' Exhibition.* The selections include *Stonehenge* by Alexander Thom and *The Cosmology of Stone Circles* by Keith Critchlow, as well as papers by many other well known researchers. This is an interesting collection which will be treasured by those who are deeply interested in Earth mysteries.

DAMES, MICHAEL. **THE AVEBURY CYCLE. Notes, bibliography, index, 240pp. T&H77, 12.95c.**
4,000 years ago, Avebury parish in South England was the metropolis of Britain; today it contains the most amazing collection of Stone Age monuments to be found anywhere in the world. This book is a unified presentation of the extent of the Neolithic achievement, making use of archaeology, comparative ethnography, folklore, placename research, and allied disciplines. As the earliest farmers, the Neolithic people were worshipers of the Great Goddess, whose seasonal aspects were commemorated with appropriate temples. Dames shows the yearly cycle to be animated with lunar climaxes and consciously synchronized with farming activities and corresponding threshold events in the human life cycle. Hundreds of plates illustrate Dames' thesis.

DAMES, MICHAEL. **THE SILBURY TREASURE. Notes, bibliography, index, 192pp. T&H76, 12.95c.**
Silbury Hill in Wiltshire, England, is the tallest prehistoric structure in Europe. Attempts in recent centuries to explain Silbury in terms familiar to our own culture have not succeeded. In this important and challenging book, Dames demonstrates that the form and purpose of Silbury is entirely consistent with the principle concern of European Stone Age communities—the cult of the Great Goddess. The hill and moat together are the Great Goddess, portrayed in the pregnant squatting attitude known from hundreds of figurines of similar antiquity. Silbury Hill is her womb, and the moat makes up the rest of her body—a figurative use of landscape which was normal in the Neolithic world. A careful, detailed study, fully illustrated with photographs and line drawings.

DOTTIN, GEORGES. **THE CELTS. 8"x9½", 142pp. Mnr77, 3.98c.**
A concise, topically arranged text, accompanied by an abundance of color and black and white photographs. An adequate introductory survey.

EVANS-WENTZ, W.Y. **THE FAIRY-FAITH IN CELTIC COUNTRIES. 11.75p.**
See the Fairies subsection of Fairy Tales.

FORDE-JOHNSTON, J. **PREHISTORIC BRITAIN AND IRELAND. Bibliography, index, 7½"x9¾", 208pp. Nor76/Den, 11.50c.**
Forde-Johnston focuses on the wide range of prehistoric structures which are still visible in the British Isles and places them in their archaeological context. The opening chapter outlines the period from Neolithic times until the Roman conquest of AD 43, and provides a structural framework for the subsequent discussion. This is followed by an account of the houses and settlements throughout the same period, and the major types of prehistoric structures discussed in later chapters. The author has incorporated the results of the most recent archaeological research and fully illustrates his discussion with photographs and line drawings.

GRAY, WILLIAM. **THE ROLLRIGHT RITUAL. 8.50c.**
See the Mysticism section.

HADINGHAM, EVAN. **CIRCLES AND STANDING STONES. Bibliography, index, 7"x10", 247pp. Dou75/SBL, 4.95p.**
Hadingham explores the megalith mysteries of early Britain from every possible angle. He summarizes the recent archaeological studies of Gerald Hawkins, Alexander Thom, Colin Renfrew, and others, and reviews the work of hundreds of local archaeologists and antiquarians. Hadingham also offers his own observations based on extensive field studies, augmented by hundreds of his drawings, maps, and photographs. This is a fascinating exploration of the most important sites and the culture of early Britain. The reader does not have to have any background in the field to enjoy the book.

HARTLEY, CHRISTINE. **THE WESTERN MYSTERY TRADITION. 171pp. TPL68, 3.90p.**
The bulk of this book is a survey of the Western mystery tradition as it has appeared historically in Britain. Ms. Hartley's discussion centers on the Druids and the Arthurian legend, though she also takes the reader back to the days of Atlantis and up to the present time. This is an interesting narrative which introduces material we have not seen elsewhere. Ms. Hartley was a student of Dion Fortune.

HATT, JEAN-JACQUES. **CELTS AND GALLO-ROMANS. Maps, chronology, notes, bibliography, index, 6½"x9½", 333pp. Nag70, 26.20c.**
A very detailed, profusely illustrated study of Celtic and Gallic archaeology. Dr. Hatt has been deeply involved in recent research and he is very qualified to present this account which begins with a study of the history of archaeological research in France and goes from there to an exploration of the methods and techniques employed by archaeol-

ogists. The bulk of the volume is devoted to an in depth analysis of the civilizations in the area from the dawn of recorded time to the fifth century AD. In addition to analyses of the cultural achievements of the people, sections are also devoted to religion, gods, and mythology.

HAWKINS, GERALD. **STONEHENGE DECODED. Appendix, index, 202pp. Del65/Fon, 2.45p.**
Hawkins is an astronomer who has attempted to decode the monument at Stonehenge through the use of a computer. His thesis is that Stonehenge was actually a sophisticated astronomical observatory, rather than a Druid temple as is commonly believed. Tables, illustrations, and photographs supplement the text and Hawkins provides a good bibliography.

HERITY, MICHAEL and GEORGE EOGAN. **IRELAND IN PREHISTORY. Notes, bibliography, index, 7½"x10", 318pp. RKP77, 26.85c.**
A scholarly reconstruction of the prehistory of Ireland, examining the economy, technology, burial customs, and arts, as well as the material record that remains of them. An abundance of line drawings and maps accompany the text. The authors are both lecturers in the Department of Archaeology at the University College, Dublin.

HERM, RICHARD. **THE CELTS. Chronology, bibliography, index, 312pp. SMP76, 12.50c.**
This is a magnificent study of Celtic civilization, beginning with prehistoric times and continuing through the period following the Roman occupation. Herm writes well. The book was number one on the German bestseller list.

HOYLE, FRED. **ON STONEHENGE. Notes, index, 6"x8", 168pp. Fre77/HeG, 6.50p.**
Hoyle, an internationally known cosmologist, presents evidence that Stonehenge was an astronomical calculator and shows how Paleolithic astronomers may have made their calculations. *The purpose of Stonehenge,* writes Hoyle, *was to predict the occurrence of eclipses.* Many illustrations and charts, including a foldout ground plan, accompany the text.

HUBERT, HENRI. **THE RISE OF THE CELTS. Plates, line drawings, maps, many notes, bibliography, index, 360pp. B&T34, 16.80c.**
This definitive volume incorporates a wealth of information on Celtic language and civilization; on the origins of the Celts; and on the Celtic people themselves. Also contains a great deal of archaeological evidence.

KINSELLA, THOMAS, tr. **THE TAIN. 10.65p.**
See the Mythology section.

LETHBRIDGE, T.C. **GOGMAGOG—THE BURIED GODS. Illustrations, index, 192pp. RKP57, 11.05p.**
Lethbridge writes about the excavation of a Neolithic chalk figure; he details the available clues, shows how they were followed up, and tells how the search ended in the discovery of two other giant figures. The greater part of the book is devoted to an analysis of the meaning of these figures, based on archaeological, historical, and biblical information. Lethbridge's findings throw light on the nature of the old gods and the old religion in Britain.

LEWIS, LIONEL. **ST. JOSEPH OF ARIMATHEA AT GLASTONBURY OR THE APOSTLE CHURCH OF BRITAIN. Appendices, notes, 211pp. Cla22, 8.40c.**
A detailed retelling of the legends surrounding St. Joseph's visits to Glastonbury, citing both traditional stories and literary and ecclesiastical authorities.

MABINOGION.
See the Mythology section for various translations of the **Mabinogion.**

MALTWOOD, K.E. **A GUIDE TO GLASTONBURY'S TEMPLE OF THE STARS. 6.70c.**
See The Grail and King Arthur section.

MARKALE, J. **WOMEN OF THE CELTS. Notes, index, 6¼"x9½", 315pp. Cre75, 17.95c.**
This is a very thorough review of the title subject. The major portion of the text is a detailed exploration of women in Celtic mythology. There is also a survey of women in Celtic societies which includes information on social life, marriage, sexual liberation, and love. Much of the

mythology cited and liberally quoted here is not generally well known. The book is well written and should be of great interest to those seeking deeper insights into Celtic society and mythology and the role of women in that society. Markale is the leading scholar in the field.

MICHELL, JOHN. **SECRETS OF THE STONES: THE STORY OF ASTRO-ARCHAEOLOGY. Illustrations, 5¾"x8¼", 96pp. Vik77, 2.95p.**
In these pages we follow the rise of an archaeological theory which relates the designs and locations of megalithic sites to the observed positions of the heavenly bodies at the time they were constructed.... Resistance to astro-archaeological theory has been intensified by the understanding that, if ancient people of Neolithic culture are credited with an astonomical science far in advance of medieval, and even in some respects of modern standards, current faith in the unique quality of our own scientific achievement is undermined. Yet evidence of a remarkably developed and widespread Stone Age science continues to accumulate.... The following essay is designed to illustrate the stages by which a new idea...promotes itself in status from lunacy to heresy to interesting notion and finally to the gates of orthodoxy.—from the introduction.

■ MICHELL, JOHN. **THE VIEW OVER ATLANTIS. Many illustrations, notes, index, 211pp. RaH72, 1.95p.**
Michell believes that we all live within the ruins of an ancient structure, whose vast size has hitherto rendered it invisible. The entire surface of the Earth is marked with traces of a gigantic work of prehistoric engineering, the remains of a once universal system of natural magic, involving the use of polar magnetism together with another positive force related to solar energy. This book contains evidence to support his theory. In particular, it describes a system of leys or lines laid out throughout the British Isles connecting religious and power sites. Numerous drawings and photographs illustrate the text. The physical evidence is pretty clear, and while Michell's hypothesis as to the meaning is speculative, it makes a lot of sense to us. We recommend this book to all who seek a greater understanding of the makeup of the cosmos.

MORGANWG, IOLO. **THE TRIADS OF BRITAIN. Introduction, lengthy glossary, bibliography, 112pp. Wdw77, 8.15p.**
The **Triads of Britain** form one of the most important contributions to our knowledge of Britain as it was before the Anglo-Saxon period. The text records the varying fortunes of the British Celts, telling of the first settlements, and the legendary rulers, legislators, bards, and cultural heroes. It also recounts the Roman invasion and occupation of Britain, the resistance of native chieftains, the period of Roman decline, and the history of the great British kings. This collection of **Triads** was put together by Iolo Morganwg, and first published in 1801. Many can be found in earlier collections, some dating to the thirteenth century; a number, however, are peculiar to Iolo and scholars are not sure whether they are his own invention. Many lovely Celtic woodcuts accompany the text.

MORRIS, JOHN. **THE AGE OF ARTHUR. Maps, notes, index, 683pp. Scr73, 17.50c.**
A full history of the British Isles from the fourth to the seventh century AD. The history of each of the four nations—England, Wales, Scotland, and Ireland—is separately traced. In a final section, Morris examines and analyzes religion, ideas, learning, economy, and society, and traces their change and evolution. This is a careful, academic study which is as thorough as anything we have seen. Morris is thoroughly familiar with his material and he has put together a readable history.

NIEL, FERNAND. **THE MYSTERIES OF STONEHENGE. 208pp. Avo75, 1.95p.**
There have been hundreds of works written on Stonehenge since the sixteenth century when the famous architect Inigo Jones became fascinated by Stonehenge and wrote the first known comprehensive study of it, illustrated with drawings that included an attempt to depict its original state. Many questions have been given satisfactory answers, precise plans have been drawn, intelligent and methodical excavations have been carried out, and a number of discoveries have been made, some of them sensational.... But important questions still remain unanswered, for one of the most bewildering aspects of that enigmatic structure is its uniqueness. Nowhere else in the world is there anything comparable to it.... I have spent thirty entire days studying Stonehenge at the site itself. Among other things, I have verified its measurements and alignments. But although my own studies were one of the factors that prompted me to write this book, it is based to a large extent on the great works of British scientists.... Most of the great works on Stonehenge contain many plans, diagrams, maps, and drawings to which the reader is often referred. This book...follows that

rule.—from the foreword. This is a well written, fascinating account. Neil is thorough in his treatment and he introduces material not readily found in other sources. This is a serious study which should be appreciated by all who are fascinated by ancient archaeology. Niel sets the stage, reviews the findings of others, and then advances his own evidence and conclusions.

NORDENFALK, CARL. **CELTIC AND ANGLO-SAXON PAINTING.** 9.95p.
See the Sacred Art section.

O'BRIEN, HENRY. **ATLANTIS IN IRELAND. Illustrations, notes, 524pp. Mul1834, 9.50p.**
Originally titled, **The Round Towers of Ireland**, this volume should be of interest to those who seek a better understanding of the life and culture of the Druids, including their monuments and religious cults. The book has been long out of print and only recently reprinted. It does not read particularly well and many of the author's ideas have been disputed by later scholars. Nevertheless, it remains an intriguing study that seems to be a work of fairly good scholarship.

PIGGOT, STUART. **THE DRUIDS. Illustrations, notes, bibliography, index, 236pp. Pen74, 3.00p.**
Druidism, according to traditional belief, was the religion of the Celts of pre-Roman Gaul and Britain, among whom the Druids were the priestly class. References to Druids by Greek and Roman writers provide much of the limited knowledge we have of their nature and characteristics, and this has been supplemented by archaeological evidence of early Celtic society. This is an interesting synoptic treatment of the source material in the area. Piggot's aim is to present the Druids to the general reader, and this he does in a good manner.

■ *REES, ALWYN and BRINLEY.* **CELTIC HERITAGE. Extensive notes, indices, 427pp. T&H61, 7.95p.**
This is an excellent, monumental work which reinterprets Celtic tradition in the light of recent advances in the comparative study of religion, mythology, and anthropology. Part one considers the distinguishing features of the various cycles of tales and the major individuals who figure most prominently in them. Part two reveals the cosmological framework within which the action of the tales takes place. Part three is a discussion of the themes of certain classes of stories which tell of conceptions and births, supernatural adventures, courtships and marriages, violent deaths, and voyages to the *Other World*, and an attempt is made to understand their religious function and to glimpse their transcendent meaning. The scholarship is excellent as is the retelling of the stories. This is the best overall work on the Celts that we have seen and we recommend it highly.

REISER, OLIVER. **THIS HOLYEST ERTHE. Photographs and line drawings, bibliography, 121pp. Prn74, 6.50c.**
An interesting, scholarly study of Glastonbury which attempts to answer the following questions: *What is the meaning of the Tor of Avalon, which has been likened to the Great Pyramid?; What is the truth about the Quest for the Holy Grail and the story of King Arthur?; Is there treasure buried in the abbey ruins or nearby, as tradition relates?; Did Christ visit Glastonbury, or St. Joseph of Arimathaea?; Is the Holy Cup of the Last Supper buried on Chalice Hill?*

RENFREW, COLIN, ed. **BRITISH PREHISTORY. Line drawings, chronology, ample bibliographies, index, 348pp. Duc74, 8.85p.**
In this authoritative study, six of Britain's leading prehistorians offer a period-by-period analysis, making full use of the latest developments in dating and the more recent archaeological discoveries.

RIMMER, ALFRED. **ANCIENT STONE CROSSES OF ENGLAND. Seventy-two woodcuts, index, 176pp. GaP1875, 8.50c.**
This remains the most complete description of the appearances and sites of the ancient stone crosses in Britain.

ROBERTS, ANTHONY. **ATLANTEAN TRADITIONS IN ANCIENT BRITAIN. Many illustrations, bibliography, index, 7¾"x10", 135pp. HPG75, 6.95p.**
The researching and writing of this book has taken more than a year, entailing extensive reading and travelling. The majority of the British sites and monuments have been personally investigated, various notes on legends and "atmosphere" being made on the spot via detailed fieldwork. The book itself is really a self-contained part of a much larger, more ornate pattern that is slowly being deciphered and which spans the whole

face of the globe. "The Lost Giants" are gradually being discovered again, for their presence lingers in the landscape as a perpetual reminder of past glory. They form physical and spiritual remnants from a lost world. It is the purpose of the speculative mythologist to reclothe the bones of the "Giants" in a semblance of their former majesty, and that has been the aim of this book as far as the British Isles are concerned. Much has been left out, much cannot yet be written, but in spite of this the work does encompass a re-reading of certain key legends and symbols that are archetypal to the human race as a whole.—from the preface.

ROBERTS, ANTHONY, ed. **GLASTONBURY—ANCIENT AVALON, NEW JERUSALEM. Notes, bibliographies, 7¾"x10", 176pp. HPG78, 8.15p.**
A collection of twelve original articles celebrating many aspects of the Glastonbury mystique. Among the subjects discussed are the Glastonbury Zodiac, the Abbey and its treasures, legendary Somerset geomancy, and the zodiac temples of southwest Britain. The contributors are the leading figures in the field. Each article is fairly technical and contains a number of illustrative diagrams and maps.

ROSS, ANNE. **EVERYDAY LIFE OF THE PAGAN CELTS. Notes, bibliography, index, 224pp. Crg70, .95p.**
By piecing together archaeological discoveries, classical references, and the later vernacular literature of Ireland, Ms. Ross recreates the life of the early Celts. She outlines the structure of their society, describes their appearance and activities. She also reviews their complex religious beliefs and practices—their temples and shrines, festivals and rites, deities and cults, and their ideas about the afterlife. Examples of Celtic art are scattered throughout the book. The text is written in a conversational style and the reader does get a good feeling for the times.

SCREETON, PAUL. **QUICKSILVER HERITAGE. Notes, index, 304pp. SBL74, 5.20p.**
Screeton is editor and publisher of **The Ley Hunter**, an English publication devoted solely to ley lines throughout the world. Here he builds on the earlier work of Watkins and Michell in presenting a comprehensive study embracing leys, prehistoric monuments, terrestrial zodiacs, astronomy, astrology, alchemy, and spiritual physics. The ley system is a network of straight lines—age old trackways and paths of a subtle energy—which run across Britain and other parts of the world. This is a fascinating study for all who are interested in understanding the magnetic and electrical properties of the Earth and learning how the ancients used these forces and how they can be applied today.

■ *SHARKEY, JOHN.* **CELTIC MYSTERIES. 8"x11", 96pp. T&H75, 6.15p.**
The last tribal culture in Europe was that of the Celtic lands, whose landscape and traditions hold echoes of the ancient religion of nature, with its emphasis on the fairy and spirit world and its symbols of death and rebirth. The mysteries begin in the frenzy of battle, where the hero is transfigured and the god appears; or in a ghostly circle of stones left by an unknown people; or in the mystic center of the Celtic cross; or in the stone heads of Gaul and Ireland, which face both ways. The ancient oral tradition that perpetuated the laws, legends, and tribal teachings through the trained memories of a group of poets and priests made the act of writing unnecessary. And, much like the prohibitions laid on the Celtic warrior heroes, which predestined their lives and

actions, the taboo on writing continued as long as the old religion lasted. Therefore it is in pictures of Celtic art, artifacts, and religious sites that the culture comes the clearest. This volume is made up of 117 illustrations, twenty-four in color. Each is fully described and the book begins with an excellent introduction summing up what is known of the Celtic mysteries and setting the stage for the art that follows.

SPENCE, LEWIS. **THE HISTORY AND ORIGINS OF DRUIDISM.** Notes, index, 178pp. Wei49, 7.95c.
An examination of the origins and practices of the Druids. Druidic theology, ritual, places of worship, and priesthood are discussed as well as their magical practices.

SPENCE, LEWIS. **THE MYSTERIES OF BRITAIN.** Illustrations, offset, spiral bound, 246pp. HeR nd, 5.00p.
A detailed investigation of the ancient British mystical tradition, associated with the Celts, which Spence believes to be of North African origin. He fully examines Celtic and Druidic traditions and draws parallels with other early civilizations.

SQUIRE, CHARLES. **CELTIC MYTH AND LEGEND.** 4.95p.
See the Mythology section.

THOM, ALEXANDER. **MEGALITHIC LUNAR OBSERVATORIES.** Many detailed drawings, maps, graphs, notes, index, 127pp. Oxf73, 16.15c.
A technical study which shows that the methods used by megalithic man for astronomical observations were more elaborate than was formerly believed. Descriptions are given of thirty-five lunar and solar sites in Britain from which accurate declinations can be obtained. Analysis of these declinations yields values of the moon's orbital inclination and parallax that are in remarkable agreement with modern values. The way in which the megalithic observers extrapolated the turning values of the declination, which could not in general be observed directly, is shown by the remains at several sites. The book includes details of the astronomical background necessary for an understanding of the moon's movements. Thom is a very careful researcher and his work is highly regarded.

THOM, ALEXANDER. **MEGALITHIC SITES IN BRITAIN.** Index, 174pp. Oxf67, 17.50c.
This book derives from a study of 500 megalithic sites in Britain. Thom establishes the megalithic yard and uses it to elucidate the geometry of the rings, ellipses, and other compound shapes that the megalithic erectors used. He shows astronomically that a sophisticated solar calendar was in use, and that extensive observations of the moon were made in its four limiting positions. Typical surveys of many sites show the kind of material on which the author's conclusions are based, and several introductory chapters are devoted to such aspects of statistics, mathematics, and astronomy as are necessary to an understanding of the analysis. The material is highly technical and the text includes a profusion of line drawings, charts, and diagrams.

THOMAS, CHARLES. **BRITAIN AND IRELAND IN EARLY CHRISTIAN TIMES, A.D. 400-800.** 110 plates, nineteen in color, drawings, maps, topically organized bibliography, index, 144pp. MGH71/T&H, 3.95p.
The four centuries between the end of the Roman occupation and the first Viking raids are the most obscure in British history. Professor Thomas recreates this era, based on his own research and personal insights. He discusses migration and settlement, the rise of Christianity, and the spread of spoken and written languages. He covers development throughout the British Isles, including Ireland, with special stress on the Celtic areas.

TREHARNE, R.F. **THE GLASTONBURY LEGENDS.** Illustrations, bibliography, 135pp. SBL67, 2.00p.
The ruins of Glastonbury Abbey are all that remain of one of the greatest monasteries of medieval England—a place shrouded in mystery and legend and said to be the site of the first Christian church in Britain, and the burial place of both the Holy Grail and King Arthur. Drawing on archaeology, history, and myth, Treharne penetrates the legends that surround Glastonbury, examines their development, and provides an insight into the world of prehistoric Britain.

UNDERWOOD, GUY. **PATTERN OF THE PAST.** Notes, index, 192pp. SBL69, 3.50p.
Guy Underwood devoted his life to the study of the prehistoric monuments and mysteries of ancient Britain. This remarkable book tells the story of his work. Underwood believed that *some powerful cosmic force which covers the surface of the earth as do gravity and light* was responsible for much of the unexplained remains. In this book he explains its influence on animal life, vegetation, and above all on early man, who harnessed it to set out the great prehistoric monuments of Britain. This is an intriguing, important work which will be of great interest to all who have followed John Michell's work. Many line drawings and photographs illuminate the text.

WATKINS, ALFRED. **THE LEY HUNTER'S MANUAL: A GUIDE TO EARLY TRACKS.** Index, 107pp. Pcl27, 5.05p.
This is a recent reprint of Watkins' pioneering manual—showing the nature and extent of prehistoric British relics and detailing how to discover them. Many illustrations, including actual site plans, are included.

WATKINS, ALFRED. **THE OLD STRAIGHT TRACK.** 129 plates, index, 256pp. SBL25, 4.20p.
This book remains the most important source for the study of the ancient straight tracks or leys that crisscross the British Isles—a system already old when the Romans came to Britain. Watkins noticed that beacon hills, mounds, earthworks, moats, and old churches built on pagan sites seemed to fall into straight lines. His investigations convinced him that Britain was covered with a vast network of straight tracks, aligned with either the sun or the path of a star. Although traces of this network can be found all over the country, the principles behind the ley system still remain a mystery.

WILLIAMS, MARY, ed. **BRITAIN: A STUDY IN PATTERNS.** Many two color illustrations and photographs, 8½"x11", 59pp. RLK71, 6.25p.
A collection of papers on British prehistory put together by members of the Research into Lost Knowledge Organization. Geometric principles and patterns are emphasized, and the authors include Keith Critchlow and John Michell. All but two of the papers deal with the pre-Christian period.

WILLIAMS, MARY, et al. **GLASTONBURY: A STUDY IN PATTERNS.** 8½"x11", 40pp. RLK69, 4.65p.
This is an excellent collection of technical papers on the mythology surrounding Glastonbury and the scientific achievement which it represents and demonstrates. Both the pre-Christian and post-Christian eras are covered. Each of the selections is fully illustrated.

WOOD, JOHN EDWIN. **SUN, MOON AND STANDING STONES.** Many illustrations, bibliography, index, 229pp. Oxf78, 14.95c.
An aura of mystery surrounds Stonehenge, Carnac, and other remains of the Late Neolithic and Early Bronze Ages. Many scientists have claimed that they are evidence that prehistoric cultures devised their own geometry and units of length, invented accurate methods of observing the sun and moon, produced a calendar, and predicted eclipses. In this book the evidence for and against the geometrical and astronomical hypotheses is collected and assessed (Wood considers the case to be proven). Dr. Wood's approach is scientific, but with a minimum of mathematics. He gives all the necessary background information and discusses several sites in detail. A final section looks at the impact of the astronomical theory on our understanding of the Neolithic and Early Bronze Ages.

■ WRIGHT, DUDLEY. **DRUIDISM.** Illustrations, bibliography, index, 192pp. EPG24, 10.50c.
Druids were members of a pre-Christian religious order of the ancient Celts of Gaul, Ireland, and Britain. The Romans massacred them in a wholesale slaughter during their conquest because they felt that the Druids were heathens performing human sacrificial ceremonies, and feared that they would interrupt the smooth running of the state. This book is a concise history of the Druids, describing their origins, beliefs, ceremonies, festivals, customs, magical practices, and affinity with other religions. Many legends about Druidic temples have come down to us, some of which are described here.

ANCIENT CIVILIZATIONS

Men have probably been interested in the past, and more particularly in origins, ever since they have been capable of conceptual thought. But for a very long time there was no attempt to look back objectively and rationally, much less to try to recover past events through their material remains. Instead, men explained their origins imaginatively, making their creation stories part of their religious beliefs. The resulting myths were historical only in so far as they were emanations of the human psyche. The Babylonians told how the creator, Ea, made men from the blood of the erring divinity, Klingu, in order that they might serve as slaves for the gods; one Egyptian myth tells how men were first shaped on the potter's wheel by the ram-god Knum; according to the Shilluk the original man was born of a white cow which came up from the Nile; the Pueblo Indians believe that mankind climbed from the underworld through the opening of Shipapu. In the ancient world how astonished they would have been to learn that the Hebrew version of the creation story as told in **Genesis** was to cause violent resistance to the findings of science thousands of years later.

A more objective approach to a study of man began with the observations made by travellers and foreign visitors. Travellers' tales have always found listeners. Whether it was Pytheas the Greek, home from his dim and misty voyage round the British Isles, Marco Polo back from the court of the Great Khan, Columbus from America, Cook from the Pacific or Gagarin and Glenn from outer space, their fellows have drawn round to hear tell of the strange things they have seen. In particular (and here the astronauts are at a disadvantage) men have delighted to learn about the ways of unknown races in order to compare these ways with their own—to wonder and to laugh at the foreigners' preposterous manner of eating and dressing, of marrying and burying, or at their peculiarities of skin colour, features and hair.

Almost exactly the same kind of curiosity and wonder have been roused by the discoveries of individuals who have explored not in space but in time. Layard and Schliemann, Botta and Mariette, Stephens, Evans and Woolley are all famous for having brought back news of unknown peoples— of peoples who did not live far away, but long ago. And although they may be felt to have lost something in being denied encounters with living men and women, they also gained immeasurably in having ventured into the past. For one thing, almost everyone has a nostalgia for the past—whether it is his own past or that of mankind. But also, while living *barbarians* and *savages* (*Ancient Britons* equally with Australian aborigines) were always felt to be oddities on the fringes of history, it was often clear that the remains of forgotten cultures recovered by the spade lay at the roots of our own civilization; were a part of the central development of world history.

There are two strong justifications for beginning an introduction to archaeology with this analogy between explorations in space and time. The first and most obvious is that until recent times the two overlapped and were sometimes almost identical. Herodotus, for example, is rightly accepted as the Father of History, yet what is now of interest to archaeology is not his heroic account of the Persian Wars, but the enthralling digressions in which he describes the many peoples inhabiting the background of his scenes. These digressions, which evidently fascinated him as much as they have fascinated his readers ever since, were generally the fruits of his own travels—or those of his many informants. It will be found, too, that many of the extracts dating from the seventeenth to the early nineteenth century come from the books of men who were first and foremost simply travellers. They noted the antiquities they saw, might even on occasion, like Stephens, stop to do a little digging, but their accounts show an equal interest in the living Arabs, Egyptians, or Mexicans who entertained or robbed them, or in the other adventures they experienced in the course of their journeys. They were archaeologists only by the way.

The second and more significant justification for the use of the analogy is that it illumines what should be the best aims of archaeology. An immense amount of labour, skill and ingenuity goes into excavation and the study of antiquities, but unless they result in the resurrection of life, all this effort is largely in vain. This has been insisted upon again and again by leading archaeologists. Sir Mortimer Wheeler has written *. . . the archaeologist is digging up, not things, but people. Unless the bits and pieces with which he deals be alive to him, unless he have himself the common touch, he had better seek out other disciplines.* Professor Grahame Clark puts it like this: *It is true that your archaeologist is compelled by circumstances to rely upon the material remains surviving from the people he is studying to arrive at any idea of their daily life; yet however much he may be preoccupied with things, often in themselves unattractive, he is really interested all the time in people.* Professor Clark perhaps too easily assumes that this is so rather than that it should be so. There are only too many lesser practitioners in the subject who— whether they lack *the common touch* or simply imagination—seem only too ready to use ever more meticulous techniques to pile up ever larger mounds of almost meaningless information.

In fact the insistence on the human values of archaeology is far more necessary today than it was in the past. Modern excavators condemn their predecessors out of hand for their lack of scientific methods and aims. But at least the old antiquaries and such early diggers as Layard were working directly to enrich their own cultures. Thus sculptures brought home from the Grand Tour might represent ignorant pillage, but they beautified fine houses and gardens. Classical remains unscientifically studied by such men as the Adam brothers led to a happy revolution in architecture and interior deocoration. The observations on Egyptian art brought back by the learned gentlemen accompanying Napoleon's armies to the Nile gave rise to all the delicious Egyptianate fantasy of the *Empire* style. Layard and Botta's discoveries in Assyria introduced a new art to all the educated public of Europe as well as putting new heart into **Bible** students. In this last they may be said to have countered the almost simultaneous discoveries of the scientists who were establishing the reality of antediluvian man and setting fundamentalist Christianity in turmoil. No, it is only today, when science can fill many pages with statistical tables giving the angles of percussion of flint implements and the like, that it has to be insisted that archaeology is first and foremost a handmaid of history.

For I must expand a little on the statements of Sir Mortimer Wheeler and Professor Clark. While certainly archaeologists must always concern themselves with revealing people and their daily lives, I believe that they must also be shown in the context of history—that is to say of change and development. Quite static studies of a family of Palaeolithic cave dwellers or of Basket Maker Indians are interesting in themselves, certainly, because of the special lure of the past. Yet one has to ask whether it is reasonable to devote so much time to them, when nobody is taking anything like the same trouble to discover and record the details of modern life—say of an agricultural worker in his cottage, of a National Service man in his barracks, or a millionaire in his penthouse. No, the interpreter of archaeological discovery must not be content with static description. He can show us a vast spectacle of movement in time, of cultures and civilizations each unique in form and style, growing, flowering, and dying. He can enable us to make comparisons between all these endlessly various manifestations of human creativity, and between them and our own. Above all, archaeological discovery can give a sense of the continuity of past and present. Despite the terrible extravagance of human affairs, the often-repeated tragedies of degeneration and destruction (which excavation has revealed to us even more clearly than written history), the long vista which we now command, from the days of the apemen to our own, enables us to watch past effort and achievement accumulating to form the present. Archaeology has revealed the cultural evolution of man.

If these are some of the aims and purposes of our subject, it also has its more spontaneous gifts and pleasures, no less important but less solemn. It has enormously enriched the art treasury of the world. Thousands of works of art, each an expression of the style of its age and place, have been unearthed and offered for our enjoyment. To enter museums where such treasures are best displayed, often the products of civilizations completely unknown a century ago, can be a most moving experience. They are ancient, yet come to us pristine from the imaginations that created them.

Finally, there is the pleasure which archaeology brings to its own devotees. It is a subject which happily bridges the chasm between the arts and sciences. It also offers equal opportunities to work indoors and out of doors, to the man of action and the man of thought or scholarship. There may be the adventure of going into remote places, of setting up camp far from the modern world and getting to know the native people in a way quite impossible for the ordinary traveler. Several excavators, particularly those writing in the nineteenth century, have left full and affectionate portraits of workmen, foremen and local worthies. Then, whatever the more austere type of modern scientific excavator may say, there is the extraordinary excitement of seeing what is going to turn up next. It is true that day after day workers may be tied to boring routine, often tormented by heat, flies, and dust—or, in Europe, by rain and mud. But then something shows in the trench or pit, it is followed up with trowel and knife and brush, it takes shape, and is finally laid bare. This kind of dramatic experience extends all the way from the uncovering of some quite humble object to the great monuments of archaeology such as the unearthing of the Sutton Hoo Treasure, the descent into the pyramid tomb at Palenque and the opening of the inner burial chambers of Tutankhamen in the Valley of the Kings.

—condensed from **The World of the Past**, *by Jacquetta Hawkes*

Atlantis

For thousands of years memories of this strange, mystical land have haunted the dreams and visions of mankind in a never ending kaleidoscope of half-remembered images and historical fragments. More than 3,000 books on this fascinating subject have been composed, published and either accepted or rejected according to the dispositions of their numerous readers. The earliest extant evidence pertaining to Atlantis is found in two dialogues of Plato known as the **Timaeus** and **Critias**. They were written about 350 BC and describe the history of a great and powerful land that once lay beyond the straits of Gibraltar, somewhere in the vast Atlantic Ocean. It is believed that Plato's famous ancestor Solon, who visited Egypt, was told the history of Atlantis by learned Egyptian priests and that he wrote an epic poem on the subject about 600 BC. Now although Plato was essentially a philosopher, his knowledge of history was extensive and, because of his fineness of perception, accurate. The modern academic scholars dismiss Plato's Atlantis as a fiction. They say it was composed to illustrate various philosophical points, but this cannot be accepted because it is well known that the ancient writers, although using personal vision, drew upon definite historical traditions. The incredible antiquity of Atlantis can next be noted, for Plato describes its devastation and sinking as happening 9,000 years before his time. Only a few years ago the archaeologists were calling this date preposterous. Now, with the advent of radio-carbon and potassium-argon dating methods, they have been forced to drastically rethink their position. Nowhere in Plato's narrative is there any reference to the more fanciful elements of Greek imagination such as gorgons, satyrs, nymphs, etc. He tells a straightforward tale of a definite historical character, dealing with a powerful and civilised people who had great knowledge of architecture, astronomy, navigation and agriculture, coupled with a highly advanced metallurgy and social organization. After Plato there are more than 100 references to Atlantis by classical historians, many of them drawing heavily on now lost source documents.

—condensed from **Atlantean Traditions in Ancient Britain**, *by Anthony Roberts*

■ *BERLITZ, CHARLES.* **THE MYSTERY OF ATLANTIS.** Illustrations, bibliography, 201pp. Grn76, 2.00p.
One of the best modern books on this intriguing subject, containing the most recent evidence and discoveries. Numerous photographs of archaeological artifacts and geographical mysteries are included in this authoritative text.

BRAMWELL, JAMES. **LOST ATLANTIS.** Appendices, notes, index, 288pp. NCP36, 3.45p.
An easy to read survey of the literature on Atlantis. Examines the writings and conclusions of authorities from Plato to Ignatius Donnelly and Lewis Spence, as well as the early twentieth century researches.

CALDWELL, TAYLOR. **ROMANCE OF ATLANTIS.** 285pp. Faw75/Fon, 1.75p.
A novel written when Ms. Caldwell was twelve and prepared for publication by Jess Stearn. The Atlantis pictured is a highly technological society that has harnessed both nuclear and solar energy, but is in moral decay. It is a caste society with factions fighting each other; in its streets are foreigners proclaiming a new god. To the north the Althustrian king plots invasion. There is a cosmic climax.

CAYCE, EDGAR. **ATLANTIS: FACT OR FICTION?** 36pp. ARE62, 1.25p.
Written by Edgar Cayce's son, this pamphlet looks at evidence for and against the Atlantis legend and goes over the information on Atlantis, from prior to 50,000 BC to its final destruction around 10,000 BC, as given in the Edgar Cayce readings.

■ *DONNELLY, IGNATIUS.* **ATLANTIS: THE ANTEDILUVIAN WORLD. Illustrations, index, 326pp. Dov1882, 5.00p.**
When originally published this book caused a stir of interest and was immediately popular. It remains so today and has been the modern keystone for all such books on the subject of Atlantis and lost continents. Donnelly has approached the subject with scientific accuracy and a precise, detailed inquiry into the mystery of man's past. It has been said that of all writers on the subject of Atlantis, Donnelly ranks next to Plato in importance and influence.

DONNELLY, IGNATIUS. **THE DESTRUCTION OF ATLANTIS: RAGNOROK, THE AGE OF FIRE AND GRAVEL. Illustrations, notes, index, 441pp. Mul71, 3.50p.**
This is the second book by the author on the subject of Atlantis and is concerned with the possible causes of the cataclysm that resulted in the continent's destruction. His pioneering theory was that a comet grazing the Earth could have been the key to the deluge which obliterated that mysterious land.

GALANOPOULOS, A.G. and EDWARD BACON. **ATLANTIS: THE TRUTH BEHIND THE LEGEND. Bibliography, index, 7¾"x10¼", 216pp. BoM69, 12.50c.**
This is a beautifully illustrated volume. The authors begin with a general survey of Atlantis theory, including a critical discussion of Plato's Atlantis. They also summarize a number of geophysical theories and facts. The last half of the book is devoted to a thorough presentation of Professor Galanopoulos' Atlantean research, investigations, and findings. He believes, and illustrates, that Atlantis could never have existed in the Atlantic, and that it must have been situated in the Aegean. His contention is that the Minoan kingdom consisted of at least two islands; one of which was Crete, and the other Atlantis. Modern day Santorini is his choice for the site of Atlantis. We do not agree with the author's premise; nonetheless, we found this to be a fascinating book. Many photographs, including some in color, as well as line drawings illuminate the text.

LUCE, J.V. **THE END OF ATLANTIS. Index, 187pp. Ban70/Grn, 2.50p.**
An erudite study which presents a picture of Santorini and its Bronze Age eruption based on the evidence accumulated by archaeologists as well as an equation, extensively documented, of Atlantis with Minoan Crete. Includes material on the recent excavations. Many full color plates and photographs supplement the text.

MAVOR, JAMES. **VOYAGE TO ATLANTIS. Many illustrations, long bibliography, 310pp. Fon69, 2.65p.**
Mavor led the scientific expeditions to Santorini which verified (at least to his satisfaction) that it was the site of Atlantis. He uncovered, on land and under the sea, a great deal of archaeological and geological evidence—all of which is discussed here in great detail. An interesting, firsthand account.

MEREJKOWSKI, DMITRI. **ATLANTIS/EUROPE. 449pp. Mul71, 3.50p.**
A novelistic exploration of the occult practices and traditions of Atlantis. The author feels that there is a comparison between the evil that overtook Atlantean civilization in its decline and contemporary Western civilization.

■ *MUCK, OTTO.* **THE SECRET OF ATLANTIS. Illustrations, notes, index, 284pp. NYT78, 12.50c.**
Muck, an accomplished German scientist, here relates the accounts of Atlantis handed down from the ancients to geophysical history to explain why Atlantis has figured so strongly in our collective memory down the ages. He states, and attempts to factually prove, that Atlantis was the greatest trauma of human history. According to Muck, Atlantis was a flourishing island empire in the area of the Azores, dominated by an awesome volcano. At 8:00 pm on June 5th, 8498 BC, the world was instantly shattered when an asteroid several miles in diameter plunged through the Earth's crust with the force of 30,000 hydrogen bombs. The globe wobbled on its axis; the island of Atlantis sank; the Gulf Stream was diverted north; the Ice Age receded. A deluge and a gigantic tidal wave wiped out human, animal, and plant life and the civilization of Atlantis vanished, leaving only fragmented folk memories of a lost paradise. Muck bases his extrapolation on scientific data from geophysical analysis and he also draws on a variety of ancient sources. We highly recommend this volume to all who are looking for an in depth study. Only time and more study can tell how accurate Muck's thesis is. In any event, his is the most believable presentation we have read—and it also makes an enthralling story.

■ *SPENCE, LEWIS.* **THE HISTORY OF ATLANTIS. Illustrations, 238+pp. Stu26, 3.95p.**
Spence devoted his life to the study of mythology and prehistory. He has written a number of books on Atlantis. This is his most comprehensive introduction to Atlantean civilization. Spence has a wonderful facility for bringing ancient cultures and events to life and he is at his best in this work. He begins with a survey of the sources of Atlantean history, including a full summary of Plato's writings on the subject. The next chapters cover, respectively, Atlantean geography, races, and rulers. There are also chapters on Atlantis in Britain, Atlantean traditions, daily life in Atlantis, Atlantean state and polity, religion in Atlantis, animal life in Atlantis, and Atlantean colonies.

SPENCE, LEWIS. **THE OCCULT SCIENCES IN ATLANTIS. Offset, spiral bound, 133pp. HeR22, 4.50p.**
A scientific and reasonable account. Much is related concerning magical practice in ancient Atlantis and the various forms it took, some lofty and others debased. The influence of Atlantis on various cults in Britain is also discussed.

STACY-JUDD, ROBERT. **ATLANTIS: MOTHER OF EMPIRES. Index, 9"x11¼", 365pp. DeV39, 20.00c.**
Stacy-Judd wrote **Atlantis** in 1939, after years of study, research, and personal exploration of Mayan ruins in the jungles of the Yucatan. Through his studies he developed the theory that the Mayas and other South American and African people were descendents of the people of Atlantis. This monumental work covers every aspect of man's development and the development of his early civilizations. Stacy-Judd was an architect and the text is replete with analyses of building design and iconography as well as many illustrations. A fascinating, well developed study.

STEIGER, BRAD. **ATLANTIS RISING. Bibliography, 220pp. SBL73, 1.75p.**
A flamboyant, journalistic account by a writer who specializes in *unexplained phenomena* and the *occult*. Many of the major theories are explored and Steiger offers some explanations of his own.

ZINK, DAVID. **THE STONES OF ATLANTIS. Bibliography, 234pp. PrH78, 9.95c.**
Since 1974 Zink has been conducting a series of underwater archaeological expeditions on the floor of the Atlantic Ocean off the island of Bimini. In this book he describes the results of his investigations and includes a large number of photographs and drawings. It is a highly personal, easy to read account. Zink is certainly not a scholar; however, he has come up with a number of interesting findings.

──────────END OF ATLANTIS SUBSECTION──────────

BELENITSKY, ALEKSANDR. **CENTRAL ASIA. Many photographs, bibliography, index, 251pp. Nag68, 26.20c.**
Belenitsky surveys the area between the Caspian and Lake Balkhash, in Turkmenistan, Uzbekistan and Kazakhstan, in which stretch the great barren foothills of the Himalayan range. These steppe lands have been the meeting place of the civilizations of East and West. This cultural intermingling is followed through the artifacts left by the various peoples. The author is with the Institute of Archaeology of the Soviet Academy of Science.

BENY, ROLOFF and ROSE MACAULAY. **PLEASURE OF RUINS. Index, 7¾"x10¼", 241pp. HRW77, 20.00c.**
An essay on the title theme by Ms. Macaulay is accompanied by 156 photographs, sixteen in color, by Beny who was inspired by the essay. The photographs encompass the whole of the ancient world, and maps

and site plans are also included. Ms. Macaulay does a wonderful job of bringing the ancient sites to life, so that the reader can often sense its decayed magnificence. In the process she offers a fair amount of ancient history. This book is as good a photographic guide to ancient world history as anything we can think of.

BERGIER, JACQUES. **EXTRA-TERRESTRIAL VISITATIONS FROM PREHISTORIC TIMES TO THE PRESENT.** 207pp. NAL74/Fut, 1.50p.
A comprehensive, documented account which identifies visitations and expands upon items that science has dismissed as nonsense or explained quickly. The author is a French scientist, and coauthor of the popular book, **Morning of the Magicians.** The British title of **Visitations** is **Mysteries of Time and Space.**

BERLITZ, CHARLES. **MYSTERIES FROM FORGOTTEN WORLDS.** Illustrations, bibliography, 225pp. Del73/Crg, 1.50p.
A presentation of facts and evidence pointing to the existence of previous great civilizations not generally recognized in orthodox history. Berlitz fits puzzle pieces together that indicate lost civilizations to have been located in America and on the continent of Atlantis, now sunk beneath the waters of the Atlantic Ocean. Many archaeological discoveries and scientific explanations are cited.

Peruvian metal founding, part of a drawing from a sixteenth century codex.

BIBBY, GEOFFREY. **FOUR THOUSAND YEARS AGO: A PANORAMA OF LIFE IN THE SECOND MILLENNIUM BC.** Illustrations, index, 441pp. RaH61, 8.95c.
There has long been a place vacant, on the history shelves of the world, for a volume covering the Second Millenium BC. That millenium is the span of time in which some of the most well-known events in man's history occurred, in which some of the most renowned persons of antiquity lived. It is the period of Stonehenge and the Hyksos, of the Minoan and Indus valley civilizations, of the Hittites and the Argonauts and the Philistines, of the Trojan War and the Exodus, of Hammurabi and Abraham, Akhenaten and Tutankhamon and Rameses the Great, Moses and Saul and Samson and Agamemnon and Theuseus and Tiglathpileser. Everyone has heard these names—and yet the history of the period remains vague, a jumble of disconnected stories. . . . We are here dealing with a thousand years. And a thousand years is, after all, but fourteen lifetimes measured by the conventional scale. . . . So alongside the tale of this thousand years are set fourteen "lifetimes"; fourteen lay figures will obtrude themselves, chapter by chapter, to point the passage of time between the events recorded. This is, of course, the device of the historical novel; but here the human actors are for the most part anonymous spectators of and participators in history.—from the introduction. This is a marvelous account which brings the times to life in a way we have not experienced before.

BLACKER, CARMEN. **ANCIENT COSMOLOGIES.** Illustrations, notes, bibliography, index, 270pp. A&U75, 25.20c.
Nine eminent scholars, each a specialist in his or her own field, seek to answer the question; what was the shape of the universe imagined by the ancient people of Egypt, Babylonia, Israel, India, China, Arabia, Greece, and Scandinavia? A remarkable range of answers is presented, and in the process the cosmological conceptions of each of these early civilizations is examined at length. A fascinating study, recommended to those who are deeply interested in the subject.

CALVANI, VITTORIA. **LOST CITIES.** 8"x9½", 144pp. Mnr76, 3.98c.
A photographic study of some of the most famous cities of antiquity. Calvani's text, while brief, gives a feeling for the culture and civilization associated with each city.

■ *CAMP, L. SPRAGUE DE.* **THE ANCIENT ENGINEERS.** Illustrations, notes, thirteen page bibliography, 450pp. RaH74/Wyn, 1.95p.
A detailed study of the engineers who *learned to exploit the properties of matter and the sources of power for the benefit of mankind.* De Camp explores the accomplishments of the engineers in Egypt, Mesopotamia, Rome, the Orient, and Europe. His narrative illuminates our knowledge of the technology of these ancient civilizations.

CAMP, L. SPRAGUE DE. **LOST CONTINENTS.** Bibliography, index, 348pp. Dov70, 3.50p.
A detailed study of the Atlantean theme in history, mythology, and literature. De Camp sorts out fact from fiction, and reports just about everything that has been written about Atlantis through the ages. This is an excellent compilation and, while we often do not agree with de Camp's generalizations, we thoroughly enjoyed reading the book.

CAMP, L. SPRAGUE DE and CATHERINE DE. **CITADELS OF MYSTERY.** Illustrations, notes, extensive bibliography, 292pp. RaH73, 1.25p.
A fascinating exploration of the ruins of twelve ancient civilizations: Atlantis, Troy, the Pyramids, Tikal, Stonehenge, Zimbabwe, Tintagel Castle, Machu Picchu, Rapa Nui, Angkor Wat, and Nan Matol. In each case the authors describe the site, review its factual and legendary history, and evaluate contemporary theories.

■ *CERAM, C.W.* **GODS, GRAVES AND SCHOLARS: THE STORY OF ARCHAEOLOGY.** Illustrations, bibliography, index, 529pp. Ban67/Pen, 2.95p.
Since the original German edition of this book was published in 1949, it has been translated into twenty-six languages and read by millions of people. . . . Originally written for the widest general reading public, its strict adherence to scientific standards has led long since to its being required reading for some college courses. . . . In the meantime, archaeology has marched on. . . . To cover these new developments, I have revised the original version and concluded the book with a summary of the most important new findings and methods.—from the foreword. This book remains the best overall survey of archaeology available.

CERAM, C.W., ed. **HANDS ON THE PAST.** Photographs, index, 434pp. ScB66, 4.95p.
The story of the world's major archaeological discoveries, in the words of the discoverers themselves. Ceram has produced an excellent volume—the selections are well organized and generally of a high quality.

CERAM, C.W. **THE MARCH OF ARCHAEOLOGY.** Chronology, index, 6½"x8¼", 350pp. RaH58, 6.95p.
A pictorial history of archaeology, containing 310 photographs, paintings, and reconstructions and a well integrated text. This is as good a study of its type as anything we know of.

CERVE, W.S. **LEMURIA: THE LOST CONTINENT OF THE PACIFIC.** Appendix, 274pp. Amo72, 7.60c.
A Rosicrucian compilation of all the tabulated and recorded facts on Lemuria and its people, prepared for the general reader.

CHARROUX, ROBERT. **THE MYSTERIOUS UNKNOWN.** Many photographs, index, 288pp. Crg73, 2.35p.
A collection of amazing facts and stories dealing with relatively unknown aspects of history, civilization, and obscure phenomena. Includes such topics as pyramid mysteries, ancient air travel and spacecraft, and the mystery of vanished continents.

CHATELAIN, MAURICE. **OUR ANCESTORS CAME FROM OUTER-SPACE. Illustrations, bibliography, 209pp. Dou78, 7.95c.**
Another in the constant stream of books on the possible extraterrestrial origin of human civilization. Chatelain, one of the scientists who conceived and designed the Apollo spacecraft, argues that astronauts from another planet in another solar system landed on Earth where they mated with Neanderthal women, thus producing the Cro-Magnon man. He bases his theory on extensive computer analysis of prehistoric remains. This appears to be as good or better than most books on the subject, and the author does introduce some new material in his analyses of the Mayan calendar, the Maltese Cross, and the Rhodes calculator.

CHILDE, V. GORDON. **THE DAWN OF EUROPEAN CIVILIZATION. Many illustrations, notes, bibliography, index, 463pp. Grn57, 2.75p.**
This is a classic work in the history of archaeological thought. From Spain to the Balkans, from the British Isles to the Aegean, from Germany to the Black Sea, Childe surveys the whole of European prehistory. In particular he analyzes the relationship between the civilized and barbarian peoples of the Old World, and defines the environmental and economic forces that shaped the varied cultures of prehistoric Europe. As Glyn Daniel said, *prehistoric archaeologists are always fond of paying lip service to the view that their job is to create prehistory out of the dry bones and broken pots of archaeology. Childe was constantly achieving this act of creation; he, more than anyone else of his generation, wrote prehistory: he made the potsherds speak and the dry bones live.*

CHURCHWARD, JAMES. **COSMIC FORCES OF MU. Many illustrations, 246pp. Spe34, 4.95c.**
A detailed explanation of the sciences as they were taught in Mu (Lemuria), with chapters on the origin of the great forces, the Earth's forces, the atmosphere, rays, the life force, specialization, the sun, and sundry phenomena. Many drawings illustrate the text. While the sources of Churchward's information have been questioned over the years, no one has ever denied the intriguing qualities of his exposition.

CHURCHWARD, JAMES. **THE LOST CONTINENT OF MU. About 286pp. Spe34, 2.15p.**
This series represents an attempt by the author to prove that a great civilization existed on Mu (Lemuria) in the central Pacific, stretching from the Hawaiian Islands to the Fijis and from Easter Island to the Marianas, and having a population in excess of sixty-four million. He believed that there was once a universal esoteric language of symbols which the ancients used in recording their secret wisdom, and that by staring at ancient symbols long enough an intuitively gifted person can conjure their meanings out of his inner consciousness and thus recover forgotten historical facts. Churchward said that he based his theory upon two sets of tablets, found in India and Mexico. His books are profusely illustrated. **Lost Continent** is the first book in the series.

CHURCHWARD, JAMES. **THE SECOND BOOK OF THE COSMIC FORCES OF MU. 269pp. Spe70, 6.70c.**
An exploration of cosmic forces as they were taught in Mu relating to the Earth. A great deal of information about the Earth's history and geology is presented along with many illustrative drawings and maps.

COHANE, JOHN. **THE KEY. Illustrations, index, 224pp. ScB73/Fon, 5.95p/2.50p.**
This is a well researched, provocative study in which Cohane asserts that two major worldwide Semitic migrations took place long before the Egyptian, Greek, Phoenician, and Carthaginian eras. These migrations demonstrate that mankind has a common origin. Cohane builds his thesis on his contention that the key to man's past is hidden in his language, and most of all in the forgotten history revealed through place names which echo from continent to continent, and in words which link together an amazing variety of civilizations. The etymology of these words and place names is analyzed at length and in the process many early civilizations are surveyed.

COTTRELL, LEONARD. **LOST CITIES. Index, 251pp. G&D57/PnB, 2.95p.**
An eminent British archaeologist and scholar narrates the story of cities and whole civilizations that have been lost for centuries. He writes in a novelistic style, recreating the life of each civilization, and he includes many quotations from original sources. The cities include Nimrud, Ninevah, Ur, Nippur, Pompeii, Chichen-Itza, Vilcabamba, Harappa, and some Babylonian sites.

DANIEL, GLYN. **THE FIRST CIVILIZATIONS: THE ARCHAEOLOGY OF THEIR ORIGINS. Sixty-one pages of plates and in text figures, notes, index, 208pp. Cro68, 4.95p.**
A pioneering investigation into the world's first seven civilizations, showing what archaeology has revealed about their origins. While the book is oriented toward the nonprofessional reader, Ms. Daniel's scholarship is impeccable and her theses should be of interest to all.

DANIEL, GLYN. **MEGALITHS IN HISTORY. Fifty-seven plates, notes, 64pp. T&H72, 9.85c.**
Transcription of a lecture on the megalithic monuments of western Europe, a subject to which Ms. Daniel has devoted many years of study. Here she sets out not to discuss megaliths in their prehistoric contexts but to show how this tradition of prehistoric buildings and the religious beliefs that inspired it have persisted through some twenty centuries into our own time.

DANIKEN, ERICH VON. **CHARIOTS OF THE GODS. 153pp. Ber71/Crg, 1.75p.**
This book and a TV show based upon it created a nationwide stir of interest in the possibility of extraterrestrial beings who have directly influenced human history. The author claims that visitors from space have frequently visited our planet and made contact with humans. He uses as evidence the numerous suggestive archaeological mysteries that exist in virtually all portions of the world, but especially in South America.

DANIKEN, ERICH VON. **GODS FROM OUTER SPACE. 166pp. Ban72, 1.50p.**
This second book by the author of **Chariots** takes up where the first book left off.

DANIKEN, ERICH VON. **THE GOLD OF THE GODS. Bibliography, 216pp. Ban74/Crg, 1.95p.**
More of the same with the addition of fascinating material on a system of caves and tunnels up to 200 miles long recently discovered in Ecuador—and filled with gold and silver treasures as well as many inscribed gold plaques. Other interesting new findings are also explored in detail. The text is illustrated with over 100 photographs and color plates as well as numerous drawings.

DANIKEN, ERICH VON. **IN SEARCH OF ANCIENT GODS. 149pp. Ban74/Crg, 1.95p.**
The subtitle of this book is, *My Pictorial Evidence for the Impossible*, and this describes it as well as anything we could say. 319 black and white and fifty-seven color pictures present the story more clearly and credibly than anything else von Daniken has written. An interpretative commentary goes along with the photographs. Whatever the merits of von Daniken's thesis, this is an impressive collection of food for thought.

DANIKEN, ERICH VON. **RETURN TO THE STARS. Many illustrations, 190pp. Crg70, 2.00p.**
Another series of von Daniken's examination of the beginnings of earthly civilization.

DRAKE, W. RAYMOND. **GODS AND SPACEMEN IN THE ANCIENT EAST. 289 item bibliography, 246pp. NAL68/SBL, 1.50p.**
Was Earth once ruled by extraterrestrial beings? This book is an attempt to answer this question affirmatively by presenting a barrage of evidence and data, both suggestive and conclusive, that has come to us from our racial past. The main emphasis is upon the rich heritage of the East that is laden with provocative hints of divinely intelligent beings from other planets.

DRAKE, W. RAYMOND. **GODS AND SPACEMEN OF THE ANCIENT PAST. 266pp. NAL74, 1.50p.**
Drake considers questions such as: does the blood of ancient spacemen flow in our veins?; were Sodom and Gomorrah destroyed by nuclear attack?; could the angel Gabriel, who foretold the birth of Jesus, have been an extraterrestrial?; did Martians, who had destroyed their own civilization, come to Earth to teach humans war?

DRAKE, W. RAYMOND. **GODS AND SPACEMEN THROUGHOUT HISTORY. Bibliography, index, 264pp. SBL75, 2.00p.**
This is hopefully the last book in this series. It is also by far the best. Here Drake assembles and analyzes the legends, folklore, and scientific or quasiscientific data that other writers have touched on to prove his thesis that extraterrestrial visitation was and is a practical reality. Drake writes very well and he reproduces a great number of fascinating tales. The book begins with a general discussion and then is divided into separate chapters on each geographical area.

DRAKE, W. RAYMOND. **GODS OR SPACEMEN? Bibliography, index, 167pp. NAL64, 1.50p.**
Eventually Drake is either going to have to change his titles and find some new material or else stop writing. With this book he seems to have run out of places to name in the title. This volume includes his hypotheses on life in the Sun, Moon, Mars, and Venus and the possible contacts between people from these planets and Earth. Drake also discusses the possibility of space gods in ancient Britain and he devotes chapters to Apollonius of Tyana and Count St. Germain.

ELLIOTT, R.W.V. **RUNES. Forty-seven illustrations, notes, bibliography, indices, 163pp. MUP63, 11.90c.**
Runic writing and runic lore are a valuable part of our heritage, revealing something of the culture and history of a period when paganism and Christianity were in conflict and the old and the new could appear side by side in a poem or on a tombstone. This book is an introduction to the study of runes in general and of English runic inscriptions in particular.

FAGAN, BRIAN, ed. **AVENUES TO ANTIQUITY. Bibliography, index, 8½"x11", 334pp. Fre76, 9.40p.**
A collection of thirty articles from **Scientific American** which highlight the major controversies, discoveries, and research in Old World and New World archaeology. The articles are individually introduced and arranged chronologically. Excellent illustrations abound.

FAGAN, BRIAN. **QUEST FOR THE PAST. Many photographs and line drawings, 7½"x9", 312pp. AdW78, 6.95p.**
This is a book about actual archaeological discoveries and remarkable archaeologists. Fagan has chosen nine of the most noted discoveries including Heinrich Schliemann and ancient Troy, Arthur Evans and the Minoans, Rene Millon and the city of Teotihuacan, and Howard Carter and Tutankhamun's tomb. He writes simply and vividly and does a good job of bringing the people and sites to life.

FINLEY, M.I., ed. **ATLAS OF CLASSICAL ARCHAEOLOGY. Glossary, index, 8¾"x11½", 256pp. MGH77/CeW, 22.50c.**
This book covers the centuries from the beginning of the first millenium BC to the end of the Roman Empire, and it ranges geographically throughout the entire classical world. Classical in this sense means the area colonized and known by the Greeks and Romans. The **Atlas** is divided into thirteen cultural and geographic sections, each of which has been planned and written by a specialist. The book is abundantly illustrated with two color maps and plans of over 100 of the major classical sites, and monochrome plates and drawings.

FLINT, MAX and OTTO BINDER. **MANKIND—CHILD OF THE STARS. Notes, index, 272pp. Faw74, 1.75p.**
I know of no work since Darwin that deserves as much attention with regard to the evolution of man.—from the introduction by Erich von Daniken. The book consists of *clues* gleaned from a wide variety of sources.

FURNEAUX, RUPERT. **ANCIENT MYSTERIES. Bibliography, 234pp. RaH76, 1.95p.**
A well organized survey of ancient mysteries. Furneaux divides his study into the following areas: *Megalitic Mysteries, Biblical Mysteries, Mysterious Peoples, British Mysteries, American Mysteries,* and *Fables and Hoaxes.* He has researched the material well and, while this is a popularization, it is a solid book.

GIMBUTAS, MARITA. **THE GODS AND GODDESSES OF OLD EUROPE, 7000-3500 BC. Notes, long bibliography, index, 303pp. UCa74/T&H, 20.00c.**
An in depth study of the naturalistic pantheon developed in *Old Europe* during the early Stone Age. These *gods* and *goddesses* are the familiars of the hunters and the fishermen, objects of worship evoked by the animal world and other natural phenomena. In support of her thesis, the author presents a unique body of illustrations depicting cult figures from the Balkan countries. She has also provided a comprehensive catalog of the objects illustrated as well as a detailed list of the principal sites where they were found.

GOODMAN, JEFFREY. **PSYCHIC ARCHAEOLOGY. Bibliography, index, 339pp. Put77, 8.95c.**
Psychic archaeology involves the ability of an individual or individuals to sense and pinpoint the ruins of an ancient civilization. Goodman himself has done a great deal of work on a site in Arizona which was discovered psychically. He relates his experiences and traces the roots of psychic archaeology through three seminal figures.

A mummy, said to be at least 4,000 years old and discovered in Arizona.

GORDON, CYRUS. **FORGOTTEN SCRIPTS: THE STORY OF THEIR DECIPHERMENT. Illustrations, notes, index, 189pp. Pen71, 1.05p.**
Professor Gordon has himself made considerable contributions to the decipherment of ancient scripts. This is a remarkably clear exposition of the history of decipherment, and a discussion of the main people involved.

HANSEN, L. TAYLOR. **THE ANCIENT ATLANTIC. Index, 8½"x11", 437pp. Amh69, 10.00p.**
Hansen presents a pictorial biography of the Atlantic Ocean, including material on the civilizations in the coastal land areas and the physical, seismological, and legendary facts about the Atlantic. This is a unique study, replete with maps and illustrations. Covers a multitude of topics.

HAPGOOD, CHARLES. **MAPS OF THE ANCIENT SEA KINGS. Illustrations, appendices, notes, bibliography, index, 315pp. Chi66, 14.50c.**
Hapgood has been researching the material presented in this fascinating narrative for many years and has collected a large and convincing amount of data and ancient maps to illustrate his thesis. Highly recommended for the serious student, and fascinating reading for all.

HAWKES, JACQUETTA, ed. **ATLAS OF ANCIENT ARCHAEOLOGY. Glossary, index, 8½"x11¼", 272pp. MGH74/H&G, 19.50c.**
This atlas traces the patterns of cultures and civilizations down to the beginning of the classical world. It is arranged according to global regions, and each region is presented by a specialist in that area. Each regional map shows cultural areas, marks a large number of archaeological sites, and is accompanied by a general introduction to the ancient

history of the region, followed by detailed descriptions, plans, and reconstructions of the most interesting monuments. Over 170 sites are described and illustrated.

HAWKES, JACQUETTA. THE ATLAS OF EARLY MAN. Index, 8¾"x11½", 256pp. SMP76/MGB, 15.00c.
This unique volume gives a comprehensive picture of the ancient world via a discussion of the concurrent developments of early history from 35000 BC to AD 500. By means of illustrated maps showing what events took place around the world simultaneously, summary time charts linking people and events across the world, a gazetteer of archaeological sites and over 1,000 drawings and photographs, the relative progress of civilization (at least in an esoteric sense) is charted. While particular emphasis is laid on the simultaneous developments in art, architecture, and technology, Ms. Hawkes also surveys the social, political, and religious forces which helped to shape them.

HAWKES, JACQUETTA. THE FIRST GREAT CIVILIZATIONS: LIFE IN MESOPOTAMIA, THE INDUS VALLEY, AND EGYPT. Illustrations, chronology, bibliography, index, 508pp. RaH73, 15.95c.
A vivid recreation of one of the great creative periods of all human history—the rise of three extraordinary pre-classic civilizations: Mesopotamia, Egypt, and the Indus Valley. Ms. Hawkes, today's foremost writer on archaeology for the layman, surveys their beginnings 5,000 years ago and shows how, in the vast and fertile flood plains of three broad, semitropical river valleys (the Tigris-Euphrates, the Nile, and the Indus), once nomadic tribesmen developed the social and economic patterns that brought them out of the Stone Age. She contrasts their life views and relationships to the world and the gods and shows what made each civilization unique.

HAWKES, JACQUETTA. PREHISTORY. Illustrations, plates, notes, bibliography, index, 404pp. A&U63, 21.45c.
This is Volume I, Part II, in UNESCO's History of Mankind: Cultural and Scientific Development series. It is concerned with man's prehistoric past. Starting with the early ape men and their first efforts to make tools, control fire, and develop language, Ms. Hawkes passes on to the emergence of *homo sapiens*, the differentiation of races, and the peopling of the Americas. The material culture, religion, and artistic creations of the latest Old Stone Age hunters are fully discussed and illustrated. Finally, Ms. Hawkes reviews the domestication of plants and animals in southwestern Asia, the spread of farming in Europe and Asia, and the origins of agriculture in the New World. She does an excellent job of presenting archaeological facts while giving insight into the human experience.

HAWKES, JACQUETTA, ed. THE WORLD OF THE PAST. S&S63, 5.95p/each.
This is a noted anthology of the history of archaeology. Most of the accounts have been written by well known archaeologists and Ms. Hawkes has also included reports of observant lay travelers like Herodotus. She presents an introduction to each section together with a discussion of the pleasures and purposes of archaeology, some of its classical errors, and modern techniques. Her introduction (long enough to be a book in itself), together with the introductory notes, provides a consecutive history of archaeological discoveries and a vast spectacle of movement in time; of cultures and civilizations, each unique in form and style, each growing, flowering, and dying. Volume I presents a panorama of the Old Stone Age and the Evolution of Man, the New Stone Age and the Beginnings of Farming, Mesopotamia, Palestine, and Egypt. Volume II surveys the ancient civilizations of Asia Minor, Greece, Italy, India, China, Easter Island, Britain, Scandinavia, eastern Europe, and the entire Western Hemisphere from the Eskimos to South America. Each volume is indexed and the two cover about 1,350 pages.

HAWKINS, GERALD. BEYOND STONEHENGE. Notes, index, 308pp. H&R75, 7.25p.
Explores many of the mysteries of ancient civilizations, using a computer as a base. Hawkins' topics include the vast linear Nazca lines in the Peruvian desert which can only be appreciated from the air; Machu Pichu and its temple; the Great Temple of Karnak, and the temple of Amon-Ra where the pharaoh made his sun observations, as well as other temples of the Nile and the Mayan ruins in Central America. He feels that anything which shows today as clearly

astronomical was known in antiquity to the builders. Fascinating scholarly speculation, with over 100 plates.

HEYERDAHL, THOR. THE ART OF EASTER ISLAND. 1,163 photographs, bibliography, index, 8½"x9", Dou75, 35.00c.
The full story of Heyerdahl's explorations on Easter Island, including his discovery of art treasures in secret caves. He devotes a great deal of space to exploring the mystery of the great stone men, with theories on why and how they were carved, transported, and raised. The historical and religious meaning of the art is also analyzed and new findings on the ancient and later history of the island and its people are explored.

HIGGINS, GODFREY. ANACALYPSIS. Illustrations, notes, index, 1,440pp. HeR1836, 40.00p/set.
This is a massive, two volume inquiry into the origin of languages, nations, and religions—the product of the author's life study. Virtually every aspect of ancient civilizations is discussed in some depth. Higgins believes that civilization came from the East and he quotes profusely from source material to prove his thesis. The only edition of this classic work that remains in print is a spiral bound, 8½"x11" book that will not hold together too well. However, it can easily be rebound and since the last regular edition cost $75.00 it can be rebound for far less than a bound edition would cost today. The presentation is out of date, but it still remains a fascinating work and an excellent historical document of the time it was produced.

HITCHING, FRANCIS. EARTH MAGIC. Bibliography, index, 320pp. S&S77/PnB, 2.50p.
A profusely illustrated investigation of megalithic man based on Hitching's own research as well as on a synthesis of recent scholarship and the theories of eminent archaeologists and speculative historians. Hitching contends that early man had a civilization of extraordinary sophistication and, in support of this thesis, he examines monuments, lunar observatories, mounds, symbols, and other artifacts. Hitching is a member of the Royal Institute of Archaeology and the Prehistoric Society and he focuses his study on Britain and Europe. The book reads well and many difficult concepts are conveyed in simple language.

HODGES, HENRY. TECHNOLOGY IN THE ANCIENT WORLD. 313pp. RaH70, 12.95c.
Hodges, Senior Lecturer in Archaeology at the University of London, is a specialist on prehistoric and ancient technology. In this book he describes, explains, and visualizes man's earliest inventions, and relates them to social developments. To illustrate his text he commissioned a remarkable series of drawings that reconstruct—from ancient writings and archaeological evidence—objects never before seen by modern man, showing, in many cases, how they were made and how they work. 265 illustrations are included in all, many of them photographs. The discussion is well organized and written in a flowing style.

HODSON, F.R., ed. THE PLACE OF ASTRONOMY IN THE ANCIENT WORLD. 8½"x12", 276pp. Oxf74, 52.60c.
Transcription of a symposium organized jointly for the Royal Society and the British Academy by D.G. Kendall, S. Piggott, D.G. King-Hele, and I.E.S. Edwards. Needless to say, the papers are technical, and they cover an astonishing range of material from all of the known civilizations, both literate and pre-literate. In addition to the papers, there are also recorded summaries of the comments made in discussion. Illustrated throughout with photographs and line drawings.

IVIMY, JOHN. THE SPHINX AND THE MEGALITHS. Many illustrations, including geometric drawings, index, 215pp. H&R75/SBL, 3.45p.
An in depth study of how the megalithic builders acquired the knowledge and skills that they possessed and why those skills and knowledge were applied in the way they were. Ivimy examines the conflicting arguments, highlights the significant facts, and then advances an original solution of his own.

JONES, GWYN. A HISTORY OF THE VIKINGS. Many illustrations, notes, bibliography, index, 528pp. Oxf68, 3.95p.
Beautifully written, bespangled with pictures and supported by a vast critical apparatus....Professor Jones has used the results of...scientific advances to build a vivid

and living picture of the Viking adventure.... Archaeology, philology, art history, palaeography, religious history and numismatics are all part of the historical discipline, and [he] has shown this admirably.—**Times Literary Supplement.**

KRUPP, E.C., ed. **IN SEARCH OF ANCIENT ASTRONOMIES.** Introduction, many illustrations, bibliography, index, 317pp. Dou78, 10.00c.
This is an extremely interesting introduction to the new science of archaeoastronomy—the study of the astronomies of ancient and prehistoric times through the discipline of archaeology. Krupp is director of the Griffith Observatory in Los Angeles and the other contributors to this volume—Alexander and Archibald Thom, John Eddy, and Anthony Aveni—are among the top men in the field. Each contributes a chapter on his own research and findings.

MCEVEDY, COLIN. **THE PENGUIN ATLAS OF ANCIENT HISTORY.** Notes, index, 8¾"x7¼", 96pp. Vik67, 4.95p.
Illustrates, in a chronological series of clearly reproduced maps, the evolution and flux of races in Europe, the Mediterranean area, and the Near East. From 50,000 BC to the fourth century AD, the maps and their accompanying commentaries trace the movements and cultural developments of the peoples in the area.

MACKIE, EVAN. **THE MEGALITH BUILDERS.** 117 illustrations, sixteen in color, index, 208pp. Dut77, 7.95p.
A survey of megalithic sites in Europe and the societies which produced them. Mackie seems to be thoroughly familiar with his material and the book, while oriented toward the general reader, is a work of good scholarship—albeit a bit dry.

MELVILLE, LEINANI. **CHILDREN OF THE RAINBOW: THE RELIGION, LEGENDS AND GODS OF PRE-CHRISTIAN HAWAII.** 183pp. TPH69, 1.95p.
A fascinating effort to capture the remaining oral tradition and secrets of the Kahunas by a native Hawaiian. Many illustrations and explanations of their sacred symbols are included.

MERRY, ELEANOR. **THE ASCENT OF MAN.** Index, 480pp. NKB63, 12.60c.
This is a spiritual review of man's civilizations throughout the world from earliest times through the Middle Ages. Ms. Merry is an Anthroposophist and is especially interested in the Celtic and early

Volcanic eruption.

Nordic cultures. She insists that Christianity is the oldest religion and her review of other cultures must be viewed in the light of this bias. Nevertheless, **The Ascent of Man** is a fascinating journey through the ancient Near East, Egypt, Greece, and India. The main characters come alive in a moving narrative; the spiritual teachings of each civilization are examined; and the text includes long quotes from sacred texts. The material is illustrated with seventy-seven beautiful paintings and photographs, over half in color.

MICHELL, JOHN. **CITY OF REVELATION.** Many illustrative diagrams, index, 205pp. RaH72/SBL, 1.75p.
Presents evidence for the view that earlier civilizations understood better than our own the natural laws controlling seasons, human behavior, and the most subtle relationships between the whole of the universe and its parts. These relationships, says Michell, are analogues of harmonic relationships in music and of the sacred geometry of the ancients. They are preserved, as he demonstrates, in the forms of the great temples of man—the cathedral of Chartres, Stonehenge, the Chapel at Glastonbury, the Great Pyramid, and others. An important work.

MICHELL, JOHN. **THE EARTH SPIRIT: ITS WAYS, SHRINES AND MYSTERIES.** 113 illustrations, twenty-two in color, 8"x11", 96pp. T&H75, 5.95p.
From earliest times men have believed that the Earth is a living creature, animated by a spirit that corresponds to the spirit in men. Science originated in the attempts of the first cultivators to adapt the roving ways of the Earth spirit to the new settled way of life. This volume illustrates the natural shrines and channels of the Earth spirit and the relics of the old, once universal science by which its powers were concentrated for the benefit of all life on Earth.

MONTGOMERY, RUTH. **THE WORLD BEFORE.** 1.95p.
See the Revealed Teachings section.

MOONEY, RICHARD. **COLONY: EARTH.** Index, 320pp. Faw74/PnB, 1.95p.
The advertising blurb on the front of this book says *This book begins where von Daniken leaves off*—and this is as good an explanation of the content as any we can think of. Mooney's style is much the same as von Daniken's: topical chapters more or less held together by a central theme, and without notes or any *factual* backup. Mooney devotes chapters to constant themes like Atlantis, the Great Pyramid, and Stonehenge—and he also has some ideas we have not seen elsewhere.

MOONEY, RICHARD. **GODS OF AIR AND DARKNESS.** 191pp. Faw75/PnB, 1.75p.
In this sequel to **Colony: Earth,** Mooney explores what happened to the colonizers. In the process he discusses the ancients' knowledge of atomic physics and suggests that a nuclear holocaust of global proportions in 5000 BC may not only have destroyed whole civilizations, but may also have changed the very climate of our planet.

MORRILL, SIBLEY, ed. **THE KAHUNAS.** 111pp. BrP68, 2.50p.
A collection of nine essays on the Kahunas, including *The Lesser Hawaiian Gods* by J.S. Emerson and *Kahunas and the Hawaiian Religion* by W.D. Alexander.

NEWSWEEK BOOKS. **ANCIENT EMPIRES.** Charts, index, 9"x11½", 160pp. Nsw73, 10.00c.
One way to know where the human race is headed is to look at where it came from. And the best way to see where it came from is with pictures. This book has pictures showing 3,000 years of history: Egypt, the Aryan invasion of India, the Exodus of the Jews, Rameses III defeating the Sea Peoples, the Great Wall of China, the Slaves' Revolt in Rome, the rise of Christianity, and the destruction of Zion. The pictures are accompanied by texts by specialists who have the ability to translate scholarly material into informative essays.

PARETI, LUIGI. **THE ANCIENT WORLD, PARTS I-III.** Maps, notes, bibliography and index (both in Part III), 1,108pp. A&U65, 21.40c/each.
This three volume set covers a key period of history—the millenium and a half between 1200 BC and AD 500, a period which witnessed the formation of the great classical civilization of the West and the emergence of the Indian and Chinese civilizations in the East. **Part I** covers 1200 BC-500 BC; **Part II,** 500 BC to the Christian era; and **Part**

III, the beginnings of the Christian era to about AD 500. Each volume begins with a summary of the main historical events of the period. The other main sections review languages and writing systems, technology, trade and science, political organization and social life, religion and philosophy, and literature and art. We recommend these books to all who seek a readable ancient history. The scholarship is impeccable and yet it does not overwhelm the reader. Many illustrations are included. The book was compiled under the auspices of UNESCO and is part of the **History of Mankind: Cultural and Scientific Development** series.

Assyrian horse-drawn chariot.

PAUWELS, LOUIS and *JACQUES BERGIER.* **THE ETERNAL MAN.** Photographs, bibliography, index, 254pp. Avo72/PnB, 1.50p.
An imaginative, popular account of the beginnings of man which greatly differs from generally accepted theories. The authors say they searched throughout the world and throughout recorded and unrecorded history for answers to universal questions.

PEPPER, ELIZABETH and *JOHN WILCOCK.* **MAGICAL AND MYSTICAL SITES.** Bibliography, index, 304pp. H&R77/W&N, 10.95c.
An often whimsical tour of sites in Europe and the British Isles which are traditionally believed to have magical powers. Many ancient stories associated with the sites are retold.

PHILLIP, BROTHER. **SECRET OF THE ANDES.** 151pp. LOG76, 4.95p.
Covers the history and work of those at the Monastery of the Brotherhood of the Seven Rays, which is situated in the Andes. According to this first person narrative, secret knowledge which has been hidden away for thousands of years is stored at this mystery school. It will be revealed *when the children of the earth have progressed enough spiritually to be allowed to use it again.* Half of the volume consists of inspirational transcripts of the hierarchy.

PHYLOS. **A DWELLER ON TWO PLANETS.** 442pp. Bor nd, 8.50c.
This document came to the author through automatic writing in 1884, when he was eighteen. Much of the narrative is concerned with the nature and activities of Atlantean civilization—government, science, and daily life. Many predictions and prophetic statements are also offered. This book and its companion volume are occult classics.

PHYLOS. **AN EARTH DWELLER RETURNS.** 510pp. Bor69, 8.50c.
A companion volume to **Dweller** which discusses many incarnations of the principal character, a former high priest of Lemuria. Topics include the mystery teachings, forces beyond magnetism, astral records, karma, inventions and their development through psychic channels, and Atlantean records.

ROBINSON, LYLE. **EDGAR CAYCE'S STORY OF THE ORIGIN AND DESTINY OF MAN.** 208pp. Ber72/Spe, 1.95p.
The first comprehensive organization and interpretation of the great psychic's vision of history from the dawn of creation to the new millenium due to arrive in 1998. At the center of Cayce's theory of history is the secret of the lost civilization of Atlantis—the primal society from which, through holocaust and migration, reincarnation and the forces of karma, Western civilization sprang.

SAUER, CARL. **NORTHERN MISTS.** Index, 204pp. TIF68, 3.50p.
The theme proposed here is the faring out to sea during the Middle Ages from Atlantic Europe. Some of the lore is of voyages of adventure in strange parts, which blend ancient myth with partly remembered events. Sagas told of real persons who got to places that may perhaps be identified today. Chronicles and geographies set down soberly what had been seen and experienced. In time, official records added their documentation.—Carl Sauer. In this volume Sauer discusses these early voyages and relates many of the old chronicles and sagas. Many maps accompany the text.

SCHUON, FRITHJOF. **LIGHT ON THE ANCIENT WORLDS.** 144pp. Prn65, 6.75c.
This is a philosophical study of the ancient world. Schuon writes extremely well (although symbolically) and his work in comparative religion and philosophy is highly regarded. Chapters on the ancient Greeks and early Christians are included as well as a very interesting essay on the nature religion of the American Indians.

SCHURE, EDOUARD. **FROM SPHINX TO CHRIST: AN OCCULT HISTORY.** 2.50p.
See the Rudolf Steiner section.

SCHWARTZ, JEAN-MICHEL. **THE MYSTERIES OF EASTER ISLAND.** 207pp. Avo75, 1.95p.
This is one of the few in depth studies of Easter Island which is approachable by the nonspecialist. Schwartz has done an excellent job of conveying some of the enigmas of Easter Island. He describes what is known about the monumental statues that dot the landscape and the script which can be likened only to that found in China and the Indus Valley. He also goes into the religious beliefs of the early islanders and the reasons for the disappearance of most of the native population. And he offers his own explanations for these mysteries, along with a review of the explanations of others. The text is filled with line drawings and photographs and a great deal of space is devoted to translations and interpretations of early writings.

SCOTT-ELLIOT, W. **THE STORY OF ATLANTIS AND THE LOST LEMURIA.** 119pp. TPH04, 8.95c.
Two classic, comprehensive studies. The information was obtained clairvoyantly. Includes large, foldout maps.

SENDY, JEAN. **THOSE GODS WHO MADE HEAVEN AND EARTH.** 191pp. Ber72, 1.25p.
Sendy's thesis stems from the Hebrew word *Elohim*, which is a plural (the gods) rather than God as it is usually translated: **Genesis** *appears as an account of the arrival of perfectly concrete Celestials, physically in our image, who behaved on earth as we can imagine our own astronauts behaving on another planet.* He treats **Genesis** as an historical narrative whose text, already ancient at the time of Christ, takes on coherence in the light of our present scientific knowledge.

SILVERBERG, ROBERT. **LOST CITIES AND VANISHED CIVILIZATIONS.** 152pp. Ban63, .95p.
Presents a general picture of Troy, Babylon, Angkor, Knossos, Chichen Itza, and Pompeii. This is an introductory, easy to read work, designed to give the general reader a taste of each civilization.

■ *SPENCE, LEWIS.* **THE PROBLEM OF LEMURIA.** Offset, spiral bound, index, 249pp. HeR33, 6.00p.
Lemuria is usually thought of as a vast Pacific continent which existed in early prehistoric times. Almost no vestiges of Lemurian civilization remain today and little has been written about it in contrast to the voluminous material on Atlantis. Spence spent his life researching ancient civilizations and in this volume he details everything he has been able to ascertain about Lemuria and attempts to document his presentation. This is far and away the most complete study ever made.

STEINER, RUDOLF. **COSMIC MEMORY: ATLANTIS AND LEMURIA.** Index, 262pp. Mul59, 2.95p.
Steiner's first written expression of a cosmology resulting from his spiritual perception. He includes essential elements of man's prehistory and early history when he forfeited divine direction for the attainment of his present self dependent freedom. Steiner traces in detail each step that man took in arriving at his present situation. He also includes material on various aspects of the universe in illustration of his belief in the insoluble link between man and cosmos. A rather difficult, though highly enlightening, philosophical work.

STONE, MERLIN. **WHEN GOD WAS A WOMAN.** 3.95p.
See the Women and Men section.

STORY, RONALD. **THE SPACE-GODS REVEALED. Many illustrations, notes, index, 157pp. H&R76, 1.75p.**
Mr. Story is to be commended for having performed the social service of writing in simple language a reasoned critique of some of the many errors in von Daniken's writing.—Carl Sagan.

SZEKELY, EDMOND. **MESSENGERS FROM ANCIENT CIVILIZATIONS. 42pp. Aca74, 2.50p.**
This is the story of canine archaeology, a method which traces the origins of civilization from studying the genealogy of various breeds of dogs.

THORNDIKE, JOSEPH, ed. **MYSTERIES OF THE PAST. Index, 8¾"x 11¼", 319pp. S&S77, 34.95c.**
A well organized, pictorial study of ancient mysteries. The selections, written by Lionel Casson, Robert Claiborne, Brian Fagan, and Walter Karp, are uniformly well researched and informative. Speculation abounds; however, unlike many of the von Daniken books and their ilk, it is informed, intelligent speculation. The book was prepared by **American Heritage** and the graphic presentation is similar to that magazine. More than 300 pictures complement and clarify the text, and many of the plates are in color.

TOMAS, ANDREW. **SHAMBHALA: OASIS OF LIGHT. Illustrations, bibliography, 175pp. SBL77, 2.35p.**
Legends of a mysterious kingdom beyond the Himalayas, of an oasis of advanced culture hidden deep in the mountains, have permeated our history for centuries. Tomas presents evidence which he says is from ancient Tibetan sources, showing that Shambhala does indeed exist, and he discusses how and why it has remained hidden down through the ages. It makes for a fascinating story, whatever its versimilitude.

TOMAS, ANDREW. **WE ARE NOT THE FIRST. Bibliography, 180pp. Ban71/SBL, 1.25p.**
Tomas' aims may be summed up as follows: to show that in former eras people possessed many scientific notions that we have today; they were more technically skilled than is generally believed; and certain advanced scientific and technical ideas of the ancients came from an unknown outside source. His narrative is illustrated, documented, and well written.

TRENCH, BRINSLEY LE POER. **FORGOTTEN HERITAGE. Many illustrations, bibliography, index, 271pp. Spe64, 6.50c.**
A provocative new study of the origins of the human race. Trench includes both archaeoanatomy and creation myths, writes well, and incorporates some fascinating concepts out of the esoteric tradition.

VITALIANO, DOROTHY. **LEGENDS OF THE EARTH: THEIR GEOLOGIC ORIGINS. Index, 318pp. Stu73, 4.95p.**
Ms. Vitaliano is a geologist who invented the term *geomythology*, which denotes the study of the actual geologic origins of natural phenomena which have long been explained in terms of myth or folklore. She feels that there are two primary kinds of geologic folklore: in one, some geologic phenomenon has inspired a folklore explanation of an actual geologic event; in the other, a garbled explanation represents an actual geologic event, usually a natural catastrophe. In the first case, Ms. Vitaliano contrasts the scientific explanation with the folklore; in the second, she examines possible sources of various myths and legends. This is a fairly technical book, with an abundance of notes.

VLAHOS, OLIVIA. **FAR EASTERN BEGINNINGS. Illustrations, bibliography, index, 298pp. Vik76, 10.95c.**
This is a well written study of Asian cultural prehistory. Ms. Vlahos'

emphasis is on the people and on their developing lifestyles. Each of the cultures is discussed separately.

WELLARD, JAMES. **THE SEARCH FOR LOST WORLDS. Notes, bibliography, 176pp. PnB75, 1.35p.**
Subtitled, *An exploration of the lands of myth and legend, including Atlantis, Sheba and Avalon,* this is a provocative, wide ranging study which examines these legendary civilizations in the light of both science and mysticism.

WHITE, PETER. **THE PAST IS HUMAN. Illustrations, index, 163pp. Tap74, 4.95c.**
An archaeologist responds to books like **Chariot of the Gods**, reviewing the relics that they claim were created by extraterrestrials, and basing his response on the latest discoveries in archaeology. Dr. White's thesis is that these mysteries can be explained by man's own actions and his evolution. The author teaches prehistory at the University of Sydney and he has aimed his presentation at the general reader.

WHITEHOUSE, DAVID and RUTH. **ARCHAEOLOGICAL ATLAS OF THE WORLD. Bibliographies, index, 6¾"x9½", 272pp. Fre75, 10.00p.**
This atlas is divided into seven sections, each prefaced by a commentary on the period or territory covered. There is also a general introduction providing a survey of the origins and growth of archaeological research. Over 100 maps are included in all, pinpointing more than 5,000 sites and accompanied by brief, explanatory texts. Superimposed on each map is a standardized grid, by means of which the exact location of every site can immediately be found by consulting the index. Symbols indicate the precise nature of the marked sites.

WILLIAMSON, GEORGE. **ROAD IN THE SKY. 248pp. Spe59, 6.60c.**
The road referred to in the title is the highway linking the stars together and moving out beyond the known universe into the infinite vastness of galactic space. Williamson presents evidence which links ancient civilizations and the mysteries of their temple rituals with the beginnings of humanity and visitations from outer space.

WILLIAMSON, GEORGE. **SECRET PLACES OF THE LION. Illustrations, 230pp. Spe58, 6.70c.**
Williamson claims that he has received a great deal of information from disincarnate identities about ancient mysteries. He discusses his information in this volume and also tells of places where this wisdom is stored and where it can be found. In the process Williamson covers a great deal of material and goes into considerable detail.

WOOLLEY, SIR LEONARD. **THE BEGINNINGS OF CIVILIZATION. Notes, bibliography, index, 541+pp. A&U63, 28.25c.**
Volume I, Part II of UNESCO's **History of Mankind** series, covering the Bronze Age. The Bronze Age saw the birth of civilization as we know it today. By the end of the period, great portions of Europe, Asia, and Africa were sparsely populated by farmers living in small but largely self sufficient settlements. A veritable revolution in man's way of life and thought began first in Mesopotamia and the Nile Valleys. This volume vividly describes that revolution and the impetus behind it. Woolley shows the gradual urbanization of civilizations, the social and economic structures of the period, the evolution of industries in pottery, glass, ivory, and textiles, and the development of science, fine arts, music, and literature. Other chapters deal with religion, education, communication, and travel. The book continues its historical scan through the end of the thirteenth century BC. Woolley includes an abundance of illustrations and plates. His writing style, though a bit dry, is quite readable.

ANCIENT EGYPT

Antiquity, vast and richly textured, cloaks the land of Egypt. In the dimness of prehistory, more than 10,000 years ago, man began to settle in the long valley ribboned by the Nile. Sustained by the life-giving river, the land prospered and, in the Fourth Millennium before Christ, burst into splendor under the first of the pharaohs. And in splendor outstanding in the ancient world, it flourished for twenty-seven centuries.

Egypt was ancient even to the ancients. It was a great nation a thousand years before the Minoans of Crete built their palace at Knossos, about 900 years before the Israelites followed Moses out of bondage. It flourished when tribesmen still dwelt in huts above the Tiber. It was viewed by Greeks and Romans of 2,000 years ago in somewhat the same way the ruins of Greece and Rome are viewed by modern man.

The great Greek historian Herodotus made a grand tour of ancient Egypt in the Fifth Century BC and wrote of *wonders more in number than those of any other land and works it has to show beyond expression great.* Later writers bore him out. Journeying the Nile, they passed the imposing mounds of the pyramids, avenues of sphinxes, slender obelisks. They were dwarfed by towering images in stone and intrigued by enigmatic hieroglyphics covering the walls of temples.

Modern man knows of many ancient and wonderful civilizations, some of them of misty origin and impressive accomplishments. What sets Egypt apart from the others?

For one thing, Egypt was one of the earliest of the ancient lands to weave the threads of civilization into a truly impressive culture. More to the point, it sustained its achievements unabated for more than two and a half millennia—a span of accomplishment with few equals in the saga of humanity.

Nature favored Egypt. The early civilizations of Mesopotamia stood on an open plain, and they spent much of their vitality in defending themselves from one another. Palestine, farther west, was largely unprotected, prey to invaders. In Egypt it was different. Desert barriers girded the Valley of the Nile and discouraged invasion; the people lived in relative security. The scattered tribes that shared the river merged into villages instead of fighting among themselves; the villages learned to cooperate in controlling the river's annual flood so that all might reap abundant harvest.

Cooperation meant organization. And it was the gift for organization, perhaps more than any other single factor, that enabled Egypt to erect a dominant, enduring state.

The first important move in this direction occurred around 3100 BC. At that time the Egyptian people, hitherto divided into two lands, Upper and Lower Egypt, found themselves under a single monarch—the first of thirty dynasties of pharaohs. They thereby became the world's first united nation and took a decisive step toward establishing a stable civilization. With the first two dynasties, which covered some 400 years, Egypt emerged from prehistoric obscurity into the full light of history. From that point on are numbered its greatest centuries. They are divided into three main eras—the Old Kingdom, the Middle Kingdom and the New Kingdom, separated by two intermediate periods when the country's fortunes were temporarily at low ebb.

Each of the three Kingdoms was characterized by accomplishments of its own. The Old Kingdom, from about 2700 BC to 2200 BC, was the period during which the great pyramids were built. With the Middle Kingdom, about 2000 BC to 1800 BC, Egypt enjoyed an expanding political strength and broader economic horizons. The New Kingdom, beginning about 1600 BC, saw the nation's zenith as a political power and its acquisition of an empire mostly in Asia. When the New Kingdom came to a close around 1100 BC, Egypt's days as a great nation were over, although pharaohs, interspersed with foreign conquerors, continued to occupy the throne until the Fourth Century BC.

The unique quality of Egyptian civilization began to emerge even under the earliest pharaohs. Political and social structure quickly crystallized into the form it was to maintain, with few interruptions, from then on. All power, in theory and to a great extent in fact, lay in the hands of the ruler. Cast in the double role of king and god, he sat enthroned at the pinnacle of society. Supporting him were the high officers to whom he delegated authority. Below them, the ranks of a vast bureaucracy rested upon the broad shoulders of workers and peasants.

The awakening of Egypt was accompanied by the introduction of writing, all-important prerequisite to successful centralized rule. Records could now be kept, instructions issued, history written down. The creators of poems, stories, essays and narratives could not entrust their works to papyrus rather than memory, and Egypt's literature was born. Methods of calculating kept pace with writing. It became possible to compute taxes with precision, to survey land, measure weights and distances, and reckon time.

With all power emanating from a single fountainhead, manpower could be amassed to tame the Nile. Under the first pharaohs, irrigation projects were launched on a grand scale; a spreading network of canals carried water to the fields, and dike systems held the river at bay and reclaimed thousands of arable acres. As the Nile's green fringe of agriculture grew ever greater, so did the material wealth of its civilization.

With spectacular suddenness, an architecture sprang up that was suitable for kings and gods. Within a century after the first pharaoh of the Old Kingdom mounted his throne, Egyptian builders had graduated from sun-baked bricks to highly sophisticated construction in stone, and their artisans were among the earliest to master this difficult technique. The same omnipotent authority that drafted mass labor for irrigation was able to recruit unlimited sinew to quarry and dress enormous blocks, and to transport them to sites beside the Nile. Within a brief span of 200 years or so, Egypt's builders had so mastered the new material that they had finished the pyramids at Gizeh, wonders of the ancient world and the mightiest royal sepulchers of all time. In succeeding centuries, Egyptian architects flanked the river from the Delta, near the Mediterranean, to lower Nubia, about 800 miles south, with stone monuments that rank with the most impressive of any age.

Sculptors carved colossal images of impassive gods or rulers in stone, and also fashioned lifesized portraits in stone, wood and copper. Painters added vivid pigments to the works of the sculptors—and also covered temple walls with stately official and religious scenes, and decorated palaces and tombs with animated frescoes. The important builings of the ancient Egyptians were brilliant with color.

Egyptians themselves were responsible for the preservation of many artifacts of their civilization because of their distinctive attitude toward death. Since they viewed death as an extension of life, they prepared for it elaborately. Any man who could afford a proper tomb spared neither energy nor expense to furnish it with the many things thought indispensable for living in the hereafter. Geography and climate assisted in the preservation process. Most of the land bordering the Nile is desert, receiving little or no rainfall. The remains of the past, blanketed by dry sand, rested undisturbed through the millennia. Even the most perishable materials—delicate fabrics, articles of fragile wood, papyrus—survived relatively unscathed.

As a result of these two factors—religion and climate—Egypt remained a huge and unique storehouse of antiquity. Its artifacts span all the periods from primitive prehistory to the sophisticated and magnificent age of the pharaohs. Scenes painted on the walls of tombs from dynastic days onward faithfully depict many details of Egyptian life. Their subjects range from the lowly tasks of farmers and servants and the joyous games of children to the pomp and ceremony that attended gods and kings. Small wooden models reproduce dwellings, ships, soldiers in battle gear; butchers, bakers and brewers in their shops. Although the tomb furnishings—clothing, musical instruments, furniture, cosmetics, tools and weapons—were for the use of the dead, all shed light on the ways of the living.

Nevertheless, in the years that followed the decline of Egypt, it was a long time before anyone saw much by this light. It was not until 1798 when Napoleon launched his conquest of Egypt that the veil began to lift. Accompanying Napoleon's troops was a small array of savants dedicated to a study of the Valley of the Nile. Under their ministrations there began to take shape a picture of a vital people endowed with great skills. The discovery by one of Napoleon's officers of the Rosetta Stone—a fragment of a stele inscribed not only in hieroglyphics but also in an Egyptian script called demotic and in Greek—provided the final key to Egypt's lost history. Its bilingual text made it possible for the philologist Jean Francois Champollion, who had devoted years to the study of ancient languages, to announce in 1822 that the enigma of the hieroglyphs had been solved: for the first time, the pictographs could be read.

—condensed from **Ancient Egypt**, by Lionel Casson

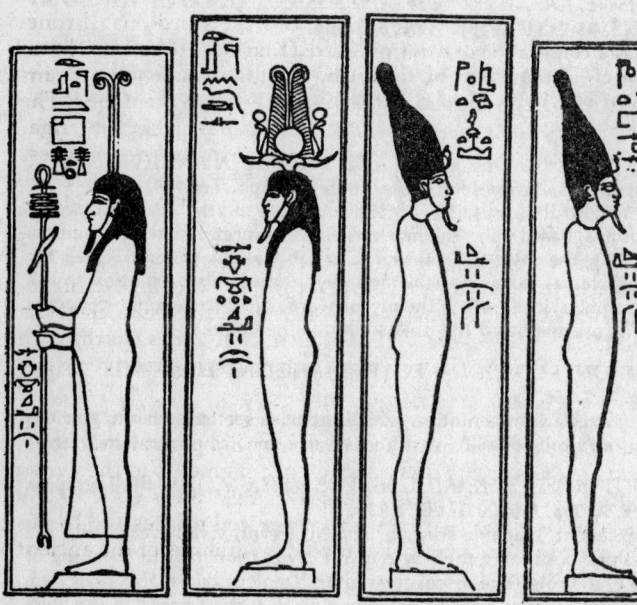

ALDRED, CYRIL. **EGYPT TO THE END OF THE OLD KINGDOM.** Bibliography, index, 143pp. MGH65/T&H, 3.95p.
A study of the development of Egyptian civilization from earliest times to the end of the Old Kingdom. It includes over 130 plates, about one-third in color, and covers every aspect of the culture of the period. The text is chronologically arranged.

ALDRED, CYRIL. **TUT-ANKH-AMUN AND HIS FRIENDS.** 8½"x11", BlB77, 2.50p.
This book combines a series of short essays on the major figures of the Eighteenth Dynasty with large line drawings (suitable for coloring) based on still-standing monuments.

BELLEROPHON. **ANCIENT EGYPT COLORING BOOK.** 8½"x11", BlB76, 1.95p.

BENAVIDES, RODOLFO. **DRAMATIC PROPHECIES OF THE GREAT PYRAMID.** 475pp. EMU61, 6.00p.
A personal interpretation of the meaning, in terms of prophecy, of the symbols found in the Great Pyramid of Gizeh. Predictions of dire circumstance live in these pages and Benavides predicts that a transformation of humanity will take place after the destruction.

BLEEKER, C.J. **EGYPTIAN FESTIVALS.** Notes, bibliography, index, 158pp. Bri67, 18.20c.
General background information followed by a detailed study of each of the most important festivals of ancient Egypt. A very scholarly study.

BLEEKER, C.J. **HATHOR AND THOTH.** Index, 171pp. Bri73, 23.80c.
Hathor represents the creative life; Thoth is the god of wisdom, who gives laws to gods and mortals, maintains the world order, and restores harmony. This is a very detailed study of the two gods, based on ancient texts and the most recent studies. The gods are discussed in each of their aspects and in the process the reader gets a good feeling for the religion and culture of the ancient Egyptians. A plethora of notes accompany the text.

BREASTED, JAMES. **DEVELOPMENT OF RELIGION AND THOUGHT IN ANCIENT EGYPT.** Introductory material, notes, index, 401pp. UPa59, 4.95p.
A masterly study of the development of religion and thought in ancient Egypt. . . . No better attempt has been made to trace, from beginning to end, the leading categories of life, thought, and civilization as they successfully made their mark on religion, or to follow religion from age to age, disclosing especially how it was shaped by these influences, and how in turn it reacted to society.—E.O. James. Over a half a century has passed since Dr. Breasted put together the lectures which were later incorporated into this book; new texts have been discovered, and the older texts are better known. Nonetheless this remain the most lucid examination of the subject.

BREASTED, JAMES. **A HISTORY OF EGYPT: FROM THE EARLIEST TIMES TO THE PERSIAN CONQUEST.** Notes, bibliography, index, 636pp. Scr09, 23.50c.
This is accepted as the standard history of the ancient Egyptians. Every aspect of the civilization and dynastic rulers is examined in great detail by Breasted, a noted Orientalist. The text is very readable and is illustrated with over 200 illustrations and maps.

BROMAGE, BERNARD. **OCCULT ARTS OF ANCIENT EGYPT.** 204pp. Wei53/APC, 4.95p.
Bromage reveals some of the esoteric practices of Egyptian priests and magicians, and explains how their magic really worked.

BRUNTON, PAUL. **A SEARCH IN SECRET EGYPT.** 287pp. Wei35/ HPG, 3.50p.
We can think of no better introduction to the esoteric philosophy of the ancient Egyptians than this book. Brunton is an excellent writer and he writes from first-hand experience. The book tells of his travels in the land of Egypt and his meetings with seers, dervishes, and fakirs. The high point of the book is Brunton's mystical experience inside the Great Pyramid; he spent the night in the King's Chamber and psychically participated in an initiation rite.

BUDGE, E.A. WALLIS. **THE BOOK OF THE DEAD.** Illustrations, index, 718pp. Stu60, 5.98c/7.95p.
The Book of the Dead is the most important of the religious writings of the Egyptians; it is also one of the oldest, parts of it dating back to the

earliest historical period. The text consists of a collection of spells and incantations, hymns and litanies, magical formulae, words of power, and prayers which were carved or painted on the walls of pyramids and tombs and on coffins and sarcophagi. The texts basically dealt with judgment and resurrection. This edition contains the most complete rendering of Budge's work on the subject. The hieroglyphs of many texts are included along with translation and extensive commentary. There is also an abundance of introductory information.

BUDGE, E.A. WALLIS. **THE DWELLERS ON THE NILE. Illustrations, index, 358pp. Dov26, 4.00p.**
A study of the life, history, religion, and literature of the ancient Egyptians. Budge's aim is to bring every aspect of their culture to life. While we do not care for his writing style and often do not agree with his interpretation of the findings, he is an excellent source.

BUDGE, E.A. WALLIS. **THE EGYPTIAN BOOK OF THE DEAD. Notes, bibliography, 534pp. Dov1895/RKP, 4.95p.**
This is not as complete an edition of the **Book of the Dead** as the edition described under that name. It contains hieroglyphic texts along with an interlinear transliteration of their reconstructed sounds, a word for word translation, and a separate smooth translation. There is also a lengthy introduction.

BUDGE, E.A. WALLIS. **THE EGYPTIAN HEAVEN AND HELL. Index, 212pp. OpC74/RKP, 5.30p.**
A recently reprinted edition of Budge's explanation to *the Guides to the Other World*: **The Theban Book of the Dead, The Book of Two Ways, The Book of What is in the Underworld (the Am-Taut) and The Book of Gates.** Budge includes explanatory material in addition to translations of the texts.

BUDGE, E.A. WALLIS. **AN EGYPTIAN HIEROGLYPHIC DICTIONARY. Introduction, 6½"x10", 1468pp. Dov20, 10.00p/each.**
This monumental two volume set contains nearly 28,000 words or terms that occur in hieroglyphic texts dating from the Third Dynasty through the Roman period, roughly from 3,000 BC to AD 600. Arranged alphabetically, each entry consists of the transliteration of the word, the word in hieroglyphs, the English meaning, and often, a literary or other textual source where the word can be found. The entries in the 915 page main dictionary include all the gods and goddesses as well as other mythological beings, and principal kings of Egypt, and geographic names. There is also a full list of the most frequently used hieroglyphic characters arranged by pictorial similarity. In the second volume, there is a 60,000 English word index.

BUDGE, E.A. WALLIS. **EGYPTIAN LANGUAGE. 254pp. Dov10/RKP, 7.50c.**
A collection of what Budge terms, *easy lessons in Egyptian hieroglyphs.*

BUDGE, E.A. WALLIS. **EGYPTIAN MAGIC. 234pp. Dov01/RKP, 2.75p.**
Budge covers the role of magic in Egyptian religion, the use of wax images and amulets, magical pictures and formulas. Combined with a study of the mythological role of magicians, this volume presents a comprehensive overview of the Egyptian hermetic system.

BUDGE, E.A. WALLIS. **EGYPTIAN RELIGION. 198pp. Crn00/RKP, 2.98c.**
A study of the ancient Egyptian's fundamental religious ideas and beliefs. Budge shows that the ideas of immortality and resurrection were the crux of Egyptian social and religious life for thousands of years.

BUDGE, E.A. WALLIS. **FIRST STEPS IN EGYPTIAN. Offset, spiral bound, 337pp. HeR1895, 7.50p.**
This book gives some fundamentals of the Egyptian language. Budge begins with a sketch of basic grammar and a vocabulary of about 500 common words. The rest of the book is devoted to a series of thirty-one texts and extracts, with interlinear transliteration and word for word translation, ending with a few untransliterated and untranslated texts with a glossary.

BUDGE, E.A. WALLIS. **THE GODS OF THE EGYPTIANS. Two volumes, 235 illustrations, 990pp. Dov04, 6.00p/each.**
A comprehensive presentation of the full pantheon of Egyptian gods and goddesses, major and minor. Dr. Budge includes information on

the origins of the ancient religion; the evolution of cults, rites, and gods; the priesthood; the sacred animals and birds; and the wisdom literature. The text is profusely illustrated with reproductions of tomb and mummy-case paintings. Many full Egyptian texts are also presented, with both hieroglyphs and translation.

BUDGE, E.A. WALLIS. **THE MUMMY. 404pp. McM72, 4.95p.**
Describes in detail the entire tradition of burial among the Egyptians, illuminating much of the ancient Egyptian culture in the process. The intricacies of mummifying are described and profusely illustrated with many examples of Egyptian hieroglyphics and accurate renderings of idols and god figures as well as a reproduction of the Rosetta Stone.

BUDGE, E.A. WALLIS. **OSIRIS AND THE EGYPTIAN RESURRECTION. Index, two volumes, 873pp. Dov11, 5.00p/each.**
Osiris, the king, was slain by his brother Set, dismembered, scattered, then gathered up and reconstructed by his wife Isis and finally placed in the underworld as lord and judge of the dead (and thus of the initiates). He was worshipped in Egypt throughout the entire period of its civilization and elements of Osiris-worship still exist today. This is the most thorough explanation ever offered of Osirism. Budge goes directly to numerous Egyptian texts and makes use of the writings of classical authors. Includes many translations of pyramid texts (often with the original hieroglyphs) and illustrations.

BUDGE, E.A. WALLIS. **TUTANKHAMEN, AMENISM, ATENISM AND EGYPTIAN MONOTHEISM. Many illustrations, introduction, index, 182pp. Crn23, 2.98c.**
A full discussion of the cult of Aten under Akhenaten, combined with essays on the reign of Tutankhamen and Tutankhamen and the cult of Aten. The volume also includes hieroglyphic texts of hymns to Amen and Aten, with translations.

CASSON, LIONEL. **ANCIENT EGYPT. Chronology, bibliography, index, 8¾"x10¾", 192pp. TLB65, 8.95c.**
An informative collection of photographic essays surveying many aspects of ancient Egyptian culture. Many of the almost 200 plates are in color and the text is readable and a work of good scholarship. Part of Time-Life's **Great Ages of Man.**

■ CHAMPDOR, ALBERT. **THE BOOK OF THE DEAD. 7¼"x10¼", 180pp. GtP66, 10.00c.**
A very readable translation, based on the same texts as Budge's, but done by a Frenchman who was considerably more learned in the esoteric aspects of the ancient text. Champdor also introduces new material, discovered since Budge's classic 1898 translation. Includes interpretative and descriptive material and over sixty pages of beautifully reproduced illustrations. If you can afford it we recommend this text rather than Budge's. Translated from the French by Faubion Bowers.

CHRISTIE, JUDITH and ROBERT JANSKY, eds. **GODS OF THE EGYPTIANS. 8½"x11", 91pp. AsA76, 7.50p.**
This is a compilation drawn from Alfred Knight's 1915 book entitled **Amentet—An Account of the Gods, Amulets, and Scarabs of the Ancient Egyptians.** Most of the major and minor gods are discussed and pictured.

CLARK, R.T. RUNDLE. **MYTH AND SYMBOL IN ANCIENT EGYPT. Illustrations, chronology, notes, index, 292pp. T&H59, 7.95p.**
An insightful discussion of the principal myths of the ancient Egyptians, based upon the most reliable interpretations of their texts. In telling the myths, Professor Clark allows the texts to speak for themselves as far as possible and pays considerable attention to the philosophical ideas which the myths were trying to express—concepts which foreshadowed the philosophy of the Greeks.

CLAYSON, RODMAN R. **EGYPT'S ANCIENT HERITAGE. 221pp. Amo71, 7.75c.**
A Rosicrucian presentation which includes sections on the Ancient Egyptian's religious life, arts and science, medicine, and family life.

■ COTTRELL, LEONARD. **THE LOST PHARAOHS. Bibliography, index, 250pp. G&D61/EvB, 3.95p.**
An excellent, readable study of ancient Egypt, vividly recreating the times and discussing the origin of the civilization and the meaning of its monuments. The discoveries of archaeologists are also reviewed. All in all, this is as good an introduction to ancient Egypt as any book

we know of. The book also includes many illustrations and selected translations.

DAVID, A. ROSALIE. **THE EGYPTIAN KINGDOMS. Glossary, bibliography, index, 8¾"x11½", 152pp. Pdn75, 5.98c.**
This is a beautifully produced, lively study, lavishly illustrated with over 230 color plates, maps, tables, and line drawings. Ms. David both summarizes the history of ancient Egypt and discusses the civilization in a fair amount of depth. Many of the most noted explorers and travellers are surveyed and important archaeological findings are examined.

DAVIES, PENELOPE and PHILIPPA STEWART. **TUTANKHAMUN'S EGYPT. Chronology, glossary, index, 96pp. SMP78, 4.95p.**
A simple, pictorial account of daily life in Egypt in Tutankhamen's time. The photographs and drawings are well reproduced and a brief comment, in big type, accompanies each one. There is also some information on the discovery of Tutankhamen's tomb.

DONADONI, SERGIO. **EGYPTIAN MUSEUM, CAIRO. Indices, 9¼"x 11¾", 176pp. Nsw69, 9.95p.**
The Egyptian Museum contains the world's most extensive collection of the arts of ancient Egypt. The volume begins with a short history of that collection by the museum's director. Donadoni includes nearly two hundred plates of the exhibits and offers an excellent commentary on the historical and artistic significance of the works and their creators.

DRURY, ALLEN. **A GOD AGAINST THE GODS. Bibliography, 326pp. Del76/Jos, 1.95p.**
This is a fine historical novel which vividly creates the life and times of Akhenaten who, 3,300 years ago, used his power as a human god-king to challenge not only the existing order of a then already ancient Egypt, but the very gods themselves, in his attempt to establish monotheism. Drury bases his account upon years of research and two trips to Egypt.

DRURY, ALLEN. **RETURN TO THEBES. 284pp. Del77, 1.95p.**
The concluding volume of Drury's story of ancient Egypt. This book recounts Tutankhamen's brief reign and Horemheb's eventual ascendency. Once again Drury has done an excellent job of recreating the royal family and the tragic and bloody period. Reading his two books helped us to get a grasp of the era that eluded us when we read standard histories.

EDWARDS, I.E.S. **THE PYRAMIDS OF EGYPT. Many illustrations, bibliography, index, 319pp. Vik72, 3.50p.**
Edwards is Keeper of Egyptian Antiquities at the British Museum. This is a description of some of the principal features of the most important pyramids. The final chapter discusses the construction methods used and the motives behind their construction. A very detailed account, revised and updated from the original 1947 edition.

■ *ERMAN, ADOLF.* **LIFE IN ANCIENT EGYPT. Topically organized, many illustrations, notes, index, 593pp. Dov1894, 6.00p.**
This is the basic sourcebook on life in ancient Egypt; a classic in its field and the basis of numerous other works. Erman covers virtually every aspect of Egyptian domestic and political life, culture, literature, religion and folk beliefs, arts and crafts, and much else. His account is detailed, but not overwhelmingly so, so readers on all levels should be able to handle the text.

FAGAN, BRIAN. **THE RAPE OF THE NILE. 7"x9", 413pp. Scr75/M&J, 8.95p.**
An entertaining, profusely illustrated account of tomb robbers, tourists, and archaeologists in Egypt over the last few centuries. Fagan has done a wonderful job of making fact more fascinating than fiction.

FAKHRY, AHMED. **THE PYRAMIDS. Index, 272pp. UCh69, 3.25p.**
Fakhry was Professor of Ancient History at Cairo University. His account of the pyramids is a good, readable academic study combining the different viewpoints of archaeologist, religious historian, engineer, architect, mathematical expert, and ordinary individual. The sequence of the pyramids is treated historically, through the grandeur of the finest examples, to the less lavish monuments at the end of the era. The dry, technical material is alleviated by excerpts from medieval historians and anecdotes about ancient personages and modern excavators. Many illustrations and diagrams are included.

FAULKNER, R.O., tr. **THE ANCIENT EGYPTIAN COFFIN TEXTS, VOLUME I. 292pp. A&P73, 22.50c.**
These texts are a collection of religious utterances written inside the large rectangular wooden coffins used for interning the wealthy. They date from the Middle Kingdom and thus help to fill the great gap between the Pyramid Texts of the Old Kingdom and the **Book of the Dead** of the New Kingdom. In general character they resemble the latter and in many cases contain the earliest versions of spells in the **Book of the Dead**.

FORD, S.H. **GREAT PYRAMID OF EGYPT. Illustrations, offset, spiral bound, 208pp. HeR73, 4.00p.**
A late nineteenth century interpretation of Piazzi Smyth's pioneering scientific work. Ford also includes quotes from and references to numerous other scientific and historical accounts.

■ *FRANKFORT, HENRI.* **ANCIENT EGYPTIAN RELIGION: AN INTERPRETATION. Thirty-one plates, index, 191pp. H&R48, 4.70p.**
This is generally considered the finest treatise on ancient Egyptian religion produced in recent years. In the preface Frankfort says that he will *go beyond the local and temporal differences in cults and dogmas, and look for those trends and qualities that seem to have shaped the character of Egyptian religion as a whole....It will appear...that the Egyptian doctrines are not without coherence. They were rooted in a single basic conviction, to wit that the universe is essentially static. The Egyptian held that he lived in a changeless world...and it informed not only his theology but also his moral and political philosophy [and] determined the forms he gave to his state and his society, to his literature and his art.*

GARDINER, ALAN. **EGYPT OF THE PHARAOHS. Chronology, notes, index, 481pp. Oxf61, 5.95p.**
Sir Alan Gardiner was long recognized as one of the world's most distinguished Egyptologists. This is an excellent general history of Egypt from the earliest times to the conquest of Alexander the Great in 332 BC. The **Times Literary Supplement** called this work, *Outstanding both for the meticulous scholarship for which the author is renowned...and for the humanity and understanding with which he approaches his subject...*

GARDINER, ALAN. **EGYPTIAN GRAMMAR. 9"x11", 482pp. A&P57, 20.00c.**
This is the finest book on the Egyptian language. Sir Alan includes a good introductory essay on the study of hieroglyphs as well as vocabularies and exercises.

GEDGE, PAULINE. **CHILD OF THE MORNING. 403pp. Faw77, 2.25p.**
This is an evocative historical novel about Hatshepsut, ancient Egypt's most brilliant female pharaoh. She ruled for more than two decades during a time of great prosperity. Her achievements and adventures were almost obliterated by her successors so that only fragments remains. Ms. Gedge has done a fine job of piecing together the historical evidence to produce a lively picture of Hatshepsut and her times.

GLUBOK, SHIRLEY and ALFRED TAMARIN. **THE MUMMY OF RAMOSE. Many photographs, bibliography, index, 7"x9", 82pp. H&R78, 6.95c.**
Ramose was a high official during the final years of the Eighteenth Dynasty. This is the story of his final day, death, and subsequent mummification. The book has been written for children and is therefore exceedingly simple.

GRANT, JOAN. **EYES OF HORUS. 406pp. Avo42, 1.75p.**
Joan Grant became aware as a child of her uncanny gift of *far memory*—the ability to recall in detail previous incarnations, both male and female, in other centuries and other lands. Her popular books, published and reviewed as historical novels, have been highly praised for their extraordinary vividness and rich detail, and are in fact the author's memories of her earlier lives. This volume is the story of her life as a young prince devoted to restoring the rule of decency in ancient Egypt's most corrupt age.

GRANT, JOAN. **LORD OF THE HORIZON. 255pp. Avo44, 1.95p.**
A young prince and his wife raise the son of the pharaoh according to the benevolent and progressive tenets of Ra during a time of violence and corruption.

GRANT, JOAN. **SO MOSES WAS BORN. 224pp. Avo52, 1.50p.**
The story of the pharaoh's court during the early years of Moses' life, and of Moses' upbringing by the brother of the pharaoh.

GRANT, JOAN. **WINGED PHARAOH. 1.75p.**
See the Occult Fiction section.

GRANT, MICHAEL. **CLEOPATRA. Illustrations, genealogical tables, chronology, index, 431pp. Grn72, 3.30p.**
This is probably the best of the recent biographies of Cleopatra. Grant is an eminent historian and he shows her as a shrewd and powerful political force whose ambitions were directed toward the restoration of the Ptolemaic empire and who was also a woman of dignity, intellect, and self interest.

■ GREEN, ROGER. **TALES OF ANCIENT EGYPT. Illustrations, 185pp. Vik67, 1.50p.**
Green has a wonderful faculty for retelling ancient tales in a way that children can appreciate and still retaining the underlying meaning of the stories. Here he begins with the story of Amen-Ra, the father of gods and men who created all the creatures of the world, and follows it with the story of how Isis searched the waters of the world for the body of her dead husband Osiris. Here, too, you will find the legends concerning the source of the Nile, journeys to the land of the dead, and much more.

GRIFFITH, F. and HERBERT THOMPSON, eds. **THE LEYDEN PAPYRUS. Long introduction, 212pp. Dov74, 2.75p.**
This papyrus is an ancient Egyptian manuscript that dates from around the beginning of the Christian era. It was probably the textbook of a practicing sorcerer in Egypt and contains many spells, incantations, and other forms of magic. In addition to purely native elements involving the gods, the manuscript shows the influence of Gnostic beliefs, and Greek and other magical traditions. A transliteration of the script is printed on facing pages with a complete translation, which includes copious explanatory footnotes.

HABACHI, LABIB. **THE OBELISKS OF EGYPT. Chronology, notes, bibliography, index, 219pp. Scr77, 12.95c.**
The pharaohs erected hundreds of obelisks, many of which have been transported outside Egypt and stand today in Western museums. Originally they were constructed as symbols of the power of the pharaoh or to honor the solar gods. In this volume Habachi, former Egyptian Chief Inspector of Antiquities, describes the production of the obelisks and explains the complex cluster of meanings that they had for the ancient Egyptians. He also tells about the pharaohs who built them and the conquerors and archaeologists who carried some of them out of Egypt. Eighty-four photographs and line drawings accompany the text.

■ HAICH, ELISABETH. **INITIATION. 366pp. See65/A&U, 6.00p.**
Ms. Haich is a European yoga teacher. **Initiation** is an autobiographical novel bringing together her present life story, with the events and experiences that contributed to her spiritual growth, and vivid recollections of her earlier life experiences as a young priestess in ancient Egypt. A story within a story emerges, describing in detail how she is prepared for initiation by the High Priest, who leads her, step by step, to an understanding of the ultimate mysteries. **Initiation** can be appreciated and enjoyed at many levels. It is a moving novel and is also the best presentation of the cosmic view of the Egyptians that we know of. The book is one of our favorites and has helped us understand many difficult concepts. Excellent diagrams illustrate the narrative.

HALL, MANLY P. **FREEMASONRY OF THE ANCIENT EGYPTIANS. 6.95c.**
See the Freemasonry section.

HARRIS, J.R., ed. **THE LEGACY OF EGYPT. Illustrations, notes, bibliography, index, 534pp. Oxf71, 14.75c.**
This is an excellent collection of scholarly essays covering the following topics: *The Calendars and Chronology; Mathematics and Astronomy; The Canonical Tradition; Technology and Materials; Medicine; Mystery, Myth and Magic; The Hieroglyphic Tradition; Language and Writing; Literature; Egypt and Israel; The Concept of Law in Ancient Egypt; Graeco-Roman Egypt; The Greek Papyri; Christian and Coptic Egypt; The Legacy to Africa;* and *The Contribution to Islam.* The essays read well.

HARRIS, JAMES and KENT WEEKS. **X-RAYING THE PHARAOHS. Notes, index, 194pp. Scr73, 4.95p.**
An account of the University of Michigan School of Dentistry's examination and analysis of a collection of mummies housed in the Egyptian Museum in Cairo. Written in nontechnical terms and well illustrated, the book provides an understanding of the civilization of ancient Egypt which is not available by any other means. A great deal of background material information on the pharaohs and their times is included.

Hermes Trismegistus

Hermes is said to be a historical personage, an Egyptian sage or succession of sages. He is associated with the Egyptian god Thoth who was the custodian of wisdom, learning, and literature. Teachings attributed to Hermes deal with astrology, priestly education, temple ritual, and medicine. The major work that bears his name, **The Divine Pymander,** is a collection of dialogues giving an account of the creation of the world. Hermes was well known to the Greeks and the philosophy of the ancients is often known today as hermetic teachings.

CHAMBERS, JOHN, tr. **THE DIVINE PYMANDER AND OTHER WRITINGS OF HERMES TRISMEGISTUS. Introduction, notes, index, 194pp. Wei1882, 3.95p.**
In addition to a careful translation of the **Pymander,** this book contains excerpts from works by Stobaeus, a fifth or sixth century Greek, and references to Hermes from the writings of the early church fathers.

EVERARD, DR. **THE DIVINE PYMANDER. 128pp. Wiz73, 6.95c.**
This is a photographic copy of the 1884 edition of this translation, which was reset verbatim from the 1650 edition, with the addition of an introduction. This was one of the earliest translations, and is still considered one of the finest.

KINGSFORD, ANNA and EDWARD MAITLAND. **THE VIRGIN OF THE WORLD: OF HERMES MERCURIUS TRISMEGISTUS. Introduction, 186pp. Wiz1884, 7.95c.**
This is a companion volume to **The Divine Pymander.** It includes **A Treatise on Initiations; or, Asclepios** as well as the title work.

RANDOLPH, P.B., ed. **DIVINE PYMANDER. 144pp. YPS71, 6.00c.**
A reproduction of Dr. Everard's translation, with explanatory prefaces.

SHRINE OF WISDOM EDITORS. **THE DIVINE PYMANDER OF HERMES TRISMEGISTUS. 53pp. ShW nd, 5.95c.**
The Pymander *is a book most choice for the elegance of its language, most weighty for the abundance of its information, full of grace and propriety, full of wisdom and mystery. For it contains the profoundest mysteries of the most ancient theology, and the arcana of all philosophy.*—Cornelius Agrippa. This is an excellent edition which presents the fundamental truths in a systematic manner.

————END OF HERMES TRISMEGISTUS SUBSECTION————

JAMES, T.G.H. **THE ARCHAEOLOGY OF ANCIENT EGYPT. Fifty-five black and white and color photographs, maps, and drawings, index, 7¼"x9½", 144pp. McK72/BoH, 4.95p.**
This history of Egypt began at least 5000 years ago, but the scientific study of its ancient remains, usually called Egyptology, was born only in 1822. In that year Jean-Francois Champollion presented the first results of his decipherment of Egyptian hieroglyphics. Over the years many different scholars have contributed to the study. This book shows how some of the great discoveries about Egypt's past have been made, and how they and others, not so spectacular, have contributed to a better understanding of obscure periods. The selections have been chosen to cover both the range of Egyptian history and the work of significant excavators.

JOHNSON, KEN. **THE ANCIENT MAGIC OF THE PYRAMIDS. Illustrations, bibliography, 158pp. S&S77, 1.75p.**
A highly simplified investigation of the inner meaning of the Egyptian pyramids, and especially of the Great Pyramid. Johnson reviews previous theories and puts forth his own explanation. It is an OK book for those who seek an inexpensive overview and it is not as provocative as the title and mass market format would have you expect. One strange omission in Johnson's bibliography is Peter Tompkins' book, the most important of all recent studies.

JORDAN, PAUL. **EGYPT: THE BLACK LAND. Index, 207pp. Dut76, 8.95p.**
This is a well written graphic presentation of early Egyptian life and culture. The emphasis is archaeological and the book is illustrated with 117 plates, some in color. The presentation is geared toward the general reader seeking an overview of ancient Egyptian civilization.

KAMIL, JILL. **LUXOR: A GUIDE TO ANCIENT THEBES. 181pp. Lon76, 5.30p.**
This well illustrated guidebook includes an excellent descriptive text on both the remains and the history of the area. Photographs and site plans abound. This is a useful book for all who wish to learn more about the rulers of the Eighteenth Dynasty.

KEES, HERMANN. **ANCIENT EGYPT: A CULTURAL TOPOGRAPHY. Illustrations, chronology, notes, bibliography, index, 392pp. UCh61, 6.95p.**
Kees was one of the foremost German Egyptologists of this century; he traveled extensively throughout Egypt over a more than fifty-year period. This volume, based on articles Kees wrote for the great German classical dictionary, is an all-embracing survey of the land and peoples of Egypt in ancient times. This is history from a geographical standpoint, and Professor Kees reveals the great extent to which the successive phases of Egypt's history have been determined and colored by the natural characteristics of the country.

LEACROFT, HELEN and RICHARD. **THE BUILDINGS OF ANCIENT EGYPT. 8"x9¾", AdW63/Hod, 8.75c.**
A profusion of line drawings and some color plates along with a simple text graphically show what life in ancient Egypt was like and especially what the buildings looked like. The construction of the buildings and their function are surveyed. The orientation is toward young people.

LEHNER, MARK. **THE EGYPTIAN HERITAGE. Notes, bibliography, 144pp. ARE74, 2.95p.**
The material in this book is based on the Edgar Cayce readings—1,159 of which contain references and information on the Ra Ta period in Egypt. The story presented in this volume has been culled from about 300 of these readings. Basically Lehner lets the readings speak for themselves, and there is little editorial comment. The bulk of the book is devoted to a description of life in the Egypt of 10,500 BC. Ra Ta, the

high priest of those times, is the central character in the drama presented by the readings. All aspects of the culture are described in detail. Cayce believes that all the later developments in science, technology, religion, and art had their foundations in this period.

LEMESURIER, PETER. **THE GREAT PYRAMID DECODED. Notes, bibliography, index, 350pp. SMP77, 12.95c.**
Basing his inquiry on a hint left by Edgar Cayce, Lemesurier draws on recent research and suggests that the pyramid's whole design derives from a simple number code. When this code is applied to the building's passages and chambers, a message starts to unfold which seems to be nothing less than an evolutionary blueprint for mankind, covering almost the whole of recorded history and stretching on to at least the fourth millennium AD. The total *read out* that the author arrives at is controversial to say the least, and the correlations between his story and ancient prophecies do nothing to add to its scientific veracity. A final section links the pyramid's picture of man's place in the universe with many religious traditions. The academicians should have fun tearing this book apart.

LEWIS, H.S. **THE SYMBOLIC PROPHECY OF THE GREAT PYRAMID. 192pp. Amo36, 7.00c.**
A penetrating look into the mysteries surrounding the Great Pyramid, its purpose, meaning, symbolism, influence, and prophecy. Includes evidence supporting beliefs of the mystery schools and their ancient use of the Great Pyramid.

LICHTHEIM, MIRIAM, tr. **ANCIENT EGYPTIAN LITERATURE, VOLUME I: THE OLD AND MIDDLE KINGDOMS. Indices, 266pp. UCa73, 3.95p.**
The most comprehensive selection of works in English translation ever to be gathered into a single collection. Ms. Lichtheim has done a wonderful, vibrant series of translations which reflect a profound understanding of Egyptian literature. The selections are arranged in chronological order to show the evolution of the literature. Notes are included on virtually every text.

LICHTHEIM, MIRIAM, tr. **ANCIENT EGYPTIAN LITERATURE, VOLUME II: THE NEW KINGDOM. Indices, 253pp. UCa76, 3.95p.**
This volume parallels the earlier work. Literary production of the New Kingdom was much larger than that of the earlier periods, and the individual works were longer. Therefore this book includes fewer selections than Volume I. Again, an abundance of notes accompany the texts.

MACAULAY, DAVID. **PYRAMID. 8.95c.**
See the Children's Books section.

MACQUITTY, WILLIAM. **RAMESSES THE GREAT. Bibliography, 8½"x11¾", 64pp. Crn78, 4.95p.**
When the Ancient Egyptians who lived in the last centuries of pharonic power looked back into their country's past for a figure of overwhelming stature they chose Ramesses II. By his buildings alone he was undoubtedly a man of exceptional achievement....In ancient story he was the king under whom remarkable things occurred.—T.G.H. James. This gorgeous book is a survey of Ramesses life and times in the form of a photographic survey of Ramesses-attributed monuments and works of art. Each of the more than forty photographs is in color and is a remarkable work of art in itself. The text is succinct; lengthy enough to inform the reader of the high points of Ramesses' career. Each of the photographs is discussed.

MANNICHE, LISE, tr. **HOW DJADA-EM-ANKH SAVED THE DAY: A TALE FROM ANCIENT EGYPT. 5.95p.**
See the Children's Books section.

MASSEY, GERALD. **ANCIENT EGYPT—THE LIGHT OF THE WORLD. Two volumes, notes, index, 905pp. Wei nd, 50.00c/set.**
Another of Massey's weighty compendiums exploring the mythology, symbolism, religion, astronomy, and origins of ancient Egypt. Massey elaborates on the Egyptian mystery tradition, the **Book of the Dead**, the Great Flood and Ark legend, and the Hebrew exodus from Egypt. He also reviews the **Gospel of St. John** in terms of the Egyptian influence apparent in the text and provides a lengthy historical investigation of the Jesus legend as it is found in ancient Egyptian sources.

MASSEY, GERALD. A BOOK OF THE BEGINNINGS—CONCERN-ING AN ATTEMPT TO RECOVER AND RECONSTITUTE THE LOST ORIGINS OF THE MYTHS AND MYSTERIES, TYPES AND SYMBOLS, RELIGION AND LANGUAGE, WITH EGYPT FOR THE MOUTHPIECE AND AFRICA AS THE BIRTHPLACE. Introduction, Egyptian-English vocabulary, notes, 1,384pp. UnB1881, 30.00c/set.
A voluminous two-volume account in which Massey offers an incredible amount of detailed information—all highly controversial. Massey was a serious scholar, but many of his conclusions and findings are supported by almost no one else.

MASSEY, GERALD. EGYPTIAN BOOK OF THE DEAD AND THE MYSTERIES OF AMENTA. Offset, spiral bound, 125pp. HeR nd, 3.50p.
A reprint of Book IV of Ancient Egypt: The Light of the World. Includes a long, interpretative introduction by Hilton Hotema.

MASSEY, GERALD. GERALD MASSEY'S LECTURES. Introduction, 294pp. Wei74, 12.50c.
A collection of lectures in which Massey contends that the gnosis of Christianity was primarily derived from Egypt through various lines of descent—Hebrew, Greek, Persian, Essenian, and Nazarene—all of which converged in Rome. As usual, Massey has to be read very carefully and it is often hard to follow his references.

MASSEY, GERALD. THE NATURAL GENESIS. Illustrations, glossary, index, boxed, 1,103pp. Wei1883, 50.00c/set.
This two volume set builds on the material Massey presented in The Book of the Beginnings. It is equally voluminous and equally hard to follow. However for those who can decipher his writings Massey is well regarded. When reading Massey it is always good to have a good symbolical dictionary handy as well as a reference book on mythology.

MCDERMOTT, GERALD. THE VOYAGE OF OSIRIS. 8.95c.
See the Children's Books section.

MENDELSSOHN, KURT. THE RIDDLE OF THE PYRAMIDS. Over 100 plates and line drawings—many in color, index, 7¼"x9¾", 224pp. HRW74/SBL, 8.95p.
Dr. Mendelssohn is a noted physicist who has devoted a great deal of time to pyramidology. The ruined state of the pyramid at Meidum led him through a series of deductions to a new theory about the purpose of the pyramids that he supports by his hypotheses of the parallel developments of pyramids in Mesoamerica. The author's thesis is not as clear or as well documented as the material in Tompkins' massive study, but does provide some interesting material and insights not available elsewhere.

MICHALOWSKI, KAZIMIERZ. ART OF ANCIENT EGYPT. Boxed, chronology, bibliography, index, 600pp. Abr nd, 75.00c.
This is the most magnificent presentation of the art of ancient Egypt that we can imagine, with 904 illustrations, including 145 in full color (many with gold leaf), plus 135 plans, elevations, sites, and diagrams, and fifteen maps and charts. The author is a distinguished archaeologist who has led excavation teams to astonishing discoveries. He writes well and the text is both informative and illuminating.

MICHALOWSKI, KAZIMIERZ. GREAT SCULPTURE OF ANCIENT EGYPT. Index, 8¾"x11¼", 191pp. Mor78, 25.00c.
A lavishly illustrated volume, with 160 plates, thirty-two in color. Michalowski reviews, analyzes, and interprets the 3000 year story of Egyptian sculpture from the vantage point of the social and cultural realities of the time and place. The author is one of the leading contemporary authorities on ancient Egyptian art.

MORAY, ANN. DAWN FALCON. 1.75p.
See the Occult Fiction section.

MORENZ, SIEGFRIED. EGYPTIAN RELIGION. Bibliography, index, 395pp. Cor73/Met, 30.25c.
Morenz is a noted Egyptologist and this is his most important work. After a general statement about religion as the center of Egyptian civilization, Morenz discusses the gods and treats the entire range of their relationship with man. He describes the complex structure of Egyptian cosmological systems and the Egyptian concept of time, and his thoughtful observations on determinism and freedom constitute in

effect an essay on moral philosophy in the ancient world. The text includes almost 100 pages of notes.

NIMS, CHARLES. THEBES OF THE PHARAOHS. Forty-nine color and fifty-one monochrome plates, notes, bibliography, index, 8¼"x 11", 208pp. Ele65, 19.95c.
For a thousand years, from 2100 BC, Thebes dominated the religious and political scene of ancient Egypt. In this magnificently illustrated volume Nims, who has spent twenty-three years in archaeological work in Egypt, reconstructs Egyptian history in the light of the latest discoveries in Thebes. He illustrates his narrative with a profusion of photographs specially taken in the tombs for this volume. The text reads well and is a work of excellent scholarship.

OSCOTT, F.L., et al. THE SECRET OF THE SPHINX. Glossary, 184pp. Spe77, 10.50c.
The introduction states that, This is not an ordinary book. The author lived more than six thousand years ago, yet his text reaches us today for the first time. The convincing message of the Pharaoh Amigdar comes to us from the etheric distances, captured by metaphysical means. His spirit has survived down the millennia in the care of the Great Sphinx.... The transmission of the message of Pharaoh Amigdar and the other people who tell their tale is the result of two years of research carried out by a group of experts in ancient writing, chemistry and engineering and is due to the extraordinary mediumistic powers of one of its members. Many line drawings and photographs accompany the text.

PACE, MILDRED. WRAPPED FOR ETERNITY. Bibliography, index, 192pp. MGH74, 9.00c.
A simple discussion of Egyptian mummies and tombs, written for older children. Ms. Pace describes the funerary rituals of the ancient Egyptians, the building of the tombs, the plundering by tomb robbers. Many photographs and line drawings accompany the text.

PECK, WILLIAM. EGYPTIAN DRAWINGS. Index, 9¾"x10½", 208pp. Dut78, 24.95c.
A full scale study of Egyptian drawing—the foundation upon which the arts of fresco, temple relief, sculpture, and architecture were built. Because the Egyptian artist's ideal was the achievement of a timeless reality, not individual artistic expression, preliminary drawings assume a special significance in Egyptian art. In the first section, Peck describes the histories, theories, tools, and techniques of Egyptian drawings and examines the interrelationship between drawing and painting, sculpture and hieroglyphics. The second section consists of a magnificent collection of 166 plates, sixteen in color, arranged by subject and fully analyzed.

PETRIE, SIR FLINDERS. RELIGIOUS LIFE IN ANCIENT EGYPT. Index, 221pp. CSq24, 8.75c.
This is a good survey, focusing on religion as a part of daily life, and in its social connections. The scholarship is fine and the writing style is unpretentious and easy to follow. The text is divided into the following chapters: The Gods and Their Temples, The Priesthood and Its Teaching, The Faith in the Gods, The Future Life, The Burial and the Tomb, The Folk Beliefs. Petrie was a noted early twentieth century Egyptologist.

PIANKOFF, ALEXANDRE, tr. THE LITANY OF RE. PUP64, 22.00c.
Contains the translations of the Litany text, the most important theological work of the New Kingdom, restored on the basis of the version on the shroud of Thutmosis III and on the walls of royal tombs; translations and descriptions of papyri that also contain the names of Re; and a theological commentary. Piankoff understands the god Re as the cosmic principle of energy, who manifests himself in the gods of the Egyptian pantheon.

PIANKOFF, ALEXANDRE, tr. MYTHOLOGICAL PAPYRI. Many plates, two volumes, 9½"x12", PUP nd, 63.85c/set.
Texts and descriptions of thirty-one mythological papyri of the twenty-first dynasty from museums in the afterworld, these documents contain many magical formulas and representations not found elsewhere in ancient Egyptian culture.

PIANKOFF, ALEXANDRE, tr. THE TOMB OF RAMESSES VI. 350 plates, two volumes, 9½"x12", PUP nd, 63.85c/set.
Texts of the nearly complete versions of the four great sacred books of the New Empire, presenting in effect a liturgical description of the cycle of birth, life, and death.

Osiris the Moon-god.

POCHAN, A. THE MYSTERIES OF THE GREAT PYRAMIDS. Many illustrations, notes, 303pp. Avo78, 2.25p.
A translation of an important French work. M. Pochan begins with a detailed description of the Great Pyramid as it now stands, including its precise dimensions. He follows with a series of major extracts from ancient, Arab, and modern sources. The next section is devoted to an analysis of theories surrounding the meaning and destiny of the Great Pyramid—the author's own and others. The book ends with a historical account of the Great Pyramid from the time of its construction up to the present, setting the date of its inception back to 4800 BC. Pochan has deeply studied the Great Pyramid, both in *sito* and through all the available literature, and he has produced a revealing narrative.

PREGER, ELFRIEDE. **ANCIENT EGYPT—A SURVEY. Eighty-five plates, thirty-nine in color, 8½"x10", 96pp. BoP75, 6.00p.**
A pictorial outline of ancient Egyptian culture based on reliable authorities and written in nontechnical language.

RANDALL-STEVENS, H.C. **ATLANTIS TO THE LATTER DAYS. 175pp. OKT66, 10.00c.**
A detailed description of the Atlantean teachings which formed the basis of Egyptian civilization. Randall-Stevens provides a detailed description of the pyramids of Gizeh—an area which he calls an *Ancient Masonic Center or University of Initiation.* The second part of the book contains five essays, reviewing the trend of world events from both a temporal and spiritual viewpoint.

RANDALL-STEVENS, H.C. **THE BOOK OF TRUTH OR THE VOICE OF OSIRIS. 201pp. OKT66, 5.00c.**
Inspirational writings received through the author from a higher intelligence accompanied by symbolically drawn pencil sketches, received in the same manner. The teaching is concerned with the theology of the ancient and prehistoric Egyptian civilizations. This is the first book in the series.

RANDALL-STEVENS, H.C. **THE TEACHINGS OF OSIRIS. OKT66, 6.00c.**
Incorporates the original teachings, inspirationally received by the author. The *Laws of Atlantis* and the *Commandments of Osi-ra-es* have been included.

RANDALL-STEVENS, H.C. **THE WISDOM OF THE SOUL. 126pp. OKT66, 6.50c.**
A book of teachings, both theoretical and practical, that try to bridge the gap between the exoteric and esoteric. The intent is to quicken human consciousness by the cultivation of higher qualities of the human soul. Present earthly conditions are outlined and suggestoins made for remedying the destructive trends in the light of certain prophecies.

REYMOND, E.A.E. **THE MYTHICAL ORIGIN OF THE EGYPTIAN TEMPLE. Illustrations, many notes, bibliography, indices, 363pp. MUP69, 22.25c.**
An in depth study of the development of the temple in late predynastic and protodynastic Egypt, based upon the author's study of original texts. This is a highly detailed, scholarly work which is only suggested to those seriously interested in the subject. Dr. Reymond is a professor of Coptic Studies in the University of Manchester.

ROCHE, RICHARD. **EGYPTIAN MYTHS AND THE RA TA STORY. Bibliography, 56pp. ARE75, 1.95p.**
This study is based on the Edgar Cayce readings. However it is not a verbatim transcript of the readings as Lehner's book is. Roche summarizes the story of Ra Ta and then goes far beyond this and focuses on Egyptian mythology and parallels between some of the early gods and later ones. Countless references are cited on each page (which tends to make the text fairly hard to read, but gives the reader an excellent idea of where to go for more information on a specific topic).

ROLFE, MONA. **INITIATION BY THE NILE. 192pp. Spe76, 7.85c.**
During the quarter of a century in which Mona Rolfe was lecturing—her twin soul and master initiate came close to earth from the planes of light, to give an understanding of life today, by drawing a picture of the teaching given in that great temple in Atlantis, from whence masters went forth to many centres on earth, carrying the teaching and building temples in which this knowledge was given. . . . These lectures. . .give a picture of conditions that gradually took shape—and slowly developed into the glory that was Egypt.—from the introduction. The teachings presented here cover a variety of topics and they give the reader a vivid picture of the teachings of Egyptian initiates.

■ *RUFFLE, JOHN.* **THE EGYPTIANS. Bibliography, index, 8½"x10", 224pp. Cor77, 12.50c.**
This is an extensive volume which is designed to bring the ancient Egyptian civilization to life for the modern reader. After dealing with the history and geography of Egypt, and its specific archaeological problems, Ruffle discusses the major artistic monuments within the context of Egyptian history, from predynastic times to the Copts. He then reconstructs the daily life of the ancient Egyptians—from laborer to pharaoh—largely through an analysis of lesser known artifacts. Subsequently he reviews the nature of the Egyptian state, farming and food production methods, fashion, language, literature, art, beliefs, customs, and funerary practices. Profusely illustrated with 181 color and black and white plates.

RUTHERFORD, ADAM. **PYRAMIDOLOGY, BOOK I: ELEMENTS OF PYRAMIDOLOGY, REVEALING THE DIVINE PLAN FOR OUR PLANET. Illustrations, 220pp. IPy57, 10.00c.**
This massive series is the product of the author's life-long research. It is the most complete work we could imagine. This volume elucidates, with many graphic diagrams and tables, the meaning of every passage and chamber in the Great Pyramid and deals with the historical chronology of the world. For serious students only!

RUTHERFORD, ADAM. **PYRAMIDOLOGY, BOOK II: THE GLORY OF CHRIST AS REVEALED BY THE GREAT PYRAMID. Illustrations, 288pp. IPy62, 12.00c.**
Covers in great detail, again with many tables and diagrams, the entire life of Jesus on Earth as portrayed and foretold in the Great Pyramid.

RUTHERFORD, ADAM. **PYRAMIDOLOGY, BOOK III: CO-OR-DINATION OF THE GREAT PYRAMID'S CHRONOGRAPH, BIBLE CHRONOLOGY AND ARCHAEOLOGY. Illustrations, 644pp. IPy66, 20.00c.**
A great mass of new material is contained in this volume. It deals with every nook and corner in the vast structure of the Great Pyramid and contains full page photographs of every passage and chamber including parts prohibited to the public. A large section is devoted to **Old Testament** chronology, and the whole work is related to recent archaeological discoveries.

RUTHERFORD, ADAM. **PYRAMIDOLOGY, BOOK IV: THE HISTORY OF THE GREAT PYRAMID AND PYRAMIDOLOGY. Illustrations, 400pp. IPy70, 18.00c.**
The most comprehensive history imaginable, including many diagrams and photographs. This is probably the most readable of any of the volumes.

■ SCHWALLER DE LUBICZ, ISHA. **HER-BAK, VOLUME I: THE LIVING FACE OF ANCIENT EGYPT. 385pp. PSm72, 8.10c.**
Ms. Schwaller de Lubicz spent a great many years in Egypt studying the ancient civilization and monuments and elucidating their mysteries. In this illuminating fictional narrative she recreates the spiritual tapestry of this ancient land. The main character is a young Egyptian lad, whose life is woven into a revealing tale of Egyptian religion and everyday life. The boy becomes apprenticed to a master craftsman and sage, and we are taken step-by-step through his life and training. This is a marvelous work which we recommend highly to all those who wish to get a feeling for the essence of ancient Egypt.

■ SCHWALLER DE LUBICZ, ISHA. **HER-BAK, VOLUME II: EGYPTIAN INITIATE. Illustrations, notes, 396pp. ITI78, 6.95p.**
This second volume presents Her-Bak's initiation into the Inner Temple and his progressive penetration of the esoteric aspects of the Egyptian mystery teachings. The events related take place between the Twentieth and Twenty-five Dynasties in the temple of Karnak. Her-Bak's story shows the evolution of one individual's life through the phases of temple training. This work is an authentic reconstruction of the sacred science and spiritual disciplines as taught in the temple of Karnak. Fifteen years' research in the temples and tombs of Egypt enabled the author to decipher the hidden meaning of hieroglyphic symbolism. The *Commentaries* appended to this volume contain a systematic exposition of the metaphysical and psychological ideas woven throughout the narrative.

SCHWALLER DE LUBICZ, R.A. **SYMBOL AND THE SYMBOLIC—EGYPT, SCIENCE AND THE EVOLUTION OF CONSCIOUSNESS. 100pp. Aut78, 3.95p.**
In this brief work, Schwaller de Lubicz examines symbolism or, rather, the symbolic method in general, not from the point of view of our contemporary use of symbols as conventional designations, abbreviations or as literary, metaphoric devices, but as the means for transmitting a precise suprarational knowledge and intuitive vision which, he contends, was a major aspect of ancient science.—from the introduction. The author explains that true progress in human thought can be made only if we call upon the symbolizing faculty of human intelligence, the faculty developed and refined in the temple culture of ancient Egypt and reflected in the Egyptian hieroglyphs.

SCHWALLER DE LUBICZ, R.A. **THE TEMPLE IN MAN: THE SECRETS OF ANCIENT EGYPT. Fifty-two plates, 132pp. Aut77, 10.00c/4.95p.**
Schwaller de Lubicz was well versed in alchemy and the hermetic tradition before he lived in Egypt. He was not an Egyptologist so his extraordinary insights have been rejected by the powers that be. Nonetheless his work is beginning to gain acceptance in certain quarters. This volume presents a summary of his findings on the Temple of Luxor. He viewed symbolic representation and imagistic writing as the only true way to transmit esoteric meaning and the only manner in which we can read the thoughts of the ancients. Schwaller de Lubicz spent more than eight years studying and analyzing the Temple of Luxor. He found that it *is indisputably devoted to the Human Microcosm. This consecration is not merely a simple attribution: the entire temple becomes a book explaining the secret functions of the organs and nerve centers.* The illustrated essays reprinted here discuss the symbolic meaning of the temple's architecture.

SEISS, JOSEPH. **THE GREAT PYRAMID: A MIRACLE IN STONE. 250pp. Mul73, 2.95p.**
This classic, published almost 100 years ago, has influenced all subsequent work on the subject. Seiss writes that, *The Great Pyramid... is a time capsule from another age.... [It] contains scientific information and clues to the knowledge that produced it. The information is contained in the measurements and proportions of the stone structure with its interior rooms and corridors, and in its orientation on the Earth and to the stars.*

SIMPSON, WILLIAM, ed. **THE LITERATURE OF ANCIENT EGYPT. 354pp. YUP72, 3.95p.**
An authoritative anthology of stories, instructions, and poetry—newly revised.

SKINNER, RALSTON. **KEY TO THE HEBREW-EGYPTIAN MYSTERY IN THE SOURCE OF MEASURES. 394pp. Wiz1875, 17.50c.**
A treatise using geometrical calculation and formula to show the esoteric intricacies of the Qabala and the ancient foundation of the **Bible** while revealing the numerological and geometrical basis for the construction of the Great Pyramid and the origins of the British inch and the ancient cubit.

SMYTH, PIAZZI. **OUR INHERITANCE IN THE GREAT PYRAMID. Twenty-four plates, index, 666pp. Mul1877, 15.00p.**
Smyth was one of the first authors to do a systematic study of the Great Pyramid and to attempt concrete mathematical correlations between its measurements and astronomy, physics, and history. He based his theses on both his own original investigations at the site and on the pioneering theories of John Taylor. This is a controversial work which forms the basis for much of twentieth century pyramidology.

STEINDORFF, GEORGE and KEITH SEELE. **WHEN EGYPT RULED THE EAST. Indices, 304pp. UCh57, 3.95p.**
An excellent overview of Egyptian history and civilization, clearly written and containing many illustrations. The authors cover the period from the Old Kingdom to the end of the Eighteenth Dynasty.

STEINER, RUDOLF. **EGYPTIAN MYTHS AND MYSTERIES. 151pp. API71, 5.95c.**
Twelve lectures on Egypt: its influence today, relation of past to present and future, cosmic events, initiation, evolution, and many other subjects.

■ STEWART, DESMOND. **THE PYRAMIDS AND SPHINX. Index, 9"x11½", 172pp. Nsw71/ReD, 12.95c.**
A beautifully produced book tracing the course of Egyptian civilization. Supplementing the narrative are some 140 illustrations—nearly one-half in full color. Colossal statues, delicately colored wall paintings, elaborate funerary objects, papyrus scrolls, and modern views of temples and ruins combine to recreate the spirit of a vanished civilization. Stewart also includes a selection of the accounts of Egyptian explorers. An excellent historical-cultural account for the general reader.

THREE INITIATES. **THE KYBALION: HERMETIC PHILOSOPHY. 223pp. YPS12, 6.00c.**
From Egypt have come the fundamental esoteric and occult teachings which have so strongly influenced philosophies of all races, and nations. This book is a study of that knowledge, the hermetic philosophy of ancient Egypt and Greece.

■ TOMPKINS, PETER. **SECRETS OF THE GREAT PYRAMID. Index, 8¼"x10¼", 416pp. H&R71, 20.00c/8.95p.**
This beautifully illustrated book presents the thousand-year drama which has centered on the mysteries of the Great Pyramid of Cheops. The author recreates the adventures and explorations of the archaeologists, treasure-hunters, soldiers, scientists, and eccentrics who have tunnelled into and studied the Pyramid over many centuries. He analyzes the various theories as to how and why the Pyramid was built; its relation to other structures of antiquity, including Stonehenge, the ziggurats of Babylon, and other pyramids; and its influence on the fields of astronomy, astrology and the occult, geodesy, and history. Recommended for all serious students.

Tutankhamen

Tutankhamen was the last pharaoh of the Eighteenth Dynasty. Very little is known of his brief reign. He died at about the age of nineteen, either of ill health or inimical forces. He is generally believed to have been either the son or brother of his predecessor, Akhenaten. During the latter's reign the old gods were totally overthrown and a new order and god, Aten, were introduced. When Tutankhamen came to power the traditional forces were again in ascendency and he was forced to accept the old gods and denounce the Aten. It was a time of great political and religious turbulence. The second of Tut's successors obliterated virtually all references to Tutankhamen and Akhenaten. Tutankhamen's tomb was discovered by Howard Carter, a British archaeologist, in 1923. Though it was not a terribly elaborate tomb, it was one of the few that was relatively unplundered. Today, it is universally considered one of the greatest finds ever made.

BRACKMAN, ARNOLD. **THE GOLD OF TUTANKHAMEN. Boxed, 9¼"x12¼", 288pp. Nsw78, 49.95c.**
This is without a doubt the most magnificent of all the books on King Tut's treasures. It contains 128 full color pages with hundreds of absolutely magnificent color plates, each of which was painstakingly taken for this book under the best possible conditions of lighting and perspective at the Egyptian Museum, Cairo. Many closeups of the detail work of each object are included and lengthy captions explore the functions and meaning of each object. An excellent text by Brackman tells the complete story of the search, discovery, and aftermath of the discovery.

BRACKMAN, ARNOLD. **THE SEARCH FOR THE GOLD OF TUTANKHAMEN. Notes, index, 197pp. S&S76, 1.95p.**
A vivid, journalistic survey of the search for the tomb of Tutankhamen, Carter's discovery, and its aftermath. The book is well researched and easy to read. Brackman also includes an excellent long bibliographic essay.

CARTER, ELIZABETH ELIOT. **VALLEY OF THE KINGS: A NOVEL OF TUTANKHAMUN. 231pp. Dut77, 7.95c.**
In this historical novel, Ms. Carter (a pseudonym) weaves together the story of Howard Carter's discovery of the tomb of Tutankhamen with the life and times of King Tut himself. She portrays Tutankhamen as a young pharaoh engaged in a mortal feud with his mother, Nefertiti. And she shows Carter involved in a quest into the culture of ancient Egypt. As might be expected, this fusion is not entirely successful; whenever the reader gets involved in one plot, he is carried off into another age and has to get totally reoriented. Still, it is an interesting attempt.

CARTER, HOWARD. **THE DISCOVERY OF THE TOMB OF TUTANKHAMEN. Index, 276pp. Dov77, 4.00p.**
Carter and his team were the ones who discovered Tutankhamen's tomb. This book, written by Carter in 1923, only a year after the discovery, captures the overwhelming exhiliration of the find, the painstaking, step-by-step process of excavation, and the wonder of it all. 104 on-the-spot photographs chronicle the phases of the discovery. The opening chapters discuss the life of Tutankhamen and earlier excavation work in the Valley of the Kings. An appendix contains fully captioned photographs of the tomb's objects. Jon M. White has written a new preface for this edition.

CARTER, HOWARD. **THE DISCOVERY OF TUTANKHAMEN'S TOMB. 8¼"x11", 84pp. MMA76, 5.95p.**
An account of Carter's discovery of King Tut's tomb, prepared under the editorial direction of The Metropolitan Museum of Art and based on Carter's own text. The book includes more than 100 photographs taken in and around the tomb and culled from the museum's own collection. The photographs are extremely well reproduced and there is enough text to give all but the most curious a full glimpse into the discovery and its aftermath.

■ CARTER, HOWARD. **THE TOMB OF TUTANKHAMEN. Notes, index, 7¾"x10", 238pp. Dut72, 5.98c.**
Between 1923 and 1933 Howard Carter wrote about his findings for British newspapers and magazines. The articles were published in installments and illustrated with an abundance of photographs. Together they form a brilliant portrait of the life and death of Tutankhamen; they also communicate the feeling of awe and excitement which spurred the archaeologists on. This volume contains the bulk of Carter's writings, complemented by Harry Burton's contemporary photographs and sixteen pages of color plates.

■ DESROCHES-NOBLECOURT, CHRISTIANE. **TUTANKHAMEN. Index, 7½"x10", 312pp. NYG63, 8.95p.**
There is a plethora of books on Tutankhamen. This is the most comprehensive one—both in terms of the number of plates (seventy-five color and 187 black and white) and the excellence of the textual material. The author and the photographer, F.L. Kenett, reconstruct Tut's early life, the ceremony of his coronation, the years of his reign, and interpret the objects found in the burial treasure.

EDWARDS, I.E.S. **THE TREASURES OF TUTANKHAMUN. 8¼"x 9½", 54pp. Vik72/Jos, 5.95p.**
An annotated catalog of an exhibition of Tutankhamen treasures held at the British museum in 1972. Includes color and black and white illustrations as well as extensive commentary on the personal and ritual possessions.

EDWARD, I.E.S. **TREASURES OF TUTANKHAMUN. Bibliography, 8½"x11", 176pp. RaH76, 8.95p.**
This is the catalog of the current exhibition which is touring the United States. Edwards includes a fine text as well as an abundance of color and black and white photographs. Each of the plates is analyzed at length and there are also introductory discussions of Tutankhamen and of the finding of his tomb.

EDWARDS, I.E.S. **TUTANKHAMUN: HIS TOMB AND ITS TREASURES. 9"x11½", RaH76, 35.00c.**
Edwards' third book on Tutankhamen. This masterwork includes not only the treasures on display in the current exhibition, but those exquisite objects considered too delicate or too large to send to America. One hundred color plates, showing us unsurpassed examples of every kind of treasure buried in the tomb, are reproduced from new photographs taken by Lee Boltin with the special cooperation of the Cairo Museum under ideal conditions never before granted. The color plates are juxtaposed with 103 historic on-the-scene photographs taken by the Metropolitan Museum observer Harry Burton throughout the six-year excavation of the tomb. Edwards provides extensive commentary on the individual treasures. The book itself is exquisitely produced.

GLUBOK, SHIRLEY, ed. **DISCOVERING TUT-ANKH-AMEN'S TOMB. 9"x10½", 144pp. McM68, 5.95c.**
An abridged version of Howard Carter's The Tomb of Tut-ankh-Amen, containing much of Carter's first-person account along with many black and white photographs.

■ MACQUITTY, WILLIAM. **TUTANKHAMUN: THE LAST JOURNEY. 8½"x11", about 60pp. Crn76/QuB, 4.95p.**
This beautifully produced volume contains both the magnificent photographs—all in color—and an excellent, concise text. We recommend the book to all who want to evoke the mystery of ancient Egypt and the death and burial of Tutankhamen. The text also includes short discussions of the major gods and goddesses of ancient Egypt.

NEUBERT, OTTO. **TUTANKHAMUN. Illustrations, 235pp. Grn57, 1.95p.**
Neubert, one of the few survivors of the Opening of the Tomb, writes a first-hand account of the splendors revealed within it and also tells a tale of the Egypt of Nefertiti and Tutankhamen.

PIANKOFF, ALEXANDRE, tr. **THE SHRINES OF TUT-ANKH-AMON. 226pp. PUP55, 5.95p.**
The first translation of the hieroglyphic texts inscribed on the four gold encrusted shrines that enclosed Tutankhamen's sarcophagus. The text consists of rituals and devotional inscriptions, including

fragments of sacred books. This volume boasts full translations of the texts, numerous diagrams, sixty-six pages of illustrations, and an introduction by Piankoff.

STREATFIELD, NOEL. **THE BOY PHARAOH: TUTANKHAMEN.** 7½"x12¼", 128pp. Jos72, 5.95c.
A simple pictorial retelling of the life and times of King Tut, designed to bring him to life for young readers. Seventeen color and many monochrome plates accompany the text.

SWINBURNE, IRENE and LAURENCE. **BEHIND THE SEALED DOOR.** 9¾"x11½", 96pp. Ath77, 12.95c.
A beautifully produced photographic discussion of the discovery of the tomb of Tutankhamen. Forty-two of the more than 100 photographs are in color, and the text is simply written—geared as it is to older children. The most unique feature of the book is a series of acetate overlays that one by one reveal the different coffins of King Tut; the final photograph showing the actual unwrapped mummy.

—————— **END OF TUTANKHAMEN SUBSECTION** ——————

VALENTINE, TOM. **THE GREAT PYRAMID.** 176pp. Pin75, 1.50p.
This is a detailed exploration of the Great Pyramid written for the general reader and based on the author's explorations into history, archaeology, astronomy, geometry, and religion. Many older works are quoted and the book is readable and well organized.

VANDENBERG, PHILIPP. **THE CURSE OF THE PHARAOHS. Notes, bibliography, index,** 252pp. S&S75/Hod, 1.75p.
More than thirty researchers and archaeologists who have excavated in Egypt since 1900 have died suddenly. Delving into the pyramids' secrets, Vandenberg discovered three principal causes for the deaths: fever with delusions, strokes accompanied by circulatory collapse, and sudden cancers that were quickly terminal. He links the deaths to several remarkable explanations while taking the reader on an excursion into ancient Egyptian history, customs, medicine, and science.

VANDENBERG, PHILIPP. **NEFERTITI: AN ARCHAEOLOGICAL BIOGRAPHY. Illustrations, bibliography,** 161pp. Lip78, 10.00c.
As the author tells it, Nefertiti was a Mitannian princess whose father sold her to the Egyptian pharaoh Amenhotep III when she was fifteen years old. Widowed at seventeen, she married his son, Amenhotep IV. Nefertiti died in poverty and loneliness, but her influence on the politics, art, and religion of her time was immeasurable. Vandenberg's account of many of the major features of Nefertiti's life does not follow the usual historical thought.

WAINWRIGHT, G.A. **THE SKY-RELIGION IN EGYPT. Notes, index,** 135pp. Gre38, 12.10c.
This is a detailed, scholarly study of a heretofore little understood aspect of ancient Egyptian religion.

WAKE, C.S. **THE ORIGIN AND THE SIGNIFICANCE OF THE GREAT PYRAMID.** 131pp. Wiz75, 6.95c.
A recent reprint of an important rare esoteric volume from 1882, with new material and additional notes.

WALTARI, MIKA. **THE EGYPTIAN.** 576pp. Ber78, 2.50p.
A vividly written novelistic account of life in ancient Egypt. As might be expected the main characters are close to the pharaoh and the novel is filled with intrigue, murder, passion, and religious strife. The novel is well done.

WEEKS, JOHN. **THE PYRAMIDS.** 8½"x8", 48pp. CUP71, 2.95p.
A profusely illustrated account covering the following topics: *Land of the Pyramids, Planning the Pyramids, The Stones, Transporting the Stones, The Building of the Pyramid,* and *The Workmen of the Pyramid.*

WHITE, J.E. **ANCIENT EGYPT. Index,** 206pp. Dov70, 3.00pp.
A well written historical view of Nile civilization illustrated with numerous photographs. Includes material about the life of the pharaoh, priest, artistocrat, architect, craftsman, and commoner in the Egypt of antiquity.

WHITE, JON MANCHIP. **EVERYDAY LIFE IN ANCIENT EGYPT. Bibliography, index,** 200pp. Put63/Bat, 2.95p.
White describes each level of Egyptian society—pharaoh, noble, priest, soldier, scribe, peasant—throughout ancient Egypt's 3,000 year history. Drawing on a wealth of archaeological evidence and supplemented by more than 100 illustrations, he discusses virtually every aspect of the civilization.

■ *WILSON, JOHN A.* **THE CULTURE OF ANCIENT EGYPT. Many illustrations, index,** 344pp. UCh51, 3.45p.
This is an interpretative work by a noted Egyptologist, based not on a stringing together of facts, but rather on his intuitive understanding of what the civilization was like: *What we have to do, then, is to learn our material as thoroughly as its vast bulk will permit; test it constantly against itself, against evidence known from other peoples and cultures, and against good common sense; then form certain tentative generalizations about ancient Egyptian culture, and, finally, apply those generalizations to the material as broad interpretations of the specific.*

YOYOTTE, JEAN. **TREASURES OF THE PHARAOHS. 205 illustrations, eighty-five in color,** 10½"x12¼", 260pp. Riz78, 35.00c.
A magnificent collection of the finest remaining examples of the enduring splendor of the pharaohs. The rash of recent books on ancient Egypt has focused almost exclusively on the treasures of Tutankhamen. Yoyotte covers all periods of ancient Egypt and he has picked out the finest examples of each era. He is a distinguished Egyptologist and he also contributes an illuminating text.

ANCIENT GREECE & ROME

For centuries Greece has exerted a peculiar enchantment over the imaginations of men. The Romans, who incorporated Greece into their empire—and in the process did not shrink from sacking its cities—were deeply impressed by it. Young Romans were sent to study at the university in Athens, and educated Romans looked to the Greeks as their masters in philosophy, science and the fine arts. Despite the Romans' confidence in their own mission and their gift for government, they felt, a little uneasily, that there was much in art, letters and thought which they could never hope to do as well as the Greeks.

When the Italian Renaissance of the 15th Century A.D. brought an intensified interest in the ancient world, Rome at first held the attention. But behind the imposing Roman facade, scholars and poets felt the presence of something more powerful and more alluring. Slowly this was disentangled from the mists of the past, and the full majesty of the Greek performance was revealed. So great was Greek prestige that Greek ideas on medicine, astronomy and geography were accepted with unquestioning faith until the 17th Century, when the birth of a new scientific spirit inaugurated the era of experiment and inquiry into which we ourselves have been born.

Even today, when we have discarded so many creeds and cosmologies, the Greek view of life excites and exalts us. Greek thought and Greek assumptions are closely woven into the fabric of our lives almost without knowing it, and for this reason alone we are right to wish to know about the Greeks, to assess the value and the scope of their achievement. No people can afford to neglect its own origins, and the modern world is far too deeply indebted to Greece to accept in unthinking ingratitude what it has inherited.

At the center of the Greek outlook lay an unshakable belief in the worth of the individual man. In centuries when large parts of the earth were dominated by the absolute monarchies of the east, the Greeks were evolving their belief that a man must be respected not as the instrument of an omnipotent overlord, but for his own sake. They sought at all costs to be themselves, and in this they were helped by the nature of their country.

Geographically, Greece was in ancient times very much what it is today: the southernmost extremity of the huge Balkan mass. A land of hard limestone mountains separated by deep valleys, it is cut almost in two by the narrow divide of the Corinthian Gulf. To the east the structure of the mainland is continued intermittently by islands, and the whole pattern is rounded off to the south by the long rampart of Crete, which has been called *the stepping-stone* of continents. Even including the islands, Greece is a small country, smaller than Florida. Moreover, this small area has never been able to support more than a few million inhabitants, and yet in the history of Western civilization it has played an enormous part.

The reason is partly geographical. In Egypt and Mesopotamia, in the great riverlands of the Nile and the Euphrates, it was easy to subject a large population to a single ruler and to see that each man performed an allotted function in a vast, unified system. But in Greece, where every district was separated from the next by mountains or the sea, central control of this kind was impossible, and men were forced to be not specialists in this or that profession but masters of a whole range of crafts and accomplishments. Each separate group was deeply aware of its own being, and within each group its members were cognizant of their responsibilities. The Greek climate, dry and exhilarating and gifted with the most magical of skies, incited to action, while the sea, which was always at hand, developed in its servants an unusual skill of both hand and eye.

Nature nursed the Greeks in a hard school, but this made them conscious of themselves and their worth. Without this self-awareness they would never have made their most important contribution to human experience: the belief that a man must be honored for his individual worth and treated with respect just because he is himself. In the words of the great Athenian statesman Pericles: *Each single one of our citizens, in all the manifold aspects of life, is able to show himself the rightful lord and owner of his own person, and do this, moreover, with exceptional grace and exceptional versatility.*

—condensed from **Classical Greece**, by C.M. Bowra

ARMSTRONG, A.H., ed. **THE CAMBRIDGE HISTORY OF LATER GREEK AND EARLY MEDIEVAL PHILOSOPHY. Notes, bibliography, indices, 731pp. CUP70, 39.70c.**
A wide ranging, detailed survey of philosophy from the Neoplatonists to St. Anselm, showing how Greek philosophy took the form in which it was known to its cultural inheritors, and how they interpreted it. The volume is divided into eight sections, each written by a different authority: *Greek Philosophy from Plato to Plotinus; Philo and the Beginnings of Christian Thought; Plotinus; The Later Neoplatonists; Marius Victorinus and Augustine; The Greek Christian Platonist Tradition from the Cappadocians to Maximus and Erigena; Western Christian Thought from Boethius to Anselm,* and *Early Islamic Philosophy.*

BAILEY, CYRIL, ed. **THE LEGACY OF ROME. Illustrations, 525pp. Oxf24, 15.95c.**
A collection of fairly scholarly essays which show the extent to which the modern world is indebted to ancient Rome. Topics include the transmission of the legacy, administration, communication and commerce, law, family and social life, religion and philosophy, science, literature, language, architecture and art, building and engineering, and agriculture.

BAMBROUGH, RENFORD, ed. **THE PHILOSOPHY OF ARISTOTLE. 432pp. NAL63, 1.95p.**
The aim of this book is to stress the importance of Aristotle's discussion of problems that still perplex and preoccupy philosophers of the modern day.... For this book I have chosen a selection from the texts of Aristotle that relate most directly to philosophical questions still being debated today. The translations are by J.L. Creed and A.E. Wardman, and Bambrough provides an introduction and commentary.

BARR, STRINGFELLOW. **THE MASK OF JOVE. Illustrations, maps, notes, index, 619pp. Lip66, 15.00c.**
An excellent history of Graeco-Roman civilization from the death of Alexander to the death of Constantine. The book is basically a history of Rome, but its underlying theme is the continued development of Greek civilization as expressed in Greek literature, reflected in Latin literature, carried on by Greek mathematicians and scientists, and recorded by Greek or Hellenized painters, sculptors, and architects. Barr writes exceptionally well and conveys his history in the form of a swiftly moving narrative. Many quotations from classical works are included.

BERG, STEPHEN and DISKIN CLAY, trs. **SOPHOCLES' OEDIPUS THE KING. 8.50c.**
See the Mythology section.

BEYE, CHARLES. ANCIENT GREEK LITERATURE AND SOCIETY. Extensive bibliography, index, 469pp. Dou75, 3.95p.

This book covers Greek literature from Homer to Thucydides, emphasizing its public nature and social function. Professor Beye analyzes many of the important individual works and describes how tragedy and history developed out of epic poetry. He also discusses how the sophistic rationalism in the late fifth century challenged the dominance of the mythopoetic tradition and the Greek tragic sense of life. A final section is devoted to the Hellenistic poets who, exalting education and the library, broke with the earlier tradition. A dry study.

BIRLEY, ANTHONY, tr. LIVES OF THE LATER CAESARS. Maps, notes, index, 336pp. Vik76, 2.95p.

This is a translation of the first part of the **Augustan History**, a collection of biographies of the emperors, possibly written as a hoax towards the end of the fourth century. Supposedly composed of the work of six different men, the collection tells of Hadrian and Antinous, the martial glory of Marcus Antoninus and the shocking depravities of Commodus and Heliogabalus. This edition is prefaced by an essay by Birley which deals with the lives of Nerva and Trajan and restores the continuity between Suetonius' **The Twelve Caesars** and the **Augustan History**.

■ **BOWRA, C.M. CLASSICAL GREECE. Bibliography, index, 8¾"x 10¾", 192pp. TLB65, 8.95c.**

This is an excellent introductory work, part of Time-Life's **Great Ages of Man** series. Bowra combines a clear text on all aspects of the Greek experience with a magnificent collection of color plates, line drawings, and maps.

■ **BOWRA, C.M. THE GREEK EXPERIENCE. Sixty-four illustrations, notes, index, 224pp. NAL57, 1.50p.**

This book is in no sense an attempt to give a comprehensive account of the Greeks and their achievements. It aims at assessing what is most characteristic and most striking in them. As such it inevitably represents my own views and is to that degree subjective.... Yet, if we are to try to form some general picture of what the Greeks were, we have to rely on our own judgment and hope that others will to some degree share it.... There is a danger that with the growth of specialization in classical scholarship we may lose our vision of the ancient world as a whole, and for this reason we must from time to time try to form general notions of it. I have set my limits roughly from the Homeric poems to the fall of Athens in 404 BC. This is a highly readable discussion, and a work of excellent scholarship.

BROWNING, ROBERT. THE EMPEROR JULIAN. Photographs, chronology, annotated bibliography, index, 268pp. UCa76, 12.50c.

The life of the Roman emperor Julian has tantalized the historian and the artist for sixteen centuries. He was certainly unique—a Greek intellectual who ruled the Roman Empire which for a century had been dominated by soldiers. Although his early and rather mysterious death brought to an abrupt end his hope of replacing Christianity with the old pagan gods, Julian became the subject of legends within a few years of his death, and was not forgotten as are most of his predecessors and followers. Browning, Professor of Classics and Ancient History at the University of London, presents a readable new picture of the life of Julian based on recent scholarship. He shows us a man of unusual ability in who is embodied all the sharpest contradictions of his age and class.

■ **BRUMBAUGH, ROBERT. THE PHILOSOPHERS OF GREECE.** Illustrations, notes, bibliography, index, 287pp. Cro64, 4.95p.

This is a very clearly written introductory survey, with individual chapters on Thales, Anaximenes, Empedocles, Heraclitus, Parmenides, Zeno, Anaxagoras, the Sophists, Socrates, Plato, and Aristotle. Dr. Brumbaugh analyzes all these philosophers, explains their works and key concepts, and demonstrates their contemporary relevance.

BURNET, JOHN. EARLY GREEK PHILOSOPHERS. Notes, index, 375pp. ACB30, 13.50c.

This is a detailed, scholarly study with chapters on the Milesian School; science and religion; Herakleitos of Ephesos; Parmenides of Elea; Empedokles of Akragas; Anaxagoras of Klazomenai; the Pythagoreans; the Young Eleatics; and Leukippos Miletos.

CALDWELL, TAYLOR. GLORY AND THE LIGHTNING. 472pp. Faw74, 1.95p.

This historical novel is based on the life of Aspasia, the beautiful and intelligent courtesan who became the companion of Pericles. It is the story of an extraordinary woman, trained since childhood in the arts of beauty and seduction, who finds herself increasingly in rebellion against the helpless position of women in ancient society. Her first lover is a rich, powerful Persian satrap; her second, and the main figure in the novel, is Pericles, the ruler of Athens at the height of its glory. A vivid account which reads well and is fairly accurate historically.

CHADWICK, JOHN. THE MYCENAEAN WORLD. Many photographs, bibliography, index, 6¾"x9½", 219pp. CUP76, 6.95c.

In 1952 the decipherment of the Linear B script revealed the Greekness of Mycenaean Greece. Now, after new discoveries and more than twenty years of intensive work, scholars are able to interpret the written documents and reconstruct from them a vivid picture of life in this remote period. Chadwick, who assisted in the original decipherment, has played a major part in these advances. He now summarizes the results of recent research and in so doing opens the door to a new world: Mycenaean Greece seen through the eyes of its inhabitants. Chadwick's account is well organized and clearly written.

COLDSTREAM, J.N. GEOMETRIC GREECE. Chronology, notes, bibliography, site index, indices, 405pp. SMP77, 33.60c.

The geometric style of pottery flourished in Greece during the ninth and eighth centuries BC—a creative time which saw the dawn of Hellenic civilization and the evolution of the Greek city state, the composition of the Homeric epics, the invention of the Greek alphabet after several centuries of illiteracy, the rebirth of figured art, the rise of the great Panhellenic sanctuaries (Olympia, Delphi, Delos), and the first exodus of the Greek colonists to the shores of southern Italy and Sicily. This is a comprehensive, illustrated study of the period, written by a leading scholar.

CORNFORD, FRANCIS. BEFORE AND AFTER SOCRATES. Notes, index, 123pp. CUP32, 2.95p.

Transcription of four lectures: *Ionian Science Before Socrates; Socrates; Plato; and Aristotle* which, as **The Times Library Supplement** said, provide *a clear insight into the development of Greek philosophy and a brilliant commentary on the Greek mind and its attitude to life. Cornford says, I have tried...to describe the Ionian science as to show why it failed to satisfy Socrates, and I have treated the systems of Plato and Aristotle as attempts to carry into the interpretation of the world the consequences of Socrates' discovery.*

COSON, DONNA. THE ANCIENT GREEK COLORING BOOK. Forty-six plates, 8¼"x11½", 96pp. Wdw77, 5.10p.

COTTRELL, LEONARD. THE BULL OF MINOS. Illustrations, bibliography, 223pp. PnB55, 1.75p.

This is a revised edition of Cottrell's noted study of the rise and development of the Minoan civilization on Crete. Cottrell writes in a popular style and vividly recreates both the prehistoric Cretan civilization and the recent archaeological investigations—especially those of Sir Arthur Evans. Many quotations from a variety of sources are included.

CUMONT, FRANZ. ASTROLOGY AND RELIGION AMONG THE GREEKS AND ROMANS. 2.00p.

See the Astrology section.

CUMONT, FRANZ. **ORIENTAL RELIGIONS IN ROMAN PAGAN-ISM. Extensive notes, bibliography, 322pp. Dov11, 3.50p.**
A detailed study of the mystery religions of the ancient Near East and of their influence on the religious life of the early Roman Empire.

D'AGOSTINO, BRUNO. **GREECE. Chronology, glossary, bibliography, index, 9¾"x13", 191pp. G&D75, 19.95c.**
This sumptuously illustrated book contains 106 color photographs depicting the splendor of Greek civilization. D'Agostino explores the Greek genius through its architecture, sculpture, and other works of art, literature, religious forms, and social structure—thus placing the monuments in their historical as well as natural context. The account begins with the precursors of the later Greek civilizations—the Minoans and Mycenaeans—then focuses on Greece emerging from its dark age after 1000 BC, traces the classic civilization, and ends with the Hellenistic world that followed Alexander the Great's conquests. The text itself is well written and provides an excellent overview.

DEVAMBEZ, PIERRE, ed. **GREAT SCULPTURE OF ANCIENT GREECE. 180 illustrations, forty in color, index, 8½"x10¾", 194pp. Mor78, 25.00c.**
No culture is as famous for its sculpture as ancient Greece. As Devambez says, *The human form was the only thing Greek art judged worthy of representation; the only thing that interested them; the only thing that could reflect divinity.* This lavishly illustrated work presents a representative selection of Greek sculpture, accompanied by a series of essays.

DILLON, JOHN. **THE MIDDLE PLATONISTS. Notes, bibliography, indices, 445pp. Cor77, 28.90c.**
Professor Dillon traces the evolution of Platonism during the last century BC and the first two centuries AD, from the age of Cicero through that of Plutarch and finally to the time of Plotinus. He groups the philosophers of the period according to trends within Platonism, rather than by themes or subjects; and much of the time he allows them to speak in their own words. An interesting, readable study.

DODDS, E.R. **THE GREEKS AND THE IRRATIONAL. Many notes, index, 332pp. UCa51, 3.95p.**
Greek culture has long been identified with the triumph of rationalism. The role of primitive and irrational forces in Greek society has been neglected or largely glossed over, even when it was obviously touched on by the Greeks themselves. In this volume, Professor Dodd examines why this is so, and in the process makes many references to ancient Greek texts. The analysis is topically arranged.

DOWRICK, STEPHANIE. **LAND OF ZEUS: THE GREEK MYTHS RETOLD BY GEOGRAPHIC PLACE OF ORIGIN. 7.95c.**
See the Mythology section.

DRAKE, W. RAYMOND. **GODS AND SPACEMEN IN GREECE AND ROME. Bibliography, index, 256pp. NAL76, 1.50p.**
Drake thinks that the gods of the classical world were in reality spacemen. And in this volume he attempts to prove his thesis, quoting liberally from classical sources in the process.

FEIBLEMAN, JAMES. **RELIGIOUS PLATONISM. Notes, index, 236pp. Gre59, 23.50c.**
Feibleman sets forth the thesis that *Plato has two philosophies and subscribed to two sets of religious ideas consistent with these philosophies. The first of Plato's philosophies—and the one for which he is chiefly known—is that of idealism.* As Feibleman says, *According to idealism, the ideas are more real than the actualities....The second and more neglected philosophy...is that of realism. According to realism, the ideas are as real, but no more real than the actualities.... The Orphic and Dionysiac cults are more consistent with idealism, the native Greek religion more consistent with realism.* Philo and Plotinus followed the idealistic version. Feibleman's aim is *to show how the two strands of religious philosophy...first arose and had their influence upon Plato, and how later men chose the one strand and developed it in a particular direction.*

FINLEY, M.I., ed. **THE PORTABLE GREEK HISTORIANS: THE ESSENCE OF HERODOTUS, THUCYDIDES, XENOPHON, POLYBIUS. Notes, 507pp. Vik59, 4.95p.**
A collection of long excerpts from the major writings of Herodotus, Thucydides, Xenophon, and Polybius—the principle Greek historians. The translations themselves read well and Finley contributes an introduction.

FLACELIERE, ROBERT. **GREEK ORACLES. 7.95c.**
See the Mythology section.

GIBBON, EDWARD. **THE DECLINE AND FALL OF THE ROMAN EMPIRE, VOLUME I. Many notes from a variety of sources, index, 964pp. RaH nd, 6.95c.**
Gibbon's masterwork, completed 150 years ago, remains the standard work. No scholar has ever come close to duplicating Gibbon and, while there have been countless discoveries since his time, the book remains startlingly up to date and relevant. When we started going through it we were amazed at how well it read; Gibbon is an excellent writer. This is an unabridged edition in three volumes, taken from the set prepared by Oliphant Smeaton. Volume I covers the period from AD 180 to AD 395.

GIBBON, EDWARD. **THE DECLINE AND FALL OF THE ROMAN EMPIRE, VOLUME II. 932pp. RaH nd, 6.95c.**
This volume covers the period from AD 395 to 1185.

GIBBON, EDWARD. **THE DECLINE AND FALL OF THE ROMAN EMPIRE, VOLUME III. Notes, index, 907pp. RaH nd, 6.95c.**
This volume covers the history of the Empire from 1185 to the fall of Constantinople in 1453.

GIBBON, EDWARD. **THE PORTABLE GIBBON—THE DECLINE AND FALL OF THE ROMAN EMPIRE. Introduction, 701pp. Vik52, 5.95p.**
A one volume abridgment of Gibbon's masterwork, edited by Dero Saunders. The reduction has been made chiefly in Gibbon's lengthy digression on the Empire's survival in the East. Saunders clearly summarizes the deleted material, thus preserving the scope and sweep of Gibbon's vast historical perspective.

GRANT, FREDERICK, ed. **ANCIENT ROMAN RELIGION. Lengthy introduction, 287pp. BoM57, 6.30p.**
A collection of primary source texts organized under the following general headings: *The Old Agricultural Religion; Foreign Influences; Philosophy and Religion; Religion under the Imperial Republic; The Augustan Restoration; Religion under the Empire;* and *The Christian Victory and the Pagan Reaction.* Much of the material is not readily available elsewhere.

GRANT, FREDERICK, ed. **HELLENISTIC RELIGIONS. 235pp. BoM53, 9.50p.**
A topically organized collection of primary source material, usually in the form of brief selections. Professor Grant also supplies a lengthy introduction.

GRANT, MICHAEL. **ANCIENT HISTORY ATLAS. Index, 7"x9½", 100pp. McM71, 6.95c.**
Eighty-seven clearly reproduced maps of the ancient Greek and Roman world. The maps are based on the most modern archaeological research and cover economic, political, and religious factors as well as political and military themes.

■ GRANT, MICHAEL. **THE ANCIENT MEDITERRANEAN. Nineteen maps, notes, bibliography, index, 394pp. Scr69, 3.95p.**
An informative and sensitive essay on the civilizations of the ancient Mediterranean world. Grant has a wonderful facility for bringing history to life and he is at his best here. The bulk of this book is devoted to Greek and pre-Greek civilization going back to prehistoric times.

GRANT, MICHAEL. **MYTHS OF THE GREEKS AND ROMANS. 2.50p.**
See the Mythology section.

GRANT, MICHAEL. **ROMAN MYTHS. 3.50p.**
See the Mythology section.

GRANT, MICHAEL. **THE WORLD OF ROME. Almost 100 illustrations, notes, bibliography, index, 342pp. NAL60, 1.50p.**
This is an excellent overview of the world of Rome by our favorite classical historian. Grant has organized his study into sections on *The Roman Empire; State and Society; Beliefs;* and *Literature and the Arts.* As with all Grant's books, this work is extremely readable and is a product of excellent scholarship.

GRAVES, ROBERT. **CLAUDIUS THE GOD. 585pp. RaH35, 3.95p.**
The second in Graves' two part recreation of the life and times of the

fourth Roman emperor. We did not enjoy this volume as much as **I, Claudius**; the personalities are less interesting than in the earlier part. This volume is concerned solely with the period in which Claudius is emperor. Three accounts of Claudius' death and Seneca's satire of Claudius are appended.

GRAVES, ROBERT. **THE GREEK MYTHS. 10.00c/5.90p/set.**
See the Mythology section.

■ *GRAVES, ROBERT.* **I, CLAUDIUS. 437pp. RaH34, 2.95p.**
This is a marvelous fictional recreation of the early Roman Empire, as narrated by Claudius, the step-grandson of Augustus. Despised as a weakling and considered an idiot because of his physical infirmities, Claudius survived the intrigues and poisonings of the reigns of Augustus, Tiberius, and Caligula to become emperor in AD 41. Graves has created a wonderful cast of characters, in particular Claudius' grandmother Livia. As **The New York Times** said, *One of the really remarkable books of our day, a novel of learning and imagination, fortunately conceived and brilliantly executed.*

GRAVES, ROBERT, tr. **SUETONIUS: THE TWELVE CAESARS. Notes, 315pp. Vik57, 2.50p.**
The Twelve Caesars of Suetonius (born AD 69), covering the Roman rulers from Julius Caesar to Domitian, remains one of the richest and most fascinating of all Latin histories. Suetonius gathered much of his information from eyewitnesses, checking his facts carefully and quoting conflicting evidence without too much bias. He loved to dwell on the scandalous and amusing incidents in the domestic lives of the Caesars, so his account is often vivid and racy.

GREEN, PETER. **THE PARTHENON. Index, 9¼"x11¾", 172pp. Nsw73, 10.00c.**
At the time of its completion the Parthenon—the great temple of Athena—was an awe inspiring testament to the splendor and might of Periclean Athens. This pictorial account uses the Parthenon as the focus for a study of Athens' ascendancy, her worldwide impact, and subsequent decline. The text is supplemented by more than 120 illustrations, over one-third in color.

GREEN, ROGER. **THE LUCK OF TROY. 1.50p.**
See the Mythology section.

GREEN, ROGER. **THE TALE OF THEBES. 2.95p.**
See the Mythology section.

GREEN, ROGER. **THE TALE OF TROY. 1.50p.**
See the Mythology section.

GREEN, ROGER. **TALES OF THE GREEK HEROES. 1.50p.**
See the Mythology section.

GRENE, DAVID and RICHMOND LATTIMORE, eds. **GREEK TRAGE-DIES. 3.45p/each.**
See the Mythology section.

GUTHRIE, W.K.C. **THE GREEK PHILOSOPHERS FROM THALES TO ARISTOTLE. Bibliography, index, 175pp. H&R50, 2.95p.**
An excellent summary of the salient features of Greek philosophy, including studies of the early cosmologies, the humanistic reaction in the second half of the fifth century BC, and the philosophies of Plato and Aristotle.

GUTHRIE, W.K.C. **THE GREEKS AND THEIR GODS. Notes, indices, 402pp. Bea54, 5.95p.**
In its review, **The New York Times** said, *Mr. Guthrie's book, which is refreshingly unpedantic in tone, is an examination of the meaning of the major gods, taken individually, and of the groups of less important divinities and semi-divinities....He is always cogent and rewarding.* This is an exceedingly readable study which should be of great interest to all students of Greek philosophy and mythology.

GUTHRIE, W.K.C. **A HISTORY OF GREEK PHILOSOPHY, VOL-UME I: THE EARLIER PRESOCRATICS AND PYTHAGOREANS. Notes, bibliography, index, 554pp. CUP71, 31.50c.**
Beginning with the infancy of Western philosophy in Ionia in the sixth century BC, Professor Guthrie discusses in turn the doctrines of Thales, Anaximander, and Anaximenes, and shows how Pythagoras

and his followers then took philosophy in a new direction. He surveys separately the related doctrine of Alcmaeon and the work of the philosopher-poet Xenophanes; and concludes with a study of Heraclitus. This is without question the most comprehensive account of ancient Greek philosophy. The text is well written and should be understandable to the general reader as well as a valuable tool for the serious scholar.

GUTHRIE, W.K.C. **A HISTORY OF GREEK PHILOSOPHY, VOL-UME II: THE PRESOCRATIC TRADITION FROM PARMENIDES TO DEMOCRITUS. Notes, bibliography, indices, 573pp. CUP65, 31.50c.**
As in the first volume, Professor Guthrie groups families of philosophers who were interested in the same things, distinguishing particularly between the natural philosophers, with their primary interest in cosmogony and the nature of matter, and the moral philosophers with their absorption in human nature and in problems of individual and social morality. This volume focuses on the natural philosophers, beginning with Parmenides and the Eleatics, going on to the work of Empedocles and Anaxagoras, and concluding with the Atomists of the fifth century.

GUTHRIE, W.K.C. **A HISTORY OF GREEK PHILOSOPHY, VOL-UME III: THE FIFTH CENTURY ENLIGHTENMENT. Notes, bibliography, indices, 560pp. CUP69, 31.50c.**
This volume deals comprehensively with the Sophists and in particular with the towering intellectual figure of Socrates (though not with Plato). It is a record of the fundamental shift of philosophical interest from the universe to man, and from investigations into the nature of the physical world to an almost total absorption in problems of human life and conduct.

GUTHRIE, W.K.C. **A HISTORY OF GREEK PHILOSOPHY, VOL-UME IV: PLATO, THE MAN AND HIS DIALOGUES (EARLIER PERIOD). Notes, bibliography, indices, 621pp. CUP75, 34.50c.**
Plato was so prolific a writer, so profoundly original in his thought, and so colossal an influence on the later history of philosophy, that Professor Guthrie needs more than one volume to discuss him fully. This volume offers a general introduction to his life and writings, and covers the so-called early and middle periods of his philosophical development up to and including the **Republic**. Volume V will cover the remaining dialogues, the letters, and the unwritten doctrines.

GUTHRIE, W.K.C. **SOCRATES. Many notes, bibliography, indices, 207pp. CUP71, 5.95p.**
This is the first part of the third volume of Guthrie's impressive history of Greek thought. Socrates dominated the controversies of the fifth century BC, as he has dominated the subsequent history of Western philosophy. Professor Guthrie offers a balanced and comprehensive picture of the man, his life, and his thought.

GUTHRIE, W.K.C. **THE SOPHISTS. Notes, bibliography, indices, 354pp. CUP71, 8.95p.**
This is the second part of the third volume of Guthrie's history of Greek thought. **The Sophists** assesses the contribution of individuals like Protagoras, Gorgias, and Hippias to the extraordinary intellectual and moral ferment in fifth century Athens. They questioned the basis of morality, religion, organized society itself, and the nature of knowledge and language; they initiated a whole series of important and continuing debates, and they provoked Socrates and Plato to a major restatement and defense of traditional values.

HALL, MANLY P. **JOURNEY IN TRUTH. 270pp. PRS45, 6.50c.**
Volume I of Hall's survey of *Idealistic Philosophy*, this volume traces the great thinkers of the classical world from Orpheus to St. Augustine and includes sections on Pythagoras, Plato, Socrates, Diogenes, Aristotle, and Plotinus.

HAMILTON, EDITH. **THE GREEK WAY. Notes, 347pp. Avo42, 1.95p.**
A collection of essays on Greek thought and art, with individual pieces on Pindar, Plato, Aristophanes, Herodotus, Thucydides, Xenophon, Aeschylus, and Euripides. Ms. Hamilton is a renowned writer on things Greek and this book is an excellent introductory survey of the major figures and ideas.

HAMMOND, N.G.L. and H. SCULLARD, eds. **THE OXFORD CLASSICAL DICTIONARY. Index, 7½"x10", 1,198pp. Oxf70, 29.95c.**
An encyclopedic compendium, with individual articles by many of the leading contemporary scholars. Every conceivable subject is covered at some length.

HAVILAND, VIRGINIA. **FAVORITE FAIRY TALES TOLD IN GREECE. 4.95c.**
See the Fairy Tales section.

HAWKES, JACQUETTA. **DAWN OF THE GODS. Bibliography, index, 7½"x10¼", 303pp. C&W68, 10.95c.**
A well written study of the beginnings of European history focusing on the culture of Minoan Crete and Mycenaean Greece. The myths and the often astonishing works of art are discussed, and the book is exquisitely illustrated with approximately 200 color and monochrome plates.

HERODOTUS. **THE HISTORIES. Maps, notes, index, 653pp. Vik72, 3.95p.**
Few facts are known about the life of Herodotus, although his personality is clearly reflected in his writings. He was born between 490 and 480 BC in Asia Minor and died in Italy in 425 BC. As a young man he traveled widely—in Egypt, Africa, and other parts of the Greek world. He has been called *the Father of History*. The main theme of his **Histories** is the heroic and successful struggle of a small and divided Greece against the mighty empire of Persia—with its underlying conflict between the absolutism of the East and the free institutions of the West. When direct evidence was lacking, Herodotus recorded popular beliefs about historical events—so he has been called *the Father of Lies* as well as *the Father of History*. His writing is often entertaining and has been the basis for much of the later scholarship. This edition contains Aubrey de Selincourt's translation, revised and introduced by A.R. Burn.

HESIOD. See the Mythology section for various translations of Hesiod.

HOMANN-WEDEKING, E. **THE ART OF ARCHAIC GREECE. Glossary, notes, index, 7¼"x9¼", 224pp. Crn68, 6.95c.**
The Archaic period in Greece, which lasted from about 1000 BC to the beginning of the fifth century, was, no less than the classical period, a time of remarkable artistic activity. At the beginning of the Archaic era, vase painting in the geometric style had already reached its full flowering, and by the fifth century black figure painting had been developed to its fullest extent, while the Attic vase painters were in command of the subtle red figure technique. Sculpture, on the other hand, did not reach its fullest expression until relatively late in the period. The latter part of the Archaic era also saw the development of the austere Doric and more elegant Ionic orders of architecture, and massive temples began to be constructed. This text is illustrated with more than fifty color plates and numerous photographs and drawings.

HOMER. See the Mythology section for various translations of Homer.

HOOD, SINCLAIR. **HOME OF THE HEROES—THE AEGEAN BEFORE THE GREEKS. Bibliography, index, 144pp. T&H67, 3.90p.**
The early civilization of Crete is the main focus of this archaeological volume. Hood has excavated widely and is primarily known for his work on Crete, particularly at Knossos. 122 plates and drawings are included, many of which are in color.

JASPERS, KARL. **ANAXIMANDER, HERACLITUS, PARAMENIDES, PLOTINUS, LAO-TZU, NAGARJUNA. Bibliography, index, 138pp. HBJ66, 3.25p.**
A collection of biographical and critical essays on each of these men, taken from Jaspers' *magnum opus*, **The Great Philosophers**, and edited by Hannah Arendt. Numerous quotations from the philosophical works of the individuals are included within the body of the text and each figure is seen as a person rather than as merely a bundle of abstract ideas. The individual accounts are very well organized.

■ *JOHNSTON, ALAN.* **THE EMERGENCE OF GREECE. 209 illustrations, 156 in color, glossary, bibliography, index, 9"x11½", 151pp. Dut76, 5.98c.**
A survey of archaic Greece up to 480 BC and the Greek colonies on the Black Sea, in Italy, and Sicily to 300 BC. The book opens with an account of the geography of the area and the political and social history of the period. This is followed by a description of the more important excavations, including recent ones. An examination of the archaeology leads to a closer look at the social structure and political development of Athens in the seventh and sixth centuries. The book ends with a discussion of the art and architecture of the period up to 480 BC.

KERENYI, CARL. **THE RELIGION OF THE GREEKS AND ROMANS. Notes, index, 303pp. Gre62, 26.20c.**
This is a very interesting study which is highlighted by a collection of 124 monochrome plates. The material is reviewed in a great deal of detail, but in a manner which should not overwhelm the general reader. It is rare to find a good study on this subject, so this volume is welcome in spite of its high price. Kerenyi was closely associated with Carl Jung and his writings reflect his Jungian approach.

KIRK, G.S., tr. **HERACLITUS: THE COSMIC FRAGMENTS. Introduction, extensive notes, indices, 431pp. CUP62, 29.50c.**
Little is known about Heraclitus' life. He was a Greek who lived in the fifth or sixth century BC and belonged to an ancient royal house. He refers to Pythagoras and Xenophanes by name and is in turn alluded to by Parmenides. We do not know the title that Heraclitus gave to his work—and it is not easy to form a clear idea of its contents. Later Greeks say that it was divided into three discourses: one dealing with the universe, one political, and one theological. His style is obscure and he was later given the nickname *the Dark*. The fragments that have come down to us resemble Taoist philosophy more than anything else. This edition provides the Greek text, a translation, and an extended study of those of Heraclitus' fragments whose subject is the world as a whole rather than man and his part in it. Professor Kirk fully discusses the fragments which he considers genuine and treats in passing others usually considered genuine, but which he considers paraphrased or spurious. This is considered the definitive edition of the **Fragments**.

KIRK, G.S. **THE NATURE OF THE GREEK MYTHS. 3.95p.**
See the Mythology section.

■ *KIRK, G.S. and J.E. RAVEN.* **THE PRESOCRATIC PHILOSOPHERS. Notes, bibliography, indices, 499pp. CUP63, 6.50p.**
This work has been universally acclaimed as the best history of pre-Socratic philosophy to appear in English since Burnet's **Early Greek Philosophy**. The judicious selection of material, the careful translation of each ancient text, and the unusually competent commentary make this the standard work for all students of early Greek philosophy. In many cases the original Greek text is provided, along with translation and commentary.

LINES, KATHLEEN, ed. **THE FABER BOOK OF GREEK LEGENDS. 8.95c.**
See the Mythology section.

Mycenaean vase, with chariots and horses.

■ LING, ROGER. **THE GREEK WORLD. 180 illustrations, 140 in color, glossary, index, 9"x11½", 152pp. Dut76, 5.98c.**
A pictorial survey of the greatest period of Greek civilization, from the fifth to the first century BC, with special emphasis on archaeological research and material remains. In an introductory chapter, Ling describes the Greek achievement in literature, philosophy, science, government, and the arts, and the role and features of the Greek city state. He next traces the history of archaeology in classical and Hellenistic Greece. The last chapters review military and political history, economics and society, and art and architecture.

LIVINGSTONE, RICHARD, ed. **THE LEGACY OF GREECE. Many illustrations, 424pp. Oxf21, 3.50p.**
This volume contains eleven essays by distinguished scholars—among whom are Gilbert Murray, W.R. Inge, Arnold Toynbee, A.E. Zimmern, Sir Reginald Bloomfield, Charles Singer, Percy Gardner, and the editor. The essays point out the lasting values of our Greek heritage in such realms as art and architecture, literature, philosophy and political thought, mathematics, and the natural sciences.

LIVY. **THE EARLY HISTORY OF ROME. Bibliography, index, 424pp. Vik71, 2.95p.**
A translation by Aubrey de Selincourt of the first five books of Livy's monumental work, beginning with the foundation of Rome and the history of the seven kings, through the establishment of the Republic and its internal struggles, up to Rome's recovery after the fierce Gallic invasion of the fourth century BC. Long introduction by Robert Ogilvie.

LIVY. **ROME AND THE MEDITERRANEAN. Maps, chronology, notes, index, 699pp. Vik76, 4.95p.**
A translation by Henry Bettenson of fifteen books from Livy's masterly **History of Rome from its Foundations**, tracing the final stages of Roman aggrandizement up to 167 BC and focusing on the defeat of the Hellenistic Kings in the three *preventive* Eastern wars, from which Rome emerged as ruler of the Mediterranean. Livy also includes information on Roman domestic affairs: the bitter feuding, the debates and oratory, Cato's celebrated Censorship, the repression in 186 BC of the subversive rites of Bacchus, and many other events. Livy writes vividly. Introduction by A.H. McDonald.

■ MCNEILL, WILLIAM and JEAN SEDLAR, eds. **THE CLASSICAL MEDITERRANEAN WORLD. 300pp. Oxf69, 2.60c.**
The readings in this volume were chosen to emphasize the distinctive character of ancient Greek (or Hellenic) civilization and to show how it met and mingled with other cultural strands as it expanded eastward and westward....The book opens with selections which illustrate the two central realities of Greek life: the polis or city-state as a basic institution...and the idea of natural law....The readings in Section II illustrate how Greek ideas met and combined with diverse elements of Near Eastern culture in the period following the conquests of Alexander....The readings in Section III present some Roman reactions to the Greek civilization encountered after Rome became the overlord, first of Greece itself, then of the entire Mediterranean basin. Each selection includes introductory material.

MERWIN, W.S. and GEORGE DIMOCK, JR., trs. **EURIPIDES' IPHIGENEIA AT AULIS. 8.50c.**
See the Mythology section.

MOURELATOS, ALEXANDER, ed. **THE PRE-SOCRATICS. Notes, bibliography, indices, 574pp. Dou74, 5.95p.**
A collection of critical essays grouped under the following general headings: *Concept Studies; Ionian Beginnings; Pythagoras and Pythagoreanism; Heraclitus; Parmenides; Xeno of Elea; Empedocles; and Anaxagoras and the Atomists.* There is also an introduction with sections keyed to each of the six parts.

MYLONAS, GEORGE. **ELEUSIS AND THE ELEUSINIAN MYSTERIES. Many photographs, glossary, notes, bibliography, index, 416pp. PUP61, 6.95p.**
Few archaeological sites have so much material, so much interest, so many problems, in such close concentration, as Eleusis. The tremendous value of this book is that it presents the whole picture, including most of the details, in a brief but solid treatment....Professor Mylonas collects, assimilates, and interprets it all: the legends and history of the sanctuary and cult, the development architecturally from Mycenaean through Roman times, the evidence pertaining to the myth and rites from archaeology and literature.—**Classical Philology.** The author is Director of the Excavations at Mycenae and is the leading scholar today on the Eleusian Mysteries.

NICHOLS, ROGER and KENNETH MCLEISH, eds. **THROUGH GREEK EYES: GREEK CIVILISATION IN THE WORDS OF GREEK WRITERS. Many illustrations, bibliography, 8½"x8¼", 144pp. CUP74, 10.95c.**
A collection of translated extracts of Greek writers from Homer to Pausanias. The extracts are topically organized with a brief linking narrative.

NILSSON, MARTIN. **A HISTORY OF GREEK RELIGION. Notes, index, 316pp. Nor52, 4.65p.**
A good academic study divided into the following chapters: *Minoan-Mycenaean Religion and its Survival in Greek Religion; Origins of Greek Mythology; Primitive Belief and Ritual; Gods of Nature and of Human Life; The Homeric Anthropomorphism and Rationalism; Legalism and Mysticism; The Civic Religion;* and *The Religion of the Cultured Classes and the Religion of the Peasants.*

NILSSON, MARTIN. **THE MYCENAEAN ORIGIN OF GREEK MYTHOLOGY. 11.00c.**
See the Mythology section.

OTTO, WALTER. **DIONYSUS: MYTH AND CULT. Introduction, plates, notes, index, 264pp. IUP65, 2.95p.**
An important analysis of the spiritual significance of ancient Greek religion. As the title suggests, Dionysus is at the center of the study and Otto makes a thorough theological survey of the Greek pantheon. This is a somewhat dry work, translated form the German by Robert Palmer.

■ PAYNE, ROBERT. **THE SPLENDOUR OF GREECE. Index, 219pp. PnB61, .95p.**
This is a well written survey of classical Greek civilization, organized according to geographical units and major sites. Payne has done a good job of bringing the civilization to life through his narrative and in the process he retells a great deal of mythology and folk history.

Plato

Plato (c.427-347 BC) was, with Socrates and Aristotle, one of the three philosophers of ancient Greece who laid the philosophical foundations of Western culture. Building on the life and thought of Socrates, whom his dialogues memorialized, Plato developed a profound and wide ranging system of philosophy that was strongly ethical, and at times even mystical in spirit, while remaining basically rationalistic. He came from a family that had long played a prominent part in Athenian politics, and it would have been natural for him to follow the same course. He declined to do so however, due to the violence and corruption of Athenian political life. Inspired by Socrates' inquiries into the nature of ethical standards, Plato sought a cure for the ills of society not in politics but in philosophy, and arrived at his fundamental and lasting conviction that those ills would never cease until philosophers became rulers or rulers philosophers. In the early fourth century BC he founded the Athenian Academy, the first permanent institution devoted to philosophical research and teaching.

BUCHANAN, SCOTT, ed. **THE PORTABLE PLATO. Lengthy introduction, bibliography, 696pp. Vik48, 5.95p.**
This volume contains the complete Jowett translation of **Protagoras, Symposium, Phaedo,** and **The Republic,** edited by Buchanan.

CORNFORD, FRANCIS, tr. **PLATO'S COSMOLOGY. Many diagrams, notes, index, 390pp. BoM37, 7.85p.**
A translation of the **Timaeus** of Plato, with running commentary. The translation is an excellent one and the commentary helps illuminate many difficult parts of the text. As might be expected from the title of the book, the **Timaeus** forms Plato's most complete cosmological presentation.

CORNFORD, FRANCIS, tr. **PLATO'S THEORY OF KNOWLEDGE.** Notes, index, 348pp. BoM57, 7.15p.
Translations, with running commentary, of the **Theaetetus** and **Sophist** of Plato—two masterpieces of his later period.

CORNFORD, FRANCIS, tr. **THE REPUBLIC OF PLATO. Introduction,** many notes, index, 395pp. Oxf41, 3.35p.
The Republic, perhaps the best known of Plato's dialogues, is an attempt to apply the principles of Plato's philosophy to political affairs. In it he interweaves the ethicopolitical, the aesthetic and mystical, and the metaphysical strands of his thought. Ostensibly a discussion of the nature of justice, the dialogue lays before us Plato's vision of the ideal state, covering a wide range of topics—social, educational, psychological, moral, and philosophical. It also includes some of Plato's most important writing on the nature of reality and his *theory of the forms.* Ms. Cornford is widely regarded as one of the finest translators of Plato of this century.

FINDLAY, J.N. **PLATO AND PLATOISM—AN INTRODUCTION.** 249pp. H&R78, 12.50c.
Professor Findlay presents a penetrating analysis of the Platonic dialogues and the whole of Plato's doctrine, based on Plato's own writings and the work of Aristotle and others who attended his academy.

■ FRIEDLANDER, PAUL. **PLATO: AN INTRODUCTION. Diagrams,** notes, index, 466pp. PUP69, 4.95p.
Professor Friedlander was one of the great Platonists of our time. In this volume he is concerned with the whole corpus of Plato's work. His approach to Plato is nonacademic, revealing Plato as concerned primarily with fundamental problems of human conduct and existence. This is an excellent introduction to Plato's writings.

GUTHRIE, W.K.C., tr. **PLATO: PROTAGORAS AND MENO.** Introduction, summaries, 158pp. Vik56, 1.95p.
The **Protagoras,** a dramatic dialogue, gives the most complete presentation to be found in Plato of the main principles of the Socratic morality. Protagoras is a Sophist who believes that his profession is the *teaching of goodness.* Socrates argues with him that the conduct of life is not teachable. The **Meno** is nominally concerned with the question of what virtue is and whether it can be taught. While the **Protagoras** keeps to the level of practical commonsense, the **Meno** leads on into the heart of Plato's philosophy—the immortality of the soul and the doctrine that learning is knowledge acquired before birth.

HACKFORTH, R., tr. **PLATO'S PHAEDO. Many notes, index, 207pp.** CUP55, 3.45p.
This celebrated dialogue describes the last conversations in prison between Socrates and his friends. Socrates' bearing in the last hours before his execution, the devotion of his friends, the admiration of his jailer, and his reasoned conviction that the human soul survives the death of the body are all portrayed with moving simplicity. Professor Hackforth includes a running commentary on the course of the argument and the meaning of the key Greek terms, and a full introduction explaining the philosophical background and the place of this work among Plato's writings.

HALL, MANLY P. **INITIATION OF PLATO. 32pp. PRS39, 1.50p.**
A translation of a prologue to a masonic comedy which summarizes the early mystery rituals of the ancient Greeks and Egyptians. There is a record in the British Museum that Plato received the Egyptian rites of Isis and Osiris in Egypt when he was forty-seven years old, and this presumption is the basis of this short play.

■ HAMILTON, EDITH and HUNTINGTON CAIRNS, eds. **PLATO: THE COLLECTED DIALOGUES INCLUDING THE LETTERS.** Notes, index, 1,768pp. PUP63, 17.55c.
This is the only complete one volume edition of Plato available in English. The editors set out to choose this collected edition from the works of all the best British and American translators of the last century, ranging from Jowett to present day scholars. The volume also contains editorial notes prefacing each dialogue by Edith Hamilton, and an introductory essay on Plato's philosophy and writings by Cairns. In the index, ample cross references are provided in order to

assist the reader with the philosophical vocabulary of the different translators.

HAMILTON, WALTER, tr. **PLATO—GORGIAS. Introduction, notes,** index, 155pp. Vik71, 1.95p.
To judge by its bitter tone, **Gorgias** was written shortly after the death of Socrates. Though Gorgias was a Sicilian teacher of oratory, the dialogue is more concerned with ethics than with the art of public speaking. The ability, professed particularly by the Sophists, to make the worst cause appear the better, struck Plato as the source of all corruption. The dialogue's chief interest lies in the clash between Socrates, the true philosopher, and Callicles, a young Athenian of the stamp of Alcibiades, who brashly maintains that might is right.

HAMILTON, WALTER, tr. **PLATO: THE SYMPOSIUM. Introduction,** notes, 122pp. Vik51, 1.95p.
In this dialogue Plato records several banquet eulogies in praise of love. Love, or *eros,* is seen as a reaching out of the soul towards eternal beauty. Various kinds of love are discussed, from the crudest to the highest. The dialogue ends with a character sketch of Socrates by Alcibiades.

JOWETT, BENJAMIN, tr. **THE DIALOGUES OF PLATO. Many notes,** 114 page index, 1,830pp. RaH1892, 40.00c/set.
A two volume set of Jowett's noted translations. This edition contains the complete text and marginal notes from the third (and last) edition of Jowett's work. The translations are extremely readable and are works of impeccable scholarship.

JOWETT, BENJAMIN, tr. **PLATO: THE REPUBLIC AND OTHER WORKS.** 552pp. Dou73, 2.95p.
The complete text of Jowett's translations of **The Republic, The Symposium, Parmenides, Euthyphro, Apology, Crito,** and **Phaedo.**

JOWETT, BENJAMIN, tr. **THE WORKS OF PLATO. 635pp. RaH28,** 5.95c.
Here, Jowett's classic translations are introduced and edited by Irwin Edman. This volume includes the following works: **Lysis, Euthyphro, Apology, Crito, Phaedo, Protagoras, Phaedrus, Symposium, The Republic,** and **Theaetetus.** The translations are good works of scholarship, though not our favorites.

LEE, DESMOND, tr. **PLATO: THE REPUBLIC. Many notes, bibliography,** 467pp. Vik74, 2.95p.
This is a readable translation with an excellent fifty-eight page introduction.

LEE, DESMOND, tr. **PLATO: TIMAEUS AND CRITIAS. Introduction,** notes, 167pp. Vik71, 1.95p.
The **Timaeus,** in which Plato attempted a scientific explanation of the universe's origin, is the earliest Greek account of a divine creation. This dialogue and its unfinished sequel, the **Critias,** has attracted great attention down through the ages as one of the main sources of the Atlantis legend. In the **Critias** Plato gives exact descriptions of an antediluvian world. Lee has appended a critical survey of Atlantean theories.

ROUSE, W.H.D., tr. **GREAT DIALOGUES OF PLATO. Pronouncing** index, 525pp. NAL56, 3.95p/1.95p.
Good translations of the complete works of **The Republic, Apology, Crito, Phaedo, Ion, Meno,** and **Symposium.**

SAUNDERS, T.J., tr. **THE LAWS. Notes, bibliography, index, 553pp.** Vik75, 3.95p.
The reader of **The Republic,** Plato's best known political work, may well be astonished by **The Laws.** Instead of an ideal state ruled directly by moral philosophers, this later work depicts a society permeated by the rule of law. Immutable laws control most aspects of public and private life, from civil and legal administration to marriage, religion, and sport. In his introduction Dr. Saunders reinterprets the whole work and also discusses the question of Plato's totalitarianism.

SHRINE OF WISDOM EDITORS. **THE HUMAN SOUL IN THE MYTHS OF PLATO.** 68pp. ShW36, 5.60c.
Plato incorporated many myths in his dialogues, and in this volume the Shrine of Wisdom has selected and arranged those relating to the nature of the human soul, together with explanatory passages. The discussion reveals many of the problems which perplex modern man: What are we? Why are we here? What is our purpose? How may we achieve it? An enlightening study.

SHRINE OF WISDOM EDITORS, trs. **TWO DIALOGUES OF PLATO: THE FIRST ALCIBIADES AND THE MENO.** Introduction, 186pp. ShW31, 5.60c.
This translation is a product of excellent scholarship and it stresses the true spiritual significance of the dialogues. The **Meno** contains a deep discussion of *innate ideas* and the **First Alcibiades** is an investigation of the true nature of man.

TAYLOR, THOMAS, tr. **THE CRATYLUS, PHAEDO, PARMENIDES, TIMAEUS AND CRITIAS.** 453pp. Wiz76, 25.00c.
Thomas Taylor's translations are universally admired by all true scholars and it is a pity that so few remain in print today. This is a limited edition reprint of the original edition of 1793 and includes all of Taylor's original notes along with some new material added by the current publisher. It is well printed and handsomely bound in gold stamped leatherette. An annotated bibliography of Taylor's works is also included.

TREDENNICK, HUGH, tr. **THE LAST DAYS OF SOCRATES.** Introduction, notes, bibliography, 200pp. Vik69, 1.95p.
This volume contains translations of four Socratic dialogues: **Euthyphro, Apology, Crito,** and **Phaedo.** The **Apology,** although it contains some imaginary dialogues, is not written in dialogue form; it professes to be the speech (or rather series of speeches) delivered by Socrates at his trial. In the **Crito** Socrates justifies his attitude toward escape and his scorn for subterfuge. The **Euthyphro** supplies a sort of prologue to the drama. It shows us Socrates awaiting his trial and informs us of the charges preferred against him. The **Phaedo,** a much later work, narrates the events and discussions of the last days in Socrates' life, and the manner of his death.

VLASTOS, GREGORY, ed. **PLATO, VOLUME I: METAPHYSICS AND EPISTEMOLOGY.** Notes, index, 338pp. Dou71, 2.50p.
A collection of critical essays illustrating the variety of approaches represented in current contributions to interpretation of Platonic thought. This volume is heavily weighted on the analytical side. All but one of its essays were written by men whose academic training was strongly philosophical.

Socrates.

VLASTOS, GREGORY. **PLATO'S UNIVERSE.** Notes, bibliography, index, 143pp. UWa75, 3.95p.
A distinguished Platonic scholar discusses the impact of the Greek discovery of the cosmos on man's perception of his place in the universe, describes the problems of his place in the universe, analyzes the problems this posed, and interprets Plato's response to this discovery. Starting with the Presocratics, Vlastos describes the intellectual revolution that began with the cosmogonies of Thales, Anaximander, and Anaximenes in the sixth century BC and culminated a century later in the Atomist system of Leucippus and Democritus. In a detailed analysis of the astronomical and physical theories of the **Timaeus,** Vlastos demonstrates Plato's role in the reception and transmission of the discovery of the cosmos. This is a fairly technical analysis.

WARRINGTON, JOHN, tr. **PLATO—TIMAEUS.** Brief introduction, notes, 153pp. Dut65, 1.95p.
A somewhat stilted, though scholarly translation of Plato's masterful creation myth.

WARRINGTON, JOHN, tr. **PLATO—THE TRIAL AND DEATH OF SOCRATES: EUTHYPHRO, APOLOGY, CRITO, PHAEDO.** Brief introduction, notes, 190pp. Dut63, 2.95p.
Readable translations of four dialogues linked together not so much by their subject matter as by the fact that they are represented by Plato as having taken place at various stages of the trial, imprisonment, and death of Socrates.

END OF PLATO SUBSECTION

Plotinus

Plotinus (204-70) holds a very important place in the history of thought—important in philosophy, more important in theology and in the development of mysticism. Heir to the great philosophies of the ancient world, those of Plato, Aristotle, and the Stoics, he borrowed from all of them the insights which he needed, but without surrendering at any point the dominant influence of Platonism. Eclectic in appearance but powerfully unified by the strength of a single pervading impulse, his system has, by various channels often obscure and often indirect, come to be and remained one of the guiding forces in the thought of the West. He is the last great philosopher of antiquity, and yet in more than one respect, and notably in the stress which he places on the autonomy of spirit, he is a precursor of modern times. He is in the West the founder of that speculative mysticism which expresses in intellectual or rather supra-intellectual and negative categories the stages and states of union with the Absolute. It is a mysticism wholly philosophical, transposed into a new key which is specifically Plotinian; and it differs very greatly from the mysticism of St. Paul or St. John with which through the centuries it runs parallel or combines, often unconsciously, though at times also it is in conflict with the **Gospel** mysticism.
—*condensed from the introduction to*
Plotinus—The Enneads, *by Stephen MacKenna*

BLUMENTHAL, H.J. **PLOTINUS' PSYCHOLOGY.** Introduction, notes, indices, 168pp. MaN71, 13.85p.
A comprehensive account of Plotinus' views on the embodied soul, concentrating on man as a living being in the sensible world, and not on his relation to a higher universe.

BREHIER, EMILE. **THE PHILOSOPHY OF PLOTINUS.** Bibliography, index, 212pp. UCh58, 10.75c.
A clear, readable exposition of the main features of Plotinus' philosophy. Topically organized and translated from the French by Joseph Thomas.

MACKENNA, STEPHEN, tr. **PLOTINUS: THE ENNEADS.** Notes, bibliography, 708pp. FaB69, 17.95c.
This is universally acknowledged as the definitive translation. It

originally appeared in five volumes between 1917 and 1930. This is the fourth edition, revised by B.S. Page—with the five volumes in one. Professor Paul Henry supplies an excellent, long introduction which discusses Plotinus' thought and compares it with philosophers both before and after him. We recommend **The Enneads** highly to all readers who wish to immerse themselves in and gain an understanding both of classical mysticism and of mystical philosophy in general. The text reads amazingly well and does not seem dated at all. This is truly timeless literature. All of Plotinus' writing is presented here.

MEAD, G.R.S. **PLOTINUS. Bibliography, 48pp. HR1895, 2.00p.**
A short sketch, originally written as an introduction to Thomas Taylor's translation of **The Enneads**. The bulk of the essay is devoted to an analysis of the philosophical system enunciated by Plotinus.

RIST, J.M. **PLOTINUS: THE ROAD TO REALITY. Notes, bibliography, index, 280pp. CUP67, 5.95p.**
This is a very good study of Plotinus' philosophy, beginning with a biographical sketch (taken basically from Porphyry's **Life**, with extensive critical commentary) and including a discussion of some of Plotinus' major concepts: *The One, The Logos, Beauty, The Descent of the Soul, Free Will, Happiness, The Self and Others,* and *Faith.* Rist concludes with a discussion of Neoplatonic faith.

TAYLOR, THOMAS, tr. **PLOTINUS ON THE BEAUTIFUL AND ON INTELLIGIBLE BEAUTY. 32pp. ShW32, 2.00p.**
Taylor is best known for his excellent translations of Porphyry and Plato. **Plotinus on the Beautiful** is translated by the editors of the Shrine of Wisdom and **On Intelligible Beauty** by Taylor.

TURNBULL, GRACE, ed. **THE ESSENCE OF PLOTINUS. Notes, bibliography, index, 323pp. Gre34, 27.55c.**
A topical arrangement of selections from Stephen Mackenna's translations of the six **Enneads** and **Porphyry's Life of Plotinus**. Ms. Turnbull also supplies an appendix citing some of the most important Platonic and Aristotelian sources on which Plotinus drew.

————————END OF PLOTINUS SUBSECTION————————

PLUTARCH. **THE AGE OF ALEXANDER. Introduction, maps, notes, 443pp. Vik73, 2.95p.**
Writing at the turn of the first century AD, Plutarch intentionally blended two cultures in his parallel lives of Greek and Roman heroes. However unreliable in places, Plutarch's readable accounts have been a prime source of much historical knowledge. The nine lives in this selection trace a crucial phase in ancient history, from the collapse of Athens to the rise of Macedonia. They include studies of Demosthenes and Phocion, the leading Athenian orators; of Agesilaus, the Spartan king, and Pelopidas, the Theban military hero; of Dion and Timoleon, the liberators of Sicily; and, above all, of three generals—Demetrius the Besieger, Pyrrhus, and Alexander the Great. Translated by Ian Scott-Kilvert.

PLUTARCH. **FALL OF THE ROMAN REPUBLIC. 361pp. Vik72, 2.95p.**
Looking back from the turn of the first century AD, Plutarch records the lives of Marius and Sulla, Crassus and Cicero, Pompey and Caesar—and in the process details the long and bloody period of foreign and civil war which marked the collapse of the Roman Republic and ushered in the Empire. Translated by Rex Warner, with introductions and notes by Robin Seager.

PLUTARCH. **MAKERS OF ROME. Maps, notes, 366pp. Vik65, 2.50p.**
For this volume, Ian Scott-Kilvert has selected nine of the Roman lives, from the earliest years of the Republic to the establishment of the Empire, to illustrate the courage and tenacity of the Romans in war and their genius for political compromise. The **Lives** are of Coriolanus, Fabius Maximus, Marcellus, Cato the Elder, Tiberius Gracchus, Gaius Gracchus, Sertorius, Brutus, and Marc Antony. Anthony and Cleopatra are discussed in an appendix.

PLUTARCH. **THE RISE AND FALL OF ATHENS. Introduction, maps, notes, 320pp. Vik60, 2.95p.**
The nine biographies chosen for this volume illustrate the rise and fall of Athens from the legendary days of Theseus, the city's founder, to

the age of Pericles and the razing of its walls by Lysander. Solon, Themistocles, Aristides, Cimon, Nicias, and Alcibiades are the other individuals studied. Translated by Ian Scott-Kilvert.

Pythagoras

Pythagoras is a shadowy figure of whom we know little from any early or reliable source, though we have full-length biographies written nearly a thousand years after his birth. He seems to have been born in Samos in the sixty century BC, to have left for political reasons, perhaps traveled as far as India (there are important links between Hindu and Pythagorean thought), and to have settled in southern Italy and formed a community there, which followed his interests in mathematics, music, mysticism and politics. Aristotle, our principle early source, prefers to speak of the Pythagoreans. The Pythagoreans were a closed religious community. Their cosmology built the world out of number, one for a point, two for a line, three for a surface, four for a solid. One was the basis, and generated a series of even and odd numbers, and with them the whole universe. Moral qualities were numbers: 4 (2x2 and 2+2) was justice, equal shares all around. A special number was 10, built up of 1+2+3+4, and containing the point, line, plane and solid. Pythagoras had discovered the mathematical basis of music, and (for instance) the fact that an octave can be expressed by the relation 1:2 (a string stopped at half its length will sound the octave above the full length). So music was involved in all life; and even the planets circling in their courses sounded the music of the spheres. Within this cosmos Pythagoreans believed in the immortality of the soul, and borrowed the Hindu doctrine of reincarnation and transmigration. The body is a tomb to be escaped from, through silence, meditation, purification and asceticism, and virtue, the love of friends and religious devotion. Purification lay in cleansing, baptism and lustration, avoidance of ritual pollution and contact with death or birth, vegetarianism and abstinence from beans and a whole series of general taboos. Membership of this sect was open to women as well as to men.
—*condensed from* **Encyclopedia of Mysticism**, *by John Ferguson*

BURKERT, WALTER. **LORE AND SCIENCE IN ANCIENT PYTHAGOREANISM. Bibliography, indices, 541pp. HUP72, 33.60c.**
This is a highly erudite study of Pythagoras and Pythagorean theory, divided into the following major sections: *Platonic and Pythagorean Number Theory, Pythagoras in the Earliest Tradition, Philolaus, Astronomy and Pythagoreanism, Pythagorean Musical Theory,* and *Pythagorean Number Theory and Greek Mathematics.* Each of these topics is considered at length, and Burkert quotes widely from a great variety of sources. This is without question the best one volume work on the subject that we know. An abundance of lengthy textual notes are included.

OLIVER, GEORGE. **THE PHYTHAGOREAN TRIANGLE. 253pp. Wiz1875, 8.95c.**
Oliver was a nineteenth century Freemason. This is a photographic reprint of his study of the Pythagorean numbers and their relations to Freemasonry.

OLIVET, FABRE D', tr. **GOLDEN VERSES OF PYTHAGORAS. 172pp. Wei1813, 3.95p.**
This edition includes the Greek text of the verses along with a French translation and then this translation is again translated into English and each verse is discussed in detail. These verses are an excellent expression of the ancient mystery teachings and d'Olivet himself was an initiate who understood the deepest meanings of these teachings.

PHILLIP, J.A. **PYTHAGORAS AND THE EARLY PYTHAGOREANISM. Notes, bibliography, index, 222pp. UTo66, 13.45c.**
Pythagoras and his followers are cast by historians in four important roles: they are reputed to have originated the mathematical disciplines, harmonics and, in a large measure, astronomy; they are said to have

Pythagoras

propounded theories of the nature of our universe to which in differing ways, Paramenides, Empedocles, Anaxagoras, and Democritus reacted; they are reputed to have made the alliance between religion and philosophy that made philosophy in the ancient world a way of life; and their thought exerted a major influence on Plato, particularly on his mathematical theories. This volume is a survey of these assertions by a noted scholar. The exposition is topically organized.

ROWE, N., tr. COMMENTARIES OF HIEROCLES ON THE GOLDEN VERSES OF PYTHAGORAS. 132pp. TPH71, 3.25p.
Translation of an important fifth century commentary. Included also are translations of the verses themselves. Each verse is followed by commentary.

SHRINE OF WISDOM EDITORS, trs. THE GOLDEN VERSES OF THE PYTHAGOREANS. 32pp. ShW nd, 4.20c.
This is the most recent translation of the verses. The aim is to make the practical teaching expounded in the verses accessible to contemporary man. A translation of the entire text is followed by translations of the stanzas, with a commentary.

STANLEY, THOMAS. PYTHAGORAS. Double column, 9"x13", 93pp. PRS70, 12.50c.
A photographic reprint of Stanley's seventeenth century study of Pythagorean philosophy and the doctrines attributed to Pythagoras and his followers.

TAYLOR, THOMAS. THE THEORETIC ARITHMETIC OF THE PYTHAGOREANS. 248pp. Wei1816, 15.00c.
For those with the mental equipment suitable for the utilization of the science of numbers as a means to knowledge and wisdom, this will serve as a major contribution. Pythagoras held that arithmetic and the numerical sciences were an approach to the divine and a way of communion with the gods. Also contained are the essentials of the Pythagorean teachings of Iamblichus, Boetius, and Nicomachus.

──────── END OF PYTHAGORAS SUBSECTION ────────

QUENNELL, PETER. THE COLOSSEUM. Over 100 illustrations, half in color, 9¼"x11½", 176pp. Nsw nd, 12.95c.
A pictorial study of the panoramic sweep of Rome's rise to power, decline, and fall—as viewed from her most impressive ruin.

RENAULT, MARY. THE BULL FROM THE SEA. 336pp. RaH62, 2.45p.
Mary Renault's recreations of life in classical Greece are among our favorite historical novels. She has a gift for storytelling and makes ancient stories seem fresh and immediate. This is the story of the hero Theseus, King of Athens. The book opens with his triumphant return from Crete after slaying the Minotaur to mount the throne left empty by the death of his father. Out of the many classical myths that surround the exploits of Theseus, Ms. Renault has fashioned a magnificent adventure novel. She includes the tale of Theseus' famous capture of the Amazon Hippolyta who became the love of his life and the crux of his fate.

RENAULT, MARY. FIRE FROM HEAVEN. 410pp. RaH69, 2.95p.
The story of Alexander the Great's life from his childhood to the age of twenty when he succeeded his murdered father, King Philip of Macedon. These years cover almost two-thirds of his short life, and to everything that is enigmatic or contradictory in his character as recorded in history, the key must lie here.

RENAULT, MARY. THE KING MUST DIE. 339pp. Ban58, 1.95p.
Out of legend and history, Ms. Renault weaves the splendid story of Theseus' early years. The core and climax of the novel is the Cretan adventure when Theseus, sent to the Bull Court, managed to vanquish his enemies and destroy the matriarchal culture of Crete.

RENAULT, MARY. THE LAST OF THE WINE. Chronology, 446pp. RaH56, 3.95p.
This is an extraordinary piece of historical reconstruction. Alexias, a young Athenian of good family, reaches manhood during the last phases of the Peloponnesian War, a time not unlike our own, when people born to a heritage of security and power felt the structure of their lives being undermined by forces that they but dimly understood. He becomes a student of Socrates and meets his lover, an older lad who is also Socrates' student. Their relationship develops against a background of expeditions, athletic games, famine, siege, and civil war. Ms. Renault also paints a wonderful picture of Socrates and his circle and of the young Plato, a friend of Alexias.

RENAULT, MARY. THE MASK OF APOLLO. Historical note, 376pp. Ban66, 1.95p.
In this novel Ms. Renault draws the reader into the world of ancient Greek theater. As the review in **The New York Times** said, *Mary Renault has few peers in the art of reconstructing and making utterly convincing the people and places of classical times....It is a superbly controlled performance.*

RENAULT, MARY. THE NATURE OF ALEXANDER. Index, 7½"x 9¾", 240pp. RaH75, 7.95p.
This is one of Ms. Renault's few nonfictional works. It is both a biography and a beautifully illustrated history. The emphasis is on a psychological understanding of Alexander. Many color photographs illustrate typical scenes in Alexander's life and double as gorgeous nature photographs. There are also a number of smaller black and white plates.

RENAULT, MARY. THE PERSIAN BOY. 419pp. Ban72, 2.25p.
In **The Fire from Heaven**, Ms. Renault followed the career of the young Alexander the Great up to his accession when he was twenty. In this book we meet him six years later and follow him to his death in a moving narrative told by his young lover and companion, Bagoas, a beautiful slave boy who became devoted to Alexander and was a definite historical personage.

RIST, J.M. EROS AND PSYCHE—STUDIES IN PLATO, PLOTINUS, AND ORIGEN. Notes, bibliography, indices, 238pp. UTo64, 33.60c. 33.60c.
Plato's thought could not easily be reduced to a system or taught systematically. It contained within itself unresolved, but—as it is the purpose of this study to demonstrate—philosophically fruitful divergences of opinion on the highest topics: the Good, the nature of love, the aim of the life of virtue....The unity of his thought consists only in certain general beliefs....Many of his successors..., including Plotinus and Origen, assumed that they could "explain" or "correct" his "system" as

though it were a compact and unified whole. Accordingly they took parts of that supposed system out of context and welded them to their own theories. In doing so, by the very production of a system that was seldom self-contradictory and indistinct in detail, they were unplatonic even when expounding parts of the Platonic corpus. To extend the meaning of "unplatonic" in this direction is somewhat unusual, but none the less meaningful. To understand in particular instances the way Plotinus and Origen handled the Platonic originals and developed Platonic themes is a major object of this book.—from the introduction.

ROSE, H.J. **A HANDBOOK OF GREEK MYTHOLOGY. 2.95p.**
See the Mythology section.

■ *ROSE, H.J.* **RELIGION IN GREECE AND ROME. Introduction, index, 326pp. H&R59, 5.30p.**
This book was originally published as two separate books: **Ancient Greek Religion** and **Ancient Roman Religion**. It is the best summary we know of what religion meant, in practice, to the ancient people of Greece and Rome. Professor Rose is a master of his subject and he has skillfully summarized a great body of material.

Poseidon slays the giant Polybotes in the presence of Gaia.

SIMON, BENNETT. **MIND AND MADNESS IN ANCIENT GREECE: THE CLASSICAL ROOTS OF MODERN PSYCHIATRY. Notes, index, 336pp. Cor78, 17.50c.**
This ambitious and complex book shows how the diverse views of mind and madness that characterize modern psychiatry were foreshadowed in the works of the ancient Greeks. Simon is a practitioner and teacher of psychiatry who has read widely and deeply in ancient Greek literature. In the major part of the book, he gives a detailed account of the representation of mind and mental illness in Greek poetry, philosophy, and medicine. He draws his examples from the Homeric epics, Greek tragedy, Plato, and Hippocrates, and quotes extensively from relevant literature.

SIMPSON, MICHAEL, tr. **GODS AND HEROES OF THE GREEKS: THE LIBRARY OF APOLLODORUS. 5.95p.**
See the Mythology section.

TACITUS. **THE HISTORIES. Introduction, maps, glossary, notes, bibliography, indices, 336pp. Vik75, 1.95p.**
In the surviving book of **The Histories**, the great Roman historian, Tacitus, writing some thirty years after the events, reconstructs the anarchy of AD 69, *that long but single year,* during which the Emperors Galba, Otho, and Vitellius briefly held power and the Emperor Vespasian established a new dynasty. Though occasionally partisan, or perhaps merely malicious, Tacitus is notable for the general accuracy with which he records a sudden, violent eruption which shook the whole edifice of the Roman Empire. Translated by Kenneth Wellesley.

TAYLOR, THOMAS. **THE ELEUSINIAN AND BACCHIC MYSTERIES. Offset, spiral bound, glossary, 196pp. HeR1875, 5.00p.**
A careful analysis of the mysteries in light of the author's lifelong study of mythology and Platonic thought.

TAYLOR, THOMAS, tr. **OCELLUS LUCANUS ON THE NATURE OF THE UNIVERSE. Introduction, 107pp. PRS76, 12.50c.**
A group of four brief translations and extracts combined originally by Taylor into one volume and all dealing with what Taylor termed *astrotheology:* **Ocellus Lucanus on the Nature of the Universe; Tarus, the Platonic Philosopher on the Eternity of the World; Julius Firmicus Maternus of the Thema Mundi;** and **Select Theorems on the Perpetuity of Time,** by Proclus. This is a facsimile reprint of the original 1831 edition.

TAYLOR, THOMAS, tr. **PORPHYRY ON ABSTINENCE FROM ANIMAL FOOD. Index, 196pp. Ctr65, 20.00c.**
Porphyry was Plotinus' leading disciple. His books were publicly burned by order of Theodosius and only a few of his treatises are still extant. The one reprinted here is his best known statement. In it he discusses the so-called pagan religion which preceded Christianity and shows how many of its tenets were the same as those of the ante-Nicean Christianity. This is an excellent presentation of the true philosophy of the ancient Greeks, and Thomas Taylor has provided a superb translation. Esme Wynne-Tyson has edited the volume and provided a lengthy critical introduction.

TAYLOR, THOMAS, tr. **SALLUST ON THE GODS AND THE WORLD AND OTHER SELECTIONS. Introduction, 185+pp. PRS76, 12.50c.**
Sallust was a Neoplatonic philosopher who flourished in the fourth century AD and is said to have written the work translated here for the Emperor Julius. This volume also has five hymns by Proclus and five by Taylor himself, along with many notes by Taylor on Sallust's text. A facsimile reprint of the original 1795 edition.

TAYLOR, THOMAS. **THOMAS TAYLOR THE PLATONIST—SELECTED WRITINGS. Illustrations, notes, bibliography, index, 549pp. PUP69, 33.60c.**
Taylor (1758-1835) prepared the first full English translation of Plato and Aristotle. He is also noted for his translations of and commentaries on Plotinus, Porphyry, and Iamblichus. This edition is edited by Kathleen Raine and G.M. Harper, both of whom supply introductory essays.

VELLACOTT, PHILIP, tr. **AESCHYLUS—THE ORESTEIAN TRILOGY. 1.95p.**
See the Mythology section.

VELLACOTT, PHILIP, tr. **AESCHYLUS—PROMETHEUS BOUND, THE SUPPLICANTS, SEVEN AGAINST THEBES, THE PERSIANS. 1.95p.**
See the Mythology section.

VELLACOTT, PHILIP, tr. **EURIPIDES—ALCESTIS, HIPPOLYTUS, IPHIGENIA IN TAURIS. 1.95p.**
See the Mythology section.

VELLACOTT, PHILIP, tr. **EURIPIDES—MEDEA, HECABE, ELECTRA, HERCULES. 2.50p.**
See the Mythology section.

VICKERS, BRIAN. **TOWARD GREEK TRAGEDY. 29.40c.**
See the Mythology section.

VIDAL, GORE. **JULIAN. Bibliography, 432pp. RaH64, 1.95p.**
An enthralling historical recreation of the turbulent life of Julian the Apostate, the nephew of the Emperor Constantine, who ascended the throne in 361 at the age of twenty-nine and was murdered four years later after an unsuccessful attempt to restore worship of the old gods.

VIRGIL. See the Mythology section for translations of Virgil.

WARNER, REX. **THE STORIES OF THE GREEKS. 7.95p.**
See the Mythology section.

WARREN, PETER. **THE AEGEAN CIVILIZATIONS. Glossary, bibliography, index, 8½"x11", 152pp. Dut76, 5.98c.**
A comprehensive account of the cultures of Crete and Mycenae beginning with Neolithic times and continuing through the collapse of the Mycenaean Empire c. 1200 BC. Dr. Warren begins with a discussion of the early archaeological pioneers and describes the civilizations which they and their successors discovered. 177 illustrations, 148 in color, illuminate the text.

WASSON, R. GORDON, CARL RUCK and ALBERT HOFMANN. **THE ROAD TO ELEUSIS: UNVEILING THE SECRET OF THE MYSTERIES. Illustrations, some in color, many notes, 126pp. HBJ78, 4.95p.**
Three integrated papers on ethnomycology—the study of the role of mushrooms in the past of the human race. Wasson is the author of three acclaimed books on the role of hallucinogenic mushrooms in human societies; Hoffman is a renowned chemist who discovered LSD; Rusk is a classical scholar specializing in Greek ethnobotany. They applied themselves to the puzzle of the Eleusinian Mysteries, and believe that they have found the solution. This is a documented, in depth study.

WATLING, E.F., tr. **SOPHOCLES—ELECTRA AND OTHER PLAYS. 1.95p.**
See the Mythology section.

WATLING, E.F., tr. **SOPHOCLES—THE THEBAN PLAYS. 1.95p.**
See the Mythology section.

WEIL, SIMONE. **INTIMATIONS OF CHRISTIANITY AMONG THE ANCIENT GREEKS. 215pp. RKP57, 9.50c.**
A collection of Simone Weil's writings on Greek thought, including both commentaries and translations. The selections range from essays on Greek mythology to discussions of Platonic thought and Pythagorean doctrine.

WHEELWRIGHT, PHILIP, ed. **THE PRESOCRATICS. Glossary, notes, index, 347pp. BoM60, 7.60p.**
The writings of the early philosophers of Greece have survived only in the form of fragments, which later Greek writers fortunately quoted. *The present volume offers in English translation a critically full collection of quotations from, and ancient testimonies about, early Greek philosophical writings, principally of the sixth and fifth centuries B.C. . . . . By "critically full" is meant that the editor's judgment has been exercised in attempting to include all such Fragments and Testimonia as are at once adequately authenticated and capable of throwing light on the doctrines in question. The usual groups of philosophers . . . are here supplemented by certain passages from Greek religious and medical writings.*—from the preface.

WILDER, ALEXANDER. **NEW PLATONISM AND ALCHEMY. Notes, 33pp. Wiz1869, 2.00p.**
A recent reprint of a Hermetic treatise fully titled: **New Platonism and Alchemy: A Sketch of the Doctrines and Principal Teachers of the Eclectic or Alexandrian School; also an Outline of the Interior Doctrines of the Alchemists of the Middle Ages**.

WITT, R.E. **ISIS IN THE GRAECO-ROMAN WORLD. Illustrations, notes, bibliography, index, 336pp. Cor71, 24.85c.**
Professor Witt believes that the cult of Isis was a potent factor in the formation of Graeco-Roman and Christian civilization. This is a wide ranging examination of that thesis. Witt cites evidence in locations as far apart as Afghanistan and Portugal, the Black Sea coast, and northern England as proof of the widespread influence of Isis and her associated divinities. His investigations are both archaeological and theological and augmented by copious references to ancient history sources.

WUNDERLICH, H.G. **THE SECRET OF CRETE. Extensive bibliography, index, 382pp. Fon74, 2.50p.**
Professor Wunderlich is a geologist who has studied Sir Arthur Evans' celebrated reconstruction of the so-called Palace of King Minos at Knossos—the legendary labyrinth where Theseus once defeated the Minotaur. One contradiction struck him after another in the established interpretation of Minoan culture. This book is his attempt to resolve the paradoxes that have obsessed the archaeological world since Evans' spectacular finds at the beginning of this century. Wunderlich suggests that the finds at Knossos represent not an isolated lost civilization, but one of the great turning points in history: the moment when the earliest Greeks turned from the ancient monumental form of the cult of the dead—such as persisted in Egypt—towards remembrance through drama, and the cult of the hero. This is an excellent study which immerses the reader in the culture of ancient Crete and its antecedents. Every aspect of the ancient Cretan civilization is examined in detail and like a good detective the author puts the clues together to form a fascinating account. Wunderlich's scholarship seems to be excellent and the account is illustrated throughout with line drawings.

ANCIENT NEAR EAST

For some years now a profound transformation has been going on in our knowledge of the ancient Near East; a transformation for which the history of European culture suggests the apt name: the Oriental Renaissance.

The transformation has been based fundamentally on archaeological data, but from archaeology it has naturally extended to literature, to religion, to art, and to the entire cultural sphere. It had its beginnings in April 1928, when a Syrian peasant, ploughing in his field, ran his share into the remains of an ancient tomb, and so discovered Ugarit. True, the earlier years of the present century had seen other important discoveries; but that of Ugarit, and those which followed, have a significance reaching beyond their own local limits, and have transformed a whole historical and cultural area. These finds are equalled only by those which in the second half of the nineteenth century first revealed the previously almost unknown peoples of the ancient Orient.

In the Oriental Renaissance we may distinguish three archaeological key discoveries: Ugarit, Mari, and the **Dead Sea Scrolls**. In all three cases the discovery was made by chance: at Ugarit, a peasant was ploughing; at Mari, some natives were burying a dead man; near the Dead Sea, a Beduin was looking for a stray sheep. In all three cases, the additions to our knowledge were revolutionary in their effect. Ugarit proved to be the site of an ancient city which had flourished for four thousand years, and had been the centre of fertile cultural exchange between the Near East and the Mediterranean islands; hundreds of texts, new in language and in script, revealed the beliefs and mythology of the peoples who preceded the Hebrews in Palestine and Syria. Mari disclosed another city of like antiquity, the centre of a state which in its heyday had held sway over a great part of northern Mesopotamia. Its diplomatic archives, containing over 20,000 docu-writing of the history of Western Asia in the first half of the second millennium B.C., and they have revolutionized our chronology by advancing our dates for ancient Western Asia by about two centuries. The **Dead Sea Scrolls** are older by several centuries than the earliest Hebrew manuscripts hitherto known; their Biblical texts are especially valuable to scholars in the field of textual criticism, while the non-Biblical texts throw a new, vivid light upon the beliefs and the ritual of the Hebrew world on the eve of the Christian era.

Ancient Oriental history is born in the two great river valleys, where the geographical conditions first allow of settled ways of life and the formation of political groupings; and it passes, first in Egypt and then in Mesopotamia, from the fragmentary stage to that of organization, from petty city or regional states to unified kingdoms.

When this phase of the process has come to fruition, the two opposed organisms begin to expand beyond their frontiers, though in different ways; for the dominant aim of the Egyptian is control over the neighboring peoples, whereas that of the Mesopotamians in annexation and dominion.

The meeting between the two forces comes about, after repeated skirmishes, towards the middle of the second millennium B.C., when the mountain peoples intervene from the north and east, and resolve the historical dualism into a plurality of acting forces. The Syrian strip takes on the main task of providing a meeting place for the powers, and around it gravitates an equilibrium of forces which continues unstable but substantially unchanged for some three centuries.

Then invasion from the sea by new peoples with weapons of iron destroys the equilibrium, and eliminates those who had built it up. But it cannot destroy the established reciprocal influence of the various parts of the Oriental world; and the connective function is assumed by the desert peoples, who abandon their primitive habitat and arrive to fill the gap left by the invasion, occupying the region destined to serve as a bridge.

When the roads are open again, the ancient chief actors of history, the peoples of the valleys, gradually reorganize and move on towards the encounter. But now Egypt does not get far, for her strength is exhausted; and Mesopotamia profits by this circumstance to achieve predominance over the whole of the ancient Orient for the first time.

Predominance, not dominion. This, and a durable unification of the entire area, is achieved only by the Persians, the last of the mountain peoples, who profit by the crisis in the centre to pour in from the periphery. Now the Near East confronts the West as a unity: here the clash comes, and here comes the end.

Such is the main course of ancient Oriental history, as viewed in time. Changing our viewpoint and considering it in space and in the conditions of the principal actors, the outstanding feature is the conflict between the peoples of the Fertile Crescent, the peoples of the desert, and the peoples of the mountains. The logical centre of this conflict is the Fertile Crescent, the land of the peoples engaged in settled agricultural life, the most prosperous, and the most coveted, region. Towards it press, with recurrent concentric movements, the nomadic bedouin of the desert on the one side, and the nomadic horsemen and hunters of the mountains on the other. Both are moved by the prospect of freedom from want.

Whenever they attain this freedom, the nomadic conditions give place to settled life, and their aspirations and policy are reversed. The settled peoples, for their part, are favoured by the geographical situation in so far as the constitution of strong states is concerned, and it is they, or the forces set up by them, that periodically determine the governing organisms of history. But it is remarkable that before the nomads they are powerless, at least to achieve a decisive success. Their operations are defensive rather than offensive; they clear the frontiers and protect their lines of communication, but their adversary always reappears, overcomes resistance, infiltrates, is assimilated —and the process begins all over again.

As a whole—to resort to an analogy from chemistry— ancient Oriental history may be regarded as a synthesis. The component elements, the reagents, are the civilizations of the valleys, Egypt and Mesopotamia, which are historically the first to establish their states and continue to have essential independence for many centuries. The substances that determine or assist the process of synthesis, the catalysts, are the peoples of the mountains and of the desert, who bring about the conjunction of the opposed forces, leading first to equilibrium, then to the domination of one side. The last of the catalysts produces the synthesis. But the elements of dissolution are already present, and the compound soon breaks down. In the general run of existence, it is always the conceptions and attitudes of a spiritual nature that seem to us to guide the course of civilization in the ancient Orient.

First and foremost there is religion, which dominates and interpenetrates every aspect of life. What is more, every aspect of life is shaped and motivated in accordance with the religion. It is this unity in religious faith which again and again appears as the dominant motive of Oriental civilizations. This is the measuring rod of them all, to an extent unparalleled, it would seem, in any other civilization of ancient times: we have to come down to the middle ages to find anything comparable in our own world. Consider, for instance, the legal institutions: religious and secular laws are mixed together without distinction, and for the man of the ancient Orient there is no sense in separating them, since they all spring from the same authority. So, too, in regard to the sciences: astronomy and astrology interpenetrate, and the Oriental sees neither the need for nor any point in separating them. Similarly in respect to art: it is the handmaid of religion, and the Near East does not conceive of free artistic creation, art for art's sake. *Render unto Caesar the things that are Caesar's, and unto God the things that are God's* is a criterion that has no place in the ancient Orient.

Even so, it would be superficial not to define more precisely, or not to make reservations with respect to, the absolute predominance of religion which has just been postulated. No one, perhaps, has put this problem better than German scholar Schmokel, who in the course of describing Sumerian beliefs asks the questions: *What did the peasant think when he was continually torn from his plough and thrust into the arduous slave gangs organized for the erection of the temples of the gods? What did king Lugalzaggisi think when his conqueror Sargon put him in a cage before the temple of the very same god who previously, through his priests, had granted him rule over the Sumerians?* We do not know, and probably never shall know. In other words, the religion we know is that of the restricted ruling class, the official state cult; we can penetrate very little beyond that into the religious world of the greater part of the people.

All this is true: but one might reply by pointing to the pilgrims whom Herodotus saw crowding the boats to go to the festival at Bubastis, with music and song; or the others of Papremis, who smote one another with maces, re-enacting the conflicts between the gods. The fact is that the question must be formulated differently: it is true that we do not know the degree to which individuals were attached to the religious life; but it is also true that official religion is accompanied by religion of a broadly popular nature, and that it is definitely on the traditional religious feeling of the people that the official cult is grafted and grows.

From the examination of ancient Oriental religions emerge certain aspects and conceptions which permeate and determine them from start to finish. In the first place, these religions are fundamentally naturalistic, based on the worship of cosmic forces. Heaven and earth and water are deified and given souls, and, as has been well said, are set as a *Thou* before the *I* which is man. Divinity is also attributed to the stars, which, with time, regulate the course of life throughout the universe. The distinctive features of the divine forces are modelled on human ones: the macrocosm is adapted to the microcosm, and the gods love and hate and make mistakes. Thus the superhuman world acquires its own patrimony of events, which to a large extent are aetiological in origin, i.e. devised in order to explain the reason for everything that is in the universe, its laws and its destinies. This is the realm of mythology. We have come across various types of myth: the myth of the creation of the world; that of the origin of labour; that of the craving for immortality; that of the journey to the other world. But one towers above them all: the vegetation myth, conveyed in the figure of the god who dies and rises again, frequently with the addition of the figure of the mother goddess, symbol of the fruitful earth.

But myth has no independent life in the ancient Orient. Before taking on literary form it is worship and ritual. The works of the gods are not presented as fantastic tales, but as real actions to which are joined those of men, who evoke and renew them dramatically. We can follow this interaction of myth and ritual particularly well in the two centres of ancient Oriental civilization, Egypt and Mesopotamia. Religious life is adapted to the cycle of the seasons, and its solemnities are basically those of seasonal change. The picture is dominated by fading and reflowering nature, the vegetation that dies and is revived. But between the two centres there is a profound difference, which we may call one of tone, and which directly arises out of opposing conceptions of the government of the universe. In Mesopotamia, where the king is a man, there is perhaps not one rite which does not reflect anxiety and fear, oscillation between pain and joy: because there is no certainty in the interpretation of the will of the gods and in man's conformity with that will. In Egypt, where a god is king, the rites have a basis of constant serenity: all is well, cannot be otherwise than well. Is it necessary to recall that fundamentally this difference of attitude reflects the different conditions of the two lands? Mesopotamia is open to invasion from the mountains and the desert, and depends for its life on uncertain rains and incalculable rivers; Egypt is cut off and protected by its desert, and nourished by a river whose floods never fail even though they vary in intensity and effectiveness.

Thus the essential object of all worship is the renewal and so the conservation of life. But in this respect, too, there is a profound difference between the two great valleys. In Mesopotamia the object is the life of nature, its fruitfulness, because the future of man is obscure, and the undeniable traces of a belief in survival present a predominantly unfavourable picture of the life to come as a wretched and distressful state of wandering. In Egypt, on the contrary, the life of nature and of man go together: the next life uninterruptedly continues that of this world with its peaceable and often joyous forms. The soul persists; the body is protected by mummification; the tomb is its home: it has been well said that the ancient Egyptian paradoxically denies the reality of death.

Such a conception of man and the universe makes the large place occupied by divination and magic in religious life easily understandable; for when the law of existence is identified as the constant relation between the *I* of man and the *Thou* of deified nature—a *Thou* which, although indeed more powerful than man, shares like characteristics with him—it is understandable that man should bend all his energies to the task of maintaining his side of that relationship, should apply his mind and the instruments which the *Thou* itself offers him to the double purpose of comprehending and controlling its energies. Divination and magic are the extreme forms of the effort made to associate the different spheres of the universe; and it is reasonable that this effort should be greater—and the corresponding literary production more extensive—where the association is more uncertain, where distinction and uncertainty predominate.

Once more, in conclusion, we must draw attention to the circumstance that the foregoing considerations apply essentially to the principal representatives of ancient Oriental civilization. Outside their spheres, two different situations can be distinguished. To some extent there is an attitude which is the same as—or if you will, imitated from—that of the greater powers, but with a less accentuated degree of development, and with embryonic features because of the limited possibilities; and there is no need to dwell on this aspect. But to some extent we have an independent attitude, a reaction, a surpassing of the pre-existing positions. Ethical monotheism, which makes its appearance in Palestine and Iran, overthrows the conception of the universe that prevails in the two river valleys, severs the divine from the natural and human plane, and attributes to it characteristics that do not repeat but sublimate human ones, and so are opposed to them. The nature cult declines, and the problem of cosmic integration is absorbed into that of the superior divine will. Even the bond of the state disappears: God in his absoluteness no longer knows any frontiers, cannot confine his attention to a single people, or share the government of the universe with other deities.

At this point, religion being divorced from the state, it is understandable that the attainment of its greatest heights is in no way conditioned by political power. On the contrary, it would seem that this last development of religion is in conflict with the state, and becomes more and more an element provoking crisis for it: just as Christianity, when it was established in Rome, led to Rome's crisis and fall.

—condensed from **The Face of the Ancient Orient**, by Sabatino Moscati

ALLEGRO, JOHN. **THE SACRED MUSHROOM AND THE CROSS.** Index, 253pp. SBL73, 1.60p.
An impressive and controversial piece of scholarship in which Allegro not only argues against the existence of Jesus Christ and the Apostles, but claims that Christianity itself—as well as Judaism and other religions of the ancient Near East—is no more than a hangover from an ancient fertility cult. Allegro quotes extensively from the **Old** and **New Testaments** and from source texts from the ancient Near East in making his case.

ANGUS, SAMUEL. **THE MYSTERY RELIGIONS AND CHRISTIANITY.** Notes, extensive bibliography, index, 383pp. Dov66, 3.95p.
When Alexander the Great completed his conquest of the Near East in 331 BC, one world died and another was born. The spiritual climate of the age found expression in the development of new types of religion. As Angus writes, *the Mystery Religions consisted essentially in the performance of rites aimed at achieving the rebirth of the spiritually dead or moribund individual and providing a means whereby he might surmount the limitations of the human condition and be released from the trammels of mortality.* This book remains, after fifty years, the classic volume on the mystery religions and their connection with the development of Christianity.

BADAWY, ALEXANDER. **ARCHITECTURE IN EGYPT AND THE NEAR EAST.** Glossary, notes, index, 7¼"x10¼", 256pp. MIT66, 26.90c.
An in depth study of the evolution of architectural design and construction in Egypt, Mesopotamia, Asia Minor and North Syria, the Levant, Elam and Persia, and Cyprus from the earliest times to the Hellenistic period. Badawy treats the achievements of each country separately. He further reviews the buildings by category: domestic, religious, funerary, and military. 400 tracings are also arranged by functional category to show the evolution of types of building within each country. Historical maps and charts are also included.

BIBBY, GEOFFREY. **LOOKING FOR DILMUN.** Illustrations, index, 405pp. NAL70, 2.25p.
Sumer has until now been considered the first high civilization of the world. But the Danish Archaeological Expedition, of which Bibby has been field director for fifteen years, has uncovered overwhelming evidence for an extensive high civilization even older than Sumer, in archaeologically virgin territory along the Persian Gulf, in the maritime highway between Mesopotamia and India. This civilization is beyond reasonable doubt the kingdom known to the Sumerians and Babylonians as Dilmun, the legendary land of immortality referred to in Assyrian records and the **Gilgamesh Epic**. This book gives us an enthralling, firsthand account of the fifteen year search for Dilmun.

BOHLIG, ALEXANDER and FREDERICK WISSE. **THE GOSPEL OF THE EGYPTIANS.** Notes, bibliography, indices, 245pp. Eer75, 36.70c.
This volume is part of the **Nag Hammadi Studies**. It contains an English translation, the full Coptic text, introductory material, and commentary. The text translated here is also known as **The Holy Book of the Great Invisible Spirit** and it is one of the most important of all the texts.

BOYCE, MARY. **A PERSIAN STRONGHOLD OF ZOROASTRIANISM.** Photographs, notes, indices, 296pp. Oxf77, 26.80c.
Ms. Boyce spent a year living in the Zoroastrian village of Sharifabad in Iran, taking part in all domestic and communal observances. This is a unique study of a highly traditionalist community which was for centuries the home of the Irani High Priest and has the oldest of all sacred fires, burning for more than 2,000 years. What the author records sheds new light on many Zoroastrian customs and ceremonies and these in turn illumine the beliefs of Zoroastrianism.

BRACKMAN, ARNOLD. **THE LUCK OF NINEVEH.** 357pp. MGH78, 20.00c.
For six centuries Nineveh was the most notorious and powerful city in the world. Yet after its demise in 600 BC, it disappeared from sight, and its exact location remained a mystery for twenty-five centuries—until it was rediscovered in the late 1840s by Austen Henry Layard. This is an extremely readable, detailed story of that discovery. Brackman is a journalist who has written a number of books on noted archaeological discoveries.

BREASTED, JAMES. **THE CONQUEST OF CIVILIZATION.** 679pp. H&R38, 16.80c.
Dr. Breasted, probably the foremost twentieth century Egyptologist, here presents the culmination of his lifetime study of the ancient world. Breasted, in addition to being a wonderful scholar and researcher, also writes well! And this volume is an excellent review of the ancient Near East. The book begins with a review of prehistory and then goes on to study the origins and early history of civilization in the ancient Near East. Next there is a detailed study of the Greeks followed by a chapter on the Mediterranean world in the Hellenistic Age and the Roman Republic and ending with a study of the Roman Empire. Many illustrations accompany the text.

BROWNE, EDWARD G. **A LITERARY HISTORY OF PERSIA.** 36.00c/each.
See the Islam section.

BRUNS, J. EDGAR. **THE FORBIDDEN GOSPEL.** 64pp. H&R76, 5.95c.
Bruns feels that much of the **New Testament** can only be understood from a Gnostic viewpoint. In this book he has compiled a gospel according to Gnosticism which depicts a Jesus radically different from the traditional picture. Here is a Jesus who commisions Judas to betray him, a Jesus who sings and dances at his Last Supper, a Jesus uttering cryptic, mystical adages. A wealth of notes documents the sources of this reconstructed gospel.

BUDGE, E.A. WALLIS. **AMULETS AND SUPERSTITIONS.** Introduction, index, 582pp. Dov30, 6.00p.
Budge presents a wealth of information on the origins of amulets and talismans of many cultures and traditions: Arab, Persian, Babylonian, Assyrian, Egyptian, Gnostic, Hebrew, Mandaean, Phoenician, and Syriac. The text is profusely illustrated with more than 300 drawings.

BUDGE, E.A. WALLIS. **BABYLONIAN LIFE AND HISTORY.** Many illustrations, bibliography, index, 312pp. CSq25, 13.45c.
A good survey, based on the best scholarship available at the time, and covering all aspects of Babylonian life, mythology, culture, and history. This is one of Budge's clearest books.

BUDGE, E.A. WALLIS. **A HISTORY OF ETHIOPIA: NUBIA AND ABYSSINIA.** Two volumes bound in one, illustrations, plates, maps, long bibliography, index, 743pp. Atp70, 42.00c.
Budge brings his excellent scholarship to this little studied (in comparison with Egypt) part of the ancient world. The material in the text is drawn from the Ethiopian Royal Chronicles and the hieroglyphic inscriptions of Egypt and Nubia; there are few inscribed buildings, obelisks, or tombs. Budge has done an admirable job in compiling all the known history, and his work has yet to be excelled in the fifty years since its original publication.

BURNEY, CHARLES. **THE ANCIENT NEAR EAST.** 195 plates, thirty-two in color, bibliography, index, 8½"x10", 224pp. Cor77, 15.00c.
A superbly illustrated introduction to Near Eastern archaeology and civilization which traces the progress of mankind over a period of some eight thousand years, from Neolithic times until the fall of the Assyrian empire in 612 BC. Burney is Senior Lecturer in Near Eastern

Archaeology at Manchester University in England. His book is geared toward the general reader and he does an excellent job of summarizing a great deal of information in a readable fashion.

BURY, J.B. et al., eds. **THE PERSIAN EMPIRE AND THE WEST. Many charts, maps, index, 723pp. CUP69, 32.50c.**
Volume IV of **The Cambridge Ancient History**. In addition to the Persian Empire, the Athenean civilization is traced in depth. Each of the chapters is written by a specialist and accompanied by an extremely complete bibliography and extensive notes.

CERAM, C.W. **THE SECRET OF THE HITTITES. Many illustrations, bibliography, index, 318pp. ScB55, 4.95p.**
The Hittite empire flourished in the second millennium BC. Until this century it was little more than a name—virtually no historical traces of it remained. Recently many archaeological discoveries have revealed significant details about the Hittite empire and the way of life of the Hittite people. This is a well written account of the archaeological discovery of the Hittite empire together with a brief history of the empire itself.

Two Mazdean priests and Tree of Life, with symbol of Ahura Mazda (wings and sun) above.

CERNY, JAROSLAV. **COPTIC ETYMOLOGICAL DICTIONARY. 350pp. CUP75, 47.50c.**

CONTENAU, GEORGES. **EVERYDAY LIFE IN BABYLON AND ASSYRIA. Illustrations, notes, bibliography, index, 339pp. Nor66/ASL, 3.95p.**
A survey of Mesopotamian civilization between 700 and 530 BC. During these years the Near East was dominated first by the Assyrians and then the Babylonians, who were to be subdued by the Persians. M. Contenau covers every conceivable aspect of Mesopotamian life. He also discusses Mesopotamian thought and religion, the doctrine of names, literature and the sciences, and religious beliefs and practices. The information has been reconstructed from a wealth of evidence, including both written records and monumental evidence. The book reads fairly well and seems to contain good scholarship.

CORY, ISAAC. **ANCIENT FRAGMENTS. Notes, index, 425pp. Wiz75, 17.50c.**
The full title of this book is **Ancient Fragments of the Phoenician, Chaldaean, Egyptian, Tyrian, Carthaginian, Indian, Persian, and Other Writers; With an Introductory Dissertation: and an Inquiry into the Philosophy and Trinity of the Ancients.** This describes the contents as well as anything we can say. The original version and the translation are printed in parallel texts. This is a photographic reproduction of the 1832 edition and many of the fragments are not found in any other work.

COTTRELL, LEONARD. **READING THE PAST. Illustrations, bibliography, index, 173pp. Den72, 3.00p.**
A popularized account which explains how the art of writing came into existence, how and why it developed among certain people while remaining at a primitive level elsewhere, how nineteenth and twentieth century scholars deciphered these ancient languages, and what we have learned about the lives, customs, and beliefs of the peoples of the ancient Near East as a result of these researches.

CUMONT, FRANZ. **THE MYSTERIES OF MITHRA. Index, 253pp. Dov03, 3.25p.**
The Mithraic religion originated in Persia and enjoyed great popularity throughout the Roman Empire, including parts of Germany and Great Britain. When Mithraism and early Christianity met, the result was a ferocious, implacable duel, whose marks can still be detected in present day Christian doctrine. This definitive discussion by a recognized authority on classical religions pieces together information from a variety of areas. Seventy illustrations accompany the text.

DARMESTER, JAMES, tr. **THE ZEND-AVESTA. Extensive introductory material, three volumes, 1,186pp. MoB1884, 30.25c/set.**
The **Zend-Avesta** is the sacred book of the Parsis (the religion of the Parsis is known today as Zoroastrianism) who flourished in Persia between the fifth century BC and the seventh century AD. Very little is known today about the Parsis. When the Muslims conquered Persia in the seventh century most of the citizens converted and the few who remained loyal to the old religion fled to India, where a small Zoroastrian population exists to this day. The first part of the **Avesta** is a compilation of religious laws and mythical tales; the second is composed of short prayers which are recited not only by the priests, but by all the faithful, at certain moments of the day, month, or year, and in the presence of the different elements. The **Avesta** itself does not profess to be a religious encyclopedia, but only a liturgical collection, and it bears more likeness to a prayer book than to the Western **Bible**.

DART, JOHN. **THE LAUGHING SAVIOR. Annotated bibliography, index, 175pp. H&R76, 7.95c.**
A journalistic survey of the discovery and significance of the **Nag Hammadi Gnostic Library**.

DAWSON, MILES, ed. **THE ETHICAL RELIGION OF ZOROASTER. 299pp. AMS31, 12.75c.**
Translations of authoritative texts on ethical conduct and religion garnered from a wide variety of sources and arranged topically. Introductions and commentary are also included.

Dead Sea Scrolls

The **Dead Sea Scrolls** are manuscripts left by an obscure cult of scholars known as the Essenes. Discovered unexpectedly in 1947 near the Dead Sea, these writings give us significant new information about the life, religious trends, and beliefs of the Jewish people around the time of Jesus. Since the discovery, scholars have been piecing together fragments of the brittle parchments and translating and interpreting the contents.

ALLEGRO, JOHN. **THE DEAD SEA SCROLLS: A REAPPRAISAL. 200pp. Vik56, 2.25p.**
Allegro, a linguist and Secretary of the Dead Sea Scrolls Fund, discusses the discoveries of the **Scrolls**, what they indicate about the life of the Jewish monastic community at Qumran, and their significance for the reinterpretation of both early Christian history and the **New Testament**.

■ *DAVIES, A. POWELL.* **THE MEANING OF THE DEAD SEA SCROLLS. Notes, 144pp. NAL56, 1.50p.**
This is the most comprehensive analysis of the **Scrolls** available, including detailed accounts of the discovery of the **Scrolls**, their dating, the Essenes, the **Scrolls** and Christian origins, and the **Scrolls** and Jesus. The material is clearly presented and illustrated. Recommended as the best overall book on the **Scrolls**.

FRITSCH, CHARLES. **THE QUMRAN COMMUNITY. Illustrations, notes, bibliography, index, 155pp. B&T56, 11.45c.**
This is a recent reprint of an important work discussing both the discovery of the **Dead Sea Scrolls** and their significance for biblical study, and fully analyzing the community out of which the **Scrolls** came. An excellent work of scholarship which covers many areas not touched upon by later scholars.

GASTER, THEODOR, tr. **THE DEAD SEA SCRIPTURES. Introductory material, indices, 596pp. Dou76, 3.50p.**
This is a newly revised edition of Gaster's definitive translation. Dr. Gaster has added all of the coherent texts published since 1964 and provides separate introductions to each new **Scroll**, as well as new translations of the **Hymns**, and paraphrases of the **Bible** narratives. Very little interpretation is included; however, the text is well annotated throughout.

KITTLER, GLENN, ed. **EDGAR CAYCE ON THE DEAD SEA SCROLLS. 205pp. War70, 1.50p.**
This volume contains material selected from the Cayce readings which bear on the **Dead Sea Scrolls** and the ancient Essenes, along with a historical reference frame to place in perspective what Cayce had to say. The **Scrolls** were not discovered during Cayce's lifetime.

TREVER, JOHN. **THE DEAD SEA SCROLLS, A PERSONAL ACCOUNT. Illustrations, notes, index, 246pp. Eer77, 5.95p.**
Dr. Trever is Director of the Dead Sea Scrolls Project at the School of Theology, Claremont, California. He was Acting Director of the American School of Oriental Research when the **Scrolls** were first unearthed. This is a revised version of his account of the initial research, intrigue, undercover negotiations, and archaeological detective work.

VERMES, GEZA, tr. **THE DEAD SEA SCROLLS IN ENGLISH. Bibliography, index, 250pp. Vik62, 3.50p.**
Faithful English translation and sensitive, scholarly interpretation of the nonbiblical **Scrolls** from the Qumran cave.

VERMES, GEZA. **THE DEAD SEA SCROLLS: QUMRAN IN PERSPECTIVE. Bibliography, index, 238pp. CWo77, 9.95c.**
A scholarly reevaluation of the **Scrolls** based on a careful study of forty-three related documents. Dr. Vermes includes chapters on *Authenticity and Dating of the Scrolls, The Qumran Library, Life and Institutions of the Sect, Identification of the Community, History of the Sect, The Religious Ideas and Ideals of the Community,* and *Qumran and Biblical Studies.*

WILSON, EDMUND. **ISRAEL AND THE DEAD SEA SCROLLS. Index, 432pp. FSG78, 5.95p.**
The **Dead Sea Scrolls** *were not discovered by archaeologists but by the Bedouin, and their importance was brought to the knowledge of the world at large, again not by an archaeologist, but by a very scholarly amateur, Edmund Wilson.—Yigael Yadin.*
The **Scrolls** of the Essenes and the history of this Jewish sect's possible antecedence to Christianity intrigued Wilson and drew him, in 1954, to Israel and the revelations contained in the newly discovered **Scrolls**. His resulting account of the **Scroll's** history and significance was first published in 1955 and revised and updated in 1969. The latter edition, along with Wilson's essay on Israel from **Red, Blond, Black and Olive** is included in this volume. Wilson's narrative is as complete as any we know of and the book often reads like a detective story.

————————END OF DEAD SEA SCROLLS SUBSECTION————————

DORIA, CHARLES and HARRIS LENOWITZ, eds. **ORIGINS: CREATION TEXTS FROM THE ANCIENT MEDITERRANEAN. 4.95p.**
See the Mythology section.

DRAKE, W. RAYMOND. **GODS AND SPACEMEN IN ANCIENT ISRAEL. Bibliography, index, 192pp. SBL76, 1.75p.**
A detailed investigation of the links between ancient spacemen and the story of ancient Israel. Drake quotes from many sources, including the

Old and **New Testaments**, to make his case. Drake is an excellent writer who has researched his material well and makes an interesting case for all of his suppositions. His books are definitely a cut above others of this ilk.

DROITON, ETIENNE, GEORGES CONTENAU and J. DUCHESNE-GUILLEMIN. **RELIGIONS OF THE ANCIENT EAST. Bibliography, 165pp. B&O59, 1.75c.**
A collection of essays examining in a nontechnical manner the salient features of the religions of ancient Egypt, Iran, and Western Asia. An adequate overview.

DURDIN-ROBERTSON, LAWRENCE. **COMMUNION WITH THE GODDESS TEMPLES OF THE NEAR AND FAR EAST. 46pp. Ces77, 2.50p.**
Details about goddess worship, temples dedicated to the goddess, and related rites in the lands of the ancient Near East and with a bit of information devoted to worship in India and the Far East. The text is continuous and not well organized, which makes the book hard to read.

EDWARDS, I.E.S., ed. **THE CAMBRIDGE ANCIENT HISTORY, PLATES TO VOLUMES I AND II. 223pp. CUP77, 25.00c.**
This companion volume contains 181 pages of plates, often three or more plates to a page.

EDWARDS, I.E.S., et al., eds. **EARLY HISTORY OF THE MIDDLE EAST. Extensive notes, chapter-by-chapter bibliography, long index, 1,081pp. CUP71, 45.00c.**
Volume I, Part Two of **The Cambridge Ancient History,** dealing with the history of the Near East from about 3000 to 1750 BC. The material is chronologically arranged and the period covered includes the Egyptian Old Kingdom and the greatest flourishing of Bablonian civilization. Every aspect of the society of the period is covered in depth and the text includes many diagrams and maps. Each of the chapters is written by a noted authority.

EDWARDS, I.E.S., et al., eds. **HISTORY OF THE MIDDLE EAST AND AEGEAN REGION. 891pp. CUP73, 45.00c.**
Volume II, Part One of **The Cambridge Ancient History,** dealing with the history of the region from about 1800 to 1380 BC. This was the era of Hammurabi in Western Asia, the Hyksos and the warrior-kings of the Eighteenth Dynasty in Egypt, and the Minoan and early Mycenaean civilizations in Crete and mainland Greece. The format of each part of the **History** is the same.

FERDOWSI. **THE EPIC OF KINGS. 450pp. RKP67, 12.95c.**
The **Shah-nama** is the national epic of Persia. Written in the tenth century, it contains the country's myths, legends, and historical reminiscences. It deals with the reign of fifty kings and queens. The beginning is the creation of the world out of nothingness; the end is the Islamic conquest of Persia. Between those times, Ferdowsi devotes a separate section to each ruler. In the present edition, Professor Reuben Levy has made a valuable prose translation, selecting the most representative parts of the original, and has provided an informative prologue. Part of the **Persian Heritage Series.**

FINEGAN, JACK. **LIGHT FROM THE ANCIENT PAST, VOLUMES I AND II. PUP59, 5.95p/each.**
The purpose of this book is to give a connected account of the archaeological background of Judaism and Christianity....The presentation...is in the form of a continuous account extending, in round numbers, from 5000 BC to AD 500....In order to give a more vivid sense of direct contact with the living past, frequent quotations are made from the ancient sources, and numerous photographs are presented,—from the preface. Volume I (312pp.) is divided into the following general sections: *Mesopotamian Beginnings, The Panorama of Egypt, Penetrating the Past in Palestine, Empires of Western Asia: Assyria, Chaldea, and Persia;* Volume II (418pp.) covers *The Holy Land in the Time of Jesus, Following Paul the Traveler, Manuscripts Found in the Sand, Exploring the Catacombs and Studying the Sarcophagi, The Story of Ancient Churches, The Principles of the Calendar and the Problems of Biblical Chronology.* This is an unusual work, intermingling history, archaeology, and the development of religion. Professor Finegan has succeeded admirably in his stated aim of thorough scholarship and readability. A general index is included with each volume along with notes.

FRANKFORT, HENRI. **KINGSHIP AND THE GODS: A STUDY OF ANCIENT NEAR EASTERN RELIGION AS THE INTEGRATION OF SOCIETY AND NATURE. Illustrations, chronology, many notes, index, 470pp. UCh78, 7.95p.**
This classic study clearly establishes a fundamental difference in viewpoint between the peoples of ancient Egypt and Mesopotamia. By examining the forms of kingship which evolved in the two countries, Frankfort discovered that beneath resemblances fostered by similar cultural growth and geographical location lay differences based partly on the natural conditions under which each society developed. The river flood which annually renewed life in the Nile Valley gave Egyptians a cheerful confidence in the permanence of established things and faith in life after death. Their Mesopotamian contemporaries, however, viewed anxiously the harsh, hostile workings of nature. This is a fully documented description, rich in quotations from original sources.

FRANKFORT, HENRI and H.A., JOHN A. WILSON, THORKILD JACOBSEN and WILLIAM A. IRWIN. **THE INTELLECTUAL ADVENTURE OF ANCIENT MAN: AN ESSAY ON SPECULATIVE THOUGHT IN THE ANCIENT NEAR EAST. Bibliography, index, 408pp. UCh77, 4.95p.**
A collection of essays originally delivered as a course at the University of Chicago. The book is divided into five sections. The Frankforts contribute introductory and concluding essays; John Wilson writes on Egypt; Jacobsen on Mesopotamia; and Irwin on the Hebrews. Each of the essays stands alone as an excellent summary of the cultures of each of the civilizations, and all the presentations flow together and complement each other. The scholarship is excellent and the essays are readable and informative.

FRYE, R.N., ed. **THE CAMBRIDGE HISTORY OF IRAN, VOLUME IV: FROM THE ARAB INVASION TO THE SALJUQS. Bibliography, index, 733pp. CUP75, 33.50c.**
This is a survey of every aspect of the civilizations which flourished in the Iranian region from the Arab conquests to the Saljuq expansion. In particular, it studies the gradual transition of Iran from Zoroastrianism to Islam, the uniting of all Iranians under one rule, the flowering into full magnificence of the Persian language, and the development of the culture which we associate today with Persia. The text includes essays on *Philosophy and Cosmology,* and on *The Religious Sciences* by S.H. Nasr, and critical selections from literature along with many notes and illustrations. This is definitely a historical textbook, and yet most of the selections read well and all of the contributors are tops in their fields.

GASTER, THEODOR, tr. **THE OLDEST STORIES IN THE WORLD. 4.95p.**
See the Mythology section.

GERSHEVITCH, ILYA. **THE AVESTAN HYMN TO MITHRA. Indices, 371pp. CUP59, 27.50c.**
This Avestan hymn, written in the fifth century BC, is the one extensive ancient literary record of the attributes, companions, and cult of the Iranian god whose worship spread—five or six centuries later—as far as Britain. Dr. Gershevitch reproduces Geldner's text and critical apparatus of the hymn, adding his own introduction, translation, and commentary. The Avestan text is faced by the English translation, and the commentary is exhaustive.

GILGAMESH EPIC. See the Mythology section for descriptions of various translations.

GOEDICKE, HANS and J.M.M. ROBERTS, eds. **UNITY AND DIVERSITY. Illustrations, notes, index, 238pp. JHU75, 19.50c.**
A series of academic essays on the history, literature, and religion of the ancient Near East. The papers in this volume were presented at a symposium at Johns Hopkins University.

GUILLAUMONT, A., et al., trs. **THE GOSPEL ACCORDING TO THOMAS. Short introduction, 62pp. H&R59, 5.95p.**
This **Gospel** was found with a number of other early Christian manuscripts in 1945, preserved for centuries under layers of dry sand in northern Egypt. Scholars believe the **Gospel** may date as far back as AD 130. It contains personal records of Jesus not available in any other source as well as a wealth of information on the Gnostics. This edition contains the original Coptic text along with a faithful English translation on facing pages.

GURNEY, O.R. **THE HITTITES. Many photographs and line drawings, notes, bibliography, index, 240+pp. Vik54, 3.95p.**
The Hittites of history were a great nation of Asia Minor, whose kings were on equal terms with those of Egypt, Babylon, and Assyria, during a period of about two hundred years in the second millennium BC. This book gives a balanced picture of what is known of the Hittites, based on the archaeological discoveries of this century.

A design using Point (Creator), Square (Power), Triangle (Love), Circle (Wisdom).

HAARDT, ROBERT. **GNOSIS. Bibliography, index, 434pp. Bri71, 43.95c.**
The most comprehensive anthology of Gnostic writings available, accompanied by extensive introductory and textual notes. Includes all the important, well known texts such as the **Gospel According to Thomas** and the **Gospel of Phillip** as well as many lesser known writings. In all, fifty texts (or excerpts therefrom) are presented.

HEIDEL, ALEXANDER. **THE BABYLONIAN GENESIS. 2.95p.**
See the Mythology section.

HOOKE, S.H. **BABYLONIAN AND ASSYRIAN RELIGION. Bibliography, index, 143pp. UOk63, 3.95p.**
This is one of the few full studies available of the religions of the ancient civilizations of the Tigris-Euphrates valley. Apart from its intrinsic interest, the religion of the Babylonians and Assyrians has an added importance because of its great influence on Hebrew religion and life. Chapters discuss the cultural background of the religion, its pantheon, rituals, mythology, religion and daily life, as well as divination techniques and astrology. An appendix offers a selection of ritual texts. Dr. Hooke is the author of many distinguished volumes on Semitic and comparative religions and is an authority on biblical archaeology.

HUOT, JEAN-LOUIS. **PERSIA. 153 illustrations, sixty-two in color, notes, bibliography, index, 219pp. Nag65, 26.20c.**
A detailed archaeological study of ancient Persia from its origins to the Achaemids.

JACOBSEN, THORKILD. **THE TREASURES OF DARKNESS. Notes, index, 273pp. YUP76, 15.00c/4.95p.**
Jacobsen is professor emeritus of Assyriology, Harvard University. In this volume he summarizes a lifetime of study. His aim is to recreate the spiritual life of ancient Mesopotamia and he succeds admirably. Jacobsen illustrates his discussion with extensive new translations from ancient sources. Both the **Gilgamesh Epic** and **Enumaelish** are studied at length and the book is illustrated. A scholarly tome, but a readable one, too.

■ *JONAS, HANS.* **THE GNOSTIC RELIGION. Many notes, index, 358pp. Bea58, 3.95p.**
A full scale study of Gnosticism, its literature, symbolic language, and main tenets, based on actual Gnostic documents and written by a noted authority in the field. Gnosticism is a little understood pre-Christian

religion that was vilified by the early Christians, forgotten for centuries, and finally resurrected in the nineteenth century. Opinions differ as to its origins; some limit it to Hellenistic Greece, others trace it to the Orient. This investigation takes all the conflicting theories into account. A very serious study.

KAUS, MULLA FIRUZ BIN. **THE DESATIR. Many notes, 192pp. Wiz75, 7.95c.**
A photographic reproduction of the original 1888 edition, which was itself a reprint of the first edition from 1818. **The Desatir** professes to be a collection of the writings of different Persian prophets from the time of Mahabad to the fifth Sasan, of whom Zoroaster was the thirteenth. The writings of these fifteen prophets are in a tongue of which no other vestige appears to remain, and which would have been unintelligible without the assistance of an ancient Persian translation. The old Persian translation was made by the fifth Sasan, who has added a commentary. There is also an extensive discussion of the **Desatir** by Anthony Troyer.

KEEL, OTHMAR. **THE SYMBOLISM OF THE BIBLICAL WORLD. Notes, 422pp. Sea78, 24.50c.**
Professor Keel's aim is to demonstrate the relationship between the motifs found in the reliefs and paintings of the ancient Near East and various forms of expression in the **Old Testament**. While standard biblical history books concentrate on geography, history, and cultural artifacts, the stress here is on the cultural milieu of the biblical world. Over 550 line drawings and photographs make the imagery visually concrete. A detailed commentary relates the illustrations to individual biblical passages. The illustrations are arranged according to the following major themes: the cosmic system, destructive forces, the temple, and representations of God, king, and cult.

KELLER, WERNER. **THE BIBLE AS HISTORY. 520pp. Ban56, 3.50p.**
A massive attempt to integrate all of the scientific and archaeological research on the history of the biblical period: *In view of the overwhelming mass of authentic and well-attested evidence now available. . .there kept hammering in my brain this one sentence: "The* **Bible** *is right after all!"*—Werner Keller. Includes an index of **Bible** references, a general index, and a long bibliography.

KELLER, WERNER. **THE BIBLE AS HISTORY IN PICTURES. 337 illustrations, chronology, bibliography, index, 7"x8¾", 360pp. Mor64, 10.95c.**
A pictorial history of biblical events in the light of archaeological finds arranged so as to give a panoramic view of biblical history. Each photograph is accompanied by an appropriate passage from the **Bible** and a variety of explanatory notes are also included.

KENYON, KATHLEEN. **ROYAL CITIES OF THE OLD TESTAMENT: JERUSALEM, MEGIDDO, HAZOR, GEZER, AND SAMARIA. 102 plates, notes, bibliography, index, 6¾"x9¼", 176pp. ScB71, 4.50p.**
A comprehensive account of the origin and development of these cities set against the background of social, political, and cultural development and the varying military and political fortunes of the Israelite kingdom.

KING, CHARLES WILLIAM. **GNOSTICS AND THEIR REMAINS. Illustrations, appendices, 500pp. Wiz73, 17.50c.**
This is a recent reprint of this important work, which first appeared in 1864 and was revised and enlarged for an 1887 edition (of which this is a photo offset copy). The emphasis here is on the esoteric, Oriental aspects of Gnosticism, and as King examines the ancient evidence, he makes many comparisons with Hermetic philosophies. A very scholarly text.

KING, L.W., tr. **ENUMA ELISH: THE SEVEN TABLETS OF CREATION. Introduction, two volumes, glossary, notes, 381pp. AMS02, 39.95c/set.**
Translations of the Babylonian and Assyrian legends concerning the creation of the world and of mankind. Both translations and reproductions of the texts are included.

KRAMER, SAMUEL. **SUMERIAN MYTHOLOGY. 2.95p.**
See the Mythology section.

■ LACARRIERE, JACQUES. **THE GNOSTICS. Bibliography, 136pp. Dut77/Owe, 3.95p.**
This is a strange and original essay—a sort of poetic meditation on the vanished Gnostics of Egypt whose total refusal to believe in the world as outlined by the Christian theologians led to their destruction. I should stress that this is more a work of literature than of scholarship, though its documentation is impeccable. It is a convincing reconstruction of the way the Gnostics lived and thought.—from the foreword by Lawrence Durrell. We got a better understanding of the Gnostics and Gnostic texts from this poetical interpretation than from anything else we have read.

■ LAROCHE, LUCIENNE. **THE MIDDLE EAST. Site plans, glossary, chronology, 10"x13", 190pp. G&D74, 19.95c.**
This text is lavishly illustrated with over 100 full color photographs and carefully reviews the main contributions of the early Middle Eastern civilizations centering around Mesopotamia. Altogether some 7,000 years are surveyed through the architecture, sculpture, literature, religious forms, and social structures of the religions that existed there. Augmenting the text and photographs are excerpts from ancient Middle Eastern tablets, inscriptions, and other records providing contemporaneous documentation of sites and personages depicted. Ms. Laroche is a noted French archaeologist, specializing in Mesopotamia.

LEHMANN, JOHANNES. **THE HITTITES: PEOPLE OF A THOUSAND GODS. Many photographs, line drawings, chronology, bibliography, index, 315pp. Vik77, 11.95c.**
With insight and scholarship, Dr. Lehmann has gathered together all the available information on the Hittites and on the archaeologists, scientific and eccentric, who have rediscovered them during the past hundred years. He begins with a description of the Stone Age peoples whom the Hittites conquered and absorbed and moves on to an analysis of everything that is known of these mysterious people. From their worship of new and existing deities—the reason they were called *People of a Thousand Gods*—to their language, art, and daily life, Dr. Lehmann dramatically recreates their civilization. His scholarship is excellent.

LLOYD, SETON. **THE ART OF THE ANCIENT NEAR EAST. 6.95p.**
See the Sacred Art section.

MACDERMOT, VIOLET. **THE CULT OF THE SEER IN THE ANCIENT MIDDLE EAST. Notes, bibliography, indices, 841pp. UCa71, 40.00c.**
Books on the ancient Near East seem to be weightier (literally) than most other sections. This is certainly a mammoth tome which is a multifaceted study of the lives, ascetic practices, and visionary experiences of a group of seers of the early Christian period, accompanied by a medico-historical commentary which aims to clarify the practice of self induced hallucinations. The material is drawn mainly from recently translated Coptic texts and a direct translation of many of the early writings is presented along with an analysis of the spiritual experience of the seers, distinguishing how these ancient religious experiences differ from contemporary psychedelic experiences.

MCNEILL, WILLIAM and JEAN SEDLAR, eds. **THE ANCIENT NEAR EAST. 274pp. Oxf68, 4.00p.**
The readings compiled in this volume all date from before 500 BC when the civilization of the Near East was still the most advanced in the world. Section I illustrates the succession of empires and some facets of their political evolution. In Section II, selections from ancient law codes have been arranged under a number of more or less arbitrary rubrics. Section III reproduces documents from three religions unique in their concept of a single god: Atenism in Egypt, the worship of Yahweh in Palestine, and Zoroastrianism in Persia. The editors supply introductory material on each selection and textual notes.

MCNEILL, WILLIAM and JEAN SEDLAR, eds. **THE ORIGINS OF CIVILIZATION. 213pp. Oxf68, 4.00p.**
This collection of readings concerns the origins of civilization in the ancient Orient. We begin with sample legends of creation that answered the naive and universal human question: How did the world begin?. . . . The main portion of the volume is organized around two themes: the nature of kingship and the relationship between men and gods. One group of readings presents Mesopotamian views on these two questions; the second does the same for ancient Egypt. . . .The editors have supplied numerous

footnotes of their own in order to aid the nonspecialist in comprehending these texts. . . .Technical discussions and scholarly references have been almost entirely omitted. This is a useful compilation. Many of the selections are not available elsewhere.

MASPERO, GASTON. **THE DAWN OF CIVILIZATION. Two volumes, many notes, index, 7¾"x11", 814pp. Ung1894, 35.00c/set.**
In the nineteenth century, Maspero stood preeminent among archaeologists. Schooled in philology, history, and the techniques of archaeology, head of the mission that eventually became the Institute Francaise de 1'Archaeologie Orientale, he possessed a prodigious knowledge of Egyptian and Chaldean culture linked to meticulous scholarship. Although later discoveries have enlarged our area of knowledge of ancient cultures, Maspero's achievement was a lasting one. This is one of his most important works, a classic study of ancient Egypt and Chaldea. Richly illustrated with line drawings of artifacts, temples, reconstructions, and maps. The translation was supervised by Maspero himself.

MASPERO, GASTON. **LIFE IN ANCIENT EGYPT AND ASSYRIA. 188 line drawings, notes, 391pp. Ung1892, 13.85c.**
Maspero was a French archaeologist who directed some of the great discoveries in Egypt during the nineteenth century. One of Maspero's most remarkable books, this is an evocation of life in two different eras: Egypt during the reign of Ramses II in the fourteenth century BC, and Assyria some seven centuries later. In his fluid, lucid style, Maspero offers new insight into the daily customs, ceremonies, and political and religious life of these two civilizations.

MEAD, G.R.S. **FRAGMENTS OF A FAITH FORGOTTEN: THE GNOSTICS, A CONTRIBUTION TO THE ORIGINS OF CHRISTIANITY. Offset, spiral bound, extensive bibliography, 633pp. HeR60, 15.00p.**
An anthology of Gnostic texts which survived in Coptic in Ethopia and Egypt, together with Mead's explanations. Though this book was written over seventy years ago, it is still considered the most reliable guide to the corpus of Gnosticism that we have. It is an unbelievably complicated, ambiguous, and difficult subject, and Mead's exposition is as lucid as could possibly be expected. The introduction by Kenneth Rexroth is correctly called *A Primer of Gnosticism*.

MELLAART, JAMES. **EARLIEST CIVILIZATIONS OF THE NEAR EAST. 108 plates, thirty in color, bibliography, index, 143pp. MGH65, 3.95p.**
A profusely illustrated anthropological study of the civilizations beginning with the tenth century BC. The author describes his own excavations as well as the discoveries of others.

MELLAART, JAMES. **THE NEOLITHIC OF THE NEAR EAST. Bibliography, index, 300pp. T&H75, 15.95c.**
The Neolithic peoples of the Near East laid the foundations upon which the civilizations of western Asia and Europe were built. The territory over which they ranged extends from the Balkans to Central Asia, and the time span of their cultures covers about 10,000 years. In spite of extensive study by archaeologists—notably the author of this book—much still remains to be learned. Dr. Mellaart has assembled and correlated the available material to provide a lucid and coherent account of the period. He has organized his work by regions, stressing the principal achievements by various cultures, making comparisons, and drawings parallels. Line drawings and photographs accompany the text throughout.

MOOREY, P.R.S. **BIBLICAL LANDS. Over 180 illustrations, almost half in color, maps, glossary, bibliography, index, 8¾"x11¼", 151pp. Pdn75, 5.98c.**
An account of the early history of the Holy Land and adjacent areas, the birthplace of Judaism, Christianity, and Islam. Dr. Moorey tells the intriguing story of how that history was gradually pieced together over the centuries and recounts how, as a result of their research, modern archaeologists have been able not only to illuminate the background of the **Old Testament** but also to reveal the remains of the civilizations of Canaan and Phoenicia. Moorey also discusses the Hebrew conquest of Palestine, the subsequent Hebrew kingdoms, and ends with a consideration of the Persian Empire up to its destruction by Alexander the Great.

MOSCATI, SABATINO. **THE FACE OF THE ANCIENT ORIENT. Plates, notes, index, Dou62, 2.95c.**
Professor Moscati, Director of the Center of Semitic Studies in the University of Rome, surveys the Near Eastern civilizations and culture as an organic whole from just before 3000 BC to the defeat of the Persians by Alexander the Great. His approach is chronological, beginning with the original civilizations of the Fertile Crescent. The text is clear and the author often includes quotations from primary source material.

MOULTON, JAMES. **EARLY ZOROASTRIANISM: THE ORIGINS, THE PROPHET, THE MAGI. Notes, indices, 484pp. Plo12, 39.50c.**
Transcriptions of a series of lectures delivered at Oxford. The lectures begin with an examination of the sources and an investigation of the religious conditions prevailing before Zarathustra. The next ones cover the prophet's reform movement and analyze his doctrine of evil and his eschatology. Two lectures are devoted to the origin and work of the Magi and one to the Fravashis. The concluding lecture illustrates the true character of early Zoroastrian concepts by comparing them with corresponding concepts in Judaism and Christianity. A collection of annotated texts from the Gathas and Greek authors completes the volume.

MOULTON, JAMES. **THE TREASURE OF THE MAGI. Notes, index, 273pp. AMS17, 22.85c.**
This is a comprehensive study of Zoroastrianism. Dr. Moulton was a well known British scholar, specializing in Iranian studies. This volume was written shortly before he left on an expedition to India where he lectured on Zoroastrianism to the Parsis. Dr. Moulton discusses the teaching of Zarathustra and his followers, the religion of the **Avesta**, and the Parsi community and its ancient and current beliefs. Many quotations from the sacred literature of the Parsis are included, and Dr. Moulton has generally done his own translating. The material in this volume reads well and the author's scholarship is still well regarded.

Gnostic amulet.

NEUGEBAUER, O. **THE EXACT SCIENCES IN ANTIQUITY. Illustrations, notes, index, 256pp. Dov69, 3.50p.**
This is the standard nontechnical coverage of Egyptian and Babylonian mathematics and astronomy, and their transmission to the Hellenistic world. After a discussion of the number systems used in the ancient Near East, Dr. Neugebauer covers Babylonian tables for numerical computation, Pythagorean numbers, and various other geometric and algebraic cases. Babylonian strength in algebraic and numerical work reveals, he feels, a level of mathematical development in many cases comparable to the mathematics of the early Renaissance in Europe—in contrast to the relatively primitive Egyptian mathematics. In the realm of astronomy, too, Dr. Neugebauer reveals a great sophistication.

OATES, DAVID and JOAN. **THE RISE OF CIVILIZATION. 160 illustrations, 123 in color, glossary, bibliography, index, 8½"x11", 152pp. Pdn76, 5.98c.**
An authoritative account of incipient agriculture and animal domestication during the Neolithic period, the rise of villages and towns, and the beginnings of civilization in the ancient Near East. The authors begin with a survey of the geography and climate of the area and the development of literate urban communities. They discuss why developments took place in particular areas and how they lead to urban living. The second half of the book provides an overview of the trade, economy, technology, and structure of society in this period as revealed through archaeology.

OPPENHEIM, A. LEO. ANCIENT MESOPOTAMIA. Plates, glossary, notes, bibliography, index, 461pp. UCh77, 6.95p.
This is one of the most valuable books on Mesopotamian civilization. Professor Oppenheim was editor in charge of the **Assyrian Dictionary** of the Oriental Institute and he made a life long study of the Mesopotamian clay tablets. In this volume he surveys virtually ever aspect of this ancient civilization and synthesizes a vast mass of philological and archaeological data. Following Oppenheim's death, his colleague Erica Reiner used the author's outline to complete revisions he had begun.

ORT, L.J.R. MANI—A RELIGIO HISTORICAL DESCRIPTION OF HIS DEVELOPMENT. Notes, bibliography, index, 296pp. Bri67, 28.35c.
This reads like a PhD dissertation. Ort begins with a survey of all past studies on Mani and his religion. He also reviews all the existing source literature on Mani and his disciples, and provides translations of the major Manichaean texts, topically arranged.

PALLIS, SVEND AAGE. MANDAEAN STUDIES. Extensive notes, 226pp. Plo26, 19.75p.
A comparison of Mandaeism and Mandaean writings with the Babylonian religion, Persian religion, Judaism, and Gnosticism.

THE PERSIAN EPIC (A RECORDING). 6.98.
A 33 1/3 rpm record of a Persian recital of the epic poem **Shah Nama (The Book of Kings)**. The Persian text and selected English translations and commentary are included in the liner notes.

PETERS, F.E. THE HARVEST OF HELLENISM. Introduction, chronology, notes, annotated bibliography, index, 800pp. S&S70, 5.95p.
A history of the Near East from the time of Alexander the Great to the triumph of Christianity. This is an extremely readable work which blends history, philosophy, religion, archaeology, and literature.

PORADA, EDITH. THE ART OF ANCIENT IRAN: PRE-ISLAMIC TIMES. 182 illustrations, sixty-one in color, maps, glossary, chronology, notes, bibliography, index, 7¼"x9¼", 279pp. Crn65, 6.95c.
This lavishly illustrated book covers the period from the first prehistoric cultures in what is now Persia up to Sassanid times. Sculpture, pottery, architecture, metalwork, and the minor arts are all surveyed against the general historical and cultural background. Professor Porada emphasizes those features of Iranian art which have endured through the centuries.

PRITCHARD, JAMES, ed. THE ANCIENT NEAR EAST. PUP75, 3.95p/each.
A two volume anthology which includes translations of primary texts and pictures on the art, architecture, religion, and daily life of the ancient Near East. The first volume was published in 1958 and the second volume takes into account discoveries since that date. Volume I (399pp.) includes most of the basic translations along with 197 plates. Volume II (318pp.) has supplementary texts as well as 110 plates. Both volumes contain notes and indices.

RAWLINSON, GEORGE. THE RELIGIONS OF THE ANCIENT WORLD. Offset, spiral bound, index, 180pp. HeR nd, 4.50p.
The material in this book is based upon lectures the author gave at Oxford during 1879-81. Professor Rawlinson was one of the best known nineteenth century ancient Near East scholars. This volume contains separate chapters on the religion of the ancient Egyptians, Assyrians, Babylonians, Iranians, Sanskritic Indians, Phoenicians, Carthaginians, Etruscans, Greeks, and Romans. Much of the material is dated, but the book remains interesting as documentation of how far we have come in our study of ancient religions.

RINGGREN, HELMER. RELIGIONS OF THE ANCIENT NEAR EAST. Notes, bibliography, index, 198pp. Wes73, 7.50c.
The majority of the material presented here is devoted to study of the Sumerian, Babylonian and Assyrian, and West Semitic religions. After outlining the literary and archaeological sources for these studies, Dr. Ringgren discusses the gods, mythology, cults as well as ideas of kingship, man, piety, ethics, and the afterlife. He has written a number of interpretative works on the **Old Testament** and here he emphasizes certain elements which are of special interest for the study of the **Old**

Testament. This is an in depth discussion, written in an easily understood manner, without an overabundance of details.

ROBINSON, JAMES, ed. THE NAG HAMMADI LIBRARY IN ENGLISH. Notes, indices, 508pp. H&R77, 16.95c.
The Nag Hammadi library is a collection of religious texts that vary widely from each other as to when, where, and by whom they were written. Even the points of view diverge to such an extent that the texts are not to be thought of as coming from one group or movement. The focus that brought the collection together is an estrangement from the mass of humanity, an affinity to an ideal order that completely transcends life as we know it, and a life-style radically other than common practice. This life-style involved giving up all the goods that people usually desire and longing for an ultimate liberation.—from the introduction. The texts are the sacred scriptures of the Gnostic sect that emerged in the ancient Near East at the time of early Christianity. The Library was rediscovered only thirty years ago, and this is the first time it has been published in full in any language. The translations were prepared by members of the Coptic Gnostic Library Project of the Institute for Antiquity and Christianity. Dr. Robinson provides an excellent introduction.

ROEBUCK, CARL. THE WORLD OF ANCIENT TIMES. Many photographs, maps, chronologies, bibliography, index, 785pp. Scr66, 9.35p.
This book surveys the history of the Near East, of Greece, and of Rome from the New Stone Age to the fourth century after Christ. . . . It is on the historical experience of this classical ancient world that this book is focused. It has seemed important to me to understand both the individual character of these peoples and also the long process of their history. Accordingly, I have placed most emphasis on social and political institutions, tried to link cultural achievements with these in an organic fashion and to mold the whole into a balanced narrative. The approach is chronological and is designed to stress the process and continuity of history rather than to interpret its achievements broadly.—from the preface.

ROUX, GEORGE. ANCIENT IRAQ. Many illustrations, maps, chronology, notes, bibliography, index, 480pp. Vik64, 3.95p.
A political, cultural, and economic history which covers the whole of Mesopotamia from the prehistoric era to Christian times. Dr. Roux describes the empires, dynasties, and religions of each millennium. He also reviews what is known today about the art, science, and literature of the Sumerians, Akkadians, Babylonians, and Assyrians. The material is well organized and presented; this is an authoritative study.

SANDARS, N.K. THE SEA PEOPLES: WARRIORS OF THE ANCIENT MEDITERRANEAN, 1250-1150 BC. 131 plates, some in color, notes, bibliography, index, 6½"x9¾", 224pp. T&H78, 12.95c.
In the latter part of the thirteenth century BC, an epoch of prosperity and relative stability in the East Mediterranean came to an abrupt end. The following years saw the collapse of Egyptian influence, the total ruin of the Hittite Empire, widespread destruction of cities throughout the Levant and, in the Aegean, the end of Mycenaean civilization. A Dark Age intervened that in the case of Greece and Anatolia lasted for more than 300 years. What caused these catastrophes? Today scholars lay much of the blame on warlike bands known to the Egyptians as the *Sea Peoples*. But who were these people? Where did they come from and vanish to? Ms. Saunders draws on extensive archaeological evidence to paint a convincing account of the Sea Peoples.

SHORE, A.F., ed. JOSHUA I-VI AND OTHER PASSAGES IN COPTIC. Notes, index of Coptic words with translation and page references, 7¾"x10¼", 76pp. HFC63, 9.00p.
A presentation of Old Testament passages in the Sahidic dialect, followed by a translation of the material as well as introductory notes on the fourth century manuscript.

SMITH, GEORGE. THE CHALDEAN ACCOUNT OF GENESIS. 12.95c.
See the Mythology section.

SZEKELY, EDMOND B. THE ESSENE TEACHINGS OF ZARA-THUSTRA. 1.80p.
See the Edmond Szekely section.

SZEKELY, EDMOND B. THE ZEND AVESTA OF ZARATHUSTRA. 100pp. Aca73, 4.80p.
Szekely's translation is from the original text. He sees the Avesta as not only a work of art, but also a universal encyclopedia, with chapters dealing with astronomy, organic gardening, health, psychology, philosophy, and religious thought. Szekely also includes portions of the pictographs that made up the original manuscript.

VELIKOVSKY, IMMANUEL. AGES IN CHAOS. Illustrations, notes, index, 340pp. Dou52, 10.00c.
A radical revision of ancient history. Taking for the starting point the simultaneity of physical catastrophes described in the book of Exodus and in Egyptian documents, Dr. Velikovsky reconstructs the political and cultural histories of the ancient world. His work greatly enriches the records of biblical history and changes the concepts of the cultural and historical progress of Egypt, Assyria, Babylonia, Greece, and other lands of the ancient East. *If Dr. Velikovsky is right, this volume is the greatest contribution to the investigation of ancient times ever written.*—Dr. Robert Pfeiffer, Harvard University.

VELIKOVSKY, IMMANUEL. OEDIPUS AND AKHNATON. Illustrations, notes, 208pp. Dou60, 8.95c.
Unraveling myth, lore, and fact, Velikovsky identifies the scene and all the personages of the Greek Oedipus legend with the life patterns of the family of the Egyptian King Akhnaten, reputedly the first monotheist during the most famous period of Egyptian history. The material is well documented and the narrative is fascinating, though Velikovsky's conclusions are controversial, to say the least.

VELIKOVSKY, IMMANUEL. PEOPLES OF THE SEA. Introduction, notes, index, 279pp. Dou77/S&J, 10.00c.
Dr. Velikovsky's long awaited continuation of his reconstruction of ancient history. Here he argues that most dates conventionally assigned to the ruling dynasties of Egypt—and thus to the most important events of ancient history as well—are widely inaccurate. The *Peoples of the Sea* are generally thought to have been barbarians from the north who swept down upon the Mediterranean, destroying the Hittite, Mycenaean, and other civilizations before being driven back by Ramses III of Egypt in the twelfth century BC. The later invasion of Egypt was thought to have been undertaken by them together with the Pereset, generally identified as the Philistines. Dr. Velikovsky presents evidence that Ramses III lived 800 years later; that the events in question took place in the first part of the fourth century BC; and that the *Peoples of the Sea* were Greek mercenaries and the Pereset were Persians. As usual, Dr. Velikovsky's theories are bound to stir up considerable controversy.

VELIKOVSKY, IMMANUEL. RAMSES II AND HIS TIME. Many illustrations, notes, index, 282pp. Dou78, 10.00c.
The more proper title for this volume would have been Ramses II and Nebuchadnezzar, since both of them play dominant roles in this volume, or in this part of history. But revealing in this way the subject of the book—and the contemporaneity of two well-known figures of antiquity, separated in conventionally written history by 700 years—would have added sensation to what is perforce a revolutionary reconstruction of the past. . . . The thesis presented and evidenced in this volume is that the so-called Hittite Empire. . .is nothing but the kingdom of the Chaldeans; further, that the pictograph script found on monuments from the western shores of Asia Minor to Babylon. . .is most probably the Chaldean script.—from the introduction.
Velikovsky makes an equally startling analysis of Ramseian Egypt in this provocative continuation of his ancient history.

WELCH, STUART. A KING'S BOOK OF KINGS: THE SHAH-NAMEH OF SHAH TAHMASP. Bibliography, 8¾"x12½", 199pp. MMA72, 18.75c.
Composed in the fifteenth century by the poet Firdowsi, the Shah-nameh or Book of Kings is Iran's central literary work, a historical epic peopled with monarchs—some of inspiring goodness, others of unmatched wickedness—handsome paladins, beautiful maidens, malevolent witches, and treacherous demons. This particular manuscript of the Shah-nameh is the most sumptuous ever produced. It contains scores of paintings of outstanding craftsmanship. About half of the 745 plates are in exquisite full color and gold. Welch contributes an

excellent introduction and an analysis of the action in each of the illustrated scenes.

WELLARD, JAMES. BABYLON. Illustrations, notes, bibliography, index, 223pp. ScB72, 2.95p.
An excellent, nontechnical discussion of virtually every aspect of Babylonian culture. Wellard begins with a summary of the great archaeologists and their findings. The next major section is devoted to the Sumerians and their art and literature. Later chapters cover the rise of Babylon, Hammurabi, social life in Babylon, the splendor and final collapse of Babylon, Babylonian Jews, and the Assyrians.

WEST, E.W., tr. PAHLAVI TEXTS, VOLUMES I-V. MoB65, 13.50c/each.
These volumes contain the only extant English translations of these texts. They are part of the Sacred Books of the East series. Each volume is over 400 pages long and each is separately indexed.

WOOLLEY, LEONARD. EXCAVATIONS AT UR. Many photographs and site plans, index, 261pp. Cro65, 2.95p.
Sir Leonard was the director of the excavations at Ur. In this book he presents a nontechnical discussion of the twelve years of digging, amplified with a complete record of the excavations and an analysis of the archaeological material unearthed at Ur. In the process he also summarizes the history of the area.

WYNNE-TYSON, ESME. MITHRAS. Notes, bibliography, index, 250pp. Ctr72, 20.00c.
The cult of Mithras was an offshoot of Zoroastrianism and was based on the idea of the perpetual warfare between light and darkness and good and evil, in which Mithras, the chief warrior, inspired and aided the most worthy rulers of the world and ensured them victory. This was the religion of the Roman legionnaires and Mithras was considered the special friend and protector of kings and soldiers, demanding in his worshipers the discipline, courage, and nonattachment necessary if the armies were to be victorious. This volume is one of the only full scale studies available.

XENOPHON. THE PERSIAN EXPEDITION. Glossary, index, 375pp. Vik72, 3.50p.
This account of the Ten Thousand, of their march into Persia to put Cyrus on the throne, their total defeat at the the battle of Cunaxa, and their heroic march back to the Black Sea, remains one of the great adventure stories of history. Even if Xenophon (c. 430-354 BC), the Athenian general and historian whose sympathies lay with Sparta, sometimes rivals Julius Caesar for self congratulation, it is impossible not to be moved by his simple narrative of courage, skill, and initiative. Translated by Rex Warner. Long introduction by George Cawkwell.

YAMAUCHI, EDWIN. PRE-CHRISTIAN GNOSTICISM. Many notes, extensive bibliography, indices, 219pp. Eer73, 7.95c.
This is a very thorough study of Gnostic thought and its relation to Christianity. Dr. Yamauchi is an authority in the field of Mandaean studies. In compiling this study he draws on and analyzes what he terms *evidences* from the following areas: Patristic, Hermetic, Iranian, Syriac, Coptic, Mandaic, and Judaic.

■ ZAEHNER, R.C. THE TEACHINGS OF THE MAGI: A COMPENDIUM OF ZOROASTRIAN BELIEFS. Notes, bibliography, index, 156pp. Oxf56/SIP, 2.50p.
This book provides a clear introduction to the main tenets of Zoroastrian dualism presented largely in the words of the Zoroastrian texts themselves. There are chapters on cosmology, the relation of man to God, the nature of religion, ethics, sacraments and sacrifice, the soul's fate at death, and eschatology. Dr. Zaehner provides minimal commentary, letting the texts speak for themselves.

ZAEHNER, R.C. ZURVAN: A ZOROASTRIAN DILEMMA. Glossary, notes, bibliography, indices, 511pp. B&T55, 23.50c.
This is Zaehner's most important and comprehensive work on Zoroastrianism, and it is also the definitive modern work on the subject. The first section is devoted to a detailed survey of Zoroastrian mythology, cosmology, and religious beliefs; the second part contains translations of a number of important texts.

ASTROLOGY

Astrology is a functional application of the awareness of the active relationship existing between the microcosm (smaller whole) and the macrocosm (greater whole). At the time when human consciousness was initially emerging from its primordial condition of undifferentiated consciousness, the mind sought to bring order and harmony to the apparent meaninglessness and confusion of human life by consciously regulating human activity with the flow of nature. Man was in a precarious position; in becoming a self-conscious individual, his contact with nature was severed; his activities could no longer follow the ebb and flow of nature. He had lost his directive instincts and had to maintain a constant fight for survival in a world filled with chaos and fear. To overcome the overwhelming forces of nature, the rudimentary intelligence of the human race had to be implemented and developed.

It was in such conditions that astrology first emerged, from an awareness of seasonal changes in the environment and the way these changes affected man's ability to survive. Gradually it was realized that with the aid of astrological knowledge one could prepare for the future by gathering food and migrating, closely following the patterns of lower animals, only on a conscious and intellectual level rather than instinctively. Regardless of how uncertain and confused one's own existence may have been, there was always order in the sky. This knowledge gave the much needed psychological and spiritual reassurance for coping with the primitive conditions. Astrology was man's first attempt to bring order within by the realization of the order of the universe.

Later, when human consciousness became more or less free from the fear of the immediate, astrology was used in the establishment of the social state, a system originally set up as a microcosm of the supreme, solar order. However, even though man had reached a state of individual consciousness, at this time astrologers were probably not concerned with the casting of birth-charts, for the tribal or national community was all-important and the individual had, for the most part, no identity or meaning outside of the community in which he was born.

It is difficult to ascertain the degree of exactness and perfection maintained by the early astrologers. We have only our present knowledge of history, psychology, and, of course, science to base our speculations on the nature of prehistoric astrology. We know astrological knowledge was used for more than strictly mundane and political purposes several thousand years ago, possibly, for example, for the invocation of spiritual and transcendental experiences. In addition we know that astrologers of at least as early as 4000 B.C. had a knowledge of celestial cycles *at least* as exact and extensive as that of the modern astrophysicist and scientific astronomer.

This knowledge was eventually lost or veiled, and astrology became, for the most part, a device for everyday success. It remained, however, a very exact instrument—or perhaps its practitioners were simply able to determine things in a very exact manner by some other means. The study of astrology was held in the highest respect by most academic institutions throughout Europe, Asia, and North Africa right up until the dawn of the *Age of Reason*—the eighteenth century, when the *sciences* to which astrology gave birth rationalized that it was invalid.

Astrology probably first became individualized around the sixth century B.C. (the time of Buddha, Lao-tzu, and Pythagoras), when a great wave of repolarization took place in man's consciousness, resulting in the transition from a physiological emphasis to a system of psychological values. It was probably around the Mediterranean and India that natal astrology first appeared openly, but it may have been practiced secretly much earlier. The practice of this type of astrology became very popular; the use of astrology by the Greeks and the Romans has been well documented. In the second century A.D., Ptolemy compiled all that was known at the time on natal astrology in his **Tetrabiblos,** and astrologers have closely followed his values and concepts ever since.

It was during the latter part of the Victorian era that astrology started to regain popularity after its decline in the eighteenth century. It met the mass media and became popularized in England through the influence of Alan Leo, and in America by Evangeline Adams and Max Heindel. Even so, the knowledge of Ptolemy was handed down in almost unaltered form, with very little question on the part of contemporary astrologers.

Today an overwhelming, yet steadily decreasing, majority of astrologers and astrological writers continue to base their work on antiquated information and values still tinged with fear and confusion. This type of astrology may have been acceptable and helpful for a humanity living in medieval times, but today's individual needs an astrology able to give meaning and purpose to the apparently meaningless and confused modern way of life. To answer this need, a small movement directed toward the re-examination and reformulation of astrological concepts and values was initiated by Marc Edmund Jones in the 1920s and further elucidated by Dane Rudhyar during the past forty years.

Astrology is firstly a discipline of mind, a technique for the development of holistic thinking. The study of the cyclic patterns of astrology places the mind in the habit of constantly perceiving things as wholes rather than as unrelated parts. An understanding of astrology makes the mind aware that what is happening at any given moment is just one point, just one moment of an entire cycle of complex and intricate relationships. It gives one an objective awareness of the unity of all things, the conscious realization that all things are in some way intimately related to everything else.

Astrology is a symbolic language in that it enables one to translate the cyclic interrelationships of all parts of any existential whole. It is the language of the holistic perception of archetypal and evolving patterns. As a symbolic language, astrology correlates everything with everything else, though the procedure of correlation varies depending upon the nature of the wholes being studied. It is a highly sophisticated system, which reduces all functional activities and experiences into a few essential categories. Symbolically, the birth-chart of an individual person is a representation of his archetypal form; it is a mandala of individual selfhood.

Astrology is indeed much like the Glass-Bead Game, as presented by Hermann Hesse in the novel of the same name. Hesse describes the Glass-Bead Game as *a universal language in which all knowledge is reduced to a single principle (which was) built up over several centuries into a universal system and language, in order to express* and bring every spiritual and artistic value and concept beneath a common denominator. Hesse was also aware of the all-significance of all things: *I understood in a flash that the language, or at least, in the spirit of the Glass-Bead Game, everything was in actual fact all significant, that each symbol and each combination of symbols led, not hither and thither, not to single examples, experiments and proofs but towards the center.* Both astrology and the Glass-Bead Game qualify as systems of universal symbolism, which may be defined as techniques that apply holistic perception to the interpretation of the dynamic relationship existing between and within all organic wholes for the purpose of revealing a universal or particular truth.

—*condensed from* **A Handbook for the Humanistic Astrologer**, *by Michael Meyer*

ABAYAKOON, CYRUS. ASTRO-PALMISTRY: SIGNS AND SEALS OF THE HAND. 20.00c.
See the Palmistry section.

ADAMS, H. EUGENE. A PRACTICAL APPROACH IN ASTROLOGICAL ANALYSIS. Offset, 8½"x11", 91pp. Ada74, 5.60p.
This is a very comprehensive study, recommended to astrologers beyond the beginning stage. Topics covered include judging planetary quality and quantity, the finality of the ascendant, the houses, planets and houses combined, and predictive astrology. The text is clearly written and illustrated with sample charts and detailed examples. There is also material on transits and solar and lunar returns.

ADDEY, JOHN. THE DISCRIMINATION OF BIRTHTYPES IN RELATION TO DISEASE. 25pp. CCL75, 3.95p.
This is a technical monograph which analyzes and graphically illustrates the extensive research Addey has done in the area.

ADDEY, JOHN, ed. HARMONIC ANTHOLOGY. 148pp. CCL76, 13.95p.
This book is intended to serve two purposes. First, it makes readily available a number of important journal articles on harmonics which are otherwise very difficult to obtain. Second, the articles selected for reprinting, arranged as they are in historical order, provide readers with a unique perspective on the evolution and development of the harmonic viewpoint in astrology.—from the preface. Charts and graphs accompany all the articles.

ADDEY, JOHN. HARMONICS IN ASTROLOGY. Notes, charts, indices, 269pp. CCL76, 15.95p.
This is the basic textbook on harmonics, written by the man responsible for developing the system. Includes information on the general theory of harmonics, on its practical applications, and on problems brought to light through the study of harmonics.

ALDRICH, ELIZABETH. DAILY USE OF THE EPHEMERIS. 8½"x11", 67pp. Hug71, 4.95p.
A complete, instructive account for the beginning astrologer.

ALLEN, GARTH. TAKING THE KID GLOVES OFF ASTROLOGY. 48pp. Cln75, 2.75p.
A collection of essays on the planets which originally appeared in **American Astrology Magazine**. The author's approach is generally positive and many of his insights are psychological in nature. Garth Allen is the *nom de plume* of Donald Bradley.

AMERICAN FEDERATION OF ASTROLOGERS. THE BASIC PRINCIPLES OF ASTROLOGY. 64pp. AFA62, 1.00p.
AFA propaganda with a good general look at astrology past, present, and future.

ANRIAS, DAVID. MAN AND THE ZODIAC. 211pp. Wei70, 3.50p.
An esoteric study which provides methods of synchronizing the planets, houses, and their mutual aspects, giving solid definitions of the signs and their decanates. Signs are discussed in relation to conscious, unconscious, and superconscious minds.

ARCANA WORKSHOPS. FULL MOON MAGIC. 16pp. ArW, 1.00p.
The material in this pamphlet is designed to supplement Alice Bailey's **Esoteric Astrology**. Included are new and full moon charts for the current year, for many different times zones, information on the three and seven year cycles, and on the esoteric rays and rulerships.

ARCANA WORKSHOPS. FULL MOON MEDITATIONS. 16pp. ArW, 2.00p.
These twelve meditations, one for each month, are designed for group use at the time of each full moon. The full moon marks the point in each month when energies not normally or usually contacted are available. At the time of the full moon it is as if a door opened wide, which at other times stands closed . . . . In the symbology of astrology, the sun represents the soul. From one point of view (ours) each sign of the zodiac represents one station upon the path of expanding consciousness.

ARCANA WORKSHOPS. THE FULL MOON STORY. 3.00p.
See the Theosophy section.

■ **ARROYO, STEPHEN. ASTROLOGY, KARMA, AND TRANSFORMATION. Illustrations, bibliography, 263pp. CRC78, 7.95p.**
This insightful book focuses on astrology as a tool for spiritual and psychological growth. Arroyo's approach is based on the idea of karma and the individual's desire for self transformation. He emphasizes the transformative and karmic significance of Saturn, Uranus, Neptune, and Pluto. He includes chapters on karma and relationship, progressions, transits, astrology in the Edgar Cayce readings, the meaning of the ascendant and its ruler, and a positive approach to Saturn and Pluto. This is an excellent work which we highly recommend to all astrologers.

■ **ARROYO, STEPHEN. ASTROLOGY, PSYCHOLOGY, AND THE FOUR ELEMENTS. Notes, bibliography, 207pp. CRC76, 5.95p.**
This is a truly excellent presentation in every sense of the word. It is subtitled, *An Energy Approach to Astrology and Its Use in the Counseling Arts.* Arroyo is a psychologist and part of this book was originally included in his Masters Thesis in psychology. The book deals with the relation of astrology to modern psychology and with the use of astrology as a practical method of understanding one's attunement to universal forces. It clearly shows how to approach astrology with a real understanding of the energies involved, and it includes practical instruction in the interpretation of astrological factors in a great deal more depth than is commonly found in astrological textbooks. The approach Arroyo takes is practical application based on the actual energies involved (air, fire, water, and earth) in all life processes. The book is dedicated to Dane Rudhyar, and Rudhyar's influence is apparent throughout. Highly recommended.

ASHMAND, J.M., tr. PTOLEMY'S TETRABIBLOS: FOUR BOOKS OF THE INFLUENCE OF THE STARS. 240pp. Sym nd, 3.95p.
A comprehensive text on the elements of astrology written in the first century AD. This translation has been made from Proclus' Greek paraphrase of Ptolemy's original text. Numerous references to the original are included, as are copious notes.

BACHER, ELMAN. **STUDIES IN ASTROLOGY, VOLUMES I-IX.** 100+pp. each, Ros nd, 1.75p/each.
This series has been compiled from articles which first appeared in **Rays from the Rose Cross** over a period of many years. They present an excellent picture of the spiritual basis of astrology as it relates to many specific cases. Many of the essays cover material which is not found in any other astrological literature.

BAILEY, ALICE. **ESOTERIC ASTROLOGY.** 742pp. LPC51, 15.00c/ 6.25p.
Astrology is described here as *the science of relationships*—the relationship existing between all living organisms within the universe. This is an excellent comprehensive account for the advanced student. The main chapter headings provide the sequence in developing study: *The Zodiac and the Rays; The Nature of Esoteric Astrology; The Science of Triangles; The Sacred and Non-Sacred Planets; Three Major Constellations; The Three Crosses; The Rays, Constellations and Planets.* An appendix summarizes and tabulates many important factors.

BAILEY, ALICE. **THE LABOURS OF HERCULES.** 2.75p.
See the Theosophy section.

BAILEY, E.H. **THE PRENATAL EPOCH.** 239pp. Wei70, 6.95c.
The prenatal epoch can be used as a method of rectification of doubtful horoscopes and for determining the actual period of human conception. This is the only work on the subject. It includes practical step-by-step instructions on working out pre-natal charts and ascendant tables.

BAKER, DOUGLAS. **ESOTERIC ASTROLOGY.** 8"x11½", Bak75, 16.00p.
The format here is the same as the earlier volumes in Dr. Baker's series, **The Seven Pillars of Ancient Wisdom.** As the title suggests this is a very thorough study of esoteric astrology, based on the pioneering work of Alice Bailey. Baker begins with a description of the nature of esoteric astrology and goes from there to an analysis of the twelve signs, the esoteric planetary rulers (which differ from the traditional ones), the twelve houses, and a final section on interpretation. As is usual with Baker's books, many interesting illustrations are included, a number in color. There is a profusion of material here, but often we are not exactly sure what Baker is saying.

BAKER, DOUGLAS. **ESOTERIC ASTROLOGY, PART II: THEORY, INTERPRETATION, AND PRACTICE.** Indices, 8"x11½", 280pp. Bak78, 20.00p.
Baker continues his scattered discussion of esoteric astrology in this volume with a survey of the importance and meaning of the seventh, eighth, and ninth houses. As usual, many illustrations and sample charts accompany the text.

BARTOLET, SAM. **ECLIPSES AND LUNATIONS IN ASTROLOGY.** Offset, 8½"x11", 60pp. AFA nd, 3.00p.
The contents of this book are valuable to those who require an introduction to the subject as well as instructions regarding procedure in the applications of lunations. Advanced students should find the various tables on eclipses and lunations useful and a good foundation for further study.

BENJAMINE, ELBERT. **BEGINNER'S HOROSCOPE MAKER AND READER.** 198pp. ChL72, 7.25p.
Complete instructions for casting a chart and guidance toward elementary interpretation.

BENJAMINE, ELBERT. **CHURCH OF LIGHT ASTROLOGICAL RE-SEARCH AND REFERENCE CYCLOPEDIA.** Over 650pp. ChL72, 7.50p/each.
These two volumes are reprints of out of print reference books written by Benjamine under the pseudonym of C.C. Zain. They are excellent resource material for the advanced student. They not only provide an abundance of technical and statistical information on astrological factors, but also offer many chart delineation suggestions. The following chapter headings give an idea of the depth of the coverage: *When and What Events Will Happen, Stellar Dietetics, How to Select a Vocation, Body Disease and Its Stellar Treatment.* The results of statistical analysis of over 5,000 natal and progressed charts are also included.

BILLS, REX. **THE RULERSHIP BOOK.** Oversize, Mac71, 12.50c.
In the symbolic language of astrology, the planets, signs, and houses are said to *rule* over everything on earth and every facet of our lives. This book presents a practical list of these correspondences, conveniently arranged alphabetically as well as by signs, houses, and planets.

BLACKMAN, EVERETT. **ASTROLOGY: WORLDS VISIBLE AND INVISIBLE.** 94pp. AFA74, 5.25p.
This is a detailed study of mundane astrology, focusing on three areas: *The Presidency*—and especially the charts of those Presidents who were assassinated or who succeeded to the Presidency due to the death of the previous president; *Cycles and Progressions;* and *New Horizons—with a Look at the U.S Chart.* The text is illustrated with numerous case studies and should be of interest to all who find astrological prediction fascinating. The material is quite recent.

BRAM, JEAN, tr. **ANCIENT ASTROLOGY, THEORY AND PRAC-TICE. Introduction, glossary, notes, bibliography, index, 347pp.** Noy75, 20.15c.
This is the first English translation from the Latin of the **Matheseos Libri VIII** of Firmicus Maternus, written in the fourth century AD. It is the most complete classical book on astrology. We have seen numerous references to it and we are delighted to have tracked down a source for it. The organization is sometimes a bit hard to follow, however the material itself is excellent and the book makes fascinating reading. All of the basic information is included and the reader gets a wonderful feeling for the times and for the changes in astrology when s/he reads the various descriptions and analyses. We recommend this volume highly to all those who are interested in the development of astrology over the centuries and also to all who are serious students and practitioners who would like a new source of information and insight.

BROWN, W. KENNETH, CHARLES and VIVIA JAYNE. **FUNDAMEN-TALS OF ASTROLOGY.** Offset, 8½"x11", 31pp. AsB nd, 3.00p.
Basic sun sign analyses—a good deal deeper than most—and information on casting a horoscope.

BRUNHUBNER, FRITZ. **PLUTO.** 8½"x11", 97pp. AFA34, 4.50c.
This book on Pluto was written soon after the planet's discovery and it remains one of the most important studies of the influences of Pluto. Brunhubner discusses the astronomical background and the mythology. He also gives careful explanations of the Plutoian forces and characteristics and its physiological effects along with information on aspects and examples of delineation.

CARELLI, ADRIANO. **THE 360 DEGREES OF THE ZODIAC.** 199pp. AFA51, 4.50p.
Illustrative meditations on each degree, with notes and historical references.

CARTER, C.E.O. **THE ASTROLOGICAL ASPECTS.** 160pp. Fow30, 4.55p.
A detailed treatise on the thirty-six possible combinations of the sun, the moon, and the seven known planets. A number of examples are given of each combination and each is treated under three headings: harmonious aspects, the conjunction, and inharmonious aspects. All terms used are well defined. Carter is a noted British astrologer of the Margaret Hone school.

CARTER, C.E.O. **AN ENCYCLOPEDIA OF PSYCHOLOGICAL AS-TROLOGY.** 199pp. TPH63, 4.25p.
This work is an attempt to produce a useful astrological Encyclopedia of Character, and, as far as data permits, of Disease. The approach is scientific and the examples are drawn from easily accessible and reliable sources such as the nativities of royalty.

CARTER, C.E.O. **ESSAYS ON THE FOUNDATIONS OF ASTROL-OGY.** Offset, 8½"x11", 106pp. Hug65, 5.95p.
A useful work, with chapters on the sun, moon, and planets; aspects and exaltations; the positive-negative polarity; aspects in terms of the signs; the Northern and Southern signs; and the houses.

CARTER, C.E.O. **INTRODUCTION TO POLITICAL ASTROLOGY.** 103pp. Fow73, 1.90p.

At the moment the horoscope of an individual...appears to be the principal field of astrological study. But actually the nativity cannot adequately be considered as isolated from the social environment, as represented astrologically by other horoscopes of greater amplitude....Sooner or later, I believe, "mundane" astrology will have to be replaced at the top of the astrological tree, and the more the state controls the individual, the truer this will be....Our subject here is political astrology, or the study in the light of astrology of politically organized and significant communities....We shall find that this study embraces, in terms of itself, most other kinds of astrology in greater or lesser degrees. This is the most comprehensive study available; well written and illustrated with many sample charts.

CARTER, C.E.O. **THE PRINCIPLES OF ASTROLOGY.** 188pp. TPH63, 3.75p.

A revised edition of a popular introductory astrology textbook. It contains a concise statement of known astrological facts as well as explanations of how these facts affect human life.

CARTER, C.E.O. **SEVEN GREAT PROBLEMS OF ASTROLOGY.** 37pp. AAs70, 1.00p.

Includes explanations of the problems and suggestions as to the lines along which they might be successfully handled.

CARTER, C.E.O. **SOME PRINCIPLES OF HOROSCOPE DELINEATION.** Offset, 8½"x11", 76pp. Hug nd, 5.25p.

An illustrative, instructive work, designed to follow **The Principles of Astrology,** and which may be read in conjunction with **The Astrological Aspects** and **The Encyclopedia of Psychological Astrology.**

CARTER, C.E.O. **THE ZODIAC AND THE SOUL.** 120pp. TPH28, 5.25c.

An inspiring philosophical work, covering many of the major aspects of astrology.

CARUS, PAUL. **CHINESE ASTROLOGY.** 2.95p.

See the Chinese Philosophy section.

CHARUBEL. **THE DEGREES OF THE ZODIAC SYMBOLISED.** 135pp. Ari07, 2.95p.

This is a reprint of one of Alan Leo's astrology manuals to which is appended a translation by Sepharial of a similar series found in **La Volasfera.** Each degree is named and a brief esoteric description is offered.

CORNELL, H.L. **ENCYCLOPEDIA OF MEDICAL ASTROLOGY.** 958pp. Wei72, 16.50c.

A comprehensive, thoroughly indexed and cross referenced text which includes general medicine-planetary influences for every condition, natural or pathological; alphabetical listings for each sign, luminary, and planet, indicating the diseases ruled by them; nonmedical information on everything that appeals to or affects our physical body and the senses.

Cosmobiology

The term cosmobiology designates those methods applied to the study of the relationship between the cosmic rhythms and life on earth. Experience has taught us that weather, climate, plant growth, natural catastrophes, and the individual's life as well are linked with the cosmic phenomena....The particular aim of cosmobiological research is to honor the knowledge of the ancient world, but at the same time to survey with a critical eye the rules of traditional astrology and incorporate modern methods, such as statistics, to the investigation of cosmobiological concepts.

—Reinhold Ebertin

AMERICAN FEDERATION OF ASTROLOGERS. **DRAWING INSTRUMENT.** 15.00.

A high precision protractor head, which can be used in any position, thus making it possible to draw all angles. The head is connected to a thirty centimeter ruler.

EBERTIN, REINHOLD. **THE ANNUAL DIAGRAM.** 152pp. EbV73, 5.50p.

A new system for setting up an annual diagram using the graphic 45° ephemeris which gives the astrologer a quick, easy, and readable picture of an entire year and enables him to ascertain when positive or negative reaction points make their appearance.

EBERTIN, REINHOLD. **APPLIED COSMOBIOLOGY. Many sample charts,** 200pp. EbV72, 10.50p.

This is one of Ebertin's most important works. In it he shows how to apply cosmobiological concepts to daily life. It is a technical book, not recommended for the beginning student.

EBERTIN, REINHOLD. **AUXILIARY TABLES FOR THE CALCULATION OF THE STELLAR POSITIONS.** 32pp. EbV nd, 1.75p.

These tables allow the student to calculate the stellar positions for a particular point in time, without the use of logarithms.

EBERTIN, REINHOLD. **THE COMBINATION OF STELLAR INFLUENCES.** 256pp. EbV72, 13.50p.

The interpretations of certain planetary constellations presented in this book are intended to provide an insight into the disposition, capabilities, aspects of character, and possibilities of fate of the individual. The reader is shown how he can combine the various aspects of his chart into a meaningful picture of himself. This book points out the stellar relationships to the biological, organic, psychological, and sociological elements. The correlations between cosmic constellations and biological events have never been so convincingly and clearly shown through example as by this method. A technical work.

EBERTIN, REINHOLD. **THE CONTACT COSMOGRAM.** 151pp. EbV74, 7.00p.

Ebertin's venture into chart comparison. As usual he has presented a method quite different from traditional astrology. His *contact cosmogram* is primarily concerned with the stellar positions at the time of birth and is brought into relation with current constellations or with a particular event. Here he shows how to set one up and gives many examples, graphically illustrated with the actual charts and discussed at length.

EBERTIN, REINHOLD. **THE COSMIC MARRIAGE.** 160pp. EbV74, 8.00p.

This is Ebertin's most extensive analysis of astrological compatibility, or *synastry.* He includes many sample charts with accompanying discussion of them. A major portion of the book is devoted to an interpretation of the stellar positions in the signs with respect to marital disposition and fate. Other chapters discuss the midpoints, significant aspects, and celestial bodies in the *house of marriage.* There are also detailed directions for comparative analysis using the 90° workboard. The writing is clearer than most of Ebertin's work.

EBERTIN, REINHOLD. **DIRECTIONS: CO-DETERMINANTS OF FATE.** 224pp. EbV76, 12.00p.

Ebertin defines directions as conditions and influences shaping life's destiny. This is a practical guide to the use of directions in chart interpretation, complete with many sample charts and case histories.

EBERTIN, REINHOLD. **GRAPHIC 45° MIDPOINT EPHEMERIS.** 2.50p.

Published annually, and available for all recent years.

EBERTIN, REINHOLD. **THE INFLUENCE OF PLUTO ON HUMAN LOVE LIFE.** 28pp. EbV70, 2.50p.

The aspects and influences of Pluto and its aspects to other planets and constellations.

EBERTIN, REINHOLD. **MAN IN THE UNIVERSE.** 103pp. EbV73, 7.00p.

An introduction to cosmobiology. Following a short history of cosmobiological concepts, the reader is made familiar with various methods of working and interpretation.

EBERTIN, REINHOLD. **90° Dial. Plastic,** EbV, 7.50.

EBERTIN, REINHOLD. **PLUTO TABELLE: 1851-2000,** 24pp. EbV75, 3.00p.

EBERTIN, REINHOLD. **RAPID AND RELIABLE ANALYSIS. 65pp. EbV70, 4.50p.**
Attempts to show by a diagnostic delineation how to pick out the vital elements from a cosmogram and to draw from them certain conclusions as to when the tendencies shown therein may make their appearance. Includes many examples of charts or cosmograms of famous people as statistical evidence.

EBERTIN, REINHOLD. **TABLES OF EVENTS—FOR THE CORRECTION OF BIRTHTIME AND PROGNOSTICATIONS. EbV nd, 3.50.**
Facilitates the correction of the solar arc directions.

EBERTIN, REINHOLD. **TRANSITS—WHAT DAY IS FAVORABLE FOR ME? 136pp. EbV71, 5.00p.**
Complete delineation of transit aspects, with real life examples and Ebertin philosophy.

EBERTIN, REINHOLD and GEORG HOFFMAN. **FIXED STARS AND THEIR INTERPRETATION. 95pp. EbV71, 6.00p.**
Presents a working basis in which to incorporate fixed stars into natal charts. In Ebertin's interpretations of fixed stars, he has tried to include many cases in order to clarify the *effects* resulting from fixed stars. The examples cited are ones relating to the radical position in the cosmogram. Very technical, not recommended for the beginning student.

HARDING, PATRICK, ed. **SYNASTRY. 79pp. AsA72, 3.00p.**
Synastry is the comparison of horoscopes for the purpose of judging the extent and character of their interaction. This is a collection of practical, graphically illustrated essays: *Synastry as Therapy* by Ingrid Lind; *Synastry, Its Principles and Practice* by Sheila Geddes; *The Synastry Problem* by Reinhold Ebertin; *A Key to Relationships* by Stephen Arroyo; and *Synastry in Depth* by Patrick Harding. Only those familiar with cosmobiology should consider this work.

■ *KIMMEL, ELEONORA and MANFRED.* **FUNDAMENTALS OF COSMOBIOLOGY. Spiral bound, 8½"x11", 84pp. CBC72, 7.65p.**
As the title suggests, this is a detailed instructional manual. Ebertin's works, even his more basic ones, have been hard for students to grasp. The Kimmels run the Cosmobiology Center in Denver and they devised this book as a correspondence course for students. The difficult material is presented in as clear a manner as seems possible and the text is profusely illustrated with tables, charts, graphs, and examples of the special cosmobiological tools—all well analyzed. Each chapter is summarized and includes an assignment for further study. If you want to learn this method without a teacher, this is the book for you.

LANDSCHEIDT, THEODOR. **COSMIC CYBERNETICS. 80pp. EbV73, 5.00p.**
A summary of concepts the author has presented in previous articles. Central themes are: the theoretical foundations of cosmobiology and their correlations with structural elements of mathematics, theoretical physics, cybernetics, and music; mathematical statistics as instruments of cosmobiological research; the forecasting of solar eruptions and natural catastrophes on Earth; and the significance of the galactic center for the interpretation of a personal cosmogram. Very technical.

LANDSCHEIDT, THEODOR. **TRANSPLUTO. EbV72, 3.50p.**
Graphic ephemeris of Transpluto's tropical zodiacal position between 1878 and 1987, geocentric and heliocentric.

REYNOLDS, JANE. **THE LIFE BLUEPRINT. 191pp. RIC78, 10.50p.**
The purpose of this book is for the student to learn how to read the natal abilities and emotional traits of the subject through the life blueprint, to evaluate the abilities and emotional traits and to counsel a person to use these abilities and emotional traits in a positive way. The student will learn how to locate the important times for the growth of these abilities and how to choose the best channeling of the energy present. The life blueprint contains the basic structure of energy surrounding each planet in the natal chart through the use of the signs of the zodiac, major aspects and midpoints.—from the introduction. Every aspect of the approach is clearly delineated. Many tables and charts.

REYNOLDS, JANE. **NATAL CHART PRINCIPLES. 98pp. RIC77, 5.95p.**
A clear explanation of the basics of natal chart erection according to the principles of cosmobiology. All the material is covered at length and each example is fully illustrated with charts and diagrams.

—————END OF COSMOBIOLOGY SUBSECTION—————

COUNCEL, PAUL. **X MARKS MY PLACE. 78pp. Dar38, 3.50p.**
This recent reprint is the only text on geographical astrology that we know of. The first section gives the theoretical background and a second one tells how to make practical applications. Astro-geographic tables and location maps are included. Many astrologers feel that correct or incorrect location according to the birth chart and progressions has a great deal to do with an individual's health, happiness, and success.

■ *CROSSLEY, PATRICIA.* **LET'S LEARN ASTROLOGY. Bibliography, 8½"x11", 96pp. ExP73, 7.50c.**
An excellent comprehensive workbook for beginning students, the clearest and best that we know of. Dr. Crossley shows how to prepare astrological charts; how to read and make use of a Table of Houses and an Ephemeris; how to understand many astrological concepts. She discusses the solar chart, aspects, rulerships and exaltations, lunations and eclipses, elements and qualities, parallels of declination, and depositing the planets. Every possible option is surveyed clearly and the text is illustrated with charts, diagrams, and special tables, including many work sheets. Highly recommended.

CROWLEY, ALEISTER. **ASTROLOGY. 224pp. Wei15, 7.95c.**
Crowley explains astrology within the context of the Western esoteric tradition. For him, the signs and planets are not mere ciphers in a mathematical calculation, but living archetypes which have developed along with the men who conceived them. Crowley also analyzes other symbolic systems such as the tarot and alchemy. Edited and annotated by Stephen Skinner.

CROWLEY, ALEISTER. **THE COMPLETE ASTROLOGICAL WRITINGS. Index, 235pp. Tdm74, 1.35p.**
This collection, edited by John Symonds and Kenneth Grant, includes, *The Treatise on Astrology*—noted for its exhaustive accounts of Neptune and Uranus—*Batrachophrenoboocosmomachia* and *How Horoscopes are Faked.*

CULPEPER, NICHOLAS. **ASTROLOGICAL JUDGMENT OF DISEASE. 135pp. AFA nd, 4.50p.**
Culpeper was a seventeenth century English physician, best known today for his **Herbal**. This is an offset reprint of his major work on disease as it relates to astrology. Many cases and specific instances are cited. The material is archaic, but some valuable insights are included.

CUMONT, FRANZ. **ASTROLOGY AND RELIGION AMONG THE GREEKS AND ROMANS. 110pp. Dov12, 2.75p.**
Reconstructs the beginnings of astrology in eighth century BC Babylonia, a full discussion of both the state of Chaldean astronomy and the motives that impelled scientists to study the stars. Also gives the history and development of early astrology in Greece, Syria, Egypt, and the Roman Empire.

DAATH, HEINRICH and H.S. GREEN. **THE ASTEROIDS. 26pp. Sym75, 1.50p.**
A reprint of a series of articles which originally appeared in Alan Leo's monthly publication **Modern Astrology** around the turn of the century.

DARLING, HARRY and RUTH OLIVER. **ASTRO-PSYCHIATRY. CSA74, 11.95c.**
The definitive work to date on criminal and abnormal psychiatry and astrology. It discusses in detail, with case histories and a wealth of diagrams, how mental problems can be recognized in birth charts. Relates abstractions of James, Freud, Adler, and Jung to specific birth chart configurations.

DARR, CLARA. **COMPARISONS. 48pp. Dar73, 5.00p.**
A follow-up to Ms. Darr's **Keys**, which analyzes the effects of another's planets falling in your natal houses, and shows how you affect others. Also has some material on the transiting planets not

included in her **Transits**. Her books are incredibly overpriced, but many of our professional customers say they are well worth having.

DARR, CLARA. **KEY TO INTER-RELATIONS. 25pp. Dar61, 2.50p.**
Guidelines for comparing horoscopes which include aspects to nodes, part of fortune, ascendant, and mid-heaven.

DARR, CLARA. **NEPTUNE IN TRANSIT WITH THE ASPECTS. 43pp. Dar75, 3.00p.**
This is the first in a projected series taking each planet through the houses and analyzing each transiting aspect in detail. The material here expands greatly upon Ms. Darr's earlier work, **Transits**.

DARR, CLARA. **NODES IN TRANSIT WITH ASPECTS. 54pp. Dar76, 3.50p.**
A detailed analysis of the transiting north and south nodes as they aspect with each of the planets and with each other.

DARR, CLARA. **TRANSITS. 126pp. Dar71, 10.00p.**
One of the most complete books on transits available. Guidelines for the six major aspects are given for each of the planets plus the sun and moon. This is Ms. Darr's most informative book.

DARR, CLARA. **URANUS IN TRANSIT WITH THE ASPECTS. 48pp. Dar76, 3.00p.**

DATON, LOIS. **LILITH. Bibliography, 71pp. LDE77, 5.98p.**
The most detailed analysis of Lilith available. Ms. Daton begins with a survey of Lilith in mythology, history, and astrology. The next two chapters are an analysis of Lilith through the signs and houses. There are also a few case studies and a biweekly Lilith ephemeris covering the years 1890-2000.

DAVIDSON, WILLIAM. **THE CARDINAL CROSS. Offset, 8½"x11", 20pp. AFA63, 2.50p.**
The transcription of a lecture which Dr. Davidson describes as follows: *An esoteric, astrological revelation of the progress of the Soul and how to determine your rank on the path of evolution. Herein dealt with are the three crosses of the horoscope, esoteric interpretation of one's malefics, and a valuable guide to the little understood Doctrine of the Rays.*

DAVIDSON, WILLIAM. **SET OF LECTURES ON MEDICAL ASTRO-LOGY. Offset, 8½"x11", 5 volumes, 266pp. AsB73, 19.50p/set.**
A transcript of nine lectures on medical astrology and health Dr. Davidson gave in 1958, which form the fullest treatment of the subject available anywhere by an authority in this field.

DAVIS, GERALDINE. **HORARY ASTROLOGY. 270pp. Sym42, 4.50p.**
A practical and comprehensive guide to the use of horary astrology in business, travel, relationships, and legal matters. The author tells when and under what aspects two conditions may arise and indicates many possible routes an individual may take in coping with the two situations. You need a basic knowledge of astrological principles to understand the technical terminology of this book.

DAVIS, JAMES. **ASTROLOGY: ESOTERIC AND PSYCHOLOGI-CAL. 164pp. CSA76, 3.95p.**
An esoteric analysis of each of the sun-ascendant possibilities in the form of descriptive phrases on probable personality limitations, transitional characteristics, and soul possibilities. A related quotation is sometimes also offered. The analysis is not terribly impressive, but it is worth glancing through if you are interested in esoteric astrology since there is little else written on the subject.

DAVIS, JAMES and JOHN RAIFSNIDER. **ASTROLOGY OF THE SEVEN RAYS. 135pp. CSA77, 2.95p.**
The astrology of the seven rays emphasizes consciousness and the evolution of consciousness. It is essentially an approach to astrology which evokes self-knowledge in the deepest sense yet strives for a clear-eyed recognition of all the limitations which obstruct that knowledge.... Esoteric Astrology... as developed in this book synthesizes modern scientific research with principles drawn from the wisdom of the East and West.... The viewpoint of esoteric astrology is that fate can be recast by the power of love, will, and intelligence.—from the introduction.

DAVISON, RONALD. **ASTROLOGY. 171pp. Arc63, .95p.**
Complete instructions for erecting a birthchart, as well as brief definitions of major astrological concepts. This book is well-regarded

by many astrologers, but we do not feel that the material is very clearly presented.

■ *DAVISON, RONALD.* **SYNASTRY: UNDERSTANDING HUMAN RELATIONS THROUGH ASTROLOGY. Index, 339pp. ASI77, 15.00c.**
An excellent comparative survey of the various techniques of horoscope comparison combined with an exposition of Davison's *relationship horoscope*, an entirely new method of chart comparison. Virtually every aspect of the subject is covered in depth and many case studies and sample horoscopes accompany the text. Recommended for all serious astrological students. Davison is one of England's foremost astrologers.

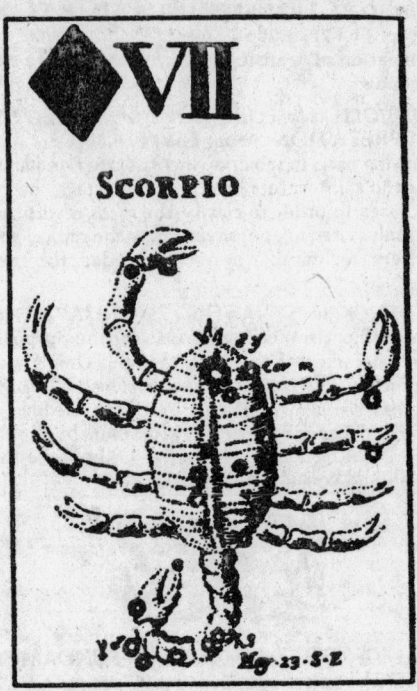

DAVISON, RONALD. **THE TECHNIQUE OF PREDICTION. 6¾"x 9½", 152pp. Fow55, 8.30p.**
Discussion and illustration of a new method of prediction which combines new measures of prediction discovered by Davison with the Arabian system of secondary directions. Numerous examples and special tables are included.

DELSOL, PAULA. **CHINESE ASTROLOGY. 248pp. War72/PnB, 1.95p.**
A lighthearted look at Chinese lunar astrology.

DELUCE, ROBERT. **COMPLETE METHOD OF PREDICTION FROM GENETHLIAC ASTROLOGY ACCORDING TO THE WESTERN SYSTEMS. Index, 211pp. ASI35, 8.75p.**
This is an important work on progressions. DeLuce includes methods of directing, extensive interpretation of planetary arcs and mundane aspects, plus many mathematical and astronomical tables. DeLuce views astrology as a tool in spiritual growth.

DOANE, DORIS CHASE. **ASTROLOGY. 300pp. AFA56, 7.75p.**
This book is the result of thirty years research into astrology based on the statistical studies of birth charts, paralleled with case histories. The book statistically shows, by tabulations of aspects, signs, and planets, certain predispositions to conditions, vocations, journeys, disease, and much else. It also has a section on stellar dynamics, a brief outline of the mathematical calculation of astrodynes, harmodynes, and discordynes, and twenty-four historical events occurring at the time of twenty-four major progressions in the chart of the U.S.A. For the advanced student.

DOANE, DORIS CHASE. **ASTROLOGY RULERSHIPS. 62pp. Fos70. 2.95p.**
Small dictionary of predictable objects and events and the astrological factors they involve.

DOANE, DORIS CHASE. **HOW TO PREPARE AND PASS AN ASTROLOGER'S CERTIFICATE EXAM.** 8½"x11", 56pp. AFA73, 4.25p.
A detailed compilation.

DOANE, DORIS CHASE. **HOW TO READ COSMODYNES.** 8½"x11", 49pp. AFA74, 4.95p.
Cosmodynes is a new term for *stellar dynamics*, which is defined as follows: *Judging the relative power, harmony and discord of the four basic factors in the natal and progressed chart—planets, signs, houses and aspects—by employing astrodynes, harmodynes, and discordynes. With cosmodynes the astrologer can determine the amount and kind of astral energy a native has at his disposal at any given time. They eliminate much of the guess work that astrologers have had to deal with in the past and aid the astrologer in determining what trends to expect from each birthchart position or progressed aspect.* This is a detailed, step-by-step description of how to use and compute them, graphically illustrated with many case studies.

DOANE, DORIS CHASE. **HOROSCOPES OF U.S. PRESIDENTS.** 159pp. AFA71, 6.25p.
Precise birth data and natal charts—with declinations—for each of the U.S. Presidents through Nixon. Includes comparative data to pinpoint astrological constants for events, vocations, and diseases, in their lives, as well as listings of important events.

DOANE, DORIS CHASE. **PROGRESSIONS IN ACTION.** 251pp. AFA77, 9.50p.
To illustrate her progression techniques, Ms. Doane uses the charts of twenty-one movie stars and well known figures. A miscellany of information on progressions is also included.

DOBYNS, ZIPPORAH. **DISTANCE VALUES,** 1971-1980. 67pp. TIA72, 1.50p.
Gives percentages of distance based on smallest and largest distances of the sun, moon, and planets from Earth. Also includes an introduction covering possible meanings and giving examples. Dr. Dobyns has a doctorate in clinical psychology and has spent over fifteen years working in the fields of humanistic psychology, parapsychology, and astrology, seeking to integrate their respective insights into the nature of man in order to facilitate self actualization and growth through self knowledge.

DOBYNS, ZIPPORAH. **EVOLUTION THROUGH THE ZODIAC.** 33pp. TIA72, 1.50p.
Subtitled, *The World-View of Astrology*, this book presents the essential meaning of the twelve signs as a symbolic portrayal of man's spiritual evolution. *The signs have been presented here primarily as a path of evolution, a spiral path of growth, but they are also the twelve sides of a complete life. In a real chart, everyone has the potential for all twelve, however limited may be the expression of some of them.* An appendix contains *house-planet-sign combinations* and *key phrases.*

DOBYNS, ZIPPORAH. **FINDING THE PERSON IN THE HORO-SCOPE.** 63pp. TIA73, 2.50p.
This is a humanistic analysis of selected topics in astrology: fixed stars, midpoints, nodes, asteroids, aspects, elements and qualities, and Saturn. Each topic is briefly discussed and illustrated with examples. An appendix presents key phrases for house-planet-sign combinations.

DOBYNS, ZIPPORAH. **THE NODE BOOK.** TIA73, 3.50p.
Table of longitudes of the nodes of the planets from a geocentric point of view from 1971-74, with a table of equivalent years to apply them to any year. Includes a discussion of the planetary nodes and the moon's nodes in the six zodiacal polarities, with illustrative examples.

DOBYNS, ZIPPORAH. **PROGRESSIONS, DIRECTIONS AND REC-TIFICATION.** 100pp. TIA75, 4.00p.
This is a detailed humanistic study, including clear directions and defining at length all the technical terms. Over half the book is devoted to an in depth analysis of the chart (or, rather, charts) of Senator Edward Kennedy as an illustration of how progressions, directions, and rectification are worked out. This section includes eighteen fold out pages—most of which are the charts of Edward, Robert, and John Kennedy. The book is an interesting presentation and the reader is given a good idea of how these techniques work and what they show.

DOBYNS, ZIPPORAH. **THE ZODIAC AS A KEY TO HISTORY.** 23pp. TIA68, 4.00p.
A presentation of the historical astrological ages, splitting them into sub-ages and explaining the rationale behind this division. Dr. Dobyns feels that this division explains the contemporary confusion over the timing of the Aquarian Age as well as other historical incidents and helps in understanding present day trends.

DODSON, CAROLYN. **HOROSCOPES OF THE U.S. STATES AND CITIES.** Bibliography, spiral bound, 8½"x11", 205pp. CaD75, 10.00p.
This is the first book to give the charts on each of the fifty states and their major cities. The charts are done by a computer and are very clear. An invaluable tool for astrologers who want an aid in selecting the best location in which to live, and in forecasting upcoming state and city changes, growth, and economic trends.

DONAT, EMMA. **ASTEROIDS IN THE BIRTH CHART.** 63pp. GeW76, 4.00p.
A discussion of the four main asteroids—which the author feels are the true rulers of Gemini—including keywords, chart examples, and a review of each of the asteroids in the signs and the houses. There's not much psychological depth here, but it is certainly good to have the meanings of the asteroids in a handy form.

DONAT, EMMA. **ASTEROIDS IN SYNASTRY.** 94pp. GeW77, 6.50p.
A detailed study of the subject, aimed at practical application and illustrated with many sample charts.

DUZ, M. **A PRACTICAL TREATISE OF ASTRAL MEDICINE AND THERAPEUTICS.** Many diagrams, offset, spiral bound, 252pp. HeR12, 5.00p.
In this book Dr. Duz presents an in depth study of the relationship between medicine and astrology.

EASTCOTT, MICHAEL. **MEDITATION AND THE RHYTHM OF THE YEAR.** 89pp. Sdl75, 1.95p.
Subtitled, *An introduction to the spiritual use of the cosmic, solar and lunar cycles which govern life on earth.* The esoteric aspects of each of the astrological signs are also discussed.

EBERTIN, ELSBETH. **ASTROLOGY AND ROMANCE.** 132pp. ASI26, 7.95c.
A recent reprint of a 1926 treatise which presents many ancient and modern astrological observations and rules of interpretation, together with over twenty male and female horoscopes. The writing style (or perhaps the translation) is quite dated but the content is often insightful. The theme is lovers and what makes them suited or not suited for each other and the whole is presented in an almost novelistic vein. The author's son, Reinhold, adds an afterword to this edition.

ELENBAAS, VIRGINIA. **FOCUS ON NEPTUNE.** Notes, 144pp. AFA77, 5.50p.
Most astrologers agree that Neptune represents all that is illusive, mystical, magical and intangible. . . . When we attempt to rationally explain that which cannot be seen, touched, or contained, it would appear that we are attempting the impossible. . . . But where, the reader may ask, do we look for the effects of this nebulous, mystical planetary force? We must look in all areas where Neptune resides and presides, and to a large extent this takes us to "never-never" land. We keep a sharp eye on all matters where there is some degree of creativity, illusion, artificiality, or that which is contrived. . . . When we discuss Neptune we discuss not only the ideals for which we are sometimes willing to die, but, more important, the values, tastes, and standards by which we are determined to live.—from the introduction.

ELENBAAS, VIRGINIA. **FOCUS ON PLUTO.** Bibliography, notes, 85pp. AFA74, 4.00p.
A book on Pluto, examining Pluto in the signs, the houses, the planets, and in aspect. The analyses are related to the historical/national scene. Basic material, well presented.

ELSNAU, MARY. **ASTROLOGER'S NOTEBOOK ON THE ASPECTS OF THE TRANSITING PLANETS.** Offset, 8½"x11", 92+pp. HeR62, 4.00p.
Basic details, often simplistically written. Includes blank space throughout for the student to add her own observations. The spiritual aspects of astrology are emphasized here.

ERLEWINE, MICHAEL and MARGARET, and DAVID WILSON. INTERFACE: PLANETARY NODES. 25pp. Cir76, 5.00p.
Tables of the interface points between the planetary nodes for the years between 1700 and 2000. The points are designed to be used in astrological work with the heliocentric coordinate system. Instructional and background material is also included.

ERLEWINE, STEPHEN. THE CIRCLE BOOK OF CHARTS. 8½"x11", 275pp. Cir72, 8.95p.
Hundreds of charts of famous and not so famous people over the ages, the majority being twentieth century figures. A good reference tool.

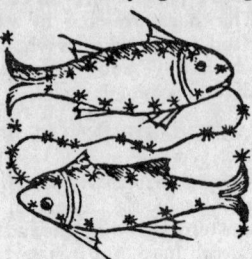

EVANS, COLIN. NEW WAITE'S COMPENDIUM OF NATAL ASTROLOGY. 252pp. Wei71/RKP, 7.95c.
The major portion of this text is devoted to a condensed ephemeris for the years 1880-1980, table of houses, latitudes and longitudes table and time changes table. The written portion of the text presents introductory material along with a discussion of planets, aspects, houses, character delineation, rival systems of house division, and instructions for casting a chart (with examples).

FLEMING-MITCHELL, LESLIE. RUNNING PRESS GLOSSARY OF ASTROLOGY TERMS. Illustrations, 102pp. RuP77, 1.95p.
An adequate glossary, covering most of the basics and defining all the terms clearly.

FOELSCH, KUNO. TRANSITS. 8½"x11", 71pp. Hug nd, 4.95p.
A clearly presented, complete treatise on the transits. Includes a review of the better known systems of astrological prediction and the character and purpose of astrological prognosis.

FURZE-MORRISH, L. THE PARALLEL IN ASTROLOGY. Vul74, 5.50p.
Furze-Morrish is one of Australia's leading astrologers. This book discusses parallels to the ascendant and progresses parallels.

GADBURY, JOHN. THE NATIVITY OF KING CHARLES. 128pp. Dar74, 4.00p.
A verbatim offset reproduction of a 1659 text, for those interested in historical research.

GALLANT, ROY. ASTROLOGY: SENSE OR NONSENSE? 6¼"x9¼", 216pp. Dou74, 5.95c.
This is an objective illustrated general account of astrology written by an astronomer. The bulk of the book is devoted to a fairly good historical survey of astrology and astrologers and early views about the zodiac. Only about one-fifth of it discusses the meaning of the signs and planets. Many illustrations are included along with a glossary and index.

GAMMON, MARGARET. ASTROLOGY AND THE EDGAR CAYCE READINGS. 85pp. ARE74, 2.50p.
Beams of knowledge about signs, planets, transits, cusps, from Mr. Cayce's superconscious.

GARRISON, OMAR. MEDICAL ASTROLOGY. 269pp. War71, 1.25p.
Presents astrology as an early warning system which enables one to prevent as well as prepare for illnesses. Medical astrology aims at preventing the occurrence of illness by identifying certain inherent physical weaknesses in the birth chart and determining the periods when one will be subject to discordant planetary influences.

GAUQUELIN, MICHEL. THE COSMIC CLOCKS. 250pp. Reg67/Owe, 3.95p.
One of the original, and undoubtedly still among the very best, scientific statistical research into the Earth's connection to her solar system. The objectively produced rational conclusions are apt to startle skeptic and devotee alike into more complete awareness of our true relation to the cosmic flow.

GAUQUELIN, MICHEL. COSMIC INFLUENCES ON HUMAN BEHAVIOR. Tables, charts, notes, 286pp. Fut74, 2.00p.
Gauquelin is a French psychologist and statistician who has devoted more than twenty years to a search for statistical proof of astrology. He and his wife have studied the birth charts of more than 27,000 people and his findings have been prepared with meticulous care. This is the most extensive and most technical presentation of his findings.

GAUQUELIN, MICHEL. SCIENTIFIC BASIS OF ASTROLOGY. Bibliography, index, 255pp. S&D69/DaL, 2.95p.
A serious and comprehensive look at astrology. Includes discussions of Jung's differentiation between astrological and parapsychological conditions, and many scientific experiments connected with astrology as well as a complete history of astrology. Recommended for the skeptic. The British title is **Astrology and Science**.

GEORGE, LLEWELLYN. A TO Z HOROSCOPE MAKER AND DELINEATOR. 813pp. LlP10, 12.95c.
One of the most popular astrology texts available—though not one of our favorites. It contains all the information necessary to erect and interpret natal and progressed charts, with complete definitions of every term used. Graphically illustrated with charts, tables, and examples, and quite comprehensive.

GEORGE, LLEWELLYN. IMPROVED PERPETUAL PLANETARY HOUR BOOK. 217pp. LlP06, 5.00p.
Each hour of the day is ruled by a planet and the nature of any hour corresponds to the nature of the planet ruling it. If you possess a Planetary Hour Book you may choose a fortunate hour to commence important undertakings....It is the object of this edition to meet the needs...of students with a practical text and tables having range from 27 to 55 degrees latitude. A great deal of explanatory material is also included.

GILBERT, PRISCILLA. POTENTIAL FULFILLED, VOLUME I: ACCIDENT PATTERNS IN THE CHART. 105pp. AFA76, 4.50p.
A detailed study accompanied by many case studies. The charts are very clear.

GILBERT, PRISCILLA. POTENTIAL FULFILLED, VOLUME II: WHAT SAVED THEM? 100pp. AFA76, 4.50p.
This second volume focuses on case studies of accidents which did not end tragically.

GLEADOW, RUPERT. THE ZODIAC REVEALED. 186pp. Wil68, 2.00p.
Explains how horoscopes have been cast over the years, and sheds light on the different interpretations given to the twelve signs of the zodiac. Also contains a listing of the signs of many famous people.

GOODAVAGE, JOSEPH. ASTROLOGY: THE SPACE AGE SCIENCE. 250pp. NAL66, .95p.
Shows the modern scientific case for the ancient wisdom of astrology. Relates astrology to the creation of the universe, astro twins, the lost continent of Atlantis, the meaning of the Great Flood myth, the mystical United States, predicting weather, earthquakes, disasters and more.

GOODMAN, DAVID. PSYCHOLOGICAL ASTROLOGY. 55pp. AFA74, 4.00p.
Dr. Goodman is a clinical psychologist who is co-director of the Astro-Psychological Consultation Center in New York, the first public professional collaboration between the two disciplines. The temperament of each sign is analyzed and a number of case studies (with charts) are given for each sign.

GOODMAN, LINDA. SUN SIGNS. 484pp. Ban68/PnB, 2.50p.
An introductory text for those whose astrology has been formed by the daily newspaper horoscope. Goes into the basics.

GORDON, HENRY. RECTIFICATION OF UNCERTAIN BIRTH HOURS. 212pp. JPA nd, 5.95p.
Rectification is always an uncertain thing and there is great controversy as to what is the best method. Gordon makes the case that a true

understanding of an individual's character will allow the astrologer to rectify a chart. His system is based on individual delineation of the rising degree and mid-heaven degree and the key word of each degree. A few application examples are also included.

GREBNER, BERNICE. **DECANATES: A FULL VIEW. 100pp. ArP77, 4.00p.**
A decant is 10° of a sign; each sign is divided into three decantes. The first represents the physical influence, the second mental, and the third spiritual. This is the most thorough discussion of decantes we have ever read. Ms. Grebner writes well and has done a good job of interpretation. The bulk of the book is devoted to sign-by-sign decante interpretations and analyses of decantes through the houses.

GREBNER, BERNICE. **LUNAR NODES. 8½"x11", 41pp. BGr73, 4.50p.**
There is almost nothing written on the nodes, so it is good to have a book-length exposition of them. Ms. Grebner seems to be coming from a positive place and her discussion should be helpful to those who seek a deeper understanding of the nodes. The nodes are individually discussed through the houses and in aspect and the general meaning of the nodes is presented. There is also some material on transits and progressions and on the astronomical explanation of the nodes. Two other sections discuss nodal points in the charts of famous people and synastry.

GREEN, H.S. **DIRECTIONS AND DIRECTING. 81pp. AFA72, 2.00p.**
The heavenly bodies are all in constant motion, so that although at birth they indicate accurately the nature of the physical vehicle and personality, they do not maintain this relationship unchanged. Day by day the signs rise and set, and the planets continue their revolutions; thus any heavenly body changes its position not only with regard to the rest that are also moving, but also in relation to the positions it and they occupied at birth . . . . This movement constitutes a direction, and will coincide with an event in the life. This small book includes chapters on calculating and interpreting directions; on the effects of directions; on solar and lunar revolutions; on transits and eclipses; and on pre-natal directions. Many examples are also presented.

GREEN, H.S. and RAPHAEL. **MUNDANE ASTROLOGY. 205pp. Sym77, 3.95p.**
Two separate books bound into one—each written in equally archaic language. The primary difference between the two is that Green classifies the body of his work by planets and Raphael, by houses. The content of the two also varies slightly.

■ GREEN, LANDIS. **THE ASTROLOGER'S MANUAL. Index, 255pp. Arc75, 6.95p.**
Green's approach is very positive and his writing style is excellent. We looked up some of the planets and signs that interested us most (the ones that are most prominent in our chart!) and we thought the descriptions were excellent. The book begins with a general discussion of the history of astrology and some of the main astrological concepts— complete with excellent long definitions. Green goes from there to a detailed analysis of the signs, both individually and in terms of the four elements. Next comes an analysis of the houses, both individually and in terms of house patterns and after that the sun, moon, and planets are discussed. Another long chapter is devoted to astrological categories and correlations. There is also an illuminating section on astrology and human relationships. Highly recommended as a basic text for the beginning student and as an aid in interpretation for all astrologers.

GREENE, LIZ. **LOOKING AT ASTROLOGY. 8½"x11½", 30pp. Scr77, 7.50c.**
A colorfully illustrated spiritual look at astrology, written for children and stressing the basics.

GREENE, LIZ. **RELATING: AN ASTROLOGICAL GUIDE TO LIVING WITH OTHERS ON A SMALL PLANET. 299pp. Wei78/Cov, 12.50c/8.00p.**
Ms. Greene uses basic astrological concepts symbolically and practically to show the ways in which people relate to one another on both conscious and unconscious levels. She refines her astrological knowledge within the framework of Jungian psychology. Unfortunately the author does not go much beyond the insights she offered in her wonderful **Saturn.** She builds on the material she has already

presented, but we were disappointed that she did not expand it more. Nonetheless, this is a fine synthesis of astrology and psychology and, while it is not everything we would like it to be, it is certainly a useful book.

■ GREENE, LIZ. **SATURN. 196pp. Wei76, 3.95p.**
Saturn symbolizes a psychic process as well as a quality or kind of experience. He is not merely a representative of pain, restriction, and discipline; he is also a symbol of the psychic process, natural to all human beings, by which an individual may utilize the experiences of pain, restriction, and discipline as a means for greater consciousness and fulfillment. This is a detailed study of Saturn which discusses the planet in each of the elemental signs and houses and surveys the aspects. There is also an extensive section on synastry. This book is a fine addition to the scanty literature on this too often misunderstood planet. The tone is generally positive throughout and the analysis is deep and spiritually oriented.

GRELL, PAUL R. **KEYWORDS. 8½"x11", 31pp. AFA70, 2.00p.**
Listing of keywords associated with all the planets, signs, and houses.

HALL, MANLY PALMER. **ASTROLOGICAL KEYWORDS. 229pp. L&A68, 2.95p.**
The keyword system is the most efficient means by which the student can analyze the implications of a horoscope as well as the most convenient method for finding the meaning of various factors in astrological charts. This is an extremely useful and timesaving work.

HALL, MANLY PALMER. **ASTROLOGY AND REINCARNATION. 45pp. PRS36, 1.75p.**
A collection of three essays: *How to Read Your Past and Future Lives; Astrology and Reincarnation;* and *Astrology and Karma.*

HALL, MANLY PALMER. **THE PHILOSOPHY OF ASTROLOGY. 91pp. PRS70, 3.00p.**
An esoteric approach which traces the philosophy of astrology throughout history.

HALL, MANLY PALMER. **PLANETARY INFLUENCE AND THE HUMAN SOUL. 32pp. PRS57, 1.50p.**
Lecture on the spiritual approach to astrology and the spiritual benefits to be gained through its study.

HALL, MANLY PALMER. **PLUTO IN LIBRA. 31pp. PRS71, 1.50p.**
A general interpretation of Pluto, with emphasis on its meaning in the sign of Libra. The influences are discussed in relation to the individual and to the United States.

HALL, MANLY PALMER. **PSYCHOANALYZING THE TWELVE ZODIACAL TYPES. 64pp. PRS37, 1.75p.**
Individual analyses of each of the signs, from Manly Hall's insightful point of view.

HALL, MANLY PALMER. **THE STORY OF ASTROLOGY. 156pp. PRS75, 6.50c.**
A general survey of astrology's development throughout time, with separate chapters devoted to the astrology of each of the following: the Orient, the Hindus, the Burmese, the Tibetans, the Greeks, the Romans, the Arabs, the Aztecs. There are also chapters on astrology as a religion and as a philosophy and on astrology and science and on astrology's place in the modern world. Much of the source material for this book was derived from rare books and manuscripts in Mr. Hall's library.

HALL, MANLY PALMER. **STUDENTS CALCULATION FORM. 8½"x 11", 11pp. PRS nd, 1.25p.**
Briefly and clearly explains the procedure for erecting a natal chart. There is not enough information given to allow an individual to learn solely from this pamphlet, however, it provides a good supplement to the material given in the general textbooks.

HAND, ROBERT. **PLANETS IN COMPOSITE. Index, 376pp. PaR75, 13.00c.**
Subtitled, *Analyzing Human Relationships,* this is a welcome addition to the scanty material in this area. Heretofore astrologers have relied on a complicated technique of chart comparison known as synastry. The composite technique was developed in Germany about thirty years ago,

and has been researched and tested quite extensively—although it is much too soon to comment on how effective and accurate the method is. The technique combines two individual charts (using midpoints) and creates a composite third chart, a chart of the relationship itself. This book contains a clear explanation of the composite technique, chapters on casting and reading the composite horoscope, five case studies illustrating the use and validity of composite charts, plus twelve chapters of delineations. There are delineations for all the planets (including sun and moon) in each house and every major aspect (conjunction, sextile, square, trine, opposition). All together there are 374 interpretations, each about 300 words. And there are also forty-one delineations of the moon's nodes.

■ *HAND, ROBERT.* **PLANETS IN TRANSIT.** 400pp. PaR76, 14.00c.
Descriptions of the typical effects associated with the transits of the planets over the factors of the natal horoscope. Transits of the sun, moon, and planets to the ascendant, M.C., planets, and houses of the chart are each described in passages averaging 300 words. Transits by conjunction, sextile, trine, and opposition are delineated. In each case emphasis is on the feelings, psychological shifts, and inner energies of the transits. Events indicated by the transit are treated as consequences of these psychological patterns, rather than as fated inevitabilities. In addition, there are introductory chapters describing the use of transits in forecasting, factors that effect timing, and various other matters. There is also an extended case study illustrating the principle set forth. Recommended.

HAND, ROBERT. **PLANETS IN YOUTH: PATTERNS OF EARLY DEVELOPMENT.** 379pp. PaR77, 13.00c.
This is the first major discussion of children and childhood in relation to astrology. Hand says that his orientation is toward viewing *the child as an adult in the process of becoming*. The first four chapters define the roles of mother and father, explain the effects of various planetary energy systems and discuss the meaning of the elements and crosses in a child's chart. The major part of the book consists of delineations of horoscope factors, written with children in mind. Every planet in every sign, house, and major aspect, as well as every rising sign, is interpreted in about 300 words that stress possibilities rather than certainties.

HAWKINS, JOHN. **TRANSPLUTO, OR SHOULD WE CALL HIM BACCHUS, THE RULER OF TAURUS.** Bibliography, 78pp. Haw76, 5.85p.
This is the most comprehensive discussion yet produced of Transpluto. Hawkins includes scientific evidence, mythology, and information on the qualities of Transpluto (or Bacchus, which is the name that Hawkins prefers). He also summarizes Bacchus in the signs and houses and gives aspects to planets and midpoints.

HEINDEL, MAX. **ASTRO-DIAGNOSIS: A GUIDE TO HEALING.** 482pp. Ros29, 5.00p.
Astro-diagnosis is the science and art of obtaining scientific knowledge regarding disease and its causes as shown by the planets, as well as the means of overcoming it. A chapter is devoted to each of the different parts of the body, with actual examples of diagnosis from the horoscope.

HEINDEL, MAX. **HOW TO CHART YOUR HOROSCOPE.** 198pp. Wil28, 3.00p.
A clear, complete textbook on the art of erecting a horoscope. Includes many tables.

HEINDEL, MAX. **THE MESSAGE OF THE STARS.** 728pp. Ros73, 9.00c/6.00p.
Heindel was one of the most noted early twentieth century astrologers as well as a leading Rosicrucian. This is a basic book, though it is not recommended for the beginning student. Contains chapters on progression, medical astrology, complete information on each planet and sign, as well as a spiritual survey of astrological history.

HEINDEL, MAX. **YOUR CHILD'S HOROSCOPE.** Two volumes, about 100pp. each, Ros73, 1.50p/each.
Case studies of the horoscopes of many children, seemingly chosen at random to show how various planetary configurations and signs and houses relate to a child's life.

HELINE, CORINNE. **THE BIBLE AND THE STARS.** 128pp. NAP71, 3.50p.
A series of esoteric lessons on the sacred science of the stars.

HELINE, CORINNE. **COSMIC HARP.** 4.95p.
See the Music section.

HELINE, CORINNE. **STAR GATES.** 4.95c.
See the Christianity section.

HELINE, CORINNE. **THE TWELVE LABORS OF HERCULES IN THE ZODIACAL SCHOOL OF LIFE.** 1.95p.
See the Mysticism section.

HICKEY, ISABEL. **ASTROLOGY: A COSMIC SCIENCE.** 7"x10", 280pp. Hic70, 13.00c.
An excellent, inspiring basic textbook—one of our favorites. Especially recommended for students interested in the karmic and reincarnational aspects of astrology. The presentation is comprehensive and very clearly written. The basic material on learning how to erect a birth chart is quite skimpy, but the explanatory, interpretative material is generally very good.

HICKEY, ISABEL. **PLUTO OR MINERVA—THE CHOICE IS YOURS.** 83pp. Hic74, 3.95p.
Pluto, the most invisible of the planets, represents the energy in us which is unknown on the surface but which works ceaselessly in the depths of our being. It rules the underworld in us as well as the highest part of us. This is a very nice analysis of Pluto: in the signs, the houses, natal aspects, transits, and its meaning. Also included are a number of letters to Isabel Hickey, with charts and responses.

HODGSON, JOAN. **WISDOM IN THE STARS.** 124pp. WET73, 2.75p.
This is a spiritual analysis of the sun signs which discusses each one as a stage of soul development. Many beautiful insights are revealed.

HOLLEY, GERMAINE. **PLUTO/NEPTUNE.** 150pp. Wei74, 3.95p.
Ms. Holley is a French astrologer who believes that the sign Pisces is ruled not by Jupiter, nor even by Jupiter and Neptune—but by Pluto and Neptune jointly. This is a detailed exposition of this theory along with a study of the role played by Pluto and Neptune in an individual's chart. There is also a very complete aspectarian for the two planets, an analysis of their tenancy in the signs and houses, and an analysis of Pisces on the house cusps. A final section explores the placement of Pluto and Neptune in the charts of the U.S., Egypt, and Israel. This is an interesting study which sheds some light on Pluto through a highly spiritual analysis.

THE HOLY ORDER OF MANS. **THE STARS OF HEAVEN.** Illustrations, 133pp. HOM75, 3.00p.
This book is a well written, spiritual discussion of the basics of astrology. The author uses mythological references and material from the ancient mystery teachings in his presentation of the signs, planets, and houses. Color correspondences are provided for each sign and planet and there is an excellent review of astrological symbolism. The astrological ages are also discussed and there is a good deal of supplementary material. All in all, a nice book for those in the path who want to get a feel for astrology.

HONE, MARGARET. **APPLIED ASTROLOGY.** 7"x10", 119pp. Fow53, 7.35c.
Companion volume to the **Modern Textbook**. Gives examples of chart interpretation with marginal astrological references, and case histories which illustrate astroanalysis. Very clearly presented interpretative work, including many diagrams.

HONE, MARGARET. **MODERN TEXTBOOK OF ASTROLOGY.** 7"x10", 315pp. Fow51, 15.40c.
One of the best all around general astrology texts, designed as a complete self study course for beginners—and also quite useful for experienced astrologers. Establishes a sound basis of knowledge. Well written. Ms. Hone was the founder of the Faculty of Astrological Studies of Great Britain and its Director for many years.

HOWELL, IRENE. **CYCLIC ASTROLOGY.** 68pp. Dar74, 3.50p.
Presents a new method for the rectification of a birth chart when the hour is not known, or only approximately known. Howell uses the ascendant as the vital point of the chart and follows its course through the natal chart in the three cycles. She gives detailed specifics here which are the fruit of six years of research and application and includes many graphic examples. Accurate rectification is one of the most difficult things in astrology and the method presented here seems to be a good clear one.

HUGHES, DOROTHY. **THE BASIC ELEMENTS OF ASTROLOGY.** 8½"x11", 37pp. AFA70, 2.50p.
Concise condensation of volumes of material. Aims at showing the beginner a wide view right from the start.

HUGHES, ROBERT. **THE SUN AND MOON POLARITY IN YOUR HOROSCOPE.** 176pp. AFA77, 6.00p.
An interpretation of the 144 possible combinations of the sun and moon signs. The approach is not found in many books and it represents an interesting way to learn how to synthesize a horoscope. Hughes seems to have a good understanding of his material.

JACOBSON, IVY. **ALL OVER THE EARTH ASTROLOGICALLY.** 215pp. Jac63, 7.00c.
Mrs. Jacobson is a very respected astrologer who has been teaching for many years. Her books often overlap each other—but each presents exciting and enlightening new concepts not discussed in a previous work. They are written for the intermediate student who is well acquainted with the mechanics of astrology but who needs further guidance in *reading the scriptures*. The main emphasis in this volume is on reading the natal and progressed chart and understanding the various aspects presented. Astrology is seen as a key to self growth and understanding. A section is devoted to transits and there is a good glossary.

JACOBSON, IVY. **THE DARK MOON LILITH IN ASTROLOGY.** 55pp. Jac61, 7.00c.
A comprehensive account for those interested in the effects of this little understood, and little seen moon. Includes a complete ephemeris for Lilith.

JACOBSON, IVY. **FOUNDATION OF THE ASTROLOGICAL CHART.** 125pp. Jac59, 7.00c.
This work is designed for use as a textbook in setting up a chart for the exact location of the planets for any given date, hour and place on earth. It also goes further, to include progressing the chart to show the advanced positions at any desired future date. The text is arranged to be learned entirely at home, without a teacher. The mathematics is very clearly presented and the text is graphically illustrated. Much of the material presented here is found in no other book we have seen. Includes questions and detailed answers to assist the student.

JACOBSON, IVY. **HERE AND THERE IN ASTROLOGY.** 215pp. Jac61, 7.00c.
The first part of this work is comprised of special sections designed to give the student...a new, different, and much simpler approach to his work with natal charts.... The second part is devoted to a system the author derived through extended research for making and interpreting event charts.

JACOBSON, IVY. **IN THE BEGINNING ASTROLOGY.** 237pp. Jac75, 10.00c.
Ivy reviews a number of little understood areas in depth including pre-natal astrology, rectification, delineation, vocational astrology, and mundane astrology. The delineation section expands upon the material she presented in her book on horary. Many sample charts illustrate her exposition and the technical instructions are excellent. We like Ivy's books alot and we are delighted with this one.

JACOBSON, IVY. **THE MELODY OF LIFE AND LOVE.** 89pp. Jac76, 5.50c.
A book of poems on astrological themes.

JACOBSON, IVY. **SIMPLIFIED HORARY ASTROLOGY.** 278pp. Jac60, 10.50c.
Horary *is the branch of Astrology in which we set up a chart for the time that a question takes shape, either seriously in the mind or put into words. The position of the planets at that moment will reveal the problem, its background, and also its final outcome or answer.* This is an excellent, detailed account of how to set up a horary chart and how to go about interpreting it. Includes an extensive section on planets and questions in each house.

JACOBSON, IVY. **THE TURN OF A LIFETIME ASTROLOGICALLY.** 8½"x11", 115pp. Jac64, 7.50p.
Presents a simplifed method for calculating primary arcs (important for pinpointing event dates in life), including all the necessary tables in larger print than usual.

JACOBSON, IVY. **THE WAY OF ASTROLOGY.** Glossary, 233pp. Jac67, 9.00c.
A fascinating account of the history of astrology; the natal chart and its development; reading the natal chart; progressions; the election chart; forecasting; and special aspects.

JANSKY, ROBERT. **ASTROLOGY AND THE FEMINIST MOVEMENT.** Offset, 8½"x11", 158pp. AsA77, 7.50p.
Analyses of the charts of sixty-two American women who have been either active in the feminist movement or who are well known personalities. A horoscope is compiled for each woman and analyzed.

■ *JANSKY, ROBERT.* **ASTROLOGY, NUTRITION AND HEALTH.** 188pp. PaR77, 4.95p.
Jansky is a trained biochemist and engineer and his main astrological interest is health and nutrition. This is both his most complete book on the subject and the most detailed analysis of nutritional astrology available. The emphasis is on ways we can use our natal horoscope to foresee and prevent health problems. Jansky explains how the signs of the zodiac relate to different parts of the body and how your natal houses correspond to your food preferences and nutritional needs. He also shows how the planetary aspects represent the flow of energy in your bodily systems, and how they can indicate potential health problems. All the information is clearly and scientifically presented.

JANSKY, ROBERT. **HOROSCOPES: HERE AND NOW.** Spiral bound, 8½"x11", AsA74, 7.50p.
This is a collection of the horoscopes of contemporary figures. The charts are accurate, with cusps and planets shown to the nearest minute of a degree—major aspects and all outstanding chart features are clearly shown. Time, place, and date of birth are indicated, and all charts are classified by planetary pattern. The book was designed to provide astrologers with living examples of such things as t-crosses, singletons, retrograde rulers, and planetary patterns as they affect the everyday life of people in today's news.

JANSKY, ROBERT. **HOROSCOPES: MUSICIANS AND COMPOSERS.** Spiral bound, 8½"x11", AsA74, 7.00p.
One hundred charts of famous composers and musicians of the past and present. The format is the same as the previous book.

JANSKY, ROBERT. **INTERPRETING THE ASPECTS.** Bibliography, spiral bound, 8½"x11", AsA74, 7.00p.
Most of the material on aspects and planetary structures simply contains definitions of what each particular pattern means without delving into the fundamental meaning of each type of aspect or structure. This excellent book studies the major aspects and their interpretations. Jansky is concerned with helping the student gain a

basic understanding which he can later apply to specific situations. This is much more than a planetary aspect dictionary. Planetary structures (the grand trine, the crosses, the yod, and the kite) are examined in greater detail here than in any other book. The aspects and structures are presented in terms of assets and liabilities, and in light of present day midpoint theory. The material is very clearly presented.

JANSKY, ROBERT. **INTERPRETING THE ECLIPSES. Offset, 8½"x11", 114+pp. AsA77, 7.50p.**
This is the most meticulous investigation of eclipses we have read anywhere. Jansky has spent years studying their effects and he includes many case histories here. A great deal of practical instructional material is also offered.

JANSKY, ROBERT. **MODERN MEDICAL ASTROLOGY. Spiral bound, 8½"x11", AsA74, 8.00p.**
This text introduces you to the technique of delineating the astrological relationship to health and disease. It shows the relationship between the planets and signs and the various parts of the body and their proper function. Vitamins and minerals are related to the planets, cell salts to the signs. Illustrated by many careful case studies, it covers such topics as birth control techniques, alcoholism, asthma, violence, conditions surrounding death, sexual preference, diabetes, and hypoglycemia. Rather than simply for diagnosis, these topics are used to illustrate the research techniques that can be used—both the classical and modern (midpoint) methods. Topically organized and graphically illustrated.

JANSKY, ROBERT. **PLANETARY PATTERNS. Spiral bound, 8½"x11", AsA74, 7.50p.**
Nearly forty years ago Marc Edmund Jones (in **Guide to Horoscope Interpretation**) described seven basic planetary distribution patterns, to each of which he ascribed certain general characteristics of self expression or temperament. Since that time his system has received wide acceptance by professional astrologers with very little change made to the original system. Jones speaks of each pattern as a *Temperament Type* with each type having a characteristic set of general traits that can be objectively observed. In this book Jansky reviews his pattern sytem, challenges certain of his ideas, and presents contemporary example charts. This is an excellent delineation tool.

JANSKY, ROBERT. **SELECTED TOPICS IN ASTROLOGY. Spiral bound, 8½"x11", AsA74, 7.50p.**
Jansky put this book together as an aid to students who have a basic working knowledge of astrology and who want to learn interpretation. It includes detailed instructions in how to use an ephemeris and discusses the meaning of retrograde planets, parallel aspects, focal determinators, the sign qualities, natural disposition, singleton planets, intercepted signs, planetary dignities, and many other not easily understood areas. The text is very clearly written and graphically illustrated.

JANSKY, ROBERT. **SYNASTRY. Spiral bound, 8½"x11", AsA74, 7.00p.**
Synastry is the study of the way in which two persons will relate to each other by comparing the planetary positions in one chart with those in the other. This book teaches a technique for making this comparison, using your own chart as the primary one. Jansky shows you how to predict both compatibilities and potential problem areas and illustrates how to deal with them through increased understanding. Well written, with graphic illustrations and sample charts.

JAYNE, CHARLES, ed. **BEST IN ASTROLOGY FROM IN SEARCH. Offset, stapled, 8½"x11", 60pp. AsB74, 4.00p.**
In Search was the first international astrological periodical. It was published from 1958-1961. The best astrologers contributed to it. The articles in this reprint are by Marc Jones, William Davidson, W. Kenneth Brown, Dane Rudhyar, Charles Carter, Pauline Messina, Edouard Symours, Ludwig Rudolph, and W.O. Sucher. Many pioneering concepts were introduced in its pages.

JAYNE, CHARLES. **HOROSCOPE INTERPRETATION OUTLINED. Offset, stapled, 8½"x11", 53pp. AsB70, 5.00p.**
Tries to correct the widespread fallacy of examining the horoscope in a piecemeal manner. The chart is interpreted first as a whole and then gradually to the *chart-in-particular*. It presupposes knowledge of the fundamentals. Included are explanations of the major components of the horoscope (i.e., the major configurations), the lights and angles and their relationships, the pivotal and singular factors, and a section on declination parallels.

JAYNE, CHARLES. **A NEW DIMENSION IN ASTROLOGY. Offset, stapled, 8½"x11", 31pp. AsB75, 2.50p.**
A technical study of nodes, eclipses, and other alignments of planets to the sun. A variety of tables are included.

JAYNE, CHARLES. **A PREFACE TO PRENATAL CHARTS. Offset, stapled, 8½"x11", 21pp. AsB75, 3.00p.**
Charles Jayne is well known for his astrological research in a variety of areas. He has done pioneering work in the area of prenatal charts and in this short volume he presents some of his findings. Illustrative examples are given for seven prenatal charts. *The basic premise is that there are stages in the "Descent of the Soul" to the body and that Charts can be made for each stage.*—from the preface.

JAYNE, CHARLES. **PROGRESSIONS AND DIRECTIONS. Offset, stapled, 8½"x11", 53pp. AsB73, 5.00p.**
The first part briefly describes progressions, secondary or major, minor, and tertiary; the second part, *new directions in astrology*, deals with the solar arcs; the third part deals with primary directions; and a fourth, very brief section, is concerned with symbolic directions. The appendix is an explanation of how to do a double interpolation. Very technical.

JAYNE, CHARLES. **THE TECHNIQUE OF RECTIFICATION. Offset, stapled, 8½"x11", 60pp. AsB72, 5.00p.**
Techniques of rectifications using mainly solar ascendant arc directions and vertical arcs. Very technical.

JAYNE, CHARLES. **THE UNKNOWN PLANETS. Offset, stapled, 8½"x11", 29pp. AsB74, 5.00p.**
This is a detailed discussion of the *unknown* planets, including their effects, and ephemerides for them.

JAYNE, VIVIA. **ASPECTS TO HOROSCOPE ANGLES. Offset, stapled, 8½"x11", 53pp. AsB74, 5.00p.**
Vivia Jayne has spent twenty of her twenty-five years as an astrologer in rectification of the horoscope angles. She discusses aspects to the ascendant, midheaven, and vertex angles and illustrates her exposition with many examples. The material presented here is not available in the texts on aspects.

JINNI and JOANNE. **DIGESTED ASTROLOGER. 60pp. ANW73, 3.00p.**
A students' guide to comprehensive natal analysis. All concepts are fully explained.

◼ JINNI and JOANNE. **THE SPIRAL OF LIFE. 160pp. ANW74, 6.95p.**
This is a very full explanation of all aspects of interpretation, in the form of an exploration of the relationship between the signs and their corresponding natural houses which reveals a dynamic growth process constantly operating in the natal chart which can be seen without the use of progressions and transits. Signs and houses are described at the level of psychological functioning, and their planetary rulerships are integrated. Major and minor aspects are explained and every planet is related to every other planet, whether in aspect or not. The lunation phases are also discussed and there is a complete listing of every type of phase aspect. In addition, Pluto and the nodes are analyzed and one section describes the effects of solar and lunar eclipses in the natal chart. The book covers a lot of ground—but it does so well and in a unique way that seems very suited to today's astrologers.

JINNI and JOANNE. **WHEN YOUR SUN RETURNS. ANW73, 3.50p.**
Volume II of the **Digested Astrologer**. The only book based on tropical astrology that teaches the math and interpretation of the solar return chart.

JINNI and JOANNE. **YOUR COSMIC MIRROR. Oversize, 18pp. ANW73, 1.50p.**
This workbook is for the purpose of helping you find greater self awareness through your own personal astrological birth chart. The techniques we use are based on concepts fully developed in **The Spiral of Life.** *In the following pages, you will find sets of key*

phrases for aspects, signs, and houses. The last section contains a form for analyzing the structure and activity of your personality through the planets that rule your natal houses and signs. There are spaces for you to write in your analysis, using the key phrases as indicated. This is a very useful tool in humanistically understanding a natal chart. The key phrases are well chosen and the material is clearly organized.

JOCELYN, JOHN. **MEDITATIONS ON THE SIGNS OF THE ZODIAC.** 277pp. Mul70, 3.25p.
This book presents the spiritual nature of the zodiac for meditation and relates it to self knowledge. The right use of these meditations enables one to achieve wholeness within oneself and in one's environment.

JOHNDRO, EDWARD. **THE ASTROLOGICAL DICTIONARY.** Offset, stapled, 8½"x11", 41pp. AFA nd, 2.00p.
The major part of this book consists of a listing of keywords for each planet. There is also material on aspects.

JOHNDRO, EDWARD. **A NEW CONCEPTION OF SUN RULERSHIP.** Offset, stapled, 8½"x11", 30pp. AFA71, 2.00p.
This is a companion volume to **Astrological Dictionary.** The material presented here is not available in any other book and it has been influential among astrologers seeking to show the relation between the native and his environment and the reactions between the individual and his society.

JOHNDRO, EDWARD. **THE STARS: HOW AND WHERE THEY INFLUENCE.** 120pp. Wei73, 6.50c.
A graphic explanation of how the latitudinal positions of the fixed stars are related to people, places, and events, as well as periodic states such as prosperity and depression.

JONES, MARC EDMUND. **ASTROLOGY: HOW AND WHY IT WORKS.** 364pp. ShP45/RKP, 2.95p.
A technical introduction to the basics of astrology, not recommended as a beginning text. Opens by showing how astrology arose from primitive man's confrontation with a world of chance and risk, and goes from there to show how the fundamentals have been developed and how they can be applied to daily life. The houses, signs, planets, and each horoscopic element are discussed at great length. Includes a large amount of interpretative material.

JONES, MARC EDMUND. **THE ESSENTIALS OF ASTROLOGICAL ANALYSIS.** 455pp. Sab60, 16.50c.
A complete exposition of the horoscope, and an explanation of how its total view becomes an approach to better understanding the human potential. Not recommended for the beginning student.

■ JONES, MARC EDMUND. **THE GUIDE TO HOROSCOPE INTERPRETATION.** 195pp. TPH72, 2.75p.
Presents a technique of interpretation which divides all horoscopes into seven simple types, which the experienced astrologer can identify at a glance, and then explains how to interpret each type. Twenty-eight horoscopes are given full preliminary delineation, to illustrate the technique, and the basis for a similar interpretation of forty-four others is provided.

JONES, MARC EDMUND. **HORARY ASTROLOGY.** 464pp. ShP43, 4.95p.
A complete horary manual which explains the mechanisms, and tells how to use them. It is an extensive philosophical work, but the techniques outlined are not as clear as some of the more modern texts such as Ivy Jacobson's or Barbara Watters'.

JONES, MARC EDMUND. **HOW TO LEARN ASTROLOGY.** 190pp. ShP41, 2.25p.
Presents a simplified method for looking at a horoscope, defining each of the elements and giving a basic approach to interpretation; and also explains chart erection in great detail. Includes a detailed glossary.

JONES, MARC EDMUND. **HOW TO LIVE WITH THE STARS.** 160pp. TPH76, 3.45p.
As is unfortunately the case with so many of Marc Jones' books, this one is both poorly written and badly organized. We feel that Jones has something to say, but is totally unable to say it in a way others can understand. In his introduction he states that this book is geared toward those who want to understand how astrology can be applied to their own lives. He also states that no knowledge of astrology is necessary for an understanding of his material. Maybe so, but we are fairly well versed in astrology and we have little or no idea of what he is trying to say. Basically Jones traces the cycles of the planets and the meaning of these cycles. He also reviews the signs and the most common symbols and focuses on transits.

JONES, MARC EDMUND. **MUNDANE PERSPECTIVES IN ASTROLOGY.** Index, 463pp. Sab75, 16.50c.
This is a major work in which we are given an intimate, sometimes tedious study of the techniques Jones has developed for studying the astrological nature of a corporate entity as well as an autobiographical study of certain years during his early career. In this latter part Jones demonstrates how the positions of the Arabian Parts and the geocentric nodes in his horoscope signaled certain events in his life. He goes on to discuss the use of and importance of the Parts and the geocentric nodes. The bulk of the book is taken up with discussion of *astrological surrogation,* Jones' term for the symbolic mantle of power given to and assumed by the central figure of any given field. The idea originates in the historic fact that until fairly recently only the rulers of nations had their horoscopes calculated, since the destiny of the citizens depended on that of their ruler. In a lengthy and important section, Jones delineates several hundred progressions and transits of Presidents Lincoln through Franklin Roosevelt according to the parallel events and decisions that took place during their terms in office. Then he introduces his version of the U.S. national horoscope, exploring it at length to demonstrate his particular techniques for mundane analysis. This is a mammoth study, often vaguely written, but containing many gems for the experienced astrologer.

JONES, MARC EDMUND. **THE SABIAN BOOK.** 389pp. Sab73, 13.50c.
A collection of letters selected from about 1200 weekly messages written by Dr. Jones to students of the Sabian Assembly, often re-edited by the author. They consist of page-long inspirational messages on everyday issues and on problems of individual aspiration. Jones feels that they present the best possible introduction to the Sabian materials.

JONES, MARC EDMUND. **THE SABIAN MANUAL: A RITUAL FOR LIVING.** 287pp. Sab57, 10.50c.
A method of personal development and self discipline through knowledge of the complete rituals of the Sabian Assembly, and an introduction to the esoteric tradition. Includes a healing ritual and a full moon ceremony.

JONES, MARC EDMUND. **THE SABIAN SYMBOLS IN ASTROLOGY.** 437pp. ShP53, 5.95p.
A comprehensive analysis of the Sabian degrees, giving the symbolical picture and interpretation for each of the 360 fundamental divisions of the zodiac. The origins and use of the symbols is explained in clear language.

JONES, MARC EDMUND. **SCOPE OF ASTROLOGICAL PREDICTION.** 461pp. Sab69, 16.50c.
A discussion of the primary, secondary and tertiary directions as projected by the horoscope. Other information includes solar and lunar returns, the problem of rectification when the precise moment of birth is unknown, and a primer of calculation.

JULIANN. **THE CALCULATOR KEY TO ASTROLOGY.** 59pp. Ari77, 4.00p.
A simple guide for the use of a calculator in preparing astrological charts, including solar returns, progressions, and other types of computations.

KEMP, CHESTER. **PROGRESSIONS.** 24pp. AAs72, 1.00p.
A detailed, clear exposition of the technique of progression. Kemp empirically studied most of the works on the subject and experimented until he came up with this precise treatise. The basis of his technique is tertiary progressions.

KENTON, WARREN. **ASTROLOGY.** Oversize, T&H74, 5.00p.
An excellent pictorial study of astrology, part of the **Art and Cosmos** series, with 146 illustrations—thirty in full color—and an excellent

thirty-two page historical survey. Each of the illustrations is well analyzed. This is the best book of this type we have seen and the illustrations are incomparable.

KEYES, KING. *MASTER GUIDE TO PREPARING YOUR NATAL HOROSCOPE.* Bibliography, index, 214pp. PrH74, 3.45p.
This is an excellent step-by-step guide, including test questions which follow each chapter and detailed, graphically illustrated anwers. It shows the beginning student how to use all of the astrological tools (with sample pages from ephemerides, tables of houses, etc.). All the necessary calculations are well explained and every possible option seems to have been covered. Includes many tables, charts, and graphs, with ample explanations.

KEYES, KING. *PARALLELS TO MIDHEAVEN AND ASCENDANT.* ChL68, 2.50p.
A parallel aspect is formed when a planet, the midheaven, or the ascendant occupy the same degree of declination. This is an eight page overpriced treatise on calculation and interpretation with *E-Z Tables.*

KEYES, KING. *PROGRESSION FORMULAS.* 12pp. AFA75, 1.25p.
It is difficult to find clear rules with examples of problems that come up in progressions. For this reason, I have written this little booklet in hopes it may solve some of these problems. I have concentrated on ten examples only, using a Raphael's Ephemeris for noon and Dalton's Table of Houses. This is a very clear presentation.

KLOCKLER, H. BARON VON. *ASTROLOGY AND VOCATIONAL APTITUDE.* 94pp. AFA28, 5.00p.
This book presents a system and structure for interpretation within the individual personality based on the author's research. Many vocations are analyzed and examples of individual charts of people in the vocation are illustrated and discussed.

KNAPP, ELSIE. *HORARY ART AND ITS SYNTHESIS.* Snd nd, 5.00p.
Ms. Knapp has been specializing in horary charts for over twenty years and in this volume she illustrates and interprets about thirty of her charts. The first section of the book reviews the technique she uses in some detail. The author was a student of Ellen McGaffery, and the latter's spiritual inclinations seem to be shared by Ms. Knapp. There is a good deal of variety in the cases presented which should help the student understand horary astrology. We do not recommend this as a basic book, but it is useful as a supplement to a more detailed text.

KOPARKAR, MOHAN. *DEGREES OF THE ZODIAC MAGNIFIED.* 199pp. Moh76, 10.00p.
Most of the degree books we have seen do not seem to fit the charts of the people around Yes! very well. This one fits better than most. That is not necessarily to say that it is any better than the others, it is just an observation and it is hard to judge astrology books on any basis other than a personal one. The analysis is basically positive and psychologically oriented.

KOPARKAR, MOHAN. *LUNAR NODES.* 95pp. Moh77, 3.95p.
This is the most comprehensive discussion of the lunar nodes available. Koparker begins with a discussion of the basic concept of the nodes and follows with chapters on karmic controls and controlling aspects. The rest of the book is devoted to analyses of nodes through the signs and the houses, aspects to the nodes in the natal chart and the progressed chart, and transiting nodes.

KOPARKAR, MOHAN. *PRECISE PROGRESSED CHARTS.* 105pp. Moh76, 4.95p.
The technique that Koparker outlines in this volume focuses on event analysis through an understanding of the potential, principle, and culminating structure of an event. The book begins with a detailed analysis of the mechanics of the technique. This is followed by a series of eleven example charts, fully analyzed. The presentation is often scattered, but the ideas are provocative. Koparker's work is based in part on Hindu astrology.

KOZMINSKY, ISIDORE. *ZODIACAL SYMBOLOGY AND ITS PLANETARY POWER.* 194pp. AFA nd, 5.00p.
A comprehensive study of the planetary influence for each degree of the zodiac in each of the signs.

A seventeenth century English woodcut showing Faust conjuring up the devil with the aid of a magic zodiac circle.

KRIYANANDA, SWAMI. *YOUR SUN SIGN AS A SPIRITUAL GUIDE.* 132pp. AnP71, 3.50p.
A beautifully written work which discusses the sun signs as they relate to human nature and soul maturity.

LAYMAN, MARVIN. *INTERVIEWING AND COUNSELING TECHNIQUES FOR ASTROLOGERS.* Offset, stapled, 8½"x11", 42pp. AsB74, 5.90p.
Layman is a minister and a sociologist who has had extensive experience in pastoral counseling using astrology. He draws on his personal experience in this volume and cites a number of case studies. Illustrated with charts.

LEACH, JUDITH. *HOW TO INTERPRET YOUR HOROSCOPE.* 168pp. H&R78, 1.95p.
A basic introduction and guide to natal interpretation, consisting mainly of keywords for each of the planets in each of the signs and houses. The information is basic and generally quite positive. This is a useful work for those who do not want to spend a lot of money on astrological texts.

LEE, DAL. *DICTIONARY OF ASTROLOGY.* 250pp. War68, 1.95p.
This is the most modern astrological dictionary available. It is geared to the nonprofessional and the definitions are not always very precise. Includes general background material.

LEINBACH, ESTHER. *DEGREES OF THE ZODIAC.* 206pp. Mac72, 6.50p.
Ms. Leinbach gives the guidelines of the influence that the degrees have shown from the behavior of individuals. The material has been gathered from the author's practical experience as an astrologer as well as from the leading authorities. Analysis of the degrees is an important part of seeing a person's chart as a whole, and this is the most complete work we have seen.

LEINBACH, ESTHER. *PLANETS AND ASTEROIDS—RELATIONSHIPS IN CONJUNCTIONS.* 8½"x11", 90pp. Vul74, 7.25p.
The strongest expression of any two planets occurs when they are conjunct. Every planets has some kind of relationship to every other planet in the chart. This is the most detailed study we have seen, exploring, in a spiritual sense, the relationship of each planet and asteroid to each other. This book can be an invaluable guide to interpretation for the professional astrologer.

LEINBACH, ESTHER. *SUN-ASCENDANT RULERSHIPS: THEIR INFLUENCE IN THE HOROSCOPE.* Vul72, 3.75p.
A detailed analysis.

LEMESURIER, PETER. **GOSPEL OF THE STARS: A CELEBRATION OF THE MYSTERY OF THE ZODIAC. Many illustrations, notes, 108pp. Com77, 6.50p.**
This is not a book on sun signs or on astrology as a means of personal prognostication; rather, it is about the zodiac as an expression of the understanding by man of his destiny through the succeeding planetary ages. The author believes that the ancients wrote the evolution of man's being in the arrangement of the stars. The symbolism of the zodiac, he is convinced, reveals to us the *limitless inner space of human consciousness*. Part One is an esoteric interpretation of the zodiacal symbology; Part Two is devoted to an analysis of the major tarot trumps.

LEO, ALAN. **ART OF SYNTHESIS. 7½"x10", 284pp. Fow68, 10.50c.**
Leo was one of the best known astrologers of the early twentieth century. His work still includes some of the most valuable insights available to the intermediate and advanced astrologer. His books synthesize his first hand experience. Leo was a Theosopist and he stresses the philosophical and intuitional aspects of astrology along with the esoteric and the psychological. The original version of this book was known as **How to Judge a Nativity, Part II**. Later it was revised and retitled. It still forms a companion volume to **How to Judge a Nativity**. This work is a detailed study of the planets as they relate to consciousness. Each of the individual planets (with the exception of Pluto) is studied, as are the sun and moon. There is also a section of sample horoscopes, including an analysis of the chart of Rudolf Steiner.

LEO, ALAN. **ASTROLOGY FOR ALL. 7½"x10", 336pp. Fow69, 9.85c.**
This is Leo's most general text, designed for the beginning student. It includes a bit of background material; an analysis of the characteristics of each of the signs; a description of the sun and moon together through the signs; and the planets in the signs. There is also a brief description of each of the degrees of each sign and tables for the place of the moon, 1850-1909. Leo is not at his best when analyzing the various signs. He often tends to negativity and excessive Victorian morality.

LEO, ALAN. **CASTING THE HOROSCOPE. 7½"x10", 353pp. Fow69, 9.40c.**
This is a guide to all the intricacies involved in chart erection—not recommended to the beginning student. The coverage is comprehensive, and includes areas not detailed in other similar works, but the format and the writing style are not as clear as some other works. Includes material on rectification, directions, methods of house division, lessons in astronomy, and sample tables.

LEO, ALAN. **THE COMPLETE DICTIONARY OF ASTROLOGY. 205pp. Wei29, 5.95p.**
This is a very confusing, disorganized volume. Most of it is in alphabetical order, but many of the entries are lengthy and it is hard to find information quickly. Alan Leo wrote the first half of the book and Vivian Robson put the second part together from notes Leo left.

LEO, ALAN. **ESOTERIC ASTROLOGY. 294pp. Wei67/Fow, 5.95p.**
An excellent presentation which examines all aspects of esoteric astrology. Covers chart interpretation in terms of reincarnation and the working out of karma in great detail.

LEO, ALAN. **HOW TO JUDGE A NATIVITY. 7½"x10", 336pp. Fow69, 9.35c.**
This is a comprehensive analysis of the individual houses as they relate to chart interpretation. Also includes material on the aspects. Leo shows how to synthesize the individual elements.

LEO, ALAN. **JUPITER, THE PRESERVER. 88pp. Wei73, 2.00p.**
An entire book devoted to the planet Jupiter. The planet is presented as the preserver of the zodiac and the unifying principle.

LEO, ALAN. **THE KEY TO YOUR OWN NATIVITY. 303pp. Wei69/Fow, 5.95p.**
This is an attempt to show how to break up the constituent parts of a natal chart and understand the significance of each detail. Leo has written this volume from the point of view of the practical astrologer with the aim in mind of teaching the beginning student how to write

out a delineation of a chart. He analyzes the sign and planet rulerships and the aspects and then he considers the material under such headings as health, occupation, finance, marriage, friends, and personal characteristics.

LEO, ALAN. **MARS, THE WAR LORD. 99pp. Wei73, 2.50p.**
Leo presents the horoscopes of ten famous people to illustrate the significant part Mars played in their lives. The illusion that Mars is utterly warlike and vindictive is corrected.

LEO, ALAN. **PRACTICAL ASTROLOGY. 224pp. Fow73, 3.60p.**
A small comprehensive astrological text, emphasizing the esoteric side of astrology. Extensive charts and text. Not recommended for the beginning student.

LEO, ALAN. **THE PROGRESSED HOROSCOPE. Index, 353pp. Wei69/Fow, 5.95p.**
This is the most detailed examination of progressions available. Includes a great deal of background information on the why of progressions in addition to detailed instructions on calculating the progressed horoscope, directions, the progressed ascendant, solar and lunar positions and aspects, solar revolutions and transits, and primary directions.

LEO, ALAN. **SATURN, THE REAPER. 108pp. Wei73, 2.50p.**
Leo stresses the planet's individualizing influence and its relationship to the last three signs of the zodiac. Saturn is seen as the bridge between higher and lower self.

LEO, ALAN. **A THOUSAND AND ONE NOTABLE NATIVITIES. Offset, spiral bound, 138pp. HeR nd, 3.00p.**
Leo gives the birthdate, house cusp, and planets' places for each of the 1,000 individuals and events. He also includes the sources of his information and a miscellany of other material.

LEWI, GRANT. **ASTROLOGY FOR THE MILLIONS. 266pp. Ban69, 10.00c/2.50p.**
Here is astrology applied to daily living; astrology applied to history; and astrology applied to your future. Includes an extensive discussion of transits, explains how to cast a horoscope and interpret, how to project the horoscope into the future, and explains planetary influences in daily life. Also has the positions of the planets from 1870-1970, and planetary projection tables through 1980, with explanations.

LEWI, GRANT. **HEAVEN KNOWS WHAT. 203+pp. Ban35, 10.00c/2.95p.**
Lewi has developed a method for casting complete natal charts without learning complicated mathematics. Tables are included here which explain the technique and provide all the necessary material. Extensive interpretive material is also provided. A very popular beginning text.

LEWIS, URSULA. **CHART YOUR OWN HOROSCOPE: FOR BEGINNER AND PROFESSIONAL. Index, 8½"x11", 192pp. G&D76, 6.95p.**
This is a concise handbook which discusses virtually every aspect of astrology. It includes basic information on chart erection and interpretation as well as information on the meaning of the planets and the houses and on chart comparison. Aspects are also discussed as are transits—both very briefly. Many tables accompany the text. An adequate, inexpensive book that touches on all parts of astrology. The information is clearly stated.

LIBRA, C.A. **ASTROLOGY: ITS TECHNIQUES AND ETHICS. Illustrations, charts, tables, 271pp. NPC76, 3.95p.**
This is a recent reprint of a classic text on astrology. We do not know the original publication date, but the text appears to date from the late nineteenth or early twentieth century. The interpretations tend to be negative, as is true with many books from that period, although this one is not as bad as some. All the basic material is included along with a great deal of information that is usually only found in more advanced texts. The presentation is spiritually-oriented and religious and karmic ideas are interspersed throughout. There is a lot of interesting material here—though we recommend it only for supplementary reading.

LILLY, WILLIAM. AN INTRODUCTION TO ASTROLOGY. 346pp. NCP72, 3.75p.
A comprehensive astrological classic. Covers all the basic material and forms an interesting contrast to modern astrological manuals for the beginning and more advanced astrological student.

LINDANGER, ALFA. YOUR SUN'S RETURN. 47pp. Mac49, 2.50p.
The technique of computing a Solar Revolution Chart with thirteen chart illustrations together with the noon date method of finding an unknown birth time and an accurate method of rectification by arcs of events.

LITTLEJOHN, FRANCES. THE DUODENARY SYSTEM OF ASTROLOGY. LjP nd, 5.25p.
The duodenary system is useful in pinpointing the influences which lead to certain events. The author developed this system and uses it extensively in her personal practice. It is especially useful in rectification. The book includes many cycle charts including ones for the solar monthly return, lunar returns, and various duodenary charts. There are also complete tables, formulas, examples, and a dictionary of aspect interpretations.

LIVINGSTON, PETER. ON ASTROLOGY. Glossary, index, 143pp. PrH74, 6.95c.
This is an excellent introductory astrology text for older children covering the history of astrology and separate analyses of the planets, signs, and houses. The text is very graphically written so that all readers can get a good feeling for the meaning of the signs, planets, houses, and many other fundamental aspects of astrology. Though the book is obviously oriented toward children in its language and illustrations, it also makes a good introduction for anyone who wants a brief overview and does not want to be overwhelmed by detail.

LLEWELLYN PUBLICATIONS. DAILY PLANETARY GUIDE. 249pp. LlP, 2.00p.
This annual volume contains a noon ephemeris, an aspectarian listing all aspects and planetary movements, a variety of tables, listing of planetary rulerships, moon tables, information on astrological birth control, folklore, and much else. -

LLEWELLYN PUBLICATIONS. MOON SIGN BOOK. 378pp. LlP, 2.25p.
An annual almanac that helps people plan their activities in accordance with the monthly lunar cycle. Packed with information including monthly weather forecasts, stock market forecasts, a farming and gardening guide, plus articles of special interest.

LOWELL, LAUREL. PLUTO. 105pp. LlP73, 2.95p.
A source book on Pluto, with charts detailing Pluto aspects arranged by planets; Pluto in the houses and the signs; transits; Plutonian correspondences, alphabetically arranged, with aspects; and a Pluto ephemeris 1851-2000.

LOWELL, LAUREL. SECONDARY PROGRESSIONS—USING THE ADJUSTED CALCULATING DATE. 91pp. Mac73, 4.75p.
A technical text by a noted astrologer, with all the necessary tables.

LYNCH, JOHN, ed. THE COFFEE TABLE BOOK OF ASTROLOGY. 8"x10½", 326pp. Vik67, 7.95p.
This is a profusely illustrated compilation of writings on astrology. It begins with a history of astrology and study of the planets, both by John Lynch. The major portion of the book is devoted to an analysis of the twelve signs of the zodiac, compiled from the writings of Alan Leo and Isabelle Pagan. There is also an essay on spiritual astrology by Zoltan Mason and a section relating palmistry to astrology. The text ends with a table of ascendants and ephemerides of the moon between 1900-1974. The book is not recommended to anyone who wants an in depth study; however, it does serve a function as a pictorial overview for the general reader. Includes many color plates.

LYNDOE, EDWARD. ASTROLOGY FOR EVERYONE. 212pp. Dut70/ Spe, 7.95c.
A basic text that includes everything for casting a chart (including ephemerides, tables of houses) and interpretative and instructional material. Not a complete presentation, but a useful beginning book for the interested student. The British title is Everyman's Astrology.

MCCAFFERY, ELLEN. ASTROLOGICAL KEY TO BIBLICAL SYMBOLISM. 192pp. Wei75, 7.95c.
A study of the esoteric wisdom in the Bible as it relates to astrology. *In this book I desire to show the different landmarks that should be passed by each believer who is on the Path. . . . Generally speaking the steps in spiritual progression may be grouped into four—corresponding to Initiation by Water, Air, Fire, and Earth.* An examination of each of these steps is followed by a discussion of each of the signs of the zodiac from biblical and psychological viewpoints. A meditation exercise of scriptural readings on the inner meaning of each sign is also provided.

MCCAFFERY, ELLEN. GRAPHIC ASTROLOGY. 303pp. Mac52, 6.75c.
A good primer for the beginning astrologer. Explains all the basic concepts and shows in great detail how to put together a natal chart and begin basic interpretation.

MCCORMICK, JOHN. THE BOOK OF RETROGRADES. 84pp. AFA75, 5.00p.
A graphic, statistical analysis of retrograde planets between 1880 and 1980 and including the following special features: what is a retrograde planet?, interpretation of the planets in retrograde, planetary group interpretation, and four sets of related tables.

MCCORMICK, JOHN. DEDUCTIVE INTERPRETATIONS OF THE NATAL HOROSCOPE. 68pp. AFA76, 4.50p.
This is a very helpful review of the houses, planets, and signs combined with a case study demonstrating *deductive interpretation*. The case study is quite lengthy and is very clearly presented. The approach is positive and the emphasis is on the inner meaning of the signs, houses, and planets and their synthesis. A good book for those who are learning interpretation.

MCCORMICK, JOHN and CAROL RUSHMAN. DEDUCTIVE INTERPRETATION OF THE PROGRESSED HOROSCOPE. 118pp. AFA77, 5.00p.
There is not much substance in this book, and certainly little or nothing on progressions. The bulk of the book is devoted to discussions of McCormick's personal philosophy and likes and dislikes.

MCDOW, SANDRA and JO ANNA GRAZIANO. THE A.C.D./L.D. METHOD OF PROGRESSIONS SIMPLIFIED. 12pp. AFA76, 1.50p.
This technique is clearly explained and examples are offered.

MACLEOD, CHARLOTTE. ASTROLOGY FOR SKEPTICS. 297pp. Tur72, 9.15c.
An excellent presentation of the basics of astrology. The author set out to write a debunking book and ended up with a rational presentation of astrology as a practical and challenging way of approaching life. The major part of the book is devoted to explanations of the planets and the signs.

MACNEICE, LOUIS. ASTROLOGY. Index, 7"x10", 351pp. Dou64, 6.95c.
The major portion of this oversize book is devoted to a survey of the history of astrology. The text is replete with photographs and drawings, many in color. Chapters on the planets and the individual signs are also included along with general instructions for erecting a chart. There is also an appendix containing tables of sidereal time (for finding ascendants) and extremely simplified tables of houses and ephemerides.

MCWHIRTER, LOUISE. THEORY OF ASTROLOGY AND STOCK MARKET FORECASTING. 207pp. ASI77, 156.00c.
A reprint of a work originally entitled, McWhirter Theory of Stock Market Forecasting. The author was an astrologer and financial analyst and she originated the theory of astrological stock market forecasting. Her technique is fully outlined in this volume.

MANILIUS. THE FIVE BOOKS OF M. MANILIUS. Spiral bound, 179pp. AFA1697, 3.75p.
Written originally at least a century and a half before Ptolemy, this work points out the influence of the Greek and Roman civilizations on astrology. All the major features of astrology as we know it today are apparent in Manilius' books, although couched in very different language. Much of the work is in the form of a poem. The translation is by T.C.

MANOLESCO, JOHN. **SCIENTIFIC ASTROLOGY.** 188pp. Pin73, .95p.
An overview of twentieth century scientifically-oriented researchers and discoveries, with brief summaries of the major books and theories and of some of the major periodical references. A scattered treatment, containing nonetheless some interesting information.

MANTHRI, CHANDRA. **THE DEGREES OF LIFE. Spiral bound, 8½"x11", 97pp. AsA74, 7.50p.**
Manthri has deeply studied the astrological methods of the ancient Egyptian and Hindu schools. The material in this volume was first printed in **Wynn's Astrology Magazine** as a series and is reprinted here for the first time. The author says that he obtained these degree readings from an old Sanskrit text. The description of each degree is full of poetic insight and the material differs considerably from all the other books on degree-by-degree analysis.

MARCH, MARION and JOAN MCEVERS. **THE ONLY WAY TO LEARN ASTROLOGY, VOLUME I. Charts, multilithed, 8½"x11", 256pp. AsA76, 9.50p.**
This is a good manual covering the basics. It evolved out of teaching manuals which the authors developed and is arranged into a series of self learning lessons. A series of test questions and answers follows each lesson. The material is clearly presented.

MARCH, MARION and JOAN MCEVERS. **THE ONLY WAY TO LEARN ASTROLOGY, VOLUME II. Offset, 8½"x11", 200pp. AsA78, 8.50p.**
A clearly written presentation of the basics of delineation, organized in the form of lessons. Many sample charts accompany the text and all of the terms are well defined. We found this an informative, easy to follow volume. The first section gives chart erection instructions. The emphasis is on self teaching and review questions are included, with answers.

MARK, ALEXANDRA. **ASTROLOGY FOR THE AQUARIAN AGE.** 400pp. S&S70, 4.95p/2.75p.
The chart, how to construct it, its division and the meaning of each aspect and sign is explained simply. Differentiates between the solar chart and the natal chart and offers interpretations that even the newest student of astrology can understand.

MASON SOPHIA and MARY LOU SHEPHERD. **LUNATIONS AND PREDICTIONS.** 68pp. ASC76, 4.00p.
A study of lunations: forecasting by the use of the new moon and the full moon. The authors briefly describe the technique. The bulk of the book is devoted to lunations in the houses, both full and new moon ones. Many case studies, with charts, illustrate the exposition.

MATCHETT, EDWARD and GEORGE TREVELYAN. **TWELVE SEATS AT THE ROUND TABLE. Photographs, 104pp. Spe76, 7.85p.**
A series of twelve meditations on the signs of the zodiac, each designed to give a deeper understanding of the concept of creative action. Sir George Trevelyan's contribution is an introductory essay on the inner meaning of the zodiac as it relates to the evolution of man.

MATTHEWS, E.C. **THE ASCENDING SIGN.** 126pp. MDC70, 4.50p.
Contains complete readings for twelve ascending signs, 144 portraits, profiles, and cartoons of the types. Also includes the sun and ascending signs of many famous people, and for those who cannot erect a chart, a simplified table of ascending signs.

MATTHEWS, E.C. **FIXED STARS AND DEGREES OF THE ZODIAC.** 78pp. MDC68, 3.00p.
Exact readings for the 360 different degrees based on a careful analysis of more than 500 horoscopes. Each degree has a keyword, or characteristic name, along with the delineation. Also points out the mathematical, musical, literary, artistic, and eccentric degrees and the planetary natures and longitudes of important fixed stars in the signs.

MATTHEWS, E.C. **STARS OF THE BIBLE.** 10.00c.
See the Bibles section.

MAYO, JEFF. **THE ASTROLOGERS' ASTRONOMICAL HANDBOOK.** 126pp. Fow65, 4.05p.
An informative reference book which is a guide towards a clearer understanding of the derivation and elements of the basic factors of astrological charting and theory.

■ MAYO, JEFF. **ASTROLOGY.** 214pp. Hod64, 2.50p.
An excellent introduction to the basics of astrology. Includes material on the signs, planets, and aspects, as well as a section on chart erection and brief essays on interpretation and progressions. Some of the deeper aspects of astrology are covered and the text is generally quite clear.

MAYO, JEFF. **HOW TO CAST A NATAL CHART. Index, 194pp. Fow67, 5.15p.**
A very clear step-by-step presentation of natal chart calculations which includes exercises at the end of each chapter (with answers) and many examples. Mayo, a student of Margaret Hone, is one of Britain's top traditional astrologers. Here he takes advantage of his many years of teaching, clearly pointing out the most common errors made by students and presenting the most detailed method of calculation and erection he has been able he has been able to devise. The mathematical sections are especially well written. Includes many sample tables and charts. Volume Three in his **Astrologer's Handbook** series.

MAYO, JEFF. **HOW TO READ THE EPHEMERIS.** 108pp. Fow66, 3.80c.
Excellent, comprehensive instructions for reading and interpreting the information in an ephemeris and a table of houses.

MAYO, JEFF. **THE PLANETS AND HUMAN BEHAVIOR.** 172pp. Fow72, 4.00c.
Explains what the sun, the moon, and the planets represent in terms of human behavior, and also correlates each cosmic body with contemporary psychological factors and the Jungian concepts of the psychic structure of man. Practical guidance in interpretation is given with the help of an example birth chart.

METZNER, RALPH. **MAPS OF CONSCIOUSNESS.** 8"x11", 160pp. McM74, 3.95p.
Down the ages, man has devised ways to free his consciousness from exterior limitations. These ancient ways, once only known to a few, have now become routes well traveled by many modern adventurers. This book shows how to use these ways, and why they operate as "maps of consciousness." The maps discussed include the I Ching, Tantra, Tarot, alchemy, astrology, and actualism. Extensive treatment of each topic, including bibliography, and references. The material on astrology encompasses two chapters and contains some of the best introductory material we have read. The material would be enlightening even to a professional astrologer. Many esoteric sources are cited.

MEYER, MICHAEL. **THE ASTROLOGY OF CHANGE. Bibliography, 280pp. Dou75, 3.50p.**
Subtitled, *Horary Astrology and Its Humanistic Applications,* this is a self contained guide to horary astrology, including an in depth discussion of the factors involved in interpreting a chart (with material on houses, signs, planetary patterns, the lunation cycle, and the Sabian symbols). Meyer also includes an actual case study showing the value of horary astrology in personal problem solving, and an extended series of appendices containing all the tables and instructions necessary to cast a horary chart. The horary (literally *of the hour*) chart is cast for the time and place that a specific crisis arises in the life of an individual and is used to uncover the potential for growth which may be found at the heart of any personal problem. Following as he does in the tradition of Marc Edmund Jones and Dane Rudhyar, Meyer's approach is spiritual and his book sheds a positive light on an aspect of astrology which so often speaks of disasters and unworkable situations on the individual level. The book is aimed at a psychological, humanistic understanding of incidents and problems in the best sense of these words.

MEYER, MICHAEL. **THE ASTROLOGY OF RELATIONSHIP. Bibliography, 263pp. Dou76, 3.95p.**
This is another of Meyer's handbooks on humanistic astrology. This one focuses on synastry (chart comparison). Explaining the significance of planets, houses, and signs in determining personal compatibil-

ity, Meyer offers a step-by-step technique for chart comparison and he includes full instructions for casting and interpreting zodiacal contact, house contact, and composite charts. As usual, Meyer's discussion is philosophical. All of the basics are included: individual analyses of each house, sign, and planet, with emphasis on their meanings in terms of synastry. A final section presents synastric analyses of the charts of Sigmund Freud and Carl Jung, George Sand and Frederic Chopin, and Madame Blavatsky and Henry Olcott.

■ *MEYER, MICHAEL.* **A HANDBOOK FOR THE HUMANISTIC ASTROLOGER.** 141 illustrations, bibliography, 380pp. Dou74, 4.95p.
A handbook for the new astrologer who is more concerned with human growth than with isolated single events. By correlating the phenomenon of the cyclic motions of the planet with the inevitable cycle of human existence, Meyer describes the unique potential focused in man and deciphers the *instructions* for realizing this potential. Charts of modern personalities are used as examples. An important new book by a close associate of Dane Rudhyar. Definitely not suggested for the beginning astrologer, despite the beguiling title. It is an excellent and a difficult book.

MILBURN, LEIGH HOPE. **PROGRESSED HOROSCOPE SIMPLI-FIED.** 170pp. AFA28, 6.00c.
The progressed horoscope indicates—for the particular time for which it is set up—the relative activity of the influences indicated in the natal chart. It is a very difficult aspect of astrology to master. This is a good, comprehensive text.

MILLER, H. DOUGLAS. **LADY, I HAVE YOUR NUMBER.** 44pp. AFA72, 3.50p.
Presents a formula for computing astrological birth control, along with tables and explanatory material.

MOORE, MARCIA. **ASTROLOGY IN ACTION.** 336pp. ArB73, 7.00c.
Illustrates the application of astrology by means of astrotypes, keywords, forty-two horoscopes, chart comparisons, and discussions of transits and progressions as means of predicting the future. The material is based on the charts of Jacqueline Kennedy Onassis, her family and friends.

■ *MOORE, MARCIA and MARK DOUGLAS.* **ASTROLOGY: THE DIVINE SCIENCE.** Bibliography, 850pp. ArB70, 20.00c.
This unique book will instruct the newcomer and illumine the expert. It contains information necessary to become an expert astrologer, including instructions for casting and interpreting a soul map. Lucid and explicit, this book is a ready reference of astrological information. An excellent compilation of insightful analysis and straightforward computation. This is the best overall text we have seen. Highly recommended for the beginning astrologer.

MORIN, J.B. **THE MORINUS SYSTEM OF HOROSCOPE INTER-PRETATION.** 109pp. AFA74, 5.00p.
In the early seventeenth century, Morin attempted to purge astrology of many of its medieval superstitions. His work (newly translated here by Richard Baldwin) forms the basis of all horoscope interpretation since his lifetime. This is a difficult work, but quite valuable for the advanced astrologer.

MORIN VILLEFRANCHE DE. **ASTROSYNTHESIS.** 192pp. Mas75, 10.00c.
This translation by Lucy Little is generally considered the clearer of the two.

MORRISON, AL. **JOHNDRO'S THEORY OF PLANETARY RULER-SHIP OF ASPECTS PER SE.** 8½"x11", 14pp. AFA72, 2.25p.
Selections from notes taken during a series of lectures that W. Kenneth Brown gave in the early 1950s on the Johndro material.

MUIR, ADA. **BOOK OF NODES AND THE PART OF FORTUNE.** 46pp. Mac30, 1.50p.
A nicely written pamphlet illuminating the meaning of these important, but little understood, features of the birth chart.

MUIR, ADA. **THE HEALING HERBS OF THE ZODIAC.** 63pp. LIP59, 1.00p.
A nicely illustrated little book which discusses the ailments common to the zodiacal signs and reviews the herbs that are most beneficial to each sign.

NAYLOR, P.I.H. **ASTROLOGY: A FASCINATING HISTORY.** 242pp. Wil67, 2.00p.
An illustrated, nontechnical account.

NOONAN, GEORGE. **SPHERICAL ASTRONOMY FOR ASTROL-OGERS.** 62pp. AFA74, 3.00p.
There is a definite need for a book to instruct astrologers in the theory and application of spherical astronomy....This booklet as written will not achieve the objective mentioned. What is presented here is a collection of formulae that will be useful to those interested in the theory of astrology. Examples are given of the use of these formulae, but no attempt is made to develop or prove them; there has been no attempt at a systematic discussion of the subject matter and its astrological implications. However this potpourri will enable those familiar with it to translate readily between the various coordinate systems in use in astronomy, and to compute such important astrological points as the MC and ascendant without having to use out of date and inaccurate tables. The knowledge of elementary algebra and trigonometry...is required to read this booklet.

NORELLI-BACHELET, PATRIZIA. **THE GNOSTIC CIRCLE.** Index, 7½"x10", 317pp. Aeo75, 12.90c.
This is a very personal exploration of esoteric astrology by a disciple of Sri Aurobindo and the Mother: *It is our intention to give as clear a picture as possible of the true purpose of astrology, and in which ways it can be an asset in the development of the spirit....The zodiac gives us a picture of this outer movement of evolution which has as its support the inherent spirit.* The emphasis here is on sacred geometry and numbers, especially three and four and combinations thereof. Many intricate diagrams illustrate the text. The presentation is complete in itself and the reader does not need a depth of astrological knowledge to be able to appreciate and understand the text. We get a very nice feeling from the book and the philosophy it

expounds and we recommend it to all who seek a deeper understanding of the true meaning of astrology.

NORELLI-BACHELET, PATRIZIA. **THE MAGICAL CAROUSEL. 146pp. AAP73, 3.75p.**
Subtitled, *A Zodiacal Odyssey,* this is a story of two children's adventure. *The children represent two complementary poles within the individual. It is also a treatment of astrology, each image evoked being a key to the deeper meaning of the signs.* The author is a resident of Pondicherry, the Aurobindo ashram in India, and the spirituality of her life is fully revealed in her discussion of each sign.

NORELLI-BACHELET, PATRIZIA. **SYMBOLS AND THE QUESTION OF UNITY. 157pp. Ser74, 5.75c.**
Every breakthrough, every Age that introduces a new element in evolution, must also bring with it a new understanding of symbols, because the way in which man reveals himself and his higher states of consciousness in symbols tells us what the stage of evolution is and the achievements of any given Age. Symbols are the language whereby man expresses his experience of God, and whereby the Supreme reveals the part and image of Himself that man is in the process of expressing. These articles were prepared originally for publication in the journal of the Sri Aurobindo Ashram. They are mainly concerned with astrological and astronomical symbols and with mythology and sacred numbers.

NORRIS, A.G.S. **TRANSCENDENTAL ASTROLOGY. 288pp. Wei30, 9.95c.**
Deals with the spiritual implications of astrology. The planetary numerals and glyphs and the lessons of the signs are delineated to enable an astrologer to link the soul to the astrological chart.

■ *OKEN, ALAN.* **AS ABOVE SO BELOW: A PRIMARY GUIDE TO ASTROLOGICAL AWARENESS. 344pp. Ban73, 1.95p.**
An excellent introduction which gives the reader a good feeling of what astrology is and how it has evolved. A fascinating section is devoted to *Astrology, Astronomy, the Earth and You,* the sidereal as well as the tropical zodiac is discussed and the material on the signs, houses, and planets is very well presented. Of all the inexpensive general texts we have seen this seems to be the most enlightening.

■ *OKEN, ALAN.* **THE HOROSCOPE, THE ROAD AND ITS TRAVELERS. Illustrations, index, 402pp. Ban74, 1.95p.**
The purpose of the present work is to present astrology, both as a spiritual path toward the expansion of one's understanding of universal law and as a practical tool for helping others through the use and interpretation of the horoscope. This book is far and away the best value that we know of as well as an enlightening addition to any astrologer's library. Includes a general section on astrology with material on the planets in the signs and houses; information on chart erection and interpretation; exercises; and analyses and sample charts for eight famous people, ranging from Carl Jung and Edgar Cayce to Joseph Stalin.

OLIVER, RUTH. **PHYSIQUE, TEMPERAMENT AND PSYCHE—AN ASTROLOGICAL APPROACH. 8½"x11", 54pp. RHO77, 5.45p.**
An in depth discussion of the title theme, based on the pioneering classification system of Dr. William Sheldon and including many chart-illustrated case histories. Ms. Oliver feels that Dr. Sheldon's method for classifying people according to body type is an effective tool for an objective understanding of the individual on any and every level.

OMARR, SYDNEY. **MY WORLD OF ASTROLOGY. 378pp. Wil65, 4.00p.**
General instructions for casting and interpreting your birth chart, interpretations of every sign, the planets, the transits, and cusps, by one of America's most noted astrologers, as well as a personal view of how astrology influences his life.

OMARR, SIDNEY. **SIDNEY OMARR'S ASTROLOGICAL REVELATIONS ABOUT YOU. 239pp. NAL73, 1.25p.**
General newspaper type sun sign analyses, more detailed than most. Also gives approximate rising signs, with commentary.

ORSER, MARY and RICK and GLORY BRIGHTFIELD. **INSTANT ASTROLOGY. 8"x8", 146pp. H&R76, 5.95p.**
This is a well organized general introductory book written in simple, clear language. It covers all the basics and the approach is positive throughout. There is a long section on compatibility and a series of *instant astrology* charts and wheels.

ORSER, MARY and RICK and GLORY BRIGHTFIELD. **PREDICTING WITH ASTROLOGY. 158pp. H&R77, 5.95p.**
The authors of **Instant Astrology** have come up with a simplified method for making personal and political predictions. Again they include a full series of tables and graphs. The presentation is oversimplified; nonetheless, the authors' approach is generally positive and the trends they help you to see can be helpful. The method is certainly not foolproof, but it is also not complete nonsense.

OSTEN, GAR. **THE ASTROLOGICAL CHART OF THE UNITED STATES: FROM 1776 TO 2141. 272pp. S&D76, 10.00c.**
A detailed study of the history of the U.S. as it can be viewed through an analysis of its natal chart, and of the effects of transiting and progressed planets. The chart on which Osten bases his study is the Gemini rising one. The material is organized chronologically and a study is made of the historical events as well as the major planetary configurations. The last part of the book is devoted to a speculative analysis of future events based on planetary activity. A number of sample charts are included.

PAGAN, ISABELLE. **FROM PIONEER TO POET OR THE TWELVE GREAT GATES. 318pp. TPH69, 12.00c.**
A fascinating, instructive introduction to the study of the science of astrology. Details the twelve signs at great length and gives summary material and an analysis of selected horoscopes of historical personages.

PALMER, LYNNE. **ABC BASIC CHART READING. 8½"x11", 52pp. AFA74, 5.75p.**
As the title suggests this is a guide to reading the horoscope. The material is more clearly and succinctly presented than in Ms. Palmer's other books. The material covered includes the houses, the aspects, and the planets (viewed in terms of discordant and harmonious). Basically the information is given in terms of key words and phrases. The author's point of view seems to be that key words provide the kernel of an idea of the chart pattern without locking the reader into too firm a conception of each particular aspect, house, or planet.

PALMER, LYNNE. **ABC OF CHART ERECTION. 8½"x11", 212pp. AFA71, 5.50p.**
A very comprehensive manual, well presented but the very amount of information may be confusing for the beginning student. We suggest it as a good book to have around to review procedures (advanced as well as beginning ones) rather than something to start with. Graphically illustrated, with numerous examples, and many helpful tables.

PALMER, LYNNE. **ABC OF MAJOR PROGRESSIONS. 8½"x11", 162pp. AFA70, 5.50p.**
A very technical work which clearly details the procedures for progressing, giving a few alternate methods and many tables. Numerous practical examples assist the student. Recommended for the advanced student.

PALMER, LYNNE. **ASTROLOGICAL COMPATABILITY. 345pp. AFA76, 9.50p.**
This is a detailed analysis of the title theme. Ms. Palmer's presentation is a great deal more lucid here than in her other books. She focuses on ways of determining the positive and negative blending of two natal charts and she offers a variety of ways for comparing the charts. Virtually every aspect of chart comparison is discussed at length and specific technical instructions are also included. The author also presents a variety of illustrative case studies.

PARCHMENT, S.R. **ASTROLOGY: MUNDANE AND SPIRITUAL. Many sample charts, 680pp. AFA33, 10.00c.**
An esoteric text which blends traditional astrological insights with information on mundane events. The style and language are a bit old fashioned.

PARKER, ELSE. **ASTROLOGY AND ITS PRACTICAL APPLICATION. 204pp. NCP27, 4.95p.**
A reprint of a spiritually-oriented basic astrology text; which includes chapters on the houses, the planets, the signs ascending, the planets in the signs and the houses, the part of fortune in the houses, aspects, and information on progressions.

PARKER, JULIA and DEREK. **THE COMPLEAT ASTROLOGER.** 9"x 11½", Ban71/MiB, 24.95c/8.95p.
A beautifully illustrated volume, covering the following information: a history of astrology, guide to the astronomy behind astrology, interpretations and progressions of the birth chart, as well as astrological tables, including ephemerides from 1900 to 1975. Not very technical.

PAUL, HELEN and BRIDGET O'TOOLE. **INTERPRETING THE HOUSES.** Offset, 8½"x11", 103pp. AsA76, 7.00p.
An individual analysis of each of the houses along with a chapter on intercepted signs. The discussion is fairly complete and includes analyses of the signs and planets in the house and the major aspects of the house. A miscellany of other information, as well.

PAUL, HELEN and BRIDGET O'TOOLE. **THE YOD AND OTHER POINTS IN YOUR HOROSCOPE.** 52pp. Vul77, 3.00p.
A detailed analysis of many infrequently discussed points including the Arabian points, the composite point, the nodal points of the planets, the midpoint, decision points, solstice point, and the vertex.

PEARCE, A.J. **TEXTBOOK OF ASTROLOGY.** Charts, graphs, 468pp. AFA70, 8.00c.
A recent reprint of an old astrological textbook. Pearce covers all the basics, and includes information illuminating even the most complex aspects of astrology. Part of the book is devoted to a critical analysis of Ptolemy's astrological teachings. There are also many spiritual references.

PELLETIER, ROBERT. **PLANETS IN ASPECT.** 346pp. PaR74, 13.00c.
Aspects are the relationship between planets in a chart. Most of the astrology texts do not devote much space to aspects, so this definitive text is a much welcomed addition to the literature. Every major aspect—conjunction, sextile, trine, opposition, inconjunction—is covered. In all over 300 aspects are discussed in comprehensive analyses. The general meanings of each major aspect are also presented. The text is fully indexed and forms an invaluable aid to the student seeking guidelines and material for chart interpretation.

PENFIELD, MARC. **AMERICA: AN ASTROLOGICAL PORTRAIT.** Bibliography, 8½"x11", 433pp. Vul76, 13.00p.
This is a very complete presentation of the charts of the cities, states, and provinces of the U.S. and Canada. Basic information on the areas discussed along with historical details are included on facing pages. The book is spiral bound. A well researched work, with easy to read charts.

PENFIELD, MARC. **AN ASTROLOGICAL WHO'S WHO.** 567pp. ArB72, 7.00c.
500 full page natal charts of well known personalities, especially calculated, checked and where necessary, rectified for this volume. Includes a chart of the aspects in each horoscope, and other explanatory material.

PENFIELD, MARC. **THE NADI SYSTEM OF RECTIFICATION.** 8½"x11", 29pp. Vul77, 4.00p.
The nadi is a Hindi system which Penfield tested on over 2,000 charts and found to be remarkably effective. In this pamphlet he summarizes the steps to be followed, gives examples of the nadi system in operation, and offers a series of tables.

PERRY, INEZ and GEORGE CAREY. **THE ZODIAC AND THE SALTS OF SALVATION.** 352pp. Wei71, 13.95c.
A definitive work which explains the relation of the mineral salts of the body to the signs of the zodiac, and esoterically analyzes and synthesizes the signs and their physico-chemical allocations.

PETULENGRO, LEON. **HERBS, HEALTH AND ASTROLOGY.** Glossary, 95pp. Kea77, 2.50p.
A gypsy records some of the ancient Romany beliefs about herbs and their links with astrology. Petulengro devotes a chapter to each zodiacal sign, specifying the herbs which best suit each native.

PUOTINEN, C.J. **COMPUTING HOROSCOPES WITH YOUR ELECTRONIC CALCULATOR.** Offset, 8½"x11", 48pp. NSP77, 4.50p.
Puotinen describes this as *a guide with simple instructions, step by step example problems, a quiz or two, chart computation forms, and information regarding time* corrections, house cusp interpolation, planetary declinations and longitudes, solar arc progressions, secondary progressions, solar and lunar return charts, biorhythms, midpoints, and calculator models.

QUIGLEY, JOAN. **ASTROLOGY FOR ADULTS.** 372pp. War69, 2.50p.
An introductory text, covering the basics of sun sign analysis plus a bit more. Each of the planets is analyzed in each of the signs and some tables are also included. It is not a terribly serious work, but does give an overview for those who are curious as to what astrology is all about. The tables can be used to figure out approximations, but should not be relied on for exact information. Ms. Quigley writes well and her analyses are generally positive.

Sagittarius the Archer.

RECHTER, CHRISTINE. **ELECTIONAL ASTROLOGY.** 8½"x11", 56pp. Lor75, 4.50p.
Electional astrology is the art of choosing the proper moment or birth time for any particular project or event. There is very little material written in this area (please note that electional astrology is not the same as horary astrology). Ms. Rechter has studied and practiced electional astrology and here she draws on her experience to present a set of workable rules in casting and interpreting an electional chart. Many sample charts and case studies are included.

RECHTER, CHRISTINE. **FINE POINTS OF DELINEATION.** 8½"x11", 65pp. Lor75, 4.50p.
This pamphlet is designed as an aid for the student who already knows the basics of chart erection and now wants some tips on interpretation. Many themes to look for and specific topics are touched on in outline form. Though by no means a comprehensive presentation, this volume does present some useful hints.

RECHTER, CHRISTINE. **VOCATIONAL ASTROLOGY.** 8½"x11", 42pp. Lor76, 4.50p.
This is a brief, not terribly enlightening presentation of the basics of vocational astrology. Unfortunately not much has been written on the subject, so if you are interested in it you might find some nuggets in Ms. Rechter's book.

REID, VERA. **TOWARDS AQUARIUS.** 124pp. Arc71, 1.45p.
Traces each of the great ages through its 2,000 year cycle, interpreting the cataclysmic events of each age in the light of the zodiac and its symbols. A large portion of the text is devoted to the coming Aquarian Age.

RICHARDSON, DALE. **PLUTONIAN PHOENIX.** 166pp. AFA74, 7.00p.
Dale Richardson is an astrological writer who is especially noted for his stock market analyses. Though this book appears from the title to be on the influence of Pluto, it is this only in part. The text is a compilation of articles Richardson has published in **Horoscope Magazine** over the last fifteen years, with updating notes appended. Many of the articles do relate to Pluto and the transits of Pluto as they have affected individuals and public events. As a unified presentation, the book does not succeed—but as a collection of randomly presented ideas, there is much of interest.

RIEDER, THOMAS. **ASTROLOGICAL WARNINGS AND THE STOCK MARKET.** Bibliography, 116pp. PPL72, 4.95p.
A study of astrology and the correlation between planetary cycles, investor confidence, and stock market patterns. All the astrological assumptions are tested against the historic performance of the Dow

Jones Industrial Average from 1899 to 1971 and only those which meet the statistical test are accepted. The ideas and concepts utilized in this study are clearly explained and the reader is provided with all the necessary information to do his own market forecasting over the next decade. The author's research and analysis is condensed in a thirty-four inch fold out graph.

ROBERTS, PRESS and IMA. TRANSITS IN PLAIN ENGLISH. 120pp. Vul74, 4.50p.
This is one of the most comprehensive books on transits. Each planet is studied in a separate chapter which begins with a listing of keywords and goes on to analyze each transit connected with that planet and the various aspects related to each particular transit. Includes transits of the full and new moon, the nodes, and the part of fortune.

ROBERTS, PRESS and IMA and DON BORKOWSKI. SIGNS AND PARTS IN PLAIN ENGLISH. Bibliography, 155pp. Vul76, 6.25p.
The title of this book is a bit deceptive. A simple listing of the contents gives a better idea of the areas covered—*Intercepted Signs in the Houses, Arabic Parts, Retrograde Planets, Cusp—Born or Borderline Individuals, The Shaping of a Chart, Qualities, Elements and Patterns, Empty Signs, Psychic Indications in the Horoscope,* and *Eclipses.* Much of the material presented here is not readily available anywhere else and the authors write with a fair amount of clarity. The book is well organized and easy to use.

ROBERTSON, MARC. COSMOPSYCHOLOGY: THE ENGINE OF DESTINY. 100pp. ANW74, 5.00p.
Describes the eight types of human personality, the supporting mechanisms in the personality that deal with self definition, self expansion, self propagation, self transformation, and self maintenance. Cosmopsychology focuses on the concept of a cycle of energy flow within which the aspects of astrology operate. It also deals with the idea of reincarnation and how the personality types are a clue to where the individual is in a cycle of incarnations. As is the case with Robertson's other books, the material is provocative and unusual. The emphasis is on the positive benefits for inner development to be gained through the study of astrology.

ROBERTSON, MARC. THE EIGHTH HOUSE. 75pp. ANW76, 3.95p.
The eighth house is the house of renewal through experience. Robertson describes this book as covering *the astrological interpretation of human change through POWERS OF THE SOUL operating through mysteries in the nature of human potential. It also takes up POWERS OF MONEY in the individual's operation in society, giving suggestions on SIMPLE TRANSITS FOR TIMING INVESTMENTS. And then there is that always fascinating perspective of human experience POWERS OF SEX, giving us the ability to transform individuality.*

ROBERTSON, MARC. NOT A SIGN IN THE SKY BUT A LIVING PERSON. 8½"x11", ANW75, 3.00p.
This booklet presents an analysis of the basic impulses moving through the eight personality types (as defined by the time of the month an individual was born) as they relate to the inner self. This analysis is derived from the lunation cycle expounded by Dane Rudhyar. Robertson also discusses the progression of the moon phases and the *natural outlets* by sign and house for expressing the energy flow and the personality type. As is the case with all of Robertson's books the material in this volume seems to be excellent—but the organization is so terrible that it is often hard to follow what is being presented. This is the first volume in Robertson's **Cosmopsychology** series.

ROBERTSON, MARC. SEX, MIND, HABIT COMPATIBILITY. ANW75, 3.00p.
Reveals how individuals attract or repel one another on the basis of their birth charts. Emphasizes the factors that show quickly whether two people will be compatible. Robertson's books are well thought of by professional astrologers.

ROBERTSON, MARC. TRANSITS OF SATURN. 8½"x11", 73pp. ANW73, 5.00c.
Considers Saturn from every conceivable viewpoint. Gives suggestions on what you can do when Saturn is moving through a sign of the zodiac, a quadrant, a house, and a conjunction cycle with a birth planet.

ROBSON, VIVIAN. AN ASTROLOGICAL GUIDE TO YOUR SEX LIFE. 140pp. Arc63, .95p.
Examines astrology and its relation to the sex life of the individual man and woman. The work is illustrated with seven horoscope charts including those of Oscar Wilde and Tchaikovsky.

ROBSON, VIVIAN. A BEGINNER'S GUIDE TO PRACTICAL ASTROLOGY. 184pp. Wei30, 3.95p.
This is an archaic study which is of more interest as a reminder of how far astrology has come in the last fifty years than anything else. All the basics are covered, including information on chart erection. The material on the planets and signs is heavily dependent on an analysis of physical types and key words. Each of the planets is analyzed in each sign and in each house. A final section is devoted to instructions on calculating directions and on interpreting them. The style is dry and often moralistic.

ROBSON, VIVIAN. ELECTIONAL ASTROLOGY. 224pp. Wei72, 7.50c.
Shows how to choose the best time, as far as astrological influences are concerned, to start a venture or undertaking. Includes general rules and principles of electional astrology; personal elections, i.e., cutting hair, buying clothes, etc.; domestic elections, i.e., employing servants, buying food, cooking; commerce and finance; friendship; medical elections; and much more. Knowledge of the basics of astrology is needed.

ROBSON, VIVIAN. THE FIXED STARS AND CONSTELLATIONS IN ASTROLOGY. 225pp. Wei69, 7.95c.
This is as systemized and as complete as possible compilation of all the information ever written about fixed stars since the Middle Ages. Includes chapters on the influence of constellations, fixed stars in natal astrology, influence of the stars and nebulae, and a chapter on the fixed stars and medieval music.

ROBSON, VIVIAN. THE RADIX SYSTEM. 110pp. Dar74, 5.00p.
An amplification of the system introduced by Sepharial in 1918 to estimate the direction of progress of an astrological chart. Ms. Robson here describes and exemplifies the Radix system, with directions on calculating a directional and minor directional chart, cuspal directions, background material on each type of direction, information on midpoints and parallels, and on converse directions. Half of the text is devoted to an analysis of the effects of directions in the signs and the planets. Includes example readings and tables.

RODDEN, LOIS. **THE MERCURY METHOD OF CHART COMPAR-ISON. 200pp. AFA73, 9.50c.**
This is a method of chart comparison between two people using the planet Mercury. Deals exclusively with the aspects of Mercury in one person's chart to the planets in another person's chart and shows that relationships can be defined with consistent accuracy by this method.

Dane Rudhyar

To me, astrology has no meaning or value except it helps man to understand better his innate potentialities, the unfolding of these potentialities, and the development of humans through the centuries with reference to the planet's biosphere within which it should operate as a harmonious force for further evolutionary growth. Indeed, as I see it, there is no such thing as astrology per se, as an independent entity having strictly defined methods of operation absolutely valid under any circumstances.

At the end of the cycle of the year all that belongs to the realm of the leaves of the yearly plants inevitably decays; but the seeds remain, as hidden centers from which the new life will spring. What humanity needs now are seed-men and women willing and ready to assume the sacred task of self-metamorphosis, individually yet in constant relation to one another.

—*Dane Rudhyar*

RUDHYAR, DANE. **THE ASTROLOGICAL HOUSES—THE SPECTRUM OF INDIVIDUAL EXPERIENCE. 208pp. Dou72, 2.95p.**
Analyzes the twelve houses in detail. Rudhyar considers them the basic astrological frame of reference from whence all else derives.

RUDHYAR, DANE. **AN ASTROLOGICAL MANDALA—CYCLE OF TRANSFORMATIONS AND ITS 360 SYMBOLIC PHASES. 392pp. RaH73, 2.45p.**
A reinterpretation of the Sabian symbols, a symbolic collection of images for each degree of the yearly cycle. It is an attempt to give meaning and significance to life experiences. *The symbols can be applied to any cycle of experience that can be conveniently divided into 360 phases.* Rudhyar feels that the book may be profitably used in the same fashion as the **I Ching.**

RUDHYAR, DANE. **ASTROLOGICAL SIGNS—THE PULSE OF LIFE. 144pp. ShP70, 2.50p.**
Rudhyar believes that each sign represents a state of human experience in which two basic forces are active. The force of day symbolizes individual uniqueness and personality, while night force represents the integration of personalities in society. In his book he discusses each of the zodiacal signs and explains how human meaning and freedom develop from an appreciation of the pulsating rhythm of the forces of night and day.

RUDHYAR, DANE. **AN ASTROLOGICAL STUDY OF PSYCHOLOGICAL COMPLEXES AND EMOTIONAL PROBLEMS. ShP nd, 4.50p.**
Rudhyarian philosophy delving into the astrological roots of parental, social, mental, emotional, and sexual complexes.

RUDHYAR, DANE. **ASTROLOGICAL TIMING: THE TRANSITION TO THE NEW AGE. 246pp. H&R69, 3.95p.**
An excellent philosophical work, originally entitled **Birth Patterns for a New Humanity;** a presentation of historical developments in the Western world combined with an account of the cycles of the precession of the Equinoxes. One of the best statements of Aquarian Age philosophy that we have read.

RUDHYAR, DANE. **ASTROLOGY AND THE MODERN PSYCHE. Notes, 182pp. CRC76, 4.95p.**
This is the most interesting of Rudhyar's recent books. He begins with an analysis of astrology and depth psychology and goes from there to a look at a number of current psychological systems. The relevance of astrology to each is fully discussed and many case histories and examples are cited. An entire chapter is devoted to an interpretation of the natal chart of Carl Jung. We recommend this book to all who are deeply interested in the psychological applications of astrology.

RUDHYAR, DANE. **THE ASTROLOGY OF AMERICA'S DESTINY. 209pp. RaH74, 2.45p.**
In this controversial work Rudhyar provides an astrological key to the social and political problems confronting our government and people. Contrary to other astrologers, he finds that the ascendant of the U.S. is Sagittarius, and this observation makes his analysis of the chart and the future of the U.S. very different from that of most other astrologers. Rudhyar provides a new context for the understanding of the events that marked the establishment of the American national identity, and for both their esoteric and exoteric meanings. Many contemporary events and future trends are discussed in the light of his examination of the birth chart. A very detailed, graphic study.

RUDHYAR, DANE. **THE ASTROLOGY OF PERSONALITY. 500pp. Dou70, 2.95p.**
Rudhyar's most important philosophical work. He seeks to present astrology mainly as a symbolic language; by reformulating its basic concepts and stressing the importance of the study of the chart as a whole rather than merely piecing together many small bits of memorized information and traditional data, he attempts to reorient and modernize the science of astrology. Highly recommended for the advanced astrologer.

RUDHYAR, DANE. **CULTURE, CRISIS, AND CREATIVITY. 4.25p.**
See the Consciousness Expansion section.

RUDHYAR, DANE. **DIRECTIVES FOR NEW LIFE. 73pp. See71, 2.25p.**
An enlightened look at the individual and how he fits into the society of the great transition.

RUDHYAR, DANE. **FROM HUMANISTIC TO TRANSPERSONAL ASTROLOGY. 77pp. See75, 2.50p.**
This is an expanded version of Rudhyar's earlier pamphlet, **My Stand on Astrology.** *This new material introduces the concept of transpersonal astrology, which develops on the foundation that humanistic astrology has built, but refers to a new, more inclusive approach to life. On the transpersonal way, everything in a birth chart is used for transformation, and the outermost planets of our known solar system—Uranus, Neptune, and Pluto—act as guides, pointing the way beyond the limits of the known.*

RUDHYAR, DANE. **THE LUNATION CYCLE. 138pp. ShP71, 3.50p.**
The cyclic relationship of the moon to the sun produces the lunation cycle; and every moment of the month and day can be characterized significantly by its position within this lunation cycle.—from the introduction.

RUDHYAR, DANE. **NEW MANSIONS FOR NEW MEN. 273pp. Ser71, 9.50c.**
This poetic work treats the science of astrology as a system of symbols by which man can understand himself and the processes of life.

RUDHYAR, DANE. **OCCULT PREPARATIONS FOR THE NEW AGE. Notes, 275pp. TPH75, 3.25p.**
This book is not about astrology per se. Rather, it is a study of man and his universe, a study that recognizes not only that the heavens affect us, and we affect the heavens, but also that the evolution of life is a cyclical process; to evaluate correctly the condition of the world today, it is necessary that we retain the long, aeonic, evolutionary view. Rudhyar includes a 1975 overview of Blavatsky's **Secret Doctrine** and a discussion of the *occult brotherhood.*

RUDHYAR, DANE. **PERSON-CENTERED ASTROLOGY. 375pp. CSA72, 5.95p.**
Six essays. The title is derived from Rudhyar's person-centered approach to astrology as opposed to the *event-oriented* approach. He distinguishes between the two and establishes a psychological and

philosophical basis for humanistic astrology. A psychologically oriented interpretation of man's relationship to himself, other people and his environment as dictated by planetary influences. A compilation of his humanistic astrology series.

RUDHYAR, DANE. **THE PLANETARIZATION OF CONSCIOUSNESS. 318+pp. ASI77, 7.95p.**
The author calls this *a book in which is expressed what I trust is a deep and vivid intuition of what existence could mean for this and coming generations of men willing to consecrate themselves to the task of building a new humanity.* It is the fruit of a lifelong creative activity and deep meditation on the nature of man and his relation to the present period of turmoil and its consequences for the future.

RUDHYAR, DANE. **THE PRACTICE OF ASTROLOGY AS A TECHNIQUE IN HUMAN UNDERSTANDING. 152pp. ShP68, 2.50p.**
This book explains clearly the basic methods and facts of astrology and shows how they can be used to attain the ultimate goal of that study: the development of human understanding.

RUDHYAR, DANE. **RETURN FROM NO RETURN. 167pp. See73, 3.00p.**
A *paraphysical novel* set in the twenty-second century which uses the medium of the novel to introduce us to a new concept of space and the possibility of integral existence beyond physical death.

RUDHYAR, DANE. **THE RHYTHM OF HUMAN FULFILLMENT— IN TUNE WITH COSMIC CYCLES. 81pp. See73, 2.50p.**
Essay on flowing with nature through the doorways of great change.

RUDHYAR, DANE. **THE SUN IS ALSO A STAR. 209pp. Dut75, 3.95p.**
Subtitled, *The Galactic Dimension of Astrology,* this is an in depth philosophical study of the trans-Saturnian planets: Uranus, Neptune, and Pluto. These planets, and especially Pluto, are the least understood of any of the planets (perhaps because they have been discovered the most recently). Rudhyar here begins with an insightful study of the solar system and of the differing scientific approaches to the universe throughout history. This theme reoccurs at various points in the book. The bulk of the material is devoted to in depth analyses of the three planets including individual analyses, a study of them in zodiacal signs, and an analysis of their interpenetrating cycles. Rudhyar has done a good job of integrating his philosophical concepts of the nature of the universe with an illuminating astrological analysis. This study of the trans-Saturnian planets is the best we know.

RUDHYAR, DANE. **TRIPTYCH. Ser68, 9.95c.**
Inspiring writing on the spiritual nature and challenge each sign presents to the individual seeking fulfillment.

RUDHYAR, DANE. **WE CAN BEGIN AGAIN TOGETHER. 233pp. See74, 5.00p.**
Subtitled, *A Re-evaluation of the Basic Concepts of Western Civilization in Terms of an Emergent Future for Mankind,* this is Rudhyar's philosophical attempt to explain where we have come from and where we are going.

WHITE, JOHN, ed. **DANE RUDHYAR: SEED MAN. 8½"x11", 28pp. HDI75, 2.50p.**
A selection from some of the many books and articles Rudhyar has written over the years along with a full biographical study—and including some of Rudhyar's art (in color) and music.

————————**END OF DANE RUDHYAR SUBSECTION**————————

RUSSELL, LESLEY. **BRIEF BIOGRAPHIES. 94pp. AAs73, 2.75p.**
This is a very interesting collection of natal charts of noted artists and writers which also includes birth data, family, physical characteristics, physical illnesses, psychological character, relationships, and a chronology of important life events.

SAINT-GERMAIN, COMTE DE. **PRACTICAL ASTROLOGY. 257pp. NPC01, 3.95p.**
The author was a noted occultist. This work presents the basic astrological principles, including chart erection, and then goes into the relationships between astrology and the tarot. Graphically illustrated.

■ *SAKOIAN, FRANCES and LOUIS ACKER.* **THE ASTROLOGER'S HANDBOOK. 461pp. H&R73/DaL, 11.95c.**
An impressive and complete introductory text on the subject of astrology. It includes the necessary information for casting the horoscope and interpreting the chart. The major portion of the work is given to delineations of each aspect. This is the best basic text that we know of for the beginning student and an invaluable aid for all astrologers. Includes a general index and a cross index of aspects. Highly recommended.

■ *SAKOIAN, FRANCES and LOUIS ACKER.* **THE ASTROLOGY OF HUMAN RELATIONSHIPS. 401pp. H&R76/DaL, 10.95c.**
This is the only major textbook that discusses the comparison of natal charts in depth. The book begins with a review of the basic principles of astrological analysis, especially as they apply to chart comparison. The bulk of the book is a study of comparative influences of the planets, by house placement and by aspects. Each of the planets is discussed individually, and at length. There is also a glossary and an excellent long index.

SAKOIAN, FRANCES and LOUIS ACKER. **THE IMPORTANCE OF MERCURY IN THE HOROSCOPE. 41pp. NES70, 2.00p.**
This pamphlet begins with a general discussion of Mercury and then goes on to analyze Mercury in each of the elements, retrograde Mercury, and Mercury in each of the houses.

SAKOIAN, FRANCES and LOUIS ACKER. **LADDER OF THE PLANETS. 27pp. NES74, 2.50p.**
This is a comprehensive essay on the correct planetary sign rulerships and exaltations, including material on the outer planets: Uranus, Neptune, and Pluto.

SAKOIAN, FRANCES and LOUIS ACKER. **MAJOR AND MINOR APPROACHING AND DEPARTING ASPECTS. 38pp. AFA74, 2.75p.**
This is an analysis of the following aspects: conjunction, opposition, sextile, square, trine, semisextile, decile, semisquare, quintile, tridecile, sesquiquadrate, biquintile, quincunx, and vigintile. First the aspect itself is discussed and then the approaching and departing and applying and separating aspects of each aspect.

■ *SAKOIAN, FRANCES and LOUIS ACKER.* **PREDICTIVE ASTROLOGY. Glossary, index, 476pp. H&R77, 12.50c.**
Sakoian and Acker have finally done it. All of their little pamphlets on transits have been consolidated into one volume! The language has been slightly altered, but the interpretative meaning remains the same. There is also additional material on the role of the aspects, the basics of the houses, planets, and signs, and much else. We recommend this book to all who seek a fuller understanding of chart interpretation.

SAKOIAN, FRANCES and LOUIS ACKER. **THAT INCONJUNCT-QUINCUNX. 57pp. NES72, 3.00p.**
Most of the books on aspects do not discuss quincunxes, or do so only very briefly. This is the only book that discusses them in detail through the planets.

SAKOIAN, FRANCES and LOUIS ACKER. **TRANSITS OF JUPITER. 72pp. NES74, 3.00p.**
Each of these pamphlets on transits first discusses the planet transiting each of the houses and then explores the transiting planet conjunct, sextile, square, trine, and in opposition to each of the natal planets.

SAKOIAN, FRANCES and LOUIS ACKER. **TRANSITS OF MARS. 55pp. NES74, 3.00p.**

SAKOIAN, FRANCES and LOUIS ACKER. **TRANSITS OF MERCURY. 80pp. NES75, 3.00p.**

SAKOIAN, FRANCES and LOUIS ACKER. **TRANSITS OF THE MOON. 60pp. NES75, 3.00p.**

SAKOIAN, FRANCES and LOUIS ACKER. **TRANSITS OF NEPTUNE. 78pp. NES72, 3.00p.**

SAKOIAN, FRANCES and LOUIS ACKER. **TRANSITS OF PLUTO. 64pp. NES72, 3.00p.**

SAKOIAN, FRANCES and LOUIS ACKER. **TRANSITS OF SATURN.** 75pp. NES72, 3.00p.

SAKOIAN, FRANCES and LOUIS ACKER. **TRANSITS OF THE SUN.** 67pp. NES75, 3.00p.

SAKOIAN, FRANCIS and LOUIS ACKER. **TRANSITS OF URANUS.** 78pp. NES73, 3.00p.

SAKOIAN, FRANCES and LOUIS ACKER. **TRANSITS OF VENUS.** 72pp. NES75, 3.00p.

SAKOIAN, FRANCES and LOUIS ACKER. **TRANSITS SIMPLIFIED.** 227pp. NES76, 10.95p.
The authors have altered and amended their earlier **Transits of...** booklets and have bound them into one volume. However, the material in this volume is in more of an outline form than the separate booklets. Each of the transiting aspects is described in terms of a series of keywords.

SAKOIAN, FRANCES and LOUIS ACKER. **THE ZODIAC WITHIN EACH SIGN.** 142pp. NES75, 5.95p.
Astrologers have often noticed the differences in personal mannerisms of people who have the same planets prominent in the same signs of their horoscopes....It is not difficult to recognize that, in terms of its quality of influence, a sign of the zodiac is not an undifferentiated continuum, but that different parts or sections of each sign have slightly, and sometimes noticeably, different influences. Several methods are used to determine the different qualities of natives born with planets placed in the same sign. The most widely known and publicized of these is the system of decantes. According to the decante system, a sign consisting of 30° of arc is subdivided into three segments of 10° each. Each of these segments has been found to have the subinfluence or overtone quality of one of the signs of the triplicity (or element) to which the sign in question belongs....Another important and highly useful method of subdividing the signs is the system of duads. By this approach each sign is divided into twelve segments of 2½° each, each segment having the subinfluence of one of the twelve signs of the zodiac.— from the introduction. A detailed discussion of the decantes and duads of each sign is presented in this manual, along with some helpful charts and general explanatory material.

SAMPSON, WALTER. **THE ZODIAC: A LIFE EPITOME.** 450pp. ASI26, 15.00c.
An effusively written study of the inner meaning of the signs of the zodiac based upon the teachings of Christianity and upon the ancient mystery teachings. The presentation is a bit hard to follow, but illuminating insights are offered and the esoteric aspects of astrology are emphasized.

SARGENT, LOIS. **HOW TO HANDLE YOUR HUMAN RELATIONS.** 77pp. AFA58, 4.50p.
A manual giving practical pointers for living in a more harmonious manner with family, friends, and associates. The suggestions and theory presented are based upon astrological considerations in conjunction with the findings of modern psychology.

SCHULMAN, MARTIN. **KARMIC ASTROLOGY, VOLUME I: THE MOON'S NODES AND REINCARNATION.** 133pp. Wei75, 3.95p.
Many astrologers believe that the moon's nodes represent karmic influences at work in an individual's current life. The South Node is symbolic of the past and the North Node represents the future potential. In this volume Schulman gives a delineation of the nodes by sign and house position and also discusses aspects to the nodes. He also presents several sample delineations, illustrating the natal charts and discussing the nodal positions. Yogananda, Gandhi, and Edgar Cayce are among the samples chosen. This volume should by no means be considered a definitive work—Schulman is a young astrologer-psychic just beginning his exploration—however it does delve into areas untouched by other books and the information Schulman comes up with is quite interesting. An appendix gives nodal positions from 1850-2000.

SCHULMAN, MARTIN. **KARMIC ASTROLOGY, VOLUME II: RETROGRADES AND REINCARNATION.** 204pp. Wei77, 4.95p.
Schulman's second offering is no better than his first. If anything it is worse because it is longer. An astrologer friend of ours described it as an astrological novel—so little sense did it make to her. But Schulman's books really sell, in part we guess because there is so little else on the subjects he writes on. If you liked his first book, you will be happy with this one.

SCHWICKERT, FRIEDRICH and ADOLF WEISS. **CORNERSTONES OF ASTROLOGY.** 342pp. Wei72, 10.00c.
Teaches the analytical and systematic approach to horoscope interpretation developed by Morin de Villefranche. Much of the material here is unique to this book. Includes many explanatory charts.

SCHWICKERT, GUSTAV. **RECTIFICATION OF THE BIRTH TIME.** 163pp. AFA54, 4.50p.
A good attempt at elucidation of the difficult task of rectification.

SEHESTED, OVE. **THE BASICS OF ASTROLOGY.** Ura73, 14.95c.
This is a basic textbook for the beginning student, including extensive material on chart erection and interpretation and a long section of tables and reference material. The coverage is very comprehensive— too comprehensive we feel. Some selective editing would have improved the book—this is especially true of the chart erection instructions. However, some people find the abundance of material helpful.

SEISS, JOSEPH. **THE GOSPEL IN THE STARS.** Offset, spiral bound, index, 522pp. HeR1884, 7.00p.
A reprint of a Christian-oriented spiritual text, covering each of the signs in depth and relating them to the biblical tradition.

SEPHARIAL. **ASTROLOGY AND MARRIAGE.** 59pp. Wei70, 3.50c.
The influence of planetary action in courtship and married life is explained. Sepharial discusses harmonizing factors, signs of happiness, signs of discord, the domestic circle, multiple marriages, and children. Case histories of assorted marriages are recorded.

SEPHARIAL. **ECLIPSES.** 112pp. Sym73, 2.95p.
The only complete treatise on eclipses in print which covers all phases of astrological significance and interpretation for application to mundane and individual affairs and charts.

SEPHARIAL. **GEODETIC EQUIVALENTS.** 61pp. AFA nd, 2.00p.
Geodetic equivalents are used in mundane astrology as aids in prediction. It has been found that the longitude and latitude of a place affects the midheaven and ascendant. The geodetic equivalent measures and adjusts these effects. This is a short exposition of the g.e., with proofs of geodetic values, a table of the g.e.'s of principal towns, and a study of sign rulership.

SEPHARIAL. **THE SCIENCE OF FOREKNOWLEDGE.** Offset, spiral bound, 160pp. HeR18, 3.00p.
Sepharial is often not the clearest writer, but his knowledge of the astrology of the ancients is unequaled. In this volume he discusses the astrology of the Hebrews and the ancient Hindus. He also focuses on Lilith and on Neptune and on the radix system as a method of future forecasting.

SEPHARIAL. **THE SILVER KEY.** 94pp. HeR nd, 3.00p.
This is an attempt of Sepharial's to see how accurate astrological prediction could be in relation to horse racing. Includes tables and detailed instructions.

SEPHARIAL. **THE SOLAR EPOCH: A NEW ASTROLOGICAL THESIS.** 90pp. Wei70, 3.50c.
Sepharial claims that man is endowed with an organism capable of responding to impulses from the solar, lunar, and terrestrial planes of existence. If we accept the validity of a horoscope applied to terrestrial life, we must also accept the reality of a further horoscope corresponding to the solar epoch. It is the latter thesis that he explores in this book.

SEPHARIAL. **TRANSITS AND PLANETARY PERIODS.** 94pp. Wei70, 3.50c.
An examination of the problems of transits: their continuity, duration, and the reasons for perceptible breaks in their action.

SEPHARIAL. **THE WORLD HOROSCOPE.** 70pp. Fou65, 7.50c.
Points out biblical references to the influences of stars and lays down the key to the study of scriptural prophecy. Includes interpretations of the world horoscope and period charts of the U.S.A.

Sidereal Astrology

When astrologers talk about the zodiac they usually mean the great circle of the ecliptic which, for all intents and purposes, is the apparent path of the sun, moon and planets around the heavens. There is only one circle of the ecliptic and hence only one zodiac, the ecliptic being as it were the backbone of the zodiac. Because a circle has no natural beginning, different points on that circle have, over the centuries, been held to constitute the beginning of the zodiac.

To talk of the tropical zodiac and the sidereal zodiac as though they were two separate and distinct zodiacs is just false thinking. The fundamental difference between the two is that they commence at different points on precisely the same circle, namely the Circle of the Ecliptic, which is divided into 360 equal parts, called degrees of longitude. So, when we reduce one zodiac to the other, we merely are altering the position of the starting point, and measuring all our longitudes from it, instead of from the former. At present, the starting point of the popular or tropical zodiac is about twenty-four degrees in advance of the sidereal zodiac, counted clockwise. Thus, in order to change from the tropical to the sidereal, all that one has to do is to subtract these twenty-four degrees from all tropical longitudes, thereby altering them into sidereal measurement.

—from **Astrological Origins**, by Cyril Fagan

AYER, V.A.K. **EVERYDAY ASTROLOGY.** 169pp. Tar58, 2.95p.
This is the clearest presentation of Hindu astrology that we have seen. The author has integrated parts of the Western system to make the computations clearer. The whole volume is oriented toward practical use and is the result of years of research and experience.

BEHARI, BEPIN. **INTRODUCTION TO ESOTERIC ASTROLOGY.** 284pp. Sag75, 7.00c.
The first part of this book deals with the occult nature of astrology, the implications of physical death, and the significance of the *Heavenly Man*. The inner meanings of the zodiacal signs are discussed in the second part, and planetary influences in the third.

BHARADWAY, BALCHAND. **ASTROLOGY OF ANNUAL READINGS.** 64pp. Sag nd, 1.50c.
The author presents a Hindu technique which is comparable to tropical astrology's solar returns.

BOYD, HELEN. **THE TRUE HOROSCOPE OF THE UNITED STATES.** Glossary, 174pp. ASI75, 7.25p.
This is a very careful analysis, based on ten years of study. Ms. Boyd feels that the true birth time of the U.S. is July 6, 1775 at 11:00 AM. She presents the chart for this time along with many charts for other possible times and important events in U.S. history. The account includes documented historical data, 100 charts, including ones for each of the U.S. birth times previously advanced by others.

BRADLEY, DONALD. **SOLAR AND LUNAR RETURNS.** 123pp. LIP nd, 3.95p.
Presents information for the beginning astrologer on casting and interpreting solar and lunar returns according to the sidereal zodiac of the constellations, an accurate system of predicting future events. The planetary positions are delineated fully, the meaning of planetary vibrations in daily life is discussed, and the text is illustrated with actual examples.

ESHELMAN, JAMES. **THE SIDEREAL HANDBOOK.** 50pp. ROS75, 4.00p.
This pamphlet discusses and instructs the reader in a variety of sidereal techniques. Step-by-step directions are given in each case and a sample chart illustrates each example.

■ *ESHELMAN, JAMES and TOM STANTON.* **THE NEW INSTANT ASTROLOGY.** Bibliography, index, 8½"x11", 184pp. APr76, 8.95c.
This is the only general textbook on sidereal astrology. All the basics are adequately covered, including terminology and chart erection.

There are also chapters on the constellations of the sun and moon, aspects and angular planets, synastry, and forecasting methods. The material is well written and clearly presented. Carl Stahl's Synetic Vernal Point Tables, 1881-2000 are appended.

FAGAN, CYRIL. **ASTROLOGICAL ORIGINS.** 224pp. LIP71, 2.95p.
Fagan, in the late 1940s and 1950s, rediscovered sidereal astrology, the type of astrology used by the ancients. This is an introductory historical treatment of its origins and development.

FAGAN, CYRIL. **THE SOLUNARS HANDBOOK.** 130pp. Cln76, 5.85p.
A collection of excerpts from a series of articles originally published in **American Astrology Magazine** between 1953 and 1970. The selections show some of Fagan's observations on human behavior in relation to the planets and give instructions on the interpretation of major planetary configurations in sidereal solar and lunar return charts.

FAGAN, CYRIL and ROY FIREBRACE. **A PRIMER OF SIDEREAL ASTROLOGY.** LjP nd, 7.35p.
This is virtually the only instructional book on the sidereal system available. The authors developed the system as we think of it today and this is their basic book. Includes detailed instructions, sample charts, tables explaining sidereal techniques, and a dictionary of aspect meanings.

GUPTA, B.S. **STARS AND HUMAN DESTINY.** Index, 234pp. Sag73, 4.50c.
The author outlines a number of formulas for predicting events after first summarizing his philosophical understanding of astrology. Many case histories accompany the text including an analysis of the horoscope of Sathya Sai Baba.

HYNES, JAMES. **THE SYNETIC VERNAL POINT TABLES.** 21pp. ROS76, 4.50p.
Full instructions for using the tables are given.

JAIN, M.C. **ASTROLOGY AND THE LAW OF SEX.** 215pp. All74, 5.00c.
A treatise by one of India's leading astrologers. Lots of strange material combined with more traditional ideas. Includes chapters on sex abnormality and sex perversion, sex potentiality and sex drive, marriage, love, and much else. Final sections discuss chart comparison and present some case studies.

JAIN, M.C. **MUNDANE ASTROLOGY.** 182pp. Sag73, 4.00c.
A review of the general principles of mundane astrology followed by studies of the planets, signs, houses, and aspects as seen in mundane astrology. There is also material on mundane maps and how to erect them, along with information on judging the maps and examples of maps. The bulk of the book is devoted to analyses of individual houses and *the planets therein*. There are also chapters on eclipses, planetary conjunctions, earthquakes, and comets.

JAIN, M.C. **THE STARS AND YOUR FUTURE.** 194pp. Sag73, 4.00c.
A study of the fixed stars in the signs, with interpretations of each degree in each sign according to the Hindu system of astrology.

KOPARKAR, MOHAN. **MATHEMATICAL ASTROLOGY.** 105pp. AFA74, 4.25p.
An interpretative presentation of the techniques of Hindu astrology. Instruction is presented in all the basic techniques and appropriate charts and diagrams are included. Special features include chapters on planetary period, chart magnification, planetary transits, planetary power, fixed stars, and marriage compatibility. The material is adequately presented, although it is hard for someone immersed in tropical (or Western) astrology to understand this system.

KOPARKAR, MOHAN. **MOON MANSIONS.** 8¼"x10¾", 92pp. Moh74, 4.50p.
Influence of moon on human beings was more prominently observed by ancient Indian astrologers than the influence of any celestial objects. Since the motion of moon relative to earth is faster than any other planet, its effects in a natal chart are to be considered very important. As the moon takes about 27 days to complete one revolution around the earth, it seemed most logical, in those days, to divide the constellation into 27 equal parts. Thus, the distance or space traveled by moon in one day is considered as a moon mansion. The 360°...when divided by twenty-seven lunar mansions, brings each

moon mansion as 13°20'.—from the introduction. This is a step-by-step handbook on reading a natal chart using the moon mansions.

KRISHNAMURTI, K.S. **KRISHNAMURTI'S EPHEMERIS. Sag70, 5.00c/ each.**
Sidereal ephemerides containing the daily positions of all the planets together with complete tables and illustrations explaining chart erection. Two volumes are available: 1941-1956 and 1957-1970.

LITTLEJOHN, FRANCES. **WHAT IS IN THE FUTURE FOR AMERICA OR THE WORLD? 15pp. LjP69, 3.25p.**
Predictions about world events and the lives of well known individuals based on sidereal astrology.

LOCKHART, GENE. **LOCKHART'S SIDEREAL EPHEMERIS OF MARS, JUPITER, SATURN, URANUS, NEPTUNE, AND PLUTO. 35pp. ROS75, 2.00p.**
Gives approximate longitudes for the first day of each month from 1900-99.

LOCKHART, GENE. **SIDEREAL EPHEMERIS. 48pp. ROS, 4.50p.**
Published annually.

MISHRA, BHAWANI. **ASTROLOGY FOR ALL. 200pp. JPH73, 2.95p.**
This is the simplest of all the books on Hindu astrology. The material is taken from ancient Sanskrit texts, adapted to the interests of the modern day. Includes information on what astrology is; on the birth chart; on the signs, houses, and planets; on the planets in the signs and in the houses; on judging the chart; on the timing of events; and on transits.

OMEGA ASSOCIATES. **SIDEREAL EPHEMERIDES. 80pp. OmA, 3.00/each.**
Gives the longitude (in the sidereal zodiac), latitude, right ascension and declination for the sun and planets daily at midnight and for the moon at both midnight and noon. Calculations done by computer. Each one also includes fifteen pages of diurnal and twelve hour logarithms. Extensive explanations and examples show how to make interpolations, calculate solar and lunar returns and progress the solar return. Available for the years 1970 on.

RAO, JAGANNATH. **PRINCIPLES AND PRACTICE OF MEDICAL ASTROLOGY. 219pp. Sag72, 4.50c.**
A Hindu discussion which demonstrates how a natal chart can indicate an individual's predisposition towards certain types of physical and mental troubles.

ROBERTSON, DOROTHY. **ESSENCE OF SIDEREAL HINDU ASTROLOGY. 188pp. BAI71, 5.95p.**
A good introductory explanation of the basics of sidereal Hindu astrology.

SHIL-PONDE. **HINDU ASTROLOGY. 333pp. Sag75, 6.00c.**
A comprehensive basic text with calculation instructions and a great deal of interpretative material.

STAHL, CARL. **BEGINNER'S MANUAL OF SIDEREAL ASTROLOGY, BOOK I. Offset, stapled, 8½"x11", Sol69, 5.00p.**
The only instructional manual in sidereal astrology chart erection available. Includes all the fundamentals necessary as well as tables and charts and logarithms. The detailed instructions are quite helpful but the student would have to be very good at math to catch on to the intricacies of the system without a teacher. Many examples of the various charts are given. The section of instructional material and charts is seventy pages, and the one with the tools is sixty-six pages.

STAHL, CARL. **BEGINNER'S MANUAL OF SIDEREAL ASTROLOGY, BOOK II. Offset, stapled, 8½"x11", 133pp. Sol73, 7.00p.**
Detailed lessons in sidereal natal interpretation gleaned from the author's eighteen years of experience with the system. Questions follow each chapter.

STAHL, CARL. **BEGINNER'S MANUAL OF SIDEREAL ASTROLOGY, BOOK III, PROGRESSIONS. Offset, stapled, 8½"x11", 132pp. Sol75, 7.00p.**
A detailed series of twenty lessons plans, with individual chapters on progressed planets and on aspects of progressed planets.

STAHL, CARL. **MINI AND MICRO-DWADASHAMSA TABLES. 8½"x11", 160+pp. Sol, 6.95p.**
A new method based on the Dwadashamsa (subdivisions of the signs) of Hindu astrology and adapted to both personal charts and cyclic charts by the Paracelsus Research Society.

STAHL, CARL. **SOLUNAR SIDEREAL EPHEMERIDES. Sol, 3.50p/ each.**
Single years, 1960-69 available. Moon positions for every six hours; right ascensions of the sun, moon, and all the planets included with logarithms.

STAHL, CARL. **THOUGHTS ON SIDEREAL ASTROLOGY. Offset, stapled, 8½"x11", 52pp. Sol73, 2.00p.**
A collection of articles from **Spica, A Review of Sidereal Astrology:** *Personally Speaking, House Meanings in Sidereal Astrology, Thoughts on Pluto, Thoughts on Neptune, Thoughts on Uranus,* and *Thoughts on Saturn.*

STAHL, CARL and GARTH ALLEN. **SYNETIC VERNAL POINT EPHEMERIDES. 8½"x11", 25pp. Sol, 1.50p.**
Tables for the years AD 1761-2000.

———————**END OF SIDEREAL ASTROLOGY SUBSECTION**———————

SIMMONITE, W.J. **THE ARCANA OF ASTROLOGY. 434pp. NPC74, 4.95.**
This is a recent reprint of one of the most noted astrological texts of the previous century. Unlike many of the other early texts there is a great deal of valuable information here for the experienced astrologer. We do not recommend this book to the beginner since both the writing style and the abundance of detail would be confusing. Each chapter is followed by a section of related questions—with the answers being given—and many of the items discussed are hard to find elsewhere. Over 100 pages of mathematical and astronomical tables are also included.

SIMMONITE, W.J. **HORARY ASTROLOGY. 8½"x11", 171pp. AFA50, 5.50p.**
A nineteenth century horary text, revised in the late nineteenth century by John Story, and revised again by Ernest Grant (of the A.F.A.) in 1950.

SMITH, HERBER. **TRANSITS. Offset, 8½"x11", 42pp. AFA nd, 4.00p.**
Dr. Smith was Evangeline Adams' teacher. Although this volume suffers from the negative language so often found in nineteenth and early twentieth century works it is still a fairly good, in depth study of the aspects of the transiting planets. The style and the words used are unusual to say the least.

■ *SORIC, JOHN.* **THE NEW AGE ASTROLOGER, VOLUME I. 324pp. StA76, 9.95c.**
This general textbook has the most spiritual bent of any we have read. We have checked charts of friends against Soric's comments on the signs, planets, and houses, and we are impressed with his comments. This book covers all the basics thoroughly and we recommend it to those who seek a sensitive introduction. Soric begins with information on the meaning of the signs, planets, and houses, and integrates philosophy into his comments. He also discusses chart calculation. The bulk of the book is devoted to analyses of the planets through the signs and the houses, rising signs, and aspects.

STAHL, CARL. **VULCAN. 104pp. Sol72, 6.00p.**
Arguments seeking to prove the existence of Vulcan, *the intra-Mercurial planet,* along with detailed tables for the calculation of its zodiacal position, published in the hope that by providing these tables more astronomers and astrologers would accept Vulcan as an actual planet.

STEARN, JESS. **A TIME FOR ASTROLOGY. 435pp. NAL71, 1.95p.**
A well written, chatty narrative, touching on many astrological subjects in a topical vein. Includes sample charts and analyses of famous people. The charts of the U.S. and of many of its presidents are also illustrated and analyzed and the whole is related to contemporary events. Includes ascendant, moon tables, and an abbreviated ephemeris for 1900-75. A good book for those with a general interest in astrology who do not want to get bogged down in detail.

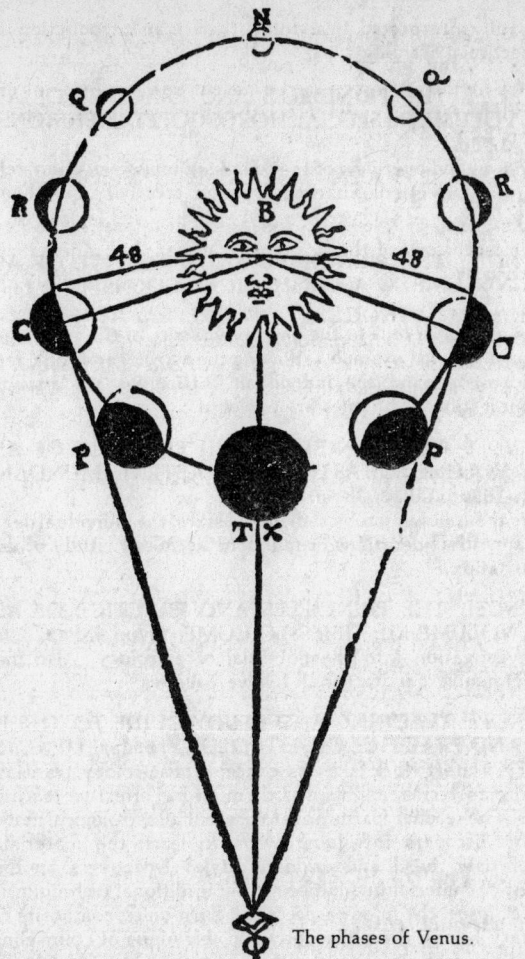

The phases of Venus.

STONE, DIANA. THE UNITED STATES' WHEEL OF DESTINY. Bibliography, 131pp. AFA76, 4.50p.
An interpretation of U.S. history in the light of esoteric mundane astrology. The suppositions that Ms. Stone introduces are entirely her own invention, and, while they are based on research, are undocumented.

STONE, KEN. ASTRODYNES. 75pp. ChL68, 4.40p.
Stone presents a numerical method of deciding important factors in chart interpretation.

STONE, KEN. DELINEATION WITH ASTRODYNES. Charts, 60pp. ChL72, 3.50p.
Gives the basics in the delineations and interpretation of astrodynes in the horoscope, concerning health, vocational selection, harmony, temperament, and compatibility.

TAYLOR, MAXINE. NOW THAT I'VE CAST IT, WHAT DO I DO WITH IT? 86pp. Tay75, 4.50p.
Ms. Taylor is an astrology teacher and she has successfully applied the material presented here with many of her students. Her basic approach tends toward an intuitive understanding of the whole chart through key words and basic sentences. The main topics include the following: the houses, signs on cusps, planets in houses, planets in signs, aspects to planets, aspects to angles, and linking planets with signs. This is a useful interpretative aid for the beginning student.

TAYLOR, MAXINE. WHAT'S A DIURNAL? 50pp. Tay76, 3.50p.
The diurnal chart is an event chart which does not show the actual event or activity but rather reveals the true nature of the event and our subjective reaction to it and takes into consideration the natal, progressed, and transiting planets. This pamphlet begins with a short discussion of diurnals followed by instructions on casting a diurnal chart. The bulk of the book is devoted to twenty-six example charts, with interpretations.

TAYLOR, MAXINE WHAT'S A RELOCATED CHART? 11pp. Tay76, 1.50p.
An individual's natal chart relocates itself every time he leaves his place of birth. The farther one goes, the greater the changes. This pamphlet gives directions for casting a relocated chart along with three example charts with interpretations.

TESSIER, ELIZABETH. THE MEANING OF THE HOUSES AND THE PLANETS. 102pp. IAS76, 4.75p.
A general survey of the houses and the planets, emphasizing the basic ideas they represent. The presentation is psychologically and symbolically-oriented and the mythological background of each of the planets is fully reviewed. A good introductory overview.

TESSIER, ELIZABETH. THE SIGNS AND THE PLANETS IN THE SIGNS. 130pp. IAS77, 4.75p.
This is an analysis of the planets in the signs. The approach is generally positive and often case studies illuminate the discussion. There is also some general information on the signs and sign groups. A useful book for those who are learning about chart interpretation.

THIERENS, A.E. ASTROLOGY AND THE TAROT. 4.95p.
See the Tarot section.

TIERNEY, BILL. PERCEPTIONS IN ASTROLOGY. 8½"x11", 75pp. Tie75, 6.00p.
This is a useful, well written study which focuses on a number of areas which are little discussed in other astrological manuals. The first section is devoted to an analysis of the major planetary configurations: grand trines, grand squares, t-squares, yods, and dissociate aspects. The second section discusses the function of retrograde planets and the transits of retrograde higher octave planets. A final section defines and interprets the hemispheres and the quadrants.

TITSWORTH, JOAN. CASE STUDIES IN HORARY ASTROLOGY. Spiral bound, 8½"x11", AsA75, 5.50p.
This book opens with a discussion of how to place the horary question by house and the strictures to reading certain charts (with example charts). This is followed by two example case studies of questions for each of the twelve houses. Each case is illustrated by the horary chart used followed by the background for the asking of the question, the actual question asked, and an in depth delineation of the horary chart for the answer to that question. The cases themselves are taken from the actual practice of several of New Jersey's leading astrologers.

TOWNLEY, JOHN. ASTROLOGICAL CYCLES AND THE LIFE CRISIS PERIODS. 51pp. Wei77, 2.95p.
We are concerned here with the regular rhythm of event patterns that individuals face, according to the dictates of their horoscopes. . . . The mathematics of celestial mechanics and traditional astrology indicate that everyone must experience certain fixed planetary cycles to which each individual may respond slightly differently, but which nonetheless retain their specific description and flavor. This book describes and, hopefully, helps to clarify these experiences that we all must share.—from the introduction.

TOWNLEY, JOHN. THE COMPOSITE CHART. 47pp. Wei74, 2.95p.
A composite chart is a horoscope of the mutual midpoints of two natal charts. It seems to describe the relationship between two (or more) people. Townley explains the how's and why's of composite technique and its possibilities and illustrates his exposition with many sample charts including Hitler and Eva Braun, Nixon and the U.S.A., the U.S. and the U.S.S.R.

TOWNLEY, JOHN. PLANETS IN LOVE: EXPLORING YOUR EMOTIONAL AND SEXUAL NEEDS. Index, 380pp. PaR78, 13.00c.
Townley delineates each of the traditional horoscope factors in terms of love and sex. He looks at an individual's love life as an expression of his whole self represented by his whole chart. **Planets in Love** contains a 300 word delineation of every planet and the ascendant in every sign, every planet in every house, and every major planetary aspect—550 delineations in all—written in terms of the native's sexual behavior and relationships.

TUCKER, WILLIAM and ELIZABETH TESSIER. CASTING HOROSCOPES PAST AND PRESENT. 94pp. IAS75, 4.75p.
This is a good introduction to the basics of chart erection. All the tools are described and the major terms are defined. The chart erection instructions are clearly presented and examples are given using several

types of systems and ephemerides. There are also interesting sections on ancient astrology, Ptolemy's contributions, the original table of houses, Tucker's system of equal house division, great quadrangles, and Tessier's sundial system.

TYL, NOEL. **THE HOROSCOPE AS IDENTITY.** 279pp. LIP74, 10.00c.
This is not part of Tyl's series. It is his first book. The material is more general than in the other books and it is just as clearly written. The approach is an understanding of the psychological basis of astrology and the text is illustrated with fifty-eight charts. Also includes extensive material on the meaning of Saturn and guidelines for interpretation. It does not overlap the presentation in the series.

■ *TYL, NOEL.* **THE PRINCIPLES AND PRACTICE OF ASTROLOGY, VOLUME I: HOROSCOPE CONSTRUCTION.** 250pp. LIP73, 3.95p.
This is a self contained volume, with tables and practice horoscope blanks. Includes step-by-step instructions on casting the chart, with details on the use of materials and examples; material on placing the planets and measuring the houses; and a calculation review. For the money this is one of the best erection manuals available.

■ *TYL, NOEL.* **THE PRINCIPLES AND PRACTICE OF ASTROLOGY, VOLUME II: THE HOUSES: THEIR SIGNS AND PLANETS.** LIP74, 3.95p.
Presents the rationale of house demarcation; the meaning of the signs and planets in each house; and derivative house readings.

■ *TYL, NOEL.* **THE PRINCIPLES AND PRACTICE OF ASTROLOGY, VOLUME III: THE PLANETS: THEIR SIGNS AND ASPECTS.** 175pp. LIP74, 3.95p.
A good concentrated study including material on the reading of aspects and dignities *at a glance* (not as easy as he makes it sound) and a brief analysis of all major aspects and sun-moon combinations. Graphically illustrated.

■ *TYL, NOEL.* **THE PRINCIPLES AND PRACTICE OF ASTROLOGY, VOLUME IV: ASPECTS AND HOUSES IN ANALYSIS.** 144pp. LIP74, 3.95p.
Much of this book is devoted to aspect patterns, hemisphere emphasis and retrogradation, and to parallels, nodes, and parts of fortune.

■ *TYL, NOEL.* **THE PRINCIPLES AND PRACTICE OF ASTROLOGY, VOLUME V: ASTROLOGY AND PERSONALITY.** 158pp. LIP74, 3.95p.
This volume systematically translates psychological theories of personality into astrological terms and techniques. Tyl's theory is illuminated through analyses of many horoscopes of well known people. This forms a valuable addition to the available material on interpretation.

TYL, NOEL. **THE PRINCIPLES AND PRACTICE OF ASTROLOGY, VOLUME VI: THE EXPANDED PRESENT.** 183pp. LIP74, 3.95p.
Tyl begins with a discussion of prediction and then goes on to clarify the main techniques of prediction: radix methods, rapport measurements, secondary progressions, and his own discovery, *factor-7 timescan.* He explains procedures for quickly estimating and corroborating important developments in the horoscope, and shows how to integrate the various predictive systems. A large part of the text is devoted to an analysis of progressed aspects. As with all Tyl books, the exposition is well presented and illustrated with sample charts.

TYL, NOEL. **THE PRINCIPLES AND PRACTICE OF ASTROLOGY, VOLUME VII: INTEGRATED TRANSITS.** 237pp. LIP74, 3.95p.
A definitive work, modernizing the rationale, analysis, and application of transit theory. Astrology is translated into behavior with many case studies illustrating every major transit. Also includes studies of solar revolution, rectification, eclipse theory, and accidents.

TYL, NOEL. **THE PRINCIPLES AND PRACTICE OF ASTROLOGY, VOLUME VIII: ANALYSIS AND PREDICTION.** 171pp. LIP74, 3.95p.
This volume sets out each step of deduction, analysis, and projection—illustrated with case studies. Radix methods, progressions, and trans-

its are fully interpreted. In addition, there is an introduction to horary and electional astrology.

TYL, NOEL. **THE PRINCIPLES AND PRACTICE OF ASTROLOGY, VOLUME IX: SPECIAL HOROSCOPE DIMENSIONS.** 206pp. LIP75, 3.95p.
Presents a good overview of the following topics: vocation, relocation, opportunity, elections, chart comparison, creativity, health problems, vitality.

TYL, NOEL. **THE PRINCIPLES AND PRACTICE OF ASTROLOGY, VOLUME X: ASTROLOGICAL COUNSEL.** 171pp. LIP75, 3.95p.
This is a detailed look at the psychodynamics of the astrologer-client relationship, with examples showing the astrologer's consideration of the horoscope and the individual. Difficulties are analyzed, and communication techniques are explored.

TYL, NOEL. **THE PRINCIPLES AND PRACTICE OF ASTROLOGY, VOLUME XI: ASTROLOGY: ASTRAL, MUNDANE, OCCULT.** 165pp. LIP75, 3.95p.
Covers the following topics: the fixed stars, the individual degrees and decanates; considerations of mundane astrology; study of death and reincarnation.

TYL, NOEL. **THE PRINCIPLES AND PRACTICE OF ASTROLOGY, VOLUME XII: TIMES TO COME.** 197pp. LIP75, 3.95p.
An investigation into the potential of astrology. Also includes a complete subject index for all twelve volumes.

TYL, NOEL. **TEACHING AND STUDY GUIDE TO THE PRINCIPLES AND PRACTICE OF ASTROLOGY.** 650pp. LIP76, 15.00c.
Noel Tyl's latest work takes the concepts of astrology, translates them into human terms, and frames them within effective teaching techniques. The teacher learns how to present all astrological material; the student discovers intriguing ways to learn the material. In his characteristic lucid and dramatic style, Tyl covers an enormous amount of material in addition to the traditional techniques: the key cycle, eclipses, the minor aspects and harmonics, composite charting, planetary hours, the philosophy and technique of counseling, mundane astrological prediction, and much more. Over 190,000 words tell how every astrological concept from beginning to advanced can be taught and learned. A glossary of over 350 terms is also included.

Uranian Astrology

The basic vocabulary of Uranian astrology consists of the six personal points and sixteen planets (Sun and Moon are not really planets). Eight of these planets exist hypothetically beyond the orbit of Neptune and are therefore called transneptunian planets. These planets (so called) were discovered astrologically by Alfred Witte and Frederich Sieggruen in this century. They have subsequently been verified in thousands of horoscopes by students of the Uranian system all over the world. Words from the Uranian vocabulary are combined together *grammatically* in ways that correspond to the arrangement found among planets in the inscription that is the horoscope chart. The tablet upon which the inscription is written is the ecliptic. The factors of Uranian astrology are arranged with respect to each other in different ways in different horoscopes, because different planets move at different rates. A particular arrangement of planets corresponds to a particular set of meaningful statements. Each horoscope is unique.

—*condensed from* **The Language of Uranian Astrology**, *by Roger Jacobson*

AMBJORNSON, K.H. **DELINEATIONS OF MUNDANE EVENTS.** 8½"x11", 22pp. Amb74, 2.50p.
Presents a technique for delineating mundane events through investigation of the axes of midheaven, sun, ascendant, moon, moon's node, or their respective 45° angles. Planetary equations found on these

axes, or combinations of planets forming a midpoint connection with these axes, will provide accurate information when precise timing has been ascertained. Planetary equations utilizing the transneptunian planets are emphasized. This pamphlet presents two case studies, analyzed in depth.

AMBJORNSON, K.H. **THE HANDBOOK OF THE 90° DISC. 218pp.** **Amb74, 9.75p.**
This handbook has been especially prepared to teach the ninety degree disc technique for finding, simply and quickly, all planetary pictures and midpoints in the natal chart. Not only is it profusely illustrated with drawings to show the methods for deriving these patterns, but it also takes the astrologer step-by-step from the simplest to the most complicated structures. An added feature...is the inclusion of practice problems with answers....While this handbook has been prepared with Uranian Astrology in mind, the material is equally useful in finding the midpoint data for the cosmic structural pictures of Ebertin cosmobiology.—from the introduction.

BRUMMUND, RUTH. **TRANSNEPTUN-EPHEMERIDE: 1890-1990.** **209pp. AFA72, 13.60p.**
Gives positions of the transneptunian planets every ten days.

CERS, ALFONS. **NEW HORIZON ASTROLOGY, PART I. 8½"x11",** **46pp. Cer72, 5.00p.**
Cers believes that Uranian astrology and cosmobiology are the astrology of the future and that the traditional techniques are obsolete. His books are instructional texts in the use of halfsums and planetary pictures. Each contains a number of guided lessons, with solutions. The instructions are not as clear as they might be; however, some of our customers have found them to be useful. The material is keyed to the basic Uranian and cosmobiological texts. This book covers the interpretation of a natal chart and also includes introductory material.

CERS, ALFONS. **NEW HORIZON ASTROLOGY, PART II. 8½"x11",** **45pp. Cer73, 5.00p.**
Covers natal chart calculations, directions, transits, investigations, interpretations, and determinations.

■ *JACOBSON, ROGER.* **THE LANGUAGE OF URANIAN ASTROL-OGY. 252+pp. UrP75, 11.05c.**
This textbook is the best so far available on this complex subject, and most of the information needed to begin to understand Uranian astrology is here. The transneptunian planets are well explained as are the Uranian house systems. The information on *planetary pictures*, the basic technique, is really excellent. Included are some simple meanings of planetary combinations. No index, unfortunately. This book has been badly needed for some time.

KICKBUSCH, ARTHUR. **SOLAR ARC TABLES. AFA, 2.35p.**

NINETY DEGREE METAL DISC. 4.50.

RUDOLPH, LUDWIG. **MEANING OF THE PLANETS IN THE HOUSES.** **35pp. UrP nd, 3.50p.**
Goes into the meanings of the planets in the houses of the various Uranian house systems, using equal houses on a 360° dial.

RUDOLPH, LUDWIG. **RULES FOR PLANETARY PICTURES. 339pp.** **UrP59, 16.65p.**
This is the basic tool for Uranian astrologers and should be bought as soon as Jacobson's book begins to be understood. It presents the basic meanings of planets (including the transneptunians) in pairs and in combination with any third planet. Essential.

RUDOLPH, UDO. **THE HAMBURG SCHOOL OF ASTROLOGY.** **23pp. UrP73, 2.00p.**
A useful explanation of the basics of Uranian astrology, planetary pictures, and house systems.

SHERMAN, SYLVIA and JORI FRANK. **URANIAN ASTROLOGY GUIDE AND EPHEMERIS. Index, ring binder, 200pp. ASO76, 14.95c.**
A discussion of the basics of Uranian astrology, including many specifics, together with an ephemeris of transneptunian planets, 1900-2000 produced by Neil Michelsen. An appendix contains tools and methods for calculating *fundamental sensitive points*, and wheels and graphs which can be reproduced.

320 DEGREE METAL DISC. 5.00.

————**END OF URANIAN ASTROLOGY SUBSECTION**————

VAN STONE, HENRY. **STUDY IN ZODIACAL SYMBOLOGY. 109pp.** **Sym74, 2.95p.**
Scholarly esoteric treatise synthesizing ancient Egyptian and Buddhist origins and significance of the symbols of the planets and zodiacal signs.

VOLGUINE, ALEXANDRE. **LUNAR ASTROLOGY. Notes, bibliog-raphy, 130pp. ASI74, 8.95c.**
Volguine is of the school of astrologers who feel that the role in astrology assigned to the moon is far smaller than it should be, taking into account the nearness of the moon and its influence on our lives. The astrology of antiquity recognized a lunar zodiac, as well as lunar houses, thus portioning out the influence of the moon into three systems similar to those of solar influence. Volguine believes that the twenty-eight *Moon Mansions* of the ancients is a system with a great deal of validity and he presents it in depth in this volume.

VOLGUINE, ALEXANDRE. **THE RULER OF THE NATIVITY. 152pp.** **ASI73, 6.95c.**
Volguine is considered France's most noted twentieth century astrol-oger. This is the first translation of his work into English. This book is devoted to an exposition of his system for finding the strength of each planet, house, sign, aspect, etc. and assigning to each a series of coefficients derived from multiple criteria, astronomical as well as astrological. His ideas are related to Hindu astrology and the book is only recommended to the expert astrologer.

VOLGUINE, ALEXANDRE. **THE TECHNIQUE OF SOLAR RETURNS.** **222pp. ASI76, 15.00c.**
A very complete discussion of solar returns divided into the following major topics: how to calculate a solar return, the relationship of the solar return to the natal chart, the meaning of the planets, signs, houses, and aspects in the solar return, and the timing of returns.

■ *VORE, NICHOLAS DE.* **ENCYCLOPEDIA OF ASTROLOGY. 444pp.** **LtA47, 4.95p.**
This is widely considered the finest astrological encyclopedia ever produced. Virtually every aspect of astrology is clearly defined and the presentation is suitable to both beginning students and advanced astrologers. Many of the entries are comprehensive articles and many tables are also included.

WADE, ELBERT. **ASTROLOGY DIAL-A-SCOPE. 79pp. Arc70, 3.50p.**
Tables and a colored wheel for finding your ascendant and moon, and material on the ascendant, sun, and moon in the signs. Seems to be generally accurate, although not very detailed.

WAKEFIELD, JUNE. **COSMIC ASTROLOGY. 149pp. CSA68, 3.00p.**
This is one of the nicest books on esoteric astrology that we know of. Ms. Wakefield writes well and manages to convey many complicated concepts. All the basics are presented and the reader gets a good feeling for the spiritual underpinings of many seemingly mundane things.

WARREN, ADRIENNE. **MEASURING COMPATIBILITY. Offset,** **8½"x11", 76pp. NSP77, 5.95p.**
Ms. Warren begins with a systematic outline of the basics of synastry and keyword aspect comparisons. The last part of the book contains a *compatibility analysis score sheet* along with instructions for using her point

system to measure compatibility. The system seems extremely detailed and takes many factors into consideration. It is hard to say how valid the results are.

WARREN, DAVID. YOUR BEST PLACE—ASTROLOGICAL RELOCATION TECHNIQUES. Offset, 8½"x11", 40pp. NSP77, 3.95p.
An extremely detailed discussion of relocation techniques, including many example charts and interpretations. Many specific techniques are suggested, along with a fair amount of interpretative material. This is the most complete discussion of the subject we have ever seen.

WATTERS, BARBARA. THE ASTROLOGER LOOKS AT MURDER. 173pp. Val69, 1.95p.
Entrancing analyses of seven famous murders.

WATTERS, BARBARA. HORARY ASTROLOGY AND THE JUDGMENT OF EVENTS. 220pp. Val73, 13.50c.
Elucidates the science of horary astrology with enormous clarity, precision, and style. Case histories that inspire study, along with definitions and guidelines make this definitely one of the best.

WATTERS, BARBARA. SEX AND THE OUTER PLANETS. 222pp. Val71, 4.95p.
A very well presented, unusual study.

WATTERS, BARBARA. WHAT'S WRONG WITH YOUR SUN SIGN. 290pp. Val70, 4.50p.
An instructive and unusual book by a noted astrologer which presents little known facets of the sun signs.

WEST, J.A. and J.G. TOONAER. THE CASE FOR ASTROLOGY. 310pp. Vik73, 1.65p.
A well written substantial account of where astrology has come from and how and why it has grown so in our time. Highly recommended for all who seek to comprehend the scientific basis of astrology. A very important introductory work.

WESTON, H.L. THE PLANET VULCAN. 35pp. AFA nd, 1.50p.
This is an analysis of all that is known about the history and nature of this unknown planet. Also includes tables.

WHITE, G. THE MOON'S NODES. 74pp. AFA27, 1.50p.
A comprehensive account of the nodes and their importance in natal astrology.

WHITMAN, EDWARD. ASPECTS AND THEIR MEANINGS: ASTRO-KINETICS, VOLUME III. 178pp. Fow70, 7.10c.
The effects of the major and minor aspects in their differing locations, together with the meanings, are dealt with in detail. Also contains a detailed description of the influence of a progressed moon and its progressed aspects as well as a chapter on world time differences.

WHITMAN, EDWARD. THE INFLUENCE OF THE HOUSES: ASTRO-KINETICS, VOLUME I. 200pp. Fow70, 7.45c.
First of a series of three books on applied astrology. The influence of each individual house of the zodiac has been analyzed and explained so that the reader may see just how to set about the delineation of a horoscope.

WHITMAN, EDWARD. THE INFLUENCE OF THE PLANETS: ASTRO-KINETICS, VOLUME II. 252pp. Fow70, 8.30c.
Explains how each of the signs of the zodiac has a definite planetary ruler and each planet is more favorably placed in certain signs and less in others. However, the planets possess both negative and positive attributes and therefore, of necessity, must rule over two signs in order that both attributes shall have full expression.

WICKENBURG, JOANNE. IN SEARCH OF A FULFILLING CAREER. 117pp. J&J77, 5.00p.
An astrological guide for understanding and fulfilling vocational needs. This is the most up to date and complete book on the subject.

WILLIAMS, DAVID. ASTRO-ECONOMICS. 8½"x11", 54pp. LIP59, 3.00p.
A detailed study of astrology and business cycles, emphasizing the development of an astrological tool to predict the turning points in mass psychology as applied to the economic field. Williams includes an extensive review of the development of economic thought regarding the business cycle in addition to his analysis of the planetary aspects as they relate to actual economic cycles. The text is illustrated with charts and diagrams, and a long bibliography is included.

WILLIAMS, DAVID. SIMPLIFIED ASTRONOMY FOR ASTROLOGERS. 8½"x11", 88pp. AFA, 3.00p.
More than simply a study of astronomical data useful to astrologers, this is a presentation of the historical ages involved in the precession of the equinoxes. Many details of each age are reviewed and related to astrology. The development of various technical aspects of astrology is also explored.

■ WILLIAMS, KATALIN. ASTROLOGY STUDY GUIDE. 8¼"x10¾", 49pp. Fos72, 5.75p.
Fine simple aid in understanding the symbolism of planets, signs, decants, and aspects. It is presented in the form of a work book, with blank space left for the student to fill in his own information. Includes many fold out pages. Highly recommended for the beginning student.

WILLIAMS, KATALIN. ON CONSTRUCTING THE NATAL HORO-SCOPE. 8¼"x10¾", 59pp. Fos74, 5.75p.
A pretty clear presentation of the mechanics of chart construction, but without many of the samples from astrological tools which are included in several of the other books. Ms. Williams' step-by-step method is well organized and seems to be a good one.

WILLIAMSEN, JAMES and RUTH. ASTROLOGER'S GUIDE TO THE HARMONICS. 435pp. CCL75, 17.95p.
This is a reference work which serves first as a comprehensive catalog of harmonic intervals in astrology, and second as a manual and index defining the meaning, application and scope of harmonic analysis. Over 16,000 harmonics are listed, cross tabulated and indexed. The volume is assembled in a steel ring binder with heavy plastic covers.

WILSON, JAMES. DICTIONARY OF ASTROLOGY. 406pp. Wei1880, 15.00c.
The definitive work, which gives explicit definitions of every aspect of astrology.

WILSON-LUDLAM, MAE. HORARY: THE GEMINI SCIENCE. 65pp. Mac73, 4.50p.
Fourteen examples of horary delineation.

WILSON-LUDLAM, MAE. INTERPRET YOUR CHART. 141pp. Mac73, 6.00p.
A detailed presentation of an excellent method for learning chart interpretation. Very comprehensive and easy to follow.

WILSON-LUDLAM, MAE. THE POWER TRIO: MARS, JUPITER, SATURN. 151pp. Mac76, 6.95p.
The bulk of this book is devoted to an in depth analysis of the three planets which Ms. Wilson-Ludlam terms the modern nucleus of the universal system of cyclic balance. All who are interested in a deeper understanding of astrology should find a great deal of interest in the author's exposition. The book begins with a summary of the basics of astrological analysis and ends with an essay on the Age of Aquarius.

WYNN. THE KEY CYCLE. Offset, 8½"x11", 55pp. AFA nd, 2.50p.
The key cycle is an aid to interpretation of daily, weekly, and monthly influences upon an individual's chart. The details of the cycle and how it was developed are presented here as well as many examples of specific interpretations using this technique.

YOTT, DONALD. INTERCEPTED SIGNS AND REINCARNATION. 55pp. Wei77, 3.50p.
According to Yott, an intercepted sign indicates that in past lifetimes we failed to develop and grow through the qualities of the sign in the affairs of the house in which it appears. In this book he examines each sign and its opposite—as interceptions always occur in pairs—in each of the zodiacal houses.

YOTT, DONALD. RETROGRADE PLANETS AND REINCARNATION. 94pp. Wei77, 3.50p.
This analysis of retrograde planets and reincarnation is based on the pioneering work of an early twentieth century astrologer, Alice Fowler, who believed that retrograde planets indicate the negative character

traits that are carried over from past lifetimes. Yott says that the retrograde planet itself is the focal point for development in this lifetime. This study considers each of the planets in retrograde as they appear in each of the houses.

ZAIN, C.C. **ANCIENT MASONRY. 416pp. ChL73, 5.95p.**
The three fold interpretation of every ritual and symbol of ancient masonry is fully explained. The astrological meaning and derivation of each symbol and its meaning, as applied to the individual and to mankind as a whole, are given along with the principle it contains as used in the unfoldment of the powers of the soul.

ZAIN, C.C. **ASTROLOGICAL SIGNATURES. 288pp. ChL73, 5.95p.**
Deals chiefly with the soul and the manner in which it makes progress; and shows why it was brought into existence, and the eventual form it will occupy. Topics include the zodiac, the mundane houses, reincarnation, and Egyptian initiation. Graphically illustrated.

ZAIN, C.C. **COSMIC ALCHEMY. 288pp. ChL46, 4.95p.**
Discusses how man is not an isolated intelligence, but rather a soul undergoing special training to perform a definite function in the cosmos. Many practical hints.

ZAIN, C.C. **DELINEATING THE HOROSCOPE. 256pp. ChL73, 4.25p.**
Explains how to read a horoscope, how to make the most of whatever natural talents are present and how to select environmental conditions that are especially favorable. It analyzes the thirty-six decants, the keywords, and the qualities of the signs and planets.

ZAIN, C.C. **DIVINATION. 224pp. ChL40, 4.25p.**
A complete analysis of every aspect of the subject, and every type of divination. Includes practical how-to suggestions.

ZAIN, C.C. **ESOTERIC PSYCHOLOGY. 384pp. ChL37, 6.95p.**
Explains how the mind is formed and the laws that govern its working are created.

ZAIN, C.C. **EVOLUTION OF LIFE. 256pp. ChL49, 4.95p.**
An account of each important evolutionary step on earth which shows the important part played by innerplane (astrological) weather, parapsychology, and psychokinesis in adaptation and natural selection.

ZAIN, C.C. **HORARY ASTROLOGY. 256pp. ChL30, 5.95p.**
Presents the math involved in erecting a horary chart as well as extensive interpretative material.

ZAIN, C.C. **IMPONDERABLE FORCES. 224pp. ChL45, 4.25p.**
Explains the destructive uses of occult forces, and how to avoid their effect when directed toward you. The forces and their antidotes are discussed in great detail.

ZAIN, C.C. **LAWS OF OCCULTISM. 224pp. ChL73, 5.25p.**
A complete presentation of the energies used by man and the substances through which they function. Topics include: occult data, astral substance, astral vibrations, doctrine of nativities, doctrine of mediumship, and spiritism.

ZAIN, C.C. **MENTAL ALCHEMY. 224pp. ChL36, 4.25p.**
Explains how what we have within ourselves is attracted from without. In order to change a diseased condition, the discord within the astral body, of which it is an external manifestation, must be healed. This course explains how to apply specific thoughts to accomplish this.

ZAIN, C.C. **MUNDANE ASTROLOGY. 320pp. ChL39, 4.95p.**
Shows how to judge the trends of large groups of people and how to erect and read cycle charts. Text includes almost 200 horoscopes.

ZAIN, C.C. **NATURAL ALCHEMY: THE EVOLUTION OF RELIGION. Illustrations, 256pp. ChL49, 5.95p.**
An esoteric discussion of the process by which both primitive and modern religions have developed.

ZAIN, C.C. **THE NEXT LIFE. 320pp. ChL64, 6.95p.**
Gives a great deal of information about the conditions to be met in the *next life*, and the activities of life after physical death.

ZAIN, C.C. **OCCULTISM APPLIED TO DAILY LIFE. 384pp. ChL nd, 6.95p.**
A very practical guide.

ZAIN, C.C. **ORGANIC ALCHEMY. 224pp. ChL44, 4.25p.**
Sets forth the formula of the *Universal Law of Soul Progression*, the Brotherhood of Light's answer to reincarnation.

ZAIN, C.C. **PERSONAL ALCHEMY. 320pp. ChL49, 5.95p.**
Sets forth the steps and methods best used to attain enlightenment. Half of the book is devoted to stellar healing.

ZAIN, C.C. **PROGRESSING THE HOROSCOPE. 256pp. ChL73, 4.25p.**
A complete explanation of how to progress and a discussion of major and minor progressions of the sun, moon, planets; angles; transits; and rectification.

ZAIN, C.C. **THE SACRED TAROT. 6.95p.**
See the Tarot section.

ZAIN, C.C. **SPIRITUAL ALCHEMY. 160pp. ChL nd, 4.75p.**
Topics include the doctrine of spiritual alchemy, seven spiritual metals, purifying the metals, transmutation, and higher consciousness.

ZAIN, C.C. **SPIRITUAL ASTROLOGY. 416pp. ChL nd, 6.95p.**
Gives a full picture of each of the forty-eight ancient constellations and sets forth the stories associated with each, the outstanding characteristics of those born under each sign, and the appropriate spiritual texts.

ZAIN, C.C. **STELLAR HEALING. 384pp. ChL47, 6.95p.**
Gives the birthchart constants and the progressed constants for 160 of the most prevalent diseases and indicates the specific stellar treatment for each disease.

ZAIN, C.C. **WEATHER PREDICTING. 224pp. ChL49, 4.25p.**
Explains how to predict the oncoming weather by astrology by using temperature, moisture, and air movement charts—and how to draw up the charts.

ZOLAR. **THE HISTORY OF ASTROLOGY. 300pp. Arc72, 7.95c.**
A complete, illustrated history from the Chaldean astrologers of 5,000 years ago to the present day.

ZOLAR. **IT'S ALL IN THE STARS. 318pp. Arc62, 2.95p.**
Mainly concerned with sun sign characteristics. Gives an interpretation for the degree in each sign, compatibility with other signs and a description of each sign as a marriage mate. Also includes a brief history of astrology and a short explanation of the planets and houses.

Calendars

The prices listed below and the descriptions are for the 1978 editions. In later years the price may vary slightly and the format may also be different—although the changes usually are not significant.

■ *CIRCLE BOOKS.* **CALENDAR. Cir, 1.75.**
Includes an ephemeris (with declination of sun and moon), moon's sign, moon's phases, lunar aspects, lunation charts, important phenomena, upper transit time of moon for every day and angle between sun and moon for every day. Also has a short introduction to basic chart configurations and explanations of symbols. Calculated for Washington, DC time.

LLEWELLYN. **ASTROLOGICAL CALENDAR. LIP, 2.95.**
This is the oldest of the astrological calendars. For each day there is data on the moon's sign, phase, and time of change, as well as the best fishing and planting dates. There is also a sign forecast based on the individual lunar cycle, a chart of the planetary transits for each month along with a section containing charts of the new and full moons and solar ingresses and a table of time zone conversions. In addition, there are several articles.

MACGREGOR, MARCIAN. **THE ASTROLOGY ANNUAL CALEN-DAR. Sym, 1.95.**
Includes all the regular information as well as many additional tables. Lists all the major aspects, tables of times of solar and lunar ingress and new and full moons, along with special dates such as eclipses, solstice dates, etc. Also includes weekly planet position charts and a listing of monthly special phenomena and a chart of the symbols and elements of of astrology. Calculated for GMT.

MACGREGOR, MARCIAN. **ASTROLOGY ANNUAL REFERENCE BOOK. Sym, 6.95p/5.95p.**
An excellent tool, equally valuable to both professional and beginning student. It is in the form of a daily diary containing the following information: all the current data for the year, graphically portrayed; space for recording daily events with daily aspectarian and weekly flat chart with planets' places, times of moon's phases and change of signs; a graphic preview of the present year consisting of a flat chart for the first day of each month; a miscellaneous reference data section; and two foldout charts.

MAYNARD, JIM. **CELESTIAL INFLUENCES CALENDAR. QPr, 2.95.**
In addition to the calendar there is an ephemeris presented in two ways: the traditional numerical tables giving sidereal time, daily longitudes, and declinations; and a graphical presentation with plotted monthly planetary motions and directions for superimposing a natal chart over the graph to see the transiting aspects. The calendar includes moon phases, times of sign change for sun and moon, times when the moon is void of course, best days for planting root and above ground crops, and daily planetary aspects. There is also a lunar planting guide along with a general introduction to the planets and aspects and how they might influence our daily lives along with many planetary tables. A pocket version is available for 1.95. Calculated for Eastern Standard Time.

══════**END OF CALENDARS SUBSECTION**══════

Sol

Ephemerides

ARIES PRESS. **THE ASTROLOGER'S EPHEMERIDES. ArP, 8.00c/each.**
Handy sized ten year volumes covering the following years: 1890-1900, 1900-1910, 1910-1920, 1920-1930, 1930-1940. Calculated for midnight Greenwich and considered to be accurate.

DIE DEUTSCHE. **BAND VI: 1971-1980. OTT, 17.00c.**
These volumes are known for their accuracy and their handy size and cloth binding. No knowledge of German is required to read them. The two main drawbacks to them are that the position of Pluto is not listed before 1960 (though separate Pluto ephemerides are available from several sources) and they do not have as many supplementary tables as Raphael's and the Rosicrucian ones. Calculated for noon Greenwich until 1930, after which they are calculated for midnight Greenwich.

DIE DEUTSCHE. **BAND II: 1890-1930. OTT, 19.00c.**

DIE DEUTSCHE. **BAND III: 1931-1950. OTT, 17.05c.**

DIE DEUTSCHE. **BAND IV: 1951-1960. OTT, 20.00c.**

DIE DEUTSCHE. **BAND V: 1961-1970. OTT, 20.00c.**

DIE DEUTSCHE. **BAND VI: 1971-1980. OTT, 20.00c.**

DIGICOMP RESEARCH CORPORATION. **TRUE LUNAR NODES. 156pp. DRC75, 4.95p.**
Daily tables of the true lunar nodes computed for midnight Greenwich and covering the years 1850-2000.

DOBYNS, ZIPPORAH. **THE ASTEROID EPHEMERIS, 1883-1999. 8½"x11", TIA77, 12.50p.**
Precise, daily positions for each of the asteroids along with a great deal of introductory material explaining the importance of the asteroids, their astronomical and mythological background, and giving brief delineations and examples in natal charts. The computations were done by Neil Michelson and the programming by Rique Pottenger.

DONAT, EMMA. **APPROXIMATE POSITIONS OF ASTEROIDS, 1900-1999. 23pp. GeW76, 2.50p.**

ERLEWINE, MICHAEL. **THE SUN IS SHINING. Introduction, instructions, 53pp. Cir75, 5.00p.**
Heliocentric charts have neither houses nor ascendants and consist largely of the various aspects and whole chart configurations formed by the planets in relation to their center...the sun.... Heliocentric astrology lends itself to quick sketches to bring out the basic configurations in effect at a given time...and the absence of a precise birthtime is not felt so strongly as with the geocentric natal chart.... The tables of positions for the outer planets from 1653-2050 were taken from the Astronomical Papers prepared for the use of **The American Ephemeris and Nautical Almanac.**

GOLGGE. **1961-1965. Bau, 7.65p.**
These are very clearly presented ephemerides, calculated for midnight Greenwich. Excellent for daily references.

GOLGGE. **1966-1970. Bau, 7.65p.**

GOLGGE. **1971-1975. Bau, 8.85p.**

GOLGGE. **1976-1980. Bau, 8.85p.**

GOLGGE. **1981-1985. Bau, 14.70p.**

HARDSIL, GEORGE. **ECLIPSES. AFA, 1.50p.**
Background material plus tables covering the years 1865-2000.

HIERATIC PUBLISHING COMPANY. **COMPLETE PLANETARY EPHEMERIS, 1950-2000 AD. Hie75, 25.00c.**
Calculated for midnight Greenwich and includes longitude and latitude tables, right ascension, and declinations.

HIERATIC PUBLISHING COMPANY. **THE CONCISE PLANETARY EPHEMERIS FOR 1950 TO 2000 AD. Hie77, 16.00c/9.00p.**
Contains the same information as in the **Complete Planetary Ephemeris** with the exception of right ascension tables. Also includes tables of lunar phases and diurnal proportional logarithms.

MACCRAIG, HUGH. **THE EPHEMERIS OF THE MOON. Mac51, 6.75c.**
Computed for Greenwich noon, covering the years 1800-2000.

MACCRAIG, HUGH. **THE 200 YEAR EPHEMERIS, 1800-2000. 420pp. Mac47, 15.00c.**
A month by month presentation of the position of the planets. This is not an ephemeris and cannot be used for calculating accurate charts; it is useful as a means for finding the approximate degrees of the planets. Includes selected longitudes and latitudes. Computed for Greenwich noon.

MICHELSEN, NEIL. **THE AMERICAN EPHEMERIS. 9½"x12", ACS76, 5.00p/each.**
Michelsen's superb ephemeris, available in ten year bands covering the following years: 1931-1940, 1941-1950, 1951-1960, 1961-1970, 1971-1980, 1981-1990.

■ *MICHELSEN, NEIL.* **THE AMERICAN EPHEMERIS, 1901-1930.** **10"x12", ACS77, 17.50c/12.95p.**
This is a companion volume to Michelsen's 1931-1980 ephemeris. The ephemeris format is exactly the same and it is equally accurate. Time and logarithm tables are included.

■ *MICHELSEN, NEIL.* **THE AMERICAN EPHEMERIS, 1931-1980, AND BOOK OF TABLES. 10"x12", 726pp. ACS76/Fow, 25.00c.**
Michelsen is well known for his excellent astrological computer programs. This ephemeris is a master work. It gives daily longitudes, latitude and declination of sun and planets at midnight, moon at midnight and noon, all moon phenomena including mean and true nodes, and a complete aspectarian. Also included are complete Placidus tables of houses, time tables, interpolation tables, and complete instructions on casting a natal horoscope. Highly recommended.

MICHELSEN, NEIL. **THE COMPLETE MIDPOINT EPHEMERIS. Spiral bound, 11"x8½", 26pp. AsB77, 2.50p.**
Published yearly.

OMEGA ASSOCIATES. **PLUTO EPHEMERIS, 1773-2000. OmA, 5.00p.**
Longitude, latitude, and declination at ten day intervals, calculated for Greenwich midnight.

PALMER, LYNNE. **PLUTO EPHEMERIS. AFA74, 10.00p.**
This is by far the most complete Pluto ephemeris available, giving daily positions for the years 1900-2000.

RAMUS, CARL. **EPHEMERIS OF THE GREAT COMETS. AFA, 2.75p.**
Covers the years 1402-1948.

RAPHAEL. **ASTRONOMICAL EPHEMERIS. Fou, 2.55/each.**
Single years, 1900-present. Calculated for noon Greenwich. Considered more accurate than the Rosicrucian ephemerides and also contains more supplementary tables. The more recent tables include a daily listing for Pluto.

RAPHAEL. **GEOCENTRIC LONGITUDES AND DECLINATIONS. 35pp. Fou nd, 1.35p.**
For Neptune, Herschel, Saturn, Jupiter, and Mars for the first of each month from 1900-2001.

ROSICRUCIAN FELLOWSHIP. **SIMPLIFIED SCIENTIFIC EPHEMERIS. Ros.**
Single years, 1900-present, 1.50/each; ten years, 1880-89, 1890-99 etc. to 1990-99, 8.00p/each. Calculated for Greenwich noon.

SIMMONS, A. LEROI. **EPHEMERIDES, 1890-1950. ArB nd, 20.00c.**
Positions of planets and the moon's nodes every day, Pluto's positions every eight days, latitudes, longitudes and time zones of major world cities. Generally considered quite accurate. Calculated for Greenwich noon.

TUCKERMAN, BRYANT. **PLANETARY, LUNAR, AND SOLAR POSITIONS, 601 BC to AD 1. 9½"x12", 341pp. APS62, 8.10c.**
Astronomical tables, prepared by computer, giving the positions at five day and ten day intervals.

TUCKERMAN, BRYANT. **PLANETARY, LUNAR, AND SOLAR POSITIONS, AD 2 TO AD 1649. 9½"x12", 842pp. APS64, 13.45c.**
Astronomical tables giving the position of the sun, moon, and major planets at ten day intervals (with five day intervals for the moon, Mercury, and Venus). The tables were prepared by computer and are extremely accurate.

————— END OF EPHEMERIDES SUBSECTION —————

General Tools

AMERICAN FEDERATION OF ASTROLOGERS. **ASTRO DISCS. AFA, 5.50/set.**
A set of four plastic templates for making chart forms, 3", 4", 5", and 6".

ASTRO NUMERIC SERVICE, ed. **AFA ASTROLOGICAL ATLAS OF THE UNITED STATES. 336pp. AFA76, 15.00c.**
The title is deceptive for no maps are included. The latitudes and longitudes for over 30,000 towns and cities are given along with time conversions. Personally, we feel that the book is overpriced and that the student would be better off with a good atlas which contains maps and which also covers the entire world—although the time conversion is a helpful feature.

CIRCLE BOOKS. **ASPECT FINDER. Cir, 2.25.**
This is the nicest of the aspectors. It has a large, easy to ready dial and is made of heavy cardboard with protective coating. Includes opposition, conjunction, square, trine, sextile, semi-square, semi-sextile, quincunx, quintile, septile, novile, bi-quintile, and sesquiquadrate. All clearly marked with orbs given for all major aspects. Reverse side gives aspect and interpretation keywords.

DERNEY, EUGENE. **LONGITUDES AND LATITUDES IN THE U.S. AFA, 6.00c.**

DOANE, DORIS CHASE. **TIME CHANGES IN CANADA AND MEXICO. AFA nd, 7.00p.**

DOANE, DORIS CHASE. **TIME CHANGES IN THE U.S.A. AFA nd, 10.00.**

DOANE, DORIS CHASE. **TIME CHANGES IN THE WORLD. AFA nd, 8.00p.**

ERLEWINE, MICHAEL and MARGARET. **ASTROPHYSICAL DIRECTIONS. 8½"x11", 140pp. Cir77, 10.00p.**
This book gives the clearest explanation of the three different coordinate systems which form the basis of astrology that we have seen. It gives explanations of every aspect of the solar system from planets and asteroids to galactic nebulae. The last section of the book consists of tables which allow you to locate all of the astronomical phenomena in your own chart. Throughout the book the Erlewines communicate the deep spiritual significance they have found in taking the whole universe into account in their study of astrology.

ESPENSHADE, EDWARD and JOEL MORRISON, eds. **GOODE'S WORLD ATLAS, 9"x11", 372pp. RMN78, 12.95c.**
In addition to being a fine atlas, this book contains the largest selection of latitudes and longitudes available anywhere.

FORREY, ALYSE. **MIDPOINT/HALFSUM LOCATOR. AIR, 8.50.**
This is an extremely well produced plastic wheel which is especially useful for those astrologers who use the cosmobiology system.

GRANT, ERNEST. **TABLES OF DIURNAL PLANETARY MOTION. 165pp. AFA nd, 5.00p.**
The purpose of this time saving tool is to provide the necessary calculations in order to find the exact positions of the planets for the given time of birth. If this table is not used the student will have to use logarithms—which are rather uncomplicated but do add extra steps and can be a source of arithmetic error.

GRANT, ERNEST. **TALES OF MIDHEAVENS, ASCENDANTS, AND SIDEREAL TIME. AFA nd, 4.25p.**

HUGHES, DOROTHY. **INSTANT ASPECTARIAN. Hug, 2.00.**

HUGHES, DOROTHY. **INSTANT HOROSCOPE DELINEATOR. Hug, 2.00.**
A quick—though not always totally accurate—way to find the ascendant.

JONES, ALLEN. **EASY TABLES. 38pp. GSR73, 3.00p.**
Includes the following: Diurnal Logarithms; Terrestrial Longitude to Longitude Time and/or Sidereal Time to Right Ascension and Celestial Longitude; Minutes and Seconds of Arc to Decimals of a Degree

and/or Decimals of a Degree to Minutes and Seconds of Arc; Corrections for Longitude Time and G.M.T. Interval. All with examples.

LIBIN, ARTHUR. **TABLES OF DIURNAL PLANETARY MOTION. 186pp. ASI75, 2.00p.**
This is a very complete set of tables, recently produced by computer and hopefully very accurate. Includes three sets of tables: I, used for calculating the apparent motion of the sun for each minute of the day, and for every three seconds of longitude within the range of the sun's apparent motion; II, covers the range of diurnal motion of the moon and all the planets; III, allows for a more precise calculation when the moon's position is given for seconds of arc (used in solar and lunar returns and cyclic charts).

LOGARITHM CARDS. AFA, .25.
A large table on heavy paper.

MAYNARD, JIM. **DIURNAL PLANETARY MOTION. 32pp. QPr75, 2.00p.**
Contains diurnal proportional logarithms, and tables of diurnal planetary motion. The tables are in three groups: solar motion, lunar motion, and planetary motion. The tables of solar motion are calculated in minutes and seconds of arc; the tables of lunar motion and planetary motion are for calculations to the nearest minute of arc.

ORBIMETRIX CO. **ASTROLOGER'S PLANETARY SLIDE RULE. OrC, 5.10**
An accurate, timesaving tool for the computation of intermediate planetary positions (longitude, latitude, declination) that takes the place of the more cumbersome diurnal logarithms or interpolation tables. It shows the proportional motion of the moon and the planets accurately to one minute of an arc and that of the sun to one-three seconds of an arc. Includes an instruction booklet.

PRESS TYPE ASTROLOGICAL SYMBOLS. AFA, 3.75/sheet.
Assorted sizes from about ⅛" to ½".

RAND MCNALLY. **THE INTERNATIONAL ATLAS. 11"x15", 557pp. RMN74, 45.00c.**
Over 300 pages of maps and the longitudes and latitudes for more than 160,000 places in the comprehensive index. We looked up the most obscure places we could think of and they were all listed!

STAHL, CARL. **TABLES OF ASCENSIONAL DIFFERENCES. 35pp. Sol, 2.00p.**
Gives a step-by-step procedure for calculating tables of ascentional differences for any latitude along with tables for Washington, DC (38°44' N Lat) and for Bay City, Michigan (43°18').

──────**END OF GENERAL TOOLS SUBSECTION**──────

Tables of Houses

ARIES PRESS. **TABLES OF HOUSES EQUATOR TO 66° NORTH LATITUDE. ArP nd, 4.00p.**
Similar to the Rosicrucian tables in format.

ASTRO NUMERIC SERVICE. **AFA TABLE OF HOUSES: CAMPANUS SYSTEM, KOCH SYSTEM, PLACIDUS SYSTEM. 8¾"x11¼", about 175pp/each. AFA77, 12.00c/each.**
Three different books, each contains clear, readable, computer derived tables covering the range of latitudes from 0°-66° and listing all cusps to one tenth of a minute of arc.

COPRIVIZA, R.C. **CAMPANUS TABLES. Spiral bound, 8½"x11", Cop73, 7.00p.**
This spiral bound book is the only complete Campanus table and it is very clearly laid out and printed. Calculations were done by an IBM computer from Equal Division of the Prime Vertical, complete from 1° to 60° North latitude.

DALTON, JOSEPH. **TABLE OF HOUSES. 8½"x11", Mac nd, 6.95c.**
Covers 22°-60° North latitude. This is the table of houses that we recommend; it is the easiest to read and is very accurate. Includes instructions.

JONES, J. ALLEN. **MECHANICS OF TABLES OF HOUSES. 8½"x11", 65pp. GSR74, 6.00p.**
Shows all necessary angles and arcs with explanations of the necessary math for Placidus, Regiomontanus, and Campanus methods of house division, with examples and diagrams. Also included in this volume is the procedure for calculating Placidian cusps for above the Arctic Circle.

KOCH. **BIRTHPLACE TABLE OF HOUSES. ASI77, 10.00c/7.50p.**
This is the house system that is used most frequently in Europe. Astrologers who use it find that they can make aspects to the house cusps. 0°-66° North latitude, with calculations for southern latitudes.

LORENZ, DONA. **TOOLS OF ASTROLOGY: THE HOUSES. 127pp. EGP73, 3.50p.**
One of the biggest arguments in astrology today is which house system to use. This book discusses nine methods of house division: Alcabitius, Campanus, Morinus, Placidus, Porphry Regiomontanus and Equal House. Each method of house division is defined and the house sizes of different methods of division are compared and illustrated. Also included are the latitudes and longitudes of over 200 urban areas of the world; sidereal time for the years 1800-2045; and separate tables for determining the longitude of the ascendant, the longitude of the medium coeli, the longitude of the sun, and the size of semi arcs.

MARR, ALEXANDER. **CAMPANUS TABLE OF HOUSES. 60pp. Sol nd, 2.50p.**
Covers 35°-46° North latitude. Mimeographed text is sometimes faint, but readable.

MICHELSEN, NEIL. **AMERICAN BOOK OF TABLES. PaR76, 5.00p.**
This book reprints the following sections from Michelsen's larger book: Placidus Tables of Houses, time tables, interpolation tables and complete instructions on casting a natal chart.

OCCIDENTAL DATA. **THE OCCIDENTAL TABLE OF HOUSES. Spiral bound, 8½"x11", 135pp. Occ72, 8.95p.**
Latitudes 0°-66° North—according to the systems of Campanus, Regiomontanus, and Placidus. Can be used for the Equal House system and tables are also valid for the southern hemisphere. The text was done by a computer.

POLICH, VENDEL. **THE TOPOCENTRIC SYSTEM WITH TABLE OF HOUSES AND OBLIQUE ASCENSION FOR ALL LATITUDES 0°-90°. Spiral bound, 9"x13", 192pp. AFA75, 15.00p.**
When the zodiacal circle is cut into twelve arcs the arcs normally come out unequally. With the topocentric system of houses they come out perfectly even. *This system turned out to be a magic one, because it not only solved the problem of true house division but also carried us along from one discovery to another until we arrived at the point where we could obtain through it astrological correlations of sudden events...with an accuracy of one second of time.*

RAPHAEL. **TABLE OF HOUSES FOR NORTHERN LATITUDES. Fou nd, 2.50p.**
0°-60° North latitude. Incredibly small print.

ROSICRUCIAN FELLOWSHIP. **SIMPLIFIED SCIENTIFIC TABLE OF HOUSES. 313pp. Ros49, 5.25p.**
0°-66° North latitude.

STAHL, CARL. **STAHL'S OCTOSCOPE TABLES OF HOUSES, CAMPANUS DOMNIFICATION. 8½"x11", 75pp. Sol74, 4.00p.**
0°-60° North latitude. Gives midheaven for each minute; ascendants for each four minutes for each degree of latitude; together with a set of tables for the Octoscope House Cusps and meridians (as well as tables for the twelve-fold houses and medians).

──────**END OF TABLES OF HOUSES SUBSECTION**──────

Astrology Subject Index

Palmer - ABC of Chart Reading
Rechter - Fine Points of Delineation
Taylor - Now That I've Cast It
Wilson-Ludlam - Interpret Your Chart

MEDICAL
Cornell - Encyclopedia of Medical Astrology
Culpeper - Astrological Judgment of Disease
Davidson - Set of Lectures on Medical Astrology
Duz - A Practical Treatise of Astral Medicine and
Therapeutics
Garrison - Medical Astrology
Heindel - Astro-Diagnosis
Jansky - Astrology, Nutrition, and Health
Jansky - Modern Medical Astrology
Zain - Stellar Healing

MUNDANE
Blackman - Astrology
Carter - Introduction to Political Astrology
Jones - Mundane Perspectives in Astrology
Osten - The Astrological Chart of the U.S.
Penfield - America
Rudhyar - The Astrology of America's Destiny
Stone - The U.S. Wheel of Destiny

PLANETS
Allen - Taking the Kid Gloves Off Astrology
Brunhubner - Pluto
Elenbaus - Focus on Neptune
Elenbaus - Focus on Pluto
Greene - Saturn
Hawkins - Transpluto
Hickey - Pluto or Minerva
Holley - Pluto/Neptune
Jayne - The Unknown Planets
Leinbach - Planets and Asteroids
Leo - Art of Synthesis
Leo - Jupiter
Leo - Mars
Leo - Saturn
Lowell - Pluto
Mayo - The Planets and Human Behavior
Rudhyar - The Sun is Also as Star
Stahl - Vulcan
Tyl - The Planets
Whitman - The Influence of the Planets
Wilson-Ludlam - The Power Trio

PROGRESSIONS AND PREDICTIONS
Bradley - Solar and Lunar Returns
Davison - The Technique of Prediction
Doane - Progressions in Action
Dobyns - Progressions, Directions, and Rectification
Jayne - Progressions and Directions
Jinni and Joanne - When Your Sun Returns
Jones - The Scope of Astrological Prediction
Kemp - Progressions
Keyes - Progression Formulas
Koparkar - Precise Progressed Charts
Leo - The Progressed Horoscope
Lowell - Secondary Progressions
McDow and Graziano - The A.C.D./L.D. Methods of
Progressions Simplified

Mason and Shepherd - Lunations and Predictions
Milburn - Progressed Horoscope Simplified
Orser and Brightfield - Predicting With Astrology
Palmer - ABC of Major Progressions
Robson - The Radix System
Tyl - The Expanded Present
Tyl - Analysis and Prediction
Zain - Progressing the Horoscope

PSYCHOLOGICAL
Arroyo - Astrology, Karma and Transformation
Arroyo - Astrology, Psychology and the Four Elements
Carter - An Encyclopedia of Psychological Astrology
Goodman - Psychological Astrology
Greene - Relating
Rudhyar - An Astrological Study of Psychological
Complexes and Emotional Problems
Rudhyar - Astrology and the Modern Psyche
Rudhyar - The Astrology of Personality
Rudhyar - From Humanistic to Transpersonal Astrology
Rudhyar - Person Centered Astrology
Tyl - Astrology and Personality

RECTIFICATIONS
Bailey - The Prenatal Epoch
Dobyns - Progressions, Directions and Rectification
Gordon - Rectification of Uncertain Birth Hours
Howell - Cyclic Astrology
Jayne - The Technique of Rectification
Lindanger - Your Sun's Return
Penfield - The Nadi System
Schwickert - Rectification of the Birth Time

TEXTBOOKS
George - A to Z Horoscope Maker and Delineator
Green - The Astrologer's Manual
Heindel - The Message of the Stars
Hickey - Astrology, A Cosmic Science
Hone - Modern Textbook of Astrology
Jones - Astrology: How and Why It Works
Leo - Astrology for All
Lewi - Heaven Knows What
Moore - Astrology: The Divine Science
Parker - Astrology and Its Practical Application
Sakoian and Acker - The Astrologer's Handbook
Sehested - The Basics of Astrology
Simmonite - The Arcana of Astrology
Soric - The New Age Astrologer

TRANSITS
Darr - Transits
Ebertin - Transits
Elsnau - Astrologer's Notebook on the Aspects of the
Transiting Planets
Foelsch - Transits
Hand - Planets in Transit
Roberts - Transits in Plain English
Robertson - Transits of Saturn
Sakoian and Acker - Predictive Astrology
Smith - Transits
Tyl - Integrated Transits

ASTRONOMY

For thousands of years people have gazed into the star-filled nighttime sky and felt a sense of mystery and wonder. Even in the most ancient times, before recorded history, people have marveled at the orderly workings of the heavens. The rising and setting of the sun, the silver moon going through its phases, the drama of an eclipse, and the wanderings of the planets among the constellations of the zodiac proved sufficient to inspire our ancestors to take up the study of astronomy.

In retrospect, the depth of insight and the dedication to knowledge demonstrated in many of these ancient civilizations is truly incredible. The architects of the pyramids and the builders of Stonehenge clearly had a great wealth of information at their fingertips, astronomical information that could only have been gathered over decades or generations of patient, careful observation. From the extensiveness of these observations it can only be concluded that ancient men and women were far more interested in astronomy than people today living in the so-called *space age*. Indeed, in a certain sense it may be said that the building of Stonehenge 5,000 years ago was a far more impressive accomplishment for humanity than traveling to the moon during the last decade. This is especially apparent when we consider the miniscule cost of our space program and how it has touched our lives. At the height of the Apollo program, the annual cost was comparable to the amount of money Americans spend each year on dog food, one third of what they spend on cigarettes, and one seventh of what they spend on liquor. Compare this with the fact that thousands of years ago urban centers, such as those found in Central America, were built with key astronomical orientations in mind.

Regardless of one's viewpoint or orientation, all knowledge of the universe must begin with some sort of observations. But few human beings are satisfied with endless observations alone. It is not enought to go out night after night and merely record the positions of the stars and planets or to take endless photographs. Instead, at some point we are all inclined to ask why things are the way they are. At some point we want to know why and how the planets move, or we want to know why galaxies have certain sizes and shapes. To various degrees, over the ages human beings have always felt that there was some level of order to the universe. The regular rising and setting of the sun over the years, or the moon going through the same phases every four weeks, implies order rather than chaos. It is this appearance of order that gives rise to the hope of finding a deeper understanding of the universe.

A collection of ideas or a hypothesis that expresses this understanding of the universe and from which astronomical observations can be explained is called a *cosmology*. Every civilization and every religion to appear on our planet has had a cosmology at the core of its teachings. The nature and content of a cosmology is profoundly dependent on the culture from which the cosmology originated. In the most ancient civilizations, cosmological ideas were said to be transmitted from the gods through high priests and occult initiates. In later times, beginning with the Greeks, people relied more on direct observations of the heavens. In view of the wide range of accepted methods for obtaining an understanding of the universe, we are not surprised by the colorful and often contradictory theories of the cosmos which were prevalent in different societies. Some of these theories consist of myths and legends that reveal far more about the universe; other ideas demonstrate a rudimentary application of what we today might call the *scientific method*. And we wonder if it is possible that thousands of years from now the astronomy and astrophysics of the twentieth century will be looked upon as fantasy and myth.

Of course, a cosmology is dependent on available observations, and no intelligent astronomer would deny that theories should be modified or even abandoned as new information comes to light. However, in a much more profound sense, a cosmology is affected by a wide range of axioms and assumptions that frequently are unexamined and unquestioned. For example, modern psychology teaches that the way in which children learn to process sensory information and formulate concepts and ideas results in a particular way of seeing the world. Thus human beings systematically exclude or include certain data according to prior psychological conditioning. And modern scientists, who with wide-eyed innocence protest their objectivity, are actually as biased as the Catholic priests who persecuted Galileo. The priests who declined Galileo's invitation and refused to look through his telescope at the moon, Venus, or Jupiter, did so simply because this was not an accepted methodology for obtaining insights into the beauty and harmony of God's universe.

We find that we are all easily seduced by modern science. After all, it works. Astronomers can calculate when the sun will rise tomorrow, and we find that at the prescribed instant the dazzling solar disk appears above the unobscured eastern horizon. Pioneer 10 sends back photographs of Jupiter, and the Apollo astronauts land on target on the moon and return safely.

Modern science is clearly mechanistic, not in the crude sense of gears and levers, but rather in terms of what is considered relevant. The only portions of reality considered truly important in modern science are those which can be measured and recorded by machines. The use of mechanical instruments such as telescopes, spectroscopes, galvanometers, and photographic film has the obvious effect of including or excluding precisely those portions of the total possible world-experience prescribed by the methodology of modern science. The inherent assumption that the true nature of reality is only that which can be recorded by machines reduces the modern scientist to the role of a *one-eyed, colorblind onlooker*.

If we are to continue on this planet as a viable species, we must formulate new paradigms on which a postindustrial science can be developed. These new directions in science must have the precision and predictive power to which we have become accustomed, yet must be permeated with an awareness of the relationships between ourselves and the universe, between the microcosm and the macrocosm. In a postindustrial society we can no longer afford the luxury of ignorance concerning the directions of science. The average citizen cannot afford to sit back, cajoled by the professional elitism of the scientist, and be uninterested in the future course of science. Conversely, the professional scientist must recognize his or her moral responsibility to inform the public, lest in the face of aggressive technology we find ourselves impotently trying to cope with the dubious *benefits* and ill-conceived applications of pure research.

Perhaps in astronomy more than in any other physical science we find the best opportunity to develop this awareness. Over the centuries many of the most important and fundamental discoveries of physical science have come from studying the universe. For example, in the motions of the planets the scientist sees the laws of mechanics revealed in their purest and simplest form, unhampered by the friction and wind resistance encountered in the laboratory. It is no wonder, then, that Sir Isaac Newton was able to set the foundation of classical mechanics from his understanding of the workings of the solar system. Therefore, by examining the frontiers of modern astronomy we might well obtain insight into the future course of science.

—condensed from **The Cosmic Frontiers of General Relativity**, by William J. Kaufmann, III

ALLEN, RICHARD H. **STAR NAMES: THEIR LORE AND MEANING.** **Bibliography, indices, 577pp. Dov1899, 5.00p.**
In this study, based on the writings of ancient astronomers, Allen discusses the names various cultures have given the constellations, the literary and folkloric uses that have been made of the stars through the centuries, and the often incredible associations that the ancients established with the stars. Each star is discussed independently.

ALLER, LAWRENCE. **ATOMS, STARS, AND NEBULAE. Index, 359pp. HUP71, 5.00p.**
This is a revised and updated version of an earlier highly praised edition by the same name, by Aller and Professor Leo Goldberg. The text is fairly technical and is geared toward the knowledgeable layman and the beginning student of astronomy. The author explains how the astronomical explorer finds the distances of stars and nebulae, and how, on the basis of atomic structure, the constitution of stars can be determined. After a brief, nonmathematical excursion into the principles of atomic physics and of optics, Aller explains in nontechnical language the physical processes at work in the interiors and exteriors of stars and discusses the evolution of stars, the production of novae and of supernovae, the interstellar medium, quasars, and pulsars. Includes many technical drawings, graphs, and photographs.

ALTER, DINSMORE, CLARENCE CLEMINSHAW, and JOHN PHILLIPS. **PICTORIAL ASTRONOMY. Glossary, index, 8¼"x10½", 328pp. Cro74, 12.50c.**
A revised edition of this classic general survey. The text is clearly written and covers all the basics. It is enhanced with numerous tables, drawings, and diagrams, as well as many large, clearly reproduced photographs. The book is well organized and makes a fine introduction to astronomy.

■ *ASIMOV, ISAAC.* **ASIMOV'S GUIDE TO SCIENCE. 945pp. H&R72/ Pen, 17.95c.**
This is an updated edition of Asimov's classic **New Intelligent Man's Guide to Science**, revised to include the latest developments in every field. This is generally considered the finest layman's account of modern science. It is an encyclopedic work, in nontechnical language, which offers a comprehensive picture of the whole of modern science, explaining the basic ideas, highlighting the important developments, and pointing out the meaning of recent scientific discoveries. With wit, enthusiasm, and clarity, Dr. Asimov tells what has been learned of the earth and its atmosphere and the space beyond; the nature of matter and the atom; the natural laws and phenomena that have shaped our technology; the living cells and the chemistry of life; the biological heritage of mankind; the human brain and human behavior. For all who are interested in understanding individual areas of science this is a volume without equal and it is one that we have found immensely helpful. It is hard to understand how Asimov can produce the quantity of books that he does and still keep the quality uniformly high—but he does. And his gift for simplifying the complex is a rare and valued one. Includes an excellent chapter-by-chapter bibliography and subject and name indices, as well as many illustrations.

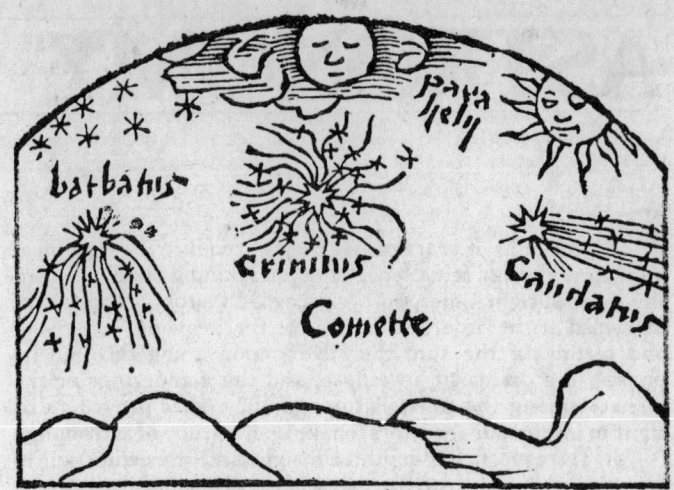

Sixteenth century woodcut of meteors and comets, from Aristotle's **Meteorologia**.

ASIMOV, ISAAC. **ASIMOV ON ASTRONOMY. Illustrations, index, 238pp. Dov75/Hod, 3.50p.**
The seventeen chapters in this book have been selected from earlier essays, updated, and enhanced with new photographs. They represent Asimov at his best.

ASIMOV, ISAAC. **ASIMOV ON PHYSICS. Illustrations, index, 206pp. Dou76, 9.95c.**
A collection of seventeen essays, selected from Asimov's earlier articles on physics and updated for this volume. As usual, Asimov's presentation is amazingly clear despite the complexity of the material.

ASIMOV, ISAAC. **THE BEGINNING AND THE END. 260pp. Dou77, 8.50c.**
A varied collection of articles by Asimov, written in his usual humorous, literate manner.

ASIMOV, ISAAC. **THE COLLAPSING UNIVERSE. Index, 204pp. S&S77/HPG, 1.95p.**
A detailed probe into black holes and their implications, along with related issues.

ASIMOV, ISAAC. **FROM EARTH TO HEAVEN. 253pp. Avo72/DoB, 1.75p.**
Here the reader is taken on an intriguing journey through basic scientific questions dealing with the earth, physics, and the universe.

ASIMOV, ISAAC. **SOLAR SYSTEM AND BACK. 253pp. Avo72, 1.50p.**
In his clear, instructive manner, Asimov examines the riddles of our solar system. Then he returns to earth to explore the vagaries of certain metals; the clues behind the disappearance of the dinosaurs; the causes and effects of chromosome aberrations; and many other areas.

■ *ASIMOV, ISAAC.* **THE UNIVERSE, FROM FLAT EARTH TO QUASAR. Index, 315pp. Avo68/Pen, 1.95p.**
Asimov's most comprehensive exploration of astronomy. Topics include the earth, solar system, stars, galaxy, age of the earth, energy of the sun, stellar evolution, galactic evolution, receding galaxies, beginning of the universe, and the edge of the universe. Well illustrated with photographs and drawings.

BAADE, WALTER. **EVOLUTION OF STARS AND GALAXIES. Index, 334pp. MIT63, 5.95p.**
An astonishing complex of facts and the relations between them is presented with unusual clarity and lucidity, in a lively, spirited tone that is, I think, unrivaled in astronomical literature... [This volume] is pervaded by the spirit of a great adventure: to grasp and to comprehend for the first time the evolution of a whole galaxy. Dr. Baade's approach was basically simple. He concentrated on detailed study of nearby systems, especially the local group of galaxies, trying with inexhaustible invention to fit together a multitude of facts....It is a pleasure to read the full story of some spectacular Baade discoveries.—**Sky and Telescope**. This is an edited transcription of a series of lectures given by Dr. Baade at Harvard Observatory in 1958. A highly technical presentation.

BERRY, ADRIAN. **THE IRON SUN: CROSSING THE UNIVERSE THROUGH BLACK HOLES. Notes, bibliography, index, 176pp. Dut77, 7.95c.**
This is a volume of informed speculation about the future. Berry envisages the establishment of a galactic empire, a society in which our descendents will be scattered through millions of worlds in orbits around countless stars. Since the stars are separated by light years of conventional travel, Berry proposes a new means of speedier transport. He feels that within the next 250 years virtually instantaneous travel will be feasible via flight through black holes. Thus he opens the book with a description of black holes. He continues with an outline of a plan to manufacture them near enough to earth to be of practical value to us.

BRACEWELL, RONALD. **THE GALACTIC CLUB: INTELLIGENT LIFE IN OUTER SPACE. Many illustrations, notes, index, 152pp. SFB76, 3.95p.**
This is a nontechnical exploration of extraterrestrial communication, space travel, and space colonization. Bracewell is an astronomer, physicist, and electrical engineer and he bases his discussion on the latest scientific findings.

BRAND, STEWART, ed. **SPACE COLONIES. 10¾"x7¼", 160pp. Vik77, 5.00p.**
A collection of articles on space colonies, most of which were originally published in **Coevolution Quarterly**. The book is organized into three sections—*Vision, Debate,* and *Space.* The *vision* section progresses from broad propaganda to technical details to anecdotes; *debate* is a collection of the most intelligent attacks on the space colony theory; and *space* is a collection of reports from astronomers and astronauts. An abundance of illustrations accompany the text.

BROWN, G. SPENCER. **LAWS OF FORM. 141pp. Crn69, 9.00c.**
John Lilly calls this book one of the most important recent works. Many other scholars, mathematicians, and philosophers have acclaimed it. The **Whole Earth Catalog** said it *should be in the hands of all young people.* We, however, cannot begin to understand it—although I admit we haven't really tried. If you are a whiz at math and calculus perhaps you'll acclaim this as a work of genius also. Intense concentration is a prerequisite.

BROWN, HUGH. **CATACLYSMS OF THE EARTH. Illustrations, index, 281pp. Mul67, 5.50p.**
Brown has spent over fifty years collecting material which led to the formulation of the theories presented here. He believes that the continual growth of the South Polar icecap, interacting with gravitational force, first produces a wobble in the earth's normal spin. Eventually, every 6,000 to 8,000 years, a sudden and radical shift of the earth's axis is caused. Continents and sea areas are rearranged, and the once tropical areas become lands of snow and ice. The great flood of Noah resulted from the last careening of the globe. This is a detailed scientific investigation of this phenomenon.

■ CALDER, NIGEL. **KEY TO THE UNIVERSE: A REPORT ON THE NEW PHYSICS. Bibliography, index, 7¾"x10¼", 199pp. Vik77/BBC, 6.95p.**
This is a lively synthesis of the latest findings in physics, astronomy, and cosmology. Calder describes how, one after another, seemingly bizarre theories have found support in the latest discoveries of high energy research and astronomy. Calder writes lucidly and he clarifies not only the breakthrough discoveries but also the broader implications of these discoveries. An abundance of color and black and white plates accompany the text.

CALDER, NIGEL. **THE RESTLESS EARTH—A REPORT ON THE NEW GEOLOGY. 7½"x10", 152pp. Vik73/Fut, 4.95p.**
Calder explores a bold new theory of the earth based on the theory of plate techtonics. Earthquakes, volcanoes, mountain ranges are all connected to a single comprehensive process—the movement of huge plates that are said to make up the earth's outer shell. The account can be understood by the layman and is beautifully illustrated with color and black and white photographs, drawings, and tables.

CALDER, NIGEL. **THE VIOLENT UNIVERSE—AN EYEWITNESS ACCOUNT OF THE NEW ASTRONOMY. 7"x9½", 160pp. Vik69/Fut, 4.95p.**
A superbly written, illustrated book which presents the current state of knowledge, investigation and speculation concerning quasars, pulsars, neutron stars, anti-matter, exploding galaxies, and gravity holes.

CALLATAY, VINCENT DE and AUDOUIN DOLLFUS. **ATLAS OF THE PLANETS. 9"x12½", 160pp. UTo74, 15.00c.**
This is a profusely illustrated account which begins with a review of the historical record of the planets and the ideas people have held about the heavens, beginning with the origins of astronomy in China and Babylon. A detailed description of the development of modern concepts of the solar system is also given. The second section describes the fundamental principles of the planetary system and the methods of determining a planet's characteristics, and it reviews major astronomical terms. The authors explain the classification of planets, planetary symbols, the celestial sphere, both true and apparent motion of planets, their brightness, and methods of measuring distance and mass. The final section—the bulk of the book—is devoted to a study of each planet. Emphasis is placed on recent discoveries made by Russian and American space probes and recent observations from all over the world. Hundreds of diagrams and photos, some in color, illustrate the text. The material is clear enough for the layman to understand yet sophisticated enought to be of value to the specialist.

■ CAPRA, FRITJOF. **THE TAO OF PHYSICS. Notes, bibliography, index, 330pp. ShP75/Fon, 20.70c/5.95p/2.95p.**
This is an amazing book which explores the parallels between the underlying concepts of modern physics and the basic ideas of Eastern mysticism. Dr. Capra gives a clear account, supplemented by diagrams and photographs, of the theories of atomic and subatomic physics, of relativity theory and of astrophysics, up to and including the most recent research, and relates the world view emerging from these theories to the mystical traditions of Hinduism, Buddhism, Taoism, Zen, and the I Ching. Dr. Capra has a remarkable gift for making the complex understandable. From his text emerges a picture of the material world not as a machine made up of a multitude of objects, but a harmonious *organic* whole whose parts are determined by their interrelations and which reflects a reality behind the world of ordinary sense perception involving spaces of higher dimensions and transcending ordinary language and logical reasoning. We are fascinated by Capra's presentation and, despite the technical nature of the material, it has been extremely popular.

CHARON, J. **COSMOLOGY. Bibliography, index, 255pp. MGH73, 2.95p.**
An excellent book for the general reader which first traces the development of scientific ideas about the universe from the Greeks to the present day, and then discusses the possible meanings of space, time, distance, and man's uniqueness in the universe. Charon reviews the controversies and gives what he feels are reasonable explanations. Many fine illustrations in color and black and white are included.

CLAYTON, DONALD. **THE DARK NIGHT SKY. 218pp. NYT75, 9.95c.**
This is a very personal, simply written account of the history of cosmology and the men who made the revolutionary steps. The author is himself an astronomer and he relates the impact these discoveries had on him intellectually. Dr. Clayton seeks to share the sense of adventure that has led him to dedicate his life to the pursuit of the meaning of the universe. The book is, as the subtitle indicates, *A Personal Adventure in Cosmology.* Many photographs illustrate the text.

DAVIES, P.C.W. **SPACE AND TIME IN THE MODERN UNIVERSE. Illustrations, 232pp. CUP77, 5.95p.**
The structure of space and time lies at the very foundation of both physical science and our perceptual experience of the world. They are concepts so fundamental that in everyday life we do not question their properties. Yet modern science has discovered situations in which space and time can change their character so drastically that remarka-

ble and unexpected phenomena occur. Dr. Davies explores the changing notions of space and time, particularly as illustrated by their application to astronomical and cosmological scenarios. He writes in a nontechnical, straightforward style.

■ *DITFURTH, HOIMAR VON.* **CHILDREN OF THE UNIVERSE.** **Illustrations, index, 301pp. Ath74, 4.95p.**
This is not merely a book of popular science. Underlying the scientific data is a philosophical premise and even an evangelical intent. Von Ditfurth has presented a very animated narrative that actually seems to ensoul the vast machinery of the universe. Nature here is often personified, and always has implications for human life. Just beneath the surface of twentieth century scientific fact we find the preoccupation with immortality; the ancient concepts of *microcosm and macrocosm*; and echoes of the *As above, so below* of hermetic philosophy. Sober as the facts may be, underlying them is von Ditfurth's recognition that science is *merely the continuation of metaphysics in another form.* This is a fascinating exploration of stars and atoms, moons and fossils, earth and man, and the reaches of the cosmos. Von Ditfurth is a noted German scientist and this book was number one on the German best seller list when it was first published there in 1972.

EDDINGTON, SIR ARTHUR. **THE EXPANDING UNIVERSE. Index, 128pp. UMP58/CUP, 1.75p.**
A detailed pioneering work by one of this century's most noted astronomers, dealing *with the view now tentatively held that the whole material universe of stars and galaxies of stars is dispersing; the galaxies scattering apart so as to occupy an ever-increasing volume.* This is a brilliant exposition of the theory of the structure of the universe, not intended for the general reader.

EDDINGTON, SIR ARTHUR. **THE NATURE OF THE PHYSICAL WORLD. Index, 380pp. UMP58/Den, 3.25p.**
To any intelligent and thoughtful reader who would know something of the trend of the finest scientific thought of today [1928], and of the bearing of the new theories of the nature of the phenomenal world on the eternal problems of philosophy and theology, it would be difficult to suggest a better or nobler introduction than this brilliant book.— **Saturday Review.**

Albert Einstein

Albert Einstein (1879-1955) was one of the truly seminal thinkers of the modern era. His theory of relativity, published when he was twenty-six, caused the greatest revolution in science since Galileo.

In Newtonian physics, if a moving object is pushed, the push speeds it up and the energy of propulsion becomes the kinetic energy of the object's motion. Repeated pushes will give increased speed, without any limit. Einstein showed that nothing can exceed the speed of light and that masses increase at high speeds. This meant that near the speed of light a push contributes only partly to increased speed, with the remainder going to increase the object's mass. The mass increase could be directly related to the energy of the push, to give the equation $E=mc^2$ (energy is equal to mass times the speed of light squared). The making of the atomic bomb, which was an application of Einstein's theory, proved that matter was merely unreleased energy, and that matter and energy were two different manifestations of a single cosmic unity.

Einstein spent his life searching for scientific proof that the whole physical universe is one continuity, a rising and falling and never ending stream. His faith in the oneness of the universe is exemplified in his statement, *I cannot believe that God plays dice with the cosmos. God is subtle, but not malicious.*

■ *BARNETT, LINCOLN.* **THE UNIVERSE AND DR. EINSTEIN.** **Diagrams, annotated bibliography, index, 128pp. Ban57, 1.75p.**
This is the clearest, most readable book on Einstein's theories ever published. Barnett discusses the problems Einstein faced, the experiments that lead to his theories, and what his findings reveal about the forces that govern the universe.

BORN, MAX. **EINSTEIN'S THEORY OF RELATIVITY. 376pp. Dov62, 4.50p.**
Born is a Nobel Laureate and one of the world's great physicists. In this book he analyzes and interprets the theory of Einsteinian relativity and presents his material in a style that is midway between vague popularizations and complex scientific presentations. High school algebra is used to explain the nature of classical physics and relativity, and simple experiments and diagrams are used to illustrate each step.

CLARK, RONALD W. **EINSTEIN, THE LIFE AND TIMES. Photographs, notes, bibliography, index, 864pp. Avo71, 2.95p.**
This perceptive and painstakingly researched book is universally considered the definitive biography of Einstein. It is also an extremely readable study.

EINSTEIN, ALBERT. **IDEAS AND OPINIONS. 377pp. Del54, 1.50p.**
This is the most definitive collection of Einstein's popular writings, gathered under the supervision of Einstein himself. The subjects include relativity, atomic war or peace, religions and science, human rights, economics and government.

EINSTEIN, ALBERT. **THE MEANING OF RELATIVITY. 168pp. PUP74/ C&H, 3.45p.**
A comprehensive paper on general relativity, including appendices on related matters including one on the *Relativistic Theory of the NonSymmetric Field.*

EINSTEIN, ALBERT, ed. **THE PRINCIPLE OF RELATIVITY. 216pp. Dov52, 3.35p.**
A collection of original papers on the special and general theories of relativity. Contributors include H.A. Lorentz, H. Weyl, and H. Minkowski.

EINSTEIN, ALBERT. **RELATIVITY. Notes, bibliography, index, 164pp. Crn61/Met, 3.00c.**
A simple presentation of both the special theory of relativity and the general theory of relativity written for those who are not conversant with the mathematical apparatus of theoretical physics.

EINSTEIN, ALBERT and LEOPOLD INFELD. **THE EVOLUTION OF PHYSICS. Index, 315pp. S&S38/CUP, 4.95p.**
A masterly exposition of physical thought since Galileo. To have presented a clear, penetrating account of the main stages in the evolution of modern physics without the use of mathematics is an extraordinary feat, and one possible only to complete masters of their subject.... Einstein and Infeld's book should do much to spread an understanding and appreciation of one of the great dramas in the evolution of human thought.— **Saturday Review.** This is probably the clearest, most understandable of Einstein's works and is recommended to the general reader.

HOFFMANN, BANESH. **ALBERT EINSTEIN: CREATOR AND REBEL. Illustrations, index, 272pp. NAL72, 2.95p.**
The author of this biography is a noted scientist who collaborated with and was a friend of Einstein. This is a very readable work, tracing Einstein's personal life from childhood and showing the development of his creativity.

———————END OF ALBERT EINSTEIN SUBSECTION———————

ENGELBREKTSON, JUNE. **STARS, PLANETS AND GALAXIES. Index, 159pp. Ban75, 1.95p.**
This is as good an introduction to the basics of the stars, planets, and galaxies as we know of for the reader who knows little or nothing about the subject and is curious, but does not want to be overwhelmed with details. Part of Bantam's **Knowledge Through Color** series and illustrated with 132 color photographs and maps.

EVANS, DAVID. **ASTRONOMY. Glossary, bibliography, index, 304pp. McK75/Hod, 5.95p.**
This is a basic book, part of the British **Teach Yourself** series, which is designed for the novice who is interested in observation with the naked eye or with the aid of simple optical instruments. All the fundamentals are presented in a clear manner. The approach is often technical, but not overwhelmingly so. There are separate chapters on the sun, the planets, the stellar universe, and on rare and common phenomena.

FANNING, A.E. **PLANETS, STARS AND GALAXIES. Index, 189pp. Dov66, 3.00p.**
This is a well written introductory survey of astronomy, with the bulk of the volume being devoted to the earth, the sun, and the other planets. There are also sections on the stars and the galaxies. The book is written for the beginner and all the material is very clearly presented, with a number of diagrams where they seem helpful and a section of photographs. Donald Menzel has completely updated the text and has included the latest discoveries.

■ FEINBERG, GERALD. **WHAT IS THE WORLD MADE OF? ATOMS, LEPTONS, QUARKS, AND OTHER TANTALIZING PARTICLES. Illustrations, glossary, bibliography, index, 307pp. Dou77, 3.95p.**
A first rate lucid explanation of many complicated scientific developments and an excellent introduction to both the achievements and paradoxes of modern physics. Feinberg is a professor of physics at Columbia University and he is a fine teacher. We found his explanations clearer than anything else we have read.

FERRIS, TIMOTHY. **THE RED LIMIT: THE SEARCH FOR THE ENDS OF THE UNIVERSE. Illustrations, bibliography, index, 287pp. Mor77, 10.00c.**
There is a need for a comprehensible, accurate, up-to-date discussion of cosmology which does not talk down to the lay reader. I believe Timothy Ferris' **The Red Limit** *is such a book. It is gracefully composed, studded with metaphors and similes of poetic clarity, and remarkably successful in conveying in words some of the content and feel of the mathematics essential to the subject. . . . For many readers who have not previously encountered modern cosmological ideas, this book will provide a two-fold revelation— about the beauty and grandeur of the universe, and about the brilliance and tenacity of the human minds that occupy an obscure corner of that universe.*—Carl Sagan.

GAMOW, GEORGE. **ONE, TWO, THREE, INFINITY. 340pp. Ban71, 1.95p.**
The book originated as an attempt to collect the most interesting facts and theories of modern science in such a way as to give the reader a general picture of the earth in its microscopic and macroscopic manifestations, as it presents itself to the eye of the scientist of today. . . . The subjects to be discussed have been selected so as to survey briefly the entire field of basic scientific knowledge, leaving no corner untouched.—George Gamow. 128 of Gamow's own drawings illustrate the text.

GARDNER, MARTIN. **THE RELATIVITY EXPLOSION. Index, 209pp. RaH76, 3.95p.**
Gardner has treated a very difficult subject with consummate skill. Without mathematics or complicated technical arguments he manages to convey the significance and basic meaning of Einstein's relativity. . . . By far the best layman's account of this difficult subject.—**Christian Science Monitor.** This is a completely revised, updated version of **Relativity for the Millions.** Excellent line drawings throughout.

GINGERICH, OWEN, ed. **COSMOLOGY +1. Charts and illustrations throughout, bibliographies, index, 8½"x11¼", 113pp. Fre77, 4.50p.**
This collection of articles from **Scientific American** presents various aspects of our search for an understanding of the universe and considers such topics as the origin of galaxies, background radiation, quasars, black holes, and nonEuclidian space.

GINGERICH, OWEN, ed. **NEW FRONTIERS IN ASTRONOMY. Notes, bibliography, index, 8½"x11", 369pp. Fre75, 7.50p.**
A collection of thirty-one articles from **Scientific American** grouped under the following general headings: *The Planetary System, The Sun, Stellar Evolution, The Milky Way, Galaxies, High-Energy Astrophysics,* and *Cosmology.* The book has been designed as supplementary reading for introductory astronomy and general science courses and the selections are generally not too technical. Many illustrations accompany each selection.

GOLDEN, FREDERIC. **QUASARS, PULSARS AND BLACK HOLES. Bibliography, index, 205pp. Scr76, 7.95p.**
In spite of the title, this is basically a clear introductory survey of astronomy by the science editor of **Time** magazine. The text is simply written and many photographs are included. The last few chapters are devoted to quasars, pulsars, and black holes.

GOODAVAGE, JOSEPH. **OUR THREATENED PLANET. Index, 302pp. S&S78, 10.00c.**
Goodavage is a science writer, specializing in the field of astrometeorology, the science of planetary weather forecasting. In this book he makes a number of alarming predictions. As he says, *Your future and mine is determined by climatic and other geological conditions that mankind has been trying to understand (or do something about) for more than a thousand years. Scientists now realize that something new, strange, and perhaps frightening is happening to Earth's weather, and that every man, woman and child on the planet is being affected.* Goodavage is also an astrologer, and astrology at times figures into his predictions.

The comet of 249 AD, from a sixteenth century woodcut.

GRIBBIN, JOHN. **OUR CHANGING UNIVERSE. Bibliography, index, 7½"x10", 160pp. Dut76/McM, 11.95c.**
A simply written pictorial account of the new astronomy. *An excellent and up-to-date picture of the universe as we currently know it after the astronomical revolution of the last quarter-century. . . clear, orderly, and I enjoyed it very much.*—Isaac Asimov. Dr. Gribbin is an experienced science writer and researcher.

GRIBBIN, JOHN. **WHITE HOLES: COSMIC GUSHERS IN THE UNIVERSE. Photographs, glossary, notes, bibliography, index, 304pp. Del77/Grn, 4.95p.**
The popular belief about black holes is that they are an *ultimate sink or plughole* to drain matter in the universe. Black holes have caught the popular imagination more than any other aspect of the new astronomy. If things drain from black holes, then by reversing a sign in the equation matter can come out of white holes. And with a little more imagination, the equations can be interpreted to suggest links between black and white holes, like tunnels forming a cosmic subway. This book, a popular exploration of such concepts, is composed of three lengthy essays: *Where Do We Come From?, Where Are We Now?, Where Are We Going?*

GRIBBIN, JOHN and STEPHEN PLAGEMANN. **THE JUPITER EFFECT. Diagrams, notes, bibliography, index, 136pp. RaH74/Fon, 1.95p.**
Two young scientists present a chilling hypothesis with astrological overtones: the forthcoming Grand Alignment of all the planets in 1982, the first such in 179 years, may well trigger a California earthquake far worse than the San Francisco catastrophe of 1906. In establishing this link between planetary motion and accumulating strain in the San Andreas Fault, the authors examine findings on the role of continental drift in earthquake tensions and the latest research into storms on the earth and on the sun. Dr. Gribbin is an editor of **Nature,** the international journal of science and Dr. Plagemann is currently working on a NASA study of upper atmosphere phenomena.

■ GUILLEMIN, VICTOR. **THE STORY OF QUANTUM MECHANICS. Illustrations, glossary, index, 348pp. Scr68, 3.95p.**
Beginning with a brief sketch of the background against which quantum theories were developed, this book presents a detailed account of the discovery of the principles of quantum mechanics as well as an evaluation of their validity and significance. The book also portrays the men whose insight and imagination led to the creation of quantum mechanics. A concluding section stresses the strong influence of quantum mechanics on metaphysics, ethics, and theology. The material is geared toward the reader who has a foundation in basic physics.

HAPGOOD, CHARLES. **THE PATH OF THE POLE. Index, 439pp. Chi70, 10.00c.**
A completely revised version of Hapgood's **Earth's Shifting Crust.** By making use of thousands of radio-carbon datings of climatic events of the last 100,000 years, Hapgood shows that the earth's outer shell has slipped over its interior—changing the relative positions of the poles—three times during that period. The last such change came at the end of the Ice Age, between 18,000 and 15,000 years ago. Good scholarship and not an overly technical presentation.

HEISENBERG, WERNER. **ACROSS THE FRONTIERS. 248pp. H&R74, 2.95p.**
The present collection of essays and addresses, which have sprung, directly or indirectly, from the author's concern with atomic physics, repeatedly leads beyond the frontiers of this domain. The reason lies in the universal character of the science of the atom. Anyone who takes it seriously, with all its consequences in philosophy, technology, and politics, has no other choice, when reflecting on these implications, than to trespass far beyond the boundaries of the field of physics proper.... The most important topics can perhaps be indicated by way of the following questions: Where is technology taking us?....What content of truth do scientific assertions possess? ....What can we learn from modern science to assist in the solution of ancient philosophical problems?—from the preface.

HEISENBERG, WERNER. **THE PHYSICAL PRINCIPLES OF THE QUANTUM THEORY. Index, 184+pp. Dov30, 3.20p.**
In this classic text, based on lectures delivered at the University of Chicago, Heisenberg presents a complete physical picture of quantum theory and covers not only his own contributions, but also those of the other pioneers in the field. A technical work, geared toward the scientist.

HEISENBERG, WERNER. **PHYSICS AND BEYOND. 257pp. H&R72, 4.50p.**
Heisenberg was awarded the Nobel Prize for his work in theoretical atomic physics and was Director of the Max Planck Institute for Physics and Astrophysics in Munich. He was one of the most noted and creative philosopher-scientists of this century. This autobiographical study should appeal to scientists and nonscientists alike and is essential reading for anyone interested in the history of physics, or in the personality of the man who had so great a share in making that history.

HEISENBERG, WERNER. **PHYSICS AND PHILOSOPHY: THE REVOLUTION IN MODERN SCIENCE. 212pp. H&R58, 5.30p.**
A fascinating and stimulating work. In the main, Heisenberg's remarks comprise a presentation of his view of the historical roots of atomic science, of the current status of quantum theory and the extent to which it constitutes a radical break with antecedent physical theories, and of the "consequences" of quantum theory on society as well as on science....It is a book which every scientist, every person interested in the history of ideas, will find profitable and enjoyable.—**Science Magazine.**

HEPPENHEIMER, T.A. **COLONIES IN SPACE. Bibliography, index, 7½"x9½", 224pp. Stk77, 12.95c.**
A fully illustrated study of space colonies, discussing the recent interest in the subject and suggesting how, with present technology, space colonization will occur. This book includes information on the architecture and design of the colonies, farming and food in space, recreation, the lunar base, power satellites to fuel the earth's energy needs, the economic importance of space colonization, and much else. Over 100 illustrations in all, including many color drawings, give concrete visual dimensions to the story. Dr. Heppenheimer is present Alexander von Humboldt Fellow at the Max Planck Institute fur Kernphysik in Heidelberg, Germany. This is a serious, scientific, and yet still readable study.

HOWARD, NEALE. **THE TELESCOPE HANDBOOK AND STAR ATLAS. Oversize, bibliography, glossary, index, 226pp. Cro75/Fab, 14.95c.**
This is a complete introduction to stargazing which combines a comprehensive discussion of telescopes with a star atlas featuring transparent map overlays. The maps show the stars seen by the naked eye and the transparencies show those visible through the telescope. An accompanying celestial gazetter groups objects by type and the characteristics of each—color, magnitude, right ascensions, and declinations—are correlated with map numbers, catalogue numbers, and names. Many astronomical study techniques are also outlined.

HOYLE, FRED. **ASTRONOMY AND COSMOLOGY. Bibliography, index, 725pp. Fre75/HeG, 17.00c.**
This is an excellent text, designed for an introductory college course. As usual Hoyle's exposition is crystal clear; the book has gotten excellent reviews and is widely used in universities. Hoyle himself states that the major differentiation between his book and the countless other good texts is his concentration on the relationship between astronomy and physics. Hundreds of line drawings and color and black and white plates illustrate the text. This is a wonderful reference book, but unless you are deeply interested in the subject and have some prior knowledge, you will not be able to take sufficient advantage of it.

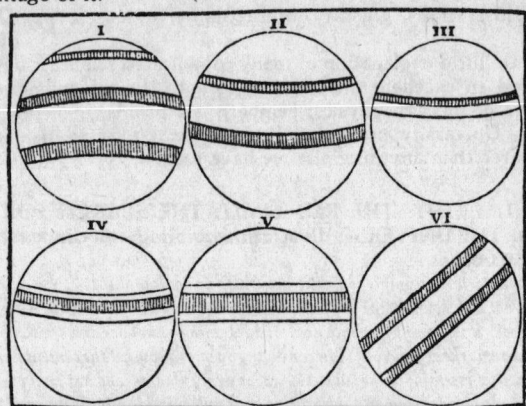

First observation of Jupiter's belts, drawings by a seventeenth century Italian Jesuit priest.

HOYLE, FRED. **FROM STONEHENGE TO MODERN COSMOLOGY. Index, 96pp. Fre72, 7.00c.**
A collection of four essays by one of the greatest astronomers of our day, which demonstrate how astronomical knowledge is one of the main indices of human culture. The first is entitled *Science and Society in Modern Times*; the second, *Stonehenge*, reviews the scientific debate concerning the significance of this astronomical marvel and advances evidence for some startling new possibilities. In the third and fourth essays, Hoyle outlines the latest developments in the continuing research into the origin of the universe.

HOYLE, FRED. **FRONTIERS OF ASTRONOMY. Index, 360pp. H&R55, 10.00c.**
Dr. Hoyle is one of the most noted astronomers of recent times besides being an excellent writer. This is one of the finest astronomy books that we know of. It opens with chapters on the earth and a review of the discoveries in physics which have contributed to astronomy's advance. There are chapters on the earth-moon system and the origin of the planets. Then follow chapters on the sun and the physical composition of the stars—with special reference to the stars as manufacturers of chemical elements and to exploding stars. The evolution of stars and galaxies is discussed and this leads into the question of the origin of the universe. Much of the information in the book has been obtained through radio astronomy. Includes over 100 photographs and line drawings. Even though the book is old, it is still an excellent survey.

■ HOYLE, FRED. **HIGHLIGHTS IN ASTRONOMY. 8"x9¼", 179pp. Fre75, 5.95p.**
Hoyle's latest book is an introduction to astronomy for the layman—a lucid overview of what astronomers know and what they seek to know. This oversize volume presents the full scope of the science: from the structure of the earth to the latest cosmological speculations—from the phases of the moon to such phenomena as pulsars and black holes. Closely integrated with the text are 142 illustrations, including nearly 100 photographs (many in color). Hoyle writes extremely well and he is thorough and yet concise. This volume presents the best general survey of astronomy that we know of. Recommended.

HOYLE, FRED. **TEN FACES OF THE UNIVERSE. Many photographs and charts, index, 7"x9¼", 207pp. Fre77, 6.95p.**
A provocative look at the frontiers of our present knowledge of ourselves, our planet, and the universe. In the course of the book, Hoyle gives readers an autobiographical sketch of his education and development as a scientist, presents details of his latest cosmological

theory—based on a radically different interpretation of astronomical data—and poses the seeming paradox that unless civilization collapses soon, humankind may be doomed.

JAKI, STANLEY. **SCIENCE AND CREATION. Notes, index, 375pp. WAP74/ScA, 16.15c.**
A systematic analysis of the birth of science. Professor Jaki begins with a detailed analysis of ancient Hindu, Chinese, Maya, Egyptian, Babylonian, and Greek cultures—all of which made significant advances in science. This is followed by studies of science in the early Christian and Arabian cultures when science came to play an increasingly larger role in society. This is a scholarly study which offers the reader a wealth of information not generally available detailing the philosophy and civilization of the various cultures as much as their cultural achievements.

JASTROW, ROBERT. **UNTIL THE SUN DIES. Many photographs and line drawings, index, 172pp. Nor77/Sou, 8.95c.**
A lively examination of the riddles of creation and life. In clear language using vivid imagery, Jastrow explores the meaning of the latest discoveries in astronomy, space exploration, and the origin of life. He also describes the forces that have shaped the human race and created human intelligence. In addition, he shows how recent discoveries have shed new light on man's place in the cosmos.

JOBB, JAMIE. **THE NIGHT SKY BOOK. 4.95p.**
See the Activities subsection of Education.

JONES, G.O., J. ROBLAT, and G.J. WHITROW. **ATOMS AND THE UNIVERSE. Vik73, 3.60p.**
Three physicists and astronomers survey the whole field of subatomic physics and modern astronomy, giving a complete guide to the structure of matter and to the age and origins of the universe. This is considered by many the outstanding book in its field and it will appeal to laymen as well as to scientists.

■ *KAUFMANN, WILLIAM.* **THE COSMIC FRONTIERS OF GENERAL RELATIVITY. Glossary, index, 7¾"x9½", 316pp. LBC77, 12.95c.**
A clear, nontechnical, up to date introduction to the incredible series of recent discoveries and speculations that have reshaped—and shaken—our thinking about the stars and the universe. It presupposes no scientific or mathematical knowledge on the reader's part, other than an enjoyment of astronomy and interest in the direction of post-Einsteinian physics and relativity. Through copious illustrations and many analogies, Dr. Kaufmann begins with a lucid introduction to the space-time qualities of Einstein's theory. After further discussing the synthesis of relativity and gravitation, Kaufmann moves on to the evolution and death of stars and what remains afterward: a white dwarf, a neutron star, or a black hole. He describes the various geometric aspects of space-time within the black hole, leading to the possible existence of antigravity universes connected to ours through the black hole. He also covers x-ray sources and such astonishing speculative developments as evaporating black holes, gravitational waves, antigravity, and space travel in and out of black holes to future and past universes. Recommended.

KAUFMANN, WILLIAM. **RELATIVITY AND COSMOLOGY. Many photographs and line drawings, glossary, index, 134pp. H&R73, 8.00p.**
A new vision of what astronomy is and what it can be unfolds to the reader of this book. From black holes to the primordial cosmic fireball radiation, from gravitational radiation to quasi-stellar sources, the reader sees the subject through the eyes of one close to the observational evidence and becomes aware of what rapidly evolving techniques can do to clear up some of the greatest of the outstanding mysteries.—John Wheeler, Princeton University. *Kaufmann has done a magnificent job of exposition; it is one of the best-written scientific books I have ever had the chance to read. It is remarkable how the fundamental ideas of such complicated, difficult subjects can be so lucidly explained by skillfully drawn analogies, without the usually encountered penalty of loose and sloppy thinking.*—L.H. Aller, University of California, Los Angeles.

KILMISTER, CLIVE. **THE NATURE OF THE UNIVERSE. Glossary, bibliography, 216pp. Dut71, 3.95p.**
A well written, comprehensive introductory account of contemporary cosmology. Includes over 150 illustrations—nineteen in color.

KOESTLER, ARTHUR. **THE SLEEPWALKERS. 624pp. G&D59/Pen, 5.95p.**
This is a generalized account of the men whose discoveries led to a radical reformulation of our vision of the universe. It is written in a lively style and is definitely designed for the nontechnical reader. The historical development of each of the movements and the prime movers is fully covered. Extensive chapter notes are included along with a bibliography and an index.

■ *KYSELKA, WILL and ROY LANTERMAN.* **NORTH STAR TO SOUTHERN CROSS. Bibliography, indices, 160pp. UHa76, 3.95p.**
This is a good presentation of all parts of the night sky which are visible from anywhere on earth. The authors take the reader through the seasons, month by month, as new constellations appear overhead and are replaced in turn by others, represented by the twelve signs of the zodiac and figures from Greek mythology. An abundance of additional material is also provided in an easily comprehensible manner. We get a better feeling for the stars that make up the night sky from this book than from any other we know. Profusely illustrated and nontechnical.

LEVITT, I.M. **BEYOND THE KNOWN UNIVERSE—FROM DWARF STARS TO QUASARS. Index, 179pp. 7"x9½", Vik74, 10.00c.**
Dr. Levitt is Director Emeritus of the Fels Planetarium and the author of many books on astronomy. Here he tells about many of the new astronomical discoveries and relates how scientists are attempting to solve the riddles they pose. Topics include white dwarfs, supernovae, neutron stars, black holes and white holes, pulsars, and quasars. The text is written for the general reader and over forty-eight pages of color illustrations are included.

LOVE, JEFF. **THE QUANTUM GODS. 10.75p.**
See the Jewish Mysticism section.

MACKEY, SAMSON. **"MYTHOLOGICAL" ATRONOMY OF THE ANCIENTS DEMONSTRATED. Glossary, notes, bibliography, 342pp. Wiz74, 15.00c.**
An offset reprint of an 1822 treatise on the spiral precession of the equinoxes, Hindu time cycles, and the zodiacal origin of myths. Also includes **The Key of Urania**. The text is mythologically-oriented, and often seems full of obscure references. It is one of the books referred to often by Blavatsky in **The Secret Doctrine**.

MACVEY, JOHN. **INTERSTELLAR TRAVEL: PAST, PRESENT, AND FUTURE. Notes, index, 270pp. S&D77, 9.95c.**
This is in intriguing, scientifically presented discussion of how we and *alien beings* may travel between the stars, the galaxies, and even into other dimensions of time and space. The author is a member of the Royal Astronomical Society and his account is free of the sensationalism that mars many similar studies. He explains how bent space, black holes, and space tunnels may bridge vast interstellar gulfs, providing time destroying short cuts for travelers to places inconceivably remote in our own universe or in others. He also surveys the problems of interstellar navigation at near light speeds, and calls into question the immutability of the Einsteinian *light velocity barrier*.

MENZEL, DONALD. **ASTRONOMY. Glossary, index, 320pp. RaH75, 20.00c.**
A beautifully presented oversize pictorial survey of astronomy and the universe. Dr. Menzel's opening chapters are a thoughtful review of the gropings and later disproved *systems* of the early astronomers. The next chapter—on atoms, atomic energy, and radiation—lays the groundwork for an understanding of the universe. The remainder of the book is a masterly description of the sun, moon, planets, asteroids, meteors, comets, stars, nebulae, galaxies, eclipses, and auroras. All the latest theories are presented and analyzed. One interesting section is devoted to an account of a star from its prenatal state to its decline. Supplementing the text are 319 photographs, diagrams, and star maps.

MENZEL, DONALD. **A FIELD GUIDE TO THE STARS AND THE PLANETS. Tables, glossary, bibliography, index, 397pp. HMC64/ WCS, 5.95p.**
This is the most complete pocket guide to the night sky ever published. The authoritative text by Dr. Menzel, former director of the Harvard College Observatory, and numerous charts, photographs, drawings, and astronomical tables convey the basic information needed by amateur astronomers. Each of the charts and sky maps appears twice,

once as seen in the telescope and again on the facing page with the names of the stars, nebulae, clusters, and other objects superimposed. These charts and the accompanying text provide the reader with a pictorial road map to sky watching with binoculars or telescope. Other sections of the book cover the solar system, the planets, and other bodies such as comets, meteors, and asteroids. There is also material on using the telescope and camera in astronomy.

MENZEL, DONALD, FRED WHIPPLE, and GERARD DEVAUCOU-LEURS. **SURVEY OF THE UNIVERSE.** 877pp. PrH70, 25.45c.
The authors of this comprehensive text are three of the most noted contemporary astronomers. This is a well written scholarly account which includes chapters on the following areas: *Astronomy and the Origins of Science, Ancient Astronomy, The Copernican Revolution, The Law of Gravitation, The Motions of the Earth, Some Tools of Astronomy, Measurements in the Solar System, Radiation and Atomic Structure, The Sun and Its Radiations, The Earth as a Planet, The Moon, The Terrestrial Planets, The Giant Planets, Asteroids and Comets, Interplanetary Debris, Space Exploration, Origin and Evolution of the Solar System, Extraterrestrial Life, Stellar Distances and Luminosities, The Spectra and Temperatures of Stars, Double Stars and Stellar Masses, The Diameters and Densities of Stars, Stellar Atmospheres, The Nucleus of the Atom, Sources of Stellar Energy, Nuclear Reactions, and Atomic Evolution, Variable Stars, The Cataclysmic Variables, Stars with Atmospheric Shells, Interstellar Matter, Star Clusters and Associations, The Milky Way, Galaxies, Radio and X-Ray Sources, Relativity and Cosmology, Cosmic Evolution and Time Scales.* This is basically a textbook and the format and style are in that vein. The whole work is illustrated with countless photographs, line drawings, and graphs. There is also an extensive chapter-by-chapter bibliography, name and subject indices, and chapter textbook questions. An overwhelming amount of information in one fat book for the serious student.

MERLEAU-PONTY, JACQUES and BRUNO MORANDO. **THE RE-BIRTH OF COSMOLOGY.** Index, 313pp. RaH76, 12.50c.
Looking back to the dawn of civilization, when man first searched the sky above him for some revelation of divine presence and human purpose, and forward to the most recent discoveries about the explosive nature of the huge galactic systems in which our tiny world exists, two leading French savants have woven together an extraordinary account. Morando and Ponty discuss in historical, philosophical, and scientific terms the three major cosmologies Western man has conceived to chart the patterns and rhythms of the universe. They begin with an exploration of the ancient world of Plato, Aristotle, and Ptolemy, seeing through their eyes the earth as the center of all things. This is followed by a review of the *classical revolution* of Galileo, Newton, and others who made the immense intellectual leap away from direct, observable experience to a new science of physics based on abstract hypotheses and laws. The final section is a study of the development of modern cosmology beginning with a discussion of Einstein's general theory of relativity. All in all, a clearly written, illuminating survey.

MITTON, SIMON, ed. **THE CAMBRIDGE ENCYCLOPEDIA OF ASTRONOMY.** Index, 10½"x10", 502pp. Crn77, 35.00c.
A comprehensive guide to modern astronomy based, in part, on information from space missions and including many NASA photographs. Every section has been written by researchers active in that particular field. The information is somewhat technical and we only recommend the book to those who want an in depth overview. An abundance of photographs, including some in color, and line drawings accompany the text.

MOORE, PATRICK. **THE A TO Z OF ASTRONOMY.** 192pp. Scr76, 2.95p.
This is a fine reference book. In over 400 entries, Moore discusses every aspect of modern astronomy and provides definitions, data, and explanations. Illustrations are interspersed throughout.

MOORE, PATRICK. **THE NEW GUIDE TO THE STARS.** Many illustrations, bibliography, index, 251pp. Nor74, 9.95c.
This is Moore's most comprehensive and readable survey of stellar astronomy. All the latest scientific findings have been taken into account and related to their historical developments. Moore discusses the true nature of stars through reference to their movements, luminosity, age, dimensions, color, and composition. He also describes the constellations in the Northern and Southern hemispheres and shows how they can be used as pathfinders to stars of special interest.

In addition, he surveys the current theories of the development of the universe and includes practical advice for the would be stargazer.

MOORE, PATRICK. **THE OBSERVER'S BOOK OF ASTRONOMY.** Index, 222pp. Scr74, 2.95p.
This is a cute little book, 4"x6"—just the right size to put in your pocket or purse when you go off stargazing. Moore is a leading astronomer and has written many books. Here he describes the stars visible at each season of the year, and in separate chapters deals with the sun, moon, and planets—together with such irregular occurrences as aurorae, comets, and shooting stars. The text is concise and clear and includes sixty-four plates, fourteen in color, and numerous text illustrations.

MOORE, PATRICK and IAIN NICHOLSON. **BLACK HOLES IN SPACE.** Index, 126pp. Nor74, 7.95c.
This is the least technical account we know of. The authors explain how black holes are formed from the collapse of large stars, how they can be detected, and how they might be the explanation for some of the mysterious occurrences in the universe, such as quasars, that continue to baffle astronomers.

■ MURCHIE, GUY. **MUSIC OF THE SPHERES.** Dov67.
A remarkably clear explanation and analysis of the latest findings about our material universe. Volume I ($3.50, 237 pages) covers the macrocosm: planets, stars, galaxies, cosmology, and much else. Volume II ($4.00, 386 pages) surveys the microcosm: matter, atoms, waves, radiation, and relativity. The index in is Volume II. This is an excellent introductory survey which we recommend highly.

NELSON, J.H. **COSMIC PATTERNS.** Illustrations, notes, 76pp. AFA74, 5.50p.
Nelson was employed to study sunspots by RCA Communications, because sunspots were believed to be the cause of magnetic storms which from time to time would disrupt shortwave radio communications. He spent almost thirty years doing detailed research and has produced very strong evidence that the planets do, when in certain arrangements, cause changes in the particular solar radiations that are associated with magnetic storms in the earth's atmosphere.

NICOLSON, IAIN. **ASTRONOMY.** Ban71, 2.25p.
A simple account, profusely illustrated in color.

OTTEWELL, GUY. **ASTRONOMICAL CALENDAR.** ACa75, 4.95.
There are a few astronomical calendars available, but this one far surpasses all the others. It is designed to be useful to both advanced and beginning astronomers. There is a sky map for each month which is exceedingly clearly drawn and represents the whole of the sky that you can see, at the convenient time for viewing in the evening. There is also a monthly solar system diagram and on the page facing each map is a comprehensive day-by-day listing of events. Extensive explanatory information is included to help the beginning astronomer and separate sections detail the following information: position, time, constellations, star designations, ecliptic, zodiac, precession, magnitudes, elongations, sun, young moon, tides, Jupiter's satellites, comets, meteors, brightest stars. There is also an excellent glossary. If you are interested in astronomy and star viewing you will definitely enjoy this calendar. Published yearly.

POSTLE, DENIS. **FABRIC OF THE UNIVERSE.** 7½"x9", 210pp. Crn76, 5.95p.
This is a basically pictorial book which has its roots in a film made by the author. Much of the remarkable photography has been preserved in this volume. Postle describes the book as one in which *teachings from the Eastern philosophic tradition...are used to illuminate some of the discoveries of Western science, especially those of particle physics....The subject of the book is not particle physics itself, but what particle physics reveals about the world. The aim throughout has been to de-mystify particle physics and to open up points of contact between it and the non-scientist. The book is as far as possible a practical one, full of recipes for action, things to make and do.* The language is as simple as possible and the exercises make many difficult concepts understandable.

RAND MCNALLY. **STAR FINDER.** Heavy board, 11"x11", RMN, 2.95p.
The large, simplified star map shows the constellations, stars to the fifth magnitude, nebulae, the Milky Way. A zodiacal dial locates constellations at various times of the year. Instructions and planet location tables are included.

RAND MCNALLY. **THE STARFINDER (GLOBE).** 16" high, RMN, 24.95.
A map of the heavens in the form of a globe which adjusts easily to place the stars in positions relating to any given time and place. Double ring mounting. Rings are tinted to match zodiac. Base is chrome plated, contrasting the dark blue globe and yellow stars. With Starfinder Handbook and Official Map of the Moon.

REY, H.A. **FIND THE CONSTELLATIONS.** 9"x11", 72pp. HMC76, 3.95p.
An excellent collection of star maps and introductory material on the heavens and on astronomy. The text is informal and makes a good introduction to the heavens for adults and children alike. The book has been critically acclaimed.

SCIENTIFIC AMERICAN. **THE NEW ASTRONOMY. Bibliography,** 246pp. S&S55, 2.95p.
A collection of twenty articles first published in **Scientific American** between 1948-55. Topics include: *structure of the universe; the shape and dynamics of space; our own galaxy; stars; the sun and its satellites;* and *photocell and radio telescope.*

◼ *SCIENTIFIC AMERICAN.* **THE SOLAR SYSTEM.** 8½"x11½", 145pp. Fre75, 5.00p.
A bound, fully indexed reprint of the September, 1975 issue of **Scientific American**—devoted to a survey of our current scientific knowledge of the sun, the planets, and interplanetary space. The articles are extraordinarily clear and are accompanied by a profusion of charts, drawings, and some of the finest photographs (many in color) we have ever seen. The selections are uniformly excellent and are appropriate for the general reader as well as for the specialist who wishes to keep up with the latest discoveries and theories in the field.

SHAPLEY, HARLOW. **GALAXIES. Index,** 242pp. HUP72, 13.45c.
This very detailed study of galaxies is the second (updated) edition of the most noted book on the subject. In addition to new sections, chapters, and a revision of terminology, there is fresh material on galactic structure, galaxies as sources of radio signals, emitting and absorbing clouds of gas and dust in and among galaxies, and quasars. The text is enhanced by many fine photographs and drawings.

SHIPMAN, HARRY. **BLACK HOLES, QUASARS, AND THE UNIVERSE. Bibliography, notes, index,** 309pp. HMC76, 12.95c.
Black holes and quasars are the latest developments in astronomy and an incredible amount of material has been written on them. This is a clearly written study of new developments in astronomy and of the new view of the universe that is emerging. The presentation is geared toward the general reader and though the topic is highly technical by nature, Shipman's exposition should be understandable to the reader who has little or no scientific background. Each topic is very fully discussed and the text is supplemented by a profusion of photographs, tables, diagrams, and line drawings.

STROMBERG, GUSTAV. **MAN, MIND, AND THE UNIVERSE.** 120pp. DeV66, 3.00p.
A noted scientist applies his knowledge of the physical world to a further understanding of the nature of life, mind, the immortality of the human soul, and God.

STROMBERG, GUSTAV. **THE SEARCHERS.** 242pp. DeV48, 4.00p.
A fine series of essays which delve into science, medicine, and philosophy and explore many aspects of the physical and nonphysical world. Topics include gravitation, vibrating atoms, expanding waves and small particles, the roots of our consciousness, and the immortal soul.

STROMBERG, GUSTAV. **THE SOUL OF THE UNIVERSE.** 312pp. Sci70, 6.00p.
Stromberg describes, in simple language, scientific discoveries concerning the nature of matter, life and mind, and their bearing on the problems of the existence of God (or, as he calls it, a World Soul), and on the age old ideas of the immortality of the soul.

SULLIVAN, WALTER. **CONTINENTS IN MOTION. Illustrations, notes, index,** 8½"x11", 399pp. MGH74, 17.95c.
Sullivan, science editor of **The New York Times**, reveals how a variety of seemingly disparate discoveries were brought together to form the revolutionary theory of *continental drift—the view of our planet as everliving, ever in flux, its continents in motion with respect to one another, carried by the creeping movements of gigantic plates of the earth's crust, clashing with one another from time to time to produce the great mountain ranges.* It casts new light on the topography of every part of the world. This is a well written account of the vast panorama opened up by the new discoveries.

TAYLOR, JOHN. **BLACK HOLES: THE END OF THE UNIVERSE? Bibliography, index,** 175pp. Avo73/Fon, 1.50p.
Dr. Taylor is Professor of Mathematics at Kings College, University of London, and has held Chairs of Physics at the University of Southhampton and at Rutgers University in New Jersey. This is the most authoritative study available on black holes. He defines black holes as burned out stars that have undergone gravitational collapse. The fate of objects, however distant from the black hole, is ultimately to fall into it, and at a later time to be crushed to death at its center. Dr. Taylor explores various theories and attempts to put the entire question into perspective.

TOBEN, BOB. **SPACE-TIME AND BEYOND.** 8½"x11", 175pp. Dut75/Wdw, 5.95p.
This is one of the best books on psi theory, on physics, and on the relation of the two areas. It is good because it is written by a person with an understanding of modern physics and ancient knowledges (in conversation with physicists Jack Sarfatti and Fred Wolf who share the same orientation) and is able to explain the world of sense experience, the world of matter and energy, as understood in quantum physics as it is connected to the world beyond sense experience, the world of psi phenomena. It is a quantum mechanical explanation of ESP, time travel and space warps. It deals with the space-time structure of consciousness and with the universal patterns that relate galaxies, planets, humans, and particles. And, though it goes into these subjects deeply, it does so in a way that is helpful in understanding them—in pictures. Over eighty percent of the central part of the book is pictures. It is the only book on advanced physics that might be mistaken for a coloring book (which it also can be). It has a technical commentary by Dr. Sarfatti, and a good annotated bibliography.

TOULMIN, STEPHEN and JUNE GOODFIELD. **THE FABRIC OF THE HEAVENS. Illustrations, index,** 285pp. H&R61, 3.75p.
*Drawing not only from scientific but also from historical and literary sources, [Dr. Toulmin and Ms. Goodfield] have illustrated the often halting, always uncertain progress of man's knowledge of the universe and its laws through half-a-dozen representative figures: Aristotle, Aristarchos, Ptolemy, Copernicus, Tycho Brahe, Kepler, and Newton. . .they have reconstructed the cultural milieu of the ancient and medieval worlds, the intellectual, emotional and social limitations that frequently misled scientists and philosophers to theories that may seem merely ridiculous to us. . . . It is the best exposition of the subject.—*E. Nelson Hayes, **Astrophysical Observatory, Smithsonian Institute.**

137

Immanuel Velikovsky

Velikovsky (born 1895) is without a doubt one of the most controversial figures of this decade. He has written on both science and history; only his books on astronomy are catalogued here, his history books are with the Ancient Near East section. In the 1940s he developed a unique model for the recent history of the solar system. His major thesis dealt with close encounters of Venus, Mars, and the Earth in historical times. He also challenged the chronology used for certain historical periods. Velikovsky has been continually attacked by the more traditional scientists who have little sympathy for his cataclysmic theories. Whether you agree with his theories or not, he has come up with a lot of interesting ideas.

GOLDSMITH, DONALD, ed. **SCIENTISTS CONFRONT VELIKOV-SKY.** Notes, bibliography, index, 183pp. Cor77, 8.95c.
At the American Association for the Advancement of Science symposium on Velikovsky's ideas, three astronomers (Carl Sagan, David Morrison, and J.D. Mulholland), a sociologist (Normal Storer), and an expert on ancient astronomical records (Peter Huber) seriously discussed and assessed Velikovsky's theories. Velikovsky himself and Irving Michelson, a physicist, defended and supported the theories. Velikovsky and Michelson did not permit their papers to be reprinted here so all that is in this volume is, as the title suggests, anti-Velikovsky. The papers have been reprinted more or less verbatim, with the exception of Dr. Sagan's, which has been slightly expanded. There is also an introduction by Isaac Asimov and a foreword by the editor discussing how both the symposium and conference came about.

GREENBERG, LEWIS. **VELIKOVSKY AND ESTABLISHMENT SCIENCE.** 150pp. Kro77, 5.00p.
Since the publication in 1950 of **Worlds in Collision** (now in its seventy-fourth printing), Velikovsky has been a favorite target of the scientific community. In 1974 a Symposium on Velikovsky was held by the American Association for the Advancement of Science. This book contains a full scale rejoinder to the arguments raised at that Symposium, beginning with Velikovsky's own address.

PENSEE EDITORS. **VELIKOVSKY RECONSIDERED.** 304pp. War76, 2.95p.
A collection of the best articles out of the many **Pensee** has published as special features on Velikovsky. Some review the history of the case, reexamine the criticism and the claims, and in the light of subsequent scientific discoveries show not only how and wherein Dr. Velikovsky was right, but also how the critics are still claiming ad hoc explanations of Dr. Velikovsky's predicted phenomena, or pretending *they knew it all along.* A number of new articles by Velikovsky himself are also included along with many charts, diagrams, and graphs. It must be remembered that **Pensee** is very pro-Velikovsky, so this is not a balanced presentation.

RANSOM, C.J. **AGE OF VELIKOVSKY.** Notes, index, 285pp. Del76, 3.95p.
Dr. Ransom has a PhD in plasma physics, is a senior editor of the journal **Kronos**, which presents discussions about Velikovsky's work, and assisted with the **Pensee** series. This book is an introduction and overview of Velikovsky's work. It contains a survey of the academic support behind his theories, and offers a defense against the more common objections to and misrepresentations of them. Both Velikovsky's astronomical and archaeological theories are reviewed.

VELIKOVSKY, IMMANUEL. **EARTH IN UPHEAVAL.** 308pp. S&S55/ SBL, 1.95p.
Documents the assertations in **Worlds in Collision.** Presents evidence from the natural sciences which indicate that these great disturbances which rocked our globe were caused by forces outside the Earth itself. The evidence is assembled from mountains and oceans, deserts and tundras and jungles, and establishes the Velikovsky theory as of prime importance in man's understanding of the Earth's past and man's own origins.

VELIKOVSKY, IMMANUEL. **WORLDS IN COLLISION.** 401pp. S&S50/ SBL, 2.50p.
A very controversial book which propounds the theory that more than once within historical times the order in our planetary system was disturbed and caused enormous cataclysms; the Earth became a primeval chaos lashed by tornados of cinders; the skies darkened; land masses were destroyed and large portions of the human race perished.

————END OF IMMANUEL VELIKOVSKY SUBSECTION————

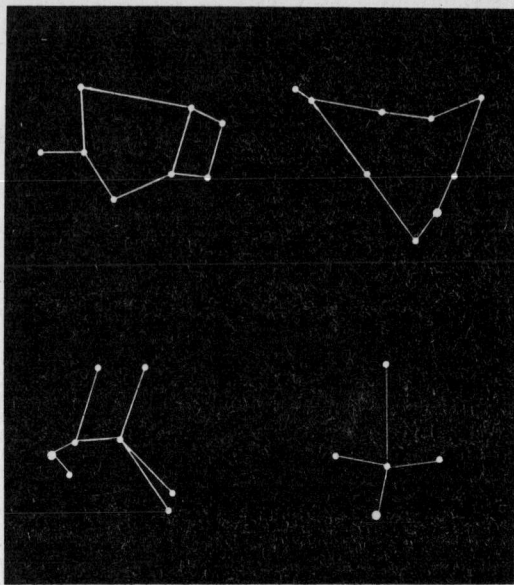

WEINBERG, STEVEN. **THE FIRST THREE MINUTES.** Illustrations, annotated bibliography, 198pp. H&R77, 8.95c.
A remarkable exploration of the origin of the universe based on the latest scientific findings and incorporating Dr. Weinberg's own theories. The entire book is devoted to a replay of the first three minutes. The author *stops the action* at frequent intervals to describe and analyze each incident. He also discusses how these findings were made. This is a fairly technical book, though it purports to be written for the nonspecialist.

WHIPPLE, FRED. **EARTH, MOON AND PLANETS.** Index, 296pp. HUP68/Pen, 2.75p.
This is a very well written account; the approach is nonmathematical and the scientific arguments are advanced in a simple but sound way. The illustrations are uniformly good and the photographs of the Earth, Moon, and Mars, taken from space vehicles, are truly remarkable. This is the third edition of this noted book and the material has been almost completely revised and updated to keep abreast of the rapid changes and discoveries in the field.

WHITNEY, CHARLES. **WHITNEY'S STAR FINDER.** 7"x8", 103pp. RaH74, 5.95p.
A field guide to the heavens created by Dr. Whitney, Professor of Astronomy at Harvard. It clearly tells, explains, and shows what is up there. And it provides a removable *locator wheel* that enables the user to identify every prominent star in the sky, on any day of the year, all over North America. Includes very detailed instructional material and an index. The locator wheel is of durable plastic.

ZEILIK, MICHAEL. **ASTRONOMY: THE EVOLVING UNIVERSE.** Glossary, index, 8¼"x9½", 529pp. H&R76, 20.00c.
This is a textbook for a university level course. It is extremely well written and incorporates all the latest developments. Much of the material here is not as accessible in most textbooks and hundreds of clearly drawn diagrams, photographs, and tables accompany the text. Professor Zeilik divides his information into the following major categories: *Man's Conception of the Cosmos, The Kingdom of the Sun, The Universe of Stars and Galaxies,* and *Cosmic Evolution.* We recommend this book to all who are seriously interested in developing their understanding of modern astronomy and cosmology.

BAHA'I

Baha'i faith is a religion founded by Mirza Husayn Ali (1817-92), generally known as Baha'u'llah, Glory of God. The word Baha'i derives from *baha* (glory, splendor) and signifies a follower of Baha'u'llah. The religion stemmed from the Babi faith—founded in 1844 by Mirza Ali Mohammad of Shiraz, known as the Bab—which emphasized the forthcoming appearance of a new prophet or messenger of God. The Babi faith in turn had sprung from Shi'ah Islam which believed in the forthcoming return of the twelfth *imam* (successor of Muhammad), who would renew religion and guide the faithful.

Baha'u'llah, who had been an early disciple of the Bab, was arrested in 1852 in connection with an unsuccessful attempt on the life of the Shah of Persia. Though he professed no knowledge of the plot, he was thrown into the Black Pit, a notorious jail in Teheran, where he became aware of his mission as a messenger of God. After his release he declared that he was the messenger of God whose advent had been prophesied by the Bab. An overwhelming majority of the Babis acknowledged his claim and thenceforth became known as Baha'is.

Before his life ended in 1892, Baha'u'llah saw his religion spread beyond Persia and the Ottoman Empire to the Caucasus, Turkistan, India, Burma, Egypt, and the Sudan. Since then the movement—still active today—has spread to virtually every country in the world. No official membership statistics for the entire Baha'i community are available. In 1971, however, Baha'is were residing in more than 50,000 localities throughout the world, with more than 100 national spiritual assemblies and no fewer than 60,000 local spiritual assemblies.

Baha'u'llah teaches that God is unknowable and *beyond every human attribute....No tie of direct intercourse can possibly bind Him to His creatures.* God has chosen to reveal himself through his messengers. In Baha'i teachings, God is, and always has been, the Creator. Therefore, there was never a time when the cosmos did not exist. Man was created by God's love *to know and worship God and to carry forward an ever-advancing civilization.* Civilization, Baha'u'llah says, has evolved to the point where unity of mankind has become the paramount necessity.

Membership in the Baha'i community is open to all who profess faith in Baha'u'llah and accept his teachings. There are no initiation ceremonies, no sacraments, no clergy. The Baha'i community is governed according to general principles proclaimed by Baha'u'llah and through institutions created by him that were elaborated and expanded by 'Abdu'l-Baha, his son and successor.

BAHA'U'LLAH. **THE KITAB-I-IQUAN—THE BOOK OF CERTITUDE. BPT31/Ron, 8.95c.**
Sets forth the grand redemptive scheme of God, reveals the oneness of religion and explains abstruse passages of Jewish, Christian, and Muslim scriptures.

BAHA'U'LLAH. **PRAYERS AND MEDITATIONS. 347pp. BPT38, 6.95c.**
A treasury of prayers and devotional passages from the scriptures of the Baha'i faith.

BAHA'U'LLAH. **THE SEVEN VALLEYS AND THE FOUR VALLEYS. 65pp. BPT75, 2.95c.**
This is one of Baha'u'llah's most important mystical works. **The Seven Valleys** is loosely based on Attar's **Conference of the Birds** and traces the seven stages of progress of the soul toward the object of its being.

The Four Valleys sets forth four divine states and the four kinds of *mystic wayfarers.*

BAHA'U'LLAH and ABDU'L-BAHA. **THE REALITY OF MAN. 61pp. BPT31, 3.95c.**
A topically arranged series of selections from the writings of Baha'u'llah and Abdu'l-Baha.

BALYUZI, H.M. **THE BAB. Notes, bibliography, index, 271pp. Ron73, 2.60p.**
This is a study of the life and ministry of one of the three central figures of the Baha'i faith. The Bab's brief ministry (1844-50) ended in his own martyrdom and that of many thousands of his followers.

BALYUZI, H.M. **BAHA'U'LLAH. 134pp. Ron nd, 2.00p.**
The first part offers a short account of the life of Baha'u'llah, describing his background and his chief writing. The second is an essay on the *eternal manifestation of God,* entitled *The Word Made Flesh.*

CONRADER, JAY and CONSTANCE, eds. **TOKENS: FROM THE WRITINGS OF BAHA'U'LLAH. 78pp. BPT73, 5.95p.**
This is a beautifully produced 8½"x11" volume which counterpoints quotations from Baha'u'llah summing up the origin and destiny of man and the meaning and purpose of his life on earth with evocative color and black and white nature photographs. All of the sources of the quotations are cited.

EFFENDI, SHOGHI, tr. **THE HIDDEN WORDS OF BAHA'U'LLAH. 52pp. BPT75, 2.95c.**
A collection of mystical verses which sum up the path all true seekers follow, according to the Baha'i faith.

ESSLEMONT, J.E. **BAHA'U'LLAH AND THE NEW ERA. Jov23, 1.75p.**
An introduction to the Baha'i faith, covering its history and teachings. Includes many quotations from Baha'i writings.

MILLER, WILLIAM MCELWEE. **WHAT IS THE BAHA'I FAITH? 151pp. Eer77, 3.95p.**
Dr. Miller spent a lifetime studying the history and theology of the Baha'i faith. The result was his definitive **The Baha'i Faith: Its History and Teachings.** This is an abridged edition of that work.

SCHAEFER, UDO. **THE LIGHT SHINETH IN DARKNESS. Notes, bibliography, 205pp. Ron77, 3.80p.**
Schaefer is a German lawyer who served as Chairman of the National Spiritual Assembly of the Baha'is of Germany for several years. This book contains translations of the following papers: *Belief and Unbelief Today, What It Means to be a Baha'i, Answer to a Theologian, The Baha'i Faith and Islam,* and *Muhammad and the West.* This is a good presentation of the contemporary Baha'i point of view.

TAHERZADEH, ADIB. **THE REVELATION OF BAHA'U'LLAH, VOLUME I. Notes, bibliography, indices, 380pp. Ron76, 5.50p.**
This is the first of a four volume definitive description of the writings of Baha'u'llah which were revealed during his forty year ministry. These *Tablets of Baha'u'llah* were recorded in Persian and Arabic and authenticated by the Founder himself. They encompass a vast range of subjects—spiritual, philosophical, social, and humanitarian. This volume covers his Baghdad writings in the years 1853-63.

TAHERZADEH, ADIB. **THE REVELATION OF BAHA'U'LLAH, VOLUME II. Notes, bibliography, indices, 493pp. Ron77, 6.75p.**
This volume covers Baha'u'llah's Adrianople writings in the years 1863-68.

TOWNSHEND, GEORGE, ed. **THE GLAD TIDINGS OF BAHA'U'LLAH. Introduction, notes, 122pp. Ron75, 2.00p.**
Extracts from the sacred writings of the Baha'is.

BIBLES

Now the **Bible**, containing the best of a great people's literature during nearly ten centuries, is regarded throughout the Western World as the most important of the world's books. But though esteemed as highly as ever, perhaps as pure literature esteemed more highly than ever, it is not read as formerly.

This work, which through the King James translation became a part of the very body of our language, which was often the one book in the possession of our pioneering ancestors, its teachings intertwined in the warp and woof of the American tradition, not always for good but unquestionably making us what we have been and are, this food of their fathers is neglected by the children. When it became no longer possible to regard the **Bible** as the literal word of God, or to turn superstitiously after the manner of the Virgilian lots to any chance text for immediate guidance in one's particular affairs, with the loss of authority came also, unfortunately, a loss of interest. Through having been made too exclusively sacred, the **Bible** forfeited momentarily its enormous secular power. With its study in the schools limited or even proscribed by sectarian jealousy, after having been virtually the whole of education, the **Bible** seemed to drop out of education altogether. In the long run, this will not matter, since one may safely prophesy that the **Bible** will outlive every sect fashioned upon it as Homer has outlived every pagan cult of Greece, but the loss to the immediate contemporary generation is incalculable.

Few things could be culturally more deplorable than that to-day the average college graduate, who fancies himself educated, should never have read the **Book of Job**, should be unfamiliar with **Isaiah**, and should hardly be able to identify those mighty men of valor, Joshua the son of Nun, Gideon, and Jephthah, or those most famous of scarlet women, Rahab, Delilah, Bath-sheba—and should not only be thus abysmally ignorant but should feel no incentive to be otherwise. For this is nothing less than a loss of racial memory, a forgetfulness of our cultural heritage that is as serious in the life of nations as is for the individual the loss of personality attendant upon certain forms of neurotic disease.

Not only deplorable but unnecessary—because the outstanding qualities of Biblical literature are precisely those that have more and more come into favor in recent years. In striking contrast to Greek literature, that of the **Bible** is marked by three great characteristics: it is collective rather than individual in inspiration and workmanship; it is realistic rather than idealistic in manner; it is free and flexible rather than constrained in form.

With the exception of the **Prophetical Books**, all those of the **Old Testament** are anonymous, and the **Prophets** belonged to a definite school with a common style; though in the **New Testament**, where the individualistic note is, of course, introduced with Christianity, authors' names have been affixed to all but one of the books; yet Mark, Luke, and Paul are the only ones of whom we have any certainty. The **Bible** as a whole is essentially folk literature in which the speakers and writers are at one with their audience, expressing the interests and collective wisdom of their group—at first, the larger group of the whole Jewish nation, later the smaller group of Christian disciples.

Like that of folk literature everywhere, the language is vividly realistic. Doubtless, among other reasons for the long continuance of the belief in the literal truth of the Scriptural narratives is the fact that they were composed with an imaginative realization of small details which makes the account of every incident seem like the report of an eye-witness. The same realistic habit of mind appears in the thought and the emotions; Jehovah was to the Jews no poetic myth or philosophic theory but the most tremendous of concrete realities to which their behavior was the appropriate response. When they ventured at all beyond the realm of orthodoxy, they went far; the Prophets actually remade the Jewish religion, while the determined skepticism of **Job** and the thorough-going pessimism of **Ecclesiastes** have few rivals in other literatures. And the one entirely secular work that strayed into the sacred canon, the Song of Songs, is the most impassioned and voluptuous of all love poetry.

Finally, though the Hebrews may have used an elementary metre in their verse, their main principle of versification was a parallelism of word, phrase, or strophe, which, though distinct from the structure of prose, was very close to it, supplying through the King James translation the ultimate basis for the free verse of Walt Whitman and the polyphonic prose of Amy Lowell. So, in these various ways, the **Bible** might be said to be almost contemporary.

—from **The Bible**, by Ernest Sutherland Bates

ADDINGTON, JACK. **THE HIDDEN MYSTERY OF THE BIBLE.** **276pp. DMd69, 7.95c.**
A study guide to understanding the spiritual and psychological messages in the **Old Testament**, written as a result of Addington's many years' search for meaning while teaching Bible classes.

ANONYMOUS. **THE BOOK OF JASHER. Oversize, 83pp. Amo nd, 7.75c.**
This is one of the long lost and long sought for sacred books which is contemporary with the **Old Testament** and which many think should have been included with the other books of the **Bible**. The original author was born during the lifetime of Moses and lived in association and companionship with him. Therefore, the first part of this edition was written by Jasher from the records and traditions that had been preserved by his ancestors. The latter part is based upon what he observed himself. For all interested in biblical history this book presents another record of the events recorded in the **Old Testament**. This is a photographic reproduction of the 1751 edition, with an introduction and notes.

ANONYMOUS. **HEBREW-ENGLISH LEXICON OF THE BIBLE.** **287pp. ScB74, 5.50p.**
A handy, concise dictionary designed to assist the student reading the **Bible** in the original Hebrew and Aramaic.

ANONYMOUS. **THE LOST BOOKS OF THE BIBLE AND THE FORGOTTEN BOOKS OF EDEN. 269pp. NAL27, 4.95p.**
You will find between these covers all the ecclesiastical writings of early Christian authorities that are known to exist, and yet were omitted from the authorized **New Testament**.—from the preface.

The Apocrypha

The **Apocrypha** consists of twelve books of the **Bible**, dating from the time of the **Old Testament**—not found in the **Hebrew Bible** and removed from the King James version by the Puritans in the seventeenth century. It is a collection of histories, romances, books of devotion, and edifying sayings and discourses, which bridges the period between the **Old** and **New Testaments**.

GOODSPEED, EDGAR, tr. **THE APOCRYPHA. 519pp. RaH38, 3.45p.**
A translation into contemporary English, part in prose, part in poetry. This is the most popular edition and includes a good introduction.

THE NEW ENGLISH BIBLE: THE APOCRYPHA. 462pp. CUP nd, 4.95c.
See review of **New English Bible** for a critique of this edition.

OESTERLEY, W.O.E. **AN INTRODUCTION TO THE BOOKS OF THE APOCRYPHA. Notes, bibliography, index, 345pp. SCK35, 10.95c.**
Oesterley is a well known **Old Testament** scholar. Here he discusses the importance of Apocryphal literature from the literary, historical, and doctrinal points of view and gives the reader some background information on the individual books.

————— END OF THE APOCRYPHA SUBSECTION —————

ASCH, SHOLEM. **IN THE BEGINNING. Illustrations, 112pp. ScB35, 4.95c.**
A simply written retelling of stories from the **Old Testament**, translated into English by Caroline Cunningham.

ASIMOV, ISAAC. **ASIMOV'S GUIDE TO THE BIBLE. Nearly 200 maps, chronology, indices, 1,358pp. Avo69, 4.95p/each.**
In this two volume set (devoted respectively to the **Old** and **New Testaments**) Asimov presents a book-by-book examination of the **Bible**. As usual he writes in an entertaining way and his scholarship is excellent. He incorporates history, religion, archaeology, and mythology into his discussion and helps to make reasonable many seemingly unreasonable biblical events.

Bibles

There are, of course, countless different editions and translations of the **Bible**. We have chosen only ones which contain both the **Old** and **New Testaments**. We have tried to offer a varied, albeit scanty selection. All the ones we have chosen are works of excellent scholarship and they are among the most noted editions available.

BATES, ERNEST, ed. **THE BIBLE DESIGNED TO BE READ AS LIVING LITERATURE. Glossary, 1,300pp. S&S36, 6.95p.**
This is a modernized arrangement of the **Bible**, basically following the King James version. Bates has edited the material for reading and enjoyment and is not overly concerned with strict theology. Over the years the **Bates Bible** (as this book is generally called) has been extremely popular. All the spelling is modernized.

CHAMBERLIN, ROY and HERMAN FELDMAN, eds. **THE DARTMOUTH BIBLE. 1,260pp. HMC50, 10.95p.**
A good, modern King James with the **Apocrypha**. Voluminous commentary on the historical background is included.

KING JAMES. **THE HOLY BIBLE: KING JAMES VERSION. NAL74, 4.95p.**
This translation was prepared under the direction of James I of England in the seventeenth century. It remains the standard against which all other translations are measured and has been the basis for countless other editions.

JONES, ALEXANDER, ed. **THE JERUSALEM BIBLE: READER'S EDITION. 1,698pp. Dou66, 5.95p.**
First published in English in 1966, this is a modern translation in clear, faithful, and beautiful language. Single column pages, including the **Apocrypha** with chronological table, measures and money tables, and maps. A recommended translation.

LAMSA, GEORGE, tr. **HOLY BIBLE. 1,262pp. Hol40, 13.95c.**
A translation from ancient Eastern (mainly Aramaic) manuscripts. Aramaic is the language of the Eastern church and it is generally felt that the Aramaic manuscripts are more authentic than those which are generally used. Lamsa himself is a native Assyrian and his translations from the Aramaic and comments on the Scriptures have aroused tremendous interest both in the U.S. and in Europe.

MAY, HERBERT and BRUCE METZGER, eds. **THE NEW OXFORD ANNOTATED BIBLE WITH THE APOCRYPHA. 1,936+pp. Oxf57, 14.95c.**
First published in 1967, this is the first edition of the **English Bible** to receive both Protestant and Catholic approval. Many aids for reading and study are provided, including introductions and page-for-page annotations. Also includes many supplementary articles and a full color map section. All articles and notes have been recently revised; cross references and an index to annotations are also included. Based on the Revised Standard version, this is designed to be an aid to all who desire a modern translation combined with outstanding study aids.

NEW ENGLISH BIBLE WITH THE APOCRYPHA. 1,824pp. Oxf71, 9.95c/6.95p.
English scholars have painstakingly collaborated on this **Bible** since 1946, comparing meaning, discussing wording and language forms, going sentence-by-sentence in an attempt to produce an edition best suited to many readers. This edition includes introductions to each part; footnotes throughout; descriptive subheadings for major divisions within each book; single column format with text printed in paragraph form and set in verse form whenever poetry occurs. The language used is that of today.

————— END OF BIBLES SUBSECTION —————

BLAKE, WILLIAM, il. **BOOK OF JOB. 8¼"x11", 73pp. Pad76, 4.95p.**
The full text of the **Book of Job**, accompanied by excellent reproductions of Blake's illustrative plates. The introduction discusses Blake and the **Bible** and Blake as a visual artist.

CAIRD, G.B. **SAINT LUKE. 271pp. Vik63, 3.50p.**
The **Gospels** all tell the story of Jesus and his ministry—each one giving the narration from a different point of view and using different sources. Luke was a second generation Christian who had ample opportunity to associate with those who had firsthand knowledge of the **Gospel** story. He was an educated man who could adapt his diction to different occasions, writing sometimes formal, classical prose, sometimes a racy narrative style, and sometimes the *Bible Greek* in which the Septuagint was written. This **Gospel** is notable for its insistence on the life, death, and teaching of Christ as a message of universal salvation addressed to all men. Included are detailed accounts of the working of the Spirit and the ministry of the angels. This book is part of the **Penguin New Testament Gospel Commentaries**. These new paragraph-by-paragraph commentaries have been written by modern scholars who are in touch with contemporary biblical theology and also with the interests of the layman. The words of the **Gospel** are interpreted in a very clear way in the light of the latest archaeological, historical, and linguistic research. Also includes indices of references, subjects, and authors, more commentary on the verses than there are verses, and a long introduction.

CERMINARA, GINA. **INSIGHTS FOR THE AGE OF AQUARIUS.** Index, 314pp. TPH73, 4.50p.
Ms. Cerminara uses biblical insights and the teachings of a variety of religious traditions to illustrate a number of practical techniques for increasing an individual's capacity for growth. Biblical references are scattered throughout the text.

CLAREMONT, LEWIS DE. **THE TEN LOST BOOKS OF THE PROPHETS.** 320pp. DPC59, 3.50p.
Ten books, bound together, which purport to reveal the secret knowledge used by Moses, Solomon, and Jesus to cure the ill and perform other miracles.

DORE, GUSTAVE. **THE DORE BIBLE ILLUSTRATIONS.** 9"x12", 256pp. Dov74/Pad. 5.00p.
Beautiful plates—241 in all—which capture the dramatic intensity of the Scriptures.

Enoch

There are two books generally attributed to Enoch: the first, generally known as **The Book of Enoch**, was unearthed in Ethiopia in 1773; the second, usually known as **The Book of the Secrets of Enoch**, is a Slavic manuscript which was found in Russia in 1895. The **Slavic Enoch** contains material which is similar to the **Ethiopian**, as well as some additional information. The **Book of Enoch** is generally considered the most notable extant apocalyptic work outside the canonical Scriptures. While it is attributed to Enoch, most scholars feel that it was written over a long period of time and by more than one individual. The ideas contained in the manuscripts form the basis for much of the later Christian mystical doctrines.

CHARLES, R.H., tr. **THE BOOK OF ENOCH.** 182pp. SCK17, 6.15p.
Charles' original translation of the **Ethiopian Enoch**, with introductory and background material provided by W.O.E. Oesterley.

CHARLES, R.H., tr. **THE BOOK OF ENOCH.** Offset, spiral bound, index, 441pp. HeR12, 5.00p.
This edition contains Charles' translation of the **Ethiopian Enoch**. Charles also provides 110 pages of introductory material and an incredible number of textual notes. Selections from the Greek Enochian fragments are also included.

CHARLES, R.H., ed. **THE BOOK OF THE SECRETS OF ENOCH.** Offset, spiral bound, index, 148pp. HeR1896, 2.50p.
A translation by W.R. Morfill of the original Slavic manuscripts. Charles supplies a forty-eight page introduction and extensive notes.

LAURENCE, RICHARD, tr. **THE BOOK OF ENOCH THE PROPHET.** 235pp. Wiz nd, 7.95c.
A translation of the **Ethiopian Enoch**. This was the translation that H.P. Blavatsky referred to in **The Secret Doctrine** and she, at least, considered it the definitive one. Includes a long introduction and an index.

MILIK, J.T., ed. **THE BOOKS OF ENOCH.** Notes, bibliography, index, 7¾"x10", 476pp. Oxf76, 83.00c.
In 1952 Dr. Milik identified the first Aramaic fragment of **Enoch** among a mass of material unearthed by the Bedouins in a cave at Qumran. Since then he has been able to recognize and to assign to positions in several distinct manuscripts a rich collection of Enochic fragments. This work provides a comparative textual and literary study of the **Aramaic Enoch** and its early versions. An extensive introduction discusses the origin and development of the various **Books of Enoch**, evaluates a number of versions, and considers the works—very different in character—attributed to Enoch from Roman times to the later Middle Ages, with special attention to Qabalistic literature. A restored text is provided, along with a complete set of plates and a lengthy commentary.

ODEBERG, HUGO, ed. **3 ENOCH OR THE HEBREW BOOK OF ENOCH.** 484pp. KTV73, 30.25c.
This text deals with the visit of Rabbi Ishamel to heaven. Metatron is his guide. At the beginning of the vision we are told of Enoch's ascension to heaven, the protest of the angels, and how Enoch became Metatron. Metatron informs Ishamel of all the secrets revealed to him and the visions that he has seen. It is through Metatron's narrative that Ishamel sees, as it were, his heavenly vision.... Metatron also shows R. Ishamel all sorts of things and reveals the divine names to him.—from the prolegomenon. This work is also known as **Sefer ha-Hekhalot.** This edition contains an introduction, commentary, and critical notes as well as the original Hebrew text.

WORK OF THE CHARIOT. **BOOK OF ENOCH.** WkC70, 12.00p.
Consists of the R.H. Charles translation of **Enoch, Book of the Secrets of Enoch**, and the **Odeberg Hebrew Book of Enoch**, along with the Hebrew text and critical notes. Also the *Shur Qoma, The Measure of the Divine Body*, from the **Book of the Angelic Secrets of the Great One.**

———— END OF ENOCH SUBSECTION ————

Angel with the Key of the Abyss by Albrecht Durer

FENTON, J.C. **SAINT MATTHEW.** 487pp. Vik73, 4.50p.
Part of the **Penguin New Testament Gospel Commentaries**. The author of **St. Matthew's Gospel** is often regarded as the most ecclesiastical and concise of the evangelists. He records Christ's teaching very fully, and shows special interest in the relation of the **Gospel** to Jewish law. Of the four **Gospels**, his is probably the best known and the one best adapted to the general reader.

FILLMORE, CHARLES. **METAPHYSICAL BIBLE DICTIONARY.** 709pp. 10.00c.
A complete index of names and places which are written about or mentioned in the **Bible**, with extensive definitions and a discussion of the allegorical meaning they hold in the story they come from.

FORRESTER-BROWN, JAMES. **THE TWO CREATION STORIES IN GENESIS.** Index, 302pp. ShP74, 3.95p.
Forrester-Brown suggests some keys to understanding the symbolic meaning of the two distinct stories of creation contained in the first three chapters of **Genesis**. He also analyzes the creation stories in the light of the ancient esoteric wisdom.

FRIELING, RUDOLF. **HIDDEN TREASURES IN THE PSALMS.** 6.50c.
See the Steiner section.

FROMM, ERICH. **YOU SHALL BE AS GODS.** 191pp. Faw66/CaL, 1.25p.
A radical interpretation of the **Old Testament** and its tradition by a noted psychologist which explores the evolution of the basic concepts of God, man, history, sin, and repentance.

GESENIUS, WILLIAM. **A HEBREW AND ENGLISH LEXICON TO THE OLD TESTAMENT. 1,144pp. Oxf nd, 37.50c.**
The most comprehensive edition available, edited by Francis Brown, S.R. Driver, and C.A. Bridges, and translated by Edward Robinson.

GINZBERG, LOUIS. **LEGENDS OF THE BIBLE. Introduction, 685pp. Jew56, 7.95c.**
This is an abridged edition of Ginzberg's **Legends of the Jews**, originally published in seven volumes. All the major biblical stories are retold here in novelistic prose. The book provides a fine means of learning about the biblical stories without having to plod through the **Bible**.

GRAVES, ROBERT and RAPHAEL PATAI. **HEBREW MYTHS—THE BOOK OF GENESIS. Index, 311pp. MGH64, 3.95p.**
The authors have analyzed sixty-one stories of cosmic forces, deities, angels and demons, giants and heroes from **Genesis** and other Hebrew and Aramaic sources in the light of modern anthropology and mythology.

GREEN, ROGER. **THE TALE OF ANCIENT ISRAEL. Illustrations, 192pp. Den69, 6.40c.**
A well written retelling of the **Old Testament** story, geared toward young readers. Green specializes in myths and here he emphasizes the mythical quality of the biblical tales.

GREENLEES, DUNCAN. **THE GOSPEL OF ISRAEL. Bibliography, index, 521pp. TPH55, 3.50c.**
A topically arranged selection of **Old Testament** material, bound together with a 144 page exploration of the history of the Jewish people and the biblical prophets. This is part of the Theosophical Society's **World Gospel Series**.

GROVE, DAISY. **THE MYSTERY TEACHING OF THE BIBLE. 120pp. TPH25, 3.75c.**
A Theosophist's look at the **Bible**, explaining the significance of certain archetypes, numbers, and names, and showing how the stories relate to man's need for God.

HALL, MANLY P. **OLD TESTAMENT WISDOM. Index, 312pp. PRS57, 10.00c.**
This is the result of years of careful biblical research. Mr. Hall gives not only facts, but also his masterful interpretation of the deeper meanings contained in the Holy Scriptures. The approach is always within the framework of comparative religion, mysticism, and their practical application.

HEIDENREICH, ALFRED. **THE UNKNOWN IN THE GOSPELS. 150pp. CCP72, 4.95c.**
A collection of seven lectures given recently by a follower of Rudolf Steiner: *The Place of the* **Gospels** *in the Religious Literature of the World; The Contrasting Stories of the Childhood of Jesus in the* **Gospels of Matthew** *and* **Luke** *and their Meaning; The Dead Sea Scrolls and the Historical Background of the* **Gospels**; *Stages of the Incarnation of Christ in Jesus; Spiritual Healing in the* **Gospels**; *Miracles; The Raising of Lazarus.* The material is fascinating and very clearly presented.

HELINE, CORINNE. **THE BIBLE AND THE STARS. 128pp. NAP71, 3.50p.**
Explores the spiritual relationships between the zodiac and the important stories of the **Bible—Genesis**, Abraham, Isaac, Jacob, the Ten Commandments, Solomon, **Job**, the Prophets, the Apostles, and **Revelations**, to name but a few.

HELINE, CORINNE. **THE MYSTERY OF THE CHRISTOS. Index, 322pp. NAP61, 5.95c.**
Deals with the Christ in his several aspects: cosmic, planetary, historical, and mystical. In these various treatments references are made to the foremost events between the annunciation and the ascension, since each one has a specific meaning relative to progressive attainment in these different phases of spiritual unfoldment.

HELINE, CORINNE. **MYSTIC MASONRY AND THE BIBLE. 75pp. NAP nd, 3.95p.**
An esoteric analysis.

HELINE, CORINNE. **MYTHOLOGY AND THE BIBLE. 75pp. NAP62, 2.00p.**
A study of biblical myths as related to those of Greece and Rome.

HELINE, CORINNE. **NEW AGE BIBLE INTERPRETATION: AN EXPOSITION OF THE INNER SIGNIFICANCE OF THE HOLY SCRIPTURES IN THE LIGHT OF ANCIENT WISDOM. NAP73.**
. . . Not representative of any one school or system of thought. The **Bible**, *the supreme spiritual textbook of life, is above all creeds, dogmas, and differences in religious beliefs. So also, this, a deeper and larger interpretation of its meaning, is offered as a manual of study for all groups, organizations, and individuals who seek to know the inner Christ and to develop increasingly the consciousness of the kingdom of Heaven within.* **Old Testament**: Volume I, 8.50c., 513pp; Volume II, 8.50c., 469pp; Volume III, 8.50c., 536pp. **New Testament**: Volume IV, 4.75c., 139pp; Volume V, 6.00c., 237pp; Volume VI, 6.00c., 262pp.

HELINE, CORINNE. **OCCULT ANATOMY AND THE BIBLE. 365pp. NAP37, 6.00c.**
Elaborates upon the idea that the mystery of the universe is expressed through the formation and birth of a child, and extended throughout the physical life of spiritual rebirths.

HELINE, CORINNE. **QUESTIONS AND ANSWERS ON THE BIBLE.** **100pp. NAP61, 2.00p.**

HELINE, CORINNE. **TAROT AND THE BIBLE. 267pp. NAP69, 4.50p.**
Although the title only mentions Tarot, this study also encompasses the Qabala and the mystic significance of the Hebrew alphabet.

HIEBEL, FREDERICK. **TREASURES OF BIBLICAL RESEARCH AND THE CONSCIENCE OF THE TIMES. 42pp. APl nd, .95p.**
Brief but detailed historical survey of the time of Christ based on the writings found in the Dead Sea Scrolls. Traces the identity of the Essene *Teacher of Righteousness*, and describes Jesus' life with his parents and their connection with the Essenes.

HODSON, GEOFFREY. **THE CHRIST LIFE FROM NATIVITY TO ASCENSION. Glossary, bibliography, index, 466pp. TPH75, 5.50p.**
Hodson continues the exploration he began in **The Hidden Wisdom in the Holy Bible**. Here he focuses on the **New Testament**, interpreting the four **Gospels** in the light of their allegorical meaning. His text is based on the King James version. *Ever must it be remembered that the wonderous story (of Jesus the Christ) was never intended to be read as a record of external events alone, but rather as a revelation of the divine within man.*

HODSON, GEOFFREY. **THE HIDDEN WISDOM IN THE HOLY BIBLE, VOLUME I. Index, 250pp. THP67, 1.95p.**
As with the scriptures of all religions, many profound meanings lie hidden beneath the literal interpretations of the **Bible**, and Geoffrey Hodson has shown that these can be discovered through an understanding of the sacred language of allegory and symbol. The more incredible and baffling some of the myths and stories appear, he points out, the more important it is to search for the underlying truths which can bring genuine insight and inspiration. For almost fifty years Hodson has lectured for and contributed to the literature of the Theosophical Society. He has carried out significant research in collaboration with physicians, physicists, anthropologists, and archaeologists, and has made many other major contributions to mankind's understanding of his unique place in the universe. This volume is a discussion of allegory and symbol in both the **Old** and **New Testaments**, with a look at the life of Jesus.

HODSON, GEOFFREY. **THE HIDDEN WISDOM IN THE HOLY BIBLE, VOLUME II. Glossary, bibliography, index, 493pp. TPH67, 4.95p.**
This is an excellent, detailed study of the **Book of Genesis**, incorporating Theosophical wisdom, the symbolism of mystic Christianity, and many insights from the Qabalistic tradition.

HODSON, GEOFFREY. **THE HIDDEN WISDOM IN THE HOLY BIBLE, VOLUME III. 365pp. TPH71, 2.95p.**
While Volume II deals with the first twenty-five chapters of **Genesis**, this one concludes the discussion of **Genesis**. The approach is the same as in the previous volume. A glossary and an index are included here.

HOLBEIN, HANS. **IMAGES FROM THE OLD TESTAMENT. Introduction, Pad76, 4.95p.**
Ninety-four woodcuts, immortalizing Holbein's visualization of biblical themes.

HOLLADAY, WILLIAM, ed. **A CONCISE HEBREW AND ARAMAIC LEXICON OF THE OLD TESTAMENT. 443pp. Eer71, 18.90c.**

KINGSLAND, WILLIAM. **THE GNOSIS AND CHRISTIANITY. Bibliography, index, 230pp. TPH70, 3.25p.**
Kingsland outlines an esoteric interpretation of Christianity which, he contends, is the same root teaching contained in the more ancient scriptures of other religions. His work is well documented and is valuable to anyone interested in a deeper study of Christianity.

KLUGER, RIVKAH. **PSYCHE AND BIBLE. 7.50p.**
See the Jungian Psychology section.

LAMBDIN, THOMAS. **INTRODUCTION TO BIBLICAL HEBREW. 7½"x11", 373pp. Scr71, 16.80c.**
This is generally considered the best contemporary biblical Hebrew grammar. The lessons are very well organized and the text can be used either with a teacher or without. It is designed for a full year's course in elementary Hebrew at the college level. Lambdin is a Harvard professor.

LAMSA, GEORGE. **MORE LIGHT ON THE GOSPEL. Introduction, index, 407pp. ABS68, 10.65p.**
Lamsa provides an explanation of over 400 **New Testament** passages.

LAMSA, GEORGE. **NEW TESTAMENT ORIGIN. 113pp. ABS76, 2.35p.**
A detailed investigation of the Aramaic origin of the **New Testament** and an analysis of the Aramaic language. Lamsa has translated many old Aramaic documents and he incorporates a great deal of original research into his exposition.

LAMSA, GEORGE. **OLD TESTAMENT LIGHT. Index, 991pp. ABS64, 9.75c.**
Detailed scriptural commentary based on passages selected from Dr. Lamsa's own translation and from the King James version.

LAMSA, GEORGE. **THE SHEPHERD OF ALL. 86pp. ABS76, 3.70p.**
An interpretation of the psalm based on Aramaic teachings and on Lamsa's knowledge of the past and present lifestyle of the people who lived in biblical lands.

MCCAFFERY, ELLEN. **AN ASTROLOGICAL KEY TO BIBLICAL SYMBOLISM. 7.95c.**
See the Astrology section.

MARSH, JOHN. **SAINT JOHN. 705pp. Vik68, 4.75p.**
Part of the **Penguin New Testament Gospel Commentaries**. Professor Marsh begins by debunking the traditional view that the author of this **Gospel** was John, the apostle. He feels that it must have been written by a later figure (this is the fourth and last **Gospel**). The main body of the commentary is an endeavor to locate John's central purpose, which was to enshrine, for a wide circle of readers, the living word of God. In this attempt he examines John's conception of history and takes a look at the similarities and the notable differences between this record and that of the **Synoptic Gospels**.

MATTHEWS, E.C. **STARS OF THE BIBLE. Oversize, 162pp. MDC nd. 10.00c.**
The main feature of this book are the eighty full page illustrations from the **Bible** illustrated by Gustave Dore. These woodcuts are not to be found anywhere else except in long out of print editions. The rest of the text consists of vaguely related biblical quotations and general, quite antiquated astrological analysis.

MEAD, G.R.S. **THE GOSPELS AND THE GOSPEL. Offset, spiral bound, 215pp. HeR nd, 5.00c.**
A collection of essays examining various aspects of the **Gospels** from a metaphysical/historical viewpoint by a noted nineteenth century scholar.

NEIL, WILLIAM. **HARPER'S BIBLE COMMENTARY. 544pp. H&R62, 4.95p.**
An aid to serious **Bible** study which follows the chronology of the **Bible** and presents commentary and background information.

NINEHAM, D.E. **SAINT MARK. 477pp. Vik69, 4.95p.**
Part of the **Penguin New Testament Gospel Commentaries**. This **Gospel** is generally acknowledged as the one which comes nearest to the events described. Although it is the least cultured and grammatical of the four, St. Mark's talent for writing narrative is indisputable. His **Gospel**, written around the themes of the Church's preaching, evinces his desire to witness Christ as the Messiah.

NORELLI-BACHELET, PATRIZIA. **THE HIDDEN MANNA. 385pp. Aeo76, 10.00c.**
An analysis of the **Gospel of John**, with the complete text and commentaries. Ms. Norelli-Bachelet concentrates on the prophetic aspects of the text, and she compares it to Eastern prophetic books.

PANAS, HENRYK. **THE GOSPEL ACCORDING TO JUDAS. 254pp. HPG77, 11.50c.**
A novelistic reconstruction of a fifth **Gospel**, tracing the development of Jesus' teachings and messianic mission through the eyes of Judas. In this account Judas is seen as Jesus' closest follower and his appointed

successor. As might be expected, Judas is seen in a very sympathetic light, and the narrative emphasizes the political motivations of Jesus' followers. An interesting, highly readable account, which offers a new perspective on this familiar story. Panas is a respected Polish novelist.

PRYSE, JAMES. **THE APOCALYPSE UNSEALED. Offset, spiral bound, 222pp. HeR nd, 3.95p.**
To most of us the **Book of Revelations** of John is exactly what it pretends to be, the hallucinations of Jesus' beloved apostle. But to James Pryse it is far more. He interprets and untangles the riddles and puzzles John devised to shield the sacred knowledge from the eyes of the profane.

PRYSE, JAMES. **THE MAGICAL MESSAGE ACCORDING TO IOANNES. Offset, spiral bound, 230pp. HeR nd, 4.50p.**
Annotated literal translation of **John's Gospel** from the Greek, with half the book containing highly mystical commentary on the esoteric substance.

PRYSE, JAMES. **REINCARNATION IN THE NEW TESTAMENT. Offset, spiral bound, 90pp. HeR1899, 2.50p.**
A short work that points out possible references to **Old Testament** characters reincarnated in **New Testament** stories.

PRYSE, JAMES. **THE RESTORED NEW TESTAMENT. Two volumes, offset, spiral bound, 800pp. HeR14, 12.50p/set.**
Pryse wants to emphasize in his translation the mystical quality of the biblical literature that can lift man's spirit above the illusions of his ego and connect him with the depth of his divinity.

RUTHERFORD, ADAM. **BIBLE CHRONOLOGY. Index, 555pp. IPy57, 18.00c.**
The most comprehensive work imaginable, covering every biblical period from **Genesis** to **Revelation** in detail. It also explains and demonstrates every known method of testing a chronological system and establishing accuracy: astronomical fixing, recorded synchronisms, observed cycles, archaeological data, and radioactivity determination. The enormous data presented here throws light on related chronologies, especially the Egyptian. Includes a great deal of background material in addition to the tables.

SINGH, CHARAN. **ST. JOHN THE GREAT MYSTIC. 172pp. RaS nd, 3.50c.**
An Indian yogi-master has written an inspiring commentary on the verses of **John's Gospel.** He explains the spiritual motivations and instructions of the words and deeds of Jesus.

STEINER, RUDOLF. **GOSPEL OF ST. JOHN. 3.50p.**
See the Steiner section.

STRONG, JAMES. **STRONG'S EXHAUSTIVE CONCORDANCE OF THE BIBLE. Oversized, 1,808pp. Abi1894, 24.30c.**
This is the most complete concordance of the **Bible** available. It includes a main concordance which lists each word in the King James version, and all passages in which it occurs; a comparative concordance which compares the King James version with the English and American revisions of 1885 and 1901; a dictionary of the **Hebrew Bible**; and a dictionary of the **Greek Testament.** Every word in the **Bible** and every passage in which it occurs is listed. Considered the standard reference work.

WESTERMANN, CLAUS. **THE BIBLE: A PICTORAL HISTORY. 8¼"x9½", 152pp. Sea77, 14.95c.**
A collection of stunning photographs of Holy Land landscapes and archaeological artifacts by Erich Lessing is accompanied by selected **Old Testament** quotations, brief descriptions of each photograph, and an introductory text by Westermann summarizing the **Old Testament** story.

BIORHYTHMS

The basics of biorhythm are easy to understand. In its simplest form, the theory states that from birth to death each of us is influenced by three internal cycles—the physical, the emotional, and the intellectual. The physical cycle takes 23 days to complete, and it affects a broad range of physical factors, including resistance to disease, strength, coordination, speed, physiology, other basic body functions, and the sensation of physical well-being. The emotional cycle governs creativity, sensitivity, mental health, mood, perceptions of the world and of ourselves, and, to some degree, the sex of children conceived during different phases of the cycle. It takes 28 days to come full circle. Finally, the intellectual cycle, which takes place over a 33-day period, regulates memory, alertness, receptivity to knowledge, and the logical or analytical functions of the mind.

On the day of birth, each of the cycles starts at a neutral baseline or zero point. From there, it begins to rise in a positive phase, during which the energies and abilities associated with each cycle are high. Gradually declining, the cycles cross the zero point midway through their complete periods. For the balance of the period each rhythm is in a negative phase in which energies are recharged and our physical, emotional, and intellectual capabilities are low, or at least somewhat diminished. We pick up increasing amounts of energy as the negative phase continues until, at the end of each cycle, the zero point is recrossed into the positive phase, and the whole process begins again.

Since the three cycles last for different numbers of days, they very rarely coincide and cross the baseline at exactly the same time (only at birth and every 58 years plus 67 or 68 days thereafter). Therefore, we are usually influenced by mixed rhythms. Some will be high while others are low; some will cross the neutral point while others have many days to go until they reach the same level; to make an even finer distinction, one rhythm may be in a stronger part of the positive phase (or a weaker part of the negative phase) than others that are going through the same phase. The result is that our behavior—from physical endurance to creativity to performance on academic examinations—is a composite of these differing rhythms. We seldom have absolutely wonderful or absolutely terrible days. We have up days, down days, and a good many in-between days, but every day can be understood in terms of a particular and almost unique combination of the three basic cycles.

—*condensed from* **Biorhythm**, *by Bernard Gittelson*

BIOMATE COMPUTER. 9.95.
The Biomate is a plastic slide rule especially designed to show at a glance the three biorhythms controlling your life. It consists of four gear wheels which you set into position following guidelines. Once set, the Biomate will show at a glance your personal biorhythms for a complete year. Each year a small adjustment will update it for the next year. The Biomate can also be used for a number of people by individually setting it each time it is used. It is easy to use and seems to work quite well—though occasionally the gears slip.

COHEN, DANIEL. **BIORHYTHMS IN YOUR LIFE.** Index, 192pp. Faw76, 1.75p.
A good historical discussion of biorhythms, with information on the initial research and all the current studies. There is also instructional material and addresses of the major sources for biorhythm supplies.

■ *GITTELSON, BERNARD.* **BIORHYTHM: A PERSONAL SCIENCE.** 186pp. War76, 2.95p.
This is the best of the books on biorhythms. The background data, proofs, and explanations are clearly presented and complete tables are included, with instructions for casting your own biorhythm.

GITTELSON, BERNARD. **BIORHYTHM SPORTS FORECASTING.** 238pp. Arc77, 2.95p.
Gittelson uses the science of biorhythms to show, through a number of case studies, why athletes have certain up and down days. He gives the biorhythm codes for thousands of athletes in every major sport, together with charts for the years 1977-79, so that sports fans can plot a given athlete's cycle.

LEWIS, H. SPENCER. **SELF MASTERY AND FATE WITH THE CYCLES OF LIFE.** 5.75c.
See the Rosicrucianism section.

LUCE, GAY. **BIOLOGICAL RHYTHMS IN HUMAN AND ANIMAL PHYSIOLOGY.** 8"x11", 183pp. Dov71, 3.50p.
Recent scientific research has shown that man, along with the rest of the animal and plant world, feels, grows, and reacts in time to various rhythms, the most common being the twenty-four hour solar day. Hundreds of experiments and observations are cited in this book, a survey of all that was known about biological rhythms as of 1970. This is a technical survey, originally prepared for the National Institute of Mental Health. Includes over fifty pages, double column, of references.

LUCE, GAY. **BODY TIME.** 411pp. SBL73, 3.30p.
An intriguing report on man's inner time clocks and the new scientific discoveries about them that could revolutionize our lives. Tells how our highs and lows can be predicted—our peaks of strength and productivity, our valleys of stress and illness. Excellent chapter on the relation of body cycles to earth and moon cycles.

■ *MALLARD, VINCENT.* **BIORHYTHMS AND YOUR BEHAVIOR.** Glossary, bibliography, oversize, 68pp. RuP76, 4.95p.
A brief explanation of the biorhythm cycles combined with a section of step-by-step instructions for computing biorhythms and many tables and blank graphs. There are also sections on comparing two or more people's biorhythms and case studies of biorhythmic data for well known public figures. Most of the book is devoted to the workbook sheets and the book is illustrated throughout.

PSI RHYTHMS. **BIO-KIT. PSI74, 4.95.**
A kit containing complete instructions for charting biorhythms, bio-curve plastic templates for the actual charting, a pad of bio-chart paper, and mathematical calculation tables.

TATAI, KICHINOSUKE. **BIORHYTHM FOR HEALTH DESIGN.** Tables, bibliography, index, 7"x10", 160pp. Jap77, 6.95p.
A detailed study, theoretical and instructive, written by a Japanese physician who has done pioneering work in the health applications of biorhythms.

THOMMEN, GEORGE. **IS THIS YOUR DAY?** Bibliography, 160+pp. Avo73, 1.75p.
This was the first extensive exploration of biorhythms published in the U.S. and it remains the most popular one. General background and explanatory information is presented along with a history of the development of the biorhythm theory. Also included are complete directions for charting biorhythms and calculation tables up to 1984.

WARD, RITCHIE. **THE LIVING CLOCKS.** Notes, index, 368pp. NAL71, 1.95p.
A well written study of biological clocks which link all living things with the rhythm of the earth, the moon, the sun, and the stars. Profusely illustrated and geared toward the general reader—and also a work of good scholarship.

BUDDHISM

Buddhism, the religion of reason and meditation and the faith of approximately one fifth of humanity, was founded by the so called *historic* Buddha, Siddhartha Gautama, a unique spiritual genius born in northeastern India at a date generally accepted as 563 B.C. Although in the land of its origin Buddhism was in time reabsorbed into the all embracing Hinduism from which is sprang, it was destined to become and remain the dominant influence in vast sections of Asia, including Ceylon, Burma, Cambodia, Thailand, Vietnam, Laos, as well as Nepal, Sikkim, Tibet, Mongolia, China, Korea and Japan. In all these countries it has had an almost incalculable effect on art, thought, literature and ways of life.

As happens with all world religions, there have accrued to Buddhism, with the passing of the two and a half millennia since its founding, the usual elaborate deification cults, superstitious rites and even, to some degree, fixed authoritative dogma. These developments bear little relation to the original precepts of the strongly pragmatic, down-to-earth, compassionate yet tough minded aristocrat who established this religious philosophy almost six centuries before the beginning of the Christian era. During the more than forty years of active ministry that followed Siddhartha Gautama's attainment of Supreme Enlightenment while seated in deep meditation under a sacred fig tree—a scene frequently depicted in Asian art—this gifted teacher took special pains to emphasize to his many devoted followers that none of them was to look upon or rely upon him as a Divine Savior or Intercessor. He had, to be sure, become a *Buddha*, but this simply meant an Enlightened or Awakened Being. In his opinion, not he, nor any other great Master or World Teacher, could do more for those who sought help about attaining salvation than merely to *show the way*; each man must find the path to final peace and knowledge through his own efforts.

Said the Buddha: *Within this very body, mortal as it is and only six feet in length, I do declare to you are the world and the origin of the world, and the ceasing of the world and the path that leads to cessation.* Another of his challenging sayings—*Look within, thou art the Buddha*—clearly indicates his psychological emphasis on humanity as the instrument of its own fate.

The Buddha made very few concessions to his fellow Indians' love of mythmaking, or to the common human desire to dwell on the miraculous and the supernatural. The world as it was seemed enough of a miracle for him, offering, as it did, the one road immediately at hand for attaining the final goal of Nirvana—release from blind appetites and the limiting sense of a *separate self*. Over and over again, with tireless patience, the Buddha—using the repetitive teaching style of the Far East in the days before written literature—expressed his belief that final illumination required only determination and ardent desire, a quickened *awareness* (a favorite Buddhist word) in thought and deed, and a sincere wish to compose human experience after more meaningful, less ego-centered patterns. Although the Buddha went forth personally to teach his doctrine of *mindfulness* as the way to enlightenment, he never failed to stress the necessity for freedom from all sacrosanct religious authority. *Believe nothing*, he said to his followers, *just because you have been told it, or it is commonly believed, or because it is traditional or because you yourselves have imagined it. Do not believe what your Teacher tells you merely out of respect for the Teacher. But whatsoever,*

after due examination and analysis, you find to be conducive to the good, and benefit, the welfare of all beings—that doctrine believe and cling to, and take as your guide.

Buddhism is sometimes described as a reform movement within an already calcifying Hinduism—comparable to Lutheranism and the European Christian Reformation many centuries later. This is an oversimplification, but it is possible to agree that millennia before Martin Luther, Siddhartha Gautama was, in effect, promulgating the principle of the *priesthood of all believers*. He took a firm stand against the growing strictures of the Indian caste system and the acceptance of inherent superiority, or inferiority, because of the circumstances of individual birth. Brahmins, he declared, did not deserve their exalted title simple because of hereditary status, but only if they lived lives that were virtuous and exemplary.

Anyone from a king to a barber who wished to listen to the Buddha's teachings, or follow him in his missionary wanderings, or join the Sangha, the formal fellowship of Buddhist disciples, was free to do so. Even women—after some hesitation—were admitted to the Sangha, whose establishment is often counted as one of the Buddha's most practical achievements, in large measure responsible for the eventual spread and continuity of Buddhist doctrine in the Asian world. The founding of an Order appears also to illustrate still further the Buddha's psychological acumen, for although he taught that each human being must tread the path to *awakening* or *deliverance* alone, he also realized what sustainment there could be in daily association with others working toward a common goal. Of the establishment of the Buddhist Sangha, Arnold Toynbee has said that it was a greater social achievement than the founding of the Platonist academy in Greece.

There are many stories illustrating the human warmth and loving-kindness of the radiant personality whose sculptured image—usually in a pose of meditation—is to the Eastern world what the Christ figure is to the Western. The Buddha's compassion was accompanied, however, by an unflinching realism whenever he addressed himself to the laws that govern earthly life. He once said, *I teach only two things, O disciples, the fact of suffering and the possibility of escape from suffering.* How could one deny the first of these *truths*, as he called them? Did not suffering begin with the very agony of birth itself, and continue through all the unavoidable complexities of human life: illness, disappointments, decrepitude, decay, death? Even love and happiness carried the dark shadow, for separation from or loss of what one loved brought suffering, as did the inability to get what one desired. There was just one escape from the meaningless maze. One must learn to conquer *tanha* (in Sanskrit, *trishna*, literally *thirst*), the ego's craving for satisfactions that could only lead to frustration, anxiety, sorrow, in face of the further indisputable truth that *impermanence is the law of all existence*. Since change and flux are a universal part of nature, does it not behoove human beings to take their emphasis off having, holding, possessing, even being this or that, and to concentrate instead on *extinguishing* the trouble-making greedy ego?

The Buddha went so far as to declare that an individual's seeming individuality, his self, was not *real* in any fixed sense, but was actually only a succession of instants of consciousness. As he lay dying peacefully in his eightieth year, fully aware that his end was near, he did not alter this uncompromising viewpoint. He was, he stated calmly to those gathered about him soon to disappear. Ananda, his favorite and grieving disciple, must wipe away his tears and accept this irrevocable fact. The members of the Sangha were not to mourn his passing but just get on with the work of spreading knowledge about the cause and cure of suffering and the attainment of enlightenment.

Immediately after the Great Demise, according to Buddhist history, a First Great Council of five hundred leading monks was held, at which the entire teaching was recited aloud, the most venerable monk repeating the rules of discipline, another giving the sermons, a third dealing with what could be called the psychology and philosophy of the Buddha's doctrine. This was the first authoritative formulation by Buddhist elders of the Great Teaching, a procedure some Buddhists have averred the Buddha himself might have deplored as apt to lead to profitless dogmatizing and to the very binding traditionalism he had criticized in Hinduism.

One hundred years after his death a Second Great Council was held in an attempt to settle certain doctrinal and interpretational differences that had grown up in the brotherhood. The third of the Great Councils was called by the most worldly and powerful early Buddhist convert, the Indian Emperor Ashoka, who ruled almost the whole of the vast Indian subcontinent during forty years of the third century B.C. This Third Council, tradition tells us, was held to *purify* the teaching and exclude certain fanciful theories that had been introduced by adherents improperly versed in the original tenets. At this Council, one thousand monks recited the entire canon during a period of nine months, and from this restating of basic principles there was laid the foundation for intensified missionary effort.

The Fourth Council, in the first century A.D., was held on the island of Ceylon, off the southern tip of India, indicating the spread of the doctrine southward. At this momentous Fourth Council the memorized scriptures—handed down for centuries by word of mouth in the classic teaching tradition of Asia—were first recorded in writing. This record, in the Pali tongue, constitutes to this day the orthodox Buddhist canon. The Fifth Council was not held until almost two thousand years later in Mandalay, Burma, in the year 1871, at which time these same Pali texts were inscribed on seven hundred and twenty-nine marble slabs placed at the foot of Mandalay Hill. The last council was held in the 1950's in Rangoon, Burma.

Almost from the beginning of Buddhist history there have been two main schools of Buddhist teaching. One branch, the Theravada, or School of the Elders (less correctly known as the Hinayana or Small Vehicle of Buddhism), is the Buddhism of such countries as Ceylon, Burma, Thailand and Cambodia. The other, the Mahayana, or Large Vehicle—which became, down the centuries, the majority sect—spread to the north and east, finally reaching China, Korea and Japan. The words *large* and *small* have reference to the respective latitudes or restrictions of doctrinal approach and the interpretations and practice of Buddhist principles. The Mahayana does not object to its designation as Large Vehicle, but the Hinayana Buddhists consider it preferable to refer to themselves as the Theravada School, or School of the Elders. In general, and briefly, the authoritarian Theravada School inclines toward a strict, even austere, personal adherence to established rules and doctrines, while the Mahayana holds that a more flexible and permissive attitude comes nearer the Buddha's true aims. As a consequence, the countries in which Mahayana Buddhism has flourished have created a far wider diversity in ways of Buddhist worship and art. Buddhism's diversity, however, rests on a basic unity comparable to the underlying unifying principles of Christianity that exist in spite of many denominational differences in interpretation and practice.

From the outset of his ministry the Buddha emphasized a Middle Way of conduct lying between self indulgence on one hand and extremes of asceticism on the other. His doctrine was based on the incontrovertible, undeniable truth about humanity's suffering, a truth that he embodies in a formula of four parts to which he gave the adjective *noble*. These Four Noble Truths, constituting what might be termed the Buddha's diagnosis of humanity's sickness, took a simple form: 1) No one can deny that existence involves a great deal of suffering for all human creatures. 2) This suffering and general dissatisfaction come to human beings because they are possessive, greedy and, above all, self centered. 3) Egocentricism, possessiveness and greed can, however, be understood, overcome and rooted out. 4) This rooting out can be brought about by following a rational Eightfold Path of behavior in thought, word and deed that will create a salutary change in viewpoint.

This Eightfold Path is the Buddha's basic formula for deliverance from the kind of crippling invalidism that comes with having a *body-identified mind*, as Gerald Heard has described mankind's general state. The eight requirements that will eliminate suffering by correcting false values and giving true knowledge of life's meaning have been summed up as follows: right views (or understanding), right purpose (or aspiration), right speech, right conduct, right means of livelihood (or vocation), right effort, right kind of awareness or mind control, and right concentration or meditation.

Even a novice could, in the Buddha's opinion, practice the first six steps. He could learn to think and speak with care and truthfulness, abide by basic moral laws, earn his living in ways that were not deleterious to himself or others, and maintain consistently the pursuit of the goal indicated in the last two steps. With the achievement of awareness and mind control, through ever deeper contemplative practices, there was bound to come a calm freedom from the unpredictable vagaries of ego drives and willful appetites. When ultimate freedom from every kind of egocentric thought and wish had been gained, the aspirant would also, inevitably, be through with the endless wheel of *becoming*. Nirvana, the supreme goal, the selfless *peace that passeth all understanding*, would then be within his reach. Apart from the major precepts involved in following the Eightfold Path, the Buddha took scant interest in precise rules for his adherents. When asked on one occasion whether a true disciple should not live a hermit's existence, he simply replied, *Whoever wishes may dwell in the forest and whoever wishes may dwell in a village.* What mattered was not where an aspirant chose to live but how well he could concentrate on the search for truth.

In place of the moral imperative *Thou shalt not*—so much a part of Judeo-Christian precepts—Buddhism in general offers a perhaps sounder psychological counsel, *It would be better if you refrained from.* This attitude is basic to both Mahayana and Theravada, much as they may differ in other matters—like Mahayana's use of intercessory rites versus the almost puritanic self reliance of the Theravada, or the former's belief in the efficacy of prayers versus the stress on *works* in the latter, and other significant differences.

But although interpretations of Buddhist doctrine may vary, the teaching that life is One is emphasized by all sects and branches of this vital religious philosophy, followed by so many hundreds of millions of people. The Oneness of all life is a truth, Buddhism asserts, that can be fully realized only when false notions of a separate self—whose destiny can be considered apart from the whole—are forever annihilated. When the individual seeker has finally acquired this supreme sense of the Oneness of all life, he has, indeed, reached the bliss of Nirvana. Freed completely of the limiting conditions connected with the sense of a personal ego, he has come to *the end of separateness.*

—condensed from **Three Ways of Asian Wisdom**, by Nancy Wilson Ross

AKIYAMA, TERUKAZU and SABURO MATSUBARA. **ARTS OF CHINA: BUDDHIST CAVE TEMPLES, NEW RESEARCHES. Map of sites, chronology, notes, 10½"x14¾", 248pp. Kod69, 35.00c.**
This book opens up a treasure house of Chinese Buddhist art that has been almost entirely inaccessible to the West. The fifth to the ninth centuries saw the highest florescence of Buddhist art in China, and it was in this period that a large number of temples—including the spectacular and monumental cave temples—were constructed throughout the country. These temples also housed treasures of Buddhist art; objects that are still being discovered today. This is the first book to present the new Chinese material on the art treasures—mainly the cave paintings—with many high quality photographs. The objects pictured in the forty-one color and 196 black and white plates have been selected from this heritage, with special emphasis on the richest and most inaccessible ones. An excellent text accompanies the plates.

ARNOLD, SIR EDWIN. **THE LIGHT OF ASIA. 154pp. TPH1879/RKP, 1.25p.**
Sir Edwin Arnold has rendered in exquisite poetic form the story of the Buddha's search, enlightenment, and teaching.

Asvaghosa

Asvaghosa was the first expounder of Mahayana Buddhism. Very little is known of his life, and even the exact date of his birth is unknown; he is thought to have lived in the first century AD. He was brought up as a Brahman and converted to Buddhism late in life. Asvaghosa was a poet and a musician as well as a philosophical mystic, and he composed the words and music of many hymns used in Buddhist monasteries. The most celebrated work attributed to him is the **Mahayana Shraddotpada** or **The Awakening of Faith in the Mahayana.**

BEAL, SAMUEL, tr. **THE FO-SHO-HING-TSAN-KING: A LIFE OF THE BUDDHA. Introduction, many notes, 417pp. MoB1883, 12.00c.**
A translation, from the **Sacred Books of the East** series, of an important early source document, attributed to Asvaghosa; translated from Sanskrit into Chinese in 420 AD. For the serious scholar.

HAKEDA, YOSHITO, tr. **THE AWAKENING OF FAITH. Long valuable introduction, extensive notes, annotated bibliography, 128pp. Col67, 3.45p.**
Professor Hakeda has supplied words which were only implied in the original and has also drawn upon the commentaries of ancient scholars, notably that of Fa-tsang.

JOHNSTON, E.H., tr. **THE BUDDHACARITA OR ACTS OF THE BUDDHA. Index, 515pp. MoB36, 10.50c.**
This work celebrates the life and teachings of the Buddha. Included here is a translation of the Sanskrit text as well as a profusion of notes and ninety-eight pages of introductory material.

JOHNSTON, E.H., tr. **THE SAUNDARANANDA OF ASVAGHOSA. Introductory material, commentary, glossary, notes, index, 294pp. MoB28, 10.50c.**
This book celebrates the conversion of Nanda, half brother of Gautama the Buddha, to Buddhism. It is written in verse. This edition includes the Sanskrit text, with an English translation.

LIBRARY OF TIBETAN WORKS. **FIFTY VERSES OF GURU-DEVOTION. Introduction, 39pp. LTW75, 2.00p.**
A translation of Asvaghosa's **Gurupancasika**, a short text discussing true guru-devotion and citing many case studies. According to the text you must have full confidence that it is possible to become enlightened, that your guru is living proof of this, and that by following the Buddha's teaching as he instructs, you can also achieve enlightenment. Only if this is so will you be able to benefit by the practices.

RICHMOND, TIMOTHY, tr. **THE AWAKENING OF FAITH. Long introduction, 96pp. UnB60, 5.00c.**
A profound and beautiful work which formulates the fundamental doctrines of the Mahayana school of Buddhism. It is considered one of the five most valuable Buddhist scriptures, occupying a place not dissimilar to the **New Testament.** This is a very readable translation.

SHRINE OF WISDOM EDITORS, trs. **THE AWAKENING OF FAITH IN THE MAHAYANA. 59pp. ShW64, 5.75c.**
A nicely written, flowing translation. The introduction includes biographical material on Asvaghosa, as well as a discussion of Mahayana Buddhism, nirvana, and adoration.

————————**END OF ASVAGHOSA SUBSECTION**————————

AUNG, MAUNG HTIN, tr. **BURMESE MONK'S TALES. Bibliography, 181pp. Col66, 14.00c.**
The **Monk's Tales** were collected in the nineteenth century as part of the general effort to strengthen the national religion and Burmese way of life under British rule. They were told by the Thingazar Sayadaw, one of the great monks of the era. These tales were modeled on the traditional Burmese folktale and they dealt with the current problems and difficulties of the clergy and laity. The Thingazar Sayadaw usually introduced his tales into his short, informal addresses, inventing the tale on the spot to illustrate a point or give advice. Other monks soon began to tell similar tales of their own. A sampling of these is given here, following the fifty-seven tales and two groups of anecdotes and dialogues attributed to the Thingazar. Aung provides an abundance of introductory and background information.

BAHM, ARCHIE. **PHILOSOPHY OF THE BUDDHA. Bibliography, 166pp. Put58, 2.75p.**
A basic introduction to Buddhist thought.

BARY, WILLIAM DE, ed. **THE BUDDHIST TRADITION IN INDIA, CHINA, AND JAPAN. Bibliography, 401pp. RaH69, 3.95p.**
An anthology, compiled from basic Buddhist writings, covering central doctrines and practices and including introductions and commentary on each selection.

BEYER, STEPHEN, tr. **THE BUDDHIST EXPERIENCE. Illustrations, 274pp. Dic74, 8.75p.**
This is an excellent anthology of Buddhist writings. Many of the pieces presented here have never been translated and most of the others are only available in archaic editions. The text is very well organized and covers all aspects of the Buddhist experience. The translations themselves are uniformly good. Both prose and poetry are included, and there is introductory and background material. The book is both a fine primer on Buddhism and a wonderful sourcebook.

BLOFELD, JOHN. **BEYOND THE GODS. 2.45p.**
See the Chinese Philosophy section.

BLOFELD, JOHN. **THE WHEEL OF LIFE. Illustrations, index, 291pp. ShP72/HPG, 6.95p.**
The Wheel of Life is Blofeld's spiritual autobiography—from his early years in England, to his life in Peking, and travels in Mongolia, Burma, and India. He frankly discusses his experiences and his ups and downs on the spiritual path. Blofeld writes extremely well and vividly conveys his impressions and encounters. We enjoy reading his books; there is nothing terribly deep here, but the reader does get a good feeling for the place and the times.

BRUN, VIGGO. **SUG, THE TRICKSTER WHO FOOLED THE MONK. 179pp. Cur76, 10.50p.**
A translation of a trickster cycle containing about twenty-seven episodes, recorded in Northern Thailand in 1971 and never before translated into a Western language. The cycle is presented in parallel text and a vocabulary contains all the Thai words in the text. A long introduction discusses the trickster cycle and its variants along with notes on the social setting and an analysis of the trickster's development throughout the tale.

BUDDHIST PUBLICATION SOCIETY. **THE BODHI LEAVES, VOLUMES I - III. BPS nd, 4.25c/each.**
Compilation of pamphlets originally published as part of **The Wheel** series. The quality of the text is uniformly excellent—although the physical production of the books could hardly be worse! Many of the selections deal with Pali texts and the Theravada point of view. Each volume is a fat little book.

BUKKYO DENDO KYOKAI. **THE TEACHING OF BUDDHA. Glossary, index, 326pp. Jap76, 6.50c.**
A topically arranged selection of Buddha's teachings, with sections on dharma, the way of practice, the brotherhood, and Buddha himself. The text is summarized into numbered paragraphs, which in turn are organized according to various subheadings. The book was put together by the Buddhist Promoting Foundation in Japan.

BURTT, E.A., ed. **THE TEACHINGS OF THE COMPASSIONATE BUDDHA. Glossary, bibliography, 247pp. NAL55/NEL, 1.50p.**
An excellent collection of the best translations of the basic texts, with introduction and commentary. A good basic book.

BYLES, MARIE. **FOOTPRINTS OF GAUTAMA THE BUDDHA. 224pp. TPH57, 1.75p.**
A narrative of the Buddha's day to day ministerial life, related in the first person by one of his disciples. In researching this story the author retraced the Buddha's pilgrimage. All sources are cited.

CARUS, PAUL. **THE GOSPEL OF THE BUDDHA. Illustrations, glossary, 287pp. OpC1894, 4.95p.**
Carus' purpose here is to compile the life story and the teachings of the Buddha into the equivalent of a **New Testament** gospel. Part of his purpose is to emphasize the *many striking coincidences in the philosophical basis as well as in the ethical applications of Christianity and Buddhism.* The book is in the form of a series of stories: first the story of the birth, life, and enlightenment of Prince Siddhartha who renounced the world and became the Buddha; then the stories of the first disciples; the establishment of the order; the first schism, the great questions and Buddha's answers, his parables, and his last days.

CARUS, PAUL. **KARMA/NIRVANA. Illustrations, 135pp. OpC73, 7.95c.**
Each of these two stories revolves around the *Four Noble Truths* preached by the Buddha. And each contains a tale within a tale, showing that good actions lead to good karma. The stories were written over seventy years ago and have been translated into many languages. They were often attributed to Leo Tolstoy (who wrote the introduction to this volume and translated them into Russian). The stories are simple and strike to the heart of Buddhist philosophy.

CHANG, GARMA. **THE BUDDHIST TEACHING OF TOTALITY. Glossary, notes, index, 300pp. PSU71/A&U, 8.00p.**
This is a study of the philosophy and literature of the Hwa Yen School of Buddhism in China. *The Chinese word Hwa Yen means "the flower-decoration" or "garland," which is originally the name of a voluminous Mahayana text:* **The Garland Sutra**. *Therefore, the teaching of this School is based mainly upon this text and draws inspiration from it. . . . Inspired by the revela-*

tion of the all-embracing Totality in this Sutra, the pioneer Hwa Yen thinkers. . .taught that the correct way of thinking is to view things through a multiple or total approach. Nothing is rejected, because in the "round" Totality of Buddhahood there is not even room for contradiction; here the inconsistencies all become harmonious. . . . The three major concepts of Mahayana—namely the Philosophies of Totality, of Emptiness, and of Mind-Only—are all merged into a unity. . . . Hwa Yen has been regarded as the "crown" of all Buddhist teachings, and as representing the consummation of Buddhist insight and thought. . . . As any pioneer work, this book does not claim to be an exhaustive study of the stupendous Hwa Yen literature. But it is my humble opinion that the gist and the essential elements of Hwa Yen teachings, especially the philosophical aspects, are all included in this volume. I have tried to avoid meticulous annotations and excessive footnotes in order to make the reading easier for the general reader. The philosophical presentation is very clear and quotations from the literature abound throughout the text in addition to the reading selections. This is a very important work.

CHATTERJEE, ASHOK. **THE YOGACARA IDEALISM. Introduction, glossary, index, 237pp. MoB76, 21.00c.**
An exposition of the metaphysics of the Yogacara school of Buddhism combined with an analysis of its logical implications. A complete picture of the school is presented and the system is seen as an original and constructive philosophy, not merely as a phase of Buddhism.

■ CH'EN, KENNETH. **BUDDHISM. Glossary, index, 297pp. BES68, 2.75p.**
This is one of the best overall works we have read. The topics include the life and teachings of the Buddha; Mahayana Buddhism; the *sangha* or monastic community; the spread of Theravada Buddhism; Buddhism in China, Japan, and Tibet; Buddhist literature and art; and Buddhism in the modern world. Each chapter is clearly written and the text includes an excellent chapter by chapter bibliography. The emphasis is academic but not overly so. This makes a good book for those who want a general introduction. Ch'en is a religion professor at Princeton University and the author of several more technical books on Buddhism.

CH'EN, KENNETH. **BUDDHISM IN CHINA: A HISTORICAL SURVEY. Glossary of Chinese, Sanskrit, and Pali terms, bibliography, index, 548pp. PUP64, 4.95p.**
Ch'en treats the entire history of Buddhism in China up to the present century and concludes with an excellent chapter on the contributions of Buddhism to Chinese culture. A scholarly work.

CH'IEN, HENG, tr. **THE ESSENTIALS OF THE DHARMA BLOSSOM SUTRA, VOLUME I. Glossary, index, 466pp. SAB74, 10.00c.**
This is the first volume of a three volume translation from the Chinese of **The Wonderful Dharma Lotus Blossom Sutra**, one of the major Mahayana texts, together with the commentary of Tripitaka Master Tu Lun. This Sutra is attributed to the Buddha and was thought to have been delivered by him near the end of his life; it is said to sum up his teaching. The commentary is based on over 350 lectures given by Tu Lun during a two year period beginning in 1968. The lectures were all recorded, later translated, and then edited to form the basis of the present commentary. Additional information has also been added.

■ CONZE, EDWARD. **BUDDHISM: ITS ESSENCE AND DEVELOPMENT. Chronology, bibliography, index, 212pp. H&R51/Cas, 2.95p.**
This is universally considered the best introductory volume in English. Here is what two noted scholars have to say about it. *There is not at present in English or in any other language so comprehensive—and at the same time so easy and readable—an account of Buddhism as is to be found in Dr. Conze's book. . . . To Dr. Conze the questions that Buddhism asks are actual, living questions, and he constantly brings them into relation both with history and with current actuality.*—Arthur Waley. *Mr. Conze's* **Buddhism** *is perhaps the best book on the subject published so far in a European language. It is a brilliant piece of work, beautifully written and dramatically successful in presenting the essentials of Buddhism, from the beginnings to the Japanese Zen schools, in less than 200 pages.*—Mircea Eliade.

CONZE, EDWARD. **BUDDHIST MEDITATION. Glossary, index, 183pp. H&R56, 2.50p.**
Conze presents his own translations of some of the most important meditational texts. The bulk of the selections have been taken from Buddhaghosa's **Path of Purity**. In an introduction he discusses the meaning of Buddhist meditation, its range and principal divisions, and relation to modern psychology.

■ *CONZE, EDWARD, tr.* **BUDDHIST SCRIPTURES. Glossary, 250pp. Vik59, 2.50p.**
Most of the writings chosen for this anthology were recorded between AD 100 and 400, the Golden Age of Buddhist literature. They include passages from the **Dhammapada**, the **Buddhacarita**, the **Questions of King Milinda**, and the **Tibetan Book of the Dead**. The collection is divided into topics.

CONZE, EDWARD. **BUDDHIST THOUGHT IN INDIA. Notes, index, 297pp. UMP62, 3.25p.**
A careful, clear exposition of the development of the fundamental ideas of Buddhism, and the form in which each sect adopted them. Deals with three forms of Buddhism: Archaic, Hinayana, and Mahayana.

CONZE, EDWARD. **FURTHER BUDDHIST STUDIES. Bibliography, index, 238pp. Cas75, 16.00c.**
A collection of six fairly long articles along with a number of shorter pieces and a series of thirty-one book reviews written between 1948 and 1967.

CONZE, EDWARD. **THIRTY YEARS OF BUDDHIST STUDIES. Notes, index, 274pp. Cas67, 10.95c.**
A collection of the most important articles written by Dr. Conze over the last thirty years, including both translations and original essays. Includes a report on recent progress in Buddhist studies; a survey of Mahayana Buddhism, based on original sources; a comparison of Buddhist and European philosophy; an essay on Buddhist saviors; and a variety of articles and translations of the **Prajnaparamita**.

CONZE, EDWARD, I.B. HORNER, DAVID SNELLGROVE and ARTHUR WALEY, eds. **BUDDHIST TEXTS THROUGH THE AGES. Glossary, 322pp. H&R54, 4.70p.**
A comprehensive anthology, topically arranged. Many of the excerpts are quite brief, but the reader is referred to important translations available elsewhere. All translations are new and some have never before appeared in English.

COOK, FRANCIS. **HUA-YEN BUDDHISM. Glossary, notes, index, 160pp. PSU77, 15.60c.**
Hua-yen is regarded as the highest form of Buddhism by most modern Japanese and Chinese scholars. This book is a description and analysis of Hua-yen, based largely on one of the more systematic treatises of its third patriarch. Hua-yen is also known as the Flower Ornament School and it was developed in China in the late seventh and early eighth centuries as an innovative interpretation of Indian Buddhist doctrines in the light of indigenous Chinese presuppositions, chiefly Taoist. This is the most comprehensive book on the philosophical system of Hua-yen ever to appear in English.

COOMARASWAMY, ANANDA. **ELEMENTS OF BUDDHIST ICON-OGRAPHY. Many illustrations, notes, 8½"x11", 127pp. MuM35, 20.40c.**
An analysis of Buddhist symbolism in historical perspective. In Coomaraswamy's view Buddhist symbolism, in both art and religion, is

but a part of the main current of Indian religion and art and has to be studied in that context.

COOMARASWAMY, ANANDA. **THE ORIGIN OF THE BUDDHA IMAGE. Seventy-three illustrations, 8½"x11", 46pp. MuM72, 19.15c.**

COWARD, HAROLD and KRISHNA SIVARAMON, eds. **REVELATION IN INDIAN THOUGHT. Notes, 300pp. Dha77, 19.95c.**
A collection of academic papers presented in honor of T.R.V. Murti and grouped around the three themes that have occupied much of Professor Murti's scholarship and teaching—*Studies in the Philosophy of Language, Studies in Buddhism,* and *Studies East and West.*

COWELL, EDWARD, MAX MULLER and J. TAKAKUSA, trs. **BUDDHIST MAHAYANA TEXTS. Notes, indices, 201pp. Dov69, 5.00p.**
Translations originally published in the **Sacred Books of the East** series: **The Buddha-karita** of Asvaghosa, the **Larger and the Smaller Sukhavativyuha**, the **Vagrakkhedika**, the **Larger and Smaller Prajna-paramita Sutras**, the **Amitayurdhyana Sutra**.

DAVID-NEEL, ALEXANDRA. **BUDDHISM: ITS DOCTRINES AND ITS METHODS. Index, 199pp. SMP39, 8.95c.**
Madame David-Neel is well known for her travels in Tibet and her extensive accounts of Tibetan Buddhism. This book is a good overview of Buddhism as taught and practiced in India, Tibet, China, and Japan. She writes not as one seeking to make converts to a particular school of Buddhism, but as an interpreter. She reviews and evaluates all the basic doctrines and tenets of the Buddhist faith and includes a number of suggestions for Westerners who seek a deeper understanding of Buddhism. A well written nontechnical account.

DAYAL, HAR. **THE BODHISATTVA DOCTRINE IN BUDDHIST SANSKRIT LITERATURE. Many notes, index, 411pp. MoB32, 13.20c.**
A comprehensive discussion of the texts and practices which deal with the Bodhisattva doctrine as expounded in the principal Buddhist literature in Sanskrit.

DEHEJIA, VIDYA. **EARLY BUDDHIST ROCK TEMPLES. Notes, bibliography, index, 7½"x10", 240pp. Cor72/T&H, 24.85c.**
Along the coastal reaches near Bombay, the flanks of the Deccan plateau have been tunnelled, carved, and polished into a series of cathedral like caves. These sanctuaries are among the most imposing and sophisticated works of Indian religious art and were, for Buddhist India, the equivalent of the great cathedrals of medieval Europe. Until now, published information about these cave temples, known as *caityas*, has been scanty and inadequate. The photographic documentation in this book, together with Dehejia's thorough analysis, offers a lucid picture of these temples. Their chronology is also discussed.

The Dhammapada

The Dhammapada consists of twenty-six poems or chapters, attributed to the Buddha himself. These verses are an almost complete presentation of Buddhist ethics, much of it in actual practice today. As the Buddhist *way of truth* (*pada*, meaning path or way; *dhamma*, the teaching), **The Dhammapada** thus offers an invaluable insight into the nature of the Buddhist mind and its response to life.

ANONYMOUS. **THE DHAMMAPADA. Commentary, notes, 139pp. CuN55, 3.95c.**
Just as a fletcher makes straight his arrow, the wise man makes straight his crooked thinking. This is difficult to guard. This is hard to restrain.

AUSTIN, JACK, tr. **THE DHAMMAPADA. 72pp. BuS45, .85p.**
As a fletcher straightens his arrow, so the wise man straightens his unsteady mind, which is so hard to control. This is a nice pocket edition, with a translation by a member of the Buddhist Society, London.

BABBIT, IRVING, ed. **THE DHAMMAPADA. 126pp. NDP36, 2.75p.**
As a fletcher makes straight his arrow, a wise man makes straight his trembling and unsteady thought, which is difficult to guard, difficult to hold back. This is a revision of Max Muller's translation. Includes an essay by Babbit, *Buddha and the Occident.*

BYROM, THOMAS, tr. **THE DHAMMAPADA.** 8½"x11", 165pp. RaH76, 5.95p.
As the fletcher whittles/And makes straight his arrows,/So the master directs/His straying thoughts. The text is lyrical, but not very faithful to the original. Photographs accompany the book; but they do little to suggest the feeling of the scripture and even as photography they are often not of very high quality.

■ LAL, P., tr. **THE DHAMMAPADA. Annotated bibliography, 184pp.** FSG67, 3.45p.
Like an archer and arrow, the wise man steadies his trembling mind, a fickle and restless weapon. This is our favorite translation. It is the most concise of the lot and was intended by Lal as a *transcreation* rather than merely another translation. Includes an introduction on the Buddha in two parts: his life and his teaching. All highly readable.

MASCARO, JUAN, tr. **THE DHAMMAPADA.** 93pp. Vik73, 1.50p.
The mind is wavering and restless, difficult to guard and restrain: let the wise man straighten his mind as a maker of arrows makes his arrows straight. This is a very nice translation. Mascaro numbers the verses and includes a lengthy introduction.

MULLER, F. MAX, tr. **THE DHAMMAPADA AND SUTTA NIPATA.** 269pp. MoB1881, 12.00c.
As a fletcher makes straight his arrow, a wise man makes straight his trembling and unsteady thought, which is difficult to guard, difficult to hold back. Part of the **Sacred Books of the East** series. Includes a critical introduction and notes.

NARADA THERA, tr. **THE DHAMMAPADA. Introduction,** 88pp. Mur54, 4.00c.
The flickering, fickle mind, difficult to guard, difficult to control, the wise person straightens, as a fletcher an arrow. Narada is a distinguished Ceylonese Buddhist scholar. His translation is faithful to the original and his extensive notes provide valuable insights from his first hand knowledge.

RADHAKRISHNAN, S., tr. **THE DHAMMAPADA. Notes, indices,** 202pp. Oxf50, 5.00c.
Just as a fletcher makes straight his arrow, the wise man makes straight his trembling, unsteady thought, which is difficult to guard and difficult to hold back (restrain). This volume includes a transliterated Pali text and commentary, and a lengthy essay, *Gautama the Buddha.*

RAJA, C. KUNHAN. **DHAMMAPADA.** 73pp. TPH56, .75p.
Mind which is shakey and fickle, hard to keep, hard to control, an intelligent person makes straight as an arrow-maker the arrow. The verses are numbered and there is a short introduction.

────── **END OF THE DHAMMAPADA SUBSECTION** ──────

DHIRAVAMSA. **A NEW APPROACH TO BUDDHISM.** 67pp. DHP72, 1.95p.
The author is a Thai meditation master, currently teaching in England. This book is a collection of discourses on the following topics: life and death; integration of the intellectual and the spiritual life; freedom and love; *Anatta*—no-self; the meditative way of life; what Buddhism has to offer the West; and the problem of conflict. He writes very clearly and his aim is to present a new approach to Buddhism and the possibilities of integrating meditational techniques into daily life. He leans towards the *vipassana* form of meditation popular in South Asia. Dhiravamsa has lectured at many universitites in the U.S. and Canada in addition to his work in England.

DHIRAVAMSA. **THE WAY OF NON-ATTACHMENT.** 6.95c.
See the Meditation section.

DONATH, DOROTHY. **BUDDHISM FOR THE WEST—THERAVADA, MAHAYANA, VAJRAYANA. Bibliography,** 146pp. MGH71, 2.45p.
A comprehensive review of Buddhist history, philosophy, and teachings. Includes an interesting section on Vajrayana (or Tibetan) Buddhism and the influence of Marpa and Milarepa. Written in a very personal style that is easy for the student to understand.

DRUMMOND, RICHARD. **GAUTAMA THE BUDDHA. Notes, bibliography, index,** 239pp. Eer74, 3.95p.
This is an unusual treatment of the life and teaching of the Buddha.

Professor Drummond interprets the man and his thought in the light of Christianity, pointing to significant relationships between Gautama's teaching and the basic tenets of Christianity. After describing the religious background out of which Gautama arose, Drummond discusses such important themes in Buddhism as the *Four Noble Truths*, the *Eight-Fold Path*, the *Middle Way, Dharma*, and *Nirvana*. In all cases the author draws a parallel between the Buddhist teaching and the teachings of Christ.

DUMOULIN, HEINRICH, and JOHN MARALDO, eds. **BUDDHISM IN THE MODERN WORLD. Notes, bibliography, index,** 368pp. McM76, 6.95p.
A survey of contemporary Buddhism in which eighteen scholars of varying nationalities and religious backgrounds examine modern movements in Buddhist nations against the background of original Indian Buddhism and attempt to show the historic effects of secularization, technology, and political ideology on the Buddhist religion. Virtually every tradition is discussed at length and, while the essays often tend to be dry, the scholarship is uniformly excellent. Notes accompany each essay and there is an excellent bibliography of English and German books.

DUTT, NALINAKSHA. **MAHAYANA BUDDHISM. Notes, index,** 310pp. MoB77, 12.00c.
A revised edition of Dutt's earlier book, **Aspects of Hinayana and Mahayana Buddhism.** This is a detailed work, which we suggest only for those who have deeply studied Buddhist literature. An abundance of technical words are used in the text and the level is quite advanced. The book is also not very clearly written.

DUTT, SUKUMAR. **BUDDHISM IN EAST ASIA. Index,** 225pp. Btk66, 13.50c.
This is a good book for the general reader, reviewing Buddhism and its development in Ceylon, Burma, Siam, Cambodia, Vietnam, China, Chinese Turkestan, Japan, and Tibet. The text is accompanied by numerous photographs and emphasizes culture as well as important individuals and movements.

EDGERTON, FRANKLIN. **BUDDHIST HYBRID SANSKRIT GRAMMAR AND DICTIONARY.** 8½"x11", 898pp. MoB53, 45.00c.
Buddhist Hybrid Sanskrit is the language in which most North Indian Buddhist works are composed. This two volume set is the first systematic grammar that has been produced.

EMILLLE MUSEUM. **DIAMOND MOUNTAIN.** 9"x12", 103pp. Eml75, 10.00p/each.
Korea is a land where mythology plays an all important role; it is also a mountainous country and throughout history people have believed in the mountain spirit. The Diamond Mountain is often considered the holiest mountain in Korea and it has been painted often through the ages. In the preface the editors say that the purpose of this two volume set is *to explore those long forgotten, popular Diamond Mountain paintings, and to interpret them in terms of Shamanism as against the past method of tying classical paintings with Buddhism or Taoism.* Most of the plates are full page and in color and the text is in both Korean and English.

EMILLLE MUSEUM and THE ROYAL ASIATIC SOCIETY. **THE LIFE OF BUDDHA IN KOREAN PAINTINGS.** 9"x12", 48pp. Eml74, 6.00p.
Buddha's Life paintings show the life of Sakyamuni from his birth to his passing, in eight stages, each painted as a separate panel. Our book explaining these paintings is, of course, an account of Sakyamuni's life in eight steps; but, rather than an historical biography, our story must be a composite of the legends that surround Sakyamuni, for the Buddha's Life paintings are really portrayals of legendary events....As for the text of this book, the narratives are based on **The Eight Stages of Buddha's Life** *....Through the woodblock prints and paintings of the Buddha's life which are presented here, one can catch the long-forgotten flavor of Korean Buddhist painting, its traditionally rich colors and fine line joined by the sense of humor we find in Korean folk painting.*—from the foreword. Both Korean and English texts are included and there are many color plates.

EMMERICK, R.E., tr. **THE SUTRA OF GOLDEN LIGHT.** 220pp. RKP70, 9.60c.
A literal translation of the Sanskrit text of the **Suvarnabhasottama Sutra** based on the J. Nobel text. The Sutra is thought to date from before the beginning of the fifth century AD and it is built up around

the idea of confession. It is an important Mahayana text and has been translated into a wide number of languages. The translator also provides an introduction and notes.

FOUCHER, A. THE LIFE OF THE BUDDHA. Notes, bibliography, 286pp. Gre63, 22.85c.
This is perhaps the definitive modern study of the life of the Buddha, based mainly on primary Indian sources. The material on the nativity includes information on the Buddha's earlier lives, some early predictions, and an analysis of his horoscope. The book is extremely well written, with photographs interspersed. Both the general reader and the scholar should appreciate this text—although the price makes it unlikely that anyone but a scholar or a library will buy the book, which is too bad, because we recommend it highly. This is a well bound, limited edition reprint.

FOZDAR, JAMSHED. THE GOD OF BUDDHA. Glossary, index, 194pp. APH73, 13.45c.
A topically arranged presentation of the major ideas of the Buddha, showing how they relate to traditional Hindu thought. The material is organized as follows—each page is divided into two columns: the right hand one presents quotations from Hindu sacred literature; on the left there is a parallel selection for the sacred literature of Buddhism. Connective commentary is interspersed, and each topic is introduced. There is also an abundance of background and explanatory material to back up the author's thesis that the Buddhist does believe in divine revelation and an eternity of divine bliss.

■ **FRAZIER, ALLIE, ed. BUDDHISM. Glossary, bibliography, 304pp. Wes69, 3.50p.**
An excellent book of readings on Buddhist religious thought and practice which brings together both interpretative essays on the Buddhist tradition by noted scholars such as Joseph Campbell, Edward Conze, D.T. Suzuki, Ananda Coomaraswamy, and Heinrich Zimmer, and selections from the sacred literature of Buddhism. The commentaries are spaced throughout the selection of primary sources, and the principles governing the selection of materials has been to include those original sources and commentaries which illuminate the fundamental themes of Buddhist thought and experience.

■ **GARD, RICHARD, ed. BUDDHISM. Notes, index, 256pp. Brz61, 6.95c.**
This introductory survey begins with an analysis of Buddhism and a discussion of its historical development and major schools. This is followed by selections which emphasize the dominant themes of the Buddhist way of life. The first describes the teachings of the Buddha and the development of Buddhism. The second is devoted to an analysis of the basic philosophy of Buddhism. The third analyzes Buddhist practices, ceremonies, and rituals. The last two sections cover Buddhist monasticism and Buddhist thought on social, political, and cultural issues. This is a useful compilation.

GETTY, ALICE. THE GODS OF NORTHERN BUDDHISM. Glossary, bibliography, index, 7½"x10½", 341pp. Tut62, 32.50c.
This study has been recognized for almost half a century as a landmark achievement of unsurpassed excellence. Since its publication it has become a rare and costly collector's item and this edition is a beautifully produced unabridged reprint of the second edition. Ms. Getty discusses in detail the major deities of the Mahayana pantheon, their symbols, and their characteristics, at the same time giving attention to the minor gods and deified historical personages. The presentation of the gods themselves is preceded by an introduction in which Joseph Deniker provides the reader with a general survey of Buddhism and its evolution and prepares him for the discussions that follow. Almost two hundred works of Northern Buddhist art are illustrated in plates, eight in color.

GODDARD, DWIGHT, ed. A BUDDHIST BIBLE. 667pp. Bea38, 7.95p.
The first Buddhist anthology and still one of the most comprehensive and scholarly. Includes selections from all schools of Buddhism.

GOLDSTEIN, JOSEPH. THE EXPERIENCE OF INSIGHT. 4.95p.
See the Meditation section.

GOMBRICH, RICHARD. PRECEPT AND PRACTICE: TRADITIONAL BUDDHISM IN THE RURAL HIGHLANDS OF CEYLON. Introduction, glossary, notes, bibliography, index, 380pp. Oxf71, 22.95c.
Buddhism is far better known as a set of doctrines than as a real working system. In his introduction, Gombrich says that his book *is intended as a contribution to the empirical study of religion, and in particular to the study of religious change.* He has based his discussion on visits to thirty-nine Sinhalese local temples and extensive interviews with thirty-four local monks. Gombrich begins with a detailed study of Buddhism and Buddhist precepts and practice.

GOVINDA, LAMA. PSYCHO-COSMIC SYMBOLISM OF THE BUDDHIST STUPA. Index, 120pp. Dha76, 4.95p.
Throughout the Buddhist cultures, the stupa has been the most pervasive and symbolic form of architecture. In early times stupas were symbols of illumination—memorials which were intended to inspire later generations to follow the path to enlightenment. Like the Egyptian pyramid, the Buddhist stupa evolved not only as a repository for the relics of revered persons, but as a universal symbol, the embodiment of all knowledge contained in a single picture of architecture. Much of Lama Govinda's knowledge about the stupa comes from his personal pilgrimages to various stupas in Ceylon, India, Nepal, and Tibet. Often he took measurements of the stupas by counting on his beads the number of steps required to circumambulate the structures. In this volume he discusses and illustrates his findings and he also reviews the relationship of the stupas to the chakras and to the traditional Buddhist stages of meditation.

GOVINDA, LAMA. THE PSYCHOLOGICAL ATTITUDE OF EARLY BUDDHIST PHILOSOPHY. Appendix, index, 176pp. Wei61/HPG, 3.50c.
Lama Govinda shows not only what the ideas of early Buddhism were, but how they came into existence and why they took the form in which we now know them. This is a brilliant summary of Pali Buddhism; and in addition it constitutes a logical approach to the problems of Mahayana and tantric philosophy. The text is clarified by a series of diagrams and charts. A very interesting interpretative work. Definitely not recommended for the student who desires simply an introduction.

GRIMM, GEORGE. **DOCTRINE OF THE BUDDHA. Bibliography, indices, 413pp. MoB58, 10.50c.**
Translation of a very scholarly German philosophical work on *truth as the theme and basis of the doctrine of the Buddha*. The study is prefaced with an introduction answering the questions: who was the Buddha, and what is a Buddha. The appendix deals with the doctrine and the metaphysics of Buddhism.

GUENTHER, HERBERT. **BUDDHIST PHILOSOPHY IN THEORY AND PRACTICE. Many notes, bibliography, index, 230pp. ShP71, 2.95p.**
An excellent philosophical treatise which traces the growth of Buddhist thought. Guenther is especially noted for his studies of the Tibetan school and the tantras. The emphasis is apparent here although all schools are treated. Clearly written, but definitely not an introductory work.

GUENTHER, HERBERT. **PHILOSOPHY AND PSYCHOLOGY IN THE ABHIDHARMA. Notes, index, 279pp. ShP76, 4.95p.**
The study of the *abhidharma* is indispensible for understanding the history of Buddhist philosophy and practice. Originally a summary of terms according to subject matters, it became systematized into a philosophical analysis of man and his world. This book summarizes the significance of the *abhidharma* and analyzes the concepts of mind and its states with reference to healthy and unhealthy attitudes toward life. Theories of perception are discussed together with the interpretation of the world on the basis of these theories as well as their critiques. The volume ends with a discussion of the path, as conceived by the various schools. Six tables analyze the structure of mind in Buddhist psychology.

HALL, MANLY P. **THE ARHATS OF BUDDHISM. 112pp. PRS53, 3.00p.**
Volume II of Hall's series **The Adepts in the Eastern Esoteric Tradition**.

HAMILTON, CLARENCE, ed. **BUDDHISM. Introduction, glossary, bibliography, index, 218pp. BoM52, 5.45p.**
An excellent collection of source readings from Buddhist literature. Over half the book is devoted to an anthology of Pali literature on the life of the Buddha and early Buddhist teachings. Other sections include selections from Sanskrit and Chinese sources, and on Japanese and Tibetan Buddhism. The translations are not the most modern; nonetheless, Hamilton has made uniformly good choices.

HAMILTON-MERRITT, JANE. **A MEDITATOR'S DIARY. Glossary, bibliography, 155pp. S&S76/Sou, 1.75p.**
This is a very personal account of the author's experience in Thai meditation temples. Ms. Hamilton-Merritt frankly reveals her struggles and her fears as well as her insights, experiences, and inner visions. She studied and practiced both *samadhi* and *vipassana* meditation and she clearly explains the differences between the two. In the process the reader gets a good feeling for the Thai temples (or *wats*) and the Buddhism of Thailand. Ms. Hamilton-Merritt is a journalist who originally came to Southeast Asia to cover the Wars. She writes well and many excerpts from her personal diary are included.

HEROLD, A. FERDINAND. **THE LIFE OF BUDDHA. 285pp. Tut54, 3.25p.**
The story of the Buddha's life told in the form of a novel and based on the author's study of Indian legends, poems, history, and literature. This account is translated from the French.

HESSE, HERMANN. **SIDDHARTHA. 122pp. NDP51, 8.00c/1.75p.**
A simple and beautiful story of a man's long quest in search of the ultimate answers to existence. A classic which forms an excellent introduction to the basic philosophy of Buddhism, and reading to savor for all.

HORNER, I.B. **WOMEN UNDER PRIMITIVE BUDDHISM. Notes, index, 415pp. MoB30, 13.20c.**
A detailed study based on early Pali sources including the Canonical literature and commentaries. The book is divided into two parts. The first depicts the lay woman in her role of mother, daughter, wife, widow, and worker. The second deals with the almswoman and reviews her admission into the order, the eight chief rules of conduct, life in the order, and **Therigatha**.

HUA, HSUAN. **BUDDHA ROOT FARM. Index, 68pp. SAB76, 3.00p.**
This is a collection of talks given during a seven day Amitabha Buddha session. One of the most widely used Buddhist meditation methods is the recitation of the name of the Buddha Amitabha of the Western Pure Land. All these talks discuss this meditation practice.

HUA, HSUAN. **THE DHARANI SUTRA. 339pp. SAB76, 10.00p.**
This is an extraordinary book of a kind rarely found in English translation.... Presented with the lively commentary of Tripitaka Master Hua...it belongs to a category of Buddhist works normally held to be secret and transmitted from Master to disciple....I cannot conscientiously recommend this book to everybody, nor was it ever intended to be "everybody's cup of tea"; but, if you...desire to become a compassionate Bodhisattva—as every Mahayana Buddhist does—then buy it!—John Blofeld.

HUA, HSUAN, tr. **ESSENTIALS OF THE SRAMANERA VINAYA AND RULES OF DEPORTMENT. Index, 103pp. SAB75, 3.95p.**
Translation of an instructional treatise written in the Ming dynasty by Lien Ch'ih and derived from the **Vinaya** texts to serve as a guide to novice monks. Commentary and introductory material are also included.

HUA, HSUAN, tr. **A GENERAL EXPLANATION OF THE BUDDHA SPEAKS OF AMITABHA SUTRA. Index, 179pp. SAB74, 5.95p.**
This is a translation, with elaborate and extensive commentary, of the Sutra in which the Buddha said that all living beings who recited his name with faith would be reborn in his *Buddhaland*, the *Land of Ultimate Bliss*. Illustrations and a great deal of background material are also included.

HUA, HSUAN. **RECORDS OF THE LIFE OF THE VENERABLE MASTER, HSUAN HUA. Photographs, 96pp. SAB73, 5.00p.**
Volume I of a projected three part work tracing the early life of the Master and presenting a vivid glimpse of the religious life of China in the first half of this century.

HUA, HSUAN. **RECORDS OF THE LIFE OF CH'AN MASTER HUA, VOLUME II. Bibliography, index, 247pp. SAB75, 6.95p.**
The second volume of Master Hsuan Hua's autobiography, tracing his life from the time he arrived in Hong Kong—where he built many monasteries and temples—to his arrival in the U.S.

HUA, HSUAN, tr. **THE SHURANGAMA SUTRA, VOLUME I. Introduction, index, 272pp. SAB77, 8.50p.**
When the Buddhadharma begins to disappear, the very first sutra to disappear will be the Shurangama. Shurangama Sutra lays bare the deviant knowledge and deviant views of those who misuse their powers. The Sutra text exposes their eccentricities and tactics so vividly that it is referred to as a "monster spotting mirror," "a demon pounding pestle," and "a demon cutting sword." It breaks up the deviant and manifests the orthodox, destroys all the heavenly demons and those of external ways, and reveals the human capacity for proper knowledge and proper views. So, if we are to protect the proper dharma, we should investigate the Shurangama Sutra, understand, and protect it.—Hsuan Hua. Extensive commentary accompanies the translation of each of the sutras.

HUA, HSUAN. **SUTRA IN FORTY-TWO SECTIONS. Index, 104pp. SAB77, 4.00p.**
In the **Sutra in Forty-Two Sections***, the Buddha exhorts his monastic disciples, and by extension all living beings, to undertake the work of renunciation. Not simply wealth, position, fame, physical pleasure, and family life, but all desire and anger, all thought, any attempt to hold on to the self and the world; all must be renounced if one is to reach the goal of the road to enlightenment.... The explanatory commentary which accompanies the text in this volume gives proof that the wisdom of the Buddha can be lived to the utmost in the modern world.*—from the introduction.

HUA, HSUAN, tr. **SUTRA OF THE PAST VOWS OF EARTH STORE BODHISATTVA. Glossary, 232pp. SAB74, 6.75p.**
From ancient times, this Sutra has been one of the most popular ones. *Earth Store* is a literal rendering of the *bodhissatva's* original Sanskrit name, *Ksitigarbha*. In the Buddhist pantheon he represents the great vow to help all sentient beings. *If I do not go to hell (to help them there) who else will go?* is the famous pronouncement of this *bodhisatva*. This is the first English translation of this Sutra. Master Hua also includes a sutra-by-sutra commentary.

HUA, HSUAN. **THE TEN DHARMAREALMS ARE NOT BEYOND A SINGLE THOUGHT. Illustrations, 34pp. SAB73, 3.00p.**
A description of the realms of being as Buddhism teaches them—from

Buddhas and *bodhisattvas* to gods, men, animals, ghosts, and beings in hell. A short text is presented, followed by commentary.

HUA, HSUAN. **THE WONDERFUL DHARMA LOTUS FLOWER SUTRA, VOLUME I: INTRODUCTION. Index, 85pp. SAB77, 3.95p.**
The Wonderful Dharma Lotus Flower Sutra *was delivered by the Buddha near the end of his teaching career to reveal the Real Dharma, the miraculous Dharma; all previous teachings are considered to be provisional—used to lead his disciples to the level where they might understand the doctrine of universal salvation contained in the Lotus teaching. For this reason, this is a most important Sutra, and a clear understanding of it is necessary for all who wish to truly understand the Buddhadharma.*—from the introduction.

HUA, HSUAN. **THE WONDERFUL DHARMA LOTUS FLOWER SUTRA, VOLUME II. Index, 323pp. SAB77, 7.95p.**
A translation of the first chapter of the Sutra, with extensive commentary by Tripitaka Master Hua.

HUMPHREYS, CHRISTMAS. **BUDDHISM. Glossary, extensive subject indexed bibliography, index, 252pp. Vik51, 2.50p.**
Traces the history and development of Buddhism and the teaching of the various schools, as well as its condition in the world today. An excellent primer. Humphreys is as qualified as any man in the West to write this material. He has been studying Buddhism and interpreting it to the West for over fifty years and has been President of the Buddhist Society of London for most of that time.

HUMPHREYS, CHRISTMAS. **BUDDHIST POEMS. 59pp. A&U71, 4.20p.**
A collection largely inspired by Buddhist themes, selected from Humphrey's finest poems over a fifty year period.

HUMPHREYS, CHRISTMAS. **THE BUDDHIST WAY OF ACTION. Glossary, bibliography, 195pp. A&U60, 4.50p.**
A record of the author's personal experience. Humphreys writes about the analysis of action, in the sense of right acting rather than right action—emphasizing the how and why of action rather than the theoretical what. Many quotations from Buddhist texts illustrate this practical treatise.

HUMPHREYS, CHRISTMAS. **THE BUDDHIST WAY OF LIFE. 224pp. ScB69/A&U, 2.45p.**
Humphreys directs his attention to the interaction between Buddhism and its growing Western following. Designed as *An Invitation for Western Readers*, the book provides an introduction to Buddhism, both its basic doctrine and its adaptability in new contexts.

HUMPHREYS, CHRISTMAS. **EXPLORING BUDDHISM. Glossary, index, 191pp. TPH74/A&U, 2.50p.**
As the title suggests, this is an exploration of a variety of aspects of Buddhism. Each of the selections is fairly short and all schools of thought are reviewed. The text begins with essays on the Buddha and his enlightenment. This section includes the review of Madame Blavatsky and Buddhism (Humphreys has been active in the Theosophical movement). Next comes a discussion of various Buddhist doctrines, followed by a survey of Buddhism in the West. The volume ends with a discussion of Buddhist practices. There is no great depth to the presentation.

HUMPHREYS, CHRISTMAS. **A POPULAR DICTIONARY OF BUDDHISM. 224pp. Cur74, 9.35c.**
A dictionary and glossary of terms covering the entire field of Buddhism. Revised and enlarged edition.

HUMPHREYS, CHRISTMAS. **SIXTY YEARS OF BUDDHISM IN ENGLAND (1907-67). 84pp. BuS68, 4.40c.**
A history and a survey of the Buddhist movement in England by the current President of the Buddhist Society.

HUMPHREYS, CHRISTMAS. **STUDIES IN THE MIDDLE WAY, BEING THOUGHTS ON BUDDHISM APPLIED. 180pp. Cur76, 8.00c.**
The Middle Way is the path between the introverted life of contemplation and the extroverted life of action in the world of men. In this volume Humphreys aims at an understanding and application of Buddhist principles in Western society, and a means whereby the Way

may be traversed. Each chapter expounds a facet of life in relation to Buddhism.

HURVITZ, LEON, tr. **SCRIPTURE OF THE LOTUS BLOSSOM OF THE FINE DHARMA. Introduction, glossary, notes, index, 449pp. Col76, 7.85p.**
The *Lotus Sutra* is one of the most influential and most popular Mahayana Buddhist texts. It emphasizes the doctrine that there is really only one path to enlightenment, the *bodhisattva* path, and the principle that the Buddha is not an individual being, but is universal in nature. Many parables are included throughout the work. This translation has been made from one of the best known Chinese versions, the **Kumarajiva** and the volume also includes translations of passages of the Sanskrit text that are omitted from the Chinese. The translation reads well and is a work of excellent scholarship.

IIJIMA, KANJITSU. **BUDDHIST YOGA. Photographs, 7¼"x10", 174pp. Jap75, 7.95p.**
Reverend Iijima begins with a theoretical discussion of the Buddhist approach to mind-body health. This is followed by a series of detailed exercises and practical techniques. The writing style is stiff and the book is not very easy to use.

IKEDA, DAISAKU. **BUDDHISM: THE FIRST MILLENNIUM. Glossary, bibliography, index, 172pp. Kod77, 7.95c.**
A well written general discussion of the early development of Buddhism, up to the time when it spread beyond the borders of India and grew into a major world religion. All the major doctrinal concerns are surveyed and the fabric of events is pieced together in a clear fashion. Translated from the Japanese by Burton Watson.

IKEDA, DAISAKU. **THE LIVING BUDDHA: AN INTERPRETATIVE BIOGRAPHY. Illustrations, glossary, 158pp. Wea76, 7.95c.**
In this work, the Buddha emerges as a man, living in a turbulent period, who was confronted with the same kinds of personal problems and social conflicts that we all face. The description of how he conquered these obstacles, the nature of his great enlightenment, and the secret of his success as a religious teacher and leader makes this an engrossing and inspiring account. The author is leader of one of the most dynamic Buddhist renewal movements in the world. His image of the Buddha grows out of his own living experience as a Buddhist and as a man of action. Translated by Burton Watson.

IRIE, TAIKICHI and SHIGERU AOYAMA. **BUDDHIST IMAGES. Glossary, 136pp. Hoi70, 3.25p.**
A beautiful pocket book containing 104 images of the Buddha, most in color. The plates are briefly described and there is a good section on Buddhist art and images.

JACOBSON, NOLAN. **BUDDHISM: THE RELIGION OF ANALYSIS. Notes, bibliography, index, 202pp. SIU66, 2.95p.**
Let it be admitted at the outset that I have tried to write a convincing modern interpretation of the teachings of the Buddha. I have written out of a conviction that Buddhism, especially in its early Theravada sources, has something significant to say to modern man. It seems to me that the West provides new ground for an appreciative understanding of what the Buddha taught. I have described this new ground as fully as possible, and I have sought to view the Buddha's teachings in this new frame of reference. This is a somewhat dry study, which should interest those looking for Western applications of Buddhist teachings.

Jataka Tales

These tales are stories of the Buddha's previous lives when he was still a *bodhisattva*, striving (that doesn't sound very Buddhist does it—but you get the idea) to accumulate a sufficient store of merit and wisdom to be able to achieve Buddhahood. They are based on traditional folklore and, whatever their intrinsic value, they illustrate the main tenets of Buddhism and are also just plain good stories.

BABBITT, ELLEN. **THE JATAKAS. 105pp. PrH40, 6.00c.**
An extremely simplified retelling of some of the main tales, geared to young readers and illustrated.

COWELL, EDWARD. **JATAKA STORIES. Three volumes, PTS nd, 57.60c/set.**
These volumes are the longest in the whole collection of *suttas*. The **Jatakas** or **Birth Stories** contain the stories of the former lives of the Buddha. In these stories the Buddha is referred to as the *bodhisattva*, since he was not yet enlightened, and he is presented sometimes as the hero, sometimes a secondary character, and at times a mere spectator. The story usually begins with the words, *At such and such a time, the "bodhisattva" was reborn in the womb of so and so,* and this permitted any story to be converted into a Buddhist **Jataka** by merely changing some human being, animal, or deity in it into the *bodhisattva*. Of the 547 **Jatakas** in the collection probably more than half were of non-Buddhist origin. They are notable as more than edifying tales to entertain audiences. They are valuable for the information which they provide concerning the early history of Buddhism as well as the social, political, and economic conditions in India. They also served as the inspiration for numerous scenes in Buddhist art.

CROFTS, TRUDY and KEN MCKEON. **THE HUNTER AND THE QUAIL. 8½"x11", Dha76, 2.95p.**
A retelling of the Buddha's past life as a wise quail in the form of a colorfully illustrated children's book.

DE ROIN, NANCY, tr. **JATAKA TALES. 7¼"x9", 84pp. HMC75, 5.95c.**
This is a lovely rendition of thirty of the **Tales,** and it is our favorite version. It is a children's book—but like so many children's books the adults probably enjoy it as much as the children; at least this adult does! The drawings are delightful and the stories themselves are told in a wonderful manner. Each is a couple of pages long and there are illustrations on almost every page. Ms. De Roin is a Buddhist.

GELLEK, NAZLI. **THE KING AND THE MANGOES. 8½"x11", 24pp. Dha75, 4.75c.**
This is part of a series of children's books. The story line in this one is as follows: wanting to save his herd of 80,000 monkeys, the Monkey King stretched his own body as far as possible to make a bridge from the mango tree to a bamboo grove nearby. But as the last monkey crossed over to safety he jumped with all his might on the king's back. Giving his own life to save his herd, the Monkey King died of a broken heart.

GELLEK, NAZLI. **THE PROUD PEACOCK AND THE MALLARD. 8½"x11", 24pp. Dha76, 4.75c.**
Having no modesty the Proud Peacock is spurned by King Mallard's daughter who turns to a young mallard wise enough not to show his feathers. The peacock is so ashamed that his voice turns hoarse. Squawking unhappily he flies away into the forest.

GELLEK, NAZLI. **THE SPADE SAGE. 8½"x11", 24pp. Dha76, 4.75c.**
In that instant, as he looked into the river, the Spade Sage found within himself the secret of happiness and became a very wise man. The king and his people looked in wonder as the Spade Sage rose into the air and called them to follow him and were taught by him how to conquer their greediness and find the secret of happiness locked within their own minds. And so it happened that a poor gardener named the Spade Sage became a wiseman and a great teacher.

KARUNARATNE, DAVID, tr. **UMMAGGA JATAKA (THE STORY OF THE TUNNEL). Notes, 224pp. Gun62, 1.50c.**
This tale is a masterpiece of medieval Sinhala literature, and one which is well known in Sri Lanka. The translator states that *neither the form of the narrative nor the style of the language has been changed in the slightest degree.*

KHAN, NOOR INAYAT. **TWENTY JATAKA TALES. Illustrations, 136pp. EWP39, 7.95c.**
This is a beautifully written retelling of some of the tales. While simplifying the narrative, Ms. Khan has endeavored to preserve the flavor of the original. Our favorite collection. Ms. Khan is the daughter of Hazrat Inayat Khan.

RHYS DAVIDS, T.W., tr. **BUDDHIST BIRTH STORIES. Notes, index, 268pp. IBH15, 12.80c.**
This volume was the first Pali text translated by T.W. Rhys Davids. This edition includes a long introductory discussion of the **Jataka Tales** by Rhys Davids, followed by his translation of a classical commentarial introduction entitled **Nidana-Katha (The Story of the Lineage).** This text is chiefly concerned with two milestones in the career of the Buddha: the moment when his conscious will to help mankind awoke,

and the time when that will had reached such perfection that he could become such a helper. The **Nidana-Katha** is a running commentary on the **Buddhavamsa (Chronicle of the Buddhas),** a canonical book, and it presents an early account of the life and mission of the Buddha. This edition has been slightly revised by Caroline Rhys Davids.

An illustration from a **Jataka,** showing the Buddha's past life as a crane.

STAMLER, SUZANNE. **THREE WISE BIRDS. 8¾"x11½", Dha76, 4.75c.**
Another of Dharma Press' colorful versions of the **Jataka Tales.**

STONE, KAREN. **GOLDEN FOOT. 8¾"x11½", Dha76, 4.75c.**
The story of the Buddha's incarnation as a deer.

WRAY, ELIZABETH, et al. **TEN LIVES OF THE BUDDHA. Glossary, extensive bibliography, 7½"x10½", 154pp. Wea72, 15.00c.**
Beautiful color reproductions of wall paintings illustrating ten of the most important **Jataka Tales.** Every detail in the pictures means something. Each of the tales is an allegory of the ten cardinal virtues to be perfected in attaining Buddhahood. Two lengthy and informative background essays complement the stories and paintings.

————————**END OF THE JATAKA TALES SUBSECTION**————————

JAYATILLEKE, K.N. **EARLY BUDDHIST THEORY OF KNOWLEDGE. Bibliography, index, 519pp. A&U63, 35.00c.**
A comprehensive study of the theory of knowledge in early Buddhism. Jayatilleke has arranged his material well and accompanies his text with extensive notes.

JAYATILLEKE, K.N. **THE MESSAGE OF THE BUDDHA. Index, 262pp. McM74, 17.25c.**
The author was one of the best known contemporary Buddhist scholars in Asia and was a professor of philosophy at the University of Ceylon until his recent death. This volume is a culmination of his life's work. Writing for both the layman and the scholar, Professor Jayatilleke provides a historical perspective on the central events of the life of the Buddha and on the roots and rise of Buddhism, and he examines the Buddha's teachings in the light of contemporary understanding. The presentation is basically devoted to Theravada Budhism. The material is topically organized and all the major schools are cited.

JOHANSSON, RUNE. **PSYCHOLOGY OF NIRVANA. Index, 138pp. A&U69, 5.15c.**
An attempt to fit all the diffuse explanations and pronouncements on nirvana in the scriptures together into a consistent picture, and to

relate this picture to modern psychology. A fascinating, scholarly comparative study by a trained Swedish psychologist who has also studied Sanskrit and Pali.

JOSHI, LALMANI. **STUDIES IN THE BUDDHISTIC CULTURE OF INDIA. Revised edition, many notes, bibliography, index, 520pp. MoB77, 20.00c.**
An authoritative study of Buddhism in India during the seventh and eighth centuries AD, the time of Nalanda University. The work is based on an examination of contemporary Buddhist, *brahmanical*, and secular literary texts; Indian epigraphic and monumental antiquities; and Chinese and Tibetan documents bearing on the period. All aspects of Buddhist faith, worship, philosophy, and culture are discussed at length.

KALUPAHANA, DAVID. **BUDDHIST PHILOSOPHY. Notes, bibliography, index, 209pp. UHa76, 5.30p.**
A fairly technical analysis of the basic philosophical teachings and historical development of Buddhism. Part I outlines the historical background out of which Buddhism arose, and examines the early teachings in both the Pali **Nikayas** and the Chinese **Agamas**. Topics such as epistemology, causality, existence, karma, morality, ethics, and nirvana are discussed in detail. Part II examines developments in the history of Buddhist thought and the emergence of the various schools of Buddhism. The development of *abhidharma* is studied through analysis of the various doctrines of the scholastics, and Mahayana is reviewed through an analysis of the Mahayana sutras. Two chapters examine *Madhyamika Transcendentalism* and *Yogacara Idealism.*

KALUPAHANA, DAVID. **CAUSALITY: THE CENTRAL PHILOSOPHY OF BUDDHISM. Notes, bibliography, index, 298pp. UHa75, 16.15c.**
A scholarly articulation, analysis, and interpretation of the doctrines of causation in Buddhist philosophy. Special attention is given to early Buddhist teachings as found in the Pali **Nikayas** and Chinese **Agamas.** *In early Buddhism,* Kalupahana maintains, *a cause is defined as "the sum total of several factors that gives rise to a consequent"—the "consequent" being the entire universe as well as a specific thing or event.*

KAVERNE, PER. **AN ANTHOLOGY OF BUDDHIST TANTRIC SONGS: A STUDY OF THE CARYAGITI. Notes, 281pp. Col77, 17.75p.**
This is a study of a small collection of songs of the mystic path. It is the first Western exposition of this material and includes both a translation and transliteration of the songs as well as an in depth analysis of their meaning and imagery.

KAWAMURA, LESLIE and KEITH SCOTT, eds. **BUDDHIST THOUGHT AND ASIAN CIVILIZATION. Notes, 335pp. Dha77, 19.95c.**
An excellent collection of scholarly essays on many aspects of Buddhism put together in honor of Herbert Guenther. The contributors are all major figures in the field and a number of the selections cover material not available elsewhere.

KERN, H. **MANUAL OF INDIAN BUDDHISM. Extensive notes, index, 145pp. MoB1898, 7.50c.**
This is a reprint of one of the earliest European studies of Buddhism. The text does not read very easily. It is based on Nepalese, Chinese, and Singhalese original sources and includes a general survey of the early literature; a study of the Buddha's life and his fundamental doctrines; a review of the *sangha* and its disciplinary and ascetic rules; and an outline of the theological and philosophical history of Buddhism.

KERN, H., tr. **SADDHARMA-PUNDARIKA OR THE LOTUS OF TRUE LAW. Extensive introduction, notes, 442pp. Dov1884, 4.50p.**
A dated translation of perhaps the single most important Mahayana Buddhist text, described as the *crown-jewel* in which *all Buddhalaws are succinctly taught.* It is almost required reading for every serious Buddhist student. This translation comes from the **Sacred Books of the East** series.

KING, WINSTON L. **IN HOPE OF NIBBANA: AN ESSAY ON THERAVADA BUDDHIST ETHICS. 284pp. OpC74, 4.95p.**
Nibbana is the Pali word for nirvana. This is a very complete treatment of the topic.

KLOPPENBORG, RIA, tr. **THE SUTRA ON THE FOUNDATION OF THE BUDDHIST ORDER. Notes, bibliography, index, 137pp. Bri73, 8.25p.**
A translation of the **Catusparisat Sutra,** giving an account of the foundation of the *fourfold order,* consisting of monks, nuns, and male and female lay disciples. It describes that part of the Buddha's life that starts with his enlightenment and ends with the ordination of his two main disciples, Upatisya and Kolita. The text describes the meditations preceding enlightenment; the attainment of the six higher knowledges and of enlightenment; the acceptance of the first lay disciples; and the Buddha's decision to preach the dharma.

KORNFIELD, JACK. **LIVING BUDDHIST MASTERS. Glossary, 332pp. UnP77, 6.95p.**
Jack Kornfield . . . has offered us in this volume a compilation of the philosophy and practice of Theravadin Buddhism interspersed with rich anecdotes and interviews— the situations through which he received his training. Jack spent much time traveling and studying in monasteries throughout Burma, Laos, Thailand, and Cambodia and conveys in his writing the profound simplicity and sustained effort that surround the practice of Theravada Buddhist meditation. Through his anecdotes he shows the way in which a practice is linked to a lineage. . . . Each teacher emphasizes a specific aspect of the transmission of the Buddha, yet each is representative of the essence of this lineage.—from the introduction by Ram Dass.

LAW, B.C. **HEAVEN AND HELL IN BUDDHIST PERSPECTIVE. Index, 163pp. BPH25, 8.00c.**
A scholarly discussion of the ideas of heaven and hell prevalent amongst the people of Northern India at the time of the Buddha, and incorporated subsequently in the Buddhist scriptures. Much of the material derives from the **Nikayas,** and Dr. Law translates and discusses many illustrative stories from the *Vimanavatthu* commentary.

LAW, B.C. **THE LIFE AND WORK OF BUDDHAGHOSA. Notes, index, 194pp. MoB21, 11.20c.**
Buddhaghosa was the most celebrated commentator of the Theravada school. This book traces both the known facts about his life and the legends that have been built up around him. Law also analyzes the origin and development of Buddhist commentaries, discusses Buddhaghosa's works and his philosophy, and surveys his successors.

LAYMAN, EMMA, ed. **BUDDHISM IN AMERICA. Glossary, notes, bibliography, index, 360pp. NeH76, 7.95p.**
This book was written with a two fold purpose in mind: (1) to meet the need for a work on Buddhism in America which would include a survey of all major Buddhist schools and sects found in the United States; (2) to present an analysis of the American Buddhist scene and American Buddhist adherents from the point of view of a psychologist and social scientist. A large part of this book is based on observation made during the spring and summer of 1972. . . . During that time I visited Buddhist groups from coast to coast, participating in rituals, meditation and other aspects of life in Buddhist centers. I also interviewed Buddhist priests representing different sects and about 300 American lay Buddhists.—from the preface. This is an interesting study.

LEGGE, JAMES, tr. **A RECORD OF BUDDHIST KINGDOMS. 168pp. Dov1886, 2.00p.**
A translation of an early fifth century account of Buddhism in India and Central Asia. Extensively annotated; the full Chinese text is reproduced.

LERNER, ERIC. **JOURNEY OF INSIGHT MEDITATION: A PERSONAL EXPERIENCE OF THE BUDDHA'S WAY. 185pp. ScB77/Tur, 3.95p.**
Eric Lerner describes this book as: *an account of a journey in time and space through the initial stages of this process. Although its locale is the somewhat exotic landscape of Asian monasteries and meditation centers, peopled by wise and very powerful teachers, its real setting is internal. The journey, as I experienced it, was one of a constantly evolving understanding, but, in essence, a very simple experience. I can only call the book an adventure story. That is the way I relate to it. Learning to die and consequently learning to live, is an adventure.*

LESTER, ROBERT. **THERAVADA BUDDHISM IN SOUTH EAST ASIA. Appendix, extensive notes, bibliography, index, 198pp. UMP73, 2.95p.**
Lester describes both the scriptural and traditional ideal, and the contemporary reality of Buddhist practice. His portrayal combines

insights of the religious historian and the cultural anthropologist. In this account, Theravada Buddhism is seen as a way of life. An interesting study.

LING, TREVOR. **THE BUDDHA. Extensive notes, bibliography, 287pp. Vik73/Pen, 2.95p.**
Ling describes the India into which the Buddha was born, recounts what is known of his life and the development of his teaching, and then follows the course of Buddhism through succeeding centuries in India and Ceylon. His emphasis is on the links between religious thought and the society in which it exists.

LING, TREVOR. **A DICTIONARY OF BUDDHISM. 277pp. Scr72, 2.95p.**
Over 200 entries provide a detailed introduction to Buddhist history, doctrine, and practice. Most entries are cross referenced and contain a bibliography. Clear and concise.

LU K'UAN YU (CHARLES LUK). **PRACTICAL BUDDHISM. Glossary, notes, index, 167pp. TPH71, 5.95c.**
A very clear outline of Buddhist doctrine combined with a discussion of meditational techniques. Luk includes translations of ancient texts and teaching stories as well as two cases of spiritual awakening by Western Buddhists. This is an excellent introduction to Buddhism.

LU K'UAN YU (CHARLES LUK), tr. **THE VIMALAKIRTI NIRDESA SUTRA. Glossary, ShP72, 157pp. 3.95p.**
This is one of the most important texts of Zen and Mahayana Buddhism. The Sutra was produced in India probably around the beginning of the Christian era. It is a philosophical discourse, full of dramatic episodes. The *bodhisattva* path—the dedicating of one's energies towards the benefit of all living things—is introduced with critical insight and rare humor.

Madhyamika

Ideas concerning the nondual nature of phenomenal existence and nirvana were first discussed in a group of Mahayana scriptures known as the **Prajna** or **Wisdom Sutras**, which developed about the beginning of the Christian era. They were further expounded in the writings of Nagarjuna, who is said to have established the Madhyamika, or the School of the Middle Way. Nagarjuna lived during the second century AD. Although there is no doubt that he is a historical person, very little is known about him, other than that he was of *brahman* parentage, and that he studied all the Hindu branches of knowledge before he was converted to Buddhism. The school he founded takes its position between the extremes of existence and nonexistence, affirmation and negation, pleasure and pain. However, he also related this middle path to the Hinayanist doctrine of dependent origination, which he paraphrases by means of the eight fold negation: *Nothing comes into being, or does anything disappear. Nothing is eternal, nor has anything an end. Nothing is identical or differentiated, nothing moves hither, nor moves anything thither.* By means of this negation he sought to explain the truth of emptiness and the unreality of all elements of existence. However, the word *sunya*, which is usually translated as empty, is also interpreted as relative. This is to say, a thing is *sunya* in that it can be identified only by mentioning its relation to something else; it becomes meaningless without these relations. Madhyamika accepts the truth that relations and dependence constitute the phenomenal world, but it also contends that one is unable to explain these relations intelligibly. In his writings, Nagarjuna proceeds to demonstrate that all relationships are false and erroneous, and on the assumption that any contradiction is proof of error, he finds contradictions in every concept. By a merciless system of logic, he proves that the whole phenomenal world is empty or unreal because it is based on relations which cannot be explained satisfactorily.

He also points out that genuine realization of the emptiness of the phenomenal world is at the same time a religious awakening, a direct intuition of the highest truth, and this spiritual intent gives the real meaning to the doctrine of emptiness. To Nagarjuna, the doctrine of emptiness is taught not as a theory but as a means (*upaya*) to get rid of all theories, thus freeing one from the world around us. By getting rid of the ignorance that binds us to the phenomenal world through the realization that this world is empty and unreal, we achieve *prajna* or intuitive wisdom, that enables us to realize the absolute truth which is unconditioned, undeterminate, and beyond thought and word.

CONZE, EDWARD. **BUDDHIST WISDOM BOOKS: THE DIAMOND SUTRA, THE HEART SUTRA. Index, 107pp. H&R/A&U, 3.30p.**
The two sutras contained in this book were written between 1,500 and 2,100 years ago and are considered by Buddhists to be the loftiest of the Buddhist writings called **Prajnaparamita**, which means *the perfection of wisdom*. The author spent twenty years translating these profound texts and writing a worthy commentary.

CONZE, EDWARD, tr. **THE LARGE SUTRA ON PERFECT WISDOM. Glossary, notes, index, 697pp. UCa75, 25.00c.**
The earliest and most influential of the Mahayana sutras had the perfection of wisdom as its main subject matter. Of these texts, the famous **Diamond** and **Heart Sutras** have been known in the West for many years, but they are merely condensations of the original **Large Sutra on Perfect Wisdom** that took shape between 50 and 200 AD in southern India. The **Wisdom Sutras** continued to be composed over a period of 600 years, and in their entirety form a large and complex body of religious literature. The volume makes the **Sutra** available in its complete form for the first time in an annotated translation and is the result of thirty-five years of close study by Dr. Conze. This is a deeply philosophical work, filled with esoteric terminology, and is recommended only to those familiar with the Buddhist tradition.

CONZE, EDWARD, tr. **THE PERFECTION OF WISDOM. Glossary, cross referenced index of topics, 325pp. FSF73, 5.00p.**
Composition of this work extended over a period of 700 years. It is considered one of the world's most important spiritual documents. It was written to be memorized by monks, and for this reason this translation is a literary rather than a literal one—aimed at bringing forth the true meaning of the document. The text is presented in two versions, verse and prose.

CONZE, EDWARD, tr. **SELECTED SAYINGS FROM THE PERFECTION OF WISDOM. 131pp. BuS55, 5.15p.**
An abundance of translations of **Prajnaparamita Sutras** has appeared in the last few years, most of them by Dr. Conze. This anthology contains selections from all important aspects of the teaching arranged under three main headings, according to whether they deal with the Buddha, the dharma, or the *sangha*. The most readable passages have been selected and technicalities have been avoided. Usually the translation is quite literal. The selections are topically arranged within the main headings. This version is probably the best introduction to **Prajnaparamita** and a helpful introduction is also included.

CONZE, EDWARD, tr. **THE SHORT PRAJNAPARAMITA TEXTS. Glossary, notes, indices, 224pp. Luz73, 14.30c.**
Translations of the following texts: **The Questions of Suvikrantavikramin (Perfect Wisdom in 2,500 Lines)**, **The Perfection of Wisdom in 700 Lines**, and **The Perfection of Wisdom in 500 Lines**. In addition Dr. Conze provides summaries of: **The Diamond Sutra (Perfect Wisdom in 300 Lines)**, **The Heart of Perfect Wisdom, The Perfection of Wisdom in a Few Words, Perfect Wisdom and the Five Bodhisattvas, The Holy and Blessed Perfection of Wisdom in 50 Lines**, and **The Perfection of Wisdom for Kausika**. In addition there are selections from **The Questions of Nagasri** and a summary of **The Sutra on Perfect Wisdom**. A final section is devoted to translations of four related tantric texts.

GONSAR TULKU and GAVIN KILTY, trs. **THE KEY TO MADHYAMIKA. 30pp. LTW76, 2.00p.**
A translation of the Fourteenth Dalai Lama's discourse on Madhyamika.

HOPKINS, JEFFREY, tr. **ANALYSIS OF GOING AND COMING.** Bibliography, 28pp. LTW76, 2.00p.
A translation of the second chapter of Chandrakirti's **Clear Worlds**, a commentary on Nagarjuna's **Treatise on the Middle Way**.

HOPKINS, JEFFREY, tr. **OCEAN OF REASONING.** 34pp. LTW74, 2.00p.
A translation of chapter two of Tsong-ka-pa's **Ocean of Reasoning**, a commentary on Nagarjuna's **Fundamental Treatise on the Middle Way**.

HOPKINS, JEFFREY and LATI RIMPOCHE, trs. **THE BUDDHISM OF TIBET AND THE KEY TO THE MIDDLE WAY.** 5.95c.
See the Tibetan Buddhism section.

HOPKINS, JEFFREY and LATI RIMPOCHE, trs. **THE PRECIOUS GARLAND AND THE SONG OF THE FOUR MINDFULNESSES.** 4.75p.
See the Tibetan Buddhism section.

HUA, HSUAN, tr. **A GENERAL EXPLANATION OF THE VAJRA PRAJNAPARAMITA SUTRA.** Illustrations, index, 186pp. SAB74, 8.00p.
The **Prajnaparamita Sutra** comprises many volumes, of which the **Vajra Sutra** is just one. *Vajra* is a Sanskrit word which essentially means an indestructible substance, usually represented by a diamond —and this Sutra is usually called the **Diamond Sutra**. This is a translation of the Sutra, with extensive commentary by Hsuan Hua and translation sof some of the traditional commentaries.

INADA, KENNETH, tr. **NAGARJUNA.** Bibliography, 214pp. Hok70, 24.75c.
A translation of Nagarjuna's major work, the **Mulamadhyamakakarika** (generally known as the **Karika**), with notes, the Romanized Sanskrit text, an introductory text on Nagarjuna's philosophy, and a long glossary.

KAWAMURA, LESLIE, tr. **GOLDEN ZEPHYR.** 4.95p.
See the Tibetan Buddhism section.

MURTI, T.R.V. **THE CENTRAL PHILOSOPHY OF BUDDHISM.** Glossary, notes, index, 356pp. A&U55, 16.15c.
This is the most comprehensive and authoritative treatise on Madhyamika. Murti covers every aspect of the subject with great clarity and thoroughness.

NAGARJUNA and SAKYA PANDIT. **ELEGANT SAYINGS.** 3.95p.
See the Tibetan Buddhism section.

RAMANAN, K. VENKATA. **NAGARJUNA'S PHILOSOPHY.** Notes, index, 409pp. MoB66, 11.35c.
Dr. Ramanan states in the introduction that his purpose is *to give as far as possible an objective and complete picture of the Madhyamika philosophy as it can be gathered from the whole of this text.* The text he refers to is the **Mana-prajnaparamita-sastra**, which is a commentary on the **Prajnaparamita Sutras** and is traditionally attributed to Nagarjuna. The original Sanskrit version of the *Sastra* has been lost and the text is preserved only in a Chinese translation. The author's main aim is not a translation— though in his exposition a great deal of the text is translated—but a deep study of the philosophical concepts found in the *Sastra*. The material is topically arranged and the author has made a valuable contribution to Buddhist studies with this volume.

ROBINSON, RICHARD. **EARLY MADHYAMIKA IN INDIA AND CHINA.** Index, 357pp. MoB65, 16.45c.
This is an important descriptive analysis of specific Madhyamika texts comparing the ideology of Kumarajiva, who translated the four Madhyamika treatises in the fourth century AD, with that of his three Chinese contemporaries—Hui-Yuan, Seng-Jui, and Seng-Chao. Dr. Robinson's presentation is highly technical and is accompanied by a profusion of notes.

SINGH, JAIDEVA. **AN INTRODUCTION TO MADHYAMIKA PHILOSOPHY.** 58pp. MoB76, 1.80p.
A brief survey which traces the rise and growth of Madhyamika philosophy and the origin, structure, development, and purpose of the Madhyamika dialectic. A number of concepts unique to Madhyamika are also discussed.

SOPA, GESHE and JEFFREY HOPKINS. **PRACTICE AND THEORY OF TIBETAN BUDDHISM.** 3.95p.
See the Tibetan Buddhism section.

STCHERBATSKY, THEODORE. **THE CONCEPTION OF BUDDHIST NIRVANA.** Glossary, indices, 264+pp. MoB77, 18.30c.
An English translation of Nagarjuna's treatises on causality and nirvana, accompanied by a translation of Candrakirti's comprehensive commentary. The book is edited by Jaideva Singh and he adds an exhaustive exploration of the historical background of Madhyamika philosophy, and an exposition of its logic and metaphysics. The original Sanskrit text is also included.

STRENG, FREDERICK. **EMPTINESS: A STUDY IN RELIGIOUS MEANING. Very complete annotated bibliography, notes, index, 252pp. Abi67, 4.95p.**
This is a fine in depth study of Nagarjuna and his interpretation of ultimate reality. Also included are translations of Nagarjuna's **Fundamentals of the Middle Way** and **Averting the Arguments**. The first two chapters on the relevance of studying emptiness, and the implications of emptiness for understanding some basic Buddhist concepts are good scholarship and fairly dry going. The rest of the book is an excellent presentation of basic Indian Mahayana Buddhism (known generally as Madhyamika) and Nagarjuna's contribution to its development. They should be accessible to the general reader but we suggest that the reader reverse the order of the chapters and read the latter two first unless s/he has excellent grounding in Indian Buddhism.

THURMAN, ROBERT, tr. **THE HOLY TEACHING OF VIMALAKIRTI.** 176pp. PSU76, 19.45c.
This is a translation of a Tibetan version of a key Buddhist sutra— previously known to the English speaking world only through translations from Chinese texts. This version is generally conceded to be more faithful to the original Sanskrit than are the Chinese texts. It is also clearer (for one thing, it summarizes each section), and more precise in its philosophical and psychological expression. Along with Nagarjuna, Vimalakirti was one of the main teachers of the Middle Way. His sutra focuses on an exposition of the central Buddhist concept of emptiness or voidness. The translation is accompanied by introductory comments; an epilogue; glossaries of Sanskrit terms, numerical categories, and technical terms, and extensive textual notes.

——————END OF MADHYAMIKA SUBSECTION——————

MATICS, MARION, tr. **ENTERING THE PATH OF ENLIGHTENMENT.** Glossary, bibliography, 318pp. McM70/A&U, 2.95p.
Contains the first complete English translation of Santideva's **Bodhicaryavatara**, a Mahayana classic which describes the *bodhisattva* vow, one of the major Buddhist concepts. Included also is an interpretation and extensive notes as well as background material which places the text within the framework of Buddhist thought. It is a beautifully written piece and the translation is excellent.

MATSUNAGA, ALICIA. **THE BUDDHIST PHILOSOPHY.** Many illustrations, extensive notes, bibliography, index, 7"x10½", 310pp. Tut69, 18.75c.
This is a detailed study of the rise and development of a theory of assimilation of the native gods in early Buddhism, particularly noting the developments occurring as this philosophy spread to China and Japan. This phenomenon is known in Japan as the *honji-suijaku* theory— the native Japanese gods are considered to be manifestations of the true nature of the various Buddhas and *bodhisattvas*. Ms. Matsunaga examines the reasons why a unity between Buddhism and the indigenous faith occurred, the results of this unity, and the specific reasons why the Japanese developed their theory. She analyzes the principal deities involved and investigates the theory's impact upon other aspects of Japanese culture.

MATSUNAMI, KODO. **INTRODUCING BUDDHISM.** Annotated bibliography, index, 304pp. Tut73, 3.95p.
The author describes himself as *a Japanese student who sets out for a journey in search of his true self.* The presentation is not the best, yet far from the worst, we have seen. The language is often stilted and it is apparent that English is not the native tongue of the author.

Dharmachakra: Veneration of Buddha turning the *Wheel of the Law.*

MOOKERJEE, SATKARI. THE BUDDHIST PHILOSOPHY OF UNI-VERSAL FLUX. Notes, index, 495pp. MoB35, 17.10c.
A systematic exposition of the philosophy of critical realism as expounded by Dignaga and his school.

MULLER, F. MAX and T. ROGERS. **BUDDHAGHOSHA'S PARABLES. Notes, indices, 378pp. Alo1870, 28.55c.**
This volume contains Captain Rogers' translation from the Burmese of **Buddhaghosha's Parables** along with an introduction by Max Muller, and Muller's translation from the Pali of the **Dhammapada.** The parables are contained in Buddhaghosa's **Commentary on the Dhammapada.**

NAKAMURA, HAJIME. **GOTAMA BUDDHA. Notes, index, 154pp. BBI77, 7.00p.**
An authoritative, concise view of the personality and life of the historical Buddha, relying upon the earliest sources rather than the later legendary biographies. Professor Nakamura objectively analyzes the facts known about the Buddha from the time of his birth, including the circumstances of his genealogy and family through his enlightenment and long years of preaching up until his death. The author also discusses the alleged Piprahwa discovery in 1898 of the Buddha's relics. The author is Professor Emeritus at Tokyo University.

NANAMOLI, BHIKKU. **A THINKER'S NOTEBOOK. 252pp. BPS nd, 3.40p.**
A collection of short thoughts and questions gleaned from this Buddhist monk's diary and papers.

NANANANDA, BHIKKHU. **CONCEPT AND REALITY IN EARLY BUDDHIST THOUGHT. Notes, index, 143pp. BPS71, 4.50p.**
The analysis of the nature of concepts constitutes an important facet of the Buddhist doctrine of Anatta ("not-self"). Buddhism traces the idea of a soul to a fundamental error in understanding the facts of experience. This ignorance....is reflected to a great extent in the words and concepts in worldly parlance....The Buddha's teachings on this particular aspect of our phenomenal existence can best be appreciated with the aid of two key words, "papanca" and "papanca-sanna-sankha," an evaluation of which is the aim of this work.

NYANAPONIKA, VENERABLE. **THE HEART OF BUDDHIST MEDI-TATION. Glossary, notes, 223pp. Wei62/HPG, 3.95p.**
An introductory treatise, divided into three parts. The first explains the basic Buddhist meditation practices. This is followed by a full translation, with explanatory notes, of **The Greater Discourse on the Foundations of Mindfulness** (the **Maha-Satipatthana-Sutta**), a review of the Buddha's teaching on the subject. There is also an anthology of translations from Pali and Sanskrit texts dealing with right mindfulness. A lucid exposition.

NYANAPONIKA, VENERABLE, ed. **PATHWAYS OF BUDDHIST THOUGHT. Notes, index, 256pp. A&U71, 8.95c.**
A collection of some of the most important essays from **The Wheel,** a series of short, authoritative paperbacks dealing with all aspects of Theravada Buddhism. Over 140 of them have been published over the years and a high standard has consistently been maintained. They include translations of portions of scriptures and commentarial works, as well as original essays on Buddhist themes related to modern life. The present essays cover some of the most important aspects of Buddhism and include discussion of such basic themes as the nature of Buddhism, Buddhist ethics and philosophical concepts, Buddhism and science, the power of mindfulness, *anatta* and *nibbana.* The Venerable Nyanaponika's writings form the central section of the book.

NYANATILOKA, VENERABLE. **BUDDHIST DICTIONARY. 225pp. Fwn72, 5.00c.**
A manual, in dictionary form, of Buddhist terminology and doctrine. All the Pali words are transliterated and many English words are given Pali equivalents. The text is fully cross referenced and seems to be quite complete. Often original sources are quoted in the explanations. This is the third edition, revised and enlarged by Venerable Nyanaponika.

OHASHI, ALAN and DEAN KOGA. **PILGRIMAGE. 9"x8", HIn77, 4.95p.**
Photographs of pilgrimage sites in India, Sri Lanka, and Nepal, along with a bit of text and instructions for making a pilgrimage.

OLCOTT, HENRY STEEL. **THE BUDDHIST CATECHISM. 138pp. TPH1881, 1.00p.**
A classic work which contains the essence of Buddhist teachings.

OVERMYER, DANIEL. **FOLK BUDDHIST RELIGION. Glossary, many notes, bibliography, index, 306pp. HUP76, 18.80c.**
A survey of Chinese folk religious sects from the Han era to the twentieth century, with an emphasis on those of Buddhist orientation. Focusing on the rituals and beliefs of prominent groups, Professor Overmyer describes how many of these sects developed their own traditions of organization, leadership, and scripture, and maintained an active congregational life over long periods of time. This analysis throws new light on the whole nature of peasant rebellions in China. Overmyer characterizes the Chinese sectarian movements as a logical extension of Buddhist evangelism.

The Pali Canon

The Pali Canon is a compendious term for the Scriptures of the Theravada—"Teaching of the Elders"—School of Buddhism, sometimes called the Southern School, which today may be found in Ceylon, Thailand, Burma, and Cambodia. The language is Pali, which was the language of Magadha, where the Buddha taught, and was carried by missionaries at some stage to Ceylon....The Canon is the slow product of an oral tradition handed down by generations of "bhikkhus" or monks, as agreed in form, so the Canon itself claims, at a Council of Elders convened soon after the Buddha's death. What happened, in the 400 years of that handing down to this large collection of remembered discourses and conversations and to the written word as "edited," no doubt, in the course of further centuries of commentary and argument, it is impossible to say.—from the introduction to **Some Sayings of the Buddha,** translated by F.L. Woodward. The Canon relates the life and teachings of the Buddha in the forty-five years of his ministry after reaching enlightenment. Virtually all of the material now available has been translated by the Pali Text Society, founded in 1881 by Dr. and Mrs. Rhys Davids. See the subsections on **Jataka Tales** and **The Dhamapada** for more Pali texts.

ANDERSEN, DINES and HELMER SMITH, eds. **SUTTANIPATA, VOL-UMES I AND III. PTS nd, 15.10/each.**
An early work which presents Buddhism not as an established monastic system, but only as an ethical religion stressing the simple virtuous life. The recluse is called upon to adhere to the moral virtues, to subdue his desires for sensual pleasures, to turn his mind away from material possessions, to have no dealings in gold and silver, and to eat only moderately.

AUNG, SHWE ZAN and CAROLINE RHYS DAVIDS, trs. **POINTS OF CONTROVERSY OR SUBJECTS OF DISCOURSE. Introduction, notes, indices, 471pp. PTS15, 28.50c.**
A translation of the **Katha-Vatthu**, the fifth among the seven books which make up the **Abhidhamma Pitaka**. As the title suggests, it is made up of subjects, with related points of discourse and quotations from Pali commentaries.

BUDDHADATTA, A.P. **CONCISE PALI-ENGLISH DICTIONARY. 302pp. CAp68, 5.00c.**

BUDDHADATTA, A.P. **THE HIGHER PALI COURSE FOR ADVANCED STUDENTS. 300pp. CAp51, 4.25c.**

BUDDHADATTA, A.P. **THE NEW PALI COURSE, PART I. 133pp. CAp62, 2.50p.**
An excellent collection of exercises designed to teach Pali to English-speaking students. A vocabulary is included.

BUDDHADATTA, A.P. **THE NEW PALI COURSE, PART II. 268pp. CAp74, 5.35p.**

BURLINGAME, E.W. **BUDDHIST LEGENDS (DHAMMAPADA COMMENTARY). 1123pp. PTS21, 51.00c/set.**
The **Dhammapada** commentary is ascribed to Buddhaghosa, one of the greatest of all the Buddhist scholastics. Burlingame does not agree with this traditional ascription and states unequivocally that the authorship is unknown. The work purports to tell us *where, when, why, for what purpose, with reference to what situation, with reference to what person or persons,* the Buddha uttered each of the 423 stanzas in the **Dhammapada**. In the process, the author of the commentary narrates 299 legends or stories. All of these are translated in this three volume set and extensive introductory material is also included along with a profusion of notes.

CONE, MARGARET and RICHARD GOMBRICH, trs. **THE PERFECT GENEROSITY OF PRINCE VESSANTARA. Notes, bibliography, 158pp. Oxf77, 33.50c.**
The selfless generosity of Vessantara, who gave away everything, even his wife and children, is the most famous story in the Buddhist world. It has been retold in many languages, pictured in the art of every Buddhist country, and has formed the theme of countless sermons, dramas, dances, and ceremonies. This volume contains a translation by Margaret Cone of the oldest extant version of the epic. The book is illustrated with a wide range of hitherto unpublished paintings from Singhalese temples, including a number in color. There is also a long introduction.

FERNANDO, K.C. **A STUDENTS' PALI-ENGLISH DICTIONARY. 125pp. Gun50, 1.95c.**
An elementary dictionary prepared for students of Pali studying in English schools and based on the Pali Text Society's dictionary.

GEIGER, WILHELM, tr. **CULAVAMSA. 802pp. PTS29, 19.20c.**
This translation contains Geiger's two volumes bound into one. The **Culavamsa** is the more recent part of the **Mahavamsa**, the national epic of Sri Lanka. The information is historical in the main part, although the original author did add a fair amount of literary elaboration. Geiger provides an introduction and many notes.

GEIGER, WILHELM, tr. **THE MAHAVAMSA. Glossary, index, 387pp. PTS12, 18.40c.**
The **Mahavamsa** is the second of the Pali Chronicles. It describes the early history of Buddhism, its introduction into Ceylon, and its progress there. It is known as *the great Chronicle* and traces the history of Buddhism in Ceylon up to the early fourteenth century AD. Much of the work is based on actual history, although some of it is pure legend. Geiger's translation is into prose and he provides a lengthy introduction and extensive notes.

GEIGER, WILHELM. **PALI LANGUAGE AND LITERATURE. 264pp. MuM43, 17.00c.**
Translated into English by Dr. Batakrishna Ghosh.

HORNER, I.B., tr. **THE BOOK OF THE DISCIPLINE. PTS38-66, 140.00c/set.**
These six volumes (I, II, III: **Vinaya, Suttavibhanga**; IV: **Mahavagga**; V:

Cullavagga; VI: **Parivara**) contain the rules which govern the conduct of the monks and nuns in the Buddhist order. They cover such things as the admission of nuns and monks, their daily activities, their communal life, their food, clothing and shelter, and their relations with the laity.

HORNER, I.B. **THE EARLY BUDDHIST THEORY OF MAN PERFECTED. Notes, indices, 328pp. Plo36, 29.30p.**
A study of the Arahan concept and of the implications of the aim to perfection in religious life in early and post canonical Pali literature.

HORNER, I.B., tr. **THE MIDDLE LENGTH SAYINGS (MAJJHIMA-NIKAYA). Three volumes, each about 400 pages, PTS54-59, 20.00c/each.**
A collection of discourses which exemplify the philosophy of the *dhamma*. Every point of this doctrine is discussed over and over again and in the process some of the greatest literary works in Buddhist literature are presented.

HORNER, I.B., tr. **THE MINOR ANTHOLOGIES OF THE PALI CANNON, PART III. Indices, 284pp. PTS75, 15.35c.**
Translations of **Chronicles of Buddhas** (Buddhavamsa) and **Basket of Conduct** (Cariyapitaka). Ms. Horner also provides extensive notes and introductory material.

HORNER, I.B. and H.S. GEHMAN, trs. **THE MINOR ANTHOLOGIES OF THE PALI CANON, PART IV. Indices, 310pp. PTS74, 15.35c.**
Translations of **Stories of the Mansions** (Vimanavatthu) and **Stories of the Departed** (Petavatthu), along with commentaries, introductory material, and notes.

JAYAWICKRAMA, N.A., tr. **CHRONICLE OF THE THUPA AND THE THUPAVAMSA. Indices, 320pp. PTS71, 20.15c.**
A translation of a comparatively late chronicle recording events belonging to a period at least fourteen centuries before its date. The Pali text is also included along with a lengthy introduction, many technical notes, and illustrations.

JOHANSSON, RUNE. **PALI BUDDHIST TEXTS. 160pp. Cur76, 10.55p.**
A simple and practical introduction to the language, consisting of texts, vocabularies, translations, and notes, and a systematic treatment of grammar.

JONES, J.J., tr. **THE MAHAVASTU. Indices, 1,318pp. PTS56, 61.60c/set.**
This three volume biography of the Buddha begins with the Buddha's previous life and carries the narration down to his establishment of a monastic order. Extensive notes.

LAW, B.C., tr. **THE DEBATES COMMENTARY. Notes, 260pp. PTS40, 12.00c.**
A translation of the **Kathavatthuppakarana-Atthakatha**. The text introduces the student to the controversies that took place between the orthodox *sangha* and other early Buddhist schools of thought.

MAHATHERA, A.P. BUDDHADATTA. **ENGLISH-PALI DICTIONARY. 588pp. PTS55, 20.80c.**

MALALASKERA, G.P. **THE PALI LITERATURE OF CEYLON. Notes, bibliography, index, Gun28, 5.00c.**
More than simply a history of Pali literature, this is also a cultural history of Sri Lanka, with chapters on the major individual figures and schools of thought.

■ *MAURICE, DAVID, tr.* **THE LION'S ROAR. Introduction, glossary, index, 255pp. Stu62, 4.95c.**
A well translated, topically organized anthology of the Buddha's teachings selected from the Pali Canon. This is an excellent work which we recommend to all who are interested in what the Buddha is purported to have said.

MULLER, E. **A SIMPLIFIED GRAMMAR OF THE PALI LANGUAGE. 159pp. BPH nd, 3.40c.**

NANAMOLI, VENERABLE, tr. **THE LIFE OF THE BUDDHA. Notes, bibliography, index, 375pp. BPS72, 13.00c.**
This **Life** has been translated and compiled by a scholar-monk and it is

based on the oldest authentic records as found in the Pali Canon. The material is presented in the form of *narrators* and *voices* who quote the Canonical material. Venerable Nanamoli has organized the material chronologically and cites his sources. The narration often lacks cohesion and we would not recommend this book as a primary account of the Buddha's life and teachings. However it is a good supplementary volume since a great deal of the material is not available in English translation elsewhere, or else is not easily obtainable.

NANAMOLI, VENERABLE, tr. **MINDFULNESS OF BREATHING.** **125pp. BPS73, 3.40p.**
"Anapansati," or "mindfulness of breathing," is among the Buddhist methods of mind training given most prominence in the Pali Canon. It was originally for his own use that the translator collected the material that follows from the Pali Canon and its commentaries. The idea was to have "under one cover," for the purpose of study, the Pali teaching of this meditation subject, omitting nothing important and eliminating repetitions.—from the introduction. Notes and background information accompany the selections.

NANAMOLI, VENERABLE, tr. **THE MINOR READINGS AND THE ILLUSTRATOR OF ULTIMATE MEANING. Indices, 383pp. PTS60, 16.00c.**
The Minor Readings is the shortest of all the books in the Pali **Tripitaka**. It is often regarded as a practical handbook whose contents represent the central doctrines of the Buddha's teaching. This is a new translation, bound together with a translation of Buddhaghosa's extensive commentary, **The Illustrator of Ultimate Meaning**.

NANAMOLI, VENERABLE, tr. **THE PATH OF PURIFICATION: VISUDDHI MAGGA. Glossary, index, notes, 935pp. ShP76, 22.95c/ 5.95p/each.**
This book, written in the fifth century, systematically summarizes and interprets the teaching of the Buddha contained in the Pali **Tripitaka** which is generally regarded as the oldest and most authentic record of the Buddha's words. This is one of the most important, if not the most important Pali text. It contains clear, detailed instructions on Buddhist doctrine and meditation. The translator was a member of a Ceylonese Buddhist monastic order for eleven years and is well known for his excellent critical translations of difficult texts. This volume is recommended to all serious students of Buddhism. The paperback edition is in two volumes.

NANAMOLI, VENERABLE, tr. **PITAKA-DISCLOSURE. Pali-English glossary, many notes, indices, 446pp. PTS64, 20.80c.**
A translation of the **Petakopadesa**, a text which sets forth a method *for composing commentaries on the Buddha's Utterance as recorded in the suttas.* The **Nettippakarana** (translated as **The Guide**) sets forth the same information, but the **Petakopadesa** is the older of the two texts.

NANANANDA, BHIKKHU. **THE MAGIC OF THE MIND. Notes, index, 92pp. BPS74, 3.40p.**
An exposition of the **Kalakarama Sutta**, a canonical discourse on the illusory nature of consciousness centering on a discussion of the *Law of Dependent Arising* as a *golden mean* which freely transcends the dualities of *existence and nonexistence* and *mind and matter.* An annotated translation of the discourse is presented, followed by a detailed exposition of the psychological and philosophical implications of the text.

NARADA, VENERABLE. **THE BUDDHA AND HIS TEACHINGS. Notes, index, 730pp. BMS73, 14.00p.**
The author of this study is a member of the Order of the Sangha and he has based his account on the Pali texts, commentaries, and traditions prevailing in Buddhist countries (especially in Sri Lanka). The first part of the book deals with the life of the Buddha; the second with the *dhamma*, the Pali term for his doctrine. The section reviewing the Buddha's life is quite vividly written and often reads like a novel. All of the terms used are clearly defined and a great deal of background information is presented. The book seems to be designed for the general reader and is easy to read. The material is presented in many short sections. All the references are cited.

NARADA, VENERABLE, tr. **A MANUAL OF ABHIDHAMMA. Index, 458pp. BPS75, 7.15p.**
A translation of the **Abhidhammattha Sangha**, with extensive commentary and notes on virtually every word and a Romanization of the Pali text. *Abhidhamma...is the higher teaching of the Buddha. It expounds the*

quintessence of His profound doctrine....In the Abhidhamma both mind and matter...are microscopically analyzed. Chief events connected with the process of birth and death are explained in detail. Intricate points of the "dhamma" are explained The Path of Emancipation is set forth in clear terms....Consciousness is defined. Thoughts are analyzed and classified chiefly from an ethical standpoint. All mental states are enumerated. The composition of each type of consciousness is set forth in detail.

NORMAN, K.R., tr. **THE ELDERS' VERSES, I: THERAGATHA. Indices, 383pp. PTS69, 21.80c.**
A new translation, based upon a considerably better Pali text than was available at the time of Mrs. Rhys Davids' work. The **Theragatha** is literally translated as *Verses of the Elders* and this volume contains translations of 1279 verses, with an abundance of notes and a lengthy introduction.

NORMAN, K.R., tr. **THE ELDERS' VERSES, II: THERIGATHA. Indices, 290pp. PTS71, 21.80c.**
A new translation of this important early work, based upon a different text than the one used by Mrs. Rhys Davids. Over half the book is devoted to introductory material and notes.

NYANAPONIKA, VENERABLE, ed. **SELECTED BUDDHIST TEXTS FROM THE PALI CANON. Many notes, about 1400pp. BPS74, 9.25c/each.**
More selections from **The Wheel**. This three volume set is devoted to translations from Pali texts. Many of the texts presented here are not available anywhere else and all the translations are by noted Buddhist scholars. Essential reading for all who are seriously interested in Theravada Buddhism.

NYANATILOKA, VENERABLE. **GUIDE THROUGH THE ABHIDHAMMA-PITAKA. Index, 192pp. BPS71, 5.10c.**
An authoritative synopsis of canonical Abhidhamma literature. The author's student, Nyanaponika, has revised and enlarged this edition.

NYANATILOKA, VENERABLE, tr. **THE WORD OF THE BUDDHA. Index, 113pp. BPS71, 2.40p.**
A systematic exposition of all the main tenets of the Buddha's teachings as found in the **Sutta-Pitaka** of the Pali Canon. The selections have been grouped topically and the original texts themselves are translated and presented, with little commentary. The translator provides a Pali pronunciation guide and a short introduction as well as a fairly lengthy bibliography.

PIYADASSI, VENERABLE, tr. **THE BOOK OF PROTECTION. Notes, introductory material, 123pp. BPS75, 4.00p.**
A translation of an anthology of selected discourses of the Buddha which was compiled centuries ago and intended to be a handbook for the newly ordained novice. The idea was that those novices who are not capable of studying large portions of the *Discourse Collection* (**Sutta-Pitaka**) should at least be conversant with the **Book of Protection**. The twenty-four discourses presented here have been selected from the five **Nikayas** (the original Pali collections of the Buddha's discourses). This is the most widely known Pali book in Sri Lanka today. It is given an important place in the Buddhist home; it is treated with veneration and kept in the household shrine so that the residents can refer to it during their devotional hour.

PIYADASSI, VENERABLE. **THE BUDDHA'S ANCIENT PATH. Notes, index, 239pp. BPS64, 5.00c.**
This is a well written account by one of the leading monks in Sri Lanka today. It is based on the Buddha's teachings as expounded in the Pali Canon and is basically an in depth discussion of the *Four Noble Truths* and the *Noble Eightfold Path*—with a full chapter devoted to an exposition of each of the *Truths* and *Paths*. There is also a concise account of the Buddha's life and an informative survey of Buddhist meditation. *This makes interesting and instructive reading, and the validity of the interpretations is not open to question. On the contrary, these interpretations, authoritative and unimpeachable, may be taken as a trustworthy guide.*—I.B. Horner, President, Pali Text Society.

RHYS DAVIDS, CAROLINE, tr. **A BUDDHIST MANUAL OF PSYCHOLOGICAL ETHICS. Indices, 456pp. PTS00, 23.20c.**
A translation of the first book in the **Abhidhamma Pitaka** entitled

Dhamma-Sangani or **The Compendium of States or Phenomena**, with an introductory essay and notes.

RHYS DAVIDS, CAROLINE, tr. **BUDDHIST PSYCHOLOGY. Glossary, index, 488pp. OrP75, 22.50c.**
A translation of **Dhamma-Sangani**, the first of the seven books of the **Abhidhamma-Pitaka**. The text reviews the elements and objects of consciousness according to Buddhist doctrine and provides an *enumeration of the "dhammas"*, i.e., an inquiry into the numerous long notes and a connection of the material with the rest of the **Pitakas**. Mrs. Rhys Davids also provides an excellent ninety-five page introduction.

RHYS DAVIDS, CAROLINE, tr. **COMPENDIUM OF PHILOSOPHY. Indices, 319pp. PTS10, 14.40c.**
A translation of the **Abhidhammattha-Sangaha**, a primer on the psychology and philosophy of Ceylon and Burma, with an introductory essay and notes by Shwe Zan Aung.

RHYS DAVIDS, CAROLINE and F.L. WOODWARD. **THE BOOK OF KINDRED SAYINGS (SAMYUTTA-NIKAYA). Bibliography, index, PTS14, 112.50c/set.**
Another collection (containing five volumes) of discourses which makes an attempt to divide the *suttas* according to different categories: a chief point of doctrine, or a class of demon or deity, or some prominent disciple of the master.

RHYS DAVIDS, T.W., tr. **BUDDHIST SUTTAS. Index, 307pp. Dov1881, 3.00p.**
The **Pali Suttas**, third and fourth centuries BC, form the earliest essential part of the Buddhist scriptures. This selection, originally published in the **Sacred Book of the East** series, presents translations of seven of the most important. The gospel of the life, works, and death of the Buddha takes up almost half the volume. Introductions discuss the age, form, and authenticity of the **Suttas**.

RHYS DAVIDS, T.W., tr. **THE QUESTIONS OF KING MILINDA. Two volumes, index, 708pp. MoB1894, 12.60c/each.**
Translations of ancient Buddhist dialogues, probably written in the second century. They provide an important supplement to the Pali Canon and help explain many of the philosophical ideas found there. Part of the **Sacred Books of the East** series.

RHYS DAVIDS, T.W. and CAROLINE, trs. **DIALOGUES OF THE BUDDHA. PTS1889, 69.00c/set.**
These three volumes, constituting in the Pali text, the **Digha** and **Magghima Nikayas**, contain a full exposition of what early Buddhists considered the teaching of the Buddha to have been. Each volume includes an index of principal subjects, proper names and Pali words discussed, and averages over 350 pages.

RHYS DAVIDS, T.W. and H. OLDENBERG, trs. **VINAYA TEXTS. MoB1885, 13.00c/each.**
A collection of regulations governing the conduct of Buddhist monks. The three texts translated are, respectively, **The Patimokkha**, **The Mahavagga**, and **The Kullavagga**. Three volumes, about 400 pages each, with extensive notes.

RHYS DAVIDS, T.W. and WILLIAM STEDE, eds. **THE PALI TEXT SOCIETY'S PALI-ENGLISH DICTIONARY. Romanized, 8½"x11", 738pp. PTS21, 28.80c.**
This is the definitive Pali dictionary.

SADDHATISSA, H., tr. **BIRTH STORIES OF THE TEN BODHISATTVAS AND THE DASABODHISATTUPPATTIKATHA. Indices, 166+pp. PTS75, 35.25c.**
A translation of a small work of late Pali literature which is the only example of a book devoted entirely to extolling the *bodhisattvas* who will be buddhas in future ages. Saddhatissa also provides a lengthy introduction and a profusion of technical notes. The Pali text is also included.

SAYADAW, MULA PATTHANA, tr. **DISCOURSE ON ELEMENTS. 203pp. PTS62, 19.20c.**
A translation of **Dhatu-Katha**, the third book of the **Abhidhamma Pitaka**, with charts and explanations. The *abhidhamma* (sometimes translated as *Higher Subtleties of the Dhamma* or *Metaphysics*) is the third

basket of the canon and its consists of seven works. It is concerned with phenomena, and uses two methods to describe phenomena: analysis and investigation of the relations of things. This volume is devoted to an in depth analysis of classification and unclassification and association and disassociation.

SOMA, VENERABLE, tr. **THE WAY OF MINDFULNESS. Notes, introduction, 207pp. BPS75, 4.30p.**
Translations of **The Discourse on the Arousing of Mindfulness**, with commentary, **The Contemplation of the Body**, and **The Contemplation of Mental Objects** (the **Satipatthana Sutta** and commentary). These are advanced texts, designed for the practicing student. The presentation is often abrupt—but this is a conscious design of the original author. Many practical topics are discussed in depth and the material here is not available elsewhere.

Preaching Buddha, Sarnath.

VAJIRANANA, PARAVAHERA MATHATHERA. **BUDDHIST MEDITATION IN THEORY AND PRACTICE. 516pp. BMS75, 8.50p.**
A general exposition of Buddhist meditational theory and practice according to the Pali Canon. An abundance of quotations from the Canon make up the bulk of the text, and the author supplies commentaries, where applicable. Introduction by Francis Story.

WOODWARD, F.L., tr. **MANUAL OF A MYSTIC. Index, 179pp. PTS16, 8.80c.**
This is a translation of Yogavachara's **Manual**, a practical working text for the aspirant in which systems of preparation and of meditation are set forth. Included are eight meditations and two exercises, all but one drawn from the **Sutta Pitaka**. This text is recommended only to the advanced student. Introduction by Mrs. Rhys Davids.

WOODWARD, F.L., tr. **THE MINOR ANTHOLOGIES OF THE PALI CANON, PART II. Indices, 224pp. PTS48, 10.40c.**
Translations of **Verses of Uplift (Udana)** and **As It Was Said (Itivuttaka)**, along with extensive notes and an introduction by Mrs. Rhys Davids.

■ *WOODWARD, F.L., ed.* **SOME SAYINGS OF THE BUDDHA. Index, 249pp. Oxf25, 3.95p.**
A selection (the only material available in paperback) of major portions of the Pali Canon, chosen and topically arranged by F.L. Woodward, a scholar who spent the last thirty years of his life translating the most important volumes of the Canon, and editing the commentaries to many others. The only way for the beginning student to even begin to approach the innumerable *suttas* contained in the Canon seems to be through the material presented here. A very well organized collection An introduction by Christmas Humphreys discusses the Canon, and sketches the life and teachings of the Buddha.

WOODWARD, F.L. AND E.M. HARE, trs. **THE BOOK OF THE GRADUAL SAYINGS (ANGUTTARA-NIKAYA). Five volumes, about 300pp. each, PTS33, 70.00c/set.**
A collection of discourses which consists of a classification according to numerical categories—that is, Section One consists of *suttas* dealing with things of which only one exists; Section Two, of things in which there are two; and so on until Section Eleven.

------END OF THE PALI CANON SUBSECTION------

PANDE, GOVIND CHANDRA. **STUDIES IN THE ORIGINS OF BUDDHISM. Notes, bibliography, index, 615pp. MoB74, 16.50c.**
A study of the rise and evolution of Buddhist doctrinal thought and literature both as an inner process and as reflected externally in the actions of individuals and monastic communities. Many individual texts are considered. A technical work.

PARDUE, PETER. **BUDDHISM. Notes, bibliography, index, 215pp. McM68, 1.95p.**
An historical introduction to Buddhist values and the social and political forms they have assumed in Asia, written in nontechnical language and organized geographically.

PARRINDER, GEOFFREY, ed. **THE WISDOM OF THE EARLY BUDDHISTS. 86pp. NDP77, 2.95p.**
A selection of traditional instruction drawn from the life of the Buddha himself. The texts selected come from the Theravada tradition and present a good picture of the Buddha's teaching. An introduction provides a lucid explanation of the background of Buddhism and a description of how the various Buddhist schools originated.

PREBISH, CHARLES, ed. **BUDDHISM: A MODERN PERSPECTIVE. Bibliography, index, 345pp. PSU75, 10.00p.**
This is a clearly written, in depth introductory text written by eight leading scholars. The volume begins with a comprehensive survey of fundamentals and goes on to include topics previously untouched in introductory texts. Buddha's life, basic Buddhist doctrines and practices, the Hinayana and Mahayana sects, Buddhist literature, schools of thought, and meditation are all thoroughly discussed. Each basket of the **Tripitaka** or Buddhist canon is discussed individually, and several of the most important Mahayana sutras are considered in detail. Much of the book is devoted to Indian Buddhism, and discussions of Buddhism in China, Japan, Ceylon, Tibet, Southeast Asia, and Korea are also included. An appendix gives the location of Buddhist groups in the U.S. and there is a fifty-two page glossary.

PREBISH, CHARLES, tr. **BUDDHIST MONASTIC DISCIPLINE. Notes, bibliography, 156pp. PSU75, 18.15c.**
Translations from the Sanskrit of two important Buddhist monastic disciplinary texts, the **Pratimoksa Sutras** of the **Mahasamghikas** and **Mulasarvastivadins**, printed on facing pages. Introductory chapters give an overview of the rise of Buddhist monasticism, analyze *Vinaya*, that portion of the Buddhist canon regulating the life of monks and nuns; provisionally identify the problems inherent in *Pratimoksa* study; and describe how the Sutras were found and edited. The texts themselves are thoroughly annotated.

PRICE, A.F. and WONG MOU-LAM, trs. **THE DIAMOND SUTRA AND THE SUTRA OF HUI-NENG. 114pp. ShP69, 2.95p.**
Translations of two classic texts. The **Diamond Sutra** is a subtle scripture which forms a part of the **Prajnaparamita** (or Wisdom texts). The **Sutra of Hui Neng**, also known as the **Platform Sutra**, is one of the basic texts of Zen Buddhism. The translations are of fine quality and the translators also supply an abundance of notes.

RAHULA, WALPOLA. **THE HERITAGE OF THE BHIKKHU. Glossary, extensive notes, index, 176pp. RaH74, 3.95p.**
An account of the Buddhist monk's life as a servant of the people's needs in his role as follower and teacher of the principles of the Buddhist doctrine. Rahula sees Buddhism as a religion of monks and laymen cooperating to improve the spiritual and material conditions of humanity rather than as a mere monastic discipline. Rahula himself received the traditional monastic training in Ceylon and held a high position in one of the leading monastic institutes there.

RAHULA, WALPOLA. **HISTORY OF BUDDHISM IN CEYLON. Illustrations, maps, notes, bibliography, index, 394pp. Gun66, 6.00c.**
This is the definitive history of Buddhism in Sri Lanka. Rahula supplies a well balanced account of the religious, social, political, and economic life of the country from the earliest days to the end of the Anuradhapura period.

■ RAHULA, WALPOLA. **WHAT THE BUDDHA TAUGHT. Illustrations, glossary, bibliography, index, 151pp. RaH77/GFG, 3.95p.**
The best presentation of the fundamental principles of the Buddha's teachings that we know of. Rahula is a Ceylonese Buddhist monk and scholar and he has based his book on the original Pali texts, which are universally accepted by scholars as the earliest extant records. This is a new, revised, and expanded edition which includes texts from the *suttas* and the **Dhammapada**.

RAHULA, WALPOLA. **ZEN AND THE TAMING OF THE BULL— TOWARDS THE DEFINITION OF BUDDHIST THOUGHT. Glossary, notes, index, 160pp. GFG78, 16.35c.**
A collection of essays on various aspects of Buddhism. *Zen and the Taming of the Bull* takes up one of the book's themes—that all the fundamental principles of Zen are already to be found in Theravada. The remaining essays fall into three sections which reexamine some of the assumptions about Buddhism current in the West. In the first section, Dr. Rahula surveys in broad outline the history of Buddhism and Buddhist attitudes in the West from pre-Christian times to the present day. In the second, some fundamental misconceptions are examined, and in the third, he considers the history of Buddhism as it pertains to Sri Lanka.

RAWDING, F.W. **THE BUDDHA. 8¼"x8", 48pp. CUP75, 2.75p.**
A pictorial introduction to the Buddha's life, main teachings, and times.

REICHELT, KARL. **TRUTH AND TRADITION IN CHINESE BUDDHISM. Many illustrations, index, 343pp. PBR28, 11.50c.**
A fairly dry, albeit comprehensive, study of Chinese Buddhism as it appeared to an early twentieth century Swedish professor. Reichelt includes chapters on the introduction of Buddhism into China and its development there, the Pure Land school, the Buddhist pantheon, literature, monastic life, and pilgrimages.

RHYS DAVIDS, T.W. **BUDDHIST INDIA. Notes, index, 347pp. MoB02, 7.50c.**
This is a well written survey of India at the time of Buddhist ascendancy. Rhys Davids discusses the kings and the clans (paying special attention to Asoka, Candragupta, and Kaniska), the villages and towns, economic conditions, and religion. He also surveys the beginnings and development of writing and the language and literature of the time. As might be expected, Rhys Davids devotes a great deal of attention to the Pali books and to the **Jataka Tales**. The book is illustrated throughout and gives the reader a good feeling for the land and the times.

ROBINSON, RICHARD. **THE BUDDHIST RELIGION. Excellent topical annotated bibliography, index, 136pp. Dic70, 6.65p.**
This book seems to have been designed as a text for a course on comparative religion. It begins with a survey of Buddhism today in the East and West. This is followed by a discussion of the life and teachings of the historical Buddha. The last two chapters review the development of Indian Buddhism and developments outside India. The material is well written and organized, although it tends to be somewhat dry. The book is quite well thought of, especially in the academic community. All the major schools of thought are covered.

ROCKHILL, W. WOODVILLE, tr. **UDANAVARGA. 250pp. OPr1883, 19.60p.**
This is a translation of a Tibetan collection of verses from the Buddhist canon which is general known as the northern **Dhammapada**. It contains 300 verses which are nearly identical to the verses of the **Dhammapada**, 150 more resemble verses of that work, and forty are either identical or similar to verses from the **Sutta Nipata**. In all, the **Udanavarga** contains thirty-three chapters of about 250 verses each, divided topically into four books. Most of the verses are seven or nine syllables. This type of verse was generally found at the end of Buddha's sermons and they were probably intended to convey to his hearers, in a few easily remembered lines, the essence of his teaching. This edition includes notes and extracts from Pradjnavarman's commentary.

ROERICH, HELENA. **FOUNDATIONS OF BUDDHISM. 146pp. AgY71, 6.95c.**
An essay on the life of the Buddha and his teachings on the problem of human existence and the cessation of suffering, by one of the founders of the Agni Yoga Society in New York.

SADDHATISSA, H. **THE BUDDHA'S WAY. Illustrations, glossary, bibliography, index, 139pp. Brz71/A&U, 1.95p.**
This is a good clear presentation of Buddha's teachings and Buddhist practices. Part I describes the life and teachings of the Buddha, what it means to become a Buddhist, and both the negative and positive aspects of Buddhist morality. Part II explains the *Four Noble Truths* which form the foundations of Buddhist philosophy. Part III is devoted to meditation and has preliminary instructions for meditation, information on the subjects for meditation, and sections on *samatha* and *vipassana* meditation. Dr. Saddhatissa also includes selections from the Pali scriptures and details of the main Buddhist history in both the East and West.

SADDHATISSA, H. **BUDDHIST ETHICS. Bibliography, index, 197pp. Brz70/A&U, 6.50c.**
A very complete scholarly work which draws heavily on the scriptures of Theravada Buddhism.

■ SADDHATISSA, H. **THE LIFE OF THE BUDDHA. Bibliography, index, 89pp. H&R76, 2.95p.**
Dr. Saddhatissa is a Ceylonese monk who has studied extensively at Western universities and is one of the leading Buddhists in Great Britain. He bases his account of the Buddha's life on the Pali Canon and on early Sanskrit texts. The day to day incidents of the Buddha's life and the allegories and parables in which he envelopes much of his teaching are presented clearly and succinctly. The teachings are topically organized. A nice, short study.

SANGHARAKSHITA, VENERABLE. **MIND REACTIVE AND CREATIVE. 21pp. Wdh71, 1.05p.**
Transcription of an interesting lecture on the mind as seen in Buddhist psychology.

SANGHARAKSHITA, VENERABLE. **THE THOUSAND-PETALLED LOTUS: AN ENGLISH BUDDHIST IN INDIA. Index, 324pp. HeG76, 12.60c.**
This is an extraordinary account of the author's years of wandering in India from village to village with a begging bowl, and of how he changed from being Dennis Lingwood to the Venerable Sangharakshita. Not only is this a moving account of a spiritual odyssey, the book also provides a unique view of small town and village life in the remoter parts of India.

SANGHARAKSHITA, VENERABLE. **THE THREE JEWELS: AN INTRODUCTION TO BUDDHISM. Notes, index, 287pp. FWO67, 2.75p.**
The three jewels are the Buddha, the dharma, and the *sangha* (the Assembly, or spiritual community). These constitute the central portion of Buddhist life, from which all other parts derive their significance, and without reference to which Buddhism itself is intelligible. The author, a Westerner who has been ordained and initiated into the three major Buddhist traditions, relates the three jewels to general Buddhist belief, its origins, practices, and schools. The book is a comprehensive and understandable guide to modern Buddhism.

SAYADAW, MAHASI. **THE PROGRESS OF INSIGHT. 67pp. BPS73, 2.15p.**
The translation by Nyanaponika Thera of an advanced treatise: *The foremost concern in this work is with a stage where, after diligent preliminary practice, the insight knowledges have begun to emerge, leading up to the highest crest of spiritual achievement, Arahantship (Sainthood).* This edition includes a Romanized version of the Pali original in addition to the translation. Introduction by Narada Thera.

SCHUMANN, HANS. **BUDDHISM. Illustrations, bibliography, index, 200pp. TPH73, 2.45p.**
This is a systematically arranged study which outlines the distinctions between three main Buddhist systems: Theravada, Mahayana, and tantra. Schumann has used original Pali and Sanskrit texts, and his work contains material on karma, conditioned orientation, meditation, dharma, nirvana, and the Yogacara School. The most unique feature of the book is a *Tabulated Synopsis* of all the systems with which the book deals, showing the source, the method, the *Interim Goal*, and the *Ultimate Goal* of each. The material is clearly presented, but is intended for students with some previous knowledge of Buddhism.

SERAGE, NANCY. **THE PRINCE WHO GAVE UP A THRONE: A STORY OF THE BUDDHA. 8¼"x7", 69pp. Cro66, 6.50c.**
This is a simple retelling of the story of the Buddha, aimed at children. Ms. Serage writes well and does an excellent job of bringing the tale to life. Delicate brush drawings accompany the text.

SHAFTEL, OSCAR. **AN UNDERSTANDING OF THE BUDDHA. Bibliography, index, 247pp. ScB74, 10.00c.**
This is a fairly critical Western view of the Buddha's teachings and of Buddhist beliefs over the centuries. Shaftel appears to be trying to see what there is in Buddhism that can be useful to the Western man. He begins with a general review of Buddhism and the Buddha's teachings and goes from there to a more detailed analysis of tantra, Zen, and nirvana. Extensive notes follow the text.

SILCOCK, T.H., tr. **A VILLAGE ORDINATION. 264pp. Cur76, 7.35c.**
Translation of a Thai poem which describes the ordination of a Buddhist monk in a rural monastery, and also discusses Thai rural culture, Buddhist religion, and life in a Thai monastery. Parallel Thai-English texts, notes, introductory material, and photographs of the ceremony.

SINNETT, A.P. **ESOTERIC BUDDHISM. 11.25c.**
See the Theosophy section.

SNELLGROVE, DAVID, ed. **THE IMAGE OF THE BUDDHA. Chronology, glossary, bibliography, index, 9"x12", 482pp. Kod78, 45.00c.**
Compiled over a period of five years under the auspices of UNESCO, this monumental work traces the many forms in which the ideal of Buddhahood has found expression over some 2,500 years in the major Buddhist countries of Asia. The text is arranged according to chronological periods and geographical areas, allowing the reader to follow the gradual evolution of Buddhist iconography as well as to recognize the characteristic features of Buddhist statuary and paintings in each Asian country. The text is complemented by a wealth of illustrative materials, over 350 black and white and color plates, figures, and maps. Each chapter is prefaced by an essay on the development of Buddhist thought in the respective period and locale.

SOOTHILL, W.E., tr. **LOTUS OF THE WONDERFUL LAW. Illustrations, glossary, index, 286pp. Cur30, 12.00c.**
An important early translation of the **Lotus Sutra** in which Soothill succeeds in his aim of making this all important Mahayana sutra more available to the general public. His translation is a work of excellent scholarship, and yet often reads like a novel. Some commentary is interspersed.

SOOTHILL, W.E. and LEWIS HODOUS. **A DICTIONARY OF CHINESE-BUDDHIST TERMS. 7½"x10½", 531pp. CWP75, 18.50c.**
This work includes Sanskrit and English equivalents and a Sanskrit-Pali index. The Chinese is not Romanized.

SPIRO, MELFORD. **BUDDHISM AND SOCIETY. Extensive bibliography, index, 493pp. H&R70/A&U, 8.00p.**
A comprehensive anthropological study of Burmese Theravada Buddhism. Many notes accompany the text.

STCHERBATSKY, THEODORE. **BUDDHIST LOGIC. Notes, index, 996pp. Dov30, 6.00p/each.**
This is the most important work on Buddhist logic ever published. The first volume covers the history of Indian and Tibetan logic up through the system of Dignaga. The second contains a translation of Dharmakirti's **Nyayabindu**, with Dharmottara's commentary. Translations from other commentaries are included in the appendices.

STCHERBATSKY, THEODORE, tr. **THE SOUL THEORY OF THE BUDDHISTS. Glossary, 109+pp. BVB76, 7.55p.**
A translation, with commentary, of the last chapter of Vasubandhu's **Abhidharmakosa** which discusses the Buddhist denial of the existence of the soul. The Sanskrit text is appended.

STORY, FRANCIS. **THE BUDDHIST OUTLOOK, VOLUME I: ESSAYS, DIALOGUES, POEMS. Index, 389pp. BPS73, 7.65c.**
Story was a British Buddhist who lived in India, Burma, and Sri Lanka for twenty-five years and deeply studied and absorbed the Buddhist philosophy of life. An autobiographical sketch is included.

■ *STRYK, LUCIEN, ed.* **WORLD OF THE BUDDHA: A READER. 479pp. Dou68, 2.95p.**
This is one of the most complete source books available and the one we recommend. The translations are uniformly excellent and Stryk has made an excellent selection of texts. Material is included on all aspects of Buddhism and Stryk provides commentaries on each text as well as a lengthy introduction.

SUJATA, ANAGARIKA. **BEGINNING TO SEE. 2.95p.**
See the Meditation section.

SURE, HENG and HENG CH'AU. **WITH ONE HEART, BOWING TO THE CITY OF 10,000 BUDDHAS. Illustrations, glossary, 176pp. SAB77, 6.00p.**
The first volume in a series of daily records of two Buddhist monks engaged in a pilgrimage between two monasteries in California. The stated goal of their journey was to influence humankind to cease all hatred and hostility and prevent disasters, wars, and suffering of all kinds. Most of the discussion focuses on mundane daily events.

SUZUKI, D.T., tr. **THE LANKAVATARA SUTRA. Many notes, index, 300pp. RKP32, 18.00c.**
The first complete translation of this important Mahayana text. The Sutra consists of a memorandum kept by a Mahayana master, in which he put down all the teachings of importance accepted by the Mahayana followers of his day. He did not try to keep them in any order—and so the text is a bit disorderly. But it can be understood with effort. A long introduction describes the general teaching of the Sutra, and the appendix contains the Sanskrit text, the three Chinese and the Tibetan versions, with their respective English translations.

SUZUKI, D.T. **MYSTICISM—CHRISTIAN AND BUDDHIST. Notes, 214pp. Gre57, 18.15c.**
A comparative study which shows that the superficial differences between Buddhism and the Christian mystical tradition, as exemplified by Meister Eckhart, are far less significant than their basic similarities. Many quotations illuminate Suzuki's treatise.

SUZUKI, D.T. **ON INDIAN MAHAYANA BUDDHISM. Bibliography, notes, 284pp. H&R68, 3.90p.**
An anthology of the best of Suzuki's essays from a variety of books, edited by Edward Conze. Conze also provides a long, illuminating introduction and a glossary.

SUZUKI, D.T. **OUTLINES OF MAHAYANA BUDDHISM. Index, 371pp. ScB63, 3.95p.**
A very complete introductory work. Alan Watts provides a long preface and gives an annotated listing of follow-up reading in various areas.

SUZUKI, D.T. **STUDIES IN THE LANKAVATARA SUTRA. 458pp. RKP30, 24.00c.**
An attempt to elucidate the teachings presented in the Sutra systematically, at the same time analyzing the contents of the Sutra itself. Includes long introduction and an extensive Sanskrit-Chinese-English glossary.

SWEARER, DONALD. **BUDDHISM. Glossary, notes, annotated bibliography, 111pp. Arg77, 2.95p.**
A simple introduction to Buddhism, divided into the following major topics: *The Birth and Growth of Buddhism, The Teachings of Buddhism,* and *The Practice of Buddhism.* Dr. Swearer writes well and he is a noted authority in the field. Many color photographs illuminate the text.

SWEARER, DONALD. **SECRETS OF THE LOTUS. 1.95p.**
See the Meditation section.

SWEARER, DONALD, ed. **TOWARD THE TRUTH. Glossary, notes, 189pp. Wes71, 2.95p.**
Selections from the writings of Buddhadasa, a widely acclaimed Thai Bhikkhu, which contribute to an understanding of contemporary Theravada Buddhism. He explains Buddhist doctrine as a practical system, open to all and his particular genius as an interpreter of Buddhism has been to relate ancient truths to our era, stressing the importance of individual personal experience.

TACHIBANA, S. **THE ETHICS OF BUDDHISM. Notes, bibliography, index, 304pp. Cur26, 12.00c.**
A didactic work, emphasizing the idea that Buddhism is a religion of moral stature—and has been since its origin—and that the morality which Buddhism particularly emphasizes is a practical one.

TAMBIAH, S.J. **BUDDHISM AND THE SPIRIT CULTS IN NORTHEAST THAILAND. Notes, bibliography, index, 388pp. CUP70, 6.95p.**
This volume represents the most extensive—and, on balance, the best—account of Thai religion published to date in English. . . . The author addresses himself at length to Buddhist cosmology, the initiation of manhood (both historically and locally), primary religious concepts "that emerge from the observation of thought and deed in the village," the expression in contemporary religious institutions of the great literary and historical traditions of Buddhism, and, finally, the belief and ritual complexes that constitute the working substance of local religion.—American Anthropologist.

TAMURA, YOSHIRO and KOJIRO MIYASAKA, eds. **THREEFOLD LOTUS STURA. Glossary, 399pp. Wea75, 19.75c/7.95p.**
The *Lotus Sutra* is revered by millions of Buddhists as containing the core and culmination of the Buddha's teaching. Together with the two shorter sutras that traditionally accompany it, **Innumerable Meanings** and **Meditation on the Bodhisattva Universal Virtue,** it comprises one of the most important scriptures of Mahayana Buddhism. Here all three scriptures are presented together for the first time in English. The latter two have never before been translated into English, while this version of the **Lotus Sutra** itself is based on the translation made by Bunno Kato and W.E. Soothill, thoroughly revised and annotated in the light of present scholarship. This excellent, readable translation is a welcome addition to the literature.

TERWIEL, BAREND. **MONKS AND MAGIC. Illustrations, glossary of Thai, Pali, and Sanskrit words, bibliography, 303pp. Cur76, 13.50p.**
The narrative describes the practice of Buddhism in a Thai rural community. The children and young adults appear largely interested in esoteric spells and magical diagrams. Full ritual knowledge is obtained by many men in their twenties. The older people practice a more traditional Buddhism. Daily life and the role that Buddhism plays in it is discussed at length and there is also an analysis of Buddhist rituals.

THOMAS, EDWARD. **THE HISTORY OF BUDDHIST THOUGHT. Notes, bibliography, index, 328pp. RKP51, 9.25c.**
A detailed, scholarly study of the development of Buddhist thought and of the various schools of Buddhism. This is basically a comparative work, topically organized, which sets forth the different lines of thought. Though the writing style is dry, the book reads well and covers material that is not readily accessible elsewhere.

THOMAS, EDWARD. **THE LIFE OF BUDDHA. Notes, bibliography, index, 321pp. RKP49, 7.50p.**
This is a scholarly, authoritative **Life,** based on Sanskrit sources and Chinese and Tibetan material in addition to the more traditional Pali source books. As is true with most studies of the Buddha's life, legend and history are intertwined. Thomas has updated the earlier material presented by such scholars as the Rhys Davids, Kern, and Oldenberg in the light of new findings in recently translated Pali texts. He also includes many translations. An important work for all seriously interested in Buddhism, but not one that we recommend to the reader who seeks only a general survey.

THUBTEN KALSANG RINPOCHE and BHIKKHU PASADIKA, trs. **EXCERPTS FROM THE SURANGAMA SAMADHI SUTRA. Notes, 60pp. LTW75, 2.80p.**
This translation of one of the most important Mahayana sutras has been prepared by two monks whose practice of the way matches their academic knowledge. John Blofeld provides an introduction.

TRUNGPA, CHOGYAM. **GLIMPSES OF ABHIDHARMA. 100pp. Pra75, 3.95p.**
The *abhidharma* is a collection of Buddhist scriptures that investigates the workings of the mind and the states of human consciousness. In this volume, based on a seminar on Buddhist psychology, Chogyam

Trungpa discusses the development of the ego as it is explained in the *abhidharma*. He says that the creation of ego is a neurotic process based on fundamental ignorance of our true situation. In this volume Trungpa shows how an examination of the formation of ego leads to a realization of confusion and also provides an opportunity to develop real intelligence. He also offers practical meditation instruction. The bulk of each of the chapters consists of questions and answers.

UPADHYAYA, K.N. **EARLY BUDDHISM AND THE BHAGAVAD-GITA. 20.00c.**
See the Gitas subsection of Indian Philosophy.

WALTERS, JOHN. **THE ESSENCE OF BUDDHISM. Bibliography, index, 164pp. Cro61, 1.75p.**
Walters, a British journalist, became converted to Buddhism during a visit to Thailand and received instruction in Buddhist practices from monks in Sri Lanka. This volume is an excellent introduction to Buddhism, covering its basic tenets and illustrating the ways in which Buddhism can be applied to the complexities of modern life. Walters writes well and speaks out of his own experience.

WARREN, HENRY, tr. **BUDDHISM IN TRANSLATIONS. 502pp. Ath1896, 6.65p.**
This volume was first printed in 1896 as part of the **Harvard Oriental Series** and remained for many years the only authoritative collection of translations from the Pali which was generally available. Warren did all the translations himself and while they are stylistically dated, this volume remains an important sourcebook for those who seek translations of the Pali texts. 102 texts of varying length are included.

WAYMAN, ALEX and HIDEKO, trs. **THE LION'S ROAR OF QUEEN SRIMALA. Glossary, bibliography of Chinese, Japanese, and Western sources, index, 142pp. Col74, 15.20c.**
This text is the chief scriptural authority in India for the theory that all sentient beings have the potentiality of Buddhahood. It was a source of inspiration for both the **Lankavatara Sutra** and the **Awakening of Faith.** The original work was written in South India in the third century AD. This is the first modern translation into English, and it has been pieced together from many existing editions and commentaries. Also included here is a very detailed fifty-seven page introduction and extensive textual notes.

WEI TAT, tr. **THE DOCTRINE OF MERE CONSCIOUSNESS. Bibliography, 7"x10½", 957pp. CWL73, 55.45c.**
This is the first complete English translation of the **Ch'eng Wei-shih Lun,** the masterpiece of the charismatic Tripitaka Master Hsuan Tsang. The text is a thorough and profound exploration of the human mind by introspection, meditation, and contemplation. Its central theme is that all sense impressions of the phenomena of the universe are illusory and that nothing exists except in the consciousness. The material is based on the insights of the ancient Buddhist scholars and mystics. Wei Tat provides an excellent long introduction and the text itself is reproduced on facing pages in both Chinese and English.

WEINER, SHEILA. **AJANTA: ITS PLACE IN BUDDHIST ART. 104 plates, notes, bibliography, index, 184pp. UCa77, 14.75c.**
Ajanta is the only extant grand site in India which combines painting, sculpture, and architecture. Carved in the period between 100 BC and AD 600, the Ajanta caves were once a Buddhist monastic center. The site is a key to the understanding of Buddhist art. Dr. Weiner presents a comprehensive view of Ajanta, assembling historical, inscriptional, numismatic, and stylistic evidence.

WELCH, HOLMES. **THE PRACTICE OF CHINESE BUDDHISM, 1900-50. Bibliography, 584pp. HUP67, 6.95p.**
A detailed, careful study which brings together a large amount of documentary material and the results of innumerable interviews Mr. Welch held with refugee monks during the four years he spent assembling material for this book.

WETERING, JANWILLEM VAN DE. **LITTLE OWL: AN EIGHTFOLD BUDDHIST ADMONITION. 8¼"x10¼", 64pp. HMC78, 6.95c.**
Buddha recommended a method that, he claimed, would lead to supreme insight or enlightenment. The method is known as the Buddhist Eightfold Path and its aspects are Right Insight, Right Intentions, Right Talking, Right Action, Right Livelihood, Right Effort, Right Awareness, and Right Meditation. The concept is that we should try and keep all aspects in mind while we live but sometimes this is not done and one aspect becomes much more important than others.—from the preface. In this children's book various animals following the Eightfold Path become caught up in one aspect and come to grief, but, as van de Wetering says, *All troubles are temporary and when the little animals meet and decide to try together a marvellous journey begins.* Delightfully illustrated by Marc Brown.

WRIGHT, ARTHUR. **BUDDHISM IN CHINESE HISTORY. Illustrations, index, 138pp. SUP59, 2.25p.**
A balanced, well written account. Includes a long section of selected further readings.

ZURCHER, E. **THE BUDDHIST CONQUEST OF CHINA. Notes, bibliography, indices, 482pp. Bri72, 72.60c/set.**
An impressive, scholarly study of the formative phase of Chinese Buddhism (from the first to the early fifth century AD) set against the background of Chinese economic, political, and intellectual developments. Zurcher bases his study on a great variety of early source material. This is a two volume set; the first volume contains the text and the second is devoted to notes, bibliography, and indices.

TIBETAN BUDDHISM

The terms Vajrayana or Tantric Buddhism are often used loosely of Tibetan Buddhism as a whole. Properly speaking, Tibetans and Mongols are Mahayana Buddhists of whom many but not all observe the Vajrayana practices derived from a special additional section found only in the Tibetan Buddhist canon. Otherwise, that version of the canon contains the usual *vinaya* (rules of conduct), sutras (discourses) and the equivalent of *abhidharma* (advanced doctrines). The part played by the Tantras in Tibetan spiritual life varies. Lamas of the Gelugpa (Yellow Hat) sect are expected to spend twenty years on sutra and scholastic study before starting on the Tantras; many of them do not get that far and never become Tantric adepts. At the opposite extreme are the Nyingmapas (one of the Red Hat sects) who are initiated into the Tantras early and spend little time on other sacred studies. However, it is true to say that all Tibetan Lamas, and most laymen, too, do follow some degree of Tantric practice, even if it amounts to no more than the visualization which is attached to the mantra *Om Mani Padme Hum*.

Buddhism was introduced into Tibet some twelve hundred years ago in a form which included the Vajrayana. The first Lamas were Indians and Tibetans who had studied at northern India's great University of Nalanda, which then had some thirty thousand students. That this form of Buddhism has persisted in Tibet and neighbouring Mongolia until today, despite Chinese rather than Indian influence on other apsects of their cultures, is because mountains and deserts offer admirable soil for the cultivation of the flowers of the Vajrayana.

The most striking characteristic of those two countries is the cruel inhospitality of their terrain. Tibet consists of high plateaux scourged by icy winds and of range upon range of mountains where frightful thunderstorms and murderous hail seem like the manifestations of demons athirst for blood. Mongolia's wideflung deserts are strewn with bleached bones and its grasslands are comfortless wastes where nomads roam. Children reared in those frightful windswept regions soon learn that life is a battle against remorseless nature. People there live in close proximity to disaster and sudden death. Being constantly menaced by danger, they have developed admirable courage and are easily moved to gaiety, but there is no shrinking from recognition of life's inherent bitterness. Man's spiritual thirst arises from two causes: intimations of a splendidly luminous, quiescent state lying beyond the weaving mists and murky clouds of the cosmic flux; and a longing to escape from an existence compounded of fleeting joys inter-mixed with inevitable boredom and suffering. Dwellers in a wilderness are brought face to face with both of these. They have a more intense awareness of the contrasting splendours and terrors of the universe than city dwellers pent within walls and living in cushioned ease; and, in Tibet especially, intima-tions of an all-encompassing glory are of almost daily occur-rence, as when the sun god dances upon pinnacles of snow; or when the traveller, after fighting his way through blizzards howling amidst slippery crags and echoing caverns, crosses the pass and gazes down upon a lake flashing turquoise and emerald amidst the shining rocks of the sunlit valley.

At those high altitudes and in that pure air, the richness of nature's colours is marvellously enhanced; so, also, man's perceptiveness. Intuitions of the dazzling reality which is their source are doubly welcome on account of present pains and terrors, which include labouring from dawn till eve to wrest a meagre harvest; seeing the ripening crops flattened to the ground by hailstones large enough to smash a man's skull, floundering amidst the ruins of homesteads toppled by earth-quakes or torrential rains, and knowing that loved ones while yet within a bowshot of home may be devoured by famished beasts or perish miserably in a blizzard.

Thus, in Tibet, all conditions are fulfilled for naked displays of violent contrasts between the forces of good and evil which elsewhere, though just as active, are less visible. The Vajrayana's vivid symbolism marvellously depicts the inter-play of contrasting forces. Strangers entering a Tibetan milieu may be inclined to doubt the loftiness of a religion in which rites and symbols play so great a part. They may carry away impressions of temples overstocked with images and sacred pictures, of people fingering their rosaries and whispering mantras even when window-shopping, of old women twirling their prayer-wheels and intoning *Om Mani Padme Hum* while riding in buses, and of processions of monks striding along to the thunder of mighty horns. There is seldom anyone at hand who can properly explain the significance of these things in English. How are they to know that the benign and night-marish figures in the sacred pictures, unlike gods and demons elsewhere, are recognized by the faithful as the products of their own minds, as symbolic representations of the phantas-magoria that haunts the threshold of human consciousness, and as personifications of the forces of passion called into being by the everlasting play of mind?

The symbols are often of great beauty, especially the *tankas* (religious paintings). The artists take great pains, grinding their own colours from mineral substances and performing the brushwork with infinite skill and patience. The mountings of the *tankas* are of rich brocade and the rollers tipped with heavy ornaments of silver filigree. Besides these, the many ritual objects and some personal and household articles are fashioned with exquisite artistry.

The reason why so many of the figures of deities and other symbols are reminiscent of the Hindu and Tibetan Bon relig-ions is that, in the old days, Buddhists used the outward forms of local faiths to make the transition to Buddhist concepts easier. This has always been the way. If Buddhism has spread through medieval Europe, we should have had Bodhisattvas and Arahans looking like Christian saints. The borrowing of externals to suit local needs does not involve any departure from Buddhist principles. In the early centuries of the Catholic Church, the same method was used. Christmas and at least one of the festivals connected with the Virgin Mary are celebrated on days that were once the feasts of pagan divinities; and in Italy one sometimes sees depictions of the Virgin with several attributes of the Goddess Diana: a sickle moon, a stag and so forth.

Of special interest to Western scholars is the faithfulness with which the system of instruction formulated at Nalanda in the early centuries of the Christian era has been preserved in Tibet. Right up to the Chinese occupation a few years ago, the courses given at Lhasa's monastic universities in such subjects as Buddhism, metaphysics, astrology, grammar, logic and medicine, as well as the manner of student debating, remained much the same as they had been at Nalanda fifteen centuries earlier. The world provides no example of another teaching system continued for half as long.

Advanced degrees from Lhasa's universities were not recklessly bestowed. The Geshe (Doctor of Divinity) degree took some twenty years and there were others that took even longer. Years of study principally devoted to methods of mind control resulted in the development of remarkable powers of extrasensory perception, of which telepathy is so common as to excite no comment in Tibet. Such powers, though deemed unimportant bi-products of Buddhist meditational and yogic practices, do provide a kind of evidence of the efficiency of the Vajrayana techniques.

In its general purpose, the Vajrayana does not differ from other forms of Buddhism or from any religious endeavour aimed not at personal survival but at negating the ego and attaining a state of unity transcending I and other. What is unique about the Tantric method is its wealth of techniques for utilizing all things good and evil to that end. Obstacles are transmuted into instruments for providing the tremendous momentum needed. Most other spiritual paths require a turning away from dark to light, whereas Vajrayana yogins welcome both demons and angels as their allies. Transcending good and evil, they transmute them both back into that pure essence from which the universe's whirling phantasmagoria is mentally created.

—condensed from **The Tantric Mysticism of Tibet**, by John Blofeld

Green Tara, from a sketch by Tendzin yongdu.

ANDERSON, MARY M. THE FESTIVALS OF NEPAL. Twenty-three pages of color plates, bibliography, index, 288pp. A&U71, 14.95c.
At the beginning of my five-year residence in Nepal I attended Nepalese festivals because they are mysterious, colorful, and fun. Soon I became absorbed in the meaning of the ancient processions and rituals, the mythological, religious and historical backgrounds of the ceremonies, and the wealth of delightful legends and folktales surrounding them. I came to see that, for the Nepalese, the continuous flow of interrelated festivals throughout the year is literally a way of life, reflecting their joys and fears, dreams and sorrows. The festivals become a calendar, marking the changing seasons, the revolving of the years and ages, giving continuity and meaning to their lives. This is a discussion of the most important festivals along with an introductory sketch of Nepalese geography, history, religion, and culture.

BELL, CHARLES. TIBET—PAST AND PRESENT. Many photographs, maps, index, 340pp. CWP24, 7.25c.
An excellent survey of Tibetan history from earliest times until the first part of the twentieth century. Sir Charles was a British civil servant in India and served for eighteen years as the British political representative in Tibet, Bhutan, and Sikkim. He spoke and wrote the Tibetan language and was quite sympathetic to the Tibetan way of life. He knew Tibetans from all walks of life, the Dalai Lama included. In this book he records anecdotes, conversations with leading Tibetans, and poetry and proverbs in addition to retelling straight history. He also involves himself in the narrative and his historical emphasis is on the more recent events.

BELL, MICHAEL, ed. THE UNPARALLELED POSTER COLORING BOOK OF TIBETAN ART. Introduction, spiral bound, 11"x16", Sto72, 3.95p.
Nineteen prints, plus a giant foldout.

BEYER, STEPHAN. THE CULT OF TARA-MAGIC AND RITUAL IN TIBET. Illustrations, notes, long bibliography, index, UCa73, 7.95p.
Dr. Beyer spent fourteen months in one of the few remaining Tibetan monasteries (in northern India). Here he draws on his experience as he attempts to formulate the processes and presuppositions of Tibetan ritual and generalize from there to the fundamental structures of Tantric meditation. The book sets out from a consideration of the cult of the goddess Tara, and demonstrates its ramifications in monastic ceremony, folklore, literature, and magic. In thus outlining the

fundamentals of the Tantric vision, Beyer deals as well with poetry, drama, medicine, divination, and art; trying to create a full statement of the life of Tibetan Buddhism. Many quotations from primary source material are included. A feeling of the living ritual of Tibetan Buddhism can come out of a careful reading of the text. This is one of the most important books on Tibetan Buddhism that has been written since the Chinese takeover.

■ **BLOFELD, JOHN. THE TANTRIC MYSTICISM OF TIBET. Illustrations, glossary, index, 257pp. Dut70/A&U, 4.45p.**
An excellent review of the practice of Tibetan Buddhism, with an emphasis on meditation techniques. The Mahayana background is given together with details of the techniques, purpose, and underlying theory of Tantric meditation. Ninety percent of the material in the book is based on the author's firsthand experience studying under Tibetan Lamas. The book forms an excellent introduction to the Buddhism of Tibet. It is very clearly written and includes both an introductory survey of the main features of the religion and a detailed presentation of the actual practices. The British title is **Way of Power**.

BRAHAM, TREVOR. HIMALAYAN ODYSSEY. Many maps and photographs, glossary, notes, index, 243pp. A&U74, 16.75c.
Braham spent much of his boyhood in India during the last years of the British raj. For about thirty years he traveled, explored, and climbed throughout the Himalayas. He has made fifteen expeditions in all. This book describes his experiences and his impressions of the Himalayan lands and peoples.

BROMAGE, BERNARD. TIBETAN YOGA. 238pp. Wei52, 6.00c.
An esoteric presentation of Tibetan magical rites and spells. Much of what Bromage writes about is the old Bon religion, rather than Tibetan Buddhism. Many specific exercises are suggested.

BURANG, THEODORE. TIBETAN ART OF HEALING. 117pp. Wat74, 5.85p.
The medicine indigenous to Tibet is highly respected throughout Central Asia and has a remarkable record of success in healing. Its philosophy and curative methods transport us into a strange web of macrocosmic and microcosmic interrelations. In contrast to the standpoint of Western research, it acquaints us with unusual spiritual foundations . . . and often displays a masterful observation of nature. The material

is divided into the following parts: *The Cosmic Humours, The Second Body, Tibetan Medical Writings, Materia Medica, Tibetan Methods of Healing, About Cancer, Mental Illness and Possession,* and *Co-operation Between Western and Tibetan Doctors.* The style is not overly technical and the general reader can gain much from this book.

CAMPBELL, JOSEPH, ed. **MY LIFE AND LIVES: THE STORY OF A TIBETAN INCARNATION. 239pp. Dut77, 4.95p.**
This is the story of Rato Khyongla Nawang Losang, a Tibetan monk of the Gelugpa sect who lived in Tibet until 1959, then fled to India with the Dalai Lama and thousands of other monks. He now lives in the United States. In his foreword Joseph Campbell says: *No one has given us anything like this full-bodied narrative picture of Tibet as it was known to its own people....Nor have we anywhere anything like this inward history of the life and disciplines of its great Buddhist monasteries and temples, hermitages and mountain retreats—any such intimate portraits of its once numerous scholar-mystics.*

CHANG, GARMA. **TEACHINGS OF TIBETAN YOGA. Notes, 128pp. Stu63, 3.95p.**
An excellent, extremely concentrated book which provides an introduction to spiritual, mental, and physical exercises. Includes an extensive discussion of *dumo,* the generating of heat in one's body, which is a major part of Tantric Buddhism. Chang is a Chinese scholar who studied in Tibet for eight years and is very well respected.

CLARK, WALTER E. **TWO LAMAISTIC PANTHEONS. 6½"x10¼", 348pp. PBR37, 63.00c.**
The present publication gives a complete reproduction of the 360 figures of the **Chu Fo P'u-sa Sheng Hsiang Tsan** *and of the 766 preserved images or inscribed pedestals...of the* **Pao-hsiang Lou Pantheon.** *The Chinese index gives the Chinese names of the figures in these two Pantheons.... The transliteration is that of Wade-Giles.*—from the introduction. There are also Sanskrit and Tibetan indices.

CONZE, EDWARD, tr. **THE BUDDHA'S LAW AMONG THE BIRDS. Commentary, notes, 65pp. Cas74, 5.85p.**
According to Buddhist belief, the *dharma* of the Buddha is not confined to men, but is taught to all kinds of beings, including animals. There is a legend that the great Bodhisattva of Mercy, Avalokitesvara, had taken among the birds the form of a cuckoo—an animal which recommends itself to the Buddhist mind by its attitudes towards family life. About three centuries ago a Lama wrote a charming little book describing how the birds of the Himalayas met under the leadership of the cuckoo on a holy mountain and how they were instructed in the Buddhist way of living and thinking. Though it is a simple and unsophisticated book, it brings home to us, better than many scholarly treatises, the overtones of the faith of Tibet. This translation has been made from the Tibetan original and includes an introduction by Dr. Conze which sketches the background of the story and gives extracts from another Tibetan work which describes the spiritual antecedents of the cuckoo.

DARGYAY, EVA. **THE RISE OF ESOTERIC BUDDHISM IN TIBET. Many notes, bibliography, indices, 284pp. MoB77, 13.85c.**
An in depth analysis of the old school of Tibetan Buddhism, the Nyingma. Dr. Dargyay shows that the history of this school goes back far earlier than Padmasambhava. Each of the two lineages—*Pronouncements* and *Concealed Treasures*—is discussed at length and the author includes biographical studies of the twenty most famous masters. Dr. Dargyay is a German Tibet specialist and is married to a Tibetan Geshe.

DAS, SARAT. **CONTRIBUTIONS ON THE RELIGION AND HISTORY OF TIBET. 210pp. Mnj1882, 11.45c.**
This is a recent reprint of a classic volume from the late nineteenth century. Das was one of the first Westerners to travel extensively in Tibet and study the religious practices.

DAS, SARAT. **INDIAN PANDITS IN THE LAND OF SNOW. 162pp. Muk1883, 6.00p.**
This is a dated transcription of a series of lectures that Das gave in the late nineteenth century which discuss Tibetan history and religion.

DAS, SARAT. **JOURNEY TO LHASA AND CENTRAL TIBET. Index, 301pp. PBR02, 14.00c.**
Das was an educator and scholar who made two trips into Tibet in 1879 and 1881-82. The account here is of his second, more extended trip. He

was well versed in Tibetan language, history, religion, and folklore and attempted to take in as much as he could in his travels. He visited Tibet at a time when foreign visits were very limited and was one of the first to report in detail on the country. He describes in the first person his travels and the people, secular and nonsecular, whom he encountered as well as the rites and ceremonies he witnessed. The text includes many foldout maps.

DASGUPTA, SHASHI. **AN INTRODUCTION TO TANTRIC BUDDHISM. 3.95p.**
See the Tantra section.

DAVID-NEEL, ALEXANDRA. **INITIATIONS AND INITIATES IN TIBET. Illustrations, appendix, 224pp. HPG58, 7.35p.**
The author, who died in 1969 at the age of 103, was a major force in spreading knowledge of the mystical and philosophical thought of Tibet. This book is a record of her observations on Tibetan Buddhist teachings and initiatory practices.

■ DAVID-NEEL, ALEXANDRA. **MAGIC AND MYSTERY IN TIBET. 320pp. Vik29/SBL, 3.95p.**
Ms. David-Neel wandered freely throughout Tibet for more than fourteen years, observing all aspects of Tibetan culture and practice. In this book she includes accounts of how Tibetan mystics aquire the ability to live naked in sub-zero temperatures; how they communicate with each other over vast distances by telepathy; how they learn to float on air, and walk on water; how they create animate objects by thinking them into existence; and much else. It is a provocative, anecdotal account, but one which gives the reader a good feeling for the land and people of Tibet. Ms. David-Neel writes extremely well.

DAVID-NEEL, ALEXANDRA and LAMA YONGDEN. **THE SECRET ORAL TEACHINGS IN THE TIBETAN BUDDHIST SECTS. 128pp. CiL64, 2.50p.**
This is a fine, short presentation of the essential features of Tibetan Buddhism. The *Madhyamika* (Middle Way) school is emphasized and meditational methods are described.

DELATTRE, PIERRE. **TALES OF A DALAI LAMA. Illustrations, 146pp. CrA71, 3.95p.**
To avoid any possible misunderstanding, let me say clearly and emphatically that this is not a biography but tales of fiction; that the human incarnation even of a Dalai Lama, including the Fourteenth...cannot in fact be so very different from other human beings, least of all as a child of tender years; that he appears here not as an individual but in a representative and symbolic capacity; and that in this book fiction is decidedly stranger than truth.—from the foreword. This is a delightful collection of tales of trance walkers, oracles, hermits, dancing masters, amorous elephants, holy men, monks, ghosts, and magical plants.

DENWOOD, PHILIP. **THE TIBETAN CARPET. Glossary, bibliography, index, 8½"x12", 110pp. A&P74, 53.75c.**
This is both a lovely and practical book. The author begins with a brief survey of Tibetan history and of Tibetans and their carpets. He follows with chapters on materials, the tools of the trade, and the carpet making process. The last chapters are devoted to discussions of traditional carpets, refugee carpets, and the origins of the craft of carpet weaving. The book is profusely illustrated with color plates, line drawings, and photographs.

DHARGYEY, GESHE NGAWANG. **TIBETAN TRADITION OF MENTAL DEVELOPMENT. Index, 239pp. LTW76, 10.00p**
A topically arranged translation of the oral teachings of a respected contemporary Tibetan monk associated with the Fourteenth Dalai Lama.

DOUGLAS, NIK. **TIBETAN TANTRIC CHARMS AND AMULETS. 9½"x12¼", 306pp. Dov78, 10.00p.**
With its belief in numerous gods, saints, demons, and protectors, Tibetan tantric Buddhism has one of the strongest amulet traditions in religious history. Although Tibetan paintings and sculptures have attracted considerable attention in the West in recent years, hardly any area of Tibetan art has been so much neglected as the field of illustrated charms and amulets. This book contains 232 full page examples of this potent and expressive art form, most in the form of diagrams or other representations of secret protective formulas. A long introduction supplies religious, philosophical, historical, and artistic background

and includes quotations from many texts. The full captions for each illustration contain complete transliterations of the liturgical phrases and detailed commentaries of its use, symbolism, and connection with other rites.

DOUGLAS, NIK and MERYL WHITE. **KARMAPA THE BLACK HAT LAMA OF TIBET. Sixteen color and many black and white plates, glossary, notes, bibliography, index, 7½"x9½", 247pp. Luz76, 22.10c.**
The Karmapa has been honored as a living Buddha in his sixteen successive incarnations. Traditionally the coming of the first Karmapa fulfilled a prophecy made by the Buddha that this emanation would appear in the world in order to alleviate the sufferings of humanity in the dark age of materialism. The Karmapa life stories—compiled from authentic Tibetan biographies and diaries and presented here for the first time in English—cover 800 years of events of great cultural and historical importance. The Karmapas were the teachers of emperors and kings and established many important monasteries and hermitages in Tibet and neighboring countries.

DOWMAN, KEITH, tr. **THE LEGEND OF THE GREAT STUPA AND THE LIFE STORY OF THE LOTUS BORN GURU. Glossary, 139pp. Dha73, 4.75p.**
The Life Story is *the life story of the Guru Padma Sambhava, mendicant, tantrika, magician, scholar, exorcist, priest, missionary, visionary, and saint....[He] traveled throughout eighth-century India before being invited to Tibet....The Guru's magical power was his primary instrument in turning the Tibetans away from the primitive fantasies of the Shamans. He brought Tibet the highly evolved techniques of yoga and meditation developed by Mahayana India and founded the original lineages of the Nyingma tradition....The story surrounding the Great Stupa is a legendary Tibetan tale of incarnation, adoration, disaster and rebirth. It is a Tibetan means of instructing the visionary along the spiritual path....The method is given in a narrative between Guru Padma Sambhava and his entourage of aspirants....The text has been used in ritual for several centuries to eradicate habitual mental reaction patterns of distortion and stupour by causing a faithful concentration upon both sound and meaning.*—from the introduction.

DRIESSENS, GEORGES, ed. **THE PRELIMINARY PRACTICES OF TIBETAN BUDDHISM. Notes, 62pp. Dus74, 2.95p.**
A clear transcription of an oral commentary on an eleventh century text by the Venerable Geshe Rabten, a contemporary Tibetan meditation master. The text begins with the *Four Contemplations*—preliminaries which set the stage for the teaching which follows. The second part presents detailed instruction in four actual practices which are especially designed for the dedicated beginning student. Tibetan teaching is immensely practical and this small volume is an excellent presentation of some basic techniques.

EKVALL, ROBERT. **RELIGIOUS OBSERVANCES IN TIBET. Notes, bibliography, 326pp. UCh64, 16.80c.**
Ekvall approaches Tibetan society anthropologically and in this study he is concerned with the Tibetan's subjective response to the particular form of Buddhism he has developed. Six religious attitudes characterize the Tibetan form of Mahayana Buddhism: faith, prayer, offering, salutation, circumambulation, and divination. In this volume the function of religious belief and ritual are studied in terms of these six attitudes and acts. The history of each is outlined and related to traditional beliefs and practices derived from the pre-Buddhist Bon cult.

EKVALL, ROBERT. **TIBETAN SKY LINES. 250+pp. FSG52, 16.40c.**
Ekvall is a missionary who grew up on the Tibetan border and speaks fluent Chinese and Tibetan. In this book he discusses the people of Tibet and the land itself, and recounts some memorable incidents which occurred during his Tibetan travels.

EVANS-WENTZ, W.Y., ed. **THE TIBETAN BOOK OF THE DEAD. Notes, index, 333pp. Oxf60, 14.95c/3.50p.**
Evans-Wentz is one of the best known Tibetan scholars. This volume, originally published in 1927, was the first book that brought Tibetan Buddhism to the general Western public. Known as the **Bardo Thodol**, it is a basic sourcebook for the teachings concerning the Clear Light, the Void, and other major features of the religion. Although the book is used in Tibet as a breviary, and read or recited on the occasion of death, it was originally conceived as a guidebook for initiates who must *die in order to be reborn.* All the basic material is here for an understanding

of the inner meaning of Tibetan Buddhism, and Evans-Wentz' scholarship is excellent; however, the book is often hard to read and the translation is not as flowing as we would like. Carl Jung has contributed a *Psychological Commentary* to this edition and Evans-Wentz himself has written a number of prefaces.

EVANS-WENTZ, W.Y., ed. **THE TIBETAN BOOK OF GREAT LIBERATION. Many beautiful plates, notes, index, 254+pp. Oxf54, 10.00c/4.95p.**
Expounds the quintessence of the supreme path and reveals the yogic method of attaining enlightenment by means of knowing the one mind, without recourse to the postures, breathings, and other techniques commonly associated with the lower yogas. This work is attributed to Padma Sambhava, and an account of his life and doctrines precedes the text. Another treasure brought to us by Evans-Wentz. Psychological commentary by Carl Jung.

EVANS-WENTZ, W.Y., tr. **TIBETAN YOGA AND SECRET DOCTRINES. Notes, index, 354pp. Oxf58, 4.95p.**
Texts of seven treatises on yoga and **The Seven Books of Wisdom of the Great Path**, with extensive commentary.

FOREIGN LANGUAGE PRESS. **TIBET TODAY. 8¾"x10", 117pp. FLP74, 2.95p.**
A pictorial document of life in Tibet today. The book consists solely of photographs, over half in color. It is obviously a propaganda document showing how wonderful life is today for the comrades in Tibet. The people are all smiles as they go about their work.

FOURTEENTH DALAI LAMA. **THE INSEPARABILITY OF THE SPIRITUAL MASTER AND AVALOKITESHVARA. 28pp. LTW75, 3.20p.**
In Buddhist teachings compassion plays an especially important part. The embodiment of compassion in Tibetan Buddhism is known as Avalokiteshvara and the Dalai Lamas are thought of as true human manifestations of Avalokiteshvara. This text is a translation of a practice composed when His Holiness was nineteen years old. The Tibetan version is also included.

FOURTEENTH DALAI LAMA. **UNIVERSAL RESPONSIBILITY AND THE GOOD HEART. 29pp. LTW76, 2.00p.**
In 1973 the Dalai Lama visited eleven European countries. The main theme he expressed was that the problems confronting mankind at the present time could be overcome by *the development of a feeling of universal responsibility, a genuine concern for the welfare of all other beings, the cultivation of a good heart.* This pamphlet contains an article based on his addresses and talks and a series of questions and answers.

FREMANTLE, FRANCESCA and CHOGYAM TRUNGPA, trs. **THE TIBETAN BOOK OF THE DEAD. Illustrations, glossary, bibliography, index, 140pp. ShP75, 12.50c/3.95p.**
Ms. Fremantle is thoroughly familiar with the Tibetan language and with this text and Chogyam Trungpa first received a transmission containing the **Bardol Thodol**, or **Book of the Dead**, at the age of eight. The translators have attempted to both make the translation as faithful to the original as possible and applicable to contemporary society. The text itself concerns the nature of the mind and its projections—beautiful or terrible, peaceful or wrathful—which seem to exist objectively and inhabit the external world. In particular it describes these projections as they appear immediately after death, when they are overwhelming since the consciousness is no longer grounded and shielded by its connection with a physical body. The text teaches how to recognize these forms and, through recognition, attain a state of enlightenment. A thorough commentary is provided by the translators.

GOVINDA, LAMA. **CREATIVE MEDITATION AND MULTI-DIMENSIONAL CONSCIOUSNESS. 11.00c/4.95p.**
See the Meditation section.

GOVINDA, LAMA. **FOUNDATIONS OF TIBETAN MYSTICISM. Bibliography, index, 297pp. Wei74/HPG, 4.95p.**
This is the most valuable book written on the subject of Tibetan mysticism. Lama Govinda has spent over twenty years in Tibetan hermitages and monasteries and his direct experience has given him a clear insight into much that has so far remained totally obscure to the outside world. Highly recommended for the serious student.

GOVINDA, LAMA. **MEDITATION. 62pp. HDI72, 2.00p.**
This pamphlet contains a series of essays by Lama Govinda: *Meditation, The Relativity of Perfection, The Magic of Words and the Power of Speech,* **The Tibetan Book of the Dead,** and *Mandala—The Sacred Circle.* A number of color paintings by Lama Govinda are also included.

GOVINDA, LAMA. **THE WAY OF THE WHITE CLOUDS: A BUDDHIST PILGRIM IN TIBET. 297pp. ShP70/HPG, 5.95p.**
Lama Govinda is a German who has spent most of his adult life in Asia and has studied a number of Buddhist traditions. He is best known for his writings on Tibetan Buddhism. This magical book is his autobiography; it is a rich mixture of prose, drawings, and photography. He is a wonderful example of a religious pilgrim. As he says, *pilgrims are religious nomads, people who go with a purpose, think as they go, move for a reason. They have a constancy in flux, patterns in variety, knowledge of the void.* We enjoyed reading his book tremendously and feel that it is a good first book for those who are curious about Tibetan Buddhism.

GOVINDA, LI GOTAMI. **TIBETAN FANTASIES. 8¾"x11½", Dha76, 4.95p.**
A collection of humorous verses and paintings composed by Li Gotami Govinda during her journey through Tibet in 1947 and 1948. They depict the ancient customs and daily life of the Tibetan people. A musical score accompanies several of the poems.

GRENARD, F. **TIBET—THE COUNTRY AND ITS INHABITANTS. 373pp. Csm74, 25.50c.**
Grenard was part of a scientific mission which was sent by the French government in the late nineteenth century to penetrate portions of Tibet which were almost inaccessible until then. The first part of the book contains the story of the journey; the second comprises an account of the manners and customs, the social and economic life, and the political conditions of Tibet. Grenard writes well. This is a more interesting study than most of the nineteenth century Tibetan travelogues.

GUENTHER, HERBERT, tr. **THE JEWEL ORNAMENT OF LIBERATION. Notes, index, 333pp. ShP59, 7.50p.**
A fine translation of a complex text which describes the special training necessary to win enlightenment and explains how the enlightened attitude is strengthened by practicing the *six perfections.* The text closes with a definition of Buddhahood and a commentary and guide to the *bodhisattva* tradition.

Yamantaka (conqueror of Yama, god of death) with bull's head.

GUENTHER, HERBERT, tr. **KINDLY BENT TO EASE US. Dha nd, 15.95p/set.**
A boxed set of Guenther's three part translation.

GUENTHER, HERBERT, tr. **KINDLY BENT TO EASE US, PART ONE: MIND. Introductory material, notes, index, 346pp. Dha75, 10.95c/ 5.95p.**
A translation of Part I of **Ngal-gso skor-gsum.** *Until now, there has been no authentic translation describing the Dzogchen teachings of the Nyingma school which are the most sophisticated and effective practices of Vajrayana Buddhism.... The subject of this book is how to attain Enlightenment. By interweaving the teachings of the Sutras and Tantras, Longchenpa beautifully summarizes all Buddhist thought. Longchenpa's presentation is very deep and meaningful, so read and study each word and sentence carefully.... Traditionally it is said that "Padmasambhava pointed to the door and Longchenpa opened it." Through his omniscient insight and untiring compassion, he inspired many followers to practice the Dzogchen teachings and to attain Enlightenment in one lifetime.—Tarthang Tulku Rinpoche.*

GUENTHER, HERBERT, tr. **KINDLY BENT TO EASE US, PART TWO: MEDITATION. Extensive notes, index, 139pp. Dha76, 10.95c/ 4.95p.**
Meditation is the theme of this second volume of Longchenpa's **Trilogy of Finding Comfort and Ease.** The practice of Dzogchen meditation presented here is considered by some to be the pinnacle of all Buddhist meditative traditions. According to Longchenpa, the aim of meditation is *to become free of the restrictive operations of the mind and to encounter directly the unparalleled radiance of pure awareness.* In this volume Longchenpa first describes the environments which are most suitable for this meditation; next, he outlines the personal qualities which are most suitable; and, finally, he distills the essence of the instruction.

GUENTHER, HERBERT, tr. **KINDLY BENT TO EASE US, PART THREE: WONDERMENT. Notes, indices, 181pp. Dha76, 10.95c/ 4.95p.**
This third volume deals with *the paradox of there being nothing and yet there is a presence.* Longchenpa addresses the central question of the meaning and scope of being. He encourages us to open up and expand our perspective and to overcome the monotony of our ordinary restricted vision.

GUENTHER, HERBERT. **THE LIFE AND TEACHINGS OF NAROPA. Appendices, extensive notes and commentary, bibliography, indices of Tibetan and Sanskrit terms, subject index, 308pp. Oxf63, 3.95p.**
In the history of Tibetan Buddhism, the Indian Naropa (1016-1100) occupies a unique position. To the present day his life is held up as an example to anyone who aspires after spiritual values, which are never realized the easy way but only after years of endless toil and perseverance. It took Naropa twelve years of ardent devotion and indefatigable service to his Guru Tilopa (988-1069) to attain his goal: overwhelming experiences of the Real in direct knowledge.... Naropa's biography, which has been translated here from hitherto unknown sources, contains a number of strictly historical data, but is pre-eminently an account of the inner development of this scholar-saint.— from the introduction.

GUENTHER, HERBERT. **TIBETAN BUDDHISM IN WESTERN PERSPECTIVE. Notes, index, 272pp. Dha77, 4.95p.**
A collection of ten articles written by Dr. Guenther between 1956 and 1975 on the subject of Tibetan Buddhism and the Buddhist Tantra. The articles represent the core insights of this prodigious scholar and are invaluable reading for all who are deeply interested in Tibetan Tantric Buddhism.

GUENTHER, HERBERT and LESLIE KAWAMURA, trs. **MIND IN BUDDHIST PSYCHOLOGY. Introduction, glossary, notes, index, 162pp. Dha75, 4.95p.**
A translation of Ye-shes rgyal-mtshan's **The Necklace of Clear Understanding,** a text which *belongs to that group of literature called Abhidharma which concentrates on the training of one's critical cognition by methods of proper inspection. The Abhidharma...is a systematic approach to understanding the world as man's horizon of meaning.—*from the preface. As Tarthang Tulku Rinpoche says, *The subject of this book is self-knowledge. That is, until we thoroughly examine the nature of our mind, we cannot really be aware of who we are or why we are here.* This is a difficult text, suggested only for those with a firm grounding in Tibetan Buddhism, although it probably would be of interest to all students of psychology.

GUENTHER, HERBERT and CHOGYAM TRUNGPA. **THE DAWN OF TANTRA. 3.50p.**
See the Tantra section.

GYATSHO, TENZIN. **THE OPENING OF THE WISDOM EYE. Many notes, index, 178pp. TPH66, 7.50c.**
An authentic account of the teachings of Tibetan Buddhism by the present Dalai Lama. He also includes a summary of the spread of Buddhism in Tibet.

HAAS, ERNST and GISELA MINKE. **HIMALAYAN PILGRIMAGE. 184 color photographs, 13¼"x9", 184pp. Vik78, 38.50c.**
Few have journeyed to the Himalayan areas that Haas has visited, and no one has photographed them with more reverence and skill. His pilgrimages to the places where Tibetan Buddhism flourishes began in 1968. Since then he and Minke have returned nine times to visit Tibetan refugee settlements in northern India as well as Bhutan, Sikkim, Nepal, and other religious centers. Against brilliant landscapes, including the world's highest mountains, Haas observes people in daily activity and in worship, crafting mandalas, participating in religious events and the most sacred festivals. While Haas photographed, Minke made careful notes of her impressions and experiences.

HALL, GEORGE, tr. **THE URGA MANUSCRIPT. 31pp. Smy49, 1.35p.**
Transcription of a letter from Do-Ring, scribe of the Panchen Lama of Tibet, to his friend concerning the inner life. This is a very carefully prepared, literal translation of a revealing document.

HAN SUYIN. **LHASA, THE OPEN CITY: A JOURNEY TO TIBET. Twenty-nine photgraphs, notes, bibliography, index, 190pp. Put77, 7.95c.**
Dr. Han spent two months in Tibet during the Fall of 1975, and she reports on her impressions here. It is a biased account which repeats much of the traditional Chinese propaganda against the old Tibetan theocracy. Nonetheless, it should be of interest to all who are fascinated by Tibetan culture, for it does bring the reader up to date on recent developments. Dr. Han begins with a review of Tibet's past history and builds up a case for the historical dependence of Tibet on China. She follows with a detailed discussion of life in today's Tibet, including many case histories.

HODGSON, B.H. **ESSAYS ON THE LANGUAGES, LITERATURE, AND RELIGION OF NEPAL AND TIBET. Notes, 346pp. Plo72, 32.00c.**
A collection of important early papers, originally published in 1841 and 1857 and based on firsthand observation and study, bound with additional papers on the geography, ethnology, and commerce of Tibet and Nepal. This edition includes a supplement of additions and corrections from Hodgson's own copy edited by Mahadeva Prasad Saha.

HOFFMAN, HELMUT. **TIBET—A HANDBOOK. Chronology, notes, 261pp. IUP75, 15.00p.**
A collection of scholarly articles on Tibet written expressly for this volume. The following chapter headings show the book's comprehensiveness: *The Geographic Setting, Tibetan and its Relation to Other Languages, Tibetan Historical Sources, The History of Tibet, The Present Political Framework of Tibet, The Religions of Tibet and Tibetan Missionary Activities, Social and Economic Structure in Traditional Tibet, Tibetan Literature, Tibetan Religious Art,* and *Tibet in Exile.*

HOPKINS, JEFFREY, tr. **PRACTICE OF EMPTINESS. 26pp. LTW76, 2.00p.**
A translation of *The Perfection of Wisdom* from the Fifth Dalai Lama's **Sacred Work of Manjusri.**

HOPKINS, JEFFREY, tr. **TANTRA IN TIBET: THE GREAT EXPOSITION OF SECRET MANTRA. Glossary, notes, bibliography, index, 252pp. A&U77, 7.75p.**
This is an authoritative translation of the first part of **The Great Exposition of Secret Mantra,** one of the principal classic texts on tantra handed down by Tsong-ka-pa, the great fourteenth century scholar and yogi who founded the Ge-luk-pa order. The Dalai Lama provides an extensive introduction to the text, summarizing the essence of tantra.

HOPKINS, JEFFREY and LATI RIMPOCHE, trs. **THE BUDDHISM OF TIBET AND THE KEY TO THE MIDDLE WAY. Notes, bibliography, index, 104pp. H&R75, 5.95c.**
This is the first volume in a new series, **The Wisdom of Tibet,** in which each volume has been chosen by the Dalai Lama and bears his own seal, certifying that it reveals a true oral tradition. The first essay contains an official introduction to Tibetan Buddhism for nonspecialists, while the second presents a meditation on emptiness. This series is an important addition to the burgeoning literature on Tibetan Buddhism both because of the clarity of its presentation and the authenticity of the textual material. Professor Hopkins has prepared the translations at the direct request of the Dalai Lama and a close associate of the Dalai Lama has reviewed them for accuracy.

HOPKINS, JEFFREY and LATI RIMPOCHE, trs. **THE PRECIOUS GARLAND AND THE SONG OF THE FOUR MINDFULNESSES. Notes, 119pp. A&U75, 4.75p.**
Book Two in **The Wisdom of Tibet** series makes available two classic poetic Buddhist texts, often memorized by monks. **The Precious Garland** is a layperson's guide to enlightenment, written for a king by Nagarjuna some 400 years after the Buddha. It is famous for its description of the *bodhisattva* path of compassion, together with its clear, concise analysis of the Buddha's teaching on emptiness. **The Song of the Four Mindfulnesses** contains a short summary of the meditational approach to enlightenment by Kaysang Gyatso, the Seventh Dalai Lama (1708-57). Both texts are in verse and the first one occupies the major part of the book.

JAMYANG KHYENTZE RINPOCHE. **THE OPENING OF THE DHARMA. 23pp. LTW76, 2.00p.**
A brief explanation of the essence of the Buddha's many vehicles according to the Tibetan teaching.

JERSTAD, LUTHER. **MANI-RIMDU: SHERPA DANCE DRAMA. Glossary, bibliography, index, 208pp. UWa69, 11.40c.**
The colorful and ancient Cham, a traditional Tibetan Buddhist dance drama, has been noted by travelers in Tibet since the eighteenth century. Here Jerstad describes the Nepalese form of Cham as he observed it among the Sherpas of northeastern Nepal. He focuses on the religious and historical message which the dances convey and includes a discussion of the Sherpas themselves. The text is liberally illustrated with photographs and line drawings.

KALU RINPOCHE. **THE FOUNDATION OF BUDDHIST MEDITATION. Notes, 32pp. LTW76, 2.00p.**
In this book, the four teachings which motivate religious practice and the attributes of the Three Jewels are explained. If one completely understands the significance of all these things, one will turn away from the Cycle of Existence and strive to procure freedom, will believe in action and result (Karma), and will either obtain Buddhahood in this life or will become free of this Cycle, etc. Moreover, when many positive qualities are cultivated, one will consolidate a basis for the Holy Dharma. So, please, don't just penetrate the significance of all these things, but, in addition, strive at Dharma practice.—from the introduction.

KARMAY, HEATHER. **EARLY SINO-TIBETAN ART. 43.70c.**
See the Sacred Art section.

KAUFMANN, WALTER. **TIBETAN BUDDHIST CHANTS. Introduction, index, 562pp. 7"x10", IUP75, 20.00c.**
This technical study presents the translation of a Tibetan liturgical songbook and of part of a textbook on Tibetan Buddhist chants. The musical scores are included along with extensive technical notations.

KAWAMURA, LESLIE, tr. **GOLDEN ZEPHYR. Introduction, glossary, bibliography, index, 185pp. Dha75, 4.95p.**
Translations from the original Tibetan of two classical works, Nagarjuna's **A Letter to a Friend** and Lama Mipham's commentary, **The Garland of White Lotus Flowers.** Nagarjuna originally wrote his **Letter** to a close friend, instructing and encouraging him to practice the dharma in his daily life. The enduring insight and conciseness of Nagarjuna's presentation prompted Lama Mipham, one of the most brilliant Tibetan Lamas of the nineteenth century, to expand the original text for the edification of his own students. In his commentary the Lama interweaves an explanation of the Buddhist path, which refers to a continual unfolding of our inner potential.

KAZAMI, TAKEHIDE. **THE HIMALAYAS. 154pp. Kod68, 4.95p.**
A pictorial travel guide to Nepal, with 110 beautiful color photographs.

KONGTRUL, JAMGON. **THE TORCH OF CERTAINTY. Notes, bibliography, indices, 179pp. ShP77, 5.95p.**
Jamgon Kongtrul was a versatile and prolific scholar of nineteenth century Tibet. He has been characterized as a Tibetan Leonardo because of his significant contributions to religion, education, medicine, and politics. In his writing, which spans the entire field of Tibetan learning, he brought together the essence of the great intellectual and contemplative traditions of Tibetan Buddhism. The volume contains a translation of a fundamental tantric text describing the *Four Foundation Practices* which all practitioners of Vajrayana Buddhism must complete. Among the subjects discussed are the nature of impermanence, the effects of karma, the development of an enlightened attitude, and devotion to the guru. This is a very practical work.

LAUF, DETLEF. **SECRET DOCTRINES OF THE TIBETAN BOOKS OF THE DEAD. Twelve full page plates, with commentary, notes, bibliography, 277pp. ShP77, 5.95p.**
The **Tibetan Books of the Dead** are a diverse collection of texts which provide insight into the nature of death and dying and suggest the importance of meditative practice and knowledge as tools for self understanding. This book is a detailed presentation of the teachings and the iconography which play a major role in the Tibetan understanding of death. It is based on Lauf's study of original texts from both the Buddhist and the Bon religions. The peaceful and wrathful deities, the mandala principle, the five Buddha families, and the six realms of existence are among the tantric doctrines Lauf examines. He also provides a psychological commentary and a comparative examination of Western investigations of consciousness, death, and dying.

LAUF, DETLEF. **TIBETAN SACRED ART. 10"x12", 131pp. ShP76, 15.00c.**
This is the finest presentation of Tibetan art and imagery that we know of. The author is a well known Swiss Tibetologist and professor of religion who teaches at the Jung Institute in Zurich. The text explains the system of beliefs which integrates polar opposites found in Tibetan art, such as the representations of multi-armed, flaming guardian dieties and sublimely composed Buddhas appearing together in the same painting. These explanations open up the remarkable paradoxes of Tibetan iconography. The volume includes eighty-six magnificent color plates and eighteen line drawings. A concise history of the development of Buddhism in Tibet supplements the text.

LIBRARY OF TIBETAN WORKS. **A COMPENDIUM OF WAYS OF KNOWING. 71pp. LTW76, 2.40p.**
The text translated here was written in the late eighteenth century and is from the Lo-rig class concerning ways of knowing. It is a technical compendium of all the major ways, written in metered verses. The selections presented in this pamphlet have been translated into prose.

LIBRARY OF TIBETAN WORKS. **DAILY RECITATIONS OF PRE-LIMINARIES. 27pp. LTW75, 2.00p.**
These preliminaries are recited in the daily classes and meditation sessions at the Library of Tibetan Works for the purpose of training the mind and accumulating merit. This volume contains the Tibetan text, transliteration, and English translation.

LIBRARY OF TIBETAN WORKS. **THE GREAT SEAL OF VOIDNESS. 27pp. LTW76, 2.00p.**
A translation of the root text for the Ge-lug/Ka-gyu tradition of *mahamudra* known as *The Main Path All Buddhas Have Traveled* and attributed to the First Panchen Lama.

LIBRARY OF TIBETAN BOOKS. **LINES OF EXPERIENCE. 23pp. LTW74, 2.00p.**
A translated condensation of the *Lam-rim Teaching of the Graded Course to Enlightenment* compiled by Je Tzong-k'a-pa. Many notes follow the text.

LIBRARY OF TIBETAN WORKS. **A SHORT BIOGRAPHY AND LETTER OF TZONG-K'A-PA. 65pp. LTW75, 2.80p.**
Je Tzong-k'a-pa was a fourteenth century reformer who founded the Gelug tradition of Tibetan Buddhism. This pamphlet includes a short

biography of him and a translation of a letter which he sent to a disciple explaining the tantric way to enlightenment.

LIBRARY OF TIBETAN WORKS. **THE STEPS OF VISUALIZATION FOR THE THREE ESSENTIAL MOMENTS. Notes, 31pp. LTW76, 2.00p.**
A translation of a short, valuable text on basic tantric practices composed by the Second Dalai Lama. It presents advanced material and should only be studied by those who have received the proper intiations.

LIBRARY OF TIBETAN WORKS. **THE THIRTY-SEVEN PRACTICES OF ALL BUDDHA'S SONS AND THE PRAYER OF THE VIRTUOUS BEGINNING, MIDDLE AND END. Glossary, 27pp. LTW76, 2.00p.**
Translations of two works by the *bodhisattva* Thogs-med bzang-po (1245-1369), a teacher of scripture and logic.

LIBRARY OF TIBETAN WORKS. **THE TIBET JOURNAL. LTW, 6.00p/each.**
A quarterly publication devoted to the presentation of scholarly and general interest articles on Tibetan culture and civilization. It is published under the auspices of the Fourteenth Dalai Lama. Each issue is about 100 pages long.

LIBRARY OF TIBETAN WORKS. **THE WHEEL OF SHARP WEAPONS. 39pp. LTW76, 2.00p.**
A translation of a Mahayana text on the training of the mind written by Dharmaraksita.

MACGREGOR, JOHN. **TIBET: A CHRONICLE OF EXPLORATION. Illustrations, notes, bibliography, index, 373pp. MoB70, 25.50c.**
MacGregor is the pen name of a U.S. diplomat, specializing in South and Central Asian affairs. This is a well written book which describes many of the Western explorers and explorations of Tibet. MacGregor himself apparently never made it to Tibet, although he did serve in northern India.

Milarepa

Milarepa has been an inspiration to Tibetans for almost ten centuries. Wronged in childhood, he left home to become apprenticed to a sorcerer, quickly became proficient in the black arts, then returned and destroyed his enemies. Struck with remorse he turned towards truth and started on the search for a teacher who would liberate him from his violent past. After various false starts, he found Marpa and persevered despite appalling hardships until Marpa eventually relented and gave him his teaching. He spent many years receiving instruction and finally returned to Tibet where he was widely recognized and gathered a large group of disciples around him. Milarepa was not only a great yogi, he was also a poet and singer—and his songs are both instructive and among the finest Tibetan literature ever produced.

CHANG, GARMA, tr. **THE HUNDRED THOUSAND SONGS OF MILAREPA. 748pp. ShP62, 6.50p/each.**
The songs of Milarepa are a synthesis of lyric beauty and profound spiritual understanding. They are one of the most important works of Tibetan Buddhism. Garma Chang provides an excellent translation as well as illuminating annotations. The glossary and index are in Volume II.

EVANS-WENTZ, W.Y., ed. **TIBET'S GREAT YOGI, MILAREPA: A BIOGRAPHY FROM THE TIBETAN. Index, 309pp. Oxf28, 4.95p.**
In Milarepa's life, the teachings of all the great yogis of India, including Gautama the Buddha, are exemplified. He is considered the prototype of everything that a great saint should be. Dr. Evans-Wentz contributed a highly informative introduction and liberal explanatory notes to this edition.

JIVAKA, LOBZANG. **THE LIFE OF MILAREPA. 185pp. Mur62, 3.50c.**
This is a skillful retelling of Evans-Wentz' original edition, designed to bring the story of Milarepa to as many people as possible. The songs,

some of the more obscure references, and some of the teaching have been omitted, but the bulk of the story remains. Jivaka's rendition is certainly more readable than Evans-Wentz' often awkward prose. A fairly long introduction summarizes the salient features of Tibetan Buddhism.

■ *LHALUNGPA, LOBSANG, tr.* **THE LIFE OF MILAREPA. Notes, 251pp. Dut77, 5.95p.**
This is the first translation of Milarepa's life to appear in half a century. Lhalungpa was born in Lhasa, Tibet, and has studied under many masters. He is presently engaged in a far reaching project of translating major texts from the Tibetan tradition. This translation is in modern language and is far superior to the earlier ones. Many of Milarepa's songs are included. Lhalungpa also provides an excellent introduction. We recommend this work highly to all who are interested in Tibetan Buddhism.

THE SONGS OF MILAREPA (A RECORDING). 6.98.
A 33 1/3 rpm recording of five of Milarepa's poems, sung in Tibetan. The songs sound more like chants and are accompanied by various percussion instruments. The voices are often hard to understand due to the poor quality of the recording. Short descriptive notes are included.

──────── END OF MILAREPA SUBSECTION ────────

MILLER, LUREE. **ON TOP OF THE WORLD. Bibliography, index, 222pp. G&D76, 10.95c.**
Biographies of five women who explored Tibet in the late 1800s: Fanny Bullock, Nina Mazuchelli, Annie Taylor, Isabella Bird Bishop, and Alexandra David-Neel. By far the most amount of space is devoted to Ms. David-Neel, the best known of the five. The reasons that they undertook the arduous exploration and their experiences in Tibet are all surveyed.

NAGARJUNA and SAKYA PANDIT. **ELEGANT SAYINGS. 115pp. Dha77, 6.95c/3.95p.**
Translations of **The Staff of Wisdom** by Nagarjuna and **A Precious Treasury of Elegant Sayings** by Sakya Pandit. Both texts are in verse.

NEWARK MUSEUM. **CATALOGUE OF THE TIBETAN COLLECTION AND OTHER LAMAIST ARTICLES, VOLUMES I-V. NwM.**
The Newark (New Jersey) Museum contains one of the finest collections of Tibetan art in the United States. They have also put together an excellent series of books on the collection. Introductory and descriptive material is included along with reproductions and detailed analysis of specific pieces. Volume I ($7.50p., sixty-eight pages) contains introductory material and definitions of terms and symbols in Tibetan art. Volume II ($7.50p., ninety pages) catalogues prayer and ritualistic objects, music and musical instruments. Volume III ($10.00p., 142 pages) focuses on images and molds, paintings, writing and printing equipment, books, and seals and documents. It has over sixty plates, many in color, including a number of full page thankas. Volume IV ($7.50., 112 pages) deals with textiles, rugs, needlework, costumes, and jewelry. Volume V ($7.50., seventy-six pages) concentrates on food utensils and tables, firemaking and tobacco utensils, travel and fighting equipment, and currency and stamps. It also contains an index to the five volumes. Each volume is 7¼"x9½" and contains many plates. Each also has its own bibliography.

NORBU, JIGME and COLIN TURNBULL. **TIBET. Illustrations, 352pp. S&S68/Pen, 4.95p.**
A portrait of the people, religion, customs, and daily life in Tibet by the elder brother of the present Dalai Lama. Norbu describes Tibetan literature, the legends and realities of its religious life, the rituals and ancient customs, and the final ordeal of the Chinese takeover. He writes well and has done an excellent job of bringing his material to life.

OAKLEY, E.S. and TARA GAIROLA. **HIMALAYAN FOLKLORE. Illustrations, notes, 363pp. RPB77, 19.85c.**
A collection of traditional folklore of Kumaon and West Nepal, personally gathered by the authors in the 1930s and divided into the following general categories: *Legends of Heroes, Wit and Wisdom, Animal Lore, Bird Folklore,* and *Ghost and Demon Lore.* A new introduction by March Gaborieau brings the material up to date.

OLSCHAK, BLANCHE, tr. **SPIRITUAL GUIDE TO THE JEWEL ISLAND. 224pp. BPu73, 10.00c.**
Translation of an important text by Konchog Tanpa Donme on spiritual experience which includes practical instructions and is written in simple and insightful language. *In our technical over-civilized phase of life, such texts, guiding to an island of spiritual jewels, may help to bring about the longed-for balance between material and spiritual values and to create mental peace and serenity, whenever the tormented mind grows restless.*—from the preface. On the left hand pages the original Tibetan calligraphy is printed, followed by the orthographical letter-by-letter transcription and the phonetical transcription. On the right hand pages, the English translation is given, followed by the German.

PAL, PRATAPADITYA. **NEPAL. Bibliography, 10"x10", 136pp. Wea75, 19.95c.**
Dr. Pal is the curator of Indian and Islamic art, Los Angeles County Museum of Art. This is the catalogue of the exhibit he put together for the Asia House Gallery in New York City. It includes about 100 paintings and bronzes gathered from all parts of the United States. Each of the pieces is illustrated, many in full color, and a full description of each is supplied. An introduction discusses Nepali art.

PALLIS, MARCO. **PEAKS AND LAMAS. Notes, index, 452pp. Wob74, 33.50c.**
A vivid narrative of the author's journeys through Tibet which illuminates both the country and the Tibetan people. Many of Pallis' encounters with Tibetans of all classes and ways of life are recounted and much of the book is devoted to an exposition of the main tenets of Tibetan Buddhism. This is a new edition, revised by Pallis and updating the story of Tibet from 1949 (the original publication date) to the present.

PALLIS, MARCO. **THE WAY AND THE MOUNTAIN. Many illustrations, 216pp. Owe60, 13.30c.**
This is a highly acclaimed survey of the Buddhism of Tibet. Pallis traveled extensively through the Himalayas in the 1930s and 1940s and did a great deal of scholarly research. This volume was written after his 1947 trip to Tibet and is basically a series of personal impressions rather than an academic study.

PILARSKI, LAURA. **TIBET: HEART OF ASIA. Illustrations, bibliography, index, 125pp. BoM74, 5.95c.**
An informative, easy to read survey of Tibetan history, culture, and religion which begins with Tibet's mythical beginnings and continues up to its present day domination by the People's Republic of China.

RABTEN, GESHE and GESHE NGAWANG DHARGYEY. **ADVICE FROM A SPIRITUAL FRIEND: TIBETAN TEACHINGS ON BUDDHIST THOUGHT TRANSFORMATION. Introduction, notes, 132pp. Vjr77, 4.00p.**
A series of practical instructions from two Tibetan Lamas. The texts on which their commentaries are based came from the great Indian synthesizer of Buddhist lineages, Dipamkara Shrijnana, or Atisha (982-1054), who transmitted them to his closest Tibetan disciples in the last years of his life. The teachings were originally transmitted very selectively and only made generally available in the twelfth century. The subject matter emphasizes practical application of the meditative experience.

RAJNEESH, BHAGWAN SHREE. **ONLY ONE SKY. 4.45p.**
See the Contemporary Spiritual Teachers section.

RECHUNG RINPOCHE, tr. **TIBETAN MEDICINE. Bibliography, index, 327pp. UCa73, 6.95p.**
English translations of important Tibetan medical texts, as well as a history of Tibetan medicine. A very extensive, illustrated treatment.

RINJING, DORJE, tr. **TALES OF UNCLE TOMPA. Oversize, 78pp. Lng75, 3.95p.**
Many people in the world, especially in the West, believe Tibet is a land of "magic saints" where all people spend their time meditating. . . . While all the stories in this book deal directly with Tibetan Buddhist culture, they also reflect the ways in which Tibetans laugh and enjoy life. The stories were told to me while I was a yak herder boy. . . . Until now, none have ever appeared in print. They were all written down by me from memory. . . . This book was written informally using plain language about sexual matters as Tibetans always do when joking in their own tongue. Sample

175

chapters include *Uncle Tompa Sells Penises at the Nunnery, Uncle Tompa Paints a Bull, Uncle Tompa Plays a Trick on his New Wife*. The book is beautifully produced, with many lovely illustrations.

ROERICH, GEORGE, tr. **THE BLUE ANNALS: THE STAGES OF THE APPEARANCE OF THE DOCTRINE AND PREACHERS IN THE LAND OF TIBET. Introduction, indices, 1,275pp. MoB49, 33.00c.**
The Blue Annals is a landmark in the historical literature of Tibet. Composed by Gos lo-tsa-ba-gZon-nu-dpal (AD 1392-1481), it is the main source of information for all later historical compilations, establishing a firm chronology of events in Tibetan history and working out in detail a list of the names of famous religious teachers and their spiritual lineage. Each of the chapters is dedicated to the history of a particular school or sect.

SHEN, TSUNG-LIEN and SHEN-CHI LIU. **TIBET: THE TIBETANS. Photographs, bibliography, index, 209pp. FSG53, 13.85c.**
Mr. Shen was a Chinese scholar who became resident Chinese Commissioner in Lhasa after World War II. He got to know the people and the civilization well and his book provides a variety of data which cannot be found elsewhere. Mr. Liu was Shen's secretary and he remained in Tibet until 1949. Together they provide us with an up to date (relatively) picture of Tibet before the Chinese invasion.

SHERRING, CHARLES. **WESTERN TIBET AND THE INDIAN BORDERLAND. Many photographs, index, 391pp. Csm74, 25.50c.**
This is a detailed description of the area, with a full discussion of all the important tribes and the religions and customs of the people. The account was written in 1906, at the time of the British hegemony—and since this text was written by an Englishman, at attitudes prevalent at that time are readily apparent. Still, there is much of interest here, both as an historical document and as a description of many customs and beliefs which retain their importance in the Himalayas and among the Tibetan refugee communities.

SHIRAKAWA, YOSHIKAZU. **HIMALAYAS. 10"x13¼", 128pp. Abr76, 18.50c.**
A pictorial exploration, with commentary, of the awesome grandeur of the world's highest mountains. Seventy-one full page color illustrations are included, along with six maps and some text.

SINGH, MADANJEET. **HIMALAYAN ART. Bibliography, 287pp. McM68, 3.95p.**
A handsome book which explains both the history of the mountain kingdoms and the complicated mythology reflected in their sacred art. 168 plates are included, almost half in color. An excellent introductory work.

SNELLGROVE, DAVID, tr. **FOUR LAMAS OF DOLPO. Many photographs, line drawings, maps, index, 352pp. Cas67, 22.20c.**
Translations of the autobiographies of four Tibetan Lamas in the land of Dolpo, which was part of western Tibet until the end of the eighteenth century. Three of them were born in the fifteenth century, and one in the seventeenth. In every case the substance of these biographies was dictated by the Lamas themselves in response to the entreaties of their disciples. They are of great importance in that they provide a direct and spontaneous account of Tibetan religious life as seen from the inside. An introduction provides the general background of conditions in Dolpo, including an account of religious beliefs. A second volume contains the original Tibetan texts, commentary, and glossary, and sells for $27.00c.

SNELLGROVE, DAVID and T. SKORUPSKI. **THE CULTURAL HERITAGE OF LADAKH, VOLUME I. Bibliography, index, 8½"x12", 160pp. Pra77/A&P, 27.50c.**
Ladakh existed as an independent western Tibetan kingdom until 1834 when it was finally taken over by the rulers of Jammu and Kashmir, thus becoming an integral part of India. It has, however, remained one of the few regions where Tibetan Buddhism and the Tibetan way of life continue to flourish. During the last twenty-six years entry has been denied to outsiders and only recently has it been possible for Western scholars to visit Ladakh. The authors of this book were the first to do so in 1974 when the ban was lifted, and they stayed there through the winter months when the passes are blocked and the religious life is especially active. This profusely illustrated volume is

A *tsen*, from a sketch by Tendzin yongdu.

the result of that visit and it focuses on the religion, culture, and artistic heritage. The bulk of the book is devoted to an examination of the monasteries.

SOPA, GESHE and JEFFREY HOPKINS. **PRACTICE AND THEORY OF TIBETAN BUDDHISM. Glossary, bibliography, index, 192pp. Grv76/HPG, 3.95p.**
This presentation of the fundamental aspects of the practice and theory of Tibetan Buddhism was prepared under the supervision of the Dalai Lama. The first section concentrates on the practice of meditation in Tibetan Buddhism and is a translation, with commentary, on the Fourth Panchen Lama's **Instructions on the Three Principal Aspects of the Path**. The second section focuses on theory and on the systems of tenets, and consists of an annotated translation of Kon-chok-jik-may-wang-po's **Precious Garland of Tenets**.

STEIN, R.A. **TIBETAN CIVILIZATION. Many illustrations, notes, bibliography, index, 316pp. SUP62/Fab, 3.95p.**
This excellent survey is based on Professor Stein's wide knowledge of all the relevant European studies and Chinese and Tibetan literature. The volume includes sections on habitat and inhabitants, history, society, religion and customs, and arts and letters.

SZEKELY, EDMOND. **PILGRIM OF THE HIMALAYAS. 31pp. Aca74, 1.95p.**
This is the story of Alexander Csoma de Koros' travels in Tibet in the early nineteenth century. He was one of the first Westerners to travel to Tibet and record his experiences and observations. He also brought back a great number of Tibetan books and was instrumental in bringing Tibetan Buddhism to the attention of Western scholars.

TARING, RINCHEN DOLMA. **DAUGHTER OF TIBET. Many photographs, index, 295pp. Mur70, 9.10c.**
The author comes from one of the oldest noble families in Tibet. Her parents died while she was still a child and she was sent to India to finish her education. She became the first Tibetan girl to learn to speak and write in English. She first married the one time commander in chief of the Tibetan army and later a prince of Sikkim, who with her, now devotes his life to caring for and educating Tibetan refugee

children. This book is the author's personal history of domestic life in Tibet in the early twentieth century, of the Chinese invasion, and her flight and life as an exile. This is an often fascinating account which reveals many details we have not read elsewhere about the land and people of Tibet.

TARTHANG TULKU, ed. **ANNALS OF THE NYINGMA LINEAGE IN AMERICA, VOLUME TWO: 1975-77. 8½"x11", about 250pp. Dha77, 12.00p.**
This study chronicles the development of Tibetan Buddhism as taught and practiced by Tarthang Tulku and his students. The first third of the book outlines the Nyingma lineage. The remainder is devoted to an exploration of the areas in which the practitioners have been active and to the projects which they have undertaken. It is basically an in house propaganda document which will be of interest to those seeking more information on the development of this school in America.

TARTHANG TULKU, ed. **CALM AND CLEAR. 4.75p.**
See the Meditation section.

TARTHANG TULKU, ed. **CRYSTAL MIRROR, VOLUME I. Illustrated with many blockprints, 7"x10", 82pp. Dha71, 3.95p.**
Crystal Mirror is a periodical put together by the Tibetan Nyingma Meditation Center. It is a uniformly excellent publication which always includes excerpts from talks by Tarthang Tulku. This issue describes the cultural and historical context of Vajrayana Buddhism, and contains biographies of Tibet's greatest teachers.

TARTHANG TULKU, ed. **CRYSTAL MIRROR, VOLUME II. Illustrated with many blockprints and line drawings, 7"x10", 89pp. Dha72, 3.95p.**
Includes an interview with Tarthang Tulku; translations of the **Vajra Guru Mantra** and of **The Teaching of the Essential Point in Three Words**; and the following philosophical articles: *Fact and Fiction in the Experience of Being* by H.V. Guenther, and Tarthang Tulku's *Judgment, Skillful Means*, and *Entering the Mandala*. This issue also has information on the Center's projects and other related material.

TARTHANG TULKU, ed. **CRYSTAL MIRROR, VOLUME III. 4.75p.**
See the Meditation section.

TARTHANG TULKU, ed. **CRYSTAL MIRROR, VOLUME IV. Illustrations, 7"x10", 281pp. Dha75, 7.95p.**
This compilation seems to get better with each year. Volume IV is divided into four parts: *History, Teachings, Culture*, and *Practice*. Part I presents three essays by Tarthang Tulku: *The Life and Liberation of Padmasambhava, The Twenty-five Disciplines of Padmasambhava*, and *Buddhism in Tibet: The Early Chronicles*. Part II is composed of a series of essays by Tarthang Tulku on various aspects of the practice entitled *Bring the Teachings Alive* and a translation by Herbert Guenther of Longchenpa's **The Natural Freedom of Mind**. Part III includes an essay by Tarthang Tulku, *Tibet: The Land, People, and Culture*, and two by Lama Govinda: *A Tibetan Buddhist Looks at Christianity* and *Pilgrims and Monasteries in the Himalayas*. In the last part Tarthang Tulku answers some questions on the practice and discusses some other things in *Opening to the Dharma*.

TARTHANG TULKU, ed. **CRYSTAL MIRROR, VOLUME V. Many photographs and line drawings, notes, bibliography, index, 7"x10", 411+pp. Dha77, 9.95p.**
The bulk of this book is devoted to Tarthang Tulku's four part *A History of the Buddhist Dharma*, containing a full history of the early and later development of Buddhism in India, the development of Buddhism in Tibet, and the Vajrayana lineages in Tibet. There are also two new translations from Longchenpa.

TARTHANG TULKU. **GESTURE OF BALANCE. 4.95p.**
See the Contemporary Spiritual Teachers section.

TARTHANG TULKU, ed. **REFLECTIONS OF MIND. Notes, 198pp. Dha75, 4.75p.**
In the summers of 1973 and 1974 the teachings of Tibetan Buddhism were introduced to a group of psychologists and mental health professionals during intensive eight-week seminars. This is a collection of essays by a number of the participants, including Charles Tart, Gay Luce, and Claudio Naranjo. They combine their professional training in Western therapeutic practices with their experiences in Tibetan Buddhism to present a picture of the vast psychological expertise of Tibetan Buddhism. Tarthang Tulku contributes a long introductory article.

TARTHANG TULKU, ed. **SACRED ART OF TIBET. Thirty-six beautiful plates, 8¼"x10½", 85pp. Dha72, 5.95p.**
The catalogue of an exhibition held a few years ago. A nice introduction on Tibetan art is included.

TARTHANG TULKU. **TIME, SPACE AND KNOWLEDGE: A NEW VISION OF REALITY. 6.95p.**
See the Contemporary Spiritual Teachers section.

TATZ, MARK and JODY KENT. **REBIRTH: THE TIBETAN GAME OF LIBERATION. 231pp. 7"x10", Dou77, 6.95p.**
Rebirth is a traditional Tibetan board game, depicting the Buddhist map of the universe in a scheme of 104 squares. Each square represents a stage of enlightenment and, with each roll of the die, one progresses toward nirvana, afloat among gods of delights, or descends to one of the hellish states, such as that of the realm of hungry ghosts. This version of **Rebirth** includes an introduction, complete instructions for playing the game, commentary for each of the 104 squares, and a full color poster sized tanka gameboard—drawn in accordance with ritual iconography.

THURLOW, CLIFFORD. **STORIES FROM BEYOND THE CLOUDS. 185pp. LTW77, 8.00p.**
An anthology of Tibetan folk tales, gathered with the support of the current Dalai Lama and published under his auspices.

Tibetan Language

The Tibetan and Burmese languages are related, although they are mutually unintelligible in their modern forms. Spoken Tibetan has developed a pattern of regional dialects and subdialects, which can be mutually understood. The dialect of Lhasa is used as a lingua franca. There are two social levels of speech—the *zhe-sa* (honorific) and *phal-skad* (ordinary); their use depends on the relative social status between the speaker and the listener. Tibetan is written in a script derived from that of Indian Gupta in about AD 600. It has a syllabary of thirty consonants and five vowels; six additional symbols are used in writing Sanskrit words. The script itself has four variations—*dbu-can* (primarily for Buddhist textbooks), *dhu-med* and *Khyug-yig* (for general use), and *bru-tsha* (for decorative writing).

BELL, CHARLES. **GRAMMAR OF COLLOQUIAL TIBETAN. 230pp. Dov19, 4.00p.**
Sir Charles Bell, who later became British resident in Lhasa, prepared this book for English speaking members of the Indian civil service as a practical introduction for the nonlinguist. It is suitable for self study and is organized in progressive lessons.

BUCK, STUART. **TIBETAN ENGLISH DICTIONARY. Introduction, 850pp. CUA69, 47.00c.**
This is an important modern work, based on the most recent scholarship and designed to be useful to contemporary students.

CSOMA DE KOROS, ALEXANDER. **A GRAMMAR OF THE TIBETAN LANGUAGE IN ENGLISH. 8½"x11", 251pp. Alt1834, 16.15c.**
This is a recent reprint of one of the earliest Tibetan grammars. *I have enumerated only those articles which I thought to be essentially required for a fundamental knowledge of this . . . language. I have gone through all the part of speech, and have given lists of them as fully as it was in my power to do, together with their derivations and variations, that the learner might at once see and perceive all the constituent parts of the Tibetan language.* Appendices illustrate and explain the letters of the Tibetan language and the alphabet.

DAS, SARAT. **AN INTRODUCTION TO THE GRAMMAR OF THE TIBETAN LANGUAGE. Oversize, 340pp. MoB nd, 13.50c.**
This generally is considered the best grammar available. Most of the text is in Tibetan and it includes exercises in the grammatical rules and specimens of composition from the standard works.

DAS, SARAT. **A TIBETAN-ENGLISH DICTIONARY.** 7¼"x9¾", 1,384pp. MoB02, 35.65c.
The most useful work available.

DHONGTHOG, T.G. **THE NEW LIGHT ENGLISH-TIBETAN DICTIONARY. 542pp. LTW73, 20.00c.**
This dictionary is designed to be easy to use and as accurate as possible. It was put together by associates of the current Dalai Lama.

GOLDSTEIN, MELVYN, ed. **TIBETAN-ENGLISH DICTIONARY OF MODERN TIBETAN. Introduction, 1,234pp. RPB75, 40.65c.**
A useful volume, prepared with a great deal of care, focusing on modern literary Tibetan. Approximately 40,000 entries.

HANNAH, HERBERT. **GRAMMAR OF THE TIBETAN LANGUAGE —LITERARY AND COLLOQUIAL. 416pp. Csm73, 25.50c.**
This grammar came out of Hannah's studies with Lama Kazi. During his lessons he took a considerable quantity of notes and after a time put them in order. Hannah does not claim that this is an original work; he is merely restating what has already been presented by others, with some corrections and modifications, and supplementing earlier work.

JASCHKE, H.A. **TIBETAN-ENGLISH DICTIONARY. 671pp. Ung81/ RKP, 25.00c.**
Includes an English-Tibetan vocabulary.

JASCHKE, H.A. **TIBETAN GRAMMAR. 126pp. Ung54, 8.00c.**
This is a well known text, first published in the late nineteenth century. This edition includes a reading exercise, with vocabulary.

KAZI, LAMA DAWASAMDUP. **AN ENGLISH-TIBETAN DICTIONARY.** 5¾"x8¾", MuM19, 25.50c.
About 20,000 entries.

——————— **END OF TIBETAN LANGUAGE SUBSECTION** ———————

TIBETAN NYINGMA MEDITATION CENTER. **TIBETAN THANKA PORTFOLIOS. Dha nd, 25.00c.**
Reproduced in full color and packaged in a gold stamped, cloth bound portfolio, these twenty paintings are a visual representation of Tibet's deeply spiritual culture. Examples of both ancient and modern styles of painting. The reproductions are fairly good.

TRUNGPA, CHOGYAM. **BORN IN TIBET. Photographs, glossary, 267pp. ShP77, 4.95p.**
Trungpa was a young man when he had to flee from Tibet. This is a moving story of his early training as a Tulku (an incarnate Lama of high rank) and his escape. Subsequent chapters bring the story up to date and summarize his experiences as a teacher in the United States. Trungpa writes extremely well and the reader gets a good feeling for the rigors of traditional Tibetan discipline.

TRUNGPA, CHOGYAM. **CUTTING THROUGH SPIRITUAL MATERIALISM. 250pp. ShP72, 4.95p.**
The record of two series of lectures given by Trungpa Rinpoche in 1972. They present an overview of the path and some warnings as to the dangers along that path. *Walking the spiritual path properly is a very subtle process.... There are numerous sidetracks which lead to a distorted, ego-centered version of spirituality.... This fundamental distortion may be referred to as spiritual materialism.... These talks first discuss the various ways in which people involve themselves with spiritual materialism.... After this tour of the sidetracks along the way, we discuss the broad outlines of the true spiritual path.*—Chogyam Trungpa.

TRUNGPA, CHOGYAM, ed. **THE FOUNDATIONS OF MINDFULNESS.** 8½"x9½", 88pp. ShP76, 3.95p.
This is the fourth volume of the **Garuda** series which is intended to constitute an ongoing encyclopedia of Buddhism. Mindfulness is the basic technique used for 2,500 years in the tradition of Buddhist meditation. Trungpa teaches an understanding of mindfulness and why it is important and very alive in the modern world. Most of the selections were written by Trungpa himself and also included is a translation of the **Satipatthana-Sutta**, one of the earliest Buddhist meditation texts. The book is heavily illustrated with photographs and line drawings.

TRUNGPA, CHOGYAM, ed. **GARUDA V: TRANSCENDING HESITATION. Many illustrations,** 8½"x9½", 104pp. ShP77, 4.50p.
An enlightening collection of essays and translations about the Buddhist way.

TRUNGPA, CHOGYAM. **MEDITATION IN ACTION. 2.25p.**
See the Meditation section.

TRUNGPA, CHOGYAM. **MUDRA. 105pp. ShP72, 2.95p.**
Mudra is a symbol, in the sense of gesture or action. It arises spontaneously, as an expression of apparent phenomena. It is not separate from that which it symbolizes. It is self evident. **Mudra** is a selection of some songs and spontaneous poems written in Tibetan and English. The volume also includes a presentation of the nine Yanas, an illustrated commentary on the classic Zen Oxherding pictures, and a translation of a Maha Ati meditation text.

TRUNGPA, CHOGYAM. **THE MYTH OF FREEDOM AND THE WAY OF MEDITATION. Illustrations, index, 190pp. ShP76, 3.95p.**
This volume is based on a series of talks given by Trungpa between 1971 and 1973. Here the idea of freedom is set in the context of Tibetan Buddhism. Spanning the gulf between the most esoteric tradition of the East and the everyday realities of American life, Trungpa shows how our attitudes, preconceptions, and even our spiritual practices can become chains that bind us to repetitive patterns of frustration and despair. He also explores the significant role that meditation plays in bringing into focus the cause of frustration and in allowing these negative forces to become aids in advancing toward true freedom. The volume ends with Trungpa's translation of a classic text: Tilopa's instructions on Mahamudra meditation to his disciple Naropa. As usual Trungpa expresses himself clearly and the text is an excellent blend of irony and seriousness.

TUCCI, GIUSEPPE. **THE THEORY AND PRACTICE OF THE MANDALA. Notes, index, 141pp. HPG61, 5.35p.**
Mandalas are complex arrangements of patterns or pictures used in Hindu and Buddhist tantrism to give expression to the infinite possibilities of the human subconscious. In this book Professor Tucci conducts a survey into the basic doctrines of the mandala. He shows how mandalas are used in religious ceremonies as a means of integration. An excellent presentation which is generally considered the finest work ever written on mandalas.

TUCCI, GIUSEPPE. **TIBET: LAND OF SNOWS. Bibliography, index,** 8"x11", 216pp. Ele73, 19.95c.
Professor Tucci is one of the few Europeans able to speak of Tibet from personal experience. Here he presents a comprehensive survey of the nation's spiritual, artistic, and social achievements. The text is illustrated with 106 plates, about half in full color. This is much more accessible than Tucci's more scholarly works and forms an excellent introduction to Tibetan civilization.

TUCCI, GIUSEPPE, tr. **TIBETAN FOLK SONGS FROM GYANTSE AND WESTERN TIBET. Introduction, eighteen plates, technical appendices, index, 9¼"x12½", 215pp. Art66, 27.75c.**
Translations of popular songs and ritual chants. The volume also includes a transliterated text of the songs and the Tibetan text of many of them.

TUCCI, GIUSEPPE. **TO LHASA AND BEYOND. Many illustrations, index, 7¼"x10½", 195pp. IPS56, 6.95p.**
An illustrated reproduction of the diary Tucci kept on his expedition to Tibet in 1948. He writes vividly and includes a description of his extended visit with the Dalai Lama. An appendix contains Dr. Regolo Moiso's *Remarks on Medicine and the State of Health in Tibet.*

TUCCI, GIUSEPPE. **TRANSHIMALAYA. Notes, bibliography, index, 239pp. Nag73, 26.25c.**
Professor Tucci has traveled extensively in Tibet and is the twentieth century authority on Tibetan culture. In this volume he reviews the present state of archaeological knowledge about Tibet and suggests possible lines of investigation once archaeological work again becomes possible in Tibet. 210 plates, thirty-three in color, illustrate the text.

TURNER, RALPH. **A COMPARATIVE AND ETYMOLOGICAL DICTIONARY OF THE NEPALI LANGUAGE. 9"x11¼", 854pp. RKP65, 72.00c.**
The standard work.

WADDELL, L. AUSTINE. **TIBETAN BUDDHISM WITH ITS MYSTIC CULTS, SYMBOLISM, AND MYTHOLOGY. Notes, bibliography, index, 583pp. Dov1895, 6.00p.**
A scholarly, very complete text. Abounds with translations of Indian and Tibetan documents and texts, summaries of important works, annotated pictorial representations, and a wealth of data.

WALDSCHMIDT, ERNST and ROSE. **NEPAL: ART TREASURES FROM THE HIMALAYAS. Bibliography, index, 7¼"x10", 160pp. Ele69, 19.95c.**
This book provides an introduction to all the phases and aspects of Nepalese art from earliest times to the beginning of the nineteenth century. The 113 illustrations, twelve in color, show archaeological finds, sculpture, painting, and manuscript and architectural details. Each of the plates is fully discussed and the introduction covers the history, civilization, and culture of Nepal.

WANGYAL, GESHE. **DOOR OF LIBERATION. Introduction, glossary, index, 323pp. Stu73, 6.95c.**
An important work by an authentic Tibetan Geshe which contains a comprehensive selection of Buddhist teachings. The translations of texts were made by the author himself; the English rendering is therefore consistently true to the Tibetan without the interpolation of Western concepts. Rather than another collection of theoretical discourses, this is a practical handbook.

WAYMAN, ALEX. **BUDDHIST TANTRAS. Illustrations, notes, bibliography, index, 255pp. Wei73/RKP, 12.50c.**
A detailed work by a renowned Sanskrit and Tibetan scholar. An introductory section discusses the Buddhist Tantra within Mahayana Buddhism and analyzes the nature of Buddhist esotericism and the early literary history of the tantras. The second section reviews the main features of this school, and the symbolism involved in its teaching. A final section presents some little known aspects of the subject including tantric teachings on astrology, the orifices of the body, female energy and symbolism, the five-fold ritual symbolism of passion, and the Tibetan canon. This is a difficult text, recommended only to those with an excellent background in the Tibetan esoteric teachings.

WAYMAN, ALEX. **YOGA OF THE GUHYASAMAJATANTRA. Notes, index, 400pp. MoB77, 30.00c.**
An in depth analysis of one of the most important Buddhist tantric texts. Wayman, an excellent Buddhist scholar, includes translations of many of the verses along with an illuminating commentary. He also translates some related texts.

WEINER, DOUGLAS. **TIBETAN AND HIMALAYAN WOODBLOCK PRINTS. 11"x16", 75pp. Dov74, 4.00p.**
Examples of woodblock prints carved by contemporary craftsmen which convey the traditional images of Buddhist deities, saints, and kings as they have been pictured over the centuries. The black and white reproductions are adequate, and captions and an introduction are included.

WILLIS, JANICE. **THE DIAMOND LIGHT. 124pp. S&S72, 2.45p.**
An introduction to Tibetan practices, especially meditation. The terminology is explained and defined, thus clarifying the significance of the technique. The instructions are quite clear and a great number of actual practices are described in detail. This is not a profound book, but it does provide a more than adequate introduction to the subject.

WINKLER, JURGEN. **NEPAL. 11¾"x12½", 227pp. Kod77, 45.00c.**
This is a magnificent collection of over 200 full page color and black and white photographs of the art, architecture, and landscapes of the Kathmandu valley. Each picture is accompanied by detailed information on the content. This book will be a treasure to all who are fascinated by Nepalese art and culture.

YESHE, THUBTEN and THUBTEN ZOPA RINPOCHE. **WISDOM-ENERGY. Photographs, annotated bibliography, 7¾"x10½", 89pp. Vjr76, 3.50p.**
Transcriptions of discourses given by two Tibetan Lamas on a lecture tour in the West.

YONGDEN, LAMA. **MIPAM. 12 original woodcuts, 349pp. Mud38, 3.95p.**
A faithful description of the Tibetan people and their ways, in the form of a novel, by a Tibetan Lama who was the adopted son of Ms. David-Neel and accompanied her on many of her travels.

ZEN BUDDHISM

During the past few years in America a small Japanese word, with a not inappropriate buzzing sound, has begun to be heard in unlikely places: on academic platforms, at cocktail parties and ladies' luncheons, and in campus hangouts. This word is *Zen*. Sometimes called a religion, sometimes *the religion of non-religion*, sometimes identified simply as a *way of life*, Zen is ancient and alien in origin, its philosophy paradoxical and complex. Its sudden Western blooming is therefore something of a phenomenon.

The applied tenets of Zen—formulations and adaptations of original Buddhist principles—lie at the root of the most unique elements in Japanese life. Zen's influence, implicit or explicit, can be traced through almost every aspect of Japan's culture from garden planning to architecture, ceremonial swordsmanship to Judo, flower arrangement to archery, poetry composition to the formal tea ceremony, painting techniques to the conventions of the theater. So complete has been Zen's infiltration for centuries that it is by now quite impossible to understand the contradictory and long-enduring civilization of this small island country without some understanding of Zen itself.

Traveling a long distance in space and time from its origins in India in the sixth century B.C., to reach Japan via China and Korea in the twelfth and thirteenth centuries A.D. (although other forms of Buddhism reached Japan as early as the sixth century A.D.), Zen Buddhism first touched American shores about 1900. After some fifty years of incubation—and ironically enough, since the war in the Pacific—it has suddenly begun to attract a growing number of enthusiastic supporters in this country, among them distinguished scientists, artists, and psychoanalysts.

From Japan some pertinent remarks on the fad side of Zen were recently offered by Chicago-born Ruth Fuller Sasaki, who has been ordained a Zen priest and is now in full charge of a Kyoto subtemple—a quite extraordinary honor for a Westerner and a woman. In an interview given at the time of her ordination in 1958 she commented: *In the Western world Zen seems to be going through the cult phase. Zen is not a cult. The problem with Western people is that they want to believe in something and at the same time they want something easy. Zen is a lifetime work of self-discipline and study.* Mrs. Sasaki went on to describe how, during her period of training, she learned to spend seven days at a time in a monk's hall sleeping only one hour a night, and sitting in meditation or contemplation for as long as eighteen hours without a break.

To know Zen, even to begin to understand it—it is necessary to practice it. And here Westerners come to a dilemma. Ruth Sasaki believes it is not possible to get at Zen's deepest roots or to rightly utilize its unique method without the aid of a master, a *guru*, to use the Indian term.

To reach the state of illumination—*satori*—and the *spiritual equilibrium* that follows, certain definite techniques are used by the Zen master and pupil. There is a form of question and answer known as the *mondo* by which ordinary thought processes are speeded up to the point of the hoped-for abrupt breakthrough into *awareness*. And then there is the *koan*, a formulation in words not soluble by the intellect alone—indeed, often quite senseless to the rational mind, a veritable *riddle*. But the *koan* contains the possible seeds of the shock that may also break open the sealed door of ordinary consciousness,

which is forever caught in the contradictory bonds of dualism, forever balancing this with that, unable to take hold of *reality* because always immersed in a series of distinctions, discriminations, and differences.

To work on a *koan* necessitates a sincere and enduring eagerness to solve it, but also—and here comes the twist, and one of the many paradoxes in which Zen abounds—you must *face it without thinking about it*. This point is stressed in the unbending effort to force the student beyond the eternally dualistic and dialectic pattern of ordinary thinking. Again and again it is emphasized that one cannot take hold of the true merely by abandoning the false, nor can one reach peace of mind or any final *answer* by argument or logic. Science might be cited as a prime example of the failure to bring solace or release through *facts*. Scientists reduce matter to molecules, molecules to atoms; they present the theory of the infinite divisibility of matter. They also assert that all life is merely force or energy. The sum total of their brilliant findings remains almost totally incomprehensible to the average mind, even to the exceptional mind that happens to be unscientific. How, then, in the modern world, ruled by conflicting theories, with global problems and personal problems forever presenting themselves for solution, can the individual ever *come to rest*, struggling as he still is—but in an ever more complex environment—with the very same basic questions of individual meaning, of the riddle of life and death, that Siddartha Gautama, the historic Buddha, faced in the sixth century B.C.?

Once you have taken up this ancient basic question of *meaning*, you are on your way to an impasse which your so-called *rational* mind cannot solve for you. And it is at this point that the Zen *koan* is presented as a sort of spiritual dynamite. But one cannot, alas, *explain* a *koan*. *Koans* are meant to be directly experienced. They are formulations on which to practice that famous *law of reversed effort* by which results are often mysteriously obtained in the hidden, unconscious depths of one's being.

A subject for meditation might be these lines from an old Japanese poem: *The cherry tree blooms each year in the Yoshino Mountains. But split the tree and tell me where the flowers are.* Or the last line from another famous Japanese poem: *Now I know my true being has nothing to do with birth and death.*

An instructor giving this line as a *koan* might question: *How can you free yourself from birth and death? What is your true being? No! No! Do not think about it! Just gaze at it closely.* Perhaps a few hints would be offered: *Zen, it is asserted, has the aim of enabling you to see directly into your own nature. Very well. Where is your true nature? Can you locate it? If you can locate it you are then said to be free of birth and death. All right, you have become a corpse. Are you free of birth and death? Now do you know where you are?* . . . . *Now your body has separated into its four basic elements. Where are you now?*

Doshin asked Sosan: *What is the method of liberation?* The master replied: *Who binds you? No one binds me. Why then*, said the master, *should you seek liberation?* Replies of this type, says Alan Watts, *seem to throw attention back upon the state of mind from which the question arises, as if to say: If your feelings are troubling you, find out who or what it is that is being troubled. The psychological response is therefore to try to feel what feels and to know what knows—to make an object of the subject. Yet this is not easy. It is indeed much like looking for an ox when you are riding on it or like an eye that sees, but cannot see itself.*

Just how far the ordinary, unaided seeker can penetrate toward the core of Zen is difficult to assess, but whichever way he seeks it—either under direct personal guidance or alone—the key to realization lies in the words *direct immediate perception*, or *direct seeing into*. The condition of enlightenment itself, and not words about that condition, are what matter in Zen. Zen masters sternly reject all the speculation, ratiocination, and verbalism so dear to the intellectual Westerner. Overemphasis on the brain, at the expense of other part of the total consciousness, can seem both amusing and amazing to Asian teachers. A Zen abbot once set before an American aspirant two sets of small legless Japanese dolls, one pair weighted in the bottom part, the other in the head part. When the pair weighted in the head were pushed over, they remained on their sides; the ones weighted in the bottom bounced back at once. The abbot roared with laughter over this illustration of the plight of Western man, forever stressing the thinking function at the expense of his totality.

Zen enlightenment, which carries with it a deep and lasting comprehension of one's place in the totality of the universe, is not easily gained—contrary to the impression of *immediacy* that many people have taken away from their cursory reading of Zen literature. Although illumination may come in a sudden flash, during which one perceives one's *self* and the rest of the world as they really are, this galvanic charge is unlikely to occur short of an extended period of disciplined personal effort. The seeker, as one Master asserts, must pursue for a very long time the problem of final *knowing* with a single-purposed ferocity and all the attendant frustrations of a *mosquito trying to bite on a bar of iron*.

Those who, to begin with, find Zen not only paradoxical and puzzling but annoying, even enraging, might profit from an old story of a certain learned man who came to a Zen master to inquire about this rare philosophy. The master politely invited his visitor to share a cup of ceremonial tea while they discoursed together. When the master has brewed the tea by the strict procedures of the tea ceremony, he began to pour the whisked green liquid into the visitor's cup and continued pouring until the cup had overflowed. Even then he went on pouring until the discomfited guest, unable longer to restrain himself, cried out in agitation, *Sir, my cup is already full. No more will go in.* At once the master put down the teapot and remarked, *Like this cup, you are full of your own opinions and speculations. How can I show you Zen unless you first empty your cup?*

—condensed from **The World of Zen**, by Nancy Wilson Ross

ANDO, SHOEI. ZEN AND AMERICAN TRANSCENDENTALISM. Notes, index, 224pp. Hok70, 11.25c.
A comparative study in which Professor Ando shows the way both Zen Buddhism and American transcendentalism look at human nature. He begins with a separate discussion of each, then follows with a comparative section, and ends with a comparison of Zen and Christianity. It is a dry, not terribly interesting book.

ANESAKI, MASAHARU. **HISTORY OF JAPANESE RELIGION. Illustrations, notes, index, 423pp. Tut30, 10.50c.**
A somewhat dated, standard, one volume history, chronologically arranged and tying the religions in with the political and historical events of each era. The text is oriented toward the general reader—although one would have to have a deep intrest in Japanese culture to want to read so much about it.

ANESAKI, MASAHARU. **RELIGIOUS LIFE OF THE JAPANESE PEOPLE. Illustrations, bibliography, 122+pp. KBS70, 3.75p.**
This is a dry survey, sponsored by the Japanese Cultural Society, with chapters on Shinto, Confucianism, Taoism, Buddhism, and Christianity. Also includes background material.

AWAKAWA, YASUICHI. **ZEN PAINTING. 9"x11½", 184pp. Kod70, 20.00c/11.95p.**
This is an integrated survey, presenting 139 of the finest masterpieces of the ink monochrome ever produced in Japan. Each of the plates and the artists is fully discussed and there is an excellent introductory essay entitled, *Brushmarks of Infinity*. Beautifully produced.

BAYRD, EDWIN. **KYOTO: JAPAN'S ANCIENT CAPITAL. Chronology, bibliography, index, 9"x11½", 172pp. Nsw74, 12.95c.**
Kyoto is the ancient capital of Japan. The imperial epoch, which began in 794 and lasted for more than 1,000 years, witnessed the emergence of a civilization that is considered one of the most refined and elegant in the world. To this day Kyoto remains the religious and aesthetic center of Japan. Imposing Buddhist temples and Shinto shrines can be found in every quarter of the city. This beautifully produced book contains a text reviewing Kyoto's history and 115 illustrations, half in color. A final section presents descriptions of the city by Westerners and Japanese, written between the twelfth century and the present.

BENARES, CAMDEN. **ZEN WITHOUT ZEN MASTERS. 127pp. AOP77, 4.95p.**
A collection of contemporary Zen parables, written in a hip style. Benares describes true Zen as neither words nor their meaning, but rather the reality behind them. The information he offers in this book is designed as a tool to help you experience that reality more fully. In addition to the parables he offers a series of meditation guides and exercises. This is an interesting attempt to help the contemporary American realize the essence of Zen.

BENEDICT, RUTH. **THE CHRYSANTHEMUM AND THE SWORD: PATTERNS OF JAPANESE CULTURE. Glossary, index, 324pp. NAL46, 3.95p.**
An anthropologist writes of the Japanese view of life and of themselves. Ms. Benedict sketches the main outlines of Japanese society, describes their ethical system, and their discipline. This is a very useful work for those who seek greater insight into the Japanese people.

BENOIT, HUBERT. **LET GO!—THEORY AND PRACTICE OF DETACHMENT ACCORDING TO ZEN. 277pp. Wei62, 4.50p.**
Benoit details an exercise by which a viewpoint similar to that which the Zen Buddhists would call *satori* is achieved. The book represents a culmination of the material in **The Supreme Doctrine** and consists of theoretical discussions about *letting go* and *ultimate realization* followed by the exercise, based on the analysis of language. The theoretical concepts presented throughout this book are often difficult to grasp—but once understood they become illuminating.

BENOIT, HUBERT. **THE SUPREME DOCTRINE—PSYCHOLOGICAL STUDIES IN ZEN THOUGHT. Index, 248pp. Vik51, 3.50p.**
Dr. Benoit, a practicing psychoanalyst, shows how Zen can liberate us from some of the sickness and anxiety that plague contemporary civilization. As Aldous Huxley states in his introduction, *this should be read by everyone who aspires to know who he is and what he can do to acquire such self-knowledge.*

BERRIGAN, DANIEL and THICH NHAT HANH. **THE RAFT IS NOT THE SHORE: CONVERSATIONS TOWARD A CHRISTIAN/BUDDHIST AWARENESS. 139pp. Bea75, 3.45p.**
Hahn led the Vietnamese Buddhist Peace Delegation in Paris; Berrigan is a Jesuit priest who had been active in the peace movement. They met at the Peace Delegation and conducted many long midnight conversations, some of which are transcribed here. The talk ranges widely over memory, eucharist, and death; exile; priests and prisoners;

self-immolation; government, economics, and religion; Jesus and Buddha; and communities of resistance.

BLACKER, CARMEN. **THE CATALPA BOW. Thirty photographs, glossary, notes, bibliography, index, 376pp. A&U75, 18.50c.**
A detailed study of shamanistic practices in Japan. Dr. Blacker describes the supernatural beings—both good and evil—with whom the shaman communicates, the complex other world geography in Japanese myth and legend, the initiatory dreams by which the shaman is elected to his task, and the ascetic practices by means of which he consolidates his powers. She goes on to discuss those shamanistic figures who survive today. Dr. Blacker has, wherever possible, witnessed and participated in the rituals and practices she writes about. She fills out the picture by drawing on mythological motifs and on the work of Japanese ethnologists.

BLOFELD, JOHN, tr. **THE ZEN TEACHING OF HUANG PO ON THE TRANSMISSION OF THE MIND. Introduction, notes, index 136pp. Grv62/BuS, 3.95p.**
An historical record of the direct teaching of a Zen master—considered one of the key works in Zen. The dialogues use the technique of a paradox to show how the experience of intuitive knowledge reveals to a man what he really is and illustrate the impossibility of communication through words. Blofeld provides an excellent translation.

BLOFELD, JOHN, tr. **THE ZEN TEACHING OF HUI HAI. Long introduction, glossary, notes, index, 160pp. Wei62/HPG, 2.95p.**
The first part of this book contains a Mahayana instruction for self realization, perception of self nature, and attainment of Buddhahood. The second part has a translation of dialogues between Hui Hai and his disciples.

BLOOM, ALFRED. **SHINRAN'S GOSPEL OF PURE GRACE. Notes, bibliography, index, 111pp. UAr65, 3.35p.**
Shinran was the founder of the True Sect of the Pure Land. This is a systematic presentation of Shinran's cardinal ideas and his contributions to the development of Pure Land thought. Bloom focuses on those doctrines which describe the human predicament, the nature of faith, the status of the believer, the nature of religious devotion, and the final destiny of the believer. Wherever possible, Shinran's own words are used in explaining his concepts.

BLYTH, R.H. **BUDDHIST SERMONS ON CHRISTIAN TEXTS. 93pp. HIn76, 2.95c.**
Christian scriptures which parallel Zen Buddhist concepts are quoted by Dr. Blyth, with commentary. An appendix gives parallel passages from Christian mystics and Zen writings.

BLYTH, R.H. **GAMES ZEN MASTERS PLAY. 169pp. NAL76/NEL, 1.50p.**
Selections from Blyth's books, edited and with an introduction by Robert Sohl and Audrey Carr. Contents include a translation, with commentary, of the **Hsinhsinming** (setting forth the basic Zen approach); a selection of the most famous *mondos* (questions and answers which differ from *koan* in that an immediate answer is demanded) of the Zen masters; an an important selection of *koan* from the **Mumonkan**, perhaps the most widely used instrument for the teaching of Zen.

BLYTH, R.H. **ZEN AND ZEN CLASSICS, VOLUME I. 126pp. Hok60, 6.95p.**
This series of essays and translations contains some of the finest material on Zen Buddhism and Japanese culture ever written in the English language. Blyth spent many years in Japan and was imbued with the spirit of Zen. The books are not terribly well organized—they are not meant to be read straight through. They are wonderful to dip into from time to time. In his own way, Blyth was also a good scholar and his writings have been accepted as authoritative. Volume I contains general introductory material on Zen and a discussion of Ch'an Buddhism up to the time of the Sixth Patriarch, with translations.

BLYTH, R.H. **ZEN AND ZEN CLASSICS, VOLUME II. Index, 224pp. Hok64, 7.25c.**
This volume purports to be the History of Zen from Eno to Ummon, that is, of the Seigen branch of the double-forked tree of Zen, but what the reader actually gets is something better, a selection of the anecdotes concerning this line of patriarchs. It was from such stories that the Hekinganroku, Mumonkan, and Shoyoroku were composed. —from the preface.

BLYTH, R.H. **ZEN AND ZEN CLASSICS, VOLUME III. 188pp. Hok70, 7.25c.**
The present volume deals with Zen from Nangaku to Rinzai and his disciples, that is, with the Nangaku branch of Chinese Zen. As with Volume Two, its companion, this is something better than a history, it is a selection of anecdotes concerning the Chinese Zen geniuses of the T'ang Dynasty. —from the preface.

BLYTH, R.H., tr. **ZEN AND ZEN CLASSICS, VOLUME IV. Introduction, notes, index, 355pp. Jap66, 15.95c.**
Blyth's translation of the **Mumonkan**, the classical *koan* anthology.

BLYTH, R.H. **ZEN AND ZEN CLASSICS, VOLUME V. Index, 225pp. Jap62, 8.50c.**
This volume contains twenty-five essays on all aspects of Zen.

BRANDON, DAVID. **ZEN IN THE ART OF HELPING. Notes, 124pp. Del76, 2.95p.**
The author is a social worker and a practicing Zen Buddhist. In this book he questions much of what passes as help for others and contends that it is in reality only a kind of egotism which succeeds in hindering them. True compassion seeks a higher and unegotistical good, and is essential to the basic practice of all *helping*. This book explores the major areas where the helping process can be illuminated by viewing it through a Zen perspective. Case studies from the author's own work accompany the text.

BUKSBAZEN, JOHN. **TO FORGET THE SELF: AN ILLUSTRATED GUIDE TO ZEN MEDITATION. Photographs, 10"x8½", 76pp. Zen77, 7.95p.**
The author has been involved with the Zen Center of Los Angeles for ten years, first as a student and then a monk. This book reflects the sitting practice of the Zen Center community and it has been written in as clear a fashion as possible. Every aspect of sitting is covered on an introductory and then on a deeper level. There are also essays on Buddhism and on community. Appendices contain an illustrated collection of exercises to help you sit, detailed instructions for making your own *zafu*, and a listing of meditation centers around the U.S. This is the most simple instruction manual we have ever seen.

BUNCE, WILLIAM. **RELIGIONS IN JAPAN—BUDDHISM, SHINTO, CHRISTIANITY. 194pp. Tut55, 2.95p.**
A general survey.

CALLAWAY, TUCKER. **ZEN WAY—JESUS WAY. Glossary, index, 262pp. Tut76, 8.50c.**
Dr. Callaway is a Christian missionary who has practiced *zazen* in Japanese temples for over twenty years. Callaway's assignment in Japan was to teach world religions and the philosophy of religions at a major Japanese university; he therefore has had extensive opportunity to compare Christianity and Zen Buddhism. Much of the book is devoted to a relating of his experiences in Zen temples. There is also a transcription of one of his conversations with D.T. Suzuki. A final section relates the teachings of Jesus to those of Zen Buddhism.

CHAMBERLAIN, BASIL. **JAPANESE THINGS. Foldout map, notes, index, 579pp. Tut71, 4.95p.**
This is a reprint of the fifth revised edition of 1905, with an updated bibliography. The book is arranged in encyclopedic fashion and covers a wide variety of subjects. The discussion is based on the author's personal observations and interpretations and many of his remarks are still applicable to modern Japan.

CHIBA, REIKO, ed. **DOWN THE EMPEROR'S ROAD WITH HIROSHIGE. 6"x4", 72pp. Tut65, 5.95c.**
A lovely, boxed volume. The Emperor's Road is the Tokaido, Japan's most famous highway. Built in 1603, it joined Kyoto—residence of the Emperor—and Edo (today's Tokyo), seat of the executive government of the shoguns. From Edo the Tokaido follows the Pacific coast, hugging the mountains that come right down to the sea. Then it turns inland across a mountain range, passes Lake Biwa, and ends at Kyoto. The scenery is magnificent. Hiroshige produced twenty versions of prints showing the fifty-three stations of the Tokaido. This book reproduces a little known version. Every second station is reproduced

in full color and fills the small pages; the alternate station is in minature and black and white. There is also some commentary on each illustration.

CHIBA, REIKO, ed. **HIROSHIGE'S TOKAIDO IN PRINTS AND POETRY. 72pp. Tut57, 4.95c.**
A boxed gift book which reproduces Hiroshige's first version of the **Tokaido**. Accompanying Hiroshige's scenes are appropriate examples of Japanese poetry in three forms: *tanka*, *haiku*, and *senryu*, plus a selection from the **Manyoshu**, Japan's earliest anthology. Unfortunately, the fifty-five individual color illustrations are tiny—2¼"x1¼".

CHIBA, REIKO. **JAPANESE SCREENS IN MINIATURE. Tut nd, 8.95c.**
Six masterpieces of the Momoyama Period, reproduced in color as actual miniature screens and contained in a gold embossed folding box. An accompanying scroll contains a discussion of Japanese screens as an art form and an evaluation of each of the screens. Each screen is 13"x6".

CHIBA, REIKO, ed. **SESSHU'S LONG SCROLL—A ZEN LANDSCAPE JOURNEY. Tut59, 6.95c.**
Sesshu's **Long Scroll** is the masterwork of the fifteenth century artist whom Japan honors as one of her greatest. Famed not only as a painter but also as a Zen priest and a great traveler, Sesshu found inspiration for his wonderful landscapes both in China and Japan. This magnificent scroll, done in ink and faint color washes, is approximately 51'x1¼' in size and depicts the procession of the seasons. It is an essentially religious painting with a strong feeling of Zen Buddhism. This reproduction is in the form of a book with continuous fanlike pages and it measures 178½"x5½". Reiko Chiba provides provides an introduction and a running commentary.

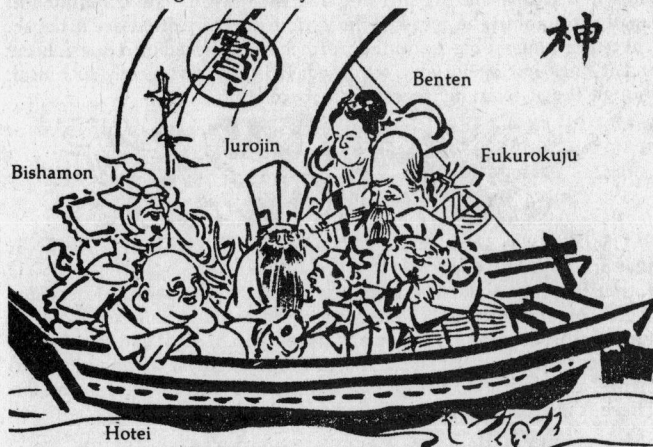

CHIBA, REIKO. **THE SEVEN LUCKY GODS OF JAPAN. 4¾"x6¾", Tut66, 5.25c.**
A beautifully produced gift book, with drawings of each of the gods and rainbow pages. The seven lucky gods are a group of deities whose origins stem from Indian, Chinese, and indigenous Japanese gods of fortune. Each of the gods has been recognized as a deity for more than a thousand years and each has had its own large following of believers.

CLAVELL, JAMES. **SHOGUN: A NOVEL OF JAPAN. 1,210pp. Del75, 2.75p.**
Shogun *is irresistible. I can't remember when a novel has seized my mind like this one. James Clavell breathes narrative. It's almost impossible not to continue to read* **Shogun** *once having opened it. Yet it's not only something that you read—you live it...possessed by the Englishman Blackthorne, the Japanese lord Toranaga and medieval Japan.... People, customs, needs and desires all become so enveloping you forget who and where you are.*—**The New York Times Book Review.**

CLEARY, CHRISTOPHER, tr. **SWAMPLAND FLOWERS. 171pp. Grv77, 3.95p.**
The first English translation of the classic writings of twelfth century Chinese Zen Master Ta Hui, which form some of the basic texts of Zen teaching. Cleary has culled the text from the voluminous selections of Ta Hui's letters, sermons, and lectures, originally published in the **Chi Yuen Lu.** Ta Hui addresses his remarks mainly to people in lay life, not to other monks. Cleary includes an introductory essay on Ch'an Buddhism and a short biography of Ta Hui.

CLEARY, THOMAS, tr. **THE ORIGINAL FACE: AN ANTHOLOGY OF RINZAI ZEN. Introduction, 158pp. Grv78, 4.95p.**
An anthology of Rinzai texts from the thirteenth to the eighteenth century. All the most important texts and masters are well represented and many lesser known works are also included. The translations are excellent.

CLEARY, THOMAS and J.C., trs. **THE BLUE CLIFF RECORDS, VOLUMES I-III. 681pp. ShP77, 20.00c/5.95p/each.**
An excellent three volume translation of this classic collection of model *koans.* 100 examples are included in all, each with extensive commentary. As it says in the introduction, **The Blue Cliff Record** *has become almost uniquely revered among Zen Buddhists as a model "koan" text, especially noted for its subtlety and profundity in both form and content.* The hardcover edition contains all three volumes bound in one.

COVELL, JON and YAMADA SOBIN. **ZEN AT DAITOKU-JI. 102 plates, including many color photographs, index, 9¼"x11½", 203pp. Kod74, 29.50c.**
Daitoku-ji, founded in the early fourteenth century, is the most important Zen temple in Japan. Yamada Sobin is the abbot of a major subtemple of Daitoku-ji and a specialist on its history. Dr. Covell is an expert both on Oriental art and on Daitoku-ji; she is also one of the few women who has been given the privilege of living there, as she has done on and off for the last forty years. Thus the authors' discussion is authoritative and their familiarity with the daily routine of the temple—its personalities, ceremonies, and festivals—affords a vivid picture of the practice of Zen.

Dogen

Dogen (1200-1253) was one of the greatest figures in the history of Zen. He is best known as the founder of the Soto school of Zen—the largest Buddhist sect in Japan today. The following quotation from one of his treatises explains the philosophy of this sect: *The burning of incense, the bowing before the Buddha's image and prayer to him, confession of sin and the reading of the Sutras are all, from the very beginning of one's discipleship, wholly unnecessary. The one and only thing required is to free oneself from the bondage of mind and body alike, putting the Buddha's own seal upon yourself. If you do this as you sit in ecstatic meditation the whole universe itself turns into enlightenment.* Soto Zen relies on deep meditation (*zazen*) rather than the use of *koans*—as in the Rinzai sect—in striving for enlightenment. English translaitons of Master Dogen's works have only recently become available.

KIM HEE-JIM. **DOGEN KIGEN—MYSTICAL REALIST. Notes, bibliography, index, 400pp. UAr75, 6.65p.**
This is an important survey of the life and thought of Dogen Kigen. This definitive study presents the widest selection available of Dogen's writings, most never before published in English translation. The selections are topically arranged and extensive commentary is included.

MASUNAGA, REIHO, tr. **A PRIMER OF SOTO ZEN. Introduction, notes, index, 119pp. UHa71, 2.95p**
This text is a translation of Dogen's brief talks and instructional comments collected together in the **Shobogenzo Zuimonki,** or the *simplified eye of the true law.* This is an excellent introduction to the form of Zen most popular in Japan today, in the words of the founder of the school.

NISHIYAMA, KOSEN and JOHN STEVENS, trs. **SHOBOGENZO: THE EYE AND TREASURY OF THE TRUE LAW, VOLUME I. Notes, index, 188pp. Jap75, 25.00c.**
This is the first complete English translation of Dogen's masterwork. The first volume contains thirty-five chapters and an introduction to Dogen's life.

YOKOI, YUHO, tr. **ZEN MASTER DOGEN: AN INTRODUCTION WITH SELECTED WRITINGS. 217pp. Wea76, 9.75c/4.75p.**
A selection of representative writings by Dogen. The translations are faithful to the original and rendered in a lucid style. They are completely annotated and supplemented by a comprehensive glossary.

In addition, the introductory section provides a penetrating and detailed evaluation of Dogen's life, thought, and writings. The bulk of the book is devoted to the twelve final sections of the **Shobo-genzo**. These were chosen because they were composed as a distinctive group shortly before Dogen's death and thus in many ways represent the culmination of his mature thought. Three independent translations round out the book: *A Universal Recommendation for Zazen; Points to Watch in Buddhist Training;* and *The Meaning of Practice Enlightenment.*

────────── **END OF DOGEN SUBSECTION** ──────────

DOI, TAKEO. **THE ANATOMY OF DEPENDENCE. Notes, 170pp. Kod73, 4.95p.**
In my opinion this is a fundamental contribution which develops the interrelationships between Japanese culture, personality development, individual psychopathology and current social stresses. Doi's familiarity with psychoanalytic psychology and social psychology gives him the background to see the relationships within all of these areas. It is a tightly reasoned work which develops logically the use of language in describing the special personality and cultural characteristics of the Japanese.—Donald Langsley, M.D.

DUMOULIN, HEINRICH. **A HISTORY OF ZEN BUDDHISM. Notes, extensive bibliography, index, 335pp. Bea59, 4.50p.**
A comprehensive, illustrated account by a Jesuit professor at Sophia University in Tokyo.

DUNN, CHARLES. **EVERYDAY LIFE IN TRADITIONAL JAPAN. Many illustrations, bibliography, index, 209pp. Tut69, 3.95p.**
It was during the approximately two and half centuries of Tokugawa rule (1600-1867) when Japanese contacts with the outside world were deliberately avoided, that the traditions behind present day Japan were consolidated. Under the overall control of the military dictator, the *shogun*, society was divided into four classes: the samurai, or warriors; the farmers; the craftsmen; and the merchants and traders. In this book Dunn describes how each class lived and also takes account of certain important groups that fell outside the formal class structure.

DURCKHEIM, KARLFRIED. **HARA. Illustrations, 208pp. Wei62, 3.95p.**
Durckheim is a philosopher and a psychotherapist. He abandons the old dualistic thinking about man in terms of body and soul, which is the hallmark of Western thought, and shows how man must always be taken as one whole. Realization of the self can never be a spiritual development alone, but must include the body. In Japan Durckheim discovered the teaching and tradition of *hara*, Japanese for the vital center. He found that through the experience of it man can be freed from his persistent conceptual thinking, which inevitably blocks his access to being. This volume includes material on the practice of *hara* and texts by three Japanese masters on *hara*. It is an unusual work, containing some fine insights.

DURCKHEIM, KARLFRIED. **THE JAPANESE CULT OF TRANQUIL-ITY. 5.35p.**
See the Meditation section.

DURCKHEIM, KARLFRIED, et al. **THE GRACE OF ZEN. 107pp. Sea77, 3.95p.**
A collection of parables, prayers, and meditations garnered from a wide variety of writers on Zen. As Durckheim says, *Zen texts are especially demanding. The closer you get to what lies behind the imagery, the more questions they raise. . . . Yet everything can suddenly become simple and lucid. . . . An objective and rational approach to Zen texts is pointless. One has to engage with them in a wholly personal way and repeatedly to allow what is said to enter within one's self and quietly to take effect on one.* Most of the passages are short and there are illustrations throughout.

DUUS, PETER. **FEUDALISM IN JAPAN. Chronology, glossary, bibliography, index, 143pp. RaH76, 5.30p.**
An academic survey of the institutions of feudal government in Japan, focusing on the relations between members of the warrior class and the institutions through which they exercised power.

EARHART, H. BYRON. **JAPANESE RELIGION. Index, 158pp. Dic74, 6.65p.**
This book was designed as a survey of Japanese religion for a college course. It is well written and chronologically arranged, beginning with the earliest religious traditions and continuing through the postwar period. Selected readings are given for each chapter and there is a long annotated bibliography.

EARHART, H. BYRON, ed. **RELIGION IN THE JAPANESE EXPERI-ENCE: SOURCES AND INTERPRETATIONS. Illustrations, 282pp. Dic74, 6.65p.**
An excellent collection of fifty-two essays on all aspects of Japanese religion from a variety of books and authors. All of the selections are quite short, and each is followed by a list of recommended readings.

EIDO SHIMANO ROSHI, ed. **LIKE A DREAM, LIKE A FANTASY: THE ZEN WRITINGS AND TRANSLATIONS OF NYOGEN SENZAKI. 128pp. Jap78, 4.95p.**
Eido Roshi is a contemporary Rinzai Zen master and Nyogen Senzaki was a Japanese Zen teacher who spent much of his life teaching in the United States. As Eido Roshi says in his introduction, *when we carefully observe the life of Nyogen Senzaki, his style of teaching and his personality, we cannot help but be impressed with how different he was from both the ancient masters and the modern teachers of Zen. He was not a hermit, nor did he choose to involve himself with traditional temple life. . . . [His aim] was to present the teachings of Buddhism and the tradition of Zen in a way that could be easily recognizable for those who . . . are interested in actualizing the practice in their everyday lives.*

ELIOT, CHARLES. **JAPANESE BUDDHISM. Notes, index, 485pp. RKP35, 21.00c.**
Sir Charles was the British Ambassador to Japan. He wrote this volume after his return to private life. Earlier he had written a monumental tome, **Hinduism and Buddhism**, based on his years of residence in the East and on his extensive study. Despite its title, this volume traces Buddhism from the time of the early Canons through India and China and its introduction into Japan. The conditions in Japan throughout the ages and the various sects are discussed in depth. There is an incredible amount of information packed into this volume and it does not seem very outdated. It is also not overly technical, though the scholarship seems to be excellent.

ENOMIYA-LASSALLE, H.M. **ZEN—WAY TO ENLIGHTENMENT. 126pp. S&W66, 5.45p.**
Father Enomiya-Lassalle is a Jesuit missionary who became interested in Zen practice during his many years in Japan. In this handbook he surveys the basic tenets of Zen and its relation to the Western religious experience. As is reflected in the title, the emphasis is on enlightenment—although the author does not offer any magical formulas. There is also an analysis of Zen prayer and practice.

FAST, HOWARD. **THE ART OF ZEN MEDITATION. 2.95p.**
See the Meditation section.

FRANCK, FREDERICK. **THE BOOK OF ANGELUS SILESIUS. 8¼"x 10½", RaH76/Wdw, 4.95p.**
Angelus Silesius was a seventeenth century Christian mystic who described his four days and nights of illumination in 304 Zen-like epigrams. Franck has newly translated more than half of these deceptively simple verses and he also provides a *running commentary* of observations by the ancient Zen masters. In an introduction Franck shows how the verses of the Silesian poet form a bridge between Eastern and Western mysticism. Delicate drawings in the style Franck used so successfully in **Zen of Seeing** ornament each page.

■ *FRANCK, FREDERICK, ed.* **ZEN AND ZEN CLASSICS: SELEC-TIONS FROM R.H. BLYTH. 308pp. RaH78/Wdw, 4.95p.**
This is a distillation of the essence of four of the five volumes of Blyth's masterwork—no portions of Volume IV, the **Mumonkan**, are included. Dr. Franck says that he has been studying Blyth's writings for twenty-five years and has selected what seems most precious to him. *My task proved to be both a delightful and a desperate one, for Blyth is not systematic, much less an academic writer. He is perhaps the first Western Zen fool. . . . He says somewhere: "To write about Zen is not difficult. What is difficult is to write by Zen. And if we don't write by Zen, we shouldn't write at all. If we don't live by Zen, there is no point in living.* Franck has attempted to bring order to Blyth's work by organizing it topically and he has illustrated the volume in his own unique style.

FRANCK, FREDERICK. THE ZEN OF SEEING: SEEING/DRAWING AS MEDITATION. 8"x11", 164pp. RaH73, 10.00c/3.95p.
This lovely handwritten and drawn book presents a way of contemplation by which all things are made new and the world is freshly experienced at each moment. *What I have not drawn, I have never really seen*, says Franck, and he goes on to show that *once you start drawing an ordinary thing, a fly, a flower, a face, you realize how extraordinary it is—a sheer miracle.* Joseph Campbell says: *Even reading it, I could feel myself getting ready for a change. It is a beautiful book, a pure book—something good to have at hand, to be opened again and fed upon.*

FROMM, ERICH, D.T. SUZUKI and RICHARD DE MARTINO. ZEN BUDDHISM AND PSYCHOANALYSIS. 180pp. H&R60/Sou, 2.95p.
Transcription of a series of lectures from a symposium on the title subject.

FUKUYAMA, TOSHIO. HEIAN TEMPLES: BYODO-IN AND CHU-SON-JI. 7½"x9½", 168pp. Wea76, 15.00c.
In the Heian period (794-1185) the advance of Buddhism in Japan inspired the creation of ever more splendid temples and works of art. It was during this period that the Pure Land sect found increasing favor with the aristocracy and the common people. The two temples illustrated in this volume were built and ornamented during the Heian period and the masterpieces of sculpture, architecture, and painting epitomized the refinement of the age. Fukuyama uses the remaining splendor of these two temples to survey the art and architecture of Pure Land Buddhism in Heian times. The discussion is richly illustrated with 167 photographs and drawings, forty-three in color.

GABB, W.J. THE GOOSE IS OUT. 121pp. BuS72, 2.55p.
All Europeans who have written on Zen and the way to it, save Mr. Gabb, have approached by means of the intellect and the normal processes of thought. This writer alone, in my experience, has found for himself and learnt to use the technique of the Chinese Masters of Zen. Here there is no thought, as we in the West regard that term, no striving to build with concept the roofless palace of no-thought. Here is a simple, humble and direct approach to each person, each thing, and each situation by a delicately poised Zen mind.—Christmas Humphreys. The first half of this book contains short pieces on Zen mind and the second, *Tales of Tokuzan*, consists of many short teaching stories.

THE GAME OF GO BOARD GAME. 12.50.

GRAHAM, DOM AELRED. ZEN CATHOLICISM. Many quotations, 228pp. HBJ63, 2.95p.
The author, a noted Benedictine monk, reflects here upon Zen and Catholicism—usually considered divergent in their rituals and philosophies—and finds many points of contact between them.

HAKEDA, YOSHITO, tr. KUKAI—MAJOR WORKS. Notes, index, 303pp. Col72, 15.10c.
Kukai (774-835), the man who introduced esoteric Buddhism into Japan, greatly influencing the culture of Heian Japan and setting the tone for all subsequent artistic expression, is generally considered the father of Japanese culture. In the first two parts of this book, Professor Hakeda examines the life and thought of Kukai both in relation to his times and to his influence down the ages. The third part consists of translations of eight of Kukai's major works. A definitive study which establishes Kukai's place in Japanese cultural history.

HAKUIN, ZENJI. THE EMBOSSED TEA KETTLE—ORATE GAMA AND OTHER WORKS. Notes, index, 197pp. A&U63, 7.75c.
Hakuin's teaching, as contained in this, his most important work, may be summed up as follows: (1) he suggests that meditation is not an *affair of the cloister* alone; rather, it is the spirit that should pervade the whole life of men; (2) Neither meditation nor any other religious practice is sufficient without a strict observance of the moral law; and (3) those who aim at spiritual maturity should take care to preserve the health of the body. This is one of the most important practical Zen handbooks and is universally highly regarded. Translated by R.D.M. Shaw.

HAKUIN, ZENJI. THE ZEN MASTER HAKUIN—SELECTED WRITINGS. Notes, bibliography, index, 253pp. Col71, 15.10c
Translated here are three works: the **Orategama, Hebiichigo,** and **Yabukoji**—the latter two have been unavailable in English. Written in the form of letters to various acquaintances, the works are in effect

sermons and lectures on the study of Zen, its relationship to other schools of Buddhism, and exortations to feudal lords to promote humane government, and other matters. Philip Yamplosky, the translator, provides—when they are readily determinable—explanations of difficult references and allusions in the texts as well as a valuable introduction.

HANH, THICH NHAT. THE MIRACLE OF MINDFULNESS: A MANUAL ON MEDITATION. 3.95p.
See the Meditation section.

HANH, THICH NHAT. ZEN KEYS. 185pp. Dou74, 1.95p.
The author is a leading spokesman of the Vietnamese Buddhist peace movement and his teaching, as presented in this book, is a response to the needs of the society and culture in which he lives. Nhat Hanh begins with a discussion of the daily regime of life in a Zen monastery and the character of Zen as practiced in Vietnam. Drawing on both historical and personal examples, he explains the central philosophical concepts of awareness, impermanence, and not-I. Many major Zen concepts are discussed in a short paragraph and some relevant teaching stories are included. Hanh often skips around in his discussion, and his exposition is not as clear as we would like. Phillip Kapleau provides a long introduction.

HARDING, D.E. ON HAVING NO HEAD: A CONTRIBUTION TO ZEN IN THE WEST. 72pp. BuS71, 2.65p.
The best day of my life—my rebirthday, so to speak—was when I found I had no head. . . . What actually happened was something absurdly simple and unspectacular: I stopped thinking. A peculiar, quite an odd kind of alert limpness or numbness, came over me. Reason and imagination and all mental chatter died down. For once, words really failed me. Past and future dropped away. I forgot who and what I was, my name, manhood, animalhood, all that could be called mine. It was as if I had been born that instant, brand new, mindless, innocent of all memories. There existed only the Now, that present moment and what was clearly given in it . . . . It took me no time at all to notice that . . . this hole where a head should have been, was no ordinary vacancy, no mere nothing. On the contrary, it was very much occupied. It was a vast emptiness vastly filled, a room that found room for everything—room for grass, trees, shadowy distant hills, and far above them snowpeaks like a row of angular clouds riding the blue sky. I had lost a head and gained a world.

HASEGAWA, SEIKAN. THE CAVE OF POISON GRASS. Notes, index, 182pp. GOP75, 3.95p.
This is a profound exposition of the **Hannya-shin-gyo Sutra**, a one page summary of the **Mahaprajnaparamita Sutra** which is widely known in Japan. All Buddhists, whatever their sect, chant this sutra on every religious occasion. The volume begins with a translation of the sutra accompanied by a transliteration of the Chinese as it is chanted in Japan. Then Hasegawa analyzes virtually every word and concept at great length and relates the material to many other Zen source texts and other aspects of Buddhist philosophy. The author is a young Rinzai Zen monk who has founded a Buddhist temple near Washington, D.C.

HASEGAWA, SEIKAN. ESSAYS ON MARRIAGE. 2.95p.
See the Women and Men section.

HEARN, LAFCADIO. **THE BUDDHIST WRITINGS OF LAFCADIO HEARN. 330pp. REr77, 8.95c.**
In his introduction, Kenneth Rexroth describes this volume as *a definitive collection of Hearn's Buddhist writings, from his exploratory days as a New Orleans journalist to his last years in Tokyo. From these essays and stories emerges a sensitive and durable vision of how Buddhism was and still is lived in Japan—the ancient Buddhist traditions, rituals, myths, and stories that are still preserved, and their effects upon the beliefs and daily life of ordinary Japanese people.*

HEARN, LAFCADIO. **GLEANINGS IN BUDDHA-FIELDS: STUDIES OF HAND AND SOUL IN THE FAR EAST. Notes, 302pp. Tut1897, 2.75p.**
Hearn, a Westerner who spent his last years in Japan, was an early interpreter of things Japanese to the West. His keen intellect and poetic imagination helped him to penetrate to the very essence of Japanese culture and thought. This volume contains a number of essays on the Buddhist theory of the nature of pleasure and the Japanese people's enjoyment of the wonders of the natural world.

HEARN, LAFCADIO. **JAPAN: AN INTERPRETATION. Notes, bibliography, index, 498pp. Tut59, 3.75p.**
A penetrating interpretation of Japanese culture and history, with chapters on Shintoism, the home and family, Buddhism, and modern perils (i.e. the Jesuits, industrialism, and education).

HEARN, LAFCADIO. **KOKORO: HINTS AND ECHOES OF JAPANESE INNER LIFE. Notes, 388pp. Tut1896, 3.95p.**
The fifteen stories and essays in this volume discuss the inner rather than the outer life of Japan. For this reason they have been grouped under the title *kokoro* (heart). The word also signifies mind, in the emotional sense; spirit; courage; resolve; sentiment; affection; and inner meaning—the same ideas as the English expression, *the heart of things.*

■ HERRIGEL, EUGENE. **THE METHOD OF ZEN. 124pp. RaH60/ RKP, 1.95p.**
Herrigel was a German professor who taught philosophy at the University of Tokyo between the Wars. In endeavoring to become a Zen mystic he subjected himself to the rigorous discipline of training with a Zen master for six years. An account of this experience is given in his now classic book, **Zen in the Art of Archery.** He died in 1955. Among his papers were found voluminous notes on various aspects of Zen. They were selected and edited in the form of short, pointed essays and collected here. This is an excellent primer on Zen culture and training. Recommended as an excellent introduction to *the method of Zen.*

■ HERRIGEL, EUGENE. **ZEN IN THE ART OF ARCHERY. 109pp. RaH53, 1.95p.**
In the case of archery, the hitter and the hit are no longer two opposing objects, but are one reality. The archer ceases to be conscious of himself as the one who is engaged in hitting the bull's eye which confronts him. The state of unconscious is realized only when, completely empty and rid of the self, he becomes one with the perfecting of his technical skill. This is a wonderful book which illumines what very often must seem to be a strange and somewhat unapproachable Eastern experience. Introduction by D.T. Suzuki.

HERRIGEL, GUSTIE. **ZEN IN THE ART OF FLOWER ARRANGEMENT. 138pp. RKP58, 3.95p.**
This is a charming book which reveals the significance and symbolism underlying flower arrangement. Mrs. Herrigel studied under a contemporary master of the art, Bokuyo Takeda. The book is illustrated throughout. Introduction by D.T. Suzuki.

HILLIER, J.R. **JAPANESE COLOUR PRINTS. Introduction, 9¼"x 12¼", 72pp. Dut71, 7.95c.**
Forty-eight color plates, reproduced in color and size as nearly as possible to the originals. The chronological sequence of the reproductions emphasizes the changes in draftsmanship and design and the emergence of a succession of great masters, from Moronobu in the late seventeenth century to Hokusai and Hiroshige in the nineteenth.

HILLIER, J.R. **JAPANESE DRAWINGS. Notes on the artists, bibliography, 8½"x9¼", 139pp. LBC65, 5.95p.**
Japanese drawings are usually impromptu, unelaborated pieces drawn freely from nature. The Japanese masters executed their drawings for the sheer joy of exhibiting brushwork—they drew flower, bird, landscape, and *genre* scenes without any illustrative intent other than to provide an occasion for aesthetic design. In their drawings the viewer can enjoy the interplay of the strong, circumscribing line contrasted against the flat silhouettes of the wash. This collection of Japanese drawings from the seventeenth to the nineteenth century presents a wide selection of outstanding works. Ninety plates are included, more than half in color. An introduction discusses Japanese drawings.

HIRAI, TOMIO. **ZEN AND THE MIND—SCIENTIFIC APPROACH TO ZEN PRACTICE. Illustrations, index, 144pp. Jap78, 9.95c.**
For about twenty years Dr. Hirai and his colleagues have been studying the psychological and physiological aspects of the mental and physical states that occur during Zen meditation. Their work has shown that Zen influences the body as well as the mind, regulating the whole organism of the body both internally and externally. This book contains a full exploration of their findings.

HIRAI, TOMIO. **ZEN MEDITATION THERAPY. 3.50p.**
See the Meditation section.

HISAMATSU, SHIN'ICHI. **ZEN AND THE FINE ARTS. Biographies, notes, index, 9"x11½", 400pp. Kod71, 32.50c.**
Dr. Hisamatsu, former Professor of Religion and Buddhism at Kyoto University, is one of the foremost scholars of Zen and the fine arts in Japan. Here he presents plates of 276 art objects which represent the creative essence of Zen expression and are drawn from the fields of painting, calligraphy, architecture and gardens, Noh drama, and tea ceremony utensils and ceramics. Dr. Hisamatsu also discusses Zen aesthetics, Zen Buddhist philosophy, and Zen fine arts. The book is exquisitely produced.

HOFFMAN, YOEL, tr. **EVERY END EXPOSED. 127pp. Aut77, 7.95c/ 3.95p.**
This is a companion volume to Hoffman's **The Sound of the One Hand.** It consists of a translation of the **Kidogoroku,** a collection of 100 *koans* selected from various older sources by the Chinese Master Kido Chigu who lived during the Sung Dynasty (960-1269). In Japan these *koans* are part of the teaching reserved for an advanced stage of practice. This edition contains Master Kido's comment on the *koan,* Hakuin's answer or substitute phrase, and a *plain saying.* Dr. Hoffman also adds his own short notes and comments.

HOFFMAN, YOEL, tr. **RADICAL ZEN: THE SAYINGS OF JOSHU. Brief introduction, 160pp. Aut78, 5.95p.**
Here, translated into English for the first time, are 458 aphorisms and *koans* from **The Sayings of Joshu,** one of the oustanding Zen texts of T'ang China.

HOFFMAN, YOEL, tr. **THE SOUND OF THE ONE HAND: 281 ZEN KOANS WITH ANSWERS. Bibliography, 323pp. H&R75, 4.95p/ 2.95p.**
The author of the original Japanese version of this book (published in 1913) considered contemporary Zen masters and most of their followers to be fakes and he hoped to reveal their *true face* through this account. The answers given here seem to fit, and the translator provides a long introduction and extensive commentary. It is a strange book, but one which may be of interest to those who seek a deeper understanding of Zen and of *koans* in particular.

HOLMES, STEWART and CHIMYO HORIOKA. **ZEN ART FOR MEDITATION. 115pp. Tut73, 3.50p.**
Reproduced here are thirty-one *landscapes of the soul* created by the great masters of ink painting in China and Japan. For the artists who painted them, they represented acts of intense contemplation, attempts to comprehend the essential nature of the universe and to penetrate to the very core of individual existence. The commentaries and the translated *haiku* accompanying the paintings are designed to work at the nonverbal level, stimulating readers to similar *transactions with the universe.* The plates are arranged by subject, with two plates illustrating each perception.

HOOVER, THOMAS. **ZEN CULTURE. Notes, bibliography, index, 262pp. RaH77/RKP, 3.95p.**
This is a simply written, revealing study of Zen which begins with an explanation of how Zen developed in Japan and the roles it played in

different periods of Japanese history. The bulk of the book is a discussion of how Zen has influenced Japanese art, architecture, literature, sports, ceramics, and theater. Photographs and plates are incorporated into the text.

HORI, ICHIRO. **FOLK RELIGION IN JAPAN. Glossary, bibliography, index, 278pp. UCh68, 4.25p.**
An examination of the organic relationship between the Japanese social structure—the family and kinship system, village and community organizations—and *folk religion* as practiced by the majority of the Japanese populace. Professor Hori discusses the Pure Land Buddhist practice called *nembutsu* and the magical custom of reciting the holy name of Amitabha. The significance of sacred mountains as the focus of beliefs in the other world, Japanese shamanism, and the survival of shamanistic tendencies in the contemporary *new religions* are also studied.

HORI, ICHIRO, ed. **JAPANESE RELIGION. Notes, 272pp. Kod72, 10.00c.**
A dry study of the religions of contemporary Japan prepared by the Japanese Agency for Cultural Affairs. Part I consists of interpretative descriptions of Shinto, Buddhism, Christianity, and *new religions.* Part II focuses on the present situation of Japan's religious organizations. Part III presents related statistical data.

HUA, HSUAN. **PURE LAND AND CH'AN DHARMA TALKS. 70pp. SAB74, 3.00p.**
A collection of discourses on Zen practice given at an extended retreat.

HUBER, JACK. **THROUGH AN EASTERN WINDOW. 121pp. SMP65, 2.95p.**
A beautifully written, very personal account of the author's experience in a Zen monastery in Japan. *Probably one of the best efforts of an American to convey to Westerners what Zen discipline is all about.*—Thomas Merton.

HUMPHREYS, CHRISTMAS. **WALK ON! 101pp. TPH47/BuS, 2.75p.**
An inspiring and yet practical book which contains hints on meditation and suggestions for understanding some of the difficulties which face the aspirant. Christmas Humphreys was the founder of the Buddhist Society of England and has been one of the most influential and prolific Western interpreters of the East.

HUMPHREYS, CHRISTMAS. **WESTERN APPROACH TO ZEN. Glossary, notes, 212pp. TPH71/A&U, 5.95c.**
A clear, detailed analysis—perfected over years of practical teaching. Advocates deep study of the Buddha's teaching, some meditation allied to character building, and then and only then, a course of mind control and development.

HUMPHREYS, CHRISTMAS. **ZEN—A WAY OF LIFE. Glossary, bibliography, 199pp. LBC62, 2.65p.**
An excellent basic account of the nature of Zen, its philosophy, and the ultimate goal of its teaching. Humphreys includes an extensive treatment of the doctrine of karma and of concentration and meditation, as well as quotations from the scriptures. The book ends with a practical system of training for the Zen way of life.

HUMPHREYS, CHRISTMAS. **ZEN BUDDHISM. 175pp. McM67, 1.95p.**
Humphreys has attempted to transfer the life of Zen to the reader by *leading the...mind to the precipice which lies between the highest thought and the humblest truth and then, by a jerk or joke, tries to push it over.* Liberal use of quotations as well as an extensive bibliography.

HUMPHREYS, CHRISTMAS. **ZEN COMES WEST: ZEN BUDDHISM IN WESTERN SOCIETY. Bibliography, index, 218pp. Cur77, 9.35c.**
Humphreys has devoted his life to teaching Zen to Westerners. In this volume he makes many of his insights and experiences available for the first time. The bulk of the book is devoted to a series of topically arranged letters to students in his Zen class, discussing themes, problems, and aspects of Zen teaching.

ISHIDA, MOSAKU. **JAPANESE BUDDHIST PRINTS. Glossary, 10½"x 13½", 195pp. Kod64, 70.00c.**
This is a magnificent book. The endpapers are of handmade rice paper and there are thirty-two handtipped color plates, each exquisitely reproduced. If these were bought individually they would cost far more than the book costs! There are also 162 gravure plates. The broad

selection of prints dates from the twelfth century to the sixteenth. Each of the color plates is fully discussed and there is also an excellent general discussion of the art of the Japanese woodblock print.

IWAMOTO, KAORU. **GO FOR BEGINNERS. 148pp. RaH72, 2.45p.**
A good introductory book which includes explanations of the rules, illustrations of the simplest techniques of good play and of some of the more difficult problems the player will encounter. Appendices include a concise list of rules, a glossary, and a list of American and international Go organizations. This is generally considered the best beginning Go book available in English. See the review of Smith's book for further explanation of the game of Go.

JAPAN TIMES. **KYOTO. Maps, 7½"x10½", 112pp. Jap71, 10.50c.**
A collection of photographs, many in color, with a brief accompanying text, showing all aspects of the city of Kyoto.

JAPAN TIMES. **NARA. 7½"x10½", 112pp. Jap72, 10.50c.**
The city of Nara is a veritable treasure chest of temples and Buddhist images. This picture book contains photographs of Nara, many in color, with a brief accompanying text and a short history of Nara Buddhist culture.

JAPANESE BUDDHIST RITUAL (A RECORDING). 8.95.
This 33 1/3 rpm record includes morning prayers chanted by a priest accompanied on a gong and drum, typical hymns sung by a congregation, and very brief examples of various gongs used in temple services. The chanting is rapid and repetitious. The hymns are slow and melancholy, and the voices have a nasal quality. Extensive notes on Buddhism; brief notes on the recording.

Japanese Language

Experts believe that the Japanese language is genetically related to Korean; it became separated from Korean more than 5,000 years ago. There is no evidence that the Japanese had their own script before they adopted the *kanji* (Chinese characters) early in the Christian era. During the several centuries after the adoption of the *kanji*, the Japanese apparently used classical written Chinese as their formal written language. As they became accustomed to the characters, however, they tried to write Japanese with them, and in the proces the *on* and *kun* of every *kanji* became established. Each *kanji* represents a Chinese word, which has its own sound and meaning. The *on* is a Japanese imitation of the Chinese sound. The *kun* is an indigenous Japanese word with a meaning similar to that of the Chinese; it is this reading that the Japanese are accustomed to give the *kanji*. Around the ninth century a Japanese cursive script began to be used, so that the symbols eventually retained little or no vestige of their original shape.

DUNN, C.J. and S. YANADA. **TEACH YOURSELF JAPANESE. Glossary, index, 310pp. McK58, 3.95p.**
A practical handbook for beginners organized into a series of lessons. Romanized spellings are used throughout, and the complexities of the language are introduced gradually.

NELSON, ANDREW. **MODERN READER'S JAPANESE-ENGLISH CHARACTER DICTIONARY. 6¼"x9¼", 1,109pp. Tut62, 19.50c.**
Beautifully produced, and universally considered the most authoritative dictionary available.

O'NEIL, P.G. **ESSENTIAL KANJI. 325pp. Wea73, 7.95c.**
A carefully integrated course for learning to read and write the 2,000 basic Japanese characters. The material is well organized and devised for either home or classroom use. The characters are shown in both brush and pen calligraphy, with the order of strokes clearly indicated for each character.

PYE, MICHAEL. **THE STUDY OF KANJI. Annotated bibliography, indices, 316pp. Hok71, 22.00c.**
This is a good modern text. The *kanji* are classified according to frequency of use rather than by the traditional arrangement of the

number of strokes needed to write them. Pye divides his exposition into the following main sections: *The Mnemonic of Shape and Sound; Non-aligned Kanji; Important Distinctions of Form; Alternative Forms of Kanji; Limited Readings;* and *Notes on Kun Readings.* A variety of other information on *kanji* is also included.

ROSE-INNES, ARTHUR. **BEGINNER'S DICTIONARY OF CHINESE-JAPANESE CHARACTERS. 557pp. Dov59, 6.50p.**
This is the most authoritative book available. It contains the 5,000 most important Japanese characters, arranged by stroke according to the standard system of 214 radicals. Under each character are printed the major compounds utilizing it, each with a pronunciation guide and English translation. A wide range of secondary aids is also included.

SAKADE, FLORENCE. **A GUIDE TO READING AND WRITING JAPANESE. 312pp. Tut61, 5.95c.**
An up to date, practical handbook with the 1,850 most essential characters, phonetic writing, writing charts, definitions, vocabulary, reading and writing exercises, and an index.

VACCARI, ORESTE. **STANDARD KANJI. 502pp. UTk77, 19.50c.**
This book contains all the characters prescribed by the Ministry of Education of Japan for use in magazines and newspapers. The *kanji* have been arranged in the order of their number of strokes; each is given in brush style and then repeated in printed style in some of its most common compound character words. The symbolic characters are given on the left side of each page; on the right are their Japanese transliteration, Chinese pronunciation, and English translations of both the single *kanji* and compound character words. This is an excellent work by one of the most noted contemporary Japanese linguistic scholars.

————END OF JAPANESE LANGUAGE SUBSECTION————

Japanese Literature

Both in quantity and quality, Japanese literature ranks as one of the major literatures of the world, comparable in age, richness, and bulk to English literature, though the course of development has been quite dissimilar. The surviving works extend from the seventh century AD to the present; during all of this time there was never a dark age, devoid of literary production. Not only do poetry, the novel, and the drama have long histories in Japan, but some literary *genres* not so highly esteemed in other countries—including diaries, travel accounts, and books of random thoughts—are also prominent. A considerable body of writing by Japanese in the Chinese classical language testifies to the Japanese literary indebtedness to China. The pure Japanese language, untainted and unfertilized by Chinese influence, contained remarkably few words of an abstract nature; but if the Japanese language was lacking in the vocabulary appropriate to a Confucian essay, it could express almost infinite shadings of emotional content. For the most part Japanese writers, far from feeling dissatisfied with the limitations of expression imposed by their language, were convinced that virtuoso perfection in phrasing and an acute refinement of sentiment were more important to poetry than the voicing of intellectually satisfying concepts. Japanese literature absorbed much direct influence from China, but the characteristic literary works are strikingly dissimilar. The tradition of feminine writing, especially of such introspective works as diaries, gave a coloring to Japanese prose quite unlike the more objective, masculine Chinese writings. Although the Japanese have been criticized for their imitations of Chinese examples, the Japanese novel in fact antedates any Chinese novels by centuries; and the theater developed quite independently. Because the Chinese and Japanese languages are unrelated the poetry naturally took different forms, although Chinese poetic examples and literary theories were often in the minds of the Japanese poets.

AKUTAGAWA, RYUNOSUKE. **TU TZE-CHUN. Boxed, 8¼"x8", Kod65, 7.50c.**
No one knows how long ago the legend of Tu Tze-chun came to Japan from China. This 1920 retelling is based on a ninth century Chinese model, though the classic tale has been considerably altered in Akutagawa's rendition. It is the story of a boy who squanders fortunes, spoils a chance to gain untold power, and eventually finds immortality by being very human. The book is beautifully produced and is illustrated with a series of unusual and exquisitely conceived woodblock prints by Matsubara Naoko.

ANDREWS, JAMES, tr. **FULL MOON IS RISING. Illustrations, preface, 94pp. BrP76, 7.50c.**
A selection of translations of Basho's travel sketches and travel *haiku.* Andrews retains the Japanese *haiku* five-seven-five form in his translations, and in the process produces stiff, unnatural renderings.

ASTON, W.G. **A HISTORY OF JAPANESE LITERATURE. Bibliography, index, 426pp. Tut1899, 4.25p.**
This is a classic work and remains one of the most readable books on the subject. Aston pioneered in the translation of Japanese literature into English and made many original contributions to Japanese studies. The periods he reviews range from the ancient days to the Meiji Restoration of 1868 when all aspects of Japanese life were being transformed.

ASTON, W.G., tr. **NIHONGI. Introduction, notes, 465pp. Tut72, 5.75p.**
This volume, often called the **Nihonshoki,** is generally considered one of the most important Japanese histories. It provides a vivid picture of a nation in formation and we see the growth of national awareness following the assimilation of Buddhism and the general Chinese and Indian influence on Japanese culture. Ritual, myth, and superstition are mingled in this account which was written down in the eighth century.

BASHO. **THE NARROW ROAD TO THE DEEP NORTH AND OTHER TRAVEL SKETCHES. Illustrations, 167pp. Vik66, 1.95p.**
This volume contains Nobuyuki Yuasa's translation of five travel sketches written, in later life, by Matsuo Basho (1644-94), one of the greatest *haiku* poets. His journeys through Japan are recorded in linked prose and verse, and the title piece of these sketches is a bid by the poet to discover a vision of eternity in nature and the ephemeral world around him. The translator also supplies an excellent, long introduction.

BENNETT, JEAN, ed. **JAPANESE LOVE POEMS. Index, 114pp. Dou76, 6.95c.**
A lovely selection of nearly 200 love poems from ancient and modern Japanese poets. The poems have been well chosen and the translations are uniformly good. The accompanying illustrations are not up to the class of the poetry—but this is a small complaint.

BLYTH, R.H., tr. **HAIKU. Jap nd, 19.95c/each.**
This exquisite set of books is cherished by all who love Japanese poetry. All of the translations are Blyth's own and he also includes the Japanese text, transliteration, and commentary. Volume I contains an introductory essay, discussions of the spiritual origins of *haiku* and its Zen-relatedness, an essay on *haiku* and poetry, an analysis of the four great *haiku* poets, and an exposition of the technique of *haiku*. Volumes II **(Spring)**, III **(Summer-Autumn)**, and IV **(Autumn-Winter)** contain translations of *haiku* evocative of each season, divided into the following sections: *The Season, Sky and Elements, Fields and Mountains, Gods and Buddhas, Human Affairs, Birds and Beasts,* and *Trees and Flowers.* Each volume is over 400 pages long and is illustrated.

BLYTH, R.H. **A HISTORY OF HAIKU. Hok64, 15.95c/each.**
This is the best full length history available. Volume I (427pp.) covers the period from the beginning up to Issa and Volume II (375pp.) continues up to the present. Blyth has chosen the best *haiku* of as many writers as possible, enabling the reader to learn by considering the failure and near hits rather than just the successes. The text includes the Japanese characters, transliteration, translation, and commentary. Brief biographical material is included on each poet. *Haiku* are poems of seventeen syllables, usually about nature.

BLYTH, R.H., tr. **JAPANESE LIFE AND CHARACTER IN SENRYU. Introduction, plates, index, 630pp. Hok60, 34.50c.**
Senryu is a form of Japanese poetry which uniquely expresses the comic spirit associated with the contradictory and paradoxical philosophy of Zen Buddhism. Zen and *senryu* matured together and all of the early *senryu* poets have, to a certain degree, the feeling of Zen. Blyth begins this anthology with a chronological survey of the great *senryu* poets. The next section is devoted to a topically arranged collection of *senryu.* Among the topics that Blyth chooses are psychology, women, domestic and daily life, and scenes of this fleeting world. A final section is devoted to *senryu* for each of the seasons. Like *haiku, senryu* are very brief and Blyth provides comments on each one, explaining its meaning and frequently providing information about the period in which it was written. The Japanese text and transliteration are also included.

BLYTH, R.H. **ZEN IN ENGLISH LITERATURE AND ORIENTAL CLASSICS. Notes, index, 457pp. Hok42, 18.50c.**
In this volume Blyth brilliantly demonstrates how the true spirit of Zen infuses the great literature of both the East and the West. In presenting his thesis that *all is good in European literature and culture is simply and solely in accordance with the Spirit of Zen,* Blyth quotes extensively from Japanese and Chinese classics and from English, German, French, Italian, and Spanish works.

BUCHANAN, DANIEL. **ONE HUNDRED FAMOUS HAIKU. 120pp. Jap73, 4.50p.**
Selections from Basho and Issa to the present, each in its original version, translated, and transliterated. Notes on the poets are included.

CHIBA, REIKO. **PAINTED FANS OF JAPAN: FIFTEEN NOH DRAMA MASTERPIECES. Introduction, bibliography, boxed, 41pp. Tut 62, 7.95c.**
A fan shaped book which contains adequate color reproductions of some of the exquisite paintings found on fans used in the traditional Japanese Noh drama. A poem accompanies each fan.

DORSON, RICHARD. **FOLK LEGENDS OF JAPAN. 3.25p.**
See the Fairy Tales section.

HARRIS, H. JAY, tr. **THE TALES OF ISE. Chronology, notes, annotated bibliography, 247pp. Tut72, 6.00c.**
Ise-monogatari (Tales of Ise), an anonymous tenth century collection of Japanese poems and prose, is revered as one of the great literary classics of Japan. A product of court life, the work gives a revealing picture of the romantic affairs, intrigues, and social standards of aristocratic society in ancient Japan. Consisting of 125 episodes, the work follows the life of a nameless hero who embodies the social ideals of the era. Each episode contains a story plus poetry in the *uta* form (five lines totaling thirty-one syllables). The text is accompanied by an introduction, explanations of the cultural, literary, and historical material relevant to each episode, and authentic woodblock prints from the first printed edition of **Ise** in 1608.

HENDERSON, HAROLD. **HAIKU IN ENGLISH. 75pp. Tut67, 2.50p.**
A simple, illustrated account in which Henderson attempts to clarify the following questions: (1) What is a Japanese *haiku*?; (2) What is, or should be, a *haiku* in English?; (3) What should an English speaking person do in order to write *haiku* in English? In dealing with these points he quotes the works of Japanese and American *haiku* writers and draws from the comments of recognized critics. An appendix contains suggestions on reading *haiku*.

HENDERSON, HAROLD, tr. **AN INTRODUCTION TO HAIKU. 200pp. Dou58, 2.50p.**
An anthology of poems and poets from Basho to Shiki. Henderson also supplies biographical information and a fair amount of commentary.

HIBBETT, HOWARD. **THE FLOATING WORLD IN JAPANESE FICTION. Twenty-three double page illustrations, notes, index, 245pp. Tut59, 3.95p.**
Among the most delightful *genres* of Japanese literature is that of the *ukiyo-zoshi,* or *tales of the floating world.* These gay stories and novels reflect the milieu of the familiar *ukiyo-e* prints, to which they offer the best possible introduction. In them we find an unsurpassed view of the manners and customs, arts and affectations, of the multifarious city life of Tokugawa Japan. That view is focused on the search for pleasure that was the hallmark of the age. This book contains a full discussion of the genre along with selected translations.

HONDA, H.H., tr. **THE KOKIN WAKA-SHU. Introduction, index, 300pp. Hok70, 11.25c.**
A tenth century anthology, compiled by imperial decree and edited by four poets. The poems reflect the delicacy of the times and the selections include seasonal songs, parting songs, love songs, and songs of sorrow.

HONDA, H.H., tr. **THE MANYOSHU. Brief introduction, index, 9"x12", 360pp. Hok67, 39.50c.**
A complete translation of the *tanka* compiled in the ninth century by imperial decree. The translation has been acclaimed as a superb work and **The Manyoshu** is generally considered one of Japan's most important poetry anthologies.

HONDA, H.H., tr. **ONE HUNDRED POEMS FROM ONE HUNDRED POETS. 110pp. Hok56, 4.95c.**
A translation of the Ogura Hyaku-nin-isshiu, a thirteenth century anthology of four-line poems. The Japanese text and transliteration are included.

HONDA, H.H., tr. **THE SANKA SHU (THE MOUNTAIN HERMITAGE). Brief introduction, 288pp. Hok71, 12.50c.**
Translations of the poems and songs of Saigyo, a twelfth century noble who renounced the world at the age of twenty-three. The poems, like so much of Japanese poetry, evoke the seasons.

HONDA, H.H., tr. **THE SHIN KOKINSHU. Brief introduction, index, 568pp. Hok70, 23.50c.**
This is a translation of the eighth and last anthology compiled by imperial command in the early thirteenth century. The songs and poems follow the seasons and the anthology also includes love songs, songs of travel, and miscellaneous songs.

HONDA, H.H., tr. **STRAY LEAVES FROM THE MANYOSHU. 102pp. Hok65, 4.50c.**
Translations of 200 poems from **The Manyoshu.**

INOUE, YASUSHI. **THE ROOF TILE OF TEMPYO. Introduction, 157pp. UTk75, 8.95c.**
This book is a novelist's view of an era long ago when thousands of Japanese embarked on perilous voyages to the Asian mainland, each with the hope of returning as a transmitter of an aspect of the dazzling culture of the Chinese T'ang Empire. The story focuses on the lives of four monks, whose dedication to learning symbolizes that of countless others who contributed to the formation of a national culture imbued heavily with influences of a new religion, Buddhism.

ISAACSON, HAROLD, tr. **PEONIES KANA: HAIKU BY THE UPASAKA SHIKI. Glossary, indices, 115pp. TAB72, 3.65p.**
Shiki (1867-1902) was the last great *haiku* master. Professor Isaacson feels that *haiku* has generally been prettified in translation, losing much

of the vigor and power of the original. In this book he has chosen over 300 poems from Shiki's many books, and arranged them by the seasons of the year to which they relate. He has tried to present the *haiku* as accurately as possible, and to do this he has transferred into the English the *haiku* articles left out by previous translators. These are the words *ya, kana,* and *keri,* which have no precise meaning in Japanese but which are essential to the form. A long biographical introduction is also included.

KATO, GENCHI and HIKOSHIRO HOSHINO, trs. **KOGOSHUI, GLEAN-INGS FROM ANCIENT STORIES. Introduction, 130pp. Cur26, 9.00c.**
This is a classic work on the origins, tenets, rites, customs, and practices of the Shinto religion, originally prepared in 807. Half the volume is devoted to a selected bibliography and critical notes.

■ *KEENE, DONALD, ed.* **ANTHOLOGY OF JAPANESE LITERA-TURE. Bibliography, 444pp. Grv55, 5.95p.**
A chronologically organized selection covering the period from the earliest times to the mid-nineteenth century. Selections are included from all the major works and Keene has made an excellent series of choices. This is as good a way as any to savor the full range of Japanese literature and see which areas you would like to delve more deeply into.

KEENE, DONALD, ed. **THE MANYOSHU. Lengthy introduction by Keene, chronology, biographical notes, indices, 444pp. Col69, 7.85p.**
The Manyoshu, compiled during the late Nara period (the latter half of the eighth century), is both the oldest and the greatest of Japanese anthologies. Included are more than 4,000 poems which reflect the Japanese life and civilization of the seventh and eighth centuries. This edition, containing 1,000 poems, has been prepared by a specially selected Japanese committee. The poets represent every level of society and a variety of verse forms are utilized.

KITAGAWA, HIROSHI and BRUCE TSUCHIDA, trs. **THE TALE OF THE HEIKE. Introduction, two volumes, index, 868pp. UTk75, 16.80p/set.**
This epic story by an unknown author depicts the rise and fall of the Heike clan and its defeat at the hands of the powerful Genji clan. It is set in the twilight years of the Heian period in the last half of the twelfth century, a time of far reaching change in Japan when the Fujiwara hegemony was waning and court factions struggled to establish claims and protect themselves through alliances with provincial military clans. The clans eventually overthrew the nobles and seized power. The Heike and the Genji were two of the strongest clans. The theme of *shoja hissui* (those who flourish are destined to fall) pervades the **Heike.**

LEWIS, RICHARD, ed. **IN A SPRING GARDEN. 1.75p.**
See the Children's Books section.

MINER, EARL. **AN INTRODUCTION TO JAPANESE COURT PO-ETRY. Glossary, index, 188pp. SUP68, 2.95p.**
The poetry written by the Japanese imperial court between 550 and 1350 is one of the great literatures of the world. The present volume is at once a condensation, reorganization, and extension (to 1500) of **Japanese Court Poetry** by the author and Robert H. Brower, the standard treatment of the subject in English. The book's five central chapters are devoted to the major court poets and their work; other chapters deal with the forms, assumptions, and themes of court poetry. Miner's emphasis is on the human and cultural values of this poetic tradition. Over 150 poems are included in both transliteration and translation. Many are joint efforts with Professor Brower; others are new translations by Miner.

MISHIMA, YUKIO. **THE WAY OF THE SAMURAI. Illustrations, 175pp. H&R77, 10.00c.**
The first English translation of Mishima's own adaptation and interpretation of **Hagakure,** the fascinating collection illustrating the way of the samurai—the traditional code of life for the Japanese. In his commentary, Mishima stresses the application of **Hagakure** to modern life and shows how it has influenced his own conduct and career.

MITFORD, A.B. **TALES OF OLD JAPAN. Notes, 429pp. Tut1871, 4.25p.**
A noted anthology of Japanese literature, including several tales of

historical origin; a collection of fairy tales and stories of superstition; fantasy tales of bewitched animals; an analysis of three Japanese sermons written by a priest belonging to the *Shingaku* sect—a group professing to combine all that is excellent in the Buddhist, Confucian, and Shinto teachings; a detailed, eyewitness account of *seppuku* (*hara-kiri*); and analyses of many traditional Japanese customs and cere-monies. Illustrated with thirty-one original Japanese woodblock prints.

MORRIS, IVAN, tr. **THE PILLOW BOOK OF SEI SHONAGON. Introduction, illustrations, descriptive appendices, notes, bibliog-raphy, 411pp. Vik67, 3.95p.**
Sei Shonagon was a court lady in tenth century Japan at the height of the Heian culture. In her **Pillow Book** she noted down all the things that attract, displease, or interest her in daily life. She was an enthusiast for good manners and good taste. This book is by far our most detailed source of factual material on the times and it is also a work of great literary beauty.

MARASAKI, LADY. **THE TALE OF GENJI. Introduction, 1,105pp. RaH76, 25.00c/10.00p.**
This is an excellent new translation of what is universally considered the finest Japanese novel. The translation is by Edward Seidensticker and it is complete. We read it as soon as it came out and were completely entertained by the narrative. The story is a very long romance, running to fifty-four chapters and describing the court life of Heian Japan, from the tenth century into the eleventh. It was probably written during the first quarter of the eleventh century and is generally considered the work of a single hand, a court lady. A great deal of lyric poetry is interspersed throughout the narrative. Virtually every Japanese artist of note has illustrated the **Genji** and the translator chose a long series of woodcuts from a seventeenth century edition of the work to illustrate his edition (almost every second page is illustrated). We are delighted with this edition and recommend it to all who love literature and would like to get a feeling for medieval Japanese court life.

MURASAKI, LADY. **THE TALE OF GENJI. Introduction, 1,135pp. RaH35, 7.95c.**
Until recently this translation by Arthur Waley was the only generally available English edition of this classic Japanese novel. Waley has made a smooth, skillful translation which reads extremely well. The major criticism seems to be that he has omitted certain important sections and included others which are of dubious origin.

MURASAKI, LADY. **GENJI MONOGATARI. Introduction, 227pp. Tut74, 3.75p.**
An abridged translation by Kencho Suematsu, the native Japanese who introduced the novel to the West almost a century ago. It is such a fine story that we recommend reading the most complete edition avail-able—Seidensticker's. For those who do not want such a lengthy version, this one is certainly adequate and the translation reads well.

PHILIPPI, DONALD, tr. **THIS WINE OF PEACE, THIS WINE OF LAUGHTER: A COMPLETE ANTHOLOGY OF JAPAN'S EARLI-EST SONGS. Introduction, 7½"x10½", 257pp. Vik68, 12.50c.**
A complete collection of Japan's earliest poetry, antedating, for the most part, strong cultural influences from the Asian mainland. The songs are arranged by type. Twenty-six photographs by Kuzunishi Sosei help set the tone of this beautifully produced book.

PIGGOTT, JULIET. **JAPANESE FAIRY TALES. 5.80c.**
See the Fairy Tales section.

PORTER, WILLIAM, tr. **THE MISCELLANY OF A JAPANESE PRIEST. Introduction, illustrations, notes, index, 216pp. Tut14, 3.95p.**
A translation of **Tsure-zure Gusa** by Kenko Yoshida, one of the classics of Japanese literature. It is a collection of brief essays on miscellaneous subjects written by a fourteenth century Buddhist priest named Kanko—a man who lived the life of a recluse without being able entirely to forget the passions and desires of this world.

PUTZAR, EDWARD. **JAPANESE LITERATURE—AN HISTORICAL OUTLINE. Introduction, bibliography, index, 278pp. UAr73, 8.75p.**
An authoritative history of Japanese literature from the early ancient period to the end of World War II. The text is well organized, though it is, of necessity, presented in almost outline form.

REXROTH, KENNETH, tr. **ONE HUNDRED POEMS FROM THE JAPANESE. 170pp. NDP55, 1.95p.**
Excellent translations of important poems, drawn chiefly from the traditional **Manyoshu, Kokinshu,** and **Hyakunin Isshu** collections. In addition there are examples of *haiku* and later forms. A Romanized version of the poems is also reproduced along with calligraphy of the poet's name. Rexroth also supplies an introduction giving basic background on the history and nature of Japanese poetry, notes on the individual poets, and an extensive bibliography.

REXROTH, KENNETH and IKUKO ATSUMI, trs. **THE BURNING HEART: WOMEN POETS OF JAPAN. 191pp. Sea77, 4.50p.**
No other literature in the world has as many women poets as Japan. The first group of poems represented here comes from the classic period, 645-1603. All are characterized by the great compression of language in the *waka* or *tanka* style of thirty-one syllables. Next come fine examples of women *haiku* poets. A final section shows how the *haiku* tradition has been carried into the twentieth century and also includes representative selections from the contemporary free verse school. More than seventy-five poets are included and the book includes biographical notes on the individual poets, an essay on Japanese women and literature, and a table of historical periods.

SADLER, A.L., tr. **THE TEN FOOT SQUARE HUT AND TALES OF THE HEIKE. Introduction, illustrations, index, 283pp. Tut28, 3.50p.**
Translations of two thirteenth century classics, the entire **Hojoki** and selections from the **Heike Monogatari**. The first is made up of the reflections of a recluse who has retired in disgust from a world too full of violent contrasts and cataclysms. The latter is the story of the Heike clan from the days of its splendor down to its tragic end, when its leaders, utterly defeated by the Minamoto clan and scorning surrender, throw themselves into the sea and perish.

A Shirabyoshi

SAIKAKU, IHARA. **COMRADE LOVES OF THE SAMURAI. Introduction, 153pp. Tut28, 2.95p.**
Saikaku, one of the most illustrious writers of the seventeenth century, excelled in describing the life of the common people and, in satirical style, the life of the samurai, who were falling from positions of grace before the money power of the merchants. The subject of money and love predominates in most of his stories. The theme of this novel is the homosexual love of samurai for samurai or of samurai for page or court boy bent on becoming samurai. To the old Japanese, such love among samurai was quite permissible and even expected. The sons of samurai families were urged to form alliances while youth lasted and often these loves matured into lifelong companionships. **Songs of the Geishas,** a verse collection unassociated with Saikaku, is appended.

SAIKAKU, IHARA. **FIVE WOMEN WHO LOVED LOVE. Long introduction, 264pp. Tut56, 3.75p.**
With love in the background, Saikaku takes five typical women of the time as his heroines and follows them in the course of their always amorous and usually illicit adventures. The five place love above all, defying the conventions of society and, when necessary, bravely meeting tragic ends imposed by a relentless moral code and their own passionate natures.

SAIKAKU, IHARA. **THE LIFE OF AN AMOROUS MAN. Introduction, 223pp. Tut63, 3.50p.**
This is Saikaku's first major work in prose. The hero is a man of wealth and Saikaku follows him from a precocious childhood to the close of his amatory career. In the process the author offers vivid character sketches of the men and women with whom his hero dallies. Translated by Kengi Hamada.

SAIKAKU, IHARA. **THE LIFE OF AN AMOROUS WOMAN AND OTHER WRITINGS. Illustrations, bibliography, index, 415pp. NDP 63, 4.75p.**
Fine translations by Ivan Morris of **Five Women Who Chose Love, The Life of an Amorous Woman, The Eternal Storehouse of Japan,** and **Reckonings that Carry Men through the World**. Morris, Chairman of the Department of East Asian Languages and Cultures at Columbia University, also provides excellent introductory material, extensive notes, and two essays on the social customs of the period.

SAIKAKU, IHARA. **THIS SCHEMING WORLD. Introduction, 128pp. Tut65, 2.95p.**
This book was published one year before Saikaku's death and represents the culmination of his perceptive genius. In structure, it is the most consolidated of his works. Most of the stories are told as incidents or episodes relating to New Year's Eve, when in those days it was the custom to balance all debits and credits for the year. At this time, the drama of life reached its climax and there were tragedies, comedies, and farces. Saikaku portrays his characters with great realism.

SAKADE, FLORENCE, ed. **JAPANESE CHILDREN'S FAVORITE STORIES. 6.25c.**
See the Fairy Tales section.

SEIDENSTICKER, EDWARD, tr. **THE GOSSAMER YEARS (KAGERO NIKKI). Long introduction, illustrations, notes, 209pp. Tut64, 3.50p.**
A translation of an autobiographical diary covering twenty-one years in the life of a mid-Heian Fujiwara noblewoman. It is the record of her unhappy marriage to her kinsman, beginning with his first love letters and ending twenty years later with their very nearly complete estrangement. The diary is in a sense her protest against the marraige system of the time and her exposition of the thesis that men are beasts.

SEKI, KEIGO, ed. **FOLKTALES OF JAPAN. 3.95p.**
See the Fairy Tales section.

STEVENS, JOHN, tr. **ONE ROBE, ONE BOWL: THE ZEN POETRY OF RYOKAN. Index, 85pp. Wea77, 3.50p.**
Ryokan was an eighteenth century Japanese hermit monk whose reclusive life and celebration of nature and the natural life bring to mind Thoreau. This book offers a representative selection of his verse in both Chinese and Japanese modes. Stevens also provides an introduction.

STEWART, HAROLD, tr. **A CHIME OF WINDBELLS. Boxed, notes, bibliography, index, 236pp. Tut69, 10.95c.**
This is Stewart's second collection of *haiku*. Here we find 365 *haiku*, with the same delicate, fragile beauty in translation as the originals written centuries ago. They are divided into the traditional four seasons, with a short section on the New Year. *Haiku* try to express what the Japanese call *mono no aware,* the *ah!-ness of things,* a feeling for natural loveliness tinged with sadness at its transience. Thirty-three *haiku* paintings help create the mood and atmosphere of the seasons. Stewart also provides an essay which discusses the spiritual and religious tradition of *haiku*. A beautifully printed and bound book.

STEWART, HAROLD, tr. **A NET OF FIREFLIES. Boxed, notes, bibliography, index, 180pp. Tut60, 11.75c.**
320 *haiku* over a span of five centuries by many of Japan's foremost

poets, as well as thirty-three color paintings—swiftly brushed sketches which provide the reader with a new dimension for understanding the elusive essence of the *haiku*. This book is quite special in its beauty and content and includes a deeply perceptive essay by the translator.

STOCK, DENNIS and DOROTHY BRITTON. **A HAIKU JOURNEY. 11½"x11½", about 125 pages. Kod74, 17.50c.**
In the seventeenth century the pilgrim poet Basho trekked to some of the most distant parts of Japan, always in wonder at his natural surroundings and the continuous cycle that propels nature in its artistry. A master of *haiku*, Basho kept a record of his impressions in prose-poetry diaries of which the most famous is **Oku no Hosomichi: The Narrow Road to the Far North.** Photographer-essayist Dennis Stock recently set out on the same path to capture in color photographic images the insights Basho expressed with words. Indeed, Basho's *haiku* and photography have much in common—a seventeen syllable *haiku* freezes the fleeting moment as does a photograph and both are candid sketches which indirectly suggest an expanse of emotion. Dorothy Britton has provided both a succinct introduction to Basho and the craft of Japanese verse, and has given us a vibrant and lyrical rendering of Basho's work which, in preserving the gentle aesthetics of the Japanese original, goes far beyond mere translation.

STRYK, LUCIEN and TAKASHI IKEMOTO, trs. **AFTERIMAGES: ZEN POEMS. 153pp. Dou72, 1.95p.**
Translations of some of the poems of Shinkichi Takahashi, the foremost Zen poet of this century, which communicate the experience of Zen and illustrate the harmony of Buddhist thought and poetic imagery. The translators provide an excellent, long, introductory essay.

STRYK, LUCIEN and TAKASHI IKEMOTO, trs. **THE CRANE'S BILL— ZEN POEMS OF CHINA AND JAPAN. 143pp. Dou73, 1.95p.**
An annotated selection grouped under general subject headings.

UEDA, MAKOTA, tr. **MODERN JAPANESE HAIKU: AN ANTHOLOGY. Introduction, 273pp. UTo76, 6.00p.**
The West has become familiar with Japanese *haiku* predominantly through the works of classical masters such as Basho and Issa. This anthology presents, in English translation, twenty *haiku* each from the work of twenty modern poets. The writers have been selected to exemplify the various trends that have dominated Japanese *haiku* in the last hundred years. The poetic translation is accompanied by the original Japanese and a word-by-word translation into English.

WALEY, ARTHUR, tr. **JAPANESE POETRY: THE "UTA". Glossary, 112pp. UHa19, 2.95p.**
The *uta* is a traditional Japanese form consisting of thirty-one syllables. Those in this collection reflect a period when poetry was just beginning to make a transition from the mystical and religious to the literary. The poems are printed in both transliterated Japanese and English and an introduction is included.

WALEY, ARTHUR, tr. **THE NO PLAYS OF JAPAN. Appendices, 270pp. Tut76, 3.95p.**
This volume contains Waley's exquisite translations of nineteen plays and summaries of sixteen more, together with a revealing introductory essay that furnishes the background for a clear understanding and a genuine appreciation of the Noh as a highly significant dramatic form. It was this volume that introduced Noh drama to the West.

WATSON, BURTON, tr. **JAPANESE LITERATURE IN CHINESE, VOLUME I: POETRY AND PROSE IN CHINESE BY JAPANESE WRITERS OF THE EARLY PERIOD. Introduction, notes, 130pp. Col75, 12.40c.**
Since very early times the Japanese literary tradition has included works written not only in Japanese but also in classical Chinese. In this volume Watson presents a selection of *kanshi* and *kambun*—Chinese poetry and prose—by Japanese writers from the mid-seventh century to 1185.

WATSON, BURTON, tr. **RYOKAN: ZEN MONK-POET OF JAPAN. 121pp. Col77, 10.00c.**
Ryokan (1758-1831), a Soto Zen monk, was a major figure in Tokugawa poetry. Though a Zen master, he never headed a temple but chose instead to live alone in a simple hut and support himself by begging. His poems are mainly a record of his daily activities—of

chores and outings to gather firewood and edible plants, of lonely snowbound winters, begging expeditions to town, meetings with friends, romps with the village children. At the same time they show us how contented, even joyous, a man can be with a minimum of material possessions, and how rich a spiritual and intellectual life he can enjoy in the midst of poverty. Eighty-three representative works are translated here and Watson also contributes an introduction.

YAMAGIWA, JOSEPH, tr. **THE OKAGAMI. Chronology, many notes, index, 488pp. Tut66, 5.25p.**
The Okagami (Great Mirror) is a Japanese historical novel written in the eleventh century. The work of an anonymous author, it covers Japanese history from 850 to 1025, when the Fujiwara family dominated Japanese government and society. Various members of the Fujiwara clan are the main characters in this novel. **The Okagami** uses the device of having two old raconteurs tell the history of their country. In lengthy appendices Yamagiwa discusses the history of Japanese narrative writing up to the rise of the historical tale and two varying texts of **The Okagami.**

YASUDA, KENNETH. **THE JAPANESE HAIKU. Notes, bibliography, 252pp. Tut57, 3.50p.**
This is a very complete study of the nature of *haiku* and its history, with illustrative examples throughout and a selection of *haiku*.

YASUDA, KENNETH, tr. **LAND OF THE REED PLAINS: ANCIENT JAPANESE LYRICS FROM THE MANYOSHU. Introduction, indices, 124pp. Tut72, 2.50p.**
Translations, with brief commentary and reproductions of the original Japanese text, of some of the most important poems included in the **Manyoshu**—the oldest and greatest anthology of Japanese poetry.

YUASA, NOBUYUKI, tr. **THE YEAR OF MY LIFE: A TRANSLATION OF ISSA'S ORAGA HARU. 142pp. UCa72, 2.45p.**
Issa is recognized together with Basho and Buson as one of the three greatest writers of Japanese *haiku*. This is a translation of **Oraga Haru,** the autobiographical record of what Issa heard, thought, and felt in the year 1819, an archetypal year that serves as a symbol for his entire life. The medium he used for his autobiography is known as *haibun*, a mixed form of *haiku* and prose, but within this form he developed an individual style distinctly his own. Yuasa also includes a lengthy introduction.

————END OF JAPANESE LITERATURE SUBSECTION————

JAPANESE TEMPLE MUSIC (A RECORDING). 6.98.
A 33 1/3 rpm record containing examples of Zen Buddhist chanting. Included are sutra chanting of the Jodo sect, a Zen priest doing solo chants, and the morning services of the Shoken sect. The chants are slow and monotonous, and are often accompanied by gongs, clappers, and conch shells. Brief descriptive notes are included.

JOHNSTON, WILLIAM. **CHRISTIAN ZEN. 109pp. H&R71, 3.50p.**
Thomas Merton and others have pleaded for the need of those of us brought up in the West to expose our Christian orientation to the insights to be found in Zen. William Johnston has responded with a workbook on the actual use of Zen meditation for precisely this purpose. The book is clear, personal, and practical. It is a personal testament that has been practiced before it was written.—Douglas Steere. This small book includes material on *koan*, the body, breathing and rhythm, and about how Zen and Christianity have met in the author and what this meeting has evoked.

JONES, EASLEY STEPHEN. **HOKUSAI'S VIEWS OF MT. FUJI. Introduction, 3¾"x5¾", 62pp. Tut65, 5.75c.**
Twenty-four full page color prints out of Hokusai's total of forty-six **Views.** The **Views,** issued between 1823 and 1830, became widely popular. Jones wrote the poems which accompany each print after a tour of duty in Japan in the 1920s. A boxed gift volume.

KAMMER, REINHARD, ed. **ZEN AND CONFUCIUS IN THE ART OF SWORDSMANSHIP: THE TENGU-GEIJUTSU-RON OF CHOZEN SHISSAI. Illustrations, notes, bibliography, 135pp. RKP78, 8.75c.**
The sword has played an important role in the Japanese consciousness since ancient times. The earliest swords, made of bronze or stone, were clearly, by their design and form, used for ritualistic purposes rather than weapons. Later swords were associated with a philosophical reinforcement, which ultimately made it one of the Zen ways. Zen

Buddhism related the correct practice of swordsmanship to exercises for attaining enlightenment and selflessness, while Confucius, emphasizing the ethical meaning, equated it to service to the state. This classic text includes a history of the development and an interpretation of Japanese swordsmanship. It describes in detail the long and intensive training, emphasizing and explaining the importance of both Zen and Confucian ideas and beliefs.

■ *KAPLEAU, PHILIP, ed.* **THE THREE PILLARS OF ZEN. Notes, index, 363pp. Bea65, 3.95p.**
One of the best introductions as well as all around books available, this rich sourcebook includes Yasutaniroshi's introductory lectures on Zen practice and his private instructions to ten Westerners studying Zen, letters and a sermon by Bassui, eight contemporary enlightenment letters, passages from Dogen, illustrations of *zazen* postures, the *oxherding* pictures, and notes on Zen vocabulary and Buddhist doctrine.

KAPLEAU, PHILIP, ed. **THE WHEEL OF DEATH: A COLLECTION OF WRITINGS FROM ZEN BUDDHIST AND OTHER SOURCES ON DEATH-REBIRTH-DYING. Glossary, 110pp. H&R71, 2.95p.**
An anthology which enables the reader to view death through the eyes of great Buddhist, Taoist, Hindu, and Western masters. The sections on rebirth and karma deal succinctly with those complex and often misunderstood doctrines.

KATO, GENCHI. **A STUDY OF SHINTO. Bibliography, index, 259pp. Cur26, 10.00c.**
A historical study of Shinto, from its origins to the present day, along with a review of its principal doctrines and practices. A scholarly presentation, which cites the major studies. Topically arranged.

KEENE, DONALD, tr. **ESSAYS IN IDLENESS: THE TSUREZURE-GUSA OF KENKO. Introduction, illustrations, bibliography, index, 255pp. Col67, 3.95p.**
Written around 1330, the **Essays**, with their timeless relevance, their homage to all the values held dear by the Japanese, and their never ending charm, hardly mirror the turbulent times in which they were born. The **Essays**, none more than a few pages in length and some consisting of but two or three sentences, treat a great variety of subjects in an anecdotal style. Kenko was a Buddhist priest and he clung to tradition, Buddhism, and the pleasures of solitude. Above all, he gives voice to the most peculiarly Japanese of all aesthetic principles: that beauty is indissolubly bound to its perishability.

KENNETT ROSHI. **HOW TO GROW A LOTUS BLOSSOM OR HOW A ZEN BUDDHIST PREPARES FOR DEATH. 296pp. ZMS77, 4.95.**
In the fall of 1975 Kennett Roshi, Abbess of Shasta Abbey and spiritual head of the Reformed Soto Zen Church, fell ill and was given only a few months to live. She entered into a period of intensive meditation, resigning all her duties and never leaving her room. For a year she continued her meditation and finally cured herself completely. In this book she describes and visually illustrates the forty-three meditations she underwent and in appendices she instructs the reader in a number of specific meditations.

KENNETT ROSHI. **THE WILD, WHITE GOOSE, VOLUME I. 219pp. ZMS77, 3.95p.**
This book is based on the diary Kennett Roshi kept during her years of study in Japan. In addition to telling the Roshi's own story, the book paints a revealing picture of life in a large Zen training monastery.

KENNETT ROSHI. **THE WILD, WHITE GOOSE, VOLUME II. 308pp. ZMS78, 4.95p.**
This is an account of Kennett Roshi's life as a junior officer in one of the largest Zen monasteries in Japan and as the abbess of her own temple in a remote mountain village. She offers glimpses of the political intrigues of a great imperial temple and rural village life in a feudal society, as well as of the events which led her to leave Japan for the U.S.

KENNETT ROSHI. **ZEN IS ETERNAL LIFE. Lengthy glossary, index, 483pp. Dha76, 5.95p.**
A practical manual. In *The Stem of the Lotus*, the first section, Kennett Roshi explains Buddhist ideas and beliefs and shows how we can put them into practice in our daily lives. The second section is devoted to a series of translations of Dogen Zenji. In the third section there is a translation of Keizen Zenji's **Denkoroku** or **Transmission of the Light**, a collection of stories showing how Zen masters have helped their disciples realize the Buddha nature within themselves. The final section contains Kennett Roshi's description of scriptures and ceremonies performed in Zen monasteries and temples.

KIKUCHI, SADAO. **HOKUSAI. 128pp. Hoi75, 3.50p.**
Hokusai produced a series of forty-six woodblock prints, which he titled *Thirty-Six Views of Mt. Fuji*. These prints, extremely famous throughout Japan, are reproduced in color in this pocketsize book. The accompanying text explores what Mt. Fuji means to the people of Japan today and what it meant in the days of Hokusai. There is also a biographical essay on Hokusai.

KIYOTA, MINORU. **SHINGON BUDDHISM—THEORY AND PRACTICE. Glossary, notes, 186pp. BBI78, 9.35p.**
A survey of the background, philosophy, and basic doctrines of Shingon Buddhism in Japan. Shingon is a tantric Buddhist sect, emphasizing the experiential awakening of the human consciousness leading to the actualization of Buddhahood within the individual. Professor Kiyota demonstrates the importance of iconography in this sect and illustrates the continuity of Shingon practice as a development of Mahayana Buddhism.

KOBAYASHI, TAKESHI. **NARA BUDDHIST ART: TODAI-JI. 7½"x 9½", 156pp. Wea75, 15.00c.**
In seventh and eighth century Japan the exuberance of a newly united nation expressed itself in the creation of works of art that still convey eloquently the vitality and religious fervor of the people who made them. The powerful motivating influence was Buddhism, and the center of artistic activity was the capital city of Nara. The most remarkable project undertaken there was the casting of the colossal bronze statue known as the Great Buddha and the construction of the great temple Todai-ji for its enshrinement. The Great Buddha and the Todai-ji form the central theme of this book, which introduces the reader to the superb creations of the Nara sculptors that survive today in the temples of the ancient capital of Japan. The text is illustrated with 208 plates, forty-eight in color.

KUBOSE, GYOMAY. **ZEN KOANS. Glossary, 274pp. Reg73, 4.95p.**
The most complete collection available in one volume. The *koans* are arranged in categories, although the editor admits that there are no real categories of *koans*; all are about finding the true self. This selection includes extensive commentary from ancient and modern sources as well as many brush paintings by Ryozo Ogura.

LANE, RICHARD. **IMAGES FROM THE FLOATING WORLD: THE JAPANESE PRINT, INCLUDING AN ILLUSTRATED DICTIONARY OF UKIYO-E. 60.00c.**
See the Sacred Art section.

LEGGETT, TREVOR, ed. **A FIRST ZEN READER. 236pp. Tut60, 3.75p.**
An anthology of texts discussing Zen theory and practice for the layman. The backbone of the book is lectures by contemporary masters, Takashina Rosen and Amakuki Sessan, who represent respectively the two main surviving transmissions of Zen—Soto and Rinzai. Also includes selections from Zen literature and a valuable *Note on the Ways* by Leggett, in which he points out how *the student keeps his Zen practice in touch with his daily life.* Beautiful illustrations help to clarify the text.

LEGGETT, TREVOR, tr. **THE TIGER'S CAVE. Illustrations, 192pp. RKP64, 5.50p.**
A selection of translations of Japanese texts which give a fascinating picture of traditional temple training and relate many stories and numerous historical incidents connected with Zen masters. The main text is an important commentary by a contemporary Soto Zen abbot on the **Heart Sutra**. Next comes a translation of the **Yasen Kanna**, a short autobiographical piece by Hakuin, the teacher, monk, and poet who revitalized Rinzai Zen in the eighteenth century. The remaining texts—two discourses by the late primate of Soto Zen, a commentary on some *koans*, and a few other short pieces—show what Zen means in Japan today.

LEGGETT, TREVOR. **ZEN AND THE WAYS. Illustrations, 271pp. ShP78, 5.95p.**
As Leggett says, *The tradition developed that Zen could be practiced in and through things like fencing, painting, flower arrangement, writing with a brush, serving tea and so on, and when so practiced they were termed Ways.* This book is made up of six parts. The first presents Zen mainly in the words of twentieth century masters and focuses on the *koan* system. The second describes the warrior Zen of the first 300 years in Japan. The third contains translations of a number of Kamakura *koans*. The fourth discusses a variety of the ways, as exemplified in the so-called *secret scrolls*, and the fifth contains excerpts from these scrolls. The final section is made up of stories of the ways in practice. All the translations are Leggett's own and the explanatory material is excellent.

LEONARD, JOHN. **EARLY JAPAN. Bibliography, index, 10"x11¾", 191pp. TLB68, 8.95c.**
This volume is part of Time-Life's **Great Ages of Man** series. It combines a lucid narrative with an abundance of color plates and black and white photographs. The text covers the period from the sixth century BC to the seventeenth century AD and the emphasis is on the origins of Japanese traditions and culture. This is an excellent introduction to Japanese cultural history.

LEVERANT, ROBERT. **ZEN IN THE ART OF PHOTOGRAPHY. 35pp. ImP69, 2.50p.**
This work goes back to the essential question of why—not just why we take photographs but why we do anything. It is a beautiful, poetic reminder that *How is only important when there is a Why.*

LINSSEN, ROBERT. **LIVING ZEN. Notes, index, 348pp. Grv58, 3.45p.**
Linssen presents Zen as *neither simply a religion nor a philosophy... but as Life itself.* The essence of Zen thought consists in suppressing mental activity; the author says that the only way to live fully in the world is to be detached from it. This work explains various Zen concepts and shows how they can be introduced into everyday living.

LU K'UAN YU (CHARLES LUK), tr. **CH'AN AND ZEN TEACHINGS, FIRST SERIES. Extensive glossary, notes, index, 255pp. HPG60, 7.35p.**
Charles Luk studied under two of the most noted Ch'an masters of his day. He now lives in Hong Kong and devotes himself to presenting *as many Chinese Buddhist texts as possible so that Buddhism can be preserved... in the West, should it be fated to disappear in the East as it seems to be.* In this series, Luk has translated the most significant literature. He clearly defines the hidden meanings and describes the practices. Luk's translations are often criticized both in terms of their accuracy and readability; however, he is doing a yeoman's job with them, making many works available to the general public that would otherwise be lost. Volume I

contains: the practice as taught by Hsu Yun, the best known modern master; translations of six representative stories (*kung-an*) of Ch'an masters—each fully explained; and a translation of the **Diamond** and **Heart Sutras** with the commentary of Ch'an Master Han Shan.

LU K'UAN YU (CHARLES LUK), tr. **CH'AN AND ZEN TEACHING, SECOND SERIES. Index, 254pp. HPG60, 7.60p.**
Contains a summary of the different methods of teaching used by the five Ch'an sects; translations and explanations of the forty *gathas* by which the essence of Ch'an was transmitted verbally from Buddha to Patriarch; and translations of the biographies of the seven founders of the five Ch'an sects, together with explanations of the *kung-ans* (or *koans*) they contain. Luk has provided an enlightening preface and a glossary.

LU K'UAN YU (CHARLES LUK), tr. **CH'AN AND ZEN TEACHING, THIRD SERIES. Preface, glossary, index, 306pp. HPG62, 9.00p.**
Translations of three important texts: **The Sutra of the Sixth Patriarch**; **The Song of Enlightenment**; and **The Sutra of Complete Enlightenment** with the Ch'an Master Han Shan's illuminating commentary. The latter, translated into English for the first time here, is the key sutra on which the meditational technique of all five Ch'an and Zen schools is still based.

LU K'UAN YU (CHARLES LUK), tr. **TRANSMISSION OF THE MIND OUTSIDE THE TEACHING. 191pp. Grv75/HPG, 2.95p.**
This is the first volume of a projected ten volume translation of the **Ku Tsun Su Yu Lu**, a compilation of Ch'an sayings and dialogues gathered by a number of disciples of each master during their stay at his monastery. The present volume contains biographies and teachings of the masters of the first, second, third, fourth, fifth, and sixth generations of the Nan Yo lineage of *Dharma descendants* of the Sixth Patriarch Hui-neng, with explanations and annotations.

MAEZUMI, HAKUYU and BERNARD GLASSMAN, eds. **THE HAZY MOON OF ENLIGHTENMENT: ON ZEN PRACTICE III. Illustrations, lengthy glossary, notes, indices, 206pp. Zen78, 4.95p.**
This volume consists of talks by Taizan Maezumi Roshi himself and by his teachers and students. *Parts one and two, "Enlightenment" and "Delusion," tell what there is to realize—what enlightenment means, what delusion means, and why Dogen Zenji says that enlightenment is delusion. The last part, "Enlightenment in Action," presents the active state of nirvana, the state of letting go and going on, as embodied in the eight awarenesses of the enlightened person.*—from the preface. This book contains an extremely clear set of teachings and we recommend it to those who are either involved or deeply interested in Zen practice.

MAEZUMI, HAKUYU and BERNARD GLASSMAN, eds. **ON ZEN PRACTICE I. 6"x9", 134pp. Zen 76, 4.00p.**
A beautifully produced collection of essays, teaching stories, discourses, and notes on *koan* study. Illustrated throughout with photographs and line drawings. The book was put together by members of the Zen Center of Los Angeles. Includes an excellent annotated bibliography.

MAEZUMI, HAKUYU and BERNARD GLASSMAN, eds. **ON ZEN PRACTICE II. Illustrations, glossary, index, 142pp. 6"x9", Zen76, 4.00p.**
An excellent collection of eleven translations and essays on various aspects of Zen practice. Three of the selections relate to Dogen, two are on *koan* practice, and a number include questions and answers.

MARCH-PENNEY, JOHN. **THE MASTER'S BOOK OF IKEBANA. Glossary, index, 9¼"x12¼", 176pp. TCP76, 16.95c.**
Ikebana is the Japanese word for flower arrangement based on ancient Japanese aesthetic. This volume traces the evolution of *ikebana* through photographs, line drawings, and text. It is beautifully produced and contains many color plates. The bulk of the book is devoted to specific suggestions for a number of arrangements combined with advice on selection of materials and the importance of symbolism.

MATSUNAGA, DAIGAN and ALICIA. **FOUNDATION OF JAPANESE BUDDHISM. Chronology, many notes, index, 670pp. BBI76, 35.90c/ set.**
This two volume set is a systematic study of the historical socio-political development of Japanese Buddhist institutions combined with

a consistent philosophical interpretation of the seemingly diverse schools of Buddhist thought. The first volume traces the period from pre-Buddhist Japan to the close of the Heian era; the second volume contains an analysis of the golden age of Japanese Buddhism. This is generally considered the most comprehensive treatment of Japanese Buddhism in any Western language. The authors write very clearly.

MERTON, THOMAS. **ZEN AND THE BIRDS OF APPETITE. 141pp. NDP68, 1.95p.**
Merton believed the study of Zen to be an attempt to reach the ground of pure, direct experience which underlies all creative thought and activity. These essays approach this experience through Japanese art and philosophy, through the Zen of D.T. Suzuki, and through the classic Zen masters themselves.

MICHENER, JAMES. **THE HOKUSAI SKETCHBOOKS: SELECTIONS FROM THE MANGA. Index, 6¾"x10½", 286pp. Tut58, 21.50c.**
Between the years 1814 and 1878 Hokusai published his **Manga** or **Sketches from Life,** a work which was destined to be one of the most popular art publications ever issued anywhere in the world. With its rich tapestry of life in Tokyo and its magical evocation of the beauties of the Japanese countryside, it gained immediate popularity in Japan and throughout the entire world. Michener has selected 187 full page plates and hundreds of text decorations from the original fifteen volumes and he also includes an illuminating introductory essay and informative captions. The plates are topically arranged.

MITCHELL, STEPHEN. **DROPPING ASHES ON THE BUDDHA. 243pp. Grv76, 4.95p.**
A record of the teachings of a living Zen master, Seung Sahn. Master Seung Sahn's students are young Americans and the dialogues set down here took place in the U.S. Thus the *koan* method may be seen applied within a modern context, in place of the more familiar setting customary in traditional literature. The dialogues are often humorous and many stories are included. Master Seung Sahn, the first Korean Zen master to teach in the U.S., is currently the director of a number of Zen communities.

MITTWER, HENRY. **THE ART OF CHABANA: FLOWERS FOR THE TEA CEREMONY. List of plants, glossary, notes, bibliography, index, 144pp. Tut74, 12.00c.**
Chabana is a simple arrangement of floral or other plant material traditionally placed in the *tokonoma,* or alcove, of the room in which the tea ceremony is performed. A few branches, a flower or two, are arranged with such delicacy that their frail beauty might disappear in a waft of wind. That very frailty contributes to Chabana's aesthetic expression, to its aura of truth and purity, and evokes an intense feeling in viewers. Mittwer traces the tea ceremony and Chabana historically, and discusses its modern application. He gives some practical guidelines and discusses at length more than 100 flowers that are suitable for Chabana, explaining how they can be used and the most appropriate seasons for their display. Forty-four illustrations, including twelve full page color drawings.

MIURA, ISSHU and RUTH FULLER SASAKI. **THE ZEN KOAN. 156pp. HBJ65, 2.95p.**
Koans are used to bring the student, without recourse to the mediation of words or concepts, to direct, intuitive realization of reality. This work first considers the nature and origin of the *koan* itself, then traces the tradition of *koan* study. A final section includes translations from the most important *koans,* giving the Chinese calligraphy, a phonetic transcription, and an English translation.

MIZUNO, SEIICHI. **ASUKA BUDDHIST ART—HORYU-JI. 8½"x 8¼", 172pp. Wea74, 15.00c.**
The monastery temple complex and its treasures at Horyu-ji represent the first great age of Buddhist art in Japan—the age that began in the mid-sixth century with the introduction of Buddhism from the Asian continent and continued until the late seventh century. The adoption of the new religion by the imperial court and the aristocracy motivated a series of changes that came to affect every phase of Japanese culture. At the same time it inspired the building of many imposing temples and the creation of the superb works of sculpture and painting that were enshrined in them. Unfortunately, none of these early temples has

survived intact, but the Horyu-ji, although considerably altered from its original state, remains today to convey the feeling of the age, and many of its treasures date from that time. 205 illustrations, including thirty-five in color, are presented here.

MOORE, CHARLES, ed. **THE JAPANESE MIND. Notes, index, 357pp. UHa67, 4.95p.**
A collection of essays on the essentials of Japanese philosophy and culture written by noted Japanese scholars. The topics range from the strictly philosophical to economics and sociology.

MORI, HISASHI. **JAPANESE PORTRAIT SCULPTURE. Glossary, bibliography, index, 7½"x10½", 150pp. Kod77, 12.95c.**
This is the only book in a Western language devoted solely to Japanese portrait sculpture. It includes a general discussion of the art form and its principal characteristics and development. Each of the 137 individual works, sixteen in color, is illustrated and discussed.

MORRIS, IVAN. **THE NOBILITY OF FAILURE—TRAGIC HEROES IN THE HISTORY OF JAPAN. Many illustrations, notes, bibliography, index, 523pp. NAL75, 4.95p.**
There is another type of hero in the complex Japanese tradition, a man whose career usually belongs to a period of unrest and warfare and represents the very antithesis of an ethos of accomplishment. He is the man whose single-minded sincerity will not allow him to make the manoeuvres and compromises that are so often needed for material success. . . . The men who appear in this book belong to many centuries and social systems and conform to no single pattern of behaviour or ideals; yet they were all "bred to a harder thing" and, taken together, they suggest the varieties of worldly defeat, the dignity it can bestow, and the reasons for its particular evocative appeal in the Japanese tradition.—from the introduction.

MORRIS, IVAN. **THE WORLD OF THE SHINING PRINCE. Bibliography, index, 351pp. RaH64, 10.95c.**
A vividly written evocation of life in the Heian culture in Japan at the time of **The Tale of Genji.** It was a narrow world, aristocratic, self centered, oblivious of other classes, provinces, countries. Yet, despite its insularity, it reached extraordinary cultural heights at a time when Europe was mired in the Dark Ages. Morris draws on many sources, including works of fiction, diaries by court ladies, and most important of all, Sei Shonagon's **Pillow Book,** the main factual document about daily life in Kyoto. He also used chronicles and journals written by male courtiers.

MUSASHI, MIYAMOTO. **A BOOK OF FIVE RINGS. 96pp. OvP74, 8.95c.**
Born in 1584, Musashi was one of Japan's most renowned warriors. He was a samurai and, by the age of twenty, had fought and won more than sixty contests by killing all of his opponents. Satisfied that he was invincible, Musashi then turned to formulating his philosophy of *the way of the sword,* and it is philosophy which is the heart of this book. **A Book of Five Rings** is also one of the most perceptive psychological guides to strategy ever written, and the philosophy behind it—influenced by Zen, Shinto, and Confucianism—can be applied to many areas of life. This is an extraordinary book which gives the reader a good idea of the ideas which influenced and guided the Japanese civilization for centuries and in which one can often find striking parallels with contemporary Western civilization. This is the first time this classic has appeared in the West, and the book includes many beautiful illustrations.

NAKATA, YUJIRO. **THE ART OF JAPANESE CALLIGRAPHY. 7¼"x9¼", 172pp. Wea73, 12.50c.**
In Japan, as in China, calligraphy has always been regarded as one of the most important art forms. This book discusses Japanese calligraphy in great depth and the text is illuminated by 184 illustrations, twenty-two in color.

NARAZAKI, MUNESHIGE. **HIROSHIGE. 7¼"x10¼", 96pp. Kod68, 8.95p.**
Hiroshige is probably the best known of the *ukiyo-e* artists. The name of this school translates as *pictures of the floating world* and its artists focused on the nature and beauty of Japan. This volume presents sixty-seven prints of Hiroshige's Japan, compiled from all the great series and famous views that he painted (with the exception of the **Fifty-three Stations on the Tokaido**). A biographical study is also included.

NARAZAKI, MUNESHIGE. **HOKUSAI. 7"x10", 96pp. Kod68, 8.95p.**
Hokusai was the most prolific of the *ukiyo-e* masters. He is noted for the special relationship between figure and landscape in his work—a perfect fusion in which neither element dominates nor is dominated. He also gives his figures a remarkable sense of life through the use of color and light. This volume reproduces the entire **Thirty-six Views of Mt. Fuji** (his most noted work), the ten prints he added to the series, and ten pages of details from the most famous of the prints in the series—all in full color. An account of his life and work is also included along with analyses of several of the prints.

NISHIMURA, ESHN. **UNSUI: A DIARY OF ZEN MONASTIC LIFE. Introduction, glossary, 6¾"x9¾", UHa73, 4.95p.**
Lovely watercolors by Giei Sato and a warm, handwritten text by Nishimura present Western readers with a realistic, nontechnical introduction to every aspect of Zen monastic life.

NITOBE, INAZO. **BUSHIDO: THE SOUL OF JAPAN. 203pp. Tut69, 4.95c.**
This neat little volume offers a thoughtful view of the ways and traditions of the Japanese samurai and the intrinsic relationship between the martial virtues of Bushido and the soul of Japan.

NOMA SEIROKU. **THE ARTS OF JAPAN, ANCIENT AND MEDI-EVAL, VOLUME I. Glossary, bibliography, 10½"x14¾", 236pp. Kod66, 50.00c.**
This splendid book is, without question, the finest work of its type that we have ever seen. It was awarded the first Society for International Cultural Relations prize for excellence of format, content and design, and for its role as a primary contribution to the furtherance of understanding between East and West. 198 plates, many in color, are exquisitely reproduced and the text does a fine job of surveying the arts of Japan in terms of the spirit of the time and place in which they were produced. Dr. Noma Seiroku has selected objects—including sculpture, painting, ceramics, architecture, lacquer, and costume—that evoke the aesthetic, spiritual, and social ideals of their original settings. We recommend this book to all who are interested in Japanese art and culture.

NORDSTROM, LOUIS, ed. **NAMU DAI BOSA: A TRANSMISSION OF ZEN BUDDHISM TO AMERICA. Illustrations, glossary, notes, bibliography, 291pp. TAB76, 6.95p.**
This is a collection of the talks and poems of three of the Japanese Zen masters—Nyogen Senzaki, Soen Nakagawa, and Eido Shimano—who introduced Zen Buddhism to America. There is also a history of the spread of the Rinzai Zen teaching in America. This is a lovely book which we recommend to all who are interested in the Rinzai tradition.

OGATA, SOHAKU. **ZEN FOR THE WEST. Illustrations, index, 182pp. Gre59, 17.45c.**
This is a well written, comprehensive, general survey of Zen thought and culture. The book has a nice feeling and it is very well bound. Included are full translations of the **Mumonkan** and the **Tao Te Ching**, a chapter on *koans*, and an account of life in a Zen monastery. It is unfortunate that the book is so expensive, because it is a good introductory work.

OKAKURA, KAKUZO. **THE BOOK OF TEA. Introduction, index, 133pp. Tut06, 5.95c/1.50c.**
A charming presentation of the distinctive personality of the Japanese through an analysis of the ancient tea ceremony. Okakura fully discusses the tea ceremony and its rigid formalities as well as the cult and patterns of belief surrounding tea and tea drinking. He also considers religious influences, origins, and history, and goes into the importance of flowers and floral arrangement in Japanese life. The hardcover edition is boxed and illustrated.

OKAZAKI, JOJI. **PURE LAND BUDDHIST PAINTING. Glossary, bibliography, index, 7½"x10½", 201pp. Kod77, 12.95c.**
Pure Land Buddhism is a branch of the Mahayana tradition emphasizing reliance on the grace of the Buddha Amitabha and birth into the Pure Land, where the faithful wait for final enlightenment. Originating in India and expanding rapidly in China, it reached full maturity in Japan, where uniquely Japanese sects were formed and Pure Land arts flourished. This book covers the development of the Pure Land school over a period of more than a millenium, up to the fourteenth century. The author focuses on Pure Land mandalas and depictions of Amitabha descending to welcome the faithful to the Pure Land. He discusses in detail the various types and rich imagery, and pursues the ramifications brought about by changing religious and social demands. 191 plates, twenty-five in color, enhance the text.

OKUDAIRA, HIDEO. **NARRATIVE PICTURE SCROLLS. 122 plates, glossary, bibliography, index, 7½"x9¼", 151pp. Wea73, 10.00c.**
Emaki, the narrative picture scrolls produced in Japan in great numbers from the tenth to sixteenth century, are both an art form and a mirror of Japanese life and customs. Picture scrolls came to Japan from China and were transformed, by the emphasis on decorative style and narrative subject matter, into a new and distinctively Japanese art. *Emaki* illustrate—usually with accompanying text—Buddhist sutras, literary works, historical accounts, moral tales, biographies, poems, fables, and legends. They range in style from the richest of coloring and decoration to simple lines in ink monochrome. In this introduction, Okudaira has chosen a number of outstanding examples of this art form.

ONO, SAKYO. **SHINTO—THE KAMI WAY. Index, 116pp. Tut62, 4.50c.**
A comprehensive, scholarly, illustrated treatment of Shinto, often called *The Way of the Gods.* As a religion, it is relatively unknown in the West, although for the Japanese, it is as old as time. It combines a personal faith in the *kami* (the sacred spirits) and a communal way of life.

POWELL, ROBERT. **ZEN AND REALITY. Bibliography, 142pp. Vik61, 2.50p.**
Transcription of a series of lectures given to the Buddhist Society in London, most only a few pages long. Powell is a scientist who has written and lectured widely on Zen, consciousness, Krishnamurti, and science. His style is fairly dry; however, he does present some unusual insights.

RAJNEESH, BHAGWAN SHREE. **AND THE FLOWERS SHOWERED. 10.95c.**
See the Contemporary Spiritual Teachers section.

RAJNEESH, BHAGWAN SHREE. **NEITHER THIS NOR THAT. 10.95c.**
See the Contemporary Spiritual Teachers section.

RAJNEESH, BHAGWAN SHREE. **NIRVANA: THE LAST NIGHT-MARE. 12.95c.**
See the Contemporary Spiritual Teachers section.

RAJNEESH, BHAGWAN SHREE. **NO WATER, NO MOON: REFLECTIONS ON ZEN.** 10.95c.
See the Contemporary Spiritual Teachers section.

RAJNEESH, BHAGWAN SHREE. **RETURNING TO THE SOURCE.** 10.95c.
See the Contemporary Spiritual Teachers section.

RAJNEESH, BHAGWAN SHREE. **ROOTS AND WINGS.** 11.00c.
See the Contemporary Spiritual Teachers section.

RATTI, OSCAR and ADELE WESTBROOK. **SECRETS OF THE SAMURAI: A SURVEY OF THE MARTIAL ARTS OF FEUDAL JAPAN.** Introduction, chronology, bibliography, index, 7½"x10½", 483pp. Tut73, 25.00c.
The definitive study of the martial arts of feudal Japan, illustrating in detail the weapons, techniques, strategies, and principles of combat of the Japanese warrior. Beginning with a panoramic survey of the tumultous early struggles for political ascendancy, the authors first outline the relentless progression of the military class toward absolute power. Then they examine each of the ancient martial arts in detail and follow their evolution through an examination of famous masters. They also discuss certain lesser known training methods that were intended to help develop a man's inner power and fuse all his energies into one concerted force. The book is profusely illustrated throughout.

REISCHAUER, EDWIN. **THE JAPANESE.** Bibliography, index, 443pp. HUP77, 15.00c.
Reischauer is University Professor at Harvard. He was born and grew up in Japan, has been a student of Japanese history and culture throughout his life, and was U.S. Ambassador to Japan from 1961-66. After placing Japan and its people in their historical and geographic setting, Reischauer weighs the paradoxes and particularities in contemporary Japanese society. He offers a penetrating analysis of the Japanese personality, identifying the ways in which the Japanese really are different from Westerners. He also provides a revealing description of the Japanese government and Japanese politics as well as an evaluation of Japan as a world power. Virtually every aspect of Japanese culture is treated in a separate chapter. This is a direct, highly readable account, richly illustrated and infused with the author's lifelong rapport with Japan.

REPS, PAUL. **BE!—NEW USES FOR THE HUMAN INSTRUMENT.** 63pp. Wea71, 3.95c.
More of Reps' delightful picture poems. All deal with ways of rediscovering our natural being.

REPS, PAUL. **GOLD AND FISH SIGNATURES.** 94pp. Tut69, 4.25p.
Spontaneous picture poems, light and gay.

REPS, PAUL. **JUICING.** 111pp. Dou78, 3.50p.
More of Reps' poems and brush stroke pictographs. *It proposes a new orienting—not kill but let—not apart but including other life forms with ours—not out-think but feel.*—from the preface.

REPS, PAUL. **SIT IN: WHAT IT IS LIKE.** 18pp. Zen75, 2.00p.
Here Reps illustrates his thoughts on Zen sitting meditation. The drawings are done with brush and ink in the Oriental style. The poems and drawings are on facing pages.

REPS, PAUL. **SQUARE SUN, SQUARE MOON.** 100pp. Tut67, 3.95p.
A collection of essays in Reps' unique style, combining verse, prose, and sketches. Reps' books are offbeat, modern approaches to Zen.

REPS, PAUL. **10 WAYS TO MEDITATE.** 4.95c.
See the Meditation section.

REPS, PAUL. **UNWRINKLING PLAYS.** 59pp. Tut65, 4.75p.
Short, illustrated plays in Reps' usual style.

■ REPS, PAUL. **ZEN FLESH, ZEN BONES.** 207pp. Dou57/Pen, 6.25c/1.95p.
This is actually four books in one, books that would surely rank high in the canon if Zen were so non-Zen as to have scriptures. **101 Zen Stories** recounts actual Zen experiences; the **Gateless Gate** is a thirteenth century collection of the mind problems used in attaining enlightenment; **10 Bulls** is a twelfth century commentary upon the stages of awareness leading to enlightenment. Illustrated with woodblock prints. Recommended as a delightful and insightful introduction to Zen. The hardcover edition is boxed and beautifully produced.

REPS, PAUL. **ZEN TELEGRAMS.** 101pp. Tut59, 3.50p.
Picture poems. If Zen works as a sudden flash of insight, so do these. Very much in the Zen tradition.

■ ROSS, NANCY WILSON. **THE WORLD OF ZEN: AN EAST-WEST ANTHOLOGY.** 362pp. RaH60, 3.95p.
The most comprehensive, accessible anthology we have seen. Includes illustrated sections on every aspect of the Zen way of life, arts, science, poetry, psychology—as well as extensive selections from translations of the basic source material. Highly recommended.

SADLER, A.L. **CHA-NO-YU: THE JAPANESE TEA CEREMONY.** Index, 286pp. Tut33, 3.95p.
This was the first English work written on the Japanese tea ceremony and it remains the most comprehensive and detailed study. This is an unabridged edition of this classic work, complete with all the original illustrations. Professor Sadler was one of the most outstanding foreign experts on Japanese culture. Here he discusses the ceremony and utensils and relates many stories of the tea masters.

SALAJAN, IOANNA. **ZEN COMICS.** 88pp. Tut74, 2.75p.
A collection of Zen stories and *koans* in comic strip form. When we first got this book we wondered whether it was any good. Some of our customers whose opinion we trusted told us that the book was really insightful and as we looked through it more carefully it did seem to be an interesting volume. One of the main tenets of Zen is not to take anything very seriously and so Zen often expresses its essence best in humor.

SAN, TENKO. **A NEW ROAD TO ANCIENT TRUTH.** Glossary, 183pp. Hor72, 5.95c.
Tenko San is the founder of *Ittoen*, a spiritual community in Japan that has had a rapid growth in the past couple of decades. He attempts to present, through parables and anecdotes, the inner meaning of the movement (whose name translates as *Garden of the Light*). The aspect of *Ittoen* which most deeply impresses visitors to it is the loving kindness which pervades the community where no harsh word breaks the harmony. The main concept of *Ittoen* is *sange*, which is not only a taking of responsibility for one's own acts, but a surrender of the sense of selfhood which is conceived as the source of evil—thus the life becomes one of selfless service and profound peace. Many personal accounts are also included. This book has been a best seller in Japan.

SANGHARAKSHITA, VENERABLE. **THE ESSENCE OF ZEN.** 62pp. FWB73, 2.75p.
Transcription of five talks by an Englishman who has had a long and deep experience of Buddhist teachings. Ordained and initiated into the three major traditions of Buddhism, Sangharakshita has spent about twenty years in the East, practicing and teaching.

SANSOM, GEORGE. **A HISTORY OF JAPAN TO 1334.** Illustrations, bibliography, index, 514pp. SUP58, 6.65p.
The brilliant synthesis in Sansom's **History of Japan** represents the culmination of the life work of the most distinguished historian writing on Japan. Written in the elegant and lucid prose that has become the hallmark of his writing, all three volumes are indispensable for serious students of Japan. Every conceivable aspect of Japanese society and cultural and political life is surveyed at length.

SANSOM, GEORGE. **A HISTORY OF JAPAN, 1334-1615.** Illustrations, bibliography, index, 445pp. SUP61, 9.35p.

SANSOM, GEORGE. **A HISTORY OF JAPAN, 1615-1867.** Illustrations, bibliography, index, 274pp. SUP63, 6.65p.

■ SANSOM, GEORGE. **JAPAN: A SHORT CULTURAL HISTORY.** Illustrations, index, 564pp. SUP52, 7.50.
This book, originally published in 1931 and revised by Sansom twice since then, remains the standard introduction to Japanese cultural history. It covers the period from earliest days to the breakdown of feudalism in the nineteenth century. The volume has been universally praised both for its scholarship and readability.

SASAKI, JOSHU. **BUDDHA IS THE CENTER OF GRAVITY. 95pp.
LaF74, 3.50p.**
Transcription of a series of lectures given by a Rinzai master who has
taught at many centers in the U.S. The lectures are based on the
Mumonkan, a thirteenth century compilation of forty-eight Zen *koans*
and commentary. Excerpts from an English translation of the text are
included along with many illustrations. Also included is a series of
questions and answers between Sasaki Roshi and individuals at the
Lama Foundation where the talks were given. The volume is beautifully produced and a pullout insert on rice paper reproduces the **Heart
Sutra** in the original Chinese characters.

SASAKI, RUTH FULLER, *tr.* **THE RECORDED SAYINGS OF LIN-
CHI. Introduction, many notes, 123pp. IZS75, 14.95c.**
A complete translation of the **Lin-chi lu**—the record of the life and
teaching of the great T'ang Dynasty Ch'an Master Lin-chi I-hsuan,
who, amid the disordered world of ninth century China, preached the
absolute dignity and freedom of man's intrinsic spirit, denying
uncompromisingly all outward forms of authority—even that of the
Buddha himself. His utterances such as the following, *Just make yourself
master of every situation, and wherever you stand is the true place*, raised a
revolutionary whirlwind in the Ch'an world of his time. The Ch'an
school which bears his name remains one of the most influential in
Japan today. The Chinese text is appended.

SASAKI, RUTH FULLER, *et al.* **A MAN OF ZEN: THE RECORDED
SAYINGS OF LAYMAN P'ANG—A NINTH CENTURY ZEN CLAS-
SIC. Illustrations, bibliography, notes, index, 109pp. Wea71, 3.50p.**
The story of P'ang's later years, during which he attained the highest
spiritual insight and came to be known as one of the leading Zen
figures of China. It is written in anecdotal style and consists of
revealing incidents involving P'ang and his family, followed by a
representative selection of his verses. A comprehensive introduction
and notes make this ancient text more meaningful today.

SATO, KOJI. **THE ZEN LIFE. 190pp. Wea66, 4.95p.**
120 pages of striking photographs and a succinct text by a Japanese
psychology professor present an absorbing account of the everyday
life of monks in Japan today. The text discusses the tradition and
creativity of the Zen monk's life and the way of enlightenment.
Included also is an account of life in a Zen influenced Tokyo commune.

SAUNDERS, E. DALE. **BUDDHISM IN JAPAN. Illustrations, glossary,
chronologies, bibliography, index, 328pp. UPa64, 3.45p.**
A survey of the history of Japanese Buddhist doctrine which provides
an historical framework which the reader may use as a point of
departure for further reading. The first part gives the general outlines
of the doctrine as it evolved in India; and the second part presents a
more detailed treatment of Buddhism in Japan from earliest times until
the twentieth century, arranged according to sects. The discussion is
dry and presented in summary fashion.

SAUNDERS, E. DALE. **MUDRA. Many line drawings, diagrams, half
tones, copious notes, bibliography, index, 7½"x10¼", 319pp. PUP60/
RKP, 24.20c.**
This is a detailed study of *mudra* (symbolic gestures or hand postures)
with particular reference to the Buddhist sculpture of Japan. Saunders
discusses the history and symbolism of each *mudra*. The eight principal
and six secondary *mudra* are emphasized.

SAWA, TAKAAKI. **ART IN JAPANESE ESOTERIC BUDDHISM.
7½"x9", 151pp. Wea72, 15.00c.**
Esoteric Buddhism flowered in ninth century Japan and upheld the
doctrine that the essence of Buddhism was never directly understandable to mankind through pure teaching. It relied greatly on ritual and
magical practices concealed from all but the initiate. Its numerous and
remarkable deities, however, became well known to the populace and
were represented over and over again in painting and sculpture. In
fact, it was through the worship of sacred images and mandalas that
devotees of the esoteric sects learned the concepts of their faith and
sought salvation in the present world. This book presents the most
outstanding of these art treasures, revealing their aesthetic values as
well as their religious connotations, and exploring the historical
background from which they derive. The text includes 182 illustrations, thirty-eight in color.

SCHLOEGL, IRMGARD, *tr.* **THE RECORD OF RINZAI. Introduction,
notes, 64pp. BuS75, 3.75p.**
Rinzai Gigen (ninth century AD) was the founder of the school of
Rinzai Zen. Rinzai's **Record** was written by his disciples; it contains his
teachings, episodes from his training, and from his teaching career.
This is a translation of the complete text.

SCHLOEGL, IRMGARD. **THE WISDOM OF THE ZEN MASTERS.
80pp. NDP76/SIP, 2.25p.**
Dr. Schloegl is the librarian at the Buddhist Society, London. This
small volume presents a fine sampling of the stories and sayings of
both Japanese and Chinese Zen masters. It is a good way to get a feeling
for Zen.

SCHLOEGL, IRMGARD, *tr.* **THE ZEN TEACHING OF RINZAI.
ShP76, 3.50p.**
Rinzai was a ninth century Chinese Zen master. His teachings were
considered eccentric, harsh, and shocking—but were intensely dynamic in their effect. He broke attachments to any ideal directly and
fiercely, and destroyed complacency by using outrageous contradictions. He founded one of the principal schools of Zen Buddhism which
flourished in China for eleven centuries, migrated to Japan in the
thirteenth century, and to America in the twentieth. This record of
Rinzai's training, teachings, and teaching career was written by his
disciples and is translated into English for the first time in this volume.

SCHLOEGL, IRMGARD. **THE ZEN WAY. 125pp. SCK77, 7.65p.**
A concise exploration of the theory and practice of Zen. Dr. Schloegl
sets out the basic Buddhist teaching based on the Buddha's teaching
and then she traces the fundamentals of the Zen way through an
account of life in a contemporary Zen monastery. She herself spent
twelve years in a Rinzai monastery. Later sections of the book discuss
the fundamentals of Zen Buddhist insight and their practical application.

SCHOMBERG, HOGETSU, *ed.* **ZEN MEDITATION. 84pp. ZMS76,
2.00p.**
A special issue of **The Journal of Shasta Abbey** devoted entirely to
meditation. *We have tried to make this book straightforward, covering all the
essentials of meditation so that the reader can begin immediately to practice it. These
articles are the fruit of many years of experience by Kennett Roshi and the priests of
Shasta Abbey in practicing and instructing others in zazen. We include articles on how
to sit, both the mental and physical aspects, how to meditate in the midst of everyday
activity, frequently asked questions, pitfalls and problems that occur, how to make a
meditation cushion bench, meditation for children, etc. accompanied by photographs
and drawings.*

■ SEKIDA, KATSUKI, *tr.* **TWO ZEN CLASSICS: MUMONKAN AND
HEKIGANROKU. Index, 413pp. Wea77, 13.50c/7.95p.**
The *koan* has been variously defined as an expression of the inexpress-
ible, a finger pointing to the moon, a verbal paradox designed to jog the
mind beyond the confines of conceptual thought. However defined,
the *koan* is one of the distinctive elements of Zen Buddhism and lies at
the heart of the Zen experience. The two works translated here,
Mumonkan (The Gateless Gate) and **Hekiganroku (The Blue Cliff
Records)**, are the best known and most frequently studied collections
of *koans*, and are among the classics of Zen literature. This is a
completely new translation of these works, accompanied by original
commentaries. It is an excellent book and we highly recommend it to all
who seek a deeper understanding of the insights of Zen Buddhism.

SEKIDA, KATSUKI. **ZEN TRAINING, METHODS AND PHILOS-
OPHY. Introduction, index, 258pp. Wea75, 8.95c/4.95p.**
*For Mr. Sekida the unquestioned basis of any serious practice of Zen is "zazen," the
exercise in which the student sits and learns to control his body and mind. A substantial
part of the book is devoted to describing how "zazen" is performed and what its effects
are....Posture, breathing, the function of the abdominal muscles, muscle tone, the
mechanisms of wakefulness and attention—all are discussed in detail in the language of
the physiologist....[Sekida] goes on to present an account of the aims of "zazen," and
of Zen training in general, that differs markedly from most of those we have hitherto
been offered.—*from the introduction. The author goes beyond the earlier
stages and discusses *kensho, samadhi*, and how one lives as well as trains
in Zen. This is an excellent work which we recommend highly to those
seriously interested in the practice of Zen. Some of the author's
personal experiences are included.

SEKIGUCHI, SHINDAI. **ZEN: A MANUAL FOR WESTERNERS.** **111pp. Jap nd, 5.85c.**
Contains many illustrations and thorough explanations that help the reader in achieving true *zazen* meditation even when the benefit of further guidance is unavailable. The author is a Buddhist priest and university professor. A comprehensive, well developed treatment.

SHAKU, SOYEN. **ZEN FOR AMERICANS.** Index, 226pp. OpC06, 3.95p.
Formerly titled, **Sermons of a Buddhist Abbot**, this is a collection of lectures given by the author on the **Sutra of Forty-Two Chapters**, one of the most important canonical books—put together into book form and translated by D.T. Suzuki. The lectures present traditional thought in a modern form. Also includes the complete text of the Sutra.

■ *SHIBAYAMA, ZENKEI.* **A FLOWER DOES NOT TALK.** 264pp. Tut70, 3.95p.
Introductory essays by a Japanese abbot. He describes the basic characteristics of Zen, the training it calls for, and Zen personality. He also presents three typical Zen writings, along with copious explanatory notes. The book is exquisitely illustrated.

SHIBAYAMA, ZENKEI. **ZEN COMMENTS ON THE MUMONKAN.** **Introduction, long glossary, index, 377pp. NAL74, 2.25p.**
The basis of this book is the **Mumonkan**, a classic collection of forty-eight *koans* commonly used in monastic training. The *koans* themselves were gathered by the thirteenth century Chinese Master Mumon and discussed first by him. Mumon also appended short poems to each of his discussions. Sharing the insights of a long life of disciplined religious seeking and teaching, Shibayama has added his own comments on the *koans* themselves and on the commentaries and poems by Master Mumon. This is an excellent work for the serious student. Through concentrated attention first to the words of Master Mumon and then to those of a modern commentator, he is led as near to a sense of what *satori* implies as is possible without actual Zen discipline and training. The English translation is done by Sumiko Kudo, a student of Shibayama.

The Sixth Patriarch (Hui-neng)

During the eighth century in T'ang China, Ch'an Buddhism grew into a sect of considerable importance. Hui-neng, the Sixth Patriarch, is revered, along with Bodhidharma, its founder, as the man who set Ch'an on the course it has followed ever since. The **Platform Sutra** is the summation of Hui-neng's teachings. Hui-neng was an illiterate commoner and his Sutra is not a book of obscure dogmas and impracticable theories. In the Sutra he declares that the way of sudden enlightenment is the essence of Buddhism, and he presents a practical path to one-pointed understanding. The Sutra was written down soon after his death by several of his disciples. We recommend this work highly to all who seek a deep understanding of Zen Buddhism.

CHAN, WING-TSIT, tr. **THE PLATFORM SCRIPTURE—THE BASIC CLASSIC OF ZEN BUDDHISM.** Many notes, index, 202pp. SJU63, 3.50p.
A fine translation, with the Chinese text on facing pages. Chan also includes an excellent, long introduction.

FUNG, PAUL and GEORGE, trs. **THE SUTRA OF THE SIXTH PATRIARCH ON THE PRISTINE, ORTHODOX DHARMA. English/Sanskrit/Chinese glossary, many notes, 187pp. BUC64, 6.00c.**
A new translation of Hui-neng's Sutra, accompanied by a number of the Patriarch's discourses and a series of answers to questions put to him about his form of Buddhism.

HUA, HSUAN, tr. **THE SIXTH PATRIARCH'S DHARMA JEWEL PLATFORM SUTRA AND COMMENTARY. 380pp. SAB71, 10.00c.**
A collection of lectures on the Sutra and its commentary, together with a fresh translation of the passages discussed. The presentation is often a bit scattered; however, it is the fullest one that we know of, and

many interesting points are raised and examined. This text should be of interest to all who are seeking a deeper understanding of the Sutra and its personal applications.

LU K'UAN (CHARLES LUK), tr. **CH'AN AND ZEN TEACHINGS, THIRD SERIES. Preface, glossary, index, 306pp. HPG62, 9.00p.**
This volume contains a complete translation of the **Platform Sutra**, along with a discussion of the life and work of Hui-neng. Full translations of two other Ch'an works are also included—**The Song of Enlightenment** and **The Sutra of Complete Enlightenment**.

SUZUKI, D.T. **THE ZEN DOCTRINE OF NO MIND. Index, 160pp. Wei49, 3.50p.**
This is an excellent discussion of the teachings of Hui-neng and the school he founded. Most of what we know of his philosophy comes from the **Platform Sutra** and Suzuki discusses this text at length and includes quotations from it as part of his exposition. Suzuki is at his best when he is either translating or discussing a specific individual or movement and this is certainly one of his finest works. It is essential reading for all who seek an understanding of the Chinese roots of Zen Buddhism.

WONG, MOU-LAM, tr. **THE SUTRA OF HUI NENG. Introduction, notes, 136pp. BuS66, 2.50p.**
This is a translation of the **Sutra Spoken by the Sixth Patriarch on the High Seat of the Treasure of the Law** (also known as the **Platform Sutra of the Sixth Patriarch**). It is accurate, albeit a bit stilted, and has been somewhat edited by Christmas Humphreys.

■ *YAMPOLSKY, PHILIP, tr.* **THE PLATFORM SUTRA OF THE SIXTH PATRIARCH. Glossary, bibliography, index, 252pp. Col67, 15.15c/6.95p.**
This is the finest translation available. Yampolsky also includes a 123 page essay on Ch'an in the eighth century, divided into the following sections: *The Formation of the Legend; The Lankavatara School; Shen-hui; The Birth of a Patriarch—Biography of Hui-neng; The Making of a Book—The* **Platform Sutra;** and *Content Analysis.* There is also a reproduction of the Tun-huang text.

–END OF THE SIXTH PATRIARCH (HUI-NENG) SUBSECTION–

SMITH, ARTHUR. **GAME OF GO.** 237pp. Tut08, 3.75p.
The Game of Go is probably the oldest intellectual game in the world. First developed in China over 3,000 years ago, the game was introduced to Japan in the eighth century. As Smith says, *Go is not merely a picture of a single battle like chess, but a whole campaign of a modern kind, in which the strategical movements of the masses in the end decide the victory. Battles occur in various parts of the board, and sometimes several are going on at the same time . . . and far reaching strategy alone assures victory.* Smith was one of the first Westerners to make a scientific study of the game, and his classic work has never been surpassed for completeness, lucidity, and general excellence. This volume includes a glossary and detailed instructions.

SMITH, BRADLEY. **JAPAN: A HISTORY IN ART. Bibliography, 9"x13", 295pp. Dou64, 12.95c.**
This beautiful book presents the history of Japan through twenty centuries—as seen, remembered, and recorded by her artists. It captures and clarifies the Japanese vision of life in its richness, delicacy, and complexity of pattern. Each of the 288 plates is faithfully reproduced in color. Each was chosen not only for its extraordinary beauty, but as a storytelling panel in a vast, dramatic, historical panorama that encompasses the rise and fall of dynasties, the sweep of religious and political movements, the flowering of the arts, and the minutiae of daily life. This is an amazing book and one of the best bargains that we know of.

SOHL, ROBERT and AUDREY CARR, eds. **THE GOSPEL ACCORDING TO ZEN. 133pp. NAL70/NEL, 1.50p.**
This is an interesting collection of essays on Zen and translations of some of the important works of Zen masters, designed to give the beginning reader a feel for what Zen is.

STATLER, OLIVER. **JAPANESE INN. 334pp. Jov61, 1.95p.**
Reading this delightful book is a fine way to painlessly learn a great deal about Japanese history and culture. Statler lived in Japan for eleven years and, while there, heard of an inn which had been at the crossroads of history from the sixteenth century to the present day. Each chapter is a sketch of important or not so important individuals who stayed at the inn and the events of their lives. In each case all the principal characters are brought to life and related illustrations accompany the text. Statler writes of emperors and bandits, warlords and merchants, actors and artists.

STISKIN, NAHUM. **THE LOOKING-GLASS GOD. 157pp. Aut71, 4.95c.**
A lucid synthesis of three seemingly irreconcilable elements—Shinto, the dogma-free pantheism of Japan; the Chinese principle of *yin* and *yang*; and Western scientific rationalism. With the aid of many graphic illustrations, Stiskin presents a new cosmology for modern man, merging *the analytic prowess of the West with the intuitive heritage of the East.*

SUZUKI, D.T. **ESSAYS IN ZEN BUDDHISM, FIRST SERIES. Notes, index, 388pp. Grv49/HPG, 5.95p.**
In 1927, when Suzuki published the first volume of his **Essays,** the Western world had little knowledge of Zen Buddhism. He, more than anyone else, is responsible for the increase in interest. He is the author of more than 100 works on Zen and Buddhism in both Japanese and English. Included here are essays on Zen training, the doctrine of enlightenment and *satori,* a history of Zen, and his commentary on *The Ox-herding Pictures,* which have long been used to illustrate the stages of spiritual progress. A long introduction is included.

SUZUKI, D.T. **ESSAYS IN ZEN BUDDHISM, SECOND SERIES. Many illustrations, notes, index, 367pp. Wei53/HPG, 5.95p.**
Includes a long essay, *The Koan Exercise,* as well as shorter pieces; *Bodhidharma;* Zen textbooks: **Pi-yen-chi** and **Wu-men-kuan;** and *Passivity in Buddhist Life.*

SUZUKI, D.T. **ESSAYS IN ZEN BUDDHISM, THIRD SERIES. Notes, index, 396pp. Wei53/HPG, 5.95p.**
A collection of profusely illustrated essays which show the evolution of Indian metaphysical ideas into a form more compatible wtih Chinese psychology. Includes a section on the relationship between Zen and the chief Mahayana sutras, the **Prajnaparamita** and the **Gandavyuha.**

SUZUKI, D.T. **THE FIELD OF ZEN. 105pp. H&R69/BuS, 1.25p.**
A selection of articles and recorded talks on a variety of subjects, originally published in the **Journal of the Buddhist Society of England.**

SUZUKI, D.T. **AN INTRODUCTION TO ZEN BUDDHISM. 132pp. Grv64, 1.95p.**
A somewhat dry overview of Zen. Dr. Suzuki begins with a response to the question, *What is Zen?* Next, he discusses various facets of Zen, ending with chapters on *Satori, Koan,* and *The Meditation Hall and the Monk's Life.*

SUZUKI, D.T. **LIVING BY ZEN. 187pp. Index, Wei50, 3.50p.**
This book was regarded by Suzuki as his second *introduction* to Zen, written many years after the first. It reinterprets Zen in the light of his later experience and reflection. Includes a general survey of Zen as well as detailed studies of *satori* and the *koan.*

SUZUKI, D.T., tr. **MANUAL OF ZEN BUDDHISM. Notes, index, 192pp. Grv60, 3.95p.**
A comprehensive anthology of Zen's most important original sources. Included are the sutras or sermons of the Buddha; the *gathas* or hymns; many *koans* and the *dharanis* or invocations to expel evil spirits. In addition, there are numerous reproductions of drawings and paintings and the recorded conversations of some of the great masters.

SUZUKI, D.T. **SHIN BUDDHISM. 93pp. A&U70, 2.70p.**
An in depth exploration of Shin Buddhism—a way of enlightenment which stems from the writings and teachings of Shinran, a remarkably charismatic thirteenth century Japanese religious prophet.

SUZUKI, D.T. **STUDIES IN ZEN. Index, 210pp. Del55, 2.45p.**
A collection of lectures and articles produced over a forty-seven year period. The volume includes general treatises on Zen, a discussion of the role of nature in Zen, analyses of *mondos,* a survey of reason and intuition in Buddhist philosophy, and much else.

SUZUKI, D.T. **THE TRAINING OF THE ZEN BUDDHIST MONK. Appendices, 161pp. Win34, 3.00p.**
A precise, scholarly picture of Zen in life—including forty-three illustrations by Zenchu Sato.

SUZUKI, D.T. **WHAT IS ZEN? 116pp. H&R71/BuS, 1.50p.**
Three essays: *What is Zen?; Self and the Unattainable;* and *The Essence of Buddhism.*

SUZUKI, D.T. **ZEN AND JAPANESE CULTURE. Sixty-nine illustrations, some of them foldouts, bibliography, index, 478pp. PUP59/RKP, 6.95p.**
After briefly explaining what Zen is, Suzuki considers in detail the various aspects of Japanese art and life that Zen has influenced: the cult of swordsmanship, the tea ceremony, *haiku,* the Japanese love of nature, and the tradition of the samurai. A delightful work, pervaded with the spirit of Zen.

SUZUKI, D.T. **ZEN BUDDHISM. 294pp. Dou56, 2.50p.**
A sampling, chosen from various Suzuki works covering the following topics: meaning of Zen; its historical background; *satori;* techniques; *The Zen Doctrine of No Mind;* Zen and philosophy; and Zen and Japanese Culture. An excellent introduction to Suzuki and to Zen.

■ SUZUKI, SHUNRYU. **ZEN MIND, BEGINNER'S MIND. 138pp. Wea70, 6.95c/3.50p.**
This book is about how to practice Zen as a workable discipline and religion, about posture and breathing, about the basic attitudes and understanding that make Zen practice possible, about nonduality, emptiness, and enlightenment. Here one begins to understand what Zen is really about. Suzuki-roshi says: *The world is its own magic*—a feeling that pervades the entire book. Here indeed is a book of intense, profound, joyous reflection. Highly recommended.

TAKADA, KOIN. **THE SPIRIT OF BUDDHISM TODAY. 125pp. Tok73, 9.95c.**
Koin Takada is one of the most influential men in Japan today. He is abbot of the Yakushi-ji and the head of the Hosso Sect of Buddhism. He feels that it is his duty to bring his religion to them. The essays translated here reflect a preaching directed toward the people in general, discussed in terms of the current state of the world. They reveal a side of Buddhism that is not well known to Western readers.

TAKAKUSU, JUNJIRO. **THE ESSENTIALS OF BUDDHIST PHILOSOPHY. Notes, index, 243pp. MoB56, 11.00c.**
This is a scholarly study of Buddhist philosophy in Japan. Professor Takakusu was the author, editor, and translator of monumental works on Buddhism. This volume, his only major work in English, is the summation of his lifetime study of Buddhist philosophy. The material originally was delivered as a series of lectures at the University of Hawaii and was edited for publication by Wing-tsit Chan and Charles Moore. Divided into fifteen chapters, the book deals with many different schools of Japanese Buddhism. Each is discussed very fully with the major individual figures and movements analyzed in depth. A

long introductory section gives the background necessary to appreciate the text. This is an excellent work for the serious student.

TAMBURELLO, ADOLFO. **JAPAN. Chronology, bibliography, index, 10"x13", 192pp. G&D73, 19.95c.**
A magnificently illustrated survey of the richness and delicacy of the traditional arts of Japan—some of which date back 7,000 years. 108 full color plates complement the text and all aspects of Japanese culture are fully covered. Part of the **Monuments of Civilization** series.

TANAKA, MINORU, tr. **BUSHIDO: WAY OF THE SAMURAI. 85pp. SnB75, 3.50p.**
This is the first English translation of a Japanese classic, **Hagakure**, which discusses the philosophy of the samurai. The text is made up of a number of short, illustrative stories and aphorisms.

TANAKA, SEN'O. **THE TEA CEREMONY. Glossary, index, 9½"x11", 214pp. Crn75, 7.95p.**
This magnificently illustrated volume by one of Japan's contemporary tea masters was written specifically to provide the Western world with a deeper understanding of the complexities and inspiration of this art form, and reveal how the discipline of the ritual leads the individual to greater understanding and appreciation of the world around him. Beginning with the twelfth century origins, Tanaka traces the practice to the present day. All the elements of the ceremony—art, architecture, *kaiseki*, occasions for the ceremony, the utensils, incense, and flowers used, and the connections between Zen and the ceremony—are discussed. Beautiful black and white and color photographs add an important dimension to the text.

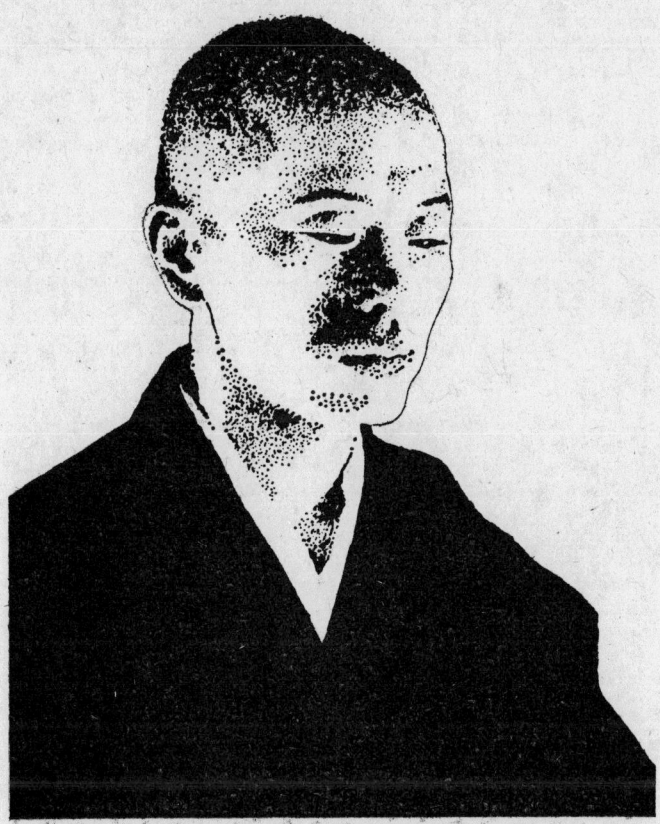

TERUKAZU, AKIYAMA. **JAPANESE PAINTING. 12.50p.**
See the Sacred Art section.

THICH THIEN-AN. **BUDDHISM AND ZEN IN VIETNAM. Notes, index, 301pp. Tut75, 12.50c.**
A comprehensive account of the history, traditions, and practices of the various Zen Buddhist schools in Vietnam and their relation to Buddhism in other Asian countries. Thich is a monk and scholar who has studied Vietnamese history in depth and intimately experienced his country's recent upheaval and chaos.

■ *THICH THIEN-AN.* **ZEN PHILOSOPHY, ZEN PRACTICE. Illustrations, glossary, 191pp. Dha75, 4.95p.**
Dr. Thich Thien-An is one of Vietnam's most influential contemporary Buddhist scholars and religious leaders. He has lived in the U.S. since 1970 and is presently the President of the College of Oriental Studies in Los Angeles. Here he presents a comprehensive survey of Zen theory and technique. He begins by tracing Zen from its historical origins, viewing it within a more general context of Buddhist thought, and from there moving on to a discussion of the union between theory and practice, sitting and action, wisdom and compassion. Each of the fourteen chapters describes a specific meditation practice, ranging from relatively simple to more complex techniques as taught by the various Zen traditions. The material is presented as clearly as Zen can be in words, and reflects the author's extensive experience as both a teacher and a practitioner. Dr. Thich relates his material to contemporary American society and each chapter includes some traditional, applicable Zen stories or one of his own discourses. A good study for both beginning and experienced students.

TSUDA, NORITAKE. **HANDBOOK OF JAPANESE ART. Extensively illustrated, bibliography, index, 526pp. Tut76, 5.50p.**
This book *offers the Westerner a comprehensive view of Japanese art through Japanese eyes.... It surveys the full range of achievement in painting, sculpture, architecture, ceramics, lacquerware, woodblock printmaking, metalwork, textiles, garden making, and other artistic fields.*—from the foreword. The approach is chronological, and the art of each historical period is introduced by the categories in which it found its most significant expression during that period.

TSUNODA, RYUSAKU, WILLIAM T. DE BARY and DONALD KEENE. **SOURCES OF JAPANESE TRADITION. Bibliography, index, 928pp. Col58, 5.60p/set.**
A massive, two volume sourcebook, illustrating Japanese thought from the earliest times and covering not only religious and philosophical speculations, but also political, economic, and aesthetic questions. The work consists of translations from a variety of sources (including some made especially for this book) as well as extensive introductory essays and commentary.

UCHIYAMA, KOSHO. **APPROACH TO ZEN. Illustrations, 122pp. Jap73, 4.25p.**
A practical guide, intended as a manual for the actual practice of *zazen*. It is written specifically for Westerners by the Roshi of a Soto Zen temple in Kyoto and offers the reader practical instruction and encouragement to go on sitting. A minimum of technical Buddhist terminology is used.

WATTS, ALAN. **THE SPIRIT OF ZEN: A WAY OF LIFE, WORK, AND ART IN THE FAR EAST. Many illustrations, bibliography, index, 128pp. Grv58/Mur, 2.95p.**
A philosophical examination of Zen as a way of life, treating the same material as in **The Way of Zen** in a less technical and less comprehensive manner. Many quotations from Zen texts are included.

■ *WATTS, ALAN.* **THE WAY OF ZEN. Notes, bibliography, index, 236pp. RaH57/Pen, 1.95p.**
A concise, lucid, and comprehensive introduction to the history and philosophy of Zen. Very rewarding reading. The best single introduction to Zen that we know of.

THE WAY OF EIHEIJI (A RECORDING). 13.98.
A two record (33 1/3 rpm) set featuring examples from many different Zen Buddhist ceremonies and rituals of the Eiheiji (*Temple of Great Peace*). This is a well regarded collection among serious scholars. Very extensive descriptive notes are included.

WEI, WU WEI. **ASK THE AWAKENED—THE NEGATIVE WAY. Index, 228pp. LBC63/RKP, 3.45p.**
Mixing parables and gentle teaching, the author presents and interprets the teachings of the six Ch'an Patriarchs and the great masters of the T'ang Dynasty, stressing the need for subjective awareness rather than objective understanding. An enlightening undertaking.

WETERING, JANWILLEM VAN DE. **THE EMPTY MIRROR. 145pp. HMC73/RKP, 3.95p/1.95p.**
An absorbing account of the year that the author spent in a Japanese

Zen Buddhist monastery. The narrative is vivid, often humorous, and sometimes disillusioning. This is the best book of its type that we have ever read.

WETERING, JANWILLEM VAN DE. **A GLIMPSE OF NOTHINGNESS: EXPERIENCES IN AN AMERICAN ZEN COMMUNITY. 184pp. S&S75/RKP, 1.95p.**
This is the story of the two weeks that van de Wetering spent in an intensive retreat. It is vividly narrated in the first person. Unlike his earlier account of struggle toward enlightenment in a Japanese monastery, here he seems to reach more of an intuitive understanding of *satori*. The reader can get a good feeling of Zen from this narrative without being overwhelmed by details which he cannot relate to his own existence.

WHITFORD, CECILIA. **JAPANESE PRINTS. 5.95p.**
See the Sacred Art section.

WIENPAHL, PAUL. **THE MATTER OF ZEN. Extensive notes, index, 6"x7¾", 162pp. NYU64, 3.95p.**
Zazen is an intense form of sitting meditation practiced by the Rinzai Zen Buddhist sect. The author is a Westerner who has studied *zazen* in Japan, and he explains the discipline step-by-step. He describes each of the aspects: sitting quietly; breathing in a certain way; counting; *koans*; as well as the role of the *roshi*, or teacher, and the Zen moral code. This is one of the few books which specifically directs the student in *zazen* and, although not the most enlightened study possible, it is adequate. Wienpahl includes chapters on the history of Zen and the relation of Zen to traditional Western metaphysics.

WOOD, ERNEST. **ZEN DICTIONARY. 165pp. Tut57/Pen, 3.75p.**
A comprehensive, practical work covering all aspects of Zen as taught and practiced both in China and in Japan. Each entry is concise and clear.

WU, JOHN C.H. **THE GOLDEN AGE OF ZEN. 322pp. NWC67, 6.50p.**
An exposition of Zen as experienced and taught by the great Zen masters of the T'ang Dynasty (619-906). Includes an excellent, long introduction by Thomas Merton, as well as many notes in Chinese.

YOSHIKAWA, ITSUJI. **MAJOR THEMES IN JAPANESE ART. 7½"x 9½", 166pp. Wea76, 15.00c.**
Both an introduction to Japanese art and an overview of its rich history, this volume serves two major purposes: to survey the development of Japanese art from its primitive beginnings down to the nineteenth century and to interpret significant aspects of its splendid and often unique achievements. Every representative trend, style, and school is covered by the text and the 175 illustrations, forty-two of which are in color.

EDGAR CAYCE

The story of Edgar Cayce's life is quite remarkable and the results of his work have had far reaching and proliferating effects. He will always be known for the trance-like state that he entered into over 16,000 times during his life and the wealth of information he gave humanity while in this state.

He had very little education as a young boy and was never very intellectual. However, even at a young age he had the amazing ability to acquire information during sleep which he retained in his memory and could reproduce verbatim. In this way, he could memorize whole texts but not know the meaning of what his mind recorded.

At a later time, but still early in his life, Cayce began entering into an unconscious trance state where he apparently had access to a universal storehouse of knowledge on all matter of subjects, including prognostications of the future. His revelations became known as *readings*. His first several thousand readings concerned medical diagnosis and therapeutical remedies. These were often done for patients suffering hundreds of miles from Cayce, whom he had neither met nor knew of in any fashion. His medicinal prescriptions were extraordinarily accurate and showed an insight into the healing processes of the body which even today is lacking in the traditional medical profession.

Later in his life Cayce began giving life readings concerning the needs of individuals and the solution of their problems. It was during one of these readings that he casually mentioned that an individual had lived a previous life in another country. Thus began a new dimension of Cayce material, as much relating to the law of rebirth was delivered during his state of trance. His prophecies relating to future events and *earth changes* have received much public attention. He accurately predicted every major international occurrence over a period of four decades and has prophesied much for the planet into the next century. Among his accurate forecasts were the death while in office of two American presidents and the emergence of the continent of Atlantis off the coast of Bimini in the late 1960's.

Another result of the Cayce material, of practical benefit to the lives of all mankind, is the synthesis and integration of the philosophy of the East with the Western and Christian traditions of dynamic living.

In his last years Cayce located his headquarters in Virginia Beach, Virginia. Today the Association for Research and Enlightment (A.R.E.), the organization founded by Cayce and continued by his son Hugh Lynn and others, is very active in many disciplines. Lectures and research projects are ongoing at the Headquarters (A.R.E., P.O. Box 595, Virginia Beach, Virginia 23451) and there are study groups in almost every major city in the U.S. and a few in other countries. Complete transcripts of every reading Cayce made are kept on file at the Association and are available to the public.

ADRIANCE, ROBERT. HIGHLIGHTS FROM THE EDGAR CAYCE READINGS. 73pp. ARE68, 1.50p.
A selection from the 254 readings which discuss how the A.R.E. should best be organized and its work conducted. The material is topically organized and can be used as a model for those wishing to start other organizations.

AGEE, DORIS. **EDGAR CAYCE ON ESP. 224pp. War69, 1.50p.**
Details how Cayce was able to tune into his subject's unconscious mind as well as the universal unconscious, how he developed his psychic ability. Other topics include telepathy, clairvoyance, auras, and prophecy.

ALLEN, EULA. **BEFORE THE BEGINNING. 74pp. ARE66, 1.75p.**
These three books by Ms. Allen form a trilogy which chronologically covers the Cayce material on creation.

ALLEN, EULA. **THE RIVER OF TIME. 76pp. ARE65, 1.75p.**

ALLEN, EULA. **YOU ARE FOREVER. 74pp. ARE66, 1.75p.**

A.R.E. PRESS. **A COMMENTARY ON THE BOOK OF THE REVELATIONS. 8½"x11", 216pp. ARE69, 5.95p.**
An in depth commentary based on a study of twenty-four discourses in which Cayce mentioned the **Book of Revelation**. Extensive quotations from the readings are included.

A.R.E. PRESS. **ECONOMIC HEALING. 29pp. ARE74, .50p.**
An investigation of the reasons for *economic illness* in individuals and in society coupled with a detailed plan for *economic healing*.

A.R.E. PRESS. **GEMS AND STONES. 1.50p.**
See the Gems and Stones section.

A.R.E. PRESS. **A SEARCH FOR GOD. 266pp. ARE50, 2.95c/each.**
These two volumes are the outcome of eleven years of work by Edgar Cayce and a study group. They represent a distillation of the practical lessons coming through in Cayce's readings and are arranged topically.

A.R.E. PRESS. **THE HANDBOOK FOR A.R.E. STUDY GROUPS. 42pp. ARE57, 1.00p.**

BAKER, M.E. PENNY. **MEDITATION—A STEP BEYOND WITH EDGAR CAYCE. 1.50p.**
See the Meditation section.

BRO, HARMON. **EDGAR CAYCE ON DREAMS. 1.95p.**
See the Dreams section.

BRO, HARMON. **EDGAR CAYCE ON RELIGION AND PSYCHIC EXPERIENCE. 265pp. War70, 1.95p.**

CARLSON, VADA. **THE GREAT MIGRATION. 1.50p.**
See the Ancient Americas section.

CARLSON, VADA. **THE VISION AND THE PROMISE. 35pp. ARE72, 1.25p.**
The story of the childhood and youth of Edgar Cayce, illustrated and told especially for children.

CARTER, MARY ELLEN. **EDGAR CAYCE ON PROPHECY. 207pp. War68, 1.50p.**
A comprehensive account of all the life readings connected with prediction as well as general material on Cayce's life and work. The material from the readings is arranged topically.

CARTER, MARY ELLEN and WILLIAM McGAREY. **EDGAR CAYCE ON HEALING. 205pp. War72, 1.50p.**
This book is about a psychic and his work in suggesting methods by which healing might come to the human body. These suggestions centered on the field of medicine and spread out over osteopathy, chiropractic, physical therapy, herbal therapy, nutrition, spiritual therapy, hypnotherapy, dentistry, and what is best described as "other methods." The major part of the book consists of Ms. Carter's narrative of the lives of several people (some critically ill) who, through Cayce's suggestions, regained their health as well as a different perspective on life. Each of Ms. Carter's accounts is followed by Dr. McGarey's

discussion of the physiological concepts and the various therapies which Cayce suggested. Dr. McGarey is Director of the A.R.E. Clinic.

CATALDO, GERALD. **A DICTIONARY.** 81pp. ARE73, 2.00p.
Definitions and comments from the Cayce readings arranged in alphabetical form.

CAYCE, EDGAR. **AURAS.** 20pp. ARE45, .75p.
This booklet is one of the few things that Edgar Cayce ever wrote. The countless books that often bear his name are merely transcriptions of his psychic readings. Cayce was without question the greatest psychic America has ever produced. He gave thousands of health readings while he was in a trance-like state. He had finely developed intuitive powers including the gift of being able to see auras easily. **Auras** was written in the last month of his life and it sums up his observations in an unusually clear manner. Each of the primary colors is discussed individually and the value of auric sight is touched on. There is also a summary color chart.

CAYCE, EDGAR. **CHANGE: EDGAR CAYCE ON THE I CHING.** 1.95p.
See the I Ching subsection of Chinese Philosophy.

CAYCE, EDGAR. **MEDICINES FOR A NEW AGE.** 47+pp. Her74, 1.75p.
This is the most detailed account of the remedies suggested in the Cayce readings. The material is alphabetically arranged by remedies and is paraphrased from the original readings with some background information on the remedy. The appropriate circulating files are cited by number (these files are available only to A.R.E. members) and manufacturers' product names for Cayce formulas are also given. Appendices contain an alphabetical listing of publications and files available from the A.R.E., and a list of products recommended in the readings that are not currently available.

CAYCE, EDGAR. **WHAT I BELIEVE.** 48pp. ARE46, 1.50p.
This autobiographical account is one of the few things that Cayce actually wrote himself.

CAYCE, EDGAR EVANS. **ATLANTIS: FACT OR FICTION.** 1.25p.
See the Ancient Civilizations section.

CAYCE, HUGH LYNN. **DREAMS: THE LANGUAGE OF THE UN-CONSCIOUS.** 2.50p.
See the Dreams section.

CAYCE, HUGH LYNN. **THE EDGAR CAYCE READER #2.** 206pp. War69, 1.95p.

CAYCE, HUGH LYNN. **FOR THESE TIMES.** 62pp. ARE64, 1.25p.
Transcriptions of five lectures by Edgar Cayce's son: *This Man Sought First the Kingdom, Clairvoyance and the Bible, Where Karma Ends and Grace Begins, Faith and Miracles,* and *Can We Break the Time Barrier.*

CAYCE, HUGH LYNN and EDGAR. **GOD'S OTHER DOOR.** 48pp. ARE58, 1.50p.
A study of the Cayce readings on life after death combined with the transcription of a lecture, *The Continuity of Life,* which Edgar Cayce gave in 1934.

CAYCE, J. GAIL. **OSTEOPATHY.** Bibliography, 11"x8½", 64pp. ARE73, 3.00p.
A comparison of various parallel concepts expressed by A.T. Still, the founder of osteopathy, and Edgar Cayce. Excerpts from both sources are examined with brief comments between the extracts. The material is topically arranged and an appendix explores several topics in further detail. *It is hoped that this survey will serve as a tool and as a foundation for expansion of the various points presented in the outline.*

CERMINARA, GINA. **MANY MANSIONS.** 1.75p.
See the Reincarnation and Karma section.

CHURCH, W.H. **A GARLAND OF WISDOM.** 35pp. ARE75, 1.25p.
Topically arranged short quotations from the Cayce readings, in an illustrated gift book format.

CRAIG, PAULA. **BUILD YOUR OWN DREAM HOUSE.** 1.25p.
See the Dreams section.

FURST, JEFFREY. **EDGAR CAYCE'S STORY OF JESUS.** 1.95p.
See the Christianity section.

GAMMON, MARGARET. **ASTROLOGY AND THE EDGAR CAYCE READINGS.** 2.00p.
See the Astrology section.

HATT, CAROLYN. **THE MAYA.** 1.75p.
See the Ancient Americas section.

JAMES, WALENE. **HANDBOOK FOR EDUCATING IN THE NEW AGE.** Notes, 100pp. ARE77, 2.50p.
Selections from the readings, along with commentary, organized around the following general topics: *Purposes and Ideals, School System, Teacher, Methods—The Mandala Principle of Learning,* and *Curriculum for Consciousness.* Quotations from other humanistically-oriented writings are interspersed.

JOHNSON, RAYNOR. **THE SITUATION OF MODERN MAN.** 76pp. ARE71, 2.00p.
Transcription of a series of lectures on the importance and unimportance of life and reorientation of being.

KIDD, WORTH. **EDGAR CAYCE AND GROUP DYNAMICS.** 54pp. ARE71, 2.00p.
Practical suggestions for A.R.E. group organization and leadership.

KITTLER, GLENN. **EDGAR CAYCE ON THE DEAD SEA SCROLLS.** 1.50p.
See the Dead Sea Scrolls subsection of Ancient Near East.

KRAJENKE, ROBERT. **THE PSYCHIC SIDE OF THE AMERICAN DREAM.** Bibliography, notes, 72pp. ARE76, 2.00p.
A unified collection of fragments from the Cayce readings, quotations from a variety of other sources, and reflections by Krajenke himself.

LANGLEY, NOEL. **EDGAR CAYCE ON REINCARNATION.** 1.95p.
See the Reincarnation and Karma section.

LEARY, DAVID. **EDGAR CAYCE'S PHOTOGRAPHIC LEGACY.** 7½"x 10½", 340pp. Dou78, 12.95c.
A photographic biography of Cayce containing over 300 photographs and clippings from the Cayce family album along with selections from his readings. Many of the photographs were taken by Cayce himself (he was a professional photographer).

LEHNER, MARK. **THE EGYPTIAN HERITAGE.** 2.95p.
See the Ancient Egypt section.

LEWIS, ROGER. **COLOR.** Bibliography, 48pp. ARE73, 1.50p.
Lewis is an artist who has studied the Cayce material on color at great length. First, he sets the stage with the scientific examination of color. Then, using the Cayce booklet, **Auras**, he shows how Cayce interpreted various colors when they appeared in the emanation of light around an individual. Because the Cayce readings associated various colors with the seven spiritual centers in the body, Lewis traces the colors on the path of the kundalini, describing the influences of the endocrine glands. Finally he looks at color from the point of view of the color psychologist. Includes many quotations from the Cayce readings.

MCGAREY, WILLIAM. **EDGAR CAYCE AND THE PALMA CHRISTI.** **134pp. ARE70, 4.95p.**
A detailed study of the use of castor oil packs as suggested in the Edgar Cayce readings and as observed in case histories from the readings and in Dr. McGarey's own practice. Cayce suggested the packs as remedies for over fifty different ailments and the results have often been remarkable.

MCGAREY, WILLIAM and GLADYS. **THERE WILL YOUR HEART BE ALSO. Index, 264pp. War75, 1.50p.**
Subtitled, *Edgar Cayce's Readings About Home and Marriage,* this is an examination of Cayce's readings on almost every aspect of love and marriage—from choosing one's mate and forming one's own marriage vows, to the proper guidance of adolescents. Cayce's advice, above all, is practical and the Drs. McGarey have been practicing medicine and counseling for over twenty years, while raising a family of their own. They dramatize Cayce's theories of choice, growth, and forgiveness with actual events from their own household and from their patients' experiences. The material is better integrated than most of the works drawn from the Cayce material. The McGareys run the A.R.E. Clinic in Arizona.

NEIMARK, ANNE. **WITH THIS GIFT: THE STORY OF EDGAR CAYCE. Fairly big print, bibliography, index, 192pp. Mor78, 6.95c.**
A simple biography of Cayce, geared toward junior high school age readers.

PATTERSON, DORIS. **VARIETIES OF ESP IN THE EDGAR CAYCE READINGS. 77pp. ARE68, 2.00p.**

PATTERSON, DORIS and VIOLET SHELLEY. **BE YOUR OWN PSY-CHIC. 83pp. ARE75, 2.00p.**
Selections from the readings, with commentary, which explain how to use your psychic abilities safely in accordance with your spiritual growth.

PETERSON, MARILYN. **NIGHTLIGHTS: A DREAM DIARY. 4.95p.**
See the Dreams section.

PURYEAR, HERBERT and MARK THURSTON. **MEDITATION AND THE MIND OF MAN. 107pp. ARE75, 2.50p.**
See the Meditation section.

READ, ANNE and CAROL ILSTRUP. **A DIET/RECIPE GUIDE. 84pp. ARE67, 2.00p.**
A collection of recipes and nutritional advice based on and gleaned from the Cayce readings.

READ, ANNE, CAROL ILSTRUP and MARGARET GAMMON. **EDGAR CAYCE ON DIET AND HEALTH. Index, 191pp. War69, 1.95p.**
Selections from the Cayce readings containing his most practical suggestions for practical diet. He emphasizes eating the right foods in the right combinations at the right time. The book also includes a series of questions and answers on vitamins, minerals, cooking methods, sleep and rest, the correct psychological attitude to eating, and other issues.

REILLY, HAROLD and RUTH BROD. **THE EDGAR CAYCE HAND-BOOK FOR HEALTH THROUGH DRUGLESS THERAPY. Index, 348pp. McM75, 10.95c/2.25p.**
Dr. Reilly is a physiotherapist who was referred many cases by Edgar Cayce and has worked with Cayce methods for some forty-five years. In this book he presents a fusion of his own knowledge and experience and Cayce's recommendations. Subjects covered include diet and nutrition, exercise, hydrotherapy, massage, internal cleansing, weight reduction, complexion and skin care, and how to age without growing old. The chapter on massage is particularly good, with extensive instructions and line drawings on how to give a massage. For followers of Cayce's health ideas, this is the most comprehensive, useful book yet to come along.

ROBINSON, LYLE. **EDGAR CAYCE'S STORY OF THE ORIGIN AND DESTINY OF MAN. 228pp. Ber72, 1.95p.**
See the Ancient Civilizations section.

ROCHE, RICHARD. **EGYPTIAN MYTHS AND THE RA TA STORY. 1.95p.**
See the Ancient Egypt section.

RUNNELS, RACHEL. **MARRIAGE AND THE HOME. 74pp. ARE73, 1.95p.**
A study of the readings approach to marriage, home, sex, parenthood, and being single.

SECHRIST, ELSIE. **DREAMS: YOUR MAGIC MIRROR. 1.95p.**
See the Dreams section.

SECHRIST, ELSIE. **MEDITATION—GATEWAY TO LIGHT. 1.50p.**
See the Meditation section.

SHARMA, I.C. **CAYCE, KARMA, AND REINCARNATION. 3.95p.**
See the Reincarnation and Karma section.

SHELLEY, VIOLET. **SYMBOLS AND THE SELF. 63pp. ARE65, 1.75p.**
A study of numbers and symbols based loosely on the Cayce readings, showing how symbolism surrounds us and enters into every aspect of our lives.

SPARROW, GREGORY. **LUCID DREAMING. 2.25p.**
See the Dreams section.

STEARN, JESS. **A PROPHET IN HIS OWN COUNTRY. 309pp. Ban74, 1.75p.**
Subtitled, *The Story of the Young Edgar Cayce.*

■ *STEARN, JESS.* **EDGAR CAYCE—THE SLEEPING PROPHET. 287pp. Ban67, 1.95p.**
A presentation of many of Cayce's predictions and prophecies, both those that have been accurate in the past and those forecast for the future. Many incidents in Cayce's life and some of his unorthodox but effective medical diagnoses and remedies are also described. A good introduction to the Cayce material, and the one we prefer.

STEINHART, LAWRENCE, ed. **EDGAR CAYCE'S SECRETS OF BEAU-TY THROUGH HEALTH. 216pp. Ber74, 1.95p.**
Because of Edgar Cayce's excellent track record in diagnosis and prescription, whatever he said about health and beauty is well worth listening to. This book collects all the relevant readings: care of skin, eyes, teeth, hair, food and exercise, physiotherapy, elimination. The last part of the book goes beyond most health and beauty books, delving into reincarnation, recycling the mental body, vibratory influences, dreams, and rejuvenation. Steinhart has done a good job of integrating the readings with other relevant information and putting it all together in an easy to read format.

■ *SURGUE, THOMAS.* **THERE IS A RIVER—THE STORY OF ED-GAR CAYCE. 384pp. Del42, 1.75p.**
The closest, most intimate portrayal of the life of America's greatest psychic, clairvoyant, and modern day prophet. The author was the only writer who actually knew Cayce personally and observed his activities. The writing style and information is very folksy, but the essential information is there. This is the first Cayce book that most people read.

THURSTON, MARK. **EXPERIMENTS IN A SEARCH FOR GOD. 139pp. ARE76, 2.95p.**
This is an in depth study of six to eight key concepts from each chapter of **A Search for God, Book I.** The analysis includes parallel material from the readings and from a variety of other sources including depth psychology, the Bible, and Eastern religions. Each essay is followed by an experiment which provides explicit instructions for applying the philosophical concept just discussed. In all, 100 essays and experiments are included along with introductory material.

THURSTON, MARK. **UNDERSTAND AND DEVELOP YOUR ESP. 2.50p.**
See the Parapsychology section.

TURNER, GLADYS and MAE ST. CLAIR. **123 QUESTIONS AND ANSWERS FROM THE EDGAR CAYCE READINGS. Index, 59pp. ARE66, 1.25p.**
Topically arranged.

WINSTON, SHIRLEY. **MUSIC AS THE BRIDGE. 1.95p.**
See the Music section.

WOODWARD, MARY ANN. **EDGAR CAYCE'S STORY OF KARMA. 1.95p.**
See the Reincarnation and Karma section.

CHILDREN'S BOOKS

If we hope to live not just from moment to moment, but in true consciousness of our existence, then our greatest need and most difficult achievement is to find meaning in our lives. It is well known how many have lost the will to live, and have stopped trying, because such meaning has evaded them. An understanding of the meaning of one's life is not suddenly acquired at a particular age, not even when one has reached chronological maturity. On the contrary, gaining a secure understanding of what the meaning of one's life may or ought to be—this is what constitutes having attained psychological maturity. And this achievement is the end result of a long development: at each age we seek, we must be able to find some modicum of meaning congruent with how our minds and understanding have already developed.

Contrary to the ancient myth, wisdom does not burst forth fully developed like Athena out of Zeus's head; it is built up, small step by small step, from most irrational beginnings. Only in adulthood can an intelligent understanding of the meaning of one's existence in this world be gained from one's experiences in it. Unfortunately, too many parents want their children's minds to function as their own do—as if mature understanding of ourselves and the world, and our ideas about the meaning of life, did not have to develop as slowly as our bodies and minds.

Today, as in times past, the most important and also the most difficult task in raising a child is helping him to find meaning in life. Many growth experiences are needed to achieve this. The child, as he develops, must learn step by step to understand himself better; with this he becomes more able to understand others, and eventually can relate to them in ways which are mutually satisfying and meaningful.

To find deeper meaning, one must become able to transcend the narrow confines of a self-centered existence and believe that one will make a significant contribution to life—if not right now, then at some future time. This feeling is necessary if a person is to be satisfied with himself and with what he is doing. In order not to be at the mercy of the vagaries of life, one must develop one's inner resources, so that one's emotions, imagination, and intellect mutually support and enrich one another. Our positive feelings give us the strength to develop our rationality; only hope for the future can sustain us in the adversities we unavoidably encounter.

As an educator and therapist of severely disturbed children, my main task was to restore meaning to their lives. This work made it obvious to me that if children were reared so that life was meaningful to them, they would not need special help. I was confronted with the problem of deducing what experiences in a child's life are most suited to promote his ability to find meaning in his life; to endow life in general with more meaning. Regarding this task, nothing is more important than the impact of parents and others who take care of the child; second in importance is our cultural heritage, when transmitted to the child in the right manner. When children are young, it is literature that carries such information best.

Given this fact, I became deeply dissatisfied with much of the literature intended to develop the child's mind and personality, because it fails to stimulate and nurture those resources he needs most in order to cope with his difficult inner problems. The preprimers and primers from which he is taught to read in school are designed to teach the necessary skills, irrespective of meaning. The overwhelming bulk of the rest of so-called *children's literature* attempts to entertain or to inform, or both. But most of these books are so shallow in substance that little of significance can be gained from them. The acquisition of skills, including the ability to read, becomes devalued when what one has learned to read adds nothing of importance to one's life.

We all tend to assess the future merits of an activity on the basis of what it offers now. But this is especially true for the child, who, much more than the adult, lives in the present and, although he has anxieties about his future, has only the vaguest notions of what it may require or be like. The idea that learning to read may enable one later to enrich one's life is experienced as an empty promise when the stories the child listens to, or is reading at the moment, are vacuous. The worst feature of these children's books is that they cheat the child of what he ought to gain from the experience of literature: access to deeper meaning, and that which is meaningful to him at his stage of development.

For a story truly to hold the child's attention, it must entertain him and arouse his curiosity. But to enrich his life, it must stimulate his imagination; help him to develop his intellect and to clarify his emotions; be attuned to his anxieties and aspirations; give full recognition to his difficulties, while at the same time suggesting solutions to the problems which perturb him. In short, it must at one and the same time relate to all aspects of his personality—and this without ever belittling but, on the contrary, giving full credence to the seriousness of the child's predicaments, while simultaneously promoting confidence in himself and in his future.

—*condensed from* **The Uses of Enchantment**, *by Bruno Bettelheim*

AARDEMA, VERNA. **WHO'S IN RABBIT'S HOUSE?** 10¼"x10¼", **Dia77, 7.95c.**
This book is illustrated by Leo and Diane Dillon in the same style as their earlier two Caldecott Medal books. In this humorous Masai tale Rabbit cannot get into her house because The Long One, hiding inside, threatens to trample her just as he tramples elephants. Various unhelpful suggestions are offered by Rabbit's friends, but in the end the solution comes from an unexpected source. The illustrations show the story presented in the form of a play performed before their fellow villagers by Masai actors wearing animal masks.

AARDEMA, VERNA. **WHY MOSQUITOES BUZZ IN PEOPLE'S EARS.** 10½"x10½", Dia75, 6.95c/2.50p.
Magnificent illustrations by Leo and Diane Dillon combined with a simple African legend make for a story that should hold any child's interest. The illustrations are unlike anything we have seen before and they have a definite African feeling. The chief colors are pastel blues, pinks, and purples on a black background. Winner of the 1976 Caldecott Medal for the most distinguished picture book for children and recipient of a number of other citations.

ALDRED, CYRIL. **TUT-ANKH-AMUN AND HIS FRIENDS.** 2.50p.
See the Tutankhamen subsection of Ancient Egypt.

BARKER, CAROL. **AN OBA OF BENIN.** 8½"x11", MCD76, 7.00c.
The day to day life of the son of a ruler of Benin, a great Nigerian kingdom of the past. Village life, hunts, religious festivals, and the making of bronze heads are described. The illustrations are colorful, done in African style, and evocative of African village life.

BARKER, CAROL. **A PRINCE OF ISLAM.** 8½"x11", MCD76, 8.00c.
Prince Omar lived in Baghdad when it was the capital of a great empire. This book is colorfully illustrated with pictures drawn in the style of Islamic art; it describes the Prince's everyday life as he explores the bazaars and quays of the city. He also visits the desert Bedouins and goes on a pilgrimage to Mecca. In addition several stories of his fighting ancestors and the life of Muhammad are told to him by his mother.

BARKER, CICELY. **A LITTLE BOOK OF OLD RHYMES.** 4¼"x7", TCP36, 1.95c.
A collection of traditional verses, rhyming games, and old songs for May Day, New Year's Day, and other festive occasions, illustrated with Ms. Barker's color paintings.

BARKER, CICELY. **THE LORD OF THE RUSHIE RIVER.** 4¼"x7", TCP38/Bla, 1.95c.
A little girl runs away from a cruel and dishonest guardian to live among the swans of the Rushie River. The birds shelter her and look after her as if she were one of their own young. Many full page color illustrations in the style of the **Flower Fairy** books.

BARKER, CICELY. **THE RHYMING RAINBOW.** 4¼"x7", TCP77, 1.95c.
An illustrated collection of some of Ms. Barker's favorite poems and songs.

BELLEROPHON. **COLORING BOOKS.** BIB, 1.95p/each.
These books are 8½"x11" and contain reproductions of illustrations from artists of the period. The illustrations often contain a lot of detail, so they are recommended only for older children. Once colored they become works of art and the books are a good way for the child to learn about other cultures. Titles available include **American Indians, Ancient Egypt, Ancient Greece, The Ancient Near East, Incas-Aztecs-Mayas, Japan, The Middle Ages,** and **The Renaissance.**

BIERHORST, JOHN, ed. **THE RING IN THE PRAIRIE.** 8½"x10½", Del70, 1.75p.
This is an evocative retelling of a Shawnee legend with exquisite, colorful illustrations by Leo and Diane Dillon. Even the landscape speaks, as images appear in trees and star faces loom from the heavens. A young brave falls in love with the daughter of a star, eventually wins her, and they live for a while on earth and have a child. After a bit she longs to return to her star father and she does so. The brave mourns her and is finally invited to come to join his wife and son. As requested, he brings along one of each kind of bird and animal that he kills in his hunting. Each star chooses one of them and is turned into that creature.

BILENKO, ANATOLE. **THE LITTLE SHEPHERD.** 7¾"x8½", 16pp. PrP74, .50p.
Translation of a Ukrainian folk tale about a little shepherd's conquest of a dragon. Colorfully illustrated.

BOLLIGER, MAX. **NOAH AND THE RAINBOW.** 8½"x11½", Cro72, 2.95p.
Lovely pastel watercolors enliven this retelling of Noah's story. The drawings convey a misty feeling—appropriate for a story that tells of a time when the world was covered with water. The text is simple and should appeal to even the youngest readers. The illustrations are by Helga Aichinger.

BOSSILEK, RAN. **THE THREE BROTHERS AND THE GOLDEN APPLE.** 8¾"x10½", PrP74, .60p.
This Russian fairy tale deals with a woman, her three sons, and their struggles to regain the golden fruit of their ancient apple tree from a monster who carries it off to the underworld. The bravery of the youngest son in his adventures through the underworld is pointed up. The illustrations have the charm of medieval tapestries.

BRANDT, KATRIN. **THE CATERPILLAR'S STORY.** 7¼"x7¾", Pen72, 1.50p.
A beautifully illustrated story of a little green caterpillar who ate his way, day after day, through leaf after leaf, and dreamed of flying. One day he rolled himself up in a leaf and went to sleep, and when he awoke he found his dream had come true. The illustrations bring the story to life and the book should be enjoyable even for very young children.

BRODSKY, BEVERLY. **JONAH: AN OLD TESTAMENT STORY.** 9½"x 9", Lip77, 8.95c.
A modern retelling of the story of Jonah, a biblical prophet who tried to run away from his responsibilities, was swallowed by a whale, and finally learned about independence, anger, and love. The simple eloquence of this retelling is complemented by Ms. Brodsky's glowing, evocative watercolors which create a feeling of Jewishness and produce a visual sense that is both ancient and modern.

BROWN, MARGARET. **WHEN THE WIND BLEW.** 5¼"x6¼", 31pp. H&R77, 3.95c.
This story should delight young children. It tells of an old lady who lived by the sea with seventeen cats and one kitten. It is a simple, warm tale and is nicely illustrated in full color.

CAMERON, ANN. **THE SEED.** 6¾"x9¼", RaH75, 5.50c.
A simple story, delicately colored in pastels, of how a seed awakens and begins to grow, finally maturing into a tree. It evokes the beauty and mystery of the natural world and is written simply, so it can be enjoyed by the smallest child.

CARLE, ERIC. **THE VERY HUNGRY CATERPILLAR.** 8½"x12", Pen76, 1.75p.
This is an innovative book which dramatizes the story of one of nature's most common yet loveliest marvels—the metamorphosis of a caterpillar into a butterfly. Die-cut pages show what the caterpillar ate on successive days, graphically introducing sets of up to ten objects and also the names of the days of the week in rotation, as well as telling the central story of the transformation of the caterpillar. The pictures are striking and bold and the text is simple and printed in clear, large type. The story of the hungry little caterpillar's progress through an amazing variety and quantity of foods should delight even the youngest readers.

CHARUSHIN, Y. **HOW THEY LIVE.** 8½"x11", PrP nd, .60p.
This is one of a series of children's picture books imported from the Soviet Union. Each is beautifully produced and is a remarkable value. The books are full color throughout. This is a simple book, suitable for the youngest child. Beautiful drawings and a short text detail the lives of the squirrel, hare, wolf, bear, zebra, camel, lion, tiger, and elephant.

CHEK, CHIA HERN. **MOONGATE COLLECTION: FOLKTALES FROM THE ORIENT.** 10¼"x7¾", Dom76, 4.95c/each.
Chek is one of Southeast Asia's best known writers of children's books. His work has won countless awards. This collection presents some of the best loved stories of the region, retold in a simple style and vividly illustrated by a Chinese artist, Kwan Shan Mei. The stories are designed to appeal to children of all ages, and they can be understood easily by young readers. Each is well bound and seems fairly indestructible. The following books make up the collection: **The Redhill** (Singapore), **The Magic Princess** (Malaysia), **The Dragon of Kinabalu** (Borneo), **The Bird Hunter** (Indonesia), **The Sun King** (Thailand), **The White Elephant** (Burma), **The Emperor and the Nightingale** (China), **Taro and His Grandmother** (Japan), **Uenuku and the Rainbow** (Maori), **The Talking Parrot** (Pakistan), **The Angry Gods** (Tibet), **The Master Chess Player** (Mongolia), and **The Wind Loves You, Aminata** (Africa).

CHUKOVSKY, KORNEI. **THE MUDDLE.** 8¾"x11", PrP76, .70p.
Nonsense rhymes about animals are accompanied by a series of colorful and amusing illustrations designed to appeal to young children.

CHUKOVSKY, KORNEI. **WONDER TALES.** 9"x11¼", PrP73, 1.70c.
A collection of four animal tales which are takeoffs on modern life. Each is in verse, accompanied by lively color illustrations.

COSGROVE, STEPHEN and ROBIN JAMES. **SERENDIPITY BOOKS.** PSS74, 7.50p/each.
Two boxed sets, each with five delightfully illustrated booklets relating a tale of an imaginary creature. The stories are colorful and boldly illustrated and the storyline is simple, and easy to follow. Even the youngest reader will love the books and we know many adults who are delighted with them. This is one of the most unusual series we have seen. Set No. 1 contains *The Muffin Muncher, Morgan & Me, Serendipity, The Dream Tree,* and *In Search of the Saveopotamas.* Set No. 2 includes *Leo the Lop, Jake O'Shawnasey, Creole, The Gnome from Nome,* and *Hucklebug.* Each booklet is 5½"x8½" and about 32 pages.

COSON, DONNA. **THE ANCIENT GREEK COLORING BOOK.** 46 plates, 8¼"x11½", 96pp. Wdw77, 5.10p.

CROFTS, TRUDY and KEN MCKEON. **THE HUNTER AND THE QUAIL.** 2.95p.
See the **Jataka Tales** subsection of Buddhism.

CUMMINGS, E.E. **FAIRY TALES.** 39pp. HBJ75, 1.75p.
These four exquisite little stories might have sprung from the consciousness of a child. They are fragmentary and luminous, delicate, and blissfully unresolved....John Eaton's illustrations are quite perfect for the book, combining line with soft washes of color.—**N.Y. Times Book Review.**

D'AULAIRE, INGRI and EDGAR. **D'AULAIRE'S BOOK OF GREEK MYTHS.** Index, 9"x12½", 192pp. Dou62, 8.95c.
This is a handsomely produced volume which retells the major and minor myths in a simple fashion and manages to retain the power of the tales. We enjoyed reading it and we know many children who have been delighted with the book. The d'Aulaires are prize-winning illustrators and there are drawings on virtually every page.

D'AULAIRE, INGRI and EDGAR. **D'AULAIRE'S NORSE GODS AND GIANTS.** Glossary, index, 9"x12½", 161pp. Dou67, 7.95c.
The Norse myths are not nearly as well known as the Greek ones. Ingri d'Aulaire is Norwegian and she has succeeded admirably in bringing these myths to life. We like the illustrations in this volume better than the ones in **Greek Myths** and the retellings are simple and nicely written. We recommend the d'Aulaires' work to all parents who want to introduce their children to mythology.

D'AULAIRE, INGRI and EDGAR. **D'AULAIRE'S TROLLS.** 9¼"x12½", 62pp. Dou72, 1.95p.
A picturebook devoted to trolls, the legendary inhabitants of the wild Norwegian mountains. The illustrations show every imaginable kind of troll and many of the illustrations are in color. Stories about the trolls accompany the drawings.

DAYRELL, ELPHINSTONE. **WHY THE SUN AND THE MOON LIVE IN THE SKY.** 9"x9", HMC68, 1.95p.
An African folktale which tells the story of how the sun and moon came to live in the sky. African tribesmen are dressed to represent the elements and the creatures of the sea. The folktale comes directly from the oral tradition, and Blair Lent does a wonderful job of recreating the African style in his illustrations. This book has been recommended by all the major children's book reviewers.

DUFF, MAGGIE. **RUM PUM PUM.** 10¼"x8¼", McM78, 7.95c.
Blackbird is preparing to make war on the king who has stolen his wife. Beating his walnut shell drum he marches down the road toward the palace. As he goes he is joined by others who have been cruelly treated: cat, stick, river, and the ants. One by one they jump into Blackbird's ear. The king tries to dispose of Blackbird but is outwitted by each of his companions, and, in the end, the good guys win out. An extremely simple retelling of an Indian folktale, suitable for the youngest children, and boldly and colorfully illustrated by Jose Aruego and Ariane Dewey.

FARMER, PENELOPE and CHRIS CONNOR. **THE SERPENT'S TEETH: THE STORY OF CADMUS.** 8"x9¾", WCS71, 4.70c.
Princess Europa was abducted by Zeus who had taken the form of a great white bull. Prince Cadmus was charged by his parents with finding his sister; when he failed, he was banished. Then he began to have many adventures, including a terrifying fight with a three-headed dragon. The story ends with his founding and populating the city of Thebes. This is a pictorial retelling of this classic Greek myth. The illustrations are bold and colorful and successfully create a feeling for the times.

FOREMAN, MICHAEL. **ALL THE KING'S HORSES.** 9"x11¼", Dut76/HHL, 7.95c.
Marvelous watercolors of depth, breadth and energy contrast with an informal, offbeat text. The main character is an Asiatic princess—but not the golden-haired, meek variety usually found in fairy tales. This one is big and dark. Her father the king wants her married to a rich man who will not scrounge off him, but the princess won't marry anyone who cannot outwrestle her. She beats everyone, including the likely hero—the huge son of a poor woodcutter. Finally she rides away on a horse, taking thousands of other horses with her, and spends the rest of her life sweeping back and forth across the whole of Asia.

FOREMAN, MICHAEL. **DINOSAURS AND ALL THAT RUBBISH.** 9"x11½", Pen72, 1.50p.
Rainbow colored watercolors plus an enchanting tale make this story one that will captivate, as well as increase ecological awareness in, young readers. A man on Earth, desiring to fly to a faraway star, ordered a rocket built no matter what the cost, but in the process nearly destroyed the Earth. The chaos awakened dinosaurs and other ancient creatures hiding deep within the Earth. These creatures restored the Earth and cavorted in their jungle paradise, eventually allowing the man to return only with his promise to treat the Earth with respect and care.

FOREMAN, MICHAEL. **PANDA'S PUZZLE AND HIS VOYAGE OF DISCOVERY.** 8¾"x11¼", Dut78, 7.95c.
Before he saw his reflection in a tin can lid, Panda lived unquestioningly on bamboo shoots and clear mountain air. But the tin can started puzzling Panda, for pictured on its label were two bears facing each other, one black, one white. *Am I a white bear with black bits or a black bear with white bits?,* he asked himself. Panda sought the answer all over the world. Everywhere he learned something different, though never

quite the answer to his question—until he realized that it did not matter at all what color he was. Foreman's pastel illustrations are delightful; there are scenes in China, India, Egypt, and America.

FUJIKAWA, GYO. **A TO Z PICTURE BOOK.** 9¼"x12¼", G&D74, 4.95c.
This is a nicely illustrated alphabet book, designed to appeal to the youngest readers. The illustrations are vivid and are brightly colored and they include a great deal of detail. Some of our favorites are a peacock and a monster.

FUJIKAWA, GYO. **MOTHER GOOSE.** 9"x12", 64pp. G&D77, 2.95p.
Simple retellings of many Mother Goose rhymes, illustrated in Fujikawa's distinctive style. Every other page is in color.

GARSHIN, V. **THE FROG WENT TRAVELLING.** 8½"x11", PrP75, .60p.
This Russian book tells of a frog who talked a group of ducks into taking him on their yearly migratory flight. The drawings are done in browns and other nature colors. The text is fairly long, although the writing style and ideas are simple.

GELLEK, NAZLI. **TALES OF THE BUDDHA.** 9"x11½", Dha, 4.75c.
This is a series of brightly colored tales of the Buddha's adventures in earlier incarnations. The stories can be read on a number of levels and many of the simple happenings have a deep symbolic meaning. See the **Jataka** subsection of Buddhism for a description of each of the individual volumes. Personally we prefer the retelling in the DeRoin version, but this format is more appropriate for young children. The following books are now available: **The Golden Foot, The King and the Mangoes, The Proud Peacock and the Mallard, The Spade Sage, Three Wise Birds.**

GEORGIOU, CONSTANTINE. **RANI: QUEEN OF THE JUNGLE.** 7¼"x10", PrH70, 5.25c.
This is a simple tale; and the book is filled with brightly colored, tapestry-like illustrations. The story tells of a small East Indian boy who adopts a tiger cub. The two become inseparable playmates, but the tiger is destined to become queen of the jungle and so they eventually part. The book is written for the youngest readers.

GINSBURG, MIRRA. **HOW THE SUN WAS BROUGHT BACK TO THE SKY.** 10½"x8½", McM75, 7.95c.
This is an adaptation of a Slovenian folktale. Grey clouds have shut out the sun for days. A family of chicks accompanied by a variety of other small animals set out to find the sun and bring it back to the sky. A series of beautifully colored full page illustrations parallel the text and spill over onto the page that has the writing. We personally love drawings of the sun and this book contains some of the finest we have seen along with a delightful set of animals.

GINSBURG, MIRRA. **MUSHROOM IN THE RAIN.** 10½"x8½", McM74, 2.50p.
It is raining and all the animals hide under a mushroom. They are amazed that there is room for them all until they realize what happens to a mushroom when it rains—it multiples! Adapted from a Russian folk tale and beautifully illustrated with a variety of animals, rainbows, multi-colored mushrooms, and much else.

GOODALL, JOHN. **CREEPY CASTLE.** All color, 7"x5¼", MGB75, 3.60c.
This is a delightful wordless book. The illustrations speak for themselves and convey a tale which should enchant small children fascinated by castles and adventure. The main characters are two nobly dressed mice and the story line follows their activities inside the castle where they encounter bats and a dragon and only just succeed in escaping. Many half size pages are overlaid and show the continuing story.

GORSLINE, MARIE and DOUGLAS. **NORTH AMERICAN INDIANS.** 8"x8", RaH77, .95p.
A colorful, pictorial account of the lives and traditions of native Americans. Very few words are used; the pictures are vivid and convey a great deal of information.

HALEY, GAIL. **A STORY, A STORY.** 7"x7", Ath70, 1.95p.
Many African stories, whether or not they are about...the "spider man," are called "Spider Stories." This book is about how that came to be. "Spider stories" tell how small, defenseless men or animals outwit others and succeed against great odds. The tale is simply written and illustrated in vivid colors. The illustrations convey a feeling of Africa and should delight small children. A Caldecott Award winner.

HEINS, PAUL. **SNOW WHITE.** 9½"x9", LBC74, 6.95c.
Trina Schart Hyman's exquisite illustrations powerfully express the conflict between good and evil. Each page glows with color, with shadings and shadows evocative of pain and sorrow, and with explosions of light and joy. The illustrations give us a better feeling for the story than we have ever had before and the translation is equally good. The language and style are simple and clear. A charming book for young readers.

HITZ, DEMI. **LU PAN—THE CARPENTER'S APPRENTICE.** 5.95c.
See the Chinese Philosophy section.

HODGSON, JOAN. **ANGELS AND INDIANS.** 48pp. WET74, 4.75c.
This is a strange book which is more obviously spiritual than most of the children's books. The first part of the book presents a series of photographs of fairies which purport to be real and discusses the young girl who made contact with the fairies. The next section is devoted to a story which illustrates what the American Indians knew about the fairies and angels in the world of light and discusses American Indian children's contact with the *Great White Spirit*. A final section shows how Indians and others from the past influence our lives today. Many brightly colored illustrations are included, but these are not of the best quality.

HODGSON, JOAN. **HULLO SUN.** 10½"x8½", WET72, 3.25c.
This book is designed to help children reach spiritual understanding and encourage them to take full advantage of their natural fantasies. Here is an example: *Hello Sun! You give us light. You make us warm. You make the trees and flowers grow. You make us happy. Thank you, Sun. Now shut your eyes and think of the Sun. Can you see the Sun with your imagination—with your inside eyes? It is shining so brightly. It makes us feel lovely and warm and happy inside. God is like the Sun. God is the Great Spirit behind the Sun. God is everywhere. God is everything but you cannot see Him with your outside eyes.* Fully illustrated with bright colors—again poorly drawn, but here it is the message that counts, not the pictures. Large print.

HUTTON, WARWICK. **NOAH AND THE GREAT FLOOD.** 8½"x11", Ath77, 7.95c.
This retelling of the Noah legend uses very few words and can therefore be read and appreciated by even the youngest readers. Hutton has reinterpreted the biblical story in watercolor paintings of remarkable beauty which succeed admirably in bringing the story to life.

JARRELL, RANDALL, tr. **SNOW-WHITE AND THE SEVEN DWARFS.** 9"x12", FSG72, 6.95c.
Nancy Burkert has painted a series of magical visions. The illustrations can be studied endlessly and new forms and creatures pop out of the amazingly detailed work. Our favorite is a forest scene where the animals are camouflaged—the more you look at the pictures, the more animals you see. The drawings themselves are extraordinary and the colors are well chosen. The one complaint we have heard about this book is that the pictures and text are not on facing pages and parents feel that children enjoy having a story read to them more when they can simultaneously look at related pictures.

JOHNSON, CROCKETT. **HAROLD AND THE PURPLE CRAYON.** 5"x6", H&R55, 3.95c.
This is one of our all time favorite books. It is an ingenious story, unlike any other we have ever seen. Harold is a small boy. He goes out for a walk with his purple crayon and thinks of a variety of things he would like to do. Whatever he thinks of he draws and follows the adventure through until he decides he would like to do something else. So then he draws his next idea with his purple crayon. And the adventures continue from page to page. It is a simple story which children of almost any age can enjoy.

KAMM, ANTONY. THE STORY OF ISLAM. 1.75p.
See the Islam section.

KENNEDY, PAUL. STAINED GLASS WINDOWS COLORING BOOK.
8"x10½", 16 plates, Dov72, 1.75p.
This coloring book is designed for older children. Kennedy has selected
and reproduced a number of actual windows from Europe. He uses
translucent paper so that, when colored, the sheet can be mounted on a
window.

KIPLING, RUDYARD. FAVORITE JUST SO STORIES. 8¼"x11¼",
71pp. G&D nd/PnB, 2.95c.
A colorfully illustrated collection of Kipling's delightful stories. The
illustrations are designed to appeal to young children.

KUBILINSKAS, KOSTAS, tr. THE FROG QUEEN. 8¼"x11¼", 82pp.
PrP74, 2.00c.
Simple poetic retellings of a number of lively folktales illustrated in
bright colors. There is no message, but the colors and the simple text
are designed to interest even the smallest child.

**LEACROFT, HELEN and RICHARD. THE BUILDINGS OF ANCIENT
EGYPT. 8.75c.**
See the Ancient Egypt section.

LEAF, MUNRO. THE STORY OF FERDINAND. 7½"x9", Vik36,
1.50p.
This story of a young bull who refused to be bull-like and aggressive
and whose greatest joy was smelling flowers has long been a favorite
with children. Black and white illustrations.

LE CAIN, ERROL. THE CABBAGE PRINCESS. 8½"x10", Fab69, 4.95c.
This story tells of a king who had a very bad temper. He complained
about everything and called everyone names. Since he was king no one
objected—until he offended a powerful enchanter and learned just
how dangerous calling names can be. Le Cain has done a marvelous job
of recreating eighteenth century court life, where exquisitely formal
costumes and settings make a piquant contrast with the very odd
experiences of those who fall under the enchanter's spell.

LE CAIN, ERROL. KING ARTHUR'S SWORD. 5.10c.
See the Grail and King Arthur section.

LEWIS, RICHARD, ed. IN A SPRING GARDEN. 8½"x10½", Del65,
1.75p.
*This picture book for all ages is a collection of classic Japanese haiku, exquisitely
illustrated by Ezra Jack Keats, winner of the Caldecott Medal, who uses with full
effectiveness his familiar style of watercolor and collage. The book, both in text and
illustrations, shimmers and glows with sensitivity, reverence for life, and earth-wise
humor.... Here indeed is a book to enjoy over and over in the viewing and the reading.*—**Los Angeles Times.**

MACAULAY, DAVID. CASTLE. Glossary, 9¼"x12¼", HMC77, 8.95c.
This book is stylistically similar to Macaulay's other works. Here he
takes us to thirteenth century England when England was attempting

to conquer Wales and the English were building impressive fortresses
with adjoining towns. Macaulay traces the step-by-step planning and
construction of both castle and town from the hiring of a skilled master
engineer to the actual test of castle defenses when hundreds of Welsh
soldiers launched a direct attack. Magnificent detailed illustrations accompany a straightforward text.

MACAULAY, DAVID. CATHEDRAL. 8.95c.
See the Sacred Geometry section.

MACAULAY, DAVID. PYRAMID. 9½"x12", 80pp. HMC75, 8.95c.
Macaulay is a teacher and designer whose two previous books have
won him overwhelming praise and international recognition. His
books are geared toward children and the text and illustrations are so
clearly presented that they are illuminating for people of all ages. Here
he graphically explains the step-by-step construction process of an
imaginary pyramid and through a concise text and detailed illustrations he explores the philosophy of life and death that led the ancient
Egyptians to construct these massive structures. We do not always
agree with his explanations of the construction and its reason for
being, but it makes a good story and helps to bring history alive.

MACAULAY, DAVID. UNDERGROUND. Glossary, 9½"x11¼", 112pp.
HMC76, 9.95c.
Surface clues—an escaping column of steam, the tip of a ladder rising
above a manhole, the rumbling of trains beneath our feet—are often
the only reminders of the complex and immense root system that
exists beneath the buildings and streets of a modern city. In this book
Macaulay takes us on a visual journey through a city's various support
systems by exposing a typical section of underground network and
explaining how its works. Inventing a site at the intersection of two
streets, he first shows the various kinds of foundation construction
that provide support for massive city buildings and then opens up the
street and sidewalk to picture the basic support systems that are so
essential to city life. Once again Macaulay's text and drawings are
exceedingly clear.

**MCDERMOTT, BEVERLY BRODSKY. THE GOLEM: A JEWISH LEG-
END.** 9¼"x12¼", Lip76, 8.95c.
This legend tells of the time that Rabbi Lev used a series of magic spells
to create the Golem out of a lump of sacred clay. He took the clay and
shaped it into the form of a man and breathed life into it by giving it the
name of God. The rabbi created the Golem to protect his people from
persecution; but the Golem became a power unto himself, more terrible than the evil he had been summoned to dispel. Finally the rabbi
had to command him to return to clay. This magical story is wonderfully illustrated with full color watercolors that evoke a sense of Jewishness and bring the simple tale to life. A Caldecott Honor Book.

**MCDERMOTT, GERALD. ANANSI THE SPIDER: A TALE FROM
THE ASHANTI.** 9¼"x7¾", HRW72, 1.95p.
Anansi the Spider is one of the great folk heroes of the world, a wise
and lovable rogue who triumphs over larger and more powerful foes.
He is a supreme mischief maker who has endless troubles. In this tale,
Anansi sets out on a long and difficult journey, helping to put the moon
in the sky. The language echoes authentic African rhythms and the
illustrations are boldly drawn in McDermott's characteristic flat, block
style. A Caldecott Honor Book.

MCDERMOTT, GERALD. ARROW TO THE SUN. 9½"x10½", Vik74,
1.95p.
McDermott has adapted a Pueblo Indian tale. The color hues are bright
and strong and the illustrations are bold, almost geometric; they really
fill up the pages and the story itself is told in only a few simple words. It
is a vibrant rendering of the universal myth of the hero's quest and it
illustrates the Indian reverence for the source of all life—the sun. A
Caldecott Award Book.

MCDERMOTT, GERALD. THE MAGIC TREE. 7½"x9", Vik73, 1.95p.
The simplicity and starkness of McDermott's shapes and colors fits
this tale from the Congo. It tells of twin boys, one handsome and one
ugly; one loved by his mother and one not. One night the unloved twin
leaves home. In the river he finds a great tree with magical leaves.
Suddenly everything he has wished for is his—beauty, wealth, and
love. After a time the boy returns home and boasts of his fortune.

MCDERMOTT, GERALD. **THE STONE-CUTTER. 7"x11", Vik75, 2.50p.**
An adaptation of a Japanese folk tale in which a man's foolish longing for power becomes a tale of wishes and dreams that can be understood on many levels. It is the story of a stonecutter who is happy with his life until a prince passes by him in a lavish procession. He wishes aloud for great wealth and the spirit who lives in the mountain hears him and transforms the stonecutter into a wealthy and powerful prince. He is happy for a while until his desire causes him to make another wish, which the spirit again grants. And so it goes until he has his final wish when he desires to become a mountain. This too is granted and the story ends as the mountain trembles when a lowly stonecutter chisels away at its feet! The illustrations' style resembles McDermott's other books.

MCDERMOTT, GERALD. **THE VOYAGE OF OSIRIS. 9¾"x11¼", Dut77, 8.95c.**
A contemporary vision of this ancient Egyptian myth. Osiris symbolized reincarnation and spiritual rebirth; the bare facts of the myth surrounding him are retold here by McDermott. The illustrator's usual luminous colors and block designs are more subtle in this work and again succeed in recreating a feeling for the characters and the story.

MCKEE, DAVID. **THE DAY THE TIDE WENT OUT. 8"x9", Cro76, 1.50p.**
This book contains some of the most delightful illustrations we have ever seen—all vividly drawn and brightly colored and designed to appeal especially to preschoolers. Only a few words are on each page. The story is humorous, telling of life on a beach and the comic interplay between beachkeeper and jungle animals. Each day during the keeper's nap the animals erect huge sand castles all over the beach and on the keeper's back; and always the tide washes the castles away before the keeper wakes. But one day the animals convinced the tide not to return—and this changed the lives of all those living on the beach.

MAIR, HENRIETTE WILLEBEEK LE. **CHRISTMAS CAROLS FOR YOUNG CHILDREN. 10¼"x9", 31pp. Fin76, 5.00c.**
A collection of twelve pastel illustrations of the Nativity, each coupled with a traditional Christmas carol. The book begins with a simple retelling of the Christmas story based on the gospels of Matthew and Luke. The illustrations are printed here for the first time.

MANNICHE, LISE, tr. **HOW DJADJA-EM-ANKH SAVED THE DAY. Cro77, 5.95p.**
This story takes place in ancient Egypt about 4,500 years ago. It was written down about a thousand years later. This translation has been made from the original Hieratic. It is printed on paper that looks like papyrus, and is made in the form of a scroll. Reading from left to right, as we do, there is a description of Egypt in the time of King Seneferu. When you read the story from right to left, as the Egyptians did, you can follow the ancient text. This is a delightful book which we highly recommend to all who wish to instill a sense of history in their children.

MAYER, MERCER. **FOUR FROGS IN A BOX. No words, 3½"x4¼", Del73, 5.95c.**
A set of four tiny books with engaging pictures which tell a story that even the smallest child can enjoy about a boy, a dog, and a frog.

MILNE, A.A. **A GALLERY OF CHILDREN. 125pp. McK25/HeG, 4.95c.**
An illustrated collection of stories about a wide variety of children.

MILNE, A.A. **THE HOUSE AT POOH CORNER. 192pp. Del28/Met, 1.25p.**
This is the second of the Pooh books and the one that introduces the character of Tigger, one of everyone's favorite Pooh characters. The original Shepard illustrations accompany this edition.

MILNE, A.A. **POOH'S POT O'HONEY. 2¾"x3¾", Dut68/Met, 6.95c/set.**
A boxed set of four little books. **Pooh Hears a Buzzing Noise and Meets Some Bees, Pooh Goes Visiting and Gets into a Tight Place, Pooh and Piglet Go Hunting and Nearly Catch a Woozle,** and **Eeyore Loses a Tail and Pooh Finds One.** Kids love both the stories and the size of the books and we have found that it is hard to part a little kid from these little books once they have seen them. The vocabulary is simple enough for a beginning reader and there are illustrations throughout.

MILNE, A.A. **A TREASURY OF WINNIE THE POOH. Del24-28, 5.00p/set.**
A boxed set of A.A. Milne's four classics—**Winnie-the-Pooh, The House at Pooh Corner, Now We Are Six, When We Were Very Young**—with the original illustrations by Ernest Shepard.

MILNE, A.A. **WINNIE-THE-POOH. 174pp. Del26/Met, 1.95p.**
Winnie-the-Pooh is one of the most famous and best loved children's characters of all times. Over one million copies of the hardcover editions of the Pooh books have been sold, along with many millions of the paperbacks. This is the first (and most popular) book in the series and it includes the original color drawings by Ernest Shepard.

MOSEL, ARLENE. **THE FUNNY LITTLE WOMAN. 9"x10", Dut72, 1.95p.**
This book has some of the most unusual and delightful illustrations we have ever seen. The story takes place in Japan and the main human character is an amazing little old woman in a kimono with chopsticks in her hair. She is great, but our favorites are the wicked *oni* whom she accidently meets when chasing a dumpling down a hole leading to the middle of the earth. She is captured by the *oni* and made their cook until she finally escapes. She likes to laugh and her *tee-he-he-he* resounds on each page. The *oni* themselves are magnificent beasts, part troll, part dwarf, and truly unlike any creature we have ever seen. They live in a magical land. We know from experience that this is a story that children will never tire of. At first they are frightened of the *oni*, but soon they become transported into the enchanted realm that Ms. Mobel and Blair Lent, the illustrator, have created. A Caldecott Award book.

MUSGROVE, MARGARET. **ASHANTI TO ZULU: AFRICAN TRADITIONS. 10"x12½", 48pp. Del76, 8.95c.**
Delightful vignettes describe the ceremonies, celebrations, and day to day customs of twenty-six African tribes. Dramatic illustrations by Leo and Diane Dillon capture the tone.

PAULUS, TRINA. **HOPE FOR THE FLOWERS. Oversized, 152pp. Pau72, 4.95p.**
This is a delightful, beautifully illustrated tale of a caterpillar who has trouble becoming what he really is (a butterfly!)—and in allegorical form it is the story of all of us who must die old before becoming born anew. The story is a wonderful one to read and then to pass on to a friend, an underground classic along the lines of **Jonathan Livingston Seagull**—but much better done.

PUSHKIN, ALEXANDER. **THE TALE OF CZAR SALTAN. 12"x9½", Cro75/Met, 5.95c.**
Many artists have been inspired by the Pushkin's poetic retellings of folktales. In the early twentieth century the great Russian painter, I. Bilibin illustrated many of Pushkin's works in books that have become collectors' treasures. The illustrations in this book are faithfully reproduced from Bilibin's originals. This story is in the style of many classic folk tales. It tells of a prince and a magically transformed swan princess and how they get together despite many obstacles.

PUSHKIN, ALEXANDER. **THE TALE OF THE DEAD PRINCESS AND THE SEVEN KNIGHTS. 8½"x11", 36pp. PrP73, .80p.**
A beautifully illustrated retelling of Pushkin's classic tale. The translation is stilted, but the pictures are well worth the price of the book.

PUSHKIN, ALEXANDER. **THE TALE OF THE GOLDEN COCKEREL. 12"x9½", Cro75/Den, 5.95c.**
The illustrations in this beautiful volume are of the same fine quality and style as the other Pushkin book illustrated by I. Bilibin. Again, Pushkin's poetic retelling has been rendered in graceful prose. This classic Russian tale tells of the time when a mighty czar grew too old to defend his realm. He calls on a sorcerer for help, promising him his heart's desire as a reward. A magical bird, a queen who was more beautiful than good, and a broken promise start a strange chain of events.

RACKHAM, ARTHUR. **MOTHER GOOSE NURSERY RHYMES. Index, 7"x8¾", 153pp. PnB13, 4.15p.**
A collection of 160 well known nursery rhymes both chosen by Rackham and superbly illustrated by him in black and white and color.

RAOUL-DUVAL, FRANCOIS. **PETALI AND GURIGOO OR HOW THE BIRDS GOT THEIR COLORS.** 10"x7½", MTI71, 3.50c.
An Amazonian legend, with some amazing illustrations. A baby snake in the jungle eats up all the vegetation and most of the denizens. He thereby acquires a truly beautiful skin and strips the jungle of all its colors. The birds—who had never been colorful—appealed to the snake to give the jungle back its colors, and he did. The birds all split up his skin and wrapped themselves in it, and magically their feathers turned the bright colors that we associate with jungle birds.

RAY, IRENE and MALLIKA GUPTA. **TALES FROM RAMAKRISHNA.** 1.50p.
See the Ramakrishna subsection of Indian Philosophy.

REY, H.A. **FIND THE CONSTELLATIONS.** 3.95p.
See the Astronomy section.

RIORDAN, JIM, tr. **MERGEN AND HIS FRIENDS: A NANAI FOLK TALE.** 8¾"x11", PrP73, 1.25p.
The tale of a hunter who befriends a number of animals and is later helped to gain his heart's desire (a beautiful maiden) by these same animals. Vividly illustrated in a tapestry-like style that evokes images of Siberia.

ROBBINS, MARIA. **MY VERY FIRST TEENY TINY STRAWBERRY PAPERBACK LIBRARY.** 2¾"x4", Lss76, 5.95p/set.
A boxed set of six little separate books. Each retells a classic fairy tale in very simple language and has an abundance of detailed illustrations by Diane Dawson. The following stories are included: *The Big Radish, Lazy Jack, The Princess and the Pea, The Mouse and the Lion,* and *The Runaway Pancake.*

SCHWARTZ, STEPHEN. **THE PERFECT PEACH.** 8½"x10¼", 48pp. LBC77, 7.95c.
This is the story of Pee-Chee, a young Oriental prince who rebels at being babied by his parents and runs away to the mountain where the gods live. He and his pet turtle cause an unending amount of trouble through their escapades until the prince is accidently turned into a peach. The verse is light hearted and should appeal to the youngest readers. The illustrations are delicate pastels in a Japanese style. There is a tremendous amount of detail in each and even nonreaders can follow the story.

SENDAK, MAURICE. **NUTSHELL LIBRARY.** 2¾"x3¾", H&R62, 4.95c.
A boxed set of four little books which is a favorite of our youngest friends. The stories are extremely simple. One describes the months, another tells two rhymed stories about each of the ten numbers, a third teaches the alphabet, while the last one tells a tale *with a moral air.*

SERAGE, NANCY. **THE PRINCE WHO GAVE UP A THRONE: A STORY OF THE BUDDHA.** 6.50c.
See the Buddhism section.

SHERLOCK, PHILIP. **ANANSI, THE SPIDER MAN.** 9"x6¼", 112pp. Cro54, 6.95c.
Anansi was a man and a spider; when things went well he was a man, but when he was in great danger he became a spider, safe in his web. By trickery and guile he always got the better of those who were much bigger than himself. Anansi's home was in the villages and forests of West Africa—and when the Africans were brought to the West Indies they brought with them the stories that they loved—the stories about Br'er Anansi and his friends. As a child growing up in Jamaica Sherlock listened to these stories, and his retelling reflects the authentic tradition. The illustrator also lived in Jamaica and knows well the background and atmosphere for these tales.

SHIVKUMAR, K. **THE KING'S CHOICE.** 8¼"x8¼", PMP71, 5.95c.
This folktale from India tells of a lion king who calls on a fox, a leopard, and a vulture to serve him. In return for his protection, they assist him in every way—advising him, running his messages, and finding his food. One day the animals invite the lion to travel to the desert so that he might try camel meat. The expedition turns into a disaster, and it is only thanks to the unwary camel that the king's life is saved. The other animals are still hungry for the taste of camel meat, and through a trick they get the poor beast to *ask* to be eaten. The lion, however, is a true king, and in the end it is his nobility that triumphs over their trickery. This simple tale is illustrated by Yoko Mitsuhashi in pastels of a primitive, Rousseau-like quality.

SHULEVITZ, URI. **DAWN.** 10½"x9½", FSG74, 5.95c.
This beautiful muted picturebook was inspired by a brief eighth century Chinese poem which tells of the coming of dawn. Only a few words accompany each watercolor, conveying a feeling of silence and the beauty of nature.

SOLASKO, FAINNA, tr. **THE WHITE DEER: A LATVIAN FOLK-TALE.** 8½"x11", PrP73, .60p.
A colorfully pictured rendition of a classic Latvian folk tale which tells of the adventures of two brothers who set off together as hunters. They soon split and one follows an enchanted white deer and eventually is turned into stone. The other becomes a herdsman and rescues the king's three daughters from three dragons. After a series of adventures he is given the hand of the youngest daughter. He eventually breaks the spell of the deer and all ends happily.

SPIER, PETER, ill. **NOAH'S ARK.** 10½"x8¼", Dou77, 6.95c.
An extraordinarily detailed, wordless version of the Noah's Ark story, winner of the Caldecott Medal. A host of animals, in all shapes and sizes, parade across the colorful pages of this brilliantly illustrated book.

STEIG, WILLIAM. **SYLVESTER AND THE MAGIC PEBBLE.** 8"x11", Dut69/AbS, 1.95p.
This is a neat story about Sylvester, a humanized donkey, and his parents. One of Sylvester's main hobbies was collecting unusual pebbles. One day he found an especially beautiful one which he soon realized had the power to grant the wishes of anyone who possessed it. By accident he wished he was a rock and this was his final wish. His parents deeply mourned his disappearance and after a year or so came upon the magic pebble and by chance wished that it would turn into a donkey—and it did! The illustrations are especially fine. All the animals are delightfully drawn and Steig has chosen beautiful bright colors. A Caldecott Award book.

STOCKTON, FRANK and MAURICE SENDAK. **THE BEE MAN OF ORN.** 7½"x9", 47pp. HRW64, 1.65p.
A wise and witty tale of an old man whose entire time is spent in the company of bees and who is told by a Junior Sorcerer that he must have been transformed from something other than his present being. The Bee-man's search for his previous existence takes him on many adventures, until he is finally given the chance to relive his life. Sendak's color drawings fill every page.

SVEND, OTTO. **TIM AND TRISHA.** 10½"x8½", Pel77, 5.95c.
Tim, a little troll, is bored because he has no one to play with—until he meets a little girl in the forest. This simple, delightfully illustrated story tells of their friendship and adventures. Geared toward the youngest children.

TURSKA, KRYSTYNA. **THE MAGICIAN OF CRACOW.** 8¾"x11¼", Mor75, 7.95c.
A beautifully illustrated retelling of a Polish legend which tells of a famous astronomer and magician who longed above all else to be the first man to visit the moon. He strikes a bargain with the devil and goes through many adventures before finally outwitting the devil and getting his wish. The illustrations are incredibly detailed and very successfully set the mood.

VAVRA, ROBERT. **LION AND BLUE.** 8½"x11", Mor74/WCS, 7.95c.
Robert Vavra's books are highly acclaimed, and among the most unusual picture books we have ever seen. Vavra saw Fleur Cowles' paintings and was convinced that they would make wonderful illustrations for a book. He convinced her too, and she agreed to the idea. The paintings are bold and bright and filled with a wonderful series of animals and of nature scenes. Vavra's story matches the brilliance of the illustrations. One of the most amazing features of the books is Vavra's use of cutouts to make one illustration serve a number of purposes. This book tells the story of a magnificent lion who grieves because he has lost his friend the butterfly; he searches the world until he and Blue, the butterfly, are reunited. We recommend these books highly for children and adults alike.

VAVRA, ROBERT. **ROMANY FREE.** 11½"x8½", 43pp. Mor77, 8.95c.
A poetic tale written around paintings by Fleur Cowles. The painting style is the same as in the other books by Vavra and Cowles and it includes a number of cut outs. The poetry does not seem to be geared toward young readers and the print is exceedingly small.

VAVRA, ROBERT. **TIGER FLOWER.** 8½"x11", Mor68/WCS, 7.95c.
An enchanting book which is the favorite of many people we know. It tells the story of Tiger Flower, King of the Grass, who lives *where everything that should be small, is big, and everything that should be big, is small.* Craig Clairborne says that **Tiger Flower** *is a volume I have read with uncommon pleasure, and I wish I could give it to every child and adult that I love. It should be required reading for everyone else.*

VINOKUROV, A. and L. SHVARTSMAN. **THE LEGEND OF THE STONECUTTER.** 8½"x11", PrP75, .75p.
This is a finely illustrated version of the classic tale of the stonecutter (see the review of McDermott's version for a short rendition). This is our favorite version. It is another one of the amazingly priced Russian children's books.

VISHIVASHRAYANANDA, SWAMI. **RAMAKRISHNA FOR CHILDREN.** 1.50p.
See the Ramakrishna subsection of Indian Philosophy.

WATTS, BERNADETTE. **RAPUNZEL.** 9½"x12½", Cro75, 6.95c.
This is a beautifully illustrated retelling of this classic tale. Ms. Watts follows the version used by the Brothers Grimm and her illustrations are executed in a combination of pastel and tempura. Though impressionistic and imaginative, they are firmly based on the actual architecture, scenery, and traditional peasant costume of the area. The story itself tells of a beautiful young maiden who is imprisoned by an evil witch and rescued, after some difficulty, by a prince who loves her truly.

WETERING, JANWILLEM VAN DE. **LITTLE OWL: AN EIGHTFOLD BUDDHIST ADMONITION.** 6.95c.
See the Buddhism section.

WILLIAMS, JAY. **EVERYONE KNOWS WHAT A DRAGON LOOKS LIKE.** 11½"x8¾", FWP76, 7.95c.
This is an enchanting book, with some of the most delightful illustrations we have seen. Mercer Mayer has created an oriental dreamworld with his amazingly detailed drawings; the landscape figures come alive, and ancient China is recreated. The tale itself points out that appearances can be deceiving. A poor gate sweeper believes that a small fat man is a dragon who can save his city from invasion and destruction, but he is the only one who believes the old man's claims. All others ignore the man/dragon and it is only because of the loyalty of the gate keeper that the dragon does save the city. The language is simple and young readers will be delighted with this tale.

WILLIAMS, MARGERY. **THE VELVETEEN RABBIT.** 6"x9", 44pp. Avo75, 3.95c/1.75p.
This is an extraordinarily popular book. *"What is REAL?"* asked the Rabbit one day.... *"Real isn't how you are made,"* said the Skin Horse. *"It's a thing that happens to you. When a child loves you for a long, long time, not just to play with, but REALLY loves you, then you become Real. It doesn't happen all at once. You become. It takes a long time. Generally, by the time you are Real, most of your hair has been loved off, and your eyes drop out and you get loose in the joints and very shabby. But these things don't matter at all, because once you are Real you can't be ugly, except to people who don't understand."* We love this strange and wonderful story and we know you will too.

WOLKSTEIN, DIANE. **THE RED LION.** 8½"x10¼", Cro77, 7.50c.
This is a book of rare beauty. Ed Young's illustrations are in the style of Persian miniatures and Ms. Wolkstein has retold this old Persian Sufi teaching story in a simple and lyric form, retaining its exotic flavor and its wisdom. It tells of a prince who ran away on the eve of his coronation because before he became king he had to prove his bravery by fighting a ferocious red lion. He finds other lions waiting for him wherever he goes. Finally he returns to the capitol for his coronation, and when he meets the red lion it is tame! Every lion who ever fought a prince of Persia had been tame; only fear made them ferocious.

WYATT, ISABEL and JOAN RUDEL. **HAY FOR MY OX.** 7.20c.
See the Waldorf Education subsection of Steiner.

YOLEN, JANE. **THE BIRD OF TIME.** 8½"x10½", Cro71, 4.50c.
Jane Yolen is our favorite storyteller (as you can see by the number of her titles that we list!). She weaves original, enchanting tales, each one different and each magical in its own way. She has the remarkable quality of picking exactly the right illustrator, so each book has an entirely different feeling. We recommend all of her books highly. Once you have read one, you are sure to want to read all the rest. They are magical enough to interest even the smallest child and older children can not get enough of them. Time is the theme of this tale. A miller's son is given the power to make time move faster and slower. He was a dreamer and believed in miracles, so he was not overawed by the gift. He used the power to rescue the king's daughter who had been captured by a fierce giant. It all ends happily: the giant is vanquished, the lad marries the king's daughter, and the bird of time is safely hidden away, never to be used again. The illustrations are in the classical style of fairy tales, with browns and greens predominating.

YOLEN, JANE. **THE BOY WHO HAD WINGS. 9"x12"**, Cro74, 5.50c.
Long ago in a small Greek village a boy was born with a beautiful set of wings. His family was amazed and uneasy, fearing that the wings were a sign of the gods' disfavor. The boy was warned to keep them covered always so that others would not know of his *differentness*. One day his herdsman father was trapped in the high mountain snows and only Aetos, with his wings, was able to save him. He almost killed himself in the process and during his recovery his wings fell off—but for an enchanted moment, he glimpsed the meaning of his gift. The illustrations are magnificent and subtle.

YOLEN, JANE. **THE GIRL WHO CRIED FLOWERS AND OTHER TALES. 7¼"x9½"**, Cro74/CSC, 7.50c.
Five masterful tales, each of which has an underlying message. There is the bittersweet story of the beautiful Olivia, who could not be happy herself, but whose sorrows brought happiness to others as her tears turned magically to flowers. There is the giant who hid the sun from the world; the proud lad who challenged the king to a contest; Vera, who had an insatiable desire for the truth; and silent Bianca whose wisdom outwitted an army and won her the hand of the king. The illustrations are by David Palladini and are stylized and quite unlike any other drawings we have seen. Again, they seem perfect for the stories.

YOLEN, JANE. **THE GIRL WHO LOVED THE WIND. 8"x10"**, Cro72, 6.95c.
An incredible set of illustrations fill these pages. The border is tawny yellow and the pictures themselves are reminiscent of Persian miniatures in their richly patterned design and beautiful colors. A king surrounds his daughter with every possible luxury and comfort and gives her an abundance of love so that she would never be sad. And lest any of the world's sorrows reach her, he had great protective walls built around the palace and the garden. But for all his care, the king could not keep the wind's voice from his daughter's ears. It sang of the world that she had never seen. Its song was sometimes harsh and sometimes sweet, like life itself. And after she had heard it the palace walls seemed to be imprisoning her. So finally the princess accepts the wind's challenge and sets forth to discover the real world for herself.

YOLEN, JANE. **AN INVITATION TO THE BUTTERFLY BALL. 8¼"x10¼"**, PMP76, 5.95c.
This is the most inventive counting book we have ever seen. The illustrations are delightful and the rhymes equally so. A different set of animals is used for each number and the work is beautifully produced. It is an excellent way to introduce even the smallest child to the numbers.

YOLEN, JANE. **THE LITTLE SPOTTED FISH. 10"x8½"**, Sea75, 7.95c.
This is a much simpler tale than most of Jane Yolen's books and therefore suitable for the youngest children. It tells of a fisherlad and of the little spotted fish that three time saves the lad's life. The tale is inspired by folklore from the British Isles. The bright illustrations complement the mood of the narrative.

YOLEN, JANE. **MILKWEED DAYS. 8"x10"**, 32pp. Cro76, 5.95c.
Milkweed days are the long, lazy late summer days that children love best. These are the days when they like to play in the sunny fragrant meadow behind the old barn. Beautiful photographs and a concise text evoke the sights, smells, and sounds of a summer day. A simple book for the beginning reader.

YOLEN, JANE. **THE SEEING STICK. 8¼"x10¼"**, Cro77, 6.95c.
Here Ms. Yolen tells a tale set in the China of long ago. An emperor is sad because his beloved daughter is blind and cannot see the beauty which surrounds her. One day a mysterious old man comes along and teaches the princess how to see with her fingers, mind, and heart. She learns and is sad no longer. It turns out that the man who teaches her to see is blind himself, but with the magic that he knows, the world is visible to both of them. The illustrations by Remy Charlip and Demetra Maraslis follow the tone of the story, beginning in pencil and, as the princess learns to see, becoming delicately colored.

YOLEN, JANE. **THE SULTAN'S PERFECT TREE. 8¼"x10¼"**, PMP77, 5.95c.
This is an elegantly illustrated tale of a sultan who loved perfection and carried this love to extremes. Everything within and without his sumptuous palace had to be perfect. But one day one of the trees outside his palace began to lose its leaves and suddenly the sultan's world was no longer perfect. After a great deal of turmoil he realized that the real world—constantly growing and changing—is far preferable to his so called perfect one. The color illustrations are muted and drawn in the Persian style.

ZAKHODER, BORIS. **THE WOLF WHO SANG SONGS. 8½"x11"**, PrP nd, .60p.
A series of Russian fables with brightly colored illustrations. The stories are about the peacock, the fox, and the wolf; the most familiar features of each are explained in the fables.

ZHELEZNOVA, IRINA. **THE LITTLE STRAW BULL. 8¾"x11"**, PrP74, .75p.
A handsomely illustrated retelling of a Ukrainian folk tale about a straw bull covered with tar that a farmer makes for his wife. The bull captures a wolf, a bear, and a fox successively and the farmer imprisons them. After they plea for freedom and make a number of promises, the farmer releases them. They fulfill their promises and all live happily ever after. The story's not much—but the illustrations are more than worth the minimal price of the book.

ZHELEZNOVA, IRINA. **WITHIN-AND-WITHOUT-WEARS-HIS-COAT-WRONG-SIDE-OUT. 8½"x11"**, PrP75, .60p.
A colorfully reproduced picture rendition of a Byelorussian folk tale. The czar sent out a call throughout his czardom which said that whoever succeeded in hiding from him would get half his czardom. This story tells of the youth who took up the call and his subsequent adventures.

CHINESE PHILOSOPHY

China is considered infinitely alien and westerners often tend to feel that understanding its mystery is beyond them. Because of China's cultural complexity and the subtle character of its arts, most western commentary misleads the reader even if only by omission—a constant difficulty when discussing things Chinese. Those of us in the West unfamiliar with eastern history and ideas are sometimes disdainful of what we have labeled the superstitious and magical mentality of the Orient. While it is certainly an odd belief that thirty-six thousand gods inhabit the human body as the ancient Chinese concluded, a bit of reading in western scientific history reveals surprisingly similar beliefs. Even as monumental a genius as Sir Isaac Newton believed, along with many seventeenth-century European scientists, that animal spirits lived within the human body. Newton described these spirits as *ethereal in nature and subtle enough to pervade the animal juices as freely as the electric forces do.* This observation is made not to credit or discredit either Chinese or western beliefs, but merely to suggest that customs that seem initially alien should rather be seen as part of that culture's growth and maturation.

Initially the growth of Taoism and Confucianism was almost coincidental; but there is little doubt that Confucian teaching was dominant throughout most of the late Chou (1112-249 B.C.), Ch'in (221-207 B.C.), and Han (206 B.C.-A.D. 220) times. Yet, it is not surprising that Lao Tzu initially won such little notice considering his belief that the man who pursues worldly recognition, who desires position in government even for the benevolent purposes Confucius believed in, was deluded and seeking vainglorious things. Indeed, Lao Tzu taught that even to write books was self-defeating because words were mere sounds, or forms of reality, and could not communicate the true realities themselves. Words were simply symbols, outward manifestations of an inner reality that could only be misrepresented. *To understand the reality of life,* Lao Tzu wrote, *one must seek it directly by discarding all superficial identifications such as words. Those dependent on outward symbols, signs, or other representations would never be able to penetrate to the essence of what is real; for simply using a word warps beyond recognition the reality it stands for.*

But Lao Tzu was not so impractical a man as to suggest that all forms of symbolism, language, and communication cease. What he pointed out was that such communication as words should not be mistaken for the thing itself, that the finger pointing at the moon not be mistaken for the moon itself. Now this idea is very well known in contemporary philosophy classes, but it must be remembered Lao Tzu was formulating his thoughts in the sixth century before the birth of Christ. Lao Tzu said, *If I am forced to define it*—as we are all forced to define and limit our inner feelings and understandings—it should be understood that such a definition is always unsatisfactory. Chuang Tzu writes in one of his anecdotes, *When the hearing stops at the ears, the mind stops at the symbol.* But if one is single-minded and listens with the mind, then learns to listen with the spirit, one begins to truly hear. In another place even Confucius, who agreed in some instances with Taoist principles, explains: *Let the hearing turn inward and let it not be interfered with the intellect or intelligence.*

Lao Tzu asked, *Why do seekers after truth not identify at once with that which moves heaven and earth and regulates nature? The move of nature, heaven, and earth is the infinite, and this infinite waits on nobody to penetrate beyond words and symbols. It can only be apprehended directly. Those who achieve identification with this infinite power of nature, one that moves the substance of life under its veils of form and physical perceptiveness, no longer desire fame or achievement of any sort. Such perfect men challenge every designation of life that limits and modifies the great principles that move life to fulfillment and its rightful place in the natural rhythm of things.* Lao Tzu and Chuang Tzu both admired the intuitive wisdom of the common man and consistently advocated a return to the simple life, to a spontaneous and truer understanding of nature. Indeed, Lao Tzu was perhaps the first philosopher to develop a true philosophy of nature. As the sinologist Cyril Birch has written, *The teachings of Taoism made it possible for a man of understanding to accomplish an identification with the world of hills and streams which is almost inconceivable to the ego-ridden westerner.*

With such a philosophy Lao Tzu was, it can be seen, not particularly thirsty for disciples or government position as Confucius seemed to be. While Confucius assiduously sought a government position so he could put his ideas into action, Lao Tzu was a discipleless sage, who quietly went his way alone, eschewing recognition. His subsequent fame, which ironically in some ways even transcended Confucius's, was based on the one five-thousand-character book he was begged to leave the world before he died (or so the tradition goes) and the advocacy of the brilliant champions who followed him

Confucius (551-479 B.C.) considered himself more of a transmitter of traditional beliefs than a creative philosopher. He believed the correct principles of past ages, the doctrines of ancient sages, had been forgotten and saw himself as a teacher with the duty of recalling people to them. The legendary sages of China were mainly concerned, as Confucius interpreted them, with the Tao or *Way* of the correct and virtuous life in governing both the self and the state. The old rituals as interpreted by Confucius were a rationalist doctrine having little to do with the supernatural and emphasized moderation in all things.

Yet always running parallel to the Confucian philosophy of social and moral concern was the visionary and isomorphic world of the Tao. While Confucianism was often stuffy, prosaic, moralistic, Taoism appealed to a strong alternative quality of fantasy in the Chinese temperament. Early Taoist writers were witty, caustic, and full of paradox, poetic vision, mystical and intuitive insights. The Confucian scholar was a commonsensical gentleman, a good family man, a conscientious bureaucrat, and a sober citizen. His Taoist counterpart would more than likely be a loner, seeking mountainous retreats instead of court or government service; he would no doubt escape official responsibilities by wandering over the hills and through the streams of China, seeking self-cultivation and cessation of his human conflicts in the simplicities of nature. The Taoist would probably drink up poetry as if it were life-sustaining air, while the Confucianist would often analyze the poem's content for its social or moral good as well as its traditionally acceptable esthetic qualities.

It is not surprising then that the gift of the Confucianist to his culture was a social, ethical, and philosophical one; while the gift of the Taoist scholars, the first great creative writers of China, was a poetic and literary one—as well as philosophical. But the Confucianists should not be misrepresented here. As Thomas Merton points out, if Kung Tzu (Confucius) was practical, it was not a strictly utilitarian pragmatism, but embodied with a *sacred sense of the "will of heaven" inscribed in the very nature of man. Kung therefore respected the Tao, but unlike the Taoists he did not concentrate on the Tao alone. He set his gaze clearly on man, and he saw that if the will of heaven was to have any meaning on earth, it would have to be in some way reflected in man's society.* In this fashion the Tao, which underlay all early Chinese philosophy, diverged into two great streams—the Tao of man in society, of the *way of right action*; and the Tao of Lao Tzu, the Tao of concentrating on self-realization, on the *axis of heaven* within oneself. This axis within is the center of man's being. It is the ultimate reality for consciousness to perceive it; the superior man is one who finds this center in himself and lives always centered upon it. Most men do not find this centering reality and spend their lives aimlessly self-seeking, amid confusion and turmoil.

—*condensed from* **Taoist Tales**, *by Raymond Van Over*

BARY, WILLIAM DE, *et. al.* **THE UNFOLDING OF NEO-CONFU-CIANISM.** Notes, index, 607pp. Col75, 22.40c.
The fourteen essays collected here explore the range and variety of Neoconfucian thought in seventeenth century China with special attention to the new growth that emerged in the transition from the Ming to the Ch'ing periods. Emphasis is placed on the flowering of Confucian thought and scholarship which occurred partly as a result of interaction with Buddhism and Taoism. These papers were originally presented at a conference on seventeenth century Chinese thought.

BARY, WILLIAM DE, WING-TSIT CHAN *and* CHESTER TAN, *eds.* **SOURCES OF CHINESE TRADITION, VOLUME I.** Chronology, notes, index, 601pp. Col60, 3.90p.
A collection of translations from Chinese sources that illustrate Chinese thought since earliest times. Most were made especially for this book. The selections cover political and economic questions, as well as philosophical and religious speculations.

BARY, WILLIAM DE, WING-TSIT CHAN *and* CHESTER TAN, *eds.* **SOURCES OF CHINESE TRADITION, VOLUME II.** Notes, index, 333pp. Col60, 3,90p.
This volume covers Chinese thought from 1839 to the present day. Topics include such modern movements as nationalism, socialism, and communism.

BASKIN, WADE, *ed.* **CLASSICS IN CHINESE PHILOSOPHY.** 737pp. LtA72, 4.95p.
A sourcebook which traces Chinese philosophy from the time of Confucius to the present. Selections from forty-eight individuals are included and the editor provides an introduction to each one. The translations are from a variety of sources. The volume is a good introductory survey and in terms of the number of different selections it is as comprehensive as any we know of. Chronologically arranged.

BINYON, LAURENCE. **THE FLIGHT OF THE DRAGON.** Notes, 86pp. Mur11, 3.85c.
Binyon's theme is that in the East, art is an approach to an understanding of life. For the Chinese there was much more to life than could immediately be seen on the surface, and the artist sought continually with the utmost economy to suggest the inner form and rhythm of things. Here Binyon presents a collection of essays on the theory and practice of art in China and Japan, based on original sources.

■ BLOFELD, JOHN. **BEYOND THE GODS: BUDDHIST AND TAO-IST MYSTICISM.** Glossary, 164pp. Dut75/A&U, 8.85c/2.45p.
Blofeld's account of his extensive travels in China and on the fringes of Mongolia and Tibet before the Communist takeover. *I have sought to describe something of what I found; for amidst much that was merely colorful rather than spiritually inspiring, I came upon certain teachings and practices that bore witness to impressive soarings of the human spirit. As far as possible I have woven into my material stories heard and personal experiences so as to offer the reader a series of insights just as I acquired them....I use [the term mysticism] to mean all that pertains to the search for intuitive experiences inaccessible to ordinary understanding and to the merging of one's being into something so exalted, so vast as to be beyond all human conceptions of divinity.* The text includes details on mystical practices and illuminating dialogue.

BLOFELD, JOHN. **BODHISATTVA OF COMPASSION.** Sixteen plates, glossary, 158pp. A&U77, 3.95p.
Kuan Yin is the Chinese goddess of love and compassion. In this book Blofeld explores the many faceted cult that surrounds Kuan Yin and the rites and rituals associated with her. Kuan Yin is sometimes depicted as a folk goddess, charming and benign, with miraculous powers; sometimes she is seen as a symbolic personification of divine compassion; and in other cases as a yogic vehicle through which it is possible to attain enlightenment and to perceive the ultimate nature of reality. The book includes new translations of a number of devotional poems and yogic texts along with detailed descriptions of contemplative meditation techniques. And, like all of Blofeld's writings, it is extremely well written, generally nontechnical, and readable.

■ BLOFELD, JOHN. **THE SECRET AND THE SUBLIME.** 217pp. Dut73/A&U, 3.95p.
An engrossing survey of all aspects of Taoism, based on Blofeld's own experiences and observations. Blofeld includes first person accounts of popular Taoism, with its lavish ceremonies, demon exorcisms, oracles, and magical happenings; Taoist yoga, with its emphasis on rejuvenation; the ancient teachings of philosophical Taoism; and mystical Taoism which aims at direct experience of the reality that lies behind the confines of conceptual thought. Blofeld has traveled widely through China and Asia and he tells of the masters he encountered and the Taoist sanctuaries he passed through. We enjoyed reading the book and got a good feeling for Taoism as it exists today.

BUSH, RICHARD. **RELIGION IN CHINA.** Glossary, notes, annotated bibliography, 96pp. Arg77, 2.95p.
A simple introduction to the religious tradition of China, covering the following general topics: *The Source of the Stream in Ancient Times; The Confucian Current; The Taoist Current; The Character of Buddhism in Ancient China;* and *Popular Folk Religion.* A series of color photographs accompanies the text.

Astrologer casting a horoscope.

CAHILL, JAMES. **CHINESE PAINTING.** 100 full color plates, bibliography, indices, 9¼"x11", 212pp. Riz77, 12.50p.
The Chinese have always regarded painting as the supreme art—the only one which demands more than mere craftsmanship can give, and pure and lyrical enough to stand on an equal footing with poetry and the contemplative thought. Chinese painting is preeminently an art of painting on silk and paper, mounted on rollers and forming vertical or horizontal scrolls. Many of China's greatest painters were also scholars and poets. This book is part of a series created by Albert Skira. The color reproductions faithfully render the fine shades and subtle nuances of Chinese art. This is a magnificent work and the quality of the accompanying text matches the excellence of the color reproductions.

CARUS, PAUL. **CHINESE ASTROLOGY.** 135pp. OpC07, 2.95p.
Much more than an astrological tract, this is a study of the major systems of Chinese occultism and thought. Carus includes many illustrations and detailed analyses of the Yih system, P'an-Ku, Feng-Shu, Lo Pan, joss sticks, as well as of astrology. This is a scholarly work which gives the historical and philosophical background of the systems discussed and includes comparisons with the systems of other civilizations.

CHAN, WING-TSIT, tr. **INSTRUCTIONS FOR PRACTICAL LIVING AND OTHER NEO-CONFUCIAN WRITINGS. Detailed introduction, notes, bibliography, index, 407pp. Col63, 22.35c.**
This volume contains the major works of Wang Yang-ming, an important Neoconfucian writer. Neoconfucianism arose in the fifteenth century and developed and transformed Confucianism under the influence of Buddhism and Taoism and dominated Chinese thought for 800 years. Wang lived in the fifteenth century and represented the idealistic wing of the tradition. The radical difference between Wang and his predecessors is that he considered knowledge and action to be one thing, while they felt the two were separate. This innate knowledge he equated with the *principle of nature.*

CHAN, WING-TSIT, tr. **REFLECTIONS ON THINGS AT HAND. Glossary, bibliography, index, 482pp. Col67, 19.60c.**
Translation of the **Chin-ssu lu**, *an anthology of Neo-Confucianism, giving in clear outline its doctrines of metaphysics, learning, ethics, literature, government, and its evaluation of great men in Chinese history and of heterodoxical systems, notably Buddhism and Taoism. Since it is the forerunner and model of the* **Hsing-li ta-ch'uan (Great Collection of Neo-Confucianism)** *which was for five hundred years the standard text for Chinese thought, its tremendous influence on Chinese philosophy can easily be imagined. In addition, just as Wang Yang-ming's* **Instructions on Practical Living** *is the major work of the idealistic wing of Neoconfucianism, so is the* **Chin-ssu lu** *the major work of the rationalistic wing.—* from the introduction. Introductory material and extensive notes are provided by the translator.

■ CHAN, WING-TSIT, tr. **A SOURCEBOOK IN CHINESE PHILOSOPHY. Glossary of Chinese characters, notes, long bibliography, 831pp. PUP63, 18.50c/5.95p.**
This massive volume covers the entire development of Chinese philosophy from pre-Confucianism to present times. Professor Chan has translated many of the selections himself (including the **Tao Te Ching**) and he provides extensive, illuminating commentary on the extracts. The selections themselves are fairly lengthy. Chan is a leading scholar and this is the definitive anthology.

CHANG CHUNG-YUAN. **CREATIVITY AND TAOISM: A STUDY IN CHINESE PHILOSOPHY, ART, AND POETRY. Many illustrations and quotations, notes, 241pp. H&R63/Wdw, 3.50p.**
A gentle, sensitive work which makes the elusive principle of the Tao available to the Western mind. It is a brilliant exposition and analysis of the relevance and applicability of the Taoist view in Chinese artistic and intellectual creativity. We recommend this study to all who are interested in Chinese culture.

CHANG, JOLAN. **THE TAO OF LOVE AND SEX: THE ANCIENT CHINESE WAY TO ECSTASY. Illustrations, bibliography, index, 7"x9¾", 136pp. Dut77/Wdw, 5.95p.**
Between the thirteenth and fourteenth centuries the Mongols who ruled China for eighty-eight years made a clean sweep of all Taoist literature except the **Tao Te Ching** *and this work of scholarship and insight is the first attempt to assemble the fragments and shards which remain into a coherent picture of Taoist teachings about the role of sexual love as a therapeutic agent for all healing . . . . Connected as love was to a notion of cosmic force emanating from the Tao Principle, the ancient attitudes did not distinguish between love sacred and love profane as we have done in the West.—* Lawrence Durrell. This is a beautifully produced book which encompasses both philosophy and practical techniques.

CHANG, KWANG-CHIH. **THE ARCHAEOLOGY OF ANCIENT CHINA. Notes, bibliography, index, 554pp. YUP77, 8.95p.**
A revised and enlarged version of Professor Chang's important study. Chang believes that there were two or possibly three parallel regional centers of early farmers in China. Each had distinctive features, but their growth processes were essentially identical, they shared common characteristics, and all were ancestral to the historical Ch'in and Han civilizations. Chang's discussion is clearly written and very thorough. The text is abundantly illustrated with photographs, maps, and line drawings.

Chinese Language

Chinese is the principle language of eastern Asia. Chinese exists in a number of varieties that are usually called dialects but that are classified as separate languages by many scholars. More people speak a dialect of Chinese than any other language in the world; the most widely spoken is Mandarin, the dialect most students undertake to study. When spoken, the dialects of Chinese are mutually unintelligible; they differ to about the same extent as the modern Romance languages. Communication between people speaking different dialects is made possible through the common link of the written character.

Unlike the Romance languages, there are four major tones in Chinese. The usage of these tones is indicative to all dialects of the Chinese language. This allows one word such as the one Romanized as *ma* to mean four different things when spoken in its respective tones. One often sees Chinese people writing out characters when conversing with others in an attempt to clarify the meaning of a spoken word.

All the Chinese dialects share a common literary language called the *wen-yen*, written in characters and based on a common body of literature. Before 1917 the formal literary language was used for almost all writing, since that date it has become increasingly acceptable to write in the vernacular style or *pai-hua* instead. In the early 1900s a program for the unification of a national language based on the Mandarin dialect, was launched. In 1956 a new system of Romanization called *pin-yin* based on the pronunication of the characters in the Mandarin dialect was devised as an educational instrument. Simultaneously, in order to make it easier to educate the illiterate people of China, the number of strokes in the most frequently used complex characters were reduced. In other words, the character was *simplified.* This system has been widely promulgated in the People's Republic of China.

CHAN, SHAW WING. **ELEMENTARY CHINESE. Complex characters, 538pp. SUP59, 20.15c.**
This is the second edition of a widely used text which provides an effective means for teaching modern Chinese at the college level. Equal emphasis is placed on developing the student's ability to read, write, and speak Chinese. Though prepared mainly for classroom use, the book can also be used by those who want to learn modern Chinese by themselves. This edition contains an index of the characters and compounds used in the text, as well as sixty lessons that provide material for building a practical vocabulary of about 2,700 words.

CHIANG YEE. **CHINESE CALLIGRAPHY. Index, 6"x9¼", HUP73, 5.95p.**
This is a very highly regarded classic introduction to Chinese calligraphy, exploring the aesthetics and the techniques of this art in which rhythm, line, and structure are perfectly embodied. The illustrations alone make the book worth owning for all who are interested in calligraphy. This third edition includes two new chapters, *Calligraphy and Painting* and *Aesthetic Principles.*

CHINA BOOKS. **ELEMENTARY CHINESE. Simplified characters, two volumes, 631pp. CBk71, 3.50p/set.**
A beginning text for those interested in Chinese as a foreign language, consisting of sixty-six lessons designed to teach everyday conversation and simple written Chinese. There is also a vocabulary at the end of the book.

CHUNG HWA BOOK COMPANY, LTD. **GENERAL CHINESE-ENGLISH DICTIONARY. 926pp. CBk66, 6.50c.**
A clearly organized, compact dictionary produced in the People's Republic of China.

COSMOS BOOKS. **A CURRENT CHINESE-ENGLISH DICTION-ARY.** Appendices, 750pp. Cos78, 9.95c.
This dictionary contains over 18,000 words, phrases, and idioms most frequently used in the political, economic, and cultural activities in the daily life of China. It also includes current scientific and technological terms. The words have been arranged in the alphabetical order of the Chinese phonetic alphabet. Homophones of the same tone are grouped according to the number of strokes in the Chinese character. This is a well produced, handy volume.

CREEL, HERRLEE, *ed.* **LITERARY CHINESE BY THE INDUCTIVE METHOD, VOLUME I. Introductory material, complex characters,** 6¾"x9¾", 228pp. UCh48, 10.10c.
This set of books is generally considered the best instruction manual on learning the Chinese written language ever produced in English. The text itself is printed in very large, clear characters and each is numbered. The bulk of each volume is devoted to notes which analyze in detail each of the characters—taking them apart and discussing their formation, the other characters that they are composed of, a translation, and extensive explanatory and etymological information. Exercise sentences and essays using vocabulary introduced by the text and notes are also presented along with an index of first occurrences of characters and compound expressions and a general index in English. The text in this volume is **The Hsiao Ching** (a classic of filial piety).

CREEL, HERRLEE, *ed.* **LITERARY CHINESE BY THE INDUCTIVE METHOD, VOLUME II. Complex characters,** 6¾"x9¾", 261pp. UCh39, 13.50c.
This volume studies selections from the **Lun Yu**.

CREEL, HERRLEE, *ed.* **LITERARY CHINESE BY THE INDUCTIVE METHOD, VOLUME III. Complex characters,** 6¾"x9¾", 338pp. UCh52, 13.50c.
The text here is **Mencius**, Books I-III.

DE FRANCIS, JOHN. **BEGINNING CHINESE. Complex characters, glossary, index,** 601pp. YUP76, 9.35p.
The most widely used text in secondary and university level courses. The text is an introduction to spoken Mandarin, in *pin-yin* Romanization. Based on a vocabulary of some 600 items, the lessons include pronunciation drills, dialogues, sentence building exercises, pattern drills, substitution tables, and a variety of learning aids. There are also special memorization exercises.

DE FRANCIS, JOHN. **BEGINNING CHINESE READER, PART I. Complex characters,** 539pp. YUP77, 9.35p.
This text is based on a new approach which takes into account the advantages of the oral-aural method but gets the student more quickly into material that he is likely to encounter in actual written Chinese. Unique features are the emphasis on compounds and their extensive use in various types of exercises. The 1,200 combinations are based on 400 characters; in all, the book contains 120,000 characters of running text. All compounds appear in illustrative sentences accompanied by English translations, in dialogue and in narrative or expository form. Characters are introduced in large size, and tables indicate the sequence of strokes used in their formation. Many charts and supplementary lessons are also included. This is considered the standard text and it is widely used in secondary and college level courses.

DE FRANCIS, JOHN. **BEGINNING CHINESE READER, PART II. Complex characters,** 507pp. YUP77, 9.35p.
The glossary and index are included in this part.

DE FRANCIS, JOHN. **CHARACTER TEXT FOR BEGINNING CHINESE. Complex characters,** 519pp. YUP76, 9.35p.
A parallel character version of **Beginning Chinese**. The texts of the companion volumes are identical: dialogues, pronunciation drills, sentence building exercises, substitution drills, and memorization exercises are printed in Chinese characters in this volume while **Beginning Chinese** offers the same lessons in English and in *pin-yin* Romanization of Mandarin. Characters are presented in large size and tables show the sequence of strokes used in their formation.

DE FRANCIS, JOHN. **CHARACTER TEXT FOR INTERMEDIATE CHINESE. Complex characters,** 434pp. YUP65, 8.00p.

DE FRANCIS, JOHN. **INTERMEDIATE CHINESE. Complex characters, glossary, index,** 554pp. YUP64, 8.00p.
A series of lessons, building on the vocabulary in **Beginning Chinese**. This volume presents a series of dialogues on everyday topics, together with an analysis of anticipated points of difficulty. Many new words and grammatical points are also introduced.

DE FRANCIS, JOHN. **INTERMEDIATE CHINESE READER, PART I. Complex characters,** 706pp. YUP67, 8.00p.

DE FRANCIS, JOHN. **INTERMEDIATE CHINESE READER, PART II. Complex characters,** 1,418pp. YUP67, 10.00p.
The glossary and index are in this volume.

◼ FENN, C.H. **THE FIVE THOUSAND DICTIONARY, CHINESE-ENGLISH.** 733pp. HUP42, 5.95p.
Used by thousands of students over the years, this pocket dictionary is generally acknowledged as a basic tool in the study of the Chinese language. Words are arranged in the alphabetical order of their Romanized form. Six columns on each page present the characters in their various forms and the Peking tone of each; the radical; the phonetic; the usual translations, indications as to whether the character is colloquial or literary, and whether it is used as a classifier, numerator, or surname; other readings of the same character; and indications as to its frequency.

FENOLLOSA, ERNEST. **THE CHINESE WRITTEN CHARACTER AS A MEDIUM FOR POETRY. Illustrations, notes,** 45pp. CiL36, 1.50p.
The old theory as to the nature of the Chinese written character (which Fenollosa and Ezra Pound, the editor of this essay, followed) is that the written character is ideogrammatic—a stylized picture of the thing or concept it represents. The opposing theory (which prevails today among scholars) is that the character may have held pictorial origins in prehistoric times but that they have been obscured in all but a very few simple cases. This essay is a full exposition of the old theory.

GILES, HERBERT. **CHINESE-ENGLISH DICTIONARY.** 1,729pp. CWP12, 37.85c.
This was a pioneering work and is still well regarded today. Includes a full radicals index. The characters are printed very clearly and many alternate meanings are given for each entry.

HSU, F.C. **CHINESE WORDS. Index,** 320pp. SAA76, 10.50c.
An etymological analysis of the Chinese language. Professor Hsu has categorized words into indicatives, pictographs, ideatives, harmonics, and combinations. In the case of each group, the first word in each grouping is the modern typescript; the second is the form of the word in the Minor Script, Hsiao Ch'uan; the third is the word as it is written today; the Chinese phonetic pronunciation is denoted by the fourth character; and, finally, the Romanized transliteration is given. This is followed by an English translation and a brief discussion of the formation of the word. The characters and words are extremely well drawn. The author also includes excellent introductory and supplemental material.

LAI, T.C. **CHINESE CALLIGRAPHY. Introduction, glossary,** 269pp. UWa73, 6.95p.
To the Chinese, calligraphy is one of the highest forms of art, the progenitor of the art of brush painting and seal engraving, and a heritage as old as the culture. This is a visual collection of samples of the calligraphy drawn from many periods and styles and chronologically arranged. Each of the selections is identified.

LEWIS, JOHN. **BOOK 1: THE CHINESE WORD FOR HORSE.** 8"x8", about 50pp. TCP76, 3.95p.
This is a neat picture book which illustrates how the appearance of Chinese characters are actually pictorial representations of the object itself. The story tells of a horse and his travels through fields and streams. The illustrations and calligraphy are done in bold face. The various characters used in the story are all briefly and clearly explained.

LEWIS, JOHN. **BOOK 2: THE CHINESE WORD FOR MAN AND WOMAN.** 8"x8", TCP78, 3.95p.
This book follows the same format as **The Chinese Word for Horse** and builds on the characters introduced there. This story introduces nine new characters.

LEWIS, JOHN. **BOOK 3: THE CHINESE WORD FOR THIEF.** 8"x8", TCP78, 3.95p.
All the words in this book are simple Chinese picture words, some of them have appeared in previous books.... If you can't see what the words mean right away you will find them explained at the back of the book.

LIN YUTANG. **LIN YUTANG'S CHINESE-ENGLISH DICTIONARY OF MODERN USAGE.** 7¼"x10¼", 1,786pp. CHK72, 61.00c.
This is a handsomely produced dictionary with a number of important innovations. Each of the characters is clearly reproduced, with Romanization. The author is especially proud of his _instant index_ system for both Chinese and English which reduces the 214 _Kanghsi_ radicals to fifty. Dr. Lin considers this his life's work. It is especially valuable as a literary dictionary, though it should be useful to all serious students of Chinese.

MATTHEWS, ROBERT. **MATTHEWS' CHINESE-ENGLISH DICTIONARY. Pronunciation guide,** 7½"x10¼", 1,250pp. HUP43, 32.15c.
This is the definitive dictionary, revised and corrected, and very clearly printed.

PAAR, FRANCIS, ed. **CH'IEN TZU WEN, THE THOUSAND CHARACTER CLASSIC—A CHINESE PRIMER. Complex characters, bibliography,** 288pp. Ung63, 12.60c.
This work, written in the sixth century AD, is China's oldest primer. It has been used for hundreds of years to teach reading to Chinese children. Chou Hsing-szu's work aims at teaching a maximum of characters in a minimum of text. By organizing a list of 1,000 characters in a somewhat coherent and rhymed form, learning was made easier and more interesting. This volume contains a summary of the text; a brief rendition, with the text in running script and a rather literal translation; a detailed version, with the text written large in four different scripts, notes on the characters, and translations into four languages.

PEKING LANGUAGE INSTITUTE. **CHINESE FOR BEGINNERS. Glossary,** 201pp. FLP76, 1.95p.
This is an excellent basic manual, compiled by the Peking Language Institute and **China Reconstructs**. It consists of twenty-four lessons as well as some general notes on Chinese characters and pronunciation.

PEKING UNIVERSITY FACULTY. **MODERN CHINESE. Simplified characters,** 269pp. Dov71, 3.50p.
This overall course in modern Chinese was designed by the faculty of Peking University and has been used successfully for the past decade in teaching English speaking students basic Mandarin Chinese. Assuming no previous training in Chinese, this course is excellent for self study, with full explanations and ample pronunciation and grammar drills throughout. The official transcription of mainland China is used, and a conversion table to the Yale and Wade systems is provided, along with a vocabulary. A set of three records designed to go along with the course is also available for $12.50—this price includes the book.

QUONG, ROSE. **CHINESE WRITTEN CHARACTERS.** 78pp. Bea68, 2.95p.
A lovely analysis and presentation of several hundred Chinese characters, grouped under key characters known as _radicals_, which, in composition, give a clue to meaning. Ms. Quong interprets the meaning of the characters and shows how conceptions of the material and spiritual world are given visible form by simple strokes arranged in an infinite number of combinations. The essence of each character is illuminated with quotations from Chinese sages.

ROSE-INNES, ARTHUR. **BEGINNER'S DICTIONARY OF CHINESE-JAPANESE CHARACTERS.** 6.50p.
See the Japanese Language subsection of Zen Buddhism.

SIMON, W. **1200 CHINESE BASIC CHARACTERS. Complex characters, appendices, index,** 332pp. LuH57, 9.00p.
This is an elementary textbook, adapted from one of the most popular manuals in use in China over the past century. The material is organized in the form of lessons and about fourteen new characters are introduced in each lesson, along with Romanization and English translations.

WEIGER, L. **CHINESE CHARACTERS. Complex characters,** 820pp. Dov15, 8.95p.
Their origin, etymology, history, classification, and significance. This is the standard text.

WILDER, G.D. and J. H. INGRAM. **ANALYSIS OF CHINESE CHARACTERS. Complex characters, indices,** 375pp. Dov34, 4.00p.
An examination of about one thousand Sino-Japanese characters, beginning with simple words like _I, you, he,_ and working through a high frequency vocabulary. For each character the text offers a printed form, and, where such exists, a seal form; a transcription of the pronunciation into modern Mandarin, including tonal indications; and an English translation. This is followed by an examination of the historical origin of the character, its semantic content, and its components, including its radical in the traditional system.

WILLIAMSON, H.R. **TEACH YOURSELF CHINESE. Complex characters,** 638pp. McK47/Hod, 4.65p.
An excellent teach-yourself manual for both written and spoken Mandarin Chinese. An introductory section covers the sounds and spelling of the language and grammar is presented through a series of dialogues. Forty dialogues (first in Roman script, then in Chinese) introduce and illustrate every aspect of everyday Chinese. Grammar notes and vocabulary are included at the appropriate points in the text and all the grammatical information is summarized at the end.

WOLFF, DIANE. **CHINESE WRITING. Bibliography,** 9¼"x7¾", 46pp. HRW75, 5.95c.
An introduction to Chinese calligraphy geared toward young readers, covering the philosophy behind this Chinese art and including a simple how-to guide for the novice. The book is well illustrated and some basic characters are fully discussed.

■ _WOLFF, DIANE._ **AN EASY GUIDE TO EVERYDAY CHINESE. Complex characters, bibliography,** 231pp. H&R74, 3.95p.
This book is designed to enable anyone to appreciate Chinese for the magnificent language it is, or to begin learning it. You can browse in it and read what interests you in any order. The English section provides background information, history of the langauge, discussion of calligraphy, and technical information such as pronunciation and sentence patterns. The Chinese section contains common everyday words, their meanings, many word derivations, and the stroke order (which is the instruction for writing each character). This is the most introductory of all the books on the Chinese language.

————**END OF CHINESE LANGUAGE SUBSECTION**————

Chinese Literature

Chinese literature is one of the major literary heritages of the world, with a number of distinctive characteristics. First of all, it has an uninterrupted history of more than 3,000 years, dating back at least to the fourteenth century BC. Second, through cultural contacts, Chinese literature has profoundly influenced the literary traditions of other Asian countries, particularly Korea, Japan, and Vietnam. Not only was the Chinese script adopted for their written language, but some writers adopted Chinese as their chief literary medium. Third, the graphic nature of the written aspect of the Chinese language has produced a number of noteworthy effects upon Chinese literature, especially poetry. Fourth, the tonal feature of the Chinese language has brought about an intimate relationship between poetry and music.

All major types of Chinese poetry were originally sung to the accompaniment of music. Chinese poetry, besides depending on end rhyme and tonal meter for its cadence, is characterized by its compactness and brevity. There are no epics of either folk or literary variety and hardly any narrative or descriptive poems that are long by standards of world literature. Stressing the lyrical, the Chinese poet refrains from being exhaustive, marking instead the heights of his ecstasies and inspiration or the depths of sorrow and sympathy. In Chinese poetry a word or two frequently indicates an allusion to a very complex thought or situation that might require paragraphs of elucidation. This explains why some poems have been differently interpreted by learned commentators and competent translators. It has also been observed that the line of demarcation between prose and poetry is much less distinctly drawn in Chinese literature than in other national literatures.

AYLING, ALAN and DUNCAN MACKINTOSH. **A FOLDING SCREEN: SELECTED CHINESE LYRICS FROM T'ANG TO MAO TSE-TUNG. Notes, index, 7½"x10¼", HeG76, 7.50p.**
A beautifully produced collection, with the Chinese text on facing pages. The bulk of the poems are from the T'ang and Sung dynasties.

BERWITT-TAYLOR, C.H., tr. **ROMANCE OF THE THREE KINGDOMS. Two volumes, boxed, 1,279pp. Tut59, 19.50c/set.**
This is regarded by the Chinese as their greatest novel. Its perennial allure springs mainly from its basis in exciting historical fact and its telling portrayal of human ambition against a background of adventure and intrigue. The **Romance** is a product of fourteenth century China, although the events it depicts occurred some centuries earlier.

■ BIRCH, CYRIL, ed. **ANTHOLOGY OF CHINESE LITERATURE, VOLUME I: FROM EARLIEST TIMES TO THE FOURTEENTH CENTURY. 500pp. Grv65, 5.95p.**
This set has been widely hailed as the best anthology of Chinese literature in English translation in recent years. Birch, chairman of the Department of Oriental Languages of the University of California, Berkeley, has drawn together the finest of existing translations. Where these have been found inadequate, new translations have been commissioned. Thus, roughly half the material is published for the first time in this volume. The selections span a 200 year period from the Chou Dynasty (1122-221 BC) to the Yuan Dynasty (1280-1367 BC). From the ancient **Songs** to the dramas of the fourteenth century, all major *genres* are represented.

■ BIRCH, CYRIL, ed. **ANTHOLOGY OF CHINESE LITERATURE, VOLUME II: FROM THE FOURTEENTH CENTURY TO THE PRESENT DAY. Introduction, bibliography, 507pp. Grv72, 4.95p.**

BONNET, LESLIE. **CHINESE FAIRY TALES. 3.90c.**
See the Fairy Tales section.

BYNNER, WITTER. **THE CHINESE TRANSLATIONS. 388pp. FSG78, 20.00c.**
This lovely volume contains **The Jade Mountain**, with an introduction by Burton Watson; **The Way of Life According to Lao Tzu**, with an introduction by David Lattimore; and Bynner's essay on Kiang Kang-hu, *Remembering a Gentle Scholar.*

BYNNER, WITTER, tr. **THE JADE MOUNTAIN. 300pp. RaH29, 2.45p.**
A beautifully translated anthology of 300 T'ang poems. Bynner also contributes a lengthy overview of Chinese poetry.

CALVIN, LEWIS and DOROTHY WALMSLEY. **WANG-WEI THE PAINTER-POET. Notes, bibliography, index, 182pp. Tut68, 6.00c.**
Wang-Wei lived during the T'ang Dynasty, the most brilliant cultural period in Chinese history. Whatever he attempted—as artist, poet, musician, doctor, official—he performed with a master's touch. He is acknowledged as the father of pure landscape painting and greatest of all his innovations is the long horizontal scroll. This is an excellent study. The authors begin with a survey of T'ang China and a life study

of Wang-Wei. The rest of the book is devoted to an analysis of his paintings, sixty-eight of which are reproduced.

CARPENTER, FRANCES. **TALES OF A CHINESE GRANDMOTHER. 3.95p.**
See the Fairy Tales section.

CHAVES, JONATHAN, tr. **YANG WAN-LI—HEAVEN MY BLANKET, EARTH MY PILLOW. Index, 118pp. Wea75, 4.95p.**
A translation of nature poems from Sung Dynasty China, accompanied by lovely illustrations and a long interpretative introduction.

CHEN, SHIH-HSIANG and HAROLD ACTON, trs. **THE PEACH BLOSSOM FAN. Introduction, notes, 333pp. UCa76, 3.95p.**
A translation of a poetic drama about national cataclysm. More than 300 years ago the Ming Dynasty, the last native Chinese imperial house, fell before rebel onslaughts, made a short lived attempt at restoration in the south, then yielded finally to the invading Manchus. Writing in the 1690s, K'ung Shang-jen was able to gather the recollections of survivors. Out of these and a multitude of documentary accounts he constructed a great historical play in the elegant southern Chinese style.

COOPER, ARTHUR, tr. **LI PO AND TU FU. 239pp. Vik73, 2.25p.**
Wonderful translations of two of China's greatest poets along with over 100 pages of information on Chinese poetry as well as analyses of each poem.

EBERHARD, WOLFRAM, ed. **FOLKTALES OF CHINA. 4.45p/1.25p.**
See the Fairy Tales section.

FOREMAN, MICHAEL and PETER HARRIS. **MONKEY AND THE THREE WIZARDS. 8.40c.**
See the Fairy Tales section.

FRANKEL, HANS. **THE FLOWERING PLUM AND THE PALACE LADY—INTERPRETATIONS OF CHINESE POETRY. Glossary, many notes, bibliography, index, 289pp. YUP76, 5.95p.**
One of the most thorough analyses for the general reader of Chinese poetry in translation. The selection—much of which has been translated by Professor Frankel himself—includes examples of all four of the major *genres* of Chinese poetry. There are many poems which have never been translated before, as well as the work of a number of lesser known but extremely interesting poets. Each poem is printed in Chinese at the bottom of the page.

GILES, HERBERT. **HISTORY OF CHINESE LITERATURE. Indices, 510pp. Ung67, 3.95p.**
A pioneering work, originally published in 1901. Professor of Chinese at Cambridge, Giles contributed more than any one scholar to Western knowledge of Chinese language and literature. This **History** remains an important work to this day and this edition includes an entirely new section covering the first half of this century by Liu Wu-Chi.

GORDON, DAVID, tr. **EQUINOX, A GATHERING OF T'ANG POETS. Introduction, notes on the translations and adaptations, biographical notes on the poets, 109pp. OUP75, 8.25c.**
I have tried to realize an ideogram specifically and in terms of its context. . . . I have condensed, expanded, abridged, used compression, ellipsis, inversion, impressionism and expressionism in an effort to directly translate the spirit of these poems (a literal translation is a pound of flesh without a drop of blood).

GRAHAM, A.C., tr. **POEMS OF THE LATE T'ANG. Notes, 173pp. Vik77, 1.95p.**
Chinese poetry achieved an unsurpassed greatness during the eighth and ninth centuries AD. This anthology includes the later poems of Tu Fu as well as a good selection of the following T'ang poets: Meng Chiao, Han Yu, Lu T'ung, Li Ho, Tu Mu, and Li Shang-yin. Graham also includes an essay on translating Chinese poetry and short biographical sketches of the poets.

HALL, MANLY P. **THE WAY OF HEAVEN. 185pp. PRS46, 6.00c.**
A collection of nine Oriental fantasies told in the manner of Chinese literature of the classical period, based on Buddhist and Taoist philosophy. Nice woodblock prints illustrate the stories.

HART, HENRY H. tr. **A CHARCOAL BURNER AND OTHER POEMS.** **Introduction, index, 253pp. UOk74, 12.00c.**
A wide ranging selection of translations of Chinese poems from many eras, from the first through the nineteenth century.

HAWKES, DAVID, tr. **THE STORY OF THE STONE, VOLUME I: THE GOLDEN DAYS. Long introduction, list of characters, genealogy, 542pp. Vik73, 4.95p.**
The Story of the Stone, better known as **The Dream of the Red Chamber,** is the great novel of manners in Chinese literature. Written in the mid-eighteenth century, it charts the glory and decline of the illustrious Jia family (a story which closely accords with the fortunes of the author's own family). The two main characters, Bao-yu and Dai-yu, are set against a rich tapestry of humor, realistic detail, and delicate poetry which accurately reflects Chinese family life. This is a wonderful translation. Hawkes says that his *one abiding principle has been to translate everything—even puns....I have assumed that whatever I find in it is there for a purpose and must be dealt with somehow or other.* The translation will eventually be complete in five volumes.

HAWKES, DAVID, tr. **THE STORY OF THE STONE, VOLUME II: THE CRAB-FLOWER CLUB. List of characters, appendices, 605pp. Vik77, 4.95p.**
The second volume of this wonderful translation.

HSIA, C.T. **THE CLASSIC CHINESE NOVEL: A CRITICAL INTRODUCTION. Introduction, glossary, notes, bibliography, index, 424pp. Col68, 5.05p.**
An in depth study of the six titles most representative of the strengths and diversity of the classic Chinese novel: **The Romance of the Three Kingdoms, The Water Margin** (or **All Men Are Brothers**), **Journey to the West** (or **Monkey**), **Chin P'ing Mei** (or **The Golden Lotus**), **The Scholars,** and **Dream of the Red Chamber.** While Hsia provides pertinent historical information, his focus is mainly critical as he examines in detail each novel's structure and style, and analyzes its major characters and episodes in relation to its moral or philosophical themes. Many Western classics are cited for comparison, and generous excerpts from each novel are included. The strong feeling that we get throughout is that Hsia does not feel that the Chinese novels compare favorably with their European counterparts.

HSIUNG, S.I., tr. **THE ROMANCE OF THE WESTERN CHAMBER (HSI HSIANG CHI). Illustrations, 326pp. Col68, 4.50p.**
For nearly eight centuries in China the play **Hsi Hsiang Chi,** based on a short story by Yuan Chen (779-831), has delighted generations of playgoers and readers. The drama relates the wooing and winning of the beautiful Ts'ui Ying-ying by a young scholar. The trio of major characters is completed by a quick witted maid who acts as go-between for the lovers. In classic style, the play ranges from prose to poetry. Yuan Chen's tale is given in an appendix. Critical introduction by C.T. Hsia.

INOUE, YASUSHI. **TUN-HUANG. Introduction, 213pp. Kod78, 8.95c.**
This novel is a romantic adventure story set in a desert kingdom in China's westernmost frontier in the eleventh century. Tun-huang gained fame in the early part of this century when some 20,000 Buddhist scrolls and manuscripts were discovered in the Thousand Buddha Caves there. Around this priceless archaeological and cultural find, and how they came to be hidden there in the first place, Inoue has woven an intricate and enthralling tale.

JENNINGS, WILLIAM, tr. **THE SHI KING. Introduction, 383pp. PBR1891, 11.50c.**
A fully annotated translation of the *poetry classic* of the Chinese. The translations are stiff and do not give the reader the sense of the original poems, though the scholarship is adequate.

KUO, LOUISE and YUAN HSI, trs. **CHINESE FOLK TALES. 4.95p.**
See the Fairy Tales section.

LEVY, HOWARD, tr. **TRANSLATIONS FROM PO CHU-I'S COLLECTED WORKS, VOLUME I: OLD STYLE POEMS. Many notes, 8¾"x12", 183pp. PRB70, 10.00c.**
Po Chu-i (772-846) was a Chinese poet of many poems but few themes. When he compiled his collection, he divided poems into the thematic categories of social criticism, quiet pleasures and moved-to-sorrow.—from the preface. This is a critical discussion and translation of many of the thematic poems, organized

topically. Levy is a sympathetic translator and his commentary is based on the most recent scholarship and thought.

LEVY, HOWARD, tr. **TRANSLATIONS FROM PO CHU-I'S COLLECTED WORKS, VOLUME II: THE REGULATED POEMS. Notes, 8¾"x12", 94pp. PRB70, 8.00c.**
Po Chu-i composed more than two thousand regulated poems, in a variety of line and stanza lengths....All of his life he composed regulated poems, and from his fifties onwards he came to favor this form almost exclusively over the free so-called old style form in which he wrote some of his best remembered poems....The regulated poems deal with the pleasures of friendship and the pains of absense, absorption in scenic splendor, keen realization of the aging process, and the acceptance and cultivation of melancholy.—from the introduction.

LIN, SHUEN-FU. **THE TRANSFORMATION OF THE CHINESE LYRICAL TRADITION: CHIANG K'UEI AND SOUTHERN SUNG TZ'U POETRY. Long introduction, glossary, notes, bibliography, index, 261pp. PUP78, 20.15c.**
Chiang K'uei was a major writer of *tz'u,* the most important poetic *genre* of the Sung Dynasty. This book explores his work and career as they exemplified the radical transformation that took place in Chinese life, art, literature, and thought at the turn of the thirteenth century.

LIU, WU-CHI. **AN INTRODUCTION TO CHINESE LITERATURE. Illustrations, chronology, notes, bibliography, index, 329pp. IUP66, 4.95p.**
A descriptive and critical account of the major accomplishments, movements, and writers of the traditional and modern periods of Chinese literature as well as translations of original writings. Unlike many works on Chinese literature, Professor Liu devotes a great deal of space to the drama and the novel, and to twentieth century literature. This book provides an adequate overview of the subject, and it should be especially interesting to those who would like to place individual works in a larger context.

■ *LIU, WU-CHI and IRVING YUCHENG LO, eds.* **SUNFLOWER SPLENDOR. 694pp. Dou75, 6.95p.**
This has been widely acclaimed as both the most comprehensive and the finest anthology of Chinese poetry in English. The volume presents the writings of over 140 poets—the chief exponents of the main schools of Chinese poetry within each major *genre* and period and covers 3,000 years from the twelfth century BC to the present day. Over fifty individuals worked on the translations, the majority of which have been especially commissioned for this volume. A general introduction, biographical introductions for each poet, textual notes, and a bibliography provide a thorough background for the reader.

MA, Y.W. and J.S.M. LAU, eds. **TRADITIONAL CHINESE STORIES: THEMES AND VARIATIONS. Introduction, notes, bibliography, 7¾"x10", 629pp. Col78, 9.45p.**
For centuries the Chinese referred to their fiction as *hsiao-shuo,* etymologically meaning *roadside gossip* or *small talk* and held it in low

regard compared to classical poetry and drama. Not until this century was the Chinese story internationally recognized as a beautiful and vital expression of the Chinese spirit. This is the most distinguished and comprehensive anthology of the rich tradition of Chinese short fiction available to the general reader. Spanning the former Han Dynasty (206 BC–AD 8) to the early Republican years, these sixty-one stories represent the five major forms of Chinese fiction: *pi-chi, ch'uan-ch'i, pien-wen, hua-pen,* and *kung-an.*

■ *MCCURDY, JOHN.* OF ALL THINGS MOST YIELDING. 8½"x 11", 128pp. RaH75, 6.95p.
Full color nature photographs are set off with Chinese poetry from all traditions and all ages. The photographs are some of the most beautiful we have seen and each poem is successfully matched to a photograph, evoking an equivalent mood.

■ *MCHUGH, FLORENCE and ISABEL.* THE DREAM OF THE RED CHAMBER. Introduction, 603pp. G&D58, 4.95p.
The first realistic novel in Chinese, **The Dream of the Red Chamber** is a vast, abundantly peopled chronicle of a noble family in the eighteenth century, a rich, powerful family that had been singled out for generations by imperial favor. The splendor of their enchanting gardens and pleasure pavilions and a daily life of the most sophisticated refinements hide the symptoms of decline and self destruction. The characters and scenes are magnificently realized: the ruling matriarch, vigorous and earthy; her son, a strict, inflexible Confucian; her grandson, the hero of the story, neurotic, effeminate, and happy only in the company of his sisters and female cousins, who live with him in the *park of delightful vision.* Yet beneath all the lively and glittering pageant is a strangely mystical mood, an all pervading sense of the transitoriness of all earthly things. Though immensely popular in China and long considered the peak of Chinese fictional literature, this novel has seemed inaccessible to the Western reader, for it presented almost insuperable difficulties to the translator. Dr. Franz Kuhn's version has been widely acclaimed and it is the basis of this English translation. The story has been cut down in size considerably for this one-volume translation, but all the essential elements remain and the novel reads extremely well. A series of lovely illustrations is included, along with an all important listing of the main characters.

■ *MCNAUGHTON, WILLIAM, ed.* CHINESE LITERATURE: AN ANTHOLOGY FROM THE EARLIEST TIMES TO THE PRESENT DAY. Introduction, index, 836pp. Tut74, 15.00c.
This is an excellent collection which presents Chinese literature as an organic development. The translations themselves are of the finest quality. The translators include Pearl Buck, Arthur Waley, Ezra Pound, and Burton Watson.

MANDEL, OSCAR. CHI PO AND THE SORCERER. 8"x11½", 85pp. Tut64, 5.50c.
A delightful story, ostensibly for children, of how young Chi Po, aided by the sorcerer Bu Fu, became the greatest painter of all China. The tale is based on the life of Ch'i Po-shih, one of China's greatest living painters, who died in 1957 at the age of ninety-six. Illustrated with a Chinese scroll in ink by Lo Koon-Chiu.

MANTON, JO and ROBERT GETTINGS. THE FLYING HORSES: TALES FROM CHINA. 6.95c.
See the Fairy Tales section.

MAYHEW, LENORE and WILLIAM MCNAUGHTON, trs. A GOLD ORCHID: THE LOVE POEMS OF TZU YEH. Introductory material, illustrations, notes, bibliography, 135pp. Tut72, 5.50c.
Translations of fourth century erotic poems written by Tzu Yeh, a wineshop girl.

MORRIS, IVAN, ed. MADLY SINGING IN THE MOUNTAINS: AN APPRECIATION AND ANTHOLOGY OF ARTHUR WALEY. Sixteen photographs of Waley, chronology of his life and writings, index, 403pp. Wal70, 12.50c.
Arthur Waley did more than any other single man to introduce Chinese and Japanese literature to the Western reader. The first part of this book consists of articles by people who had a close knowledge of Waley and his work: his relatives, friends, fellow authors, and students (Morris himself was a student of Waley). The second—and longest—section is an anthology of Waley's writings, and Morris includes his own favorite pieces as well as a number of lesser known selections. Both poems and prose passages are represented.

OBATA, SHIGEYOSHI, tr. THE WORKS OF LI PO, THE CHINESE POET. Bibliography, 275pp. PBR35, 10.00c.
Fine translations of 132 of Li Po's brief poems. The Chinese text of each poem is included along with annotation. There is also a lengthy introduction and biographical notes.

REXROTH, KENNETH, tr. LOVE AND THE TURNING YEAR. Bibliography, 140pp. NDP70, 2.25p.
Subtitled, *One Hundred More Poems from the Chinese,* it includes works by sixty different poets, from the third century to the present. The translations themselves are uniformly excellent and retain the flavor of the originals.

REXROTH, KENNETH, tr. NEW POEMS. Index, 87pp. NDP74, 2.95p.
This book includes many poems translated from the Chinese, along with a miscellany of other work.

REXROTH, KENNETH, tr. ONE HUNDRED POEMS FROM THE CHINESE. Bibliography, 160pp. NDP71, 1.95p.
Thirty-five poems by Tu Fu (713-770) make up the first part of this volume. Rexroth follows with a selection of poets from the Sung Dynasty (tenth to twelfth century), much of whose work is not available elsewhere in English. There is also a general introduction, and biographical and explanatory notes on the poets and poems.

REXROTH, KENNETH and LING CHUNG, trs. THE ORCHID BOAT: WOMEN POETS OF CHINA. Bibliography, 165pp. Sea72, 4.50p.
A representative collection of Chinese women's poetry in translation, ranging from the legendary earliest court poetry of courtesans, palace women, and Taoist priestesses to works by contemporary Chinese living in both the East and West. Appendices include notes on poems, an introductory essay on Chinese women and literature, and a table of Chinese historical periods.

ROBERTS, MOSS, tr. THREE KINGDOMS. Introduction, many illustrations, index, 343pp. RaH76, 4.95p.
An abridged translation of the great Ming epic, **Three Kingdoms** by Lo Kuan-chung. The story depicts the conflict between chivalry and statecraft during the twilight of the Han empire. Earlier English versions of the epic were turgid and so the work was known mainly to Chinese specialists. This is an eminently readable translation which makes the book more accessible to general readers. The story is fascinating, as it says in the introduction, *The vast canvas of* **Three Kingdoms** *is crowded with stories and peopled with kings and courtiers, peasants, soldiers, sorcerers, scholars. Its themes of power, loyalty, and social obligation appear and vanish, only to surface again in a different context and with ironically altered significance. Its scale of time is dynastic rather than individual: men's acts overtake them, but then run beyond their personal destinies until the flow of history absorbs them all.*

ROBINSON, G.W., tr. POEMS OF WANG WEI. Introduction, 144pp. Vik73, 1.95p.
Wang Wei (AD 699-761) was one of China's greatest poets, especially noted for his descriptions of landscape and the beauties of country life.

SACKHEIM, ERIC, tr. ...THE SILENT ZERO, IN SEARCH OF SOUND...Notes, 191pp. Vik68, 3.95p.
An anthology of Chinese poetry from earliest times through the sixth century AD. The quality of the translations is uniformly excellent; Sackheim's stated aim is to preserve as much *verbal fidelity* as possible. An essay on translation appended to the poems summarizes much that has been written on the subject through extensive direct quotation from writers of many different cultures and periods.

SCHAFER, EDWARD. THE DIVINE WOMAN: DRAGON LADIES AND RAIN MAIDENS IN T'ANG LITERATURE. Glossary, notes, bibliography, index, 199pp. UCa73, 10.00c.
Schafer remarks: *Throughout Chinese history dragons have been powerful water spirits, concealing themselves in tiny pools as frogs or minnows, until they chose to transform themselves into magnificent sky-striders and to herd the rain-clouds through heaven to bring fertilizing rain to the parched earth. They had close affinities with ancient Chinese goddesses of rivers and lakes....The rain and fertility goddess who had the most successful career in Chinese literature was the Divine Woman of Wu Shan. This book is named for her. She flashed in and out of rainbows...to dazzle and*

seduce prehistoric kings, thus guaranteeing the fertility of their queens and of the nation's crops. She continues to appear down through the centuries as a favorite figure in semi-erotic poetry.... This book tells of the Divine Woman under many names and enchanting aspects—poetic, mystifying, haunting, alluring, or didactic.

SIE, CHEOU. **A BUTTERFLY'S DREAM AND OTHER CHINESE TALES. 5.50c.**
See the Fairy Tales section.

SNYDER, GARY. **RIPRAP, AND COLD MOUNTAIN POEMS. 61pp. FSF65, 2.00p.**
Snyder, a respected young American poet, has made a deep study of Eastern and especially Taoist philosophy. This orientation is apparent in all of his poems. This volume includes his fine translation of **Cold Mountain Poems** by a T'ang Dynasty poet.

TSAO HSUEH-CHIN. **A DREAM OF RED MANSIONS, VOLUME I. Twelve color illustrations, 600pp. FLP78, 14.95c.**
A new translation of this classic eighteenth century novel, prepared in the People's Republic of China by Yang Hsien-yi and Gladys Yang. This version will be complete in three volumes; Volume I contains the first forty chapters. The story provides a dramatic picture of the decline of the old feudal order through the lives of four great families of the Ching Dynasty. It is a wonderful tale, and we are delighted to see another complete translation being prepared.

TSAO HSUEH-CHIN. **DREAM OF THE RED CHAMBER. 349pp. Dou58, 2.95p.**
This is a revised, greatly edited and abridged edition of Chi-chen Wang's definitive translation—a work which was described by Arthur Waley as *singularly accurate...the work of adaptation skillfully performed.* We do not like this version very much; it is too condensed. The editor has simply taken the first sentence of each paragraph—and sometimes he skipped many paragraphs, all of which makes the story very confusing; you never know why people are acting the way they are. However, if you do not like reading long novels, this will give you a feeling for the story and the time.

WALEY, ALISON. **DEAR MONKEY. 223pp. Bla73, 7.35c.**
This is an abridgment by Arthur Waley's wife, Alison. The story really comes alive in this retelling and we actually like it better than Waley's original version. A profusion of delightful woodcuts illustrate the text.

WALEY, ARTHUR, tr. **CHINESE POEMS. 213pp. A&U76, 5.25p.**
A collection of Waley's favorite Chinese poems, some selected from previously published works and some translated here for the first time.

WALEY, ARTHUR. **LIFE AND TIMES OF PO CHU-I. Extensive notes, index, 237pp. A&U49, 9.25c.**
A biographical study of Po Chu-i (772-846) combined with a social history of the early ninth century in China. Translations in whole or in part of about 100 poems by Po Chu-i are also included.

■ *WALEY, ARTHUR, tr.* **MONKEY. 306pp. Grv43/Pen, 4.95p.**
This classic combination of picaresque novel and folk epic, which mixes satire, allegory, and history, is one of the most popular books in China. It is the story of the roguish Monkey and his encounters with major and minor spirits, gods, demigods, demons, monsters, and fairies. Waley has given us a wonderful translation of Wu Ch'eng-en's novel.

WALEY, ARTHUR, tr. **THE NINE SONGS. Index, 65pp. CiL55, 2.50p.**
In ancient China the shaman was prophet, healer, dancer, and singer, sometimes regarded as an outcast, though treated always with high consideration. In these songs, known in China for well over 1,000

years, the always fleeting relationship of shaman and spirit is seen as that of lovers who come together and then part. Waley includes a commentary on the various deities whom the shaman served, and gives a general account of shamanism in China, in addition to his translations.

WALEY, ARTHUR. **THE POETRY AND CAREER OF LI PO. Indices, 133pp. A&U50, 5.75c.**
Li Po (701-62) is one of China's greatest poets. This is the most complete study of his life and work available in any language. Dr. Waley presents Li Po's life against the background of contemporary history and he emphasizes the poet's devotion to Taoism. Taoists often sought religious inspiration in wine and through wine Li Po often reached the ecstatic state which is reflected in his mystical poems. Translations of some of his poems are included within the text.

WALEY, ARTHUR, tr. **TRANSLATIONS FROM THE CHINESE. Illustrations, notes, 325pp. RaH19, 1.95p.**
This volume contains all the poems from Waley's two famous collections, **170 Chinese Poems** and **More Translations from the Chinese**. The poems translated here are both ancient China's finest and Waley's most evocative work. One can get a good feeling for the essence of ancient China from this collection.

WALEY, ARTHUR. **YUAN MEI. Notes, index, 227pp. SUP57, 2.95p.**
A biographical study of this eighteenth century Chinese poet. Waley includes a number of his own translations of Yuan Mei's poems. In **The New York Times Book Review**, Kenneth Rexroth made the following comment: *I wish everyone who reads this review would go out and buy the book. I wish every American poet would read and ponder it long. The poems are beautiful, the biography is absorbing.*

WANG HSING-PEI. **MONKEY SUBDUES THE WHITE-BONE DEMON. 6¾"x10", 110pp. FLP64, 1.95p.**
This picture story book is based on an episode from **The Pilgrimage to the West**, quite possibly the most popular Chinese novel ever written. The line drawings in this version are in the traditional Chinese style and the book itself is a product of the People's Republic of China. Nine-tenths or more of each page is devoted to drawings.

WATSON, BURTON, tr. **CHINESE LYRICISM: SHIH POETRY FROM THE SECOND TO THE TWELFTH CENTURY. 236pp. Col71, 3.95p.**
The *shih* is a lyric form using a predominantly five or seven character line. Some 200 poems, illustrating the most important formal, stylistic, and thematic developments in the growth of *shih* poetry, are presented here in new translations by Professor Watson. The major poets such as T'ao Ch'ien and Po Chu-i are not extensively treated, making it possible to devote more space to poets of the six Dynasties and Sung eras. The accompanying background material—critical, historical, or biographical—is given in notes to particular poems and in brief essays.

WATSON, BURTON, tr. **COLD MOUNTAIN. Introduction, notes, 118pp. Col62, 2.95p.**
A collection of 100 poems by Han-shan. It is one of the earliest and most important works of Chinese Buddhist poetry and is especially influential in the later literature of Zen. The poems are important both as vivid descriptions of the wild mountain scenery in Han-shan's home, and as metaphors of the poet's search for spiritual enlightenment and peace.

WATSON, BURTON. **EARLY CHINESE LITERATURE. Introduction, chronology, index, 306pp. Col62, 4.95p.**
Chinese literature has flowered brilliantly in three fields: history, philosophy, and poetry. Dr. Watson here provides an account of Chinese literature from the time of the Chou Dynasty, which began around 1100 BC and ended in 249 BC, to the middle of the later Han Dynasty, which extended from AD 25 to 220. He describes the masterpieces of the period and quotes at length from them. Many of these works are of unknown or doubtful authorship; for known authors, Dr. Watson provides biographical information. The text is divided into three separate sections—history, philosophy, and poetry.

WATSON, BURTON, tr. **KOJIRO YOSHIKAWA'S AN INTRODUCTION TO SUNG POETRY. Notes, 191pp. HUP67, 11.45c.**
The enormous corpus of Sung (960-1279) poetry has remained largely unstudied and only the most famous of the numerous poets, Su Tung-p'o, has been extensively written about and translated. Sung poetry

explored directions which T'ang writers had shunned or ignored, and deliberately strove for new effects and values. The most significant Sung poets concentrated on the concerns of daily life and society as a whole and expressed more explicit philosophical ideas. As Yoshikawa says, *T'ang poetry could be likened to wine, Sung poetry to tea....Tea is less stimulating, bringing to the drinker a quieter pleasure, but one which can be enjoyed more continuously.* Yoshikawa is one of the world's outstanding scholars of Chinese literature.

WATSON, BURTON, tr. **THE OLD MAN WHO DOES AS HE PLEASES, POEMS AND PROSE BY LU YU. Introduction, notes, 141pp. Col73, 11.25c.**
Lu Yu (1125-1210) was among the most prolific of Chinese poets, having left behind a collection of close to 10,000 poems as well as miscellaneous prose writings. His poetry, often characterized by an intense patriotism, is also notable for its recurrent expression of a carefree enjoyment of life. The present volume offers a selection of sixty-three of Lu Yu's works; Watson concentrates upon those which provide, with an abundance of succinct and evocative detail, characteristic glimpses of the poet's daily life.

WATSON, BURTON, tr. **SU TUNG-PO. 149pp. Col65, 3.90p.**
Su Shih, better known by his literary name Su Tung-p'o, was the greatest poet of the Sung Dynasty. This book contains Watson's translations of more than eighty poems. The selections include examples of the *shih* form, the *tz'u* (originally lyrics written for well known tunes), and the *fu* (prose poem). Watson also supplies an introduction and notes.

WILHELM, RICHARD, tr. **CHINESE FOLKTALES. 5.95c.**
See the Fairy Tales section.

WRIGGINS, SALLY. **WHITE MONKEY KING. 123pp. RaH77, 5.95c.**
This is an illustrated retelling of the adventures of Monkey, taken out of a portion of China's greatest folk novel, **Journey to the West.** This story is best known in Arthur Waley's version. Ms. Wriggins presents only the first part, in which the mischievous monkey acquires god-like powers and creates havoc in heaven. A sequel will describe the journey to India. The story reads well and should capture the fancy of older children.

WU, JOHN C.H. **THE FOUR SEASONS OF T'ANG POETRY. Illustrations, index, 225pp. Tut72, 7.75c.**
This is a superlative survey of the Golden Age of Chinese poetry, based on the author's study of nearly 50,000 poems written by more than 2,000 poets. Dr. Wu interprets the poems with deep understanding and captures the spirit of the age. Many poems are included in whole or in part.

YIP, WAI-LIM, tr. **WANG WEI: HIDING THE UNIVERSE. 6¾"x8¾", 136pp. Vik72, 4.95p.**
This is an exquisite edition of Wang Wei's poems, with the original Chinese on facing pages with the trannslation. Delicate paintings from the **Mustard Seed Manual** are scattered throughout and the translator offers an essay, *Wang Wei and Pure Experience.* The quality of the translations is excellent.

YU, ANTHONY, tr. **THE JOURNEY TO THE WEST, VOLUME I. Notes, 542pp. UCh77, 31.50c.**
The Journey to the West has enjoyed great popularity since its first publication in the late sixteenth century. It is best known to English readers in Arthur Waley's version, **Monkey.** Professor Yu's edition is the first complete translation in English. The fantastic tale recounts the sixteen year pilgrimage of the monk Hsuan-tsang, who journeyed to India to bring back more than 600 items of Buddhist scripture. In the narrative, the pilgrim monk is accompanied by four animal disciples endowed with superhuman abilities. The story involves assaults on the monk by demons and monsters and his deliverance by his disciples with the assistance of appropriate deities. Yu is a Chinese scholar and he includes both the prose narration and verse sections. Volume I includes an excellent introduction to the work as a whole, followed by an annotated translation of the first twenty-five chapters.

ZINER, FEENIE. **CRICKET BOY. 6.95c.**
See the Fairy Tales section.

──────END OF CHINESE LITERATURE SUBSECTION──────

CHING, JULIA. **TO ACQUIRE WISDOM: THE WAY OF WANG YANG-MING. Glossary, notes, bibliography, index, 399pp. Col76, 19.60c.**
A comprehensive analysis of the philosophy of Wang Yang-ming, an important Ming Dynasty sage. Dr. Ching begins with a general discussion of truth and ideology in the spiritual and intellectual traditions out of which emerged Wang's own body of ideas. His thought is then traced within the context of Confucian orthodoxy and as it moves away from it, within the orbit of thought constructed by Wang himself. Ideas and concepts central to his philosophy are explained and analyzed. A final section contains translations of Wang's philosophical essays and poems. Appendices include brief surveys of the Yang-ming schools in Japan and Korea.

Chuang Tzu

Chuang Tzu (399-295 BC) lived 200 years after Lao Tzu. Using parables and anecdotes, allegory and paradox, he set forth the early ideas of what was to become Taoism. Central in these is the belief that only by understanding Tao (the Way of Nature) and dwelling in its unity can man achieve true happiness and be truly free, in both life and death. *To him, nature is not only spontaneity but nature is a state of constant flux and incessant transformation. This is the universal process that binds all things into one, equalizing all things and all opinions. The pure man makes this oneness his eternal abode, in which he becomes a "companion" of Nature and does not attempt to interfere with it by imposing the way of man on it. His goal is absolute spiritual emancipation and peace, to be achieved through knowing the capacity and limitations of one's own nature, nourishing it, and adapting to the universal process of transformation. He abandons selfishness of all descriptions, be it fame, wealth, bias or subjectivity. Having attained enlightenment through the light of Nature, he moves into the realm of "great knowledge" and "profound virtue."*

FENG, GIA-FU and JANE ENGLISH, trs. **CHUANG TZU: INNER CHAPTERS. 8½"x11", 162pp. RaH74, 7.95c/3.95p.**
A companion volume to the translators' earlier book on Lao Tzu, also including lovely photographs and calligraphy. The format does not seem to work quite as well as in the earlier book since the material translated here is much longer than Lao Tzu's chapters, but it is still a beautiful work which would make a fine gift and is a good introduction to the inspired writings of Chuang Tzu. The seven *Inner Chapters* presented here are accepted by scholars as being definitely the work of Chuang Tzu; another twenty-six chapters are of questionable origin—they are interpretations and developments of his teaching and may have been added by later commentators.

GILES, HERBERT, tr. **CHUANG TZU: TAOIST PHILOSOPHER AND CHINESE MYSTIC. Introduction, notes, index, 335pp. A&U26, 13.75c/8.95c.**
This is a complete edition of Chuang Tzu's writings. Giles was an

excellent scholar, but not the best translator for a writer like Chuang Tzu. His style is too stilted to recreate Chuang Tzu's flowing narrative. The translation combines prose and poetry, but it is mainly prose. The cheaper edition is from Taiwan.

MERTON, THOMAS, ed. **THE WAY OF CHUANG TZU.** 159pp. NDP65/A&U, 4.00c/1.75p.
Working from existing translations, Father Merton has composed a series of personal versions from his favorites among the sayings of Chuang Tzu—a recreation of an ancient sage by a contemporary poet. Includes an introduction on the meaning of Taoism for the West today. Illustrated with early Chinese drawings.

RAJNEESH, BHAGWAN SHREE. **THE EMPTY BOAT.** 12.95c.
See the Contemporary Spiritual Teachers section.

RAJNEESH, BHAGWAN SHREE. **WHEN THE SHOE FITS.** 5.25p.
See the Contemporary Spiritual Teachers section.

WALTHAM, CLAE. **CHUANG TZU: GENIUS OF THE ABSURD.** Pronunciation guide, index, 398pp. G&D71, 1.50p.
An arrangement of Chuang Tzu's writings, based on the Legge translation. Ms. Waltham has edited Legge's often ponderous prose, so this is much more readable than the original.

■ *WATSON, BURTON, tr.* **CHUANG TZU, BASIC WRITINGS.** 140pp. Col64, 3.90p.
An excellent prose translation of the seven *inner chapters* which form the heart of Chuang Tzu's book, three of the *outer chapters*, and one other one. Watson does a wonderful job of recapturing Chuang Tzu's spirit and message. An illuminating, long introduction places Chuang Tzu in relation to Chinese history and thought.

WATSON, BURTON. **THE COMPLETE WORKS OF CHUANG TZU.** 397pp. Col68, 24.75c.
An excellent translation, probably the most scholarly and also most readable available. Watson also provides extensive annotations and an enlightening introduction.

──────────END OF CHUANG TZU SUBSECTION──────────

Confucius

Confucius (551-479 BC) is known as the molder of Chinese civilization. He believed that man *can make the Way (Tao) great*, and not that *the Way can make man great*. To this end he advocated a good government that rules by virtue and moral example rather than by punishment or force. For the family, he particularly stressed filial piety and for society in general, proper conduct or *li* (propriety, rites).

BAHM, ARCHIE. **THE HEART OF CONFUCIUS.** Notes, bibliography, 159pp. SIU69, 2.95p.
An interpretation of the two most basic Confucian classics—**Genuine Living** and **Great Wisdom.** Nearly half of the book consists of Bahm's clear explanations of key Confucian terms. It is an excellent introduction to Confucian thought. Illustrated with Ming Dynasty Confucian prints.

CHING, JULIA. **CONFUCIANISM AND CHRISTIANITY.** Notes, bibliography, index, 270pp. Kod77, 12.50c.
A comparative study, beginning with the historical encounter between Christianity and Confucianism in the seventeenth century. Ms. Ching examines similarities and differences inherent in certain common themes. This is a detailed study which will be most appreciated by scholars and students of comparative religion. The author was born in China and is presently a professor of comparative philosophy at Yale University. Her field is Chinese philosophy and the emphasis in this volume is on Confucianism.

■ *CH'U CHAI and WINBERG CHAI.* **CONFUCIANISM.** Glossary, notes, bibliography, index, 208pp. BES73, 2.95p.
This is an excellent survey of Confucianism, with material on its origins, development, great exponents, and domination of Chinese

thought for over 2,500 years. Introductory material characterizes Confucianism in Chinese history and briefly discusses the Confucian classics. The body of the book consists of nine chapters, in chronological and historical sequence, each devoted to a major exponent or phase of the Confucian school. In addition, each chapter is preceded by a general survey of the background against which the individual developed his version of what Confucius taught. The text also includes biographical studies of the leading exponents and critical commentary on their writings and doctrines.

CREEL, HERRLEE. **CONFUCIUS AND THE CHINESE WAY.** Very extensive notes, bibliography, index, 354pp. H&R49, 4.40p.
A fine portrait of Confucius the teacher, the scholar, and philosopher-reformer. Indispensible for all interested in fully understanding Confucian thought.

FINGARETTE, HERBERT. **CONFUCIUS—THE SECULAR AS SACRED.** 82pp. H&R72, 2.60p.
A scholarly attempt to discern the deepest meanings of Confucian thought and apply it to our own time.

FONTENAY, CHARLES. **THE KAYEN OF FUTZE.** Many illustrations, 8"x10½", 83pp. CSP77, 5.95p.
A retelling of twenty-eight brief teaching stories, attributed to Confucius and emphasizing the different reality which the author feels Confucius was describing.

■ *KAIZUKA, SHIGEKA.* **CONFUCIUS.** Chronological table, index, 192pp. A&U56, 3.80c.
This is a very readable review of Confucius the man, and his life, philosophy, and times. It seems to cover all the material a general reader would want to know about Confucius and Confucian ideas and the scholarship seems to be good. If you just want to read one book on this subject, this is the one we would recommend.

LEGGE, JAMES, tr. **CONFUCIUS: THE CONFUCIAN ANALECTS, THE GREAT LEARNING, AND THE DOCTRINE OF THE MEAN.** 503pp. Dov1893, 4.50p.
This volume contains the entire Chinese text of each book in large characters, and beneath them Legge's full translation. More than 125 pages of introductory material supply excellent background information. The volume also includes a complete dictionary of all the Chinese characters in the book, with definitions, grammatical comments, and place locations. This is the most scholarly translation available, but far from the most readable.

LEGGE, JAMES, tr. **THE FOUR BOOKS.** PBR23, 20.00c.
The definitive translation of the most important Confucian texts. Each page is divided into three parts: in the key section is the original Chinese text in large characters; the middle contains Legge's English translation; and on the bottom are his extensive textual notes. We recommend Legge only to the serious student.

■ *LIN YUTANG, ed.* **THE WISDOM OF CONFUCIUS,** 290pp. RaH38, 4.95c.
This is the best overall collection of Confucius' writings available. The text includes material on education, music, ethics, politics, and social order, as well as his aphorisms and some of Mencius' writing. This edition also has 100 pages of introductory material on the life of Confucius and the character of Confucius and Confucian ideals.

MCNAUGHTON, WILLIAM, ed. **THE CONFUCIAN VISION.** 168pp. UMP74, 2.95p.
The editor has done new translations of the crucial passages from the **Five Classics** and the **Four Books** as well as selections from royal proclamations, folk songs, and literature. The volume is organized to reveal the central ideas of the *Confucian vision.* Dr. McNaughton also provides background material and commentary as well as extensive notes.

OKUMURA, NOBUYOSHI, tr. **A BOOK OF HEAVEN AND THE EARTH.** Foreword, illustrations, notes, 212pp. UTk73, 14.50c.
A collection of stories, each of which is built around a chapter or chapters from the **Analects** and illustrates some facet of Confucian thought. The tales thus take their inspiration, and often their wording, directly from the sayings of Confucius as recorded by his disciples.

POUND, EZRA, tr. **THE CLASSIC ANTHOLOGY DEFINED BY CONFUCIUS. Introduction, 240pp. HUP54/Fab, 2.95p.**
A translation of the 305 odes of the **Classic Anthology.** These poems are among the best known of all Chinese poetry and, while they date from the fifth century BC and before, they retain their freshness. Pound has done a magnificent job with his translation and has managed to recapture the essence of the original poems.

POUND, EZRA, tr. **CONFUCIUS. Introduction, 288pp. NDP47/Owe, 4.45p.**
Pound's noted translations with commentary, of three basic Confucian texts: **The Great Digest (Ta Hsio), The Unwobbling Pivot (Chung Yung),** and **The Analects (Lun-yu).** For the first two the Chinese characters are printed.

SMITH, D. HOWARD. **CONFUCIUS. Notes, bibliography, index, 254pp. Grn74, 3.00p.**
A balanced, enjoyable account which illuminates the man, his teaching, and influence. Setting the stage with a description of the ancient hierarchical tradition into which Confucius was born, Smith relates Confucian thought to what went before. He shows how the doctrines of filial piety, duty to state, propriety, education, tradition, tolerance, and moral persuasion were affected by competing philosophical schools, and explains Confucianism's peaceful coexistence with the rival systems of Buddhism and Taoism. A good introduction for the general reader.

SOOTHILL, W.E., tr. **THE ANALECTS OF CONFUCIUS. 1,033pp. PBR10, 7.50p.**
This volume includes long essays on the ancient history of China and the life and times of Confucius. The Chinese text is presented, along with a translation and extensive commentary. An added feature of this text is the ninety-three page index of characters arranged according to their radicals—with the characters, Romanization, translation, and cross references to the **Analects.** Soothill was President of the Imperial University of China.

WALEY, ARTHUR, tr. **THE ANALECTS OF CONFUCIUS. Many notes, index, 252pp. RaH38, 2.45p.**
Waley is the translator of a vast body of Oriental classics. This is thought of as the best English version of the **Analects.** It is more readable than Legge's, though perhaps not as scholarly. An extensive introduction gives the social and political background of this work, an analysis of key terms, and a careful study of the book and its interpretations.

WALEY, ARTHUR, tr. **THE BOOK OF SONGS. Introduction, notes, index, 358pp. Grv37, 3.95p.**
The Book of Songs is one of the five Confucian classics and is more generally known as **The Confucian Odes.** Confucius and his followers used the songs as texts for moral instruction and as examples of the highest wisdom. The songs deal with a variety of subjects including courtship, marriage, warriors, agriculture, dynasties, and friendship.

WARE, JAMES, tr. **THE SAYINGS OF CONFUCIUS. Introduction, index, 127pp. NAL55, 1.25p.**
Translation of 450 brief conversations and observations of the great sage.

WILHELM, RICHARD, tr. **CONFUCIUS AND CONFUCIANISM. 181pp. HBJ31/RKP, 1.65p.**
A translation of **The Life of Confucius** from a second century BC text, the **Shih-Chi,** or **The Historical Records,** by Sse-Ma Ch'ien. Wilhelm includes commentaries on the text and gives the reader a concise survey of the man and his teachings.

WRIGHT, ARTHUR, ed. **THE CONFUCIAN PERSUASION. Notes, index, 400pp. SUP60, 3.45p.**
*This extensive survey maintains a balanced perspective in its diagnosis of the degree of Confucian inspiration or influence in social, cultural, and political attitudes and developments in the course of Chinese history. . . . By virtue of its content and format this is a welcome addition to any collection of works relating to China.—*Journal of the Royal Central Asian Society *(London).*

WRIGHT, ARTHUR, ed. **CONFUCIANISM AND CHINESE CIVILIZATION. Extensive notes, 381pp. SUP64, 3.95p.**
These essays are meant to illustrate the effects of the Confucian world view and its associated patterns of behavior on the development of Chinese civilization. They also suggest the Confucian tradition's capacity for adaptation, as well as some of its inner variety. This volume is a selection of the best essays from the three books that Wright edited on Confucianism.

——————**END OF CONFUCIUS SUBSECTION**——————

COOPER, J.C. **TAOISM: THE WAY OF THE MYSTIC. Notes, 128pp. Wei72/TPL, 3.50p.**
A philosophical discussion of the mystical elements of Taoism. Cooper was brought up in North China and learned about Taoism and Buddhism there. She writes well and gives the reader a good feeling of the essential elements of Taoism through chapters on the Tao, *te, yin-yang,* the *pa kua,* Chuang Tzu and the sages, *wu-wei,* the great triad, art, and symbolism.

CREEL, HERRLEE. **THE BIRTH OF CHINA. Illustrations, notes, index, 406pp. Ung37, 13.00c.**
A dry survey of the formative period of Chinese civilization, focusing on the two earliest dynasties, Shang and Chou. Virtually every aspect of these dynasties is discussed at length, from political history to religion, literature, and daily life. Despite the age of the text, recent archaeological discoveries have not outdated the information too much.

CREEL, HERRLEE. **WHAT IS TAOISM? AND OTHER STUDIES IN CHINESE CULTURAL HISTORY. Notes, index, 192pp. UCh70, 12.00c.**
A collection of eight papers published between 1954 and 1968. Dr. Creel is one of the most distinguished contemporary Chinese scholars.

DAWSON, RAYMOND, ed. **THE LEGACY OF CHINA. Illustrations, notes, index, 411pp. Oxf64, 4.15p.**
An unusual, very interesting collection of essays covering the following general topics: *Western Concepts of Chinese Civilization; Philosophy and Religous Thought; Literature; The Heritage of Chinese Art; Science and China's Influence on the World* (a seventy-five page essay by Joseph Needham); *The Chinese and the Art of Government;* and *China and the World.*

ELVIN, MARK. **THE PATTERN OF THE CHINESE PAST. Notes, topical index, 346pp. SUP73, 3.95p.**
A comprehensive history of the social and economic development of pre-modern China.

FAWDRY, MARGUERITE. **CHINESE CHILDHOOD: A MISCELLANY OF MYTHOLOGY, FOLKLORE, FACT AND FABLE. Chronology, notes, bibliography, index, 7¾"x10", 192pp. BES77, 10.95c.**
In 1973 Pollock's Toy Museum in London organized a small exhibit of Chinese Childhood. As we set to work to prepare the catalogue, we realized that not only were we indebted to China for the invention of gunpowder, silk, paper, porcelain, the wheelbarrow, the magnetic navigational compass and other technical discoveries listed in the history books, but for many other more delightful things also: for roses and pandas; for tops and diabolos; for spillikins, puppets, puzzles, kites. . . . This picture book is the result of our researches into the world of Chinese childhood. Hundreds of plates, including many in color, enhance the text.

FU, MARILYN and WEN FONG, eds. **THE WILDERNESS COLORS OF TAO-CHI. 10¼"x14", MMA73, 16.00c.**
Tao-chi regarded nature as the source of his creativity. Unlike his contemporaries, the orthodox painters of the late seventeenth and early eighteenth century who viewed nature through the styles of earlier Sung and Yuan masters, Tao-chi experienced nature directly and intuitively. Beginning in his youth, he wandered over the peaks of southern China, seeking their inspiration. In maturity, he was able to transmute his visions of nature into works of both monumental and intimate format. In the wilderness, Tao-chi felt his consciousness merging with the mountains and rivers; while painting flowers, he identified himself with their natural purity and symbolic qualities. —from the introduction. This boxed work contains full page color reproductions of twelve of his paintings, with commentary.

FUNG YU-LAN. **A HISTORY OF CHINESE PHILOSOPHY, VOLUME I: THE PERIOD OF THE PHILOSOPHERS. Chronology, notes, bibliography, index, 490pp. PUP52, 30.25c.**
The original Chinese version of this work was published in 1934 in China. Since its appearance, it has not only been accepted by Chinese scholars as the most important contribution yet made to the study of their country's philosophy, but it remains the most complete work on

the subject that has been written in any language. The work is notable for its logical presentation and stress upon the evolution and interrelationship of the schools of thought. At the same time, its extensive use of direct quotations from the thinkers being discussed makes it something of an anthology as well as a history of Chinese philosophy. Volume I covers the period of the philosophers, from the beginnings to around 100 BC.

FUNG YU-LAN. **A HISTORY OF CHINESE PHILOSOPHY, VOLUME II: THE PERIOD OF CLASSICAL LEARNING. Notes, bibliography, index, 808pp. PUP53, 26.90c.**
Volume II covers the period of classical learning, from the second century BC to the twentieth century AD, and includes a lengthy section on Buddhism.

■ FUNG YU-LAN. **A SHORT HISTORY OF CHINESE PHILOSOPHY. Notes, extensive topic-by-topic bibliography, index, 350pp. McM48, 4.95p.**
A comprehensive adaptation of Dr. Fung's monumental two volume history. Attempts to give a systematic account of Chinese thought as a whole, from its beginnings to the present day. Dr. Fung is a scholar who is extremely well thought of by his countrymen.

FUNG YU-LAN. **THE SPIRIT OF CHINESE PHILOSOPHY. Notes, index, 238pp. RKP47, 6.00p.**
This is a good survey of Chinese philosophy. Many of the individuals discussed are not well known and the presentation is uniformly excellent. The following chapter headings should give you an idea of the contents: *Confucius and Mencius; The Philosophers Yang Chu and Mo Ti; The Dialecticians and Logicians; Lao Tzu and Chuang Tzu; The Yi Scripture Amplifications and the Chung Yung; The Han Scholars; The Mystical School; The Inner Light School (Ch'an Tsung) of Buddhism;* and *The Neo-Confucianist Philosophy.*

GERNET, JACQUES. **DAILY LIFE IN CHINA ON THE EVE OF THE MONGOL INVASION, 1250-1276. Notes, index, 254pp. SUP62, 2.95p.**
Gernet has given us not only a valuable study in society, but also a fascinating picture of a lively and brilliant society on the very eve of its destruction....One can only applaud the skillful way in which scraps of information from dozens of sources...have been pieced together to form a glittering mosaic....Every aspect of life during this period is treated with meticulous exactitude.—**Journal of Southeast Asian History.**

GOODRICH, L. CARRINGTON. **A SHORT HISTORY OF THE CHINESE PEOPLE. Listing of Chinese characters, illustrations, chronology, notes, bibliography, index, 305pp. H&R69, 6.65p.**
This is a well regarded survey of Chinese history and culture from earliest times to the Republic. This volume is basically a straight political history, with little or no discussion of philosophical and religious movements. Goodrich was a professor of Chinese at Columbia University for many years. He writes very well.

GRANET, MARCEL. **THE RELIGION OF THE CHINESE PEOPLE. Notes, bibliography, index, H&R75, 8.00p.**
An important early sociological study in the Durkheimian tradition, originally published in 1922 and only recently translated from the French. It is based on Granet's personal study and observation. The text is divided into sections on peasant religion, feudal religion, the official religion, religious revivals, and religious sentiment in modern China.

■ GROUSSET, RENE. **THE RISE AND SPLENDOUR OF THE CHINESE EMPIRE. Map, notes, index, 312pp. UCa52, 3.85p.**
This is a wonderful history of China. Grousset subtly interweaves cultural, political, and economic strands into a balanced whole that is a joy to read. We never imagined a survey could be so fascinating; we finally have a feeling for all the dynasties and the different rulers. Grousset was a member of the French Academy and, for his day, the most persuasive writer on Far Eastern history and art. We recommend this book highly to all who are interested in Chinese culture.

GUMP, RICHARD. **JADE: STONE OF HEAVEN. Countless illustrations, bibliography, index, 260pp. Dou62, 10.00c.**
Jade has very special qualities. This book details the legendary and romantic mystery with which it is surrounded, including its place in

Chinese religious ritual. Long before the creation of Earth, before rivers ran and men spoke and the valleys echoed with thunder, jade existed, according to one Chinese legend. Another says that when China was invaded by the Tartar barbarians, the Imperial Dragon shed tears of sorrow, and these petrified into jade. **Jade** is a blend of practical information on the handling, carving, and buying of jade along with a collection of legends of the stone's history.

HALL, MANLY P. **THE SAGES OF CHINA. 113pp. PRS57, 3.00p.**
An exploration of some of the most important sages. Many handsome line drawings and woodblock prints illustrate the text.

HALL, MANLY P. **THE WHITE BIRD OF TAO. 8½"x11", 51pp. PRS64, 4.00p.**
A metaphorical treatise that gives the reader a feeling for Taoism.

HAN FEI TZU. **BASIC WRITINGS. Introduction, notes, index, 142pp. Col64, 2.80p.**
Han Fei Tzu was a third century BC philosopher of the Legalistic school who produced the final and most readable exposition of its theories. His handbook for the ruler deals with the problems of preserving and strengthening the state. There are sections on the way of the ruler, standards, the use of power, punishment and favor, and dangers to be avoided. This is an excellent translation by Burton Watson.

HAY, JOHN. **MASTERPIECES OF CHINESE ART. Thirty-one color plates, 9¼"x12¼". NYG74, 8.95c.**
The forty-eight plates in this book illustrate some of the finest achievements of China's artists and craftsmen in the major fields of her artistic tradition, such as metalwork and ceramics, calligraphy and painting, sculpture and carving. The selection ranges from the twelfth century BC to the eighteenth century AD. It is arranged, not by chronology or medium, but according to the inspirations and aspirations that were a recurring concern of Chinese artists.

HITZ, DEMI. **LU PAN, THE CARPENTER'S APPRENTICE. Many line drawings, 6¼"x8¾", PrH78, 5.95c.**
Lu Pan (fifth century BC) was the greatest of all Chinese artisans and possessed all the characteristics the Chinese people held most sacred. He became not only a master craftsman, but an architect, engineer, and inventor. The carpenter's manual which he wrote is still in existence today. This simple story (for young children) of Pan's apprenticeship with his master captures the essence of traditional Chinese values.

HSU, CHO-YUN. **ANCIENT CHINA IN TRANSITION: AN ANALYSIS OF SOCIAL MOBILITY, 722-222 BC. Illustrations, notes, bibliography, index, 248pp. SUP65, 3.95p.**
A lucid and vigorous analysis of ancient China in its most eventful period of transition. Hsu quanitifies data on social mobility, synthesizes textual and archaeological evidence, and uses modern sociological concepts.

HSUN TZU. **HSUN TZU: BASIC WRITINGS. Introduction, many notes, index, 187pp. Col63, 3.95p.**
Hsun Tzu was a fourth century Confucian who differed from Mencius by asserting that the nature of man is originally evil. His philosophical works outline methods of self improvement to counteract this evil. This is an extremely readable and authoritative translation by Burton Watson, one of our favorite translators.

HSUN TZU. **THE WORKS OF HSUNTZE. Index, 336pp. CWP28, 5.60c.**
A topically arranged selection of all the writings definitely attributed to Hsun Tzu as well as some whose authenticity is doubtful. As the translator, Homer Dubs, says, *I have felt that it is more important to make the translation accurate and even literal than to make it literary.*

HUANG, AL and SI CHI KO. **LIVING TAO. 8½"x11", 96pp. CeA76, 5.95p.**
In a beautiful combination of calligraphy, quotations from ancient Chinese texts, and striking photographs, tai ch'i master Al Huang evokes the most subtle principles of Taoism.

HUCKER, CHARLES. **CHINA TO 1850: A SHORT HISTORY. Many maps, index, 171pp. SUP78, 3.95p.**
A simple overview of the evolution of Chinese civilization from

earliest times to 1850. Professor Hucker weaves together chronologically all aspects of Chinese life and culture, broadly surveying general history, socioeconomic organization, political institutions, religion, philosophy, art, and literature.

HUGHES, E.R., tr. **CHINESE PHILOSOPHY IN CLASSICAL TIMES. 385pp. Dut42, 5.00c.**
Selections from the writings and recorded sayings of thirty Chinese philosophers who lived between the seventh century BC and the end of the first century AD. The translations have almost all been done by Hughes himself and he often includes long extracts. Introductory material prefaces most of the selections and there are notes throughout. Hughes was a Reader in Chinese Philosophy and Religion at Oxford and he has a thorough knowledge of his field. Much of the material translated here is not readily found elsewhere. A general introduction is also included.

I Ching

The **I Ching** or **Book of Changes** is an oracular work dating back more than 3,000 years. Its core is a series of sixty-four symbolic figures called hexagrams, each of which is one of the possible combinations of six broken and or unbroken parallel lines. Broken lines stand for *yin*, the dark, feminine, receptive, negative principle, while unbroken lines stand for *yang*, the light, masculine, creative, positive principle. Each hexagram is an aspect of life or a life situation. Each line shows a different aspect of the situation, pictured by the hexagram. Associated with each hexagram are commentaries which expound on its meaning.

Carl Jung considered the **I Ching** to be based on as valid an experimental method of investigation as Western science. He called the principle involved synchronicity, which means the occurrence at the same time of two events which though unconnected by cause and effect, are nonetheless related.

The **I Ching** transcends its divinatory function to become a philosophical guide to Chinese thought, both Confucian and Taoist.

■ BLOFELD, JOHN. **I CHING. 228pp. Dut65/A&U, 2.75p.**
Emphasis is on the divining aspects of the oracle. Traditional commentaries are omitted. Blofeld succeeds in his stated purpose and his rendering is exceptionally clear. The introductory material is perhaps the best anywhere. However, without the commentaries, this version cannot stand alone for the serious student.

CAYCE, EDGAR. **CHANGE—THE I CHING. 70pp. ARE71, 1.75p.**
Apparently Edgar Cayce never commented on the **I Ching**. Some of his followers herein compare pertinent extracts from the Cayce readings with the concepts of the sixty-four hexagrams.

DHIEGH, KHIGH ALX. **THE ELEVENTH WING. 295pp. Del74, 3.25p.**
Despite the author's presumption in entitling this work, this volume fills a long standing need. It goes significantly beyond the scope of a how-to or introductory volume and conveys a real sense of the inner dynamics of the **I Ching** as a universal prototype. Moreover, the final chapter, notes, and the extensive bibliography afford a view of current interest in the **I Ching**. Mechanical devices and many visual aids are used. Highly recommended to those interested in a deep understanding of the **I Ching**.

DOUGLAS, ALFRED. **THE ORACLE OF CHANGE: HOW TO CONSULT THE I CHING. 239pp. Ber71/Pen, 2.95p.**
A simple introductory translation. Nothing weighty is attempted, nonetheless every word is to the point and the message of the **I Ching** comes through. Ample introductory material is included, as well as information on how to consult the oracle.

HOOK, DIANA. **THE I CHING AND MANKIND. Index, 172pp. RKP75, 10.95c.**
This is a deep study of the philosophy of the **I Ching**, pointing out its significance in today's world. Ms. Hook discusses the connections

between the **I Ching** and the Qabala, numerology, astrology, tarot, and world religions. She also deals with the laws governing growth and decay, health and sickness, attraction and repulsion—both magnetic and sexual—and the general pattern of life as set out in the **I Ching**. By means of charts and diagrams, she clearly and simply explains the two fundamental arrangements of the trigrams. The sequences of the hexagrams are also fully dealt with, as are the mutations of one hexagram into another. Many difficult concepts are well presented here.

■ HOOK, DIANA. **THE I CHING AND YOU. 149pp. Dut73/RKP, 4.25p.**
A thorough guide and introduction to the **I Ching**, and a must for any reference shelf. This book is chiefly distinguished by its many and varied diagrams and appendices. Especially useful for interpretation is the extended appendix on the nature and qualities of the eight trigrams as seen under various experience headings.

The dragon-horse of the **I Ching**.

LEE, JUNG YOUNG. **THE I CHING AND MODERN MAN. Notes, index, 8½"x11", 236pp. UnB75, 8.95c.**
A survey of the metaphysical and cosmological implications of the **I Ching** in various areas of contemporary life.

LEE, JUNG YOUNG. **PATTERNS OF INNER PROCESS. 221pp. Stu76, 5.95p.**
The primary purpose of this book is the rediscovery of the deeply spiritual and esoteric meanings of Jesus' teachings in our contemporary setting. This rediscovery is based on the new understanding of Jesus' teachings in the **Gospel** *and the intensive study of the* **I Ching**, *or* **Book of Changes**, *with the help of quantam mechanics, depth psychology and mathematical principles in our time. In this book Jesus and the* **I Ching** *are united and the religions of the world are brought together with new sciences and psychic phenomena.*

LEE, JUNG YOUNG. **THE PRINCIPLE OF CHANGES: UNDERSTANDING THE I CHING. 8½"x11", 302pp. UnB71, 10.00c.**
A workman-like effort to expose the principle of change which underlies the *working* of the **I Ching**. Much emphasis is given to understanding how meaning is derived from the structure of the original written characters of the Chinese language. Pedantic and ponderous at times, the effort is broad in scope and remains worthwhile.

LEGGE, JAMES, tr. **I CHING. 448pp. Ban1899, 4.95p/1.95p.**
The original version of the Legge translation from the **Sacred Books of the East** series. The structure and format of the volume are faithful to the ancient rather than the modern arrangement of material. This translation was aimed at nineteenth century Sinologues and those who desire to read the **I Ching** as pure literature. A serious student can approach this version by way of the study guide appended by Ch'u Chai and Winberg Chai. Not suitable for divination or casual use.

MCCLATCHIE, CANON. **CLASSIC OF CHANGE.** 473pp. CWP1876, 14.50c.
This is a photographic reproduction of the first English translation of the I Ching (1876)—of interest more as an historical document than for its literary merit, though it appears as if Wilhelm drew from the text for his definitive translation. The author was an American missionary in China and his introductory material (as well as aspects of the text) reflects the *white man's burden* approach to intercultural understanding. The Chinese text (in large characters) and the translation are presented on opposite pages, and many traditional commentaries are included, also with parallel texts. Includes a good deal of background material.

MELYAN, GARY and WEN-KUANG CHU, trs. **I-CHING: THE HEXAGRAMS REVEALED. Bibliography, 182pp. Tut77, 7.50c.**
This translation is the least philosophical of any. The orientation is entirely toward the divinatory meaning of the hexagrams. *Our goal is to open up the use of the* I Ching *as an oracle to the nonspecialist, giving him a modern context in which to ask his questions.* It is an adequate translation, but the true meaning of the I Ching is lost in this kind of presentation.

MILLER, TERRY. **IMAGES OF CHANGE: PAINTINGS ON THE I CHING.** 8½"x11", 135pp. Dut76, 9.95p.
This beautiful book of color paintings is designed to serve as an inspirational companion to the study of the I Ching. Terry Miller has created a graphic picture for each of the sixty-four hexagrams, based on the Wilhelm/Baynes translation. The editor, Hale Thatcher, has selected key phrases and fragments from this translation so as to outline some of the basic themes in each of the hexagrams and to relate them to the appropriate paintings. Comments on the illustrations appear at the bottom of each page.

REIFLER, SAM. **I CHING.** Introduction, 285pp. Ban74, 1.95p.
A modernized transcreation which loses virtually all the I Ching's symbolic meaning. For divination only.

RICHMOND, NIGEL. **THE LANGUAGE OF THE LINES: THE I CHING ORACLE.** 178pp. Wdw77, 8.15p.
Rather than a translation of the I Ching, this is an oracular interpretation of the *langauge of the lines* of each hexagram. Each line is interpreted and analyzed individually and the author also discusses the hexagram in terms of the following factors: pattern, nature, form. It is a bit of a strange work and is too modernized for us. Yet it should be of interest to those who are looking for contemporary ways to apply the ancient wisdom embodied in the I Ching in their daily lives. An ample amount of introductory and explanatory material is included.

SCHOENHOLTZ, LARRY. **NEW DIRECTIONS IN THE I CHING.** Illustrations, index, 157pp. UnB75, 7.95c.
An exploration of geometry, mathematics, and metaphysical meanings in the I Ching. This is not a translation; rather, it is an informal exploration of themes and patterns. Some interesting ideas are presented, although this is by no means a deep study.

SHERRILL, W.A., ed. **THE ASTROLOGY OF THE I CHING.** Index, 443pp. Wei76/RKP, 15.00c.
This is an interesting, controversial work, edited from Dr. W.K. Chu's translation, demonstrating how the sixty-four hexagrams represent the sum total of forces acting on the Earth at any moment of time. The hexagrams are derived from the base time when the Earth and all other planets of our solar system were in a straight line. Individuals also have a hexagram which changes according to cosmic laws. This book contains a series of predictions based on this theory. We do not quite understand what it is all about or how valid it might be. Some deep study is involved before you can use the book.

SHERRILL, W.A. and W.K. CHU. **AN ANTHOLOGY OF I CHING.** Index, 257pp. RKP77, 17.95c.
A collection of fourteen essays focusing on ways the I Ching can be and has traditionally been used for divinatory and predictive purposes. The authors have studied and worked with the I Ching for many years.

SHIMANO, JIMMES. **ORIENTAL FORTUNE TELLING.** 170pp. Tut56, 3.95p.
A parlor game approach to the Book of Changes. Translated from the Japanese to English.

SIU, R.G.H., tr. **THE PORTABLE DRAGON: THE WESTERN MAN'S GUIDE TO THE I CHING.** 463pp. MIT68, 6.95p.
A brilliant new translation aimed specifically at the modern Westerner. Illustrative literature is substituted for the traditional commentaries and provides excellent reading in its own right. Useful for a meditative approach to the I Ching. Although not a definitive rendering, the quality of this effort is very high.

SUNG, Z.D. **THE SYMBOLS OF YI-KING.** CWP34, 5.90c.
An attempt by the author to demonstrate logically how the I Ching works. Heavy going.

SUNG, Z.D., ed. **THE TEXT OF THE YI-KING.** Introduction, 395pp. CWP35, 7.25c.
The original Chinese text of each line, with the Legge translation and extensive commentary. The characters in the original text have a direct bearing on the symbolism of the lines, so this edition should be helpful to those familiar with Chinese. The appendices are also included.

VAN OVER, RAYMOND, ed. **I CHING.** Notes, 444pp. NAL71/NEL, 1.95p.
An excellent backup volume to the Wilhelm/Baynes version. Van Over lifts the scholarly Legge translation from its difficult format and renders it accessible to the ordinary reader. In addition, the running commentary, entitled *Legge's Notes*, is based essentially on sources not covered in the Wilhelm/Baynes version and adds significantly to the total expository material available. The only way to go with Legge.

WILHELM, HELLMUT. **CHANGE—EIGHT LECTURES ON THE I CHING.** 111pp. PUP60/RKP, 2.95p.
I Ching basics by the son of the master translator. He reveals something of the spirit of the book and affords a perspective for learning to interpret the oracle. Required reading for all who desire a deep understanding of the I Ching.

WILHELM, HELLMUT. **HEAVEN, EARTH, AND MAN IN THE BOOK OF CHANGES.** Notes, index, 241pp. UWa77, 12.95c.
Hellmut Wilhelm is the son of Richard Wilhelm. Like his father he is regarded as a preeminent authority on the I Ching. This book is made up of transcriptions of a series of lectures originally delivered between 1951 and 1967 at the Eranos conferences of scholars in Switzerland. Six of the seven papers appear in English for the first time in this volume. The following lecture titles give a good idea of the subject matter covered: *The Concept of Time, The Creative Principle, Human Events and Their Meaning, The "Own City" as the Stage of Formation, The Interaction of Heaven, Earth, and Man, Wanderings of the Spirit,* and *The Interplay of Image and Concept.*

■ WILHELM, RICHARD and CARY BAYNES, trs. **I CHING—BOOK OF CHANGES.** 802pp. PUP61, 10.50c.
A truly inspired translation. Wilhelm surely tapped the same levels of inspiration as did the original authors. This is the principal, definitive English language version and the most complete in its running commentaries. Extensive introduction by Carl Jung. Without equal.

──────────END OF THE I CHING SUBSECTION──────────

JENYNS, SOAME. **A BACKGROUND TO CHINESE PAINTING.** Illustrations, bibliography, index, 231pp. ScB66, 3.95p.
A brief, highly readable account of the religious and social setting within which Chinese painting must be studied. The major sections cover *The Influence of Religion, The Relation to Calligraphy, The Patronage of the Throne, The Choice of Materials and Technique, The Treatment of Landscape and the Human Figure,* and *The Use of Bird, Flower, and Animal Motives.* Jenyns is a member of the Department of Oriental Antiquities at the British Museum.

KALTENMARK, MARK. **LAO TZU AND TAOISM.** Bibliography, index, 158pp. SUP69, 1.95p.
A well written, comprehensive account for the general reader. Includes biographical information and philosophical analyses of Lao

Tzu, Chuang Tzu, and other major Taoist masters, as well as a clear presentation of the Taoist religion.

KESWICK, MAGGIE. **THE CHINESE GARDEN. 250 illustrations, forty in color, 9"x12", 200pp. Riz78, 29.50c.**
In the East, Chinese gardens are a lost art form; in the West, they are likely to call up the image of a Japanese garden with its exquisite arrangements of stone and moss, manicured pines and dry streams. Chinese gardens are really quite different. Luxuriant, intricate, an apparent haphazard of hills, trees, water, and rock piles, these gardens are, for many foreigners, incomprehensible. But to an attentive eye they reveal a profound and ancient view of the world and of man's place in it. Many gardens have survived in China and they are once again open to the public. Ms. Keswick was the daughter of the chairman of the Sino-British Trade Council and she visited China often. This insightful book is illustrated with her own photographs.

Lao Tzu

No one can hope to understand Chinese philosophy, religion, government, art, medicine...without a real appreciation of the profound philosophy taught in this little book. [Tao] is the One which is natural, eternal, spontaneous, nameless and indescribable. It is at once the beginning of all things and the way in which all things pursue their course. When this Tao is possessed by individual things, it becomes its character or virtue. The ideal life for the individual, the ideal order for society, and the ideal type of government are all based on it and guided by it. As a way of life, it denotes simplicity, spontaneity, tranquility, weakness, and most important of all, non-action ("wu-wei"). By the latter is not meant literally "inactivity" but rather "taking no action that is contrary to Nature"—in another words, letting Nature take its own course.—Witter Bynner.

This philosophy is embodied in a classic of about 5,250 words called the **Tao-te ching (Classic of Way and Its Virtue).** It is a combination of poetry, philosophical speculation, and mystical reflection. Lao Tzu tells of the deep harmony of life and how we may attune our beings with it, and of the way of life one in tune with the Tao would have: *Always calm, always clear, he opens the dreamworld to eyes newborn.* More commentaries have been written on it than on any other Chinese classic. After 2,000 years and hundreds of translations, Lao Tzu remains our friendly companion.

Lao Tzu

BAHM, ARCHIE, tr. **TAO TEH KING—INTERPRETED AS NATURE AND INTELLIGENCE. Extensive bibliography, 126pp. Ung nd, 2.45p.**
That which is most yielding eventually overcomes what is most resistant. That which is not becomes that which is. Acting without coercing or being coerced is best. Guiding by example rather than by words or commands is most successful. Such simple truths are hard to understand. Bahm provides a long, interpretative section in which he discusses key ideas and arranges quotations which summarize Lao Tzu's theories on various topics.

BLAKNEY, R.B., tr. **THE WAY OF LIFE: LAO TZU. 134pp. NAL55/ NEL, 1.50p.**
The softest of stuff in the world penetrates quickly the hardest; insubstantial, it enters where no room is. By this I know the benefit of something done by quiet being; in all the world but few can know accomplishment apart from work, instruction when no words are used. Each chapter is paraphrased directly underneath the translation. Includes a long introduction which places the text in historical perspective and discusses key concepts.

■ *BYNNER, WITTER, tr.* **THE WAY OF LIFE ACCORDING TO LAO TZU. 76pp. Put44, 1.50p.**
As the soft yield of water cleaves obstinate stone, so to yield with life solves the insoluble: To yield, I have learned, is to come back again. But this unworded lesson, this easy example, is lost upon me. Our all time favorite translation—a perfect rendering of a perfect work. Many beautiful illustrations and a fine introduction are included.

CHANG CHUNG-YUAN. **TAO: A NEW WAY OF THINKING. Introduction, notes, bibliography, 253pp. H&R75, 3.95p/2.50p.**
The meekest in the world penetrates the strongest in the world. As nothingness enters into that-which-has-no-opening. Hence, I am aware of the value of non-action and of the value of teaching with no words. As for the value of non-action, Nothing in the world can match it. The translation of each chapter is accompanied by a lengthy commentary on the application of the thoughts to contemporary life. Chang draws many parallels between the **Tao Te Ching** and the philosophy of Martin Heidegger.

CH'U TA-KAO, tr. **TAO TE CHING. Many notes, 96pp. Wei37/A&U, 2.00p.**
The non-existent can enter into the impenetrable. By this I know that non-action is useful. Teaching without words, utility without action.—Few in the world have come to this. This translation was originally issued by the London Buddhist Society and was made from a hitherto unused edition of the text. A terse, beautiful rendition—one of our favorites.

■ *FENG, GIA-FU and JANE ENGLISH, trs.* **LAO TSU: TAO TE CHING. 176pp. RaH72/Wdw, 10.00c/4.95p.**
The **Tao Te Ching** has been translated more frequently than any work except the **Bible.** This fresh translation of the ancient Chinese classic offers the essence of each word and makes Lao Tzu's teaching immediate and alive. The philosophy is simple: Accept what is in front of you without wanting the situation to be other than it is. Study the natural order of things and work with it rather than against it, for trying to change what is only sets up resistance. If we watch carefully, we will see that work proceeds more quickly and easily if we stop *trying,* if we stop putting in so much extra effort, if we stop looking for results. In the clarity of a still and open mind, truth will be reflected. In other words, simply be. This is an 8½"x11" album, illustrated with delicate full page nature photographs and the Chinese calligraphy of the text. It is one of the most beautiful works we have seen.

GILES, LIONEL, tr. **THE SAYINGS OF LAO TZU. Introduction, 60pp. Mur05, 3.50c.**
The softest things in the world override the hardest. That which has no substance enters where there is no crevice. Hence, I know the advantage of inaction. Conveying lessons without words, reaping profit without action—there are few in the world who can attain to this. The translation is divided into topical chapters, each incorporating a few of the original ones. Part of the **Wisdom of the East** series.

LAU, D.C., tr. **TAO TE CHING. 192pp. Vik63, 1.95p.**
Do that which consists in taking no action; pursue that which is not meddlesome; savour that which has no flavour. Make the small big and the few many; do good to him who has done you an injury. Lay plans for the accomplishment of the difficult before it becomes difficult; make something big by starting with it when small. This volume has almost 100 pages of supplementary material, including a

glossary, an analysis of the text, and a discussion of the nature of the work.

MACKINTOSH, CHARLES, tr. **TAO. 79pp. TPH26, 1.25p.**
The weakest thing in all the world is water; yet its play, between the rocky ledges whirled, grinds the hard rock away. Poetic translation by a Theosophist.

MEDHURST, C.S., tr. **THE TAO-TEH-KING. 166pp. TPH05, 2.25p.**
The world's weakest drives the world's strongest. The indiscernible penetrates where there are no crevices. From this I perceive the advantages of non-action. Few indeed in the world realize the instructions of the silence, or the benefits of inaction. Extensive comments and notes follow each chapter and there is a good deal of introductory material. The translator was a missionary to China.

RAJNEESH, BHAGWAN SHREE. TAO: THE THREE TREASURES. 12.95c/each.
See the Contemporary Spiritual Teachers section.

SHRINE OF WISDOM EDITORS. THE SIMPLE WAY OF LAO TSE—AN ANALYSIS OF THE TAO TEH CANON. 55pp. ShW24, 5.60c.
A flowing, clear rendition in which the stanzas are regrouped according to subject matter, and short commentaries are appended. The Shrine of Wisdom is a group which publishes the classics of East and West in an effort to show the universal teaching underlying all religions.

SUZUKI, D.T. and PAUL CARUS, trs. **THE CANON OF REASON AND VIRTUE. Introduction, index, 209pp. OpC13, 1.95p.**
The world's weakest overcomes the world's hardest. Non-existence enters into the impenetrable. Thereby I comprehend of non-assertion the advantage. There are few in the world who obtain of non-assertion the advantage and of silence the lesson. This edition has several unique features: the complete Chinese text; full commentary; a biography of Lao Tzu by Sze-Ma-Ch'ien, the Chinese Herodotus; and a table of references.

SUZUKI, D.T. and PAUL CARUS, trs. **LAO TZE—TREATISE ON RESPONSE AND RETRIBUTION. 139pp. OpC06, 2.95p.**
A generally unknown work, sometimes attributed to Lao Tzu. The main thrust of the work can be seen in the title which translates to mean that *in the spiritual realm of heaven there is a response to our sentiments, finding expression in a retribution of our deeds.* This text contains a long introduction, the Chinese text with parallel verbatim translations of each character, a rendition in English, and explanatory notes. Several Taoist folktales are also translated.

■ **WALEY, ARTHUR,** tr. **THE WAY AND ITS POWER: A STUDY OF THE TAO TE CHING AND ITS PLACE IN CHINESE THOUGHT. 257pp. Grv58/A&U, 4.95p.**
What is of all things most yielding can overwhelm that which is of all things most hard. Being substanceless it can enter even where there is no space. That is how I know the value of action that is actionless. But that there can be teaching without words, value in action that is actionless, few indeed can understand. An excellent, long introduction gives a sketch of Chinese prehistory, early philosophy, and literature. Much commentary. Considered the definitive translation by scholars.

WU, JOHN C.H. and PAUL SIH, trs. **LAO TZU—TAO TE CHING. 115pp. SJU61, 3.00p.**
The softest of all things overrides the hardest of all things. Only nothing can enter into no-space. Hence, I know the advantages of non-Ado. Few things under heaven are as instructive as the lessons of silence, or as beneficial as the fruits of non-Ado. The text in Chinese characters is on the left hand side of the page and the translation is on the right.

───────── END OF LAO TZU SUBSECTION ─────────

LATOURETTE, KENNETH. THE CHINESE, THEIR HISTORY AND CULTURE. Indices, 726pp. McM64, 16.80c.
This is generally accepted as the best single introduction to Chinese history and civilization. Because of the way geography and natural resources have determined the Chinese outlook since early times, Professor Latourette begins with a detailed description of the physical setting from which the civilization emerged. More than half the book is devoted to a readable survey of Chinese history from prehistoric times to the modern day. Postrevolutionary history is only briefly touched on; the bulk of the narrative is devoted to the dynasties. The

concluding portion of the book discusses, in separate chapters, the leading features of the culture—religion, art, language, literature, government, and economic and social life. Impressive chapter-by-chapter bibliographies are an important feature of the book.

LAUFER, BERTHOLD. JADE: A STUDY IN CHINESE ARCHAEOLOGY AND RELIGION. Bibliography, index, 284pp. Dov12, 5.00p.
Jade played a significant role in the cultural life of ancient civilizations. This book is a history of jade through 3,000 years of Chinese cultural development. Focusing upon the impact of dynastic change in relation to religious, artistic, and social thought, Laufer details the significance of jade objects characteristic of many periods. The text quotes extensively from original Chinese sources and includes a wealth of folklore. Illustrated with 204 photographs and drawings as well as sixty-eight plates.

LEE, SHERMAN E. CHINESE LANDSCAPE PAINTING. 4.95p.
See the Sacred Art section.

LEGEZA, LASZLO. TAO MAGIC. 8½"x11", 126pp. RaH75, 4.95p.
A collection of full page plates illustrating Chinese calligraphy and Taoist magic diagrams, talismans, and charms. In his commentary Legeza explores the Taoist belief in the spiritual powers of calligraphy and the beautiful secret scripts which were designed to protect the mystery of the Tao.

LEGGE, JAMES, tr. **LI CHI: BOOK OF RITES. Boxed, notes, indices, 1,047pp. UnB67, 25.00c/set.**
Li Chi is one of the Five Classics, the Confucian texts which have been the cultural foundations of Chinese civilization for over 2,000 years. *Chi* means miscellany or encyclopedia and *li* means ceremonial, ceremonies, etiquette, good manners, personal dignity, decency, moral conduct, and much else depending upon the circumstances in which the word is used. **Li Chi** gives detailed instructions on how to act on ceremonial occasions and how to conduct the ceremonies. This tranlsation is the definitive one and Ch'u Chai and Winberg Chai—both distinguished Chinese scholars and the editors of this two volume set—have added extensive introductory material.

LEGGE, JAMES, tr. **THE TEXTS OF TAOISM, PART I. Many notes, index, 395pp. Dov1891, 4.00p.**
Translations of the entire **Tao Te Ching** and selections from Chuang Tzu as well as a long introduction discussing the differences among Taoism, Confucianism, and Buddhism; the authorship of the **Tao Te Ching**; and the meaning of Tao in Chinese thought. Legge is far from our favorite translator. Part of the **Sacred Books of the East** series.

LEGGE, JAMES, tr. **THE TEXTS OF TAOISM, PART II. Index for both parts, 340pp. Dov1891, 4.00p.**
Translations of the **Thai-Shang Tractate of Actions and their Retributions,** selections from Chuang Tzu, and several shorter works—many of which can be found in English only in this collection.

LI CHI. THE BEGINNINGS OF CHINESE CIVILIZATION. Fifty plates, bibliography, index, 130pp. UWa57, 2.95p.
The archaeological site of Anyang is the largest and most important in China. Dr. Li Chi was the director of excavations there. This volume is a transcription of three lectures which describe the findings of his thirty year effort.

LIN YUTANG. IMPERIAL PEKING. Notes, bibliography, index, 8"x11", 227pp. Ele61, 19.95c.
In Peking, the ancient capital of China, Confucian, Buddhist, and Taoist temples intermingle with imperial palaces, pagodas, and pavilions. This book surveys Peking's history, art, and architecture in a coherent fashion. 119 plates, including many color prints, as well as an abundance of line drawings, accompany the text. As with all of Lin's writings, the text is flowing and quite readable.

LIN YUTANG. THE IMPORTANCE OF LIVING. Chinese vocabulary, index, 475pp. Put37, 3.95p.
This is perhaps Lin's best known work. In it he distills Chinese attitudes on a variety of subjects, their way of life, and their philosophy. The passages discuss conversation, travel, enjoying food, reading, appreciating nature, the creative impulse, the importance of all our daily habits, and much else. Dr. Lin spent much of his life in China.

LISTER, R.P. **MARCO POLO'S TRAVELS IN XANADU WITH KUBLAI KHAN.** 201pp. Cre76, 16.95c.
Marco Polo was twenty-five when he arrived at Xanadu, Kublai Khan's summer palace. From this meeting a relationship grew which lasted seventeen years. Marco Polo was insatiably curious and never missed an opportunity to explore Kublai Khan's empire. His account of what he saw was disbelieved by his fellow Italians after his return, but subsequent scholarship and comparison with Chinese sources have revealed him to be a remarkably accurate observer. This edition is beautifully illustrated with many line drawings and plates, including some in color.

LORENTZ, H.A. **A VIEW OF CHINESE RUGS FROM THE SEVEN-TEENTH TO THE TWENTIETH CENTURY. Notes, bibliography, 9"x11", 216pp. RKP72, 54.95c.**
A definitive work, sketching the geographical, historical, and artistic background of Chinese rugs. Lorentz demonstrates (through ninety-five color and sixty monochrome plates) the symbolic colors of Chinese rugs, the materials and techniques used in their manufacture, their development, and the ways in which they differ from all other Oriental rugs. East Turkestan rugs are illustrated and examined for comparison.

LU K'UAN YU (CHARLES LUK). **THE SECRETS OF CHINESE MEDI-TATION.** 3.95p.
See the Meditation section.

LU K'UAN YU (CHARLES LUK), tr. **TAOIST YOGA, ALCHEMY AND IMMORTALITY. Diagrams, glossary, 199pp. Wei70/HPG, 3.95p.**
An excellent translation of a comprehensive course of Taoist yoga, put together from the writings of ancient patriarchs and sages. Very detailed instructions are included. Luk provides a lengthy introduction.

LU YU. **THE CLASSIC OF TEA. Illustrations, 117pp. LBC74, 8.50c.**
Lu Yu lived in the eighth century in China. He is so deferred to throughout Chinese history in the matter of tea that sacrifices have been made to him as the *god of tea.* In this, his major work, he teaches the reader how to manufacture tea, to lay out the *equipage,* and to brew it properly. This edition by Francis Carpenter is the first full translation.

MACFARQUHAR, RODERICK. **THE FORBIDDEN CITY: CHINA'S ANCIENT CAPITAL. Bibliography, index, 9"x11½", 172pp. Nsw72, 12.95c.**
A history of Peking which reproduces through 150 illustrations, one-third in color, the art and architecture of the splendid imperial city. Many photographs and maps also illuminate the volume and the text discusses the history of the forbidden city from its founding in the eighth century to the present day. One section presents literary descriptions of the city. A beautifully produced book.

Mencius

MACGOWAN, J. **HISTORY OF CHINA. Index, 661pp. Cur06, 18.90c.**
The Imperial History of China is neither more nor less than the History of China, as it has been written during successive ages, by the authorized historians of the Empire. This work, together with the writings of Confucius and Mencius, are the only truly authentic sources from which the story of this long-lived nation can be obtained.... Ever since the Han dynasty (206 BC-AD 25) historians have been appointed by royal edicts to write the history of their times, and no one but themselves has ever been allowed to look upon what they have written....As each document was written it was deposited in an iron-bound chest, which remained locked up till that dynasty had ceased to rule.—from the preface. This history is solely based on these sources and begins with the mythic period.

MCNAUGHTON, WILLIAM, ed. **THE TAOIST VISION. 90pp. UMP71, 1.95p.**
Translations which illuminate Taoist concepts. Included are the most relevant passages from the **Tao Te Ching** and Chuang Tzu and a selection of Chinese, Japanese, and Western philosophy.

MCNEILL, WILLIAM and JEAN SEDLAR, eds. **CLASSICAL CHINA. 288pp. Oxf70, 4.15p.**
An anthology of texts, with introductory material, on ethics, politics, history, Confucianism, Taoism, Buddhism, and poetry. Selections from all the major works are included and there is an introduction to each along with a general preface.

Mencius

Mencius (372-289 BC) is second only to Confucius in reputation as a moralist and philosopher. The record of his teachings and conversations with princes who sought his counsel, or disciples who gathered around him for instruction, forms the fourth of the Confucian **Four Books**. He drew out the implications of Confucius' moral principles, and reinterpreted them for the harsh conditions of the time in which he lived, when Confucian doctrine was threatened by the doctrines of Legalism. His stress is on the individual conscience.

DOBSON, W.A.C.H., tr. **MENCIUS. Introduction, 233pp. UTo63, 6.40p.**
A topical arrangement of Mencius, annotated and written in modern prose. The text has been translated in its entirety. *A new translation of this great classic has long been wanted and Mr. Dobson was especially qualified to make it....[He] has produced an excellent rendering.*—**Journal of Asian Studies.**

LAU, D.C., tr. **MENCIUS. Glossary, 280pp. Vik70, 2.95p.**
A very readable translation (and our favorite), accompanied by 122 pages of historical, analytical, and introductory material.

LEGGE, JAMES, tr. **THE WORKS OF MENCIUS. 587pp. Dov1895, 6.00p.**
This translation is in three parts: large Chinese characters at the top of the page, English translation in the middle, and explanatory notes at the bottom. Includes a long index of Chinese characters and phrases as well as a wealth of introductory material, including historical background and quotations from Confucian and anti-Confucian texts.

RICHARDS, I.A. **MENCIUS ON THE MIND. 190pp. RKP64, 9.70c.**
This is a very scholarly study which reviews Mencius' psychological thought and discusses the problems of translating his ideas (and Chinese, non-Western ideas in general) into terms comprehensible by and useful to the Western rational thinker. An appendix presents psychological passages from Mencius, with characters followed by Romanization and an English translation.

——————END OF MENCIUS SUBSECTION——————

MO TZU. **BASIC WRITINGS. Introduction, index, 146pp. Col63, 3.65p.**
Mo Tzu (fifth century BC) was an important political and social thinker and, at least until the third century BC, a formidable rival of the Confucianists. He advocated universal love, honoring and making use of worthy men in government, and identifying with one's superior as a means of establishing uniform moral standards. This is a translation by Burton Watson.

MOORE, CHARLES, ed. **THE CHINESE MIND. Notes, index, 377pp. UHa67, 4.95p.**
An anthology of articles on the essentials of Chinese philosophy and culture written by noted modern scholars. Appears to have been produced for the college trade.

MORGAN, EVAN, tr. **TAO: THE GREAT LUMINANT. Commentary, notes, 399pp. CWP33, 5.90c.**
This is a collection of translations of essays by Huai Nan Tzu, a noted Taoist commentator who wrote extensively on Lao Tzu's **Tao Te Ching**. This is the only edition of his work that we know of in English.

MOTE, FREDERICK. **INTELLECTUAL FOUNDATIONS OF CHINA. Chronology, bibliography, index, 153pp. RaH71, 5.30p.**
An academic study of intellectual history in pre-imperial China, stressing the main outlines of intellectual life and analyzing the central figures and schools of thought.

MUNGELLO, DAVID. **LEIBNIZ AND CONFUCIANISM: THE SEARCH FOR ACCORD. Glossary, notes, bibliography, index, 212pp. UHa77, 13.45c.**
In the closing years of the seventeenth century, one of the most brilliant modern European philosophers became actively involved in the search for intellectual and spiritual accord between Europe and China. Leibniz entered the *Rites Controversy* on the side of the Jesuits, who had achieved positions of remarkable proximity to the Chinese throne. Yet less than forty years later the Papacy ruled against the Jesuits at Rome, and in China there was a growing distrust of the Christian missionaries by the monarchy. Professor Mungello discusses Leibniz' interpretation of Chinese (largely Neoconfucian) philosophic notions and concepts and quotes extensively from his writings.

MUNRO, DONALD. **THE CONCEPT OF MAN IN EARLY CHINA. Notes, bibliography, index, 268pp. SUP69, 2.95p.**
This is a stimulating examination of the Confucian and Taoist conceptions of human nature. Munro is a trained philosopher as well as a specialist in Chinese studies; he frequently compares Chinese ideas with Western classical philosophy, especially Plato.

NAESS, ARNE and ALASTAIR HANNAY, eds. **INVITATION TO CHINESE PHILOSOPHY. Notes, 182pp. SUB72, 14.55p.**
A fine collection of essays by some of Europe's best scholars. The selections cover many aspects of Chinese thought, including Confucianism, Taoism, Neoconfucianism, and Ch'an Buddhism. The authors quote extensively from primary texts. Despite the title, this is a work geared toward those already interested in Chinese philosophy who wish to deepen their understanding.

NEEDHAM, JOSEPH. **THE GRAND TITRATION: SCIENCE AND SOCIETY IN EAST AND WEST. Notes, bibliography, index, 350pp. A&U69, 20.15c.**
Needham has been studying the history of Chinese science for more than thirty years. Between the first and fifteenth centuries the Chinese, who experienced no Dark Ages, were generally far in advance of Europe. Throughout those centuries and ever since, the West has been profoundly affected not only in its technical processes but in its very social structures by discoveries and inventions emanating from China and East Asia. In a series of essays, reprinted here with over fifty illustrations, Dr. Needham explores China's early lead and Europe's later overtaking.

NEEDHAM, JOSEPH. **SCIENCE AND CIVILIZATION IN CHINA, VOLUME II: HISTORY OF SCIENTIFIC THOUGHT. Notes, bibliography, index, 7¼"x9¾", 696pp. CUP74, 47.50c.**
An extremely original and thought provoking—though sometimes controversial—analysis.

NEEDHAM, JOSEPH. **SCIENCE AND CIVILIZATION IN CHINA: VOLUME V, PART TWO, CHEMISTRY AND CHEMICAL TECHNOLOGY. Plates, notes, almost 200 pages of bibliography, index, 7¼"x9¾", 542pp. CUP75, 35.00c.**
From a mass of hitherto obscure and puzzling source materials, Dr. Needham provides an overview of the rise of the ancient Chinese alchemical tradition. He traces three roots: the pharmaceutical-botanical search for macrobiotic plants; the metallurgical-chemical practices for making artificial gold; and the medical-minerological use of inorganic substances in therapy. He and his collaborators try to reconstruct exactly what the old Chinese alchemists were doing in their laboratories, what they thought they were doing, and what general theories they developed about the physico-chemical world. This is the most detailed, scholarly account we know and is an indispensible reference work for scholars.

NEEDHAM, JOSEPH. **SCIENCE AND CIVILIZATION IN CHINA: VOLUME V, PART THREE. 118 pages of bibliography and indices, 7¼"x9¾", 516pp. CUP76, 42.00c.**
This is the latest volume of Dr. Needham's immense study. This part traces the history of alchemy and early chemistry in China from its origins in the fifth century BC until the time of its fusion with world chemical knowledge. The presentation is highly technical and accompanied by a profusion of notes and many quotations from primary and secondary sources. Some beautiful illustrations accompany the text.

NEEDHAM, JOSEPH. **WITHIN THE FOUR SEAS: THE DIALOGUE OF EAST AND WEST. Chronology, notes, index, 229pp. A&U69, 10.00c.**
Dr. Needham is one of the world's leading experts on the Chinese culture and state, especially the history of science and technology in China. He lived there for four years during World War II and has returned several times since the Revolution. This is a collection of addresses and lectures written over a twenty-five year period, and of poems he wrote in China on Chinese themes.

POLO, MARCO. **THE TRAVELS. Long introduction, maps, notes, index, 380pp. Vik58, 2.95p.**
This is a good translation by R.E. Latham of Marco Polo's account of his travels from the Polar Sea to Java and from Zanzibar to Japan.

■ RAWSON, PHILIP and LASZLO LEGEZA. **TAO: THE EASTERN PHILOSOPHY OF TIME AND CHANGE. 8"x11", 128pp. T&H73, 5.30p.**
This is a beautiful pictorial survey of the major elements of Taoism, with 196 illustrations, thirty-three in color. The plates are all fully commented upon and arranged topically. An excellent general introduction summarizes the main tenets and cultural aspects of Taoism. This is an inspiring book which gives the reader a good feeling for all aspects of Taoism.

RONAN, COLIN A. **THE SHORTER SCIENCE AND CIVILIZATION IN CHINA: VOLUME I. Many illustrations, bibliography, index, 336pp. CUP78, 19.95c.**
An abridgment of Joseph Needham's monumental series. The present book covers the material treated in Volumes I and II of Dr. Needham's original work. The reader is introduced to the country of China, its history, geography, and langauge. The major part of the book is devoted to the history of scientific thought in China. Ronan also includes an extensive description of the milieu in which arose the schools of the Confucians, Taoists, Mohists, Logicians, and Legalists. He carries Chinese scientific thinking up to the Chinese Middle Ages and the impact of the sceptical tradition and Buddhist and Neoconfucian thought.

ROREX, ROBERT and WEN FONG, eds. **EIGHTEEN SONGS OF A NOMAD FLUTE: THE STORY OF LADY WEN-CHI. Boxed, 11"x 10". MMA74.**
An exquisite reproduction of a fourteenth century handscroll from the collection of the Metropolitan Museum of Art. Related poems and commentary are included. More than half of the panels are printed in color, the rest are in a brown duotone.

ROWLEY, GEORGE. **PRINCIPLES OF CHINESE PAINTING. Forty-seven plates, index, 8½"x11", 132pp. PUP59, 4.95p.**
A series of essays written around the themes of subject matter and its interpretation and style. To explain what makes a painting Chinese, Professor Rowley penetrates into the Chinese way of looking at life, and he has produced a profound, illuminating document. This is a fine book which should be invaluable to students who seek to deepen their understanding of the principles of Chinese art. An excellent feature of the text is the author's examination of a number of individual works.

SASO, MICHAEL. **TAOISM AND THE RITE OF COSMIC RENEWAL. Many illustrations, notes, bibliography, 120pp. WSU72, 5.40p.**
An in depth discussion of the annual cycle of events in the religious and

social life of a Chinese town or city. A large part of the book is devoted to an analysis and description of the annual *Chiao* festival.

SASO, MICHAEL. **THE TEACHINGS OF TAOIST MASTER CHUANG.** Introduction, illustrations, notes, bibliography, indices, 330pp. YUP78, 17.50c.
Until his death in 1976, Master Chuang, a descendant of thirty-five generations of Taoist priests, taught and practiced in Taiwan. In this book Saso recounts the history of religious Taoism, as Chuang understood it, and describes the role that Chuang, as a Taoist priest, played in the social patterns of a modern Chinese town. He also faithfully records Master Chuang's rituals of black magic, meditation, and exorcistic thunder magic.

SASO, MICHAEL and DAVID CHAPPELL, eds. **BUDDHIST AND TAOIST STUDIES,** I. Illustrations, index, 174pp. UHa77, 12.75p.
The present work, comprising five essays and an extended bibliography, mainly emphasizes Taoist studies....The underlying theme of the book, however, is neither Buddhism nor Taoism, but the manifestation of these two religious movements in China. Buddhism and Taoism are essential ingredients of that third entity which often goes unnamed, the religious beliefs of the men and women of traditional China. Whether called folk religion or Chinese popular religion or simply the belief system of the Chinese people, the basic structure of Chinese religious thought must be sought in neither the Pure Lands of Buddhism nor the esoterica of Taoism, but in the popular yin-yang five element cosmology of the masses.

SCHAEFER, EDWARD. **ANCIENT CHINA.** Bibliography, index, 10"x 11¾", 191pp. TLB67, 7.95c.
This is part of Time-Life's **Great Ages of Man** series. Like the other volumes, it is profusely and exquisitely illustrated with color plates and black and white photographs. The text shows the development of Chinese culture, science, and religion, and traces Chinese civilization from the earliest times to the tenth century. It serves as a fine introduction to ancient China.

SCHARFSTEIN, BEN-AMI. **THE MIND OF CHINA.** Illustrations, notes, bibliography, index, 181pp. Del74, 2.95p.
The China of this book is the China of tradition....The book therefore has a soberly magical aim, to enter into the consciousness that traditional Chinese art, literature, history, and philosophy have kept alive....I have hardly dealt with the early, formative philosophies of China, with Buddhism, or with the popular literature....I have concentrated instead on a few subjects and a limited time, roughly the second millennium AD. This is a detailed study of this millennium, analyzing the customs, culture, and beliefs of the educated ruling class. Scharfstein is an Israeli philosophy professor.

SHRINE OF WISDOM EDITORS. **THE CLASSIC OF PURITY.** 7pp. ShW34, .80p.
This is an important early Taoist text, attributed to Ko Hsuan, which is a treatise on the Way of Attainment through the purifying of the mind and the stilling of desires.

SHRINE OF WISDOM EDITORS. **THE HISTORY OF THE GREAT LIGHT.** 36pp. ShW60, 1.20p.
A classic Taoist text.

SHRINE OF WISDOM EDITORS. **YIN FU KING.** 21pp. ShW60, 1.50p.
Another important early Taoist text, attributed to Huang Ti, the Yellow Emperor. Its theme is the importance of integrating man's inner and outer nature. As usual the Shrine of Wisdom has given us a beautiful translation, with commentary.

SIH, PAUL, ed. **THE HSIAO CHING.** Bibliography, 81pp. SJU61, 1.50p.
The term *hsiao*, generally translated as *filiality*, represents one of the most basic social and religious concepts of the Chinese people. As it says in the introduction, *The systematic teaching of filiality in China to the very young is done by means of the Confucian Classic of Filiality or the* **Hsiao Ching.** In this classic we find the sphere of *hsiao extended to embrace almost everything that is desirable in human conduct.* This edition has the Chinese text on facing pages with the translation. The **Hsiao Ching** is the finest text for the beginner in Chinese language studies. Less than 400 characters are used, and all are of fundamental importance for understanding classical Chinese. The translation is by Sister Lelia Makra.

SIREN, OSVALD. **THE CHINESE ON THE ART OF PAINTING.** Notes, index, 259pp. ScB63, 3.95p.
An authoritative handbook which gives us the history and philosophy of Chinese art as it unfolded in the stated intentions and reflections of the artists themselves. Siren presents the writings of Chinese painter-critics from the fourth through the nineteenth centuries. He also examines their aesthetic aims and ideals in relation to various schools of Chinese religion and philosophy. The selections are arranged according to the historical sequence of dynasties.

SIU, R.G.H. **CHI: A NEO-TAOIST APPROACH TO LIFE.** Notes, index, 352pp. MIT74, 4.95p.
The form of this book suggests a Chinese classic. A brief, epigrammatic text is followed by a series of more extended commentaries. Siu's ultimate goal is to reveal the *ch'i*, an untranslatable word whose essence can be thought of as an ever changing, but never ceasing flowing and confluence of time, light, and life. Dr. Siu is a scientist, and the scientific aspects of the subject are emphasized—although there is a strong underlying mystical current.

SIU, R.G.H. **THE TAO OF SCIENCE.** Bibliography, index, 192pp. MIT57, 3.95p.
Written by a Chinese/American scientist, this is an excellent essay on the nature and limitations of Western science and Eastern wisdom, considering in practical detail the theoretical basis of each and the best means of integrating the two. Siu advocates the cultivation of intuitive aesthetic sensitivity synthesized with Western rational methods of cognition.

SIVIN, NATHAN. **CHINESE ALCHEMY.** Notes, bibliography, index, 363pp. HUP68, 23.50c.
Professor Sivin is a professionally trained historian of science, specializing in the Chinese scientific tradition. He begins with a discussion of what questions about Chinese alchemy are likely to be most fruitful and what attempts have been made to solve them; follows with a study of Taoist hagiography; and then presents a definitive study of an important seventh century handbook of alchemical recipes—a collection of formulas for the preparation of elixirs and methods for making scarce natural products. This is an important work in the history of science; it does not deal with alchemy from a spiritual point of view.

SMITH, BRADLEY and WAN-GO WENG. **CHINA: A HISTORY IN ART.** 8½"x12½", 295pp. Dou nd, 12.95c.
This handsome volume is as good a place to begin a study of Chinese art as any we can think of. There are 305 plates, all in full color and beautifully reproduced. The text traces Chinese art through the ages and also surveys the cultural milieu out of which it emerged.

SMULLYAN, RAYMOND. **THE TAO IS SILENT.** Notes, bibliography, 237pp. H&R77, 4.95p.
This is a wonderful, illuminating volume which joyfully opens up the inner meaning of Taoism. To Smullyan, Taoism means a state of inner serenity combined with an intense aesthetic awareness, and it is Taoism in this sense that he is writing about. This is a book about life rather than a treatise on Chinese philosophy. Smullyan presents a series of essays and thoughts inspired by the Taoist viewpoint. The following selection gives a feeling for his approach: *Eastern discipline*

enables you to fall asleep rather than take a nap. Eastern discipline trains you to allow yourself to sleep when you are sleepy; Western discipline teaches you to force yourself to sleep whether you are sleepy or not. The following maxim I think is the quintessence of Taoist philosophy: "The Sage falls asleep not/because he ought to/Nor even because he wants to/But because he is sleepy."

SOOTHILL, W.E. **THE THREE RELIGIONS OF CHINA. Notes, index, 272pp. Cur29, 9.35c.**
An examination of the interrelationships among Buddhism, Confucianism, and Taoism, and their effects upon Chinese life and thought.

SPENCE, JONATHAN. **EMPEROR OF CHINA: SELF PORTRAIT OF K'ANG-HSI. Illustrations, notes, bibliography, index, 7½"x8", 255pp. RaH74, 4.95p.**
This book is an excursion into the imperial world of K'ang-hsi, who was Emperor of China from 1661-1722. The purpose of the journey is to gauge the dimensions of his mind: What inner resources did he bring to the task of governing China? What did he learn from the world around him, and how did he view his subjects? What gave him joy and what made him angry, how did time pass for him, onto what did his memory fasten? How did a descendent of conquering Manchu warriors adapt to the Chinese intellectual and political environment—and how was he affected by new currents of Western scientific and religious thought that Jesuit missionaries brought to his court?—from the introduction. A beautifully produced work, organized thematically.

STEELE, JOHN, tr. **THE I-LI OR BOOK OF ETIQUETTE AND CEREMONIAL. Illustrations, notes, indices, 266pp. CWP17, 6.75c.**
This is a recent reprint of Volume I of Steele's translation of this important early work. *It supplies illustrative matter from the doing and sayings of Confucius and his contemporaries; reviews of ceremonial practice under the three great dynasties, Hsia, Yun, and Chou; philosophical dissertations on the meaning of various ceremonial observances; and notes proper on ceremonial practice.*—from the introduction.

SULLIVAN, MICHAEL. **THE ARTS OF CHINA. 303 plates, including many in color, bibliography, index, 7"x9¾", 287pp. UCa77, 7.95p.**
This is a newly revised edition of the best general book on Chinese art. Sullivan presents a balanced picture of the arts of China from the Stone Age to the present day. He is concerned not only with art, but with Chinese philosophy, religion, and culture, and he places the arts in their political and social context. This revision includes information on all the most recent discoveries as well as the results of Sullivan's own visits to China in 1973 and 1975. The book is extremely well organized and comprehensive.

SUN TZU. **THE ART OF WAR. Notes, bibliography, index, 214pp. Oxf63, 3.50p.**
Sun Tzu's essays on the art of war, written in China more than a thousand years ago, are the earliest of known treatises on the subject. They have never been surpassed in comprehensiveness and depth of understanding, and might well be termed the concentrated essence of wisdom on strategy and the conduct of war. This translation by Samuel Griffith is considered definitive and the translator also contributes an explanatory introduction and selections from the many commentaries in the Chinese language.

SUZUKI, D.T. and PAUL CARUS, trs. **YIN CHIH WEN. Index, 48pp. OpC06, 1.35p.**
A translation of **The Tract of the Quiet Way**, an important Chinese religio-ethical tract, little known in the West but widely read and studied in China. The text includes notes, commentary, and introductory and background material.

SZE, MAI-MAI, tr. **THE MUSTARD SEED GARDEN MANUAL OF PAINTING. 8½"x8½", 641pp. PUP63, 8.95p.**
This is the definitive manual of Chinese painting, first issued in the seventeenth century. There are over 400 examples of brushwork, ranging form the single stroke of a blade of grass or a flower petal to the composition of a tree, village, or mountain. These examples help not only to clarify the text but also to enunciate the principles and standards of the Tao of painting and to demonstrate how the traditions were handed down from period to period. Ms. Sze also provides an introduction, chronology, and an appendix in which the basic terms of Chinese painting are analyzed and illustrated by means of their ideograms and, in many cases, the earlier pictograph forms. We highly

recommend this text to all who are interested in learning Chinese painting techniques. An abridged version is available for $3.45p.

THOMPSON, LAURENCE. **CHINESE RELIGION. Notes, index, 157pp. Dic75, 6.65p.**
A well written, textbook-like survey, divided into the following sections: *The World View of Chinese Philosophy; Proto-Science and Animistic Religion; The Family—Kindred and Ancestors; The Community—Gods and Temples; The State—Emperors and Officials; The Individual—Buddhism and Taoism; The Festival Year;* and *The Disruption of the Tradition.* Each section is clearly divided up to make reading easier and is followed by an annotated list of recommended readings.

THOMPSON, LAURENCE, ed. **THE CHINESE WAY IN RELIGION. Notes, 241pp. Dic73, 8.00p.**
Selected readings and translations divided into the following general topics: *The Ancient Native Tradition; Taoism; Buddhism; Religion of the State; Family Religion; Popular Religion;* and *Religion Under Communism.* The selections are uniformly excellent and the volume itself is well organized. A great variety of points of view are represented.

TU WEI-MING. **CENTRALITY AND COMMONALITY: AN ESSAY ON CHUNG-YUNG. Glossary, notes, 180pp. UHa76, 6.75p.**
Chung-yung, *commonly known as the* **Doctrine of the Mean,** *is a central document in the Confucian tradition. . . .My approach. . .is interpretative rather than exegetical. . . .My task, then, has not been to advocate a fundamentalist position on* **Chung-yung** *but to explicate the text through interpretation; since interpretation in this particular connection is not the imposition of a fixed notion of rationality on the text, but a process of opening oneself up to the text.*—from the preface.

■ VAN OVER, RAYMOND. **TAOIST TALES. Bibliography, 250pp. NAL73/NEL, 2.25p.**
This is a wonderful collection of Taoist tales, parables, anecdotes, *koan,* and poems written over many centuries by Taoist masters. They provide an understanding of Taoism in the one manner that Taoism recognizes—direct experience with its living nature. In so doing, they provide invaluable insight into Chinese philosophy in addition to some compelling literature. Van Over has selected translations from many sources and he also provides a long, good introduction.

WALEY, ARTHUR, tr. **LI CHIH-CHANG: THE TRAVELS OF AN ALCHEMIST. Notes, index, 117pp. Gre31, 17.80c.**
This is a translation of the **Hsi Yu Chi,** the record of the journey of the Taoist Ch'ang-Ch'un from China to the Hindukush at the summons of Chingiz Khan, as recorded by his disciple, Li Chih-Ch'ang. The most interesting feature of the book lies in its successive pictures of widely varying customs and races, and its portrait of Taoism in the time of the early Mongol Empire. Waley provides a lengthy introduction.

■ WALEY, ARTHUR. **THREE WAYS OF THOUGHT IN ANCIENT CHINA. Notes, bibliography, index, 209pp. Dou39/A&U, 2.50p.**
Consists chiefly of extracts from Chuang Tzu, Mencius, and Han Fe Tzu, illustrating the three conflicting points of view in Chinese philosophy in the fourth century BC—the Taoist, the Confucianist, and the *Realist.* A very good selection by a noted scholar.

WALTHAM, CLAE. SHU CHING: BOOK OF HISTORY. Introduction, notes, index, 294pp. GEd71, 3.45p.
This is a modernized version of the classic James Legge translation. The **Shu Ching** is one of the three oldest Chinese books, covering 1,700 years from 2357 BC to 631 BC, and discussing all aspects of daily life and the affairs of state.

WARE, JAMES, tr. ALCHEMY, MEDICINE AND RELIGION IN THE CHINA OF AD 320: THE NEI P'IEN OF KO HUNG. Notes, bibliography, index, 388pp. MIT66, 20.15c.
In the China of the fourth century AD, alchemy, medicine, and religion were so closely interrelated as to form a single study. This work, in effect, is a compendium of the state of knowledge and the mode of life open to the initiated in Ko Hung's time. In particular, it recounts the actual ways of Taoism as they would have existed until fairly recent times—an extraordinary amalgam of mystical insight, wild speculation, superstition and legend, disciplined observation, and intellectual control. Ko Hung was apparently the first to break the taboo against putting this strictly oral tradition of a secret Qabala into writing. A monumental work.

WATSON, BURTON, tr. BASIC WRITINGS OF MO TZU, HSUN TZU AND HAN FEI TZU. Notes, 452pp. Col63, 15.10c.
Watson's translation of the most important writings of these three philosophers along with an introduction which discusses the place of each in Chinese history and thought.

WATSON, BURTON, tr. COURTIER AND COMMONER IN ANCIENT CHINA: SELECTIONS FROM THE HISTORY OF THE FORMER HAN BY PAN KU. Introduction, notes, index, 282pp. Col74, 6.75p.
Pan Ku's celebrated and influential **History of the Former Han** has been a model for dynastic history since its appearance in the first century AD. The narrative is rich in detail and characterized by a purity and economy of style. Covering the period from 206 BC to AD 23, the work consists of annals, chronological tables, treatises, and biographies, the last of which often include excerpts from writings by the subjects of the biographies. Watson has translated ten chapters from the biography section, including the lives of imperial princes, generals, officials, and some lesser figures: a court jester, wandering knights, court ladies, and concubines.

WATSON, BURTON, tr. RECORDS OF THE HISTORIAN: CHAPTERS FROM THE SHIH CHI OF SSU-MA CH'IEN. Introduction, 365pp. Col69, 5.65p.
A translation of eighteen chapters and one brief excerpt from the **Shih chi**. Thirteen of these are taken from Watson's two volume **Records of the Grand Historian of China**, which contains material relating to the Han Dynasty (206 BC–AD 220). To these have been added five chapters dealing with the preceding Chou (c. 1123-256 BC) and Ch'in (221-207 BC) Dynasties. Ssu-ma Ch'ien was the official court historian in the late second century and early first century BC. His history is generally considered the first great Chinese historical work.

WATSON, WILLIAM. ANCIENT CHINA: THE DISCOVERIES OF POST LIBERATION ARCHAEOLOGY. 9½"x7", 108pp. LBC74, 3.95p.
A study of the development of Chinese art up to the Yuan Dynasty, based on the scholarship and findings of post-revolutionary Chinese archaeology. This introductory survey includes many plates, and Watson relates the works of art to what is known of the society that produced them. Watson is Professor of Chinese Art and Archaeology at London University and has traveled to China in recent years.

WATT, JAMES, ed. THE TRANSLATION OF ART: ESSAYS ON CHINESE PAINTING AND POETRY. 7¾"x10¾", 216pp. UWa76, 15.00c.
A collection of illustrated essays prepared for a special art issue of **Renditions**, a publication of the Centre for Translation Projects, The Chinese University of Hong Kong. The selections cover most periods of Chinese art and interpret its every aspect, particularly in relation to poetry. 109 pictures are illustrated and some are also shown blown up in sections; a number of color plates are included. The contributors include the some of the most distinguished scholars and translators in the field.

WATTS, ALAN. TAO: THE WATERCOURSE WAY. Notes, bibliography of works in Chinese and English, 160pp. RaH75, 2.95p.
Watts draws upon the ancient writings of Lao Tzu and Chuang Tzu, the **I Ching**, as well as the modern studies of Joseph Needham, Lin Yutang, and Arthur Waley. This final book, written in collaboration with Al Chung-liang Huang, is a survey of Taoism, documented with many examples from the literature and illustrated with Chinese calligraphy. Opening with a chapter on the Chinese written language, the author goes on to explain what is meant by *Tao* (the flow of things), *wu-wei* (not forcing things), and *te* (the power which comes from this). There are long chapters on each of these important concepts. When Watts died in 1973 the book was almost completed. It was finished by Huang, a friend and colleague who attended and codirected the discussions and lectures out of which the book came. Huang has also supplied much of the extensive calligraphy presented throughout the book. This is by no means the definitive textbook that its publishers claim it to be, but it is an interesting exposition of selected major topics and is geared toward both the general reader and the specialist.

WEBER, MAX. THE RELIGION OF CHINA: CONFUCIANISM AND TAOISM. Introduction, glossary, notes, index, 351pp. McM64, 6.65p.
A classic sociological study of virtually every aspect of ancient Chinese religious, political, and cultural life.

WELCH, HOLMES. TAOISM: THE PARTING OF THE WAY. Chronology, bibliography, index, 195pp. Bea57, 4.95p.
This is the finest overall account of Taoism available. Welch is an excellent scholar and his interpretative text reads extremely well. He includes a lengthy discussion of the **Tao Te Ching**, with selections from various translations.

WERNER, E.T.C. MYTHS AND LEGENDS OF CHINA. 29.55c.
See the Mythology section.

■ *WILHELM, RICHARD.* THE SECRET OF THE GOLDEN FLOWER. 149pp. HBJ31/RKP, 2.45p.
Essentially a practical guide to the integration of personality—hailed by Carl Jung as a link between the insights of the East and his own psychological research. The original text is translated and there is extensive commentary, including almost eighty pages by Jung. Also includes the **Book of Consciousness and Life**, a Chinese meditation text, with commentary. Numerous plates and illustrations are included. One of the most important basic texts. Recommended.

WILLIAMS, C.A.S. OUTLINES OF CHINESE SYMBOLISM AND ART MOTIFS. Introduction, notes, index, 501pp. Dov41, 5.00p.
A beautifully produced, alphabetically arranged handbook of Chinese symbolism based on the early folklore and illustrated throughout. All the important terms are accompanied by their Chinese version.

CHRISTIANITY

Today there is a ferment of interest, a positive search for the immediacy of religious experience. Where is this to be found? With the Jesus People and the Pentecostalists, or at points further East—or West, depending on which way you start? With the Hindus, the Buddhists, the Taoists, the Sufis? All these in various ways have something to offer, it would appear, that the institutional Church does not have. Admittedly we cannot be content with religion at second hand; yet maybe there is something we can still learn from past ages, something that underlies all the enduring religious traditions. It is the primacy of those gifts of mind and heart, insight and compassion (often denied to the brilliant and clever, even to the fervently *religious*), which, to the degree that they form a person's way of life, mark him out as in line with what has been taught by the masters of the spiritual life throughout the centuries.

The Christian Church still professedly upholds an immensely significant tradition: it cherishes in one of its oldest formulas *verbum Domini traditum vel scriptum, the word of the Lord that has come down to us either orally or in the scriptures.* But what, after all, is this Christianity that was handed down? The situation is pretty well documented from, say 150 A.D.; though up to then, and subsequently, the Christian message has been variously interpreted. But what before then? Nobody knows for sure— and that is one of the factors accounting for the confusion in the Church today. Because Christianity—unlike Hinduism or Mahayana Buddhism—claims to be a religion rooted in history, in what actually happened on this earth, it stands or falls by the person and message of Jesus of Nazareth as he lived and died in early-first-century Palestine. Who was this Jesus?

Many churchmen will still answer the question by citing the official creeds or examining the **Bible** in the light of those creeds. That will hardly do today. We now know, as certainly as such matters can be known, that the four gospels draw upon earlier sources. They present Jesus as faithfully as their several authors knew how, but with a variety of readers and some underlying theological purpose in mind. The evangelists were concerned, not merely to tell it as it was—this they could hardly know—but also to meet the inquiries, the needs and aspirations, of the believing communities among which the gospels circulated. Thus it is not too extravagant a question to ask, Would those who encountered Jesus as he actually operated in Galilee and Judea, supposing them to be alive today, recognize him more clearly as portrayed in the **Fourth Gospel** than (allowing for the very different medium) in *Jesus Christ Superstar?*

Then Saint Paul appears on the scene. With him emerges the question, arising from our earliest sources and still not satisfactorily answered, What is Christianity? The headquarters of the primitive Church was at Jerusalem—and so it remained until that city was destroyed by the Romans in the year 70 A.D. Included in the destruction was the disappearance of whatever written records existed of the Jerusalem Church; but that it did not accept at his own valuation the message of Paul can be gathered from the **New Testament** evidence. The members of the early Jerusalem community regarded Jesus, whom they had personally known, as a crucified prophet. They believed that he had risen from the dead, thereby establishing his Messiahship, and that he would shortly appear again as the Son of Man to destroy the Roman tyranny and establish forever the Kingdom of God.

Saint Paul went further than this: he attached to the crucifixion a saving value that extended to Gentiles as well as Jews. His vision was of the resurrected Christ who made possible a new mode of existence for all men. Paul would have had everyone enjoy his own ecstatic experience of the risen Jesus. In his attempts to bring this about he preached a message in a way that would be acceptable not only to Jews—it was unwelcome, even repugnant, to many of them—but to those already influenced by the current religious philosophies of the Graeco-Roman world.

To take an outstanding example: one of Paul's chief themes is known as the *mystical body of Christ,* of which all believers are members. This has affinities with the Stoic philosophy of which Seneca, a contemporary of Paul, was a notable representative. Seneca lays emphasis on the relationship that exists between all human beings. We should not aim at self-sufficiency, as many of the Stoics did, but at helping others and forgiving those who have injured us. We live best when we live for others. He stresses the need for active benevolence. *Nature itself bids me be of use to men,* he says, *whether they are slave or free, freed men or free born. Wherever there is a human being there is room for benevolence.* And again: *See that you are beloved by all while you live and regretted when you die.*

By assimilating in part such philosophies as a revived Pythagoreanism and Neo-Platonism, Christian thinkers gave depth to the Church's teaching and articulated a doctrine of spiritual inwardness. But if an esoteric spiritual tradition was kept alive within the Church, the demands of popular religion were fully met. Christians were instructed in a definite belief system by means of a *rule of faith* propounded by the ecclesiastical hierarchy; the pagan *mysteries* were replaced by a Christian liturgy and a series of grace-bestowing sacraments. From its early beginnings the life of the Church was extrovert, outward looking—first, to the coming of the Kingdom, then, progressively, to adjusting its relations with the Roman Empire, to meeting persecution, to organizing its own methods of government, to conducting its ritual, to converting the heathen, to dealing with heresies, to political maneuvering as an established religion; and, today, to interdenominational dialogue.

Could it be that Christianity has now exhausted the possibilities of corporate extroversion, and that the Church's chief need is to turn inward? It is the institutionalized, outward-looking Church that is in danger of falling apart today. Is its *sacred tradition*—to use the phrase—again being manifested among the Jesus People and the Pentecostalists? In part, perhaps, and all honor to the genuine religious content there. But they, like all devotees, must surely beware of the dangers of elitism, the illusion that somehow they are chosen spirits not quite like the rest of us. Transient emotional euphoria is a poor guide to the heart of religion. Furthermore, I would think that any revival of biblical fundamentalism is to promote a retrograde Christianity. Paradoxically, the need today, I suggest, is not to focus on what is distinctively Christian: salvation history, theories of redemption, conventional orthodoxies—but to show how Christianity manifests through history, as emerging in space and time, a religion that is eternal.

Perhaps we can best do this by considering briefly, though in some depth, not so much religion about Jesus but the religion of Jesus. He is reported to have pointed to what this was in the biblical language familiar to his hearers: they were to love God with all their heart, soul, mind, and strength—that is to say, in modern terminology, they were to identify totally with God, and similarly, through God-dedication, with their neighbor. Taken separately, these requirements are to be found in pre-Christian Judaism; though Jesus may have been the first to link them explicitly together. At any rate they bring us to the roots of all the higher religions. From these roots have sprung flowers that may differ from one another in appearance but whose nature is the same. Four fundamental doctrines, neatly summarized by Aldous Huxley, underlie the religions of the East:

First: the phenomenal world of matter and of individualized conscious-ness—the world of things and animals and men and even gods—is the manifestation of a Divine Ground within which all partial realities have their being, and apart from which they would be nonexistent.

Second: human beings are capable not merely of knowing about the Divine Ground by inference; they can also realize its existence by a direct intuition, superior to discursive reasoning. This immediate knowledge unites the knower with that which is known.

Third: man possesses a double nature, a phenomenal ego and an eternal self, which is the inner man, the spirit, the spark of divinity within the soul. It is possible for man, if he so desires, to identify himself with the spirit and therefore with the Divine Ground, which is of the same or like nature with the spirit.

Fourth: man's life on earth has only one end and purpose: to identify himself with the eternal self and so come to the knowledge of the Divine Ground.

Hints of these very doctrines can be discovered, at least in embryo, in the earliest Christian writings as their authors sought acceptance in the Hellenistic world. First: we find Saint Paul making the point to the community of believers at Corinth: *We look not to the things that are seen but to the things that are unseen; for the things that are seen are transient, but the things that are unseen are eternal.* Second: not only Jesus, conceived as God's incarnate Word, must be known, but God himself: *And this is eternal life, that they know thee the only true God. . . .*Third: the phenomenal ego must yield to the eternal self: *For whoever would save his life will lose it; and whoever loses his life for my sake and the gospel's will save it.* Experientially, Saint Paul implies, God's spirit testifies to our spirit that we are his children. And in a later **New Testament** document we find the hope expressed that *you may escape from the corruption that is in the world because of passion, and become partakers of the divine nature.* Fourth: finally, the great eschatological climax: that God may be all in all, *everything to every one.*

Something must now be said more specifically about the possibilities of direct religious experience within the Christian tradition. *Mysticism* is the term often employed in this context to describe what cannot really be described, but I shall use the word more customary in the West, at least among Catholic spiritual writers—*contemplation.*

If we look up the words *contemplation* or *contemplate* in a modern dictionary, we find the meaning given as *to view or consider with continued attention.* What is implied here is that there is some object of our contemplation. Saint Thomas Aquinas, for one, would not disagree: for him contemplation is an act of the intellect, though it has its roots in man's affectivity. He thinks of it, of course, as being God-directed. Moreover, for Thomas, those who are called contemplatives devote their whole lives to their objective. Their life-style involves self-discipline—particularly, he thinks (following the monastic tradition), abstention from sexual intercourse—and it is largely made up of reading the scriptures, meditation, and prayer. None of this has been outmoded today. But a lot of water has

flowed under the theological and philosophical bridges since the thirteenth century, and we must take account of it if we are to discuss the matter in terms that make sense to our contemporaries.

Was Aquinas, following in the footsteps of Plato and Aristotle, too intellectualist about it all? Underlying his thought, as I understand it, is the effort to make God real to ourselves—or better, so to dispose ourselves that God becomes consciously the greatest reality for us. And here we get beyond any faculty psychology—intellect and will and so on—to the involvement of the whole personality. Thus we may rephrase *contemplation of God* as *God-realization*: the true contemplative is the God-realized person, or at least one who is on the way to that state. And here we find ourselves, I think, in harmony with the thought both of traditional Hinduism—for which *realization* is the perfect state—and of certain Christian existentialists of today.

In Indian thought, it is worth mentioning, God-realization takes place according to the variety of people's temperaments. One person may be inclined to a life of devotion—pouring him/herself out in acts of adoration, prostrations before the Godhead or one of its manifestations, given over to interior aspirations, vocal prayers, some meaningful ritual or liturgy. Another person may give him/herself selflessly to active good works, a concern for the betterment of society, relief of the needy or destitute, trying to bring about, or move a little nearer to, one world instead of our present three. Finally, a third person may be concerned with God-realization in its most direct form: by a deepening awareness, an expansion of consciousness, trying to achieve, or disposing him/herself to, the highest degree of insight and compassion: so that, in Christian terms, *it is no longer I who live, but Christ who lives in me.*

Any one of these three ways, if practiced selflessly, can bring about God-realization. They are not mutually exclusive—it is often a question of emphasis—and they can overlap; but there are good grounds for distinguishing between them. Each, needless to say, has its pitfalls and dangers. The way of devotion can lapse into mere routine, an obsessive piety, a mechanical, even superstitious, carrying-out of a set program of observance. The way of active good works can degenerate into mere busy-ness, and at worst, a thrust for power, an itch to organize other people's lives. The way of deepening awareness can dissolve into an ego-trip, a quest for self-satisfaction, and an indifference to our neighbor's problems and difficulties. But I think that the masters of the spiritual life, both East and West, would agree that these risks have to be taken—and particularly the risks attending the most worth-while objective—what Buddhists call *seeing into one's own nature*—since the wisdom that ensues is the most effective source of any fruitful activity.

When it comes to communicating with the ultimate reality we call God, we are at the same time concerned with our own deepest self. Not our superficial empirical ego, which we are all too ready to distinguish from every other ego, but the ground of our being in which all humanity is kin, of which we are always at least implicitly aware but which can never be the object of direct conceptual knowledge. *Let me know myself,* says Saint Augustine; *let me know Thee.*

God is never to be known directly, only through some form of his self-manifestation. The metaphor of *the vision of God,* therefore, should not suggest to our minds a positive flash of insight. What is indicated is the condition in which we regard our cognitive powers as a kind of clearing in being, when, through the deepest self-awareness, we become the *locus* where being is lit up and becomes unconcealed.

Let us bring this line of thought a little closer to expressing the God of traditional Christianity, and we might add, to the ultimate reality of Hinduism. Consider the doctrine of the

Holy Trinity: to the Father can be appropriated the source of all being; to the Son, the Logos, belongs infinite consciousness; to the Spirit pertains the joy that flows from love without limit. *To be, to know, to find joy,* correspond to the *sat, cit, ananda*—the Being, Consciousness, Bliss—of the **Upanishads**. This doctrine is echoed without variation, though in existential terms, in one of the aphorisms of Saint John of the Cross: *In order to be All, do not desire to be anything. In order to find the joy of All, do not desire to enjoy anything.*

Let me conclude with the observation that our religious *experience* is of small account to anyone but ourselves. Only that of which it is the by-product can in some degrees be transmitted. Christianity's one authentic message is to proclaim that God and our neighbor be loved—utterly. Transposed into Buddhist terms, may we not say, take care of wisdom and compassion, and *nirvana* will look after itself? The genetic code indicates that we are heirs of the ages, traditionalists despite ourselves. Facing reality with all the mental clarity and honesty we can achieve, dynamically accepting and responding—that is what a life that makes sense is about. And for some reason we cannot quite understand, it appears that this is the only way to happiness.

—condensed from Graham's essay in **Sacred Tradition and Present Need**, *by Needleman and Lewis.*

Mexican Indian stone sculpture of the crucified Christ.

ABHISHIKTANANDA. **PRAYER. Notes, 81pp. Wes67/SCK, 2.45p.**
A distillation of Christian wisdom on the union with God through prayer. The author was a French Benedictine priest who spent much of his adult life in India. The book is widely read by Indian Christians who find it a good combination of traditional Indian teachings and Christianity.

AELDRED OF RIEVAULX. **FOR CRIST LOVE. 87pp. MaN65, 2.75p.**
This is a collection, edited by D. Anselm Hoste, of prayers of Saint Aelred of Rievaulx. The Latin text and English translation are presented on facing pages and the prayers are topically arranged. The translations are by Sister Rose de Lima. The editor provides an introduction.

AELRED OF RIEVAULX. **ON SPIRITUAL FRIENDSHIP. Introductory material, notes, index, 144pp. Cis74, 4.00p.**
Aelred of Rievaulx was a twelfth century English monk who was one of the earliest Cistercian leaders and writers. In this work he reflects on friendship on both the natural and supernatural plane and discusses the qualities of a true friend.

AJIBOLA, J.O. **THE SECRET SCHOOL OF JESUS. 75pp. Day72, 1.20p.**
A selection of quotations from the **Gospels** on the title theme, with commentary. The phrase *secret school* is used in the sense that after Jesus had preached in synagogues and in other public places where his twelve disciples had listened to him, he still called them separately to some secret and lonely places where he gave them more intensive instructions concerning the secrets of the kingdom of Heaven.

AKHILANANDA, SWAMI. **HINDU VIEW OF CHRIST. Notes, bibliography, index, 291pp. BrP49, 3.75p.**
Christ is accepted as God incarnate in Hinduism as well as in Christianity. Swami Akhilananda stresses the agreement of the two religions on the model of life imparted by Christ—a model that each individual can grasp through his own experience. This way of life is considered throughout the book's chapters on Christ's teachings and spiritual practices, the Cross, the spirit of Easter, and the dynamics of spiritual power.

ALLEGRO, JOHN. **THE SACRED MUSHROOM AND THE CROSS. 1.60p.**
See the Ancient Near East section.

Apollonius of Tyana

If Apollonius really lived, he was an ascetic Greek philosopher of the early part of the first century AD, who traveled through Asia to India absorbing much of the Eastern mystical tradition. A Roman empress instructed the writer Philostratus, a Greek sophist, to write a biography of him, and it is speculated that her motive for doing so stemmed from her desire to counteract the influence Christianity was having on Roman civilization. The biography portrays a figure much like Christ in temperment and power and claims that Apollonius performed certain miracles. It is believed that most of the biography is based more on fiction than on fact. Many of the pagans in the Roman Empire believed what was written, and it kindled religious feeling in many of them. To honor and worship Apollonius, they erected shrines and other memorials throughout the Empire.

CONYBEARE, F.C., tr. **PHILOSTRATUS: THE LIFE OF APOLLONIUS OF TYANA, VOLUMES I AND II. HUP50, 9.40c/each.**
This two volume set is part of the **Loeb Classical Library**. It contains an introduction as well as a translation of the entire text, with the original Greek on facing pages. Each volume has its own index. Volume I, 608 pages; Volume II, 624 pages.

EELLS, CHARLES, tr. **LIFE AND TIMES OF APOLLONIUS OF TYANA. Notes, index, 263pp. AMS23, 19.50c.**
A scholarly translation of Philostratus.

JONES, C.P., tr. **PHILOSTRATUS: LIFE OF APOLLONIUS. Notes, index, 255pp. Pen70, 1.20p.**
This is a well translated version of Philostratus' biography. A great deal of introductory material is also included.

MEAD, G.R.S. **APOLLONIUS OF TYANA: THE PHILOSOPHER-REFORMER OF THE FIRST CENTURY A.D. Many notes, bibliography, offset, spiral bound, 159pp. HeR01, 4.00p.**
Subtitled, *A critical study of the only existing record of his life with some account of the war of opinion concerning him and an introduction on the religious associations and brotherhoods of the times and the possible influence of Indian thought on Greece.*

TREDWELL, DANIEL. **A SKETCH OF THE LIFE OF APOLLONIUS OF TYANA. Notes, spiral bound, 360pp. HeR1886, 6.00p.**
A biographical sketch, based on many early sources and extensively documented—although it is hard to document the life of this shadowy figure.

——— **END OF APOLLONIUS OF TYANA SUBSECTION** ———

ASHE, GEOFFREY. **THE VIRGIN. 6.60p.**
See the Mythology section.

ATTWATER, DONALD. **A DICTIONARY OF SAINTS. 362pp. Vik65, 3.95p.**
An alphabetical reference book detailing the lives and legends of over 750 saints, from Christ's apostles to the men and women who have been canonized in recent times—with full details of their work, their feast days, emblems, and dates of canonization.

St. Augustine of Hippo

St. Augustine (354-430) was the dominant personality of the Western church of his time. He is generally recognized as the greatest thinker of early Christian times. He fused the religion of the **New Testament** with the Platonic tradition. As a young student he first became interested in philosophy; his early faith was Manichaeism. Disillusioned with Manichaeism, he turned to Neoplatonism, where he found solutions to his problems about the being of God and the nature and origin of evil. He converted to Christianity in 386 and became a bishop in 396.

BETTENSON, HENRY, tr. **CITY OF GOD. Fifty-one page introduction, index, 1,148pp. Vik72, 7.95p.**
St. Augustine incorporated Platonism (as interpreted by Plotinus) into Christianity. The **City of God** was inspired by the fifth century sacking of Rome, an event which Augustine regarded as retribution for the worship of false gods by *educated pagans*. God's real purpose in creating the world, Augustine maintains, was the building of the heavenly city and the events of history are mere moments in the implementation of a divine plan. The first half of the book reviews the sufferings of Rome throughout history, with Augustine asking where the Roman gods were during these bloody events. In the second half he turns from history to the need to found another city based on Christian love. Countless digressions present his ideals of social order in a universal religious society.

BOURKE, VERNON, ed. **CITY OF GOD. Introduction, 545pp. Dou50, 2.95p.**
An abridgment of Augustine's monumental work.

DODS, MARCUS, tr. **THE CITY OF GOD. Indices, 907pp. RaH50, 6.95c.**
A modern translation, with many notes and biblical cross references. Introduction by Thomas Merton.

PINE-COFFIN, R.S., tr. **CONFESSIONS. Introduction, notes, 347pp. Vik61, 2.50p.**
From Augustine's own account, he lived a life of sin until his conversion to Christianity at the age of thirty-two. Twelve years later he gave a personal account of his search for truth in **Confessions**. His analysis of the emotional side of the Christian experience remains unsurpassed. The work is also intensely revealing of the man himself. This is a very readable translation.

RYAN, JOHN, tr. **THE CONFESSIONS OF ST. AUGUSTINE. Bibliography, index, 429pp. Dou60, 2.45p.**
This is a good translation and the edition contains extensive notes and an introduction.

————END OF ST. AUGUSTINE OF HIPPO SUBSECTION————

BAILEY, ALICE. **FROM BETHLEHEM TO CALVARY. 3.75p.**
See the Theosophy section.

BAILEY, ALICE. **THE REAPPEARANCE OF THE CHRIST. 3.25p.**
See the Theosophy section.

BAKER, EVE. **THE MYSTICAL JOURNEY: A WESTERN ALTERNATIVE. Notes, annotated bibliography, 121pp. Wdw77, 5.45p.**
This is a simply written examination of the Western contemplative tradition, a path which the author feels has great potential for those who seek what she calls *the transformation of the self*. Throughout the book, Ms. Baker quotes from many important Christian saints. She also discusses why this Western tradition is more relevant for Westerners than the mystical paths of the East.

BELL, H. IDRIS and T.C. SKEAT, eds. **FRAGMENTS OF AN UNKNOWN GOSPEL AND OTHER EARLY CHRISTIAN PAPYRI. Index, 68pp. BMP35, 14.65c.**
A verbatim reproduction, with translation and a great deal of commentary, of papyri dating from the middle of the second century.

Bernard of Clairvaux

Bernard of Clairvaux towered over the society of twelfth century Europe. A brilliant preacher and a polished writer, he counseled kings and rebuked popes. He moved in the complicated affairs of men with a dexterity which brought him acclaim and adversaries, yet he exhorted Christians to turn from wordly affairs to serve God. He remains a man of paradoxes. He crisscrossed Europe while insisting that monks had no place outside their monasteries. He persuaded two kings to take up a Crusade against the Moslems, yet he preached that persuasion and not force should be used against infidels. A profound mystic, Bernard sought, above all and in all, to be with God and to bring all men to experience of God.
—*from the introduction to* **On the Song of Songs, Volume I**, *by Bernard of Clairvaux*

ANDERSON, JOHN D. and ELIZABETH KENNAN, trs. **FIVE BOOKS ON CONSIDERATION: ADVICE TO A POPE. Notes, bibliography, index, 221pp. Cis76, 12.50c.**
Bernard of Clairvaux was one of the most influential medieval clerics. He trained hundreds and established an extensive monastic network. This network was paralleled by another one of ecclesiastical officials ranging from bishops to a pope, who were trained as monks in Bernard's monastery. Despite his larger role in ecclesiastical politics, his first responsibility was to teach and discipline his monks—even monks who left his direct presence received a flood of advice. This volume contains suggestions on papal reform given to one of his own monks who was raised to the papal throne. He examines in detail the practical and theoretical demands of the papal office and discusses ways in which such mundane duties can be incorporated into the spiritual life.

CONWAY, M. AMBROSE and ROBERT WALTON, trs. **TREATISES, II. Introduction, notes, bibliography, index, 142pp. Cis74, 8.95c.**
The two treatises recorded here, *The Steps of Humility and Pride* and *Loving God*, are Bernard of Clairvaux's best known and most popular works. They are also among the finest examples of medieval monastic literature, incorporating both practical suggestions and mystical vision. As an abbot and director of souls, Bernard took care to lead his monks gently but firmly from the first faltering impulse toward God to the very threshold of divine vision.

LECLERCQ, JEAN, ed. **BERNARD OF CLAIRVAUX. Bibliography, 267pp. Cis73, 11.95c.**
A collection of essays on the life and work of Bernard of Clairvaux and on related topics put together by a group of Cistercian monks.

LECLERCQ, JEAN. **BERNARD OF CLAIRVAUX AND THE CISTERCIAN SPIRIT. Illustrations, chronology, bibliography, index, 179pp. Cis76, 4.00p.**
A revealing biographical study of the man and his teaching. Leclercq writes well and he has done a good job of bringing Bernard and his times to life. Many selections from Bernard's writings are included.

MERTON, THOMAS. **THE LAST OF THE FATHERS. Bibliography, index, 123pp. Gre54, 12.10c.**
This is a biographical study of the life and work of Saint Bernard of Clairvaux, including a translation of the Encyclical Letter, **Doctor Mellifluus**.

PENNINGTON, M. BASIL, ed. **ST. BERNARD OF CLAIRVAUX.** Notes, 391pp. Cis77, 14.95c.
A collection of studies commemorating the eighth centenary of St. Bernard's canonization.

WALSH, KILIAN, tr. **ON THE SONG OF SONGS, VOLUMES I AND II.** Notes, Cis71/76, 4.00p/each.
The sermons recorded in these volumes are among the most famous and beautiful examples of medieval scriptural exegesis. An introduction by Jean Leclercq is included in each volume. The first surveys the expressions St. Bernard made of his faith, while the second discusses whether the sermons were originally written texts or a series of delivered sermons.

WARD, BENEDICTA, ed. **THE INFLUENCE OF ST. BERNARD.** Notes, 162pp. Cis76, 5.50p.
Six essays on various aspects of Bernard's influence: his primary relationship with God; his monastic life and teaching; the dispute with Abelard and the relationship of theology to life; and the influence of his teaching on Cistercian elements in the legend of the Holy Grail.

————**END OF BERNARD OF CLAIRVAUX SUBSECTION**————

BERRIGAN, DANIEL and THICH NHAT HANH. **THE RAFT IS NOT THE SHORE: CONVERSATIONS TOWARD A CHRISTIAN/BUDDHIST AWARENESS.** 3.45p.
See the Zen Buddhism section.

BESANT, ANNIE. **ESOTERIC CHRISTIANITY.** Notes, index, 284pp. TPH01, 3.50p.
Discourses on the esoteric background and spiritual meanings in the Christian legends by this noted Theosophist. Ms. Besant also relates Christianity to Indian philosophy.

BETTENSON, HENRY, tr. **THE EARLY CHRISTIAN FATHERS.** Introduction, notes, index, 317pp. Oxf56, 6.65p.
A selection from the writings of the fathers from St. Clement of Rome to St. Athanasius, covering the entire Ante-Nicene period. Bettenson has selected passages which display as fully as possible the thought of the early fathers, especially on the great doctrinal questions. The selections are well organized and each father is discussed chronologically.

BETTENSON, HENRY, tr. **THE LATER CHRISTIAN FATHERS.** Notes, index, 301pp. Oxf70, 6.05p.
Selections from the writings of Basil the Great, Gregory of Nyssa, Jerome, Augustine of Hippo, Cyril of Alexandria, and other church fathers of the century and a quarter following the Council of Nicaea (AD 325). Their central concerns were formulating the doctrine of the Trinity after the Nicene conclusions, and enunciating the doctrine of the divinity and humanity of Christ. In his lengthy introduction, Bettenson individually discusses each of the fathers.

BLYTH, R.H. **BUDDHIST SERMONS ON CHRISTIAN TEXTS.** 2.95p.
See the Zen Buddhism section.

Jacob Boehme

Evelyn Underhill called Boehme *one of the most astonishing cases in history of a natural genius for the transcendent.* Nicholas Berdyaev described Boehme as *Beyond a doubt . . . one of the greatest of Christian gnostics. I am using the word not in the sense of heresies . . . but to indicate a wisdom grounded in revelation and employing myths and symbols rather than concepts—a wisdom much more contemplative than discursive.* Boehme was a German Lutheran, the son of a farmer who lived the first part of his life as a shepherd and later became a shoemaker. He was completely uneducated and claimed that his writings reflect only what he was taught through direct experience of God. A truly giant figure in the spiritual tradition, he has greatly influenced Angelus Silesius, William Blake, John Milton, Isaac Newton, William Law, and many others.

BOEHME, JACOB. **MYSTERIUM MAGNUM. Two volumes,** notes, index, 849pp. Wat24, 54.60c/set.
This book was written by Boehme the year before he died, at a time when his powers of expression had developed to their fullest. Taking the general form of an interpretation of **Genesis,** it far outstrips those confines, touching among other matters upon the meaning of the **New Testament** and, from the first sentence, leading to the heart of the universal experience of all mystics: *When we consider the visible world with its essence and consider the life of the creatures, then we find therein the likeness of the invisible, spiritual world, which is hidden in the visible world as the soul in the body; and we see thereby that the hidden God is nigh unto all and through all, and yet wholly hidden to the visible essence.*

BOEHME, JACOB. **THE SIGNATURE OF ALL THINGS. Introduction,** 295pp. Cla69, 8.40c.
A collection of selected writings, including the title piece, *Of the Supersensual Life,* and *A Dialogue Between Two Souls.*

BOEHME, JACOB. **SIX THEOSOPHIC POINTS.** 208pp. UMP70, 2.25p.
Philosophic discussion of aspects of the growth of good and evil and mystical points such as *the blood and water of the soul.* Includes an introductory essay by Nicholas Berdyaev.

ERB, PETER, tr. **THE WAY TO CHRIST. Lengthy introduction,** notes, index, 325pp. Pau78, 6.95p.
This is an excellent new translation of this classic work. As Erb says, **The Way to Christ** *provides the best introduction to [Boehme's] thought and spirituality. A collection of nine separate treatises, its parts were written late in his career and reflect his final theological position, a position established not aside from his earlier work, but on it. . . . The book was intended to serve as a meditation guide. Boehme believed that his writing had come from the Spirit. It was intended to direct his fellow-believers back to the Spirit as he had been directed.*

HARTMANN, FRANZ. **THE LIFE AND DOCTRINES OF JACOB BOEHME.** 337pp. Mul29, 6.50p.
This is a very useful, edited compilation of Boehme's writings, topically organized and combined with a study of his life and work.

LIEM, ANN. **JACOB BOEHME: INSIGHTS INTO THE CHALLENGE OF EVIL.** Bibliography, 32pp. PHP77, 1.20p.
A clear analysis of Boehme's life and writings, divided into the following major topics: *The Life of Boehme, The Nature and Manifestation of God, Salvation and Regeneration, The Problem of Free Will,* and *Practical Applications.*

————**END OF JACOB BOEHME SUBSECTION**————

BOLSHAKOFF, SERGIUS. **RUSSIAN MYSTICS. Introduction, glossary, bibliography,** 233pp. Cis76, 18.75c.
The author of this unusual book has given it too modest a title. It is in fact not only an introduction to the lives, the spirituality and the writings of the great mystics, many of whom are unknown in the West, but it is also at the same time a clear and practical outline of Russian monastic history. The journey which the reader now begins is not without excitement, for it takes him into new territory, the silence of the great Russian forests . . . —Thomas Merton

BOUYER, LOUIS. **A HISTORY OF CHRISTIAN SPIRITUALITY, VOLUME I: THE SPIRITUALITY OF THE NEW TESTAMENT AND THE FATHERS. Many notes, indices, 560pp. Sea63, 17.50c.**
This is a readable and erudite history, written for the nonspecialist and specialist alike. In the first part of this volume, Father Bouyer pays special attention to the Jewish foundations of Christianity before examining in detail the teaching and influence of Jesus, the primitive church, St. Paul, the **Synoptic Gospels**, the Johannine writings, the Epistle to the Hebrews, and the epistles linked with the names of Peter, James, and Jude. In Part Two, the author describes and discusses the spirituality of the first Christian generations, the martyrs, the problem of *gnosis* in its different manifestations, the different schools of monasticism and mysticism in Eastern and Western Christianity, and the writings and teachings of the fathers, concluding with St. Benedict.

BOYD, ANNE. **THE MONKS OF DURHAM. 48pp. CUP75, 2.75p.**
A pictorial description of life in a fifteenth century monastery.

BRIANCHANINOV, IGNATIUS, **ON THE PRAYER OF JESUS. 114pp. Wat65, 6.15p.**
Bishop Brianchaninov was one of the great theologians of the Russian Orthodox Church. This volume contains his thoughts on the *Prayer of Jesus*, a method of thought control and concentration in the form of a spiritual exercise. The first references to this prayer are contained in the **Philokalia**. The *Jesus Prayer* is first repeated aloud again and again, making it a continuous background to one's life; the next step is to say the prayer silently, and concentrate on it as it is being thought; when complete concentration has been attained the prayer enters the heart and lives itself with every heartbeat. Alexander d'Agapeyeff provides an illuminating introduction. Translation by Father Lazarus.

BUNYAN, JOHN. **THE PILGRIM'S PROGRESS. Notes, 377pp. Vik65, 1.95p.**
Penning the lines of characters such as Mercy, Christian, Obstinate, and Goodwill, Bunyan searches through the land of the **Bible** to try and find answers to the thoughts that troubled his mind. First published in 1678, this book has remained a classic of religious and allegorical literature. This volume is edited, with a long introduction by Roger Sharrock.

CALDWELL, TAYLOR *and JESS STEARN.* **I, JUDAS. 371pp. Ath77/NEL, 2.50p.**
Judas Iscariot, the archetypal betrayer, is viewed by the authors from an entirely new perspective. In **I, Judas**, they have created a new gospel, allowing Judas to speak for himself and reveal the causes and motivations for his own actions. Here Judas is seen as himself betrayed, both by the Romans and by the Jewish Sanhedrin who promised that Jesus, if brought to trial, would be acquitted of all charges of treason. Judas believed in Jesus' divinity and saw him as the savior of the Jewish people. He therefore allowed himself to be misled because he hoped that when openly challenged, Jesus would be forced to assert, once and for all, his Messianic role.

CAUSSADE, JEAN-PIERRE DE. **ABANDONMENT TO DIVINE PROVIDENCE. 119pp. Dou75, 1.95p.**
A great Christian spiritual classic. Caussade outlines the means to attain holiness through total surrender of the soul to God and complete cooperation with his will in all things. He emphasizes that we must embrace the present moment, for it provides *an ever-flowing source of holiness.* Total acceptance of the present moment and all the activities of that moment is the single most important concern of the soul seeking God. All things are sent by God, writes Caussade, and however troublesome they are, they will—if accepted gladly—lead us surely and quickly to holiness. The translation is by John Beevers, who also supplies introductory remarks.

CHADWICK, HENRY. **THE EARLY CHURCH. Topical bibliography, index, 304pp. Vik67, 3.95p.**
A detailed study of Christianity from earliest times through the fourth century, focusing on important individuals and movements.

CHADWICK, HENRY *and JOHN OUTTON, eds.* **ALEXANDRIAN CHRISTIANITY. Introduction, notes, indices, 475pp. Wes54, 7.95p.**
Selected translations from the writings of Clement of Alexandria and Origen, influential church fathers of the second century. These two fathers helped integrate Greek philosophy into Christianity. They also did much to provide the philosophical basis for Christian asceticism which was later to find expression in the monastic orders.

CHITTY, DERWAS, *tr.* **THE LETTERS OF ST. ANTHONY THE GREAT. Introduction, 41pp. Cis75, 1.50p.**
St. Anthony (251-356) was one of the best known desert fathers. These letters have been traditionally attributed to him, and they represent the quintessence of his teaching. This is the first time they have appeared in English.

CLISSOLD, STEPHEN, *ed.* **THE WISDOM OF THE SPANISH MYSTICS. 88pp. NDP77, 2.95p.**
The great flowering of Catholic mysticism in sixteenth century Spain has had a lasting effect on that country's religious life. This book provides a selection of maxims and excerpts from the writings of over twenty visionaries. Represented here are such well known figures as St. John of the Cross, St. Teresa of Avila, and St. Ignatius Loyola. Many lesser known mystics are also included and an introduction places each one in the historical and cultural context of a Christian Spain triumphant in its nearly 800 year struggle with its Muslim adversaries, and outlines their relation to the central Catholic mystical tradition.

The Cloud of Unknowing

The unknown author of this classic work was probably an English country parson of the late fourteenth century. The book's main theme is that *all thoughts, all concepts, all images must be buried beneath a cloud of forgetting, while our naked love (naked because divested of thought) must rise upward toward God hidden in the cloud of unknowing.*—William Johnston.

JOHNSTON, WILLIAM, *tr.* **THE CLOUD OF UNKNOWING. 195pp. Dou73, 1.75p.**
This is the translation we like the best. The Middle English has been rendered into modern English without losing the flavor of the original. Father Johnston is an authority on fourteenth century spirituality and in particular, on the writings of this author. He provides a lengthy introduction and also includes a translation of the same author's other principal work, **The Book of Privy Counseling**—a short but moving treatise on the way to enlightenment through a total loss of self and consciousness only of the being of God. Notes at the end cross reference the books to the **Collected Works of St. John of the Cross.**

NIEVA, CONSTANTINO. **THIS TRANSCENDING GOD. Notes, bibliography, index, 296pp. Fud71, 5.95c.**
An in depth analysis of **The Cloud of Unknowing.** Nieva discusses both the work itself and the mystical nature of its anonymous author. This is the most detailed exposition of **The Cloud** we have ever seen.

PROGOFF, IRA, *tr.* **THE CLOUD OF UNKNOWING. 243pp. Del57, 2.95p.**
Progoff, a student of Jung, provides up to date psychological comments and interpretation of this classic. He has studied **The Cloud** in detail and shares his knowledge of idiomatic expressions and the various subtleties of meaning in the original language to help us feel more clearly the writer's wisdom and to understand his advice on transcending the cloud and finding the true God.

UNDERHILL, EVELYN, *ed.* **THE CLOUD OF UNKNOWING. 270pp. Wat12, 6.85c.**
An edited, modernized version of the British Museum manuscript. Recommended only to those who want the edition most like the original. Includes an introduction by Ms. Underhill.

WOLTERS, CLIFTON, *tr.* **THE CLOUD OF UNKNOWING. Bibliography, 144pp. Vik65, 2.25p.**
A readable, modern translation. Includes a long introduction.

——**END OF THE CLOUD OF UNKNOWING SUBSECTION**——

COLLEDGE, ERIC. **MEDIEVAL MYSTICS OF ENGLAND. Index, 309pp. Scr61, 6.65p.**
A representative volume which includes writings of seven of the best known figures of England's medieval period along with an excellent introduction. The selections include **The Mirror of Love** by St. Aelred

of Rievaulx, **The Mirror of Holy Church** by St. Edmund Rich, **I Sleep and My Heart Wakes** by Richard Rolle, **The Book of Privy Counsel** by the author of **The Cloud of Unknowing**, **The Scale of Perfection** by Walter Hilton, **Revelations** by Juliana of Norwich, and excerpts from **The Book of Margery Kempe.**

CORBISHLEY, THOMAS. **THE PRAYER OF JESUS.** 143pp. Mow76, 2.00p.
There are not a few books on the prayers of Jesus, commentaries on the Lord's Prayer, on the other passages in the gospels where he speaks of prayer or himself prays. The purpose of this book is to attempt to get behind the utterances of Jesus to his own spirit of prayer; what we might call his prayerlife.—from the introduction. The first section of this book examines the experience of prayer; the second looks at prayer in the life of Jesus the man; and a third studies the chief prayers attributed to Jesus in the **Gospels** and brings out their contemporary relevance.

DANIELOU, JEAN. **GOSPEL MESSAGE AND HELLENISTIC CULTURE.** Notes, bibliography, indices, 550pp. Wes73/DLT, 17.50c.
An academic history of early Christian doctrine before the Council of Nicaea. Danielou's aim is to uncover the basic origins and development of Christian doctrine. Translated from the French.

DANIELOU, JEAN. **THE ORIGINS OF LATIN CHRISTIANITY.** Bibliography, indices, 527pp. Wes77, 25.00c. The third and final volume in Professor Danielou's massive study of early history doctrine before the Council of Nicaea. This one covers the following major topics: Latin Judaeo-Christianity, Christianity and Latin culture, the Latin fathers and the **Bible**, and Latin theology. Many translations of primary works are included along with surveys of all the major individual figures and schools of thought.

DANIELOU, JEAN. **THE THEOLOGY OF JEWISH CHRISTIANITY.** Glossary, notes, bibliography, indices, 462pp. Wes64, 22.50c.
An analysis of early church doctrine based on information from the **Dead Sea Scrolls**, Gnostic texts, and Hebraic sources. This is the first volume in Danielou's excellent history of early Christian doctrine before the Council of Nicaea.

Dante Alighieri

Dante (1265-1321) is the greatest poet of Europe and is generally acclaimed with Shakespeare and Goethe as one of the universal geniuses of western European literature. Dante was also a prose writer, rhetorician, theorist of his own Italian vernacular literature, moral philosopher, and political thinker. By writing his masterpiece, **The Divine Comedy**, in Italian rather than Latin he influenced decisively the evolution of European literature away from its origins in Latin culture and toward the expression of a new civilization. The poem itself is the greatest Christian epic. It is a profound vision of the medieval Christian world in terms of the principal problems with which it was most interested: man's moral obligation to be; the relationship between reason and faith; the value of learning and poetry as the means of understanding the supernatural; the reaching of the metaphysical through analysis of reality; and the understanding of Christian revelation through theological study. Dante began working on **The Divine Comedy** in 1308, after a period of intense political life and exile. A poet above all, he felt that only in poetry would he be able to express fully his dream of a spiritual and civilized renewal of the whole of humanity.

CARLYLE, JOHN A., THOMAS OKEY, and P.H. WICKSTEED, trs. **DANTE: THE DIVINE COMEDY. Introduction, illustrations, many scholarly notes, genealogical tables, bibliography, 646pp. RaH50, 3.95p.**
A classic prose translation which is clear and accurate, though the language is a bit archaic.

CARY, HENRY, tr. **DANTE'S INFERNO. Many notes, 8½"x 11", 183pp. G&D76, 6.95p.**
This is a finely reproduced version of the nineteenth century edition of

The Inferno, illustrated by Gustave Dore. A complete translation of **The Inferno** is included.

CIARDI, JOHN, tr. **THE DIVINE COMEDY. Introduction, notes, 619pp. Nor70, 14.95c.**
A one volume edition of Ciardi's masterful translation of Dante's great trilogy.

CIARDI, JOHN, tr. **THE INFERNO. 288pp. NAL54, 1.75p.**
The Inferno presents a visionary journey through the nine circles of Hell, where anguished men and women expiate earthly sins of lust and greed, malice and betrayal, in varying degrees of torment. It is a classic account of the way of an individual soul from sin to Purgatory and the truths Dante revealed in the Middle Ages still pertain in today's confused world. This is an excellent poetic translation with introductory and background material and notes.

CIARDI, JOHN, tr. **THE PARADISO. 388pp. NAL70, 1.50p.**
Having passed through Hell and Purgatory, Dante is led through the upper sphere wherein lie the sublime truths of divine will and purpose. This is the most mystical of the three books and the symbols of medieval Christianity mingle with those of classic antiquity; the boundaries of science, religion, and art are dissolved by a passionate unity of vision.

CIARDI, JOHN, tr. **THE PURGATORIO. 380pp. NAL61, 1.75p.**
In this volume (the second) Dante describes his journey to the renunciation of sin. It is the journey upward toward God, and from the top of Purgatory Dante rises to enter the presence of God with a purified soul. In Purgatory individuals cleanse themselves of the seven deadly sins and rejoice as they prepare to receive divine love.

DORE, GUSTAVE. **THE DORE ILLUSTRATIONS FOR DANTE'S DIVINE COMEDY. 9"x12", 143pp. Dov76, 4.50p.**
These illustrations were Dore's personal favorite work and they are generally regarded as one of his best efforts. This volume reproduces with excellent clarity all 135 plates that Dore produced for **The Inferno, Purgatorio, and Paradiso**. Each plate is accompanied by appropriate lines from the Henry Wadsworth Longfellow translation of Dante's work.

LUKE, HELEN. **DARK WOOD TO WHITE ROSE: A STUDY IN MEANINGS IN DANTE'S DIVINE COMEDY. 4.50p.**
See the Jungian Psychology section.

MILANO, PAOLO ed. **THE PORTABLE DANTE. Long introduction, notes, 704pp. Vik69, 4.95p.**
This volume contains Laurence Binyon's complete verse translation of **The Divine Comedy** along with the entire Rossetti version of **The New Life**, and letters, shorter poems, and selected prose.

SAYERS, DOROTHY, tr. **THE DIVINE COMEDY, VOLUME I: HELL. Glossary, 346pp. Vik49, 2.25p.**
This is a fine poetic translation of **The Inferno**, accompanied by extensive commentary and a lengthy introduction.

SAYERS, DOROTHY, tr. **DIVINE COMEDY, VOLUME II: PURGATORY. Bibliography, 387pp, Vik55, 2.95p.**
A verse translation of the least known portion of Dante's trilogy, again including an excellent, long introduction, many commentaries, and an extensive glossary.

SAYERS, DOROTHY and BARBARA REYNOLDS, trs. **THE DIVINE COMEDY, VOLUME III: PARADISE. 400+pp. Vik62, 2.50p.**
This poetic translation is of the same superb quality as Ms. Sayers' other volumes. Ms. Reynolds finished the work after Ms. Sayers' death. A long introduction, extensive commentaries, lengthy glossary, and a fold out *organization of Paradise* chart are included.

———END OF DANTE ALIGHIERI SUBSECTION———

DAVID, ALEXANDER. **JESUS THE CHRIST—HIS SECOND COMING: PROPHECIES, VISIONS, VISITATIONS. 225pp. Wat77, 7.80p.**
Brother Alexander David believes he has been given the job of informing people that Christ's Second Coming is imminent. He digs out many of the biblical passages relating to the Second Coming,

compares them to others concerned with the present day, and interprets the passages in the light of certain visionary experiences he has undergone. He says there will be a third world war fought in the Middle East, against a global background of deteriorating economic and social conditions and the effect of a major cosmic event, perhaps a comet. After this *Christ will return in glory, to reign on earth as King under God.* The first part of the book contains biblical prophecy; the second reveals some of the visions and visitations which have inspired the author.

DE JAEGHER, PAUL, ed. **AN ANTHOLOGY OF CHRISTIAN MYSTI-CISM. 192pp. Tpg77, 7.95c.**
This excellent anthology includes selections from the writings of John of Ruysbroeck, Henry Suso, Richard Rolle, John Tauler, Juliana of Norwich, St. Catherine of Siena, Walter Hilton, St. Catherine of Genoa, St. Teresa of Avila, St. John of the Cross, St. Francis de Sales, Augustine Baker, Louis Lallemant, John Joseph Surin, Mary of St. Teresa, and John Peter de Caussade. The translations are from a wide variety of sources and are uniformly good.

Dionysius the Areopagite

Dionysius was believed to have lived in the first century and to have been converted by St. Paul in Athens. About 500 some writings appeared in his name; many believe these to be forgeries written by a Christian Neoplatonist. Whatever their source, they became of decisive importance for the theology and spirituality of Eastern Orthodoxy and Western Catholicism.

ROLT, C.E., tr. **DIONYSIUS THE AREOPAGITE: THE DIVINE NAMES AND THE MYSTICAL THEOLOGY. Indices, 230pp. SCK 20, 10.25p.**
This is a somewhat archaic translation of all of Dionysius' extant writings. Extensive notes accompany the text.

SHRINE OF WISDOM, eds. **THE DIVINE NAMES. 91pp. ShW57, 5.60c.**
In this treatise the writer gathers together and explains a number of the symbolic Names by which the nature of the Supreme and Absolute God is revealed in the Scriptures of the Old and New Testaments. . . . Dionysius speaks of two aspects of the nature of the Supreme God—the undifferentiated and the differentiated. . . . The consideration of each of these Attributes or Names is accompanied by a philosophical exposition of its nature and its relation to the universe and the human soul which, by turning to the Divine in prayer, opening the mind to true illuminations of His nature, and imitating, as far as possible, the Divine activity, may ultimately be led upward to union with God.—from the introduction. No one knows who Dionysius was; however, nearly every great medieval scholar made use of his writings, and his authority came to be almost final.

SHRINE OF WISDOM, eds. **MYSTICAL THEOLOGY AND THE CELESTIAL HIERARCHIES. 73pp. ShW65, 5.60c.**
This is a great classic which is little known today and which contains the very essence and foundation of true Christian mysticism.

——END OF DIONYSIUS THE AREOPAGITE SUBSECTION——

EBERLE, LUKE, tr. **THE RULE OF THE MASTER. Notes, bibliography, 291pp. Cis77, 12.95c.**
A collection of ancient monastic rules compiled in the ninth century by Benedict of Aniane, *a veritable rule of life encompassing the entire existence, material and spiritual of the monastic community and the individuals within it. By turns are treated the monks' virtues and the monastery's organization, grand perspectives of Christian life and minor details of observance—and these not at all cursorily or by allusion. . . but at length and in depth. . . .No less characteristic is the care the Master took to order and inter-relate the various parts of the book.*—from the preface.

Meister Eckhart

Eckhart (1260-1327) was the greatest German speculative mystic, the founder of the school of *Rhineland Mystics,* and the ancestor of German Protestantism, romanticism, idealism, and existentialism. He was essentially a preacher, and his most significant works are transcripts from sermons he delivered in medieval German. Some of his bold expressions about the soul's union with God were condemned by the Inquisition. Although his philosophy amalgamates Greek, Neoplatonic, Arabic, and scholastic elements, it is unique. His doctrine, sometimes abstruse, always arises from one simple personal mystical experience to which he gives a number of names. The teachings of the mature Eckhart describe four stages of the union between the soul and God: dissimilarity, similarity, identity, breakthrough. At the outset, God is all, the creature is nothing; at the ultimate stage, *the soul is above God.* The driving power of this process is detachment.

BLAKNEY, RAYMOND, tr. **MEISTER ECKHART. 330pp. H&R41, 4.50p.**
This book contains up to date versions of a full selection of his sermons, as well as the first modern rendering of Eckhart's defense at being branded a heretic, notes, and some historical perspective.

KELLEY, C.F. **MEISTER ECKHART ON DIVINE KNOWLEDGE. Notes, index, 300pp. YUP77, 24.85c.**
The writings of the medieval theologian known as Meister Eckart were widely regarded as heretical in his own time, and certain of his doctrines were condemned by the church in 1328. In Kelley's view Eckhart was misunderstood then and he has been misunderstood ever since. To comprehend his teachings it is necessary, Kelley believes, only to follow Eckhart's own injunction to *think principially,* that is, from the standpoint of the infinite principle, as if one were in the mind of God. Eckhart believed that to do so was both possible and imperative because of the extremely close relationship between man and God. Kelley, a former Benedictine monk, has devoted thirty years to the study of Eckhart.

SCHURMANN, REINER, tr. **MEISTER ECKHART: MYSTIC AND PHILOSOPHER. Introduction, notes, bibliography, index, 283pp. IUP78, 17.50c.**
New translations of eight key sermons, with extensive commentary, which show the relevance and use of some of Eckhart's ideas in contemporary thought, especially that of Heidegger and D.T. Suzuki. Schurmann explores the mystical doctrines of Eckhart's writings, places them in their context in the history of philosophy, and compares them with other medieval formulations. He illuminates Eckhart's sources in Aristotelian and Neoplatonic philosophy and at the same time emphasizes what is original in his teachings. Perhaps the most powerful part of Schurmann's exegesis is his analysis of the uniqueness of Eckhart's language and usage, which he employs to clarify the special meaning and message of Eckhart.

——END OF MEISTER ECKHART SUBSECTION——

EDWARDS, TILDEN. **LIVING SIMPLY THROUGH THE DAY. Illustrations, 233pp. Pau77, 5.95p.**
Edwards is an Episcopal priest who has been active in ecumenical work and involved in many spiritual traditions. He begins this volume with an account of his own spiritual odyssey and then takes the reader

through certain basic windows of the day: waking, praying, relating, serving, eating, playing, aching, and sleeping. Each window is but a different facet of the same diamond through which we can see and participate in the uniting Ground, in the Holy One who shines through us all. He observes that, *we cannot control this "shining through" in us. That is a matter of grace, of gift. But we can learn to pay simple attention to what is happening; to be "recollected" in our deeper identity, rather than lost and scattered on the complex surface of the day.*

ELCHANINOV, ALEXANDER. **THE DIARY OF A RUSSIAN PRIEST.** 255pp. Fab67, 7.95c.
Fragments from the diary of a Russian emigre priest who died in 1934. He was deeply rooted in the spiritual and ascetic tradition of the Orthodox Church and at the same time closely in touch with the intellectual movements of his own day. He writes on themes of universal concern and relates orthodox spirituality to concrete life situations.

ELDER, E. ROZANNE, ed. **THE SPIRITUALITY OF WESTERN CHRISTENDOM.** Notes, 252pp. Cis76, 7.95p.
The essays in this collection were originally presented as lectures during a three week workshop at which scholars from several academic disciplines explored the roots and expressions of Western spirituality by analyzing specific persons within the tradition. Scholar in residence during the workshop was Jean Leclercq. The individuals discussed include Dionysius the Areopagite, Augustine of Hippo, Bernard of Clairvaux, William of St. Thierry, Francis of Assisi, Martin Luther, and John Calvin.

FAIRWEATHER, WILLIAM. **AMONG THE MYSTICS. Index,** 145pp. TTC36, 2.25c.
A dry exploration of the basic features of Christian mysticism accompanied by discussions of some of the most important Christian mystics.

FEDOTOV, G.P., ed. **A TREASURY OF RUSSIAN SPIRITUALITY.** Bibliography, 501pp. S&W50, 8.40p.
Representative selections from Russian Orthodox spiritual writing from the eleventh to the twentieth century. The material is well translated and the selections are often quite lengthy.

St. Francis of Assisi

Born to comfort and a world of ease; he rejected both—embraced poverty, disease, suffering, with ecstasy and joy. And so he caught the imagination of the world that had to believe that the weak, the sick, the hungry would inherit heaven, that there was virtue in suffering. And in his own lifetime St. Francis became a mythic figure, curing the sick, feeding the hungry, gloating almost in his own pain as a precious gift of God. He reidentified the Christian message in a vivid human way with the teaching of Christ. Also he managed—just—to stay within the confines of the Catholic Church and therefore helped to generate one of its periods of reform and renewal. He and his little band of brothers, and his sister, Ste. Claire, lived haphazaardly the life of religious ecstasy and practice. But he, too, had his St. Paul in Brother Elias, who formalized the movement, turning St. Francis into the Franciscans—one of the great crusading powers of the late Middle Ages.
—*from the introduction to* **St. Francis of Assisi,** *by Morris Bishop*

ARMSTRONG, EDWARD. **ST. FRANCIS: NATURE MYSTIC. Notes,** index, 270pp. UCP73, 5.95p.
Though St. Francis (1182-1226) is closely identified with the love of nature, this interest has been dealt with only incidentally by previous scholars. Mr. Armstrong's study of the nature stories and the manner of their incorporation in the Franciscan legend sheds light on our understanding of the saint, the outlook of his age, and the character of the movement he created. He contends that the church, both before and after St. Francis, failed to understand the contribution that nature mystics could make to it and stresses that delight in nature as God's

handiwork and compassion for all living things is an integral part of the Christian heritage. Each of the animals that St. Francis came in contact with is detailed in legend and in a chapter devoted to it, as well as in the more general material.

■ BEDOYERE, MICHAEL DE LA. **FRANCIS.** 288pp. Fon62, 1.95p.
A beautifully written biographical study which brings to life Francis the man and the main incidents in his life. It is a moving book, dramatically describing St. Francis' inner and outer struggles without ever becoming sentimental or romantic. This is one of the best biographies for the general reader.

BISHOP, MORRIS. **ST. FRANCIS OF ASSISI. Introduction, index,** 237pp. LBC74, 3.95p.
This is a very well written biographical study, aimed at giving the general reader a feeling for St. Francis and the environment in which he lived. Bishop was a classical scholar, specializing in French and Italian history and literature.

■ BROWN, RAPHAEL, tr. **THE LITTLE FLOWERS OF SAINT FRANCIS.** 359pp. Dou58, 2.45p.
This book was written 100 years after the death of St. Francis to try to capture the true spirit of his life and the Franciscan way for the followers of that time. It has come to us as the classic gospel of the great saint. This edition contains twenty chapters never published in English before, and is considered the definitive presentation of these legends. It also includes a long, enlightening introduction on the background of the book and its historical significance; a biography of St. Francis and biographical sketches of the principle characters in the book; and notes, appendices, and a bibliography. In addition, the texts of the following works are included: *The Five Considerations on the Holy Stigmata, The Life of Brother Juniper, The Life of Brother Giles,* and *The Sayings of Brother Giles.*

CHESTERTON, G.K. **ST. FRANCIS OF ASSISI.** 158pp. Dou24, 1.75p.
A biographical study in which the author's own feelings and interpretations are intermingled with the narrative of Francis' life. This has been a consistently popular book and is quite well regarded.

■ CUNNINGHAM, LAURENCE, ed. **BROTHER FRANCIS. Introduction,** 20lpp. OSV72, 1.25p.
This is a topical anthology of writings by and about St. Francis. The book begins with some interpretations of St. Francis and then goes on to give selections from **Little Flowers.** Other chapters include *Francis of Assisi and Nature, Francis on Poverty and Solitude, Francis and Women, Francis the Mystic,* and *The Prayers of St. Francis.* Each is illustrated by several essays, all from different authors. Cunningham's tapestry gives the reader an excellent feeling for St. Francis the man and for his teachings and life.

ENGLEBERT, OMER. **ST. FRANCIS OF ASSISI. Index,** 627pp. FHP65, 8.50c.
This classic biography has been edited by Raphael Brown and Ignatius Brade, two noted Franciscan scholars; they have also added eight appendices and many notes. There is a 110 page research bibliography as well.

EVERYMAN'S LIBRARY EDITION. **SAINT FRANCIS OF ASSISI. Introduction, bibliography,** 410pp. Dut73/Den, 9.95c.
Translations of **The Little Flowers, The Mirror of Perfection,** and **St. Bonaventure's Life of St. Francis.** It is not clear who the translators are, but these translations do seem to be works of good scholarship. The complete text of each is offered.

FAHY, BENEN, tr. **THE WRITINGS OF ST. FRANCIS OF ASSISI. Bibliography, index,** 200pp. FHP64, 4.95c.
Translations of *The Rule and Life of the Friars Minor, I Decided to Send You a Letter, The Spirit of Holy Prayer and Devotion,* and a number of lesser writings. Placid Hermann provides a lengthy introduction and notes.

GOUDGE, ELIZABETH. **ST. FRANCIS OF ASSISI.** 288pp. Hod59, 2.25p.
A novelistic reconstruction of the life, work, and thought of St. Francis. *My only excuse is that I wanted to write it so much that I had to, my hope is that it may serve to introduce St. Francis to a few who do not know him well and perhaps make them want to know him better.* The narrative reads well and this is probably the easiest way to get a feeling for the man.

JORGENSEN, JOHANNES. **ST. FRANCIS OF ASSISI. Detailed notes, index, 354pp. Dou12, 2.45p.**
This is the most detailed of all the countless biographies of St. Francis. Jorgensen, one of Europe's most distinguished authors, spent years researching this material. In addition to being a work of impeccable scholarship, the biography reads well.

KAZANTZAKIS, NIKOS. **ST. FRANCIS. 379pp. S&S62, 4.95p.**
This is a highly personal recreation of the life of St. Francis by one of the twentieth century's most passionate writers. The presentation is more dramatic than the other biographical studies.

THE LITTLE FLOWERS OF ST. FRANCIS (A RECORDING). 7.55.
A nice 33 1/3 rpm recording of selections from St. Francis' writings. Included are his sermon to the birds, his conversion of a wolf, his stigmatization, and two selections from **The Life of Friar Juniper.**

MOCKLER, ANTHONY. **FRANCIS OF ASSISI: THE WANDERING YEARS. Notes, index, 256pp. Dut76, 9.95c.**
In this important new biography, Mockler, by examining all the relevant contemporary sources for Francis' life, convincingly explains much that has seemed paradoxical about St. Francis' life and behavior. He carefully details the social, political, and religious background to Francis' early life and subsequent teaching. He shows how various crucial influences such as the possible Cathar leanings of his father and the traditions of courtly love and knightly prowess, colored Francis' thinking and shaped his often outrageous behavior. A carefully researched, penetrating study.

MOORMAN, JOHN. **RICHEST OF POOR MEN: THE SPIRITUALITY OF ST. FRANCIS OF ASSISI. 110pp. OSV77, 2.95p.**
In this book no attempt is made to tell the story of the life of St. Francis, as this has been done so often. All that is attempted here is to describe certain aspects of his life and his personality and ideals, using mainly the sources written by himself, or by those who actually knew and loved him or who wrote about him shortly after his death.—from the foreword.

THOMAS OF CELANO. **SAINT FRANCIS OF ASSISI. Introduction, many notes, index, 459pp. FHP63, 3.25p.**
A translation from the Latin of Thomas of Celano's **First** and **Second Life of St. Francis,** along with **Selections from his Treatise on the Miracles of Blessed Francis.**

TIMMERMANS, FELIX. **THE PERFECT JOY OF ST. FRANCIS. 276pp. Dou55, 2.50p.**
A biography which reveals a deep understanding of the man and offers a penetrating interpretation of the ideals and humor which have made Francis so appealing throughout the ages. It reveals the whole man: poet, ascetic, servant of the poor, and miracle worker. Translated into English by Raphael Brown.

TRETTEL, EFREM. **FRANCIS. Many photographs, 224pp. FHP75, 4.95p.**
A simple, illustrated review of St. Francis' life and work which was originally compiled for an Italian radio broadcast.

———END OF ST. FRANCIS OF ASSISI SUBSECTION———

FRANCIS DE SALES, SAINT. **INTRODUCTION TO THE DEVOUT LIFE. Introduction, 261pp. Dut61, 5.00c.**
A dry translation, part of **Everyman's Library,** of a book that is generally considered the finest and most usable devotional classic to come out of the Catholic Renaissance. It penetrates into the universal human condition and gives guidance for an active life in the midst of the world's problems and needs.

FRANCIS DE SALES, SAINT. **INTRODUCTION TO THE DEVOUT LIFE. Introduction, many notes, index, 315pp. Dou66, 2.45p.**
A readable, modern translation by John Ryan, generally considered the finest available.

FRANCK, FREDERICK. **THE BOOK OF ANGELUS SILESIUS. 4.95p.**
See the Zen Buddhism section.

FRIELING, RUDOLF. **THE ESSENCE OF CHRISTIANITY. 31pp. CCP71, 1.00p.**
A mystical presentation of Christian cosmology, written by a follower of Rudolf Steiner's Anthroposophy.

FULLERSON, MARY. **BY A NEW AND LIVING WAY. 88pp. ShP63, 2.50p.**
An interpretation of the inner meaning of the sacrament of the Last Supper.

FULLERSON, MARY. **THE FORM OF THE FOURTH. 86pp. ShP71, 2.50p.**
A sequel to **By a New and Living Way,** discussing how man can combat the inimical forces in the world and focusing on the **Book of Daniel.**

FURSE. MARGARET. **MYSTICISM: WINDOW ON A WORLD VIEW. 5.95p.**
See the Mysticism section.

FURST, JEFFREY. **EDGAR CAYCE'S STORY OF JESUS. 413pp. Ber68/Spe, 1.95p.**
This compilation brings together the story of Jesus, as found scattered throughout the Cayce readings. Furst also supplies commentary on the selections. Topics include *In the Beginning, On Soul Development, The Essenes, The Nativity, The Early Years and Ministry, Crucifixion and Resurrection, The Early Church,* and *The Church of Laodicea.* The nature of the readings and the language used in them does not make this work the clearest story available, but many insights are offered.

GARDNER, EDMUND. **THE CELL OF SELF-KNOWLEDGE. Introduction, index, 157pp. CSq66, 5.40c.**
A collection of seven mystical treatises by Richard of St. Victor, St. Catherine of Siena, Margery Kemp, and Walter Hilton—first printed in 1521.

GASCOIGNE, BAMBER. **THE CHRISTIANS. Index, 7"x10", 304pp. Mor77/CaL, 17.50c.**
There are two ways of writing a short book on a vast subject. One is the potted survey, where everyone appears in the index but very little is added about them in the text. The other is a more impressionistic approach. It is the way of a photographer, choosing certain significant images to suggest a broader scene. And it is the way best suited to the text of an illustrated book, highlighting certain moments at the price of excluding others. We have chosen thirteen themes, each rich in material for both the camera and the pen, which together span the 2,000 years of Christian history. Such a book must deal in concrete terms. **The Christians** *is therefore about people, events and places rather than theory or theology. It is, we hope, less exhaustive than survey: but more real.* Over 250 photographs, many in color, are included.

GIBRAN, KAHLIL. **JESUS, THE SON OF MAN. 216pp. RaH28/HeG, 8.95c.**
Gibran extends his sensitive imagination into the realm of Jesus' day to day life, writing stories as they might have been told to him by people who knew and loved and learned from Jesus in the flesh.

GOSWAMI, SHYAM SUNDAR. **JESUS CHRIST AND YOGA. 143pp. Fow nd, 6.00c.**
An examination of Christ's life by an Indian yogi, pointing out the disciplines and ways in which Jesus sustained and developed his life force and great power of love in order to lead us to that divine inner being where we can truly be ourselves.

GRAHAM, DOM AELRED. **CONTEMPLATIVE CHRISTIANITY. Index, 140pp. Sea74, 6.95c.**
Dom Aelred Graham looks at religious belief in the church and discusses what formal Christianity can gain from an understanding of Eastern meditational practice. Graham is a Benedictine monk who has studied in Japan, Thailand, and India.

GRAHAM, DOM AELRED. **ZEN CATHOLICISM. 2.95p.**
See the Zen Buddhism section.

GRANT, MICHAEL. **JESUS: AN HISTORIAN'S REVIEW OF THE GOSPELS. Glossary, notes, index, 261pp. Scr77, 12.50c.**
Almost all our information about Jesus is found in the four **Gospels**. The **Gospels** probably reached their final form between thirty-five and sixty-five years after Jesus' death. One major problem with the **Gospels** is deciding which portions refer authentically to the career and teaching of Jesus, and which are subsequent additions or inventions. In this book Professor Grant looks at the **Gospels** with an historian's eye, treating them in exactly the same way as he would any other work of ancient literature capable of yielding historical information. The picture which emerges is in some respects a new and unfamiliar one. There was no *gentle Jesus, meek and mild*, says Dr. Grant—nor was Jesus a political revolutionary, as is so often claimed. Jesus ruthlessly subordinated his every act and thought to the success of his great mission. This is a believable, readable account.

GRANT, ROBERT. **EARLY CHRISTIANITY AND SOCIETY. Notes, bibliography, indices, 233pp. H&R77, 10.00c.**
Dr. Grant is Chairman of the Department of New Testament and Early Christian Literature and Humanities at the University of Chicago Divinity School. Here he takes a scholarly look at the relationship of the early Christian church to the surrounding Roman society. The book is based exclusively on original source material and is extensively documented.

GREELEY, ANDREW. **THE MARY MYTH: ON THE FEMININITY OF GOD. Photographs, notes, 236pp. Sea77, 12.95c.**
Greeley, a theologian, uses classic prose, poetry, and art to show that Mary is not only a symbol of the feminine component of the deity, but that she represents the deeply human insight that God is *passionately tender, seductively attractive, irresistibly inspiring and graciously healing.* He points out that Mary is also part of a tradition of female deities, all of whom reflect the human conviction that the Ultimate has feminine as well as masculine characteristics.

GWATKIN, HENRY, tr. **SELECTIONS FROM EARLY CHRISTIAN WRITERS ILLUSTRATIVE OF CHURCH HISTORY TO THE TIME OF CONSTANTINE. Index, 218pp. Cla1897, 3.60c.**
The original Greek and Latin of the texts are on facing pages with the English translation.

HALL, MANLY P. **THE MYSTERY OF THE HOLY SPIRIT. 1.75p.**
See the Mysticism section.

HALL, MANLY P. **THE MYSTICAL CHRIST. Index, 253pp. PRS51, 7.00c.**
A discussion of the ministry of Christ and his principle teachings. Hall draws on the ancient mystery teachings in his presentation.

HEER, FRIEDRICH, ed. **THE FIRES OF FAITH. Index, 9⅛"x11⅛", 160pp. Nws73, 10.00c.**
A survey of the period between AD 312 and AD 1204, emphasizing the turbulent spiritual leaders and movements of the time. Sixteen are studied in depth and these include St. Patrick, who strengthened the Christian Church in Ireland; William the Conqueror; Muhammad; Eric the Red, who introduced Christianity to Greenland; and St. Benedict, who provided a lasting model for monasticism. Supplementing the text are about 300 illustrations, nearly one third in full color, as well as numerous charts, maps, and diagrams.

HEIDENREICH, ALFRED, ed. **THE CATACOMBS. 7½"x10½", 112pp. CCP62, 5.50c.**
The art which can today be found in the Catacombs represents the truest picture available of early Christianity before it became the established religion of the Roman Empire. This collection of sixty-eight color and black and white plates is accompanied by discussions of the spirit and quality of early Christianity, and a detailed structural and symbolic examination of the Catacombs themselves. Heidenreich is an Anthroposophist.

HEINDEL, MAX. **THE ROSICRUCIAN CHRISTIANITY LECTURES. Index, 374pp. Ros39, 4.50p.**
Twenty far ranging lectures on diverse topics relating to a central theme of Christianity and personal evolution. Of interest mainly to metaphysicians.

HELINE, CORINNE. **THE BLESSED VIRGIN MARY. 125pp. NAP71, 5.95c.**
An inspirational volume. Ms. Heline discusses both the historical Mary and the eternal feminine archetype. This interpretation is suggested only to those who are interested in the Western esoteric tradition.

HELINE, CORINNE. **STAR GATES. 198pp. NAP65, 4.95c.**
A discussion of the Christian mystery. Ms. Heline outlines the spiritual significance of the seasons in Christ's ministry as well as the activities of the angelic kingdom.

HOLY ORDER OF MANS. **BOOK OF THE MASTER JESUS, VOLUMES I-III. HOM74, 3.50p/each.**
A vividly written spiritual interpretation of the life and ministry of Jesus. Many quotations from the scriptures are included and the material is presented in chronological order. Volume I covers Jesus' early life, Volume II begins with his ministry, and Volume III traces his life as a teacher through his ascension. Each is about 230 pages long.

HOLY ORDER OF MANS. **THE GOLDEN FORCE. 120pp. HOM75, 3.00p.**
An integrated selection of teaching on living in harmony with the universe that God created and understanding one's purpose in the universal scheme.

HOLY ORDER OF MANS. **THE GOLDEN NUGGETS. 266pp. HOM72, 3.50p.**
A wide ranging anthology of insights into the *reality of the experience of life* by a metaphysical Christian order. The format is topical, and each section is short, so many areas are covered.

HUGEL, FRIEDRICH VON. **THE MYSTICAL ELEMENT OF RELIGION AS STUDIED BY SAINT CATHERINE OF GENOA AND HER FRIENDS. Two volumes, index, 928pp. Cla23, 28.00c/set.**
I was attracted at first, and I became more and more interested later on, in the saint of Genoa, not because of any immediately practicable suggestions furnished by her for my own life or that of others, but by certain rich and spiritual graces and deep and delicate doctrines hardly to be found elsewhere in as clear an articulation. Then, too, there was her outlook . . . which raised the whole great question as to the need and place of history and institutions in the spiritual life. And, finally, I here found rarely clear contrasts between genuine contemplative states and the more or less simply psycho-physical conditions which dogged them—conditions clearly perceived by the Saint, and by her alone, to be "maladif" and merely the price paid for the states which alone were of spiritual worth and significance. Evelyn Underhill calls this book the best work on mysticism in the English language.

HUMBER, THOMAS. **THE SACRED SHROUD. Illustrations, bibliography, 222pp. S&S77, 1.95p.**
A detailed, easy to read discussion of the shroud of Turin. Humber cites and evaluates all the evidence.

IGNATIUS, SAINT. **THE SPIRITUAL EXERCISES OF ST. IGNATIUS. Introduction, 200pp. Dou64, 1.95p.**
This volume, one of the great masterpieces of ascetical theology, is the fruit of the saint's own experiences and meditations and was used to

guide himself and others toward spiritual perfection. Since St. Ignatius completed the **Exercises** in 1533, they have been universally recognized as a brilliant and inspired guide to the development of a deeper Christian spirituality. They were intended to be useful to people in all states of life and spiritual conditions. This is a modern translation by Anthony Mottola.

IGNATIUS, SAINT. **THE SPIRITUAL EXERCISES OF ST. IGNATIUS LOYOLA.** Introduction, 124pp., ACB63, 3.95c.
In this book the translator, Father Thomas Corbishley, has made a deliberate attempt to find alternate renderings for many of the most hackneyed phrases of Christian ascetic writing. His goal is to present St. Ignatius' thoughts in language which will bring out his meaning most effectively and faithfully.

IVES, PHILIP, ed. **THE NATIVITY IN STAINED GLASS.** 8.95p.
See the Sacred Art section.

JASPERS, KARL. **ANSELM AND NICHOLAS OF CUSA.** Bibliography, index, 188pp. HBJ66, 3.50p.
The bulk of this volume is devoted to Nicholas of Cusa; the section on Anselm only covers twenty-five pages. Nicholas' basic ideas are very fully discussed in an organized, textbook-like manner and a great deal of background information on the man and the times is offered. An excellent work of scholarship. Extracted from Jaspers' **The Great Philosophers**, Volume II.

St. John of the Cross

St. John of the Cross (1542-1591) was a close associate of St. Teresa of Avila and was one of the first members of the Discalced Order of Carmelite friars which she founded. During his life he was noted for the rigor of his conduct, and for his emphasis on internal meditation and silent prayer. He is regarded by many as Spain's major poet as well as one of the greatest Catholic mystics.

As Kieran Kavanaugh says, *St. John gives witness to the sublime realities of the mystical life and of experiential union with God. However, John was also a theorizer and was able to make use of his philosophical, theological, and scriptural background in constructing a doctrinal synthesis of the spiritual life. But the purpose of his theory was to help clarify the issues for his readers and assist them in their journey up the mount of perfection to the perfect union with God. For John, God is like fire and man like a cold, damp, and dark log of wood. Through a process of purification and transformation effected by the fire of God's life, man can be gradually converted from his darkness and take on the properties of God's own fire, the light of His wisdom and the heat of His love....In his major works...St. John of the Cross treats mainly of how one reaches perfection (or union with God), and of the life of divine union itself. In brief, this union is reached through the practice of the theological virtues, which purify the soul and unite it with God. The life of union with God is a life of perfect faith, hope, and charity.*

BARNSTONE, WILLIS, tr. **THE POEMS OF ST. JOHN OF THE CROSS.** Notes, bibliography, 124pp. NDP68, 1.95p.
Barnstone provides an illuminating introduction in addition to his translation of the poems. The original Spanish version is on facing pages.

BRENAN, GERALD and LYNDA NICHOLSON. **ST. JOHN OF THE CROSS.** Notes, bibliography, index, 233pp. CUP73, 6.50p.
This is the only full biography available which includes the complete poems in both Spanish and English. Brenan covers St. John's childhood and education, his association with St. Teresa, his imprisonment, torture, and escape, and his final official disgrace and death. He writes with great sensitivity. The translations by Lynda Nicholson give the reader something very near the poems' literal prose sense, yet catch in many places the rhythm and intonation of the original. The Spanish version is on the facing page.

CAMPBELL, ROY, tr. **POEMS OF ST. JOHN OF THE CROSS.** 90pp. G&D67, 1.95p.
A bilingual collection.

HAMILTON, ELIZABETH, ed. and tr. **THE VOICE OF THE SPIRIT.** 128pp. OSV76/DLT, 2.95p.
Ms. Hamilton combines an introduction to the life and work of St. John of the Cross with excerpts from his major writings; **The Ascent of Mount Carmel, The Dark Night of the Soul, The Spiritual Canticle,** and **The Living Flame of Love**.

■ *KAVANAUGH, KIERAN and OTILIO RODRIGUEZ, trs.* **THE COLLECTED WORKS OF ST. JOHN OF THE CROSS.** 740pp. ICS64, 5.95p.
Kieran Kavanaugh is a professor of spiritual theology at the Carmelite College of Theology and Otilio Rodriguez is a Spanish scholar who has a thorough familiarity with the works of St. John. This volume is carefully done; the two men spent years preparing and editing it. The introduction is comprehensive and incorporates the most recent historical, doctrinal, and literary studies, mostly in French and Spanish. Included here are full translations of all the major works: **The Ascent of Mount Carmel, The Dark Night, The Spiritual Canticle,** and **The Living Flame of Love**; the minor works; and poetry, with parallel Spanish/English texts. This is the translation for any reader seeking a clear, understandable statement of St. John's teachings. Includes extensive commentary.

PEERS, E. ALLISON, tr. **ASCENT OF MOUNT CARMEL.** 478pp. Dou58, 2.45p.
Peers is the most noted translator of the works of both St. John and St. Teresa of Avila. His translations are considered very faithful and very well written and he supplies excellent introductions and notes. *On the opening page of the* **Ascent** *St. John indicates the nature of his treatise by declaring his intention to explain how one reaches the high state of perfection. This assertion at the outset plainly marks the practical character of the book. It is a work which describes the path to be followed in order to reach the perfection, which he chooses to call union with God....In addition to setting down rules, the* **Ascent** *gives a keen analysis of the principles which support them.*—Kieran Kavanaugh. Peers' introductory material is nearly 100 pages long.

PEERS, E. ALLISON, tr. **THE COMPLETE WORKS OF ST. JOHN OF THE CROSS.** 1,454pp. ACB74, 28.50c.
All three volumes of Peers' definitive translation bound into one, along with introductory material, bibliography, and indices. The book includes **The Ascent of Mount Carmel, The Dark Night of the Soul, Spiritual Canticle,** and **Living Flame of Love**, along with a miscellany of poems, letters, and minor writings.

PEERS, E. ALLISON, tr. **COUNSELS OF LIGHT AND LOVE.** 95pp. B&O53, 2.95p.
A collection of the following short writings, generally attributed to St. John of the Cross: *The Nine Cautions, Four Counsels to a Religion for the Attainment of Perfection, Sayings of Light and Love,* and *Prayer of a Soul Enkindled with Love,* as well as a number of poems and letters. Thomas Merton supplies a lengthy introduction.

PEERS, E. ALLISON, tr. **DARK NIGHT OF THE SOUL.** 193pp. Dou58, 2.95p/1.75p.
A great and lasting work in the mystical tradition dealing with various stages experienced by the contemplative aspirant and the accompanying characteristics of each progressive stage. St. John's most famous work.

PEERS, E. ALLISON, tr. **THE LIVING FLAME OF LOVE.** 272pp. Dou62, 1.95p.
This is a poem with a commmentary. The poem is the song of a soul that has reached a highly perfect love within the state of transformation. Its stanzas refer to transient, intense, actual unions experienced by one advanced within this state of transformation. The commentary by St. John gives a general summary of each stanza, detailed discussions of each verse, and many doctrinal explanations.

PEERS, E. ALLISON, tr. **SPIRITUAL CANTICLE.** 520pp. Dou61, 2.95p.
This book is a gift of God to man...one of the loveliest poems that the human heart has ever conceived, or the human mind expressed....All can find much in it to instruct and inspire them; and many who have devoted their lives to the love of God count it among the dearest of their possessions.—E. Allison Peers.

POEMS OF ST. JOHN OF THE CROSS (A RECORDING). 6.98.
This 33 1/3 rpm record contains thirteen poems read very effectively in English. Commentary on the poems and the texts of the poems

themselves, in both Spanish and English, are included in the liner notes.

STEUART, R.H.J., ed. **MYSTICAL DOCTRINE OF ST. JOHN OF THE CROSS. 192pp. S&W34, 3.50p.**
It is the peculiar merit and value of the present work that the author has assembled in logical order, in a chain of which each link is an advance in demonstration upon the preceding one, the very words which the saint himself used in elucidation of his own doctrine.—from the introduction. The English translation used in this version is David Lewis'. It is not as flowing as some of the later ones, but it is considered accurate and reasonably faithful to the original. This volume includes portions of **The Ascent of Mount Carmel, The Dark Night of the Soul, The Living Flame of Love,** and **The Spiritual Canticle.**

ZIMMERMAN, BENEDICT, ed. **THE DARK NIGHT OF THE SOUL. Indices, 210pp. Cla24, 8.00c.**
The works of St. John have at times been suppressed and there are various manuscripts, differing slightly in content. Zimmerman has attempted to present all the texts of the most ancient copies of **The Dark Night,** with notes in both Spanish and English. The translation is not as flowing as Peers' and Kavanaugh's, but the introductory and background material are often useful for the serious student.

————END OF ST. JOHN OF THE CROSS SUBSECTION————

JOHN OF FORD. **SERMONS ON THE FINAL VERSES OF THE SONG OF SONGS, I. Notes, 268pp. Cis77, 14.95c.**
This translation by Wendy Beckett is the first vernacular edition of John of Ford's commentary on the **Song of Songs.** John of Ford was a twelfth century Cistercian abbot who wrote his commentary with the avowed purpose of leading souls to the love of God which enflamed him. Other Cistercians, Bernard of Clairvaux and Gilbert of Hoyland, had written commentaries on the first five chapters of the **Song of Songs.** John of Ford completed the Cistercian commentary. Hilary Costello contributes a lengthy introductory essay.

JOHN OF RUYSBROECK. **JOHN OF RUYSBROECK. Notes, 291pp. CCl74, 16.80p.**
This is a recent reprint of Evelyn Underhill's edited version of C.A. Wynschenk Dom's translation. Three of his most important works (**The Adornment of the Spiritual Marriage, The Sparkling Stone,** and **The Book of Supreme Truth**) are included here. Jan van Ruysbroeck is the greatest of the Flemish mystics, and must take high rank in any list of Christian contemplatives and saints. This is the only edition currently in print and the only English translation extant of this fourteenth century mystic. It is important reading for all who are deeply interested in mystical insights and in contemplation. In addition to the translations, there is a long introduction by Ms. Underhill.

JOHNSTON, WILLIAM. **CHRISTIAN ZEN. 3.50p.**
See the Zen Buddhism section.

JONES, FRANKLIN, ed. **SPIRITUAL INSTRUCTIONS OF ST. SERAPHIM OF SANOV. 94pp. DHP73, 2.50p.**
St. Seraphim (1759-1833) is one of the greatest saints of the Eastern Orthodox tradition. He applied himself to Christian and, in particular, Eastern Christian spiritual techniques, including the *prayer of the heart,* but the intensity of his life, realization, and spiritual work places him among those transcendent spiritual beings who stand outside tradition, orthodoxy, dogma, and history. This volume includes an introduction to his life and work by A.F. Dobbie-Bateman and a translation of the *Conversation of St. Seraphim with Nicholas Motovilov.* This text is a report of an actual experience, written by a devotee which describes direct transmission of spiritual consciousness and force.

Juliana of Norwich

Juliana of Norwich (1342-1416) was a celebrated English mystic whose **Revelations of a Divine Love** is generally considered one of the most remarkable documents of medieval religious experience. It came out of an experience in 1373 when she was healed of a serious illness after experiencing a series of visions of Christ's suffering. She wrote two different accounts of this experience; the second, longer version was composed twenty or thirty years after the first. **Revelations** spans the most profound mysteries of the Christian faith, including the problem of predestination, the foreknowledge of God, and the existence of evil. The clarity and depth of her perception, the precision and accuracy of her theological presentation, and the sincerity and beauty of her expression, reveal a mind and personality of exceptional strength and charm. In writing down her revelations, she hoped that all who read them would heartily thank God *for his endless love, mercy and goodness and guide us to everlasting bliss.*

COLLEDGE, EDMUND and JAMES WALSH, trs. **SHOWINGS. Bibliography, long index, 369pp. Pau78, 6.95p.**
This is the most authoritative translation available of both the long and short version of Juliana's revelations. The text is printed in large type and translated into contemporary English. The translators also provide an abundance of textual notes as well as a lengthy introduction analyzing the text and the place of Juliana's teaching in Catholic spirituality. In a preface Jean Leclercq addresses himself to the question, *Why is this an important work today?*

MASTRO, M.L., DEL, tr. **REVELATIONS OF DIVINE LOVE. Bibliography, 240pp. Dou77, 2.45p.**
This is an excellent new translation, based on the later and longer version of **Revelations,** restating the substance and feeling of the work in contemporary language. Mastro includes a seventy-nine page introduction examining Juliana the woman, her message, and the manuscript sources for **Revelations.**

REYNOLDS, MARIA, ed. **A SHOWING OF GOD'S LOVE. Introductory material, glossary, notes, 156pp. S&W58, 5.15p.**
This is a *Shorter Version* of **Sixteen Revelations of Divine Love.** This shorter version is generally thought to have been written down soon after the visions occurred, while the longer version includes additional teaching that she received. It is a more personal, and less formal work than the longer one. The language in this version has been modernized somewhat—although it retains a strong flavor of the original.

WALSH, JAMES, tr. **THE REVELATIONS OF DIVINE LOVE OF JULIANA OF NORWICH. 210pp. ACB61, 3.95p.**
In this edition Father Walsh has retained the original Middle English vocabulary, syntax, and idiom and has simply modernized the spelling and punctuation of the longer version manuscripts. He also contributes an excellent, long introduction.

WOLTERS, CLIFTON, tr. **REVELATIONS OF DIVINE LOVE. Bibliography, 213pp. Pen66, 2.50p.**
A fine, accurate translation which retains the cadences of the original work. Wolters also supplies a lengthy introduction.

————END OF JULIANA OF NORWICH SUBSECTION————

JURGENS, WILLIAM. **THE FAITH OF THE EARLY FATHERS, VOLUME I. Indices, 474pp. Ltu70, 6.75p.**
A sourcebook of theological and historical passages from the writings of the Ante-Nicene and Nicene eras.

KADLOUBOVKSY, E. and G.E.H. PALMER. **THE ART OF PRAYER. 287pp. Fab66, 10.95c.**
This is a collection of texts on prayer, drawn from Greek and Russian sources. The spiritual teaching of the Orthodox Church appears here in its classic and traditional form, but expressed in unusually direct and vivid language. The material was compiled by Igumen Chariton of Valamo.

KADLOUBOVSKY, E. and G.E.H. PALMER, trs. **EARLY FATHERS OF THE PHILOKALIA. 421pp. Fab54, 13.95c.**
This book is drawn from the great collection of writings of fathers of the Orthodox Church which was compiled in the eighteenth century under the title, **Philokalia.** This volume contains a representative collection of writings from between the third and seventh centuries, embracing the immense scope of the doctrines, knowledge and practices of saints who reached the highest levels of spiritual attainment.

KADLOUBOVSKY, E. and G.E.H. PALMER, trs. UNSEEN WARFARE. 280pp. Mow52, 8.85p.
A translation of the Spiritual Combat and Path to Paradise of Lorenzo Scupoli as edited by Nicodemus of the Holy Mountain and revised by Theophan the Recluse. Scupoli was a sixteenth century Venetian priest and Nicodemus and Theophan were both fathers of the Eastern Church. The work is rich in its references to the teachings of the Eastern and Western Churches on the spiritual combat which is the road to perfection. As Theophan says in his foreword, *The arena, the field of battle, the site where the fight actually takes place is our own heart and all our inner man. The time of battle is our whole life.* This edition contains a sixty-nine page introduction by Professor H.A. Hodges.

KADLOUBOVSKY, E. and G.E.H. PALMER, trs. WRITINGS FROM THE PHILOKALIA ON THE PRAYER OF THE HEART. 420pp. Fab51, 13.95c.
This is the most popular of the Philokalia books. In their writings the fathers show the way to awaken and develop attention and consciousness. They also discuss the *Jesus Prayer* at length and illustrate the means of acquiring training in what the fathers called *the art of arts and the science of sciences*, leading a man toward the highest perfection open to him. We highly recommend this work to all who are interested in the spirituality of the Eastern Church.

KAISER, A. FABER. JESUS DIED IN KASHMIR: JESUS, MOSES AND THE TEN LOST TRIBES OF ISRAEL. Notes, bibliography, index, 192pp. Cre77, 9.95c.
Kaiser has assembled an arresting body of evidence which supports a completely new conception of Jesus. He has found a group of people living in Kashmir today who call themselves the *Children of Israel* and who venerate a tomb they attribute to Christ. Among them is a man who claims to be a direct descendent of Jesus. Kaiser examines the evidence to show that Christ survived the ordeal of the Cross, went East, founded the *Children of Israel*, married, had children, and died of old age, fulfilling his mission on Earth. This is a fascinating study which should appeal to all who seek more information on Christ's last years.

KAZANTZAKIS, NIKOS. THE LAST TEMPTATION OF CHRIST. 506pp. S&S60, 4.95p.
In order to mount to the cross, the summit of sacrifice, and to God, the summit of immateriality, Christ passed through all the stages which the man who struggles passes through. This is why his suffering is so familiar to us; that is why we share it.... Every part of Christ's life is a conflict and a victory. He conquered the invincible enchantment of simple human pleasures; he conquered temptations, continually transubstantiated flesh into spirit, and ascended....—Nikos Kazantzakis. This is a fascinating novelistic rendition of the last years of Jesus' life.

KAZANTZAKIS, NIKOS. SAVIORS OF GOD. Introduction, notes, 146pp. S&S60, 2.95p.
I am writing Spiritual Exercises, a mystical book wherein I trace a method by which the spirit may rise from cycle to cycle until it reaches the supreme Contact. There are five cycles, Ego, Humanity, Earth, the Universe, God. I describe how we ascend all these steps, and when we reach the highest how we live simultaneously all the previous cycles.... The search itself—upward, and with coherence—perhaps this is the purpose of the Universe. Purpose and means become identified... God is the supreme expression of the unwearied and struggling man. This book is a collection of poetic aphorisms on the spiritual life and on union with God.

KELLY, J.N.D. EARLY CHRISTIAN DOCTRINES. Notes, index, 523pp. H&R78, 6.95p.
A revised edition of a standard history of the first great period in Christian thought, thoroughly updated in the light of the latest historical findings. Dr. Kelly outlines the development of each doctrine in its historical context and lucidly summarizes the genesis of Christian thought from the close of the apostolic age to the Council of Chalcedon in the fifth century. He includes extensive discussions of the doctrine of the Trinity, the authority of the Bible, the nature of Christ, salvation, original sin and grace, and the sacraments.

KELSEY, MORTON. HEALING AND CHRISTIANITY. Notes, bibliography, index, 409pp. H&R73, 5.95p.
A comprehensive history of sacramental healing in the Christian Church from biblical times to the present. Kelsey has been influenced by the psychology of Carl Jung.

KELSEY, MORTON. MYTH, HISTORY, AND FAITH. Notes, 185pp. Pau74, 4.95p.
Kelsey, an Episcopal minister, theologian, Jungian analyst, and educator, invites his readers to rediscover their ancient heritage of symbol making. *Life without myth,* he says, *is likely to be dead and sterile, while religion without myth is a flat, rational substitute for the real thing.... Myth and rituals that spring from it provide the meeting ground on which the nonphysical half of reality makes contact with men.* From this perspective, Kelsey takes a new look at the meaning of the individual, a sense of history, the problems of evil, conversion, Jesus, prayer, and sacrament.

KELSEY, MORTON. THE OTHER SIDE OF SILENCE: A GUIDE TO CHRISTIAN MEDITATION. 5.95p.
See the Meditation section.

KEMP-WELCH, ALICE, tr. THE TUMBLER OF OUR LADY AND OTHER MIRACLES. Introduction, notes, 153pp. CSq66, 6.00c.
An offset edition of a collection of medieval French miracle stories. The medieval tone of the language has been retained and a number of woodblock prints are included.

Thomas a Kempis

For more than five centuries The Imitation of Christ has been acclaimed by people of every faith and belief as one of the greatest spiritual writings of all times. After the Bible it is probably the best known and most influential book in Christendom. Its author, Thomas a Kempis (1380-1471), has a wide knowledge of the scriptures and classical philosophy, and although most of his life was spent in a Dutch monastery, he also possessed a deep understanding of human nature. His acquired wisdom convinced him of man's complete dependence on God's love and the futility of life without it.

EVERYMAN'S LIBRARY. THE IMITATION OF CHRIST. 227pp. Dut60/Den, 2.25p.
A dry translation into modern English.

GARDINER, HAROLD, tr. THE IMITATION OF CHRIST. 236pp. Dou55, 1.75p.
Even though this is labeled a modern version, the translation has an archaic flavor. Gardiner also provides an introduction.

KNOTT, BETTY, tr. **THE IMITATION OF CHRIST. Notes, bibliography, 253pp. Fon63, 1.60p.**
This is a vivid, modern translation. Ms. Knott's introduction is the most complete of any we have seen.

MCELROY, PAUL, ed. **THE IMITATION OF CHRIST. 61pp. PPP65, 2.50c.**
An abridged gift edition, with illustrations.

SHERLEY-PRICE, LEO, tr. **THE IMITATION OF CHRIST. Introduction, notes, 217pp. Vik52, 2.50p.**
My purpose in attempting a completely new version is to provide an accurate, unabridged, and readable modern translation, and thus to introduce this spiritual classic to a wider public.

──────────**END OF THOMAS A KEMPIS SUBSECTION**──────────

LAMSA, GEORGE. **THE HIDDEN YEARS OF JESUS. 149pp. ABS68, 2.50p.**
In an introductory essay Lamsa speculates on Jesus' early life, the years between the ages of twelve and thirty. He asserts that Jesus spent these unknown years at home in Nazareth, one of thousands of young men of similar background about whom we know nothing. The bulk of the book is devoted to parallel **New Testament** and **Old Testament** texts which depict the essence of Jesus' teaching. The two parts of the book do not seem to be related in any way.

LAMSA, GEORGE. **MY NEIGHBOR JESUS IN THE LIGHT OF HIS OWN LANGUAGE, PEOPLE, AND TIMES. Introduction, 166pp. ABS32, 2.00p.**

LANG, D.M. **THE BALAVARIANI. Introductory material, illustrations, notes, index, 187pp. UCa66, 8.00c.**
Throughout medieval Christendom, the *Edifying Story of Barlaam and Josaphat* was accepted as the classic exposition of the ideals of Christian monasticism and asceticism, renunciation of the world and of all human desires and passions. Modern research over the last century has shown that this tale is in reality an adaptation of the legendary biography of Guatama Buddha, in particular the episodes of his miraculous birth, the *four omens*, the *great renunciation*, and his last mission and death. This is a translation of the full Georgian text of the eldest Christian version.

LANTERO, ERMINE. **FEMININE ASPECTS OF DIVINITY. 32pp. PHP73, .85p.**
A brief analysis of the title theme, heavily based on biblical themes.

William Law

Law (1686-1761), an English churchman, was the author of influential works on Christian ethics and mysticism. His chief contribution lies in his delineation of the Christian ethical ideal for human life and its actualization through the disciplined practices of private mysticism.

LAW, WILLIAM. **A SERIOUS CALL TO A DEVOUT AND HOLY LIFE. 158pp. Wes75/Den, 2.45p.**
An edited, abridged version of an eighteenth century devotional classic which was designed to prod indifferent Christians into making an honest effort to live up to what they professed to believe.

LAW, WILLIAM. **THE SPIRIT OF PRAYER, THE SPIRIT OF LOVE. 301pp. Cla67, 8.00c.**
A deep discussion of the timeless communication between God and man.

MORRISON, MARY, ed. **WILLIAM LAW: SELECTIONS ON THE INTERIOR LIFE. 40pp. PHP62, 1.20p.**
A topically organized selection of Law's writings.

TIGHE, RICHARD. **A SHORT ACCOUNT OF THE LIFE AND WRITINGS OF THE LATE REVEREND WILLIAM LAW. Offset, spiral bound, 114pp. HeR1826, 7.00p.**
A reprint of an archaic study of the life and work of William Law bound

together with the author's analysis of Law's propositions relating to the glory and extent of the kingdom of God.

WALKER, A.K. **WILLIAM LAW: HIS LIFE AND HIS WORK. Notes, bibliography, index, 287pp. SCK73, 23.50c.**
A detailed study of Law's character and the whole of his work.

──────────**END OF WILLIAM LAW SUBSECTION**──────────

Brother Lawrence

Brother Lawrence was a seventeenth century Carmelite monk whose only concern was to live in the presence of God. He was deeply convinced that prayer is not saying prayers, but a way of living in which all we do becomes prayer. For Brother Lawrence the practice of the presence of God was not a practice for a few moments a day, not even for a few hours. For him, it permeated every moment of his day and every act of his life. His book is a collection of conversations, letters, and spiritual maxims gathered together by the superior of the monastery in which Brother Lawrence spent his life. It is a classic work which has been a gentle friend and guide for countless souls.

ATTWATER, DONALD, tr. **THE PRACTICE OF THE PRESENCE OF GOD. 6¼"x8", 127pp. Tpg74, 7.95c.**
A gift edition of Brother Lawrence's classic. Attwater's translation is readable and modern and there is a fair amount of introductory material. The book is illustrated with period woodblock prints.

DELANEY, JOHN, tr. **THE PRACTICE OF THE PRESENCE OF GOD. 112pp. Dou77, 2.25p.**
This is the most contemporary translation of Brother Lawrence's work, simply and well presented. The edition includes an introduction that reviews what is known about Lawrence's life, how the book came to be, and its ongoing relevance throughout the ages.

PETER PAUPER PRESS. **THE PRACTICE OF THE PRESENCE OF GOD. PPP63, 2.50c.**
An abridged, illustrated gift edition.

──────────**END OF BROTHER LAWRENCE SUBSECTION**──────────

LEADBEATER, C.W. **THE CHRISTIAN CREED: ITS ORIGIN AND SIGNIFICANCE. 3.00p.**
See the Theosophy section.

LEADBEATER, C.W. **THE SCIENCE OF THE SACRAMENTS. 12.95c.**
See the Theosophy section.

LEVI. **THE AQUARIAN GOSPEL OF JESUS THE CHRIST. 270pp. DeV07, 6.95c/3.50p.**
This is the story of Jesus' life and ministry. It was revealed to the author after years of meditation and probing into the *akashic record*. The book is written in biblical style and language and sheds light on Jesus' life between childhood and his Jordan River baptism. It is an incredibly detailed text and Levi tends to repeat the same information over and over again. Those with an inclination toward esotericism praise the book highly.

C.S. Lewis

Lewis was one of the most influential writers on Christianity of this century. He converted to Christianity in 1931 and from then until his death in the mid-1960s, he wrote and lectured extensively on nondoctrinal Christianity. In addition to theology, he also wrote science fiction and juvenile literature.

GIBB, JOCELYN, ed. **LIGHT ON C.S. LEWIS. 181pp. HBJ65, 2.45p.**
A collection of essays on Lewis' life and thought by prominent writers

and educators—most of whom knew him. These short pieces give a clear image of the man.

GILBERT, DOUGLAS and CLYDE KILBY. **C.S. LEWIS: IMAGES OF HIS WORLD. Many color photographs, 11"x9¼", 192pp. Eer73, 8.95p.**
In this award winning volume, a professional photographer and a professor of English literature—both long time students and admirers of C.S. Lewis—have collaborated to offer a composite portrait of Lewis. Much of the text is in Lewis' own words. Professor Kilby traces Lewis' long and ultimately unsuccessful struggle to find joy apart from God, and goes on to show the mature Lewis, dedicated to proclaiming and defending the faith he had once denied.

GREEN, ROGER and WALTER HOOPER. **C.S. LEWIS—A BIOGRA-PHY. Index, 320pp. HBJ74, 3.95p.**
This is the first biography of C.S. Lewis, written with full access to family papers and to Lewis' diaries, letters, and manuscripts. It provides a complete record of his life. It is also an account of Lewis' intellectual work, discussing the books that molded him and the genesis of his own writings. Throughout is the theme of Lewis' conversion from atheism to Christianity. The narrative reads well.

HOLMER, PAUL. **C.S. LEWIS: THE SHAPE OF HIS FAITH AND THOUGHT. 126pp. H&R76/SIP, 3.95p.**
This is a revealing series of essays. Lewis' great insight, according to Professor Holmer, was in understanding the special role that literature can play in drawing the reader into new constellations of emotion and belief. More immediate and more memorable than his formal theological works, Lewis' poetry, fiction, articles, and letters became powerful instruments in the service of Christianity. To demonstrate the substance of his strong and persistent appeal, Holmer analyzes Lewis' entire published works.

HOOPER, WALTER, ed. **POEMS: C.S. LEWIS. 141pp. HBJ64/CSC, 2.95p.**
Although C.S. Lewis never published a book of verse during his lifetime, he wrote poetry from the age of fourteen. There is a great variety in the subjects of these poems—God and the pagan deities, unicorns and spaceships, nature, love, age, and reason.

LEWIS, C.S. **CHRISTIAN REFLECTIONS. Introduction, 190pp. Eer67, 2.95p.**
In this collection of essays edited by Walter Hooper, Lewis reflects on Christianity and literature, culture, ethics, futility, petitionary prayer, music, and much else.

LEWIS, C.S. **THE FOUR LOVES. 192pp. HBJ60/Fon, 2.45p.**
A warm, personal book in which Lewis describes the four basic kinds of human love—affection, friendship, erotic love, and the love of God. **The Four Loves** *deserves to become a minor classic as a modern mirror of souls, a mirror of the virtues and failings of human loving.*—**The New York Times Book Review.**

LEWIS, C.S. **GEORGE MACDONALD—AN ANTHOLOGY. Intro-duction, 191pp. McM47, 4.95c.**
A compilation of MacDonald's theologically-oriented writings. Each of the 365 selections—one for each day of the year—contains a world of Christian thought and feeling compressed into a few words.

LEWIS, C.S. **GOD IN THE DOCK: ESSAYS ON THEOLOGY AND ETHICS. Introduction, index, 346pp. Eer70, 3.95p.**
A collection of essays and letters written over a twenty-four year period—almost all of them published here in book form for the first time. Drawn from a wide variety of sources, the collection is designed to illustrate the many different angles from which we are able to view the Christian religion. Edited by Walter Hooper.

LEWIS, C.S. **THE GREAT DIVORCE. 128pp. McM46/Fon, 1.25p.**
Blake wrote the Marriage of Heaven and Hell....I have written of their divorce.—C.S. Lewis. Philosophy in the form of a novel.

LEWIS, C.S. **THE GRIEF OBSERVED. 151pp. Ban61/Fab, 1.95p.**
A very revealing personal account of the desolation that Lewis felt after the loss of his wife and the inner turmoil that he went through on his way back to life.

LEWIS, C.S. **THE JOYFUL CHRISTIAN. 249pp. McM77, 7.95c.**
127 selections from fifteen of Lewis' theological works, thematically arranged.

LEWIS, C.S. **MERE CHRISTIANITY. 190pp. McM52/Fon, 1.95p.**
A revised and enlarged edition, with a new introduction, of three books: **The Case for Christianity, Christian Behavior,** and **Beyond Personality.**

LEWIS, C.S. **MIRACLES, Index, 192pp. McM47/Fon, 1.95p.**
An extended study of the possibility and probability of miracles, which cites the available historical evidence and incorporates Lewis' own beliefs.

LEWIS, C.S. **THE PILGRIM'S REGRESS. Introduction, 201pp. Eer43, 2.45p.**
Though the dragons and giants of this fable are different from those of Bunyan, the allegory performs its old function of enabling its author to say with brevity and simplicity what would otherwise have demanded a full length philosophy of religion; and in Lewis' skillful hands it becomes no less effective a Christian apologia than Bunyan's.

LEWIS, C.S. **PRAYER: LETTERS TO MALCOLM. 124pp. Fon64, 1.50p.**
C.S. Lewis' last book, *A book full of wisdom, of bitter honesty and of deep clarity. It nowhere tells us how to pray but...stimulates afresh that hunger and thirst for God without which we should never pray at all.*—J.B. Phillips.

LEWIS, C.S. **REFLECTIONS ON THE PSALMS. 128pp. Fon58, 2.25p.**
Lewis relates the **Psalms** to their triple background: the ancient Judaic religion which produced them, the age of Christ when they took on new meanings, and our daily experience in the modern world. This was the first religious book Lewis wrote after an interval of ten years.

LEWIS, C.S. **THE SCREWTAPE LETTERS. Introduction, 187pp. McM61/Fon, 1.95p.**
Screwtape is a professional devil and self described undersecretary of the department of temptation. The story gradually unfolds as a series of explicit directives and plans through which Screwtape's nephew Wormwood may subvert and twist human strivings toward love, charity, and wisdom, manipulating the human soul to his own diabolical ends. This edition is bound with **Screwtape Proposes a Toast.** This is one of Lewis' most popular books.

LEWIS, C.S. **SURPRISED BY JOY. 247pp. HBJ55/Fon, 2.95p.**
A frank autobiography which tells of Lewis' conversion from atheism to Christianity and discusses the early part of his life.

LEWIS, C.S. **TILL WE HAVE FACES. 313pp. Eer56, 2.95p.**
This was C.S. Lewis' last novel before his death in 1963, and the book he himself regarded as his best. Critics have said that the book has the stature of a religious classic, the intensity and eloquence of a powerful novel, and the provocative quality of a psychological drama.

LEWIS, C.S. **THE WEIGHT OF GLORY AND OTHER ADDRESSES. 68pp. Eer49, 1.25p.**
A transcription of lectures on Christian themes delivered to a diverse set of audiences. The British edition is entitled **Transposition and Other Essays.**

LEWIS, C.S. **THE WORLD'S LAST NIGHT. 113pp. HBJ60, 1.95p.**
Seven essays discussing the efficacy of prayer, the various usages of the phrase *I believe,* the meaning of words like *culture* and *religion,* the interplay of *good work* and *good works,* the religious implications of life on other planets, and the doctrine of the Second Coming. **Screwtape Proposes a Toast** is also included.

LEWIS, W.H., ed. **LETTERS OF C.S. LEWIS. 308pp. HBJ66, 4.95p.**
Also includes a memoir by the editor, Lewis' brother.

———————————— END OF C.S. LEWIS SUBSECTION ————————————

LEWIS, H. SPENCER. **THE MYSTICAL LIFE OF JESUS. Index, 320pp. Amo29, 6.45c.**
Detailed history of Jesus' background and activities, not spoken of in the **New Testament** writings. The information purports to come from

ancient, secret records kept by the Rosicrucians since before the appearance of Jesus.

LEWIS, H. SPENCER. **THE SECRET DOCTRINES OF JESUS. Index, 237pp. Amo37, 6.45c.**
Insights into the being and personality of Jesus. Lewis outlines Jesus' role in the larger drama of undercover organizations attempting to free men's souls from eternally repressive power structures.

LOSSKY, VLADIMIR. **MYSTICAL THEOLOGY OF THE EASTERN CHURCH. Notes, index, 252pp. Cla57, 10.65c.**
It is our intention, in the following essay, to study certain aspects of eastern spirituality in relation to the fundamental themes of the Orthodox dogmatic tradition. In the present work, therefore, the term "mystical theology" denotes no more than a spirituality which expresses a doctrinal attitude.

MACGREGOR, GEDDES. **REINCARNATION IN CHRISTIANITY. 4.50p.**
See the Reincarnation and Karma section.

MCKEON, RICHARD, ed. **SELECTIONS FROM MEDIEVAL PHILOSOPHERS, VOLUME I. Introduction, 395pp. Scr29, 2.95p.**
Selections from the writings of St. Augustine, Boethius, John Scotus Eriugena, St. Anselm, Peter Lombard, Peter Abelard, Robert Grosseteste, the Pseudo-Grosseteste, and Albert the Great.

MCNEILL, JOHN **THE CELTIC CHURCHES, Notes, bibliography, index, 6"x9¼", 289pp. UCh74, 16.15c.**
A comprehensive study of Celtic Christianity from AD 200-1200. The major saints are discussed in detail and the missionary activities are also examined.

MALHERBE, ABRAHAM and EVERETT FERGUSON, trs. **GREGORY OF NYSSA—THE LIFE OF MOSES. Notes, indices, 224pp. Pau78, 6.95p.**
Gregory of Nyssa, a spiritual master of the fourth century, was born as the general persecution of Christianity was ending. The translators regard him as the most brilliant of the three Greek Cappadocian Fathers (the other two were Gregory's brother, St. Basil the Great, and St. Gregory Nazianzen). Jean Danielou says that Gregory was the founder of mystical theology in the church—though this is a controversial view. **The Life of Moses** reflects Gregory's spiritual sense of the scriptures. He maintained that the ultimate purpose of the **Bible** was not its historical teachings, but its capacity for elevating the soul to God. In this work he also synthesizes the earlier Hellenistic and Jewish traditions. The translators supply a lengthy introduction.

MALONEY, GEORGE. **MAN, THE DIVINE ICON. Notes, 232pp. DvP73, 3.50p.**
Father Maloney begins with chapters on the patristic point of view and on Christ—the logos, image of God the father. The rest of the book consists of separate discussions of the concepts of image and its likeness in the thought of the following early fathers: St. Irenaeus,

Clement of Alexandria, Origen, St. Athanasius, St. Basil the Great, St. Gregory Nazianzen, St. Gregory Nyssa, and St. Cyril of Alexandria.

MARTIN, RALPH. **WORSHIP IN THE EARLY CHURCH. Notes, index, 144pp. Eer64, 2.95p.**
An examination of how the earliest Christians worshiped God.

MASSEY, GERALD. **THE HISTORICAL JESUS AND THE MYTHICAL CHRIST. Spiral bound, glossary, notes, index, 233pp. HeR nd, 6.00p.**
An esoteric work dealing with the allegorical symbolism of the **Gospels** and incorporating many Gnostic insights.

MEAD, G.R.S. **THE HYMN OF JESUS—ECHOES FROM THE GNOSIS. 75pp. TPH07/Wat, 1.00p.**
A collection of verses believed to be among the earliest of Christian literature. These very possibly were the basis for communal services among the original families of Christ.

MERRY, ELEANOR. **EASTER—THE LEGENDS AND THE FACTS. Index, 153pp. NKB67, 4.05c.**
A profound discussion of the spiritual foundations of Easter, based on the ancient mystery teaching and reviewing related material in the old Celtic legends of the Holy Grail and the story of Parzival, and in Goethe's **Faust**. A moving presentation which makes the true meaning of this holy day come alive. Ms. Merry is an Anthroposophist.

Thomas Merton

Thomas Merton (1915-68) was a promising poet and writer during his college and post-collegiate years, but, on his own admission, he was a disorganized personality searching for meaning in life. After a rather sudden conversion to Catholicism . . . he entered a Trappist monastery in 1941, seeking to isolate himself completely from society in the hope of finding God in solitude and prayer. He did, however, under monastic obedience, continue his writing from within the monastery. For close to twenty-seven years he maintained this isolation despite the fact that publication of his autobiography, **The Seven Storey Mountain** (1948), brought him great literary prominence. His early monastic writings were on strictly religious and monastic themes. . . . Though he remained a strictly cloistered monk until just before his sudden death in 1968, from about 1958 on his writings disclose a vastly expanded social consciousness, and a much broader awareness of man's place and function in the world. The general context of his life shifted so that he became publicly concerned about social problems and the impact of social change on man's relationship to God and to his neighbor. From the vertical, other-worldy devotion of his earlier works, Merton shifted his emphasis to a direct, horizontal, deeply engaged, often militant concern for the critical situation of man in the world.—F.J. Kelly, **Man Before God**. In his later years Merton also moved away from the strict Catholic viewpoint, and into more sympathy with the Buddhist way of life. This was due in part to the influence of his close friend, D.T. Suzuki. Merton was one of those rare Western minds who was entirely at home in Asian experience. The Asian trip during which Merton had his fatal accident was, many thought, an attempt to break out of the cloister and become more actively involved in the world. Some even felt that he was prepared to renounce his Catholicism and become a Buddhist.

BAILEY, RAYMOND. **THOMAS MERTON ON MYSTICISM. Notes, 275pp. Dou75, 1.95p.**
Bailey movingly recreates Merton's journey toward union with God. He traces the evolution of Merton's faith and includes conversations between Mertón and his associates, excerpts from his letters and journals, and some heretofore unpublished material. *I have only one desire . . . to disappear into God, to be submerged in His peace . . . .*—Thomas Merton.

BURTON, NAOMI, PATRICK HART and JAMES LAUGHLIN, eds. **THE ASIAN JOURNAL OF THOMAS MERTON. 4.45p.**
See the Comparative Religion section.

HART, BROTHER PATRICK, ed. **THE MONASTIC JOURNEY. Notes, 197pp. SAM77, 2.95p.**
Merton wrote several books on monasticism as well as many shorter essays and articles on the monastic life, describing its beauty and its essentials: an appreciation of the value of silence, solitude, prayer, and purity of heart. This book reflects his mature thoughts on both community monastic living and the solitary life. The first three pieces describe something of the mystery of the monastic vocation and make a strong statement on the basic verities of the monastic way of life. The middle section discusses monastic themes in detail, and the book ends with a moving monograph in praise of solitary life.

HART, BROTHER PATRICK, ed. **THOMAS MERTON, MONK. Woodcuts, 230pp. Dou74, 1.95p.**
Hart was Merton's private secretary, and is therefore uniquely qualified to bring together this composite monastic view of the man. The result is a moving, forceful, and honest appraisal of Merton. *The articles and poems chosen for this volume were written by monks and nuns from Europe and America, most of whom knew [Merton] personally. They bear witness to Merton's contemplative vision, and reflect the monastic frame of reference for his influence as a spiritual force in the fifties and as a social critic and bridge-builder between East and West in the sixties.*—from the introduction. Includes an essay by James Fox, Merton's abbot for twenty years, as well as a bibliography of all Merton's works.

HIGGINS, JOHN. **THOMAS MERTON ON PRAYER. Notes, bibliography, 200pp. Dou75, 1.95p.**
A comprehensive study of Merton's thoughts on prayer which reflects the full scope of his contemplative life and his writings on every aspect of prayer. To place Merton's idea of contemplative prayer in its full perspective, Higgins explores the two central forces of Merton's spirituality: man's search for God and his discovery of God through love shared with other individuals.

KELLY, FREDERICK. **MAN BEFORE GOD: THOMAS MERTON ON SOCIAL RESPONSIBILITY. Notes, 301pp. Dou74, 7.95c.**
An in depth study which reveals Merton's concept of religious man and also the shift in his concerns from religious to secular problems such as the threat of nuclear annihilation, war and peace, nonviolent alternatives for social change, modern trends towards dehumanization, Christian renewal and ecumenism, and Oriental spirituality. Topics include an excellent study of the man and his writings; Merton as a social critic; religious man in his writings; and the social dimension and concerns of religious man.

■ *MCDONNELL, THOMAS, ed.* **A THOMAS MERTON READER. 516pp. Dou38, 2.95p.**
Here in one volume are important selections from Merton's major and lesser known writings, beginning with his first book, **The Seven Storey Mountain**, and concluding with material from his **Asian Journal**. The anthology clearly reflects Merton's own personal spiritual growth and development. Merton speaks on many themes: war, love, peace, Eastern thought and spirituality, monastic life, art, the **Psalms**, contemplation, and solitude. This new edition of the **Reader** is a most welcome volume and an excellent way to gain exposure to Merton's thought.

MCINERNY, DENNIS. **THOMAS MERTON: THE MAN AND HIS WORK. 128pp. Cis74, 9.35c.**
A sympathetic portrayal of Merton by one of his fellow Cistercian monks. The book begins with a brief biography, then discusses Merton the writer and the difficulty he had coming to terms with himself as a writer. The third chapter is devoted to Merton the poet, and to his poetry, and the fourth to the central importance of monasticism in Merton's life. McInerny also analyzes Merton's role as social critic and the main ideological and cultural currents that influenced his thought.

MERTON, THOMAS. **THE ASCENT TO TRUTH. Notes, 252pp. B&O51, 3.95p.**
An inspirational discussion of ultimate truth—which Merton sees as being a realization of God reached through deep contemplation. The bulk of the book is devoted to a brilliant exposition of the doctrines of St. John of the Cross.

MERTON, THOMAS. **BREAD IN THE WILDERNESS. Notes, 140pp. Ltu54, 2.05p.**
A collection of meditations and insights on the **Psalms**.

MERTON, THOMAS. **THE COLLECTED POEMS OF THOMAS MERTON. Index, 1,046pp. NDP77/SlP, 37.50c.**
This volume includes all of Merton's published verse along with sections of uncollected poems, humorous verse, and poems in French with some English translations. Fragments of other works are also included.

MERTON, THOMAS. **CONJECTURES OF A GUILTY BYSTANDER. 350pp. Dou65, 2.45p.**
Merton describes his book as *a personal and monastic meditation, a testimony of Christian reflection in the mid-twentieth century, a confrontation of twentieth century questions in the light of a monastic commitment, which inevitably makes one something of a bystander.*

MERTON, THOMAS. **CONTEMPLATION IN A WORLD OF ACTION. 396pp. Dou71/A&U, 2.95p.**
In this book, Merton presents his finest and clearest statements on the monastic life. . . . His concern was for the fullest and most complete contemplative life and, though his other writings discussed the results of that life, it is in the twenty-one essays of this book that we are asked to consider directly the contemplative life. . . .—**The New York Times Book Review**.

MERTON, THOMAS. **CONTEMPLATIVE PRAYER. 115pp. Dou68/DLT, 1.75p.**
Looking from many sides, Merton shows the value of this nonactivity in breaking through the barriers of overorganized rituals into spiritual reality and meaning.

MERTON, THOMAS. **DISPUTED QUESTIONS. 216pp. FSG53, 3.95p.**
Eleven essays, rich in meditative insights about various esoteric and exoteric aspects of the Christian philosophy. Merton discusses love, government, spiritual art, and the views and doctrines of several well known historical personages.

MERTON, THOMAS. **FAITH AND VIOLENCE. Index, 300pp. UND68, 4.65p.**
A collection of essays which reflect the turbulence of the 1960s in the U.S. Merton tries to show how Christian teaching and practice can help us deal with contemporary problems. He believes that the *faithful* are as prone to violence as any other people.

MERTON, THOMAS. **GEOGRAPHY OF LOGRAIRE. Notes, 153pp. NDP68, 2.75p.**
This is Merton's final testament as a poet, completed a few months before he set out on his final Asian journey. The text lacks final editing, but it is substantially a completed, self contained work. Lograire is first of all a country of the imagination, but it is also a person—Merton himself—for its geography is the map of his mind. The charting in the poem is his search for self location. Sections of personal experience are set against passages reimagined from anthropological and historical texts, material that Merton chose for its mythological character to illustrate the general experience of mankind.

MERTON, THOMAS. **LIFE AND HOLINESS. 119pp. Dou62, 1.95p.**
This is intended to be a very simple book, an elementary treatment of a few basic ideas in Christian spirituality. Hence it should be useful to any Christian, and indeed to anyone who wants to acquaint himself with some principles of the interior life as it is understood in the Catholic Church. Nothing is said here of such subjects as "contemplation" or even "mental prayer." And yet the book emphasizes what is at once the most common and the most mysterious aspect in the Christian life: grace, the power and the light of God in us.—from the introduction.

MERTON, THOMAS. **THE LIVING BREAD. 124pp. B&O56, 4.10p.**
Merton views the Eucharist as being the sacrament of love and in this series of meditations he makes love his theme as he discusses the true meaning of Christianity. As he says, *To find God one must first be free. . . . To conquer the forces of death and despair, we must unite ourselves mystically to Christ who has overcome death and who brings us life and hope. . . . This book is not a defense of a doctrine, but a meditation on a sacred mystery.*

MERTON, THOMAS. **MY ARGUMENT WITH THE GESTAPO. 259pp. NDP68, 3.95p.**
This is the earliest of Merton's full length prose works. It tells of the adventures of a young man, clearly identified by the name Thomas Merton, who travels from America to Europe to report on the war with Germany from the viewpoint of a poet. It is not, however, an autobiographical work.

MERTON, THOMAS. **THE NEW MAN. Notes, 175pp. FSG62/B&O, 3.95p.**
This is one of Merton's most important mature works on the spiritual life. He discusses how we can live a full, religious life in a world that is as increasingly out of touch with real humanity as it is out of touch with God. Merton is concerned with our knowing who we really are and with what we must do if we are to find our true selves again. *It is a spiritual disaster,* he says, *for a man to rest content with his exterior identity . . . . . Since we are made in the image and likeness of God, there is no other way to find out who we are than by finding, in ourselves, the divine image.* To this theme of the true nature of man, Merton joins an exploration of the attitude contrary to the Christian and summarizes it by applying the Prometheus myth to the present age.

MERTON, THOMAS. **NEW SEEDS OF CONTEMPLATION. 297pp. NDP61, 2.45p.**
A much enlarged, revised version of **Seeds of Contemplation**, one of Merton's most widely read and best loved works. For Father Merton, *Every moment and every event of every man's life on earth plants something in his soul . . . . Most of these unencumbered seeds perish and are lost, because men are not prepared to receive them: for such seeds as these cannot spring up anywhere except in the good soil of freedom, spontaneity and love.*

MERTON, THOMAS. **NO MAN IS AN ISLAND. 197pp. Dou55/SlP, 1.95p.**
Sixteen essays centering around the reality behind the quote used in the title.

MERTON, THOMAS. **OPENING THE BIBLE. 84pp. Ltu70, 4.15c.**
To open a book at all is to question it, to ask what one may find in it. What kind of book is the **Bible**? *This question is the sort any reader implicitly asks of any book. The purpose of this booklet is to consider some of the special questions and problems which surround the* **Bible** *itself.*—Thomas Merton.

MERTON, THOMAS. **SEASONS OF CELEBRATION. 249pp. FSG65, 3.25p.**
A collection of essays containing Merton's reflections on the seasons, or cycles, of the liturgical year. Words, songs, ceremonies, signs, and movements of worship all have their place in opening up the heart and mind, as he says, to *a new spirit of openness, in which the priest is open to his people, and they are open to him and to one another.*

MERTON, THOMAS. **THE SECULAR JOURNAL. Introduction, 285pp. FSG59/SlP, 3.95p.**
This book contains a transcription of the journal in which Merton recorded his private thoughts between the ages of twenty-four and twenty-six. It covers the time from shortly after his conversion to Catholicism to his decision to become part of the Abbey of Gethsemani. The journal offers us a picture of Merton's appreciation of the secular world as well as his ongoing examination of his commitment to religion.

MERTON, THOMAS. **THE SEVEN STOREY MOUNTAIN. 512pp. Dou48/SlP, 2.45p.**
Merton's autobiography, written early in his career. It is not a personal work; rather, Merton describes his struggle to realize the spirit of God and his meditational insights. This was the work that first brought Father Merton to the public's eye.

MERTON, THOMAS. **THE SILENT LIFE. Index, 192pp. FSG57/SlP, 2.95p.**
Merton wrote this book ten years after he took monastic orders and he describes it as *a meditation on the monastic life by one who, without any merit of his own, is privileged to know that life from the inside . . . who seeks only to speak as the mouthpiece of a tradition centuries old.*

MERTON, THOMAS. **SPIRITUAL DIRECTION AND MEDITATION. 121pp. Ltu60, 2.80c.**
This book consists of an essay which originally appeared in a magazine article and has been revised and considerably expanded. It was designed to stir up the reader's desire to meditate. A number of comments from Christian mystics are interspersed.

MERTON, THOMAS. **THOUGHTS IN SOLITUDE. 124pp. FSG58/B&O, 2.95p.**
These pages were written. . .at times when the author, by the grace of God and the favor of his Superiors, was able to enjoy special opportunities for solitude and meditation. . . . This does not imply that the notes are subjective or autobiographical. They are in no way intended as an account of spiritual adventures. As far as the writer is concerned, there was no adventure to write about, and if there had been, it would not have been confided to paper in any case. These are simply thoughts on the contemplative life, fundamental intuitions which seemed, at the time, to have a basic importance.—Thomas Merton.

MERTON, THOMAS, tr. **THE WAY OF CHUANG TZU. 1.75p.**
See the Chuang Tzu subsection of Chinese Philosophy.

MERTON, THOMAS. **WHAT IS CONTEMPLATION? Illustrations, 8¼"x4", 78pp. Tpg50, 3.95p.**
The only way to find out anything about the joys of contemplation is by experience, writes Merton. *We must taste and see that the Lord is sweet.* This is a reprint of an early, introductory work which serves as a guide for the beginner and lets him know what to expect as he moves into this essential Christian experience. As he says, *When you begin the life of contemplation you have left the beaten path are are traveling by paths that cannot be charted and measured.* Merton quotes from a number of the great Christian teachers.

MERTON, THOMAS, tr. **THE WISDOM OF THE DESERT. 81pp. NDP60/SlP, 1.95p.**
This translation of the writings of the hermits who turned their backs on a corrupt society remarkably like our own was one of Merton's favorites among his own books. Merton deeply identified with the legendary fourth century Christian fathers who sought solitude and contemplation in the deserts of the Near East.

MERTON, THOMAS. **ZEN AND THE BIRDS OF APPETITE. 1.95p.**
See the Zen Buddhism section.

RICE, EDWARD. **THE MAN IN THE SYCAMORE TREE. 192pp. Dou70, 2.45p.**
This biography, subtitled, *The Good Times and Hard Life of Thomas Merton,* was written by one of Merton's closest friends. Rice not only tells the story of Merton from his childhood through his monastic years up to his fateful Far Eastern trip, but he writes more frankly and realistically than Merton, as a Trappist, was able to. The reader can get a good feeling for Merton the man from this volume. It is full of photographs from all periods of Merton's life along with some of Merton's own drawings.

SUSSMAN, CORNELIA and IRVING. **THOMAS MERTON. Bibliography, index, 175pp. McM76, 6.95c.**
A moving biography based on Merton's published works and on discussions with those who knew him. The tone is personal and analytical and the authors' aim is to bring Merton to life. Not a definitive study, but a highly readable, informative one geared toward the general reader.

THOMAS MERTON STUDIES CENTER. **THREE ESSAYS. 24pp. Ucr71, 4.00p.**
Three brief essays: *Thomas Merton Studies Center* by Monsignor Horrigan; *Concerning the Collection in the Bellarmine College Library* by Thomas Merton; and *In Search of Thomas Merton* by John Howard Griffin.

—————**END OF THOMAS MERTON SUBSECTION**—————

MOMMAERS, PAUL. **THE LAND WITHIN: THE PROCESS OF POSSESSING AND BEING POSSESSED BY GOD ACCORDING TO THE MYSTIC JAN VAN RUYSBROECK. Notes, 143pp. FHP75, 6.95c.**
An analysis based on the entire corpus of van Ruysbroeck's writings.

MONTGOMERY, RUTH. **COMPANIONS ALONG THE WAY. 256pp. Pop74, 1.95p.**
Dictated by Arthur Ford (through automatic writing) in 1973—after his death—this is the story of an incarnation Ford and Montgomery had shared 2,000 years ago when she was born as the third sister of Lazarus and Ford was their father, the Rabbi Jeremiah. The account is full of previously unpublished revelations of Jesus' life and ministry. It also details *group karma*, the transmigration of groups or *clusters* of souls to physical bodies at approximately the same time. Ford tells of nine other meetings on Earth from the Palestinian incarnation to the nineteenth century.

MUGGERIDGE, MALCOLM. **JESUS—THE MAN WHO LIVES. 7½"x 9¾", 192pp. H&R75/Fon, 6.95p.**
This is an extraordinary retelling of Jesus' life and mission accompanied by plates selected from the finest Christian art and Muggeridge's excellent commentary. Muggeridge has written widely on Christian themes and this is generally acknowledged as his greatest achievement.

NICHOLAS OF CUSA. **THE VISION OF GOD. 152pp. Ung28, 2.75p.**
Nicholas was an ordained churchman dedicated to reform. As one might imagine in fifteenth century Europe this turned out to be an extremely taxing chore. Fortunately, as his writing clearly shows, suffering and discouragement strengthened him in faith, hope, and great love of God.

NICOLL, MAURICE. **THE NEW MAN. 2.95p.**
See the Gurdjieff and the Work section.

OTTO, RUDOLF. **THE IDEA OF THE HOLY. Notes, index, 253pp. Oxf50, 8.95c.**
In this book I have ventured to write of that which may be called "non-rational" or "supra-rational" in the depths of the divine nature..... This book, recognizing the profound import of the non-rational for metaphysic, makes a serious attempt to analyse all the more exactly the "feeling" which remains where the "concept" fails, and to introduce a terminology which is not any the more loose or indeterminate for having necessarily to make use of "symbols."

PARRINDER, GEOFFREY. **JESUS IN THE QUR'AN. 5.95p.**
See the Qur'an subsection of Islam.

PAUL, FATHER. **MEMOIRS OF A MYSTIC. 87pp. HOM74, 2.25p.**
A collection of spiritual poetry by the leader of The Holy Order of Mans.

St. Paul

Paul was a first century Jew who, after being a bitter enemy of the Christian Church, became its leading missionary and possibly its greatest theologian. He was a Roman citizen whose education must have been strictly Jewish. Converted through a vision on the road to Damascus, he accepted his call to be the apostle to the Christians. He was active in missionary work for the rest of his life and many believe that Christianity would never have survived if it had not been for him—or, if it had, would have assumed a very different form.

CALDWELL, TAYLOR. **GREAT LION OF GOD: A MAJOR NOVEL ABOUT ST. PAUL. Introduction, 673pp. Faw70, 1.95p.**
A dramatic recreation of the life of St. Paul. Caldwell sees him as a man whose entire life was overshadowed by a sense of sin and a desire for forgiveness. She shows the forces that made him a righteous persecutor of the early Christians and led him to discover his identity—and his God—on the road to Damascus.

GRANT, MICHAEL. **SAINT PAUL. Glossary, notes, index, 250pp. Scr76, 4.15p.**
Grant, a historian with a wonderful gift for prose, describes Paul not as

a figure of myth but as a person. He reviews the **Epistles** and many of the earliest Christian documents, surveys the material on Paul's four evangelical journeys, and discusses the reasons for Paul's conversion. This is as interesting and informative a biography as we can imagine.

SCHWEITZER, ALBERT. **THE MYSTICISM OF PAUL THE APOSTLE. Indices, 411pp. Sea31, 5.95p.**
A detailed survey, topically organized and including an extensive number of quotations from the **New Testament** and from other Christian writers.

SHRINE OF WISDOM, *eds.* **A SYNTHESIS OF THE TEACHINGS OF ST. PAUL. 39pp. ShW22, 3.00p.**
The teachings are topically arranged and cover the following areas: the Holy Trinity; spirit, soul, and body; the law; and the redemptive graces and virtues.

————————END OF ST. PAUL SUBSECTION————————

PERIGO, GRACE, *tr.* **LETTERS OF ADAM OF PERSEIGNE. Index, 207pp. Cis76, 11.95c.**
Adam was abbot of the Cistercian monastery at Perseigne in the late twelfth century. Through his letters he counseled clerics and kings, nuns and nobles, and many others. He was himself the son of a serf and nothing is known for certain of the education by which Adam rose from the peasantry. Here his letters are preceded by a lengthy essay by Thomas Merton, *The Feast of Freedom: Monastic Formation According to Adam of Perseigne.* Fifteen letters are transcribed in all.

PONTICUS, EVAGRIUS. **PRAKTIKOS—CHAPTERS ON PRAYER. Introduction, notes, bibliography, index, 190pp. Cis70, 7.95c.**
Through [Evagrius Ponticus] the whole of an ancient wisdom, both theoretical and practical, has been transmitted and inserted into life. His texts were at once a terminus and a starting point. They were the culmination of his own experiences, the meeting point of all the trends of his period. At the same time they were the starting point of a new phase in evolution which has never ceased to go forward....Simple men of God recognize in his writings a description of their own problems and difficulties and discover in them also solutions to them.—Jean Leclercq, an important contemporary monastic scholar.

PRABHAVANANDA, SWAMI. **THE SERMON ON THE MOUNT ACCORDING TO VEDANTA. 1.50p.**
See the Vedanta subsection of Indian Philosophy.

RADICE, BETTY, *tr.* **THE LETTERS OF ABELARD AND HELOISE. Long introduction, maps, notes, index, 309pp. Vik74, 2.50p.**
The grim tale of Abelard and Heloise has echoed down from the twelfth century as one of the world's great love stories. These staunch Christians, as their letters reveal, found a path through self pity into acceptance of a changed but lasting relationship. Whilst Heloise attained fame for her learning and administrative genius as an abbess, Abelard became an inspired teacher in Paris and the foremost logician of his day. This translation includes Abelard's account of his misfortunes; four of their personal letters; the *letters of direction,* in which he advises her how to adapt the rule of Benedict for women; correspondence between Heloise and Peter the Venerable; and two of Abelard's hymns.

RAJNEESH, BHAGWAN SHREE. **COME FOLLOW ME. 12.95c/each.**
See the Contemporary Spiritual Teachers section.

RAJNEESH, BHAGWAN SHREE. **THE MUSTARD SEED: A LIVING EXPLANATION OF THE SAYINGS OF JESUS FROM THE GOSPEL ACCORDING TO THOMAS. 5.95p.**
See the Contemporary Spiritual Teachers section.

RAMACHARAKA, YOGI. **MYSTIC CHRISTIANITY. 268pp. YPS07/ Fow, 6.00c.**
An American immersed in Indian culture makes a detailed examination of the historical events and perspectives surrounding Jesus' life and ministry, and their meaning in terms of man's ultimate realization.

REINHOLD, H.A., *ed.* **THE SOUL AFIRE—REVELATIONS OF THE MYSTICS. 480pp. Dou73, 2.45p.**
Presents a wide view of the feelings and thoughts of the most mystical Christians who have ever lived. Selected writings from a magnificent collection of souls, arranged into relevant categories showing the history and depth of spiritual devotion in the West.

RINALDI, PETER. **IT IS THE LORD. Photographs, 124pp. War72, 1.50p.**
Rinaldi has studied the shroud of Christ for more than forty years. Here he offers twenty-five possible explanations to disprove its validity, tells of his research along that line, and shows why the objection does not hold up. He then offers his own theory and definitely states that the shroud is genuine.

ROBERTS, ALEXANDER and JAMES DONALDSON, eds. **THE ANTE-NICENE FATHERS, VOLUME I. 610pp. Eer1885, 12.00c.**
This is an excellent series. The books are beautifully bound and quite reasonably priced and the translations are not readily available elsewhere. Each volume has double columns, many notes, and a variety of indices. This one includes the writings of the following fathers: St. Clement, Mathetes, Polycarp, Ignatius, Barnabas, Papias, Justin Martyr, and Irenaeus (the first six of whom are generally known as the Apostolic Fathers).

ROBERTS, ALEXANDER and JAMES DONALDSON, eds. **THE ANTE-NICENE FATHERS, VOLUME II. 629pp. Eer1885, 12.00c.**
This volume presents the writings of the fathers of the second century: Hermas, Tatian, Athenagoras, Theophilus, and Clement of Alexandria. About two thirds of the book are devoted to Clement's writings.

ROBERTS, ALEXANDER and JAMES DONALDSON, eds. **THE ANTE-NICENE FATHERS, VOLUME III. 745pp. Eer1885, 12.00c.**
This volume is devoted to the writings of the founder of Latin Christianity, Tertullian.

ROBERTS, ALEXANDER and JAMES DONALDSON, eds. **THE ANTE-NICENE FATHERS, VOLUME IV. 703pp. Eer1885, 12.00c.**
Selections from the fathers of the third century: Tertullian, Minucius Felix, Commodianus, and Origen.

ROBERTS, ALEXANDER and JAMES DONALDSON, eds. **THE ANTE-NICENE FATHERS, VOLUME V. 706pp. Eer nd, 12.00c.**
This volume contains lengthy selections from four third century fathers: Hippolytus, Cyprian, Caius, and Novation.

ROBERTS, ALEXANDER and JAMES DONALDSON, eds. **THE ANTE-NICENE FATHERS, VOLUME VI. 579pp. Eer nd, 12.00c.**
More writings from third century fathers: Gregory Thaumaturgus, Dionysius the Great, Julius Africanus, Anatolius, Archelaus, Alexander of Lycopolis, Peter and Alexander of Alexandria, Methodius, Arnobius, and a number of minor writers.

ROBERTS, ALEXANDER and JAMES DONALDSON, eds. **THE ANTE-NICENE FATHERS, VOLUME VII. 600pp. Eer1886, 12.00c.**
Selections from the writings of the following third and fourth century fathers: Lactantius, Venantius, Asterius, and Dionysius. This volume also contains apostolic teaching and constitutions, the homily ascribed to Clement, and early liturgies.

ROBERTS, ALEXANDER and JAMES DONALDSON, eds. **THE ANTE-NICENE FATHERS, VOLUME VIII. 827pp. Eer51, 12.00c.**
This final volume has more writings of the third and fourth century fathers along with a lengthy selection from the **Apocrypha** and the Decretals. The editors include the testament of the twelve patriarchs, excerpts of Theodotus, epistles concerning virginity, pseudo-Clementine literature, and the memoirs of Edessa.

SADHU, MOUNI. **THEURGY: THE ART OF EFFECTIVE WORSHIP. 263pp. A&U65, 11.50c.**
Theurgy had its birth in ancient Egypt, and from there passed to the Neoplatonists, who taught worship of their gods and nature spirits in order to obtain favors and good luck. With the coming of Christianity into the Graeco-Roman world, the methods of theurgy were duplicated. This thematic book outlines a number of these methods and powerful prayers.

SANFORD, JOHN. **THE KINGDOM WITHIN. Bibliography, index, 226pp. Lip70, 7.95c.**
The truth of Christianity applies to the whole of life, but in our time the Christian message is often proclaimed only in its relevance to the social situation or to the institutional life of the Church. This book is an attempt to balance this outwardly oriented emphasis by showing the inner meaning of Jesus' sayings; that is, their relevance to the unfolding of the whole personality which is within us all. The reader will find here an interpretation of the sayings of Jesus which emphasizes their meaning for his personal, individual life and development.—from the preface.

SARAYDARIAN, H. **CHRIST—AVATAR OF SACRIFICIAL LOVE. 7¼"x10¼", 128pp. AEG74, 6.00c.**
Christ—Avatar of Sacrificial Love *is written to show the uniqueness of Christ, as the World Teacher, as the Path leading to the Brotherhood of men, and to innermost Reality within man and universe.* The work is very inspirational and includes many quotations from the works of Alice Bailey.

SMITH, MARGARET. **AN INTRODUCTION TO MYSTICISM. Notes, 126pp. SlP31, 3.50p.**
This is an important work, devoted basically to the Christian mystical tradition. Ms. Smith begins with a chapter on the nature and meaning of mysticism and follows with essays on Hebrew and Jewish mysticism, mysticism in the **New Testament**, in classical times, in the early Christian Church, in medieval England, and in Italy, Spain, Germany, and Flanders. There is also a discussion of mystics of the early Middle Ages and mysticism in the Orient. Quotations from primary texts are interspersed. Ms. Smith writes in an archaic manner and uses too much capitalization for our taste. Nonetheless, she has many outstanding insights.

SMITH, MORTON. **JESUS THE MAGICIAN. Many notes, bibliography, 220pp. H&R78, 12.50c.**
Jesus the magician was the figure seen by most ancient opponents of Jesus; Jesus the Son of God was the figure seen by that party of his followers who eventually triumphed; the real Jesus was the man whose words and actions gave rise to these contradictory interpretations. Jesus the Son of God is pictured in the **Gospels***; the works that pictured Jesus the magician were destroyed in antiquity after Christians got hold of the Roman empire. We know the lost works only from fragments and references, mostly in the works of Christian authors. Hence modern scholars, trying to discover the historical Jesus behind the* **Gospel** *legends, have generally paid no attention to the evidence for Jesus the magician and have taken only the* **Gospels** *as their sources. The bias of their work is understandable. This book is an attempt to correct this bias by reconstructing the lost picture from the preserved fragments and related material, mainly from the magical papyri, that* **New Testament** *scholarship has also generally ignored.*—from the preface. Smith is a professor of ancient history at Columbia University.

SOPHRONY, ARCHIMANDRITE. **HIS LIFE IS MINE. Introduction, 128pp. Mow77, 2.15p.**
The spiritual testimony of this Russian Orthodox desert monk.

SOPHRONY, ARCHIMANDRITE. **THE MONK OF MOUNT ATHOS. 124pp. Mow73, 3.30p.**
Mount Athos, *a holy mountain* barred to *female animals, women, eunuchs, and those without beards,* has been the focal point of orthodox monasticism since the first monastery was founded in 963. In its heyday, the monastic population numbered 40,000, but after World War I the population fell sharply. This is an account of the life and teachings of Staretz Silouan, a member of this Russian monastic community. At Mount Athos, Staretz Silouan's long years of tireless striving gave him a personal experience of Christianity identical with that of many of the ascetic fathers.

SOPHRONY, ARCHIMANDRITE. **WISDOM FROM MOUNT ATHOS. 127pp. Mow74, 3.30p.**
A translation of the writings of Staretz Silouan (1866-1938). His disciple Sophrony edited the work from a variety of notes which the Staretz penciled on odd scraps of paper. Sophrony also contributes a foreword.

SQUIRE, AELRED. **ASKING THE FATHERS. Notes, index, 249pp. Pau73, 5.95p.**
Squire traces the main lines of the teaching of the great spiritual masters of the past in terms of both method and form. The material is arranged thematically and each subject is discussed at length, with quotations from many of the masters.

STEINER, RUDOLF. **CHRIST IN TWENTIETH CENTURY. 20pp. API71, .95p.**
Translation of a lecture discussing the differing views of Christ over the centuries. Rudolf Steiner has written extensively on Christianity and Christian themes and is probably the best twentieth century

exponent of the mystical aspects of Christianity. We have just included a few of his works in this section: see the Steiner section for the rest of his books.

STEINER, RUDOLF. **CHRISTIANITY AS MYSTICAL FACT. 195pp. API47, 2.95p.**
Steiner's interpretation of many famous ancient myths. He also explains how the writings of Christianity restate and personalize the message of the old stories.

STEINER, RUDOLF. **FROM JESUS TO CHRIST. 184pp. RSP73, 5.50c.**
This is the favorite book of some of the people we know who are deeply into Steiner. Steiner sees the Christ event as a continuous happening, something that becomes different in the twentieth century from what it was in the first, and which will be still different in the future. This idea is developed here in a variety of ways. An especially interesting selection discusses the characteristics of the two different Jesus children spoken of by St. Luke and St. Matthew. Another one studies the whole relation of the Christ Being to that of Jesus the man. Ten lectures are transcribed here.

STEINER, RUDOLF. **THE MYSTERIES OF THE EAST AND OF CHRISTIANITY. 77pp. RSP43, 2.75p.**
These four lectures given by Steiner in Berlin in 1913 delve into the realm of spiritual realities underlying life on Earth and how and why we should strive to see them more clearly as our main life's activity; and how most of us in one way or another get wrapped up and tied down in life's illusions rather than it's truth.

STRONG, MARY, ed. **LETTERS OF THE SCATTERED BROTHER-HOOD. 190pp. H&R48, 4.95c.**
A collection of mystical messages of inspiration. Fragmentary quotations are interspersed through the text which bear witness to the likeness of spiritual experience throughout the ages.

SUARES, CARLOS. **THE PASSION OF JUDAS. 116pp. ShP73, 2.95p.**
According to Suares, Judas was not weak and sinful; on the contrary, he was strong and selfless in fulfilling his destiny as Christ required. This work, written as a play following very closely the **Gospel of John**, dramatizes this point.

Pierre Teilhard de Chardin

Teilhard (1881-1955) was a French priest-scientist who spent much of his life in China. He achieved a remarkable unity between his spiritual life and his scientific pursuits—but his spiritual writings never received the approval of the church and consequently none of his books was published until after his death. He was exiled from France by the church because of his heretical ideas and traveled to sites of geological and paleontological interest, developing his theories about man and his place in the universe. He finally settled in China, as Director of the Peking Geological Service, where he remained for twenty years. Throughout his life he was a prolific writer. As there were few intellectually compatible people in Peking at this time he often found himself experiencing deeply the meaning of solitude. He also conducted a voluminous correspondence with several friends in the West. In 1946 he returned to Paris, where he lived and worked with his fellow Jesuits. He was allowed to publish only scientific papers and was forbidden to lecture in public except on purely scientific matters. In spite of this he became one of the most sought out and discussed men in Paris and his books were circulated in manuscript form in scientific and religious circles. He spent most of his last years in the United States. After his death his written works were no longer under the jurisdiction of the church and they began to be released for publication. Since then his position as a seminal thinker has been proclaimed worldwide. The primary concern of Teilhard's life was to study *the area where God and the cosmos come together*, to seek and to reveal the unity underlying religion and science, spirit, and matter.

His experience and reflection during fifty years of professional research on five continents impelled him to formulate and then project into the future of the laws that he believed have governed evolution in the past. *The past*, he wrote in 1945, *has revealed to me how the future is built*. Our human task is to build that future. Evolution, says Teilhard, is in man's hands. Indeed, without our strenuous and immediate cooperation evolution on this planet, and with it life itself, may come to an end. Looking into the future Teilhard sees the long ascent, matter-life-thought-spirit, coming to its consummation in a radiant and loving suprapersonal center on which the whole of evolution converges. He calls that center Omega.

Some who wish to learn more about Teilhard may be tempted to take up his masterwork, **The Phenomenon of Man**, first. We would advise against this. A wiser plan would be to start in low gear with an introduction to his life and work by another author, then move on to some of his correspondence, after that one of his more introductory writings on his spiritual thought and his scientific vision.

BRUTEAU, BEATRICE. **EVOLUTION TOWARD DIVINITY. Many quotations, notes, bibliography, index, 270pp. TPH74, 10.00c.**
In developing his synthesis of contemporary science and traditional religion, Teilhard created a number of ideas and images which find more or less close parallels in the various strands of Hindu philosophy. Teilhard, however, was not only unaware of these similarities but even denounced Hinduism as a system and an outlook fundamentally inimical to the world view he was setting forth. Dr. Bruteau has been a director and vice-president of the American Teilhard de Chardin Association, and did her doctoral dissertation on the philosophy of Sri Aurobindo. In this volume she refutes Teilhard's criticisms and produces a brilliant comparison of the points of view represented by Teilhard and Hindu thought.

HANSON, ANTHONY, ed. **TEILHARD REASSESSED. Notes, index, 184pp. DLT70, 7.00c.**
Transcription of papers delivered at a symposium of critical studies in the thought of Teilhard, attempting an evaluation of his place in contemporary Christian thinking.

HUMAN DIMENSIONS INSTITUTE. **TEILHARD DE CHARDIN: A CRITIQUE. Photographs, 8½"x11", 26pp. HDI76, 2.00p.**
A collection of essays, poems, and a painting which highlight various aspects of Teilhard de Chardin's monumental work and illustrate the diversity of it.

KOPP, JOSEPH. **TEILHARD DE CHARDIN: A NEW SYNTHESIS OF EVOLUTION. 72pp. Pau64, 1.45p.**
A clear and careful introductory examination of Teilhard's life and works as they relate to evolution.

LUBAC, HENRI DE. **THE FAITH OF TEILHARD DE CHARDIN. Notes, 215pp. ACB65, 4.85c.**
Henri de Lubac was a close friend of Teilhard, a fellow Jesuit, and one of the most notable theologians in France today. The first part of this book is an introduction to Teilhard's thought, focusing on the sources of his inspiration; the second discusses current misinterpretations.

■ *LUKAS, MARY and ELLEN.* **TEILHARD: THE MAN, THE PRIEST, THE SCIENTIST. Notes, index, 360pp. Dou77, 10.00c.**
This is a major biography which probes into the man behind the vision—revealing new insights into his personal life and motivations, the men and women he knew, and his successes and disappointments. The Lukases have geared their narrative toward the general reader and one need not have studied Teilhard's work to be intrigued by the man as he is presented here. This is an important, readable study which we recommend to all who are interested in Teilhard's thought.

TEILHARD DE CHARDIN, PIERRE. **ACTIVATION OF ENERGY. 410pp. HBJ63, 2.95p.**
Essays from 1939 to 1955 which extend and develop the theme begun in **Human Energy.**

TEILHARD DE CHARDIN, PIERRE. **BUILDING THE EARTH. Bibliography, 116pp. Avo69, 1.25p.**
A collection of six essays, well translated, which serve as a good introduction to Teilhard's philosophy. The book also includes a good basic study of Teilhard's life and work by John Kobler.

TEILHARD DE CHARDIN, PIERRE. **CHRISTIANITY AND EVOLUTION. Index, 255pp. HBJ71, 2.95p.**
Nineteen essays which blend theological speculation with practical applications.

TEILHARD DE CHARDIN, PIERRE. **THE DIVINE MILIEU. Index, 160pp. H&R68/Fon, 2.95p.**
This is considered Teilhard's most important spiritual work and the key to his religious and meditational ideas. The vision presented here is universal in its application.

TEILHARD DE CHARDIN, PIERRE. **THE FUTURE OF MAN. Index, 332pp. H&R69/Fon, 3.95p.**
As the title suggests, this book presents a view of man, his evolution, and his relations with the Earth and universe. The material is more approachable than most of Teilhard's writing and it includes a seminal chapter on the formation of the *Noosphere.*

TEILHARD DE CHARDIN, PIERRE. **HOW I BELIEVE. 91pp. H&R69, 1.25p.**
I have tried to pin down, in what follows, the reasons for my faith as a Christian, with the shades of emphasis it bears, and also its limitations or difficulties.

TEILHARD DE CHARDIN, PIERRE. **HUMAN ENERGY. Index, 191pp. HBJ69/WCS, 2.95p.**
The six major essays collected in this volume were written during the 1930s. They develop further many of the concepts central to Teilhard's thought that had appeared earlier in **The Phenomenon of Man** and **The Divine Milieu** and form a good overview of Teilhard's thought in many areas.

TEILHARD DE CHARDIN, PIERRE. **HYMN OF THE UNIVERSE. 164pp. H&R61/Fon, 1.95p.**
In this, the most mystical of Teilhard's works, we see the poetic and visionary side of this man of prayer more intensely revealed than in his more scientific works. Teilhard glorifies and praises matter as the incarnate divine substance veiling the Christ principle of divinity.

TEILHARD DE CHARDIN, PIERRE. **LET ME EXPLAIN. 189pp. H&R70/Fon, 2.45p.**
J.P. Demoulin has selected and arranged this compilation of central passages from Teilhard's most important works in an effort to summarize the whole of Teilhard's thought in one volume. In 1948 Teilhard himself drew up an outline of what he considered the stages, the directions, and the major elements of his thought and this outline has guided M. Demoulin in his choice of extracts. The material is topically arranged and this edition includes an introduction, notes on Teilhard's vocabulary, an annotated bibliography, and an index. Presents a good overview for the beginning reader.

TEILHARD DE CHARDIN, PIERRE. **LETTERS FROM A TRAVELLER. Illustrations, index, 380pp. H&R68/Fon, 2.45p.**
These letters, written mainly from China but also throughout Teilhard's worldwide travels, form a wonderful introduction to the man and his thought. This edition also includes over sixty pages of background material in three essays by Sir Julian Huxley, Father Pierre Leroy, and Claude Aragonnes.

TEILHARD DE CHARDIN, PIERRE. **MAN'S PLACE IN NATURE. 120pp. Fon56, 2.50p.**
The aim of this work is to try to define experientially the phenomena of the human being by determining structurally and historically his present position in relation to the other forms the cosmos has assumed.

TEILHARD DE CHARDIN, PIERRE. **ON HAPPINESS. 93pp. H&R66/WCS, 4.95c.**
Happiness comes through personal growth, love, union with another (or others), and through commitment to a larger cause, says Teilhard. This small book contains a lecture on happiness given in Peking in 1928, plus three wedding addresses.

TEILHARD DE CHARDIN, PIERRE. **ON LOVE. 95pp. H&R67/WCS, 4.95c.**
Excerpts from most of Teilhard's major works which briefly but thoroughly outline his thoughts on love.

TEILHARD DE CHARDIN, PIERRE. **ON SUFFERING. 120pp. H&R75/WCS, 4.95c.**
Extracts from Teilhard de Chardin's writings on the title theme, bound into a little gift book.

TEILHARD DE CHARDIN, PIERRE. **THE PHENOMENON OF MAN. Notes, index, 320pp. H&R55/Fon, 4.50p.**
Many consider this Teilhard's most important work, containing the quintessence of his thought. Its subject could be described as the surging evolution of the world from the primal stuff of the universe, through life, to consciousness and man. Sir Julian Huxley provides a long introduction.

TEILHARD DE CHARDIN, PIERRE. **THE PRAYER OF THE UNIVERSE. Notes, 191pp. H&R73/Fon, 1.25p.**
A selection of essays from **Writings in Times of War** (World War I). This mystical contemplation of the works of God was written while Teilhard was a stretcher bearer in the War and later edited.

TEILHARD DE CHARDIN, PIERRE. **TOWARD THE FUTURE. Index, 224pp. HBJ75/Fon, 3.95p.**
Essays which come out of Teilhard's concern to reveal the true meaning of our age and stimulate the *sense of man and the sense of the Christian.*

TOWERS, BERNARD. **TEILHARD DE CHARDIN. Bibliography, 46pp. Kno66/Lut, 1.75p.**
An introduction to Teilhard's life, thought, and significance. Part of a series entitled **Makers of Contemporary Theology.**

WILDIERS, N.M. **AN INTRODUCTION TO TEILHARD DE CHARDIN. Notes, index, 191pp. Fon68, 1.20p.**
Wildiers is a Belgian theologian and general editor of the official French text of the works of Teilhard. This volume is a concise, straightforward, lucid introduction to Teilhard the man, the visionary philosopher, the scientist, and the priest. It is an excellent, nontechnical introduction which emphasizes the unity of Teilhard's thought.

————— **END OF TEILHARD DE CHARDIN SUBSECTION**—————

St. Teresa of Avila

St. Teresa (1515-82) and St. John of the Cross lived and worked in close cooperation. They took it as their mission in life to reform the existing monasteries, to found new ones, and reintroduce the full rigor of the religious life which they considered proper for the cloister. To this end they worked in collaboration against the most determined opposition. The two saints lived to see the subsidence of the opposition to their work and bring it to a successful conclusion. St. Teresa is probably the best known female saint and is considered one of the greatest women in history. She was a prolific writer and is best known for her **Autobiography** in which she observed the different stages of her mystical life.

She is a mystic—and more than a mystic. Her works, it is true, are well known in the cloister and have served as nourishment to many who are far advanced on the Way of Perfection, and who, without her aid, would still be beginners in the life of prayer. Yet they have also entered the homes of millions living in the world and have brought consolation, assurance, hope and strength to souls who, in the technical sense, know nothing of the life of contemplation. Devoting herself, as she did, with the most wonderful persistence and tenacity, to the sublimest task given to man—the attempt to guide others toward perfection—she succeeded so well in that task that she is respected everywhere as an incredibly gifted teacher, who has revealed, more perhaps than any who came before her, the nature and extent of those gifts which the Lord has laid up in this life for those who love Him.—E. Allison Peers.

HAMILTON, ELIZABETH, tr. **SERVANTS OF LOVE. Bibliography, 104pp. OSV75/DLT, 2.75p.**
A topically organized collection of quotations from the writings of St. Teresa accompanied by an introductory essay on her life and work.

KAVANAUGH, KIERAN and OTILIO RODRIGUEZ, trs. **THE COLLECTED WORKS OF ST. TERESA OF AVILA, VOLUME I. Notes, index, 413pp. ICS76, 4.95p.**
This is a long awaited masterful new translation. The first volume includes *The Book of Her Life, Spiritual Testimonies,* and *Soliloquies.* Each is preceded by an introduction and the introduction to *The Book of Her Life* is thirty pages long. An excellent work of scholarship which also reads exceptionally well.

PEERS, E. ALLISON, tr. **THE AUTOBIOGRAPHY OF ST. TERESA OF AVILA (THE LIFE OF TERESA OF JESUS). 399pp. Dou60, 2.45p.**
This autobiography, written at the express command of St. Teresa's confessors to give an accurate and detailed account of her spiritual progress, has been a treasured spiritual legacy since its publication. The first part of the book is autobiographical in the ordinary sense: it describes the author's early life and education, the inner conflicts which she experienced, and the crisis which ended in her resolve to *seek perfection and walk in the way of prayer.* After a section which describes the contemplative life under the figure of the four waters, each of which corresponds to one stage of spiritual progress, St. Teresa returns to her description of her inner life. Her concern is not to theorize, but to attract others to the love of God.

PEERS, E. ALLISON, tr. **THE COMPLETE WORKS OF ST. TERESA. Index, 1,292pp. S&W43, 27.50p.**
A three volume edition of Peers' definitive translation, accompanied by a lengthy introduction and notes.

PEERS, E. ALLISON, tr. **INTERIOR CASTLE. 235pp. Dou61, 2.25p.**
This book is one of the most celebrated books on mystical theology. It is the most sublime and mature of St. Teresa's works, and one reads in it the full blossoming of a thoroughly humble and exquisitely divine nature, whose inspiration touches even those who do not know her name or anything she did. **Interior Castle** tells the story of a soul as one travels through the mystical mansions and nears the center of life, which is love, and the innermost truth, which is God.

PEERS, E. ALLISON, tr. **THE WAY OF PERFECTION. 280pp. Dou46, 1.75p.**
In an attempt to reform the order of nuns to which she belonged, St. Teresa set down one of the finest and most sublime of the timeless classics on the practice of spiritual prayer for a life lived for pure love of the divine. One who follows closely St. Teresa's example will discover that humility and self sacrifice are more potent forces than any illusions imaginable.

—————END OF ST. TERESA OF AVILA SUBSECTION—————

TERRY, MILTON, tr. **THE SIBYLLINE ORACLES. Many notes, index, 292pp. AMS1899, 16.80c.**
A translation of a collection of oracular prophecies in which Jewish or Christian doctrines were allegedly confirmed by a sibyl (legendary Greek prophetess). The prophecies were actually the work of certain Christian and Jewish writers from 150 BC to AD 180. In the **Oracles** the sibyl proved her reliability by first predicting events that had recently occurred. She then predicted future events and set forth doctrines peculiar to Hellenistic Judaism or Christianity. Many early Christian theologians thought the works were the genuine prophecy of the sibyls, and were greatly impressed by the way in which their doctrines were confirmed by external testimony. The compositions were collected into a single manuscript in the Byzantine period.

St. Therese of Lisieux

A girl dies when she is twenty-four years old at a small Carmel in the heart of Normandy....The body of Sister Teresa was taken to the municipal cemetary, accompanied by a few friends; nobody else took any notice. The grave was scarcely filled in when the fragrance of her goodness found its way out; everybody began to talk about her, first in one province, then in another, in France and all over Europe, in the Old World and in the New; her name was on the lips of believers and infidels....Why should she have been chosen when there were so many others who had died about that time whose virtues had been demonstrated concretely and in public, servants of the poor, missionaries, apostles, martyrs, godly men and women of all kinds? "Teresa! Sister Teresa!" It was all Teresa. But what had she done for us during her life? Anything we could see? Anything we could touch? Nothing. Or nothing that we knew, anyway. And yet everybody was calling to her. It was enough that she had said, "I will spend my heaven doing good upon earth." That saying was snatched up, repeated, broadcast. But could it be believed? It was believed; it had to be. Why did it have to be? That is a matter of love, and love cannot be explained. . . .

We should have to go back to the heroic ages of Christianity to find another saint so spontaneously and unanimously acclaimed and so quickly recognized by the Church. She attained the altar almost before she was in the waiting-room: the intervals which Rome requires before confirming the virtues of even the best qualified of her children were shortened for her, and only fifty years elapsed between her birth in 1873 and her glorification in 1923. For the last twenty years of this half century the whole world, its heart full of joy and its hands of gifts had hailed her and called upon her with unparalleled steadfastness. And to the question of what great events, what heavenly favours, what miracles, prophecies, visions during her life account for this extraordinary popularity, the answer is, her silence, her obscurity, her very inexistence. She lived hidden, unknown except to a few friends and relatives, and to her dying day her apostleship remained a secret within the walls of a convent. That is the greatest, the clearest, and the most overpowering of her miracles, or of the miracles done on her behalf. There is no purely natural explanation to be found for the acclamation which she received. Moreover, no such explanation would suffice; not even, in my opinion, the **Story of a Soul**, that record of her confidences which was translated into almost every language the day after her death.

—*from* **The Secret of the Little Flower**, *by Henri Gheon*

BEEVERS, JOHN, tr. **THE AUTOBIOGRAPHY. 125pp. Dou57, 1.95p.**
Twenty-eight years after Therese's death she was officially canonized, and almost immediately recognized as one of the most holy of all the saints. Obviously the light of love which she displayed in such a short life was of incredible quality.

BEEVERS, JOHN. **STORM OF GLORY: THE STORY OF ST. THERESE OF LISIEUX. 196pp. Dou49, 1.95p.**
A moving biographical portrait presenting St. Therese's life and teachings.

CLARKE, JOHN, tr. **ST. THERESE OF LISIEUX—HER LAST CONVERSATIONS. Photographs, indices, 333pp. ICS77, 5.95p.**
The complete record of St. Therese's last words and actions. The conversations are given verbatim and some of her final letters are also included along with an abundance of introductory material.

CLARKE, JOHN, tr. **STORY OF A SOUL: THE AUTOBIOGRAPHY OF ST. THERESE OF LISIEUX. Introduction, many notes, 306pp. ICS75, 4.95p.**
A full edition of the **Autobiography** taken from an unedited version of the original work. A fresh new picture of the saint is presented here and much valuable information is added to that previously available. This translation reads very well.

GHEON, HENRI. **THE SECRET OF THE LITTLE FLOWER. 124pp. S&W34, 2.40p.**
At the beginning of this biographic study, M. Gheon admits that his book is intended for those, Catholics or not, who resist St. Therese's attraction, as he once did. He reviews his personal experience, from skeptic to admirer, and he recounts the main events and places in St. Therese's life, ending with her glorification.

JOHNSON, VERNON. **SPIRITUAL CHILDHOOD: A STUDY OF ST. TERESA'S TEACHING. Notes, 224pp. S&W53, 4.20p.**
Johnson says that the purpose of this book *is to try to develop the teaching of St. Teresa of Lisieux in its relation to our holy faith and to the Sacred Scriptures.* This teaching is best summed up in a saying from the **Gospel of St. Matthew**: *I say to you, unless you be converted and become as little children, you shall not enter into the kingdom of Heaven.* The author discusses the main tenets of St. Therese's faith and message.

KNOX, RONALD, tr. **AUTOBIOGRAPHY OF A SAINT: THERESE OF LISIEUX. Notes, 256pp. Fon58, 2.15p.**
This is a lucid and definitive translation of the edition of St. Therese's autobiography put together by Father Francoise de Sainte Marie at the request of the Carmel of Lisieux. Mr. Knox is remarkably sensitive to the original work, so much so that an exact translation becomes a positive interpretation as well. The sublimity and simplicity of the *little flower* comes to life and the often awkward wording of translations is completely absent here.

MOTHER AGNES OF JESUS, ed. **THE STORY OF A SOUL: ST. THERESE OF LISIEUX. Notes, 188pp. ACB51, 1.90p.**
Mother Agnes was St. Therese's sister and she edited this autobiography at her sister's request. Her goal was to clarify the original manuscripts and give them greater coherence and continuity as a single work. This edition is translated by Father Michael Day, who also comments on the details of the original composition and the editorial work done by Mother Agnes.

O'MAHONEY, CHRISTOPHER, ed. and tr. **ST. THERESE OF LISIEUX BY THOSE WHO KNEW HER. Notes, 287pp. OSV75, 3.95p.**
The testimony of fifteen people who knew St. Therese personally, gathered soon after her death.

SHEED, F.J., tr. **COLLECTED LETTERS OF ST. THERESE OF LISIEUX. Introduction, index, 364pp. S&W72, 8.40p.**

─────── END OF ST. THERESE OF LISIEUX SUBSECTION ───────

TRATNER, GERALD. **THE MYSTERY TEACHINGS AND CHRISTIANITY. 208pp. TPH69, 1.75p.**
An examination of biblical stories and of Jesus' teachings, showing that they have been written as psychological aids to those seeking truth.

Evelyn Underhill

Evelyn Underhill (1875-1941) was a lifelong Anglican who was also attracted by Roman Catholic piety and religious experience. Her writings helped establish mystical theology as a respectable discipline among contemporary intellectuals.

ARMSTRONG, CHRISTOPHER. **EVELYN UNDERHILL: AN INTRODUCTION TO HER LIFE AND WRITINGS. Extensive bibliography, index, 326pp. Eer75/Mow, 8.95c.**
A full study which also discusses the influences on Ms. Underhill's thought and contains a good deal of previously unpublished material.

BARKWAY, LUMSDEN and LUCY MENZIES, eds. **AN ANTHOLOGY OF THE LOVE OF GOD. 220pp. Mow53, 6.50p.**
In making the selection we have been guided by words of commendation which [Ms. Underhill] gave to a volume of readings from Baron von Hugel: "All the extracts are of substantial length; there are no snippets; no mere fine sayings." And we hope the same verdict may be passed on this volume as she passed on that: "It should give countless readers a true initiation into this rich and closely woven thought....It contains the very essence of its great author's love and wisdom, and offers to those willing to accept it the real and costly food of eternal life." The anthology is topically organized.

UNDERHILL, EVELYN. **ESSENTIALS OF MYSTICISM. 245pp. AMS20, 20.15c.**
Ms. Underhill gives a hundred page discourse on the meaning, purpose, and value of mysticism, especially as expressed in the Christian tradition, and devotes the rest of the book to illustrating her thesis through discussions of noted mystics such as Plotinus, Juliana of Norwich, and St. Teresa of Avila.

UNDERHILL, EVELYN. **MYSTICISM. Index, 519pp. Dut61, 4.95p.**
Ms. Underhill's most important work. The first section, *The Mystic Fact,* explains the relation of mysticism to vitalism (her term) and psychology; the second, *The Mystic Way,* describes the awakening, purification, and training of the self in its ascent on the path leading to *the blessedness of Unitive life.* An appendix contains an historical sketch of European mysticism and the most complete topical bibliography we have seen.

UNDERHILL, EVELYN. **MYSTICS OF THE CHURCH. Bibliography, index, 260pp. Cla25, 8.00c.**
A classic work in which Ms. Underhill not only shows the historic development of Christian mysticism and its influence on the church, but also gives a deep insight into the spiritual growth of the individual mystics—their struggles, achievements, and influence. The book covers the whole development of the church from St. Paul to the present century. This is as good a review of the Christian mystics as we know of and we welcome its recent reprinting.

UNDERHILL, EVELYN. **PRACTICAL MYSTICISM. 169pp. Dut15, 1.45p.**
Introduces the methods and practice of mysticism to those who have no prior knowledge of the subject. What mysticism is and what it has to offer the average person, how it helps to solve problems, how it increases efficiency, and how it can harmonize with the duties and ideals of an active life.

UNDERHILL, EVELYN. **THE SPIRITUAL LIFE. 142pp. H&R36, 5.95c.**
This is one of the great classics of twentieth century Christian spirituality. Ms. Underhill's inspiring words have helped thousands to enter into renewed communion and cooperation with God. She begins with the central question: *How, in the crowded hours of modern life, can one develop a technique of spiritual living in harmony with God?* The answer, she suggests, lies in locating the spiritual possibilities underlying everyday life.

─────── END OF EVELYN UNDERHILL SUBSECTION ───────

WADDELL, HELEN, tr. **THE DESERT FATHERS. Notes, 209pp. UMP36/Con, 3.95p.**
The Desert Fathers were fourth century Christians who fled from the tyranny of organized religion into the desert where they founded their own movement based on gentleness and mercy. This volume contains introductory material along with translations of the major writings of the fathers and their history. This is the fullest collection of their writings available. It is beautifully translated.

WAITE, ARTHUR EDWARD, ed. **THE UNKNOWN PHILOSOPHER: LOUIS CLAUDE DE ST. MARTIN. 464pp. Mul nd, 2.95p.**
A collection of St. Martin's writings combined with a biographical study. *We must realize the deep incisive significance of this man, without whom Harder, Goethe, Schiller and the German romantics cannot be imagined....One feels that in his works there is an enormous amount of still undiscovered wisdom.—* Rudolf Steiner.

WARD, BENEDICTA, tr. **THE SAYINGS OF THE DESERT FATHERS. Introduction, glossary, bibliography, indices, 245pp. Cis75, 7.50p.**
The men and women of whom the Sayings speak were Christians who received the challenge of the **Gospel** *with all earnestness and wanted to respond to it uncomprisingly, as generously as God, with their whole selves. Some built their whole life on one Word of the* **Gospel,** *some on one glimpse of Eternity seen in the eyes, the behavior, the whole personality of an Elder. Men of high rank in the world and of high culture came to monks without any worldly knowledge because "they knew not the first letters of the book of Wisdom which the others possessed."—*from the introduction. This is the definitive collection of these fragments, and they are presented in their entirety, alphabetically arranged.

WARNER, MARINA. **ALONE OF ALL HER SEX: THE MYTH AND THE CULT OF THE VIRGIN MARY. Notes, bibliography, index, 435pp. RaH76/QuB, 7.95c.**
This is an interesting study of the Virgin Mary which reveals her in many guises from antiquity to the present day. Ms. Warner tries to make the reader understand why Mary is a supremely important figure, and what she really is—a dynamic historic entity both deliberately created by the church to meet its own needs, and at the same time instinctively formed by simple human needs. Ms. Warner's approach is historical, mythological, and psychological and a wealth of illustrations accompany the text. The author also includes a variety of poems that illustrate man's passionate feelings about the Virgin in every century.

WATHERN, AMBROSE. **SILENCE. Notes, bibliography, 258pp. Cis73, 10.95c.**
An exploration of the dimensions of silence as a part of everyday life, as a necesary form of self discipline, as a manner of prayer, and as a method of communication. Father Warren draws upon the experiences of a number of Benedictine monks in his discussion.

WATTS, ALAN. **MYTH AND RITUAL IN CHRISTIANITY. Extensive glossary, index, 262pp. Bea68, 3.95p.**
A retelling for modern readers of many of the most noted Christian myths. The material is well written and the reader gets a good feeling for the festivals of the Christian year. Many illustrations, including reproductions of some illuminated manuscripts.

WAY, ROBERT. **THE WISDOM OF THE ENGLISH MYSTICS. 86pp. NDP78, 4.55p.**
The bulk of this book is devoted to a randomly selected and organized anthology of English mystical writings, each about a paragraph long. Way begins the book with a survey of the English mystical tradition.

The Way of the Pilgrim

This work was written by an unknown nineteenth century Russian peasant. It tells of his constant wrestling with the problem of *how to pray without ceasing.* He wanders over the steppes of Russia in search of the answer to this question until finally his intense quest is over and he attains the object of his love and surrenders himself wholly to it. This is a unique work which helps the reader understand the soul of Eastern Christianity. It is also a practical work, full of devotional guidance for those who wish to use the *Jesus Prayer.*

BACOVCIN, HELEN, tr. **THE WAY OF A PILGRIM AND THE PILGRIM CONTINUES HIS WAY. Introduction, notes, 196pp. Dou78, 2.45p.**
This is a new translation of this moving work, written in flowing modern language.

FRENCH, R.M., tr. **THE WAY OF THE PILGRIM AND THE PILGRIM CONTINUES HIS WAY. Introduction, maps, notes, 254pp. Sea52, c7.50/3.95p/1.75p.**
This fine translation is the work which introduced the writings of this unknown pilgrim to the English speaking world. Each of the translations offers a somewhat different feeling, and each is excellent. French writes vividly and does a wonderful job of conveying the essence of the pilgrim's faith.

——END OF THE WAY OF THE PILGRIM SUBSECTION——

WEIL, SIMONE. **GATEWAY TO GOD. 160pp. Fon74, 1.95p.**
An illuminated collection of essays and *pensees* on the love of God by a woman who incorporated the mystic vision into her daily life. Edited by David Rapier.

WEITZMANN, KURT. **LATE ANTIQUE-EARLY CHRISTIAN PAINTING. 8"x11", 128pp. Brz76, 9.95p.**
Reproductions and discussions of a number of illuminated manuscripts from this period including such famous works as **The Cotton Genesis, The Vienna Genesis,** and **The Rosanno Gospels.** Forty-eight plates in four colors plus gold and many additional illustrations.

WELCH, JANE. **THE KNOWN AND UNKNOWN LIFE OF JESUS CHRIST. 418pp. YPS24, 7.00c.**
The following subtitle describes the contents and approach as well as anything we can say: *Giving accounts of his travels and wonderous works during the entire thirty-five years of his manifestation on earth, together with the correspondence with, and demonstration of, the two fundamental sciences, Astrology and Numerology, by which all suns and worlds were created and placed by the Father on High, before ever the earth was formed; and which contain the basis of the understanding of the hidden knowledge given to man in the Scriptures, and without which the* **Bible** *is a closed book.*

WHEELER, ERIC, tr. **DOROTHEOS OF GAZA: DISCOURSES AND SAYINGS. Index, 259pp. Cis77, 4.95p.**
Dorotheos of Gaza was a Desert Father who wrote in a simple, approachable manner. His discourses and psychological stories form an excellent introduction to the rich spiritual universe of the deserts of Egypt, Palestine, and Syria. Wheeler includes a lengthy introduction.

WHONE, HERBERT. **CHURCH, MONASTERY, CATHEDRAL. Line drawings throughout, 191pp. Com77, 8.95c.**
An encyclopedic description, alphabetically arranged, of all major architectural features in the Christian tradition. Whone relates these artistic forms to the spiritual convictions and traditions which inspired them.

WILES, MAURICE and MARK SANTER, eds. **DOCUMENTS IN EARLY CHRISTIAN THOUGHT. 278pp. CUP75, 5.95p.**
A representative selection of extracts from the writings of the early Christian fathers. The extracts, for the most part newly translated by the editors, are arranged topically under the following headings: *God, Trinity, Christ, Holy Spirit, Sin and Grace, Tradition and Scripture, Church, Sacraments, Christian Living, Church and Society,* and *Final Goal.* They are of sufficient length to show the distinctive flavor of each writer. Annotation has been kept to a minimum, but each main section has a short introduction.

William of St. Thierry

William was a twelfth century Benedictine abbot who led a reform movement aimed at greater simplicity. He resigned his post in middle age, and became a Cistercian monk in order to experience at first hand the austere way of life he had come greatly to admire in his friend Bernard of Clairvaux. A gentle spirit and a fine theologian, William reveals his deepest aspirations in his works and attempts to explain to himself and others the way by which men could come to see *the face of God*. His importance as a writer of theological treatises and counsels on the spiritual life has been realized only in the past half century, after generations of obscurity.

ANDERSON, JOHN D., tr. **THE ENIGMA OF FAITH. Bibliography, index, 122pp. Cis74, 7.95p.**
This book is a work of William's mature period and is one of his finest treatments of the profundities of Christian belief. The translation is the first English one and Anderson also includes a careful analysis of the sources used by William in its composition.

BERKELEY, THEODORE, tr. **THE GOLDEN EPISTLE. Introduction, notes, bibliography, index, 150pp. Cis76, 4.00p.**
The Golden Epistle has been ascribed to several different authors, most notably Bernard of Clairvaux. Today its author is known to be William of St. Thierry. It is a practical guide to the spiritual life which has been translated into many languages and read by countless persons among both the clergy and the laity.

DECHANET, JEAN MARIE. **WILLIAM OF ST. THIERRY. Notes, bibliography, index, 182pp. Cis72, 10.95c.**
A biographical study of the man and his work by a Benedictine monk.

PENELOPE, SISTER, tr. **ON CONTEMPLATING GOD, PRAYER, MEDITATIONS. Notes, bibliography, index, 199pp. Cis70, 4.00p.**
Three highly personal works, written while William was abbot of the Benedictine monastery of St. Thierry, reflecting his deepening spiritual life and the hope, frustrations, and joys he met. In **Meditations**, the longest piece, the reader becomes acutely aware of the difficult personal struggle which had overtaken him and which would lead him to resign his office and enter the more austere and contemplative life of the Cistercians. Jacques Hourlier and J.M. Dechanet supply lengthy introductions to each of the texts.

SHEWRING, WALTER, tr. **GOLDEN EPISTLE OF ABBOT WILLIAM OF ST. THIERRY. 176pp. S&W73, 7.00c.**
This was the first English translation and the edition includes an extensive introduction by Abbot Justin McCann as well as many notes.

————**END OF WILLIAM OF ST. THIERRY SUBSECTION**————

WILLIAMS, CHARLES. **THE DESCENT OF THE DOVE: A SHORT HISTORY OF THE HOLY SPIRIT IN THE CHURCH. Chronology, notes, index, 254pp. Eer39, 3.95p.**
A history of Christianity, focusing on the work of the Holy Spirit in the church throughout the centuries. Williams believes that *All of Christendom is held together by the web of exchange in which man is united with his contemporaries and with former generations by practising the principle of coinherence which involves substitution, sacrifice, forgiveness, and reconciliation.* Williams shows how the principle of coinherence has been developed and expressed through the course of history.

WILSON, IAN. **THE SHROUD OF TURIN. Many illustrations, notes, 284pp. Dou78, 2.25p.**
The shroud of Turin is believed by many to be the cloth in which Christ was buried. This book details the mystery surrounding the shroud. Since it appeared in Europe in the 1350s, it has been condemned by many as a fraud. But modern scientific analysis has shown that all the markings on the cloth conform to the accounts of Christ's death and burial as recorded in the **New Testament**. This is the most complete and authoritative discussion of the shroud that we know of. Every possible aspect is considered and the narrative is well documented.

WINKWORTH, SUSANNA, tr. **THEOLOGICA GERMANICA. Introduction, notes, 134pp. Wat1893, 6.15p.**
In his preface to the 1518 edition of this book, Martin Luther wrote: *No book hath ever come into my hand, whence I have learnt, or would wish to learn more of what God, and Christ, and man and all things are.... God grant that this book may be spread abroad.* The treatise was discovered by Luther and published under his auspices. This translation is into modern English.

ZARNECKI, GEORGE. **THE MONASTIC ACHIEVEMENT. 128 illustrations, nineteen in color, bibliography, index, 144pp. MGH72, 3.95p.**
In the medieval period Western civilization was kept alive only in the monasteries. After the breakup of the Roman Empire they preserved the vestiges of classical literature and art; during the Middle Ages they provided the educated elite which administered Europe; and up to the fifteenth century they constituted centers of influence and enterprise that no secular institution could rival. Tension was inevitable and the orders went through a variety of reform movements. Professor Zarnecki is one of the world's leading medieval art historians and here he vividly recreates and draws on the immense riches of monastic art and architecture.

COMPARATIVE RELIGION

Throughout history and beyond in the dark recesses of men's earliest cultures, religion has been a vital and pervasive feature of human life. To understand human history and human life it is necessary to understand religion, and in the contemporary world one must understand other nations' ideologies and faith in order to grasp the meaning of life as seen from perspectives often very different from our own.

But religion is not something that one can see. It is true that there are temples, ceremonies, religious art. These can be seen, but their significance needs to be approached through the inner life of those who use these externals. Consider the ceremony of baptizing a baby. How can we understand it, save by knowing what the idea of baptism means to Christians and by knowing the hopes and feelings of those who participate in the occasion? We must see the way in which the externals and inner meanings of religion are fused together. This is why the history of religions must be more than the chronicling of events: it must be an attempt to enter into the meanings of those events. So it is not enough for us to survey the course which the religious history of mankind has taken: we must also penetrate into the hearts and minds of those who have been involved in that history.

Religion is a doubly rich and complex phenomenon. Not only has it the complexity indicated by this need to hold together its outer and inner aspects, but it also has existed and exists in a variety of forms of faith. There are many religions to be discovered in the world. The study of these is a fascinating and stimulating task, for not only is this variety a testimony to the richness of the religious sense and imagination of mankind, and often—though by no means always—to the nobility of the human spirit, but also it gives rise to some profoundly important questions about the truth of religion.

—condensed from **The Religious Experience of Mankind**, *by Ninian Smart*

ADAM, MICHAEL. **WANDERING IN EDEN.** 8½"x11", 115pp. **RaH76/Wdw, 4.95p.**
This volume is divided into three sections: *The Way of the Body, The Way of Emptiness,* and *The Way of Things.* As a whole it represents Adam's attempt to relate traditional Eastern concepts to Western religion, art, and science. The book is beautifully produced and 109 illustrations illuminate the narrative. Many quotations from sacred texts and masters are also included.

AMORE, ROY. **TWO MASTERS, ONE MESSAGE—THE LIFE AND TEACHINGS OF GAUTAMA AND JESUS.** Notes, bibliography, index, 208pp. **Abi78, 5.95p.**
Dr. Amore illustrates the similarities between the lives and teachings of Jesus and Gautama Buddha. He explains why so many of the stories about the two masters are remarkably similar; discusses the common ethics of the two (such as purity of mind and nonviolence); considers the hypothesis that Buddhism influenced the New Testament; and reveals matters on which Jesus and Gautama differ. Published by a Christian press.

ANDERSON, NORMAN, ed. **THE WORLD'S RELIGIONS.** Index, 244pp. **Eer75, 3.95p.**
An academic survey by a number of Christian scholars of Judaism, Islam, Hinduism, Buddhism, Shinto, and Confucianism. The essays are well organized and they delve deeper into the scholarly aspects of the religions than most general studies.

ANSLEY, DELIGHT. **THE GOOD WAYS. Illustrations, index, 223pp. Cro59, 5.95c.**
A simple, well organized comparative religion text for older children. Ms. Ansley describes the religions that have dominated the world from earliest times: those of Egypt, Greece, Palestine, India, and China, and those based on the teachings of Muhammad, the Buddha, and Jesus. She includes a brief biography of the founder of each faith, and recounts the legends that have been superimposed on historical facts. Her religious conviction is expressed in the following words: *Religions may be compared to a series of roads on which human beings are traveling. Our road is not the only one. There are others, starting from different places and going through different territory, but they all lead toward the same goal.*

ARBERRY, A.J., ed. **RELIGION IN THE MIDDLE EAST. 45.00c/set.**
See the Islam section.

BAHM, ARCHIE. **THE WORLD'S LIVING RELIGIONS. Bibliography, index, 384pp. SIU64, 3.25p.**
This is a dry, factual presentation of the basic features of Hinduism, Jainism, Buddhism, Vedantism and Yoga, Taoism, Confucianism, Shintoism, Judaism, Christianity, Islam, and Humanism. The book is keyed toward giving the general reader a feeling for the religions without overwhelming him with details. Bahm has made a deep, albeit general, study of a number of Eastern traditions and has translated some key texts.

BALLARD, MARTIN. **WHO AM I?—A BOOK OF WORLD RELIGIONS. Many photographs, 175pp. HPG71, 3.95p.**
A very simple, illustrated account of the teachings of Taoism and Confucianism, Hinduism, Buddhism, Judaism, Christianity, and Islam. The emphasis is on what these religious traditions mean in practice to their followers and how they affect each individual's life.

BALLOU, ROBERT. **THE PORTABLE WORLD BIBLE. Glossary, notes, 624pp. Vik44, 4.95p.**
An excellent compilation which presents the reader with the essential scriptures of the world's eight major religions. The only explanatory material is the notes at the end of the selections. This is an abridged version of Ballou's original work.

■ BANCROFT, ANNE. **RELIGIONS OF THE EAST. Notes, topical bibliography, index, 7¼"x10", HeG74, 256pp. 13.95c.**
This is a beautifully illustrated, clearly written presentation of the essence of Hinduism, Buddhism, Tibetan Buddhism, Zen Buddhism, and Sufism. The mystical aspects of these traditions are emphasized and Ms. Bancroft makes use of poetry and legends to convey the essence common to their teachings. We feel that this book is the best introduction to the religions of the East available.

BANCROFT, ANNE. **TWENTIETH CENTURY MYSTICS AND SAGES. Illustrations, glossary, bibliography, index, 352pp. Reg76/HeG, 4.95p.**
A nicely written survey of nineteen contemporary spiritual leaders: Aldous Huxley, Alan Watts, Thomas Merton, Teilhard de Chardin, Krishnamurti, Gurdjieff, Sak Subuh, Meher Baba, Maharaj Ji, Ramana Maharshi, Maharishi Mahesh Yogi, Chogyam Trungpa, Dhiravamsa, Martin Buber, Dion Fortune, Rudolf Steiner, Douglas Harding, Don Juan, and Mother Teresa. Each individual is fully discussed—some at greater length than others—and the presentation is definitely more enlightened than is usually the case with surveys of this type. We like Ms. Bancroft's style very much.

BARY, THEODORE DE and AINSLIE EMBREE, eds. **A GUIDE TO ORIENTAL CLASSICS. 199pp. Col64, 4.50p.**
Classics of the four major traditions—Islamic, Indian, Chinese, and Japanese—are included in this bibliographic guide. The works listed range from history, philosophy, and religion to poetry, drama, and

fiction. Under each classic there is a list of translations, complete or partial, into English and other Western languages, with annotations, followed by a list of secondary readings and a series of topics for discussion.

BESANT, ANNIE. SEVEN GREAT RELIGIONS. 274pp. TPH70, 3.00c.
Transcription of a collection of eight lectures delivered to an audience of Hindus at the Theosophical Society in Madras, India. They are popularized expositions of the major tenets of Hinduism, Buddhism, Zoroastrianism, Christianity, Jainism, Sikhism, Islam, and Theosophy.

BHARATI, AGEHANANDA. THE LIGHT AT THE CENTER: CONTEXT AND PRETEXT OF MODERN MYSTICISM. Notes, bibliography, index, 254pp. REr76, 4.95p.
Bharati is both a trained social scientist and an initiate into a Hindu monastic order. This is a rigorous, academic analysis of both mysticism and the Eastern mystical movements which have been popularized in the West. Bharati raises some interesting points and demonstrates a thorough knowledge of the subject, but the book is tough going and needs to be studied rather than read straight through.

BRANDON, S.G.F., ed. DICTIONARY OF COMPARATIVE RELIGION. Indices, 7"x10¼", 704pp. Scr70, 37.00c.
This fine sourcebook includes information on almost every topic we can think of related to comparative religion and ancient cultural traditions, East and West. The explanations are clear and succinct and there are many cross references and suggestions for further reading. A good reference tool for anyone who is building a significant library in this field.

BRANDON, S.G.F. MAN AND HIS DESTINY IN THE GREAT RELIGIONS. Many notes, lengthy bibliography, indices, 456pp. MUP62, 21.00c.
A historical and comparative study, originally delivered as a series of lectures at Oxford University. Dr. Brandon does a good job of introducing and summarizing a wide body of information in a readable manner. He includes essays on Egypt, Mesopotamia, the Hebrews, Greek culture, Christianity, Islam, Iran, India, Buddhism, and China as well as a lengthy introduction.

BRANDON, S.G.F. RELIGION IN ANCIENT HISTORY. Notes, annotated bibliography, index, 422pp. A&U69, 23.50c.
An illustrated collection of twenty-five essays. The first discusses the origin of religion. This is followed by surveys of the religious ideas of ancient Egypt, Mesopotamia, Palestine, Greece, and Iran; essays on ideas such as creation, death, time, the soul, and the judgment of the dead; and studies of figures such as Osiris, Akhenaten, Job, and Zarathustra. The latter half of the book deals with religious ideas, events, and individuals in the first three centuries AD, particularly Jesus and early Christianity.

BRANTL, GEORGE, ed. THE RELIGIOUS EXPERIENCE. Two volumes, boxed, 1162pp. Brz64, 17.40c/set.
A representative selection of writings on the four modes or stages of religious experience: the way of immanence in which God is found inward to nature and identified...with what man finds of value in this world;...the way of transcendance in which the infinity of God is asserted;...the atheistic and the agnostic position;...and the possibility of a new way of experience in which transcendance and immanence come together in such a way as to avoid the problems inherent in their separation.—from the introduction. Brantl has chosen his selections from a wide range of writings and provides an introduction to each one.

BURCKHARDT, TITUS. SACRED ART: EAST AND WEST. 7.15p.
See the Sacred Art section.

BURTON, NAOMI, PATRICK HART and JAMES LAI. THE ASIAN JOURNAL OF THOMAS MERTON. Excellent descriptive glossary, bibliography, 353pp. NDP73/SIP, 4.45p.
The personal remarks, observations and thoughts of this modern mystic and humanitarian thinker as recorded by himself during his travels in Asia prior to his untimely death. The deeply spiritual understanding of this evolved soul is revealed in his inclusive grasp of the underlying unity of the world's religions and all genuine approaches to a more enlightened consciousness. Includes his last letters and written thoughts before his death.

CAPRA, FRITJOF. THE TAO OF PHYSICS. 5.95p/2.95p.
See the Astronomy section.

CASSIRER, ERNST. LANGUAGE AND MYTH. Index, 113pp. Dov46, 2.00p.
Cassirer analyzes the nonrational thought processes that comprise culture. He demonstrates that beneath both language and myth there lies an unconscious grammar of experience, whose categories and canons are not those of logical thought. He shows that this prelogical logic is not merely an undeveloped state of rationality, but something basically different, and that this archaic mode of thought still has enormous expression through language, poetry, and myth. In these essays Cassirer discusses such seemingly diverse concepts such as the metaphysics of the Bhagavad Gita, the Melanesian concept of mana, modern poetry, ancient Egyptian religion, and symbolic logic.

CHAN, WING-TSIT, et al. THE GREAT ASIAN RELIGIONS. Glossary, bibliography, index, 429pp. McM69, 9.35p.
An anthology of some of the most important sacred texts, along with extensive commentary. The authors all teach Eastern religion courses at the university level and this anthology has been prepared to serve as a text for an introductory course. Both the translations and the commentary are uniformly excellent and the book is well organized.

COX, HARVEY. TURNING EAST: THE PROMISE AND PERIL OF THE NEW ORIENTALISM. Bibliography, index, 192pp. S&S77/AIL, 3.95p.
Cox is a noted Christian theologian and presently a professor at the Harvard Divinity School. He became curious about the neo-Oriental wave which he observed in Boston and set out to investigate what it means to turn East. In the process he became actively involved in all of the religious movements he was studying and even took up the regular practice of a Tibetan Buddhist meditational technique. In the end, though, he was brought back to a closer understanding of Christianity. This is a sympathetic, albeit dry, account of the current Eastern involvement of many Americans. Cox focuses on what individuals actually draw from their practices and it is as good a place as any for parents to start to understand what attracts their children to the various movements.

Mircea Eliade

Professor Eliade is one of the leading scholars of today in the fields of comparative religion and mythology. There is a discussion of his life and work in the mythology section.

ELIADE, MIRCEA. DEATH, AFTERLIFE, AND ESCHATOLOGY. Bibliography, 120pp. H&R74, 2.50p.
Part three of From Primitives to Zen.

ELIADE, MIRCEA. FROM MEDICINE MEN TO MUHAMMAD. Bibliography, 232pp. H&R74, 2.50p.
Part four of From Primitives to Zen.

ELIADE, MIRCEA. FROM PRIMITIVES TO ZEN. Bibliography, indices, 670pp. H&R67, 8.95p.
A thematic sourcebook on the history of religions which includes what Professor Eliade feels to be the essential documents from all the important religious traditions—with the exception of Christianity and Judaism—arranged according to recurrent themes. As Eliade says, It seems to me that only by reading a certain number of religious texts related to the same subject (cosmogony, initiation, myths on the origin of death, etc.) is a student able to grasp their structural similarities and their differences. Recently this text has been split up into a number of individual volumes; we recommend getting this one volume edition rather than the smaller volumes. That is how Eliade originally put it together and the material makes more sense as a whole unit.

ELIADE, MIRCEA. GODS, GODDESSES, AND MYTHS OF CREATION. Bibliography, 174pp. H&R74, 3.50p.
Part one of From Primitives to Zen.

ELIADE, MIRCEA. IMAGES AND SYMBOLS. Notes, index, 189pp. SAM52, 3.95p.
We have seen that myths decay and symbols become secularized, but that they never disappear, even in the most positivist of civilizations. Symbols and myths come from

such depths: they are part and parcel of the human being, and it is impossible that they should not be found again in any and every essential situation of man in the Cosmos.— from the foreword. This book is a collection of studies in religious symbolism. The essays are enlightening as they show how man has been influenced by these archetypes throughout history and their continuing role in the psyche of modern man.

ELIADE, MIRCEA. **MAN AND THE SACRED. Bibliography, 186pp. H&R74, 2.50p.**
Part two of **From Primitives to Zen.**

ELIADE, MIRCEA. **NO SOUVENIRS: JOURNAL, 1957-1969. Index, 357pp. H&R77, 15.00c.**
This is a revealing collection of fragments from Eliade's journal. It includes notes on works in progress, reflections on encounters with other notable figures, insights into the human condition, travelogues, and much else.

ELIADE, MIRCEA. **OCCULTISM, WITCHCRAFT, AND CULTURAL FASHIONS. Notes, index, 148pp. UCh76, 3.95p.**
Six essays: *Cultural Fashions and the History of Religions, The World, the City, the House, Mythologies of Death, The Occult and the Modern World, Some Observations on European Witchcraft,* and *Spirit, Light, and Seed.*

ELIADE, MIRCEA. **PATTERNS IN COMPARATIVE RELIGION. Notes, indices, 501pp. NAL63/StW, 4.95p.**
This is a study of the nature of religion based on the beliefs and systems of individuals and groups rather than on historical, categorical, or chronological approaches. Topics include: *The Sky and Sun Gods; The Structure and Morphology of the Sacred; The Sun and Sun-Worship; The Moon and Its Mystique; The Waters and Water Symbolism; Sacred Stones; The Earth, Woman and Fertility; Agriculture and Fertility Cults; Sacred Places; Sacred Time and the Myth of Eternal Renewal;* and *The Strucutre of Symbols.*

ELIADE, MIRCEA. **THE QUEST: HISTORY AND MEANING IN RELIGION. Index, 180pp. UCh69, 3.95p.**
A collection of essays on themes common to different religious experiences and beliefs. Eliade's hope in writing this work (and all his others) is to develop an awareness of the place of the history of religion in a secularized society.

ELIADE, MIRCEA. **THE SACRED AND THE PROFANE: THE NATURE OF RELIGION. 256pp. HBJ57, 2.95p.**
Eliade traces manifestations of the sacred from primitive to modern times, in terms of space, time, nature and the cosmos, and life itself. He shows how the total human experience of the religious man compares to that of the nonreligious and observes that even modern men who proclaim themselves to live in a completely profane world are still unconsciously nourished by the memory of the sacred, in camouflaged myths and degenerated rituals. Chapter-by-chapter bibliography.

ELIADE, MIRCEA and JOSEPH KITAGAWA, eds. **THE HISTORY OF RELIGIONS. Many notes, 172pp. UCh59, 2.45p.**
A collection of detailed, scholarly essays on methodology for the study of religion, especially on the university level.

KITAGAWA, JOSEPH and CHARLES LONG, eds. **MYTHS AND SYMBOLS: STUDIES IN HONOR OF MIRCEA ELIADE. Notes, index, 438pp. UCh69, 15.45c.**
A collection of important original essays focusing on Eliade's continuing effort to delineate the multidimensional character of myths and symbols as specific forms of the religious perception of mankind. The volume is divided into three sections: phenomenological and methodological, historical, and literary studies. Also included is a short account of Eliade's life, as well as a complete bibliography of his works in many languages. The contributors, well known scholars from all over the world, include Giuseppe Tucci, Gershom Scholem, Georges Dumezil, Ernst Junger, and E.M. Cioran.

———————— **END OF MIRCEA ELIADE SUBSECTION** ————————

ELLWOOD, ROBERT. **MANY PEOPLES, MANY FAITHS: AN INTRODUCTION TO THE RELIGIOUS LIFE OF MANKIND. Illustrations, annotated bibliography, index, 7"x9½", 378pp. PrH76, 13.65c.**
Ellwood says that he has endeavored *to encapsulate in nontechnical language something of the total human experience, made up as it is of an inseparable combination of conceptual, worship, and social factors, of religious life past and present.* This is a

readable study which does convey something of the essential feeling of each of the religious traditions.

ELLWOOD, ROBERT, ed. **READINGS ON RELIGION FROM INSIDE AND OUTSIDE. Thematically organized, 351pp. PrH78, 7.95p.**
An anthology of essays on the world's religions, touching on history, psychology, symbolism, mythology, sociology, and religious practices. The selections include classical writers like Apuleius and St. Augustine; renowned scholars like Marx, Freud, Piaget, Tillich, and Levi-Strauss; and countless less known authors.

Pu-tai, laughing pot-bellied monk.

ELLWOOD, ROBERT. **RELIGIOUS AND SPIRITUAL GROUPS IN MODERN AMERICA. Notes, bibliography, addresses of groups, 334pp. PrH73, 9.35p.**
A broad and generally sympathetic, survey of the vast range of non-Judeo-Christian religions, from Theosophists and Rosicrucians to Transcendental Meditation and Krishna Consciousness. Useful reading for anyone who wants to get his bearings among all the cults and movements in our present spiritual renaissance.

ELLWOOD, ROBERT, ed. **THE WORDS OF THE WORLD'S RELIGIONS: AN ANTHOLOGY. 431pp. PrH77, 10.30p.**
This is the most comprehensive anthology we have ever seen of source writings and critical essays. Professor Ellwood has done an excellent job of selecting and organizing his material and, wherever possible, he has chosen modern translations. The religions of the ancient world are well represented and the selections illustrate the roots of the great modern religious traditions. The critical essays and selections from contemporary literature give the reader a good feeling for the living significance of the religion being discussed.

EPSTEIN, PERLE. **ORIENTAL MYSTICS AND MAGICIANS. 151pp. Dou75, 5.95c.**
This is an excellent book for parents who would like their children to learn about Eastern philosophy. A chapter each is devoted to the religious ideas and movements of India, Japan, Tibet, and China. There are also separate chapters on Sri Chaitanya, the Zen Master Hakuin, Milarepa, and Sri Ramakrishna. The book is well illustrated with photographs and drawings.

FARUQI, ISMAIL, ed. **HISTORICAL ATLAS OF THE RELIGIONS OF THE WORLD. Index, 8½"x11", 368pp. McM74, 20.95c.**
This is the most extensive historical atlas of religion ever published. Sixty-five maps, including areas never before mapped, portray practically everything which lends itself to cartographic interpretation. Maps illustrate the origins and distribution of religions, and the locations of sacred cities, sites, and temples. Also highlighting the material are numerous photographs and drawings. Accompanying essays by noted scholars present the history of each religion, its growth and interaction with space and time, and the relation of one religion to another. The material is very well organized and each section includes extensive bibliographic references. An appendix traces the chronology of each religion discussed.

FAUSSET, HUGH. **THE FLAME AND THE LIGHT. Bibliography, 232pp. TPH58, 3.75p.**
This is a sensitive philosophical survey of religion based on Fausset's academic study and his inner experience. He draws parallels between the religious cultures of the East and West and focuses on Buddhism and Indian philosophy. We recommend this book to those who seek an understanding of the underlying meaning of religion rather than a purely academic study.

FEIBLEMAN, JAMES. **UNDERSTANDING ORIENTAL PHILOSO-PHY. Bibliography, index, 252pp. NAL76, 1.95p.**
A survey of the philosophies of India, China, and Japan from the dawn of recorded time to the modern era. It is an adequate work for those who seek an overview. Feibleman writes clearly and has organized his material fairly well.

FRAZIER, ALLIE, ed. **CHINESE AND JAPANESE RELIGIONS. Glossary, bibliography, 272pp. Wes69, 3.50p.**
This is Volume III of the editor's *Readings in Eastern Religious Thought.* Here Ms. Frazier is mainly concerned with the major movements in China and Japan. The book is designed to bring together in one volume the primary religious texts of the two countries along with significant secondary readings that shed light upon these traditions. The translations are chosen for their clarity and the emphasis is on those that would be of most value to the beginning student. Background material on each selection is included along with a survey of each of the religions. The contributors are noted scholars from within the several religious systems.

■ *FROST, S.E., JR., ed.* **THE SACRED WRITINGS OF THE WORLD'S GREAT RELIGIONS. 416pp. MGH72, 3.95p.**
This selection covers Hinduism, Zoroastrianism, Taoism, Confucianism, Jainism, Buddhism, Judaism, Christianity, Islam, Shinto, Sikhism, Mormonism, and Christian Science. The treatment of each religion begins with a general introduction describing the religion's origin, its founder, the location and number of its adherents, and the great books that constitute its scripture. This is followed by selections from the scripture itself. Passages of some length are included rather than brief excerpts, so that the reader can grasp the context and thereby appreciate the full message of the teaching. A topical index enables the reader to make comparisons between the views of the various faiths on specific matters.

GAER, JOSEPH. **HOLIDAYS AROUND THE WORLD. 5.95c.**
See the Fairytales section.

GAER, JOSEPH. **WHAT THE GREAT RELIGIONS BELIEVE. Bibliography, index, 205pp. NAL63/NEL, 1.25p.**
A brief account of the basic beliefs of Hinduism, Jainism, Buddhism, Taoism, Shinto, Judaism, Christianity, Islam, Zoroastrianism, Confucianism, and Zen Buddhism—with selections from their sacred literature. This is the most simplified overview we know of.

GASKELL, G.A. **DICTIONARY OF ALL SCRIPTURES AND MYTHS. 844pp. Crn60, 15.00c.**
The most definitive study of the origin, nature, and meaning of the sacred language of the scriptures and myths connected to the various religions of the world. Over 5,000 entries including numerous quotations from authoritative sources. Completely cross referenced.

GRAHAM, DOM AELRED. **THE END OF RELIGION: AUTOBIO-GRAPHICAL EXPLORATIONS. Notes, index, 292pp. HBJ71, 2.85p.**
An exploration of the meaning and nature of religion and the role of the church in the contemporary world. Dom Graham is one of the few theologians in the West who, over a long period of time, has sought to bring to Christians an awareness and understanding of Hinduism and Buddhism.

GUIRDHAM, ARTHUR. **THE GREAT HERESY: THE HISTORY AND BELIEF OF THE CATHARS. 183pp. Spe77, 8.25c.**
Dr. Guirdham has devoted much of his life to a study of the Cathars, a little known sect commonly referred to as the Albigenes. Catharism was considered heretical and was wiped out by the Catholic Church during the Inquisition. In medieval times Catharism was well established in Northern Italy and Southern France. Cathar records and literature were ruthlessly destroyed by the Church. This is a readable exposition of most of what is known today about them. The later part of the book contains a series of teachings which Dr. Guirdham received from discarnate entities, which he feels are analogous to the teachings of the Cathars.

HEBBLETHWAITE, BRIAN. **EVIL, SUFFERING, AND RELIGION. Bibliography, index, 115pp. Haw76, 3.95p.**
For those who wish to believe in a loving God, the presence of evil and suffering in the world has always been a stumbling block to both faith and reason. This book surveys the different ways in which religions have attempted to cope with the problem. It is a serious, theological exploration of the issue, though not a technical one.

HICK, JOHN, ed. **TRUTH AND DIALOGUE IN WORLD RELIGION. Index, 164pp. Wes74/SIP, 5.95c.**
An analysis of the conflicting *truth-claims* among religions—all of which purport to have the final answer. The book consists of a series of essays by noted scholars both in the field of comparative religion (e.g. R.C. Zaehner, Geoffrey Parrinder) and in specific religious areas (e.g. Trevor Ling, Kenneth Cragg), discussing the views of various religions toward the truth represented by all religion as well as by the individual religion studied.

HIXON, LEX. **COMING HOME: THE EXPERIENCE OF ENLIGHT-ENMENT IN SACRED TRADITIONS. Bibliography, 233pp. Dou78, 2.95p.**
An illuminating series of essays on a variety of spiritual teachers and sacred traditions. Hixon is himself deeply involved in spiritual work and his writing comes from the heart. He includes chapters on Ramakrishna, Ramana Maharshi, the Zen Ox-herding pictures, Plotinus, Hasidic masters, St. Paul, the I Ching, and a number of other subjects. The thread that runs through the book is the potentiality of enlightenment.

HUME, ROBERT. **THE WORLD'S LIVING RELIGIONS. Bibliography, index, 335pp. TTC59, 5.40c.**
This is a completely revised edition of a standard work on comparative religion which has gone through more than twenty-five printings. Dr. Hume is a Christian and this is apparent throughout his discussion of the thirteen major world religions. He covers the origin, sacred scriptures, history, and chief values of each one. The material is clearly dated; its chief interest lies in the picture it presents of where the Western study of comparative religion was in the early twentieth century.

JASPERS, KARL. **SOCRATES, BUDDHA, CONFUCIUS, JESUS. Bibliography, index, 104pp. HBJ62, 1.75p.**
A scholarly overview of these four individuals. Each is considered individually and the appraisal is divided into sections on life, thought, influence, and personality. A good summary, though on the dry side.

KAUFMANN, WALTER. **RELIGIONS IN FOUR DIMENSIONS. Notes, bibliography, index, 7"x10", 448pp. Cro76, 8.95p.**
The four dimensions Professor Kaufman refers to are existential, aesthetic, historical, and comparative. 240 illustrations—183 in color—represent the aesthetic and existential dimensions of the ten religions he discusses. The historical and comparative dimensions are presented in a series of chapters. The focus is mainly on Asia, since that is where most of the religions were born. This is an excellent work of scholarship which also deeply invovles the reader.

KITAGAWA, JOSEPH. **RELIGIONS OF THE EAST. Notes, bibliography, indices, 351pp. Wes68, 3.95p.**
This is a sociologically-oriented study of religion, discussed within the framework of the national community. Essays include: *Chinese Religions and the Family System; Hinduism and the Caste System; Buddhism and the Samgha; Islam and the Ummah;* and *Japanese Religions and the National Community.* Dr. Kitagawa is a Professor of the History of Religions both in the Divinity School and the Department of Far Eastern Languages and Civilizations at the University of Chicago. This is designed to provide a general orientation to the religions discussed, relating the structure and development of the *holy communities* to historical events and culture.

LANDAY, JERRY. **DOME OF THE ROCK. Bibliography, index, 9"x11½", 172pp. Nws72, 12.95c.**
Jerusalem's ancient Temple Mount, now dominated by the Dome of

the Rock, is sacred to Jews, Christians, and Moslems. This is a study of the Holy City, focusing on its most famous monument. Manuscript illuminations, statuary, ancient maps, and modern diagrams complement the text—along with numerous photographs. 120 illustrations are included in all—one half in full color. There is also a section *Jerusalem in Literature*. This volume will be especially appreciated by those who are interested in Islamic architecture.

LEE, JUNG YOUNG. **COSMIC RELIGION.** 109pp. H&R73, 2.95p.
This book is often difficult to follow. Lee has taken on an ambitious task in his desire to show how the achievements of Western culture and the teachings of Jesus appear to a man whose basic attitude derives from Taoist philosophy. Lee organizes his discussion topically and covers subjects such as: creation, sin, salvation, prayer, spirit, family, time, liberation and freedom, love, and anxiety.

MCCASLAND, S. VERNON, GRACE CAIRNS, and DAVID YU. **RELIGIONS OF THE WORLD.** Notes, bibliography, index, 778pp. RaH69, 18.75c.
A well written college-level textbook, covering both ancient and contemporary religions in all parts of the world. Each of the major religions is discussed at length and its history is traced.

MARTIN, MALACHI. **THE NEW CASTLE.** 209pp. Dut74, 3.95p.
This is a fascinating study of a few times in history when a transcendental vision came to a number of societies. Martin, a former Jesuit scholar well versed in Oriental philosophy, describes what people and places were like before the vision touched them, the nature of each vision, the tangible changes it wrought, and what remains of its promise. It includes penetrating critiques of the central artistic creations that were the concrete manifestations of each vision: the Islamic Arabesque, Byzantine mosaics, Gothic cathedrals, the temple of Angkor Wat, and even the American skyscrapers. Martin also provides insights into the character, feelings, and actions of the leaders and the general populace who shared their vision. The civilizations discussed include Mecca, Jerusalem, Constantinople, Rome, Peking, Angkor Wat, Wittenberg, and Peru, Indiana (wherever that is).

MEHTA, P.D. **THE HEART OF RELIGION.** Glossary, notes, bibliography, index, 346pp. Com76, 21.00c.
Mehta draws on more than fifty years of study and practice in this interpretation of the meaning of spiritual evolution—which he sees as the realization of the transcendent. In his discussion he distills teachings from the **Vedas, Upanishads, Bhagavad Gita, Zohar,** and the **Qabala**; from the reported sayings of the Buddha, Moses, Jesus, and Zarathustra; and from the contemporary message of Krishnamurti. Mehta also considers the teacher-disciple relationship, evil and suffering, karma, dying, revelation, communion, eternity, and science. The primary theme, though, is the implications of living a balanced, religious life. The book is often heavy going, though it is well written and informative, and not too overwhelming.

MIDDLETON, JOHN, ed. **GODS AND RITUALS.** Notes, bibliography, index, 478pp. UTx67, 9.35p.
A scholarly collection of readings on the beliefs and practices of primitive religions. The selections focus on Africa and many of the religions discussed are little known in the West.

MIRSKY, JEANNETTE. **HOUSES OF GOD.** Index, 7½"x9", 232pp. UCh65, 7.95c.
Religions vary, but religion itself is universal. This variety and universality are well reflected in this informed text and 300 illustrations.... Ranging from Stonehenge and the caves of Lascaux, from Fujiyama and Sinai, Aztec temples, Chinese pagoda shrines and medieval cathedrals to the Georgian chapels of New England and the spare, modernistic churches of contemporary Europe, this volume reveals the way in which men of all ages, in both East and West, have expressed their religious attitudes in buildings or in sacred sites.—**The New York Times Book Review.**

■ *MOORE, ALBERT.* **ICONOGRAPHY OF RELIGIONS.** Notes, bibliography, index, 9⅛"x10", 337pp. For77, 25.00c.
This is a comprehensive, comparative study of religious iconography. Moore begins with an introductory chapter and goes on to separate discussions of primal religions, polytheism in ancient religions, the Hindu tradition, Buddhism and Jainism, the religions of East Asia, Judaism and Islam, and Christianity. The analysis is clear and succinct and 248 excellent line drawings and photographs accompany and

amplify the text. We learned a great deal from Moore's informative text and we feel that this is far and away the best introduction to the subject.

MOORE, CHARLES, ed. **PHILOSOPHY AND CULTURE, EAST AND WEST.** Notes, index, 844pp. UHa62, 23.50c.
A collection of forty-five scholarly papers and public lectures delivered at the Third East-West Philosophers' Conference held in Hawaii in 1959. The conference was devoted exclusively to the attempt to achieve mutual understanding. Outstanding authorities explain their own cultures and philosophical traditions in fairly technical language.

MOORE, CHARLES, ed. **THE STATUS OF THE INDIVIDUAL IN EAST AND WEST.** Notes, index, 627pp. UHa68, 23.50c.
A collection of papers originally delivered at the Fourth East-West Philosophers' Conference held at the University of Hawaii in 1964. The meeting focused on one theme: the comparative status of the individual in the major philosophical and cultural traditions of Asia and the West. One particular aspect of the over all topic is presented and extensively discussed in each of six sections—metaphysics, methodology, religion, ethics, social thought and practices, and legal and political thought and institutions.

MOORE, GEORGE. **HISTORY OF RELIGIONS.** Two volumes, bibliography, index, 1768pp. TTC20, 16.80c/set.
This is a more than adequate presentation. Dr. Moore was Professor of the History of Religion at Harvard and he is thoroughly familiar with his material. Nonetheless he is an American Christian, so aspects of the religions he discussed are not always comfortable for him. This is a very complete text and it reads well. We enjoyed going through the books and learned a great deal from them. The first volume covers the religions of the ancient Near East and the Orient and the second is devoted to Judaism, Christianity, and Islam. The writing style is not excessively academic, though the scholarship appears to be excellent.

Greuter's engraving of the Trinity as a triangle and circle held by God.

MURPHY, GARDNER and LOIS., eds. **ASIAN PSYCHOLOGY.** Index, 253pp. H&R68, 3.95p.
An exploration of the main currents of psychological thought in the East which illustrates the special insights and contributions of Asia through a judicious selection of both ancient and modern writings. The editors link the various passages with explanatory introductions, setting them in historical perspective, and providing interpretations. The book is divided into sections on the psychology of India, China, and Japan. It is an unusual compilation, which includes a great amount of source material. We recommend this highly to those who are interested in the psychology of religions.

NAKAMURA, HAJIME. **PARALLEL DEVELOPMENTS.** Notes, 587pp. Kod75, 28.00c.
Nakamura is a respected philosopher who has taught at many of the leading universities in the world. In this volume he presents an

unusual approach to the history of thought in a variety of cultures. *These cultures are not treated separately, one after another, as is usually done in histories of thought. Rather the emphasis is upon such problems as the concept of God, the question of immortality, the controversy over universals, the nature of orthodoxy and heterodoxy, the problem of moral values, and many others. The thought of the various cultures is collected around such problems. The discussion is carried on with amazing erudition. There are thousands of quotations and references. And yet the work is not ponderous or directed solely to the specialist.*—Charles Morris.

NAKAMURA, HAJIME. **WAYS OF THINKING OF EASTERN PEOPLES.** Extensive notes, index, 6"x9", 712pp. UHa64, 5.95p.
Professor Nakamura...sets out to analyze, with rigor and objectivity, the characteristic thought-patterns of four Asian peoples as these are revealed in their languages, their logic, and their cultural products. In this analysis he speaks neither of an "Oriental mind" nor of an undifferentiated "West." Rather he speaks of the Indians, the Chinese, the Tibetans, and the Japanese out of an understanding of their distinctive cultures and histories.—from the introduction.

NEEDLEMAN, JACOB. **THE NEW RELIGIONS.** 245pp. S&S72, 3.50p/ 1.50p.
In lucid and informative terms, Needleman, examines the ways in which the traditional Western religions have failed modern man and how Eastern religions offer their followers the practical means for improving the quality of their lives. He offers a comprehensive picture of the most significant new movements, portraits of their leaders, and a glimpse into the experience of some of their adherents.

NEEDLEMAN, JACOB. **A SENSE OF THE COSMOS.** Index, 178pp. Dut75, 3.50p.
Needleman presents a critical evaluation of modern science against the background of the ancient spiritual traditions.... There are several points on which I disagree with Needleman, but I have found almost every page of his book thought provoking and stimulating, and many of his ideas extremely lucid and enlightening....I want to strongly recommend **A Sense of the Cosmos** *to every reader seriously interested in our present cultural situation.*—Fritjof Capra, author of **Tao of Physics**.

NEEDLEMAN, JACOB, ed. **THE SWORD OF GNOSIS.** Notes, 464pp. Vik74, 4.95p.
A collection of essays first printed in the English quarterly **Studies in Comparative Religion**, and written by noted continental scholars including Frithjof Schuon, Rene Guenon, Marco Pallis, Abu Bakr Siraj Ad-Din, Martin Lings, Titus Burckhardt, Seyyed Hossein Nasr, and Leo Schaya. The selections include: *The Spiritual Function of Civilization; Cosmology and Modern Science; Discovering the Interior Life; Remarks on the Enigma of the Koan; Living One's Karma; The Language of the Birds; Perennial Values in Islamic Art; The Influence of Sufism on Traditional Persian Music; The Meaning of the Temple;* and much else. The mission of the contributors is to illuminate the universal truths upon which all authentic religions are based and this they do very well. The articles tend to be scholarly.

NEEDLEMAN, JACOB and DENNIS LEWIS, eds. **ON THE WAY TO SELF KNOWLEDGE: SACRED TRADITION AND PSYCHOTHERAPY.** 251pp. RaH76, 3.95p.
The aims and disciplines of a variety of sacred traditions and of psychotherapy are explored in a series of essays by eminent psychotherapists and spiritual leaders including the editors and Thomas Malone, Michel Salzmann, Tarthang Tulku, James Hillman, Robert de Ropp, Viktor Frankl, and A.C. Robin Skynner. The authors discuss the synthesis of the disciplines and the benefits and dangers of this synthesis. The essays were originally presented as part of a lecture series and this original intent is apparent in the collection. Questions and answers follow each one. The selections themselves are not overly academic and some of the material discussed is not readily available elsewhere.

NEEDLEMAN, JACOB and DENNIS LEWIS, eds. **SACRED TRADITION AND PRESENT NEED.** 146pp. Vik75, 10.00c.
Excerpts from a lecture series given in San Francisco in 1973. The general topic was *Has the "spiritual revolution" lost its direction in a profusion of innovations? In our haste to reject outworn religious forms, customs, and ideals, have we overlooked the truths that have guided traditional life and thought since time immemorial? And can the ancient traditions cut through our present confusion and speak anew to Western man's need?* These were the lectures: *The New Religions*—Jacob Needleman, *Christianity in Dialogue with Zen*—William Johnston, *Tibetan Buddhism: The Way of Inward Discovery*—Lobsang Lhalungpa, *The Samkhya of India*—Lizelle Reymond, *Sufism and the Spiritual*

Needs of Contemporary Man—S.H. Nasr, *Contemplative Christianity*—Dom Aelred Graham, *Myth, Symbol, and Tradition*—P.L. Travers, and *Two Vedantas*—Philippe Lavastine.

PARRINDER, GEOFFREY. **ASIAN RELIGIONS.** Bibliography, index, 138pp. Oxf57, 2.50p.
A clearly written introductory survey of Islam, Buddhism, Indian, Chinese, and Japanese religions. All the important information is presented succinctly and the individuals, main movements, and texts are all discussed.

PARRINDER, GEOFFREY. **AVATAR AND INCARNATION.** Notes, bibliography, index, 296pp. Fab70, 7.95c.
Parrinder begins this in depth exposition with an examination of the Hindu belief in avatars—especially Krishna and Rama—as it can be seen in the classical texts, medieval devotional literature, and modern criticism. He also surveys other Indian belief systems. The next section contains a thorough exposition of Islamic and Christian teachings, emphasizing the parallels between the doctrine of incarnation and avatar doctrine.

PARRINDER, GEOFFREY. **A DICTIONARY OF NON-CHRISTIAN RELIGIONS.** Illustrations, bibliography, 320pp. Wes71/Hol, 10.95c.
This is a very useful, comprehensive compilation, covering the whole field of religions of the world (with the exception of Christianity). It enables the student to find instant definitions, provides him with cross references that connect many of the subjects, shows common themes of religious perception, and links theology, religion, and mythology. Thousands of entries define and explain deities, beliefs, practices, philosophies and philosophers, sacred objects, rituals, names and places, gods and goddesses, and a myriad of other topics. We found this an excellent tool in putting this book together. The concise explanations offered here are often either not available elsewhere or else require a lot of digging to come up with.

PARRINDER, GEOFFREY. **MYSTICISM IN THE WORLD'S RELIGION.** Notes, bibliography, index, 218pp. Oxf76/SlP, 2.95p.
The purpose of this book is to introduce the great religions in their mystical expressions. It does not profess to include all mystics, for even in one religion that would be impossible in one book, but selections are given from many teachers in original versions or from reliable translations, as these throw light on what mystics themselves believe has happened to them.... For over forty years I have collected books on religion in Asia and Africa; I have often made reference to mystical teachings, but this is my first venture into a full scale study of the subject. Behind it there is not only reading, discussion, and criticism, but personal conviction and experience.

PARRINDER, GEOFFREY. **THE WORLD'S LIVING RELIGIONS.** Photographs, bibliography, index, 207pp. PnB64, 2.00p.
A lively survey of the world's living religions, showing how each is suited to the society in which it is found. In addition to reviewing all the major religions, Professor Parrinder discusses minor sects such as the Jains, Sikhs, and Parsis. He also looks at the contemporary religious scene in Australia, in Africa, and among the American Indians. The American edition of this book is called **The Faiths of Mankind**.

PARRINDER, GEOFFREY. **WORSHIP IN THE WORLD'S RELIGIONS.** Bibliography, index, 239pp. LtA61, 3.50p.
Professor Parrinder sets out to answer the following questions about various religions: What is the nature of their worship?, What is their faith and prayer?, How do they appear to their worshipers? He is concerned not with histories or philosophies but with worship as seen and shared by the laity: the temples, concepts of God and other spirits, objects of reverence, sacred books, festivals, pilgrimages, and prayers —both public and private. All the major Eastern sects are covered along with several lesser known ones.

RADHAKRISHNAN, S. **EAST AND WEST IN RELIGION.** Index, 146pp. A&U33, 3.15c.
Transcriptions of five lectures dealing primarily with the attitudes and approaches to religious life characteristic of the East and West.

RADHAKRISHNAN, S. **EASTERN RELIGIONS AND WESTERN THOUGHT.** 402pp. Oxf39, 5.30p.
Radhakrishnan, distinguished statesman, educator, and philosopher, is the author of many books on Indian philosophy. He has served as President of India. This book describes the leading ideas of Indian

philosophy and traces the probable influence of Indian mysticism upon Greek and Christian thought.

RADHAKRISHNAN, S. **AN IDEALIST VIEW OF LIFE. Notes, index, 279pp. A&U37, 2.25p.**
Dr. Radhakrishnan believes that *science is a system of second causes, which cannot describe the world adequately, much less account for it.* In this book he draws upon this idea, first by examining the modern intellectual ferment and vain attempts to find a substitute for religion. He then discusses the nature and validity of religious experience, drawing on both Eastern and Western thinking. Finally he presents his vision of man's evolution and the continuing emergence of ever higher values.

RADHAKRISHNAN, S. **RELIGION AND CULTURE. 176pp. JPC68, 2.40p.**
Radhakrishnan discusses the various facets of religion and culture and their application to life in the present day world.

RADHAKRISHNAN, S. **RELIGION AND SOCIETY. Index, 148pp. A&U48, 4.30c.**
Transcription of five lectures on the title theme. Dr. Radhakrishnan's discussion is affected by the recent Second World War and the Indian independence movement.

RADHAKRISHNAN, S. et al, eds. **A HISTORY OF PHILOSOPHY, EASTERN AND WESTERN. Notes, index, two volumes, 1,119pp. A&U52, 33.55c/set.**
A broad review of man's philosophical quest from the dawn of history to the present day, edited by a board made up of four Indian philosophers. Virtually every school of philosophical thought, Eastern and Western, is discussed at least in passing, and many are given lengthy treatments.

Central lotus section of a *taizo-kai* (womb-circle).

RAMAKRISHNA VEDANTA CENTRE. **WOMEN SAINTS OF EAST AND WEST. Index, 274pp. RVC55, 6.50c.**
A collection of essays; each selection describes the struggles and difficulties, the spiritual disciplines and realizations, of the women saints portrayed, so that the reader might feel drawn to the divine ideal which they attained, and glimpse their fervor of soul. The life of the Holy Mother, Sri Sarada Devi, who like Ramakrishna taught that all religions are paths to God, is the inspiration behind this volume. Each essay is written by an individual who has been inspired by the life and work of the saint discussed. The main body of the work is devoted to Hinduism, with additional sections on Buddhism and Jainism, Christianity, Judaism, and Sufism.

RICE, EDWARD. **EASTERN DEFINITIONS. Illustrations, 443pp. Dou78, 10.00c.**
A collection of excellent, concise definitions of the major individuals, writings, and schools of thought. An excellent handbook for those involved in the study of an Eastern discipline.

■ RICE, EDWARD. **THE FIVE GREAT RELIGIONS. Index, 248pp. Ban73, 1.95p.**
Rice is an outstanding photographer who has travelled widely throughout the world. In this highly readable survey he brings to life the world view of Buddhism, Hinduism, Islam, Judaism, and Christianity. He discusses their origins, social frameworks, ethics, and scriptures, and explores their mystical aspects and traditions—leading the reader toward an understanding of each faith's inner meaning. We highly recommend this volume to those who want a glimpse into the essence of the great world religions. Countless photographs accompany the text.

RINGGREN, HELMER and AKE STROM. **RELIGIONS OF MANKIND. 468pp. For67, 4.25p.**
The authors are Swedish professors of religion. This is a concise, extraordinarily complete study, treating all the religions of the world in terms of both their history and their present vitality in faith and in life. The text is somewhat dry and is only recommended to those looking for a thorough study of uniformly high quality. It is certainly the most complete one volume survey we have ever read. An abundance of further reading suggestions follow each chapter.

■ ROSS, NANCY WILSON. **THREE WAYS OF ASIAN WISDOM: HINDUISM, BUDDHISM, AND ZEN AND THEIR SIGNIFICANCE FOR THE WEST. Glossary, extensive bibliography, 222pp. S&S66/ Fab, 5.95p.**
Our personal favorite. This is a layman's explanation of the three religions, and the arts that grew from them. The text is beautifully written and profusely illustrated, and includes many selections from sacred literature.

SCHOEPS, HANS-JOACHIM. **THE RELIGIONS OF MANKIND: THEIR ORIGIN AND DEVELOPMENT. Index, 356pp. Dou66, 2.95p.**
This is a concise, careful discussion of a great body of material. Professor Schoeps begins with a highly academic discussion of aspects and problems in the study of the science of religion. The rest of the book is divided into the following major sections: *Extinct Religions Outside of Europe*—Babylonia, Persia, Egypt, and Pre-Columbian America; *Extinct Religions within Europe*—the Teutons, the Celts, and Slavs, the Greeks, and the Romans; *The Great Religions of the East*—Hinduism, Buddhism, Tibetan Buddhism, and the religions of China and Japan; and *The Religions of Biblical Revelation*—Judaism, Islam, and Christianity. Each of the discussions is as thorough as the space permits, and not overly dry.

SEEGER, ELIZABETH. **EASTERN RELIGIONS. Bibliography, index, 214pp. Cro73, 7.95c.**
A well written discussion of Hinduism, Buddhism, the religions of China, and Shinto directed toward older children, and suitable for anyone wishing a simple, clear overview. Quotations from the sacred literature of each religion are included as well as many lovely photographs. This is the nicest book of this type that we know of and we feel that it would be an excellent introduction to Eastern philosophy for a child.

SHAH, SIRDAR IKBAL ALI, ed. **ORIENTAL LITERATURE. 416pp. Oct37, 8.55p.**
An anthology of literature (mainly poetry) from Afghanistan, Arabia, China, India, Iran, Japan, and Turkey. Mystical philosophy is emphasized in the selection.

SHAH, SIRDAR IKBAL ALI, ed. **THE SPIRIT OF THE EAST. 276pp. Dut73, 2.95p.**
The author is a noted Sufi scholar and father of Idries Shah. This is a collection of some of the most important source material from Muslim, Parsee, Hindu, Hebrew, Confucian, and other traditions. Shah presents the translations without any further explanatory material. The selections were chosen not only for their particular worth but also for the way they each illuminate the particular virtues of each tradition.

SMART, NINIAN. **THE RELIGIOUS EXPERIENCE OF MANKIND.** Bibliography, index, 735pp. Scr69, 9.35p/4.60p.
This is a philosophical examination of the religious experience of the peoples of India, the Far East, and the Near East. Each of the religions is examined independently and selections from each one's sacred scriptures are quoted. All of the major movements in world religion and the main individuals are discussed. This is a serious study, geared toward the general reader, in which Professor Smart shows how religions grow and change and affect each other just as living organisms do. This is an excellent first book for those seriously interested in the comparative study of religions.

SMITH, HUSTON. **FORGOTTEN TRUTH.** Index, 182pp. H&R76, 2.95p.
A philosophical exploration of the unity underlying all religious traditions. Dr. Smith writes that *It is as if an invisible geometry has everywhere been working to shape them to a truth that in the last resort is single.* He believes that the current emphasis on science in the West is a deviation from tradition and this deviation is due to a misunderstanding of science. Here he seeks to show how science and these traditions can and should interrelate. This is a highly personal document, based on Dr. Smith's observations and experience. Many quotations from sacred texts and scientific documents are included.

■ *SMITH, HUSTON.* **THE RELIGIONS OF MAN.** Notes, annotated bibliography, index, 371pp. H&R65, 3.50p/1.95p.
This is generally considered the best overall comparative study available, emphasizing the meaning these religions carry for the lives of their adherents. The traditions include Hinduism, Buddhism, Confucianism, Taoism, Islam, Judaism, and Christianity. *This is a book about religion that exists . . . not as a dull habit but as an acute fever. It is about religion alive. And whenever religion comes to life it displays a startling quality; it takes over. All else, while not silenced, becomes subdued and thrown without contest into a supporting role.*—from the introduction. An excellent academic account, ideal for both the general reader and the student of comparative religion.

SMITH, MARGARET. **THE WAY OF THE MYSTICS.** 3.95p.
See the Islam section.

STAAL, FRITS. **EXPLORING MYSTICISM.** Illustrations, glossary, bibliography, index, 242pp. UCa75, 4.95p.
Staal argues that mysticism can best be explored through mystical experiences. Relating mystical phenomena to drugs, ritual, religion, and philosophy, he concludes that we are only beginning to explore a domain of the mind as complex as many areas of physics or biology, but as yet barely touched by psychology and the humanities.

The Star of David.

STRENG, FREDERICK. **UNDERSTANDING RELIGIOUS MAN.** Index, 132pp. Dic69, 8.00p.
An academic study of religious experience divided into the following main sections: *methods used to understand religious life, four traditional ways of being religious, modes of human awareness used to express religious meaning.* Annotated bibliographic selections follow each chapter.

STROUP, HERBERT. **FOUNDERS OF LIVING RELIGIONS.** Glossary, bibliography, index, 256pp. Wes74, 4.25p.
This is an excellent introduction to the lives and teachings of Vardhamana (Jainism), Gautama (Buddhism), Nanak (Sikhism), Lao Tzu (Taoism), Confucius (Confucianism), Zoroaster (Zoroastrianism), Jesus (Christianity), and Muhammed (Islam). Dr. Stroup focuses on biography rather than theology or philosophy. He reports in detail what is known or believed regarding the founder's birth, family connections, early life experiences, education and calling, gathering of disciples and converts, journeys to promulgate the new faith. In addition, Dr. Stroup includes descriptions of each religion and its relationship to other religions.

STUART, VINCENT, ed. **MAITREYA 6, ORDER.** Illustrations, 103pp. ShP77, 4.50p.
A collection of articles presenting the idea of order as a spiritual sytem in which things proceed according to definite laws. The contributors represent many different paths including the Gurdjieff Work, Christianity, the Jewish mystical tradition, Tibetan Buddhism, and Hinduism. Some of the better known authors are Maurice Nicoll, Karlfried Graf von Durckheim, Herbert Guenther, and John Blofeld.

TAGORE, RABINDRANATH. **THE RELIGION OF MAN.** 239pp. Bea31/A&U, 3.95p.
Very personal thoughts on human life in its relation to the divine and the nature and being of God.

TANNER, FLORICE. **THE MYSTERY TEACHINGS IN WORLD RELIGIONS.** 192pp. TPH73, 2.45p.
Drawing from the inner doctrines of all the world's religions, the author shows that man's basic truth—which is the way to full self consciousness at every level of his being—lies hidden in every faith, whatever the superficial differences might be.

TOMLIN, E.W.F. **THE ORIENTAL PHILOSOPHERS.** Notes, index, 323pp. H&R50/HPG, 2.75p.
The aim of this book is twofold: to provide a straightforward account of the life and work of the great thinkers of the Orient, and to attempt to show, in terms intelligible to the ordinary reader, with what remarkable insistence the greatest of these thinkers dwell upon common themes. Oriental here includes the Egyptians, Babylonians, and Israelites as well as the Asian religious leaders.

TOYNBEE, ARNOLD, ed. **HALF THE WORLD: THE HISTORY AND CULTURE OF CHINA AND JAPAN.** Notes, bibliography, index, 9"x12", 368pp. T&H73, 29.95c.
This beautifully illustrated study contains 530 plates—160 in color—and a text written by thirteen noted scholars. The work begins with a chapter on Chinese writing. This is followed by a discussion of the political and social history of China to the end of the Manchu era along with accounts of China's religion, philosophy, science, and literature. This section ends with a discussion of how the whole civilization was carried to Korea, Vietnam, Tibet, and Japan—leading to a roughly parallel treatment of Japanese history up to the Menji Restoration. The last chapters show how China and Japan have grown out of their past. Integral to the book, and outstanding in their own right, are the illustrations. Two researchers, specially qualified in original studies, spent over a year tracing documents, paintings, and works of art to form a unique collection—much of it hitherto unpublished.

VAN OVER, RAYMOND, ed. **EASTERN MYSTICISM, VOLUME I: THE NEAR EAST AND INDIA.** 426pp. NAL77, 2.50p.
An excellent anthology of many primary writings on Hinduism, Buddhism, Zoroastrianism, Jainism, Sikhism, Islam, and Sufism. The text is well organized and the selections blend beautifully. Many of the translations have been selected from older versions, and are not our favorites. Nonetheless this is a useful anthology for those seeking a flavor of the sacred texts of these religions. Van Over also provides an introduction and commentary.

WATTS, ALAN. **THE ART OF CONTEMPLATION.** 8¼"x11", 18pp. RaH72, 3.45p.
Alan Watts is universally regarded as one of the most penetrating and above all, readable interpreters of Eastern philosophy to Western readers. The author of some twenty books, his life and work reflect the interests of a whole generation. He is one of the first writers one reads when he becomes interested in Eastern thought. This book contains an essay on contemplation, handwritten and drawn by Watts.

WATTS, ALAN. **BEHOLD THE SPIRIT.** Extensive bibliography, 257pp. RaH47, 1.95p.
Calls for a reconciliation between Western and Eastern religions. F.S.C. Northrop called it *one of the best—in fact the only first-rate book in recent years in the field of religion.*

WATTS, ALAN. **BEYOND THEOLOGY—THE ART OF GODMAN-SHIP. Notes, index, 244pp. RaH64, 1.95p.**
The reader must be assured it is far from my intention to debunk, to give offense, or to hold sacred things up to ridicule. For your author is acting, not in the role of the Devil, but in the capacity of the Court Jester. . . . The function of the Fool was to keep his monarch human and, with luck, even humane, by a judicious unstuffing of his pomposity and by keeping alive his sense of humor—the essence of which is laughter at oneself. This is a theological work which aims at an understanding of what religion, and especially Christianity, truly means to the individual.

WATTS, ALAN. **THE BOOK ON THE TABOO AGAINST KNOWING WHO YOU ARE. 146pp. RaH66/SBL, 1.95p.**
Probably the most popular and famous of Watts' work. **The Book** delves into the cause and cure of the illusion that the self is a separate ego, housed in a bag of skin, which confronts a universe of alien physical objects. Watts here restates Vedanta philosophy in terms understandable to the Western mind. Recommended first reader on Watts.

WATTS, ALAN. **CLOUD-HIDDEN: WHEREABOUTS UNKNOWN, A MOUNTAIN JOURNAL. 179pp. RaH68/SBL, 1.95p.**
Watts intends this to be a bedside book which can be read backwards, forwards, or any way one likes. He discusses following the Tao (flowing where the stream takes you), the nature of ecstasy, karma and reincarnation, astrology, tantric yoga, and much else.

WATTS, ALAN. **DOES IT MATTER. 125pp. RaH68, 1.95p.**
Essays on man's relation to materiality.

WATTS, ALAN. **THE ESSENCE OF ALAN WATTS. 217pp. CeA77, 4.95p.**
A collection of edited transcripts of videotaped lectures made by Watts in the last years of his life. The material in this volume was originally produced as a series of small books, each selling for almost the same price as this compilation. Many aspects of Watts' philosophical thought are covered in the book's chapters on ego, God, meditation, nothingness, death, time, the nature of man, and the cosmic drama. A related photograph faces each page of the text.

WATTS, ALAN. **IN MY OWN WAY. 388pp. RaH72/CaL, 2.95p.**
This fascinating autobiography is an absorbing discussion of Watts' ideas, beliefs, and inward and outward experiences—all brought together with a whimsical lack of concern for chronology or tiresome statistics.

WATTS, ALAN. **THE JOYOUS COSMOLOGY: ADVENTURES IN THE CHEMISTRY OF CONSCIOUSNESS. 101pp. RaH62, 1.95p.**
The best description we have seen of drug trips. The heightening of consciousness ranges all the way from aesthetic insights into nature to a philosophical view of existence as a comedy at once diabolical and divine.

WATTS, ALAN. **PSYCHOTHERAPY EAST AND WEST. Notes, bibliography, 206pp. RaH61/CaL, 1.95p.**
This is an excellent discussion of the common ground between Western psychology and Eastern mysticism. As usual Watts writes clearly and expresses his ideas through a great number of examples. This is one of our favorite Watts' books.

WATTS, ALAN. **THE SPIRIT OF ZEN. 2.95p.**
See the Zen Buddhism section.

WATTS, ALAN. **THE SUPREME IDENTITY. Bibliography, 199pp. RaH72/Wdw, 1.95p.**
An essay on Oriental metaphysics and the Christian religion.

WATTS, ALAN. **TAO: THE WATERCOURSE WAY. 2.95p.**
See the Chinese Philosophy section.

WATTS, ALAN. **THIS IS IT AND OTHER ESSAYS. Notes, 158pp. RaH60, 1.95p.**
The six essays in this volume all deal with the relationship of mystical experience to ordinary life. Also included is Watts' pamphlet **Beat Zen, Square Zen, and Zen.**

WATTS, ALAN. **THREE: THE WAY OF ZEN, NATURE, MAN, AND WOMAN, PSYCHOTHERAPY EAST AND WEST. Notes, bibliography, index, 659pp. RaH77, 15.00c.**
Three of Watts' most popular books bound into one volume.

WATTS, ALAN. **THE TWO HANDS OF GOD. 1.95p.**
See the Mythology section.

WATTS, ALAN. **THE WAY OF ZEN. 1.95p.**
See the Zen Buddhism section.

WATTS, ALAN. **THE WISDOM OF INSECURITY. 152pp. RaH51/HPG, 1.65p.**
This book proposes a complete reversal of all ordinary thinking about the present state of man. The critical condition of the world compels us to face this problem: how is man to live in a world in which he can never be secure, deprived, as many are, of the consolations of religious belief? The author shows that this problem contains its own solution—that the highest happiness, the supreme spiritual insight and certitude are found only in our awareness that impermanence and insecurity are inescapable and inseparable from life.—**Book Exchange** (London).

WEDECK, HARRY E. and WADE BASKIN. **DICTIONARY OF PAGAN RELIGIONS. 363pp. Stu71, 3.95p.**
A brief discussion of the cults, rites, and rituals associated with polytheistic religions, from the Stone Age to the present.

WILBER, KEN. **THE SPECTRUM OF CONSCIOUSNESS. Notes, bibliography, index, 374pp. TPH77, 5.75p.**
This is a deep, often difficult book which James Fadiman, a noted transpersonal psychologist, calls *the most sensible, comprehensive book about consciousness since Williams James.* Wilber suggests that consciousness establishes a multiplicity of aspects as it steps down into time and space. Thus, as a spectrum, it can be studied legitimately on one or more of its wave lengths. Viewing consciousness in this way, he shows how seemingly disparate disciplines such as Christianity, Hinduism, Buddhism, and gestalt therapy each speak to a different wave level of awareness. Therefore, though each necessarily has its own unique coloration, each is valid and valuable in its own way.

■ *YOHANNAN, JOHN, ed.* **A TREASURY OF ASIAN LITERATURE. Notes, 432pp. NAL56, 1.95p.**
Translations of selections from some of the best known Eastern classics including the **Panchatantra**, the **Gulistan** of Sa'di, the **Mathnawi** of Rumi, **The Thousand and One Nights**, **The Tale of the Genji**, the **Mahabharata**, the **Shahnamah**, the **Tao Te Ching**, the **Divan** of Hafiz, the **Bhagavad Gita**, and the **Qur'an**. Many shorter poetic and prose pieces are also included. The translators are uniformly excellent—Sir Richard Burton, R.A. Nicholson, Arthur Waley, and M.M. Pickthall, to name just a few. We recommend this book highly to all who are looking for an introductory survey of Eastern sacred literature. The editor provides an abundance of introductory material.

ZAEHNER, R.C., ed. **THE CONCISE ENCYCLOPEDIA OF LIVING FAITHS. Illustrations, topical bibliography, index, 8"x10", double column, 431pp. Bea59/HPG, 6.95p.**
The term encyclopedia in the title is deceptive. This volume presents a fairly complete introductory survey of the world's religions, each chapter written by an authority. The articles are concise and tend to be fairly lively. The bulk of the book is devoted to the Eastern religions and sects, and many of the selections are not covered in most general texts. There is also an excellent five-part discussion of Christianity, and chapters on Judaism, Islam, and Zoroastrianism.

ZAEHNER, R.C. **HINDU AND MUSLIM MYSTICISM. Notes, index, 242pp. ScB60, 3.75p.**
A comparative analysis of the major tenets of Hinduism and Islam. The two are discussed separately, but with constant reference to each other, as well as to Western thought. All the important individuals in each religion are reviewed along with the major texts. Professor Zaehner's presentations tend to be scholarly and dry, with an emphasis on the dry and the reader should not expect to get a feeling for either of these mystical traditions. It is an academic study, albeit a good one.

ZAIN, C.C. **NATURAL ALCHEMY, EVOLUTION OF RELIGION. 5.95p.**
See the Astrology section.

CONSCIOUSNESS EXPANSION

The scale of the universe is awesome. Our sun, which is more than a million times greater in volume than the earth, is, as everyone knows, only a tiny speck in the unimaginable vastness of the Milky Way. Hundreds of billions of such suns make up this galaxy, most of them far greater in size than our own. And the galaxy itself is but a tiny speck among countless billions of galaxies that occupy the cosmos that science perceives.

Each sun is an ocean of energy, one tiny fraction of which is enough to animate the life of our earth and everything that exists upon it. Every second there pours forth from the Sun an amount of energy equal to four million tons of what we call matter. Since the planets of suns capture so little of this energy, all of outer space is in reality a plenum of force that is largely invisible to us, yet life-giving.

To set our minds reeling, it is enough to contemplate the bare distances that astronomy has measured. Light, traveling at 186,000 miles a second takes eight minutes to reach us from the sun—but four years from the nearest star, 27,000 years from the center of the Milky Way, and 800,000 years from the galaxy Andromeda. Yet Andromeda is now considered a member of what is called the local cluster of galaxies, beyond which lie countless stars and groupings of stars thousands of times more distant from us than Andromeda.

As with size, energy and distance, so with the reaches of time. Astronomers say the earth is some five billion years old, which means that the entire history of mankind, as we record it, is but a fraction of a second in the time scale of the earth.

It is no exaggeration to say that in this picture of the universe man is crushed. Within cosmic time he is less than the blinking of an eye. In size he is not even a speck. And his continued existence is solely at the mercy of such colossal dimensions of force that the most minor momentary change in these forces would be enough to obliterate instantly the very memory of human life.

Ancient man's scale of the universe is awesome, too, but in an entirely different way, and with entirely different consequences for the mind that contemplates it. Here man stands before a universe which exceeds him in quality as well as quantity. The spheres which encompass the earth in the cosmological schemes of antiquity and the Middle Ages represent levels of conscious energy and purpose which surround the earth much as the physiological function of an organ such as the heart surrounds or permeates each of the separate tissues which comprise it, or as the captain's destination encompasses or pervades the life and activity of every crewman on his ship.

In this understanding, the earth is inextricably enmeshed in a network of purposes, a ladder or hierarchy of intentions. To the ancient mind, this is the very meaning of the concept of organization and order. A cosmos—and, of course, the cosmos—is an organism, not in the sense of an unusually complicated industrial machine, but in the sense of a hierarchy of purposeful energies.

In the Hermetic writings the hierarchical structure of the cosmos resembles that of an organism: cell in the service of tissue; tissue in the service of organ; organ in the service of the whole (governed by a supreme consciousness or intelligence). At each level of being there are *gods* or *angels* or, to use less uncomfortable language, *purposeful energies*. From this point of view, the ancient spatial descriptions of the cosmos are meant to be understood symbolically.

Likewise, the word *sphere,* used in describing the forces and purposes at different levels, is never meant merely to be taken literally. The very idea of the circularity of movement in *the heavens* can be understood to mean not only the encompassing nature of these progressively higher influences, but their eternal nature. The circle is, among many things, a symbol of that which *eternally recurs,* that which is not subject to time and change as we know them.

Obviously, there is a great difference between contemplating a universe which exceeds me in size alone or in intricacy alone, and one which exceeds me in depth of purpose and intelligence. A universe of merely unimaginable size excludes man and crushes him. But a universe that is a manifestation of great consciousness and order *places* man, and therefore calls to him.

So much is obvious, for a conscious universe is the only reality that can include human consciousness. And only when I am completely included by something does the need arise for me to understand my relationship to it in all the aspects of my inner and outer life. Only a conscious universe is relevant to the whole of human life.

Undoubtedly, one contributing factor in our misunderstanding the cosmos of the ancient teachings is our habitual assumption that a conscious universe is somehow more comforting, a psychological crutch. Giorgio de Santillana speaks to this in **Hamlet's Mill:**

[*Man*] *is unable to fit himself into the concepts of today's astrophysics short of schizophrenia. Modern man is facing the nonconceivable. Archaic man, however, kept a firm grip on the conceivable by framing within his cosmos an order of time and an eschatology that made sense to him and reserved a fate for his soul. Yet it was a prodigiously vast theory, with no concessions to merely human sentiments. It, too, dilated the mind beyond the bearable, although without destroying man's role in the cosmos. It was a ruthless metaphysics.*

Ruthless not in the sense of hostile to human hope, as many scholars have concluded by applying modern presuppositions to the interpretation of these ancient texts which speak of Nature as replete with *demons* and *darkness.* The universe of the traditional teachings, such as Hinduism and Judaism, is *ruthless* in that it is *ruthlessly responsive* to what man demands of it and of himself. For whatever man expects from external reality reflects what he asks or fails to ask of himself.

We must explore this thought further, for it can help us to see why the idea of a conscious universe appears to modern man as naive, as either a daydream or a nightmare. Science, as we know it, searches the universe for order and pattern. To pursue this search carefully, objectively, the scientist struggles to be free of his feelings, his inclinations to believe. He may follow hunches—what he calls *intuitions*—but in the final analysis he wishes for proofs that will compel the intellect, and only the intellect. The entire organization of modern science, the community of experimenters and researchers, the teaching of science in the schools, the training of specialists, is based on this ideal of proof that compels the mind.

Looked at in this way, we may conclude that the practice of modern science is based on a demand for human fragmentation, the division between thought and feeling. Searching for an outer unity, the scientist demands of himself an inner disunity. Perhaps *demands* is not the right word. We should simply say that in his practice the scientist endorses the division and inner fragmentation from which all of us suffer in our daily lives.

We now see why a conscious universe makes no sense to modern science. In the ancient teachings, higher mind or consciousness is never identified with thought associations, no matter how ingenious they may be. If these teachings speak of levels of reality higher than human thought, they are referring, among other things, to an order of intelligence that is inclusive of thought. Consciousness is another word for this power of active relationship or inclusion. Can the power to include ever be understood through a process of internal division and exclusion? Fascinated by the activity of thinking, and drawn to it to the extent of psychological lopsidedness, is it any wonder that we modern scientific men almost never directly experience in ourselves that quality of force which used to be called the Active Intellect, and which in the medieval cosmic scheme was symbolized by a great circle that included the entire created universe?

I realize that our task would be much easier if from now on we could be working with a precise definition of the word *consciousness*. But it is important to stay flexible toward this question of the nature of consciousness. The word is used these days in so many different ways that out of sheer impatience one is tempted to single out one or another aspect of consciousness as its primary characteristic. The difficulty is compounded by the fact that our attitude toward knowledge of ourselves is like our attitude toward new discoveries about the external world. We so easily lose our balance when something extraordinary is discovered in science or when we come upon a new explanatory concept: Immediately the whole machinery of systematizing thought comes into play. Enthusiasm sets in, accompanied by a proliferation of utilitarian explanations, which then stand in the way of direct experiential encounters with surrounding life.

In a like manner, a new experience of one's self tempts us to believe we have discovered the sole direction for the development of consciousness, aliveness or—as it is sometimes called—presence. The same machinery of explanatory thought comes into play accompanied by pragmatic programs for *action*. It is not only followers of the new religions who are victims of this tendency, taking fragments of traditional teachings which have led them to a new experience of themselves and building a subjective and missionary religion around them. This tendency in ourselves also accounts, as we shall see later, for much of the fragmentation of modern psychology, just as it accounts for the fragmentation in the natural sciences.

In order to warn us about this tendency in ourselves, the traditional teachings—as expressed in the **Bhagavad-Gita**, for example—make a fundamental distinction between *consciousness* on one hand and the *contents of consciousness* such as our perceptions of things, our sense of personal identity, our emotions and our thoughts in all their color and gradations on the other hand.

This ancient distinction has two crucial messages for us. On the one hand, it tells us that what we feel to be the best of ourselves as human beings is only part of a total structure containing layers of mind, feeling and sensation far more active, subtle and encompassing (like the cosmic spheres) than what we have settled for as our best. These layers are very numerous and need to be peeled back, as it were, or broken through one by one along the path of inner growth, until an individual touches in himself the fundamental intelligent force in the cosmos.

At the same time, this distinction also communicates that the search for consciousness is a constant necessity for man. It is telling us that anything in ourselves, no matter how fine, subtle or intelligent, no matter how virtuous or close to reality, no matter how still or violent—any action, any thought, any intuition or experience—immediately absorbs all our attention and automatically becomes transformed into *contents* around which gather all the opinions, feelings and distorted sensations that are the supports of our secondhand sense of identity. In short, we are told that the evolution of consciousness is always *vertical* to the constant stream of mental, emotional and sensory associations within the human organism, and comprehensive of them (somewhat like a *fourth dimension*). And, seen in this light, it is not really a question of concentric layers of awareness embedded like the skins of an onion within the self, but only one skin, one veil, that constantly forms regardless of the quality or intensity of the psychic field at any given moment.

Thus, in order to understand the nature of consciousness, I must here and now in this present moment be searching for a better state of consciousness. All definitions, no matter how profound, are secondary. Even the formulations of ancient masters on this subject can be a diversion if I take them in a way that does not support the immediate personal effort to be aware of what is taking place in myself in the present moment.

—*condensed from* **A Sense of the Cosmos**, *by Jacob Needleman*

AJAYA, SWAMI, ed. **FOUNDATIONS OF EASTERN AND WESTERN PSYCHOLOGY. 125pp. Him77, 1.95p.**
A somewhat technical, dry study of the differing views on the question of human development between Eastern and Western psychologists.

■ *ANDERSON, MARIANNE and LOUIS SAVARY.* **PASSAGES: A GUIDE FOR PILGRIMS OF THE MIND. 8¼"x11", 221pp. H&R73/Tur, 5.95p.**
This large, extensively illustrated book gives many practical exercises for reaching altered states of consciousness without drugs. The exercises are clearly presented and relatively easy to follow. The techniques, involving mainly relaxation and self hypnosis coupled with fantasy, are similar to those used by Silva Mind Control. Innumerable quotations add to the reader's enjoyment.

ARKLE, WILLIAM. **A GEOGRAPHY OF CONSCIOUSNESS: A PHILOSOPHY OF HUMAN COMMUNICATION. 10.20c.**
See the Gurdjieff and the Work section.

BACH, RICHARD. **ILLUSIONS: THE ADVENTURES OF A RELUCTANT MESSIAH. 144pp. Dia77/PnB, 6.95c.**
Bach's first book since **Jonathan Livingston Seagull** is a mystical adventure about two vagabonds who meet in the fields of midwest America. Each is doing what he really wants to do. They go through a series of *what ifs* and create a number of illusory sequences. In the process they look at the way many of us could live and the way some of us do.

BACH, RICHARD. **JONATHAN LIVINGSTON SEAGULL. 127pp. Avo70/Tur, 1.75p.**
An illustrated account of a seagull everyman's quest for self identity. This was the great hit of a few years ago and if you are one of the few who are not familiar with the book, the photographs and accompanying text have been a delight to millions of people.

BALLENTINE, RUDOLPH, ed. **SCIENCE OF BREATH. 108pp. Him76, 1.95p.**
This is an extremely complete discussion of breath and of the possibilities for psychological control of breathing and thereby of one's energy. The authors of the essays are all students of Swami Rama—the Indian yogi who underwent a series of experiments at the Menninger Foundation—and Swami Rama himself contributed one of the selections. An introductory essay discusses breath, and this is followed by essays on *Anatomy and Physiology of Breath, The Psychology of Breath, The Five Pranas,* and *Breath Awareness and Meditation.* The information is culled from Eastern scriptures and teachings and from Western psychological theories.

BATESON, GREGORY. **STEPS TO AN ECOLOGY OF MIND. 530pp. RaH72, 2.95p.**
The central idea in this book is that we create the world that we perceive, not because there is no reality outside our heads. . . but because we select and edit the reality we see to conform to our beliefs about what sort of world we live in. . . . For a man to change his basic, perception-determining beliefs. . . he must first become aware that reality is not necessarily as he believes it to be. This is an integrated collection of some of Bateson's most important essays. The writing style is fairly technical and Bateson has developed his own vocabulary. The book is often slow going, but many important insights are presented.

BATESON, GREGORY, et al. **ABOUT BATESON. Bibliography, 250pp. Dut77/Wdw, 4.95p.**
Bateson is one of the most important and least understood thinkers of the twentieth century. He originated the double bind theory of schizophrenia, was the first to apply cybernetic theory to the social sciences, and made important biological discoveries about such non-human species as the dolphin. In **About Bateson** seven individuals have contributed original essays containing their own interpretations of and reactions to Bateson's work. The book concludes with an afterword by Bateson, in which he presents his latest thinking.

BENITEZ, FERNANDO. **IN THE MAGIC LAND OF PEYOTE. Notes, index, 238pp. War75, 1.95p.**
Benitez is the first non-Indian to travel and live with the Huicholes. Here he recounts the sacred peyote hunt which he relived with them. It is a fascinating and perceptive account which includes a fair amount of anthropological data.

BENTOV, ITZHAK. **STALKING THE WILD PENDULUM: ON THE MECHANICS OF CONSCIOUSNESS. 151+pp. Dut77, 4.95p.**
The back cover of this book is filled with words of praise from a variety of well known authors. John Lilly says that *This book is a beautiful presentation of the elements of consciousness, creation, and matter. Bentov's range and his beautifully simple diagrams should make this a delightful textbook for the new generation. His theory of consciousness' velocity as greater than light and spread throughout the universe generates a consistent theory of omnipresence and omniscience which is intriguing. His style is clear, his substance is humorous—a fun-teasing book by a participant-meditation-neutral-observer/creator.* Bentov certainly ranges far in his analysis and includes both theoretical and practical material.

BERRY, WENDELL. **THE UNSETTLING OF AMERICA, CULTURE AND AGRICULTURE. Notes, 238pp. Avo77, 4.95p.**
Berry is a poet, teacher, and farmer—to use one of his own words, a nurturer. **The Unsettling of America** is his personal, dramatic inquiry into the way in which we use the land that sustains us. For the roots of our attitude toward farming, Berry goes back to the industrial revolution, which promised freedom from toil, and to the conquistador mentality that ruled the settlement of North America, treating land, resources, and ultimately people as infinitely expendable. Good farming, Berry argues, is a cultural development and a spiritual discipline. But we have become estranged from the land—and from the intimate knowledge, love, and care of it. Berry sees this as of a piece with the estrangement of generations, of the sexes, of urban and rural society, of neighbors. This is a provocative work of passion, eloquence, and conviction.

Biofeedback

Biofeedback training has been developed in the last decade as a technique to allow us to tune into our bodily functions and, eventually, to control them. In a typical session a subject is hooked up to a machine which can amplify one or another of his body signals and translate them into readily observed phenomena, a flashing light or the movement of a needle. Dr. Barbara Brown, a leading researcher, has the following concept of biofeedback: *Body processes generate specific electrical waves; these can be measured by electronic sensors and reported by an indicator. By watching the indicator we can follow what goes on inside us. Some sensors feed back temperature and other body changes, but the electric indicators do most of the work. This sensory feedback to the mind amounts to intimate communication with the body, and we seem to be able to control any activity we can monitor.*

BOXERMAN, DAVID and ARON SPILKEN. **ALPHA BRAIN WAVES. Bibliography, index, 116pp. CeA75, 4.95p.**
This is the most comprehensive study of alpha for the layman available (not on par with Brown's definitive **New Mind, New Body**). First the authors review what alpha is and how individuals respond to it. They then go on to discuss the potentials of alpha and the major uses of it to date. A final section gives diagrammatic instructions for building biofeedback machinery.

■ *BROWN, BARBARA.* **NEW MIND, NEW BODY. Notes, thirty-one page bibliography, index, 277pp. Ban74/Hod, 2.95p.**
Dr. Brown is Chief of Experiential Psychology at the Veterans Hospital, Sepulveda, California, and a lecturer in the Department of Psychiatry at the UCLA Medical Center. She opened up the field of biofeedback research in the mid-sixties and has done most of the pioneering research. In this definitive study she reports her own and associates' research and describes many experiments in detail.

BROWN, BARBARA. **STRESS AND THE ART OF BIOFEEDBACK. Bibliography, index, 309pp. Ban77, 2.25p.**
Following up on **New Mind, New Body**, Dr. Brown here presents the first comprehensive formulation of how to use biofeedback to treat a variety of illnesses and, especially, to relieve conditions related to stress. She also outlines a number of related concepts and psychotherapeutic measures. This is a technical work which outlines clinical procedure. Nonetheless, the interested layman should be able to understand the material.

GREEN, ELMER and ALICE. **BEYOND BIOFEEDBACK. Bibliography, index, 382pp. Del77, 4.95p.**
Since 1964 Elmer and Alice Green have been engaged in pioneering studies of biofeedback at the Menninger Foundation in Kansas. This volume is both an autobiography and a report on work in progress. After a detailed, firsthand report on the effects of biofeedback training on various diseases and conditions such as high blood pressure, migraine, gastrointestinal disorders, epilepsy, and cerebral palsy, the Greens move on to some of its broader implications. The idea of self regulation, of voluntary control over one's own mind and body, is the central thread as they examine creativity, meditation, states of consciousness, the role of the mind in cancer therapy, the powers of psychics, healers, and yogis, and much else. Many case histories are included.

KARLINS, MARVIN and LEWIS M. ANDREWS. **BIOFEEDBACK: TURNING ON THE POWER OF YOUR MIND. Many case histories, bibliography, index, 183pp. War72/SBL, 1.95p.**
This is a simple, anecdotal account of biofeedback research.

KETTELKAMP, LARRY. **A PARTNERSHIP OF MIND AND BODY. Illustrations, index, 96pp. Mor76, 5.95c.**
A general discussion of the mechanics of biofeedback written for younger readers, although we are not sure many young people would be interested in the subject. This book is good for anyone who seeks a simple explanation of the subject.

SCHWARTZ, GARY and JACKSON BEATTY, eds. **BIOFEEDBACK: THEORY AND RESEARCH.** Illustrations, notes, indices, 477pp. AcP77, 33.25c.
A scholarly overview of recent developments in biofeedback. The selections concentrate on biofeedback as a scientific tool in both basic and clinical research. Some discuss therapeutic applications and others cover theoretical issues.

--------------END OF BIOFEEDBACK SUBSECTION--------------

BLAKEMORE, COLIN. **MECHANICS OF THE MIND.** Bibliography, index, 7"x10", 216pp. CUP77, 7.95p.
This book is based on a series of lectures (on the current state of knowledge about the human brain) which Dr. Blakemore gave on the BBC in 1976, supplemented with 184 illustrations, many in color. Dr. Blakemore describes the mechanisms of sensation, sleep, memory, and thought. He also discusses the philosophical questions of human consciousness, the evolution of thinking about body and mind, and relationship between art and perception, and the origin and functions of language.

BOONE, J. ALLEN. **KINSHIP WITH ALL LIFE.** 157pp. H&R54, 3.95p.
A presentation of the author's experiences with animals ranging in size from a camel to a fly. Each of the thirty-four chapters discusses a different animal.

BOONE, J. ALLEN. **THE LANGUAGE OF SILENCE.** 139pp. H&R70, 3.95p.
More stories of Boone's communication with animals.

BRONOWSKI, JACOB. **THE ASCENT OF MAN.** Bibliography, index, 7"x9¾", 448pp. LBC73, 8.95p.
This book was lauded by critics and was an instant best seller when it first appeared as a companion to Bronowski's acclaimed television series. It is an exciting, graceful, splendidly illustrated investigation which offers a new perspective on both science and on civilization itself.

BROWNE, HARRY. **HOW I FOUND FREEDOM IN AN UNFREE WORLD.** 368pp. Avo73, 2.25p.
Discussion of the various traps we fall into which keep us from being free, along with detailed recommendations on how to break free. *From this man's love of freedom, then, has come this book, a gift of power and of joy for whoever yearns to be free.*—Richard Bach. Very practical suggestions.

BRY, ADELAIDE. **DIRECTING THE MOVIES OF YOUR MIND: VISUALIZATION FOR HEALTH AND INSIGHT.** Bibliography, 189pp. H&R78, 8.95c.
A simple, straightforward account of the many ways visualization is being clinically used today. Ms. Bry also includes a number of exercises showing how anyone can use visualization.

CALDWELL, W.V. **LSD PSYCHOTHERAPY: AN EXPLORATION OF PSYCHEDELIC AND PSYCHOANALYTIC THERAPY.** Very extensive bibliography, index, 319pp. RaH68, 3.95p.
A detailed discussion divided into two parts. The first, based on the author's interviews and research, is a survey of modern treatment in the United States and abroad. The second is devoted to the description and classification of basic, universal images and fantasies as they manifest themselves under the hallucinogens.

CALLENBACH, ERNEST. **ECOTOPIA.** 167pp. Ban75, 1.95p.
A utopian novel about Ecotopia, an independent nation comprising what used to be northern California, Oregon, and Washington. It is an underground classic in which many ecological dreams are realized. The narrative is told by an American newspaper reporter who is the first official American allowed to visit Ecotopia in the twenty years since independence. As he reports on the realities of life in Ecotopia he becomes more and more drawn to the state. An intriguing, enjoyable book for all who are interested in possibilities for the future.

CALVINO, ITALO. **COSMICOMICS.** 153pp. HBJ68, 2.50p.
Calvino is a contemporary Italian writer who has been compared to Jorge Luis Borges and Gabriel Garcia Marquez. This collection of short stories is translated by William Weaver. The stories tell about the

evolution of the universe. Calvino makes characters out of mathematical formulas and simple cellular structures. They disport themselves among galaxies, experience the solidification of planets, move from aquatic to terrestrial existence, play games with hydrogen atoms, and have a love life. During the course of the stories Calvino toys with ideas of continuous creation, the transformation of matter, and the expanding and contracting reaches of time and space. An unusual collection, to say the least.

CARLSON, RICK, ed. **THE FRONTIERS OF SCIENCE AND MEDICINE.** Notes, 224pp. Reg75, 3.95p.
Transcription of a collection of papers delivered at a conference on the title theme. The following selections give a good idea of the coverage: *Consciousness and Commitment*—Werner Erhard, *Is Primitive Medicine Really Primitive?*—Lyall Watson, *Biofeedback and Voluntary Control of Internal States*—Elmer Green, *The Role of Psychics in Mental Diagnosis*—Norman Shealy, *The Role of the Mind in Cancer Therapy*—Carl Simonton, and *In-depth Studies of Uri Geller*—Andrija Puharich.

Carlos Castaneda

Since the publication of **The Teachings of Don Juan** in the early 1970s, Castaneda has become something of a cult hero. Countless arguments have taken place over whether Don Juan actually exists, and virtually every aspect of Castaneda's writings and personal life has been scrutinized. Castaneda himself has kept an extremely low profile; he virtually never appears announced in public and his whereabouts are kept hidden. He wrote the first book as a graduate student at UCLA and he remains on the staff there. One of the books, **Tales of Power**, was actually accepted as his doctoral thesis. We are certainly not competent to judge the veracity of Castaneda's work. In terms of our own knowledge of the field, there is a high degree of versimilitude in all the books, and Don Juan's teaching is certainly in the tradition of the native populations of Mexico and the American southwest. In any event, the books themselves are often delightful reading and the teaching comes through loud and clear, though often garbed in allegory and apocryphal tales. The books themselves have been incredibly popular with a broad spectrum of people and each has been on the best seller list.

CASTANEDA, CARLOS. **DON JUAN QUARTET.** S&S77/Pen, 13.95p/7.95p/set.
A boxed set containing **Journey to Ixtlan**, **A Separate Reality**, **Tales of Power**, and **The Teachings of Don Juan**.

CASTANEDA, CARLOS. **JOURNEY TO IXTLAN.** 315pp. S&S72/Pen, 2.95p/1.95p.
The third volume in the continuing saga of Don Juan. **Teachings** was very good, **A Separate Reality** was even better, and this one transcends them both. It has nothing to do with drugs—it is about the basic spiritual lessons Don Juan was trying to show Carlos; earlier Carlos was too busy trying to see everything in terms of drugs to see them. *When you see there are no longer any familiar features in the world. Everything is new, Everything has never happened before. The world is incredible!...there is really no way to talk about it. Seeing...is learned by seeing.*

CASTANEDA, CARLOS. **THE SECOND RING OF POWER.** 316pp. S&S77/Hod, 9.95c.
Don Juan does not appear in Castaneda's latest book. In his place is Dona Soledad, a woman who turns her powers against Castaneda and almost consumes him. Dona Soledad has been trained by Don Juan and transformed by his teachings from a bent, gray haired old woman into a sensual, lithe figure of awesome power; a sorceress whose mission is to test Carlos by a series of terrifying tricks. Dona Soledad, drawn out of the shadows of a defeated and meaningless life by Don Juan, has become a warrior, a hunter, and a *stalker of power*. She and her *girls* are part of a small, closed society in which the teachings of Don Juan have become a way of life, touching and explaining every aspect of the world and totally altering the relationships among them. In this book Carlos

learns that the teachings and message of Don Juan can and must be transformed into real life. Those who were absorbed with Castaneda's earlier books will be delighted with this one.

CASTANEDA, CARLOS. **A SEPARATE REALITY: FURTHER CONVERSATIONS WITH DON JUAN.** 317pp. S&S74/Pen, 3.95p/1.95p.
At the end of the first book Carlos was so freaked out by the world of *non-ordinary reality* that he decided to go back to UCLA and his academic womb and never resume his apprenticeship. That resolve did not last long and in this volume he resumes going deeper into Don Juan's world of mystical sensation and perception, learning to *see* beyond the surface realities of life.

CASTANEDA, CARLOS. **TALES OF POWER.** 287pp. S&S74/Pen, 2.95p/1.95p.
The fourth book in Don Juan's continuing reeducation of Carlos. All of the material presented in the previous books has been merely the preparation for **Tales of Power,** in which Don Juan's task of making Carlos *a man of knowledge* and *a man of power* is brought to a conclusion in a series of dazzling exploits, visions, and lessons, ending in *the sorcerer's explanation,* which is at once an initiation and a deeply moving farewell.

CASTANEDA, CARLOS. **THE TEACHINGS OF DON JUAN: A YAQUI WAY OF KNOWLEDGE.** 276pp. S&S68/Pen, 3.25p/2.25p.
An account of nonordinary states of reality experienced through natural psychedelic substances, in the deserts of Mexico, with a strange and profound old man who has become a legend, myth, and teaching power throughout America and the world. In this first book the text reads a bit like an anthropology PhD dissertation (which it was intended to be)—and there are technical appendices. But Carlos' apprenticeship makes fascinating reading.

MILLE, RICHARD DE. **CASTANEDA'S JOURNEY.** Notes, bibliography, index, 206pp. Cap76/Spe, 4.95p.
This is the most extensive scholarly analysis yet made of the philosophy expressed in Castaneda's books. De Mille also discusses Castaneda's academic career and the sources of his writings, both mundane and spiritual. He is generally critical of Castaneda and implies that the whole series of books is just one big hoax. Despite this bias, de Mille often comes up with some interesting insights.

NOEL, DANIEL, ed. **SEEING CASTANEDA.** Notes, bibliography, 250pp. Put76, 3.95p.
An anthology, drawn from the best writing about Castaneda, including that of Joyce Carol Oates, Theodore Roszak, and Joseph Chilton Pearce. The range of essays is wide and Castaneda is often viewed in them as a seminal philosopher.

———————END OF CARLOS CASTANEDA SUBSECTION———————

COHEN, SIDNEY. **DRUGS OF HALLUCINATION.** 217pp. Grn65, 1.65p.
The results of a twelve-year objective study. Topics covered include the early use of LSD as an inducer of *model psychoses* and its present use in psychotherapy; its effects on subjects under controlled conditions; many firsthand accounts of LSD induced transcendental experiences. Includes a chemical breakdown of the hallucinogens. A very scientific study.

DEIKMAN, ARTHUR. **PERSONAL FREEDOM.** Notes, 163pp. Ban76/Sou, 1.95p.
A challenging view of reality, and how we have been deceived and deceive ourselves in regard to it. Dr. Deikman takes us on a path he has himself followed, helping us to discover the deeper realities within ourselves, thereby gaining new energy and serenity. A highly personal book, conveying a hopeful and provocative message.—Carl Rogers. Dr. Deikman is a pioneer in the scientific investigation of the psychological effects of meditation. His papers have appeared in **The Nature of Human Consciousness** and **Altered States of Consciousness** and in leading journals. His approach to both Eastern and Western psychologies is sensitive and perceptive. The British title is **On Finding Your Way to the Real World.**

DI CYAN, ERWIN. **CREATIVITY: ROAD TO SELF-DISCOVERY.** Lengthy bibliography, index, 256pp. Jov78, 1.95p.
This simple, practical book shows you how to unlock your inborn creativity. The author analyzes every facet of creativity and offers a great number of specific techniques.

FLUGELMAN, ANDREW, ed. **THE NEW GAMES BOOK.** 8¼"x9¼", 193pp. Dou76, 4.95p.
By all means let us cherish the traditional sports for their many beauties, their unplumbed potential, and for the certainty they afford. But we have signed no long-term contract to suffer their extremes. The time has come to move on, to create new games with new rules more in tune with the times, games in which there are no spectators and no second-string players, games for a whole family and a whole day, games in which aggression fades into laughter.—George Leonard. This book presents sixty new games, descriptively illustrated with over 250 photographs and extensive commentary.

FRENCH, PETER, ed. **PHILOSOPHERS IN WONDERLAND.** Notes, 388pp. LlP75, 9.95p.
This volume is hard to classify. It is subtitled, *Philosophy and Psychical Research,* but we do not feel that it fits in very comfortably with the parapsychology books. It is basically an anthology of classical and contemporary philosophical writings on consciousness. It is an interesting, albeit technical study, which covers many little discussed and less understood areas.

FUNDERBURK, JAMES. **SCIENCE STUDIES YOGA.** Glossary, notes, bibliography, index, 271pp. Him77, 5.95p.
An extremely detailed report of Dr. Funderburk's studies on the effect of yoga on physiological systems. He has systematically extracted the different elements of methodology and collated effects under the respective physiological systems. A large share of the data is presented in graphic form. *I know of no other summary of yoga research that gives the data so objectively and in a form for such ready reference. The book doubtless will be of considerable importance to therapists and teachers, and should be most valuable in stimulating further research.*—Barbara Brown.

FURST, PETER. **HALLUCINOGENS AND CULTURE.** Illustrations, notes, bibliography, index, 206pp. C&S76, 4.95p.
Dr. Furst demonstrates with a wealth of cross-cultural and historical data and some of his own first-hand experiences the often decisive role hallucinogens have sometimes played, and continue to play, in the maintenance of social systems in the traditional world, and their positive role in rituals of religion or initiation, mythology and symbolism, and in art, as well as in psychotherapy and curing of physical ills.—Norman Zinberg, MD, Professor, Harvard University.

GOLAS, THADDEUS. **THE LAZY MAN'S GUIDE TO ENLIGHTENMENT.** 80pp. See74, 2.00p.
A small jewel. Do not be put off by the title—it is a trusted companion for thousands. *There is a paradise in and around you right now, and to be there you don't have to make a move.... You can open yourself to the diamondlike perfection of everything you see and feel. If you don't think it can happen that easily, just be loving, moment by moment, and trust that it will come to you.*

GROF, STANISLAV. **REALMS OF THE HUMAN UNCONSCIOUS.** Illustrations, bibliography, index, 255pp. Vik75, 4.95p.
This is probably an important technical contribution to the literature in the field of human potential, especially as seen through the extensive LSD research that has recently taken place. It is a bit hard for us to judge since something about the format of the book and its general style does not invite casual perusal and no one around here is interested enough in the subject to wade through the mass of material presented. But if you are, this seems to be a definitive volume by one of the pioneering academic researchers. Dr. Grof supplies countless case histories, especially his experiences utilizing LSD for emotional therapy and in terminal cancer patients.

HAAS, ERNST. **THE CREATION.** 11"x7½", 159pp. Vik71, 8.95p.
The story of creation has inspired poetry, painting, and music throughout the ages. In these pages it is told through color photographs, arranged in flowing sequences to represent the elements, the seasons, and the creatures living on Earth. A magnificent volume.

HARNER, MICHAEL, ed. **HALLUCINOGENS AND SHAMANISM.** Notes, index, 196pp. Oxf73, 2.95p.
Ten studies explore the widespread practice of invoking a trance state to perceive and manipulate supernatural forces. The researchers have succeeded in penetrating the mystical experience by taking the hallucinogens themselves, and participating in native ceremonies. Primitive cultures in various parts of the world are explored.

HATTERSLEY, RALPH. **DISCOVER YOURSELF THROUGH PHO-TOGRAPHY.** 8¼"x10¾", 320pp. M&M71, 9.95p.
This is a very unusual photographic technique book which uses 239 photographs to illustrate the points made. The main subjects include the following: *Free Your Creative Mind, Understand Your Aesthetic Sense, Discover Both Sides of Yourself, Discover Your Own Secret Symbols,* and *Photography May Be a Practice of Religion for You.* An emphasis is placed on analyzing your feelings toward others from the pictures you take of them. Hattersley suggests many practical exercises, based on his years of teaching experience.

HISEY, LEHMANN. **KEYS TO INNER SPACE.** Bibliography, 252pp. Avo74, 1.95p.
Half of this book is devoted to brief analyses of self hypnosis and meditation, the tarot, rhythmic breathing, color and sound, astrology, polarity vs. duality, the Tao and acupuncture, Gurdjieff's teachings, the LSD experience, and the *chakras.* The material presented in this section is too scanty to be of value to anyone but a beginning student. The fascinating material is in the second section where Mark Prophet, a *deep trance* medium, gives an account of life after death—reproduced and documented from actual tapes.

HUMAN DIMENSIONS INSTITUTE. **CONSCIOUSNESS.** Notes, 52pp. HDI74, 2.00p.
This pamphlet focuses on consciousness research and the nature of human consciousness; the explorations are both theoretical and applied. Contributors include John White and Lama Govinda.

HUXLEY, ALDOUS. **THE DOORS OF PERCEPTION AND HEAVEN AND HELL.** 185pp. H&R54/PnB, 2.50p.
Huxley explores the mind's remote frontiers and the unmapped areas of human consciousness in this analysis of his psychedelic experience. A classic in the field.

HUXLEY, ALDOUS. **THE HUMAN SITUATION.** Index, 261pp. H&R77/C&W, 10.00c.
An edited transcription of a series of sixteen lectures delivered by Huxley in 1959 at the University of California at Santa Barbara. This is a very contemporary book which views many specific topics as part of a larger whole. The following lecture titles give a good idea of the coverage: *Integrate Education, Man and His Planet, More Nature in Art, The Population Explosion, How Original is Original Sin?, War and Nationalism, The World's Future, The Individual Life of Man, The Ego, The Unconscious, Language, Art, Man and Religion, Natural History of Visions,* and *Latent Human Potentialities.*

HUXLEY, ALDOUS. **ISLAND.** 295pp. H&R62/PnB, 1.50p.
Huxley's final major work; the summation of his life views on what an ideal society would be like. The form is a utopian novel and the island is a South Seas paradise which is isolated from the rest of the world. Many think that Huxley's Pala is actually the island of Bali. Much of the material in the novel was revealed to Huxley through his use of LSD and other psychedelics. It is a fascinating story and is not particularly didactic.

HUXLEY, ALDOUS. **MOKSHA.** Notes, index, 336pp. Sto77, 12.95c.
An authoritative compilation of Huxley's writings on psychedelics and the visionary experience, spanning the years from 1931 to 1963. The editors have gathered selections from a number of Huxley's books as well as magazine articles, interviews, correspondence, and scientific papers. The material is well organized, allowing the reader to grasp the growth of Huxley's vision and understanding.

HUXLEY, ALDOUS. **THE PERENNIAL PHILOSOPHY.** Excellent bibliography, index, 306pp. H&R44/CaL, 3.95p.
Perennial Philosophy is primarily concerned with the one, divine Reality substantial to the manifold world of things and lives and minds...it cannot be directly and immediately apprehended except by those who have chosen to fulfill certain conditions, making themselves loving, pure in heart, and poor in spirit. Huxley traces this philosophy through East and West and includes excerpts from texts.

HUXLEY, LAURA. **BETWEEN HEAVEN AND EARTH.** Bibliography, 320pp. Avo75/C&W, 1.95p.
This is a sequel to **You are Not the Target: Recipes for Living and Loving:** *The purpose of these Recipes...is to stimulate a keener insight into our multiple nature and a realization that our conflicting characteristics are desirable*

advantages rather than burdens. One group of recipes shows that it is the synchronization of will, imagination, and body that gives meaning to life. Another, *All Living Is Relationship,* explores the author's fundamental interest. *Nutrition, Transformer of Consciousness,* is the title of another group, and additional recipes develop an awareness of vibrations and auras, and of the powerful influence of our thoughts. Ms. Huxley's writing style is very clear and the *recipes* are generally quite practical.

HUXLEY, LAURA. **THIS TIMELESS MOMENT.** 308pp. CeA68, 4.95p.
A glimpse of Aldous Huxley's last years. Includes material on psychedelics and a fascinating chapter on his use of LSD while dying.

HUXLEY, LAURA. **YOU ARE NOT THE TARGET.** 277pp. Wil63, 3.00p/1.95p.
Recipes (exercises) for living and loving. Very practical stuff.

IZARD, JANET. **MANDALA COLORING PAD.** 11"x10¾", Dou nd, 2.95p.
A collection of about thirty designs on detachable pages.

JANOV, ARTHUR and E. MICHAEL HOLDEN. **PRIMAL MAN: THE NEW CONSCIOUSNESS.** Illustrations, notes, index, 532pp. SBL75, 6.60p.
A major exploration of the levels of consciousness and how they operate. The results of Janov's research at the Primal Research Laboratory and the latest research in both psychology and neurology are reviewed. Each of the chapters is a separate, albeit related, essay. An important topic is the effect of neurosis on the brain and what happens to the brain and body during a primal. Many case studies are cited. This should be an interesting book for those who are deeply interested in the brain and its functioning.

JAYNES, JULIAN. **THE ORIGIN OF CONSCIOUSNESS IN THE BREAKDOWN OF THE BICAMERAL MIND.** Notes, indices, 467pp. HMC76, 12.95c.
Jaynes is a psychologist; he bases this provocative book on recent laboratory studies of the brain and a reading of archaeological evidence. Jaynes' thesis is that ancient people could not think as we do today and were therefore not conscious. Unable to introspect, they experienced auditory hallucinations—for example, hearing the voices of gods—which, coming from the brain's right hemisphere, told an individual what to do in times of stress. This ancient way of thinking is known as the bicameral mind. Only catastrophe and cataclysm forced mankind to learn consciousness, and that happened only 3,000 years ago. Consciousness is therefore grounded in the physiology of the brain's right and left hemispheres. In the latter part of the book Jaynes examines three forms of consciousness—the bicameral man; modern, problem solving man; and contemporary throwbacks to bicamerality.

JOHARI, HARISH. **LEELA: THE GAME OF SELF-KNOWLEDGE.** 6.65p.
See the Indian Philosophy section.

KARAGULLA, SHAFICA. **BREAKTHROUGH TO CREATIVITY.** Good bibliography, 286pp. DeV67, 7.95c.
An important study by a neuropsychiatrist. Presents experimental evidence of *sensitives* who could see into and through the human body, observing states of health and disease that correlated with medical findings. Others could see energy exchange among individuals in a group, and observe the giving or sapping of others' energy. Many fascinating examples.

KATZ, MICHAEL, WILLIAM MARSH and GAIL THOMPSON, *eds.* **EARTH'S ANSWER.** 7"x9", 229pp. H&R77, 6.95c.
A collection of edited talks from two conferences at Lindisfarne focusing on the transformation of the individual, the creation of new communities, decentralization and world order, evolution and the strategies of consciousness, and planetary culture and the new image of humanity. The contributors are all individuals who are deeply involved in creating the new planetary cultures and they come from a wide variety of disciplines.

KEEN, SAM. **VOICES AND VISIONS.** 218pp. H&R74, 1.95p.
A collection of interviews which Keen did for **Psychology Today** over the last few years, originally printed in the magazine. His subjects

include Norman O. Brown, Herbert Marcuse, Joseph Campbell, John Lilly, Carlos Castaneda, Oscar Ichazo, Stanley Keleman, Ernest Becker, and Roberto Assagioli. Keen's style, as he expresses it, is *asking questions, posing problems, talking, listening.* He begins each conversation with a background essay on the individual—and the material in these essays is some of the best in the book. All in all, the conversations provide a great deal of insight into some of the most important contemporary philosophers.

KEYS, JAMES. **ONLY TWO CAN PLAY THIS GAME. 144pp. Crn72, 6.00c.**
This is a sensitive, personally revealing book. Using prose, poetry, philosophy, and satirical humor Keys shares the joys, sadness, and strivings of one person seeking another, despite the repressions and wrong emphasis of our society. James Keys is the pen name of G. Spencer Brown, a British philosopher. *Very few people would write such a book, and fewer could. This is a rare document, of high quality, and those who cherish such things, will appreciate it.*—R.D. Laing.

KLEPS, ART. **MILLBROOK: THE TRUE STORY OF THE EARLY YEARS OF THE PSYCHEDELIC REVOLUTION. 355pp. Ben77, 4.95p.**
An account of the Leary years at Millbrook by one of the country's leading social and ecclesiastical satirists. Always entertaining, he is also informative and never inhibited. Anyone interested in the Millbrook episode in modern history will find that he must cope with this tome.—Walter Houston Clark.

KOBERG, DON and JIM BAGNALL. **THE UNIVERSAL TRAVELLER: A SOFT-SYSTEMS GUIDE TO CREATIVITY, PROBLEM-SOLVING, AND THE PROCESS OF REACHING GOALS. Many illustrations, index, 8½"x11", 128pp. Kau74, 5.95p.**
A scattered compendium of interesting and not so interesting ideas.

KOBERG, DON and JIM BAGNALL. **VALUES TECH. Bibliography, index, 8½"x11", 240pp. Kau76, 6.95p.**
Values Tech *is a portable school contained entirely within the pages of this book....The work involves establishing criteria, determining meaning, choosing, selecting, and deciding between things. It includes comparing the options in life with your personal intentions for a good life and, in general, coming to grips with the value and worth of the bits and pieces of your experience.*—from the introduction. The layout and presentation are scattered and the book does not appeal to us, but some people we know have found the material extremely helpful.

KOESTLER, ARTHUR. **ACT OF CREATION. Notes, bibliography, index, 751pp. PnB64, 4.00p.**
Koestler argues that the scientist's insight is similar to the artist's act of creation, and that they share certain psychological conditions. Examining the common factors in scientific, artistic, and comic creations, he draws examples from psychology, Eastern mysticism, biology, and literature which yield *the moment of truth* in the creator's achievement. Discussing the nature of genius, he defines the process by which ability evolves into a completed work, and finds similarities to the creative process throughout the entire animal kingdom. This is a valuable compendium of psychological and scientific information for the layman.

KOESTLER, ARTHUR. **THE GHOST IN THE MACHINE. Notes, bibliography, index, 400pp. GEd67/HPG, 3.95p.**
This is a discussion of contemporary life, emphasizing the individual and his place in society. Among the topics Koestler covers are words and language, memory, forgetting, evolution, and man's brain.

KOESTLER, ARTHUR. **THE HEEL OF ACHILLES. Notes, 273pp. PnB74, 2.65p.**
A collection of Koestler's essays, 1968-73, about which he has written: *In spite of their diversity, these essays were intended as variations on certain themes, and are grouped accordingly. The first section has as its leitmotif the predicament of man...the section called "Nothing But...?" attacks the prevailing materialistic philosophy....The last essay, dealing with certain disastrous aspects of Gandhi's life and philosophy—which are largely unknown to the public—is intended to redress the balance by stressing the dangers of taking shortcuts from Western materialism to Eastern mysticism.*

KRAMER, JOEL. **THE PASSIONATE MIND: A MANUAL FOR LIVING CREATIVELY WITH ONE'S SELF. 120pp. CeA74, 3.95p.**
This book represents years of talking with people about the fundamental problems of living. It is a collection of transcribed and edited lectures. It is also an expression of my own inner inquiry.... What we are going to do in these talks, which are ideally not monologues at all, but discussions, dialogues between you and me, is to examine fundamentally the nature of what it is to be a human being. In order to do this, it is necessary for us to actually look at ourselves as we are. That's not such an easy thing to do because we have all kinds of ideas about what an individual ought to be or should be; all kinds of desires as to what we want to be.... It is not possible to see clearly anything at all, until we come into contact with ourselves.

LAMB, F. BRUCE. **WIZARD OF THE UPPER AMAZON. 223pp. HMC74, 3.95p.**
Wizard...*is an extraordinary document of life among a tribe of South American Indians at the beginning of the century. For many readers the most compelling sections of the book will be the descriptions of the use of...the "yage" or "ayahuasca" of the Amazon forests. This powerful hallucinogen has long been credited with the ability to transport human beings to realms of experience where telepathy and clairvoyance are commonplace....Manuel Cordova, the narrator...is now an old man, well-known as a healer in Peru. He attributes his powers to his time as a captive among the Amahuaca Indians, in particular to intensive training sessions conducted under the influence of "ayahuasca."*—Andrew Weil. This is an illuminating, entertaining tale which should especially appeal to Castaneda aficionados.

LANDE, NATHANIEL. **MINDSTYLES/LIFESTYLES. 8½"x11", 495pp. PSS76, 7.95p.**
Everything you could possibly want to know and more about Eastern religion, the new consciousness movements, body work, psychology, the frontiers of healing, and much else. Each of the selections is brief and covers the subject well. Sources for additional information are cited and there are also a number of interviews with well known individuals. Color illustrations by Corita Kent are interspersed. The book is much better than we expected it to be.

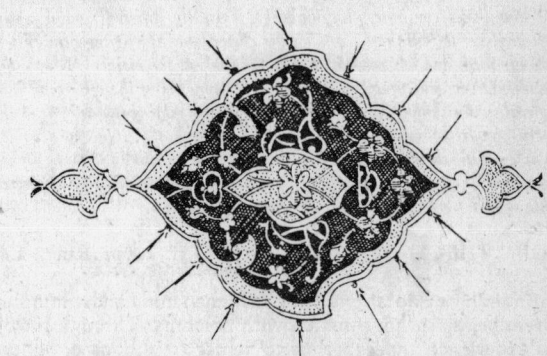

LEARY, TIMOTHY. **EXO-PSYCHOLOGY. 134+pp. Pce77, 6.95p.**
In his preface, Leary describes this book as *a simple-minded attempt to provide a galactic perspective of biological evolution on and from this planet, present[ing] hundreds of neogenetic ideas for which the human species is now ready. The transmission is presented in larval muscular-symbol-unites (laryngeal-manual) although. the topics discussed are post-larval, electromagnetic, and quantum-mechanical. The reader should expect, therefore, that his conditioned symbol-system is going to be jolted with unexpected and novel symbol combinations. This is exactly the situation that will exist when we begin living in space colonies and when Higher Intelligence begins to communicate with a species of Domesticated Primates like the human race.* Each of the twenty-four stages that Leary discusses is illustrated.

LEARY, TIMOTHY. **NEUROPOLITICS. 7"x10", 160+pp. Pce77, 6.95p.**
A study of *The Sociobiology of Human Metamorphosis* divided into two sections, *The Twilight of Terrestrial Politics* and *The Dawn of Extraterrestrial Politics.* Leary's recent books are overly technical and this one is extremely paranoid.

LEARY, TIMOTHY, RALPH METZNER and RICHARD ALPERT. **THE PSYCHEDELIC EXPERIENCE: A MANUAL BASED ON THE TIBETAN BOOK OF THE DEAD. 8"x9¼", 191pp. Stu64, 3.95p.**
A recreation of **The Tibetan Book of the Dead** in the form of a psychedelic trip guide analyzing the stages one passes through during the experience.

LEARY, TIMOTHY, RALPH METZNER and **RICHARD ALPERT. THE PSYCHEDELIC EXPERIENCE: A MANUAL BASED ON THE TIBETAN BOOK OF THE DEAD (A RECORDING). 7.98.**
A 33 1/3 rpm record containing readings from **The Psychedelic Experience**. The passages were selected to serve as a guide during the *Going Out* (side one) and the *Coming Back* (side two) phases of a psychedelic session. Detailed, descriptive notes focus on the use of the **Tibetan Book of the Dead** and other sacred books as guides to altered states of consciousness.

LEE, PHILIP, et al. **SYMPOSIUM ON CONSCIOUSNESS. Notes, 182pp. Vik76, 2.95p.**
As the title suggests, this is a collection of papers presented at the annual meeting of the American Association for the Advancement of Science in 1974. The contributors were Philip Lee, Robert Ornstein, David Galin, Arthur Deikman, and Charles Tart—each of whom is trained in a different discipline. The papers are pretty technical.

LEONARD, GEORGE. THE TRANSFORMATION—A GUIDE TO THE INEVITABLE CHANGES IN HUMANKIND. 258pp. Del72, 2.95p.
Deals with an alternate system of perceiving and being. *After all the journeying*, says Leonard, *all the pain and joy, we may discover that the transformation was difficult to grasp, not because it was so far away, but because it was so very near. To find the immense world of delight, is, in the end, to come home again, where it always was.* A beautifully written book which will appeal to all who see our culture dying, and who are experiencing a new way of being. It is a book of hope.

LESHAN, LAWRENCE. ALTERNATE REALITIES. Notes, 232pp. RaH76/ SIP, 1.95p.
This book is a "work in progress".... The central idea...is that we human beings invent reality as much as we discover it, and that if this is comprehended, we have a wide choice as to how we invent it and therefore, what sort of world we live in. There are, the thesis continues, a number of basically different, valid ways of organizing whatever is "out there," and we can choose from among these the ones that will satisfy our needs and advance us toward our goals at the moment. Many of our personal and interpersonal problems seem to arise from using the wrong method of construing reality to accomplish a particular task, or from mixing two or more methods without being aware of what we are doing. This thesis also seems to provide an acceptable and useful solution to the "impossible paradox" of ESP, and to the problems of "survival" of the personality after biological death and of the existence or nonexistence of spirit entities.—from the introduction.

LILLY, JOHN. THE CENTER OF THE CYCLONE. 200pp. Ban72/C&B, 1.95p.
Lilly continues his explorations into the human mind and communication system begun in his research with dolphins. Through his own personal experience and experiments under conditions of solitude, confinement, LSD, and mystical inspiration, he provides a scientific account of how the mind operates on various levels of consciousness. He demonstrates how an individual can self program such spaces and create the principles that govern thoughts and behavior. The last chapters detail his experiences in Arica, Chile, with Oscar Ichazo.

LILLY, JOHN. THE DEEP SELF. Notes, 320pp. S&S77, 9.95c.
Lilly sums up his empirical observations about what he terms *isolation therapy*. The book begins with Lilly's discussion of his physical isolation experience in the tank and with reprints of a number of papers on isolation previously published. Next follows information on tank construction, manufacture, and use. More than 100 pages are devoted to transcripts of the experiences of people using the tanks, including excerpts from Lilly's previously published personal observations. There are also a number of technical appendices. As with all of Lilly's recent work, this book is often unreadable. Lilly has trouble following the basic rules of English grammar and this greatly lessens the clarity of his writing style. He also quotes extensively from his own earlier works and tends to be repetitive.

LILLY, JOHN. LILLY ON DOLPHINS. Illustrations, notes, bibliography, index, 515pp. Dou75, 3.50p.
This is a revised, one volume edition of **Man and Dolphin** and **The Mind of the Dolphin**. Here, Lilly describes his ground breaking attempt to communicate with dolphins and discusses his findings.

LILLY, JOHN. PROGRAMMING AND META-PROGRAMMING IN THE HUMAN BIOCOMPUTER. 160pp. Crn67, 4.95p.
Deals with the theory and methods behind Lilly's personal work as expressed in **Center of the Cyclone** and the dolphin books. The text was originally written as a summary report to a government agency and therefore the language is quite dry. An interesting, well organized presentation if you can relate to the language used.

LILLY, JOHN. THE SCIENTIST: A NOVEL AUTOBIOGRAPHY. 210pp. Lip78, 10.00c.
The most recent of John Lilly's third person autobiographical accounts, as well as the most extensive. It probably has more information than anyone other than Lilly's most ardent fans would like to know. As with all of his books in the last few years, the language is stilted and convoluted and Lilly's immense ego comes strongly through. Unfortunately, there seem to be more books to come, witness his final sentence: *A new book also seems to be gestating; so life continues, etc., etc., etc., to its future ending.* Another book would be fine if he has something to say, but unfortunately all of his books since **Center of the Cyclone** are simple rehashes.

LILLY, JOHN. SIMULATIONS OF GOD. 288pp. Ban75, 2.25p.
My purpose is to present the simulations, the models, the belief structures of others as objectively and as accurately as I can....If you will agree to look for and explore basic beliefs with me, I can, despite my own limits, point out ways to take off on your own search, directions to look in, and methods of integrating the new as you find it....I ask you to consider and think about what I write, make what you can yours, and let the rest go for a while....We shall enter the sacred realms of self, religion, science, philosophy, sex, drugs, politics, money, crime, war, family, and spiritual paths. We shall enter with no holds barred, with courage, with a sense of excitement.—from the introduction. This is a fairly technical exploration, which needs to be read slowly and carefully.

LILLY, JOHN and **ANTOINETTE. THE DYADIC CYCLONE. Bibliography, 287pp. S&S76, 8.95c.**
This is a disappointing volume in which Lilly and his wife discuss both their relationship and their work together. Actually, hardly anything about Antoinette is revealed. Most of the book is by and about John Lilly and the book is filled with his *I did this, I did that*. It is also badly written and extremely repetitious. What is revealed about John and his work is not very interesting and covers no new ground.

LOW, ALBERT. ZEN AND CREATIVE MANAGEMENT. Notes, bibliography, index, 255pp. Dou76, 3.50p.
Out of his considerable experience in management and Zen, Albert Low brilliantly diagnoses what lies behind the dilemmas and conflicts bedeviling the world of management....I know of no other book that so capably reconciles the seemingly disparate worlds of industry and Zen, or that speaks with the authority of this one. [This] is a profoundly wise book that needs to be read by managers, executives, and manual workers alike.—Phillip Kapleau.

MCCARROLL, TOLBERT. EXPLORING THE INNER WORLD. Illustrations, notes, topical bibliography, 223pp. NAL74, 1.50p.
A manual of growth techniques, for individuals and groups, that bridges contemporary humanistic psychology and ancient spiritual traditions, East and West. Among the topics are the use of a daily journal; working with inner imagery and dreams; listening to ourselves through art experiences and other tools of self exploration; meditation; working in self exploration groups; and the relationship between self knowledge and spiritual growth.

MCCARROLL, TOLBERT. NOTES FROM THE SONG OF LIFE. 144pp. CeA77, 4.95p.
This is a collection of inner dialogues which I want to share with others who are as spiritually stubborn as I am. These pieces were written down over a seventeen-month period. They came as interior urgings, usually early in the morning following a day during which I had engaged in intensive spiritual direction with a group or individual....I strongly urge you not to read more than one chapter a day. This book provides the framework for a month of reflections. Some of the topics are seasons, God, prayer, peace, detachment, anger, judging, yielding, simplicity, pain, fear planting, and love. A photograph accompanies each reflection.

MCGLASHAN, ALAN. SAVAGE AND BEAUTIFUL COUNTRY. 174pp. Sto67/C&W, 3.95p.
This beautifully written book explores the tantalizing possibilities of the human imagination. Developing the concept of psychological outer

space, McGlashan urges us to seek salvation in our dreams, to discover total reality in the pull of opposites, to reawaken our senses to myth and magic. Laurens van der Post calls this one of the most important books of this time and many have echoed that sentiment.

MCINTYRE, JOAN, ed. **MIND IN THE WATERS: A BOOK TO CELEBRATE THE CONSCIOUSNESS OF WHALES AND DOLPHINS. Many illustrations, index, 8½"x11½", 240pp. Scr74, 6.95p.**
A compendium of information drawn from mythology, poetry, natural history, and the most advanced scientific findings.

MASTERS, ROBERT and JEAN HOUSTON. **MIND GAMES: THE GUIDE TO INNER SPACE. 246pp. Del70/Tur, 3.45p.**
The authors describe and instruct the reader in many mental exercises they have developed through practical group work to alter, explore, and regulate human consciousness. The volume includes exercises for entertainment, education, ecstasy, and self exploration. We have never heard of many of them before and the individuals who have tried them say that they really work. This has been an extremely popular book.

MATSON, KATINKA. **PSYCHOLOGY TODAY OMNIBOOK OF PERSONAL DEVELOPMENT. 500pp. Mor77, 5.95p.**
An encyclopedic collection of short articles on theories and methods of personal development and exploration. Nearly every category and individual we can think of is mentioned and adequately explored. The spiritual quest is as well represented as the psychological. Bibliographical references are included at the end of every essay.

MAY, KARL. **ARDISTAN AND DJINNISTAN. 654pp. Sea77, 12.95c.**
This book is an allegory on the development of the human soul and the ultimate fate of the entire human race. While on a peace mission to an Oriental despot, a traveling scholar and his companion are captured in an armed rebellion which overthrows the tyrant as well. Banished to the City of the Dead, the three men discover the long buried secrets of a truly humane civilization. The despot stands trial in a terrifying court before the reanimated victims of his ancestors. He expiates his guilt, accepts responsibility for the past, puts down the rebellion, and renounces aggression. After a series of volcanic eruptions, nature once again transforms the desert into paradise, symbolically blessing a new order of universal peace. This is a beautifully written, thoughtful novel. It incorporates many insights as to the true nature of man into a romantic adventure story.

MERRELL-WOLFF, FRANKLIN. **PATHWAYS THROUGH TO SPACE —A PERSONAL RECORD OF TRANSFORMATION IN CONSCIOUSNESS. 228pp. War73, 1.95p.**
For anyone who is generally seeking to experience the spaces of higher consciousness I know of no other single work which so beautifully instructs and describes the pathways and the discipline.—John Lilly. The author is a scientist, but he has written in language that laymen can understand. This is a guide to be read a little at a time and slowly digested. It is arranged in the form of a diary and each entry is titled. An important contribution to modern mystical literature.

MERRELL-WOLFF, FRANKLIN. **PHILOSOPHY OF CONSCIOUSNESS WITHOUT AN OBJECT. 265pp. Crn73, 8.50c.**
Reflections on the nature of transcendental consciousness. Because the author is well versed in both Oriental and Occidental schools of philosophy and is also quite familiar with the domain of higher mathematics characteristic of our Western scientific spirit, his philosophical presentation is an integration of East and West. In fact, this book might be regarded as a pioneer effort in clearing the way for Western man to rediscover the truth of his own cultural heritage. The narrative is very personal as Merrell-Wolff shares with the reader his lifelong search for *realization*.

METZNER, RALPH, ed. **THE ECSTATIC ADVENTURE. 306pp. McM68, 6.95c.**
Thirty-eight people from a broad spectrum of backgrounds and beliefs discuss their experiences with hallucinogenic drugs. Some of the trips are hell, others ecstasy. Metzner introduces each account and explains the religious, sociological, and historical background of psychedelics.

■ METZNER, RALPH. **MAPS OF CONSCIOUSNESS. Illustrations, notes, 8½"x11¼", 161pp. McM71, 7.95c/3.95p.**
Metzner says, *Down the ages, man has developed ways to free his consciousness from external limitations. These ancient ways, once known to only a few, have now* become routes well-traveled by many modern adventurers. This book shows how to use these ways, and why they operate as maps of consciousness. The maps Metzner discusses include the I Ching, Tantra, Tarot, alchemy, astrology, and actualism (a modern synthesis in which he is very involved). Each of the individual essays is a masterpiece and represents one of the clearest expositions of the subject we have ever read. In every case Metzner integrates modern psychological and spiritual insights into his exposition. We recommend the book highly to all who are interested in any or all of these disciplines.

■ MISHLOVE, JEFFREY. **ROOTS OF CONSCIOUSNESS. Many notes, index, 8½"x11", 375pp. RaH75, 9.95p.**
As the title suggests, this is an exploration of consciousness throughout the ages divided into three increasingly technical sections. Section I, *History of the Exploration of Consciousness*, includes discussions of the rituals and major figures in ancient civilizations (primarily Western), the medieval period, the Renaissance (when alchemy and the original Rosicrucians flowered), the Age of Reason, and the nineteenth century. Section II, *Scientific Approaches to Consciousness*, presents the principal individuals, research, and findings in extrasensory perception, out-of-the-body experiences, psychic healing, firewalking, psychokinesis, life within death and death within life, other worlds, and the physiological mechanisms of consciousness. Section III, *People, Places, and Theories*, is more scientifically-oriented. It includes some fascinating material by Arthur Young under the general heading of *The Reflexive Universe*, along with a detailed overview of modern physics; and it ends with *Practical Applications of Psi*. This is a well organized, up to date sourcebook. An incredible amount of material is presented in a lively, instructive manner. **Roots of Consciousness** can be considered a textbook of consciousness as it has evolved from the esoteric teachings of ancient and medieval man down to present day scientific and quasi-scientific explorations. The text has over 300 black and white photographs and diagrams and sixty-six color illustrations.

MURPHY, MICHAEL. **GOLF IN THE KINGDOM. 205pp. Del72/SBL, 2.95p.**
Murphy founded the Esalen Institute. This is the story of time he spent with a Scottish golf pro for whom *the hidden but accessible meaning of the game became a metaphor for all the possibilities of transcendence that reside in the human soul. . . . A revelation of all in golf that connects with the inner spirit of a player, and the personal record of a man brought into transforming touch with his own expanding awareness.* One does not have to be a golfer to find this journal enlightening.

MURPHY, MICHAEL. **JACOB ATABET: A SPECULATIVE FICTION. 216pp. CeA77, 4.95p.**
Murphy's "fictional" account of Atabet's experiments in penetrating the mysteries of the human body may well turn out to be the best factual map we have of the direction that will be taken by the medicine and mysticism of the twenty-first century.—Sam Keen.

■ MUSES, CHARLES and ARTHUR YOUNG, eds. **CONSCIOUSNESS AND REALITY. Notes, 472pp. Avo72, 2.45p.**
Muses is the editor of the **Journal for the Study of Consciousness** and Young is the founder of the Foundation for the Study of Consciousness. Together they have assembled an extraordinary collection of articles on the developments in human consciousness. The selections span many scientific disciplines and cultures and are written by the most knowledgeable researchers available. Sample topics and authors include: *Trance Induction Techniques in Ancient Egypt*—C. Muses; *Recognition of Reincarnation and the Supra-Physical Body*—D. Kelsey and Joan Grant; *The Place of Consciousness in Modern Physics*—Eugene Wigner; and *Man's Potential* —Charles Lindbergh. This is far and away the best collection of articles that we know of and we recommend it highly, both to the layman and the professional.

NARANJO, CLAUDIO. **THE HEALING JOURNEY. Notes, index, 235pp. RaH73, 1.95p.**
Describes Naranjo's recent healing work using several new drugs in combination with more traditional forms of psychotherapy. These drugs—MDA, MMDA, harmaline, ibogaine—are *mind manifesting* in that they facilitate access to otherwise unconscious processes, feelings, and thoughts without the changes in thinking characteristic of the hallucinogens. They accelerate the process of analysis and allow the patient to see the problems which have made him ill.

NARANJO, CLAUDIO. **THE ONE QUEST. Notes, index, 243pp. Wdw72, 5.20p.**
An examination of the practices of religion, education, and psychotherapy all over the world and through many epochs. Naranjo's main concerns are salvation, deliverance, enlightenment, healing, and self actualization as taught in both ancient and modern systems. He seeks to show how the traditional and modern systems converge and what we can learn from each.

OATLEY, KEITH. **BRAIN MECHANISMS AND THE MIND.** 180 **illustrations, glossary, bibliography, index, 216pp. Dut72/T&H, 3.95p.**
Includes a description of the current study of the brain, an exposition of the elements of neurobiology, and analyses of forms of perception, behavior, learning, memory, language and thought, and an essay on artificial brains.

O'CONNOR, ELIZABETH. **OUR MANY SELVES: A HANDBOOK FOR SELF-DISCOVERY. 201pp. H&R71, 3.95p.**
Ms. O'Connor is on the staff at an experimental church; however, her exercises are eclectic and go far beyond traditional Christian doctrine. She says that they are meant not to guide the reader along someone else's path, but to help him find his own. The book also includes some essays and selections from writings the author has found useful, grouped with an appropriate exercise.

ORNSTEIN, ROBERT. **THE MIND FIELD. Illustrations, notes, 152pp. S&S76, 1.95p.**
Anyone reading Ornstein's work should bear in mind that he is a student of Idries Shah. His critiques of other disciplines and consciousness movements can be understood better with this knowledge in mind. In this book he attacks the promoters of what he terms self improvement packages. *I have attempted to write a book that is not primarily for the academic community.... There is little technical or academic jargon. The book is short, its ideas and conclusions distilled. It is not a textbook but a personal essay on the results of investigations undertaken, originally, for myself.* Many Shah-like teaching stories are included.

ORNSTEIN, ROBERT, ed. **THE NATURE OF HUMAN CONSCIOUSNESS. Extensive bibliography, index, oversize, 514pp. Fre73, 8.00p.**
Articles and essays are included from such diverse sources as the I Ching, Sufi literature, and neurophysiological essays on the brain. Among the contributors are William James, Michael Polanyi, Charles Tart, Aldous Huxley, Lama Govinda, Idries Shah, Robert Assagioli, Carl Jung, and David Sobel. The tone is generally pretty academic and the selections run the gamut from sheer technocratic language which only an expert in the field could comprehend to more philosophical essays. All the contributors are considered tops in their field. This is basicaly a textbook on the *new consciousness.*

ORNSTEIN, ROBERT. **ON THE EXPERIENCE OF TIME. Notes, bibliography, index, 126pp. Vik70, 2.95p.**
Dr. Ornstein is a research psychologist in neuropsychiatry who is especially noted for his right hemisphere, left hemisphere brain research. Here he discusses some of his earlier research on experimental analyses of the time experience. He disavows the generally assumed *inner clock* explanation and postulates a cognitive information processing approach. This is a technical work which recounts several experiments and summarizes the findings.

ORNSTEIN, ROBERT. **THE PSYCHOLOGY OF CONSCIOUSNESS. Notes, bibliography, index, 243pp. Vik72, 1.95p.**
Dr. Ornstein's basic analysis of the empirical research which has indicated that there are significant differences in the functioning of the two hemispheres of the brain. He sees Western thought as left hemisphere dominated, oriented toward rationality. Eastern thought, on the other hand, is primarily influenced by the right hemisphere. Ornstein integrates this information with meditative exercises and other ways of expanding awareness such as biofeedback. This is an interesting, often technical study.

ORR, LEONARD and SONDRA RAY. **REBIRTHING IN THE NEW AGE. 246pp. CeA77, 5.95p.**
Rebirthing is a technique invented by Orr. The individual who is being rebirthed immerses himself in a hot tub and remembers and re-experiences his birth in order to eliminate primal trauma and trans-

form the subconscious impression of birth into a gentle, awakening event. The process can also be used to transform thoughts and desires into positive realities. As might be expected, the technique is a controversial one, with many advocates and detractors. In this volume Orr and one of his rebirthers describe the technique, offer a variety of case histories, and discuss many related techniques and principles. One of the chapters is devoted to Orr's ideas on creating an abundant supply of money.

OYLE, IRVING. **TIME, SPACE AND THE MIND. 156pp. CeA76, 4.95p.**
Dr. Oyle runs a healing clinic in California and is actively involved in holistic health. In this book he presents a philosophical basis for some of the new consciousness ideas and illustrates a variety of ways holistic healers deal with mind-body distress signals. Eastern philosophy, medical research, and modern particle physics are all incorporated into his discussion. A scattered, stream of consciousness book which contains some interesting insights.

PAYNE, BURYL. **GETTING THERE WITHOUT DRUGS. Illustrations, bibliography, 212pp. Wdw74, 6.65p.**
A collection of exercises and techniques for expanding ordinary consciousness and transcending the here and now. Payne has worked with these exercises for many years and has done a fine job of outlining them; we know people who have had a great deal of success with them. Payne's writing style is informal and he expresses himself clearly. The bulk of the exercises can be done alone or with friends and generally no outside instruction is called for. In addition to the chapters on gateways to expanded consciousness, there are two more scientific sections—*Breaking the Shackles of Time* and *Transcending "I."* Here Payne does an excellent job of restating many complicated physical and psychological concepts. All in all, this is an informative, often entertaining and enlightening book, and one which we enjoyed.

PEARCE, JOSEPH CHILTON. **THE CRACK IN THE COSMIC EGG. Extensive notes, bibliography, index, 219pp. S&S71/LyP, 1.95p.**
This is a moving voyage of personal discovery. Pearce emphasizes the similarity of processes which produce discovery and invention in the physical sciences to such phenomena as firewalking, the dream life of aborigines, the transformations of reality evidenced in the life of Jesus, and the teachings of Castaneda's Don Juan. He feels that significant learning and achievement emerge out of the vast reservoirs of human experience, vision, and potential, and do not come from repeating formulas of obsolete data parading as scientific truth.

PEARCE, JOSEPH CHILTON. **MAGICAL CHILD: REDISCOVERING NATURE'S PLAN FOR OUR CHILDREN. 10.00c.**
See the Education section.

PEARSON, JOHN. **BEGIN SWEET WORLD. 8½"x11", 112pp. Dou76, 5.95p.**
Stunning color nature photographs, with related poems by children on facing pages.

PEARSON, JOHN. **THE SUN'S BIRTHDAY. 8½"x10", 110pp. Dou73, 5.95p.**
Sometimes the familiarity of life surrounding us creates a veil, and we cease to see it in its living, eloquent state. We need to borrow for a day the fresh vision of the photographer artist who by intent exploration, by keen attentiveness, by lingering meditation, rediscovers for us the life and illuminated beauty of each object of his magic lens.... John Pearson has such a vision and the loving attentiveness which causes clouds to swirl, waves to emit light, and sand to carry messages. His vision offers us a way to commune with nature and the deepest rhythms in ourselves.—Anais Nin.
The color photographs in the volume are all full page and often accompanied by poetic phrases.

PELLETIER, KENNETH and CHARLES GARFIELD. **CONSCIOUSNESS EAST AND WEST. Excellent bibliography, 318pp. H&R76, 4.95p.**
This is the most comprehensive array of Western scientific approaches to altered states of consciousness. Anyone interested in psychology can learn a great deal from this review of the Western literature, and scientists, themselves, will begin to see some of the major changes in approach and method that are needed for the next step in the study of consciousness.—Gay Luce. Most of the essays are fairly technical.

PENFIELD, WILDER. **THE MYSTERY OF THE MIND. Bibliography, index, 142pp. PUP75, 3.45p.**
A scientific study by a leading researcher which describes the current state of knowledge about the brain and asks to what extent recent

findings explain the action of the mind. The central question, he points out, is whether man's being is determined by his body alone or by mind and body as separate elements. Before suggesting an answer, he gives an account of his experience as a neurosurgeon and scientist observing the brain in conscious patients.

PHILLIPS, MICHAEL. **THE SEVEN LAWS OF MONEY. Index, 206pp. RaH74, 3.95p.**
This is a neat book which presents practical ideas that work. Phillips' seven laws tell you how to live with money—how to get it, care for it, and forget it. These are his seven laws: *Do It! Money Will Come When You Are Doing the Right Thing; Borrowing Has Its Own Rules: Records, Budgets, Saving, Borrowing; Money is a Dream: A Fantasy As Alluring As the Pied Piper; Money is a Nightmare: In Jail, Robbery, Fears of Poverty; You Can Never Really Give Money Away; You Can Never Really Receive Money As A Gift;* and *There Are Worlds Without Money.* Many case histories and lots of folksy talk accompany each law.

PINES, MAYA. **THE BRAIN CHANGERS. Index, 223pp. NAL73, 1.95p.**
A journalistic report on brain research being done all over the United States by biologists, chemists, psychologists, surgeons, and engineers. Includes material on controlling brain waves, on memory, and on actual ways of altering brain functions. Many case studies are cited and explored.

PIRSIG, ROBERT. **ZEN AND THE ART OF MOTORCYCLE MAINTENANCE. 412pp. Ban74/Crg, 2.50p.**
This is a remarkable, moving autobiographical account that has been acclaimed in rave reviews throughout the country, including **Psychology Today** and **The New York Times Book Review.** On one level it is the story of a cross country motorcycle trip taken by the author and his son. While they ride, Pirsig delivers *an old-time series of popular talks* which cover many topics from a search for how to live, an inquiry into *what is best,* through the creation of a philosophical system that reconciles science, religion, and humanism. On another and connecting level, the book is the story of Pirsig's visit to the *forgotten tomb of his past* and his confrontation there with the ghost of his former self, a brilliant questioning man who under the burden of his pursuit of ideals went mad, was institutionalized, underwent shock therapy, died—and has now returned.

PORTER, JEAN. **PSYCHIC DEVELOPMENT. Illustrations, 55pp. RaH74, 2.75p.**
The most important experience which I want for you is that of joyousness as you move through these various journeys, inwardly and outwardly. Become, again, like a little child eager to explore new worlds of experience, looking for the positive and the beautiful and accepting what you find there as a discovery of a new treasure. Use this book to guide you through your explorations. Trust the experiences you have, and own them. And remember, this is only a beginning of a process of your own development. Your psychic abilities will increase as you use them.—from the introduction. This book details, in clear, simple fashion, ways to develop the psychic abilities that all of us have. Ms. Porter has used all of the explorations detailed here in her classes.

PORTUGAL, PAMELA RAINBEAR. **A PLACE FOR HUMAN BEINGS. 7¼"x10", about 150pp. PoP74, 5.75p.**
This is a lovely, handwritten, and handcolored account of being in the world and living, loving. Here are a few quotes: *Love your enemy—he's just a friend in disguise. He's just the (a) part of you you can't express; You can have a once-in-a-lifetime day, or night, any time you slow down enough to notice it; Karma: you get what you make. Bitches get bitched at. Thieves get ripped off. Cheaters get cheated. Lovers get loved; Stop wasting time wondering if you made a wrong turn. There are no wrong turns, only lack of awareness of where we are going. You are on the right track; Truth does not last. it reoccurs. like blades of grass. almost always similar. almost always different. almost always new and changing. and quite often beautiful.*

PROGOFF, IRA. **AT A JOURNAL WORKSHOP. 320pp. DHL75, 5.95p.**
Dr. Progoff is a depth psychologist, trained in analytical (Jungian) psychology. He has *evolved a remarkable method that uses the intensive journal to unify the personality and effectively achieve a kind of self-therapy. He begins by eliminating the idea of the journal as a literary achievement so that anyone from any walk of life with any degree of education could complete a "mirror image" of his life and character, make a synthesis of experiences and dreams and arrive at a self-*

creation. . . . With this book anyone can learn to extract meaning from his life.—Anais Nin. The book is a basic text on the method. It presents the concepts and techniques as they have emerged over the years and details the exercises which individuals can practice. All terms and principles are fully explained.

PUHARICH, ANDRIJA. **THE SACRED MUSHROOM. Appendices, Dou59, 2.95p.**
An early classic concerning the famous *sacred mushroom* known by botanists as *Amanita Muscaria,* used for thousands of years as a psychedelic and religious agent. Puharich describes his own investigation as well as his extraordinary association with Harry Stone, a sensitive, who in a deep trance defined the long lost ritual of the mushroom and its effects on human consciousness.

RAINER, TRISTINE. **THE NEW DIARY. Bibliography, index, 323pp. Tar78, 9.95c.**
Diary writing has become an increasingly popular activity. To answer a need for more knowledge about it I taught a course with my friend Tristine Rainer. . . . We taught the diary as an exercise in creative will; as an exercise in synthesis; as a means to create a world according to our wishes, not those of others; as a means of creating the self, of giving birth to ourselves. We taught diary writing as a way of reintegrating ourselves when experience shatters us, to help us out of the desperate loneliness of silence and the anxieties of alienation. . . . Now Tristine has written a perceptive and revolutionary work that will share the immense wealth of new knowledge she has learned from the diary with all those who are seeking inner harmony and creative freedom.—Anais Nin.

RAMA, SWAMI AND SWAMI AJAYA. **EMOTION TO ENLIGHTENMENT. 171pp. Him76, 3.95p.**
As we expand our awareness, we slowly move from a world of ever-recurring conflicts, discord and suffering, both internally and in our interpersonal relations, to a gradually spreading sense of abiding joy and harmony with all that is. This book is a description of the developmental process which leads to this transformation.—from the introduction. The exposition is based on Western psychology and on the insights of Eastern mysticism.

RAMA, SWAMI, RUDOLPH BALLENTINE and SWAMI AJAYA. **YOGA AND PSYCHOTHERAPY. Illustrations, notes, index, 359pp. Him76, 11.95c/6.96p.**
An in depth study by three men who have spent their adult lives integrating modern psychology and psychotherapy with Eastern, and especially Hindu, philosophy. Chapter one deals with the physical body and how working with it through various kinds of exercises affects the psychological makeup. The second chapter covers breath and energy. The third contrasts the Western method of observing the mind by observing behavior with the yogic method of studying it through the direct experience of introspection using meditational techniques. The fourth chapter goes beyond the mind to take a look at the systems of Western psychology that have studied altered states of consciousness. The fifth discusses various *states of bliss;* while the sixth compares this consciousness with the state of psychosis with which it is sometimes confused—since both depart radically from ordinary awareness. The last chapter is a detailed study of the *chakras,* seven energy centers in the body. The *chakras* are defined and there is a discussion of the behavior manifested when energy is focused at each. An unusual and very interesting study.

RATHBUN, HARRY. **CREATIVE INITIATIVE. Illustrations, 175pp. CIv76, 4.95p.**
This book is written for people who feel deeply the need for a rational, solid, workable basis for their lives. The principles set forth here are universal. They are the product of many people's experience, and they have proven practical and rewarding for those who have lived by them. . . . The process with which this book deals is the hero's journey found in the wisdom myths of all peoples. This is the life's journey which every human being has to take. For a successful outcome it is crucial that the correct guideposts be followed. The pages that follow present those guideposts.—from the introduction. This is a well organized book, with a Christian orientation.

RICHARDS, M.C. **CENTERING IN POTTERY, POETRY, AND THE PERSON. Illustrations, 8¼"x7", 159pp. WUP62, 3.95p.**
A marvelous Zen-like melange of jokes, proverbs, anecdotes, poems, folktales, myths, and personal experiences. Ms. Richards reaches out directly and disturbingly toward inert portions of ourselves, which we suddenly find vulnerable, mysterious, and alive.

RICHARDS, M.C. **THE CROSSING POINT. 245pp. WUP66, 4.50p.**
This new volume brings together a major selection of Miss Richards' more recent statements. Prepared at different times for different audiences, they are one in their central concerns: the ongoing quest for total understanding of self and universe, for mutual respect and love, for integrity and fulfillment. She includes material on the concept of karma, the nature of language, the growth of the nonmaterialistic consciousness, and much else.

ROPP, ROBERT DE. **CHURCH OF THE EARTH: THE ECOLOGY OF A CREATIVE COMMUNITY. 280pp. Del74, 2.95p.**
This is the most personal book that de Ropp has written. It is a journal, cast in the form of essays, chronicling the life in his spiritual community in northern California. This book also reflects his religious and philosophical thoughts: man's position in the universe; ways of *inner development* along the lines suggested by Gurdjieff; the need to know death and challenge; and the spiritual benefits of living close to the Earth. The later chapters clearly reflect the same theme developed in **The Master Game:** the continuing search for a higher state of being.

ROPP, ROBERT DE. **DRUGS AND THE MIND. Bibliography, index, 302pp. Del76, 3.95p.**
This is a revised edition of de Ropp's classic work, incorporating a great deal of new information (it was first published in 1957) and rearranging the subject matter. De Ropp is a biochemist who has carried out extensive research in the fields of mental health and drugs which affect behavior.

ROPP, ROBERT DE. **THE MASTER GAME: PATHWAYS TO HIGHER CONSCIOUSNESS BEYOND THE DRUG EXPERIENCE. 2.45p/1.75p.**
See the Gurdjieff and the Work section.

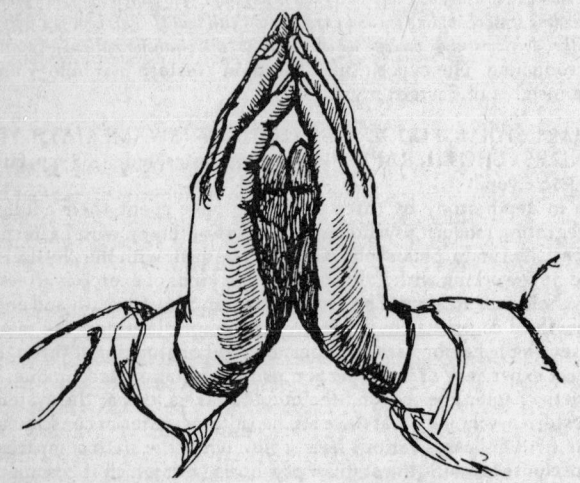

ROPP, ROBERT DE. **SEX ENERGY. 236pp. Del68, 2.45p.**
De Ropp examines the sexual behavior of plants, insects, and animals and the role of sex energy in human behavior from both a physiological and historical point of view. He ends the book with a call for a *sane sex society.*

ROSE, STEVEN. **THE CONSCIOUS BRAIN. Glossary, many notes, index, 343+pp. RaH73, 4.95p.**
A fascinating discussion of the functioning of the human brain and the brain's relationship to the mind. Rose is a neurobiologist and he clearly states what he and his colleagues are finding out about the ways in which man thinks, knows, remembers, feels, sleeps, and wakes. The book is very well organized and clearly presented and is extensively illustrated with superb diagrams and visualizations.

ROSENFELD, ALBERT, ed. **MIND AND SUPERMIND. Bibliography, index, 312pp. HRW77, 9.95c.**
A collection of articles which originally appeared in the **Saturday Review** over the last few years. They are divided into the following general headings: *Expanding the Limits of Consciousness, Inside the Brain,* and *The Spectrum of Psychotherapy.* The contributors include many of the most noted writers and authorities in their fields. Rosenfeld is science editor of **Saturday Review.**

ROSENFELD, EDWARD. **THE BOOK OF HIGHS. Bibliography, 8¼"x11", 273pp. NYT73, 4.95p.**
A compilation of 250 ways to alter your consciousness without drugs. The methods are derived from every conceivable source (including some we have never heard of). They involve: *just yourself, help from others,* and *devices and machines.* A fascinating surface account. Most of the entries include a section on access which details the best material (books, etc.) on the subject.

ROSZAK, THEODORE. **UNFINISHED ANIMAL. Index, 271pp. H&R75/ Fab, 3.45p.**
We are in the midst of a religious renaissance, but it is religion by any other name and every other name that binds our attention. The spiritual impulse of the time steps beyond the boundaries of religious tradition all together to become psychotherapy, sensory awareness, parapsychology, consciousness research, psychedelic tripping, bioenergetics, occult science. Roszak calls this phenomena the *Aquarian frontier* and feels that the exploration of this frontier represents *a transformation of the human personality which is of "evolutionary" proportions, a shift of consciousness fully as epoch-making as the appearance of speech or the tool-making talents. . . .* from the introduction. This is an interesting, albeit scattered, exploration of this frontier.

RUBIN, JERRY. **GROWING (UP) AT 37. 208pp. War76, 1.95p.**
This is a very personal, candid account of Rubin's experiences in the human potential movement detailing many of the therapies he went through including est, rolfing, and the Fischer-Hoffman process. Rubin discusses who he was and why he was that way, as well as who he is today and where he is going.

RUDHYAR, DANE. **ASTROLOGICAL TIMING—THE TRANSITION TO A NEW AGE. 3.95p.**
See the Astrology section.

RUDHYAR, DANE. **CULTURE, CRISIS, AND CREATIVITY. Notes, index, 227pp. TPH77, 4.25p.**
In this book Rudhyar suggests that there comes a time, when for the sake of our spiritual heritage, we should consider breaking away from established patterns and values that have been imposed upon us through our culture. He says that *Spirit creates, culture reproduces,* and goes on to suggest that *the process of civilization is one of transcendence, and transcendence implies crisis; just as the act of walking implies a fall from a position of equilibrium and a recovery. Dissatisfaction, fall, recovery are inherent in the process of civilization; and Man, archetypically is the Civilizer.* As usual, Rudhyar writes from on high, and his philosophical fantasies are often not easy to understand.

RUDHYAR, DANE. **DIRECTIVES FOR A NEW LIFE. 2.25p.**
See the Astrology section.

RUDHYAR, DANE. **THE RHYTHM OF HUMAN FULFILLMENT. 2.50p.**
See the Astrology section.

RUDHYAR, DANE. **WE CAN BEGIN AGAIN. 5.00p.**
See the Astrology section.

RUSH, ANNE KENT. **MOON, MOON. 7.95p.**
See the Women and Men section.

SAGAN, CARL. **THE DRAGONS OF EDEN: SPECULATIONS ON THE EVOLUTION OF HUMAN INTELLIGENCE. Illustrations, glossary, bibliography, index, 263pp. RaH77/Hod, 2.25p.**
This is a lucid, often fascinating study of the inner world of the mind. Sagan explains how human beings evolved, who our ancestors and their competitors were, how our brains and the brains of other animals work, and why other intelligent beings will be sufficiently like us intellectually to permit interstellar communication. In the process of his exposition, Dr. Sagan makes excursions into myth and legend and their relationship to recent scientific discoveries. He also speculates on the implications of these discoveries, and on what the next steps in human evolution may be.

SAMUELS, MIKE and HAL BENNETT. **SPIRIT GUIDES. 55pp. RaH74, 1.45p.**
For centuries people have called their feelings and secret thoughts "inner voices." I will discuss how these inner voices can have their own personalities, called spirit guides, and how these guides can be used to tap energies which are in all people. . . . You go to your

inner world all the time: when you pause to think; when you daydream; when you ponder a complex question. Often a kind of mental conversation takes place. There is a voice which you associate with you, your self, and a second voice that responds to you. The second voice is a spirit guide. These inner conversations take you on a journey into your imagination. On these journeys, your spirit guide can help you make full use of your inner world.

■ *SAMUELS, MIKE and NANCY.* **SEEING WITH THE MIND'S EYE: THE HISTORY, TECHNIQUES AND USES OF VISUALIZATION.** 8½"x11", 348pp. RaH75, 10.95p.
The human mind is a slide projector with an infinite number of slides in its library, an instant retrieval system, and an endlessly cross refer- enced subject catalogue. The inner images we show ourselves form our lives—whether as memories, fantasies, dreams or visions. Inner images supply the creative force in art, spirituality, psychology, healing, parapsychology and daily life, but they have never been studied comprehensively. Here Dr. Samuels, the author of the **Well Body Book**, presents such a study. The book itself is filled with illustrations; the material is topically arranged; and each chapter is followed by bibliographic entries. Visualization, as presented in this book, is a set of concepts and techniques drawn from historical as well as contemporary sources, in every aspect of life, that seeks to reinstate the reader to an understanding of the nature of his visual processes and their importance in his life.

SCHUL, BILL. **THE PSYCHIC POWER OF ANIMALS.** Index, 223pp. Faw77, 1.75p.
A journalistic presentation of documented cases of animals with psychic abilities.

SCHUMACHER, E.F. **A GUIDE FOR THE PERPLEXED.** Notes, 147pp. H&R77/CaL, 3.95p.
One way of looking at the world as a whole is by means of a map, that is to say, some sort of plan or outline that shows where various things are to be found. . . . My map or guidebook is constructed on the recognition of four Great Truths—or landmarks— which are so prominent, so all-pervading, that you can see them wherever you happen to be. . . . The guidebook. . .is about how "Man lives in the world." This simple statement indicates that we shall need to study (1) "The world"; (2) "Man"—his equipment to meet the world; (3) His way of learning about the world; and (4) What it means to "live" in this world. These are the areas that Dr. Schumacher covers in his study, drawing on the teachings of all the great world religions.

SCHUMACHER, E.F. **SMALL IS BEAUTIFUL: ECONOMICS AS IF PEOPLE MATTERED.** Notes, 313pp. H&R73/SBL, 4.50p.
This is a landmark book which is without doubt the most unusual economic treatise we have ever read. Schumacher is a British econo- mist who has worked extensively in the field he calls *intermediate technology* and in this book he weaves together threads from Galbraith and Gandhi, capitalism and Buddhism, science and psychology, and many other seemingly disparate disciplines. In countless examples and case histories, Schumacher shows how his concepts are both possible approaches and the only sensible ones.

SHAPIRO, DEANE H., tr. **PRECISION NIRVANA.** Illustrations, glos- sary, notes, index, 367pp. PrH78, 5.95p.
Shapiro blends the spiritual techniques of the East—especially Zen Buddhism—with Western self management skills as developed by the behavioralists and others. It is as strange an amalgam as any we have seen. Above it, the book is practically-oriented. Shapiro's goal is to teach Westerners how to use the ways of Zen to develop flexibility and centeredness, and Western techniques to identify and alter ingrained behavior patterns that are self defeating and self limiting. The book is not very clearly written and the instructional material is often hard to follow.

SILVA, JOSE. **THE SILVA MIND CONTROL METHOD.** Technical appendices, index, 208pp. S&S77, 2.25p.
This is Jose Silva's long awaited account of the meditation system he developed. He discusses what the system can do and has done and includes many case studies and testimonials.

SILVERMAN, DAVID. **READING CASTANEDA.** Bibliography, 124pp. RKP75, 3.95p.
The Teachings of Don Juan is here used as an initial springboard to introduce students to some of the central epistemological concerns of social science. By examining the difficulties of communication between

Don Juan and his apprentice, Dr. Silverman highlights the nature of several assumptions built into the concepts of our own culture. As might be expected, this is a dry, sociological study.

SLATER, PHILIP. **THE WAYWARD GATE: SCIENCE AND THE SUPERNATURAL.** Bibliography, 256pp. Bea77, 8.95c.
In this book Slater is attempting to guide the reader to the belief that alternate realities do exist. He argues that we limit our possibilities of experience and understanding to a pathetically narrow range. As he says, *I think it would be helpful to build a few bridges between ordinary and nonordinary ways of thinking about experience; to reduce the discordance between our ways of treating material and spiritual reality. . . . Science is pitted against spirituality, East against West, and most of us stumble through each day equipped with a junkheap of contradictory theories, all of which we firmly believe and just as firmly disregard. . . . To speak of a psychic or spiritual realm is only a verbal convenience, a convention. There is no such realm just as there is no material realm.* This is a sympathetic account.

SMITH, ADAM. **POWERS OF THE MIND.** Notes, excellent bibliog- raphy, 418pp. RaH75/WHA, 2.25p.
This book by the author of **The Money Game** and **Supermoney** was welcomed with a lot of fanfare. We wondered how an individual who did not seem to know anything or have any interest in consciousness would portray it in his *sure-fire best seller.* The title of the book and the chapter headings did not alleviate our doubt. However the content does, once the reader gets beyond the flashy words. Smith is an excellent writer and he seems to have delved quite seriously into this new (to him) world. He comes out with an enjoyable, informative, in depth analysis of these movements. He has explored and personally experienced each of the things that he writes about. We might not always agree with his impressions, but we are glad that he is getting involved and turning many other people on in the process (or off as the case may be). Some of the areas covered include Transcendental Meditation, biofeedback, est, Arica, Rolfing, Zen Buddhism, and parapsychology.

SMITH, FREDERICK. **JOURNAL OF A FAST.** Bibliography, 216pp. ScB76, 7.95c.
This is the inner journal of the thirty days that the author fasted. It is an extraordinary record of his odyssey to the innermost recesses of his being. While fasting he approaches a pure state of spiritual awareness and as he ponders the meaning of what he is sensing he relates his insights to those of some of the great mystics.

SOMMER, ROBERT. **THE MIND'S EYE.** Notes, index, 230pp. Dia78, 9.95c.
In this book Professor Sommer shows that most of us use only a small part of our perceptual capabilities in our daily life. While we are born with the ability to think using information from all our senses, our schooling—rather than developing this capability—inhibits us by teaching us to limit our mental inputs almost exlusively to words and abstract ideas. The result is that we have become a society of verbalizers rather than visualizers. Sommer outlines simple exercises which enhance visual ability. He is a professor of psychology and environmental studies at the University of California, Davis; here he draws on his own work with architects and urban planners to explain how visual thinking can help to make the buildings and spaces we design more pleasing and responsive to our needs.

STAFFORD, PETER. **PSYCHEDELICS ENCYCLOPEDIA.** Illustra- tions, index, 412pp. AOP77, 7.95p.
A wealth of information about one of the most controversial issues of modern times. It is written with clarity that will be appreciated by the general public, and so rich in content that even professionals in the field will find it a valuable source of data.—Dr. Stanislav Grof.

STEARN, JESS. **THE POWER OF ALPHA THINKING: MIRACLE OF THE MIND.** Index, 251pp. NAL76, 1.95p.
An exploration of Stearn's own experiences with alpha thinking and a presentation of techniques. A journalistic work, replete with case studies.

STEVENS, JOHN. **AWARENESS: EXPLORING, EXPERIMENTING, EXPERIENCING.** 3.50p/2.25p.
See the Gestalt Therapy subsection of Humanistic Psychology.

■ *TART, CHARLES, ed.* **ALTERED STATES OF CONSCIOUSNESS.** **Bibliography, indices, Dou69, 4.95p.**
A classic, the first major serious treatment of human consciousness. Tart collected articles from a wide range of sources to show the broad scientific dimensions of this field. Topics include drugs, yoga, self hypnosis, meditation, brain wave research, and dream consciousness. A scholarly book with forty pages of notes.

TART, CHARLES. **ON BEING STONED—A PSYCHOLOGICAL STUDY OF MARIJUANA INTOXICATION. Bibliography, 328pp. S&B73, 7.95c.**
A very complete study—the first in which the subjects, 150 experienced marijuana smokers, were in a natural social situation.

TART, CHARLES. **STATES OF CONSCIOUSNESS. Bibliography, index, 316pp. Dut75, 4.95p.**
Tart's writing style always seems overly academic. Nevertheless, he is without question one of the leaders in the field of consciousness research and this is an important work which outlines the research that he has been doing in a variety of areas and discusses the implications of his findings. Basically he is presenting a systems approach to altered states of consciousness and the discussion itself is definitely geared to the sophisticated reader.

■ *TART, CHARLES, ed.* **TRANSPERSONAL PSYCHOLOGIES. Bibliography, name and subject indices, 502pp. H&R75/RKP, 6.95p.**
This is an excellent collection of eleven essays: Charles Tart—*The Physical Universe, the Spiritual Universe, and the Paranormal* and two other long essays; Claire Owen—*Zen Buddhism;* Daniel Goleman—*The Buddha on Meditation and States of Consciousness;* Haridas Chaudhuri—*Yoga Psychology;* Kathleen Riodan—*Gurdjieff;* John Lilly—*The Arica Training;* Robert Ornstein—*Contemporary Sufism;* William McNamara—*Psychology and the Christian Mystical Tradition;* and William Gray—*Patterns of Western Magic.* Each contributor has practiced the area discussed as a personal discipline and presents its psychological rather than religious significance. The individual essays are very well done and are a good overview of the areas discussed.

TAYLOR, JOHN. **THE SHAPE OF MINDS TO COME. Bibliography, index, 304pp. Grn74, 1.30p.**
A lucid examination of the latest research into the workings and potential of the human mind, exploring the effects and value of drugs, extrasensory perception, hypnosis, dreams and sleep, mind control, personality engineering, and much else. Professor Taylor is a noted British scientist whose work often tends to be highly technical. This is his only book geared specifically toward the layperson.

TENHOUTEN, WARREN and CHARLES KAPLAN. **SCIENCE AND ITS MIRROR IMAGE. Illustrations, notes, bibliography, index, 253pp. H&R73, 10.00p.**
This is an interesting study which correlates scientific concepts with aspects of the esoteric tradition. It reads like a textbook (which it is) and does a good job of showing how rational many seemingly irrational concepts can be. The text deals in the greatest depth with the Tarot, the **I Ching**, native American traditions, and consciousness. This is an excellent work for those imbued with the rational, scientific viewpoint who seek an understanding of other ways of viewing reality.

TEYLER, TIMOTHY. **ALTERED STATES OF AWARENESS. Bibliography, index, 8½"x11", 140pp. Fre54, 4.95p.**
A collection of technical articles published in **Scientific American** between 1954 and 1972 and divided into three sections: *Brain and Awareness; Altered States of Awareness: Internal Control;* and *Altered States of Awareness: External Control.* Each selection is very fully illustrated in the usual **Scientific American** manner and complete with notes.

THOMPSON, WILLIAM IRWIN. **AT THE EDGE OF HISTORY. Notes, index, 252pp. H&R71, 2.95p.**
Thompson is a noted historian/philosopher who has taught at several major universities in the U.S. and Canada. After this book was written he dropped out of the university system and founded his own alternative community, Lindisfarne (PO Box 1395, Southampton, NY 11968) incorporating educational and spiritual techniques and teachings from many disciplines, East and West. *At the edge of history the future is blowing wildly in our faces, sometimes brightening the air and sometimes blinding us. To get a sense of where we are going, I tried to see out through the geographical limits of my own experience to the spaces of our contemporary culture where the millennial imagination of the future is interrupting the daily news of the present.*

THOMPSON, WILLIAM IRWIN. **DARKNESS AND SCATTERED LIGHT. Notes, 190pp. Dou78, 3.95p.**
Transcriptions of four talks: *Beyond Civilization or Savagery, The Meta-industrial Village, The Return of the Past,* and *The Future of Knowledge.* Thompson is a cultural historian who is deeply involved in what he terms *the study and realization of a new planetary culture.*

THOMPSON, WILLIAM IRWIN. **EVIL AND WORLD ORDER. Notes, 116pp. H&R76, 2.95p.**
A collection of essays: *Meditation on the Dark Ages, Past and Present; We Become What We Hate; Three Wise Men of Gotham; Occulture: Out of Sight, Out of Mind; Introductions to Findhorn; Freedom, Evil, and Comedy; The Ends of Art;* and *Evil and World Order.* The general tone of all the selections is negative.

THOMPSON, WILLIAM IRWIN. **PASSAGES ABOUT EARTH. Notes, index, 206pp. H&R73/HPG, 1.95p.**
Continuing the searching study of contemporary society begun in **At the Edge of History,** Thompson discusses the new planetary culture he sees emerging from the cracks in the old industrial civilization. **Passages** begins with the author's decision to leave the bureaucracy of modern university life (his material here is the most illuminating we have read anywhere on the problems of the university) and it ends with his founding of a new cultural and educational center, Lindisfarne. In between he explores and analyzes some of the most important alternative cultures present today. Two of the most fascinating chapters recount his experiences during visits to the ancient British monastery of Lindisfarne and the New Age Scottish colony, Findhorn.

TOBEN, BOB. **SPACE-TIME AND BEYOND. 4.95p.**
See the Astronomy section.

TOD, IAN and MICHAEL WHEELER. **UTOPIA. 8¾"x11½", 160pp. Crn78, 6.95p.**
A beautifully produced pictorial study of utopian ideals and their actual manifestations throughout history from earliest times to the present day. The authors have done a good job of garnering a wide variety of material and they include hundreds of unique illustrations, many in color.

TOMPKINS, PETER and CHRIS BIRD. **THE SECRET LIFE OF PLANTS. Many notes, long bibliography, index, 402pp. Avo73/Pen, 1.95p.**
An excellent, comprehensive account. The authors begin by describing recent discoveries in plant research, including the latest Russian work, Cleve Backster's studies in plant communication, and the work of scientists from various disciplines. They go on from there to trace and analyze experiments and theories from the past, including extensive surveys of the pioneers of plant research. Their narrative is extensively documented.

WATSON, LYALL. **GIFTS OF UNKNOWN THINGS. 249pp. Ban77/Hod, 2.25p.**
Watson, a biologist, recounts the story of his voyage to a small volcanic island in Indonesia, where he shared the extraordinary daily life of the islanders. The inhabitants of this island accept as everyday reality phenomena that are terrifying, miraculous, and inexplicable to the average Westerner. Theirs is a world in which magical feats are regularly experienced as normal occurrences and skills, and where extrasensory perception, psychic healing, precognition, and even the survival of death are possible. Watson blends his scientific knowledge with his imagination to explore explanations that are compatible with the ever changing theories of biology and physics, and in the process he gives us a lively nature travelogue.

■ *WATSON, LYALL.* **SUPER NATURE. Notes, bibliography, index, 335pp. Hod73, 1.95p.**
The supernatural is usually defined as that which is not explicable by the known forces of nature. Supernature knows no bounds. Too often we see only what we expect to see; our view of the world is restricted by the blinkers of our limited experience; but it need not be this way. Supernature is nature with all its flavors intact, waiting to be tasted. I offer it as a logical extension of the present state of science, as a solution to some of the

problems with which traditional science cannot cope, and as an analgesic to modern man. Watson is a scientist and naturalist who demonstrates a sound, scientific basis for many psychic and supernatural phenomena. He documents his case with an impressive array of scientific literature. An utterly fascinating book for the layman and scientist alike. We recommend it highly.

WEIL, ANDREW. **THE NATURAL MIND: A NEW WAY OF LOOK-ING AT DRUGS AND THE HIGHER CONSCIOUSNESS. Bibliog-raphy, index, 219pp. HMC72/Pen, 2.95p.**
The author is a physician who has been studying mind-altering drugs for more than ten years in settings as diverse as Harvard University, Haight-Ashbury, the National Institute of Mental Health, and the Amazon basin. His thesis is that *altered states of consciousness, consciously entered, seem to be doors to ways of using the mind that are better than those we follow most of the time.*

WENGER, WIN. **HOW TO INCREASE YOUR INTELLIGENCE. Bibliography, 172pp. Del75, 1.50p.**
There is a misconception that we are born with a certain intelligence and are trapped forever in the narrow range that is determined to be our "IQ." The truth of the matter is that unless we are taught how to use our brains, unless we fully understand how our brains work and how they relate to intelligence, we may never even approach truly intelligent functioning. Within all of us is the potential for genius. It is there for us to develop, to explore, to enjoy. . . . This is what this book is all about: utilizing the full range of human intelligence.—from the introduction.

■ WHITE, JOHN, ed. **FRONTIERS OF CONSCIOUSNESS. Notes, 366pp. Avo74, 2.50p.**
A very readable, comprehensive collection of twenty-two articles on the full spectrum of consciousness research. Among the contributors are psychologists, physicists, parapsychologists, philosophers, and behavioral scientists. The topics discussed include transpersonal psychology; the nature of madness; biofeedback; meditation research; psychic research; paraphysics; biotechnology; the neurosciences; eco-logical consciousness; space travel and extraterrestrial life; and death as an altered state of consciousness. All of the articles are written by experts and each topic is introduced by White, who also supplies a listing of suggested reading for each area.

■ WHITE, JOHN, ed. **THE HIGHEST STATE OF CONSCIOUSNESS. 484pp. Dou72, 3.50p.**
A collection of essays by a great variety of people, which attempts to find the common denominators of the experience. Some of the think-ers approach the subject as a mystical religious experience; others de-scribe it in physiological or psychological terms. The juxtaposition of these essays establishes a meaningful dialogue. Includes an excellent introductory piece by the editor on *What is the highest state of consciousness.*

WHITE, JOHN and JAMES FADIMAN, eds. **RELAX. 253pp. Del76, 1.95p.**
A collection of thirty-six essays and selections from longer works, all of which give practical step-by-step relaxation exercises and a great deal of philosophy. The authors include Herbert Benson, Aldous and Laura Huxley, Elmer Green, Bernard Gunther, Anne Kent Rush, and Hans Selye.

WHITE, JOHN and STANLEY KRIPPNER, eds. **FUTURE SCIENCE: LIFE ENERGIES AND THE PHYSICS OF PARANORMAL PHENOMENA. 598pp. Dou77, 4.50p.**
An excellent sampling of essays and selections from longer works on the title theme. The editors have carefully chosen and arranged their selections to present as comprehensive a view as possible of this new field. All of the major authors, researchers, and points of view are represented. A listing of related organizations, books, and periodicals is appended.

WILLIAMS, PAUL. **APPLE BAY: LIFE ON THE PLANET. 191pp. War76, 3.95p.**
This is the story of Williams' experience in a wilderness commune as he and a group of friends try to put the ideals of **Das Energi** into practice.

WILLIAMS, PAUL. **COMING. 100pp. Ent77, 2.95p.**
More of Williams' poetry, messages like the following: *Coming = being/ = you and me/together/again/for the first time/forever; it all comes back; Your smile moves me; It's important to be alone.*

WILLIAMS, PAUL. **DAS ENERGI. 150pp. War73, 3.95p.**
A collection of epigrams about living and being. Like most books of its type, it is hard to describe. The tone and the message are more serious than most we have seen. Here are some samples: *And one day, like any other day, finally tired of waiting for the help that never comes, make a rope, tie it to a rock, throw it up, pull yourself out, and walk away. The first law of the economics of energy is: you get what you need. . . . So don't worry about freezing or starving to death before you get this new world figured out; there's nothing to figure out; it just happens to you. Most people prefer blindness. But most people are a dying race.*

WILSON, ROBERT ANTON. **COSMIC TRIGGER: FINAL SECRETS OF THE ILLUMINATI. Notes, index, 269+pp. AOP77, 4.95p/1.95p.**
We think the blurb on the back of this book describes it as well as anything we can say: *Fact surpasses fantasy as Robert Anton Wilson explores Space Migration, psychedelics, immortality, the Gurdjieff Work, Crowley Magic, meditation, UFO contact and more in the most outrageous journey of our time,* **COSMIC TRIGGER**. *Wilson, best-selling author of the* **ILLUMINATUS** *trilogy, bares his ultimate secret in a . . . non-fiction sequel. A pan-galactic mix of Von-negut, Joyce and Burroughs, Robert Anton Wilson focuses the myths and fables of our age through the lens of expanded consciousness as* **COSMIC TRIGGER** *casts the shadows away with penetrating insight and scathing humor.*

WRIGHT, AUSTIN. **ISLANDIA. 954pp. NAL44, 5.95p.**
This is an underground classic, only recently reprinted, of a Utopian country and the experiences of a young American there. The ideals expressed by the characters here and their ancient civilization should be of interest to all those looking for alternative ways to live and be.

YOUNG, ARTHUR. **THE GEOMETRY OF MEANING. 4.95p.**
See the Sacred Geometry section.

YOUNG, ARTHUR. **THE REFLEXIVE UNIVERSE. Index, 293pp. Del76/Wdw, 6.95p.**
In **The Reflexive Universe**, *Arthur Young reveals his new intuitive insights into the great myths of mankind, as well as into the freshly minted facts and theories of modern science. For the rapidly evolving person searching for a bridge between old knowledge and new knowledge, this book provides a new path.*—Andrija Puharich. This is a technical study of the evolution of consciousness which incorporates a great deal of scientific information and insights, basically in the realms of chemistry and biology. Line drawings illuminate the text. A fascinating work which incorporates many philosophical insights.

ZINBERG, NORMAN, ed. **ALTERNATE STATES OF CONSCIOUS-NESS. Notes, bibliography, index, 304pp. McM77, 20.00c.**
A collection of technical papers on altered states of consciousness, written by well known researchers such as Andrew Weil, Jerome Singer, Charles Tart, and Arthur Deikman. The avowed purpose of the collection is to establish altered states of consciousness as a legitimate subject for scientific inquiry.

CONTEMPORARY SPIRITUAL TEACHERS

All the diverse schools, from analytical psychology through the humanistic and transpersonal disciplines to the most esoteric concepts of mysticism, no matter how different they appear outwardly, have essentially the same purpose. Each in its own way and within its own limits reveals to you the nature of your psyche; and many hint at your relation to the universe. All of them, no matter how different they appear, provide you with some realization of an essentially single truth. As the Vedas proclaim, *The Truth is one, only the sages call it by different names.*

But it's all those different names that cause confusion; and the seemingly different practices too. Because if not in the long run, at least in the short run, their differences produce different results. With so many books, psychologists, encounter leaders, yogis, mind-training organizations and mystery schools abounding, there's no problem finding something or someone to help you plumb the depths of your psyche or to guide you to the greatest spiritual heights. The real problem is to find the best ones specifically suited to you.

Abraham Maslow once said that the majority of people, those whom he considered *normal*, weren't even interested in self-realization. But he did single out some people as being spiritual seekers whom he considered more highly developed than *normals*. Similarly, the ancient mystery schools spoke of different degrees of spiritual evolution. To some extent they, like Freud, attributed the differences in people to experiences they have during their present lifetimes. But most of what you are, according to mystic tradition, was accumulated over hundreds of previous lives. It is said that your complexes, your drives, everything that makes up your personality is founded in what you experienced in this and past incarnations. That, of course, is what Hindus call karma. The Judeo-Christian concept of original sin as being an inherent human characteristic is another way of looking at karma. It might be likened more to Carl Jung's archetypes. But whichever of these concepts best expresses reality, they all imply one thing: You have something hidden in you that makes you what you are right now. For you to evolve spiritually, that something must change. It has to be worked through. So whether that something is Freudian complexes, past incarnations, original sin or archetypes, *karma* seems like a good word to express it. And self-analysis, good deeds, repentance, surrender—all of these are ways of purging your karma.

There is also something in karma that urges certain people more than others to seek self-realization. There is something in karma that determines your degree of spiritual evolution, just as the degree you have evolved spiritually influences how you receive any specific type of psychic or spiritual training. So there can be no guarantee that any form of training will automatically put you into any specific psychic state.

Generally, most people discover their real human nature before they are ready to tackle their higher selves. True, you can have peak experiences while purging yourself, and a few rare people can bypass the purgative process through fervent worship, through Bhakti yoga. But for most it is a step by step

process of cleaning out the personal garbage to clear a path to Cosmic Consciousness. And all of this requires effort. How much of yourself are you willing to give to do it? How much will you sacrifice in money, time, repetitious practice and subordination to a guru—even all your worldly possessions to enter monastic life? Is your act of giving up going to be unduly unpleasant? Does it seem like too great a sacrifice? If so, maybe you are shooting too high.

On the other hand don't aim too low. That happens to so many people, mainly because of lack of exposure. Perhaps you have an inner karmic urge for spiritual growth that is alive and strong, but is lying dormant. Maybe it needs exposure to spiritual ideals, to people with high motivations and to inspiring philosophies. Perhaps it needs but one spark to ignite it into flames of activity. Remember what the Buddha said about right living and associating with people of a spiritual nature. Vedantists are emphatic on this. They say never blindly accept what someone else tells you. You have to experience in order to really understand. The Sufis sum up the same thing with the simple statement *He who tastes knows.*

No one method is better than another. Each has its function for specific situations and for specific people. Of the numerous growth and mystical schools, there are nearly infinite combinations of techniques and philosophies to suit almost any personality and any degree of spiritual development you may have attained. More than likely, there is some teacher or group or school just right for you. So usually it isn't wise to rush in and join the first organization you run across. Don't be hasty. It's so easy to get excited about something that seems exotic or esoteric, especially if you investigate only superficially. Then if you make the wrong choice, you could waste a lot of time. Worse, you could become so turned off by your misadventure that you might drop out of the growth game altogether.

So leaders and teachers advise that you learn as much about an organization or method as you reasonably can. Investigate more than one organization if you like. Read material about their philosophies and the memberships. Talk with former students. Talk with teachers. Do you trust them? What are their credentials? Do their theories square with your understanding of psycho-spiritual development? Look at the product of their training. What is the attitude of their pupils? Observe members of the group on their own premises. Are they open, happy and enthusiastic about their work? Are they tolerant? Or are they dogmatic, pretentious and on ego trips, claiming theirs is the only way? If so, you will be expected to embrace the teachings unquestioningly. That's not to say that's wrong if you can do it. But a lot of people can't.

Many organizations or forms of instruction have names or make claims that don't exactly define what they really teach. Sometimes it's hard to know what you will get before you put up your money or time. So make sure you know what you are getting into before investing large sums of money, and more important, too much time. Since you are interested in controlling your mind, determine whether the instructor really understands mental functioning, or is just parroting the organization's line.

Don't be put off by *minor* details of a teaching that may not square with your logic, especially if the scheme as a whole looks good. Most people have difficulty distinguishing between the methods of an organization and its philosophy. So if they can't buy the philosophy, they automatically reject the techniques. Yet most philosophies, especially those pertaining to gods, the cosmos, and creation, are often based on centuries-old lore no longer compatible with modern thought. Techniques, on the other hand, are observable and measurable. They are material-world reality. So let them be your guide. No one really knows what electricity is, but who buys batteries based on the manufacturer's theory of electrostatics? Besides, if you listen or read extensively enough you will find that many diverse philosophies are really just different ways of saying the same thing. Who cares so long as the techniques to bring about the phenomena work?

The most important thing to do on the path to self-realization is to take the first step. If you aren't sure how far to go or which path you want to take, try several programs. See what the different approaches are like. Get a *feel* for them. Don't select solely on logic. Let your inner senses guide you. It's not really difficult to select what is right if you let your feelings in on the decision. You will be drawn to what's right.

Once you have selected a path that can take you to a goal that appeals to you, *stick* with it. At least stick with it long enough to give it a chance. If your needs are answered, fine; that's where you belong. If not, in six months or more you may want to change. But a word of caution. In most trainings some students reach a plateau, a stage where progress seems to stop, where they become totally discouraged, where they hate the work. They don't like the people in the movement. Many feel above the teachings. But if they don't drop out too soon, most discover they have unknowingly slipped into a higher state of consciousness. It's as if all the negativity is a product of their metamorphosis, only to vanish when the transformation is complete. Then their new state is one where personal consciousness has met cosmic consciousness. They cannot turn back. Try as they may to regain it, their material world is never again the same. They have discovered a basic truth. They know now that reality is different.

So wherever you live the psycho-spiritual movement is growing and growing fast. Many old schools of self-realization are expanding, and new ones are constantly springing up. Superficially they may seem quite different, but they really aren't. As the Hindus say: *Cattle are of different colors, but all milk is alike; systems of faith are different, but God is one.*

That describes the self-realization movement succinctly. Another way would be to liken it to a huge mountain, a mountain with tremendous diversities in landscape. On the plain around its base are scattered many camps full of all types of people. From each camp the mountain looks different, and in these camps are guides who know at least one path up the mountain. But all the paths seem different, and some go higher than others. A few routes follow canyons and rocky streams. Others cross broad grasslands or meander through rich forests. Some are said to be fast approaches to the top, but they scale steep escarpments. Some trails are easier and traverse many types of countryside, with lots of stopping places on the way. Many trails interconnect. As the trails near the summit they get closer together and their landscapes become more similar. The vegetation looks more alike and the high altitude makes you equally giddy on all of them. A few of the paths go all the way to the summit where they meet and become one—as do the climbers. The summit is where the snowy peak merges with swirling white clouds; where earth and heaven join; where man finally awakens and meets his Being; where there is nothing but oneness in the universe. This is the limit of the world of illusion—the end of individuality. It is where the cosmos begins.

And all of us can climb at least one path up that mountain. All we have to do is start.

—*condensed from* **Awakening, Ways to Psycho-Spiritual Growth**, *by C. William Henderson*

BHAJAN, YOGI. THE EXPERIENCE OF CONSCIOUSNESS. 140pp. KRI77, 3.50p.
Transcriptions of a series of talks given on a wide range of subjects. Many practical suggestions are offered.

BHAJAN, YOGI. THE TEACHINGS OF YOGI BHAJAN. 193pp. Haw77, 5.95p.
Yogi Bhajan is the founder and chief religious authority of the 3HO organization. His goal in life has been to introduce the ideals and way of life of the Indian Sikhs to the West. This is a compilation, topically arranged, of his thoughts on a wide variety of topics.

DASS, BABA HARI. HARIAKHAN BABA—KNOWN, UNKNOWN. 93pp. SrR75, 1.95p.
This small book is a compilation of stories about one of the greatest and most mysterious of India's saints, who is known by several names, according to the region in which he appeared.—from the foreword. Baba Hari Dass collected all these stories himself.

DASS, BABA HARI. SILENCE SPEAKS. Illustrations, glossary, 213pp. SrR77, 4.95p.
Baba Hari Dass is a monk who practices continual silence. He has developed the skill of saying a great deal in the fewest possible words, writing them down on his chalkboard. In 1971 he came to the U.S. and since then he has been holding weekly meetings with people interested in the philosophy and practice of yoga. These gatherings consist of an exchange of questions and answers. The teachings found in this book are drawn from these meetings, from letters to students, and from his philosophical writings.

DASS, BABA HARI. THE YELLOW BOOK. Crn74, 3.50p.
These sayings were first collected from the chalkboard of Baba Hari Dass during his first two visits to the Lama Foundation. Baba Hari Dass was first introduced to most of us by Baba Ram Dass in **Be Here Now**. The teachings and stories have Ashtanga Yoga as their foundation. Included here are the original quotations and later comments that Baba Hari Dass made on the quotations.

DHARMA SARA. BETWEEN PLEASURE AND PAIN. 159pp. DSP76, 3.95p.
This is a beautifully produced collection of information on *The Way of Conscious Living* by disciples of Baba Hari Dass. The volume includes thoughts on spirituality, the chakras, yogic practices, marriage, health, yoga psychology, and the yoga of love. Many questions and answers are included and the whole work is very well put together. Much of the material is clearer than we have seen it put anywhere else. Illustrated throughout.

EMERY, STEWART. ACTUALIZATIONS. 237pp. Dou78, 4.95p.
Emery was the first person other than Werner Erhardt to lead the est training. Three years ago he left est to form a similar type of program which he calls Actualizations. This book contains a full exploration of the process. The following chapter headings should give the reader a good idea of the approach: *How We Got to be the Way We Are; The Transformation of our Relationship with Ourselves; Our Relationship with our Parents; The Transformation of our Relationship with our Body; Without Communication, there is Nothing.* And so on. Many feel that the Actualizations training is more attuned to the human element than est.

est

In an **East West Journal** interview Werner Erhard, est's founder, described est as *a sixty-hour experience which opens an additional dimension of living to transform the level at which you experience life so that living becomes a process of expanding satisfaction.... My notion of what happens in the training is that the individual is given an opportunity to create original experiences, or to re-create original experiences.... It is definitely a way past the mind. It transcends the mind. Actually, what I would really say...is that it blows the mind.*

BRY, ADELAIDE. **EST: 60 HOURS THAT TRANSFORM YOUR LIFE.** **233pp. Avo76, 1.95p.**
Adelaide Bry did a great job. The book is readable, accurate and gives a balanced view of est. Adelaide has demonstrated her integrity as a writer by extensive research, verifying the quotes she uses, checking and rechecking her facts; and by stating her opinion as opinion rather than fact. I support the author.—Werner Erhard.

FENWICK, SHERIDAN. **GETTING IT: THE PSYCHOLOGY OF EST.** **Notes, 191pp. Vik76, 2.50p.**
Dr. Fenwick is a trained psychotherapist and is currently on the faculty of the psychology department of Columbia University. Her study of est is both more critical and more technically informative than the other est books. Dr. Fenwick did participate in the training and she offers her view of what happened and what the est process is. She also evaluates many of the claims made by both the est organization and by est graduates—always with a critical eye. She is above all a psychologist and this is apparent in her condemnation of est's instant therapy.

FREDERICK CARL. **EST: PLAYING THE GAME THE NEW WAY.** **215pp. Del74, 3.95p.**
Frederick took est and has remembered his experience phenomenally well. This is a retelling of the high points of est and should provide an excellent review for those who have taken the training and a taste of the training for those who are curious. All the philosophy is here and some of the exercises. The est organization tried to prevent the publication of this volume because it reveals many details of the training.

HARGROVE, ROBERT. **EST. 239pp. Del76, 1.95p.**
What I'm doing in my book is sharing my experiences of the training, the seminar programs, and the est organization; re-creating that experience as it happened.... The training made it possible for me to take all the things I had known as intellectual concepts and bright ideas and have them become experiences for me so that they became real in my life....est was like a laser; it took all the light in the rainbow and condensed it into a single beam. Hargrove is the former publisher of the **East West Journal.**

■ *RHINEHART, LUKE.* **THE BOOK OF EST. Notes, 286pp. HRW76, 4.95p.**
Luke Rhinehart has written an engaging, dramatic re-enactment of the est training. He brilliantly communicates to the reader both a sense of being in the training room and the spirit of what takes place there.—Werner Erhard, founder of est. This is a vivid recreation of the training which has been thoroughly checked for accuracy by the est organization.

—————— **END OF EST SUBSECTION** ——————

GASKIN, STEPHEN. **THE CARAVAN. Unpaginated, RaH72, 2.95p.**
Traces the journey of Stephen Gaskin and his students on a cross-country speaking tour of colleges and churches. It contains the edited tape recordings of the meetings on the road along with lots of pictures. Stephen Gaskin's message is how to get high by telling the truth. The message comes on loud, strong, and clear.

GASKIN, STEPHEN. **SUNDAY MORNING SERVICES ON THE FARM, VOLUME I. 160pp. BPC77, 3.95p.**
Transcriptions of Stephen's talks, each followed by a selection of questions and answers. Many photographs.

GASKIN, STEPHEN. **THIS SEASON'S PEOPLE. 167pp. BPC76, 2.50p.**
Stephen Gaskin is the spiritual leader of a large Tennessee community known as the Farm. This is a collection of his teachings. The book is produced in a slick, hip way and quotations from Stephen and photographs of life on the Farm are interspersed throughout along with decorative art. With each book, the members of the Farm seem to be getting more professional. Stephen's message remains the same: grow up, be straight, be responsible.

GOLD, E.J. **THE JOY OF SACRIFICE—SECRETS OF SUFI WAY.** **Many photographs and line drawings, 257pp. IDH78, 5.95p.**
E.J. Gold runs The Institute for the Harmonious Development of the Human Being in California, a school modeled along Gurdjieffian lines. His methods are sometimes harsh, many times blatant. He speaks of himself as a Sufi and often stresses that he is a direct successor to Gurdjieff—a claim which is questioned, to put it mildly, by true Gurdjieffians. He is something of a mystery man and seems to delight in that role. His teaching is somewhat eclectic, drawing on techniques from a variety of disciplines. The first half of this book contains a lengthy statement of his essential teachings and beliefs. The second section is devoted to a number of chapters individually outlining the message of a number of the twentieth century's best known teachers and masters.

GREENFIELD, ROBERT. **THE SPIRITUAL SUPERMARKET. 277pp.** **Dut75, 3.95p.**
Greenfield has written extensively for **Rolling Stone** and the general writing style of that publication is apparent in this narrative. This is a frank, open look at some of the best known spiritual gurus in the U.S. today. A large part of the book is devoted to a detailed critique of Guru Maharaj-ji. A fascinating section explores Millenium 73—the gathering that took place in Houston. Other chapters discuss Stephen Gaskin, Sri Chinmoy, Ram Dass, Kriyananda, and the Lama Foundation. The account is all in the first person and all the leading characters come to life in the narrative.

HENDERSON, C. WILLIAM. **AWAKENING: WAYS TO PSYCHO-SPIRITUAL GROWTH. 255pp. PrH75, 3.95p.**
An in depth exploration of the most important growth groups, metaphysical schools, and Eastern spiritual organizations in the U.S. It is topically arranged and within each topic there is an introductory section and then a four to ten page write-up of each group describing its history, specifying what is taught, training methods, cost, and where to find local training centers. The material has been gathered from interviews with members and leaders of these groups, and from the author's personal experience. The expositions are objective, and, at least for the groups that we know of personally, factual. A fascinating account for those on the path who want to know more about specific groups and find out about ones that they have not heard of before.

ICHAZO, OSCAR. **THE HUMAN PROCESS FOR ENLIGHTENMENT AND FREEDOM. 120pp. Ari76, 3.95p.**
Transcription of a series of five lectures given to Arica students in advanced training. As Ichazo says, *The aim of these lectures is to answer the questions: What is mind? What is reason? What is consciousness? What is history? and What is the Arica system?* The answers to these questions are not as clearly presented as we would wish.

JOHN, BUBBA FREE. **BREATH AND NAME. Photographs, suggested readings, 275pp. DHP77, 5.95p.**
A collection of essays, comprising a detailed explanation of the spiritual practices taught by Bubba Free John. The book is topically arranged, though all the practices are reducible to one idea: devote yourself totally to your master.

JOHN, BUBBA FREE. **THE PARADOX OF INSTRUCTION. 326pp.** **DHP77, 5.95p.**
There are few precedents for **The Paradox of Instruction** *in the previous literature of human religion and spirituality. In this principal source text of his Teaching, Bubba Free John elucidates all the philosophical and esoteric matters that must be considered in spiritual or real life. But Bubba is not a mere intellectual or speculative philosopher. His writings, like all his actions, only express the elegance and conscious intensity of Divine Ignorance, of God-Realization, which is his constant Enjoyment. His communication speaks directly to the human heart, requiring intelligence, feeling, and constant attention to all who would listen.—from the* introduction. A suggested reading list is appended.

JOHN, BUBBA FREE. **THE WAY THAT I TEACH: TALKS ON THE INTUITION OF ETERNAL LIFE. Photographs, 261pp. DHP78, 5.95p.**
A collection of talks on Bubba's approach to the spiritual way. Questions and answers are included with a number of the talks.

KEYES, KEN. **HANDBOOK TO HIGHER CONSCIOUSNESS. 160pp. LLC72, 4.95c/2.95p.**
One of the best step-by-step guidebooks we have encountered. We recommend it as a basic textbook for all who are seeking ways to overcome their addictions and become loving, peaceful, wise, and free of the constant barrage of unpleasant emotional feelings. Its message is *love everyone unconditionally—including yourself.* It combines the spiritual insights of the East with the concepts of Western humanistic psychology, particularly Maslow and Perls and is therefore recommended for people in the human potential movement who are interested in moving on.

KEYES, KEN and BRUCE BURKAN. **HOW TO MAKE YOUR LIFE WORK OR WHY AREN'T YOU HAPPY. 190pp. S&S76, 1.95p.**
Keyes outlines his *twelve pathways to higher consciousness, unconditional love and happiness* in simple terms. Cartoons make up half of the book.

Krishnamurti

One cannot talk of Krishnamurti's teaching because he does not set himself up as a teacher; one cannot talk of his philosophy because he would not call himself a philosopher. He himself says that his words are merely a mirror in which to see ourselves. Indeed, Krishnamurti's thought illumines, with however rich a variety, a great central fact: namely, that for each individual human, problems can be solved in only one way—for and by himself.

As a small child, Krishnamurti was recognized by Annie Besant and C.W. Leadbeater as a teacher, who, like the Buddha and Christ, would show the way out of the world's confusion. He was given an extensive education in the West and a religious organization for him to lead was established. At his installation he dissolved the organization, saying *I maintain that Truth is a pathless land and you cannot approach it by any path whatsoever, by any religion, by any sect. That is my point of view and I adhere to that absolutely and unconditionally.*

ALCYONE. **AT THE FEET OF THE MASTER. TPH nd, 1.00c/1.25p.**
When he was a boy, involved with the Theosophical Society, Krishnamurti wrote down the precepts for right living contained in this book. They have been a source of inspiration and guidance to thousands of people. As an adult, Krishnamurti disclaimed the work and said it was written through him. It is totally unlike his adult writing.

BENJAMIN, HARRY. **BASIC SELF-KNOWLEDGE. 167pp. Wei71, 3.95p.**
Benjamin draws parallels between the teachings of Krishnamurti and Gurdjieff.

KRISHNAMURTI, J. **THE AWAKENING OF INTELLIGENCE. Fifteen photographs, Avo73/Glz, 2.75p.**
A master work of completely new material which comprehensively covers Krishnamurti's teachings since 1967. The talks and dialogues across America, Europe, and India have been taken from tapes.

KRISHNAMURTI, J. **BEGINNINGS OF LEARNING. 254pp. H&R75/ Pen, 10.00c.**
A collection focused on Krishnamurti's educational beliefs: *When we stop learning in our relationship, whether we are studying, playing, or whatever we are doing, and merely act from the knowledge we have accumulated, then disorder comes.* The first half consists of discussions between Krishnamurti, students, and staff at Brockwood School; the second expands his talks to parents and teachers into short essays.

KRISHNAMURTI, J. **BEYOND VIOLENCE. 175pp. H&R75/Glz, 2.95p.**
Talks and discussions on the urgent need for change in human values.

KRISHNAMURTI, J. **COMMENTARIES ON LIVING. 250pp. each, TPH56-60/Glz, 3.25p/each.**
A series of commentaries taken from Krishnamurti's notebooks in which he touches upon many human problems—our hopes, fears, illusions, beliefs, and prejudices—and in the simplest language seems to pierce to their roots. Three volumes.

KRISHNAMURTI, J. **EDUCATION AND THE SIGNIFICANCE OF LIFE. 125pp. H&R53, 4.95c.**
An exquisite book that penetrates to the core of the problems of education. Krishnamurti has been deeply involved in a number of schools and he has taught and lectured at length on the role and purpose of the teacher, the interrelation of the school staff, and the necessary qualities of the true teacher.

KRISHNAMURTI, J. **THE FIRST AND LAST FREEDOM. 288pp. H&R54/Glz, 3.95p.**
A collection of essays and lengthy answers to questions, summing up the essential features of Krishnamurti's philosophy. Much of the material in this book was actually written for it—most of Krishnamurti's books are simply transcriptions of his talks. Introduction by Aldous Huxley.

KRISHNAMURTI, J. **THE FLIGHT OF THE EAGLE. 156pp. H&R71, 2.95p.**
I say one can live. . .only when one knows how to be free from all the stupidities of one's life. To be free from them is only possible in becoming aware of one's relationship, not only with human beings, but with ideas, with nature, with everything. One of our favorite selections.

KRISHNAMURTI, J. **FREEDOM FROM THE KNOWN. 124pp. H&R69, 2.95p.**
In this volume Krishnamurti shows how people can free themselves from the tyranny of the expected—no matter what their age. And, by first changing themselves, people can then change the whole structure of society and their relationships.

KRISHNAMURTI, J. **THE IMPOSSIBLE QUESTION. 190pp. H&R73/ Pen, 2.25p.**
Here Krishnamurti speaks of various aspects of living, and each of these talks is followed by a dialogue. Topics include fear and pleasure, the act of looking and truly seeing, religion, and mechanical thoughts.

KRISHNAMURTI, J. **KRISHNAMURTI ON EDUCATION. 189pp. H&R74, 3.95p.**
These talks form the most complete presentation to date of Krishnamurti's thoughts on education. Krishnamurti acknowledges the importance of developing the intellect and also continually stresses the

necessity of a heightened awareness of the inner and outer world. The following are some of the main topics he covers: knowledge and intelligence, image making, behavior, freedom and order, denial, sensitivity, competition, violence, fear, and meditation.

KRISHNAMURTI, J. **KRISHNAMURTI'S NOTEBOOK. 256pp. H&R76, 10.00c.**
For a seven-month period a number of years ago Krishnamurti kept an intimate daily record of his perceptions, observations, and states of consciousness. The record starts and ends abruptly and Krishnamurti has never revealed what prompted him to begin it since he had never kept such a notebook before and has not kept one since. Though the entries are hardly ever personal, the reader can get a better feeling for the man himself than in any other book that we know of. The wellspring of Krishnamurti's teaching is also apparent throughout.

KRISHNAMURTI, J. **LIFE AHEAD. 191pp. H&R63, 3.50p.**
Talks addressed particularly to young people, emphasizing the essentials of right education.

KRISHNAMURTI, J. **THE ONLY REVOLUTION. 175pp. H&R70, 1.95p.**
Transcriptions of talks on interior change given by Krishnamurti in India, California, and Europe. Edited by Mary Lutyens.

KRISHNAMURTI, J. **THE PENGUIN KRISHNAMURTI READER. 251pp. Pen64, 2.10p.**
Another excellent introduction to Krishnamurti's thought, divided into three sections: *Problems of Living, For the Young,* and *Questions and Answers.* Extracts from **The First and Last Freedom, Life Ahead,** and **This Matter of Culture.**

KRISHNAMURTI, J. **THE SECOND PENGUIN KRISHNAMURTI READER. 318pp. Pen73, 2.25p.**
This volume incorporates **The Urgency of Change** and **The Only Revolution,** two of Krishnamurti's most popular and influential books. In it he comes to grips with the problems that beset the individual's search for happiness and discusses the difficulties of living peacefully in an increasingly hostile world.

KRISHNAMURTI, J. **TALKS AND DIALOGUES. 252pp. Avo68, 2.25p.**
Transcription of ten talks and six dialogues, delivered at Saanen in the summer of 1967. The subjects cover the entire corpus of Krishnamurti's philosophy.

■ *KRISHNAMURTI, J.* **THINK ON THESE THINGS. H&R70, 2.25p.**
This book consistently outsells all the other Krishnamurti books three or four to one. It is definitely many people's favorite collection and is as good a place to learn Krishnamurti's philosophy as any of his books.

KRISHNAMURTI, J. **TRUTH AND ACTUALITY. 171pp. H&R77/Glz, 6.95c.**
A collection of both talks and dialogues. It opens with three discussions taken from a longer series with David Bohm, Professor of Theoretical Physics at London University. In this section Krishnamurti discusses the problem of truth and reality as it appears to our consciousness. In the main part of the book Krishnamurti considers how man's consciousness is made up of all sorts of misconceptions about the *me* or ego center, and how solidly it is conditioned.

KRISHNAMURTI, J. **THE URGENCY OF CHANGE. 154pp. H&R70/Glz, 1.95p.**
In these talks Krishnamurti enters into dialogue with people who often find themselves unable to cope with the world, with other people, and with themselves. He makes practical suggestions and covers a variety of specific topics including awareness, fear, relationship, conflict, morality, love and sex, perfection, suffering, belief, dreams, and much else.

KRISHNAMURTI, J. **YOU ARE THE WORLD. 175pp. H&R72, 1.95p.**
In oneself lies the whole world, and if you know how to look and learn, then the door is there and the key is in your hand. Nobody on Earth can give you either that key or the door to open, except yourself. Talks at American universities.

LUTYENS, MARY. **KRISHNAMURTI. Chronology, notes, index, 337pp. Avo75/Mur, 2.25p.**
This is a personal account of the first thirty-eight years of Krishnamurti's life which traces his development from the days when, as a boy in India, he was heralded by the leaders of the Theosophical Society as the vehicle for the coming messiah until, as a young man with extraordinary conviction, he was able to make a clean ideological break from the individuals and organizations that sought to confine him to a traditional messianic role. Related partly in Krishnamurti's own words, this book reveals his many doubts and difficulties, as well as his achievements. It discusses his close relationship with Annie Besant and with C.W. Leadbeater and the trauma and loneliness involved in his spiritual maturation and his special position. Ms. Lutyens' mother was Krishnamurti's chief confidante in those early years, and with this book his letters to Lady Emily Lutyens and his own account of the spiritual experience which changed his life are published for the first time. Mary Lutyens has edited four collections of Krishnamurti's work.

MEHTA, ROHIT. **THE NAMELESS EXPERIENCE. 473pp. MoB76, 11.35p.**
A comprehensive analysis of all aspects of Krishnamurti's teaching—his philosophy, psychology, and practice of no practice.

──────── END OF KRISHNAMURTI SUBSECTION ────────

LOZOWICK, LEE. **IN THE FIRE. Photographs, 249pp. IDH78, 5.95p.**
Lozowick is the leader of a spiritual community in New Jersey. He says that he awoke one morning in 1975 to find himself *awake* and an individual who could transmit ultimate truth to his followers through words and by his very presence. This is a collection of his thoughts on gurus, the Godlife, personal responsibility, existence, the meaning of life, and much else, arranged in the form of short, personal, connected essays.

MANDELKORN, PHILIP, ed. **TO KNOW YOUR SELF: THE ESSENTIAL TEACHINGS OF SWAMI SATCHIDANANDA. Introduction, 264pp. Dou78, 3.95p.**
Swami Satchidananda is one of the best known and most respected yoga masters in the U.S. today. In this compilation of teachings and stories, he offers guidance for everyday problems in family life and business, and shows how to realize universal consciousness.

MARTIN, JAMES. **ACTUALIZATIONS: BEYOND EST. 208pp. SFB77, 8.95c.**
Stewart Emery, the founder of Actualizations, is a former long time est instructor. Like est it is a synthesis of many disciplines, and a great deal is taken from the est experience itself. Martin says that Actualizations is a *heart trip* in comparison with est's *head trip.* This book contains a detailed review of the Actualizations seminar Martin attended, recording the author's reactions and his observation of others. Many case histories are included, showing the effect of Actualizations training in a number of specific areas inlcuing marriage, sex, and work.

MISRA, L.K., ed. **SWAMI RAMA OF THE HIMALAYAS. Him76, 2.95p.**
A photographic sketch, accompanied by a selection of Swami Rama's aphorisms.

Bhagwan Shree Rajneesh

Rajneesh is an enlightened master living in India. When he speaks on Zen, he is a Zen master; when he speaks on Lao Tzu, he is a Taoist master; when he speaks on tantra, he is a tantric master. Incorporating in his teachings the essence of all the great religions, he is defined by none of them. He tells us that religion is not something separate from life. It is life itself, and to be religious is to live life to its fullest, to celebrate the existence.

His approach is psychological not philosophical. He responds to the individual needs of his thousands of disciples

from all over the world, giving to one a Tibetan technique, to another a bioenergetic technique, and to still another a meditation technique or psychotherapeutic technique that he himself has devised.

His books are mainly direct transcriptions of the daily lectures he gives. He speaks on a wide variety of subjects and whatever his subject, he speaks out of his own inner knowing and brings the ancient scriptures to life. Some of the books are edited in prose and some in poetry.

RAJNEESH, BHAGWAN SHREE. **ABOVE ALL, DON'T WOBBLE—A DARSHAN DIARY. 450pp. RaF76, 15.95c.**
Part of a continuing series of books that record, in words and photographs, the unique experience of being face to face with a living master. Every evening for an hour and a half, Rajneesh holds darshans for a small group of disciples and visitors. These books record his response to each individual's needs, problems, and progress, and they show how a true master works. The books contain 120 photographs, many in color.

RAJNEESH, BHAGWAN SHREE. **THE ALCHEMY OF CELEBRATION (A RECORDING). 7.00.**
A 33 1/3 rpm. record. Side one consists of excerpts from a question and answer session. Side two contains meditation music, played on electronic instruments.

RAJNEESH, BHAGWAN SHREE. **AND THE FLOWERS SHOWERED. 276pp. RaF75, 10.95c.**
A collection of talks Bhagwan Rajneesh gave on Zen and on the early Zen masters. Many of the teaching stories are repeated and interpreted by Rajneesh in the light of his own philosophy. And, as with all of Rajneesh's discourses, the title topic is only a starting point for his philosophical digressions. He uses these Zen stories as the early Zen masters used them—to teach, to poke, to prod, to trick you into your own inner knowings.

RAJNEESH, BHAGWAN SHREE. **BE REALISTIC: PLAN FOR A MIRACLE—A DARSHAN DIARY. Photographs, 403pp. RaF77, 15.95c.**
Bhagwan's responses to questions from disciples. Many areas are covered and Rajneesh provides an abundance of suggestions.

RAJNEESH, BHAGWAN SHREE. **THE BOOK OF THE SECRETS. RaF77, 10.95c/each.**
A five volume series on the ancient tantric scripture known as **Vigyana Bhairava Tantra.** In this scripture, Lord Siva gives the 112 methods of meditation which are the basis of all the meditation techniques in the world. Rajneesh discusses both traditional and modern derivations of

these techniques and shows that tantra is the path of surrender and of total acceptance to whatever life offers. Volume I is available in a paperback edition for $3.95. Each volume is about 400 pages.

RAJNEESH, BHAGWAN SHREE. **COME FOLLOW ME, VOLUMES I-IV. 250pp. RaF76, 12.95c/each.**
Rajneesh speaks on the Christ. He says that Christ consciousness, Buddhahood, enlightenment, are various names of the same ultimate realization, the same state of knowing. As he discourses on Christ's teachings, the teachings come alive.

RAJNEESH, BHAGWAN SHREE. **DANG DANG DOKO DANG: TALKS ON ZEN. 278pp. RaF77, 12.95c.**
Transcriptions of ten talks delivered in 1976. *Dang dang doko dang is the sound of the gong beaten by the Master. It symbolizes the poetic quality special to Zen. It indicates what cannot be expressed. Whenever you are again becoming victims of theories, dogmas, doctrines, philosophies, say, "dang dang doko dang."*

RAJNEESH, BHAGWAN SHREE. **THE EMPTY BOAT. 400pp. RaF nd, 12.95c.**
Discourses on Chuang Tzu. *Such is the perfect man: his boat is empty. Empty of what? Empty of the "I". Empty of the ego. Empty of somebody there inside. Here Rajneesh speaks of the emptiness he shares with Chuang Tzu and all enlightened masters.* Edited as poetry.

RAJNEESH, BHAGWAN SHREE. **THE GRASS GROWS BY ITSELF. 220pp. DeV78, 4.50p.**
Sitting silently, doing nothing. Spring comes...and the grass grows by itself. Rajneesh uses these words of the ancient Zen master, Zenerin, to lead one deeper and deeper into the mysteries of Zen. Edited as poetry.

RAJNEESH, BHAGWAN SHREE. **HAMMER ON THE ROCK—A DARSHAN DIARY. 450pp. RaF76, 15.95c.**
The first volume in a series of books on the experience of darshan with Rajneesh. See the review of **Above All, Don't Wobble** for more details on the series.

RAJNEESH, BHAGWAN SHREE. **THE HIDDEN HARMONY. 300pp. RaF76, 10.95c.**
Eleven talks based on the **Fragments** of Heraclitus. Rajneesh says that if Heraclitus had been born in India, he would have been known as a Buddha. But because Greek philosophy is based on Aristotelian concepts of logic, Heraclitus could not be understood. Heraclitus spoke as a poet, reconciling opposites and creating mysteries out of the obvious. Rajneesh brings the poetry of Heraclitus' wisdom to light.

RAJNEESH, BHAGWAN SHREE. **I AM THE GATE. 203pp. H&R77, 3.95p/1.95p.**
In the discourses contained in this volume given in the spring of 1971, Bhagwan Shree talks extensively about how he works with his disciples. Not only does he talk about the techniques he uses, and the esoteric meaning behind them, but he uses his very words as a technique to push one beyond mind, beyond intellect.—from the introduction.

RAJNEESH, BHAGWAN SHREE. **JUST LIKE THAT. 450pp. RaF75, 10.95c.**
For ten days Rajneesh was a Sufi, bringing rare insight to ten chosen Sufi stories. The true tradition of Sufi learning lies in the rapport between master and disciple. These talks, edited as poetry, give the reader an opportunity to experience this intimate transfer, a transfer that is beyond words. Bhagwan says: *Let me repeat the Sufi saying: Simply trust. Do not the petals flutter down just like that?*

RAJNEESH, BHAGWAN SHREE. **MEDITATION: THE ART OF ECSTASY. 224pp. H&R76, 3.95p/2.50p.**
The basic text on the teachings and meditation techniques of Rajneesh. The need for meditation techniques that start out from a psychotherapeutic base is discussed and an extensive description and analysis is given of both traditional techniques and new methods that have been devised by Bhagwan specifically for the needs of the modern seeker.

RAJNEESH, BHAGWAN SHREE. **THE MUSTARD SEED: A LIVING EXPLANATION OF THE SAYINGS OF JESUS FROM THE GOSPEL ACCORDING TO THOMAS. 518pp. H&R75/SIP, 5.95p.**
A collection of talks in which Rajneesh explains texts selected from **The Gospel According to Thomas.** This is one of the most popular Rajneesh books.

RAJNEESH, BHAGWAN SHREE. **THE MYSTIC EXPERIENCE. 545pp. MoB77, 14.95c.**
Transcriptions of eighteen discourses on kundalini given in 1970. Many questions and answers are included.

RAJNEESH, BHAGWAN SHREE. **NEITHER THIS NOR THAT. 265pp. RaF75/SIP, 10.95c.**
In these talks Bhagwan expands and illuminates the sutras of Sosan, a Zen Patriarch. These brief scriptures, called **Verses on the Faith Mind**, are the only words Sosan ever uttered and as such are very powerful. Bhagwan illuminates these words in the light of present day experience. *We will be talking about Sosan and his words. If you listen attentively suddenly you will feel a release of silence within you. These words are atomic, they are full of energy. Whenever a person who has attained says something, the word becomes a seed, and for millions of years the word will remain a seed . . . and will seek a heart.*

RAJNEESH, BHAGWAN SHREE. **NIRVANA: THE LAST NIGHT-MARE. 350pp. RaF76, 12.95c.**
Ten talks on Zen stories, followed by questions and answers. Rajneesh says that nirvana and enlightenment are the ultimate desire which must be dropped. Here and now is the only goal.

RAJNEESH, BHAGWAN SHREE. **NO WATER, NO MOON: REFLEC-TIONS ON ZEN. 246pp. SIP75, 10.00c.**
A series of talks based on ten Zen stories. Rajneesh transforms what at first glance seem to be nothing more than humorous anecdotes into a direct perception of Zen.

RAJNEESH, BHAGWAN SHREE. **NOTHING TO LOSE BUT YOUR HEAD—A DARSHAN DIARY. Many photographs, 401pp. RaF77, 15.95c.**
An informal collection of dialogues between Rajneesh and his disciples.

RAJNEESH, BHAGWAN SHREE. **ONLY ONE SKY. 250pp. Dut76, 4.45p.**
These lectures are based on Tilopa's **Song of Mahamudra**, a rare document that is at the heart of tantra. Rajneesh shares with the reader the rich meanings of this miraculous text. Each part is unravelled to expose the intricate threads of paradox which weave the complex web of tantra. Bhagwan has said that the time is ripe now for a tantric explosion in the West; we are faced with a world that will move into either madness or meditation.

RAJNEESH, BHAGWAN SHREE. **THE PSYCHOLOGY OF THE ESO-TERIC: THE NEW EVOLUTION OF MAN. 160pp. H&R78, 3.95p.**
What Bhagwan is talking about in these discourses is nothing less than the creation of a new man . . . a climate in which Buddhahood can begin to flower. For that to happen, he says, we must accept man in his totality.—from the introduction.

RAJNEESH, BHAGWAN SHREE. **RETURNING TO THE SOURCE. 400pp. RaF76, 10.95c.**
Zen is a meeting of all that is beautiful in Buddha and all that is beautiful in Lao Tzu, Rajneesh says. *That is why there is nothing like Zen. Two streams—tremendously powerful, tremendously beautiful, literally of the unknown—come to a meeting. There has never been such a meeting before. Other religions have met, but they have met as enemies. This meeting of Buddha's teaching with Taoism is out of love.* Edited as poetry.

RAJNEESH, BHAGWAN SHREE. **ROOTS AND WINGS. 475pp. RaF75, 11.00c.**
Discourses based on eleven Zen stories, followed by questions and answers. *Religion has always been against the roots (the world) and for the wings (renunciation). But without the roots the tree cannot flower.* Edited as poetry.

RAJNEESH, BHAGWAN SHREE. **THE SEARCH: TALKS ON THE TEN BULLS OF ZEN. Illustrations, 274pp. RaF77, 12.95c.**
The ten Zen bulls comprise ten moods in the total unfolding of life, each one expressed in poetry, prose, and picture. They have the amazing quality of being earthy and aethetic but at the same time transcendental. . . . Rajneesh has drawn the Zen bulls in a series of ten discourses. . . . He invites you to feel the presence of the bull, to see the bull within you. He invites you each to catch the bull and tame it.—from the introduction.

RAJNEESH, BHAGWAN SHREE. **TAO: THE THREE TREASURES. 350pp. each, RaF76, 12.95c/each.**
Talks on fragments from the **Tao Te Ching** by Lao Tzu. *When I talk on Lao Tzu, I speak as if I am speaking on my own self. With him my being is totally one.* Four volumes, edited as poetry.

RAJNEESH, BHAGWAN SHREE. **THE TRUE SAGE. 300pp. RaF76, 12.95c.**
The discourses in this volume are based on five hasidic tales and Rajneesh uses these stories as tools to transmit that understanding which is beyond words, beyond intellect. The chief characteristic of the hasidic movement was the emergence of different communities around a true sage or *zaddik*. The presence of the *zaddik* served as an inspiration for the people in the community, for he was living proof of everyone's possibility to live in God. Rajneesh feels that he is a modern day *zaddik*, creating a situation for his disciples to grow through, to learn through. Edited as poetry.

RAJNEESH, BHAGWAN SHREE. **THE ULTIMATE ALCHEMY. Each volume is 420pp. long, RaF76, 12.95c/each.**
Two volumes on the **Atma Pooja Upanishad (Worship of the Self)**. Most books on the Upanishads are scholarly commentaries about the possible meaning of these ancient scriptures. Bhagwan doesn't comment on them, he responds to them. And he says that he has chosen to respond to the **Atma Pooja** *simply because I have fallen in love with it. Firstly, it is the shortest of the Upanishads. It is just seedlike—potent, pertinent, with much in it. Every word is a seed with infinite possibilities, so you can echo it and re-echo it infinitely. And the more you ponder over it and allow it to enter you, the more new significances will be revealed.*

RAJNEESH, BHAGWAN SHREE. **UNTIL YOU DIE. 270pp. RaF76, 12.95c.**
Ten discourses on Sufi anecdotes and teaching stories. *The whole of my effort is to help you move towards the heart, because only through the heart will you be reborn. Nobody can be reborn until he dies.*

RAJNEESH, BHAGWAN SHREE. **VEDANTA: SEVEN STEPS TO SAMADHI. 420pp. RaF76, 12.95c.**
On the **Akshya Upanishad**, an ancient Hindu scripture which outlines a practical and life affirming path for the spiritual seeker. Because these discourses were given at a meditation camp Bhagwan conducted, alternating with his discussion of the Upanishads is much practical information about meditation techniques.

RAJNEESH, BHAGWAN SHREE. **WHEN THE SHOE FITS. 400pp. DeV78, 5.25p.**
When the shoe fits, the foot is forgotten. When the belt fits, the belly is forgotten. When the heart is right, for and against are forgotten. Bhagwan uses **The Way of Chuang Tzu** by Thomas Merton as the text on which he bases these discourses. *Chuang Tzu is a rare flowering because to become nobody is the most difficult, most impossible, most extraordinary thing in the world. The ordinary mind hankers to the extraordinary. That is part of its ordinariness. The extraordinary starts only when you don't hanker after extraordinariness. Then the journey has started. Then a new seed has sprouted.* Edited as poetry.

RAJNEESH, BHAGWAN SHREE. **YOGA: THE ALPHA AND THE OMEGA. 240pp. each, RaF76, 12.95c/each.**
Eight volumes of discourses on the **Yoga Sutras** of Patanjali.

———END OF BHAGWAN SHREE RAJNEESH SUBSECTION———

RAM DASS. **BE HERE NOW. Glossary, 8"x8", over 300pp. Crn71, 3.33p.**
Ram Dass is, without a doubt, the most popular native born American guru; this is his bible. We do not know of anyone on the spiritual path today who has not read and been touched by **Be Here Now**. It is usually one of the first things someone reads when they get interested in the path. The book begins with the transformation of Richard Alpert from a hip Harvard professor experimenting with LSD to a genuine seeker in India. Everyone knows that story too well for us to repeat it here. The center of the book, *From Hindu to Ojas—The Core Book*, is a collection of illustrated lessons—pure light which unravels the lessons we must share on our journey into consciousness. The final section, *Cookbook for a Sacred Life*, contains insights into daily life, dietary suggestions, yoga asanas, sample reading lists, and much more.

RAM DASS. **GRIST FOR THE MILL. 174pp. UnP77, 3.95p.**
These words are pulled forth from me by you. I have no identification with them, this book is just the transcript of words spoken to us listening, demanding that they be spoken. So whose book is it? When beautiful music is played on a violin, would you go up and thank the violin? I'm just the mouthpiece for a process. What you're doing when you read this book is you're touching your self. Forget me, I am a passing show. You're

touching yourself.—Ram Dass. This transmission is interwoven from lectures, retreats, articles, and interviews given by Ram Dass during 1974-76 throughout the U.S.

RAM DASS. **JOURNEY OF AWAKENING: A MEDITATOR'S GUIDEBOOK. 2.95p.**
See the Meditation section.

RAM DASS. **THE ONLY DANCE THERE IS. Index, 180pp. Dou74, 2.95p.**
This book contains transcripts of lectures Ram Dass gave at the Menninger Foundation in 1970 and at Spring Grove Hospital in Baltimore in 1972. The style is very personal and there are also sections of questions and answers. Much of the material covered here is not included in **Be Here Now**, so this volume is well worth reading. The teaching, as usual, is clear and enlightening.

RAMA, SWAMI. **MARRIAGE, PARENTHOOD AND ENLIGHTENMENT. 108pp. Him77, 1.95p.**
A collection of the following essays: *From Sexual Attraction to Understanding, The Aim of Life, Children, Stages of Growth,* and *Spiritual Fulfillment.* Swami Rama is a sympathetic writer and he expresses his ideas in ways which are easy for Westerners to understand.

RUDI. **SPIRITUAL CANNIBALISM. Photographs, 207pp. OvP78, 4.95p.**
Rudi was an American spiritual teacher who died a few years ago. In this book he outlines the concept of spiritual work and describes his practice and teachings. Rudi says that, *The title,* **Spiritual Cannibalism,** *attempts to put into perspective the relationship of human beings to one another. When we eat fruit, the skin provides roughage essential to our growth. In human relationships, too, roughage is essential. The total person must be consumed to support life in its depth—to allow for creative interchange between a human being and God. We cannot limit our intake to the qualities that are easy to take—we must welcome those that force us to change the pattern we have been able to deal with in the past. We must come to understand that everything is part of perfection and must be taken in a state of surrender; it must be digested and transcended. Life must be consumed whole—with all its tensions, pain, and joy.*

SATCHIDANANDA, SWAMI. **BEYOND WORDS. Illustrations, 7½"x9¼", 182pp. HRW77, 5.95p.**
This collection of puns, parables, philosophy, and stories distills the essence of Swami Satchidananda's message. The material has been topically edited from talks.

TARTHANG TULKU. **GESTURE OF BALANCE. Illustrations, 182+ pp. Dha77, 4.95p.**
This book is the result of a Tibetan lama's encounter with American culture. Tarthang Tulku explains that most of our problems are created by subtle mental attitudes—feelings of bewilderment, separateness, and meaninglessness which constantly tax our energies. One of the most effective methods to overcome this anxiety and to heal ourselves is meditation. Through meditation we learn to examine our minds and hearts, to develop warm, positive feelings, and to contact—beyond words and concepts—a more sensitive level of awareness. The natural expression of this meditative awareness is balance—balance between our bodies and minds, ourselves and our world. This lovely book interweaves insights into the human condition and methods for unfolding human potential that have been developed over centuries in Tibet with the textures of our own American experience. It is a practical book which includes many exercises and a number of dialogues between Tarthang Tulku and his students.

TARTHANG TULKU. **TIME, SPACE, AND KNOWLEDGE: A NEW VISION OF REALITY. 348pp. Dha77, 6.95p.**
It would seem that now is the time for a new venturing out, for a vision which would integrate and unite all aspects of being, thereby inspiring a broad, open-ended, and vigorous appreciation of life. Space and Time themselves have now presented such a vision, and I hope that it will be helpful to the contemporary world. Once our perspective is sufficiently open, all experience can be seen as the dynamic play of Space, Time, and Knowledge.... We can then directly experience our Being, which expressed itself as a dynamic and complete freedom. In this way we can discover what it means to be truly human.—from the introduction. In addition to a philosophical exposition, this book contains thirty-five exercises for developing our awareness. These techniques are different from anything else we have seen. Though Tarthang Tulku is a Tibetan lama, the exercises and philosophical underpinning are designed to appeal to those who have been brought up in the Western empirical tradition. This is a book which demands study and attention if the reader is to benefit from the approach. Many full color crystalline illustrations are interspersed throughout, along with a number of line drawings.

TRUNGPA, CHOGYAM. **CUTTING THROUGH SPIRITUAL MATERIALISM. 4.95p.**
See the Tibetan Buddhism section.

TURIYASANGITANANDA (ALICE COLTRANE). **MOMENT ETERNAL. 53pp. Wei53, 2.95p.**
Alice Coltrane is widely known as an accomplished musician. She is also a spiritual teacher and in this book she tells of her spiritual initiation, revelations, and austerities.

DIVINATION

As far as we can go back in the history of recorded time, man has been interested in his future. Divination is simply another word for prognostication, prediction, prophecy or fortunetelling.

Some of those methods used in the past have died out completely and some have never been so popular as today. To many these beliefs seem absurd, but if in a stone or amulet man finds peace, security, luck and above all protection from his unknown fears often labelled *The Evil Eye*, then it is no more absurd, and certainly less detrimental, than modern tranquilizers.

Be it a plant, piece of wood or the pronouncements of some oracle, wizard or medium, it often brings luck to the owner for he has faith in it, and it has always been said that *Faith* moves mountains.

In any case, looking into the future as a profession has always had its adherents, for from time immemorial the demand has been there. We are all born naked into an alien world, but some, by accident of birth, having position or wealth, are better endowed than others to survive the rigours of earth life. Many seek to weight the scales in their favour by obtaining a glimpse of the future and what it will bring, and this is where divination comes in.

—*condensed from* **Divination**, *by Mary Anderson*

ACHAD, FRATER. **CRYSTAL VISION THROUGH CRYSTAL GAZING.** 128pp. YPS23, 6.95c.
An esoteric treatise on the real value of crystal gazing, including many practical instructions.

ANDERSON, MARY. **DIVINATION: HOW TO USE UNUSUAL METHODS.** Bibliography, 63pp. Wei74/TPL, 1.00p.
A concise study of many methods of divination with chapters on divination by the elements, the shape of things to come, signs and omens from plants, and divination by stones and bones. Part of the **Paths to Inner Power** series.

ATKINSON, WILLIAM. **PRACTICAL PSYCHOMANCY AND CRYSTAL GAZING.** 93pp. YPS08, 1.00p.
Atkinson was later known as Yogi Ramacharaka. Here he gives a series of practical lessons.

FABIA, MADAME. **THE BOOK OF FORTUNE TELLING.** Illustrations, index, 510pp. Arc72, 3.95p.
This is a detailed study of four techniques: palmistry, fortune telling by cards; phrenology; and dream analysis. Each is discussed at length, though not much depth or insight is incorporated into the analyses.

FITZGERALD, DONALIE. **EDITH L. RANDALL'S YOUR PLACE IN THE CARDS.** 535pp. BoM74, 7.95p.
Ms. Randall believes that the seemingly random construction of our familiar deck of playing cards is anything but accidental. It follows a strict mathematical symbology that corresponds to the mathematical laws on which the universe was founded. Symbolically decorated cards were used for fortune telling before they were used in games of chance. The unique system presented in this book was developed more than fifty years ago by Randall, a professional astrologer. According to her formula, each birthdate in the year has a corresponding card, and each card in turn has a ruling planet. One of these cards represents each individual and by studying the cards, Ms. Randall said, you can learn a great deal about yourself. This is a detailed presentation of the Randall system.

GIBSON, WALTER and LITZKA. **THE COMPLETE ILLUSTRATED BOOK OF DIVINATION AND PROPHECY.** Glossary, index, 268pp. NAL73/Sou, 2.25p.
The Gibsons have written many volumes on psychic phenomena, witchcraft, and other similar areas. This is their newest effort. Like their other books, this is basically a how-to, self help book. Topics include use of the mystic oracle, divination by numbers, what today can mean to you, tasseomancy, tarot, divination with playing cards, and palm reading.

HALL, MANLY P. **STUDIES IN CHARACTER ANALYSIS.** 87pp. PRS58, 1.75p.
Sections on phrenology, palmistry, physiognomy, and graphology. Includes many diagrams and gives a good general view of each subject. An excellent introduction.

MAR, TIMOTHY. **FACE-READING.** 175pp. NAL74, 1.50p.
A clearly written exposition of Chinese physiognomy. Each of the parts of the face is analyzed in detail and many line drawings accompany the text. The last third of the book is devoted to a photographic analysis of noted individuals. This book has been surprisingly popular.

MELVILLE, JOHN. **CRYSTAL GAZING AND CLAIRVOYANCE.** 92pp. Wei1896, 1.95p.
Clear instructions for the use and care of the crystal.

OPHIEL. **THE ORACLE OF FORTUNA.** 129pp. Pea70, 3.50p.
Ophiel discusses this system of divination through and by symbols. Four symbols, each with a key word, are presented and thoroughly explained. The appendix contains color plates of the planet symbols and directions for drawing them.

RANDALL, EDITH and FLORENCE CAMPBELL. **SACRED SYMBOLS OF THE ANCIENTS.** Spiral bound, 8½"x11", 198pp. Sym47, 9.95p.
This is a fascinating study of the mystical significance of the fifty-two *playing cards*. Each card is analyzed at length. The study forms a method of character analysis based on numerical and astrological correspondence e using the playing cards as keys. Each of the fifty-two cards symbolizing a particular type of person. A complete description of the different types, their birthdates, and variants is detailed in addition to the significance of suit, number, astrological rulership, etc. Includes spread charts.

ZAIN, C.C. **DIVINATION.** 4.25p.
See the Astrology section.

DREAMS

What is a dream? Some seem totally trivial, like the idle meanderings of a brain off-duty, and it is not surprising that skeptics say they are best forgotten. But others cannot be so easily dismissed. There are the very frightening ones we wish we could pass off as *only dreams*, as parents urge their children to do with nightmares, but often their impression is so strong that the memory continues to haunt us for years. There are other dreams of such beauty and joy that we would not have missed them, and still others so vivid that we wonder whether they could be visions of another world or glimpses into some previous incarnation. A few actually predict the future. Is there anything they all have in common?

Although science is still a long way from having any comprehensive understanding of dreams, one finding has emerged pretty firmly from modern research, namely that the majority of dreams seem in some way to reflect things that have preoccupied our minds during the previous day or two. Sometimes this is easy to see, but it is equally true even of those fantastic dreams that seem worlds away from our ordinary life and thoughts, like being chased down the street by a tiger or conversing with a dead person. Dreams express themselves in a special kind of picture language; and once this is understood it will be seen that the tiger symbolized someone or something we found frightening the day or so before the dream, while the dead person appeared in order to give tangible expression to some idea he gave us long ago, an idea of immediate relevance to our present life. Dreams reflect not only actual happenings, but also a whole host of thoughts and feelings that passed us by during the day because we were too busy or unwilling to catch them.

In fact, the dreaming mind may be compared to a movie director, picking up things from waking life that need more attention than we have given them, and reflecting on them in depth by composing stories in which flashbacks, cartoon-style pictures, and all kinds of other devices are used to express what we are feeling deep down inside about ourselves, other people, and the quality of our lives generally. And this alone, even if we went no further, would be an excellent reason for not merely brushing dreams aside, for is there any human being whose life would not be improved by a little additional reflection?

Just what the dreaming process achieves if we sleep right through the dream and never remember it, no one knows. There is probably some basis to the ancient idea of being able to tackle life's difficulties better simply by *sleeping on them*, though we can only speculate about how this works. What we do know is that when dreams are remembered, and their reflections-in-depth are understood, a whole new dimension of wisdom and insight is added to life, bringing greater sanity, meaning, and humor into our existence.

One of the commonest questions I am asked is whether the time and effort necessary to understand the picture language of dreams would not be better spent giving straight rational thought to our problems. The answer is that until the dreaming mind brings to our notice all the subtle feelings, vibes, and impressions we have missed during waking life, we are in no position even to evaluate the problems, let alone solve them. A detective with only half the facts of a case at his disposal is unlikely to unravel a mystery, however much reason and commonsense he brings to bear on it. That is why

mankind's age-old fascination with dreams was rooted in wisdom, however much it may have been sidetracked into superstition and mystification.

The price our civilization has paid for its heavy concentration on rational thought was nicely brought out in a story told by Jung of a conversation with a chief of the Pueblo Indians called Ochwiay Biano. Jung asked the chief's opinion of the white man and was told that it was not a high one. White people, said Ochwiay Biano, seem always upset, always restlessly looking for something, with the result that their faces are covered with wrinkles. He added that white men must be crazy because they think with their heads, and it is well known that only crazy people do that. Jung asked in surprise how the Indian thought, to which Ochwiay Biano replied that naturally he thought with his heart.

In our culture we not only train our children to think with their heads, but we actively discourage them from listening to their hearts, even though we pay lip service to the power of feelings in human life. When someone behaves out of character, apparently disregarding the dictates of reason and commonsense, we nod wisely and perhaps murmur the famous words of Pascal, *The heart has its reasons which are unknown to the head*—understanding for a moment why it is that so many of our own well-laid plans go astray. But most of the time we have a deep distrust of feeling and emotion, fearing that they will rule our lives if we allow them to flow. In fact, the opposite is the case, for emotion causes trouble only when denied expression. A healthy life is one in which head and heart cooperate without either trying to put the other down. In modern colloquial terms, a person who lives this way is *together*.

It is precisely because dreams help us get ourselves together that I have called them *thoughts of the heart*, although it would be more accurate to say that dreams show us some of our heart thoughts—specifically those we have neglected during the day to our possible disadvantage or danger. . . . As Jung put it, *In each of us there is another whom we do not know. He speaks to us in dreams and tells us how differently he sees us from the way we see ourselves. When, therefore, we find ourselves in a difficult situation to which there is no solution, he can sometimes kindle a light that radically alters our attitude—the very attitude that led us into the difficult situation.*

In all cases, irrespective of what kind of message they have for us, it is important to remember that dreams reflect something in or on our minds at the time of the dream. Even when they reveal deep, long-standing problems, or touch on higher transcendental issues, they always show how these things are hitting us now, at the present moment in time. And to understand a dream properly it is necessary to see how it relates to some event or preoccupation of the past day or two.

If a dream takes us back to childhood or introduces someone we used to know well but with whom we are no longer involved, it is always because these past events are in some way relevant to a present concern, and it is this reference to the present that constitutes the dream's meaning. While knowing about the past may help a lot in tackling basic life problems, it is essential to know how these problems are affecting our lives at the moment, for it is in the present, in the actual circumstances of life here and now, that we have to get ourselves together. Edgar Cayce, who believed that some dreams give visions of earlier incarnations, still insisted that such dreams must be interpreted in terms of the dreamer's present life situation, for he held that dreams bring us memories of this life or of earlier lives only when such memories are relevant to the needs of the here and now.

The thoughts of the heart have access to a vast storehouse of memories we have accumulated throughout our lives, and it is uncanny to discover from dreams just how precise some of these memories are. If you take note of the dates of your dreams, for example, you will find that some of them seem to be commemorating an anniversary, by throwing up a picture of an event that happened on that very day exactly a year, or sometimes many years ago. This frequently happens with deaths and traumatic stress situations of the past, and it means that the memory is still somehow affecting our lives. It is as if our hearts go on mourning such anniversaries even though our heads have forgotten all about them, and this can sometimes extend to making us physically ill on a certain date each year without our consciously connecting the symptoms with the anniversary. When dreams bring such events to our conscious attention, they are in effect asking us to consider why we are holding on to the unhappiness of the past, and the answer is almost always that we are using the past to avoid having to live fully in the present, perhaps because we fear being hurt again or because it brings some drama to an otherwise empty existence. In my experience such dreams usually show us our fears about the present as well as commemorating the past, and so help us to break free for the future. More commonly, dreams bring us memories of past events to warn us not to repeat the same mistakes in a present situation or to spur us on to more positive thinking about a related present problem. For this purpose they can call up any past event that happens to be relevant at the time, but if a convenient anniversary is at hand they will often make use of it.

The power of the dreaming mind to show us the thoughts of the heart that have passed us by during the day, with all their vast array of associated memories and fantasies, comes first and foremost from the fact that the sleeping brain is not having to pay attention to the outside world. Over and above this, however, the dreaming mind is able to bypass the prejudices and social pressures that so often prevent us from facing the thoughts of the heart straightforwardly in waking life. The dreaming mind cuts right through the pretension and self-deceptions of the waking mind, riding roughshod over many of our most cherished illusions and showing our feelings for what they really are.

But even this is probably not the whole story about the power of dreams. Brain-wave records indicate that the dreaming brain is even more active than the waking brain, which may mean that it is capable of more work in a given amount of time. My hunch is that the dreaming brain is in a state similar to that produced by the ingestion of psychedelic drugs, when a person experiences things very much more deeply than usual. Computer experts would say that more information per unit time is being *processed* by the brain. Dreaming may show the brain running over the experiences of the previous day or two at a faster rate than in waking life, bringing to our attention all manner of things we have felt or perceived subliminally but have simply not been able to register consciously. This could also account for the dramatic vividness and *exaggeration* of feelings in dreams, both pleasant and unpleasant.

Only further research will show whether this theory of dreaming consciousness is correct, but there can be no doubt that the dreaming mind does offer us a remarkable in-depth review of our lives on a regular night-by-night program, which will enrich and expand us if only we pay attention to it.

—*condensed from* **The Dream Game**, *by Ann Faraday*

BRO, HARMON. EDGAR CAYCE ON DREAMS. 223pp. War68, 1.95p
Many related selections from the seemingly endless library of Cayce readings. This volume should be read after Hugh Lynn Cayce's; it builds on the material presented there and includes many practical exercises. Dr. Bro himself provides a number of insights based on his work in depth psychology and he is the only trained social scientist to have written on Cayce. There is less direct quoting from the readings here than in most of the books, which makes this book more readable than many.

BRUCE, ROBERT. **LACANDON DREAM SYMBOLISM, VOLUME I: DREAM SYMBOLISM AND INTERPRETATION. Extensive notes, 132pp. EdE75, 6.90p.**
The Lacandon Indians live in the Yucatan peninsula in Mexico and are descended from the Mayas. They have an intricate system of dream interpretation which they consider prophetic. The author is an anthropologist who spent a few years living in the Lacandon jungle. In his study he hopes to illuminate the nature of symbolism itself among the Lacandons and thereby gain a deeper understanding into the mindset and belief systems that created the great Maya civilization. Bruce begins this study with a review of the general principles of dream interpretation and symbolism. This is followed by a series of actual dream prophecies, with interpretation and confirmation. The bulk of the volume is devoted to an analysis of the cosmological meaning of the symbolism.

CARTWRIGHT, ROSALIND. **NIGHT LIFE: EXPLORATIONS IN DREAMING. Bibliography, index, 148pp. PrH77, 2.95p.**
A straightforward exploration of dreaming as a psychological process. Drawing on experimental studies conducted in dream research labs, Ms. Cartwright explains our physiological and psychological need to dream, and shows the direct correlation between REM sleep—the dreaming phase—and awakening refreshed and rested after sleep. She analyzes actual dreams and relates dream content to events and emotions which prevail in the waking state. She also investigates the connection between hallucinations, dreams, and madness; offers techniques for improving dream recall; and examines the problem solving function of dreams.

CAYCE, HUGH LYNN. **DREAMS, THE LANGUAGE OF THE UNCONSCIOUS. 94pp. ARE62, 2.50p.**
Includes some of the material derived from the Cayce readings as well as other essays by A.R.E. researchers: *A Psychic Interprets His Dreams*, and *Working with Dreams as Recommended by the Edgar Cayce Readings.*

CORRIERE, RICHARD and JOSEPH HART. **THE DREAM MAKERS. Notes, index, 222pp. Ban77, 1.95p.**
Two psychologists apply their clinical work, laboratory research, and personal exploration to their discovery of breakthrough dreams. They believe that an individual is active and fully aware in a breakthrough dream and they contend that these dreams guide the dreamer toward a fuller, more conscious life. In this book the authors cite case histories and introduce their *Dream Maker Approach*, a step-by-step discussion of how to have breakthrough dreams and how to understand and grow from them.

COLTON, ANN REE. **WATCH YOUR DREAMS. 414pp. NAP73, 10.00c.**
Ms. Coulton has been actively researching the spiritual significance of dreams for many years. In this book she thoroughly explains the

various types of dreams and their accompanying symbols. A detailed and highly instructive account.

COXHEAD, DAVID and SUSAN MILLER. **DREAMS: VISIONS OF THE NIGHT. 8"x11", 96pp. T&H76, 7.95p.**
A beautifully presented pictorial exploration of dreams and *visions of the night* in various cultures and through the ideas of analytical psychology. 110 illustrations, twenty-four in color. Part of the **Art and Cosmos** series.

CRAIG, PAULA. **BUILD YOUR OWN DREAM HOUSE. 44pp. ARE74, 1.25p.**
A dream book for children, based in part on the Edgar Cayce readings. The first part is a general analysis of dreams; the second contains topically arranged blanks for the child to fill in the words or symbols that pertain to a specific object; and the third is a form for making a simplified dream diary.

CRISP, TONY. **DO YOU DREAM? 352pp. Dut71, 4.75p.**
This is a general survey of dream theory and symbolism combined with a dream dictionary. Crisp explains in a simple and practical way how we can gain insight into our dreams and shows how each dream represents something different for each individual. This is not a terribly profound book, but it is serviceable as an introductory overview. The emphasis is on self understanding and Crisp incorporates many current dream theories and supplies a number of suggestions for using your dreams.

DEMENT, WILLIAM. **SOME MUST WATCH WHILE SOME MUST SLEEP. Index, 160pp. S&S72, 4.95p.**
I do feel that my book is a satisfactory and authoritative introduction to the sleep field, readable in an evening or two without inducing drowsiness. At the end, the reader will have some awareness of the major problems of sleep research and the overall complexity of sleep and dream processes as well as a few ways in which knowledge of sleep might be personally helpful. If the book stimulates a desire for further exploration, the Reader's Guide at the end of the book contains a fairly substantial number of suggestions for additional reading. Dement has done extensive sleep research at Stanford University and he reports on his findings in detail.

DUDLEY, GEOFFREY. **DREAMS, THEIR MYSTERIES REVEALED. 64pp. Wei69/TPL, 1.25p.**
An overview.

DUDLEY, GEOFFREY. **HOW TO UNDERSTAND YOUR DREAMS. Index, 109pp. Wil57, 2.00p.**
A general account of the symbolism in different types of dreams, aimed at the individual who wants the simplest exposition possible.

■ *FARADAY, ANN.* **THE DREAM GAME. Bibliography, index, 398pp. H&R74/Pen, 1.95p.**
Dr. Faraday is a noted psychologist. She has written this book in response to many requests for a comprehensive, step-by-step manual on how to understand and use dreams. The first two parts set out the ground rules for keeping a dream diary and understanding the symbolism of dreams. The third part, *Games for Advanced Players*, is based mainly on the author's research over the past two years. Her approach to dreams is based on the pioneering work of Freud and Jung as well as the techniques developed by Calvin Hall, Edgar Cayce, and Fritz Perls.

■ *FARADAY, ANN.* **DREAM POWER. Bibliography, index, 334pp. Ber72/PnB, 1.95p.**
This is an excellent exploration of dreams by a British dream researcher who has trained in hypnotherapy, Freudian analysis, and Jungian depth psychology. The book begins with an outline of modern experimental dream research relevant to dream interpretation and goes on to review the theories of Freud and Jung in this light, drawing from Dr. Faraday's own experiences with patients. She also reviews the more modern approaches to dreams of Calvin Hall and Fritz Perls, who, in very different ways, sought to make dream interpretation more accessible to the average person. Against this background, she describes the method she herself developed in her dream study groups. The book concludes by showing how dreams may be used in all realms of life for greater self awareness.

FREUD, SIGMUND. **THE INTERPRETATION OF DREAMS. Notes, bibliography, index, 768pp. Avo65/Pen, 2.95p.**
This book, first published in 1900, marked the beginning of dream interpretation as we know it today. Many of the theories advanced by Freud in this seminal exploration are still well considered today and are the basis for much of the later work. This translation by James Strachey is the definitive one, incorporating all the alterations, additions, and deletions Freud made over a thirty year period. The detailed commentary and scrupulous cross referencing enable the reader to understand clearly the development of Freud's thought.

FROMM, ERICH. **THE FORGOTTEN LANGUAGE. 263pp. Grv51, 2.95p.**
Interesting discussion by an important modern psychological thinker of Jung's, Freud's, and his own concepts of the nature of the language of the dream. Fromm also relates his concepts to the interpretation of myths, fairy tales, rituals, and the novel.

■ *GARFIELD, PATRICIA.* **CREATIVE DREAMING. Extensive notes, index, 281pp. RaH74/Fut, 2.25p.**
This is a very popular recent book. Dr. Garfield explains how to keep a dream diary; develop control over what you dream; how to plan for *creative dreaming*; practice self suggestion; and how to learn from the experiences of people in other cultures. *You can start dreaming creatively tonight....As you succeed in establishing creative dreaming you will increase your capacity for concentration and recall. You will build a capacity for coping with fear producing dream situations that carries over into the waking state. You will experience pleasurable adventures in your dreams. You will understand yourself better....You will find support and help for waking problems....And all this may be just the beginning.*

GREEN, CELIA. **LUCID DREAMS. 194pp. HHL68, 9.10c.**
A dream is called lucid when the dreamer is aware that he is dreaming and has some degree of voluntary control over the subsequent course of his dream, similar to out-of-the-body experiences. This book is based on case material in the possession of the Institute of Psychophysical Research, and on published accounts of lucid dreams and related phenomena. The sources are all cited.

GUMPERTZ, ROBERT. **DREAM NOTEBOOK. 8"x11", 222pp. SFB76, 7.95p.**
This is a type of blank book for recording dreams. Fanciful pale purple illustrations form the background to each page and a dream-oriented quotation is printed in an upper corner.

HALL, CALVIN. **THE MEANING OF DREAMS. Notes, index, 244pp. MGH66, 3.50p.**
Dr. Hall, Director of the Institute of Dream Research, shows how the dreamer transforms his inner thought into symbols, into a play in which he is author, director and property man, and actor. Dr. Hall's work is quite highly regarded and he writes simply and clearly. This book is a good overview.

HALL, CALVIN and VERNON NORDBY. **THE INDIVIDUAL AND HIS DREAMS. 207pp. NAL72/NEL, 1.95p.**
A good presentation of techniques for scientifically recording and analyzing dream sequences, developed by the authors from years of research. Includes chapters on types of dreams, content, symbols, consistencies, dreams and waking behavior, and a section on analyzing one's own dreams.

HALL, MANLY P. **AN INTRODUCTION TO DREAM INTERPRETATION. 33pp. PRS55, 1.75p.**
Transcription of one of Mr. Hall's lectures.

HALL, MANLY P. **STUDIES IN DREAM SYMBOLISM. 70pp. PRS65, 4.00p.**
Transcriptions of a series of classes. Topics include the dream process, sleep, self instruction through dreams, dream symbols, dreams as mystical experiences and as warnings.

HARTMANN, ERNEST. **THE FUNCTIONS OF SLEEP. Bibliography, index, 198pp. YUP73, 2.95p.**
Hartmann begins with a review of historical and contemporary theories of the functions of sleep and of recent research in sleep deprivation and synchronized (nondreaming) and desynchronized

(dreaming) sleep. Citing his own studies, he investigates the reasons for variable sleep patterns and finds that sleep requirements are influenced by differences in personality, as well as age, life style, and mental state. He then explores the effects on sleep of psychological stress, physical and intellectual activity, and the use of drugs and of other chemicals. The different kinds of tiredness and the role of dreaming in sleep are also studied. This is a sophisticated theoretical presentation, not intended for the layman.

HIRSCH, S. CARL. **THEATER OF THE NIGHT. Bibliography, index, 123pp. RMN76, 6.95c.**
An exploration of dreams written for young readers. Hirsch discusses the creative potential of dreams and looks in on dream and sleep laboratories throughout the world, describing some of the most innovative experiments currently being performed. Many first person accounts are included.

JONES, RICHARD. **THE NEW PSYCHOLOGY OF DREAMING. Notes, index, 238pp. Vik70, 2.95p.**
Jones sets out to reevaluate Freud's original dream theory in the light of the current use of sophisticated laboratory instruments and tests the theory against subsequent theoretical and empirical developments. In effect he has modern psychologists such as Ullman, Angyal, Erikson, Lowy, Piaget, and Hall in a dialogue with Freud, Jung, and Adler.

JUNG, C.G. **DREAMS. 356pp. PUP74, 3.95p.**
This is a collection of some of Jung's most important dream-related writings, composed of selections from **Freud and Psychoanalysis, The Structure and Dynamics of the Psyche, Psychology and Alchemy,** and **The Practice of Psychotherapy.** The book is divided into four parts: *Dreams and Psychoanalysis, Dreams and Psychic Energy, The Practical Use of Dream Analysis,* and *Individual Dream Symbolism in Relation to Alchemy* (including material on the symbolism of the mandala). Fully illustrated throughout, with a very complete index. See the Jung section for more background on his theories.

LEADBEATER, C.W. **DREAMS. 67pp. TPH1898, 1.25p.**
A study of what dreams are and how they are caused. Includes reports of the author's experiments in the dream state.

MACKENZIE, NORMAN. **DREAMS AND DREAMING. 341pp. Van65, 15.00c.**
A fully illustrated discussion of the origin and meaning of dreams. The first section provides an historical survey of dream theories from antiquity to the present—from the idea that dreams were the work of

gods and demons to the latest scientific discoveries about the nature of dreams. The second part reviews psychological concepts of the dream, and the third discusses modern dream research and clinical experiments with *mind revealing drugs.* Many of the more than 300 plates are in color.

MCLEESTER, DICK. **WELCOME TO THE MAGIC THEATER. Illustrations, oversize, 123pp. FFT76, 3.00p.**
An annotated collection of ideas and theories about dream work. The first section is a series of pieces by the author covering topics such as the potential value of dreams, remembering and recording your dreams, and working on dreams. The main part contains an extensive annotated bibliography with excerpts from many of the sources mentioned and a variety of quotations. The sources are organized into types of dream work and a listing (with addresses and personal comments) of the main people working in the field of dreams. A useful reference for all interested in working with dreams.

MAHONEY, MARIA. **THE MEANING IN DREAMS AND DREAMING. Index, 256pp. Stu66, 3.95p.**
This is the best nontechnical review of Carl Jung's dream theory. Ms. Mahoney begins by reviewing Jung's basic dream theories. She goes on to an analysis of archetypes and symbols as seen by Jung and an interpretative analysis of Jung's theories on the persona, the shadow, and the anima and animus. The next section outlines techniques for dreaming and integrating dreams. Final chapters discuss compensatory or complementary dreams, reductive dreams, reactive dreams, prospective dreams, somatic dreams, telepathic dreams, and archetypal dreams.

O'NELL, CARL. **DREAMS, CULTURE, AND THE INDIVIDUAL. Index, 88pp. C&S76, 2.50p.**
A fairly technical discussion of the significance of dreams in human cultural experience, emphasizing ways social and behavioral scientists can utilize dreams in their various approaches to the study of man.

PETERSON, MARILYN. **NIGHTLIGHTS: A DREAM DIARY. ARE77, 4.95p.**
A spiral bound dream notebook, with lined pages facing a photograph and a quotation from one of Edgar Cayce's readings on dreams.

REED, HENRY, ed. **SUNDANCE COMMUNITY DREAM JOURNAL. ARE77, 3.25p/each.**
Reed introduces this journal as follows: *You'll find poetry and art in our journal, along with facts and theories. And because the sharing and comparing of personal experience is at the root of the research process we call science, you'll also find several personal testimonies....Perhaps these testimonies will stimulate some interesting research projects for us to try.* Volume I, numbers one and two, are available thus far. Each is about 140pp.

REGUSH, JUNE and NICHOLAS. **DREAM WORLDS: THE COMPLETE GUIDE TO DREAMS AND DREAMING. 180pp. NAL77, 1.75p.**
A compendium of experiments and explorations for understanding, interpreting, and controlling your dream world. The authors have collected their suggestions from a wide variety of sources.

ROHEIM, GEZA. **THE GATES OF THE DREAM. 5.95p.**
See the Mythology section.

SANFORD, JOHN. **DREAMS: GOD'S FORGOTTEN LANGUAGE. Notes, 223pp. Lip68, 8.95c.**
An exploration of the relationship between dreams and religious experience, drawing on modern psychology and biblical scholarship. The case material comes from the author's counseling (he is an Episcopal rector). A great deal of attention is also devoted to Jungian dream theories. Sanford's intention is *to show the extraordinary at work in the ordinary—to point out the spiritual overtones of meaning which are inherent in the simplest dreams of the most ordinary people.* Originally published by the Jung Institute in Zurich.

■ *SECHRIST, ELSIE.* **DREAMS: YOUR MAGIC MIRROR. 255pp. War68, 1.95p.**
A comprehensive account based on a study of the Edgar Cayce dream readings, explaining the moral, spiritual, and practical meanings of dream incidents and symbols and giving practical step-by-step instruction in dream interpretation. Includes interpretations of hundreds of actual dreams on a great variety of subjects.

SEGAL, JULIUS and GAY LUCE. **SLEEP. Notes, extensive bibliography, index, 364pp. Jov66/HeG, 1.95p.**
An absorbing account of all that is known about sleep: how it affects and renews the body and mind, the nature of dreams and dreaming, and much else. The account is based on the author's scientific research and includes material on REM sleep, alpha waves, biological rhythms, and sleep learning.

SHERWOOD, JANE. **THE FOURFOLD VISION. 224pp. Spe65, 4.00p.**
An interesting study of dreaming and verge-of-sleep experiences. The author uses psychological and scientific discoveries and combines them with information learned by her automatic writing to suggest a coherent theory of the nature of consciousness.

SINGER, JEROME. **THE INNER WORLD OF DAYDREAMING. Bibliography, index, 273pp. H&R75/A&U, 3.45p.**
An interesting study which explores the deeper meaning of daydreams. Singer, a Yale psychologist, contends that daydreams—besides providing spontaneous enjoyment and relief from monotony or frustration— serve as *rehearsals for future action,* a way in which *we can explore a great range of future possibilities without necessarily committing ourselves through action to irrevocable consequences.* The British title is **Daydreaming a Fantasy.**

SPARROW, GREGORY. **LUCID DREAMING. 59pp. ARE76, 2.25p.**
Lucid dreaming is simply the experience of becoming aware that one is dreaming while in the dream. The author, in compiling these selections from the Edgar Cayce readings, notes that Cayce himself did not refer directly to this phenomenon, but since the term itself is a recent one, that is understandable. In tracing Cayce's references to the subject of lucid dreaming, Sparrow studies the selections which refer to astral and out-of-the-body experiences. He also offers extensive commentary.

ULLMAN, MONTAGUE and STANLEY KRIPPNER. **DREAM TELE-PATHY. 2.95p.**
See the Parapsychology section.

WEBB, WILSE. **SLEEP: THE GENTLE TYRANT. Index, 180pp. PrH75, 3.95p.**
A study of the psychology of sleep. The first two chapters are descriptions of the *dimensions and organization of sleep.* The next seven chapters report on and analyze variations in sleep under different conditions. This is followed by two chapters on insomnia and its treatment and an evaluation of the effects of variations in sleep on behavior. Final chapters are devoted to dreams, a review of why we sleep, and answers to the most frequently asked questions about sleep.

WHITE, ROBERT. **THE INTERPRETATION OF DREAMS. Introduction, many notes, index, 259pp. Noy75, 18.90c.**
A translation with commentary of the **Oneirocritica** by Artemidorus, a second century work on dreams which was frequently mentioned by both Freud and Jung. The author was a dream interpreter by profession and the most outstanding characteristic of this volume is its rational, practical approach. The approach is quite serious and while the examples are clearly mythological and classical, today's dreamer can find much to relate to. The exposition is an excellent one and the material is well organized.

ZELLER, MAX. **THE DREAM—THE VISION OF THE NIGHT. 6.00p.**
See the Jungian Psychology section.

EDUCATION

If humankind is to last beyond the next century, then the massive competitive value structure in which people see only the parts of the puzzle of global survival must be dismantled and replaced. This value structure, which pits man against man in competition over limited resources, must give way to an understanding that the earth's limited resources must be shared by all if any are to survive. In a society based on human values, man's most precious resource is his fellow man. If the school has a function for the future, it is to teach our young these human values, these survival skills.

Let there be no mistake about what this means for the classroom. There can be no preaching. Just as skill at tennis is learned by playing tennis, skill at interdependence is learned by working interdependently, and skill at love is learned through loving. It is the teacher's role to foster human values by creating learning opportunities where human values will come into play. And, perhaps even more difficult for the teacher, it is also his role to live by the values he is teaching.

Fortunately for teachers, human values are skills, no less than computation or public speaking: accordingly, they can be learned, with hard work, practice, and perseverance. Yet no skill can be taught in an atmosphere which fails to take account of each student's basic needs for safety, belongingness, love, respect, and self-esteem—as well as the individual's needs for information, knowledge, and wisdom. The boredom and alienation which pervade our schools signify a craving for the satisfaction of those basic needs.

It is the school's chief function to fill these needs, and in filling them to produce individuals who cannot be bored: individuals who have too high a regard for themselves and too clear a view of the needs of society to find themselves with nothing to do. It is the school's function to produce individuals who cannot feel isolated in the midst of mankind, who have the ability to seek out and initiate friendships and associations, the understanding to take part in collaborative efforts, the wisdom to ask for and to give love. It is the school's chief function to produce socially-self-actualizing people, to use Abraham Maslow's phrase.

The school should be a place where each student can develop as an individual and at the same time use his powers to further the larger activities of the group. Unfortunately, as our schools are now set up, most students are trained to develop into rigid, self-interested, and dependent people. Our schools often emphasize passive submission to authority rather than independent thought; conformity rather than diversity; neatness rather than creativity. This schools' exercise of power is often arbitrary rather than responsive to student needs—most demonstrably in the formulation of the curriculum and in determining how and what to grade. All these facts of school life leave their stamp on the student. All support the values of submission to and dependence on authority.

Creative thinking dies in an authoritarian atmosphere, thrives in an atmosphere of psychological freedom and security. When one feels free to speculate, to toy with ideas, to think outrageous and bizarre thoughts, without the threat of lowered self-esteem or the withdrawal of respect, love, friendship, or protection, then one is free to create. When one feels outside forces attempting to control, coerce, limit, or evaluate his thinking, then one feels threatened, and his creative energy is siphoned off into responding to the threat.

Carl Rogers has identified three psychological conditions which foster creativity. The first is *openness to experience*, being continually aware of new perceptions as they come in. The second is *an internal locus of evaluation*. This is perhaps the most fundamental condition for fostering creativity. For the creative individual, the value of his product is not determined by the praise or criticism of outside agents, but by himself. My product is satisfying to me. It fills my basic needs for self-respect, for self-expression, for joy. The third condition is *the ability to play*, to toy with the world. This implies an ability to live for the moment without regard for future consequences. Living for the moment enhances the ability to be open to new experience, to go off on a wild goose chase, to follow a hunch.

How can we imbue the classroom with these conditions that foster creativity? What can we do to allow for spontaneous play and internal evaluation? The answer is not in merely letting everyone do his own thing. The answer lies with the teacher: the teacher who takes delight in novelty, in ambiguity, in absurdity; the teacher who fosters an atmosphere of joy and play and helps supply the materials, words, colors, music, costumes; the teacher who steadfastly refuses to evaluate the creative output of the student, and who helps the student to be strong enough to rely on his own internal evaluation. In the classroom of such a teacher, creativity flourishes.

The distinguishing mark of the creative person is that he can see old problems in new ways. This means accepting, encouraging, and delighting in the new, the different, the unusual. We must educate our young people to think creatively. We must educate them not to see the world as a series of givens, of single right answers, of pre-ordained limitations. We must educate them to survive by teaching them survival skills—by teaching them how to live by human values.

—*condensed from* **Human Values in the Classroom**, *by Robert and Isabel Hawley*

Activity Books

Children have an insatiable curiosity to explore and experience everything around them. It is a whole new world for them and they are not jaded to its wonders as so many adults are. Many parents would like to direct the child's desire to learn and so a great number of books have been written on the subject. Many are excellent and we know countless children who have been delighted with the ones we list. Most are written for children to look through, and are fully illustrated. A parent's ingenuity can often go just so far, so it is helpful to have additional resources.

ALLISON, LINDA. **BLOOD AND GUTS.** 7½"x10" 127pp. 76, 4.95p.
You are many things. You are miles of blood vessels, billions of cells, hundreds of muscles, many thousands of hairs. You are a system of levers, pumps, and bellows. You are electrical charges and chemical reactions. You are a furnace, filters and a fancy computer with a huge memory bank. You are a finely tuned organism with more parts than there are people in New York City. When you think about it, you're pretty incredible. This is a book to help you explore the amazing territory that is inside the bag you live in that you call your skin. It is a book of things to do. It will show you experiments to try, tests to take, tools to make that will help you see and feel and hear what is going on inside. You'll amaze yourself. Illustrated with line drawings

throughout. Part of **The Brown Paper School** series. A delightful, unique book.

ALLISON, LINDA. **THE REASONS FOR SEASONS.** 7½"x10", 125pp. LBC75, 4.95.
This is a neat book, a hundred or so different exercises written and designed for kids and adults to work at together—or just for kids to work with. *This is a book about the trip that the earth makes around the sun. It explains the reasons for seasons. Plus a whole lot more. Inside you will find stuff to do, things to make, ideas to think about, stories to read, and things to inspect, collect, and give away.* All the instructions are clear and the book is illustrated throughout. The material is roughly organized according to things to do in different seasons.

ALLISON, LINDA. **THE SIERRA CLUB SUMMER BOOK.** 8"x8¼", 160pp. Scr77, 4.95p.
This book is for anyone looking for a way to spend a summer day....It tells what's going on in the heavens to make it hot down here on earth. It has stories about animals and instructions for growing weird plants. There are directions for making collections of your natural finds. It has craft projects like knob knitting and basic whittling with a pocketknife. There are hints on sleeping out and getting acquainted with nighttime critters and flitters; plus ways to keep cool, good stuff to send away for, games to play, and toys to make; not to mention projects to get wet with at the beach, and things to think about while you're getting there. It is simply written and illustrated with many line drawings.

BARATTA-LORTON, MARY. **WORKJOBS...FOR PARENTS.** 8½"x 11", 115pp. AdW75, 3.95p.
During the past several years I have been making learning tasks for the children in my classroom built around a single concept I wanted my children to work with. These manipulative skills are designed to help children develop language and numbers skills, as well as more general skills such as hand-eye coordination, observing, seeing relationships, and making judgments....I have selected those activities from the original classroom edition of **Workjobs** *that seem to be the most appropriate for parents to make and use at home.* Each activity includes a general description, ideas for getting started, ideas for follow-up discussion, and a picture of a child doing the activity.

■ *BLAKE, JIM and BARBARA ERNST.* **THE GREAT PERPETUAL LEARNING MACHINE.** Index, 9¼"x11½", 308pp. LBC76, 7.95p.
A whole earth catalog for kids and their parents, subtitled, *being a stupendous collection of ideas, games, experiments, activities, and recommendations for further exploration.* This is far and away the best book we know of its type. It is well organized and lavishly illustrated and is divided into the following general headings: *nature and ecology, science, math, arts and crafts, music and movement, ourselves,* and *language.*

BOGOJAVLENSKY, ANN and DONNA GROSSMAN, et al. **THE GREAT LEARNING BOOK.** Index, 11"x8¼", 164pp. AdW77, 8.50p.
This book is about bringing the real world into the classroom. Its emphasis is practical. It identifies resources for stimulating learning that not many people had previously thought of as appropriate for students to explore in schools. It suggests ways to use these resources and is intended to encourage you to use your own creativity.—from the introduction. The suggestions are extremely varied and include many ideas we have not seen elsewhere. In each case the experience is first outlined and any necessary background information is offered. The discussion includes sections on skills and outcome, materials, and preparation and sequence. Case studies and follow-ups are given. The selections are topically organized.

BOSTON CHILDREN'S MEDICAL CENTER. **WHAT TO DO WHEN "THERE'S NOTHING TO DO".** Index, 186pp. Dia68, 1.95c.
Childcare experts suggest 601 play ideas for babies, toddlers, and two to six year olds using ordinary household items. The ideas are illustrated and arranged according to age groups.

BRAGA, JOSEPH and LAURIE. **CHILDREN AND ADULTS.** Index, 310pp. PrH76, 10.95c.
A fine idea book of *activities for growing together* arranged according to recommended ages and covering the period from birth to six years. Each of the ideas is very fully explored and the descriptive material is divided into the following parts: *participants, materials, explanation* (in steps), *purpose,* and *variations.* A very creative, well planned presentation. Includes an annotated resource list as well as a chapter on learning and growing with children. We get a very good feeling from this book. The Bragas are both developmental psychologists.

BURNS, MARILYN. **THE BOOK OF THINK (OR HOW TO SOLVE A PROBLEM TWICE YOUR SIZE).** 7½"x10", 128pp. LBC76, 4.95p.
This book is about what to do when you are puzzled, or perplexed, or stumped, or can't get there from here. It is about using your noggin. It is about being smart even when you feel dumb. This book is about how to think even when you know you are fresh out of ideas. This is a nicely illustrated collection of ideas, suggestions, and exercises. Part of **The Brown Paper School** series.

BURNS, MARILYN. **I AM NOT A SHORT ADULT: GETTING GOOD AT BEING A KID.** Profusely illustrated, 7½"x10", 125pp. LBC77, 4.95p.
Maybe you've noticed that some of the grownups in your life act like being a kid is mostly about getting ready to be an adult. People who think that way believe that your kidhood is a time for getting ready....This is a book about being a kid now, not preparing for later. Later is going to come no matter what....This book says that there are some things about your life that you control and there are some things about your life that you don't control. That's mostly when grownups take over and decide things for you and about you. This book won't change that. But it can help you take a sharp look at how your life is shaped just because you are a kid, along with some clues about what you might do about that. This book says that if you explore being a kid now in as many ways as you possibly can, you'll be ready for later anyway.

BURNS, MARILYN. **THE I HATE MATHEMATICS BOOK.** 7½"x10", 127pp. LBC75, 4.95p.
This book is for nonbelievers of all ages. It was written especially for kids who have been convinced (by the attitudes of adults) that mathematics is (1) impossible, (2) for those smart kids who can't play stickball, and (3) no fun anyhow. But this book will also do wonders for parents, teachers, or any adult who likes kids. This book says that mathematics is nothing more (nor less) than a way of looking at the world and is not to be confused with arithmetic. The content of mathematics is the same as the content of any kid's life. Why not? In this book you'll find several hundred mathematical events, gags, magic tricks, and experiments to prove it. Beautifully produced, with an abundance of drawings.

CANEY, STEVEN. **KIDS' AMERICA.** 8½"x11", 414pp. WPC78, 6.95p.
A profusely illustrated collection of activities, projects, and adventures.

CANEY, STEVEN. **STEVEN CANEY'S PLAY BOOK.** 9"x8¼", many photographs and drawings, 230pp. WPC75, 4.95p.
Caney is a well known designer and consultant on toys and educational materials. *The book contains more than seventy activities and projects to do, to make, and to play with wherever children are. They use only discards and inexpensive materials found around the house, or at places kids often visit—things like straws, paper cups, cardboard, old tires, pencil and paper, wood scraps, playing cards, and art materials....While all are complete projects in themselves, each provides incentive, and stimulates the imagination for further self-starting play.*—from the foreword.

CANEY, STEVEN. **TOY BOOK.** 9"x8¼", 176pp. WPC72, 3.95p.
This was Caney's first book. Here he tells how to make a variety of toys. He supplies information on the materials needed and instructions on the construction as well as a general description of the toy. Fully illustrated with photographs and line drawings. This has been a very popular book.

CANFIELD, JACK and HAROLD WELLS. **100 WAYS TO ENHANCE SELFCONCEPT IN THE CLASSROOM: A HANDBOOK FOR TEACHERS AND PARENTS.** 7"x9¼", 253pp. PrH76, 8.75p.
This is an excellent sourcebook, coherently written and arranged. It should help sensitize the classroom teacher to the human needs of each of his or her students, as well as provide a rich and comprehensive variety of exercises, experiments and approaches which can be adapted readily to the teacher's unique teaching needs. I recommend it strongly.—George Brown.

CARDOZO, PETER. **THE SECOND WHOLE KID'S CATALOGUE.** 8½"x11", 256pp. Ban77, 7.50p.
This book replaces Cardozo's first one, now out of print. Again it outlines a variety of projects for kids and includes an abundance of information on where to write for things and where to look for further information. It is designed for older kids, although children of all ages will be able to participate in most of the projects. The material is topically organized and illustrated throughout. The catalogue has activities in every field we can think of and it includes activities for both indoors and outdoors.

CASS, JOAN. **HELPING CHILDREN GROW THROUGH PLAY.** 166pp. ScB71, 9.00c.
Delves into the meaning and significance of child's play and its major role in the formation of personality and character. *Play is as necessary and important to a child as the food he eats, for it is the very breath of life to him, the reason for his existence and his assurance of immortality.* Different methods and styles of play are discussed with suggestions for stimulating and improving the quality of child's play and enhancing the materials used.

COLE, ANN, et al. **I SAW A PURPLE COW AND 100 OTHER RECIPES FOR LEARNING.** 96pp. 9¼"x8¾", LBC72, 2.95p.
A multi-colored delightfully illustrated workbook containing many innovative ideas for preschoolers and elementary students.

COLE, ANN, et. al. **A PUMPKIN IN A PEAR TREE: IDEAS FOR TWELVE MONTHS OF HOLIDAY FUN. Many colorful illustra-tions, bibliography,** 9¼"x8¾", 112pp. LBC76, 4.95p.
Holidays have always been times of feasting, singing, dancing, and exchanging gifts, but they have a serious side, too, and understanding something about their true origins will help us to appreciate how and why each is celebrated. **A Pumpkin in a Pear Tree** *offers a chance to sample a variety of ways to enrich our holiday enjoyment...[It] is an imaginative activity book that...features an easy to follow recipe format. The materials required are generally found around the house...We have searched for activities that involve the whole family, bridging the generations by offering something for everyone, from toddlers to grandparents. A delightful presentation, in the same format and style as* **Purple Cow.**

CROFT, DOREEN and ROBERT HESS. **AN ACTIVITIES HANDBOOK FOR TEACHERS OF YOUNG CHILDREN. Illustrations, spiral bound,** 8½"x11", 207pp. HMC75, 11.00p.
This is a sophisticated, extremely complete handbook. All of the activities come from actual classroom experience and may be used either as central elements of a curriculum or as supplementary programs. Most are tailored for early education programs, but they can also be easily used at home. The major sections are devoted to language abilities, science, the arts, pre-math experiences, and cooking. The activities are clearly presented, each contains a good introduction, and each is followed by an excellent annotated reading list.

FIAROTTA, PHYLLIS. **SNIPS, SNAILS AND WALNUT WHALES.** 9"x8¼", 283pp. WPC75, 4.95p.
This is a book of nature crafts for children. It shows how nature provides the artist or craftsman with raw materials as well as the sense of form, color, and harmony from which all beautiful or useful things are born. In making the projects found here, your children explore the relationship between natural things and the created object and come to know nature better while learning to use it in new and imaginative ways....All specific measurements (inches and feet) are omitted, leaving the total creative process to the young artisan. Drawings accompany each craft project, and in some cases step-by-step illustrations are included.—from the foreword.

FIAROTTA, PHYLLIS. **STICKS AND STONES AND ICE CREAM CONES.** 9"x8⅛", 319pp. WPC73, 4.95p.
A step-by-step presentation of more than 120 craft projects, toys, and games for children. Fully illustrated with photographs and line drawings throughout. This is a very popular book.

FIAROTTA, PHYLLIS and NOEL. **BE WHAT YOU WANT TO BE. Index,** 8½"x11", 304pp. WPC77, 5.95p.
The Fiarottas suggest ways that kids can dress up and pretend to take part in thirty-four occupations through more than 275 craft projects. In the process the kids can learn about what is involved in these occupations. Clear instructions and lots of illustrations.

FIAROTTA, PHYLLIS and NOEL. **PIN IT, TACK IT, HANG IT.** 9"x8¼", 288pp. WPC75, 4.95p.
Hundreds of carefully explained, illustrated bulletin board activities. The authors have done a good job of selecting interesting activities and writing them up in a lively fashion.

FIAROTTA, PHYLLIS and NOEL. **THE YOU AND ME HERITAGE TREE: ETHNIC CRAFTS FOR CHILDREN. Many illustrations,** 9"x8¼", 283pp. WPC76, 4.95p.
Step-by-step instructions for more than 100 craft projects drawn from twenty-two different ethnic traditions. A good way to help kids learn about other cultures.

FLEMMING, BONNIE and DARLENE HAMILTON. **RESOURCES FOR CREATIVE TEACHING IN EARLY CHILDHOOD EDUCATION.** 8½"x11", 738pp. HBJ77, 17.40p.
An excellent manual which we recommend highly to those involved in early childhood education. *The book combines a quick reference for basic information about a great many subjects and a practical, scannable format. It is perforated and three-hole punched so that it can be used in a loose-leaf binder....A section of the book describes games, dramatic play props, music and art accessories, and playground equipment that can be inexpensively made by the teacher. Commercial games, records, and their manufacturers, as well as a concise bibliography, are also included. The book deals with a variety of subjects presented as guides and grouped under the general headings Self Concept, Families, Family Celebrations, Seasons, Animals, Transportation, and The World I Live In.*—from the introduction.

FOUKE, GEORGE. **FIRST BOOK OF SPACE MAKING.** 64pp. GeB74, 2.95p.
An 8½"x11" book containing step-by-step instructions for making various kinds of geometric forms. The illustrations are large and the directions are clear.

GORDON, IRA. **BABY LEARNING THROUGH BABY PLAY. Many illustrations,** 8¼"x11", 121pp. SMP70, 3.95p.
A collection of exercises designed to develop a baby's motor skills and awareness of his or her environment. We are not really sure that a baby needs these exercises, but if you want a book like this, this one seems as good as any. The exercises are arranged according to age (the book covers the period up to age two).

GORDON, IRA, BARRY GUINAGH, and R.E. JESTER. **CHILD LEARN-ING THROUGH CHILD PLAY. Well-illustrated,** 8¼"x11", 116pp. SMP72, 3.95p.
The years between two and four are special because so much happens in the child's use of speech and language. The child uses language not only to extend his intellectual development but also as a way of knowing and handling his feelings. Of special importance at this time is the way in which parents and other adults play with, work with, and care for him....The purpose of this book is to provide specific, concrete, realistic learning opportunities for you to present to a child in a positive and loving fashion....Their primary aim is to foster intellectual and language development. Included are suggestions for involving other children...so that the child will have opportunities for both a one to one relationship with an adult and interaction with other children.

HAWLEY, ROBERT and ISABEL. **DEVELOPING HUMAN POTEN-TIAL: A HANDBOOK OF ACTIVITIES FOR PERSONAL AND SOCIAL GROWTH. Bibliography,** 92pp. ERA75, 5.80p.
The purpose of this book is to give teachers and other group leaders specific activities to use for the following purposes: First, to develop the creative potential of their students. Second, to help young people become more aware of their own totality of being—of their impact on other people and things and upon themselves, and of the nature and extent of outside influences and forces which shape their lives. Third, to help young people to take conscious control over their lives so that they can become more effective as persons. Fourth, to combat the spectator-consumer psychology which is so prevalent in today's culture. This is an extremely practical handbook.

HENDRICKS, GAY and THOMAS ROBERTS. **THE SECOND CENTER-ING BOOK.** 344pp. PrH77, 4.95p.
A follow up to Ms. Hendricks' extremely successful earlier book showing how to use meditation, dreams, fantasy, and other techniques to help children become relaxed, alert, and whole. Both verbal and nonverbal activities are included, all of which are geared toward helping children get in touch with their minds, emotions, and bodies. The material is geared toward parents, teachers, and counselors. The last 100 pages are devoted to an excellent annotated bibliography and resource guide. We recommend this book heartily to all who are interested in transpersonal education.

■ *HENDRICKS, GAY and RUSSELL WILLS.* **THE CENTERING BOOK.** 180pp. PrH75, 3.95p.
There is a feeling of balance, a feeling of inner strength that we feel when we are centered. To feel centered is to experience one's psychological center of gravity—a solid integration of mind and body.... This book contains activities that people use to help themselves feel centered; all of the techniques can be used in the classroom and in the home, and they can be used by people of all ages....Schools place a great deal of emphasis on the development of cognitive, rational, and intellectual processes. To balance this emphasis, **The Centering Book** *provides the core of a curriculum for the development of affective, intuitive, and creative processes in students...(in addition) this book can...be used in the home to provide a set of activities that parents and children can use to explore new levels of awareness together. The sources of the activities include yoga, Zen, movement, imagery, relaxation training, the Senoi people of the Central Malay Peninsula, and the Sufi tradition.* This is a wonderful collection, very well put together and complete with detailed instructions, clear descriptions of the exercises, and illustrations where applicable. The table of contents reads as follows: *Basic Centering, Relaxing the Mind, Expanding Perception, Relaxing the Body, Working with Dreams, Imagery, Stretching the Body, Movement and Dance,* and *Storytelling.* There is also a topical listing of recommended books.

JOBB, JAMIE. **THE NIGHT SKY BOOK.** 7½"x10", 127pp. LBC77, 4.95p.
Many people know stars and planets by name. You can too. To help you become familiar with the night sky, this book is divided into five parts. Part One tells how people find directions using the stars, even when they're lost at sea. Part Two shows how to find your place on earth or any other globe. Part Three tells about the zodiac, the moon, and time. Part Four sizes up the solar system. And Part Five looks at stars and other sights in the night sky. Clocks, sticks, rocks, record players, and other everyday objects can show you a lot about the stars. But the best way to learn about the stars is to watch them. Turn out the lights and go outside. The book is part of **The Brown Paper School** series and is profusely illustrated.

JORDE, PAULA. **THE KIDS DO IT BOOK.** 8½"x11", 70pp. GIP76, 3.95p.
An excellent collection of projects and activities that a parent can use with preschoolers to help shape their intellectual and emotional development. Includes chapters on the following topics: *sensory aware-ness, getting ready to read and write, learning math concepts, discovery through science, creating through art and music,* and *what's cooking.* This is a revised, expanded, and updated version of **Living and Learning with Children.** Illustrated throughout.

KOHL, JUDITH and HERBERT. **THE VIEW FROM THE OAK: THE PRIVATE WORLDS OF OTHER CREATURES.** Index, 7¼"x9", 112pp. Scr77, 4.95p.
There are many different worlds on our planet, and this book explores the strange and marvelous ways in which a variety of living crea-tures—ranging from whales to spiders—experience space, sense time, and communicate with others of their kind. It is based on a science called ethology, the study of how an animal behaves in its habitat. The Kohls have included activities and illustrations designed to help the reader enter these different worlds through an understanding of the senses of the animals themselves. Reading this book took us into extraordinary spaces and greatly increased our understanding of the other living beings on this planet.

MCDIARMID, NORMA, MARI PETERSON and JAMES SUTHERLAND. **LOVING AND LEARNING.** Glossary, bibliography, index, 309pp. HBJ75, 3.95p.
Working on the premise that it is the emotional component which provides the basis for a child's intellectual and social development, the authors show how love, physical contact, and simple interaction with a baby or toddler will foster the child's curiosity and lead to an emotional stability that will have a profound effect on his later life. The emphasis is on play as a learning stimulus and the book includes many activities, exercises, and games to stimulate a child from shortly after birth to the age of three. It describes yoga exercises, new reading techniques, feeling and touching games, and ways to make musical instruments, puppets, and books. The material is arranged according to the age of the child.

MACLATCHIE, SHARON. **GARDENING WITH KIDS.** Index, 233pp. Rod77, 7.95c.
If the idea of gardening with your children turns you on then this is the book for you....Each chapter, whether about how to get started with summer vegetables, how to beat the bugs, or how to garden indoors, offers every child something he can do....Whatever your gardening skill, begin first by remembering how a child experiences the world, then participate with him. Many photographs ac-company the text.

MADARAS, LYNDA. **CHILD'S PLAY.** 152+pp. Pce77, 6.95p.
An imaginative collection of games and toys and things to do which young children can enjoy and learn from. The first chapter explains how to put a playgroup together. Photographs and children's line drawings accompany each suggested activity, along with ample instructions. Ms. Madaras suggests many activities that we have not seen in other books.

MAID, AMY and ROGER WALLACE. **NOT JUST SCHOOLWORK: NEW DIRECTIONS IN WRITTEN EXPRESSION.** 8½"x11", 201pp. Man76, 11.70p.
This is a humanistic approach to the development of writing skills and creative writing which is designed to help students create expressions which arise out of their actual life experiences. The book is handwrit-ten and can be used by the student himself. It is divided into four major sections that focus on the many possibilities of creative thinking: perceptions of the world, creative story writing, spelling, writing the news, holidays, moods, and science fiction.

MARZOLLO, JEAN. **SUPERTOT.** Index, 9¼"x6¼", 167pp. H&R77, 11.95c.
What makes one to three year olds both wonderful and frustrating is that they want to learn about everything...if they can get their hands on it, if they can just see it they are interested. To them, the world is brand new, and they are experiencing it for the first time. By the time they are three years old, they will have spent more than a thousand days examining what's around them; they will have absorbed a good deal of information and come to some conclusions of their own about the fruits of learning, conclusions that may stay with them for the rest of their lives. Unfortunately, some children will conclude that our curiosity leads to trouble and that questions annoy adults. [Others] will have concluded that learning is a busy and joyful business that brings personal rewards as well as appreciation and encouragement from the people they love. This book provides a collection of stimulating play situations for one to three year olds. It is the best book we have seen on the subject. An abundance of illustrations accompany the text.

MARZOLLO, JEAN and JANICE LLOYD. **LEARNING THROUGH PLAY.** Index, 9¼"x6¼", 211pp. H&R72, 3.45p.
Learning Through Play *is an all-day, every-day book aimed at the parents of preschool children. It is a deft translation of the weightiest and most advanced findings of educational scientists into a lighthearted collection of games, projects, amusements and conversational gambits designed to stimulate and satisfy the preschooler's twin appetites for fun and knowledge....The dozens of activities listed in the book are divided into eleven chapters corresponding to what the authors call basic skill-families: The Five Senses, Language Development, Pre-reading, Understanding Relationships, Sorting and Classifying, Counting and Measuring, Problem Solving, Exploring, Creativity, Self-Esteem,* and *Physical Growth.* The activities are described well and the book is illustrated throughout.

MAXIM, GEORGE. **LEARNING CENTERS FOR YOUNG CHIL-DREN.** Bibliography, 169pp. Har77, 7.95p.
The core of this book consists of scores of blueprints for specific learning centers in a variety of subject areas. These activities are designed to build concepts and skills, while promoting creativity and growth in attitudes and values. The activities have been successfully used in many classroom situations with children between the ages of five and thirteen. Many simple drawings illustrate the activities.

NICKELSBURG, JANET. **NATURE ACTIVITIES FOR EARLY CHILD-HOOD. Illustrations, bibliography, 11"x8½", 167pp. AdW76, 7.50p.**
A collection of forty-four projects and activities which are designed to help children develop their senses, sharpen their powers of observation, and expand their appreciation of nature by experiencing their natural surroundings directly. The book is divided into the following major sections: outdoor group projects, projects with small animals, indoor projects, watching things, looking for things in the ground, and projects with plants. The text uses fairly simple terms; however, very young children could not read the book themselves. Most of the projects are ones in which the children would need a minimum of adult guidance.

PETRICH, PATRICIA and ROSEMARY DALTON. **THE KIDS' ARTS AND CRAFTS BOOK. Hand lettered, index, 8¼"x5¼", 184pp. Nit75, 4.95p.**
An imaginative collection of arts and crafts suggestions—all of which are simple enough for a young child to make on his or her own. Each of the suggestions is well explained and every page is illustrated with color and black and white drawings. Where adult help is needed, this is noted and some general instructions are offered.

PETRICH, PATRICIA and ROSEMARY DALTON. **THE KIDS' GARDEN BOOK. Index, 8½"x5¼", 184 pp. Nit74, 3.95p.**
A hand drawn, brightly colored book which gives simple instructions for a number of things that kids can do both with outdoor gardening and with houseplants. Lots of excellent hints are included as well as basic information about the tools needed and how to care for a great variety of plants.

SABO, JUDIE and CHRISTINA HARRISON. **ART EXPRESSIONS FOR YOUNG HANDS. Bibliography, 8½"x8½", 125pp. PFP76, 6.95p.**
Say Yes! to art . . . and teach young people to say yes too. Children see vibrant compositions in Nature. They are aware of texture, color, and shape at a very early age. Some are inspired to communicate what they see and feel by creating a tangible expression of an idea out of material things. . . . To help others experience art and say yes to art is why this book is. We do not intend this book to be an all-in-one study of the many art forms that exist. Rather, it is a compilation of experiences that we found to be valuable in our classrooms. . . . All of the art expressions in this book are experientially oriented. The doing of the art becomes the most important learning tool. This is far and away the best book of this type we have ever seen. All the exercises are clearly presented and the book is illustrated throughout.

SAVA, S. **LEARNING THROUGH DISCOVERY FOR YOUNG CHILDREN. 156pp. MGH75, 7.95c.**
A practical, well written book, designed as a handbook for teachers as well as a guide for parents. Dr. Sava begins by tracing the pioneering efforts of Montessori, Gesell, Bloom, Hunt, Piaget, and others. The major part of the book is devoted to a section entitled *activity centers*. This is divided into eight chapters and it details practical activities in the following areas: creative play, art and sculpture, cooking, woodworking, language, numbers, music and movement, and nature and science. The book is well produced and photographs are interspersed. There is also an excellent nineteen page bibliography. This is an excellent toolbook for the preschool teacher.

SCHNEIDER, TOM. **EVERYBODY'S A WINNER. 7½"x10", 139pp. LBC76, 4.95p.**
Right now a lot of people are changing their minds about playing sports. There are new games. There are new ways to play the old ones. And maybe most important, there are new ways to think about winning and losing. It turns out that winning might have more to do with what you learn and how you feel than it does with ribbons or prizes or being best. It turns out that maybe everybody is a winner—or could be. This book tells about new games and new ideas and what they might mean to you.—from the introduction. Like all **The Brown Paper School** *books, this is a delightful, fully illustrated volume.*

SHAKESBY, PAUL. **CHILD'S WORK. 8½"x11", 112pp. RuP74, 4.95p.**
In one sense, this is a book about homemade toys which offer sound education as well as good fun and enjoyable work for your child. Yet on another level, the true subject of these pages is the relationship between parent and child. For it is only through your involvement in making the toys and using them with your child that this book will fulfill its purpose. . . . If you enjoy being with your child, sharing the experiences of learning, growth and discovery, then you will appreciate the kind of involvement this book demands. This is a well laid out and extremely well illustrated manual with sections covering sensory awareness, manual dexterity, size, shape, and form, numbers, and language. Suggested age groups are given for the activities.

SINGER, DOROTHY and JEROME. **PARTNERS IN PLAY: A STEP-BY-STEP GUIDE TO IMAGINATIVE PLAY IN CHILDREN. Recommended reading and listening lists, index, 215pp. H&R77, 10.95c.**
The human imagination is still one of the great untapped resources for the development of the growing child's ability to learn, to evolve a sense of self, and simply to enjoy the pleasures of his or her own creative capacities. . . . This book has grown out of extensive research by ourselves and others and our own direct involvement with preschoolers. We have explored a range of exercises and games to help preschool children expand their imaginative horizons and enjoy their own play more. . . . Our format consists of brief general discussions of the importance of different aspects of make-believe play and imagination in healthy growth, followed by a series of specific exercises or games. A delightful book.

SPARKMAN, BRANDON and JANE SAND. **PREPARING YOUR PRE-SCHOOLER FOR READING: A BOOK OF GAMES. Index, 7"x9½", 117pp. ScB77, 7.95c.**
A collection of eighty-four visual games and fifty-six listening games, all designed to improve children's visual and auditory skills. The activities are presented in sequential order and are illustrated.

STEIN, SARA. **THE KIDS' KITCHEN TAKEOVER. 9"x8¼", 208pp. WPC75, 4.95p.**
The Kids' Kitchen Takeover *is more than a compilation of recipes for children. This book contains a variety of child-tested ideas for hours of pleasure in the kitchen. There are things to do which require nothing more than supplies found in any pantry; there are experiments with leftovers; there are projects to do outdoors; there are tricks to play; there are pets to keep; there are plants to grow; and plenty of craft suggestions. . . . The craft, design, and sculpture projects included give the kids freedom to use their own imaginations. We've only mentioned exact amounts, times, and temperatures where it was absolutely necessary. . . . There are enough things to do in this book to interest your children from ages five through twelve.*

WILKINS, MARNE. **LONG AGO LAKE: A CHILD'S BOOK OF NATURE LORE AND CRAFTS. Many excellent illustrations, bibliography, index, 160pp. Scr78, 5.95p.**
Ms. Wilkins spent her childhood summers in the Wisconsin north country and was close friends with Chippewa Indian boys. In this wonderful book she retells her memories and shares the skills and knowledge she obtained. She includes information on plants and birds, meadows and prairies, forests and trees, and much else. She also provides instructions on how to make pine needle baskets, clay pots, rush mats, and more than thirty other crafts. This is a unique book, rich in lore and practical advice and written in a simple, interesting way.

──────END OF ACTIVITY BOOKS SUBSECTION──────

AKMAKJIAN, HIAG. **THE NATURAL WAY TO RAISE A HEALTHY CHILD. Bibliography, index, 318pp. HRW75, 4.95p.**
While we do not agree with all the advice that is offered on these pages, a great many useful suggestions are made. The book is based on the author's professional experience and it is the result of the hundreds of questions the author has been asked by parents. His major thesis is that the key to a baby's mental health is the dependable emotional availability of his parents. The book is written in a nontechnical style and covers a lot of ground.

ASHTON-WARNER, SYLVIA. **SPEARPOINT. 222pp. RaH72, 1.95p.**
Ms. Ashton-Warner's **Teacher** has profoundly influenced the education of small children around the world and she has been invited to observe and consult with schools in England, Israel, and Asia. Recently she was invited to bring her *organic teaching* to an American experimental school in Colorado. In this book she pours out her impressions, feelings, and intuitions about the American children she worked with, their teachers, their schooling, and their world.

ASHTON-WARNER, SYLVIA. **TEACHER. Illustrations, 191pp. Ban63, 1.50p.**
Miss Ashton-Warner believes that she has discovered a method of teaching that can make the human being naturally and spontaneously peaceable. Agressiveness, an "instinct" without which wars could not arise or be conducted, is the name we give to mental or emotional reactions caused by the frustration of the child's inherited drives: self-preservation and sexual gratification. Education as normally practiced throughout

the world ignores these main interests. By recognizing and even welcoming their presence in the child and making them the foundation of an "organic" method of teaching, these interests can be allowed expression and be at the same time moulded into patterns of constructive delight. This is a first person account of what happened in the classes that Ms. Ashton-Warner taught in New Zealand for twenty-four years. It is considered a landmark work.

AUROBINDO, SRI and THE MOTHER. **ON EDUCATION. 2.00p.**
See the Indian Philosophy section.

AXLINE, VIRGINIA. **DIBS IN SEARCH OF SELF. RaH64, 1.75p.**
Dibs is a perceptive study of a disturbed adolescent; it is the portrait of a little boy achieving under therapy a successful struggle for identity. To anyone who has, or expects to have, contact with small children, this book is a deeply moving experience.

BARTH, ROLAND. **OPEN EDUCATION AND THE AMERICAN SCHOOL. Index, notes, 320pp. ScB72, 3.95p.**
Barth is the principal of an elementary school in Newton, Massachusetts, and was formerly Assistant to the Dean of the Harvard Graduate School of Education. This account is solidly rooted in the author's own personal experience and academic research and is considered one of the best accounts of open education available. Barth begins with a theoretical analysis of some assumptions about learning and knowledge. The next section is devoted to a discussion of the teacher and the open classroom. This is followed by a case study of what actually happened at the school Barth is at. A final section investigates the principal and the open classroom. There is also an excellent fifty-plus page annotated bibliography of books and curriculum materials (including addresses).

BENNETT, HAL. **NO MORE PUBLIC SCHOOLS. 137pp. RaH72, 2.95p.**
A complete step-by-step guide and idea book. It includes materials and information one would need for withdrawing one's child from public school, starting one's own school, gathering essentials, structuring the day, and operating efficiently. Also includes a bundle of ideas and suggestions for operating a school on limited funds.

BERENDS, POLLY. **WHOLE CHILD/WHOLE PARENT. Index, 301pp. H&R75, 6.95p.**
Besides providing a sound philosophical interpretation of the early child-rearing years, **Whole Child/Whole Parent** offers practical guidelines for the construction, purchase, and use of specific toys, books, learning materials, and nursery equipment. Included are annotated bibliography of direct mail catalogues, toy making, and play activity books, and nearly 500 books for children under four. The book is 8½"x9" and topically organized under the following headings: *spirit; happiness and fulfillment; freedom; unity; beauty; truth;* and *love.* The material is garnered from a wide variety of sources and the text includes many relevant quotations. A well done, unusual book.

BLAKE, HOWARD. **CREATING A LEARNING CENTERED CLASSROOM. Bibliography, 338pp. Har77, 8.95p.**
A teacher who attempts to teach the same things to each of his students at the same time and expects them to learn at the same pace and in the same way is being totally unrealistic. Children do not learn by being talked at; they need to explore, to question, to experiment, and to formulate their own solutions. By creating learning centers, a teacher does much more than organize the classroom—he deals effectively with children's individual needs. This book discusses learning centered teaching, both the theory and the practice. Blake tells you how to get started, choose a model that suits you, organize and manage your classroom, keep track of each child's progress and much more. Sample learning centers in all curriculum areas are included.

BLESSINGTON, JOHN. **LET MY CHILDREN WORK. 184pp. Dou74, 2.95p.**
An informally written account of the state of formal and informal education in the U.S. today. Blessington, an educator and a parent, feels that the changes that have taken place are basically cosmetic and much still remains to be done. The book suggests the major flaws and presents some constructive and creative plans for resolving them.

BORTON, TERRY. **REACH, TOUCH AND TEACH. Illustrations, 213pp. MGH70, 3.95p.**
The title of this book, by one of the most sane and humane teachers around, could not be more apt. This is a powerful description of a way of teaching that really does have the personal development of kids as its central purpose. Moving and practical. Includes an excellent selection of firms and resources.

BOWER, T.G.R. **THE PERCEPTUAL WORLD OF THE CHILD. Illustrations, notes, bibliography, 90pp. HUP77, 2.95p.**
Professor Bower takes the reader on a tour through the ingenious experiments that have given psychologists new insight into the perceptual world of the child. These experiments have revealed an extremely sophisticated perceptual system that permits the infant to see an organized three dimensional world right from the start. This system is also extraordinarily vulnerable during development. It needs the proper sights and sounds to grow on, just as the muscles need appropriate exercise. Bower demonstrates that these needs have important implications for the way in which we provide stimulation for normal infants, as well as for our efforts to overcome sensory deficiencies in handicapped children.

BRAGA, JOSEPH and LAURIE. **GROWING WITH CHILDREN. Bibliography, 205pp. PrH74, 2.95p.**
A humanistically-oriented study of childrearing relating the parents' growth to their children's development. The needs, capabilities, and limitations of children from birth to six years are studied, the most noted authorities are cited, and many practical hints from the authors' own experiences as parents and as developmental psychologists are offered.

BRAZELTON, T. BERRY. **INFANTS AND MOTHERS. Index, 7"x10", 296pp. Del69, 6.95p.**
This is a pictorial month-by-month study of the development of a baby in its first year. Three general types are individually studied: quiet, active, and average. Individual infants are traced, giving continuity to the narrative. The aim is to show parents different ways that an infant can develop.

BRAZELTON, T. BERRY. **TODDLERS AND PARENTS. Many photographs, index, 7"x10", 267pp. Del74, 6.95p.**
Utilizing the format that was so successful in his earlier work, Dr. Brazelton explores the period between one year and two and a half years when children are struggling for independence and often challenging the patience and understanding of everyone around them, as well as growing, changing, and learning very swiftly. Each chapter is a realistic family profile, recreating with tenderness and humor the life of one particular small child and the brothers and sisters, parents, or other adults shaping his or her life. Woven into the narrative are Dr. Brazelton's professional insights and advice.

BROWN, GEORGE I. **HUMAN TEACHING FOR HUMAN LEARNING. 298pp. Vik71, 2.95p.**
In this humanistic manual of education, the author is concerned with the feeling and thinking content of the child's learning. This approach to learning is called confluent education and deals with the total integration of feeling and thinking and the quality and results of their interaction. One purpose of the book is to demonstrate that school can be a place where both teachers and students can have a richer, deeper, and more meaningful experience of growth in learning.

BROWN, GEORGE I., ed. **THE LIVE CLASSROOM. Bibliography, 306pp. Vik75, 3.50p.**
The book contains theory illustrated by practice, and practice underlined by theory or explanation. These teaching and learning practices take as their philosophical base a combination of several theories of learning and growing: gestalt therapy (here termed Gestalt Awareness Training) and Roberto Assagioli's psychosynthesis. The authors share their own classroom experiences. The range is from first grade through high school and covers a variety of subjects including science, social studies, mathematics, English, art, and foreign languages.

BUCKMAN, PETER, ed. **EDUCATION WITHOUT SCHOOLS. 134pp. Sou73, 2.10p.**
A collection of essays which show how education can be a lifelong process of exploring and discovering the workings of the world. Their purpose is not merely to make out a case against schools, but to point to ways in which a true education can be pursued without them. Contributors include Ivan Illich and a number of noted British educators.

CAPLAN, FRANK, ed. **PARENTS' YELLOW PAGES. 7"x10¼", 511pp. Dou77, 7.95p.**
This alphabetical resource directory was put together by the Princeton Center for Infancy. Every area we can think of is covered at length and innumerable suggestions are made for further information on a particular subject.

CAPLAN, FRANK and THERESA. **THE POWER OF PLAY. Bibliography, index, 334pp. Dou73, 3.95p.**
An exposition of the belief, supported by leading psychologists, that play is a child's natural way of life, developing the child's intelligence, skills, and general capacity to grow, as well as encouraging self discovery and self confidence. The book also covers the various phases of physical and mental development throughout childhood. The authors were the founders of Creative Playthings.

CARMICHAEL, CARRIE. **NON-SEXIST CHILDRAISING. Notes, bibliography, 174pp. Bea77, 9.95c.**
In the last ten years the women's movement has raised the consciousness of the nation. Laws have been changed, the language has been altered, and old habits have been challenged. Parents who believe in the equality of the sexes are breaking important new ground in the method of childraising. Alone or in small groups, these feminist mothers and fathers are working to develop techniques to raise children into fair-minded, nonsexist adults. . . . Essentially this book is a report on how the project of rearing nonsexist children is going. . . . My sources are parents and feminist families all over the country. . . . They shared with me the techniques they are using, their successes, their theories. . . . My sources are the psychologists, psychiatrists, pediatricians, and educators who deal with these frontier families.

CASTILLO, GLORIA. **LEFT-HANDED TEACHING: LESSONS IN AFFECTIVE EDUCATION. Annotated bibliography, 249pp. HRW78, 8.00p.**
Traditionally, public schools have had as their main focus the development of

cognitive skills. But today many experts. . .insist that the development of cognitive skills is not enough. They say that we also need to deal with the affective dimensions of students—their interests, concerns, fears, anxieties, joys, and other personal and emotional reactions they bring to the learning situation. . . . The goal of this book is not to have teachers use their right or left hands exclusively in teaching, but to equip them to use both with equal skill; not to teach cognitive or affective lessons but to have cognitive and affective dimensions available in each and every learning situation.—from the preface. Sample lessons are included in many study areas.

COFFIN, PATRICIA. **1, 2, 3, 4, 5, 6—HOW TO UNDERSTAND AND ENJOY THE YEARS THAT COUNT. 159pp. McM72, 4.95p.**
A lovely, 8"x11" photographic and word essay about the development of the author's daughter from one to six. The daughter, now eighteen, offers her own comments. The theme is how the human traditions of family love are the sources of the child's own humanity, her capacity to love and to embrace the values of the human community.

COHEN, DOROTHY. **THE LEARNING CHILD—GUIDELINES FOR PARENTS AND TEACHERS. 360pp. RaH72, 2.45p.**
Gives commendable answers to such questions as: how does a child learn?, why is the seventh year such a turning point in the child's life?, what are the limits to learning at any given age?, etc. The entire presentation is stimulating and challenging and the research and qualified resources utilized, such as Piaget and the author's own experience as a child development instructor, lend credibility and authoritativeness to the author's conclusions. A highly recommended guidebook for both parents and teachers.

DENNISON, GEORGE. **THE LIVES OF CHILDREN. 308pp. RaH69, 1.95p.**
A journal of the author's experiences with twenty-three children in a small New York private school: *. . .there is no book that I know of that shows so well what a free and humane education can be like, nor is there a more eloquent description of its philosophy.*—Herbert Kohl.

DODSON, FITZHUGH. **HOW TO PARENT. 457pp. NAL70, 2.25p.**
Many of today's parents were raised in what is referred to as the permissive generation. Things have now come full circle and these new parents are looking for effective ways to discipline their children. Dr. Dodson is a psychologist and he has a positive and humanistic approach to childrearing, witness the following quotation: *Your child's self concept is the mental image he has of himself. How successful he will be in school and in later life will depend upon how strong and positive his self concept is. Remember that our ultimate goal in disciplining a child is to help him become a self-regulating person, and that the extent to which he will become self-regulating will depend upon the strength of his self-concept.* A long annotated list of recommended reading is included.

DUNN, JUDY. **DISTRESS AND COMFORT. Photographs, notes, index, 127pp. HUP77, 2.95p.**
One of the first serious questions any new parent must deal with is *Why is my baby crying?* Ms. Dunn takes this question as a starting point, shows how experienced parents answer it, and moves on to many other areas including the following: what is it about a parent's comforting behavior that actually soothes the child? Do the speed and quality of a parent's response to a baby's cries affect her intellectual or emotional development? The information is based on extensive research.

ELIAS, J. **CONSCIENTIZATION AND DESCHOOLING: FREIRE'S AND ILLICH'S PROPOSALS FOR RESHAPING SOCIETY. Bibliography, 170pp. Wes76, 12.95c.**
This is the first book to give an extended analysis of Freire's and Illich's ideas that emphasizes the religious dimension of their thought. Elias portrays both men as reformers, Christian humanists, social critics, theorists of different kinds of revolution, and constructive theorists of education.

ERNST, KEN. **GAMES STUDENTS PLAY (AND WHAT TO DO ABOUT THEM). Notes, bibliography, 127pp. CeA72, 4.50p.**
Ernst is a California high school teacher who studied under Eric Berne for ten years. In this book he uses the transactional analysis model to solve problems in schools—problems about students, parents, teachers, and administrators. Many case histories based on his own experience are included.

FABER, ADELE and ELAINE MAZLISH. **LIBERATED PARENTS, LIB-ERATED CHILDREN. Index, 238pp. Avo74, 1.95p.**
This is a description of the practical application of Dr. Hiam Ginott's nonviolent method of communication: instead of threats, choices are offered; cooperation is invited, not demanded; children's feelings are accepted rather than denied.

FANTINI, MARIO, ed. **ALTERNATIVE EDUCATION: A SOURCE BOOK FOR PARENTS, TEACHERS, STUDENTS AND ADMINIS-TRATORS. Bibliography, index, 517pp. Dou76, 4.50p.**
A collection of basically professional papers divided into the following sections: *The Alternative Movement, Free and Independent Alternative Schools, Alternatives Within the System, Implementation of Public School Alternatives, Developing Alternatives District-wide: Minneapolis Story, Evaluating Alternatives, Financing Alternative Schools, Politics,* and *Teacher Preparation for Alternative Schools.*

FLYNN, ELIZABETH and JOHN LAFASO. **DESIGNS IN AFFECTIVE EDUCATION. Index, 8½"x11", 358pp. Pau74, 10.00p.**
This volume is organized in terms of 126 different teaching strategies in a recipe-like format (purpose, group size, time suggested, general directions, materials required, and procedure). Selections include themes of communication, freedom, happiness, life, peace, love, valuing, responsibility, work, prejudice, dreaming, futuring, ecology, senses, conflict, family, meditations, marriage, death, life styles. This is a very well presented innovative book for junior and senior high teachers.

FRAIBERG, SELMA. **EVERY CHILD'S BIRTHRIGHT: IN DEFENSE OF MOTHERING. Notes, 175pp. H&R77, 8.95c.**
During the first six months, a baby learns the rudiments of the language of love, based on embraces, eye contact, smiles, and vocalizations of pleasure and distress. In this book Professor Fraiberg shows us how love is born and how it may die in infancy, and makes a moving affirmation of the enduring and irreplaceable value of mothering. **Every Child's Birthright** raises the question of what it is that all infants need and have a right to expect in the way of motherly love and care. In answering, the authors shows how a child's capacity to respond to the world and his ability to value himself and love others, depends on the forging of a bond of love between the child and the person committed to nurturing him. This is a sensitive, evocative account, full of wisdom and practical advice.

FRAIBERG, SELMA. **THE MAGIC YEARS. Index, 318pp. Scr59, 3.95p.**
To a small child, the world is an exciting and sometimes frightening and unstable place. In **The Magic Years**, Ms. Fraiberg takes the reader into the mind of the child, showing how she confronts the world, and learns to cope with it. With great warmth and perception, she discusses the problems at each stage of development and reveals the qualities—above all, the quality of understanding—that can provide the right answer at critical moments. This is a remarkable study of early childhood development.

Paulo Freire

In the course of a few years, the thought and work of the Brazilian educator Paulo Freire have spread from the Northeast of Brazil to an entire continent, and have made a profound impact not only in the field of education but also in the overall struggle for national development. At the precise moment when the disinherited masses in Latin America are awakening from their lethargy and are anxious to participate, as Subjects, in the development of their countries, Paulo Freire has perfected a method for teaching illiterates that has contributed, in an extraordinary way, to that process. In fact, those who, in learning to read and write, come to a new awareness of selfhood and begin to look critically at the social situation in which they find themselves, often take the initiatve in acting to transform the society that has denied them this opportunity of participation.

—*Richard Schaull*

BROWN, CYNTHIA. **LITERACY IN THIRTY HOURS: PAULO FREIRE'S PROCESS IN NORTHEAST BRAZIL. Illustrations, 47pp. WRP75, 1.20p.**
In the Center for Open Learning and Teaching in Berkeley, California, a number of teachers are attempting to incorporate Paulo Freire's ideas into their own practices. Ms. Brown is one of these teachers and she gives an account of Freire's work in Brazil. This is followed by interviews with two of her colleagues, Herbert Kohl and Brenda Bay.

COLLINS, DENIS. **PAULO FREIRE—HIS LIFE, WORKS, AND THOUGHT. Notes, 94pp. Pau77, 2.45p.**
An introduction to the life and ideas of Freire, providing an overview of his educational theories and a discussion of his emphasis on problem posing and consciousness raising for the poor. Collins is director of education for the California Province of Jesuits and he draws parallels between Freire's work and the Church movement of liberation theology.

FREIRE, PAULO. **EDUCATION FOR CRITICAL CONSCIOUSNESS. 164pp. Sea73, 2.95p.**
The first English translation of two of Freire's major studies: *Education as the Practice of Freedom* and *Extension or Communication.* These were developed as the result of his efforts in the field of adult literacy in Brazil and his studies of the practice of agricultural extension in Chile, but they extend in reference to all social *helping* relationships.

FREIRE, PAULO. **EDUCATION: THE PRACTICE OF FREEDOM. 176pp. WRP74, 2.60p.**
Two essays in which Freire explains and develops the theory and practice behind his revolutionary educational ideas. The first is a concise account of how the method was brought into being and used with the illiterate peasants of Brazil. The second essay examines the way in which Western attempts to develop third world countries are in fact a form of cultural domination, and contrasts the genuine dialogue where educator and pupil are together humanized in the act of transforming their world.

FREIRE, PAULO. **PEDAGOGY IN PROCESS: THE LETTERS TO GUINEA-BISSAU. Illustrations, notes, 178pp. Sea78, 8.95c.**
A firsthand account of the most comprehensive attempt yet to put into practice Freire's concept of education within a total societal setting. During 500 years of colonial rule, Guinea-Bissau on the West African coast had only fourteen university graduates; and when the Portuguese withdrew in 1974, ninety percent of the adult population was illiterate. As a result, the new government faced an enormous task if it were to take educating its citizens seriously. And so, they invited Freire to collaborate in what was literally a grass roots literacy campaign.

FREIRE, PAULO. **PEDAGOGY OF THE OPPRESSED. 186pp. Sea68, 3.95p.**
Freire evolved a theory for the education of illiterates, especially adults, based on the conviction that every human being, no matter how ignorant or submerged in the *culture of silence,* is capable of looking at his world in a dialogical encounter with others, and that provided with the

proper tools for such an encounter he can gradually perceive his personal and social reality and deal critically with it. As the illiterate learns, his world becomes radically transformed and he is no longer willing to be a mere object responding to changes occurring around him. This is Freire's basic book, outlining his theory and his experiences.

──────END OF PAULO FREIRE SUBSECTION──────

GARVEY, CATHERINE. **PLAY.** Illustrations, notes, annotated bibliography, index, 133pp. HUP77, 2.95p.
Professor Garvey discusses why children play and contends that what is most remarkable about play is that it stimulates reality without being bound by it. The playing child is buffered from the ordinary consequences of his behavior, and this buffering provides a natural laboratory in which to experiment with actions, utterances, and social roles he has not yet mastered. The author's exposition ranges from anecdotes to detailed linguistic analyses and precise timings of video taped play sessions.

GINANDES, SHEPARD. **THE SCHOOL WE HAVE.** Bibliography, 272pp. Del73, 2.75p.
I find this to be a fascinating account of the way in which a school has gradually been built which really meets the needs of young people today. While the group at the School is composed primarily of disturbed adolescents and young people, the principles evolved in working with them contain highly significant lessons for everyone in all of the helping professions and for teachers of young people.—Carl Rogers. Dr. Ginandes is a psychiatrist who is director of the school. His study is based on case histories and actual scenes from day to day operations of the school.

GLASSER, WILLIAM. **SCHOOLS WITHOUT FAILURE.** 255pp. H&R 69, 2.95p.
Working from the premise that today's schools are designed for failure, the author deals with the teaching process and ways to make the classroom more relevant. He examines the shortcomings of the education system itself and the role it plays in causing the failure of its students. He offers practical suggestions toward introducing involvement, relevance, and thinking into the school.

GOODELL, CAROL, ed. **THE CHANGING CLASSROOM.** 340pp. RaH73, 1.95p.
A wide selection of pioneering classroom techniques and educational philosophies in the words of leading figures in the field.

GOODLAD, JOHN, et al. **TOWARD A MANKIND SCHOOL.** Annotated bibliography, index, 204pp. MGH74, 7.95c.
Dr. Goodlad and his coauthors organized an experimental school at the University Elementary School, UCLA, to find ways to put their humanistic concepts into schooling. This book identifies some of their basic ideas and their possible meaning for education and schooling, and contains the authors' reflections on the project and its implications for the future. The project was aimed at both a group of elementary school children and a group of teachers. This is a dry, scholarly, descriptive text. Includes almost fifty pages of annotated bibliography.

GOODNOW, JACQUELINE. **CHILDREN DRAWING.** Notes, annotated bibliography, index, 159pp. HUP77, 3.95p.
Educators and psychologists have often puzzled over what it is about the child's mind, eye, and hand that lead him to draw as he does. In this book Professor Goodnow offers several hypotheses and backs up her views with a readable account of her extensive research. Over seventy examples of children's drawings are included.

GORDON, IRA. **BABY TO PARENT, PARENT TO BABY.** Illustrations, 8¼"x11", 105pp. SMP77, 4.95p.
This is a practical guide to loving and learning in a child's first year. Gordon often writes simplistically; nonetheless, he offers genuinely positive advice and comes up with many interesting suggestions.

GORDON, THOMAS. **PARENT EFFECTIVENESS TRAINING.** Bibliography, index, 334pp. NAL70, 5.95p.
P.E.T. was devised to help parents become more responsive to their children. It has been successfully used by many thousands throughout the country. This is a comprehensive discussion of the technique. Many case studies are included.

GORDON, THOMAS. **P.E.T. IN ACTION.** 367pp. S&S76, 2.50p.
An investigation of what happens when P.E.T. is applied in the home. Includes interviews with parents and a variety of case studies.

GORDON, THOMAS. **TEACHER EFFECTIVENESS TRAINING.** 382pp. S&S74, 9.95c.
T.E.T. (Teacher Effectiveness Training) evolved from P.E.T. (Parent Effectiveness Training) which is now taught by over 5,000 instructors. Teachers and administrators began to hear from parents about what they had learned in P.E.T., and asked that the course be given to their districts' teachers, so that they could apply the same communication skills and conflict resolution methods to students in the classroom. A special course was designed for school teachers. This book presents the same principles, skills, and methods that were developed, refined, and tested in Dr. Gordon's inservice work with teachers in the T.E.T. course. Many of the illustrations and case histories have been drawn from these teachers. The orientation is on developing practical skills rather than on abstract educational concepts.

GRAUBARD, ALLEN. **FREE THE CHILDREN—RADICAL REFORM AND THE FREE SCHOOL MOVEMENT.** 306pp. RaH72, 2.45p.
The author has combined his knowledge and experience with the ideas of many other outspoken leaders of educational reform to penetrate into the triumphs and failures of the movement. He analyzes much of the current literature on the subject written by such notables as John Holt, A.S. Neill, and George Leonard, and places the radical school reform movement in the context of a wide political and cultural viewpoint.

GROSS, BEATRICE and RONALD, eds. **WILL IT GROW IN A CLASSROOM?** Bibliography, 332pp. Del74, 3.25p.
The book is a joy. I started reading it sitting in an airport waiting room and that first gorgeous mad story made me laugh out loud. I get a great deal of mail from lonely, discouraged teachers who write me how defeated they feel in trying to change the established order. The book breaks through that anomie with encouragement and practical ideas and reinforcement. Thanks for a great experience!—Eda LeShan. Every article was written by a teacher and every one was written out of personal experience. Among the contributors are some of the best known teachers in the United States—John Holt, Herbert Kohl, Miriam Wasserman, for example.

HALL, BRIAN. **THE DEVELOPMENT OF CONSCIOUSNESS.** Diagrams, annotated bibliography, index, 282pp. Pau76, 5.95p.
This book is about values. It formulates a theory of values that offers you, the reader, an overall construct . . . a meaning structure out of which you can understand the nature of values and how they may be utilized within the educational process. The book is the result of Dr. Hall's work at The Center for the Exploration of Values and Meaning. A great deal of technical instructional material is included in this detailed analysis along with case studies. The emphasis is on an integration of affective and cognitive learning.

HALL, BRIAN. **VALUE CLARIFICATION: A GUIDEBOOK.** Well-illustrated, 8"x10", 253pp. Pau73, 7.95p.
A basic manual of exercises and strategies: the companion volume to the Sourcebook. The book is divided into four parts: I, an introduction, giving definitions of a value, value ranking, and value indicators; II, presents forty-nine *strategies* (techniques) for students, teachers, and professionals; III, details six complete workshops for training people in the value clarification process; and IV, deals with those issues which will enable value clarification techniques to be used in the classroom. The exercises are presented in a recipe-like format.

HALL, BRIAN. **VALUE CLARIFICATION: A SOURCEBOOK.** Illustrations, annotated bibliography, index, 8"x10", 306pp. Pau73, 7.95p.
The basic text for understanding the theory of values underlying Dr. Hall's methodology of value clarification. The book also contains a variety of practical techniques designed to engage the reader in the process of clarifying his or her own values. Many case studies are presented along with supportive material.

HALL, BRIAN and MARY SMITH. **VALUE CLARIFICATION: A HANDBOOK FOR CHRISTIAN EDUCATORS.** Annotated bibliography, 8"x10", 269pp. Pau73, 7.95p.
Provides a theological basis for understanding the possibilities and limitations of the effective use of value clarification in religious

education. Includes case studies of the methodology, with applications for parish renewal, liturgy, and prayer life.

HAWLEY, ROBERT and ISABEL. **HUMAN VALUES IN THE CLASS-ROOM. Annotated bibliography, index, 282pp. Har75, 4.95p.**
The Hawleys set forth a humanistic approach to teaching and learning which focuses on the prime values of love, trust, cooperation, and tolerance. To foster the development of values, the teacher creates learning opportunities where values come into play. This book presents practical ways to create such opportunities. The authors delineate a sequence of theoretical and practical ideas for creating a classroom climate which promotes personal and social growth. Included are scores of specific activities, procedures, and suggestions which have proven their worth in classroom use. They also address such issues as the need for positive focus in teaching, the merits of grading as a means of evaluation, and what to do about discipline and behavior problems.

HAWLEY, ROBERT and ISABEL. **WRITING FOR THE FUN OF IT. Bibliography, index, 116pp. ERA74, 4.65p.**
This book is subtitled, *An Experience-Based Approach to Composition* and it contains over sixty activities which stimulate written expression in a wide variety of forms. This approach is based on the authors' personal experience as teachers and emphasizes the development of critical thinking skills in gathering and organizing information and choosing appropriate modes of written expression.

■ *HENDRICKS, GAY and JAMES FADIMAN, eds.* **TRANSPERSONAL EDUCATION. Bibliography, 191pp. PrH76, 3.95p.**
The authors provide original lesson plans that put transpersonal psychology theory to work in a typical classroom situation. The contributors (ranging from Aldous Huxley to Krishnamurti to Jean Porter and George Leonard) tell how to help students get in touch with themselves and their creative abilities. Selections explain how to incorporate activities such as dreamwork, fantasy, and body awareness into an exciting and individualized curriculum. The approaches are wide ranging and all aim at helping students and teachers understand their inner self better.

HENTOFF, NAT. **DOES ANYBODY GIVE A DAMN? Index, 224pp. RaH77, 8.95c.**
This is a provocative analysis and exposition of public schools that work. Hentoff focuses on a remarkable diversity of teachers and principals in the public schools who refuse to allow their students to give up on themselves.

HERNDON, JAMES. **THE WAY IT SPOZED TO BE. 198pp. Ban68, 1.50p.**
The personal record of one ill fated year in a metropolitan ghetto school, ninety-eight percent Black, ninety-nine percent *deprived*, and 100 percent chaotic. It tells how the educational bureaucracy, the schools, and life itself in our big cities are all rigged against the students who can't take it—the ones we call *deprived*. *The most accurate description so far in print of ghetto school-children and the forces (teachers and administrators) lined up against them.*—Nat Hentoff.

HERTZBERG, ALVIN and EDWARD STONE. **SCHOOLS ARE FOR CHILDREN. 232pp. ScB71, 2.45p.**
Written by two American elementary school principals, this book is a valuable attempt to bring the reality of the open school method of learning into more extensive consideration. The authors relate their experiences and communicate to the reader an understanding of the immense potential of this method. They suggest practical means of adapting the medium of the open classroom to the needs and temperament of American society.

HOLT, JOHN. **ESCAPE FROM CHILDHOOD. 225pp. RaH74/Pen, 1.75p.**
John Holt has been called a prophet in the educational wilderness. He has written extensively and his books have been very influential. Holt has been a teacher for more than twenty years. This book, subtitled *The Needs and Rights of Children*, is an examination of the way society systematically denies young people responsible choices, while expecting them to assume this same responsibility at an arbitrarily determined age.

HOLT, JOHN. **FREEDOM AND BEYOND. 276pp. Del72/Pen, 2.75p.**
Holt explores certain fallacies in human thinking and assumption, which create unreasonable behavior and irrational social perspectives. Excellent selection of recommended readings, films, and other source material.

HOLT, JOHN. **HOW CHILDREN FAIL. 181pp. Del64/Pen, 1.95p.**
Holt attacks the coercive, mindless, fear producing techniques of our schools—techniques that blunt the normal drive to experience and learn.

HOLT, JOHN. **HOW CHILDREN LEARN. 156pp. Del67/Pen, 2.45p.**
A series of observations about the mechanisms of learning as actually witnessed by the author. The obvious conclusion is that children most assuredly do come into the world equipped to explore, discover, and learn.

HOLT, JOHN. **INSTEAD OF EDUCATION. Notes, bibliography, 250pp. Dut76, 3.45p.**
Subtitled, *Ways to Help People Do Things Better*, this book shows how we can turn our whole society into a place of genuine learning. Holt proposes expanding the creative uses of facilities we already have, adding new facilities that will serve more people for less money (like neighborhood printing presses), and using people to their fullest capacity—for example, matching skilled people with those who want to learn that skill). A very positive approach to improving both our educational system and society in general.

HOLT, JOHN. **THE UNDER-ACHIEVING SCHOOL. 207pp. Del69/Pen, 2.25p.**
A collection of short essays, lectures, and insights written down by the author over a period of several years.

HOLT, JOHN. **WHAT DO I DO MONDAY? 318pp. Del70/Pen, 2.95p.**
Holt makes the reader look at himself and the world and his understanding of the world in new ways. He gives many practical examples of how the experience of learning might be made more meaningful and might retain more of its wondrous quality for both child and adult.

HOWE, LELAND and MARY. **PERSONALIZING EDUCATION. Long bibliography, index, 574pp. Har75, 5.95p.**
Subtitled, *Values Clarification and Beyond*, this is a clear practical explanation of just how and why the valuing process can be made to permeate the total educational process. The four part elaboration of techniques for personalizing education focuses on (1) human relationships,(2) goals in the classroom, (3) the curriculum, and (4) classroom organization and management. The book contains well over 100 specific techniques and worksheets. An excellent sourcebook for the teacher.

ILLICH, IVAN. **AFTER DESCHOOLING, WHAT? 162pp. H&R73, 1.95p.**
Illich has written in many fields and has had a deep impact upon the cultural and educational revolution. In this volume he probes into the possible consequences of the disestablishment of institutionalized schooling. A number of critics add their own thoughts to his essays.

ILLICH, IVAN. **CELEBRATION OF AWARENESS. 181pp. Dou69, 1.95p.**
Illich seeks to arouse man's sleeping consciousness to an appreciation of the potential for a wondrous future if humanity can break the shackles that hold us in bondage to an obsolete past.

ILLICH, IVAN. **DESCHOOLING SOCIETY. 167pp. H&R71, 1.95p.**
This is an important study which exposes the massive failures of our educational system. As usual, Illich is not easy to read, but his argument is clear and straightforward. Things must change. Rather than just complain about what is wrong, he outlines what can and must be done—and his ideas are both visionary and immensely practical.

ILLICH, IVAN. **TOOLS FOR CONVIVIALITY. 110pp. H&R73, 1.50p.**
Illich chooses the term *conviviality* to designate the opposite of industrial productivity. He intends it to mean creative intercourse among persons, and the intercourse of persons with their environment, and this in contrast with the conditioned response of people to the demands made upon them by others, and by a manmade environment.

ILLICH, IVAN and ETIENNE VERNE. **IMPRISONED IN THE GLOBAL CLASSROOM. Bibliography, 63pp. WRP76, 1.20p.**
This essay contains Illich's most recent thoughts on educational matters.

JAMES, WALENE. **HANDBOOK FOR EDUCATING IN THE NEW AGE. 2.50p.**
See the Edgar Cayce section.

JANOV, ARTHUR. **THE FEELING CHILD. 285pp. S&S73/SBL, 2.95p.**
Dr. Janov draws on his vast experience with patients in primal therapy and the research done at the Primal Institute to formulate ways of bringing up emotionally healthy children. He deals with a broad range of problems common to childrearing, from daydreaming, excessive whining, and fear of the dark, to the consequences of divorce, punishment, and childhood sexuality. He shows how parents can fulfill the psychological and physiological needs of their children to bring both parent and child in touch with their own feelings in an environment free from neurotic pain.

JONES, PHILIP and SUSAN. **PARENTS UNITE! 270pp. S&S76, 9.95c.**
Detailed advice by a former editor of **The American School Board Journal** on how parents can band together and *pit parent power against teacher power, school bureaucrats and politicians.* Every conceivable topic is discussed.

JONES, SANDY. **GOOD THINGS FOR BABIES. 8¼"x10½", 125pp. HMC76, 4.95p.**
A catalogue and sourcebook of safety and consumer advice about products needed during the first twenty-four months of life. Over 250 items are illustrated in all, with complete mail order information.

KELLY, MARGUERITE and ELIA PARSONS. **THE MOTHER'S ALMA-NAC. Illustrations, bibliography, index, 7½"x10", 288pp. Dou75, 4.95p.**
This is an informative guide to child care for preschoolers based on the authors' own experience with their families and the experience of their friends. *We have divided [the book] into three parts, but the first is perhaps the most important because it covers the realities of family life—not just the routine...but how you teach your child to become independent and self-disciplined....In the second section we consider the influences that give this enrichment....Finally, there are avenues of expression you offer your child which we cover in our last section. Here we tell about the traditional arts and drama and crafts; the experiments your child can make in science and reading...the skills of the kitchen and the workshop and the garden...We like this book a lot and friends who have small children recommend it.*

KHAN, HAZRAT INAYAT. **EDUCATION: FROM BEFORE BIRTH TO MATURITY. 3.95p.**
See the Islam section.

KIRSCHENBAUM, HOWARD, RODNEY NAPIER, and SIDNEY SIMON. **WAD-JA-GET. Notes, 315pp. Har71, 2.95p.**
A discussion of grading and its effects on students written by three professors of education who have had firsthand contact with this problem in all its manifestations. All possible alternatives are examined in detail.

KOHL, HERBERT. **MATH, WRITING AND GAMES IN THE OPEN CLASSROOM. 252pp. RaH74/Met, 2.45p.**
Kohl gives practical suggestions for teachers and parents on developing new and imaginative ways to teach. The section on writing describes the techniques that Kohl used in getting children to write stories, fables, and poetry by encouraging them to rely on their own experiences and their own language. The largest part of the book, *Games and Math*, is an analysis of the ways in which games can be used for teaching. He describes games and learning ideas and shows how playing these games can stimulate children's imagination and thinking so that they can comprehend complex concepts. Kohl includes clear and practical suggestions on setting up a classroom game center, and a list of materials needed. The book also has more than 150 illustrations and an annotated list of recommended reading.

KOHL, HERBERT. **ON TEACHING. Notes, index, 185pp. Ban76, 2.25p.**
This book is for people thinking about becoming a teacher as well as for people in teacher training and for people who are in the classroom and think of themselves as still learning how to teach. It is about the specifics of working with children and developing curriculum material. It is also about educational politics, the social structure of the school, and the ways in which the feelings we have as adults affect the work we do in school. It is a putting together of the things I have seen and thought about and tried over the past fifteen years in regular public schools and alternative schools, with children from kindergarten through senior high school.—from the preface.

KOHL, HERBERT. **THE OPEN CLASSROOM. 116pp. RaH69/Met, 1.95p.**
A clear practically presented guide to open classroom teaching techniques. Chapters are included on starting the year, actual operational classroom examples, discipline, and other specific problems.

KOHL, HERBERT. **READING, HOW TO. 224pp. Ban73/Pen, 1.95p.**
Proclaiming that reading is no more difficult than walking or talking, and that all persons can learn to read effectively or can improve their skills, the author proceeds to suggest techniques that will facilitate reading ability.

KOHL, HERBERT. **THIRTY-SIX CHILDREN. 224pp. NAL67/Pen, 1.25p.**
A first person account of what it is like to be a white teacher in a public school in Harlem. Kohl really cares and this is obvious from the narrative presented here.

KOZOL, JONATHAN. **THE NIGHT IS DARK AND I AM FAR FROM HOME. Notes, 253pp. Ban75, 2.25p.**
A chilling indictment of our public school system as a center for systematic, intentional brainwashing which teaches children too well how to obey—and not to think, question, and disobey. Many case histories are included.

KRAMER, EDITH. **ART AS THERAPY WITH CHILDREN. Color and black and white plates, illustrations, index, 234pp. ScB71, 5.50p.**
Edith Kramer has worked as art therapist in a variety of settings with children suffering from just about every known emotional or social disorder....Her true and practical understanding stems from a deep knowledge of psychoanalysis combined with the skill and intuition of an artist and the humane love of a born teacher. The book deals with such subjects...as sense of identity, feelings of emptiness, interpretation of reality, ambivalence, aggression, defenses, sublimation. It is organized around these ideas, and richly documented with case material—from the introduction. This is a useful study of a little explored field.

KRAMER, EDITH. **ART THERAPY IN A CHILDREN'S COMMUNI-TY. Bibliography, index, 257pp. ScB58, 8.95p.**
As it says in the introduction, *Art Therapy, as evolved by Edith Kramer, engages the creative process, through painting, towards the goals of overall personality growth and rehabilitation.* This book is an interpretative study of Ms. Kramer's work in a community of emotionally disturbed boys. The exposition is both theoretical and practical, and many case histories document the generalizations. Some of the illustrations and case histories are included in Ms. Kramer's other books; however, there is a great deal of new material here.

KRISHNAMURTI, J. **EDUCATION AND THE SIGNIFICANCE OF LIFE. 4.95c.**
See the Contemporary Spiritual Teachers section.

KRISHNAMURTI, J. **KRISHNAMURTI ON EDUCATION. 3.95p.**
See the Contemporary Spiritual Teachers section.

LEONARD, GEORGE. **EDUCATION AND ECSTASY. 239pp. Del68/ Mur, 3.45p.**
This is a thought provoking book that attacks many traditional educational concepts and celebrates the joy of learning and living. Leonard is an important figure in the human potential movement and here he selectively explores ways in which we can deepen and improve the educational environment we offer our children. Many examples and practical suggestions are included.

LIEDLOFF, JEAN. **THE CONTINUUM CONCEPT. 177pp. RaH77, 7.95c.**
This is a pioneering study based on Ms. Liedloff's two and a half years of living among Stone Age Indians in the South American jungle. She found that the Indians understood innate human expectations and tendencies and were allowed to follow their natural continuum of development. As she says, *We are now fairly brought to heel by the intellect; our inherent sense of what is good for us has been undermined to the pont where we are barely aware of its working and cannot tell an original impulse from a distorted one. But I believe it is possible to start as we are, lost and handicapped, and still find a way back.* In this book she discusses how the Indians live with and educate their young and shows how these ways of being can be adapted to contemporary *developed* society.

MANN, JOHN. **LEARNING TO BE. Notes, bibliography, index, 281pp. McM72, 5.30p.**
Subtitled, *The Education of Human Potential,* this book explores new learning methods such as psychosynthesis, Tai Chi Ch'uan, tantric yoga, and breathing exercises in the hope of designing an *internal curriculum* which will help children develop their feelings as well as their intellects. Professor Mann has adapted many humanistic awareness and sensitivity techniques for classroom use and related them to basic human functions. This is a dry, academic account which contains some good ideas which can be followed up in greater depth elsewhere.

MARIN, PETER, VINCENT STANLEY and KATHRYN MARIN, eds. **THE LIMITS OF SCHOOLING. 150pp. PrH75, 2.45p.**
Provides a close look at education's most radical departures by giving selections from the writings of some of the nation's most active alternative educators. Includes essays by George Dennison, Jonathan Kozol, Paul Goodman, Ivan Illich, John Holt, Herbert Kohl, Sylvia Ashton-Warner, and James Herndon.

MARSH, L. **ALONGSIDE THE CHILD. Index, 154pp. H&R70/ABC, 2.45p.**
This is a warm, well written discussion of experiences in an English primary school modeled on the open classroom system. Included are chapters on specific areas such as painting, mathematics, writing, using books, and discovery approaches. There is also information on using teaching areas, organization, and on the school and the community. Many photographs of classrooms and children's work are included.

■ *MILLE, RICHARD DE.* **PUT YOUR MOTHER ON THE CEILING. 175pp. Vik73, 2.95p.**
This is a collection of imaginative children's games (printed in large type so children can use the book themselves). The games are designed for two people, only one of whom may be a child. Each game has a short introduction that gives some idea of what the game is about and establishes a reference point in reality for that game. The game ends with questions which allow the child to complete the game in a way that satisfies him. The individual games progress from easy to hard, but they can be done in any order and we have gotten excellent reports from our customers who have used the book with children. This is a unique book which puts the participating adult in touch with the most neglected and enjoyable parts of her children and herself.

MILLER, JOHN. **HUMANIZING THE CLASSROOM: MODELS OF TEACHING IN AFFECTIVE EDUCATION. Notes, index, 189pp. HRW76, 7.95p.**
Miller integrates a number of teaching approaches in affective education—values clarification, synectics, confluent education, meditation, and psychosynthesis—and suggests a framework in which to organize these approaches based on their focus and on the amount of

framework associated with each. This is a valuable tool book for those teachers interested in practicing humanistic education.

Maria Montessori

Maria Montessori was one of the most eminent and influential figures in the field of education during the past century. She became a practicing physician in Rome, one of the first women to achieve such a specialized status in her country. She later left the field of medicine for what she felt was her true life purpose: the study and improvement of the education of the child.

She patterned her philosophy and techniques upon her understanding of the mysteries of childhood. Her methods revolutionized education throughout the world and she introduced many new principles for her schools based on her conception of the child as a soul with a profound potential.

■ *HAINSTOCK, ELIZABETH.* **TEACHING MONTESSORI IN THE HOME: THE PRE-SCHOOL YEARS. Bibliography, 117pp. NAL68, 3.95p.**
One of Montessori's pioneering achievements was to recognize the importance of a child's first six years of development. It is during this time that a child's powers of absorption are at their highest and lifelong attitudes and patterns of learning are firmly formed. This book contains a selection of techniques, exercises, and easy to make Montessori materials. Ms. Hainstock includes reading and writing, mathematics, sensory awareness, and practical life skills. The presentation is well organized and the book has been highly acclaimed.

HAINSTOCK, ELIZABETH. **TEACHING MONTESSORI IN THE HOME: THE SCHOOL YEARS. Illustrations, annotated bibliography, 176pp. NAL71, 3.95p.**
A companion volume to Ms. Hainstock's first book which serves as a guide for more advanced learning. It deals with math and language development, the two basic disciplines. Realizing that most children have problems in these areas, the author has adapted exercises from actual Montessori classroom activities to supplement and implement your child's education in these subjects, regardless of what type of school he attends. The exercises are graduated, to increase ability.

KRAMER, RITA. **MARIA MONTESSORI: A BIOGRAPHY. Illustrations, notes, index, 410pp. Put76, 4.50p.**
A long overdue definitive biography. Ms. Kramer draws on Montessori's own works, what others have written about her, and the memories of those still living who knew and worked with her. This is a study of the Montessori method as much as of Montessori herself.

LILLARD, PAULA. **MONTESSORI: A MODERN APPROACH. Notes, index, 191pp. ScB72, 2.75p.**
Maria Montessori describes this book as *not just a popular introduction in Montessori education. It is a well-chosen and coordinated presentation of its basic principles and techniques, preceded by a historical survey of its vicissitudes in the States and a preface giving a flash of a classroom at work, and ending with some considerations of its present-day value plus a perspective of ongoing research. . . . Its particular merit is its use for those working in the field of education. . . . [The author] lets, as it were, Maria Montessori speak for herself.*

■ *MALLOY, TERRY.* **MONTESSORI AND YOUR CHILD: A PRIMER FOR PARENTS. Bibliography, 95pp. ScB74, 3.95p.**
The first three sections of this lovely hand drawn book ask simple questions: What is your child really like? What does your child need? How can you help your child? The last section describes ideas used in Montessori preschool education. An illustrated appendix shows some of the Montessori materials mentioned in the text and gives concrete guidance to parents. The author is director of a Montessori school in California. This is the best primer for parents on the Montessori method that we have ever seen.

MONTESSORI, MARIA. **THE ABSORBENT MIND. Index, 316pp. Del67, 3.95p.**
A fascinating analysis of the physical and psychological aspects of a child's growth during the first six years. It is during this period that the

child acquires a knowledge of motor coordination, language, work and play habits, social adjustments, and the beginnings of routines that will set the pattern of her life. This is a sensitive, intuitive discussion of these first six years, and takes spiritual growth into account as well.

MONTESSORI, MARIA. **THE CHILD IN THE FAMILY. 160pp. Avoc56/PnB, 1.50p.**
A chief principle of Montessori's technique is that a child must have the liberty to mold her own personality. This and other fundamental insights and beliefs are discussed in this volume.

MONTESSORI, MARIA. **CHILDHOOD EDUCATION. 136pp. NAL55, 2.95p.**
A general philosophical discussion of the basic principles of the Montessori method and an attempt to answer both the criticisms and the serious misconceptions that have arisen about it.

MONTESSORI, MARIA. **THE DISCOVERY OF THE CHILD. 339pp. RaH62, 1.95p.**
A basic book on the author's methods with a selection of pictures of children at work in a Montessori school.

MONTESSORI, MARIA. **DR. MONTESSORI'S OWN HANDBOOK. Photographs, 189pp. ScB14, 3.90p.**
This handbook was written by Dr. Montessori herself as a practical guide to her method of teaching young children. Most aspects of her work are covered.

MONTESSORI, MARIA. **EDUCATION FOR A NEW WORLD. 89pp. TPH46, 5.00c.**
An exploration of the methods for the education of a child from birth through the third year. This book was published by a Theosophical press and Montessori preaches a bit more than usual here. The influence of the recently concluded Second World War is also apparent.

MONTESSORI, MARIA. **FROM CHILDHOOD TO ADOLESCENCE. Index, 141pp. ScB73, 2.75p.**
The emphasis in this work is on the needs and moral characteristics of the child between seven and twelve years of age. A number of chapters focus on specific educational approaches and the study of chemistry is especially emphasized.

MONTESSORI, MARIA. **THE MONTESSORI ELEMENTARY MATERIAL. 421pp. ScB17, 3.45p.**
An intensive discussion of the body of knowledge that is to be put before the elementary school child. Almost half the book is devoted to Ms. Montessori's original techniques for teaching grammar. The successive steps in learning reading meaningfully are also discussed in detail as are arithmetic, geometry, and music. The teaching materials for these subjects are illustrated and their use described.

MONTESSORI, MARIA. **THE MONTESSORI METHOD. 376pp. ScB12, 4.50p.**
This book is the most complete rendition of the application of Montessori's principles. It covers all phases of development and all areas of instruction.

MONTESSORI, MARIA. **THE SECRET OF CHILDHOOD. 216pp. RaH60, 1.95p.**
The author reveals her deep understanding of childhood. She points out that all children have an inborn urge to learn and that learning is a spontaneous action of their growth.

MONTESSORI, MARIA. **SPONTANEOUS ACTIVITY IN EDUCATION. 383pp. ScB65, 3.75p.**
This is a fundamental text in the theory and practice of producing the right environment for children who are learning through their own developing mastery of experiences. Key sections are devoted to *Experimental Science, Attention,* and *Intelligence* as fundamental problems in education. The text includes many case studies. The material was written after Dr. Montessori had been teaching for quite a while and therefore contains some advanced text. This should not be considered an introductory volume.

MONTESSORI, MARIA. **TO EDUCATE THE HUMAN POTENTIAL. 124pp. TPH48, 5.00c.**
This book follows **Education for a New Age**; its style is similar to that volume. It is designed to help teachers envision the child's needs after the age of six. The first chapters are mainly psychological, showing the child's changed personality and the teacher's corresponding need for a change of approach. The rest of the book contains a discussion of the creation of life on earth and of the early civilizations.

MONTESSORI, MARIO. **EDUCATION FOR HUMAN DEVELOPMENT: UNDERSTANDING MONTESSORI. Notes, index, 134pp. ScB76, 7.95c.**
The author is a psychoanalyst who is Dr. Montessori's grandson. He surveys Montessori's ideas from philosophical, psychological, and educational points of view and relates her discoveries to present day concerns. This is a somewhat technical volume which covers areas not treated in other works on Montessori, especially her concern in helping the young to understand and respect nature and to see man as part of it.

OREM, R.C., ed. **MONTESSORI. 263pp. Put74, 3.25p.**
Orem has assembled a layman's guide to Montessori that answers many questions parents have about the method. Both the practical aspects (the day to day operations of a typical school) and the philosophical roots are discussed in easy to comprehend terms. The first essay offers Montessori as a *strategy* for much needed educational reforms. In the second section, Montessori *tactics* as employed in a variety of Montessori schools are described. The third section includes six articles exploring topics such as the home, discipline, flexibility, public education, language, and arts—each in relation to contributions made by the Montessori method.

■ OREM, R.C., ed. **A MONTESSORI HANDBOOK. 192pp. Put66, 2.45p.**
Half of this book consists of **Dr. Montessori's Own Handbook**, the only authentic practical manual of the Montessori method, and the other half contains new material on current Montessori theory and practice. The book integrates Dr. Montessori's writings with up to date commentary and is designed to be useful for both practicing teachers and interested parents. Each section of the Montessori text is introduced by an interpretative commentary and accompanied by a brief essay relating that particular aspect of Montessori to current educational practices. An appendix provides a guide to what to look for in a good Montessori school. Recommended as a primer.

OREM, R.C., ed. **MONTESSORI AND THE SPECIAL CHILD. 232pp. Put69, 3.65p.**
The Montessori method has been successful in educating the special child—the intellectually gifted and the mentally retarded as well as handicapped and emotionally disturbed children. Orem and a number of other experts explain and demonstrate a variety of Montessori techniques. Many case studies are included along with a variety of practical techniques.

OREM, R.C. and MARJORIE COBURN. **MONTESSORI: PRESCRIPTION FOR CHILDREN WITH LEARNING DISABILITIES. 188pp. Put78, 8.95c.**
The authors draw on Montessori's philosophy, principles, materials, and methods, and adapt them to the special needs of children with learning disabilities.

STANDING, E.M. **MARIA MONTESSORI: HER LIFE AND WORK. Photographs, 370pp. NAL57/NEL, 1.50p.**
The author was a close friend and associate of Montessori for many years.

————END OF MARIA MONTESSORI SUBSECTION————

MOUSTAKAS, CLARK. **CHILDREN IN PLAY THERAPY. Notes, index, 237pp. RaH53, 1.75p.**
Moustakas presents the methods and materials used at the Merrill-Palmer School in Detroit—a playroom equipped with toys and materials chosen in part for their symbolic content, arranged in an unstructured fashion, and reserved for the child to use and interpret in his own way, without the judgment or interference of the supervising adult and without restrictions other than those of safety. He also

discusses the attitudes and attributes of the therapists and illustrates them, and the techniques of play therapy, through a number of case histories containing both verbatim materials and commentary.

MOUSTAKAS, CLARK. **WHO WILL LISTEN? Notes, bibliography, 147pp. RaH75, 2.25p.**
An exploration of the communication problem between parents and children in which Moustakas contends that simply by listening to children, parents can come to understand their hidden needs, fears, joys, and frustrations.

MOUSTAKAS, CLARK and CERETA PERRY. **LEARNINGTO BE FREE. 184pp. PrH73, 2.95p.**
The authors present guidelines for setting up an educational environment in which active learner participation, learner initiated experiences, the one to one relationship of play therapy, and open discussion groups make the child a decision maker in his own education. Many case studies are included and there are bibliographies of children's books and professional books, a list of supplemental materials and resources, and an index.

A.S. Neill

Neill's famous Summerhill school, which was a unique experiment when started, has greatly altered the approach to childhood education. Much has been written about Neill's ideas and his radical philosophy of childrearing, both critical and complimentary. His writings, thoughts, and practices have deeply stirred thoughtful people everywhere. No doubt, the Summerhill school and its success have shattered many of the old assumptions about what is proper or necessary in education. His principal book, **Summerhill**, with an introduction by Erich Fromm, is very stimulating, and the provocative ideas are sure to evoke a strong response from the reader, either sympathetic or otherwise.

Neill's philosophy of Summerhill is really the belief that children must be free and unoppressed and that if they are allowed this liberty, within an environment of understanding, their innate impulse will be to interact and live cooperatively and constructively. They will, naturally and spontaneously, learn, study, and grow. Thus coercion, punishment, suppression, and authoritarianism are removed and the child can be himself and can express his individuality in an atmosphere of happiness without inhibiting psychological burdens being forced upon him. Neill died in 1973 at eighty-nine.

HEMMINGS, RAY. **CHILDREN'S FREEDOM—A.S. NEILL AND THE EVOLUTION OF THE SUMMERHILL IDEA. 218pp. ScB73, 3.45p.**
An absorbing examination which traces the progression of Neill's thought and the evolving manifestations of his ideas. Neill's ideas are discussed in relation to current education reform ideas and are placed in a sociological and political frame of understanding and influence.

NEILL, A.S. **FREEDOM, NOT LICENSE. 187pp. Har66, 3.95p.**
Advice to parents and educators on how to raise their children and cope with common (and uncommon) problems of growing children. Written as answers to questions by Americans.

NEILL, A.S. **SUMMERHILL. 412pp. S&S60/Pen, 4.95p.**

————END OF A.S. NEILL SUBSECTION————

NEWMAN, RUTH. **GROUPS IN SCHOOLS. Bibliography, 286pp. S&S74, 4.95p.**
Dr. Newman examines the group dynamics of the school world—the administration, the staff, the parents, and the children—to explain why some children thrive in the school, why some fail, and what can be done to change the schools for the benefit of all children. The author has done a great deal of study of group behavior and has also done practical work with groups. She believes that an understanding of the groups in the schools is essential in providing an environment where change can take place.

NEWMARK, GERALD. **THIS SCHOOL BELONGS TO YOU AND ME. Bibliography, index, 432pp. Har76, 5.95p.**
This book describes a new kind of learning community where students, parents, teachers, staff, and administrators are turned on to learning and to each other. The discussion is based on the Tutorial Community Project in Los Angeles and many of the experiences of those involved in the project are cited at length. A systematic, detailed plan for the total redesign of a school community is also offered.

NYQUIST, E. and C. HAWES, eds. **OPEN EDUCATION—A SOURCE-BOOK FOR PARENTS AND TEACHERS. 371pp. Ban72, 1.95p.**
A comprehensive compilation of educational methods by a large number of contributors. A helpful and idea-stimulating collection that provides one of the best overviews available.

PEARCE, JOSEPH CHILTON. **MAGICAL CHILD: REDISCOVERING NATURE'S PLAN FOR OUR CHILDREN. Notes, bibliography, index, 372pp. Dut77, 10.00c.**
In this book Pearce argues that, from birth, the child has only one concern—to learn all that there is to learn from the world that he is a part of. He says that this planet is the child's playground and nothing—neither adult values nor concepts of normal growth—should interfere with the child's play. Raised in this way, the *magical child* is capable of learning anything and of becoming a balanced, unencumbered adult. In the West, we have traditionally started thwarting the child's natural instincts very early. The alarming rise in autism, hyperkinetic behavior, and adolescent suicide are the most extreme examples of the unhappy results of our childrearing methods. As George Leonard says, *This is the brilliant, provocative, humane synthesis we've been waiting for. I hope* **Magical Child** *is read by every parent and parent to be, every educator, everyone interested in the future of our society.*

Jean Piaget

Jean Piaget is the Swiss psychologist whose name will forever be inextricably associated with the study of the crucial stage of childhood. He has perhaps done more than anyone else to clarify the complex psychology of the period. His research and conclusions are significant breakthroughs in understanding human personality development. The concepts Piaget has developed are often complex and the terminology involved somewhat specialized. Nonetheless, his work represents the most scientifically precise and verifiable observation and theory on the developmental psychology of childhood.

FURTH, HANS. **PIAGET FOR TEACHERS. Glossary, 163pp. PrH70, 6.65p.**
A professional manual detailing the educational implications of Piaget's theory of knowledge, emphasizing practical applications.

■ FURTH, HANS and HENRY WACHS. **THINKING GOES TO SCHOOL: PIAGET'S THEORY IN PRACTICE. Notes, index, 314pp. Oxf74, 9.95c.**
This is an excellent manual showing how to prepare children to develop their full potential as thinking human beings. The book sets forth a curriculum which is based upon clinical work conducted since 1952, and upon a work-study project carried out at the Tyler School in West Virginia. At the Tyler School the project classroom was marked by laughter, discussion, activity, and movement. There was freedom, but it was freedom within structure. The child was permitted to perform at the level which most challenged his ability and interest. This was accomplished through a series of specially designed activities or games. How to perform these games at home or in the classroom is the heart of this book. More than 175 games or activity situations are described in detail. This is generally considered the best practical manual on Piaget education.

PHILLIPS, JOHN L., JR. **THE ORIGINS OF INTELLECT: PIAGET'S THEORY. Illustrations, bibliography, indices, 232pp. Fre75, 5.00p.**
The works published by Piaget and his associates during the past forty-five years constitute the largest available source of information about the cognitive development of children. This book is a general summary

of Piaget's theory, written at a relatively nontechnical level. This is a new edition which takes into account new developments in the practical use of Piaget's theory.

PIAGET, JEAN. **THE CHILD AND REALITY. Index, 182pp. Vik73, 1.95p.**
How do children learn to perceive the world around them? How do they learn to coordinate their muscles? To speak? To hold notions of right and wrong? Piaget has made answering these questions his life's work. This book is comprised of nine essays in which Piaget offers an exposition of his answers to those questions—answers which in turn form his now famous theory of the stages of intellectual development through which all children pass. This is a good general overview of Piaget's major theories.

PIAGET, JEAN. **THE CHILD'S CONCEPTION OF PHYSICAL CAU-SALITY. Index, 309pp. LtA60/RKP, 2.50p.**
An in depth exploration of the conception of material force and the system of physics peculiar to the child. The results of practical experiments are discussed and the volume is divided into sections on the explanation of movement, prediction and explanation, explanation of machines, and the child's conception of causality and reality.

PIAGET, JEAN. **THE CHILD'S CONCEPTION OF THE WORLD. Notes, indices, 444pp. Grn29, 4.00p.**
A classic study of the child's notions of reality and behavior focusing on two essential standpoints: the modality of child thought and the significance of explanations put forward by the child, i.e. the child's notion of causality. The material is based on Professor Piaget's observation of his own children and his innumerable interviews with school children.

PIAGET, JEAN. **THE CONSTRUCTION OF REALITY IN THE CHILD. 434pp. RaH54/RKP, 1.65p.**
In the words of Gardner Murphy, *The unique contribution of Jean Piaget seems to me to be in the sensitive and imaginative way in which he has explored the inner world of the child's thought; the child's way of understanding the world, the social order and himself; and the long process of development from the infantile to the adult way of thinking.*

PIAGET, JEAN. **THE GRASP OF CONSCIOUSNESS. Notes, index, 367pp. HUP76, 4.95p.**
In this volume, Piaget turns his attention to the development of the child's awareness of his own action. He reports the results of experiments conducted at the Center of Genetic Epistemology in Geneva to distinguish between the child's ability to perform the actions required by a simple task and the child's understanding of the rationale behind the action. Taking a broad view of his results, Piaget shows that they reveal several stages in the slow and gradual development of the child's conceptualization of his actions. In analyzing each stage, he argues that the child's concept of his own action must be actively reconstructed from his experience.

PIAGET, JEAN. **THE MORAL JUDGMENT OF THE CHILD. Notes, indices, 410pp. McM65/Pen. 4.95p.**
This classic study examines a problem that stands at the heart of society—how does a child distinguish between right and wrong. Piaget and his co-workers conducted a number of experiments and the results are reported here along with detailed analysis. The volume concludes with a comparison of Piaget's findings with related social psychology and sociology theories.

PIAGET, JEAN. **SCIENCE OF EDUCATION AND THE PSYCHOL-OGY OF THE CHILD. 180pp. Vik69/Lon, 2.95p.**
A biting attack upon the educational techniques in use today. Piaget criticizes the outmoded and obsolete methods of the public school systems which ignore the mental and emotional growth of the child. He feels educators must concentrate on the child they seek to help rather than upon educational theory.

PIAGET, JEAN and BARBEL INHELDER. **THE PSYCHOLOGY OF THE CHILD. 159pp. H&R69, 5.30p.**
Designed to serve as a definitive summary of Piaget's work, this book is concerned with the growth of consciousness and behavior patterns up to the stage of adolescence.

PULASKI, MARY ANN. **YOUR BABY'S MIND AND HOW IT GROWS: PIAGET'S THEORY FOR PARENTS. Notes, bibliography, index, 219pp. H&R78, 8.95c.**
A photographically illustrated description of ways parents can apply Piaget's theory to the stage-by-stage cognitive growth of their children from birth to the age of three. This is an extremely clear, accessible account.

RICHMOND, P.G. **INTRODUCTION TO PIAGET. Index, 120pp. H&R70/RKP, 3.95p.**
A short, clearly written, general introduction to Piaget's theories. Among the topics Professor Richmond discusses are the process of intellectual development, the development of thought from the sensorimotor to the operational stage, the progression from concrete to formal operations, and learning and teaching from a Piagetian viewpoint.

SCHWEBEL, MILTON and JANE RALPH, eds. **PIAGET IN THE CLASS-ROOM. Notes, index, 319pp. H&R73, 4.95p.**
Instead of being restricted in scope to the statement of general concepts, the various chapters provide details of factual situations and teaching practices in the school environment...and the authors demonstrate a thorough comprehension of children's intelligence and knowlege.—Jean Piaget.

SIME, MARY. **A CHILD'S EYE VIEW. Index, 7½"x9½", 144pp. H&R73/T&H, 10.00c.**
This book examines the implication of Piaget's theories based on the author's years of experience working with the theories. It begins by outlining the fundamental tenets of Piaget about a child's intellectual growth and basic concept development, and describes the reactions of

some primary school children to some of his tests. The second section illustrates the paths by which young children learn to reason logically, while the third explores the progress of logical thinking as the child matures. Piagetian tests are used throughout to illustrate the stages of normal intellectual development and to pinpoint their lack of synchronization with chronological age. Illustrated appendices describe projects carried out in junior high schools. The book is illustrated with diagrams, reproductions of children's work, and photographs.

─────────END OF JEAN PIAGET SUBSECTION─────────

POSTMAN, NEIL. **CRAZY TALK, STUPID TALK. Bibliography, index, 287pp. Del76, 3.95p.**
Postman attacks two of the oldest nemeses of the human race: crazy talk and stupid talk. Stupid talk is a language that does not work because of the inappropriateness of its tone, vocabulary, or assumptions. Crazy talk is talk that gets its work done but promotes purposes that are unreasonable, trivial, or evil. We are all burdened by such self defeating ways of talking. Postman feels that learning to recognize them is a first step toward defusing their power. He explains that, by bearing in mind crazy talk and stupid talk are all learned responses, we can also unlearn them.

POSTMAN, NEIL and CHARLES WEINGARTNER. **LINGUISTICS. Bibliography, 209pp. Del66, 2.45p.**
The linguistics approach is used extensively in today's schools. The book begins with a survey of linguistics and then goes on to an examination of linguistics and grammar, usage, semantics, lexicography, and reading. A detailed study geared toward the English teacher.

POSTMAN, NEIL and CHARLES WEINGARTNER. **THE SCHOOL BOOK. 308pp. Del73, 3.45p.**
The first part of this book contains a history of school criticism in the past fifteen years, a discussion of ways schools can change, have changed, and are likely to change; and a series of questions for parents to ask in evaluating their children's schools. The second part is descriptions of people and terms important in the school world, recent important legal decisions, and resources for further study.

POSTMAN, NEIL and CHARLES WEINGARTNER. **THE SOFT REVOLUTION. 181pp. Del71, 1.95p.**
A grab bag of strategies for students.

POSTMAN, NEIL and CHARLES WEINGARTNER. **TEACHING AS A SUBVERSIVE ACTIVITY. 218pp. Del69, 3.25c.**
A stimulating presentation which exposes the sham methods that have gone by the name of teaching and education and which so dominate our schools even today. The authors contribute valuable suggestions for introducing real discovery into our education methods.

RENFIELD, RICHARD. **IF TEACHERS WERE FREE. 158pp. Del69, 2.25p.**
Contends that teachers might be entirely different if they saw their task as to help learning happen instead of trying to make it happen.

ROBERTS, THOMAS, ed. **FOUR PSYCHOLOGIES APPLIED TO EDUCATION. Notes, bibliography, index, 7"x10", 588pp. ScP75, 12.75p.**
A massive tome. In four separate sections, four psychologies—Freudian, behavioral, humanistic, and transpersonal—are presented with some of their applications to education. The editor provides an introduction to each section and he has done an excellent job in choosing the selections. It is a technical volume designed for the professional educator and as such it makes a fine contribution to the literature in the field.

ROWEN, BETTY. **LEARNING THROUGH MOVEMENT. 87pp. TCP 63, 4.70p.**
The material for this booklet has been gathered from my experiences as a classroom teacher in the elementary school and in nursery school, and as a dance teacher. Chapters include: *Developing Creativity through Movement, Language and Movement, Creative Movement as an Aid to Social Learning, Movement as an Aid in Mastering Number Concepts, Creative Movement in the Science Program, Creative Movement and Personality.* Also includes recommended readings, songs, poems, and recordings to be used in conjunction with the movement techniques described.

RUBIN, THEODORE. **JORDI/LISA AND DAVID. 144pp. RaH62, 1.50p.**
Two essays which movingly reveal the inner life of mentally troubled children.

RUDOLF, MARGUERITA. **FROM HAND TO HEAD. Bibliography, index, 159pp. ScB73, 3.95p.**
This handbook for teachers of preschool programs emphasizes learning from physical contacts and under congenial conditions. A number of specific learning programs are outlined and many case histories and anecdotes are included.

SCHAFFER, RUDOLPH. **MOTHERING. Photographs, notes, bibliography, index, 120pp. HUP77, 2.95p.**
A psychological study based on a variety of modern studies of the minute to minute interactions between mother and child. Professor Schaffer argues that the essence of good mothering lies not in rigid schedules or floods of stimulation, but in the sensitivity and receptivity of the mother.

SCHMUCK, RICHARD and PATRICIA. **A HUMANISTIC PSYCHOLOGY OF EDUCATION. Bibliography, index, 399pp. MPC74, 7.95p.**
In this book, we grapple with ways of humanizing schools by using theory and research available from the social sciences—social psychology in particular.... It is meant to be practical: to shed light on what humanized schooling means, what humanized schools look and feel like, and, most important, how such schools can be created. Although it undoubtedly will be used primarily in professional courses...we intend it to be read also by individual educators, parents, students, and citizens interested in our schools.

SCHRANK, JEFFREY. **TEACHING HUMAN BEINGS. 192pp. Bea72, 3.95p.**
An idea book filled with possibilities for making any classroom a real place of learning and discovery. It serves the purpose of being a resource catalogue as well as a mine of practical ideas. This book takes for granted that schools and classrooms need to be greatly changed and makes a practical step in that direction. Many high school teachers feel that this is an extremely useful resource book.

SILBERMAN, CHARLES. **CRISIS IN THE CLASSROOM. Notes, index, 567pp. RaH70/W&W, 2.45p.**
Subtitled, *The Remaking of American Education,* this has been an extremely influential book. *One of the most significant statements on education since World War II. To one of the most important and urgent problems of modern society, Mr. Silberman has brought a unique combination of perceptive inquiry, broad scholarship, and deep personal concern.*—John Fischer, President, Teachers' College, Columbia University.

SILBERMAN, CHARLES, ed. **THE OPEN CLASSROOM READER. 789pp. RaH73, 2.95p.**
A companion to **Crisis in the Classroom,** containing sixty-five selections from American, Canadian, and English sources, plus a general introduction by Mr. Silberman and his running commentary explaining why each selection has been made and how it fits into the overall framework. Each selection presents practical explanations and detailed descriptions of classroom activities and methods, interspersed with theoretical discussions.

SIMON, SIDNEY, ROBERT HAWLEY, and DAVID BRITTON. **COMPOSITION FOR PERSONAL GROWTH. Bibliography, index, 184pp. Har73, 5.95p.**
This book presents a detailed program for teaching composition skills to students in grades seven through twelve. Through guided activities and a wide range of written assignments, this approach attempts to promote the student's awareness of self, his ability to relate positively to others and translate his values into meaningful actions. The authors include many specific suggestions and techniques to stimulate students to exchange ideas about themselves and each other. The material is clearly presented and designed for practical classroom use.

SIMON, SIDNEY, LELAND HOWE, and HOWARD KIRSCHENBAUM. **VALUES CLARIFICATION. 397pp. Har72, 5.95p.**
An inciseful book. The authors' goal is to involve students in practical experiences, making them aware of their own feelings, ideas, and beliefs, so that the choices and decisions they make are conscious and deliberate ones based on their own value systems. The technique outlined here has been widely—and successfully—used throughout the world.

SIMON, SIDNEY and SALLY OLDS. **HELPING YOUR CHILD LEARN RIGHT FROM WRONG.** 223pp. MGH76, 2.95p.
This is a self help manual for parents to aid in establishing moral values and emotional self awareness in children, based on the principles of values clarification. The authors explain why values themselves cannot be taught, but how parents can teach children a process for arriving at their own values. A system is developed through game-like strategies which can help children examine their feelings about friendship, money, work, honesty, and much else. The program is designed to teach children to examine life rationally, weigh alternatives, foresee consequences, cope with the complex world, and prepare to lead joyful and rewarding lives.

SKUTCH, M. and W. HAMLIN. **TO START A SCHOOL.** Many photographs, 147pp. LBC71, 2.45p.
The story of a housewife in Stamford, Connecticut, who started an *Early Learning Center* devoted not only to learning, but to the awareness of how wonderful it is to learn.

SMETHURST, WOOD. **TEACHING YOUNG CHILDREN TO READ AT HOME.** Index, 237pp. MGH75, 7.95c.
This seems to be the most thorough of the many books on this subject. The author has had extensive experience in the teaching field and also as a father. Part I summarizes the history of home reading. Part II develops a step-by-step teaching program, including suggestions for materials. A final section offers a buyer's guide to available teaching material and a reading list.

STANFORD, GENE. **DEVELOPMENT EFFECTIVE CLASSROOM GROUPS.** Bibliography, 287pp. Har77, 5.95p.
A practical guide for teachers, this book offers activities and games which help convert a class of individuals into an effective learning group. Dr. Stanford introduces the teacher to the theory and strategies of group dynamics—a technique which he says enhances learning, minimizes discipline problems, and promotes personal growth. He also analyzes how children operate in groups and examines their patterns of communication and their methods of decision making.

STEINER, RUDOLF. Rudolf Steiner (see our section on his books) was one of the most innovative and creative thinkers of the twentieth century. His conception of man and universe (anthroposophy) has detailed explanations of the scientific application of spiritual principles to all areas of human endeavor. His ideas led naturally into the all important area of childhood education, for Steiner realized that there could be no regeneration of human civilization without a technique, philosophy and practice of education that dealt with the whole human being, emotional, mental, and spiritual. The application of Steiner's ideas in education has come to be known as Waldorf Education (after the first school with that name). The philosophy and approach is centered in the understanding of the child as an evolving human soul with unlimited potentiality. Education then becomes an art whereby the highest, truest, and most beautiful is drawn out of the child and he learns to express his unique, divine individuality in a socially, artistically, and creatively constructive manner. For a description of specific books, see the Waldorf Education subsection in the Steiner section.

STERN, DANIEL. **THE FIRST RELATIONSHIP: MOTHER AND CHILD.** Photographs, notes, bibliography, index, 149+pp. HUP77, 3.95p.
This book focuses on the details of the way mother and infant behave together, and particularly on the playful, apparently frivolous episodes that accompany and modulate their daily routines. Professor Stern argues that these episodes are more than just fun—rather, they are designed to teach the infant about the nature of the social world he will soon enter. Carefully analyzing high speed motion pictures of babies and mothers interacting, Stern offers many examples demonstrating how mothers instinctively instruct infants in *the ways of things human.*

TIMMERMAN, TIM. **GROWING UP ALIVE.** Bibliography, 250pp. Man75, 9.35p.
A collection of exercises and suggestions on humanistic education for the pre-teen, written for teachers. This book begins with a philosophical discussion of how to implement the plans in the book. The major emphasis of the book is on a *how* section divided into two parts: methodology—skills which need to be learned and practiced by students and teachers; and plans—suggestions for learning activities.

TIMMERMAN, TIM and JIM BALLARD. **STRATEGIES IN HUMANISTIC EDUCATION, VOLUME I.** Bibliography, 145pp. Man75, 7.00p.
An in depth examination of a series of words that are important to the process of growing and living. The authors, using these words as stimuli to their thinking, have generated activities and ideas for use in the classroom.

TIMMERMAN, TIM and JIM BALLARD. **STRATEGIES IN HUMANISTIC EDUCATION, VOLUME II.** 237pp. Man76, 9.35p.
The first part of this book outlines eight different strategies for conducting humanistic education activities: S-I-P-A self growth plan, forced choice, rank order, inventories, spectrum, support groups, and energizers. The second section concentrates on activities, divided into eleven themes. All of the skills and strategies outlined in the how-to section are implemented in each of the theme's curricula.

WHITE, BURTON. **THE FIRST THREE YEARS OF LIFE.** Annotated bibliography, index, 298pp. Avo75, 4.95p.
Probably no living person knows more about what happens during the first three years of life than Dr. Burton White, Director of Harvard University's world famous Pre-School Project. And now, for the first time, Dr. White has made his knowledge available in book form to the general reader. The book is a detailed guide to the intellectual and emotional development of the very young child. Dr. White divides the first thirty-six months into seven successive developmental phases, paying special attention to the critical fifth and sixth phases. For each phase he provides both a comprehensive description of the characteristic physical, emotional, and mental developments of which parents must be aware and a detailed list of instructions concerning childrearing practices, parental strategies, and even toys and equipment. This is an excellent book which we cannot recommend too highly.

WICKES, FRANCES. **THE INNER WORLD OF CHILDHOOD.** 8.00p.
See the Jungian Psychology section.

WURMAN, RICHARD. **THE YELLOW PAGES OF LEARNING RESOURCES.** 8½"x11", 94pp. MIT72, 1.95p.
A new look at how to learn about living from simply taking a closer look at all the many things that go on around us. The book opens up the sense of discovery and introduces a new way of looking at things, a new perspective and awareness of the many things in our culture from which we can learn. Contains information and suggestions about learning from such things as airports, restaurants, tree stumps, candy, money, telephones, cemeteries, libraries, etc.

FAIRY TALES

Fairy tales are the purest and simplest expression of collective unconscious psychic processes. Therefore their value for the scientific investigation of the unconscious exceeds that of all other material. They represent the archetypes in their simplest, barest and most concise form. In this pure form, the archetypal images afford us the best clues to the understanding of the processes going on in the collective psyche. In myths or legends, or any other more elaborate mythological material, we get at the basic patterns of the human psyche through an overlay of cultural material. But in fairy tales there is much less specific conscious cultural material and therefore they mirror the basic patterns of the psyche more clearly.

In terms of Jung's concept, every archetype is in its essence an *unknown* psychic factor and therefore there is no possibility of translating its content into intellectual terms. The best we can do is to circumscribe it on the basis of our own psychological experience and from comparative studies, bringing up into light, as it were, the whole net of associations in which the archetypal images are enmeshed. The fairy tale itself is its own best explanation; that is, its meaning is contained in the totality of its motifs connected by the thread of the story. The unconscious is, metaphorically speaking, in the same position as one who has had an original vision or experience and wishes to share it. Since it is an event that has never been conceptually formulated he is at a loss for means of expression. When a person is in that position he makes several attempts to convey the thing and tries to evoke, by intuitive appeal and analogy to familiar material, some response in his listeners, and never tires of expounding his vision until he feels they have some sense of the content. In the same way we can put forward the hypothesis that every fairy tale is a relatively closed system compounding one essential psychological meaning which is expressed in a series of symbolical pictures and events and is discoverable in these.

After working for many years in this field, I have come to the conclusion that all fairy tales endeavour to describe one and the same psychic fact, but a fact so complex and far-reaching and so difficult for us to realize in all its different aspects that hundreds of tales and thousands of repetitions with a musician's variations are needed until this unknown fact is delivered into consciousness; and even then the theme is not exhausted. This unknown fact is what Jung calls the Self, which is the psychic totality of an individual and also, paradoxically, the regulating center of the collective unconscious. Every individual and every nation has its own modes of experiencing this psychic reality.

Different fairy tales give average pictures of different phases of the experience. They sometimes dwell more on the beginning stages, which deal with the experience of the shadow and give only a short sketch of what comes later. Other tales emphasize the experience of animus and anima and of the father and mother images behind them and gloss over the preceding shadow problem and what follows. Others emphasize the motif of the inaccessible or unobtainable treasure and the central experiences. There is no difference of value between these tales, because in the archetypal world there are no gradations of value for the reason that every archetype is in its essence only one aspect of the collective unconscious as well as always representing also the whole collective unconscious.

We read in Plato's writings that old women told their children stories—*mythoi*. Even then fairy tales were connected with the education of children. In later antiquity Apuleius, a philosopher and writer of the second century A.D., built into his famous novel **The Golden Ass** a fairy tale called *Amor and Psyche*, a type of beauty and the beast story. This fairy tale runs on the same pattern as those one can nowadays still collect in Norway, Sweden, Russia and many other countries. It has therefore been concluded that at least this type of fairy tale (that of a woman redeeming an animal lover) has existed for 2,000 years, practically unaltered. But we have even older information, because fairy tales have also been found in Egyptian *papyri* and *stelai*, one of the most famous being that of the two brothers, Anup (i.e., Anubis) and Bata. Its runs absolutely parallel to the two brother-type tales, which one can still collect in all European countries. We have written tradition for 3,000 years and, what is striking, *the basic motifs have not changed much*. Until the seventeenth and eighteenth centuries, fairy tales were—and still are in remote primitive centres of civilization—told to adults as well as to children. In Europe they used to be the chief winter-time form of entertainment. In agricultural populations fairy tale-telling became a kind of essential, spiritual occupation.

It was this religious search for something which seemed lacking in official Christian teaching that first induced the famous brothers Jakob and Wilhelm Grimm to collect folk tales. Before then, fairy tales suffered the same fate as the unconscious itself, which was taken for granted. People take it for granted and live on it, but do not want to admit its existence. They make use of it—for instance, in magic and talismans. If you have a good dream, you exploit it, but at the same time you do not take it seriously. For such people a fairy tale or a dream does not need to be looked at accurately but may be distorted; since it is not *scientific* material, one can just as well spin a little around it and one has the right to pick what suits one and to discard the rest.

That same strange unreliable, unscientific, and dishonest attitude has for a long time prevailed towards fairy tales. So I always tell students to look up the original. You can still get editions of the Grimm fairy tales in which some scenes have been omitted and those from other fairy tales inserted. The editor or translator is sometimes impertinent enough to distort the story without taking the trouble to make a footnote. They would not dare do that with the Gilgamesh Epic or a text of that kind, but fairy tales seem to provide a free hunting ground where some feel free to take any liberty.

The brothers Grimm wrote down fairy tales literally, as told by people in their surroundings, but even they could sometimes not resist mixing a few versions, though in a tactful way. They were honest enough to mention it in footnotes or in their letters to Achim von Arnim. But even the Grimms did not yet have that scientific attitude, which modern folklore writers and ethnologists try to have, of taking down a story literally and leaving the holes and paradoxes in it, dreamlike and paradoxical as they may sound.

The collection of fairy tales which the Brothers Grimm published was a tremendous success. There must have been a strong unconscious emotional interest, for like a mushroom growth other editions popped up everywhere, such as the collection of Perrault in France. In every country people began to make a basic collection of their national fairy tales. At once everybody was struck by the enormous number of recurrent themes. The same theme, in thousands of variations, came up again and again in French, Russian, Finnish, and Italian collections.

—condensed from **Interpretation of Fairy Tales**, *by Marie Louise Von Franz*

AARDEMA, VERNA. **BEHIND THE BACK OF THE MOUNTAIN: BLACK FOLKTALES FROM SOUTHERN AFRICA. 5.95c.**
See the African Philosophies section.

Aesop's Fables

Aesop is the name traditionally assigned to the author of a collection of Greek fables; he is almost certainly a legendary figure. The main difference between fables and fairy tales, other than sheer length, is that there can be no good fable with human beings in it and no good fairy tale without them. In a fable, all the characters are totally impersonal and simply represent stereotypes. Fables are also almost always about animals. Aesop's is the classic collection of fables and it set the style for all that were to follow. All the tales are short (no more than a paragraph), there is absolutely no character development, and a moral is appended to each one.

BEWICK, THOMAS, il. **THE FABLES OF AESOP. 400pp. Pad75, 6.95p.**
A very complete collection of the fables, illustrated by one of the nineteenth century's most noted engravers. The plates are small and detailed and do not particularly appeal to us. Over 250 woodcuts are included in this edition. This is an unabridged reproduction of the first edition of 1818.

HANDFORD, S.A., tr. **FABLES OF AESOP. Illustrations, notes, 250pp. Vik64, 2.95p.**
Translations of 207 of the fables attributed to Aesop along with an introduction tracing the history of fables and discussing Aesop himself. Handford is a wonderful storyteller.

JACOBS, JOSEPH, ed. **THE FABLES OF AESOP. Introduction, notes, index, 223pp. ScB1894, 2.45p.**
Jacobs was one of the most accomplished nineteenth century folklorists. In this volume his graceful retelling of Aesop is combined with an extensive series of line drawings by Richard Heighway, classic illustrations which help bring the fables to life.

MILLER, J.P. **TALES FROM AESOP. 8"x8", RaH76, .95p.**
This is a retelling of six of the fables. The book is very fully illustrated with brightly colored drawings simple enough to be enjoyed by even the smallest child. There is a fair amount of text, and it is designed to be read to the child.

SPRIGGS, RUTH, ed. **THE FABLES OF AESOP. 8½"x11", 116pp. RMN75, 5.95c.**
This is a fully illustrated (mainly in color) collection of 143 fables, specially retold and illustrated for children between the ages of six and twelve.

WRIGHT, FREIRE and MICHAEL FOREMAN. **BORROWED FEATHERS AND OTHER FABLES. 8¼"x8¼", RaH78, 3.95c.**
Simple new versions of seven of Aesop's most popular fables, illustrated in shimmering watercolors.

—————END OF AESOP'S FABLES SUBSECTION—————

AFANAS'EV, ALEKSANDR. **RUSSIAN FAIRY TALES. Notes, index, 662pp. RaH45, 12.95c/5.95p.**
This is the only comprehensive edition available in English of the classic Russian folk and fairy tales collected by Afanas'ev, the Russian counterpart to the brothers Grimm. This collection introduces the Russian versions of such universal fairy tale figures as witches and heroes, soldiers and fishermen, peasants and kings, beggars and thieves; as well as such unique Russian creations as Koshchey the Deathless, Baba Yoga, the Swan Maiden, and the splendid Firebird. These immortal tales are a storehouse of psychological and historical experience. An excellent commentary is included as well as many fine illustrations by Alexander Alexeieff.

ALEXANDER, LLOYD. **THE BLACK CAULDRON. 229pp. Del65, 1.50p.**
Book two in the Prydain chronicles. The story becomes more heroic here as the quest now is aimed at destroying the black cauldron in which evil Arawn created his terrible army of deathless warriors from stolen bodies.

ALEXANDER, LLOYD. **THE BOOK OF THREE. 224pp. Del64, 1.25p.**
This is the first book in Alexander's chronicle of the land of Prydain, a series inspired by Wales and Welsh mythology. Those who have enjoyed LeGuin, Tolkien, and Walton will also like Alexander's series. The language is simplified and the books are quite obviously aimed at older children. This book is a tale of enchantement, of good and evil. Young Taran, an assistant pig-keeper, sets out on a hazardous mission to save his land from the forces of evil and encounters many strange adventures.

ALEXANDER, LLOYD. **THE CASTLE OF LLYR. 206pp. Del66, 1.25p.**
Book three of the Prydain chronicles. Princess Eilonwy must leave her kingdom to go to the Isle of Mona for training. Because she possesses magical powers she is sought out by the most evil enchantress in the land. Shortly after her arrival something sinister befalls her. Her friends realize her peril and set out on a terrifying mission to rescue her.

ALEXANDER, LLOYD. **THE HIGH KING. 304pp. Del68, 1.50p.**
The final book in the Prydain chronicles. The most powerful weapon in the kingdom has fallen into the hands of Arwan, the death-lord. Taran, his friends, and Prince Gwydion raise an army to march against Arwan's terrible cohorts. The book ends with a successful battle and the proclamation of Taran as High King of Prydain.

ALEXANDER, LLOYD. **TARAN WANDERER. 272pp. Del67, 1.50p.**
Book four of the Prydain chronicles. Taran goes on a quest to find out his true parentage. After many adventures he is sent by three wily enchantresses to consult the Mirror of Llunet for the answers he is seeking, with the cryptic promise that *the finding takes no more than the looking.*

ALEXANDER, LLOYD. **TIME CAT. Illustrations, 191pp. Avo63, 1.25p.**
A delightful collection of adventures, filled with excitement and excellent imagery. Gareth, Jason's magical cat, has the power to transport the two across time into ancient Egypt, Rome, Peru, and anywhere else he chooses. The book tells of some of Jason and Gareth's adventures in other times and places.

ALEXANDER, LLOYD. **THE TOWN CATS. 126pp. Dut77, 7.50c.**
A collection of eight tales in the traditional style about cats who outwit, outmaneuver, and often outclass the humans with whom they come into contact. A series of detailed charcoal drawings by Laszlo Kubinyi accompany the tales.

ANDERSEN, HANS CHRISTIAN. **THE COMPLETE FAIRY TALES AND STORIES. Introduction, boxed, notes, index, 1125pp. Dou74, 16.95c.**
A definitive collection, translated by Erik Christian Haugaard.

ANDERSEN, HANS CHRISTIAN. **DULAC'S THE SNOW QUEEN AND OTHER STORIES. 7"x9½", 144pp. Dou75, 7.95c.**
Andersen was a contemporary of the brothers Grimm. Unlike the latter, he wrote his own tales; while they reflect traditional Scandinavian folklore themes, they are his own creations. He is one of the best known folklorists and his stories are represented in all the major collections. Five of Hans Christian Andersen's most loved fairy tales—*The Snow Queen, The Nightingale, The Emperor's New Clothes, The Little Mermaid,* and *The Wind Tale*—illustrated with fifteen color pictures by Edmund Dulac, one of the most famous illustrators of the early twentieth century.

ANDERSEN, HANS CHRISTIAN. **FAIRY TALES, ILLUSTRATED BY ARTHUR RACKHAM. 7¼"x10¼", 288pp. Crn32, 5.98c.**
Rackham selected the tales included in this volume and each one is illustrated with many line drawings and some color prints.

ANDERSEN, HANS CHRISTIAN. **THE FIR TREE. 38pp. H&R70, 7.95c.**
Deep in the forest lived a little fir tree. He was surrounded by sunlight, singing birds, and sweet flowers. Children would come to see him; they thought he was the prettiest tree of them all. Yet, the little fir was not content. He longed to grow, and to find something grander, something greater in life. Then he would be happy—or so he thought. This classic tale is exquisitely illustrated by Nancy Ekholm Burkert with detailed color paintings and drawings.

ANDERSEN, HANS CHRISTIAN. **HANS ANDERSEN'S FAIRY TALES. 7"x8¾", 308pp. PnB13, 3.45p/each.**
A two volume collection of the most popular fairy tales by Andersen superbly illustrated by W. Heath Robinson in color and black and white.

ANDERSEN, HANS CHRISTIAN. **THE NIGHTINGALE. 9¾"x11", 34pp. H&R65, 7.95c.**
This version of Andersen's classic tale is illustrated with exquisite full page, double spread paintings by Nancy Ekholm Burkert. The illustrations are delicately colored and filled with detail. They bring the story to life and recreate the ancient Chinese court. Ms. Burkert is our favorite illustrator and we highly recommend her books. We are not as pleased with Eva Le Gallienne's somewhat stilted retelling, however it is an adequate rendition. The story tells of an emperor of China and his joyous possession of, first a real nightingale, and then a singing, jeweled fake one.

ANGULO, JAIME DE. **INDIAN TALES. 3.45p/1.75p.**
See the American Indian Religion section.

THE ARABIAN NIGHTS.
For descriptions of a variety of editions of **The Arabian Nights** see the Islam section.

AUNG, MAUNG HTIN and HELEN G. TRAGER. **A KINGDOM LOST FOR A DROP OF HONEY AND OTHER BURMESE FOLKTALES. Glossary, 7¼"x9¼", 96pp. PMP68, 5.95c.**
Though no two of these folktales are very much alike, they reveal qualities that many Burmese people have: a directness, almost bluntness, yet restraint and courtesy. Also, you come on unexpected things, like surprise endings and surprise characters....If humor were lacking these wouldn't be Burmese tales, for Burmese people enjoy laughter. They have a keen sense of the ridiculous; they delight in preposterous, incongruous situations, and are able to laugh at themselves....A type of tale included here in several variations is one in which there is discord or argument.... The parties in the dispute voluntarily seek out an individual with a cool heart and wise head....True to Burmese Buddhist tradition, their decisions must be directed at the reestablishment of harmony, rather than at establishing guilt or meting out punishment.—from the foreword. The tales are illustrated with lovely block prints.

BABBITT, ELLEN. **THE JATAKAS. 6.00c.**
See the **Jataka Tales** subsection of Buddhism.

BAIN, R. NISBET, tr. **TURKISH FAIRY TALES. Illustrations, introduction, 285pp. Dov1896, 2.50p.**
The Turkish tales are a curious blend of Eastern and Western elements which turns them into stories that are extraordinarily bizarre and beautiful. The tales are reminiscent at times of the **Arabian Nights** and at other times of the tales of the brothers Grimm. They are filled with magic carpets and magic mirrors, animals and birds with extraordinary powers, great journeys, and magical people—the peris. Seventeen tales from Asia Minor are followed by four from Rumania which reflect a blend of Magyar, Slavonic, Romance, and Turkish elements. This book was compiled at a time when Turkey's ancient oral tradition was still very much alive.

BANG, MOLLY. **THE BURIED MOON AND OTHER STORIES. 6¼"x8¼", 64pp. Scr77, 5.95c.**
Five mysterious tales from the folk literature of India, Germany, China, England, and Japan. Each has at its core the buried moon inside us all which only experience, effort, and trust will enable us to find and set free. Many magical illustrations accompany the tales.

BATO, JOSEPH. **THE SORCERER. 171pp. McK76, 6.95c.**
The paintings found on the walls of prehistoric caves in Lascaux, France, have long been considered the work of the earliest magicians—men whose talents at depicting the world around them gave them special powers over the beasts and the elements. From these paintings, the author has drawn the story of a young Stone Age boy who becomes apprenticed to a sorcerer. He becomes a painter and soon his power surpasses even that of the old sorcerer.

BAUER, JOHN, il. **GREAT SWEDISH FAIRY TALES. Many color plates, 7¼"x9¼", 249pp. Del73, 6.95p.**
The favorite fairy tales of generations of Swedish children are combined in this anthology with pictures by Sweden's greatest illustrator of fairy tales, Bauer. Gentle and malicious trolls, knights in search of princesses, elks and bears and other creatures of the deep northern forests, stream through this enchanted world. Bauer adds his own vision to these perennial stories. His gnarled, shaggy trolls, mossy forest caverns, and slender medieval knights on stallions in the moonlight seem to express the essence of Scandinavian tradition and imagination. Holger Lundbergh, the translator of these stories, is the grandson of Helena Nyblom, a famous Danish storyteller.

BAUMANN, HANS. **HERO LEGENDS OF THE WORLD. Illustrations, 153pp. Den75, 7.40c.**
A collection of myths and folk tales from Eastern Europe, Siberia, Africa, Asia, Australia, and the Americas. Many of the selections are not terribly well known. The themes are heroism, the conflict with evil, the search for what is right, and the protection of others. This is a flowing, well written retelling, geared toward young readers.

BETTELHEIM, BRUNO. **THE USES OF ENCHANTMENT. Notes, bibliography, index, 339pp. RaH76/Pen, 3.95p.**
This is a masterful examination which opens the reader up to the real content of the great fairy tales. Dr. Bettelheim shows how, beneath their surface shimmer of palaces and princesses, fairies and witches, wishes and spells, they deal in the profoundest ways with the emotional turmoils of childhood—with feelings of smallness and helplessness, with the terrifying perceptions of outward dangers, with the even more terrifying anxieties the child feels possessed by, with the mystery of the outside world, and with the child's deepest questions about self and about the future. He also shows how fairy tales help children cope with their emotions and their world and how they reveal the child, subconsciously to him or herself. Over half the book is devoted to a detailed examination and retelling of some of the best known stories. Here Dr. Bettelheim shows specifically how the tales work to support and free the child.

BRIGGS, KATHERINE. **BRITISH FOLKTALES. 315+pp. RaH77/RKP, 10.00c.**
This volume is culled from Dr. Briggs' massive 2,558 page **Dictionary of British Folk-Tales**. The folk narratives in this collection are divided into five groups: fables and exempla, fairy tales, jocular tales, novelle,

and nursery tales. The selections include stories about bogies, devils, dragons, fairies, ghosts, witches, giants, and the supernatural; as well as local and historical legends, origin myths, and legends of saints. Dr. Briggs is past president of the English Folklore Society.

BRIGGS, KATHERINE and RUTH TONGUE, eds. **FOLKTALES OF ENGLAND. Glossary, bibliography, indices of motifs and tale types, 208pp. UCh65, 2.95p.**
An excellent collection, divided into wonder tales, legends, and jocular tales. The editors provide a brief discussion of the origin of each tale as well as a lengthy introduction.

BROCKETT, ELEANOR. **TURKISH FAIRY TALES. Illustrations, 198pp. Mll63, 5.95c.**
These stories have an affinity with both the traditional legends and folklore of the Orient and the fairy tales of Europe. They have on the whole a background of peasant life and agricultural labor, rather than the piety of the mosque and the guile of the bazaar, although these too play their part in giving these stories their unique character. This is a varied collection, retold by Ms. Brockett.

CARPENTER, FRANCES. **TALES OF A CHINESE GRANDMOTHER. Many illustrations, 272pp. Tut73, 3.95p.**
A rich treasury of Chinese folklore is represented in these tales told against the vivid and realistic background of the Ling household and its life in the China of the early twentieth century. It is the aged grandmother who tells the tales, sometimes on festive occasions to the assembled family, but more often to her two grandchildren. Ms. Carpenter herself traveled extensively in China.

CARROLL, LEWIS. **ALICE IN WONDERLAND. 80pp. SMP76, 4.95p.**
An 8½"x11" version, with the illustrations of John Tenniel.

CARROLL, LEWIS. **ALICE'S ADVENTURES IN WONDERLAND 7½"x9¾", 162pp. Vik07, 6.95c.**
Alice in Wonderland is one of those classic tales which, while it is generally considered a children's story, has as much appeal to adults as it does to children. This edition includes Arthur Rackham's wonderfully detailed illustrations in color and black and white.

CARROLL, LEWIS. **ALICE'S ADVENTURES IN WONDERLAND AND THROUGH THE LOOKING GLASS. 347pp. Vik62, 1.95p.**
This volume contains the text of the first edition of both works, with ninety-two illustrations by John Tenniel. There is also ample introductory material.

CARROLL, LEWIS. **THE ANNOTATED ALICE. Bibliography, 8¼"x11", 352pp. Crn nd/Pen, 5.98c/3.95p.**
This is the only edition of Carroll's two masterpieces, **Alice's Adventures in Wonderland** and **Through the Looking Glass**, that contains the full text together with all of the original John Tenniel illustrations in their correct places, and that adds to this a full annotation running concurrently with the text.

CARRUTH, JANE. **MY WORLD OF FAIRY TALES. 7½"x10¼", 220pp. RMN76, 5.95c.**
An illustrated collection of stories from Perrault, Grimm, and Andersen. There are color pictures on every page and the quality of the illustrations is uniformly good. The retellings are well done and designed to appeal to young readers.

CARTER, ANGELA, tr. **THE FAIRY TALES OF CHARLES PERRAULT. Introduction, 159pp. Glz77, 8.00c.**
New translations of Perrault's ten stories; faithful to the simplicity and charm of the originals. Perrault's late seventeenth century compilation contains some of the best known of all fairy tales: *Cinderella, Little Red Riding Hood, Puss in Boots, Bluebeard,* and *Sleeping Beauty.* Etchings by Martin Ware illustrate the stories.

CHRISTIANSEN, REIDAR, ed. **FOLKTALES OF NORWAY. Long introduction, glossary, bibliography, indices, 333pp. UCh64, 4.95p.**
Often lacking the clear episodic structure of folktales about talking animals and magic objects, legends grow from retellings of personal experiences. Christiansen isolated some seventy-seven legend types, and many of these are represented here in absorbing stories of St. Olaf, hidden treasure, witches, and spirits of the air, water, and Earth. The ugly, massively strong, but slow witted trolls are familiar to English speaking readers. Less well known, but the subject of an enormous number of legends are the more man-like yet sinister *huldre-folk* who live in houses and try to woo human girls. All the tales reflect the wildness of Norway, its mountains, forests, lakes, and sea, and the stalwart character of its sparse population.

CLASK, ANN. **THE SECRET OF THE ANDES. 120pp. Vik52, 1.25p.**
This is the story of an Inca boy who lives in a hidden valley high in the mountains of Peru with an old llama herder. The boy is of royal blood and he is the *chosen one*—but all this is unknown to him until the end of the story. The book tells of his life and how he learned the ancient religious teachings and practices. A Newbery Award Book.

COATSWORTH, ELIZABETH. **THE CAT WHO WENT TO HEAVEN. 7¾"x9¼", 63pp. McM58, 5.50c/1.95p.**
This is the story of a little cat who came to the home of a poor Japanese artist and, by humility and devotion, brought him good fortune. When the artist was commissioned to paint the death of the Buddha for the village temple, the artists drew all the animals who came to receive the blessing of the dying Buddha. The cat sat by and begged to be included—even though the cat alone of all the animals had refused to accept the teachings of the Buddha—and finally the compassionate artist did include her, thus bringing about a miracle. Illustrated throughout. Winner of the 1931 Newbery Medal.

COLUM, PADRAIC. **THE BOY APPRENTICED TO AN ENCHANTER. 150pp. McM20, 4.95c.**
This is a collection of magical fantasy tales. It consists of three interrelated tales on the title theme and tells of Eean, a fisherman's son, who is apprenticed to Merlin and has many adventures, performing magical deeds and vanquishing a series of enemies. Fine line drawings illuminate the narrative.

COLUM, PADRAIC, ed. **A TREASURY OF IRISH FOLKLORE. Introduction, index, 640pp. Crn67, 7.95c.**
An excellent collection of stories, traditions, legends, humor, wisdom, ballads, and songs—over 300 stories and thirty songs in all. Colum is Irish and he first heard many of these stories from his grandmother. He was later involved with William Butler Yeats, Lady Gregory, and many others in the Irish Renaissance.

COURLANDER, HAROLD and GEORGE HERZOG. **THE COW-TAIL SWITCH AND OTHER WEST AFRICAN TALES. 5.95c.**
See the African Philosophies section.

DASENT, G.W., tr. **EAST O' THE SUN AND WEST O' THE MOON. 433pp. Dov70, 4.00p.**
This is one of the basic collections of fairy tales. Most editions of the work are incomplete, often reprinting a small fraction of the fifty-nine stories that Dasent translated from the great collection of Scandinavian folktales gathered by Asbjornsen and Mod in the mid nineteenth century. This is a full unabridged edition of all the stories. Many traditional illustrations are also included.

DEROIN, NANCY. **JATAKA TALES: FABLES FROM THE BUDDHA. 5.95c.**
See the **Jataka Tales** subsection of Buddhism.

DICKINSON, WILLIAM. **BORROBIL. Illustrations, 174pp. Vik44/Pen, 1.50p.**
Two children enter a dark, mysterious wood where they meet Borrobil, a white wizard. He takes them back in time and leads them through a variety of adventures including a dragon fight and a battle between the White King of Summer and the Black King of Winter.

DORSON, RICHARD. **FOLK LEGENDS OF JAPAN. Many illustrations, introduction, bibliography, indices, 256pp. Tut62, 3.25p.**
The true folk legend, is distinguished from fairy tale or literary embellishment, as one of the sure keys to a people's beliefs, customs, and ways of thinking. Japan possesses more such legends than does any Occidental country. This book contains a representative collection of over 100 folk legends, selected by a distinguished Japanese folklorist, drawn from expert Japanese transcriptions of oral legends, and carefully translated. The legends are grouped thematically and each is carefully annotated.

EAGER, EDWARD. **HALF MAGIC. Illustrations, 217pp. HBJ54, 1.75p.**
Four young children who have been reading the books of E. Nesbit stumble on a magical world of their own. They take turns making wishes and their wishes lead them into incredible adventures.

EBERHARD, WOLFRAM, ed. **FOLKTALES OF CHINA. Extensive notes, 309pp. UCh65, 4.45p/1.25p.**
Although folktale themes are an important part of Chinese literature, the scientific collection of folktales began in China only with the nationalist movement which followed World War I. Many facets of Chinese life and culture are revealed in these stories of city gods and magicians, thieves and beggars, serpents and tigers, treacherous ministers and dutiful sons. This collection of seventy-nine stories is drawn from Eberhard's 1937 landmark work, supplemented by six newly translated tales from Communist China. Historical notes for each tale and indexes of motifs and types add to the book's usefulness.

ELLIOT, GERALDINE. **THE LONG GRASS WHISPERS: A BOOK OF AFRICAN FOLKTALES. 139pp. ScB39, 2.95p.**
All through the African day men and women, children and animals, on their way to the maize gardens, to the water holes, to the hunting grounds, to the forests, pass through the long grass. What happens there to beasts and men cannot be spoken of in the daylight. But at night the people gather round the flickering fire, within the dark circle of the hut, to hear the grandmother as she leans against the hut pole, telling how the animals live and talk. Her imagination and her personality illuminate the ancient stories with her own turns and phrases. The story is the same, but its telling is ever changing, for the long grass whispers its secrets anew to each hearer.—from the foreword. Each tale is delightfully illustrated.

ELLIOT, GERALDINE. **THE SINGING CHAMELEON. Illustrations, pronunciation guide, 171pp. RKP57, 5.00c.**
A collection of animal stories woven around the proverbs and customs of Central Africa. With most African tribes the chameleon is highly unpopular, and he is blamed for the fact that the Bantu are black. The Anyanja, however, have a proverb: *If your face is ugly, learn to sing* and Ms. Elliot has made her chameleon follow this advice. He does this well and so earns the right to be a *Teller of Tales* and a *Singer of Songs*. The stories in this book are, for the most part, either told by or to him.

ELLIOT, GERALDINE. **WHERE THE LEOPARD PASSES. 141pp. ScB49, 2.95p.**
A delightful collection of African fables which point up human foibles through the tricks of animals. This is one of the most popular collections of African folk tales. A series of charming illustrations accompany the fables.

ERDOES, RICHARD, ed. **THE SOUND OF FLUTES AND OTHER INDIAN LEGENDS. 5.95c.**
See the American Indian Religion section.

Fairies

Fairies are supernormal beings who, skilled in magic, can become invisible, change shape and size, and bewitch or aid human beings. Fairies were said to live far longer than men, but had no souls and perished utterly at death. While some are of human size and appearance, the flower fairies of Devon were minute beings, some only three inches high. Once feared as dangerous and powerful, they were euphemistically called *the gentle people* or *the good neighbors*; to refer to them by name gave them power over the speaker. One who visited fairyland might return with scattered wits, or a new lease on life, or he might find that long years had elapsed in his apparently short absence. Fairies were often resorted to for their healing powers, and they in turn frequently sought human mid-wives. Fairy men sometimes took human wives, or a fairy woman might consent to marry a man. One of the fairies most dreaded habits was stealing human babies and substituting a changeling or fairy child, so that it might have the benefit of human milk. Some fairies were agriculturists, cattle keepers, weavers, and woodworkers. Others, such as brownies, attached themselves to human families as helpers. There were also nature fairies, who haunted woods, moorlands, and rivers. Such were the Scandinavian trolls and the German wood women. Various theories purport to account for the widespread and persistent belief in fairies. One is that it derives from an actual memory of Neolithic peoples who precariously survived in isolated communities after conquest by other peoples. With their superior knowledge of the countryside and of native gods, they might be credited with magic, and they might also help, harm, or intermarry. Another suggestion is that the belief springs from legends of pagan gods and nature spirits, whose worship was suppressed under Christianity. Gaelic fairy lore can best be explained by this theory. In any case, fairies and little people have been sighted and discussed down the ages in a wide variety of cultures and they remain a persistent element of world folklore.

ARROWSMITH, NANCY. **FIELD GUIDE TO THE LITTLE PEOPLE. Illustrations, notes, bibliography, index, 296pp. FSG77/MGB, 3.95p.**
As the title suggests this is a delightful compendium of folklore and descriptions of the inhabitants of elfland (elves is the generic term the author prefers). Each of the seventy-nine entries sets out the lineage, habitat, appearance, and general characteristics of the species concerned. This information is followed by case histories, forming a rich compendium of folk tales.

BARKER, CICELY. **THE FAIRY'S GIFT. Color illustrations, TCP46, 1.95c.**
This is the story of a little girl who wishes she had a different necklace for every day of the year. For reasons of their own, the fairies decide to make her wish come true and they present her with an extraordinary treasure trove of fairy jewels that changes her life beyond all expectations. Originally published under the title **Groundsel and Necklaces.**

BARKER, CICELY. **FLOWER FAIRY BOOKS. Each book is about 50pp. TCP nd/Bla, 1.95c/each.**
This series of books has delighted children and adults alike for many years. Each of the pictures of the fairies is full page and beautifully colored. The personality of each fairy comes across and each is totally unlike the others. A poem accompanies each drawing. The following books are available: **A FLOWER FAIRY ALPHABET** (2.95p), **FLOWER FAIRIES OF THE AUTUMN, FLOWER FAIRIES OF THE GARDEN, FLOWER FAIRIES OF THE SPRING, FLOWER FAIRIES OF THE SUMMER, FLOWER FAIRIES OF THE TREES,** and **FLOWER FAIRIES OF THE WAYSIDE.**

BRIGGS, KATHERINE. **AN ENCYCLOPEDIA OF FAIRIES: HOB-GOBLINS, BROWNIES, BOGIES, AND OTHER SUPERNATURAL CREATURES. Bibliography, index, 493pp. RaH76/Pen, 4.95p**
This is a unique reference work in which the reader learns not only about the appearance and customs of the varied inhabitants of the fairy world, but also can read short essays on questions such as the fairy economy, their food, sports, and varying sizes and powers. Every conceivable topic is discussed at length. And there are illustrations too! Dr. Briggs is one of England's most prominent folklorists.

BRIGGS, KATHERINE. **THE FAIRIES IN TRADITION AND LIT-ERATURE. Illustrations, notes, bibliography, index, 271pp. RKP67, 6.50p.**
An excellent study of the fairy faith, divided into the following general topics: _The Fairy Peoples, Traffic with the Fairies,_ and _Some Literary Fairies._ Dr. Briggs is quite possibly the most qualified scholar to write about fairies; she is the author of numerous definitive works on British folk tales. She includes a number of eyewitness accounts, as well as quotations from a wide variety of literary sources.

DOYLE, ARTHUR CONAN. **THE COMING OF THE FAIRIES. 196pp. Wei21, 3.95p.**
We all know about the author through his master detective Sherlock Holmes, yet few realize that Sir Arthur was an enthusiastic occultist who lectured throughout Europe and in America on higher metaphysical and psychic subjects. He was quite knowledgeable in the hidden side of nature as exemplified in this series of articles and letters by Doyle and others. Controversial photographs are included of fairies and nymphs.

EVANS-WENTZ, W.Y. **THE FAIRY FAITH IN CELTIC COUNTRIES. Many notes, index, 462pp. Smy77, 11.75p.**
First published in 1911, **The Fairy-Faith** has become a classic on the subject. Its theme, as Kathleen Raine says in her foreword, is _the other-world of the Celtic race as this can be discovered in the fairy-lore common to all the Celtic countries. . . . In their beliefs and traditions about the fairy-world the Celts have retained elements of their pre-Christian religion._ [_They have_] _preserved elements of the religion of a learned caste, the Druids, whom Pythagoras himself honored as custodians of secret knowledge. Elements of earlier and later faiths and local circumstances have coloured this immemorial doctrine of the unseen world only superficially. . . . The old religion is grounded in the unchanging nature of things visible and invisible common to all traditions . . . the universe is held to be living. The visible is but the outer aspect of the one life, diverisifed into spiritual beings, energies, and agencies of all kinds._

GARDNER, EDWARD. **FAIRIES. 53pp. TPH45, 8.25c.**
A record of clairvoyant observations of brownies, elves, gnomes, mannikins, sea spirits, fairies, sylphs, and angels. Includes the famous Coltinghley photographs purporting to be of actual fairies, as well as extensive interpretative material.

GELDER, DORA VAN. **THE REAL WORLD OF FAIRIES: A TRUE, FIRST PERSON ACCOUNT. 120pp. TPH77, 3.25p.**
Dora Van Gelder was brought up in the East, where the visible and the invisible world impinge upon one another and interpenetrate in a manner and to an extent strange and incredible to Western habits of thought. Her parents were gifted with the same clairvoyant power which she possesses, and in her young girlhood she was under the tutelage of C.W. Leadbeater. . . . The folklore of all nations abounds in stories of creatures of the air and of the water who are induced by love of a mortal to take human shape and incur human experience while still maintaining their contact with their own world and the denizens of that world. . . . Preposterous as such an idea may seem to the conventional thinker, it is the only one, to my mind, which at all explains Dora.— Claude Bragdon. Ms. Van Gelder describes seven different types of fairies on the basis of her personal perceptions.

HUYGEN, WIL and RIEN POORTVLIET. **GNOMES. 9¾"x12¼", 212pp. Abr77, 17.50p.**
This is an absolutely delightful book which will appeal to adults as well as children. We loved going through it! Poortvliet is Holland's most popular illustrator and every page is filled with his color drawings, maps, and diagrams. Huygen is a science writer, and he brings verisimilitude to this natural history of gnomes. Every aspect of gnome

life is discussed and illustrated in a factual manner. Did you know that gnomes rub noses in both greeting and farewell? Or that gnome couples always have twins? We follow the daily life of the whole gnome family as they go about their rounds and learn of their alliances with various animals, their use of medicinal herbs, their courtship habits, the ways they use natural energy, and an incredible assortment of other tidbits!

LARKIN, DAVID, ed. **FAERIES. 251 illustrations, 228 in color, 8¼"x 12", 208pp. Abr78, 17.50c.**
An exquisitely illustrated, delightful exploration of the fairy world, with information on all the fairy types—elves, gnomes, leprechauns, dryads, pixies, and others. Larkin includes a wonderful selection of fairy myths, legends, folklore, and fantasy. The book was put together in response to the success of **Gnomes** and it is equally well done.

MACMANUS, DIARMUID. **IRISH EARTH FOLK. Illustrations, photographs, 192pp. DAC59, 6.95c.**
A straightforward account of fairylore in present day Ireland. MacManus states that all of his histories are well authenticated, factual accounts. The author begins with a general survey of the little folk; the rest of the book is devoted to actual reports of sightings.

—————————**END OF FAIRIES SUBSECTION**—————————

FOREMAN, MICHAEL and PETER HARRIS. **MONKEY AND THE THREE WIZARDS. 8"x9¾", WCS76, 8.40c.**
This delightful tale is based on a single episode from the epic adventure, **Journey to the West,** written in China about 400 years ago. Still the best read novel in the Far East, **Journey to the West,** is also known in English by the name given to its main character, Monkey. **Monkey and the Three Wizards** tells the story of how Monkey's powers are challenged by three powerful wizards. With amazing oneupmanship Monkey outwits all three of them in a series of spectacular magic contests that explode one after the other. Foreman is one of our favorite illustrators. His pastel drawings and watercolors fill each page and are wonderfully evocative, recreating the magic of the story and the land. Harris, the translator, is a Chinese scholar.

FRANZ, MARIE-LOUISE VON. **INDIVIDUATION IN FAIRY TALES. 8.45p.**
See the Jungian Psychology section.

FRANZ, MARIE-LOUISE VON. **INTERPRETATION OF FAIRYTALES. 5.60p.**
See the Jungian Psychology section.

FRANZ, MARIE-LOUISE VON. **PROBLEMS OF THE FEMININE IN FAIRYTALES. 7.85p.**
See the Jungian Psychology section.

FUJIKAWA, GYO. **FAIRY TALES AND FABLES. 9¼"x11¼", 124pp. G&D70, 5.95c.**
This is a nicely illustrated collection of many of the best known fables and fairy tales. The pictures are vivid and are designed to appeal to the youngest readers. The retellings follow the traditional style and are generally short.

GAER, JOSEPH. **THE FABLES OF INDIA. 4.95c.**
See the Indian Philosophy section.

GAER, JOSEPH. **HOLIDAYS AROUND THE WORLD. Illustrations, index, 212pp. LBC53, 5.95c.**
This is a lively discussion of the major holy days of the Chinese, Hindu, Jewish, Christian, and Muslim faiths. The folklore surrounding each holy day is fully discussed and its historical origin is also presented.

GALE, JAMES, S., tr. **KOREAN FOLK TALES: IMPS, GHOSTS, AND FAIRIES.** 244pp. Tut13, 3.25p.
Translations of two noted collections of Korean tales—those of Im Bang (seventeenth century) and Yi Ryuk (fifteenth century). As Gale says, *To anyone who would like to look somewhat into the inner soul of the Oriental, and see the peculiar spiritual existences among which he lives, the stories will serve as true interpreters, born as they are of the three great religions of the Far East, Taoism, Buddhism, and Confucianism.*

GRAHAME, KENNETH. **THE WIND IN THE WILLOWS.** 259pp. Scr54/Met, 3.95p.
This is the nicest edition of this classic work—and it is also one of our all time favorite books. The illustrations are by Ernest Shepard and they do a wonderful job of bringing Kenneth Grahame's memorable characters to life. Reading this book is an excellent way to gain a finer appreciation of the role which animals play in the balance of nature. And, whatever the underlying value, this is one of the best animal stories we know of.

GREEN, ROGER, ed. **OTHER WORLDS.** Introduction, illustrations, 6½"x10", 261pp. HHL76, 12.00c.
A nice collection of tales which take the reader into legendary lands—some of great beauty and others of great danger. Writers such as C.S. Lewis, Andrew Lang, Mrs. Molesworth, George Webbe Dasent, and Joseph Jacobs have all contributed to this anthology, and there are some superb retellings by Green.

GREGORY, LADY. **VISIONS AND BELIEFS IN THE WEST OF IRELAND.** Introduction, 365pp. Oxf20, 15.15c.
This is Lady Gregory's masterwork of Irish and Gaelic folklore. She spent many years researching the material quoted in the first person and the recollections are quite vivid. Lady Gregory herself provides a connective narration along with a great deal of background material.

GREGORY, LADY. **THE VOYAGES OF ST. BRENDAN THE NAVI-GATOR AND TALES OF IRISH SAINTS.** Introduction, 116pp. Smy71, 1.95p.
A collection of stories of Irish Christian saints. Lady Gregory also includes a variety of wonder stories.

Jacob and Wilhelm Grimm

The brothers Grimm were lawyers who lived during the end of the eighteenth and the beginning of the nineteenth century. They were serious, scholarly men who were fascinated by German history and particularly by the history of the German language which contained so many traces of the past in everyday speech. The land they lived in then was very different from the Germany of today. Instead of one country, Germany was a mass of small kingdoms ruled by hereditary dukes and princes who lived in castles on the shores of lakes or in the beautiful dark forests. Almost every district had its own dialect and a special store of local wisdom and history contained in tales and folklore about former days. The brothers devoted much of their lives to collecting and transcribing many of these traditional tales. Their collections remain the best known and most authoritative ones to this day. *Told by generation after generation, the traditional stories projected the deepest wishes of the folk, generalized diverse characters into a few types, selected the incidents that would most strikingly illustrate what heroes and heroines, witches, enchanters, giants and dwarfs, the haughty, the envious and the unfaithful were capable of.*—from the introduction to the Pantheon edition. Today we think of these tales as mainly for children—but down through the ages they have appealed to many adults.

ALDERSON, BRIAN and MICHAEL FOREMAN. **THE BROTHERS GRIMM—POPULAR FOLK TALES.** Notes, 7"x10", 192pp. Dou78, 8.95c.
This is a delightful volume, containing thirty-one stories. In making his translation Alderson has remained faithful to the original oral source of the stories by capturing the folk tale manner so often missing in other versions. His stories read extremely well are enlivened by twenty-six full color plates by Michael Foreman, one of our favorite illustrators. Foreman's illustrations are delicately colored, detailed pastels.

CARLE, ERIC. **ERIC CARLE'S STORYBOOK: SEVEN TALES BY THE BROTHERS GRIMM.** 8½"x11¼", 94pp. Wts76, 5.95c.
Full color, vivid illustrations on every page along with large type make this book a perfect introduction to the Grimms' folktales for very young readers. Carle's illustrations have a geometric feeling to them and his drawings and bright colors are loved by children.

LE CAIN, ERROL. **THORN ROSE.** 10¾"x7¾", Vik75, 1.95p.
A magical collection of illustrations in Le Cain's inimitable style bring this classic fairy tale to life. The story of **Thorn Rose** is a better known as **The Sleeping Beauty.** Le Cain has a wonderful ability to capture details and he uses color in a subtle and extremely effective way.

MAGOUN, FRANCIS and ALEXANDER KRAPPE, trs. **THE GRIMM'S GERMAN FOLK TALES.** Foreword, 682pp. SIU60, 6.95p.
This is a highly acclaimed new translation of all the stories. The stories are presented with literal faithfulness and the original style is captured. People who have deeply studied the stories feel that this is the definitive collection. German and English title indices are included.

MANHEIM, RALPH, tr. **GRIMMS' TALES FOR YOUNG AND OLD: THE COMPLETE STORIES.** Index, 643pp. Dou77, 12.50c.
Since the times have caught up with the **Tales,** *since there was no longer any reason to rationalize or bowdlerize them, and since they are such wonderful stories, I thought the time had come to attempt a new translation that would be faithful to the Grimm brothers' faithfulness. I have tried to use a simple, natural language, though when the original waxes literary . . . I wax with it. I have tried to capture the tones of the various narrators. And, by no means least, I have paid close attention to descriptive detail, because the tellers of these stories were close observers and even their wildest fantasies, not to mention their comedies of village life, are set in houses, streets, and landscapes with which they were thoroughly familiar. Manheim is one of the most distinguished contemporary German translators and this is a very successful work.*

PANTHEON BOOKS. **THE COMPLETE GRIMM'S FAIRY TALES.** 878pp. RaH44, 12.95c/5.95p.
For many years this was the only complete edition of the tales available. The stories are presented in a lively style and the edition has been highly praised. Many fine line drawings are included and two noted mythologists, Joseph Campbell and Padraic Colum, supply illuminating commentaries and introductory material.

PUFFIN BOOKS. **GRIMM'S FAIRY TALES.** 268pp. Vik48, 1.75p.
A simple and accurate retelling of some of the best loved stories. The edition is designed for children and the translation is by Sir Walter Scott.

RACKHAM, ARTHUR. **GRIMM'S FAIRY TALES.** 7½"x9½", 127pp. Vik73/HeG, 6.95c.
Twenty stories, chosen especially for their appeal to young readers and illustrated with Rackham's delightful drawings.

SEGAL, LORE and RANDALL JARRELL, trs. **THE JUNIPER TREE AND OTHER TALES FROM GRIMM.** 332pp. FSG73, 4.95p.
A beautiful volume of fresh translations of twenty-seven of the tales which the translators and Maurice Sendak, the illustrator, felt were the most significant. The translations are both graceful and faithful to the original text. The selections include some of the best known stories as well as a number of lesser known ones. Sendak's amazingly detailed line drawings are quite possibly his finest work.

WILLIAMS-ELLIS, AMABEL. **GRIMM'S FAIRY TALES AND MORE GRIMM'S FAIRY TALES.** About 180pp. each. PnB59, 1.20p/each.
Simple, lively retellings of many of the tales, including a number of those not frequently anthologized. Evocative line drawings accompany the text.

————END OF THE BROTHERS GRIMM SUBSECTION————

HARRIS, JOEL CHANDLER. **THE COMPLETE TALES OF UNCLE REMUS. Introduction, glossary, 907pp. HMC55, 17.50c.**
There has been a strong backlash against the Uncle Remus stories recently as people have become more aware of stereotypes in literature. The popularity of the stories has certainly been affected by this change in public consciousness. When we were first looking for children's books to stock in our bookshop a customer whose opinions we respect said that we should definitely have Uncle Remus because these stories represent one of the purest forms of African folklore available today—despite the dialect and the Southern trappings. This edition includes the complete tales of Brer Rabbit, Brer Fox, Brer B'ar, and all the other animal tales which Harris made famous. All the fine original line drawings are also included.

HARRIS, JOEL CHANDLER. **UNCLE REMUS. Introduction, 208pp. ScB1880, 2.95p.**
An illustrated selection of some of the most beloved Brer Rabbit stories.

HARRIS, ROSEMARY. **THE CHILD IN THE BAMBOO GROVE.** 7½"x10", Plp71, 6.95c.
This story is a favorite in Japan. It tells how a lonely old bamboo cutter found a tiny child inside a bamboo reed, how she grew up to be a young woman of exceptional beauty, how she disposed of her tiresome suitors by setting them impossible tasks, and how she at last left the Earth to return to her true home. Ms. Harris has retold the story with an enchanting blend of wit and fantasy, and Errol Le Cain's illustrations are both magically beautiful and remarkably true to the spirit of Japanese art.

HARRIS, ROSEMARY. **THE FLYING SHIP.** 7½"x10", Fab75, 4.95c.
Another exquisitely illustrated collaboration of Ms. Harris and illustrator Errol Le Cain. This classic folk tale tells of a Russian czar who loved his only daughter so much that he could not bear her to marry and leave him. Se he decreed that no suitor should marry her unless he came for her in a flying ship. Well, as might be expected in a fairy tale, such a suitor does arrive, a simple lad accompanied by three magical helpers. The czar set the suitor three tasks, each more impossible than the last. With the help of his companions, Peter is equal to them all, and so he and the princess wed and live happily ever after.

HARRIS, ROSEMARY. **THE KING'S WHITE ELEPHANT.** 7¾"x10", Fab73, 2.50p.
White elephants were higly valued in Siam. It was the custom for the Supreme King to own one and its presence was thought to bring benefits to the whole country. But there was once a Supreme King who had no white elephant—so it was no surprise when his armies began to be defeated. The Royal Washerwoman declared that she could wash a grey elephant white and the king took up her boast. This is a delicate story, exquisitely illustrated by Errol Le Cain.

HARRIS, ROSEMARY. **THE LITTLE DOG OF FO.** 6½"x8½", Fab76, 4.95c.
Long, long years ago and a far, far space away all kinds of animals were commanded not to kill. The command came from Fo, whom we know as the Buddha, and all the animals obeyed it. Even the lions fed on lilybuds and brought up their cubs on honey, roots, and flowers. But the time came when a little lion wearied of his diet, and killed a gazelle. This story tells of how the little lion made amends for his crime and won back the favor of Fo. Color illustrations by Errol Le Cain give an oriental feeling to the narrative.

HARRIS, ROSEMARY. **THE MOON IN THE CLOUD.** 171pp. Pen68, 1.50p.
This story takes place in Noah's time when, other than Noah and his wife, there was only one deserving couple in Israel. This couple undertakes a dangerous journey to Kemi (Egypt) in search of cats and lions for Noah's ark. The story itself blends an Old Testament flavor with incidents of the Egyptian Old Kingdom. As always, Ms. Harris is a wonderful storyteller.

HARRIS, ROSEMARY. **SEA MAGIC AND OTHER STORIES OF ENCHANTMENT.** 188pp. McM74, 9.35c.
Ten stories, based on legends from East and West. As Ms. Harris says, *In all of them something, someone; wholeness; wisdom; blessing; another person who perhaps represents a kind of anima or animus figure; or even the swallowing of someone else's father to make strong magic, is the goal. . . . None are meant to be read as correct*

folktale versions, but simply as fresh interpretations of old tales. Ms. Harris writes extremely well and she has made a wonderful selection. The British edition of this book is called **The Lotus and the Grail**.

HARRIS, ROSEMARY. **THE SHADOW ON THE SUN.** 189pp. Fab70, 3.90c.
This is a sequel to **The Moon in the Cloud**, telling what happened when Reuben and his wife and all the animals returned to Egypt after the great flood. Again, the daily life is recreated and fully commented on by the animals.

HART, DAVID. **THE PSYCHOLOGY OF A FAIRY TALE.** 32pp. PHP77, .95p.
David Hart is a Jungian analyst who has a special interest in the spiritual and psychological meaning of fairytales. In this pamphlet he discourses on one of Grimm's tales, *Ferdinand the Faithful and Ferdinand the Unfaithful*, and shows it to be an example of evil and its integration into life.

HAVILAND, VIRGINIA. **FAVORITE FAIRY TALES TOLD IN GREECE.** 7"x9½", 91pp. LBC70, 4.95c.
A collection of eight tales, with color illustrations by Nonny Hogrogian. Ms. Haviland is head of the Children's Book Section of the Library of Congress. She has retold the stories in a simple, colorful fashion, designed to appeal to young readers. Dragons and fairies are frequent characters in the tales.

HEUSCHER, JULIUS. **A PSYCHIATRIC STUDY OF MYTHS AND FAIRYTALES: THEIR ORIGIN, MEANING, AND USEFULNESS.** 20.10c.
See the Jungian Psychology section.

HIGGINS, JAMES. **BEYOND WORDS: MYSTICAL FANCY IN CHILDREN'S LITERATURE. Notes, 112pp. TCH70, 4.35p.**
This exploration focuses on works by J.R.R. Tolkien, W.H. Hudson, Antoine de Saint-Exupery, George MacDonald, and C.S. Lewis. Higgins asserts that the works of these authors and others like them, as well as the classic fairy tales, appeal to the inner child and respect the integrity of childhood.

HITCHCOCK, ETHAN. **THE RED BOOK OF APPIN: A KEY TO THE INTERPRETATION OF FAIRY TALES AND FOLKLORE.** 301pp. PRS1865, 15.00c.
In his introduction, Manly P. Hall says that, *Hitchcock was one of the first Western thinkers to explore the abstract realm of archetypal symbolism. He realized intuitively that fairy tales and folklore. . .often had secret meanings and that they stimulated the thoughtful mind to explore the mysterious world of the subconscious . . . . The key which Hitchcok provides unlocks a treasury of legendry and lore as it is applied to such epics as the Arthurian Cycle or* **The Song of Roland**. *These are transformed into Mystery Dramas. The fables of Aesop and La Fontaine take on new dimensions of meaning and the semi mythological accounts in early scriptural writings take on a new significance. Each separate fairy tale reveals some aspect of the Ageless Wisdom and the veiled account of man's perilous journey in search of eternal truth.*

HOLME, BRYAN, ed. **TALES FROM TIMES PAST.** 7¾"x9¼", 176pp. Vik77, 10.00c.
This is a magnificent collection of fairy tales. Many of the most delightful tales have been included and each is illustrated by a different famous artist. Holme has chosen the illustrator he felt was best suited to each story and his artists include Edmund Dulac, George Cruikshank, Eleanor Vere Boyle, Kate Greenaway, Kay Nielsen, Harry Clarke, Maxfield Parrish, Charles H. Bennett, Richard Doyle, along with Dore, Crane, and Rackham. Many of the illustrations are in full color.

HUME, LOTTA, ed. **FAVORITE CHILDREN'S STORIES FROM CHINA AND TIBET.** 8"x7", 119pp. Tut62, 7.50c.
This is an extraordinary collection of traditional legends and stories. Ms. Hume lived in China for twenty-two years and immersed herself in the culture. She was especially impressed by the stories her neighbors told their children. Nineteen of them have been collected here in a format designed especially to appeal to children. A well known Chinese artist has supplied over ninety illustrations, twelve in color.

We love to read these stories, many of which are filled with animals that speak and play tricks on each other and humans who perform magical acts. There is a delightful illustration on virtually every page which children can look at while the story is read to them.

JACOBS, JOSEPH. **CELTIC FAIRY TALES. Preface, notes, 279pp. Dov1892, 3.00p.**
Jacobs (1854-1916) was a leading British folklorist. His collection captures the special vision and color and the unique magic of the Celtic folk imagination. The twenty-six stories in this volume present many wonderful characters and incidents. The stories are often long and detailed and Jacobs has included characteristic samples of every type. Eight full page plates and thirty-seven drawings are included.

JACOBS, JOSEPH. **ENGLISH FAIRY TALES. Sixty-five line drawings, preface, notes, 276pp. Dov1898, 3.00p.**
Forty tales, including many familiar ones like *Jack and the Beanstalk* and quite a few lesser known ones. The style of the retelling is excellent and this book has been loved by children and adults for generations.

JACOBS, JOSEPH. **INDIAN FAIRY TALES. Forty-six illustrations, preface, notes, 280pp. Dov1892, 3.00p.**
A selection of stories from India. Included are many **Jataka Tales** from a variety of other collections. As usual, Jacobs has made a fine selection and the stories are geared toward children.

JACOBS, JOSEPH. **MORE CELTIC FAIRY TALES. Illustrations, preface, notes, 237pp. Dov1894, 2.95p.**
Twenty more tales.

KHAN, NOOR INAYAT. **TWENTY JATAKA TALES. 7.95c.**
See the **Jataka Tales** subsection of Buddhism.

KIM SO-UN. **THE STORY BAG: A COLLECTION OF KOREAN FOLK TALES. Illustrations, 239pp. Tut55, 3.25p.**
A good collection of folktales, oriented toward young readers. Translated by Setsu Higashi.

KINGSLEY, CHARLES. **THE HEROES. 201pp. McM54, 4.95c.**
This volume, subtitled, *Greek Fairy Tales,* is an illustrated retelling—in simple language—of some of the most noted Greek myths. Kingsley writes well and the main characters and events come to life in his portrayal.

KINGSLEY, CHARLES. **THE WATER-BABIES. 7"x8¾", 142pp. PnB73, 3.45p.**
A superb reproduction of the famous 1915 edition of this much loved classic, in which a careful abridgment of Kingsley's story is beautifully illustrated by Mabel Lucie Attwell with numerous line drawings and eight color plates.

KIPLING, RUDYARD. **JUST SO STORIES. 248pp. ScB02, 2.75p.**
This is a collection of modern fables which Kipling originally created for his own daughter. They are simple tales which are designed to be read aloud. The language is archaic and many of the images come from outside a child's normal world, but all the tales are exciting and involve the child in a wonderful fantasy world. Some of the titles should give an idea of the content: *How the Camel Got His Hump, How the Leopard Got His Spots, How the First Letter Was Written, The Elephant's Child.* This edition contains Kipling's own illustrations, with captions.

KIPLING, RUDYARD. **JUST SO STORIES, ANNIVERSARY EDITION. 9"x13", 112pp. Dou72, 9.95c.**
Etienne Delessert's bold and imaginative full color drawings make this the finest edition of the **Just So Stories** we can imagine. The illustrations are modern and yet retain all the essential elements of the stories themselves.

KIPLING, RUDYARD. **NEW ILLUSTRATED JUST SO STORIES. 10½"x11½", 84pp. Dou52, 7.95c.**
Vivid unsophisticated color illustrations accompany the stories.

KUO, LOUISE and YUAN HSI, trs. **CHINESE FOLK TALES. Map, glossary, chronology, 175pp. CeA76, 4.95p.**
A simple retelling of many of the most loved tales, with illustrations and a short introduction to each one.

KURTI, ALFRED, tr. **PERSIAN FOLKTALES. Notes, 216pp. Bel71, 5.95c.**
Fine versions of twenty-one folktales, anecdotes, and tales from Persian literature. The tales are well written and are based on scholarly collections of folklore made within the last hundred years.

KYBER, MANFRED. **THE THREE CANDLES OF LITTLE VERONICA. 5.50p.**
See the Rudolf Steiner section.

LANG, ANDREW, ed. **FAIRY BOOKS. Dov nd.**
Lang's renditions of classic fairy tales are the best known and most popular versions available today. Many complain that he cleaned up the texts too much, but most people love his books. The stories are from a variety of sources and each of the books is complete and unabridged. The following books are available: **BLUE** (3.50p), **BROWN** (3.00p), **CRIMSON** (3.00p), **GREEN** (3.00p), **GREY** (3.00p), **LILAC** (3.50p), **OLIVE** (3.00p), **ORANGE** (3.00p), **PINK** (3.00p), **RED** (3.50p), **VIOLET** (3.50p), and **YELLOW** (3.00p).

LANG, ANDREW. **FAVORITE ANDREW LANG FAIRY TALE BOOKS. 1,471pp. Dov1890-04, 14.00p/set.**
A boxed set containing the blue, yellow, red, and green fairy books—all in all 164 stories and 439 illustrations.

LANG, ANDREW. **THE RAINBOW FAIRY BOOK. 252pp. ScB67, 3.95p.**
A selection of thirty-seven tales drawn from Lang's color fairy books, originally published between 1889 and 1910. A number of them will be familiar to most children, though there are a few new ones. Edited by Kathleen Lines with illustrations by Margery Gill and an epilogue by Roger Lancelyn Green.

LE GUIN, URSULA. **THE EARTHSEA TRILOGY. Ban78, 5.25p/set.**
A boxed set.

LE GUIN, URSULA. **THE FARTHEST SHORE. 197pp. Ban72/Pen, 1.75p.**
The final volume in the **Earthsea Trilogy**, an award winning classic of high fantasy that has been compared with Tolkien and C.S. Lewis' **Narnia** stories. In this book the story of a hero's quest, is repeated as the prince and the archmage set out to confront their own pasts, meet unknown dangers, and test the ancient prophecies.

LE GUIN, URSULA. **ORSINIAN TALES. 209pp. Ban76, 1.95p.**
Eleven beautifully written tales about people who feel they are being torn apart by massive forces in society and fight courageously to remain whole.

LE GUIN, URSULA. **THE TOMBS OF ATUAN. 146pp. Ban71/Pen, 1.95p.**
This is the second volume in the trilogy. The heroine is a young priestess who has had everything taken away from her and becomes a high priestess to the ancient and nameless powers of the Earth. She is living in the middle of the desert when her vigil is interrupted by a thief who is seeking the great treasure that surrounds her in the tombs. The thief is in reality a young wizard on a quest. They join together and she escapes from her lonely life.

LE GUIN, URSULA. **A WIZARD OF EARTH SEA. 205pp. Ban70/Pen, 1.95p.**
This is the first volume of the **Earthsea Trilogy**. It tells of a young boy who goes off on a quest and meddles with the dark forces before he is strong enough to withstand them. It is pure fantasy, with deep underlying significance—as is the case with the whole trilogy.

LEWIS, C.S. **THE CHRONICLES OF NARNIA. Boxed set, McM56/Pen, 12.50p/set.**
These seven books are the passport into an enchanted magical land and wondrous happenings. We recommend the books highly for people of all ages. In the first book the children enter through a wardrobe into Narnia and learn how Aslan, the noble lion, freed Narnia from the spell of the white witch. The second discusses Prince Caspian and his army of talking beasts. In the third Caspian, now king, sails through magic waters. The fourth book tells of Prince Rilian's escape from the emerald witch's underground kingdom. The next tale is about how a talking

horse and a boy prince saved Narnia from invasion. The sixth tells how Aslan created Narnia and gave speech to its animals. And the final reveals how evil came to Narnia and Aslan led his people to a glorious new paradise.

LEWIS, C.S. **SPACE TRILOGY. 764pp. McM46, 5.95p/set.**
The books which make up this trilogy, **Out of the Silent Planet, Perelandra,** and **That Hideous Strength,** appear, on the surface, to be fantasy stories in the science fiction mold. But, like all of Lewis' writing, there is a deep core of meaning in them and they can be viewed as one way of understanding the Christian quest. Of course, they are also fine works of fantasy which have enchanted countless readers.

LINDOW, JOHN. **SWEDISH LEGENDS AND FOLKTALES. Long bibliography, index, 232pp. UCa78, 10.95c.**
A collection of about 100 legends. Shorter and less complex than fairy tales, such legends were far more popular in the Swedish oral tradition and were related closely to the everyday lives of the community. The legends in this book deal primarily with the supernatural and are indicative of Swedish folk beliefs widespread in rural areas until fairly recently. The stories are presented in three categories: stories about *This World* (the physical environment, fate and portents, disease), *The Other World* (nature beings, including giants, trolls, forest, sea, and household spirits and their interaction with humans), and *The World of Religion.* The tales were collected from the oral tradition, in most cases as verbatim field recordings. A lengthy general introduction and notes on each of the stories are also included.

LUTHI, MAX. **ONCE UPON A TIME—ON THE NATURE OF FAIRY TALES. Notes, index, 179pp. IUP70, 2.95p.**
An absorbing collection of essays which reveal the important role of fairy tales in our lives. Luthi approaches fairy tales and related genres (local legends and saints lives) as works of art, forms of pure fiction richly imbued with poetic symbolism. In each chapter he singles out one or two tales for discussion, and each stands as a model for some particular way or combination of ways—sociological, psychological, structural, or stylistic—of exploring the meanings and social function of traditional tales and of illuminating their symbolism and structural dynamics. This is an excellent study which we recommend to all who are interested in deepening their appreciation of fairy tales. This edition includes a lengthy introduction and additions to the notes by Francis Lee Utley, a leading authority.

MACDONALD, GEORGE. **THE COMPLETE FAIRY TALES OF GEORGE MACDONALD. 288pp. ScB61, 3.95p.**
MacDonald was one of the main early figures in modern fantasy writing. He lived in the nineteenth century and influenced C.S. Lewis, J.R.R. Tolkien, and Charles Williams. This volume contains the following tales: *The Light Princess, The Giant's Heart, The Shadows, The Carasoyn, Little Daylight, Cross Purposes, The Golden Key,* and *The Day Boy and the Night Girl.* Introduction by Roger Lancelyn Green and illustrations by Arthur Hughes.

MACDONALD, GEORGE. **THE GIFTS OF THE CHILD CHRIST. Two volumes, 593pp. Eer73, 7.95p/set.**
This edition includes all of MacDonald's stories and fairy tales—except for several longer ones which are readily available elsewhere. Mac-Donald himself said that *I do not write for children, but for the childlike, whether of five, or fifty, or seventy-five.* Glenn Sadler, the editor, provides an introduction.

MACDONALD, GEORGE. **THE GOLDEN KEY. 86pp. FSG67/BoH, 5.95c/1.25p.**
This is often considered MacDonald's most magical book. It tells of a boy and a girl and their mysterious life together. This edition includes illustrations by Maurice Sendak and an afterword by W.H. Auden.

MACDONALD, GEORGE. **THE LIGHT PRINCESS. 110pp. FSG69/ BoH, 5.95c/1.25p.**
A new, unabridged edition of this tale. It is the story of a king, a queen, a baby princess, and a witch. The witch sets a spell on the child which causes her to lose her ability to flow with the laws of gravity. She floats constantly and can never touch the ground. After many adventures and trials, the love of her parents overcomes the curse. Illustrations by Maurice Sendak.

MACDONALD, GEORGE. **PHANTASTES AND LILITH. 420pp. Eer64, 3.95p.**
MacDonald's two most famous works, bound together in one volume.

MACDONALD, GEORGE. **THE PRINCESS AND CURDIE. 221pp. Vik1882/Bla, 1.50p.**
This story begins a year after Curdie, the miner's son, saved the princess from the goblins. The kingdom is still in peril and Curdie is called to court and given a special task. Before he goes to carry out his mission, the princess' great-great-grandmother gives him the rare and magical gift of knowing the true nature of every person whose hand he grasps. And so he sets out, accompaneid at times by the princess, and always by a new companion who was the ugliest person anyone had ever seen—and also the most faithful friend possible.

MACDONALD, GEORGE. **THE PRINCESS AND THE GOBLIN. Vik1872, 1.50p.**
A story in the classic fairy tale style which tells of a little princess who lives in an ancient castle in a wild and lonely mountainous region. Her father has left her to go off on a serious mission and she is attacked by the goblins who live underneath her land. She is saved by a boy miner. A classic tale about the battle between good and evil.

MANTON, JO and ROBERT GITTINGS. **THE FLYING HORSES: TALES FROM CHINA. Illustrations, 127pp. HRW77, 6.95c.**
Simple retellings of twenty-seven Chinese stories, ranging in time from the earliest popular legends and creation stories to a twentieth century account of the Revolution.

MEGAS, GEORGIOS, ed. **FOLKTALES OF GREECE. Long introduction, many notes, glossary, bibliography, indices, 344pp. UCh70, 4.95p.**
For 2500 years the folklore of Greece has cast its spell over the Western world. In recent times Greek folklorists have sought to build a bridge back to Homer and Herodotus by demonstrating that many folk beliefs, tales, and songs still in currency were already a part of the oral tradition that the epic poets themselves inherited. The folk narratives in this collection, selected from more than 22,000 varients, have been faithfully recorded in the vernacular. Thus they retain the verve of imagination, the power of expression, and the narrative grace of the Greek people. The tales are grouped by type. Megas is the foremost folklore scholar in Greece and president of the Greek Folklore Society. Translated by Helen Colaclides.

METAYER, MAURICE, tr. TALES FROM THE IGLOO. 127pp. SMP72, 4.95p.
A collection of tales from the oral tradition of the Copper Eskimos, a people who occupy the harsh and forbidding land along the Canadian Arctic coast. These traditional legends and fables reveal a view of man, nature, and the supernatural very much influenced by the realities of their often difficult lifestyle. Each story is illustrated with traditional color drawings.

NARDINI, BRUNO. FABLES OF LEONARDO DA VINCI. 8½"x11¼", 128pp. Hub73, 7.95c.
A collection of fables which Leonardo particularly liked. These fables are written down in his notebooks and it is usually not clear what the original source was. Many of them are not found in other collections and the full color illustrations which appear on virtually every page are exquisitely executed. Included are some of the most delightful animals we have seen anywhere along with some beautiful nature scenes.

NESBIT, EDITH. THE ENCHANTED CASTLE. 239pp. Den64, 4.20p.
Three children wander into an enchanted garden in a magical castle and find a fourth child. Their adventures begin as the stone monsters in the garden come to life and many other unexpected things happen. This is one of the most popular of all Ms. Nesbit's books. Illustrations throughout, some in color.

NESBIT, EDITH. FAIRY STORIES. Illustrations, 188pp. BnL77, 7.10c.
Ms. Nesbit's original fairy stories are less well known than her timeless children's books. This collection of them is edited by Naomi Lewis and it shows how delightfully she used the genre. She followed the lines of traditional fairy tales and imposed their pattern on everyday modern British life. Most of these stories originally appeared in magazines; this is their first appearance in a book collection. Ms. Lewis provides a foreword and introductory notes.

NESBIT, EDITH. FIVE CHILDREN AND IT. Nicely illustrated, 215pp. Vik02, 1.50p.
"It" was a Psammead, which looked a little like a monkey but had eyes which came out on stalks like a snail's, and it was furry all over. Five children found it when they were digging in a sandpit. It was thousands of years old. It gave them a wish a day, but whatever they wished for was guaranteed to fade at sunset, when everything went back to normal. One difficulty was to think of really good wishes; another was to avoid saying thoughtlessly at the critical moment, "Oh, I wish...!" and getting something they did not really want at all. Every wish brought them into difficulties.... This is an old and tried favorite. Between nine and twelve is a good first time for it, but plenty of children read (or have it read) at eight, and people in their sixties still reread it.—from the preface.

NESBIT, EDITH. THE PHOENIX AND THE CARPET. Illustrations, 250pp. Vik04, 1.25p.
The same children have more adventures with a magic carpet which transports them wherever they wish to go. Inside the carpet is a strange egg from which hatches the phoenix, an ancient and honorable bird, but not much easier to handle than the Psammead.

NESBIT, EDITH. THE STORY OF THE AMULET. Illustrations, 281pp. Vik06, 1.50p.
At the end of **Five Children and It** the children promised not to ask the Psammead for another wish as long as they lived, but expressed half a wish to see it again some time. They found it again, badly mistreated, in a pet shop and their adventures started all over again. They were led to an amulet—half of it actually—which contained strong magic and which they used to try to find the other half. The amulet took them back to ancient Egypt and Babylon, they visited Atlantis, and they saw Julius Caesar. But none of these adventures ran smoothly and they were always afraid of losing the amulet or forgetting the word of power and thus being stuck in another era.

NIELSEN, KAY. EAST OF THE SUN AND WEST OF THE MOON. 7½"x10", 108pp. Dou14, 7.95c.
A retelling of some classic Norwegian folk tales. The illustrations are among the most inspired we have seen. They not only capture the mystery and melancholy of the Nordic tales, but also have unexpected qualities of elegance and refinement. Includes both wood block prints and full color drawings.

NIELSEN, KAY. KAY NIELSEN. 8¾"x12", 85+pp. Ban75, 5.95p.
A collection of forty of Nielsen's best known and most successful, full color illustrations. Nielsen belonged to the Golden Age of book illustration and his work has never been surpassed. The book has been edited by David Larkin.

NIELSEN, KAY. THE UNKNOWN PAINTINGS OF KAY NIELSEN. Introduction, 9"x11¼", 98pp. Ban77, 7.95p.
A marvelous collection, edited by David Larkin, of forty-two full color plates created to illustrate a new translation of **A Thousand and One Nights**, but never published. The magic of these tales combines marvelously with Nielsen's enchanting drawings and adds new dimensions to this frequently illustrated, classic work.

NIVEDITA, SISTER. CRADLE TALES OF HINDUISM. 2.50p.
See the Indian Philosophy section.

NOY, DOV, ed. FOLKTALES OF ISRAEL. Introduction, glossary, bibliography, indices, 245pp. UCh63, 4.25p.
Dov Noy is on the faculty of the Hebrew University, Jerusalem. He established the Israeli Folktale Archives to record oral tales known to citizens of Israel coming from many countries. This volume contains a selection of seventy-one tales from the first 2000 collected in the Archives. Both religious and secular tales are represented, and some can be traced back to biblical times. Translated by Gene Baharav.

OPIE, IONA and PETER, eds. THE CLASSIC FAIRY TALES. Bibliography, index, 7"x10", 255pp. Oxf74, 13.95c.
Designed primarily for adults, this book presents twenty-four of the best known fairy tales in the exact words in which they were first published in English. The stories are lavishly supported by illustrations—more than forty of them in color—that show how the tales have been visualized in popular and juvenile literature since the time of their first publication. The work of the finest illustrators of the nineteenth and twentieth century has been selected. For each tale, the Opies provide an historical introduction, showing the development of the story, citing parallels in other countries and other centuries, and noting the changes in the tales over the ages.

O'SULLIVAN, SEAN, ed. **FOLKTALES OF IRELAND. Long introduction, glossary, notes, bibliography, indices, 364pp. UCh66, 4.45p.**
This selection of Gaelic folktales, drawn from the original manuscripts in the archives of the Irish Folklore Commission, is mainly composed of international or national tales with a peculiarly Irish flavor. The collection contains eight long tales of kings and warriors; religious tales of saints and sinners, which blend pagan and Christian sources; tales of the Otherworld and preternatural powers of witches and magicians; and tales of the wise, the foolish, and the strong. The tales are grouped by type.

OZAKI, YEI THEODORA. **JAPANESE FAIRY BOOK. 308pp. Tut04, 3.50p.**
Twenty-two stories, especially retold for young readers and beautifully illustrated. The Eastern mood is captured in these tales about magical animals, serpent-dragons, undersea kingdoms, magic chariots, and much more.

PAREDES, AMERICO, tr. **FOLKTALES OF MEXICO. Notes, bibliography, index, 365pp. UCh70, 4.95p.**
An excellent cross section of Mexican folktales, ranging across social classes and time. Dr. Paredes is a professor in the department of English and anthropology as well as a member of the graduate faculty in the Folklore Program at the University of Texas and was formerly editor of the **Journal of American Folklore**. His renderings are both products of excellent scholarship and eminently readable tales which retain the flavor of Mexican Spanish. An introduction sketches the major events and influences in the development of modern Mexico and serves as a background against which the tales can be understood.

PERRAULT, CHARLES. **CINDERELLA. 9¾"x7¼", Vik72, 1.50p.**
The exquisite illustrations by Errol Le Cain in this book make this far and away our favorite version of this classic tale. The illustrations, which are beautifully colored and incredibly detailed, do an excellent job of capturing the flavor of the story.

PERRAULT, CHARLES. **PERRAULT'S FAIRY TALES. 8"x11", 117pp. Dov69, 2.50p.**
The original eight stories from Perrault's 1697 volume. These were among the earliest versions of some of our most familiar fairy tales and are still some of the few classic retellings of these perennial stories. This edition also includes thirty-four extraordinary full page engravings by Gustave Dore—who in many cases created the pictorial image we associate with the stories.

PERRAULT, CHARLES. **THE SLEEPING BEAUTY. 10"x7½", Cro76/HeG, 6.95c.**
A new translation by David Walker, illustrated by him in dreamlike, earthtone illustrations.

PIGGOTT, JULIET. **JAPANESE FAIRY TALES. 192pp. Mll72, 5.80c.**
The culture of Japan is one of the most ancient in the world, and the richness of its folklore is well represented in this collection of thirteen tales. Ms. Piggott grew up in Japan and is an authority on Japanese history and legend. This is a fine collection, nicely illustrated.

RACKHAM, ARTHUR. **ARTHUR RACKHAM FAIRY BOOK. 271pp. Crn78, 3.98c.**
Twenty-three stories from Perrault, Grimm, Andersen, **The Arabian Nights**, and traditional English sources personally selected by Rackham and illustrated by him in color and black and white.

RACKHAM, ARTHUR. **FAIRY TALES FROM MANY LANDS. 7¾"x 9½", 122pp. Vik16/HeG, 6.95c.**
Thirteen tales, each told in a form characteristic of the country it represents. The tales come from Japan, England, Belgium, Scotland, Serbia, Wales, Russia, Portugal, France, Italy, and Ireland. Many color illustrations and line drawings are included.

RACKHAM, ARTHUR. **ONCE UPON A TIME: THE FAIRY TALE WORLD OF ARTHUR RACKHAM. 296pp. Vik72, 14.95c.**
A collection of Rackham's personal favorites, including 110 illustrations, thirty-five in color.

RANKE, KURT, ed. **FOLKTALES OF GERMANY. Long introduction, many notes, bibliography, indices, 290pp. UCh66, 3.95p.**
Ranke is the outstanding folklore scholar in Germany today. This is the first major collection of German folktales to appear in English since the translation of the stories gathered by the brothers Grimm. The tales are organized by type. Translated by Lotte Baumann.

RUGOFF, MILTON, ed. **PENGUIN BOOK OF WORLD FOLK TALES. Illustrations, index, 752pp. Vik49/Pen, 5.95p.**
A rich collection which includes both familiar stories and those from rare and unusual sources. Rugoff has picked what he feels is the most readable version of each tale. The book is divided into nineteen representative world areas: African, American, American Indian, Arabian and Turkish, Chinese, Egyptian, English; Finnish, French, German, Greek, Indian, Irish, Italian, Jewish, Latin American, Russian, Scandinavian, and Spanish. As you can see by the areas, the Western world is definitely the primary source for this collection. All categories of folk tales are included.

RUSKIN, JOHN. **THE KING OF THE GOLDEN RIVER. 4¾"x6½", 68pp. Dov1889, 1.50p.**
This is a complete rendition of Ruskin's tale, illustrated with drawings by Richard Doyle.

RUSKIN, JOHN. **THE KING OF THE GOLDEN RIVER. 10¼"x11¼", Mor78, 8.95c.**
This is a wonderful timeless tale. Gluck is a kind, young innocent who has two wicked brothers. The brothers are punished by natural forces and Gluck's goodness is rewarded. The tale is chock full of those themes which are associated with fairy tales: good versus evil, dwarfs and spirits, nature personified, virtue triumphant, and, of course, a happy ending. It is a story in the classic style, handsomely illustrated by Krystyna Turska, which should delight all who love fairytales.

RYDER, ARTHUR, tr. **THE PANCHATANTRA. Introduction, 470pp. UCh25, 5.95p.**
The word **Panchatantra** means the *Five Books*. Each of the five books is independent, consisting of a framing story with numerous inserted stories, told by one or another of the characters in the main narrative. The majority of the main characters are animals who have a fairly constant character. The animals often quote verses from the sacred writings to justify their actions. It is now believed that the original work was composed in Kashmir about 200 BC—at this date, however, many of the individual stories were already ancient. The text that is translated here dates from AD 1199. The fables have traveled the world and are the forerunners of many tales that we associate with other cultures. They are noted for their realism and pervasive humor.

SAINT-EXUPERY, ANTOINE DE. **THE LITTLE PRINCE. 113pp. HBJ43/PnB, 5.95c/1.50p.**
This is an enchanting, elusive fable which is loved by children and adults alike. The Little Prince lived alone on a tiny planet no larger than a house. He owned three volcanoes, two active and one extinct. He also owned a flower, unlike any other flower, of great and inordinate pride. It was this pride that ruined the serenity of the Little Prince's world and started him on the interplanetary travels that brought him to earth, where he learned the secrets of what is really important in life from a talking fox. Fully illustrated, in color and black and white.

SAKADE, FLORENCE, ed. **JAPANESE CHILDREN'S FAVORITE STORIES. 8"x7", 120pp. Tut58, 6.25c.**
A collection of twenty of Japan's most popular children's stories. These delightful tales are true expressions of Japanese character and customs and the more than ninety illustrations, twelve in color, by one of Japan's most noted illustrators of children's books add to the appeal. There is an enchanting illustration on virtually every page, helping to hold the child's interest while the story is read to him. A beautifully produced volume.

SANDBURG, CARL. **ROOTABAGA STORIES, PART I. Illustrations, 237pp. HBJ23, 1.95p.**
One does not normally think of Sandburg as a writer of fairy tales. Nonetheless, his **Rootabaga Stories** are a delightful collection of pure nonsense and rare beauty of thought and expression. They were written for children and reflect much that is uniquely American.

SANDBURG, CARL. **ROOTABAGA STORIES, PART II.** 224pp. HBJ23, 1.75p.

SEDGWICK, PAULITA. **MYTHOLOGICAL CREATURES.** Bibliography, HRW74, 6.95c.
A remarkable book which includes illustrations and descriptions of over 400 fantastic mythological creatures. Each of the entries is a story in itself and the language and style are geared toward children. An amazing series of illustrations which should delight older children.

SEKI, KEIGO, ed. **FOLKTALES OF JAPAN.** Glossary, bibliography, 242pp. UCh63, 3.95p.
A representative sampling of tales from the Japanese oral folk tradition. Some are known in over a hundred current versions, and a number can be traced back to classical examples set down over a thousand years ago. Widespread, deep rooted beliefs and traditions are reflected in these tales. Professor Seki is the leading folklore scholar of Japan and has compiled the standard classification of Japanese tales. The tales are translated by Robert J. Adams. Historical notes and indices of motifs and types are included along with introductory material and a variety of notes.

SHAH, AMINA. **FOLK TALES OF CENTRAL ASIA.** Introduction, glossary, 148pp. Oct70, 6.00c.
Eighteen very readable tales, compiled from the oral tradition of Central Asia by Idries Shah's sister.

SHULEVITZ, URI and ARTHUR RANSOME. **THE FOOL OF THE WORLD AND THE FLYING SHIP.** 10¾"x9¾", FSG68, 7.95c.
The Fool of the World, a peasant looked down on by his parents, wins the hand of the Czar's daughter after overcoming enormous obstacles with the aid of a wise old man and seven supernaturally talented companions. It is a Russian tale and the illustrations are vividly drawn in a Russian style. This book won a Caldecott Medal in 1969 as the most distinguished American picturebook for children.

SIE, CHEOU. **A BUTTERFLY'S DREAM AND OTHER CHINESE TALES.** 91pp. Tut70, 5.50c.
An exquisite collection of simple, universal tales. From romance to tragedy, from the emperor to the hermit, they run the gamut of human emotions and types. The renditions in this volume are excellent and they present a penetrating picture of ancient China. Each tale has an appropriate evocative color illustration by Chi Kang, China's greatest living classical artist.

STEIG, WILLIAM. **ABEL'S ISLAND.** 119pp. Ban76, 1.75p.
Abel is a mouse who has always been secure in his home and life. One day furious flood waters carry him off and dump him on an uninhabited island. Despite his resourcefulness, Abel can not find a way to get back home. Days, weeks, and months pass, and slowly Abel's soft habits disappear. His time on the island brings him a new understanding of the world he is separated from. Faced with the daily adventure of survival he is moved to reexamine his old lifestyle and he discovers new strength in himself and the potentiality of a new, more meaningful way of life once he returns to the mainland. A beautifully illustrated, entertaining, and illuminating book.

STEVENSON, ROBERT LOUIS. **THE TOUCHSTONE.** 6¾"x8¾", 48pp. Mor76, 6.95c.
An elder son goes in search of the touchstone of truth that is to win him a beautiful princess and a kingdom. He collects many false touchstones before, at last, he finds the true one. But when he returns home to claim his princess, he discovers that his brother has married her. His sorrow is deep until the touchstone reveals brother and princess for what they are—shallow and false—and he sees that happiness and self fulfillment lie in truth and understanding and not in princesses and kingdoms. Illustrations by Uri Shulevitz add inspired beauty to the text.

THOMPSON, STITH. **THE FOLKTALE.** Notes, bibliography, indices, 520pp. UCa46, 15.00c/6.95p.
This informative study is divided into four major sections: Nature and Forms of the Folktale, The Folktale from Ireland to India, The Folktale in a Primitive Culture—North American Indian, and Studying the Folktale. In the first section Thompson shows the importance of the folktale in society as the narrative form still used by the great majority of people. The second part contains an account of all the well known folktales now current in Western countries, with a brief account of their history and dissemination. The final section has a survey of studies and theories of folklore. This is a well organized, comprehensive volume which should be of interest to those who are making an in depth study of folktales.

THOMPSON, STITH, ed. **TALES OF THE NORTH AMERICAN INDIANS.** 3.95p.
See the American Indian Religion section.

J.R.R. Tolkien

Tolkien (1892-1973) was an eminent British scholar and philologist who achieved fame with his richly inventive trilogy, **The Lord of the Rings.** For most of his life he was a professor of Anglo-Saxon and English literature at Oxford and he was the author of a number of scholarly works. His great epic contains a world of fantasy, convincing in its precisely imagined detail and inner consistency, written in a prose and with the rhythms and strengths of Norse saga and Anglo-Saxon poetry.

NOEL, RUTH. **THE MYTHOLOGY OF MIDDLE EARTH.** Glossary, notes, bibliography, index, 208pp. HMC77, 4.95p.
A revealing study of Tolkien's mythology and its relationship to the myths of the ancient world, especially Nordic and Celtic myths. The book is divided into four parts: themes, places, beings, and things. Many intriguing parallels are found.

TOLKIEN, J.R.R. **THE HOBBIT.** 287pp. RaH38/A&U, 2.50p.
The enchanting prelude to **The Lord of the Rings**, where Tolkien first created the imperishable world of fantasy called Middle Earth and the charming hobbits. The tale tells of Bilbo, the hobbit's search for the ancestral home of the dwarfs, of Gandalf the Wizard, and of the magical ring that Bilbo acquires.

TOLKIEN, J.R.R. **THE HOBBIT, AN ILLUSTRATED EDITION.** 11"x11¾", 220pp. Abr77, 8.95p.
A collection of 230 full color illustrations and cinematic sequence drawings based on the animated film by Arthur Rankin, Jr. and Jules Bass, accompanied by the complete original text. The illustrations are a bit too cartoony for our tastes; nonetheless, the book should appeal to

those who want pictures of all the wonderful characters Tolkien created.

TOLKIEN, J.R.R. **THE LORD OF THE RINGS. Illustrations, index, 1,530pp. RaH65/A&U. 30.00c/10.00p/set.**
This is a boxed edition of this great fantasy classic which chronicles Middle-Earth and tells of the successful attempt to save the land from the dark forces. A delightful series of creatures take part in the tale: hobbits, wizards, dwarfs, elves, and men. The story should be well enough known so that there is no need to repeat it here. Boxed set, including all four volumes.

TOLKIEN, J.R.R. **THE SILMARILLION. Glossary, index, 365pp. HMC77/A&U, 10.95c.**
The Silmarillion is the core of all Tolkien's work. He wrote on it throughout his life, altering it continuously. His son Christopher put the present book together after Tolkien's death. This collection of tales and legends clearly sets the stage for all Tolkien's other works. For this is the story of the creation of the world and of the events of the First Age. It is the ancient drama to which the characters in **The Lord of the Rings** look back, and in whose events some of them took part. **The Silmarillion** is the history of the rebellion of the elves against the dark gods, their exile from their home and return to Middle-Earth, and their war, hopeless despite their heroism, against the Great Enemy. The book includes several other shorter works, including *Of the Rings of Power*, which is the connecting link to **The Lord of the Rings**.

END OF J.R.R. TOLKIEN SUBSECTION

TOLSTOY, LEO. **FABLES AND FAIRY TALES. Introduction, bibliography, 157pp. NAL62, 2.95p.**
Tolstoy wrote fables and fairy tales throughout his adult life. The stories gathered in this book date from his early manhood to his last years. The form was cherished by him for its purity, simplicity, and directness; most of the fables and tales collected here were originally written for the primers he prepared to teach peasant children to read.

TOLSTOY, LEO. **STORIES FOR CHILDREN. Illustrations, 8¾"x11", 41pp. PrP65, 1.00p.**
A collection of thirteen of Tolstoy's stories, translated into simple language.

TOTH, MARIAN DAVIES. **TALES FROM THAILAND. Illustrations, glossary, 183pp. Tut71, 7.15c.**
Thailand abounds with folktales and legends, telling how the people lived in the ancient past, when the gods still spoke to men. This collection of Thai folktales recreates the magic of the original stories. Animal and bird stories are included along with stories of the Thai people and their Buddhist religion. There is also a section on *Thailand and Her People*.

TRAVEN, B. **THE CREATION OF THE SUN AND THE MOON. 65pp. FSG68, 3.95c.**
This beautiful Mexican legend tells the story of a young Indian hero who saves mankind by rekindling the sun after it has been extinguished by the spirits of evil. A second legends tells how this Indian's son, with the aid of a rabbit, creates a moon to provide man with light by night. Simply retold and illustrated throughout.

TRAVERS, P.L. **ABOUT THE SLEEPING BEAUTY. 6½"x8½", 111pp. MGH75, 7.95c.**
P.L. Travers has made a lifelong study of fairy tales and legends. Of all of them, it is **The Sleeping Beauty** that has fascinated her the most. *Who is she, this peerless beauty, this hidden sleeping figure that has kindled the imagination of so many generations?* Travers reflects. *We find ourselves compelled to ask: What is it in ourselves that at a certain moment suddenly falls asleep? Who lies hidden deep within us? And who will come to wake us, what aspect of ourselves?* In this unique book, exquisitely illustrated by Charles Keeping, she has given us her own magical version of **The Sleeping Beauty** as well as an essay in which she meditates on the meaning and mystery of fairy tales. She has also collected five traditional versions of the tale, and uses them to show the variations on the theme.

TREVINO, ELIZABETH BORTON DE. **BEYOND THE GATES OF HERCULES. 255pp. FSG71, 4.95c.**
An imaginative story of life on Poseidon, one of the islands of the lost Atlantis. Ms. Borton de Trevino tells of the Archers, the island's leading family. The Archers tend the sacred flower the saffron, and they know of the prophecy that tragedy will invade their homeland. Among the six children of the family are Atlanta, promised since birth to the sea priestesses, who retains the ancient gift of reading and transmitting thoughts, and Baka, whose brillance coupled with pride destines him for tragedy.

UNESCO. **FOLKTALES FROM ASIA FOR CHILDREN EVERYWHERE, BOOK ONE. 7½"x10", 53pp. Wea75, 4.95c.**
This series of folk tales is an excellent one. Through the stories children in Western cultures can get a good feeling for the other cultures. The selections presented in this series are entirely authentic, having been selected, retold, and illustrated by writers and artists from each of the Asian countries. The stories are simple and timeless and present the real flavor of Asia. Each is beautifully illustrated in bright colors. The stories in this volume come from Bangladesh, India, Iran, Korea, Laos, Singapore, Thailand, and Viet Nam.

UNESCO. **FOLKTALES FROM ASIA FOR CHILDREN EVERYWHERE, BOOK TWO. 7½"x10", 53pp. Wea75, 4.95c.**
Stories from Indonesia, Japan, Khmer, Malaysia, Nepal, Pakistan, Philippines, and Sri Lanka.

UNESCO. **FOLKTALES FROM ASIA FOR CHILDREN EVERYWHERE, BOOK THREE. 7½"x10", 59pp. Wea76, 5.95c.**
Stories from Afghanistan, Burma, Indonesia, Iran, Japan, Pakistan, Singapore, Sri Lanka, and Viet Nam. This volume has our favorite stories.

UNESCO. **FOLKTALES FROM ASIA FOR CHILDREN EVERYWHERE, BOOK FOUR. 7¼"x9½", 64pp. Wea76, 5.95c.**
Tales from Bangladesh, Cambodia, India, Korea, Laos, Malaysia, Nepal, the Philippines, and Thailand.

UNESCO. **FOLKTALES FROM ASIA FOR CHILDREN EVERYWHERE, BOOK FIVE. 7½"x9¾", 59pp. Wea77, 6.50c.**
Seven stories from India, the Philippines, Pakistan, Japan, Malaysia, Burma, and Iran.

UNESCO. **FOLKTALES FROM ASIA FOR CHILDREN EVERYWHERE, BOOK SIX. 7½"x9¾", 59pp. Wea77, 6.50c.**
Seven tales from Korea, Afghanistan, Indonesia, Thailand, Nepal, Singapore, and Sri Lanka.

WAITE, ARTHUR. **THE QUEST OF THE GOLDEN STAIRS. 176pp. NPC74, 2.95p.**
An allegory of the exploration and discovery of an individual's innermost being. Set in a mystical *other world*, it tells of the quest of a noble prince in search of fame and fortune. Fairies and magic abound throughout the narrative.

WALEY, ALISON. **DEAR MONKEY. 223pp. Bla73, 7.35c.**
This is a delightful abridgment of Arthur Waley's classic translation of one of China's most famous and best loved folktales. Monkey is an amazing character who is created out of a stone monkey and who somehow obtains great powers, including immortality. He challenges the gods, is eventually vanquished and punished, and only set free as a companion on a dangerous quest to bring back the Buddhist scriptures from India to China. Monkey is valiant and intrepid and he and his compatriots have many strange and exciting adventures. A series of excellent woodblock prints illustrate the story.

WALTON, EVANGELINE. **THE FOUR BRANCHES OF THE MABINOGION. Four volumes, introduction, 1006pp. RaH36, 6.95p/set.**
These books are not only the best fantasies of the twentieth century, but also great works of fiction. They are actual retellings of the diverse legends of **The Mabinogion** *in novel form...dealing with Good and Evil...and the nature of love.*—**The Saturday Review**. **The Mabinogion** is the classic Welsh book of mythology. The books are also available individually for 1.95p/each—(1) **Prince of Annwn**; (2) **The Children of Llyr**; (3) **The Song of Rhiannon**; (4) **The Island of the Mighty**.

WANG HSING-PEI. **MONKEY SUBDUES THE WHITE-BONE DEMON. 1.95p.**
See the Chinese Literature subsection of Chinese Philosophy.

WARNER, SYLVIA TOWNSEND. **KINGDOMS OF ELFIN.** 222+pp. Del77, 4.95p.
A rich and imaginative collection of magical tales, some traditional and some Ms. Warner's own inventions.

WELLS, BENJAMIN. **THE SEARCH FOR THE KING.** 334pp. SRe76, 6.95c.
A collection of stories written by disciples of Meher Baba and subtitled, *Stories for All God's Children.* The following preface sets the tone for the stories: *O reader! begin this book with care for it may be the start of a long search, the Search for the King. Each story has its own clues about where to find Him. You will love some of the stories, you may be puzzled by others, but you can learn from them all, for each one is special. How? Each one is a gift to you from the heart of a friend. The friends who wrote these stories live in the East and the West, and they know children from all over the world...and each one sat down and wrote a special story for you.*

WHITE, E.B. **CHARLOTTE'S WEB. Nicely illustrated,** 184pp. H&R52/Pen, 1.50p.
In all of White's books the animals come magically to life and there is an underlying moral. This one tells the story of a little girl who loved a little pig named Wilbur, and of Wilbur's close friend Charlotte, a beautiful grey spider who lived with Wilbur in the barn. As the story progresses, Charlotte saves the life of Wilbur with the aid of a rat who never did anything for anybody unless there was something in it for him. It is a good story, and one that children love.

WHITE, E.B. **STUART LITTLE.** 131pp. H&R45, 1.50p.
The adventures of Stuart Little, a mouse who was born into a human family. It is an endearing story for young and old, full of wit and wisdom and amusement. Wonderful illustrations add to the appeal.

WILDE, JANE FRANCESCA. **ANCIENT LEGENDS OF IRELAND.** 359pp. Smy1888, 4.80p.
When this book first appeared, William Butler Yeats wrote of it, *We have here the innermost heart of the Celt in moments he has grown to love through years of persecution, when, awakening himself almost with dreams, and hearing fairysongs in the twilight, he ponders on his soul and on the dead. Here is the Celt, only it is the Celt dreaming.*

WILHELM, RICHARD, tr. **CHINESE FOLKTALES. Notes,** 215pp. Bel71, 5.95c.
A delightful collection of fifty tales, based on scholarly collections of folklore made within the last 100 years. These folktales belong partly to the myths of Confucianism and Buddhism, and partly to historical times, when heroes, saints, and rulers assume magical powers. Other stories deal with the continual warfare between good and evil spirits, which can be resolved only with the help of humans.

WOLKSTEIN, DIANE. **THE MAGIC ORANGE TREE AND OTHER HAITIAN FOLKTALES.** 6¾"x9¼", 220pp. RaH78, 6.95c.
In Haiti African and European cultures have blended to form a distinct way of life. The folklore tradition is very much alive there and the stories in this volume were collected firsthand by Ms. Wolkstein. They are wonderous tales. An orange tree grows at the command of a child, a fish speaks, a bone sings, animals turn into humans and return to being animals again. The magical in all of life becomes real and strangely natural. Ruling over all of these beings are the great forces that shape and transform their destinies: Papa God, General Death, and the spirits who hold sway in voodoo ceremonies. Each story is further illuminated by introductory notes which tell of the actual circumstances of the storytelling in which Ms. Wolkstein first heard the tale. Illustrations by Elsa Henriquez.

WRIGGINS, SALLY. **WHITE MONKEY KING.** 5.95c.
See the Chinese Literature subsection of Chinese Philosophy.

WYATT, ELIZABETH. **SEVEN-YEAR-OLD WONDER BOOK. Illustrations,** 189pp. DLP58, 5.95p.
Seven-Year-Old Wonder Book *is what we grown-ups might call a collection of fairy tales. But to Sylvia, a sensitive and imaginative girl of six-going-on-seven, it is a very real and a very special experience....From the very first page, you and your children will be enthralled by her vivid imagery and tales of mystery, magic, and mythical creatures like snow birds, fairy princesses, witches, gnomes, and even the Dragon. For that great majority of us concerned with the human condition, this special book also has a message. Woven throughout each story...is the profound, humanistic Waldorf School philosophy [see the Steiner section] which stresses our kinship with nature, our inherent creativity, our higher levels of consciousness, and our need to take things one at a time.*—from the introduction.

WYATT, ISABEL and JOAN RUDEL. **THE KING AND THE GREEN ANGELICA.** 10.55c.
See the Waldorf Education subsection of Rudolf Steiner.

YEATS, WILLIAM BUTLER, ed. **FAIRY AND FOLK TALES OF IRELAND.** 406pp. McM73, 13.50c.
A representative collection of Irish folk tales, bringing together stories recorded by writers over the last two hundred years which cover every aspect of Irish folklore: fairies, changelings, leprechauns, the Pooka, the Banshee, ghosts, witches, fairy doctors, Tir-na-n'og, saints, priests, the devil, giants, animals, kings, queens, robbers, druids. The authors represented include Crofton Croker, Sir William Wilde and Lady Wilde, Lover, Carleton, Allingham, Hyde, and Yeats himself. Kathleen Raine has written a special foreword to this volume, tracing Irish folklore.

YEATS, WILLIAM BUTLER. **MYTHOLOGIES.** 3.95p.
See the Yeats subsection of Mysticism.

YOLEN, JANE. **THE HUNDREDTH DOVE AND OTHER TALES.** 7½"x9", 64pp. Cro77, 7.50c.
A collection of seven short stories with universal themes. One tells of the pain of Oedipal love and rejection; several are concerned with various kinds of love and separation. The title story raises the issue of obedience and loyalty so blind it leads a faithful servant to destroy what he and his master prize most; another, though expressed lightheartedly, is a serious exploration of the real nature of happiness. Charcoal drawings by David Palladini accompany the stories.

YOLEN, JANE. **THE MAGIC THREE OF SOLATIA. Illustrations,** 172pp. Cro74, 6.95c.
The magic three are three magical buttons which grant the wisher one desire apiece. They are the web that connects this haunting four-part novel of fantasy, magic, romance, and enchantment. The main characters are Dread Mary, part witch and part mermaid, who teaches her magic to Solatia; Solatia herself; Solatia's son; and Blaggard, the evil king who is also a powerful sorcerer. We love this story and if you are moved by fantasy, you will love it too. Ms. Yolen is a great storyteller.

YOLEN, JANE. **THE MERMAID'S THREE WISDOMS.** 112pp. CWo78, 6.95c.
A moving novel of twelve-year-old Jess and Melusina the mermaid. By accident Jess sees Melusina; because she has been seen by a landperson Melusina has broken the strictest law of the merfolk. In punishment she is banished from her undersea home and sent to live on land. Jess finds her lying on the sand and the two become friends. Ink and pencil drawings illustrate the tale.

YOLEN, JANE. **THE MOON RIBBON AND OTHER TALES. 54pp. Cro76, 6.95c.**
A collection of six stories, told in a traditional style. Proud princesses, wicked stepmothers, magical spirits, wise fools, and fair maidens are all present in these beautifully written stories, each of which has an underlying theme. Love nourishes, says one; belief can be stronger than truth, warns another; the finding is in the seeking, philosophizes a third. The title story is a classic tale of goodness and evil triumphing over evil and greed; the final tale is a powerful plea for tolerance and understanding.

YOLEN, JANE. **THE TRANSFIGURED HART. 86pp. Cro75, 5.95c.**
A young boy catches sight of a white hart and this changes his whole world. He hopes to tame the hart and in his quest he ventures into enchanted woods. A young girl is also trying to tame the hart and they get to know each other. As hunting season approaches they try hard to save the hart (really a unicorn) from the hunters. This tale is not quite as magical as some of Ms. Yolen's other books.

YOLEN, JANE. **THE WIZARD ISLANDS. 7¼"x10¼", bibliography, index, 115pp. Cro73, 7.95c.**
Mysteries and islands seem to be natural companions. In this book Jane Yolen brings her storytelling gift to both fact and fancy as she tells of ghost-haunted islands, pirate islands, and legendary islands such as Atlantis. Two excellent chapters tell of the Galapagos Islands and Easter Island. The illustrations include photographs, old documents, and newly drawn maps. For older children.

ZHELEZNOVA, IRINA. **THE SUN PRINCESS AND HER DELIVERER. 8½"x11", PrP nd, .90p.**
A magnificently illustrated retelling of this classic Lithuanian folk tale. The writing style is not graceful, but the pictures and the design make up for this.

ZHELEZNOVA, IRINA. **VASILISA THE BEAUTIFUL. 9¼"x11¾", PrP76, 1.50p.**
An exquisitely illustrated Russian fairy tale, retold in the classic style. Vassilisa is a beautiful young woman, with a wicked stepmother, stepsisters, and a magical doll. After many trials she ends up marrying the tsar. The illustrations are beautifully drawn, mutely colored, and filled with detail. They are in the style of Arthur Rackham and Edmund Dulac and each is fine enough to stand by itself as a print.

ZHELEZNOVA, IRINA and BERNARD ISAACS. **THE FIRE BIRD. 8¼"x11¾", PrP nd, 3.25c.**
A beautifully produced collection of six Russian fairy tales: *The Fire Bird, The Frog Tsarevna, Chestnut-Grey, Emelya and the Pike,* and *Vasilisa the Beautiful.* Each of the pages is bordered all around by a delicate design and every fourth page is a full page color plate. The retelling reads well and some of the most beloved stories have been chosen. This is as good an introduction to the genre as we know of.

ZINER, FEENIE. **CRICKET BOY. 8¾"x11¼", 40pp. Dou77, 6.95c.**
Long ago in China tiny crickets which sang in the night were held in high esteem. Men of every rank and station kept them as pets, and cricket fights were one of the most popular spectator sport. This lovely story tells of Scholar Hu, an honorable but poor peasant who takes great pride in his crickets. The emperor hears of the fame of one of them and expresses a wish to match his champion against Scholar Hu's. Scholar Hu's son tries to help him and in the process kills his father's cricket. In horror, he kills himself too. But all ends well. Scholar Hu finds another champion cricket who does beat the emperor's, he is granted a wish, and the wish comes true when his son regains life. Illustrated by Ed Young with exquisite color paintings in the Chinese style.

FREEMASONRY

Modern Freemasonry is concerned with good fellowship and charity. It is founded on the *practice of moral and social virtue*, and Freemasons are under obligation to help their fellow Masons in distress. They have a number of signs, consisting chiefly of passwords, handgrips, and other signals, by which they recognize each other, and also a cryptic alphabet and complicated rituals which have to be learned by heart and must not be disclosed. Their principal symbols are the tools of the stonemason's trade, such as the compass and set-square, but nowadays the Society has no connection with building or architecture.

Of the peculiar beliefs associated with Freemasonry, the most prominent is that Masonic brethren possess certain secrets *of vital importance* in relation to building, so that this secret knowledge has had great influence upon the development of architecture all over the world, and enabled their predeccesors to design and build the great cathedrals of the Middle Ages which are among the architectural wonders of the world.

It is also claimed that Freemasonry has existed from the earlier times, that it was involved with the building of Solomon's Temple in Jerusalem, and even that Solomon and Hiram of Tyre were Grand Masters of the then existing brotherhood. Freemasonry has also been associated with Noah's Ark and the Tower of Babel, Moses, Nebuchadnezzar and the Knights Templar, but it is upon the legend of the building of Solomon's Temple that the rituals of modern Freemasonry are based. These legends are not taken very seriously outside Freemasonry, but are generally regarded as further innocent mystifications which add conviviality to masonic gatherings. However, these traditions cannot be dismissed out of hand, particularly since they derive from existent ancient manuscripts known as the **Old Charges** which relate to the masonic brotherhoods of the Middle Ages, some of which date from the fourteenth century.

Whatever its biblical antecedents, Freemasonry as it is known today originated during the great church-building period which extended from about A.D. 600 for approximately a thousand years. During that time there were in several countries guilds or brotherhoods of masons specializing in the building of churches, castles, and great houses. These guilds were responsible for cathedrals such as Canterbury, Salisbury, and Winchester, as well as for many old parish churches. Customarily their guilds entered into contracts with the ecclesiastical authorities known as *lodges* until the work was completed.

No individual architect can be named as the designer of the great cathedrals built prior to 1355. These were not the work of any individual, but of an order (the Freemasons) which planned, built, and adorned them. The masons were strictly controlled by their Masters and Wardens, and, while in any country other than their own, they were exempt from taxes and to some extent from the laws of that country. It is said that for this reason they were known as *free* masons; and because freemasons had to travel from place to place, often in foreign countries, it was necessary that they should be able to identify each other without having to furnish evidence of skill or initiation, and thus be able to claim hospitality from brother masons whenever necessary. For this purpose certain secret words and signs were formulated, so that these could be understood by other initiated masons only.

The church-building age died out near the end of the sixteenth century, and subsequently the freemasons were engaged mainly on secular work. At the beginning of the seventeenth century the masons' lodges began to accept as members men who possessed no qualification for admission on the usual grounds of hereditary or building apprenticeship. These persons were known as *accepted* or *speculative* masons, and were thus distinguished from the craftsmen or *operative* masons who were fully initiated into the masonic mystery and secrets. The passwords, signs, and peculiar phrases used by the old masons were disclosed to the speculative masons, but not the *vital secrets.* Many speculative masons seem to have joined the brotherhood in order to learn the famous secrets and, disappointed at not being initiated into the esoteric knowledge, withdrew from the fraternity in consequence.

It is this possession of esoteric knowledge which appears to form the real distinction between the modern Freemason and the old free mason. Ultimately, the operative element appears to have generally retired from participation in the activities of the masonic lodges. Freemasons recognized by the brotherhood as operative masons do, however, still exist, and there is evidence that certain architects and priesthoods still understand the principles which underlay the ancient system, and that they train initiates in order that the secrets of the order will not be lost. A number of churches and other structures erected during the last two hundred years, some in quite recent times, display peculiarities which prove that freemasonry in its original sense retains its imprint.

—*condensed from* **The Pattern of the Past**, *by Guy Underwood*

BAILEY, FOSTER. **THE SPIRIT OF MASONRY. 2.75p.**
See the Theosophy section.

CASTELLS, F. DE P. **THE GENUINE SECRETS IN FREEMASONRY: PRIOR TO A.D.1717. Index, 327pp. Lew71, 10.00c.**
A speculative, esoteric study whose thesis is that Freemasonry is Qabalism in another garb. The detailed text shows how each item of the masonic ceremonial has been derived from the Qabala. The author has done a tremendous amount of research and written many books—of which this is the culmination. His scholarship seems to be excellent, and while his thesis is controversial, he makes a good case for it. The reader does not have to know much about the Qabala to follow the presentation.

CHAILLEY, JACQUES. **THE MAGIC FLUTE: MASONIC OPERA. 9.75c.**
See the Music section.

COIL, HENRY. **COIL'S MASONIC ENCYCLOPEDIA. 781pp. Mac61, 22.50c.**
This is the newest masonic encyclopedia. Coil is a life long mason and he spent many years compiling the material. A great deal of historical material is included and many of the individual entries read like essays. This is considered the definitive work.

■ COIL, HENRY. **A COMPREHENSIVE VIEW OF FREEMASONRY.**
Bibliography, index, 258pp. Mac73, 6.00c.
This is an excellent study which discusses all aspects of Freemasonry
and covers its development throughout the world from the earliest
times to the present.

COIL, HENRY. **FREEMASONRY THROUGH SIX CENTURIES.** Bibliography, index, 721pp. Mac68, 16.50c/set.
This two volume set is a comprehensive, historical study.

DENCE, A.F. **AN INTERPRETATION OF CRAFT FREEMASONRY.**
42pp. Lew nd, 1.60c.
An exposition of the true meaning of the first, second, and third degree
initiatory rituals. Vividly written.

DUNCAN, MALCOLM. **DUNCAN'S RITUAL OF FREEMASONRY.**
281pp. McK76, 4.65p.
*The purpose of this work is not so much to gratify the curiosity of the uninitiated as to
furnish a guide for the neophytes of the Order, by means of which their progress from
grade to grade may be facilitated. Every statement in the book is authentic.*—from
the preface.

DYER, COLIN. **SYMBOLISM IN CRAFT FREEMASONRY.** 178pp.
Lew76, 19.80c.
An in depth analysis of the symbols used in masonic rites, based on
Dyer's extensive research. The material is well organized and Dyer
includes information not readily available elsewhere.

GARVER, WILL. **BROTHER OF THE THIRD DEGREE.** 377pp.
Bor1894, 8.95c.
A fictional portrayal of a young man's struggle to attain ranking as an
initiate of the third degree in a mystery school. Garver includes many
details of masonic work and practices.

HALL, MANLY P. **DIONYSIAN ARTIFICERS.** 105pp. PRS36, 5.50c.
This is a reprint of a rare masonic monograph, **Dionysian Artificers** by
Hippolyto Da Costa, with extensive notes by Manly Hall. Over half
the book is devoted to Mr. Hall's detailed interpretation of **The Myth of
Dionysius.** Both texts discuss how the laws of nature and the moral
rules deduced from them were explained in allegories, which we call
myths, and were impressed on the memory by the mystery ceremonies.
Hall interprets the central myth of the Dionysian mysteries and
explains the secret metaphysical doctrines of this cult.

336

HALL, MANLY P. **FREEMASONRY OF THE ANCIENT EGYP-
TIANS.** Notes, 366pp. PRS65, 6.95c.
An in depth interpretation of the Freemasonry of the ancient
Egyptians as set forth in the teaching of the state mysteries. Among
the subjects Hall discusses are Egyptian magic, the Osirian cycle, the
secret doctrine of Egypt, and the initiation of Plato.

HALL, MANLY P. **LOST KEYS OF FREEMASONRY.** 100pp. Mac23,
3.75c.
A concise exploration of all aspects of masonry: *The true Masonic Lodge is a
Mystery School, a place where candidates are taken out of the follies and foibles of the
world and instructed in the mysteries of life, relationships, and the identity of that germ
of spiritual essence within, which is, in truth, the Son of God, beloved of his father.*—
from the introduction.

HALL, MANLY P. **MASONIC ORDERS OF FRATERNITY.** 112pp.
PRS50, 5.75c.
A survey of Freemasonry, in the form of short biographies of some of
the principal seventeenth and eighteenth century individuals and
movements. Written in a simple style and illustrated throughout.

HAYWOOD, H.L. **THE NEWLY MADE MASON.** 220pp. Mac48,
5.00c.
A clear summary of Freemasonry. Includes history, philosophy, and
information on the day to day workings of the orders.

HELINE, CORINNE. **MYSTIC MASONRY AND THE BIBLE.** 173pp.
NAP63, 3.95p.
An esoteric interpretation.

HODSON, GEOFFREY. **AT THE SIGN OF THE SQUARE AND
COMPASS.** 8.95c.
See the Theosophy section.

HORNE, ALEX. **KING SOLOMON'S TEMPLE IN THE MASONIC
TRADITION.** Index, 352pp. Wil72/ACP, 5.00p.
A detailed, speculative study based on academic research and on
extracts from masonic rituals and legends.

KNIGHT, G. NORMAN and FREDERICK SMYTH. **THE POCKET
HISTORY OF FREEMASONRY.** Index, 348pp. Mll77, 8.60c.
A description of theories which account for the histories of English,
Scottish, and Irish Freemasonry from the earliest times to the present
day.

LEADBEATER, C.W. **GLIMPSES OF MASONIC HISTORY.** Offset,
spiral bound, notes, index, 393pp. HeR26, 8.50p.
An esoteric analysis, based on Theosophical teachings and divided into
the following general topics: the Egyptian, Cretan, Jewish, Greek, and
Mithraic mysteries; craft masonry in medieval times; operative masonry in the Middle Ages; the Scottish rite; and the co-masonic order.

LEADBEATER, C.W. **THE HIDDEN LIFE IN FREEMASONRY.** Offset,
spiral bound, illustrations, index, 382pp. HeR26, 10.00p.
An exploration of all aspects of the esoteric side of masonry, written to
give the brethren a fuller understanding of the mysteries of the craft.

MACKEY, ALBERT. **MACKEY'S REVISED ENCYCLOPEDIA OF
FREEMASONRY.** Mac09, 37.50c/set.
This three volume set is considered the best overall work available.

■ NEWTON, JOSEPH. **THE BUILDERS: A STORY AND STUDY OF
MASONRY.** Illustrations, notes, bibliography, index, 345pp. Mac51,
6.50c.
This is one of the best overall introductions to masonry available
today. Newton divides his material into three parts: prophecy, history,
and interpretation. The first part is the most interesting to us. Here
Newton surveys early references to the masonic tradition in mankind's
early history, tradition, and mythology. In the second part, Newton
traces the masonic order through the centuries—from the building of
the Temple of Solomon to the modern day. The final section is an
excellent exposition of the faith of masonry, focusing on its philosophy, religious meaning, and relationship to the individual and state.

NEWTON, JOSEPH. **RELIGION OF MASONRY.** Notes, annotated
bibliography, 160pp. Mac27, 3.75c.
This is generally considered the best presentation of the subject ever
written.

OLIVER, GEORGE. **THE PYTHAGOREAN TRIANGLE. 8.95c.**
See the Pythagoras subsection of Ancient Greece and Rome.

PERCIVAL, HAROLD. **MASONRY AND ITS SYMBOLS. 73pp. WdF52, 3.00p.**
This valuable little book should be in the possession of every sincere Mason who desires more LIGHT on and a truer understanding of the symbols of Masonry, of the ceremonies in which he takes part, and of their deep esoteric significance.—from the introduction.

ROBERTS, ALLEN. **THE CRAFT AND ITS SYMBOLS. 101pp. Mac74, 5.00c.**
Why this book? Because symbolism is the life-blood of the Craft. It is what distinguishes Freemasonry from other fraternal organizations. It is the principal vehicle by which the ritual teaches Masonic philosophy and moral lessons. Masonic symbolism is unique. I was asked to write this book....[It] was felt there was a definite need for a modern approach. A book with illustrations (old and new) which would help the newly raised Master Mason to a better understanding of the meaning and teachings of the ceremonies through which he had recently passed. A book written simply without the profuse occult meanings....And, yet, a volume to inspire him, make him eager to pursue his Masonic education that he might learn more of the glorious teachings of our Craft for his further enrichment in his daily pursuits.—from the preface.

ROBERTS, J.M. **THE MYTHOLOGY OF SECRET SOCIETIES. Notes, index, 478pp. Grn72, 4.00p.**
An often fascinating survey of the revolutionary secret societies which existed in all parts of Europe in the eighteenth and early nineteenth centuries. Roberts throws light on the shifting alliances between the groups and discusses the lives and work of many of the most notable figures. Dr. Roberts is a historian and he has produced both a work of excellent scholarship and a highly readable illumination of the secret societies and their times.

RONAYNE, EDMOND. **RONAYNE'S HANDBOOK OF FREEMA-SONRY. Offset, spiral bound, 584+pp. HeR24, 8.00p.**
A revised edition of this definitive lodge manual, containing a thorough exposition of all the signs, grips, passwords, and hiero-glyphics used by Freemasons, along with information on the proper manner of opening, closing, and conducting the lodge. There are also chapters on the correct method of conferring the three degrees of ancient craft masonry: entered apprentice, fellow craft, and master mason. A dissertation on chapter masonry is appended.

STEINMETZ, GEORGE. **FREEMASONRY—ITS HIDDEN MEANING. 218pp. Mac48, 5.75c.**
A spiritual interpretation of the esoteric work of the masonic lodge. Steinmetz carefully and systematically analyzes the lectures and symbols of the first three degrees and reviews true masonic philosophy.

STEINMETZ, GEORGE. **THE LOST WORLD—ITS HIDDEN MEAN-ING. Bibliography, index, 262pp. Mac53, 3.50c.**
A correlation of the allegory and symbolism of the ancient mystery teachings and the **Bible** with Freemasonry.

STEINMETZ, GEORGE. **THE ROYAL ARCH. 145pp. Mac46, 3.50c.**
An esoteric interpretation of the royal arch degree. Steinmetz is one of the most respected masonic writers and he is best known for his deep understanding of the symbolic meaning of all aspects of the craft.

THOMSON, KATHARINE. **THE MASONIC THREAD IN MOZART. 12.60c.**
See the Music section.

WAITE, A.E. **A NEW ENCYCLOPEDIA OF FREEMASONRY. Notes, index, 950pp. UnB70, 9.98c.**
A comprehensive view of the history, literature, and myths of Freemasonry, together with explanations of masonic ritual and symbolism.

WARD, A.H. **MASONIC SYMBOLISM. 110pp. TPH23, 2.25c.**
A series of short papers originally prepared for delivery at lodge meetings. The symbolism connected with the first three degrees is discussed at length and there is also material on *the lost word.*

WESTCOTT, W. WYNN. **THE ISIAC TABLET OR THE BEMBINE TABLE OF ISIS. 10¾"x13½", 20+pp. PRS76, 12.50c.**
The Isiac Tablet is a mysterious relic of ancient times which some think was originally produced in the fourth century BC. This monograph by Westcott critically discussed it along modern Hermetic lines. It is an extremely rare work, of which only 100 copies were originally printed and which has just been reprinted in a limited edition. Manly Hall feels that the tablet is of Gnostic origin.

ZAIN, C.C. **ANCIENT MASONRY. 416pp. ChL38, 5.95p.**
See the Astrology section.

GEMS & STONES

For many ages investigation and research has been primarily centered upon the plant and animal kingdoms in pursuit of the energies and healing qualities contained therein. However the mineral kingdom of nature has not been brought forward nor understood in all that is or all that it can be utilized for. Mostly this kingdom has been totally ignored or there have been centered around it, myths, misconceptions and other facets of human nature such as glamour and greed. Only a handful of persons have attempted to peel away some of the aura of mystery which surrounds the earthly dominion of the Celestial Gem.

Let us begin here by saying that since all things are of the One Universal Energy, everything that physically exists is an external manifestation of an energy form, or vibratory rate, or combination of rates. The mineral kingdom manifests the lowest vibratory rate on the third dimensional Earth plane. Therefore the mineral kingdom is the building block of which all things on the physical plane are made, be it vegetable, animal or human in nature. This can be equated with the body framework that holds the flesh, muscles and other necessities sustaining life together.

With this understanding, we can then see that our physical vehicle or body is a compound form of organic mineral. Since the Earth and all of us are one, for we are of the Earth and of the elements of the Earth while here, the Earth itself is like a physical body made up of the same elements which compose every other manifested form. It therein has a network of veins and arteries leading to the *heart center* and other key areas of the Earth body. These veins and arteries are made up of large collections of minerals such as are found in mines and lead deep into the Earth. The various crystals found in rich mineral veins can be likened unto the individual corpuscles that travel or transmit upon those arteries.

Each mineral crystal has its own special individual influence, function and vibration. Inherent within the evolution of the mineral kingdom exists the vibratory rates that heal, energize, attune and uplift the spirit of our very inner beings. There are no two crystals alike as indeed there are no two atoms that are identical. Each gem or mineral is a crystallized sound vibration which emits its own unique individual musical note. This can be *heard* by discerning ears especially in the proximity of large mineral collections.

—from **Healing Stoned**, by Joel Glick and Julia Lorusso

CAYCE, EDGAR. **GEMS AND STONES. 50pp. ARE60, 1.75p.**
A comparative study of the scientific properties and occult aspects of twenty-two gems, stones, and metals, based on Cayce's life readings and arranged topically.

CROW, W.B. **PRECIOUS STONES. 64pp. Wei nd/TPL, 1.25p.**
A popular account which details the history and uses of the stones and their healing and magical properties.

EVANS, JOHN. **MAGICAL JEWELS OF THE MIDDLE AGES AND THE RENAISSANCE. Notes, indices, 264pp. Dov22, 3.00p.**
Belief in the virtues of amulets, talismans, and rare stones dates back to the beginnings of recorded history. This belief was especially prevalent in the Middle Ages. In this scholarly work, Joan Evans, expert on the Middle Ages and former librarian at Oxford University, undertakes a thorough study of this belief in England. Her sources are medieval lapidaries and astrology. Appendices contain the Latin text of the material she cites.

■ FERNIE, WILLIAM. **OCCULT AND CURATIVE POWERS OF PRECIOUS STONES. 486pp. Mul07, 4.50p.**
This is our most popular book on gems and stones. Dr. Fernie was a physician and his life's work is reflected in this volume. The best known gems and metals are discussed at length and a great deal of background information is also supplied. Folklore is incorporated into the discussion and the book is fully indexed. This is the most comprehensive treatment of precious and semi-precious stones and metals available.

■ GLICK, JOEL and JULIA LORUSSO. **HEALING STONED. 92pp. MiP76, 5.50p.**
This is the only modern discussion of the therapeutic properties of gems and minerals that we know of. The authors are spiritual teachers and this vibrance is evident in their presentation. Every conceivable aspect of each gem is considered. This is an excellent compilation which we highly recommend.

HODGES, DORIS. **HEALING STONES. 72pp. Hia61, 2.50p.**
A discussion of the twelve most common precious stones followed by information on *four stones of hidden healing*: azurite, malachite, lazurite, and chrysocolla.

KUNZ, G.F. **THE CURIOUS LORE OF PRECIOUS STONES. 410pp. Dov13, 5.00p.**
Dr. Kunz was America's foremost gemologist and this is the definitive collection of traditional gem lore. The material presented here is derived from a great number of sources—oral, ancient lapidary manuals from the Middle Ages, Greek and Roman geographic accounts, archaeological discoveries in Egypt, Oriental gem books, and much else. Among the topics covered are the following: the use of gems as amulets and talismans, carved and engraved magical stones (including scarabs), luminous stones, crystal balls and crystal gazing, the religious use of gems in many traditions, birth stones, the astrological meaning of precious stones, and the therapeutic value of gems.

MELLA, DOROTHEE. **THE LEGENDARY AND PRACTICAL USE OF GEMS AND STONES. Bibliography, spiral bound, 8½"x11", 22pp. Dml76, 3.95p.**
The information in this booklet is the distillation of the stories and legends of centuries. The practicing arts of the ages, as well as the knowledge of the mystics, have been synthesized into these pages in order to present a composite and practical guide to the use of gems and stones in our world of here and now. This is a neatly designed pamphlet which discusses thirty-two different gems and stones in a simplified manner. It is a fine short overview containing as much as most people would like to know.

STEWART, NELSON. **GEM STONES OF THE SEVEN RAYS. Notes, index, 119pp. HeR39, 3.00p.**
To the ceremonialist. . .precious stones are especially valuable as wave-meters transmitting specialised psychic-qualities, and this little book groups some forty-seven mineral species and varieties under the Seven Rays. The main physical features are given for each stone, and in most cases some historical or ethnological notes are added, often with a bearing on the Ray quality of the stone. In addition, the preliminary chapters gather together modern Theosophical statements concerning the Mineral Kingdom.—from the preface

WRIGHT, RUTH and ROBERT CHADBOURNE. **GEMS AND MINERALS OF THE BIBLE. 160pp. Kea70, 3.95p.**
A medley of information, folklore, and history drawn from a variety of sources. Sixty-two gems and minerals are discussed.

GRAIL & KING ARTHUR

The *matiere de Bretagne* which formed the theme and incident of so much of medieval literature of the twelfth and early thirteenth centuries appears to hark back, at any rate in part, to a corpus of Celtic myth and legend preserved in Ireland, Wales, and to some degree in Cornwall, and cross-fertilized by constant contact between the indigenous populations. How the figure of Arthur came to be connected with this material is far from clear. It would seem that at some stage legends woven round a hero of the British resistance to the Saxon hordes became incorporated in the older pagan heritage. Indeed these legends may have proved so resistant to time and change partly because they were the culture of a subject people.

The Saxons seem to have shown very little interest in these stories sung or recited by Welsh bards, nor do we hear anything about them under the Norman kings, too busy establishing their grip on the conquered land. With the accession of the Plantagenets, however, things change: court life becomes more civilized, Eleanor of Aquitaine brings from France her poets and her minstrels, her love of life and letters. Perhaps, too, Henry II found it politic to foster past tales of British glory to rival the lustre which the legend of Charlemagne conferred on the kings of France.

Be that as it may, Geoffrey of Monmouth produced shortly after 1130 what a contemporary chronicler somewhat acidly described as *the fables about Arthur which he took from the ancient fictions of the Britons and increased out of his own head.* He followed this up a little later by a book called the **Vita Merlini**. Most scholars no longer attribute to Geoffrey of Monmouth the prime role he was once thought to have had in the propagation of the Arthurian legends. Perhaps his Latin prose conferred a certain respectability on these *ancient fictions.* Certainly the dates of his works are important, for before him there was nothing, and the trickle he started soon became a flood. In 1155 a Norman poet called Wace translated Geoffrey's Latin into French. Within the next thirty years the Tristan romances, the lais of Marie de France and the romances of Chretien de Troyes had all seen the light of day.

Undoubtedly the Norman Conquest was a central factor in that it spread the French language and culture right across England to the marches of Wales and opened the gates of French courts first in Britain and then on the Continent to Welsh bards and story-tellers eager to peddle their wares. The same period saw the opening up of the routes to the East with the two-way traffic created by the Crusades. The courts of Northern France found themselves therefore at one of the crossroads of history where ideas, themes, subject-matter, much of it old but all of it novel, could intermingle and create fresh patterns, forming a new and exciting mould into which so much literary activity was to be poured.

But what of the Holy Grail itself? The legend represents the Grail as the dish in which Christ ate the paschal lamb with His apostles and which was brought to Britain by Joseph of Arimathea, the first missionary to this island. The tradition attributing possession of this relic to Joseph of Arimathea goes back to the apocryphal Evangelium Nicodemi; the link between Joseph, the Grail vessel and an early Christian settlement at Glastonbury is found in a work composed around the year 1200 by a French knight called Robert de Boron, though where

and how he came by the tale remains a mystery. The Grail vessel is also associated with a miraculous lance which many identify as the lance of Longinus, with which Christ's side was pierced on the cross.

Once these precious relics had come to Britain their custody devolved upon a line of Grail-keepers, known as the Fisher Kings, descendants of Joseph of Arimathea. The Grail was preserved in their Castle of Corbenic, enveloped in mystery and hidden from the sight of such adventurous knights as went in search of it.

This brief account shows the Grail vessel in the light of a Christian relic. It seems however almost certain that its origins were very far from Christian. Chretien de Troyes first introduced the legend into France with his **Conte del Graal**, written in 1190. Here we have a Grail Castle and a Grail-keeper, a large platter with mysterious attributes, a bleeding lance, and a question that must be asked in order to heal a wounded king and restore fertility to his land. There are indeed Christian overtones, in that this platter contains a host which is the sole food of the wounded king. Underneath, however, one can clearly discern the outlines of an ancient Celtic myth describing the visit of a mortal hero to an otherworldly palace. This myth in its different versions has certain constant elements: the maimed king who has usually been wounded with his own sacred sword or lance; the barren land (in primitive times it was popularly believed that the fertility of a domain was related to the potency of its ruler, and the maimed king is generally represented as wounded *through the thighs*; traces of this belief still persisted in twelfth-century France); the extraordinary dangers to be surmounted in the quest for the palace; the question that must be asked in order to heal the king and loose his kingdom from its enchantment. Each of these factors, with the exception of the redeeming question (which is still an essential element in all the versions portraying Perceval as the hero of the quest), is present in the Christian version, and it is quite clear that ancient legendary material has been reinterpreted to make it relevant to a society whose beliefs, philosophy and relationships were far removed from those of the ancient Celts.

The key that unlocks the door of the allegory is the meaning embodied in the Holy Grail. The Grail itself is the symbol of God's grace. At once the dish of the Last Supper, the vessel which received the effusion of Christ's blood when His side was pierced, and in the text both chalice and ciborium, its *secrets* are the mystery of the Eucharist unveiled. Now whereas grace is freely given to all men, it is dispensed to each individual soul in the measure in which he is capable of receiving it, and only the wholly dedicated, the pure in heart can attain to that ecstatic union where they may contemplate in love what *the heart of man cannot conceive nor tongue relate.*

—*condensed from* **The Quest of the Holy Grail,** *by P.M. Matarasso*

ACHAD, FRATER. **THE CHALICE OF ECSTASY: A MAGICAL AND QABALISTIC INTERPRETATION OF THE DRAMA OF PARZIVAL. 82pp. YPS23, 6.95c.**
Achad retells the legend as interpreted by Richard Wagner and comments on its esoteric meaning. Many quotations from the drama are included.

BEARDSLEY, AUBREY. BEARDSLEY'S ILLUSTRATIONS FOR LE MORT D'ARTHUR. 171pp. Dov72, 4.00p.

BLAISDELL, FOSTER and MARIANNE KALINKE, trs. EREX SAGA AND IVENS SAGA. Introduction, notes, index, 111pp. UNP77, 12.05c.
Translations of two sagas from the medieval Scandinavian branch of the Arthurian literary tradition. Directed toward a general audience and unencumbered by excessive scholarliness.

CABLE, JAMES, tr. THE DEATH OF KING ARTHUR. 235pp. Vik71, 2.50p.
Set at the end of the Arthurian world, this translation of La Mort le Roi Artu is a French romance of the thirteenth century. The story begins with a Round Table depleted in numbers after the quest of the Holy Grail. It goes on to tell of Lancelot and Guinevere and the treacherous Mordred and ends with the last battle of Arthur and Lancelot at Salisbury.

CHRETIEN DE TROYES. ARTHURIAN ROMANCES. 393pp. Dut75/ Den, 2.95p.
Chretien was, as far as is known, the first person to recount in verse the romantic adventures of Arthur's knights; and, more than any other individual, he is responsible for having established the Arthurian legend as a major branch of European literature. His works present the most complete expression we possess from a single author of the ideals of French chivalry. Chretien lived in the twelfth century. The translation is into prose and this edition includes an introduction and notes by D.D.R. Owen.

ESCHENBACH, WOLFRAM VON. PARZIVAL. 493pp. RaH61, 3.45p.
Parzival, an Arthurian romance completed by von Eschenbach in the first years of the thirteenth century, is one of the foremost works of German literature and a classic work on the Grail. The most important aspects of human existence, worldly and spiritual, are presented against the panorama of battles and tournaments and Parzival's long search for the Grail. The world of knighthood, of love and loyalty and human endeavor despite the cruelty and suffering of life, is constantly mingling with the world of the Grail, affirming the inherent unity between man's temporal condition and his quest for something beyond human existence. This translation by Helen Mustard and Charles Passage is the definitive one. The translators also provide a fifty-six page introduction.

EVANS, SEBASTIAN, tr. HIGH HISTORY OF THE HOLY GRAIL. Introduction, 388pp. Cla69, 8.00c.
A translation of the first volume of **Perceval le Gallois ou le conte du Graal,** the most complete book of the Grail known today, the original manuscript of which dates from the thirteenth century. Every aspect of the legend is discussed at length and the narrative is in the form of a story. The language is archaic.

■ **GREEN, ROGER. KING ARTHUR AND HIS KNIGHTS OF THE ROUND TABLE. 282pp. Vik53, 1.50p.**
A retelling of twenty-two of the stories, aimed at children but fine for all who wish to read the stories. Green writes well and the enchantment is retained in his recreation. A beautifully illustrated book.

HAAR, J.T. KING ARTHUR. Illustrations, 160pp. CRs73, 6.95c.
A simple retelling of some of the major stories about the life of King Arthur, geared toward junior high aged readers.

HALL, LOUIS. THE KNIGHTLY TALES OF SIR GAWAIN. Bibliography, 188pp. NeH76, 4.95p.
A collection of seven tales about Sir Gawain. The book begins with a general introduction and each tale has its own introduction describing the particulars of the manuscript from which it originated and defining the medieval position on the basic issues presented by the tale. The translations are in modern English.

HALL, MANLY P. ORDERS OF THE QUEST: THE HOLY GRAIL. 101pp. PRS49, 5.75c.
A survey of the Western mystery tradition in *the period extending from the collapse of the pagan Mysteries to the end of the Age of Chivalry.* Each of the main societies and individuals is briefly discussed.

HELINE, CORINNE. MYSTERIES OF THE HOLY GRAIL. 128pp. NAP73, 2.95p.
A deeply esoteric exposition of the roots of the Grail story and the legends that grew up around it. Ms. Heline believes that the Grail story represents the path of the soul through various initiations into greater consciousness.

HOPE-MONCRIEFF, A.R. THE ROMANCE OF CHIVALRY. Many illustrations, index, 447pp. NCP76, 4.95p.
This is a fine early twentieth century selection of chivalric romances drawn from all parts of Europe. The author retells the exploits of King Arthur and his knights, of Charlemagne, Roland and Oliver, Huon of Bordeaux, Ogier the Dane, Amadis of Gaul, and many other heroic tales. The stories read fairly well, though it is apparent that they were written down some time ago.

■ **JENKINS, ELIZABETH. THE MYSTERY OF KING ARTHUR. Index, 7½"x9½", 224pp. Put75/Jos, 20.00c.**
A sumptuously illustrated, well researched account of all that is known today about Arthur. Exploring every aspect of the myth, Ms. Jenkins discusses the Round Table, the Holy Grail, Glastonbury, the tragedy of Lancelot and Guinevere, and much else. She recounts the development of these concepts over the years and notes the political significance of the Arthur story. Fascinating reading for those who would like to learn more about Arthur. Ninety-six illustrations, sixteen in color, are included.

LANG, ANDREW, ed. KING ARTHUR, TALES OF THE ROUND TABLE. 182pp. ScB02, 1.95p.
A facsimile edition, with the original illustrations by H.J. Ford. Lang, writing in simple language, has retold thirteen of the best known legends associated with the Arthurian cycle.

LANIER, SIDNEY, ed. THE BOY'S KING ARTHUR. 321pp. Scr24, 3.95p.
This is a retelling of Malory, written in simple language and including the stories of King Arthur, Lancelot, Sir Gareth of Orkney, Sir Tristram, Sir Galahad and Sir Percival and the quest of the Holy Grail, the fair maid of Astolat, and the death of Arthur. Many lovely color drawings by N.C. Wyeth accompany the text.

LE CAIN, ERROL. KING ARTHUR'S SWORD. 8¾"x11½", Fab68, 5.10c.
This story, which is suggested by the Arthurian legends but does not attempt to follow them closely, tells how King Arthur received a magic

sword from the Lady of the Lake, and how his wicked sister Morgana le Fay tried to use it against him. The illustrations are remarkable. The delicately romantic quality of some scenes, the startling dramatic impact of others, and the abundance of finely wrought detail create a fairy tale world of extraordinary charm.

MALORY, SIR THOMAS. **LE MORTE D'ARTHUR. 532pp. Crn62, 4.75c.**
Le Morte d'Arthur, originally published in 1485, was the first coherent history of Arthur from his magical birth to his dramatic death. Malory collected all the legends and myths and attempted to judge their historical veracity. His account is still considered the definitive one and all later scholars have relied heavily upon it—although later research has shown it to be in error on a number of counts. It is a classic work which many have heard of but few have read due to the elaborate and obscure nature of medieval rhetoric. This edition is rendered in a modern idiom and includes an introduction by Robert Graves.

MALORY, SIR THOMAS. **LE MORTE D'ARTHUR. Introduction, glossary, 866pp. Dut06, 3.50p/each.**
This two volume set contains an unabridged edition of Malory's masterwork, the principal English contribution to the Arthurian cycle.

MALORY, SIR THOMAS. **LE MORTE D'ARTHUR. Glossary, 9"x 11¼", 590pp. SMP72, 50.00c.**
This exquisitely produced volume includes the full edition of Malory's book along with over 1,000 reproductions from 362 black and white Beardsley drawings. Some of the drawings are delicate and detailed; others are massed black and white portrayals of mood. This is a facsimile of the third edition, with addenda.

MALTWOOD, K.E. **A GUIDE TO GLASTONBURY'S TEMPLE OF THE STARS. Illustrations, bibliography, 129pp. Cla64, 6.70c.**
The author believes that it is now possible to localize the Arthurian Grail legends by means of aerial photographs of the area between Glastonbury and Somerton. The prehistoric earthworks and artifical water courses in that area appear from the air to delineate enormous effigies resembling zodiacal creatures arranged in a circle. Maltwood studies each of the representational images as if it were a zodiacal sign and makes an in depth analysis of the symbolism and the legends that derived from the giant natural form. Appropriate quotes from **The High History of the Holy Grail** are included.

MARKALE, J. **KING ARTHUR—KING OF KINGS. Notes, bibliography, index, 242pp. Cre77, 24.95c.**
This is the definitive work to date on Arthur and his times. By means of historical, geographical, and literary deduction, he recreates the real King Arthur, the Celtic warrior who organized the resistance to the Saxon onslaught in fifth century England. Markale's knowledge of Celtic history has enabled him to reconstruct precisely the world in which Arthur lived and to define the place which Arthur occupied in such a world. A long section of the book is devoted to a thorough analysis of Arthurian literature. Virtually every extant early work is summarized and analyzed and many of the legends are retold in full. Markale also analyzes the development of the Arthurian myth and retells the saga of Arthur as it appeared in the earliest sources. Markale is professor of Celtic history at the Sorbonne and the greatest living authority on the Celtic past. In the process of his analysis, Markale traces British history from the fifth century through the Dark Ages. This is a readable account which we recommend highly to all who are deeply interested in the Arthurian romances and in Celtic Britain.

MATARASSO, P.M., tr. **THE QUEST OF THE HOLY GRAIL. 304pp. Vik69, 2.50p.**
The translation of an important thirteenth century work which vividly discusses the adventures of Arthur's knights in their search for the Holy Grail. In the process the author didactically presents the Christian ideals and fuses Christian symbolism and Celtic legend. The translator provides a long introduction and extensive notes.

MONACO, RICHARD. **PARSIVAL OR A KNIGHT'S TALE. Illustrations, 343pp. McM77, 4.95p.**
A modern retelling, in the form of a novel, of the quest for innocence and the struggle against evil. This version should appeal to fantasy lovers. All the essential elements of the original story remain.

MORDUCH, ANNA. **THE SOVEREIGN ADVENTURE. 196pp. Cla70, 8.40c.**
The Sovereign Adventure endeavors to show that the story of the Grail in all its different versions is neither romantic fiction nor the property or tradition of one race. It belongs to mankind and every race of men has its own Grail story.... We hope that this book will send many of the young out as Grail knights of our time, strong, enlightened and tolerant.... They can all share in the sovereign adventure, the quest for man's goal and the finding of the way that leads to it.

NUTT, ALFRED. **STUDIES ON THE LEGEND OF THE HOLY GRAIL WITH SPECIAL REFERENCE TO THE HYPOTHESIS OF ITS CELTIC ORIGIN. Notes, indices, 295pp. CSq65, 10.00c.**
An important late nineteenth century work. Nutt retells and analyzes many of the Arthurian romances and discusses varying accounts of the same romance.

POWYS, JOHN COWPER. **A GLASTONBURY ROMANCE. 1,136pp. PnB55, 6.95p.**
An epic novel that recreates the eternal legend of the Grail. Colin Wilson calls this Possibly the greatest novel of the twentieth century, and one of the great masterpieces of all time. Powys explores, in his own words, the effect of a particular legend, a special myth, a unique tradition, from the remotest past in human history, upon a particular spot on the surface of this planet together with its crowd of inhabitants of every age and of every type of character....Its heroine is the Grail. Its hero is the Life poured into the Grail. Its message is that no one Receptacle of Life and no one Fountain of Life poured into the Receptacle can contain or explain what the world offers us.

PYLE, HOWARD. **THE STORY OF THE CHAMPIONS OF THE ROUND TABLE. 6½"x9¼", 347pp. Dov05, 3.50c.**
This companion volume to Pyle's earlier book retells the stories of three of the most colorful Arthurian figures: Sir Lancelot, Sir Tristan, and Sir Percival. Pyle's books are generally considered the most readable available and time has not dated them. Fifty illustrations illuminate the text. The style is geared toward young people.

PYLE, HOWARD. **THE STORY OF KING ARTHUR AND HIS KNIGHTS. 6"x9¼", 329pp. Dov03, 3.50p.**
A vividly written retelling of the adventures of King Arthur and his knights. All the major stories are included. This is considered the

definitive children's version of the Arthurian legend—though some of the more recent works probably speak better to contemporary youth. Forty-one excellent drawings by Pyle accompany the text.

RACKHAM, ARTHUR, il. **THE ROMANCE OF KING ARTHUR AND HIS KNIGHTS OF THE ROUND TABLE. 6¼"x9¼", 530pp. Crn17, 4.98c.**
This abridgment of Malory's version is done by Alfred Pollard and accompanied by thirty-two illustrations, half in color, by Arthur Rackham.

SAYERS, DOROTHY, tr. **THE SONG OF ROLAND. Lengthy introduction, notes, 206pp. Vik37, 2.50p.**
The **Song of Roland**, as Dr. Sayers remarks in the introduction to this fine verse translation, is *the earliest, the most famous, and the greatest of those Old French epics which are called Songs of Deeds.* Writing around the end of the eleventh century, and recalling an actual disaster in 778, the anonymous poet describes in detail the betrayal and slaughter by Sarcens of the rear guard of Charlemagne's army under Roland at Rencevaux and Charlemagne's bitter revenge.

SCHACH, PAUL, tr. **THE SAGA OF TRISTRAM AND ISOND. Notes, 148pp. UNP73, 3.00p.**
This is the first English translation of **Tristram's saga**, which in turn is a Norwegian adaptation of the French **Tristan** of Thomas of Brittany. It is the only complete edition of the Thomas branch of the Tristan legend, and a knowledge of it is essential for the reconstruction of its source, of which only a fraction is extant. This is a faithful translation. Professor Schach's introduction compresses a great amount of invaluable background information.

STEINBECK, JOHN. **THE ACTS OF KING ARTHUR AND HIS NOBLE KNIGHTS. 378pp. RaH76, 4.95p.**
This book has received a lot of critical attention since its publication. For a time in the 1950s Steinbeck was almost obsessed with the stories of King Arthur, especially Malory's version of the tales. His desire in this volume was to set the stories down in modern language, neither omitting nor adding anything. He began to do this, based on the Winchester manuscript of Malory, and he has fully succeeded in his aim. This is the best retelling of the stories that we know of. For some reason he stopped writing and went on to other things, so his version of Malory remains incomplete. Nonetheless, this edited version of what he did finish is now available along with transcripts of letters which he wrote about the manuscript in progress.

STEWART, MARY. **THE CRYSTAL CAVE. 384pp. Faw70/Hod, 1.75p.**
This novel brings the legend of Merlin to life. It is the story of his childhood, his mystical visions, and the manner in which he developed. Ms. Stewart has given us a fascinating tale. She does not claim to be presenting a serious study—yet the reader can get as good (or better) a feel of fifth century Britain from this book as from any of the more scholarly works.

STEWART, MARY. **THE HOLLOW HILLS. 447pp. Faw73/Hod, 1.95p.**
This is our personal favorite of all the books on Arthur. Mary Stewart is an enthralling writer and she has created a wonderful story which takes us through Arthur's childhood and young manhood up to the time when he becomes king. And again Merlin plays a leading role. Must reading for all those who would like to know more about Arthur and Merlin.

STONE, BRIAN, tr. **SIR GAWAIN AND THE GREEN KNIGHT. 185pp. Vik59, 1.95p.**
The tale of Sir Gawain is one of the best known of the Arthurian romances. This version was written in the fourteenth century and is considered a masterpiece of medieval alliterative poetry. In the poem Sir Gawain triumphs against almost insuperable odds. This edition includes sixty-eight pages of interpretative and background material and a twenty page introduction.

SUTCLIFF, ROSEMARY. **TRISTAN AND ISEULT. 138pp. Vik74/HeG, 1.50p.**
The tragic love story of Tristan and Iseult is today intimately associated with the Arthurian cycle. It is as old as the oldest stories of

King Arthur and like them, far older than any of the written versions we have today. In its distant beginnings, **Tristan** was a Celtic legend and it only became joined to the King Arthur stories quite late in medieval times. This version is written in a simple style and is geared toward older children. Line drawings accompany the text.

WACE, ROBERT and LAYAMON. **ARTHURIAN CHRONICLES. Introduction, 276pp. Dut62/Den, 3.50p.**
Along with Geoffrey of Monmouth, Wace and Layamon were the most important twelfth century Arthurian chroniclers. This is a verse translation by Eugene Mason of Wace's **Roman de Brut** and Layamon's **Brut**. Each gives a different view of the events in the Arthurian legends.

WAITE, A.E. **THE HIDDEN CHURCH OF THE HOLY GRAIL. 724pp. YPS09, 17.50c.**
I am about to set forth after a new manner, and chiefly for the use of English mystics, the nature of the mystery which is enshrined in the old romance-literature of the Holy Grail....The task will serve...on the one hand...to illustrate the deeper intimations of Graal literature, and, on the other, certain collateral intimations which lie behind the teachings of the great churches and are, in the official sense, as if beyond their ken.

WEIGAND, HERMANN. **WOLFRAM'S PARZIVAL. Notes, index, 210pp. Cor69, 16.80c.**
A collection of five essays, originally published as separate articles. They provide a minute analysis of the **Parzival** text together with a careful consideration of sources and analogous works.

WESTON, JESSIE. **FROM RITUAL TO ROMANCE. Notes, index, 217pp. Dou57, 2.95p.**
The Grail Story is not...the product of imagination, literary or popular. At its root lies the record, more or less distorted, of an ancient Ritual, having for its ultimate object the initiation into the secret of Life, physical and spiritual. Ms. Weston is an eminent medieval scholar and here she has applied the discoveries of cultural anthropology to the literature of medieval legend and romance. This book is best known as the one which inspired the basic symbolism of T.S. Eliot's **The Waste Land**.

WHITE, T.H. **THE BOOK OF MERLYN. 7¼"x10¼", 157pp. Ber77/CSC, 2.25p.**
This manuscript was written at the time that White was putting **The Once and Future King** together and he intended it to be the final section of that book, yet this portion was never published. This is a slightly edited version of the manuscript that White prepared. White wrote at a time when he was preoccupied with thoughts of World War II, and this is reflected in the story. The tale begins with an aged King Arthur sitting alone in his tent, awaiting his last battle. Merlin enters to give Arthur one last lesson in life, and the king is whisked away to meet again with the Animal Council to which Merlin had introduced him as a boy. Arthur hears many anti-war arguments from the animals and is himself transformed into an ant and a wild goose. Ultimately Arthur returns to the battle lines and attempts a truce, after which he is accidentally killed. White also tells the fate of some of the other major characters. This is a poetic work which includes some of White's finest writing. A number of delightful pen and ink drawings accompany the text and Sylvia Townsend Warner wrote the introduction.

WHITE, T.H. **THE ONCE AND FUTURE KING. 639pp. Ber39/CSC, 2.75p.**
A novelistic recreation of Arthur's childhood and his reign as king. This is the most popular contemporary retelling and was the basis for **Camelot**.

WILLIAMS, CHARLES and C.S. LEWIS. **TALIESSIN THROUGH LOGRES/THE REGION OF THE SUMMER STARS/ARTHURIAN TORSO. 384pp. Eer74, 5.95p.**
Taliessen Through Logres and **The Region of the Summer Stars** contain Williams' Grail poems, a reworking of the theme of the Holy Grail into a poetic myth of unusual wisdom and contemporary significance. The **Arthurian Torso** is composed of two works: **The Figure of Arthur**, Williams' prose study of the Arthurian legend, and **Williams and the Arthuriad**, Lewis' commentary on the poems and the prose study.

GRAPHOLOGY

Character traits change in individuals as changes take place in a culture. These changes reveal themselves in handwriting, even though it takes a long time for a new set of ideas or habits to wear a groove in one's inner consciousness. If an individual's handwriting shows a receptivity to new experiences and changes, an examination of specimens written over a period of years will clearly show the person's development or regression.

The way in which the individual writes, just as the manner in which he shakes hands, laughs, walks, and makes unconscious gestures, tells you much more than his words alone. Handwriting is a composite picture of the way a person's mind works, how his thinking affects his emotions, what his attitude is toward life and other human beings.

In Europe, and especially Germany, graphology has always been studied in connection with the subject of psychology. In the United States it has been taken less seriously until the recent arrival of many students of this science. Slowly but surely, it is moving into the realm where it belongs as a valuable psychometric tool in assisting psychiatrists and psychologists in their diagnoses. Along with other projective techniques, such as the Rorschach Ink Blot Test, an analysis of a subject's handwriting is being used to throw further light on his character structure and certain habit patterns which may not be readily discerned by other tests.

Graphology has also come to be used as an aid in vocational guidance for students entering upon careers; in personnel selection for business firms and banks; and in discerning whether men and women are suited for each other in marriage.

Since there are so many details to consider when analyzing a handwriting, it is best to systematize your approach. These are the fundamentals of handwriting analysis.

Pen Pressure—The pressure relates to the senses and to some extent reveals the vitality of the individual. It will be heavy, medium-heavy, *muddy*, medium-light, light, or extremely light so that it appears hair-like. Observe the writer's vitality—is he robust, athletic, delicate, supersensitive, unhealthy?

Slant—As Dr. Alfred Adler, the famous Viennese psychologist, said: *Handwriting points the way from me to you.* It follows that the slant of an individual's handwriting will express whether his way is one of ardor, affection, reserve or withdrawal. There is the extreme rightward-flowing handwriting; the moderate right angle; the vertical, moderate backhand; and the extreme left-slanted backhand. In the slant (or slope) you discover whether the person is outgoing, extroverted, leaning toward people; or the opposite, which is reserved, introverted, unsocial or even antisocial.

Size—The size of the writing gives us clues to the individual's manner of approaching a situation. Does he generalize or observe details? The size really represents the kind of lens through which a person sees. Is it unusually large, large, medium-large? (All three sizes give a clue to a degree of exhibitionism). Or is it *normal*, which does not particularly strike the eye? This is the size most people write. The smaller the writing, the better the powers of concentration.

Basic line—Whether the lines run uphill, downhill or in both directions relates to the writer's point of view and his spirits. Is he optimistic, buoyant, cheerful, euphoric? Or skeptical, depressed, temporarily unhappy, suffering from melancholia, suicidal? Sometimes lines veer upward but words hang down either in the middle of a sentence or at the end of many sentences. You may see temporary or chronic depression, morbidity, hopelessness in these signs. The downhill writer is often the skeptic whose attitude arises from self-doubt. Downhill writing is often a warning of depleted vitality, forerunner to a breakdown.

Margins and Spacing—The width or narrowness of margins and spacing between words determine the width or narrowness of a person's mind, his aesthetic reactions, whether he is a clear or muddled thinker, whether he is economical or extravagant. There may be wide spacing between letters in words, between the words, or between the lines. Or there may be no appreciable space between any of these. If the writing is poorly spaced in every respect so that it looks disturbed, you are probably dealing with a mentally and emotionally disturbed person.

t Bars—They are extremely important in determining how much will power, drive, energy, determination (or a lack of these) the writer has and how much he uses. The t bars reveal whether he is aggressive, persistent, compulsive; or weak, timid, vacillating, indecisive, passive, neurotic. In the t bar you will see clues to emotional immaturity; to whether the writer lives in the past or drives his energy ambitiously toward the future. Many handwritings will show a variety of t bars, all of which have special meanings. The t bar, together with other horizontal strokes, shows the extent of the writer's balance—how he copes with life's situations.

i Dots—The i dots, considered in combination with the t bars and other letter formations, show, among other things, retentiveness or lack of it, imagination, humor and critical faculties. Are the dots high, close to the letter, wavy, pointed, circled?

Small Letters (the abc's)—Observe these in conjunction with other signs. Are they printed, copybook style, open or closed, angular or rounded or both? They indicate conformity to rules, mental development, caution, generosity and other personality traits.

Capitals—The capital letters denote taste and pride. Are they ornate, simple, printed, old-fashioned, artistic, open at the top or closed tightly with a loop? Do they start with an incurve or an outgoing flourish; are they rounded or angular? Do capital letters appear where small ones would normally be?

Loops—Upper and lower loops have a special significance. Notice whether they are wide, narrow, compressed, ragged at the top, very high; whether the lower ones are exaggerated and run into the line below. Are they the outstanding feature in the entire handwriting? Do they have a *broken back* look? Or is there, instead of loops, a single stroke—the uppers in the letters l, h, k, the lower ones in y's and g's? Breaks in loops, both upper and lower, reveal the presence of a physical impairment.

Zones—Divide the writing into three zones: upper, middle, and lower. The upper zone (loops especially) symbolizes the person's ideals, fantasy life, set of principles, standards; the middle zone concerns his approach to reality, how he deals with practical problems; the lower zone gives us clues to his physical demands, sexual potency, primitive impulses, materiality. Balance the three zones, as you would a mathematical problem. They will give you clues to more about the person than meets the eye..

Initials and Terminals—Initial strokes, often unnecessary, show attention to detail. The terminals, too, give valuable clues. Are they long, wavy, curving upward or downward, abrupt, blunt, or do letters end with a long horizontal line that has a hook on it? The terminals (or finals) are clues to how much *give* the person has. Taken in conjunction with other signs and strokes, terminals give us important clues to many traits of character.

Speed (rhythm)—Indicative of energy, it tells you how much the person expends in the way he does things as well as how he thinks—whether slowly or quickly. The person who thinks more quickly than his hand can record may leave out some letters in words or slur a word ending in *ing*. He writes as though recording his thoughts in shorthand. There are two kinds of speedy writing—distinct and indistinct. The distinct writer slows down his thinking in order to conform; the indistinct writer can't bother with conforming but goes ahead and expresses himself, later rearranging his thinking to make it all into a comprehensible pattern. The slow thinker appears to draw every letter and the speed, therefore, is slowed down. He is also careful of punctuation, unless he is illiterate or negligent. Uneven speed produces letters lacking in uniformity and may be corroborated by other signs of disturbance in the writing. Writing that is too speedy shows anxiety, which is further revealed in a going over or patching up of letters or words. Words crossed out in a messy looking specimen tell us the person is in an emotional mess. Writing in anger will show uneven pen pressure, blunt downstrokes, thick t bars, and the speed will be evident if you try to imitate the writing. When you have learned to estimate the speed of a person's writing you will know something about his energy output: whether he is lazy, indolent, indecisive because of tension, or, at the other extreme, whether he is a human dynamo.

Connecting Strokes—A word is either connected in its letter format or it is broken up. When the entire writing is connected, with even words joined together, consecutive reasoning or logic is revealed. The person may also be literal-minded. If breaks appear, this is the sign of intuition. Where the handwriting is entirely broken up, looking like printing but not printing, it is the *inspirational hand*. Many poets, artists, and dancers print consistently. So do engineers. Connected writing combined with breaks in some words shows that the writer is capable of logic, yet possesses some intuition.

Punctuation—Careful punctuation indicates the writer's attention to details. Such care may be evident in the writing of an intelligent person. However, the person concerned with larger issues, with essences rather than details, may be careless in both punctuation and spelling, yet have a high intelligence rating. It is wise, therefore, to withhold judgment until the handwriting has been categorized according to which intellectual group the person belongs in. One sure conclusion we can draw from the person who punctuates carefully is that he is obedient to the rules taught and often follows them to the letter. Careless punctuation, on the other hand, often shows a person who makes his own rules and can't be bothered with details, especially if someone else demands they be followed.

Signature—The way a person signs his name gives an important clue to his personality. It is the face shown to the outside world, the facade that is presented, and it may be at variance with the *real* person.

—condensed from **The Psychology of Handwriting**, *by Nadya Olyanova*

BUNKER, M.N. WHAT YOUR HANDWRITING TELLS YOU. 243pp. NeH31, 8.95c.
A pioneering study by one of the leaders in the field of graphoanalysis. Well known personalities of the thirties are used as case studies. The book is designed to teach the general principles so that they can be applied in daily life.

FALCON, HAL. **HOW TO ANALYZE HANDWRITING. Many illustrations, index, 159pp. S&S64, 1.95p.**
Dr. Falcon has been a practicing graphologist for over thirty years. Here he explains the basic techniques he uses and quotes from many sources. The text is directly written to the reader and seems to be a good overall survey of the basics. There seems to be more depth here than in many of the general books.

FRENCH, W. **YOUR HANDWRITING AND WHAT IT MEANS. 240pp. NPC74, 2.95p.**
Formerly titled, **The Psychology of Handwriting**. Each chapter contains some of the underlying principles of handwriting psychology as applied to some phase of human endeavor and such information as is relative to characteristic traits, aptitudes, and talents.

■ *GARDNER, RUTH.* **A GRAPHOLOGY STUDENT'S HANDBOOK. 137pp. LIP73, 4.95p.**
Material covered in detail includes strokes, margins, spacing, line and letter leanings, script size, and pen pressure. Space is left for the student to add information as it is acquired. Also includes removable transparencies which assist in the calculation of the degrees of various factors. This is the best practical text we have seen both for self study and group instruction.

GREEN, JANE. **YOU AND YOUR PRIVATE I. Bibliography, 299pp. LIP75, 4.95p.**
Ms. Green is a social worker who uses graphology as a supplementary diagnostic tool, focusing on the personal pronoun *I* as a unique expression of personality. Numerous case histories show how she does in depth personality analyses on the basis of handwriting samples. As with most graphology books the author seems to get carried away with what she sees in each squiggle—however, as an additional psychological tool graphology has proven its usefulness. This is a serious study.

HARRISON, PHYLLIS and D. MATCHAN. **HELPING YOUR HEALTH THROUGH HANDWRITING. Bibliography, index, 203pp. Jov77, 1.75p.**
The authors are both experienced handwriting analysts. In this volume they focus on graphoanalysis and graphotherapy—the science of detecting physical and emotional illness through handwriting analysis. Many exercises are suggested along with information on how to understand what your handwriting reveals and what you can do about it.

HEAL, JEANNE. **YOU AND YOUR HANDWRITING. Index, 6¾"x 8¾", 118pp. Pel73, 5.95c.**
A clear, straightforward account of the basics of handwriting analysis, illustrated with an abundance of sample writing.

HOLDER, ROBERT. **YOU CAN ANALYZE HANDWRITING. Index, 256pp. NAL58, 1.50p.**
Holder presents a clear technique for analyzing handwriting. The presentation is psychologically-oriented and many specifics are cited. The book seems to be as comprehensive as any we have seen and is a good value for the price. Fairly advanced material is also included.

HUGHES, ALBERT. **WHAT YOUR HANDWRITING REVEALS. Bibliography, 123pp. Spe70, 7.00c.**
This is one of the better handwriting analysis books. All the standard information is included and clearly presented—often in outline form. The author also covers the scientific basis, the nature of character and personality from both Freudian and Jungian points of view, how this correlates with graphological findings, and much else. There is also an index containing 211 character traits, a table of 174 characteristics in their negative and positive aspects, and seventy-two samples of handwriting.

MANN, PEGGY. **THE TELLTALE LINE. 72pp. McM76, 6.95c.**
A very simplified guide to the science of handwriting analysis. Written for older children. Practical instructions are included.

MARCUSE, IRENE. **GUIDE TO PERSONALITY THROUGH YOUR HANDWRITING. Bibliography, index, 190pp. Arc62, 1.45p.**
Dr. Marcuse is one of the foremost contemporary graphologists and this book is considered a classic. She tells us the history and development of graphology: in the field of child psychology, in vocational guidance, in marriage counseling, in personnel, selection, in criminal detection, and in abnormal psychology. There is also instructional material on the technique of graphology. The text is illustrated throughout with handwriting samples.

MARLEY, JOHN. **HANDWRITING ANALYSIS MADE EASY. 183pp. Wil67, 2.00p.**
A practical, comprehensive guide to character and human behavior as discovered through graphology.

■ MEYER, JEROME. **THE HANDWRITING ANALYZER. 101pp. S&S53, 4.95p.**
A recent reprint of a classic text, first written in 1927 and revised in 1953, which includes many samples and techniques along with a series of see-through charts which can be used as diagnostic aids. This is about as comprehensive a technique manual as we have seen and it even includes an index to characteristics.

OLYANOVA, NADYA. **HANDWRITING TELLS. 370pp. Wil36/Owe, 3.00p.**
Ms. Olyanova was one of the pioneers in the science of graphology and was instrumental in getting it generally accepted as a significant tool in character and personality analysis. This is a classic volume in which she illustrates the broad range of application the science covers.

OLYANOVA, NADYA. **THE PSYCHOLOGY OF HANDWRITING. 224pp. Wil60, 2.00p.**
A more recent volume, covering the same material as the other, but adding many new insights garnered from years of application.

■ PATERSON, JANE. **INTERPRETING HANDWRITING. Bibliography, index, 95pp. McK76, 4.95p.**
This book covers all the basics of handwriting analysis clearly, with an abundance of illustrative material. The presentation is very readable. This is an excellent introductory book.

■ ROMAN, KLARA. **HANDWRITING: A KEY TO PERSONALITY. 382pp. RaH52/QuB, 4.95p.**
This volume has a great deal more substance than most books on handwriting analysis. Ms. Roman is an internationally known psychological handwriting expert. Here she combines an introductory survey of the art of handwriting analysis with an excellent advanced study of analysis techniques and implications. Her approach can be utilized for both normal and disturbed personalities. A well organized study, illustrated with many handwriting samples.

SARA, DOROTHY. **HANDWRITING ANALYSIS. 158pp. H&R67, 1.75p.**
A simple, straightforward introduction which is well organized and covers all the basics. A fine work for those seeking a simple presentation of what handwriting analysis is all about.

SINGER, ERIC. **A MANUAL OF GRAPHOLOGY. 244pp. Hip49/Duc, 4.95p.**
This is a reissue of three of Singer's books, bound in one volume: **Graphology for Everyman, The Graphologist's Alphabet,** and **A Handwriting Quiz Book.** Singer writes very well and this volume is an excellent introduction for the general reader. All aspects are well covered and the quiz at the end should be helpful to those who seek to test their knowledge.

SOLOMON, SHIRL. **KNOWING YOUR CHILD THROUGH HIS HANDWRITING AND DRAWINGS. 189pp. Crn78, 8.95c.**
This book shows parents and teachers how to recognize a child's inner feelings from his handwriting and drawings. Ms. Solomon was a consultant to the Palm Beach County Public Schools and the Juvenile Court and she is the first fully trained graphologist to analyze children. In this book she includes hundreds of writing and drawing examples from a wide spectrum of children, along with a comprehensive analysis.

WHITING, ELDENE and PETER BLAZI. **TRAITMATCH. Bibliography, 152pp. Vul77, 10.00c.**
Ms. Whiting is past president of the American Handwriting Analysis Foundation. This volume is subtitled, *Discovering Occupational Personality Through Handwriting Analysis,* and its emphasis is on ways to find specific personality traits for specific job needs through handwriting analysis. The material is well organized and the book is replete with handwriting examples.

GURDJIEFF & THE WORK

In most of the major cities in the Western world you can, if you make a serious attempt to do so, find a group of people who are, as they say, *in the work*—that is, who attempt, together and as individuals, to function more consciously and harmoniously by studying the ideas and practicing the techniques given by George Ivanovitch Gurdjieff. Gurdjieff groups generally avoid publicity. They do not proselytize. They are relatively invisible in the world, being as hard to find as a particular piece of hay in a haystack because their members lead ordinary lives while devoting themselves to their inner work. This work is designed to engage many aspects of human functioning: it involves a wide range of activities including intellectual study, self-observation, daily meditation, sacred dances or *movements*, cooperative efforts, and, more often than not, manual labor performed under special conditions.

The extraordinary being and *rascal sage* to whom all this activity is due devoted his life to the study of Eastern esoteric teaching and the translation of the knowledge of theory and practice he acquired into forms assimilable by people living in the Occidental world. He was careful to create a fog around himself during his lifetime, just as Don Juan, another man of knowledge, was to recommend to all who tread the path. Thus we know relatively little about Gurdjieff, and although some information can be pieced together from more or less reliable sources, the specific influences on and sources of his teaching will probably remain as mysterious as he intended them to be.

He was born in the 1870s in Alexandropol, in the Caucasus region of what is now Russia, of a Greek father and an Armenian mother. Some insist that December 28, 1877, his passport date of birth, is accurate, and yet his own reports of his age and the events of his life seem to point to an earlier birthdate, perhaps about 1872. When he was still a boy his family moved to Kars, where he had the good fortune to become the student of Dean Borsh of the Russian Military Cathedral, who, with Gurdjieff's own father, became an important influence on his development. According to Gurdjieff these two men were chiefly responsible for his *irrepressible striving to understand clearly the precise significance, in general, of the life process on earth of all outward forms of breathing creatures and, in particular, of the aim of human life in the light of this interpretation.* He lived in a place that was particularly rich ground for unearthing answers to such perennial questions, or at least for finding clues. Kars and the surrounding region lying between the Black and Caspian Seas had been invaded and occupied by many different peoples and was, at the time of Gurdjieff's formative years, a place of great cultural ferment owing to the interpenetration of Christian, Armenian, Assyrian, Islamic, and even Zoroastrian sources.

There was considerable knowledge about Christian ritual and practice to be had in Kars, and Gurdjieff learned much about the ancient symbolism of the liturgy and the techniques of rhythmic breathing and mental prayer that were still part of the orthodox monk's religious duty. Yet, despite the fertility of his native land and the religious tradition into which he was born, he was not at all satisfied with the progress of his understanding of the basic question he had posed himself. He went in search of knowledge.

Accompanied by a band of friends who called themselves *Seekers after Truth*, Gurdjieff set off, in his teens or early twenties, toward the east in wanderings through Central Asia and to such far-flung regions as Ethiopia and the Solomon Islands. During these travels he was undoubtedly in contact with esoteric circles in several Islamic orders, most notably the Sarmouni and the Naqshbandi, and it is to these Sufi sources that much of his teaching can be traced. The central symbol of the Gurdjieff work, the enneagram, is certainly of Sufi origin, and it is fairly well established that many of the sacred dances done as meditations in movement by students of Gurdjieff were also inspired by Sufi contacts, most particularly the Sarmouni.

Sufi teachings certainly contributed much to Gurdjieff's thought in ways that can be noted more or less exactly. Another esoteric influence was also important, though less easily specified. This was the Vajrayana Buddhism of Tibet.

Very little is known about the period in Tibet and Central Asia, which may have lasted from the early 1890s until perhaps 1910 or 1912, except that Gurdjieff was on the track of archaeological and religious keys to unlock the secrets of his *fundamental question.* He carried on his researches into lamaism and prelamaistic practice, into *tekkias* and monasteries where ancient knowledge was preserved, and even, it seems likely, into Siberian shamanism, often referred to as the original matrix from which religions developed. Apparently, during these wanderings, Gurdjieff pieced together a world view that he found satisfactory and became aware of his mission: to bring this understanding of the *terror of the situation* and the possible way out to the Western world.

The next time Gurdjieff's whereabouts are certain is the year 1915, when he first appeared as a teacher in the Russian towns of St. Petersburg and Moscow. There he found, or was found by, Peter Ouspensky, the man who was to become Plato to his Socrates. Ouspensky had himself just returned from travels in search of genuine esoteric knowledge, and was amazed to find that what he had been looking for was in his native land, and, in fact, in his hometown.

Ouspensky was impressed. Gurdjieff, alien as he still was to the Westernized Russian mind, was presenting ideas in a way that rang true, that threw new light on basic questions about man in relation to the universe, levels of consciousness, the human condition, mortality and immortality, and the possibility of self-realization—and he was encouraging and even insisting upon personal verification. So Ouspensky joined a group of Gurdjieff's followers who were meeting secretly in Moscow and worked with them until the group disbanded under the threat of revolution. A number of his Russian students fled west with Gurdjieff and finally—after five years of hardship—settled in Paris.

The decade from 1923 to 1933 was spent in intense work with students at the Institute, during which time Gurdjieff tested and revised a system of study, self-observation, physical work, and exercise aimed toward the reconciliation and union of the three basic human functions of thinking, feeling, and physical activity. Many pupils came to stay at the Institute, including such notables as Katherine Mansfield (who died there), A.R. Orage, Maurice Nicoll, and the de Salzmanns. Gurdjieff, however, made no distinctions on the basis of eminence, and whoever came to study with him could be sure to be required to make consistent and intense efforts and also to be exposed to Gurdjieff's particular style of work on ego reduction, which involved planned interpersonal friction and the public acknowledgment, if not actual ridicule, of personal patterns of malfunction. Every moment at the *Prieure*, as the chateau was called, was regarded as an opportunity for developing self-awareness and attuning personal attitudes—from work in the gardens, to housebuilding, to cooking and cleaning as well as in the more formal instruction. Mealtimes were particularly likely to produce talk and teaching by Gurdjieff, who would often end a dinner with toasts to specific members of the group as various kinds of idiots—round idiots, square idiots, compassionate idiots, and nineteen other varieties. These celebrations of individual personality weaknesses were part of the attempt, carried on by Gurdjieff on many fronts simultaneously, to invalidate and detoxify patterns of conditioning so that the student's more essential nature could begin to appear.

This period of intense work included exhibitions and lectures in Europe and America. It was punctuated by a serious accident which occurred while Gurdjieff was driving alone in a powerful car, and from which physicians were amazed to see him recover. He began, while still recuperating, to give some of his attention to writing and eventually completed his three major works, which consist of ten books divided into three series. Of these the first series **All and Everything**, and the second series, **Meetings with Remarkable Men**, are available. The third work, **Life is Real only Then, When "I Am"**, has been privately printed.

The years between 1933 and 1949, when he died in Paris, marked a new phase of Gurdjieff's activity in which he closed the Prieure and traveled widely, starting new groups in several American cities. At the time of his death he may have had several hundred pupils, mainly in New York and Paris. Ouspensky had broken sharply with him and had died before him, leaving a group of students committed to Ouspensky's version of the work in London. Gurdjieff's writings were practically unknown, and his influence on European thought and culture, apart from the deep impressions made on his pupils, was virtually nil.

Yet now the students of his teachings number in the thousands. His birthday is ritually celebrated on the first day of the year according to the Russian calendar, January 13, with festivities, music, and sacred dances, and the anniversary of his death, October 29, is honored with Russian Orthodox memorial services. The ideas Gurdjieff offered to the Western world continue to ring true. The growth of his influence must be due, at least in some measure, to the current resurgence of interest in self-realization that has led those suffering from what Jung called *holy neurosis* to seek out spiritual guidance wherever it is authentically present. In part, however, it must be due to the fact that Gurdjieff was successful, at least in a considerable degree, in the effort he made to translate Eastern methods and ideas related to the unfolding of man into terms that were specifically evocative for Westerners. Whether he was *the first emissary to the West* from a great Middle Eastern teaching school, as he has been called by some, or whether he was working under his own auspices, he undertook the heroic task of the cultural translation of esoteric ideas, and his efforts deserve the consideration—and perhaps even the gratitude—of post-industrial seekers after truth who, tired of what the material world, the world of business and even the world of academia can offer, turn inward to find reality.

—*condensed from Kathleen Riordan Speeth's essay in* **Transpersonal Psychologies**, *edited by Charles T. Tart*

ANDERSON, MARGARET. **THE STRANGE NECESSITY. 223pp. Hor69, 7.50c.**
This is the last volume in Ms. Anderson's autobiography, covering the period in which she worked closely with Gurdjieff. A very personal, literary account which discusses the people and things the author knew.

ANDERSON, MARGARET. **THE UNKNOWABLE GURDJIEFF. 212pp. Wei62/RKP, 3.95p.**
An evocation of Gurdjieff written in a simple manner by one of his students which passes over the biographical facts about Gurdjieff and concentrates on his teaching. Ms. Anderson writes *of what he said when I was there to hear him say it; of what he taught us, how he taught it, and what effect it had not only upon me but upon my friends since each of us experienced it differently.*

ARKLE, WILLIAM. **A GEOGRAPHY OF CONSCIOUSNESS. 240pp. Spe74, 10.20c.**
While Arkle is not a Gurdjieffian the ideas he presents here about cosmology and man's mechanical nature are quite similar to those taught by Gurdjieff. One of the most interesting features of this book is Arkle's careful analysis of different *circuits* (corresponding to Gurdjieff's *centers*). There is also a good discussion of consciousness and the self. Other chapters cover sin, justice, education, religion, astrology, the will, beauty, and the atomic field. Many diagrams illustrate the text. Foreword by Colin Wilson.

BENJAMIN, HARRY. **BASIC SELF KNOWLEDGE. 167pp. Wei nd/ APC, 3.95p.**
A very simple introduction to Gurdjieff, with some parallels to Krishnamurti's thinking.

BENNETT, J.G. **CREATIVE THINKING. 116pp. CSP64, 2.95p.**
Bennett was in touch with Gurdjieff and Ouspensky for more than thirty years. He is the author of more than twenty books on scientific, philosophical, and religious subjects—many of which reflect his grasp of Gurdjieff's teachings and their importance in the contemporary world. Fluent in the languages of Central Asia, Mr. Bennett was one of the few Anglo-Americans who could converse with Gurdjieff in his native tongue. In the last years of his life he founded and ran a school in England set up along lines suggested by Gurdjieff's school in France. His followers have a practical ongoing school, Claymont, in West Virginia. In this book Bennett discusses the need to set free the instrument of thinking so that creative thought can occur. He makes a number of practical suggestions and says that the key idea is that in order to think, you must not think.

BENNETT, J.G. **THE DRAMATIC UNIVERSE, VOLUME I: THE FOUNDATIONS OF NATURAL PHILOSOPHY. Glossary, indices, 576pp. CSP56, 9.95p.**
The four volumes in this series are the outcome of Bennett's lifetime study and represent the culmination of his adult philosophical insights. He changed toward the end of his life, so the series does not represent his final viewpoint, but it certainly must be considered his *magnum opus* both in terms of sheer bulk and the time devoted to its composition. The books are suitable only for those who are mathematically inclined—Bennett was, after all, a mathematician. The books are all well indexed and cross referenced. In Volume I the discussion centers on a twelve term systematics of the universe which is based on twentieth century scientific discoveries.

BENNETT, J.G. **THE DRAMATIC UNIVERSE, VOLUME II: THE FOUNDATIONS OF MORAL PHILOSOPHY. Glossary, indices, 384pp. CSP61, 9.95p.**
In this second volume we pass from the Domain of Fact, where everything is knowable, to the Domain of Value, where nothing can be known and where we must rely upon faculties other than sense-perception and mental contacts if our explorations are to be fruitful. Bennett's approach is through the study of multi-term systems carried as far as systems with five independent terms. As he says, From Will as triad and Being as tetrad, we come to postulate Spirit, as the source and fulfillment of potentialities hence associated with the pentad . . . . Once we associate the meaning of certain key words—such as wholeness, difference, relatedness, order, potentiality—with the right kind of system, metaphysical thinking loses many of its terrors.

BENNETT, J.G. **THE DRAMATIC UNIVERSE, VOLUME III: MAN AND HIS NATURE. Glossary, indices, 361pp. CSP66, 9.95p.**
Contains extensive sections on the structure of the world, values, anthropology, the human life cycle, and human societies. This material is combined with recent research through the new disciplines of systematics (described in the second volume) and value theory.

BENNETT, J.G. **THE DRAMATIC UNIVERSE, VOLUME IV: HISTORY.** Glossary, indices, 441pp. CSP66, 9.95p.
This volume applies to history the conclusions of the earlier volumes regarding the nature of time and the *Laws of Universal Transformation.* The basic hypothesis is that *Intelligent Direction distinguished history from mere happenings.* The evidence for this is examined for all stages of evolution. The book ends with a forecast of the course of history in the next one thousand years.

BENNETT, J.G. **ENERGIES: MATERIAL, VITAL, COSMIC.** 145pp. CSP64, 3.95p.
This volume contains a collection of scientific interpretations of personal experiences which are a bit less complex than those presented in **The Dramatic Universe.** As it says in the introduction, Bennett *shows how depth psychology, mysticism and religious experience connect with modern theories of Energy Force Fields and Vital Structures, and the later chapters devoted to Consciousness, Creativity and Love open new vistas towards understanding man and the universe as a complete harmonious structure.*

BENNETT, J.G. **THE ENNEAGRAM.** 64pp. CSP74, 2.95p.
The enneagram is an ancient symbol of profound significance. The understanding of its use has been passed down through spiritual brotherhoods for over 2,000 years. During his travel in search of teachers of wisdom, Gurdjieff found the enneagram used as a method of passing on traditional teachings. Since his first contact with Gurdjieff, Mr. Bennett has studied and worked with the enneagram. Here he uses everyday situations to illustrate the working of this symbol as well as to show its deeper significance, revealing possibilities of using it to come to an understanding of the principles underlying the laws of the universe. Part of the **Transformation of Man** series.

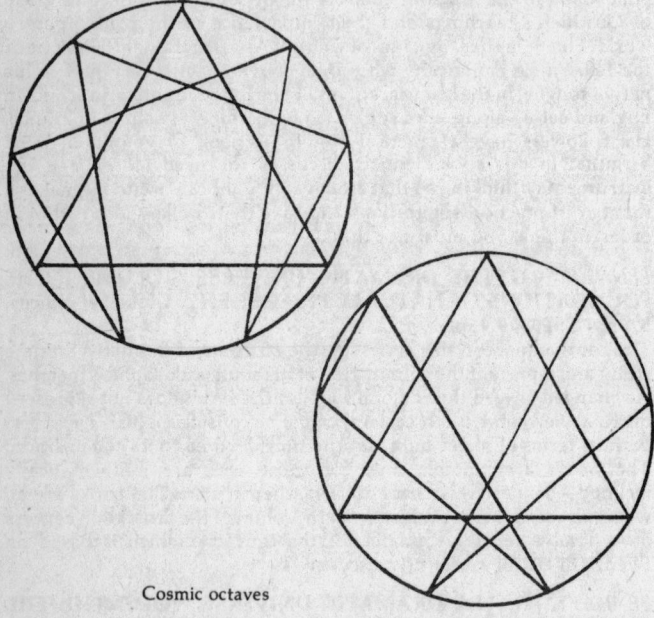

Cosmic octaves

BENNETT, J.G. **EXISTENCE.** 74pp. CSP77, 3.25p.
Number two of Bennett's **Studies from the Dramatic Universe.** The book consists of transcriptions of talks along with a series of questions and answers.

BENNETT, J.G. **THE FIRST LIBERATION.** 35pp. CSP76, 1.95p.
Number one of a series of books, **Sherbourne Theme Talks,** taken from tape recordings of meetings at Sherbourne House between 1972 and 1975. The theme discussed in this book is the idea of overcoming likes and dislikes as the first practical step out of the dream world that most of us live in. A series of questions and extensive answers follows the theme talk.

BENNETT, J.G. **FOOD.** 50pp. CSP77, 1.95p.
One of the **Sherbourne Theme Talks** series, this pamphlet incudes a transcription of Bennett's discourse on what it really means to eat— not simply on the physical or even psychological level, but also in the spiritual sense. A number of questions and answers are also included.

■ *BENNETT, J.G.* **GURDJIEFF: MAKING A NEW WORLD.** Illustrations, index, 320pp. H&R73/Tur, 3.95p.
This is the only major biographical study of Gurdjieff and it is a book which we highly recommend to all who are interested in the Work. Bennett sets out to inquire whether Gurdjieff was an isolated phenomenon or part of a tradition that for centuries 'has been concerned with the destiny of mankind. In the first part of the biography he traces the *masters of wisdom* and explores Gurdjieff's personal search and mission. Much of the information revealed here has not been written about elsewhere and, since Bennett traveled widely in Central Asia, he was in a unique position to explore this avenue. Later chapters survey Gurdjieff's Insititute, writings, teaching style, and central concepts. This is a well written, illuminating volume.

BENNETT, J.G. **GURDJIEFF TODAY.** 47pp. CSP74, 2.95p.
Part of the **Transformation of Man** series, this is a reprint of a talk that Bennett gave in 1973 and expresses better than anything else how Bennett felt the Work and the Gurdjieffian tradition relate to present day world conditions and needs. The material is clearly presented and there is also a section of questions and answers which delve more deeply into several relevant areas.

BENNETT, J.G. **GURDJIEFF: A VERY GREAT ENIGMA.** 100pp. Wei73/CSP, 2.75p.
Transcripts of three lectures dealing with Gurdjieff's background and boyhood environment, the sources of his teaching, and his instructional methods.

BENNETT, J.G. **HAZARD.** 147pp. CPS76, 3.25p.
This is number one of the series, **Studies from the Dramatic Universe,** which presents transcriptions of talks that Bennett gave on material from **The Dramatic Universe.** The discussion in this book centers on the idea that hazard—the moment of choice, the grasping of an opportunity, the risk without guarantee—is the key to understanding the nature of existence and the working of our lives.

BENNETT, J.G. **HOW WE DO THINGS.** 69pp. CSP74, 2.00p.
This book is based on a series of lectures on the human functions which discuss how our bodies are made and how their structure influences our behavior. Topics include automatism, sensitivity, spontaneity and consciousness, and the role of vital energies in our lives.

BENNETT, J.G. **THE IMAGE OF GOD IN WORK.** 74pp. CSP76, 2.95p.
In these talks Mr. Bennett discusses God as a force manifesting itself in the universe. *God, Life and Demiurgic Intelligence are all beyond the ordinary world of things and persons. They belong to a reality that is more than personal. Suprapersonal reality is hard to see and hard to express; but it really matters to us because it affects the meaning of our lives....This book is about finding the suprapersonal realities in practice.*—from the introduction. Part of the **Transformation of Man** series.

BENNETT, J.G. **INTIMATIONS: TALKS WITH J.G. BENNETT AT BESHARA.** Glossary, 111pp. Bes75, 3.95p.
Beshara is a Sufi school and center in England which was located close to Bennett's school, Sherbourne. *The talks which comprise this book exemplify the depth and universality of [Bennett's] vision, and yet, they retain a clarity and simplicity of expression that is hard to equal. The knowledge which we are shown here relates in all cases to the primary and unique position of man, with his capabilities of self-consciousness and self-perfection.*—from the introduction. There is more reference to Sufism here than in most of Bennett's writings. A series of questions and answers follows each talk.

BENNETT, J.G. **IS THERE "LIFE" ON EARTH: AN INTRODUCTION TO GURDJIEFF.** 156pp. Sto73, 3.95p.
Transcriptions of four lectures delivered by Bennett in London during the last weeks of Gurdjieff's life: *The Needs of a New Epoch, Gurdjieff: The Man and His Work, Work on Oneself,* and *Gurdjieff's Writings.* The volume also includes an introduction and selected passages from the three books of **All and Everything.**

BENNETT, J.G. **JOURNEYS IN ISLAMIC COUNTRIES, VOLUMES I AND II.** 123pp. CSP76, 3.95p/each.
In 1953 J.G. Bennett undertook a long journey. This volume is an edited version of the detailed diary that he kept and sent to friends, relatives, and students back in England. Part of the purpose of his

journey was to study *tekkes* and meeting places from an architectural point of view—so these details play a large part in his descriptions. The first volume discusses his journey from Konya through Syria to the Holy Land; the second covers his encounters with the Mevlevi dervishes and his exploration of the northeastern corner of Turkey.

BENNETT, J.G. LONG PILGRIMAGE: THE LIFE AND TEACHING OF THE SHIVAPURI BABA. Rai75/Tur, 4.95p.
The Shivapuri Baba was one of the most remarkable sages of our time. Bennett met him for the first time when he was well over one hundred and had several discussions with him before he died in 1963 at the age of 137. These conversations are recorded here and they present a vital discipline and guide to *right living* that incorporates many traditions. The book begins with the account of an amazing thirty-five year journey the Shivapuri Baba set out on at the end of the nineteenth century. It was undertaken after he had lived in seclusion for thirty years. During his travels he met personally with monarchs and heads of state including Queen Victoria and Theodore Roosevelt as well as with spiritual and cultural leaders. An important book for all seriously interested in work on themselves.

BENNETT, J.G. THE MASTERS OF WISDOM. 256pp. Tur76, 10.25c.
Bennett was working on this book at the time of his death. It is more or less completed, but his estate would not permit a final editing, so the text does not read very well. Because of his intimate lifelong contact with Central Asian brotherhoods, Bennett is uniquely qualified to write of them and their mission. In this book he does just that. These were the groups that Gurdjieff studied under and whose techniques he taught. These brotherhoods also directed Bennett's work throughout his life.

BENNETT, J.G. MATERIAL OBJECTS. 56+pp. CSP77, 1.95p.
We are trying to wake up from a dream world. This has to be done before we can begin to realize our own destiny. There is a spurious kind of inner life that is dreaming and useless imagination. In front of material objects we can assess our true situation. Do we see them? Do we use them responsibly? Do we have any contact with them? Any freedom of attention to direct towards them and their working in our world? If we are asleep, material objects become our masters. If we are to begin to be awake we must understand how to be worthy masters of the material world.—J.G. Bennett. Number three of the **Sherbourne Theme Talks**.

BENNETT, J.G. NEEDS OF A NEW AGE COMMUNITY. Notes, 99pp. CSP77, 2.95p.
A collection of talks on the title theme given by Bennett to students at his academy. He felt that new communities run along Fourth Way lines were a vital part of the future and he hoped that many of his students would become involved in such communities. This book also includes two of his lectures on the Sermon on the Mount. Part of the **Transformation of Man** series.

BENNETT, J.G. NOTICING. 48pp. CSP76, 1.95p.
Unless we notice, we cannot be in a position to choose or act from ourselves. It is a transition from one state of existence to another....Noticing is the opening of possibilities.—J.G. Bennett. Number two of the **Sherbourne Theme Talks**.

BENNETT, J.G. THE SEVENFOLD WORK. Index, 122pp. CSP75, 2.95p.
The material in this monograph developed out of talks given by Mr. Bennett at Sherbourne. The Work is resolved into a spectrum of seven lines which are applicable to past and present practice and experience, and probably valid for the future. All the aspects of the Work are discussed, and while this is not a complete presentation, there could never be a complete written presentation, since material such as this cannot be explained in books but must be transmitted from person to person. Part of the **Transformation of Man** series.

BENNETT, J.G. SEX. 85pp. CSP75, 2.95p.
In this book I will be talking about the action of sex in us with little reference to the power of love. We shall have to spend some time looking at how the sexual energy affects the workings of our bodily and physical apparatus, and the role that it plays in the transformation of the energies which constitute our being....To understand something, we must try and see it as a whole in all its diversity. Sex in human life is all or any one of the following: a disease and a source of illusion; a means of reproduction and the perpetuation of the species; a regulator of our psychic energies, or a way towards union of will. All of these must be taken into account if we wish to understand the operation of sex in our lives and what is possible in our human communities. The last chapter...is an attempt to sketch the requirements for right sexual life in the truly progressive society.

BENNETT, J.G. A SPIRITUAL PSYCHOLOGY. 251pp. CSA64/CSP, 6.95c.
An edited, expanded transcript of talks given at a seminar. Bennett presents a framework in which the spiritual and natural elements in human experience can be distinguished and yet related, and indicates ways in which spiritual development can be realized. Bennett includes some autobiographical material.

BENNETT, J.G. TALKS ON BEELZEBUB'S TALES. 147pp. CSP77, 4.50p.
Bennett's attempt to help his students understand the significance of Gurdjieff's masterpiece. The talks collected here are representative of Bennett's expositions from 1949-1974. Part of the **Transformation of Man** series.

BENNETT, J.G., ed. VALUES. 166pp. CSP51, 4.50p.
A collection of thirty-eight essays and translations from a wide variety of sources. The selections were chosen to be read and studied individually each week in a Work group and each ends with a meditation upon the theme: *Forms are different but Truth is One*. The pieces include extracts from Nicholson's **Mathnawi**, various **Upanishads**, the **Tao Te Ching**, and Suzuki's **Essays on Zen**.

BENNETT, J.G. WHAT ARE WE LIVING FOR? 167pp. CSP65, 4.50p.
A searching look at the quality of contemporary life and a discussion of the necessity for the reestablishment of the balance between the inner and outer man.

BENNETT, J.G. WITNESS. Photographs, 385pp. Tur74, 5.95p.
A revised, updated version of Bennett's autobiography, including two new chapters which cover the last part of his life and include information on his work at Sherbourne, his school in England. It is as frank as we can imagine any autobiography being, telling of his false starts and failures as well as his more successful experiences. Bennett encountered and worked with many of the great spiritual leaders of this century. He discusses them all here and emphasizes his relationship with Gurdjieff, Ouspensky, and Work groups. This is a fascinating account which we recommend to all who are interested in the Work.

BUTKOVSKY-HEWITT, ANNA. WITH GURDJIEFF IN ST. PETERSBURG AND PARIS. 157pp. Wei78, 7.50c.
Ms. Butkovsky-Hewitt was one of Gurdjieff's first pupils in the days before the Russian revolution. She evokes the excitement and atmosphere of those early days when Gurdjieff and his few pupils would meet in a cafe and he would direct them along new lines of spiritual development. After some time she and the other disciples moved into a communal house which Gurdjieff bought for the group. Many years after the revolution she met Gurdjieff again in Paris and resumed her studies. All those involved in the Gurdjieff Work will be interested in this account of Gurdjieff's early teaching. There is a great deal here that has not been described in other books.

COLLIN, RODNEY. THE MIRROR OF LIGHT. 89pp. Wat59, 5.20p.
A beautiful little book, composed of notes found among Collin's papers after his death. It is impossible to say which he wrote himself and which came from other sources. He had collected them as material for those who have passed beyond the preliminary stage of self-study. *The Fourth Way is the balanced combination of the three traditional ways of re-union with God—those of physical, mental and emotional control. It is the development of the whole man, situated in the ordinary circumstances of daily life and dedicated to the realization of his highest possibilities.*

■ **COLLIN, RODNEY. THE THEORY OF CELESTIAL INFLUENCE. Index, 374pp. Wat73, 8.95p.**
A complex scientific reconstruction in one particular form and in one particular language of the body of ideas given by Ouspensky, profusely illustrated with charts and diagrams. It is an attempt to assemble all the knowledge and experience of today into a single whole which would explain their relation to the universe and their possibilities within it. Collin's conclusion is that the purpose of everything in the universe, from sun to cell, is the attainment of a higher level of consciousness. Without that, whatever the accumulation of *facts*, there is no growth in

knowledge or real understanding. Collin's cosmology is clearly presented and geared toward the scientific/intuitive mind of the person seeking to awaken and to understand. Highly recommended.

COLLIN, RODNEY. **THE THEORY OF CONSCIOUS HARMONY.** Glossary, bibliographical note, 224pp. Wat58, 8.45p.
In 1948 Collin moved to Mexico to carry on his study and practice of the ideas he received from Ouspensky and Gurdjieff. During the next few years he corresponded with many people, from varied walks of life and from all over the world. Most of these individuals were seeking guidance in the Gurdjieff teachings and the letters represent a sustained attempt to see problems of the individual path and of related study groups in a very broad perspective. After his death in 1956 the letters were collected, edited, and topically arranged in this book.

COLLIN, RODNEY. **THEORY OF ETERNAL LIFE.** 134pp. Wat74, 10.00c.
A fascinating theoretical study of death and *man's being in the invisible world between life and death.* Collin has reviewed the ancient teachings on this subject and presents his view of the eternal recurrence. He illustates his account with diagrams and quotations. Every word counts in this illuminating study—and each rereading brings new insights.

DAUMAL, RENE. **MOUNT ANALOGUE. Introduction,** 106pp. Vik59, 2.95p.
This is an unfinished narrative of a quest to the top of a symbolic mountain, representing the knowledge which can be passed on to other seekers. As Daumal says, Mount Analogue represents the concept *that between learning and teaching there exists no secure or stationary zone of knowledge. To know means to be learning or to be teaching; there is no middle way.*

GAGE, ANNE. **THE ONE WORK—A JOURNEY TOWARDS THE SELF.** 137pp. Wat61, 4.80p.
A very personalized intuitive account of the author's visits to Benares, Arunachala, Angkor Wat, Ajanta, Borobodur, and Bali. She is able to evoke real meaning from the shrines and temples of the past, and from the teachers of today, not only as a scholar, but as a human being on a quest for enlightenment. The book includes long dialogues with the holy men and teachers she encountered.

GURDJIEFF, GEORGE I. **ALL AND EVERYTHING: BEELZEBUB'S TALES TO HIS GRANDSON.** 1,238pp. Dut50/RKP, 12.95c/10.50p.
Gurdjieff made an extraordinarily detailed examination of the human conditioning process. He pointed out that the conditioning of each individual creates major distortions in the way that the mental, physical, and emotional centers of a person interrelate. One or another of the centers come to typify the conditioned personality, instead of all the centers being in harmonious balance. In other words, one person may be primarily intellectual, while another is primarily emotional or physical. When the centers were in balance—a very rare occurrence—new intuitive powers beyond the faculties of the rational mind would develop. Higher emotions would also come into being, superceding the lower emotions of anger, jealousy, envy, and fear. As this work on oneself was taking place, something called *self remembering* would also develop. The individual will have a growing relation to the universe, and an intuition of the cause and effect relationships which surround us and, among other things, determine the conditioning of ourselves and others. The goal of Gurdjieff's work was to wake man up so that he does not sleepwalk through life. To accomplish this, Gurdjieff and his students developed many exercises and techniques. Gurdjieff taught and worked in the West for about thirty years and his ideas have been very influential, especially in intellectual circles. Work groups are still active all over the world. **Beelzebub's Tales** is Gurdjieff's major book, a monumental work which Gurdjieff says is designed *to destroy, mercilessly, without any compromises whatever, in the mentations and feelings of the reader the beliefs and view, by centuries rooted in him about everything existing in this world.* The book is written in the form of a myth on a cosmic scale, showing how human life is growing steadily more empty of meaning. Gurdjieff traces, with compassion and often humor, the history of man on this planet and the causes of alienation from the real sources of life. He integrates his conception of man into a new, universal science embracing all fields of thought and endeavor in every period of human history. This book should only be tackled by those with at least some familiarity with the Gurdjieff Work. It is allegorical and often difficult going. Gurdjieff read the

manuscript to his students and whenever an idea appeared too clear or simple he said that he would *bury the bone deeper*—and he did! The paperback is in three volumes; the hardcover in one.

Gurdjieff

GURDJIEFF, GEORGE I. **GUIDE AND INDEX TO GURDJIEFF'S ALL AND EVERYTHING.** 680pp. TsP73, 9.95c.
This is an excellent aid for those who want to study certain topics in **Beelzebub.** Many ideas and words are listed in alphabetical order, with subheadings under the main one, explanatory phrases, and page references. There is also a page correlation for the paperback edition. The book was prepared by members of a Gurdjieff group in Toronto.

GURDJIEFF, GEORGE I. **HERALD OF COMING GOOD: FIRST APPEAL TO CONTEMPORARY HUMANITY.** 87pp. Wei74, 3.50p.
Gurdjieff's first book, and the only one published (in 1933) during his lifetime. An early attempt to get his teachings into written form.

■ GURDJIEFF, GEORGE I. **MEETINGS WITH REMARKABLE MEN.** 314pp. Dut69/RKP, 13.35c/3.95p.
Meetings consists of a series of stories, each bearing as its title the name of one of the men Gurdjieff knew in his early life including his father, and masters whom he met in his travels. *As he grew up, his urge to understand the meaning of human life became so strong that he attracted a group of "remarkable men"—among whom were engineers, doctors, archaeologists....In search of a knowledge which they were certain had existed in the past but of which almost all traces seemed to have disappeared, he set out with them to explore many countries in the Middle East and Central Asia....If Gurdjieff speaks of himself, he does so to serve his life-long purpose. It is apparent that this is not an autobiography in the strict sense of the word. For him the past is not worth recounting except in so far as it can serve as an example. In these tales of adventure what he suggests are not models for outward imitation, but a completely new way of facing life, which touches us directly and gives us a foretaste of another order of reality.*—from the introduction. The book also includes background prefaces and a long rambling final essay by Gurdjieff, *The Material Question,* in which he reviews his activities, financial and otherwise, since coming to Europe. Most readers feel that this book is easier to read than **Beelzebub,** so, even though it is the second series of **All and Everything,** it is often read first. And it can be read on the surface as an entertaining narrative—although that certainly was not what Gurdjieff had in mind when he wrote it.

GURDJIEFF, GEORGE I. **NIMBUS—THE CREATION STORY AC-
CORDING TO MR. G.** 182pp. IDH nd, 4.95p.
We have put Gurdjieff down as the author of this book because the
unnamed editor attributes it directly to him. It is published by E.J.
Gold's press and more than likely authored by Gold himself. Gold likes
to think of himself as a direct spiritual descendent of Gurdjieff—a view
which is questioned—to put it mildly—by those who actually studied
with Gurdjieff. The style of the book and the vocabulary employed is
reminiscent of Gurdjieff's writing, though the story itself is set in
contemporary times. The whole novel can be looked upon as something of a pun on **Beelzebub**.

GURDJIEFF, GEORGE I. **SECRET TALKS WITH MR. G.** 170pp.
IDH78, 4.95p.
Another book which is attributed by the unnamed editor to Gurdjieff,
but which most likely was written by E.J. Gold. The material
transcribed here certainly does sound like Gurdjieff's own words and
the selections provide an adequate overview of the essence of his
philosophy. The talks purport to be ones delivered to a specially formed
group of pupils in the U.S. and they cover all aspects of the Work.

GURDJIEFF, GEORGE I. **VIEWS FROM THE REAL WORLD.** 288pp.
Dut74, 3.95p.
A collection of talks and lectures that Gurdjieff gave in the period from
1917-33. Gurdjieff did not permit his pupils to take notes while they
were working with him—so these selections are made up of carefully
selected notes made by various students shortly after the actual talks
were given. Some of the selections are followed by questions and
answers and the selections themselves allow the reader a glimpse of
Gurdjieff's own techniques and how he applied his theories in various
contexts. This should not be read as a first book by someone seeking to
understand Gurdjieff and his system, but it is excellent supplementary
reading for all who have had some exposure to the system. The talks
are wide ranging and, at least for this reader, many concepts are
expressed and illustrated better in this selection than anywhere else.
Also included is a translation of the aphorisms which Gurdjieff had
inscribed above the walls of the study house at his Institute, as well as
Glimpses of the Truth, a long essay on Gurdjieff and his ideas written by
one of his Russian pupils around 1914. This contains germs of what is
developed more fully in **In Search of the Miraculous**, along with a more
personal approach toward the ideas and their application.

HARTEN, MARJORIE VON. **A WAY OF LIVING.** 86pp. CSP74, 2.50p.
A discussion of the author's experiences with Gurdjieff and Ouspensky. Ms. von Harten was intimately associated with the Work throughout her life, was a member of the New York Orage group and
Ouspensky's English groups, and was closely involved in J.G. Bennett's
work at Coombe Springs.

HARTMANN, THOMAS DE. **OUR LIFE WITH MR. GURDJIEFF.**
134pp. Vik64, 1.65p.
A very personal account of the years (1917-1929) that de Hartmann
and his wife spent studying under Gurdjieff. This is one of the only
accounts of the first years of Gurdjieff's teaching as well as the best
one. Its aim is to tell about the way Gurdjieff worked with his students
and to convey an idea of the Work and its relation to man. De
Hartmann was a noted composer.

HULME, KATHRYN. **UNDISCOVERED COUNTRY—IN SEARCH
OF GURDJIEFF.** 306pp. LBC66, 3.95p.
Ms. Hulme was one of a small group of women with whom Gurdjieff
worked intensively during the thirties and forties. All of the women
were writers or incipient authors (Ms. Hulme is best known for **The
Nun's Story**) and Gurdjieff used a number of unique techniques with
them. This personal memoir centers on the author's years with
Gurdjieff and contains many valuable insights into his teaching style as
well as a brilliant evocation of *a very wise old man sitting in his rich pantry of
food and thoughts telling his students to know thyself.*

LEFORT, RAFAEL. **THE TEACHERS OF GURDJIEFF.** 151pp. Wei63,
2.45p.
A record of a journey which purports to trace the sources of Gurdjieff's
teachings, following clues provided in his writings. Rumor has it that
Idries Shah is the true author of this book. It is very anti-Gurdjieff, or
at least anti the Gurdjieff movements of today. Each of the sages that

the author found stated that Gurdjieff's teachings—as interpreted by
various disciples—are a dead end to today's seekers. Central concepts
in Sufi philosophy are well described.

MAIRET, PHILIP. **ORAGE: A MEMOIR.** 129pp. UnB66, 6.00c.
Orage was a noted English literary critic who, as a mature man, left his
work to serve a stern apprenticeship under Gurdjieff in France and
then, for seven years, was a missionary in the U.S. of the gospel
according to Gurdjieff—only to have his position of authority totally
destroyed by Gurdjieff. He finally returned to the work he had been
doing before he joined Gurdjieff, though he never criticized Gurdjieff
in any way. Along with Ouspensky and Nicoll, Orage was one of
Gurdjieff's most able students. This memoir is written by a close
associate of his last years and this edition contains extensive after-
thoughts, written thirty years after the book's initial publication.

NICOLL, MAURICE. **LIVING TIME AND THE INTEGRATION OF
LIFE.** Notes, bibliography, index, 252pp. Wat52, 8.90p.
Maurice Nicoll was a noted physician and an early believer in
psychological medicine. He was closely associated with Carl Jung for
many years, met Ouspensky in 1921, and studied with both Ouspensky
and Gurdjieff. He became a teacher of the system in 1931 and was
formally named as Ouspensky's successor after the latter left England
for the United States. Nicoll's interpretations are especially valuable
because he applied the system's concepts to the interpretation of
psychology and Christian scripture. **Living Time** is Nicoll's major
philosophical statement, containing his ideas about time, higher levels
of consciousness, and the possibilities of changed time sense leading to
a changed sense of oneself. Many quotations from relevant literature
are included.

NICOLL, MAURICE. **THE NEW MAN: AN INTERPRETATION OF
SOME PARABLES AND MIRACLES OF CHRIST.** 152pp. Vik50/
Wat, 9.55c/2.95p.
Nicoll believes that all sacred writings contain an outer and inner
meaning. As he says, *behind the literal words lies another range of meanings,
another form of knowledge.* Penetrating to this inner knowledge, Nicoll
finds that the **Gospels** are about transcending the violence that
characterizes mankind's present level of being. He includes many
scriptural quotations.

NICOLL, MAURICE. **PSYCHOLOGICAL COMMENTARIES ON
THE TEACHINGS OF GURDJIEFF AND OUSPENSKY. Wat.**
These commentaries come out of Dr. Nicoll's own understanding of
the practical application of Gurdjieff's teaching. They take the form of
weekly papers to members of his groups who were scattered all over
the world. In the papers Nicoll expounds the fundamental ideas of the
system with clarity so that the reader is helped toward an understanding of the efforts required to reach a level of comprehension and
integration. These volumes contain many deep insights which we have
not read elsewhere. The volumes can be read in any order. We
recommend them highly to all students involved in the Work. **Volume
I: 1941-43**, (373pp.), $16.95c; **Volume II: 1944-45**, (402pp.), $16.95c;
Volume III: 1945-48, (449pp.), $16.95c; **Volume IV: 1948-51**, (277pp.),
$14.25c; **Volume V: 1951-53**,(263pp.), $17.00c.

NOTT, C.S. **JOURNEY THROUGH THIS WORLD: MEETINGS
WITH GURDJIEFF, ORAGE, AND OUSPENSKY.** Index, 271pp.
Wei69/RKP, 6.95c.
A gossipy, self centered account of Nott's relationship with Gurdjieff,
Ouspensky, and Orage and of the influence of their teachings on his
life and lifestyle. Nott does not come across as the most enlightened of
men. The book also contains a summary of Gurdjieff's booklet, **Herald
of Coming Good.**

NOTT, C.S. **TEACHINGS OF GURDJIEFF—JOURNAL OF A PUPIL.**
Index, 228pp. Wei61/RKP, 7.95c.
The earlier of Nott's autobiographical accounts. Nott, a young seeker,
met Gurdjieff in New York and was convinced by seeing the sacred
dance demonstrations that at last he had found the way he was looking
for. He spent time at the Prieure and also participated in Orage's New
York group. Much of the book consists of transcriptions of Orage's
discourses (including commentary on **Beelzebub**) and records of
Gurdjieff's sayings and doings—compiled from the voluminous diaries
Nott kept.

ORAGE, A.R. **CONSCIOUSNESS. 86pp. Wei74, 2.25p.**
Orage was a leading English critic and essayist, praised as one of the leading minds of his day by no less than George Bernard Shaw. He became exposed to Gurdjieff by Ouspensky in the early 1920s and became, after Ouspensky split from Gurdjieff, Gurdjieff's leading pupil. He went to New York and set up groups there. His success in the United States gave Gurdjieff the financial support he needed to continue his activities. After a few years Gurdjieff told Orage not to teach any longer and disbanded Orage's groups. Even so, Orage remained close to Gurdjieff until his death a couple of years later. This book contains a transcription of four lectures on the nature of consciousness and on animal, human, and superhuman consciousness.

ORAGE, A.R. **ON LOVE—WITH SOME APHORISMS AND OTHER ESSAYS. 72pp. Wei74, 1.95p.**
Four essays written after Orage came into contact with Gurdjieff's system—*On Love, On Religion, What is the Soul?*, and *Talks with Katherine Mansfield at Fountainbleau*. The aphorisms were given out in his talks to the groups in New York, 1924-30. Includes a detailed biography of Orage.

ORAGE, A.R. **PSYCHOLOGICAL EXERCISES AND ESSAYS. 123pp. Wei74, 1.95p.**
Over 200 *practical exercises which were used for years in classes consisting of students varying in age from twelve to sixty. The results were observed and checked and the conclusion is that the exercises, at first utterly impossible, became with practice relatively easy; and that along with the increased facility in the exercises themselves, the facility in the use of the mind upon ordinary exercises is enormously increased.* The fifteen essays are on topics such as *How to Learn to Think, Can Intuition be Acquired?, On Daily Dying, Doing as One Likes.*

OUSPENSKY, P.D. **THE FOURTH WAY. Index, 437pp. RaH57/RKP, 21.00c/3.95p.**
Ouspensky was a noted Russian mathematician and writer. After journeying through Europe, the Middle East, and South Asia in a quest for knowledge, he met Gurdjieff in 1915 in Russia and began studying with him. At the time Ouspensky was already a respected scientist and philosopher, and author of a couple of important books. From 1915 on, his interest was centered on the practical study of methods for the development of consciousness in man. After the Russian revolution he moved to London and began a series of lectures which led to the establishment of study groups concerned with Gurdjieff's system. Ouspensky split with Gurdjieff in the early 1920s over personality differences, but he remained faithful to the system and continued to teach it in Britain and the United States until his death in 1947. **The Fourth Way** consists of verbatim extracts from talks given by Ouspensky between 1921 and 1946, with questions and answers. Ouspensky had a prodigious memory and Gurdjieff himself commented upon its accuracy. The first chapter contains a general survey of the fundamental concepts of the system, each of which is amplified subject-by-subject in the specific order Ouspensky followed with his students. This is an essential volume for those deeply interested in the Work.

■ *OUSPENSKY, P.D.* **IN SEARCH OF THE MIRACULOUS. Illustrations, index, 387pp. HBJ49/RKP, 22.75c/3.95p.**
This is the most complete presentation of Gurdjieff's entire system. Every idea is dealt with at length and explained in as clear a language as possible. It is often hard to understand and almost no one comprehends it all on first (or even second) reading. But if you are interested in the Gurdjieff Work you will be fascinated by his cosmology. The text consists mainly of transcriptions of lectures Gurdjieff gave in Russia, with some additional material from the early years in France before the split with Ouspensky. This is a must for those who are seriously interested in the system.

OUSPENSKY, P.D. **A NEW MODEL OF THE UNIVERSE: PRINCIPLES OF THE PSYCHOLOGICAL METHOD IN ITS APPLICATION TO PROBLEMS OF SCIENCE, RELIGION, AND ART. Illustrations, index, 508pp. RaH34/RKP, 8.95c/2.95p.**
This book was written following Ouspensky's search for the wisdom teachings and teachers and before he met Gurdjieff. Ouspensky analyzes and restates the ancient teachings and connects them with modern physics and philosophy. He includes chapters on *Esotericism and Modern Thought, The Fourth Dimension, Superman, Christianity and the New Testament, The Symbolism of the Tarot, Yoga, The Study of Dreams and Hypnotism,*

Experimental Mysticism, A New Model of the Universe, Eternal Recurrence and the Laws of Manu, and *Sex and Evolution.* There are also sketches of various masters he met in his travels. It is easier reading than the rest of Ouspensky's *ouvre* and quite fascinating.

■ *OUSPENSKY, P.D.* **THE PSYCHOLOGY OF MAN'S POSSIBLE EVOLUTION. 135pp. RaH73/RKP, 10.95c/1.95p.**
Transcription of a series of lectures designed by Ouspensky as an introductory course for those who came to study with him in London and New York and revised shortly before his death, to be published after **In Search of the Miraculous**. This is the most simple presentation available of the basics of Gurdjieff's system and forms a good first reader.

OUSPENSKY, P.D. **THE SYMBOLISM OF THE TAROT: PHILOSOPHY OF OCCULTISM IN PICTURES AND NUMBERS. 1.75p.**
See the Tarot section.

OUSPENSKY, P.D. **TALKS WITH A DEVIL. 155pp. RaH72/Tur, 5.95c.**
The first translation of two stories, written in 1914, which express Ouspensky's belief that man's chief error is to believe that the material world is the only reality. Two problems are examined. The first is conscious evil and is illustrated by the story of an inventor who does harm particularly when he intends to do good and cannot bring himself to accept the disastrous consequences of his own work of genius. It is an allegory of modern man faced with the consequences of the miracles of science and technology. The second problem is brought out by the suggestion that the devils are interested in man only when he makes an effort to escape. Only a few people can recognize that the price of doing the right thing is inevitably to expose oneself to opposition and even to the threat of destruction. Edited and introduced by J.G. Bennett.

OUSPENSKY, P.D. **TERTIUM ORGANUM—A KEY TO THE ENIGMAS OF THE WORLD. Notes, index, 351pp. RaH39/RKP, 21.25c/2.95p.**
Ouspensky's second book, written before his encounter with Gurdjieff. In it he formulates a philosophy based on the mathematical concept known as the fourth dimension, the fourth form of the manifestation of consciousness—the intuitional. This work is an attempt to formulate a new logic which will deal with this higher consciousness, a bold attempt to reorganize all knowledge. It is a heavy book that requires of the reader the ability to handle mathematical concepts.

PAUWELS, LOUIS. **GURDJIEFF. 456pp. Wei54, 5.95p.**
A critical survey of various students' experiences with the Work. Includes both positive and negative reactions as well as long extracts from diaries and letters. Pauwels himself had a terrible experience with Gurdjieff which almost led to his death, so this colors the reporting.

PETERS, FRITZ. **GURDJIEFF REMEMBERED. 160pp. Wei74, 2.25p.**
Peters and his brother lived at the Prieure as boys and got to know Gurdjieff fairly well. This book describes Peters' later encounters with Gurdjieff in Paris, New York, and Chicago. It is a chatty account, without much of interest to the serious reader—though one does get a feeling for Gurdjieff's methods of instruction.

POGSON, BERYL. **THE WORK LIFE. Index, 142pp. Ced75, 10.00p.**
Beryl Pogson studied the Work for many years under Maurice Nicoll. Before his death Dr. Nicoll authorized her to teach. She began with meetings in London and Sussex and soon added residential sessions of intensive work. The meetings were not formal lectures followed by questions. Frequently Ms. Pogson would ask for a question at the beginning, and would then allow the discussion to take its course from the question asked. This book is a record of some of these discussions. The selections are organized according to the time of year in which the discussion took place.

POGSON, BERYL. **WORK TALKS IN BRIGHTON, 1936-1966. 92pp. Ced nd, 4.00p.**
A topically arranged selection.

POPOFF, IRMIS. **THE ENNEAGRAMA OF THE MAN OF UNITY. 7½"x10", 106pp. Wei78, 4.50p.**
Work with the enneagram was and is an important part of the Gurdjieff Work. In this book Ms. Popoff illustrates her Work group's work with the enneagram. The group's aim was to study the

movements of the enneagram in life situations which range in scope from sewing a dress and weeding a garden to complex subjects such as *The Descent of the Holy Spirit* and *The Man of Unity*. Each situation is illustrated through the movements of the enneagram—an all-embracing symbol which helps us understand the eternal laws of the universe. This study is unlike anything else we have read in the entire corpus of Work literature. Ms. Popoff studied with both Ouspensky and Gurdjieff and, since their death, has lead a Work group.

POPOFF, IRMIS. **GURDJIEFF: HIS WORK ON MYSELF, WITH OTHERS, FOR THE WORK. Illustrations, index, 198pp. Wei73, 5.95c.**
Ms. Popoff mainly worked with Ouspensky's group in New York and it is the experiences in that group and the work she continues to do today that she reconstructs here. This is a very subjective account, and the experiences she recounts are not found in any of the other personal accounts, most of which are by pupils who studied in Europe. Of special interest is the vivid picture she gives of the exercises and the meaning of the enneagram.

REMDE, HENRY. **THE ART IN A CRAFT. Illustrations, oversize, 36pp. TsP75, 4.95p.**
A spiritual study of what is required to become a true craftsman. If a craft can be a vehicle for inner understanding, this book points the way. It draws us past technical competence towards an awareness—on another level—of the three inner laws of craftsmanship.

REYMOND, LIZELLE. **TO LIVE WITHIN. 1.75p.**
See the Indian Philosophy section.

ROPP, ROBERT DE. **CHURCH OF THE EARTH. 2.95p.**
See the Consciousness Expansion section.

ROPP, ROBERT DE. **THE MASTER GAME: PATHWAYS TO HIGHER CONSCIOUSNESS BEYOND THE DRUG EXPERIENCE. Illustrations, notes, bibliography, index, 252pp. Del68/PnB, 2.75p.**
De Ropp studied with Ouspensky and Gurdjieff and has been teaching the system (with modifications) for a number of years. In this volume he restates the essence of the system in modern terms and uses contemporary examples to elucidate the often difficult conceptual framework. His stated aim is to show that one does not need drugs to achieve higher consciousness; it can be attained through work on oneself.

■ *SPEETH, KATHLEEN.* **THE GURDJIEFF WORK. Notes, bibliography, 114pp. AOP76/Tur, 4.95p/1.95p.**
This is the only publication which summarizes the philosophical basis of the Gurdjieff Work in a few simple chapters. And therein lies its greatest promise and failure. Ms. Speeth has been involved in the Work her whole life and she writes earnestly and from the heart. And her presentation is an accurate one. However, it is so summarized that it loses much of its meaning. The words seem merely to be words and

the true meaning has simply to be accepted but cannot be understood. Nonetheless, this is a useful work and many of the diagrams cannot be readily found elsewhere. There is also information on the practical application of the Work and photographs of the sacred movements along with a miscellany of other information.

TRAVERS, P.L. **GEORGE IVANOVITCH GURDJIEFF. TsP73, 1.20p.**
A brief biographical sketch which indicates some of the broad currents in Gurdjieff's teaching.

■ *WALKER, KENNETH.* **THE MAKING OF MAN. Bibliography, index, 170pp. RKP63, 5.95c.**
An autobiographical account of the time Walker spent studying under Ouspensky and Gurdjieff as well as his encounters with Maurice Nicoll. He transcribes various talks as well as incidents. There are chapters on *Special Movements and Dance, Gurdjieff as a Teacher,* and *The Death of Gurdjieff,* as well as a commentary on **All and Everything.** Another excellent presentation.

■ *WALKER, KENNETH.* **A STUDY OF GURDJIEFF'S TEACHING. 216pp. Wei74/CaL, 3.50p.**
Walker was a British physician who studied Gurdjieff's system for many years, first under Ouspensky, and then under Gurdjieff himself. He expounds in outline the ideas themselves, with the help of diagrams, and compares them with kindred ideas obtained from scientific, religious, and philosophical sources, both Eastern and Western. Though he acknowledges that *formulation and printing squeeze out of the spoken word [Gurdjieff's teaching was essentially oral] almost all of its vitality,* Walker has made as clear and thoughtful a presentation as we have seen. Recommended as the best introduction to Gurdjieff for those who do not want to plunge into the rigors of **In Search.**

WALKER, KENNETH. **VENTURE WITH IDEAS. 192pp. Wei51/Spe, 5.95c.**
Walker's first attempt, newly reprinted, to illustrate the impact Gurdjieff's and Ouspensky's ideas had upon him, trained as he was in the scientific method. The book *is the chronicle of a journey through the bewildering inner world of ideas, a journey in which I was fortunate enough to have two remarkable men as guides.* A clear, personal presentation.

WELCH, LOUISE. **THE OLD MAN RIDES A BICYCLE. 30pp. TsP72, 2.95p.**
A children's book, written by a member of the Toronto Gurdjieff group, that presents a young boy's journey of exploration into reality.

WELCH, WILLIAM. **WHAT HAPPENED IN BETWEEN. 219pp. Brz72, 6.95c.**
This is the autobiography of a physician who has had a lifetime involvement with the Gurdjieff Work. He personally knew both Gurdjieff and Ouspensky and attended Gurdjieff as a physician during his last days. Dr. Welch's philosophy of medicine reflects his inner work.

HUMANISTIC PSYCHOLOGY

There is now emerging over the horizon a new conception of human sickness and of human health, a psychology that I find so thrilling and so full of wonderful possiblities that I yield to the temptation to present it publicly even before it is checked and confirmed, and before it can be called reliable scientific knowledge.

The basic assumptions of this point of view are:

1. We have, each of us, an essential biologically based inner nature, which is to some degree *natural*, intrinsic, given, and, in a certain limited sense, unchangeable, or, at least, unchanging.

2. Each person's inner nature is in part unique to himself and in part species-wide.

3. It is possible to study this inner nature scientifically and to discover what it is like—(not *invent*—*discover*).

4. This inner nature, as much as we know of it so far, seems not to be intrinsically or primarily or necessarily evil. The basic needs (for life, for safety and security, for belongingness and affection, for respect and self-respect, and for self-actualization), the basic human emotions and the basic human capacities are on their face either neutral, pre-moral or positively *good*. Destructiveness, sadism, cruelty, malice, etc., seem so far to be not intrinsic but rather they seem to be violent reactions against frustration of our intrinsic needs, emotions and capacities. Anger is *in itself* not evil, nor is fear, laziness, or even ignorance. Of course, these can and do lead to evil behavior, but they needn't. This result is not intrinsically necessary. Human nature is not nearly as bad as it has been thought to be. In fact it can be said that the possibilities of human nature have customarily been sold short.

5. Since this inner nature is good or neutral rather than bad, it is best to bring it out and to encourage it rather than to suppress it. If it is permitted to guide our life, we grow healthy, fruitful, and happy.

6. If this essential core of the person is denied or suppressed, he gets sick sometimes in obvious ways, sometimes in subtle ways, sometimes immediately, sometimes later.

7. This inner nature is not strong and overpowering and unmistakable like the instincts of animals. It is weak and delicate and subtle and easily overcome by habit, cultural pressure, and wrong attitudes toward it.

8. Even though weak, it rarely disappears in the normal person—perhaps not even in the sick person. Even though denied, it persists underground forever pressing for actualization.

9. Somehow, these conclusions must all be articulated with the necessity of discipline, deprivation, frustration, pain, and tragedy. To the extent that these experiences reveal and foster and fulfill our inner nature, to that extent they are desirable experiences. It is increasingly clear that these experiences have something to do with a sense of achievement and ego strength and therefore with the sense of healthy self-esteem and self-confidence. The person who hasn't conquered, withstood and overcome continues to feel doubtful that he could. This is true not only for external dangers; it holds also for the ability to control and to delay one's own impulses, and therefore to be unafraid of them.

Observe that if these assumptions are proven true, they promise a scientific ethics, a natural value system, a court of ultimate appeal for the determination of good and bad, of right and wrong. The more we learn about man's natural tendencies, the easier it will be to tell him how to be good, how to be happy, how to be fruitful, how to respect himself, how to love, how to fulfill his highest potentialities. This amounts to automatic solution of many of the personality problems of the future. The thing to do seems to be to find out what one is really like inside, deep down, as a member of the human species and as a particular individual.

The study of such self-fulfilling people can teach us much about our own mistakes, our shortcomings, the proper directions in which to grow. Every age but ours has had its model, its ideal. All of these have been given up by our culture; the saint, the hero, the gentleman, the knight, the mystic. About all we have left is the well-adjusted man without problems, a very pale and doubtful substitute. Perhaps we shall soon be able to use as our guide and model the fully growing and self-fulfilling human being, the one in whom all his potentialities are coming to full development, the one whose inner nature expresses itself freely, rather than being warped, suppressed, or denied.

The serious thing for each person to recognize vividly and poignantly, each for himself, is that every falling away from species-virtue, every crime against one's own nature, every evil act, *every one without exception records itself* in our unconscious and makes us despise ourselves. Karen Horney had a good word to describe this unconscious perceiving and remembering; she said it *registers*. If we do something we are ashamed of, it *registers* to our discredit, and if we do something honest or fine or good, it *registers* to our credit. The net results ultimately are either one or the other—either we respect and accept ourselves or we despise ourselves and feel contemptible, worthless, and unlovable. Theologians used to use the word *accidie* to describe the sin of failing to do with one's life all that one knows one could do.

This point of view in no way denies the usual Freudian picture. But it does add to it and supplement it. To oversimplify the matter somewhat, it is as if Freud supplied to us the sick half of psychology and we must now fill it out with the healthy half. Perhaps this health psychology will give us more possibility for controlling and improving our lives and for making ourselves better people. Perhaps this will be more fruitful than asking *how to get "unsick."*

How can we encourage free development? What are the best educational conditions for it? Sexual? Economic? Political? What kind of world do we need for such people to grow in? What kind of world will such people create? Sick people are made by a sick culture; healthy people are made possible by a healthy culture. But it is just as true that sick individuals make their culture more sick and that healthy individuals make their culture more healthy. Improving individual health is one approach to making a better world. To express it in another way, encouragement of personal growth is a real possibility; cure of actual neurotic symptoms is far less possible without outside help. It is relatively easy to try deliberately to make oneself a more honest man; it is very difficult to try to cure one's own compulsions or obsessions.

The classical approach to personality problems considers them to be problems in an undesirable sense. Struggle, conflict, guilt, bad conscience, anxiety, depression, frustration, tension, shame, self-punishment, feeling of inferiority or unworthiness—they all cause psychic pain, they disturb efficiency of performance, and they are uncontrollable. They are therefore automatically regarded as sick and undesirable and they get *cured* away as soon as possible.

But all of these symptoms are found also in healthy people, or in people who are growing toward health. Supposing you should feel guilty and don't? Supposing you have attained a nice stabilization of forces and you are adjusted? Perhaps adjustment and stabilization, while good because it cuts your pain, is also bad because development toward a higher ideal ceases?

In a word if you tell me you have a personality problem I am not certain until I know you better whether to say *Good!* or *I'm sorry*. It depends on the reasons. And these, it seems, may be bad reasons, or they may be good reasons.

An example is the changing attitude of psychologists toward popularity, toward adjustment, even toward delinquency. Popular with whom? Perhaps it is better for a youngster to be *unpopular* with the neighboring snobs or with the local country club set. Adjusted to what? To a bad culture? To a dominating parent? What shall we think of a well-adjusted slave? A well-adjusted prisoner? Even the behavior problem boy is being looked upon with new tolerance. Why is he delinquent? Most often it is for sick reasons. But occasionally it is for good reasons and the boy is simply resisting exploitation, domination, neglect, contempt, and trampling upon.

Clearly what will be called personality problems depends on who is doing the calling. The slave owner? The dictator? The patriarchal father? The husband who wants his wife to remain a child? It seems quite clear that personality problems may sometimes be loud protests against the crushing of one's psychological bones, of one's true inner nature. What is sick then is not to protest while this crime is being committed. And I am sorry to report my impression that most people do not protest under such treatment. They take it and pay years later, in neurotic and psychosomatic symptoms of various kinds, or perhaps in some cases never become aware that they are sick, that they have missed true happiness, true fulfillment of promise, a rich emotional life, and a serene, fruitful old age, that they have never known how wonderful it is to be creative, to react aesthetically, to find life thrilling.

The question of desirable grief and pain or the necessity for it must also be faced. Is growth and self-fulfillment possible at all without pain and grief and sorrow and turmoil? If these are to some extent necessary and unavoidable, then to what extent? If grief and pain are sometimes necessary for growth of the person, then we must learn not to protect people from them automatically as if they were always bad. Sometimes they may be good and desirable in view of the ultimate good consequences. Not allowing people to go through their pain, and protecting them from it, may turn out to be a kind of overprotection, which in turn implies a certain lack of respect for the integrity and the intrinsic nature and the future development of the individual.

—*condensed from* **Toward a Psychology of Being**, *by Abraham Maslow*

ABELL, RICHARD. **OWN YOUR OWN LIFE.** Index, notes, 254pp. Ban76, 1.95p.
The techniques and exercises presented here are a synthesis of transactional analysis, gestalt therapy, nonverbal techniques, and traditional psychoanalytic procedures. Dr. Abell is a psychiatrist who became dissatisfied with analytic methods and participated in a number of experimental therapeutic workshops which changed him profoundly. He describes his own experiences and tells how he incorporates the techniques into his own practice. Many case histories are included and special attention is given to the moments when therapeutic breakthroughs take place.

AGEL, JEROME. **ROUGH TIMES. 243pp. RaH73, 1.65p.**
A collection of essays attacking therapy as a means of social control and discussing ways therapists can become agents of social change.

ANDERSON, WALT, ed. **THERAPY AND THE ARTS. 219pp. H&R77, 4.95p.**
In this volume I want to try to make clear the natural similarities between art and therapy: by stressing that these two lines of human activity flow out of similar—if not identical—sets of human needs and aspirations, it will be easier to show why therapy and the arts are again drawing closer together. Use of the arts in therapy is not a gimmick; it is a natural and effective pipeline to rich sources of feeling and meaning. The arts and the therapies are logically related enterprises: they are tools of consciousness, paths of development of the human mind.—from the introduction. A collection of essays.

ARASTEH, A. REZA. **TOWARD FINAL PERSONALITY INTEGRATION. Notes, index, 308pp. JWS75, 9.10p.**
A dry, often difficult to follow, psychological study which draws on the author's experiences both as a psychiatrist and a Sufi scholar. *I hypothesize that in every culture the formalistic cultural self (the dominant superego) leads man to the rational state characterized by the dominant ego, and when rationality has reached its end, (as in the West now), it can, if guided, ripen into wisdom—an experiential state. I give supportive evidence from the life experiences of a number of individuals from the East and West who have broken through rationality, conformity, and the world of conceptualization, and have regained experiential naturalness.*

ASSAGIOLI, ROBERTO. **THE ACT OF WILL. Notes, index, 288pp. Vik73/Wdw, 2.95p.**
A development of some of the concepts presented in **Psychosynthesis**. Here Assagioli emphasizes the human will which he defines as a constructive force guiding intuition, impulse, emotion, and imagination toward complete realization of the self. He proposes a set of exercises that train the will for *optimum use at all levels of existence—from the personal to the transpersonal and reaching into the realm where the individual will merges with the universal will.* Thus transfigured, the will becomes a central part of a *coherent psychology of joy.* Dr. Assagioli writes very clearly.

■ ASSAGIOLI, ROBERTO. **PSYCHOSYNTHESIS. Index, 323+pp. Vik65/Tur, 2.95p.**
Psychosynthesis is a psychological and educational approach for recognizing and harmonizing the many, often conflicting, elements of our inner life. It is a developmental process based on a positive conception of man within an evolving universe. Starting with each person's existential situation as he perceives it, personal growth is organized into a process aiming at the integration of personality and the emergence of an effective unifying center of being and awareness, the Self. The practical work of psychosynthesis chooses in each situation the appropriate progressive activities among many techniques and methods available. Some of these are: guided imagery, movement, self-identification, creativity, gestalt, meditation, training of the will, symbolic art work, journal-keeping, ideal models, and development of intuition. The emphasis is on fostering an ongoing process of growth that can gain momentum and bring about a more joyful, balanced actualization of one's life.—**The Esalen Catalog.** Assagioli was an Italian psychiatrist who formulated the concept of psychosynthesis in response to what he felt was the partial answer provided by traditional psychoanalysis. This is the basic book and it includes both theoretical material and many practical exercises. We recommend Assagioli's work highly.

ASSAGIOLI, ROBERTO. **THE PSYCHOSYNTHESIST. Illustrations, 8½"x11", 28pp. HDI74, 2.00p.**
A special issue of **Human Dimensions Magazine** devoted to Assagioli and including the following articles by him: *The Impact of a Presence, BioPsychosynthesis, The Technique of Evocative Words, Life as a Game and Stage Performance (Role Playing), Symbols of Transpersonal Experiences, Smiling Wisdom, The Conflict between the Generations and the Psychosynthesis of the Human Ages.* Also includes some biographical material. Provides a good survey of Assagioli's major ideas.

BACH, GEORGE and RONALD DEUTSCH. **PAIRING. 318pp. Avo70, 1.95p.**
A book about intimacy, how to establish it and keep it going. A handbook for singles who want to learn to get along better with the opposite sex.

BACH, GEORGE and HERB GOLDBERG. **CREATIVE AGGRESSION.** Notes, index, 337pp. Avo74/Cov, 1.95p.
A popularly written account which details how individuals can express their natural anger constructively. The techniques are clearly presented and many people have found them extremely useful.

BACH, GEORGE and PETER WYDEN. **THE INTIMATE ENEMY.** 384pp. Avo68, 2.25p.
An original approach for using domestic quarrels constructively—how to fight with your mate but fight fair.

BACK, KURT. **BEYOND WORDS. Bibliography, index, 287pp. Vik73, 1.75p.**
A fairly academic survey of the encounter movement, tracing its development and growth, detailing the techniques that make it up, and assessing its overall impact.

BALDWIN, CHRISTINA. **ONE TO ONE: SELF-UNDERSTANDING THROUGH JOURNAL WRITING. Bibliography, 202pp. EvC77, 6.95c.**
The journal is a way of connecting. The journal is a connection of the self with the self. The journal sets up an inner dichotomy so that one part may write and one part may read. And since the journal connection between the two parts is interior, it fosters an increased sense of awareness of personal psychology. It becomes a way of observing survival. It becomes an instrument of survival.—from the introduction. In this book Ms. Baldwin shares excerpts from her own journal entries and discusses the development of a process for journal writing.

BANDLER, RICHARD and JOHN GRINDER. **THE STRUCTURE OF MAGIC, I. Glossary, bibliography, 225pp. S&B75, 7.95c.**
This is an excellent manual for practicing therapists. *What we have attempted to do...is not to create a new school of psychotherapy but rather to make understandable and learnable some of the language skills of some of the world's most talented psychotherapists. We do this in a way which shows both the simplicity and the similarities of the techniques of these seemingly divergent therapists. Our hope is that this work will begin the long overdue process of sharing the resources of all those who are involved in finding ways to help people have better, fuller and richer lives and relationships with those they love. Our approach to this was to distill and formalize the patterns of therapeutic interaction which are common to some of the leading clinicians of the many schools of psychotherapy. By formalizing these patterns, our belief is that they will become available as a tool for people—helpers to have access to the resources of these therapeutic wizards. If you are someone who wishes to have more tools and resources as a people-helper, we wrote this book for you.*

BANDLER, RICHARD, JOHN GRINDER and VIRGINIA SATIR. **CHANGING WITH FAMILIES. 202pp. S&B76, 13.40c.**
The process of writing this book was, for the three of us, an opportunity to change and grow and integrate parts of our experience of doing family therapy and individual therapy. We came to understand explicitly how the communications skills we use in those contexts applied to writing this book together. Taking three very different models of the world, three different types of background, we found a way to use those same communication skills to communicate with each other and then finally to translate the communication we found effective among the three of us onto paper.

BERNHARD, YETTA. **HOW TO BE SOMEBODY. 95pp. CeA75, 3.95p.**
Despite the title, this is not a how to book in the strictest sense of the words. The editors have selected universal questions based on the fact that many of us, at some time or another in our lives, have felt unloved, isolated, friendless, lonely, or depressed. My friend and respected colleague, Yetta Bernhard, addresses herself to these questions in a down-to-earth, common sense manner....If you have ever felt any of the kinds of feelings reflected by the questions in the pages that follow, this book can do much more than entertain or edify you. It is quite possible that if you can hear what she is saying, you will be able to change your opinion of yourself.—Virginia Satir.

BERNHARD, YETTA. **SELF-CARE. Glossary, bibliography, index, 227pp. CeA75, 6.95p.**
I think that Yetta Bernhard addresses herself to the central issue which is how to define, to limit, and to make specific your every-day interpersonal negotiations with the people with whom you live....Another outstanding contribution of her book is the specific and practical methods she offers....Implied in her book is the assumption that human beings in daily work with one another will meet conflict and differences as part of the givens of being human. Coping with this difference in the way that Yetta demonstrates is a central point in the development of maintenance and self-care.—Virginia Satir.

BUGENTAL, JAMES, ed. **CHALLENGES OF HUMANISTIC PSYCHOLOGY. Index, 7"x10", 376pp. MGH67, 12.75p.**
A collection of readings organized under the following general headings: *The Nature and Task of Humanistic Psychology, The Human Experience, Research Areas and Methods, Some Research Projects, The Growthful Encounter,* and *The Reunion of Psychology and the Humanities.* This is a textbook and the readings are uniformly technical.

BUHLER, CHARLOTTE and MELANIE ALLEN. **INTRODUCTION TO HUMANISTIC PSYCHOLOGY. Bibliography, index, 128pp. Wad72, 6.65p.**
A systematic formulation of the goals, methodology, and theoretical bases of humanistic psychology divided into the following chapters: *Science and culture, The historical roots of humanistic psychology, Theoretical concepts, Humanistic psychology as related to contemporary culture,* and *The importance of humanistic psychology in the contemporary perspective: Applications and innovations in psychotherapy and education.*

FADIMAN, JAMES and ROBERT FRAGER. **PERSONALITY AND PERSONAL GROWTH. Indices, 7½"x9½", 510pp. H&R76, 18.75c.**
This is the best textbook in transpersonal psychology that we know of. The authors begin with separate chapters on the major figures in twentieth century psychology: Sigmund Freud, Carl Jung, Alfred Adler, Wilhelm Reich, Fritz Perls, William James, B.F. Skinner, Carl Rogers, and Abraham Maslow. Each of these discussions is clear, well organized, and illuminating. Quotations from the writings of each man are included in the margin. A final section is devoted to an introduction to Eastern theories of personality, with separate chapters on Zen Buddhism, yoga and the Hindu tradition, and Sufism. Elizabeth Lloyd has contributed an appraisal of women in psychoanalytic theory and an annotated bibliography on the psychology of women. Annotated bibliographies follow each chapter.

FADIMAN, JAMES and DONALD KEWMAN, eds. **EXPLORING MADNESS. Notes, bibliography, index, 236pp. Wad73, 6.65p.**
This book presents many innovative and, in some cases, radical ideas for the investigation, understanding, and treatment of madness. Included are personal and literary accounts of madness, theoretical positions, and research findings. Our intention is to present the contributions of individuals who extend or go beyond current conceptions in abnormal psychology—to survey alternative models that emphasize inner experience in the development of further theories and research. Many of the writers view madness as an altered state of consciousness that causes certain perceptual, emotional, and behavioral changes; however, each viewpoint is based on a different way of exploring and interpreting the experience.—from the preface.

FRANKL, VIKTOR. **THE DOCTOR AND THE SOUL. Bibliography, 318pp. RaH65, 2.45p.**
Dr. Frankl sets forth the principles of existential psychiatry, which hold that man's search for a meaning in existence is a primary facet of his being. If the search is unrequited, it leads to neurosis. He emphasizes man's spiritual values and says that the role of the therapist is to help the patient discover a purpose in his life. This is the second, expanded edition which includes revisions and an added chapter.

FRANKL, VIKTOR. **MAN'S SEARCH FOR MEANING. 226pp. S&S59/Hod, 1.75p.**
Frankl is the founder of logotherapy, or existential analysis, which grew out of his three years in Auschwitz concentration camp where he survived because of the strength of his goals. His approach is based on man's search for and need for meaning in life and in whatever he does. *Logotherapy…makes the concept of man into a whole…and focuses its attention upon mankind's groping for a higher meaning in life.* The first half of this book is a chilling yet fascinating account of Frankl's concentration camp experience. The second presents the basic concepts of logotherapy. A good introduction.

FRANKL, VIKTOR. **PSYCHOTHERAPY AND EXISTENTIALISM. 249pp. S&S67/Pen, 3.95p.**
Collected papers on logotherapy. Only recommended to those seriously interested in the subject.

FRANKL, VIKTOR. **THE UNCONSCIOUS GOD. Notes, bibliography, index, 161pp. S&S75/Hod, 2.95p.**
A central feature of logotherapy is the idea that an awareness, conscious or unconscious, of a God within is essential to man's humanity. Through his own psychiatric practice Dr. Frankl has found that even the repression of religiosity in a patient does not conceal a belief within. In fact, a more intense denial frequently reflects an equally intense acknowledgment of God. This book is an updated translation of a volume originally written in 1948, including current empirical evidence.

FRANKL, VIKTOR. **THE UNHEARD CRY FOR MEANING: PSYCHOTHERAPY AND HUMANISM. Notes, lengthy bibliography, index, 191pp. S&S78, 9.95c.**
Dr. Frankl expands his discussion to the philosophical concomitants of logotherapy; to its relationship to the more traditional therapies; to the light it sheds on selected areas of contemporary life; and to a detailed presentation of logotherapy's central clinical strategies, paradoxical intention, and dereflection.

FRANKL, VIKTOR. **THE WILL TO MEANING. 181pp. NAL69/Sou, 2.95p.**
A survey of the foundations of logotherapy and its applications.

FROMM, ERICH. **THE ART OF LOVING. 148pp. H&R56/A&U, 2.95p.**
This is a classic volume. Dr. Fromm calls love the answer to all the problems of human existence and discusses self love, brotherly love, motherly love, erotic love, and love of God.

FROMM, ERICH. **TO HAVE OR TO BE. Notes, bibliography, index, 229pp. H&R76, 8.95c.**
This volume summarizes Fromm's lifetime study. His thesis is that two modes of existence are struggling for the spirit of wo/mankind: the having mode, which concentrates on material possession, acquisitiveness, power, and aggression and is the basis of such universal evils as greed, envy, and violence; and the being mode, which is based in love, in the pleasure of sharing, and in meaningful and productive rather than wasteful activity. Dr. Fromm sees the having mode bringing the world to the bring of psychological and ecological disaster and he outlines a program for change.

FROMM, ERICH. **MAN FOR HIMSELF: AN INQUIRY INTO THE PSYCHOLOGY OF ETHICS. Notes, index, 256pp. Faw47, 1.95p.**
My experience as a practicing psychoanalyst has confirmed my conviction that problems of ethics cannot be omitted from the study of personality, either theoretically or therapeutically. The value judgments we make determine our actions, and upon their validity rests our mental health and happiness….I have written this book with the intention of reaffirming the validity of humanistic ethics, to show that our knowledge of human nature does not lead to ethical relativism but, on the contrary, to the conviction that the sources of norms for ethical conduct are to be found in man's nature itself; that moral norms are based upon man's inherent qualities, and that their violation results in mental and emotional disintegration.

FROMM, ERICH, D.T. SUZUKI and RICHARD DEMARTINO. **ZEN BUDDHISM AND PSYCHOANALYSIS. 1.95p.**
See the Zen Buddhism section.

GALE, RAYMOND. **WHO ARE YOU? Notes, bibliography, index, 177pp. PrH74/CaL, 2.95p.**
Subtitled *The Psychology of Being Yourself,* this volume is part of a series of books on humanistic psychology. Gale describes the task of becoming and growing, and explains how each of us must assume responsibility for realizing our full potential.

GAYLIN, WILLARD. **CARING. Notes, bibliography, index, 208pp. RaH76, 7.95c.**
Dr. Gaylin's study is written in response to the recent theorizing about man as primarily aggressive and destructive. He draws on the most recent scholarship in psychology and biology to show that an impulse for caring is biologically programmed in man, and that man is uniquely and fundamentally a caring creature. He demonstrates that this impulse is essential to the survival of the species and is our natural and imperative response to the prolonged helplessness of the young. Dr. Gaylin suggests that we should recognize, encourage, and nurture this impulse. He emphasizes our need for attachments to individuals and to the community at large and shows that the need for attachment is so crucial that our individual selves are formed in large part by the means by which we secure this attachment.

GEBA, BRUNO. **VITALITY TRAINING FOR OLDER ADULTS. Bibliography, 106pp. RaH74, 5.95c.**
We need to change our attitude about growing old. Through an invigorating attitudinal change, new values can be created. They can lay the foundation for a new mythology of aging. The initiative for this change must come from older adults. There is no time to look outside ourselves for help. The solution must come from within us. By allowing yourself to experience yourself growing old, you will discover your own solutions and will act accordingly. And that is what Vitality Training is all about: a method which assists in changing a person's defeatist attitude into a vital one. It is a gentle way—a way of going with life, of going with growing old and all that is associated with it.

Gestalt Therapy

Gestalt therapy was originated by Fritz Perls (who died in 1970). It is more than a philosophy, it is a philosophy of life which involves needs and desires and being fully responsible for one's own actions. It centers on the reality of what is instead of the abstraction of what we think should be or might be. The philosophy is capsulized in Perls' Gestalt Prayer:

> *I do my thing, and you do your thing.*
> *I am not in this world to live up to your expectations*
> *And you are not in this world to live up to mine.*
> *You are you, and I am I.*
> *And if by chance, we find each other, it's beautiful.*
> *If not, it can't be helped.*

FAGAN, JOEN and IRMA SHEPHERD, eds. **GESTALT THERAPY NOW. Index, notes, bibliography, 341pp. H&R70, 3.50p.**
This is an authoritative collection of articles on the theory, techniques, and applications of gestalt therapy. This is probably the most extensive presentation of all the aspects of gestalt that has ever been published. Twenty-two different practitioners present their ideas and experiences. The material is geared toward the practicing therapist. Portions of this book have been separately reprinted in **What is Gestalt Therapy?** and **Life Techniques in Gestalt Therapy** ($1.95 each).

LATNER, JOEL. **THE GESTALT THERAPY BOOK. 243pp. Ban73, 1.95p.**
A holistic guide to the theory, principles and techniques of gestalt therapy. In straightforward prose it shows the reader how gestaltists understand human events, health and illness, and growth. Includes an excellent up to date bibliography. Dr. Latner is a gestalt therapist in San Francisco.

PERLS, FRITZ. **EGO, HUNGER AND AGGRESSION. 273pp. RaH47, 2.95p.**
Fritz's first book, a fairly technical introduction to the basics of gestalt therapy. It is not as interesting as his later books.

PERLS, FRITZ. **THE GESTALT APPROACH AND EYE WITNESS TO THERAPY.** 214pp. Ban73, 1.95p.

These are Fritz's two last works, uncompleted at his death. He wrote **The Gestalt Approach** because he was no longer satisfied with his two earlier theoretical works, **Ego, Hunger and Aggression** and **Gestalt Therapy.** In the intervening twenty years he had integrated a great deal from Eastern religions, meditation, psychedelics, and body work. After the section on theory, **Eye Witness** consists of transcripts of films of Fritz working with patients, each with an introduction that highlights the lessons to be learned.

■ *PERLS, FRITZ.* **GESTALT THERAPY VERBATIM.** 306pp. Ban69, 3.50p/2.25p.

In this book, Perls gives a clear explanation in simple terms of the basic ideas of gestalt therapy, followed by verbatim transcripts of complete therapy sessions with explanatory comments. It is probably the best introductory book to this method of therapy, and is certainly one of the most interesting to read.

PERLS, FRITZ. **IN AND OUT OF THE GARBAGE PAIL.** 296pp. Ban69, 4.00p/2.25p.

This is Fritz Perls' autobiography, in which he applies his theory of focusing on awareness and writes *whatever wants to be written.* Partly in poetic form, often playful, sometimes theoretical, the book is a many faceted mosaic of memories and reflections on this life—in the past and at the moment—and on the origins and continuing development of gestalt therapy.

PERLS, FRITZ and PATRICIA BAUMGARDNER. **LEGACY FROM FRITZ.** 218pp. S&B75, 7.95c.

The first part of this book is devoted to transcriptions of a series of mini-lectures which Perls gave shortly before his death. Next there is an edited transcription of his actual work with people from his earliest days at Esalen to his last period at Lake Cowichan. The second half of the book is a personal document about Patricia Baumgardner's months of training with Perls during the last months of his life.

PERLS, FRITZ, RALPH HEFFERLINE, and PAUL GOODMAN. **GESTALT THERAPY.** 470pp. Del51/Pen, 3.95p.

This collaboration is perhaps the single most important book on gestalt therapy. A unique feature is a series of eighteen experiments on sharpening the body senses, integrating awareness, changing anxiety into excitement, mobilizing the muscles, and much else. The second part is devoted to an in depth exposition of the theory underlying the practice of gestalt therapy.

POLSTER, ERVING and MIRIAM. **GESTALT THERAPY INTEGRA-TED.** Notes, index, 347pp. RaH73, 2.95p.

The Polsters are among the group of second generation gestaltists who learned from, further developed, and refined the work of Fritz and Laura Perls. This book, subtitled *Contours of Theory and Practice,* has been widely acclaimed as probably the best current presentation of gestalt therapy. It is a serious and scholarly work which is well written and very clearly organized. The authors explain the basic principles, develop new concepts, reformulate older ones, and show, through case studies, how all of these elements come together in the therapeutic practice.

RHYNE, JANIE. **THE GESTALT ART EXPERIENCE.** Oversized, illustrations, index, 216pp. Wad73, 17.40c.

Ms. Rhyne is an art therapist. Here she focuses on direct and immediate experiential insights gained through creating art that expresses and clarifies an individual's personal problems and potential. The emphasis is on exploring one's present life style and discovering possibilities for self actualization. The author presents simple directions for art activities designed for individuals and groups in therapeutic and educational settings. The book is divided into four sections: *Art Experience in Therapeutic Growth Processes, Art Experience for Contact and Communication, Using the Gestalt Art Experience for Yourself,* and *Using the Gestalt Art Experience with Others.*

■ *ROSENBLATT, DANIEL.* **THE GESTALT THERAPY PRIMER.** 188pp. H&R75, 1.95p.

This book is intended as a first taste, a small bite, a slice of what gestalt therapy is like. In a real session with a gestalt therapist, what happens is cooked up for just you. Here, since I didn't know you, I will invent what might happen between us, so that you can

gain some idea of the kind of thinking and the kind of techniques that are used to help you to grow, to get in touch with your feelings, to explore hidden parts of yourself, to become whole. . . . This book is deliberately small and short. That is because you are asked to do the experiments by yourself. If you will put the book down and do the experiments, much more will happen. The book is illustrated throughout.

ROSENBLATT, DANIEL. **OPENING DOORS.** 144pp. H&R75, 1.95p.

*This book is a strong gestalt, a successful integration of theory and practice, of explanation and expression, into an intensely personal style of communication. Daniel Rosenblatt's precise and, at the same time, imaginative and flowing use of language in dialogue and metaphor makes exciting and enjoyable reading. It is the most painless and least superficial introduction to gestalt therapy. I recommend this book to all serious students and practitioners of psychotherapy as well as to the general public.—*Laura Perls.

SCHIFFMAN, MURIEL. **GESTALT SELF THERAPY.** 223pp. STP71, 3.50p.

A very personal book that can be used by persons without any background in psychology. Helps you to know yourself, to be truly aware of the opposing forces within you, to deal with your search for identity, self discipline, judgmental attitude, need to control, failure, depression, loneliness, etc.

SCHIFFMAN, MURIEL. **SELF THERAPY.** 166pp. STP67, 2.45p.

An earlier work on the same subject.

SIMKIN, JAMES. **GESTALT THERAPY MINI-LECTURES.** Notes, 124pp. CeA76, 3.95p.

Simkin was a long time student, friend, and colleague of Fritz Perls and he is often referred to as the co-founder of gestalt therapy. In this book he demonstrates the applications of gestalt therapy to ordinary life situations and discusses self-expression, taking responsibility, resentment and guilt, anxiety, love/hate, and much else. The writing style is informal and case histories abound.

SMITH, EDWARD, ed. **THE GROWING EDGE OF GESTALT THERAPY.** Notes, index, 255pp. Stu77, 5.95p.

An excellent collection of essays on gestalt therapy divided into the following major sections: *Historical Background, Further Explications of Gestalt Therapy, Gestalt Therapy and Jungian Psychology, Gestalt Therapy Integrated with Other Techniques and Systems, Gestalt Therapy and Eastern Philosophy,* and *A Summing Up.* All of the major figures are represented.

STEVENS, BARRY. **DON'T PUSH THE RIVER.** Illustrations, 268pp. RPP70, 3.50p.
A lovely first person account of Ms. Stevens' therapeutic integration of gestalt therapy, Zen, and Krishnamurti. She has been extremely effective in deepening and expanding her patients' personal experience and helping them work through difficulties. As she says, *We have to turn ourselves upside down and reverse our approach to life.*

STEVENS, JOHN. **AWARENESS: EXPLORING, EXPERIMENTING, EXPERIENCING.** 309pp. Ban71, 3.50p/2.50p.
This is a very popular book. Detailed instructions lead the reader through more than 100 experiments, helping expand her awareness of herself, her surroundings, and her interaction with others.

STEVENS, JOHN, ed. **GESTALT IS.** 277pp. Ban75, 3.50p/2.50p.
This book is a collection of writings on gestalt therapy. It contains all of Fritz Perls' previously published uncollected papers....The Perls papers were originally published in the 1950s and 1960s, and Van Dusen's articles originally appeared in the 1960s. These papers show important aspects of the development of gestalt during that period. All of the other articles were either published within the past five years, or were written for this book. They show some of the developments that are now taking place in the theory and practice of gestalt. These articles have been chosen simply on the basis of our preference. To us, they are the clearest, most interesting, original and vital of current writing on gestalt.—from the introduction. Stevens is the son of Barry Stevens, a well known gestalt therapist, and he was the original publisher of Perls' books.

——————— **END OF GESTALT THERAPY SUBSECTION** ———————

GILLIES, JERRY. **FRIENDS: THE POWER AND POTENTIAL OF THE COMPANY THAT YOU KEEP.** Annotated bibliography, 254pp. H&R76, 2.95p.
This is an informal, practical guide which shows you how to discover what your friends really mean to you and what roles they play in your life. Gillies has had extensive experience as a group leader in the human potential movement and he brings this experience to bear in the exercises and case studies that make up **Friends.**

William Glasser

William Glasser conceived reality therapy after judging classical psychiatric treatments to be generally futile. At the core of his approach is the formula of the three r's: reality, responsibility, and right and wrong. According to Glasser the way to fulfill basic human needs is to live realistically, responsibly, and rightly. Reality therapy has been used in schools and hospitals as well as in more traditional therapeutic situations.

BASSIN, ALEXANDER, THOMAS BRATTER, and RICHARD RACHIN, eds. **THE REALITY THERAPY READER: A SURVEY OF THE WORK OF WILLIAM GLASSER.** Index, 701pp. H&R76, 15.00c.
A collection of articles on all aspects of reality therapy, divided into six sections: *Glasser the Man, Theory, Practice, Education, Corrections,* and *Role Playing.* The selections have been gathered from books, popular magazines, and journals, and there is also some original material.

GLASSER, WILLIAM. **THE IDENTITY SOCIETY.** Index, 254pp. H&R75, 1.95p.
This volume carries Dr. Glasser's ideas about reality therapy into the field of sociology. He examines almost all varieties of human motivation and behavior, applying his theory and knowledge most specifically to aspects of modern life such as childrearing, criminal justice, hospitals, welfare, and maladjustment. Revised edition.

GLASSER, WILLIAM. **POSITIVE ADDICTION.** 159pp. H&R76, 7.95c.
A detailed presentation of Dr. Glasser's thesis that it is possible to become *addicted* to positive behavior. These positive addictions can strengthen a person so that he can overcome negative addictions, and lead a more integrated and rewarding life. In his investigations Dr. Glasser found more *PA* devotees among runners and meditators, and so he explores these activities in depth. He also discusses the steps to positive addiction, its manifestations and benefits. Many case studies are included.

GLASSER, WILLIAM. **REALITY THERAPY.** 189pp. H&R65, 2.95p.
Reality therapy has been developed over many years by Dr. Glasser. Its requirements—an intense personal involvement, facing reality, rejecting irresponsible behavior, and learning better ways to behave—bear little resemblance to conventional therapy and produce markedly different results. Whether the patient thinks he is Napoleon, is running berserk, or has nervous headaches, the common cause is inability to fulfill his two essential needs: to love and be loved, and to feel worthwhile to himself and to others. The first part of this book explains reality therapy and contrasts it with conventional treatment. The second part illustrates it in practice and includes many case studies.

——————— **END OF WILLIAM GLASSER SUBSECTION** ———————

GORDON, THOMAS. **L.E.T.: LEADER EFFECTIVENESS TRAINING.** Index, 278pp. Wyd77, 10.95c.
Dr. Gordon presents a comprehensive set of leadership tools and shows how leaders can apply these new methods to many kinds of groups. The material is based on his experience with thousands of leaders trained in his L.E.T. classes. The tone and techniques resemble those he has put forth in P.E.T.

GREENBERG, IRA, ed. **PSYCHODRAMA.** Index, 511pp. Sou74, 7.15p.
Psychodrama is a therapeutic approach which involves acting out your significant *others* as well as yourself. By playing different roles, an individual gains new perspective on relationships. This anthology presents the most important articles and essays that have been written on the subject and on its creator, J.L. Moreno, M.D. Theory, history, biography, and practical methods are presented, and the approach itself is evaluated. Most of the selections are fairly technical and the book is oriented toward professionals.

GRINDER, JOHN and RICHARD BANDLER. **THE STRUCTURE OF MAGIC, II.** Bibliography, 198pp. S&B76, 7.95c.
In this volume the authors bring their skills as model builders to the area of nonverbal communication. They extend their explicit model of verbal communication created in Volume I of this series, using the patterns of verbal form as a way of helping the reader to identify and use the patterns of nonverbal communication. Many practical techniques and a great deal of background information are presented.

HALEY, JAY. **PROBLEM-SOLVING THERAPY.** 285pp. H&R76, 4.95p.
A collection of specific skills and techniques based on Haley's approach of causing a change in the patient's behavior that will clearly alleviate a symptom or eliminate a problem. Haley's therapy is family-, rather than individual-oriented. A number of case histories are included.

HARPER, ROBERT. **THE NEW PSYCHOTHERAPIES.** Bibliography, index, 178pp. PrH75, 3.45p.
Short summaries of the major therapeutic systems that have arisen in recent years. The therapies are grouped by type and individual therapies in each grouping are compared and contrasted. A bibliography is given which covers the major books in the field. The material is clearly presented.

HOFFMAN, BOB. **GETTING DIVORCED FROM MOTHER AND DAD.** 222pp. Dut76, 7.95c.
This book is by the founder of the Fisher-Hoffman Process, a new alternative therapy. Hoffman believes that we can only experience selfless or genuine love once we have grown up and gotten our parents out of our systems. The process begins with bringing out all our open or hidden resentment toward both parents for their part in our unhappiness. This is followed by a reconciliation with them, combining an understanding of their negative effects on us with the realization that they were similarly affected by their parents. In this way Hoffman believes we become able to leave behind our *negative emotional child* and accept the adult responsibility of real loving. This is a complete exploration of the process and it includes many case studies.

HOPSON, BARRIE and CHARLOTTE. **INTIMATE FEEDBACK.** Bibliography, notes, 222pp. NAL73, 1.50p.
Subtitled, *A Lover's Guide to Getting in Touch with Each Other,* this is a collection of exercises and information on marital patterns based on

the authors extensive work with couples in the human potential movement. Quotations from various authorities are also included.

HOWARD, JANE. **PLEASE TOUCH.** 274pp. Del70, 2.95p.
Jane Howard set out to experience every possible form of encounter. This is her report on what she saw happen to others—and what happened to her.

HUDSON, LIAM. **HUMAN BEINGS: THE PSYCHOLOGY OF HU-MAN EXPERIENCE.** Notes, index, 232pp. Dou75/CaL, 2.95p.
This book is designed to serve as an introductory text, an invitation to approach the discipline of psychology in a certain way. The view of psychology that it advances seems to me to have two virtues that more conventional approaches lack. It has immediate human relevance, in that it is about people and the lives they lead. . . . And it is integrative, creating connections between traditions and styles of thought that have in the past been treated as separate: the artistic as well as scientific; the biological as well as the cultural. For the heart of psychology lies, I believe, in interpretative argument: in the effort to make sense of what people think and do.

HUYCK, MARGARET. **GROWING OLDER.** Bibliography, index, 191pp. PrH74, 2.95p.
A collection of essays on all aspects of aging, explaining the biological and psychological changes that take place and showing how to best deal with these changes.

JAFFE, DENNIS, ed. **IN SEARCH OF A THERAPY.** 154pp. H&R75, 3.25p.
The contributors to this book all practice therapy in certain ways based on certain values, experiences, and commitments each of them will relate. The purpose of bringing their accounts together is, however, to shed light on the nature of the basic choices and definitions of the work we call therapy. . . . This book presents personal answers. . . not in theoretical form, but as they evolved in the work and growth of each of the contributors.

JANOV, ARTHUR and E. MICHAEL HOLDEN. **PRIMAL MAN: THE NEW CONSCIOUSNESS.** 6.60p.
See the Consciousness Expansion section.

JANOV, ARTHUR. **THE PRIMAL REVOLUTION.** 285pp. S&S72/SBL, 3.95p.
An exploration of how primal therapy works, as seen through case studies and the thoughts of its founder.

JANOV, ARTHUR. **THE PRIMAL SCREAM.** 446pp. Del70/SBL, 3.95p/1.95p.
Janov presents a revolutionary new approach to psychological thinking—primal therapy—and, through case histories, gives documented evidence for the elimination of lifetime ailments, both psychological and physical. Primal therapy forces a patient to relive core (primal) experiences, i.e. those moments in infancy and childhood which he found too painful to endure and took refuge in the comfortable half-world of neurosis.

JOURARD, SIDNEY. **DISCLOSING MAN TO HIMSELF.** Notes, bibliography, index, 245pp. Lit68, 3.95p.
This is a continuation of material presented in **The Transparent Self**. Again, Jourard discusses the importance of revealing oneself and not hiding behind veils and personas. A technical study by one of the major figures in humanistic psychology. For professionals or well read laymen only.

JOURARD, SIDNEY. **HEALTHY PERSONALITY.** Notes, index, 370pp. McM74, 19.50c.
Some ways of behaving in the world are life-giving to the person and not destructive to other people, to animals, or to the environment which supports us all. These are ways I call healthy personality. Not only do these ways enhance life and health for the person, they also stimulate, or at least do not impede, the growth and actualization of his more desirable possibilities. . . . In this book I have presented what we have learned in psychology—through clinical experience and through research in laboratories and natural settings—about healthy personality. . . . The two previous editions of this book were entitled **Personal Adjustment**. *This is a greatly expanded version.*

JOURARD, SIDNEY. **SELF-DISCLOSURE.** Tables, notes, bibliography, indices, 255pp. JWS71, 21.50c.
Man's behavior is visible, his experience is not. Yet it is man's experience that is the subject of great fascination to everyone. We want to know what a man means by his behavior, what he is saying to us and to the world by his deeds. The only way we can know what a man is experiencing is if he discloses his experience to us in language we can understand. This book reports research we have done on some of the factors involved in a person's willingness to let others know his experience. It is a book about self-disclosure. . . . This book offers a record of the way in which an idea for research came into being, and how one person used it, alone, and with help.—from the preface.

JOURARD, SIDNEY. **THE TRANSPARENT SELF.** 245pp. Lit71, 4.95p.
A detailed discussion of the following question: *Shall we permit our fellow man to know us as we now are, or shall we seek instead to remain an enigma, wishing to be seen as something we are not?*

KEEN, SAM. **BEGINNINGS WITHOUT END.** 142pp. H&R75, 3.95p.
During three years of intense inner turmoil and change I wrote, almost daily, memos to myself. Whenever I found a way to move from despair to hope, or numbness to anger, or sorrow to laughter I tried to capture the insight in an aphorism, a paragraph, a story or an essay. This book began from notes and fragments I left beside the trail to mark my journey. When I was past the crisis, I retraced my steps and filled in descriptions of the roads and twisting lanes that led me from one point to the next. I share this log of my travels because I think it may be helpful to others who are on a similar adventure. Each person's journey involves both unique circumstances and a common map. My particular path is only a variation of a way that is universal. . . . This book is offered to anyone who feels the need to begin again. It is not so much the story of my journey as it is a report of places where I found an oasis, a helping spirit, a devouring demon, a rushing river or a tree with magical apples.

KEEN, SAM and ANNE VALLEY FOX. **TELLING YOUR STORY.** 159pp. NAL73, 1.50p.
The techniques of storytelling and the psychology which underlies them rest on a discovery of the obvious: that what all persons have in common is their uniqueness. Every person has a story to tell. . . . We were all raised by an intimate group that had traditions, values, rites of passage, ceremonies and legends. We feel nameless and empty when we forget our stories. . . . Find the unconscious and make it conscious, find an audience for the untold tales, and you will discover you are already living a rich mythical life. What most of us lack is only the permission to tell stories that are our own birthright. . . . Journey back into the past, ahead into your future, and out into cosmic time. Discover a few of your many selves. Keen presents guidelines and sample stories.

KENT, IAN and WILLIAM NICHOLLS. **I AMNESS: THE DISCOVERY OF THE SELF BEYOND THE EGO.** Bibliography, 274pp. BoM72, 2.95p.
An interesting synthesis of a variety of religious and psychological techniques, both Eastern and Western. The authors have been conducting workshops in British Columbia over the past few years—workshops which are designed to help individuals in their search for an authentic personal identity. They begin with a brief description of the current social situation in North America. This is followed by a critical examination of psychiatry and religion in its contemporary form—both of which have failed, the authors feel, in their goal of helping an individual confront his soul and recover an awareness of the *precious person within him*. The bulk of the book is devoted to a presentation of their own philosophy and a variety of specific techniques gleaned from Eastern and Western philosophical thought and most apparently influenced by Martin Buber and Zen Buddhism.

KEYES, MARGARET. **THE INWARD JOURNEY.** Many illustrations, index, 121pp. CeA74, 4.95p.
My concern here is to describe in practical detail how I use art materials with the nonartist, the client who has come into therapy with some very specific questions and problems. Some of these questions are similar to your own for they are the questions of anyone who seeks to understand himself, his thoughts, his feelings and actions. These art processes, originally developed in work with troubled clients, I have used in workshops with teachers, students, ministers, and a range of people who simply wished to know themselves more deeply and who found these methods useful. An excellent presentation. Ms. Keyes' background is in Jungian psychology and she has also worked with Eric Berne and Fritz Perls.

KOPP, SHELDON. **BACK TO ONE: A PRACTICAL GUIDE FOR PSYCHOTHERAPISTS. Notes, bibliography, index, 165pp. S&B77, 7.95c.**
This book is a detailed description of how I do therapy. I offer it only as a guide. These are not the ways to work. They are simply my ways of working. They need not be yours, though some may suit your own path. I offer it to encourage you to become ever clearer about the fundamentals of your own style of work. To free oneself from the bondage of attachments to its results, it is necessary to be clear about the work. When we do not concentrate one-pointedly on the basic work, we pay attention instead to the patient's "progress," or to our own ego-bound "Look how well (or badly) I'm doing" trip. Neither path benefits the patient or the therapist. At the point of impasse, the only thing that helps is to go "back to one." But to find your way back, you must first know what "one" is "for you."—Sheldon Kopp.

KOPP, SHELDON. **GURU. 180pp. S&B71, 6.95c.**
In **Guru,** Washington psychologist Kopp distills the wisdom of gurus from many times and settings: from primitive tribes, ancient Greece and Rome, Judaism and Christianity, the Renaissance world and the Orient, even children's tales, science fiction, and the psychedelic scene. In the closing chapters, Dr. Kopp takes his place as a latter day guru with some profound thoughts on life and loving and change and death and rebirth. Kopp writes as he lives; directly with poetry, simply yet with profundity, mystically yet with immediacy, firmly yet with warmth.

KOPP, SHELDON. **THE HANGED MAN. Notes, bibliography, 256pp. S&B74, 7.95c.**
The theme of this personal account is that each of us has a dark side which we must get in touch with in order to become realized beings. *I would turn myself, my patients, and my readers toward those hidden unconscious recesses of ourselves, away from which we have been turned by science, civilization, and conventional wisdom.* Dr. Kopp uses a tarot card to highlight the subject of each chapter and he illustrates his narrative with myths, dreams, and stories from countless traditions and ages. He also presents case studies from his psychiatric practice. A well written, moving account.

KOPP, SHELDON. **IF YOU MEET THE BUDDHA ON THE ROAD, KILL HIM. 183pp. Ban72/SIP, 1.95p.**
This book, subtitled, *The Pilgrimage of Psychotherapy Patients,* uses the framework of the **Cantebury Tales** to recount the spiritual pilgrimages of people today, as seen by their therapist, and—in the course of all this—Kopp's own pilgrimage.

KOPP, SHELDON. **THE NAKED THERAPIST. Bibliography, 255pp. EdI76, 8.95c.**
An exploration of the phenomena of embarrassment and shame, documented and exemplified by some of Dr. Kopp's own personal and professional experiences and a collection of autobiographical descriptions of similar experiences of other psychotherapists.

KOPP, SHELDON. **NO HIDDEN MEANINGS. 9"x10", S&B75, 4.95p.**
Photographs by Claire Flanders illustrate Kopp's *An Eschatalogical Laundry List: A Partial Register of the 927 (or was it 928?) Eternal Truths.* Our poster of this (see illustration) has been one of our most popular items.

KOPP, SHELDON. **THIS SIDE OF TRAGEDY. Notes, index, 236pp. S&B77, 7.95c.**
Dr. Kopp uses the metaphor of theater to illustrate the funny, the foolish, and the profound stuff out of which our lives are made. He deftly weaves together the relationship between the sometimes dramatic, sometimes silly, sometimes tragic experiences of his patients and the corresponding occurrences that take place behind the footlights. As with all of Dr. Kopp's books, this one is masterfully written and contains profound insights into the human character.

KOVEL, JOEL. **A COMPLETE GUIDE TO THERAPY. Glossary, notes, index, 303pp. RaH76/Pen, 5.95c.**
As the title suggests, this is an exploration of a variety of therapies from psychoanalysis and behavioralism to transactional analysis, gestalt therapy, primal therapy, and many other contemporary movements. Dr. Kovel is a professor of psychiatry and he has written and lectured widely on the social implications of psychoanalysis. His precises of each of the therapies are objective and the historical origins and pros and cons of each are examined. Other aspects of the therapeutic relationship are also discussed.

R.D. Laing

R.D. Laing is one of the best known and most influential of the *anti-psychiatrists.* In his first work, **The Divided Self** (1960), he viewed much of *madness* not as a disease but as a reasonable adjustment to an unreasonable environment. In **Self and Others** and **Sanity, Madness and the Family,** he enlarged on this, looking at the schizophrenic family which created and cast out into a mental institution the young person who would not adapt to the doublebind situation forced upon him. By 1964 he began to view schizophrenia as one stage in a natural psychic healing process which, if successful, could lead to entry into a realm of *hyper-sanity.* Psychiatric medicine offered, at best, a mechanistic bungling of this potential process; at worst, it drove its patients insane with its chemicals, surgery and regimentation. Laing founded a therapeutic community at Kingsley Hall in London to provide a sympathetic setting for the patients' inner voyage. In his more recent writings, Laing has become both more socially committed and more mystical. He compares psychotic and psychedelic experiences. It is not the psychotic who has the split personality, it is the so-called *normal* person: alienation and splitting are indeed the basic conditions for our repressive normality and its apparatus of anti-human institutions. Laing thus can be seen as possibly the most influential spirit behind the whole radical therapy movement.

BARNES, MARY. **TWO ACCOUNTS OF A JOURNEY THROUGH MADNESS. Illustrations, notes, 374pp. RaH71, 1.95p.**
What an extremely rich book this is—how it combines a personal drama of redemption from "madness" with a profound revolutionary statement on how a free community of souls can interact for the good of its individuals; how it sets forth the theories of the charismatic R.D. Laing without reducing them to sterile syllogisms....But what I found particularly moving is the faith the book expresses in the resiliency of the human spirit; that no matter how damaged the soul, there remains a part of it that always grows toward wholeness...and that no behavior, however bizarre or seemingly empty it may seem, is without order and meaning or beyond the reach of love.—**The New York Times.**

BOYERS, ROBERT, et al. **R.D. LAING AND ANTI-PSYCHIATRY. 310pp. H&R71, 1.95p.**
A collection of serious essays about Laing's ideas and his influence.

COLLIER, ANDREW. **R.D. LAING: THE PHILOSOPHY AND POLITICS OF PSYCHOTHERAPY. Notes, bibliography, index, 224pp. RaH77, 3.95p.**
A critique of Laing's thought focusing on Laing's writings in relation to the three theoretical traditions from which it stems: Marxism, psychoanalysis, and existentialism.

EVANS, RICHARD. **R.D. LAING: THE MAN AND HIS IDEAS. Index, 255pp. Dut76, 3.95p.**
Transcription of a long dialogue Evans had with Laing in which Laing covers a wide range of subjects—his debt to Freud and Gregory Bateson, his true position on schizophrenia, mysticism as an aid to understanding, his concept of therapy as practiced at Kingsley Hall. Also includes a biographical essay by Peter Mezan and a hitherto unpublished study by Laing of Kallman and Slater's genetic theory of schizophrenia. Evans also provides a long introduction.

FRIEDENBERG, EDGAR. **R.D. LAING. Bibliography, index, 118pp. Vik73, 1.95p.**
A critical examination of Laing, part of the **Modern Masters** series, which discusses Laing's revolutionary theories and their implications not only in psychiatry but in politics and culture as well.

HOWARTH-WILLIAMS, MARTIN. **R.D. LAING: HIS WORK AND ITS RELEVANCE FOR SOCIOLOGY. Bibliography, index, 218pp. RKP77, 10.00p.**
A rigorous, comprehensive review of Laing's work and theoretical development. Howarth-Williams believes that Laing's insights into

such controversial issues as the divided self and the politics of the family are of an importance that transcends their basis in clinical psychiatry and that they have special significance for sociology. The author illuminates the internal coherence of Laing's aims through the various stages of his work and shows how his ideas have been shaped by consistent philosophical presuppositions and influences. He also explores Laing's involvement in nonpsychiatric realms such as politics and Eastern philosophy. The book reads like a PhD dissertation.

LAING, R.D. **CONVERSATIONS WITH ADAM AND NATASHA.** **158pp. RaH77/AlL, 6.95c.**
Transcriptions of dialogues between Laing and his two youngest children, designed to show how children's thoughts and personalities develop. There's nothing at all deep in the content, just an example of how the children react to various life situations.

LAING, R.D. **THE DIVIDED SELF. 218pp. Vik60, 2.50p.**
Laing's first book and the one most people consider his best. His basic desire is to make madness, and the process of going mad, comprehensible. A provocative study. If you're going to read just one Laing book, this is the one you should choose.

LAING, R.D. **DO YOU LOVE ME? 87pp. RaH76/Pen, 1.75p.**
Subtitled, *An Entertainment in Conversation and Verse*, this book resembles **Knots** more than any other of Laing's books. The emphasis, as always, is on the human situation on the level of the individual.

LAING, R.D. **THE FACTS OF LIFE. 153pp. RaH76/Pen, 1.95p.**
In this book I've tried to portray some facts of my life and world. What is here is sketches of my childhood, first questions, speculations, observations, reflections on conception, intra-uterine life, being born and giving birth: allusions to behavior and experience of adults which seem to belong to the same class as traumatic neuroses. They make us wonder: the adult content of the adult misery seems to have the form or mold of intra-uterine and birth catastrophes—can this be possible? I continue to muse over the ways in which structural configurations emerge into two sets of elements, mythological and embryological.

LAING, R.D. **KNOTS. 90pp. RaH70/Pen, 1.65p.**
They are playing a game. They are playing at not playing a game. If I show them I see they are, I shall break the rules and they will punish me. I must play their game, of not seeing I see the game. **Knots** is unlike any other book, consisting of a series of powerful, witty, unexpected, dialogue-scenarios, revealing Laing's insights into the intricacies of human relationships and the way we tie ourselves into knots.

LAING, R.D. **THE POLITICS OF EXPERIENCE. 190pp. RaH67/Pen, 1.95p.**
The condition of alienation, of being asleep, of being unconscious of being out of one's mind, is the condition of the normal man. Society highly values its normal man. It educates children to lose themselves and to become absurd, and thus to be normal. Normal men have killed perhaps 100,000,000 of their fellow men in the last fifty years. We are not able even to think adequately about the behavior that is at the annihilating edge. But what we think is less than what we know; what we know is less than what we love; what we love is so much less than what there is.

LAING, R.D. **SELF AND OTHERS. 192pp. Vik71, 2.50p.**
This is a thoroughly revised edition of a book originally published in 1962. In the first part Laing examines different modes of experience as forms of relationships. In the second part he considers key patterns of interaction, especially those which characterize certain key forms of disturbance.

LAING, R.D. and D.G. COOPER. **REASON AND VIOLENCE. 184pp. RaH64, 1.95p.**
This is an introduction to the thought of the great French existentialist, Jean-Paul Sartre. Laing and Cooper see in him one of the most radical thinkers of the century, a man who has brought about a revolution in man's understanding of himself.

LAING, R.D. and A. ESTERSON. **SANITY, MADNESS AND THE FAMILY. 282pp. Vik64, 2.95p.**
To prepare this report, Drs. Laing and Esterson conducted and recorded a series of interviews with eleven patients, drawing on parents and relatives. In this way the authors dramatically exposed the cross-currents of affection, hatred, and indifference within the family, which go far to explain the *why* of madness.

——————— **END OF R.D. LAING SUBSECTION** ———————

LAZARUS, ARNOLD. **IN THE MIND'S EYE. Index, 210pp. Ath78, 6.95c.**
A self-help treatise on *imagery therapy*, a technique pioneered by the author to help individuals direct their imagination and will and become more effective in life. Many case histories and step-by-step exercises are included.

LIBO, LESTER. **IS THERE LIFE AFTER GROUP? Bibliography, index, 148pp. Dou77, 1.95p.**
What a refreshing delight to find a knowledgeable, thoughtful book on encounter. After the rash of archly condescending, put down books written by people with scant acquaintance with the field, it is a pleasure to read Lester Libo's wise, informed account of his extensive experience with this valuable social phenomenon. . . . He has taken a major step toward restoring encounter to its important place in the human quest. A splendid book.—Will Schutz.

LUCE, GAY GAER. **BODY TIME. 3.30p.**
See the Biorhythms section.

LUTHMAN, SHIRLEY. **DYNAMIC FAMILY. Bibliography, 250pp. S&B74, 7.95c.**
A practical text on family therapy by a student of Virginia Satir, rich with examples, anecdotes, and case histories drawn from the author's professional experience. The book begins with a discussion of her theories on growth, both individual and within the family context. The next sections review treatment concepts and techniques. Final sections discuss the development of the family therapist and give many practical ideas.

MCWATERS, BARRY, ed. **HUMANISTIC PERSPECTIVES: CURRENT TRENDS IN PSYCHOLOGY. Index, 256pp. Wad77, 9.35p.**
A collection of fairly specialized essays grouped under the following headings: *Broadening Images of the Self, New Modes of Being Together,* and *Emerging Sociocultural Forms.*

Abraham Maslow

Maslow, who died in 1970, is regarded as the father of humanistic psychology and the human potential movement. He had the revolutionary idea of studying the healthiest people he could find—rather than the most neurotic ones. As he once said, *mankind, throughout history, has looked for guiding values, for principles of right and wrong. But he has tended to look outside of mankind, to a God, to some sort of sacred book perhaps, or to a ruling class. What I am doing is exploring the theory that you can find the values by which mankind must live, and for which man has always sought, by digging into the best people in depth....If under the best conditions and in the best specimens, I simply stand aside and describe in a scientific way what these human values are, I find values that are old values of truth, goodness and beauty, and some additional ones as well—for instance, gaiety, justice, and joy.*

GOBLE, FRANK. **THE THIRD FORCE—THE PSYCHOLOGY OF ABRAHAM MASLOW. 222pp. Vik70, 8.95c.**
This is a condensation of Maslow's ideas, distilled from his five books and over a hundred articles, in language understandable to the layman. It is a good place to start in studying Maslow and humanistic psychology. Maslow coined the term *third force psychology* to distinguish it from the Freudian and behavioristic approaches.

MASLOW, ABRAHAM. **THE FARTHER REACHES OF HUMAN NATURE. 429pp. Vik71, 2.95p.**
This first posthumous work serves as an extension of Maslow's classic **Toward a Psychology of Being**. It is a wide ranging synthesis of his inspiring and influential ideas on biology, synergy, creativity, cognition, the hierarchy of needs, and the role of science in the expanding study of human nature. In this book he has touched upon all the key concepts of his work and life over the past forty years.

MASLOW, ABRAHAM. **MOTIVATION AND PERSONALITY. Notes, bibliography, indices, 399pp. H&R70, 15.45p.**
A fully revised edition of Maslow's classic work on what he terms self actualization theory. This is a technical work and is appropriate only for those well versed in personality theory and humanistic psychology.

MASLOW, ABRAHAM. **RELIGIONS, VALUES, PEAK EXPERIENCES. 131pp. Vik64, 1.95p.**
Argues that the religious experience is a rightful subject for scientific investigation and, conversely, the scientific community will see its work enhanced by acknowledging and studying the species-wide need for spiritual expression which, in so many forms, is at the heart of *peak experiences* reached by healthy, fully functioning persons.

■ MASLOW, ABRAHAM. **TOWARD A PSYCHOLOGY OF BEING. 250pp. Lit68, 4.95p.**
This is Maslow's basic book. We recommend it highly to all those interested in self-actualization and growth.

WILSON, COLIN. **NEW PATHWAYS IN PSYCHOLOGY: MASLOW AND THE POST-FREUDIAN REVOLUTION. 268pp. NAL72/Glz, 1.95p.**
Wilson considers Maslow second in importance only to Freud among twentieth century psychologists. To place Maslow in his proper professional perspective, Wilson surveys the history of psychology from David Hume through Freud and Jung, placing special emphasis on Maslow's true forerunner, William James, who recognized that *higher* forms of consciousness are natural to man. After discussing Maslow's life and ideas, he also surveys the work of Frankl, Assagioli and other post-Freudian psychologists.

——— END OF ABRAHAM MASLOW SUBSECTION ———

MAY, GERALD. **SIMPLY SANE. 130pp. Pau77, 7.95c.**
May is a practicing psychiatrist. He says that this book describes *an almost universal human myth...which says that people are objects, to be built, fixed, improved upon, and that life is a ladder of achievement, accomplishment and attainment. The book emphasizes how this myth has led countless people into seemingly interminable struggle and despair. He also says that psychotherapy is a child of the* myth, and also has helped to foster it, and he discusses ways in which we can live fuller, more satisfying, and less complicated lives.

MAY, ROLLO. **THE COURAGE TO CREATE. Notes, 143pp. Ban75/WCS, 1.95p.**
All my life I have been haunted by the fascinating questions of creativity. Why does an original idea in art and science "pop up" from the unconscious at a given moment? What is the relation between talent and the creative act, and between creativity and death?....I have asked these questions not as one who stands on the sidelines, but as one who himself participates in art and science....These chapters are a partial record of my ponderings. They had their birth as lectures given at colleges and universities. I had always hesitated to publish them because they seemed incomplete—the mystery of creation still remained. I then realized that this "unfinished" quality would always remain, and that it is part of the creative process itself.

MAY, ROLLO, ed. **EXISTENCE. 445pp. S&S58, 3.95p.**
Regarded as the most important, complete and lucid account of the existentialist approach to psychology. Classic case histories and writings of the leading spokesmen of the existential analytic movement have been selected to define the approach which seeks to understand mental illnesses not as deviations from the conceptual yardstick of the psychiatrist but as deviations in the structure of the particular patient's existence.

MAY, ROLLO, ed. **EXISTENTIAL PSYCHOLOGY. Exhaustive annotated bibliography, 126pp. RaH69, 4.35p.**
A collection of fairly technical essays by May, Herman Feifel, Abraham Maslow, Carl Rogers, and Gordon Allport.

MAY, ROLLO. **LOVE AND WILL. 352pp. Del69/Fon, 3.95p.**
The heart of our dilemma, according to May, is our failure to understand the real meanings of love and will, their sources, and their interrelation. An important book.

MAY, ROLLO. **MAN'S SEARCH FOR HIMSELF. 239pp. Del53/Sou, 3.95p.**
Here May examines the neuroses afflicting modern men and women. With uncommon wisdom he probes the hidden layers of personality to reveal the core of man's integration—the ability to choose, judge, and act.

MAY, ROLLO. **THE MEANING OF ANXIETY. Bibliography, index, 445pp. Nor77, 12.95c.**
Since the first edition of this book appeared in 1950, there has been an enormous amount of research and interest in anxiety....Our knowledge has increased but we have not learned to deal with [anxiety]. Though the concept of normal anxiety, as advanced in the first edition..., has been generally accepted, the implications of it have not been faced....Anxiety has a meaning. Though part of this meaning can be destructive, another part can also be constructive....I believe a bold theory is necessary....I propose that this theory be founded on the definition that anxiety is the "experience of Being affirming itself against Nonbeing." The latter is that which would reduce or destroy Being, such as aggression, fatigue, boredom, and ultimately death. I have rewritten this book in the hope that its publication will aid in the forming of this theory of anxiety.

MAY, ROLLO. **POWER AND INNOCENCE. Notes, index, 283pp. Del72/Fon, 2.95p.**
Dr. May argues that powerlessness is just as corrupting as is power—when people feel impotent they are likely to become either violent or sick. This lies at the root of the rise of violence in our society. We have made a virtue of powerlessness because we have been in the habit of thinking of power only in its negative forms—in terms of aggressors and victims. But, Dr. May shows, *power is the birthright of every human being. It is the source of his self-esteem and the root of his conviction that he is...significant.*

MAY, ROLLO. **PSYCHOLOGY AND THE HUMAN DILEMMA. Notes, 221pp. Lit67, 5.50p.**
These essays, most of which were written in the past four years, have a common theme. It arises out of the great variety, richness, and span of human experience—a vast spectrum shown, for example, by man's capacity for admirable reason on the one hand and the far reach of his irrational behavior on the other, the joy and productivity of which he is capable and his ever-present proclivity for despair and self-defeat. The very extent and range of this spectrum, I propose, introduces certain distinguishing characteristics into human consciousness, some of which we shall discuss in this book under the term "dilemma"....The word "dilemma" is not used here in its technical sense....I use it rather as referring to polarity or paradox.—from the foreword.

MAYEROFF, MILTON. **ON CARING. 106pp. H&R71, 1.50p.**
To care for another person, in the most significant sense, is to help him grow and actualize himself. . . . Through caring for certain others, by serving them through caring, a man lives the meaning of his own life. In the sense in which a man can ever be said to be at home in the world, he is at home not through dominating, or explaining, or appreciating, but through caring and being cared for. This small book is destined to become a classic.

MISSILDINE, HUGH. **YOUR INNER CHILD OF THE PAST. 317pp. S&S63, 9.95c.**
Somewhere, sometime, you were a child. This is one of the great obvious, seemingly meaningless and forgotten common denominators of adult life. . . . Your childhood, in an actual, literal sense, exists within you now. It affects everything you do, everything you feel. These childhood feelings and attitudes influence, often actually determine and dominate your relations. . . . They can interfere with your ability to work or to love. Such feelings may be a significant part of your fatigue, your inability to relax, your irritating headaches, your upset stomach. . . . The child you once were can balk or frustrate your adult satisfactions, embarrass and harass you, make you sick—or enrich your life. This is a detailed exploration, based on Dr. Missildine's extensive study and experience.

MISSILDINE, HUGH and LAWRENCE GALTON. **YOUR INNER CONFLICTS—HOW TO SOLVE THEM. 345pp. S&S74, 8.95c.**
A development of the material in Dr. Missildine's earlier book. Patterns of living and being as well as of experience are identified and specific suggestions are made for counteracting each pattern. Guidelines are presented for achieving an awakened sense of self-confidence and the freedom to explore and develop abilities and talents and to pursue more meaningful relationships.

MONTAGU, ASHLEY. **TOUCHING. Notes, index, 395pp. H&R78, 10.00c.**
This book is about the skin as a tactile organ very much involved, not only physically but also behaviorally, in the growth and development of the organism. The central referent is man, and what happens or fails to happen to him as an infant by way of tactile experience, as affecting his subsequent behavioral development, is my principal concern here. . . . The first edition of this book has gratifyingly found a large audience. The present edition incorporates much new information concerning the vital importance of touch from birth to old age.—from the preface.

MOUSTAKAS, CLARK. **CREATIVITY AND CONFORMITY. Notes, index, 157pp. Lit67, 5.00p.**
This book takes a stand in behalf of individuality and creativity and discusses the consequences of widespread conformity in modern life. An effort is made to evolve a meaningful understanding of creativity, self-growth, and self-renewal and to show that significant strides in knowledge and awareness are essentially the reflection of a light which is kindled from within the self and not from external sources.—from the foreword.

MOUSTAKAS, CLARK. **FINDING YOURSELF, FINDING OTHERS. 120pp. PrH74, 3.95p.**
This illustrated, oversized volume contains quotations from leading figures in the human potential movement.

MOUSTAKAS, CLARK. **LONELINESS. 107pp. PrH61, 2.95p.**
Loneliness is an intrinsic condition of human existence. This study of existential loneliness reveals that—beyond the first pangs of desolation, out of the terror of despair—human beings have found a key to deeper insight and keen perception of the world in which they live. Moustakas encourages the reader to make a penetrating investigation of his own solitude.

MOUSTAKAS, CLARK. **LONELINESS AND LOVE. 146pp. PrH72, 2.45p.**
Reveals how periods of loneliness and solitude can help a person move toward more authenticity, more honesty, and therefore more meaningful love relationships with his fellow human beings.

MOUSTAKAS, CLARK, ed. **PORTRAITS OF LONELINESS AND LOVE. Oversize, 95pp. PrH74, 2.95p.**
A blend of photographs and sensitive poetry and prose which evokes the depth and impact of the emotions we experience. Most of the writing is Moustakas'.

MOUSTAKAS, CLARK, ed. **THE SELF: EXPLORATIONS IN PERSONAL GROWTH. 302pp. H&R56, 3.95p.**
A collection of essays by Erich Fromm, Gordon Allport, Karen Horney,

C.G. Jung, A.H. Maslow, Carl Rogers, and others which, according to Moustakas, *portrays the fundamental unity of personality and presents a framework for understanding healthy behavior. The emphasis is on knowing, exploring, and actualizing the self.*

MOUSTAKAS, CLARK. **THE TOUCH OF LONELINESS. 112pp. PrH75, 2.45p.**
Dr. Moustakas definitely seems to be guilty of writing the same book over and over again. This is his newest attempt. It is a collection of letters received by the author in response to his earlier books—letters which detail many individuals' experience of loneliness. Also included are some letters Moustakas wrote to himself in times of crisis and a review of his own recent experiences with loneliness.

MOUSTAKAS, CLARK. **TURNING POINTS. Notes, 133pp. PrH77, 3.45p.**
Moustakas views turning points as times of crisis and challenge which significantly alter the world in which a person lives. This book contains accounts of Moustakas' own experiences and the experiences of others and offers insights into the universal feelings of loneliness, fear, and self doubt that often accompany change. He suggests ways in which we can benefit from these turning points.

MURPHY, GARDNER. **HUMAN POTENTIALITIES. Notes, bibliography, index, 352pp. Vik58, 3.95p.**
Dr. Murphy, a leading psychologist, traces the development of man from the simple, biologically motivated mammalian, through the more complex organism evolving from interaction with its cultural mold, to the next stage of human growth in which, Dr. Murphy foresees, man's creative drive will transcend his biological and cultural inheritances to open the way for a broad, free expression of his capacity for love and knowledge. This is a fairly technical account which is definitely not light reading.

MURPHY, GARDNER and MORTON LEEDS. **OUTGROWING SELF-DECEPTION. Bibliography, index, 175pp. H&R75, 13.45c.**
An exploration of techniques for testing one's assumptions about oneself and the world—from everyday methods (such as logic and learning to listen to what others are telling you) to more specialized approaches, such as analysis, biofeedback, sensitivity training, yoga, Eastern philosophy. In addition the authors examine the lives of men who *changed the world*—Freud, Darwin, Einstein, and others—showing the methods they used to confront (and triumph over) their own self deceptions.

MURPHY, GARDNER and LOIS, eds. **ASIAN PSYCHOLOGY. 3.95p.**
See the Comparative Religion section.

NARANJO, CLAUDIO and ROBERT ORNSTEIN. **ON THE PSYCHOLOGY OF MEDITATION. Vik71/A&U, 2.50p.**
See the Meditation section.

O'CONNOR, ELIZABETH. **OUR MANY SELVES: A HANDBOOK FOR SELF DISCOVERY. 201pp. H&R71, 3.95p.**
Written from a Christian activist point of view, this book contains a series of practical exercises to help the reader understand his or her own life and evolve a program of continuing growth. On the path to self realization, the book moves from confession, to identification with those one has criticized, to creative suffering. The author's comments are buttressed by readings from a wide range of sources which integrate the findings of contemporary psychology with ancient discoveries in the life of the spirit.

O'NEILL, NENA and GEORGE. **OPEN MARRIAGE. Notes, bibliography, 286pp. Avo72/SBL, 2.25p.**
This book came out when the idea of open marriage was just beginning to be discussed in the media. It was an immediate best seller and has remained a popular book, although the ideas it expresses are today not the slightest bit revolutionary. The O'Neill's got divorced recently, so their *open marriage* did not seem to work.

O'NEILL, NENA and GEORGE. **SHIFTING GEARS. Notes, bibliography, 280pp. Avo74, 1.95p.**
A popular account which gives practical guidelines and advice on achieving your full potential in today's rapidly changing world, by making crucial changes in yourself, your relationships, your job, and your whole way of life. In short, how you can keep growing. The advice is often simplistic, but many have found it to be helpful.

OTTO, HERBERT, ed. **LOVE TODAY.** 272pp. Del72, 2.75p.
Love Today had its beginnings when the American Psychological Association undertook the study of love in the twentieth century and chose *Love as a Growth Experience* for the theme of a recent annual meeting. Twenty professionals from various disciplines were invited to examine the meaning of love and this is a transcription of these papers.

OTTO, HERBERT and JOHN MANN, eds. **WAYS OF GROWTH—APPROACHES TO EXPLORING AWARENESS.** 229pp. Vik68, 2.95p.
A collection of various articles: general personal expressions on the theme; accounts of new methods requiring professional background and training before they can be successfully applied; and approaches that the reader can directly apply to his own life. Most of the authors come out of the human potential movement.

PESSO, ALBERT. **EXPERIENCE IN ACTION.** 270pp. NYU73, 13.10c.
A description of psychomotor therapy, a technique developed by Pesso and his wife Diane. Psychomotor can be described as follows: movement is isolated into three modalities—reflex, voluntary, and emotional—and accommodators, usually other group members, provide an appropriate responding environment that encourages emotional free association. Since most of the material that emerges relates to the past and to parents, the negative accommodators represent negative aspects of the parents, while the positive accommodators represent new archetypal parents. This provides a structure within which catharsis may be achieved followed by new and more positive experiences. This volume presents psychomotor theories, illustrated with examples from actual sessions.

PESSO, ALBERT. **MOVEMENT IN PSYCHOLOGY.** 233pp. NYU69, 13.10c.
The basic book of psychomotor, outlining the theories and the techniques. Neither of the Pesso books is easy to read and we have a hard time following what is being presented. If you are familiar with the technique, the books will probably be quite helpful.

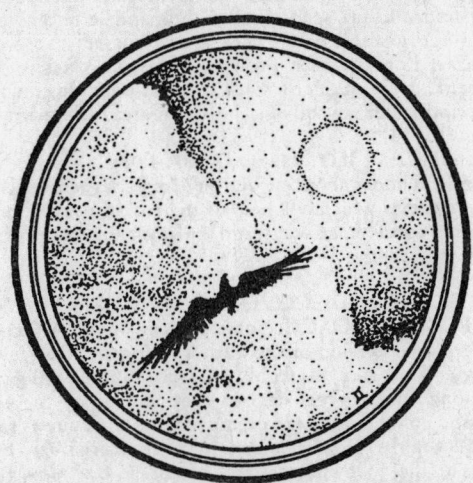

fears, and incestuous fantasies that link family members to each other and are apt to cause psychological distress at pivotal points in the life cycles of families. Pincus and Dare have been associated for many years with the work of the Tavistock Clinic in London. In this book they develop an important new perspective for understanding the emotional patterns of family life and draw on many therapeutic case histories.

PIAGET, JEAN. **MAIN TRENDS IN PSYCHOLOGY.** 72pp. H&R70, 2.00p.
Does the mind retain its own identity independent of its biological origins and its involvement with society, or is its reality inevitably confined to these two connecting areas?....These are the two problems which we shall find underlying all the perspectives and it is for me a great privilege to present them. Small type.

PINCUS, LILY and CHRISTOPHER DARE. **SECRETS IN THE FAMILY.** Notes, index, 159pp. RaH78, 8.95c.
The authors focus on the network of unconscious beliefs, longings,

PRATHER, HUGH. **I TOUCH THE EARTH, THE EARTH TOUCHES ME.** Dou72, 2.95p.
This book, like the one which preceded it, evolved....The entries...exhibit the same curious pattern I saw in my last book: that every time I think I have learned something, my life seems to deliberately set about contradicting it. Yet the contradiction is never absolute; it is more a quarter turn than a whole. And so I am left with this belief: that there are no answers, only alternatives.

PRATHER, HUGH. **NOTES ON LOVE AND COURAGE.** Dou77, 3.95p.
Another selection of Prather's highly personal diary entries, written in poetic form. Those who liked his earlier books will be equally moved by this one.

PRATHER, HUGH. **NOTES TO MYSELF.** Ban70/LyP, 1.95p.
Cogent and incisive short paragraphs, personal yet general, about living, feelings and experience, behavior and relationships. These serve both as beginnings for the reader's exploration of his own experiences, and as thoughtful and insightful reminders about them.

ROGERS, CARL. **A THERAPIST'S VIEW OF PERSONAL GOALS.** 30pp. PHP60, 1.20p.
Dr Rogers is best known for his development of *client-centered therapy*, an approach in which the patient is considered a person capable of the growth necessary to realize certain potentials inherent in the human being. The goal of Rogerian therapy is self-actualization. Rogers also made a comprehensive study of the patient-therapist relationship and outlined a methodology and process of group therapy. He is one of the most important figures in the human potential movement. This pamphlet contains a transcription of a lecture on the title theme.

ROGERS, CARL. **BECOMING PARTNERS: MARRIAGE AND ITS ALTERNATIVES.** Annotated bibliography, 243pp. Del72/Con, 3.25p.
This is a transcription of a series of interviews done by Dr. Rogers. They have been edited slightly and arranged to give the reader a series of perceptions of relationships, breakdowns, and restructurings in a wide variety of partnerships, both traditional and nontraditional. Dr. Rogers comments briefly on each situation.

ROGERS, CARL. **CLIENT-CENTERED THERAPY: ITS CURRENT PRACTICE, IMPLICATIONS, AND THEORY.** Notes, index, 572pp. HMC51/Con, 13.35p.
In this book there is a clear exposition of procedures by means of which individuals who are being counseled may be assisted in achieving for themselves new and more effective personality adjustments. It deals with the nature of this important and subtle therapeutic process and with related counseling problems. This is not a static guidebook to monuments of past thinking. It is rather a current synthesis and a dynamic integration of successful techniques of general counseling and of counseling procedures in special situations.—from the introduction.

■ *ROGERS, CARL.* **ON BECOMING A PERSON.** 424pp. HMC61/Con, 4.95p.
In the few years since it was first published, this study of personal growth and creativity has established itself as a classic work, posing such fundamental questions as: What is the meaning of personal growth? Under what conditions is growth possible? How can one person help another? What is creativity and how can it be fostered?

ROGERS, CARL. **ON ENCOUNTER GROUPS.** 174pp. H&R70/Pen, 2.50p.
Clear, lucid, simple, evocative, Carl Rogers' book is the only one that I have seen that communicates to the layman what an encounter group is, what it looks like, what it feels like, what the different approaches are about. This is a beautiful and straightforward book. It is far and away the best general book on encounter groups in existence. Everything I ever wanted to say to a group leader or to a prospective member is here.—Philip E. Slater.

ROGERS, CARL. **CARL ROGERS ON PERSONAL POWER.** Notes, 299pp. Del77/Con, 4.95p.
Throughout his career as a therapist, Rogers has found that when people come in contact with and accept their inner strength, exciting new ways of living emerge. When they are trusted to make choices, and find the courage to make responsible decisions, they begin to change their worlds. In this book Dr. Rogers presents case histories of many people who have been able to tap that power, moving through obstacles and becoming as alive and creative as they were born to be.

He discusses what factors help release personal potential and challenges the usual concepts on which our society is based—that power is power *over*, that strength is the strength to *control*. This is the most important of Rogers' recent books.

ROGERS, CARL and BARRY STEVENS. **PERSON TO PERSON: THE PROBLEM OF BEING HUMAN. 293pp. S&S67/Sou, 3.00p/1.95p.**
This book is intended for anyone who is interested in it: anyone who is not interested should not read it. That is a simple statement of what this book is chiefly about: the importance of choosing for ourselves, regardless of what anyone else tells us is good or bad.

ROSE, ANTHONY and ANDRE AUW. **GROWING UP HUMAN. 125pp. H&R74, 2.25p.**
This is primarily a practical book. Nonetheless there are some theoretical threads weaving through it. Foremost is our unbending faith in the worthiness of the person....Out of this...grows a series of correlative assumptions: that the individual is educable, that relationships are resilient, that transcendence is within reach. The book begins with chapters on seeking and on trust. These are followed by chapters on the individual, relationships, and community. The material is well written and a great number of exercises accompany the text. The exercises themselves are clearly presented and quite unusual.

ROWAN, JOHN. **ORDINARY ECSTASY. HUMANISTIC PSYCHOLOGY IN ACTION. Index, 234pp. RKP76, 3.75p.**
Rowan was trained as a social psychologist and he is currently chairperson of the Association for Humanistic Psychology in the United Kingdom. This is a dry study of the field of humanistic psychology. The book reads like a PhD dissertation and is organized like one—perhaps it even is one. It is typed rather than typeset and includes a large number of annotated references and bibliographical notes. Rowan discusses the major theories underlying the humanistic psychology movement and their application in eight different fields. Many examples are cited, most from British cases.

RUBIN, THEODORE. **THE ANGRY BOOK. 223pp. McM69, 1.95p.**
This book by a former president of the American Institute of Psychoanalysis urges people to get out their anger rather than repress it and possibly cause depression, insomnia, psychosomatic illness, frigidity, etc. Simply and soundly written.

SATIR, VIRGINIA. **CONJOINT FAMILY THERAPY. Bibliography, index, 220pp. S&B67, 8.00p.**
This is a revised edition of Ms. Satir's first book. The material is geared toward teaching and training in the field of family practice. It is a fairly technical work which includes a great deal of anecdotal as well as practical material.

SATIR, VIRGINIA. **MAKING CONTACT. CeA76, 3.95p.**
Ms. Satir is generally considered the finest family therapist practicing in the U.S. today. She has devised a number of innovative techniques which are used throughout the therapeutic community. This is a lovely book which explores ways in which people contact each other and suggests ways that these contacts can be more positive. A number of techniques developed in her workshops are included along with some sound philosophical suggestions and poetic principles. A practical compendium which is also an inspiration and a joy to read.

SATIR, VIRGINIA. **PEOPLEMAKING. 306pp. S&B72, 5.95p.**
The book is written so clearly, and with so much humanity, that it will be useful to the layman as well as the professional. In simple language free of jargon Satir presents her concepts about self-worth, communication, and the family in the form of case histories, anecdotes, and a strikingly effective series of communication games that illuminate her research findings.—**Psychotherapy and Social Science Review**.

SATIR, VIRGINIA. **SELF ESTEEM. Handwritten, CeA75, 2.95p.**
Illustrated, schmaltzy poems like the following: *When I review later how I looked and sounded, what I said and did, and how I thought and felt, some parts may turn out to be unfitting.*

SCHEFLEN, ALBERT. **BODY LANGUAGE AND SOCIAL ORDER. 210pp. PrH72, 3.45p.**
Through text and many photographs, Scheflen shows that body language, combined with spoken language, primarily serves to control human behavior and maintain the social order. He describes greeting, courting, and other social behavior and analyzes how territorial and dominance behavior determine the mobility of individuals and groups within the social hierarchy.

SCHULTZ, D. **GROWTH PSYCHOLOGY. Notes, 156pp. Lit77, 5.50p.**
This textbook focuses on the theoretical rationales or models that attempt to define the nature of the healthy personality. It is intended as a supplementary text for courses in personal adjustment and for those who are interested in a nontechnical introduction to the healthy personality as seen through humanistic psychology. Seven models of the healthy personality are discussed: those of Gordon Allport, Carl Rogers, Erich Fromm, Abraham Maslow, Carl Jung, Viktor Frankl, and Fritz Perls. Each theorist offers his unique view of and prescription for psychological growth and fulfillment.

SCHUTZ, WILLIAM. **JOY. 252pp. Grv67, 1.95p.**
One of the first books about encounter groups, largely concerned with methods or games which will help us to break through our defenses, rigidities, and accustomed ways, and find joy in new ways of relating to ourselves and others.

SEVERIN, FRANK, ed. **DISCOVERING MAN IN PSYCHOLOGY: A HUMANISTIC APPROACH. Notes, indices, 344pp. MGH73, 10.70p.**
A greatly revised version of the author's **Humanistic Viewpoints in Psychology**. This is a textbook, incorporating readings by many experts along with a great deal of commentary by the editor. The readings and commentary are organized in a continuous fashion and the result is a fairly readable document. Severin organizes his material according to the following general headings: *Underdeveloped Areas in Psychology, An Image of Man, Values in Psychology,* and *In Search of a Human Science.* Bibliographies and discussion topics follow each chapter.

SHAPIRO, STEPHEN and HILARY TYRKA. **TRUSTING YOURSELF: PSYCHOTHERAPY AS A BEGINNING. Bibliography, 127pp. PrH76, 2.45p.**
An exposition of the role of therapy and of the client-therapist relationship. *The biggest step we can take toward knowing and trusting ourselves is trusting another person to help us. This book is no substitute for that step. Rather, it helps clarify why we cannot just look at ourselves, read books, and change.*

SHEPARD, MARTIN. **THE DO-IT-YOURSELF PSYCHOTHERAPY BOOK. 178pp. Dut73, 3.95p.**
This is a helpful book, written for people interested in growth and for unhappy people who might be tempted to try helping themselves before they pay somebody to help them. The advice throughout is simple and sound and there are many neat exercises. The book is written in a humorous vein and this helps us to grow and not to dwell on our sorrows.

SHOSTROM, EVERETT. **FREEDOM TO BE.** Bibliography, index, 173pp. Ban72, 1.75p.
Most of us, because of early experiences, have cut off one or more of the polarities in our attempts to experience and express ourselves. Whereas being self-actualized may be defined as the total expression of our unique beings, most of us are only partial in this ability to be fully ourselves. Hopefully, however, this book can help us to become more total in our expression, to become more and more self-actualizing.—from the introduction.

SHOSTROM, EVERETT. **MAN THE MANIPULATOR.** Bibliography, index, 205pp. Ban67, 1.95p.
According to Shostrom, man is a manipulator who needs to become aware of the manipulative styles of relating to others. He is also a person who needs therapeutic goals which are comprehensible and which will motivate and excite him to live his life to its fullest potential. This book attempts to provide a model which meets these two needs. *I believe that this is a significant book. Laymen and professionals alike will find it interesting and challenging. I believe this book will serve as a layman's guide to many of the principles of gestalt therapy....I am proud to have been [Dr. Shostrom's] teacher and therapist.*—Fritz Perls.

SIEGLER, MIRIAM and HUMPHREY OSMOND. **MODELS OF MADNESS, MODELS OF MEDICINE.** Notes, index, 254pp. H&R74, 2.95p.
It is a valuable book for, like a good road map, it lays out before the reader all the alternative routes which may be taken to understanding "mental illness"....The reader is left with the feeling that he understands more after finishing the book, something which can be said about few books in this field.—E. Fuller Torrey.

SMITH, GERALD. **COUPLE THERAPY.** 150pp. McM71, 1.95p.
Contains forty-seven exercises the author has used with married couples at Esalen and elsewhere. For example, asking a couple to plan something together, like what to do Sunday afternoon, reveals how they deal with power, who is in charge, how they communicate, etc. This last is a central concern of the book.

SPITZER, ROBERT, ed. **TIDINGS OF COMFORT AND JOY.** 305pp. S&B75, 4.95p.
Dr. Spitzer is the publisher of Science and Behavior Books. In this anthology he contributes two lengthy essays about contemporary world problems and presents excerpts from the following Science and Behavior books: Virginia Satir's **Peoplemaking,** Fritz Perls' **The Gestalt Approach and Eyewitness to Therapy,** Raven Lang's **The Birth Book,** and Sheldon Kopp's **If You Meet the Buddha on the Road, Kill Him.**

STEINER, CLAUDE, ed. **READINGS IN RADICAL PSYCHIATRY.** Index, notes, 202pp. RaH75, 4.95p.
Dr. Steiner's *Manifesto* signaled the emergence of a new group of radical psychiatrists on the West Coast who challenge the most cherished beliefs and practices of extended individual psychotherapy still so widely used today. This group, which has been gaining increasing attention, developed its ideas and recorded its experiences in its own publication, **The Radical Therapist.** The most seminal of the writings which appeared in this publication have been collected in this anthology.

SUGERMAN, SHIRLEY. **SIN AND MADNESS: STUDIES IN NARCISSISM.** Notes, bibliography, index, 184pp. Wes76, 5.95p.
[My] studies in the self have led me to an understanding of sin, as it is traditionally defined, and madness, in a more contemporary idiom, as correlative modes that reflect the human situation in a similar way. Later Eastern studies suggested images of man that relate to and reflect a similar understanding of the human condition and of man's existential relationship to being....Furthermore, psychoanalytic work and studies over a long period of time led to the practical, concrete, and specific understanding of our condition as narcissism, as well as to the therapeutic possibilities inherent in that understanding. Finally, all the paths that I followed in my search for understanding led to the image of Narcissus as the metaphor of the human condition....My awareness of these deep connections and my desire to put all the strands together...have resulted in this volume.—from the preface.

SUTICH, ANTHONY and MILES VICH, eds. **READINGS IN HUMANISTIC PSYCHOLOGY.** Notes, bibliography, index, 455pp. McM69, 6.65p.
A collection of twenty-four articles, the majority of which were originally published in the **Journal of Humanistic Psychology.**

SZASZ, THOMAS. **THE MANUFACTURE OF MADNESS.** Extensive bibliography, index, 383pp. H&R70, 3.45p.
It is widely believed today that just as some people suffer from diseases of the liver or kidney, others suffer from diseases of the mind...and that "mental patients" because of their supposed incapacity to "know what is in their best interests," must be cared for by their families or the state, even if that care requires interventions imposed on them against their will....In vain does the alleged madman...reject treatment and hospitalization as forms of torture and imprisonment; his refusal to submit to psychiatric authority is regarded as a further sign of his madness. In this medical rejection of the Other as a madman, we recognize...his former religious rejection as a heretic.—from the preface. Szasz and Laing are the two strongest voices urging us to view madness as a socially determined disease. This is a serious, careful, and well documented study comparing our present treatment of madness with our former treatment of witches. *In actuality, Institutional Psychiatry is a continuation of the Inquisition. All that has really changed is the vocabulary and the social style...the only hope for remedying the problem of "mental illness" lies in weakening—not in strengthening—the power of Institutional Psychiatry. Only when this peculiar institution is abolished will the moral powers of uncoerced psychotherapy be released.*

SZASZ, THOMAS. **THE MYTH OF PSYCHOTHERAPY.** Notes, index, 260pp. Dou78, 8.95c.
In this volume Dr. Szasz, a practicing psychiatrist, turns his attention to psychotherapy. He believes that it is both illogical and immoral to classify psychotherapy as a medical treatment. Shedding new light on the work of Freud and Jung, he demonstrates that what we now call psychotherapy is actually religion, or rhetoric, or repression, or a combination of all three. He shows how what was once regarded as the cure of sinful souls has been transformed into the cure of sick minds. He feels that we should return psychotherapy to its original and rightful place as the *talking cure.* A provocative analysis which raises some important questions.

SZASZ, THOMAS. **SCHIZOPHRENIA. Notes, technical appendices, index, 251pp. H&R76, 10.00c.**
In this book I shall try to show how schizophrenia has become the Christ on the cross that psychiatrists worship, and in whose name they march in battle to reconquer reason from unreason, sanity from insanity; how reverence toward it has become the mark of psychiatric orthodoxy, and irreverence toward it the mark of psychiatric heresy; and how our understanding of both psychiatry and schizophrenia may be advanced by approaching this "diagnosis" as if it pointed to a religious symbol rather than to a medical disease.

TORREY, E. FULLER. **THE DEATH OF PSYCHIATRY. Notes, bibliography, index, 234pp. Vik74, 2.50p.**
Dr. Torrey presents a reasoned review of the mythology of mental illness and the persecutory practices of psychiatry....His work should help to make psychiatric barbarities couched in the idiom and imagery of mental care morally more distasteful and hence politically less useful. I commend his courage and recommend his book.—Thomas Szasz, M.D.

Transactional Analysis

The unit of social intercourse is called a transaction. If two or more people encounter each other in a social aggregation, sooner or later one of them will speak, or give some other indication of acknowledging the presence of the others. This is called the *transactional stimulus*. Another person will then say or do something which is in some way related to this stimulus, and this is called the *transactional response*. Simple transactional analysis is concerned with diagnosing which ego state implemented the transactional stimulus, and which one executed the transactional response. The simplest transactions are those in which both stimulus and response arise from the Adults of the parties concerned....Next in simplicity are Child-Parent transactions....Both of these transactions are *complementary*; that is, the response is appropriate and expected and follows the natural order of healthy human relationships....The first rule of communication is that communication will proceed smoothly as long as transactions are complementary...[and] communication is broken off when a *crossed transaction* occurs.

—condensed from **Games People Play***, by Eric Berne*

BARNES, GRAHAM, ed. **TRANSACTIONAL ANALYSIS AFTER ERIC BERNE. Notes, index, 558pp. H&R77, 15.50c.**
This book documents the growth and developments in transactional analysis that have taken place since Berne's death in 1970. In this authoritative work, leaders of the classical, cathexis, and redecision schools have contributed separate chapters, each of which explains a particular theoretical orientation and clinical approach. Chapters by other authors reveal how they have drawn upon, moved beyond, or passed over the teachings and practices of the schools in their personal and professional development.

BERNE, ERIC. **BEYOND GAMES AND SCRIPTS. Illustrations, annotated bibliography, glossary, 352pp. Ban76, 2.50p.**
A one volume selection of Berne's major writings on transactional analysis which covers the entire range of his ideas.

BERNE, ERIC. **GAMES PEOPLE PLAY. Notes, index, 192pp. Grv64/Pen, 2.95p.**
Subtitled, *The Psychology of Human Relationships*, this was the first book that brought transactional analysis to the general public. It was on **The New York Times** best seller list for over two years. *Most people, in most of their family and business relationships, are constantly playing games with each other. What's more, they are striving—often unconsciously—for an emotional "payoff" which is startlingly different from what they might rationally expect to get from winning or losing their game.—Eric Berne.* Here Dr. Berne presents and explains 120 of these games and describes the *antigame* which liberates an individual from each game.

BERNE, ERIC. **INTUITION AND EGO STATES. Illustrations, bibliography, index, 199pp. H&R77, 4.95p.**
Eric Berne does more in these pages than penetrate the mysteries of intuition. He explains the fascinating course that leads him to found a whole psychotherapeutic system, transactional analysis (TA)....These eight papers trace the story, from his early experiments with intuition...to the evidence (by way of primal imagery, primal judgment, and ego imagery) that each of us is not just one personality but a combination of three, Parent, Adult, and Child, all residing in one skin.—from the preface.

BERNE, ERIC. **A LAYMAN'S GUIDE TO PSYCHIATRY AND PSYCHOANALYSIS. Glossary, index, 342pp. Grv57/Pen, 1.95p.**
An entirely revised and updated edition of Berne's first book, **The Mind in Action**. As the title suggests, the presentation is nontechnical and the coverage is comprehensive; the book itself is about the human mind and the human being as the psychiatrist sees them.

BERNE, ERIC. **PRINCIPLES OF GROUP TREATMENT. Glossary, index, 397pp. Grv66/Oxf, 4.95p.**
A systematic treatise on the use of transactional analysis in groups which draws on the author's more than twenty years of clinical experience as well as information provided by hundreds of other group therapists. The first part of the book describes how to set up a group therapy program and discusses the four most common methods of group therapy. The second part focuses on transactional analysis: its principles and techniques and its relationship to other forms of treatment. This book is geared toward the professional.

BERNE, ERIC. **SEX IN HUMAN LOVING. Diagrams, index, 282pp. S&S70/Pen, 1.95p.**
A long look at the title theme, based on the principles of transactional analysis. Every aspect of the subject is touched on.

BERNE, ERIC. **THE STRUCTURE AND DYNAMICS OF ORGANIZATIONS AND GROUPS. Illustrations, glossary, index, 350pp. Grv63, 2.50p.**
Berne offers a systematic framework for the therapy of ailing groups and organizations. An elementary clinical vocabulary is employed, and technical notes are kept separate from the text.

BERNE, ERIC. **TRANSACTIONAL ANALYSIS IN PSYCHOTHERAPY. 270pp. Grv61/Sou, 1.95p.**
A technical analysis for the practicing therapist. Includes a clear description of the process and its technical applications, diagrams, notes, and indices.

BERNE, ERIC. **WHAT DO YOU SAY AFTER YOU SAY HELLO? 458pp. Ban72/Crg, 2.25p.**
Here Dr. Berne talks about the scripts that people follow compulsively throughout their lives, and how they can break out of them and achieve freedom and fulfillment.

BRY, ADELAIDE. **T.A. FOR FAMILIES. 167pp. H&R76, 1.50p.**
Subtitled, *Using Transactional Analysis for a Happier Family Life*. This is a simplistic series of books, all with the same format (a picture or drawing on the left hand page, a transactional analysis-related saying on the right).

BRY, ADELAIDE. **T.A. GAMES. 115pp. H&R75, 1.50p.**
Subtitled, *Using Transactional Analysis in Your Life.*

BRY, ADELAIDE. **THE T.A. PRIMER. 151pp. H&R73, 1.50p.**
A profusely illustrated, basic introduction to the three personas—parent, adult, and child—that make up each of us, and how our personas interact with those of others to make us feel good or bad.

ERNST, KEN. **PRE-SCRIPTION: A TA LOOK AT CHILD DEVELOPMENT. Bibliography, index, 127pp. CeA76, 4.50p.**
Ernst is a California high school teacher who studied with Eric Berne for ten years. This is the most complete book on transactional analysis in the classroom that we know of. Many practical suggestions are offered along with a series of case studies.

ERNST, KEN. **TA STORIES FOR KIDS. 124pp. CeA77, 3.95p.**
An illustrated collection of *question, observe, and answer stories* that teach transactional analysis concepts to children.

HALLETT, KATHRYN. **A GUIDE FOR SINGLE PARENTS. Glossary, bibliography, 122pp. CeA74, 3.95p.**
A family therapist shows how, by means of transactional analysis,

personal loss such as divorce, separation, desertion, or death can provide growth rather than paralysis and despair.

HARRIS, THOMAS A. **I'M OK, YOU'RE OK. 317pp. Avo67, 2.25p.**
A clearly written, general presentation of the basics of transactional analysis. This is the most popular of all transactional analysis books.

JAMES, MURIEL. **BORN TO LOVE. 209pp. AdW73, 3.95p/2.25p.**
Applies transactional analysis to church activities and relationships. Can be read by one person or used in church study groups. Well illustrated.

JAMES, MURIEL. **THE OK BOSS. 153pp. Ban75, 2.25p.**
Using transactional analysis concepts, Dr. James explains how our bossing style is related to certain *OK* and *not OK* aspects of our personality. She tells how our OK sides can be nurtured and developed to make us better bosses, feel better about being bossed, and bring about changes in the way people boss us. Many cartoon-like illustrations are included.

JAMES, MURIEL. **TRANSACTIONAL ANALYSIS FOR MOMS AND DADS. Bibliography, 148pp. AdW74, 3.95p.**
Shows how a parent or teacher can use transactional analysis to recognize unpleasant feelings and behavior and turn them into pleasant ones and provides new insights into the giving and receiving of *strokes* among members of a family. Line drawings throughout.

JAMES, MURIEL. **WINNING WITH PEOPLE: GROUP EXERCISES IN T.A. AdW73, 3.95p.**
An 11"x8½" workbook designed to accompany **Born to Win.**

■ *JAMES, MURIEL and DOROTHY JONGEWARD.* **BORN TO WIN. 301pp. AdW71, 4.95p.**
Primarily concerned with transactional analysis, the book also uses gestalt-oriented experiments to show the reader a useful way to discover the many parts of his personality, to integrate them, and to develop a core of self confidence. **Psychology Today** calls it *the clearest and most up to date statement of current thinking in transactional analysis, and easily the best of the popular books.*

JAMES, MURIEL and LOUIS SAVARY. **THE HEART OF FRIENDSHIP. 205pp. H&R76, 3.95p.**
A guide to the art of making and keeping friends utilizing principles developed in transactional analysis.

JAMES, MURIEL and LOUIS SAVARY. **A NEW SELF: SELF THERAPY WITH TRANSACTIONAL ANALYSIS. Many illustrations, 348pp. AdW77, 5.95p.**
A collection of exercises and scripts *designed to lead you through a process that is both educational and therapeutic. It is educational because it helps you become aware of what you need to change. It is therapeutic because it shows you how you got to be the way you are and how to carry out your program of self-change.*

JAMES, MURIEL and LOUIS SAVARY. **THE POWER AT THE BOTTOM OF THE WELL. Notes, 160pp. H&R74, 3.95p.**
Subtitled, *TA and Religious Experience.* Includes exercises which specifically apply the principles to life situations.

JONGEWARD, D. and D. SCOTT. **WOMEN AS WINNERS. 5.95p.**
See the Women and Men section.

STEINER, CLAUDE. **SCRIPTS PEOPLE LIVE. Bibliography, index, 394pp. Ban74, 2.25p.**
Dr. Steiner was a close collaborator with Eric Berne in developing the principles of transactional analysis. This book has more substance to it than most of the transactional analysis books. Steiner begins with a survey of the development of transactional analysis and a biographical essay on Berne. The rest of the book is devoted to the transactional analysis of life scripts. Both theoretical material and practical exercises are presented.

TANNER, IRA. **LONELINESS: THE FEAR OF LOVE. 143pp. H&R73, 1.75p.**
Transactional analysis applied to loneliness.

——**END OF TRANSACTIONAL ANALYSIS SUBSECTION**——

ULMAN, ELINOR and PENNY DACHINGER, eds. **ART THERAPY—IN THEORY AND PRACTICE. 415pp. ScB75, 15.00c.**
This collection brings together in book form the most important thinking, discussion, and experience in the field of art therapy. The articles are culled from **The American Journal of Art Therapy.** This is a very comprehensive presentation of every aspect of the field, with articles on the visual arts in education, rehabilitation, and psychotherapy. Many color and black and white plates illustrate the text.

VERNY, THOMAS. **INSIDE GROUPS: A PRACTICAL GUIDE TO ENCOUNTER GROUPS AND GROUP THERAPY. Resource guide with addresses, index, 262pp. MGH74, 3.95p.**
I hope in the following pages to strike a balance between an objective assessment of what these groups are all about and how they function and a subjective expression of my own feelings about their strengths and shortcomings. I have sought to write a practical, straightforward guide for those who wish to find out about the different approaches to groups and to derive the most benefit from a group once they have joined it.

WEINBERG, GEORGE. **SELF-CREATION. 228pp. SMP78, 8.95c.**
As Dr. Weinberg says in the first chapter, *this book will make only one claim, but it's almost as large a claim as I can imagine: This book will help you to see what you are, how you become the way you are, and how to change the way you are. But, for all its aspirations, this book cannot change you. Only you can change you. Because only you created you. What the book can do is to help you to change yourself. By explaining precisely how you created—and are constantly re-creating—yourself.* This is a revealing account, which advises the reader in many areas. It is simplistic, but nonetheless quite well done of type.

WOOD, JOHN. **HOW DO YOU FEEL? 203pp. PrH74, 2.95p.**
This is a uniquely personal book. I believe anyone reading it will become more aware of the vast unknown world which lies within each one of us. He will find himself more able to be, and to express those fragile things we call "feelings." It will encourage the reader to be more fully a person.—Carl Rogers.

WYCKOFF, HOGIE, ed. **LOVE, THERAPY AND POLITICS. Index, 309pp. Grv76, 4.95p.**
A collection of articles which originally appeared in the first year of **Issues in Radical Therapy.** Many of the articles focus on sex role programming as well as the radical ways to combat them. The articles are especially concerned with ways to overcome the oppression that we have internalized.

YABLONSKY, L. **PSYCHODRAMA. Index, 293pp. H&R76, 10.95c.**
Dr. Yablonsky has directed or participated in several thousand psychodrama sessions and he was an associate—both student and colleague—of the founder of psychodrama, Dr. J.L. Moreno. *Psychodrama is a natural and automatic process. Everyone at some time has an inner drama going on in his mind.... Many people are able to act out these internal psychodramas in the reality and activity of their external life.... For most people, psychodrama can provide a unique opportunity for externalizing their internal world onto a theatrical stage of life; and, with the help of the group present at a session, emotional conflicts and problems can often be resolved. A basic theme of this book is that of psychodrama as a happening or as a productive experience rather than exclusively as a therapeutic method.*—from the book.

ZUNIN, LEONARD. **CONTACT. 271pp. RaH74/TaF, 2.45p.**
What two people communicate during their first four minutes of contact is so crucial that it will determine whether strangers will remain strangers or will become friends, lovers, or lifetime mates. This book deals with those four minutes: what often happens and what can happen.

INDIAN PHILOSOPHY

One might at first attempt a geographical definition of Hinduism by recognizing in it the totality of religious forms which originated and developed on Indian soil. It would then be necessary to exclude Buddhism, which in ancient days spread across a large part of Hindustan and still remains very much alive in some areas of the continental borderlands. It would also be necessary to exclude Jainism, which has today about one and a half million followers although in the past it was, relatively at least, more widespread. Other religious groups would also have to be excluded: six million Christians, Jews and Zoroastrians, and some twenty-five million fetishists and animists, who one might say participate in varying degrees in certain elementary forms of Hinduism.

In relation to the mass of the Indian population, which at present numbers approximately four hundred million, these groups are practically negligible both statistically and culturally. This is not the case, however, with Islam. Since the eleventh century Islam has steadily drawn millions of persons from the Hindu community; and even today, in spite of the creation of Pakistan as a Muslim state within the subcontinent, Islam has some thirty-five million followers in the Indian Union. As for Sikhism, or the religion of the Sikhs, it may be considered a religious movement at the extreme limits of Hinduism: it is not considered a heresy.

To confine Hinduism to the circumference of India, however, would be to bypass the missionary character of this religion in the past. In the so-called Hinduization of southeast Asia, Indian religious influences combined with indigenous elements and in the course of time were assimilated by Buddhism, Islam or some form of national religion. In this way Hinduism has had a profound influence, especially in Cambodia, ancient Champa and Bali. One should also recall that there are Hindus in Ceylon (among the Dravidian population), in Nepal, in Pakistan (an inestimable number) and in Indian settlements scattered all over the world.

Can one rather define Hinduism by its elements? Actually, this will have to be done; but in attempting to find such a unifying definition we run the risk of generalizing to such an extent that we fail to grasp the infinite diversity of forms which constitute Hinduism.

The primitive foundation of Hinduism was in part of Indo-European origin; the framework at least was such, while the content was largely indigenous or was modified on the spot. The Aryan tribes which invaded India during the second millennium before our era brought with them a body of religious belief which was already well organized and which survived in classical Hinduism—at the cost of many modifications. This *Aryan* religion (that is, Indo-European on Indian soil) had already been sifted out during the so-called Indo-Iranian intermediary period. It was at the end of this period that a separation occurred between the original religion of Iran (pre-Zoroastrian) and what was to become the Vedic religion in northwestern India.

To this ancient foundation was added a succession of influences which made Hinduism a religion quite different from that of the Aryan invaders. Most of these new developments took place during historical time. The main stages were the appearance of great philosophical speculations and the fixation of the *Smrti* (at the beginning of the Christian era), the first fragmentation into sects (first and second centuries A.D.),

the appearance of *bhakti* (ca. 600-800 A.D.), and Tantrism (since 800 A.D.). The main outline of all these movements existed, however, as early as the Vedic period.

It is possible, too, and even probable that Hinduism assimilated some pre-Aryan, or at least non-Aryan institutions which were inherited from local cults and modified with the primitive Indian data as the basis. The prehistorical civilization of the Indus basin (Mohenjo-Daro and Harappa), which dates from the beginning of the second millenium before Christ, testifies to some of the characteristics by which we can identify a proto-Hinduism: an image of the Mother Goddess, a horned god in the posture of a Yogin, and ritual emblems of vegetal or animal character.

Hinduism is indeed a complex and rich religion. No founder's initiative, no dogma, no reform has imposed restrictions on its domain; on the contrary, the contributions of the centuries have been superimposed without ever wearing out the previous layers of development.

In fact, according to what phenomena one considers, Hinduism can appear either as an extrovert religion of spectacle, abundant mythology and congregational practices or as a religion which is profoundly interiorized. To the first view belong the activities of the sects, the *bhakti* movement, and the worship of the cow, in which some find the concrete symbol of Hinduism; here, too, could be included the principle of nonviolence, at least in its social application. To the view of Hinduism as an interior life belong the paths of spiritual progress, the quest for liberation, the tendency to renunciation, and finally the intensive concentration on problems which in other cultures are more often reserved for theologians or philosophers. Hinduism, which is eminently popular in its practices and external manifestations, is essentially also a religion of the learned: it cannot be understood if the *Vedanta* and the *Samkhya* have not been fully comprehended or if, at the outset, there is no idea of the immense network of symbolism which underlies and links together all Indian thought.

Finally, Hinduism characterizes society as a whole. The caste system with its various *stages* of existence is part of Hinduism. Life is looked upon as a rite; there is no absolute dividing line between the sacred and the profane. In fact, there is no Hindu term corresponding to what we call *religion*. There are *approaches* to the spiritual life; and there is *dharma*, or *maintenance* (in the right path), which is at once norm or law, virtue and meritorious action, the order of things transformed into moral obligation—a principle of which governs all manifestations of Indian life.

When, it may be asked, did Hinduism begin? A reply to this question can only be indirect: Hinduism began at the time when the original activity of the Vedic ritual came to an end, when the old Vedic framework was lost. We may date this occurrence, perhaps, between the sixth and fourth centuries B.C. From this perspective, a text or a religious manifestation is designated as Hindu as long as it does not reveal any trace of division into schools or of the ancient liturgical patterns. Such was the position immediately before our era of the Epics, the ethico-juridical literature and the Aphorisms (*Sutras*) which served as the basis for grand speculations.

The situation, however, is not quite so clear, for just as there was an undercurrent of Hinduism in Vedism, so there are Vedic survivals in classical Hinduism. The name of

Brahmanism is sometimes given to the oldest of the learned forms of Hinduism. But taking everything into consideration, it is preferable to look upon Hinduism as a whole without looking for superficial subdivisions. On this interpretation Vedism is considered the most ancient form of Hinduism. Certainly Vedism cannot be neglected since all that follows it is inexplicable without it.

If we are to look for a global characterization of Hinduism, we could (as was recently suggested) consider it the very type of a religion of renunciation. Certainly Hinduism could exist without those who renounce, but it would remain singularly impoverished and would be as if deprived of its crest. Many of the elements of the religion seem to have been created for the man who has withdrawn from mundane life, or they were later modified for his needs. This could explain the evolution of the theory of *karma* and of transmigration, perhaps too the development of *bhakti* and (by a kind of reversal) of Tantrism. On a general plane, we can consider as effects of renunciation both Indian pessimism and the escapist tendency, which may go so far as to reject the elementary exigencies of religion. It is all an affair of the individual. Hinduism does not know the opposition which is found in Buddhism between a well-developed monastic milieu and a secular environment; consequently a Hindu, even if he belongs to a group, considers himself alone to be responsible for his salvation.

—*from* **Hinduism**, *by Louis Renou*

ABHEDANANDA, SWAMI. HOW TO BE A YOGI. 188pp. VdP55, 2.75c.
This is an excellent presentation of the science and practice of different types of yoga, along with their philosophy and psychology. Two introductory chapters discuss true religion and what yoga is. The next chapters are devoted to different types of yoga: hatha, raja, karma, bhakti, and jnana. The two final chapters discuss the science of breathing and *Was Christ a Yogi?* Swami Abhedananda was a direct disciple of Sri Ramakrishna.

AJAYA, SWAMI, ed. LIVING WITH THE HIMALAYAN MASTERS: SPIRITUAL EXPERIENCES OF SWAMI RAMA. Many photographs, 515pp. Him78, 13.95c.
Born in 1925 to a learned Brahmin family in the Himalayas, Swami Rama was ordained a monk at a young age. In his early manhood he traveled from monastery to monastery, studying and living with more than 120 sages. He later taught the **Upanishads** and Buddhist scriptures in Indian schools and monasteries and received many high honors. More recently, he studied Western psychology, philosophy, and medicine in Europe. After he came to the U.S. he became a consultant at the Menninger Foundation, involved in a project called *Voluntary Control of Internal States*. This informal book recounts his life story, emphasizing his years in India, and the spiritual teaching and experiences he encountered.

AKHILANANDA, SWAMI. HINDU PSYCHOLOGY: ITS MEANING FOR THE WEST. Notes, bibliography, index, 228pp. BrP46/RKP, 3.75p.
A comparison of Western and Eastern schools of thought, with emphasis on meditation, intuition, extrasensory perception, and methods of superconscious experience. Swami Akhilananda emphasizes the importance of developing the superconscious state as a means of integrating the total personality.

AKHILANANDA, SWAMI. HINDU VIEW OF CHRIST. 3.75p.
See the Christianity section.

AKHILANANDA, SWAMI. SPIRITUAL PRACTICES. 225pp. Sta74, 8.50c.
Swami Akhilananda founded the Ramakrishna Vedanta Society in Boston and was an active minister from 1926-62. In this book he stresses that in our scientific age, verification of the existence of the ultimate reality or God is the main objective of real religion. He points out that only by this direct and immediate experience of God can our personalities be integrated and society harmonized. The handbook is illustrated with details from his personal experiences and from the lives of his spiritual teachers.

ANANDAMURTI, SHRII SHRII. BABA'S GRACE. Illustrations, glossary, 197pp. AMa73, 2.95p.
A collection of discourses by the spiritual leader of the Ananda Marga organization. Each of the selections is short and the translation is clearly done. The emphasis is on the journey of the soul.

ANANDAMURTI, SHRII SHRII. THE GREAT UNIVERSE. Illustrations, 271pp. AMa73, 3.25p.
Discourses discussing the problems that beset modern mankind: governmental corruption, economic injustice, overpopulation, crime—and offering practical solutions to them.

ARNOLD, SIR EDWIN, tr. LIGHT OF ASIA AND THE INDIAN SONG OF SONGS (GITA GOVINDA). Introduction, glossary, 253pp. JPH49, 1.60p.
Two classic translations, bound in one volume.

ARYAN, K.C. and SUBHASHINI. HANUMAN IN ART AND MYTHOLOGY. 10"x10", 80pp. RPr75, 60.00c.
Hanuman is known as the perfect servant. He played a large role in the **Ramayana** and is today worshiped by followers from many traditions. He was proficient in all the *shastras*: fine arts, sciences, philosophy. All the facets of his manysided personality have been brought out in this volume. Hanuman has inspired not only Indian artists and artisans but also those of Nepal, Burma, Indonesia, Thailand, Bali, Java, and many other areas. Certain yantras and mantras associated with Hanuman have also been included in this volume along with over 200 plates, some in color. A chapter on mythology and folklore relates various episodes from Hanuman's life.

ASHBY, PHILIP. MODERN TRENDS IN HINDUISM. Glossary, notes, index, 152pp. Col74, 11.20c.
Ashby begins this survey with an historical discussion of Hinduism as a religious and philosophical system. The bulk of the book is devoted to its diversification in the nineteenth and twentieth centuries. The great modern religious and social leaders—Aurobindo, Ramakrishna, Vivekananda, and Gandhi—are evaluated in terms of their liberalizing influence on Hinduism. There are also studies of contemporary Indian youth and their changing attitudes toward the Hindu faith and of the Radha Soami Satsang sect (followers of Charan Singh). Concluding chapters discuss the role of Hindu religion and culture in Indian politics and the promise of Hinduism for the future.

Sri Aurobindo

Sri Aurobindo was a great knower of God who exemplified a way of spiritual integration that combined the noblest truths of the East and West. Although born in Calcutta, he was given a Western education and was actually sheltered from the influence of mystic India by his Anglicized father. At seven he moved to England where he lived and studied until the age of twenty. He manifested a brilliant intellect and great aptitude for reading, devouring volumes of books with nearly verbatim comprehension. His fertile mind was nourished by the Western rational tradition and he soon mastered Greek and Latin as well as English. Ironically, he was forbidden to learn his native tongue and thus his mother country remained remote.

At twenty he went to India and was soon immersed in the task of liberating that country from foreign control. He was appalled at the condition of the masses and through the medium of newspaper articles he urged the immediate release of the proletariat from the bondage of oppression. His deep insight made him aware that India's political problems stemmed largely from her apathy, passivity, negligence, and even cowardice. He was a man of action and he sought a means to rouse the languor of his sleeping countrymen.

During this time, he read the numerous sacred writings of India with the same relish and avid intensity that he had applied to his studies of Western literature. But it was not until he had witnessed an actual demonstration of the powers wielded by the individuals proficient in the science of yoga that he was aroused to the possibility of using these less tangible means to accomplish his ends.

The young revolutionary plunged into the practice of yoga eager to find the key that would enable him to relieve the suffering of the people he loved. But his was a unique yoga formed from the practical, action-oriented side of his nature joined with the fathomless spiritual realizations that were soon to be his. His political activities led to his arrest and during the days of trial and imprisonment his diligent efforts led to supernal realizations and recognitions of divine unity.

Aurobindo realized that true liberation was an experience of consciousness, but simultaneously he knew that the key to discovering the greatness of being was through diligent activity. This was not the restless cogitation of frenzied motion, but was rather the action of self discovery. Unlike other systems of yoga that resulted in the upward surge of the kundalini energy from the base of the spine, Sri Aurobindo's integral yoga resulted in the downflow of creative, inspirational energies from supramental centers of one's being.

Later in his life, Aurobindo was joined by a French woman who soon became known as The Mother and who helped carry on the work. Sri Aurobindo and The Mother became powerful forces for good in the world and their new age message of brotherhood and liberty have caught the imagination and the heart of people throughout the world. A city called Auroville has been started in India to embody their philosophy of human unity and to demonstrate the oneness of mankind.

AUROBINDO, SRI. **BASES OF YOGA. 168pp. SAA36, 1.50p.**
Extracts from letters to disciples. Selections chosen are considered especially helpful to aspirants seeking an understanding of the practice of yoga.

AUROBINDO, SRI. **THE FOUNDATIONS OF INDIAN CULTURE. 414pp. SAA59, 5.50c.**
Systematically sets forth the spiritual basis of Indian culture, with reference to Western religion, spirituality, art, and literature.

AUROBINDO, SRI. **THE FUTURE EVOLUTION OF MAN. Notes, bibliography, 157pp. TPH71, 2.25p.**
Extracts from **The Life Divine, The Human Cycle,** and **The Synthesis of Yoga.**

AUROBINDO, SRI. **THE FUTURE POETRY AND LETTERS ON POETRY, LITERATURE AND ART. 561pp. SAA72, 7.50c.**

AUROBINDO, SRI. **A GATEWAY TO SRI AUROBINDO'S THOUGHTS. 61pp. SAA72, 1.25p.**
Extracts from **The Life Divine, The Human Cycle,** and **The Synthesis of Yoga,** arranged to present Sri Aurobindo's vision of man's future.

AUROBINDO, SRI. **THE HOUR OF GOD. 74pp. SAA73, 1.65p.**
Compiled from manuscripts, consisting mainly of notes intended for fuller treatment.

AUROBINDO, SRI. **THE HUMAN CYCLE, THE IDEAL OF HUMAN UNITY, WAR AND SELF-DETERMINATION. 654pp. SAA71, 7.50c.**
A trilogy on the psychology of social development, mankind's search for true unity, and how life and society may be remolded in the truth of the spirit to express the greatest harmony of individual freedom and social unity.

AUROBINDO, SRI. **LETTERS ON YOGA, VOLUME I. 502pp. SAA71, 6.00c.**
These three volumes present a complete picture of Aurobindo's philosophy and its practical application. The short pieces presented here are often easier to comprehend than the material in **The Synthesis of Yoga.**

AUROBINDO, SRI. **LETTERS ON YOGA, VOLUME II. 587pp. SAA71, 7.00c.**

AUROBINDO, SRI. **LETTERS ON YOGA, VOLUME III. 686pp. SAA71, 8.00c.**

AUROBINDO, SRI. **THE LIFE DIVINE. Sanskrit glossary, two volumes, SAA73, 10.00p/set.**
Aurobindo's philosophical *magnum opus,* 1,070 pages on his vision of the spiritual life.

AUROBINDO, SRI. **LIGHTS ON YOGA. Sanskrit glossary, 104pp. SAA35, 1.50p.**
Extracts from letters to disciples.

AUROBINDO, SRI. **MAN—SLAVE OR FREE. 48pp. SAA66, 1.00p.**
Eight essays.

AUROBINDO, SRI. **MORE LIGHTS ON YOGA. 113pp. SAA73, 1.50p.**
More extracts.

AUROBINDO, SRI. **THE MOTHER. 4"x5½", 62pp. SAA28, .75p.**
Extracts from Aurobindo's writings on The Mother and her purpose on Earth.

AUROBINDO, SRI. **THE MOTHER. 495pp. SAA72, 8.50c.**
An essay on The Mother, with Aurobindo's letters on the identity, purpose and working of The Mother, and his translation of her **Prayers and Meditations** and interpretations of some of her prayers and conversations.

AUROBINDO, SRI. **THE PROBLEM OF REBIRTH. 2.25p.**
See the Reincarnation and Karma section.

AUROBINDO, SRI. **RIDDLE OF THIS WORLD. 98pp. SAA33, 1.25p.**
Originally issued as answers to questions raised by disciples and others.

AUROBINDO, SRI. **SAVITRI: A LEGEND AND A SYMBOL. 816pp. SAA73, 7.50p.**
His (unfinished) epic poem is based on an episode in the **Mahabharata** and records in mantric poetry his vast spiritual experience and Savitri's struggle with and final victory over death. Includes Aurobindo's letters on the poem.

AUROBINDO, SRI. **SRI AUROBINDO ON HIMSELF. 513pp. SAA72, 7.50c.**
Compiled from notes and letters. *It would be only myself who could speak of*

things in my past giving them their true form and significance. In my view, a man's value does not depend on what he learns, or his position or fame, or what he does, but on what he is and inwardly becomes. Includes letters on himself and The Mother.

AUROBINDO, SRI. **THE SYNTHESIS OF YOGA.** 872pp. SAA73, 8.00p.
Each side of the Yoga dealt with separately, with all its possibilities and indications as to how they meet so that one starting from knowledge could realize Karma and Bhakti and so on with each path. Presents the four parts of his Integral Yoga: *The Yoga of Divine Works; The Yoga of Integral Knowledge; The Yoga of Divine Love;* and *The Yoga of Self-Perfection.* One of Aurobindo's most important writings.

AUROBINDO, SRI. **THOUGHTS AND APHORISMS.** 125pp. SAA58, 1.50p.

AUROBINDO, SRI and THE MOTHER. **COLLECTIVE YOGA.** 75pp. SAA74, 1.75p.
Extracts dealing directly with collective discipline.

AUROBINDO, SRI and THE MOTHER. **THE DESTINY OF MAN.** 269pp. SAA69, 3.00p.
A compilation covering the following topics: *evolution and spiritual transformation, reason, towards Supermind, gnostic being, divine life, how man can realize his destiny, yoga.*

AUROBINDO, SRI and THE MOTHER. **ON EDUCATION.** 118pp. SAA56, 2.00p.
They insist that one must understand human psychology in order to adequately teach and learn. This includes the understanding of the human mind in all its stages (infant, adolescent, adult) and an integration and development of the human personality equipment and its proper relationship to the divine soul within us all.

AUROBINDO, SRI and THE MOTHER. **A PRACTICAL GUIDE TO INTEGRAL YOGA.** 345pp. SAA55, 4.50p.
A compilation on nearly all aspects of the yoga.

AUROBINDO, SRI and THE MOTHER. **THE TEACHING OF SRI AUROBINDO.** 76pp. SAA64, 1.50p.
Extracts arranged to present the teaching in a clear manner, including chapters from **The Mother**, and essays on meditation, psychological perfection, living from within, physical education, sex, food, prayers.

AUROPUBLICATIONS. **AUROVILLE: THE FIRST SIX YEARS.** 102pp. Aur74, 3.75p.

CHAUDHURI, HARIDAS. **BEING, EVOLUTION, AND IMMORTALITY.** Notes, index, 217pp. TPH74, 2.75p.
An outline of the author's *integral philosophy* which reinterprets the ancient teachings for the modern age. Portions of the book were originally published as **The Philosophy of Integralism.** Chaudhuri was a close disciple of Sri Aurobindo.

■ DONNELLY, MORWENNA. **FOUNDING THE LIFE DIVINE.** Glossary, notes, 176pp. DHP55, 3.95p.
Sri Aurobindo is undoubtedly one of the most important twentieth century Indian philosophers and he is also one of the least understood. His books are hard to comprehend and—while there is an abundance of literature about him and his work—there has been little written on a truly basic level. This book is billed as an introduction to Aurobindo's Integral Yoga and we feel that it succeeds well in its stated aim. There are many quotes from Aurobindo's works and a fair amount of explanatory material. The exposition is topically organized and it reads well.

GANDHI, KISHOR, ed. **THE NEW AGE.** 647pp. SAA77, 7.50p.
A transcription of speeches at the seminars and conferences of the New Age Association, an organization founded in Pondicherry under The Mother's guidance. The selections cover the years from 1964 to 1972.

■ MCDERMOTT, ROBERT, ed. **THE ESSENTIAL AUROBINDO.** Glossary, bibliography, index, 200pp. ScB63, 3.95p.
Extracts from some basic writings of Sri Aurobindo, giving his concept

of spiritual and human evolution, his vision of man's destiny, the Integral Yoga, the implementation of his vision by The Mother, with extracts from her writings on education and Auroville. Includes a life sketch by McDermott. An excellent introduction.

■ MCDERMOTT, ROBERT, ed. **THE MIND OF LIGHT.** Excellent introduction, long annotated bibliography, 128pp. Dut71, 2.50p.
The best general introduction to Sri Aurobindo's system, for it concentrates in a brief space his entire cosmic and transcendent vision.

THE MOTHER. **THE MOTHER ON SRI AUROBINDO.** 15pp. SAA61, 2.00p.
A discussion of the identity and purpose of Sri Aurobindo.

THE MOTHER. **PRAYERS AND MEDITATIONS.** 42pp. SAA62, 1.50p.
Selected and translated from The Mother's diaries by Sri Aurobindo.

THE MOTHER. **QUESTIONS AND ANSWERS.** SAA, 10.00c/each.
Questions asked at The Mother's class for students and disciples at the ashram. Volume I: 1950-51; Volume II: 1956; Volume III: 1957-58. Each volume is almost 400 pages long.

THE MOTHER. **WHITE ROSES.** 152pp. SAA nd, 2.50p.
Letters to a disciple on various aspects of the yoga, and inspirational notes.

NIRODBARAN. **CORRESPONDENCE WITH SRI AUROBINDO.** Photographs, 356pp. SAA69, 6.00c.
The author was a doctor who served as secretary and attendant to Aurobindo. The material covers a wide range of subjects.

NIRODBARAN. **TALKS WITH AUROBINDO.** SAA nd.
Material taken from the author's notebooks covering the post-1938 period. Volume I: 385 pages, 3.00p; Volume II: 256 pages, index, 4.50c; Volume III: 257 pages, index, 4.00c.

NIRODBARAN. **TWELVE YEARS WITH SRI AUROBINDO.** 289pp. SAA72, 4.00p.
Personal glimpses of Aurobindo, The Mother, the ashram, etc., from 1938 to 1950.

NORELLI-BACHELET, PATRIZIA. **THE GNOSTIC CIRCLE.** 12.90c.
See the Astrology section.

NORELLI-BACHELET, PATRIZIA. **THE MAGICAL CAROUSEL.** 3.75p.
See the Astrology section.

NORELLI-BACHELET, PATRIZIA. **SYMBOLS AND THE QUESTION OF UNITY.** 5.75c.
See the Sacred Art section.

PANDIT, M.P. **DICTIONARY OF SRI AUROBINDO'S YOGA.** 315pp. SAA66, 6.00c.
A comprehensive dictionary of the ideas, concepts, principles, Sanskrit and special English words used by Aurobindo, defined in his own words.

PANDIT, M.P. **GEMS FROM SRI AUROBINDO.** 913pp. SAA nd, 7.50c/set.
Four volumes of brief extracts from Aurobindo's prose and poetry on a wide range of subjects, arranged alphabetically.

PANDIT, M.P. **SRI AUROBINDO ON THE TANTRA.** 47pp. SAA67, 1.00p.
Compiled from writings on Integral Yoga, kundalini, *chakras*, worship, mantra, *japa*, and much else.

PURANI, A.B. **EVENING TALKS WITH SRI AUROBINDO.** SAA.
Recorded by one of the early disciples, covering a wide range of topics. Series I: 325 pages, index, 6.50c; Series II: 351 pages, index, 5.65c; Series III: 320 pages, 5.95c.

■ SATPREM. **SRI AUROBINDO OR THE ADVENTURES OF CONSCIOUSNESS.** Photographs, index, 381pp. H&R68, 4.95p.
Written by a Westerner, this biography of Sri Aurobindo sets forth his spiritual realizations in terms of his own life and the life of man the

mental being—the yoga, the supramental consciousness and transformation. Highly recommended as an introduction to Sri Aurobindo's vision and work.

SRI AUROBINDO ASHRAM. **GLOSSARY OF TERMS IN SRI AUROBINDO'S WRITINGS. Introduction, 314pp. SAA78, 10.00c.**
A definitive study. Each word or phrase is discussed at length.

───────── END OF SRI AUROBINDO SUBSECTION ─────────

BANERJEE, N.V. **THE SPIRIT OF INDIAN PHILOSOPHY. Bibliography, index, 380pp. Cur75, 15.75p.**
An academic examination which discusses Indian epistemology, metaphysics, ethics, and religious philosophy. Dr. Banerjee was head of the philosophy department at the University of Delhi for many years.

BANERJEE, P. **EARLY INDIAN RELIGIONS. Notes, bibliography, index, 253pp. VPH73, 13.60c.**
A comprehensive survey of India's religious history during the period between 185 BC and AD 300.

BASHAM, A.L. **THE WONDER THAT WAS INDIA. Bibliography, index, 6½"x10", 589pp. Grv54/Fon, 6.95p.**
An encyclopedic picture of Indian culture, civilization, social and political structure, art, language, and literature. Over 200 half tone illustrations and a number of specialized appendices are also included. This is an extremely informative account, thought it is often not the most interesting reading. It is a good deal for the price, for those who want a comprehensive overview.

BASHAM, A.L., et al. **SOURCES OF INDIAN TRADITION. 946pp. Col58, 12.60p/set.**
Source material that illustrates Indian and Pakistani thought since earliest times. The traditions represented include Buddhism, Jainism, Hinduism, Sikhism, and Islam. Recent movements such as nationalism, liberalism, socialism, and religious revivals are also included. A massive two volume collection, with an extensive bibliography.

BEHARI, BANKEY. **BHAKTA MIRA. 190pp. BBU71, 1.25p.**
A biographical sketch of Mira Bai along with a critique of her songs and the Sanskrit text and English translation of 112 of her poems.

BEHARI, BANKEY. **MINSTRELS OF GOD. Two volumes, 342pp. BBU70, 3.10p/set.**
Writings by and about a variety of spiritual figures who are associated with Brindaban in India: the gopis, Mira Bai, Andal, Jaideo, Bilwamangal, Surdas, Narsi Mehta, Chandidas, Vidyapata, Chaitanya, Tukaram, and Tulsidas. Most of the texts are not readily available elsewhere and Behari's translations read very well. The Sanskrit is included at the end of each volume and Behari also provides a long introduction.

BEHARI, BANKEY. **SUFIS, MYSTICS AND YOGIS OF INDIA. 384pp. BBU62, 3.00p.**
This book is meant to show the Path pursued by the Saints who realized God in one Life, and thereby to guide aspirants after God-realisation who have a similar desire to get His Vision and thereby emancipation in this present life.—from the introduction. Behari provides about 100 pages of excellent introductory material, a bibliography, and extensive quotations from saints such as Kabir, Nanak, Ramdas, and Shankaracharya. The entire text is also included in Sanskrit.

BENNETT, J.G. **LONG PILGRIMAGE. 4.95p.**
See the Gurdjieff and the Work section.

BERREMAN, GERALD. **HINDUS OF THE HIMALAYAS. Photographs, notes, bibliography, index, 497pp. UCa72, 4.95p.**
An informative ethnographic account of village India, focusing on a single area and discussing in detail one village, Sirkanda. The features it describes and the processes it analyzes are generally representative of other regions of South Asia.

BESANT, ANNIE. **INDIAN IDEALS IN EDUCATION, RELIGION AND PHILOSOPHY AND ART. 1.50c.**
See the Theosophy section.

BHARDWAJ, S.M. **HINDU PLACES OF PILGRIMAGE IN INDIA. Bibliography, index, UCa73, 16.95c.**
A very scholarly study of the nature of the interconnections between the Hindu sacred places of different levels and their pilgrim fields in both spatial and social dimensions. The book begins with a survey of pertinent literature on the Hindu holy places, and is followed by an attempt to establish a direct continuity of the broad spatial pattern of Hindu sacred places from the time of the **Mahabharata** to the modern period.

BHATTACHARYA, DEBEN, tr. **LOVE SONGS OF VIDYAPATI. Notes, index, 148pp. Grv69/A&U, 2.95p.**
Vidyapati, a fourteenth century Bengali poet, is regarded as one of the greatest of all Indian poets. Vidyapati's songs concern the love and lovemaking of Krishna and Radha, the major erotic figures of Indian mythology and literature. This volume contains 100 of Vidyapati's songs. An introduction by W.G. Archer describes the circumstances in which he wrote the songs and explains their meaning and significance. A series of thirty-one plates shows how themes analogous to Vidyapati's were illustrated in Indian miniature painting.

BOUQUET, A.C. **HINDUISM. Notes, bibliography, index, 160pp. HPG49, 6.15p.**
This survey goes far beyond most introductions in the depth of its presentation. The exposition is historical, beginning with the Vedic age and culminating with Indian political independence. All the major movements, deities, and spiritual leaders are discussed and quotations from sacred texts and other source material are interspersed.

BOYD, DOUG. **SWAMI. 350pp. RaH76/HPG, 10.00c.**
Doug Boyd spent several months in India in 1973 and 1974, and over two months as a personal assistant to Swami Rama during a series of psychophysiological tests at the Menninger Foundation in Kansas. The first third of this book is a detailed study of Swami Rama, including verbatim recordings of conversations between the swami and others at the Institute and a discussion of the tests he underwent and their results. The rest of the book is devoted to a series of portraits of various Indian holy men whom Boyd encountered in his travels. A vividly written account.

BROOKS, ROBERT and VISHNU WAKANKAR. **STONE AGE PAINTING IN INDIA. Bibliography, index, 8¾"x11½", 126pp. YUP76, 20.15c.**
A greater number and variety of Stone Age paintings are found in the sandstone caves of central India than in any other region of the world. The oldest of these paintings probably date from the Upper Paleolithic period, over ten thousand years ago, and cave paintings continued to be made until the recent past. Indian Stone Age art has remained largely unexplored and this is the first book length discussion of the subject. The text explores who painted the pictures, why they painted, and the relationships between painting and other artistic traditions. The book is profusely illustrated, with thirty pages in color and many duotones. Technical appendices are also provided.

BROUGH, JOHN, tr. **POEMS FROM THE SANSKRIT. Lengthy introduction, index, 151pp. Vik68, 1.95p.**
An anthology of secular poems written between the fourth and tenth centuries AD.

BRUNTON, PAUL. **A SEARCH IN SECRET INDIA. 313pp. Wei34/HPG, 4.50p.**
The story of Brunton's quest for the truly sacred in India, which he found embodied in Ramana Maharshi. *I have titled this book* **Secret India** *because it tells of an India which has been hidden from prying eyes for thousands of years, which has kept itself so exclusive that today only its rapidly disappearing remnants are left.*

BUHLER, GEORGE, tr. **THE LAWS OF MANU. Many notes, index, 582pp. MoB1886, 12.00c.**
Translation of an important early Indian document which presents the basic moral and social code for the Hindu way of life. This edition includes extracts from important commentaries. Part of the **Sacred Books of the East** series.

BUITENEN, J.A.B. VAN, tr. **TALES OF ANCIENT INDIA. 260pp. UCh59, 2.45p.**
This admirably produced and well-translated volume of stories from the Sanskrit takes the Western reader into one of the Golden Ages of India.... The world in which the tales are set is one which placed a premium upon slickness and guile as aids to success.... Merchants, aristocrats, Brahmins, thieves and courtesans mingle with

vampires, demi-gods, and the hierarchy of heaven in a series of lively or passionate adventures. The sources of the individual stories are clearly indicated; the whole treatment is scholarly without being arid.—**The Times Literary Supplement**.

CARROLL, DAVID. THE TAJ MAHAL. 12.95c.
See the Sacred Art section.

CHAKRAVARTI, PULINBIHARI. ORIGIN AND DEVELOPMENT OF THE SAMKHYA SYSTEM OF THOUGHT. Bibliography, index, 343pp. OrB75, 28.70c.
A scholarly work which discusses some of the fundamental topics of Samkhya and traces the system's evolution and growth. This study is based entirely on a detailed examination of the original texts. Sanskrit words (not transliterated) are interspersed throughout and many of the notes are in Sanskrit.

CHAPMAN, TOM and ERIKA PETIGURA. DELHI AND AGRA. Kod74, 3.50p.
A descriptive travel guide illustrated with eighty-two color photographs.

CHETHIMATTAM, JOHN. CONSCIOUSNESS AND REALITY: AN INDIAN APPROACH TO METAPHYSICS. Notes, bibliography, index, 238pp. Orb71, 5.95c.
A dry, academic discussion of the Indian approach to the question of god and reality. Dr. Chethimattam asserts that in the East, the ultimate can only be arrived at through self awareness or consciousness. The first part of this book examines the historical background of the various schools of Indian thought, while the second shows how elements of all these schools can be synthesized into one school of typically Indian thought.

CHINMAYANANDA, SWAMI, tr. ASHTAVAKARA GEETA. CPT72, 5.75c.
A translation of an illuminating text which records *the universal insight and spiritual experiences which a seeker gathers during moments of his intense meditation.*

CHINMAYANANDA, SWAMI. A MANUAL FOR SELF-UNFOLD-MENT. 97pp. Chn75, 2.95p.
Swami Chinmayananda has the wonderful ability to take complicated concepts and distill their essence. His translations of the sacred scriptures are among our favorites; he writes clearly and well. This volume is an edited edition of his teachings put together by a disciple, with the Swami's own assistance. The bulk of the book presents practical teachings on the spiritual path and on various techniques of self discovery and self awareness. Many Sanskrit terms are used and all are thoroughly defined. There is also a short review of Hinduism.

CHINMAYANANDA, SWAMI, tr. THOUSAND WAYS TO THE TRANSCENDENTAL: VISHNU SAHASRANAAMA. Notes, index, 266pp. CPT69, 4.00c.
The *sahasranaama* are the thousand names of Sri Narayan, the immutable self, each one a pointer indicating the direction towards which the mind's attention should turn in order to detect and apprehend divine reality. In essence, the text is a collection of 1,000 meditation exercises, with extensive commentary. The Sanskrit text, transliteration, translation of individual words, and translation of each stanza are included.

COOMARASWAMY, ANANDA. THE DANCE OF SHIVA: ON INDIAN ART AND CULTURE. Many illustrations, index, 182pp. FSG47, 3.25p.
Fourteen excellent essays, illuminating the Indian way of life by one of its most respected interpreters.

■ *COOMARASWAMY, ANANDA and SISTER NIVEDITA.* **MYTHS OF THE HINDUS AND BUDDHISTS. Illustrations, 414pp. Dov13, 3.95p.**
A collection of the most important Indian myths, taken mainly from the **Mahabharata** and the **Ramayana**, with additional ones from the **Puranas** and **Vedas** and assorted narratives of Krishna, Buddha, and Siva. This is universally considered the finest one volume introduction to Indian mythology ever prepared.

CRAVEN, ROY. A CONCISE HISTORY OF INDIAN ART. Index, 252pp. Oxf76, 6.95p.
Professor Craven traces Indian art from its beginnings in the Indus

Valley, through the masterpieces of Buddhist and Hindu art, to the coming of Islam, the Mogul culture, and the golden age of Indian miniature painting. In the process he discusses Hindu mythology and Indian mysticism and delves into the complex symbolism of the various art forms. 200 well chosen illustrations, thirty in color, accompany the text.

DANIELOU, ALAIN. HINDU POLYTHEISM. Bibliography, index, 7¾"x10¼", 491pp. PUP64/RKP, 20.00c.
A detailed, scholarly work which seeks to explain the significance of the most prominent Hindu gods as envisaged by the Hindus themselves. Principal topics are the polytheistic philosophy, the Vedic gods, the Great Trinity (Vishnu, Siva, Brahma), the goddess (Shakti) and the secondary gods, forms of worship, and representations. Numerous illustrations are included. The appendix contains transcriptions of the Sanskrit texts which are quoted in translation.

DARIAN, STEVEN. THE GANGES IN MYTH AND HISTORY. Illustrations, notes, bibliography, index, 235pp. UHa78, 9.95c.
From its origins high in the Himalayas, the Ganges flows through the holy cities and great plains of northern India to the Bay of Bengal. In a country where the red heat of summer inspires prayer for the coming monsoon, the life giving waters of the Ganges have assumed legendary powers in the form of the Hindu goddess Ganga, the source of creation and abundance. Pilgrims flock to her shores to cleanse and purify themselves, cure ailments, and die that much closer to paradise. Darian writes of the human experience and the legendary myths that surround the Ganges.

DASGUPTA, SURENDRANATH. HINDU MYSTICISM. 188pp. Ung27, 3.45p.
A systematic introduction, designed for the general reader. Dasgupta begins with an analysis of *sacrificial mysticism* in Vedic times and goes from there to chapters on the *mysticism of the* **Upanishads**, *yoga mysticism, Buddhistic mysticism,* and *classical forms of devotional mysticism.* Numerous references to the sacred literature are incorporated into the text.

DASGUPTA, SURENDRANATH. A HISTORY OF INDIAN PHILOS-OPHY. Notes, bibliography, index, 2,494pp. MoB22, 57.00p/set.
An exhaustive study in five volumes. Every school of thought and movement is discussed at length. This is universally considered the definitive study of Indian philosophy.

DASGUPTA, SURENDRANATH. INDIAN IDEALISM. Index, 229pp. CUP33, 3.95p.
[For] *students of philosophy who are at a loss where to begin in their search for the main principles that have influenced philosophical speculation in India . . . this book will be of great value. The style is extremely lucid and easy to read, with the result that so abtruse a subject is made not only interesting but also popular without being denuded of its peculiar depth. . . . We commend this book to every student of serious thought.—* **Times** *of India. The main topics are Beginnings of Indian Philosophy, Upanishadic Idealism, Buddhist Idealism, and The Vedanta and Kindred Forms of Idealism.*

DATE, V.H. THE YOGA OF THE SAINTS. Index, 270pp. MuM74, 10.05c.
Dr. Date's book, originally entitled, **Analysis of Spiritual Experience**, is an elaboration of the thesis he presented as a PhD candidate at Bombay University. He traces all aspects of the spiritual life, using his direct experience and the experiences of the great saints as his models. Often heavy going, but some good insights are included.

DAYA, SISTER. THE GURU AND THE DISCIPLE. 124pp. VdC76, 2.95p.
In April, 1919, Georgina Jones Walton, the aristocratic daughter of a United States senator, met Swami Paramananda, a young monk of the Ramakrishna Order of India. Two months later she joined his small monastic community in Boston and became known as Sister Daya. **The Guru and the Disciple** *is her personal account of her struggles and strivings and of the way her teacher dealt with them.*—*from the introduction.*

DEVI, SRIMATA GAYATRI. ONE LIFE'S PILGRIMAGE. Many photographs, 342pp. VdC77, 4.95p.
Addresses, letters, and articles by the first Indian woman to teach Vedanta in the West.

DIMOCK, EDWARD, tr. **THE THIEF OF LOVE: BENGALI TALES FROM COURT AND VILLAGE. Good readable translations, glossary, 316pp. UCh63, 3.95p.**
One of the richest of India's regional languages is Bengali, spoken today by over seventy-five million people. The medieval period of Bengali extends from the thirteenth through the eighteenth century and includes an immense oral literature as well as numerous manuscripts. Professor Dimock has chosen stories representing two important genres: village and court poetry. Folk legends combining the exotic, the homely, and the shrewd contrast strongly with the extract from a religious epic, **Manasa Mangal**, which shows the gods afflicting but ultimately blessing their human victims.

DIMOCK, EDWARD, et al. **THE LITERATURES OF INDIA: AN INTRODUCTION. 292pp. UCh74, 16.80c.**
Six experts review the representative genres of Indian literature. Each contributor writes in depth about the area of his particular interest, treating it in the light of traditional Indian canons of literary criticism and poetics and presenting its cultural background. The material is arranged topically and excerpts in translation are provided to clarify concepts, themes, and premises.

DOWSON, JOHN. A CLASSICAL DICTIONARY OF HINDU MYTHOLOGY. Alphabetically arranged, Sanskrit and general indices, 430pp. RKP72, 10.00c.
It is not clear when this book was originally produced, but from the typeface it appears to have been in the late nineteenth or early twentieth century. It remains the standard work. The entries are quite extensive and all aspects of the mythology and religion are well covered. Short descriptions of the most frequently mentioned Sanskrit books are also included.

DWIVEDI, R.C., ed. **THE CONTRIBUTION OF JAINISM TO INDAN CULTURE. Notes, indices, 323pp. MoB75, 15.20c.**
India's leading Jain scholars contributed to this volume; the areas covered include language and literature, religion, philosophy and ethics, fine arts and sciences, history, and culture. Extensive quotations from the appropriate Jain texts are included and the material is in both Sanskrit and English.

EDGERTON, FRANKLIN, tr. **THE PANCHATANTRA. 151pp. HPB65, 1.50p.**
A scholarly translation of this classic instructive collection of Indian folklore. The book was originally published as part of the UNESCO Collection and includes many notes and an excellent introduction. The translation itself reads well. Many familiar tales and fables originally appeared in this collection.

ELIADE, MIRCEA. YOGA: IMMORTALITY AND FREEDOM. 558pp. PUP69/RKP, 4.45p.
This is the most important and exhaustive single volume study of the major ascetic techniques available in English. It is a wide survey of the various phases of yoga: the **Yoga Sutras** of Patanjali; yogic techniques (e.g. concentration on a single point, postures, respiratory discipline); and yoga in relation to Brahmanism, Buddhism, tantra, Oriental alchemy, mystical eroticism, and shamanism. Fully indexed with a fifty page list of references cited and extensive annotation. Highly recommended for the serious student.

ELIOT, CHARLES. HINDUISM AND BUDDHISM. Notes, index, 1,284pp. RKP21, 36.95c/set.
A massive historical survey in three volumes, covering both the major individuals and philosophical schools. The book reads well and is an excellent reference for those seriously studying the religions of India.

EMBREE, AINSLIE, ed. **THE HINDU TRADITION. Bibliography, index, 351pp. RaH66, 2.95p.**
A comprehensive anthology of basic writings which range in time from the **Rig Veda** to the writings of Radhakrishnan. Selections are preceded by introductory material. Many deal with Indian social life, political relationships, and love, as well as religion.

FAIRSERVIS, WALTER. THE ROOTS OF ANCIENT INDIA. Line drawings and photographs, notes, bibliography, index, 513pp. UCh75, 7.95p.
A major accomplishment, certain to remain a standard of reference for many years. It offers a most comprehensive, detailed, and richly-illustrated review of South Asian prehistory to the time of the Buddha.—**American Anthropologist.** Professor Fairservis succeeds admirably in bringing the ancient cultures to life.

FEUERSTEIN, GEORG. THE ESSENCE OF YOGA. Notes, bibliography, index, 224pp. RaH76/HPG, 3.95p.
A psychohistorical examination of yoga within the framework of its contribution to the development of Indian civilization, focusing on the variety of ways that yoga has been used to expand consciousness and on its philosophical and practical application to contemporary society. Translations from relevant texts are included.

FEUERSTEIN, GEORG and **JEANINE MILLER. YOGA AND BEYOND. Notes, index, 189pp. ScB71/HPG, 2.95p.**
A collection of essays which outline the philosophical basis of Indian philosophy and yoga, particularly in its classical form. The authors quote extensively from sacred literature, especially the **Vedas**. In fact, their discussion is overwhelmingly based on Vedic thought. This is not recommended as an introduction—it is a technical work. The British edition is entitled, **A Reappraisal of Yoga**.

FRAUWALLNER, ERICH. HISTORY OF INDIAN PHILOSOPHY. Two volumes, glossary, bibliography, index, 665pp. MoB73, 24.00c/set.
This is one of the most authoritative texts available, written by a noted German Indologist.

FRAZIER, ALLIE, ed. **HINDUISM. Glossary, 272pp. Wes69, 3.50p.**
A collection of readings on Hindu religious thought and practice, including both interpretive essays and selections from the sacred literature. The book begins with a general essay by Heinrich Zimmer on the meeting of East and West and goes from there to essays on the formative stages of the Hindu religion and selections from the **Rig** and **Atharva Vedas**, the **Bhagavad Gita**, and the **Upanishads**. There are also essays on samkhya yoga by Mircea Eliade, and one on Vedanta by Paul Deussen and selections from the **Jain Sutras**, with commentary. Most of the translations are from the nineteenth century and are of good scholarship, though not as flowing as some of the more recent ones. All in all, this is a good collection.

FULLER, J.F.C. YOGA. Illustrations, 148pp. YPS25, 6.00c.
An esoteric examination of yoga and Indian metaphysics by a student of Yogi Ramacharaka. Fuller discusses yogic practices in the light of the Western esoteric system and the Qabala. He includes chapters on Vedanta, raja yoga, mudras, and the esoteric bodies of man. There is also some reference to Buddhism.

GAER, JOSEPH. THE FABLES OF INDIA. Bibliography, 175pp. LBC55, 4.95c.
The fables which are retold here have been selected from three collections: the **Panchatantra**, the **Hitopadesa**, and the **Jatakas**. All the stories are *beast fables*—that is, stories about animals who have human emotions and human failings. Gaer has done a fine job of recreating the ancient fables. The narrative reads well and older children should enjoy the book. There are nice illustrations throughout. The introduction discusses fables.

Mohandas Gandhi

In 1947, after centuries of foreign rule, India won its independence from Great Britain—not through violence, but through years of intense, patient opposition based on love. The architect of this was the *professional revolutionary* M.K. Gandhi, whom a reverent nation called *Mahatma* or *Great Soul*: a little man in a loincloth, weighing less than 100 pounds and worth only two dollars in material possessions at the time of his death who had managed to translate the perfect love of the **Sermon on the Mount** and the **Bhagavad Gita** into effective action.

EASWARAN, EKNATH. GANDHI THE MAN. Index, 7½"x9½", Nil78, 6.95p.
This is a beautifully written and produced, highly personal study of Gandhi the man. Easwaran knew Gandhi personally and his own life incorporates many of Gandhi's ideals. In this volume he brings Gandhi

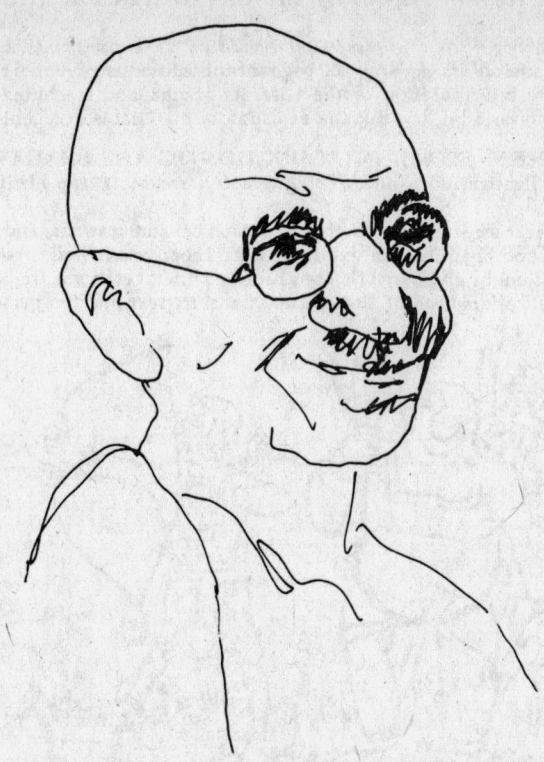

to life in a way we have not experienced before. Countless beautiful photographs illuminate the text and quotations from Gandhi's own writings are interspersed.

FISCHER, LOUIS, ed. **THE ESSENTIAL GANDHI. 369pp. RaH62, 2.95p.**
A detailed self portrait—in Gandhi's own words—of his mind, heart, and soul. Essays from all periods of his life are included.

GANDHI, MOHANDAS. **AN AUTOBIOGRAPHY. Index, 543pp. Bea57, 5.95p.**
A highly personal, self critical account, subtitled, *The Story of My Experiments with Truth.* Its narrative goes only as far as 1921, and is primarily concerned with Gandhi's spiritual development rather than his public political activity.

GANDHI, MOHANDAS. **THE HEALTH GUIDE. Glossary, index, 223pp. Css65, 3.95p.**
Gandhi's detailed suggestions on every aspect of bodily health and diet.

GREEN, MARTIN. **THE CHALLENGE OF THE MAHATMAS. Index, 271pp. H&R78, 10.95c.**
A comparative study of the teachings of Tolstoy and Gandhi—the two men, Green says, who have offered the most potent spiritual challenge to that restless expansionist fever which has always been a driving force of Western civilization. Green explores the relevance of their ideas to contemporary times.

IYER, RAGHAVAN. **THE MORAL AND POLITICAL THOUGHT OF MAHATMA GANDHI. Glossary, notes, index, 462pp. Oxf73, 4.95p.**
An authoritative work which elucidates the central concepts in Gandhi's moral and political thought and brings out the subtlety, potency, and universal import of Gandhi's political ethic in theory and practice. The study is enriched by allusions to a wide range of political thinkers, both classical and modern.

■ *MEHTA, VED.* **MAHATMA GANDHI AND HIS APOSTLES. Index, 271pp. Vik77, 3.50p.**
Mehta spent several years traveling through India, Afghanistan,

Bangladesh, England, and Austria, talking with relatives and disciples of Gandhi. From these conversations and an enormous body of research, he has fashioned a biographical portrait unlike any other. It shows the man, the leader, and his life. This is an important work which we consider the definitive biography of Gandhi. The man himself comes alive in these pages in a way that he does not elsewhere—including in his autobiography.

MERTON, THOMAS, ed. **GANDHI ON NON-VIOLENCE. Index, 83pp. NDP64, 1.50p.**
Selections from Gandhi's *Non-Violence in Peace and War.* In a long introduction Merton shows how Gandhi linked the thought of the East and West in his search for universal truth, and how, for him, nonviolence sprang from realization of spiritual unity in the individual.

POWER, PAUL, ed. **THE MEANINGS OF GANDHI. Notes, 199pp. UHa71, 11.40c.**
A collection of papers which came out of a 1969 conference at the East-West Center of the University of Hawaii, marking the centenary of Gandhi's birth. The participants were scholars of different training and viewpoints; the selections discuss Gandhi as both a man and a public actor and delve into his main ideas.

VASTO, LANZA DEL. **GANDHI TO VINOBA. Glossary, 231pp. ScB74, 8.95c.**
A comprehensive analysis of the life, work, and thought of Vinoba—one of Gandhi's most influential disciples and the teacher of del Vasto.

VASTO, LANZA DEL. **WARRIORS OF PEACE. 236pp. RaH74, 2.45p.**
Lanza del Vasto is the leader of the nonviolent movement in France. In 1948 he founded the Community of the Ark, a nonsectarian working order of men and women who put nonviolent principles into practice in their daily lives. **Warriors of Peace** contains his most important writings and discourses on the techniques of nonviolence.

WOODCOCK, GEORGE. **MOHANDAS GANDHI. Bibliography, index, 133pp. Vik71, 1.95p.**
A critical survey of Gandhi's life and work.

————**END OF MOHANDAS GANDHI SUBSECTION**————

GERBER, WILLIAM, ed. **THE MIND OF INDIA. Extensive bibliography, 285pp. SIU67, 3.95p.**
A topical anthology of Indian philosophical thought from ancient times to the twentieth century. Gerber has chosen his selections very carefully and he includes a wide variety of translators and writers. Each section begins with a succinct explanation of the particular philosophy's place in Indian history, and short biographies of the philosophers.

Gita

The **Gita** is often called the **Bible** of India. It is a portion of the **Mahabharata** (the great Hindu epic) and is recognized as embodying the highest and noblest truths of Eastern philosophy. The scene is a battlefield and the contestants are symbolic of the struggle between the higher and lower self in every man. Its form is that of a dialogue between Krishna and his disciple Arjuna. Emphasis is given to the discharge of spiritual duties as an effective discipline for the realization of God. Countless generations have been inspired and uplifted by the wisdom of the **Gita**.

ABHEDANANDA, SWAMI. **THE BHAGAVAD GITA. 1,028pp. RVM69. 15.25c/set.**
In 1907 Swami Abhedananda delivered a series of sixty-four discourses on the **Gita** before sophisticated American audiences. Thirty-two of them have been collected here, critically edited and annotated. Virtually every idea expressed in the **Gita** is fully discussed. Swami Abhedananda expresses himself very clearly and most of his analogies are derived from Western sources. He also keeps his usage of Sanskrit terminology to a minimum.

ARNOLD, SIR EDWIN, *tr.* **THE SONG CELESTIAL: A POETIC VERSION OF THE BHAGAVAD GITA.** 154pp. TPH1885, 2.50p/1.25p.
The poets rightly teach that Sannyasa is the foregoing of all acts which spring out of desire; and their wisest say Tyaga is the renouncing of fruits of acts. This is a classic rendition and the one which first popularized the **Gita** in the West.

AUROBINDO, SRI. **ESSAYS ON THE GITA.** 575pp. SAA70, 7.00c.
Almost all spiritual problems have been dealt with in the **Gita** *and I have tried to bring out all that fully in the* **Essays.**

AUROBINDO, SRI, *tr.* **THE MESSAGE OF THE GITA. Index,** 340pp. SAA38, 4.50p.
Aurobindo's interpretation of the **Gita,** one of his many works on the subject. With Sanskrit text, translation, and notes.

BESANT, ANNIE, *tr.* **BHAGAVAD GITA. Extensive index,** 223pp. TPH1895, 2.50c.
Sages have known as renunciation the renouncing of works with desire; the relinquishing of the fruit of all actions is called relinquishment by the wise. Noted for its close adherence to the original Sanskrit.

BUITENEN, J.A.B. VAN, *tr.* **RAMANUJA ON THE BHAGAVAD-GITA. Index,** 200pp. MoB68, 10.50c.
Ramanuja commented on virtually every word and sentence of the **Gita.** Van Buitenen's translation is a condensation which retains all of Ramanuja's most significant statements. He also supplies an abundance of his own notes.

CHINMAYANANDA, SWAMI. **GEETA FOR CHILDREN.** 171pp. CPT67, 2.50p.
Sannyasa is the Renunciation of Ego and its desire-prompted Activities while Tyaga is the abandonment of all anxieties to enjoy the fruits-of-action. This translation is not written in a language that young children can easily understand but rather is intended as a guide to parents for explaining the **Gita** to their children. Each chapter recommends a few stanzas which the children may memorize and chant and there are questions suggesting areas for discussion.

CHINMAYANANDA, SWAMI. **THE HOLY GEETA.** 1,156pp. CMT nd, 12.00c.
The sages understand SANNYASA to be "the renunciation of works with desire"; the wise declare "the abandonment of the fruits of all actions" as TYAGA. This is one of our favorite editions and combines an exceptionally careful textual analysis and commentary with an excellent translation. There is a constant attempt to bring forth from each verse not only its obvious meaning, but also its hidden import. The Sanskrit text is included and the edition is beautifully bound and a great deal sturdier than most Indian books.

DATE, V.H. **BRAHMA-YOGA OF THE GITA. Index,** 687pp. MuM71, 22.50c.
Renunciation of actions which are motivated by desires, the sages know as Sannyasa. The wise have called the giving up of the fruits of all actions, as Tyaga. Dr. Date is a well known contemporary Indian scholar who has written a number of important volumes. Here he expounds at length on the philosophy of the **Gita.** Years of deep study went into this exposition. Sankara's commentary on the **Gita** is cited and quoted often.

EASWARAN, EKNATH. **THE BHAGAVAD GITA (A RECORDING).** 3.00.
Easwaran, a disciple of Gandhi and the founder of a spiritual community in California, reading the Sanskrit text and his own English translation. He also includes commentary. A 33 1/3 rpm record.

EASWARAN, EKNATH. **THE BHAGAVADGITA FOR DAILY LIVING. Index,** 433pp. Nil73, 12.95c.
A translation of the first six chapters. *Sri Easwaran's commentary on the* **Bhagavad Gita** *differs from any of those existing at present. Since, in common with Gandhi, he sees the battlefield described in the* **Gita** *as symbolic of interior warfare between narrow self seeking and selfless divine realization, Easwaran's commentary is concerned not with textual criticism or historical exposition but with practical and specific ways whereby this spiritual battle may be won.*—Elizabeth Nottingham. Both the Sanskrit text and the translation of each stanza are presented.

EDGERTON, FRANKLIN, *tr.* **THE BHAGAVAD GITA.** 202pp. HUP44, 2.95p.
The renouncing of acts of desire sages call renunciation. The abandonment of action-fruits the wise call abandonment. 100 pages of this edition are devoted to an extensive interpretation of the **Gita,** its origins, and teaching. The translation is a bit dry, but the explanatory material is excellent.

FEUERSTEIN, GEORG. **INTRODUCTION TO THE BHAGAVAD GITA. Illustrations, notes, bibliography, index,** 191pp. HPG74, 10.00p.
A penetrating analysis of the philosophical implications and the cultural and historical context of the **Gita.** Feuerstein is well versed in Indian thought and Sanskrit literature; his interpretations are based on a critical analysis of the original Sanskrit text and his personal experience with the teachings.

ISHERWOOD, CHRISTOPHER *and* SWAMI PRABHAVANANDA. **BHAGAVAD GITA: THE SONG OF GOD (A RECORDING).** 7.98.
Zia Mohyeddin reads the Isherwood-Prabhavananda translation and Isherwood reads his own introduction. A 33 1/3 rpm record.

JHUNJHUN WALA, *ed.* **THE GITA. Glossary,** 270pp. SAA74, 4.50p.
The sages have known as Sannyasa the laying aside of actions born of desire; Tyaga is the name given by the wise to the entire abandonment of the fruit of action. This edition contains Sri Aurobindo's translation and his comments as well as the original Sanskrit text. There is also a selection from Aurobindo's **Essays on the Gita.**

JOHNSTON, CHARLES, *tr.* **BHAGAVAD GITA.** 132pp. Wat08, 3.25c.
The renouncing of works done through desire, sages have called Renunciation; and the wise have declared that ceasing from all desire of personal reward for one's work is Resignation. General introduction and an introduction to each chapter.

■ LAL, P., *tr.* **THE BHAGAVADGITA.** 107pp. WrW65, 10.10c/1.95p.
Renunciation means the giving-up of desire-laden action; it also means abandonment of action's fruits. A terse, beautiful rendition.

MAHARISHI MAHESH YOGI. **ON THE BHAGAVAD-GITA.** 494pp. Vik67, 2.95p.
The first six chapters with the original Sanskrit text, an introduction, and a commentary relating the text to meditational techniques.

MASCARO, JUAN, *tr.* **THE BHAGAVAD GITA.** 122pp. Vik62, 1.95p.
The renunciation of selfish works is called renunciation; but the surrender of the reward of all work is called surrender. Includes a long introduction but no textual commentary. Verses are numbered.

NIKHILANANDA, SWAMI, *tr.* **THE BHAGAVAD GITA. Introduction, glossary,** 226pp. RVC44, 3.00c.
The renunciation of works induced by desire is understood by the sages to be sannyasa, while the surrender of the fruits of all works is called tyaga by the wise.

NIKHILANANDA, SWAMI, *tr.* **THE BHAGAVAD GITA.** 382pp. RVC44, 5.95c.
The same translation and the following special features: an introduction to the philosophy of the **Gita,** a summary of the **Mahabharata,** and notes and comments based on the commentary of Sankara.

NIKHILANANDA, SWAMI and T.M.P. MAHADEVAN. **THE BHA-GAVAD-GITA (A RECORDING). 6.98.**
Swami Nikhilananda reads portions of his translation of the **Gita** and Mahadevan reads Sanskrit selections from the **Ramayana** and **Brahma Sutra** as well as a few hymns. The descriptive notes have both English and Sanskrit texts. A 33 1/3 rpm record.

PARAMANANDA, SWAMI, tr. **SRIMAD BHAGAVAD GITA. 162pp. VdC74, 2.75p.**
The Sages declare that the renunciation of actions with desire (for fruits) is Sannyasa, and the learned declare that the relinquishment of the fruits of all actions is Tyaga. This is a very clear translation and is the favorite of many. Paragraphs are numbered and there is a short introduction.

PARRINDER, GEOFFREY. **THE BHAGAVAD GITA. 124pp. Dut75/SIP, 2.95p.**
Renouncing actions of desire is what Renunciation meant, abandoning rewards of acts the wise have called Abandonment. Includes textual notes and references, and an appendix summarizing the chapters. *The purpose is to provide a popular yet accurate rendering, which will help readers to memorize important verses and understand the teachings.* Parrinder is one of England's most distinguished scholars of Hindu literature.

■ *PRABHAVANANDA, SWAMI and CHRISTOPHER ISHERWOOD, trs.* **THE SONG OF GOD, BHAGAVAD GITA. 191pp. VdP44/NEL, 3.75c/1.50p.**
The sages tell us that renunciation means the complete giving-up of all actions which are motivated by desire. And they say that non-attachment means abandonment of the fruits of action. An interpretation rather than a straight translation. The most popular **Gita**, it is highly recommended for its readability, clarity, and insight. Introduction by Aldous Huxley.

PREM, SRI KRISHNA. **THE YOGA OF THE BHAGAVAT GITA. Glossary, 224pp. Vik38/Wat, 1.65p.**
The point of view from which this book has been written is that the **Gita** *is a textbook of Yoga, a guide to the treading of the Path. By Yoga is here meant not any special system called by that name...but just the path by which man unites his finite self with Infinite Being. It is the inner Path of which all these separate yogas are so many one sided aspects.*

PUROHIT, SWAMI SHRI, tr. **THE BHAGAVAD GITA. 8½"x11", 183pp. RaH77, 10.00c/5.95p.**
A new edition of Purohit's translation accompanied by photographs of life in India and the East by Curt Bruce. The Sanskrit version of each stanza is presented alongside the translation.

PUROHIT, SWAMI SHRI, tr. **THE GEETA. 95pp. Fab35, 1.95p.**
The sages say that renunciation means foregoing an action which springs from desire; and relinquishing means the surrender of its fruit.

■ *RADHAKRISHNAN, S., tr.* **BHAGAVAD-GITA. 384pp. H&R48/A&U, 8.25c/4.95p.**
The wise understand by renunciation the giving up of works prompted by desire: the abandonment of the fruits of all works, the learned declare, is relinquishment. A classic work by one of the most noted contemporary Indian philosophers. Sanskrit text, English translation, and extensive commentary as well as an excellent, long, introductory essay are included.

RAGHAVACHAR, S.S. **SRI RAMANUJA ON THE GITA. Introduction, 236pp. SRM69, 2.25p.**
An in depth examination of Ramanuja's commentary on the **Gita**.

RAMACHARAKA, YOGI, tr. **BHAGAVAD GITA OR THE MESSAGE OF THE MASTER. 184pp. YPS30, 4.00c.**
The sages have told us that the principle of Sannyasa, or Abstaining from Action, lieth in the forsaking of all Action which hath a desired object; and that the principle of Tyaga, or Renunciation of Fruits of Action, lieth in the forsaking of all the fruits of every Action.

RAMDAS, SWAMI. **GITA SANDESH: MESSAGE OF THE GITA. 124pp. BBU66, 2.25p.**
A chapter-by-chapter discussion of the philosophical message of the **Gita**. Krishna's message is restated in modern terms and the exposition is aimed at seekers on the path.

ROY, DILIP, tr. **THE BHAGAVAD GITA. Index, 190pp. IBC74, 15.75c.**
The sages hold that the repudiation/Of all acts motivated by desire/Is renunciation
(*sannyasa*) *and the disclaimer/Of the fruits of action is (tyaga) non-attachment.* Dilip Roy is a singer and a musician and one of Sri Aurobindo's leading disciples. In addition to the translation, Roy offers the reader a series of thoughts inspired by the message of the **Gita**.

SARAYDARIAN, H. **BHAGAVAD GITA. Introduction, numbered verses, 96pp. AEG74, 6.00c.**
Renunciation is performed when a man acts without the desire of fruits. Abandonment is performed when all the fruits are given up. Saraydarian says that he did this translation while *in deep reflection and meditation, pondering on each Sanskrit word and phrase until the spirit behind the words was seen, grasped, and put into form.*

SHASTRI, HARI PRASAD, tr. **TEACHINGS FROM THE BHAGAVAD GITA. 96pp. ShS35, 1.65c.**
True renunciation consists in renouncing all selfish activities, and also the fruits of other activities, as offerings to God. Includes a nice introduction.

SHRINE OF WISDOM EDITORS. **A SYNTHESIS OF THE BHAGAVAD GITA. 72pp. ShW27, 4.95c.**
This version is specially prepared for the seeker of the significance of the Indian teachings in respect to the *good life,* and therefore the passages in the poem are rearranged under the headings of the five *margas* or *paths to perfection.* A very interesting translation.

STANFORD, ANN, tr. **THE BHAGAVAD GITA. Long introduction, numbered verses, notes, 172pp. Sea70, 3.95p.**
You praise renunciation of works/And again you say perform them./Krishna, tell me for certain/Which one is the better of these?/Renouncing, and work with discipline/Both lead to the best. But of these/Work with discipline surpasses/The renunciation of works. This is a verse translation by a poetess. Malcolm Crowley has called it *undeniably the best translation of the* **Gita** *ever done in English.*

STEINER, RUDOLF. **OCCULT SIGNIFICANCE OF THE BHAGAVAD GITA. 142pp. API68, 5.50c.**
Nine lectures.

The Dance of Siva.

SWARUPANANDA, SWAMI, tr. **SHRIMAD BHAGAVAD-GITA.**
430pp. AdA72, 3.50c.
*The renunciation of Kamya actions, the sages understand as Sannyasa; the wise declare
the abandonment of the fruit of all works as Tyaga.* The Sanskrit text is included
and individual works are defined. The translator is a disciple of Swami
Vivekananda.

THOMAS, EDWARD, tr. **THE SONG OF THE LORD: BHAGAVAD-**
GITA. 128pp. Mur31, 2.50c.
*The giving up of actions that involve desire the sages know as renunciation; the
abandonment of the fruit of all actions the wise call abandonment.* Includes a good
introduction.

UPADHYAYA, K.N. **EARLY BUDDHISM AND THE BHAGAVAD-**
GITA. Notes, bibliography, index, 567pp. MoB71, 20.00c.
A critical and comparative philosophical analysis of the teachings of the
Buddha as found in the early stratum of the Pali Canon and those of
Krishna as embodied in the **Bhagavad Gita**. It is the first time that
these two foundational works have been brought together for
comparative treatment.

VIRESWARANANDA, SWAMI, tr. **SRIMAD BHAGAVAD GITA.**
Index, 536pp. RVM48, 1.25p.
*Sages understand the renouncing of actions that fulfill desires as renunciation
(Sannyasa), and the learned declare the abandoning of the fruit of all actions as
relinquishment (Tyaga).* This edition includes the Sanskrit text and
translation as well as Sridhara's gloss on the **Gita** known as **Subodhini**.

ZAEHNER, R.C., tr. **THE BHAGAVADGITA. Lengthy introduction,**
index, 489pp. Oxf69, 4.95p.
*To give up works dictated by desire, wise men allow (this) to be renunciation; surrender
of all the fruits that (accrue) to works discerning men call self-surrender.* A
transliterated version of each stanza accompanies the translation
along with definitions and expositions of specific words and ideas and a
lengthy stanza and chapter commentary. This is a very scholarly
version, somewhat lacking in the spirit of the original, but containing
an abundance of valuable information for understanding the subtler
points of the text.

———————— END OF GITA SUBSECTION ————————

■ GOETZ, HERMANN. **THE ART OF INDIA. Glossary, chronology,**
bibliography, index, 283pp. Crn59, 6.95c.
This handsome book traces Indian art—including architecture, painting, sculpture, and handicrafts—from its origin in the late Stone Age to
the most recent developments. This is an excellent work which should
appeal to specialists and the general reader alike. Accompanying the
text are over sixty handtipped color plates and several maps. The
author has spent his lifetime studying Indian art.

GOETZ, HERMANN. **MIRA BAI: HER LIFE AND TIMES. 46pp.**
BBU66, .95p.
A biographical sketch of this widely loved fifteenth or sixteenth
century saint and poetess. Little is known about the details of her life;
this biography recreates Mira Bai's life by means of a critical analysis of
all the available information.

HAICH, ELISABETH, ed. **THE DAY WITH YOGA. 85pp. ASI77, 2.50p.**
A different creative energy is at work on each day of the week. Nature
and all living creatures are influenced by these vibrations. In this book
Ms. Haich has carefully chosen quotations which show us how we can
attune ourselves to the vibrations of each day. Most, but not all, of the
quotations are from Indian philosophers.

HAICH, ELISABETH and SELVARAJAN YESUDIAN. **YOGA AND**
DESTINY. 80pp. ASI66/A&U, 4.95c.
Transcripts of a series of lectures: *Yoga and Destiny, Yoga and Self-Healing,
How to Become a Yogi, Yoga in Today's Struggle for Existence,* and *A Few Words
About Magic.*

HAMBLY, GAVIN. **CITIES OF MUGHUL INDIA. Glossary, bibliog-**
raphy, index, 8¾"x11¼", 168pp. Ele nd, 19.95c.
The splendor and opulence of the courts of the great Moguls at Delhi
and Agra confirmed for the European explorers who went there in the
sixteenth century all their wildest dreams of the inexhaustible wealth
of the East. Between 1526 and 1712 the Mogul emperors, Turks by

origin but with Mongol, Persian, and Hindu blood in their veins, ruled
the greater part of the Indian subcontinent. This is a lively account of
the three great cities of Mogul India—Delhi, Agra, and Fatehpur
Sikri—illustrated with 128 magnificent photographs by Wim Swaan of
architectural landmarks, miniatures, and *objets d'art,* seventy-one of
which are in color.

HIRIYANNA, M. **THE ESSENTIALS OF INDIAN PHILOSOPHY.**
Glossary, notes, index, 216pp. A&U49, 10.00p.
A scholarly, thorough account of Indian philosophy, providing interpretation and criticism. An introductory chapter summarizes Vedic
religion and philosophy, and then Indian thought is considered in
chapters dealing respectively with the early post-Vedic period and the
age of the systems.

HIRIYANNA, M. **OUTLINES OF INDIAN PHILOSOPHY. Notes,**
index, 419pp. A&U32, 10.75p.
This is a scholarly tome, based upon lectures which the author
delivered at the Mysore University in India over a period of many
years. Every doctrine of Indian philosophy and each of the major
periods are covered at length. It is an excellent work for those desiring
a textbook approach to Indian philosophy.

HOPKINS, EDWARD, ed. **HINDU POLITY: THE ORDINANCES OF**
MANU. Lengthy introduction, 446pp. Kly1884, 9.20c.
An edited reprint of Arthur Coke Burnell's translation of the ordi-
nances or laws of Manu. An abundance of notes accompany the text.

■ HOPKINS, THOMAS. **THE HINDU RELIGIOUS TRADITION.**
Excellent chapter-by-chapter annotated bibliography, index, 166pp.
Dic71, 8.75p.
An excellent historical and chronological survey of the thoughts,
values, and religious practices of the Hindu population of India: where
they came from, how they developed, what they are now, and where
they are heading. This is written by a professor and seems to have been
designed as a basic text for a survey course. The material is well
written and organized and the student gets a good idea of the religious
tradition and its development.

JACOBI, HERMANN, tr. **JAINA SUTRAS. 750pp. MoB1884, 10.10c/**
each.
The Jain religion developed in India at about the same time as
Buddhism did, during a period of Hindu decline. It has had continuing
importance in India to the present day—though it has never been as
significant a movement as Hinduism or Buddhism. This two volume
set, from the **Sacred Books of the East** series, contains the most
important classical sutras, along with an extensive introductory essay.

JOHARI, HARISH. **LEELA: THE GAME OF SELF-KNOWLEDGE.**
143pp. Put75, 6.65p.
This ancient game is to the Hindu tradition what the **I Ching** *is to the Chinese, and,
in both, chance plays a vital part. The game of Leela is centuries old. The version used as
the basis for this translation was brought to this country in 1969 by Harish Johari, a
distinguished Sanskrit scholar, poet, artist, and composer. He created the Commentaries on each of the seventy-two squares of the gameboard in a form Western readers could
understand. With them American readers can now play the Leela game and discover
through this unique Hindu psychological tool, the nature of their hidden selves.—*
from the preface. A gameboard is included.

■ JOHNSON, CLIVE, ed. **VEDANTA. Glossary, bibliography, 284pp.**
Ban71/H&R, 2.50c.
This is an excellent anthology for those seeking an introduction to the
sacred literature of the Hindus and to the writings and philosophy of
India's contemporary saints and spiritual leaders: Sri Ramakrishna,
Gandhi, Tagore, Sri Aurobindo, and Ramana Maharshi. Selections are
included from the **Vedas**, the **Upanishads**, the **Ramayana**, the **Maha-
bharata**, the **Bhagavad Gita**, Sankara, the **Bhakti Sutras** of Narada, the
Yoga Sutras of Patanjali, the **Laws of Manu**, and the **Bhagavata
Purana**, along with verses from some of the most noted Indian mystic
poets. Recommended for those desiring an introductory overview.
The translations are usually from the most readable editions.

JOHNSON, DONALD and JEAN. **GOD AND GODS IN HINDUISM.**
88pp. Com72, 5.20c.
An illustrated, concise presentation of the nature of God according to
the Hindus and the role played by deities in Hinduism throughout the

ages. Each of the major deities is examined and many plates are included.

JOHNSTON, E. **EARLY SAMKHYA. Index, 198pp. MoB37, 6.00c.**
The descriptions of Samkhya before the formulation of the classical system of Isvarakrsna are contained in a large number of contradictory and vague texts. Johnston begins with an introduction in which he describes the sources and defines methods. The next sections are basically made up of original source material in the following areas: origins, *prakrti*, life and the soul, and theoretical principles of Samkhya philosophy. Extensive textual notes are included which help bring the material together, and the author attempts to account for the contradictions.

Kabir

Kabir was one of India's most beloved poets and mystics. He lived in the fifteenth century. Both Sufis and Hindus claim him as their own, but his joyous teachings transcend all such boundaries and categories. Kabir was not a recluse or an ascetic. He was a weaver and a family man and it was from out of the heart of the common life that he sang his rapturous lyrics of divine love. His dislike of all institutional religion was obvious. *The simple union with Divine Reality which he perpetually extolled, as alike the duty and the joy of every soul, was independent both of ritual and of bodily austerities; the God whom he proclaimed was neither in Kaaba nor in Kailash. Those who sought Him needed not to go far; for He awaited discovery everywhere, more accessible to the washerwoman and the carpenter than to the self-righteous holy man. Therefore the whole apparatus of piety, Hindu and Moslem alike—the temple and mosque, idol and holy water, scriptures and priests—were denounced by this . . . clear-sighted poet as mere substitutes for reality; dead things intervening between the soul and its love.*—from **Songs of Kabir**, by R. Tagore.

BLY, ROBERT. **THE KABIR BOOK. Illustrations, 71pp. Bea77, 7.95c/ 3.95p.**
Other than the Tagore/Underhill translation, this is the only English version of Tagore's intensely religious poetry. Bly feels that Tagore's Victorian English was simply not equal to Kabir's directness, spontaneity, and irreverent humor, so he set out to rework the Tagore translation into more contemplative language. He includes forty-four poems, some of which originally appeared in shorter books.

TAGORE, RABINDRANATH. **SONGS OF KABIR. 145pp. Wei15/ McM, 2.25p.**
Despite the criticisms quite justifiably made by Robert Bly and others, Tagore's translation of Kabir's songs remains the standard work. The reader can get a good idea of Kabir from the book and can always let his imagination and heart fill in the rest.

VAUDEVILLE, CHARLOTTE. **KABIR, VOLUME I. Extensive notes, bibliography, 354pp. Oxf74, 32.25c.**
There has been to this day no critical translation of the bulk of Kabir's verses and hardly any attempt at studying him for himself, against the background of his own time and tradition. The present work is a step in that direction. It aims at filling what is felt as a serious gap in our knowledge of Indian religious tradition and mysticism, by translating whatever can be considered "authentic" in Kabir's utterances and also by carefully sifting and analysing the various data which can be gathered to this day about Kabir himself, his words and his time.

───────── END OF KABIR SUBSECTION ─────────

KAPOOR, O.B.L. **THE PHILOSOPHY AND RELIGION OF SRI CAITANYA. Notes, bibliography, index, 258pp. MuM77, 23.20c.**
A comprehensive, critical, comparative study of all aspects of the philosophy and religion of Sri Caitanya, one of the main representatives of the bhakti school of Indian philosophy.

KESHAVADAS, SANT. **SAINTS OF INDIA. 100pp. TCR75, 3.50p.**
A lively discussion of a variety of Indian saints who lived in the thirteenth, fifteenth, sixteenth, and seventeenth centuries. The order of presentation is chronological.

KINSLEY, DAVID. **THE SWORD AND THE FLUTE. Notes, bibliography, 176pp. UCa75, 12.00c.**
An in depth, scholarly study of the transcendent dimensions of Krishna and Kali. Kinsley feels that these two gods dramatically express central truths of the Hindu religious tradition. He seeks to demonstrate that the divine form is redemptive—whether it is apprehended in terrible or in divine form. Many quotations from the sacred scriptures back up his thesis.

KIRK, JAMES. **STORIES OF THE HINDUS. Glossary, bibliography, 287pp. McM72, 2.95p.**
This is a collection of myths, legends, popular dramas, and tales. These stories, writes Kirk, *are not primarily important religious texts, but they employ many of the assumptions, attitudes, and unsophisticated forms of the Hindu Religion.* Kirk has tried to introduce Hinduism to the reader in the same way that the young Hindu child is introduced to his heritage. Part I contains stories which portray the assumptions and ideals of Hindu culture in rather general terms. The stories in Part II have a more specifically religious content and many of them are highly devotional in nature. Those in Part III tell of the principal gods, Vishnu and Siva, in their various incarnations. Commentary is also included.

Krishna

The god Krishna is uniquely Indian. He embodies some of the most attractive things about that ancient civilisation. The heroic spirit of the old Sanskrit epics is found in Krishna's adventures as warrior and dragon-slayer. The wisdom of the yogis is embodied in the instruction Krishna gives to his friend Arjuna, which is set out in the **Gita**. Also in Krishna we find the exoticism of the East, as shown in his rich life as a Raja, and his harem of 16,000 concubines, and the warm-hearted earthiness, which is especially found in Indian culture, is met with in Krishna's hilarious youthful pranks, when he lived a life of irredeemable mischief among the cowherds of Braj. But perhaps most typical of all, and the most popular and striking quality of Krishna, as he is worshipped today in India, is the luscious eroticism of his life with his milkmaids in the forests of Vrindavan.

—*Nigel Frith*

BHATTATIRI, MEPPATHUR. **NARAYANEEYAM: BHAGAVATA CONDENSED. 407pp. SRM76, 7.50c.**
A masterly summary of the subject matter dealt with in the **Bhagavata Purana**. Sanskrit text, English translation, and doctrinal notes are included along with a forty-four page introduction by the translator, Swami Tapasyananda.

COHEN, S.S., tr. **SRIMAD BHAGAVATA. 376pp. CPT65, 2.00p.**
This is a condensation of the original longer work, bringing out all the instructions and stories and cutting out some of the repetition. This book is basically a series of stories about the life (and loves) of Krishna and contains some of the most famous tales about him. Other stories are interspersed. The translation flows well and is quite faithful to the original.

DIMOCK, EDWARD and DENISE LEVERTOV, trs. **IN PRAISE OF KRISHNA. Notes, 95pp. Dou67, 1.95p.**
Songs from the Bengali.

■ FRITH, NIGEL. **THE LEGEND OF KRISHNA. 237pp. ScB76, 7.95c.**
A modern retelling of Krishna stories gathered together from nearly every major classic of Hindu literature, providing a continuous narrative of Krishna's exploits. In novelistic style, Frith portrays Krishna in all his guises—mischievous youth, lover, mighty warrior, and great teacher. All the major Indian gods and Vedic myths are woven into the narrative. This is a welcome addition to the Krishna literature. Frith teaches poetry at Oxford University.

KEYT, GEORGE, tr. **GITA GOVINDA: SONG OF LOVE. 123pp. HPB40, 12.60c/1.95p.**
The love of Radha and Krishna has been the inspiration for countless

works of art, music, and literature in India. The **Gita Govinda** is a twelfth century poem about their love and it is probably the most popular account. The hardcover edition is on fine paper and is beautifully illustrated.

LAMBERT, H.M., ed. **JNANESHVARI. Notes, 357pp. A&U67, 6.95c.**
This is a lengthy religious work in a form of rhythmic prose by the Marathi saint Jnaneshvar, who lived in the western region of India towards the end of the thirteenth century. He completed this poetic presentation of Hindu teachings at the age of nineteen. It is a source of devotional literature for those who have dedicated their lives to Krishna. This is the first half of an English translation. A second and concluding volume is to follow.

MCGREGOR, R.S., tr. **NANDDAS: THE ROUND DANCE OF KRISHNA AND UDDHAV'S MESSAGE. Index, 146pp. Luz73, 14.00c.**
The poems translated here for the first time into English are the principal works of Nanddas, one of the foremost Krishna poets of north India. Nanddas lived in the sixteenth century, during the last truly creative period in the evolution of Krishna worship. In these poems he expresses the essential spirit of Krishna devotionalism as it was to be felt from his time onwards. McGregor provides a lengthy critical introduction and notes.

MADHAVANANDA, SWAMI, tr. **UDDHAVA GITA OR THE LAST MESSAGE OF SHRI KRISHNA. Index, 382pp. AdA71, 2.75c.**
A translation of chapters six to twenty-nine of the eleventh book of the **Srimad Bhagavatam**, with the original Sanskrit text and notes.

MILLER, BARBARA, tr. **LOVE SONG OF THE DARK LORD: JAYADEVA'S GITAGOVINDA. 145pp. Col77, 3.95p.**
A translation of Jayadeva's work which concentrates on Krishna's love for the gopi Radha. Intense earthly passion is the example Jayadeva uses to express the complexities of divine and human love. The love songs are an important part of Indian devotional music and literature, and the poem itself is a major subject in medieval Rajput painting. An introduction places the poem in the context of Indian culture and literature and includes background on the poet and analysis of the poem's structure and symbolism.

RAMAKRISHNANANDA, SWAMI. **SRI KRISHNA: PASTORAL AND KING-MAKER. 122pp. SRM73, 1.00p.**
Transcription of two lectures summarizing the main events in the life of Krishna and the major thrust of his teaching.

SANYAL, J.M., tr. **THE SRIMAD BHAGAVATAM. Two volumes, index, 1,450pp. MuM73, 42.50c/set.**
A scholarly translation of the **Srimad Bhagavatam**, emphasizing those portions which deal with the life and feats of Krishna. This book contains the most Krishna stories of any Sanskrit work. The translation is into fairly flowing English.

SINGER, MILTON, ed. **KRISHNA: MYTHS, RITES, AND ATTITUDES. Notes, bibliography, index, 277pp. UCh66, 2.95p.**
A collection of essays which examine Krishna the divine herdsman and mischievous child. Singer analyzes poetry, legends, myths, and rites which have dramatized his deeds and described his world.

WILSON, FRANCES, ed. **THE LOVE OF KRISHNA. Indices, 472pp. UPa75, 38.00c.**
An English translation, with the transliterated Sanskrit text on facing pages, of the **Krsnakarnamrta**, a medieval Sanskrit devotional anthology of stanzas in praise of the youthful Krishna. The translation has been derived from a collation of more than seventy manuscripts. Ms. Wilson also includes a lengthy introduction and an abundance of critical notes.

──────────── **END OF KRISHNA SUBSECTION** ────────────

Kundalini Yoga

The physical and subtle bodies meet at certain points known as *chakras*, meaning wheels. They represent psychic vortices or powerhouses of force. Many *chakras* exist throughout the body, but all are controlled from seven major centers, which some modern exponents equate with the ductless glands. The energizing of the *chakras* is the specific goal of kundalini yoga. Learning the art of arousing the kundalini is a long and arduous process involving many exterior and interior exercises, including asanas, mudras (hand gestures), pranayama, mandalas, and mantras. The cultivation of two kinds of breath is important. One generates in the subtle body and one in the physical; one moves downward and one upward along the spinal column. At a given moment the two breaths are impacted and the full force of colliding energies is directed toward the kundalini. This results in the closing of the two side arteries in the spinal column and the opening of the middle one, whereupon a series of extraordinary events is precipitated. The kundalini, aroused, begins to tremble, uncoils itself from its home at the base of the spine, and begins its journey upwards, piercing each *chakra* through the middle and causing its petals to open. Each *chakra* as it opens contributes to the awakening of a particular faculty, and thus stage-by-stage the practitioner becomes progressively enlightened.

ARUNDALE, GEORGE. **KUNDALINI: AN OCCULT EXPERIENCE. 118pp. TPH62, 3.00c.**
The author describes the awakening of consciousness as kundalini moves from its base in the human body through the force centers, causing illumination of universal life, light, sound, and power.

BERNARD, RAYMOND. **THE SERPENT FIRE. Offset, stapled, 8½"x 11", 100pp. HeR59, 4.00p.**
Subtitled, *The Awakening of Kundalini: Secret Yoga Methods of Rejuvenation Through Awakening a Mysterious Power at the Base of the Spine, known as Kundalini or the Serpent Fire, and Causing it to Ascend to the Brain, Which it Energizes and Vitalizes.* Detailed instructions, but watch out, it can be dangerous.

KRISHNA, GOPI. **THE AWAKENING OF KUNDALINI. Introduction, 141pp. Dut75, 3.25p.**
Gopi Krishna believes that planted in human beings is a powerful reservoir of psychic energy which, when roused to activity in the state of Kundalini, can lead to transcendental states of consciousness, genius, and supernormal psychic powers. In the state of Kundalini the reproductive system recoils on itself and transfers energy to the brain. We can learn to activate Kundalini only through devoted meditation and yogic exercises.—from the introduction. This book is Gopi Krishna's fullest exploration of the phenomena of kundalini. He tries to make his exposition as practical as possible and emphasizes the scientific aspects.

KRISHNA, GOPI. **KUNDALINI: THE EVOLUTIONARY ENERGY IN MAN. 252pp. ShP67, 4.50p.**
A fascinating autobiographical account of what happens to the mind and body when the kundalini is aroused spontaneously, after many years of yogic discipline. It is told in a sincere and simple way. Besides describing the perils, upheavals, and final balanced entry into another dimension, the book also gives some of the traditional Hindu theories about this force.

KRISHNA, GOPI. **THE RIDDLE OF CONSCIOUSNESS. 156pp. KRF76, 3.95p.**
A collection of prophetic, revelatory poetry about the future prospects of mankind on Earth.

KRISHNA, GOPI. **THE SECRET OF YOGA. 207pp. MoB72, 7.20c.**
An exploration of yoga and its source of energy, kundalini, in the light of modern scientific knowledge. Gopi Krishna views kundalini as the key to enlightenment and cosmic consciousness in the sense Richard Bucke discussed. This metamorphosis brings about a tremendous increase in intellectual stature, which Gopi Krishna says is **The Secret of Yoga.** This is the most difficult of his books.

KUNDALINI RESEARCH INSTITUTE. **KUNDALINI MEDITATION MANUAL. 8¼"x11¾", 64pp. KRI77, 3.50p.**
A series of over forty meditation exercises and techniques accompanied by explicit instructions and barely adequate line drawings.

KUNDALINI RESEARCH INSTITUTE. **KUNDALINI: YOGA/SADHANA GUIDELINES. 8½"x10", 112pp. KRI76, 5.00p.**
This manual contains thirty basic exercises and fifteen meditations. The instructions are detailed and accompanied by step-by-step illustrations.

NARAYANANANDA, SWAMI. **THE PRIMAL POWER IN MAN OR THE KUNDALINI SHAKTI. 155pp. NUY50, 8.20p.**
An extremely detailed study, based on Tantric teachings. It is good to have some knowledge of Indian philosophy before beginning this volume, although the Sanskrit terminology is kept to a minimum.

PANDIT, M.P. **KUNDALINI YOGA. 3.00c.**
See the Tantra section.

RELE, VASANT. **THE MYSTERIOUS KUNDALINI. Glossary, bibliography, 113pp. TSC60, 2.60p.**
The chief interest in this book consists in the description of the modification at will of certain physiological processes by a Yogi. It has a distinct value as describing and illustrating the physical training of the Yogi, and interpreting the difficult pseudoanatomical descriptions of the Tantric Texts.—Sir John Woodroffe.

RIEKER, HANS-ULRICH. **THE YOGA OF LIGHT: HATHA YOGA PRADIPIKA. Illustrations, glossary, 203pp. DHP71/A&U, 4.95p.**
In Indian philosophy it is generally understood that hatha yoga is one distinct path to liberation and raja yoga another. This text shows a rare and fruitful combination of the two paths. This is the first time that the full text has been translated into English. This ancient text is written in an extremely terse and often highly symbolic language. Rieker's excellent commentaries help a great deal. The text is concerned mainly with various postures and breathing exercises, and it also discusses kundalini at great length.

SANELLA, LEE. **KUNDALINI—PSYCHOSIS OR TRANSCENDENCE. Notes, index, 112pp. HSD76, 3.95p.**
An exploration of kundalini, synthesizing concepts and observations from anthropology, Eastern philosophy, and Western medical science. Dr. Sanella is a psychiatrist and he worked with patients who have undergone the kundalini awakening process. Fifteen medical case histories are included. He also discusses how to distinguish manifestations of the kundalini awakening process from psychosis. A previously unpublished paper by Itzhak Bentov, a physicist, examining the physiological processes which accompany kundalini experiences, is appended.

■ SIVANANDA, SWAMI. **KUNDALINI YOGA. 272pp. DLS35, 3.60c.**
This is the best exposition of the theory and practice of kundalini yoga that we have seen. Includes an excellent summary chart of the *chakras* and many other clear, helpful illustrations. The first 120 pages present background and theoretical material and the last 200 give detailed, practical exercises for raising the kundalini (along with preliminary exercises).

WHITE, JOHN, et al. **KUNDALINI: CATASTROPHE OR CREATIVE CONSCIOUSNESS? 8½"x11", 31pp. HDI76, 2.00p.**
A collection of essays from a number of disciplines and spiritual movements. Far and away the most varied selection available.

WOODROFFE, SIR JOHN. **THE SERPENT POWER. 5.00p.**
See the Tantra section.

———————END OF KUNDALINI YOGA SUBSECTION———————

KUNHAN RAJA, C. **SOME FUNDAMENTAL PROBLEMS IN INDIAN PHILOSOPHY. Index, 430pp. MoB74, 15.00c.**
A survey of Indian philosophy from the **Vedas** to the medieval period. The author's fundamental thesis is that, in essentials, there is no confict between ancient philosophical thought and modern scientific thought, and that there is only a progression accompanied by appropriate revision of views with the change of time and environment. Part I is a discussion of the three modes of knowing: direct experience, inference, and authority. Part II is a survey of the formation of the world and its constituent parts as expounded in different systems of Indian philosophy; Part III is a review of man and his destiny.

KUTUMBIAH, P. **ANCIENT INDIAN MEDICINE. Glossary, notes, index, 285pp. OLL62, 9.20p.**
This is a comprehensive picture of ancient Indian medicine written by an Indian physician who is well versed in the ancient Indian medical classics. A fifty-two page introduction traces the origin and development of ancient Indian medicine. The rest of the book is devoted to a presentation of the treatment techniques of the ancient Indians and much practical information is included. The book is more detailed than most individuals would want, and it is also not very clearly written.

LAL, P., tr. **GREAT SANSKRIT PLAYS IN MODERN TRANSLATION. 416pp. NDP64, 4.45p.**
The beauty of classical Indian drama has been obscured for most readers by the stilted style of the existing nineteenth century translations. Lal, a fine poet and translator, has produced new versions which bring across the richness and vitality of the originals. This volume contains **Shakuntala** by Kalidasa, **The Toy Cart** by King Shudraka, **The Signet Ring of Rakshasa** by Vishakadatta, **The Dream of Vasavadatta** by Bhasa, **The Later Story of Rama** by Bhavabhuti, and **Ratnavali** by Harsha. Lal also provides an introduction on the history and aesthetic theory of Sanskrit drama, individual prefaces for each play, a phonetic guide, and a bibliography.

LANNOY, RICHARD. **THE SPEAKING TREE: A STUDY OF INDIAN CULTURE AND SOCIETY. Extensive bibliography and index, 492pp. Oxf71, 4.95p.**
This is an excellent, sociologically-oriented study of Indian culture and society *with the chief aim of identifying the origins of the nation's contemporary problems. Though generally manifested in economic terms, these have their root causes in the historical development of India's system of values and thought, as reflected in its cultural and social organization.* The study traces Indian culture from antiquity to the present and is illustrated with many photographs. Lannoy has lived, studied, and worked in India during much of the past two decades.

LANNOY, RICHARD and HARRY BAINES. **THE EYE OF LOVE IN THE TEMPLE SCULPTURE OF INDIA. 12.50c.**
See the Sacred Art section.

LAW, B.C. **HISTORICAL GLEANINGS. Index, 101pp. MoB22, 8.00c.**
A collection of six academic essays: *Taxila as a Seat of Learning in Sanskrit and Pali Literature, The Wandering Teachers at the Time of the Buddha, The Influence of the Five Heretical Teachers on Jainism and Buddhism, Buddhaghosa's Commentaries, The Licchavis in Ancient India,* and *Buddha and Niganthas.*

LIPSKI, ALEXANDER. **LIFE AND TEACHING OF SRI ANANDA-MAYIMA. 84pp. MoB77, 6.30c.**
A summary of the teachings and presence of a contemporary Indian holy woman.

MCCARTNEY, JAMES. **YOGA: THE KEY TO LIFE. Illustrations, 241pp. HPG69, 4.50p.**
Provides a good, general outline of yoga philosophy, surveying first hatha yoga; then going on to a discussion of concentration, meditation, and contemplation; and then reviewing the less familiar aspects of karma, mantra, bhakti, raja, and jnana yoga. Each chapter concludes with appropriate exercises.

MCDERMOTT, ROBERT and V.S.NARAVANE, eds. **THE SPIRIT OF MODERN INDIA. Glossary, bibliography, index, 337pp. Cro74, 2.45p.**
This book establishes the historical context in which Indian thinkers of the past 100 years have developed their ideas, and shows how these ideas comprise a coherent vision which is at once Indian and contemporary. The editors focus on writings by Ramakrishna, Vivekananda, Tagore, Gandhi, Nehru, Radhakrishnan, and Sri Aurobindo. The selections are topically arranged and contain introductory and background material.

MCNEILL, WILLIAM and JEAN SEDLAR, eds. **CLASSICAL INDIA. 307pp. Oxf69, 3.35p.**
A collection of source readings classified according to subject matter under four headings: 1) *artha,* or the practical skills of public and private life; 2) *kama,* or sense gratification; 3) *dharma,* or law and righteousness; and 4) *moksha,* the means of transcending the commonsense world of things. A good selection of translations.

The Mahabharata

The **Mahabharata**, an ancient and vast Sanskrit poem that traditionally runs to 100,000 couplets, is the most important Indian literary work in existence. This remarkable collection of epics, legends, romances, theology, and ethical and metaphysical doctrine is representative of the history and culture of the entire Hindu civilization. The **Bhagavad Gita**, for example, is but one of its component parts. Begun perhaps in the twelfth century BC by an unknown author, the epic spans a period of history that saw the rise and spread of Buddhism, Indian political and economic expansion, and the transformation of the ancient Vedic religion into Hinduism. This was also the period of the development of the principal philosophical schools and the rise of the worship of Vishnu and Siva. The core of the **Mahabharata** is formed by stories of an epical struggle between two branches of a royal family. The five Pandava brothers spend many years and experience countless adventures in vying with their one hundred contentious cousins for rule of the land.

■ BUCK, WILLIAM, tr. **THE MAHABHARATA. 370pp. UCa73, 10.95c/4.95p.**
Buck's redering is not a translation. Instead, he has retold the story so that the modern reader will be able to know the epic in terms of modern life as well as in terms of its origins. Although he greatly condensed the story, he remained faithful to its spirit and underlying truth, reflecting the original sequence of events, and conveying the flavor by using traditional narrative techniques.

BUITENEN, J.A.B. VAN, tr. **THE MAHABHARATA: I, THE BOOK OF THE BEGINNING. Index, 539pp. UCh73, 26.00c.**
This is the first volume in what will ultimately become a multi-volume edition encompassing all eighteen books of the **Mahabharata**. Professor van Buitenen has based his translation on the definitive Poona edition of 1933-66. He provides the reader with a wealth of material for understanding the text including summaries of sections, notes, chapter-by-chapter cross references, and much else. This volume incorporates the first of the eighteen books and serves as an introduction to the following ones.

BUITENEN, J.A.B. VAN, tr. **THE MAHABHARATA: II, THE BOOK OF THE ASSEMBLY HALL AND III, THE BOOK OF THE FOREST. Index, 875pp. UCh75, 44.35c.**
Translations of the second and third books.

DANGE, S.A. **LEGENDS IN THE MAHABHARATA. Notes, index, 423pp. MoB69, 14.00c.**
A scholarly discussion of the most important legends and folktales recorded in the **Mahabharata**, with special reference to the legends of Garuda, Kaca, and Amrtamanathana. Dange cites and questions the traditional views about the legends, suggests new interpretations, and establishes a fresh link between the Vedic and epic Puranic traditions on the one hand and current folk beliefs and customs on the other. Many of the tales are retold in full or part.

GOLDMAN, ROBERT. **GODS, PRIESTS AND WARRIORS. Notes, bibliography, index, 207pp. Col77, 13.50c.**
Members of the priestly clan known as the Bhargavas appear throughout Indian mythological literature from the earliest Vedic to the latest Puranic text. The **Mahabharata** provides the most extensive treatment of Bhargava mythology. In this book Goldman examines the complex Bhargava submythologies deliberately worked into the fabric of this great epic by early Bhargava redactors. The Bhargavas were an unconventional race whose behavior often deviated from the norms set forth in the dharma literature of their fellow Brahmans. They were preoccupied with death, violence, and sorcery, and were often hostile to the gods. Many of their central myths are retold and analyzed in this volume.

HILTEBEITEL, ALF. **THE RITUAL OF BATTLE. Many notes, index, 368pp. Cor76, 26.20c.**
An academic study of Krishna as he is portrayed in the **Mahabharata**. Professor Hiltebeitel interprets Krishna's role within the framework of the multi-dimensional epic and maintains that the **Mahabharata**—and especially Krishna's role in it—is the tradition of Indo-European epics and mythology, yet specifically reshaped in the Indian context. He also shows that the main symbolism of the epic centers on the themes of warfare and world renovation as interpreted through the ritual medium of the Brahamanic sacrifice.

NARASIMHAN, C.V., tr. **THE MAHABHARATA: AN ENGLISH VERSION BASED ON SELECTED VERSES. 254pp. Col65, 3.95p.**
The best scholarly one volume English translation of this great epic poem. Includes a glossary of persons, places, and transliterated Sanskrit words, as well as genealogical tables which show the relationship of the Kauravas and the Pandavas, and an index of chapters and verses correlated to the original Sanskrit text.

NARAYAN, R.K. **THE MAHABHARATA. Introduction, illustrations, glossary, 202pp. Vik78, 12.50c.**
A shortened modern prose version by one of India's greatest novelists. This is an excellent rendition, successfully designed to appeal to the modern reader. We enjoyed Narayan's version immensely.

■ RAJAGOPALACHARI, C. **MAHABHARATA. 332pp. BBU51, 3.95p.**
A simple retelling which speaks to the readers in their own language. Recommended as the best introduction.

RAO, SHANTA RAMESHWAR. **THE MAHABHARATA. 229pp. OLL74, 2.85c.**
A novelistic recreation and condensation of the main story of the epic. Ms. Rao retells the story vividly. For those who wish to get a feeling for the content without being overwhelmed with details, this is as good a place to start as any we can think of.

ROY, PRATAP, tr. **THE MAHABHARATA. MuM76, 280.50c/set.**
This is a new edition of Roy's pioneering translation, still considered the best complete translation available. The set is in twelve volumes and each is about 500 pages long.

────── **END OF THE MAHABHARATA SUBSECTION** ──────

MAHADEVAN, T.M.P. **TEN SAINTS OF INDIA. Index, 159pp. BBU65, 2.00p.**
Short biographical studies of Tirujnana Sambandhar, Tirunavuk-karasu, Sundaramurti, Manikkavackar, Nammalvar, Andal, Sankara, Ramanuja, Sri Ramakrishna, and Ramana Maharshi. All but one of these saints are from south India.

MARTIN, E. OSBORN. **THE GODS OF INDIA. Notes, index, 344pp. IBH13, 16.00c.**
This book retells many of the Vedic and Puranic myths and also includes many minor myths. The author's intent is to treat all of the Indian gods equally; the gods are seen and discussed in many of their aspects. This is as good a general survey of Hindu mythology as any we know.

MEHTA, RAKSHA, tr. **THE SONG OF A THOUSAND NAMES. Wat76, 5.20p.**
A newly translated selection of Sanskrit verses, originally chanted to ward off dangerous influences and bring prosperity. A drawing accompanies each two verses and the transliterated Sanskrit text is also included.

MICHELL, GEORGE. **THE HINDU TEMPLE: AN INTRODUCTION TO ITS MEANING AND FORMS. 22.50c.**
See the Sacred Geometry section.

MISHRA, RAMMURTI. **FUNDAMENTALS OF YOGA. Line drawings, 238pp. Dou59/LyP, 2.50p.**
This is an excellent beginning text on yogic philosophy. Dr. Mishra is an endocrinologist who has taught Indian philosophy at a variety of American colleges. The book was originally written to serve as a textbook for his classes. Topics include the *chakras* and the kundalini, opening the third eye, breathing, and much else. The exercises are all carefully explained; however, the text is replete with Sanskrit terms, and the reading is slow going despite the clear exposition. A good glossary is included.

MONIER-WILLIAMS, M. **RELIGIOUS THOUGHT AND LIFE IN INDIA. Notes, 532pp. MuM74, 22.50c.**
First published in 1883, this is still the most comprehensive general survey that we know of. Monier-Williams is a well known Sanskrit scholar and while the reader needs to keep the date the book was written in mind, he will find the text both informative and well written.

MOOR, EDWARD. **THE HINDU PANTHEON. 582pp. PRS76, 40.00c.**
This book, originally published in 1810, was one of the first and most complete expositions of the religious iconography of India. The work is comparatively free of Western influence, as Moor spent a good part of his adult life in the East. Each of the major figures is discussed in a separate chapter and over 100 plates follow the text. This is a beautifully produced 9¼"x12¼" volume.

MOORE, CHARLES, ed. **THE INDIAN MIND. Notes, index, 469pp. UHa67, 3.95p.**
A middle of the road explanation of the fundamentals of the Indian mind as expressed in its great philosophies, religions, and social thought and practices. The essays in this volume were originally presented at four East-West Philosophers' Conferences between 1939 and 1964.

Swami Muktananda

Swami Muktananda is an Indian guru who has a large American and European following. He is of the bhakti or devotional tradition and practices what he calls siddha yoga. He initiates disciples by *shaktipat*, a process whereby he transfers his energy for an instant to the new disciple. In colloquial terms, he zaps them. The swami has traveled throughout the West and lived in the U.S. for a couple of years. His Indian ashram is in Ganeshpuri, near Bombay.

AMMA. **SWAMI MUKTANANDA PARAMAHANSA. Glossary, 104pp. SYD69, 1.50p.**
A biographical study written by one of Muktananda's close disciples and edited and revised by other disciples.

JOHN, BUBBA FREE, ed. **THE SPIRITUAL INSTRUCTIONS OF SWAMI MUKTANANDA. Introduction, epilogue, 30pp. DHP74, 1.50p.**
The text of this book is in the form of an intimate letter written by Swami Muktananda in 1968 in which he describes the nature and goal of spiritual life, its experiences, and its benefits, and also goes into the meditational techniques which he advocates.

MUKTANANDA, SWAMI. **AMERICAN TOUR, 1970. 103pp. SYD74, 2.95p.**
Muktananda's style is especially informal in this series of talks. He includes many teaching stories and discusses aspects of the spiritual life.

MUKTANANDA, SWAMI. **GETTING RID OF WHAT YOU HAVEN'T GOT. Glossary, 45pp. SYD74, 1.45p.**
A collection of Muktananda's talks and conversations, including a bit of personal advice given to individuals. The reader can get a good feeling of Muktananda's technique through the introductory material to each selection and there are also short pieces by Ram Dass and Claudio Naranjo.

MUKTANANDA, SWAMI. **LIGHT ON THE PATH. 119pp. SYD72, 2.95p.**
A collection of several short works, each dealing with specific aspects of the path of siddha yoga. Topics include spiritual initiation, the relationship of guru and disciple, the nature of God, the path of devotion to the guru, and meditation on oneness with the divine.

MUKTANANDA, SWAMI. **MUKTESHWARI II. Glossary, 200pp. SYD73, 2.95p.**
A series of poems on the spiritual life.

MUKTANANDA, SWAMI. **THE NECTAR OF CHANTING. 151pp. SYD75, 3.50p.**
Contains both the Sanskrit transliteration and the English translation of chants, mantras, prayers, and texts sung in Muktananda's ashrams all over the world. Includes the **Guru Gita** and the **Hymn to the Glory of Siva.** Muktananda stresses chanting as one of the main aspects of spiritual practice because it has such a purifying effect on the entire atmosphere as well as on the person who is chanting.

MUKTANANDA, SWAMI. **PLAY OF CONSCIOUSNESS. Long glossary, 295pp. SYD74, 5.95p.**
Muktananda's autobiography. He relates his experiences on the path to realization: his fears, his physical contortions, his development of supernormal abilities, and his ecstatic states. A frank record of a fascinating spiritual journey.

MUKTANANDA, SWAMI. **SADGURUNATH MAHARAJ KI JAY. 8¼"x11¼", 216pp. SYD76, 10.00p.**
110 black and white and 100 color pictures of Muktananda, plus a text selected from Muktananda's 1974 talks in Australia.

MUKTANANDA, SWAMI. **SATSANG WITH BABA, VOLUME I. 348pp. SYD74, 4.95p.**
Questions and answers between Muktananda and Western disciples living in his Indian ashram. The answers are specific and practical and the topics covered include work, marriage, meditation, and much else.

MUKTANANDA, SWAMI. **SATSANG WITH BABA, VOLUME II. SYD76, 4.95p.**
More questions and answers from the Ganeshpuri ashram.

MUKTANANDA, SWAMI. **SIDDHA MEDITATION. 117pp. SYD76, 3.00p.**
Siddha Meditation is understanding that everything you see, touch, hear, smell, taste, imagine, think, dream, or in any way experience is made of the same divine consciousness, which is your Self. In this volume Swami Muktananda comments on the **Siva Sutras** and other ancient texts, all of which he feels reveal the essence of siddha meditation.

SHANKAR. **MUKTANANDA, SIDDHA GURU. Glossary, 65pp. SYD76, 1.95p.**
An informal introduction to Muktananda and his teachings by one of his disciples.

SWARD, ROBERT, ed. **CHEERS FOR MUKTANANDA. Glossary, 64pp. Sof76, 4.95p.**
An anthology of photographs and poetry expressing the love that disciples feel for Swami Muktananda.

■ *ZWEIG, PAUL, ed.* **MUKTANANDA. Glossary, 173pp. H&R76, 3.95p.**
The chapters of this book contain the principal aspects of Swami Muktananda's teaching, as he expressed them in many dozens of talks throughout the United States during the two and a half years he spent here. Although I call the chapters essays, they are in fact based on transcripts of the talks themselves which I have edited so that important ideas are developed continuously in each chapter. . . . Each chapter is followed by a number of questions which people have asked Baba from time to time, and the answers that he has given to clarify his teaching by connecting it to specific problems of feeling and behavior.

───── **END OF SWAMI MUKTANANDA SUBSECTION** ─────

MULLER, MAX. **SIX SYSTEMS OF INDIAN PHILOSOPHY. Notes, index, 510pp. CSS71, 10.20c.**
Professor Muller was the general editor of the **Sacred Books of the East** series and was responsible, through that series, for bringing the wisdom of the East into more general recognition in the West. Here he presents a scholarly study of Indian philosophy. The scholarship is excellent, but the text is often hard going—especially since this is a translation of the original German version.

NAKAGAWA, TSUYOSHI. **INDIA: CENTURIES OF YOUTH. 154pp. Kod73, 3.95p.**
A beautiful little travel guide with many color plates and an informative text.

Narada

Try as we might, we have not been able to find any hard facts on Narada's life. All we know is that he is presumed to be a historical personage and is known to history as the author of a sutra propounding the doctrine of unceasing love of God, a path generally known as bhakti. This approach demands neither great knowledge of philosophy nor total renunciation of the world.

CHINMAYANANDA, SWAMI, tr. **NARADA BHAKTI SUTRA. 197pp. CPT70, 4.00c.**
Translations of each sutra, with extensive commentary. Includes the Sanskrit text, translations of individual words, and a translation of the whole sutra. As usual, Chinmayananda's translation is excellent and his commentary is enlightening.

PRABHAVANANDA, SWAMI, tr. **NARADA'S WAY OF DIVINE LOVE: THE BHAKTI SUTRAS. Glossary, 189pp. VdP71, 5.25c.**
By his clear translation of each sutra and commentary, illustrated by quotations from scriptures and examples from lives of holy men of many religious traditions, Swami Prabhavananda provides an invaluable aid for spiritual aspirants. Introduction by Christopher Isherwood.

SHASTRI, HARI PRASAD, tr. **THE NARADA SUTRAS: THE PHILOSOPHY OF LOVE. 3¾"x5¾", 102pp. ShS47, 1.75p.**
A fine translation accompanied by a full commentary. This is our favorite translation.

TAIMNI, I.K., tr. **SELF-REALIZATION THROUGH LOVE. 94pp. TPH75, 3.75c.**
This volume includes the Sanskrit text, transliteration, English translation, and extensive commentary. Taimni also provides introductory comments on the Hindu path of devotion.

TYAGISANANDA, SWAMI, tr. **NARADA BHAKTI SUTRAS. 306pp. SRM72, 1.95p.**
Each sutra is followed by a word for word translation and a sentence expressing the whole thought. A separate section contains extensive notes which discuss the aphorisms and recommended practices.

───────── **END OF NARADA SUBSECTION** ─────────

NIKHILANANDA, SWAMI. **HINDUISM: ITS MEANING FOR THE LIBERATION OF THE SPIRIT. 189pp. SRM68, 3.95c.**
A very complete survey of the religious and philosophical beliefs of the Hindus, based on Vedantic teachings.

NIKHILANANDA, SWAMI. **MAN IN SEARCH OF IMMORTALITY: TESTIMONIALS FROM THE HINDU SCRIPTURES. 107pp. RVC68, 4.95c.**
Five articles on the immortality of the soul. The scriptures cited and quoted record the experience of the enlightened seers *who see truth directly, as fruit lying in the palm of one's hand can be seen. This experience is not the monopoly of any particular seer, but the heritage of all, irrespective of time, place and creed.*

NIVEDITA, SISTER. **CRADLE TALES OF HINDUISM. Illustrations, 319pp. AdA07, 2.50p.**
A collection of traditional Indian nursery tales whose authenticity has been carefully checked by the translator, a disciple of Swami Vivekananda. The collection includes most of the best loved tales and the language is well suited to reading to children.

NIVEDITA, SISTER. **FOOTFALLS OF INDIAN HISTORY. 264pp. AdA56, 1.25p.**
An interesting study of some aspects of Indian history from the point of view of their impact on the Indian mind and the character of the Indian people. Sister Nivedita was an English disciple of Swami Vivekananda.

O'FLAHERTY, WENDY. **ASCETICISM AND EROTICISM IN THE MYTHOLOGY OF SIVA. Notes, index, 386pp. Oxf73, 34.60c.**
A scholarly examination of a wide range of Indian texts—Vedic, Puranic, classical, modern, and tribal—in the light of a dialectic pattern of interlocking motifs which center upon the myths of Siva. The author thus offers both a case study of an applied method of dealing with hundreds of related myths and an analysis of the historical development of the Indian approach to an enduring human dilemma—the conflict between spiritual aspirations and human desires.

■ *O'FLAHERTY, WENDY.* **HINDU MYTHS. Introduction, glossary, 358pp. Vik75, 2.95p.**
This new selection and translation of seventy-five seminal myths

spans the wide range of classical Indian sources, from the serpent slaying Indra of the **Vedas** (c. 1200 BC) to the medieval pantheon—the phallic and ascetic Siva, the maternal and bloodthirsty goddess Kali, the mischievous child Krishna, and the many minor gods, demons, rivers, and animals sacred to Hinduism. The traditional themes of life and death are set forth and interwoven with many complex variations which give a kaleidoscopic picture of the development of almost three thousand years of Indian mythology. Ms. O'Flaherty's translations could not be better.

O'FLAHERTY, WENDY. **THE ORIGINS OF EVIL IN HINDU MYTHOLOGY. Notes, bibliography, index, 422pp. UCa76, 16.50c.**
This is the first comprehensive study of the problem of evil in Indian thought. Dr. O'Flaherty marshals more than 1,000 myths from the earliest levels of Indian thought through contemporary tribal traditions, grouping and analyzing them according to the villain in each plot—occasionally abstractions such as time, fate, or necessity, but more often anthropomorphic figures of gods, demons, or (rarely) men. All the myths are newly translated by the author and illuminated by mutual comparison—one myth explaining the other—and through a hermeneutical approach which draws upon textual exegesis and a study of the ritual context of Indian religion.

OMAN, JOHN. **THE MYSTICS, ASCETICS AND SAINTS OF INDIA. Notes, index, 303pp. OrP nd, 13.50c.**
A detailed, scholarly, early twentieth century study of Indian asceticism tracing the tradition throughout history up to the time of publication. There is also a great deal of scholarly information on Hindu *sadhus* and on various spiritual movements.

ORGAN, TROY. **THE HINDU QUEST FOR THE PERFECTION OF MAN. Notes, seventy-one page bibliography, indices, 449pp. OUP70, 16.45c.**
An in depth discussion which looks at Hinduism as a *sadhana*, a discipline for the actualizing of human potentialities. Organ sees Hinduism as a *sadhana* which seeks to guide man to integration, spiritualization, and liberation. He views man's nature as a becoming, not a being; hence the human ideal is perfecting, not perfection. This is a readable, scholarly study which is designed for those with a fairly good knowledge of Hindu philosophy.

■ *ORGAN, TROY.* **HINDUISM, ITS HISTORICAL DEVELOPMENT. 425pp. BES74, 3.50p.**
This is an excellent textbook presentation of Hinduism which traces its historical development and within this historical context reviews and summarizes the major religious and reform movements. Each of the important individuals and individual movements is dealt with in a clear way and all the Sanskrit terms are well defined. The early background (up to the time of Sankara's Vedantist, nondualist movement) is discussed in the greatest depth. There are extensive notes and an excellent chapter-by-chapter bibliography, as well as an index. Recommended to those desiring a readable, not overly detailed, academic overview.

OSBORNE, ARTHUR. **THE INCREDIBLE SAI BABA. 128pp. HPG58, 4.00p.**
Sai Baba was a very eccentric Indian saint who died in 1918, but is still worshiped daily by many. He taught neither a specific philosophy nor any special means for God realization. He was especially known for the unending miracles he performed. This volume contains his life, teachings, miracles, and anecdotes: *I give people what they want in the hope that they will begin to want what I want to give them.* This book discusses the original Sai Baba—not to be confused with the current Indian guru.

PARAMANANDA, SWAMI. **SECRET OF RIGHT ACTIVITY. 84pp. VdC64, 2.50c.**
A modern restatement of the philosophy of karma yoga, written by a monk of the Ramakrishna Order.

PARAMANANDA, SWAMI. **SELF-MASTERY. 84pp. VdC61, 2.50p.**
A treatise on gaining control over our faculties and ending internal discord through surrender to the supreme will.

PARRINDER, GEOFFREY. **THE INDESTRUCTIBLE SOUL. Index, 116pp. H&R73, 4.25p.**
For over 3,000 years much thought has been devoted in India to the idea of the eternal and indestructible soul or self of man. This book discusses different Indian teachings about the soul and its destiny, its relationship to God or the absolute, its transmigration, and its final goal of nirvana or bliss. Professor Parrinder illustrates the different teachings with quotations from many texts. He is Professor of the Comparative Study of Religions at the University of London, has studied Indian beliefs for over forty years, and is the author of countless books on the subject.

Patanjali

Patanjali's **Yoga Sutras (Aphorisms)** are not the original exposition of a philosophy, but a work of compilation and reformulation. What he did was to restate yoga philosophy and practice for the man of his own period. But what was his period? And who was he? Hardly anything is known about him. As for the date of the **Sutras,** the guesses of scholars vary widely, ranging from the fourth century BC to the fourth century AD. *The simplest meaning of the word sutra is "thread." A sutra is, so to speak, the bare thread of an exposition, the absolute minimum that is necessary to hold it together.... Only essential words are used.... There was a good reason for this method. Sutras were composed at a period when there were no books. The entire work had to be memorized and so it had to be expressed as tersely as possible. Patanjali's* **Sutras,** *like all others, were intended to be expanded and explained.*—**How to Know God.** Patanjali's **Sutras** remain the best exposition of raja yoga we have, and they are highly recommended.

ABHEDANANDA, SWAMI. **THE YOGA PSYCHOLOGY. 239pp. RVM67, 3.95c.**
A transcription of a series of lectures which Swami Abhedananda delivered to sophisticated American audiences in 1924. The material has been carefully edited. All facets of Patanjali's psychological system are fully discussed.

BAILEY, ALICE. **THE LIGHT OF THE SOUL: ITS SCIENCE AND EFFECT. 475pp. LPC27, 4.75p.**
An esoteric restatement of the **Yoga Sutras,** with extensive commentary.

BESANT, ANNIE. **AN INTRODUCTION TO YOGA. 167pp. TPH08, 2.25c.**
A series of lectures designed to prepare students for study of the **Yoga Sutras.**

DASGUPTA, SURENDRANATH. **YOGA AS PHILOSOPHY AND RELIGION. 200pp. MoB nd, 11.55c.**
An exposition of the philosophical and religious doctrines found in Patanjali's **Yoga Sutras**, as explained in the commentaries of Vyasa, Vacaspati, Vijnana Bhiksju, and others. It is a comprehensive analysis which assumes that the reader is familiar with the content of the **Sutras**, Sanskrit terminology, and Hindu philosophy. An excellent work for the advanced student.

DAVIS, ROY EUGENE, tr. **THIS IS REALITY. Glossary, 211pp. CSA62, 3.95p.**
An updated commentary on the eternal wisdom contained in the **Sutras**. Davis was a student of Yogananda.

ELIADE, MIRCEA. **PATANJALI AND YOGA. Chronology, annotated bibliography, index, 222pp. ScB62/Wdw, 3.45p.**
A survey of the **Yoga Sutras** and of their subsequent influence. All the major commentaries are cited and quoted and various Indian theories of yoga are discussed. While Eliade's exposition is interesting, he seems to miss the heart of what the **Sutras** express. This is an important, but disappointing study. Beautifully illustrated.

JOHNSTON, CHARLES, tr. **THE YOGA SUTRAS OF PATANJALI. 127pp. Wat12, 6.15c.**
This translation emphasizes the application of the **Sutras** for Western man. The commentary is often stilted; nonetheless, Johnston does capture the spirit of the original work.

MEHTA, ROHIT. **YOGA: THE ART OF INTEGRATION. 470pp. TPH75, 11.75c.**
A commentary on the **Yoga Sutras** which emphasizes self awareness, observation, revitalization of the senses, and reeducation of the mind. Mehta is a Theosophist.

MISHRA, RAMMURTI, tr. **YOGA SUTRAS: THE TEXTBOOK OF YOGA PSYCHOLOGY. 554pp. Dou63/LyP, 2.95p.**
An authoritative, recent translation, with thorough interpretation and commentary by Mishra, a respected Sanskrit scholar. He provides both the Sanskrit transliterated text and the translations as well as a long introduction on the philosophy of yoga, and a glossary. The commentaries are very detailed and incorporate many Sanskrit terms. An excellent work for the serious student.

■ *PRABHAVANANDA, SWAMI and CHRISTOPHER ISHERWOOD,* trs. **HOW TO KNOW GOD: THE YOGA APHORISMS OF PATANJALI. 166pp. NAL53/NEL, 2.95c/1.25p.**
A beautiful, absorbing translation, and our personal favorite by far. *In this translation we have not only provided a commentary but expanded and paraphrased the aphorisms themselves, so that each one becomes an intelligible statement in the English language....Our commentary is mainly our own work. However we have followed the explanations of the two ancient commentators, Bhoja and Vyasa. We have also quoted frequently from...Swami Vivekananda.* Highly recommended.

PRAKASH, SWAMI SATYA. **PATANJALA RAJA YOGA. Notes, index, 347pp. Cnd75, 14.00c.**
A technical, scientific restatement and interpretation of the yogic techniques presented in Patanjali's **Yoga Sutras**. Swami Prakash was head of the Department of Chemistry at the University of Allahabad and his scientific background is evident throughout this work. The bulk of the book is devoted to practical exercises.

RAJNEESH, BHAGWAN SHREE. **YOGA, THE ALPHA AND THE OMEGA. 12.00c/each.**
See the Contemporary Spiritual Teachers section.

TAIMNI, I.K., tr. **THE SCIENCE OF YOGA. Extensive commentary, Sanskrit text, transliteration, English translation, index, 461pp. TPH61, 3.95p.**
A clear, intelligible presentation of the **Sutras** from a spiritual and philosophical point of view in the light of both ancient and modern thought. This is many people's favorite version.

■ *VIVEKANANDA, SWAMI.* **RAJA YOGA. Glossary, 305pp. RVC55, 3.50c/1.75p.**
A wonderful commentary on the **Sutras** which captures the essence of the text. Swami Vivekananda was a close disciple of Sri Ramakrishna and one of the twentieth century's most enlightened interpreters of the **Yoga Sutras**. He focuses on methods of concentration and discusses the liberation of the soul from the bondage of the body.

■ *WOOD, ERNEST, tr.* **PRACTICAL YOGA, ANCIENT AND MODERN. 244pp. Wil48, 2.00p.**
Wood has studied yoga and Sanskrit for over forty-five years. He has made his life's work the interpretation of ancient Indian wisdom to the West. In his presentation of the **Sutras** he has rearranged the order of the sections to make them more intelligible. His translation is clear and direct and his commentary is very enlightening. Next to **How to Know God**, we feel that this is the most illuminating version for the average reader—the two complement each other quite well. When reading an ancient text in translation it is often good to read more than one version as each translator has his own viewpoint and brings out nuances in the work.

WOODS, JAMES. **THE YOGA SYSTEM OF PATANJALI. 424pp. MoB14, 18.30c.**
An extensive philosophical study, including a full translation of the **Sutras** and many notes. This is the most scholarly of any of the translations—and also the most weighty.

——————— **END OF PATANJALI SUBSECTION** ———————

PEREIRA, JOSE, ed. **HINDU THEOLOGY: A READER. Extensive notes, index, 558pp. Dou76, 3.50p.**
This is a collection of translations of important Hindu theological documents. Most of the translations are not to be found elsewhere so this is a good resource book for serious students of Hinduism, especially those interested in the impact of Hindu theology on Western thought.

PRABHAVANANDA, SWAMI. **THE ETERNAL COMPANION: BRAHMANANDA, HIS LIFE AND TEACHINGS. 301pp. VdP44, 3.95p.**
Swami Brahmananda was regarded by Sri Ramakrishna as his spiritual son. The teachings given here are taken from diaries and private notes on informal talks. They are simple, direct, and full of practical counsel regarding meditation and the inner life.

PRABHAVANANDA, SWAMI. **THE SPIRITUAL HERITAGE OF INDIA. Long bibliography, index, 361pp. VdP63, 3.50p.**
Illuminating discussions of the **Vedas, Upanishads, Bhagavad Gita,** Buddhism, Jainism, and India's six systems of thought. Includes liberal quotations from scriptures and supplemental writings. Swami Prabhavananda also discusses the lives and ideals of the greatest Indian philosophers.

PRABHAVANANDA, SWAMI, tr. **SWAMI PREMANANDA: TEACHING AND REMINISCENCES. 157pp. VdP57, 2.95p.**
Enlightening teachings of a close personal disciple of Sri Ramakrishna.

PRABHAVANANDA, SWAMI. **VEDIC RELIGION AND PHILOSOPHY. 172pp. SRM nd, 2.00c.**
A discussion of the **Vedas, Upanishads,** and **Gita** combined with a general description of Indian philosophy.

PRABHAVANANDA, SWAMI. **YOGA AND MYSTICISM. 53pp. VdP68, 1.25p.**
Transcription of four lectures.

PULIGANDLA, RAMAKRISHNA. **FUNDAMENTALS OF INDIAN PHILOSOPHY. Glossary, notes, bibliography, index, 363pp. Abi75, 6.95p.**
An academic survey of the major Indian philosophical schools: Carvakism, Jainism, Buddhism, Samkhya, Yoga, Vaisesika, Nyaya, and Vedanta. A final chapter discusses the philosophical contributions of Sri Aurobindo and Radhakrishnan. It is a pretty dry account, though the scholarship is certainly adequate.

S. Radhakrishnan

Radhakrishnan, distinguished statesman, educator, and philosopher, is the author of countless books on Indian philosophy and he has done excellent translations of many of the sacred texts.

MCDERMOTT, ROBERT, ed. **RADHAKRISHNAN. 344pp. Dut70, 3.75p.**
This is an excellent selection of Radhakrishnan's most significant writings. Includes essays on Tagore, Gandhi, and Nehru, selections of Radhakrishnan's personal philosophy, and surveys of major themes in Indian philosophy. McDermott provides extensive explanatory material as well as a fine annotated bibliography and glossary.

MUNSHI, K.M. and R.R. DIWAKAR, eds. **RADHAKRISHNAN READER. Index, 680pp. BVB69, 11.50c.**
A representative selection of Radhakrishnan's writings, intended to give an idea of his thoughts on philosophy, education, and religion. This is the most comprehensive anthology available.

RADHAKRISHNAN, S. **THE HINDU VIEW OF LIFE. 92pp. McM71/ A&U, 1.95p.**
Transcription of four lectures on the title theme.

RADHAKRISHNAN, S. **INDIAN PHILOSOPHY. Voluminous notes, index, 1,545pp. A&U29, 40.85c/set.**
This two volume set is Professor Radhakrishnan's *magnum opus* and, as the title suggests, it reviews every aspect of Indian philosophy from the Vedas through the Advaita Vedanta of Sankara and the theism of Ramanuja and Vaisnava in great depth—with extensive citations and quotations from pertinent literature. This is a book that every good library should have; however, the treatment of each topic is probably more extensive than most individuals would want.

RADHAKRISHNAN, S. **OUR HERITAGE. 156pp. HPB73, 2.35p.**
Dr. Radhakrishnan examines Indian culture as a whole and shows how this heritage affects the India of today. His main topics include the legacy of Sanskrit, the **Mahabharata** and the **Bhagavad Gita**, Sankara, the Buddha, Ramakrishna and Vivekananda, Gandhi, and Nehru.

RADHAKRISHNAN, S. **RECOVERY OF FAITH. 187pp. HPB67, 1.80p.**
Our age is still in desperate need of that which religion alone can give. Dr. Radhakrishnan gives his answer to man's need for a new faith. Examining a wide field of religious thought, he discusses the faiths that men have lived by, and shows how, out of these enduring expressions, a faith can be achieved which transcends religious dogma and narrow sectarianism.

RADHAKRISHNAN, S. **RELIGION AND CULTURE. 176pp. HPB68, 1.50p.**
An ecumenical view of religion and culture and their application to life in the world today.

■ RADHAKRISHNAN, S. and CHARLES MOORE, eds. **A SOURCE-BOOK IN INDIAN PHILOSOPHY. Notes, bibliography, index, 669pp. PUP57, 5.95p.**
An excellent work, the finest collection available. The authors begin with the **Rig Veda** and end with writings from the twentieth century. They include the full text of Radhakrishnan's fine translation of the **Gita** as well as translations from many lesser works. Some commentary is also included. We recommend this anthology to all who are studying Indian philosophy.

——— END OF S. RADHAKRISHNAN SUBSECTION ———

RAJAGOPALACHARI, C. **HINDUISM: DOCTRINE AND WAY OF LIFE. 101pp. BBU70, 1.50p.**
A brief survey of some of the main doctrines and tenets of Hinduism.

RAMA, SWAMI. **LECTURES ON YOGA: EIGHT LESSONS ON YOGA. 126pp. Him nd, 3.00p.**
A clear presentation of the following topics: *What is Yoga?, Yama and*

Niyama, Asanas and their Therapeutic Value, Pranayama, Nadhishodhanam, Concentration, Mind and Its Analysis, What is Meditation?, and *Samadhi.* The Sanskrit terms are well defined in the text.

RAMA, SWAMI. **YOGA AND PSYCHOTHERAPY. 11.95c/6.95p.**
See the Consciousness Expansion section.

Yogi Ramacharaka

These works are generally considered among the clearest and most comprehensive on the subject of Oriental Occult Philosophy ever offered to the Western World. **Fourteen Lessons** and **Advanced Course** may be read first to afford a basic understanding. However, the Yoga System is scientifically separated into a number of different branches or phases, i.e., Raja Yoga is mental development, Gnani Yoga is the development of intellect and wisdom, Hatha Yoga is physical development and well-being. Bhakti Yoga is spiritual development and Karma Yoga is development through deeds and work. The term Yoga is neither mystical nor mysterious in any sense. It is derived from the Sanskrit root yug, literally meaning to yoke or unite the separate, innate forces of Man.—Yogi Ramacharaka. Yogi Ramacharaka, who was an American from Iowa, wrote under at least two additional names: William Atkinson and Bhikshu.

ATKINSON, WILLIAM. **MEMORY CULTURE: THE SCIENCE OF OBSERVING, REMEMBERING AND RECALLING. 92pp. YPS03, 6.00c.**
A presentation of theory and exercises for developing memory and eye perception.

ATKINSON, WILLIAM. **MIND POWER. 441pp. YPS12, 7.00c.**
This is Ramacharaka's most comprehensive work on the subject—it incorporates the material in **Secret of Mental Magic** and **Mental Fascination**. The material is clearly stated and very practical. This is one of his most popular books.

ATKINSON, WILLIAM. **PRACTICAL MENTAL INFLUENCE AND MENTAL FASCINATION. 96pp. YPS nd, 1.00p.**

ATKINSON, WILLIAM. **PRACTICAL MIND READING. 97pp. YPS10, 1.00p.**
A course of lessons on thought transference, telepathy, mental currents, mental rapport, etc.

ATKINSON, WILLIAM. **PRACTICAL PSYCHOMANCY AND CRYSTAL GAZING. 93pp. YPS nd, 1.00p.**

ATKINSON, WILLIAM. **REINCARNATION AND THE LAW OF KARMA. 6.00c.**
See the Reincarnation and Karma section.

BHIKSHU. **BHAKTI YOGA. 148pp. YPS30, 5.50c.**
Bhakti Yoga is that branch or form of the Yogi Philosophy specially suited to those whose religious nature is largely developed and who prefer to grow into an understanding and union with the Absolute by the power of Love—by the inspiration that comes from the love of some conception of God and some form of worship that may accompany that conception of Deity. This is a series of twelve detailed lessons on every aspect of the yoga.

BHIKSHU. **KARMA YOGA. 138pp. YPS28/Fow, 5.50c.**
A detailed treatise in the form of a series of lessons, geared toward the general reader.

MUKERJI, A.P. **YOGA LESSONS FOR DEVELOPING SPIRITUAL CONSCIOUSNESS. 191pp. YPS11, 5.50c.**
A collection of practical lessons on the title theme.

RAMACHARAKA, YOGI. **ADVANCED COURSE IN YOGI PHILOSOPHY AND ORIENTAL OCCULTISM. 337pp. YPS nd/Fow, 6.00c.**
Lessons include: an extensive analysis of **Light on the Path**; a discussion of the branches of yoga; dharma, the yoga philosophy of ethics or right action; and a presentation of the higher yogic scientific and metaphysical principles.

RAMACHARAKA, YOGI. **FOURTEEN LESSONS IN YOGA PHILOSOPHY.** YPS03/Fow, 6.00c.
Lessons include: *The Human Aura, Thought Dynamics, Clairvoyance, Human Magnetism, Occult Therapeutics, The Astral World, Spiritual Cause and Effect,* and *Death and the Afterlife.*

RAMACHARAKA, YOGI. **THE HINDU YOGI BREATHING EXERCISES.** 48pp. YPS nd, 3.00c.
A collection of Yogi Ramacharaka's writings on breath and development exercises.

RAMACHARAKA, YOGI. **LESSONS IN GNANI YOGA.** YPS06/Fow, 6.00c.
What is known as Gnani Yoga deals with the scientific and intellectual knowing of the great questions regarding Life and what lies back of Life—the Riddle of the Universe.

RAMACHARAKA, YOGI. **THE LIFE BEYOND DEATH.** 6.00c.
See the Reincarnation and Karma section.

RAMACHARAKA, YOGI. **THE PHILOSOPHIES AND RELIGIONS OF INDIA.** 359pp. YPS30/Fow, 6.00c.
The discussion is from the *occult* point of view.

RAMACHARAKA, YOGI. **THE PRACTICAL WATER CURE.** 123pp. YPS37/Fow, 2.00p.
A comprehensive survey of various water cures practiced in India and the Orient.

RAMACHARAKA, YOGI. **RAJA YOGA.** 248pp. YPS06/Fow, 6.00c.
This book presents a series of lessons for development of mental concentration.

RAMACHARAKA, YOGI. **SCIENCE OF BREATH.** 88pp. YPS04/Fow, 4.00c.
A complete manual of the oriental breathing philosophy of physical, mental, psychic, and spiritual development.

RAMACHARAKA, YOGI. **THE SCIENCE OF PSYCHIC HEALING.** 190pp. YPS09/Fow, 6.00c.
A simple, introductory explanation of healing through the understanding of natural laws and cooperation with them. Many theories are introduced to acquaint the reader with various aspects of healing.

——————— **END OF YOGI RAMACHARAKA SUBSECTION** ———————

Sri Ramakrishna

Sri Ramakrishna (1836-1886) devoted his life to an intensive career of experimentation in the field of religious experience: he had a vision of Kali, an aspect of God worshiped by Hindus as the Divine Mother of the Universe; he ventured into other branches of Hinduism and experienced Sri Rama, Sri Krishna, and the **Tantras**, gaining insight into the nondualism of Advaita Vedanta as expounded by Sankara. He never learned to read or write and his beliefs are known to us through **The Gospel**, notes taken by *M*, one of his disciples. He preached the message set down in the **Rig Veda**: *Truth is One but the Wise have given it different names,* a gospel of truly universal love and universal understanding of all religions. This *madman of God* spent almost half his life in a state of religious ecstasy and each experience brought him new awareness of the absolute God. As *M* quoted him: *I have practiced all religions—Hinduism, Islam, Christianity—and I have also followed the paths of the various sects of Hinduism . . . and I have found that it is the same God toward whom all are turned, along different roads. . . . You have to pass along these various roads in the practice of each religion once. Everywhere I see men who dispute in the name of religion. . . . But they do not stop to think that he who is called Krishna is also called Siva, and that he is also called Primal Force or Jesus or Allah. . . . The substance is One under different names, and each man is looking for the same substance.*

ADVAITA ASHRAMA. **THE LIFE OF SRI RAMA KRISHNA.** Index, 511pp. AdA24, 4.95c.
A biography compiled from various sources by monks of the Ramakrishna Order.

ADVAITA ASHRAMA. **TEACHINGS OF SRI RAMAKRISHNA.** 344pp. AdA nd, 2.25p.
An excellent compilation, arranged topically. A systematic, condensed presentation of Ramakrishna's teaching in his own words.

ANONYMOUS. **SAYINGS OF SRI RAMAKRISHNA.** Index, 402pp. SRM71, 1.95c.
A topically organized collection of 1,120 sayings, including parables. The book claims to be the most exhaustive collection available and includes an introduction summarizing the life and work of Sri Ramakrishna.

BUDHANANDA, SWAMI. **SRI RAMAKRISHNA: A BIOGRAPHY IN PICTURES.** 9"x11½", 108pp. AdA76, 15.00c.
Authentic photographs of Ramakrishna, his disciples and associates, and the sites associated with his life.

GAMBHIRANANDA, SWAMI, ed. **THE APOSTLES OF SHRI RAMAKRISHNA.** 401pp. AdA66, 2.95c.
Short studies on the lives, work, and teachings of Sri Ramakrishna's sixteen major disciples.

GHANANANDA, SWAMI. **SRI RAMAKRISHNA AND HIS UNIQUE MESSAGE.** 174pp. RVC70, 2.75p.
A discussion of Ramakrishna's most important philosophical statements, clearly presented and designed to be pertinent to modern day seekers. The practical application of his ideas is stressed.

■ *ISHERWOOD, CHRISTOPHER.* **RAMAKRISHNA AND HIS DISCIPLES.** Photographs, index, 432pp. S&S64, 4.95p.
This is the best introductory work on Ramakrishna that we know of. Isherwood has been involved in the Vedanta Society of California and the love he feels for Ramakrishna comes across. His discussion focuses on Ramakrishna, the man and his teachings. He also includes excellent portraits of many of Ramakrishna's personal disciples. We recommend this book to all who want to get a feeling for Indian philosophy.

M. **THE GOSPEL OF SRI RAMAKRISHNA.** Extensive glossary, index, 1,063+pp. RVC42, 12.95c.
M, one of the intimate disciples of Sri Ramakrishna, recorded his conversations with disciples, devotees, and visitors. M was present during all the conversations in the main body of the book and he received firsthand reports of those in the appendix. He has produced a unique book which relates his master's teaching in detail, as well as the small happenings of each day—all with complete fidelity. Swami Nikhilananda has made a literal translation. He has purposely retained the repetitions of teachings and parables. Nikhilananda also includes a lengthy introduction in which he acquaints the reader with the master's life, the systems of Indian religious thought intimately connected with his teaching, people who came into contact with him, and much else.

■ *M.* **THE GOSPEL OF SRI RAMAKRISHNA (ABRIDGED).** 615pp. RVC42, 5.00c.
The same fine translation—but abridged by one third. The continuity and completeness of the teachings remain unaffected; only the repetitions and unfamiliar references have been eliminated. Nikhilananda has retained his excellent introduction and glossary.

NIKHILANANDA, SWAMI. **HOLY MOTHER—BEING THE LIFE OF SRI SARADA DEVI, WIFE OF RAMAKRISHNA.** 334pp. RVC62, 4.50c.
The Holy Mother came to Ramakrishna when she was five and later lived with him for fourteen years. He trained her for her future role as his spiritual successor. To her disciples she was a mother and teacher, and also the embodiment of divinity. This book may be regarded as a companion volume to Sri Ramakrishna's **Gospel.**

RAMAKRISHNA, SRI. **TALES AND PARABLES OF SRI RAMAKRISHNA.** 316pp. SRM43, 2.50c.
A delightful, exhaustive collection. Includes a long introduction on Ramakrishna's life and teaching.

Ramana Maharshi

Ramana Maharshi was born in 1879. At seventeen he attained enlightenment through a remarkable experience: he underwent the death of his physical body while remaining in full consciousness. Following this transformation he left his home and was drawn to the sacred hill of Arunachala. He never left it. In the ashram which soon formed around him he taught the purest form of Advaita Vedanta (nondualism) through the discipline of self inquiry.

COHEN, S.S. **REFLECTIONS ON TALKS WITH RAMANA MAHARSHI. Glossary, 202pp. SRT71, 1.80p.**
A topically arranged discussion, based on direct quotations from Ramana Maharshi.

JONES, FRANKLIN, ed. **THE HEART OF THE RIBHU GITA, AS TAUGHT BY RAMANA MAHARSHI. Illustrations, 34pp. DHP73, 2.50p.**
The **Ribhu Gita** is a legendary mystical text which is said to represent the teaching given to the sage Ribhu by God himself in the form of the Lord Siva. This is a selection of verses which represent a summation of its central teaching.

MAHADEVAN, T.M.P. **RAMANA MAHARSHI. Notes, 186pp. A&U 77, 5.25p.**
Dr. Mahadevan is one of the most distinguished contemporary Indian philosophers and the author of many books on Hindu thought and Advaita Vedanta. He is also the Director of the Center for Advanced Study in Philosophy at the University of Madras. In this book he explores the life and teachings of Ramana Maharshi and analyzes Maharshi's major writings. This is a detailed study which is not suitable as an introduction to Ramana Maharshi unless the reader is thoroughly grounded in Hindu philosophical thought.

MAHADEVAN, T.M.P., tr. **RAMANA MAHARSHI AND HIS PHILOSOPHY OF EXISTENCE. Glossary, index, 190+pp. SRT59, 2.15p.**
Translations of Maharshi's **The Forty Verses** and **The Supplement**, with extensive commentary and introductory material. Dr. Mahadevan also includes a series of essays on the significance of Maharshi's life and teachings as well as a short biography. The Tamil of the two texts is included in an appendix.

MUDALIAR, A. DEVARAJA. **DAY BY DAY WITH BHAGAVAN. 405pp. SRT68, 3.60c.**
A record of Maharshi's talks, taken from Mudaliar's diary.

NARASIMHA, B.V. **SELF REALIZATION. 271pp. SRT68, 2.50p.**
A biographical study, which emphasizes Maharshi's teachings and includes quotations from his discourses.

OSBORNE, ARTHUR, ed. **THE COLLECTED WORKS OF RAMANA MAHARSHI. Glossary, 188pp. Wei59/HPG, 3.50p.**
An anthology of all Maharshi's writings, including his translations of classic texts, Sankara's work, and a portion of the **Gita**.

OSBORNE, ARTHUR. **RAMANA MAHARSHI AND THE PATH OF SELF KNOWLEDGE. Glossary, 207pp. Wei56/HPG, 3.95p.**
The most comprehensive and readable account of Maharshi's life and teachings.

OSBORNE, ARTHUR, ed. **THE TEACHINGS OF RAMANA MAHARSHI. Index, 195pp. Wei62/HPG, 3.95p.**
Contains many actual conversations with those who sought Ramana Maharshi's spiritual guidance. They cover the whole religious and spiritual field from basic theories about God and the nature of man to advice about the conduct of our daily lives. Expressed in the form of questions and answers. The material is well arranged by subject and there are helpful editorial comments.

RAMANA MAHARSHI. **MAHARSHI'S GOSPEL. 92pp. SRT69, 2.75p.**
A series of topically arranged questions and answers on a variety of subjects related to the spiritual quest. The interchange is between Maharshi and some of his devotees.

RAMAKRISHNANANDA, SWAMI. **GOD AND DIVINE INCARNATIONS. 135pp. SRM70, 1.50p.**
A well integrated compilation of the speeches and discourses of one of Swami Ramakrishna's main disciples.

RAY, IRENE and MALLIKA GUPTA. **TALES FROM RAMAKRISHNA. 58pp. AdA75, 1.50p.**
When Sri Ramakrishna was teaching people he often used to tell them stories to help them grasp his point. He loved telling these stories and at that time his room would be filled with joy and laughter. Adults enjoy them as good stories, and they also enjoy the inner teaching. Children enjoy them as good stories, teaching or no teaching. This is a delightful retelling of some of the most loved stories, designed with many joyful illustrations for children and meant for readers of all ages.

SARADANANDA, SWAMI. **RAMAKRISHNA: THE GREAT MASTER. Glossary, index, 960pp. SRM52, 19.75c.**
Interpretative account of Sri Ramakrishna's life, spiritual disciplines, and teachings, closely analyzed by one of his intimate disciples. Sourcebook for all other biographies.

TAPASYANANDA, SWAMI. **SRI SARADA DEVI—THE HOLY MOTHER. Photographs, glossary, chronology, index, 469pp. SRM69, 4.50c.**
This book includes both a biography of the Holy Mother and a selection of conversations setting forth her teachings. This is the most exhaustive work available on the Holy Mother. The biography is written by Swami Tapasyananda and the conversations are translated by Swami Nikhilananda.

VISHIVASHRAYANANDA, SWAMI. **RAMAKRISHNA FOR CHILDREN. 9¾"x7¼", 39pp. RVM75, 1.50p.**
A simply written account of some of the major incidents in Sri Ramakrishna's life. Color drawings throughout.

YOGESHANANDA, SWAMI. **THE VISIONS OF SRI RAMAKRISHNA. Index, 150pp. SRM73, 2.25c.**
Swami Yogeshananda has carefully, conscientiously, collected the records of Sri Ramakrishna's transcendental experiences that have heretofore lain scattered throughout the histories of his life, and presented all that are available—from the most profound to the seemingly slight. The result is a glowing, indeed dazzling, display.—from the foreword.

——— **END OF SRI RAMAKRISHNA SUBSECTION** ———

RAMAN, A.S. **TALES FROM INDIAN MYTHOLOGY. Line drawings, 123pp. ICA61, 3.60c.**
A simple retelling of twelve stories and legends which have been passed down in the oral tradition.

SADHU, MOUNI. **IN DAYS OF GREAT PEACE. 3.00p.**
See the Meditation section.

SARASWATI, SWAMI, tr. **TALKS WITH RAMANA MAHARSHI. 655pp. SRT58, 5.40c.**
An extensive collection of questions and answers from 1935-39.

SHAMBHALA PUBLICATIONS. **THE SPIRITUAL TEACHINGS OF RAMANA MAHARSHI. 135pp. ShP72, 3.95p.**
A topically organized collection of Maharshi's thoughts and instruction, arranged in a question and answer format. The two major books reproduced here are **Spiritual Instruction** and **Maharshi's Gospel**. An essay by Carl Jung is also included.

——————— **END OF RAMANA MAHARSHI SUBSECTION** ———————

RAMANUJAN, A.K., tr. **SPEAKING OF SIVA. Long introduction, notes, 199pp. Vik73, 2.25p.**
A collection of lyric expressions of love for Siva, written in the tenth century.

The Ramayana

The **Ramayana** is one of the two great Sanskrit epic poems. It is thought to have been composed by the sage Valmiki about the fourth century BC. *It may sound hyperbolic, but I am prepared to state that almost every individual among the five hundred millions living in India is aware of the story of the* **Ramayana** *in some measure or another. Everyone of whatever age, outlook, education, or station in life knows the essential part of the epic and adores the main figures in it— Rama and Sita. Every child is told the story at bedtime. Some study it as part of a religious experience, going over a certain number of stanzas each day, reading and rereading the book several times in a lifetime. The* **Ramayana** *pervades our cultural life in one form or another at all times, it may be as a scholarly discourse at a public hall, a traditional story-teller's narrative in an open space, or a play or dance-drama on stage. . . . Everyone knows the story but loves to listen to it again. One accepts this work at different levels; as a mere tale with impressive character studies; as a masterpiece of literary composition; or even as a scripture. As one's understanding develops, one discerns subtler meanings; the symbolism becomes more defined and relevant to the day to day life. The* **Ramayana** *in the fullest sense of the term could be called a book of "perennial philosophy."*—R.K. Narayan.

BAPU. **RAMAYANA: THE STORY OF RAMA. 7¼"x8¼", 71pp. ICA74, 3.50p.**
Comic book style and color illustrations, accompanied by a short, simple text. For the youngest readers. Follows Valmiki.

BESANT, ANNIE. **SHRI RAMACHANDRA. 2.25c.**
See the Theosophy section.

BUCK, WILLIAM, tr. **RAMAYANA. Illustrations, 416pp. NAL76, 14.95/2.50p.**
A well written one volume retelling of the major episodes.

■ *COLLIS, MAURICE.* **QUEST FOR SITA. 162pp. Put47, 1.95p.**
A novelistic retelling of the central section of the **Ramayana**. If we had to choose just one book to introduce a friend to the story of the **Ramayana** it would be this one. Collis has chosen the most exciting episodes of the tale and has recreated them in an engrossing fashion. Accompanying the text is a series of extraordinary line drawings.

DUTT, ROMESH, tr. **THE RAMAYANA AND THE MAHABHARATA. 333pp. Dut10/Den, 2.95p.**
A very condensed poetic version of the epics.

GRIFFITH, RALPH, tr. **RAMAYANA OF VALMIKI. Notes, index, 590pp. CSS1875, 27.50c.**
A translation into rhyming octosyllabic couplets. Griffith wrote in the last half of the nineteenth century and is best known for his translations of the Vedic Hymns. To say that this translation is dated is to speak kindly of it. It is interesting as a document of its times, but it is hardly one that we would choose to read.

KHAN, BENJAMIN. **THE CONCEPT OF DHARMA IN VALMIKI RAMAYANA. Notes, bibliography, index, 287pp. MuM65, 9.00c.**
This study is calculated to show to the present generation how in this age of seething doubts we may still draw inspiration from that ancient epic and how most of the problems that are baffling modern society can be solved by understanding and following the precepts held out by it. It also shows how the Western Ethics compare with the ancient ethical notions of the **Ramayana**.—from the introduction.

KRISHNAMURTI, G. **THE ADVENTURES OF RAMA. 127pp. Tdm75, .95p.**
A simple retelling of highlights from the epic, geared toward young readers.

MAZUMDAR, SHUDHA, tr. **RAMAYANA. Glossary, 540pp. OLL58, 5.50c.**
A translation of the Bengali version of the **Ramayana**. The story is retold in simple, modern prose and the translator has succeeded admirably in making this ancient story come alive for the modern reader.

■ *NARAYAN, R.K.* **THE RAMAYANA—A SHORTENED MODERN PROSE VERSION OF THE INDIAN EPIC. Introduction, illustrations, 173pp. Vik72/C&W, 2.50p.**
Narayan is considered India's leading English novelist. His **Ramayana** was inspired by a Tamil version written by an eleventh century poet called Kamban. It is less a translation than a new retelling, in terms that will help the modern reader to appreciate its rich lore.

RAGHAVACHARYA, T. SRINIVASA. **GEMS FROM RAMAYANA. Sanskrit text, English translation, 186pp. BBU71, 1.50p.**
This book contains almost all the *neeti slokas* or moral sayings culled out of the **Srimad Valmiki Ramayana**.

SARMA, D.S. **SRIMAD RAMAYANA: THE STORY OF THE PRINCE OF AYODHYA. 385pp. SRM46, 2.75c.**
This is a literary retelling of the story of the **Ramayana**. All the main details and events remain. The writing style is somewhat stilted, though the book does read fairly well and the language is simple.

SEEGER, ELIZABETH. **THE RAMAYANA. Introduction, 261pp. Den69, 9.35c.**
This is a lively retelling of the major portions of the epic. This rendition

is based on Shastri's translation and was written especially for young people. Illustrated with color plates and line drawings.

SHASTRI, HARI PRASAD. **THE RAMAYANA OF VALMIKI. Three volumes, many notes, index, 1,797pp. ShS62, 31.20p/set.**
The most readable, complete edition available in English. Recommended for all who wish to get the full flavor of the epic.

───────── **END OF THE RAMAYANA SUBSECTION** ─────────

RAWSON, PHILIP. **EROTIC ART OF INDIA. 8"x11", 85pp. Uni77, 6.95p.**
Forty full page color paintings are beautifully reproduced. Rawson includes a short commentary on each along with an overview of the Indian epics of the sixth to the third century BC which were the inspiration for the paintings.

■ *RENOU, LOUIS, ed.* **HINDUISM. Notes, bibliography, index, 226pp. Brz61, 6.95c.**
An excellent introduction to Hinduism. Renou has selected a wide variety of classical and modern texts—from the earliest known hymns, epics, and moral treatises through the writings of Tagore, Gandhi, and Radhakrishnan, and arranged them chronologically. Each is prefaced by an introduction. The final section discusses the role of Hinduism in Indian society. The transcriptions are taken from the works of noted scholars.

RENOU, LOUIS. **RELIGIONS OF ANCIENT INDIA. Index, 147pp. ScB53, 1.95p.**
M. Renou is Professor of Sanskrit and Indian Literature at the Sorbonne. This is a very concise discussion of the early religious movements in India. The emphasis is on an understanding of the major texts and of the mythology.

REYMOND, LIZELLE. **MY LIFE WITH A BRAHMIN FAMILY. 192pp. Vik58, 1.75p.**
Ms. Reymond lived with a Brahmin family in India from 1947 to 1953. In this book she describes each member of the family, from their great uncle Maharaj, who sat naked in contemplation on his tiger skin, to the family guru and the grandchildren. She discusses her adjustment as a cultured Frenchwoman to life in the Himalayas and skillfully recreates the atmosphere. This is an extremely readable account.

REYMOND, LIZELLE. **SHAKTI. 64pp. RaH74, 5.00c.**
A moving description of the very nature of *shakti*—a concept at the heart of the Hindu tradition. It is, Ms. Reymond says, *the active and conscious force of God, the glory of the absolute; shakti is the Presence, invisible and constant, which sustains the world, linking form and name.* Illustrated with Tantric drawings by Madhur Jaffrey.

REYMOND, LIZELLE. **TO LIVE WITHIN. 271pp. Vik69/A&U, 1.75p.**
This is a deceptive book. We once took it with us on a trip thinking that it would be light reading. It is not. The first half is an account of the five years Ms. Reymond spent in a Himalayan hermitage. The second contains her master's thoughts on the path, consciousness, awakening, life in death, and much else. It is a clear, beautiful work which we found engrossing. We found the philosophy to be reminiscent of Gurdjieff's teaching.

RIEPE, DALE. **THE NATURALISTIC TRADITION IN INDIAN THOUGHT. Glossary, notes, bibliography, index, 319pp. UWa61, 9.35c.**
A detailed study of a little explored area. Most books on Indian philosophy concentrate on the mystical and idealistic aspects of the Indian traditions. This is the only one that we know of that is solely devoted to Indian early naturalistic tendencies. The Hindu, Jain, and Buddhist schools are all included.

RYDER, ARTHUR, tr. **THE PANCHATANTRA. Introduction, 470pp. UCh25, 5.95p.**
The word *Panchatantra* means *five books.* Each of the five is independent, consisting of a framing story with numerous inserted stories, told by one or another of the characters in the main narrative. The majority of the main characters are animals who have a fairly constant character. The animals often quote verses from the sacred writings to justify their actions. It is now believed that the original work was composed in Kashmir about 200 BC—at this date, however, many of the individual stories were already ancient. The text that is translated here dates from AD 1199. The fables have traveled the world and are the forerunners of many tales that we associate with other cultures. They are noted for their realism and pervasive humor.

SAHUKAR, MANI. **SAI BABA: THE SAINT OF SHIRDI. Photographs, glossary, 65pp. DHP77, 3.95p.**
A study of the life and teachings of Sai Baba of Shirdi—an early twentieth century holy man who should not be confused with Sathya Sai Baba.

───────────────────────────────

Sanskrit Language ──────────

Sanskrit is the classic literary language of the Hindus, an old Indo-Aryan tongue from which the Prakrits and the modern Indo-Aryan languages evolved. Vedic Sanskrit, based on a dialect of northwestern India, was used from about 1500 BC to about 200 BC. Classical Sanskrit overlapped with Vedic somewhat, dating from about 500 BC to AD 1000. Sanskrit continues to be a learned and sacred language in India today. The vehicle of a rich literature written prior to the fifteenth century, Sanskrit is now written in the Devanagari script and is widely used in India as a scholarly second language, with a status similar to that of Latin in medieval Europe.

APTE, VAMAN. **PRACTICAL SANSKRIT-ENGLISH DICTIONARY. MoB65, 42.00c.**
This is a revised and enlarged version of V.S. Apte's masterwork *which has attempted to give in 1200 closely printed pages . . . matter at least equal in point of quantity to that given by Professor Monier-Williams in his Dictionary, but in point of quality more reliable, varied, and practically useful.*—from the preface. The dictionary is highly regarded. This edition is printed on poor quality paper and the Sanskrit is often hard to read.

APTE, VAMAN. **STUDENT'S ENGLISH-SANSKRIT DICTIONARY. 501pp. MoB20, 8.55c.**
Apte's dictionaries are generally considered the best reasonably priced volumes available.

APTE, VAMAN. **STUDENT'S SANSKRIT-ENGLISH DICTIONARY. 664pp. MoB1890, 12.30c.**
A comprehensive compilation which covers virtually every discipline and field of study.

BARBORKA, GEOFFREY. **GLOSSARY OF SANSKRIT TERMS. 76pp. PoL72, 1.25p.**
With a pronunciation key.

BLUE MOUNTAIN CENTER OF MEDITATION. **A GLOSSARY OF SANSKRIT. 24pp. Nil70, 2.00p.**
A glossary of the terms that are most commonly found in the spiritual traditions of India. A clear copy of the original Sanskrit word is included, along with transliteration. There is also a bit of information on the Sanskrit alphabet. The explanations are clear.

COULSON, MICHAEL. **SANSKRIT. 523pp. McK76, 7.95p.**
Carefully graded chapters explain the basics of Sanskrit grammar and style with exceptional clarity. Exercises are also included, most of which use only sentences taken directly from works in Sanskrit. The text has an appendix on prosody, extensive vocabularies, and full keys to the main exercises. Part of the **Teach Yourself** series.

EDGERTON, FRANKLIN. **BUDDHIST HYBRID SANSKRIT GRAMMAR AND DICTIONARY. 50.65c/set.**
See the Buddhism section.

EDGERTON, FRANKLIN, ed. **BUDDHIST HYBRID SANSKRIT READER. 76pp. MoB53, 4.50c.**
A companion to the editor's dictionary. A number of classical works are presented in transliterated form.

GONDA, JAN. **A CONCISE ELEMENTARY GRAMMAR OF THE SANSKRIT LANGUAGE. 152pp. UAl66, 9.45c.**
This is a very good grammar, translated and amended by Gordon Ford. The primary objective of the author was to make it possible for students to acquire a good measure of command over the Sanskrit language in as short a time as possible, either in the classroom or privately. With this in mind, he has provided twenty translation exercises and thirteen Sanskrit readings, together with a glossary of all words used. The Sanskrit is all transliterated.

KALE, M.R. **A HIGHER SANSKRIT GRAMMAR. 160pp. MoB1894, 5.70p.**
The present Grammar has been prepared with a view to meet the growing wants of the Indian University students. The University examiners have been, of late, evincing a desire to exact a more thorough knowledge of the obscurer and therefore more difficult parts of Sanskrit Grammar, than was required formerly. Mr. Kale has based his work on the style and format of the classical Sanskrit literature and his text includes many special features. He has relied on many of the older works, and has tried to incorporate the best features of each in an attempt to present as complete a grammar as possible.

LANMAN, CHARLES. **A SANSKRIT READER. Many notes, 421pp. HUP1884, 20.15c.**
In making my selections from the various Sanskrit writings, I have had two practical aims in view: first, to provide abundant material for thorough drill in the language of the classical period; and secondly, to furnish a brief introduction to the works of the Vedic period, Mantra, Brahmana, and Sutra. There is also a complete vocabulary which aims at teaching the student how to trace every word back to its root and to trace every signification back to the radical idea. The words in the vocabulary are transliterated. This is generally considered one of the best readers available.

LEIDECKER, KURT. **SANSKRIT: ESSENTIALS OF GRAMMAR AND LANGUAGE. 150pp. TPH76, 4.50c.**
Sanskrit grammar is highly complex and it is not easy to master it.... Standard grammar books on Sanskrit are available... but the beginner may find them difficult. Here is an attempt not only to the lead the serious student through a short cut to the structure of the Sanskrit language, but also to help him to have a general understanding of the vocabulary through the method of starting from the root. —from the introduction.

MACDONNELL, ARTHUR. **A PRACTICAL SANSKRIT DICTIONARY. 8¾"x11", 392pp. Oxf24, 25.20c.**
A well printed, clearly presented work, with transliteration, accentuation, and etymological analysis. Excellent definitions.

MACDONNELL, ARTHUR. **SANSKRIT GRAMMAR FOR STUDENTS. 282pp. Oxf27, 11.35c/6.00c.**
This has been considered the definitive introductory grammar for generations. All the usual features are included and the whole work is extremely well organized. Includes verb lists, information on Vedic grammar, and indices.

MONIER-WILLIAMS, M. **ENGLISH-SANSKRIT DICTIONARY. 872pp. MoB nd, 37.50c.**
The most complete available.

MONIER-WILLIAMS, M. **A SANSKRIT-ENGLISH DICTIONARY. 9"x11¼", 1,370pp. Oxf1899, 59.00c.**
The recommended dictionary for the serious scholar.

PANDIT, M.P. **GLOSSARY OF SANSKRIT TERMS IN SRI AUROBINDO'S WORKS. 84pp. SAA66, 2.25c.**
Excludes Vedic words, for which there is another glossary, and translations from the **Upanishads**. English equivalents are almost wholly in Aurobindo's own words.

PERRY, EDWARD. **A SANSKRIT PRIMER. 240pp. Col36, 14.00c.**
The Primer can be finished by earnest students in sixteen or seventeen weeks, reckoning three lessons per week, with here and there an hour for review. After than Lanman's **Sanskrit Reader**, *an introduction to which this work is partly intended to be, should be taken up. Students are strongly recommended to provide themselves with Whitney's* **Sanskrit Grammar** *at the outset.* All the usual basic features are included and exercises follow each lesson. A romanized Sanskrit-English glossary is provided.

SIVANANDA, SWAMI. **YOGA VEDANTA DICTIONARY. 190pp. MoB73, 1.80p.**
Definitions of technical terms geared toward helping the spiritual aspirant understand yogic and Vedantic texts. Includes a pronunciation guide. The Sanskrit terms are transliterated.

SURYAKANTA, DR. **SANSKRIT-HINDI-ENGLISH DICTIONARY. 7½"x10", 703pp. OLL75, 49.50c.**
A unique trilingual dictionary by a contemporary Indian academician.

■ TYBERG, JUDITH. **FIRST LESSONS IN SANSKRIT GRAMMAR AND READING. 240pp. EWC64, 6.50p.**
A simplified, yet comprehensive and inspiring text designed by a disciple of Sri Aurobindo for those who wish to delve into the ancient scriptures of India. Includes many verses from the **Bhagavad Gita** and **Upanishads**.

■ TYBERG, JUDITH. **LANGUAGE OF THE GODS. 254+pp. EWC70, 8.95c.**
Contains the interpretation of some 2,000 Sanskrit spiritual, philosopical, and religious terms. A stress has been given to the verb roots of the words, since they are the essential carriers of the meaning of the words as originating in the spiritual element of the universe. Designed for students who would like to become familiar with the meaning and symbolic truths contained in Sanskrit words.

TYBERG, JUDITH. **SANSKRIT KEYS TO THE WISDOM RELIGION. 4.00p.**
See the Theosophy section.

The syllable *om*.

USHA, BRAHMACHARINI. **A RAMAKRISHNA-VEDANTA WORDBOOK. 87pp. VdP62, 1.35p.**
Six hundred terms and proper names most important in the vocabulary of today's student of Vedanta, defined and pronunciation indicated. —from the introduction.

WHITNEY, WILLIAM. **THE ROOTS, VERB-FORMS AND PRIMARY DERIVATIVES OF THE SANSKRIT LANGUAGE. 263pp. MoB1885, 6.00p.**

WHITNEY, WILLIAM. **SANSKRIT GRAMMAR. Indices, 571pp. HUP1889, 21.50c/16.50p.**
This is universally considered the definitive grammar. Every possible aspect of the subject is covered in depth and the instructional material is fairly clear, although the presentation is dated.

——— **END OF SANSKRIT LANGUAGE SUBSECTION** ———

SARMA, D.S. **ESSENCE OF HINDUISM. 121pp. BBU71, 1.15p.**
A concise survey of some of the major elements of the Hindu faith divided into the following general topics: *Hindu Scriptures, Hindu Rituals and Myths, Hindu Ethics, Hindu Theism,* and *Hindu Philosophy.*

SARMA, D.S. **HINDUISM THROUGH THE AGES. 312pp. BBU56, 2.40p.**
Sarma begins with a general survey of Hinduism. The bulk of the book is devoted to late nineteenth and twentieth century individuals and movements. Included are separate chapters on each of the following: *Ram Mohun Roy and the Brahmo Samaj, Ranade and the Prarthana Samaj, Swami Dayananda and the Arya Samaj, Tilak, Annie Besant and the Theosophical Society, Sri Ramakrishna, Swami Vivekananda, Tagore, Gandhi, Sri Aurobindo, Ramana Maharshi,* and *Radhakrishnan.*

Sathya Sai Baba

A very popular present day guru who purports to be the reincarnation of the original Sai Baba, India's most beloved twentieth century saint. To some he is thought of as a god, to others he is a siddha (a man who performs miracles, but has little real power or spiritual distinction). Thousands follow him and his miracles are legendary.

BENJAMIN, SOLOMON. **SELECTED JEWELS. Glossary, 105pp. SSS71, 1.25p.**
A selection of poems inspired by the author's contact with Sathya Sai. The style is often narrative.

DEVI, INDRA. **SAI BABA AND SAI YOGA. 149pp. MGB75, 3.10p.**
In the beginning of this book Indra Devi explains that the practice of sai yoga *involves not only physical and mental but moral and spiritual aspects as well. It is primarily designed to produce a contemplative and meditative attitude of mind at the time of performing the Asanas... without diminishing or interfering with their beneficial effects upon the body.*

GOKAK, V.K. **SRI SATHYA SAI BABA: THE MAN AND THE AVATAR. 308pp. Abh75, 3.90p.**
One of Sathya Sai's chief disciples discusses the personality, philosophy, work, sayings and writings, and impact of his master. This is an extremely complete—albeit unobjective—presentation.

MURPHET, HOWARD. **SAI BABA, MAN OF MIRACLES. Index, 211pp. Wei73/Mll, 3.95p.**
A journalistic survey focusing on the miracles Sai Baba has performed since childhood. Many case studies are included. The account is entirely uncritical.

RUHELA, S.P. and DUANE ROBINSON, eds. **SAI BABA AND HIS MESSAGE. Glossary, bibliography, 350pp. VPH76, 2.75p.**
Subtitled, *A Challenge to the Behavioral Sciences,* this volume presents a number of essays analyzing Sai Baba's potential influence in the realms of education, family life, community life, psychotherapy, and religion. Many of the contributors are followers of Sai Baba and all are influenced by his being and his ideas.

■ *SANDWEISS, SAMUEL.* **SAI BABA: THE HOLY MAN AND THE PSYCHIATRIST. Many color photographs, glossary, 240pp. BDP75/ Spe, 4.25p.**
Sandweiss is an American psychiatrist who became dissatisfied with traditional therapeutic techniques and journeyed to India to see what he could learn from the approach of the Indian gurus. While there he became deeply involved with Sathya Sai Baba. *This book is an attempt to describe my direct observation and personal experience of some of these powers. It is the outcome of a soul's struggle to comprehend phenomena in which the West does not generally believe. I have tried to prepare the Western reader for the alien territory which he will encounter here and to relate what I observed to psychiatric concepts with which most of us are at least somewhat familiar.... Who is Sai Baba? If his powers are genuine, how can he lead one deeper into the innermost mysteries of our existence? These were the basic questions with which I started my search....I invite you to join my journey toward this holy man...to explore an exciting and inspirational realm of human possibility through this enigmatic figure.* This is a very personal account. The second half of the book is devoted to a reproduction of key passages from Sathya Sai's writings and speeches.

SATHYA SAI BABA. **BHAGAVAN SRI SATHYA SAI BABA IN AMRITSAR—SIMLA—DELHI. 79pp. SSS75, 1.35p.**
Transcriptions of Sai Baba's discourses on his April, 1975 trip to these cities. Some background information is also included.

SATHYA SAI BABA. **BHAGAVATHA VAHINI. 338pp. SSS70, 3.60p.**
Sathya Sai's retelling of the *Srimad Bhagavatam.* He also includes episodes from other ancient texts which detail events in Krishna's life. Written in a novelistic style. Sathya Sai claims to be an incarnation of Krishna.

SATHYA SAI BABA. **CHINNA KATHA. 184pp. SSS75, 1.70p.**
A selection of stories and parables from Sathya Sai's discourses.

SATHYA SAI BABA. **DHARMA VAHINI. SSS nd, 1.90p.**
Teachings on morality.

SATHYA SAI BABA. **DHYANA VAHINI. 76pp. SSS nd, 1.75p.**
Translation of a series of discourses on meditation.

SATHYA SAI BABA. **GEETHA VAHINI. SSS nd, 3.60p.**
Teachings on the **Bhagavad Gita.**

SATHYA SAI BABA. **JNANA VAHINI. SSS nd, 2.25p.**
Teachings on wisdom.

SATHYA SAI BABA. **PRASANTHI VAHINI. 92pp. SSS62, 1.90p.**
Transcription of a series of discourses. *The Syllable Pra in Pra-santhi means, expanding, enlarging, vikasa; and so Prasanthi means that type of Santhi. That is to say, the absence of Desire and Anger, Greed and Hatred.*

SATHYA SAI BABA. **PREMA VAHINI. 97pp. SSS70, 1.25p.**
Transcription of a series of discourses on bhakti yoga or *inner peace through love,* as Sathya Sai phrases it.

SATHYA SAI BABA. **SANDEHA NIVARINI. 122pp. SSS75, 1.35p.**
A collection of dialogues on the spiritual path between Sathya Sai and his disciples.

SATHYA SAI BABA. **SATHYA SAI GEETA. Glossary, 67pp. SSS68, 1.00p.**
A small booklet which summarizes Sathya Sai's main teachings and his view of Indian philosophy.

SATHYA SAI BABA. **SATHYA SAI SPEAKS, VOLUMES I-IX. SSS.**
Verbatim transcriptions of discourses. I (1956-60), 2.95p; II (1960-62), 3.60p; III (1963-64), 3.60p; IV (1964-65), 4.50p; V (1965-67), 4.50p; VI (1967-68), 4.50p; VII (1968-71), 4.95p; VIII, 3.00p; IX, 3.00p.

SATHYA SAI BABA. **SATHYAM SHIVAM SUNDARAM, PARTS I-III. SSS.**
Sathya Sai's autobiography, in three parts. Part I covers the period from his birth to 1926, 3.60p; Part II covers the years 1926-1961, 3.60p; and Part III covers the years from 1961-72, 3.95p.

SATHYA SAI BABA. **SONGS OF SRI SATHYA SAI BABA. 89pp. SSS nd, .95p.**
The Bhajans presented here are songs, traditionally sung in praise of God during congregational worship.—from the introduction. The transliterated text and translation are on facing pages.

SATHYA SAI BABA. **SUMMER SHOWERS IN BRINDAVAN. SSS.**
Each summer Sathya Sai invites hundreds of high school students from all over India to Brindavan and has educators instruct them in matters relating to morality, spiritual living, and service to others. He also gives frequent discourses. Three sets of summer discourses have been transcribed: 1972, 4.50p; 1973, 3.60p; and 1974, 3.60p.

SATHYA SAI BABA. **TEACHINGS OF SRI SATHYA SAI BABA. 144pp. CSA74, 1.25p.**
A topically arranged collection of Sai Baba's teachings. Each selection is very short.

SATHYA SAI BABA. **TRUTH—WHAT IS TRUTH? 192pp. SSS75, 1.75p.**
A selection from Sathya Sai's discourses.

SATHYA SAI BABA. **UPANISHAD VAHINI. 78pp. SSS70, 1.75p.**
Teachings on spiritual discipline.

————— **END OF SATHYA SAI BABA SUBSECTION** —————

■ SEN, K.M. HINDUISM. 153pp. Vik61, 1.95p.
A good introduction to the nature and functions of Hinduism for those who have no previous knowledge of the subject. Includes extracts from the scriptures.

SERRANO, MIGUEL. THE SERPENT OF PARADISE. 184pp. RKP72, 6.30p.
A very readable account of Serrano's pilgrimage through India. He discusses the people, holy places, and saints that he encounters, and reveals his personal reactions.

SHANKARANARAYANAN, S. SRI CHAKRA. Many illustrations, notes, 123pp. SAA73, 4.25c.
This is an obscure work, based at least in part on the teachings of Sri Aurobindo. Shankaranarayanan discusses the true meaning of the nine *chakras* that make up the *Sri Chakra*.

SHARMA, CHANDRADHAR. A CRITICAL SURVEY OF INDIAN PHILOSOPHY. Extensive topical bibliography, index, 415pp. MoB73, 6.00c.
An important treatise on the different systems of Indian philosophy based on original sources. Each system, from the Vedas to Sri Aurobindo, is analyzed in depth and Sharma has quoted from the original sources on almost all fundamental points.

SHASTRI, HARI PRASAD, tr. ADVADHUT GITA. 40pp. ShS68, 1.60c.
The word Gita means a song. The Indian holy Scriptures were written in songs, and each was attributed to a great sage, or to an Incarnation of God, called an Avatara.... The Avadhut Gita is a special classic which is meant for the use of those advanced students of Indian metaphysics who have learnt self-control to an appreciable extent.... It is for those who practice detachment in daily life, and are eager to realise God at any cost.—from the introduction.

SHASTRI, HARI PRASAD. THE HEART OF THE EASTERN MYSTICAL TEACHINGS. Glossary, 320pp. ShS48, 4.25p.
An account of the life of a modern mahatma, Sri Dada of Aligarh. In dialogues with pupils he expounds his teaching in different ways, appropriate to their understanding.

SHASTRI, HARI PRASAD. THE WORLD WITHIN THE MIND. 142pp. ShS37, 1.95p.
Extracts translated from the Indian classic, Yoga Vasishtha, a work of unusual charm. Both philosophical and practical teachings are given by the sage Vasishtha to his pupil Rama.

SHASTRI, HARI PRASAD. YOGA. Glossary, 96pp. Foy57, 2.50c.
Shastri comes from a long line of Brahmin scholars and is well versed in Sanskrit and in the classical philosophy of India, as well as in Chinese, Japanese, and Persian languages and literatures. This is an excellent treatise on the philosophy and practice of yoga and includes illustrative passages from yoga literature, biographical sketches of three yogis, and a glossary.

SHASTRI, J.L., ed. THE BHAGAVATA-PURANA. 1,012pp. MoB76, 15.00c/set.
The first two volumes of the Sanskrit text, accompanied by a profusion of notes. The rest of the Purana is due to be published in the next few years.

SHASTRI, J.L., ed. THE LINGA-PURANA. Notes, index, 841pp. MoB73, 30.00c/set.
A complete translation of the Sanskrit text, in two volumes. *It derives its name from the fact that it reveals the supreme lord, Siva in his "niskala" (attributeless) and "sakala" (qualified) forms, recounts his emblems, qualities, exploits and incarnations, narrates legends on the origin and importance of the Linga—his phallic idol, dwells upon the merit of installing and consecrating it, describes the ritual and philosophical principles of the Linga cult and embodies sermons and dissertations on the glory of the Linga image.*—from the introduction.

SHASTRI, J.L., ed. THE SIVA-PURANA. Extensive introduction, notes, index, 2,174pp. MoB70, 60.00c/set.
This is a complete translation of the Sanskrit text, in four volumes. Primarily concerned with Saivite religion, philosophy, and ethics, this Purana is a source of ancient Indian geography, history, and sociology.

Sikh Religion

The Sikh religion was founded in the fifteenth century by Guru Nanak. At that time India was ruled by Mogul princes. Nanak's family were Muslims and his teachings form a deliberate bridge between the Hindu and Muslim faiths. It is ironic that Nanak himself preached nonviolence since the Sikhs today are associated with militancy. The Sikh faith quickly grew in popularity and by the time of the sixth guru, Gobind Singh, they began to be persecuted by the ruling Moguls. It was at that time that they took to arms to defend themselves. Today the Sikh religion remains one of the most popular faiths in India.

CHADDA, H.C., ed. SEEING IS ABOVE ALL. 8"x8", 112pp. SKP77, 3.00p.
A photographic study of Sant Darshan Singh's first Indian tour. Darshan Singh is the successor to Kirpal Singh.

GREENLEES, DUNCAN. THE GOSPEL OF THE GURU-GRANTH SAHIB. Many notes, bibliography, 563pp. TPH75, 7.50c.
A translation of the Gospel based on the Jap Ji and portions of the Guru Granth, combined with a 293 page introductory essay.

JOHNSON, JULIAN. PATH OF THE MASTERS. 617pp. RaS39, 4.65c.
Presents a comprehensive description of Charan Singh and his yogic system as well as details on the previous Sikh masters who presented the Radha Soami system to the world. This is considered an excellent work for all who seek to understand the Indian spiritual tradition and what it is like to follow a master. Includes practical techniques.

JOHNSON, JULIAN. WITH A GREAT MASTER IN INDIA. 241pp. RaS71, 3.55c.
Letters based on upon the observations and experiences of the author during the year and a half he spent with Sawan Singh. Includes a section on the Radha Soami system.

KAUR, PREMKA. PEACE LAGOON. 223pp. SpC72, 5.50p.
Sacred songs attributed to Guru Nanak, Guru Amar Das, Guru Ram Das, Guru Arjun, and Guru Gobind Singh.

KOHLI, SURINDAR. A CRITICAL STUDY OF ADI GRANTH. Notes, bibliography, index, 403pp. MoB61, 15.00c.
A scholarly study which was written as the author's doctoral dissertation, which is how it reads. Much of the book is devoted to translations of important passages, with commentary.

MCLEOD, W.H. THE EVOLUTION OF THE SIKH COMMUNITY. Glossary, notes, bibliography, index, Oxf76, 11.75c.
Sikh history has traditionally been regarded as a paradox. Beginning in the early sixteenth century as a system of interior devotion, Sikhism emerged into prominence during the eighteenth century as a clearly defined belief laying stress upon martial prowess and external symbols. McLeod seeks to demonstrate that there is in fact no paradox. In a series of five essays he examines the history and sacred literature of the Sikhs, showing that the evolution of the community has in reality been a logical and consistent process.

MCLEOD, W.H. GURU NANAK AND THE SIKH RELIGION. Glossary, notes, bibliography, index, 268pp. Oxf68, 8.40p.
This is an absorbing study of Guru Nanak's life and teachings. The analysis is both highly readable and a work of exacting scholarship. Guru Nanak's teachings constitute the basis and substance of the Sikh religion and an understanding of them and of the man responsible for them is requisite to an understanding of Sikhism.

MANSUKHANI, GOBIND SINGH, ed. HYMNS FROM THE HOLY GRANTH. 119pp. HeP75, 2.75p.
The Sanskrit is given, along with transliteration and translation.

SCOTTI, JULIET and RICKI LINKSMAN. KIRPAL SINGH: THE STORY OF A SAINT. 8½"x11", 110pp. SKP77, 3.95p.
A collection of miracle stories about the life and teachings of Kirpal

Guru Nanak

Singh, written by two of his disciples and geared toward children. Many drawings accompany the text.

SEADER, RUTH, ed. **THE TEACHINGS OF KIRPAL SINGH, VOLUME II: SELF-INTROSPECTION MEDITATION. Notes, 188pp. SSB75, 3.00p.**
Teachings on the title theme, compiled and edited from the writings of Kirpal Singh.

SEADER, RUTH, ed. **THE TEACHINGS OF KIRPAL SINGH, VOLUME III: THE NEW LIFE. 192pp. SSB76, 2.50p.**
A topically arranged compilation from the writings of Kirpal Singh. Unfortunately there is no apparent order to the entries, although there is a table of contents.

SINGH, CHARAN. **DIVINE LIGHT. 386pp. RaS67, 6.00c.**
*The book is in two parts—the first dealing with the Path of the Saints which all perfect Masters have revealed in all ages, climes and countries. . . . In the second part are excerpts from letters to seekers and disciples dealing with their day to day personal problems, material and spiritual.—*from the introduciton. Charan Singh is the current master of the Radha Soami (or Sant Mat) sect of the Sikhs.

SINGH, CHARAN. **LIGHT ON SANT MAT. Glossary, index, 432pp. RaS58, 4.50c.**
The first section of this book contains Charan Singh's explanation of what Sant Mat truly is; the rest contains some of his correspondence with disciples throughout the world.

SINGH, CHARAN. **THE PATH. 148pp. RaS nd, .75p.**
The first half of **Divine Life** is presented here. Devotees of this faith suggest that this volume is the best one to start with.

SINGH, CHARAN. **QUEST FOR LIGHT. 321pp. RaS72, 3.95c.**
Excerpts from letters written by the master to his disciples.

SINGH, CHARAN. **SPIRITUAL DISCOURSES. 254pp. RaS64, 3.70c.**
Transcription of discourses on a variety of topics.

SINGH, GOPAL, ed. **THE RELIGION OF THE SIKHS. 199pp. APH71, 6.40c.**
A topically organized compilation of selections from the sacred literature of the Sikhs, with commentary.

SINGH, GURSARAN. **JAPJI: THE MORNING PRAYER OF THE SIKHS. 291pp. ARS72, 9.00c.**
This work includes the full text of the **Jap Ji**, in Gurmukhi script and English translation—with an extensive interpretation in the light of modern thought. The author suggests that Guru Nanak's mission was

not to found any new faith; what he wanted was to create a new society based on the principles of truth, tolerance, and equality.

SINGH, HARBANS. **GURU NANAK AND THE ORIGINS OF THE SIKH FAITH. 247pp. APH69, 11.00c.**
This is the most extensive biographical study available. Every aspect of Nanak's life and teachings is discussed at length. Also includes selections from his major writings.

SINGH, HUZUR. **PHILOSOPHY OF THE MASTERS. RaS67.**
A very complete presentation of the teachings from the present line whose current master is Charan Singh. An abridged one-volume edition is available for $3.75c and the following individual volumes are also in print: II, Spiritual Discipline—Mental, 3.35c; III, Worship and Prayers, 3.55c; IV, The Lord, The Sound Current, The Name of God, and Ambrosia, 2.75c; V, Devotional Music, and The Master and His Characteristics, 2.75c.

SINGH, KIRPAL. **THE CROWN OF LIFE: A STUDY IN YOGA. 255pp. RuS61, 3.00p.**
Includes an exhaustive analysis of Patanjali's yoga system, studies of all yogas currently practiced in India, an explanation of Sankara's philosophy, and a complete presentation of the surat shabd yoga of which the author was an exponent.

SINGH, KIRPAL. **GODMAN. 191pp. RuS67, 2.00p.**
A thorough study of the origin, mission, and nature of masters of the highest order.

SINGH, KIRPAL. **A GREAT SAINT, BABA JAIMAL SINGH: HIS LIFE AND TEACHINGS. 146pp. RuS60, 2.00p.**
This great saint was the master of Baba Sawan Singh, the spiritual master of both Charan Singh and Kirpal Singh. Includes an excellent glossary.

SINGH, KIRPAL. **THE HOLY PATH. Notes, 94pp. RuS74, 2.00p.**
This is Volume I of **The Teachings of Kirpal Singh.** It includes essays on various aspects of the spiritual path, selected from his major writings.

SINGH, KIRPAL, tr. **JAP JI: THE MESSAGE OF GURU NANAK. Glossary, notes, 215pp. RuS59, 2.25p.**
The bulk of this volume is devoted to Kirpal Singh's introductory comments. The translation itself is more than adequate and extensive commentary is also included.

SINGH, KIRPAL. **NAAM OR WORD. 335pp. RuS60, 3.00p.**
A poetic, carefully drawn study of the expression of God, *Naam*, word, or *Logos*, the aspect of God that at once creates and sustains the universe. Numerous quotations from Hindu, Buddhist, Islamic, and Christian sacred writings demonstrate the universality of the concept.

SINGH, KIRPAL. **THE NIGHT IS A JUNGLE. 358pp. RuS75, 8.95c.**
A selection of discourses prepared especially for Western audiences.

SINGH, KIRPAL. **PRAYER: ITS NATURE AND TECHNIQUES. 153pp. RuS59, 1.50p.**
All forms and aspects are discussed, from the most elementary and dualistic to the ultimate stage of *praying without ceasing,* where all life is a prayer. Includes specific prayers from all religious traditions.

SINGH, KIRPAL. **SURAT SHABD YOGA: THE YOGA OF CELESTIAL SOUND. 71pp. ImP75, 2.50p.**
Surat shabd yoga, translated as the *yoga of the celestial sound,* is the practice that Kirpal Singh taught. Here he presents an introduction to the practice.

SINGH, KIRPAL. **THE WAY OF THE SAINTS. Color and black and white photographs, 402pp. RuS76, 6.00p.**
A restatement of *Sant Mat* taken from the talks and letters of Kirpal Singh. The contents range from basic introductory talks to intimate explanations of subtle spiritual points. The volume also includes a biography of Kirpal Singh's master, Baba Sawan Singh.

SINGH, KIRPAL. **THE WHEEL OF LIFE. 1.95p.**
See the Reincarnation and Karma section.

SINGH, K. and S.V. **HOMAGE TO GURU GOBIND SINGH.** 100pp. JPH66, 2.30p.
A short, popularized, biographical study.

SINGH, SANGAT, tr. **JAPJI. Notes,** 128pp. HPB73, 1.80p.
A nice, concise translation, with a fair amount of introductory material.

SINGH, SARDAR. **SCIENCE OF THE SOUL.** 287pp. RaS59, 3.30c.
A collection of discourses and excerpts from letters and talks.

SINGH, SAWAN. **SPIRITUAL GEMS. Index,** 458pp. RaS65, 4.00c.
A collection of excerpts taken from letters written by Sawan Singh to seekers and disciples in America and Europe during the period from 1919 to 1948.

SINGH, SHANT, tr. **NANAK THE GURU.** 180pp. OLL70, 3.40c.
A comprehensive account of Nanak, the man, reformer, and universal prophet.

SINGH, TRILOCHAN, et al. **THE SACRED WRITINGS OF THE SIKHS. Glossary, index,** 288pp. Wei73/A&U, 3.50p.
This is the only paperback containing many selections from the **Adi Granth.** Also includes material from the **Dasm Granth.** These translations are excellent. Part of the UNESCO Collection.

TRUMPP, ERNEST, tr. **THE ADI GRANTH.** 7¼"x10½", 853pp. MuM 1877, 45.00c.
The **Adi Granth** is the most sacred book of the Sikhs and the authoritative scriptural work. The present version includes writings by all the ten Sikh gurus and also the *banis* of thirty-six Hindu and Muslim saints who lived between the twelfth and the seventeenth centuries. This is the only complete edition of the **Adi Granth** that we know of. It also includes extensive introductory material.

WASON, KATHRYN. **THE LIVING MASTER.** 316pp. RaS66, 3.50c.
Ms. Wason's impressions of life with Charan Singh.

───────**END OF SIKH RELIGION SUBSECTION**───────

SINGH, PURAN. **THE STORY OF SWAMI RAMA.** 297pp. Kly74, 8.10c.
Swami Ram Tirtha was one of the greatest philosophers and humanitarians of modern India. He believed that the Indian people had lost touch with their ancient wisdom and worked with missionary zeal to help them regain the faith. He felt that this could be done by the sixfold path: action, love, knowledge or law, fearlessness, purity, and yoga (a word which he considered to be synonymous with contemplation or concentration). He also followed the religion of nature and looked upon the many aspects of nature as his coreligionists. This biography includes selections from his letters and writings.

SIVANANDA, SWAMI. **DIVINE NECTAR.** 377pp. MoB76, 15.00c.
A topically arranged compilation of aphorisms and sayings of Swami Sivananda on a variety of topics.

SIVANANDA, SWAMI. **FOURTEEN LESSONS IN RAJA YOGA.** 135pp. DLS53, 1.90p.
A thorough, practical discussion of raja yoga.

SIVANANDA, SWAMI. **GYANA YOGA.** 267pp. MoB44, 2.10p.
A discussion of discipleship, the yoga of wisdom, the doctrine of maya, and practical aspects of yogic philosophy. The appendix contains the text of the **Ribhu Gita,** Sri Rama's instructions to Hanuman, and several ancient stories.

SIVANANDA, SWAMI. **JAPA YOGA.** 192pp. DLS72, 1.90p.
Japa is the repetition of any mantra or name of the Lord. This is a comprehensive treatise on japa yoga.

SIVANANDA, SWAMI. **PRACTICAL LESSONS IN YOGA.** 248pp. DLS38, 3.10p.
Swami Sivananda is without a doubt the most prolific writer on spiritual matters the twentieth century has produced. His books are extremely popular in India. He is the guru of two well known American gurus: Swami Satchidananda and Swami Vishnudevananda. In this book he presents twelve lessons on yoga and its objects, yoga *sadhana*,

yogic discipline, yogic diet, obstacles in yoga, yoga asanas, concentration, meditation, and *samadhi*.

SIVANANDA, SWAMI. **PRACTICE OF KARMA YOGA.** 324pp. MoB65, 4.55p.
A comprehensive treatise, discussing all aspects of the subject.

SIVANANDA, SWAMI. **PRACTICE OF YOGA. Glossary,** 479pp. DLS70, 4.55p.
Subtitled, *A comprehensive introduction to the definition, ethics, psychology and the science of yoga in its various branches of approach.* This seems to be the most complete of Sivananda's general yoga books.

SIVANANDA, SWAMI. **RELIGIOUS EDUCATION.** 365pp. DLS60, 2.85p.
Despite the title, this book contains a series of essays on various aspects of the spiritual life.

SIVANANDA, SWAMI. **SADHANA.** 755pp. MoB58, 9.45p.
This is one of Swami Sivananda's major works. He discusses Hindu psychology and psychological processes and includes information on all types of practices. A very complete account.

SIVANANDA, SWAMI. **THE SCIENCE OF PRANAYAMA.** 142pp. DLS75, 1.90p.
A detailed work on the science and the practice of pranayama, a very important aspect of yogic practice.

SIVANANDA, SWAMI. **SURE WAYS FOR SUCCESS IN LIFE AND GOD-REALIZATION.** 352pp. DLS70, 2.70p.
This is one of Sivananda's most popular practical works. Topics include *Culture of Will and Memory; Raja Yoga; Psychic Influence; Cultivation of Virtues; Eradication of Negative Qualities;* as well as a number of short guides for day to day living.

SIVARAMURTI, C. **THE ART OF INDIA. Glossary, chronologies, bibliography, index,** 9½"x12¼", 602pp. Abr77, 75.00c.
Sivaramurti is the former director of the National Museum in New Delhi. Superb illustrations and comprehensive reference materials combine with the author's incisive text to make this a landmark work. Nearly 1,000 photographic plates, 180 in color, are provided—almost all were specially commissioned for this book. Nearly 200 line drawings portray the gestures and motifs common in Indian art. A separate section, illustrated with thirty-one ground plans and over 300 plates, contains detailed descriptions of over 130 archaeological sites.

SLATER, WALLACE. **RAJA YOGA.** 106pp. TPH68, 1.75p.
Presents the basic technique of raja yoga in a graded, practical, do it yourself course divided into ten lessons. The instructions include posture, breathing, right attitudes, and methods of meditation.

THE SOUNDS OF YOGA-VEDANTA: A DOCUMENTARY OF LIFE IN AN INDIAN ASHRAM (A RECORDING). 7.98.
This 33 1/3 rpm recording tries to convey to the listener the sounds of a typical day at the Sivananda ashram. Included on the first side are portions of temple services, yoga classes, and lectures by Swami Sivananda. Side two contains selections from the evening *satsang*. There is little solid information about life in the ashram; rather, the album attempts to convey the feelings and impressions generated there.

STOOKE, H.J. and K. KHANDALAVALA. **THE LAUD RAGAMALA MINIATURES. Bibliography,** 66pp. Cas53, 14.25c.
Towards the beginning of the seventeenth century, there grew up in India a type of painting for which no exact parallels exist in the West. This art served to illustrate a particular form of poetry—a form which aimed less at poetic description than at rendering the mood and sentiment behind the traditional forms of Indian music. Poetry, painting, and music were thus brought into a new relationship.—from the introduction. This volume presents and describes a sequence of eighteen pictures, eight in color.

STUTLEY, M.E.L. and J.D. **HARPER'S DICTIONARY OF HINDUISM. Cross references, maps, illustrations, notes, index,** 7½"x10", 416pp. H&R77, 30.00c.
An exhaustive study which concentrates on classical Hinduism through the fourteenth century when the religion became fully formulated and after it had absorbed Buddhism in India. Both major

and lesser known terms, gods, goddesses, and legends are clearly explained. The presentation is comprehensive but not overwhelmingly so. Hinduism is seen not only in its religious aspects, but also in terms of the social, economic, and political conditions of the times. Many sources and parallels—both mythological and etymological—have been drawn upon. The authors devoted over seventeen years to the preparation of this definitive volume.

TADDEI, MAURIZIO. **INDIA. 169 plates, many in color, notes, bibliography, index, 263pp. Nag70, 26.20c.**
An archaeological study of early Indian civilization which incorporates the latest findings and, while a work of excellent scholarship, is not overly technical.

TADDEI, MAURIZIO. **MONUMENTS OF ANCIENT CIVILIZATION: INDIA. Chronology, bibliography, index, 9¾"x13", 191pp. G&D78, 19.95c.**
In his introduction, Taddei says, *We are to approach India from a very special angle: through a consideration of its ancient great monuments. These will principally be temples, monasteries, sanctuaries cut out of rock, stupas, sculptures, and relief carvings—mostly with religious associations and, as a group, comprising the major remains of artistic interest that ancient India offers to archaeology. But we shall not be limited in our examples, any more than we shall be confined by the political boundaries of contemporary India.... Among the various goals of this study... will be the search for the historic roots of what at times appear to be the constants of Indian thought.* Taddei's clear, insightful text is accompanied by a series of excerpts from ancient Indian texts and over 100 stunning color photographs.

TAGORE, RABINDRANATH. **COLLECTED POEMS AND PLAYS. Index, 578pp. McM36, 14.40c.**
Contains the complete text of the following works: **Gitanjali, The Crescent Moon, The Gardener, Chitra, Fruit-Gathering, The Post Office, Lover's Gift, Crossing, Stray Birds, The Cycle of Spring, The Fugitive,** and **Sacrifice.** Many shorter poems and plays are also included.

TAGORE, RABINDRANATH, tr. **GITANJALI. 123pp. McM13, 1.45p.**
Prose translations of a collection of Indian song offerings. Tagore's best known work. Introduction by W.B. Yeats.

TAGORE, RABINDRANATH. **THE LATER POEMS OF RABINDRANATH TAGORE. Glossary, index, 142pp. Cro74/Owe, 3.95p.**
None of the poems in this collection has been published in English before. The translator, Aurobindo Bose, was a personal friend and pupil of Tagore. He also contributes a good introduction.

TAGORE, RABINDRANATH. **LOVE POEMS OF TAGORE. Introduction, glossary, 189pp. HPB75, 2.75p.**
This is the first English translation of these poems.

TAGORE, RABINDRANATH. **A TAGORE READER. 414pp. Bea66, 5.95p.**
Tagore (1861-1941) was hailed during his lifetime as the living embodiment of Indian culture and its greatest spokesman. This volume includes selections from his most important writings—including poetry, short stories, fables, drama, and philosophy. Some of his letters are also included. The selection was made by his former literary secretary.

TAHTINEN, UNTO. **AHIMSA: NON-VIOLENCE IN INDIAN TRADITION. Notes, bibliography, index, 160pp. HPG76, 13.20c.**
A comprehensive analysis of *ahimsa* as it appears in the **Jaina Sutras**, Buddhism, and the **Vedas**, and as it has been exemplified in the twentieth century by Mahatma Gandhi. Tahtinen also includes an analysis of *himsa*, or violence.

TAIMNI, I.K. **GAYATRI. 202pp. TPH74, 3.25c.**
The japa of Gayatri is an integral part of sandhya, the daily practice of the Hindus.... The Gayatri mantra which is the chief element in Gayatri upsana or sandhya as it is usually called occurs in all the four Vedas and also in Tantras and is referred to in superlative terms by many Rishis.—from the introduction. This is the fullest exploration in print of *gayatri* and the *gayatri* mantra. Taimni is a Theosophist.

TAIMNI, I.K. **GLIMPSES INTO THE PSYCHOLOGY OF YOGA. 426pp. TPH73, 6.50c.**
A very complete discussion which builds upon the material Taimni

presented in **Science of Yoga** (see the Patanjali subsection). The major topics are the nature of reality, consciousness, mind, and matter. Taimni uses a lot of Sanskrit terminology.

TAIMNI, I.K., tr. **ULTIMATE REALITY AND REALIZATION. 229pp. TPH76, 5.95c.**
A Theosophically-oriented translation of the **Siva Sutra**, with Sanskrit text, transliteration, and commentary.

THAPAR, ROMILA and PERCIVAL SPEAR. **A HISTORY OF INDIA. Bibliography, index, Vik73.**
This is an excellent summary of Indian history, in two volumes. The first (381pp. 3.50p) traces the evolution of India from the establishment of Aryan culture about 1000 BC to the coming of the Moguls in AD 1526. The second volume (292pp., 3.95p) deals with both the Mogul and British periods. The book discusses the many manifestations of Indian culture, as seen in religion, art, and literature, and in ideas and institutions.

THOMAS, P. **EPICS, MYTHS, AND LEGENDS OF INDIA. 282 plates, index, 8¾"x11½", 152pp. TSC73, 32.30c.**
A topically arranged pictorial presentation of the mythological systems and cosmology of the Hindus, Buddhists, and Jains. The text is well written and organized and should appeal to both the general reader and the specialist.

UBAN, SUJAN SINGH. **THE GURUS OF INDIA. Photographs, bibliography, 175+pp. Fin77, 9.50c.**
Uban was a major general in the Indian army who, though raised a Sikh, devoted his life to acquiring a broad understanding of the spiritual and contemplative disciplines found on the Indian subcontinent. General Uban personally knew all of the gurus and spiritual teachers he discusses here, and he faithfully records both his own impressions of them and anecdotes he has heard from others. Among the gurus covered are Yogananda, Swami Sivananda, Sathya Sai Baba, Maharishi Mahesh Yogi, Kirpal Singh, Swami Muktananda, and the Dalai Lama.

Upanishads

The **Upanishads** form the concluding portion of the Hindu scriptures, the **Vedas**; and their philosophy, called Vedanta (*anta* meaning *the end of*) is the basis of all Hindu systems of religious thought, both dualistic and nondualistic. Originating hundreds of years before Christ, they record the mystical experiences of saints and sages. All ask and answer this one question: *What is that, knowing which, everything else is known?* And all attempt to solve the problems of the origin, nature, and destiny of man and the universe.

ALSTON, A.J., tr. **REALIZATION OF THE ABSOLUTE. 285pp. ShS69, 7.55c.**
This is a translation of the **Naiskarmya Siddi** of Sri Suresvara. Sri Suresvara was an immediate pupil of Sankara and he lived in the eighth century. He called his work *a compendium containing the essence of the entire Upanishadic teaching.* This edition contains the transliterated Sanskrit text and a full commentary.

AUROBINDO, SRI. **A GUIDE TO THE UPANISHADS. 143pp. SAA67. 3.50c.**

AUROBINDO, SRI, tr. **THE UPANISHADS. 541pp. SAA72, 7.50c.**
A collection of essays on Upanishadic philosophy and translations of the thirteen major **Upanishads** as well as translations of some early Vedantic texts. The Sanskrit is included and the translation is into simple, rhythmic English. Commentaries are included with each text.

BESANT, ANNIE. **THE WISDOM OF THE UPANISHADS.** 95pp. TPH07, 2.50c. A collection of lectures by this noted Theosophist.

CHINMAYANANDA, SWAMI, tr. **AITREYA UPANISHAD.** 135pp. CPT nd, 3.50c.
Swami Chinmayananda's translations are especially noted for their clarity. He provides the original Sanskrit verses, with transliteration, accompanied by the meanings of individual words, followed by a complete discourse on each verse.

CHINMAYANANDA, SWAMI, tr. **ISA VASYOPANISHAD.** 153pp. CPT nd, 3.50c.

CHINMAYANANDA, SWAMI, tr. **KAIVALYOPANISHAD.** 121pp. CPT nd, 3.50c.

CHINMAYANANDA, SWAMI, tr. **KATHOPANISHAD.** 273pp. CPT nd, 4.50c.
This is generally considered one of the major **Upanishads**.

CHINMAYANANDA, SWAMI, tr. **KENOPANISHAD.** 158pp. CPT nd, 3.50c.

CHINMAYANANDA, SWAMI, tr. **MUNDAKOPANISHAD.** 150pp. CPT nd, 2.75c.

CHINMAYANANDA, SWAMI, tr. **PRASNOPANISHAD.** 166pp. CPT nd, 3.50c.

CHINMAYANANDA, SWAMI, tr. **TAITTREYA UPANISHAD.** 217pp. CPT nd, 4.25c.

DEUSSEN, PAUL. **THE PHILOSOPHY OF THE UPANISHADS.** Many notes, index, 429pp. Dov06, 5.00p.
A clear, detailed statement of the Upanishadic system of thought. Deussen includes a history of the **Upanishads**, a full exposition of the system emergent from them, and a discussion of parallel Western concepts. A first rate work for the scholar.

EASWARAN, EKNATH, tr. **THE KATHA UPANISHAD.** 28pp. Nil70, 2.00p.
A beautifully written poetic rendition. Includes a short introduction.

EASWARAN, EKNATH, tr. **THREE UPANISHADS.** 35pp. Nil73, 2.00p.
Poetic renditions of the Isa, Manduka, and Shvetashvatara Upanishads. Easwaran writes beautifully.

HUME, ROBERT, tr. **THE THIRTEEN PRINCIPAL UPANISHADS.** Bibliography, indices, 588pp. Oxf31, 5.95p.
This was considered the definitive collection for many years. It seems a bit stiff and dated to us. This edition is fully annotated and includes an appendix of recurrent and parallel passages in the principal **Upanishads** and the **Gita** as well as a discussion of translation techniques.

ISHERWOOD, CHRISTOPHER. **SELECTIONS FROM THE UPANISHADS (A RECORDING).** 9.98.
Isherwood reads lengthy selections from nine **Upanishads** translated by Swami Prabhavananda and Frederick Manchester. The text of the selection along with summaries of each of the **Upanishads** is included with the liner notes. Two 33 1/3 rpm records.

LEGGETT, TREVOR, tr. **THE CHAPTER OF THE SELF.** 190pp. RKP78, 7.95c.
In one of the oldest Indian law books (before 300 BC) there is a chapter on the realization of the universal self through yogic practice. It contains verses from an early **Upanishad** which is now lost. Sankara wrote a commentary on this *chapter of the self*, setting out the respective roles of the **Upanishad** texts and yoga practice. This translation also contains details on yoga practice from Sankara's commentary on Patanjali's **Yoga Sutras**. Leggett studied under Dr. Hari Prasad Shastri for twenty years. He supplements his translations with stories, commentary, and practice suggestions.

MASCARO, JUAN, tr. **THE UPANISHADS.** 143pp. Vik65, 1.95p.
Includes the full texts of six **Upanishads** and parts of six others. Mascaro also gives us an excellent introductory essay. A good basic translation for the general reader.

MULLER, F. MAX, tr. **THE UPANISHADS, VOLUME I.** 420pp. Dov1878, 4.50p.
This is one of the most scholarly translations available—and to our taste also one of the least enlightening. This was a landmark volume when it was first written in the nineteenth century, a part of Muller's **Sacred Books of the East** series. This volume contains a 100 page introduction and the **Chandogya, Kena, Aitareya, Kausitaki,** and **Vejasaneyi Upanishads.**

MULLER, F. MAX, tr. **THE UPANISHADS, VOLUME II.** 401pp. Dov1884, 4.50p.
Sixty page introduction plus the following **Upanishads**: Katha, Mundaka, Taittreya, Brihadaranyaka, Svetasvatara, Prasna, and Maitrayani.

■ NIKHILANANDA, SWAMI, tr. **THE UPANISHADS.** 388pp. H&R63, 5.70p.
An abridgment of Nikhilananda's fine translations. Certain portions of the texts have been omitted and the notes and explanations have been condensed. An excellent comprehensive glossary and a long introduction discussing the nature of Brahman, the soul and rebirth, Hindu ethics, and other aspects of Vedanta philosophy have been added.

NIKHILANANDA, SWAMI, tr. **THE UPANISHADS, VOLUME I.** 319pp. RVC49, 6.50c.
This translation in four volumes is both literal and graceful, preserving the dignity and flavor of the original. The extensive accompanying notes, based on the commentaries of Sankara, explain abstruse texts. Each **Upanishad** has its own introduction and a glossary is appended to each volume. Volume I contains an outline of Upanishadic thought, the metaphysics, and the psychology of Hinduism. Includes **Katha, Isa, Kena,** and **Mundaka.**

NIKHILANANDA, SWAMI, tr. **THE UPANISHADS, VOLUME II.** 390pp. RVC52, 6.50c.
Contains a long study of Hindu ethics as well as the following **Upanishads**: Svetasvatara, Prasna, and Mandukya. The introduction discusses Hindu ethics.

NIKHILANANDA, SWAMI, tr. **THE UPANISHADS, VOLUME III.** 392pp. RVC57, 6.50c.
The **Aitareya,** and the **Brihadaranyaka,** the most extensive and, by general consideration, the most important **Upanishad.**

NIKHILANANDA, SWAMI, tr. **THE UPANISHADS, VOLUME IV.** 406pp. RVC59, 6.50c.
The **Taittreya** and the **Chhandogya Upanishads.** The **Taittreya** is regarded as the sourcebook of Vedanta philosophy, and the **Chhandogya** is one of the oldest and most authoritative. Both discuss meditation and ways to realize the true self.

PANDIT, M.P., tr. **THE UPANISHADS: GATEWAYS OF KNOWLEDGE.** 260pp. Gan68, 4.00c.
General introduction to the **Upanishads** by a disciple of Sri Aurobindo as well as a translation and detailed study of the **Isa, Kena,** and **Taittreya.**

PARAMANANDA, SWAMI, tr. **THE UPANISHADS.** 154pp. VdC19, 3.00c.
A fine concise translation of the **Isa, Katha, Kena,** and **Mundaka Upanishads,** with commentary. Swami Paramananda was a disciple of Swami Vivekananda.

PARRINDER, GEOFFREY. **THE WISDOM OF THE FOREST.** 94pp. NDP75/SIP, 1.95p.
In this new version I have tried to make things as plain as possible, in straightforward English and using the narrative fully. Some passages have been shortened and some of the repetition reduced. But in the main this book presents the most important teachings and nearly all the narrative faithfully. A fine introduction for the general reader.

■ PRABHAVANANDA, SWAMI and FREDERICK MANCHESTER, trs. **THE UPANISHADS: BREATH OF THE ETERNAL.** Short introduction, 210pp. VdP47, 3.50c/1.50p.
Major portions of the twelve principal **Upanishads**. An eloquent translation which captures the sense, beauty, and spirit of the original.

PREM, SRI KRISHNA. THE YOGA OF THE KATHOPANISHAD.
264pp. Wat55, 7.40c.
The Kathopanishad is an exposition of the ancient road that leads from death to immortality. Being a real road, the knowledge of it is not confined to any one religious tradition. The aim of this commentary is to bring out the fact that it is a road known to a few over the world and that, though their descriptions have varied in detail, they all refer to what is recognizably the same experience.—from the introduction.

RADHAKRISHNAN, S., tr. THE PRINCIPAL UPANISHADS. Bibliography, 952pp. A&U53, 29.40c.
The most scholarly and at the same time readable text available. Eighteen of the principal **Upanishads** are given here in Roman script, along with a very valuable introduction, English translation, and illuminating notes. The introduction discusses every aspect of Upanishadic thought.

RAMACHARAKA, YOGI. THE SPIRIT OF THE UPANISHADS.
85pp. YPS07, 4.00c.
A collection of texts, aphorisms, and sayings from the **Upanishads**, compiled from over fifty translations.

SHASTRI, HARI PRASAD, tr. ASHTAVAKRA GITA. Notes, 67pp.
ShS49, 2.00c.
The word "Gita" means song. . . . The Ashtavakra Gita . . . expresses the highest Teachings of the Upanishads, and embodies the philosophical thought of the Sages Yajnavalkya and Varmadeva. It does not give an exposition of the truth by logical reasoning, but a description of the bliss experienced by an illuminated Saint. . . . Each verse is a text for meditation; the whole work has a magic of its own, which elevates and exalts the mind and grants glimpses of the transcendental region.—from the introduction.

SHASTRI, HARI PRASAD. WISDOM FROM THE EAST. 238pp. ShS nd, 3.75p.
A series of lectures which contain the essence of Upanishadic teaching.

SIRCAR, MAHENDRANATH. HINDU MYSTICISM ACCORDING TO THE UPANISHADS. Index, 344pp. MuM74, 15.60c.
A thoughtful collection of twenty-six essays on the title theme covering almost every aspect of Upanishadic and mystical thought. The author was a philosophy professor in Calcutta. The essays read well and virtually no Sanskrit terms are included, so even students who have little knowledge of Hindu philosophy can easily immerse themselves in the text.

YEATS, WILLIAM BUTLER and SWAMI SHRI PUROHIT. THE TEN PRINCIPAL UPANISHADS. 159pp. McM37/Fab, 2.95p.
A free translation of ten **Upanishads** by an English and an Indian poet.

──────── **END OF UPANISHADS SUBSECTION**────────

VARENNE, JEAN. YOGA AND THE HINDU TRADITION. Illustrations, notes, bibliography, index, 263pp. UCh76, 4.95p.
This is an excellent work by a distinguished French scholar. Professor Varenne presents the theory of classical yoga through quotations from the sacred Hindu texts, with extensive commentary. He begins with a brief discussion of the history and structures of Indian religious thought. The cosmology is discussed and the structure of Indian society is analyzed. The next section is a topically arranged commentary on a variety of yogic exercises. There is also a fine discussion of kundalini yoga and tantra. A final section contains a translation of the **Yoga Darshana Upanishad**.

VATSYANA. THE KAMA SUTRA. 252pp. Dut64/PnB, 5.50c/1.95p.
Richard Burton's translation of the Hindu classic on physical love. A long introduction is included.

Vedanta

Vedantic philosophy is probably the most influential of the Indian philosophical systems. Its springs from the **Upanishads** and its central thesis is the Upanishadic doctrine of *brahman*. The founder of the system was Badarayana whose **Brahma Sutra** (also called the **Vedanta Sutra**) makes up, along with the **Upanishads** and the **Bhagavad Gita**, the foundation of the Vedanta system. In the 555 sutras an attempt is made to systematize the teachings of the **Upanishads**. These sutras, which consist of two or three words each, can not be understood without a commentary. The different commentators develop different interpretations in the light of their own preconceived opinions. The three outstanding commentaries on the **Vedanta Sutras** are those of Sankara (ninth century), Ramanuja (eleventh century), and Madhva (thirteenth century), and their forms of Vedanta are known respectively as *advaita* (nondualism), *vishishtadvaita* (nondualism qualified by difference), and *dvaita* (dualism). Sankara's interpretation, because his commentary is one of the earliest and perhaps the most thorough, is usually assumed to be the Vedanta. All Vedantists agree that the world is the manifestation of *brahman*, that knowledge of *brahman* is the *marga* (path) which leads to liberation, and that *brahman* can be known only through the *sruti* teachings of the **Upanishads**. They differed regarding the nature of *brahman*, how *brahman* causes the world to be, the nature of the world, the relation of the individual self to *brahman*, and the condition of the self in the liberated state.

BHATTACHARYYA, K.C. SEARCH FOR THE ABSOLUTE IN NEO-VEDANTA. Bibliography, index, 203pp. UHa76, 14.80c.
The search for the absolute is the central concern of Vedanta philosophy. The three essays reprinted here are the major works of the three phases in the development of Bhattacharyya's philosophical thought, in which he defines the absolute as *Indefinite*, as *Subject*, and as *Alternation*, respectively. The volume is edited by George Burch, who also contributes a lengthy introduction.

CHARI, S.M. ADVAITA AND VISISHADVAITA. Glossary, notes, bibliography, index, 220pp. MoB61, 9.00c.
An exposition of Vedanta Desika's **Satadusani**, a polemic classic of *visishadvaita vedanta* devoted to criticism of the doctrines of *advaita vedanta*. The arguments found in the sixty-six vedas of the original text are brought together, analyzed, and discussed in a systematic manner under a number of broad headings.

CHATTERJI, MOHINI, tr. VIVEKA-CHUDAMANI OR CREST-JEWEL OF WISOM OF OF SRI SAMKARACARYA. 228pp. TPH32, 3.50c.
Chatterji was a nineteenth century Theosophical writer. This volume includes the Sanskrit text and English translation, with no commentary.

CHINMAYANANDA, SWAMI, tr. ATMA BODH. 137pp. CPT nd, 3.50c.
A fine translation of Sankara's **Self Knowledge**. Chinmayananda writes beautifully and conveys the essence of the original. This work forms an excellent introduction to Vedantic thought. Includes the Sanskrit text, transliteration, and a translation of individual words, along with a stanza-by-stanza translation of the text and extensive commentary.

CHINMAYANANDA, SWAMI, tr. HYMN TO SRI DAKSHINA-MOORTHY. 132pp. CMT68, 2.00c.
Of all the hymns of Sri Sankara, Sri Dakshinamoorthy Stotra is the shortest, but, at the same time, in its philosophical import, subtlety of expression, and confident assertion, it is one of the most inspired works of the Advaita philosopher. On a small canvas, Sankara has with unerring dexterity crammed all the arguments of the Nondualists

against the preachers of Dualism.—from the introduction. Includes translation, Sanskrit text, transliteration, and an in depth commentary on each stanza.

CHINMAYANANDA, SWAMI, tr. **TALKS ON VIVEKACHUDAMI, THE CREST JEWEL OF DISCRIMINATION.** 596pp. CPT nd, 8.00c/set.
An excellent two volume translation and commentary.

CHINMAYANANDA, SWAMI. **VEDANTA THROUGH LETTERS.** 231pp. CPT nd, 3.50c.
A collection of replies to letters from a variety of people.

COHEN, S.S. **ADVAITIC SADHANA.** Index, 92pp. MoB75, 9.00c.
Translations of three important texts: **Advaitic Sadhana**, the **Mandukya Upanishad**, and the **Atma Bodha** of Sankara. Notes and comments follow each stanza and the whole book is designed as a treatise on self knowledge and understanding.

DATE, V.H. **VEDANTA EXPLAINED.** 958pp. MuM54, 30.00c/set.
A scholarly and faithful translation of Sankara's commentary on the **Brahma Sutras.** Includes the original Sanskrit text along with transliteration, and translation of key phrases. The translation is sutra-by-sutra and is very complete. Dr. Date is a noted contemporary Indian scholar.

DEUSSEN, PAUL. **THE SYSTEM OF THE VEDANTA. Many notes, indices of names, terms, and quotations,** 513pp. Dov12, 4.00p.
Vedanta is notoriously difficult to expound, and the student is sometimes hard pressed to find an exposition that is both adequate and easily intelligible. It is the opinion of many scholars that Dr. Deussen, a noted German philosopher and Sanskritologist, has prepared one of the finest expositions of the Vedanta of Sankara by working with the **Vedanta Sutras** of Badarayana and Sankara's commentaries on them. The text is complete and authoritative, yet so clear in its organization and exposition that the reader can follow it without too much difficulty.

DEUTSCH, ELIOT. **ADVAITA VEDANTA—A PHILOSOPHICAL RECONSTRUCTION. Bibliography,** 114pp. UHa68, 1.95p.
Covers the basic metaphysical, epistemological, and ethical ideas of Vedanta in an organized manner.

DEUTSCH, ELIOT and J.A.B. VAN BUITENEN, trs. **A SOURCE BOOK OF ADVAITA VEDANTA. Bibliography, index,** 344pp. UHa71, 20.25c.
A collection of English translations of the major Sanskrit writings of the most important Vedantic philosophers, together with extensive background information.

DEVARAJA, N.K. **AN INTRODUCTION TO SANKARA'S THEORY OF KNOWLEDGE. Index,** 230pp. MoB72, 8.40c.
A comprehensive analysis of the title theme, with direct reference to Sankara's major philosophical works. An introduction discusses Sankara's place in Indian philosophy.

GAMBHIRANANDA, SWAMI, tr. **BRAHMA-SUTRA BHASYA OF SANKARACARYA. Sanskrit notes, index,** 920pp. AdA72, 9.50c.
A reliable, unabridged translation of the **Sutras** and of Sankara's commentary by a senior monk of the Ramakrishna Order. The Sanskrit text of each sutra is included.

GRIFFITHS, BEDE. **VEDANTA AND THE CHRISTIAN FAITH.** 99pp. DHP73, 1.95p.
Griffiths is an English Benedictine monk who founded a contemplative community in India in 1955. His book is a capsulization of the spiritual and mystical tradition of India combined with a parallel description of the mystical and spiritual tradition of the Christian West. Includes quotations from the **Gospels** and the **Upanishads** along with the author's personal experiences.

ISHERWOOD, CHRISTOPHER. **AN APPROACH TO VEDANTA.** 72pp. VdP63, 1.00p.
Isherwood describes his impressions of the Vedanta Society in California in the 1940s and discusses what attracted him to Vedanta and how he became a devotee. He also discusses the translations he made with Swami Prabhavananda.

ISHERWOOD, CHRISTOPHER, ed. **VEDANTA FOR MODERN MAN. Index,** 441pp. NAL45, 1.50p.
A collection of essays and aricles which relate Vedantic to modern thought. Separate phases of the philosophy and techniques are discussed in sixty-one selections.

ISHERWOOD, CHRISTOPHER, ed. **VEDANTA FOR THE WESTERN WORLD.** 453pp. VdP45/A&U, 5.95c.
Essays by individuals such as Aldous Huxley, Rabindranath Tagore, Swami Prabhavananda, and many others.

MAHADEVAN, T.M.P. **THE PHILOSOPHY OF ADVAITA. Glossary, notes, index,** 313pp. Com77, 11.70c.
The Vedantist philosophy of *advaita* suggests that the nature of the self (*atman*) is at one with the ultimate reality (*brahman*). This is a systematic presentation of *advaita* philosophy, along the lines originally expounded by Bharatitirtha Vidyaranya, one of the most celebrated teachers to follow Sankara. The information is topically arranged and Mahadevan includes chapters on ways of knowing, truth and error, the nature of reality, experience, and illusion.

MAHADEVAN, T.M.P., tr. **SELF-KNOWLEDGE. Introduction, index,** 112pp. Com77, 7.80c.
A beautifully produced translation of Sankara's **Atma Bodha,** one of Sankara's key works. Sankara says that real nature is hidden by five *sheaths of illusion*, and the key to dissolving these sheaths is discrimination of the real from the unreal and the removal of ignorance by knowledge.

MADHAVANANDA, SWAMI, tr. **VIVEKACHUDAMANI OF SHRI SHANKARACHARYA. Sanskrit and English indices,** 232pp. AdA21, 2.15p.
The Sanskrit text of the **Crest Jewel** along with a stanza-by-stanza translation and notes on certain terms.

MUDGAL, S.G. **ADVAITA OF SANKARA: A REAPPRAISAL. Notes, bibliography, index,** 205pp. MoB75, 12.00c.
An attempt to bring out the impact of Buddhism and Samkhya on Sankara's philosophical thought and account for the inherent contradictions in his two-tiered philosophy (transcendentalism vs. theism). A deeply philosophical work, suitable only for those with an excellent background in Indian thought.

MURTY, SATCHIDANANDA. **REVELATION AND REASON IN ADVAITA VEDANTA. Index, notes,** 384pp. MoB59, 12.00c.
The author deals in great detail with texts from the earliest **Upanishads** *of seventh or sixth century B.C., to the last great dialectic texts of sixteenth and seventeenth centuries A.D. This is of great interest since many of these texts have not been translated.... The treatment is fair and adequate.... [The text] also discusses the treatment of revelation and reason in the other five most important Indian philosophical systems and their criticism of Advaita Vedanta...[and] contains the author's own criticism and rejection of the Advaita Vedanta and his arguments in favor of theism.*—**The Journal of the Asia Society.**

■ *NIKHILANANDA, SWAMI, tr.* **SELF-KNOWLEDGE.** 243pp. RVC67, 5.00c.
A translation of Sankara's **Atma Bodha** which sets forth the knowledge of the *atman* or the self, to which all other forms of knowledge are secondary. The long introduction gives a detailed account of Vedanta, both in its theoretical and practical aspects, covering different phases of man's progressive thought, beginning with dualism, passing through the qualified nondualism, and ending in absolute nondualism, in which one experiences the total identity of the soul, the universe, and the Godhead.

NIKHILANANDA, SWAMI, tr. **VEDANTASARA. Sanskrit and English, glossary,** 136pp. AdA49, 1.50p.
A translation of Sadananda's treatise on Vedanta, one of the best and most widely read introductory books on the subject.

NITYASWARUPANANDA, SWAMI, tr. **ASTAVAKRA SAMHITA.** **Index, 224pp. AdA69, 1.95p.**
This text, also known as the **Astavakara Gita**, is a short treatise on *advaita vedanta*. It consists of a dialogue between a great sage, Astavakara, and his disciple, Janaka. This edition includes the Sanskrit text with word for word translation, English rendering, commentary, and an introduction.

PARAMANANDA, SWAMI. **VEDANTA IN PRACTICE. 110pp. VdC08, 1.50p.**
The aim of these lectures is to show us how to avail ourselves of the great principles of Vedanta, so that they will become part of our daily lives; to teach us how we can put them into practice and live by them every moment of our existence.—from the preface. Swami Paramananda was a direct disciple of Swami Vivekananda.

PRABHAVANANDA, SWAMI. **THE SERMON ON THE MOUNT ACCORDING TO VEDANTA. 110pp. VdP63/NEL, 2.95c/1.50p.**
In the form of a part-by-part commentary, the entire Sermon and Christ's teachings are compared with those of Vedanta.

■ *PRABHAVANANDA, SWAMI and CHRISTOPHER ISHERWOOD; trs.* **THE CREST-JEWEL OF DISCRIMINATION WITH A GARLAND OF QUESTIONS AND ANSWERS. 162pp. NAL71/NEL, 2.95c/1.50p.**
A translation of Sankara's best known work, describing the transcendental knowledge of *brahman* and the way to achieve it through concentration. The book serves as an excellent introduction to Sankara's philosophy of nondualism in the form of a dialogue between a teacher and his disciple.

RADHAKRISHNAN, S., tr. **THE BRAHMA SUTRA: THE PHILOSOPHY OF SPIRITUAL LIFE. Index, 606pp. A&U60, 12.25c.**
This sutra is known as the **Brahma** since it deals with the doctrine of *brahman*; as the **Vedanta** since it sets forth a systematic account of Vedanta—the final aim of the **Veda**; and the **Sariraka**, due to its discussion of the embodiment of the unconditioned self. In the 555 sutras an attempt is made to systematize the teachings of the **Upanishads**. In this volume Dr. Radhakrishnan surveys twelve different commentators, though he bases his discussion primarily on Sankara's commentary. Half this volume is devoted to an in depth discussion of the sutra and its varied topics; the rest contains the text, translation, and notes.

RAJNEESH, BHAGWAN SHREE. **VEDANTA: SEVEN STEPS TO SAMADHI. 12.00c.**
See the Contemporary Spiritual Teachers section.

RAMACHANDRAN, T.P. **DVAITA VEDANTA. 132pp. Com77, 7.80c.**
The *dvaita* school challenged the *advaita* primarily on the grounds that the latter championed intellect only, discounting the role of human emotion and will and the need for religion and ethics. This is a comprehensive exposition of the *dvaita* view of the nature of knowledge, metaphysics, and religious practice.

SHARMA, B.N.K. **THE BRAHMASUTRAS AND THEIR PRINCIPAL COMMENTARIES. Two volumes, notes, index, 938pp. BVB71, 33.15c.**
This is the first work on the **Sutras** to give parity of treatment to the three principal traditions of interpretation by placing them in close thematic relation to each other and allowing them to speak for themselves. Many minor commentators are also reviewed. An important work for all who seek a deep understanding of Vedantic philosophy.

SHASTRI, HARI PRASAD, tr. **DIRECT EXPERIENCE OF REALITY. Glossary, 88pp. ShS75, 3.00p.**
A translation, with commentary, of verses from the **Aparokshanubhuti** of Sankara, outlining the essence of the latter's exposition of *advaita vedanta*.

TATTWANDA, SWAMI, tr. **THE QUINTESSENCE OF VEDANTA. 191pp. AdA70, 2.75c.**
A translation of Sankara's **Sarva-Vedanta-Siddhanta-Sarasangraha** which, *as its name implies, is a compendium and a precise restatement of all that has*

been thought of and set down about the Self from a purely philosophical viewpoint.—from the preface. The text is presented in both Sanskrit and English.

THIBAUT, GEORGE, tr. **THE VEDANTA SUTRAS OF BADARAYANA. WITH SANKARA'S COMMENTARY. Two volumes, copious footnotes, 945pp. Dov1890, 10.00p/set.**
The definitive English translation, originally part of the **Sacred Books of the East** series. Also includes a translation of Sankara's exhaustive commentary as well as a comprehensive 128 page introduction and summary by the translator.

THIBAUT, GEORGE, tr. **THE VEDANTA SUTRAS WITH THE COMMENTARY OF RAMANUJA. Many notes, index, 811pp. MoB04, 12.00c.**
This is the only unabridged translation of Ramanuja's commentary that we know of. *The present translation...claims to be faithful on the whole, although I must acknowledge that I have aimed rather at making it intelligible and, in a certain sense, readable than scrupulously accurate.*—from the introduction.

VIDYARANYA, SWAMI, tr. **PANCHADASI: A VEDANTA CLASSIC. 486pp. ShS54, 6.95c.**
A classic text which serves as a logical and dialectical exposition of the metaphysics of Vedanta and also details practical meditation techniques. Translated into English by H.P. Shastri.

VIVEKANANDA, SWAMI. **ADVAITA VEDANTA: THE SCIENTIFIC RELIGION. 68pp. AdA52, .65p.**
Transcription of an important lecture Vivekananda gave on *advaita vedanta*.

WOOD, ERNEST. **THE GLORIOUS PRESENCE. 320pp. TPH51, 2.75p.**
A topically organized distillation of Vedantic philosophy which is built around Sankara's commentaries on the **Vedanta Sutras**, the **Gita**, the **Upanishads**, and some of his shorter works. Wood also includes a translation and explanation of Sankara's **Ode to the South-Facing Form**, a series of meditations.

WOOD, ERNEST, tr. **THE PINNACLE OF INDIAN THOUGHT. 161pp. TPH67, 1.45p.**
Translation of Sankara's **Crest Jewel**, with extensive commentary, by a noted Western scholar who spent many years studying in India. Includes a long introduction.

———— END OF VEDANTA SUBSECTION ————

Brahma as the Creator, facing four directions.

Vedas

The word *Veda* means wisdom. Wisdom in this case means absolute, intuitive, and esoteric wisdom as distinguished from discursive knowledge, either rational or empirical. The word *Veda* is used both to designate the entire early literature of the Hindus and the earliest collection of hymns, sacrifices, and prayers. We shall use the term only in the latter sense. The **Vedas** consist of four collections (*samhitas*) known as the **Rig**, the **Sama**, the **Yajur**, and the **Atharva**. The first is the oldest, largest, and most important; indeed it is so important that it is sometimes known simply as **The Veda**. The **Vedas** are not the folklore of a primitive, animistic, and nature worshiping people, as has sometimes been thought. They are the work of sophisticated priests seeking riches, success, long life, power, safety, posterity, food, and women for their patrons. The formula is quite simple: praise the god, and then petition the god for benefits. The **Vedas** are hopelessly confusing if they are approached as encyclopedias of information about the earliest form of Hinduism, but if they are examined as records of the religious experiences, practices, experiments, and thoughts of these early Hindus, they can prove to be immensely valuable. The **Vedas** are also interesting for the light they shed on the gods who came to the fore in later Hinduism.

AUROBINDO, SRI, tr. **HYMNS TO THE MYSTIC FIRE.** 607pp. SAA nd, 10.00c.
Hymns to Agni from the **Rig Veda**, in Sanskrit with an esoteric English translation, and an introduction on the problem of translating the **Vedas** and the doctrine of the mystics.

AUROBINDO, SRI. **KEY TO VEDIC SYMBOLISM.** 123pp. SAA67, 4.00c.
A useful, topically organized study covering most of the major concepts, ideas, and individual figures.

AUROBINDO, SRI. **THE SECRET OF THE VEDA.** 581pp. SAA71, 7.50c.
A discussion of the significance and symbolism of the Vedas and the origins of Aryan speech. Translations of selected hymns from the **Rig Veda**, with commentary, are also included.

BISSOONDOYAL, BASDEO. **THE ESSENCE OF THE VEDAS AND ALLIED SCRIPTURES.** 154pp. JPH66, 1.80p.
Includes long extracts, arranged topically, and a good introduction.

BLOOMFIELD, MAURICE, tr. **HYMNS OF THE ATHARVA-VEDA. Introduction, notes,** 780pp. MoB1897, 7.50c.
The **Atharva Veda** is the last of the **Vedas**. It is mainly a book of spells and incantations designed to assist people who were possessed with a fear of evil spirits. Many of its stanzas (or *suktas*) are to be used with magical plants, potions, lotions, and drugs. The chief significance of this **Veda** in India today is that it is the basis of Ayurvedic medicine. The classic book of medicine and health is called the **Ayurveda**, and it is a supplement to the **Atharva**. This translation is a part of the **Sacred Books of the East** series.

BLOOMFIELD, MAURICE. **THE RELIGION OF THE VEDA. Notes, index,** 315pp. AMS08, 12.75c.
Transcription of a series of six lectures, with some amplification. Bloomfield covers the development of the Vedic religion from its origins in prehistoric nature myths to its appearance in the **Upanishads.**

BOSE, ABINASH, tr. **HYMNS FROM THE VEDAS. Notes, index,** 387pp. APH66, 16.15c.
We feel that this is the best single-volume translation of selected hymns from all the four Vedas. The original Sanskrit text is also given on facing pages. Dr. Bose's emphasis is on the poetic and spiritual values, on the inner life of the early Aryans, and their contact with the realities of material existence. He shows no preoccupation with the external forms and rituals of Vedic worship. The selections are topically arranged and Dr. Bose also provides an excellent long introduction.

CHATTERJI, J.C. **THE WISDOM OF THE VEDAS.** 99pp. TPH73, 3.95c.
A simplified, systematic presentation of the Vedic system of thought.

DUMEZIL, GEORGES. **THE DESTINY OF A KING. Index,** 155pp. UCh73, 13.40c.
An extensive and scholarly commentary on the biography of Yayati—a central figure in the **Zend Avesta** and the **Rig** and **Atharva Vedas**. Both the Zoroastrian and the Vedic mythological elements are examined at length. Detailed notes accompany the text.

FOUR VEDAS (A RECORDING). 25.00.
Subtitled, *The Oral Tradition of Hymns, Chants, Sacrificial and Magical Formulas,* this two record set includes examples from various Vedic traditions still practiced in India. Featured on the first record are typical examples from some of the more isolated traditions, and rare pieces from the main traditions. The second is devoted to the main portions of the Nambudiris of Kerala, a small, almost inaccessible tradition from southwest India. Only three of the selections were recorded in a studio, and many were done on a small tape recorder, so the quality often leaves much to be desired. Very detailed and extensive descriptive notes.

GONDA, J. **THE VEDIC GOD MITRA. Indices,** 147pp. Bri72, 25.40c.
An exhaustive study of all that can be surmised about Mitra's character, functions, and relationships with other gods and with various aspects of the natural world. Many quotations from Vedic texts are included.

GONDA, J. **THE VISION OF THE VEDIC POETS. Extensive notes, indices,** 372pp. Mou63, 36.75p.
A scholarly, technical study which discusses the major Vedic concepts and quotes from the **Hymns** themselves—both in English translation and transliteration. For serious students only.

GRIFFITH, RALPH, tr. **THE HYMNS OF THE ATHARVAVEDA. Two volumes, notes, index,** 1,035pp. CSS1894, 15.00c/set.
A comprehensive selection with copious notes. The style is stilted, but there is no other edition that even comes close to this one in terms of completeness and excellence in scholarship.

GRIFFITH, RALPH, tr. **HYMNS OF THE RIGVEDA. Notes, index,** 728pp. MoB1889, 22.80c.
A new, revised edition of this classic work—one of the few authentic translations available in English.

GRISWOLD, H.D. **THE RELIGION OF THE RIGVEDAS. Notes, index,** 415pp. MoB71, 9.00c.
A scholarly survey written in the first decade of the twentieth century. The first section details the origin and development of the Indo-European and Indo-Iranian religion, emphasizing the early concepts of the Godhead, demonology, and the priesthood. The culture of the Vedic tribes is also examined. The second section discusses the traits of the major and minor Vedic gods and the eschatology of the **Rig Veda**. The final section examines the impact of Vedic religion on later Hindu religious thought.

HALL, MANLY P. **THE ADEPTS IN THE EASTERN ESOTERIC TRADITION, PART I: THE LIGHT OF THE VEDAS.** 111pp. PRS52, 3.50p.
A summary study by one of the twentieth century's most prolific writers on these matters.

JOLLY, JULIUS, tr. **THE INSTITUTES OF VISHNU. Index,** 348pp. MoB1880, 10.10c.
A translation of the **Vishnu Smriti**, which many scholars feel is really the ancient **Dharma Sutra** of the Karayaniyakathaka Sakha of the **Black Yajur Veda**. Part of the **Sacred Books of the East** series.

KEITH, ARTHUR. **THE RELIGION AND PHILOSOPHY OF THE VEDA AND UPANISHADS. Two volumes, notes, index,** 708pp. MoB nd, 24.00c/set.
The most comprehensive, scholarly treatment available. Topics include the following: *The Sources; The Gods and Demons of the Veda; Vedic Ritual; The Spirits of the Dead;* and *The Philosophy of the Veda.* Many appendices. Part of the **Harvard Oriental Series**.

KEITH, ARTHUR, tr. **RIG VEDA BRAHMANAS. Indices, 567pp. MoB20, 12.00c.**
Translations of the *Aitareya* and *Kausitaki Brahmanas* of the **Rig Veda,** both of which are extremely important for an accurate understanding of the ancient traditions of the Vedic period. Dr. Keith also includes extensive notes and a 103 page introduction. Originally published in the **Harvard Oriental Series.**

KEITH, ARTHUR, tr. **THE VEDAS OF THE BLACK YAJU SCHOOL. Two volumes, notes, index, 832pp. MoB14, 4.50c/set.**
The **Yajur Veda** is a priestly handbook containing both mantras and prose directions for the performance of sacrifices. Here Keith provides a translation of a portion of it, the *Taittiriya Samhita* along with a running commentary and an elaborate introduction.

KNIPE, DAVID. **IN THE IMAGE OF FIRE. Many notes, long bibliography, index, 187pp. MoB75, 10.00c.**
This is a penetrating study of Vedic man's religious experience of fire and heat. It is a portrayal of the complex system of religious expressions that developed in ancient India from man's intimate relationship with the element fire. Utilizing the full corpus of Vedic literature, the author ranges from the mysteries of the great Vedic sacrifices through the Brahmanical doctrine of correspondences to Upanishadic identities and yogic techniques, demonstrating the ritualized control of cosmic heat (*tapas*) which eventually became the hallmark of asceticism. Related expressions of fire and heat are drawn from ancient Iran, Scandinavia, and European Christianity. This work was the author's PhD thesis from the University of Wisconsin and it reads like one.

KUNHAN RAJA, C., tr. **ASYA VAMASYA HYMN (THE RIDDLE OF THE UNIVERSE). Many notes, 223pp. Gan56, 5.00c.**
A translation of one of the finest hymns in the **Rig Veda.** The original Sanskrit text is included.

Bull found on a seal from Mohenjo-Daro.

KUNHAN RAJA, C. **POET-PHILOSOPHERS OF THE RIG VEDA. Notes, 360pp. Gan63, 7.95c.**
A study of the lives and teachings of the most important Vedic poets along with a survey of the story of creation and evolution as described in the hymns. Thirteen important hymns are translated in an appendix, and the transliteration is given along with translations of individual words.

KUNHAN RAJA, C. **THE QUINTESSENCE OF THE RIG VEDA. 160pp. Tar64, 2.25c.**
A prose summary of the narrative of the **Vedas** written in a novelistic style and including a good general introduction.

LE MEE, JEAN, tr. **HYMNS FROM THE RIG VEDA. 11"x8½", 236pp. RaH75/CaL, 12.50c/5.95p.**
This lovely book presents translations of twelve hymns, designed to make generally available for the first time one of the major scriptures of mankind, and to suggest something of its profundity and magnificence. The book was put together by the same people who did the Gia Fu Feng edition of **Lao Tzu** and **Chuang Tzu.** It is illustrated with evocative full page photographs facing each stanza. The Sanskrit text is also given, and there is an introduction to each hymn and a general

introduction which tells of the Vedic tradition and sets the stage for the hymns which are presented. The unusual photographs make this a wonderful gift for all—even those not on the spiritual path.

MACDONELL, ARTHUR. **THE BRIHAD-DEVATA. Two volumes, many notes, 582pp. MoB04, 4.50c/set.**
A summary of the deities and myths of the **Rig Veda.** Includes Sanskrit text and English translation.

MACDONELL, ARTHUR. **VEDIC MYTHOLOGY. Many notes, index, 189pp. MoB1898, 10.50c.**
A detailed study which is almost impossible to follow due to the poor organization and poor typography of the text. An amazing amount of material is condensed into these pages if you can plow through them. We wish you luck!

MACDONELL, ARTHUR. **A VEDIC READER FOR STUDENTS. Index, 294pp. Oxf17, 2.15c.**
Thirty hymns, comprising just under 300 stanzas, taken from the **Rig Veda,** with Sanskrit text, transliteration, translation, explanatory notes, introduction, and vocabulary. An adequate knowledge of classical Sanskrit is necessary before attempting this volume.

MULLER, F. MAX. **THE VEDAS. 163pp. IBH nd, 6.40c.**
A survey written by the man who first brought the **Vedas** to the attention of the West. It remains one of the most comprehensive general presentations available—though it is far from stimulating. The text is organized under the following general headings: *The* **Veda** *and the* **Zend-Avesta,** *What is the* **Veda?** *Hymns of the* **Vedas** (including some translations), *The Religion of the* **Veda,** *Vedic Deities,* and *The* **Veda** *and Vedanta.*

MULLER, F. MAX, tr. **VEDIC HYMNS. Two volumes, 1,180pp. MoB1891, 24.00c/set.**
An important early translation of the hymns, accompanied by a veritable profusion of notes. Part of the **Sacred Books of the East** series.

NICOLAS, ANTONIO DE. **MEDITATIONS THROUGH THE RIG VEDA: FOUR-DIMENSIONAL MAN. Many notes, index, 301pp. ShP76, 5.95p.**
Original translations combined with an in depth analysis of Vedic hymns. Dr. de Nicholas shows how the insights of modern physics apply to the world view expressed in the **Vedas.** He also probes into the language of the **Rig Veda,** which he describes as the language of existence and nonexistence, the language of images and sacrifices, and the language of embodied vision.

PANIKKAR, RAIMUNDO, tr. **MANTRAMANJARI, THE VEDIC EXPERIENCE. Illustrations, indices, 800pp. UCa76, 25.00c.**
An annotated selection of texts from the **Rig Veda,** from the *Brahamanas* (prayers and rituals of sacrifice), from the *Aranyakas (Forest Treatises* which set forth the spiritual ideals and speculations of those who have renounced the world), and the **Upanishads.** Each of the sections is fully introduced and there is also a general introduction as well as a glossary.

PHILLIPS, MAURICE. **THE TEACHING OF THE VEDAS. Notes, index, 239pp. Sem1894, 17.00c.**
An academic study which, although not clearly written, does contain material not readily available elsewhere.

SAMPURNANAND, SRI, tr. **THE ATHARVA VEDA: VRATYAKANDA. 67pp. Gan56, 1.50p.**
Sanskrit text and translation, with extensive commentary. An introduction discusses the **Vedas.**

VIDYALANKAR, SATYAKAM, tr. **WISDOM OF THE VEDAS. 130pp. HPB74, 2.00p.**
A simple modern translation of 108 hymns from the four **Vedas.** The Sanskrit text is also included.

WHITNEY, WILLIAM, tr. **ATHARVA-VEDA-SAMHITA. Two volumes, 1,208pp. MoB nd, 24.00c/set.**
Original text, translation, and notes.

————— **END OF VEDAS SUBSECTION** —————

VEQUAUD, YVES. **THE WOMEN PAINTERS OF MITHILA. 8"x11",** **112pp. T&H77, 8.95p.**
Mithila is a province of Bihar in northeast India. It is only the women of Mithila who paint. They use vivid colors applied with simple brushes made of bamboo and raw cotton and produce vigorous and distinctive art. The subjects of Mithila paintings are traditional: tantric scenes, Krishna and his flute, Siva with his wives, the lingam and the yoni, scenes from the **Ramayana.** An excellent introduction by Vequaud discusses Mithila painting at length. Eighty-eight illustrations, sixty in two and four colors, are included.

VITSAXIS, VASSILIS. **HINDU EPICS, MYTHS AND LEGENDS IN** **POPULAR ILLUSTRATIONS. 7¼"x10", 110pp. Oxf77, 12.75c.**
A simple discussion of the main Hindu myths and legends, illustrated with a series of forty-four color plates which exactly reproduce popular posters sold throughout India.

Swami Vivekananda

Swami Vivekananda (1863-1902) was Ramakrishna's leading disciple and he is the great interpreter of the eternal Vedanta for modern man in the West as well as the East. As the dynamic representative of Hinduism at the World Parliament of Religions in Chicago in 1893 he proclaimed the truth of all religions, the divinity of the soul, and the oneness of all existence. He, more than any other individual, introduced Indian philosophy to the U.S. In the course of a short life, of which only ten years was devoted to public activities, Vivekananda composed his four classic volumes on yoga—all of which are outstanding treatises on Hindu philosophy. In addition, he delivered innumerable lectures, wrote ceaselessly, acted as spiritual guide to the many seekers who came to him for instruction, and organized and led the Ramakrishna Monastic Order.

ADVAITA ASHRAMA. **TEACHINGS OF SWAMI VIVEKANANDA.** **298pp. AdA71, 1.95p.**
An excellent compilation of many aspects of Vivekananda's teaching, in the form of direct quotations, topically arranged. An excellent introduction to the man and his philosophy.

NIKHILANANDA, SWAMI. **VIVEKANANDA, A BIOGRAPHY. 357pp.** **AdA75, 2.95c.**
This is a very readable biographical study, dealing mainly with the period during and following Vivekananda's first trip to the United States.

ROLLAND, ROMAIN. **THE LIFE OF VIVEKANANDA AND THE** **UNIVERSAL GOSPEL. 382pp. AdA53, 2.95c.**
A biographical study which presents a graphic account of Vivekananda's life and teachings.

VIVEKANANDA, SWAMI. **BHAKTI YOGA. 113pp. AdA nd, 1.00p.**
This is a comprehensive treatise on the yoga of love and devotion.

VIVEKANANDA, SWAMI. **THE COMPLETE WORKS OF SWAMI** **VIVEKANANDA. AdA.**
Volume I (543pp., 4.95p): Contains karma yoga, raja yoga, and twenty-one lesser lectures and discourses (among them are selections on the **Gita** and breathing); Volume II (535pp., 4.95c): Contains jnana yoga, reports from American newspapers, and practical Vedanta and other lectures; Volume III (558pp. 4.95p): Contains bhakti yoga, para bhakti (or supreme devotion), reports from American newspapers, and lectures from Colombo to Almora; Volume IV (534pp., 4.95p): Contains prose and poems, original works as well as translations, seventeen lectures on bhakti yoga, discourses, and six addresses; Volume V (554pp. 4.95c): Contains epistles, interviews, notes from lectures and discourses, questions and answers, conversations and dialogues (recorded by disciples), and prose and poems both original and translated; Volume VI (535pp. 4.95c): Contains ten lectures and discourses, notes of class talks and lectures, prose and poetic writings, and epistles; Volume VII (542pp., 4.95c): Contains inspired talks,

conversations, and dialogues, translation of writings, notes of class talks and lectures, and epistles; Volume VIII (558pp., 4.95c): Discourses on jnana and raja yoga, lectures on Buddha's message to the world, women of India, discipleship, and Vedanta, as well as original prose and poetry.

VIVEKANANDA, SWAMI. **INSPIRED TALKS. Glossary, 259pp.** **RVC58, 3.50c/2.00p.**
A lecture on Sri Ramakrishna, as well as conversations with friends and disciples.

VIVEKANANDA, SWAMI. **JNANA YOGA. Glossary, 317pp. RVC55,** **3.50c/2.00p.**
Contains the essence of the Vedanta philosophy, and describes the wisdom of the **Vedas,** the **Upanishads,** and the **Gita.**

VIVEKANANDA, SWAMI. **KARMA YOGA. 131pp. AdA nd, 1.00p.**

VIVEKANANDA, SWAMI. **KARMA YOGA AND BHAKTI YOGA.** **Glossary, 316pp. RVC nd, 3.50c.**
Describes the method of reaching perfection through daily work and of sublimating human affection into divine love. Also includes essays on the **Ramayana** and the **Mahabharata.**

VIVEKANANDA, SWAMI. **MEDITATION AND ITS METHODS.** **127pp. VdP76, 3.50p.**
A collection of extracts from the collected works of Swami Vivekananda discussing what religion is, why it is of vital concern to us, and how we must practice it to make it part of our lives. Edited by Swami Chetanananda.

VIVEKANANDA, SWAMI. **RAJA YOGA. 280pp. RVC55, 3.50c/1.95p.**
Refer to the discussion earlier in this section under Patanjali.

VIVEKANANDA, SWAMI. **THE YOGAS AND OTHER WORKS.** **978pp. RVC53, 14.95c.**
Swami Vivekananda provided rational interpretations of such eternal truths as the divine nature of the soul, the oneness of man, and the harmony of religions. The present volume includes the unabridged texts of **Jnana Yoga, Raja Yoga, Karma Yoga, Bhakti Yoga,** and **Inspired Talks,** the Chicago address, lectures, poems, letters, a glossary, and a biography of Swami Vivekananda by his disciple, Swami Nikhilananda.

——— END OF SWAMI VIVEKANANDA SUBSECTION ———

WEBER, MAX. **THE RELIGION OF INDIA. Notes, index, 400pp.** **McM58, 3.95p.**
A pioneering study of the formative influence of Hinduism and Buddhism on Indian society, written from a sociological point of view. Weber's central concern was the obstacles that traditional beliefs presented to industrialization and modernization. This in depth presentation has not been surpassed in the more than fifty years since its publication.

WELCH, STUART. **IMPERIAL MUGHAL PAINTING. 9.95p.**
See the Sacred Art section.

WERNER, KAREL. **YOGA AND INDIAN PHILOSOPHY. Notes,** **bibliography, index, 204pp. MoB77, 12.00c.**
Indian philosophy has preserved its special character, particularly its closeness to man's life and its concern for his destiny, mainly owing to its relation to Yoga.—from the introduction. This book is a dry survey of the mutual relationship between yoga and Indian philosophy. Many of the major schools are discussed at length.

WHEELER, MORTIMER. **EARLY INDIA AND PAKISTAN. Notes,** **index, 241pp. T&H68, 9.10c.**
A well researched archaeological survey. Hundreds of photographs and line drawings accompany the text and each is fully discussed. The material is chronologically organized.

WILKINS, W.J. **HINDU MYTHOLOGY. Illustrations, index, 518pp.** **Cur00, 10.65c.**
This is a very complete study. The deities are described, discussed, and classified in so far as possible according to the words of the Hindu scriptures and the period in which they appear most often. The

classification is designed to give the reader a good overview of Hindu mythology.

WILKINS, W.J. MODERN HINDUISM. Index, 423pp. Cur00, 10.65c.
As the reader can see by the copyright date, this is hardly a modern study. Nonetheless, it does have several interesting features and is useful as an historical picture of academic thought on Hinduism in the late nineteenth century. The book is designed as a companion to the author's work on Hindu mythology and the major topics are as follows: life and worship, morals, woman, caste, sects, death, and future life. The writing style itself is more in a popular rather than scholarly vein.

WILSON, HORACE. THE VISHNU PURANA—A SYSTEM OF HINDU MYTHOLOGY AND TRADITION. PPu nd, 58.00c.
A monumental work by one of the greatest Sanskrit scholars of the mid-nineteenth century. Recently republished.

WOOD, ERNEST. SEVEN SCHOOLS OF YOGA, AN INTRODUCTION. 115pp. TPH76, 2.25p.
The seven kinds of yoga which Wood discusses are the raja yoga of Patanjali, the karma and buddhi yogas of Sri Krishna, the jnana yoga of Sankara, hatha yoga, laya yoga, bhakti yoga, and mantra yoga. This is a philosophical exposition which clearly summarizes information not readily available elsewhere. The text is oriented toward Westerners unfamiliar with Hindu terminology.

WOOD, ERNEST. YOGA. 272pp. Vik59, 1.75p.
A complete analysis of yogic philosophy based largely upon the leading classical books and supplemented by the author's own experiences. Bibliography and glossary are included. A scholarly work, yet useful for anyone interested in the subject.

YAMUNACHARYA, M. RAMANUJA'S TEACHINGS IN HIS OWN WORDS. 180pp. BBU70, 1.25p.
An introduction to the teachings of Ramanuja, written in his own words and based mainly on his *magnum opus*, **Sri Bhasya** and the **Bhagavad Gita Bhasya.** A biographical sketch and an outline of his philosophy and theology are also included.

YESUDIAN, SELVARAJAN. SELF RELIANCE THROUGH YOGA. 243pp. A&U75, 5.25p.
An autobiographical account of the author's childhood and youth in India, the inner guidance which he received, and other memories. Within this loose framework, practical instruction, legends and ancient stories, and sequences of questions are gathered together. Many beautiful illustrations are included in this fascinating account.

YESUDIAN, SELVARAJAN and ELISABETH HAICH. RAJA YOGA. 160pp. A&U56, 5.00p.
This book was originally entitled **Yoga Uniting East and West.** It is a practical introduction to yoga as it actually is by two noted practitioners. The examples utilized come from the **Bible** rather than from the holy books of the Orient. It is very clearly written and illustrated and Sanskrit vocabulary is avoided. Topics include *What is Yoga? The Path of the Orient, The Path of the Occident, The Two Paths Meet.*

Paramahansa Yogananda

Yogananda was the first great Indian master to live in the West for a long period and he was instrumental in introducing Indian thought and practices to Americans. His **Autobiography** is one of the first things a person reads when he becomes interested in spiritual work. A selection of Yogananda records is also available. They are reviewed in the Chanting and Singing subsection of the Records section.

KRIYANANDA, SWAMI. O GOD BEAUTIFUL (A RECORDING). 5.95.
Swami Kriyananda and members of Ananda Cooperative Village sing chants composed by their guru, Paramahansa Yogananda. The chants are in English, have simple tunes, and are easy to follow. A 33 1/3 rpm record.

KRIYANANDA, SWAMI. THE PATH: AUTOBIOGRAPHY OF A WESTERN YOGI. Photographs, index, 658pp. AnP77, 3.95p.
The bulk of this autobiography is devoted to the period during which Swami Kriyananda lived as a disciple of Paramahansa Yogananda. Many hitherto unpublished stories about Yogananda are included and the reader is afforded a rare glimpse into what it is like to be the disciple of a great master. In the final section Kriyananda emerges as a teacher in his own right and the founder of a highly successful spiritual community. This is an informal, personal portrait of man's search for truth.

KRIYANANDA, SWAMI. THE ROAD AHEAD. 140pp. AnP74, 1.95p.
An edited collection of prophecies on future world events which Yogananda made at the end of his life.

KRIYANANDA, SWAMI. STORIES OF MUKUNDA. Illustrations, AnP76, 3.50p.
A collection of true episodes from the early life of Yogananda. Swami Kriyananda, a close personal disciple of Yogananda, compiled these stories from reminiscences of Yogananda himself and firsthand accounts gathered from his childhood friends.

MATA, SRI DAYA. IS MEDITATION ON GOD COMPATIBLE WITH DAILY LIFE? (A RECORDING). 7.95.
Sri Daya Mata speaks of the life and teachings of Yogananda. A two record set (33 1/3 rpm).

MATA, SRI DAYA. ONLY LOVE. 277pp. SRF76, 6.50c.
Sri Daya Mata is the leader of the Self Realization Fellowship, the organization founded by Paramahansa Yogananda. She was a disciple for twenty-one years and today carries on the work he introduced into the U.S. This volume presents her personal philosophy and her hints for living a life filled with the love of God.

■ **YOGANANDA, PARAMAHANSA. AUTOBIOGRAPHY OF A YOGI. Many photographs, 591pp. SRF46/HPG, 6.95c/1.95p.**
This is the first time that an authentic Hindu Yogi has written his life story for Western readers. Describing in vivid detail many years of spiritual training under Sri Yukteswar, the author has here revealed a fascinating and little known phase of modern India. He explains with scientific clarity the subtle but definite laws by which yogis perform miracles and attain self mastery. A book about yogis by a yogi. *This unusual life-document is certainly one of the most revealing of the depths of the Hindu mind and heart, and of the spiritual wealth of India, ever to be published in the West.*—W.Y. Evans-Wentz.

YOGANANDA, PARAMAHANSA. COSMIC CHANTS. Spiral bound, 106pp. SRF nd, 3.50p.
Chants for awakening man's consciousness of the omnipresent Lord. Words in English, and music of sixty songs: original compositions by

Yogananda and adaptations by him of ancient Hindu *bhajans* (devotional melodies). An introduction explains musical notation. Foreword by the author on the sacred art of chanting to God.

YOGANANDA, PARAMAHANSA. **HOW YOU CAN TALK WITH GOD. 32pp. SRF57, .95p.**

YOGANANDA, PARAMAHANSA. **THE LAW OF SUCCESS. 32pp. SRF44, .95p.**

YOGANANDA, PARAMAHANSA. **MAN'S ETERNAL QUEST. Glossary, notes, 501pp. SRF75, 7.95c.**
A collection of some of the weekly talks Yogananda gave between 1931 and his death in 1952 on a variety of subjects, all related to seeking and knowing God within oneself and developing along the spiritual path. The messages are often inspirational and should be welcomed by the thousands who have read and absorbed his **Autobiography**. In general, no knowledge of Indian philosophy or Yogananda's work is necessary for an understanding of the material presented here.

YOGANANDA, PARAMAHANSA. **METAPHYSICAL MEDITATIONS. 115pp. SRF74, .95p.**
Thoughts that bestow divine peace. Includes an inspiring foreword on meditation. Pocket size edition.

YOGANANDA, PARAMAHANSA. **PARAMAHANSA YOGANANDA: IN MEMORIAM. 125pp. SRF nd, 1.50p.**

YOGANANDA, PARAMAHANSA. **SAYINGS OF YOGANANDA. 126pp. SRF nd, 2.95c.**
Illuminating answers to questions about the meaning and purpose of life.

YOGANANDA, PARAMAHANSA. **SCIENCE OF RELIGION. 101pp. SRF53, 2.50c.**
A clearly written exposition of man's inescapable search for God.

YOGANANDA, PARAMAHANSA. **SCIENTIFIC AND HEALING AFFIRMATIONS. 76pp. SRF74, .95p.**
Explains healing potency of thought, will, feeling, and prayer.

YOGANANDA, PARAMAHANSA. **SPIRITUAL DIARY. SRF nd, 2.25p.**
An inspiring quotation for each day, taken from the writings of Yogananda and Sri Yukteswar.

YOGANANDA, PARAMAHANSA. **WHISPERS FROM ETERNITY. 274pp. SRF35, 3.00c.**
Heartfelt prayers that convey to man an infinite hope.

YUKTESWAR, SWAMI SRI. **THE HOLY SCIENCE. 77pp. SRF74, 2.95c.**
A profound treatise, by Yogananda's guru, on the underlying unity of the **Bible** and the Hindu scriptures. The Sanskrit rendition of each sutra is followed by its English translation and then by the commentary of Sri Yukteswar.

—— **END OF PARAMAHANSA YOGANANDA SUBSECTION** ——

ZAEHNER, R.C., tr. **HINDU SCRIPTURES. Introduction, glossary, 328pp. Dut66, 3.50p.**
Dry academic translations, beginning with hymns from the **Rig** and **Atharva Vedas**. The next and largest section is devoted to the **Upanishads**; the shorter ones are translated *in toto* and there are selections from others. The **Bhagavad Gita** is translated in the final section.

ZAEHNER, R.C. **HINDUISM. Annotated bibliography, index, 210pp. Oxf62, 2.95p.**
An academic introduction which focuses on the key Hindu concepts of *veda, brahman, moksha, god, dharma, bhakti* (devotion), and encounter. Professor Zaehner feels that these concepts underlie the changing surface of the Hindu tradition and stresses that a thorough understanding of them will help the student reach an intuitive understanding of Hindu religion and philosophy. Zaehner is not our favorite writer, but he is at his best in this volume. Our main complaint against him is that he does not seem to either like or truly understand the Eastern mentality. However, his scholarship is impeccable.

ZIMMER, HEINRICH. **THE ART OF INDIAN ASIA. Notes, bibliography, index, about 1,000pp. PUP55, 65.00c/set.**
This mammoth, boxed, two volume set was Zimmer's major work. He was working on it at the time of his death and it was completed and edited by Joseph Campbell. It consists of an excellent text emphasizing the mythology of Indian art and its transformations, plus 614 plates. The entire second volume is devoted to the plates and some are interspersed throughout the first. This is generally considered the definitive work on Indian art.

ZIMMER, HEINRICH. **MYTHS AND SYMBOLS IN INDIAN ART AND CIVILIZATION. Index, notes, 318pp. PUP46, 3.95p.**
A comprehensive, scholarly interpretation of the key motifs of India's legend, myth, and folklore, illustrated with seventy plates.

ZIMMER, HEINRICH. **PHILOSOPHIES OF INDIA. Illustrations, notes, fine bibliography, 687pp. PUP51/RKP, 5.95p.**
A monumental and scholarly work, prepared by Joseph Campbell from the extensive notes left by Zimmer. Divided into three sections: *Eastern and Western Thought and their Meeting; Success, Pleasure, and Duty;* and *Jainism, Sankara, Yoga, Brahmanism, Buddhism, Tantra.*

INSPIRATION

The time has come for the greatest idea in the world to take possession of your consciousness. It is a simple idea, but when you open up your mind and let it in, you'll never be the same again. It will destroy old false concepts and replace them with new ones. It will eventually remove fear and worry from your life. It will release you from chronic nervous tensions, restore your self-confidence, give you a more positive attitude, and enable you to face things you've been running away from, for years!

All the great, successful men and women in this world have made use of this idea. It has been the dominant idea in their lives. Without it they could never have been great, in their way, or successful.

What is this idea?

It is the realization that what you picture in your mind, if you picture it clearly and confidently and persistently enough, will eventually come to pass in your life!

That's it! Oh, of course, there's a little more to it than that. But boiled down to the very essence, the wise men said it all when they said: *As a man thinketh in his mind and in his heart so is he!*

When this idea first hit me it knocked me down for the count. I had been blaming the other fellow, circumstances beyond my control, for the mess I was in. I just knew I hadn't been responsible for all the unhappy experiences I had undergone. Well, anyway, it helped salve my many hurts to pretend that I hadn't been to blame. But deep down within, I think I had finally begun to realize that the way I thought and felt about things had some connections with what was happening to me.

If I got up in the morning, depressed and convinced it was going to be a bad day, it more often than not turned out a bad day. At first I thought I was psychic, that I could tell in advance what was going to happen. It took a long time and I took a lot of unnecessary punishment before it dawned on me that there is a universal law in the mental realm, *like always attracts like*, and that I had been creating what happened to me by wrong thinking.

Looking around me, I saw happy men and women to whom happy things were happening. They got up in the morning expecting good things to come to them—and good things did!

Sometimes these happy people had unhappy experiences, but I noticed that they didn't let these experiences get them down. They got up the next day expecting more good things to happen, and sure enough more good things did!

Before my awakening came, this always amazed me. I even resented it. Why should just a different mental attitude make so much difference?

I didn't know then that there is a mighty force in the world which scientists call electro-magnetism. I didn't know that everything in the universe is electro-magnetic in nature, that the laws of attraction and repulsion operate electro-magnetically; that when you assume a positive or negative attitude of mind, you get a positive or negative result; that there is no such thing as an accident in life—that everything happens in direct accordance with the laws of cause and effect!

—condensed from **TNT—The Power Within You**, by Claude Bristol and Harold Sherman

ACHAD, FRATER. **ANCIENT MYSTICAL WHITE BROTHERHOOD.** 174pp. CSA74, 3.50p.
This book is prepared with a sacred reverence to the Great Spiritual Teachers who have preceded us in life on earth and whose endless task is to point to the base of reference for mankind, to which he must become oriented.... The chapters of this book represent a record of such guidance which has come to certain individuals who were sincerely seeking it, not for self alone, but to share that knowledge.

ACHAD, FRATER. **MELCHIZEDEK TRUTH PRINCIPLES.** 196pp. DeV63, 4.00p.

ALLEN, JAMES. **AS A MAN THINKETH.** G&D nd/Fow, 2.50c/1.95c.
A classic inspirational book and one of the most popular.

ANDERSON, U.S. **THE GREATEST POWER IN THE UNIVERSE.** 270pp. Wil71, 4.00p.
Anderson's books are considered to be among the clearest and best available. In this one he delves into many new areas such as alpha waves, *chakras*, reading the aura, and generally expanding awareness.

ANDERSON, U.S. **THE SECRET OF SECRETS.** 252pp. Wil58, 4.00p.

ANDERSON, U.S. **SUCCESS CYBERNETICS: PRACTICAL APPLICATIONS OF HUMAN CYBERNETICS.** 241pp. Wil66, 2.00p.

ANDERSON, U.S. **THREE MAGIC WORDS.** 318pp. Wil54, 3.00p.
People who are into inspirational literature love this book and often buy copies to give to their friends.

ANONYMOUS. **BROTHERHOOD.** 106pp. Wll27, 2.25p.
Thoughts on *The Voice, The Call to Service, A Voice Crying in the Wilderness, He Is To Come, Leaders, Evil, The Enemy,* and *The Kingdom of Heaven,* by the author of **The Impersonal Life.**

ANONYMOUS. **THE IMPERSONAL LIFE.** 167pp. Wll44, 3.50c.
This little book...is intended to serve as a channel or open door through which you may enter into the Joy of your Lord, the Comforter promised by Jesus, the living expression in you of the Christ of God.—from the introduction. The book contains practical instruction on a variety of topics including thinking and creating, the word, good and evil, authority, mediums and mediators, masters, and much else.

ANONYMOUS. **THE WAY OUT.** 154pp. Wll71, 3.50p.
Four essays written by the author of **The Impersonal Life:** *The Way Out, The Way Beyond, Wealth,* and *The Teacher.* More practical instruction.

ANONYMOUS. **THE WAY TO THE KINGDOM.** 345pp. DeV32, 4.00p.
Subtitled, *Being Definite and Simple Instructions for Self-Training and Discipline, Enabling the Earnest Disciple to Find the Kingdom of God and His Righteousness.* By the author of **The Impersonal Life.**

BACH, MARCUS. **THE POWER OF PERCEPTION.** 156pp. Haw51, 2.75p.
Dr. Bach discusses the art of perception through an examination of such subjects as insight, reflection, awareness, perception, inspiration, recognition, intuition, receptivity, empathy, consciousness, expectation, and apprehension. He also provides hints for finding one's own potential.

BACH, MARCUS. **QUESTIONS ON THE QUEST.** 159pp. H&R78, 6.95c.
Dr. Bach has a popular column in **Unity** magazine where he responds to queries posed him by spiritual seekers. For this volume, Dr. Bach has selected and topically organized many thought provoking inquiries and has shaped his answers.

409

BRISTOL, CLAUDE and HAROLD SHERMAN. TNT—THE POWER WITHIN YOU. 238pp. PrH54, 2.95p.
Many of our customers feel that this book formed the basis of Silva Mind Control and it contains a good, detailed presentation of Mind Control teachings.

CRUM, JESSIE K. **THE ART OF INNER LISTENING. 96pp. TPH75, 1.25p.**
Jessie K. Crum speaks of inspirational listening through which she discovered and freed the soul of a poet—her own. In this fascinating book she explores her personal experiences, showing how, when and why she was able to tap heretofore unimagined wisdom, grace, even genius, which in her case found its expression in writing.—from the foreword.

DAVIS, ROY EUGENE. **HOW YOU CAN USE THE TECHNIQUE OF CREATIVE IMAGINATION. 107pp. CSA77, 2.50p.**
Davis believes that *man can alter his circumstances and change his lot in life by intentionally controlling his mental attitude and states of consciousness.* In this book he outlines practical methods toward that end.

DAVIS, ROY EUGENE. **SECRETS OF INNER POWER. 191pp. Fel64, 2.95p.**
Davis was a disciple of both Yogananda and Neville and his books synthesize the philosophy of both.

DAVIS, ROY EUGENE. **STUDIES IN TRUTH. 165pp. CSA69, 3.00p.**
A number of observations containing practical suggestions and insightful messages for the daily search for self realization.

DAVIS, ROY EUGENE. **TIME, SPACE AND CIRCUMSTANCE. 140pp. Fel73, 2.95p.**
In this volume Davis summarizes and restates his teaching in a number of important areas including health and healing, meditation, the extension of awareness, and higher vision. As is true with all of Davis' books, the material is oriented toward self transformative techniques for the individual.

DAVIS, ROY EUGENE. **WITH GOD WE CAN. 256pp. CSA78, 4.95p.**
A collection of articles originally published in Davis' **Truth Journal**. The tone and content can be summed up with the following quote from one of the pieces: *There is an intelligent power that runs this universe and we can learn to fully cooperate with it. Being made in the image and likeness of God our destiny is to enter into an intimate relationship with God.*

DUMONT, THERON. **ADVANCED COURSE IN PERSONAL MAGNETISM. YPS16, 6.00c.**

DUMONT, THERON. **THE ART AND SCIENCE OF PERSONAL MAGNETISM. YPS30, 6.00c.**

GOLDSMITH, JOEL. **THE THUNDER OF SILENCE. 5.95c.**
See the Reincarnation and Karma section.

HICKEY, ISABEL. **IT IS ALL RIGHT. 141pp. Hic76, 7.00c.**
Ms. Hickey is a very well known astrologer who is noted for her spiritual and karmic approach to astrology. This volume is a collection of her thoughts on a variety of subjects related to the spiritual life. *This book goes forth with the prayer that it will bring healing, hope and understanding to my brothers and sisters everywhere. It is written from my heart to yours . . . no matter what happens in the world of appearance IT IS ALL RIGHT. Right for that moment in time and space—right for the growth of the individual concerned.—from the introduction.*

HOLMES, ERNEST. **THE SCIENCE OF MIND. 667pp. DMd38, 10.00c.**
Holmes was the founder of the New Thought school of Christianity, an important early twentieth century movement which is still active today. This is the movement's bible.

HOWARD, VERNON. **ESOTERIC ENCYCLOPEDIA OF ETERNAL KNOWLEDGE. 256pp. TPL74, 7.45c.**
Here Howard reveals how to achieve three objectives: solving daily problems, ending unwanted experiences, and winning self command. In his discussion he presents and analyzes 200 *guides to a new life* which are arranged in alphabetical order.

HOWARD, VERNON. **THE MYSTIC MASTERS SPEAK! Index, 283pp. Wei74, 7.50c.**
This book is for anyone who wants to escape from the trap. There is a way out. And you can find it. I assure you of this. This book contains the concentrated wisdom of the ages. In this power-packed volume are all the answers you need for winning a New Life. Its solutions are simple, accurate, helpful. . . . It shows you how to abolish fear and loneliness, what to do about painful problems with other people, how to achieve ease, confidence, and a self-independence beyond your fondest dreams.

HOWARD, VERNON. **THE MYSTIC PATH TO COSMIC POWER. 258pp. PrH67, 2.95p.**

HOWARD, VERNON. **PATHWAYS TO PERFECT LIVING. 214pp. S&D69, 3.95p.**
A detailed guide to a happy, fulfilled life, replete with case histories and written in an extremely simple style.

HOWARD, VERNON. **PSYCHO-PICTOGRAPHY: THE NEW WAY TO USE THE MIRACLE POWER OF YOUR MIND. 202pp. PrH65, 3.45p.**

MURPHY, JOSEPH. **THE COSMIC ENERGIZER. 214pp. PrH74, 3.45p.**

MURPHY, JOSEPH. **LIVING WITHOUT STRAIN. 156pp. DeV59, 3.00p.**

MURPHY, JOSEPH. **MAGIC OF FAITH. 35r MCP54, 1.50p.**

MURPHY, JOSEPH. **MENTAL POISONS AND THEIR ANTIDOTES. 28pp. DeV58, 1.00p.**

MURPHY, JOSEPH. **MIRACLE POWER FOR INFINITE RICHES. 221pp. PrH72, 2.95p.**

MURPHY, JOSEPH. **PEACE WITHIN YOURSELF. 221pp. DeV56, 5.00p.**
The meaning of the **Book of John**.

MURPHY, JOSEPH. **THE POWER OF YOUR SUBCONSCIOUS MIND. 224pp. PrH63, 3.45p.**
The most popular of all Murphy's books.

MURPHY, JOSEPH. **PRAY YOUR WAY THROUGH IT. 171pp. DeV58, 3.00p.**
The inner meaning of the revelations of St. John.

MURPHY, JOSEPH. **PRAYER IS THE ANSWER.** 190pp. DeV56, 3.00p. The meaning of the sacraments.

MURPHY, JOSEPH. **PSYCHIC PERCEPTION: THE MAGIC OF EXTRASENSORY POWER.** 242pp. PrH71, 2.95p. An inspirational text which instructs the reader on the practical applications of ESP in every conceivable field.

MURPHY, JOSEPH. **SPECIAL MEDITATIONS FOR HEALTH, WEALTH AND LOVE.** 64pp. ChD52, 1.50p.

MURPHY, JOSEPH. **TELEPHYSICS: MAGIC POWER OF PERFECT LIVING.** 230pp. PrH73, 2.95p.

MURPHY, JOSEPH. **WITHIN YOU IS THE POWER.** 277pp. DeV77, 6.00p.
Murphy offers a potpourri of meditational and relaxation exercises along with many biblical quotations. The title expresses the theme of the book.

MURPHY, JOSEPH. **YOUR INFINITE POWER TO BE RICH.** PrH68, 3.45p.

NELSON, RUBY. **THE DOOR OF EVERYTHING.** DeV nd, 3.50p.

NEVILLE. **IMMORTAL MAN.** 253pp. CSA77, 4.95p.
A highly inspirational discussion of the role of God in the universe and the nature of man's operant power.

NEVILLE. **RESURRECTION.** 226pp. DeV66, 5.50p.
Neville was the teacher of many of the other authors in this section including Joseph Murphy and Roy Davis.

OPHIEL. **THE ART AND PRACTICE OF GETTING MATERIAL THINGS THROUGH CREATIVE VISUALIZATION.** 120pp. Wei67, 3.50p.
A simply written, illustrated account, replete with many specific guidelines.

RUSSELL, LAO. **GOD WILL WORK WITH YOU—BUT NOT FOR YOU.** 270pp. DeV55, 6.00c.

RUSSELL, WALTER. **THE MESSAGE OF THE DIVINE ILIAD.** Two volumes, 400+pp. DeV48, 20.00c/set.

SHERMAN, HAROLD. **HOW TO KNOW WHAT TO BELIEVE.** 224pp. Faw76, 1.50p.
A personal exposition, based on Sherman's life experiences and including many case studies.

SHERMAN, HAROLD. **HOW TO TAKE YOURSELF APART AND PUT YOURSELF TOGETHER AGAIN.** 192pp. Faw71, 1.50p.
Sherman's books are very clearly written and usually contain less hype than those of other writers in the field.

SHERMAN, HAROLD. **KNOW YOUR OWN MIND.** 160pp. Faw53, 1.50p.

SHERMAN, HAROLD. **THE NEW TNT, MIRACULOUS POWER WITHIN YOU.** PrH66, 7.95c.

SHERMAN, HAROLD. **YOUR POWER TO HEAL.** 223pp. Faw72, 1.50p.
An excellent overview of healing techniques and important healers, including practical suggestions and case studies.

SKARIN, ANNALEE. **BEYOND MORTAL BOUNDARIES.** 342pp. DeV69, 4.95p.
As Ms. Skarin says, *Death is the dreary, back-door entrance into the other world. It is the servant's entrance. But there is a great front door of glory for those who OVERCOME.*

SKARIN, ANNALEE. **THE BOOK OF BOOKS.** 333pp. DeV72, 2.50p.
This is the newest of Ms. Skarin's books as well as the most comprehensive.

SKARIN, ANNALEE. **THE CELESTIAL SONG OF CREATION.** 212pp. DeV62, 3.75p.

SKARIN, ANNALEE. **TO GOD THE GLORY.** 196pp. DeV56, 3.75p.

SKARIN, ANNALEE. **MAN TRIUMPHANT.** 253pp. DeV66, 3.75p.

SKARIN, ANNALEE. **SECRETS OF ETERNITY.** 287pp. DeV60, 3.75p.

SKARIN, ANNALEE. **THE TEMPLE OF GOD.** 224pp. DeV58, 3.75p.

SKARIN, ANNALEE. **YE ARE GODS.** 343pp. DeV52, 2.50p.

TRINE, RALPH WALDO. **IN TUNE WITH THE INFINITE.** 171pp. BoM08/BeL, 2.95p.

WEED, JOSEPH. **COMPLETE GUIDE TO ORACLE AND PROPHECY METHODS.** 222pp. PrH71, 2.95p.
Weed's books are very popular, practical manuals which deal with a great variety of subjects. This is his newest one.

WEED, JOSEPH. **PSYCHIC ENERGY—HOW TO CHANGE DESIRE INTO REALITY.** 216pp. PrH70, 3.45p.

WEED, JOSEPH. **WISDOM OF THE MYSTIC MASTERS.** 208pp. PrH68, 3.45p.
The emphasis is on healing techniques as the author covers the panorama of information regarding the human body, karma, birth-death-reincarnation, the power of thought, the law of cycles, the power of prayer, telepathy, psychic energy, and psychic projection.

WIEHL, ANDREW. **CREATIVE VISUALIZATION.** 112pp. LIP58, 2.95p.
Subtitled, *How to Unlock the Secret Powers of Mind and Body for Full Self-Realization and Happiness.*

ISLAM

The word Islam has several meanings. In the traditional sense, as used by Muslims, it connotes the one true divine religion, taught to mankind by a series of prophets, each of whom brought a revealed book. Such were the **Torah**, the **Psalms**, and the **Gospel**, brought by the prophets Moses, David and Jesus. Muhammad was the last and greatest of the prophets; and the book he brought, the **Qur'an**, completes and supersedes all previous revelations.

In this sense, the Jewish prophets and heroes before Christ, and the Christians before Muhammad, were all Muslims—apart from those who had corrupted the revelations vouchsafed to them and gone astray. More commonly, the term Islam is restricted to the final phase of the sequence of revelations—that of Muhammad and the **Qur'an**. Here again there is a range of meanings, which should be, but are not always, distinguished. In the first instance Islam means the religion taught by Muhammad himself, through the **Qur'an** and through his own precept and practice. By extension, it is used of the whole complex system of dogma, law and custom, which was elaborated, on the basis of his teachings and of others ascribed to him, during the centuries after his death.

In a still wider sense the word Islam is often used by historians, and especially non-Muslim historians, as the equivalent not of Christianity but of Christendom, and denotes the whole rich civilization which grew up under the aegis of the Muslim empires.

The basic religious precepts of the **Qur'an** are already contained in the early chapters, those revealed at Mecca before the migration of the Prophet and his followers to Medina. They teach that there is one God, omnipotent and omniscient, creator of all that exists; that it is the duty of men to submit themselves completely to the will of God; that those who rebel against the prophets sent by God to guide them and who persist in their unbelief are punished both in this world and the next; that after death there is a heaven and a hell where the good are rewarded and the wicked chastised; that at the end of time and the end of the world, there will be a resurrection of bodies and a universal judgment.

The **Qur'an** may be supplemented as a source of guidance by *hadith* (*Sayings*), the technical name for reports concerning the actions and utterances of the Prophet, who is believed by Muslims to have been divinely inspired in all that he did and said. These were therefore handed down by oral tradition and later committed to writing in collections which have an authority among Muslims second only to that of the **Qur'an** itself.

Qur'an and *hadith* form the basis of the *shari'a*, the Holy Law. This great corpus, lovingly elaborated by successive generations of jurists and theologians—where the law is seen as enacted by God and promulgated by a prophet, the two are not clearly distinguished—is one of the major intellectual achievements of Islam, and in many ways the fullest and richest expression of the character and genius of Islamic civilization. Unlike other systems of law, it does not rest primarily on the legislative acts of governments, though the decisions of the Prophet and of those who governed the Islamic community after him, as transmitted by tradition, contributed significantly to its development. Its source, for Muslims, is revelation, manifested through the **Qur'an** and *hadith*, and then amplified and interpreted through the work of the jurists. In this work, they relied on tried and tested methods of reasoning and interpretation. Since the doctors of the Holy Law were not state officials but private citizens, their rulings were not formally binding, nor were they unanimous.

The *shari'a* covers all aspects of the public and private, communal and personal lives of the Muslims. In some of its provisions, especially those relating to property, marriage, inheritance and other matters of personal status, it is a normative code of law, which men were expected to obey and society to enforce; in others, more especially in its prescriptions, it is rather a system of ideals towards which men and society were presumed to aspire and strive. Muslim scholars divided the law into two main parts, one concerned with the minds and hearts of the believers; that is, with dogmatics and individual morality; the other with external acts in relation to God and to man; that is, with worship and with civil, criminal and constitutional law. The purpose of both was to define a system of duties fulfilment of which would enable the believer to live a righteous life in this world and prepare himself for the next.

Of the body of Islamic observances, five are regarded as central and fundamental. The first of these is the *shahada* or Testimony, the profession of faith, in which the Muslim testifies that there is no God but God and that Muhammad is the Prophet of God. This assertion of the unity and uniqueness of God and of the mission of Muhammad is the basic creed of Islam, and most Muslim theologians agree that any man who subscribes to it may be regarded as a Muslim. This simple formula remains the irreducible minimum of belief to which all who would call themselves Muslims must subscribe.

The second of the five pillars of Islam is prayer. This is of two kinds. One, *du'a'*, is a personal, spontaneous, prayer, not bound by any rules or rituals. The other, *salat*, is the set ritual prayer to be offered with prescribed words and motions five times every day at sunrise, mid-day, afternoon, sunset, and evening. This is a religious obligation of all adult Muslims, both men and women, except those incapacitated by illness. The worshipper must be in a state of ritual purity, in a ritually clean place and facing in the direction of Mecca, the birthplace of the Prophet. The prayer itself consists of the profession of faith and some passages from the **Qur'an**. The times for the prayer are indicated by the *adhan*, or call to prayer, usually given from the top of the minaret of the mosque.

The word mosque comes from the Arabic *masjid*, literally a place of prostration. The primary purpose of the building was indeed communal prayer. But it would be misleading to describe the mosque as the Islamic equivalent of the Christian church or the Jewish synagogue. As a place of worship, the mosque is indeed the equivalent of these. But, in another sense, it is the successor of the Roman forum and of the Greek agora. The mosque was not only a place of public prayer but also the centre of Muslim society, especially in the new towns created by the Muslims after the conquests. The pulpit of the mosque was the platform from which important decisions and announcements were proclaimed, such as the appointment and dismissal of officials, the first appearance of new rulers or governors, statements of policy, important news of war and conquest and other major events. In the earliest cities, the mosque, the government offices and the military cantonments were all grouped together in a sort of central citadel, and it was the ruler or governor in person who made important pronouncements from the pulpit. It was customary for the speaker in the pulpit to hold a sword, staff or bow, symbolizing the sovereignty and supremacy of Islam.

The mosque is not open only at offical prayer times. It is always open for meditation, study and spontaneous prayer and also for other business of various kinds. In early times it often served as a court of justice, since the law of Islam was the holy law, and law and religion were inseparably intermingled. The mosque also served as a place of study, a school, and later was frequently linked with a seminary in which not only the **Qur'an** but the rest of Muslim learning was taught. From the earliest times, many mosques had schools attached to them and the practice arose of maintaining these by pious endowments.

The interior of the mosque is simple and austere. There is no sanctuary and no altar, since the Islamic religion has no sacraments, no mysteries, no priestly office. The imam is a leader in prayer, and any Muslim knowing the prayers and the ritual may act in this way. If one may speak of the mosque as the equivalent of the church in the sense of a building and a place of worship, there is in Islam no equivalent of the Church as an institution.

The third pillar of Islam according to the traditional reckoning is pilgrimage—the *hajj*. At least once in his lifetime every Muslim is required to go on pilgrimage to the two holy cities in Arabia, and to re-enact the migration of the Prophet from Mecca to Medina. Women may go with the permission of their husbands and with a safe escort. Those who are unable to go may entrust this duty to others on their behalf, even by testament. This annual pilgrimage, which brings together Muslims from many different lands in a single act of devotion, is one of the most potent unifying factors in the world of Islam. To comply with this requirement of their faith, every year vast numbers of Muslims from every part of the Muslim world, men and women of many races and of different social strata, leave their homes and undertake a long and frequently arduous journey to participate in a single, joint act of devotion. These journeys are quite different from the mindless, aimless collective migrations of Antiquity and the Middle Ages, in that each such journey is voluntary and individual—a personal act following a personal decision and resulting in a series of wide-ranging personal experiences.

The fourth pillar is fasting. This refers to the fast of Ramadan, the ninth month of the Muslim year, which all adult Muslims, men and women, are required to observe with the exception of the aged and the sick. For the whole of the month of Ramadan, believers must abstain from sunrise till dusk from food, drink and sexual relations. During the night, special prayers are recited.

The fifth and last of the five pillars is the *zakat*, a financial contribution paid by Muslims to the community or to the state. Originally a charitable levy collected from the believers for pious purposes, it was transformed into a kind of tribute or tax whereby converts to Islam gave formal expression to their acceptance of the authority of Islam and their allegiance to the Muslim state.

—condensed from **Islam and the Arab World**, by Bernard Lewis

ABDEL-KADER, ALI HASSAN, tr. THE LIFE, PERSONALITY, AND WRITINGS OF AL-JUNAYD. Notes, 276pp. Luz76, 6.55p.
A detailed study of this ninth century mystic. The Arabic text of some of his writings is included along with a translation and in depth analysis of his personality and writings. Part of the **Gibb Memorial Series.**

ABDUL, M.O.A. **ISLAM AS A RELIGION. 101pp. IPB74, 2.80p.**
A thematic study of the doctrine and principles of Islam, with quotations from the Qur'an interspersed. The text was written for Muslim high school and university students in Africa.

ABUN-NASR, JAMIL. **THE TIJANIYYA. Notes, bibliography, index, 204pp. Oxf65, 12.00c.**
The Tijaniyya is a mystical Sufi order which has had considerable political activity and influence. This study covers the theological controversies over Tijani doctrines as well as the history of the movement up to the present. The order is most influential in Maghriban and West Africa.

AHMAD, AZIZ. **AN INTELLECTUAL HISTORY OF ISLAM IN INDIA. Notes, bibliography, index, 236pp. EUP69, 11.40c.**
An historical survey of the religious and cultural impact of Islam on the Indian subcontinent. Professor Ahmad first considers Indian Islamic culture as an integral part of the Muslim world. He discusses Sunni orthodoxy, the Shi'i sects, Messianic movements, orthodox Sufism, and much else. He then examines the effect on Indian Islam of its interaction with Hinduism. He covers, in addition to theology, the fine arts and literature. Many illustrations are included.

AHMAD, FAZL. **HEROES OF ISLAM SERIES. MuA74, 1.35p/each.**
This is a nice series of short books, written especially for Muslim youth. Each one contains a biographical study of a major Islamic figure and is over 100 pages long—1: Muhammad, the Prophet of Islam; 2: Abu Bakr, The First Caliph of Islam; 3: Omar, The Second Caliph of Islam; 4: Othman, The Third Caliph of Islam; 5: Ali, The Fourth Caliph of Islam; 6: Khalid Bin Walid, The Sword of Islam; 7: Muhammad Bin Qasim; and 8: Mahmood of Ghazni.

ALI, AMEER. **THE SPIRIT OF ISLAM. Notes, bibliography, index, 586pp. C&W22, 12.35c.**
In the following pages I have attempted to give the history of the evolution of Islam as a world religion; of its rapid spread and the remarkable hold it obtained over the conscience and minds of millions of people within a short space of time. The impulse it gave to the intellectual development of the human race is generally recognized. But its great work in the uplifting of humanity is either ignored or not appreciated; nor are its rationale, its ideals, and its aspirations properly understood. It has been my endeavor in the survey of Islam to elucidate its true place in the history of religions. The first half of the book describes the life and ministry of Muhammad; the second discusses the religious spirit of Islam. This volume was originally published in 1890 and revised and enlarged in 1902 and 1922. It is a classic and is not overly scholarly.

Muhyiddin Ibn al-'Arabi

Ibn 'Arabi (1164-1240) is universally considered one of the greatest mystical Islamic philosophers. He was born in Spain during the height of the Golden Age of Islam and spent his early years there. He later lived in several Middle Eastern countries and traveled widely. He was a prolific writer and his teaching has been a source of inspiration to practically every Sufi that came after him. Even Rumi is said to have come under his influence. Outside the Islamic world 'Arabi's influence reached Christian philosophers and mystics of the Middle Ages.

AFFIFI, A.E. **THE MYSTICAL PHILOSOPHY OF MUHYID DIN IBNUL 'ARABI. Notes, index, 233pp. MuA38, 7.50c.**
This work is divided into four chapters dealing with the whole of Ibnul 'Arabi's mystical philosophy, i.e., his ontology, doctrine of the Logos, epistemology, psychology, mysticism, religion, ethics, eschatology and aesthetics, and an appendix in which a rough outline is given of the main sources which seem to me to have influenced Ibnul 'Arabi's thought. . . . The material on which the work is based is drawn from twenty-three works by Ibnul 'Arabi, principally his **Futuhat** *and* **Fusus**. This volume was originally part of the **Gibb Memorial Series** and Affifi was a student of R.A. Nicholson. This is an excellent pioneering study, which helps to make many of 'Arabi's difficult philosophical doctrines understandable.

■ *AUSTIN, R.W.J., tr.* **SUFIS OF ANDALUCIA: THE RUH AL-QUDS AND AL-DURRAT AL-FAKHIRAH. 173pp. UCa74, 10.75c.**
Biographical sketches describing the lives and teaching of some Sufi masters of the twelfth and thirteenth centuries from Muslim Spain and North Africa. The sketches come from two works by the celebrated Muslim Sufi, Muhyiddin Ibn al-'Arabi—these are among the few works of this great master available in English. There is, in addition, an extensive account of 'Arabi's life and work. This book provides, in a most inspiring way, many insights into the teachings and practices of the Sufis. Includes in depth annotation.

BURCKHARDT, TITUS. **MYSTICAL ASTROLOGY ACCORDING TO IBN 'ARABI. Notes, 52pp. Bes77, 3.00p.**
An excellent distillation of the essential symbolism underlying spiritual astrology. Translated from the French by Bulent Rauf.

■ *BURCKHARDT, TITUS, tr.* **WISDOM OF THE PROPHETS (FUSUS AL-HIKAM). Glossary, notes, 146pp. Wei76, 4.50p.**
This is a translation of what is probably the most significant and influential of all 'Arabi's books. It is the nucleus of his teaching, expressing the particular standpoint and teaching of each of the major prophets from Adam to Muhammad. The work is beautifully written and the translation itself is as accurate and evocative as any we could imagine. 'Arabi's concept of a totally unified and unifying spiritual perspective is expressed well. We urge all who are deeply interested in both Sufism and the mystical aspects of all religions to dip into this volume.

CORBIN, HENRY. **CREATIVE IMAGINATION IN THE SUFISM OF IBN 'ARABI. Many notes, long bibliography, index, 390pp. PUP58, 23.50c.**
A penetrating analysis of 'Arabi's life and doctrines. The text includes translations of a number of 'Arabi's major works, with commentary and extensive background information. Professor Corbin is the leading contemporary 'Arabi specialist. We recommend this volume to all serious students of Sufism.

HUSAINI, S.A.Q. **IBN AL 'ARABI. 109pp. MuA49, 1.50p.**
This book begins with a biographical study of 'Arabi and then reviews his writings and his philosophy. While there is no depth of analysis, this is the only volume that briefly reviews 'Arabi's work. The scholarship seems adequate.

HUSAINI, S.A.Q., tr. **THE PANTHEISTIC MONISM OF IBN AL-'ARABI. Notes, index, 268pp. MuA70, 6.00c.**
The bulk of this volume is devoted to topically arranged translations of 'Arabi's writings. Each section begins with introductory remarks by the author, followed by the Arabic text and then the translation. All of 'Arabi's major doctrines are included. The selections have been made from the **Futuhat**, the **Fusus**, and 'Arabi's poetry. The volume begins with a short history of pantheism, including information on the pantheistic schools which preceeded 'Arabi. There is also a life study of 'Arabi and a good deal of background material. A number of the topics presented here are not dealt with in any other book on 'Arabi.

WEIR, T.H., tr. **IBN 'ARABI: "WHOSO KNOWETH HIMSELF...". Notes, 27pp. Bes76, 3.95c.**
A translation of a portion of 'Arabi's **Treatise on Being (Risale-t-ul-wujudiyyah)**, prepared with the collaboration of The Muhyiddin Ibn 'Arabi Society.

———END OF MUHYIDDIN IBN AL-'ARABI SUBSECTION———

The Arabian Nights

The Book of a Thousand and One Nights, popularly known as **The Arabian Nights**, is a composite work consisting of popular stories originally transmitted orally and developed over several centuries, with material added somewhat haphazardly at different periods and places. As in much medieval European literature the stories—fairytales, romances, legends, fables, parables, anecdotes, and exotic adventures—are set within a frame story. Its theme is that the sultan Shahryar, after discovering that during his absences his wife has been regularly unfaithful, kills her. Then, loathing all women he decides to marry a new wife each evening and have her executed in the morning. He pursues this course of action until the only women left in the kingdom are the vizier's daughters. The elder, having devised a scheme to save herself and others, insists that her father give her in marriage to the sultan. Each evening she tells a wondrous story, leaving it incomplete and promising to finish it the next night. The stories are so entertaining and the sultan so eager to hear the end, that he puts off her execution from day to day until 1,001 nights have passed and at the conclusion of that period the death decree was withdrawn. Though the names of its chief characters are Iranian, the frame story is probably Indian, and the largest percentage of names is Arabic. The tales' variety and geographic range of origin—India, Iraq, Iran, Egypt, Turkey, and possibly even Greece—make single authorship unlikely. The tales have almost become part of Western folklore. They depict a fabulous and fanciful world of jinns and sorcerers, but their bawdiness, realism, and variety of subject matter also firmly anchor them to everyday life.

BURTON, RICHARD, tr. **THE BOOK OF THE THOUSAND NIGHTS AND A NIGHT. Out nd, 59.95c.**
This is a sixteen volume unexpurgated edition of Burton's masterwork, originally privately printed by the Burton Club and generally regarded as the only complete and authoritative edition. Both **The Arabian Nights** and the **Supplemental Nights** are included and the books are handsomely bound with simulated gold and silver stamping. The Burton translation is universally regarded as definitive and we are delighted that this magnificent set is now generally available at such a bargain price. The volumes are 6¼"x9¼" and together come to over 5,000 pages.

■ *DAWOOD, N.J., tr.* **TALES FROM THE THOUSAND AND ONE NIGHTS. Introduction, illustrations, 406pp. Vik73, 2.95p.**
This is our favorite one volume translation of **The Arabian Nights**. Dawood has done an excellent job of recapturing the tone and feeling of the original and he has not oversimplified the stories. From the Lane edition.

DIXON, E., ed. **FAIRY TALES FROM THE ARABIAN NIGHTS. 343pp. Den51, 6.35c.**
A well written retelling of the stories. The language is geared toward

young readers and there are many line drawings and eight color plates. This edition is selected from the Galland 1821 translation, slightly abridged and altered.

LANE, E.W., tr. **BEST SELECTIONS FROM THE ARABIAN NIGHTS ENTERTAINMENTS. 471pp. Har76, 4.95p.**
Next to Richard Burton, Edward Lane is the best known of the many English translators of **The Arabian Nights**. This is a selection of some of the stories. Woodcuts by William Harvey accompany the text.

LANG, ANDREW, ed. **THE ARABIAN NIGHTS ENTERTAINMENTS. Thirty-three full page plates and thirty-four smaller drawings, 440pp. Dov1898, 3.50p.**
This edition of **The Arabian Nights** has been especially edited for children and told in a manner that children can enjoy. Twenty-six tales are presented here, including the full *Voyages of Sinbad the Sailor, Aladdin and the Lamp, The Enchanted Horse*, and some of the other most popular tales. The vivid illustrations which H.J. Ford provided for the original text have been retained here.

WIGGIN, KATE and NORA SMITH, eds. **THE ARABIAN NIGHTS. 350pp. Scr09, 3.95p.**
A well written, easy to read retelling of nine of the major tales, with illustrations by Maxfield Parrish. Technically this is a handsome volume with large print.

WILLIAMS-ELLIS, AMABEL. **THE ARABIAN NIGHTS. 348pp. Bla57, 7.80c.**
This is a beautifully produced volume, illustrated throughout with line drawings and color plates. Twelve stories are included, each in a complete version; notes on the sources and history follow the narrative.

──────── **END OF THE ARABIAN NIGHTS SUBSECTION** ────────

Arabic Language

Arabic is a Semitic language spoken by more than 100 million people in a large area including North Africa, most of the Arabian Peninsula, and parts of the Middle East. Arabic is the language of the **Qur'an** and is the religious language of all Muslims. Literary Arabic, usually called Classical Arabic, is essentially the form of the language found in the **Qur'an**, with some modifications necessary for its use in modern times; it is uniform throughout the Arab world. Colloquial Arabic includes numerous spoken dialects, some of which are mutually unintelligible. Most of the dialects have been strongly influenced by the literary language. The earliest known written Arabic is a royal funerary inscription dating from AD 328.

BEESTON, A.F.L. **ARABIC HISTORICAL PHRASEOLOGY. 186pp. CUP69, 6.95p.**
A companion volume to Beeston's **Written Arabic**, containing exercise material taken from historical writing in modern Arabic.

BEESTON, A.F.L. **WRITTEN ARABIC. Index, 117pp. CUP68, 6.50p.**
This is a very clear introduction to the essential features of modern written Arabic. Beeston excludes the mass of linguistic detail contained in traditional Arabic grammars which assume that the student wishes to master all aspects of the language. Instead, he provides for a sound understanding of abstract literature on scholarly subjects, in contrast to manuals teaching a quick understanding of journalistic Arabic.

CACHIA, PIERRE. **THE MONITOR: A DICTIONARY OF ARABIC GRAMMATICAL TERMS, ARABIC-ENGLISH, ENGLISH-ARABIC. 198pp. LdL73, 13.35c.**

COWAN, DAVID. **MODERN LITERARY ARABIC. 215pp. CUP58, 8.50p.**
The lessons are written in nontechnical language, and include many examples as well as numerous translation exercises. Since the fundamental grammar of written Arabic has hardly changed at all during the

last thirteen centuries, this book also serves as an introduction to the classical language. This grammar is considered to be quite a good one.

COWAN, J.M., ed. **ARABIC-ENGLISH DICTIONARY. 1,117pp. SLS76, 8.50p.**
An unabridged edition of the highly acclaimed Hans Wehr **Dictionary of Modern Written Arabic**. *Its comprehensiveness and reliability as well as its clear presentation of the material have made it the principal aid for the study of written Arabic. Indeed, for the student and the younger (Western) scholar, it seems to have superceded—at least to a large degree—all other lexical aids.*—**Journal of the American Oriental Society**. Unfortunately the printing quality is not very good and the Arabic script is often hard to read.

ELIAS, ELIAS and EDWARD. **ELIAS' POCKET DICTIONARY— ENGLISH-ARABIC. Eli nd, 4.65c.**

ELIAS, E.A. and EDWARD. **ELIAS' PRACTICAL GRAMMAR AND VOCABULARY OF COLLOQUIAL ARABIC. 103pp. Eli nd, 1.30p.**
A collection of thirty gradual lessons. The vocabulary for each lesson is listed at the top of each page and the translation exercise faces the exercise in transliterated Arabic. A complete vocabulary is appended, referencing each word to the lesson in which it first occurred.

HAYWOOD, J.A. and H.M. NAHMAD. **A NEW ARABIC GRAMMAR OF THE WRITTEN LANGUAGE. Index, 867pp. HUP65, 26.90c.**
This is a revised edition of the grammar of the same name originally published in 1962. It replaces Thatcher's **Arabic Grammar**, which it is based on, and has a vocabulary of almost 4,000 words. The supplement contains a number of new features including selections from the **Qur'an**, fables, stories, newspaper extracts, and portions from classical and modern Arabic writings. This is above all a practical grammar, not an advanced reference work like Wright's; it is meant for the beginner and should suffice for the first two or three years of study.

RAUF, MUHAMMAD ABDUL. **ARABIC FOR ENGLISH SPEAKING STUDENTS. 444pp. Isl75, 16.15p.**
I assumed that the student is an absolute beginner, and I go along with him on the road very slowly in the early stages until he gradually builds up some basic knowledge for proceeding at a faster rate. The method adopted here is as follows: (a) The lesson begins by giving a sample for the uses of the topic to be discussed and taught, in a clear and tabulated form. (b) This is followed by "Notes" in which observations are derived from the examples in the table. (c) At the end of the Notes, a summary of information gained in the lesson is given to reinforce the student's understanding. (d) The lesson is concluded by an exercise to help in digesting the rules.... This book is basically a work on grammar, not an Arabic reader.

SALMONE, H. ANTHONY. **AN ADVANCED LEARNER'S ARABIC-ENGLISH DICTIONARY. 1,461pp. LdL1889, 33.60c.**
This excellent work also includes an English index.

SOMMER, F.E. **THE ARABIC WRITING IN FIVE LESSONS. 20pp. Ung42, 1.70p.**
A clear presentation, with practical exercises and a key.

STEINGASS, F. **A LEARNER'S ARABIC-ENGLISH DICTIONARY. 1,258pp. LdL72, 40.30c.**
Contains more than 40,000 words.

THATCHER, G.W. **ARABIC GRAMMAR OF THE WRITTEN LANGUAGE WITH KEY. 560pp. Ung nd, 15.50c.**
A comprehensive, well respected grammar which covers all aspects of written and spoken Arabic. The material is organized into lessons and vocabularies are included. This is an old work, but it remains one of the best.

TRITTON, A.S. **TEACH YOURSELF ARABIC. Index, 296pp. McK43, 3.95p.**
The script and grammar of the classic language are clearly explained in a series of carefully graded lessons, each of which contains many examples and exercises. The author has many years of experience teaching Arabic and has developed a number of excellent techniques.

WRIGHT, W., tr. **A GRAMMAR OF THE ARABIC LANGUAGE. Indices, 468pp. CUP64, 16.95p.**
A translation from the German of Caspari's grammar, edited with numerous additions and corrections. It is considered the definitive

volume and includes sections on orthography and pronunciation, the verb, the noun, the adjective, numerals, prepositions, adverbs, and conjunctions. It also includes a review of syntax and prosody. Two volumes bound in one.

——————— END OF ARABIC LANGUAGE SUBSECTION ———————

ARBERRY, A.J., tr. THE DOCTRINE OF THE SUFIS. Introduction, notes, index, 207pp. CUP35, 4.95p.
A translation of the Kitab al-Ta'arruf li-madhhab ahl al-tasawwuf of Kalabadhi, a fourth century philosopher. This volume has been generally accepted as an authoritative textbook on Sufi doctrine and practice, and commentaries have been written on it by a number of eminent scholars. The opening section discusses the meaning and derivation of the term Sufi and enumerates the names of the great Sufis. The next part contains a statement of the tenets of Islam, as accepted by the Sufis—the author emphasizing that Sufism lies within and not without the bounds of orthodoxy. The next sections illustrate *the stations of the Sufis* (such as fear, hope, love) and the technical terms used by them to designate the true mystical experience. The book concludes with the descriptions of Sufi phenomena and miraculous dispensations.

ARBERRY, A.J. ORIENTAL ESSAYS. 261pp. A&U60, 6.50c.
A collection of portraits (one a self portrait) of seven English Islamic scholars: Simon Ockley, Sir William Jones, E.W. Lane, E.H. Palmer, E.G. Browne, and R.A. Nicholson.

ARBERRY, A.J., ed. RELIGION IN THE MIDDLE EAST. Glossary, notes, bibliography, index, 1,345pp. CUP69, 45.00c/set.
These two volumes survey Judaism, Christianity, and Islam, and their relationships during the last hundred years. Since Arberry is an Islamic scholar he includes Central Asia, India, Pakistan, and parts of Africa in his discussion. While primarily concerned with religion, the work also follows the interaction of ethnic, economic, political, social, and cultural factors. The background and history of the three religions are described; the distribution of sects and communities is studied; and each religion is discussed in terms of its doctrinal, legal, social, political, and cultural aspects. Arberry is the general editor of the work and the individual subject editors are E.I.J. Rosenthal, Judaism; M.A.C. Warren, Christianity; and C.F. Beckingham, Islam.

ARBERRY, A.J. REVELATION AND REASON IN ISLAM. 122pp. A&U57, 5.20c.
A transcription of three lectures Arberry gave on the title topic. He reviews the conflict and examines the attempts made to resolve the dilemma. Many references are cited.

ARBERRY, A.J. SHIRAZ. Bibliography, index, 191pp. UOk60, 5.95c.
Shiraz, an ancient Persian city, is known as the city of saints and poets. *In these essays I have sought to isolate the elements which have made Shiraz immortal, and I have diagnosed those elements to be the worship of beauty and the love of beautiful things; the vision of beauty as an eternal spirit transcending and yet informing phenomena, giving a purpose to life, and a consolation in the midst of life's incalcuable calamities. I have tried to body forth these abstractions in the lives and works of saints and poets who are the great glory of Shiraz.*

ARBERRY, A.J., tr. A SUFI MARTYR. Notes, 101pp. A&U69, 10.10c.
A translation of The Apologia of Ain al-Qudat al Hamadhani, composed in 1131 while he was in jail, in a vain attempt to overthrow his death sentence. It gives a fascinating account of his life and works.

■ ARBERRY, A.J. SUFISM. Notes, index, 141pp. A&U50, 6.00c.
This is the best short survey of Sufism that we know. Each of the major individuals and orders is reviewed and the development of Sufi doctrines is traced. Professor Arberry illustrates his treatise with extensive quotations from the literature, including selections from all the major poets and philosophers.

ARNOLD, SIR EDWIN. PEARLS OF THE FAITH OR ISLAM'S ROSARY. 152pp. MuA61, 1.75p.
A verse enumeration of the ninety-nine names of Allah. Appended to each is an illustrative legend, tradition, or comment, and occasionally a paraphrase of the Qur'an.

ARNOLD, THOMAS. PAINTING IN ISLAM. 4.00p.
See the Sacred Art section.

ASHRAF, MUHAMMAD. SALAT OR ISLAMIC PRAYER BOOK. 49pp. MuA71, .75p.
An illustrated description of the main prayers of Islam, with introductory material.

ATIL, ESIN. ART OF THE ARAB WORLD. Notes, 9¾"x9¾", 155pp. MIT75, 20.15p.
This is the catalogue of an exhibition at the Freer Gallery of Art in Washington, D.C. Eighty magnificent full page color plates are reproduced and fully discussed. An historical text accompanies the plates.

Farid al-Din Attar

Attar (1142-1221) is one of the greatest Sufi poets. He was very prolific, having written, according to one account, forty treatises and over 100,000 lines of poetry. Modern scholars usually consider between nine and twelve of the works attributed to him to have actually been written by him. Rumi knew Attar and was greatly influenced by his work. Rumi himself states: *The Seven Cities of Love did Attar traverse/We are still in the curve of one alley.* Attar's poetry was steeped in mystical love for the Creator and his creations. Attar wrote in many forms.

ARBERRY, A.J., tr. MUSLIM SAINTS AND MYSTICS. 287pp. RKP66, 10.00c.
A translation of the Tadherat al-Auliya (Memorial of the Saints), Attar's best known prose work. This is an account of the lives of 142 Sufi saints, accompanied by philosophical material. The beauty of the work lies in the fact that it brings out the obstacles that often surmount mystics when they tread the path, and details how these saints met with these difficulties. In this edition Professor Arberry has shortened the work, only presenting the lives of ninety-six saints, and concentrated on the biographies. The selections start with Hasan of Basra (642-728) and finish with al-Shebli (759-846), whose death marks the end of the formative period of Sufism. Attar writes vividly, and all readers (even those not versed in Sufism) should find the biographical studies entertaining and enlightening. Arberry has provided an excellent translation, along with a bibliography and notes for each section and an introduction. Part of the Persian Heritage series.

BEHARI, BANKEY, tr. TADHKARATUL-AULIYA OR MEMOIRS OF SAINTS. 245pp. MuA65, 5.40c.
This translation does not read quite as well as Arberry's, nor is it as well organized. However, more of Attar's philosophical speculations are presented, and some of the sixty-two selections in this edition are different from the ones Arberry chose. The translation is definitely adequate and if we did not have Arberry's to compare it to we would probably be very pleased with this one. Dr. Behari is a noted scholar and translator and he supplies excellent introductory material.

BOYLE, JOHN, tr. THE ILAHI-NAMA OR BOOK OF GOD. Introduction, notes, bibliography, index, 414pp. MUP76, 26.50c.
Professor Boyle's fully annotated translation is the first into English of the Book of God, one of Attar's most important works. It is one of several *mathnavis*, or narrative poems in rhymed couplets, in which he illustrated Sufi doctrines by means of allegories and anecdotes. It tells the story of a king who has six sons, each of whom he invites to tell him his heart's desire. The king's reply to each son—in a series of lively tales that form the main body of the work—is the same: their hearts are fixed on material and transient things, whereas true happiness is to be attained only by pursuing the spiritual and the eternal.

NOTT, C.S., tr. THE CONFERENCE OF THE BIRDS: A SUFI FABLE. Glossary, 155pp. Wei54/RKP, 4.50c/3.95p.
A prose translation of Mantiq ut-tair, Attar's great philosophical poem. The work is a collection of illustrative, instructive tales and fables. *O you who have set out on the path of inner development, do not read my book only as a poetical work, or a book of magic, but read it with understanding; and for this a man must be hungry for something, dissatisfied with himself and this world. He who has not smelt the perfume of my discourses has not found the way of lovers.* This is one of the most popular books on the Sufi tradition. Nott's translation is from a French version rather than the original Persian.

———— END OF FARID AL-DIN ATTAR SUBSECTION ————

AZZAM, ABD-AL RAHMAN. THE ETERNAL MESSAGE OF MUHAMMAD. Index, 297pp. DAC64, 6.50c.
Azzam was a distinguished Arab diplomat and Muslim scholar. He begins this book with a short biographical sketch of Muhammad. Drawing on years of study, he then examines the origins and development of monotheistic religion as expressed by Muhammad and the social, economic, and constitutional requirements of a Muslim state. The book is less about the prophet as a man than it is a restatement and analysis of traditional Muslim beliefs as they can be perceived in the world today.

■ BAKHTIAR, LALEH. SUFI. 9½"x10", Avo76, 5.95p.
An exploration of the inner world of Sufism in the form of 120 illustrations, thirty in color, which focus on the forms and rhythms of Islamic art and architecture. An illuminating text accompanies the photographs.

BALYUZI, H.M. MUHAMMAD AND THE COURSE OF ISLAM. Illustrations, glossary, notes, bibliography, index, 474pp. Ron76, 16.95c.
This is both a biography of the prophet and a history of Islam from the years of his mission to the nineteenth century. The discussion reads well and is comprehensive and yet succinct. Most of the major sources are cited and often quoted, and the religious history is discussed as fully as the political. Balyuzi has done an especially fine job of making the major figures come alive.

BAMBOROUGH, PHILIP. TREASURES OF ISLAM. Many color plates, index, 160pp. Arc76, 4.60p.
A pictorial survey of the art of the Islamic world, along with an historical analysis of the Islamic artistic tradition.

BARKER, CAROL. A PRINCE OF ISLAM. 8.00c.
See the Children's Books section.

BAWA, GURU. THE DIVINE LUMINOUS WISDOM THAT DISPELS THE DARKNESS. 288pp. GBF72, 4.95p.
Guru Bawa is a Sufi teacher from Sri Lanka who has spent some time in the U.S. This book contains a series of answers that he gave to students visiting his ashram. They are in the form of simple parables and deal with the most fundamental questions of life and death.

BAWA, GURU. THE GUIDEBOOK TO THE TRUE SECRET OF THE HEART, VOLUME I. Glossary, 256pp. GBF76, 3.95p.
This book is a series of Graces given as discourses....They were expressed in Tamil...and translated into English....The meanings of this book are found through our own efforts, through a going in to the Heart and in the Remembrance of God's Grace. It is not a book about what we see. It is a book to understand who is seeing. The normal process of absorption in the distracting senses, the configurations of thought, and the willing forgetfulness of God's Presence must be suspended in order to

grasp this work....These are transmissions of an exalted teaching—the Complete Teaching—...the Guide is That which reveals and unveils the hiddenness.—from the preface.

BAWA, GURU. THE GUIDEBOOK TO THE TRUE SECRET OF THE HEART, VOLUME II. Glossary, 232pp. GBF76, 3.95p.
A second selection of Guru Bawa's discourses.

BAWA, GURU. SONGS OF GOD'S GRACE. 160pp. GBF73, 2.95p.
English translations of songs which convey moments of ecstatic communion with God.

BAWA, GURU. TRUTH AND LIGHT. 143pp. GBF74, 2.50p.
Transcriptions of conversations Guru Bawa held over the radio that distill his own brand of the universal wisdom teachings. Some questions and answers are included.

BEHARI, BANKEY. SUFIS, MYSTICS, AND YOGIS OF INDIA. 1.95p.
See the Indian Philosophy section.

BENNETT, J.G. JOURNEYS IN ISLAMIC COUNTRIES, VOLUMES I AND II. 3.95p/each.
See the Gurdjieff and the Work section.

BENY, ROLOFF. PERSIA. Bibliography, index, 10"x12", 367pp. NYG75, 55.00c.
This is a beautifully produced volume, distilling the essence of Persian culture with grace and sensitivity. The volume was commissioned by the Empress of Iran, and so reflects a desire to make the Persian heritage as significant as possible, which it does very well. The book is divided into four main themes: *Light, Life, The Sacred Place,* and *The Domain of Kings.* The text is filled with exquisite color photographs, drawings, and calligraphy. Much of the written material is on brown paper with gold lettering. Seyyed Hossein Nasr, a leading Persian scholar, examines his country's culture in an essay and anthology which trace the literary and spiritual development of Persian history. Prose and poetry, selected from Persian literature, harmonize with magnificent images of the land, the people, and its artistic and cultural heritage. Illustrated with 228 color plates and many engravings, with long notes on each of the plates.

BINYON, LAURENCE. PERSIAN MINIATURE PAINTING. 6.00p.
See the Sacred Art section.

BLUNT, WILFRID and WIM SWAAN. ISFAHAN, PEARL OF PERSIA. Notes, bibliography, index, 8"x11", 208pp. Ele66, 29.95c.
Isfahan is one of the most beautiful of all the Islamic cities—and yet it is not well known. This magnificent volume recounts the history of the city from its beginnings to the present day. Blunt describes all the principal buildings and his text is augmented by thirty-six color plates and fifty-five monochrome ones.

BOURGOIN, J. ARABIC GEOMETRIC PATTERNS. 4.50p.
See the Sacred Art section.

BOURGOIN, J. ISLAMIC PATTERNS: AN INFINITE DESIGN COLORING BOOK. 8¼"x11", 48pp. Dov77, 1.50p.
A collection of patterns based on Islamic art designs.

BROWN, JOHN P. THE DARVISHES; OR ORIENTAL SPIRITUALISM. Introduction, notes, 520pp. FrC nd, 23.50c.
An extremely detailed account, written in somewhat archaic language and first published in 1868. Edited by H.A. Rose.

BURCKHARDT, JOHN. TRAVELS IN ARABIA. Map, 493pp. FrC1829, 45.00c.
A recent reprint of Burckhardt's pioneering study of the holy areas of

the Arabian Peninsula, including the holy cities of Mecca and Medina, which are off limits to non-Muslims, Burckhardt was one of the first Westerners to visit this sacred land and, until the publication of Richard Burton's work, the only individual to write about the area in detail. The author does a fine job of bringing the people and their customs to life and he does not insert as much unrelated material as Burton.

BURCKHARDT, TITUS. **ALCHEMY. 3.25p.**
See the Alchemy section.

■ *BURCKHARDT, TITUS.* **ART OF ISLAM: LANGUAGE AND MEANING. 9½"x12", 228pp. WIF76, 27.50c.**
This is far and away the most magnificent book on Islamic art we have seen, with over 200 color plates and 100 half tones and line drawings. The text itself is excellent and Burckhardt is one of our favorite authors. Here he states that Muslim art is a sacred art and its masterpieces are outward manifestations of the religious beliefs of Islam. From this standpoint he studies the flowering of Islamic art, its mosques, crafts, and cities, and illustrates his theme with carefully selected photographs.

■ *BURCKHARDT, TITUS.* **AN INTRODUCTION TO SUFI DOC-TRINE. Index, 155pp. TPL59, 5.85p.**
An excellent account, illuminating many of the most subtle aspects of Sufi thought and practice. Burckhardt writes extremely well and, as a practicing Sufi, is thoroughly versed in the subject matter. His discussion is based heavily on the philosophy of 'Arabi.

BURCKHARDT, TITUS, tr. **LETTERS OF A SUFI MASTER. Introduction, 48pp. Prn69, 2.35p.**
Mulay al-'Arabi ad-Darqawi, the author of these letters, was the founder of the Darqawi Order of Sufis, a Moroccan branch of the great Shadhili Order. The spiritual radiation of the shaikh al-Darqawi brought about a sudden great flowering of Sufism in Morocco, Algeria, and beyond, and several of his direct disciples became outstanding masters themselves. These letters were compiled by the shaikh himself and the translation is based on two nineteenth century manuscripts.

BURCKHARDT, TITUS. **MOORISH CULTURE IN SPAIN. 200 plates and illustrations, chronology, bibiliography, index, 232pp. A&U70, 16.45c.**
A monumental study of the character and achievements developed during 800 years of the Muslim dominance of Spain.

■ *BURKE, O.M.* **AMONG THE DERVISHES. Bibliography, 203pp. Dut73/Oct, 3.95p.**
We recommend this as a first reader for those who want to get a true picture of Sufism in practice. Burke states that he *resolved to travel to as many Eastern lands as my resources would permit, to spend as much time as might be needed, to look for and record as much as possible about the Sufis.* Traveling as a dervish and staying at secluded Sufi monasteries, he became immersed in Sufism and this book is a record of many of his experiences. Burke writes vividly. We enjoyed reading his book enormously. Burke is now a student of Idries Shah.

BURTON, RICHARD. **THE KASIDAH. 128pp. Oct74, 5.50c.**
The **Kasidah** or **Lay of the Higher Laws** was composed by Sir Richard in 1853 on his return journey from Mecca. He comments upon Western methods of thought, modern theories and philosophies, from the Sufi point of view.

BURTON, RICHARD, tr. **THE PERFUMED GARDEN. Notes, 271pp. Ber63, 2.25p.**
The Perfumed Garden is the most celebrated Persian manual of erotic technique. It reveals the Muslim attitude of reverence for the sexual act and for the divine power that is released through it. It is also a philosophical work.

BURTON, RICHARD. **PERSONAL NARRATIVE OF A PILGRIMAGE TO AL-MADINAH AND MECCA. Index, 955pp. Dov1893, 5.00p/each.**
Sir Richard (1821-90) was one of the great traveler-explorers of history. Successfully posing as a wandering dervish, he gained admittance to the holy Kaabah and to the tomb of the prophet at Medina and participated in all the rituals of the *hadj* (pilgrimage). He is still one of the very few non-Muslims to visit and return from Mecca.

Above all, Burton was a sharp observer—of character, customs, and physical surroundings. These pages contain a treasury of material on Arab life, beliefs, manners, and morals; detailed descriptions of religious ceremonies and mosques; and a variety of ethnographic, geographical, and economic information. This two volume edition gives us a vivid picture of the region and its people.

CARTWRIGHT, FAIRFAX. **THE MYSTIC ROSE. 216pp. Wat76, 6.85p.**
Sir Fairfax was a diplomat and he traveled widely in Eastern countries. Here he distills from his experience and contacts with traditional sources a deeply poetic vision of life in which worldly and spiritual wisdom interweave. The book is subtitled, *A Fragment of the Vision of Sheikh Haji Ibrahim of Kerbela,* and it takes the form of a continuous narrative.

CHAPMAN, J.A., tr. **MAXIMS OF ALI. Introduction, 97pp. MuA46, 1.35p.**
Ali was Muhammad's son in law and was considered one of the great men of his day. A well known orator and spokesman, his sermons and speeches were collected soon after his death. This is a topically arranged translation of some of the most popular ones.

CHRISTOPHER, JOHN B. **THE ISLAMIC TRADITION. Notes, annotated bibliography, index, 207pp. H&R72, 8.00p.**
An introductory text, briefly discussing the following major topics: *The Arabian Setting, The Prophet, The Teachings of Islam, The Pillars of the Faith, The Law and the State, Orthodoxy and Heterodoxy, Sufism, Philosophy, Science, The Arts and Literature,* and *The Modern Challenge.* Professor Christopher provides a good overview.

CORBIN, HENRY. **SPIRITUAL BODY AND CELESTIAL EARTH. Notes, bibliography, index, 369pp. PUP77, 21.75c.**
Corbin, a distinguished authority on Iranian Islam, analyzes interrelated themes in Iranian religion, beginning with the angelology of Mazdaism and its links to the Islamic Shi'ite concept of *hurqalya,* the realm of creative imagination. Discussion of these themes forms a prelude to a second part of the book, which presents selected texts by eleven Persian mystics that have never before been translated into a Western language. A foreword to the text summarizes the lives and works of the Shi'ite masters who developed different aspects of this central theme in their teachings and schools. The texts include an important extract from 'Arabi.

COULSON, N.J. **A HISTORY OF ISLAMIC LAW. Glossary, notes, bibliography, index, 264pp. EUP64, 6.75c.**
Presents a broad picture of the nature of Islamic law.

CRAGG, KENNETH. **THE HOUSE OF ISLAM. Questions for further study and discussion, glossary, chronology, notes, bibliography, index, 158pp. Dic75, 6.65p.**
This is a good academic survey of the religious life of Islam with chapters on *Islamic Cosmology, Muhammad, The* **Qur'an,** *Law, Liturgy and the Sufic Path,* and *Ummah* (the spiritual community of Islam). The format is definitely that of a textbook but the material reads better than most textbooks.

CRAGG, KENNETH. **WISDOM OF THE SUFIS. 94pp. NDP76/SLP, 2.75p.**
This is a nice selection. Professor Cragg begins with a discussion of the religion of the Sufis and their poetic literature. He explains how Sufism grew out of the severe and uncompromising theological dogma of medieval orthodox Islam. The prayers and legends included are divided into four sections—the first three examine the task, search, and goal of the Sufi mystic, and the last discusses the significance of the Quranic prayer, *Thou Lord of the Worlds.*

CRITCHLOW, KEITH. **ISLAMIC PATTERNS. 9.95p.**
See the Sacred Geometry section.

CRONE, PATRICIA and MICHAEL COOK. **HAGARISM. Notes, bibliography, indices, 277pp. CUP77, 18.50c.**
The authors present a new theory of the origins of Islam and a novel analysis of the formation of Islamic civilization. The sources cited point to a very intimate link between the earliest form of Islam and Judaic messianism.

CROOKE, WILLIAM. **ISLAM IN INDIA. Illustrations, glossary, notes, bibliography, index, 414pp. Cur21, 12.00c.**
An archaic study, written in the early nineteenth century, of the manners, social habits, customs, and religious rites of the Muslims in India. Every conceivable aspect of their life is discussed at length.

DARKE, HUBERT, tr. **THE BOOK OF GOVERNMENT OR RULES FOR KINGS. Introduction, notes, index, 288pp. RKP78, 15.50c.**
A translation of a classic eleventh century Persian text on behavior and conduct in government, extensively revised from the first edition.

DE BOER, J.J. **THE HISTORY OF PHILOSOPHY IN ISLAM. 224pp. Dov03, 2.75p.**
A very comprehensive account, covering the major philosophers, their teachings, and the historical background of the Islamic system.

DOI, A. RAHMAN. **THE CARDINAL PRINCIPLES OF ISLAM. Bibliography, index, 201pp. IPB72, 5.40p.**
This book deals with the Islamic practices according to the Maliki Madhhab as practiced in the Maghreb, Upper Egypt, and West Africa. As the title suggests, all major tenets of the Islamic faith are clearly covered. There is also a comprehensive analysis of Islamic faith and practices.

EATON, RICHARD. **SUFIS OF BIJAPUR, 1300-1700: SOCIAL ROLES OF SUFIS IN MEDIEVAL INDIA. Many illustrations, glossary, notes, bibliography, index, 390pp. PUP78, 33.60c.**
The Sufis have generally been viewed as standing more or less apart from the social order. Professor Eaton contends to the contrary that the Sufis were an integral part of their society, and that an understanding of their interaction with it is essential to an understanding of the Sufis themselves. This is an extremely detailed examination of Professor Eaton's thesis.

ELAHI, MAQBOOL, tr. **THE 'ABYAT' OF SULTAN BAHOO. Introduction, notes, 398pp. MuA67, 3.00c.**
Sultan Bahoo (1630-91) was a well known Indian mystic, author of well over 100 books on aspects of mysticism and religion. It is in his **Abyat** that his beliefs about the fundamentals of mysticism find their most impressive expression. This is a bilingual Punjabi/English edition, divided into parts and translated into verse, expressing the true mystic's love of God.

EL-SAID, ISSAM and AYSE PARMAN. **GEOMETRIC CONCEPTS IN ISLAMIC ART. 9½"x12", 160pp. WIF76, 27.30c.**
This volume shows how knowledge of simple geometric principles led Muslim craftsmen to produce intricate and beautiful patterns and provided a measuring system needed in other art forms. These patterns are illustrated by over 150 of the author's original drawings and by photographs of their architectural application.

ESIN, EMEL. **MECCA THE BLESSED, MADINAH THE RADIANT. 113 illustrations, over half in full color, notes, index, 8"x11", 222pp. Ele63, 29.95c.**
For thirteen centuries, the cities of Mecca and Medina have been closed to non-Muslims; this work contains the first comprehensive description and photographic documentation of them to appear in the West. The author and the photographer are both Turkish Muslims who were given special permission by the Saudi authorities to travel in the area and take photographs. Ms. Esin is an expert on Islamic art. Her text for this volume embraces all historical and cultural aspects of the holy cities, from the legends of prehistory up to the present day.

ETTINGHAUSEN, RICHARD. **ARAB PAINTING. 12.50p.**
See the Sacred Art section.

■ FARAH, CAESAR. **ISLAM. Glossary, notes, bibliography, index, 306pp. BES68, 2.95p.**
This is a well written textbook type analysis of Islam as a religion as well as a system and ideology. It traces the history and growth of Islam, the role of Muhammad as prophet and man, the significance of the **Qur'an**, the fundamentals of Islamic beliefs and observances, the dynamism and resiliency of the religion, and its status in the world today. Quotations from the sacred literature are interspersed throughout the text.

FARUQI, BURHAN. **THE MUJJADDID'S CONCEPTION OF TAWHID. Introduction, index, 146pp. MuA43, 3.75c.**
A careful, detailed study of the conception of *tawhid*, or the unity of Being and of all Beings, in the thought of Shaikh Ahmad Sirhindi (who is generally called the Mujjaddid-i Alf-i-Thani). Shaikh Ahmad was the first and greatest among the mystics of Islam who expressly and strenuously opposed the pantheistic concept of *tawhid*, an idea which was almost universal among Muslim mystics. Dr. Faruqi has been careful to define all the terms used and he provides extensive textual annotation.

■ FARZAN, MASSUD. **THE TALE OF THE REED PIPE. 104pp. Dut74, 1.95p.**
Professor Farzan has taught at universities in the U.S. and here he provides a guide to the main concepts of Sufism. Part I, *What is Sufism, Who is a Sufi*, includes a short general introduction and a selection from the writings of Al-Ghazali, Attar, Shams-e Tabrizi, Rumi, and Sa'di. Part II, *The Practice of Sufism*, includes selections from some of the Sufi masters discussing the following topics: *Repentance, Dreams, Zikr, Jami on the Practice of Sufism, Ghazali on the Practice of Sufism, Sufi Dance and Music*, and *Psychic Phenomena*. Part III, *Treasure in the Ruins*, presents some traditional teaching stories. Part IV, *Sufism East and West*, is a translation of Muhammad Iqbal's writings on the *Idea of Individuation*. A very simple overview of some of the main Sufi ideas and writings.

■ FEILD, RESHAD. **THE LAST BARRIER: A JOURNEY THROUGH THE WORLD OF SUFI TEACHING. Illustrations, 183pp. H&R76/Tur, 3.95p.**
This is an enjoyable, novelistic retelling of the author's quest for enlightenment. Reshad meets a dervish in England and follows him to Turkey where he undergoes an often grueling apprenticeship. The story of his time in Turkey is reminiscent at times of Castaneda's interactions with Don Juan, and Reshad is very much the foil. Toward the end of his journey Reshad meets a master and learns what it really means to immerse himself in God. The reader is caught up in the plot and in the process learns a great deal about Sufi practice.

■ FRIEDLANDER, IRA. **THE WHIRLING DERVISHES. Glossary, bibliography, 8¼"x11", 160pp. McM75/Wdw, 15.00c/4.95p.**
This photographic study is a good introduction to the practice of Sufism. It is an account of the Sufi order known as the Mevlevis (or whirling dervishes) and its founder, the poet and mystic Mevlana Jalalu'ddin Rumi. The author is an American Sufi who is also a writer and an excellent book designer, and this photographic study reflects well on both of those abilities. It begins with a general study of the Sufi, goes on to an account of the life and spiritual development of Rumi, and ends with a detailed presentation of the whirling dervish ceremony and its background. The photographs are evocative of the ceremony's atmosphere and captions explain each one.

FRYE, RICHARD. **THE GOLDEN AGE OF PERSIA. Maps, glossary, notes, bibliography, index, 303pp. Wdf75, 33.60c.**
In the middle of the seventh century the ancient Persian civilization was conquered by the Arabs. In this book, Professor Frye presents a brilliant account of the mutually enriching fusion of the ancient traditions of Iran and the culture of Islam, especially during the seventh to tenth centuries. A leading world specialist on Iran, the author definitively explains how the Arabs and Islam changed the entire Iranian cultural world and how Islam in turn was transformed by the cultures of the East. He takes into account the latest research on the period, and makes use of original sources in all languages relevant to the subject.

GEERTZ, CLIFFORD. **ISLAM OBSERVED. Notes, bibliography, index, 144pp. UCh68, 2.45p.**
In four brief chapters I have attempted both to lay out a general framework for the comparative analysis of religion and to apply it to a study of the development of a supposedly single creed, Islam, in two quite contrasting civilizations, the Indonesian and the Moroccan.—from the preface. In Morocco, the Islamic conception of life came to mean activism, moralism, and intense individuality, while in Indonesia the same concept emphasized aestheticism, inwardness, and the radical dissolution of personality.

al-Ghazali

Al-Ghazali (1058-1111) was born in Persia and wrote in both Persian and Arabic. He studied under the greatest theologian of his age, al-Juwayni, and at thirty-three was appointed professor at the university in the capital—one of the most distinguished positions in the academic world of his day. A few years later he underwent an internal crisis and came to feel that his way of life was too worldly to have any hope of eternal reward. He left Baghdad and took up the life of a wandering ascetic. Though later he returned to the task of teaching, the change that occurred in him at this crisis was permanent. He was now a religious man, not just a worldly teacher of religious sciences.

Al-Ghazali has sometimes been acclaimed in both East and West as the greatest Muslim after Muhammad, and he is by no means unworthy of that dignity. His greatness rests above all on two things: (1) He was the leader in Islam's supreme encounter with Greek philosophy—that encounter from which Islamic theology emerged victorious and enriched, and in which Arabic Neoplatonism received a blow from which it did not recover. (2) He brought orthodoxy and mysticism into closer contact; the orthodox theologians still went their own way, and so did the mystics, but the theologians became more ready to accept the mystics as respectable, while the mystics were more careful to remain within the bounds of orthodoxy.—W. Montgomery Watt.

ALI, SYED, tr. **SOME MORAL AND RELIGIOUS TEACHINGS OF AL-GHAZALI. Index, 182pp. MuA44, 2.00p.**
This small work includes a good study of Ghazali's life and work along with a topically divided list of his writings. The bulk of the book presents extracts from **Ihya 'Ulum al-Din (The Revival of Religious Sciences),** one of his most important philosophical treatises. The volume ends with some extracts from **Minhaj-ul-Abidin,** said to be Ghazali's final work.

AVERROES. **THE INCOHERENCE OF THE INCOHERENCE. Introduction, notes, indices, 629pp. Luz54, 25.60c/set.**
A translation from the Arabic of **Tahafut al-Tahafut** by Simon Van Den Bergh. The two volume set is a refutation of al-Ghazali's major attack on philosophers and philosophy. The substance of Ghazali's attack is incorporated in this volume and Averroes follows point for point the arguments Ghazali uses and tries to refute them. Averroes' systematic discussion relies heavily on the Greek philosophers.

BAGLEY, F.R.C., tr. **GHAZALI'S BOOK OF COUNSEL FOR KINGS. Notes, biographical index, 270pp. Oxf71, 20.50c.**
This is one of the masterpieces of Persian literature, though it was long known in an Arabic version made some decades after Ghazali's death. The book consists of two parts. The first sets forth the proper beliefs which a good ruler should hold, and contains a valuable Islamic creed. The second gives advice, mainly ethical but partly practical, concerning proper conduct by the good ruler, and desirable qualities in ministers, secretaries, and wives. All these counsels are exemplified in anecdotes and aphorisms, attributed to famous Muslim kings and sages and Greek philosophers. A long introduction by the translator discusses the book's background and Ghazali's place in Muslim political thought.

FARIS, NABIH AMIN, tr. **THE BOOK OF KNOWLEDGE. Introduction, notes, bibliography, index, 252pp. MuA66, 7.50c.**
A translation of the **Kitab al-Ilm,** the opening part of **The Revival of Religious Sciences.** Here Ghazali defines what constitutes true knowledge, its relation to religious faith, and the abuses of academic learning.

FARIS, NABIH AMIN, tr. **THE FOUNDATIONS OF THE ARTICLES OF FAITH. Bibliography, index, 146pp. MuA63, 4.50c.**
The **Ihya 'Ulum al-Din** is divided into four quarters. The first deals with the acts of worship, the second with the usages of life, the third with the destructive matters of life, and the fourth with the saving matters of life. Each of these four quarters comprises ten books (*kitab*). The present work is the second book in the first quarter, the **Kitab Qawa'id al-Aqa'id.** It deals with the foundations of the articles of faith and is generally considered the most important part of the first quarter.

FARIS, NABIH AMIN, tr. **THE MYSTERIES OF FASTING. 52pp. MuA68, 1.80p.**
The practice of fasting as a spiritual discipline is both ancient and widespread, found in virtually all religious traditions. Al-Ghazali, a fourteenth century poet and mystic, wrote this piece to discuss fasting from the Islamic point of view, rather than strictly from a health standpoint. Fasting *stands alone as the only act of worship which is not seen by anyone except God. It is an inward act of worship performed through sheer endurance and fortitude...it is a means of vanquishing the enemy of God, Satan, who works through the appetites and carnal lusts.*

FARIS, NABIH AMIN, tr. **THE MYSTERIES OF PURITY. Bibliography, 103pp. MuA66, 3.00p.**
A translation of Book III of the first quarter of the **Ihya.** In his preface the translator states that this volume is not one of the more profound contributions of Ghazali; however, it is an integral part of the text and it is his desire to translate the entire **Ihya.** The material in this book should be especially valuable to those interested in cleansing and purifying their physical bodies. Part of the text gives detailed instructions on making ablutions.

FIELD, CLAUD tr. **THE ALCHEMY OF HAPPINESS. 136pp. MuA64, 1.80p.**
Ghazali was a practical mystic. His aim was to make men better by leading them away from a parrot-like repetition of orthodox phrases to a real knowledge of God. The constituents of alchemy are the knowledge of the self, the knowledge of God, the knowledge of the world as it really is, and the knowledge of the next world as it really is.

FIELD, CLAUD, tr. **THE CONFESSIONS OF AL GHAZALI. 69pp. MuA nd, 1.05p.**
This is a translation of a short autobiographical work in which Ghazali reviews important events in his life and discusses many aspects of his philosophy and the ways he arrived at many of his major insights.

GARDNER, W.H.T., tr. **MISHKAT AL-ANWAR (THE NICHE FOR LIGHTS). MuA nd, 2.25p.**
A translation of an intimate statement which reveals Ghazali's inner life and esoteric thought.

HOLLAND, MUHTAR, tr. **AL GHAZALI: ON THE DUTIES OF BROTHERHOOD. 95pp. OvP76, 5.95c.**
A translation of one of Ghazali's most important examinations of ethics and personal conduct.

KAMALI, SABIH, tr. **TAHAFUT AL-FALASIFAH (INCOHERENCE OF THE PHILOSOPHERS). Notes, index, 267pp. MuA58, 7.20c.**
I decided to write this book in order to refute the ancient philosophers. It will expose the incoherence of their beliefs and the inconsistency of their metaphysical theories.... This book will set forth the doctrines of the ancient philosophers as those doctrines really are.... This book is going to demonstrate that the ancient philosophers, whose followers the atheists of our day claim to be, were really untainted with what is imputed to them. They never denied the validity of the religious laws. On the contrary, they did believe in God, and did have faith in His messengers.

QUASEM, MUHAMMAD. **THE ETHICS OF AL-GHAZALI. Notes, bibliography, index, 273pp. MAQ75, 12.30p.**
This is the most exhaustive account available of al-Ghazali's ethical thought. It is a revised version of the author's PhD dissertation and it was put together under the supervision of Professor W. Montgomery Watt. Dr. Quasem begins with an examination of the nature and

characteristics of al-Ghazali's ethical system. The rest of the book is devoted to an in depth presentation of the system in its entirety, with particular references to background concepts and underlying principles. The author draws only on those works which have been unanimously accepted as authentic—works which generally belong to the later part of al-Ghazali's life when his ethical views reached their culmination and took their final shape.

SHEHADI, FADLOU. **GHAZALI'S UNIQUE UNKNOWABLE GOD. Many notes, bibliography, index, 132pp. Bri64, 26.15c.**
Subtitled, *A Philosophical Critical Analysis of Some of the Problems Raised by Ghazali's View of God as Utterly Unique and Unknowable.* This is a very scholarly work, which quotes extensively from Ghazali's work.

SHERIF, MOHAMED AHMED. **GHAZALI'S THEORY OF VIRTUE. Extensive notes, long bibliography, index, 218pp. SNY75, 20.15c.**
A study of Ghazali's ethical thought as shown in his extensive treatment of the virtues and their relation to the ends of life and each other. This is a scholarly presentation which is exceedingly well organized.

STADE, ROBERT, tr. **NINETY-NINE NAMES OF GOD IN ISLAM. 138pp. Day70, 2.50p.**
A translation of the major portion of al-Ghazali's *Al-Maqsad Al-Asna. Among Muslims and students of Islam it is common knowledge that the beads of the Muslim rosary ("subha") are ninety-nine in number and that the individual adherent of the Islamic faith regularly uses them in his worship life. As he fingers the individual bead, he quietly and reverently repeats the ninety-nine names of God that are particularly familiar to him.*—from the introduction. In this work Ghazali discusses in detail the ninety-nine names that he regularly used.

UMARUDDIN, MUHAMMAD. **THE ETHICAL PHILOSOPHY OF AL-GHAZALI. Preface, bibliography, index, 346pp. MuA62, 9.00c.**
The term Ethics...is used by al-Ghazali...in a much wider sense than is usually done by modern ethical writers. It includes all the activities of man, religious as well as social, consequently there are many topics included in the present work which would have been omitted in a book dealing strictly with ethics. But such an omission would have presented a distorted picture of al-Ghazali's ethical theory. My aim in this work is to present the basic principles and the practical implications of al-Ghazali's ethical theory, and to reconstruct the whole system of his thought as presented in his works.... The presentation...in this book is based on al-Ghazali's original works in Arabic, particularly the **Ihya** *and the* **Mizan al-'Amal.** This is a very carefully presented, clearly written study, with ample notes.

WATT, W. MONTGOMERY, tr. **THE FAITH AND PRACTICE OF AL-GHAZALI. Index, 155pp. MuA53, 6.50c.**
The first of the books here translated, **Deliverance from Error (al-Munqidh min ad-Dalal)**, is the source for much of what we know about al-Ghazali's life. It is autobiographical, yet not exactly an autobiography. It presents us with an intellectual analysis of his spiritual growth, and also offers arguments in defense of the view that there is a form of human apprehension higher than rational apprehension, namely, that of the prophet when God reveals truths to him. The second selection is a translation of the introduction to the **Ihya**, *The Beginning of Guidance.* It deals with the *purgative way* and directs the reader to the larger work for what lies beyond that. The ideal he establishes resembles that of a monastic order with a very strict rule, and the forces of evil and superstition are prominent in his exposition. Watt supplies introductory material and notes.

WATT, W. MONTGOMERY. **MUSLIM INTELLECTUAL. Notes, bibliography, index, 223pp. EUP63, 8.50c.**
This is an excellent biographical study of al-Ghazali which looks at his life and thought as a whole within the context of the times in which he lived.

ZAYD, ABDUL-R-RAHMAN ABU, tr. **AL-GHAZALI ON DIVINE PREDICATES AND THEIR PROPERTIES. Introduction, index, 146pp. MuA70, 6.00c.**
In Islam, the question of the *divine attributes* has been treated from various perspectives. This volume presents a critical and annotated translation of the chapters of **Al-Iqtisad Fil-i'tiqad** which discuss the logical aspects of this question. It is Ghazali's major work on the subject.

——————— **END OF AL-GHAZALI SUBSECTION** ———————

GIBB, H.A.R. **MOHAMMEDANISM. Chapter-by-chapter annotated bibliography, index, 144pp. Oxf70, 3.95p.**
Dr. Gibb was Director of the Center for Middle Eastern Studies at Harvard University and the author of many books. Here he presents an historical survey of the growth and influence of Islam. The life of the prophet, the teachings of the Qur'an, the expansion of Islam in Asia and Africa, Sufism, and the problems which Islam confronts in the modern world are all reviewed. The tone is dry and academic though the presentation does not overwhelm the reader with a mass of details. This is as good a short overview as we know of.

GIBB, H.A.R. and J.H. KRAMERS, eds. **SHORTER ENCYCLOPAEDIA OF ISLAM. 7"x10½", 671pp. Bri53, 38.75c.**
An edited version of the articles contained in the first edition and supplement of the **Encyclopedia of Islam** which relates particularly to the religion and law of Islam. The majority have been reproduced without alteration. A number have been shortened or revised, and a few new articles have been added. Each of the entries is extremely complete. A definitive study. Bibliographical references follow each entry.

GILANI, HAZRAT. **FUTUH AL-GHAIB (THE REVELATIONS OF THE UNSEEN). 236pp. MuA58, 3.00p.**
Gilani was an important Sufi saint, known generally as the Saint of Baghdad. This collection of eighty of his discourses is one of the most highly regarded works in the Islamic world. His teaching is both esoteric and exoteric, directed toward aspirants on the path, and is eminently practical. This is a translation by M. Ahmad and includes introductory material and a life sketch.

GILSENAN, MICHAEL. **SAINT AND SUFI IN MODERN EGYPT. Notes, bibliography, index, 248pp. Oxf73, 20.50c.**
A detailed study of the sociology of religion focusing on the Sufi Orders of contemporary Egypt as the author observed them during two years in Cairo. He examines and attempts to explain the transformation of the Orders in Egypt since the turn of the century. The bulk of the book is devoted to an analysis of the only modern Egyptian Order which has succeeded, in however limited a way, in expanding its membership and activities: the *Hamidiya Shadhiliya.* It differs from more traditional orders in its emphasis on comprehensive direction and control over its members.

GOHLMAN, WILLIAM, tr. **THE LIFE OF IBN SINA (AVICENNA). Many notes, long bibliography, index, 163pp. SNY74, 26.90c.**
This is the first complete Arabic text and English translation of the eleventh century philosopher's autobiography with its continuation by one of his pupils. The translation is based on recently discovered manuscripts; the Arabic text and English translation are on facing pages.

GOICHON, A.M. and M.S. KHAN. **THE PHILOSOPHY OF AVICENNA. Notes, bibliography, 129pp. MoB69, 5.10c.**
Avicenna was the first Arab to create a philosophical system which is complete and whole. He had a profound and lasting influence on both Eastern and Western philosophers. This book is an expanded version of a series of lectures the author gave, based entirely on Arabic and Persian original sources.

GOLDZIHER, IGNAZ. **MUSLIM STUDIES, VOLUME I. Index, 254pp. SNY66, 20.15c.**
This study, originally published in German at the end of the last century, is considered one of the works which laid the foundations for the study of Islam as a religion and a civilization. This volume discusses the reaction of Islam to the ideals of Arabic tribal society and the attitudes of early Islam to the various nationalities that they conquered (especially the Persians). The volume culminates in a study of the Shu'ubiyya movement which represents the reaction of the newly converted peoples, and again especially the Persians, to the idea of Arab superiority. The second volume of **Muslim Studies** is reviewed with the works on *hadith.* A good third of this volume is devoted to annotations.

GOODWIN, GODFREY. **ISLAMIC ARCHITECTURE: OTTOMAN TURKEY. 8¼"x7¾", 192pp. Scp77, 8.40p.**
A photographic study of Ottoman architecture, showing how it first appeared and tracing its development up to the baroque period. There

is an introduction as well as comments on each plate. Some of the photographs are in color.

GRABAR, OLEG. **THE FORMATION OF ISLAMIC ART. 131 plates, bibliography, index, 307pp. YUP73, 6.95p.**
A collection of seven essays related to each other through a question defined in the first essay: *if it exists at all, how was Islamic art formed?* Among the specific topics considered are the following: *The Land of Early Islam, Islamic Attitudes Toward the Arts, Islamic Religious Art, Islamic Secular Art,* and *Early Islamic Decoration and the Idea of an Arabesque.* Professor Grabar's goal is to give a nontechnical presentation and in this he has succeeded masterfully, without sacrificing the exacting scholarship for which he is known.

GRAY, BASIL. **PERSIAN PAINTING. Bibliography, indices, 9½"x11", 190pp. Riz77, 12.50p.**
Running parallel to the evolution of Christian art in the West, the art of book illumination in Iran began in the fourth century and developed uninterruptedly until the fifteenth. Miniature painting and calligraphy emerged as one of the most characteristic art forms of Islamic Persia, and they played a more important role than they did in the West. Gray discusses the historical development of Persian painting and a magnificent collection of eighty color reproductions accompanies his text. This book is part of a series created by Albert Skira.

GRUNEBAUM, G.E. VON. **MEDIEVAL ISLAM. Notes, index, 385pp. UCh53, 4.65p.**
This book has grown out of a series of public lectures....It proposes to outline the cultural orientation of the Muslim Middle Ages, with eastern Islam as the center of attention. It attempts to characterize the medieval Muslim's view of himself and his peculiarly defined universe, the fundamental intellectual and emotional attitudes that governed his works, and the mood in which he lived his life. It strives to explain the structure of his universe in terms of inherited, borrowed, and original elements, the institutional framework within which it functioned, and its place in relation to the contemporary Christian world.

GRUNEBAUM, G.E. VON. **MUHAMMADAN FESTIVALS. Bibliography, notes, 112pp. Cur76, 7.90c.**
A systematic study of the religious festivals of the Islamic world which focuses on the essential and typical elements of Islamic ritual.

▨ GUILLAUME, ALFRED. **ISLAM. Glossary, bibliography, index, 210pp. Vik54, 2.25p.**
An excellent survey of the Islamic world. Professor Guillaume deals in turn with Muhammad; the Qur'an; the evolution of Islam as a system of faith, law, religion, and philosophy; the varying schools of thought and the intense devotional life that has grown up within them; and the changes taking place in the contemporary Islamic world.

Hadith

The *hadith* consists of the sayings and practices of the prophet and his immediate companions. Its contents not only complement the Qur'an and explain the vague passages therein, but also provide guidance on matters on which the Qur'an is silent; thus the *hadith* has become the second source of law in Islam. The *hadith* is also a source of information on the development of Islamic thought and contains most of the basic ideas which later Muslim scholars drew upon with regards to the conduct of daily life as well as social, political, and cultural institutions.

ABDUL, M.O.A. **THE PROPHET OF ISLAM. 120pp. IPB72, 2.90p.**
The bulk of this text is devoted to a survey of the basic and most important traditions relating to law and theology which are known as *hadith.* Abdul includes a discussion of the origin, transmission, contents, and arrangement of *hadith,* information on the classification of *hadith* collections, and a presentation of the **Forty Traditions of Al-Nawawi,** including Arabic text, transliteration, and translation. There is also a short biography of the prophet.

ABDUL, M.O.A., *tr.* **THE SELECTED TRADITIONS OF AL-NAWAWI. 90pp. IPB73, 3.20p.**
The selections presented here consist of traditions from almost all the

important, recognized, Sunnite collections of *hadith* and cover a variety of topics relating to every possible aspect of Muslim life—religious, social, cultural. An introductory chapter reviews the development of *hadith* literature and subsequent chapters contain the Arabic text, transliteration, translation, and commentary on each of the forty selections. Abdul has attempted, through his commentaries, to make *hadith* relevant to contemporary life.

ALI, MAULANA MUHAMMAD. **A MANUAL OF HADITH. Notes, 420pp. Cur78, 14.00c.**
An excellent thematic manual. Each chapter is preceded by appropriate verses from the **Qur'an** and includes a long note summarizing the teachings of the **Qur'an** and *hadith* on the subject. The Arabic text and English translations are in parallel columns.

DOI, A. RAHMAN. **INTRODUCTION TO THE HADITH. Index, 155pp. IPB71, 4.25p.**
A topical discussion of the major laws promulgated in the *hadith.* Each selection is first presented in the Arabic script, followed by a transliteration and translation, and ending with a short commentary.

FRIEDLANDER, SHEMS. **SUBMISSION—SAYINGS OF THE PROPHET MUHAMMAD. 8"x9¼", 144pp. H&R77, 5.95p.**
A beautifully produced collection of *hadith,* with parallel English and Arabic texts and numerous, evocative photographs. Each of the ninety-nine names of Allah is reproduced in calligraphic form.

GOLDZIHER, IGNAZ. **MUSLIM STUDIES, VOLUME II. Extensive notes, index, 378pp. SNY71, 30.90c.**
A recent translation of Goldziher's famous study on the development of the *hadith,* in which he shows that the *hadith* reflects the various trends of early Islam, and describes its collection and the subsequent literature devoted to it. An additional essay discusses the cult of saints, which though contrary to the spirit and the letter of the earliest Islam, played an important part in its subsequent development.

IBRAHIM, EZZEDIN and DENYS JOHNSON-DAVIES, trs. **AN-NAWA-WI'S FORTY HADITH. Introduction, 127pp. DAK77, 7.00c.**
An-Nawawi lived in Syria in the thirteenth century. His brief compilation of *hadith* is generally regarded as the most popular anthology. This volume contains the original Arabic text on facing pages with the translation. The translation reads well and is a work of excellent scholarship. The book is well produced.

IMAM 'ABD AR-RAHIM IBN AHMAD AL-QADI. **ISLAMIC BOOK OF THE DEAD. 165pp. Diw77, 6.00p.**
The main portion of this book is a translation of **The Fire and the Garden** by Imam 'Abd ar-Rahim ibn Ahmad al-Qadi, a collection of *hadith.* There also are a few short essays on death, a brief instruction in death related practices, and an excerpt from **The Miracles of the Way** from the **Diwan** of Shaykh Muhammad ibn al-Habib.

KARIM, FAZLUL, *tr.* **AL-HADIS. Extensive introductory material, notes, 2,960pp. TBH nd, 50.00c/set.**
An English translation in four volumes, with commentary, of **Mishkat-ul-Masabih,** arranged into thematic chapters. In many cases the Arabic text is included in a parallel column. Related sayings from many classical writers are integrated into the text.

KHAN, MUHAMMAD Z., *tr.* **GARDENS OF THE RIGHTEOUS. Notes, index, 352pp. Cur75, 14.00c.**
A fine translation of a concise collection of *hadith.*

ROBSON, JAMES, *tr.* **MISHKAT AL-MASABIH. Introduction, glossary, notes, bibliography, indices, 1,473pp. MuA75, 31.25c/set.**
This two volume set is based on the most authentic and reliable *hadith* literature and shows the prophet's attitude towards various aspects of religious and social life. Virtually every imaginable topic is authoritatively presented and the discussion is in depth. This is an extremely important book for all who are seriously interested in the Islamic way of life as taught by the prophet.

SIDDIQI, ABDUL, *tr.* **SAHIH MUSLIM. Introduction, index, 1,638pp. MuA75, 55.00c/set.**
This is a mammoth four volume translation of one of the most authentic and exhaustive collections of the traditions of the prophet, narrated by his companions and originally compiled under the title

Al-Jami'-Us'Sahih by Imam Muslim. This edition also includes extensive commentary and many notes based on original sources along with brief biographical sketches of major *hadith* narrators. A welcome addition to the literature and a must for all serious Islamic scholars and practitioners.

─────── **END OF HADITH SUBSECTION** ───────

Hafiz

Hafiz' spiritual greatness and mental power proceeded from that mystical consciousness which in him attained perfection. That path of life of which Sana'i, Attar, Rumi, and Sa'di had spoken each in turn and in his own way, was by Hafiz described in language that plumbs the depths of feeling and soars to the heights of expression.... So deeply immersed was he in the mystical unity, that in every ode and lyric, whatever its formal subject, he included one or more verses expressive of this lofty theme.... His true mastery is in the lyric (*ghazal*). In Hafiz' hands the mystical lyric on the one hand reached the summit of eloquence and beauty, and on the other manifested a simplicity all its own.... In short words he stated ideas mighty and subtle.... It is evident that the master's lyrics come straight from the heart; each poem is a subtle expression of the poet's innermost thoughts.

—*A.J. Arberry*

ARBERRY, A.J., *ed.* **HAFIZ: FIFTY POEMS. Index, 187pp. CUP53, 21.00c.**
Here Arberry presents poetical translations of Hafiz' poems done by fourteen different people. This has the double object of exhibiting the various aspects of Hafiz' style and thought, and of showing how various English scholars have translated his poetry. Professor Arberry also supplies a long introduction and biographical and critical notes on the texts. The poems are presented in full in the original Persian script and then the translations follow. The translations are considered among the finest available and while not as many poems are here as in Clarke's monumental work, they are generally much more readable.

ARYANPUR, ABBAS, *tr.* **POETICAL HOROSCOPE OR ODES OF HAFIZ. 6¾"x9¾", EPI65, 14.70c.**
This is a recent Iranian translation of the **Odes** which includes a biographical sketch, a glossary, and the English translation on facing pages with the Persian script. The translations are often quite literal and are certainly not the best we have read. Each is followed by a short interpretative paragraph. The tone seems more racy than mystical and the color illustrations interspersed throughout add to this impression.

CLARKE, WILBERFORCE, *tr.* **THE DIVAN-I-HAFIZ. 1,011pp. Oct1891, 56.75c/set.**
This remains the only complete prose translation of Hafiz' masterwork. Lt. Clarke's style is often stilted and the translation is not the finest work of scholarship. Nonetheless, it is certainly adequate. Many notes on Sufism and critical and explanatory remarks are included. A beautifully bound, limited edition.

NAKOSTEEN, MEDHI, *tr.* **THE GHAZALIYYAT OF HAAFEZ. Notes, bibliography, 390pp. EEP73, 17.50c.**
An excellent poetic translation, with Nakosteen's beautiful calligraphy of the Persian text on facing pages. This volume contains the following additional features: a long introduction on the life and work of Hafiz and his place in Persian literature; a discussion of the structure, contents, and origin of the *ghazal* (sonnet); and notes on the sources. The edition is limited to 300 copies.

─────── **END OF HAFIZ SUBSECTION** ───────

HALL, MANLY P. **THE MYSTICS OF ISLAM. 107pp. PRS75, 3.50p.**
This is an excellent review of the Islamic mystical tradition. Hall begins with a discussion of the mystical visions and insights of Muhammad and in the process gives us an informative summary of the main features of the prophet's life and experiences—including a discussion of the Qur'an. The next sections cover the rise of Islam, the Caliphs, religious philosophy, and the foundations of Islamic mysticism.

HAQ, M. ANWARUL. **THE FAITH MOVEMENT OF MAWLANA MUHAMMAD ILYAS. Notes, bibliography, index, 210pp. A&U72, 18.50c.**
The Faith Movement originated in a small area south of Delhi, India, in 1927 and has now spread across the world It claims to be one of the largest religious movements in the history of Islam. Ilyas' simple goal was to teach Muslims true Islam: to revive the Islamic way of life prescribed by God and practiced by the prophet and his companions. He emphasized practice and personal involvement. Since he was a Sufi, he based his movement on Sufi teaching and ceremonies, though he made certain changes. He kept his movement free from political influences, and it is a tribute to him that Muslims of different political views could work together. This book presents a detailed study of the life, work, and thought of Ilyas.

HAWI, SAMI. **ISLAMIC NATURALISM AND MYSTICISM. Extensive notes, bibliography, index, 295pp. Bri74, 29.50c.**
A detailed philosophical study of Ibn Tufayl's **Hayy Bin Yaqzan** divided into the following sections: *Philosophical and Literary Background and the Methodical Structure of the Treatise; Naturalism, The Beginning of All Philosophizing;* and *The Existence of God and His Attributes and The Nature and Unity of the Phenomenal World.*

HIRASHIMA, HUSSEIN. **THE ROAD TO HOLY MECCA. 130pp. Kod72, 3.50p.**
A beautiful little travel guide, filled with color plates.

HISKETT, MERVYN. **THE SWORD OF TRUTH: THE LIFE AND TIMES OF SHEHU USUMAN DAN FODIO. Illustrations, notes, index, 216pp. Oxf73, 4.00p.**
In the late eighteenth and early nineteenth centuries an Islamic revolutionary movement arose in Hausaland (now part of northern Nigeria) that was to have profound influence on the subsequent history of the area. At its center was a Muslim divine and literary figure named Shehu Usuman dan Fodio. The success of the holy war to which the movement gave rise led directly to the establishment of the Fulani theocratic state in Hausaland, and has had continuing influence on the society's way of life. Using native sources in both Arabic and Hausa, Dr. Hiskett presents the shehu's life and times as they appeared

to eyewitnesses and participants. He emphasizes the effect of the shehu's Islamic upbringing, his intellectual set and world view, and his ideological motivation.

HITTI, PHILIP. **THE ARABS. Index, 274pp. GEd70/MGB, 4.95p.**
This short history is condensed from the author's definitive larger study, and the material has been revised thoroughly for this edition. The emphasis is on social and cultural history rather than political. This book is an excellent introduction to the Arab world.

HITTI, PHILIP. **ISLAM, A WAY OF LIFE. Maps, bibliography, index, 198pp. GEd70, 2.95p.**
An excellent overview of Islam divided into sections on Islam the religion, the state, and the culture. Professor Hitti knows his material well and expresses his understanding clearly. All major features of Islamic civilization are discussed. It is basically an academic work, geared toward the general reader, and the presentation is somewhat dry.

HOAG, JOHN. **ISLAMIC ARCHITECTURE. 513 illustrations, including 192 diagrams, plans, and reconstructions, glossary, index, 10"x11¼", 424pp. Abr77, 37.50c.**
An impressive examination of the variety and vast sphere of influence of Islamic architecture. Professor Hoag focuses on the two major facets of the architecture: the congregational mosque with its lofty minaret and the sumptuous caliphal palace with inner courtyards, fountains, and gardens.

HODGSON, MARSHALL. **THE VENTURE OF ISLAM, VOLUME I: THE CLASSICAL AGE OF ISLAM. Glossary, bibliography, index, 544pp. UCh74, 7.95p.**
This volume analyzes the world before Islam, Muhammad's challenge (570-624), and the early Muslim state of 625-692. Professor Hodgson then reviews the classical civilization of the High Caliphate, discussing such topics as the bloom of Arabic literary culture, Muslim personal piety, and the dissolution of the absolute tradition. There is also a section on the Islamic vision in religion. This is a very detailed, scholarly study, which reads like a textbook (which, in a way it is, since it grew out of the course that Hodgson taught for many years at the University of Chicago).

HODGSON, MARSHALL. **THE VENTURE OF ISLAM, VOLUME II: THE EXPANSION OF ISLAM IN THE MIDDLE PERIODS. Maps, glossary, notes, bibliography, index, 615pp. UCh74, 7.95p.**
A detailed investigation of the period from the mid-tenth century to the beginning of the sixteenth, a time when an international Islamic civilization was being established.

HODGSON, MARSHALL. **THE VENTURE OF ISLAM, VOLUME III: THE GUNPOWDER EMPIRES AND MODERN TIMES. Maps, glossary, notes, bibliography, index, 471pp. UCh74, 7.95p.**
A description of the second flowering of Islam: the establishment of the Safavi, Timuri, and Ottoman empires.

HOLT, P.M., ANN LAMBTON and *BERNARD LEWIS, eds.* **THE CAMBRIDGE HISTORY OF ISLAM. Notes, bibliography, index, 1,894pp. CUP70, 39.50p/set.**
This four volume set is the most comprehensive and ambitious collaborative survey of Islamic history and civilization yet to appear in English.

HOURANI, GEORGE, tr. **AVERROES: ON THE HARMONY OF RELIGION AND PHILOSOPHY. Introduction, notes, index, 128pp. Luz61, 6.65p.**
Translation of an important work in which Averroes sets out to show that the scriptural law of Islam does not altogether prohibit the study of philosophy by Muslims, but, on the contrary, makes it a duty for those people gifted with the capacity for scientific reasoning.

HUGHES, THOMAS. **A DICTIONARY OF ISLAM. 750pp. TBH1885, 26.00c.**
A systematic exposition of the doctrines of the Muslim faith in the form of a concise and comprehensive account of the doctrines, rites, ceremonies and customs, together with the technical and theological terms, of the Islamic religion. Also includes biographical sketches of some of the most noted figures, many illustrations and appropriate quotations from the **Qur'an.**

HUSSAIN, AHMED. **THE PHILOSOPHY OF FAQIRS. 70pp. MuA40, 1.80p.**
A discussion of the two schools of *tasawwuf*: the Monistics, who identify God with nature; and the Positivistics, who differentiate God from nature.

HUTT, ANTHONY. **ISLAMIC ARCHITECTURE: NORTH AFRICA. 8¼"x7¾", 192pp. Scp77, 8.40p.**
This book traces the development of Islamic architecture in North Africa from its simple beginnings in the eighth century to the splendors of the fourteenth and the age of the Barbary Corsairs. An introductory text plus 136 plates, some in color and each one annotated, are included.

HUTT, ANTHONY and *LEONARD HARROW.* **ISLAMIC ARCHITECTURE: IRAN I. Introduction, 8¼"x7¾", 192pp. Scp77, 8.40p.**
An analysis of the origins of Islamic architecture in Iran. The editors have selected 136 plates (some in color) to illustrate the various techniques and ideas which led to the glories of seventeenth century Iranian architecture.

Muhammad Iqbal

Iqbal (1877-1938) was an Indian poet and philosopher, best known for his influential efforts to establish a separate Muslim state, eventually realized in the nation of Pakistan. Today he is acclaimed as the symbolic father of Pakistan. He wrote eleven volumes of poetry as well as scores of essays and letters and urged upon his followers spiritual regeneration based on the love of man and God. His approach toward Islam was unorthodox.

ARBERRY, A.J., tr. **COMPLAINT AND ANSWER OF IQBAL. 79pp. MuA55, 1.20p.**
Verse translations of the **Shikwa** and the **Jawab-i-Shikwa**. These are among the most popular of Iqbal's poems and were the first to bring him fame. The central theme of both is the decay of Islam from its former greatness, and the measures to be adopted if it was to regain its authority and vitality.

ARBERRY, A.J., tr. **JAVIA-NAMA. Introduction, extensive notes, bibliography, 151pp. A&U66, 3.95c.**
This is an excellent translation of Iqbal's greatest work, the **Javid-nama**. In imitation of the prophet of Islam, the poet soars through the spheres, encountering on his heavenly journey many great figures of history with whom he holds converse.

ARBERRY, A.J., ed. **NOTES ON IQBAL'S ASRAR-I KHUDI (THE SECRETS OF THE SELF). Introduction, 57pp. MuA52, .90p.**
These are notes by Iqbal himself which were not included in the revised edition of the **Asrar-i-Khudi** and which Professor Arberry feels throw light upon important aspects of the work.

ARBERRY, A.J., tr. **PERSIAN PSALMS. Introduction, 135pp. MuA48, 3.00c.**
A translation of Iqbal's **Zabur-i-Ajam**, which was written in the Persian *ghazal* or lyric. Iqbal did an excellent job of making this ancient form express his philosophy with the simple language for which he is noted.

ASHRAF, MUHAMMAD. **THUS CONFERRED SATAN. Glossary, notes, bibliography, index, 360pp. TBH74, 8.50c.**
An interpretation of Iqbal's message; with its many peculiar features, this work attempts at an interpretation of the message of the great poet-philosopher from a fresh realistic angle, containing an illuminating introduction as also a sufficiently annotated translation of Iqbal's most instructive Urdu poem.—from the title page.

HUSSAIN, M. HADI, tr. **THE NEW ROSE GARDEN OF MYSTERY AND THE BOOK OF SLAVES. Introduction, 182pp. MuA69, 1.95p.**
The New Rose Garden (Gulshan-i-Raz-i-Jadid) was composed by Iqbal in response to Shabistari's **The Secret Garden**. The latter was written in reply to a series of fifteen questions on mystical philosophy propounded by an inquirer. Iqbal's poem has nine questions, covering the same material. This is a verse translation which reads quite well. A

second selection, **Bandagi Namah,** is translated in blank verse. It describes the arts, music, and religion of slave nations and the architecture of free nations.

IQBAL, ALLAMA. **THE RECONSTRUCTION OF RELIGIOUS THOUGHT IN ISLAM.** Index, 207pp. MuA75, 2.25c.
This is a transcription of a series of lectures which Iqbal gave on the title theme. In his *reconstruction* the great philosopher took both the philosophical traditions of Islam and the more recent developments in human knowledge into consideration.

MALIK, HAFEEZ, ed. **IQBAL: POET-PHILOSOPHER OF PAKISTAN.** Notes, bibliography, index, 466pp. Col71, 19.70c.
This is the definitive study of Iqbal, divided into sections on his political thought, philosophy, attitude toward Islamic mysticism, and poetry. There is also a lengthy biography. Each of the pieces has been written by an authority and many quotations from Iqbal's writings are included.

NICHOLSON, REYNOLD, tr. **THE SECRETS OF THE SELF.** 179pp. MuA40, 2.25c.
A translation of **Asrar-i-Khudi,** a philosophical poem exploring the doctrine of unity. This edition was revised by Nicholson in the light of corrections suggested by Iqbal himself. The translator also supplies ample introductory material and notes.

————— **END OF MUHAMMAD IQBAL SUBSECTION** —————

Islamic Literature

Strictly speaking there is no such thing as Islamic literature. There is Arab literature, Persian literature, Urdu literature, and Turkish literature. Since the dominant faith in all these countries is Islam it seemed sensible to us to group them all together in this one section. The literature of these various countries represents an amalgam of national and cultural traditions. Most of the books listed here are important classical works—although some are more recent and others come out of the folklore tradition. In a number of cases we list a number of books by one author (such as Attar or Rumi) and so we have categorized all his books together in a separate section.

AHMED, ALI. **THE GOLDEN TRADITION.** Index, 286pp. Col73, 5.50p.
An anthology of Urdu poetry from the fourteenth to the beginning of the twentieth century. The introduction contains a comparative study of Urdu and English poets and poetic movements; a discussion of the techniques and characteristics of Urdu poetry, its particular forms and schools; and a survey of the literary and philosophical background of the eighteenth and nineteenth centuries. There is also a short sketch of each poet.

ARBERRY, A.J. **ARABIC POETRY: A PRIMER FOR STUDENTS.** Biographical and textual notes, 174pp. CUP65, 7.95p.
Professor Arberry begins with a long introduction on the development, nature, forms, and rhythms of Arabic poetry. The main body of the book is an anthology of Arabic poems in the original, ranging from the sixth century to the present day, and giving examples of the work of thirty of the greatest Arab poets. Each poem has a literal English translation on the facing page.

ARBERRY, A.J. **ASPECTS OF ISLAMIC CIVILIZATION.** 409pp. UMP64, 2.95p.
This selection of translated passages from the most highly regarded works of Islamic literature illustrates the development of Islamic civilization from its origins in the seventh century to the present. The anthology is made up of selections from Arabic and Persian writers such as Hafiz, Sa'di, Rumi, Omar Khayyam, Ibn al-Farid, Avicenna, and Ibn Hazm—and from such works as the **Qur'an** and the **Masnavi.** This is a very good collection.

ARBERRY, A.J., ed. **FITZGERALD'S SALAMAN AND ABSAL.** 213pp. CUP56, 11.95c.
The poem, by Jami, tells with much digression and courtliness of Salaman (born to Solomon without the aid of a woman and meant to live the same way) and Absal, his nurse, who fell in love and eloped with him to a desert isle. Solomon discovered them and subjected them to a trial by fire in which Absal was consumed. This edition includes introductory material and three translations: a literal one by Arberry and two different ones by Fitzgerald.

ARBERRY, A.J., tr. **THE MYSTICAL POEMS OF IBN AL-FARID.** 7½"x10", 130pp. HFC56, 15.00p.
Translation of major poems accompanied by notes summarizing the contents of each poem and elucidating the form and meaning of the individual verses. Ibn al-Farid was a twelfth century Arabic poet who wrote some of the finest mystical poetry ever produced. This volume does not include **Nazm al-suluk.**

ARBERRY, A.J., tr. **THE POEM OF THE WAY. Introduction, notes, bibliography,** 7½"x10", 88pp. HFC52, 12.00p.
A translation of Ibn al-Farid's **Nazm al-suluk,** a poem whose theme is *the mystic's quest for and realization of his identity with the spirit of Muhammad, and thereby the absorption of his individual personality into the Unity of God.*

ARBERRY, A.J., ed. **POEMS OF AL-MUTANABBI. Many notes,** 155pp. CUP67, 18.30c.
Al-Mutanabbi (AD 915-965), though universally considered among the greatest of the Arab poets, has seldom been translated or discussed outside Arab countries. This study uses the same format as Arberry's **Arabic Poetry** and is intended to supplement that text. The introduction discusses al-Mutanabbi's life, style, influence, and critics. There follows a selection from his poems, in the original Arabic, with a literal English translation on the facing page.

■ *ARBERRY, A.J., tr.* **THE RUBAIYAT OF OMAR KHAYYAM AND OTHER PERSIAN POEMS.** 223pp. Dut54, 2.65p.
An anthology of verse translations from the classical period. Includes passages by Rumi, Sana'i, Hafiz, and from the **Shah-nama** and the **Rubaiyat.**

ARYANPUR, MANOOCHEHR. **A HISTORY OF PERSIAN LITERATURE. Extensive bibliography, index,** 347pp. Kay73, 8.85p.
The author has tried to give a general survey of Persian literature, complemented, on the one hand, with brief sketches of relevant Persian history and, on the other, with longer sections in which the work of major writers is examined. Considerations of space have made it necessary to bridge many areas and to omit many names. A detailed history of Persian literature . . . demands several volumes and more than a single man's lifetime. All translations used in this book are by the author unless otherwise stated. As far as footnotes are concerned, the policy has been to reduce them to a minimum and give them, whenever practical, within the text itself. Despite the author's disclaimers, he has done an excellent job in this volume. The major figures and minor ones are surveyed at some length and the quotations from the literature are abundant.

BAIN, R. NISBET, tr. **TURKISH FAIRY TALES.** 2.50p.
See the Fairy Tales section.

BODROGLIGETI, A.J.E. **HALIS'S STORY OF IBRAHIM.** 100pp. Bri 75, 20.60p.
The Story of Ibrahim *is a literary-artistic exposition of the belief, widely held by the Sufis, that the believer's attention must be turned entirely to Allah, that it cannot be divided or shared with "anything but Allah". . . . The Lord, displeased by what he regards as Mohammed's excessive love for his son Ibrahim, requests the Prophet to sacrifice his son if he wishes to retain the guardianship of his Community and the concomitant right to intercede for it on the Day of Resurrection. Mohammed . . . does not hesitate to carry out Allah's request, and yet, like everyman, he finds it difficult to sacrifice the pleasures of this life—here represented by Ibrahim—for the higher*

spiritual pleasures associated with the Divine Being. This is a religious legend which minstrels recited. The edition includes a large photographic reproduction of the original late Chagatay Turkic script, transliteration, English translation, introduction, glossary, and notes.

BROCKETT, ELEANOR. **TURKISH FAIRY TALES.** 5.95c.
See the Fairy Tales section.

BROWNE, EDWARD G. **A LITERARY HISTORY OF PERSIA. CUP 06,** 36.00c/each.
This is the definitive study. Volume I covers the period from the earliest times until Firdawsi; Volume II from Firdawsi to Sa'di; and Volume III the Tartar Dominion (1265-1502). Quotations are included throughout as are notes. There is also an excellent bibliography and an index. Each volume is about 550 pages long.

CHELKOWSKI, PETER. **MIRROR OF THE INVISIBLE WORLD: TALES FROM THE KHAMSEH OF NIZAMI.** 8½"x12", 127pp. **MMA75,** 15.00c.
This is the finest version available of the exquisite Persian miniature paintings which were produced to illustrate Nizami's romantic stories. In this edition Chelkowski has written an English adaptation of each of the tales as well as an introduction to and commentary on each story. Each of the miniatures is reproduced in color and gold and a number of details from each is also reproduced in the same manner. The stories themselves are delightful and it is easy to understand why they have been a favored theme of Persian artists.

DANNER, VICTOR, tr. **IBN 'ATA'ILLAH'S SUFI APHORISMS.** 102pp. **Bri73,** 18.30c.
This is a translation of **Kitab al-Hikam.** *The main theme of the* **Hikam** *is...Gnosis....In other words, instead of being a purely objective exposition of Oneness of Being, that doctrine is here deliberately "aimed" at the reader so that he may experience it as a continual knocking on the doors of his intelligence. Bound up with this is the theme of "adab" which...may be translated "pious courtesy." Gnosis is not merely an act of the intelligence; it demands a total participation; and "adab" in its highest sense is the conformity of the soul, in all its different facets, to the Divine Presence....We have here, in this little volume, one of the great basic texts of Islamic mysticism.*—Martin Lings. Danner also provides a study of the life and work of Ibn 'Ata'illah, background and introductory material, glossary, extensive notes, and a bibliography.

DAVIS, F. HADLAND, tr. **THE PERSIAN MYSTICS—JAMI.** 103pp. **MuA46,** 1.50p.
Nurrudin Abdur Rahman Jami (1414-1492) was a great Persian mystical poet. This volume includes a short biographical sketch followed by abridged translations and selected passages from his most noted works: **The Story of Salaman and Absal**, **The Teaching of the Lawaih**, **The Story of Yusuf and Zulaikha**, and **The Baharistan** or **Abode of Spring**.

FARZAN, MASSUD. **ANOTHER WAY OF LAUGHTER. Dut73,** 2.35p.
A collection of over 100 examples of Sufi humor in the form of short tales, written by such masters as Rumi, Attar, Sa'di, and Jami. The translator and editor is a native Persian now teaching Persian culture at Columbia University.

FATEMI, NASROLLAH, FARAMARSZ, and FARIBORZ. **SUFISM.** Notes, index, 243pp. **ASB76,** 16.10c.
A collection of essays on Sufi thought and on the writings of al-Ghazali, Rumi, Sa'di, Hafiz, Nizami Ganjai, and Omar Khayyam. Each of the pieces is clearly written and does a good job of summing up the topic. A good introduction to some of the greatest Sufi poets, with quotations from their works.

FUZULI. **LEYLA AND MEJNUN.** 350pp. **A&U70,** 8.25c.
In the Islamic world the love story of Leyla and Mejnun is as famous as Romeo and Juliet in the English speaking world. This edition is part of the UNESCO series. It provides a thorough introduction to the Leyla and Mejnun theme and the various forms in which the story has appeared by one of the leading authorities on the poem, Professor Alessio Bombaci, and an extremely readable translation by Madame Sofi Huri.

GIBB, H.A.R. **ARABIC LITERATURE: AN INTRODUCTION. Notes, bibliography, index,** 192pp. **Oxf63,** 3.35p.
This is a revised edition of Professor Gibb's acclaimed survey. It is written for both the general reader and the specialist and covers the period from 500 to 1800. Gibb was Professor of Arabic at Oxford and Director of the Center for Middle Eastern Studies at Harvard.

GIBRAN, KAHLIL. **THE PROPHET.** 96pp. **RaH23,** 5.00c.
Islam might seem to be a strange category for this Christian mystic. However, Gibran wrote in Arabic and came out of a tradition similar to many Sufis. And **The Prophet** seems to fit as well here as anywhere else. (That's the advantage of having an author index—we can put things where we feel they fit best, and those who do not agree can still find their favorite works.) **The Prophet** is Gibran's masterpiece and it has sold over four million copies in the U.S. alone. It is mystical poetry at its finest and if you have not read it, we recommend that you do. You cannot help but be moved by the majesty and beauty of the language and the imagery. Twelve mystical drawings by Gibran illustrate the text. **The Prophet** is available in both a regular size and pocket size edition. A deluxe, boxed version is also available for $10.00.

KRITZECK, JAMES, ed. **ANTHOLOGY OF ISLAMIC LITERATURE.** Bibliography, 379pp. **NAL64,** 4.95p.
As the title suggests, this is a comprehensive anthology of Islamic literature from the rise of Islam to the nineteenth century. The selections cover both prose and poetry and the translations are interspersed with commentary and introduced by biographical information. The arrangement of the material is chronological. On the whole the quality of translation seems to be good, although this varies with individual selections. The translations date from both the nineteenth and twentieth centuries.

KURTI, ALFRED, tr. **PERSIAN FOLKTALES.** 5.95c.
See the Fairy Tales section.

LEDERER, FLORENCE. **THE SECRET ROSE GARDEN OF SA'ID-UD-DIN (MAHMUD SHABISTARI).** 74pp. **MuA69,** 3.60c.
A poetic translation of this classic Persian work. The translation does not flow; the language sounds archaic.

LEVY, REUBEN. **AN INTRODUCTION TO PERSIAN LITERATURE.** Index, 194pp. **Col69,** 13.45c.
Levy begins with the historical setting, discussing the various geographical, political, and religious forces that influenced the development of Persian literature. He goes on to examine the main trends of that literature from ancient times to the present, illustrating his comments with his own translations of many of its forms. Appendices contain biographical and bibliographical information.

LICHTENSTADTER, ILSE. **INTRODUCTION TO CLASSICAL ARABIC LITERATURE.** Notes, index, 416pp. **ScB76,** 6.50p.
The first section consists of a long introductory survey of the history of Arabic literature from pre-Islamic times through its high period in the Middle Ages. Both religious and secular literature are discussed. The rest is devoted to a representative selection of the literature itself, beginning with some pre-Islamic poetry and including, among many other things, a portion of Ishaq's **Life of Muhammad** (the definitive early study), philosophical writings of Ghazali, and much else.

MORIER, JAMES. **THE ADVENTURES OF HAJJI BABA OF ISPAHAN.** Illustrations, 404pp. **Har nd,** 5.95p.
A collection of picturesque rogue tales written by an early nineteenth century British diplomat who spent much of his life in Persia and the Middle East. The tales form a continuous narrative and present a wonderful picture of life in those times. The book gained immediate popularity and has remained continually in print.

MORRIS, LAWRENCE and RUSTAM SARFEH, trs. **MUNAJAT.** 109pp. **KMM75,** 5.00c.
A translation of the intimate prayers of Khwajih 'Abd Allah Ansari, an eleventh century poet, mystic, and commentator on the **Qur'an.** These prayers are considered to be among the masterpieces of Persian mystical literature. *The original meaning of the word Munajat was simply a private conversation. In time this came to include the idea of inward speech with God, which in turn grew into that of silent and fervent prayer. Certainly in this work...we are dealing with prayer of the most fervent and wholehearted kind. Yet the original*

idea of a single conversation still lingers. For, in what appear to be separate prayers, Ansari is actually exploring...every aspect of his relationship to God.—from the introduction. The Persian text of each prayer is on a facing page.

MORRISON, GEORGE, tr. **VIS AND RAMIN. Introduction, notes, 366pp. Col72, 16.80c.**
This Persian poem was composed in the eleventh century AD by Fakhr ud-Din Gurgani. It is a romantic epic and one of the earliest of its kind in Persian literature. The story bears a resemblance to the legend of Tristan and Isolde, following the adventures of a pair of lovers who go against countless odds to be together. This is a prose translation.

NAIMY, MIKHAIL. **THE BOOK OF MIRDAD: A LIGHTHOUSE AND A HAVEN. 185pp. Wat48, 8.20p.**
A skillful blend of legend, mysticism, philosophy, and poetry. Addressing himself to the age-old esoteric question of *the whence, whither, and wherefore of Man,* Naimy seeks and finds answers in man himself. Through a beautifully written narrative, Mirdad leads his everyman from the consciousness of the divided self to the superconsciousness of the undivided self. *Spread out,* says Mirdad to his disciples, *until there are no regions where you are not. Spread out until the whole world be wherever you may chance to be. Spread out until you meet God wherever you meet yourselves. Spread out. Spread out.*

NAIMY, MIKHAIL. **A NEW YEAR. 103pp. Bri74, 8.35p.**
A collection of stories, autobiographical notes, and poems selected from Naimy's finest work.

NAKOSTEEN, MEHDI, tr. **RETURN TIES OF EXISTENCE OF HATEF OF ISFAHAN. 7¼"x10¼", EEP76, 25.00c.**
Sayid Ahmad Hatef (eighteenth century) was among the last classical Sufi poets of Iran. His strophe poem translated here (**The Tarji'band**) is a pantheistic interpretation of existence. The edition is limited to two hundred copies, numbered, autographed, and beautifully bound.

NAKOSTEEN, MEHDI, tr. **THE RUBIYYAT OF BABA TAHIR ORYAN OF HAMADAN. 54pp. EEP67, 12.50c.**
Oryan, an eleventh century Persian poet, was considered one of the most noted mystics of his time. This volume includes introductory and comparative material, and Persian calligraphy of the text.

NAKOSTEEN, MEHDI, tr. **A TALE OF CATS AND MICE. EEP nd, 12.50c.**
A free and interpretative translation of the fourteenth century Persian satirist Obeyd of Zaakan, beautifully illustrated and including the Persian text and introductory material. Limited edition.

NICHOLSON, REYNOLD. **A LITERARY HISTORY OF THE ARABS. Bibliography, index, 537pp. CUP07, 12.95p.**
The Arabs during a thousand years or more produced one of the richest and most extensive literatures of the world, embracing fine poetry on subjects as diverse as the fierce desert life and the sophistication of the royal court; *belles lettres* (learned essays and satires); religious, mystical and philosophical writings; and a huge compendia of history, biography, and geography. For over sixty years, the best account in English of this vast output has been Nicholson's **Literary History**, and it is likely that its supremacy will long unremain unchallenged.

PELLAT, CHARLES, ed. **THE LIFE AND WORKS OF JAHIZ. Glossary, 286pp. UCa69, 12.75c.**
Al-Jahiz, who lived in the eighth and ninth centuries, was one of the most famous and prolific of Arab prose writers. He is known for his works of *adab* and his religious and political polemics as well as his literary works of social satire. *For the majority of literate Arabs al-Jahiz remains, if not a complete buffoon, at least something of a jester...for he never fails, even in his weightiest passages, to slip in anecdotes, witty observations and amusing comments....He deliberately aimed at a lighter touch, and his sense of humour enabled him to deal entertainingly with serious subjects.* In this book Professor Pellat, indisputably the greatest Jahiz authority, has selected the best as well as the most characteristic of Jahiz' writings, prefacing them with an assessment of his life and works.

SANA'I, HAKIM. **THE ENCLOSED GARDEN OF THE TRUTH. 300pp. Wei08, 12.50c.**
Sana'i (1118-1152) was an important Persian writer and mystic. The core of this work is an interpretation of the Sufi philosophy regarding prayer and the adoration of God. This edition is edited and translated by Major J. Stephenson and is considered the best one available. A copy of the original Persian text is appended. This is an important work for all who are interested in Sufism.

SANA'I, HAKIM. **THE WALLED GARDEN OF TRUTH. 74pp. Oct74, 2.95p.**
This is an abridged translation by David Pendlebury, a student of Idries Shah, which gives a feeling of the original. It is based on the study of Stephenson's translation and is designed to appeal to modern readers.

SHAH, AMINA. **FOLK TALES OF CENTRAL ASIA. 148pp. Oct70, 6.00c.**
Stories from the oral tradition collected by the author (the sister of Idries Shah) in her travels. Delightful tales.

SHAH, AMINA. **TALE OF THE FOUR DERVISHES OF AMIR KHUSRU. 144pp. Oct76, 13.50c.**
This is a retelling of an allegory which was originally told to the great thirteenth century Sufi teacher Nizamuddin Awliyya by his disciple, a Persian poet, when he was ill. On his recovery Nizamuddin placed a benediction on the book, and it is widely believed that the recitation of this tale will restore health to the ailing.

SHAH, SIRDAR IKBAL ALI. **ORIENTAL LITERATURE. 7.20p.**
See the Comparative Religion section.

STOREY, C.A. **PERSIAN LITERATURE, VOLUME I, PART I: QUR'-ANIC LITERATURE; HISTORY. Notes, 820pp. Luz70, 21.00c.**
A detailed, technical bibliographical study, covering all the major works and individual figures.

——— **END OF ISLAMIC LITERATURE SUBSECTION** ———

ISLAMIC LITURGY: SONG AND DANCE AT A MEETING OF DERVISHES (A RECORDING). 7.98.
This 33 1/3 rpm record includes verses from the **Qur'an**, prayers, and praise to Muhammad. There are no instruments and the songs often sound like prayer chants. Descriptive notes give translations and transliterations of songs and a brief description of the accompanying dances and movements. This album is only recommended to those seriously interested in Sufi ceremonies.

JALBANI, G.N. **TEACHINGS OF SHAH WALIYULLA OF DELHI. Notes, bibliography, index, 259pp. MuA73, 4.25c.**
The shah was an eighteenth century Indian reformer who was versed in both the esoteric and exoteric sciences. His slogan was *back to the* **Qur'an**, and he felt that he had been selected to deal with a scientific age where people were not disposed to accept everything at face value. He did not follow any of the established schools and subjected the findings of all the schools to a thorough investigation based on the **Qur'an** and the *hadith*—what conforms to them both, he accepts, the rest he rejects outright.

KAMAL, AHMAD. **THE SACRED JOURNEY, BEING PILGRIMAGE TO MAKKAH. 216pp. A&U61, 12.60c.**
The volume includes the laws pertaining to Pilgrimage, and whenever the author approaches a facet or aspect of the Pilgrimage he provides an insight into the origin and the rituals. In brief, within these pages, you will find the complete ceremony of Pilgrimage, its laws and observances, and implicit therein, an appeal to Muslims to unite and thrust out of bondage, with a warning against discord and its perils. Both the Arabic text and translation are included.

KAMM, ANTONY. **THE STORY OF ISLAM. 6"x9". Din76, 1.75p.**
This is a colorful, pictorial presentation of the main features of Islamic civilization and history. The accompanying text is simply written and the book is basically for children, although it would be an adequate brief introduction for anyone.

KARIM, FAZLUL. **THE RELIGION OF MAN. 384pp. TBH39, 6.50c.**
The essence of this tract is that Islam is the religion and way of life ideally suited to the needs of modern man. Karim quotes from a variety of sources to prove his thesis. The bulk of the book is thematically arranged.

KEDDIE, NIKKI, ed. **SCHOLARS, SAINTS, AND SUFIS—MUSLIM RELIGIOUS INSTITUTIONS SINCE 1500. Many notes, index, 401pp. UCa72, 20.00c.**
A collection of sixteen scholarly papers dealing with the social role of religious institutions in the Muslim world, this volume attempts to provide a view of these institutions as functional groups playing an important role in Muslim society and politics.

Ibn Khaldun

Ibn Khaldun was a fourteenth century Arab historian who founded a special science to deal with the problems of history and culture based on the philosophies of Plato and Aristotle and their Muslim followers. He is known as one of the fathers of modern social science and cultural history.

MAHDI, MUHSIN. **IBN KHALDUN'S PHILOSOPHY OF HISTORY. Many notes, bibliography, index, 325pp. UCh57, 4.25p.**
This is a detailed investigation of Khaldun in the light of what he himself wrote and taught and in its relations to modern social science. A very scholarly account.

ROSENTHAL, FRANZ, tr. **THE MUQADDIMAH. 479pp. PUP67, 5.95p.**
Edited and abridged by N.J. Dawood, this version makes Khaldun's essential ideas more accessible to the general reader.

ROSENTHAL, FRANZ, tr. **THE MUQADDIMAH: AN INTRODUCTION TO HISTORY. Long introduction, notes, bibliography, index, 1,698pp. PUP67, 67.20c/set.**
This is the earliest critical study of history in the Muslim world, and one of the earliest extant anywhere, written by Ibn Khaldun in 1377 as the preface to a book of world history. It has since become known as a self contained work, treating in almost encyclopedic detail the general problems of the philosophy of history and relating the information to the Islamic tradition. This is the first English translation. Three volumes, boxed.

-----------------END OF IBN KHALDUN SUBSECTION-----------------

KHAN, ALI MAHDI. **THE ELEMENTS OF ISLAMIC PHILOSOPHY. Index, 147pp. MuA47, 2.35p.**
A discussion of Islamic philosophy and philosophers based on original texts and including a survey of the development of Sufism.

KHAN, EBRAHIM, ed. **ANECDOTES FROM ISLAM. Glossary, bibliography, 479pp. MuA60, 9.00c.**
A selection of short teaching stories culled from a great variety of sources (the editors claim that over five hundred are represented) from all parts of the Islamic world and from its major leaders.

Hazrat Inayat Khan

Inayat Khan was born in 1882 in Baroda, in a family who had been well-known musicians for several generations. When he was twenty he began travelling all over India, giving concerts, lectures and private lessons.

When he came to Hyderabad his aptitude to follow the spiritual path was recognized and he lived there from 1903 till 1907 as a disciple of his Sufi master. His sense of the brotherhood of men was deepened and connected to his religious foundations, for as a mystic he was able to understand the truth that all originates in one source. When his master died, Inayat travelled as a pilgrim throughout India, Ceylon and Burma, at the same time giving concerts, which met with an increasing measure of success. But his master had enjoined him not only to work to bring all Indians together, but also to unite people of East and West.

In 1910 he travelled to America with his brothers, musicians like himself. He gave concerts and lectures in America, France and Russia and met the prominent artists of the time. Between 1914 and 1920 he was in London, founding the universal Sufi Movement to make known *the idea of unity which is at the root of everything.*

He expressed this truth in such a way that people from a Western background notwithstanding all outward differences could take the steps to understand his message. He had to give up his music, but his Movement grew.

From 1920 till 1926 he travelled in Europe and America, followed by an increasing number of disciples. He founded Sufi centres in twelve countries, meeting fame and admiration, but also misunderstanding and resistance. Towards the end of 1926 Inayat Khan returned to India and he died the following year in Delhi.

—*Elisabeth de Jong-Keesing*

JONG-KEESING, ELISABETH DE. **INAYAT ANSWERS. 258pp. EWP77, 9.50c.**
Ms. de Jong-Keesing describes her approach in this book as follows: *I should cite Inayat's answers to questions, and these questions I could arrange systematically, thus sketching an outline of his philosophy and aims, at the same time showing as much of his personality and the way he spoke as the written word can convey.* This volume is fully indexed and contains a chronological survey of Inayat Khan's work.

JONG-KEESING, ELISABETH DE. **INAYAT KHAN. Glossary, notes, 302pp. EWP74, 7.95c.**
This is the most complete biographical study of Inayat Khan available. Ms. de Jong-Keesing worked closely with surviving members of his family and with his associates in the Sufi movement. The material is well written and covers Inayat Khan's entire life, with the greatest emphasis being given to his mystical experiences.

KHAN, HAZRAT INAYAT. **THE BOOK OF HEALTH. 106pp. SPC74, 3.95p.**
A collection of teachings on the spiritual aspects of healing, originally intended only for Inayat Khan's students. Khan discusses the following topics: the basic laws governing the mind's influence over the body; the psychological nature of disease; the development and application of healing power; and methods of healing.

KHAN, HAZRAT INAYAT. **THE COMPLETE SAYINGS OF HAZRAT INAYAT KHAN. Index, 299pp. SOP78, 5.25p.**
As Pir Vilayat says in his introduction, *the sayings and aphorisms . . . represent a crystallization of flashes of thought arising from the depths of Hazrat Inayat Khan's consciousness busy meeting the day to day problems of his pupils. Therefore they cut right into life while giving verbal expression to the way things look in the perspective of a realized being, or what he would call the Divine Consciousness, because that is what happens when one has outstretched the personal outlook.* These sayings originally appeared in three books: **Gayan, Vadan, Nirtan; Aphorisms;** and **The Bowl of Saki.**

KAHN, HAZRAT INAYAT. **EDUCATION. 127pp. SPC75, 3.95p.**
The volume includes a wealth of knowledge and insight into the upbringing of infants and children, leading to a greater understanding of the young soul on its journey to maturity.

KHAN, HAZRAT INAYAT. **MUSIC. 101pp. EWP62, 3.95p.**
Touches on the themes of music as related to life, to man, to the

universe and to creation. Topics include: *Music of the Spheres, The Mystery of Sound and Colour, The Psychic Influence of Music,* and *The Aid of Music in Spiritual Development.*

KHAN, HAZRAT INAYAT. **THE MYSTICISM OF SOUND. 2.50p.**
See the Music section.

KHAN, HAZRAT INAYAT. **THE PALACE OF MIRRORS. 65pp. SPC35, 2.95p.**
A collection of short essays dealing *with the "mirroring" faculty, a specific quality of mind, which often passes unobserved under the "rust" of the usual, emotional and logical, processes. It is only recently that this faculty has come to be recognized on a wider scale under different technical terms, such as synchronicity, gestalt, nonsequential thinking or self-remembering.*—from the introduction.

KHAN, HAZRAT INAYAT. **THE SOUL WHENCE AND WHITHER. Index, 190pp. SOP77, 4.95p.**
This volume contains Inayat Khan's teaching on the inner laws of manifestation. He reveals life to be a far vaster journey than merely that between our physical birth and death, and unveils a whole new dimension of reality. The material in this book was prepared from lectures given in 1923.

STAM, K.D. **RAYS. Glossary, 148pp. EWP27, 6.95c.**
This book has been written by one of the close collaborators of the great Sufi master, Pir-o-Murshid Hazrat Inayat Khan.... In these memories the accent is not so much on the historical sequence of events, but rather on the atmosphere of the great teacher and how he spoke and behaved in various life-circumstances. The book was written shortly after the death of Murshid Inayat Khan and not a word has been changed.... The book radiates reverence and should be read as a book of meditation.—from the foreword.

STOLK, SIRKAR VAN. **MEMORIES OF A SUFI SAGE: HAZRAT INAYAT KHAN. 205pp. EWP67, 4.95p.**
The purpose of the present work was simply to share with the reader some part, some breath, of the fragrance of Hazrat Inayat Khan's teachings, so that those who felt drawn to them might be moved to gather the real flowers from his own books.

——— **END OF HAZRAT INAYAT KHAN SUBSECTION** ———

KHAN, KHAN, tr. **THE SECRET OF ANA'L HAQQ. Glossary, notes, 199pp. MuA35, 4.50c.**
A topically arranged translation of **Shadat-i-Shaykh Ibrahim**, the teachings of a tenth century Muslim saint which expound the secret doctrine of *how God is manifest in man*, in the form of short, detached sayings. These sayings are commentaries on the esoteric teachings of some verses of the **Qur'an**.

KHAN, MUSHARAFF. **PAGES IN THE LIFE OF A SUFI. 155pp. SPC32, 6.30c.**
The author recounts his youth in India and tells of his experiences with maharajas and wandering dervishes. He also speaks of the relationship between master and disciple, spiritual healing, his travel experiences with Inayat Khan, and the practices of Sufis, Hindus, and Muslims. An entertaining, often illuminating account.

KHAN, PIR VILAYAT. **TOWARD THE ONE. 400pp. H&R74, 10.00p.**
Pir Vilayat's *magnum opus,* an enlightening presentation of Sufi practices, teachings, and transcripts of his lectures in Europe and America, as well as some completely new material. Filled with drawings, designs, and photographs, and printed on oatmeal paper. Includes a 24"x36" poster folded into the book to reproduce the chapter entitled, *Heart.*

KHATIBI, ABDELKEBIR and MOHAMMED SIJELMASSI. **THE SPLENDOUR OF ISLAMIC CALLIGRAPHY. 174 illustrations, fifty-four in color, notes, 9¾"x12¼", 254pp. Riz76/T&H, 45.00c.**
This is a splendid book indeed! Calligraphy, the art which combines visual image and written word, achieves its most brilliant expression in the work of the Islamic peoples. Islamic calligraphy takes its inspiration from a belief in the divine origin of Arabic writing, the medium through which the Quranic revelation was transcribed by followers of the prophet. Thus the calligrapher's purpose is spiritual as well as aesthetic. In this book the authors assemble the most exquisite examples of calligraphic scripts and show the interdependence of script and page decoration. The photographs show whole pages, single sentences, and even details of certain letters.

KHATTAK, MUSTAFA, ed. **ISLAM, THE HOLY PROPHET, AND THE NON-MUSLIM WORLD. 197pp. TBH76, 8.00c.**
An anthology of writings by Western authors on various aspects of Islam. Khattak has made a wide selection and he includes pieces from the eighteenth century through the twentieth.

Omar Khayyam

Khayyam, best known as the author of the **Rubaiyat,** was an eleventh century mathematician. The *rubaiyat* is a traditional Persian verse form of poems built of quatrains. Omar's **Rubaiyat** is a collection of poems, each written on a particular occasion and constituting a complete poem in itself. The poems exalt sensual pleasure as the sole aim of life, thereby departing from the prevailing mystical tradition. The **Rubaiyat** was introduced to the West through Edward Fitzgerald's Victorian translation.

ARBERRY, A.J. **THE ROMANCE OF THE RUBAIYAT. 239pp. A&U59, 6.85c.**
A facsimile reprint of Edward Fitzgerald's first edition with notes by Arberry on its origin and step-by-step evolution as well as an extensive introduction.

BOWEN, JOHN, tr. **A NEW SELECTION FROM THE RUBAIYAT OF OMAR KHAYYAM. Notes, 175pp. A&P76, 7.95c.**
Bowen here translates into prose and verse sixty out of over 1,000 quatrains attributed to Omar Khayyam. Fitzgerald's version is on facing pages for comparison. In his introduction, Bowen discusses the problems that face a modern translator of Khayyam. We much prefer Bowen's translations to Fitzgerald's. Each quatrain is illustrated.

DASHTI, ALI. **IN SEARCH OF OMAR KHAYYAM. Glossary, bibliography, index, 276pp. Col71/A&U, 17.95c.**
This is a biographical study of Omar Khayyam by a noted Persian scholar, translated into English by L.P. Elwell-Sutton. A major problem facing anyone seeking to study this twelfth century poet is

that there is no conclusive evidence to prove which of the many quatrains attributed to Khayyam are authentic. Ali Dashti therefore constructs a picture of the poet from references found in the works of writers of his day or immediately after, and from Khayyam's own works on philosophy, mathematics, and astronomy—of which the authenticity is not questioned. Using this portrait as a touchstone, Dashti draws up a list of some hundred quatrains which are in keeping with Khayyam's character and translates them for this volume. A final section studies Khayyam's religious and philosophical beliefs.

FITZGERALD, EDWARD, tr. **RUBAIYAT OF OMAR KHAYYAM.** **110pp. Dou1859, 1.95p.**
Fitzgerald, writing in 1859, has supplied an adaptation rather than a strict translation. It is the most popular version available. This edition includes biographical and critical introductions.

NAKOSTEEN, MEHDI, tr. **THE RUBAIYYAT OF OMAR KHAYYAM.** **258pp. EEP73, 16.50c.**
A new translation in quatrain form by a noted Iranian scholar. This is a lovely, flowing translation and it includes Nakosteen's calligraphy of the original Persian facing each page, extensive notes, and an excellent bibliography. Collectors' edition, limited to 300 copies.

————— END OF OMAR KHAYYAM SUBSECTION —————

KHUSHAIM, ALI. **ZARRUQ THE SUFI. Notes, bibliography, 218pp. GCP76, 12.00c.**
Zarruq was a jurist who lived during the second half of the fifteenth century; he also was the founder of a Sufi order and is best known as one of the orthodox Sufi masters whose main concern was alleviating the misunderstanding which had occurred in Islamic thought between jusrisprudence and Sufism. This book surveys Zarruq's activities and his influence as a Sufi.

KLEIN, F.A. **THE RELIGION OF ISLAM. Notes, 241pp. Cur06, 9.35c.**
A topically arranged study-discussion of the major doctrines of Islam. Each of the topics is explored at some length and more are discussed here than in any other book we know. The exposition is often hard to follow and Islamic terms are interspersed throughout. It seems that more space is devoted to notes than to the text itself. Includes such things as contracts, marriage, debt, prayer, hell, and much else.

LANDAU, ROM. **MOROCCO. Chronology, bibliography, index, 8¾"x11¼", 160pp. Ele67, 19.95c.**
A beautifully produced study of Morocco's three main cities— Marrakesh, Fez, and Rabat—illustrated with over 100 photographs by Wim Swaan, many in color. Both the text and photographs concentrate on the surviving architectural monuments.

LANE-POOLE, STANLEY. **STUDIES IN MOSQUE. Notes, 288pp. TBH1883, 8.00c.**
A collection of essays written in an antiquated style: *The Arabs before Islam, Mohammad, Islam, The Koran, The Brotherhood of Purity, The Persian Miracle Play,* and *Sabians and Christians of St. John.* Lane-Poole was a respected nineteenth century Islamic scholar.

LEACROFT, HELEN and RICHARD. **THE BUILDINGS OF EARLY ISLAM. 8"x10", index, 40pp. Hod76, 6.40c.**
A simply written study, designed for older children. All aspects of the buildings are discussed and the book is illustrated with many fine line drawings and a number of color plates.

LEFORT, RAFAEL. **THE TEACHERS OF GURDJIEFF. 2.45p.**
See the Gurdjieff section.

LEWIS, BERNARD, ed. **ISLAM. Glossary, bibliography, index, 644pp. H&R74, 8.00p/each.**
This two volume set traces the history of Islam in the Middle Ages from its inception in the time of the prophet Muhammad to the capture of Constantinople in 1453. Translations from Arabic, Persian, and Turkish sources—many previously unavailable in English—trace the broad philosophical and geographical perimeters of the Islamic world. Volume I analyzes the political structure of the Islamic world and the expansion of that world through war. Theoretical and descriptive material augments the narration. Volume II focuses on the religious, cultural, and social life of the medieval Muslim world. The selections

are topically organized and each section is preceded by brief comments by the editor. The volumes themselves are well edited.

■ *LEWIS, BERNARD, ed.* **ISLAM AND THE ARAB WORLD. 9¾"x12", 360pp. RaH76/T&H, 15.98c.**
A beautifully produced exploration of Islamic culture which contains nearly 500 illustrations—photographs, paintings, illuminated manuscripts, tapestries, and maps—almost half of them in full color. Thirteen eminent specialists discuss in turn the origins and history of the Islamic faith, the achievements of Islamic artists, architects, and poets, Islamic history, and the great Islamic nations. The British title is **World of Islam.**

LEWIS, SAMUEL. **THE JERUSALEM TRILOGY. 6½"x9½", 335pp. PrP75, 5.95p.**
Three long poems which Murshid Sam considered his most important literary effort. The volume is subtitled, *Songs of the Prophets,* and this is just what the poems are. They are entitled **The Day of the Lord, What Christ? What Peace?,** and **Saladin.** An introduction and an extensive glossary accompany each poem and there are many illustrations throughout.

LINGS, MARTIN, tr. **A SUFI SAINT OF THE 20TH CENTURY: SHAIKH AHMAD AL-'ALAWI, HIS SPIRITUAL HERITAGE AND LEGACY. 242pp. UCa61/A&U, 2.95p.**
The author allows the Sufis to speak for themselves, and, in a series of unusual texts mainly translated from the Arabic, provides a vivid picture of life in a North African Sufi order. Against this background stands the Algerian shaikh who headed the order until his death in 1934. The final chapters reproduce selections from his writings.

■ *LINGS, MARTIN.* **WHAT IS SUFISM? Notes, index, 133pp. UCa75/ A&U, 2.45p.**
This is the best introduction to Sufism that we know. Lings has written extensively on the subject and he presents his exploration in a clear, thorough, authoritative manner. He begins with a general discussion of the originality and universality of Sufism and goes from there to a study of *The Book* (the **Qur'an**) and *The Messenger* (Muhammad). Other chapters consider *The Heart, The Doctrine,* and *The Method,* and a final one traces *Sufism through the Ages.*

MCNEILL, WILLIAM and MARILYN WALDMAN, eds. **THE ISLAMIC WORLD. 485pp. Oxf73, 5.30p.**
A sourcebook of political, historical, religious, and literary readings from AD 600 to the present day. The material is chronologically arranged and each historical epoch is introduced. Comments and notes for each section are also included. The readings are well selected and give a good total picture of Islamic culture through the ages.

MANSUR AL-HALLAJ. **THE TAWASIN. 81pp. Diw74, 3.95p.**
This is the first volume in a new series of translations of classical Sufi texts. This volume is a translation of one of the greatest texts on *tawhid* (the *unity of reality*) and a contemporary text by a renowned Sufi from Fez, Morocco. Also included is the **Commentary on the Song Purification** by Sidi Fudul al-Hawari as-Sufi. The various *ta-sins* translated are arranged by subject and are in the form of short paragraphs. The teaching is very clear if the reader is familiar with Islamic terminology and philosophical ideas. The book is beautifully produced.

MARTIN, B.G. **MUSLIM BROTHERHOOD IN 19TH CENTURY AFRICA. Notes, bibliography, index, 278pp. CUP76, 25.15c.**
The Muslim brotherhoods were first formed in the twelfth century; by the eighteenth century their importance began to decline due to the steady growth of European influence in Africa. The nineteenth century saw a religious revival under the aegis of the Muslim brotherhoods. Professor Martin considers the social and political aspects of this revival. He focuses on eight Sufi brotherhoods and their leaders. These brotherhoods run the gamut from militancy through social reformers to those who totally resisted change. This is an excellent scholarly study.

MAY, KARL. **IN THE DESERT. 411pp. Sea77, 10.95c.**
In the Desert is one of a series of novels in which May explores the Islamic world of the late nineteenth century. A German scholar and his friend are traveling in the North African desert when they come across the body of a murdered Frenchman. In trying to solve the mystery of

this murder and while pursuing the guilty parties, they uncover an international network of criminals which spans the entire Ottoman empire. The dramatic action takes the reader through many countries and offers an excellent introduction to Islamic culture, customs, and religious beliefs. May's interest as a storyteller was always in the symbolic meaning of time and place, and he was almost obsessed with the cradleland of the three great monotheistic religions.

Meher Baba

Meher Baba (his name means *Father of Compassion*) was born in India in 1894. Between the years of 1913 and 1921 the five Perfect Masters (Sadgurus) of that time led him to realize his identity and universal mission as the Avatar of the age. After working intensively with an intimate group of disciples for some years, Baba began to observe silence in 1925, and throughout the remaining four decades of his spiritual activities he never uttered another word. From his work in India and the East with the mad, infirm, and poor and with spiritually advanced souls to his contact with thousands of people in the West, Meher Baba has awakened innumerable persons to the quest for higher consciousness and their own ultimate reality. Declaring that his work had been completed 100 percent to his satisfaction and that the results of that work would soon begin to manifest, Meher Baba dropped his body on January 31, 1969.

ADRIEL, JEAN. **AVATAR. MBI47, 2.95p.**
This colorful biography, written by one of Baba's early Western disciples, gives the reader a vivid acquaintance with Meher Baba the man. Besides telling Baba's life story, the author relates his personal experience with him. It includes Baba's visit to Hollywood and his encounters with all manner of seekers, both famous and ordinary.

ANZAR, NAOSHERWAN. **THE BELOVED. 8"x10¼", glossary, 153pp. Shr74, 10.00c.**
This is a pictorial, biographical study of Meher Baba. The narrative is clear, readable, and interspersed with anecdotes. Meher Baba is seen in his childhood; in his first contact with his spiritual masters; during his much publicized visits to the West; on his travels by foot throughout India; in the periods of deep seclusion; and in his close contact with people of all classes and religions throughout the world. The text was put together by a disciple and reflects the love that his disciples feel for him.

BARKER, ELSA. **SONGS OF A VAGROM ANGEL. 55pp. SRe68, 2.75c.**
Spiritual poems by a disciple of Baba.

BRABAZON, FRANCIS. **IN DUST I SING. 162pp. MBI74, 2.95p.**
The poetry in this volume is based on material that Baba gave to Brabazon, his close disciple. The form is based on the Persian *ghazal*. The content is *the relationship between the Lover and the Beloved—a relationship that is never wholly fulfilled until the loved ceases to exist in himself and passes away in the Beloved.*

BRABAZON, FRANCIS. **JOURNEY WITH GOD. 35pp. Shr71, 1.25p.**
A collection of love poems written to Baba by the author, selections from Baba's discourses in India, and a note on the *God-Man.*

■ COHEN, ALLEN, *ed.* **THE MASTERY OF CONSCIOUSNESS. Notes, 222pp. H&R77, 3.95p.**
This volume focuses on methods of spiritual development as explained by Meher Baba. We can think of no better single work for those who seek an understanding of Meher Baba's practical techniques. The information is topically organized and the bulk of the material consists of quotations from Meher Baba's own writings. A final section discusses reactions to Meher Baba and the Meher Baba movement—again using many of the master's own words. There is also a glossary and the finest annotated bibliography on Meher Baba we have seen.

DESHMUKH, C.D., *ed.* **SPARKS OF THE TRUTH FROM THE DISSERTATIONS OF MEHER BABA. 95pp. Shr66, 1.75p.**
Twenty dissertations, including practical hints and guidance to aspirants, expositions of eternal truths concerning the nature of the soul and the meaning of life, and some hitherto unknown sayings of Baba.

DONKIN, WILLIAM. **THE WAYFARERS: MEHER BABA WITH THE GOD-INTOXICATED. 512pp. SRe48, 10.95c.**
This is a meticulous account of Meher Baba's work between 1922 and 1946 with the *God intoxicated*—spiritually advanced souls who, overcome by the power of their inner vision, drown in the ecstasy of the experience.

DUCE, IVY. **HOW A MASTER WORKS. Glossary, bibliography, 778pp. DMd75, 17.95c.**
Murshida Duce is the present leader of the organization founded by Baba. In this book she presents answers to questions of interest to all spiritual seekers—such as Who am I? What am I doing here? How do I grow spiritually? She also discusses authentic spiritual practice and integrating the mystical with the practical. The bulk of the book is an illustration of Baba's work with his disciples—both in India and the West. A long supplementary section contains excerpts from Meher Baba's writings which illustrate the principles with which she is concerned. A wide range of topics has been selected—from the dynamics of reincarnation to the poetry of divine love; from a spiritual perspective on the occult to the specifics of everyday spiritual practice.

DUCE, IVY, *ed.* **SUFISM. 58pp. SRe nd, 1.00p.**
Four essays on various aspects of Sufism as seen by Meher Baba and his disciples.

DUCE, IVY. **WHAT AM I DOING HERE? 112pp. SRe66, 1.20p.**
Murshida Duce draws here on the teachings of Meher Baba in her discussion of a variety of topics including the planes of existence, the bodies, reincarnation and karma, the spirit world, and the Avatar.

FREDERICK, FILIS, *ed.* **THE LIFE DIVINE. Photograph index, 79pp. Awa71, 2.00p.**
This is a special photographic issue of **The Awakener**, a journal devoted to Meher Baba. Selected short essays accompany the pictures which show Baba in every imaginable (for him anyway!) situation.

HOPKINSON, TOM and DOROTHY. **MUCH SILENCE. Bibliography, 191pp. DMd75/Mll, 7.95c.**
The Hopkinsons knew Meher Baba personally and have been his disciples for many years. This is the most complete biographical study of him. It is straightforward and is directed toward general readers who are curious about Baba but do not want to wade through some of the more detailed volumes of his teachings. The authors include a summary of the teaching.

MEHER BABA. **THE ADVANCING STREAM OF LIFE. 200pp. MBI69, 2.00p.**
A comprehensive sampling of excerpts and discourses from Baba's published works, including some which are currently out of print. The material covers a vast range of spiritual subjects.

MEHER BABA. **BEAMS FROM MEHER BABA ON THE SPIRITUAL PANORAMA. 116pp. SRe58, 2.00c.**
A collection of questions, answered by Baba, arising from ideas in **God Speaks**. The simplified responses in this volume illuminate some of the more difficult concepts in the latter work.

MEHER BABA. **DARSHAN HOURS. 72pp. Beg71, 1.95p.**
A record of conversations which took place between Meher Baba and disciples who visited him in India in 1960. Baba, as was his custom, conducted his *conversations* through the use of gesture-language, which was translated by his closest disciples.

■ MEHER BABA. **DISCOURSES. Three volumes, 546pp. SRe67, 5.95p/set.**
A major work, dictated on Baba's alphabet board. They *are the practical guide for the aspirant as he slowly finds his way back to Oneness.* This is the standard edition of **Discourses**. The editing of each discourse was carefully examined and approved by Meher Baba. Every aspect of

Baba's teaching is contained herein, and the collection is arranged topically. **Discourses** and **God Speaks** are his major philosophical statements.

MEHER BABA. **THE EVERYTHING AND NOTHING. 115pp. MBI63, 1.95p.**
These are in many ways the most vital and profound of all Baba's discourses. Certainly they are the most poetic. With frequent flashes of humor, Baba highlights the essence of spirituality through rich parables, anecdotes, and vibrant images.

MEHER BABA. **THE FACE OF GOD. 14pp. Shr71, 1.25p.**
A small volume which has quotations from Baba faced with drawings of him.

MEHER BABA. **GOD SPEAKS—THE THEME OF CREATION AND ITS PURPOSE. Glossary, notes, 334pp. DMd73, 15.00c.**
This is Baba's most advanced philosophical statement. It deals with the mechanics of the universe and how consciousness develops through various stages. The material is illustrated with various charts to make it more comprehensible. This is a revised edition in which certain new points and corrections indicated by Meher Baba have been made. There are also some additions to the supplement, some of the charts have received minor but necessary changes, and five more charts have been included.

MEHER BABA. **LIFE AT ITS BEST. 106pp. Dut57, 1.95p.**
A collection of messages given by Baba during his visit to the United States in 1956. The style is succinct and penetrating and touches on all aspects of Baba's teaching.

MEHER BABA. **MEHER BABA IS LOVE: MESSAGES FOR CHILDREN, 4 TO 100. 11"x8½", Shr61, 5.00p.**

MEHER BABA. **THE PATH OF LOVE. 102pp. Wei76, 3.95p.**
A compilation of Baba's teachings on a variety of topics organized under the following general headings: *God and God-Man, Aspects of the Path,* and *The Art of Discipleship.* The selections are fairly lengthy.

NATU, BAL. **GLIMPSES OF THE GOD-MAN, MEHER BABA, VOLUME I: 1943-48. Glossary, 420pp. SRe77, 6.95p.**
Bal Natu was an Indian schoolteacher who was given the privilege of being allowed to visit Baba at any time. During many of his visits, Baba asked him to take notes of Baba's meetings with devotees. In this book, Bal Natu traces the development of his relationship with Baba and gives glimpses into the master's way with his disciples. Bal also traces Baba's daily activities and contributes many anecdotes.

PURDOM, C.B., ed. **GOD TO MAN AND MAN TO GOD. 287pp. Shr75, 3.95p.**
This is a reprinting of Purdom's edited and condensed version of the original edition of Meher Baba's discourses. It differs from **Discourses** by being more compact (thirty-two discourses in one volume as opposed to forty-five discourses in three volumes) and less authoritative (not benefiting from the review procedures used in the editing of **Discourses**).

PURDOM, C.B. **THE GODMAN: THE LIFE, JOURNEYS AND WORK OF MEHER BABA WITH AN INTERPRETATION OF HIS SILENCE AND SPIRITUAL TEACHING. 464pp. Shr64, 6.95c.**
This is the most complete biography of Meher Baba available. It describes in detail the various phases of his life, journeys, and spiritual work up to the late 1960s.

PURDOM, C.B. **THE PERFECT MASTER. Index, 333pp. Shr76, 3.95p.**
A biography of Meher Baba's early years, first published in 1937, and long out of print. This was the first biography of Baba to appear in the West. It discusses the period from 1911 to 1936 in a great deal of depth.

SHIFRIN, ADAH. **THE FLOWER OF CONTEMPLATION. 66pp. Shr65, 1.70p.**
A small book of spiritual thoughts dedicated to Baba's forty years of silence and including a short biographical sketch.

■ *STEVENS, DON, ed.* **LISTEN, HUMANITY. 262pp. H&R57, 3.45p.**
An American businessman reports vividly on his experience with Baba in India and Baba's answers to questions on life, death, suicide, war, love, avatarhood, and much else. Of all the books about Baba, this is probably the most comprehensible and interesting introduction.

STEVENS, DON, et al, eds. **TALES FROM THE NEW LIFE WITH MEHER BABA. 191pp. Beg76, 3.95p.**
Some of Meher Baba's closest disciples recount their memories of their experiences with Baba and of his teaching.

WATSON, RICHARD. **MEHER BABA AND SUFISM: A PERSONAL VIEW. 26pp. SRe nd, 1.00p.**

———— **END OF MEHER BABA SUBSECTION** ————

MILSON, MENAHEM, tr. **A SUFI RULE FOR NOVICES. Long introduction, glossary, bibliography, 93pp. HUP75, 2.50p.**
This is the first translation of a twelfth century guide to the Sufi way of life, the **Kitab Adab al-Muridin** of Suhrawardi, founder of one of the oldest and largest Sufi orders. A manual of ethics, addressed to novices and laymen, this work spells out in detail the *adab* or rules of conduct—general rules of such matters as eating, companionship, hospitality, and specific ones dealing with particular situations. The concluding section is on ethical dispensations—permitted departures from the rules.

MITCHELL, GEORGE, ed. **ARCHITECTURE OF THE ISLAMIC WORLD: ITS HISTORY AND SOCIAL MEANING. Bibliography, index, 8¼"x10¾", 288pp. Mor78, 50.00c.**
Islamic architecture makes an immediate impact, with its monumental forms, rich colors, and profuse ornamentation. But the architecture has a beauty and meaning that goes much deeper than its outward impressiveness. The grandeur of these buildings cannot be fully appreciated without understanding a great deal about Islamic life. In this volume eight Islamic specialists place Islamic architecture in its cultural setting, revealing its relationship to Islamic society. This is a definitive study, magnificently illustrated with 758 plates, 112 in color.

MOREWEDGE, PARVIZ. **THE METAPHYSICS OF AVICENNA. Indices, 371pp. Col73/RKP, 19.70c.**
A critical exposition of one text of Avicenna, the great Persian philosopher who lived from 980-1037. The text is his **Metaphysica** in the **Danish Nama-i ala-i (The Book of Scientific Knowledge)**. In addition to a translation, this edition includes a critical commentary on the major arguments found in the text, and notes and references to other texts of his as well as to relevant texts of Greek philosophers, particularly Aristotle, Plotinus, and Proclus. There is also a glossary of the key terms in the **Metaphysica**, with their Persian, Arabic, Greek, and Latin equivalents where necessary. Part of the **Persian Heritage** series.

Muhammad

Muhammad (570-632) was the founder of the religion of Islam and of the Arab Empire, and the initiator of religious, social, and cultural developments of monumental significance in the history of mankind. He was born in Mecca and became a merchant, marrying at the age of twenty-five, a rich older widow. He received his prophetic call in about 610 and, after proclaiming his message publicly, began his religious activities among the members of his own clan. The appearance of Meccan opposition about 615 and the withdrawal of his clan's protection about 619 caused him to seek aid elsewhere. In 620 he began negotiating with clans in Medina, leading to his emigration (*hijrah*) there in 622, along with many of his followers. He achieved a number of military victories, which seemed a divine vindication of his prophethood and, finally, in 628 forced the Meccans to acknowledge his political authority and grant him concessions. His Muslim following grew rapidly and in 630 he entered Mecca with 10,000 men. He also formed alliances with nomadic tribes scattered throughout the peninsula and left, on his death, most of Arabia united, ready to spread the faith to neighboring countries.

ABBOTT, NABIA. **AISHAH: THE BELOVED OF MOHAMMED.** Notes, index, 230pp. Arn42, 20.15c.
This is the only full length biography of Aishah, Muhammad's child wife. Aishah was the daughter of Abu Bakr and was an important influence on Muhammad in the last years of his life, as well as being significant in her own right following his death.

'ABD AL-QADIR AS-SUFI. **THE WAY OF MUHAMMAD.** Illustrations, 248pp. Diw75, 5.95p.
A topically arranged presentation of the practice and teaching given to the Islamic world by Muhammad. Numerous quotations from the Qur'an and Islamic masters illuminate the commentary. The book is written by an English Muslim living in a community that follows the *sunna* and is from the line of transmission of the Habibiya-Shadhiliyya Tariqa. This is an extremely complex work, only recommended to those who are deeply versed in the Sufi tradition.

■ *ANDRAE, TOR.* **MOHAMMED—THE MAN AND HIS FAITH.** Notes, index, 274pp. H&R36, 5.30p.
This is a good standard biography which, though published many years ago, has retained both its popularity and its relevance. This was a pioneering book in that it was the first to apply the principles of the psychology of religion to the certain facts of Muhammad's life and character. Andrae begins with a survey of Arabia at the time of Muhammad and then discusses the period from Muhammad's childhood to his prophetic call. The next two sections are devoted to Muhammad's religious message and his doctrine of revelation. From there the author reviews the conflict with the Quraish and Muhammad as the ruler in Medina. A final section is a psychological study of Muhammad's personality. This volume reads well and remains the best general biography that we know of.

BODLEY, R.V.C. **THE MESSENGER: THE LIFE OF MOHAMMED.** Glossary, bibliography, index, 378pp. Gre46, 19.85c.
Bodley is a Westerner who lived among the Arabs of the Sahara Desert for seven years. He became immersed in a culture which still follows Muhammad's teachings faithfully. Here he presents the picture of Muhammad which he absorbed and in the process he has given us the most readable account of the prophet's life and work that we know of. The orientation is not toward Oriental scholars or theologians—though the account seems to be a work of excellent scholarship.

CRAIG, H.A.L. **BILAL.** 158pp. Qtb77, 5.95p.
Bilal, a black Abyssinian slave and the first muezzin in Islam, was one of the early followers of Muhammad. This is an historical novel, ostensibly written by Bilal as an old man living in Damascus and looking back fondly on his days with Muhammad. He remembers the great events of his life—the sufferings and glories of early Islam—and recalls his slavery and torture and the spiritual companionship of the prophet. Craig wrote the screenplay for the film **Mohammad—Messenger of God**, and many color photographs from that movie accompany the narrative.

GLUBB, JOHN. **THE LIFE AND TIMES OF MUHAMMAD.** Bibliography, index, 416pp. S&D70, 2.95p.
Glubb spent almost sixty years in the Arab countries and had a great deal of contact with illiterate tribesmen whose lives are not very different from their ancestors in Muhammad's time. With this in mind, Sir John has written a study of Muhammad which is designed to give the general reader a good feeling for Muhammad the man; his trials, the wars he fought, his exile, and his ultimate achievements. Many maps are included along with a great deal of background material. Glubb writes vividly and brings the times to life in this volume.

HUSAIN, ATHAR. **PROPHET MUHAMMAD AND HIS MISSION.** Notes, bibliography, index, 224pp. APH67, 7.05c.
A study of the prophet's life and work which aims at presenting the reader with as comprehensive a picture of his personality as it can be seen through his message and his life. Husain uses passages from the Qur'an to illustrate the message of Islam and the personality of the prophet. The reader can also get a good feeling for the times from this study.

JEFFERY, ARTHUR, ed. **ISLAM: MUHAMMAD AND HIS RELIGION.** Glossary, notes, bibliography, index, 270pp. BoM58, 6.00p.
Jeffery begins this anthology with writings on the prophet and the Qur'an. The rest of the book is organized according to the conventional six articles of belief and five practical duties, concluding with some material illustrative of the devotional side of Islam. The selections are all drawn from writers who follow the old classical system of traditional Islam.

KARIM, FAZLUL. **THE IDEAL WORLD PROPHET: MUHAMMAD.** 470pp. TBH35, 6.50c.
This book does not contain in detail the events that took place in the life of the Holy Prophet of Arabia, but chiefly deals with the various phases of his life and with his teachings in connection thereto. That the Holy Prophet is the greatest ideal for a human being in all aspects of life and that he was sent by God as the last world teacher for the guidance of ever-warring humanity, will be seen, I hope, from a close and careful study of this book.—from the preface.

KHAN, SYED. **ESSAYS ON THE LIFE OF MUHAMMAD.** Introduction, many foldout charts and chronologies, TBH69, 6.50c.
This is a recent reprint of a rare nineteenth century biography of Muhammad. Sir Syed wrote his study to counterbalance Sir William Muir's misleading **Life of Muhammad**. His work is a product of careful scholarship and should be read by all who are deeply interested in the teachings of the prophet. The original English text has been revised and corrected for this edition.

LANE-POOLE, STANLEY, tr. **TABLE-TALK OF THE PROPHET MUHAMMAD.** Notes, 206pp. MuA66, 2.70p.
The aim of this little volume is to present all that is most endearing and memorable in the public orations and private sayings of the Prophet Muhammad in such a form that the general reader may be tempted to learn a little of what a great man he was and of what made him great. Some of the material is derived from the Qur'an—but from a chronological and topical arrangement of material rather than the scattered way that Muhammad's message is presented in the Holy Book. The other material comes from his recorded speeches and from sayings traditionally attributed to him dealing with the most minute and delicate circumstances of life. Lane-Poole has done a good job of translating his material and he also has written an excellent, long introduction.

RODINSON, MAXINE, tr. **MOHAMMED.** Glossary, annotated bibliography, index, 381pp. RaH74/Pen, 3.95p.
This is basically a political biography of Muhammad which approaches Islam as an ideology which galvanized a fragmented and nomadic society. M. Rodinson reviews the major events of Muhammad's life in the light of this thesis and backs up his discussion with excellent scholarship and an assortment of notes. The text itself reads well and is not cluttered with too much obvious scholarship. For those interested in this aspect of Muhammad's life and work this is as good a survey as we know of.

SARWAR, HAFIZ. **MUHAMMAD.** Index, 448pp. MuA61, 7.50c.
This is one of the few biographies of Muhammad available in English which was written by a Muslim. *This book attempts to show the path of success in life by most carefully collecting the facts of Muhammad's (peace be upon him) life and setting them up as an Example to all mankind. . . . The learned author is an expert student of the* **Qur'an** *and the chief events of the Holy Prophet's life are explained by quotations from the* **Holy Qur'an.** *. . . This biography depicts Muhammad as a man—the greatest MAN who ever lived on this earth.*

SEGUY, MARIE-ROSE. **THE MIRACULOUS JOURNEY OF MA-HOMET: MIRAJ NAMEH.** 8¼"x11¾", 158pp. Brz77, 35.00c.
The **Miraj Nameh** is a mystical legend describing the marvelous or apocalyptical visions that marked the stages of the miraculous ascension in the course of which, one night, Muhammad reached the throne of God. This is a reproduction of a sumptuous fifteenth century manuscript, decorated with sixty-one splendid illuminations of the successive stages of Muhammad's journey, first through the heavenly regions peopled with angels, and then through the infernal world of shadows haunted by demons who torture the damned. Some believe that Dante's **Divine Comedy** was influenced by this work since, as early as 1264 there were both French and Latin translations available. Mme. Seguy discusses the origin and meaning of the manuscript and comments on each of the fifty-eight double page golden plates.

WAHAB, SYED. **THE SHADOWLESS PROPHET OF ISLAM.** 148pp. MuA49, 3.60c.
Subtitled, *A Treatise on the Spiritual Aspect of the Prophet's Life and Spiritualism of Islam as Taught By Him.* Muhammad's prophecies and the supernatural events surrounding his life are emphasized.

WATT, W. MONTGOMERY. **MUHAMMAD AT MEDINA.** Extensive notes, index, 432pp. Oxf56, 20.00c.
An in depth, scholarly study of the second half of Muhammad's life, mainly emphasizing the political and social aspects of his career. Watt is one of the most respected contemporary historians.

WATT, W. MONTGOMERY. **MUHAMMAD: PROPHET AND STATES-MAN.** Notes, bibliography, index, 250pp. Oxf61, 3.95p.
This is an abridgment of Watt's fine study, **Muhammad at Medina,** with some additional material. The book opens with a background chapter on the birth and early life of the prophet in Mecca. Dr. Watt tells of Muhammad's call to prophethood as a result of his visions and recounts the writing down of the prophet's revelations in the **Qur'an** (with an explanation of some of its passages); Muhammad's betrayal, expulsion from Mecca, and migration to Medina; and his rise to political power in Arabia. Throughout, Dr. Watt makes clear the social and political background out of which Islam was born, especially the influence of Judaism and Christianity. This book is addressed to a wider public than Watt's more detailed and specialized earlier volumes and is written in a clear, interesting manner.

——————— **END OF MUHAMMAD SUBSECTION** ———————

MYERS, EUGENE. **ARABIC THOUGHT AND THE WESTERN WORLD.** Bibliography, index, 156pp. Ung64, 2.45p.
This is a survey of Islamic philosophers and translators during the Golden Age of Islam. Myers points out that the philosophical traditions of the Greeks were not known in Europe during the Dark Ages and when they again became known in Europe it was only in Arabic translation. Myers discusses the major figures in the Islamic Golden Age and devotes special attention to Ghazali, Ibn 'Arabi, and Ibn Khaldun. He begins with a survey of the early scholars—ninth and tenth century—and then goes on to discuss Islamic scholarship in the eleventh and twelfth centuries. Other chapters are devoted to the translations which were made into Arabic between the seventh and eleventh centuries and to the impact of these translations in the West.

NAFZANI, SHANKH. **THE GLORY OF THE PERFUMED GARDEN.** Indices, 134pp. Spe75, 2.75p.
An English translation of that part of **The Perfumed Garden** which is missing from Sir Richard Burton's translation. This first appeared in 1886 and it is known that two years later Burton set to work on a new version, this time bypassing the French source he has used before and translating directly from an Arabic manuscript. After he died his wife, shocked by the material, burned his translation. The document translated in this volume is crude and coarse at times, at others sensitive and understanding, reflecting the Arabic culture that it comes out of. The translator of this version is not named.

NAKOSTEEN, MEHDI. **MULLA'S DONKEY AND OTHER FRIENDS.** 6"x9", 149pp. EEP74, 8.50p.
Professor Nakosteen's adaptations of many of the shortest Nasrudin stories—most of which are not in the three Idries Shah Nasrudin books.

NAKOSTEEN, MEHDI. **SUFISM AND HUMAN DESTINY AND SUFI THOUGHT IN PERSIAN POETRY.** Notes, bibliography, index, 246pp. EEP77, 12.50p.
The two surveys presented here . . . propose to provide an historic overview of the Sufi Path and Goal, along with an evaluation of their drawbacks and contributions in Book One; and an analysis of Sufism in Persian poetry supported by a selective anthology of Sufi poems from nine poets, whose "Diwans" . . . embody Sufi verses, in Book Two.— from the foreword.

■ NASR, SEYYED HOSSEIN. **IDEALS AND REALITIES OF ISLAM.** Index, 184pp. Bea66/A&U, 3.95p.
In six chapters dealing with Islam, the **Qur'an,** the prophet, the *shari'a* or divine law, the *tariqah* or Sufism, Sunnism and Shi'ism, Nasr discusses the major aspects of the Islamic tradition, making frequent comparisons with other religions. In each case the traditional Islamic doctrines and beliefs are explained in the light of contemporary thought, and each chapter is accompanied by an annotated bibliography of the works of both Muslim and Western scholars. Nasr is a very noted Iranian scholar and educator.

NASR, SEYYED HOSSEIN. **ISLAM AND THE PLIGHT OF MODERN MAN.** Notes, bibliography, index, 173pp. Lon75, 22.95c.
Professor Nasr examines and expounds in detail the contemporary spiritual situation in his own country, Iran, as well as in the rest of the Arab world. He shows how there is a profound struggle between the Islamic tradition and Western ideologies and philosophical currents such as Marxism, evolutionism, and existentialism. He also criticizes those *Muslims who have already attempted to modify their religion in order to reconcile it with other beliefs and ideas. Professor Nasr argues that the Arab world will be best served by a return to what he terms "the Divine Truth" embodied in the* **Qur'an.**

NASR, SEYYED HOSSEIN. **ISLAMIC SCIENCE: AN ILLUSTRATED STUDY.** 9½"x12", 272pp. WIF76, 27.50c.
The first fully illustrated study of Islamic science published in the West. Professor Nasr examines many branches of science, including cosmology, geography, astronomy, alchemy, medicine, and agriculture, and discusses them and the role of science within the context of the Quranic revelation. Includes 135 color plates and over 100 halftones and line drawings.

NASR, SEYYED HOSSEIN. **SACRED ART IN PERSIAN CULTURE.** 23pp. Gol76, 7.10p.
An extremely clear analysis of the title theme.

■ *NASR, SEYYED HOSSEIN.* **SCIENCE AND CIVILIZATION IN ISLAM. Notes, bibliography, index, 384pp. NAL68, 3.50p.**
This is the only one volume work in English which discusses every branch of Islamic science and approaches it not from the Western viewpoint but as it is understood by the Muslims themselves. Islamic science, known to the West principally for its influence on the development of European scientific thought, occupied a central position within the Muslim culture. Through historical and morphological analysis, as well as excerpts from texts, Dr. Nasr conveys to Western readers the content and spirit of Islamic science. His introduction surveys the religious, metaphysical, and philosophical concepts of Islam. Succeeding chapters cover the entire scientific spectrum from cosmography, mathematics, and medicine to alchemy and theology, as well as the interaction of these with related schools of thought.

NASR, SEYYED HOSSEIN, tr. **SHI'ITE ISLAM. Bibliography, index, 267pp. SNY75/A&U, 20.15c.**
A translation from the Persian of Muhammas Husayn al-Tabataba-i's comprehensive statement of the history and beliefs of the Shi'ite religion. Edited, and includes an introduction and notes (many of which form a running commentary on the text).

NASR, SEYYED HOSSEIN. **SUFI ESSAYS. Notes, index, 184pp. ScB72/A&U, 3.75p.**
This book combines scholarly research into certain aspects of Sufi doctrines with a penetrating account of the spiritual and metaphysical message and significance of Sufism as a living spiritual tradition. Nasr, probably the leading scholar of Sufism today, places special emphasis on the pertinence of Sufi teachings to the most acute contemporary problems and draws on his intimate knowledge of Sufi literature in Arabic and Persian as well as his firsthand knowledge of the Sufi tradition itself in this excellent study. We recommend all of Nasr's books highly—although not on the introductory level.

NASR, SEYYED HOSSEIN, et al. **RE-ORIENTATION OF MUSLIM PHILOSOPHY. 50pp. PPC65, 4.50p.**
A collection of short essays on the title theme by S.H. Nasr, B.H. Siddiqi, D.M. Azraf, and M.S. Shaikh—together with an introduction by the editor which ties the selections together.

NICHOLSON, R.A. **IDEA OF PERSONALITY IN SUFISM. 105pp. MuA64, 3.00c.**
My chief purpose was to show by means of examples chosen from the literature, that Sufism is not necessarily pantheistic but often bears the marks of a genuine personal religion inspired by a personal God.

NICHOLSON, R.A., tr. **KASHF AL-MUHJUB OF AL-HUJWIRI. Introduction, notes, index, 463pp. Luz11, 7.65p.**
A translation of the oldest Persian treatise on Sufism. Al Hujwiri discusses some of the basic concepts of Sufism, eminent Sufis, and Sufi sects. This is an excellent text and many of the ideas the author discusses have not been expressed better in any other place. Nicholson has done a fine job with the translation. **Gibb Memorial Series.**

NICHOLSON, R.A. **THE MYSTICS OF ISLAM. 168pp. ScB14/RKP, 2.45p.**
Nicholson is one of the most noted Persian scholars of this century. He gives an outline of Sufism here and describes some of the basic principles, methods, and characteristic features of the inner life. Many quotations are included, mainly in the author's own fine versions of the original Arabic and Persian.

NUMANI, SHIBLI. **"AL-FAROOQ": LIFE OF UMAR THE GREAT. Introduction, notes, index, 295pp. MuA43, 4.80c.**
After the Holy Prophet...Omar is universally acknowledged as the first great Conqueror, Founder and Administrator of the Muslim Empire. It was during his Caliphate that Islam planted its banners far beyond the confines of the Arabian peninsula. This great military and administrative genius is up till now believed to be a miracle in himself, for he not only founded a great Empire but gave that solidarity to it which remained unshaken for centuries. This edition was translated by Maulana Zafar Ali Khan, a well known scholar. It is the only major biographical study of Omar available in English.

NURBAKHSH, JAVAD. **IN THE TAVERN OF RUIN. 136pp. KNP78, 3.95p.**
Seven essays on Sufism by the present master of the Nimatullahi Order of Sufis. Many beautiful insights are offered on the Sufi path and way of life. The author quotes extensively from the great Sufi teachers and poets.

PALMER, E.H. **ORIENTAL MYSTICISM. Glossary, index, Oct1867, 5.45c.**
The following work is founded upon a Persian MS, treatise by 'Aziz bin Mohammed Nafasi, but I have endeavoured to give a clearer and more succinct account of the system than would have been afforded by a mere translation. This is a good presentation of the basic cosmological system of Sufism. A classic work, recently reprinted.

PERLMANN, MOSHE. **IBN KAMMAUNA'S EXAMINATION OF THE THREE FAITHS. Many interpretative notes, index, 160pp. UCa71, 14.25c.**
Written in 1280 by a Jew of Baghdad, this essay systematically examines the creeds, arguments, and counterarguments of the three monotheistic faiths—Judaism, Christianity, and Islam. The book offers an excellent summary of the Arabic literature and lore of interfaith disputations and provides insight into the mentality of medieval scholars. The translator's introduction places Ibn Kammuna in his historical and theological context.

Persian Language

Persian is a member of the Iranian branch of the Indo-Iranian language family; it is the official language of Iran and is widely used in Afghanistan. Written in Arabic script, modern Persian also has many Arabic loanwords and an extensive literature. Old Persian died out in approximately the third century BC; Middle Persian was spoken from the third century BC to the ninth century AD. Middle Persian has a varied literature, embracing both the Zoroastrian and Manichaean religious traditions. Pahlavi was the name of the official Middle Persian language of the Sasanian Empire.

ELWELL-SUTTON, L.P. **ELEMENTARY PERSIAN GRAMMAR. Index, 225pp. CUP72, 9.95p.**
Provides a simple grammatical framework for contemporary written Persian based on the characteristic idiom and phraseology of the language as it is used in newspapers, magazines, and novels. The student is introduced to Persian script from the first lesson. Words are fully vocalized in the early lessons, but vowels are progressively discarded—they are, however, shown in the vocabulary. The letter forms of printed Persian are used in the exercises and two appendices give examples of commonly used cursive scripts. The examples and exercises require only a limited vocabulary of fairly commonly used words—about 1,500 in all. Pronunciation guides are also given and there is a key to the lessons at the end of the book, along with a Persian-English vocabulary.

LAMBTON, A.K.S. **PERSIAN GRAMMAR. Index, 300pp. CUP57, 9.95p.**
With her unrivalled knowledge of the Persian language, Professor Lambton has produced a work that will long remain the standard textbook. As was to be expected, the treatment of pronunciation and the spoken language is particularly excellent...an extremely useful work for which teacher and student will be equally grateful.— **Journal of the Royal Asiatic Society.** Although it is primarily for the contemporary Persian language, the book also serves as an excellent introduction to the classical language.

LAMBTON, A.K.S. **PERSIAN VOCABULARY. 406pp. CUP64, 10.95p.**
This is a companion volume to Professor Lambton's **Persian Grammar.** It is mainly intended for the student of contemporary Persian and it will also be a useful handbook for those who wish to read classical Persian literature. The Persian-English and English-Persian sections contain a wide range of the more common words and phrases.

MACE, JOHN. **TEACH YOURSELF MODERN PERSIAN. 263pp. McK71, 3.95p.**
A clearly written manual which covers Persian script, grammar, and vocabulary. Exercises are included at the end of each section and there is Persian-English, English-Persian vocabulary.

PALMER, E.H. **A CONCISE DICTIONARY OF THE PERSIAN LANGUAGE.** 363pp. RKP02, 8.25c.
A classic.

STEINGASS, F. **A COMPREHENSIVE PERSIAN-ENGLISH DICTIONARY.** 1,548pp. RKP73, 51.00c.
A revised, enlarged, and newly reconstructed version of Johnson and Richardson's **Persian-Arabic-English Dictionary.**

———————— END OF PERSIAN LANGUAGE SUBSECTION ————————

PETERS, F.E. **ALLAH'S COMMONWEALTH. Glossary, chronology, notes, annotated bibliography, index,** 800pp. S&S73, 19.95c.
This is an excellent scholarly (and quite readable) history of Islam in the Near East, AD600-1100. *The format of this book is what the Arabs called an "era work," the setting-down of deeds, chiefly those of a political nature, along a chronological line established by the succession of Caliphs, their vassals and their ministers. But I have attempted something more, an excursion into another literary genre known to the Arabs as the "book of refinement." The Arabs' "refinement"... was a generous term in that it eventually came to embrace the sum of manners and learning appropriate to the Muslim gentleman. And although there is rich material available on the manners of the early Muslim, the emphasis here is upon his literary learning, what the educated Muslim knew and thought about man, the world and Islam. His culture is in his books...and some of the most important of them have been opened again here and their contents displayed in the appropriate context.* This is a secular history, and an excellent one. And since Islam itself has such a strong religious and philosophical basis these elements play a large role in the narrative presented here.

PETERS, F.E. **ARISTOTLE AND THE ARABS: THE ARISTOTELIAN TRADITION IN ISLAM. Introduction, notes, bibliography, index,** 326pp. NYU68, 13.45c.
Greek science and philosophy, known to the Arabs as *falsafah*, were the single most important influence in the shaping of the intellectual life of Islam. Aristotelianism was the strongest feature of that legacy, and the Muslims fashioned from it an elaborate structure that was in part Hellenic and in part the offspring of their own tradition. The marks of Islamic Aristotelianism can be detected in almost every branch of Islamic learning, in method as well as substance. Dr. Peters, a recognized authority on the subject, provides the first real synthesis of it. Many translations from primary sources are included.

PICKTHALL, M. **CULTURAL SIDE OF ISLAM.** 202pp. MuA61, 2.70p.
Pickthall is a respected Islamic scholar whose translation of the **Qur'an** is generally considered one of the finest available. This volume is the transcription of a series of lectures which reveal important points about Islamic culture. Many pertinent quotations from the **Qur'an** and other writings of the prophet are included.

The Qur'an

The **Qur'an** (Arabic for *The Recital*) is the earliest and by far the finest work of Classical Arabic prose. For Muslims it is the infallible word of God, a transcript of a tablet preserved in Heaven, revealed to the prophet Muhammad by the angel Gabriel. Except in the opening verses and some passages in which the prophet or the angel speaks in the first person, the speaker throughout is God.

The **Qur'an** preaches the oneness of God and emphasizes divine mercy and forgiveness. God is almighty and all knowing, and though compassionate toward his creatures, He is stern in retribution. He enjoins justice and fair dealing. The most important duties of the Muslim are faith in Allah and His apostle, prayer, almsgiving, fasting, and (if possible) pilgrimage to Mecca.

In preparing the contents of the **Qur'an** for book form its editor or editors followed no chronological sequence. Its chapters were arranged generally in order of length, the longest coming first and the shortest last. Various scholars have attempted to arrange the chapters in chronological order, with varying success.

ABDUL, M.O.A. **THE HOLY BOOK OF ISLAM. Index,** 140pp. IPB73, 3.50p.
An introduction to the **Qur'an** based on an examination of selected verses. Abdul presents a number of Quranic chapters and includes the original Arabic script, transliteration, translation, and commentary. In addition he discusses the following topics: the revelation of the **Qur'an**, Quranic form and contents, Quranic legislations on foods and drinks, moral and ethical teachings, and Quranic commentaries.

■ ALI, A. YUSUF, tr. **THE HOLY QUR'AN. Index,** 1,862pp. Isl nd, 16.80c.
This is far and away the most magnificent translation available. Ali includes extensive commentary on almost every line and the Arabic text is in facing columns. The scholarship is impeccable and the book itself is exquisitely produced.

AMIR-ALI, HASHIM. **THE MESSAGE OF THE QUR'AN. 7"x10",** 500pp. Tut74, 25.00c.
Dr. Ali is a noted Muslim scholar who has devoted his heart and intellect to transcribing the **Qur'an** into poetic English that would convey the depths of the Quranic message to today's readers. In this volume he presents a complete translation of the **Qur'an** which combines his intellectual integrity with a wide knowledge and personal experience. Textual notes discuss certain Quranic problems which have baffled scholars over the centuries and the author's solutions. The text is accompanied by introductory material and appendices. The volume is beautifully bound, with illustrations and the full Arabic text. The translation reads very well.

ARBERRY, A.J., tr. **THE KORAN INTERPRETED. Index,** 358pp. McM55/A&U, 7.95p.
Dr. Arberry is generally considered to be the leading Islamic scholar of this century and his translation of the **Qur'an** to be the finest one by a non-Muslim, and the one that comes closest to conveying the impression made on Muslims by the original. He follows the traditional arrangement of the *suras*. An interesting preface compares the English translations of the **Qur'an** over the years.

AZAD, MAWLANA. **THE TARJUMAN AL-QUR'AN, VOLUME I. Extensive introductory material, index,** 248pp. APH62, 10.75c.
This is a scholarly and readable book which is devoted to a translation and interpretation of the first chapter of the **Qur'an**. The translation itself is interspersed with the commentary. The book was originally written in Urdu and this fine English translation is by Syed Abdul Latif. Azad's scholarship is well regarded throughout the Islamic world and his aim is to give to the Quranic word the interpretation it was originally meant to bear, as understood by the contemporary followers of the prophet.

AZAD, MAWLANA. **THE TARJUMAN AL QUR'AN, VOLUME II. Index,** 531pp. APH67, 11.45c.
This volume is a translation of and commentary on chapters II to VIII.

BELL, RICHARD, tr. **THE QUR'AN. Two volumes, index,** 709pp. TTC37, 19.20c/set.
In this translation the *suras* are kept in their original order, but the contents of each one have been critically rearranged according to Bell's interpretation of how they should read. Bell also shows which parts of the material have been added later. Extensive notes and commentary accompany each *sura*.

BURTON, JOHN. **THE COLLECTION OF THE QURAN. Notes, bibliography, index,** 273pp. CUP77, 17.95c.
An academic analysis of early Islamic traditions concerning the collection of the Quranic material. Dr. Burton provides an in depth analysis of the subject, including quotations from many other writers and a wealth of detail.

CRAGG, KENNETH. **THE EVENT OF THE QUR'AN. Glossary, indices,** 208pp. A&U71, 15.10c.
*Separate events in the Islamic Scriptures are not hard to arrange and to chronicle—a lonely brooding in the caves and hills of Mecca, a tenacious vocation in the teeth of heavy odds, emigration to a new city as the watershed of the story, energy in leadership, vindication, success. But what was the event of the whole? How should we understand the coming together of personal charisma, poetic eloquence, Arab consciousness, and vibrant theism, into the single phenomenon of the **Qur'an**? What is the inner story of*

the prophethood which Islam receives as the final, cumulative revelation from God? How did the setting of time and territory and tradition enter into its metaphors and condition its contents? How should its relation to the present time be read in its original time? These are the questions which make the theme of this study. In aiming to be scholarly they have a duty to more than scholarship. The text includes many quotations from the Qur'an, along with detailed notes.

CRAGG, KENNETH. **THE MIND OF THE QUR'AN. 209pp. A&U73, 10.85c.**
Cragg takes up a number of central Quranic themes; life and time, God and man, mercy and forgiveness, death and eternity, and sets them within the context of the Qur'an itself. The object of this work is to determine how the Qur'an is received in contemporary Islamic society and whether its philosophy is integrated into the society.

DAR AL-KORAN AL-KAREEM. **KORAN. 5"x3½", DAK nd, 10.00c.**
A beautifully produced all Arabic Qur'an. It is boxed and gold embossed, and, while pocket size, is extremely readable.

■ DAWOOD, N.J., tr. **THE KORAN. 431pp. Vik74, 2.95p.**
A very readable translation in which the traditional arrangement of verses has been abandoned. The sequence presented here begins with the more biblical and poetic revelations and ends with the much longer, and often more topical, chapters. A translation for the general reader.

DOI, A. RAHMAN. **INTRODUCITON TO THE QUR'AN. Bibliography, index, 134pp. IPB71, 3.90p.**
Professor Doi begins with a study of the compilation, contents, and importance of the Qur'an. He follows with a discussion of the Meccan and the Medina *suras* and a comparison of them. The largest section is devoted to selections from the Qur'an, including the Arabic script, transliteration, translation, and commentary. In a final section he discusses some of the most important Quranic moral and ethical teachings.

GATJE, HELMUT. **THE QUR'AN AND ITS EXEGISIS. Notes, bibliography, index, 330pp. UCa76, 20.00c.**
A translation of key passages of the Qur'an (following Arberry's version) and its classical and modern commentaries. The book shows the teachings of the Qur'an and the views of later commentators on such topics as revelation, Allah, Muhammad, angels and *jinn*, eschatology, and Muslim beliefs and duties. It also discusses the Quranic view of other religious communities, particularly the *People of the Book*. There are also chapters on mystical, philosophical, and Shi'ite Quranic exegesis. This volume has been translated from the German and edited by Dr. Alford Welch.

GAUHAR, ALTAF, tr. **TRANSLATIONS FROM THE QUR'AN. Index, 184pp. IIS75, 13.40c/6.60p.**
An illuminating discussion of certain key passages from the Qur'an, along with translations of many of these passages. Gauhar is a Muslim and he made the translations at a time when the only book he had access to was the Qur'an. His comments show the true meaning of the Quranic teachings for one man. He also discusses the meaning of the Qur'an and suggests how it can best be read and understood.

GREENLEES, DUNCAN. **THE GOSPEL OF ISLAM. 211pp. TPI|48, 4.00c.**
The Gospel of Islam is not a translation of the Glorious Qur'an . . . . *This little book is meant only as an introduction or a guide-book to the Scripture itself, whose arrangement does not make quick reference easy for the general reader. So I have chosen beautiful, striking and typical passages from all parts of the Book and woven them into a logical sequence in short sections, each on a certain topic, and then completely translated afresh from the Arabic original. To help the reader to refer to the original context of each passage, the reference to chapter and verse . . . is printed after it.*

HINGORA, Q.I. **THE PROPHECIES OF THE HOLY QUR'AN. 173pp. MuA64, 3.15p.**
A presentation of the major prophecies, topically arranged and in composite form.

HUSAIN, ASHFAQUE. **THE QUINTESSENCE OF ISLAM. Introduction, notes, 92pp. TBH nd, 2.60c.**
A summary of the commentary of Maulana Abul Kalam Azad on *Al-Fateha*, the first chapter of the Qur'an. This opening chapter is variously referred to by Muslims as *the most prominent in the* Qur'an, *the essence of the* Qur'an, *the sufficient, the treasure.* The prominence of this chapter is due to the fact that it is not only the introduction to the Qur'an, but its essence.

KHAN, MUHAMMAD Z., tr. **THE KORAN. Cur70, 673pp. 13.20c.**
This is an excellent translation which is a great deal more readable than most. Rather than duplicate the verse patterns of the original, Khan structures the material through verse paragraphs that combine groups of verses which capture the feel of the Arabic but do not sacrifice clarity of meaning. The Arabic text and English translation are printed in parallel columns to facilitate comparisons and cross references. Khan has drawn upon the most up to date scholarship in Arabic and Quranic studies to enrich the accuracy of the translation. The translator is not only a noted Islamic scholar but has also had a distinguished political career: first as Foreign Minister of Pakistan, then as head of the Pakistani delegation to the United Nations, and presently as President of the International Court of Justice. Beautifully bound, with excellent introduction and index.

LINGS, MARTIN. **THE QURANIC ART OF CALLIGRAPHY AND ILLUMINATION. 9½"x12", 256pp. WIF76, 63.00c.**
A beautiful book which reveals the superb workmanship of Quranic calligraphy, its history, and differing styles. The color reproductions cover over 200 pages and are all from the best manuscripts extant, include the use of gold, and are of outstanding quality.

LINGS, MARTIN and YASIN SAFADI. **THE QUR'AN. Glossary, bibliography, index, 7½"x9¾", 98pp. WIF76, 6.95p.**
The catalogue of an exhibition of the Qur'an, arranged by the British Library in cooperation with the World of Islam Festival Trust and featuring a splendid display of calligraphic and illuminated manuscripts from many countries. The selections are organized according to the historical developments of the art of Quranic illumination and calligraphy throughout the period from the eighth to the nineteenth century. Each of the 164 plates is fully discussed and twenty-four are reproduced in color.

MERCHANT, MUHAMMAD. **A BOOK OF QURANIC LAWS. 206pp. MuA47, 4.45p.**
A selection of verses on some of the fundamental principles of Islam arranged under the following subject headings: *Doctrine of the Unity of God; Prayers and Alms; Fasts; Hadj; Food, Drinks, and Games—Lawful and Unlawful; Marriage; Divorce; Inheritance; Usury;and Purdah.*

MERCIER, HENRY, tr. **THE KORAN. Introduction, index, 349pp. Luz56, 6.95p.**
This is the only paperback translation which also includes the Arabic text and transliteration. The volume is also very nicely laid out and the translation appears to be a good one.

MUHTAR-KATIRCIOGLU, MAHMUD. **THE WISDOM OF THE HOLY QUR'AN. Notes, 206pp. TBH nd, 6.50c.**
A selection of verses from the Qur'an conveying the moral, religious, and social philosophy of Islam. The book contains about one fifth of the verses in the Qur'an. Extensive introductory material is also included. English translation by John Naish.

PALMER, E.H., tr. **THE QUR'AN. Extensive introduction, notes, 730pp. MoB1880, 12.00c/each.**
A dry, scholarly, two volume translation which gives little feeling for the original work. Part of the **Sacred Books of the East** series.

PARRINDER, GEOFFREY. **JESUS IN THE QUR'AN. Indices, 187pp. Oxf65, 5.95p.**
A scholarly study of the Quranic teachings about Jesus. Dr. Parrinder approaches Islam as a religion akin to Christianity and explores in detail all the ninety-three verses in the Qur'an in which Jesus is mentioned, setting them in the context of the book as a whole. He also cites parallels to the **Gospels** where applicable.

PENRICE, JOHN. **DICTIONARY AND GLOSSARY OF THE KORAN. Revised edition, 7½"x10", 174pp. Cur76, 10.55c.**
The Qur'an is one of the most complex and difficult works in any language. The wealth of commentaries and interpretations of individual passages testifies to the subtlety and complexity of both language and syntax and the resulting ambiguities of meaning. This volume was

originally published in 1873. In it Penrice, a distinguished scholar, seeks to provide *a clue of elucidation to the intricate passages of the Koran*. Through painstaking and detailed analysis, he clarifies the more ambiguous passages, drawing upon grammatical as well as linguistic references.

PICKTHALL, MARMADUKE, tr. **THE GLORIOUS KORAN. Index, 1,768pp. A&U76, 40.30c.**
This is a magnificent volume which combines Pickthall's fine rendering with an Arabic text reproduced from the original Hyderabad edition, based on the famous **Royal Koran** which many regard as the most beautiful example of Arabic script ever produced. The Arabic and English are on facing pages and the translator also provides extensive notes and an excellent introduction.

■ *PICKTHALL, MARMADUKE, tr.* **THE MEANING OF THE GLORIOUS KORAN. Index, 456pp. NAL70/A&U, 2.50p.**
*The aim of this work is to present to English readers what Muslims the world over hold to be the meaning of the words of the **Koran**, and the nature of that Book....It may be claimed that no Holy Scripture can be fairly presented by one who disbelieves its inspiration and its message; and this is the first English translation of the **Koran** by an Englishman who is a Muslim. Some of the translations include commentation offensive to Muslims, and almost all employ a style of language which Muslims at once recognize as unworthy. The **Koran** cannot be translated....The Book is here rendered almost literally and every effort has been made to choose befitting language. But the result is not the **Glorious Koran**....It is only an attempt to present the meaning of the **Koran**—and peradventure something of the charm—in English.... Before publication the work has been scrutinized word by word and thoroughly revised in Egypt with the help of one whose mother-tongue is Arabic, who has studied the **Koran** and who knows English; and when difficulties were encountered the translator had recourse to perhaps the greatest living authority on the subject. This is the most popular modern translation among the Muslims.*

ROBERTS, ROBERT. **THE SOCIAL LAWS OF THE QUR'AN. Index, 138pp. Cur74, 9.00c.**
A straightforward presentation of Quranic teachings as they affect everyday life and as a guide to social conduct.

RODWELL, J.M., tr. **THE KORAN. Introduction, notes, index, 517pp. Dut09, 2.75p.**
The main feature of this translation is Rodwell's chronological arrangement of the *suras*, which enables the reader to trace the development of the prophet's inspiration. The translation itself is a good work of scholarship, but not as readable as some of the more recent versions. Rodwell himself was not a Muslim and this is reflected in his presentation.

SHAH, AHMAD. **MIFTAH-UL-QURAN: CONCORDANCE AND COMPLETE GLOSSARY OF THE HOLY QUR'AN. 7"x9½", 383pp. TBH06, 16.50c/set.**
A two volume set.

SIDDIQUI, ABDUL HAMEED, tr. **THE HOLY QUR'AN, VOLUME I. Index, 7"x9½", 410pp. TBH77, 16.00c.**
An excellent translation, by a noted Muslim scholar, of the following *suras: Al-Fatihah, Al-Baqarah, Al-Imran,* and *An-Nisa.* The Arabic text is in parallel columns and there are extensive explanatory notes.

STANTON, H.U. **THE TEACHING OF THE QUR'AN. 136pp. B&T19, 13.45c.**
A comprehensive sketch of Quranic theology, topically oraganized and accompanied by a lengthy glossary and subject index.

WATT, W. MONTGOMERY. **COMPANION TO THE QUR'AN. Glossary, index, 355pp. A&U67, 14.70c.**
A useful work, based on the Arberry translation and designed to help readers by giving essential background information and explaining allusions. Professor Watt uses numbered verses, so his volume can be used with any translation.

──────── **END OF THE QUR'AN SUBSECTION** ────────

RAJNEESH, BHAGWAN SHREE. **JUST LIKE THAT. 12.00c.**
See the Contemporary Spiritual Teachers section.

RAJNEESH, BHAGWAN SHREE. **UNTIL YOU DIE. 12.00c.**
See the Contemporary Spiritual Teachers section.

RAUF, MUHAMMAD ABDUL. **ISLAM, FAITH AND DEVOTION. Illustrations, notes, 133pp. IPB74, 7.55p.**
This work begins with a chapter on the Muslim creed, but the main part of the work deals with the rituals of prayers, alms, fasting and pilgrimage, through which the individual and community seek companionship with God. These chapters are specially designed for adult Muslims who have no access to the original Arabic sources.—from the introduction.

RAUF, MUHAMMAD ABDUL. **THE SACRED TEXTS OF ISLAM. 97pp. IPB74, 7.75p.**
An introductory discussion of the **Qur'an** and the *hadith.* Dr. Rauf begins with historical notes on the two texts and then presents ten sample sections from each, with full analysis and explanatory notes. Both the original Arabic and an English translation are included, along with a transliteration and definition of each individual word.

REDHOUSE, JAMES, tr. **LEGENDS OF THE SUFIS. 137pp. TPH76, 3.95p.**
A selection of anecdotes taken from **Menaqibu'L'Arifin** written by a historian, Shemsu-'D-Din Ahmed, El Eflaki in 1353. El Eflaki was a Mevlevi dervish and a disciple of Rumi's grandson. This collection of stories and legends of events in the lives of Rumi and other Mevlevis is profound and sometimes miraculous and contains a timeless wisdom. Preface by Idries Shah.

RICE, DAVID. **ISLAMIC ART. 6.95p.**
See the Sacred Art section.

RICE, DAVID. **ISLAMIC PAINTING: A SURVEY. Bibliography, 202pp. EUP71, 13.45c.**
This book concentrates on less familiar aspects of Islamic painting, including its early developments. Only two of the nine chapters discuss the paintings of the famous age which developed in Persia between 1400 and 1600. Professor Rice is thoroughly familiar with his material and he has prepared an excellent survey. Eighty-one plates, including some in color, accompany the text. The quality of the reproductions is only fair.

ROBINSON, B.W. **PERSIAN DRAWINGS. 5.95p.**
See the Sacred Art section.

RODITI, EDOUARD. **THE DELIGHTS OF TURKEY. 184pp. NDP77, 4.45p.**
Twenty witty tales, set for the most part in Asia Minor, where the centuries long mingling of Turks, Armenians, Greeks, and Jews has produced a vibrant, diverse culture. The tales are often bawdy or fanciful in the manner of **The Arabian Nights**; others are more poignant in style, as we meet pasha, princess, and peasant, become privy to the intrigues of an Ottoman harem, or follow the merchant caravans on their journeys east. The collection is arranged thematically.

ROGERS, MICHAEL. **THE SPREAD OF ISLAM. Glossary, bibliography, index, 8¾"x11½", 152pp. Pdn76, 5.98c.**
A comprehensive study of the early history and architecture of Islam, covering the period from Islam's beginnings in the seventh century AD to the year 1500. Using architectural history as a framework, Rogers builds up a picture of the secular and religious life of the medieval Muslim. He also includes detailed descriptions of some of the most noted palaces, shrines, and mausolea. An introductory section is devoted to the historical development of Islam. The book is illustrated with 153 photographs, maps, and drawings, 104 in color.

Jalal al-Din Rumi

Rumi, who lived during the thirteenth century in what is now Turkey, is the greatest mystical poet of Persia, and perhaps the greatest of any language. His vast body of poetry includes the **Mathnawi**, a lengthy epic of religious mysticism, and more than three thousand lyrics and odes, many of which came to him while he was in a state of trance.

Rumi lived the quiet life of a religious teacher until the age of thirty-seven, when he came under the influence of a wandering dervish, Shams Tabriz. After a time Rumi's jealous disciples drove Shams away, but Rumi's transformation into a state of religious ecstasy was permanent. Torrents of poetry poured from him. To symbolize the search for the lost Divine Beloved, now identified with Shams, Rumi invented the famous whirling, circling dance of the Mevlevi dervishes and under the impact of the passionate moment, uttered a stream of quatrains and lyrics which his disciples recorded. These poems were thereafter chanted as accompaniment to the dervishes' sacred dance. Rumi opens a new world of spiritual experience. *God is One but religions are many* runs the Sufi teaching. The influence of his example, his thought, and his language has been powerfully felt through all the succeeding centuries.

ARASTEH, A. REZA. **RUMI THE PERSIAN, THE SUFI. Notes, index, 196pp. RKP65, 6.30p.**
Arasteh presents a systematic study of Rumi's rebirth into a total being who expressed the ideas of religious tolerance and presented the idea of love as the fundamental creative force. By studying elements of Persian culture, as well as Rumi's writings, Dr. Arasteh reveals the characteristics of maturity, the qualities of final integration in identity, health, and happiness that underly Rumi's life and work.

■ *ARBERRY, A.J., tr.* **THE DISCOURSES OF RUMI. Many notes, 276pp. Wei61/Mur, 4.95p.**
These discourses are the raw materials out of which the **Mathnawi** was fashioned and like the **Mathnawi** they *represent the impromptu outpourings of a mind overwhelmed in mystical thought, the multifarious and often arrestingly original and beautiful images welling up unceasingly out of the poet's overflowing consciousness.* Profoundly instructive stories and parables.

■ *ARBERRY, A.J., tr.* **MYSTICAL POEMS OF RUMI. Introduction, notes, index, 202pp. UCh68, 2.95p.**
This is the best collection of Rumi's lyrics. Arberry has carefully chosen two hundred from the 1,500 odes and lyrics—representing a planned selection which includes poems of various styles and degrees of difficulty. If you want to read just one book on Rumi this is the one we suggest. He was above all a mystical poet, and it is through these poems that he revealed his soul and the profundity of his thought.

DAVIS, F. HADLAND. **THE PERSIAN MYSTICS: RUMI. 107pp. MuA67, 1.50c.**
The first part of this monograph is devoted to an analysis of Sufism, with sections on its origins, nature, and influence as well as a study of the early Sufis and an analysis of the *Religion of Love*. The next part reviews the life and work of Rumi and discusses the main influences on him. This is followed by selections from the **Divani Shamsi Tabriz** and the **Masnavi**.

HAKIM, K.A. **METAPHYSICS OF RUMI. Bibliography, 157pp. IIC65, 1.35c.**
This is a detailed, scholarly study with extensive quotations from Rumi's own work—in Persian and in English translation. Hakim includes chapters on *The Nature of the Soul, The Problem of Creation, Evolution, Love, Freedom of the Will, The Ideal Man, The Survival of Personality, God,* and *Sufi Pantheism.*

IQBAL, AFZAL. **LIFE AND WORK OF RUMI. Notes, bibliography, index, 321pp. MuA74, 7.50c.**
Until the publication of the present volume no attempt has been made to write for the general public a biography and aesthetic appreciation of the man who enriched humanity with such splendid and massive contributions to literature and thought.... The author of this excellent monograph...has read deeply the extensive writings of Rumi, and what others have said on the subject in ancient and modern times....I recommend this book warmly; it is a pleasure to read, and it holds the key to further delight for those many who will be encouraged by it to study further the immortal poetry of Rumi.—A.J. Arberry. Selections from Rumi's work are included in the text.

NICHOLSON, REYNOLD, tr. **DIVANI SHAMSI TABRIZ. Notes, 126pp. Rai73, 2.95p.**
When Shamsi met Rumi he took his books and threw them in a pool of water saying "Now you must live what you know." When a disturbed Rumi moved to save his books Shamsi told him that the theoretical knowledge in his hands was meaningless but if they meant so much to him he could remove them from the pool and they would be dry. Rumi declined and the two men embraced. To the jealousy of Rumi's students...the two merged as one being....Rumi was the teacher, the prophet, and Shamsi the enigmatic catalyst who knows and knows that he knows.—from the introduction. Shamsi was first driven from Konya by the students of Rumi and finally murdered by the students after Rumi in his loneliness brought him back to Konya. The poems in this volume were written after Shamsi's death in dedication to him, and they represent some of Rumi's finest work. This edition includes a good introduction and illustrations.

NICHOLSON, REYNOLD, tr. **THE MATHNAWI. Luz.**
Nicholson's volumes on the **Mathnawi** are considered the definitive edition. They were edited and translated from the oldest available manuscript and contain an abundance of critical notes and commentary. Volumes I (16.40c), III (out of print), and V (20.00c) contain the Persian texts of the **Mathnawi**—each incorporating two books. Volumes VII (14.50c) and VIII (17.30c) form Nicholson's complete commentary on the work. The translation is in three volumes which sell for 7.30p each. Part of the **Gibb Memorial Series**.

NICHOLSON, REYNOLD, tr. **RUMI, POET AND MYSTIC, 1207-1273: SELECTIONS FROM HIS WRITINGS. 190pp. A&U50, 7.95c.**
Beautiful and faithful translations of Rumi's last works of poetry. Covers a variety of subjects, illuminated by Professor Nicholson's notes on Sufi doctrine and experience. An introduction traces Rumi's life, literary output, and philosophy.

NICHOLSON, REYNOLD, tr. **SELECTED POEMS FROM THE DIVANI SHAMSI TABRIZ. Index, 422pp. CUP1898, 9.95p.**
This is the definitive edition of Professor Nicholson's translation of Rumi's poems dedicated to his friend and mentor Shams Tabriz. The Persian text and the translation are on facing pages. There are extensive notes on each poem as well as a number of technical appendices and a lengthy introduction.

WHINFIELD, E.H., tr. **TEACHINGS OF RUMI: THE MASNAVI. 342pp. Dut73/Oct, 3.95p.**
This is the only abridged English edition of Rumi's masterpiece. The translation does not match Nicholson's, but the price difference is considerable.

——— **END OF JALAL AL-DIN RUMI SUBSECTION** ———

Sa'di

Sa'di (c1213-1292) was one of the greatest figures in Persian classical literature. Very few hard facts are known about his life. All of the information we have comes from autobiographical references and anecdotes in his writings. He received a classical Islamic education and, at an early age, wandered abroad through Anatolia, Syria, Egypt, and Iraq. He also refers to travels in India and Central Asia, but these cannot be confirmed. When he reappeared in his native Shiraz he was an elderly man and he remained there for the rest of his life. His two best known works, the **Bustan** and **Gulistan**, were published in 1258 and 1259 respectively. Sa'di is also remembered as a great panegyrist and lyricist, and the author of a number of masterly odes portraying human experience. He also wrote in Arabic.

EASTWICK, EDWARD, tr. **THE ROSE GARDEN OR GULISTAN OF SA'DI.** 267pp. Oct1852, 6.00p.
This is Sa'di's most popular work, and the one for which he is best known. It was written about the same time as the **Bustan** and complements the latter work. The book consists of a series of instructive and often humorous prose stories. The great beauty of Sa'di's style lies in his simplicity and his work (and especially this book) remains among the most read and the most beloved literature in the Islamic world.

EDWARDS, A. HART, tr. **THE BUSTAN OF SA'DI. Introductory material, notes,** 147pp. MuA nd, 1.80c.
The translation reads well and this is probably a better edition to begin with than Wickens' because you can read the stories straight through without being constantly interrupted by annotations. Part of the **Wisdom of the East** series.

SCHOLEY, ARTHUR, tr. **THE DISCONTENTED DERVISHES.** 7"x9", 136pp. Deu77, 11.50c.
A collection of seventy-four stories selected from the **Gulistan** and the **Bustan,** topically arranged and retold in a simple style. This is the only popularly written edition of Sa'di available. The book is nicely produced and a number of line drawings by William Rushton accompany the text.

THYLMANN, KARL. **GULISTAN OF SA'DI.** 8½"x10½", ShP77, 4.95p.
A highly ornamental, illustrated collection of simple, readable translations. Delicate, detailed line drawings and borders fill the pages and bring the tales to life. Thylmann lived in the late nineteenth century and he illustrated this book for young children, in order to keep them amused.

WICKENS, G.M., tr. **THE BUSTAN OF SA'DI: MORALS POINTED AND TALES ADORNED. Introductory material, notes,** 344pp. UTo74, 37.00c.
Sa'di's **Bustan** is one of the best known moralistic poems in the whole of Persian literature, and this translation is the first fully annotated modern English edition. It is part of the **Persian Heritage** series. The text mixes anecdotes with precepts and illustrations of the proper life in its presentation of moral lessons. There is a good deal of variety within the poems as each of the 160 poems is a separate tale. The narrative reads well and the message is often cloaked within an entertaining tale.

END OF SA'DI SUBSECTION

SALIK, S.A. **THE EARLY HEROES OF ISLAM. Notes, index,** 426pp. TBH nd, 18.00c.
A political history of the early days of Islam and the major figures of the period: Muhammad, Abu Bakr, Omar, Othman, and Ali.

SALMIN, MOHAMMAD. **FATIMA: THE LADY OF LIGHT.** 191pp. TBH38, 6.50p.
Fatima was the only daughter of Muhammad and she is considered the embodiment of truth, virtue, modesty, and ideal womanhood. This is a badly written survey of all that is known about her life.

SAUNDERS, J.J. **A HISTORY OF MEDIEVAL ISLAM. Maps, chapter-by-chapter bibliographies, index,** 234pp. RKP65, 9.75c.
A thoughtful introductory survey of the history of the Middle East from the rise of Islam to the Mongol conquests, explaining and indicating the main trends of Islamic historical evolution during the Middle Ages.

■ SAVORY, R.M., ed. **INTRODUCTION TO ISLAMIC CIVILIZATION. Glossary, annotated bibliography, index,** 7½"x10", 212pp. CUP76, 6.95p.
A wide ranging general introduction to Islamic civilization from its origins to the present day. The book begins with a section on the geographic, ethnic, and linguistic background of the Middle East, continues with an historical resume of the Islamic period, and moves on to the core chapters on the religious, philosophical, and legal foundations of Islamic society and its contributions to world civilization in the fields of literature, art, science, and medicine. The selections are written in clear and nontechnical language and there are illustrations throughout.

■ SCERRATO, UMBERTO. **ISLAM. Index,** 9½"x12½", 192pp. G&D76/CaC, 19.95c.
A monumental pictorial investigation of Islamic civilization illustrated with 106 color photographs, maps, drawings, and charts. Also includes an anthology of Islamic texts and a history of Islamic civilization. An excellent survey for the general reader.

SCHACHT, JOSEPH and C.E. BOSWORTH, eds. **THE LEGACY OF ISLAM. Photographs, notes, bibliography, index,** 550pp. Oxf74, 18.75c.
The Legacy of Islam *takes Islam in the sense of a civilization, not merely a religion. . . . Thus in addition to chapters on Islamic theology, philosophy, and mysticism, and on Islamic religious law and constitutional theory, it contains others—and they are the majority—on aspects of Islamic political, economic, and cultural history, on Islamic art and architecture, and on Islamic medicine, science, and music. Although it was the responsibility of the editor to assemble a harmonious team of contributors, no rigid uniformity of opinion, or agreement with the opinion of the editor, have been imposed, and each author is responsible for his or her contribution exclusively. The same persons and the same subjects are occasionally discussed in more than one chapter; this follows from the fact that they are of importance to more than one aspect of the* **Legacy of Islam.**—from the introduction. The contributors are all experts in their fields.

■ SCHIMMEL, ANNEMARIE. **MYSTICAL DIMENSIONS OF ISLAM.** 526pp. UNC75, 7.00p.
Dr. Schimmel is a professor of Indo-Muslim Culture at Harvard University and is very well known for her translations. Here she gives us an excellent balanced historical treatment of Sufism from its beginnings through the nineteenth century. After exploring the origins of the mystical movement in the meditations of orthodox Muslims on the **Qur'an** and the prophetic tradition, the author then discusses the development of its different stages. Particular emphasis is placed on spiritual education and on Sufi psychology and Sufi orders. Professor Schimmel examines mystical poetry in Arabic, Persian, Turkish, Sindhi, Punjabi, and Pashto and provides selected translations. She also demonstrates how Sufi ideals permeated the whole fabric of Muslim life, providing the average Muslim—villager or intellectual—with the virtues of perfect trust in God and the loving surrender to God's will. This book reads very well and, while the scholarship is impeccable, we also get the feeling that the author has more than an academic knowledge of her subject. This is the best overall account of Sufism that we have seen and we recommend it highly. The bibliography is quite extensive, notes accompany the text, and there are indices of names, places, and subjects.

SCHUON, FRITHJOF. **ISLAM AND THE PERENNIAL PHILOSOPHY. Index,** 228pp. WIF76, 10.25p.
Schuon considers the relationships and diversities between all true religions and their metaphysical unity. He also discusses the connections between Shi'ism and Sunnism within Islam and reflects on the dilemma of evil and the Quranic promise for the afterlife.

■ SCHUON, FRITHJOF. **UNDERSTANDING ISLAM. Many notes, index,** 159pp. Vik61/A&U, 1.45p.
Schuon's purpose is to explain the basics of the Islamic belief. In achieving this aim, he considers four essentials: the nature of the

Muslim perspective, the doctrine about and the function of the Qur'an, the role of the prophet, and Sufism. An excellent introductory volume, highly recommended.

SEMAAN, KHALIL ASH-SHAFI'I'S RISALAH. 96pp. MuA61, 1.80p.
Ash-Shafi'i lived in the eighth century. Al-Risalah was the first book written on Islamic jurisprudence and criticism and it is still one of the most important works on the subject. This volume presents a summary of the main points in the work, along with a short biographical study of the author.

SHABISTAN, MAHMUD. THE SECRET GARDEN. 81pp. Dut74/Oct, 2.25p.
We know very little about the life of the author...but his work is important out of all comparison...because it is a compendium of Sufi terminology in the form of question and answer. A fourteenth century work, arranged topically. Includes an introductory essay on Sufi thought.

SHAH, IDRIES. THE BOOK OF THE BOOK. Oct nd, 5.85c.
Shah was born into a noble Afghan family that traces its descent back to the prophet. He is the most visible Sufi master in the West today and has his own school in England. In his travels throughout the Middle East, Shah collected a massive number of tales, aphorisms, and teaching stories. He has made an excellent series of contemporary renderings which have been published in many different books. The purpose of these tales is not merely to entertain—though entertaining they are—but also to provide concrete examples of nonlinear thinking. This volume is basically a blank book, although there are a number of stories on the first few pages.

SHAH, IDRIES. CARAVAN OF DREAMS. 207pp. Vik68/QuB, 1.95p.
A nice selection of writings: stories of Rumi and Mulla Nasrudin, proverbs, short fables, and longer pieces.

SHAH, IDRIES. THE DERMIS PROBE. 191pp. Dut71/CaL, 3.75p.
Another collection of short stories and anecdotes.

SHAH, IDRIES. DESTINATION MECCA. Many photographs, 183pp. Oct57, 14.20c.
Shah's only travel guide, containing a wealth of information, including philosophical material.

SHAH, IDRIES. THE EXPLOITS OF THE INCREDIBLE MULLA NASRUDIN. 159pp. Dut72/PnB, 2.95p.
Shah's three Nasrudin books are the most popular of any of his volumes. Nasrudin is a bit of a rogue and gets into all kinds of incredible situations. His appeal is as universal and timeless as the truths he illustrates. Many delightful illustrations accompany the teaching stories collected here.

SHAH, IDRIES. THE MAGIC MONASTERY. 208pp. Dut72/PnB, 3.95p.
Differs from its predecessors in that it contains not only traditional tales but also stories especially written by Shah to complete the book as *a course in nonlinear thinking.*

SHAH, IDRIES. ORIENTAL MAGIC. Many illustrations, categorized annotated bibliography, 206pp. Dut56/Grn, 3.75p.
Here Shah surveys and analyzes the many varieties of magical rites and beliefs practiced in the Orient. He covers Jewish magic, Egyptian magic, the contribution of the Arabs, magic and alchemy in India, love magic, wonder workers of Tibet, and much else.

SHAH, IDRIES. PLEASANTRIES OF THE INCREDIBLE MULLA NASRUDIN. 220pp. Dut71/PnB, 2.95p.
A collection of teaching stories—outstanding both as an anthology of humor and as a book of Sufi wisdom. Stories by Rumi, Jami, and Attar. Our personal favorite. Highly recommended, these small tales will add pleasure to everyone's life. Includes whimsical drawings.

SHAH, IDRIES. REFLECTIONS: FABLES IN THE SUFI TRADITION. 146pp. Vik68, 2.50p.

SHAH, IDRIES. THE SECRET LORE OF MAGIC. Many illustrations, 316pp. Stu58/Mll, 3.95p.
Includes the entire text of the four **Books of the Secrets of Albertus Magnus,** the **Book of the Spirits,** the **Almadel,** the **Book of Power,** the **Clavicle and the Testament,** and many other ancient **Grimores.**

SHAH, IDRIES. THE SUBTLETIES OF THE INIMITABLE MULLA NASRUDIN. 176pp. Dut73/CaL, 2.95p.
The newest collection of the wisdom of Nasrudin.

SHAH, IDRIES. THE SUFIS. Notes, bibliography, index, 451pp. Dou71/Wyn, 2.95p.
The most comprehensive account of Sufism available. Includes chapters on the great Sufi masters, the dervishes, and details of the metaphysical philosophy underlying Sufi practices. Recommended only for the reader desiring a full account of Sufism. Introduction by Robert Graves.

SHAH, IDRIES. TALES OF THE DERVISHES: TEACHING STORIES OF THE SUFI MASTERS OVER THE PAST 1000 YEARS. 220pp. Dut70/PnB, 2.95p.
On one level these tales can be read as enchanting fables or folklore. However, their true function has been as Sufi teaching stories used by dervish masters to instruct their disciples in the mysteries of Sufism. This collection contains stories from Persian, Arabic, Turkish, and other cultures.

SHAH, IDRIES. THINKERS OF THE EAST: TEACHINGS OF THE DERVISHES. 198pp. Vik71, 1.95p.
Another collection of teaching stories.

■ *SHAH, IDRIES.* THE WAY OF THE SUFI. 288pp. Dut70/Pen, 3.45p.
This is the best single primer on Sufism. Shah includes an excellent anthology of classical writings, an essay on the study of Sufism in the West, information on the four major Sufi orders, many teaching stories, and much else.

SHAH, IDRIES. WISDOM OF THE IDIOTS. 179pp. Dut71/Oct, 2.75p.
Collection of narratives of the action philosophy of the Sufi thinkers, who called themselves idiots, in contrast to the many self styled wisemen.

SHAH, IDRIES, et al. THE ELEPHANT IN THE DARK AND OTHER WRITINGS ON THE DIFFUSION OF SUFI IDEAS IN THE WEST. Bibliography, 160pp. Dut76, 3.95p.
A collection of essays which give a good sense of the relevance of

Sufism to Western thought. Some of the selections have been written by Shah himself; others discuss Sufism in general and Shah's work in particular. Originally entitled, **The Diffusion of Sufi Ideas in the West**.

SHAH, SIRDAR IKBAL ALI. **ISLAMIC SUFISM.** 299pp. Wei nd, 2.50p.
An excellent survey discussing various aspects of Sufism, including an extensive analysis of music in Sufism and of Sufi practices. The author is Idries Shah's father.

SHAH, SIRDAR IKBAL ALI. **THE SPIRIT OF THE EAST.** 2.95p.
See the Comparative Religion section.

SHARDA, S.R. **SUFI THOUGHT. Notes, bibliography, index,** 312pp. MuM74, 19.15c.
A detailed study of Punjabi Sufism. Includes comparisons between this form of Sufism and Hindu mystical philosophies and a study of its impact on Punjabi literature.

SHARIB, ZAHURUL. **KHAWAJA GHARIB NAWAZ.** 162pp. MuA61, 3.75c.
This is a biographical study of the great twelfth century saint and scholar of the Chishti Order. The book also contains excerpts from some of his writings and discourses.

SHEIKH, SAEED. **STUDIES IN MUSLIM PHILOSOPHY. Notes, bibliography, index,** 262pp. MuA69, 4.50c.
The first third of this scholarly work is devoted to an exposition of the four principal philosophical movements of the early medieval period. The rest of the volume devotes a chapter each to the group of thinkers who were known during the same period as the *Philosophers*, i.e. those under the influence of Greek philosophy.

SHERWANI, NAWAB. **LIFE OF ABU-BAKR. Index,** 200pp. MuA47, 3.75p.
This is a very readable study of the life and important works of the first caliph of Islam. Most of the book details Abu Bakr's battles and conquests, as that was basically what his life was devoted to. Translated from the Urdu by S.M. Haq.

SINGH, BAIJNATH. **LETTERS FROM A SUFI TEACHER.** 133pp. Wei08, 2.75p.
This is an excellent collection of letters on Sufi teachings, presenting the main principles so that the individual can integrate them into his daily life. Centering on spiritual development, they effectively demonstrate that the differences between spiritual and everyday life are imaginary. Spiritual understanding is shown to be one of the surest methods of harmonizing inner and outer life, making it possible for men to use worldly duties and human relationships as tools for inner development and bridges to divine union. In the letters the student is given a thorough introduction to the nature of discipleship, self awareness, and understanding of the human condition. The letters cover the heart of Islamic teaching as well as any material we know of.

SIRAJ ED-DIN, ABU BAKR. **THE BOOK OF CERTAINTY.** 108pp. Wei52, 2.25p.
Our aim has been to express in the language of Sufism some of the universal truths which lie at the heart of all religions. Each chapter serves as a commentary upon some verse or verses of the **Qur'an**. *The book is also based on various sayings of the Prophet, and to a certain extent upon a Quranic commentary attributed to Muhyiddin ibn 'Arabi.*

SMITH, MARGARET. **RABI'A THE MYSTIC AND HER FELLOW SAINTS IN ISLAM. Notes, bibliography, indices,** 245pp. Rai28, 4.95p.
The biographical sources for Rabi'a are fragmentary and this is the only complete study available. It is a valuable book for all who are interested in the Sufi tradition, since Rabi'a was one of the greatest Islamic saints. The volume also includes an account of the place of women in Islam. Many quotations from primary and secondary sources are interspersed throughout.

SMITH, MARGARET. **THE WAY OF THE MYSTICS: THE EARLY CHRISTIAN MYSTICS AND THE RISE OF THE SUFIS. Bibliography, index,** 288pp. SlP31, 3.95p.
In the early centuries after Christ, the Islamic religion was growing and Sufism was beginning to develop. In this volume Ms. Smith shows the relationship of the Sufis and their teaching to the already existing mysticism found in the early Christian Church of the Near and Middle East. She surveys the mystical thought and teaching which is found in both Christian and Sufi writings and quotes extensively from the writings of early Christian and Sufi mystics. A scholarly study, originally entitled **Studies in Early Mysticism in the Near and Middle East**.

SMITH, WILFRED CANTWELL. **ISLAM IN MODERN HISTORY. Notes, index,** 327pp. PUP57, 3.45p.
Smith says that *This is a study of a people in the turmoil of the modern world. The Muslim community in our day, like the rest of mankind, is in serious transition. What distinguishes it is that its members face the perplexities and opportunities of modernity as heirs of a unique tradition. Their society is characterized by a faith, Islam, and a great past. What is happening to the community and to the faith is the attempted subject of this book.* This is a remarkable book, filled with insight and wisdom; Smith has spent many years in Islamic countries.

SORDO, ENRIQUE. **MOORISH SPAIN. Bibliography, index,** 8"x11", 223pp. Ele63, 29.95c.
An examination of the political and cultural achievements of the Moors as seen in the principal cities of Andalucia: Cordoba, Seville, and Granada. Most of the book is devoted to Granada, where the Moorish spirit reached its greatest heights. There is a fine text which is accompanied by a spectacular series of full page illustrations, thirty-two in color and forty-eight in black and white.

STEWART, DESMOND. **THE ALHAMBRA. Chronology, index,** 9"x 11¾", 172pp. Nsw74/ReD, 11.95c.
The Alhambra is the last and finest Muslim monument in Spain. From 711 until 1492 Iberia was largely in Islamic hands. For part of this long period, there was peaceful intermingling of Muslim, Christian, and Jew under tolerant caliphs, culminating in a rich cultural potpourri. Many of the discoveries and speculations of Islamic Spain occurred at a time when the rest of Europe was mired in the Dark Ages and fueled the later Christian Renaissance. It is doubtful that anywhere in the world there are buildings that so completely express the spirit of an entire civilization as does the Alhambra. Here, embraced by austere walls, the achievements and aspirations, the fears and fantasies of Muslim Spain are embodied in a scattering of buildings that are a miracle of grace and fancy. More than 100 illustrations, nearly half in color, are the main feature of this history of Islamic Spain and its best known monument. They range from vistas and closeups of the Alhambra itself to art and artifacts of the period. A special section contains writings about the Alhambra from the sixteenth century to the present.

STODDARD, WILLIAM. **SUFISM. Bibliography, index,** 91pp. Wei76/ TPL, 6.95c.
This volume is designed as a summary of the mystical doctrines and methods of Islam. The presentation is exceedingly brief and not as clear as we might wish. Many of the major terms are discussed and Sufism is related to the Western mystical tradition and to other Eastern religions. The appendix presents a series of short quotations.

SUBHAN, JOHN. **SUFISM: ITS SAINTS AND SHRINES.** 412pp. Wei38, 8.50c.
Presents material on Islamic mysticism and its saints—material which has heretofore only been available in Persian and Urdu literature. He outlines the general principles of Sufism, considers the teachings which are the basis of Sufi practice, the introduction of Sufism in India, the Sufi attitude toward Hinduism, and discusses the religious orders.

SUFI CEREMONY: RIFA' CEREMONY (A RECORDING). 6.98.
A 33 1/3 rpm record of an actual celebration of the Rifa'iyya Sufi Order in South Africa. Participants in the ritual celebration achieve a trancelike state which makes them oblivious to pain and able to perform remarkable feats. The album is unclear as if recorded from a distance. Descriptive notes are included.

SUHRAWARDI, SHAHAB-U'D-DIN. **THE 'AWARIF-U'L-MA'ARIF.** **310pp. MuA1891, 6.75c.**
Idries Shah has said that this volume contains an excellent summary of the thought and action of the dervishes. The book was written by Shaikh Shahab-u'd Din Umar b. Muhammad Suhrawardi (1144-1234), the founder of an order of dervishes, and Lt. Clarke, the translator, was himself a dervish.

TOWNSON, DUNCAN. **MUSLIM SPAIN. Glossary, 8¼"x8", 48pp. CUP73, 3.45p.**
A pictorial presentation.

TRIMINGHAM, J. SPENCER. **A HISTORY OF ISLAM IN WEST AFRICA. Chronology, notes, index, 271pp. Oxf62, 4.70p.**
Dr. Trimingham is not attempting to write a history of West Africa, but rather to show the way in which Islam spread and moulded the history of the western Sudan. His thesis is that a fundamental change occurred towards the end of the eighteenth century in Islam's relationship to the indigenous African civilizations, a change which transformed it into a social and political force and helped usher in a new age.

TRIMINGHAM, J. SPENCER. **THE SUFI ORDERS IN ISLAM. Glossary, index, 281pp. Oxf71, 3.50p.**
This is the first attempt in this century to study the orders through which the organizational aspect of the Sufi spirit was expressed within the context of Islamic society. Trimingham shows how they developed and changed, traces their relationship to the unfolding of mystical ideas, and describes their rituals and ceremonial practices. Finally, he assesses the influence of these Sufi orders upon Islamic society in general. Supplementing the text is a very extensive bibliography, including sources in the Oriental as well as European languages.

ULLMANN, MANFRED. **ISLAMIC MEDICINE. Illustrations, notes, indices, 152pp. EUP78, 12.75c.**
An analysis of the specific character of Islamic medicine, concentrating on certain of its basic aspects. After a brief account of the development of Islamic medicine and its transmission to Europe, Ullmann goes on to explain some of its main characteristics—its system of human physiology, its ideas about the nature of disease and how infection is transmitted, its rules for diet and the use of drugs. A final chapter explains the relation of *rational medicine* to the occult and astrology.

UNESCO COLLECTION. **MUSICAL SOURCES—ZIKR: ISLAMIC RITUAL, RIFA'IYYA BROTHERHOOD OF ALEPPO (A RECORDING). 7.65.**
This is a well recorded 33 1/3 rpm transcription of a Sufi ceremony. Side one builds up a state of exaltation leading up to the *zikr.* Side two presents an abridgment of a *zikr,* ecstatic religious chanting by a group of Sufis.

VALIUDDIN, MIR. **THE ESSENTIAL FEATURES OF ISLAM. 573pp. MoB nd, 9.00c.**
This is a fairly scholarly study delineating the main features of Islam, as revealed in the **Qur'an** and presented by the prophet, in terms of their practical application. Dr. Valiuddin is head of the Department of Philosophy at Osmania University in India. He includes many quotations from the sacred literature, including the **Qur'an**. The approach incorporates the psychological, the mystical, and the practical. All of the major Islamic schools of thought and practice are reviewed quite thoroughly.

VALIUDDIN, MIR. **LOVE OF GOD: THE SUFI APPROACH. Notes, 205pp. SPC68, 3.40p.**
An interesting attempt to analyze and determine the nature of love as understood in a sublime sense. The text is filled with quotes in English and in Persian from the works of eminent Sufis reflecting their own experiences, sentiments, and intuitive feelings.

VALIUDDIN, MIR. **THE QURANIC SUFISM. 216pp. MoB77, 13.50c.**
A penetrating study of Sufism, suggested only to those who are already well versed in the literature. Valiuddin divides his discussion into the following major topics: *What is Sufism?, Worship in Islam, Transcendence and Immanence, Tanazzulat—The Descent of the Absolute, Self-Determinism, Good and Evil,* and *Divine Presence.* The author includes many quotations from the sacred literature.

WADDY, CHARIS. **THE MUSLIM MIND. Illustrations, notes, 223pp. Lon76, 17.65c.**
Dr. Waddy has compiled a useful survey of Muslim attitudes and thought on a wide variety of topics from international relations through family life. The information is well organized and is derived from copious quotations from Islamic sacred literature, from contemporary Islamic writing, and from the author's personal interviews with Muslims.

WADE, DAVID. **THE ISLAMIC COLOURING BOOK. 8½"x11½", Wdw76, 5.35p.**
A nice collection of geometric designs with wide lines for coloring, accompanied by quotations from Sufis on facing pages.

WADE, DAVID. **PATTERN IN ISLAMIC ART. 20.00c.**
See the Sacred Art section.

WATNEY, JOHN. **TRAVELS IN ARABY OF LADY HESTER STANHOPE. Index, 294pp. Cre75, 16.95c.**
Lady Stanhope was William Pitt's niece. In the early nineteenth century she traveled extensively throughout the Arab world on her own, at a time when few Westerners ventured into the uncharted Arab lands. She adopted the customs, language, and dress of her Arab companions, and had a multitude of adventures. Near the end of her life her reputation was so great that not even the Sultan dared defy her. This volume often reads like a novel and it includes many period drawings, including some in color.

WATT, W. MONTGOMERY. **THE FORMATIVE PERIOD OF ISLAMIC THOUGHT. Notes, bibliography, index, 436pp. EUP73, 12.50c.**
This massive study represents Professor Watt's major single contribution to Islamic studies to date. It covers the ground of his earlier **Free Will and Predestination in Early Islam**, though it greatly modifies and extends the plan of that work. Watt makes a more radical critique of the sources than has hitherto been attempted. The main sections are as follows: *The Kharijites, Proto-Shi'ite Phenomena under the Umayyads, The General Religious Movement, God's Determination of Events, Faith and Community, The Establishment of the Abbasids, The Attraction of Reasoning, The Great Mu'tazilites, The Polarity of Sunnism and Shi'ism,* and *The Maturing of Sunnite Theology.*

WATT, W. MONTGOMERY. **THE INFLUENCE OF ISLAM ON MEDIEVAL EUROPE. Notes, index, 133pp. EUP72, 8.75c.**
Professor Watt describes how Islamic culture gradually made its way into Western Europe through trade contracts and political presence in Spain and Sicily. He contrasts Arab achievements in mathematics, astronomy, medicine, logic, and metaphysics with the knowledge of science, philosophy, and medicine in Europe. An appendix contains a listing of English words derived from Arabic.

WATT, W. MONTGOMERY. **ISLAM AND THE INTEGRATION OF SOCIETY. Notes, index, 302pp. NUP61, 16.15c.**
An excellent academic discussion of the title theme.

WATT, W. MONTGOMERY. **ISLAMIC PHILOSOPHY AND THEOLOGY. Notes, bibliography, index, 209pp. EUP62, 8.50c.**
A technical work; Watt reviews the relevant literature, looks at the contemporary position of studies in this field, notes the main controversies, and points to some of the chief gaps.

WATT, W. MONTGOMERY. **THE MAJESTY THAT WAS ISLAM. Index, 276pp. S&J74, 10.95c.**
This is a detailed study of the Islamic world between AD 661 and 1100. Watt looks at the civilization as a whole, showing the close inter-twining of literature and religion with politics. The volume is clearly written; however, the abundance of material is probably more than the general reader would want to know. An excellent subject organized bibliography and over fifty illustrations are included.

WELCH, STUART. **PERSIAN PAINTINGS. 9.95p.**
See the Sacred Art section.

WESINCK, A.J. **MUSLIM CREED: ITS GENESIS AND HISTORICAL DEVELOPMENT. Notes, index, 311pp. FrC32, 22.50c.**
A comprehensive study of the historical development of Muslim dogmatics, consisting for the most part of translations of, and commentaries on, the creed in its various forms. The discussion is historical rather than systematic, although there are a number of systematic, introductory chapters.

■ *WILLIAMS, JOHN A. , ed.* **ISLAM. Pronunciation guide, notes, index, 256pp. Brz61, 6.95c.**
A well organized anthology of the finest translations of essential Islamic texts. Williams provides excellent, integrative material and has organized his collection into the following general topics: *The* **Qur'an**: *The Word of God; The Hadith: The News of God's Messenger; The Law: Fiqh; Shari'a; Sufism: The Interior Religion of the Community; Kalam: The Statements of the Theologians;* and *The Dissidents of the Community.*

WILLIAMS, JOHN A., ed. **THEMES OF ISLAMIC CIVILIZATION. Notes, annotated bibliography, index, 382pp. UCa71, 15.75c.**
This book illustrates the thematic and archetypal ideas that moulded Muslim minds and were expressed in Islamic institutions of government, law, and culture. Each chapter demonstrates, by means of selections from works of history, law, poetry, philosophy, and letters, a set of attitudes commonly found in Islam. Within each chapter the texts, arranged chronologically, represent works from early Islam to modern times. The editor provides a running commentary on the texts—many of which have been translated here for the first time.

WILLIAMS, L.F.R., ed. **SUFI STUDIES: EAST AND WEST. Dut74/Oct, 3.95p.**
Twenty-four world scholars offer, in tribute to Idries Shah, analyses of Sufism from the literary, scientific, religious, and historical points of view. The contributors include, in addition to Persian and Arab specialists, a Chinese expert on the Middle East, a Coptic-Christian savant, a Hindu monk who has made Sufism a major study, Jewish scholars, and members of both the Sunni and Shia persuasions in Islam.

WOLFSON, HARRY. **THE PHILOSOPHY OF THE KALAM. Notes, bibliographies, 805pp. HUP76, 40.30c.**
Kalam, an Arabic term meaning speech, and hence discussion, was applied to early attempts in Islam to adduce philosophic proofs for religious beliefs. It later came to designate a system of religious philosophy which reached its highest point in the eleventh century; the masters of *kalam*, known as *mutakallimun*, were in many respects the Muslim equivalent of the Christian church fathers. Professor Wolfson studies the *kalam* systematically, unfolding its philosophical origins and implications and observing its repercussions in other religions. He scrutinizes Islamic texts and shows how Quranic teachings were constantly interwoven with ideas from Greek and Oriental philosopies, Judaism, and Christianity, as Islamic thought developed.

JEWISH MYSTICISM

For the Jew, community and religious observance are one. The mystic cannot isolate himself from his fellow men even in his esoteric practices, for the core of his faith, the divine revelation at Sinai, appeared not to one man, but to a community numbering six hundred thousand souls. The Jewish mystical experience has remained communal ever since. Suffering and persecution have infused it with hopes for messianic redemption; exile has imbued it with nationalism. When foreign tyrants were not busy exterminating the Jewish community, then false Messiahs and internal heresy seekers were doing their best to destroy the mystic vision from within. In the seventeenth century Smyrna-born Sabbatai Zevi, a self-proclaimed Messiah, succeeded in uprooting entire Jewish communities throughout Europe and the Near East. Envisioning immediate redemption at his hands, ecstatic bands followed their manic-depressive leader to Turkey. Those who returned home often found themselves broken, penniless nomads. Those who continued in their blind belief turned to license and apostasy. In the name of mystical redemption, Sabbatai Zevi (who finally converted to Islam) almost succeeded in destroying Jewish mysticism once and for all.

For more than a hundred years after this debacle, true followers of the mystical tradition practiced in secret, until, in the eighteenth century, they emerged as European Hasidim. And then, during the decaying Hasidic dynasties which followed, cults again sprang up around one master, a *tzaddik* whose supply of divine grace was believed powerful enough to transform an entire community of moonstruck devotees. Men threw up their jobs, donned exotic clothing, and exhibited exotic behavior in the name of their *tzaddik*; they carried him through the streets on a palanquin and let their families go in want, without even the basic necessities, in order to serve the needs of the master. This kind of worship was very un-Jewish, since Jews traditionally find it hard to submit to the absolute mental tyranny of another human being. Great teachers have always been revered among them, but the Jew was never to kneel before a *graven image*—even if it was the projected saintly image of his spiritual master. Yet the Jews continued to display a penchant for teacher worship that is still apparent today.

Because of its communal nature, Jewish mystical practice presents a double burden: one must not only learn to cleave to God, but he must take the entire community, the entire creation, with him! And, in order not to destroy them en route, he must be perfect. With Moses as his model, the Jewish mystic must concentrate on God in his every daily act, with his every breath; but he must always come down from the *high place* and live among the people as well. By *yoking* himself to God he develops a power of love so great that he brings the godly influx into this imperfect world of men.

From the earliest times the practice of Jewish mysticism has been secret. In eleventh-century Spain a philosopher named Ibn Gabirol labeled these secret oral teachings *Kabbalah*, or *tradition*. All Jewish mystical practice since then falls under the heading of *Kabbalah*. But that should not mislead us, for the same spiritual life style and practice, the same involvement with community predominated regardless of time or culture long before the eleventh century of the Common Era. But the Kabbalists did their work only too well. Fearful of persecution from within and without the Jewish community, they buried an already esoteric tradition even deeper. The complicated diagrams and mystic texts that pass for Kabbalah today were often deliberately distorted in order to confuse the uninitiated eye. The tradition was itself passed down orally from master to disciple, thus insuring its integrity on the one hand and providing personal guidance on the other. In the thirteenth century in Spain much of it came to light in written form in a book called **Zohar** (**Book of Splendor**), which supposedly described the exploits and teachings of Rabbi Simeon bar Yohai, a first-century sage and master Kabbalist. Yet even this *explication* of kabbalistic beliefs and practices leaves both laymen and scholars hardly more informed about its practical application than they were before.

Kabbalah is not an intellectual discipline, nor is it—like the **Talmud**—a rational exegesis of Jewish Law. It is first and foremost a mystical practice, but one that is fully dependent on, and integrated with, Judaism as a whole. Trying to practice kabbalistic *meditation* without understanding its foundation in the **Torah** (the **Pentateuch**) would be like trying to fly without wings. One cannot even begin to live the mystical life as a Jew without a knowledge of Hebrew, for the very stuff of its contemplation is the language of the **Torah**. Various Kabbalists have used the individual letters comprising chapter and verse as subjects for meditation. Contrary to most other spiritual disciplines which urge the seeker to get away from it all, to retire to a quiet place in the country and meditate, the Jewish mystic is urged to start living in the midst of worldly activity in a new way. He begins with the advice of the talmudic sages who urge him to *eat bread with salt, drink water moderately, sleep on the ground, lead a close life, and study hard.*

Different masters have interpreted this injunction in different ways. The dispersion of the Jews has made a consistent school of mystical practice almost impossible. The wonder is that, despite the scattered and often culturally incompatible populations, Jewish mystical practices are so similar. Hebrew as a common language undoubtedly helped. Ancient mystics placed great emphasis on visionary experience and contemplation. Sephardic Jews concentrated more on the prophetic aspects of meditation and on the Jews as a holy community. European mystics elevated prayer to divine status. With the **Pentateuch** and Laws as its guide, the Kabbalah has flourished—sometimes darkly and sometimes brilliantly—for over five thousand years. Often so incorporated into the everyday life of the Jews that it has gone unnoticed, mysticism once again appears to be enjoying a popular resurgence. Since it is almost entirely centered on the words of its great masters and on their personal approaches to its implementation in Jewish life, the Kabbalah can best be understood through the teachings themselves.

—*from* **Kabbalah: The Way of the Jewish Mystic**, *by Perle Epstein*

445

ABELSON, J. IMMANENCE OF GOD IN RABBINICAL LITERA-TURE. Many notes, index, 399pp. SHP12, 14.50c.
In a long introduction Abelson explains what is meant by the idea of the *Immanence of God* and what the Rabbinical literature consists of. Later chapters discuss the concept and the major ideas involved in it as it appears throughout the literature.

ABELSON, J. JEWISH MYSTICISM. Bibliography, index, 190pp. SPH13, 6.75c.
Dr. Abelson combines his wide acquaintance with Rabbinical literature with thorough research into all sources of Jewish mystical teaching to trace the development and summarize the teachings of the Qabala. He begins with a study of the mystical tradition as found in the **Old Testament** and in the teachings of the Essenes. From there he discusses the Merkabah (Chariot) mysteries. The next two chapters are devoted to the teachings of Philo and to the *Kingdom of Heaven*. Then he gets into the heart of the Qabalistic tradition, with material on the **Sepher Yetzirah**, the **Zohar**, the *sephiroth*, and the soul. Dr. Abelson expects his readers to have a general familiarity with his terminology and sources, so this does not make too good an introduction for the general reader.

ABULAFIA, ABRAHAM. THE PATH OF NAMES. 75pp. Tre76, 4.00p.
A collection of translations and adaptations by Bruria Finkel, Jack Hirschman, David Meltzer, and Gershom Scholem from the writings of Abraham ben Samuel Abulafia, a thirteenth century Sephardic Qabalist. Much of this work is concerned with the meaning of the tetragramaton.

ACHAD, FRATER. THE ANATOMY OF THE BODY OF GOD—BEING THE SUPREME REVELATION OF COMIC CONSCIOUS-NESS. 111pp. Wei69, 10.00c.
A complicated attempt to help the finite mind of man comprehend the infinite by means of many geometric drawings based on extensions of the Tree of Life. Achad's books are very intricate and esoteric; we have never been able to get much from them.

ACHAD, FRATER. THE EGYPTIAN REVIVAL OR THE EVER-COMING SON IN THE LIGHT OF THE TAROT. 123pp. Wei69, 10.00c.
A miscellany of thoughts and illustrations centered on the Western mystery tradition. Achad discusses the symbolism of the tarot trumps according to his *reformed astrological order*, offers a summary of the earliest human traditions, and much else.

ACHAD, FRATER. QBL OR BRIDE'S RECEPTION: A SHORT QABALISTIC TREATISE ON THE TREE OF LIFE. 152pp. Wei69, 10.00c.
This is the first book in Achad's series, as well as the most important one for students of the Qabala. He deals with the formation of the Tree of Life, the paths, correspondences in the Hebrew alphabet, the tarot, numbers, symbols, the macrocosm and microcosm. A long appendix is devoted to Achad's *reformed astrological order*. Many detailed illustrations —some in color. Achad uses a large number of Hebrew words; most are translated.

ARYEH, ISAIAH and JOSHUA DVORKES, eds. THE BAAL SHEM TOV ON PIRKEY AVOTH. 176pp. Fld74, 10.00c.
A selection of the Baal Shem Tov's writings on the *Ethics of the Fathers*, including thoughts, interpretations, and explanations.

ASHLAG, RABBI YEHUDA. KABBALAH—TEN LUMINOUS EMA-NATIONS. 131pp. RCK73, 10.00c.
An interpretation of the *sephiroth* or Heavenly Attributes according to the system of Rabbi Yitzhak Luria. Also contains the Hebrew to English text of Luria's **Tree of Life**. Rabbi Ashlag is the author of a twenty-one volume translation of the **Zohar** from Aramaic into Hebrew, with commentary. He is the founder of the Research Center for the Kabbalah in Jerusalem. There is a long introduction by Dr. Philip Gruberger, the present director of the Center.

BAHYA IBN PAKUDA. THE BOOK OF DIRECTION TO THE DUTIES OF THE HEART. Indices, 480pp. RKP73, 18.75c.
A translation of an important eleventh century Arabic work in which Bahya investigates the motivation of Judaic religious practice and embarks on a philosophical enquiry into the nature of God, religion,

and man. The book shows the influence of both Islamic mysticism and Neoplatonism. Professor Menahem Mansoor, the translator, also supplies a long introduction and many notes.

BAKEN, DAVID. SIGMUND FREUD AND THE JEWISH MYSTICAL TRADITION. Notes, index, 448pp. Bea58, 4.95p.
In a provocative study Baken, himself a well known psychologist, argues that the roots of Freudian psychoanalysis can be found in the history of Judaism and particularly in the Jewish mystical tradition. He begins by reviewing the background of Freud's development of psychoanalysis. Next he delves deeply into the Jewish mystical tradition, with chapters on the Qabala, the **Zohar**, the Sabbatai Sevi, and Hasidism. In the third part he develops the Moses theme in the thought of Freud; and in a fourth section, discusses the devil theme as it appears in the literature and as it was understood by Freud. Finally, he integrates Freudian psychoanalysis with the Qabala.

■ **BAND, ARNOLD, tr. NAHMAN OF BRATSLAV—THE TALES. Bibliography, indices, 359pp. Pau78, 6.95p.**
The body of this work is comprised of thirteen tales attributed to Rabbi Nahman of Bratslav, one of the most renowned early Hasidic masters and probably the greatest of the Hasidic storytellers. These tales are presented in a form which is both readable and true to the originals. Band also provides an introduction and commentaries.

BARDON, FRANZ. THE KEY TO THE TRUE QUABBALAH. 270pp. Rug74, 12.00c.
An excellent discussion of Qabalistic Hermetics, illustrated with an abundance of drawings. We suggest this book only to those who are well versed in the Western mystery tradition.

BARON, SALO and JOSEPH BLAU, eds. JUDAISM: POSTBIBLICAL AND TALMUDIC PERIOD. Introduction, glossary, notes, 271pp. BoM54, 6.00p.
A good selection of primary source writings. The translations tend to be somewhat dry.

■ **BEN-AMOS, DAN and JEROME MINTZ, eds. and trs. IN PRAISE OF THE BAAL SHEM TOV. Introduction, 382pp. IUP70, 4.50p.**
A translation of the earliest collection of legends about the founder of Hasidism. The translators also supply notes, indices, a glossary, and a chart of the legends and their sources. The translations themselves are well done and the legends form a moving portrayal of the Baal Shem Tov.

BLOCH, CHAYIM. THE GOLEM: MYSTICAL TALES FROM THE GHETTO OF PRAGUE. 244pp. Mul72, 2.25p.
The Golem stories originated in the ghettos of medieval Germany and the Golem theme has provided the inspiration for a wealth of stories, plays, novels, and occult studies up to the present day. The Golem is a mystical servant created to serve his people in their sufferings. This is a collection of some of the most noted tales.

BLOOM, HAROLD. KABBALAH AND CRITICISM. 127pp. Sea75, 6.95c.
Bloom is a literary critic who has written studies on Yeats, Blake, and Shelley. He begins this study with a brief review of major Qabalistic concepts. The bulk of the book is devoted to an analysis of the great Qabalistic commentators and the *revisionary ratios* they employed. Unless the reader is quite familiar with Qabalistic literature, this book will have little meaning.

BOND, FREDERICK and THOMAS LEA. GEMATRIA. 127pp. TPL77, 7.45p.
Each letter of the alphabet in *gematria* possesses a number that helps to establish a numerical link between one apparently different word or phrase and another, and this with a third, and so on. This continuing link is the basis of the esoteric channels of wisdom known as *gematria*. This is a highly detailed, technical study of *gematria*, incorporating many diagrams.

Martin Buber

Buber (1878-1965) was originally a fervent Zionist and worked closely with Theodor Herzl and Chaim Weizmann. He became deeply involved in a study of Hasidism, the mystical movement that swept Eastern European Jewry in the eighteenth and nineteenth centuries, and is considered largely responsible for the revival of interest in this tradition. He also wrote many traditional philosophical works.

BUBER, MARTIN. **I AND THOU.** Index, 185pp. Scr70/TTC, 2.95p.
This is generally considered Buber's most important philosophical work. In dialogical form Buber analyzes our relationships with others, God, and the universe as a whole. This is an excellent translation by Walter Kaufmann, a distinguished writer and philosopher in his own right, who was close to Buber. Professor Kaufmann has added a prologue and a wealth of informative footnotes to clarify obscurities.

BUBER, MARTIN. **KINGSHIP OF GOD.** 228pp. H&R56, 2.45p.
This is the most important of Buber's **Old Testament** studies and is considered a landmark in contemporary biblical scholarship. An excellent translation by Richard Scheimann, with many notes.

BUBER, MARTIN. **THE KNOWLEDGE OF MAN.** Index, 186pp. H&R65, 3.95p.
The essays in this volume represent the culmination of Buber's philosophical study of what is peculiar to man as man. The book is edited by Maurice Friedman and contains a long introductory essay by him. There is also, in the appendix, a dialogue between Martin Buber and Carl Rogers on the patient-therapist relationship.

BUBER, MARTIN. **THE LEGEND OF THE BAAL-SHEM.** 223pp. ScB55, 4.75p.
This book consists of a descriptive account and twenty stories. The descriptive account speaks of the life of the Hasidim, a Jewish sect of eastern Europe which arose around the middle of the eighteenth century and still continues to exist in our day in deteriorated form. The stories tell the life of the founder of this sect, Rabbi Israel ben Eliezer, who was called Baal-Shem, that is, the master of God's name, and who lived from about 1700 to 1760. . . . But the life about which we shall learn here is not what one ordinarily calls the real life. I do not report the development and decline of the sect; nor do I describe its customs. I only desire to communicate the relation to God and the world that these men intuited, willed, and sought to live. I also do not enumerate the dates and facts which make up the biography of the Baal-Shem. I build up his life out of his legends, which contain the dream and the longing of a people. . . . I have received it from folk-books, from note-books and pamphlets, at times also from a living mouth. . . . I have received it and told it anew. . . . I bear in me the blood and the spirit of those who created it, and out of my blood and spirit it has become new.—from the introduction. The text includes an extensive glossary.

BUBER, MARTIN. **MEETINGS.** 115pp. OpC73, 7.95c.
Autobiographical fragments. Dr. Maurice Friedman's famous Buber bibliography is appended.

BUBER, MARTIN. **MOSES.** Notes, index, 226pp. H&R46, 5.30p.
In this book a fascinating attempt is made to depict the historical Moses. The work is rich in brilliant comment. He has profound things to say on the flight of Moses to Midian, where he met with a life resembling that of his ancestors; on the Burning Bush, where he saw fire, but no form; on Moses before Pharaoh, as the first historical instance of prophet versus king; on the contrast between Moses summoned by God, and Balaam, made use of by Him. The style is invariably clear, precise, and dignified. This is a book to be read, re-read, and treasured.—David Daube, Regis Professor Oxford University.

BUBER, MARTIN. **ON JUDAISM.** 242pp. ScB67, 5.50p.
Twelve essays written between 1909 and 1951, covering every aspect of the Jewish religion.

■ BUBER, MARTIN. **THE ORIGIN AND MEANING OF HASIDISM.** 254pp. Hor60, 7.50c.
This volume is the culmination of Buber's lifetime recreation and interpretation of Hasidism. All aspects of the tradition are reviewed and the material is very clearly presented. Professor Buber's work is less concerned with defining theoretical concepts than with pointing to an image of man and a way of life.

BUBER, MARTIN. **TALES OF THE HASIDIM, EARLY MASTERS.** Glossary, index, 355pp. ScB47, 4.95p.
The mystical religious enthusiasm which swept through eastern Europe in the eighteenth century expresses itself in stories and epigrams by and about the Hasidic masters. These two volumes are the largest collection generally available of these stories. Buber has done an excellent job of compiling and retelling the tales.

BUBER, MARTIN. **TALES OF THE HASIDIM, LATER MASTERS.** Glossary, index, 352pp. ScB48, 2.95p.
The later masters were more concerned with the problems of everyday life, so their stories are often less flighty and more practical.

BUBER, MARTIN. **THE TALES OF RABBI NACHMAN.** 214pp. Sou56, 4.50p.
Rabbi Nachman. . . is perhaps the last Jewish mystic, says Martin Buber. He stands at the end of an unbroken tradition whose beginning we do not know. . . . I have not translated these stories of Rabbi Nachman, but retold them in all freedom, yet out of his spirit as it is present to me. Includes some remarks on Jewish mysticism.

BUBER, MARTIN. **TEN RUNGS: HASIDIC SAYINGS.** Notes, index, 126pp. ScB47, 1.75p.
The various ways in which men struggle to perfect themselves are the rungs of Hasidic lore. Of them it is said: *No limits are set to the ascent of man, and to each and everyone the highest stands open. Here it is only your personal choice that decides.* As Buber says, *This book contains a small selection of Hasidic sayings of this nature. They all revolve around a single question: How can we fulfill the meaning of our existence on earth? And so, dear reader, these pages are not concerned with the mysteries of heaven, but with your life and mine, in this hour and the next. These sayings were scattered through hundreds of books, in versions largely distorted in the speeches and writings of the disciples who transmitted them. I have selected, reduced to the quintessence of meaning, and arranged them according to major themes.* Most of the selections are a paragraph in length.

BUBER, MARTIN. **THE WAY OF MAN.** 41pp. Stu50, 1.50p.
A collection of six short essays discussing the way of man according to the teachings of Hasidism and clarifying some major aspects of this teaching.

GLATZER, NAHUM, ed. **THE WAY OF RESPONSE.** Bibliography, 223pp. ScB66, 3.95p.
A comprehensive anthology of Buber's writings, topically arranged and focused around the motif of response: *Buber's man is a responding man. Response establishes him as a person. . . . Nietzsche's dictum that "in the end one experiences only oneself" is counterposed by Buber's view that it is the other through whom I become fully I: if with my whole being I enter into a relationship with him.—* from the preface. The selections are generally fairly short and are clearer than much of Buber's philosophical writings.

SCHLIPP, PAUL and MAURICE FRIEDMAN, eds. **THE PHILOSOPHY OF MARTIN BUBER.** Index, 831pp. OpC67, 33.60c.
A collection of descriptive and critical essays on Martin Buber's philosophy by a distinguished group of philosophers and scholars. Virtually every aspect of Buber's thought is covered; the only notable omission is social philosophy. The volume also includes *Autobiographical Fragments* written by Buber and a topically arranged collection of Buber's *Replies to My Critics.* There is also a forty-two page bibliography.

————— END OF MARTIN BUBER SUBSECTION —————

BUTLER, W.E. **MAGIC AND THE QABALAH.** 107pp. Wei64, 4.95p.
A very clear presentation of the subject, designed for those of us not trained in an esoteric school. A general introduction gives as good a background to the Qabala as we have read, and specific chapters relate it to psychism, the astral plane, and modern psychology. Later chapters deal with the Qabala and the Tree of Life in more detail, without getting totally beyond comprehension.

CHALEB, RABBI. **THE SIXTH AND SEVENTH BOOKS OF MOSES.** 190pp. DeV nd, 6.00c.
These two books are translated from the Hebrew and contain many spells and mystic seals and signets.

COHEN, GERSON, tr. **SEPHER HA-QABBALAH: THE BOOK OF TRADITION.** Index, 423pp. Jew67, 8.50c.
A history of the social and cultural climate of Jewish Spain during the golden age of medieval Hebrew literature, written soon after the exile

of the Jews from southern Spain in the twelfth century. Abraham Ibn Daud composed the work to prove that Rabbinic tradition was the fulfillment of the revelation in scripture. This edition includes the original text, a translation, commentary, analysis, and extensive introductory material.

COHEN, SEYMOUR, *tr.* **SEFER HAYASHAR: THE BOOK OF THE RIGHTEOUS. Notes, 318pp. KTV73, 16.80c.**
A bilingual edition of this thirteenth century classic, which deals largely with the creation of the world, and contains many unusual concepts. Among them is an answer to the question of why God created the wicked as well as the righteous. There are chapters on love and fear of God, the relations between man and his fellow men, repentance, prayer, and good deeds. The influence of both Greek and Arabic philosophers is evident. Many feel that the anonymous author is a Qabalist who hid beneath the mask of a writer of a conventional ethical tract.

CORDOVERO, RABBI MOSES. **THE PALM TREE OF DEBORAH. Bibliography, 133pp. SHP60, 9.35c.**
Rabbi Cordovero was one of the most profound and systematic exponents of the teachings of the **Zohar** and a leading figure in the circle of mystics for which sixteenth century Safed in Palestine was renowned. This book is an ethical treatise devoted to the Qabalistic significance and application of the *Imitation of God.* Little space is devoted to an exposition of Qabalistic teachings—the reader is presumed to have a background in the Qabala before entering into this essentially ethical work. Cordovero explores his theme through Qabalistic literature, especially with reference to the *sephiroth,* and through Rabbinic ethical literature. The text includes a forty-five page introduction and extensive notes by the translator, Louis Jacobs.

CROWLEY, ALEISTER. **777 AND OTHER QABALISTIC WRITINGS OF A. CROWLEY. 296pp. Wei73, 10.00c.**
A new edition containing **Gematria, Liber 777,** and **Sepher Sephiroth** (consisting of Hebrew words with English translation). Includes an introduction by Israel Regardie, and much additional material.

DE LANGE, NICHOLAS. **APOCRYPHA: JEWISH LITERATURE OF THE HELLENISTIC AGE. Long introduction, bibliography, index, 254pp. Vik78, 12.50c.**
As the second century AD drew to a close there appeared to be general agreement that the **Old Testament** consisted of a single unit made up of twenty-four books. But for several hundred years before that time, a number of other writings were considered by many to be a part of the **Bible.** Dr. de Lange brings us back to the earlier concept in this collection of apocryphal writings, many translated into English for the first time. Going beyond this narrow view of the **Apocrypha** as the portions of the Greek **Bible** not found in the Hebrew, he draws instead upon the whole body of anonymous Jewish literature of the Hellenestic age, literature diverse in origin, language, style, and content. The collection sheds light on Jewish life, thought, and belief during the period between the end of the biblical era and the rise of Rabbinic Judaism.

DENNING, MELITA *and* OSBORNE PHILLIPS. **THE SWORD AND THE SERPENT. 264pp. LIP75, 10.00c.**
A presentation of the practical applications of the Qabala as taught in modern day Western mystery schools. The first part of the book is devoted to an in depth analysis of the five emanations. The second part explores the paths and the channels of force, and the final part details practical exercises and techniques. The text also includes eleven full page diagrams and twenty-three tables of correspondences. The emphasis is on magic rather than mystical teachings.

DIMONT, MAX. **JEWS, GOD, AND HISTORY. Chronologies, annotated bibliography, index, 472pp. NAL62/WHA, 1.95p.**
This is generally considered the best one volume history of the Jewish people. Dimont begins with pre-Mosaic times and continues up to the establishment of the State of Israel. He writes extremely well, so well in fact that the book often reads like a novel.

DRESNER, SAMUEL. **THE ZADDIK. 312pp. ScB60, 3.45p.**
The *zaddik* was an individual who had attained the highest degree of spiritual solitude and was capable of being alone with God, but who

Qabalistic Square

was, at the same time, at the true center of his community. He was a saint, a mystic, and a holy leader and was created by the crisis in eighteenth century Judaism that produced the Hasidic movement. This is a study of the doctrine of the *zaddik* told through the medium of the writings of Rabbi Yaakov Yosef of Polnoy. Some of the original Hebrew text is reproduced in the notes.

EFROS, ISRAEL. **ANCIENT JEWISH PHILOSOPHY: A STUDY IN METAPHYSICS AND ETHICS. Notes, index, 199pp. Blo64, 5.80p.**
A scholarly study in two parts. Part I discusses the philosophy of religion reflected in ancient Hebrew literature and Part II surveys the philosophy of biblical ethics. Many biblical quotations are integrated into the text.

EPSTEIN, ISIDORE. **JUDAISM. 349pp. Vik59, 3.95p.**
A history of the philosophy more than a history of the people, this book traces the rise, growth, and development of the beliefs, teachings, and practices of Judaism.

■ EPSTEIN, PERLE. **KABBALAH: THE WAY OF THE JEWISH MYSTIC. Glossary, bibliography, 189pp. Dou78, 6.95c.**
If any book on Jewish mysticism and the Qabala can be said to be comprehensible to the layman, this is it. Dr. Epstein has done an excellent job of synthesizing the essence of the tradition and presenting it in an understandable form, while avoiding oversimplification. The first half of the book covers the Hasidic tradition, and the second is devoted to Qabalistic practices and history.

FINKELSTEIN, LOUIS, *ed.* **THE JEWS: THEIR RELIGION AND CULTURE. Bibliographies, index, 568pp. ScB71, 11.05p.**
This book is the first comprehensive description of Judaism and the Jews. While avoiding the anatomical structure and purely alphabetical organization of an encyclopedia, it is designed as a readable and unified sketch. . . . The principal relevant facts concerning the people of Israel and its faith are summarized in a succession of essays. . . . The book includes the first compact history of the Jews written by scholars specializing in several fields; an appreciation of the role of Judaism in world culture, seen from a wide variety of disciplines and skills; an initial effort toward a demography of Jews in America; and a brief outline of the Jewish religion.—from the introduction.

FLEER, GEDALIAH. **RABBI NACHMAN'S FIRE. 110pp. SHP75, 4.95p.**
Subtitled, *An Introduction to Breslover Chassidus,* this is the first attempt to present the many facets of the Breslover doctrine (named after Rabbi Nachman of Breslov) by a follower rather than an outsider. The first section is a detailed yet concise biography of Rabbi Nachman and a study of the times in which he lived. The second section is a collection of the Rabbi's thoughts in the areas of both man's relationship to man and his relationship to God.

FOHRER, GEORG. **HISTORY OF ISRAELITE RELIGION. Notes, indices, 416pp. Abi72, 15.75c.**
This is the most comprehensive study of Israelite religion that we know of. Dr. Fohrer is a professor of the **Old Testament** at a German university. The subject is treated chronologically to the end of the **Old Testament** period, and there is a full consideration of other ancient Near Eastern texts. The study is heavy on scholarship; therefore the text cannot be read idly but is recommended only to the interested student. The author's discussion is combined with many quotations from relevant literature.

■ FORTUNE, DION. **THE MYSTICAL QABALAH. 319pp. BnL35, 11.85c.**
This is generally considered the finest in depth study of the Qabala ever made. Ms. Fortune writes extremely well and expresses herself as clearly as we could hope, considering the complexity of the subject matter. She begins with a general discussion of the Qabala and then devotes separate chapters to the supernals, the Tree of Life, and each of the *sephiroth* and paths. Astrological and tarot correspondences are suggested, wherever applicable. An excellent book which we recommend highly.

FRANCK, A. **THE KABBALAH. Illustrations, 224pp. Crn1843, 2.98c.**
A clear, simplified exposition of Qabalistic philosophy. Separate chapters deal with the **Sepher Yetzirah**, the **Zohar**, and the Qabalistic conception of God, the world, and the human soul. In other chapters Franck discusses the authenticity and antiquity of the Qabala and its philosophical resemblances to other schools. This is a good introduction to the Qabala.

GERSH, HARRY. **THE SACRED BOOK OF THE JEWS. 256pp. S&D68, 2.95p.**
An excellent basic introduction to Judaism's most revered texts. Includes accurate, concise summaries of some of the more complicated material and translations of original source material.

GEWURZ, ELIAS. **THE HIDDEN TREASURES OF THE ANCIENT QABALAH. 43pp. YPS18, 4.00c.**
An esoteric interpretation of Qabalistic material, written by a close associate of Yogi Ramacharaka.

GEWURZ, ELIAS. **THE MYSTERIES OF THE QABALAH. 99pp. YPS22, 4.00c.**
More of the same, with chapters on the Hebrew alphabet and its hieroglyphical significance, initiation, and the soul of the Qabala.

GINSBURG, CHRISTIAN. **THE ESSENES, THE KABBALAH. Many quotations, glossary, 245pp. Wei1863/RKP, 6.95c.**
Two essays, one devoted to a treatise on the history and doctrines of the Essenes, a Jewish monastic order that predicted the coming of Christ long before he was born. The essay on the Qabala is quite scholarly and centers on its meaning, major texts, and Qabalistic schools down through the ages.

GOITEIN, S.D., ed. **FROM THE LAND OF SHEBA: TALES OF THE JEWS OF YEMEN. 142pp. ScB73, 3.45p.**
The culture of the Yemenite Jewry is a unique fusion of the religious and ethical tradition with the folk attitudes of the Orient. The tales in this volume are often reminiscent of **The Arabian Nights**. Professor Goitein collected many of these tales firsthand and he includes a lengthy introduction surveying the history of Yemenite Jewry.

GONZALEZ-WIPPLER, MIGENE. **A KABBALAH FOR THE MODERN WORLD. Bibliography, 171pp. Ban74, 1.95p.**
This is the first scientifically-oriented presentation of the Qabalistic system. Ms. Gonzalez-Wippler integrates the developments in modern physics with the ancient tradition and shows how similar the two world conceptions are. A fascinating part of her study traces the meaning of the letters of the Hebrew alphabet. This is a very good introduction to the Qabalistic teaching. The material is clearly presented and well illustrated. The beginning student can get a feeling of what the Qabala is from this text and can decide which areas he would like to explore in more depth—without becoming overwhelmed by a great number of amorphous metaphysical concepts.

GORION, EMANUEL BIN, ed. **MIMEKOR YISRAEL: CLASSICAL JEWISH FOLKTALES. Three volumes, boxed, introduction, notes, index, 1,598pp. IUP75, 50.00/set.**
A collection of 1,080 tales arranged into four books: *National Tales, Religious Tales, Folktales,* and *Oriental Tales.* Virtually every aspect of Jewish life, both religious and secular, is covered in these tales. The religious tales volume includes selections from the **Zohar**, the **Talmud**, and Hasidic writings. The folktales volume is arranged thematically. The translations and retellings are uniformly excellent. This definitive collection should be of interest to all who wish to delve deeply into the Jewish literary heritage.

GRAY, WILLIAM. **THE LADDER OF LIGHTS. 230pp. Hel68, 7.95c.**
The Tree provides the means for receiving Innerworld contacts with types of consciousness normally inaccessible to the ordinary human mind. It is from and through these sources that the Teaching comes. Nor is this an automatic process, but the result of hard and painstaking work in all worlds. Qabalism is not for the lazy, the ineffectual, or the indifferent occultist. It offers a living pattern which must be experienced, not merely looked at.... Since the essential meaning of the Qabalah is contained in the Tree of Life, it is to the Tree that we must turn for all information.... The Qabalistic Tree and its associations may be likened to a well designed crossword puzzle with clues. The entire meaning and value of the puzzle lies with the mental exercise involved in its construction and solution.—William Gray. This is an in depth analysis of the *sephiroth*.

GRAY, WILLIAM. **THE TALKING TREE. Illustrations, 573pp. Wei77, 17.50c.**
This is a companion volume to **The Ladder of Lights**. Gray presents an exhaustive and systematic analysis of the paths of the Tree of Life. He begins with a survey of the nature of the Tree and a discussion of the plan and purpose of the paths. Then he devotes a chapter each to a detailed analysis of the thirty-two paths, including information on their correlations with the major arcana of the tarot.

GRAY, WILLIAM. **THE TREE OF EVIL. 119pp. Hel74, 6.95c.**
This volume is based on the Qabalistic Tree of Life. It deals with the *anti-principles* or opposites of the Tree termed *Qlippoth* (literally translated as *harlots, shells,* or *demons*). The book consists mainly of a study of the power of evil and how it came into being along with a series of methods for coping with evil through the use of the Tree of Life and other techniques derived from the Qabala and the Western mystery tradition.

GREEN, ARTHUR and BARRY HOLTZ, trs. **YOUR WORD IS FIRE. Introduction, notes, 138pp. Pau77, 1.95p.**
A selection of topically arranged verse teachings of the Hasidic masters on contemplative prayer.

GRUBERGER, PHILLIP, ed. **KABBALAH: TEN LUMINOUS EMANATIONS, VOLUME II. 203pp. RCK73, 7.95c.**
This is a very intricate treatise divided into two sections: *Inner Light* and *Inner Reflection*—both of which are basically commentaries on the *sephiroth* taken from the writings of Rabbi Isaac Luria, with a long explanatory glossary and series of questions and answers provided by Rabbi Yehuda Ashlag. The main theme is a detailed analysis of the ten *sephiroth* in their dual aspects as line and circle. Only those students quite familiar with Qabalistic literature are advised to venture into this book.

HALEVI, Z'EV BEN SHIMON. **ADAM AND THE KABBALISTIC TREE. Index, 333pp. HPG74, 12.35p.**
Adam Kadmon is the Universe made after a likeness to God, the allegorical figure abstracted by Kabbalists into the diagram called the Tree of Life. This metaphysical

presentation **is** *a comprehensive formulation of universal principles and processes. Based upon the divine aspects and their relationships, the Tree describes the archetypal design on which the Universe is modelled. The same template applies throughout all the lesser worlds, so that even the tiny species of mankind, indeed a single human being, is directly related to the original Adam by virtue of faithful replication.* This book begins with an exposition of the Tree and from there goes into an exploration of the four *worlds* present in every human being. Beginning with the body, the process and laws of biology are related Qabalistically, so that the connection between the body and the psyche is demonstrated. This is followed by a detailed study of the psyche's anatomy. The latter part of the book is concerned with the awakening of the soul and its growing consciousness of the *upper Qabalistic Worlds of Creation and Emanation.* The conclusion describes the progress of man into *the realm of the Spirit and the Presence of the Divine.* This is a very interesting, clearly presented exposition of the study of man as seen by contemporary Qabalists, and is illustrated with many useful drawings of the Tree.

HALEVI, Z'EV BEN SHIMON. **AN INTRODUCTION TO THE CAB-ALA—TREE OF LIFE. 196pp. Wei72/HPG, 3.95p.**
First, Halevi traces its history, and outlines the metaphysical background to the Tree. He then applies the material to examples observable in everyday life. These range from the structure of government, the hierarchy of the church, and the economic system, to the manner in which a love affair develops, and birth, life, and death. The final part is devoted to a detailed study of man and his spiritual aims and possibilities. This exposition is in modern terms and helps the reader gain an understanding of how to use the Tree.

HALEVI, Z'EV BEN SHIMON. **A KABBALISTIC UNIVERSE. Illustrations, index, 220pp. Wei77/HPG, 5.00p.**
An account of the origin and the cosmic scheme of creation as seen through the Tree of Life. Halevi sets out the macrocosmic order with its differing levels of reality, the hierarchy of beings and their functions, and many related topics. Much of the book is devoted to an esoteric analysis of the purpose of the universe as it unfolds in the grand scheme. As usual, Halevi puts forward a number of intriguing ideas and relates his discussion to contemporary thought.

HALEVI, Z'EV BEN SHIMON. **THE WAY OF KABBALAH. Glossary, index, 224pp. Wei76/HPG, 5.00p.**
An esoteric study which begins by examining some differing ways that the Qabala has been viewed and studied through the ages. Many historical accounts are shown to be allegories of the human condition. The latter part of the book consists of a series of detailed studies of the disciplines involved in Qabalistic study. Many diagrammatic Trees of Life illustrate the text and are used as focal points for the exposition—showing the different stages the student passes through on the path to ultimate knowledge. An interesting presentation which attempts to make the Qabalistic teaching relevant to our age.

HALL, MANLY P. **CABBALISTIC KEY TO THE LORD'S PRAYER. 32pp. PRS64, 1.75p.**
An esoteric interpretation of the meaning of the Lord's Prayer as it can be understood through the application of Qabalistic and Hermetic wisdom.

Hebrew Language

Hebrew is a Semitic language spoken in Palestine in ancient times. It was supplanted in the third century BC by the western dialect of Aramaic, but continued to be used as a liturgical and literary language. It was revived as a spoken language in the nineteenth and twentieth centuries and is the official language of Israel. Hebrew borrowed many words from Aramaic, Greek, Latin, and Persian. Modern Hebrew, based on the biblical language, contains many innovations designed to meet modern needs; it is the only colloquial speech based on a written language. Characteristic of Hebrew is the use of word roots consisting of three consonants, to which vowels are added to derive words of different parts of speech and meaning. The language is written from right to left in a

Semitic script of twenty-two letters. These letters have often been given mystical correspondences and they play an important part in the Qabala and the tarot.

GESENIUS, WILLIAM. **GESENIUS' HEBREW GRAMMAR. 614pp. Oxf nd, 31.60c.**
Edited and enlarged by E. Kautzsch, revised in accordance with the twenty-eighth German edition (1909) by A.E. Crowley; with a facsimile of the Siloam inscription and a table of alphabets.

HARRISON, R.K. **TEACH YOURSELF BIBLICAL HEBREW. 217pp. McK55/Hod, 4.50p.**
This is an extremely clear volume designed for beginners wishing to learn biblical Hebrew. In format, it is a basic grammar; however, the emphasis is on biblical usage and vocabulary. This volume is part of the British series **Teach Yourself Books**—a highly regarded series of manuals.

LAMBDIN, THOMAS. **INTRODUCTION TO BIBLICAL HEBREW. 7½"x11", 373pp. Scr71, 20.10c.**
This is generally considered the best contemporary biblical Hebrew grammar. The lessons are very well organized and the text can be used either with a teacher or without. It is designed for a full year's course in elementary Hebrew at the college level. Lambdin is a Harvard professor.

SAWYER, JOHN. **A MODERN INTRODUCTION TO BIBLICAL HEBREW. Vocabulary, indices, 230pp. RKP76, 10.00p.**
A comprehensive description of the basic structure of biblical Hebrew grammar and syntax, emphasizing the meaning of the Hebrew. Each chapter begins with a set of Hebrew sentences, taken as a rule verbatim from the Hebrew **Bible**. These examples are then analyzed and each feature described. The analysis is followed by a summary of the material covered in the chapter, and there is often a table presenting some of it in graphic form. Each chapter ends with exercises in which the 300 most frequently occurring items of biblical Hebrew vocabulary are introduced at the rate of fifteen per chapter.

SIVAN, REUVEN and EDWARD LEVENSTON. **THE NEW BANTAM-MEGIDDO HEBREW AND ENGLISH DICTIONARY. 693pp. Ban75, 1.95.**
This is the most recent one volume dictionary. The authors are noted Israeli philologists and educators. Includes 46,000 entries with a concise explanation of the essentials of Hebrew grammar.

YEHUDA, EHUD BEN and DAVID WEINSTEIN. **BEN-YEHUDA'S ENGLISH-HEBREW, HEBREW-ENGLISH DICTIONARY. Pocket-sized, 678pp. S&S61, 1.95p.**
This book is considered the finest low priced dictionary available. It is derived from the eight volume **Dictionary and Thesaurus of the Hebrew Language** by the author's father. Over 30,000 entries are included along with explanations of grammar and pronunciation.

——— **END OF HEBREW LANGUAGE SUBSECTION** ———

HESCHEL, ABRAHAM. **THE SABBATH. Notes, 118pp. FSG51, 2.95p.**
This is a profound meditation on the nature and celebration of the Sabbath. Its thesis is that Judaism is a religion of time, not space, and the Sabbath symbolizes the sanctification of time, so that *the Sabbaths are our great cathedrals.* They represent a day of separation from space and the material things that fill it, a day of devotion to the eternal.

HIRSCHMAN, JACK, tr. **THE BOOK OF NOAH. Tre75, 2.50p.**
The Book of Noah is a section of the **Sefer ha-Raziel**, a classic book of medieval Qabalistic magic. Two additional invocation hymns from **Raziel** are also included.

HIRSCHMAN, JACK and ALEXANDER ALTMANN, trs. **THE THREE TRACTS—ELEAZER OF WORMS. Notes, Tre75, 3.00p.**
Eleazer ben Judah of Worms was a thirteenth century Qabalist, Talmudist, and religious poet who was responsible for popularizing the doctrines of German Hasidism. He was influenced by various Oriental traditions connected with *Merkavah* mysticism and the **Sepher Yetzirah.**

HOELLER, STEPHAN. **THE ROYAL ROAD. 2.95p.**
See the Tarot section.

JACOBS, LOUIS. **HASIDIC PRAYER. Notes, index, 195pp. ScB72, 3.95p.**
A systematic study of the methods of prayer of the Hasidic community. Rabbi Jacobs discusses such matters as contemplative and ecstatic prayer, quotes copiously from the writings of the Hasidim to illustrate his analysis, and draws parallels with the practices of other religious traditions.

JACOBS, LOUIS, ed. **HASIDIC THOUGHT. 256pp. Beh76, 5.30p.**
An anthology of authentic texts—some written down by the Rebbes themselves, others transcribed by their students and disciples—which present a picture somewhat at variance with the legend that has grown up around the Hasidic masters. We recommend this book to all who are interested in the Hasidic tradition. Professor Jacobs includes commentary on each selection.

JACOBS, LOUIS, tr, **JEWISH ETHICS, PHILOSOPHY AND MYSTICISM. Glossary, 182pp. Beh69, 5.30p.**
The depth and variety of Jewish belief and its expression is explored here through translations of the works of the great medieval Jewish thinkers—Maimonides, Gersonides, Luzzato, Saadya, Bachya, and others. In another section of the book, Jacobs surveys the mystical strain in Judaism, from medieval times to the present and includes selections from the writings of Rav Kook, a modern mystic. He also includes commentary on each selection.

JACOBS, LOUIS. **JEWISH MYSTICAL TESTIMONIES. Glossary, bibliography, 279pp. ScB76, 7.95p.**
This book presents a number of mystical texts, in translation, ranging from the earliest period down to the twentieth century. Each text is prefaced by an introduction and followed by a comment. Wherever possible, the texts have been allowed to speak for themselves. This is an excellent collection which includes many hard to find texts. Most of the translations were done by Jacobs.

KASDIN, SIMON. **THE ESOTERIC TAROT: THE KEY TO THE CABALA. 1.95p.**
See the Tarot section.

KATZ, STEVEN. **JEWISH IDEAS AND CONCEPTS. Glossary, notes, bibliography, 340pp. Ket77, 12.50c.**
In the preparation of this volume two goals were kept in mind. The first was to present an accurate, informative, rich picture of Jewish thought which could serve as the basis for a proper understanding of Judaism. Accordingly, we have endeavored to extract the salient features of those Jewish concepts which form the building blocks of the Jewish intellectual tradition, especially as they concern the relationship between God and the Jew, which is the cornerstone of the Jewish experience. Our second related but distinct goal was to bring to the surface the uniquely Jewish understanding of concepts which Judaism shares with its theological offspring, Christianity and Islam, as well as most of the world's religions. . . . The approach used in organizing this volume has been a topical one, examining each concept under discussion as it is found in the different historical strata of Jewish thought.

KENTON, WARREN. **THE ANATOMY OF FATE. 192pp. HPG78, 9.00p.**
Using practical astrological examples in conjunction with Qabalistic principles, Kenton places the study of astrology in the context of a universal scheme. He describes in detail the operation of cosmic influence within the psyche and how we are tuned as individuals and so move in resonance to planetary interplay.

KLAPHOLTZ, YISROEL, ed. **TALES OF THE BAAL SHEM TOV, VOLUMES I AND II. Glossary, 486pp. Fld70, 6.25c/each.**
This two volume set is the largest collection of tales of the Baal Shem Tov. They are all taken from reliable sources and include both stories and biographical sketches. The retellings are all in a modern style and read well. In addition, Klapholtz supplies excellent introductory material.

KNIGHT, GARETH. **EXPERIENCE OF THE INNER WORLD. 11.00c.**
See the Mysticism section.

KNIGHT, GARETH. **A PRACTICAL GUIDE TO QABALISTIC SYMBOLISM. Illustrations, notes, index, 541pp. Wei65, 17.50c.**
As the title suggests, this is an analysis of the practical meaning of the Qabala. The first section is devoted to an extensive analysis of the Tree of Life and the *sephiroth*. The second second contains the most

detailed analysis we have seen of the twenty-two paths which join the *sephiroth*, taking into account Hebrew alphabetical correspondences. A large part of this volume deals exclusively with the tarot, tracing its history and suggesting varying systems of correspondences with the Tree of Life. The emphasis throughout is on the practical applications of the teaching and a final chapter is devoted to techniques for *working the Tree.* A very clear presentation which we recommend highly.

KRAKOVSKY, RABBI LEVI. **KABBALAH: THE LIGHT OF REDEMPTION. 267pp. RCK70, 9.00c.**
An introduction to basic Qabalistic concepts, from the Research Institute of the Kabbalah in Jerusalem. Rabbi Krakovsky emphasizes the origin and essence of the Qabala. Not suggested as a general introduction.

KRAKOVSKY, RABBI LEVI. **THE OMNIPOTENT LIGHT REVEALED. Index, 106pp. YeP nd, 4.00c.**
This is a review of some of the major themes of the Qabala. Rabbi Krakovsky seems out to prove that all the wisdom of the world is contained in the Qabala and goes a bit overboard in his hyperbole. There is not much in his presentation that cannot be found elsewhere in a less dramatic form.

KRAMER, SIMON. **GOD AND MAN IN THE SEFER HASIDIM. Bibliography, 285pp. Blo66, 8.10c.**
The **Sefer Hasidim** (Book of the Pious) by Rabbi Judah ben Samuel of Ratisbon is a thirteenth century book on Jewish ethics and morals. Much has been written about it in Hebrew, Yiddish, and German—but little of this material is available in English. The book embraces a multitude of subjects from the conduct of men in relation to God and to each other and worship and prayer to business regulations, table manners, and the care of animals. Dr. Kramer, President of Hebrew Theological College in Chicago, presents a full review of the material in the **Sefer Hasidim**, arranged topically. Extensive chapter notes are included.

KUSHNER, LAWRENCE. **THE BOOK OF LETTERS. Oversize, 64pp. H&R75, 6.95c.**
More than just symbols, all twenty-two letters of the Hebrew alphabet overflow with meanings of their own. Rabbi Kushner draws from ancient Judaic sources, weaving Talmudic commentary, Hasidic folk tales, and Qabalistic mysteries around the letters. Each letter is illuminated and, together with the comments, is presented in the author's original calligraphy, recalling the look and feel of ancient medieval manuscripts. For those who want to understand the Judaic spiritual heritage better this beautiful text should be very illuminating.

■ *KUSHNER, LAWRENCE.* **HONEY FROM THE ROCK: VISIONS OF JEWISH MYSTICAL RENEWAL. 152pp. H&R77, 8.95c.**
In this book Kushner attempts to reveal the world of Jewish mysticism to readers who are little aware of this tradition. He presents a selection of autobiographical tales, age-old legends, and biblical quotations which usher the reader through each of the ten gates of mystical experience, *from the wilderness of preparation, through learning to recognize messengers of Most High, to the ultimate union with the Creator.* It is a subtle and absorbing book; Kusher has produced a very successful work.

LANGER, JIRI. **NINE GATES. 297pp. Blo61, 5.30c.**
The author, as a youth in Prague in the days before World War I, took leave of his family and went to live among the Hasidim. This book grew out of his experience and his life as a Hasid. The reader is given a vivid picture of this lifestyle and of the people: their ecstasies, austerities, feasts, and the all pervading Rebbe, purveyor of esoteric wisdom. Just as the life of the Hasidim is filled with stories by and about the Hasidic masters, so too is this narrative interwoven with the same stories. This volume should be a delight to those readers seeking a deeper insight into the lifestyle and meaning of the Hasidim. There is a long introduction by Langer's brother.

LEVI, ELIPHAS. **THE BOOK OF SPLENDORS. 191pp. Wei73, 8.95c.**
Levi is a noted nineteenth century Hermeticist who wrote several books on the Qabala, of which this is considered the best. It has only recently been translated into English. Part I provides the actual Qabalistic text, with an explanation of the resemblance between Qabalism and Freemasonry. Part II shows the connection among

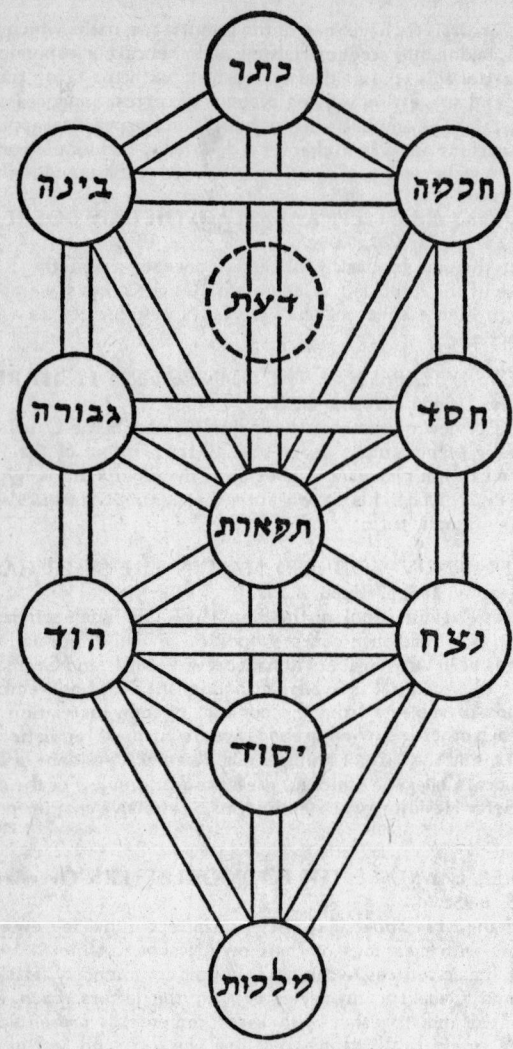

Tree of Life

Qabalism, numerology, and the tarot. In an appendix, Papus supplies a summary of Levi's doctrines and teachings, and extensive information on Levi's disciples.

LEVI, ELIPHAS. THE GREAT SECRET. 188pp. Wei75, 10.00c.
This is a sequel to **The Book of Splendors.** Here Levi discusses evil and its manifestations.

LEVI, ELIPHAS. THE MYSTERIES OF THE QABALAH. 285pp. Wei74, 10.00c.
This volume is a commentary on Ezekiel's **Prophecies** and the **Apocalypse of St. John.** In each case the text itself is reproduced (although not in one place) along with a survey of its esoteric meaning. A profusion of drawings and emblems illustrate the text. Despite the high sounding title, this can by no means be considered a definitive study of the Qabala. In fact, the Qabala and the Tree are only referred to in passing in the text and only in an illustrative way. A border around each page makes the book fairly hard to read and the presentation itself is scattered.

■ **LEVIN, MEYER. CLASSIC HASIDIC TALES. Introduction, 357pp. Vik75, 3.95p.**
This collection is considered to be the finest English version of the authentic Hasidic tales. The text is divided into two parts. The first relates stories of the Baal Shem Tov and the second contains the parables of his grandson, Rabbi Nachman. The tales are well written and retain the flavor of the original. Illustrations are interspersed.

LOVE, JEFF. **THE QUANTUM GODS. Bibliography, 253pp. Com76, 10.90c.**
This is an unusual book which explores the origin and nature of matter and consciousness from the point of view of the ancient Qabalists. The ideas of modern quantum physics and relativity theory are also used to explain these ancient laws. The book is often difficult going—but well worth the effort if you are interested in creation and consciousness and can follow Qabalistic and quantum concepts (a tall order indeed!). Diagrams and charts accompany the exposition.

LUZZATTO, RABBI MOSES. **GENERAL PRINCIPLES OF THE KAB-BALAH. 232pp. RCK70, 8.50c.**
Luzzatto was an eighteenth century Qabalistic scholar. His most important contribution was the detailed analysis of the *sephiroth* contained in this volume. Another work for the serious student from the Kabbalah Research Center.

MAHARAL OF PRAGUE. **THE BOOK OF DIVINE POWER. Glossary, index, 103pp. Fel75, 5.00p.**
This is a collection of three essays on the **Torah** literature which discuss the diverse aspects and levels of reality, and their interrelationship. The concepts of the ancient sages of Israel are expressed in contemporary terms and an illustrated appendix explains the fundamentals of classical and modern relativity which corresponds to the teachings of the **Torah.**

Moses Maimonides

Maimonides was unquestionably the foremost intellectual figure of medieval Judaism. Born in Cordova, Spain, forced at an early age to conceal his faith, he emigrated to Morocco and then Palestine before settling in Egypt where financial necessity compelled him to study medicine and where he eventually became personal physician to Saladin. Although his medical skills were renowned and his writings in this field were widely studied throughout the Western world, Maimonides' primary interest was theology. He devoted ten years to preparing the **Mishnah Torah** and fifteen years to **The Guide for the Perplexed**—the first written in Hebrew, the second in Arabic. These studies of Jewish law were originally considered radical in their efforts to reconcile religious and scientific thought, but later became pillars of traditional Jewish faith.

FRIEDLANDER, M., tr. **THE GUIDE FOR THE PERPLEXED. 473pp. Dov56, 5.00p.**
This book is concerned mainly with finding a concord between the religion of the **Old Testament** and its commentaries and Aristotelian philosophy. Rather than being a philosophical treatise, it is designed to liberate men from the tormenting perplexities arising from their literal understanding of the **Bible.** This edition contains an unabridged photographic reproduction of the second revised edition of Friedlander's early twentieth century translation from the Arabic along with the translator's long introduction on Maimonides' life and work and a summary of the **Guide.** The translation has aged fairly well. There is an index of scriptural passages cited.

GOODMAN, LENN, tr. **RAMBAM. Bibliography, index, 462pp. ScB75, 5.95p.**
Maimonides was known by the acronym *Rambam.* In a long introduction Dr. Goodman details Maimonides' life and evaluates his role in history and theology. He also includes new translations from the **Mishnah Torah** and **The Guide for the Perplexed**, arranging the excerpts topically. He adds commentary and analysis to clarify the complexities and provides historical and religious background as well.

PINES, SHLOMO, tr. **THE GUIDE OF THE PERPLEXED. 762pp. UCh63, 15.20p/set.**
This two volume set is widely considered the best translation available. This edition has the additional advantage of providing extensive introductory material and notes by Professor Pines of Hebrew University, and the late Leo Strauss, a leading authority on Maimonides.

ROSNER, FRED, tr. **MAIMONIDES' COMMENTARY ON THE MISH-NAH, 249pp. Fel75, 10.70c.**
An English translation of Moses Maimonides' entire introduction to his **Commentary on the Mishnah**, as well as an English version of his commentary on the first tractate of the **Mishnah**, tractate *Berachoth*. In his introduction Maimonides provides an historical account and description of the development of the Oral Law (**Mishnah** and **Gemara**). From there he makes a lengthy digression into the subject of prophecy. He then classifies the various types of laws contained in the **Mishnah**. There is also a dissertation on knowledge and wisdom and understanding of the purpose of the world and of all that is contained therein. Literally hundreds of footnotes accompany the text.

YELLIN, DAVID and ISRAEL ABRAHAMS. **MAIMONIDES: HIS LIFE AND WORKS. Bibliography, index, 228pp. SHP72, 7.95c.**
This is a revised edition of an important work which originally appeared in 1903. The notes and bibliographic sources have been updated, reflecting the scholarship of the last seventy years; supplementary notes provide material not touched upon by the original authors and elaborate upon the original notes. This is still considered one of the best biographical studies of Maimonides available.

——— END OF MOSES MAIMONIDES SUBSECTION ———

MATHERS, S.L. MACGREGOR, tr. **THE BOOK OF THE SACRED MAGIC OF ABRAMELIN THE MAGE. 316pp. Dov00/TPL, 3.50p.**
This is the best description of *angelic magic* that we know of. It is a translation of a fifteenth century manuscript in which the author, a Qabalist, describes a tour that he made of the world, visiting sorcerers, magicians, and Qabalists, and estimating their powers and virtues. The system he presents is based mostly on Hellenistic theurgy of the Iamblichan sort, but with Jewish increments from the Qabala. He explains the qualifications needed to become a magician, and the activities which must be regularly practiced. Specific instructions are included on developing various powers including clairvoyance, divining metals, healing, and much else. A number of symbols, including various magic squares, are reproduced and explained in the text.

MATHERS, S.L. MACGREGOR, tr. **THE KABBALAH UNVEILED. Many diagrams, 341pp. Wei26, 10.00c**
Contains translations of the following books of the **Zohar: The Book of Concealed Mystery, The Greater Holy Assembly, The Lesser Holy Assembly,** with extensive notes and explanations. In a long introduction, Mathers answers such questions as: what is the Qabala?; who was its author?; what are its general teachings?; its subdivisions?; why a new translation? His is one of the most readable and extensive translations.

MECKLER, DAVID, tr. **MIRACLE MEN. 320pp. Blo64, 5.30c.**
A collection of tales of the Baal Shem Tov and his disciples. The stories in this collection are not found in most of the other books—in fact the Hasidic tales must number in the thousands because with the exception of a few very noted ones all the collections we know of seem to have vastly different stories. The translation appears to be fairly good.

MELTZER, DAVID, ed. **THE SECRET GARDEN: AN ANTHOLOGY IN THE KABBALAH. 238pp. Sea76, 12.95c.**
A compilation of many of the most important Qabalistic texts including the **Sepher Yetzirah**, the **Sepher ha-Bahir**, the **Shiur Qoma**, and the **Keter Malkhut**, as well as selections from the works of Moses Cordovero, Moses de Leon, Eleazer of Worms, and Hayyim Vital. Many of the works translated here are not available elsewhere and the quality of the translations is uniformly excellent.

MINTZ, JEROME. **LEGENDS OF THE HASIDIM. Glossary, notes, bibliography, index, 462pp. UCh68, 5.95p.**
The Hasidim arrived in New York in great numbers in the 1940s and 1950s. Unlike the usual immigrants they have preserved their orthodox culture and have renewed their rich oral literature of legends, parables, philosophical sayings, and historical accounts. Professor Mintz describes the mores and the history of the present community and analyzes the cultural content of the more than 370 tales which are included in this work. He explores the intimate relationship existing between Hasidic tale and Hasidic law, ritual, value, and social structure.

He discusses the role of the Rebbe, the upbringing of children, the role of women, the relationship of magic and mysticism, and the social interactions of the various groups with each other and with the outside world. The book is illustrated with many photographs and goes farther than any previous study in English in revealing the inner dynamics and spirit of the New York Hasidic community.

MULLER, ERNST. **HISTORY OF JEWISH MYSTICISM. Bibliography, index, 197pp. YeP nd, 4.00c.**
The object of this work is to give a comprehensive survey of the history of Jewish mysticism—one which shall cover the whole field and not only that part commonly known as Cabbalah. It also includes the contacts of Jewish with non-Jewish mysticism. While other works deal with various aspects of the subject in far greater detail, this work aims particularly at placing in their proper perspective the mystical spirit of the **Bible** *itself, the mystical tendencies in the apocalyptic literature and the allegorical exegesis of the* **Bible** *and the existence of an ancient esoteric lore closely connected with the popular Agada....The notes contain much historical and other information supplementary to the text, while the appendix fills out the picture given in the text by a selection of passages from the original works which speak for themselves.—from the* introduction.

MYER, ISAAC. **QABBALAH. Index, 470pp. Wei1888, 15.00c.**
Deals extensively with the philosophical writings of Avicebron, an eleventh century Qabalistic scholar. Avicebron was noted for the connections he made with Oriental scholarship such as the sacred Hindu texts and the **Tao Te Ching**. His translations discuss karma, meditation, esoteric and exoteric knowledge and wisdom, and the Chinese Qabala. Includes many excerpts from the Qabala and the **Zohar**.

NAHMAD, H.M., ed. **A PORTION IN PARADISE AND OTHER JEWISH FOLKTALES. 170pp. ScB70, 2.95p.**
A well edited collection, with individual introductions to each of the stories. Nahmad has divided the tales into the following sections: *Tales of the Prophet Elijah, Tales of David and Solomon, The Wisdom and Folly of Women, The Righteous and the Pious, Tales of Wit and Wisdom,* and *The Golem.*

NEUGROSCHEL, JOACHIM, ed. and tr. **YENNE VELT. Notes, 710pp. S&S76, 6.95p.**
A collection of short, well translated works of Jewish fantasy and occult. The popularity of this set has been surprising to us.

NEUSNER, JACOB. **THE LIFE OF THE TORAH. Glossary, 252pp. Dic74, 8.00p.**
The Life of the Torah *is a source book intended to convey, so far as it is possible through the experience of merely reading a book, some of the meanings contained within the Jewish religious tradition....What I offer here is the chance to enter into the imaginative religious life of the pious Jew. I want you to know how Jews pray—or, at least, the words they say; how they confront* **Torah** *in synagogue worship and in response to its message; how they examine their souls on the Days of Awe and celebrate the Sabbath and festivals of the Jewish year. I want you to know what it means for a Jew to live according to the* **Torah***....I present glimpses into the lives of some of the great rabbis.* The book is extremely well organized and the selections are uniformly excellent.

NEUSNER, JACOB. **THE WAY OF TORAH: AN INTRODUCTION TO JUDAISM. Index, 143pp. Dic74, 6.65p.**
A good textbook summary of the major features of the Jewish religion divided into the following sections: *The Mythic Structure of Classical Judaism, Torah: A Way of Living,* and *Continuity and Change in Modern Times.* The presentation is quite straightforward and quotations from important source books are included. There is also an excellent, long, topically arranged bibliography.

NEWMAN, LOUIS, tr. **THE HASIDIC ANTHOLOGY. Bibliography, index, 576pp. ScB34, 5.95p.**
A topically arranged collection of the tales, proverbs, and paradoxes by which the Hasidic masters conveyed their wisdom to their disciples. Newman has translated the selections directly from the original Hebrew, Yiddish, and German texts. The sayings here form a striking complement to the more consciously literary compilation of Martin Buber. Newman's introduction provides a guide to the history of Hasidism, its doctrines, leaders, and literature.

NEWMAN, LOUIS, tr. MAGGIDIM AND HASIDIM: THEIR WISDOM. 303pp. Blo62, 6.45c.
This is a collection of the wise sayings, aphorisms, epigrams, reflections, and comments of folk preachers, Hasidic religious leaders, and Rabbis. The material has been garnered from a wide variety of sources and is topically arranged in alphabetical order. Each selection is headed and the entire book is fully indexed—all of which makes it a very handy book to use if you are seeking information on a particular subject or a story related to a particular idea. Newman also supplies an introduction. He has chosen his material carefully and well.

NOVECK, SIMON, ed. GREAT JEWISH PERSONALITIES IN ANCIENT AND MEDIEVAL TIMES. Glossary, notes, bibliography, index, 351pp. BnB59, 5.30p.
This is a nice collection of short biographical studies of Moses, David, Jeremiah, Philo, Akiba, Saadia, Halevi, Maimonides, Rashi, Abravanel, the Baal Shem Tov, and Vilna Gaon. Each essay has been prepared by a well known scholar. This volume is part of the B'nai B'rith Great Books series.

NOY, DOV, ed. FOLKTALES OF ISRAEL. 4.25p.
See the Fairy Tales section.

OESTERLEY, W.O.E. and THEODORE ROBINSON. HEBREW RELIGION. Indices, 448pp. SCK37, 10.95c.
A scholarly study of the origin and development of the Hebrew religion based upon modern Old Testament scholarship. This is by far the most comprehensive discussion of the subject we could imagine, tracing the religion from earliest times through the Greek period.

OLIVET, FABRE D'. THE HEBRAIC TONGUE RESTORED. 822pp. Wei21, 25.00c.
In this prodigious work of Fabre d'Olivet, which first appeared in 1815, he goes back to the origin of speech and rebuilds upon a basis of truly colossal learning the edifice of primitive and hieroglyphic Hebrew, bringing back the Hebraic tongue to its constitutive principles by deriving it wholly from the Sign, which he considers the symbolic and living image of the generative ideas of language.—from the foreword. The bulk of the book is devoted to material which resembles a traditional Hebrew grammar—although d'Olivet's interpretations are far from traditional. The last 346 pages present a translation of Genesis, based on the principles set out in the grammar, and giving literal, hieroglyphic, and figurative meanings along with an esoteric commentary.

OPHIEL. THE ART AND PRACTICE OF CABALLA MAGIC. Illustrations, 152pp. Pea76, 5.00p.
The latest of Ophiel's popular how-to manuals. Despite the title, this is not strictly about the Qabala. Ophiel interjects a great deal of chatty, extraneous material and his organization and clarity leave much to be desired.

PAPUS. THE QABALAH: SECRET TRADITION OF THE WEST. 384pp. Wei77, 15.00c.
Papus (1865-1916) was one of the greatest French occultists and was instrumental in popularizing many of Eliphas Levi's theories. This is his most important work on the Qabala. It is not a book for someone who wants an overview, but rather for those who seek a deeper insight into specific topics. The volume also includes Papus' translation of the Sepher Yetzirah, Levi's Ten Lessons on the Qabalah, an extensive Qabalistic bibliography, parts of Rabbi Drach's rare treatise La Cabbale des Hebreux, and a profound analysis of the Rabbi's theories.

PICK, BERNHARD. THE CABALA. 115pp. OpC03, 3.30p.
Of all the books we have reviewed so far on the Qabala, this one reads the easiest. That does not mean that it is the best—it is just that we have sat here for what seems like days looking into these obscure volumes and trying to figure out how to express their essences. And it is not easy because the Qabala is an exceedingly complex subject. Pick presents an historical review of the Qabala and studies its meaning in the light of its time and place. He begins with a survey of the name and origin and goes from there to analyses of the pre-Zohar period, the Zohar, and the post-Zohar period. This is followed by a study of Qabalistic doctrines and a mystical interpretation of the text.

PULLEN-BERRY, H.B. QABALISM. 167pp. YPS25, 10.00c.
An interpretation which deals with the Qabala as the most ancient secret wisdom and relates it to Hermetic philosophy.

RABIN, CHAIM. QUMRAN STUDIES. Indices, 135pp. ScB57, 3.95p.
Professor Rabin examines the connection and continuity between Pharisean Judaism and the Dead Sea Scrolls. He postulates the theory that the Qumran community is at the point of transition between Pharisean and Rabbinic Judaism. A technical work which was originally given as a series of lectures.

RAJNEESH, BHAGWAN SHREE. THE TRUE SAGE. 12.00c.
See the Contemporary Spiritual Teachers section.

RANKIN, O.S. ISRAEL'S WISDOM LITERATURE. Notes, index, 287pp. TTC36, 6.10c.
A discussion of Israel's wisdom literature from the point of view of the influence it has had upon the growth and content of world theological and religious thought.

REGARDIE, ISRAEL. THE GARDEN OF POMEGRANATES: AN OUTLINE OF THE QABALA. 160pp. LlP70, 3.95p.
A survey of Qabalistic teachings, emphasizing their magical applications. Information on the tarot, numerology, and esoteric symbology is also included.

REGARDIE, ISRAEL. THE TREE OF LIFE. 284pp. Wei69, 4.50p.
This is an occult interpretation and explanation of the meaning of the Tree, with instructions on its use for students on the path. A great deal of general philosophical material is also presented, much of which relates to magic.

RICHARDSON, ALAN. INTRODUCTION TO THE MYSTICAL QABALAH. 63pp. Wei74/TPL, 1.25p.
An extremely simplified review of the applications of the Qabala to magical work, with some background and explanatory material and many practical exercises.

RINGGREN, HELMER. ISRAELITE RELIGION. Chronology, notes, indices, 406pp. For66, 5.95p.
Professor Ringgren is an internationally known scholar in Old Testament and comparative religion studies. In this volume he presents an in depth history of the Israelite religion during the period of the monarchy. He is writing for the general reader rather than the specialist. He has organized his material topically within a chronological sequence and his narrative gives the reader an excellent feeling for the period. As might be expected, the presentation is a bit dry, but not overly so.

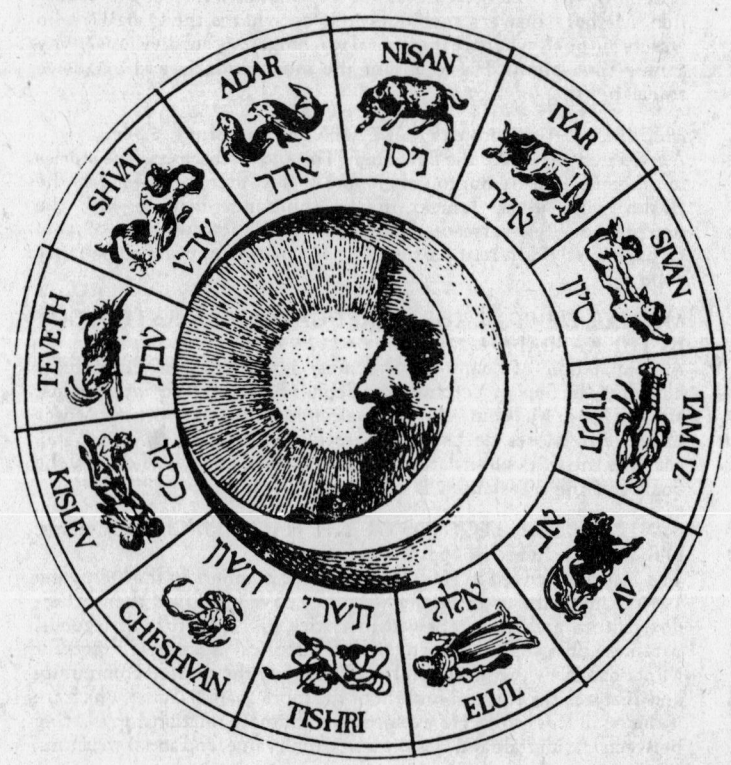

ROTHENBERG, JEROME, ed. **A BIG JEWISH BOOK. Introduction, illustrations, many notes, 679pp. Dou78, 12.95c.**
A selection of poems and visions of the Jewish people from tribal times to the present. More than 200 poems are included in all, many newly translated or uncovered. The works range from those of biblical and classical Hebrew poets to the early *Merkabah* mystics and Qabalists. Every kind of poem imaginable is offered—picture poems, oral and sound poems, number poems, meditation poems, and much else.

SAFRAN, ALEXANDRE. **THE KABBALAH. Glossary, notes, 341pp. Fel75, 14.70c.**
Dr. Safran is the Chief Rabbi of Geneva, Switzerland, and former Chief Rabbi of Rumania. He is a leading world rabbinical figure and was the leader of the Jewish underground during World War II. In addition to his political activities he is regarded as a profound and original thinker. This, his most important work, is a scholarly attempt to show the unity and continuity of Jewish tradition and an examination of the interaction between the body of the Law and the stream of the mystical tradition of the Qabala. The approach is basically philosophical and not overly esoteric.

SANDMEL, SAMUEL. **JUDAISM AND CHRISTIAN BEGINNINGS. Notes, bibliography, index, 327pp. Oxf78, 19.95c.**
Sandmel, Professor of Biblical and Hellenistic Literature at Hebrew Union College-Jewish Institute of Religion, traces the history, institutions, and religious ideas of Judaism from 200 BC to AD 175. It is a nontechnical account which focuses on the formation and consolidation of Synagogue Judaism, both in its Jewish and Christian manifestations. Sandmel reviews a wide variety of religious writings and describes all the major individuals.

SCHACHTER, ZALMAN. **FRAGMENTS OF A FUTURE SCROLL: HASIDISM FOR THE AQUARIAN AGE. Bibliography, 174pp. LOG75, 3.95p.**
So you meet in these pages, Reb Zalman, gourmet and master chef. You simply cannot find anybody around more determined to put it all together—a Gurdjieff number vibration with a Kabbalistic name; the **I Ching** *with the Sefirot. What concoctions. Only somebody who is himself the possessor of a formidable appetite, open to experimentation, and innately creative can make a respectable attempt. . . . You will find a translation of a Kabbalistic prayer, a Yiddish poem, a Hasidic tale. It's good stuff, hard to come by, delightful and urgently needed. . . . Purists will complain that the reader is not given a chance to distinguish between authentic tradition and Zalman Schachter. Well organized personalities will feel that the fragments offered in these pages are uneven in quality and rather arbitrarily strung together. . . . So let there be light, even if it be accompanied by a bit of chaos, inasmuch as it also results in these kind of "fragments."*—from the foreword by Herbert Weiner.

■ *SCHAYA, LEO.* **THE UNIVERSAL MEANING OF THE KABBALAH. Index, 180pp. Vik71, 1.95p.**
A profound study of the Qabala. Schaya relates the metaphysical basis of Judaism to the religions of the East, to Christianity, and to all the great spiritual traditions. He has organized his discussion extremely well and has done an excellent job of clarifying complex material. We recommend this as the best introductory work on the Qabala for the general reader.

SCHOLEM, GERSHOM. **JEWISH GNOSTICISM, MERKABAH MYSTICISM, AND TALMUDIC TRADITION. Notes, 136pp. KTV65, 5.30p.**
A slightly enlarged version of a series of lectures on Jewish mysticism in the early Talmudic period which Dr. Scholem delivered under the auspices of The Jewish Theological Seminary of America in 1957. Appendices contain a new interpretation of an Aramaic inscription, an essay on two magical formulae, a previously unpublished *Merkabah* text, and **Mishnath Shir ha-Shirim**, by Professor Saul Lieberman.

SCHOLEM, GERSHOM. **KABBALAH. Notes, bibliography, index, 492pp. NAL74, 5.95p.**
Dr. Scholem is one of the major figures, if not the major, in modern Jewish scholarship. He has been with the Hebrew University, Jerusalem, since 1923 and is presently Professor of Mysticism and Qabala as well as president of the Israeli Academy of Sciences and Humanities. In this volume he presents a summary of his life's studies. Though the approach is academic, the presentation is not overly technical and should be understandable to most general readers. Professor Scholem begins with a study of the historical development of the Qabala and

goes from there to an exploration of the basic ideas of the Qabala. This section is well organized and topically arranged. Part II, what Scholem terms, *Topics*, is a lengthy exploration of nineteen major subjects, themes, and movements. Each of these discussions is self contained and illuminating—though the technical detail at times gets overwhelming as is understandable when one considers the amount of material that is being covered. Part III presents short biographical studies of sixteen major Qabalistic personalities. The text also includes some notes, a glossary, and an index. Some critics have been disappointed with this book, but we feel fairly good about it. While it does not definitively cover all aspects of the subject, it is hard to see how any one book can. And while it is not the most exciting book we have read, it is readable and reasonably easy to follow.

SCHOLEM, GERSHOM. **MAJOR TRENDS IN JEWISH MYSTICISM. Extensive notes, bibliography, 424pp. ScB41, 5.95p.**
This is an outline of the principal features of Jewish mysticism in the form of an analysis of some of its most important phases. Stress is placed on the analysis and interpretation of mystical thought and a great deal of space is devoted to the Qabala.

SCHOLEM, GERSHOM. **THE MESSIANIC IDEA IN JUDAISM. 376pp. ScB71, 5.95p.**
Scholem clarifies the Messianic concept and analyzes its transformation in the Qabala up to the paradoxical versions it assumed in the Sabbatian and Frankist movements, when sin became a vehicle of redemption.

SCHOLEM, GERSHOM. **ON THE KABBALAH AND ITS SYMBOLISM. Notes, index, 216pp. ScB65, 2.95p.**
An illuminating discussion of a variety of topics: the relationship between mysticism and established religious authority; the mystics' interpretation of the **Torah** and their attempts to discover the hidden meaning underlying scripture; the tension between the philosophical and mystical concept of God; the ritual of the Qabalists; the symbolism employed in mystical religion; and the idea of the Golem.

SCHOLEM, GERSHOM. **SABBATAI SEVI—THE MYSTICAL MESSIAH. Notes, index, 1,000pp. PUP73, 9.50p.**
A detailed and masterful account of the Sabbatian movement from its inception to the founder's death which not only illuminates an extraordinary phenomenon in Jewish history, but is a major contribution to the general study of Messianic movements and their theologies. This English translation by R.J. Werblowsky is fully illustrated and presents many new facts, and enlarges and corrects the earlier Hebrew edition.

SEPHARIAL. **THE KABALA OF NUMBERS. 4.95p.**
See the Numerology section.

Sepher Yetzirah

The **Sepher Yetzirah** is a Jewish mystical treatise dating some believe from the second century BC, though incorporating later material. According to the text all that exists emanates from the one God, as the flame from the candle. All multiplicity originates in unity. All has come from God and must return to Him; He is revealed in and through the universe, is immanent and at the same time transcendent. The text gives an account of the ten *sephiroth* or divine powers which emanate from God. The *sephiroth* is a Qabalistic term for the regions or spheres emanating from God: crown, wisdom, intelligence, love, power, compassion, steadfastness, majesty, foundation, and kingdom. They are linked together as a vital organism.

FRIEDMAN, IRVING, tr. **THE BOOK OF CREATION. 60pp. Wei77, 2.95p.**
Irving Friedman's even-handed and lucid presentation of **The Book of Creation** *will be a considerable help to any contemporary person approaching the Judaic tradition as part of a serious search for self knowledge. It preserves the great mystery of the Kaballah and of the inner meaning of the* **Torah***, without encouraging subjective fantasy. This is a straightforward translation of the* **Sepher Yetzirah***,*

accompanied by extensive notes and commentary. In a final chapter, Friedman attempts to extract practical instructions from the text.

KALISH, ISIDOR, tr. **SEPHER YEZIRAH. Introduction, Hebrew-English glossary, many notes, 57pp. Sym1887, 1.75p.**
An English translation, with the Hebrew text on facing pages.

MORDELL, PHINEAS. **THE ORIGIN OF LETTERS AND NUMERALS ACCORDING TO THE SEFER YETZIRAH. 71pp. Wei14, 2.50p.**
There is no book in Jewish literature that is so difficult to understand as the **Sefer Yetzirah**. . . . *After many years of study, I reached the conclusion that the* **Sefer Yetzirah**, *as the earliest Hebrew grammar, contains not only the fundamental rules of Hebrew orthography, but also an account of the origin of letters and numerals. This account of it is my present purpose to set forth.* The text includes notes, diagrams, and portions of the **Sepher** in Hebrew-English translation.

STENRING, KNUT, ed. **THE BOOK OF FORMATION (SEPHER YETZIRAH). 63pp. KTV23, 6.65p.**
This translation of the **Sepher Yetzirah** has been extensively annotated. The notes will be very useful for all who seek an understanding of this esoteric document. An appendix contains an analysis of the twenty-two paths of wisdom and their correspondence with the Hebrew alphabet and the tarot symbols. A number of diagrams are also included. Introduction by Arthur Edward Waite.

SUARES, CARLOS. **THE SEPHER YETSIRA. 150pp. ShP76, 4.95p.**
This **Sepher** is the key work of the Qabalistic tradition and is a seed formula revealing the basic structure of energy. Suares, using a revealed cipher, breaks and explains this formula. In the process he discusses *the original astrology according to the Qabala and its zodiac* and explores what this astrology reveals about the inner life.

WORK OF THE CHARIOT. **BOOK OF FORMATION. Stapled, 8½"x11", WkC71, 4.00p.**
This volume includes the Hebrew text of the **Book of Formation** in both Ezra square Hebrew and the original Gefer. There is also a good translation, detailed notes, many diagrams and charts, and the text of the **Shuo Kua**, a similar ancient Chinese treatise.

———— **END OF SEPHER YETZIRAH SUBSECTION** ————

SIEGEL, RICHARD, ed. **THE JEWISH CATALOG. 319pp. Jew75, 5.95p.**
A collection of source material on every aspect of Jewish life—ideas about what to do and how to go about doing it. Both religious and cultural ideas are presented and this 8¼"x10¾" volume is illustrated throughout. If you are interested in learning more about what it means to be Jewish, you should enjoy this book.

SINGER, ISAAC. **THE HASIDIM. 8¾"x11¼", Crn73, 10.00c.**
A text by Isaac Singer and over seventy drawings, etchings, and lithographs by Ira Moskowitz bring the Hasidim to life. Their inner devotion, mystical preoccupations, and religious fervor are revealed as they practice their religion and go about their everyday life.

STRASSFELD, SHARON and MICHAEL. **THE SECOND JEWISH CATALOG: SOURCES AND RESOURCES 8½"x11", 464pp. Jew76, 7.50p.**
Extends the discussion of Jewish observances and customs and offers further suggestions on how to go about making them part of your daily life. The book is profusely illustrated and ranges across such topics as the Jewish life cycle, synagogue and prayer, sex and sexuality, medicine, education, and much else. The emphasis throughout is on the proper ways to act as a Jew within the Jewish community. A sixty-four page supplement, *The Jewish Yellow Pages*, is appended, alphabetically listing services, products, and institutions throughout the country.

STURZAKER, DOREEN and JAMES. **COLOUR AND THE KABBALAH. 9.50c.**
See the Tarot section.

STURZAKER, JAMES. **KABBALISTIC APHORISMS. 128pp. TPH71, 6.95c.**
The Mystical Kabbalah is a glyph or symbol system which consists of the Tree of Life and the twenty-two Major Arcana of the Tarot cards. . . . Contained within this

glyph are the basic qualities that make and keep life moving. . . . This book of Kabbalistic Aphorisms has been compiled to suit the needs of all.—from the text. The volume begins with a series of general aphorisms on the Qabala and goes from there to sections of individual aphorisms for each of the *sephiroth*. The second part of the book begins with a series of general aphorisms on the tarot and follows with sections of individual aphorisms for each of the major arcana. Every one of the *sephiroth* and major arcana sections includes about fifty aphorisms so the reader can make his selection depending upon the needs of the day. Many people have found these aphorisms quite useful in their daily meditations.

The Talmud

The **Talmud** is a collection of early biblical discussions with the comments of generations of teachers who devoted their lives to a study of the Scriptures. It is an encyclopedia of law, civil and penal, human and divine. It is more, however, than a mere book of laws. It records the thoughts, rather than the events, of a thousand years of the national life of the Jewish people; all their oral traditions, carefully gathered and preserved. . . . Accepted as a standard study, it became endeared to the people, who, as they were forbidden to add to or diminish from the law of Moses, would not suffer the work of their Rabbis to be tampered with in any manner. As it was originally compiled it has been transmitted to us. . . . At the first view, everything, style, method, and language, seems tangled and confused. The student, however, will soon observe two motives or currents in the work; at times harmonious, at times diverse; one displaying the logical mind, which compares, investigates, develops, and instructs; the other, imaginative and poetical. The first is called *Halachah* (Rule), and finds a vast field in the Levitical and ceremonial laws; the other takes possession of the ethical and historical portions of Holy Writ. It is called *Hagadah*, or Legend, not so much in our present acceptance of the term, as in the wider sense of a saying without positive authority, an allegory, a parable, a tale. The **Talmud** is divided into two parts, **Mishna** and **Gemarah**. They are continued works of successive Rabbis. . . . It was called oral or unwritten law, in contradistinction to the **Pentateuch**, which remained under all circumstances the immutable code, the divinely given constitution, the written law.
—from **The Talmud**, by H. Polano

ADLER, MORRIS. **THE WORLD OF THE TALMUD. Notes, bibliography, 156pp. ScB63, 2.95p.**
A basic guide to the **Talmud** and to its historic and cultural background. This volume is one of a series of **Hillel Little Books**, developed by the B'nai B'rith Hillel Foundation. Rabbi Adler has done a good job of organizing and clearly presenting a series of often complex ideas. Selected summaries of Talmudic material are included.

COHEN, A. **EVERYMAN'S TALMUD. Notes, index, 444pp. ScB49/Den, 6.95p.**
This is a comprehensive summary of the **Talmud**, beginning with a chapter explaining its history and makeup and continuing with an exploration, by subject, of its major teachings in the following order: *The Doctrine of God, God and the Universe, The Doctrine of Man, Revelation, Domestic Life, Social Life, The Moral Life, The Physical Life, Folklore, Jurisprudence, The Hereafter*. This is by no means an exhaustive treatment. Each of the topics could easily be expanded into a volume. However a sufficient number of extracts are offered to give the reader a good idea of Talmudic doctrine on a variety of themes without overwhelming him with an indigestible abundance of material. This seems to be the best one volume summary available.

CORRE, ALAN, ed. **UNDERSTANDING THE TALMUD. Notes, 480pp. KTV75, 8.00p.**
An extremely varied collection of essays on history, culture, and religious life as each relates to the **Talmud** and to Talmudic doctrine.

GOLDIN, JUDAH, tr. **THE LIVING TALMUD. 247pp. NAL55/NEL, 1.75p.**
This is a translation of **Pirke Abot** (The Wisdom of the Fathers), a collection of the sayings of the Synagogue Fathers, maxims which summarize the anguish, ecstasy, and understanding they had experienced in their penetrating study and practice of the Law. The sages quoted here lived between the fifth century BC and the third century AD. Included in this edition, too, are the first English translations of many of the classical commentaries on the **Pirke Abot**, made by generations of Talmudic scholars.

LIPMAN, EUGENE. **THE MISHNAH. 318pp. ScB70, 3.95p.**
The material here has been newly translated and is designed to present significant and representative passages with a traditional commentary, and to illustrate the role of this classic text in the evolution of Jewish law and of Judaism in general. Unfortunately the material is not topically arranged so the reader interested in a particular subject has no way to locate material relevant to his interest except through the index and it is hard to say how complete that is. Extensive commentary is included with each selection.

MIELZINER, MOSES. **INTRODUCTION TO THE TALMUD. 415pp. Blo68, 13.45c.**
This book, originally published in 1894, was the first comprehensive introductory work on the **Talmud** in the English language. Since then many other works have been published, yet Mielzner's scholarly study has stood the test of time and, while at times dated in its approach, remains one of the best works available today. Every aspect of the **Talmud** and Talmudic thought is surveyed. Some knowledge of the Hebrew language is needed for an appreciation of the book because many untranslated Hebrew words and phrases are interspersed throughout. Additional notes and bibliographic entries are included in this edition, along with extensive indices.

POLANO, H., tr. **THE TALMUD. 383pp. Wrn73, 5.50c.**
This is an excellent translation of some of the most important sections of the **Talmud**. The selections are from its commentaries, teachings, poetry, and legends, and all of them read uniformly well. The translator also supplies a fine introduction detailing the nature and scope of the **Talmud**.

■ STEINSALTZ, ADIN. **THE ESSENTIAL TALMUD. Index, 296pp. Ban76/Crg, 2.95p.**
Rabbi Steinsaltz is head of the Israeli Insitute for Talmudic Publications. He is currently preparing a new edition of the **Talmud** in Hebrew. In this volume he restates the major Talmudic teachings in a modern fashion and also includes a great deal of background and introductory material. The material is topically arranged. The book reads well and is as good an introduction as any book we know of.

───────── END OF THE TALMUD SUBSECTION ─────────

The Torah

The **Torah** is broadly defined as the divine revelation given to the Jewish people. It is more often used in a restricted sense, synonymous with the **Pentateuch**—the first five books of the **Old Testament**—traditionally ascribed to Moses, the recipient of the original revelation of Mt. Sinai. The term **Torah** is also used to designate the entire Hebrew **Bible**. **Torah** is also understood to include both the oral law and the written law. Rabbinic commentaries on and interpretations of both oral and written law have been viewed by some as extensions of sacred oral law, thus broadening still further the meaning of the **Torah**, so that it also designates the entire body of Jewish laws, customs, and ceremonies. The written **Torah**, in the restricted sense of **Pentateuch**, is preserved in all Jewish synagogues on handwritten parchment scrolls that reside inside the ark of the Law. They are removed and returned to their place with special reverence. Readings from the **Torah** form an important part of Jewish religious services.

JEWISH PUBLICATION SOCIETY, trs. **THE TORAH. 393+pp. Jew62, 6.75c.**
This is a new translation, which completely revises the original 1917 work. It is considered the definitive edition and includes notes and background material. The text reads well and is very nicely bound.

RUNES, DAGOBERT. **WISDOM OF THE TORAH. 300pp. Stu67, 2.25p.**
Presents the **Torah** as a book of philosophy and literature containing the following types of material: legendary tales, historical books, ritualistic books, prophetic sermons, and philosophical and poetic works. The translation is based on the King James version of the **Bible**.

WEINBERG, NORBERT. **THE ESSENTIAL TORAH. 344pp. Blo74, 10.50c.**
Rabbi Weinberg has written this volume to help individuals understand the words of the **Torah**. Each chapter is an exhaustive review of the weekly **Torah** selection, including a retelling in modern language of the basic story, a selection from the classical commentaries, and a synopsis of each prophetic section. This volume should be especially helpful for those attending services regularly and it can also be useful for all self study programs. The text is very well written.

───────── END OF THE TORAH SUBSECTION ─────────

UNTERMAN, ALAN. **THE WISDOM OF THE JEWISH MYSTICS. 84pp. NDP/SIP, 2.45p.**
A nice selection of stories and sayings drawn mainly from the Hasidic masters. An initial essay examines Qabalistic thought and retells some Qabalistic stories.

VAUX, ROLAND DE. **ANCIENT ISRAEL—RELIGIOUS INSTITUTIONS. 317pp. MGH61, 2.95p.**
This is a very detailed study of Israelite life in **Old Testament** times written primarily for the nonspecialist. De Vaux is a distinguished archaeologist who has spent years researching the material he presents here. Every aspect of ancient Israel's religious institutions is covered in depth. Abundant biblical references are included in the text along with a bibliography and several indices.

WAITE, A.E. **THE HOLY KABBALAH. Many long notes, index, 620pp. Stu60, 6.95p.**
A massive study, extensively indexed, tracing Qabalistic history, literature, and philosophy down through the ages and reviewing various students of the Qabala as well as relating the Qabala to other channels of secret tradition. This is considered to be one of the best books on the Qabala—suitable for the beginning or advanced student.

WAITE, A.E. **THE SECRET DOCTRINE IN ISRAEL. Notes, index, spiral bound, 346pp. HeR nd, 6.00p.**
This is Waite's most advanced and thorough look at the inner teachings of the Qabalistic tradition, especially as they are expressed in the **Zohar**. In the process much of the content of the **Zohar** is reviewed and summarized, and its main doctrines and tenets are analyzed.

■ WEINER, HERBERT. **9½ MYSTICS: THE KABBALA TODAY. 342pp. McM69, 1.95p.**
This is a welcome attempt to present the Qabalistic teachings and the Jewish mystical tradition in an accessible way—and an attempt at which Rabbi Weiner succeeds admirably. *This book records a search for the life secrets of a mystical tradition sometimes known as the Kabbala. It describes a series of encounters wherein individuals and groups who claim intimate acquaintance with*

this tradition are challenged to relate their hidden wisdom to problems of our day. It also contains a great deal of historical and technical information about Jewish mysticism, but frankly, anyone interested in a purely objective, scholarly account of this latter subject will be better served by other books; this journal is on a more personal and popular level.

WESTCOTT, W. WYNN, ed. **AESCH MEZAREPH OR PURIFYING FIRE. Offset, stapled, 60pp. HeR1894, 3.00p.**
Subtitled, *A Chymico-Kabalistic Treatise Collected from the* **Kabala Denudata** *of Knorr von Rosenroth.* It is an allegorical text which relates Qabalistic teachings to the alchemical process.

WIESEL, ELIE. **FOUR HASIDIC MASTERS AND THEIR STRUGGLE AGAINST MELANCHOLY. Introduction, maps, chronology, notes, 157pp. UND78, 10.65c.**
In this sequel to **Souls on Fire,** Wiesel brings to life four great charismatic leaders of the Hasidic movement—Pinhas of Koretz,Barukh of Medzebozh, the Holy Seer of Lublin, and Naphtali of Ropshitz. Wiesel shows how, inspired, they became a source of inspiration. They communicated joy and fervor to men and women who needed joy and fervor to endure and even to survive. And yet these masters, who moved others to joy, seemed to struggle with melancholy and at times with despair. In all of them a common obsession emerges: to combat sorrow with exuberance, to overcome despair with prayer, to defeat resignation by kindling a greater light, a more exalted faith in God and his creation.

WIESEL, ELIE. **MESSENGERS OF GOD: BIBLICAL PORTRAITS AND LEGENDS. 237pp. RaH76, 8.95c.**
A moving retelling of biblical lore. Wiesel has succeeded quite well in his aim of illustrating the relevance of these ancient tales to our time and of conveying his perceptions of what the tales meant to earlier generations. Included are chapters on Adam, Cain and Abel, Isaac, Jacob, Joseph, Moses, and Job.

■ WIESEL, ELIE. **SOULS ON FIRE. 280pp. RaH72, 1.65p.**
A consummate work of art. Out of the lives and legends of Hasidic masters, out of the tales of their suffering and joy, out of the dread and darkness through which they reached for God—out of all these Elie Wiesel has fashioned a work that makes these men and their times come brilliantly alive.—Chaim Potok.

WORK OF THE CHARIOT. **BOOK OF THE NAMES. 8½"x11", WkC71, 12.00p.**
A copy of the **Book of Adam,** explaining creation and discussing and illustrating the 128 names of God. A supplement shows how to use the text for practical Qabalistic meditation. A fat book.

WORK OF THE CHARIOT. **SIFRA DETZNIUTHA. Stapled, 8½"x11", WkC71, 2.00p.**
A new translation of the central portion of the **Book of Splendor.**

WORK OF THE CHARIOT. **TREE OF LIFE, BRANCHES I-X. Stapled, 8½"x11", WkC70, 3.00p.**
A translation of the mystical teachings of Rabbi Isaac Luria, a sixteenth century Qabalist. Includes the Hebrew text and many diagrams illustrating the complex mystical patterns set forth in the text.

WRIGHT, WAYNE, ed. **THE CHICKEN PRINCE AND OTHER OLD TALES OF CABALA. Introduction, 76pp. Rhi77, 3.75p.**
A collection of nine lengthy Hasidic teaching stories, told in a modern style and illustrated wtih woodcuts and intricate borders around each page.

The Zohar

The **Zohar** or **Book of Splendor,** is a Qabalistic work written mainly in the Aramaic language. It takes the form of a commentary on the **Pentateuch** and is intended to reveal the hidden meaning of the biblical narrative and the divine commands. It is a complete thesaurus of Jewish mysticism, theosophy, and occult traditions....The **Zohar** in its present form first appeared in Spain as a compilation by Moses de Leon of Avila, who claimed that the original work had been revealed to Simeon ben Jochai, a saintly Jew of the second century.... Whatever its origin, it is certain that the **Zohar** exerted a powerful influence on Jewish life in medieval ghettoes and opened up new vistas of spiritual worlds.

—from the introduction to **The Zohar**
in Moslem and Christian Spain, *by Ariel Bension*

BENSION, ARIEL. **THE ZOHAR IN MOSLEM AND CHRISTIAN SPAIN. Bibliography, index, 276pp. SPH32, 15.75c.**
We know of no better study of the **Zohar** (or **Book of Splendor**) than this book. It is well written and presents a coherent picture of the spirit and atmosphere to which the mystics of Spain's Golden Age were subjected in addition to detailing the world view of the **Zohar** and the major figures involved in it. Bension begins with a general survey of Jewish life in Spain; the next chapter is devoted to an exposition of the Spanish mystics, with a detailed study of their main concerns. The final two chapters in this section present an in depth exploration of the similarities in the work of the Spanish mystics of the three faiths— Jewish, Christian, and Muslim. The second and longest section is devoted to a discussion of the **Book of Splendor** itself. The first chapter analyzes the **Zohar** and its role in Jewish life and discusses its history, content, and the tradition that it stemmed from. The next chapters are basically concerned with the text of the **Zohar** itself and the story it has to tell. A final section reveals what happened to Sephardic mysticism after the exile. Bension himself is in the direct line of descent from these original Sephardic mystics and a great deal of this information comes from the oral tradition. He has also done a lot of historical research. The reader needs little or no background to be able to appreciate and understand the material presented here.

BERG, PHILIP, ed. **AN ENTRANCE TO THE ZOHAR. 164pp. RCK74, 11.00c.**
This is a discussion of a number of the basic concepts dealt with in the **Zohar,** based on the translations and teachings of Rabbi Yehuda Ashlag.

SCHOLEM, GERSHOM, ed. **ZOHAR, THE BOOK OF SPLENDOR: BASIC READINGS FROM THE KABBALAH. 122pp. ScB74, 1.95p.**
A selection from the extensive writings which make up the vast **Zohar.** The historical setting of the **Zohar** and its literary characters are discussed in an introduction.

SPERLING, HARRY and MAURICE SIMON, trs. **THE ZOHAR. Five volumes, glossary, 2,127pp. 42.50c.**
This is one of the only two complete editions of the **Zohar** available in English—the other is considerably more expensive and contains the same translation as this edition.

——————— **END OF ZOHAR SUBSECTION** ———————

JUNGIAN PSYCHOLOGY

To write about C.G. Jung's effect both in and on the culture of our day and to do justice to the subject is an uncommonly difficult assignment. As a rule, outstanding individuals are influential chiefly or exclusively in their own professional fields. In Jung's case, however, his original, creative discoveries and ideas had to do with the whole human being and have therefore awakened echoes in the most varied areas outside that of psychology: his concept of synchronicity, for example, in atomic physics and Sinology; his psychological interpretation of religious phenomena, in theology; his fundamental view of man, in anthropology and ethnology; his contributions to the study of occult phenomena, in parapsychology—to mention only a few instances. Because Jung's work encompasses so many varied fields of interest, his influence on our cultural life has made itself felt only gradually and, in my opinion, is still only in its beginnings. Today, interest in Jung is growing year by year, especially among the younger generation. Accordingly, the growth of his influence is still in its early stages; thirty years from now we will, in all probability, be able to discuss his work in a very different terms than we do today. In other words, Jung was so far ahead of his time that people are only gradually beginning to catch up with his discoveries. There is also the fact that his perceptions and insights are never superficial, but are so astonishingly original that many people must overcome a certain fear of innovation before they are able to approach them with an open mind. Furthermore, his published works include an enormous amount of detailed material from many fields, and the reader must work through this wealth of information in order to be able to follow him. Jung once remarked that *anything that is good is expensive. It takes time, it requires your patience and no end of it.*

Since this was the spirit in which he worked, it is not surprising that Jung's influence is slow in making itself felt. The reader must give close attention to his patient reflections, involving the painstaking elucidation of much factual material, in order to understand what Jung is aiming at.

In addition to the above considerations there is a further characteristic which distinguishes both Jung's personality and his work quite fundamentally from all other cultural achievements up to the present time. This lies in the fact that the unconscious was intensely constellated in him and so also constellates itself in his readers, for Jung was the first to discover the spontaneous creativity of the unconscious psyche and to follow it consciously. He allowed the unconscious to have its say directly in what he wrote, especially in his later work. (*Everything I have written has a double bottom,* he said once.) So that the reader does find a logically understandable argument on the one hand, but on the other finds himself at the same time exposed to the impact of that *other voice,* the unconscious, which may either grip him or frighten him off. That *other voice* can, among others factors, be heard in Jung's special way of reviving the original etymological meanings of words and of allowing both feeling and imaginative elements to enter into his scientific exposition.

These circumstances make it difficult to assess Jung's impact on our world with any accuracy. This impact was, and is even today, two-fold: the effect of his personality and of his work on the one hand, and on the other the impact of that greater entity, the unconscious, to which he was so committed.

Unlike many important men and women, Jung bothered very little about the recognition of his work by the public, and he cared less and less about it as he grew older. At the same time he made every possible effort to formulate his ideas in a generally understandable way, so as to make them accessible to his fellow men. The very large correspondence he left behind him, the innumerable letters in which he made every effort to explain his standpoint to the many people who wrote to him with various questions, all testify to this. He did it partly to avoid being left alone and isolated with his ideas, but still more because he was convinced that the fate of the Western world depended to a considerable extent on the realization of those ideas. For as he saw it, it is not only the single individual who is liable to psychic illness, as a result of a wrong attitude toward the unconscious; the same thing can also happen to nations as a whole. This touches on still another point which adds to the difficulty of giving an adequate description of Jung's impact on our culture: his work reaches beyond the academic sphere into all the other areas of life. Jung was interested not only in the specific illnesses of the soul, but even more in the mystery of the human psyche itself, which is the source of *all* human activities. No house was ever built, no work of art ever created, no scientific discovery ever made, no religious rite ever observed without the participation of the human psyche. Even the atomic bomb, which may one day annihilate all of us, had its origin in the psyche of a few physicists. Anything which can be discovered about those natural laws which hold good in the human psyche will also be valid for all aspects of human existence. We can even say that the humanities, the natural sciences, religions, arts, as well as both the sociological and the individual behavior of human beings, appear in an entirely new light as a result of the discovery of the unconscious. Both the value we set upon our culture and the values we see in it, and perhaps, too, its very survival, depend directly upon a *right* or *wrong* understanding of the unconscious.

Strangely enough, Jung's discoveries were less accepted—or were accepted more slowly—in his own profession, academic psychiatry, than in many others. Leaders in other scientific fields were the first to make fruitful use of his discoveries and ideas, and it has always been the individual person who reacted to what he found in Jung's work. Jung has never been fashionable; his work has never been the source of any sort of -isms; he always rejected movements and slogans. Two celebrations were held in his honor on his eightieth birthday. For the first occasion, invitations were sent to a carefully selected list of guests, all of whom were official representatives of his psychology. This was a rather stiff event, which tired him. To the evening party, however, anyone who wanted to see the great man was admitted: students, patients, Jung's gardener, neighbors from Bollingen. In short, a great variety of *important* and *unimportant* people came to offer their congratulations at this second party. The atmosphere was warmly human and animated, and Jung stayed longer than had been anticipated. On the way home he said, *Yes, those are the people who will carry on my work, single individuals who are suffering and seeking, and who try to take my ideas seriously in their own lives, not the ones who satisfy their vanity by preaching them to others.*

—*condensed from* **C.G. Jung, His Myth in Our Time**, *by Marie-Louise von Franz*

ADLER, GERHARD. **THE LIVING SYMBOL. Illustrations, notes, bibliography, index, 475pp. PUP61/RKP, 16.50c.**
A detailed study of a case of neurosis and its analytical treatment, showing the basic pattern of the individuation process and the practical application of Jung's theories. Includes patients' drawings and paintings.

■ ADLER, GERHARD. **STUDIES IN ANALYTICAL PSYCHOLOGY. Illustrations, notes, index, 250pp. Put69/Hod, 1.95p.**
This is a review of the main concepts of analytical psychology by one of the most eminent Jungian analysts. *Not only on account of the lucidity of its exposition, but also because of its wealth of illustrative case histories, this book fills a gap in psychological literature. It gives both the professional and the psychologically minded layman a welcome set of bearings in territory which—at any rate to begin with—most people find rather hard of access. But the examples drawn direct from life offer an equally direct approach, and this is an aid to understanding. I would like to recommend this book most cordially to the reading public.*—C.G. Jung.

Union of fire and water.

ADLER, GERHARD and ANIELA JAFFE, eds. **C.G. JUNG LETTERS, 1: 1906-50, 621pp. PUP73, 20.00c.**
Jung's correspondence with such notable figures as Sigmund Freud, Karl Abraham, Hermann Hesse, Mary Mellon, Henry A. Murray, Victor White, Richard Wilhelm, Heinrich Zimmer, and others. The editors provide extensive annotations.

ADLER, GERHARD and ANIELA JAFFE, eds. **C.G. JUNG LETTERS, 2: 1951-61. 625pp. PUP75, 20.00c.**
A selection from Jung's copious correspondence during the last decade of his life, characterized by profound statements on philosophy and religion and moving letters on personal and human themes. With a full index of the two volumes.

BENNETT, E.A. **WHAT JUNG REALLY SAID. 186pp. ScB67, 2.95p.**
An incisive analysis of the development of Jung's work and thinking from his early experiments and meetings with Freud through his ideas of personality analysis and classification, the collective unconscious, dreams, active imagination, alchemy, and psychotherapy. A good brief general overview of Jung's ideas.

BENZ, ERNST, ADOLF PORTMAN, et al. **COLOR SYMBOLISM. Notes, index, 202pp. Spr77, 7.25p.**
Transcriptions of six papers delivered at the 1972 Eranos Conference: *Colour Sense and the Meaning of Colour from a Biologist's Point of View, Concepts of Colour and Colour Symbolism in the Ancient World, White, Red, and Black: Colour Symbolism in Black Africa, Color in Christian Visionary Experience, Color and the Expression of Interior Time in Western Art,* and *The Elimination of Colour in Far Eastern Art and Philosophy.*

■ CAMPBELL, JOSEPH, ed. **THE PORTABLE JUNG. Introduction, chronology, notes, index, 692pp. Vik71, 10.00c/4.95p.**
This is the most comprehensive anthology of Jung's writings available. *I have opened this anthology with papers introducing elementary terms and themes of Jung's psychology. Once acquainted with these, the reader will be prepared to range at will through* **The Collected Works**; *and my second aim, consequently, has been to provide a usable guide to that treasury of learning. For Jung was not only a medical man but a scholar in the grand style, whose researches, particularly in comparative mythology, alchemy, and the psychology of religion, have inspired and augmented the findings of an astonishing number of the leading creative scholars of our time.... My final aim, accordingly has been to provide such a primer and handbook to Jung's writings that if a reader will proceed faithfully from the first page to the last, he will emerge not only with a substantial understanding of Analytical Psychology, but also with a new realization of the relevance of the mythic lore of all peoples to his own psychological "opus magnum" of Individuation.*—from the introduction. The translations are all taken from the **Collected Works** and Campbell supplies an excellent introduction. Campbell himself is a noted scholar and was a close friend and associate of Jung.

CARUS, CARL. **PSYCHE. 94pp. Spr70, 5.60p.**
The name Carus appears often in Jung's writings when he speaks of precursors to the theory of the unconscious. This translation of Part I of **Psyche**, entitled *The Unconscious,* was made by a number of individuals; there is also a precis of Parts II and III by Murray Stein. An introduction by James Hillman examines the parallels between Jung and Carus.

CASTILLEJO, IRENE DE. **KNOWING WOMAN: A FEMININE PSYCHOLOGY. 188pp. H&R73, 2.95p.**
This book presents a unique approach to self understanding for all women. As Ms. Castillejo says, *A woman today lives in perpetual conflict. She cannot slay the dragon of the unconscious without severing her own essential contact with it, without in fact destroying her feminine strength and becoming a mere pseudo-man. Her task is a peculiarly difficult one. She needs the focused consciousness her animus alone can give her, yet she must not forsake her woman's role of mediator to man. Through a woman, man finds his soul. She must never forget this. Through a woman, not through a pseudo-man. Through man, woman finds the animus who can express the soul she has never lost. Her burning need is to trust her own diffuse awareness, to know what she knows and to learn to speak of it, for until it is expressed she does not wholly know it.* Ms. de Castillejo is a noted Jungian psychologist. *I love this book. It is very wise and very pertinent for women today.*—Anais Nin.

CHRISTOU, EVANGELOS. **THE LOGOS OF THE SOUL. 105+pp. Spr76, 4.45p.**
A philosophical discussion of the soul as seen from the psychological, intuitive, and scientific points of view. Christou delves deeply into his subject and comes up with a number of intriguing insights.

COHEN, EDMUND. **C.G. JUNG AND THE SCIENTIFIC ATTITUDE. Bibliography, index, 179pp. LtA75, 2.95p.**
The content of this monograph bears little resemblance to the idea invoked by the title. It is basically a fairly simplistic, somewhat dull study of Jung's beliefs on a wide number of topics. As might be expected, the ideas are little more than summarized. Cohen often allows Jung to speak for himself through extensive quotations and he has arranged his material topically. Dr. Cohen is a psychology professor who studied at the C.G. Jung Institute in Zurich.

COX, DAVID. **THE TEACHINGS OF C.G. JUNG. 191pp. H&R68, 1.95p.**
A very simplified synopsis of Jung's psychological thought. The first chapters discuss psychology in general and review contemporary theories other than those of Jung. The next chapters elucidate the central concepts of Jungian psychology and a final one details the author's own experiences in Jungian analysis (as a patient, not an analyst). This is a basic primer, designed for those who wish some understanding of Jungian thought. Only the psychological aspects are discussed.

CROOKALL, ROBERT. **THE JUNG-JAFFE VIEW OF OUT-OF-THE-BODY EXPERIENCE. 2.85p.**
See the Out-of-the-Body Experiences section.

DAVIES, ROBERTSON. **THE DEPTFORD TRILOGY. Vik78, 5.85p/set.**
A boxed set of **Fifth Business, The Manticore,** and **World of Wonders.**

DAVIES, ROBERTSON. **FIFTH BUSINESS. 266pp. Vik70, 1.95p.**
This is the first volume of a powerful fictional trilogy, in the form of a memoir of a Canadian schoolteacher. It is Jungian in the sense that Jungian psychology influences Davies both as a man and a writer. This is generally considered the best of the trilogy and it can stand alone as the story of a rational man who discovers that the marvelous is only another aspect of the real.

DAVIES, ROBERTSON. **THE MANTICORE. 310pp. Vik72, 1.95p.**
This is the story of a man's experiences in Jungian analysis in Switzerland. It reveals how analysis proceeds and how the psychiatrist and the patient cope with and learn from the emerging symbols. We got a better feeling for the process of Jungian analysis from this novel than we have from anything else we have read. As with the other books in this trilogy, it is not necessary to read all of them.

DAVIES, ROBERTSON. **WORLD OF WONDERS. 316pp. Vik75, 1.95p.**
The life story of a master illusionist and magician forms the central core of the concluding volume of Davies' trilogy.

DONINGTON, ROBERT. **WAGNER'S RING AND ITS SYMBOLS. 6.95p.**
See the Music section.

■ EDINGER, EDWARD. **EGO AND ARCHETYPE. Sixty-three plates, notes, index, 304pp. Vik72, 3.95p.**
Edinger is a psychiatrist who is presently Chairman of the New York Institute of the Jung Foundation. This is a remarkably lucid synthesis of Jung's basic ideas in the form of a detailed journey through art, religion, legend, and folklore into the deepest regions of the psyche. Part I surveys the changing relations between the ego and the archetypal psyche at different stages of development. Part II explores the ways the ego can relate to symbolic imaging and describes some of the categories of experience an individual encounters. In Part III the goal of individuation and its symbolism is discussed and a remarkable series of dreams is presented.

ERANOS YEARBOOKS. **VOLUME I: SPIRIT AND NATURE. 514pp. PUP54/RKP, 14.00c.**
The yearly Eranos Conferences have been conducted at Ascona, Switzerland since 1933; at each conference, some of the world's best minds meet at a round table and share ideas. The papers delivered at the conferences represent a unique contribution to the unfolding understanding of mankind and come out of a wide variety of disciplines. Jung was one of the initial supporters of the conferences and an honored guest almost every year. The papers in this volume include *The Spirit in Fairy Tales, The History of the Spirit in Antiquity, The Spirit of Science, The Spirit of Psychology, The Indian Conception of Psychology,* and *The Transformation of the Spirit in the Renaissance.*

ERANOR YEARBOOKS. **VOLUME II: THE MYSTERIES. 492pp. PUP55/RKP, 16.50c/5.95p.**
The papers in this volume are concerned with manifestations of the spiritual impulse in sacred traditions, both modern and ancient. Some of the individual selections include *The Orphic Mysteries and the Greek Spirit, The Ancient Mysteries in the Societies of their Times, The Transformation of the Ancient Mysteries and their Most Recent Echoes, The Mysteries of Osiris in Ancient Egypt,* and *The Pagan and Christian Mysteries.*

ERANOS YEARBOOKS. **VOLUME III: MAN AND TIME. Index, 434pp. PUP57/RKP, 13.50c.**
The contributors to this volume include Mircea Eliade, Hellmut Wilhelm, C.G. Jung, and Erich Neumann. Essays include *Time and Eternity in Indian Thought, The Concept of Time in the Book of Changes, The Relation of Time to Death, Time in Islamic Thought,* and *Transformation of Science in Our Age.*

ERANOS YEARBOOKS. **VOLUME IV: SPIRITUAL DISCIPLINES. 527pp. PUP60/RKP, 14.00c.**
Participants include Eliade, Martin Buber, Heinrich Zimmer and Carl Jung. Essays include *The Significance of Indian Tantric Yoga, Spiritual Guidance in Contemporary Taoism, Psychology of Ancient Mexican Symbolism, Contemplation in Christian Mysticism,* and *The Position of Art in the Psychology of our Times.*

ERANOS YEARBOOKS. **VOLUME V: MAN AND TRANSFORMATION. 433pp. PUP64/RKP, 15.00c.**
Among the authors represented in this volume are D.T. Suzuki, Paul Tillich, Jean Danielou, Heinrich Zimmer, and Mircea Eliade. The selections include *The Birth of a New Consciousness in Zen, Symbols in Ancient Byzantine Mysticism,* and *Immortality, Death, and Rebirth in the Light of India.*

ERANOS YEARBOOKS. **VOLUME VI: THE MYSTIC VISION. 500pp. PUP68/RKP, 14.00c.**
This volume contains papers on the title theme by Ernesto Buonaiuti, Wilhelm Koppers, Heinrich Zimmer, and other noted scholars.

EVANS, RICHARD. **JUNG ON ELEMENTARY PSYCHOLOGY. Index, 252pp. Dut76, 3.95p.**
An updated transcription of Evans' extensive series of dialogues with Carl Jung, originally published under the title, **Conversations with Carl Jung.** The emphasis is almost totally on Jung's psychological ideas; his more metaphysical concepts are hardly touched on. The dialogues have been thematically edited.

EVANS-WENTZ, W.Y. **THE TIBETAN BOOK OF THE DEAD. 3.95p.**
See the Tibetan Buddhism section.

EVANS-WENTZ, W.Y. **THE TIBETAN BOOK OF THE GREAT LIBERATION. 4.95p.**
See the Tibetan Buddhism section.

■ FORDHAM, FRIEDA. **AN INTRODUCTION TO JUNG'S PSYCHOLOGY. Introduction, glossary, notes, index, 159pp. Vik66, 2.50p.**
Ms. Fordham is a Jungian analyst. She worked closely with Jung and his wife in the preparation of the first edition of this book. Jung himself had the following to say about the final product: *She has delivered a fair and simple account of the main aspects of my psychological work. I am indebted to her for this admirable piece of work.* We agree and to this day the book remains the best simple introduction to Jungian psychology. The author begins with a general analysis of analytical psychology and from there devotes chapters to Jung's major themes: *Psychological Types, Archetypes of the Collective Unconscious, Religion and the Individuation Process, Psychotherapy, Dreams,* and *Psychology and Education.* A final chapter, *Jung on Himself,* was added after the publication of **Memories, Dreams, and Reflections,** and it contains a biographical study culled from that volume and other material.

FORDHAM, MICHAEL. **CHILDREN AS INDIVIDUALS. Illustrations, notes, bibliography, index, 223pp. JFP69/Hod, 12.10c.**
Dr. Fordham was the first Jungian to apply the concept of analytical patterns to the study of child development. This book is a radically revised version of his original work, **The Life of Childhood.** It is a study of child maturation, expressed through comprehensive investigation of the self and individuation in childhood. Dr. Fordham's extensive analytical practice with children of all ages has provided a rich store of case material including play behavior, drawings, fantasies, and dreams.

FORDHAM, MICHAEL. **NEW DEVELOPMENTS IN ANALYTICAL PSYCHOLOGY. Foreword by Jung, notes, index, 228pp. RKP57, 17.35c.**
A collection of essays by a child psychologist who was closely associated with Jung. A number of the selections focus on child analysis and ego development, others discuss archetypes, synchronicity, imagery, and transference.

FORDHAM, MICHAEL. **THE SELF AND AUTISM. Notes, index, 311pp. HeG76, 20.85c.**
An elaboration of ideas presented in Fordham's earlier works on maturation in infancy and its psychopathology. Many case studies and practical techniques are included.

FORDHAM, MICHAEL, *et al.* **ANALYTICAL PSYCHOLOGY: A MODERN SCIENCE. Notes, index, 219pp. HeG73, 7.75c.**
A collection of papers in which the authors explore and discuss some of the basic theoretical concepts in Jungian psychology as these have been understood and developed by analytical psychologists in London.

FRANZ, MARIE-LOUISE VON. **AURORA CONSURGENS. 31.50c.**
See the Alchemy section.

FRANZ, MARIE-LOUISE VON. **INDIVIDUATION IN FAIRY TALES. Index, 189pp. Spr77, 8.45p.**
An analysis of the bird motifs in six fairy tales: **The White Parrot** (Spain), **The Bath Badgerd** (Persia), **Prince Hassan Pasha** (Turkestan), **The Bird Flower Triller** (Iran), **The Nightingale Gisar** (Balkan), and **The Bird Wehmus**. In the process of her analysis Dr. von Franz summarizes the storyline of each tale.

FRANZ, MARIE-LOUISE VON. **INTERPRETATION OF FAIRY TALES. 159pp. Spr73, 5.60p.**
This is Dr. von Franz's basic volume on fairy tales. She includes a review of the literature, an examination of various theories and interpretations of fairy tales, a detailed study of one tale, and an exploration of shadow, animus, and anima motives in the tales. Once this volume is digested, the reader can move on to one of the more detailed studies. Dr. von Franz writes clearly and presents an abundance of examples to back up her theories.

FRANZ, MARIE-LOUISE VON. **C.G. JUNG: HIS MYTH IN OUR TIME. Long bibliography, index, 366pp. LBC75/Hod, 15.00c/4.95p.**
Each individual's life follows a pattern which, from the point of view of analytical psychology, represents the myth or archetypal outline of the inner and outer events of one's own biography. The book refers to such a pattern in the life of Jung. Dr. von Franz, who worked closely with Jung for over twenty-five years, traces the development of basic Jungian concepts such as the collective unconscious, archetypes, psychological types, active imagination, the creative instinct, and the process of individuation from their origin in specific dreams Jung had throughout his life (and which he discusses in his autobiography) to their eventual empirical documentation in the voluminous books and papers he published over a period of sixty-five years. This is neither an academic biography of Jung nor a primer of Jungian thought. Rather, it is a history of the growth and development of one man's creative powers during a lifetime of dialogue with the unconscious. Dr. von Franz is one of the founders of the C.G. Jung Institute in Zurich and this is an important, though quite technical addition to the literature on Jungian psychology and its founder.

FRANZ, MARIE-LOUISE VON. **NUMBER AND TIME. Notes, bibliography, index, 342pp. NUP74/HPG, 18.80c.**
Jung's work in his later years suggested that the seemingly divergent sciences of psychology and modern physics might, in fact, be approaching a unified world model in which the dualism of matter and psyche would be resolved. He believed that the natural integers are the archetypal patterns that regulate the unitary realm of psyche and matter, and that number serves as a special instrument for man's becoming conscious of this unity. In this volume Dr. von Franz explores Jung's hypothesis. Her discussion draws on material from Eastern studies, ethnology, archaeology, and mythology, as well as natural sciences and mathematics. The book includes explorations of the psychological aspects of mathematics, a discussion of number as a psychophysical energy pattern, and a description of mandalas. In addition she develops Jung's theory of synchronicity. Written in a clear style and replete with illustrations which help make the mathematical ideas visible.

FRANZ, MARIE-LOUISE VON. **PATTERNS OF CREATIVITY MIRRORED IN CREATION MYTHS. Index, 250pp. Spr72, 8.80p.**
A psychological interpretation of twelve motifs in the cosmogonies of peoples from North and South America, Africa, the Near East, and other parts of the world. In this lecture series, one of the longest and most significant of her seminars, Dr. von Franz examines the motifs of

The Two Creators, Deus Faber, The First Victim, World Egg, Primordial Man and Fire, Chains of Generations, Seeds of the World, and Creation through Meditation. An aim of these lectures is to help the individual recognize creation themes in dreams as they relate to individual creativity.

FRANZ, MARIE-LOUISE VON. **PROBLEMS OF THE FEMININE IN FAIRYTALES. 194pp. Spr72, 7.85p.**
A collection of the edited transcriptions of a series of twelve lectures exploring the feminine psychology of women and men in the archetypal patterns of fairy tales from many lands. Dr. von Franz draws practical psychological counsel from these archetypes and gives us several case studies showing their application. There is also a discussion of symbolic themes and images that appear in dreams and fantasies.

FRANZ, MARIE-LOUISE VON. **A PSYCHOLOGICAL INTERPRETATION OF THE GOLDEN ASS OF APULEIUS. 188pp. Spr70, 6.65p.**
A study of the archetypal pattern of transformation as depicted in the classical novel about Lucius, the young Roman who was turned into an ass, had many adventures, and then went through the Isis mysteries. Dr. von Franz also presents the original *Eros and Psyche* story, as a tale within a tale. She gives the reader a wealth of scholarly amplification, insights, and anecdotes, and the whole account is related to basic theories of analytical psychology. The material in this volume was taken from a series of lectures Dr. von Franz gave at the Jung Institute in Zurich and a final section of the book contains questions and answers from the lectures.

FRANZ, MARIE-LOUISE VON. **SHADOW AND EVIL IN FAIRYTALES. 284pp. Spr74, 9.00p.**
This volume joins together two distinct lecture series, *Shadow* and *Evil*, to present these major motifs as they are depicted in fairy tales. As with all of Dr. von Franz' other books, the material is relevant to an individual's darkness today. A thorough index of images and motifs is also included.

FRANZ, MARIE-LOUISE VON and JAMES HILLMAN. **LECTURES ON JUNG'S TYPOLOGY. 150pp. Spr71, 6.65p.**
A collection of two lecture series, one by Dr. von Franz, the other by James Hillman. Dr. von Franz discusses the interior functioning of Jung's eight psychological types and gives examples of psychological pitfalls and potentials drawn from her analytical practice. Dr. Hillman's lectures differentiate feeling from other psychological acts and expose some misconceptions about feeling, the *anima*, and the mother complex.

FREY-ROHN, LILIANE. **FROM FREUD TO JUNG. Notes, bibliography, index, 358pp. Del74, 3.95p.**
Dr. Frey-Rohn began her own psychological career in 1936 under the supervision of Dr. Jung. As one of his closest colleagues, she collaborated with him in many of his investigations, especially in the fields of medieval astrology and synchronicity. This volume presents a comparative study of the psychology of the unconscious as seen in the work of Freud and Jung. The basic view of Jung, that the psyche is a totality seeking to realize itself, stands in sharp contrast to Freud's mechanistic view of it as the effect of prior causes. Hence Freud stresses the self transcending aspects of man's nature. The last part of the book is devoted to an analysis of the development of Jung's ideas subsequent to the death of Freud, particularly his concept of archetypes.

FROMM, ERICH. **THE FORGOTTEN LANGUAGE: AN INTRODUCTION TO THE UNDERSTANDING OF DREAMS, FAIRY TALES, AND MYTHS. 3.95p.**
See the Dreams section.

GRINNELL, ROBERT. **ALCHEMY IN A MODERN WOMAN. Notes, index, 175pp. Spr73, 6.95p.**
This is a case study similar to Jung's exposition of a young scientist's dreams in **Psychology and Alchemy**. Looking at dreams and symptoms, and illuminating their meanings in the light of alchemical and Gnostic parallels, the author penetrates into the hidden collective background of a *modern woman* and investigates the archetypal movements and thoughts in the recesses of her soul. This is a very interesting study, quite unlike anything we have ever seen before.

GUGGENBUHL-CRAIG, ADOLF. **MARRIAGE DEAD OR ALIVE.**
5.05p.
See the Women and Men section.

GUGGENBUHL-CRAIG, ADOLF. **POWER IN THE HELPING PRO-**
FESSIONS. 158pp. Spr76, 5.30p.
Most professions serve the health and well being of mankind in one way or another. But the activities of the doctor, priest, teacher, psychotherapist, and social worker involve very specialized and deliberate attempts to help the unfortunate, the ill, those who have somehow lost their way. In the following chapters I should like to describe how and why the members of these "ministering professions" can also do the greatest damage—harm caused directly by their very desire to help. I work as a medical psychotherapist, so, only in writing of doctors and psychotherapists have I tried to explore in detail the possibility of overcoming the fundamental problems of their professions.

HALL, CALVIN and VERNON NORDBY. **A PRIMER OF JUNGIAN**
PSYCHOLOGY. Index, 150pp. NAL73/NEL, 1.50p.
This is a well written summary of the main features of Jung's work. The primer begins with a biographical study of Jung and goes from there into analyses of Jung's psychological and personality theories. There is also a guide to reading Jung, with suggestions for introductory reading in various subject areas.

HALL, NOR. **MOTHERS AND DAUGHTERS. Notes, 41pp. Rus76,**
2.75p.
A collection of reflections on the archetypal feminine heavily based on mythology.

■ *HANNAH, BARBARA.* **JUNG, HIS LIFE AND WORK. Notes,**
index, 376pp. Put76/Jos, 4.95p.
This is a full scale study of Jung's life and work by a pupil, friend, and close associate for more than thirty years. It is a lucid, penetrating account that stresses the essential wholeness of the man and traces the difficult path by which that wholeness was achieved. In writing this memoir, Ms. Hannah was conscious that much of what she knew about Jung would die with her unless she committed it to writing. So she has made every attempt to tell all she knows and in the process many aspects of Jung's personal life are revealed. We recommend this book heartily to all who seek a deeper understanding of the man and his formative experiences and thoughts.

HANNAH, BARBARA. **STRIVING TOWARD WHOLENESS. Notes,**
bibliography, 316pp. JFP71/A&U, 12.60c.
This is a study of the psychic processes in individuals which move them to strive for wholeness of personality and integration of all their innate capacities. Since this inner drama manifests itself with special intensity in the lives of creative individuals, Ms. Hannah has taken for the heart of her work the biographies and literary productions of five major English novelists—Robert Louis Stevenson, Mary Webb, Charlotte, Emily, and Anne Bronte—and one nonliterary artist, Branwell Bronte, whose life was interrelated with that of his three sisters.

HARDING, M. ESTHER. **THE 'I' AND THE 'NOT-I'. Bibliography,**
index, 254pp. PUP65/Cov, 3.45p.
Dr. Harding was one of the leading American Jungian analysts for many years. This volume contains a number of general essays on Jung's concept of ego development and his personality theory. Dr. Harding places particular emphasis on his concepts of the collective unconscious, anima, animus, shadow, and archetypes.

HARDING, M. ESTHER. **PSYCHIC ENERGY: ITS SOURCE AND ITS**
TRANSFORMATION. Good bibliography, index, 497pp. PUP63,
4.95p.
Harding analyzes the transformation of instinctive drives into constructive or detrimental living patterns. She also discusses the transformation of these energies in the development of higher consciousness. The study is based mainly on Jung's ideas but not notably derivative.

HARDING, M. ESTHER. **THE WAY OF ALL WOMEN. Bibliography,**
index, 332pp. H&R70/HPG, 3.95p.
This has been acclaimed as one of the best books available on feminine psychology since it first appeared in 1933. This edition has been brought up to date in various ways by the author and new sections on old age and friendships between men and women have been added. Other major sections discuss work, marriage, maternity, and the psychological relationships between a woman and her family and friends, both male and female. Dr. Harding is a Jungian psychologist who is best known for her work with women and families. She stressed the need of a woman to work toward her own wholeness and develop the many sides of her nature and emphasized the importance of unconscious processes.

HARDING, M. ESTHER. **WOMAN'S MYSTERIES, ANCIENT AND**
MODERN. 285pp. H&R35/HPG, 3.95p.
A fascinating psychological interpretation of the feminine principle as portrayed in myth, story, and dreams, integrated with a discussion of the inner life of women.

HART, DAVID. **THE PSYCHOLOGY OF A FAIRY TALE. 1.20p.**
See the Fairy Tales section.

HENDERSON, JOSEPH and MAUD OAKES. **THE WISDOM OF THE**
SERPENT. Notes, index, 314pp. McM63, 1.95p.
A Jungian psychiatrist and an anthropologist explore the meanings and manifestations of death through ritual, religion, and myth. They feel that the knowledge that man must die is the force that drives man to create. The tribal initiation of the shaman and the archetype of the serpent exist universally in man's experience, exemplifying the death of the Self and a rebirth into a transcendent, unknowable life. The authors trace the images and patterns of psychic liberation through personal encounter, the cycles of nature, spiritual teachings, religious texts, myths of resurrection, poems, and epics. This is a fascinating study and is extensively illustrated.

HERZOG, EDGAR. **PSYCHE AND DEATH: MYTHS AND DREAMS**
IN ANALYTICAL PSYCHOLOGY. 224pp. JFP67, 10.00c.
An account of the changing forms of man's images of death as man himself has changed and developed, which reveals that the images of ancient and primitive peoples reappear with startling similarity in contemporary dreams.

HEUSCHER, JULIUS. **A PSYCHIATRIC STUDY OF MYTHS AND**
FAIRYTALES: THEIR ORIGIN, MEANING AND USEFULNESS.
Notes, bibliography, index, 440pp. Tho74, 20.10c.
This is an informative study. Dr. Heuscher's approach is Jungian and he offers both theoretical remarks and analyzes individual tales at length. Many of the archetypal meanings he suggests are not ones that had occurred to us previously, and he stresses what, to us, are the most significant points of each tale. The author's thesis is that the imagery of fairy tales may help an individual's quest for harmony and wholeness and counteract the overly intellectual stress of our society.

HILLMAN, JAMES. **EMOTION. Notes, bibliography, indices, 328pp.**
RKP60, 15.60c.
A slightly revised version of Hillman's doctoral dissertation, which is both an anthology of emotion theories and a critical analysis of different ways of thinking about emotion.

HILLMAN, JAMES. **LOOSE ENDS: PRIMARY PAPERS IN ARCHE-**
TYPAL PSYCHOLOGY. 212pp. Spr75, 7.20p.
A collection of twelve papers and talks divided into two categories, *Themes* and *Theories.*

HILLMAN, JAMES. **THE MYTH OF ANALYSIS. Index, 313pp.**
H&R72, 4.95p.
Analysis will be ended when we discover what myth it is enacting, a discovery which may not come all at once but which occurs as insights reveal the relation of analysis to soul-making. For soul-making is what binds us there, fascinated: not just the diagnosis of what is wrong, not even the cure of our sickness, but the potential in analytical psychology for soul-making....Part One develops this perspective and gives credit to the creative power of analysis....Part Two could be subtitled, "The End of the Unconscious." Its focus is on the analyst as professional; its theme, psychological language. The focus of Part Three is on analytical consciousness; its theme, analysis and its goal. This is a very detailed study, drawing heavily on mythological themes and archetypes.

HILLMAN, JAMES. **RE-VISIONING PSYCHOLOGY. Extensive notes,**
index, 283pp. H&R75, 3.95p.
This volume focuses on the soul as the rightful concern of psychology. In an introductory section Hillman attempts to define and describe what he means by the soul. In the chapters that follow he develops the

main lines of the soul-making process, nourished by the accumulated insights of the Western experience, extending from the Greeks through the Renaissance and the Romantics to Freud and especially to Jung. In the process he draws on mythology, philosophy, history, and religion, and on the ideas of the major individual figures in the field of depth psychology. As he says *All depth psychology has already been summed up by this fragment of Heraclitus: "You could not discover the limits of the soul (psyche), even if you traveled every road to do so; such is the depth (bathun) of its meaning (logos)."*

HILLMAN, JAMES. **SUICIDE AND THE SOUL. Bibliography, index, 192pp. Spr76, 5.55p.**
An in depth psychological analysis of all aspects of suicide, including a full discussion of the role of analysis and analysts in suicide. Although this is ostensibly a practical treatise, it also reveals the profound differences between the strictly medical model of therapy and one that engages the soul.

HOCHHEIMER, WOLFGANG. **THE PSYCHOTHERAPY OF C.G. JUNG. Notes, bibliography, index, 168pp. JFP69, 8.00c.**
Dr. Hochheimer is one of the few non-Jungians to write sympathetically about Jung. He is a practicing analyst and Director of the Institute for Pedagogical Psychology of the School of Education in Berlin. He integrates his experience as an analyst with a review of the main tenents of Jungian psychology, and his discussion includes extensive quotations from Jung's own writings.

HOWES, ELIZABETH and SHEILA MOON. **THE CHOICEMAKER. Notes, index, 221pp. TPH73, 3.95p.**
The authors are practicing psychotherapists who have done advanced study at the C.G. Jung Institute in Zurich. They contend that the ability to make choices is both our privilege and our responsibility. This ability is the basic difference between us and so-called unthinking creatures. Through dreams, myths, the **Bible**, and Jungian psychology, the authors explore how we can make choices and what the right choices are.

JACOBI, JOLANDE. **COMPLEX/ARCHETYPE/SYMBOL IN THE PSYCHOLOGY OF C.G. JUNG. Many notes, bibliography, index, 243pp. PUP59, 3.95p.**
Dr. Jacobi was a founding member of the C.G. Jung Institute in Zurich and an associate of Dr. Jung's for many years. In this lucid volume she presents a comparative examination of three central, interrelated concepts in analytical psychology. The first part of the book is devoted to individual analyses of complex, archetype, and symbol. The second section has a detailed interpretation of one dream, showing how these concepts can be analyzed.

JACOBI, JOLANDE. **MASKS OF THE SOUL. 97pp. Eer76, 2.95p.**
A collection of essays which Dr. Jacobi says *are not intended to impart specialized knowledge. They are only spotlights to illumine some of the dark corners of the soul and can, in fact, be used as a guide to everyday life.* An introduction surveys Dr. Jacobi's life and work.

JACOBI, JOLANDE, ed. **PSYCHOLOGICAL REFLECTIONS. 395pp. PUP70, 3.95p.**
An anthology of selections from Jung's writings between 1905-61, edited from over 100 works and arranged under the following headings: *The Nature and Activity of the Psyche, Man in his Relation to Others, The World of Values,* and *On Ultimate Things.*

JACOBI, JOLANDE. **THE PSYCHOLOGY OF C.G. JUNG. Index, 226pp. YUP73/Hod, 3.95p.**
The first edition of this work appeared in 1940 and it has been revised and updated eight times to adapt it to Jung's most recent findings and to present the material in a clearer form. Dr. Jung wrote the following in a preface to the first edition: *My endeavours in psychology have been essentially pioneer work, leaving me neither time nor opportunity to present them systematically. Dr. Jacobi has taken this difficult task upon herself with a happy result, having succeeded in giving an account free from the ballast of technical particulars. This constitutes a synopsis that includes or at least touches upon all essential points, so that it is possible for the reader...to orient himself readily whenever needful.* This book is well written, however it should not be considered as a general introduction to the reader who is merely interested in getting a feeling for Jung's work. The emphasis is on theoretical and practical applications, and the text is both scholarly and

comprehensive. Wherever possible Dr. Jacobi has used Jung's own words. She has also included a series of nineteen *pictures from the unconscious* and several diagrams as well as a short biographical sketch and a plethora of textual notes. The text also includes the most extensive bibliography we have seen.

JACOBI, JOLANDE. **THE WAY OF INDIVIDUATION. Notes, bibliography, index, 186pp. Hod67, 4.00c.**
According to Dr. Jung, individuation is man's potentiality to come to fullest awareness of his psyche and thus to achieve wholeness. In the light of her studies and of her own practical experience, Dr. Jacobi contrasts the difference between the natural growing process and that deepened by methodical and analytical insight. She draws on myths and religious rituals, and on initiation ceremonies. Particular emphasis is placed on the phases of transition between the first and second halves of life, and on the distinction between the characteristics and goals of each period. This edition includes a biographical sketch of Dr. Jacobi.

The fountain of life as *fons mercurialis.*

JACOBSOHN, HELMUTH, MARIE-LOUISE VON FRANZ, and SIEGMUND HURWITZ. **TIMELESS DOCUMENTS OF THE SOUL. Notes, index, 275pp. NUP68, 14.10c.**
Within the covers of this small book are three extraordinary documents.... When we hear, through Professor Jacobsohn's new interpretative translation, a world-weary Egyptian of four thousand years ago speaking with his "soul" and wrestling with the problem of suicide, we can rediscover a connection both to him in that time and to this theme in ourselves today. So, too, when we read the dreams of Descartes, or the visionary text of the Hasidic Maggid, we hear examples of man in dialogue with the voice of the unconscious. Although widely disparate in time and place and content, these three papers stem from the same root. They have one experience in common. They tell of the inroads of the unconscious into consciousness and of the attempts of the conscious personality to come to terms with this other force in the psyche.—James Hillman.

JAFFE, ANIELA. **FROM THE LIFE AND WORK OF C.G. JUNG. Notes, 146pp. Hod71, 5.30c.**
Dr. Jaffe was Jung's private secretary for many years and had access to all his papers. It was to her that he dictated **Memories, Dreams, Reflections.** We found the most interesting essay in this collection to be a sensitive portrait of Jung in his last years. There is also a very good review of Jung's alchemical work. The other two essays discuss *Parapsychology: Experience and Theory* and *C.G. Jung and National Socialism.* The collection is most valuable as a highly personal account of Jung and some of his major ideas and life events.

JAFFE, ANIELA. **THE MYTH OF MEANING IN THE WORK OF C.G. JUNG.** 186pp. Vik71, 2.25p.
In this book Dr. Jaffe has singled out for special study one thematic complex from the profusion of ideas in Jung's work: *What is the meaning of life and of Man?*

JOHNSON, ROBERT. **HE!** 92pp. H&R76/DLT, 1.95p.
This volume is a contribution to understanding masculine psychology, based on the legend of Parzival and his search for the Grail. Jungian psychological concepts are the basis of Johnson's interpretation.

JOHNSON, ROBERT. **SHE!** 92pp. H&R 76, 1.95p.
This is a retelling of the story of Amor and Psyche. Johnson feels that this myth is one of the best elucidations of the psychology of the feminine personality and his interpretation reflects this belief.

JUNG, C.G. **ANALYTICAL PSYCHOLOGY.** 240pp. RaH68, 1.95p.
Transcription of the Tavistock Lectures given by Jung in 1935: *These lectures provide an extremely clear, readable, and at times amusing exposition of Jung's theories. In them Jung not only describes his views on the structure of the mind, giving lucid accounts of his psychological types, of the personal and collective unconscious and of archetypes, but also explains vividly his techniques of dream analysis and active imagination and the role played by transference in analytic therapy.*—Charles Rycroft, **The New York Review of Books**. The lectures were delivered to professionals and questions and answers follow each one.

JUNG, C.G. **ANSWER TO JOB.** 136pp. PUP69/RKP, 3.45p.
Jung's very personal attempt to deal with the question of evil in terms of the significance of theological concepts in man's psychic life. Part of Volume II of the **Collected Works**.

JUNG, C.G. **THE COLLECTED WORKS, VOLUME I: PSYCHIATRIC STUDIES.** 285pp. PUP70/RKP, 11.00c.
This series is the definitive edition of Dr. Jung's writings, translated from the German by R.F.C. Hull. Each volume is 6"x9" and contains a bibliography and index. A full listing of the papers included in each volume is available in many of the works by Jung including **Memories, Dreams, Reflections**. This volume contains Jung's earliest writings, including his first publication, *On the Psychology and Pathology of So-Called Occult Phenomena*. The papers date from 1902 through 1905.

JUNG, C.G. **THE COLLECTED WORKS, VOLUME II: EXPERIMENTAL RESEARCHES.** Charts, tables, 661pp. PUP73/RKP, 17.50c.
Includes Jung's famous word association studies in normal and abnormal psychology, two lectures on the association method given in 1909 at Clark University, and three articles on psychophysical researches from American and English journals in 1907 and 1908.

JUNG, C.G. **THE COLLECTED WORKS, VOLUME III: THE PSYCHOGENESIS OF MENTAL DISEASE.** 325pp. PUP72/RKP, 9.50c.
Nine studies, including *The Psychology of Dementia Praecox* and *The Content of the Psychoses*. The book reflects the development of Jung's thinking through the years on the nature of mental illness. Many essays discuss schizophrenia. Jung's work in this area was important background to his development of the theories of psychic energy and the archetypes.

JUNG, C.G. **THE COLLECTED WORKS, VOLUME IV: FREUD AND PSYCHOANALYSIS.** 388pp. PUP70/RKP, 13.50c.
The substance of Jung's published writings on psychoanalysis and its founder between 1906 and 1916, and two later reassessments.

JUNG, C.G. **THE COLLECTED WORKS, VOLUME V: SYMBOLS OF TRANSFORMATION.** 597pp. PUP67/RKP, 16.00c/5.95p.
A complete revision of **Psychology of the Unconscious** (originally published in 1911-12), one of Jung's most influential works and the first important statement of his independent position. The essays discuss symbolic parallels from religion, mythology, ethnology, art, and literature, and the concept of the libido as mainly psychic energy from the unconscious expressed as conscious symbols. Over 100 plates and line drawings illustrate the text.

JUNG. C.G. **THE COLLECTED WORKS, VOLUME VI: PSYCHOLOGICAL TYPES.** 632pp. PUP71/RKP, 15.00c/5.95p.
This is a new translation of one of the most important of Jung's longer works. The volume also contains an appendix of four shorter papers on psychological typology published between 1913 and 1935. The system

of personality types developed by Jung was central to his work because, as he says, *it is one's psychological type which from the outset determines and limits a person's judgment.* There is also a great deal of material on the spiritual activity of the psyche.

JUNG, C.G. **THE COLLECTED WORKS, VOLUME VII: TWO ESSAYS ON ANALYTICAL PSYCHOLOGY.** 369pp. PUP53/RKP, 13.50c/ 3.95p.
Essays which state the fundamentals of Jung's psychological system: *On the Psychology of the Unconscious* and *The Relations Between the Ego and the Unconscious*, with their original versions in an appendix. Historically these writings mark the end of Jung's intimate association with Freud and sum up his attempt to integrate the psychological schools of Freud and Adler into a comprehensive framework.

JUNG, C.G. **THE COLLECTED WORKS, VOLUME VIII: THE STRUCTURE AND DYNAMICS OF THE PSYCHE.** 606pp. PUP69/RKP, 17.50c.
Eighteen studies span some forty years and illustrate the development of Jung's ideas. Arranged in thematic groupings and including the following important works: *On Psychic Energy, On the Nature of the Psyche,* and *Synchronicity.*

JUNG, C.G. **THE COLLECTED WORKS, VOLUME IX, PART I: THE ARCHETYPES AND THE COLLECTIVE UNCONSCIOUS.** 474pp. PUP69/RKP, 15.00c.
Twelve studies on the archetypes, illustrated with paintings by analytical patients. Three essays set the theoretical framework, six describe specific archetypes, and three define the process of individuation. Includes Jung's study of mandalas.

JUNG, C.G. **THE COLLECTED WORKS, VOLUME IX, PART II: AION: RESEARCHES INTO THE PHENOMENOLOGY OF THE SELF.** 356pp. PUP68/RKP, 15.00c.
A late work, devoted to the archetype of the self and its traditional historical equivalent, the Christ figure. Extensive references to Christian, Gnostic, and alchemical symbolism are included along with summations of the concepts of the ego, the shadow, and the anima and animus.

JUNG, C.G. **THE COLLECTED WORKS, VOLUME X: CIVILIZATION IN TRANSITION.** Illustrations, 630pp. PUP70/RKP, 15.00c.
Essays bearing on the contemporary scene and the relation of the individual to society, including papers written during the twenties and thirties focusing on the upheaval in Germany, and two major works of Jung's last years, *The Undiscovered Self* and *Flying Saucers*. The essays discuss our unconscious premises and the need for self knowledge to avoid being overcome by social pressures.

JUNG, C.G. **THE COLLECTED WORKS, VOLUME XI: PSYCHOLOGY AND RELIGION, WEST AND EAST.** 712pp. PUP69/RKP, 15.00c.
Eight essays on Western religion (mainly Christian) and its psychological components, including *Answer to Job*; and six on Eastern religion, including forewords to the **I Ching**, Suzuki's **Introduction to Zen Buddhism**, and works on yoga, meditation, and Tibetan Buddhism.

JUNG, C.G. **THE COLLECTED WORKS, VOLUME XII: PSYCHOLOGY AND ALCHEMY.** 16.50c.
See the Alchemy section.

JUNG, C.G. **THE COLLECTED WORKS, VOLUME XIII: ALCHEMICAL STUDIES.** 15.00c.
See the Alchemy section.

JUNG, C.G. **THE COLLECTED WORKS, VOLUME XIV: MYSTERIUM CONIUNCTIONIS.** 16.50c/6.50p.
See the Alchemy section.

JUNG, C.G. **THE COLLECTED WORKS, VOLUME XV: THE SPIRIT IN MAN, ART, AND LITERATURE.** 176pp. PUP66/RKP, 9.50c/2.95p.
In the nine essays that comprise this volume, written between 1922 and 1941, Jung's attention was directed mainly to the qualities of personality that enable the creative spirit to introduce radical innovations into realms as diverse as medicine, Oriental studies, the visual arts, and literature. The source of artistic creativity in archetypal structures is also considered. The individuals discussed include Paracelsus, Freud, Picasso, Richard Wilhelm, and James Joyce.

JUNG, C.G. **THE COLLECTED WORKS, VOLUME XVI: THE PRACTICE OF PSYCHOTHERAPY. Illustrations, 406pp. PUP66/ RKP, 14.50c.**
Essays on aspects of analytical therapy, specifically the transference, abreaction, and dream analysis, which form an excellent introduction to Jung's psychological thought. Also contains an essay, *The Realities of Practical Psychotherapy,* found among Jung's posthumous papers.

JUNG, C.G. **THE COLLECTED WORKS, VOLUME XVII: THE DEVELOPMENT OF PERSONALITY. 243pp. PUP70/RKP, 10.00c.**
Papers on child psychology, education, and individuation, underlining the overwhelming importance of parents and teachers in the genesis of the intellectual, feeling, and emotional disorders of childhood. The final paper deals with marriage as an aid or obstacle to self realization.

JUNG, C.G. **THE COLLECTED WORKS, VOLUME XVIII: THE SYMBOLIC LIFE. 400pp. PUP76/RKP, 22.50c.**
This volume is a miscellany of writings that Jung published after the **Collected Works** had been planned, minor and fugitive works that he wished to assign to a special volume, and early writings that came to light in the course of research. It opens with three important longer works: *The Tavistock Lectures* (1935), *Symbols and the Interpretation of Dreams* (Jung's last work, 1961), and *The Symbolic Life.* These are followed by some 120 shorter works arranged on the model of the **Collected Works** and including forewords, reviews, addresses, and letters.

JUNG, C.G. **CRITIQUE OF PSYCHOANALYSIS. Index, 260pp. PUP75, 3.45p.**
Extracted from Volumes Four and Eighteen. Includes *The Theory of Psychoanalysis, Psychoanalysis and Neurosis, Freud and Jung: Contrasts,* and other papers critical of orthodox psychoanalysis published between 1912 and 1953.

JUNG, C.G. **DREAMS. Plates, bibliography, index, 354pp. PUP74, 3.95p.**
Extracts from Volumes Four, Eight, Twelve, and Sixteen, including *The Analysis of Dreams, On the Significance of Number Dreams, General Aspects of Dream Psychology, On the Nature of Dreams, Individual Dream Symbolism in Relation to Alchemy,* and *The Practical Use of Dream Analysis.*

JUNG, C.G. **FLYING SAUCERS: A MODERN MYTH OF THINGS SEEN IN THE SKY. Notes, index, 184pp. PUP59, 3.95p.**
Jung's concern is not with the reality or unreality of UFOs, but rather with their effect on the human psyche. He focuses on the significance of the fact that UFOs are currently sighted in such great numbers. This leads him to a consideration of UFOs as *visionary rumors* or projections of unconscious psychic contents. He includes chapters on UFOs in dreams and in modern painting and also surveys the previous history of the UFO phenomenon. His interpretation of UFOs as archetypes is often both impressive and convincing.

JUNG, C.G. **FOUR ARCHETYPES: MOTHER/REBIRTH/SPIRIT/ TRICKSTER. 182pp. PUP69/RKP, 2.95p.**
Extracted from Volume Nine, Part I and including *Psychological Aspects of the Mother Archetype, Concerning Rebirth, The Phenomenology of the Spirit in Fairytales,* and *On the Psychology of the Trickster-Figure.*

JUNG, C.G. **THE FREUD/JUNG LETTERS. 693pp. PUP74/RKP, 17.50c/6.95p.**
Contains the entire extant correspondence between the founder of psychoanalysis and his chosen heir. A detailed annotation identifies more than 400 persons, 500 publications, and the many literary and topical allusions in the more than 350 letters.

■ JUNG, C.G., *ed.* **MAN AND HIS SYMBOLS. Illustrations, notes, index, 7¾"x10½", 320pp. Dou64, 7.95c/1.95p.**
At the age of eighty-three, Jung worked out the complete plan for this book, including the sections that he wished his four closest associates to write. He devoted the closing months of his life to editing the work and writing his own key section. Throughout the book, Jung emphasizes that man can achieve wholeness only through a knowledge and acceptance of the unconscious—a knowledge acquired through dreams and their symbols. More than 500 illustrations complement the text and provide a unique *running commentary* on Jung's thought. Most of these illustrations are omitted from the paper edition.

JUNG, C.G. **MANDALA SYMBOLISM. 131pp. PUP59, 3.95p.**
Jung's discovery of the mandala provided the key to his entire system: *The self, I thought, was like a monad which I am, and which is my world. The mandala represents this monad, and corresponds to the microcosmic nature of the psyche.* This volume is taken from Volume Nine, Part I of the **Collected Works** and contains two important papers on mandala symbolism, with many full color illustrations, and a useful popular summary of the subject.

■ JUNG, C.G. **MEMORIES, DREAMS, REFLECTIONS. Index, 445pp. RaH63/Fon, 15.00c/2.95p.**
Jung's work, with its copious disclosures of his inner life, is perhaps as near as one can get to a literary confession—profuse in subjective materials, dreams, premonitions, projections, but relatively bare of data about more commonplace external events.— Lewis Mumford. This autobiographical account was edited and in part transcribed by Aniela Jaffe from Jung's conversation. A fascinating document, and probably the best introduction to Jung.

JUNG, C.G. **MODERN MAN IN SEARCH OF A SOUL. 254pp. HBJ33/RKP, 2.95p.**
A collection of essays on dream analysis, the primitive unconscious, the relationship between psychology and religion, the spiritual problem of modern man, and the differences between the theories of Jung and Freud.

JUNG, C.G. **ON THE NATURE OF THE PSYCHE. 174pp. PUP60, 3.95p.**
A difficult work which summarizes Jung's basic theoretical position. Illustrations from religion, anthropological data, and symbolistic studies clarify Jung's notions of the unconscious, its relationship to consciousness, the collective unconscious and the archetypes. Extracts from Volume Eight of the **Collected Works**.

JUNG, C.G. **THE PSYCHOANALYTIC YEARS. Index, 174pp. PUP74, 2.95p.**
Extracts from Volumes Two, Four, and Seventeen.

JUNG, C.G. **PSYCHOLOGY AND THE EAST. 214pp. PUP78, 3.95p.**
This volume contains Jung's commentaries on **The Secret of the Golden Flower, The Tibetan Book of the Dead,** and **The Tibetan Book of the Great Liberation;** his forewords to Suzuki's **Introduction to Zen Buddhism** and the **I Ching;** and a miscellany of other papers, originally published in Volumes Ten, Eleven, Thirteen, and Eighteen of **The Collected Works**.

JUNG, C.G. **PSYCHOLOGY AND EDUCATION. 158pp. PUP54, 3.45p.**
Jung repeatedly underlined the importance of parents and teachers in the genesis of the intellectual, feeling, and emotional disorders of childhood. Other aspects discussed in this volume are psychic conflicts in the child, gifted children, and the significance of the unconscious in education. Extracts from Volume Seventeen of the **Collected Works**.

JUNG, C.G. **PSYCHOLOGY AND THE OCCULT. Bibliography, 177pp. PUP77, 2.95p.**
A collection of papers taken from Volumes One, Eight, and Eighteen of the **Collected Works**.

JUNG, C.G. **PSYCHOLOGY AND RELIGION. Many notes, 131pp. YUP38/RKP, 2.95p.**
Using a wealth of material from ancient and medieval Gnostic, alchemical, and mystical literature, Jung discusses the religious symbolism of unconscious processes and the possible continuity of religious forms that have appeared and reappeared through the centuries.

JUNG, C.G. **PSYCHOLOGY OF DEMENTIA PRAECOX. Index, 236pp. PUP60, 3.95p.**
Extracted from Volume Eight of the **Collected Works**.

JUNG, C.G. **THE PSYCHOLOGY OF THE TRANSFERENCE. 206pp. PUP66, 2.95p.**
Jung gives an authoritative account of his handling of the transference between analyst and patient in the light of his conception of the archetypes and man's inner life, and drawing a close parallel between the modern psychotherapeutic process and the symbolical pictures in a

sixteenth century alchemical text, the **Rosarium philosophorum**. Excerpted from Volume Sixteen of the **Collected Works**.

JUNG, C.G. **SYNCHRONICITY. Index, 142pp. PUP73/RKP, 2.95p.**
Extracted from Volume Eight, containing a parapsychological study of the meaningful coincidence of events, extrasensory perception, and similar phenomena.

JUNG, C.G. **THE UNDISCOVERED SELF. 113pp. LBC58/RKP, 2.95p.**
Many authors have written whole books and countless papers in an attempt to make clearer Dr. Jung's gigantic insights. We have all failed. But with this little book...Dr. Jung has achieved, at the age of eighty-three, what no one else could. Any literate layman can understand it and, in so doing, will gain a good clear comprehension of Dr. Jung's basic concept. READ IT.—Phillip Wylie.

JUNG, C.G. **THE VISIONS SEMINAR. Twenty-eight illustrations (most in color), index, 355+pp. Spr76, 20.70p/set.**
The original edition of this book consisted of about 2,000

mimeographed pages bound in eleven volumes. The material in the original edition had been assembled and edited by Mary Foote from her notes. She later revised the first part, in consultation with Jung himself. The first volume of this edition is a reproduction of this revised version. The second has been revised by Patricia Berry, following the pattern that had already been established. The seminars took place in late 1930 and the visions which provide the material under discussion came from an American woman in her thirties.

JUNG, C.G. and CARL KERENYI. **ESSAYS ON A SCIENCE OF MYTHOLOGY. Notes, bibliography, index, 208pp. PUP63/RKP, 3.45p.**
Interesting, suggestive essays by Jung and the classical scholar Carl Kerenyi on the archetypes of the child and the Maiden Goddess. The themes join in the Mysteries of Eleusis where the mother-daughter goddess bears a divine child.

JUNG, EMMA. **ANIMUS AND ANIMA. Notes, 94pp. Spr72, 4.10p.**
Two important esays: *On the Nature of the Animus* and *The Anima as an Elemental Being.* Ms. Jung expresses the idea of the anima and animus better in these two works than we have seen anywhere else in the vast Jungian literature.

KELSEY, MORTON. **DREAMS—A WAY TO LISTEN TO GOD. 1.95p.**
See the Dreams section.

KERENYI, CARL. **ASKLEPIOS: ARCHETYPAL IMAGE OF THE PHYSICIAN'S EXISTENCE. 18.10c.**
See the Mythology section.

KERENYI, CARL. **DIONYSOS: ARCHETYPAL IMAGE OF INDE-STRUCTIBLE LIFE. 40.30c.**
See the Mythology section.

KERENYI, CARL. **ELEUSIS: ARCHETYPAL IMAGE OF MOTHER AND DAUGHTER. 19.50c/9.95p.**
See the Mythology section.

KERENYI, CARL. **HERMES: GUIDE OF SOULS. 6.65p.**
See the Mythology section.

KERENYI, CARL. **ZEUS AND HERA: ARCHETYPAL IMAGE OF FATHER, HUSBAND, AND WIFE. 20.15c.**
See the Mythology section.

KERENYI, CARL, et al. **EVIL. Notes, index, 279pp. NUP67, 14.10c.**
In the conviction that the human problems subsumed under evil form the dark background that is largely responsible for man's anxiety, and that it is more important today than ever before to gain deeper insights into this subject, the C.G. Jung Institute in Zurich invited eight eminent scholars to analyze evil from the perspective of their own particular discipline and interests. The contributors to this volume include Carl Kerenyi, Geo Widengren, Victor Maag, Marie-Louise von Franz, Martin Schlappner, Liliane Frey-Rohn, Karl Lowith, and Karl Schmid.

KLUGER, RIVKAH. **PSYCHE AND THE BIBLE. Notes, 143pp. Spr74, 6.00p.**
Three lectures on **Old Testament** themes. The first, and longest one, *The Idea of the Chosen People: A Contribution to the Symbolism of Individuation,* takes up a controversial biblical concept and convincingly elucidates its psychological depths. *King Saul and the Spirit of God* examines the **Book of Samuel** regarding Saul's madness and the relation between the spirit of God, divine prophecy, and melancholy. *The Queen of Sheba* presents a study of the legends concerning King Solomon and the Queen of Sheba, a mysteriously symbolic figure from the South. The information presented in these lectures is based on analytical experience and **Old Testament** research.

KLUGER, RIVKAH. **SATAN IN THE OLD TESTAMENT. Notes, index, 191pp. NUP67, 9.40c.**
In this monograph, Rivkah Kluger investigates Satan from a psychological viewpoint which leads to far reaching reflections on the nature of the God-image in the **Old Testament**. Satan is seen here as the inner enemy, fundamental to consciousness, which arises from tension. Satan's final purpose is seen as the development of self limitation through self opposition. This paper formed a separate section of the German edition of one of Jung's books, **Symbolik des Geistes**, the other parts of which are now in Volumes Nine, Eleven, and Thirteen of his **Collected Works**.

LASZLO, VIOLET DE, ed. **THE BASIC WRITINGS OF C.G. JUNG. Introduction, notes, bibliography, index, 575pp. RaH59, 5.95c.**
A collection of Jung's writings grouped into the following major sections: *On the Nature and Functioning of the Psyche, On Pathology and Therapy, On the Religious Function,* and *On Human Development.* The volume is designed as a basic reader and it fulfills this function quite well. The psychological side of Jung's writings is emphasized rather than the archetypal.

LASZLO, VIOLET DE, ed. **PSYCHE AND SYMBOL. Introduction, notes, bibliography, 397pp. Dou58, 3.50p.**
A selection of Jung's writings focusing on symbology, archetypal psychology, and Eastern philosophy. The volume includes five chapters from **Aion**; *The Phenomenology of the Spirit in Fairy Tales, The Psychology of the Child Archetype, Transformation Symbolism in the Mass;* two chapters from *The Interpretation of Nature and the Psyche;* and Jung's commentary on the **I Ching, The Tibetan Book of the Dead,** and **The Secret of the Golden Flower.**

LAYLARD, JOHN. A CELTIC QUEST: SEXUALITY, AND SOUL IN INDIVIDUATION. Notes, index, 254pp. Spr75, 8.25p.
This is a depth psychology study of the **Mabinogion** legend of Culhwch and Olwen. It includes information interconnecting Greek myth, boar culture in exotic societies, questions of incest and marriage, and one's personal individuation. This is a fascinating study of a classic ancient Welsh saga.

LAYLARD, JOHN. THE VIRGIN ARCHETYPE. Notes, bibliography, 132pp. Spr72, 5.60p.
Two complicated papers, originally delivered at Eranos Conferences, *The Incest Taboo and the Virgin Archetype*, and *On Psychic Consciousness*.

LOPEZ-PEDRAZA, RAFAEL. HERMES AND HIS CHILDREN. Illustrations, notes, 151pp. Spr77, 6.70p.
An extremely difficult, rewarding book which, as James Hillman says, *stands by itself in a field of its own making, the field of archetypal psychopathology.... **Hermes and His Children** opens to insight some of the most obscure phenomena of psychotherapy and human character.*

LUKE, HELEN. DARK WOOD TO WHITE ROSE: A STUDY IN MEANINGS IN DANTE'S DIVINE COMEDY. Glossary, notes, 167pp. DvP75, 4.50p.
More than anything else we have ever read, this book brings out the true inner meaning of Dante's masterwork and illustrates how fruitful analytical psychology can be in the study of symbolic material. Ms. Luke analyzes in depth the symbolism in the books and devotes separate chapters to each of the major themes. Many quotations from the Sayers translation are also included.

McGUIRE, WILLIAM and R.F.C. HULL, eds. C.G. JUNG SPEAKING. Index, 501pp. PUP77/RKP, 14.50c.
A collection of more than fifty talks with Jung, ranging from transcripts of interviews to memoirs written by friends and notable personalities. The material is presented in chronological order and covers the period from 1912 to shortly before Dr. Jung's death in 1961.

MAHONEY, MARIA. THE MEANING IN DREAMS AND DREAMING. 3.95p.
See the Dreams section.

MARTIN, P.W. EXPERIMENT IN DEPTH: A STUDY OF THE WORK OF JUNG, ELIOT AND TOYNBEE. Index, 274pp. RKP55, 3.95p.
Jung, Eliot, and Toynbee have each explored—from the different standpoints of psychology, poetry, and the study of history—the dynamic potentialities of the deep unconscious, the immense creative and destructive forces latent in the human psyche. The potentialities have hitherto been seen principally in their destructive aspect, as a means of achieving absolute power. The purpose of this book is to investigate whether and how they can be used creatively. This is an excellent study.

MEIER, CARL. ANCIENT INCUBATION AND MODERN PSYCHOTHERAPY. 172pp. NUP67, 8.40c.
Through this study we see that the illnesses of the soul and its healing do not change much through time. Therefore, as the author implies, one essential aspect of the archetypal root of psychotherapy is provided by the attitudes and practices of ancient incubation. The rituals of incubation, at the core of which was sleeping within a religious preserve for the purpose of receiving healing dreams and visions, are here succinctly described so that the perceptive reader can make the connections between the classical procedures in antiquity and the events of modern psychotherapy.... Professor Meier brings to his work not only his experience as a practicing medical analyst, but a passion for the past, especially for research in Greek religion.—from the preface by James Hillman.

MEIER, CARL. JUNG'S ANALYTICAL PSYCHOLOGY AND RELIGION. 81pp. SIU59, 2.95p.
A transcription of a series of four lectures Dr. Meier gave to a group of theologians, which were designed to serve as an introduction to Jungian theory. They emphasize the basics, especially as they apply to the place of religion in psychology. Dr. Meier also offers many insights into Jung's view of religious experience.

MOON, SHEILA. A MAGIC DWELLS. 4.40p.
See the American Indian Religion section.

MOONEY, LUCINDI. STORMING EASTERN TEMPLES: A PSYCHOLOGICAL EXPLORATION OF YOGA. Notes, bibliography, index, 212pp. TPH76, 4.25p.
A not terribly successful discussion of the parallels between the approaches of analytical psychology and the Eastern philosophical and Western mystical tradition. Many interesting concepts are introduced. Unfortunately, though, Ms. Mooney does not write succinctly and clearly. Our eyes got tired wading through her long sentences and even longer paragraphs and we lost the thread of the ideas she was trying to present. Ms. Mooney is an American Indian and the best sections come out of her personal discussion of shamanism. There are a number of other illuminating areas and the book is well worth going through if you are deeply interested in the subject.

NEUMANN, ERICH. AMOR AND PSYCHE—THE PSYCHIC DEVELOPMENT OF THE FEMININE. Notes, 181pp. PUP56, 2.95p.
Contains both the tale of Amor and Psyche and an interesting analysis of its spiritual and mythical background which suggests a fresh view of the psychic life of women. Neumann was the one among Jung's pupils who was most creative in building on Jung's work and carrying it forward in new explorations and syntheses.

NEUMANN, ERICH. THE ARCHETYPAL WORLD OF HENRY MOORE. Notes, bibliography, 7¾"x10¾", 138pp. PUP59/RKP, 15.45c.
An illustrated discussion of the art of British sculptor Henry Moore from the viewpoint of analytical psychology. Two prime motives characterize Moore's art. The first is his deep concern with the feminine and the second is the development in form from a more or less naturalistic approach to one that is semiabstract or at least, nonnaturalistic. These two interrelated principles of content and form are the basis of Neumann's application of the concepts of analytical psychology to Moore's art. The work unfolds around the cardinal themes of mother and child and the reclining figure, both supreme expressions of the archetypal feminine. 107 halftones of Moore's sculpture illuminate the discussion.

NEUMANN, ERICH. ART AND THE CREATIVE UNCONSCIOUS. Notes, 232pp. PUP69/RKP, 3.45p.
Four essays, *Leonardo da Vinci and the Mother Archetype, Art and Time, A Note on Marc Chagall,* and *Creative Man and Transformation.* Neumann discusses the nature of art in relationship to the collective consciousness; the time and place, and the individual artist.

NEUMANN, ERICH. THE CHILD. 221pp. H&R73/Hod, 2.95p.
Neumann's final work; an examination of the structure and dynamics of the child's development of ego and individuality. Neumann

progresses from the primal relationship of a child and mother through to the emergence of the *ego-self constellation* via the child's relationship to his own body, his self, the thou, and being in the world.

NEUMANN, ERICH. **DEPTH PSYCHOLOGY AND A NEW ETHIC.** Notes, index, 158pp. H&R69, 2.95p.
To Neumann the basic problem of modern man is the problem of evil: conventional ethics have proved incapable of containing or transforming its destructive forces.... Awareness of evil challenges the individual: he has to learn to realize, acknowledge, and live with his own dark side. Instead of suppressing, or repressing, the shadow and consequently projecting it outside, it has to be integrated. Only thus can modern man achieve fuller consciousness and a higher degree of integration; the ambiguity of one's own existence, the awareness of both positive and negative forces within the individual and the collective becomes the point of departure for a new ethical attitude.—from the foreword by Gerhard Adler.

NEUMANN, ERICH. **THE GREAT MOTHER.** 424pp. PUP63/RKP, 5.95p.
An exploration of the manifestation, in myths and symbols both ancient and modern, of the primordial image of the Great Mother. *Neumann's creative intuition has enabled him to read in these records of the past a content and meaning that throws a beam of light on the psychological history of mankind.—M. Esther Harding.* The text includes 185 pages of illustrative plates.

NEUMANN, ERICH. **THE ORIGINS AND HISTORY OF CONSCIOUSNESS.** Many illustrations, notes, bibliography, index, 517pp. PUP54/RKP, 4.95p.
An original and creative interpretation of the relations between psychology and mythology. According to Neumann's thesis, individual consciousness passes through the same archetypal stages of development that marked human consciousness as a whole. Half the book is devoted to an analysis of the mythological stages in the evolution of consciousness and the other half to the psychological stages in the development of personality.

ODAJNYK, VOLODYMYR. **JUNG AND POLITICS.** Index, 205pp. H&R76, 4.95p.
Jung never wrote a treatise that systematically defines the implications of his psychological theories for politics. His views on the subject are dispersed throughout his works, although a number of books and essays are closely concerned with politics, either explicitly or by implication and logical extension. Hence, this book represents a compilation of those of Jung's ideas that have political and/or social implications, gleaned from his voluminous writings on various subjects, a comparison of those ideas with Freud's, and a consideration of just what Jung's ideas imply for the social and political future of humanity.—from the preface.

PERRY, JOHN WEIR. **THE FAR SIDE OF MADNESS.** Notes, bibliography, index, 177pp. PrH74, 2.75p.
Dr. Perry is a Jungian psychoanalyst and a lecturer at the Jung Institute in San Francisco. In this volume (and in his psychiatric work) he concentrates not on the causes or chemistry of schizophrenia, but instead on our empathetic understanding of the individual's inner processes. Perry calls his work a study of the intrapersonal process between the patient and the therapist and he shows that the so-called abnormal ideas and imagery of the schizophrenic actually reveal archetypal patterns common to all persons that are merely made manifest in this altered state of consciousness. Knowledge of these patterns offers the therapist a key to helping the patient to a natural reorganization of the psyche.

PERRY, JOHN WEIR. **THE LORD OF THE FOUR QUARTERS.** 1.50p.
See the Mythology section.

PERRY, JOHN WEIR. **ROOTS OF RENEWAL IN MYTH AND MADNESS.** Notes, bibliography, index, 268pp. JBP76, 17.40c.
Dr. Perry shows that when medication is avoided during acute psychotic episodes the patient experiences a legitimate altered state of consciousness in which he tries to reorganize his inner self. The images that the patient describes are symbols of emotional disturbances and can provide a healing experience. These are remarkably similar among patients and reflect the classical symbols found in ancient myth and ritual. Dr. Perry provides an historical background to the renewal process as seen in myth and ritual drama and shows how the symbols are still projected in the modern psyche. He includes many quotations from related texts as well as a number of case histories.

PHILIPSON, MORRIS. **OUTLINE OF A JUNGIAN AESTHETICS.** Notes, bibliography, index, 223pp. NUP63, 12.00c.
A systematic, critical inquiry into the accessibility of analytical psychology for the problems of aesthetics. Part I sets forth Jung's interpretation of the nature of symbolism. In the second part Philipson discusses the implications that Jung himself draws from his psychology for the philosophy of art. The final section is devoted to an evaluation of Jung's contributions to aesthetics and a discussion of lines for possible development of epistemology.

POST, LAURENS VAN DER. **JUNG AND THE STORY OF OUR TIME.** 276pp. RaH76/Pen, 3.95p.
Jung and the author had a close friendship lasting sixteen years. In this biographical study the evolution of Jung's creative beliefs and the impact of his personality are surveyed in reconstruction of conversations that touch on examples of Jung's ideas and attitudes while exploring interests shared by the two men. In putting together this book van der Post has used the many hours of interviews conducted for his now-famous BBC television film, **The Story of Carl Gustav Jung** in addition to his personal remembrances and letters.

PROGOFF, IRA. **AT A JOURNAL WORKSHOP.** 5.95p.
See the Consciousness Expansion section.

PROGOFF, IRA. **DEATH AND REBIRTH OF PSYCHOLOGY.** Bibliography, 285pp. MGH56, 2.95p.
Dr. Progoff is one of the most successful contemporary interpreters of analytical psychology. He has developed his own variation which he calls depth psychology. This book is a synthesis of the central concepts in the seemingly diverse psychological systems of Freud, Jung, Adler, and Rank.

PROGOFF, IRA. **DEPTH PSYCHOLOGY AND MODERN MAN.** 304pp. MGH59, 2.95p.
Depth psychology considers that what a person professes to believe, or what he thinks he believes is not as important as what he experiences. Depth psychology is concerned, therefore, not with new doctrines for modern man, but with providing ways of experience by which each person, according to his individual nature, can relate himself in actuality to the ultimate realities of life.

PROGOFF, IRA. **THE IMAGE OF AN ORACLE.** 372pp. GtP64, 9.45c.
In 1957 Eileen Garrett, the foremost medium of her time in the West, asked Dr. Progoff if he, based on his studies in depth psychology, could explain to her the nature and meaning of the voices that spoke through her. Dr. Progoff embarked on months of research during which he held conversations with the various figures who spoke through Mrs. Garrett when she was in trance. This book contains transcripts of twelve of these conversations. To these conversations Dr. Progoff applied the methods of depth psychology in an endeavour to discover the meaning of the voices within the total personality of Mrs. Garrett.

PROGOFF, IRA. **JUNG, SYNCHRONICITY AND HUMAN DESTINY.** Bibliography, index, 244pp. Del73, 2.95p.
This volume, in process for twenty years, was discussed and worked on with Jung himself. It is a lucid exposition and interpretation of the profound, but complex concept of synchronicity and provides an hypothesis to approach areas of human experience inaccessible to our accepted categories of cause and effect thinking. Includes material on the I Ching.

PROGOFF, IRA. **JUNG'S PSYCHOLOGY AND ITS SOCIAL MEANING.** Index, 313pp. Dou53, 2.50p.
An introduction to Jung's ideas and some discussion of their significance for our thinking about the individual and society.

PROGOFF, IRA. **THE STAR/CROSS: A CYCLE OF PROCESS MEDITATION.** 79pp. DHL72, 2.95p.
Process Meditation is an active approach to meditation that draws upon both Eastern and Biblical resources, but relates specifically to the context of Western civilization. It provides a means of working with all phases of the cycle of life, the high and the low, the active and the quiet.... A cardinal principle of Process Meditation is the recognition that spiritual life is not separate from everyday experience.... Bear in mind as you use these meditations that their purpose is to enable you to deepen your own experience in your own terms. Their effect comes not from the meaning of the specific symbols, but in the way in which those symbols generate an inward momentum that draws each person

into his own depths.—from the introduction. Each of the meditations consists of a group of verses on a particular theme.

PROGOFF, IRA. **THE SYMBOLIC AND THE REAL. 256pp. MGH63/ Cov, 2.95p.**
In this book the advanced conceptions of depth psychology are brought to bear upon the fundamental human problems of modern civilization. The result is a perspective and program of psychological practice for individuals and groups by which the modern person can establish contact with the deepest levels of his being.

PROGOFF, IRA. **THE WELL AND THE CATHEDRAL. 3.95p.**
See the Meditation section.

PROGOFF, IRA. **THE WHITE ROBED MONK: A CYCLE OF PROCESS MEDITATION. 77pp. DHL72, 2.95p.**

ROSCHER, WILHELM and JAMES HILLMAN. **PAN AND THE NIGHTMARE. Notes, 143pp. Spr72, 6.45p.**
An English translation of **Ephialtes: A Pathological-Mythological Treatise on the Nightmare in Classical Antiquity** by Wilhelm Roscher together with **An Essay on Pan, Serving as a Psychological Introduction to Roscher's Ephialtes** by James Hillman.

SANFORD, JOHN. **HEALING AND WHOLENESS. Notes, index, 169pp. Pau77, 5.95p.**
Sanford, a Jungian analyst and Episcopal priest, describes this book as *a composite of many sources, enriched by the sufferings and discoveries of the people who have consulted me over the years, the insights into healing given to me by many mentors, and the fruit of my own personal search for healing. It also draws upon insights into healing from wells ancient and modern: ancient Greek healing mysteries, the lore of shamanism, the wisdom of the American Indian, the healing emphasis in early Christianity, and the very modern perspective on healing furnished by C.G. Jung. The hope is that the reader will, through this book, see a little more clearly where healing comes from and where he or she as a person can learn to help himself or herself.*

SERRANO, MIGUEL. **EL/ELLA. 75pp. RKP72, 3.50p.**
This is an allegory of man's search for unity; it explores a mythic reality that transcends the conflicting dualities—man/woman, black/white, young/old—that divide man from nature and against himself. El/Ella is divided into three sections, which reflect the spiritual journey-quest as it has been experienced in the Himalayas, the Pyrenees, and the Andes. Part One deals mainly with the rites of Tantric love. Part Two is concerned with the Cathars, an order of medieval mystics in Provence whose dualistic belief in the existence of absolute evil as well as absolute good led to their extermination as heretics in the so-called Albigensian Crusade. Part Three deals with the Andes and, again, a secret order to which the central characters, a man and a woman, belong.

SERRANO, MIGUEL. **C.G. JUNG AND HERMAN HESSE, A RECORD OF TWO FRIENDSHIPS. 120pp. ScB66/RKP, 1.95p.**
Sets forth records of conversations and correspondence between Serrano (a Chilean writer) and Jung and Hesse.

SERRANO, MIGUEL. **THE SERPENT OF PARADISE. 6.30p.**
See the Indian Philosophy section.

SERRANO, MIGUEL. **THE ULTIMATE FLOWER. Illustrations, 102pp. ScB69/RKP, 9.95c.**
A mystical and poetic account of a man's search for things which do not really exist but which are more real than reality. Based on a conversation with Jung on the nature of the Self.

SERRANO, MIGUEL. **THE VISITS OF THE QUEEN OF SHEBA. 61pp. RKP60, 5.00c.**
This book is an extraordinary piece of work. It is dreams within dreams, highly poetic. The poetic genius has transformed the primordial material into almost musical shapes.—C.G. Jung.

SINGER, JUNE. **ANDROGYNY: TOWARD A NEW THEORY OF SEXUALITY. Notes, bibliography, index, 383pp. Dou76/RKP, 3.95p.**
Scientists and mystics throughout history have realized that every human being is the carrier of complementary life energies. Given a variety of names these energies interact in everyone, regardless of sex. Androgyny involves recognizing the eternal flux of these opposing energies within us. On a journey that takes us through Taoism,

Gnosticism, mythology, alchemy, Qabalism, Tibetan Tantrism, and Jungian psychology, Dr. Singer shows how crucial the awareness of the androgynous soul has been to those who are inquiring into the mysteries of the human being. She also discusses the interplay of opposing energies as seen in modern science. This is the most thorough discussion we have ever seen on the subject. Dr. Singer ends with a practical discussion of the range of choices by which people can identify themselves, secure that the masculine/feminine interaction within each individual is not only normal but the dynamic factor in their wholeness.

SINGER, JUNE. **BOUNDARIES OF THE SOUL: THE PRACTICE OF JUNG'S PSYCHOLOGY. Notes, bibliography, index, 514pp. Dou72, 2.95p.**
As an analyst, Dr. Singer follows Jung's lead, stressing the unconscious rather than the conscious, the mystical rather than the scientific, the creative rather than the productive, the religious rather than the profane. This is an excellent work which gives an insight into all aspects of psychotherapy.

Stag and unicorn, symbolizing soul and spirit.

SPRING PUBLICATIONS. **SPRING 1970. 217pp. Spr70, 9.45p.**
SPRING originated in 1940-41 as a collection of papers from the Analytical Psychology Club of New York. In 1960 it was transformed into a printed magazine and in 1970 **SPRING** appeared as an expanded yearbook, the only *Annual of Archetypal Psychology and Jungian Thought,* with emphasis on new insights and criticism, translations, and hitherto unpublished writings by and about C.G. Jung. The series is edited by James Hillman.

SPRING PUBLICATIONS. **SPRING 1974. 302pp. Spr74, 8.45p.**

SPRING PUBLICATIONS. **SPRING 1975. 304pp. Spr75, 8.35p.**
This volume includes Jung's psychological commentary on Kundalini Yoga, Zimmer's *The Chakras of Kundalini Yoga, Reflections on the Horoscope of C.G. Jung,* and much else. The contributions to this series are uniformly excellent—though often on quite obscure subjects.

SPRING PUBLICATIONS. **SPRING 1976.** 218pp. Spr76, 8.80p.

SPRING PUBLICATIONS. **SPRING 1977.** Notes, 222pp. Spr77, 8.35p.
Fifteen papers and essays.

STERN, PAUL. **C.G. JUNG: THE HAUNTED PROPHET. Index,**
267pp. Del76, 3.95p.
This is the only biography of Jung which is critical. Stern emphasizes
the conflicts in Jung's life and sees him as an incipient madman who
was wily enough to creatively use his madness. Many features of
Jung's life are explored which are not surveyed elsewhere. The book is
well researched and the criticisms are not sensational in tone.

STORR, ANTHONY. **C.G. JUNG.** 119pp. Vik73/Fon, 1.95p.
A critical study which focuses primarily on Jung's intellectual life and
the formation of his major ideas. Dr. Storr also explores Jung's
biography, in particular his association with and subsequent diver-
gence from Sigmund Freud.

ULANOV, ANN. **THE FEMININE IN JUNGIAN PSYCHOLOGY
AND IN CHRISTIAN THEOLOGY.** Notes, index, 358pp. NUP71,
16.15c.
*I have followed a carefully planned sequence of presentation and analysis, beginning
with Jung's approach to the psyche, and following with a discussion of what can be
gathered concerning the nature of the feminine. Out of this I have drawn conclusions
that seem to me to be inescapable for what we call religious experience.*

ULANOV, ANN and BARRY. **RELIGION AND THE UNCONSCIOUS.**
Notes, index, 287pp. Wes75, 12.00c.
*This book is about the pains and pleasures of human interiority, and some special ways
of dealing with both. The ways are those of religion and the appointed—some might say
the self appointed—guardians of the unconscious, depth psychology. The pains are the
pains that accompany our efforts to find peace and ease in the world and that almost
invariably attend our attempts to define your own identity or the identities of others.
They are the pains of relationship approached but never quite achieved or of
relationship achieved and then broken. . . . They are, in sum, the pains that in religion
are associated with sin and moral transgression and in depth psychology with neurosis
and psychosis.*—from the introduction.

VITALE, AGOSTO, et al. **FATHERS AND MOTHERS.** 142pp. Spr73,
5.00p.
A collection of papers examining family matters from an archetypal
angle.

WATKINS, MARY. **WAKING DREAMS.** Notes, bibliography, indices,
186pp. H&R76, 3.45p.
Waking Dreams *is the first complete book on the whole subject of interior imagery
and the activity of fantasying. Further, it is the only work on imagination that is
historical, critical, and therapeutically practical at once. Still further, it is the best book
on the new psychology of images because Mary Watkins writes so well!*—James
Hillman. The book includes studies in myth, religion, and literature
and, while it is often somewhat technical, Ms. Watkins offers a number
of practical exercises and techniques.

WHEELWRIGHT, JOSEPH, ed. **THE REALITY OF THE PSYCHE.**
Illustrations, notes, 316pp. JFP68, 12.00c.
A collection of the eighteen papers presented at the Third Inter-
national Congress for Analytical Psychology.

WICKES, FRANCES. **THE INNER WORLD OF CHILDHOOD. Index,**
325pp. Cov66, 8.00p.
This is a revised edition of a classic examination of the crucial
relationship between parent and child. *Her penetrating studies of children
have opened up a new world of understanding. To her, the child is a person possessing
innately the right to be "individual" and to experience the world about him in the light
of his own subjective experience. . . . [The] child psychologist needs to have at least in
some measure Frances Wickes' sensitivity, wisdom, and love.*—M. Esther Harding.
The book is based on Dr. Wickes own experiences with her patients
and many case studies are included. This revised edition follows up
some of the cases from the first edition of more than forty years ago.
Introduction by Carl Jung.

WICKES, FRANCES. **THE INNER WORLD OF CHOICE.** Notes,
bibliography, 336pp. PrH76, 3.95p.
This is a powerful, well written volume. In 1954-55, when Dr. Wickes
presented seminars on Choice and Decision at the Jung Institute in
Zurich, Jung himself asked her to enlarge her material into book form.
This volume shows how the unconscious mind constantly challenges
us to grow, psychologically and spiritually, and to act to free ourselves
from fear, apathy, and dependence. The author reviews all the major
tenets of Jungian psychology and illustrates her narrative with case
histories from her own practice. Jung's ideas of the woman in man and
the man in woman are especially well presented and there is also an
excellent discussion of archetypal imagery in dreams and folklore.

WILLEFORD, WILLIAM. **THE FOOL AND HIS SCEPTER: A STUDY
IN CLOWNS AND JESTERS AND THEIR AUDIENCE.** Illustrations,
many notes, index, 287pp. NUP69, 16.10c.
An analytical analysis of fools and instances of folly from a wide variety
of sources from the late Middle Ages to the present time. Willeford
says that *In describing fools and folly I am concerned with questions of why. Why is
the fool, as bumpkin, merrymaker, trickster, scourge, and scapegoat, such an often
recurring figure in the world and in our imaginative representations of it? Why do
fools from widely diverse times and places reveal such striking similarities? Why are
we, like people in many other times and places, fascinated by fools?*

YUNGBLUT, JOHN. **SEEKING LIGHT IN THE DARKNESS OF THE
UNCONSCIOUS.** Notes, 24pp. PHP77, 1.20p.
Yungblut is an Episcopal minister who has been engaged for many
years in counseling along Jungian lines. His personal synthesis of
psychology and mysticism is what he discusses in this essay.

ZBINDEN, HANS, et al. **CONSCIENCE.** Notes, index, 221pp. NUP70,
10.00c.
This book brings together seven different perspectives on the phenomenon of the human conscience. The essays were originally
presented as individual lectures under the auspices of the C.G. Jung
Institute, Zurich.

ZELLER, MAX. **THE DREAM—THE VISION OF THE NIGHT.** 183pp.
CGJ75, 6.00p.
A collection of analytical papers, lectures, and vignettes, all revised for
this book. Zeller has been a Jungian analyst since 1938 and has been
instrumental in the growth of Jungian psychology in Los Angeles.
Many of the selections focus on dreams and visions and others cover
the whole range of symbolic understanding.

MEDITATION

Meditation is a tool to help solve problems and achieve goals in our daily lives. But many people who have acquired the tool of meditation never really use it! They not only waste this valuable resource; they also run into some difficulty reconciling their daily lives with their meditative experiences. Creative meditation is an *active* form of meditation that begins as a specific practice or exercise but eventually becomes a way of life.

It is foolhardy to use any tool without becoming well acquainted with it. And this is as true of meditative techniques as it is of the proper use of a chain saw. We cannot expect to maximize its effectiveness and minimize its dangers until we learn all we can about it. The first thing to know is what the tool is used for.

Practitioners of passive meditation become charged with energy by remaining quiet and receptive. Frequently, the first thing that happens as a result of this exercise is what humanistic psychologists have called *peak experiences*. These are described as experiences of bliss, joy, expanded awareness, or deep spirituality. When asked to explain how their meditating affects them, these practitioners will often respond, *I don't know exactly, but I feel great*. Yet the only change in their lives is that they can occasionally exalt in the memory of the peak experience.

As they continue to meditate, less desirable phenomena begin to occur. They can become terrified by overwhelming feelings of alienation and loneliness. Visions of demons and battles with threatening forces begin to fill the world in which they first glimpsed heaven. At this point, many people begin to doubt that they are meditating correctly. If they become too doubtful or frightened, they may stop meditating. When their meditation ceases to produce appearances of someone like Jesus Christ or Krishna, disappointments and anxiety overwhelm them. The result of their efforts is that after a brief blooming, the joy of life has again disappeared. People who once walked around with their eyes raised to the sky suddenly start looking very depressed. Ask them if they are still meditating, and they will say, *No. It just doesn't work for me*. If they have the courage to try it again, they usually become very fidgety. What has happened is that they have allowed all the energy to come in and to charge them up, but they have not done anything with it. The result? The bound energy affects them in a negative way, first emotionally and then physiologically.

People who are unable to integrate the negative experiences of meditation with the peak experiences have never learned what meditation really is. They have the idea that meditation will bring them closer to reality or God or that it will bring them peace of mind. But they have specific expectations about what these experiences should be. From that perspective, passive meditation becomes a form of worship, and the worshiper wants to see only the positive aspects of God. When this meditator experiences a vision of both positive and negative—the creative and the destructive cycle of the universe—he or she cannot cope with it. This problem is avoided when a meditator goes beyond a passive role and interacts with the imagery in meditation.

Creative meditation is not the receptive silence that most people expect meditation to be. Meditation is the action of becoming a mediator between opposites—between *the above and the below*, cosmos and man, and positive and negative. When I meditate, I am responsible for the task of integrating everything that happens during my meditation, whether a peak experience or a traumatic one. I try to see beyond the conceptual evaluation that my reasoning mind makes for each experience, and I search for ways to apply my meditation to the situations confronting me in daily life. To meditate, then, is to be a responsible mediator.

To me, the additional *t* in the word *meditation* is an image of the tau cross, an ancient symbol of responsibility and commitment. In early Egyptian religion, neophytes, were required to undergo the ordeal of being tied to the cross. This was part of the ceremony that initiated them into the mysteries of Osiris. This gesture of total commitment to the responsibility that accompanies knowledge was expected before the truth was unveiled to them. To become initiates, they had to act upon their knowledge, not just receive it. In this way, they became mediators instead of worshipers.

I am not introducing this example in order to deny the importance of worship. But I do wish to point out that there is a difference between worship by practicing the presence and worship by adoration. The first brings you into a dynamic union with what you worship; adoration keeps you separated from it. All too often, we think that being religious means that we adore God at a certain time and place and in a certain form. To me, this is as misleading as the notion that meditating is sitting passively and waiting for enlightenment.

I have found that I need to worship all the time. How? I see value in things to which I otherwise might not have given value—in the flower, the trees, the clouds, the trash can. I see value in everything and worship it because it is part of everything, but I never idolize it. I need to live God, cosmos, and universe, not separate myself by sitting, gazing, and saying hallelujah. Worship means being actively involved and interacting. We can be mediators when we worship and when we meditate. When we take this active role, we live it every moment, not just at predesignated times. Everything in life is affected, especially our health and our state of mind.

—*condensed from* **Voluntary Controls**, *by Jack Schwarz*

AJAYA, SWAMI, ed. **MEDITATIONAL THERAPY. 99pp. Him77, 2.95p.**
The five chapters which comprise this book focus on the use of yoga and meditation in the treatment of stress, drug dependency, tension headaches, anxiety and a variety of psychosomatic dysfunctions....Each of the chapters is a report of recent clinical experiences carried out by professionals associated with the Himalayan Institute.—from the introduction.

ALDER, VERA STANLEY. **THE FIFTH DIMENSION. 220pp. Wei40, 3.50p.**
An esoteric discussion of what meditation is and how it works. Ms. Alder sees meditation as part of a complete way of life which will help humanity as a whole to advance. Step-by-step instructions are also included.

ARYA, USHARBUDH. **SUPERCONSCIOUS MEDITATION. 141pp. Him74, 3.00p.**
Dr. Arya is a leading disciple of Swami Rama and the founder and principal teacher of the Meditation Temple in Minneapolis. This is a detailed exposition of a traditional Indian meditation technique which

is geared toward the Westerner. A great deal of background philosophy is included with the text and basic and more advanced techniques are presented.

BAILEY, ALICE. **LETTERS ON OCCULT MEDITATION. 375pp. LPC22, 4.00p.**
Given to a group of students over a period of years. These letters describe the technique of occult meditation, which includes the establishment of correct alignment of the personality with the inner spiritual entity or soul and the resulting soul contact and inspiration.

BAKER, DOUGLAS. **MEDITATION. Over 200pp. Bak75, 16.00p.**
The format here is identical to Baker's other oversize volumes and there is an equal amount of full color and black and white illustrations. This is Volume II of his **Seven Pillars of Ancient Wisdom** series, an extensive treatise on meditation: its nature, types, stages in individual meditation, techniques, and effects. The material is all discussed at great length and the approach is esoteric. The exercises are clearly presented and visualization material accompanies them.

BAKER, M.E. PENNY. **MEDITATION—A STEP BEYOND WITH EDGAR CAYCE. Bibliography, 166pp. Pin73, 1.50p.**
An in depth look at meditation based entirely on what Cayce taught through his readings. The material is logically organized and contains extensive quotations from the Cayce readings.

BALLENTINE, RUDOLF, ed. **THE THEORY AND PRACTICE OF MEDITATION. 97pp. Him75, 1.95p.**
A collection of essays on meditation by a variety of Indian intellectuals associated with Swami Rama. The selections are fairly clear, although a great number of Sanskrit words are used.

BENSON, HERBERT. **THE RELAXATION RESPONSE. Bibliography, index, 158pp. Avo75/WCS, 2.25p.**
In the midst of all the blather about mind cures and faith healing and the angry refutations of both, Dr. Herbert Benson has written an unsentimental, astonishingly sensible book about stress, relaxation and how certain techniques known to religious people for eons can actually help ordinary people to better health. There is no legerdemain here, just good research, solid reasoning and good sense. This book will not end the causes of stress in anyone's life. That may be impossible. But it may help many of us to live with stress more comfortably and maybe even to live longer because we do.—Harvey Cox.

BLOFELD, JOHN. **MANTRAS: SACRED WORDS OF POWER. 117pp. Dut77/A&U, 4.50p.**
Mantras are sacred formulas used for meditation in India, China, and Tibet. Their precise meaning and the way they work have long been surrounded by an aura of secrecy in order to guard against distortion and abuse. Blofeld here explains the significance and operation of these sacred words of power and a number of his experiences with mantric practice are recounted. We always enjoy reading Blofeld's books. Eight color plates accompany the text.

BLOFELD, JOHN. **THE TANTRIC MYSTICISM OF TIBET. 4.95p.**
See the Tibetan Buddhism section.

BOWNESS, CHARLES. **THE PRACTICE OF MEDITATION. 63pp. Wei71/TPL, 1.25p.**
A practical guide to meditation which includes preparatory steps and answers to many often wondered questions. Very clearly written.

BROOKE, AVERY. **DOORWAY TO MEDITATION. 7"x9", 111pp. Vin73, 4.95p.**
This is a lovely, thoughtful book about praying, and being, and approaching God, and meditating. The text is handwritten and is accompanied by many pictures. Rather than saying what meditation is or what meditating means, Brooke gives the reader an idea of what the meditative life is. He is saying that meditation and prayer can be found and practiced in all forms of daily life and every act can be a manifestation of the love of God. This book can be a wonderful gift for someone whom you want to turn on to a more contemplative life.

BROOKE, AVERY. **HOW TO MEDITATE WITHOUT LEAVING THE WORLD. 7"x9", 96pp. Vin75, 3.95p.**
Subtitled, *A step-by-step description of how to learn and teach meditation in the Judaeo-Christian tradition,* this is a wonderfully clear manual which

teaches meditation with extensive references to the **Bible.** The text is not overly theological and should be an excellent tool for those who are uncomfortable with the Eastern emphasis in most meditation manuals.

BRUNTON, PAUL. **THE QUEST OF THE OVERSELF. 230pp. Wei37/HPG, 3.50p.**
Brunton, a noted occultist, outlines ways in which an individual can penetrate deeply into regions of higher consciousness, thereby gaining greater insight, illumination, and spiritual fulfillment. The discussion is mainly theoretical, though some practical advice is included.

BRUNTON, PAUL. **THE SECRET PATH. 2.25p.**
See the Mysticism section.

■ CARRINGTON, PATRICIA. **FREEDOM IN MEDITATION. Notes, index, 406pp. Dou77, 3.50p.**
This is an excellent study of meditation by a practicing psychologist. Dr. Carrington combines pioneering scientific research on meditation with sound psychological theory, and she offers a fine set of guidelines for enriching the meditative experience. Dr. Carrington regularly practices meditation herself, so she often speaks from personal experience. We recommend this book to all who seek a lucid and thorough account of the meditative experience.

Vara mudra.

CONZE, EDWARD. **BUDDHIST MEDITATION. 2.50p.**
See the Buddhism section.

COOKE, GRACE. **THE JEWEL IN THE LOTUS. 156pp. WET73, 3.50c.**
Grace Cooke is the medium through whom White Eagle delivers his teaching. In this volume she develops the material presented in her first book on meditation and draws on the accounts of some of her students. A section of the book is devoted to an analysis of the symbols brought to light during meditation. The book also includes teaching from White Eagle, offering a practical, deeply inspiring picture of the place of meditation in everyday life. Ms. Cooke's work is inspiring and illuminating and is especially recommended to those who prefer the Western, Christian-oriented approach.

COOKE, GRACE. **MEDITATION. 167pp. WET55, 3.50c.**
An inspirational book which sets forth in a clear and straightforward style a safe method of meditation and spiritual unfoldment which can be practiced alone or in groups. Mrs. Cooke's spiritual guide is known as *White Eagle* and much of his practical philosophy is incorporated in this book.

DECHANET, JEAN-MARIE. **YOGA AND GOD. 169pp. SPL74, 3.45p.**
This is a nicely written treatise which incorporates both the Christian and the Hindu tradition and also gleans some material from current research on consciousness. The bulk of the book is devoted to an analysis of human nature and of the problems confronting contemporary man. This is followed by a discussion of Kundalini and its ascent and a general survey of meditational practices. A number of specific exercises are offered and the material here differs from anything we have read elsewhere.

DHIRAVAMSA. **THE WAY OF NON-ATTACHMENT. 156pp. ScB75, 6.95c.**
The author is a Thai monk who teaches in England and the U.S. This book is subtitled, *The Practice of Insight Meditation,* and it is designed to present the basic principles in a way that is accessible to the modern Western mind. All of the chapters are short and virtually no Pali terms are used. The main concepts are clearly presented and Dhiravamsa has a good way of using metaphors to make his presentation clearer. All

the techniques are related to living in the modern world and integrating the practice with one's daily life. This is an excellent handbook and on the whole it is the clearest instruction manual in insight meditation we have seen—although it is no more than an introductory treatise. An appendix summarizes the principles of insight meditation.

DOWNING, GEORGE. **MASSAGE AND MEDITATION.** 85pp. RaH74/Wdw, 1.95p.
Downing is the author of our most popular massage book. *This book's point of view is...that massage and meditation are in key aspects very much alike. Beyond that, the two activities can be put together in ways which give new depth to both. And you yourself can begin to experience what it can be to integrate the two. You can do this easily, independently of how much previous experience you have or haven't had with either.* Both philosophy and practical instructions are included in this little volume.

DUMONT, THERON. **THE POWER OF CONCENTRATION.** 183pp. YPS18, 5.00c.
This exposition centers on the powers and riches that can be obtained by focusing and concentrating the mind. Practical guidance is given.

DURCKHEIM, KARLFRIED. **HARA.** 3.95p.
See the Zen Buddhism section.

DURCKHEIM, KARLFRIED. **THE JAPANESE CULT OF TRANQUILITY.** 5.35p.
See the Zen Buddhism section.

EASTCOTT, MICHAEL. **THE SILENT PATH.** 166pp. Wei69/Wdw, 3.50p.
An excellent discussion of various aspects of the meditative experience. Eastcott includes chapters on vision, concentration, the planes of consciousness, and different types of meditation—reflective, receptive, creative, and prayerful. Eastcott is a student of Alice Bailey (see the Theosophy section) and the influence of the Bailey teachings is apparent in his exposition.

EASWARAN, EKNATH. **THE MANTRAM HANDBOOK.** Bibliography, index, 260pp. Nil77, 5.00p.
The mantram is a holy word which helps us to calm or still our mind and bring every mental process under our complete control—not just on the conscious level, but on the unconscious as well. It is a technique which has been used in all the world's religions. In this book Easwaran discusses what the mantram is and suggests how we can make the mantram a part of our daily life. A number of the great mantrams are discussed at length and Easwaran chooses his examples from numerous religions. He also discusses the use of mantram in specific instances. This is an illuminating account.

FAST, HOWARD. **THE ART OF ZEN MEDITATION.** Pce77, 2.95p.
A simple collection of photographs and direct instructions for Zen meditation, combined with some introductory thoughts on Zen.

GARDNER, ADELAIDE. **MEDITATION—A PRACTICAL STUDY.** 116pp. TPH68, 1.45p.
Deals with the background, methods, progressive stages and obstacles to meditation. Includes a section on group meditation and various meditational exercises. A Theosophical approach.

GOLDSMITH, JOEL. **THE ART OF MEDITATION.** 154pp. H&R56, 6.95c.
A regular program of daily meditations which will help a person realize his oneness with God and find a clearer view of himself and his world. A Christian, inspirational approach.

GOLDSTEIN, JOSEPH. **THE EXPERIENCE OF INSIGHT.** Bibliography, 181pp. UnP76/HPG, 4.95p.
This is the record of the instruction, commentary, humor, and questions and answers of a month long meditation course given by Goldstein, an outstanding teacher of *vipassana* (southern Buddhist insight meditation). The instructions and discourses are extraordinarily clear and the book follows the organization of the retreat so that students can follow the day by day progression of instruction. *Because of my deep respect for Joseph, I am truly delighted that the West is to be blessed by his teaching.*—Ram Dass.

■ GOLEMAN, DANIEL. **THE VARIETIES OF MEDITATIVE EXPERIENCE.** Bibliography, index, 155pp. Dut77, 3.50p.
Goleman, associate editor of **Psychology Today**, spent two years in India and Ceylon studying meditation and has taught courses on meditation at Harvard. This is a thorough, readable exploration which begins with a general discussion of the meditative experience. Goleman points out that the meditator can choose from many paths; every major religious tradition has its own form of meditation. He describes the different maps of a dozen meditative paths, including those of Tibetan Buddhism, Sufism, Christianity and Judaism. By comparing these paths, Goleman shows that, despite their seeming diversity, they share a basic unity of method and goal. Foreword by Ram Dass.

GOVINDA, LAMA. **CREATIVE MEDITATION AND MULTI-DIMENSIONAL CONSCIOUSNESS.** Notes, index, 306pp. TPH76/A&U, 11.00c/4.95p.
Lama Govinda is a German who has spent most of his adult life in Asia and has held posts in a variety of Indian universities. He is best known for his excellent monographs on Tibetan Buddhism. *This is not a book to teach meditation or to lay down rules and techniques, it is rather the fruit of a lifelong study and practice of contemplation and action in the spirit of Buddhism against the background of contemporary problems of East and West alike....It is hoped that this book will be a bridge between these two worlds, not a manual or a mere source of information, but an incentive for others to cross the bridge in both directions.*—from the preface. The format of the book is a series of essays on a variety of subjects related to the contemplative life. A number of the Lama's color paintings are also reproduced.

GOVINDA, LAMA. **MEDITATION.** 3.00p.
See the Tibetan Buddhism section.

GUENTHER, HERBERT, *tr.* **KINDLY BENT TO EASE US, PART TWO: MEDITATION.** 4.95p.
See the Tibetan Buddhism section.

HAMILTON-MERRITT, JANE. **A MEDITATOR'S DIARY: A WESTERN WOMAN'S UNIQUE EXPERIENCES IN THAILAND TEMPLES.** 1.75p.
See the Buddhism section.

HANH, THICH NHAT. **THE MIRACLE OF MINDFULNESS: A MANUAL ON MEDITATION.** Illustrations, 107pp. Bea76, 3.95p.
Hanh is a Zen Master and a poet. Most of this book is devoted to short, beautifully written essays on mindfulness and to teaching stories. The last part briefly describes thirty-two practical concentration and relaxation exercises.

HANSON, VIRGINIA, *ed.* **APPROACHES TO MEDITATION.** 147pp. TPH73, 2.50p.
Writers familiar with meditation from different religious and philosophical backgrounds, both East and West, contributed to this work. Among them are Lama Govinda, Chogyam Trungpa, I.K. Taimni, and Simons Roof. Includes different approaches for people of varying temperaments. A good selection.

HANSON, VIRGINIA, ed. **GIFTS OF THE LOTUS.** 191pp. TPH74, 1.50p.
A book of daily meditations taken from the sacred literature of many traditions. The sources for each meditation are given.

HAPPOLD, F.C. **THE JOURNEY INWARDS.** Annotated bibliography, 142pp. Kno68/DLT, 3.95p.
A sensitive introduction to the practice of contemplative meditation. Happold describes his book as *a simple and practical introduction to a type of prayer through which we can endeavour to make this journey inwards, into that deep centre of being where we may realize that transcendent yet immanent Source of all being which men call God.* A number of practical exercises are offered and, while the Christian experience is emphasized, Happold draws on Eastern mysticism as well and shows how the two traditions interface.

HIRAI, TOMIO. **ZEN MEDITATION THERAPY.** 103pp. Jap75, 3.95p.
Hirai is a Japanese psychiatrist specializing in psychophysiology. He has done extensive study of seated Zen meditation in connection with brain waves and he applies Zen to the treatment of neuroses. His work has been quite influential in Japan. This book presents a synthesis of his findings and also includes practical techniques and exercises.

HITTLEMAN, RICHARD. **RICHARD HITTLEMAN'S 30 DAY YOGA MEDITATION PLAN.** 9"x7½", 216pp. Ban78, 6.95p.
An extremely clearly presented day-by-day meditation guide. During the daily twenty minute sessions you learn and apply many meditation techniques—breathing, visualization, *yantra*, mantra, and asanas. The value of each technique is discussed and photographs illustrate each daily routine. Suggestions for continuing meditation are also offered.

HUMPHREYS, CHRISTMAS. **CONCENTRATION AND MEDITATION.** 242pp. Vik35/Wat, 2.50p.
The basic principles of mind development, presented by a leading figure in world Buddhism. The student is guided through successive levels of concentration and meditation. Physical and mental exercises, the objects of thought, and underlying philosophical ideas are described at every stage. No knowledge of Buddhist thought is necessary to understand these teachings. *The ultimate aim of this progressive course in mind development is to bring the student to a point of spiritual attainment beyond which this or any other text would not presume to lead.*

HUMPHREYS, CHRISTMAS. **THE SEARCH WITHIN.** Bibliography, 160pp. Oxf77, 3.95p.
A progressive course of twelve theme meditations, designed to encourage the student to meditate throughout the day. Each of the courses consists of an introductory passage written by Humphreys followed by a selection of related quotations from the sacred literature of many religions.

INGRAHAM, E. **MEDITATION IN THE SILENCE.** 59pp. USC nd, 1.00p.
This little book is presented to the student as a textbook covering the principles and practices of the silence. The endeavor is to make clear the various points involved in the practice of the silence, and to render the benefits of that practice clear to every student. Inasmuch as the silence is fundamentally for the purpose of bringing man into an understanding relationship with God, it is a form of prayer....The effectiveness of prayer does not depend on the form followed, but on the spirit involved....Let us study together the simple means by which we may commune with God and the ways by which we may most effectively appropriate the blessings that He has had for us since the beginnings of time.—from the foreword.

JOHNSTON, WILLIAM. **SILENT MUSIC. Glossary, bibliography, index,** 190pp. Fon74, 4.00p.
Johnston is an Irish Jesuit with a degree in mystical theology who has taught at Sophia University in Tokyo for the past twenty years. He is the author of a number of books which combine Zen with Christian mysticism. He begins this study with a survey of the latest scientific research into altered states of consciousness, brainwaves, and biofeedback, and draws out their implications for the practice of meditation. He then outlines the ways, common to any religious traditions—Eastern and Western—by which one enters into the deeper states of consciousness. He also touches on the therapeutic value of meditation and its potential in the healing of the body and the mind, and on the *passive energy* one can get from meditation. This is an excellent presentation of the mystical potential of meditation for the betterment of humanity and a welcome and unique addition to the literature.

JYOTIRMAYANANDA. **MEDITATE THE TANTRIC YOGA WAY.** 4.75p.
See the Tantra section.

■ KELSEY, MORTON. **THE OTHER SIDE OF MEDITATION: A GUIDE TO CHRISTIAN MEDITATION. Notes,** 314pp. Pau76/SCK, 5.95p.
Kelsey is a nationally known theologian, psychologist, and educator. In this book he provides both a rationale and a method of Christian meditation. Kelsey begins with a general survey of meditation, discussing the relation of psychological types to the inner life and the problem of the intimacy that is involved in meditation. The second part lays out one by one the elements of the atmosphere in which it is possible for Christian meditation to grow and develop. In part three he considers several ways in which the individual can prepare to get into the practice of meditation. Part four reviews the importance of understanding the experiences which are gained and sought in meditation. Here Kelsey looks at the nature and uses of images,

especially as found in dreams, and then at other ways of awakening imagination. He also discusses our need for historical tradition and ritual, the reasons for keeping a journal, and the need for spiritual direction. Finally, he shows how to go about doing meditation, using biblical stories, dream images, and other images. The last sections are devoted to analyses of healing prayer and examples of meditations which have arisen spontaneously over the years. This book has a very nice feeling to it and we recommend it highly to all who are interested in Christian meditation. Kelsey writes with depth of understanding and expresses himself clearly.

LERNER, ERIC. **JOURNEY OF INSIGHT MEDITATION: A PERSONAL EXPERIENCE OF THE BUDDHA'S WAY.** 3.95p.
See the Buddhism section.

■ LESHAN, LAWRENCE. **HOW TO MEDITATE. Notes,** 210pp. Ban74, 1.95p.
This is an excellent practical guide to meditation. Drawing upon the meditational practices of such disciplines as Zen, Sufism, and yoga, and on Christian and Jewish mysticism, LeShan describes specific exercises and programs ranging from breath counting and simple mantras to group movement and sensory awareness. LeShan is a practicing psychologist and a noted parapsychological researcher. Recommended as a basic primer.

LUK, CHARLES (LU K'UAN YU). **SECRETS OF CHINESE MEDITATION. Glossary,** 231pp. Wei64/HPG, 3.95p.
Lu K'uan Yu has devoted his life to presenting as many Chinese Buddhist texts as possible to the Western world. He is among the foremost scholars. Here he presents long extracts from ancient and modern classics in which the emphasis is practical so that the reader can pick out and use that which most appeals to him. Ch'an, Mahayana and Taoist methods are included. Two chapters are devoted to Taoist yoga. An excellent work for the serious seeker.

MANGALO, BHIKKU. **THE PRACTICE OF RECOLLECTION.** 26pp. BuS70, 1.40p.
The Practice of Recollection (Satipatthana) is one of the basic practices of Buddhism. Buddhism is rightly famous amongst the family of religions for its clarity and its undogmatic, practical approach to the question of the realization of the Truth. It is not surprising therefore that we find right at the heart of Buddhism a stress on the need for training the mind to a greater awareness and clarity. This is done by the simple, yet eminently reasonable and practical expedient of keeping the mind focused on the present, on what is, here and now....The practice of recollection has the...advantage that, once one has acquired the habit, it can and indeed should be practiced at all times and throughout the day, whatever one's occupation.—from the foreword.

■ MATA, ANJANEE. **MEDITATION CARDS.** Anj75, 3.95p.
This packet of forty-nine cards is about the neatest way to get into meditation that we know of. The cards themselves have a lovely feel to them both in terms of the handwriting and the message, and the approach should be welcome by those who have unsuccessfully tried to get into the more traditional books. It is nice when someone takes a subject that has been written about endlessly and transforms it. The material goes far beyond meditation into all kinds of exercises for expanding awareness and each individual can pick out the exercises that particularly appeal to her at a given moment by selecting out certain cards. The instructions themselves are excellent and they give a good idea of the spiritual background of the exercises without being unnecessarily heavy. We are delighted with the idea and with the cards and we recommend them highly.

MAY, GERALD. **THE OPEN WAY: A MEDITATION HANDBOOK.** 182pp. Pau77, 8.95c.
One might easily remark, *What could be the possible need for another meditatin text?* There certainly is an abundance of written information on meditation. But little of it is practical and designed for genuine self learning. We therefore felt a growing pleasure as we went through Dr. May's book. It is, above all, designed to take the mystery and difficulty out of meditation. So many people get bogged down early in their meditational practice or never begin to practice at all because of the mystique that surrounds the subject. Dr. May draws away the veil and shows how exciting and easy it is to make meditation a part of one's own daily routine. He is a practicing psychiatrist who has involved

himself in many different spiritual traditions. In this volume he shares the insights he has gained. He writes in a lively fashion and introduces an abundance of introductory techniques.

MUKERJI, SWAMI. **SPIRITUAL CONSCIOUSNESS. 191pp. YPS11, 6.00c.**
This is a fairly scattered Indian treatise on some of the more basic ways to attain spiritual consciousness. The highly moralistic text reflects the spirit of the time it was written and it may seem unnecessarily heavy to contemporary readers. Some good insights are presented and exercises are included—however the material is not very clearly organized and we definitely do not suggest this as an instructional manual.

NARANJO, CLAUDIO and ROBERT ORNSTEIN. **ON THE PSYCHO-LOGY OF MEDITATION. Notes, 248pp. Vik61/A&U, 2.50c.**
Two innovative psychologists here unite their work in an examination of both the spiritual ground of all forms of meditation and the implications for modern psychology of the manifold approaches to meditation. A very clear presentation. Recommended especially for those schooled in humanistic psychology.

NARAYANANANDA, SWAMI. **THE SECRETS OF MIND-CON-TROL. 221pp. NUY76, 6.85p.**
A text on mind control loosely based on Patanjali's **Yoga Sutras**. Many practical techniques are given. The orientation is Hindu and many Sanskrit words are included in the text.

NYANAPONIKA, VENERABLE. **THE HEART OF BUDDHIST MEDI-TATION. 3.95p.**
See the Buddhism section.

OKI, MASAHIRO. **MEDITATION YOGA. Glossary, index, 174pp. Jap78, 9.95c.**
A dry, not terribly inspiring account the meditational teachings presented in a variety of yoga texts. There is something about the book that has made us not want to review it for weeks. Oki is a well known teacher and we are sure that what he has to say about both meditation and yoga is valuable. He suggests many practical techniques and exercises and explains all his suggestions thoroughly.

PARAMANANDA, SWAMI. **CONCENTRATION AND MEDITA-TION. 130pp. VdC74, 2.25p.**
Swami Paramananda, a disciple of Swami Vivekananda, was one of the first Indian teachers to come to the U.S. He founded the Boston Vedanta Centre in 1909 and a monastic community in California in 1923—both of which are still active centers under the direction of his disciples. His teaching is clear and is practically-oriented and, while it represents a traditional Hindu approach, Western philosophy is well integrated. The emphasis here is on philosophy, although techniques and inspirational thoughts also abound. Short excerpts from sacred texts are interspersed throughout.

PARAMANANDA, SWAMI. **SILENCE AS YOGA. 82pp. VdC74, 2.25p.**
In ancient India the yogi who sought to realize his divine self would retreat to the seclusion of the forest or to the quiet of a Himalayan cave. Today's spiritual aspirant sits down to meditate amongst the noise of modern society. In the series of lectures presented here Swami Paramananda discusses this problem and stresses that true silent is achievable if an individual can enter completely within himself so that he will not be disturbed or distracted by any external commotion.

PARAMPANTHI, SWAMI. **CREATIVE SELF TRANSFORMATION THROUGH MEDITATION. 157pp. Ata74, 4.95p.**
Despite the fact that the author of this volume is an Indian, it is very Western-oriented and presents a good course of study for those who want to learn about meditation without a teacher. The Swami begins with a review of the benefits of meditation, and discusses what meditation is. Then some *preliminary steps toward meditation* are presented along with a preview of meditational techniques. Once the background is given the author sets out a six week graduated program, each with a number of variations which can be creatively adapted to individual preferences and lifestyles. Some might put this down as *peace of mind* meditation, but if that is what you want, this book is as good as any we know of. The directions are clear and the philosophical material is fairly straightforward.

PROGOFF, IRA. **THE STAR/CROSS: A CYCLE OF PROCESS MEDI-TATION. 2.95p.**
See the Jungian Psychology section.

PROGOFF, IRA. **THE WELL AND THE CATHEDRAL. 166pp. DHL77, 3.95p.**
The Well and the Cathedral *is a meditative text that assists the process of personal centering by providing a way inward not limited to particular doctrines. . . . It provides a way of personal practice and inner discipline that enables an individual to reach progressively deeper levels in meditation.* **The Well and the Cathedral** *lends support and prepares the way. It truly serves as an entrance to meditation, opening the path inward whether to enter oriental meditation, Christian prayer and contemplation, or Hebraic worship. As an Entrance Meditation,* **The Well and the Cathedral** *opens a doorway into a large house of spiritual experience and it lets each of us choose our own room. The text is written in poetic form and introductory material is also included.*

PROGOFF, IRA. **THE WHITE ROBED MONK: A CYCLE OF PRO-CESS MEDITATION. 77pp. DHL72, 2.95p.**

PURYEAR, HERBERT and MARK THURSTON. **MEDITATION AND THE MIND OF MAN. 107pp. ARE75, 2.50p.**
This is a psychologically-oriented examination of the Edgar Cayce readings on meditation. It is not intended to be a definitive text, but, rather, to show how the universal principles and laws can be applied. Frequent references to Lama Govinda's **Foundations of Tibetan Mysticism** and **The Secret of the Golden Flower**, an ancient Taoist text, give the reader an idea of the universal quality of the information which came through the Christ-oriented superconsciousness of Edgar

Cayce. The text is divided into the following sections: *Fundamental Concepts of the Nature of Man, The Nature of the Mind, Meditation, The Pattern and the Power, Ideals*. A final section presents a systematic approach to meditation from the Edgar Cayce readings. This is the most detailed presentation of the Cayce material on meditation available.

RAJNEESH, BHAGWAN SHREE. **MEDITATION: THE ART OF EC-STACY. 3.95p/2.50p.**
See the Contemporary Spiritual Teachers section.

■ *RAM DASS.* **JOURNEY OF AWAKENING: A MEDITATOR'S GUIDEBOOK. Many illustrations, bibliography, 409pp. Ban78, 2.95p.**
Ram Dass is without question the best known American spiritual teacher. He has studied and practiced a variety of meditation techniques for many years. In this informal, anecdotal account he shares his understanding, explores a number of meditational techniques—mantra, prayer, singing, visualization, and sitting—and suggests how you can find a method and guidance suitable for you. He offers advice on tools and resources, pitfalls to avoid, and realistic expectations. Many short quotes from spiritual teachers are scattered throughout the exposition. Almost half the book is devoted to an up-to-date directory for the U.S. and Canada of groups that teach meditation and available retreat facilities.

REPS, PAUL. **TEN WAYS TO MEDITATE. 57pp. Wea69, 4.95c.**
Ten (or twenty-two depending on how you count them) picture poems which, in the words of Aldous Huxley, *will take one further towards the realization of the ancient self knowledge than all the roaring or pathetic eloquence of generations of philosophers*.

RIEKER, HANS-ULRICH. **THE SECRET OF MEDITATION. 176pp. Wei55/HPG, 3.95p.**
*The great advantage of this book is its concreteness. One gets the "feel" of meditation from it, learns to know it as something which is not "a strange world of its own". "For everything which disturbs our lives also disturbs meditation; and everything which helps meditation also helps our tranquility and our success in daily life." Three appendices deal with "Meditation in Japanese Zen Buddhism," "Meditation in the Wonderland of Tibet," and ..."Meditation in Christianity." Taken all in all, this is the ideal book to put in the hands of an intelligent friend who wants to know what this Buddhism business is all about. It is also a book for all Buddhists to read and reread.—*The Middle Way. This is a practical, helpful book, written by a Buddhist monk of Swiss origin.

ROOF, SIMONS. **GREATNESS OF BEING. 8½"x11", 149pp. MSE73, 7.50p.**
An excellent guide to beginning and intermediate meditation from a point of view which encompasses all religions and philosophies. Meditation, study, and service are discussed in detail; there are many chapters devoted to special exercises in the disciplines. Appendices deal with daily meditation forms and an integrated schedule of daily work. The emphasis is on meditation as a way of life leading to *greatness of being* rather than as an isolated phenomenon. Includes many quotations from other sources.

ROZMAN, DEBORAH. **MEDITATING WITH CHILDREN. Oversize, 63pp. UTP75, 5.95p.**
This is an unusual text which outlines practical techniques for introducing meditation to children. The exercises are presented in detail and the instructional material is very clear. The text is quite spiritual and is written in a language which should appeal to children. There are exercises for both individuals and groups. This is a very good book which can be used by itself and also serve as a base from which a teacher or parent can work in developing more individualized techniques.

ROZMAN, DEBORAH. **MEDITATION FOR CHILDREN. Bibliography, 151pp. CeA76, 4.95p/1.75p.**
Ms. Rozman teaches meditation to public school children in classroom settings. This is an excellent manual which presents a variety of techniques. It is written both for parents' use and also for children to read and follow themselves. Specific, direct instructions are given in concentration and meditation and a variety of other awareness and yogic exercises are also discussed. The book is illustrated throughout. There are also sections on meditating with the whole family. This is the best of Ms. Rozman's two books.

SADHU, MOUNI. **CONCENTRATION: GUIDE TO MENTAL MASTERY. 219pp. Wil59, 3.00p.**
A practical sequel to **In Days of Great Peace**. The central idea is to give the reader real knowledge of his mind and the methods of directing it as a tool of his consciousness. After some explanatory chapters, the student is introduced to the exercises. Sadhu uses an eclectic method, taking material from both Western and Eastern sources.

SADHU, MOUNI. **IN DAYS OF GREAT PEACE. 212pp. Wil52, 3.00p.**
The author, a disciple of Ramana Maharshi, describes how he mastered the techniques of *jnana* yoga and achieved the transcendent spiritual state (*samadhi*). This is probably the best attempt by a European to describe without technicalities what *samadhi* is, what meditation is about, and why Indians worship their gurus. The author's rare facility for describing his own mental and spiritual states enables him to pass on to the reader his knowledge and enthusiasm. The book is written around contemporary diary entries with flashbacks to an earlier life. It is an authentic autobiographical account of life with Ramana Maharshi, an inspired Hindu yogi, and explains convincingly how such a man can teach through silence. First book in trilogy: **In Days/Concentration/Samadhi**.

SADHU, MOUNI. **MEDITATION. 350pp. Wil67, 3.00p.**
A continuation of material presented in **Concentration** and its companion volume, **Samadhi**. This should not be considered an introductory work. Its aim is to give the student a manual, from which he may be able to obtain reasonable theoretical knowledge of the subject, plus a systematic guide for the development of practical abilities in himself. Includes introductory exercises, beginning, intermediate, and advanced meditations as well as a final section on an introduction to contemplation. The meditations are taken from all the world's scriptures and are well presented and easy to follow.

SARAYDARIAN, H. **THE SCIENCE OF MEDITATION. 364pp. AEG71, 9.00c.**
An extremely esoteric, practical discussion of meditation geared toward *leading the aspirant from the unreal to the real, from darkness into light, and from death to immortality*. Saraydarian writes well and includes detailed instructions and guidelines for group meditation and full moon meditation. Suggested for those comfortable with the Alice Bailey school of thought.

SAYADAW, MAHASI. **THE PROGRESS OF INSIGHT. 2.15p.**
See the Buddhism section.

SCHOMBERG, HOGETSU, ed. **ZEN MEDITATION. 2.00p.**
See the Zen Buddhism section.

■ *SCHWARZ, JACK.* **THE PATH OF ACTION. 155pp. Dut77, 3.50p.**
Jack Schwartz is a healer who has devoted his life to sharing techniques for the expansion of consciousness. He has participated, both as a researcher and a subject, in a number of studies on the voluntary control of internal states. In this book he draws on his own practice and teaching to present a unique synthesis of Eastern and Western thought that focuses on an active meditative practice. His approach to meditation is one that can be lived rather than contemplated. As a teacher he has opened doors for those who never before have been involved in spiritual work and through this book he will surely help open many more. This is an inviting, illuminating volume and one which we recommend highly.

■ *SCHWARZ, JACK.* **VOLUNTARY CONTROLS: EXERCISES FOR CREATIVE MEDITATION AND FOR ACTIVATING THE POTENTIAL OF THE CHAKRAS. 158pp. Dut78, 4.95p.**
A clearly explained collection of practical exercises for creative meditation and for activating the potential of the chakras. Schwarz includes exercises and techniques we have not seen elsewhere along with helpful preparation suggestions. An excellent work. Introduction by Gay Luce.

SECHRIST, ELSIE. **MEDITATION—GATEWAY TO LIGHT. 52pp. ARE64, 1.50p.**
An inspirational treatise by a woman closely associated with the Edgar Cayce work.

SHADDOCK, E.H. **AN EXPERIMENT IN MINDFULNESS. 158pp. Wei58/HPG, 2.95p.**
Describes Shaddock's practice of *satipatthana*, a Buddhist exercise in mindfulness, under a Burmese meditational master, Mahasi Sayadaw. This is not a dry text book, but a living account of the three weeks he spent at the center, the people he met, what he did and the effect it had upon him. Recommended for those who get bogged down in books full of Sanskrit and Pali terms.

SHASTRI, HARI PRASAD. **MEDITATION, IT'S THEORY AND PRACTICE. 64pp. ShS36, 1.50p.**
Clear instructions on meditation for both the beginner and the more advanced student. Includes the psychological and spiritual principles on which meditation is based.

SIVANANDA, SWAMI. **CONCENTRATION AND MEDITATION. Glossary, 423pp. DLS54, 5.75c.**
A very practical text detailing the steps to the meditative state, including excellent information on the theory and practice of concentration; the preliminaries for meditation; the practice of meditation; kinds of meditation; physical, mental and higher obstacles in meditation; and meditational experiences. Sivananda was one of the most noted Swamis of this century and was the guru to Swamis Satchidananda and Vishnudevananda. He writes very clearly and to the point.

SIVANANDA, SWAMI. **THOUGHT POWER. 152pp. DLS63, 1.90p.**
An analysis of thought power: its physics and philosophy; its laws and its dynamics; functions, values and uses; development; varieties of thoughts; methods of thought control; thought-transcendence; and thought-power and God realization. Includes philosophy and practical instruction.

SMITH, BRADFORD. **MEDITATION: THE INWARD ART. 224pp. Lip63, 3.50p.**
A Quaker's treatise on meditation: what it is and how to do it, the different forms of meditation, group meditation and Quaker meetings. Sample meditations.

SUJATA, ANAGARIKA. **BEGINNING TO SEE. UnP75, 2.95p.**
A collection of epigrams about living in the world by an American who was a Buddhist monk and now runs the Stillpoint Institute: *thoughts are not necessarily connected with reality. That is why the Buddha taught us to be aware of them before we are influenced by them....To be free we must be comfortable in being someone, anyone or no one at any time in any place....Each morning, if we commit ourselves to finding the truth of every situation then miracles will come to us all day*

long....Your pain can be the breaking of the shell which encloses your understanding. The book is handwritten and illustrated and is filled with many gems.

SUZUKI, SHUNRYU. **ZEN MIND, BEGINNER'S MIND—INFORMAL TALKS ON ZEN MEDITATION AND PRACTICE. 5.95c/3.50p.**
See the Zen Buddhism section.

SWEARER, DONALD. **SECRETS OF THE LOTUS. Glossary, 235pp. McM71, 1.95p.**
Discusses meditation within both the *satipatthana* (Theravada) and *zazen* (Zen) traditions, employing classical texts with explanatory commentary and contemporary exposition. A final chapter discusses the responses of university students to an experimental meditation workshop employing these techniques.

TARTHANG TULKU, ed. **CALM AND CLEAR. 111+pp. DhP73, 4.75p.**
Translations of two Tibetan meditational texts. They were especially chosen to make the depth and subtlety of Tibetan Buddhism available to the West. Both texts are short, relatively simple, practice-oriented, and emphasize a step-by-step development which begins at the most fundamental level. A long introduction and extensive commentary on the root verses help to clarify the teaching. A beautiful presentation.

TARTHANG TULKU, ed. **CRYSTAL MIRROR, VOLUME III. 4.75p.**
See the Tibetan Buddhism section.

TEMPLE, SEBASTIAN. **HOW TO MEDITATE. 177pp. Rad71, 7.50c.**
A practical collection of meditation and mind control techniques. A large part of the book is devoted to an in depth discussion of the kundalini. Temple has gathered together more techniques than we have seen anywhere else and he does a good job of explaining them. Recommended only to those who favor an esoteric approach.

Transcendental Meditation

Transcendental Meditation, or TM as it is usually called, is a term coined by Maharishi Mahesh Yogi for his technique which draws on the innate ability of the nervous system to rid itself effortlessly of stress and fatigue. Each practitioner is given a *mantra*, which is supposed to be expressly chosen for the individual. This *mantra* is the vehicle for the mind to relax and reach another state of consciousness. TM has been extremely popular in the U.S., there are many hundreds of thousands of meditators. A great deal of scientific research on TM has also been conducted and it is widely used in businesses and schools.

BLOOMFIELD, HAROLD, et al. **TM: DISCOVERING INNER ENERGY AND OVERCOMING STRESS. Index, 290pp. Del75, 1.95p.**
There has been an incredible outpouring lately of books about meditation in general and Transcendental Meditation in particular. This is the most extensive *authorized* treatise on the subject and it has been very popular, even reaching the best seller list. This, like all the other TM books is not a how-to manual, rather it is a description of the technique, its applications, and its effects from a psychological and physiological point of view. All of the authors have had extensive experience with TM and they present a scholarly study, backed up by charts, diagrams, and references.

CAMPBELL, ANTHONY. **SEVEN STATES OF CONSCIOUSNESS. Bibliography, 181pp. H&R74/Glz, 1.95p.**
Subtitled, *A Vision of Possibilities Suggested by the Teaching of Maharishi Mahesh Yogi*, this is a fine exploration of the common ground between science and mystical religion, illustrated by quotations from the Maharishi's writings and the literature of mysticism, as well as from scientists and humanistic psychologists such as Maslow. The author has been practicing TM since 1967 and he incorporates his personal experiences into the exposition.

CAMPBELL, ANTHONY. **TM AND THE NATURE OF ENLIGHTENMENT. Notes, bibliography, index, 223pp. H&R75, 1.95p.**
This volume goes far beyond most of the usual treatises on TM and delves into an examination of the dangers inherent in the rigid

separation in the Western world between the spiritual and the material and how this dichotomy can be resolved. It is a sophisticated presentation which reveals some of the complexities of the Maharishi's thought and of the TM process. Modern science and mystical thought are examined in depth and reconciled. An interesting study, originally published in Great Britain as **The Mechanics of Enlightenment**.

CHAPMAN, A.H., et al. **WHAT TM CAN AND CANNOT DO FOR YOU. Bibliography, index, 208pp. Ber76, 1.50p.**
The format of this book is questions and answers. The main author is a psychiatrist who is familiar with the technique of TM and with its possible benefits in a wide variety of areas. He poses many questions and then answers them, and the answers are based on both his personal experience with patients and on the TM research which has been conducted over the last few years. It is one man's opinion, but the book should be interesting to those who seek a deeper insight into the benefits of TM.

DENNISTON, DENISE and P. MCWILLIAMS. **THE TM BOOK. 224pp. War75, 1.95p.**
This account is illustrated with many simple line drawings, graphs, and tables. The material is usually in the form of questions and answers and is divided into the following areas: *What TM Is Not, What TM Is, What TM Does, Learning TM* (this section says that you must learn it personally from a trained teacher, and it does not explain how to learn it), and *TM—Solution to All Problems*. The book is very well thought of by the TM organization and it does seem to give a better feel for the approach and its basis than any other work we have seen. It is a good presentation as long as you do not mind books with a lot of hype.

EBON, MARTIN, ed. **MAHARISHI. 165pp. NAL68, 1.50p.**
A collection of essays and articles on *his life/his times/his teachings/his impact* from a variety of sources.

FOREM, JACK. **TRANSCENDENTAL MEDITATION. 274pp. Dut74/ A&U, 3.50p.**
This is *the* approved introduction to TM and the Science of Creative Intelligence. Forem traces the growth of Maharishi's worldwide movement, explains the principles of SCI in great detail, and reviews the scientific research on TM. He also points out the practical application of TM and SCI and draws parallels between the teachings of Maharishi and the insights of modern day physics, education, psychology and other disciplines. Forem began practicing TM in 1967 and has been teaching it since 1970.

GOLDBERG, PHILIP. **THE TM PROGRAM. Glossary, bibliography, index, 192pp. HRW76, 3.95p.**
Another *authorized* report on TM by a long time TM teacher which surveys what TM is, how it works, and what it does. Goldberg succeeds in his goal of making the process come alive and he includes many case studies and personal impressions. This seems to be as good a way as any to get an introduction to TM. It is easy reading and is neither overly taxing nor terribly enlightening. None of the TM books claims to be enlightening; their aim is first and foremost to turn people on to the benefits of TM.

HEMINGWAY, PATRICIA. **THE TRANSCENDENTAL MEDITATION PRIMER. Notes, index, 382pp. Del75, 1.95p.**
This is a very personal account of the author's experience in Transcendental Meditation. The technique, introductory and advanced lectures and initiation are all explored in depth. From there Ms. Hemingway reviews the benefits she and others experienced in the following areas: energy and stress, sleep, work, creativity, overcoming destructive habits, physical impact, sex and love, relating to others, and learning. A final section discusses the residence course and asanas (or postures). While the author is obviously pro-TM, she still gives a fairly objective account backed up with the latest research findings. And the personal, first person style makes for easy reading.

JEFFERSON, WILLIAM. **THE STORY OF THE MAHARISHI. Bibliography, 128pp. S&S76, 1.50p.**
A short sketch of the Maharishi and his movement.

KOLLANDER, KATHY. **TM IS FOR KIDS TOO! 8½"x7¼", CeA77, 3.95p.**
A simple, illustrated introduction to the practice of TM. The book is

written in story form. Ms. Kollander began meditation at the age of eight, became a TM teacher, and wrote this story at the age of twelve.

KROLL, UNA. **THE HEALING POTENTIAL OF TRANSCENDENTAL MEDITATION. Notes, bibliography, 176pp. Kno74/DLT, 3.95p.**
Dr. Kroll is an English physician who has written on spiritual healing and prayer and on topics related to the Christian church. Here she explores the similarities and differences between TM and Christian prayer and strongly advocates the benefits of TM. She also explores and reacts to the claims of the TM organization from the standpoint of a Christian and a medical doctor. The approach of this volume differs greatly from the other books on TM.

MAHARISHI MAHESH YOGI. **TRANSCENDENTAL MEDITATION. 320pp. NAL63, 3.95p/1.50p.**
This is the Maharishi's basic book, originally entitled, **The Science of Being and the Art of Living**. There is nothing specifically on the TM technique. The book is a restatement of ancient Vedic wisdom in the light of modern thought. It is topically organized and divided into many short sections.

MARCUS, JAY. **TM AND BUSINESS. Index, 263pp. MGH77, 9.95c.**
The subtitle of this book, *Personal and Corporate Benefits of Inner Development*, describes the contents as well as anything we could say. Marcus cites personal interviews, corporate case studies, and research reports to show how TM systematically enhances the abilities most needed in business situations.

■ *NEW THOUGHT EDUCATION SOCIETY.* **TEACH YOURSELF TRANSCENDENTAL MEDITATION. 3½"x5½", 35pp. NTE76, 2.50p.**
What is contained in this manuscript is everything you need to know to practice transcendental meditation except the experience. You will have to provide that yourself by simply following the step-by-step instructions enclosed. Inside you will find complete introductory material, the mechanics of the mantra, a list of genuine mantras, guidelines for meditation, and simple step-by-step instructions. The information enclosed is, to the best of our knowledge, completely accurate. It was gathered from three sources: 1) our own experience with Transcendental Meditation; 2) our interviews with other students; and 3) information "leaked" to us by a former teacher of Transcendental Meditation.

RUSSELL, PETER. **THE TM TECHNIQUE. Notes, index, 195pp. RKP76, 3.95p.**
This is a well written, philosophical discussion of TM which is many levels above most of the other books on the subject. The author, a long time TM teacher, is also an intelligent man who discusses TM and meditation in general in light of his academic knowledge of theoretical physics and psychology. Consciousness, creativity, and psychological balance are all discussed in depth and the possible benefits of TM in each area is fully surveyed. This is by far one of the most interesting of the TM books—to us, at least. A number of diagrams accompany the text and Russell cites all the research on TM that has been and is currently being done.

TRUCH, STEPHEN. **THE TM TECHNIQUE AND THE ART OF LEARNING. Index, 250pp. LtA77, 4.95p.**
This book advocates the use of TM in our schools and other educational institutions. Truch explains the nature of stress, the harmful effects of distress, and shows the efficacy of TM in stress situations. Many specific studies and instances are cited and there are copious notes.

WHITE, JOHN. **EVERYTHING YOU WANT TO KNOW ABOUT TM INCLUDING HOW TO DO IT. Glossary, bibliography, 191pp. S&S76, 1.95p.**
The title speaks for itself though it doesn't really tell how to do it. It is more critical than most accounts and does include instruction, of sorts. It is also fairly well written.

—END OF TRANSCENDENTAL MEDITATION SUBSECTION—

TRUNGPA, CHOGYAM, ed. **THE FOUNDATIONS OF MEDITATION. 3.95p.**
See the Tibetan Buddhism section.

TRUNGPA, CHOGYAM. **MEDITATION IN ACTION. 74pp. ShP69, 2.25p.**
Chogyam Trungpa is the former abbot of a Tibetan monestery. He is a meditation master in the Kagyupa and Nyingmapa lineages and he has established two meditation centers: Tail of the Tiger in Vermont and Karma Dzong in Boulder, Colorado. This book is a classic on the subject of meditation, recommended by teachers of all paths. It presents various aspects of meditation in a very clear manner.

TRUNGPA, CHOGYAM. **THE MYTH OF FREEDOM AND THE WAY OF MEDITATION. 3.95p.**
See the Tibetan Buddhism section.

VIVEKANANDA, SWAMI. **MEDITATION AND ITS METHODS. 3.50p.**
See the Indian Philosophy section.

WATTS, ALAN. **THE ART OF CONTEMPLATION. 8¼"x11", 18pp. RaH72, 3.45p.**
A manuscript handwritten by Watts, with his doodles—a reprint of a limited edition work.

WATTS, ALAN. **MEDITATION. 63pp. CeA74, 3.95p/1.25p.**
Thoughts to meditate upon plus a series of illustrations. It is a pretty gift book rather than a full treatment of the subject. Many associated topics are discussed such as incense and chanting.

WHITE, JOHN, ed. **WHAT IS MEDITATION. 276pp. Dou74, 2.95p.**
A good selection of essays on various methods of meditation written by experienced meditators which gives the reader a comparative approach so that s/he can experiment with different techniques and then delve more deeply into whichever one feels best. Practical techniques as well as theory are offered. Contributors include: Alan Watts, Swami Chinmayananda, Gopi Krishna, Claudio Narajo, Robert de Ropp, Chogyam Trungpa, and Joel Goldsmith.

WILLIS, JANICE. **THE DIAMOND LIGHT—AN INTRODUCTION TO TIBETAN BUDDHIST MEDITATION. 2.45p.**
See the Tibetan Buddhism section.

WOOD, ERNEST. **CONCENTRATION. 154pp. TPH49, 1.50p.**
A practical manual by a Theosophist who has written extensively on yoga and Indian philosophy. It outlines the art of concentration and mind control as a first step leading to the deeper experience of meditation. Many exercises are included.

MUSIC

At no period of man's existence upon this earth does he appear to have been without music. The harps that have been brought to light from the royal graves of Ur are silent but eloquent witnesses, six thousand years after they were buried with their royal masters, that a highly developed and highly esteemed art of music flourished at the very beginning of history. Concerning prehistoric music, a music whose power and effect we of today should have to call supernatural, we have testimony in the mythologies of many peoples, both in the East and the West. Modern anthropology tells of the far from primitive music of the so-called primitive cultures. Many investigators assume that human speech was originally a sort of chant, and that it was only in the course of evolution that the two branches separated into the language of words and the language of tones. The world of man has never been a world without tone.

Among the various experiences of our senses, tone is the only one that belongs exclusively to life. Light and color, sound, odor, and taste, solidity, fluidity, and gaseousness, rough and smooth, hot and cold—all these are also to be found in nonliving nature. Only life can produce tones. Living beings, out of themselves, add tone to the physical world that confronts them; it is the gift of life to nonliving nature. A scientist, the first man to tread another planet, not knowing if he would find organic life there or not, would only need to hear a tone and his question would be answered.

Sounds are uncrystallized tones, tones that have not yet been realized. May we not assume that it was the sounds in nature—the sound of wind, of water in all its forms, of electric discharges, the rustling of leaves rather than the sight of their growth and fall—which aroused in sensitive minds the idea of a nature alive in all its parts? A completely soundless nature (which is something other than a silent nature—silence is a condition of sound as sleep is a condition of life) could hardly have been felt as alive. The mere contemplation of the motion that accompanies these sounds does not suffice; motion merely seen hardly calls up the impression of life so directly. The image of the soundlessly circling constellations is not an image of life to us. It was not the motion of the spheres but their *harmony*, their sounding together, of which men talked when they thought of the universe as alive. It seemed to them that the universal life must reveal itself as something audible rather than visible. Perhaps it is carrying the antithesis too far if we say that man attains the inwardness of life by hearing and its outwardness by seeing. Yet it seems more than mere chance that it was among a people so deeply anchored in the visible as the classic Greeks that the idea should be conceived of a supreme being which, in absolute immobility, intangibility, and uniformity, represented the direct opposite of everything living. The peculiar melancholy of the Greeks, too, their feeling for the ephemeral, for the element of transitoriness in life, may be connected with their living so much more in the visible than in the audible. In any case, the road to the heart of the living is more difficult, more circuitous, by way of the visible than of the audible.

We are led to similar considerations if we observe certain differences in the behavior of blind and deaf people. The quietness, the equanimity, the trust, one might almost say the piety, so often found in the blind are in strange contrast to the irritability and suspicion encountered among so many of the deaf. The contrast cannot but be termed strange, because actually we should expect the opposite behavior. After all, it is the blind man—so we should think—he whose deficiency practically cuts him off from the world, who must feel in solitary confinement within himself. Yet it is not the blind man who shows the typical reaction of the prisoner, the man spied upon, who must always be upon his guard; it is the deaf man, whose most important organ of connection with the outside world has remained unimpaired. It seems as if, by the very fact that the blind man trusts himself to the guidance of ear instead of eye, other modes of connection with the world are revealed to him, modes that are otherwise overshadowed by the dominance of the eye—as if, in the realms with which he thus comes into contact, man were less alone, better provided for, more at home, than in the world of visible things to which the deaf man is directed and to which an element of foreignness always clings.

The world in which we usually live, the world of our everyday existence—and not only of our everyday existence—is a world of visible things. The sense of sight has constructed it; the eye is our guide in it. Into it we integrate the impressions of the other senses; our speech, our actions, our thinking, are largely formed and oriented upon its pattern. One might almost suppose, and many do suppose, that the visible world is our entire milieu. We integrate even the audible into the frame of the visible—with one exception: music. Only in music, the art of tone, where the audible is, as it were, alone with itself, comes to itself, is the frame of the visible world broken through. Music does not integrate itself into the world of the eye.

When we open our eyes on the world we see objects: things that confront us, are directed toward us, close in on us. Tones carry outward; lead us away with them. That music is a window opening in the world of objects that closes in on us, a window through which we can look out from our world, men have always felt. The great thoughts that in all times have been thought about music all center upon this point; they are all suggested by this wonderful power of music to be a window. Philosophers of ancient China and classic Greece, mystics of late antiquity, Fathers of the Church, thinkers of the Renaissance, of the Reformation, of the Romantic Period, may differ widely in their speculations as to *where* music leads us. But concerning one thing—that music does cross a decisive frontier; that we find its most essential nature in this crossing, this transcendence—all who have ever thought about music are of one mind, as indeed they are too in finding that this transcendence occurs nowhere else in the same way, with the same directness.

—*condensed from* **Sound and Symbol: Music and the External World**, *by Victor Zuckerkandl*

BLACKING, JOHN. **HOW MUSICAL IS MAN?** Illustrations, 118pp. UWa73, 6.65p.
An exploration of the role of music in society and culture, and of society and culture in music. Blacking is a social anthropologist and ethnomusicologist and he draws his examples from Western music and from the music of the Transvaal Venda people.

BRACE, GEOFFREY and IAN BURTON. **LISTEN! MUSIC AND NATURE. Bibliography, 8½"x8", 66pp. CUP76, 3.95p.**
This is an unusual book which discusses the sounds, signs, language, music, and magic, of nature; and the first musical instruments. It is written in simple language and extensively illustrated.

CHAILLEY, JACQUES. **THE MAGIC FLUTE. Notes, bibliography, index, 359pp. Glz72, 9.00c.**
A thorough exploration of the libretto and the music of Mozart's opera which uncovers the hidden significance of the characters and situations and relates them to each other and to the esoteric tradition from which they emanate. Chailley traces the deep and far reaching influence of Freemasonry in Mozart's time, and its influence on Mozart himself. He outlines what he calls the cosmogony of the libretto, turning as it does on the struggle between two antagonistic ideas. The meaning of the opera gradually becomes clear, in terms of symbols and myths. A final section gives a detailed, scene by scene analysis of the opera, both music and libretto, which links all the parts together. Chailley is Professor of the History of Music at the Sorbonne.

DONINGTON, ROBERT. **WAGNER'S RING AND ITS SYMBOLS. Notes, bibliography, index, 342pp. Fab74, 6.95p.**
This book is about the poetical and musical symbols in Wagner's **Ring***; and what Wagner brought, with all the suggestive artistry at his disposal, into symbolical and artistic consciousness, I as a critic am trying to bring some small stage further on towards intellectual and analytical consciousness. In both the music and the myth, there are connections which can be analyzed and parallels which can be drawn.—*from the introduction. Donington has made a thorough analysis of the mythological framework of each part of the Ring cycle in terms of archetypal and analytical psychology. The book has received critical acclaim.

GASTON, E. THAYER. **MUSIC IN THERAPY. Notes, bibliography, indices, 511pp. McM68, 10.95c.**
A comprehensive survey of theory, research, techniques, and clinical practice which is designed as a basic text for students of music therapy. In thirty-nine chapters grouped under ten parts, the sixty contributors —each writing in areas in which s/he is most expert—provide a complete discussion of all aspects of music therapy.

HALL, MANLY P. **THE THERAPEUTIC VALUE OF MUSIC. 45pp. PRS55, 1.75p.**
Transcription of a lecture on music therapy as practiced in a variety of cultures from ancient times to the present. Emphasis is placed on the Greek and Egyptian usages.

■ *HAMEL, PETER.* **THROUGH MUSIC TO THE SELF: HOW TO APPRECIATE AND EXPERIENCE MUSIC ANEW. Illustrations, bibliography, 228pp. Com78, 16.25c.**
It is my purpose in the following pages to reveal and to research the elements of a new musical integration. In the course of the various chapters, whatever the starting points of their respective researches, an attempt will be made to stretch a great arc: from, on the one hand, contemporary theories and new approaches to composition in the realm of group improvisation, via the no longer ignorable encounter with nonEuropean music, magic, mantra and ritual, to the astonishing and nowadays demonstrable parallels between the laws of acoustics and the human psyche—taking in musical meditation, self experience through breathing, singing and playing, and a variety of tried and tested exercises for individual and group work.

HANSLICK, EDUARD. **THE BEAUTIFUL IN MUSIC. 141pp. BoM57, 4.00p.**
This work, originally published in 1854, *deals with the major problems of musical aesthetics:the aim of music, its intrinsic nature, the relation between music and reality, and the role of the listener. Throughout, Hanslick's main objective is the refutation of the popular and still prevalent theory that feelings or emotions are the substance of musical sounds, and that the composer expresses his affective life in his music so that the listener shares in it. He denies that music is a language of the emotions or, by implication, of persons, places, things, events, or ideas.—*from the introduction. This is a translation by Gustav Cohen of the seventh edition of 1885.

HEINDEL, MAX. **THE MUSICAL SCALE AND THE SCHEME OF EVOLUTION. 96pp. Ros49, 1.50p.**

An African *malinka*.

HEINDEL, MAX. **MYSTERIES OF THE GREAT OPERAS. Index, 176pp. Ros21, 3.50p.**
An esoteric analysis of **Faust, Parsifal, The Ring of the Neibelung, Tannhauser,** and **Lohengrin.**

HELINE, CORINNE. **BEETHOVEN'S NINE SYMPHONIES AND NINE SPIRITUAL MYSTERIES. 77pp. NAP71, 3.95p.**
A unique description of the spiritual significance of Beethoven's great compositions in their relation to the nine spiritual mysteries.

HELINE, CORINNE. **COLOR AND MUSIC IN THE NEW AGE. 139pp. NAP64, 2.95p.**
A fascinating volume which includes chapters on the color significance of the zodiacal signs, the presence and absence of color, color therapy (an extensive account), the cosmic aspects of color, the psychology of color in everyday living, color and music correlated with the seasons and the time of day, and occult effects of music.

HELINE, CORINNE. **THE COSMIC HARP. 99pp. NAP69, 4.95c.**
*The whole solar sytem is one vast musical instrument. . . . The signs of the zodiac may be said to be the sounding board of the cosmic harp and the seven planets are the strings; they emit different sounds as they pass through the various signs and therefore, they influence mankind in a diverse manner.—*Max Heindel. This book analyzes both the signs and noted musicians born under them.

HELINE, CORINNE. **ESOTERIC MUSIC, BASED ON THE MUSICAL SEERSHIP OF RICHARD WAGNER. 274pp. NAP, 5.95c.**
An original portrayal of the music of Wagner as the expression of

grand, celestial rhythms and harmonies brought to earth for human inspiration. Wagner's striking conceptions convey the depth of the human soul and reveal the drama of the ancient temple mysteries in a new way.

HELINE, CORINNE. **HEALING AND REGENERATION THROUGH MUSIC. 40pp. NAP68, 1.75p.**
A fine introduction to the philosophy behind the therapeutic and beneficial effects of music with some practical suggestions and methods for applying the techniques.

HELINE, CORINNE. **MUSIC—THE KEYNOTE OF HUMAN EVOLUTION. 144pp. NAP65, 4.95c.**
A beautiful explanation of the importance of music and its role as a symbol of human evolution. All manifestations can be expressed as portions of a cosmic symphony, says the author, who with keen insight and a depth of understanding explores the history of music, its expression in various cultures and times, and its significance and potential at the dawn of a new era.

HELMHOLTZ, HERMANN. **ON THE SENSATIONS OF TONE. Technical appendices, notes, index, 576pp. Dov1885, 7.75p.**
A classic work, bridging the gap between the natural sciences and music theory. The first two parts deal with the physics and psychology of music, the third contains the author's theory on the aesthetic relationship of musical tones. The text is amplified with graphs, diagrams, tables, and musical examples.

HODSON, GEOFFREY. **MUSIC FORMS: SUPERPHYSICAL EFFECTS OF MUSIC CLAIRVOYANTLY OBSERVED. 8½"x11½", 55pp. TPH76, 12.00c.**
The main purpose for which the investigations here recorded were carried out was to discover the different effects produced by the performance of music upon the adjacent matter of the superphysical worlds.—from the preface. Both Hodson and Dr. Gordon Kingsley, a noted musician, listened to various pieces of classical music. Dr. Kingsley commented upon each one from a technical standpoint and Hodson recorded his clairvoyant observations. Later Hodson got an artist to produce color pictures of his observations, and these are included here. An additional section reproduces an essay by Dr. Hans Jenny, **The Sculpture of Vibrations**.

JEANS, SIR JAMES. **SCIENCE AND MUSIC. Many illustrations, index, 258pp. Dov37, 3.50p.**
This is an excellent physical analysis of musical sounds. The discussion begins with an explanation of the development of the human faculty of hearing. It is established that each sound can be represented by a curve. An examination of the general properties of sound curves follows. Questions on the transmission and reproduction of sound curves are answered in a discussion of tuning forks and pure tones. The various methods of producing sound, and the qualities of the sound produced, are further discussed as they relate to vibrations of strings and harmonics, and vibrations of air. Harmony and discord are also considered. In the final chapters on the concert room and hearing, the discussion focuses on the transmission of sound from its source to the eardrum and from the eardrum to the brain. A general theory of acoustics is also covered as well as acoustical analyses.

KHAN, HAZRAT INAYAT. **MUSIC. 3.95p.**
See the Islam section.

KHAN, HAZRAT INAYAT. **THE MYSTICISM OF SOUND. Stapled, 94pp. HeR23, 2.00p.**
Every Sacred Scripture, every Holy Picture, every spoken word produces the impression of its identity upon the mirror of the soul, but Music stands before the soul without producing any impression whatever of either name or form of this objective world, thus preparing the soul to realize the Infinite. This small treatise is excerpted from Khan's larger work with the same name and is divided into the following topics: the silent life, vibrations, harmony, name, form, rhythm, music, abstract sound.

MCCLAIN, ERNEST. **THE MYTH OF INVARIANCE: THE ORIGIN OF THE GODS, MATHEMATICS, AND MUSIC FROM THE RIG VEDA TO PLATO. Glossary, index, 227pp. ShP76, 5.95p.**
This is quite possibly the most difficult book to review (and read) we have yet seen. This quotation from McClain's conclusion describes the book as well as possible: *Harmonical analysis is a technique for synthesizing the tonal, arithmetical, and geometrical imagery of ancient civilizations. It aims at the reconstruction of the esoteric diagrams which give the sacred symbols of particular cultures their enduring and magical powers and furnish philosophy with a ground of certainty. The technique is applicable to all cultures which considered tone and number twin keys to the secrets of the universe. . . . Harmonical analysis exploits the world's fascination with number and with those correlations between tone and number which we call acoustical theory, but which a former age of innocence considered to be cosmology.* Diagrams and quotations from sacred literature abound.

MERRIAM, ALAN. **THE ANTHROPOLOGY OF MUSIC. Notes, index, 369pp. NUP64, 14.80c.**
This book is an attempt to fill the gap which exists in ethnomusicology; to provide a theoretical framework for the study of music as human behavior; and to clarify the kinds of processes which derive from the anthropological, contribute to the musicological, and increase our knowledge of both conceived within the broad rubric of human behavior.—from the preface. This is an obviously technical work for the specialist, though it is not written in an overly academic manner.

MEYER, LEONARD. **EMOTION AND MEANING IN MUSIC. Notes, index, 318pp. UCh56, 3.95p.**
An excellent study which should be read by those who want deeper insights into music listening, performing, and composing. Many examples are included.

MEYER-BAER, KATHI. **MUSIC OF THE SPHERES AND THE DANCE OF DEATH: STUDIES IN MUSICAL ICONOLOGY. 24.20c.**
See the Sacred Art section.

NORDOFF, PAUL and CLIVE ROBBINS. **THERAPY IN MUSIC FOR HANDICAPPED CHILDREN. 168pp. Glz71, 4.35c.**
Music therapy is increasingly being used in the treatment of handicapped children. The authors are experienced music therapists and their book consists of vivid descriptions of their work, the way they go about it, and children's reactions to it. In this book they concentrate on work with the most challenging children: autistic, mongols, aphasoids, children with brain damage, and children who are physically as well as mentally crippled. An illustrated appendix contains individual music therapy sessions.

RECK, DAVID. **MUSIC OF THE WHOLE EARTH. Bibliographies, index, 8½"x11", 545pp. Scr77, 9.95p.**
This is a massive exploration of the richness of sound, instruments, and music from many different cultures and a great variety of musical traditions. Tribal, folk, and classical music from all parts of the world are included. Reck discusses the mythical origins of music, endangered music, the ecology of sound, music in relation to art, magic, ritual, theater, dance, life styles, and much else. There are also sections on the anatomy and mechanics of music, and information on how to make a variety of unusual instruments. It is a bit of a hodge podge, but a unique book. Profusely illustrated with photographs, drawings, maps, and diagrams.

SACHS, CURT. **THE RISE OF MUSIC IN THE ANCIENT WORLD, EAST AND WEST. Notes, index, 324pp. Nor43, 21.45c.**
An in depth, scholarly history of music from ancient times to the middle ages. Dr. Sachs covers the musical styles and systems of virtually every major early culture and shows the parallels between many apparently different systems. We recommend this book only to those who are involved in a serious study of comparative music.

SCOTT, CYRIL. **MUSIC: ITS SECRET INFLUENCE THROUGHOUT THE AGES. 208pp. Wei nd/TPL, 3.95p.**
A fascinating investigation into the esoteric implications of music. Scott, himself a noted composer, first discusses pure music, inspiration and invention in the sphere of Western music; and then the music of the Deva (spirit intelligences) is considered in relation to the occult constitution of man and the lives and work of various composers. A historical section traces the beginnings of music and religion and their combined effects on classical civilizations. Includes a good bibliography.

SESSIONS, ROGER. **THE MUSICAL EXPERIENCE OF COMPOSER, PERFORMER, LISTENER. 127pp. PUP50, 2.95p.**
This book must be read slowly, carefully, and twice. The author deals with the indisputable but oft forgotten idea that the musical process is an absolute and indivisible whole; that the duties and actions of composer, performer, and listener must be welded

into one to produce a truly musical experience. Each of these three forces . . . is accorded a chapter of wise discussion and often superb insight.—**Christian Science Monitor**. The material was originally prepared for a lecture series.

STEBBING, LIONEL, ed. **MUSIC—ITS OCCULT BASIS AND HEALING VALUE. 8"x10", 212pp. NKB58, 9.10p.**
An excellent, comprehensive selection of writings on music in the light of Rudolf Steiner's Spiritual Science (see Steiner section) by people in diverse disciplines.

STEBBING, LIONEL, ed. **MUSIC THERAPY. 8"x10", 96pp. NKB76, 7.70p.**
This compilation is arranged according to ailments and also has a few longer articles. The contributors are almost all followers of Rudolf Steiner's spiritual science and Steiner's research is included. Each of the selections is only a paragraph or so long.

STRAVINSKY, IGOR. **POETICS OF MUSIC. 149pp. HUP42, 2.50p.**
Six lessons which provide a glimpse into the thought processes of Stravinsky's mind. Topics include the phenomenon of music, the composition of music, music typology, leading Russian musicians, and the performance of music.

SULLIVAN, J.W.N. **BEETHOVEN, HIS SPIRITUAL DEVELOPMENT. 183pp. RaH27, 1.95p.**
I am concerned with Beethoven's music solely as a record of his spiritual development. I believe that in his greatest music Beethoven was primarily concerned to express his personal vision of life. This vision was, of course, the product of his character and experience.

SZEKELY, EDMOND. **LUDWIG VON BEETHOVEN. 23pp. Aca73, 1.75p.**
Szekely thinks of Beethoven as a superman, a hero, a revolutionary—or, as he says, *a Prometheus of the modern world, suffering, creating, and eternal.* This short study is divided into the following chapters: *The Enchanted Prometheus, Hero and Revolutionary, His Musical Ancestors, His Life, His Works, The Fifth Symphony, The Ninth Symphony* and *The Last Days.*

THOMPSON, KATHERINE. **THE MASONIC THREAD IN MOZART. Glossary, notes, bibliography, index, 207pp. L&W77, 12.60c.**
Mozart was an active Freemason; he wrote several pieces for masonic occasions, and his last opera, **The Magic Flute**, is unmistakably a masonic work. This book focuses on the masonic inspiration and ideas in Mozart's symphonies and concertos. It follows the chronological order of the development of Mozart's work and it is illustrated with numerous musical examples. The book is pubished by a Marxist press, and this emphasis is often apparent.

WHONE, HERBERT. **THE HIDDEN FACE OF MUSIC. Index, 128pp. Glz74, 7.20c.**
A series of essays which attempt to lead the reader into the deeper implications of music. By looking beyond the musical interval as it appears on paper, Whone sees that the laws which govern the composition and playing of music are the same laws which govern the composition of man, nature, and the universe. Everything has a symbolic meaning; and it is the symbolism inherent not only in the instruments with which we play our music but also in the various parts of the human body, which he discusses in these essays. Whone is a well known violinist and teacher.

WINSTON, SHIRLEY. **MUSIC AS THE BRIDGE. 68pp. ARE72, 1.95p.**
Selections from the Cayce readings which reveal what Cayce had to say about music in all its forms. Ms. Winston provides connective material.

WIORA, WALTER. **THE FOUR AGES OF MUSIC. Plates, bibliography, index, 233pp. Nor65, 2.95p.**
Professor Wiora sees all music falling chronologically into four periods: the prehistoric age; the age of the high cultures of antiquity, both East and West; the age of the predominance of Western music; and music in the technological and industrial age. He treats the different world musical styles as manifestations of response to the same human needs, thus accounting for the appearance of similar types of music in regions widely separated in space and time.

ZUCKERKANDL, VICTOR. **MAN: THE MUSICIAN. Bibliography, index, 383pp. PUP73, 4.95p.**
Zuckerkandl regards the phenomenon of musicality as a trait common to all human beings and analyzes at length the ways in which we perceive music. He examines the processes involved in our sensitivity to tone, dynamic tone qualities, musical movement, and the structure of musical works, and also includes detailed analyses of particular pieces of music.

ZUCKERKANDL, VICTOR. **THE SENSE OF MUSIC. Index, notes, 246+pp. PUP59, 4.45p.**
This is a detailed study which could easily be used as a textbook. The material is very clearly presented and, while it is recommended only to those who are deeply interested in music, it does contain a great deal of basic information. The information is divided into the following general categories: melody, texture and structure, meter and rhythm, polyphony, harmony, and harmony and melody.

ZUCKERKANDL, VICTOR. **SOUND AND SYMBOL: MUSIC AND THE EXTERNAL WORLD. Notes, bibliography, index, 399pp. PUP56, 4.95p.**
Mr. Zuckerkandl believes that music has a special kind of reality; it is outside us, it takes place in the external world, but it is neither a physical phenomenon nor a projection of psychic states; we cannot trace what we hear in music to the properties of sound waves, nor can we call it a hallucination in which psychological responses become objectified. Music conceived in this way has important implications for metaphysical philosophy: it insists upon a broad conception of the external world, and the examples it provides of motion and time and space become as significant as those of science.—**The Musical Quarterly**

MYSTICISM

What is mysticism? The word *mystic* has its origin in the Greek mysteries. A mystic was one who had been initiated into these mysteries, through which he had gained an esoteric knowledge of divine things and been *reborn into eternity*. His object was to break through the world of history and time into that of eternity and timelessness. The method was through initiation ceremonies. Through the mysteries the initiated entered into something holy and numinous, a secret wisdom about which it was unlawful for him to speak. The word *mystery* (*mysterion*) comes from the Greek verb *muo*, to shut or close the lips or eyes.

In the course of time the word mysticism came to have an extended, indeed a different meaning. In that syncretism of Greek and Oriental philosophy which occurred in the centuries immediately preceding the birth of Christ, known as Neoplatonism, it came to mean a particular sort of approach to the whole problem of reality, in which the intellectual, and more especially the intuitive, faculties came into play. As a result of the fusion of Christian and Neoplatonist ideas in the early centuries of the Christian era, a system of so-called mystical theology came into existence, which was one of the main foundations of Christian mysticism.

To speak more generally, mysticism has its fount in what is the raw material of all religion and is also the inspiration of much of philosophy, poetry, art, and music, a consciousness of a *beyond*, of something which, though it is interwoven with it, is not of the external world of material phenomena, of an *unseen* over and above the seen. In the developed mystic this consciousness is present in an intense and highly specialized form.

The mystical element enters into the commoner forms of religious experience when religious feeling surpasses its rational content, that is, when the hidden, non-rational, unconscious elements predominate and determine the emotional life and the intellectual attitude. In the true mystic there is an extension of normal consciousness, a release of latent powers and a widening of vision, so that aspects of truth unplumbed by the rational intellect are revealed to him. Both in feeling and thought he apprehends an immanence of the temporal in the eternal and the eternal in the temporal. In the religious mystic there is a direct experience of the Presence of God. Though he may not be able to describe it in words, though he may not be able logically to demonstrate its validity, to the mystic his experience is fully and absolutely valid and is surrounded with complete certainty. He has been *there*, he has *seen*, he *knows*.

Not only have mystics been found in all ages, in all parts of the world and in all religious systems, but also mysticism has manifested itself in similar or identical forms wherever the mystical consciousness has been present. Because of this it has sometimes been called the Perennial Philosophy. Out of their experience and their reflection on it have come the following assertions:

1. This phenomenal world of matter and individual consciousness is only a partial reality and is the manifestation of a Divine Ground in which all partial realities have their being.

2. It is of the nature of man that not only can he have knowledge of this Divine Ground by inference, but also he can realize it by direct intuition, superior to discursive reason, in which the knower is in some way united with the known.

3. The nature of man is not a single but a dual one. He has

not one but two selves, the phenomenal ego, of which he is chiefly conscious and which he tends to regard as his true self, and a non-phenomenal, eternal self, an inner man, the spirit, the spark of divinity within him, which is his true self. It is possible for a man, if he so desires and is prepared to make the necessary effort, to identify himself with his true self and so with the Divine Ground, which is of the same or like nature.

4. It is the chief end of man's earthly existence to discover and identify himself with his true self. By so doing, he will come to an intuitive knowledge of the Divine Ground and so apprehend Truth as it really is, and not as to our limited human perceptions it appears to be. Not only that, he will enter into a state of being which has been given different names, eternal, salvation, enlightenment, etc.

Further, the Perennial Philosophy rests on two fundamental convictions:

1. Though it may be to a great extent atrophied and exist only potentially in most men, men possess an organ or faculty which is capable of discerning spiritual truth, and, in its own spheres, this faculty is as much to be relied on as are other organs of sensation in theirs.

2. In order to be able to discern spiritual truth men must in their essential nature be spiritual; in order to know That which they call God, they must be, in some way, partakers of the divine nature; potentially at least there must be some kinship between God and the human soul. Man is not a creature set over against God. He participates in the divine life; he is, in a real sense, united with God in his essential nature.

This is the faith of the mystic. It springs out of his particular experience and his reflection on that experience. It implies a particular view of the nature of the universe and of man, and it seems to conflict with other conceptions of the nature of the universe and of man which are also the result of experience and reflection on it.

In the world, constituted as it is, men are faced not with one single truth but with several truths, not with one but with several pictures of reality. They are thus conscious of a *discord in the pact of things*, whereby to hold to one truth seems to be to deny another. One part of their experience draws them to one, another to another. It has been the eternal quest of mankind to find the one ultimate Truth, that final synthesis in which all partial truths are resolved. It may be that the mystic has glimpsed this synthesis.

—*condensed from* **Mysticism**, *by F.C. Happold*

ALDER, VERA STANLEY. **THE FIFTH DIMENSION. 3.50p.**
See the Meditation section.

■ *ALDER, VERA STANLEY.* **THE FINDING OF THE THIRD EYE. 187pp. Wei38/HPG, 3.50p.**
One of the best overall introductions to the field of the esoteric sciences. The author employs her rare gift of accurate summarizing and couples it with vision and an inclusive grasp of today's problems. A practical application of the Ageless Wisdom teachings to enrich our lives both individually and collectively is outlined by a survey of breathing, color, diet, astrology, numbers, and sound, plus essential information concerning the inner path.

ALDER, VERA STANLEY. **THE INITIATION OF THE WORLD. 251pp. Wei39/HPG, 3.75p.**
As a short, comprehensive sketch of that body of teachings called the

Ageless Wisdom or Perennial Philosophy, this book is easily one of the best. Includes excellent chapters on reincarnation, evolution, initiation, the Hierarchy, Shamballa, and the passage of the secret wisdom down the ages. Closes with a comparison of those teachings with the recent discoveries of modern science.

ALDER, VERA STANLEY. **THE SECRET OF THE ATOMIC AGE.** **191pp. Wei58/HPG, 3.50p.**
Ms. Alder surveys man's *emergence from the chrysalis of matter into the illimitable regions of his own being.* Her discussion revolves around the problem of releasing the atomic energy which comprises the essential human being. This process of liberation transforms man into an immortal, according to the author.

ALDER, VERA STANLEY. **WHEN HUMANITY COMES OF AGE.** **233pp. Wei56/HPG, 3.50p.**
The human race hovers on the verge of extraordinary possibilities and achievement. We are coming out of our adolescence and entering adult maturity. With this as her theme, the author outlines man's history by revealing the inner secrets which conditioned it. She gives us practical suggestions and information that can lead to a more fulfilled life while aiding in the dissolution of much that today holds the human family in bondage to an obsolete past.

ALDER, VERA STANLEY. **WISDOM IN PRACTICE. 177pp. Wei70/** **HPG, 3.00p.**
Ms. Alder feels that wisdom and love are the same thing; they are divine energies and states of consciousness available to all humans. If we focus on these energies, mankind will be led out of its current period of conflict. In this book, Ms. Alder suggests the way in which we can and should develop love and wisdom.

ANGEBERT, JEAN-MICHEL. **THE OCCULT AND THE THIRD REICH.** **Bibliography, index, 325pp. MGH74, 3.95p.**
Rather than merely another book on occultism and Hitler's Third Reich, this is an excellent survey of the ancient mystery tradition in western Europe. The volume begins with an account of the search for the Grail and a clear explanation of the meaning of the Grail and the neopagan crusade against it. This is followed by a review of the Aryan myth, a study of the development of *gnosis* (or supreme knowledge) in the Zoroastrian and Manichean schools, and an analysis of Christianity and *gnosis*. Another chapter reviews the centers of initiation and secret esoteric orders. A final section shows how all the previously discussed material led directly to the rise of Hitler. It begins with a full discussion of Nietzche and *superman*, followed by an interpretative analysis of Wagner. After this there is a review of the secret origins of Nazism and the Hitlerian cosmogony. Final sections relate some of the esoteric events during Hitler's hegemony. This is a fascinating and serious study, with extensive textual annotations. Jean-Michel Angebert is the joint signature of Michel Bertrand and Jean Angelini, two French scholars who have extensively researched the role of mystic cults in European history. Lewis Sumberg, the translator, holds his doctorate in French medieval history and literature from the University of Paris.

ANRIAS, DAVID. **THROUGH THE EYES OF THE MASTERS. 87pp.** **Wei32/RKP, 6.50c.**
An intriguing book that contains sketched portraits of ten *masters of the wisdom*, with a message from each of them concerning different aspects of modern life and the spiritual path.

ARGUELLES, JOSE. **THE TRANSFORMATIVE VISION. Notes, bibliography, index, 368pp. ShP75, 8.95p.**
The Transformative Vision combines history and myth, psychology and art, to provide a major new assessment of the role of creativity in human behavior. Man's *psyche*—the primary intuitive being—is seen in conflict with his *techne*—the side that creates order. When these two sides of man's nature are in harmony, the author explains, aesthetic activity flourishes. Dr. Arguelles traces the history of human expression from the Renaissance to the present, arguing that modern history is characterized by an increasing repression of man's pyschic self by the technical side of his nature.

ASHE, GEOFFREY. **THE ANCIENT WISDOM. Illustrations, notes, bibliography, index, 232pp. MGB77, 11.90c.**
This is an extremely interesting survey which lends evidence to *an*

Ancient Wisdom far back in history, or prehistory, scattering seeds of mental growth in early societies we already know. Ashe also discusses whether these ancient sources are still active, so that human knowledge or powers may presently be heightened by fresh infusions. He considers all the possible evidence in an organized fashion and makes an excellent case for his thesis that the ancient wisdom is, in fact, a reality.

BACHEMAN, WILLIAM. **THE STEINERBOOKS DICTIONARY OF** **THE PSYCHIC, MYSTIC AND OCCULT. Illustrations, 235+pp.** **Mul73, 2.25p.**
The newest of the metaphysical dictionaries, and also the most concise. The definitions are clear and the cross references ample.

BAKER, DOUGLAS. **ANTHROPOGENY. 8"x11½", Bak75, 14.00p.**
An esoteric history of man's origins, divided into sections on man, time, fossils, cosmogenesis, the coming of man, and the early root races. The format is the same as Baker's other big books and as usual there is an abundance of illustrations, both color and black and white, and some foldout charts.

BAKER, DOUGLAS. **ESOTERIC PSYCHOLOGY. Index, 8"x11½",** **168pp. Bak75, 14.00p.**
A detailed, albeit scattered, analysis of esoteric psychology based on the seven rays and divided into the following sections: *The Need for an Esoteric Psychology; The Seven Rays—Their Nature, Origin, and Function; Rays of Aspect, Rays of Attribute;* and *Ray Analysis.* The format is the same as Baker's other big books and many color illustrations are included.

BAKER, DOUGLAS. **THE JEWEL IN THE LOTUS. About 250pp.** **Bak74, 14.00p.**
Volume I of **The Seven Pillars of Ancient Wisdom**, a series of 8"x12" illustrated accounts. Dr. Baker's books are a bit hard to describe. The illustrations are generally in full color and deal with all aspects of esoteric psychology, including information on the *chakras,* rays, color, sound, and magnetism. The material on the seven rays is as extensive as any we have seen and the illustrations make the text more comprehensible. Baker seems to come out of the Theosophical-arcane tradition and he is a physician, so a knowledge of occult anatomy is incorporated into the text.

BAKER, DOUGLAS. **THE OPENING OF THE THIRD EYE. Many line drawings and a few color plates, 128pp. Bak nd, 3.95p.**
Baker begins with a survey of the references to the third eye

throughout history and *the nature of the material oui of which the third eye is fashioned*. This is followed by a discussion of *the equipment that fashions it*, and a detailed presentation of the techniques for opening the third eye.

BAKER, DOUGLAS. **THE POWERS LATENT IN MAN. 94pp. AqP77, 3.95p.**
Related essays on a variety of subjects including heart transplantation, etheric matter, gifted children, telepathy, the aura, hypnotism, psychokinesis, and magnetism.

BAKER, DOUGLAS. **THE PSYCHOLOGY OF DISCIPLESHIP. Many color plates and line drawings, index, 8"x11¼", 283pp. Bak76, 15.00p.**
A scattered, though somewhat interesting presentation divided into the following sections: *The Operation of Natural Law, The Psychology of the Super-Gifted, The Psychology of Stress, The Unconscious and the Superconscious,* and *Individuation and Personality Integration.*

BAKER, DOUGLAS. **THE SEVEN RAYS—KEY TO THE MYSTERIES. Illustrations, 126pp. AqP77, 5.00p.**
An esoteric analysis of what Baker calls *Seven Ray Psychology*. Baker includes information on the nature and qualities of the rays.

BAKER, DOUGLAS. **SHAKESPEARE: THE TRUE AUTHORSHIP, VOLUME I. Illustrations, 8"x11¼", 119pp. Bak76, 10.00p.**
An esoteric survey based on Dr. Baker's extensive personal research. Many quotations from the writings attributed to Shakespeare are interspersed.

BAKER, DOUGLAS. **THE SPIRITUAL DIARY. Many illustrations, 8"x11¼", 116pp. Bak77, 14.00p.**
Dr. Baker describes this book as not an autobiography *but a textbook for esoteric students seeking to express themselves more fully about subjective matters as a preliminary to their acting subjectively in the inner planes after their initiations.* He describes his first initiations and discusses the experiences and books which led to his awakening.

BAKER, DOUGLAS and CELIA HANSEN. **IN THE STEPS OF THE MASTER. Many color plates and line drawings, notes, bibliography, 8"x10½", 189pp. Bak77, 12.00p.**
A study of discipleship divided into the following sections: *The Jewelled Way, Exercises in Disidentification, The Disciplines of Discipleship, Disciplines of the Mind,* and *The Fifth State.*

BLAIR, LAWRENCE. **RHYTHMS OF VISION. Notes, index, 320pp. War76/PaL, 2.50p.**
This is an important book which falls outside a restricted category and encompasses many disciplines. Dr. Blair is basically discussing energies in all forms of life and the correspondences between man and the natural world. He analyzes many of the phenomena generally classified under the rubric of the *occult* and shows how similar the ancient teachings are to the discoveries of scientists over the ages. Perhaps the most illuminating section of the book is Blair's extensive discussion of number and form, much of which is based on the Anthroposophical teachings of Rudolf Steiner and his disciples. While Blair has done a fine job of researching and compiling a great deal of material, his presentation is scattered and not nearly as clearly written as we would like. Many beautiful illustrations are included.

William Blake

William Blake was born in London in 1757. He was a visionary from birth. Blake never attended school. He began drawing as a child, and apprenticed to an engraver at a young age. This training was to stand him in good stead. When no one else would publish his books, he made them himself. In fact, all of his books except one were what he called *Illuminated Printing*: hand drawn, engraved, and then colored by Blake and his wife. The art and the lettering form a whole and often the letters flow into and become part of the illustration—this combined with Blake's deliberately archaic language sometimes make his exact words unclear. But perhaps this, too, is part of the style.

Blake's basic purpose in all his work was the discovery and recording of new truths about the human soul. These truths are often couched in a language and style which even the most serious student is hard put to understand. So that the reader had to put aside all previous conceptions, Blake invented his own mythology, his own style. He was not content to be read mindlessly or easily enjoyed—he wanted to force his reader to think along with him. Blake heartily embraced the idea that the ancients concealed the divine mysteries under symbols: *What is Grand is necessarily obscure to Weak men. That which can be made Explicit to the Idiot is not worth my care.* Blake's thought was *to open the immortal Eyes of Man inwards, into the Worlds of Thought.* He believed a thought to be wholly true only the first time it is said. Blake's readers must dig, participate actively; thus Blake deliberately wrote unclearly, scattered clues throughout his writings. Even his simplest and clearest statements have vast implications behind them. He was so far ahead of his time that we are just beginning to understand and appreciate him. Many of his once strange theories are now commonplace to psychologists.

Blake is a monumental figure, whose unique combination of art and literature is his timeless contribution to our understanding of the human psyche.

BINDMAN, DAVID. **BLAKE AS AN ARTIST. Glossary, notes, indices, 7"x10", 256pp. Dut77/PhP, 18.95c.**
A full scale survey and evaluation of Blake's work by an art historian who specializes in Blake and in English art. Dr. Bindman traces Blake's ideas as they develop in his art, and explores in depth the effects —both personal and professional—of influential contemporaries. He encompasses all phases of Blake's work, including the illuminated books, and emphasizes the essential unity of Blake's apparently diverse activities as poet, artist, prophet, and craftsman. Over 200 illustrations accompany the text.

BINDMAN, DAVID. **THE COMPLETE GRAPHIC WORKS OF WILLIAM BLAKE. 9½"x13", Put78, 45.00c.**
This superbly produced volume encompasses Blake's entire artistic career, from his apprenticeship to an engraver to his last, uncompleted work. It is unfortunate that none of the 765 plates is in color, since color was such an intricate part of his work.

BLAKE, WILLIAM, il. **BOOK OF JOB. 4.95p.**
See the Bibles section.

BLAKE, WILLIAM. **THE MARRIAGE OF HEAVEN AND HELL. Oxf75, 7.95p.**
This is considered by many to be Blake's most important philosophical work. The twenty-seven plates have been very carefully reproduced in color and Sir Geoffrey Keynes, doyen of Blake scholars, has written the introduction and a commentary on each plate. Also included are enlargements in color of the interlinear drawings. This is the first time that this work has been made available in the form in which Blake intended it to be read. As Keynes says, *Through freely using satire and paradox, Blake gives in this book some of the most explicit statements of his mental attitudes. . . .Blake gave the qualities, Good and Evil, meanings opposite to their usual acceptation. . .Angels and Devils change places, Good is Evil, Heaven is Hell.*

BLAKE, WILLIAM. **SONGS OF INNOCENCE. 64pp. Dov71, 2.00p.**
A color facsimile edition which reproduces Blake's color plates. This edition is based on one of the more brightly colored versions of **Songs of Innocence**. A typographical reprint of the poems follows the plates.

BLAKE, WILLIAM. **SONGS OF INNOCENCE AND OF EXPERIENCE. 115pp. Oxf67, 8.95p.**
A reproduction, accurate and in the same size as the original, of the fifty-four color plates Blake made for these poems. The text of each poem is given in letterpress on the verso of each plate and a commentary by Sir Geoffrey Keynes, editor of Blake's **Complete Writings**, follows at the end of the book. Sir Geoffrey also wrote the introduction.

BLUNT, ANTHONY. **THE ART OF WILLIAM BLAKE. Bibliography, index, 7"x9¼", 122pp. H&R59, 5.95p.**
This is a general introduction to Blake's art, including summaries of his major doctrines and separate studies of each of his major works. A

series of over 100 plates follows the text. The reproductions are fairly good. The text is as simplified as possible and many quotations from the actual writings are included.

BOGEN, NANCY. **THE BOOK OF THEL. Index, 8¾"x11¼", 96pp. BUP71, 15.00c.**
The Book of Thel has long been considered one of the most readable and beautiful of Blake's prophetic works. It is also the first prophetic work that Blake issued as an illuminated manuscript. The text in this edition is based on a collation of the seventeen extant copies of **Thel** engraved and printed by Blake himself. And, facing this text, the delicately handcolored plates of the New York Public Library copy are reproduced with exceptional fidelity. An extensive introduction provides the first total view of **Thel**, a poem about which there has been wide critical disagreement. Previous interpretations are evaluated and a new one is proposed. A commentary accompanies each plate.

BRONOWSKI, JACOB, ed. **WILLIAM BLAKE. Introduction, index, 251pp. Vik58, 2.50p.**
This is a good selection of many of Blake's major poems and parts of his longer works as well as some of his letters. Both the early lyric poems and the later prophetic works are included.

BRONOWSKI, JACOB. **WILLIAM BLAKE AND THE AGE OF REVOLUTION. Sixteen plates, notes, index, 207pp. RKP65, 7.90p.**
This is a revised version of Dr. Bronowski's **William Blake: A Man Without a Mask**. The focus is on an interpretation of Blake's art and poetry in the context of the Revolutionary period during which he was working. Bronowski writes extremely well and he quotes extensively from Blake's writings.

DAMON, S. FOSTER. **A BLAKE DICTIONARY: THE IDEAS AND SYMBOLS OF WILLIAM BLAKE. 7¾"x11¼", 484pp. BUP65, 25.00c.**
Damon assembles, synthesizes, and interprets the clues to Blake's meaning that are scattered throughout the body of his entire work, both literary and graphic. Some of the articles are extensive and contain material not readily available elsewhere, such as essays on the cathedral cities, Jacob Boehme, Thomas Taylor, the *eyes of God*, and Job. Others, such as those on painting and poetry, are limited to what Blake himself said on the subject. Textual diagrams explain a number of complex Blakean concepts and there is also a selection of Blake's illustrations. The entries are alphabetically arranged. This volume is a must for anyone who seeks to understand the complexities in Blake's work.

DAMON, S. FOSTER. **BLAKE'S GRAVE. 11¾"x14¼", 42pp. BUP63, 10.00c.**
Blake's illustrations for Robert Blair's **The Grave**, arranged as Blake directed and with an introduction and individual commentaries by Damon. Reproduced actual size.

DAMON, S. FOSTER. **BLAKE'S JOB. Introduction, 8¾"x11¼", 66pp. BUP66, 10.00c.**
Blake's series of twenty-two **Illustrations of the Book of Job**, flawlessly reproduced in full scale from the original proofs in the Harvard College library and accompanied by Damon's individual commentaries.

DAMON, S. FOSTER. **WILLIAM BLAKE: HIS PHILOSOPHY AND SYMBOLS. Notes, index, 501pp. PSm24, 18.15c.**
An extremely comprehensive study which begins with a general analysis of Blake's symbolic and metaphysical thought and follows with a detailed analysis of each of Blake's major works.

■ DAVIS, MICHAEL. **WILLIAM BLAKE: A NEW KIND OF MAN. Bibliography, index, 250pp. UCa77/Ele, 6.95p.**
This is a definitive biographical study of Blake and an exposition of his developing creative vision. It is the best general study available and includes many quotations from his letters and poetry as well as sixty-nine plates, eleven in color.

ERDMAN, DAVID. **BLAKE: PROPHET AGAINST EMPIRE. Illustrations, notes, index. 604pp. PUP77, 5.95p.**
Blake was, above all, a poet of social vision and in this volume Professor Erdman, a Blakean scholar, provides a methodical study of Blake's thought and art in relation to the history of his own times. As Erdman says, *Blake thought of himself as a prophetic bard with a harp that could prostrate tyranny and overthrow armies—or, more simply, as an honest man uttering his opinion of public matters. And although he often veiled his opinion or elaborated it into a complex symbolic fabric having little to do with public matters on many of its levels of meaning, it has been possible to trace through nearly all of his work a more or less clearly discernible thread of historical reference.*

■ ERDMAN, DAVID, ed. **THE ILLUMINATED BLAKE. Introduction, notes, index, 10½"x8¼", 415pp. Dou74/Oxf, 7.95p.**
The wedding of poetry and painting in Blake's illuminated works was the result of his desire that readers be spectators as well. This volume presents for the first time an edition of the entire illuminated canon, each plate selected for clarity of detail from among Blake's several original etched and painted copies, and each accompanied by descriptive and interpretative commentary by Erdman. All but the largest plates are reproduced in their original sizes. The commentary is uniformly excellent and this volume is probably the best single one for those interested in his imagery. Unfortunately, all the plates are in black and white with the exception of the cover—although color reproductions would make the cost of the volume prohibitive.

ERDMAN, DAVID, ed. **THE NOTEBOOK OF WILLIAM BLAKE. Indices, 9¼"x10½", 227pp. Rdx77, 22.15c.**
A photographic, typographic facsimile of Blake's notebook, in a newly improved version. Blake inherited the notebook from his brother in 1787 and filled it over the years with emblems and portraits, large and small sketches, lyrics, epigrams, parts of essays, memoranda, instructions, and comments on his contemporaries. He also used it for trial designs and draft poems. Erdman contributes ample background information.

ERDMAN, DAVID, ed. **THE POETRY AND PROSE OF WILLIAM BLAKE. Notes, index, 6"x9¼", 932pp. Dou65, 7.95p.**
A completely annotated collection which has been hailed as one of the best available texts. Erdman has used modern aids such as infrared photography, microphotography, and a powerful magnifying glass to help decipher the manuscripts. He has also recovered many suppressed or altered passages, especially in **Jerusalem**. Eighty-two pages of critical commentary by Harold Bloom are included in this volume.

ERDMAN, DAVID, ed. **THE SELECTED POETRY OF BLAKE. Introduction, 332pp. NAL76, 2.50p.**
An excellent selection of Blake's poems, taken from all periods of his life and from both major and minor works. Erdman is one of the finest current Blake scholars.

ESSICK, ROBERT and JENIJOY LABELLE, eds. **NIGHT THOUGHTS OR, THE COMPLAINT AND THE CONSOLATION. 8½"x11", 124pp. Dov75, 4.00p.**
A reproduction in its entirety of the four sections of Edward Young's poem **Night Thoughts**, illustrated with forty-three designs by the young William Blake. Blake's images of angels, spirits, poets, sensuous women, life, death, reason, truth, and so on reveal his artistic vision in its early stages. The editors contribute extensive commentary on the plates.

FRYE, NORTHRUP. **FEARFUL SYMMETRY: A STUDY OF WILLIAM BLAKE. Illustrations, notes, index, 462+pp. PUP69, 3.95p.**
According as we agree or disagree with Mr. Frye's contention we shall decide finally on the supremacy of his book. In following the structure of Blake's total vision and relating it to the thought of his age he has triumphantly carried out a task which, given the giant shape of the material, cannot help being immense. His cadences, by sheer explanatory devotion, approach the sonorities of Blake's own.—**Times Literary Supplement**.

GODDARD, HAROLD. **BLAKE'S FOURFOLD VISION. PHP56, .85p.**
Transcription of a lecture on the title theme, originally delivered in 1935.

KAZIN, ALFRED, ed. **THE PORTABLE BLAKE. Index, 713pp. Vik68/Pen, 4.95p.**
This is an excellent selection of much of Blake's work including selections from **Poetical Sketches**; the complete texts of **Songs of Innocence** and **Songs of Experience**; verses and fragments of poems from the years 1793-1810; selections from his letters; **The Prophetic Books** (this is the longest section); selections on art, money, and the age; some of his last works, including **The Book of Job** (with its illustrations); and selections from Crabb Robinson's reminiscences. Kazin also provides a fifty-five page introduction.

KEAY, CAROLYN. **WILLIAM BLAKE: SELECTED ENGRAVINGS.** Some color plates, 8½"x11½", 84pp. SMP75, 9.95p.
A selection of engravings from almost all of Blake's major projects, including designs from early works like **Songs of Innocence**, the grandiose images of the prophetic books, and his brilliant illustrations to Dante and **The Book of Job**. In addition, there is a small number of engravings by contemporary craftsmen after original designs by Blake. A brief introduction summarizing Blake's personal, philosophical, and artistic principles is included.

KEYNES, GEOFFREY, ed. **BLAKE: COMPLETE WRITINGS. 944pp. Oxf74, 9.35p.**
This is the definitive edition of Blake's writings. The writings are printed in chronological sequence, with a section of Blake's letters at the end, followed by notes. This edition includes substantive corrections and additions, lines are numbered, and Blake's designs are reproduced where they are essential to an understanding of the text. Sir Geoffrey prepared the first edition of Blake, in three illustrated volumes, in 1925.

KLONSKY, MILTON. **WILLIAM BLAKE: THE SEER AND HIS VISIONS. Index, 9"x12", 142pp. Crn77/OPL, 6.95p.**
Klonsky begins this book with an essay on Blake's life and visions. The essay is adequate, but nothing special. The heart of the book, however, is special. It consists of over eighty-five plates, thirty-two in color, presented together with the poetry and biblical passages that inspired them.

Plate from the **Book of Urizen**: Urizen struggling in the waters of materialism.

MITCHELL, W.J.T. **BLAKE'S COMPOSITE ART: A STUDY OF THE ILLUMINATED POETRY. Notes, index, 301pp. PUP78, 22.15c.**
Poem and picture unite in Blake's illuminated books, yet a unified interpretation of them has been hindered by barriers between the disciplines of art history and literary criticism. Here Professor Mitchell makes an important advance by examining the illuminated books as coherent works of art, treating pictorial style and iconography, poetic form and theme, as they contribute to the larger organic whole. He shows that Blake's originality stems from his ability to assimilate and transform a wide variety of traditional techniques. 112 illustrations are appended to the book.

OSTRIKER, ALICIA, ed. **WILLIAM BLAKE: THE COMPLETE POEMS. Glossary, indices, 1,071pp. Vik77, 7.95p.**
This new edition of Blake's poems is very completely annotated. It is always good to look at more than one version of a Blake poem; since many are handwritten, the interpretation of which words he actually used varies from editor to editor.

PALEY, MORTON. **ENERGY AND THE IMAGINATION. Notes, index, 282pp. Oxf70, 15.15c.**
This book proposes to study the thought of William Blake as it developed from the works of his early maturity through his great culminating statement, **Jerusalem***. I have tried to see Blake in his time, and as having a deliberately chosen relationship to certain intellectual and literary traditions of the past. The principal aim is not the tracing of specific sources, but the provision of a background against which the unique figure of Blake stands more clearly outlined. . . . I have focused on two concepts, Energy and the Imagination, and have tried to show how these were defined in the several phases of Blake's thought.—from the preface.*

PALEY, MORTON. **WILLIAM BLAKE. Glossary, notes, index, 8¾"x 11¼", 192pp. Dut78, 19.95c.**
This introduction to Blake as both poet and artist includes 161 illustrations, sixteen in color. Paley, one of the world's foremost Blake specialists, is coeditor of **Blake**, an illustrated quarterly. The text is as clear as we can expect any writing on Blake's complex *oeuvre* to be.

PLOWMAN, MAX, ed. **BLAKE'S POEMS AND PROPHECIES. Introduction, illustrations, notes, bibliography, 475pp. Dut27/Den, 2.95p.**
Includes the full texts of the following works: **Songs of Innocence** and **Songs of Experience**, **The Book of Thel**, **The Marriage of Heaven and Hell**, **Visions of the Daughters of Albion**, **Milton**, **Jerusalem**, and **The Gates of Paradise**. This volume also contains most of the works that remain in manuscript, including **The Last Judgment**, **The Everlasting Gospel**, and nearly forty other poems. The **Poetical Sketches** are also presented.

THE POETRY OF WILLIAM BLAKE (A RECORDING). 9.95.
Here on this record, we can but hint at the vast expanses over which the extraordinary spirit of William Blake ranged. We have tried to represent as much of his various poetic writings, from the first **Poetical Sketches***, which appeared in 1738, the* **Songs of Innocence***, from 1789, and the contrasting* **Songs of Experience***, 1794; and on the second side, the later works. A high quality 33 1/3 rpm record, read by four people. Short, descriptive notes are included.*

THE POETRY OF BLAKE READ BY SIR RALPH RICHARDSON (A RECORDING). 7.55.
A 33 1/3 rpm record of readings from **Songs of Innocence**, **Songs of Experience**, and other poems. Liner notes are included.

RAINE, KATHLEEN. **BLAKE AND ANTIQUITY. Ninety-one plates, bibliography, 176pp. PUP77, 5.95p.**
Transcription of a series of lectures drawn from Ms. Raine's masterwork, **Blake and Tradition**, and containing the essential theme of the larger work—Blake's indebtedness to the Neoplatonic and other sources within the canon of the Western esoteric tradition.

RAINE, KATHLEEN. **BLAKE AND TRADITION. 194 illustrations, eleven in color, notes, bibliography, index, 838pp. PUP68/RKP, 40.00c/set.**
In this erudite study, Ms. Raine takes as her starting point the traditional language of symbolic discourse, which may be traced in unbroken continuity from the Orphic theology, through Neoplatonic, Gnostic, and Hermetic writings and the iconography of Christian art. Assuming that Blake was a prophet of that wisdom, Ms. Raine sets out to discover what sources were available to him. This two volume boxed set is based on her Mellon lectures.

■ *RAINE, KATHLEEN.* **WILLIAM BLAKE. Index, 216pp. Oxf70/RKP, 6.95p.**
This is without question the finest popularly priced edition of Blake's art available. Ms. Raine is a well known Blake scholar and her fine text is supported by 156 plates, many in color. The reproduction is excellent.

SABRI-TABRIZI, G.R. **THE HEAVEN AND HELL OF WILLIAM BLAKE. Notes, bibliography, index, 361pp. L&W73, 11.40c.**
This book, published by a Marxist press, contains the most thorough

study yet attempted of Blake's entire system of social ideas. Sabri-Tabrizi believes Blake to have been *a social critic who opposed class society and its philosophical systems.* His text demonstrates *the consistent materialism of Blake in his opposition against Church and State and all forms of exploitation.* The author focuses on key ideas in **The Marriage of Heaven and Hell** and he thoroughly examines Blake's relationship with Swedenborg in order to prove his thesis that Blake's use of Swedenborgian images was designed to expose the latter's class bias and reactionary outlook.

TODD, RUTHVEN. **WILLIAM BLAKE THE ARTIST. Over seventy-five plates, index, 158pp. Dut71, 2.25p.**
This is a detailed study of Blake's technical achievements as an artist.

──────────END OF WILLIAM BLAKE SUBSECTION──────────

BRENNAN, J.H. **ASTRAL DOORWAYS. Many illustrations, 115pp. Wei71/TPL, 6.50c.**
A clear, absorbing presentation of concentration and visualization exercises which must be perfected before the reader attempts an astral journey. These are followed by the four main *doorways* through which one arrives on the astral plane, namely the five *tattva* symbols, the tarot, the Qabala, and the **I Ching**. Brennan devotes a chapter to the use of hypnosis, either alone, or in conjunction with one of the other *doorways*. Ways of heightening the astral experience are also discussed.

BRENNAN, J.H. **AN OCCULT HISTORY OF THE WORLD. Bibliography, index, 320pp. Fut76, 2.40p.**
Brennan surveys the broad sweep of human evolution from an esoteric standpoint and compares the scientific explanations with the myths and mysteries put forward by those who have studied what he terms *the occult.* A well organized survey which draws on a wide variety of sources.

BRUNTON, PAUL. **HERMIT IN THE HIMALAYAS. 188pp. Wei37/HPG, 3.50p.**
Dr. Brunton was a British journalist who developed an interest in comparative religion, mysticism, and philosophy. He traveled extensively in the Orient, living among yogis, mystics, and holy men. His accounts are among the most enlightening and readable available. This volume is a blend of narrative, travel, and profound spiritual experience. Illuminating hints on yoga and the mystical practices of the East are conveyed to the reader against the backdrop of scenic descriptions and personal thoughts.

BRUNTON, PAUL. **THE HIDDEN TEACHINGS BEYOND YOGA. 365pp. Wei41/HPG, 4.95p.**
I have to put up with the fact that this new book is so different in character and tone from those which have preceded it that the general reader is going to have a difficult time should he plunge into it with the lightheartedness with which he may have plunged into the others. Its pages made hard writing for me and must make harder reading for others. It needs sustained and concentrated attention, demands keen thinking, and propounds tough problems....I deliberately emphasized the insufficiencies of ordinary mysticism, the defects of ordinary yogis and the mistakes commonly made by meditators.

BRUNTON, PAUL. **THE INNER REALITY. 244pp. Wei39/HPG, 3.50p.**
This work has been selected and expanded from addresses privately given before small audiences on four continents. Absolute clearness of exposition was sought rather than elaborate treatment of theme. Topics include: *What is God?; A Sane Religion; Practical Help in Yoga; Psycho-Spiritual Self Analysis; The Scripture of the Yogis; Errors of the Spiritual Seeker; The Gospel According to John;* and *The Mystery of Jesus.*

BRUNTON, PAUL. **A MESSAGE FROM ARUNACHALA. 144pp. Wei36/HPG, 3.00p.**
Arunachala hill in southern India is a holy place and has a long tradition as such. It is where Ramana Maharshi, Brunton's teacher, spent his adult life. In this volume Dr. Brunton applies Maharshi's teaching in a Western context, emphasizing the doctrine, *know thyself.*

BRUNTON, PAUL. **THE QUEST OF THE OVERSELF. 3.50p.**
See the Meditation section.

BRUNTON, PAUL. **A SEARCH IN SECRET EGYPT. 3.50p.**
See the Ancient Egypt section.

BRUNTON, PAUL. **A SEARCH IN SECRET INDIA. 4.50p.**
See the Indian Philosophy section.

BRUNTON, PAUL. **THE SECRET PATH. 128pp. Dut35/HPG, 2.25p.**
Brunton's first book, a practical spiritual handbook. *He presents a system of practice and meditation that should open new vistas of livingness for those who would glory in the consciousness of the immortal spiritual essence or Over-Self. Each of us who practices this secret inner way can become a disseminator of true light, can change himself and thus become fit to change others.*—Alice Bailey.

BRUNTON, PAUL. **THE SPIRITUAL CRISIS OF MAN. 224pp. Wei52/HPG, 3.50p.**
A detailed look at contemporary man's plight, with suggestions for transcending the materialism and intellectualism of our day.

BRUNTON, PAUL. **THE WISDOM OF THE OVERSELF. 276pp. Wei43/HPG, 3.75p.**
A broad discussion of the spiritual value of sleep and dreams, intuition, and meditation. Brunton also touches on the universality of the mind and the infinity of time and space.

BUCKE, RICHARD. **COSMIC CONSCIOUSNESS. Notes, index, Dut01, 2.95p.**
A classic study in the evolution of the human mind. In reviewing the mental and spiritual activity of the human race, Dr. Bucke discovers that at intervals certain individuals have appeared who are gifted with the power of transcendental realization or illumination. He devotes a chapter to the life and work of each of these individuals and provides excellent interpretative material.

CASE, PAUL. **THE GREAT SEAL OF THE UNITED STATES: ITS HISTORY, SYMBOLISM, AND MESSAGE FOR THE NEW AGE. 34pp. BuA35, 2.00p.**
A highly esoteric interpretation of Qabalistic and Hermetic teachings.

CAVENDISH, RICHARD, ed. **THE ENCYCLOPEDIA OF THE UNEXPLAINED. 8¾"x11¼", 304pp. MGH74/RKP, 17.95c.**
This is a unique reference book on all aspects of the esoteric sciences and parapsychology. The articles are written by experts in the area and are often in depth accounts giving background that is not readily available anywhere else. They are alphabetically arranged, cross referenced, and well illustrated. An index of people and book titles cites those too obscure to be covered by the extensive cross referencing and a bibliography lists over 500 titles. At first glance this appears to be another flashy book on the occult—but this impression is wrong. This is a useful addition to all serious collections of books in the area.

CHENEY, SHELDON. **MEN WHO HAVE WALKED WITH GOD. Illustrations, annotated bibliography, index. 402pp. Del45, 3.45p.**
A sequence of fully developed biographical and interpretative studies of individual mystics from Lao Tzu and the Buddha through Plato and Plotinus and Jacob Boehme to Brother Lawrence and William Blake. An excellent work for the general reader.

CROW, W.B. **THE ARCANA OF SYMBOLISM. 96pp. Wei70/TPL, 5.00c.**
Includes symbology from classical mythology, the **Old** and **New Testaments**, the Qabala, the tarot, the **Qur'an**, the elements, the planets, and the zodiac.

DAVIDSON, GUSTAV. **A DICTIONARY OF ANGELS, INCLUDING THE FALLEN ANGELS. Appendix, bibliography, 7½"x10", 386pp. McM67, 4.95p.**
A work of remarkable scholarship, the fruit of some fifteen years of research in Talmudic, Gnostic, Qabalistic, apocalyptic, patristic, and legendary texts, among works of art and a range of literature. *Delightful reading and a unique reference work.*—Isaac Bashevis Singer. The sources for each entry are given and the bibliography is twenty-four pages long (in double columns). Profusely illustrated.

DAVIS, ROY EUGENE. **DARSHAN—THE VISION OF LIGHT. 204pp. CSA71, 3.95p.**
This is the revealing account of Davis' spiritual life. Many incidents and events of Yogananda's life are reported as well as the intimate revelations of the author's deep inner life.

DAVIS, ROY EUGENE. **THIS IS REALITY. 3.95p.**
See the Patanjali subsection of Indian Philosophy.

DAY, HARVEY. **OCCULT ILLUSTRATED DICTIONARY. 156pp. Oxf76/K&W, 9.25c.**
This is a very complete dictionary, with clearly written entries. Unfortunately the book is not in paperback and is fairly expensive for its size. The volume is totally cross referenced and the entries are very up to date.

DILLARD, ANNIE. **HOLY THE FIRM. 76pp. H&R77, 6.50c.**
In 1975 Ms. Dillard took up residence on an island in Puget Sound, in a wooden room furnished with *one enormous window, one cat, one spider and one person.* For the next two years she asked herself questions about time, reality, sacrifice, death, and the will of God. In this volume she speculates on the answers to her questions. She uses as few words as possible and each has countless intuitive meanings. This is a deep book which invites endless reflection.

DILLARD, ANNIE. **PILGRIM AT TINKER CREEK. 279pp. Ban74, 1.95p.**
This is a mystical journey into the world of nature which has been immensely popular, has won a Pulitzer Prize, and has been compared by many to Thoreau's **Walden.** *One day I was walking along Tinker Creek thinking of nothing at all and I saw the tree with the lights in it. I saw the backyard cedar where the mourning doves roost charged and transfigured, each cell buzzing with flame. I stood on the grass with the lights in it, grass that was wholly fire, utterly focused and utterly dreamed. It was less like seeing than like being for the first time seen, knocked breathless by a powerful glance. . . . I had been my whole life a bell, and never knew it until at that moment I was lifted and struck.*

DRURY, NEVILLE. **THE PATH OF THE CHAMELEON. 162pp. Spe73, 8.75c.**
A profusely illustrated volume which traces the sacred esoteric tradition underlying all the great religions as well as the Western magical tradition. It explains the ways in which man seeks, in a very real sense, to become a god, to be spiritually reborn, and describes the journey of the soul.

DURCKHEIM, KARLFRIED. **THE WAY OF TRANSFORMATION: DAILY LIFE AS SPIRITUAL EXERCISE. 104pp. A&U71, 8.95c/5.95p.**
A wonderful jewel whose aim is to show that daily life, especially its routine, can be used for growth and can itself be lived as a spiritual exercise: *Every moment is the best of all opportunities,* runs an old Buddhist saying.

EMERSON, RALPH WALDO. **EMERSON'S ESSAYS. Introduction, 465pp. Cro51/Den, 3.95p.**
This collection contains the complete first and second series of the **Essays** and includes his most important and sensitive writing. The essays show Emerson to be both a vigorous thinker and a profound mystic with a strong love of retirement from life, contemplation of the sublime and mystic, and self reliance.

EMERSON, RALPH WALDO. **THE PORTABLE EMERSON. 664pp. Vik46, 4.95p.**
Presents a good cross section of his work, including essays from his three books (**Programs, The Ways of Life,** and **People**), and selections from his poems, journals, and letters. The volume is edited by Mark van Doren, who supplies notes throughout and an introduction.

EMERSON, RALPH WALDO. **THE SELECTED WRITINGS OF R.W. EMERSON. 955pp. RaH50, 6.95c.**
This is the most comprehensive anthology of Emerson's work. The volume includes his complete essays and representative selections from his poems, addresses, sermons, biographical sketches, and miscellaneous works. Edited by Brooks Atkinson.

EPICTETUS. **THE ENCHIRIDIAN. Introduction, bibliography, 39pp. BoM48, 1.90p.**
Epictetus was born in Greece in the first century AD. He spent a considerable part of his life in Rome, first as a slave, and then as a teacher of the Stoic philosophy of which he is perhaps the best exponent. This is a brief summary of the basic ideas of Stoic philosophy and an introduction to the techniques required to transform Stoic

philosophy into a way of life. It has been studied and widely quoted by philosophers down the ages.

EPICTETUS. **EPICTETUS. 178pp. PhL74, 6.00c.**
This is an attempt to present Epictetus' **Discourses** in a form easily accessible to the modern reader. John Bonforte has taken them, as translated by Higginson, and reframed them into a series of dialogues in contemporary English, on contemporary themes.

FAUSSET, HUGH. **THE LOST DIMENSION. 80pp. Wat66, 3.35p.**
A profound interpretation of the spiritual quest and the search for God within. Fausset has written a number of books on ancient Indian philosophy and his viewpoint is apparent in this volume.

FERGUSON, JOHN. **AN ILLUSTRATED ENCYCLOPEDIA OF MYSTICISM AND THE MYSTERY RELIGIONS. Illustrations, bibliography, 228pp. Sea77, 14.95c.**
A well researched, alphabetically organized handbook, which should be of great use to those studying comparative religion and mysticism. Most of the major individuals, schools, and concepts are adequately covered.

Findhorn

There have been stories about Findhorn where people talk to plants with amazing results: stories of vegetable and flower gardens animated by angelic forms; forty pound cabbage, eight foot delphiniums, and roses blooming in the snow; people heard talking to plants and angels in a casual and informal way; a land where nothing is impossible and legends are reborn. What I found seems larger than a forty pound cabbage. Fairies and elves seem tame stuff compared to what one experiences there. Findhorn may be a manifestation of a light and power which could transform our planet within a lifetime, or it could be an illusory bubble on the troubled waters of the world civilization that will burst leaving no traces.—Paul Hawken. Since its founding fifteen years ago, the Findhorn Community, situated in Scotland on a sandy peninsula jutting into the North Sea, has been visited and written about by many. The site developed from a trailer park into a garden flourishing with over 128 varieties of vegetables, fruits, and herbs. It is one of the most enduring and certainly the most famous new age community. Findhorn also has conducted a wide educational program which has had outreach into many other communities. *One radiant energy pervades and gives rise to all life. While it may speak to us through plants, nature spirits or the human beings with whom we share life on this planet, all are reflections of the deeper reality behind and within them. Myth has become reality in the Findhorn garden, not to present us with a new form of spiritualism, but to offer us a new vision of life, a vision of unity. Essentially, the devas and nature spirits are aspects of our own selves, guiding us toward our true identity, the divine reality within. The story of the garden is the celebration of this divine life in its myriad forms. May the joy we experience in participating in this celebration deepen our commitment to revealing the total beauty of ourselves and of all life around us.*—**Findhorn Garden Book.**

CADDY, EILEEN. **FOOTPRINTS ON THE PATH. 150pp. FiP76, 3.50p.**
The inspirational writings in this book had their origin as Eileen Caddy . . . listened to the voice of the God within. Many years ago that voice had come to her at a time of great uncertainty and unhappiness, and through the years it has been her constant guide and stimulus and hope . . . . The messages cannot be classified, for they are living truths which are as complex and varied as life itself . . . . Read each sentence as being spoken to you, and applying to you. See where it does apply, and what steps you can then take in the light of what it has shown.—from the introduction.

CADDY, EILEEN. **THE SPIRIT OF FINDHORN. 139pp. H&R76/Fow, 6.95c.**
Eileen shares some of the uplifting messages that have inspired and guided the Findhorn Community over the years and the faith that translated those visions into gardens, buildings, and a community. A biographical study by one of the members of the community is also included. The messages themselves are in the form of poetry and are illustrated with line drawings.

DIVINA. **THE LIVING SILENCE. 104pp. FiP71, 4.50p.**
Divina is also known as Dorothy MacLean and she is best known as a resident of the Findhorn Community. *The contents of this book are messages I received by the still small voice within, generally during the quiet of the early morning. They come with an awareness of meaning and feeling which I then put into words. They have been edited slightly and arranged in their present style.* The messages are presented in the form of short poems.

DIVINA. **WISDOMS. 60pp. FiP72, 2.50p.**
These messages were received from the inner divinity at various quiet moments in 1971. They have been left in their original order and form, in the knowledge that they can be as helpful to others as they were to me. The messages are in prose.

EDWARDS, ALEXIS. **GUIDELINES. 92pp. FiP74, 3.25p.**
A collection of messages, poetry, and songs received in daily meditation, and emerging from and expressing his experiences at that time. Illustrated with abstract photographs and line drawings.

ELIXIR. **GOD SPOKE TO ME. 119pp. FiP73, 4.50p.**
The Findhorn Community was founded and developed in obedience to the voice of God within, through daily messages received by Elixir in times of silent meditation. This volume presents selections from the guidance she received in the period between 1969-71.

FINDHORN COMMUNITY. **THE FINDHORN GARDEN BOOK. Oversize, 180pp. H&R75/Tur, 10.00c/5.95p.**
This is the only account of Findhorn which has been written and photographed by the community itself. This book tells of the transformation of a tiny group into the strongest new age community anywhere, and the philosophy which sustains the community. Over 150 beautiful photographs illustrate the text.

HAWKEN, PAUL. **THE MAGIC OF FINDHORN. Illustrations, 216pp. Ban75/Fon, 10.00c/2.25p.**
This is a fascinating account of Findhorn, written by the man who first brought American public attention to the community. As Hawken says, *I can appreciate that much of what you will read will seem implausible and incredible. I do not ask you to believe this account, for it is only written through one man's eyes. Every aspect of creation has as many realities as perceivers.* Hawken lived in Findhorn for a number of months and he writes about every aspect of the community's life. We recommend this volume to all who are interested in new age communities in general and Findhorn in particular.

SPANGLER, DAVID. **FESTIVALS IN THE NEW AGE. 92pp. FiP75, 3.25p.**
Festivals have played an important part in the life of people in all ages. In this book Spangler explores the meaning of the four seasonal festivals which have been celebrated since ancient times: Christmas, Spring Equinox, Midsummer, and Michaelmas. He feels that celebrating these festivals can be a means of psychologically and spiritually unifying man and his environment and the purpose of this book, as he sees it, is to help individuals participate in these holy days. The book itself is beautifully produced, with multicolored pages.

SPANGLER, DAVID. **LAWS OF MANIFESTATION. 92pp. FiP75, 2.50p.**
By applying the laws of manifestation (the principles of attracting to oneself, through love, whatever materials, energy, or help are needed to promote wholeness or further growth), Findhorn has expanded from one small caravan on a sand dune into a large community. This book was written by Spangler at a time when the community was seeking a greater understanding of the nature of manifestation and it is a lucid statement of the principles involved.

SPANGLER, DAVID. **REVELATION, BIRTH OF A NEW AGE. 256pp. Rai76, 5.95p.**
Spangler has been active in new age groups for most of his adult life. For three years he was a codirector of Findhorn, in charge of the community's educational projects. This is his best known book, outlining his thoughts on the emergence of a new consciousness within humanity, which will be the foundation for a new age and a new planetary culture. Spangler received the information through revelation, and some quotations from his source are included. He stresses the power present in each person to transform his world and bring the new age into being.

──────────**END OF FINDHORN SUBSECTION**──────────

FORTUNE, DION. **APPLIED MAGIC. 110pp. Wei62/APC, 5.95c.**
A selection of previously unpublished writings in which the practical application of magical and occult techniques is stressed. Topics include the group mind, the psychology of ritual, the circuit of force, three kinds of reality, nonhumans, a magical body, and the occult field today. There is also an excellent, long, esoteric glossary.

FORTUNE, DION. **ASPECTS OF OCCULTISM. 87pp. Wei62/APC, 3.95p.**
A collection of nine essays, each illuminating a different aspect of occultism. Ms. Fortune includes information on the aura and the astral plane, the sacred centers, Christianity and reincarnation, and the Godhead. There is also a bit of meditation instruction.

FORTUNE, DION. **THE COSMIC DOCTRINE. 157pp. Wei66/APC, 6.00c.**
The many facets of life on Earth as well as on higher planes are touched upon with some consideration of the great laws and principles which govern evolution and all forms of planetary expression. An informative, well written outline of the fundamental precepts of the esoteric sciences and the living body of knowledge which is the fountain of human philosophy, inspiration, and wisdom.

FORTUNE, DION. **THE ESOTERIC ORDERS AND THEIR WORKS. Offset, stapled, 8½"x11", 68pp. HeR nd, 2.50p.**
In all ages and among all races there has existed a tradition concerning certain esoteric schools or fraternities, wherein a secret wisdom unknown to the generality of mankind might be learnt, and to which admission was obtained by means of an initiation in which tests and ritual played their part.... The training given in occult schools is designed to produce the adept, a human being who, by intensive training, has raised himself or herself beyond the average development of humanity.... Not much can be told concerning this training, and not many are suitable for it, but enough has been said to give food for thought.—from the introduction.

FORTUNE, DION. **THE ESOTERIC PHILOSOPHY OF LOVE AND MARRIAGE. 96pp. Wei67/APC, 3.75p.**
Ms. Fortune believes that the higher aspects of sexual energy are essential to the development of the perfect man, and she warns of the dangers inherent in the ignorant handling of these unseen forces. She also explains at length the esoteric doctrines relating to sex.

FORTUNE, DION. **THE MYSTICAL QABALAH. 11.85c.**
See the Jewish Mysticism section.

FORTUNE, DION. **PRACTICAL OCCULTISM IN DAILY LIFE. 66pp. Wei35/APC, 3.50p.**
Helpful suggestions for applying principles of occult science. Emphasis

is laid upon the importance of attitude, character, keen judgment, and concentration. Advice is given on remembering past incarnations, working out karma, and the uses and limitations of divination.

FORTUNE, DION. **PSYCHIC SELF DEFENSE. 210pp. Wei30/APC, 3.95p.**
Complete firsthand descriptions of psychic attacks, and practical instruction in methods of diagnosis, detection, and defense. A very detailed account of every aspect, and the only book available on the subject.

FORTUNE, DION. **SANE OCCULTISM. 192pp. Wei67/APC, 3.95p.**
Deals with the many pitfalls of occultism, describing both the dangers and the safeguards. Topics include the left hand path, astrology, past lives, prophecy and divination, group karma, Eastern methods and Western bodies, and secrecy in occult fraternities.

FORTUNE, DION. **THROUGH THE GATES OF DEATH. 94pp. Wei68, 3.75p.**
A survey of ancient esoteric teachings which show that death is not something to be feared.

FORTUNE, DION. **THE TRAINING AND WORK OF AN INITIATE. 126pp. Wei30/APC, 3.95p.**
The Western esoteric systems derive from three main sources: Qabalistic, Egyptian, and Greek. From these roots an unbroken tradition of initiation has been handed down from adept to neophyte. The complete system is discussed here. This volume is a complementary work to **The Esoteric Orders and Their Work.**

FURSE, MARGARET. **MYSTICISM: WINDOW ON A WORLD VIEW. Notes, indices, 220pp. Abi77, 5.95p.**
Dr. Furse sees mysticism more as a philosophy or world view than as an experience. She begins this volume with a sketch of the Eastern mystical tradition. The bulk of the book is devoted to a thorough examination of Christian mysticism, beginning with an analysis of its sources and stressing modern interpretations, in particular those of Evelyn Underhill, William Inge, and Friedrich von Hugel. A chapter is also devoted to a comparative study of Meister Eckhart and St. Teresa of Avila.

GAYNOR, FRANK, ed. **DICTIONARY OF MYSTICISM. 209pp. Wdw53, 5.20p.**
Over 2,200 short definitions, covering a wide variety of disciplines including astrology, Eastern philosophy, alchemy, and mythology.

GRAY, WILLIAM. **THE ROLLRIGHT RITUAL. 166pp. Hel75, 8.50c.**
The famous Stone Circle of the "Rollrights" in Oxfordshire. . .is well known to folklorists. . . .This account. . .is the outcome of many years of personal contact with the Stones themselves on "Inner" levels of investigation. . . .In a normal and natural way, the Stones spoke through their own symbology of what they stood for in the past, and how this infallibly indicates the future we could expect if we are willing to follow the Pattern they laid out so long ago. Since the enquirer in this case was a working magical ritualist, the Stones revealed their ancient ritual structures translated into timeless terms of truth with the most startling spiritual significance and an intense impact of authenticity.

GUENON, RENE. **CRISIS OF THE MODERN WORLD. 131pp. Luz42, 5.30p.**
Guenon believes that the crisis of our times is the degradation of knowledge and perversion of the intellect. In this book he outlines why he believes that this is so and makes a number of suggestions as to what we can do to ameliorate conditions.

GUENON, RENE. **THE REIGN OF QUANTITY AND THE SIGNS OF THE TIMES. Notes, index, 363pp. Vik53, 2.65p.**
This is an attack on the scientific orientation of the modern world. Guenon looks back to an ancient wisdom, once common to both East and West, but now almost entirely lost. Contemporary civilization itself—with its industrial societies and illusory notions of progress—is his target. In particular, he shows that today's sciences and social sciences are dominated by a quantitative approach, that they neglect the idea of quality. To this reign of quantity he opposes the sacred metaphysics of the ancients, which he sees as rooted in divine truth.

GUENON, RENE. **SYMBOLISM OF THE CROSS. Notes, 148pp. Luz58, 10.50c.**
The cross, which is the particular theme of this study, is a universal traditional symbol which is far from being confined to Christianity, central though it may be to that religion. This is a scholarly study which reviews the symbolism of the cross in all the world's religions.

HAICH, ELISABETH. **INITIATION. 6.00p.**
See the Ancient Egypt section.

HAICH, ELISABETH. **SEXUAL ENERGY AND YOGA. 158pp. ASI72/ A&U, 5.00p.**
An analysis of sexual energy and sexual activity, including suggestions on ways to transmute this energy into a higher union with the Godhead. Many specific practices are outlined—all of which are designed to help the practitioner reach a mystical state. The sexual instinct is traced throughout history and mythology. Ms. Haich is often a bit heavy handed.

HALL, MANLY P. **THE ADEPTS IN THE EASTERN ESOTERIC TRADITION, PART I: THE LIGHT OF THE VEDAS. 111pp. PRS52, 3.50p.**
Manly P. Hall has devoted his life to the study of comparative religion and philosophy, and he has been writing extensively since he was in his teens. In his books he emphasizes the practical aspects of philosophy as they apply to daily living. He restates the ancient wisdom teachings in a clear, readable fashion. This series deals with those individuals seeking to ascend, through conscious spiritual development, up to the hierarchy. Hall feels that the adept tradition came to the world through the migrations of the Aryan people, hence it is fitting that he begin this series with the **Vedas.**

HALL, MANLY P. **THE ADEPTS IN THE EASTERN ESOTERIC TRADITION, PART II: THE ARHATS OF BUDDHISM. 112pp. PRS53, 3.00p.**

HALL, MANLY P. **THE ADEPTS IN THE EASTERN ESOTERIC TRADITION, PART III: THE SAGES OF CHINA. 113pp. PRS57, 3.50p.**

HALL, MANLY P. **THE ADEPTS IN THE EASTERN ESOTERIC TRADITION, PART IV: THE MYSTICS OF ISLAM. 107pp. PRS75, 3.50p.**

HALL, MANLY P. **ADVENTURES IN UNDERSTANDING. 218pp. PRS69, 18.95c.**
The verbatim notes of eight lectures dealing with the practical problems of modern living.

HALL, MANLY P. **AMERICA'S ASSIGNMENT WITH DESTINY. 119pp. PRS51, 5.75c.**
The story of the unfolding of the esoteric tradition in the Western Hemisphere. The work begins with the rites and mysteries of the Mayas and Aztecs; parallels are drawn between the miracles of the North American Indian priests and those of the fakirs of India; an account is given of the Incas and their possible contact with Asia; and finally, the settlement in the U.S. is discussed at great length. A much more interesting account than Hall's **Secret Destiny of America.**

HALL, MANLY P. **CODEX ROSAE CRUSIS. 20.00c.**
See the Rosicrucianism section.

HALL, MANLY P. **COLLECTED WRITINGS, VOLUME II. Illustrations, 316pp. PRS59, 6.50c.**
This volume, unfolding a basic theme, presents eight sages and seekers of the modern (sixteenth to twentieth century) world: Nostradamus, Francis Bacon, Johann Comenius, Jacob Boehme, Comte de St. Germain, William Blake, Thomas Taylor, and Gandhi.

HALL, MANLY P. **COLLECTED WRITINGS, VOLUME III. 303pp. PRS62, 6.50c.**
Includes the following essays and poems: Atlantis, An Interpretation; The Sacred Magic of the Qabala; The Riddle of the Rosicrucians; Universal Reformation of Trajano Bocalini; Zodiackos: The Circle of Holy Animals; and An Essay on the Fundamental Principles of Operative Occultism.

HALL, MANLY P. **FIRST PRINCIPLES OF PHILOSOPHY. 199pp. PRS42, 6.75c.**
An informal study of philosophy, an attempt to rescue the wisdom of the ancients from scholasticism's ponderosity, covering metaphysics, logic, ethics, psychology, aesthetics, and theurgy.

HALL, MANLY P. **GREAT BOOKS ON RELIGION AND ESOTERIC PHILOSOPHY.** 85pp. PRS66, 2.00.
Most of the books in this listing are long out of print. However, Mr. Hall's description of the topics and his introductory material on building a library are often fascinating.

HALL, MANLY P. **THE GURU.** 142pp. PRS58, 4.50c.
A story of the holy or mystic life in India, as told by a disciple reminiscing upon many years of association with his Hindu teacher.

HALL, MANLY P. **HEALING: THE DIVINE ART.** 341pp. PRS71, 9.90c.
A fascinating account which traces the history of healing from the earliest times and discusses the major figures in the field. Hall analyzes various types of healing and relates the whole to esoteric psychology, physiology and anatomy, including material on the etheric bodies of man and nature, the human will, the factor of consciousness, and the energies underlying the physical processes of the body. There is a special section on the pineal gland and on the effects of mental attitudes on health. The book concludes with a group of case histories, showing how the individual causes many of his health problems, and discussing techniques for self help.

HALL, MANLY P. **THE INNER LIVES OF MINERALS, PLANTS AND ANIMALS.** 31pp. PRS73, 1.75p.
Transcription of a lecture on the title theme.

HALL, MANLY P. **INVISIBLE RECORDS OF THOUGHT AND ACTION.** 62pp. PRS69, 1.75p.
Two essays, bound in one volume. The title selection discusses the theory and practice of psychometry and the other essay is entitled, *The Use and Abuse of the Natural Psychic Powers within Us and Around Us.*

HALL, MANLY P. **IS EACH INDIVIDUAL BORN WITH A PURPOSE?** 32pp. PRS60, 1.75p.
Reprinted from lecture notes.

HALL, MANLY P. **LECTURES ON ANCIENT PHILOSOPHY.** 513pp. PRS29, 10.75c.
Although complete in itself, this volume is designed to complement **Secret Teachings**. It includes two series of lectures on symbolism and the ancient mysteries and is an effort to clarify the subject of classical pagan metaphysics.

HALL, MANLY P. **LOST KEYS OF FREEMASONRY.** 3.75c.
See the Freemasonry section.

494

HALL, MANLY P. **MAN: GRAND SYMBOL OF THE MYSTERIES.** Extensive index, 7¾"x10½", 254pp. PRS72, 12.50c.
A new edition of Hall's fascinating essays on occult anatomy, profusely illustrated with woodcuts and line drawings. Includes chapters on *The Macrocosm and the Microcosm; The Story of the Cell; The Brain and the Release of the Soul; The Heart; The Seat of Life; The Spinal Column and the World Tree (The Tree of Life); Kundalini; The Pineal Gland; Sight*, and much else. Hall relates his material to the ancient mystery teachings and as usual incorporates a great deal of fascinating philosophy.

HALL, MANLY P. **THE MEDICINE OF THE SUN AND MOON.** 32pp. PRS72, 1.75p.
A well written philosophical treatise on the principles behind the Chinese concept of healing.

HALL, MANLY P. **MYSTERY OF THE HOLY SPIRIT.** 32pp. PRS74, 1.75p.
A treatise on the Holy Spirit in Western and Eastern religious philosophies.

HALL, MANLY P. **THE MYSTICAL CHRIST.** 8.00c.
See the Christianity section.

HALL, MANLY P. **THE OCCULT ANATOMY OF MAN.** 36pp. PRS57, 1.75p.

HALL, MANLY P. **OLD TESTAMENT WISDOM.** 10.00c.
See the Bibles section.

HALL, MANLY P. **PATHWAYS OF PHILOSOPHY.** 253pp. PRS47, 6.50c.
An enlightening journey tracing the passage of Platonic wisdom from the days of the Grecian Golden Era through the centuries until modern time. The influence of this philosophy is shown in the lives and words of such great men as Diogenes, Paracelsus, Francis Bacon, Boehme, and Emerson. Volume II of Hall's survey of *idealistic philosophy.*

HALL, MANLY P. **THE PHOENIX.** Ninety-one magnificent illustrations, 9"x14", 175pp. PRS75, 13.90c.
An illustrated review of occultism and philosophy, covering the following topics: *Blavatsky; Meditation; Concentration and Retrospection; Comte de St. Germain; Cycle of Transmigration; The Great Pyramid;* and *The Ladder of Souls (mystery of the descent of the spiritual man into the body).*

HALL, MANLY P. **QUESTIONS ANSWERED ON THE PROBLEM OF LIFE.** 269pp. PRS37, 7.90c.
In the course of many years of lecturing and teaching, a great number of questions have come to me for solution and explanation. I have classified these questions into general groups for greater convenience in answering. In the present work, the questions have been so worded as to cover as many angles as possible of the subject treated. The answers are derived from the philosophies and religions of many nations and ages. The teachings of most of the world's great spiritual and intellectual leaders are incorporated into the commentary material.

HALL, MANLY P. **SECRET DESTINY OF AMERICA.** 200pp. PRS42, 7.95c.
Mr. Hall has gathered fragments of little known history which indicates that the seeds of democracy were planted here 1,000 years before the beginning of the Christian era. He traces these ideas through the birth of the American state.

■ *HALL, MANLY P.* **SECRET TEACHINGS OF ALL AGES.** Profusely illustrated, 9"x14", 254pp. PRS62, 27.50c/9.95c.
An encyclopedic outline of masonic, Hermetic, Qabalistic, and Rosicrucian symbolical philosophy—a comprehensive survey and interpretation of the esoteric teachings concealed within the rituals, allegories, and mysteries of all ages. This is Hall's major work and we recommend this fascinating compilation highly. The illustrations alone are worth the price of the book and the text can be studied for years. Every aspect of the occult sciences is covered in depth and even in the areas where we have the most knowledge, Hall's presentation is invariably enlightening.

HALL, MANLY P. **SECRET TEACHINGS OF ALL AGES, GOLDEN ANNIVERSARY EDITION.** 12"x18½", 254pp. PRS77, 95.00c.
A recent republication of the original edition of **Secret Teachings** which includes fifty-four color plates and over 200 black and white ones. It is an absolutely magnificent volume.

HALL, MANLY P. **SELF-UNFOLDMENT BY DISCIPLINES OF RE-ALIZATION.** 221pp. PRS42, 8.00c.
The theme of this book is that ilumination is as natural as life itself. Its purpose is to develop awareness and thoughtfulness so that it becomes part of you. Hall outlines in detail various practical exercises and discusses the theory behind them.

HALL, MANLY P. **SPIRITUAL CENTERS IN MAN.** 53pp. PRS29, 1.75p.
This pamphlet, originally entitled **An Essay on the Fundamental Principles of Operative Occultism,** takes off from the question asked in its first paragraph: _What must I do to unfold the divine powers latent within myself?_ To answer this question, Hall defines and discusses the fundamental principles upon which mystery schools down through the ages have been established. He takes a step-by-step approach to spiritual development and suggests a number of possible directions. The book contains black and white reproductions of the three prints published by Mr. Hall.

HALL, MANLY P. **SURVEY COURSE IN PHILOSOPHY.** PRS60, 4.00p.
This is a twelve lesson course based upon the introduction to **Secret Teachings,** with a series of questions following each lesson. Bound in a looseleaf notebook. Each lesson is about seven pages long.

HALL, MANLY P. **SYMBOLISM OF LIGHT AND COLOR.** 32pp. PRS76, 1.75p.
A philosophical survey which includes an analysis of historical and religious references to light and color and a summary of Hall's ideas on the subject.

HALL, MANLY P. **TWELVE WORLD TEACHERS.** 254pp. PRS37, 7.50c.
A summary of the lives and teachings of Akhenaten, Hermes, Orpheus, Zoroaster, the Buddha, Confucius, Lao Tzu, Plato, Jesus, Muhammad, Padhmasambhava, and Quetzalcoatl. An excellent introductory survey.

HALL, MANLY P. **WORDS TO THE WISE.** 169pp. PRS63, 7.50c.
A collection of essays based on the author's extensive experience as a teacher which explain metaphysics and give practical instruction to the neophyte.

HAMMARSKJOLD, DAG. **MARKINGS.** 222pp. RaH64, 7.50c.
A remarkable record of the spiritual life of Hammarskjold, a noted public official and former Secretary General of the United Nations. He described the manuscript as a _sort of white book concerning my negotiations with myself and with God._

HANSON, VIRGINIA, ed. **THE SILENT ENCOUNTER.** 240pp. TPH74, 2.75p.
This is a collection of essays on the mystical experience by writers from varying backgrounds and experiences. Some of the essays were originally published as part of a special set of issues of **The American Theosophist.** The coverage is quite comprehensive and most of the selections are good.

■ _HAPPOLD, F.C._ **MYSTICISM.** 407pp. Pen63, 3.95p.
An excellent work in two parts: a study, designed as an introduction to the anthology and covering all of the topics in the anthology; and an excellent anthology covering all aspects of Eastern thought, the Christian mystics (including many of the lesser known ones), and the Sufis. Each selection is accompanied by introductory paragraphs on the text. Highly recommended.

HEARD, GERALD. **THE FIVE AGES OF MAN: THE PSYCHOLOGY OF HUMAN HISTORY.** Glossary, bibliography, 393pp. Crn63, 8.50c.
An encyclopedic survey of the historical development of man which utilizes present psychological insights as well as historical records of previous civilizations and geological transformations. Heard's thesis is that man's consciousness has so far evolved in five stages. In each stage man was beset by a specific crisis or ordeal under which he either broke down or devised a psychophysical method of initiation and so was able to grow into the next stage of consciousness. Each of the stages is discussed at length. This is a hard book to categorize. It integrates traditional psychology with Jungian insights and mythological and esoteric information. There is also some sociology and biology thrown in!

HEARD, GERALD. **TRAINING FOR THE LIFE OF THE SPIRIT.** Introduction, 171pp. Mul75, 2.95p.
Heard was a twentieth century mystic who devoted his life to writing, teaching, and the contemplative life. He was closely associated with Aldous Huxley; the two eventually settled in southern California where they became involved with Christopher Isherwood, Swami Prabhavananda, and the Vedanta Society. This is a collection of short essays on contemplation, prayer, and religion in daily life. Heard writes clearly and expresses many deep concepts in exceedingly simple language.

HELINE, CORINNE. **MAGIC GARDENS.** 122pp. NAP44, 4.95c.
Every flower bears a starry imprint, declared Paracelsus. From the Zodiac came the veritable secrets of God. The Star Angels are transmitters, and flowers become symbols of their communicators. The closer our communion with the angels, the deeper will be our understanding of the mysteries of the plant kingdom and the greater our realization of the spiritual ministry of the world of flowers.

HELINE, CORINNE. **THE TWELVE LABORS OF HERCULES.** 69pp. NAP44, 1.95p.
The twelve labors set forth in perfect sequence the twelve steps in the passage of the sun through the zodiac, and represent at the same time the way of attainment for the aspirant. This study also correlates the labors of Hercules with the life of the biblical Samson.

HELINE, THEODORE. **AMERICA'S DESTINY.** 50pp. NAP37, 1.00p.
According to the prophetic promise of the Great Seal it is the destiny of the U.S. to bring forth a New Order of the Ages. This booklet discusses the symbolism of the seal and the esoteric background of this country.

HELINE, THEODORE. **THE ARCHETYPE UNVEILED.** 24pp. NAP65, 1.00p.
An illustrated study of the sound patterns formed by the creative word.

HESSE, HERMANN. **DEMIAN.** 147pp. Ban25/PnB, 1.75p.
This is a moving portrait of a young man's growing awareness of his own identity and of his powers. It is one of Hesse's most popular works and is the one that is usually read first.

HESSE, HERMANN. **THE GLASS BEAD GAME.** 570pp. Pen72, 3.00p.
A translation of Hesse's final work (also known as **Magister Ludi**). It is a difficult philosophical work. _The Glass Bead Game is an act of mental synthesis through which the spiritual values of all ages are perceived as simultaneously present and vitally alive._ The game itself is the focal point and _raison d'etre_ of an entire province, a utopian society devoted wholly and exclusively to affairs of the mind and imagination.

HESSE, HERMANN. **THE JOURNEY TO THE EAST.** 118pp. FSG56/PnB, 1.45p.
Hesse's classical narrative of his hero's modern day quest. Many have acclaimed this the most accessible of Hesse's mature ponderings.

HESSE, HERMANN. **NARCISSUS AND GOLDMUND.** 312pp. FSG30/Pen, 3.95p.
A beautifully written tale of a young boy's spiritual development and his relationship with another young man who becomes his mentor and guide.

HESSE, HERMANN. **STEPPENWOLF.** 252pp. HRW29/Pen, 3.95p/1.95p.
It seems to me that of all my books **Steppenwolf** _is the one that was more often and more violently misunderstood than any other . . . . The Treatise and all those spots in the book dealing with matters of the spirit, of the arts and the immortal men oppose the Steppenwolf's world of suffering with a positive, serene, superpersonal and timeless world of faith. This book. . .tells of griefs and needs; still it is not a book of a man despairing, but of a man believing._—Hermann Hesse.

HESSE, HERMANN. **THE WORLD OF HERMANN HESSE.** Ban nd, 9.15p.
A boxed set of **Magister Ludi, Steppenwolf, Narcissus and Goldmund, Siddhartha,** and **Demian.**

HIERONIMUS, ROBERT. THE TWO GREAT SEALS OF AMERICA. Bibliography, 50pp. Svt73, 2.50p.
This is a detailed history and interpretation, including many illustrations and quotations from source material.

HOFFSTEIN, ROBERT. THE ENGLISH ALPHABET: AN INQUIRY INTO ITS MYSTICAL CONSTRUCTION. 117pp. Kae75, 7.95c.
Hoffstein believes that the English alphabet is a code which, when unraveled, tells the story of mankind. In this book he analyzes hundreds of words in light of his esoteric concepts and groups his analyses according to a sampling of simple letter combinations.

HOWARD, MICHAEL. THE RUNES AND OTHER MAGICAL ALPHABETS. 96pp. Wei78, 8.85c.
In Norse society the runes were consulted before any undertaking, and the rune master was looked upon as a direct link between the god Odin and his mortal followers. Runic spells were also used to curse enemies, bring good fortune, and as love charms. This book discusses writing, the origin of runes, the rune masters, casting the runes, runic survivals, medieval magical alphabets, and the Enochian script.

HUXLEY, FRANCIS. THE WAY OF THE SACRED. Index, 7¾"x10½" (hardcover edition), 320pp. Del74/Ald, 7.95c/2.25p.
This is an exploration of the rites, symbols, beliefs, and taboos which have come to be considered sacred. Through the sacred, man tries to achieve communion with the divine, and also with his own physical nature. He sets apart, physically or ritually, things that overwhelm him. In particular, Huxley explores the symbolism of the sacred, because it is only in symbolic terms that the sacred can be approached. He presents 307 illustrations, thirty-two in full color, which show some of the objects that men have singled out in their search for the sacred and some of the ways men and women have represented in art the world that is apart, sacred, and divine. The text is geared toward the general reader; however, some knowledge of mythology would be helpful in understanding the references.

ISRAEL, MARTIN. AN APPROACH TO MYSTICISM. Bibliography, 49pp. ChF74, 1.10p.
This is a clearly written, general survey of mysticism in both the East and the West, with emphasis on the Christian tradition. The reader can get as good a feeling of the mystical experience from this volume as from any other that we know of.

ISRAEL, MARTIN. AN APPROACH TO SPIRITUALITY. 49pp. ChF71, 1.10p.
Another collection of lectures, this time more oriented toward the Christian experience. The following are the main topics: *Spirituality in the World; Revelation Through Relationships; The Vision of God; The Place of Discipline; Prayer and Meditation; The Dark Night of the Soul;* and *The Spiritual Life.*

ISRAEL, MARTIN. THE POWER OF THE SPIRIT IN EVERYDAY LIVING. 32pp. ChF nd, .70p.
A transcription of three Christian-oriented lectures on relationship and prayer.

JAMES, WILLIAM. THE VARIETIES OF RELIGIOUS EXPERIENCE. 416pp. McM61/Fon, 1.95p.
A classic of philosophical, religious, and scientific thought: *The problem I have set myself is a hard one:...to make the hearer or reader believe, what I myself invincibly do believe, that, although all the special manifestations of religion may have been absurd (I mean its creeds and theories), yet the life of it as a whole is mankind's most important function.*

JASPERS, KARL. SPINOZA. Bibliography, 120pp. HBJ66, 2.75p.
A detailed study of Spinoza's (1632-77) life and work, taken from Jaspers' **The Great Philosophers**, topically arranged and including many quotations from Spinoza's own writings. The book is well organized—often too well organized, in the Germanic tradition, so that the text does not flow. A tremendous amount of material is crammed into these pages.

KNIGHT, GARETH. EXPERIENCE OF THE INNER WORLDS. Illustrations, bibliography, 254pp. Wei75, 11.00c.
The material in this volume was designed for a course in Christian Qabalistic magic. The first half of the book presents a general review of the Western mystery tradition drawing on biblical sources, the traditions of the ancient Near East, Arthurian and Grail legends, and alchemy. The second half presents practical teachings on various aspects of Western occultism, including material derived from the Qabala and the work of Agrippa, Dee, Bruno, Campanella, the Rosicrucians, Kircher, Fludd, and others. There is also a personal record of the occult work conducted by Knight over the last ten years. Practical exercises are given at the end of each chapter. Knight's work is very well thought of. He integrates his material well and his practical teaching is quite easy to follow.

KNIGHT, GARETH. THE OCCULT. 103pp. K&A75, 6.50c.
An introduction to the occult in two parts: a historical survey of the occult and an occult glossary with recommended reading.

KNIGHT, GARETH. OCCULT EXERCISES AND PRACTICES. Bibliography, 68pp. Wei nd/APC, 1.25p.
A beginner's guide to practical occultism, giving basic exercises in developing clairvoyance, clairaudience, astral projection, attracting opportunities, recovering memories of past incarnations, projecting etheric force, breathing, relaxation, meditation, magical visualization, spiritual exercises, and prayer.

KUESHANA, EKLAL. THE ULTIMATE FRONTIER. 224pp. Stl63, 2.25p.
A very popular account of the ancient brotherhoods and their profound, worldwide influence during the past 6,000 years. The why, whence and whither of human existence are explored and many mysteries are elucidated in layman's terms.

LABASTILLE, ANNE. WOODSWOMAN. Photographs, 284pp. Dut76, 3.95p.
A poetic description of a young woman's life in the log cabin she built herself in the Adirondack wilderness. Ms. LaBastille sensitively describes the changing seasons and her environment and allows the reader to sense what it feels like to be alone with nature.

LANDAU, ROM. GOD IS MY ADVENTURE. Index, 255pp. A&U35, 1.95p.
Landau was a spiritual seeker who was very serious about his quest. He got to know the individuals he discusses in this volume quite well in many instances and recounts many firsthand conversations. This is a fascinating account which gives personal glimpses into many spiritual leaders. Landau seems to be the closest and most sympathetic toward Rudolf Steiner and Krishnamurti and the most critical of Gurdjieff. Other individuals discussed at length are Count Keyserling, Stefan George, Meher Baba, George Jeffreys, Dr. Frank Buchman, and P.D. Ouspensky. This book was a best seller in the 1930s.

LEUBA, JAMES. THE PSYCHOLOGY OF RELIGIOUS MYSTICISM. Notes, index, 348pp. RKP29, 16.50c.
An academic study in which Professor Leuba seeks to demonstrate that, although it is difficult to find a satisfactory answer to all problems raised by mystical life, they are nevertheless explicable *in the same sense, to the same extent and by the same general principles as any other fact of consciousness.* He begins with an examination of mystical experiences in early societies and then concentrates on the Christian mystical tradition.

LONG, MAX FREEDOM. GROWING INTO LIGHT. 177pp. DeV55, 5.00c.
In the first part of the twentieth century Long lived in Hawaii and studied the ancient psychological practices of the Hawaiian Kahuna priests. At that time there were only a few priests left and the tradition was dying off. Long gained their trust and managed to understand and

codify their complex system. He spent the remainder of his life writing about Kahuna psychology and studying parallels with other ancient cultures. This book contains readings, exercises, and affirmations to help an individual put the principles of the Kahunas to work in his own life.

LONG, MAX FREEDOM. **THE HUNA CODE IN RELIGIONS. 367pp. DeV65, 8.00c.**
This book is the fruit of Long's years of comparative study. He traces principles similar to the Kahunas back 4,000 years to ancient Egypt, then identifies them in the **Old Testament** and later in the **Gospels;** next he shows how they were carried to India and China and from there to Polynesia where the code language was preserved for almost twenty centuries. Long also reports on a number of amazing things which he discovered by applying the code to a variety of secret teachings. This volume includes an extensive dictionary of the Hawaiian language.

LONG, MAX FREEDOM. **INTRODUCTION TO HUNA. 79pp. EsP45, 2.50p.**
This recently reissued volume was the first work which Long published on his researches. It summarizes the material that he presented more fully in his later works and is especially thorough in its discussion of the Huna system.

LONG, MAX FREEDOM. **PSYCHOMETRIC ANALYSIS. 118pp. DeV 59, 5.00c.**
Discusses psychometric analysis of human character and mentality, especially as revealed through an instrument called the biometer.

LONG, MAX FREEDOM. **THE SECRET SCIENCE AT WORK. 343pp. DeV53, 7.50c.**
Describes the work of the Huna Research Associates in proving the validity of the Huna principles and the practical use of them today, as well as much new information on allied lines.

■ LONG, MAX FREEDOM. **THE SECRET SCIENCE BEHIND MIRACLES. 408pp. DeV48, 7.00c.**
This is the basic book on Huna. In it, Long tells about the authentic miracles performed by the Kahunas of Hawaii: instant healing, changing the future for the better, control of winds and weather. From

a long study of the language used by the Kahunas, Long discovered in the roots of significant words, clues to the secret knowledge held by the miracle workers. They understood and used a system of psychology undreamed of by our modern psychologists. They knew and used three kinds of vital mental forces, including that which is responsible for all hypnosuggestive phenomena. They generated these forces with ease, working with three levels of consciousness. To manipulate these forces they made use of three kinds of invisible substances of which we know almost nothing, although one form of it has often been seen partly solidified in seance rooms as *ectoplasm*. Their knowledge explains many of the mysteries of psychic phenomena. A fascinating account, highly recommended.

LONG, MAX FREEDOM. **SELF-SUGGESTION AND THE NEW HUNA THEORY OF MESMERISM AND HYPNOSIS. 117pp. DeV58, 5.00c.**
A comprehensive discussion of the practical applications of Huna, based on the research conducted by Long's Huna Research Associates.

M. **THE LORD GOD OF TRUTH WITHIN. 390pp. YPS41, 12.00c.**
Before entering the portal of his Great Initiation, our Brother was preparing this Supplement to **The Dayspring of Youth**. *His notes form the text. Scan well this quartz, for Mystic Gold may nugget in a flash. Such is the Cryptic Elemental Code.*—from the introduction.

MAGRE, MAURICE. **THE RETURN OF THE MAGI. 224pp. SBL31, 1.75p.**
This is a discussion of the life and work of the initiates and initiategroups: Apollonius of Tyana, the unknown master of the Albigenses, Christian Rosenkreutz and the Rosicrucians, the Knights Templars, Nicholas Flamel, St. Germain, and Madame Blavatsky and the Theosophists. Magre writes well and he seems to have done a thorough research job.

MENDL, R.W.S. **REVELATION IN SHAKESPEARE. Index, 223pp. C&B64, 4.40p.**
This is an authoritative study of the supernatural, spiritual, and religious elements in Shakespeare's works. Hitherto these aspects have been only partially discussed, usually in relation to specific plays. Here Mendl presents a comprehensive analysis which quotes amply from the plays.

NASR, SEYYED HOSSEIN. **MAN AND NATURE. Index, 153pp. A&U68, 4.00p.**
The thesis presented in this book is simply this: that although science is legitimate in itself, the role and function of science and its application have become illegitimate and even dangerous because of the lack of a higher form and knowledge into which science could be integrated and the destruction of the sacred and spiritual value of nature. To remedy this situation the metaphysical knowledge pertaining to nature must be revived and the sacred quality of nature given back to it once again. Nasr is best known for his writings on Sufism.

OPHIEL. **THE ART AND PRACTICE OF THE OCCULT. 170pp. Wei67, 3.50p.**
Ophiel calls this his basic book on the foundations of occult knowledge. Magical rituals and meditations are revealed and the reader is taught how to become a Gnostic, or *one who knows*. With this deeper knowledge comes power over nature.

OTTO, RUDOLF. **MYSTICISM: EAST AND WEST. Notes, index, 282pp. MCM32, 2.95p.**
A scholarly comparison of the classic types of Occidental mysticism, as interpreted by Meister Eckhart, with the Oriental system as interpreted by Sankara. Otto examines conformities in the doctrines of salvation, ways of knowledge, soul, creation, and religion, as well as the many differences—notably those concerned with ethical conduct.

PAUWELS, LOUIS and JACQUES BERGIER. **MORNING OF THE MAGICIANS. 416pp. Avo60/May, 1.75p.**
A probe into many aspects of our recent history and our complex civilization with esoteric explanations for such diverse events as Hitler's leap to power and atomic energy development. It touches a vast range of scientific, social, historical, and occult topics and yet retains a lightness that other books on such subjects lack.

PERCIVAL, HAROLD. **THINKING AND DESTINY. 1,014pp. WdF46, 7.95p.**
The book explains the purpose of life. That purpose is not merely to find

happiness . . . neither is it to save one's soul. The real purpose of life . . . is this: that each one of us will be progressively conscious in ever higher degrees in being conscious . . . of nature, and in and through and beyond nature. By nature is meant all that one can ever be made conscious of through the senses.—from the introduction.

PHILLIPS, DOROTHY, ELIZABETH HOWES and LUCILLE NIXON, eds. **THE CHOICE IS ALWAYS OURS. Bibliography, index, 492pp. TPH75, 1.95p.**
This is a very wide ranging anthology of short pieces about the spiritual path from religious and psychological sources. The selections are arranged into eleven major topical groups covering virtually every topic that we can think of. An incredibly large number of different writers are included. All in all this is a good anthology, with some pieces of course better than others, but with a generally high standard. There is something for everyone here.

PLYM, DON and THEA. **A MACRO-PHILOSOPHY FOR THE AQUARIAN AGE. 158pp. MDC70, 2.00p.**
It is the purpose of this book to present the larger macrocosmic view or philosophy of life in which the real causes and, thus, the real solutions of all human problems can be seen and considered. . . . An old way of life . . . is dying: But a new age is being born. . . . This book is designed to aid man in his adaptations to the new age by presenting the foundation for world peace and unity—macro philosophy.

PONCE, CHARLES. **THE GAME OF WIZARDS. Illustrations, 240pp. Vik75, 2.50p.**
Ponce sets out to show that the esoteric sciences reflect the symbolic structures of the subconscious mind. In his discussion he reviews alchemy, the **I Ching**, the Qabala, the tarot, and astrology at some length, though in a scattered way. Many of the classic writers are quoted and their main theories analyzed. A separate chapter is devoted to each of the esoteric sciences. The book is an adequate overview of the subject, but not something that we can get really excited about.

PREM, SRI KRISHNA. **INITIATION INTO YOGA. 128pp. TPH76, 3.25p.**
Sri Krishna Prem was an Englishman who went to India in the early 1920s to teach at Lucknow University and remained there for the rest of his life. He became immersed in Indian culture and was an excellent vehicle for transmitting the insights of the East into language that Westerners could understand. This is a disparate collection of essays written just before and during the first years of World War II. All the essays are applicable to the problems of human life. His close friend, Sri Madhava Ashish, contributes a long introductory sketch about the author and his life work.

RAVENSCROFT, TREVOR. **THE SPEAR OF DESTINY. Illustrations, 362pp. Crg73, 1.60p.**
A fascinating account of the occult aspects of Hitler's rise to power, based largely on reports of Dr. Walter Stein, who had intimate knowledge of Hitler's occult activities and became a confidential advisor to Churchill after his escape from Germany. The text ranges beyond the direct history into discussion of the Grail legend, Rudolf Steiner, **The Secret Doctrine**, the origin of the Aryan race in Atlantis, and much else. None of the material is documented.

REGARDIE, ISRAEL. **THE MIDDLE PILLAR. 162pp. LIP70, 3.95p.**
Subtitled, *A Co-Relation of the Principles of Analytical Psychology and the Elementary Techniques of Magic.*

REGARDIE, ISRAEL. **THE ROMANCE OF METAPHYSICS. 288pp. NAP46, 7.95c.**
Regardie wrote this book in 1942 in an attempt to establish certain points of relationship between the various metaphysical philosophies and modern psychology. He presents a comprehensive discussion of Christian Science, New Thought (I.N.T.A. and Neville), Unity, and more modern approaches to enlightenment.

REGARDIE, ISRAEL. **TWELVE STEPS TO SPIRITUAL ENLIGHTENMENT. Bibliography, 90pp. Wei75, 3.50p.**
A step-by-step guide to spiritual development, beginning with physical exercises (body awareness, relaxation, and rhythmic breathing) and continuing through a series of techniques designed to unite the student with the Godhead. This is an extremely esoteric discussion; Regardie was a student of Aleister Crowley.

Nicholas Roerich

Roerich (1874-1947) was one of the greatest mystics of the twentieth century. He was Russian and for many years he taught in Russia. After the revolution he came to the United States and established a number of institutions. His aim was to bring humanity together through education and culture. He was a poet and painted many mystical works (some of which are on exhibition today at the Nicholas Roerich Museum in New York City). He traveled throughout the world and spent a great deal of time in the East and his philosophy is heavily Eastern-oriented. He called his system *Agni Yoga*. Agni Yoga is the yoga of fire. Fire symbolizes life, knowledge, feeling, and action. In terms of consciousness, this is the yoga which deals with intuition, immediate inner perception, direct insight, instant understanding. *All preceding Yogas, given from the highest sources, took as their basis, a prescribed quality of life. And now, at the advent of the age of Maitreya is needed a Yoga comprising the entire life; all embracing, evading nought. . . . You may suggest to me a name for the Yoga of life, but the most precise name will be Agni Yoga. It is precisely the element of fire which gives to this Yoga of self sacrifice its name. While in other Yogas the dangers were diminished through exercise, in the Yoga of fire the perils are increased. Because fire as an all-binding element manifests itself everywhere and thereby admits realization of the subtlest energies. . . . This is the most unifying Yoga, exacting its obligation to construct the entire life in conformation to a discipline, externally imperceptible. If this irreplaceable discipline will not be regarded as chains but will turn into the joy of responsibility, we can consider the first Gates open. When the cooperation with the far-off worlds is realized, then will the second Gates unbar. And when the foundation of evolution will be understood, the bolts will fall from the third Gates. And finally, when the supremacy of the densified astral body is realized, then the locks of the fourth Gates unbolt. Paralleled with this ascent the central fires of knowledge are kindled and amidst the lightning of subtlest energies, unfold this straight knowledge.*—**Agni Yoga**.

AGNI YOGA SOCIETY. **AGNI YOGA. 403pp. AgY54, 10.75c.**

AGNI YOGA SOCIETY. **AUM: SIGNS OF AGNI YOGA. AgY36, 10.75c.**

AGNI YOGA SOCIETY. **BROTHERHOOD. 318pp. AgY37, 10.75c. 10.75c.**

AGNI YOGA SOCIETY. **COMMUNITY. AgY26, 12.60c.**

AGNI YOGA SOCIETY. **FIERY WORLD, VOLUME I. 424pp. AgY48, 10.75c.**

AGNI YOGA SOCIETY. **FIERY WORLD, VOLUME III. 356pp. AgY48, 10.75c.**

AGNI YOGA SOCIETY. **HEART. AgY32, 10.75c.**

AGNI YOGA SOCIETY. **INFINITY, VOLUME I. AgY30, 12.60c.**

AGNI YOGA SOCIETY. **INFINITY, VOLUME II. AgY30, 10.75c.**

AGNI YOGA SOCIETY. **LEAVES OF MORYA'S GARDEN, VOLUME I: THE CALL. 159pp. AgY24, 10.75c.**

AGNI YOGA SOCIETY. **LEAVES OF MORYA'S GARDEN: VOLUME II: ILLUMINATION. 250pp. AgY25, 10.75c.**

PAELIAN, GARABED. **NICHOLAS ROERICH. Bibliography, 110pp. AEG74, 6.00c.**
Dr. Paelian wrote his doctoral thesis on the teachings of Roerich, and this material forms the basis of this book. The book discusses the sources of Roerich's inspiration, his life work, and his contribution to modern education. Extensive quotations from Roerich's writings accompany the text.

ROERICH, NICHOLAS. **FLAME IN CHALICE. 106pp. AgY29, 6.75c.**
A collection of poems: *In the poetry of Roerich . . . there is a fullness and expansion*

of consciousness, a vibration of light and color, a sense of prophecy and ongoing, of search, discovery and fulfillment that is as much part of his singing word as of the colors and contours of his brush.—from the introduction.

ROERICH, NICHOLAS. HIERARCHY. Index, 280pp. AgY33, 10.75p.
Hierarchy is not coercion, it is the law of the Universe. It is not a threat, but the call of the heart and a fiery admonition directing toward the General Good. Thus, let us cognize the Hierarchy of Light.

ROERICH, NICHOLAS. THE INVINCIBLE. 395pp. AgY74, 10.75c.
A wide ranging collection of essays discussing the ancient teachings, fairy tales, general philosophy, and much else.

ROERICH, NICHOLAS. MOTHER OF THE WORLD. AgY56, 3.40p.

ROERICH, NICHOLAS. WOMAN. 69pp. AgY58, 3.40p.

————**END OF NICHOLAS ROERICH SUBSECTION**————

ROLFE, MONA. MAN—PHYSICAL AND SPIRITUAL. 285pp. Spe77, 5.60c.
A collection of articles on esoteric subjects originally delivered as lectures over a period of twenty-five years. The teachings deal with a wide variety of subjects including the nature of man and his purpose on Earth, the healing of the body and soul, the linking up of the distant past with the future to give a vision of the future, pre-Christian Celtic teachings, Druidic science, and musical sound and the development of the soul.

ROOF, SIMONS. ABOUT THE AQUARIAN AGE. 8½"x11", 61pp. MSE71, 3.95p.
The books by Simons Roof restate the ancient esoteric teachings in a fresh manner that is pertinent and applicable to this time period. As the title suggests, this book discusses the coming of the Aquarian age and the Aquarian outlook. Other chapters review evolution, reincarnation and karma, the kingdoms of life, Aquarian psychology and Aquarian values, and much else.

ROOF, SIMONS. THE AQUARIAN DISCIPLES. 8½"x11", 50pp. MSE70, 3.95p.
Sets forth the goal and purpose of the Aquarian disciples in our age— the emphasis being on a fresh outlook, a greater sense of group consciousness, and an identity with both humanity and nature.

RUDHYAR, DANE. OCCULT PREPARATIONS FOR THE NEW AGE. 3.25p.
See the Astrology section.

RUSSELL, GEORGE W. (AE). THE CANDLE OF VISION. Introduction, 186pp. TPH65, 2.25p.
This book is generally considered one of the most important records of the mystic life ever written. *Rarely and more rarely does any artist or poet interest himself in the processes of his mental and spiritual life.... Only readers who can recall some experiences similar to those described by "AE" will find themselves able to accept the work for what it is—a statement of uncommon fact; and only those who have developed their intuition to some degree will be able to appreciate the spirit of truth in which* **The Candle of Vision** *is written.*—A.R. Orage. Russell was an Irish mystic who was a key figure in the great Irish literary renaissance and was greatly influenced by the ideas of the Theosophical movement. This volume includes chapters on dreams, meditation, imagination, and much else.

SADHU, MOUNI. WAYS TO SELF REALIZATION. 242pp. Wil62, 3.00p.
Observations concerning the inner life, its practices and external demonstration; some intimate recollections of the author's experiences with Ramana Maharshi, the modern Indian saint; and helpful insights on such subjects as eternity, the fourth dimension, marriage, and occult experiences.

SALINGER, J.D. FRANNY AND ZOOEY. 202pp. Ban55, 1.95p.
Salinger's books all deal, in one way or another, with the spiritual crisis confronting modern man. He explores this problem primarily through the Glass family, all of whom are intelligent and sensitive enough to suffer greatly from modern life. This book deals with a crisis in Franny, youngest member of the family, who is troubled by the injunction to

pray without ceasing which she has read in **The Way of the Pilgrim**. Her older brother Zooey helps to resolve this crisis by outlining her responsibilities to her profession as an actress, and to a world of people in which each of us is a Christ. The story is beautifully told with both pathos and humor. It is Salinger's most popular work, and quite possibly his best.

SALINGER, J.D. NINE STORIES. 198pp. Ban53, 1.75p.
The stories in this book were written before any of Salinger's novels. Each is a little gem, carefully constructed and as enigmatic and thought provoking as the Zen *koan* which introduces the collection. The opening story, *A Perfect Day for Bananafish*, tells the story of Seymour Glass' suicide in Miami Beach at the age of thirty-one. Seymour is to become the central figure of the Glass family as Salinger further develops his theme of spiritual crisis. The final story, *Teddy*, is a concise and beautiful explication of Advaita Vedanta.

SALINGER, J.D. RAISE HIGH THE ROOF BEAM, CARPENTERS. 213pp. Ban63, 1.75p.
Seymour is the most important figure in the Glass family. His brother Buddy, a writer who narrates both parts of this book, calls him, *a ringding enlightened man, a God-knower*. For his brothers and sisters, understanding Seymour's suicide becomes the key solving the puzzle of the world. In the first part of the book, Buddy describes Seymour's wedding day, and the second part is *a thesaurus of undetached prefatory remarks about him.*

SARAYDARIAN, H. COSMOS IN MAN. 278pp. AEG73, 10.00c/8.00p.
Saraydarian was born in Asia Minor and has devoted his life to a search for the source of ancient teachings. He lived and worked with Sufis, Christian mystics, and teachers from the esoteric tradition. He is a student of the Arcane school and his teachings resemble those of Alice Bailey, though his writings are free from her obfuscation. In this volume Saraydarian outlines new age concepts of the cosmos and its relation with man. He includes chapters on superhuman and monadic evolution, the aura and the etheric body, the cosmic rays, and advanced meditation techniques. He also includes special meditations on the cosmic plan, the art of healing, sources of spiritual energy, and much else.

SARAYDARIAN, H. FIVE GREAT MANTRAMS OF THE NEW AGE. 45pp. AEG75, 1.50p.
A transcription and discussion of the following prayers: *The Great Invocation, The Sons of Men Are One, Affirmation of a Disciple, The Gayatri,* and *The Prayer to Shamballa.*

SARAYDARIAN, H. THE HIDDEN GLORY OF THE INNER MAN. 105pp. AEG75, 6.00c.
A revised edition of **The Magnet of Life**, Saraydarian's first attempt at a comprehensive explanation of the nature of the human soul and its expression through the personality. The explanations and teachings are clear and precise as far as the vocabulary and the material permits. The text includes quotations from many sources including Agni Yoga and Theosophy.

SARAYDARIAN, H. THE SCIENCE OF BECOMING ONESELF. 319pp. AEG69, 9.00c.
Saraydarian presents clear explanations of many difficult esoteric subjects along with a series of exercises designed to lead the reader into expanded consciousness. Includes many diagrams clarifying the more difficult material and definitions of all the unusual terminology.

SARAYDARIAN, TORKOM. THE LEGEND OF SHAMBALLA. 166pp. AEG76, 8.00p.
An illustrated epic poem, retelling the legend.

SATPREM. BY THE BODY OF THE EARTH OR THE SANNAYASIN UNENDING HISTORY. 345pp. H&R78, 5.95p.
A mystical novel by a disciple of Sri Aurobindo. The narrative tells of a spiritual voyage. Nil, the wanderer, embarks on an unending search through a haunting, shifting landscape for *something other*—a new world free of the mechanics and strictures of the mind. When Nil does attain cosmic consciousness he realizes that he has achieved Olympian detachment at the price of severing all contact with the nourishing Earth. So he continues his search.

SCHARFSTEIN, BEN-AMI. **MYSTICAL EXPERIENCE. Notes, index, 195pp. Vik73, 2.50p.**
This is a fairly academic survey of the mystical experience which begins with a review of the rationale for and defenses of mysticism and goes from there to an analysis of various mystical techniques. A final chapter is devoted to an exploration of *The Eleven Quintessences of the Mystical State.* This is a very readable book and in terms of Professor Scharfstein's aims as we see them, it is quite a successful one. One cannot expect to get a glimpse of the mystical experience from a book—but with this qualification in mind the general reader and the psychologist can get a good overview of the subject from this volume.

SCHUON, FRITHJOF. **GNOSIS: DIVINE WISDOM. 151pp. Prn59, 7.15p.**
Gnosis, as defined by Schuon, is wisdom made up of knowledge and sanctity. In this book he expounds on the subject through an analysis of the great spiritual traditions. As G.E.H. Palmer, the translator, says, *Many passages in the book...make clear the distinction, often nowadays obliterated, between knowledge acquired by the discursive mind and the higher knowledge which comes of intuition by the Intellect, the term Intellect having the same sense as in Plotinus or Eckhart.* Schuon collaborated for over twenty years with Rene Guenon and was named by Ananda Coomaraswamy as one of the very few who are qualified to interpret authentically Oriental doctrines.

SCHUON, FRITHJOF. **LOGIC AND TRANSCENDENCE. 273pp. H&R75, 6.65p.**
Huston Smith had this to say about Schuon: *The man is a living wonder; intellectually a propos religion, equally in depth and breadth, the paragon of our time. I know of no living thinker who begins to rival him.* Schuon's philosophical writing is excellent; however, it is recommended only to those who are well versed in comparative religion and mystical philosophy. Many of his references are fairly obscure. This is a collection of essays on a variety of subjects, each one independent of the others. Schuon writes very clearly and quotes from source material. Many foreign words are used with the body of the text, although they are usually defined in the notes.

SCHUON, FRITHJOF. **STATIONS OF WISDOM. Notes, 157pp. Prn61, 7.15p.**
This is a profound study of a wide range of metaphysical, doctrinal, and practical matters. Schuon's insights into the great religious traditions are, in the final chapter, united into a picture of the six essential aspects of spiritual wisdom, which he says can be found in every true and complete way.

SCOTT, CYRIL. **THE INITIATE IN THE DARK CYCLE. 232pp. Wei32/RKP, 4.50p.**
This is the second sequel to **The Initiate**, continuing the teaching and the personal impressions.

SCOTT, CYRIL. **THE INITIATE IN THE NEW WORLD. 302pp. Wei35/RKP, 4.95p.**
Sequel to **The Initiate**, offering further glimpses of the master interwoven with excerpts from his discourses.

SCOTT, CYRIL. **THE INITIATE: SOME IMPRESSIONS OF A GREAT SOUL. Introduction, 396pp. Wei20/RKP, 5.95p.**
The first of three volumes which present the unfolding story of a fascinating and mysterious personality. Scott maintains that mahatmas and masters do not all live in seclusion; they are to be found by those who know how to seek them. The leading character in these books is an adept who lived and worked among his fellow men, but elected to hide his true identity.

SHRINE OF WISDOM. **IDEAL PHILOSOPHY. 123pp. ShW65, 1.60p.**
What is Ideal Philosophy? In brief, it is that which enables the sincere thinker progressively to approach and understand the nature and purpose of the universe, including himself and his fellow man. This is a very clear presentation of this philosophy, with chapters on purpose, ideas, morality, science, religion, and philosophy.

SPALDING, BAIRD. **LIFE AND TEACHINGS OF THE MASTERS OF THE FAR EAST. DeV55, 4.00c/each.**
These five volumes present the teaching Spalding received in his journeys (on the astral plane?) to India. No one was ever sure whether the masters he spoke about were still in their bodies or not. Many went with him on his *tours* to India, but no one reported seeing his masters.

Whatever their source, the teachings presented in these volumes are clear and oriented toward illuminating Western man. Some of our customers consider them to be among the best collections of teachings available.

SPENCE, LEWIS. **AN ENCYCLOPEDIA OF OCCULTISM. 440pp. Stu60, 7.95p.**
A compendium of information on occult science, mysticism, individuals, and general metaphysics. First published in 1920, this volume is still considered the most comprehensive available—although the entries are not often as juicy with gossip as Cavendish's. The listings give bibliographical references and the text includes a number of plates. This book is an important reference work for libraries.

STARCKE, WALTER. **THE GOSPEL OF RELATIVITY. 111pp. H&R73/ Tur, 3.95p.**
This book was written during the 1970's, not long before the end of the world. It was written by one of those who had a great struggle of his own trying to face the crisis....I submit this book because it is valuable to see how the truths which eventually led to the freedom of mankind were voiced at that time....I was one of the young who survived. This book was written by one of my teachers, and I am grateful because, although he was barely on the edge of understanding, he helped me to find out who I am. A well illustrated, interesting essay-novel.

SUZUKI, D.T. **MYSTICISM: CHRISTIAN AND BUDDHIST. 18.15c.**
See the Buddhism section.

Emanuel Swedenborg

Swedenborg (1688-1772) was a Swedish visionary who started out as a scientist but in later life turned increasingly to a study of the relationship of soul to body. At about the age of thirty-five he began to have visions, developed clairvoyant faculties, and communicated with disincarnate souls. He asserted that his symbolic interpretation of scripture, **The Word Explained**, was dictated to him through automatic writing. He developed a vast, pantheistic theosophy which he expounded in the eight volumes of **Arcana Coelestia** and other works. According to Swedenborg the scriptures must be understood in a spiritual or mystical sense, according to a law of correspondences by which natural things are united to spiritual ones. The real world is made up of three religions: the heavens, the hells, and the world of spirits. It is our world that judgment takes place and all acts are judged by intention. For Swedenborg, God is one in person and essence; there is a trinity of attributes: Love (the Father), Wisdom (the Son), Energy (the Spirit). This trinity is found in Jesus, and for Swedenborg Jesus is God and much of his mysticism centers on Jesus. Following his death, Swedenborg's followers set up the Church of the New Jerusalem, a group which is active to this day.

SWEDENBORG, EMANUEL. **DIVINE LOVE AND WISDOM. 293pp. Swe1851, 1.25p.**
An interpretation of the universe as a spiritual or psychophysical cosmos which discusses God's role in the creation of the cosmos and the human being.

SWEDENBORG, EMANUEL. **DIVINE PROVIDENCE. Indices, 429pp. Swe1851, 1.00p.**
A powerfully personal testimony to the truth that God created his universe because of the infinite need of His nature to give life and joy....It is by fighting the limitations, temptations, and failures of the world that we reach our highest possibilities.—Helen Keller.

SWEDENBORG, EMANUEL. **HEAVEN AND HELL. 426pp. Swe76, 1.95p.**
This is generally considered to be Swedenborg's greatest work. In it he gives a comprehensive description of life in what he calls the *hereafter* based on his actual experiences in the spiritual realm and on his visions. He describes a highly organized heavenly life, universal speech, how we enter into the next world, sacred and profane love, the world of the spirits, and many other matters.

SWEDENBORG, EMANUEL. **HEAVENLY SECRETS (ARCANA CELESTIA), VOLUME I.** 823pp. Swe1837, 1.00p.
A massive investigation of the spiritual and symbolic meaning of the biblical book of **Genesis**.

SWEDENBORG, EMANUEL. **THE SPIRITUAL LIFE/THE WORD OF GOD.** 159pp. Swe1896, .50p.
Extracts from **The Apocalypse Explained**, surveying the essence of spiritual living.

SWEDENBORG, EMANUEL. **SWEDENBORG'S JOURNAL OF DREAMS.** Index, 110pp. Swe77, 2.25p.
This is a translation of Swedenborg's private journal, a document which he never intended to publish. It was kept during the time when his life was changing rapidly and he was becoming more and more in touch with his inner life.

■ *VAN DUSEN, WILSON.* **THE PRESENCE OF OTHER WORLDS: THE FINDINGS OF EMANUEL SWEDENBORG.** Notes, 255pp. H&R74, 1.95p.
I had pursued all the principal writers in psychoanalysis and psychotherapy. Only Carl Jung even approached the stature of Swedenborg. Swedenborg knew personally . . . that Self which Jung knew only by speculation on its symbolic manifestations. . . . My purpose is simple, to bring Swedenborg within the reach of many. . . . There are a number of keys to aid this grasp. It is necessary to understand the age and circumstances in which he worked. He lived at the dawn of science in the eighteenth century. He had mastered all the sciences of his day. Though the strange richness of his later psychological-spiritual findings would later get him labeled as either a great mystic or a madman, he never changed fundamentally from the scientist who simply wanted to understand and describe the whole of existence. When he finished all the known outer world, he started to work on the mind. . . . Swedenborg was looking for God within. . . . As he became a more appropriate instrument through . . . changes, the Hand of the Divine became more apparent. Finally . . . he was introduced into heaven and hell. Perhaps many down through time had had glimpses of the worlds beyond this one, but Swedenborg was to have free and relatively constant access for many years.— from the introduction. This is an excellent study of Swedenborg, and Van Dusen seems to have achieved his aim of making this great mystic accessible to the general reader. He also gives us an annotated guide to Swedenborg's writings.

WARREN, SAMUEL, *ed.* **A COMPENDIUM OF SWEDENBORG'S THEOLOGICAL WRITINGS.** Indices, 816pp. Swe1865, 5.00c.
A topically organized collection of passages from Swedenborg's writings.

──────**END OF EMANUEL SWEDENBORG SUBSECTION**──────

THOREAU, HENRY DAVID. **THE ILLUSTRATED WALDEN.** Index, 387pp. PUP73, 4.95p.
This is a complete rendering of the text accompanied by a beautiful selection of photographs by Herbert Gleason and an historical introduction by J. Lyndon Shanley. **Walden** is universally considered one of the most sensitive portraits of the natural world ever written.

THOREAU, HENRY DAVID. **THE NATURAL MAN.** Introduction, 4"x5¾", 136pp. TPH78, 2.50p.
A topically arranged anthology of very short pieces from Thoreau's writings. Edited by Robert Epstein and Sherry Phillips.

THOREAU, HENRY DAVID. **THE PORTABLE THOREAU.** Introduction, 704pp. Vik64, 4.95p.
This volume contains the complete text of **Walden** along with lengthy selections from **A Week on the Concord and Merrimack Rivers**; sections from **The Maine Woods** and the **Journal**; a number of Thoreau's most characteristic essays, including *Civil Disobedience*; eighteen of his poems; and a miscellany of other writings.

THREE INITIATES. **THE KYBALION.** 6.00c.
See the Ancient Egypt section.

TREVELYAN, GEORGE. **A VISION OF THE AQUARIAN AGE.** 162pp. Cov77, 12.85c.
This book is an attempt to present a spiritual world view—a new hierarchy of values which will hopefully impart a sense of deeper meaning to life in a difficult age. . . . The spiritual world-view is a vision of wholeness, an apprehension of the essential unity of all life. Increasingly, our minds and hearts are recoiling from the concept that the universe is a mere dead mechanism of gaseous bodies turning through infinite aeons, with life but a chance accident for a brief span on this tiny planet. In more and more minds today, there is a deepening conviction that the whole is alive and is the work of Mind, of some Intelligence. Behind all outwardly manifested form is a timeless realm of absolute consciousness. It is the great Oneness underlying all the diversity, all the myriad forms of nature.

UNDERHILL, EVELYN. **MYSTICISM.** 4.95p.
See the Christianity section.

UNDERHILL, EVELYN. **PRACTICAL MYSTICISM.** 2.95p.
See the Christianity section.

WAITE, A.E. **LAMPS OF WESTERN MYSTICISM.** 330pp. Mul73, 2.75p.
In the light of the author's conviction that this is the most opportune moment in history to discover higher levels of consciousness and unveil the deeper aspects of man's being, this work relates the mystical journeys of a number of prominent figures of Western civilization.

WAITE, A.E. **THE OCCULT SCIENCES.** 292pp. UnB74, 7.95c.
According to Waite, this volume embraces *in a compressed and digested form, the whole scope of occult knowledge, expressed in the language of a learner.* Topics include magical practices, alchemy, divination, astrology, Qabala, mystics, Rosicrucians, Freemasons, mesmerism, spiritualism, and Theosophy.

WAITE, A.E. **STUDIES IN MYSTICISM AND CERTAIN ASPECTS OF THE SECRET TRADITION.** Offset, spiral bound, 360pp. HeR06, 10.00p.
A collection of essays on aspects of the mystical tradition and on leading mystics and occultists.

WHITMAN, WALT. **LEAVES OF GRASS.** 781pp. RaH1892, 5.95c.
This is an unabridged edition, with an illustration at the begining of each chapter.

WILSON, COLIN, *ed.* **DARK DIMENSIONS.** 206pp. WHA77, 7.95c.
An anthology of essays on Rasputin, Gurdjieff, Madame Blavatsky, Nikola Tesla, Aleister Crowley, Uri Geller, Mesmer, and Nostradamus. The selections are of a fairly high caliber.

WILSON, COLIN. **THE OCCULT.** Bibliography, index, 601pp. RaH71/May, 4.95p.
An interesting overview of the Western mystery tradition. Wilson begins with a section stressing the connection between creativity and psychic sensitivity. The next major part is devoted to a history of the leading Western mages and adepts. The third section contains information on witchcraft, vampirism, spiritualism, and much else. In the

last chapter Wilson takes up the metaphysical questions that arise out of occultism, and concludes with a discussion of the nature of man's latent powers. It is a gossipy account which probably includes more information than most readers would like to know.

WILSON, COLIN. **POETRY AND MYSTICISM.** 79pp. CiL69, 2.00p.
Wilson compares the poet's moment of luminous inspiration with the similar moment experienced by the mystic. He feels that mystical experience and poetic inspiration can be pursued scientifically and learned as one learns a foreign language. His thesis is a bit ingenuous and not one with which we agree; nonetheless, it is an interesting argument.

William Butler Yeats

No one can fully comprehend the poetry of Yeats (1865-1939) without taking into account his deep and lifelong preoccupation with occultism and mysticism. In one of his letters he wrote: *The mystical life is the centre of all that I do and all that I think and all that I write.* As a young man Yeats became involved in Theosophy. After a few years he was initiated into the Hermetic Order of the Golden Dawn and he learned about the Qabala, astrology, and Rosicrucianism—all of which were to play a major part in his poetry. He was also part of the Irish literary renaissance and the mystical ideas of the Celts were restated in many of his poems.

BACHEHAN, H.R. **W.B. YEATS AND OCCULTISM.** Illustrations, notes, bibliography, 296pp. Wei74, 7.95c.
This is the only systematic treatise available which analyzes the impact that Western and Eastern occultism had upon Yeats' creative work. The text reads like a scholarly paper and is accompanied by a profusion of notes. Many quotations from Yeats' work are included.

ELLMANN, RICHARD. **THE IDENTITY OF YEATS.** Chronology, notes, index, 367pp. Oxf64, 4.95p.
This classic study of Yeats' verse examines the poet's choice of literary direction and his development of theme, symbol, style, and pattern. Ellmann, a professor of English literature at Oxford, has made an extensive study of Yeats. Here he recreates Yeats' ways of thinking, seeing, and writing. This is an illuminating work which should interest all students of Yeats.

ELLMANN, RICHARD. **YEATS: THE MAN AND HIS MASKS.** Introduction, notes, index, 341pp. McM48, 4.95p.
This is an excellent survey of all aspects of Yeats' life and works. Ellmann reconstructs the poetic and intellectual growth of this highly complex personality. He bases his study in part on some 50,000 pages of unpublished material left by Yeats at his death, which he examined during a year's stay in Ireland. Many poems and letters discovered in those manuscripts are printed here for the first time. As Edmund Wilson said, *The book helps fill in the picture of a complex and fascinating man, and it will probably prove indispensable for the serious study of the subject.*

FLANNERY, MARY. **YEATS AND MAGIC: THE EARLIER WORKS.** Notes, bibliography, index, 165pp. Smy77, 19.50c.
Throughout his career, Yeats devoted much time and energy to the unification of poetry and magic, and it is clear that all his life he associated poetry with myth, intuition, and the magical world. This book is a study of Yeats' developing ideas on poetry and the poet, and the relationship of these to his belief in and practice of magic. It shows how his poetry and magic are vitally related to each other, and how, in the years prior to 1914, his ideas about them grew together.

HARPER, GEORGE. **YEATS' GOLDEN DAWN.** Index, 332pp. H&R74, 26.25c.
Although all serious students of Yeats are aware that he belonged to the Golden Dawn for most of his mature lifetime, George Harper is the first to make a thorough study of the intellectual climate which nurtured his interest and a thorough assessment of the significance of Yeats' involvement upon his art and theory. The book is based primarily on unpublished manuscripts from the library of W.B. Yeats. A number of related documents are printed in appendices and a profusion of notes accompany the text.

QAMBER, AKHTAR. **YEATS AND THE NOH.** Notes, bibliography, 161pp. Wea74, 8.95c.
Introduced to the Noh through the ground breaking translations of Ernest Fenollosa and Ezra Pound, Yeats discovered in the highly stylized dance-plays of medieval Japan the use of dramatic techniques that would allow him to realize his vision of a new theater of poetic symbolism. He felt that this theater would be diametrically opposed in feeling and form to the predominant realism of contemporary European drama and would evoke the bardic tradition of Ireland's heroic past. This volume begins with a definition of Yeats' place as a playwright. Next, Qamber outlines the nature and history of the Noh drama and follows with a detailed analysis of how Yeats used Noh elements. The full texts of four plays are reprinted in the appendix: two of Yeats' and two Noh plays in the Fenollosa/Pound translation.

RAINE, KATHLEEN. **DEATH-IN-LIFE AND LIFE-IN-DEATH.** Notes, 63pp. Dol74, 7.00p.
A detailed analysis of two of Yeats' poems. Ms. Raine, a noted Blake scholar, defines Yeats' philosophy of the continuation and growth of the soul as revealed in *Cuchulain Comforted* and *News for the Delphic Oracle.* She also shows Yeats' debt to his predecessors, especially Blake and Plotinus, and reveals the deep faith that Yeats had in those principles which shaped his life and art. The text is illustrated by plates from Blake and others.

ROSENTHAL, M.L., *ed.* **SELECTED POEMS AND TWO PLAYS OF WILLIAM BUTLER YEATS.** Index, 275pp. McM62, 3.50p.
A selection of 195 poems representing the essential poetic achievement of Yeats in the years 1889 through 1939, printed from the most reliable texts, and in the sequence set by Yeats himself. The two plays are **Calvary** and **Purgatory.** The editor provides notes, a glossary, and an introduction which surveys Yeats' development, life and thought, techniques, and use of symbolism.

SHERRARD, PHILIP. **W.B. YEATS AND THE SEARCH FOR TRADITION.** Notes, 21pp. Gol75, 4.70p.
Transcription of a lecture on Yeats' sources, originally delivered at Oxford.

YEATS, WILLIAM BUTLER. **THE AUTOBIOGRAPHY OF WILLIAM BUTLER YEATS.** Index, 404pp. McM65, 3.95p.
A very intense, personal account ranging over fifty-eight years, from Yeats' earliest memories to his winning of the Nobel Prize. All who are moved by his poetry should be fascinated by this account. Yeats' prose style is excellent.

YEATS, WILLIAM BUTLER. **THE COLLECTED POEMS OF WILLIAM BUTLER YEATS.** Index, 480pp. McM56, 9.95c.
The definitive edition, with Yeats' final revisions.

YEATS, WILLIAM BUTLER. **MYTHOLOGIES.** 375pp. McM59, 3.95p.
A collection of stories based on Irish country beliefs, traditions, and folktales and originally published in three collections entitled **The Celtic Twilight**, **The Secret Rose**, and **Stories of Red Hanrahan**. A concluding section of essays reveals Yeats' own speculations on and experiences of the supernatural and his philosophy of *self* and *not self.*

YEATS, WILLIAM BUTLER. **A VISION.** 305pp. McM37, 3.95p.
A system of supernaturally revealed images, acquired through Mrs. Yeats' efforts at automatic writing, gave Yeats both a method by which he was able to categorize humanity and a method for dealing with history. Eventually Yeats found in these communications the metaphors for poetry he sought. **A Vision** is essential to any understanding of many of his most notable poems. It also contains some of the most penetrating and beautiful prose that Yeats ever wrote.

————**END OF WILLIAM BUTLER YEATS SUBSECTION**————

ZAEHNER, R.C. **MYSTICISM: SACRED AND PROFANE.** Notes, bibliography, index, 256pp. Oxf57, 3.95p.
A scholarly, not very exciting analysis of various types of praeternatural experience ranging from the sensations produced by such drugs as mescaline to the mystical states described by the Christian and Islamic mystics and the various schools of mystical thought in India.

MYTHOLOGY

Not until the later centuries did reflective minds see in mythology any of the significance that we have come to see in it. The Italian philosopher of the seventeenth century, Vico, knew that the heroes of myth—Hercules, whose arms could rend the mountains, Lycurgus and Romulus, law-givers, who in a man's lifetime accomplished the long work of centuries—were creations of the collective mind. When man craved for men-like gods he had his way, Vico showed us, by combining in an individual, by incarnating in a single hero, the ideas of a whole cycle of centuries. Then came Goethe who maintained that *the earlier centuries had their ideas in intuitions of the fancy, but ours bring them into notions. Then the great views of life were brought into shapes, into gods; to-day they are brought into notions.* In our day, one who loved and studied the mythologies of diverse peoples, wrote:

There are two nouns in the Greek language which have a long and interesting history behind them; these are "mythos" and "logos." Originally they had the same power in ordinary speech; for in Homer's time they were used indifferently, sometimes one being taken, and sometimes the other, with the same meaning that Word has in our language. . . . Logos grew to mean the inward constitution as well as the outward form of thought, and consequently became the expression of exact thought—which is exact because it corresponds to universal and unchanging principles—and reached its highest exaltation in becoming not only the reason in man, but the reason in the universe—the Divine Logos, the Son of God, God Himself. . . . Mythos meant, in the widest sense, anything uttered by the mouth of man—a word, an account of something, a story understood by the narrator. . . . In Attic Greek, Mythos signified a prehistoric story of the Greeks. The application of the word Myth among scholars is plain enough up to a certain point; for from being a myth of Greece only, it is now used to mean a myth of any tribe of people on earth. . . . The reason is of ancient date why myths have come, in vulgar estimation, to be synonymous with lies; though true myths—and there are many such—are the most comprehensive and splendid statements of truth known to man. A myth, even when it contains a universal principle, expresses it in special form, using with its peculiar personages the language and accessories of a particular people, time, and place; persons to whom this particular people, with the connected accidents of time and place, are familiar and dear, receive the highest enjoyment from the myth, and the truth goes with it as the soul with the body.

From these sayings of Vico's, of Goethe's, of Jeremiah Curtin's, we learn something of the inner significance of mythology. Then we may turn to a specialist who can show us how to distinguish myths from fables and from incidents in romance and epic narrative. *I maintain,* writes Bronislaw Malinowski, *that there exists a special class of stories, regarded as sacred, embodied in rituals, morals, and social organization, and which form an integral and active part of primitive culture. These stories live not by idle interest, not as fictitious or even as true narrative, but are to the natives a statement of primeval, greater, and more relevant reality, by which the present life, fates, and activities of mankind are determined, the knowledge of which supplies man with the motive for ritual and moral actions, as well as indications of how to perform them.*

It is natural to begin with things Egyptian. But the stories that we have from the mythology of that great civilization are all fragmentary; for the most famous of them we have to go to a Greek work—to Plutarch's treatise on Isis and Osiris. The greater part of Egyptian mythology dealt with the appearance, disappearance, and reappearance of the Sun, and with descriptions of the World of the Dead.

The Babylonian religion was on a higher level than the Egyptian, which, according to Maspero, one of the greatest of Egyptologists, was close to the animism and fetichism of the African tribes. Yet the Sumerians and Babylonians, compared with the Egyptians, had a very faint conception of a life beyond the grave. *They imagined the lower world to be a place of darkness, where the departed, retaining their consciousness, were condemned to lie motionless for ages, under the stern rule of a goddess who reigned in that world.* Then Professor Rostovtzeff goes on to say: *The hymns and prayers addressed to the gods of Babylon and Assyria are full of religious inspiration and unfeigned religious feeling. The Babylonians in their epic poetry sought to explain the mighty secrets of nature, connected with the life of gods and men.*

Their stories of the struggles of the gods against Chaos and the monsters produced by Chaos, of Gilgamesh's adventures, of Ishtar's descent into the World of the Dead, are comparable to nothing else but their sculptures—those carvings in which kings and soldiers, horses and lions, chariots and spears, are rendered with such power as seems to us terrifying. We owe the preservation of the Babylonian and Sumerian stories, in a large measure, to an Assyrian king of the neo-Babylonian epoch, to Ashur-bani-pal, who reigned in Nineveh B.C. 668.

At the time when the Assyrian kings of the neo-Babylonian epoch were publishing the Babylonian mythological cycles, and when Egyptian and Greek mythologies were flourishing, the original Persian or Iranian mythology was being stopped in its growth; afterwards nearly all records of it were destroyed. This happened in the reign of Darius (sixth century B.C.), through the rise of the Mazdean or Zoroastrian dualism which, accepted by the king and the governing classes, had the effect of depriving the old mythology of all value and significance.

The Zoroastrian dualism represented a religion that was on a higher level than the religions of Egypt and Babylon. Says Professor Rostovtzeff: *Like the Hebrew prophets, Zoroaster reached the conception of a single spiritual god, Ormuzd or Ahura Mazda, in whom the principle of good is personified, while the evil principle is embodied in Ariman or Angra Mainyu. The two principles strive eternally in life and nature, and in the struggle men take part. Man is responsible for his actions, good and bad; he is the master of his fate; his will determines his line of conduct. If he struggles against evil, confesses God, and cares for the purity of his body and soul, then, after four periods, of three thousand years each, in the world's history, when the time shall arrive for final victory of good over evil and of Ormuzd over Ariman—the general resurrection of the dead and the last judgment will assure him his place among the saved and the righteous.*

The Persian religion had strong influence upon both Judaism and early Christianity: a king who was the champion of early Zoroastrianism ended the Babylonian captivity and enabled the Jews to reconstitute themselves as a religious body; the star of the Nativity was hailed by the Magi who were Persians and Zoroastrians. This religion in the form of the worship of one of the angelic powers of Zoroastrian theology, Mithra, spread through the West during the late Roman Empire, and made itself a powerful rival of young Christianity. Mithra, identified with the Sun, had a cult that was fostered by the Roman military guild, it is known that as far west as Britain there was a temple built to him. Present-day Christianity, on the side of ceremony and ritual, has elements that have come into it from its one-time closeness to Mithraism.

The original mythology of Iran or Persia is supposed to have been of the type that existed in Aryan India around 1000 B.C.—the mythology of the **Vedic Hymns**. Many names out of the oldest strata of Iranian traditions can be equated with names in the **Vedic Hymns**.

The Jewish stories that have once come down to us in the **Haggadah** are more akin to the Persian than they are to any other stories. Their monotheism seems to be nominal, veiling a real dualism. Thus, God creates the Angels on the second day *lest man believe that the Angels assisted God in the creation of the heavens and the earth.* This suggestion of rivalry is in many of the stories: God is on one side, the Angels on the other. The Angel Samael who becomes Satan is, in his opposition to the Most High, like Angra Mainyu in relation to Ahura Mazda. The stories that form the **Haggadah** were developed between the second and the fourteenth century of our era.

Little remains to be said on the subject of Greek mythology. But it is worthwhile repeating some sentences written by Miss Jane Harrison: *All men, in virtue of their humanity, are image-makers, but in some the image is clear and vivid, in others dull, lifeless, wavering. The Greeks were the supreme ikonists, the greatest image-makers that the world has ever seen, and, therefore, their mythology lives on today.*

It is important to separate the Greek and Latin mythologies: Iuppiter, though akin to, is not the same as Zeus; Iuno is not the same as Hera. Minerva is not the same as Athena, Neptune is not the same as Poseidon. *The Romans worshipped not gods, not dei,* writes Miss Jane Harrison, *but powers, numina: These numina were only dim images of activities. They had no attributes, no life histories; in a word, no mythology. We must always remember that mythology, the making of images, is only one and, perhaps, not the greatest factor in religion. Because the Romans were not ikonists, it does not follow that they were a people less religious than the Greeks. The contrary is probably true. A vague something is more awe-inspiring than a known something.*

Celtic mythology is known to us only in the fragments that have come down to us through Irish (Gaelic) and Welsh (Brythonic) romances. Of the mythology of the Continental Celts we know nothing: *On the Continent the Celtic tribes came in contact with the rich and highly organised Graeco-Roman mythology, and discarded their own mythic romance. In the British Isles Celtic mythic romance escaped the destructive influence of Rome, was spared by Christianity, and served, almost down to the present day, as a backbone and rallying centre to the peasant lore about the fairies, which is substantially the old agricultural faith, preserved in rude and crude form, and partly reshaped by the fierce opposition or the insidious patronage of Christianity. Gaelic peasant lore only differs from that of other parts of Europe, because Gaeldom has preserved, in a romantic form, a portion of the pre-Christian mythology. Thanks to the fact that this mythology enters largely into the Arthurian romance, the literature of modern England has retained access to the fairy realm, and has been enabled to pluck in the old wonder-garden of unending joy fruits of imperishable beauty.*

In Ireland a learned class who took pride in preserving the relics of the national past, wrote down histories and romances that contained mythological material. We have these histories and romances in documents of the eleventh and twelfth centuries, the **Book of Leinster** and the **Book of the Dun Cow**: the material on which they are based is of a much earlier period. In Wales a material less copious and more distorted, was, between 1080 and 1260, shaped into the romances that we know in the **Mabinogion**.

The Celts were known in the ancient world for their positive beliefs concerning the survival of the soul. They appear to have had a conception of a Happy Otherworld which was similar to that of the early Greeks: *Although from fifteen hundred to two thousand years separate the earliest recorded Greek and Irish utterances in a form, substantially speaking, yet extant, yet both stand on much the same stage of development, save that Ireland has preserved, with greater fulness and precision, a conception out of which Homeric Greece had already emerged. Examination of the mythologies due to other Aryan races, or rather, to prejudge nothing, to peoples speaking Aryan tongues equally with the Greeks and Irish, reveals the remarkable fact that Greeks and Irish alone have preserved the early stage of the Happy Otherworld conception in any fulness.*

The Celtic religion appears to have been the worship of the Powers of Life and Increase: *In Greece the Powers of Life and Increase, worshipped by the primitive agriculturists, are but one element in the completed Hellenic Pantheon, and this has been subjected to so much change, to such enlargement and glorification, as to be well-nigh unrecognizable. In Ireland, to judge by extant native texts, these powers must have constituted the predominant element of the Pantheon, and cannot have departed very widely from their primitive form. . . . In the main mythology had for its "dramatis personae" the agricultural Powers of Life and Increase, in the main it was made up of stories of which the ultimate essence and significance were agricultural.*

The same authority [Alfred Nutt] offers the following conclusions on the subject of Celtic mythology as it is revealed in the Irish romances: *The features common to Greek and Irish mythology belong in the earlier known stage of Aryan mythical evolution, and are not the result of influence exercised by the more upon the less advanced race. Survivals in Greece, they represent the high-water mark of Irish pre-Christian development; hence their greater consistency and vividness in Ireland. Fragmentary as they may be in form and distorted as it may be by its transmission through Christian hands, we thus owe to Ireland the preservation of mythical conceptions and visions more archaic in substance if far later in record than the great mythologies of Greece and Vedic India.*

The mythology out of which the Finnish stories come belonged to the Finno-Ugric stock which includes the Finns and their near relations the Esthonians, and the more remotely related Lapps and Hungarians. We know this mythology through the folk-epic of Finland, the **Kalevala**, and the Magic Songs of the Finns and the Esthonians. As we have them now, the Finno-Ugric traditions reflect a definite locale—the land of forests and lakes of North Europe. Until the last century these traditions existed in peasant memory and speech. Scattered parts of the poem that is now known as the **Kalevala** were published in 1822 by Zacharias Topelius. Elias Lonnrot collected the remainder and arranged the twenty-two or twenty-three thousand verses into fifty runes. The metrical form in which the **Kalevala** has come down has been imitated by Longfellow in Hiawatha. It is startling to realize that a mythology existed on the lips of a European people in our time. There has been, of course, a Christian influence on the traditions out of which the folksongs that make the **Kalevala** have come. A large part of this poetry had its rise in the Middle Ages and Catholicism had an influence on a few incidents.

When we realize that in France, Britain, and Ireland, Christianity had been established for six hundred years before it was introduced into Iceland and the Scandinavian countries, we are aware of what a long lifetime the mythology of northern Europe had in comparison, let us say, with the mythology of Celtic Britain and Ireland. The Icelandic mythology is part of the Scandinavian which is again part of the mythology of the Germanic people. It had a separate development in Norway, and a separate development, perhaps, in Iceland where the records that we have of it were made. Iceland, at the time, was the centre of the Scandinavian world. As shaped in the Icelandic poems and stories, this mythology has been influenced by Christianity. Of the great poem that tells of the creation of the world and the gods, the **Voluspo**, the latest translator, Mr. Henry Adams Bellows, writes: *That the poem was heathen and not Christian seems almost beyond dispute; there is an intensity and vividness in almost every stanza which no archaizing Christian could possibly have achieved. On the other hand, the evidences of Christian influence are sufficiently striking to outweigh the arguments of*

Finnur Jonsson, Mullenhof, and others who maintain that the **Voluspo** *is purely a product of heathendom. The roving Norsemen of the tenth century, very few of whom had as yet accepted Christianity, were nevertheless in close contact with Celtic races which had already been converted, and in many ways the Celtic influence was strongly felt.*

We owe our knowledge of this mythology to the **Poetic** and **Prose Eddas**—the first a collection of poems celebrating the gods and heroes of the olden times, and the second a handbook giving an account of the gods and the old system of divinity, with a number of separate stories about the gods and heroes. Scholars now agree that the poems that make up the **Poetic Edda** were shaped between 900 and 1050. The **Prose Edda** was composed by an Icelandic scholar, Snorri Sturluson, about the year 1220. The rediscovery of this mythology was hailed by the whole Germanic world, and treated as a racial inheritance: it lives as no other European mythology lives today through the expression it has been given in the tragic music of Richard Wagner's **Ring** operas.

India's is the most heavily mythologized of civilizations; the mythology revealed in its literature is threefold. There is, first of all, that of Aryan India which has connections with the mythologies of Persia, Greece, and Italy: because we know it through the **Vedic Hymns** (shaped between 1200 and 800 B.C.), we name it the Vedic mythology. Then comes a mythology which nominally arises out of the **Vedas** but which is quite different in idea and outlook: this is the Brahmanical, the living mythology of India, revealed to us in the enormous epics which were shaped about the fourth century B.C., the **Ramayana** and the **Mahabharata**. Buddhism, a movement which originally aimed at simplifying the Brahmanical system, added new entities to the country's mythology: out of it came a mythology connected with beings who incarnate from period to period in order to redeem mankind: the stories of these incarnations and of the efforts of the Buddhas-to-be to attain enlightenment are its subjects; connected with it are cycles of animal-stories which tell of the incarnations of Buddha in animal forms. Unlike Persia, unlike Europe, India never had her mythology displaced by movements such as Zoroastrianism or Christianity.

There is not in China, as there is in India and there was in Greece, any dramatization of divine activities—at least, not in literature; there is no Chinese Hesiod, nor Homer, nor Valmiki. The Chinese people seem to have had no curiosity about their origin which could be thought of as the origin of mankind; the philosophers have concerned themselves with ethics and politics, and the poets with human relations and the influences of nature. According to Confucius's disciples, the subjects on which the master inclined to speak were *extraordinary things, feats of strength, disorder and spiritual beings*. This attitude, transmitted to the literate classes, did away with interest in mythology. Undoubtedly, Chinese popular traditions contain a variety of stories about personages who might be regarded as mythical. But such stories are so prosaic and fantastic, so literal and ingenious, that we have no way of retelling them with becoming seriousness. To literate Chinese the universe has been created and is sustained by impersonal forces; that which makes a mythology—personification of supernatural powers and their identifications with some of the interests of mankind—is not conceived of by them.

The widely spread Kanaka or Maori people have a rich and remarkably homogeneous mythology: the same divine beings figure in stories told in most of the islands of the Pacific Ocean. *We find,* writes Miss Martha Warren Beckwith, *the same story told in New Zealand and Hawaii, scarcely changed, even in name.* In one sense, practically all Polynesian stories are mythological, for, to quote Miss Beckwith again: *Gods and men are, in fact, to the Polynesian mind, one family under different forms, the gods having superior control over certain phenomena . . . the supernatural blends with the natural exactly the same way as to the Polynesian mind gods relate themselves to men, facts about one being regarded as, even though removed to the heavens, quite as objective as those which belong to the other, and being employed to explain social customs and physical appearances in actual experience.* The Polynesians, like the ancient Egyptians, thought of the soul as being double: a part of it could go wandering and be brought back, or be taken away and restored by spells of sorcerers.

The two great civilizations of America, the Middle American and the South American, appear to have had their rise about the same time, and in each a period of decadence seems to have set in just before the advent of the European conquerors. We have much less information about the civilization we name Inca than the one we name Aztec. Most of what we know about the antiquities of Peru comes from the writings of Garcilasso de la Vega, whose father was Spanish and whose mother was Peruvian, and who regarded himself as a descendant of the Incas and an interpreter of their traditions. The mythological survivals of the Incas are so scanty that any story that has even a slight connection with their mythology, and that has some portion of their imagination in it, is of interest.

In regarding Central America and Mexico as a single cultural area, I accept the authority of Eduard Seler, who, grouping Guatemala, Yucatan, and the area that includes Mexico City together, writes: *The unity of this entire region of ancient civilization is most clearly expressed by the calendar, which these people considered the basis and alpha and omega of all high and occult knowledge.* According to this view, the Mayan, the Toltec, and the Aztec are varieties of a single culture. The most dramatic rendering of the mythology belonging to this culture is in a book written in Guatemala, in a Mayan language, some time in the seventeenth century. This is the **Popul Vuh**. The Spanish version of the native text was translated into French by the Abbe Brasseur de Bourbourg, and our main knowledge of this curious and exciting book is derived from this translation.

As we look upon the powerful sculptures of the Aztecs and their compact drawings we get the impression of a strangely earthbound civilization: it was as if all the figures were rooted; in some of the drawings hands are in movement, but it is like the movement of branches of trees, and we can never think of the faces as being lifted to the skies. In their mythology we have the impression of thought which can never become abstract. This literalness leaves theirs the most terrible of the religions connected with any of the great civilizations. Always they wanted rain, and they strove to give example to the rainmaking deities by pouring out human blood. They sacrificed thousands of human victims every year; every Aztec ceremony culminated in human sacrifice. Some things, however, can be said for this religion: *Students of religious phenomena not infrequently show distaste for the deeper consideration of the Mexican faith, not only because of the difficulties which beset the fuller study of this interesting phase of human belief in the eternal verities, but also, perhaps, because of the "diabolic" reputation which it has achieved, and the grisly horrors to which it is thought those who examine it must perforce accustom themselves. It is certainly not the most obviously prepossessing of the world's religions. Yet if due allowance be made for the earnestness of its priests and people in the strict observance of a system the hereditary burden of which no man or generation could hope to remove, and the religion of the Aztecs be viewed in a liberal and tolerant spirit, those who are sufficiently painstaking in their scrutiny of it will in time find themselves richly rewarded. Not only does it abound in valuable evidences for the enrichment of the study of religious science and tradition, but by degrees its astonishing beauty of colour and wealth of symbolic variety will appeal to the student with all the enchantment of discovery. The echoes of the sacred drum of serpent-skin reverberating from the lofy pyramid of Uitzilopochtli, and passing above the mysterious city of Tenochtitlan with all the majesty of Olympian thunder, will seem not less eloquent of the soul of a vanished faith than do the memories of the choral chants of Hellas. And if the recollection of the picturesque but terrible rites of this gifted, imaginative, and not undistinguished people harrows the feelings, does it not arouse in us that fatal consciousness of man's helplessness before the gods, which primitive religion invariably professes and which reason almost seems to uphold?*

The pueblo-dwelling Indians, of whom the Zuni are the chief representatives, belong to a stage of culture that the great civilizations of Middle and South America had come directly out of. And as in Middle and South America, the whole form of Zuni culture, the whole trend of Zuni religious thought, is conditioned by the cultivation of maize.

—*condensed from* **Myths of the World**, *by Padraic Colum*

ALFRED, WILLIAM, W.S. MERWIN and HELEN MUSTARD, trs. MEDIEVAL EPICS. 590pp. RaH59, 5.95c.
Complete translations into modern idiom of four works: **Beowulf, The Song of Roland, The Nibelungenlied,** and **The Cid.** Only the latter is translated into verse. Each is preceded by the translator's introduction, which is both a critical evaluation and a discussion of the historical and technical aspects of the poem.

ALLEN, LOUIS A. TIME BEFORE MORNING: ART AND MYTH OF THE AUSTRALIAN ABORIGINES. Many color plates, notes, index, 7¾"x10", 318pp. Cro75, 18.95c.
This marvelously illustrated collection of the myths and legends of the aboriginal inhabitants of Australia's Arnhem Land gives the reader a glimpse into a culture that only emerged from the Stone Age. The tales were mostly collected in the field by Allen and are illustrated with reproductions of the bark paintings and carved figures used by the aborigines in their sacred ceremonies.

ASHE, GEOFFREY. THE VIRGIN. Illustrations, notes, index, 262pp. RKP76, 6.60p.
There is no clear historical basis for the cult of the Virgin Mary in the **Gospels,** yet the worship of Mary has often risen to a height where she overshadows her son. Ashe has written an exciting book which seeks to account for the facts and touches on many aspects of mythology, theology, and the spirituality of women. Beginning with the background in prehistory and the worship of the mother goddess, Ashe goes on to scrutinize what is known of Mary herself from a fresh point of view. In the second half of the book he shows that Mary's return—the return of the goddess in this new form—began not in the church but outside of it. A provocative study.

ASTON, W.G. NIHONGI. 5.75p.
See the Japanese Literature subsection of Zen Buddhism.

BACHOFEN, J.J. MYTH, RELIGION AND MOTHER RIGHT. Glossary, notes, bibliography, index, 366pp. PUP67, 4.45p.
This selection from the works of Bachofen offers chapters on symbols and myths. The central part is the investigation of the religious and juridical character of Matriarchy in the Ancient World—a theme that is inseparably linked with the name of Bachofen.—from the introduction. This edition is translated by Ralph Manheim and includes fifty-seven pages of introductory material by George Boas and Joseph Campbell.

BAKER, DOUGLAS, ed. LEMPRIERE'S CLASSICAL ENCYCLOPAEDIA OF GREEK AND ROMAN MYTHOLOGY, VOLUME I (A-C). 8"x11¼", Bak77, 14.00p.
The first volume in a projected five volume set—the first four of which will reprint this classic work and the fifth will give the esoteric psychology and philosophy behind the myths. An abundance of color plates and line drawings accompany the text. Lempriere's work is possibly the most complete ever done.

BAKER, DOUGLAS, ed. LEMPRIERE'S CLASSICAL ENCYCLOPAEDIA OF GREEK AND ROMAN MYTHOLOGY, VOLUME II (D-L). Illustrations, 8"x11¼", 151pp. Bak nd, 15.00p.

BARTH, EDNA. CUPID AND PSYCHE. 7¼"x9¼", 64pp. Sea76, 6.95c.
A retelling for young readers of this classic love story. Psyche is a mortal princess who is so beautiful that even Venus is jealous of her. Venus commands her son Cupid to fly to Earth and put an evil spell on the princess. But Psyche's incredible beauty makes Cupid forget his mother's wishes. He and Psyche fall in love and go through many trials before they are united. Vividly illustrated with Grecian watercolor washes.

BECKWITH, MARTHA. HAWAIIAN MYTHOLOGY. Notes, index, 608pp. UHa40, 6.95p.
Ms. Beckwith has lived in Hawaii since she was a young girl and has devoted her life to the study of Hawaiian mythology and folklore. In this comprehensive volume she translates all the major myths and legends and many of the minor ones. She maintains the feeling of the orally transmitted texts. This is a classic contribution to Hawaiian folklore and ethnology.

BEER, RUDIGER. UNICORN—MYTH AND REALITY. Index, 8"x 8½", 215pp. Lit77, 14.95c.
The unicorn has fascinated both storyteller and artist for thousands of years. In this beautifully produced study Beer shows how the unicorn has been pictured throughout the ages and discusses what it symbolizes. The unicorn's image is brought to life through references to Eastern and Western literature and reproductions of 161 plates from ancient illustrated manuscripts, tapestries, sculptures, woodcuts, engravings, church decorations, and architectural basreliefs.

Beowulf

The first major poem in English literature, **Beowulf** tells the story of the life and death of the legendary hero Beowulf in his three great battles with supernatural monsters. Beowulf is an example of the heroic spirit at its finest, the ideal Anglo-Saxon warrior aristocrat. The epic poem celebrates both his magnificent courage in his battles with Grendel, Grendel's mother, and the dragon, and his leadership and loyalty in dealing with his fellow men. At the same time, the poem is a deeply felt elegy for the passing of such virtues, and takes an essentially tragic view of man's fate in an uncertain world.

ALEXANDER, MICHAEL, tr. BEOWULF. Chronology, notes, bibliography, index, 176pp. Vik73, 1.50p.
An excellent verse translation; the text retains the flavor of the original Old English. Alexander includes a lengthy introduction.

CHICKERING, HOWELL, tr. BEOWULF. Notes, bibliography, 403pp. Dou77, 4.95p.
This is the only modern dual language edition of **Beowulf** available. Chickering's new translation with accompanying Old English text allows the reader the chance to encounter **Beowulf** as poetry. His translation is fresh and lively, and his *Guide to Reading Aloud* helps the

modern reader discover the sound of the original without having to study Old English. His introduction and extensive commentary incorporate recent scholarship and provide historical and literary background. The commentary also includes alternative translations of difficult passages and discussions of major critical problems.

MORGAN, EDWIN, tr. **BEOWULF. Glossary, 128pp. UCa52, 1.95p.**
In this translation Professor Morgan has sought a modern idiom that is free of archaism and a verse form that is accentual and unrhymed and only occasionally alliterative. This translation into modern English retains the dignity and lyrical quality of the original. In his lengthy introduction Morgan critically reviews the fifteen verse translations of **Beowulf** which, within the past hundred years, have preceded his own.

SUTCLIFF, ROSEMARY. **DRAGON SLAYER. 108pp. Vik61, 1.25p.**
This is an illustrated prose retelling of the epic, written for older children and retaining the flavor of the original.

WRIGHT, DAVID, tr. **BEOWULF. Introductions, glossary, notes, 122pp. Vik57, 1.95p.**
A prose translation.

──────────────END OF BEOWULF SUBSECTION──────────────

BERG, STEPHEN and DISKIN CLAY, trs. **SOPHOCLES' OEDIPUS THE KING. Introduction, glossary, many notes, 155pp. Oxf78, 8.50c.**
A prose translation of this most famous of all Greek tragedies. The translators emphasize the intensity of the spoken language and have produced an intense, vivid work. Oedipus is a king of Thebes who unwittingly killed his father and married his mother. The action of this tragedy takes place immediately before and after Oedipus finds out about his parentage and his incest. His wife/mother kills herself, he blinds himself, and goes off into a disgraced exile.

BIERHORST, JOHN, tr. **BLACK RAINBOW: LEGENDS OF INCAS AND MYTHS OF ANCIENT PERU. 7.95c.**
See the Ancient Americas section.

BIERHORST, JOHN. **THE RED SWAN: MYTHS AND TALES OF THE AMERICAN INDIANS. 7.95p.**
See the American Indian Religion section.

BLACKER, CARMEN and MICHAEL LOEWE, eds. **ANCIENT COSMOLOGIES. 25.20c.**
See the Ancient Civilizations section.

BRINTON, DANIEL. **MYTHS OF THE AMERICAS. 5.50p.**
See the Ancient Americas section.

BULFINCH, THOMAS. **BULFINCH'S MYTHOLOGY. Introduction, illustrations, glossary, notes, index, 980+pp. Cro70, 9.95c.**
Bulfinch's versions of the ancient myths are by far the best known and most widely read of any modern versions. This complete edition includes **The Age of Fable, The Age of Chivalry,** and **Legends of Charlemagne.**

BURLAND, C.A. **MYTHS OF LIFE AND DEATH. Bibliography, index, 7½"x9½", 256pp. MGB74, 11.95c.**
This is a beautifully produced volume which explores mythical themes from all the major civilizations and shows the interface between them. The selections are topically organized and illustrated with well over 100 plates, many in color. Reading this book is a good way to get a feeling for mythology and myths without being overwhelmed by details.

CAMPBELL, JOSEPH. **THE FLIGHT OF THE WILD GANDER. Illustrations, notes, index, 248pp. GEd60, 3.95p.**
An enlightening collection of six essays in which Professor Campbell explores the origin and meaning of myths from many angles and discusses a number of myths in depth. We have found the collection very useful for a better understanding of mythic expression and of myths in general.

■ *CAMPBELL, JOSEPH.* **THE HERO WITH 1,000 FACES. Illustrations, notes, bibliography, index, 416pp. PUP49, 18.50c/3.95p.**
Despite their infinite variety of setting, incident, and costume, the myths of the world offer only a limited number of responses to the

riddle of life. Campbell presents the composite hero here. Apollo, the Buddha, and numerous other protagonists of folklore and religion enact simultaneously the various phases of their common story. The relationship of their timeless symbols to those rediscovered in dreams by contemporary depth psychology is a starting point for interpretation. This is then compared with the words of spiritual leaders such as Jesus, Lao Tzu, and Muhammad. From behind a thousand faces the single hero emerges, archetype of all myth and of man's eternal struggle for identity.

■ *CAMPBELL, JOSEPH.* **THE MASKS OF GOD, VOLUME I: PRIMITIVE MYTHOLOGY. Notes, index, 504pp. Vik59/Sou, 15.00c/4.95p.**
This is an excellent series which we recommend highly to all who are seriously interested in mythology. Campbell writes extremely well and integrates information from a number of disciplines. As Erich Fromm said, *I consider this, as his other books, of outstanding importance and scholarship, clarity and depth.... Anyone truly interested in the science of man...will find these books a wealth of data, penetratingly analyzed and written.* This volume focuses on the primitive roots of mythology through an examination of the most recent discoveries in archaeology, anthropology, and analytical psychology.

■ *CAMPBELL, JOSEPH.* **THE MASKS OF GOD, VOLUME II: ORIENTAL MYTHOLOGY. Notes, index, 561pp. Vik62/Sou, 15.00c/4.95p.**
An exploration of Eastern mythology as it developed into the distinctive religion of Egypt, India, China, and Japan.

■ *CAMPBELL, JOSEPH.* **THE MASKS OF GOD, VOLUME III: OCCIDENTAL MYTHOLOGY. Notes, index, 564pp. Vik64/Sou, 15.00c/4.95p.**
A systematic and fascinating comparison of the themes that underlie the art, worship, and literature of the Western world.

■ *CAMPBELL, JOSEPH.* **THE MASKS OF GOD, VOLUME IV: CREATIVE MYTHOLOGY. Notes, 730pp. Vik68/Sou, 15.00c/4.95p.**
An illuminating discussion of the inner history of modern man, spanning our entire philosophical, spiritual, and artistic traditions since the Dark Ages, and focusing on modern man's unique position as the creator of his own mythology.

CAMPBELL, JOSEPH. **THE MYTHIC IMAGE. Notes, index, 9¼"x 12¼", 563pp. PUP74, 45.00c.**
Dr. Campbell has devoted his life to a study of the mythology of the world's high civilizations and is considered the most noted expert in the field. He has produced many definitive volumes, and this mammoth tome, in addition to being a summation of his life's work, is the last volume of the **Bollingen Series** and it sums up and enlarges on much of the work that the series has done in exploring the innumerable facets of symbology as revealed through religion, mythology, psychology, and the arts. Here Campbell presents nearly 450 color and black and white illustrations of mythic art from Mesopotamian, Egyptian, Indian, Chinese, European, and Olmec cultures covering five millennia. Starting with the relation of dreams to myth, Campbell distinguishes two orders of myths: that of the relatively simple, nonliterate folk traditions, and that of the infinitely more complex literate civilizations that culminated in the triad of the world's greatest religions, Buddhism, Christianity, and Islam. He traces the development of the mythologies and, with text and pictures, demonstrates the important differences between Oriental and Occidental interpretations of dreams and life. Ideas of space, time, cosmology, the sacrificed god, and transformation and transmutation are presented through narrative and image. An extraordinarily beautiful volume.

CAMPBELL, JOSEPH, ed. **MYTHS, DREAMS, AND RELIGION. 255pp. Dut70, 2.75p.**
A transcription of eleven related lectures delivered under the auspices of the Society for the Arts, Religion, and Contemporary Culture on one topic, *Myth and Dream.* Five of these speakers were theologians, three psychiatrists, two Orientalists, and one a student of comparative mythology.

CAMPBELL, JOSEPH. **MYTHS TO LIVE BY. 291pp. Vik72/Sou, 6.95p.**
In this edited transcription of a series of talks, Campbell focuses on popularly confused notions about myths and demonstrates how particular myths continue to reflect human needs. He relates myths to

Zen Buddhism, schizophrenia, LSD, the moon walk, the confrontation of East and West in religion, and much else.

CICERO. **THE NATURE OF THE GODS. Glossary, notes, index, 277pp. Vik72, 2.25p.**
A translation by H.C.P. McGregor of Cicero's **De Natura Deorum.** Cicero (106-43 BC) turned to philosophy at the end of his oratorical and political career, and in this volume he discusses timeless questions such as the following: Is there a God? If so, what is he like? Does he answer prayers or interfere in human affairs? Does he know the future? J.M. Ross provides a lengthy introduction.

CLARK, R.T. RUNDLE. **MYTH AND SYMBOL IN ANCIENT EGYPT. 7.95p.**
See the Ancient Egypt section.

COLUM, PADRAIC. **THE CHILDREN OF ODIN. 271pp. McM20, 6.95c.**
A recreation of the Norse myths. These myths are very different from the classical Greek myths. The gods and the giants battle and there are witches and dragons and all kinds of mythological beasts. The stories are exciting and keep the reader's interest. The print is fairly large and delightful line drawings accompany the narration. This volume has been extremely popular over the years and it is our favorite retelling of these myths—most versions of which seem incredibly dry. All the important stories are included.

COLUM, PADRAIC. **THE GOLDEN FLEECE. 316pp. McM21, 6.95c.**
Padraic Colum has a wonderful faculty for blending the separate strands of Greek mythology into one tale. In this book he relates the strange and wondrous adventures of Jason and his Argonauts. The rendition is oriented toward children and is illustrated throughout. The tone itself is not overly juvenile.

■ COLUM, PADRAIC. **MYTHS OF THE WORLD. Introduction, index, 357pp. G&D30, 3.50p.**
Well written renditions of the most important myths from the following traditions: Egyptian, Babylonian, Persian, Jewish post-Christian period, Greek, Roman, Graeco-Roman, Celtic, Finnish, Icelandic, Indian, Chinese, Japanese, Polynesian, Peruvian, Central American and Mexican, and Zuni. Many of the myths are not readily available elsewhere and this is an excellent cross-section of a great many traditions. We enjoy reading Colum's books.

COOMARASWAMY, ANANDA and SISTER NIVEDITA. **MYTHS OF THE HINDUS AND BUDDHISTS. 3.95p.**
See the Indian Philosophy section.

COURLANDER, HAROLD. **TALES OF YORUBA GODS AND HEROES. 6.95c.**
See the African Philosophies section.

COURLANDER, HAROLD. **A TREASURY OF AFRICAN FOLKLORE. 14.95c.**
See the African Philosophies section.

D'AULAIRE, INGRI and EDGAR. **D'AULAIRE'S BOOK OF GREEK MYTHS. 7.95c.**
See the Children's Books section.

DAVIDSON, H.R. ELLIS. **GODS AND MYTHS OF NORTHERN EUROPE. Glossary, index, 250pp. Vik64, 2.50p.**
This is the only popular treatment of Northern European mythology that we know of. It is the work of a scholar who specializes in Norse and Germanic mythology. All the important gods and goddesses are discussed. In addition to a retelling of many of the stories, there is a fair amount of interpretative material. The myths are topically arranged and the renditions read well.

DORIA, CHARLES and HARRIS LENOWITZ, eds. **ORIGINS: CREATION TEXTS FROM THE ANCIENT MEDITERRANEAN. Bibliography, 380pp. Dou76, 4.95p.**
This is a scholarly introduction to the cosmological ideas of the ancient peoples of the whole of the Mediterranean world. Most of the texts are in verse and very little commentary is included. Jerome Rothenberg provides a preface.

DOWRICK, STEPHANIE. **LAND OF ZEUS: THE GREEK MYTHS RETOLD BY GEOGRAPHICAL PLACE OF ORIGIN. Introduction, index, 247pp. Dou74, 7.95c.**
A collection of tales of the Greek gods and heroes, narrated in modern prose and arranged according to the places where they were originally told. Where there were several versions, Ms. Dowrick has selected her personal favorite. We are not really sure that this regrouping contributes anything notable; nonetheless, this is a readable edition of the major myths.

DOWSON, JOHN. **A CLASSICAL DICTIONARY OF INDIAN MYTHOLOGY. 10.00c.**
See the Indian Philosophy section.

DUMEZIL, GEORGES. **GODS OF THE ANCIENT NORTHMEN. Many notes, index, 195pp. UCa73, 12.50c.**
An English translation of some of the most important and representative of Dumezil's writings in the field of Germanic mythology. Dumezil is without question the premier scholar in the field of Indo-European mythology and culture, and his work, while not widely known, has been highly influential. Excellent introductory material is included. The work is edited and translated by Einar Haugen.

DURDIN-ROBERTSON, LAWRENCE. **COMMUNION WITH THE GODDESS PRIESTESSES. 46pp. Ces76, 2.40p.**
A badly written, often confusing comparative study of goddess priestesses in most of the major ancient civilizations.

DURDIN-ROBERTSON, LAWRENCE. **THE GODDESSES OF CHALDEA, SYRIA, AND EGYPT. 440pp. Ces75, 6.30p.**
A detailed account, arranged by area, but not alphabetically within the areas, giving the following information: name, etymology, genealogy, offices and titles, associated places, and folklore and legends about the individual. An extensive index helps somewhat to relieve the confusion about the lack of alphabetical order among the entries (although the index itself is not always 100 percent accurate).

Mircea Eliade

Mircea Eliade and Joseph Campbell stand at the forefront of the study of mythology in the twentieth century. While Campbell's emphasis is on the psychological meaning of myths, in the Jungian sense, Eliade stresses the basic religious nature of all myths and his writings are considerably more academic than Campbell's. Many more of Eliade's works are described in the Comparative Religion section. *On the one hand, Eliade entertains the notion of the "ambivalence of the sacred," which is an ongoing recognition of the practical reality (concreteness) of an object that has become a sacred symbol....On the other hand, Eliade understands the existential function of myth as an art form, which is both an act of creative thought and an effort to make a "world" out of often chaotic natural reality. Yet Eliade's distinctive approach as historian of religion is best understood when we notice the pervasive attention that he gives to the element of religious experience in both myth and ritual as symbolic realities. He thus calls our attention to something in the life of primitive peoples that is critically important beyond the anthropological confirmation that they are indeed human beings with the art of common sense and a remarkable inclination toward myth-making. Eliade, in sum, insists that behind and beyond the linguistic structure and pragmatic function of myths lies the conception, gestation, and birth of myth out of the depths of genuine religious experience.*
—from the introduction to Beane and Doty's **Reader.**

BEANE, WENDELL and WILLIAM DOTY, eds. **MYTHS, RITES, SYMBOLS: A MIRCEA ELIADE READER. Notes, 493pp. H&R76, 3.95p/ each.**
I should like to express my deep gratitude to the editors of this volume....They have gone to a great deal of trouble in excerpting selections from various publications that have spanned the last forty years, and I believe that they have been enormously successful in choosing passages that effectively and honestly present my central ideas on the interpretation of religious ideology, behavior, and institutions....I am delighted with their choice of texts, and their careful editing has made them uniformly accessible

for the use of the nonspecialist.—Mircea Eliade. Both volumes include the same introductory material. Volume I is divided into the following sections: *The Structure of Myths, The Greatness and Decadence of Myths, Cosmogonic Myth and Sacred History, Sacred Time and Myths, Varieties of Sacred Time, Intercommunication, Ritual Performance, Mythic Archetype, The Sacred and the Profane, Entering the Cosmos and the Society, Forming and Recreating, Reflecting and Maintaining the Sacred.* Volume II covers the following material: *Prestige and Power of the Sacred Specialist, The Shaman as Specialist Par Excellence, Women's Mysteries, Men's Mysteries, Classical and Christian Mysteries, Mysticism: Yoga and the Mystic Light, The Nature and Function of Religious Symbolism, World-Patterning Symbols, Symbols for Transitions in Life, Symbols Concerning Paradise.*

ELIADE, MIRCEA. **THE FORBIDDEN FOREST.** 611pp. UND78, 25.45c.
In a journal entry, Eliade refers to this book as *the best one I have written.* It is his major novel and is available in English for the first time. Eliade presents the *forbidden forest* as the collective myth of the Romanian people and the symbol of their salvation. In the novel the forest represents, in overt form, the psychic ideal of characters who seek to escape the world of historical time for an eternal plane. The story takes place in the years 1936-48, during which time the hero pursues his hope for immortality. The novel is rich in symbolism and resonates with themes drawn from Eliade's store of mythological, religious, and philosophical lore.

ELIADE, MIRCEA. **MYTH AND REALITY.** Notes, bibliography, index, 212pp. H&R63, 3.50p.
An important work on the nature and significance of myths—ranging from the ancient Egyptians and classical Greeks to the works of Picasso and James Joyce. Aimed at the general reader.

ELIADE, MIRCEA. **THE MYTH OF THE ETERNAL RETURN OR COSMOS AND HISTORY.** Many notes, bibliography, 201pp. PUP54/RKP, 2.95p.
This is an essay on mankind's experience of history and its interpretation, beginning with a study of the traditional or mythological view, and concluding with a comparative estimate of modern approaches. *I consider it the most significant of my books; and when I am asked in what order they should be read, I always recommend beginning with* **The Myth of the Eternal Return.**

ELIADE, MIRCEA. **MYTHS, DREAMS AND MYSTERIES.** Notes, index, 254pp. H&R57/Fon, 3.95p.
The central theme of this book is the meeting and confrontation of the two types of mentality which might be called the traditional and the modern; the first being characteristic of man in archaic and Oriental societies, the second of man in modern societies of the Western type. This is a detailed analysis of each, and of their encounter. Includes reference notes.

ELIADE, MIRCEA. **RITES AND SYMBOLS OF INITIATION: THE MYSTERIES OF BIRTH AND REBIRTH.** Notes, index, 181pp. H&R58, 4.70p.
Here Eliade takes on particular subject, the almost universal prevalence in human culture of some force of initiatory rite and custom, and treats it in a way that is at once scholarly and interpretative. This book is not merely a collection of data, but also a profound attempt to discern the underlying meaning and purpose of initiation. Includes many source notes.

ELIADE, MIRCEA. **SHAMANISM.** Notes, excellent bibliography, index, 622pp. PUP64/RKP, 4.95p.
A brilliant treatise on the characterization and peculiarities of shamanism, including a definition of this phenomenon of man's religious fervor. The book contains a compilation and description of shamanistic rituals, practices, and techniques in a variety of different cultures.

ELIADE, MIRCEA. **THE TWO AND THE ONE.** 223pp. H&R62/WCS, 3.95p.
A scholarly comparison of religious experiences and beliefs which synthesizes psychology, anthropology, and religion.

──────── **END OF MIRCEA ELIADE SUBSECTION** ────────

Brynhilde in the house of flame.

ELIOT, ALEXANDER. **MYTHS.** Bibliography, index, 10"x13", 320pp. MGH76, 39.95c.
This is a beautifully produced retelling of many of the major myths, arranged thematically and revealing the striking recurrence of basic motifs in widely differing mythologies the world over. The book begins with chapters by Mircea Eliade and Joseph Campbell. Eliade introduces the reader to the historical development of the interpretation of myth and discusses the meaning of myths. Campbell traces the emergence of the basic mythologies and follows their historical and geographical development in both archaic nonliterate societies and highly literate civilizations. Over 1,300 illustrations, many in color, accompany the text. The discussion is far from an in depth one—but the work succeeds in its aim of being an introductory, albeit expensive, survey.

EVANS, BERGEN. **DICTIONARY OF MYTHOLOGY.** Cross references, index, 333pp. Del70, 1.50p.
A fairly comprehensive dictionary, emphasizing the myths of Greece and Rome and also covering Norse mythology, the Arthurian legends, and the most often encountered figures from Egyptian and Babylonian mythology. The material is alphabetically arranged and the entries are fairly short.

EVSLIN, BERNARD. **HERACLEA—A LEGEND OF WARRIOR WOMEN.** Illustrations, 257pp. FWP78, 9.95c.
The legend of a gigantic young woman, whose exploits astonished both gods and mortals, was told thousands of years ago when the people worshiped a mother goddess and the principle of female dominance was sacred. Later, in the days of the fierce Hellenic warriors, the tale emerged as the myth of Heracles, the hero of Greek mythology celebrated for his strength and power. Here Evslin has recreated the legend in its original form—the myth of the warrior goddess, Heraclea. This is a vividly written tale, designed for older children.

FARMER, PENELOPE and CHRIS CONNOR. **THE SERPENT'S TEETH.** 4.70c.
See the Children's Books section.

FLACELIERE, ROBERT. **GREEK ORACLES.** Illustrations, notes, index, 102pp. Ele76, 7.95c.
In antiquity divination was esteemed as an official institution. It was obligatory for political and military leaders to consult the oracle, *to take the auspices*, before embarking upon any enterprise unless they were prepared to be accused of irresponsibility or, in case of failure, of having failed to seek guidance from the gods. This book is an examination of the Greek attitude toward divination.

FRANZ, MARIE-LOUISE VON. **PATTERNS OF CREATIVITY MIRRORED IN CREATION MYTHS.** 8.80p.
See the Jungian Psychology section.

FRANZ, MARIE-LOUISE VON. **A PSYCHOLOGICAL INTERPRETATION OF THE GOLDEN ASS OF APULEIUS.** 7.55p.
See the Jungian Psychology section.

James Frazer

Frazer (1854-1941) was a British anthropologist, folklorist, and classical scholar, best known as the author of **The Golden Bough: A Study in Magic and Religion**. This work was published in 1890 in twelve volumes and reissued abridged in one volume in 1922. Its underlying theme is Frazer's theory of a general development of modes of thought from the magical to the religious and, finally, to the scientific. His distinction between magic and religion (magic meaning an attempt to control events by technical acts based upon faulty reasoning, religion being an appeal for help to spiritual beings) has been basically assumed in much anthropological writing since his time. Although his evolutionary sequence of magical, religious, and scientific thought is no longer accepted and Frazer's broad general psychological theory has proved unsatisfactory, it enabled him to synthesize and compare a wider range of information about religious and magical practices than has been achieved by any other single anthropologist. **The Golden Bough** directed attention to the combination of priestly with kingly office in the *divine kingships* widely reported in the ancient world. According to Frazer, the institution of divine kingships derived from the belief that the well being of the social and natural orders depended upon the vitality of the king, who must therefore be slain when his powers began to fail him and be replaced by a vigorous successor.

DOUGLAS, MARY and SABINE MACCORMICK, *eds.* **THE ILLUSTRATED GOLDEN BOUGH.** 9¾"x7½", Dou78, 14.95c.
In this new abridgment of the original thirteen volume edition, the editors have selected passages that give the modern reader a full appreciation of Frazer's theories and the evidence he collected to support them. 166 pages of plates, sixteen in color, accompany the text, providing a unique visual reflection of Frazer's panorama of the vanished life of primitive man.

FRAZER, JAMES. **FOLKLORE IN THE OLD TESTAMENT.** Long index, 523pp. Har75, 5.95p.
Frazer has compiled all the sections of **The Golden Bough** which are concerned solely with the stories and customs of the **Old Testament** and included them in this volume. He also provides counterparts of these stories from a variety of other cultures, showing the universality of psychic experience which evoked these tales. For example, there are stories of a great flood from at least twenty different cultures, none of which were likely to have had anything at all to do with the ancient Hebrews. The volume is topically organized and contains an amazing amount of different myths and stories. The book was put together sometime in the last century and was out of print for quite a long time.

FRAZER, JAMES. **THE GOLDEN BOUGH. Index,** 864pp. McM22, 12.95c/7.95p.
A monumental survey of ancient man which shows that, contrary to the popular thought, he was enmeshed in a nightmare of magic, taboos, and superstitions. This work describes ancient man's primitive methods of worship, sex practices, magic, strange (to us) rituals and festivals. The tone of this volume is very much that of *the white man's burden*—but it is a greatly respected classic. This edition was abridged by Frazer himself and is considered the authorized version. A complete thirteen volume edition of this classic is available for $200.00.

GASTER, THEODOR. **THE NEW GOLDEN BOUGH. Introduction, notes, index,** 859pp. NAL59, 2.50p.
A modernized, readable abridgment. We prefer this version—while it is not as authoritative as Frazer's own, it is a work of impeccable

scholarship and it is written in a lively style. If you are deeply interested in Frazer's work, it would probably be helpful to have both versions, since they do contain somewhat different selections.

──────── **END OF JAMES FRAZER SUBSECTION** ────────

FROMM, ERICH. **THE FORGOTTEN LANGUAGE: AN INTRODUCTION TO THE UNDERSTANDING OF DREAMS, FAIRY TALES, AND MYTHS.** 3.95p.
See the Dreams section.

GASTER, THEODOR, *tr.* **THE OLDEST STORIES IN THE WORLD. Foreword, index of motifs,** 248pp. Bea52, 4.95p.
A collection of myths and legends of Babylonian, Hittite, and Canaanite cultures. Though these are some of the oldest stories extant they are not well known because many have been discovered only recently. Professor Gaster attempts to bring the tales to life with the aid of comparative material, and to recapture the host of ideas and associations which the tales originally evoked. The myths are all based on Gaster's own translations.

Gilgamesh Epic

The origins of this ancient Sumerian epic extend back to the third millennium BC, 1,500 years before Homer. It was miraculously preserved on clay tablets which were deciphered in the last century. The epic tells of the adventures of the king of Uruk and his fruitless search for immortality and of his friendship with Enkidu, a wild man from the hills. It also includes a legend of the Flood which agrees in many details with the biblical story of Noah.

HEIDEL, ALEXANDER, *tr.* **GILGAMESH EPIC AND OLD TESTAMENT PARALLELS. Many notes,** 269pp. UCh46, 3.75p.
A translation and interpretation of the **Gilgamesh Epic** and related Babylonian and Assyrian documents. Heidel compares them with corresponding portions of the **Old Testament** to determine the inherent historical relationship of Hebrew and Mesopotamian ideas.

MASON, HERBERT, *tr.* **GILGAMESH.** 126pp. NAL70, 1.50p.
A verse narrative which makes the age old story come alive. Some background material is also included which discusses Sumerian mythology as well as aspects of the epic itself.

SANDARS, N.K., *tr.* **THE EPIC OF GILGAMESH. Excellent long introduction, glossary,** 127pp. Vik72, 1.95p.
A straightforward prose version.

──────── **END OF GILGAMESH EPIC SUBSECTION** ────────

GIRARD, RENE. **VIOLENCE AND THE SACRED. Notes, bibliography, index,** 333pp. JHU77, 23.50c.
An anthropological and literary examination of myth and ritual in human society, demonstrating that violence pervades all forms of the sacred and lies at the basis of religion. Girard draws deeply on Greek myth and tragedy and on the rites of tribal peoples in all parts of the world to show fundamental similarities in religious thought and observance. Reappraisals of the psychoanalytic theories of Freud and the structural anthropological theories of Levi-Strauss form a crucial part of the book.

GLEASON, JUDITH. **ORISHA: THE GODS OF YORUBALAND.** 5.25c.
See the African Philosophies section.

GODOLPHIN, F.R.B., *ed.* **GREAT CLASSICAL MYTHS. Introduction, glossary, index,** 500pp. RaH64, 5.95c.
A collection of Greek myths made up of translations of Greek and Roman poetry. All of the major myths are included.

GOODRICH, NORMA. **MEDIEVAL MYTHS. Index,** 232pp. NAL61, 1.95p.
This collection compares the national heroes of Spain, England, France, Russia, Austria, Hungary, and the Scandinavian countries at a

time when the countries were emerging from barbarism to encounter the civilizing influences of ancient cultures. The influence of these myths on literature, folklore, and philosophy is apparent throughout the history of Europe.

GOULD, CHARLES, et al. **THE DRAGON. Illustrations, 8½"x11¾", 104pp. Wdw77, 6.95p.**
Throughout history dragons have played a role in the myth and folklore of all cultures. Whether well disposed towards mankind or implacable adversaries, they have always been symbols of elemental and superhuman power. This book contains essays detailing the appearance of the dragon in the natural histories and records of the ancient world. Appendices present a selection of pieces from classical and Chinese authors followed by essays on the medieval and mythical dragon.

■ *GRANT, MICHAEL.* **MYTHS OF THE GREEKS AND ROMANS. Genealogical tables, sixty-four pages of photographs and plates, maps, notes, bibliography, index, 464pp. NAL62, 2.50p.**
In this volume Grant does a great deal more than simply retell the myths; in fact, those looking solely for the stories will be disappointed with this book. Grant does trace each of the major Greek and Roman myths and many of the minor ones, and he gives lengthy renditions based on the best classical sources. He also discusses the historical and mythic backgrounds into which each myth fits, making extensive use of the theories of anthropologists, historians, and psychoanalysts. This is an illuminating work which we found extremely valuable in our study of mythology. We highly recommend it to all those who are looking for this kind of approach.

GRANT, MICHAEL. **ROMAN MYTHS. Maps, notes, bibliography, index, 310pp. Scr71, 3.50p.**
Like all of Grant's work, this is an excellent volume. The book begins with a survey of the sources of the Roman myths. This is followed by sections on Aeneas and Romulus, and on the mythology of the Roman kings and the Roman Republic. A final chapter explores the character of Roman mythology.

GRAVES, ROBERT, tr. **THE GOLDEN ASS. Introduction, 315pp. FSG51/Pen, 3.45p.**
A modern translation of the story of Lucius Apuleius, a young man who encountered many strange adventures, including one when he offended a priestess of the White Goddess and for his offense suffered the indignity of being turned into an ass. How Apuleius supported his misfortune and how he contrived at last to appease the goddess and resume his human form make up the body of the tale.

GRAVES, ROBERT. **THE GREEK MYTHS. Maps, index, 784pp. Brz55, 10.00c/5.90p/set.**
A masterwork which covers creation myths, the legends of the birth and lives of the great Olympians, the Theseus, Oedipus, and Heracles cycles, the Argonaut voyage, the tale of Troy, and much else—two hundred sections in all! All the scattered elements of each myth have been assembled and many variants are recorded. References to the classical sources and copious indices make the volumes invaluable to the scholar. A full commentary on each myth explains and interprets the classical version in the light of today's archaeological and anthropological knowledge. Graves' versions are not as much fun to read as some others but the books are excellent works of scholarship and immensely helpful to those seeking a deeper understanding of the myths. The hardcover edition is in one volume, the paperback is in two.

GRAVES, ROBERT. **HEBREW MYTHS. 3.95p.**
See the Bibles section.

GRAVES, ROBERT. **THE WHITE GODDESS: HISTORICAL GRAMMAR OF POETIC MYTH. Notes, indices, 424pp. FSG48, 4.95.**
[T]*his remains a very difficult book, as well as a very queer one, to be avoided by anyone with a distracted, tired or rigidly scientific mind....My thesis is that the language of poetic myth anciently current in the Mediterranean and Northern Europe was a magical language bound up with popular religious ceremonies in honor of the Moon goddess, or Muse, some of them dating from the Old Stone Age, and that this remains the language of true poetry. The language is called myth and is based on a few simple, magical formulas, and has been kept as a close secret for thousands of years by her initiates.*

GREEN, ROGER. **A BOOK OF MYTHS. 192pp. Den65, 7.50c.**
A good collection of myths retold for older children and drawn from ancient Egypt, Babylon, Phoenecia, Crete, and from the Hittite and Phrygian kingdoms. Some of the myths are familiar, but more are not. As is usual with Green, the stories read extremely well and illustrations are included throughout.

GREEN, ROGER. **THE LUCK OF TROY. Line drawings, 174pp. Vik61, 1.50p.**
This is a continuation of Green's excellent retelling of the Greek myths. The hero of this story is Nico, the young son of Helen who is carried off from his homeland of Sparta when his mother is kidnapped. The story begins ten years after the capture, when the war between Troy and Sparta is well underway. Even though Nico is too young to fight for Sparta he vows to assist in some way, and he does so by helping Odysseus smuggle a black stone statue out of Troy—a statue which legend says grants the city which holds it free from conquest. The retelling is geared toward young readers.

GREEN, ROGER. **MYTHS OF THE NORSEMEN. 208pp. Vik60, 1.50p.**
A wonderful, illustrated retelling of all the surviving myths, molded into one continuous narrative. This is labeled a children's book, and it makes fascinating reading for all. It is certainly the most interesting version, in terms of sheer readability, that we know. Illustrations by Brian Wildsmith.

GREEN, ROGER. **THE TALE OF THEBES. Illustrations, maps, 115pp. CUP77, 2.95p.**
The Tale of Thebes is a chronicle rather than a story, a collection of tales joined to each other by their connection with Thebes and by the influence, both a blessing and a curse, of the necklace of Harmonia. Thebes has proved as rich as or richer than Troy in supplying great stories for the poets and tragedians. Green retells the tale of Thebes in a continuous narrative and makes careful use of all the available classical sources.

GREEN, ROGER. **THE TALE OF TROY. Illustrations, 215pp. Vik58, 1.50p.**
In this volume Green retells the story of Troy in vivid detail, bringing the protagonists to life. Green draws on all the available sources and writes in a simple style. We like his books a lot.

GREEN, ROGER. **TALES OF ANCIENT EGYPT. 1.50p.**
See the Ancient Egypt section.

■ *GREEN, ROGER.* **TALES OF THE GREEK HEROES. 205pp. Vik58, 1.50p.**
A simple retelling of the tales and legends of ancient Greece from the time of the Golden Age of the Heroes up to the Trojan War. Geared toward older children and nicely illustrated throughout. Green presents the myths as the early Greeks themselves thought of them and his retellings are an excellent introduction to Greek mythology for people of any age.

GREGORY, LADY. **CUCHULAIN OF MUIRTHEMNE. Notes, bibliography, 272pp. Smy11, 6.65p.**
Yeats described this book of Irish mythology as *the best that has come out of Ireland in my time....Perhaps I should say that it is the best book that has ever come out of Ireland; for the stories which it tells are a chief part of Ireland's gift to the imagination of the world.* Yeats may have been a bit overenthusiastic—after all, Lady Gregory was one of his closest literary friends. Nonetheless, it is an important collection and was a sourcebook for Yeats' poems and plays.

GREGORY, LADY. **GODS AND FIGHTING MEN. Notes, 370pp. Smy70, 9.35p.**
First published in 1904, this is a companion volume to **Cuchulain**. It is divided into two parts: the first deals with Lugh, Mananaan, the children of Lir, and the coming of the Tuatha de Danaan to Ireland; the second relates the stories of Finn MacCumhal, the Fianna and their exploits, Oisin, and Diarmuid and Grania. Again, there is a preface by Yeats and this edition contains all of Lady Gregory's final corrections.

GREGORY, LADY. **THE KILTARTAN BOOKS. 213pp. Smy71, 10.40c.**
This volume contains the final versions of all three **Kiltartan Books**: **Poetry, History,** and **Wonder**. All are written in the Kiltartan idiom

and, as Lady Gregory says, the contents of the second two have been put down exactly as she heard them. Padraic Colum has contributed introductory material and notes.

GRENE, DAVID and RICHMOND LATTIMORE, eds. **GREEK TRAGE-DIES, VOLUME I. 298pp. UCh60, 3.45p.**
This series contains selections from **The Complete Greek Tragedies.** Each play contains a new introduction by Professor Lattimore. The series has been universally commended as the finest modern set of translations. Volume I contains Richmond Lattimore's translation of Aeschylus' **Agamemnon**; David Grene's translations of Aeschylus' **Prometheus Bound**, Sophocles' **Oedipus the King**, and Euripides' **Hippolytus**; and Elizabeth Wyckoff's translation of Sophocles' **Antig-one.**

GRENE, DAVID and RICHMOND LATTIMORE, eds. **GREEK TRAGE-DIES, VOLUME II. 295pp. UCh60, 2.95p.**
Lattimore's translations of Aeschylus' **The Libation Bearers** and Euripides' **The Trojan Women**; Grene's translation of Sophocles' **Iphigenia in Tauris**; and Emily Vermeule's translation of Euripides' **Electra.**

GRENE, DAVID and RICHMOND LATTIMORE, eds. **GREEK TRAGE-DIES, VOLUME III. 318pp. UCh60, 3.45p.**
Lattimore's translations of Aeschylus' **The Eumenides** and Euripides' **Alcestis**; Grene's translation of Sophocles' **Philoctetes**; Robert Fitzgerald's translation of Sophocles' **Oedipus at Colonus**; and William Arrowsmith's translation of Euripides' **The Bacchae.**

▣ *HAMILTON, EDITH.* **MYTHOLOGY. Index, 335pp. NAL40/NEL, 8.95c/3.95p/1.95p.**
This is one of our favorite retellings of the classical myths. Ms. Hamilton writes extremely well and she has drawn her composite version of the myths from a number of classical sources. The book is well organized and all the important myths are included, along with many lesser known ones.

HARLEY, TIMOTHY. **MOON LORE. Notes, index, 311pp. Tut1885, 3.95c.**
A compendium of mythology and folklore about the moon and lunar superstitions, written in a tongue in cheek fashion.

HATTO, A.T., tr. **THE NIBELUNGENLIED. Glossary, 403pp. Vik69, 2.95p.**
Composed nearly 800 years ago by an unnamed poet, the **Nibelungenlied** is the principal literary expression of the Germanic heroic legends. This great epic poem of murder and revenge recounts with strength and directness the progress of Siegfried's love for Kriemhild, the wedding of Gunther and Brunhild, the quarrel between the two queens, Hagen's treacherous murder of Siegfried, and Kriemhild's eventual revenge. This is the material that Wagner used in his **Ring Cycle.** This is an excellent prose translation, including over 100 pages of introductory and background material.

HEIDEL, ALEXANDER. **THE BABYLONIAN GENESIS. Illustrations, notes, 166pp. UCh51, 2.95p.**
A complete translation of all the published cuneiform tablets of the various Babylonian creation stories from both the Semitic Babylonian and Sumerian material. Each account is preceded by a brief introduction on the age and provenance of the tablets and the aim and purpose of the story. Also included is a translation and discussion of two Babylonian creation stories written in Greek. The final chapter presents a detailed examination of the Babylonian creation accounts in their relation to **Old Testament** literature.

HENDERSON, JOSEPH and MAUD OAKES. **THE WISDOM OF THE SERPENT. 1.95p.**
See the Jungian Psychology section.

Hesiod

Not a great deal is known about the details of Hesiod's life. He lived in the eighth century BC and was one of the earliest Greek epic poets and the first man in Western civilization to embody precepts or instructions in poetry. Hesiod, through his epics, serves as a useful counterpoint to Homer's more glamorous portrayal of the early classical world. Hesiod is essentially serious and describes the gloomier side of life. **Theogony** is a dramatic history of the birth of the gods and the origin of the world, focusing on the bloody power struggle between Uranus, Cronus, and Zeus. **Works and Days** is a combination of agricultural advice, moral maxims, and social and political comment, and in it Hesiod demonstrates the sad lot of mankind down through the ages. **The Shield of Herakles** and a number of other works are often attributed to him. **Theogony** is clearly both the earliest epic and his major work.

EVELYN-WHITE, H.G., tr. **HESIOD: THE HOMERIC HYMNS AND HOMERICA. Long introduction, notes, index, 705pp. HUP14, 9.40c.**
A good, scholarly translation, with the original Greek text on facing pages. This is the most complete edition of Hesiod. **Loeb Classical Library.**

LATTIMORE, RICHMOND, tr. **HESIOD: THE WORKS AND DAYS, THEOGONY, THE SHIELD OF HERAKLES. Introduction, genealogical tables, illustrations, glossary, index, 241pp. UMP59, 4.95c.**
Mr. Lattimore writes the most accurate verse translations in the language. They have a tracing paper literalness that hitherto seemed impossible, and the freshness of a scientific invention. He is not only closer to the Greek than any prose, but also more readable.—Robert Lowell. We agree heartily with Lowell's opinion; we find Lattimore's translations extremely readable.

WENDER, DOROTHEA, tr. **HESIOD AND THEOGNIS. Introduction, glossary, notes, 170pp. Vik73, 1.95p.**
Verse translations of **Theogony** and **Works and Days** as well as Theognis' **Elegies.** The latter, composed some two centuries later than Hesiod, range from serious theological questioning to intensely personal love lyrics. The quality and accuracy of the translation is more than adequate, though it is not our favorite.

─────── END OF HESIOD SUBSECTION ───────

HIGGINSON, THOMAS. **TALES OF ATLANTIS AND THE EN-CHANTED ISLANDS. Notes, 275pp. NPC77, 3.95p.**
A varied collection of legends about the enchanted islands of the Atlantic in which myth and folklore are mixed with scraps of facts and actual accounts of ancient explorers. Higginson includes Plato's account of Atlantis, tales from British, Welsh, and Celtic literature, Icelandic sagas, and many other stories. This is a reprint of an older work, originally entitled **Tales of the Enchanted Islands of the Atlantic.**

HODGES, MARGARET. **THE OTHER WORLD: MYTHS OF THE CELTS. Illustrations, bibliography, 176pp. FSG73, 5.95c.**
To the ancient Celts, filled as they were with a deep sense of mysticism and the supernatural, communication with visitors from other planes

seemed natural. The Celts' real world was so entwined with their supernatural one that tales of the gods became mixed with stories of the ancient kings and with stories of folk heroes. In this book Ms. Hodges retells ten of the most magical of the Celtic myths. The language is simple and the style is geared toward older children.

Homer

When referring to Homer, one generally means the poet or poets primarily responsible for the **Iliad** and **Odyssey**, the two great epic poems of ancient Greece. Very little is known of him beyond the fact that his was the name attached by the Greeks themselves to the two great poems. These two epics provided the basis of Greek education and culture throughout the classical age and, indeed, formed the backbone of human education down to the time of the Roman Empire and the spread of Christianity. The Greeks regarded the great epics as something more than works of literature; they knew much of them by heart and valued them not only as a symbol of Hellenic unity and heroism but also as an ancient source of moral and even practical instruction. The **Iliad** is not only a distillation of the whole protracted war against Troy, but also an exploration of the heroic ideal in all its self-contradictoriness—its insane and grasping pride, its magnificent but animal strength, its ultimate if obtuse humanity. Out of a single episode in the tale of Troy—Achilles' withdrawal from the fighting and his return to kill the Trojan hero Hector—Homer created a timeless tragedy. His characters are heroic but their passions and problems are human and universal, and he presents them with compassion, understanding and humor against the harsh background of war. The **Odyssey** tends to be blander in expression and less vigorous in the progress of the action, but it presents an even more complex and harmonious structure than the **Iliad**. The main elements are the situation in Ithaca, where Odysseus' wife and son are powerless before her suitors as they despair of Odysseus' return; the son's secret journey to Peloponnese for news of his father, and his encounters there; Odysseus' countless adventures after leaving Troy; and his dramatic homecoming.

COLUM, PADRAIC. **THE CHILDREN'S HOMER: THE ADVEN-TURES OF ODYSSEUS AND THE TALE OF TROY. 248pp. McM18, 8.95c.**
This is our favorite children's version of Homer. Colum is a masterful writer and his prose holds the rhythm, charm, and warmth of the storyteller's voice. Many line drawings accompany the text.

EVSLIN, BERNARD. **GREEKS BEARING GIFTS. Illustrations, 324pp. FWP76, 9.95c.**
A lively retelling of some of the major stories from the epic tales of Achilles, the Trojan War, and Ulysses. The language is simple and vivid, as suits a book written primarily for older children.

FITZGERALD, ROBERT, tr. **THE ILIAD. Introduction, 595pp. Dou74, 2.95p.**
A highly acclaimed poetic rendition. Fitzgerald has translated the epic into blank verse.

FITZGERALD, ROBERT, tr. **THE ODYSSEY. 507pp. Dou61, 2.95p.**
This is a translation into blank verse. *Fitzgerald's new* **Odyssey** *deserves to be singled out for what it is—a masterpiece. At last we have an* **Odyssey** *worthy of the original. What Fitzgerald brings back is, first of all, that crucial and elusive quality of freshness and delight so conspicuously absent from other translations.*—the **Nation**. Fitzgerald also includes background information.

KIRK, G.S. **HOMER AND THE EPIC. Notes, index, 251pp. CUP65, 8.00p.**
This is a shortened version of Kirk's detailed study, **The Songs of Homer.** Professor Kirk states that his purpose is *to develop a comprehensive and unified view of the nature of the* **Iliad** *and* **Odyssey,** *of their relation to the oral heroic poetry of the Greek Dark Age and beyond, and of their creation as monumental*

poems by two great singers in the eighth century B.C. This is a remarkable study which combines excellent scholarship with clear, nontechnical writing.

■ LATTIMORE, RICHMOND, tr. **THE ILIAD. Introduction, glossary, index, 527pp. UCh51, 2.95p.**
An excellent verse translation, capturing the essence of Homer's epic and transforming it into a modern work.

■ LATTIMORE, RICHMOND, tr. **THE ODYSSEY OF HOMER. Intro-duction, glossary, 374pp. H&R67, 3.95p.**
This verse translation of Homer's epic has been universally acclaimed as the best translation available. It is the one most frequently used in classes, and is our favorite version. Lattimore strikes an almost perfect balance between vivid, fast moving narrative and epic formality. The language is vigorous and fresh and the images are Homer's own.

LESSING, ERICH. **THE VOYAGES OF ULYSSES. 11½"x13", 282pp. HKG65, 50.00c.**
This is a sumptuous photographic interpretation of Homer's classic, illustrated with 115 full color plates. The book is divided into six sections: an essay on the voyages of Ulysses by Michel Gall, selections from **Ithaka, der Peloponnes** and **Troja** by Heinrich Schliemann, a photographic journey in the path of Ulysses by Erich Lessing, the **Odyssey** in ancient art by Hellmut Sichtermann, the forms and techniques of Greek pottery painting, and an essay on Ulysses by C. Kerenyi. There is also a detailed pictorial and literary index by C. Kerenyi.

REEVES, JAMES. **THE VOYAGE OF ODYSSEUS. 192pp. Bla73, 8.40c.**
A vivid retelling of Odysseus' ten year homeward journey, written for older children. A number of nice line drawings in a Greek style accompany the text.

RIEU, E.V., tr. **THE ILIAD. 491pp. Vik50, 2.25p.**
A very well composed prose rendition, accompanied by introductory material and a glossary.

RIEU, E.V., tr. **THE ODYSSEY. 365pp. Vik46, 1.95p.**
A sensitive prose translation, with a good introduction.

WEIL, SIMONE. **THE ILIAD OR THE POEM OF FORCE. 39pp. PHP56, 1.20p.**
A translation, by Mary McCarthy, of Ms. Weil's essay on the title theme, written in 1940 after the fall of France. Ms. Weil focuses on heroic force and traces the story of the **Iliad** with this theme in mind. Many quotations from the **Iliad** accompany the commentary.

─────────END OF HOMER SUBSECTION─────────

HOOKE, S.H. **MIDDLE EASTERN MYTHOLOGY. Notes, index, 199pp. Vik63, 3.95p.**
An account, based on primary sources, of the mythology of the Sumerians, Babylonians, Egyptians, Ugarites, Hittites, Canaanites, and Hebrews. Professor Hooke also discusses the nature and function of myth very fully and devotes a chapter to mythological elements in the **New Testament.**

JACKSON, KENNETH, tr. **A CELTIC MISCELLANY. Glossary, 343pp. Vik51, 2.95p.**
An anthology of poetry and prose. Includes passages on Celtic magic, religion, love, nature, and various adventure stories, as well as various kinds of poetry.

JONES, GWYN. **KINGS, BEASTS AND HEROES. Many illustrations, notes, bibliography, index, 201pp. Oxf72, 9.50c.**
This is an exploration of the storytelling art of three ancient literary works: the Old English verse epic **Beowulf;** the Welsh prose romance **Culwch and Olwen;** and the Norse legendary **King Hrolf's Saga.** Professor Jones defines their nature and assesses their importance, not only in the light of modern critical assumptions, but also in regard to the aims and expectations of their makers and first audiences.

JUNG, C.G. and CARL KERENYI. **ESSAYS ON A SCIENCE OF MYTHOLOGY. 3.45p.**
See the Jungian Psychology section.

KERENYI, CARL. **ASKLEPIOS. Fifty-eight plates, notes, bibliography, index, 7½"x10¼", 178pp. PUP59/RKP, 18.10c.**
An investigation of the archetypal significance of the *Divine Physician* in the course of an exploration of the sacred sites of his cult.

KERENYI, CARL. **DIONYSOS: ARCHETYPAL IMAGE OF INDE-STRUCTIBLE LIFE. 146 plates, notes, bibliography, index, 7½"x 10¼", PUP75/RKP, 40.30c.**
An historical account of the religion of Dionysos from its origins in the Minoan culture down to its transition to a cosmopolitan religion in the late Roman Empire.

KERENYI, CARL. **ELEUSIS: ARCHETYPAL IMAGE OF MOTHER AND DAUGHTER. Sixty-five plates, notes bibliography, index, 6½"x9¼", 290pp. ScB67/RKP, 19.50c/9.95c.**
A complete examination of the Eleusian Mysteries that draws upon archaeology, history, art, and literature and considers their relation to Greek mythology and human nature.

KERENYI, CARL. **THE GODS OF THE GREEKS. Introduction, indices, 304pp. T&H51, 7.50p.**
Drawing on a wealth of sources, from Hesiod to Pausanias and from the **Orphic Hymns** to Proclus, Professor Kerenyi provides a clear and scholarly exposition of all the most important Greek myths. The narrative is lively and highly readable and is complemented by an appendix detailing the references to all the original texts and illustrations taken from vase paintings. An exhaustive study which is more psychologically-oriented (in the Jungian sense) than other retellings of the Greek myths.

KERENYI, CARL. **HERMES: GUIDE OF SOULS. Notes, 110pp. Spr76, 6.65p.**
A collection of essays on all aspects of Hermes. Both the classical tradition and the Greek view are fully discussed and ample quotations from classical texts accompany the presentation. Kerenyi is undoubtedly an important writer, especially to those interested in an analytical approach to mythology—but we often find his works hard to follow and a bit overwhelming in their detail.

KERENYI, CARL. **HEROES OF THE GREEKS. Notes, index, 563pp. T&H59, 8.50p.**
The heroes of Greek mythology preoccupied the minds of the ancient Greeks no less than the gods themselves. This is a scholarly, narrative retelling of all that is known about some of the individual heroes, based on original sources and complemented throughout by illustrations from vase paintings and genealogical tables of mythical figures.

KERENYI, CARL. **ZEUS AND HERA: ARCHETYPAL IMAGE OF FATHER, HUSBAND, AND WIFE. Illustrations, notes, bibliography, index, 7½"x10¼", 229pp. PUP75/RKP, 20.15c.**
A study of the relationship between gods and the mortals who worshiped them. The origins of the Greek religion are discussed and Homer's role in decisively shaping the mythological tradition is emphasized.

KING, WILLIAM. **AN HISTORICAL ACCOUNT OF THE HEATHEN GODS AND HEROES. 264+pp. Ctr65, 6.00p.**
This is an archaic retelling of many of the ancient Greek myths, originally published in 1710 and reproduced here in an unaltered form. A new preface and introduction are also included.

KINGSLEY, CHARLES. **THE HEROES. 4.95c.**
See the Fairy Tales section.

KINSELLA, THOMAS, tr. **THE TAIN. Thirty-one brush drawings, maps, detailed notes, 283pp. Oxf69, 10.65p.**
A translation of the **Tain Bo Cuailnge**, centerpiece of the eighth century Ulster cycle of heroic tales and Ireland's nearest approach to a great epic. This translation is based on the partial texts in two medieval manuscripts and includes a group of related stories which prepare for the action of the **Tain**.

KIRK, G.S. **MYTH: ITS MEANING AND FUNCTIONS IN ANCIENT AND OTHER CULTURES. Notes, index, 311pp. UCa70, 3.85p.**
This is a rewarding study which is both erudite and readable. As Professor Kirk says, he *attempts to come to grips with a set of widely ranging but connected problems concerning myths: their relation to folktales on the one hand, to* rituals on the other; the validity and scope of the structuralist theory of myth; the range of possible mythical functions; the effects of developed social institutions and literacy; the character and meaning of ancient Near-Eastern myths and their influence on Greece; the special forms taken by Greek myths and their involvement with rational modes of thought; the status of myths as expressions of the unconscious, as allied with dreams, as universal symbols, or as accidents of primarily narrative aims.

KIRK, G.S. **THE NATURE OF GREEK MYTHS. Notes, bibliography, 331pp. Vik75, 3.95p.**
Kirk is a renowned classical scholar and is presently Professor of Greek at Cambridge. This is a discussion and interpretation of both the fundamental characteristics and meaning of the Greek myths. Professor Kirk recounts some of the most important myths and carefully considers both the development and function of Greek mythology, from its original beginnings as the oral tradition of a structured society to its ultimate role as a key element of philosophy. His presentation relies heavily on contemporary scholarship and he gives us a detailed review of the five major modern theories of myth. He also reviews the historical background of the Greek myths.

KRAMER, SAMUEL, ed. **MYTHOLOGIES OF THE ANCIENT WORLD. Notes, bibliography, index, 480pp. Dou61, 2.95p.**
Using the most up to date translations of primary material, ten leading scholars survey ancient mythologies. Included in this volume are the following: *Mythology in Ancient Egypt*—Rudolf Anthes; *Mythology of Sumer and Akkad*—Samuel Kramer; *Hittite Mythology*—Hans Guterbock; *Canaanite Mythology*—Cyrus Gordon; *Mythology of Ancient Greece*—Michael Jameson; *Mythology of India*—W. Norman Brown; *Mythology of Ancient Iran*—M.J. Dresden; *Myths of Ancient China*—Derk Bodde; *Japanese Mythology*—E. Dale Saunders; and *Mythology of Ancient Mexico*—Miguel Leon-Portilla. Many quotations from the primary myths are included in the selections and the essays are uniformly informative and well written.

KRAMER, SAMUEL **SUMERIAN MYTHOLOGY. Notes, index, 135pp. UPa44, 5.00p.**
No people has contributed more to the culture of mankind than the Sumerians, and yet it has been only in recent years that our knowledge of them has become at all accurate or extensive. [This book is]...our first authoritative sketch of the great myths of the Sumerians, their myths of origins, of creation, the nether world, and the deluge. The book is profusely illustrated with particularly fine photogrphas.—Theophile Meek.

LARSEN, STEPHEN. **THE SHAMAN'S DOORWAY: OPENING THE MYTHIC IMAGINATION TO CONTEMPORARY CONSCIOUS-NESS. Illustrations, notes, 256pp. H&R76, 3.95p.**
An exploration of the myths that are relevant to today's world, combined with an examination of the techniques of consciousness that we can best use to relate to them. Larsen states his indebtedness to

Joseph Campbell in the preface, and Campbell's influence can be felt throughout the book. The mythic examples are drawn from contemporary society and related to the more ancient traditions and theories.

LEACH, MARIA, ed. FUNK AND WAGNALLS STANDARD DICTIONARY OF FOLKLORE, MYTHOLOGY AND LEGEND. Long index, 7½"x10¼", 1,251pp. Cro72, 19.95c.
This is without a doubt the finest work of this type that we know of. The over eight thousand entries are essays in themselves. This is a revised one volume edition of the original work, complete and uncut. The entries are uniformly excellent and while the Western tradition is emphasized the coverage of Eastern mythology and religion is quite complete. We recommend this volume to everyone who is studying mythology and religion in any depth. The entries read well and are extremely informative, and have been prepared by noted scholars.

LEEMING, DAVID. MYTHOLOGY. Bibliography, index, 8"x10", 192pp. Nsw76, 10.00c.
A topically arranged pictorial survey of mythology divided into the following general areas: *Primitive Fears, Universal Understandings; Man, Myth, and History; The Psychological Perspective; The Hero with a Thousand Faces; The Mythmakers;* and *Mythology Today.* 184 beautiful illustrations are included, one-third in color. A final section presents excerpts from a variety of creation myths.

LINES, KATHLEEN, ed. THE FABER BOOK OF GREEK LEGENDS. Illustrations, annotated bibliography, indices, 6"x9½", 268pp. Fab73, 8.95c.
Simple retellings of twenty-five of the most popular Greek myths. Some of the selections are from Charles Lamb, Andrew Lang, Roger Lancelyn Green, and Rosemary Sutcliff; others were especially prepared for this volume. The renditions are geared toward young readers.

LOPEZ-PEDRAZA, RAFAEL. HERMES AND HIS CHILDREN. 6.70p.
See the Jungian Psychology section.

Mabinogion

The **Mabinogion** has come to be accepted as a composite title for eleven medieval Welsh prose tales which came out of the oral tradition. Although influenced by the growth and development of the Arthurian legend on the continent, these tales are essentially native in origin and they preserve much of the color and flavor of the early Celtic world. The combination of fact and fantasy, of myth, history, and folklore in the **Mabinogion** conjures up a magical, enchanted world which is nonetheless firmly rooted in the forests, hills, and valleys of ancient Wales.

BOWEN, OLWEN. TALES FROM THE MABINOGION. Illustrations, glossary, 157pp. Van69/Glz, 5.95c.
Ms. Bowen has done a fine job of retaining the rhythm and feeling of the original tales while writing in a style geared toward older children. This collection contains tales of Prince Pwyll, the children of Llyr, Ludd son of Beli, and King Arthur's knights.

FORD, PATRICK, ed. and tr. THE MABINOGI AND OTHER MEDIEVAL WELSH TALES. Introduction, glossary, notes, index, 217pp. UCa77, 2.45p.
A modern, readable translation of the **Four Branches of The Mabinogi**, the tales of Pwyll, Branwen, Manawydan, and Math. The remaining stories in this collection spring from the same tradition, and together they present the core of the ancient Welsh mythological cycle. Professor Ford includes only those stories that have remained unadulterated by the influence of the French Arthurian romances.

■ *GANTZ, JEFFREY, tr.* THE MABINOGION. Index, 311pp. Vik76/Pen, 2.95p.
This is a fine new translation which is written in a modern style and yet retains the flavor of the original. Gantz has a doctorate in Celtic languages and literatures from Harvard. Short introductions to each of the tales and a fine general introduction are also included.

JONES, GWYN and THOMAS, trs. THE MABINOGION. Introduction, notes, 327pp. Dut74/Den, 2.50p.
A good translation of eleven stories from the Welsh **Mabinogion**: *The Four Branches of the* **Mabinogi**—*Pwyll, Branwen, Manawydan;* and *Math;* four independent native tales—*The Dream of Macsen, Wledig, Lludd and Llefelys, Culhwch and Olwen* (the earliest Arthurian tale in Welsh), and *The Dream of Rhonabwy* (a romantic look back into the heroic age of Britain); and three romances—*The Lady of the Fountain, Peredur,* and *Gereint Son of Erbin* (later Arthurian stories with abundant evidence of Norman influences). The translations are fairly dry and they are well regarded in terms of scholarship.

LAYLARD, JOHN. A CELTIC QUEST. Glossary, index, 254pp. Spr75, 8.25p.
An in depth psychological study of the **Mabinogion** legend of Culhwch and Olwen which retells the main tales, with extensive commentary.

WALTON, EVANGELINE. THE FOUR BRANCHES OF THE MABINOGION. 6.95p/set.
See the Fairy Tales section.

──────── END OF MABINOGION SUBSECTION ────────

MACCULLOCH, J.A. THE CELTIC AND SCANDINAVIAN RELIGIONS. Indices, 180pp. Gre48, 13.45c.
An excellent overview discussing the people, their worship, mythic heroes and mythological writings, religious ideas, and cosmology. Very clearly written and well organized.

MACKENZIE, DONALD. THE MIGRATION OF SYMBOLS AND THEIR RELATION TO BELIEFS AND CUSTOMS. Many line drawings and plates, notes, index, 235pp. AMS26, 10.75c.
An in depth philosophical and mythological discussion focusing on the swastika, the spiral, and ear and tree symbols.

MACLAGAN, DAVID. CREATION MYTHS. Bibliography, 8½"x11", 96pp. T&H77, 7.95p.
Every culture, no matter how simple, has left us some framework to account for the origin and nature of the world's life-structures—even if it is not explicitly titled a creation myth. Myths account for the laws of nature as well as the laws of men; they describe the cosmos in human, and man in cosmic terms. In fact, they point back to the moment before such distinctions existed—through words and images they point to a past which is always present, a creative process which is life itself. This volume discusses and illustrates through 149 plates, nineteen in color, the basic themes of creation myths and shows how we can relate our scientific concepts to these ancient images.

MAGNUSSON, MAGNUS. HAMMER OF THE NORTH: MYTHS AND HEROES OF THE VIKING AGE. Bibliography, index, 9"x12¼", 128pp. Put76/OPL, 12.95c.
Magnusson is an Icelander by birth and he has translated a number of the old Icelandic sagas. This beautifully produced volume juxtaposes over 120 color photographs with a text explaining the motivations, beliefs, and heroic aspirations of the ancient Norsemen. The book gives a graphic account of the Viking vision, in which the gods, dwarfs, and elves figure in stories ranging from lighthearted intrigues to the grim but inevitable Ragnarok. In this final conflict, the chosen warriors who had fallen in battle would rise up to fight while the world shattered and burst into flame around them.

MARKALE, J. WOMEN OF THE CELTS. 17.95c.
See the Ancient Britain section.

MARRIOTT, ALICE and CAROL RACHLIN. AMERICAN INDIAN MYTHOLOGY. 1.75p.
See the American Indian section.

MARRIOTT, ALICE and CAROL RACHLIN. PLAINS INDIAN MYTHOLOGY. 1.75p.
See the American Indian Religion section.

MERCATANTE, ANTHONY. GOOD AND EVIL. Illustrations, index, 256pp. H&R78, 10.95c.
An exploration of the origin and meaning of good and evil as it appears in world mythology and folklore. Mercatante focuses on separate

traditions in each chapter and he retells many related myths. He also includes a fifty page annotated bibliography.

MERWIN, W.S. and GEORGE DIMOCK, JR, trs. **EURIPIDES—IPHI-GENEIA AT AULIS. Introduction, glossary, notes, 125pp. Oxf78, 8.50c.**
Iphigeneia depicts the first step in the fall of the House of Atreus. Agamemnon sacrifices his daughter to appease the gods on his way to the Trojan war. The point Euripides is making in this tragedy is that political ambition and an artificial aristocratic ethic seduced the Greeks into destroying their own children and their good fortune in brutal military adventures. Merwin's language superbly conveys the broad range of emotional and moral tones with which Euripides has invested his play.

MIDDLETON, JOHN, ed. **MYTH AND COSMOS. Notes, bibliography, index, 368pp. UTx67, 8.00p.**
A well organized collection of readings in mythology and symbolism. Included are essays on the *Creator Spirit* and on various beliefs in intermediaries between the spiritual power and men, including deities, priests, prophets, shamans, and others. The selections cover a wide variety of cultures and, while the scholarship is uniformly excellent, they are not overly technical.

MORFORD, MARK and ROBERT LENARDON. **CLASSICAL MYTHOL-OGY. Bibliography, index, 498pp. McK71, 9.35p.**
What makes this excellent primer on classical mythology particularly attractive for undergraduate teaching is the balanced blend of source material in translation, of judicious comments on major trends in ancient religion, and of the highly desirable emphasis, documented by pertinent illustrations and quotations, on the reception of classical myths in European art and literature.—Alfred Henrichs, University of California, Berkeley. A very well organized, comprehensive presentation.

MURRAY, HENRY, ed. **MYTH AND MYTHMAKING. 375pp. Bea59, 4.95p.**
A collection of essays by Joseph Campbell, Mircea Eliade, Jerome Bruner, Marshall McLuhan, Henry Murray, and others along with selections from the writings of Mark Schorer, Georges Sorel, and Thomas Mann. Both traditional and modern perspectives on myth are provided.

NELSON, RALPH, tr. **POPOL VUH. 3.95p.**
See the Ancient Americas section.

NEUMANN, ERICH. **AMOR AND PSYCHE: THE PSYCHIC DEVEL-OPMENT OF THE FEMININE. 2.95p.**
See the Jungian Psychology section.

NEUMANN, ERICH. **THE GREAT MOTHER. 5.95p.**
See the Jungian Psychology section.

NILSSON, MARTIN. **THE MYCENAEAN ORIGIN OF GREEK MY-THOLOGY. Introduction, index, 273pp. UCa32, 11.00c.**
Professor Nilsson was the first scholar to recognize the Mycenaean origin of Greek mythology and of many other aspects of Greek culture. Today his theory is accepted without question. This volume contains transcriptions of the major series of lectures he delivered on the subject. Despite the often technical nature of the material, the book reads well and retains its cohesiveness.

NIVEDITA, SISTER. **CRADLE TALES OF HINDUISM. 2.50p.**
See the Indian Philosophy section.

O'FLAHERTY, WENDY. **HINDU MYTHS. 2.95p.**
See the Indian Philosophy section.

OVID. **METAMORPHOSES. Introduction, index, 364pp. Vik55, 2.95pp.**
Ovid (43 BC-AD 17) was among the most sophisticated of Latin writers; he was also a storyteller. **Metamorphoses**, a poem in fifteen parts, is a rich collection of tales culled mainly from Greek and Roman myths and folktales. All of the tales have one element in common—they all deal with transformations: chaos changed into ordered harmony, animals turned into stone, men and women who become trees or animals, stones or stars. Ovid's book has been the source for

countless other works down the ages. Translated into prose by Mary Innes.

OVID. **METAMORPHOSES. Glossary, index, 416pp. IUP55, 2.95p.**
A verse translation by Rolfe Humphreys of Ovid's masterwork.

PARKER-RHODES, FREDERICK. **WHOLESIGHT—THE SPIRIT QUEST. 30pp. PHP78, 1.35p.**
Parker-Rhodes, a Quaker, writes that this pamphlet *gathers up some of the threads of my abiding concern for Wholesight, in the belief that this is the most urgent need of man today. If we cannot find coherence among religion, science, art, and politics, all these will come to nothing.... My aim, therefore, is to show by myths and stories how we may gain a little fluency in that forgotten tongue.*

PERRY, JOHN WEIR. **THE LORD OF THE FOUR QUARTERS. Illus-trations, index, 272pp. McM66, 1.50p.**
A Jungian psychiatrist traces the archetypes of the royal sacred father-king through the myths of the Nile, the ancient Near East, Indo-European ancient cultures, ancient China, and the ancient Americas. The volume is well organized and includes a profusion of quotations from primary myths. A fascinating study, though often fairly dry. Many notes and an excellent, topically-oriented, long bibliography are also included, along with an extensive introduction.

PUHVEL, JEAN, ed. **MYTH AND LAW AMONG THE INDO- EURO-PEANS. Notes, bibliography, 286pp. UCa70, 13.50c.**
A collection of papers given at a symposium held at the University of California, Los Angeles, focusing on Indo-European comparative mythology.

RADIN, PAUL, ed. **AFRICAN FOLKTALES. 5.95p.**
See the African Philosophies section.

RADIN, PAUL. **THE TRICKSTER: A STUDY IN AMERICAN INDIAN MYTHOLOGY. 3.45p.**
See the American Indian Religion section.

RECINOS, ADRIAN and DELIA GOETZ, trs. **POPOL VUH: THE SA-CRED BOOK OF THE ANCIENT QUICHE MAYA. 9.95c.**
See the Ancient Americas section.

REES, ALWYN and BRINLEY. **CELTIC HERITAGE. 7.95p.**
See the Ancient Britain section.

RIEU, E.V., tr. **APOLLONIUS OF RHODES—THE VOYAGE OF ARGO. Introduction, glossary, 216pp. Vik59, 1.95p.**
The **Argonautica** of Apollonius—written in the third century BC—is the only full remaining account of Jason's voyage in quest of the Golden Fleece. Though Apollonius used the manner and matter of the epic, he wrote from a personal viewpoint, as a critical observer.

ROBINSON, HERBERT and KNOX WILSON. **MYTHS AND LEGENDS OF ALL NATIONS. Index, 256pp. LtA76, 2.95p.**
Short summaries of many of the major world myths, arranged geographically.

ROHEIM, GEZA. **THE ETERNAL ONES OF THE DREAM. Notes, index, 283pp. IUP45, 5.40p.**
A psychoanalytic interpretation of Australian myth and ritual. All the major myths are discussed and analyzed at length. The analysis is Freudian rather than Jungian in tone and this is clearly a scholarly work. The following are some of the major topics: *The Meaning of Totemic Myth; The Dual Heroes; The Origin of Circumcision; The Phallic Ritual; The Concentric Circle and the Fertility Rite; Destruction and Restitution; The Rainbow Serpent; Wandering Ancestors;* and *The Totem Sacrament.* A great deal of background information is also included.

ROHEIM, GEZA. **THE GATES OF THE DREAM. Notes, index, 562pp. IUP52, 6.50p.**
This monumental work, alas, the author's swan song, crowns her life's work.... While the story suggests dream theory, the bulk of the volume is devoted to the application of the dream theory to anthropology and to the psychoanalytic interpretation of myth and folklore. In this respect it will serve as a sourcebook of the first order.... It is crammed to capacity with anthropologic material, showing an almost fabulous erudition and encyclopedic knowledge of the mythologies of all times and all parts of the earth, reminiscent of James Frazer and W. Wundt.—**American Journal of Psychotherapy.**

ROHEIM, GEZA. **THE RIDDLE OF THE SPHINX. Notes, index, 312pp. H&R74, 5.30p.**
An in depth study of Central Australian primitives which focuses on the totemic mythology and rituals of the tribes of this area and on their demon beliefs, fairy tales, and magic. There is a detailed psychoanalytic interpretation of the rites and customs. An introduction by Werner Muensterberger and Christopher Nichols discusses Roheim and psychoanalytic anthropology.

ROLLESTON, T.W. **MYTHS AND LEGENDS OF THE CELTIC RACE. Illustrations, glossary, index, 457pp. Lem34, 26.50c.**
This is an extremely comprehensive selection of Celtic myths, grouped by subject and well retold. Rolleston includes an abundance of background information to put the myths into perspective and make them more comprehensible.

ROSE, H.J. **A HANDBOOK OF GREEK MYTHOLOGY. Bibliography, indices, 372pp. Dut59, 2.95p.**
A comprehensive, concise manual. Rose briefly retells the myths and analyzes their content at length. An abundance of notes follow each chapter. It is a somewhat dry study and a work of excellent scholarship.

Sagas

Broadly speaking, a saga is a form of medieval Icelandic prose which tells a story or relates an historical event. More narrowly, a saga is a piece of legendary or historical fiction in which the author has attempted an imaginary reconstruction of the past organized according to certain aesthetic principles. Usually the story centers around a hero and sagas can be classified in three ways: king's sagas, legendary sagas, and sagas of Icelanders. The sagas form the only remaining coherent picture of early Scandinavian history and cosmology. Icelandic historians seem to have started writing accounts of their country's past toward the end of the eleventh century.

Hermod's farewell to Baldur.

DASENT, G.W., tr. **THE STORY OF BURNT NJAL. Index, 382pp. Dut11/Den, 5.00c.**
A translation of Njal's Saga. We prefer the Magnusson and Palsson version, but this one is certainly adequate. The Icelandic saga has been put into modern English and all of the numerous characters come alive as they go about their everyday pursuits. *Burnt Njal* is an alternate title and it is thought to be an allusion to the matter of his death. Professor E. Turville-Petre provides an introduction.

FELL, CHRISTINE, tr. **EGIL'S SAGA. 256pp. Den75, 12.00c.**
For a description of this saga, see the Palsson edition. This translation is faithful to the original and includes John Lucas' versions of the many poems in the saga. A lengthy introduction and many notes accompany the translation and there are also genealogical tables, maps, and indices.

FOX, DENTON and HERMANN PALSSON, trs. **GRETTIR'S SAGA. Introduction, maps, index, 218pp. UTo74, 4.50p.**
This is a fine translation of the last of the great Icelandic sagas. It tells of the life and death of Grettir, a great rebel, individualist, and romantic hero viewed unromantically. Grettir spends his childhood violently defying authority; as a youth of sixteen he kills a man and is outlawed; all the rest of his life he devotes, with remarkable composure, to fighting more and more formidable enemies. He pitches himself against bears, berserks, wraiths, trolls, and finally, it seems, the whole population of Iceland. Yet he is not a bloodthirsty killer, only a man who is totally unwilling to compromise. As a result of his desire for freedom, he becomes increasingly isolated, although he wishes to live in society, and indeed can hardly bear solitude. Driven back and forth from Iceland to Norway, harried around Iceland, he continually flees subjection and confinement only to find a perilous freedom beset both by the external hazards of a new land and the internal hazards of loneliness and pride. He escapes to freedom and finds destruction and finally meets his death on the top of an unscalable island near the northern tip of Iceland. This translation is unexpurgated and in unarchaic English, and it reads beautifully.

HIGHT, G.H., tr. **THE SAGA OF GRETTIR THE STRONG. Introduction, glossary, notes, index, 288pp. Den72, 2.40p.**
A somewhat dry translation.

JOHNSTON, GEORGE, tr. **THE SAGA OF GISLI. Maps, index, 159pp. UTo63, 3.95p.**
This saga tells the story of a man and his family who came to Iceland from Norway about 950. About 960 Gisli, the central figure, was outlawed for killing his brother-in-law, and lived in hiding for about thirteen years until he was finally caught and killed. Around this history, the author has spun a web of conflicting passions. Gisli is portrayed both as a man of strength and courage and as a poet and dreamer tormented by nightmarish visions which gradually sap his will to resist. The translation retains the distinctive traces of the rhythm and texture of the original. Introduction and notes by Peter Foote.

JONES, GWYN, tr. **EIRIK THE RED AND OTHER ICELANDIC SAGAS. Introduction, 4"x6", 334pp. Oxf61, 5.95c.**
Fine translations of Hen-Thorir, The Vapnfjord Men, Thorstein Staff-Struck, Hrafnkel the Priest of Frey, Eirik the Red, Thidrandi whom the Goddesses Slew, Authun and the Bear, Gunnlaug Worm-tongue, and King Hrolf and His Champions. The sagas have been translated in their entirety.

KIRBY, W.F., tr. **KALEVALA: THE LAND OF HEROES. Glossary, notes, 689pp. Dut07, 5.00c/each.**
This is a verse translation of this epic, in two volumes.

LAING, SAMUEL, tr. **SNORRI STURLUSON, HEIMSKRINGLA: THE OLAF SAGAS. Dut64, 6.75c/each.**
Sturluson is the outstanding literary figure in thirteenth century Iceland. In **Heimskringla** he surveys the whole course of Norwegian history, beginning with the legendary era and continuing through the end of the twelfth century. Sturluson drew on both all the available written works and on the oral tradition in making his compilation. He blended his material extremely well and was faithful to his sources. Volume I contains a general introduction along with **King Olaf Trygvesson's Saga, The Tale of the Greenlanders**, and the first part of the **Saga of King Olaf the Saint**. Volume II continues the **Saga of King Olaf** and includes a variety of technical appendices. This translation has been revised by Jacqueline Simpson, who also provided the introduction. Each volume is about 250 pages long.

MAGNUSSON, MAGNUS and HERMANN PALSSON, trs. **KING HARALD'S SAGA. 187pp. Vik66, 1.95p.**
1066 was not only the start of the Norman era in England; it effectively closed the Viking era as well. Less than three weeks before the Battle of Hastings, Harold of England defeated and killed the giant Harald Hardradi of Norway at Stamford Bridge in Yorkshire. **King Harald's Saga**, written by the Icelandic historian Snorri Sturluson, records the turbulent life of Harald, a warrior who served and fought in every

corner of Europe, from Russia to Sicily, and tells how the last of the great Vikings was rewarded, for his claim to the English throne, with _seven feet of English soil_. The translators provide a lengthy introduction, maps, genealogical tables, and a glossary.

MAGNUSSON, MAGNUS and HERMANN PALSSON, trs. **LAXDAELA SAGA. Forty-two page introduction, maps, long glossary, chronology, 272pp. Vik69, 2.95p.**
A thirteenth century Icelandic saga which is best known for its tragic love triangle. The Icelandic ideas of property and of courtly chivalry are clearly presented. This has been the most popular of all the medieval sagas over the centuries.

MAGNUSSON, MAGNUS and HERMANN PALSSON, trs. **NJAL'S SAGA. Long introduction, maps, glossary, chronology, 378pp. Vik60, 2.95p.**
A late thirteenth century Icelandic prose saga based on historical events in Iceland in the tenth century. It describes a fifty-year blood feud from its violent beginnings to its tragic end in a spare, simple style. It is generally considered the mightiest of all the Icelandic prose sagas.

MAGNUSSON, MAGNUS and HERMANN PALSSON, trs. **THE VINLAND SAGAS: THE NORSE DISCOVERIES OF AMERICA. 124pp. Vik65, 1.95p.**
The two medieval Icelandic sagas translated in this volume tell of the discovery of America by Norsemen five centuries before Columbus. The sagas describe how Eirik the Red founded an Icelandic colony in Greenland and how his son, Leif the Lucky, later sailed south to explore and, if possible, exploit the chance discovery by one of his men of an unknown land which is today believed to have been North America.

MAGOUN, FRANCIS. **THE KALEVALA. Introduction, glossary, index, 437pp. HUP63, 21.50c.**
The Kalevala, which means _Land of the Heroes_, is Finland's national epic, a collection of tales about magical heroes first told in song and collected by Elias Lonnrot in the nineteenth century. The songs are not unified and the epic is not of the usual type. This is a scholarly verse translation of Lonnrot's expanded second edition.

PALSSON, HERMANN, tr. **HRAFINKEL'S SAGA AND OTHER STORIES. Lengthy introduction, maps, 137pp. Vik71, 2.95p.**
All seven stories in this volume date from the thirteenth century, and exemplify the outstanding qualities of realistic fiction in medieval Iceland. Three of the stories are set in the pastoral society of Iceland and four, written without firsthand knowledge of Scandinavia, describe the adventures of Icelandic poets and peasants in the royal courts of Norway and Denmark.

PALSSON, HERMANN and PAUL EDWARDS, trs. **EGIL'S SAGA. Introduction, maps, glossary, chronology, 254pp. Vik76, 2.50p.**
Probably written about 1230 by Snorri Sturluson, Egil's Saga offers a panoramic view of the Viking world from the middle of the ninth century to the end of the tenth. It is dominated throughout by the demonic influence of its hero, Egil, and the influence of his god, the many faced Odin. Few sagas can match it for its monumental presentation of a central figure, portraying both the inner life and the deeds of Egil from early childhood to death. Of enormous physical strenth and with something of the troll in his nature, Egil is, by turns, killer, drunkard, miser, poet, wanderer, farmer, lawyer, and sorcerer. This is our favorite translation.

PALSSON, HERMANN and PAUL EDWARDS, trs. **EYRBYGGJA SAGA. Long introduction, notes, 198pp. UTo73, 10.00c.**
Of all the various records of Icelandic history and literature, wrote Sir Walter Scott, _there is none more interesting than_ **Eyrbyggja Saga**. Probably composed soon after 1250, its central figure is Snorri the Priest, _a very shrewd man with remarkable foresight, a long memory, and a taste for vengeance_, whose friends found him a wise counselor, but whose enemies learned to dread his advice. During his lifetime (963-1031), Iceland officially adopted Christianity, and, although formerly a pagan priest, Snorri did more than anyone else to persuade his fellow countrymen to question the value of their ancestral faith. The saga has a complex structure in which eerie ghost stories are interwoven with sober and realistic accounts of life in Iceland a thousand years ago.

PALSSON, HERMANN and PAUL EDWARDS, trs. **HROLF GAUTREKSSON. Introduction, 148pp. UTo72, 6.00c.**
A translation of a fourteenth century Icelandic novel in which features of the sagas of earlier centuries are seen in the process of blending with the conventions and characteristics of the European romance. The story takes the reader from Scandinavia to Russia, to England and Ireland, through a world of primitive Christianity in which people who are still unmistakably Vikings live in a strangely chivalrous society of jousts, feasts, and courtly love. The underlying moral theme centers on moderation and excess.

PRESS, MURIEL, tr. **THE LAXDALE SAGA. Introduction, indices, 330pp. Dut64, 5.00c.**
This saga was written in the west of Iceland about 1250; it is the second Icelandic saga (**Egil's Saga** was the first) to be conceived and executed on a grand scale. The chief characters were historical Icelanders of the tenth and eleventh centuries and the story is a compound of verifiable history, local tradition, and artistic invention. The central tragic motif is a triangle love—the woman is in love with the man who is not her husband, but she urges her husband to bring about the death of the man she loves.

SYNGE, URSULA. **LAND OF HEROES: A RETELLING OF THE KALEVALA. 222pp. Ath78, 9.35c.**
In this lyrical prose retelling of the song cycles, Ms. Synge sets forth the adventures of three heroes who were rivals for the hand of the lovely Maiden of Pohja. The maiden's mother is a sorceress and she sets each of the suitors almost impossible tasks. _The heroes themselves are magicians rather than warriors, and their magic is the magic of song, involving miraculous journeys and miracle escapes; they are larger than life-size, liars and rogues, boastful and vainglorious, but they are on the side of the gods, finally only vanquished when Christianity comes to Finland._—from the introduction.

TAYLOR, PAUL and W.H. AUDEN, trs. **THE ELDER EDDA. Glossary, index, 173pp. RaH69/Fab, 7.95p.**
The **Poetic** or **Elder Edda** is a compilation made about AD 1200 of earlier Icelandic poems on cosmology, mythology, and the stories of the Norse heroes. Together with the **Prose** or **Younger Edda**, it is the chief source of our knowledge of Scandinavian mythology. This translation is the result of a collaboration between a distinguished scholar and a major poet who has always felt a deep instinctive sympathy for these masterpieces. The result succeeds superbly in conveying the power, sharpness, and precision of the original. Professors Peter Salus and Peter Taylor provide an excellent introduction.

YOUNG, JEAN, tr. **SNORRI STURLUSON, THE PROSE EDDA. Introduction, notes, index, 131pp. UCa54, 2.45p.**
A twelfth or thirteenth century collection and arrangement of the pagan deities, myths, and legends of the past—with many quotations from the **Poetic Edda**. Though Sturluson himself was a Christian he had a strong interest in the past and wanted to present as complete an account of it as was possible.

————————— **END OF SAGAS SUBSECTION** —————————

SANTILLANA, GIORGIO and HERTHA VON DECHEND. **HAMLET'S MILL: AN ESSAY ON MYTH AND THE FRAME OF TIME. Illustrations, many notes, bibliography, index, 528pp. God69, 6.95p.**
Since the time of the Greeks, mythology and science have developed separately. The authors of this book contend that myth was a preliterate form of science, and that the gods and places of myth were but ciphers for celestial activity, a language for the perpetuation of complex astronomical data. It is a bold theory and one which the authors document in great detail through their analysis of the mythology of East and West. This is a provocative work which should interest all those who seek to deepen their understanding of the role myth plays in civilization.

SEDGWICK, PAULITA. **MYTHOLOGICAL CREATURES. 6.95c.**
See the Children's Books section.

SHEPARD, ODELL. **THE LORE OF THE UNICORN. Twenty-three plates, notes, index, 213pp. A&U30, 6.95c.**
A storehouse of unicorn lore gleaned from mythology, folklore, literature, art, medicine, and many other areas.

SIMPSON, MICHAEL, tr. **GODS AND HEROES OF THE GREEKS: THE LIBRARY OF APOLLODORUS. Illustrations, bibliography, index, 319pp. UMa76, 5.95p.**
The Library of Apollodorus, probably composed in the first century AD, is the only Greek handbook of mythology to survive antiquity, and it is a major source of our knowledge of Greek myths. Beginning with the birth of the gods and ending with the death of Odysseus, the **Library** traces the destinies of such great mythic figures as Prometheus, Oedipus, Heracles, Daedalus, and the heroes of the Trojan War. Sir James Frazer called the **Library**, *an accurate record of what the Greeks in general believed about the origin and early history of the world and their race.* This translation captures the simplicity and straightforwardness of the original. Extensive notes consider literary, structuralist, and psychoanalytic interpretations and modern versions of the myths; discuss the classical works in which they appear; and explore modern reactions.

SMITH, GEORGE, tr. **THE CHALDEAN ACCOUNT OF GENESIS. Index, 335pp. Wiz1876, 12.95c.**
Translations from cuneiform tablets unearthed at Nineva recounting the creation, the fall of man, the deluge, the tower of Babel, the Babylonian fables, and legends of the gods. The texts show a surprising parallel to the **Old Testament**.

SPENCE, LEWIS. MYTHS AND LEGENDS OF THE NORTH AMERICAN INDIANS. 5.50p.
See the American Indian Religion section.

SQUIRE, CHARLES. CELTIC MYTH AND LEGEND. Bibliography, index, 462pp. NPC05, 4.95p.
This is one of the most comprehensive studies of Celtic mythology, legend, and poetry ever produced. It has been out of print for many years and only recently been reprinted. Both the ancient Gaelic and British Celts are represented as are all the chief characters of Celtic mythology. The stories are well written and commentary is interspersed. Included are tales about the Gaelic gods and the giants they battled, the heroes of the **Mabinogion**, and the ancient British epics down through King Arthur and his knights.

TAYLOR, THOMAS. ELEUSINIAN AND BACCHIC MYSTERIES. 5.00p.
See the Ancient Greece and Rome section.

TAYLOR, THOMAS, tr. **THE FABLE OF CUPID AND PSYCHE. 172pp. PRS77, 12.50c.**
A facsimile, limited edition of Taylor's translation, originally published in 1795 and including Taylor's original introduction.

TRIPP, EDWARD. THE MERIDIAN HANDBOOK OF CLASSICAL MYTHOLOGY. Index, 646pp. Cro70, 5.95p.
A comprehensive, alphabetically arranged handbook of Greek and Roman mythology. The myths are retold as completely as possible in one place, so the narrative does not have to be pieced together out of several entries. All significant versions of each myth are given and the accounts are drawn almost exclusively from original sources, all of which are fully cited. The entries include not only characters and events, but nearly all the places mentioned in the myths, the constellations named for mythological personages, and brief descriptions of the principal classical works. Plentiful cross references are provided. There are also several maps and a pronunciation key.

VELLACOTT, PHILIP, tr. **AESCHYLUS—THE ORESTEIAN TRILOGY. Introduction, pronunciation guide, verse translation, index, 203pp. Vik59, 1.95p.**
What is justice? How is it related to vengeance? Can justice be reconciled with the demands of religion, the violence of human feeling, the forces of fate? These questions, which puzzled thoughtful Athenians in the decades after the battle of Marathon, provided the theme for **Agamemnon**, **The Choephori**, and **The Eumenides**—the grim tragedies that make up the **Oresteian Trilogy**. In these plays Aeschylus takes as his subject the bloody chain of murder and revenge within the royal family of Argos—a chain finally broken only after the intervention of the goddess Athena.

VELLACOTT, PHILIP, tr. **AESCHYLUS—PROMETHEUS BOUND, THE SUPPLIANTS, SEVEN AGAINST THEBES, THE PERSIANS. Introduction, verse translation, notes, 159pp. Vik61, 1.95p.**
Aeschylus (525-c.456 BC) was the first of the great Greek tragedians. The four plays presented in this volume—together with the **Oresteian Trilogy**—are all that survive of his work. **The Persians** is set against the Athenian victory at Salamis, which took place only eight years before the play was written. In **Seven Against Thebes** the two sons of Oedipus are relentlessly pursued to their death by a family curse. In **The Suppliants** and **Prometheus**, conflict of principles is resolved by rational compromise.

VELLACOTT, PHILIP, tr. **EURIPIDES—ALCESTIS, HIPPOLYTUS, IPHIGENIA IN TAURIS. Long introduction, verse translation, notes, 189pp. Vik74, 1.95p.**
Euripides (484-407 BC) is seen in the three plays in this volume as the skeptical questioner of his age. **Alcestis**, an early play in which a queen agrees to die to save her husband's life, is cast in a tragic vein, although it contains passages of satire and even comedy, while **Iphigenia in Tauris**, with its apparently happy ending, melodramatically reunites the ill fated children of Agamemnon. **Hippolytus**, however, is pure tragedy—the fatal impact of Phaedra's unreasoning passion for her chaste stepson.

VELLACOTT, PHILIP, tr. **EURIPIDES—MEDEA, HECABE, ELECTRA, HERCULES. Introduction, verse translation, notes, 205pp. Vik63, 2.50p.**
Medea, the story of Medea's horrible revenge for the infidelity of Jason, the hero of the Argonauts, is Euripides' earliest surviving tragedy; **Hercules** is one of his later plays. In **Hecabe** and **Electra** he again underlies the wickedness of revenge. An outspoken critic of society and the gods, Euripides was at his most eloquent on the theme of human suffering, and one of the most lyrical of all the dramatists.

VICKERS, BRIAN. TOWARDS GREEK TRAGEDY. Illustrations, many notes, bibliography, index, 683pp. Lon73, 29.40c.
This is a fresh and fundamental reevaluation of the whole corpus of Greek tragedy. Professor Vickers' main argument is that Greek tragedy is not a remote or metaphysical experience, but a representation of human conflict and suffering. Reacting against the tendency of

modern interpreters of Greek tragedy to treat the plays in isolation from their cultural context, Vickers reconstructs those social and religious attitudes which were most important to the plays. Turning to Greek mythology, Vickers begins by analyzing the many conflicting modern psychological and anthropological approaches to myth, and he shows that not all of them are appropriate to Greek mythology. He sees the Greek myths as being heavily influenced by the social and religious attitudes he discusses early in the book.

VIRGIL. **THE AENEID. Introduction, biographical note, cast of characters, 394pp. Scr51, 3.95p.**
This is a verse translation by Rolfe Humphreys.

VIRGIL. **THE AENEID. Introduction, maps, glossary, bibliography, 364pp. Vik58, 2.50p.**
A prose translation by W.F. Jackson Knight of Virgil's (70-19 BC) epic which describes the legendary origin of the Roman nation. It tells of the Trojan prince Aeneas, who escaped, with some followers, after Troy fell, and sailed to Italy. They settled there and laid the foundations of Roman power. The **Aeneid** was commissioned by Augustus Caesar and the text emphasizes Rome's destiny as the ruler of the world. Virgil's tone and style follow the pattern set by Homer.

■ *WARNER, REX.* **THE STORIES OF THE GREEKS. Introduction, illustrations, 415pp. FSG67, 7.95p.**
This is a one volume edition of Warner's three highly praised books on the gods, heroes, and wars of ancient Greece: **Men and Gods, Greeks and Trojans,** and **The Vengeance of the Gods. Men and Gods** is a retelling of thirty-two Greek legends, mostly taken from Ovid. Homer's **Iliad** is the main source for **Greeks and Trojans.** In **The Vengeance of the Gods** all the stories are taken from the plays of Euripides and Aeschylus. This is a delightful work which we recommend to all who are interested in Greek mythology.

WATLING, E.F., tr. **SOPHOCLES—ELECTRA AND OTHER PLAYS. Introduction, notes, 218pp. Vik53, 1.95p.**
A fine verse translation of four plays: **Electra,** Sophocles' presentation of part of the Orestean legend; **Women of Trachis,** a work remarkable for the human versimilitude imparted to a near repulsive piece of mythology; **Philoctetes,** a portrayal of the struggles of right against might; and **Ajax,** an exploration of the theme of the fallen great man.

WATLING, E.F., tr. **SOPHOCLES—THE THEBAN PLAYS. Introduction, notes, 168pp. Vik47, 1.95p.**
These three plays by Sophocles (496-406 BC), though they are all based on the legend of the royal house of Thebes, were written at different periods and dramatize different themes. **Antigone** is the tragedy of a woman ruled by conscience, an overconfident king, and a young man tormented by conflicting loyalties; **King Oedipus** is a vast

portrait of a tragic hero; and **Oedipus at Colonus** completes the story with the legend of the passing of the aged king. The translation is into verse.

WATTS, ALAN. **THE TWO HANDS OF GOD. Twenty-three plates, notes, bibliography, index, 256pp. McM69, 1.95p.**
A fascinating exploration and exposition of the myths of polarity, those crucial symbolic relationships such as light and darkness, good and evil, which illustrate the inner unity of opposites. These mythological themes, centering on the idea that explicit opposition conceals implicit unity, are illustrated by a treasury of stories and myths from Chinese, Indian, Egyptian, Iranian, and early Christian sources.

WERNER, E.T.C. **MYTHS AND LEGENDS OF CHINA. Illustrations, glossary, index, 475pp. Arn22, 29.55c.**
This is one of the most extensive collections available of Chinese myths. Werner prepared his versions from the original Chinese texts and he is faithful to the sources. His retellings also read well and he includes a great deal of introductory and background material.

WHITE, T.H., ed. and tr. **THE BESTIARY. Many notes, bibliography, index, 296pp. Put54/CaL, 2.95p.**
This is a translation of a twelfth century Latin bestiary, illustrated with over 125 plates drawn from the original medieval manuscripts. The sources go back to the distant past and come out of a great variety of traditions. The British title is **Book of Beasts.**

WILKINS, W.J. **HINDU MYTHOLOGY. 10.65c.**
See the Indian Philosophy section.

ZIMMER, HEINRICH. **THE KING AND THE CORPSE TALES OF THE SOUL'S CONQUEST OF EVIL. 338pp. PUP48, 4.95p.**
A group of popular stories from East and West, linked to one another by their common concern for the problem of man's eternal conflict with the forces of evil. Zimmer's commentary discloses the meanings within each apparently unrelated symbol and suggests the philosophical wholeness of this assortment of myth. Beginning with a tale from **The Arabian Nights,** the theme unfolds through legends from Irish paganism, medieval Christianity, the Arthurian cycle, and early Hinduism.

ZIMMER, HEINRICH. **MYTHS AND SYMBOLS IN INDIAN ART AND CIVILIZATION. 3.95p.**
See the Indian Philosophy section.

ZIMMERMAN, J.E. **DICTIONARY OF CLASSICAL MYTHOLOGY. 319pp. Ban64, 1.95p.**
This is the best inexpensive dictionary we know of. Zimmerman includes over 2,000 entries covering all aspects of classical mythology. Pronunciation guides and cross references are also included.

NUMEROLOGY

Numerology is the science of numbers or vibrations and was one of the sciences practiced by men of great wisdom in ages long past. They realized that everything is made up of vibrations. They knew that this universal law applied to people as well as to things and that it could be used to determine a great deal about individuals. It is in fact part of what makes us individuals. Each number has its own vibratory influence and therefore its own characteristics. Through a few simple rules and formulas we can begin to see how these influences come into play in our lives and have a definite influence over us.

Numerology is the belief that a person comes into a life at a certain time and with a certain name, not as a matter of chance but as a matter of choice, and that from these things much can be told about the person and his life. Even if you cannot agree with the idea that your birth name and birth date are not a matter of chance, there is no reason to argue with the theory that they have a definite effect upon your life, and upon this fact numerology is based. You may be surprised to find out just how much your numbers can tell about you and your life. It may tell you some things that you already know, others that you only suspected, and some things that you have only thus far hoped were true. This information is based upon calculations made from the numbers derived from the birth date and from the letters of the name given at birth. Not only can much be told from one's name at birth, but also from nicknames and name changes made through life.

Numerology gives us a chance to see ourselves better, to realize just what talents and abilities we possess, what our limitations are, what we are here to do and how best to accomplish that destiny, what jobs we are best qualified for, what lessons we came into this lifetime to learn, and what debts we are here to pay off. We can learn about situations and people, what forces rule us, what our greatest area of power is, the cycles of our life and the vibrations governing them, our challenges, what each year holds in store for us, and what it is best for us to do and not do.

Part of the beauty of numerology is that you do not have to study long and hard before you can begin to put what you have learned to use. You can quickly learn a few basic facts and formulas that will immediately help you to begin to understand yourself and others better. From there, you can go to learn more and more up to any point you wish. Of all the sciences, it is probably one of the easiest to learn. If you can add, or even just count on your fingers for that matter, you are able to use numerology.

In numerology we work with the numbers 1 through 9 and the master numbers 11, 22, and 33. The master numbers are never reduced, but all other two or more digit numbers are reduced to one digit. For instance, if we have the number 25, we add the 2 and 5 together: $2 + 5 = 7$. So the number we work with is 7. With years, such as 1941, we add all of the digits together: $1 + 9 + 4 + 1 = 15$. Then we must add the 1 and 5 together: $1 + 5 = 6$. Thus the number we work with is 6. The exception to this rule would be in the case of such dates as 1948, where the sum would be 22. As this is a master number, it is not reduced.

Each letter of the alphabet has its own number or vibratory influence. In the numbers from 1 to 9 are to be found all of the experiences that life can present. Here are to be found

all the things we must learn about, and in one life or another we carry all of the vibrations in each of the positions in our chart. Each number has both positive and negative aspects, because nothing is all positive or all negative. The master numbers are far more powerful than the other nine numbers in both positive and negative aspects. When you find these numbers in your chart you must take care and watch closely, lest they begin to produce the negative aspects of these vibrations. The negative aspects of the master numbers are far more destructive than the negative aspects of the others.

No number is ever limited to what it is, neither is a person limited by the numbers in his or her chart unless that is his or her choice. If we learn to attune ourselves to the highest aspects of any vibration, we can elevate that vibration to the one above it, so that there really is no limit to the heights we can achieve. We have only to set a goal and begin to work toward it, discarding any thoughts of limitations we may have, for in truth the only limitations we have are in our own minds. You have the ability to be anything that you would like to be, and numerology can help to show you the way to reach your goal. Your today is a product of your yesterday, and so your tomorrow will be a product of your today. Let's get on with building a better tomorrow, and the time to start is right now.

—condensed from **It's All In Your Numbers**, *by Kathleen Roquemore*

ANDERSON, MARY. NUMEROLOGY—SECRET POWER OF NUMBERS. 64pp. Wei72/TPL, 1.25p.
An introductory survey, with sections on the meaning of numbers, words and numbers, meaning of the birthday, divining with numbers.

ANONYMOUS. ADVANCED NUMEROLOGY. Offset, 8½"x11", 90pp. Hug nd, 6.25p.
A collection of notes gathered from a variety of sources.

■ AVERY, KEVIN. THE NUMBERS OF LIFE: THE HIDDEN POWER IN NUMEROLOGY. 312pp. Dou77, 3.95p.
This is an extremely comprehensive guide to numerology which is both spiritual and practical. Avery has studied and taught astrology and the Qabala in addition to numerology and he integrates both of these into his discussion. He also writes clearly and incorporates many case histories. Main topics include personality, habits, soul urge, expressions in life, potential problems, and the past, present, and future. This is a revised and enlarged version of an earlier work published under the same title.

BOSMAN, LEONARD. THE MEANING AND PHILOSOPHY OF NUMBERS. 187pp. HPG32, 4.85p.
This is a spiritual analysis of numbers. Bosman is a theosophist and in this book he discusses the implications of each number from one to ten, showing that they represent cosmic and creative processes. He writes in an archaic style and incorporates information from ancient Egypt and Greece.

BUTLER, CHRISTOPHER. NUMBER SYMBOLISM. Notes, bibliography, index, 198pp. RKP70, 9.95c.
This book traces the history of numerological allegory from its beginnings in Greece and its appearance in early biblical exegesis, to its effect upon the syncretic philosophical and scientific thought of the Renaissance. According to Butler, the numerological tradition had three main elements—a cosmological science of creation according to numbers, a belief that the numbers of the **Bible** had an allegorical significance, and a symbolic arithmology connected with magic, the occult, and astrology. This study is a far cry from the usual books on

numerology, and all who are interested in a deep understanding of the meaning of numbers should find it a welcome addition to the literature.

■ *CAMPBELL, FLORENCE.* **YOUR DAYS ARE NUMBERED. 246pp. Gat nd, 4.50p.**
This has been considered *the* basic numerology text. Every aspect of the subject is clearly discussed and the book is well organized. Recommended as a good beginners' manual.

CHEIRO. **BOOK OF NUMBERS. 188pp. Arc64/Crg, 1.50p.**
Cheiro clearly demonstrates how the science of numbers may be applied to your own life and affairs. He gives the numerical value of birth dates, names, etc., and he shows how to calculate from these figures the most propitious times for important decisions and transactions. Cheiro was mainly noted for his palmistry books, but all of his work is well regarded.

COATES, AUSTIN. **NUMEROLOGY. Index, 127pp. Stu74, 2.95p.**
This volume presents a very sophisticated system developed by the author, based on forty years of experience and personal observation. Coates is a British foreign service officer and has spent most of his adult life in the East. He feels that his system is in accord with the I Ching and with Buddhist principles. The text is graphically illustrated and presented very clearly. Many case studies.

HELINE, CORINNE. **THE SACRED SCIENCE OF NUMBERS. 110pp. NAP71, 3.50p.**
A series of lessons on the spiritual significance of numbers one through thirteen. Ms. Heline is best known for her writings on the esoteric significance of the **Bible** and of music.

HITCHCOCK, HELYN. **HELPING YOURSELF WITH NUMEROL—OGY. 238pp. PrH72, 3.45p.**
This is a highly informative volume, especially for those who are interested in the self help approach. The author is a theosophist and a member of Astara (a metaphysical organization), so she includes spiritual values in her exposition. The instructions are easy to follow and a great deal of material is introduced.

HITCHCOCK, HELYN. **YOUR NUMBER PLEASE. 163pp. Sag73, 3.50p.**
Esoteric guidelines for running your life according to the dictates of the author's interpretation of numerology. Some of the book is highly simplistic, and some sections present unusual and interesting material.

HOUSTON, HELEN and J. WALTON. **THE SECRET IN YOUR NAME AND YOUR NUMBER AND DESTINY. Offset, 8½"x11", 51pp. Hug nd, 4.95p.**
Two essays, discussing the spiritual meaning of the numbers and their vibratory power. The material which the authors discuss here is not available in any other volume that we know of.

JAIN, M.C. **BIRTHDAY NUMEROLOGY. 87pp. Sag73, 5.00c.**
Jain is a well known Indian astrologer. He began his study of numerology to help those, who know their date of birth but not their exact time, forecast their future and cycles of emotion. The system he discovered after twenty-five years of research he terms "birthday numerology" and in this book he describes it in detail. Many charts are included along with case studies and instructional material. For those to whom this sounds interesting, let us make the following comment: Hindu astrology, palmistry, and numerology books are written for Indians and often can not be easily understood by Westerners.

JORDAN, JUNO. **NUMEROLOGY: THE ROMANCE IN YOUR NAME. 297pp. DeV65, 8.95c.**
A complete course in numerology for the serious student. Dr. Jordan was a numerologist for Hollywood stars and this tone is apparent in her exposition. Virtually every aspect of numerology is discussed at length and many case histories are included.

KNAPP, ELSIE. **NUMBERS MEAN MORE THAN YOU THINK. 49pp. Snd74, 1.50p.**
An unusual system of numerological prediction is out-lined in this book and its rationale explored. It's based on a system of arrows originally devised by Pythagoras.

KOZMINSKY, ISIDORE. **NUMBERS—THEIR MEANING AND MAGIC. 100pp. Wei nd/HPG, 2.95p.**
The first half describes the symbols and meanings of numbers; the second half discusses the numerical values of letters, the Qabala of Pythagoras, prophesying, and colors, metals and gems which harmonize with numbers.

LAURIE, JOHN. **THE SCIENCE OF NUMEROLOGY THROUGH THE LAW OF VIBRATION. Offset, stapled, 8½"x11", 75pp. HeR59, 3.00p.**
A study of the spiritual values of the numbers as they relate to the soul's development. Included are chapters on cycles and marriage. Some interesting ideas are presented, but Laurie does not write well and his exposition is scattered.

MENNINGER, KARL. **NUMBER WORDS AND NUMBER SYMBOLS. Index, 6⅞"x9⅞", 480pp. MIT69, 9.95p.**
This is a wide ranging scholarly work which recounts the global development of numbers throughout history. Menninger presents many examples of how numbers and numerals, in the course of their evolution, have come to reflect the cultural style, the linguistic patterns, and the conceptual outlook of their makers and users. In addition to the more academic uses of numbers, he also discusses the mystical, numerological, and religious significance of numbers. Anyone with a deep interest in numbers will find this a fascinating survey. It is profusely illustrated with photographs and line drawings and the writing style is not technical.

MOORE, GERUN. **NUMBERS WILL TELL. 178pp. G&D73, 2.95p.**
Those who are deeply interested in numerology feel that this is one of the best books available. Moore himself is a well known numerologist and his presentation here is exceedingly clear. His system is based on Pythagoras and on Cheiro and like them, he uses the Chaldean alphabet. Every conceivable aspect of daily life in which numbers play a part is discussed and step-by-step directions are given for choosing favorite numbers.

OJHA, ASHUTOSH. **NUMEROLOGY FOR ALL. 188pp. HPB73, 2.00p.**
A complete presentation of the Indian science of numbers. A great deal of space is devoted to astrological correspondences.

OMARR, SYDNEY. **THOUGHT DIAL. 172pp. Wil58, 3.00p.**
Omarr devised the *thought dial* as a means of probing into an individual's subconscious. The technique, as he outlines it here, is simple and is based on a special number symbolism. The system resembles horary astrology in part and it can also be used to answer any number of pending questions. The system itself is hard to describe, and we do not totally understand it. But if you are interested, the book appears to give fairly complete instructions along with a great number of case studies.

■ *ROQUEMORE, KATHLEEN.* **IT'S ALL IN YOUR NUMBERS. Index, 312pp. H&R75, 12.50c.**
This is the most comprehensive book on numerology that we have seen. It is well written, organized, and covers many areas in depth that are either not dealt with in other books or are just briefly touched on. First, Ms. Roquemore presents information on the basic characteristics of numbers, how to interpret them, and how to calculate what your numbers are. From there she goes on to discuss what numerology has to say about the self (the inner and outer), the life cycles, and much else. The author takes a very spiritual approach in her presentation and integrates numerology with the other esoteric sciences. If you have been interested at all in numerology, this book should help you immensely in gaining insight into what your numbers mean in every aspect of your life.

SEPHARIAL. **FORTUNE TELLING BY NUMBERS. 70pp. Sag73, 1.50p.**
A qabalistic interpretation which is far more serious than the title would have you believe. The book is divided into chapters on the properties of numbers, the day planet, the hour planet, name and numbers, the magic square, and phonetic values.

SEPHARIAL. **THE KABALA OF NUMBERS. 388pp. NPC nd, 4.95p.**
This is a classic study on the esoteric significance of numbers. Sepharial studied the systems of the ancients and discovered that for them the laws governing the whole of nature and the underlying spiritual world are traceable only in terms of numbers. This is a fascinating, comprehensive study and is indispensible for the serious student of metaphysics. Includes diagrams, tables, examples, practical instruction, and historical material.

SEPHARIAL. **THE NUMBERS BOOK. 128pp. Fou57, 4.35c.**
An introductory study for the general student, clearly written, with both practical and interpretative material. Topics include the mysticism of numbers, names and numbers, numbers and characters, and divination by numbers.

SILCOCK, GRACE. **COSMOLOGY OF NUMBERS. 93pp. Sag73, 2.00p.**
An esoteric analysis of the vibratory power of each of the nine primary numbers.

VALLA, MARY. **THE POWER OF NUMBERS. 214pp. DeV71, 3.95p.**
A compilation of lessons in numerology as taught by the author. Her analysis of a number in each of its five positions derived from the birth date and name has been based on notes taken during thirty years of private counseling and research. The discussion is quite different from the other books we have seen and includes the general vibrations of the number, the soul path, destiny, mental image, and other aspects. An interesting philosophical/spiritual work.

VARLEY, DESMOND. **SEVEN, THE NUMBER OF CREATION. Many illustrations, index, 179pp. Bel76, 12.00c.**
Why, out of all possible numbers, should special significance be attached to the number seven? Why are there seven days in a week, seven wonders of the ancient world, seven seas, seven virtues, and seven sins? Seemingly trivial questions like these set Varley searching for the origins of the special qualities of the number seven. His quest led to some unexpected areas of investigation, ranging from medieval alchemy to ancient Sumerian mathematics, from comparative religion to psychology, and from astrology to world wide creation myths. This is a fascinating study which should appeal both to those interested in numerology and in mythology—about as diverse a field as any we can think of.

WESTCOTT, W. WYNN. **NUMBERS: THEIR OCCULT POWER AND MYSTIC VIRTUES. 127pp. TPH1890, 5.25c.**
A scholarly, yet readable overview of numerology through the ages. Includes excellent material on Pythagoras and Pythagorean views of numbers and the qabalistic view of numbers. The majority of the book details the properties of numbers according to the **Bible**, the Talmud, the Pythagoreans, the Romans, Chaldeans, Egyptians, Hindus, medieval musicians, Hermetic students and Rosicrucians.

OCCULT NOVELS

There are an almost unlimited number of books which could be classified as occult fiction, depending on how broadly you defined the genre. We have limited our selection to classic books by the most enduringly popular authors. The quality of the novels varies; however the ones we have chosen are representative of the field. Many novels are listed elsewhere in **Inner Development**—Hermann Hesse and J.D. Salinger are in Mysticism; novels on King Arthur such as Mary Stewart's are in the Grail and King Arthur section; historical novels can be found scattered throughout, in whichever section correlates to their content; certain fictional writers such as George MacDonald are listed in Fairy Tales; and there are long Chinese, Islamic, and Japanese literature listings in their corresponding sections, as well as a smattering of other literature in other chapters.

ALEXANDER, THEA. **2150 AD—A MACRO LOVE STORY. 168pp. War71, 1.95p.**
A visionary novel about the future of mankind, told from the viewpoint of a young man living in the uncertain world of 1970 who visits the world of 2150 during his sleep-dream state. The tone of the book is hopeful as it glances into the near future when humanity develops a new dimension of parapsychological awareness and evolves into a magnificent race possessing god-like attributes.

ASHE, GEOFFREY. **THE FINGER AND THE MOON. 251pp. Grn73, 1.60p.**
This is a strange novel which originated in a study of myth and magic—extending the insights of Carl Jung and Robert Graves and evaluating the ideas of modern magicians. It takes place in England and focuses on the *mysteries of Britain.* Ashe himself is a well known archaeologist, specializing in the early history of Britain and in the Arthurian legends. This is his first and only novel.

BALZAC, HONORE DE. **SERAPHITA. 179pp. Mul76, 2.50p.**
Seraphita *is one of the great occult novels of the world. Permeated with wisdom, a highly prophetic book, at the same time it is the keystone of the entire structure of Balzac's prolific writings. Balzac himself referred to it as* **Le Livre Mystique,** *the mystical book, but it is not merely an expression of his personal mystical views, for it reveals profound true Rosicrucian secrets of the inner life and spiritual potentials inherent in every human being.—from the introduction.*

COLLINS, MABEL. **THE IDYLL OF THE WHITE LOTUS. 152pp. TPH13, 1.25p.**
The ensuing pages contain a story which has been told in all ages and among every people. It is the tragedy of the Soul. Attracted by Desire, the ruling element in the lower nature of Man, it stoops to sin; brought to itself by suffering, it turns for help to the redeeming Spirit within; and in the final sacrifice achieves its apotheosis and sheds a blessing on mankind.

CORELLI, MARIA. **ARDATH. Amh nd, 2.00p.**
Maria Corelli's books are among the most popular mystical, visionary novels ever written. Long out of print, many of the books are now available.

CORELLI, MARIA. **BARABBAS—A DREAM OF THE WORLD'S TRAGEDY. 317pp. Amh nd/Met, 3.50p.**

CORELLI, MARIA. **FREE OPINIONS, FREELY EXPRESSED. Offset, spiral bound, 353pp. HeR05, 6.50p.**
Ms. Corelli's thoughts on *Certain Phases of Modern Social Life and Conduct.*

CORELLI, MARIA. **THE LIFE EVERLASTING. 439pp. Bor nd/Met, 5.95p.**
This love story is one of Ms. Corelli's most popular books.

CORELLI, MARIA. **THE MURDER OF DELICIA. Offset, spiral bound, 274pp. HeR1896, 6.00p.**

CORELLI, MARIA. **A ROMANCE OF TWO WORLDS. 324pp. Mul73, 3.50p.**
This is considered Ms. Corelli's masterpiece, written when she was twenty-two and depicting her spiritual and psychic experiences.

CORELLI, MARIA. **A SONG OF MIRIAM AND OTHER STORIES. Offset, spiral bound, 236pp. HeR nd, 4.50p.**

CORELLI, MARIA. **THE SORROWS OF SATAN. 264pp. Amh nd/Met, 3.50p.**

CORELLI, MARIA. **SOUL OF LILITH. Amh nd/Met, 3.50p.**

CORELLI, MARIA. **THE STRANGE VISITATION. Offset, spiral bound, 188pp. HeR nd, 3.50p.**

CORELLI, MARIA. **TEMPORAL POWER. 258pp. Amh nd, 3.00p.**

CORELLI, MARIA. **THE YOUNG DIANA—AN EXPERIMENT OF THE FUTURE. Offset, spiral bound, 381pp. HeR18, 7.00p.**

GRANT, JOAN. **EYES OF HORUS. 1.75p.**
See the Ancient Egypt section.

GRANT, JOAN. **FAR MEMORY. 285pp. Crg56, 1.60p.**
Joan Grant became aware as a child of her uncanny gift of *far memory*—the ability to recall in detail previous incarnations, both male and female, in other centuries and in other lands. Her books, published as historical novels, have been praised for their extraordinary vividness and rich detail, and are in fact Ms. Grant's memories of her earlier lives. This is her autobiography, focusing on her early years.

GRANT, JOAN. **LIFE AS CAROLA. 271pp. Avo39/Crg, 1.50p.**
The story of Carola's life in sixteenth century Italy as the illegitimate child of an Italian nobleman.

GRANT, JOAN. **LORD OF THE HORIZON. 1.75p.**
See the Ancient Egypt section.

GRANT, JOAN. **RETURN TO ELYSIUM. 303pp. Avo47/Crg, 1.50p.**
Lucina lived in Greece, then went to Rome and founded a mystic cult. Not content with this she died and finally discovered an existence that transcended death.

GRANT, JOAN. **SO MOSES WAS BORN. 1.50p.**
See the Ancient Egypt section.

GRANT, JOAN. **WINGED PHARAOH. 310pp. Ber38, 1.75p.**
In ancient Egypt, a pharaoh who had extrasensory powers and received special training as a priest was called a *winged pharaoh.* This novel is the first hand story of an Egyptian princess who becomes such a ruler. This vividly written story is Joan Grant's most popular book.

LARSEN, J. ANKER. **THE PHILOSOPHERS STONE. 379pp. Wal24, 4.50p.**
A perceptive and straightforward account of the lives of many people venturing on diverse spiritual paths which the **New York Times**

described as having *the effect of illuminating the soul of the reader. Dark places and marshy places, hazy recesses of the spirit, seem to open and brighten under the influence of this remarkable book.* Larsen was a Danish novelist and mystic.

LLOYD, JOHN. **ETIDORPHA OR THE ENDS OF THE EARTH.** Introduction, illustrations, 381pp. S&S1895, 1.95p.
An underground occult classic which tells of a man who, after violating an ancient taboo, has to redeem himself by undergoing a rite of passage deep into the heart of the Earth—a land populated by faceless humanoid creatures and intoxicating colored growths—where time vanishes and life itself becomes ecstatic.

LYTTON, EDWARD. **VRIL: THE POWER OF THE COMING RACE.** 248pp. Mul72, 2.25p.
An Englishman of the last century gives his view of the future of mankind when men have released and controlled some of their vast inner powers. It is a vision of caution and warning to a civilization that would develop a material paradise and neglect its spiritual responsibility.

MORAY, ANN. **DAWN FALCON.** 336pp. Faw73, 1.75p.
A historical novel of intrigue in the time of Nefertari, a Nubian concubine who longed to be Queen and High Priestess in Ancient Egypt. Nefertari is the main character in the drama and her lovers are two brothers who control the land of Egypt, one a warrior and the other the ruling priest and head of state.

RAMPA, MAMA SAN. **PUSSYWILLOW.** 159pp. Crg76, 2.00p.
Lobsang's wife Mama San tells of life with her famous husband and their five Siamese cats.

RAMPA, T. LOBSANG. **AS IT WAS!** 191pp. Crg76, 2.00p.
Rampa retells his life story, beginning with the predictions made at his birth based on an astrological reading.

RAMPA, T. LOBSANG. **BEYOND THE TENTH.** 158pp. Crg69, 2.00p.
Rampa's occult novels are the most popular ones we know of. People always seem to buy a few of them at a time and are soon back for others. Rampa, an Englishman, contends that a Tibetan lama is writing of his life through him, and had in fact fully occupied his body following a slight concussive accident. In this, his tenth book, he gives advice and teachings on the care of man's physical and spiritual form, and in the process answers many questions often asked by his readers.

RAMPA, T. LOBSANG. **CANDLELIGHT.** 174pp. Crg73, 2.00p.
Most of the letters Rampa receives are full of questions about all aspects of metaphysics: pendulums, dowsing, how to levitate, how to teleport, etc. Here he answers many of these questions and discusses many other topics ranging from God and good and evil to acupuncture and the press.

RAMPA, T. LOBSANG. **THE CAVE OF THE ANCIENTS.** 223pp. RaH63/Crg, 1.50p.
The sequel to **The Third Eye,** this is the story of Rampa's life in remote Himalayan lamaseries where he learned some of the ancient wisdom: the meaning of life and death; the secrets of hypnotism, telepathy and clairvoyance, the relationship between the mind and the brain.

RAMPA, T. LOBSANG. **CHAPTERS OF LIFE.** 223pp. Crg67, 2.00p.
Detailed predictions and comments on the events taking place in the astral world.

RAMPA, T. LOBSANG. **FEEDING THE FLAME.** 190pp. Crg71, 2.00p.
It is said "It is better to light a candle than to curse the darkness." In my first ten books I have tried to light a candle, or possibly two. In this, the eleventh book, I am trying to Feed the Flame. More answers to questions on a wide variety of topics.

RAMPA, T. LOBSANG. **THE HERMIT.** 159pp. Crg71, 2.00p.
A young monk receives the wisdom of the ages from an old blind hermit.

RAMPA, T. LOBSANG. **I BELIEVE.** 175pp. Crg77, 2.00p.
This book is nonfiction, rather than a novel, though it is written in the same style as Rampa's other books. He sets down his beliefs about life after death and in the process gives his opinions about a variety of other topics.

RAMPA, T. LOBSANG. **LIVING WITH THE LAMA.** Crg64, 2.00p.

RAMPA, T. LOBSANG. **THE RAMPA STORY.** 216pp. Ban60, 2.00p.
Rampa presents the teachings given to him by the Tibetan, emphasizing the ramifications of the human personality and ego and the realities of reincarnation.

RAMPA, T. LOBSANG. **THE SAFFRON ROBE.** 198pp. Crg66, 2.00p.
The story of Rampa's youth in the lamasery of Tibet and a presentation of the teachings of Buddhism.

RAMPA, T. LOBSANG. **THE THIRD EYE.** 219pp. RaH56/Crg, 1.95p.
Rampa's first book, in which he describes his spiritual training and the painful physical operation whereby his third eye was opened.

RAMPA, T. LOBSANG. **THE THIRTEENTH CANDLE.** 173pp. Crg72, 2.00p.
Rampa's thirteenth book, emphasizing healing and life after death. Includes a section of *wise sayings* taken from all his books.

RAMPA, T. LOBSANG. **TWILIGHT.** 204pp. Crg75, 2.25p.
Rampa here answers some of the many questions he has received on a variety of subjects including UFOs, astral travel, the aura, marriage and divorce, the law of karma, hypnotism, and much else.

RAMPA, T. LOBSANG. **WISDOM OF THE ANCIENTS.** 158pp. Crg65, 2.25p.
Most of this book consists of a dictionary of the occult, following which are supplements on breathing, stones, foodstuffs, and exercises.

RAMPA, T. LOBSANG. **YOU FOREVER.** Crg65, 2.00p.
Presents a special course of instruction in psychic development and metaphysics.

WILLIAMS, CHARLES. **ALL HALLOW'S EVE.** 291pp. FSG48, 4.50p.
The book's introduction by T.S. Eliot provides an excellent overview of Williams' work.

WILLIAMS, CHARLES. **DESCENT INTO HELL.** 222pp. Eer37, 3.25p.
The **New York Times** speaks of Williams' novels as *satire, romance, thriller, morality and glimpses of eternity all rolled into one.* Williams excels in descriptions of supernatural (or out-of-this-world) experiences such as many people have had on occasion but have been unable to put into words. There are pages which describe, with a frightful clarify, the deterioration and damnation of the human soul, and pages which reveal the triumphant struggle toward salvation. Williams was above all a Christian and this comes clearly through in all his writings.

WILLIAMS, CHARLES. **THE GREATER TRUMPS.** 2.95p.
See the Tarot section.

WILLIAMS, CHARLES. **MANY DIMENSIONS.** 269pp. Eer31/Fab, 3.65p.

WILLIAMS, CHARLES. **THE PLACE OF THE LION.** 206pp. Eer33/Fab, 2.95p.

WILLIAMS, CHARLES. **WAR IN HEAVEN.** 256pp. Eer30/SBL, 3.65p.

OUT-OF-THE-BODY EXPERIENCES

In our action-oriented society, when a man lies down to sleep, he is effectively out of the picture. He will lie still for six to eight hours, so he is not *behaving, thinking productively*, or doing anything *significant*. We all know that people dream, but we raise our children to regard dreams and other experiences occurring during sleep as unimportant, as not *real* in the way that the events of the day are. Thus most people are in the habit of forgetting their dreams, and, on the occasions when they do remember them, they usually regard them as mere oddities.

What are we to make of a person who takes exception to this general belief, who claims to have had experiences during sleep or other forms of unconsciousness that were not only impressive to him, but which he feels were *real*?

Suppose this person claims that on the previous night he had an experience of flying through the air over a large city which he soon recognized as New York. Further, he tells us that not only was this *dream* intensely vivid, but that he knew at the time that it was not a dream, that he was really in the air over New York City. And this conviction that he was really there sticks with him for the rest of his life, despite our reminding him that a sleeping man couldn't really be flying by himself in the air over New York City.

Probably we will ignore a person who makes such a report, or we will politely (or not so politely) inform him that he is becoming a little weak in the head or crazy, and suggest that he see a psychotherapist. If he is insistent about the reality of his experience, especially if he has other strange experiences too, we may with the best of intentions see about committing him to a mental hospital.

Our *traveler*, on the other hand, if he is smart, will quickly learn not to talk about his experiences. The only problem with that, as I have found from talking to many such people, is that he may worry about whether he's going crazy.

For the sake of argument, let's make our *traveler* even more troubling. Suppose in his account he goes on to say that after flying over New York City for a while he flew down to your apartment. There he saw you and two other people, unknown to him, conversing. He describes the two people in detail, and mentions a few things about the topic of conversation occurring in the minute or so he was there.

Let's suppose he is correct. At the time he had his experience, you were holding a conversation on the topic he mentions with two people who fit our *traveler's* descriptions. What do we make of things now?

The usual reaction to a hypothetical situation of this type is that it is all very interesting, but as we know that it couldn't possibly happen, we needn't seriously think about what it might mean. Or we might comfort ourselves by invoking the word *coincidence*. A marvelous word, *coincidence*, for relieving mental upsets!.

Unfortunately for our peace of mind, there are thousands of instances, reported by normal people, of exactly this sort of occurrence. We are not dealing with a purely hypothetical situation.

Such events have been termed traveling clairvoyance, astral projection, or, a more scientific term, out-of-the-body experiences (OOBEs). We can formally define an OOBE as an event in which the experiencer (1) seems to perceive some portion of some environment which could not possibly be perceived from where his physical body is known to be at the time; and (2) knows at the time that he is not dreaming or fantasizing. The experiencer seems to possess his normal consciousness at the time, and even though he may reason that this cannot be happening, he will feel all his normal critical faculties to be present, and so knows he is not dreaming. Further, he will not decide after awakening that this was a dream. How, then, do we understand this strange phenomenon?

If we look to scientific sources for information about OOBEs we shall find practically none at all. Scientists have, by and large, simply not paid any attention to these phenomena. The situation is rather similar to that of the scientific literature on extrasensory perception (ESP). Phenomena such as telepathy, clairvoyance, precognition, and psychokinesis are impossible in terms of the current physical world view. Since they can't happen, most scientists do not bother to read the evidence indicating that they do happen; hence, not having read the evidence, their belief in the impossibility of such phenomena is reinforced. This kind of circular reasoning in support of one's comfortable belief system is not unique to scientists by any means, but it has resulted in very little scientific research on ESP or OOBEs.

In spite of the lack of *hard* scientific data, there are still a number of definite conclusions one can make from reading what material there is.

First, OOBEs are a universal human experience, not in the sense that they happen to large numbers of people, but in that they have happened all through recorded history, and there are marked similarities in the experience among people who are otherwise extremely different in terms of cultural background. One can find reports of OOBEs by housewives in Kansas which closely resemble accounts of OOBEs from ancient Egyptian or oriental sources.

Second, the OOBE is generally a once-in-a-lifetime experience, seemingly experienced by *accident*. Illnesses sometimes bring it about, especially illnesses which are almost fatal. Great emotional stress sometimes brings it about. In many cases, it simply happens during sleep without our having any idea of what might have caused it. In very rare instances it seems to have been brought about by a deliberate attempt.

Third, the experience of an OOBE is usually one of the most profound experiences of a person's life, and radically alters his beliefs. This is usually expressed as, *I no longer believe in survival of death or an immortal soul, I know that I will survive death*. The person feels that he has directly experienced being alive and conscious without his physical body, and therefore knows that he possesses some kind of soul that will survive bodily death. This does not logically follow, for even if the OOBE is more than just an interesting dream or hallucination, it was still occurring while the physical body was alive and functioning and therefore may depend on the physical body. This argument, however, makes no impression on those who have actually had an OOBE. Thus regardless of what position one wants to take on the *reality* of the OOBE, it is clearly an experience deserving considerable psychological study. I am certain that our ideas concerning the existence of souls have resulted from early experiences of people having OOBEs. Considering the importance of the idea of the soul to most of our religions, and the importance of religion in people's lives, it seems incredible that science could have swept this problem under the rug so easily.

Fourth, the OOBE is generally extremely joyful to those who have it. I would make a rough estimate that between 90 and 95 per cent of the people who have this experience are very glad it occurred and find it joyful, while 5 per cent are very frightened by it, for the only way they can interpret it, while it is happening, is that they are dying. Later reactions of the person as he attempts to interpret his OOBE can be rather negative, however. Almost every time I give a speech on this subject, someone comes up to me afterwards and thanks me for talking about it. They had had the experience some time before, but had no way of explaining it, and worried that they were going *crazy.*

Fifth, in some instances of OOBEs the description of what was happening at a distant place is correct and more accurate than we would expect by coincidence. Not the majority, by any means, but some. To explain these we must postulate either that the *hallucinatory* experience of the OOBE was combined with the operation of ESP, or that in some sense the person really was *there.* The OOBE then becomes very real indeed.

—*condensed from* **Journeys Out of the Body**, *by Robert A. Monroe*

BAKER, DOUGLAS. **THE TECHNIQUES OF ASTRAL PROJECTION. Many illustrations, 93pp. Wei74, 3.95p.**
A detailed, comprehensive account with sections on the nature of astral projection, its types and stages, techniques for projecting, and the astral world itself. Baker writes from personal experience as well as scientific study and he includes many historical examples. His techniques section is one of the clearest we have seen.

BATTERSBY, H.F.P. **MAN OUTSIDE HIMSELF. Bibliography, 102pp. UnB69, 4.95c.**
A survey of the literature and experiences of the pioneers of astral projection.

BLACK, DAVID. **EKSTASY: OUT OF BODY EXPERIENCES. Twenty-one page bibliography, index, 243pp. BoM75, 7.95c.**
An eminently sensible and comprehensive job on a difficult subject. . . . Ekstasy has more than literary merit. It provides a clear overview of the out-of-the-body experience. . . . Black's research has gone far. His account of the work done at major scientific centers around the country is quite good, and he laces it with engaging asides about the lives of various scientists and subjects. . . . A good springboard for your flight into an intriguing problem.—John White. To our knowledge this is the only review of the recent scientific experiments with OOBEs. The text is well written and is fascinating to read.

BORD, JANET. **ASTRAL PROJECTION. Bibliography, 64pp. Wei73/APC, 1.25p.**
An overview, including case histories and information on when projection happens and what it feels like.

CROOKALL, ROBERT. **CASEBOOK OF ASTRAL PROJECTION. Bibliography, 160pp. UnB72, 7.95c.**
Dr. Crookall is a scientist who has spent more than thirty years studying astral projection. He has done pioneering research and here he brings the number of cases he has studied up to 746. Over 200 are included in this volume together with detailed notes and critical discussion.

CROOKALL, ROBERT. **THE JUNG-JAFFE VIEW OF OUT-OF-THE-BODY EXPERIENCES. Glossary, notes, bibliography, index, 134pp. ChF70, 2.40p.**
A detailed analysis of five out-of-the-body experiences studied by Ms. Jaffe, Carl Jung's personal secretary. This is followed by some cases taken directly from Dr. Jung's writings and personal experiences, with Dr. Crookall's interpretations. Appendices provide interpretations of the psychedelic experience based on Timothy Leary's manual and a review of the experimental corroboration of astral projection.

CROOKALL, ROBERT. **OUT-OF-THE-BODY EXPERIENCES: A FOURTH ANALYSIS. Notes, bibliography, 219pp. UnB nd, 3.95p.**
Cases and discussion dealing almost exclusively with *doubles.* Related information from various cases is introduced.

CROOKALL, ROBERT. **THE STUDY AND PRACTICE OF ASTRAL PROJECTION. 231pp. UnB60, 3.95p.**
A record of 160 out-of-the-body experiences, divided into various categories, as well as about 100 pages of interpretative and theoretical material.

CROOKALL, ROBERT. **THE TECHNIQUES OF ASTRAL PROJECTION. Extensive bibliography, 111pp. Wei64, 5.95c.**
A practical manual, containing precise descriptions of various techniques. Extensive quotations and page references to the basic books in the field make the actual reading slow, but are extremely helpful to those desiring further research in specific areas.

■ GREENHOUSE, HERBERT. **THE ASTRAL JOURNEY. Bibliography, index, 359pp. Avo74, 1.95p.**
This is the best account of the evidence for out-of-the-body experiences that we know of. The text is very well written and the experiences discussed are more interesting than most. From the accounts of such historical figures as Aristotle, Goethe, Admiral Byrd, and Ernest Hemingway, through out-of-the-body travels by primitive shamans, to firsthand reports by contemporary Americans, Greenhouse describes in detail the *why* and *how* of astral projection. He also provides the most up to date accounts of the breakthroughs in four ESP laboratories in the last few years, where scientists are getting hard evidence that astral projection is indeed a reality. In addition, the author carefully examines the criteria for a valid astral projection experience and the physical and psychological conditions that make it possible to project. Greenhouse, a member of the American Society for Psychical Research, has participated in many of its experiments, and has personally experienced out-of-the-body travel.

HOLROYD, STUART. **PSYCHIC VOYAGES.** 8"x10½", 144pp. Dou77, 8.95c.
A popularly written pictorial account of out-of-the-body experiences. Holroyd describes various kinds of astral travel, ties them in with beliefs about the powers of saints and shamans, and recounts a number of sensational case histories. He also examines related phenomena. Over 100 color plates accompany the text. The format reminds us of encyclopedias sold in grocery stores.

KING, FRANCIS, ed. **ASTRAL PROJECTION, MAGIC AND AL-CHEMY.** 253pp. Wei71, 6.95c.
Containing advanced inner teachings of the Golden Dawn, this is a collection of manuscripts circulated among members with detailed instructions and illustrations on imagination and willpower, astral projection, esoteric psychology, alchemy, Hermetic wisdom, higher magic, and Rosicrucian adeptship. The book also includes explanatory notes for some of the more technical material.

LEADBEATER, C.W. **THE ASTRAL PLANE.** 183pp. TPH33, 2.75c.
A detailed investigation of the astral plane as a whole—covering every aspect in a clear, concise manner.

■ MONROE, ROBERT. **JOURNEYS OUT-OF-THE-BODY.** 279pp. Dou71, 3.95p.
In 1958, Monroe, a Virginia businessman, began to leave his body at night and travel to locales far removed from the physical and spiritual realities of life. He began taking systematic notes from the beginning—and his is a very rational account. With this book he hopes to pass his experiences to others so that they will not have to go through some of the confusion and terror he did while learning on his own. He includes practical instructions on how to initiate the out-of-the-body experience. Many cases are cited and there is a great deal of explanatory material. We recommend this book for those with a general interest as well as for all who desire a scientific presentation. It is also the most interesting of the lot, overall.

MOSER, ROBERT. **MENTAL AND ASTRAL PROJECTION.** 56pp. EsP74, 2.00p.
This book gives detailed instructions on how to project, and stresses the dangers involved in projection. Various techniques are outlined. Moser teaches these techniques in a school he runs in Arizona.

MULDOON, SYLVAN. **THE CASE FOR ASTRAL PROJECTION.** 173pp. ArP36, 3.00c.
A casebook of projections, written down to strengthen the scientific case for astral projection. Muldoon has not included his own experiences.

MULDOON, SYLVAN and HEREWARD CARRINGTON. **THE PHE-NOMENA OF ASTRAL PROJECTION.** Bibliography, 222pp. Wei51/HPG, 3.75p.
A theoretical book, written twenty years after **Projection**, in which the authors discuss the scientific issues involved. A large portion of the book is devoted to case studies, grouped according to the cause of projection.

■ MULDOON, SYLVAN and HEREWARD CARRINGTON. **THE PRO-JECTION OF THE ASTRAL BODY.** 316pp. Wei70/HPG, 4.50p.
Dr. Carrington is a noted psychical researcher and Sylvan Muldoon has been having frequent out-of-the-body experiences since he was twelve. They have collaborated on this work and the results are fascinating as well as instructive. All aspects of the astral plane, sleep, dreams, and voluntary and involuntary projection are discussed. The personal accounts are vivid and Muldoon's instructions on how to project and what the dangers are, are very clear. Carrington discusses the historical and scientific aspects. This is probably the basic book for those interested in astral projection.

OPHIEL. **THE ART AND PRACTICE OF ASTRAL PROJECTION.** 122pp. Wei75, 3.95p.
Gives the occultist all the necessary information about the art of astral projection as well as simple and concise directions on how to project in a safe manner. Four techniques are explained, each building on knowledge gained in the former one. A very clear presentation—though we do not recommend it to the scientifically inclined.

PANCHADASI, SWAMI. **THE ASTRAL WORLD: ITS SCENES, DWELLERS, AND PHENOMENA.** 94pp. YPS nd, 1.00p.
Every aspect of the astral world and related phenomena seems to be touched on in this account. A good overview.

POWELL, ARTHUR. **THE ASTRAL BODY AND OTHER ASTRAL PHENOMENA.** Index, 252pp. TPH65, 7.95c/2.75p.
This is a synthesis of theosophical information on the astral body of man, together with a description and explanation of the astral world and its phenomena. Topics include colors, kundalini, thought forms, sleep life and dreams, after death life, the astral plane and astral entities, rebirth, clairvoyance, and much else. An extremely complete treatment.

POWELL, ARTHUR. **THE ETHERIC DOUBLE.** Twenty-four diagrams, index, 135pp. TPH64, 1.45p.
This is the first volume in a series dealing with the inner structure of man. Powell has consolidated the information obtained from a large number of books, a list of which is given, arranging the material, which covers a vast field and is exceedingly complex, as methodically as possible. Much of the material came from the works of Leadbeater and Besant. The etheric double is a subtle body of fine matter which extends slightly beyond the physical body. It is said to be the transformer of energy and is also known as the health aura. This volume contains material on prana, the body's centers, kundalini, birth, death, healing, mediumship, magnetism, and much else.

ROGO, D. SCOTT, ed. **MIND BEYOND THE BODY.** 365pp. Vik78, 2.95p.
A technical investigation of out-of-the-body experiences, divided into the following general sections: On Being Out-of-Body, Laboratory Investigations, Reports from Gifted Subjects, and Can We Explain the Out-of-Body Experience? Some of the most noted researchers working today have contributed to this volume.

SHAY, J.M. **OUT OF BODY CONSCIOUSNESS.** 50pp. WAO72, 2.95p.
This is the most thorough yet concise manual for the practice of astral projection that we have seen. It provides both an excellent introduction and in depth explanations of the processes and mechanisms of projection. Shay outlines a step-by-step training program. He then presents seven methods of projection, each summarized, including a description of the actual experience. The book is poorly produced and it is saddle stitched rather than bound.

SMITH, SUSY. **THE ENIGMA OF OUT-OF-THE-BODY TRAVEL.** 189pp. NAL65/NEL, 1.25p.
A reporter's well documented study of fifteen different types of projection, including case studies and background material and the most extensive chapter-by-chapter bibliography we have ever seen.

TURVEY, VINCENT. **THE BEGINNINGS OF SEERSHIP.** Index, 240pp. UnB69, 4.95c.
Turvey was one of the first men in modern times who claimed to have taught himself how to leave his body, astrally travel to places he had never been, and come back and report what he had seen. This is his personal story. It includes material on clairvoyance and prophecy as well as astral projection. Introduction by Leslie Shepard.

WALKER, BENJAMIN. **BEYOND THE BODY.** 232pp. RKP74, 3.95p.
In examining the elements that lie beyond the body, Walker analyzes the traditional and contemporary data in the light of psychology, metaphysics, and science. He describes the various methods for inducing astral projection, and the circumstances in which spontaneous out-of-the-body experiences might occur, when the second body is separated from the physical. His account is supported by information from folklore, anthropology, occultism, psychical research, and firsthand testimony. A well written, comprehensive account with an excellent bibliography and index.

YRAM. **PRACTICAL ASTRAL PROJECTION.** 253pp. Wei67, 2.45p.
This is a practical technique book on astral projection, but it is much more than a simple how-to book or a collection of experiences. It deals with all manner of existence on the astral and material plane, as well as man's place in the universal order. It is recommended reading for anyone interested in a philosophical treatment of the psychic world.

PALMISTRY

The human hand is a map of life. It reveals the potential of an individual, indicates events which have happened or will happen in his life and provides an accurate assessment of both his psychological and physiological make-up. Such information, however, can come only as a result of a careful and comprehensive study of the hand.

Hand analysis is a science; it is also an art. It is a systematic body of knowledge with fundamental laws which must be clearly understood; its real value lies in the proper application of these laws, in the ability of the palmist to balance what are perhaps contradictory markings before coming to a final judgement on the character and destiny of the individual.

Chirology is the name we give today to the technique of hand interpretation. It comprises two distinct systems of analysis: cheirognomy, which is the study of the shape of the hand, finger formations, skin texture etc.; and cheiromancy, or the study of the lines and markings engraved on the palmar surface of the hand. It would be wrong, however, to assume that these two parts are independent of each other. In fact, the information acquired through one method can be assessed only with reference to that acquired through the other; there can be no true analysis unless one takes into account this interdependence.

Chirology originated in the East, and it is there that the art still has its real home. The Chaldeans, the Persians, the Chinese and the Indians seem to have an ancient chirological tradition, and in the South of India the art is kept alive and practised daily in every town and village.

Although the West is becoming increasingly inquisitive about the predictive chirological technique, the study was regarded as a fringe activity for many centuries and is only now gaining the respect which it deserves. The oldest treatise on the subject is supposed to have been written by the Greek philosopher Aristotle, and there is evidence that palmistry was practised during Roman times. The study was given great impetus during the closing decade of the last century.

Chirology then achieved further respectability with the work of Dr. Carl Jung. Though physicians in the East have always considered the physiological aspects of the hand in their diagnostic work, Jung can be regarded as the first Western pioneer in this respect. An outstanding clinical psychologist, he was not only a great scholar but a man of infinite wisdom. To help clinical research, he kept an open mind and investigated the potential significance of chirological indications. He certainly would not have continued to use the findings of Julius Spier, the hand analyst, for a quarter of a century unless he had discovered data valuable for his work. Jung himself observed that *the totality conception of modern biology, which is based on the evidence of a host of observations and research, does not exclude the possibility that hands whose shape and functioning are so intimately connected with the psyche, might provide revealing and therefore interpretable expressions of psychical peculiarity, that is, of the human character.*

—condensed from **The Art of Hand Analysis**, by Mir Bashir

ABAYAKOON, CYRUS. ASTRO-PALMISTRY: SIGNS AND SEALS OF THE HAND. 8½"x11", 190pp. ASI75, 20.00c.
This is a new book which includes a great deal of information not readily available elsewhere. The author supplies a profusion of well marked line drawings of sample hands. Astrological correspondences are noted and the explanatory information is very complete. Abayakoon gets carried away at times with his symbols, but all in all this is a fine presentation which would be helpful to both beginning and advanced students.

ANDERSON, MARY. **PALMISTRY: YOUR DESTINY IN YOUR HANDS. Illustrations, 64pp. Wei73/APC, 1.25p.**
A fine overview of palmistry, covering all the basics. If you are just slightly curious as to what palmistry is all about, this is as good a place to find out as any.

■ *BASHIR, MIR.* **THE ART OF HAND ANALYSIS. Index, 269pp. Mll73, 8.85p.**
This is the most comprehensive recent study of the art and science of palm reading. Bashir is a Pakistani, now living in London, and is widely regarded as one of the most noted contemporary palmists: *The human hand is a map of life. It reveals the potential of an individual, indicates events which happened or will happen in his life and provides an accurate assessment of both his psychological and physiological make-up. . . . Hand analysis is a science; it is also an art. It is a systematic body of knowledge with fundamental laws which must be clearly understood; its real value lies in the proper application of these laws, in the ability of the palmist to balance what are perhaps contradictory markings before coming to a final judgement on the character and destiny of the individual.*—from the introduction. Every aspect of analysis is very clearly and well covered and there are many line drawings and a section of palm prints.

BENHAM, W.G. **THE LAWS OF SCIENTIFIC HAND READING. 650pp. Haw46, 15.00c.**
This is an essential work for the serious student, containing prints and photographs of many interesting hands. The section on chirognomy is more valuable than the section on cheiromancy, which appears to be based more on reasoning than on systematic observation.

■ *CHEIRO.* **LANGUAGE OF THE HAND: THE CLASSIC OF PALMISTRY. 224pp. Arc64/Crg, 1.95p.**
This is the most popular introductory book. Cheiro was a well known twentieth century occultist, best known for his writings on numerology and palmistry. This is the most comprehensive of his individual books, covering all the basics and including an abundance of palm prints and line drawings.

CHEIRO. **PALMISTRY FOR ALL. 143pp. Arc69/Crg, .95p.**
A profusely illustrated introductory account which explains precisely how to interpret the meaning of the lines of the hands as well as the significance of the shape of the hand, thumb, and fingers.

CHEIRO. **READ YOUR PAST, PRESENT AND FUTURE. Illustrations, 109pp. Sag73, 2.25p.**
A good basic book which contains a number of interesting insights.

COMPTON, VERA. **PALMISTRY FOR EVERYMAN. Illustrations, index, 149pp. Sag69, 5.00c.**
This is an extremely detailed study which should prove useful to intermediate and advanced students.

COTTON, LOUISE. **PALMISTRY AND ITS PRACTICAL USES. 112pp. Sag70, 4.00c.**
An interesting study which contains a number of astrological comparisons. A selection of biblical references is appended.

FRITH, HENRY. **PALMISTRY SECRETS REVEALED. 127pp. Wil52, 2.00p.**
This is a good general work, describing the meanings of the most commonly found marks and lines on the hand, and what each line means in relation to other factors. Frith is one of Britain's foremost palmists. Easy reading for those who simply want to get an idea of what palmistry is all about.

GETTINGS, FRED. **PALMISTRY MADE EASY. 156pp. Wil66, 2.00p.**
Covers palmistry in a very general way, including specific case histories, many palm prints and an annotated bibliography of the most
important palmistry books.

HIPSKIND, JUDITH. **PALMISTRY, THE WHOLE VIEW: A HUMAN-
ISTIC GUIDE TO INNER AWARENESS. 239pp. LlP77, 4.95p.**
This book presents a psychological approach to hand analysis which
goes far deeper than many traditional studies. The illustrations are
barely adequate, though the text more than makes up for this
shortcoming. This is an excellent work for all who seek to increase
their understanding of palmistry. As the title suggests, the approach is
holistic.

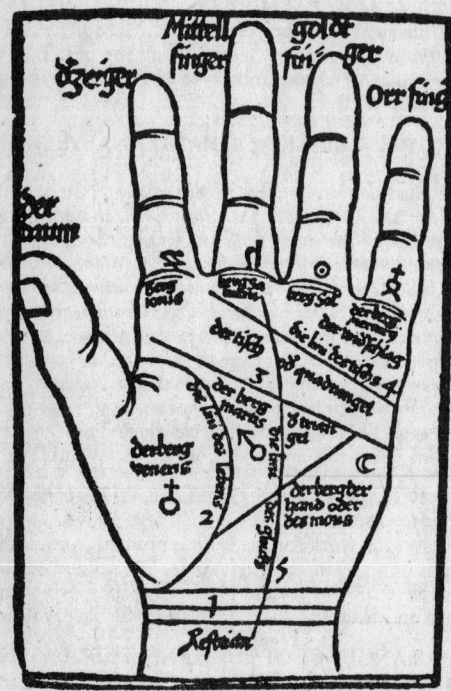

■ *HUTCHINSON, BERYL.* **YOUR LIFE IN YOUR HANDS. Bibliography, 254pp. SBL67, 2.25p.**
An excellent basic guide, emphasizing the psychological approach and
discussing facets of palmistry we have not read about elsewhere. Palm
prints and line drawings accompany the text. Includes information on
palmistry and health.

JAQUIN, NOEL. **THE HAND OF MAN: A PRACTICAL TREATISE
OF THE SCIENCE OF HAND READING. Line drawings, index,
268pp. Sag67, 6.00c.**
This is an interesting study which covers psychology, disease, and
health. Jaquin is often overly philosophical; nonetheless, he presents
material not available elsewhere.

JAQUIN, NOEL. **THE HAND SPEAKS. 143pp. Sag41, 6.00c.**
*My aim in writing this book is to show you how to discover the controlling forces of
your destiny, your character, your health, your sex life, from your hand, or more
precisely from its imprint. For this end I have given you a series of sixty-seven imprints,
reproduced by the most technically perfect method available, with analysis and
conclusions.*

JAQUIN, NOEL. **THE HUMAN HAND: THE LIVING SYMBOL.
Index, 173pp. Sag70, 4.50c.**
Jaquin is a very well known British palmist who emphasized psychological understanding in his work and developed a number of pioneering theories. His books contain useful insights for the practicing
palmist, and other disciplines are incorporated into his exposition. This
book develops Jaquin's thesis that *the human hand reveals with detailed
exactitude the psychological composition of the individual.* Many case studies are
included and the illustrations are in the form of palm prints.

JAQUIN, NOEL. **SIGNATURE OF TIME. Line drawings, notes, index,
237pp. Sag70, 4.00c.**
Another of Jaquin's psychological studies. He devotes individual
chapters to the basic factors of human character, emotions, and *the
signature of time.* Jaquin seems to know a lot, but he is often preachy and
pseudo-scientific.

PSYCHOS. **THE COMPLETE GUIDE TO PALMISTRY. 158pp. Arc59,
.95p.**
A general manual, with extensive interpretative material, but poor
illustrations.

ST. GERMAIN, COMTE DE. **THE PRACTICE OF PALMISTRY.
416pp. Wei nd, 8.95c.**
A simple but very comprehensive book on the study of palms written
in an encyclopedic fashion. Recommended for the beginning student as
well as the advanced palmist. Profusely illustrated with over 1,000
drawings, this book is a detailed, practical manual with a wealth of
information.

ST. HILL, KATHARINE. **THE GRAMMAR OF PALMISTRY. Illustrations, 96pp. Sag73, 4.00c.**
This is a good outline of the basics of palmistry. Its approach is pretty
standard and no new material is offered.

SEN, K.C. **HAST SAMUDRIKA SHASTRA: THE INDIAN SCIENCE
OF HAND READING. 256pp. TSC60, 6.80c.**
Mr. Sen is an Indian who has devoted his life to the study of palmistry.
He brings together all the important theories here rather than
presenting his own. The illustrations are not very good, but the
interpretations are extensive and clearly presented. This text delves
into areas not covered by other books.

SHERIDAN, JO. **WHAT YOUR HANDS REVEAL. Many line drawings and handprints, 131pp. Grn63, .95p.**
Ms. Sheridan is a professional British palmist and her book forms a
good general introduction. The fingers, mounts, and lines are all
discussed at length and there is also a section entitled *Love in Your Hands.*
The book is very clearly written.

STEINBACH, MARTEN. **MEDICAL PALMISTRY. 192pp. NAL75,
1.50p.**
A complete survey of medical palmistry, with many diagrams and clear
descriptive material. A final chapter discusses common ailments and
the related signs to look for.

THOMSON, PEGGY. **ON READING PALMS. Index, 72pp. PrH74,
1.25p.**
A simple, illustrated book covering all the basics and written in a
language designed to appeal to young readers.

WOLFF, CHARLOTTE. **THE HUMAN HAND. Twenty-four palm
prints, glossary, bibliography, index, 172pp. Sag nd, 5.00c.**
Dr. Wolff is a physician and her work in palmistry emphasizes the
scientific, medical aspects of the subject. Her main topics are the place
of the hand in science; the form of the hand; the physical qualities of
the hand and the nails; and the lines of the hand. There is a great deal of
material here that we have not read elsewhere.

PARAPSYCHOLOGY

Impossible things, as history constantly reminds us, have an uncanny way of becoming possible when given enough time. Of course, it is seldom the events themselves which change, only our attitude toward them. Such a change of heart is particularly evident today in the field of parapsychology, the ambitious discipline which deals with many events once tainted by occultism and talk of the supernatural. In terms of present-day research the field can be conveniently divided into five major categories: telepathy—the direct interchange of information between two or more minds; clairvoyance—the acquisition of information by a mind from an inanimate object—for example, deciphering the contents of a sealed letter; precognition—the acquisition of information about some future event by a mind; psychokinesis—the placing of an object in motion by volition alone; psychic healing—treatment of disease by an *unconventional* interaction between a *healer* and a patient.

These five phenomena are referred to collectively as *paranormal events* or, to use a shorter and increasingly popular expression, *psi events* (the term *psi* is borrowed from physics where it denotes an intangible field or immaterial substratum of matter.) It should be made clear that dubbing these five phenomena *paranormal* does not imply that they have some sort of supernatural origin, nor does calling the mode of perception through which a person becomes aware of such information *parasensory* imply some unearthly talent. The prefix *para* is used merely to indicate that the precise mechanism underlying the phenomena lies beyond our present understanding of normal sensory perception.

Today more than a dozen university laboratories, even more research centers, and the federal government are actively engaged in parapsychological research. The researchers are conventionally trained physicists, chemists, neurobiologists, psychologists, psychiatrists, and physicians—each bringing the powerful tools of a specific discipline to the psi challenge. Under this interdisciplinary attack paranormal phenomena, for the first time in history, are beginning to relinquish their secrets—secrets which are already changing our views of humankind and human interactions with the universe.

Some scientists are working under the premise that parasensory abilities are latent within us all and concentrating their studies on ordinary people, not psychics. Through hypnosis, drugs, dream experiments, and modern techniques of sensory bombardment and deprivation, these researchers are finding that certain mental states are more conducive to parasensory happenings than others.

Other laboratories are focusing on individuals who possess manifest psychic talents. While a psychic mentally transmits an image or levitates an object from across the room, today's psi researchers do more than just observe and statistically record the success or failure of such feats as their predecessors once did. In modern experiments the psychic subject is wired to a complex array of physiological monitoring equipment which continuously follows the rise and fall of such parameters as blood pressure, respiration rate, the skin's electrical conductivity, and brain-wave emanations. Scientists are finding that the acquisition of parasensory information, whether through telepathy, clairvoyance, or precognition, the motion of objects by psychokinesis, and the efforts of the psychic healer are all accompanied by measurable, and sometimes gross, psychophysical alterations in the human body.

Still other researchers are measuring lactate levels, enzyme activity, and blood hemoglobin values in the bodies of their subjects as they seek evidence of fundamental changes in body chemistry that might accompany paranormal phenomena. The question today is no longer whether parasensory perception is real or imaginary, but under what conditions it manifests itself. And once these variables are known, be they particular brain-wave patterns, muscular relaxations, or hormonal secretions, can one learn to induce them at will through biofeedback training to awaken psychical abilities?

In seeking to understand new and unusual phenomena, scientists search for models, theoretical frameworks which will embrace their observations. Only when a model can be constructed which houses the phenomena is the scientist comfortable with them. Only then does he have an intellectual grasp of their nature, a means of predicting their occurrence and a margin of control over their behavior.

Up until the mid-1800s many scientists thought they had the ultimate, all-embracing model of the physical world in the mechanics of Isaac Newton. It was a powerful formalism which in its simplicity rendered the reeling of heavenly bodies around the celestrial sphere no more mysterious than the falling of an apple to the ground. Newton's mechanics survived two hundred and fifty years and fostered a smug, if somewhat naive, confidence that was eventually shattered by the atomistic views of Max Planck and Einstein's notions on cosmology. Shortly after the turn of the century, Planck and Einstein showed that the Newtonian model of the physical world was really only an approximate paradigm, fine when used to explain and predict common, everyday interactions between relatively large objects moving at slow speeds, but totally inadequate to handle the extremes of size and speed found in the subatomic and super-cosmologic worlds. These realms had their own canon of laws and logic.

As we know, the twentieth-century model of the physical world houses some arcane concepts: space is not Euclidian but curved so that parallel lines intersect; mass is not a solid, tangible constant, but a property that increases as a body is accelerated; time, under various conditions, appears to slow down, speed up, stop, and flow backwards; even the notion of cause-and-effect, the commonsense cornerstone of the Newtonian model, simply does not hold in the subatomic world. In building the modern physical edifice, scientists of this century learned an important lesson: reality has more than one meaningful face; what we observe is not necessarily what really is. Planck summed it up when he said: *Modern Physics impresses us particularly with the truth of the old doctrine which teaches that there are realities existing apart from our (normal) sense perceptions, and that there are problems and conflicts where these realities are of greater value for us than the richest treasures of the world of (normal) experiences.*

In this century we have witnessed a total restructuring of our views of nature, and now we are beginning to see a complete revamping of our views of ourselves. It comes with the willingness of scientists to study, for the first time in history, human beings in altered states of consciousness, and to observe and record systematically the events which spring naturally from these mental states.

In the past, Western science's model of consciousness was a narrow one indeed, made up of two states, wakefulness and slumber. The mentation of a child who sees *hidden analogies between cabbages and kings* was regarded as pure nonsense. The visions and voices reported by Eastern mystics were called delusions. Hypnotic consciousness was looked upon as a curious but uninformative state. Dream consciousness, a universal experience, was regarded as a nonsensical succession of flashbacks, bizarre and improbable incidents, really no more than a collection of subliminal paraphernalia.

Today's scientists realize that these seemingly irrational mentations, with their peculiar logics and strange distortions of space and time, offer a wealth of information on the nature of humans and their untapped potential. This broader model of human consciousness, which includes the continuum of altered states, has provided a home for parapsychological phenomena.

In 1902 William James made a plea for an expanded notion of consciousness. The plea fell on deaf ears then, but it is enlightening now to compare James's words with those of Planck quoted above, for the physicist and the psychologist, each in his way, was saying the same thing: *Our normal waking consciousness... is but one special type of consciousness, whilst all about it, parted from it by the flimsiest of screens, there lie potential forms of consciousness entirely different. We may go through life without suspecting their existence; but apply the requisite stimulus, and at a touch they are here in all their completeness.... No account of the universe in its totality can be final which leaves these other forms of consciousness quite disregarded... they forbid a premature closing of our account with reality.*

We have come to realize that in this larger paradigm of consciousness our paranormal side is just as much a part of human nature as any of our other faculties. We are more than the mere composite of our wakeful perceptions, for the purely *wakeful person* is only half human. Perhaps as research into the paranormal accelerates, the day will come when the prefix *para* will be dropped altogether. After all, it is only an admission of our present inability to grasp the full spectrum of things that are humanly possible.

—*condensed from* **Supersenses**, *by Charles Panati*

ABHEDANANDA, SWAMI. **LIFE BEYOND DEATH. 240pp. RVM44, 5.25c.**
This is a critical study of spiritualism and especially of the spiritualist phenomena that were so popular in the nineteenth century. Swami Abhedananda presents the Vedantic point of view and discusses life

after death, rebirth of the soul, spirit communication, mediumship, and much else. It is an interesting presentation which serves as a good counterpoint to most spiritualist literature.

AGEE, DORIS. **EDGAR CAYCE ON ESP. 1.95p.**
See the Edgar Cayce section.

ARMSTRONG, NEVILLE, ed. **HARVEST OF LIGHT. 260pp. Spe76, 8.70c.**
This is a collection of essays on the paranormal which have been published in the last fifteen years in the journal of the College of Psychic Studies. The authors cover a wide spectrum and the essays themselves illustrate the impact of paranormal events and paranormal thinking. The editor is the publisher of Neville Spearman, Ltd.

ASHBY, ROBERT H. **THE GUIDE BOOK FOR THE STUDY OF PSYCHICAL RESEARCH. 190pp. Wei72/HPG, 3.50p.**
An essential source book for the serious student. Includes an excellent essay on the nature of psychical research; extensive annotated bibliographies for both the beginning and advanced student as well as many additional listings; a chapter detailing procedures for sitting with a medium; a section enumerating the resources in England and the U.S. available to the student; biographical sketches of important figures in the movement; and an excellent glossary.

■ *BOWLES, NORMA and FRAN HYNDS.* **PSI SEARCH. Listings of centers of psi research in the U.S., lavishly illustrated, glossary, notes, bibliography, index, 8½"x10½", 168pp. H&R78, 6.95p.**
The authors originally gathered the material presented here for an exhibit at the California Museum of Science and Industry. They later expanded their findings into this excellent introductory survey of the entire field of parapsychology. This is an extremely readable account, covering the history of psi, its traditional associations, and virtually every aspect of current psi research. We highly recommend this book to all who are interested in psi.

BROWN, MICHAEL H. **P.K.—A REPORT ON PSYCHOKINESIS. Glossary, bibliography, 318pp. Mul76, 5.95p.**
A journalistic discussion of psychokinesis, focusing on case studies of scores of people who have demonstrated various aspects of PK.

■ *BUTLER, W.E.* **HOW TO DEVELOP CLAIRVOYANCE. 64pp. Wei68/APC, 1.25p.**
A very practical outline—highly recommended as such.

BUTLER, W.E. **HOW TO DEVELOP PSYCHOMETRY. 63pp. Wei71/APC, 1.25p.**
Psychometry is the power to measure and interpret the *soul of things,* picking up the hidden vibrations and impressions which have been recorded upon material objects. Includes a good amount of background material as well as practical suggestions.

BUTLER, W.E. **AN INTRODUCTION TO TELEPATHY. 64pp. Wei75/APC, 1.25p.**
The newest of Butler's practical treatises.

■ *CARRINGTON, HEREWARD.* **YOUR PSYCHIC POWERS AND HOW TO DEVELOP THEM. 358pp. Cau73/APC, 4.95p.**
Carrington was a noted psychic researcher and he has presented an excellent detailed instruction manual, based on first hand research and study over decades. Because of its wide scope it is also a complete conspectus of the whole range of psychic phenomena—psychometry, seeing the aura, telepathy, clairvoyance, automatic writing, spiritual healing, trance mediumship, materialization, astral projection and many other areas of parapsychology. This fine work has been out of print for many years and only recently reissued. Recommended as a good introduction to the field.

CHANEY, ROBERT. **ADVENTURES IN ESP. Illustrations, 137pp. Ata65, 4.50p.**
A very simply written practical guide, with information on ESP, clairvoyance, psychometry, intuition, visualization, vocalization, and vitalization. A positive, self help approach is taken.

COLTON, ANN REE. **ETHICAL ESP. 367pp. APC71, 8.95c.**
A clairvoyant discusses lower and higher ESP, the root races and their psychic powers, zodiacal powers and the glands, and related topics.

COOKE, GRACE. **THE NEW MEDIUMSHIP. 91pp. WET65, 2.75c.**
A comprehensive presentation by a noted English medium.

CRAWFORD, DR. QUANTZ. **METHODS OF PSYCHIC DEVELOP-MENT. 102pp. LIP73, 3.95p.**
This book gives you the absolute basics of psychic development—the philosophy you must know to understand the phenomena involved, exercises that prepare you and then open your psychic centers, and then the techniques for controlling and using these new powers. The exercises are all simple. . . . —from the introduction. Perhaps the exercises are too simple. We recommend extensive spiritual development before attempting to harness these powers—and caution and moderation at all times.

CUMMINS, GERALDINE. **SWAN ON A BLACK SEA: A STUDY IN AUTOMATIC WRITING, THE CUMMINS-WILLETT SCRIPTS. 168pp. RKP65, 6.50c.**
The value and quality of these scripts has been assessed quite differently by various parapsychologists, but they are clearly among the most important mediumistic material published. The introduction is perceptive and valuable.

CURTIS, ROBERT. **ON ESP. Glossary, index, 86pp. PrH75, 5.95c.**
This is a simply written survey of parapsychology geared toward older children and covering the following topics: what is ESP, mental telepathy, clairvoyance and precognition, psychokinesis, travels in dreams, faith healing, and modern brain research.

DEAN, STANLEY, ed. **PSYCHIATRY AND MYSTICISM. Illustrations, notes, index, 446pp. NeH75, 15.00c.**
This is an excellent anthology of writings based on a series of three panel-symposia on psychic phenomena held at the 1972, 1973, and 1974 annual meetings of the American Psychiatric Association. The book is divided into four sections, the first of which is a compilation of papers on metapsychiatry, mysticism, parapsychology, psi phenomena, telepathy, and precognition. The second section deals with the energy fields of man, electromagnetism, Kirlian photography, meditation, and biofeedback. Section three includes papers on positive and negative aspects and public health implications of psychic healing and shamanism. The final section considers transcendental and transpersonal experiences (with and without drugs) of nonpsychotics compared to the sensory capacity of psychotics.

DOUGLAS, ALFRED. **EXTRA SENSORY POWERS: A CENTURY OF PSYCHICAL RESEARCH. Notes, bibliography, index, 392pp. OvP76, 15.95c.**
This is the most comprehensive historical survey we know of. Virtually all the major figures and movements are discussed at length in an objective manner and somehow the abundance of information never seems overwhelming.

EDMONDS, SIMEON. **ESP, EXTRASENSORY PERCEPTION. 204pp. Wil65, 2.00p.**
A review of much of the research in the field, written for the layperson by a well known psychic. Each chapter is followed by references.

EDMONDS, SIMEON. **HYPNOTISM AND PSYCHIC PHENOMENA. Notes, bibliography, 177pp. Wil61, 3.00p.**
This is a very complete study which incorporates the author's own extensive research with a historical survey and chapters on induction and on the general phenomena of hypnosis. The connection of hypnosis with paranormal phenomena is emphasized and various chapters discuss hypnosis in relation to different forms of psi.

EDMUNDS, H. TUDOR. **PSYCHISM AND THE UNCONSCIOUS MIND. 254+pp. TPH68, 2.75p.**
A collection of articles from the **Science Group Journal** of the English Theosophical Research Centre. Includes very interesting studies on etheric vision, radiation, psychic perceptivity, psychometry, auras, telepathy, radiesthesia, and human consciousness.

EHRENWALD, JAN. **THE ESP EXPERIENCE: A PSYCHIATRIC VALIDATION. Bibliography, index, 320pp. H&R78, 13.95c.**
Dr. Ehrenwald is a highly respected psychiatrist. In this book he takes a responsible look at the evidence and explains how much so-called psi phenomena are corroborated by psychiatric and psychoanalytic findings. He believes that conventional ESP laboratory research has little relevance to the human condition, and therefore concentrates on real life psi incidents. He traces the roots of ESP to the mother-child relationship, and then looks at psi manifestations in crises, in the psychoanalytic situation, in mental illness, in genius, and in various altered states of consciousness. Many case histories are included.

FODOR, NANDOR. **ENCYCLOPEDIA OF PSYCHIC SCIENCE. Oversize, 416pp. Stu66, 7.95p.**
A vast, comprehensive survey covering the entire field up to 1933, its date of publication. Hundreds of articles and biographies. Every conceivable subject is covered, often in great detail, and each entry is cross referenced. It is an altogether fascinating work, the only one of its kind, which provides, in effect, a whole library on the subjects concerned. We recommend it highly.

GARRETT, EILEEN. **AWARENESS. 308pp. GtP43, 5.00c.**
An excellent presentation of Ms. Garrett's concept of the universal nature of human consciousness and the laws relating to this consciousness in action. Topics include sleep and dreams, hypnosis and suggestion, dissociation and awareness, the breath and color, the way inward, perception and communication, and death and survival.

GARRETT, EILEEN. **TELEPATHY—IN SEARCH OF A LOST FACULTY. Bibliography, 210pp. GtP41, 4.00c.**
A clear, subjective explanation of telepathy, probing its origins, its manifestations, and its functions.

GARRETT PUBLICATIONS. **BIOGRAPHICAL DICTIONARY OF PARAPSYCHOLOGY. 371pp. GtP64, 12.00c.**
A comprehensive international study.

GELLER, URI. **URI GELLER: MY STORY. 282pp. War75, 1.95p.**
The autobiography of the well known Israeli psychic who can bend metal, repair broken watches, propel objects across a room or make them dematerialize by direct mind action. Recounts his experiences of growing up with ESP and his recent, and now famous, experiments at the University of London and Stanford Research Institute. Good descriptions of contemporary psi research in which the basic concepts of science are being questioned. Photographs of Uri, leading psi researchers, and of metal bending experiments.

GOODMAN, JEFFREY. **PSYCHIC ARCHAEOLOGY. 8.95c.**
See the Ancient Civilizations section.

GRIS, HENRY and WILLIAM DICK. **THE NEW SOVIET PSYCHIC DISCOVERIES: A FIRSTHAND REPORT ON THE LATEST BREAKTHROUGHS IN RUSSIAN PARAPSYCHOLOGY. Photographs, index, 324pp. PrH78, 10.95c.**
Not since **Psychic Discoveries Behind the Iron Curtain** was published in 1970 has there been such a comprehensive book on the Soviet Union's all out attempt to investigate and harness the powers of the human mind. In six separate visits to the USSR, the authors used special contacts in the Kremlin as well as the parapsychology underground to obtain unprecedented interviews with Russians involved in all related fields.

GUIRDHAM, ARTHUR. **A FOOT IN BOTH WORLDS. 244pp. Spe73, 6.00c.**
A doctor's autobiography of psychic experience which shows clearly the consistent purpose of the psychic entities which have intervened in his life. The story shows the systematic way Guirdham was prepared by his experiences.

HANSEL, C.E.M. **ESP, A SCIENTIFIC EVALUATION. Notes, bibliography, 263pp. Scr66, 2.45p.**
A good history of the statistical approach to psi research in which extensive tabulations of card guesses and dice throws are made in order to verify factual nature of telepathy, clairvoyance, and psychokinesis.

HAPGOOD, CHARLES. **VOICES OF SPIRIT THROUGH THE PSYCHIC EXPERIENCE OF ELWOOD BABBITT. Glossary, index, 338pp. Dia75, 8.95c.**
Babbitt is a trance medium who purports to have the spirits of famous persons such as Mark Twain, Einstein, and Wordsworth speaking through him. He is known for his *life readings,* in which he looks back through an individual's previous lives and offers advice based on his clairvoyant knowledge. Professor Hapgood has been studying Babbitt

and his work for over eight years. In this book he offers full length transcripts of the communications which have come through Babbitt and interprets his spiritual teachings. He also relates the phenomenon of trance mediumship to recent research in parapsychology.

HARDY, ALISTER, ROBERT HARVIE and ARTHUR KOESTLER. **THE CHALLENGE OF CHANCE. Notes, index, 309pp. RaH73, 2.95p.**
A marine biologist from Oxford and a psychologist from London University report on experiments in the telepathic transmission of line drawings and pictures to two hundred subjects. Additional comments by Arthur Koestler.

HAYNES, RENEE. **THE SEEING EYE, THE SEEING I. Bibliography, 224pp. SMP76/HPG, 8.95c.**
A journalistic discussion of psi which cites many case studies and connects them to many of the extraordinary events of history. Ms. Haynes' focus is on perception and she shows how an awareness of the paranormal can lead us to fuller, more enriching lives.

HOLROYD, STUART. **PSI AND THE CONSCIOUSNESS EXPLOSION. Notes, index, 235pp. Tap77/BoH, 9.95c.**
This is an important work in which Holroyd discusses the recent breakthroughs in psi research and places them in context with larger issues. He asserts that a new scientific paradigm is emerging which must and will include parasensory phenomena. The book is well researched and thought provoking.

HUDSON, THOMSON. **THE LAW OF PSYCHIC PHENOMENA. 409pp. Wei1892, 2.95p.**
An important early study. Hudson was the first to correlate all psychic phenomena and systematically classify it.

HUSON, PAUL. **HOW TO TEST AND DEVELOP YOUR ESP. Bibliography, index, 215pp. SBL75, 1.95p.**
Huson discusses ESP training procedures and tells of ways of using ESP in daily life. He includes a concise review of college courses on psi, a glossary of parapsychology terms, and a guide to technical journals.

■ *JOHNSON, RAYNOR.* **THE IMPRISONED SPLENDOUR. Bibliography, index, 424pp. TPH53/Hod, 5.75p.**
One of the most widely read syntheses of science, psychical research, philosophy, and religion yet produced. Dr. Johnson has the advantage of a first rate mind, thorough scientific training, many years of teaching, broad and deep interests in psychical research and mysticism, and an almost unique ability to pull disparate strands of data and approaches together into a significant whole. Highly recommended.

JOHNSON, RAYNOR. **PSYCHICAL RESEARCH. Bibliography, 176pp. Cro55, 1.75p.**
A clear, readable, and thorough introduction. The explanations are illustrated with some well chosen examples from the annals of psychical research; the problems inherent in the discipline are discussed; and guidelines as to the evaluation of evidence are given.

KARDEC, ALLAN. **THE BOOK OF MEDIUMS. 456pp. Wei70/ACP, 5.95p.**
If there exists an encyclopedia on the subject of spiritualism and mediumship, this is it. The entire field is approached with a practical and scientific attitude by one who was intimately knowledgeable on the subject. This and the **Law of Psychic Phenomena** are the most noted nineteenth century texts.

KOESTLER, ARTHUR. **THE ROOTS OF COINCIDENCE. Notes, bibliography, 159pp. RaH72/PnB, 1.95p.**
Brings together in an intriguing and persuasive way the various strands of psychical research, mysticism, biology, physics, and philosophy. This is one of the most impressive syntheses of parapsychology's discoveries and purview with those of physics yet to appear. Essential reading for the scientifically-oriented student.

KRIPPNER, STANLEY. **SONG OF THE SIREN. Notes, index, 328pp. H&R75, 3.95p.**
Krippner is one of the most noted writers and researchers in the field of parapsychology. He has been involved in this study for most of his adult life and in this account he charts that involvement over the last twenty years in an informal manner. This is a survey of the developments in parapsychology during that period as seen through

the life and *adventures* of one man. Many of the main individuals, experiments, and findings are reviewed in an informal way. Krippner attended conferences and traveled in the USSR and Czechoslovakia and he reports in depth on his experiences. His most extensive experience was at the Maimonides Dream Lab—and this is also discussed. An interesting nontechnical account.

LEADBEATER, C.W. **CLAIRVOYANCE. 226pp. TPH1899, 3.00c.**
A highly developed clairvoyant discusses the theoretical and philosophical basis of clairvoyance. Leadbeater writes very clearly.

LESHAN, LAWRENCE. **THE MEDIUM, THE MYSTIC AND THE PHYSICIST. Notes, bibliography, 284pp. RaH66, 1.95p.**
Dr. LeShan, a researcher on the paranormal and psychic healing, examines the Clairvoyant Reality (as he terms it) from three supposedly separate viewpoints—those of the medium, the mystic and the physicist—and finds each view startlingly similar. An important book.

MCCONNELL, R.A. **ESP CURRICULUM GUIDE: A SCIENTIST EXAMINES THE REALITY OF ESP. 128pp. S&S70, 1.95p.**
The author, actively engaged in ESP research, hopes to provide a means by which interested persons can teach a relevant and exciting presentation of this field. He outlines the most important books and gives exact procedures for classroom or home experiments. Scientifically oriented, but suitable for the general reader.

MAETERLINCK, MAURICE. **THE UNKNOWN GUEST. 340pp. UnB15, 7.95c.**
The *guest* in the title is the faculty in man that connects him with paranormal phenomena which in this case are premonitions, haunted houses, and the Elberfeld Horses that could apparently communicate with men and perform arithmetic calculations.

MANNING, MATTHEW. **IN THE MINDS OF MILLIONS. 174pp. WHA77, 9.50c.**
An often absorbing story of Manning's immense psychic abilities. It is written in the first person and includes reports of some of the countless experiments in which he has participated along with a narration of many of the more interesting events of his recent life.

MEEK, GEORGE. **FROM ENIGMA TO SCIENCE. Photographs, 199pp. Wei73, 6.95c.**
The author has devoted several years to traveling over much of the globe making a study of the paranormal. He has made an effort to focus the findings of psychical research, parapsychology, physics, astronomy, psychiatry, biochemistry, medicine, physiology, and occult literature on an explanation of man's psi ability. This is a scattered account which contains some useful and interesting material.

MERRY, ELEANOR. **SPIRITUAL KNOWLEDGE. 115pp. NKB35, 4.75c.**
A sensitive and insightful guide to the understanding of parapsychological phenomena written from an Anthroposophical viewpoint.

MITCHELL, EDGAR. **PSYCHIC EXPLORATION. Glossary, index, 708pp. Put74, 5.95p.**
A monumental work divided into twenty-nine chapters on every area of psychic research—each written especially for this book by a noted scientist. Most of the articles are fairly technical and are accompanied by notes.

MONAHAN, EVELYN and TERRY BAKKEN. **PUT YOUR PSYCHIC POWERS TO WORK. Index, 148pp. NeH73, 8.95c.**
Ms. Monahan teaches parapsychology at Georgia State University.

This book contains many exercises which she developed for her classes as well as some theoretical and explanatory material.

■ *MOSS, THELMA.* **THE PROBABILITY OF THE IMPOSSIBLE.** Notes, index, 394pp. NAL74/RKP, 4.95p.
Written by one of the leading researchers in Kirlian electrophotography, the book presents a parapsychologist at work in her laboratory and in the field. She explores the assumptions of parapsychologists and shows how the scientific psychical researcher attempts to recreate, capture, and analyze the elusive phenomena of the paranormal. She leads the reader along a continum from everyday experiences through events that only happen rarely and under special circumstances on to the seemingly impossible experiences of both well known and little-heralded psychics. She convincingly presents arguments for a psychic world as real as the material one. Several Kirlian photographs are included.

MUHL, ANITA. **AUTOMATIC WRITING.** Bibliography, 193pp. GtP63, 4.50c.
Dr. Muhl is a psychiatrist who has applied the method of automatic handwriting to an understanding of her patients' psychic processes over a period of more than thirty years. In this volume she presents the results of her experiences emphasizing the psychological meaning of the experiments. Many case studies are included.

OPHIEL. **THE ART AND PRACTICE OF CLAIRVOYANCE.** 137pp. Wei69, 3.50p.
Everyone has clairvoyant powers; this book tells how to use and develop them further. Ophiel teaches the basis of clairvoyance, use of the Tree of Life and the basic elements in directing your clairvoyance to work through mental images and their associations.

OSBORNE, ARTHUR. **THE EXPANSION OF AWARENESS.** 272pp. TPH61, 1.95p.
A profound study of Osborne's quest for the meaning of life and his investigation of extrasensory perception, the implications of telepathy, and the possibility of survival and rebirth. These questions lead to a discussion of the purpose of existence, the validity of mystical experience, and the achieving of deeper awareness and enlightenment. An excellent account which includes one of the most complete bibliographies we have seen.

OSBORNE, ARTHUR. **THE FUTURE IS NOW.** 250pp. TPH61, 2.50p.
A complete treatment of precognition, including a review of scientific studies and of the existing explanations.

OSBORNE, ARTHUR. **MEANING OF PERSONAL EXISTENCE IN THE LIGHT OF PARANORMAL PHENOMENA, REINCARNATION, AND MYSTICAL EXPERIENCE.** 214pp. TPH66, 3.95c.
A discussion of the implications of supernormal phenomena such as clairvoyance, clairaudience, precognition, and telepathy, with an investigation of the possibility of reincarnation and mystical experience. Well researched and highly informative.

OSTRANDER, SHEILA and LYNN SCHROEDER. **HANDBOOK OF PSYCHIC DISCOVERIES.** Index, 308pp. Ber74/SBL, 2.25p.
A collection of how-to projects, all fully explained and explored. Virtually every conceivable area is covered and many of the experiments can be conducted without any instrumentation. The projects are topically arranged and the book is illustrated throughout.

OSTRANDER, SHEILA and LYNN SCHROEDER. **PSYCHIC DISCOVERIES BEHIND THE IRON CURTAIN.** 448pp. Ban70/SBL, 2.25p.
The authors traveled to the Soviet Union in 1967 to attend a conference on ESP. This is the story of what they read, saw, and heard. Includes material on mental telepathy, hypnotism, faith healing, precognition, psychokinesis, auras around plants and animals, brain control, astrological birth control, levitation, sightless vision, dowsing, acupuncture, prophecy, psychotronics—the list goes on and on. The treatment in each case is quite thorough. Many references.

PANCHADASI, SWAMI. **CLAIRVOYANCE AND OCCULT POWERS.** 319pp. YPS16, 6.00c.
A complete set of occult lessons, prepared by an associate of Yogi Ramacharaka.

PATTERSON, DORIS. **VARIETIES OF ESP IN THE EDGAR CAYCE READINGS.** 77pp. ARE68, 2.00p.
Formerly titled **The Unfettered Mind.**

PEARCE-HIGGINS, J.D. and WHITBY, G.S., eds. **LIFE, DEATH AND PSYCHICAL RESEARCH.** Bibliography, 272pp. Wei73, 5.95p.
A collection of essays written on behalf of The Churches' Fellowship for Psychical and Spiritual Studies, divided into sections on the nature and scope of psychical phenomena and the **Bible** and psychic phenomena.

PROGOFF, IRA. **THE IMAGE OF AN ORACLE: A REPORT ON RESEARCH INTO THE MEDIUMSHIP OF EILEEN J. GARRETT.** 9.45c.
See the Jungian Psychology section.

PUHARICH, ANDRIJA. **BEYOND TELEPATHY.** 340pp. Dou62/PnB, 2.95p.
First published in 1962, this is still one of the very best books available on the subject. It presents a coherent theory of psychical research, and discusses its relation to such phenomena as ESP, astral projection, yoga, and shamanism. A very scientific, well annotated collection of studies.

RANDALL, JOHN. **PARAPSYCHOLOGY AND THE NATURE OF LIFE.** Notes, index, 266pp. H&R75/SBL, 3.95p.
A dry, technical study. Randall is a biologist and here he focuses on the relation (or lack thereof) between parapsychological findings, biology and the natural world. The book traces the rise of the mechanist-reductionist theory of life from the time of Darwin to the present day and points out the psi phenomena which do not appear to be explicable in terms of that limited theory.

REYES, BENITO. **SCIENTIFIC EVIDENCE OF THE EXISTENCE OF THE SOUL.** 251pp. TPH70, 2.45p.
A very well documented Theosophical text, including many case studies and an extensive bibliography.

RHINE, J.B. **EXTRA-SENSORY PERCEPTION: A CRITICAL SURVEY.** Twenty-one technical appendices, many tables, extensive notes, index, 463pp. BrP40, 3.95p.
This is perhaps the most comprehensive presentation of the statistical approach to ESP investigation as developed in the Duke University laboratories under Dr. Rhine. It details the mathematical and experimental methods, criticism and evidence, and the nature of ESP.

RHINE, LOUISA. **ESP IN LIFE AND LAB.** 275pp. McM67, 1.50p.
This is the second of Dr. Rhine's valuable collections of spontaneous

cases taken from over 10,000 which she has gathered. The author analyzes about eighty instances after categorizing them. She is known as a common sense authority who weighs cases within the context of their specific occurrence as well as within that of their bearing on major issues in psychical research.

RHINE, LOUISA. **MIND OVER MATTER: PSYCHOKINESIS. 390pp. McM70, 2.95p.**
Reports the studies from 1934 to the present, from experiments with cards and coins to such new targets as one-celled creatures and plants. Also included are various speculative paranormal occurrences. A serious and comprehensive report by one of the world's leading parapsychologists.

RHINE, LOUISA. **PSI—WHAT IS IT? Notes, index, 247pp. H&R75, 1.95p.**
At last there is a book about psi that is completely scientific yet thoroughly entertaining. I can think of no better way to introduce people to parapsychology than to have them read **PSI: What Is It?**—Stanley Krippner.

ROGO, D. SCOTT. **EXPLORING PSYCHIC PHENOMENA. Bibliography, index, 168pp. TPH76, 3.75p.**
This is an interesting survey of some of the latest advances in the scientific exploration of parasensory phenomena. All of the major fields are covered in separate chapters and there are quotations from individual papers and reports along with a variety of case studies. A well documented, readable book.

ROGO, D. SCOTT. **PARAPSYCHOLOGY—A CENTURY OF IN-QUIRY. Notes, index, 319pp. Del75, 1.75p.**
This comprehensive book traces the attempts to bring scientific methods and critical observation to the study of psi phenomena in the work of such men as Cesare Lombroso and Sir Oliver Lodge. Rogo gives detailed accounts of breakthroughs such as Rhine's laboratory work with ESP and psychokinesis. He also covers current work on out-of-the-body-experience, psychedelics, alpha training, and the possibilities of animal psi research.

SHAY, J.M. **HOW TO DEVELOP ESP. 53pp. WAO74, 2.00p.**
A detailed, highly simplified instruction manual in the form of subsequent lessons which covers virtually every aspect of parasensory awareness.

SHERMAN, HAROLD. **HOW TO MAKE ESP WORK FOR YOU. 208pp. Faw64, 1.95p.**
A popular introductory account.

SHERMAN, HAROLD. **YOUR MYSTERIOUS POWERS OF ESP. 239pp. NAL69, 1.25p.**
Sherman reviews the evidence for paranormal phenomena, presents many case studies, and discusses various aspects of the topic.

SINCLAIR, UPTON. **MENTAL RADIO. 285pp. McM30, 1.95p.**
This volume inspired the modern scientific investigation of extrasensory phenomena. It is the account of the experiments performed by Sinclair's wife, Mary Craig Kennedy. It explains step-by-step the methods she used for spontaneous concentration and relaxation which opened her up to receiving telepathic messages and seeing pictures on hidden cards.

SMITH, SUSY. **HOW TO DEVELOP YOUR ESP. 286pp. Pin72, 1.25p.**
A popularized account by a noted journalist.

SMITH, SUSY. **LIFE IS FOREVER. Bibliography, 256pp. Del74, 1.75p.**
A journalistic collection of *reports from beyond death* in the form of case studies of communications which the participants allege actually occur. Susy Smith is a prolific writer and she is also a good reporter.

SPRAGGETT, ALLEN. **ARTHUR FORD: THE MAN WHO TALKED WITH THE DEAD. Bibliography, index, 301pp. NAL73, 1.50p.**
A sympathetic journalistic survey of the life and extraordinary powers of Arthur Ford, a famous twentieth century psychic. The book includes many transcriptions of conversations which Ford is alleged to have had with long-dead individuals.

STEARN, JESS. **ADVENTURES INTO THE PSYCHIC. 240pp. NAL69, 1.50p.**
A well written popular account, which includes many case histories.

STEVENSON, IAN. **TELEPATHIC IMPRESSIONS. Bibliography, index, 206pp. UPV70, 9.00c.**
Dr. Stevenson begins this volume with a summary of 160 cases which he has previously published and examined for authenticity. He follows with detailed studies of thirty-five new cases.

SWANN, INGO. **TO KISS EARTH GOOD-BYE. Bibliography, index, 217pp. Del75, 1.95p.**
Ingo Swann has written an extraordinarily good book on the nature of consciousness, his first encounters with psychic experiences, the history of psychic research, what it is like to be a subject in remote sensing experiments, and how he affected a sensitive magnetic device through several types of shielding.

TARG, RUSSELL and HAROLD PUTHOFF. **MIND REACH: SCIENTISTS LOOK AT PSYCHIC ABILITY. Illustrations, charts, notes, index, 255pp. Dia77, 8.95c.**
The authors are physicists with impressive credentials. Both are senior researchers in the Electronics and Bioengineering Laboratory of the Stanford Research Institute. *This book is a clear, straightforward account of a set of successful experiments that demonstrate the existence of "remote viewing," a hitherto unvalidated human capacity.*—Margaret Mead. A general survey of parapsychology and a detailed review of the experimental technique are also included.

TART, CHARLES. **LEARNING TO USE EXTRASENSORY PERCEPTION. Notes, bibliography, index, 184pp. UCh76, 3.95p.**
This is a serious, important book which argues that the usual ways of testing for ESP are inadvertently designed to extinguish rather than to strengthen ability. Tart and his students, using a basic learning theory approach (which he discusses in detail), found a considerable level of ESP ability, and they also demonstrated that some subjects can learn to improve their abilities.

■ *TART, CHARLES.* **PSI—SCIENTIFIC STUDIES OF THE PSYCHIC REALM. Illustrations, bibliography, index, 254pp. Dut77, 4.95p.**
Dr. Tart has devoted much of his energy over the last twenty years to studying various aspects of psi and the paranormal. In this book he goes beyond the usual arguments for or against the existence of the paranormal, and discusses what we know about the nature of psi, how it works, the proper conditions for testing it, and what implications it has for our understanding of ourselves. Using rigorous laboratory methods, Dr. Tart has achieved some remarkable positive results with psi. He shares many of these experiments and their results with us here.

TAYLOR, JOHN. **SUPERMINDS. Bibliography, index, 183pp. War75/PnB, 1.95p.**
Dr. Taylor has specialized in elementary particle physics, cosmology, and brain research, and is generally concerned with promoting a wider understanding of the new frontiers of science. This is a fairly technical study, although the numerous photographs and the good layout make it approachable to general readers. The major part of the book is devoted to an analysis of the *Geller effect*—named after Uri Geller, who can bend metal objects by rubbing them or concentrating on them. Dr. Taylor believes that this phenomenon is due to the electromagnetic force field, and he details why this is so. He also speculates on methods of investigating other aspects of ESP and concludes with an absorbing account of his experiment with Uri Geller. The book has received a good press and for those interested in the subject it is an excellent addition to the available literature.

TENHAEFF, W.H.C. **TELEPATHY AND CLAIRVOYANCE. Notes, index, 161pp. Tho65, 16.80c.**
A scholarly study in which Dr. Tenhaeff describes the mechanisms of memory and amnesia and then relates these mental functions to those apparently involved in telepathy, proscopy (future memory), possession, and reincarnation. The author was among the first to undertake systematic psycho-diagnostic research into the personality structures of people with psi abilities. There are descriptions and photographs of his investigation of telepathic relationships between kindergarten children and their teachers.

THOULESS, ROBERT. **FROM ANECDOTE TO EXPERIMENT IN PSYCHICAL RESEARCH. 193pp. RKP72, 10.00c.**
A series of sketches of points of interest within the field by a noted psychologist. Includes much material not touched upon in other books. Recommended for the serious scholar. Many references.

THURSTON, MARK. **UNDERSTAND AND DEVELOP YOUR ESP.** Illustrations, bibliography, 88pp. ARE77, 2.50p.
A collection of highly practical exercises which take off from selections in the Cayce readings, but which often go far afield from the original statements. Some very interesting techniques are suggested.

ULLMAN, MONTAGUE and STANLEY KRIPPNER. **DREAM TELE-PATHY—SCIENTIFIC EXPERIMENTS INTO THE SUPERNATU-RAL.** 300pp. Vik73, 2.95p.
The first book to present and analyze the results of scientifically controlled experiments in telepathic dreaming. The authors head the Dream Laboratory of New York's Maimonides Medical Center. They conducted experiments over a ten-year period to determine if a person acting as an *agent* could transfer his thoughts to the mind of a sleeping *subject*, thereby altering or influencing the subject's dreams. The results are recorded here in great detail, along with much other interesting material.

UPHOFF, WALTER and MARY JO. **NEW PSYCHIC FRONTIERS.** Notes, index, 278pp. Smy75, 10.50c.
Written as an aid to discussion group leaders, students and instructors, this book reviews the full range of psychic phenomena: telepathy, guides, ghosts, direct voice. It also has a thirty page directory of groups world-wide doing research on these topics.

VASILIEV, L.L. **EXPERIMENTS IN DISTANT INFLUENCE.** Technical appendices, notes, 281pp. Dut76/Wdw, 5.95p.
This is a landmark book which records Dr. Vasiliev's remarkable experiments on hypnotic suggestion through telepathy. In these experiments Vasiliev showed conclusively that distant influence can be demonstrated experimentally, and further showed that such remote influence is not affected by the kind of metallic screening that would block radio signals. He thus exploded the former hypothesis that some sort of mental radio (radio-type electromagnetic waves) explains telepathy. Dr. Vasiliev was Chairman of the Physiology Department at the University of Leningrad until his death in 1966. This book was originally entitled **Experiments in Mental Suggestion.** Anita Gregory provides an excellent introduction.

VISHITA, SWAMI BHAKTA. **GENUINE MEDIUMSHIP: THE INVISIBLE POWERS.** 277pp. YPS19, 6.00c.
A very complete account of every aspect of the subject, including many practical suggestions on how to develop various mediumistic powers. Written by an associate of Yogi Ramacharaka.

VISHITA, SWAMI BHAKTA. **SEERSHIP.** 384pp. YPS nd, 6.00c.
A comprehensive collection of very practical lessons.

WICKLAND, CARL. **THIRTY YEARS AMONG THE DEAD. NPC24/PsP, 4.95p.**
Wickland was a medical doctor who communicated with departed spirits for over thirty years, with his wife as the medium. He recorded the spirit communication verbatim and presents a large body of it in this volume. This is a classic work, long unavailable in unabridged form and only recently reprinted.

WILSON, COLIN. **STRANGE POWERS.** 146pp. RaH73/SBL, 1.95p.
While writing **The Occult** Wilson became fascinated by the powers of some of the people he interviewed. In this book he tells about three such people: a dowser who can leave his body, a retired nurse through whom spirits write messages about the future, and a man whose reincarnation has been documented.

WOLMAN, BENJAMIN, ed. **HANDBOOK OF PARAPSYCHOLOGY.** Glossary, notes, index, 988pp. VNR77, 39.15c.
This is the definitive text to date on scientific parapsychology. The articles have been written by noted authorities and the information is organized under the following major headings: *History of Parapsychology; Research Methods in Parapsychology; Perception, Communication, and Parapsychology; Parapsychology and Physical Systems; Parapsychology and Altered States of Consciousness; Parapsychology and Healing; Survival of Bodily Death; Parapsychology and Other Fields; Parapsychology Models and Theories; Soviet Research in Parapsychology.* There is also an annotated listing of suggested readings.

WORRALL, AMBROSE and OLGA. **EXPLORE YOUR PSYCHIC WORLD.** 144pp. H&R70, 3.95p.
The Worralls are two of the most noted healers of this century. Here they give practical suggestions on how to develop one's psychic abilities.

YOUNG, SAMUEL. **PSYCHIC CHILDREN.** Index, 182pp. S&S77, 1.75p.
A collection of anecdotes and case histories of children with psychic abilities. Young also includes practical advice to parents on how to handle a child who displays psychic abilities.

PROPHECY

In early society a prophet was usually a priest who had the ability to look into the future and read its portents. In most instances these utterances were made in an ecstatic condition. The prophets of ancient Israel were religious leaders who occupied themselves, in great measure, with the calm statement of future political events. Prophecy in ancient times was then thought of as a direct utterance of the deity, taking man as his mouthpiece. Modern prophecy, as exemplified in the books which follow, is secular; the prophet doubtless feels some divine inspiration, but he generally speaks as an individual not as a representative of religion or state. The greatest prophet of modern times was Nostradamus (1503-66). His prophecies were extremely obscure, perhaps accounting for their popularity since they can be interpreted in many ways. His book of prophecies is one of the few books which has been continually in print since 1555. In the twentieth century most of the prophecy has centered around coming Earth changes and predictions of disasters. The best known and most accurate of modern-day prophets was Edgar Cayce. Countless books have been written that deal directly or indirectly with his prophetic statements; they are listed in his own section.

ASSOCIATION OF THE LIGHT MORNING. **SEASON OF CHANGES, WAYS OF RESPONSE. Notes, 290pp. Her74, 4.95p.**
A psychic interpretation of the coming changes in, on, and about the Earth and the corresponding transformations within man. The prophecies and teachings recorded here were received by a psychic in Virginia Beach, Va. over the period of about a year. The Earth changes are of a radical nature and they are discussed in detail. The second half of the book contains an explanation of how man might best respond to these changes and transform himself.

CARTER, MARY ELLEN. **EDGAR CAYCE ON PROPHECY. 1.50p.**
See the Edgar Cayce section.

THE LUSSON TWINS. **THE BEGINNING OR THE END. 113pp. Don75, 5.95c.**
Prophets since biblical times (and especially recent ones like Nostradamus and Edgar Cayce) have pointed out that the last quarter of the twentieth century will be a critical one for the human race. The predictions have been ones of famine, revolution, earthquakes, tidal waves, and nuclear holocaust. This book presents a series of detailed predictions including: a complete map and timetable for land changes in the next twenty-five years; the shape of economic, sociological, theological, political, and topographical transformations to come; plans for a survival community and a city of the future; and new directions in science and medicine.

PRIEDITIS, ARTHUR. **THE FATE OF THE NATIONS. Bibliography, 428pp. LIP74, 12.95c.**
Prieditis restates many of the most noted political prophecies from the sixteenth century to the present and analyzes both their veracity and meaning. Many views of the future are cited. This is a comprehensive study which is rather badly organized.

ROBERTS, HENRY, tr. **THE COMPLETE PROPHECIES OF NOSTRADAMUS. 350pp. Crn69, 7.95c.**
This is the only unabridged edition of the predictions of the world's most noted prophet. Included are the original French text, an English translation, and the translator's interpretation of each prophecy. Roberts relates the visions to actual and future world events. Those looking for clear cut predictions will not find them in Nostradamus' writings (nor in the writings of virtually any prophet)—the messages are often couched in obscure and ambiguous language.

VAUGHAN, ALAN. **PATTERNS OF PROPHECY. Notes, index, 266pp. Del73/Tur, 1.50p.**
This is the most scientific study of prophecy that we know of. Vaughn himself is a prophet as well as a writer and researcher. He believes that each individual has an inner or psychic blueprint, much like the physical RNA-DNA blueprint, and that prophets have the ability to recognize and read these blueprints. In this volume he synthesizes the concepts of synchronicity and coincidence, archetypal roles, prophetic dreams, and psi fields, to formulate a plausible explanation for prophecy. In the process he recounts his experiences in the development of prophetic abilities and scrutinizes the prophecies of others.

WOLDBEN, A. **AFTER NOSTRADAMUS. 186pp. Fon72, 1.60p.**
Traces the course of prophecy down the ages, mostly from documents which have hitherto been almost unknown. Sources include the Vedas, the Great Pyramid, La Salette, Garabandal, St. Damiano, and Nostradamus. The text is topically arranged, and this adds to its interest since a theme can be followed and considered in depth.

RECORDS

There are, of course, tens of thousands of records available —with thousands of new ones issued each year. We have selected representative recordings in the following areas: East Asian music, South and Southeast Asian music, Near Eastern music, Tibetan music, meditation and movement, and chanting and singing. We also include a miscellaneous selection of records which we feel fit in our with our general coverage, but not into one of the specific areas. Our emphasis is on classic music, or music with religious overtones. We have not chosen any Western classical recordings since that is such a broad field and classical records are generally available. The selection possibilities within our areas are seemingly endless; we have tried to pick out the best examples of each type of recording. Our criteria vary—sometimes we consider the label, other times the individual artist or producer, or else the theme of the composition. We have attempted as straightforward an analysis as possible of each recording, usually simply saying what the album consists of and staying away from critical evaluations since musical tastes are so personal.

Chanting and Singing

The recordings in this section are representative of a new, popular sound which can best be described as spiritual folk or rock music. The words are spiritual and the rhythms are often lively, though sometimes the recordings are quite solemn. Many times the performers are followers of a particular guru or spiritual teacher.

COSMIC CELEBRATION. 6.00.
The Cosmic Celebration is written and narrated by Pir Vilayat Inayat Khan and produced and performed by his students. As the liner notes say, *The* **Cosmic Celebration** *is a vast pageant which embodies the aims underlying all religious rituals, that which has drawn man to the spiritual life since the beginning of time: it creates a psychological environment in which human beings are able to recollect the cosmic drama behind all earthly events.*

KRIYANANDA, SWAMI. **O GOD BEAUTIFUL. 5.95.**
See the Yogananda subsection of Indian Philosophy.

KRIYANANDA, SWAMI. **SONGS OF THE SOUL. 5.95.**
Traditional songs in Hindi, Bengali, and Sanskrit, and modern songs in English are sung by Swami Kriyananda and members of the Ananda Cooperative Village, accompanied on sitar and *tabla* (drums). Kriyananda's voice is pleasant to listen to.

MORNING STAR. 5.95.
Melodic, devotional songs by students of Swami Muktananda.

MUHAIYADDEEN, BAWA. **INTO THE SECRET OF THE HEART. 6.98.**
Spiritual songs sung in Tamil and Arabic with English translations as part of the liner notes. Guru Bawa is a Ceylonese monk who lives in the U.S. and whose teachings are similar to those of the Sufis. The recording quality is not terribly good and Guru Bawa's voice is high pitched and not soothing to listen to.

SIDDHA. 6.98.
Spiritual folk music, far better than most albums of its type. The lead singer has a fine voice and the music is pleasing to the ear. The words are good too. Liner notes, including the lyrics of each song.

SUFI CHOIR. **CRYING FOR JOY. 5.95.**
An album by the Sufi Choir including *Garden of Allah, Jesus Was A Shepard, Krishna Song, Cryin' For Joy,* and *24th Psalm.* Lyrics are included.

SUFI SONG AND DANCE. 5.95.
A collection of songs and dances featuring the Sufi Choir and members of the San Francisco Sufi Community. A twenty-two page booklet that contains the words, music, and dance instructions is included.

TEMPLE MUSIC AND CHANTS WITH SRI SWAMI RAMA. 8.95.
Chants by Swami Rama and his students, accompanied by bells, drums, and sitar. An explanation of each chant is provided. In some cases it is possible to chant with the album, though some selections are complex and difficult to follow without printed words.

TREASURY OF GREGORIAN CHANTS. 7.99.
A three record set featuring the Vienna Choir of the Vienna Hofburg Kapelle. Includes examples of all the important types of chants.

A TREASURY OF GREGORIAN CHANTS, SERIES I. 7.99.
A four record set. The chants are performed by monks from several monasteries. A good recording.

A TREASURY OF GREGORIAN CHANTS, SERIES II. 7.99.
A four record set of chants featuring the Deller Consort, an English group which is world famous for its excellent performances. Includes liner notes.

WINDS OF BIRTH. 5.95.
Spiritual folk/rock by a group of musicians and singers from Findhorn, led by David Spangler, and called The New Troubadours. Very pleasant and melodious songs. Our most popular record of songs.

YOGANANDA. **CHANTS AND PRAYERS. 4.95.**
A recording of the voice of Paramahansa Yogananda singing devotional chants in English and Bengali.

YOGANANDA. **I WILL BE THINE ALWAYS. 4.95.**
This album and the two following feature selections from Yogananda's book **Cosmic Chants.** On this album the chants are sung by a choir of nuns from the Self Realization Order.

YOGANANDA. **IN THE LAND BEYOND MY DREAMS. 4.95.**
Organ renditions of twelve of Yogananda's chants.

YOGANANDA. **SONG OF MY HEART (CHANTS AND POEMS). 4.95.**

YOGANANDA. **WHEN THY SONG FLOWS THROUGH ME. 4.95.**
Monks of the Self Realization Order sing chants by Yogananda.

——END OF CHANTING AND SINGING SUBSECTION——

East Asian Music

The East Asian musical tradition is generally thought of as one of the four main traditions—the other three are South Asia, the Near East, and Europe. In classical East Asian music there is a conscious theoretical basis and a sense of repertoire; the performer is often—though not always—a professional. The tonal vocabulary of twelve tones generated in a cycle of fifths is a common factor in the music of the area. The emphasis is on melody supported by rhythm, with little interest in harmonic accompaniment such as is found in the Western classical style. No matter how large an ensemble may be, the individual instruments are meant to be heard. This differs from the orchestral sound ideal, popular in Western classical music, in which the intention is to merge the sounds of the individual instruments. The common tendency is for East Asian music to be word or pictorially oriented. Such orientations are obvious in the many vocal and dance forms of Asia; but with a few notable exceptions one also finds that purely instrumental music will be attached through its title to a literary movement or a scene. Perhaps this relates to a general sensitivity to nature in East Asian culture as a whole. The main instruments (using their Chinese names) are the *cheng* (a zither with thirteen to sixteen silk strings), the *chin* (similar to the *cheng*, with only seven strings), the *hsiao* (vertical bamboo flute), the *hsun* (small egg-shaped wind instrument, held in both hands as it is played), the *lo* (large gongs), the *nan-hu* (a two-string violin with a long neck), the *pa* (cymbals), the *pipa* (a pear-shaped lute), the *sheng* (a gourd with thirteen to seventeen bamboo pipes set in it, each with its own reed), and the *ta-pan* (castinets).

Japanese music can be considered as a national tradition set in the satellite category of the general East Asian music culture. Korea served as a bridge to Japan for many Chinese musical ideas as well as exerting influence through its own forms of court music. The island isolation of Japan allowed it to develop its own special characteristics without the intense influences of the Chinese giant or the Mongols so evident in other mainland cultures. The indigenous religion of Japan, Shinto, was closely connected with the legendary legitimacy of the emperor. Thus, special Shinto music was devised for use in imperial shrines. In Japan such Shinto music is called *kagura*. The basis of Buddhist classical music and hence the core of Buddhist influence of Japanese music is found in the theory and practice of chanting known generically as *shomyo*. Such a tradition came originally from foreign Buddhist missionaries and next from Japanese converts studying in China. The thirteen stringed zither with movable bridges called the *koto* is one of the basic instruments of the Japanese ensembles. Another important instrument is the *shakuhachi* or end-blown flute, a variant of the Chinese *hsiao*. The beautiful introverted sounds of *shakuhachi* music seem closer to Buddhist chant then to other instrumental forms.

A BELL RINGING IN THE EMPTY SKY. 4.96.
A short album (less than thirty minutes) of two classic Japanese songs played on the *shakuhachi*. Very beautiful music. Descriptive notes.

BUDDHIST CHANTS. 11.95.
A two record set containing two albums also sold and reviewed individually: **Japanese Temple Music** and **Zen, Goeika and Shomyo Chants**. An eleven page pamphlet of descriptive notes is included.

BUDDHIST DRUMS, BELLS AND CHANTS. 7.98.
Selections from services of the temples of Kyoto, Japan featuring solos on a drum, large temple bells, and chanting and singing by both men and women. Not for the casual listener. Brief descriptive notes.

THE CHENG. 7.98.
Solos on the *cheng* by two masters of the Northern and Southern traditions of ancient China. The music is light and pleasant. Descriptive notes.

CHINA'S INSTRUMENTAL HERITAGE. 7.98.
Eleven folk songs covering periods from the fourteenth century to the present. The music has a light and airy quality, the melodies are simple, and the sounds of the instruments are delicate and pleasing. Instruments include the *cheng, hsiao, sheng, hsun,* and *nan-hu*. Descriptive notes are included.

CHINESE BUDDHIST MUSIC. 7.98.
Examples of rituals, chants, prayers, and hymns, accompanied by bells, gongs, and other percussion instruments. Again, not an album for the casual listener.

CHINESE CLASSICAL MASTERPIECES FOR THE PIPA AND CHIN. 6.98.
Evocative mood music played by Lui Tsun-Yen, the only accomplished *pipa* and *chin* player in the West. Each of the selections is a solo recording.

CHINESE CLASSICAL MUSIC. 7.98.
Selections featuring several classical instruments in solo performances. The instruments are the *nan-hu, pipa, chin,* and *hsiao*. The music is beautiful, but the recording is very poor. Short descriptive notes.

CHINESE DRUMS AND GONG. 6.98.
In addition to the drums and gongs, this album features flutes, the *cheng, pipa,* and *sheng*. The drums and gongs are not emphasized as much in the songs as the title would indicate. Like much of the Chinese classical music the selections have a delicate quality. Brief descriptive notes.

CHINESE TAOIST MUSIC. 7.98.
Chanting by Taoist priests, usually accompanied by bells, gongs, and drums. Percussion instruments are used to set tempo and give emphasis to the chants, though there is often a randomness to their use similar to the chants of Tibet. The chants have a nasal sound with little descernable melody. Descriptive notes are included.

EXOTIC MUSIC OF ANCIENT CHINA. 7.98.
Songs played on two of China's oldest instruments, the *pipa* and the *chin*. Side 1 is devoted to the *pipa*, and the music typically involves very rapid complex plucking, with simple melodies. The songs on Side 2, played on the *chin*, are slower and, with the *chin's* richer sounds, are more thoughtful. Descriptive notes.

JAPANESE BUDDHIST RITUAL. 8.95.
See the Zen Buddhism section.

JAPANESE MASTERPIECES FOR THE SHAKUHACHI. 7.98.
Music played on the *shakuhachi* by masters from Japan. Descriptive notes.

JAPANESE TEMPLE MUSIC. 7.98
See the Zen Buddhism section.

THE KOTO MUSIC OF JAPAN. 4.96.
Six representative styles of traditional *koto* music performed by Japan's greatest living *koto* masters. In four of the pieces the *koto* is the solo instrument and the *shakuhachi* and *shamisen* accompany the *koto* in the others. The *koto* is Japan's best known instrument and it is associated with traditional courtly music. The music is melodious and the recording quality is good.

MUSIC FROM KOREA, VOLUME I: THE KAYAKEUM. 7.50.
This album features the *kayakeum*, an ancient Korean instrument related to the Chinese *cheng*. It has several long strings passing over curved bridges and it emits a wide range of tones. It is accompanied by an hourglass-shaped drum called the *changko*. The music is delicate and precise, and sounds like classical Chinese music. Descriptive notes.

Ch'in.

SHIGIN. 8.95.
Shigin is an art form developed in Japan in the mid 1800's. It is a crossing of Chinese poetry (*shi*) with the Japanese *samurai* spirit which results in very forceful, intense recitations requiring . . . *complete involvement and considerable energy*. Each piece is sung by a single person occasionally accompanied by gongs, *shakuhachi*, and wire string *koto*. Very extensive notes.

TRADITIONAL MUSIC OF JAPAN. 6.70.
This record is the most melodious of our classical Japanese collection. The quality of the recording is excellent and the listener gets a good feeling for the variety of traditional Japanese musical sounds. The performers are members of the Ensemble of Traditional Musical Instruments of Japan. The main instruments are the *koto*, the *shakuhachi*, and the *tzuzumi*.

UNESCO COLLECTION: MUSICAL SOURCES OF JAPAN. 7.65.
A recording of a ceremony of the Shingon sect that involves hymns, both individual and group chanting, and gongs, bells, conches, and even wooden staffs struck against pillars. The quality of the recording is very good. Brief descriptive notes.

ZEN, GOEIKA, AND SHOMYO CHANTS. 7.98.
Three forms of Japanese Buddhist chants: the Zen chants are rapid and unemotional, *goeika* is the chanting of short poems by groups of men or women, and the *shomyo* sound very similar to Gregorian chants. Brief descriptive notes.

──────END OF EAST ASIAN MUSIC SUBSECTION──────

Meditation and Movement

Down through the ages music has served as an accompaniment to spiritual activity. It is often an integral part of the spiritual technique, enhancing the effects of a particular exercise. Music also helps the body and mind attune to universal cadences. Much of classical music, both Western and Eastern, can serve as an excellent accompaniment to meditation. The records we list here are specifically designed for meditation or else seem to us to be good aids. There are also a number of spoken instructional recordings, often with musical background.

ANDREWS, JOEL. **MAY THE LOVE, THE LIGHT, THE POWER. 5.00.**
A beautiful album of harp music by Joel Andrews. A mellow accompaniment for meditation.

ANDREWS, JOEL. **THE VIOLET FLAME. 6.00.**
Andrews is a concert harpist who has developed a combination of notes, chords, intervals, and patterns which link the outer sound with inner essence and help bring about healing on physical, emotional, etheric, and mental levels. During the Winter Solstice, 1976, he and a small group gathered for a meditation to invoke, anchor, and broadcast the *Transmutive Seventh Ray Activity of the Violet Flame Through the Medium of Music*. This album is a result of that meditation. Both words and music are included. Liner notes.

BENDER, RUTH. **YOGA RECORDS. 5.95/each.**
These three records, **Yoga for Beginners, Yoga for Intermediates, Yoga for Advanced** provide excellent instruction in some of the more basic *asanas* as well as a graduated program of intermediate and more advanced exercises. Ms. Bender was a student of Selvarajan Yesudian.

EASWARAN, EKNATH. **MEDITATION. 4.00.**
An album by Eknath Easwaran, founder of the Blue Mountain Center of Meditation in Berkley. Side one, entitled *The Three Stages of Meditation*, discusses what takes place during meditation. Side two provides instruction in meditation. Easwaran quotes from the Sufi Rumi, the seventeenth century mystic Thomas Traherwe, Jesus, and retells various Hindu tales.

ENVIRONMENTS. DISC FOUR: ULTIMATE THUNDERSTORM AND GENTLE RAIN IN A PINE FOREST. 7.98.
On side one the intensity of a thunderstorm is captured; played softly it actually becomes soothing. Side two contains a very gentle, relaxing

sound; occasionally insects and birds can be heard, but the primary sound is that of a summer rain gently dripping on pine needles. All of the Environments records are of extremely high quality and have been carefully reproduced under real conditions.

ENVIRONMENTS. **DISC FIVE: ULTIMATE HEARTBEAT AND WIND IN THE TREES. 7.98.**
Side one, *Ultimate Heartbeat*, is a psychologically based sound environment designed to extent and intensify the physical act of making love. It can also be utilized to deepen a meditational experience. Side two reproduces one of the most beautiful sounds in nature—a soft breeze gently rustling the leaves of a grove of trees on an autumn day. There are a few songbirds in the background. This recording is very useful in neutralizing most disturbing noises found in the home.

ENVIRONMENTS. **DISC SIX: DAWN AND DUSK IN THE OKE-FENOKEE SWAMP. 7.98.**
The Okefenokee is an enormous swamp between southeast Georgia and northern Florida which contains some of the most primitive jungle on the North American continent. Sounds in the swamp range from grumbling alligators to vast choruses of insects, bullfrogs, and aquatic birds. The melodic character of these sounds changes dramatically with the time of day and the seasons, and creates a unique orchestration of natural sound. The sounds are at their zenith early in the morning and late at night, when the cacophony of the swamp is almost deafening. The two sides of this recording were taped in exactly the same location approximately ten hours apart.

ENVIRONMENTS. **DISC SEVEN: INDUCED MEDITATION. 7.98.**
This particular ENVIRONMENTS release has been designed to aid the meditative process through the use of highly refined, carefully researched sounds which improve the results of meditation with no additional effort or training on the part of the meditator.—from the liner notes. An entirely different type of sound is offered on each side. *Intonation* is the sound of hundreds of male and female voices chanting in a complex and subtle manner. The sound is experienced on many levels and the basic flow carries you along with the voices. *Summer Cornfield* is the sound of a sea of summer insects. It forms an excellent background for sustained contemplation.

ENVIRONMENTS. **DISC EIGHT: WOOD-MASTED SAILBOAT AND A COUNTRY STREAM. 7.98.**
Side one recreates virtually all the sounds and sensations of a sea voyage, making the room you are in seem to be an actual sailing ship. Side two reproduces the tranquil sound of a babbling brook, with the hum of insects and the song of an occasional bird. The recording is highly conducive to a calm, relaxed atmosphere.

HALPERN, STEPHEN. **"I": A COSMIC ATTUNEMENT. 7.98.**
This album of original compositions by Stephen Halpern played on instruments such as the electric piano, electric flute, trumpet, saxophone, and electric violin is intended to inspire a meditative state. Halpern describes it as *an interpretation of the concordance of sounds produced by the motions of the heavenly bodies in relation to human harmonics*. We find it quite pleasant and it does evoke some feeling of the music of the spheres.

HALPERN, STEPHEN. **SPECTRUM SUITE. 7.98.**
Meditation music played on various electronic instruments. Mild and unobtrusive.

HALPERN, STEPHEN. **STARBORN SUITE. 7.98.**
This is Halpern's third album. The liner notes describe it as *a continuation of Halpern's innovative exploration of music that provides a sound means of tuning in to our cosmic connection, while creating an effortless and enjoyable relaxation experience here on Earth. . . . Listeners describe it was "crystal petals tinkling in the solar wind" and "the kind of music you hear in your dreams."*

HITTLEMAN, RICHARD. **YOGA FOR HEALTH, FIRST ALBUM. 8.75.**
This two record set contains four separate practice sessions. Hittleman's instructions are extremely clear and the exercises he suggests include the most basic ones. Forty-nine illustrations are also included, depicting various stages of all the exercises.

HITTLEMAN, RICHARD. **YOGA FOR LIFE RECORD ALBUMS. 8.75/each.**
A somewhat commercial presentation of a yoga program developed by Richard Hittleman, one of the best known popularizers of yoga in the

U.S. today. He has a long running television series on yoga and has written many books. Each album is a two record set. The first set includes a short introduction, suggestions on how to best work with the albums, and the beginning postures. The second consists of instructions in more advanced postures. The instructions are clear and easy to follow. A book of photographs illustrating the postures is included with each album.

HITTLEMAN, RICHARD. **YOGA MEDITATION. 5.95.**
A short introduction to meditation followed by seven simple meditations. These include meditation with the breath, the ear, the voice, and deep relaxation.

HORN, PAUL. **INSIDE. 7.98.**
An improvisational performance recorded under the dome of the Taj Mahal. The only instrument used is the flute, with an occasional vocal accompaniment. The acoustics of the dome provide some striking echo effects. A beautiful and popular album.

HORN, PAUL. **PAUL HORN INSIDE THE GREAT PYRAMID. 11.98.**
In the extensive liner notes that accompany this two record set Paul Horn describes his experience as he began to play the flute in the King's Chamber of the Great Pyramid: *The echo was wonderful, about eight seconds. The chamber responded to every note equally. I waited for the echo to decay and then played again. Groups of notes would suspend and all come back as a chord. Sometimes certain notes would stick out more than others. It was always changing. I just listened and responded as if I were playing with another musician. I hadn't prepared anything specific to play. I was just opening myself to the moment and improvising. All of the music that evening was that way—totally improvised. Therefore, it is true expression of the feelings that transpired.* Horn played both the alto and C flute and in one case he sang. Listening to the recording takes us into another dimension. All those who are moved by flute will find this recording an incredible experience.

INNER VOYAGE. 12.00.
Lynn Sereda is an educational psychologist who is adept at yogic techniques. Over the last few years he has been involved in formulating a variety of self integrative techniques which are designed to help unify the psyche. This two record album has been put together to help initiate the listener into one of these techniques which Sereda calls *Sav-asana yoga. Sav* refers to a corpse-like state and this is a pose in which the participant attempts to relax and progressively loosen the musculature of the entire body so that he can become more in touch with his inner being. Throughout most of the recordings Sereda speaks in a slow, calm way. In some parts he is accompanied by meditative music, usually in an Eastern style.

INTERDIMENSIONAL MUSIC THROUGH IASOS. 7.20.
This is a recording of cosmic sounds designed to take the listener into new dimensions and unite him with the creator. The music is both meditative and healing, and it vibrates at a number of different octaves. It is electronic, but not offensively so. Iasos has composed, arranged, and played all the selections himself and we feel he has succeeded admirably in his goal.

KRIYANANDA, SWAMI. **MEDITATIONS. 5.95.**
The listener is guided through two fifteen to twenty minute meditations. The instructions are clear and the music played on sitar and tanpura is very conducive to relaxation and meditation.

KRIYANANDA, SWAMI. **YOGA FOR SELF AWARENESS. 9.95.**
A two record set. After a short introduction, a series of breathing exercises is presented. Yoga postures follow and take up the bulk of the albums. A short meditation is next. The last side of the records consists of meditational chants. The instructions are easily followed by the listener and the background music is gentle and soothing.

RADHA, SWAMI SIVANANDA. **MANTRAS: SONGS OF YOGA. 7.65.**
Sung and played on the harmonium by Swami Sivananda Radha, a female disciple of Swami Sivananda, the *mantras* have simple melodies and appear easy to learn. A pamphlet is included that gives the meaning and background of each *mantra.*

RADHA, SWAMI SIVANANDA. **RELAXATION. 7.65.**
A course in relaxation based upon the yogic posture called *savasan* or posture of the corpse. *The purpose of this record is to give you the basic principles*

of the technique so that once you have mastered them, you will be able to practice it on your own....[This technique] tries to stimulate you to: physically relax your body, mentally rest your mind and surrender, spiritually expand your consciousness.* Side one stresses healing, side two, creativity.

SIMONS, ESTELLE. **YOGA USA, A CLASS FOR BEGINNERS. 5.98.**
It has been my privilege to study Hatha Yoga with many of the finest instructors of our day....Now, in retrospect, I realize that of all these dedicated servers, no one has been of greater personal assistance to me than Estelle Simons. I am, therefore, delighted that this recording will make it possible for students everywhere to hear Estelle's compelling, but also soothing voice and to profit by her supremely competent guidance. I wholeheartedly recommend her system and her unique presentation to all who aspire to tread the path of Yoga to a more vital and wholesome way of life.—Marcia Moore. Photographs of the postures are included.

SIMONS, ESTELLE. **YOGA USA, INTERMEDIATE CLASS. 5.98.**
Ms. Simons teaches the following postures: sun pose, shoulder stand fish, hand/knee pose, plough, cobra, locust, bow, moon pose, relaxation pose. Photographs are included.

—END OF MEDITATION AND MOVEMENT SUBSECTION—

Miscellaneous

AFRICA: WITCHCRAFT AND RITUAL MUSIC. 4.96.
This album presents a variety of East African music including healing rituals, tribal initiations, traditional folk songs, and wedding and funeral songs. The music ranges from simple beating on drums and bells to melodious songs with a reggae sound played on a six-string harp. Other instruments include flutes, horns, mouth harps, and rattles. Descriptive notes.

BAHIA: TRADITIONAL MUSIC AND MOMENTS OF BRAZIL. 12.50.
A portfolio of evocative color photographs is boxed with an extraordinary record of Brazilian folk music. The selections range from festival music with thousands of people singing to Brazilian cowboys singing on horseback as they herd their cattle. The record captures the pulsating African rhythms which make up Brazilian music.

COLTRANE, ALICE. **ETERNITY. 6.98.**
Six progressive jazz selections, all but one written and arranged by Alice Coltrane and drawing heavily on her spiritual experiences. Ms. Coltrane's impression of the message of each piece is included on the album cover. The main instrument is the organ, although virtually every wind and string instrument is represented somewhere in the album. A feeling of worship and devotion permeates the music.

FIESTAS OF PERU. 4.96.
Examples of festival music featuring both instrumentals and vocals. Some selections are tuneful and lively with a Latin flair; others are seemingly without rhythm or melody. Instruments include harp, guitar, violin, accordian, flutes, and drums. Descriptive notes.

THE FLUTES OF THE INCA EMPIRE: LOS CALCHAKIS. 6.70.
A variety of flutes still widely played in the Andean Cordillera are the main instruments. These include the *rondador,* the *antara,* and the *siku*— all belonging to the family of panpipes. The flutes are thought to date from Inca times but the melodies are those which are traditionally associated with Latin American music. Most of the selections are instrumental, although there is a bit of vocal background on some. The music is often melodic and moving and at times is discordant. Liner notes.

INDIOS FLUTES, HARPS, AND GUITARS. 6.70.
Festive Latin American peasant music, with pleasant melodies and good syncopation. Mostly instrumental, with some background vocals.

JARRETT, KEITH. **THE KOLN CONCERT. 11.98.**
A two record set, recorded live in 1975. Jarrett is one of the most popular contemporary jazz pianists and he is at his best here. It may seem a bit odd for us to list this recording, but we really like it. We find that listening to Jarrett takes us into other, deeper dimensions much more effectively than most of the so-called meditation albums.

JARRETT, KEITH. STAIRCASE. 11.98.
This two record set is Jarrett's first solo piano recording since **The Koln Concert.** Like the latter it is improvisational and forms an excellent background sound for meditation or spiritual work.

KINGDOM OF THE SUN—PERU'S INCA HERITAGE. 4.96.
This album features traditional songs of the Andean Indians, both vocal and instrumental. The songs have nice melodies but the rhythms are often ragged and disconcerting. Instruments include harps, violins, guitars, accordians, flutes, and drums. Descriptive notes.

MUSTAPHA TETTEY ADDY. 7.98.
A *master drummer of Ghana* plays songs of Africa on several types of drums and bells, occasionally singing as he plays. The quality of the recording is good. A nice album for those who are into drums. Descriptive notes.

RELIGIOUS MUSIC OF ASIA. 8.95.
A sampler of the musical traditions of the major religions of the Near East, India, and East Asia. The thirteen pieces include an Islamic call to prayer, a Hindu wedding chant, a Chinese Buddhist priest chanting, and a selection from a Zen monastery morning service. A good (though very general) introduction to music of this part of the world. Descriptive notes are interesting and informative.

SZEKELY, EDMOND. SYMPHONY OF ANCIENT MEXICO. 5.80.
The liner notes say, *Composition and rendition from Precolumbian sources and instruments by Edmond B. Szekely and Norma Jean Nilsson.* The instruments sound like those found in a modern orchestra, and passages of the symphony give the impression of being electronically manipulated. There are also several passages with voices. Overall, the recording is pleasant to listen to.

———— END OF THE MISCELLANEOUS SUBSECTION ————

Near Eastern Music

Except in the brotherhoods such as the dervishes, Muslim religious music is relatively curtailed because of the opposition of religious leaders. It falls into two categories: the call to prayer, or *adhan* or *azan*, by the *mu'adhdhin* or muezzin, and the cantillation of the **Qur'an.** Both developed from relatively solemn cantillation to a variety of forms, both simple and highly florid. The cantillation of the **Qur'an** reflected the ancient Arabic practice of declamation of poetry, with careful regard to word accents and inflections and to the clarity of the text. Yet it was possibly also influenced by early secular art songs. Even in its most complicated aspects, Islamic music is traditional and transmitted orally. Although a musical notation exists, little written music survives. Notation was largely unnecessary, for virtuoso performance depended on improvisation, and musicians were not eager to share their compositions with others. Islamic music is monophonic—i.e., it consists of a single line of melody. In performance everything is related to the refinement of the melodic line and the complexity of rhythm. The notion of harmony is completely absent, although occasionally a simple combination of notes, octaves, fifths, and fourths, usually below the melody notes, may be used as ornamentation. Among the elements contributing to the enrichment of melody are microtonality (the use of intervals smaller than a Western half-step or lying between a half-step and a Western whole-step) and the variety of intervals used.

As the fourth is the basic melodic frame, theorists organized the intervals and their nuances into genres, or small units, combining genres into larger units, or systems. More than 130 systems resulted; on these are based the musical scales of the modes. The scale of the mode can thus be broken down into small units that are of importance in the formation of melodies. A *maqam* or *mode* is a complex musical entity given distinct musical character by its scale, small units, range and compass, predominant notes, and pre-existing typical melodic and rhythmic formulas. It serves the musician as rough material for his own composition. The Arabic term *maqam* is replaced by *dastgah* in Persia, *naghmah* in Egypt, and *tba* in North Africa.

Instrumental music is not considered an independent art from vocal music except in Persia, where it is cultivated for its own sake. The most favored instrument of ancient Near Eastern civilization, the harp, was gradually overshadowed by both long- and short-necked lutes (*ouds*). Other important instruments include the *argul* (a double clarinet—two cylindrical pipes, each with a single reed), the *busoq* (a long-necked lute, with six strings grouped into three pairs), the *dombach* or *zarb* (a goblet-shaped wooden hand drum), the *gasba* (bamboo flute), the *ghaita* (a short double-reed oboe), the *kamadja* or *kamachen* (a four-stringed version of the violin played upright on the knee), the *lira* (recorder), the *nai* (a two-feet long bamboo flute), the *rebab* (a two-string violin), the *santour* (a dulcimer with seventy-two strings played with light wooden mallets), the *tabi* (a general term for drums, both cylindrical and kettle-shaped), and the *tar* (a six-string lute with a long neck).

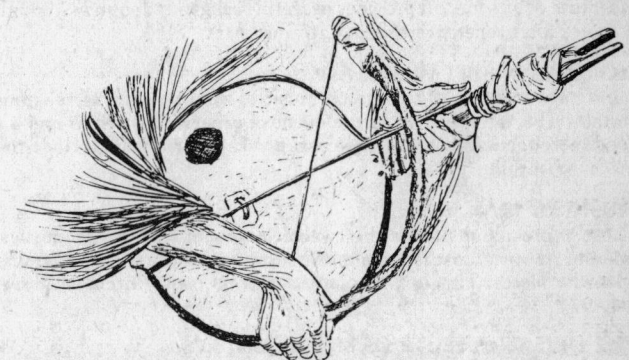

ARAB MUSIC. 7.98/each.
These two volumes feature Egyptian folk music. Vocal selections, all on side one of Volume I, are lively songs sung by women and accompanied by such instruments as the *oud, rebab, argul,* and *tabla.* The instrumentals, which comprise the rest of the albums are performed on the *oud, nai,* and *tabla.* The pieces are melodic and make for pleasant listening.

CLASSIC ARABIC MUSIC: A RECITAL OF MUWASHAHAT. 7.98.
In the Middle Ages Arabic music reached a high degree of development and sophistication in terms of musical forms, both vocal and instrumental. The songs of medieval Spain (known as *muwashahat*) are examples of the Arabic art song at its best and it is these songs which are performed on this album. Both the instrumentals and vocals are melodious and enjoyable to listen to. Most of the cuts are vocal, with instrumental backing. The main instruments are the *kanun*, lute, *nai,* and *rig.* Liner notes.

CLASSIC FLUTE OF SYRIA. 8.60.
The main instrument on this recording is the *nai,* an ancient bamboo flute which has been used by Sufis and other intiates over the thirteen centuries of Islamic civilization. The music is largely improvisational—coming from both the artist's inspiration and the vibrations he receives from the assemblage around him—and is based on *maqams* or traditional musical forms. The flutist, Selim Kusur, is permanent soloist for Syrian radio and TV. The album has a haunting, almost sighing quality. Very extensive liner notes in French.

CLASSIC LUTE OF IRAQ. 8.60.
The Oriental lute, or *oud,* is the ancestor of the modern lute and the guitar. This record, consisting of meditations (or improvisations) on traditional Arabic themes, sounds faintly reminiscent of Flamenco music to our untutored ears. The performer, Munir Bachir, has been a professor at the Baghdad Institute of Fine Arts, directed his own

schools of music in Iraq and Libya, and has made many successful tours in Europe and America. The sound quality is excellent. Extensive liner notes in French.

COPTIC MUSIC. 7.98.

The Copts are Egyptian Christians. Their services are all vocal and choral, with no instrumentation. The Coptic ceremonies sound similar to the liturgical music of the West. Extensive notes, translation, transliteration, and the services in the original Coptic are included.

EPITAPH FOR AN EGO: SACRED DANCES OF THE WAHSHI DERVISHES. 5.95.

This is a recording of music composed for sacred dances and movements. The music is rhythmic and of the dervish tradition.

EXOTIC MUSIC FOR THE OUD. 6.98.

The three major instruments on this melodious recording are the *oud*, the *sultania*, and the *sarod*. Most of the compositions are solos and while they do sound somewhat exotic, they all have pleasant harmonies.

ISLAMIC LITURGY: SONG AND DANCE AT A MEETING OF DERVISHES. 7.98.

See the Islam section.

LUTH TRADITIONAL—SYRIE. 8.60.

A melodic recording of six pieces of traditional Syrian lute music. Like most lute or *oud* music it provides peaceful background sound—though it seems a bit repetitive to our untrained ears.

MOROCCAN SUFI MUSIC. 7.98.

Sufis have traditionally relied on music to attain a state of religious ecstacy. This is a selection of the music of several Sufi orders and is a good introduction to traditional Sufi music. Instruments include the *ghaita, tabla, gasba*, and *lira*.

MUSIC OF IRAN. 6.98/each.

These three albums cover the twelve *dastgahs* of the Persian musical system. As with most Persian music short poems are sometimes sung with the pieces. This is a scholarly series by Iran's foremost *santour* player.

THE ORIENTAL FLUTE OF MOROCCO. 6.75.

A selection of traditional pieces played by Hmaoui Abd el Hamid, one of Morocco's greatest living flutists. The main instruments are the *nai*, the *kanun*, the lute, and the *darbouka*. As with all traditional Islamic music, there is a religious overtone to the pieces and there is often a melancholy quality. Includes pieces invoking the songs of the Muezzin, who fives times a day sounds his invitation to prayer, and two marriage themes. Liner notes.

THE OUD. 7.98.

This is a very beautiful album, entirely instrumental with solos and pieces played with a small ensemble (clarinet, flute, bass, and percussion). The selections come from several Middle Eastern countries.

A PERSIAN HERITAGE—CLASSICAL MUSIC OF IRAN. 4.96.

Partly composed, partly improvised, the classical music of Persia is preponderantly instrumental. The words of both composed and improvised singing are usually taken from the classics of Persian literature and from the poetry of Sufism. The improvisations, which form the central portions of performances, are based on a model, the *radif*, which a student must memorize painstakingly before he may improvise upon it. Most of the *radif* has no meter and follows a speech-like rhythm, but it also contains metrical pieces which normally have a drum accompaniment. There are twelve modes or *dastgahs* which form the basis for the *radif*. This album features a combination of composed and improvised music, primarily instrumental, performed on four classical Persian instruments: *santour, tar, kamachen*, and *zarb*.

PERSIAN LOVE SONGS AND MYSTIC CHANTS. 7.98.

A woman sings sixteen Persian songs both acapella and with flute and fingerdrum accompaniment. She has a rich voice and the songs range from lively to melancholy. English translations of the songs are provided.

THE PERSIAN SANTUR—MUSIC OF IRAN. 4.96.

Four pieces—three include the singing of Persian poetry, the fourth is instrumental. Accompanying the *santour* are the violin and *dombach*.

SUFI CEREMONY: RIFA' CEREMONY. 6.98.

Recording of an actual celebration of the Rifa'iyya Sufi order in South Africa. Participants in the ritual celebration achieve a trance state which makes them oblivious to pain and able to perform remarkable feats. The album is unclear, as if recorded from a distance. Descriptive notes.

THE TAR. 7.98/each.

Classical and contemporary pieces with occasional accompaniment by the *dombach* and *zarb*. Volume I is instrumental, Volume II includes several vocal pieces derived from the Sufi tradition. The music and chants have a gentle melancholy feeling.

TRADITIONAL LUTE OF IRAQ. 8.60.

The Oriental lute is also known as the *oud*. This is a very well produced, melodic recording on which the lute is the sole instrument. Extensive liner notes in French.

UNESCO COLLECTION. THE ARABIAN MUSICAL SOURCES— ARABIAN MUSIC: MAQAM. 7.65.

Examples of improvisational music built around the *maqam*, a tonal structure with a musical role similar to the Persian *dastgah* or Indian *raga*. The album has both vocal and instrumental selections, with each piece featuring a single instrument. Instruments used are the *nai, oud, busaq, kamadja*, and *rebab*. This album, like all the albums in the UNESCO Collection Musical Sources, is of excellent quality.

UNESCO COLLECTION. ISLAMIC MUSICAL SOURCES—ISLAMIC RITUAL FROM YUGOSLAVIA. 7.65.

Selections from an Islamic ceremony as celebrated by a Yugoslavian dervish brotherhood. Group chanting accompanied by various percussion instruments is the basis of the service. Descriptive notes included.

———— END OF THE NEAR EASTERN MUSIC SUBSECTION————

South and Southeast Asian Music

The wide field of musical phenomena in this area ranges from relatively simple two- or three tone melodies of some of the hill tribes in central India to the highly refined classical music heard in the concert halls in the large cities. This variety reflects the heterogeneous population in terms of race, religion, language, and social status. In the villages, music is not just a form of entertainment but is an essential element in many of the activities of daily life and plays a prominent part in most of the rituals. These include life-cycle events, such as birth, initiation, marriage, and death; events of the agricultural cycle; and a variety of work songs. Much of this music could be described as functional, for it serves a utilitarian purpose; for instance, a harvest song might well give thanks to the gods for a bountiful harvest, but ensure that the next harvest will be equally fruitful. These songs are usually sung by everyone participating in the activity; they are often sung in the form of leader and chorus, and the musical accompaniment, if any, is generally provided by drone instruments (those sustaining or reiterating a given note or notes), usually of the lute family, or percussion instruments. Occasionally, a flute or fiddle might also accompany the singers.

Most areas are visited by religious mendicants, many of whom travel around the countryside singing devotional songs, accompanying themselves either with a one-, two-, or three-stringed lute that generally provides only a drone or with a frame (tamborine-like) drum. During certain religious festivals, the villages might be visited by a travelling band of players who enact some of the mythological episodes connected with the festival. Such performances are accompanied by music and may also include dances.

In the cities many different forms of music can be heard. Of these, the best known in the West are the classical music of North India, including Pakistan, sometimes called Hindustani music, and that of South India, or Karnatic music. Both classical systems are supported by an extensive body of literature and elaborate musical theory. Classical music is based on two main elements, *raga* and *tala*. The word *raga* is derived from a Sanskrit root meaning *to color*, the underlying idea being that certain melodic shapes, involving specific intervals of the scale, produce a continuity of emotional experience and *color* the mind. Since neither the melodic shapes nor their sequence are fixed precisely, a *raga* serves as a basis for composition and improvisation. Indian music has neither modulation (change of key) nor changing harmonies; instead the music is invariably accompanied by a drone that establishes the tonic, or ground note, of the *raga* and usually its fifth (i.e., five notes above). These are chosen to suit the convenience of the main performer, as there is no conception of a fixed pitch. While a *raga* is primarily a musical concept, specific *ragas* have acquired, particularly in North Indian music, a number of extramusical elements and are associated with particular periods of the day, seasons of the year, colors, deities, and specific moods.

The second element of Indian music, *tala* is best described as time measure and has two main constituents; the duration of the time measure in terms of time units that vary according to the tempo chosen; and the distribution of stress within the time measure. *Tala*, like *raga*, serves as a basis for composition and improvisation.

Indian classical music is generally performed by small ensembles of not more than five or six musicians. Improvisation plays a major part in a performance, and great emphasis is placed on the creativity and sensitivity of the soloist. A performance of a *raga* usually goes through well defined stages, beginning with an improvised melodic prelude that is followed by a composed piece set in a particular time measure. The composition is generally quite short and serves as a frame of reference to which the soloist returns at the conclusion of his improvisation. There is no set duration for the performance of a *raga*. A characteristic feature of North Indian classical music is the gradual acceleration of tempo, which leads to a final climax.

CLASSICAL INDIAN MUSIC. 5.00.
Indian music is alien and incomprehensible to many. On this record Yehudi Menuhin provides a number of introductory talks, each designed to help Westerners understand and appreciate classical Indian music. Each talk is clear and succinct and is followed by a related selection of *ragas*. The performers are among India's finest and the record quality is uniformly excellent. The instruments are the *veena* and the *mridangam*.

CLASSICAL MUSIC OF INDIA: INSTRUMENTAL. 7.65.
Examples of Northern Indian instrumental music. Instruments used are the *shanai, sarangi, tabla, sitar, sarod*, flute, and an Indian adaptation of the Western guitar. A good recording. Descriptive notes.

DHYANAM/MEDITATION. 4.96.
South Indian vocal music accompanied by violin, *tamboura*, and *mridangam*. The performance is described as an *elaborate improvisation*. The voice has a pinched nasal quality. Descriptive notes.

DRUMS OF THAILAND. 8.95.
This is an authentic recording which features a number of different styles of Thai music performed on a variety of drums and accompanied by a percussion ensemble. Each of the ten selections is fully discussed in the liner notes.

FESTIVALS OF THE HIMALAYAS. 4.96.
Examples of local festival music from the area between Kasmir and Tibet. The chanting is more melodic than the chanting of Tibet and Kasmir though the influence of these areas is clear. Instruments used are oboes, flutes, *gyaling*, drums, and cymbols. Descriptive notes.

GOLDEN RAIN. 4.96.
Side one has examples of the Balinese orchestral style of music known as *Gamelan*, emphasizes complex rhythms played on gongs, cymbols, drums, flutes, and xylophones. Side two is a recording of the famous *Balinese Monkey Chant*, a strange primitive sounding ceremony performed by 200 men. It reenacts a part of the **Ramayana** epic. Descriptive notes.

HORN, PAUL. PAUL HORN IN INDIA. 7.98.
This two record set was recorded in India in early 1967 during the period when Paul Horn was studying to become a teacher of transcendental meditation. The first two sides feature musicians who were students of Ravi Shankar, and Shankar himself suggested which *ragas* the group might play and composed three original melodies based on ancient *ragas* especially for the album. One vocal selection is included. Sides three and four feature Kashmiri musicians who were favorites of Maharishi Mahesh Yogi. This is a lovely recording, and one which we treasure. Horn's flute blends with the traditional Indian instruments and carries the listener through a singular experience. The album has excellent background music for meditation.

INDIAN DRUMS. 9.95.
This is the nicest recording of Indian drums we have ever heard. It's rhythm should appeal even to those who do not generally care for Indian music. The main instruments are the *tabla, sarod*, and *tamboura*.

THE INDIAN SITAR: THE LANGUAGE OF THE RAGA. 6.70.
This is one of the nicest sitar recordings we have ever heard. Pramod Kumar is the main performer and the pieces on this recording are his own compositions. He is accompanied by *tamboura* and *tabla*.

THE JASMINE ISLE. 4.96.
Orchestral music from Java—much more sedate than the music of neighboring Bali. Javanese music features unusual rhythms, but simple melodies. Several types of xylophones, gongs, and drums are used. Descriptive notes.

KALPANA IMPROVISATIONS. 4.96.
Four selections, three of which are instrumental, and the fourth an Indian Kathak dance. The dancer, telling a story through mime, chants a rhythm in nonsense syllables, then stamps the same rhythm with ankle bells. Instruments used on the record are the *sarod* and *tabla*. The album is pleasant to listen to, the rhythms draw you into the music, and the *sarod* has a light flowing sound to it.

KASHMIR—TRADITIONAL SONGS AND DANCES. 4.96.
This is a good introduction to the music of this province. Most of the music is vocal with no solos except in the religious music. A favorite musical form is the *chakki* in which the lead singer sings a verse that is then picked up by the group. The songs have strong rhythms and at times are very melodic. All songs are accompanied by a variety of instruments including the *santour, saz-i-kashmir, sitar, surnai, sarangi, rebab*, and various percussion instruments.

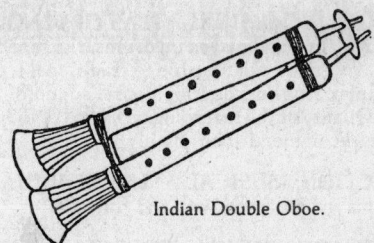
Indian Double Oboe.

KHAN, USTAD ALI AKBAR. RAGA: MIYAN KI TODI, RAGA: ZILLA-KAFI. 7.65.
An album containing improvisations on two classical Indian *ragas* (melodic patterns) by India's leading master of the *sarod*. Other instruments include *tabla* and *tamboura*. Very brief descriptive notes.

MASTER OF THE BAMBOO FLUTE: SACHDEV. 6.50.
This is a lovely recording of North Indian instrumental music. Sachdev is a fine musician who has studied under a number of masters. In this

record he performs an evening *raga* in a devotional mood. The bamboo flute is the main instrument and is accompanied by a *tabla, tamboura,* and *swar-peti.*

MUSIC FROM THE MORNING OF THE WORLD. 4.96.
Examples of the Balinese orchestral style, *Gamelan.* Descriptive notes.

MUSIC FROM THE SHRINES OF AJMER AND MUNDRA. 7.98.
Selections of the type of music played in courtyards and public areas. Because this music is meant to be played outdoors it is supposed to have less of the subleties and gradual development typical of Indian music, though to our Western ears it still sounds complex. Percussion instruments and the *mashak* are prominent. Other instruments include the *nagara, tabla,* and *shahnai.*

PALLAVI: SOUTH INDIAN FLUTE MUSIC. 4.96.
This album features the *kural* accompanied by violin, *mridangam,* and *tamboura.* The music has the complex melodies and rhythms typical of Indian music. A pleasant listening experience, especially for those who enjoy the flute.

RELIGIOUS MUSIC OF INDIA. 8.98.
A sampling of music and chants from different areas and periods. A record for the serious student, the descriptive notes have very technical musical discussions of each piece, translations and transliterations of the songs, and a brief description of their place in Indian religious life. A musical score for each song is included.

SARANGI, THE VOICE OF A HUNDRED COLORS. 4.96.
Three instrumental pieces from the Northern India Hindustani tradition, made familiar to Western audiences by Ravi Shankar. Instruments used in addition to the *sarangi* are the *tabla* and *tamboura.* The album has a subdued mellow sound and is very pleasant background music.

SHAKTI WITH JOHN MCLAUGHLIN. **A HANDFUL OF BEAUTY. 7.98.**
An interesting recording which should appeal to John McLaughlin fans. Indian blue grass music is as close as we can come to describing the sound. Many of the instruments and compositions are Indian, but the arrangements are definitely Western.

SHANKAR, RAVI and ALI AKBAR KHAN. **RAVI SHANKAR AND ALI AKBAR KHAN, A DHUN AND A RAGA. 6.70.**
A *dhun* is a melodic pattern created by Shankar and a *raga* is the preeminent Indian melodic form. Ali Akbar Khan is the best known and one of the most brilliant contemporary *sarod* players, and Shankar is a celebrated sitarist.

SHANKAR, RAVI and ANDRE PREVIN. **CONCERTO FOR SITAR AND ORCHESTRA. 7.98.**
This is a melodic concerto which combines the often discordant (at least to Western ears) elements of classical Indian music with classical Western music. The result is clearly Indian, but the music appeals to many who are not used to traditional Indian music. We like this album a lot and in general we are not very turned on by Indian music.

UNESCO COLLECTION: MUSICAL ATLAS OF BENGAL. 7.65
Traditional folk music sung and played on drums, flutes, cymbals, and lutes. The songs have a close relationship to traditional Indian music, with its quick complex rhythms and high nasal sound of the voices. Descriptive notes. Quality of the recording on all the UNESCO albums is excellent and we recommend them highly.

UNESCO COLLECTION: MUSICAL ATLAS OF INDIA. 7.65.
Traditional songs played on the *shahnai* and flute.

UNESCO COLLECTION: MUSICAL SOURCES OF INDIA. 7.65/ each.
Three albums of North Indian music are available: **Vocal Music, Instrumental Music—Sitar, Flute, Sarangi,** and **Instrumental Music— Vina, Vickitra Vina, Sarod, Shahnai.** In **Vocal Music** each side is devoted to the development of a single traditional style of singing, in which the voice is often used as an instrument, sometimes wailing in a mournful way, sometimes clucking or making unusual noises. The songs are accompanied by traditional instruments. The two instrumental albums each feature the instruments listed in their titles, as well as the *tabla* and *tamboura.* Though the rhythms and melodies are strange to Western ears the music is pleasant and graceful. All three albums have descriptive notes.

YOGA MUSIC OF INDIA. 6.98.
A collection of devotional chants, in the Vedantic tradition, accompanied by drums and *veena.* Transliteration of the chants and their general meaning are provided so that the listener may chant with the recording. Due to the complexity of the chants and the quality of the recording, chanting with the album would seem to be very difficult.

END OF SOUTH AND SOUTHEAST ASIA MUSIC SUBSECTION

Tibetan Music

Tibetan music has a long history of written notation. This notation, for liturgical chants, consists of neumes—i.e., symbols representing melodic contour rather than precise pitch, similar to the earliest music writing of medieval Europe. Also distinctive is the metaphysical aspect of Tibetan Buddhist music, related to the Buddhist philosophy. Each instrument of the monastery orchestra, as well as the drawn-out tones of chant, is believed to represent an externalized form of the *mantras,* or sounds inherent in the human body, accessible otherwise only through steadfast meditation. For the monks, such music is a basic aid to devotion and prayer. Musical styles vary somewhat among the sects of Tibetan Buddhism, but the basic approach and instruments are the same.

The monastery instruments typify the crossroads position of Tibet. Some, such as the large cymbals, stem from China, while others (the majority), such as the conch-shell trumpet and handbells, can be traced to Indian influence and are found as instruments of Buddhist worship as far away as Japan. Still other instruments, such as the large oboe and the ten-foot metal trumpet, are perhaps Near Eastern in origin. One wind instrument, the short trumpet made from a human leg bone, seems to be of purely local invention. Similarly, the structure of the music seems basically Tibetan. It is founded on a principle of greatly prolonged dense, deep sounds, such as unison long and short trumpets with oboe, or the seemingly endless bass chant of groups of monks, whose long, drawn-out notes are punctuated by sharp, extended bursts of percussion. Each monk is said to be able to sing two or even three notes simultaneously. Much of this music emerges from monasteries only at festival time, when the great *cham* dramas, which may last several days, are performed. These plays, which generally show the triumph of Buddhism over Bon, the earlier shamanistic religion of Tibet, may involve hundreds of musicians in the guise of masked dancers with drums, backed by a large temple orchestra.

CHO-GA, TANTRIC MUSIC OF TIBET. 6.95.
An anthology of Buddhist chants and ritual music. Three chants are heard in their entirety, the rest are excerpts. Several short instrumental pieces are included, and the chants are occasionally accompanied by drums and bells. Most of the chants are interesting and easy listening. Instruments include *dung-chen, gyaling, rolmo, nga-bom,* and *damaru.* The quality of the recording is good. Short descriptive notes.

PADMASAMBAVA CHOPA. 6.98.
This is an edited version of the four hour *chopa* (ritual) held in the Himalayan regions of Tibet. The purpose of the ritual is to *dispel undesirable states of being.* Chanting and instrumental sections alternate throughout the ceremony. The tone of the entire ritual is dark and melancholy and it is understandable that this ritual has often been associated with the black magic aspects of this region. Drums, bells, and horn instruments (*dung-chen* and *dung-kar*) are used. Descriptive notes.

SONGS AND DANCES OF NEPAL. 8.95.

Twenty-two popular and traditional folk songs recorded during an American Himalayan expedition. The songs are sung unaccompanied or with drums, bells, and *damyan*. They are often tuneless and sound like prayer chants. The recordings were done on location in tents, homes, and in the open fields.

SONGS AND MUSIC OF TIBET. 8.95.

A selection of songs, instrumentals, and chants. The chants are a deep monotone. The vocal selections, many with bells and drums, often sound similar to the music associated with the American Plains Indians. Other selections have an Oriental quality. Instruments include flute, *gyaling* and *dung-kar*.

TIBETAN BELLS. 5.98.

The timbre of a Tibetan bell is unique, often a haunting echo of long duration which takes the listener into distant spaces. The bells in this album are authentic ones which were collected and assembled in the East by the artists, Henry Wolff and Nancy Hennings. It takes a while to get used to the unusual rhythms of this music.

TIBETAN BUDDHISM: THE RITUAL ORCHESTRA AND CHANTS. 4.96.

Rituals of the Drukpa Kagyu Order. The ritual orchestra consists of a pair of *shawms*, a pair of five-foot long horns, a pair of longer horns with very large bells, a pair of conches, a pair of human thighbone trumpets, two sets of cymbals, drums, and handbells. Usually the orchestral interlude marks the end of each section of a *sadhana* and is the time when the actual visualization is performed. Three invocations are included on this record. Good liner notes.

TIBETAN BUDDHISM: TANTRAS OF GYUTO MAHAKALA. 4.96.

Excerpts from a tantric rite of the Gelug tradition, one of the four main traditions of Tibetan Buddhism. This particular rite is the *mahakala* (*Great Black Lord of Transcending Awareness*) *sadhana*. The rite consists primarily of chanting accompanied by cymbals and drums with an occasional instrumental interlude featuring a pair of *radong*. The chanting is slow, sustained gutteral tones, with cymbals and drums seemingly used at random. Descriptive notes.

TIBETAN BUDDHISM: TANTRAS OF GYUTO SANGWA DUPA. 4.96.

In this recording forty lamas and monks chant a recitation of part of the text of the tantra which, in its entirety, lasts over seven hours. Generally speaking, what is heard here falls into three categories. The brief passages for solo voice mark the beginning either of a chapter or of a new major section within a chapter. The text of the tantra is then presented in metrical chanting. The long sustained chords are the concluding words of verses describing specific meditations. This tantra is concerned with discovering the self existing sacredness of the universe. The rite is performed here by unaccompanied voices. Excellent liner notes.

TIBETAN BUDDHIST RITES—VOLUMES ONE, TWO, AND THREE. 7.98/each.

These three recordings provide a wide variety of examples of Tibetan religious and folk music. The selections are usually short, with an average of fifteen per album, and include instrumentals, songs, and chants from various rituals, dances, and processionals. Most of the music sounds very unusual, with slow deep monotone, and loud, quick, rhythmless interludes that startle the listener. Instruments include *gyaling, dung-kar, kang-dung, dung-chen, nga-bom, nga-chung, rom,* and *damaru*. The descriptive notes are nontechnical and interesting.

TIBETAN MYSTIC SONG. 7.98.

Examples of songs, developed by wandering mystics, which combine Indian religious doctrine and the folk imagery and traditions of Tibet. The songs are sung unaccompanied and sound like liturgical chants. Descriptive notes, including translations of the songs.

TIBETAN RITUAL MUSIC. 7.98.

Religious music of Tibet involves both chanting and instrumental playing. *The chanting, executed with exceedingly deep and constricted voice, embraces the repetition of canonical texts and the invocation of the gods. The instrumental music provides interludes between the chanted portions of the service.* The chanting is usually gutteral, and sometimes sounds like Gregorian chants. The music is seemingly without melody or rhythm. This album has five selections; and the instruments include *gyaling, dung-kar, kang-dung, dung-chen,* and various percussion instruments.

TIBETAN SONGS OF GODS AND DEMONS: RITUAL AND THEATRICAL MUSIC OF TIBET. 7.98.

A collection of ritual and theatrical music that includes chants that are more like liturgical prayers than the deep gutteral sounds associated with Tibet, and songs that have an Oriental feeling about them. Instruments include the *gyaling, dung-kar,* and various percussion instruments. Detailed descriptive notes.

UNESCO COLLECTION. MUSICAL SOURCES OF TIBET—TIBETAN RITUAL. 7.65

A complete Tibetan ritual that includes all the characteristics of Tibetan religious services: disembodied gutteral chanting, group chanting, sudden loud discordant noises, bells, gongs, and drums. The quality of the recording is excellent. Descriptive notes.

REINCARNATION & KARMA

Proof of the existence of life before birth and after death, though well investigated and documented, finds little attention in our scientific and professional, let alone our religious communities. Meanwhile, we exist with a nagging doubt: does our earthly journey justify all our pain and disappointment if we have no sense of its meaning and purposeful direction? Does it make sense to be alive if we are nothing but begrudging functionaries in a maze of accidental happenings? If we cannot face this question, we usually take refuge in some religious or philosophical doctrine and hope for the best. But a faith which cannot recreate us here can hardly sustain us in and beyond the hour of death.

Here lies a crucial problem. How can we know about a possible existence of ours before we were born or after we have died? Obviously, there is a wealth of facts and data which could be scientifically registered and accepted. More than scientific evidence is needed here, namely a new and different attitude toward life and death. The question of our attitude toward life and death is not an after-death issue, but one that faces us here and now. Can we let go of our prejudices and fears in order to open our hearts to the body of life, even if it will change us into new creatures?

Lamentable as our present Western indifference to reincarnation is, no argument or attempt to persuade will easily change it. In the past, reincarnation as a theory or phenomenon has interested mainly those who tend to be given to philosophical speculation. The issue that is of crucial importance to us all centers around the actual significance of life and whether or not we perceive it accurately. Whether our lives make sense beyond our individual short existence is the question here. We must ask ourselves to what extent we are blindfolded in our present awareness of the full dimension of life. Reincarnation raises and answers this question. Herein lies its extraordinary value.

It is indeed possible to break through the barrier of death and to grasp the lasting meaning of our awareness of ourselves. But if we accept our present existence as merely a link in the total evolution of the universe from crude vegetation to highly differentiated awareness, then our attitude toward living will change as well. Our task in life is no longer to justify ourselves through the accumulation of possessions and prestige. Reincarnation suggests that we fulfill this mission of our present earthly life by refining our inner and outer awareness. The challenge of reincarnation lies in eliciting man's ability to fulfill his potential as an individual instead of building his external world out of machines and organizations. No longer is the alternative ascetic denial of the world while waiting for a pleasant heaven, or total submission to worldly lust and power while losing one's soul. Now we are asked to become masters of our world by growing in our sovereign awareness of ourselves and in our influence on human evolution.

Reincarnation emphasizes that each of us is in the process of emerging as a conscious particle through which the universe reaches toward meaningful, harmonious self-awareness. Each one of us must find his purposeful place in the total movement toward a universal order which is both firmly planted in our understanding of the past and boldly open to a vision of what will yet be our destiny in the ages to come.

Is this idle, wild speculation? No more and no less than it was to envision the supplanting of the Roman Empire by a Galilean sect, with its peculiar world view, or to anticipate the Renaissance discovery of vast, non-European continents. In every case of such a breakthrough into wider dimensions of awareness, man's self-understanding and his recognized place in the world had to change. Our expansion into outer space is no different. The further man reaches into unknown territories, the more solid must be his realistic self-appreciation. Reincarnation allows us the opportunity to make the presently needed readjustment in man's self-understanding. It does not offer wishful and unfounded speculation about what will happen after death. Rather it lifts the veil that ordinarily covers the past before our last birth so that we can better understand ourselves. As a result, our whole vista is changed and we no longer orient ourselves by the often questionable values of our present circumstances.

Reincarnation allows us to understand our place and mission in this present existence through a recognition of what we have been in previous lives. The human life is not a one-shot affair during which we had better make our mark by excelling in whatever might be most lucrative or prestigious at the moment. Natural and human history is not a senseless bungle of meaningless accidents. We are like a thread in a broadly woven tapestry of universal evolution. Not merely mankind in general, but you and I as conscious particles have an enduring significance. In previous incarnations we may already have achieved a certain level of self-awareness. Recapturing our knowledge of the past gives us a better chance to participate in the universal movement toward higher awareness and more constructive interaction with others.

—condensed from **Reincarnation, Key to Immortality**, *by Marcia Moore and Mark Douglas*

ABHEDANANDA, SWAMI. **DOCTRINE OF KARMA—A STUDY IN ITS PHILOSOPHY AND PRACTICE. 137pp. RVM44, 2.75c.**
Discusses the law of causation and how individuals can transcend it through yoga. A clear work by a noted philosopher-monk of the Ramakrishna order.

ABHEDANANDA, SWAMI. **REINCARNATION. 99pp. RVM00, 2.00c.**
Lucid, illuminating discussions on reincarnation, transmigration, evolution, and the law of karma.

ATKINSON, WILLIAM. **REINCARNATION AND THE LAW OF KARMA. 249pp. YPS08/Fow, 6.00c.**
A philosophical discussion of the concept of reincarnation, tracing it through history. Later in his life Atkinson was known as Yogi Ramacharaka. This is one of the most popular reincarnation books.

AUROBINDO, SRI. **THE PROBLEM OF REBIRTH. 189pp. SAA52, 2.25p.**
A very complete philosophical treatment of reincarnation and karma by one of the greatest philosophers of twentieth century India.

BENNETT, COLIN. **PRACTICAL TIME TRAVEL. 64pp. Wei71/ACP, 1.25p.**
Clear, practical instructions for various methods of traveling back to past lives. Also contains related material of a more philosophical nature which makes interesting reading.

BERNSTEIN, MOREY. **THE SEARCH FOR BRIDEY MURPHY. 352pp. S&S56, 1.95p.**
This is the true story of a Colorado housewife's recollections under hypnosis of a previous existence in eighteenth century Ireland. When the case first became known almost twenty years ago it was an instant sensation and it remains the best documented case of its type to this date.

BESANT, ANNIE. **DEATH AND AFTER. 100pp. TPH1893, 1.95c.**
A survey of man's being and his abodes after physical death. Ms. Besant is a Theosophist and she believes that a person's desires, character, and evolutionary stage determine the nature of his after death experiences.

BESANT, ANNIE. **KARMA. 83pp. TPH1895, 2.00c.**
A full discussion of the law of karma. According to Eastern tradition, as interpreted by the Theosophists, karma is the law of cause and effect. We are each responsible for our thoughts, words, and actions and these determine our life potentialities.

BESANT, ANNIE. **REINCARNATION. 95pp. TPH1892, 2.25c.**
Is the ancient tradition regarding the progressive birth of the human soul in numerous physical bodies an actual fact or just a fantasy? This small manual is designed to furnish the public with a simple explanation of the Theosophical teachings.

BESANT, ANNIE. **A STUDY IN KARMA. 75pp. TPH12, 2.25c.**
A Theosophical treatise.

BRENNAN, J.H. **FIVE KEYS TO PAST LIVES. 63pp. Wei71/ACP, 1.25p.**
Practical, clearly presented techniques.

CERMINARA, GINA. **MANY LIVES, MANY LOVES. 170pp. NAL63/ NEL, 1.50p.**
An exploration of developments in the field of reincarnation and parapsychology.

CERMINARA, GINA. **MANY MANSIONS. 240pp. NAL67/Spe, 1.50p.**
Cases and interpretative material taken from Edgar Cayce's readings. One of the most popular books on reincarnation.

CERMINARA, GINA. **THE WORLD WITHIN. NAL57, 1.25p.**
Deals with the implications of reincarnation, stressing the hope and promise it holds out to man.

■ *CHALLONER, H.K.* **THE WHEEL OF REBIRTH. 285pp. TPH69, 3.50p.**
This is perhaps the most fascinating of all the works on this subject, for it is a vivid portrayal of a whole series of incarnated lives by the one who lived them. The author projected her consciousness, with guidance, into the past to recall these experiences. The thread of events controlled by the law of cause and effect is made clearly visible, and the story itself makes for enjoyable reading.

COLLIN, RODNEY. **THE THEORY OF ETERNAL LIFE. 10.00c.**
See the Gurdjieff section.

COOKE, GRACE. **THE ILLUMINED ONES. 160pp. WET66, 6.00c.**
Ms. Cooke, guided by White Eagle, has *thought back* into two past lives: in ancient Egypt and in South America. The lives are narrated in detail and spiritual guidance is unfolded. We do not like this work as much as **Wheel of Rebirth.**

COOPER, IRVING. **REINCARNATION. 2.95c.**
See the Theosophy section.

FIORE, EDITH. **YOU HAVE BEEN HERE BEFORE. 253pp. Put78, 8.95c.**
Hypnotic regression is one of the latest techniques developed for ameliorating psychological problems. In this book Dr. Fiore, a practicing psychologist, offers her explanation of how past lives and present problems are linked, and includes many case histories of patients who have been cured through past life regression.

GAUNT, BELLE and GEORGE TREVELYAN, eds. **A TENT IN WHICH TO PASS A SUMMER NIGHT. Index, 140pp. Cov77, 5.30p.**
An anthology of the visions of life after death selected from the works of many of the West's greatest poets and writers and organized topically. Most of the selections are fairly short and Ms. Gaunt succeeds in interrelating them.

GLASKIN, G.M. **WINDOWS OF THE MIND. 267pp. Del74/Wdw, 1.35p.**
Glaskin discovered that memories of other incarnations exist in our brains and by using a combination of massage and mental exercises these memories can be brought into consciousness. He and his friends had amazing experiences with the technique, many of which are recounted here along with a description of the process.

GOLDSMITH, JOEL. **THE THUNDER OF SILENCE. 192pp. H&R61, 5.95c.**
An inspirational Christian text on karmic law and living the good life.

GRAHAM, DAVID. **THE PRACTICAL SIDE OF REINCARNATION. Index, 210pp. PrH76, 8.95c.**
This is a straightforward presentation surveying all aspects of reincarnation and focusing on case studies, and on the practical benefits which can be obtained from investigating past lives. The book is well written and we found it vastly more interesting and informative than most books on the subject. One section discusses a series of case histories of groups of people who simultaneously recall a shared existence in the past. Graham also discusses psychiatrists and other therapists who are successfully using reincarnation therapy with their clients.

GRANT, JOAN and DENYS KELSEY. **MANY LIFETIMES. 203pp. Crg76, 2.00p.**
Joan Grant is best known for the novels she writes about remembered experiences from past lives. Dr. Kelsy, her husband, is a psychiatrist who specializes in exploring the problems of his patients as far back as infancy and prenatal existence. The two have been working together since 1958 and exploring the possibilities of past lifetimes that may still affect certain people today. This book presents a variety of case histories as well as the thoughts of both Kelsey and Grant.

GROF, STANISLAV, HUGH LYNN CAYCE, and RAYNOR JOHNSON. **DIMENSIONS OF DYING AND REBIRTH. 79pp. ARE77, 2.50p.**
Transcription of a series of papers from a 1976 A.R.E. conference: *Transitions: Birth, Death, and Rebirth* by Dr. Grof; *The First Ten Minutes After Death* by Cayce; and *The Wheel of Birth and Death* by Johnson. A panel discussion between the three is also transcribed.

GUIRDHAM, ARTHUR. **THE CATHERS AND REINCARNATION. 204pp. TPH70, 3.75p.**
A factual record of a woman's memories of her incarnation in the thirteenth century. Guirdham is a psychiatrist who has carefully traced many of her memories and proven them to be accurate. A fascinating account of life in the Middle Ages as well as an interesting psychological study.

GUIRDHAM, ARTHUR. **THE LAKE AND THE CASTLE. 427pp. Spe76, 14.70c.**
This book continues the narrative begun in Dr. Guirdham's **We Are One Another**. Here he tells how the group of Cathars first assembled in ancient Rome and maintained its loyalty to its basic dualistic beliefs in Celtic Christian Cumberland and as French sailors in the Napoleonic era. He also describes the manner in which information on his past lives was communicated to him and the ways in which he verified this information. A number of visionary experiences are recounted and the book also provides a great deal of information on the cult of Mithras and the seventh century Celtic Church.

GUIRDHAM, ARTHUR. **WE ARE ONE ANOTHER. 227pp. Spe74, 10.35c.**
This book describes how a group of people who had lived together in the thirteenth century reassembled in the twentieth in a small area in western England. Guirdham records constant, sometimes day to day contact with the next world, and is careful always to verify the evidence provided by the four spirit guides. Again, the Cathers play a role in the book.

HALL, MANLY P. **ASTROLOGY AND REINCARNATION. 45pp. PRS36, 1.50p.**

HALL, MANLY P. **FROM DEATH TO REBIRTH. PRS72, 4.00p.**
A clear, excellent work in three parts. The first discusses separation from the physical body at the time of death, the second examines various beliefs about life apart from the physical body, and the third explains the procedures by which a reincarnating entity returns to the physical world. Both Eastern and Western teachings are included.

HALL, MANLY P. **PAST LIVES AND PRESENT PROBLEMS AND HOW TO PREPARE FOR A FORTUNATE REBIRTH. 60pp. PRS64 1.75p.**
Transcripts of two lectures.

HALL, MANLY P. **REINCARNATION: THE CYCLE OF NECESSITY. 217pp. PRS39, 7.90c.**
A classic treatment of various aspects of the doctrine of rebirth. There are extensive references to and quotations from traditional sources as well as the most extensive bibliography we have seen on the subject. Many of the topics are not touched upon at such great length in the rest of the literature. Manly Hall is one of the most noted American philosophers of our day.

HALL, MANLY P. **RESEARCH ON REINCARNATION. 46pp. PRS64, 1.75p.**
A philosophical compilation.

HANSON, VIRGINIA, ed. **KARMA. 140pp. TPH75, 2.50p.**
A collection of essays on all aspects of karma by a variety of Theosophical authors.

■ *HEAD JOSEPH and S.L. CRANSTON, eds.* **REINCARNATION: THE PHOENIX FIRE MYSTERY. Notes, index, 639pp. Crn77, 10.00c.**
An anthology of writings on reincarnation selected from all cultures and from earliest times to the present day. The editors consulted works of religion, science, psychology, philosophy, art, and literature in preparing their anthology. This is far and away the most comprehensive and best organized compilation we have seen. Each of the selections is prefaced with comments and there is extensive commentary relating one selection to another and providing necessary background information.

HODSON, GEOFFREY. **REINCARNATION: FACT OR FALLACY. 84pp. TPH67, 1.00p.**
An excellent presentation of the doctrine of reincarnation or law of rebirth as a plausible and at times necessary fact of human existence. Hodson examines prevalent criticisms and investigates reincarnation in the light of Christianity and the Bible.

HOWE, QUINCY. **REINCARNATION FOR THE CHRISTIAN. Annotated bibliography, 112pp. Wes74, 4.95c.**
A historical and theological presentation. Good scholarship; geared to the general reader.

HUMPHREYS, CHRISTMAS. **KARMA AND REBIRTH. 110pp. Mur43, 5.00c.**
A presentation by this noted Buddhist scholar which incorporates teachings from the scriptures of the Hindus and Buddhists and Theosophical writings. Humphreys writes very clearly.

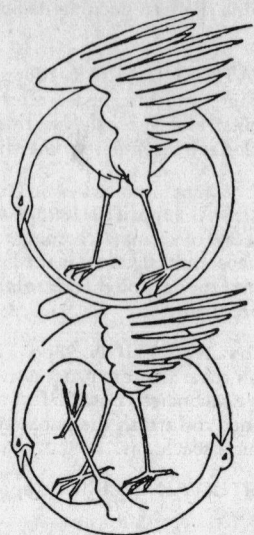

JOHNSON, RAYNOR. **LIGHT OF ALL LIFE. Illustrations, 8½"x11", 30pp. HDI76, 2.50p.**
Transcriptions of a series of lectures given for the Human Dimensions Institute centering around the theme of reincarnation, karma, the certainty of survival of death, and the soul's great journey.

JONES, GLADYS. **FLOWERING TREE. Bibliography, 316pp. NAP65, 6.95c.**
This is in many ways a different book. It has a haunting and intriguing kind of beauty, and the subject of reincarnation and karma is handled with considerable understanding.—Hugh Lynn Cayce. Ms. Jones is a psychic and she has a wonderful gift for conveying a whole squence of symbols in the form of parables.

JONES, GLADYS. **REINCARNATION, SEX AND LOVE. 185pp. NAP71, 6.95c.**
An application of ancient beliefs to the problems of today. Includes a large number of the author's poems.

LANGLEY, NOEL. **EDGAR CAYCE ON REINCARNATION. 286pp. War67, 1.95p.**
Cases selected from the readings.

LEADBEATER, C.W. **THE LIFE AFTER DEATH—AND HOW THEOSOPHY UNVEILS IT. 73pp. TPH12, 2.25c.**

LEWIS, H. SPENCER. **MANSIONS OF THE SOUL—THE COSMIC CONCEPTION. 332pp. Amo30, 7.75c.**
A very complete presentation of the Rosicrucian Order's reincarnational beliefs.

MACGREGOR, GEDDES. **REINCARNATION AND CHRISTIANITY. Notes, annotated bibliography, index, 201pp. TPH78, 4.50p.**
An exhaustive inquiry into the role of rebirth in Christian thought. Dr. MacGregor analytically reports important comments by some of the world's greatest Christian figures, and he presents philosophical, scientific, and biblical evidence in support of his appraisal. Dr. MacGregor is Professor Emeritus of Philosophy at the University of Southern California. This is a work of excellent scholarship.

MONTGOMERY, RUTH. **COMPANIONS ALONG THE WAY. 1.95p.**
See the Christianity section.

MONTGOMERY, RUTH. **HERE AND HEREAFTER. 175pp. Faw68, 1.75p.**
A popularized account consisting basically of case histories.

MOORE, MARCIA. **HYPERSENTIENCE.** 223pp. Ban76, 1.95p.
The purpose of this book is to show that you can recall your former lifetimes and can help others to do likewise. Hypersentience is a method of inducing an altered state of consciousness which affords valuable new insights into the nature of man and the universe. As such, it is very similar to meditation. The technique can be practiced by any open minded investigator. All that is required is respect for the power of the human mind and common sense. I have tried to impart all that I know of this safe, easy, and uncomplicated system because my experience has shown that people are capable of putting it to good use.—from the introduction.

■ *MOORE, MARCIA and MARK DOUGLAS.* **REINCARNATION: KEY TO IMMORTALITY. Extensive bibliography,** 394pp. ArB68, 10.00c.
This is an excellent collection of case histories (often of noted people), with interpretative material and the overall theme that the soul does incarnate and grow from life to life. Includes many quotations and material on what the conception of reincarnation means in our lives and *how to die correctly.* The case histories are arranged topically and make fascinating reading and the book as a whole makes a convincing argument for reincarnation. The authors are noted astrologers.

NETHERTON, MORRIS and NANCY SHIFFRIN. **POST LIVES THERAPY.** 191pp. Mor78, 8.95c.
Dr. Netherton, founder of the Institute for Past Life Awareness, claims, *When you behave inappropriately—that is, when what you are doing is not handling your life to your own satisfaction—you are reliving an unresolved past life incident.* Almost every therapy assumes that traumas from the past influence the present. The book outlines a system of past life therapy in which the unconscious mind is probed and a flood of traumatic events that go back into a past life are unleashed. The discussion includes numerous case histories of patients whose problems have been revealed and treated through the use of this therapy.

NIKHILANANDA, SWAMI. **MAN IN SEARCH OF IMMORTALITY: TESTIMONIALS FROM THE HINDU SCRIPTURES.** 4.95c.
See the Indian Philosophy section.

PARAMANANDA, SWAMI. **REINCARNATION AND IMMORTALITY.** 102pp. VdC61, 2.25c.
Swami Paramananda integrates Vedantic philosophy with Christianity and writes in an inspiring manner. He discusses karma as well as reincarnation in this volume.

PELT, GERTRUDE VAN. **THE DOCTRINE OF KARMA.** 58pp. PoL74, 1.75p.
A Theosophical manual, with quotations from a number of the major books.

PERKINS, JAMES. **EXPERIENCING REINCARNATION. Glossary, bibliography, index,** 202pp. TPH77, 3.95p.
I am using memory experiences that forcibly stirred an awakening in me to this astonishing rhythm of life through which one recaptures what was known previously. In myself, fragments of memory later developed into a full conception of the great universal cycle of human birth. But nothing can describe the spiritual freedom experienced with the realization that one is living immortally—now—as the law of reincarnation reveals when understood. For fifteen years Perkins was the National President of The Theosophical Society in America.

PERKINS, JAMES. **THROUGH DEATH TO REBIRTH.** 124pp. TPH61, 1.95p.
A Theosophical presentation of the stages the soul passes through between the cycles of death and rebirth, presented in the form of a series of short essays on a variety of topics.

PRYSE, JAMES. **REINCARNATION IN NEW TESTAMENT.** 2.50p.
See the Bibles section.

QUERIDO, RENE. **QUESTIONS AND ANSWERS ON REINCARNATION AND KARMA.** 2.95p.
See the Steiner section.

RAMA, SWAMI. **FREEDOM FROM KARMA.** Him73, 2.50p.
Swami Rama and his teachings have been popular recently in the U.S., especially in the Midwest. He expresses his views on karma and daily right action here.

RAMACHARAKA, YOGI. **THE LIFE BEYOND DEATH.** 192pp. YPS09/Fow, 6.00c.
A clear, comprehensive presentation of *the other side.* Includes a discussion of the planes of life; the soul's slumber and awakening; astral plane and its geography; astral religious experiences; astral communications, companionship, and occupation; and beyond reincarnation.

RUTTER, OWEN. **THE SCALES OF KARMA.** 207pp. Wei30, 2.95p.
Includes material from the world's religions as well as a general exposition of the subject.

RYALL, EDWARD. **BORN TWICE.** 214pp. H&R74, 10.00c.
The author chronicles his *other life,* when he was a farmer in seventeenth century England, and includes a wealth of details. Introduction by Ian Stevenson.

SHARMA, I.C. **CAYCE, KARMA, AND REINCARNATION.** 177pp. H&R75, 3.95p.
Dr. Sharma is an Indian philosophy professor. Here he clarifies many of Edgar Cayce's ideas by developing parallels with Hindu thought.

SHERMAN, HAROLD. **YOU LIVE AFTER DEATH.** 205pp. Faw49, 1.50p.
A well written, inspirational presentation of the soul, the spirit body, the afterlife, our link with the infinite, preparing for death and for future lives, and much else. Sherman is a very popular writer in this field and his books are well thought of.

SINGH, KIRPAL. **THE WHEEL OF LIFE: THE LAW OF ACTION AND REACTION.** 100pp. MoB, 1.80p.
Complete explanation of the law of karma and how it works. Includes a discussion of the relation of the vegetarian diet and ethical living to karma, and a demonstration of the nullifying effect of karma on a life of self surrender.

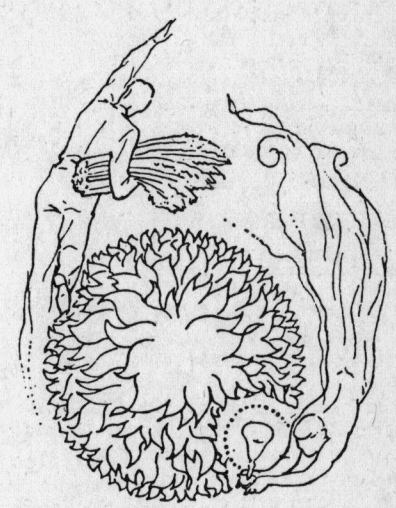

STEARN, JESS. **A MATTER OF IMMORTALITY.** 300pp. NAL76, 1.95p.
Jess Stearn reports the details of the past lives of a famous medium, Maria Moreno, as they have been revealed to her under deep hypnosis. As she recalls them, Stearn describes the roles played in these previous incarnations by her present guides and spiritual helpers. In addition, Moreno—through Stearn—discusses astral medicine and the ways in which it is used to alleviate pain and illness on the physical plane. Many celebrated people, past and present, are part of Ms. Moreno's story and the account itself is highly personal.

STEVENSON, IAN. **INDIA: CASES OF THE REINCARNATION TYPE, VOLUME I: TEN CASES IN INDIA. Glossary, index,** 388pp. UPV75, 26.90c.
A collection of detailed reports. Each begins with a summary of the

case and its investigation. Stevenson then gives background about the persons interviewed and information relevant to the subject's statements about the previous life he claims to remember. This part of the report is based almost exclusively on firsthand testimony taken during field interviews and includes commentary helpful to those unfamiliar with Indian culture. The comments also report and analyze discrepancies in the testimony. Stevenson then discusses the weak and strong features of the case and concludes each report with information on the development of the subject after the childhood period when memories and related unusual behavior were at their peak. The methodology used in the investigation of the cases is outlined in the introduction.

STEVENSON, IAN. **TWENTY CASES SUGGESTIVE OF REINCARNATION. 362pp. UPV74, 20.00c.**
This is the most noted collection of case studies ever published. Stevenson is a psychiatrist who carefully researched the material presented here for a number of years. He first presents the cases and then a general discussion of the material. All sources are fully documented. Recommended for the serious student.

STEINER, RUDOLF. **MANIFESTATIONS OF KARMA. 4.50p.**
See the Steiner section.

STORY, FRANCIS. **REBIRTH AS DOCTRINE AND EXPERIENCE. Index, 292pp. BPS75, 6.00c.**
Story was a Buddhist scholar who devoted over twenty years to investigations of cases of rebirth. His analyses were systematic and he always integrated his deep knowledge of Buddhism with his case studies. He died before completing even preliminary work on this book; it was compiled by his associate, the Ven. Nyanaponika, from field notes and essays. While it is at best an uncompleted book, it remains one of the most important contributions to an understanding of the rebirth phenomenon that is available today. Introduction by Ian Stevenson.

VIVEKANANDA, SWAMI. **KARMA YOGA. 131pp. AdA74, 1.00p.**
An excellent treatise on all aspects of the subject from the Hindu perspective.

WACHSMUTH, GUENTHER. **REINCARNATION. 14.00c.**
See the Steiner section.

WOODWARD, MARY ANN. **EDGAR CAYCE'S STORY OF KARMA. 283pp. Ber72, 1.95p.**
During his lifetime, Cayce gave more than 14,000 readings, one third of which were devoted to metaphysical areas and revolved around the central theme of reincarnation. From these discourses Ms. Woodward has selected those most related to his theory of karma and has arranged the readings topically, with commentary interspersed.

WRIGHT, LEOLINE. **REINCARNATION. 113pp. TPH75, 2.25p.**
A Theosophical manual, with quotations from some of the most important books.

ZAIN, C.C. **THE NEXT LIFE. 6.95p.**
See the Astrology section.

philosophy. After a biographical and historical introduction, Michel examines Bruno's theory of the universe in all its aspects. Focusing on the poetry and dialogues, he interprets Bruno's cosmology in the light of concepts inherited from ancient times and demonstrates that Bruno's work embodies a systematic philosophy of nature that is compatible in many ways with twentieth century thought. This is an important work which should be welcomed by all Renaissance scholars and those with a deep interest in alchemy.

MURRAY, PETER and LINDA. **THE ART OF THE RENAISSANCE. 6.95p.**
See the Sacred Art section.

ROSS, JAMES BRUCE and MARY MCLAUGHLIN, eds. **THE PORTABLE RENAISSANCE READER. Introduction, 756pp. Vik68, 5.95p.**
Selections from more than 100 writers, thematically arranged and covering all the major aspects of Renaissance writing and thought.

SHUMAKER, WAYNE. **THE OCCULT SCIENCES IN THE RENAISSANCE. Many notes, bibliography, index, 305pp. UCa72, 16.00c.**
This scholarly study offers a summary and analysis of five esoteric systems: astrology, natural or white magic, witchcraft, alchemy, and the meditative philosophy associated with Hermes Trismegistus. To many Renaissance men, these systems were considered sources of truth about the meaning and order of human life. The author's primary aim is to enlarge the modern comprehension of these systems. The text is well illustrated.

SINGLETON, CHARLES, ed. **ART, SCIENCE, AND HISTORY IN THE RENAISSANCE. Index, 8¾"x11½", 453pp. JHU67, 27.00c.**
The papers in this volume were the result of a year long seminar on the title theme held at Johns Hopkins. They were originally delivered as lectures, though they read more like scholarly essays. Extensive notes and plates accompany each paper. The selections are topically arranged under three major headings: *Art and Music, Science,* and *History.*

WALKER, D.P. **THE ANCIENT THEOLOGY. Notes, index, 276pp. Duc72, 13.65p.**
A scholarly discussion of a group of theologians and philosophers and of the various phases of a tradition which began with the early church fathers, was revived and transformed in the Renaissance, and began slowly to die in the seventeenth century. The individuals range from Ficino, Savonarola, Herbert of Cherbury, and Leibniz, to many little known authors. Frances Yates describes the book as *a masterly exercise in precise scholarship.... The work of a scholar of absolute reliability and integrity, it makes available a wealth of material for those interested in the new history of thought, and uncovers the real roots of continuity between the Renaissance and the seventeenth century.*

WALKER, D.P. **SPIRITUAL AND DEMONIC MAGIC. Detailed notes, index, 244pp. UND58, 6.65p.**
The change in attitude toward Renaissance thought which has taken place in recent years rests largely on a new understanding of Renaissance Neoplatonism. Rather than being merely a somewhat mystical and Christianized revival of Platonic idealism arising from the rediscovery of the works of Plato and his early followers, it included a deep interest in the magical and mystical writings attributed to ancient sages such as Zoroaster and Hermes. As Frances Yates has noted, it was Walker's book which first provided a firm basis for this major reinterpretation. In a precise, scholarly manner, Walker traces the history of a tradition of Neoplatonic magic, as exemplified by Ficino, and the spiritual magic which grew out of that tradition. He demonstrates how demonic magic, combined with medieval planetary magic, led to the magic of Agrippa and Paracelsus, and how spiritual magic dissolved into something else: music and poetry and orthodox and unorthodox Christianity. At the end of the sixteenth century, the two strands of the tradition came together again and thus entered into important movements of the seventeenth century. A chapter is devoted to each of the major individual figures.

YATES, FRANCES. **THE ART OF MEMORY. Illustrations, many notes, bibliography, index, 400pp. UCh66/RKP, 5.95p.**
The study of memory in its lowest form was undertaken to produce better oratory skills; in a more advanced form it helped to transmit knowledge before the invention of movable type and the widespread reproduction of written records; in its highest form it was a meditational science that used hierarchies of angels and cosmologies of the physical and superphysical worlds to remind an individual of the principles behind the arts and sciences. In this detailed account, Ms. Yates follows memory study through Greek and Latin sources to the Middle Ages and Renaissance and the works of Camillo, Lull, Bruno, and Fludd.

YATES, FRANCES. **ASTRAEA. Illustrations, notes, index, 6¼"x9½", 269pp. RKP75, 15.95c.**
Dr. Yates examines the images and symbolism of monarchy, and especially the myth of Astraea. Astraea reigned in the Golden Age but left the Earth when men grew evil. She symbolizes a rule of universal peace and justice in an ideal empire. In this study Dr. Yates concentrates on the symbolism used by Queen Elizabeth I who pictured herself as the Virgin Queen of a Golden Age of reformed imperial rule. She also surveys the pageantry of chivalry around the Queen and discusses related symbology in the works of Shakespeare and Spenser. The French monarchy in the Renaissance is reviewed as well.

YATES, FRANCES. **GIORDANO BRUNO AND THE HERMETIC TRADITION. Extensive illustrations and notes, index, 478pp. UCh64/RKP, 26.90c.**
This book looks at the sixteenth century cosmology of Bruno from its sources in the writings of Hermes Trismegistus, Ficino's natural magic, Pico della Mirandola and cabalist magic, Pseudo-Dionysus and the theology of a Christian magus, and the work of Cornelius Agrippa. Yates writes very well, and while her approach is fairly academic her scholarship is excellent and she makes the often dry material come alive.

YATES, FRANCES. **MAJESTY AND MAGIC IN SHAKESPEARE'S LAST PLAYS: A NEW APPROACH TO CYMBELINE, HENRY VIII, AND THE TEMPEST. Notes, index, 150pp. ShP72, 4.95p.**
Ms. Yates explores religious and philosophical implications of the later Shakespearean works and shows how Shakespeare's dramas were influenced by the Hermetic tradition in European thought.

YATES, FRANCES. **THE ROSICRUCIAN ENLIGHTENMENT. Illustrations, extensive notes, index, 284pp. ShP72/Grn, 5.95p.**
This is a historical analysis of the **Rosicrucian Manifestos,** mysterious documents published in Germany in the early seventeenth century. Dr. Yates reveals that the **Manifestos** were connected with movements stirred up by John Dee in Bohemia during the reign of Queen Elizabeth, and with contemporary movements in southern Germany which culminated in the short lived reign of Frederick, the *Winter King* of Bohemia. The time period covered by this study is a phase in the history of European culture that was intermediate between the Renaissance and the so called scientific revolution. Amongst the personages and themes discussed here are Johann Andreae, John Dee and Robert Fludd, Comenius and Hartlib, Boyle's *Invisible College,* the rise of the Royal Society and of Freemasonry. Major figures like Francis Bacon, Descartes, and Newton are seen in new context. Rosicrucianism, as seen in this volume, represents a stage in which the Hermetic-Qabalistic tradition received the influx of another Hermetic tradition, that of alchemy.

YATES, FRANCES. **A THEATRE OF THE WORLD: A STUDY OF JOHN DEE. Notes, index, 243pp. UCh69/RKP, 3.45p.**
In this volume Dr. Yates touches upon the Vitruvian influences in Tudor and Jacobean England in their relation to Renaissance philosophy and outlook. The book centers primarily on John Dee and Robert Fludd, with particular reference to evidence in their works of the influence of Vitruvius. She suggests that the London public theaters, including the Globe, were an adaptation of the ancient theater as described by Vitruvius; that is, a theater with cosmological proportions which expressed a Renaissance outlook on man and the universe.

YATES, FRANCES. **THE VALOIS TAPESTRIES. Notes, index, 8¾"x 11¼", 189pp. RKP75, 20.95c.**
A detailed historical investigation of the meaning of the Valois Tapestries. Dr. Yates describes how the tapestries arose out of Catherine d'Medici's marvelous series of festivals at the court of the Valois in the sixteenth century. These festivals were intended to bring together hostile religious factions. Since the festivals were constantly interrupted by renewed outbreaks of the French religious wars, the only record of this *lost moment in history* is the tapestries. Dr. Yates shows how it is possible to interpret them as a vision of life and history. Plates of the tapestries accompany the text.

REVEALED TEACHINGS

We must premise that the source of all this material is a matter for each to decide for himself. It may originate in Betty—in which case she is more of a wonder than any of us has supposed. She may, by this mechanism, tap some wide source of wisdom, some reservoir, some *universal mind*. Or, in this state of divided consciousness she may come into touch with *race consciousness*, the stored or accumulated experience of humankind. Or, finally, the source may be what it purports to be, distinct discarnate intelligences. Each is free and welcome to adopt any hypothesis that appeals to him.

But the material is here: it did not exist before as a formulated thing, either in our minds or in our reading. It came to us—and still comes—in the manner I have set down. That much is indubitable fact.

Assuming the sources as from invisible intelligences, the technique of the communication is a fascinating speculation. Early in the game it became abundantly evident that it is not so simple as talking into a telephone. In the beginning were inconsistencies in statement; sometimes direct misstatements and contradictions. There were irrelevant trivialities or absurdities. There were blank failures to give simple replies to simple questions. It was almost impossible to get any adequate explanation for these things. It took considerable faith and perserverance not to have quit in disgust.

When one sees the pencil moving in automatic writing, or hears the voice in spoken communication, one asks questions in the expectation of receiving simple and direct answer, as though the discarnate intelligence were actually holding the pencil in full control, or were talking as one talks through a telephone. Except as to the simplest ideas, such accuracy rarely occurs. Ordinarily, when one presses for a concrete statement of fact, or a detailed description of conditions, he gets either evasion, a flat assurance that the thing is too complicated or difficult to be told, or else the required details are given but are awkward, absurd, or contradictory to what has been given elsewhere through other stations with at least equal authority. Even a simple yes or no is difficult to elicit.

This is especially true of the personal type of thing; which is the usual approach to these super-normal—not supernatural —matters. If the seeker sticks at that, he is up a blind alley. It may be all right as a start: but only as a start.

This is what I conceive happens:

The Invisibles have no direct powers to manipulate our physical substance, though at times they may appear to do so. Their ability to levitate tables, for instance; or to move a pencil in automatic writing; or to jerk our limbs about; or to appear to speak by direct control of another all depend on their ability to impress an idea on a portion of the station's mind. That portion of the station's mind, in turn, so manipulates the necessary physical mechanism as to approximate the result desired. This rule I conceive to be invariable.

The portion of the station's mind with which we are dealing we will have to call the subconscious. That has become a sort of wastebasket word into which we dump everything we do not understand, but it will have to do. It is not a distinctly separate mind from the conscious intellect. They are both one Mind. It is the submerged portion, the part below the threshold. In some the threshold is higher or lower than in others; and likewise the threshold can be raised or lowered by effort and development. This subconscious portion, broadly speaking, receives impression, idea, emotion, inspiration, which it lifts to the conscious intellect to be fitted into expression. It does just that constantly in everyday life.

Now this subconscious mind is the only point of contact with the Invisibles. They cannot affect our physical selves nor our physical environment except through it. I make this statement in full appreciation of many phenomena in apparent contradiction. And as they cannot intervene directly on us physically, so they cannot intervene directly on us as to our consciously intellectual part. They must impress what they want on the submerged subconscious of the station, which in turn reports that impression to the conscious intellect for expression.

At just that point the difficulty lies.

Let us assume a specific case of a sort apparently at variance with this theory. An Invisible desires to communicate in direct words. The subject matter, the details, of that communication, are *prepared* in such a manner as to make an impression on the station's subconscious as accurately as possible. The method of impression is a trifle obscure. We have been told of it in various ways.

Recording my thought on your brain, was one attempt, *How I reach you. The clearer you understand it, the better you can co-operate. Reckon first on receptivity. Presuppose receptivity. Without that there is the merest chance of succeeding. Reckon next on desire from both ends. Registration is accomplished by means of the mating of sensitized consciousness superimposed; something like the making of a color print.*

Roughly speaking, the general preparation which you make through admitting the possibility of communication is the sensitizing which admits of the impress from this end. For this reason systematic preparation or seeking is almost certain to insure results. The preparation of the plates is your part.

After the impression is received, it must be translated. This is done by that part of the mind which we use constantly in everyday life, the intellectual part. (But not, of course, with the conscious knowledge of the station.) In the case of both automatic writing and spoken communication it is more or less divorced temporarily from conscious active thinking, so that the words seem, and are, independent of the station's will. Nevertheless, that is the part that does the translating. It must do so in accordance with its equipment. If the equipment is limited, the translation is limited. One cannot strike typewriter keys that do not exist. It should be added that in most human beings there exists vastly more equipment than is ever under conscious control at any one time. Hypnotism proves this. But nothing beyond that equipment can be expressed. If an idea totally outside it is offered, it can either be conveyed only partially and by analogy, or it cannot be conveyed at all.

Consider the case of an absolutely unlettered, untravelled solitary cast away as a child on a desert island. Bring to his subconscious mind an accurate impression of, say the essence of modern rapid transportation—motors, locomotives, airplanes—and demand of his intellect a report of that impression. He must translate it in terms of the birds of the air, the beasts of the field, the fish of the sea, or his own two feet. If anyone were present to receive that report, he might get a highly poetic analogy, but hardly much idea of the reality. And if he had just come from another island where bullock carts—and nothing else—were known; with his head full of an authentic *revelation* of winged carts, or bullocks of incredible swiftness breathing fire and smoke, he would be justified in throwing up both hands and calling it all bunk.

This matter of translation may be conceived to be one of basic difficulty. A great deal of distortion also comes in by what we call *coloring*,—the arbitrary though unintentional intervention of the station's own thinking mind. That is fairly common, and is pretty well recognized. The mind seizes a fragment of the genuine impression and, by association of ideas, goes galloping off with it in the grooves of habit, constructing out of past experience a more or less coherent statement that is genuine only in a fragment at inception. At its worst it results in complete falsity. At its best it modifies and distorts.

Let us now examine the apparent method by which these impressed ideas are translated by the station.

Everybody is familiar with the type of mind that reacts in conventional phrase to any common sentiment. We call them *bromides*. It is like touching a button: one knows exactly what to expect. That is the simplest possible example of what takes place. Certain ideas automatically attract certain forms of expression. Present the idea and the expression follows. Betty once said; *Queer how I hunt for words. I have a magnet and the proper word climbs up.* Often she will snap her fingers and cry impatiently: *Word wanted! Word wanted!*

In the unicellular rudimentary mind—if such can be imagined—there might be only one expression-response, so that the translation of any certain ideas would be invariable, even though inadequate. But as a matter of fact even the most simple-minded station has in store at least a dozen words any one of which might fit, and all of which report for duty, so to speak. That happens in everyday life. When it does so happen we have, we say, to *make a choice of words*. It is the same thing here, only there is not only a choice of words to be made, but also what might be called a choice of concepts.

In ordinary circumstances this choice is left by the Invisibles almost entirely to the station. Sometimes it is done deliberately, I believe, in order to get the gist of the matter over with a minimum of difficulty. In nine cases in ten, however, in my opinion, the Invisibles cannot help themselves. The human habit of expression is too strong for them. They can make the impression, but then the thing runs away from them. This is especially true with undeveloped or partially developed stations,—people who suddenly discover a pencil writing for them. The sequence is a premature rushing into print, with more *basic discrepancies* and attendant bewilderment and disbelief. For when the matter of translation is wholly or partially left to the station, it necessarily is tinged with the station's habit of thought. It becomes ecclesiastic through the formally religious; or fuzzy through the emotional; or highfalutin' through the sentimental; or even ungrammatical through the illiterate.

We have said that the *choice of words* was generally perforce or intentionally left to the station. We have discussed the perforce. It has seemed to me also that much of the time the Invisibles have deliberately refrained from much, if any, supervision. This happens when the station's equipment is sufficiently adequate to the impression, either because his habit of mind fits the subject matter, or because he is sufficiently in harmony with the Invisible to be exquisitely sensitive to refinements of meaning. That results in great fluency. It is a method most often allowed when the subject is very general, or of no especial importance, or in ordinary conversational exchange.

But, again, the form of translation may make a great deal of difference. Then from the flock of words that rises to the magnet of the idea impressed, the Invisible may make a choice.

In Betty's case that choice is made by elimination, by negation of one after the other that she would select until the suitable one presents itself. I imagine that is always the case. The result is more accurate, but it is also more halting. When an absolutely literal statement is in order,—what we call dictation—it is very slow. It is slow when Betty reports in her own person what is supplied her. It is slow when the Invisibles, apparently speaking in their own persons, desire to make a measured statement. The whole equipment of the station is at their disposal—vocabulary, experience, intellectual ideas, habits of mind and phrase, mental reactions, beliefs, wisdom and knowledge—as the words in a dictionary are at the disposal of those who would write. These materials are capable of being arranged in any pattern or sequence, to express in their combinations, perhaps, ideas entirely unknown to the station. But they can be so arranged only by the rejection of those not desired from that portion of them that automatically rises to meet the stimulus of the impression.

In all of the foregoing I have purposely instanced the simplest types of communication. There are many. The most striking and rapid is that in which the station seems *possessed* by the Invisible, using gestures, turns of phrase, even tones of voice not his own. It is sometimes impossible to believe, in spite of the evidence of one's eyes, that another personality is not before one. Joan, of *Our Unseen Guest*, is wonderful that way.

Nevertheless, as I see it such apparent *possession* is not incompatible with the hypothesis. Description of the process—impression on the subconscious; a rising of apposite material for translation to the conscious; a selection by suppression of all but the exact form desired—may be likened to a sloweddown moving picture. All the movements of the action stand out singly and painfully. But in some cases it is possible that the station may be far enough developed, or so sympathetically *en rapport* with the Invisible, that the film is speeded up. The mechanism moves as smoothly and promptly as the parts of an engine. The impress is formed, made, translated, almost in one movement, as it were; and with that major impression come minor impressions—perhaps intentionally, perhaps involuntarily—of personality and mannerism. These, too, the station seizes and translates into speech or action. We have the impersonation. Yet I believe if Joan's process could be slowed down for inspection,—as the moving picture is slowed down—it would be found to comprise the sequence I have outlined in my hypothesis. And even Joan does slow down at times to the point of the most deliberate and tentative dictation when some technical matter requiring absolute verbal accuracy is to be said.

Or take another type, that of the station who pronounces words unknown to him. Cases have been reported of communications in foreign languages with which the station was alleged to be unacquainted. There is no reason why sounds should not be impressed and translated as well as words; and a proper combination of those sounds as syllables would form words unknown to the station. That would imply an extremely delicate process, and the development of enormous skill, control, sensitiveness and receptivity. In principle it should be possible. We are yet at very crude beginnings. Certainly the little group around Bell, jubilant over distinguishing faintly a single jumbled sentence across the space of two rooms, could have no vision of hearing a whisper four thousand miles.

—*condensed from* **The Betty Book**, *by Stewart Edward White*

ASSOCIATION OF THE LIGHT MORNING and THE FELLOWSHIP OF THE INNER LIGHT. **THE SPIRITUAL DIMENSION OF MARRIAGE. 48pp. Her75, 1.75p.**
A series of channeled communications received over a period of a year and topically arranged according to the following general headings: *Preparation for Marriage, In the Marriage,* and *The Family Experience.* Practicality is emphasized.

DARBY and JOAN. **OUR UNSEEN GUEST. 320pp. Bor20, 3.95p.**
In the first decades of the twentieth century the psychic realm entered a new stage. Things were said from *the other side* not merely for the sake of comfort or assurance, or even ethical and religious instruction, but for realization of a universal truth that philosophers and scientists have been seeking to establish through the centuries. This truth postulates one—and only one—basic reality, a fundamental something from which everything stems. In **Our Unseen Guest** this long sought reality is isolated as consciousness—*the highest expression known to man of a single common denominator.* This book was widely read and was very influential. The material in Stewart Edward White's books and the Seth books by Jane Roberts continue this excellent teaching.

DOUGLAS, NIK. **THE BOOK OF MATAN—AUTOMATIC WRITING FROM THE BRINK OF ETERNITY. 200pp. Spe77, 14.70c.**
The extraordinary writings here presented are in the form of a complete story. This tells of a young man's search for truth and illumination through a series of awesome mystical experiences which permeate his life.... This story was written in fifteen concentrated sessions over a period of forty days.... The story tells how Matan travels from place to place in search of peace, truth and inner illumination. He experiences strange happenings and visions, undergoing an inner transformation. There are a series of revelations which teach him how to live.... Matan communicates his experiences to others and creates several forest communities.—from the introduction. Many color collages and illustrations of the original manuscript.

FORD, ARTHUR. **THE LIFE BEYOND DEATH. Index, 224pp. Ber71, 1.50p.**
Ford was one of the best known twentieth century trance mediums. In this book he reveals information on the quality, substance, and content of life on other planes of existence.

HAMMOND, ALAN. **A GIFT FROM THE MASTER. 93pp. IWP78, 6.95p.**
Color photographs taken on a pilgrimage to the East accompany thoughts on the way of Eckankar and quotations from the Eck masters.

MATHERS, J.H. and LENORA HUETT. **THE AMNESIA FACTOR. Glossary, bibliography, index, 169pp. CeA75, 4.95p.**
Lenora Huett is a gifted medium; J.H. Mathes, an airline pilot and UFO investigator who, through her, contacted his two guides. About two-thirds of the book consists of Mathes' experiences and related ideas and questions. The rest is composed of the guides' answers. Mathes had a prior interest in **The Urantia Book** and the Seth books, and quite a bit of the discussion relates to the kind of cosmological ideas found in them. In fact, there is specific information given by the guides about Seth. The title refers to the idea that when we come into this plane of existence we are given amnesia about our larger selves so that we will play the game and gain the most experience we can while on Earth.

MONTGOMERY, RUTH. **THE WORLD BEFORE. 288pp. Faw76, 1.95p.**
Arthur Ford and Ms. Montgomery's other spirit guides have dictated the story of creation and the lost worlds of Atlantis and Lemuria to her via automatic writing. This is a detailed account of much of the information she received.

MONTGOMERY, RUTH. **A WORLD BEYOND. 176pp. Faw71, 1.50p.**
Arthur Ford's own account of life in the next stages of existence beyond the portal that man calls death, transmitted through his friend, Ruth Montgomery.

NADA-YOLANDA. **ANGELS AND MAN. 138pp. MAM74, 6.00c.**
The relationships and the responsibilities between the angelic and the man kingdoms are of great importance, yet are not understood by Earthman. Instead of divine truths, man here has been plied with man-made conceptions, descriptions, definitions and fallacies through writings and paintings. The purpose of this book is to present a true revelation of this subject.... The eleven discourses are the actual words of the seven archangels as channeled vocally through Nada-Yolanda.... The glossary contains explanations of 145 possibly unfamiliar terms.

NADA-YOLANDA. **EVOLUTION OF MAN: SPIRITUAL-MENTAL-PHYSICAL. Glossary, 160pp. MAM71, 6.00c.**
Presents material designed to help man understand his past experience with the Earth and the solar system and to see what lies ahead. Topics include *The Biblical Record, The Fall of Man, Sonship with God, Man's Bodies, Environmental Relationships, Free Will, Soul, Good and Evil, Devolution and Re-evolution.*

NADA-YOLANDA. **HOW TO DO ALL THINGS—YOUR USE OF DIVINE POWER. 144pp. MAM70, 5.00c.**
A metaphysical textbook explaining methods whereby one can achieve spiritual understanding. Recommends reliance upon the inherent divine power and infinite spiritual resources to be found within each individual.

NADA-YOLANDA. **MARK AGE PERIOD AND PROGRAMS. 350pp. MAM70, 10.00c.**
This is the first Mark Age book, containing excerpts of the channeled communications. It provides a comprehensive coverage of the hierarchical plan and program as presented through Mark Age concerning the nature, powers, history and development of man and the plan to begin a new level of spiritual evolution. This is the basic text and includes a comprehensive glossary.

NADA-YOLANDA. **1000 KEYS TO THE TRUTH. Index, 157pp. MAM76, 5.00p.**
These one-sentence spiritual guidelines for the Latter Days and the Second Coming are based entirely on the interdimensional channelings of prophetess Nada-Yolanda of Mark Age, and are not in any way derived from the channelings or the teachings of any other person or group on Earth.—from the introduction.

NADA-YOLANDA. **VISITORS FROM OTHER PLANETS. 10.00c.**
See the UFOs section.

NEWBROUGH, JOHN. **THE OAHSPE BIBLE. Glossary, index, 8"x10", 921pp. Amh1892, 15.00c.**
This book was supposedly transmitted to Newbrough by archangelic beings. The text concerns the 24,000 year history of the Earth as well as the occurrences in the spiritual world during the same period. It is written in biblical style English and includes photographic reprints of portraits of evolved spiritual beings.

ROBERTS, JANE. **ADVENTURES IN CONSCIOUSNESS. Index, 296pp. PrH75, 3.45p.**
Aspect psychology ... accepts as normal the existence of precognitive dreams, out-of-body experiences, revelatory information, alterations of consciousness, peak experiences, trance mediumship, and other psychological and psychic events.... I utilize different levels of awareness to examine the nature of the psyche and its reality.... I've also examined my own trance material, and from my side of consciousness scrutinized Seth's reality as it appears in my experience, and in his behavior and writings. This is the fullest exploration Jane has made of her work with Seth and how this work has altered her psychological thought.

ROBERTS, JANE. **THE EDUCATION OF OVERSOUL SEVEN. 226pp. S&S73/Cov, 1.95p.**
With **The Education of Oversoul Seven**, *Jane Roberts brings us a great bright sad funny dream, set before waking in ink and paper. We have a strange feeling, as Seven learns, that it is us learning too—that it is us flickering back and fort' across centuries discovering what Now is; in and out of bodies discovering who we've been all along, as though we've somehow done this before, and forgotten. In the adventures of Seven and in the dream of this book it's almost as if, for a long happy moment, we can remember.*—Richard Bach.

■ *ROBERTS, JANE.* **THE NATURE OF PERSONAL REALITY. 523pp. PrH75, 8.95c/5.95p/2.75p.**
Seth's main idea is that we create our personal reality through our conscious beliefs about ourselves, others, and the world. Following this is the concept that the "point of power" is in the present, not in the past of this life or any other. He stresses the individual's capacity for conscious action, and provides excellent exercises designed to show each person how to apply these theories to any life situation.—from the introduction. This is the second book Seth has written by himself, and, as you can see from the quotation above, he brings many of the theoretical concepts presented in **Seth Speaks** down to the practical level. As usual, he speaks clearly and to the point.

ROBERTS, JANE. **PSYCHIC POLITICS. Index, 376pp. PrH76, 8.95c.**
An informal presentation of more of Jane's insights and advice. She delves into the psyche and into the ways in which we can get in touch with our inner beings. Many case studies and transcriptions of conversations are included. The book is not by Seth; however, Seth contributes many of the insights and is the inspiration for the whole study.

■ *ROBERTS, JANE.* **THE SETH MATERIAL. 304pp. PrH70, 8.95c/3.95p/2.25p.**
This is a result of the combined work of medium Jane Roberts and her cooperation with an out-of-body teacher named Seth. The philosophy presented is profound and yet easily understandable. It was selected as the best of a continuous presentation of material on dreams, health, reincarnation, astral projection and man's subconsious and his relation with his creator. Included are pictures of the author during her sessions and discussion of efforts to establish that Seth was indeed a separate entity and not part of Roberts' subconscious. One of the best introductions to the entire field that we know.

■ *ROBERTS, JANE.* **SETH SPEAKS. 505pp. PrH72, 7.95c/5.95p/2.50p.**
In this century there have been many presentations of ultimate truth through revelation. This we believe is the best. It was dictated by Seth in the form of a book over a period of two years and required virtually no editing. If you are just getting into this field and want to hear the case for Seth, read **Seth Material** first. If you are ready to get into the real teaching, start here. Topics include reincarnation, how thoughts form matter, the soul and the nature of its consciousness, death experiences and after death experiences, the multidimensional God, probable systems, men and gods, alternate presents and multiple focus, the meaning of religion, and much else. Highly recommended.

ROBERTS, JANE. **THE UNKNOWN REALITY: VOLUME ONE OF A SETH BOOK. Index, 296pp. PrH77, 8.95c.**
According to Seth each of us lives a series of infinitely expanded lives in which all possible choices are fully explored. Yet of all those probabilities, we normally focus on only one that we consider *real*. It is the enormous storehouse of *roads not taken* that Seth discusses in this book and that he calls the *unknown reality*. As he says, *The individual self must become aware of far more reality; it must allow its identity to expand to include previously unconscious knowledge. Your species is in a time of change—you are now poised on a threshold from which the race can go many ways. Potentials within the body's mechanisms, not as yet used, can immeasurably enrich the race and bring it to levels of spiritual, psychic, and physical fulfillment. But if some changes are not made, the race will not endure. . . . I am suggesting ways in which the unknown reality can become a known one.* Jane's husband, Robert Butts, contributes extensive notes, providing additional background on Seth's discussion of their personal lives as well as parallels and cross references to earlier works.

ROBERTS, JANE. **THE WORLD VIEW OF PAUL CEZANNE: A PSYCHIC INTERPRETATION. Index, 264pp. PrH77, 7.95c.**
Almost anyone will tell you that Paul Cezanne's thoughts died with his body, and that with the brain's crumbling, his thoughts and dreams disintegrated. But his World View, composed of his thoughts and feelings, still exists. Cezanne's thoughts are as alive as ever, his psychological picture of the world as brilliant and vivid as ever. It exists as surely in the psychological environment as his pictures do in physical reality. In a manner of speaking, this World View has been impressed on Jane Roberts mind.—from the introduction by Seth. The selections in this volume focus on creativity and on Cezanne's particular vision and practical techniques.

SOLOMON, PAUL. **EXCERPTS FROM THE PAUL SOLOMON TAPES. 149pp. Her74, 6.00c.**
Virginia Beach, last home of Edgar Cayce, seems to spawn similar types of psychic activity. Paul Solomon (not his real name) appeared on the psychic scene in 1972 and now has his own Fellowship of the Inner Light and gives readings on healings, past lives, and predictions. This book has information on Atlantis and Lemuria, diet and health, sex, healing, spiritual growth, and world prophecy. Soloman sounds a lot like Edgar Cayce in this book, including his convoluted style which makes for difficult reading. The book, **Season of Changes**, is also believed to be by Paul Solomon.

STANFORD, RAY. **CREATION. 36pp. AUM66, 2.00p.**
A study of the origins of man and his prehistory as explained through the unconscious mind of Ray Stanford.

STANFORD, RAY. **FATIMA PROPHECY. 194pp. AUM72, 7.95c.**
Apparitions of the *Mother of Jesus* have been recorded throughout history. The message of modern Marian apparitions seems to have become focused on certain urgent matters, both spiritual and humanistic. The purpose of this book is to present accurate accounts of the more impressive, recent apparitions and offer an interpretation of their message and meaning. Most of the text was given in the form of psychic readings through Stanford's unconscious mind. Includes a glossary and photographs of some of the apparitions.

STANFORD, RAY. **SPEAK, SHINING STRANGER. 252pp. AUM75, 8.95c.**
An extensive selection of readings given through Ray Stanford, one of the most noted present day mediums and the main force behind the Association for the Understanding of Man. The readings discuss healing, meditation, marriage, death, the nature and proper function of psychic communications, and much else. Stanford provides an introduction.

STANFORD, RAY. **THE SPIRIT UNTO THE CHURCHES. 8½"x11", 223pp. AUM77, 8.50p.**
Transcription of a series of readings given through Stanford, a well known psychic. *These readings deal with the physical, mental, and spiritual aspects of the human endocrine glands and their supraphysical counterparts, which yogis referred to in ancient times as "chakras" (Sanskrit for "wheels").*—from the foreword. Each of the glands is discussed in a separate chapter. This new edition includes a chapter, written by Stanford, on the application of the information given in the readings. There is also a correlation chart of the seven centers.

STEIGER, BRAD, ed. **WORDS FROM THE SOURCE. Index, 168pp. PrH75, 7.95c.**
Over the years Louis has delivered readings on a great variety of subjects while in a trance state. The readings come from an entity which calls itself the Source. Steiger has selected the most significant of this trance material and has arranged it topically. The information presented contains a wealth of insights and every conceivable area is covered at some length. The Source relates his material very clearly and he can best be compared to Seth in terms of both his information and his style.

TWITCHELL, PAUL. **ANITYA. 89pp. IWP69, 6.95c.**
Twitchell referred to himself as an *Eck Master* and described Eckankar as *the science of soul travel or the ability to lift one's consciousness to higher dimensions or planes where one may realize the divine consciousness of his soul. Eckankar means co-worker with God and supplies many answers to the deeper questions of human life and the possibility for direct experience of spiritual truth.* This book is a handwritten, illustrated compilation of Twitchell's writings, designed especially for contemplation. Topics include love, truth, God, light, sound, soul, and Eck spirit.

TWITCHELL, PAUL. **COINS OF GOLD. IWP39, 7.95c.**
A collection of mystical poems.

TWITCHELL, PAUL. **DIALOGUES WITH THE MASTER. 256pp. IWP70, 2.95p.**
A series of spiritual discourses dictated to Twitchell by Rebazar Tarzs, an ageless emissary for Eckankar. They give advanced training in the secret science of Eckankar.

TWITCHELL, PAUL. **THE DRUMS OF ECK. 220pp. IWP70, 5.95p.**
An historical novel, telling of a man's search for God, and of how he finally finds the path of Eckankar.

TWITCHELL, PAUL. **ECKANKAR: COMPILED WRITINGS, VOLUME I. 195pp. IWP75, 6.95c.**
Designed as an introductory volume and including the texts of **Introduction to Eckankar**, **All About Eck**, and **Eck and Music** along with a number of other essays.

TWITCHELL, PAUL. **ECKANKAR DICTIONARY. 160pp. IWP73, 4.95c.**
Alphabetically arranged definitions of terms used in the Eckankar books.

TWITCHELL, PAUL. **ECKANKAR: ILLUMINATED WAY LETTERS,** 1966-1971. 270pp. IWP75, 6.95c.
Discussions of many topics, written monthly by Twitchell and sent out to members and friends.

TWITCHELL, PAUL. **ECKANKAR: KEY TO SECRET WORLDS.** 254pp. IWP69, 2.00p.
The basic guide to the mastery of the ancient science of soul travel as well as the most popular Twitchell book. Step-by-step techniques. Extensive glossary of Eckankar words and terms.

TWITCHELL, PAUL. **THE ECK-VIDYA—THE ANCIENT SCIENCE OF PROPHECY. Cross references, extensive index,** 237pp. IWP72, 8.95c.
Practical instructions on the ancient method of reading the akashic records and predicting the future. Also contains information on the cycles of man, chemical affinities between people, sacred symbols and numbers.

TWITCHELL, PAUL. **THE FAR COUNTRY.** 247pp. IWP70, 5.95p.
A discourse by the Eck Master Rebazar Tarsz on how to get beyond the physical world. Includes information on overcoming materialistic attachments, gaining God realization, and finding oneself in this world.

TWITCHELL, PAUL. **THE FLUTE OF GOD.** 173pp. IWP70, 2.95p.
A summary of the essential features of Eck.

TWITCHELL, PAUL. **HERBS.** 189pp. IWP71, 1.95p.
A compendium of hundreds of herbs, giving their ancient and modern uses, their health giving and occult powers. A very complete account which relates herbs to the philosophy of Eckankar.

TWITCHELL, PAUL. **IN MY SOUL I AM FREE.** 190pp. IWP nd, 1.95p.
A biography of Twitchell by Brad Steiger. Includes material on Eck as an organization as well as a discussion of its elements and procedure.

TWITCHELL, PAUL. **LETTERS TO GAIL. About** 170pp. each, IWP73, 6.95c/each.
A two volume collection of letters Twitchell wrote to his wife prior to their marriage instructing her in the spiritual works of Eckankar and covering a great many other topics. One letter consists of a diverse collection of recommended readings.

TWITCHELL, PAUL. **THE SHARIYAT-KI-SUGMAD. Two volumes,** 400pp. IWP71, 6.95p/each.
The title of these books is translated as *The Way of the Eternal.* It is the ancient scripture of Eckankar. *Every phase of life in both matter worlds and the highest planes is discussed. One will find within these pages an answer to every question man has ever devised to ask the greater ones. All that which is Truth is here now, within these pages.*

TWITCHELL, PAUL. **THE SPIRITUAL NOTEBOOK.** 219pp. IWP71, 5.95p.
Discusses theoretical and practical doctrines of Eckankar and gives a history of the movement and its offspring.

TWITCHELL, PAUL. **STRANGER BY THE RIVER.** 175pp. IWP70, 5.95p.
A dialogue between Rebazar Tarzs and one of his *chelas* (followers). The *chela* raises questions and his master answers them and reveals *the divine light* of Eck.

TWITCHELL, PAUL. **TALONS OF TIME.** 188pp. IWP74, 2.95p.
In **Talons of Time,** *Peddar Zaskq describes an amazing journey undertaken with Sharir, the Magician of Lo. Their mission is to rescue the soul of John Skally, being held prisoner by Kal Niranjan, and to retrieve the Sacred Diary which contains the secret of Time. They travel to the land of the Time Makers, a land beyond time and space, encountering fascinating beings and adventures, until Peddar alone faces Kal himself and the Talons of Time.*

TWITCHELL, PAUL. **THE TIGER'S FANG.** 181pp. IWP67, 3.95p.
An autobiographical account of Paul Twitchell's initiation into Eckankar and his experience as an initiate.

TWITCHELL, PAUL. **THE WAY OF DHARMA.** 244pp. IWP70, 3.95p.
A novel which outlines the basics of Eckankar.

TWITCHELL, PAUL. **THE WISDOM OF ECK.** 87pp. IWP72, 2.00p.
A collection of quotations taken from Twitchell's writings and covering the basic precepts of Eckankar.

Urantia

The **Urantia Book** is a massive, anonymous, received document which details the story of the universe and galaxy, the history of Urantia (the Earth), and the life and teachings of Jesus. It is the most comprehensive account of the universe and the cosmic plan imaginable.

BEDELL, CLYDE. **CONCORDEX OF THE URANTIA BOOK.** 439pp. Bed74, 12.00c.
This volume should be immensely helpful to all those seriously studying the **Urantia Book.**

SADLER, WILLIAM. **APPENDICES TO A STUDY OF THE MASTER UNIVERSE.** 372pp. SSF75, 20.15c.
These **Appendices** expand on the information presented in Sadler's earlier work.

SADLER, WILLIAM. **A STUDY OF THE MASTER UNIVERSE.** 150pp. SSF68, 12.00c.
This is a development of some of the key concepts in the **Urantia Book** based on years of study and contemplation.

URANTIA FOUNDATION. **URANTIA.** 7½"x10¼", 2,097pp. UrB55, 26.00c.
This is the basic—and only—document on Urantia. We know some people (a few) who have read it several times and say that it contains the wisdom of the ages. If you have a lot of time for concentrated study-and good eyes!—read it and find out.

────────**END OF URANTIA SUBSECTION**────────

WHITE, RUTH and MARY SWAINSON. **GILDAS COMMUNICATES.** 222pp. Spe71, 5.60c.
Gildas is an inner guide who communicates through an English woman. This is a book of his teachings concerning the new age.

WHITE, RUTH and MARY SWAINSON. **SEVEN INNER JOURNEYS.** 216pp. Spe74, 7.85c.
This is an account of *the emergence of Gildas in Ruth White's* consciousness, including information on the training, psychological and spiritual purification that she has gone through in order to become a clearer channel.

■ *WHITE, STEWART EDWARD.* **THE BETTY BOOK.** 302pp. Dut30/ PsP, 3.50p.
This book is the record, condensed, of the excursions of Betty, a psychic intimately known to me and of absolute integrity, into the world of other-consciousness—and of communications received by her from forces which I have ventured to call the invisibles. These excursions, made in a condition of trance or otherwise, began in the year 1919 and have continued ever since. They are recorded in the following pages with no idea of adding to the existing literature of automatic writing and kindred phenomena; but in the belief that, as embodying a workable philosophy of life, they may be of aid to seekers after spiritual life.—S.E. White.

WHITE, STEWART EDWARD. **THE GAELIC MANUSCRIPTS. Spiral bound, 8½"x11", 154pp. PaP74, 11.20p.**
The material in this volume was collected by White just before his death and the manuscript was privately printed. White himself seems to have been the channel through which the material was given. The book needs editing, but the basic material is often quite enlightening and it is more sophisticated than most *received communications.* Many advanced ideas are presented and the whole work seems designed to resolve long standing questions such as man's relation to the cosmos, the meaning of conflict and of pleasure and pain, the purpose of existence, the pitfalls on the spiritual path, and much else.

■ *WHITE, STEWART EDWARD.* **THE UNOBSTRUCTED UNI-VERSE. 320pp. Dut40, 2.95p.**
The communication presented here was channeled to White by his wife Betty six months or so after her death. We feel that it presents the best report on what it is like *on the other side* that we know of. The presentation is straightforward and is not embellished. Forty actual conversations are reproduced, along with White's running commentary. This is truly a classic and we recommend it highly to all those who seek a deeper understanding of the ultimate meaning of it all. White's work was a forerunner of the material that Seth presents and those who find Seth enlightening will also appreciate Betty's teaching. Betty's transmission is especially clear since she had the experience of both receiving and transmitting communications.

WHITE EAGLE. **THE GENTLE BROTHER. 69pp. WET68, 2.25c.**
White Eagle is a member of the White Brotherhood—a group which has been transmitting from century to century the inner truths which have been revealed to man. He has been speaking through the mediumship of Grace Cooke for nearly fifty years. His presentations are always clear and to the point and his writings are very popular—especially in England—and are inspirationally-oriented. This book is a collection of short extracts to be used for daily guidance in living the spiritual life.

WHITE EAGLE. **GOLDEN HARVEST. 62pp. WET58, 2.25c.**
Guidance for the aspirant as s/he treads the spiritual path, and passes through the tests along the way.

WHITE EAGLE. **MORNING LIGHT—ON THE SPIRITUAL PATHS. 62pp. WET57, 2.25c.**
This book was one of the first that White Eagle transmitted. It sets forth the reason for life on Earth and tells how man descended from higher realms into the confined life of incarnation on Earth to obtain various experiences and to achieve, in the end, enlightenment.

WHITE EAGLE. **THE PATH OF THE SOUL. WET59, 2.75c.**
White Eagle discusses the great initiations of every soul on its journey toward perfection, as exemplified in the life of Jesus.

WHITE EAGLE. **THE QUIET MIND. 100pp. WET72, 2.25c.**
A small pocket book of White Eagle's sayings.

WHITE EAGLE. **SPIRITUAL UNFOLDMENT, I. Index, 143pp. WET61, 2.75c.**
White Eagle's practical advice and guidance on how to develop psychic and spiritual gifts, including healing.

WHITE EAGLE. **SPIRITUAL UNFOLDMENT, II. Index, 109pp. WET69, 2.75c.**
Discourses on the nature and work of man's unseen companions in the fairy and angelic kingdoms, and how man can train himself to see and cooperate with them.

WHITE EAGLE. **SUNRISE. 62pp. WET58, 2.25c.**
White Eagle discourses on how man, while on Earth, can build a bridge between the two worlds so that death cannot separate him from those he loves.

WHITE EAGLE. **WISDOM FROM WHITE EAGLE. Index, 99pp. WET67, 2.75c.**
A collection of talks to students, with practical advice on spiritual matters, meditation, and life in the world today.

ROSICRUCIANISM

The student of the history of occultism and the esoteric teachings, and even the average reader of current books and magazines, finds many references to *The Rosicrucians*, a supposed ancient secret society devoted to the study of occult doctrines and the manifestation of occult powers. But when such a person seeks to obtain detailed information concerning this supposed ancient *order* he finds himself baffled and defeated. Before acknowledging the futility of the quest, however, he usually investigates one or more so-called *orders* having as a part of their title the word *Rosicrucian*, only to find himself invited to join such *order* upon the payment of a fee or fees ranging from a small amount in some cases to quite large amounts in others, each *order* claiming to be the *only original order*, and asserting that all the others are base imitators.

The truth is that there is not in existence, and never has been in existence, any popular occult order sanctioned by the real Rosicrucians, which anyone may join upon payment of fees, large or small, just as he may join any of the better known fraternal organizations of which there are so many. The true Rosicrucians have no formal organization, and are held together only by the ties of common interest in the occult and esoteric studies, and by the common acceptance of certain fundamental principles of belief and knowledge. This unorganized *order* has members in all walks of life, and in all countries, and its members never announce themselves as *Rosicrucians* to the general public. Admission to this unorganized *order* is never granted upon the payment of a fee, and is possible only upon the request and recommendation of three members in good standing who have themselves been members for a certain period of time, and who have attained a certain degree of proficiency in the attainment of the esoteric knowledge, and in demonstrating the principles discovered by them under the direction of certain higher adepts in the arcane wisdom.

The modern interest in the Rosicrucian Teachings dates back to the early part of the seventeenth century. At that time there were rumors of the existence of a society known as *The Brothers of the Rosy Cross*, the officers and meeting places of which were not known to the public. The mysterious society was severely attacked by the ecclesiastical authorities and others, and was as vigorously defended by those who were interested in the general subject of occultism and the esoteric teachings. There were many spurious and counterfeit *orders* established during the following century, and for that matter in nearly every century since, but none have been able to show an undoubted connection with the original order.

The legend concerning the origin of the order—true in some respects, but erroneous in others—was as follows: That a certain Christian Rosenkreutz, a German nobleman who had donned the robes of a certain order of monks, had visited India, Persia, and also Arabia, and had returned bringing with him a certain Secret Doctrine obtained from the sages and seers of those Oriental lands. He was said to have established the original Rosicrucian Brotherhood about 1425, its existence not becoming generally known until nearly two hundred years afterward. The true Rosicrucians, however, recognize this legendary tale as being merely a cleverly disguised recital of the real facts of the establishment of the unorganized order, which must be read between the lines, aided by the spectacles of understanding, in order that its real import may be grasped.

What is known as *The Secret Doctrine of the Rosicrucians* is an extensive body of esoteric teaching and occult lore which has been transmitted from Master to Student, from Hierophant to the new Initiate, for countless generations. Seldom has any part of the Secret Doctrine been committed to writing, or exposed to public view on the printed page, until the present generation. Previous to that time the little that was written, or printed, concerning this body of teachings was disguised in the vague terms of alchemy and astrology, so that the same would have one meaning to the average reader and another and closer meaning to those who possessed the key to the mystery.

The Secret Doctrine of the Rosicrucians is believed by those best informed to have been built up gradually, carefully, and slowly, by the old occult masters and adepts, from the scattered fragments of the esoteric teachings which were treasured by the wise men of all races. The legend runs that these fragments of the Secret Doctrine were the scattered portions of the old esoteric teaching of ancient Atlantis—the bits of the great mass of the Atlantean occult teachings which were scattered in all directions by the great cataclysm which had destroyed that great continent. The few survivors of the Atlantean civilization carefully preserved these Fragments of Truth, and passed them on to their chosen students and capable descendants.

The old Masters who made it the object of their lives to gather together once more these scattered fragments, and to thus reconstruct the Occult Doctrine of the Atlanteans, found a portion of their material in Egypt, in India, in Persia, in Chaldea, in Medea, in China, in Assyria, and in Ancient Greece, and also in the mystic records of the Hebrews, such as the Kaballah and the **Zohar**. The common source, however, may be regarded as distinctly Oriental. The great philosophies of the East, in fact, may be said to have been built upon the base of these still more ancient teachings. Moreover, the great Grecian Secret Teachings are believed to have been based upon knowledge obtained from this same common source. So, at the last, the Secret Doctrine of the Rosicrucians may be said to be the Secret Doctrine of Atlantis, transmitted through the descendants of the people of that great centre of occult knowledge.

—*condensed from* **The Secret Doctrine of the Rosicrucians,** *by Magnus Incognito*

ALLEN, PAUL. **A CHRISTIAN ROSENKREUTZ ANTHOLOGY.** 45.35c.
See the Alchemy section.

BULWER-LYTTON, EDWARD. **ZANOI: A ROSICRUCIAN TALE.** 410pp. Mul71, 6.95p.
A well researched, fictional account of Rosicrucians during the days of the French Revolution. The novel is in seven parts, giving an indication of a sevenfold path of spiritual development lying behind the story. The book, originally published in 1842, has been consistently popular.

COOPER-OAKLEY, ISABEL. **THE COUNT OF SAINT-GERMAIN.** Good bibliography, 248pp. Mul70, 2.50p.
This is regarded as perhaps the most important sourcebook on the life and work of the Comte. The author traveled widely in search of the original material presented here. Personal diaries and private records as well as the so-called Mitchell papers are among the previously untapped sources. Cooper-Oakley provides deep insight into the

history of eighteenth century masonry, the work of the Rosicrucians and alchemists, and the life and work of Christian Rosenkreutz.

■ HALL, MANLY P. **CODEX ROSAE CRUCIS.** 10"x14", 113pp. **PRS38, 20.00c.**
After reading the recent histories of the Order, I feel that Rosicrucianism needs a restatement. As no other apologist has appeared, I have ventured this present treatise to clarify the subject from the injustices heaped upon it by friends, foes, and impartial historians. This is the definitive work, very extensively illustrated with color and black and white reproductions of old plates. Half the book is devoted to an exact reproduction of the D.O.M.A. manuscript, with a complete English translation and a chapter on Hall's opinions concerning the symbols. A magnificent, illuminating work, highly recommended.

HALL, MANLY P. **THE MOST HOLY TRINOSOPHIA OF THE COMTE DE ST. GERMAIN.** Commentaries, notes, 220pp. PRS62, **12.50c.**
St. Germain prepared this work for the instruction of his own disciples in the Qabalistic, Hermetic, and alchemical mysteries. This unique work is now for the first time translated and published from the original manuscript. The great Illuminist, Rosicrucian, and Freemason who termed himself the Comte de St. Germain is without question one of the most baffling personalities of modern history. His activities are traceable for the more than 100 years between 1710-1822. When once asked about himself, he replied that his father was the Secret Doctrine, and his mother the Mysteries. Includes a photostatic facsimile of the original manuscript.

HEINDEL, MAX. **ANCIENT AND MODERN INITIATION.** 148pp. **Ros31, 3.00p.**
Heindel was the founder of the Rosicrucian Fellowship, headquartered at Mount Ecclesia, Oceanside, California. There is a dispute between this fellowship and AMORC over who the true Rosicrucians are. Heindel said that he was *an authorized messenger of the Elder Brothers of the Rose Cross, who are working to disseminate throughout the Western world the deeper Spiritual meanings which are both concealed and revealed within the Christian religion.* This book contains a discussion of the general plan of initiation for humanity as outlined in the mystery teachings of all ages.

HEINDEL, MAX. **ETHERIC VISION AND WHAT IT REVEALS.** 110pp. Ros65, 1.50p.
The material in this booklet is a reprint (with some revisions and additions) of monthly lessons sent out by The Rosicrucian Fellowship to its members, and is a summary of studies and researches conducted by students in the Esoteric Section of the Fellowship. It presents material that elsewhere is available only in Besant's and Leadbeater's **Occult Chemistry** and includes material on the chemical ether, the life ether, the light ether, and the reflecting ether. The presentation is extremely clear and the material is very helpful for the student seeking a full picture of the cosmos.

HEINDEL, MAX. **FREEMASONRY AND CATHOLICISM.** 110pp. **Ros19, 2.50p.**
Subtitled, *An exposition of the cosmic facts underlying these two great institutions as determined by occult investigation.*

HEINDEL, MAX. **GLEANINGS OF A MYSTIC.** 196pp. Ros22, 4.00p.
An aggregate of writings on the mystical path by one who made practical in his life the basic precepts of spiritual living. Includes helpful information and suggestions concerning marriage, the coming Christ, and the new age.

HEINDEL, MAX. **MYSTERIES OF THE GREAT OPERAS.** 3.50p.
See the Music section.

HEINDEL, MAX. **NATURE SPIRITS AND NATURE FORCES.** 43pp. **Ros37, 1.00p.**
This is a correlation of material from many of Heindel's books.

HEINDEL, MAX. **OCCULT PRINCIPLES OF HEALTH AND HEALING.** 248pp. Ros38, 4.50p.
A treasury of material concerning the health and healing of the human organism as considered from the occult point of view. Discusses specific ailments as well as the origin, functions, and proper care of the physical vehicle.

The temple of the Rosy Cross, a symbolical figure designed by Theophilus Schweighardt Constantiens in the seventeenth century.

HEINDEL, MAX. **THE ROSICRUCIAN CHRISTIANITY LECTURES.** 374pp. Ros39, 4.50p.
The lectures presented here were first delivered by Heindel during November of 1908. They represent the direct teaching of the Elder brothers of the Rosicrucian order which he received in 1907-08. Topics include: *The Riddle of Life and Death, Spiritual Sight and Spiritual Worlds, Sleep, Dreams, Trance, Life and Activity in Heaven, Astrology, The Angels as Factors in Heaven, The Mystery of the Holy Grail,* and much else of interest to seekers on the path.

■ HEINDEL, MAX. **THE ROSICRUCIAN COSMO-CONCEPTION.** 702pp. Ros09, 6.00c/4.00p.
Heindel's most important work, giving a complete outline of the Western wisdom teachings. It contains a comprehensive outline of the evolutionary processes of man and the universe, correlating science with religion. Part I is a treatise on the visible and invisible world, and the method of evolution, rebirth, and the law of cause and effect. Part II takes up the scheme of evolution in general and the evolution of the solar system and the Earth in particular. Part III discusses Christ and his mission, future development of man, initiations, and esoteric training. The paperback edition contains only a topical index; the cloth one has an alphabetical index also.

HEINDEL, MAX. **THE ROSICRUCIAN MYSTERIES.** 155pp. Ros11, 3.50p.
A survey of some of the Rosicrucian doctrines and conceptions concerning the nature of man and his relationship to the universe. Discusses some of life's problems with their solutions and gives a view of life and death.

HEINDEL, MAX. **THE ROSICRUCIAN PHILOSOPHY IN QUESTIONS AND ANSWERS.** Fully indexed, 1,107pp. Ros47, 7.00p/each.
The questions contained in these two volumes were answered by Heindel in his magazine, **Rays from the Rose Cross,** 1913-19. The answers are often quite detailed and sometimes include illustrations.

HEINDEL, MAX. **TEACHINGS OF AN INITIATE.** 203pp. Ros27, 4.00p.
Touches upon a wide variety of subjects, including the World War in the light of spiritual misunderstanding, the esoteric significance of Easter, and the scientific method of spiritual unfoldment.

LEWIS, H. SPENCER. **ESSAYS OF A MODERN MYSTIC. Amo, nd, 7.55c.**
Lewis was the founder of AMORC (The Ancient Mystical Order of Rosicrucians) in San Jose, California, the most popular of the contemporary Rosicrucian groups. AMORC advertises widely and has an extensive following. Lewis' books are extremely practical and are also easy to read. This volume contains a collection of essays on integrating spiritual practices into daily life.

LEWIS, H. SPENCER. **MENTAL POISONING. 104pp. Amo37, 6.65c.**
Lewis discusses black magic, the psychology of mental reactions, the processes of the human mind, and methods of administering mental poisons.

LEWIS, H. SPENCER. **ROSICRUCIAN PRINCIPLES FOR THE HOME AND BUSINESS. 256pp. Amo29, 6.45c.**
Outlines the principles of practical Rosicrucianism which are applicable to the solution of everyday problems.

LEWIS, H. SPENCER. **ROSICRUCIAN QUESTIONS AND ANSWERS. 329pp. Amo29, 6.45c.**
Based on the teachings of AMORC, the questions cover a broad gamut of philosophical inquiry. Also included is a history of the Rosicrucian order.

LEWIS, H. SPENCER. **SELF MASTERY AND FATE WITH THE CYCLES OF LIFE. Index, 253pp. Amo29, 6.45c.**
Through his extensive experience in the business world and as a leader of the Rosicrucian movement, Lewis developed a system which he says brings *to any business man or woman the necessary "key" for the understanding of the peculiar fluctuations, changes and unexpected occurrences that arise in all personal and business affairs, and bring problems, trials, and tribulations of grave concern.* He begins with introductory chapters explaining the system and follows with details on the various cycles and conditions which affect our personal and business affairs, our health, and our hopes and ambitions.

An unusual, clearly written account, illuminated with many case histories and practical examples.

LEWIS, H. SPENCER. **A THOUSAND YEARS OF YESTERDAYS. 75pp. Amo20, 6.65c.**
An explanation of the manner in which a soul undergoes the process of reincarnation, written in story form with the mystic principles woven into the content.

MAGNUS INCOGNITO. **THE SECRET DOCTRINE OF THE ROSICRUCIANS. 256pp. YPS nd, 6.00c.**
A very comprehensive account of the beliefs of the Rosicrucians, including information on *The Soul of the World, The Universal Androgyne, The Planes of Consciousness, The Sevenfold Soul of Man, The Soul's Progress, The Aura and Auric Principles,* and *The Seven Cosmic Principles.*

■ *WAITE, A.E.* **THE BROTHERHOOD OF THE ROSY CROSS. Notes, index, 654pp. UnB73, 10.00c.**
Waite was not a member of this order, but in his philosophy he identified himself closely with the ancient beliefs espoused by the Rosicrucians. This is a very complete account of the origins of Rosicrucianism, its original doctrines and their unfolding and changing, its relationship to Freemasonry, and much else. Includes biographical material on the most noted Rosicrucians, including a full chapter on Robert Fludd. This text includes extensive source and explanatory notes. A massive effort. Waite tends to be a bit ponderous at times since he includes all the research he can garner—but is generally well respected.

■ *WAITE, A.E.* **THE REAL HISTORY OF THE ROSICRUCIANS. 311pp. Mul1887, 7.95p.**
Another of Waiter's in depth studies. In addition to the strictly historical and interpretative material Waite provides individual chapters on some of the most important Rosicrucian figures and translations of some important documents.

SACRED ART

When historians of art apply the term *sacred art* to any and every work that has a religious subject, they are forgetting that art is essentially form. An art cannot properly be called *sacred* solely on the grounds that its subjects originate in a spiritual truth; its format language also must bear witness to a similar origin. Such is by no means the case with a religious art like that of the Renaissance or of the Baroque period, which is in no way distinct, so far as style is concerned, from the fundamentally profane art of the era; neither the subjects which it borrows, in a wholly exterior and as it were literary manner, from religions, nor the devotional feelings with which it is permeated in appropriate cases, nor even the nobility of soul which sometimes finds expression in it, suffice to confer on it a sacred character. No art merits that epithet unless the forms themselves reflect the spiritual vision characteristic of a particular religion.

Every form is the vehicle of a given quality of being. The religious subject of a work of art may be as it were superimposed, it may have no relation to the formal *language* of the work, as is demonstrated by Christian art since the Renaissance; there are therefore essentially profane works of art with a sacred theme, but on the other hand there exists no sacred work of art which is profane in form, for there is a rigorous analogy between form and spirit. A spiritual vision necessarily finds its expression in a particular formal language; if that language is lacking, with the result that a so-called sacred art borrows its forms from some kind of profane art, then it can only be because a spiritual vision of things is also lacking.

Every sacred art is founded on a science of forms, or in other words, on the symbolism inherent in forms. It must be borne in mind that a symbol is not merely a conventional sign. It manifests its archetype by virtue of a definite ontological law; as Coomaraswamy has observed, a symbol *is* in a certain sense that to which it gives expression. For this very reason traditional symbolism is never without beauty: according to the spiritual view of the world, the beauty of an object is nothing but the transparency of its existential envelopes; an art worthy of the name is beautiful because it is true.

It is neither possible nor even useful that every artist or craftsman engaged in sacred art should be conscious of the Divine Law inherent in forms; he will know only certain aspects of it, or certain applications that arise within the limits of the rules of his craft; these rules will enable him to paint an icon, to fashion a sacred vessel or to practise calligraphy in a liturgically valid manner, without its being necessary for him to know the ultimate significance of the symbols he is working with. It is tradition that transmits the sacred models and the working rules, and thereby guarantees the spiritual validity of the forms. Tradition has within itself a secret force which is communicated to an entire civilization and determines even arts and crafts the immediate objects of which include nothing particularly sacred. This force creates the style of a traditional civilization; a style that could never be imitated from outside is perpetuated without difficulty, in a quasi-organic manner, by the power of the spirit that animates it and by nothing else.

In no traditional doctrine does the idea of the Divine Art play so fundamental a part as in the Hindu doctrine. For *Maya* is not only the mysterious Divine Power which causes the world to appear to exist outside the Divine Reality, so that it is from her, from *Maya*, that all duality and all illusion spring: she is also in her positive aspect the Divine Art which produces all form. In principle she is not other than the possibility contained in the Infinite of limiting Itself, as the object of Its own *vision*, without Its infinity being thereby limited. Thus God manifests Himself in the world, yet equally He does not so manifest Himself; He expresses Himself and at the same time keeps silence.

From the Christian point of view God is similarly *artist* in the most exalted sense of the word, because He created man *in His own image*. In Christianity the divine image *par excellence* is the human form of the Christ; thus it comes about that Christian art has but one purpose: the transfiguration of man, and of the world which depends on man, by their participation in the Christ.

That which the Christian view of things grasps by means of a sort of loving concentration on the Word incarnate in Jesus Christ, is transposed in the Islamic view into the universal and the impersonal. In Islam the Divine Art—and according to the Koran God is *artist (musawwir)*—is in the first place the manifestation of the Divine Unity in the beauty and regularity of the cosmos. Unity is reflected in the harmony of the multiple, in order and in equilibrium; beauty has all these aspects within itself. To start from the beauty of the world and arrive at Unity—that is wisdom. For this reason Islamic thought necessarily attaches art to wisdom, or on science, the function of science being the formulation of wisdom in temporal terms. The purpose of art is to enable the human environment, the world in so far as it is moulded by man, to participate in the order that manifests most directly the Divine Unity. Art clarifies the world; it helps the spirit to detach itself from the disturbing multitude of things so that it may climb again towards the Infinite Unity.

According to the Taoist view of things the Divine Art is essentially the art of transformation: the whole of nature is ceaselessly being transformed, always in accordance with the laws of the cycle; its contrasts revolve round a single centre which always eludes apprehension. Nevertheless anyone who understands this circular movement is thereby enabled to recognize the centre which is its essence. The purpose of art is to conform to this cosmic rhythm. The most simple formula states that mastery in art consists in the capacity to trace a perfect circle in a single movement, and thus to identify oneself implicitly with its centre, while that centre remains unspecified as such.

In so far as it is possible to transpose the notion of *Divine Art* into Buddhism, which avoids all personification of the Absolute, it can be applied to the beauty of the Buddha, miraculous and mentally unfathomable as it is. Whereas no doctrine concerned with God can escape, as far as its formulation is concerned, from the illusory character of mental processes, which attribute their own limits to the limitless and their own conjectural forms to the formless, the beauty of the Buddha radiates a state of being beyond the power of thought to define. This beauty is reflected in the beauty of the lotus: it is perpetuated ritually in the painted or modelled image of the Buddha.

In one way or another all these fundamental aspects of

sacred art can be found, in varying proportions, in each of the five great traditions just mentioned, for there is not one of them that does not possess in its essentials all the fullness of Divine Truth and Grace, so that in principle it would be capable of manifesting every possible form of spirituality. Nevertheless, since each religion is necessarily dominated by a particular point of view which determines its spiritual *economy*, its artistic manifestations, being naturally collective and not isolated, will reflect this point of view and this economy each in its own style. It is moreover in the nature of form to be unable to express anything without excluding something, because form delimits what it expresses, excluding thereby some aspects of its own universal archetype. This law is naturally applicable at every level of formal manifestation, and not to art alone; the various Divine Revelations on which the different religions are founded are also mutually exclusive when attention is directed to their formal contours only, rather than to their Divine Essence which is one. Here, again the analogy between *Divine Art* and human art becomes apparent.

—condensed from **Sacred Art In East and West**, *by Titus Burckhardt*

AKIYAMA, TERUKAZU *and* SABURO MATSUBARA. **ARTS OF CHINA: BUDDHIST CAVE TEMPLES, NEW RESEARCHES. 35.00c.**
See the Buddhism section.

ALEXANDER, J.J.G. **ITALIAN RENAISSANCE ILLUMINATIONS. 8½"x11", 119pp. Brz77, 9.95p.**
The intellectual, moral, spiritual, and artistic rebirth of Europe, the revival of ancient classical influences, the rise of a new impulse in culture, in literature, and art, arose in Italy during the early part of the fifteenth century, and there was a transformation in book illumination. The unreal creatures of the Middle Ages became men and women of flesh and blood; the modeling of flesh became three dimensional; the medieval censorship of nakedness was discarded. This volume includes forty representative plates, in full color and glowing with gold, selected from the major manuscripts of the Renaissance. Professor Alexander also contributes an introduction and commentaries on the individual folios.

ANDREAE, BERNARD. **THE ART OF ROME. Bibliography, index, 900 illustrations, 159 in color, boxed, 10"x12¼, 656pp. Abr78, 85.00c.**
A magnificent and comprehensive work on Roman art and architecture, bringing together all recent scholarship in the field.

ARANO, LUISA. **THE MEDIEVAL HEALTH HANDBOOK. Oversize, 156pp. Brz76, 20.00c.**
The illuminated manuscripts known as **Tacuinum Sanitatis** were medieval handbooks of the late 1300's and early 1400's which illustrated and explained the effects of foods, flowers, winds, waters, seasons, and even human emotions upon a person's health. This boxed book contains reproductions from five of the most important **Tucuina**, along with a descriptive text. 291 plates, forty-eight in color.

ARGUELLES, JOSE *and* MIRIAM. **MANDALA. 10¾"x8¼", 140pp. ShP72, 7.95p.**
The mandala as a symbol of the wholeness of the total experience of reality is a basic form—an expression of many of man's highest ideals. It has appeared throughout man's history, serving as a universal and essential symbol of integration, harmony, and transformation. This profusely illustrated, beautiful volume presents the philosophical,

religious, psychological, and artistic basis of the mandala. Extensive bibliography.

ARNOLD, THOMAS. **PAINTING IN ISLAM. Illustrations, index, 7"x9¼", 159pp. Dov28, 4.00p.**
Unlike Christianity and Buddhism, which have traditionally exalted the pictorial arts, Muslim orthodoxy has been hostile to the painter and his handiwork. Representation of the human figure and of other living things is deemed imitative of the creative activity of God, and is thus condemned by sacred law. Nevertheless, since the time of the earliest caliphs, painters have practiced their art—though usually within palace confines. This volume puts Islamic painting in its social and religious context and examines its relation to Islamic civilization in general.

ARYAN, K.C. *and* SUBHASHINI. **HANUMAN IN ART AND MYTHOLOGY. 60.00c.**
See the Indian Philosophy section.

ASHTON, ROBERT *and* JOZEFA STUART. **IMAGES OF AMERICAN INDIAN ART. 6.95p.**
See the American Indian Religion section.

ATIL, ESIN. **ART OF THE ARAB WORLD. 20.15p.**
See the Islam section.

AUBERT, MARCEL. **THE ART OF THE HIGH GOTHIC ERA. Chronology, bibliography, index, 227pp. Crn65, 6.95c.**
The soaring lines of the great Gothic cathedrals bear living witness to the piety of the Middle Ages. This book traces the Gothic style between 1220 and 1350. All the major cathedrals are discussed in terms of the architecture, sculpture, and paintings. The text is illustrated with fifty-five colored plates, twenty-four black and white illustrations, and sixty-five drawings. The reproductions are excellent and each plate is fully commented on.

AVRIL, FRANCOIS. **MANUSCRIPT PAINTING AT THE COURT OF FRANCE, THE FOURTEENTH CENTURY (1310-1380). Introduction, 8"x11", 119pp. Brz78, 9.95p.**
Fourteenth century French illuminated manuscripts have been characterized as being striking examples of varied fluid styles, expressive of narrative and enhanced by light and delicate modeling. Incidental drolleries often show a direct and tender observation of the natural characteristics of birds, beasts, insects, and flowers. In a number of the major manuscripts we find an intriguing new feature: the figures are no longer painted in full color, as is the rest of the miniature, but are portrayed in pale, semilucent monochrome or *grisaille*. Avril, of the Bibliotheque Nationale in Paris, has selected forty of the finest examples and he includes a description of each one.

AWAKAWA, YASUICHI. **ZEN PAINTING. 11.95p.**
See the Zen Buddhism section.

AYMES, CLEMENT. **THE PICTORIAL LANGUAGE OF HIERONYMUS BOSCH. Bibliography, index, 9½"x12½", 124pp. NKB75, 13.50c.**
In recent years there has been a willingness to recognize in the paintings of Bosch a spiritual content and message rather than a mere phantasmagoria of sexual and satanic ideas. This volume, written by an Anthroposophist, reveals the secrets of Rosicrucian philosophy and spiritual teachings hidden in Bosch's mysterious works. Reproductions (in color and black and white) of Bosch's major and minor works are included, with detailed commentary; his most noted works are broken down and their various parts analyzed. A fascinating study.

BAIN, GEORGE. **CELTIC ART. 9"x12", 159pp. Dov51, 4.00p.**
The construction principles of Celtic art were rediscovered in the middle of this century by Bain. Until then the intricate knots, interlacements, and spirals used in illuminating Celtic literature and decorating craftwork and jewelry seemed almost impossible. In this pioneering work he shows how simple principles, no more difficult than those in needlepoint, were used to create some of the finest artistic works ever seen. Step-by-step procedures carefully introduce the rules and method of Celtic knot work and the well known designs from the great manuscripts and stone work. Altogether over 225 different patterns are presented, with modification suggestions, 110

artifacts, and a great number of letters. Explanatory material accompanies the illustrations.

BAYLEY, HAROLD. THE LOST LANGUAGE OF SYMBOLISM. 411pp. BnL12, 18.50c.
Bayley surveys the results of his lifetime study of the origin of letters, words, names, fairy tales, folklore, and mythologies. The information the author presents is not in a readily accessible format, unfortunately, but the approach is unusual and reflects the inner meaning of the symbols. The book includes 1418 line drawings and is fully indexed. Esoteric information is emphasized.

BEUNINGEN, CHARLES VAN. THE COMPLETE DRAWINGS OF HIERONYMOUS BOSCH. Introduction, sixty-four plates, including four color pages, 8½"x11½", SMP73/Acd, 6.95p.

BINYON, LAURENCE, J.V.S. WILKINSON and BASIL GRAY. PERSIAN MINIATURE PAINTING. Introduction, nine color plates, appendices, bibliography, indices, 226pp. Dov33, 6.00p.
Three experts examine and discuss the collection of Persian miniatures assembled for the Exhibition of Persian Art in London in 1931. 225 of the pictures are reproduced here, together with background information, descriptions, analyses, and evaluations, not only of the paintings shown but of Persian art as a whole. All periods and schools are represented. This is both a definitive treatise and a magnificent introduction to the subject.

BLAKE, WILLIAM.
See the Blake subsection of Mysticism for descriptions of books on Blake's art.

BOISSELIER, JEAN, et al. THE HERITAGE OF THAI SCULPTURE. 60.00c.
See the South and Southeast Asia section.

BORD, JANET. MAZES AND LABYRINTHS OF THE WORLD. Bibliography, index, 8"x10", 181pp. Dut75, 6.95p.
Ms. Bord's reseaches have uncovered an astonishing variety of mazes and labyrinths. In this volume she surveys their many forms throughout history and from thirty-five different countries. The 268 illustrations are all commented upon.

The Virgin of Vladimir.

BOURGOIN, J. ARABIC GEOMETRICAL PATTERN AND DESIGN. 8"x10¾", 211pp. Dov1879, 4.50p.
By forbidding the representation of the human figure the Muslim religion pushed Islamic art along a path much different than that of traditional European art. Islam translates artistic impulse into elaborate geometric patterns and linear designs which became perfected over the centuries. This book contains 190 examples which exhibit the wide range of this geometrical art.

BROOKS, ROBERT and VISHNU WAKANKAR. STONE AGE PAINTING IN INDIA. 20.15c.
See the Indian Philosophy section.

BURCKHARDT, TITUS. ART OF ISLAM: LANGUAGE AND MEANING. 25.00c.
See the Islam section.

BURCKHARDT, TITUS. SACRED ART, EAST AND WEST. Profusely illustrated, 160pp. Prn67, 7.15p.
A work of wide scope, covering Hindu, Christian, Islamic, Buddhist and Far Eastern art—conveying the distinctive characteristic of each, while at the same time emphasizing their unity of principle. Every sacred art is deeply rooted in the religion in which it originates, and plays an indispensible part in preserving the character and continuity of the sacred civilization connected with that religion.

CADET, J.M. THE RAMAKIEN: THE STONE RUBBINGS OF THE THAI EPIC. 29.50c.
See the South and Southeast Asia section.

CARROLL, DAVID. THE TAJ MAHAL. Notes, bibliography, index, 9"x11½", Nsw72, 11.95c.
The Taj Mahal is the artistic jewel of the Mogul Empire in India. It stands today as an exquisitely wrought memorial both to the love match that gave it life and the artisans who entirely covered with inlaid designs executed in some thirty-five varieties of semiprecious stone; its portals are framed by intricate calligraphic inscriptions; and its formal gardens are a triumph of the landscape architect's craft. About 120 illustrations, nearly half in color, supplement this history of the Mogul Dynasty.

CAVENDISH, RICHARD. VISIONS OF HEAVEN AND HELL. Notes, bibliography, index, 9¾"x12½", 128pp. Crn77, 6.95p.
This is a pictorial presentation of the way various cultures view heaven and hell. The book is divided into the following sections: *life after death, paradise and heaven, the perfect existence, the underworld,* and *the abyss of hell.* Over fifty full page color plates and many black and white ones illuminate the text.

CHELKOWSKI, PETER. MIRROR OF THE INVISIBLE WORLD: TALES FROM KHAMSEH OF NIZAMI. 15.00c.
See the Islam section.

CIRLOT, J.E. A DICTIONARY OF SYMBOLS. Index, 454pp. PhL71/RKP, 20.15c.
This is considered the definitive work on symbology. It is an invaluable tool for all who seek to understand esoteric literature, especially graphically represented traditions such as alchemy and the tarot. The dictionary is also illuminating in dream analysis. It is arranged alphabetically by subject and the individual analyses are often in depth essays on the topic, complete with relevant quotations and cross references. Many illustrations are also included. The individual entries range from esoteric topics such as the chakras and the elements to mythological characters and themes. An excellent tool for all students and readers.

COHEN, JOAN. ANGKOR: MONUMENTS OF THE GOD-KINGS. 45.00c.
See the South and Southeast Asia section.

COOK, ROGER. TREE OF LIFE. 8"x11", 128pp. T&H74, 5.95p.
The Tree of Life, appearing in an infinite variety of forms in the symbolism of the great world religions, mythology, and folklore, is a universal symbol for the inner directions of the cosmic process and its goal: the unity of mankind and the world. Revealing the living presence of a transcendent power which mankind has traditionally both feared

and adored, *the Tree embodies in its seasonal transformations the perpetual renewal of the cosmos from a sacred source at the center-of-the-world.* The Tree of Life appears as a perennial focus of man's inner world in both the Judeo-Christian and Islamic traditions. This book traces the Tree throughout these traditions with 165 illustrations, thirty-one in full color and all descriptively analyzed, and excellent introductory material.

COOMARASWAMY, ANANDA. **THE ARTS AND CRAFTS OF INDIA AND CEYLON. Index, 272pp. FSG13, 2.95p.**
The life of Ananda Coomaraswamy was dedicated to interpreting the East to the West. In this book he surveys two thousand years of creation in the Indian subcontinent and shows that the arts and crafts reflect many different ways of life and complex ways of vision. 225 illustrations are included and Hindu, Buddhist, and Mongol art are all discussed.

COOMARASWAMY, ANANDA. **CHRISTIAN AND ORIENTAL PHILOSOPHY OF ART. Bibliography, 146pp. Dov43, 2.25p.**
A collection of nine essays covering a variety of themes. The book was originally entitled **Why Exhibit Works of Art?**

COOMARASWAMY, ANANDA. **LE CORPS PARSEME D'YEUS. 11¼"x15", ARM77, 75.00c.**
A folio volume, beautifully printed on fine paper and boxed, presenting a number of color examples of how the image of *the body studded with eyes* has been interpreted down the ages and throughout the world. Ananda Coomaraswamy provides an introduction and commentaries on the plates.

COOMARASWAMY, ANANDA. **HISTORY OF INDIAN AND INDONSIAN ART. 6.00p.**
See the South and Southeast Asia section.

COOMARASWAMY, ANANDA. **ON THE TRADITIONAL DOCTRINE OF ART. Notes, 24pp. Gol77, 7.10p.**
A beautifully produced essay, containing material not available elsewhere.

COOMARASWAMY, ANANDA. **THE ORIGIN OF THE BUDDHA IMAGE. 8½"x11", 42pp. MuM72, 19.15c.**
A detailed analysis which shows that the Buddha image originated out of pre-existing Indian forms. The text is extensively annotated and is illustrated with seventy-three different images of the Buddha.

COOMARASWAMY, ANANDA. **THE TRANSFORMATION OF NATURE IN ART. Glossaries, notes, bibliography, 255pp. Dov34, 3.75p.**
A deeply philosophical work on Asiatic art principles. Coomaraswamy begins with an examination of Indian and Chinese treatises on aesthetic theory and art manuals. He follows this with a review of the medieval European aesthetic in terms of the fourteenth century mystic Meister Eckhart. Further chapters investigate, through Indian texts, the psychology of the Indian viewer of art as well as the origin and use of images in India.

CRAVEN, ROY. **A CONCISE HISTORY OF INDIAN ART. 6.95p.**
See the Indian Philosophy section.

CRITCHLOW, KEITH. **ISLAMIC PATTERNS. 9.95p.**
See the Islam section.

DONADONI, SERGIO. **EGYPTIAN MUSEUM, CAIRO. 9.95p.**
See the Ancient Egypt section.

EMILLLE MUSEUM. **DIAMOND MOUNTAIN. 10.00p/each.**
See the Buddhism section.

EMILLLE MUSEUM. **THE SPIRIT OF THE KOREAN TIGER. 10½"x 14", 28pp. Eml72, 4.25p.**
A lovely collection of traditional Korean paintings in which tigers are a central figure. The paintings are bold in technique and colorful and the accompanying text contains a good explanation of the art.

EMILLLE MUSEUM and THE ROYAL ASIATIC SOCIETY. **THE LIFE OF BUDDHA IN KOREAN PAINTINGS. 6.00p.**
See the Buddhism section.

ENCISO, JORGE. **DESIGN MOTIFS OF ANCIENT MEXICO. 166pp. Dov47, 2.50p.**
A collection of 766 vigorous designs, divided into the following sections: geometric motifs, natural forms and flora, the human body, and artificial forms. Very clear, black reproductions.

ENCISO, JORGE. **DESIGNS FROM PRE-COLUMBIAN MEXICO. 116pp. Dov71, 2.00p.**
A sourcebook of 300 clearly reproduced designs, each of which was found on a small round clay object. Each of the plates is captioned.

ETTINGHAUSEN, RICHARD. **ARAB PAINTING. Bibliography, indices, 9½"x11", 209pp. Riz77, 12.50p.**
It is generally assumed that the Islamic religion totally prohibited the representation of the human figure. This is generally true, although, as this book illustrates, figural painting did exist in the Arab world. The eighty-one color plates in this volume have been reproduced from illuminated manuscripts and monuments. The book is part of a series created by Albert Sirka and both the quality of the reproductions and the accompanying text are uniformly excellent.

FEDER, NORMAN. **AMERICAN INDIAN ART. 35.00c.**
See the American Indian Religion section.

FENOLLOSA, ERNEST. **EPOCHS OF CHINESE AND JAPANESE ART. 174 full page plates, 665pp. Dov13, 4.00p/each.**
Professor Fenollosa was the founder of the modern study of Chinese and Japanese art. This two volume set is his most important work and it remains one of the best surveys of the political, philosophical, and social backgrounds of Far Eastern art available. The information is chronologically presented, though it necessarily skips around between the two cultures.

FOKKER, NICOLAS. **ORIENTAL CARPETS FOR TODAY. Index, 7¼"x10¾", 135pp. Dou73, 4.95c.**
An encyclopedic introduction to Oriental carpets, illustrated with sixty full page color plates of all the major types of carpets. Each of the carpets pictured is discussed individually and there is also some general information.

FUKUYAMA, TOSHIO. **HEIAN TEMPLES: BYODO-IN AND CHUSON-JI. 15.00c.**
See the Zen Buddhism section.

GANS-RUEDIN, ERWIN. **THE SPLENDOUR OF PERSIAN CARPETS. 252 full color illustrations, 9¾"x10", 552pp. Riz78, 85.00c.**
Carpet making, whether woven or tufted, is an ancient folk art common to most civilizations. Nowhere in the world has it achieved such originality and technical virtuosity as in Iran. For centuries the carpet has been central to Persian culture. The author, an internationally known carpet expert, has written what may become the definitive work on the subject. In addition to describing each step in the actual making of the carpet, he explains the meaning of the decorative motifs, cryptic signs and symbols. Each carpet illustrated here is accompanied by the size and number of knots per square inch, the type of material and dyes used, and its date, location, and origin.

GOVINDA, LI GOTAMI. **TIBETAN FANTASIES. 4.95c.**
See the Tibetan Buddhism section.

GRABAR, OLEG. **THE FOUNDATION OF ISLAMIC ART. 6.95p.**
See the Islam section.

GROSLIER, BERNARD. **THE ART OF INDOCHINA. 6.95c.**
See the South and Southeast Asia section.

HALL, JAMES. **DICTIONARY OF SUBJECTS AND SYMBOLS IN ART. Cross references, illustrations, bibliography, 345pp. H&R74/ Mur, 6.95p.**
This is a fine work which complements Cirlot's excellent volume. The emphasis here is on the biblical and classical themes on which European art is based. Mythology is also covered in detail, though esoteric symbology is not touched upon in any depth. All of the entries are clear and cover the material quite well.

HARTHAN, JOHN. THE BOOK OF HOURS. Genealogy, bibliography, index, 9"x12¼", 192pp. Cro77/T&H, 29.95c.
In the Middle Ages, before timekeeping became mechanized, the hours indicated inexact portions of the day devoted to the fulfillment of business or religious duties. Because the display of piety was not exclusively the province of the clergy, the devout and status-conscious lay society required personal prayerbooks—**Books of Hours**—in which to follow, in their own manner, the Church's daily program of devotion. Material splendor was considered appropriate to the expression of spirituality, and each worshipper, according to his means, spent unstintingly for the glorification of his **Book of Hours**. So popular were **Books of Hours** that they comprise the largest category of illuminated manuscripts to survive from the Middle Ages and the Renaissance. In these books—created by scribe and painter—religion, art, and secular life were combined in a unique synthesis. No two are alike. This volume is an anthology of more than ninety manuscript pages—nearly half of which have never before been reproduced—from thirty-four of the books. They are reproduced in full color and retain the hues of the originals. The selection represents a diversity of styles, periods, regions, and masters. Harthan contributes an extensive introductory text and a lengthy commentary on each of the plates.

HEER, FRIEDRICH. THE FIRES OF FAITH. 10.00c.
See the Christianity section.

HETL-KUNTZE, H. FAR EASTERN ART. Index, 150pp. Del67, 1.45p.
A collection of 128 full color plates which survey Chinese and Japanese art from the fourth century BC to the present. Each of the plates is discussed in an accompanying paragraph and a general introduction surveys the development of Far Eastern art. The quality of the reproductions is not always tops, but for the money this is a useful work.

HILLIER, J.R. JAPANESE COLOUR PRINTS. 7.95c.
See the Zen Buddhism section.

HILLIER, J.R. JAPANESE DRAWINGS. 5.95p.
See the Zen Buddhism section.

HISAMATSU, SHIN'ICHI. ZEN AND THE FINE ARTS. 32.50c.
See the Zen Buddhism section.

IRIE, TAIKICHI and SHIGERU AOYAMA. BUDDHIST IMAGES. 3.25p.
See the Buddhism section.

ISHIDA, MOSAKU. JAPANESE BUDDHIST PRINTS. 70.00c.
See the Zen Buddhism section.

IVES, PHILIP, ed. THE NATIVITY IN STAINED GLASS. 9½"x12¾", 64pp. Wal77, 8.95p.
A magnificent assembly of eight luminous full page color transparencies combined with many photographs and a lucid commentary. Many related biblical quotations are also included.

JENYNS, SOAME. A BACKGROUND TO CHINESE PAINTING. 3.95p.
See the Chinese Philosophy section.

KANDINSKY, WASSILY. CONCERNING THE SPIRITUAL IN ART. Illustrations, 92pp. Dov47, 2.25p.
This is one of the only books on this subject and it is an illuminating work that also contains a great deal of information on colors.

KARMAY, HEATHER. EARLY SINO-TIBETAN ART. Chronology, notes, bibliography, index, 8¼"x12", 144pp. A&P75, 43.70c.
This book presents a series of dated woodcuts and bronzes from the lamaist tradition of China and Tibet of the early thirteenth to fifteenth centuries. Each of the plates is individually discussed and there is extensive background information.

KIRUCHI, SADAO. HOKUSAI. 3.25p.
See the Zen Buddhism section.

KOBAYASHI, TAKESHI. NARA BUDDHIST ART: TODAI-JI. 15.00c.
See the Zen Buddhism section.

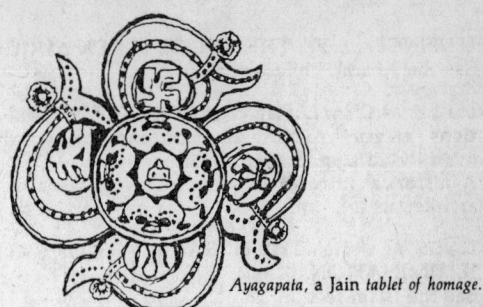
Ayagapata, a Jain *tablet of homage.*

KOCH, RUDOLF. THE BOOK OF SIGNS. 104pp. Dov30, 2.00p.
A collection of primitive and medieval symbols all redrawn by the author, with a hand written text discussing their meaning.

KUBLER, GEORGE. THE ART AND ARCHITECTURE OF ANCIENT AMERICA. 36.90c.
See the Ancient Americas section.

KUBLER, GEORGE. THE SHAPE OF TIME: REMARKS ON THE HISTORY OF THINGS. Index, 136pp. YUP62, 2.95p.
Arising from the study of art history, this book presents a radically new approach to the problem of historical change. Kubler draws upon new insights in fields such as anthropology and linguistics and replaces the notion of style with the idea of a linked succession of works distributed in time as recognizably early and late versions of the same action. The result is a view of historical sequence aligned on continuous change more than upon the static concept of style. This is an important work which helps the student reformulate traditional ideas.

LANE, RICHARD. IMAGES FROM THE FLOATING WORLD: THE JAPANESE PRINT, INCLUDING AN ILLUSTRATED DICTIONARY OF UKIYO-E. 560 illustrations, 32 in color, bibliography, index, 10"x11". Put78, 60.00c.
This magnificent volume presents the master Japanese print makers and their masterpieces—portraits, Kabuki scenes, landscapes, and erotics that form an incomparable pictorial record of Japanese life from the sixteenth to nineteenth centuries.

LANNOY, RICHARD and HARRY BAINES. THE EYE OF LOVE IN THE TEMPLE SCULPTURE OF INDIA. Bibliography, 160pp. Grv76, 12.50c.
A personal exploration of the experience and meaning of the profound, enigmatic sexuality which is firmly rooted at the very center of India's spiritual tradition. Forty-five half tone drawings accompany the text.

LAPINER, ALAN. PRE-COLUMBIAN ART OF SOUTH AMERICA. 50.00c.
See the Ancient Americas section.

LAUDE, JEAN. THE ARTS OF BLACK AFRICA. 3.45p.
See the African Philosophies section.

LAUF, DETLEF. TIBETAN SACRED ART. 15.00c.
See the Tibetan Buddhism section.

LEE, SHERMAN E. CHINESE LANDSCAPE PAINTING. 7"x9¼", 161pp. H&R nd, 4.95p.
A good presentation of the basic principles of Chinese landscape painting, illustrated with 108 reproductions. Lee begins with a general discussion and then devotes separate chapters to the beginnings of landscaping and landscape painting in the Sung, Yuan, Ming, and Ch'ing dynasties. The text analyzes the major individual painters and schools and a critique is offered for each illustration.

LEHNER, ERNST. SYMBOLS, SIGNS AND SIGNETS. Bibliography, 8"x10¾", 221pp. Dov50, 4.00p.
This is an excellent collection of noncopyrighted art which will be invaluable to anyone doing layout work. We use this book extensively in all the material we produce. The material is divided into thirteen sections: *Symbolical Gods and Dieties; Astronomy and Astrology; Alchemy; Magic and Mystic; Church and Religion; Heraldry; Monsters and Imaginary Figures; Japanese Crests; Marks and Signets; Watermarks;* and *Printer's Marks.* All the symbols have full explanatory notes.

LEUZINGER, ELSY. **THE ART OF BLACK AFRICA. 29.50c.**
See the African Philosophies section.

LEVEY, MICHAEL. **THE WORLD OF OTTOMAN ART. 107 illustra-tions, eleven in color, glossary, chronology, bibliography, index, 6½"x9¾", 152pp. Scr75, 10.95c.**
A historical introduction to the development of Ottoman art and architecture.

LINGS, MARTIN. **THE QURANIC ART OF CALLIGRAPHY AND ILLUMINATION. 52.00c.**
See the Islam section.

LIPSEY, ROGER, ed. **COOMARASWAMY: SELECTED PAPERS VOL-UME I: TRADITIONAL ART AND SYMBOLISM. Plates, notes, index, 618pp. PUP77, 40.00c.**
Coomaraswamy was a cardinal figure in twentieth century art history and in the cultural confrontation between East and West. His writings—about 1,000 items in all—range over the visual arts, aesthetics, literature, religion, metaphysics, and sociology. The essays selected for Volumes One and Two were written during the years 1932-47, when Coomaraswamy was curator in the Department of Asiatic Art at the Boston Museum of Fine Arts, where he built the first large collection of Indian art in this country. The essays in Volume One discusses various aspects of the art. There are two paradigms of the work of art in Coomaraswamy's writing: the religious icon and the useful object. The icon is a *support of contemplation*; the useful object is conceived both as physically efficient and metaphysically linked to the inner life of a person.

LIPSEY, ROGER, ed. **COOMARASWAMY: SELECTED PAPERS, VOL-UME II: METAPHYSICS. Indices, 496pp. PUP77, 40.00c.**
A collection of essays on Eastern and Western philosophy including a number of previously unpublished writings.

LLOYD, SETON. **THE ART OF THE ANCIENT NEAR EAST. Index, 302pp. Oxf61/T&H, 6.95p.**
Long before the beginnings of written history, the Near East gave birth to works of monumental sculpture and painting. By the time Athens was bursting into flower as a center of Western culture, Egypt, Mesopotamia, and their neighbors could look back on nearly twenty-five centuries of continuous artistic development. This volume has 249 plates, many in color, and a great deal of commentary.

LORENTZ, H.A. **A VIEW OF CHINESE RUGS FROM THE SEVEN-TEENTH TO THE TWENTIETH CENTURY. 54.95c.**
See the Chinese Philosophy section.

MACFARQUHAR, RODERICK. **THE FORBIDDEN CITY: CHINA'S ANCIENT CAPITAL. 12.95c.**
See the Chinese Philosophy section.

MACLAGAN, DAVID. **CREATION MYTHS. 7.95p.**
See the Mythology section.

MALE, EMILE. **THE GOTHIC IMAGE: RELIGIOUS ART IN FRANCE OF THE THIRTEENTH CENTURY. Notes, bibliography, indices, 438pp. H&R13, 5.95p.**
To the Middle Ages art was didactic. All that it was necessary that men should know—the history of the world from the creation, the dogmas of religion, the examples of the saints, the hierarchy of the virtues, the range of the sciences, arts and crafts—all these were taught them by the windows of the church or by the statues in the porch....But the meaning of these profound works gradually became obscure.— from the preface. Male systematically unveils the meaning of these works of art, based on his own intensive study and on the research of others. Many plates accompany the text.

MEREDITH-OWENS, G.M. **PERSIAN ILLUSTRATED MANUSCRIPTS. Glossary, index, 56pp. BMP65, 3.65p.**
A brief survey of the art of Persian book illumination, accompanied by twenty-four plates, eight in color.

MEREDITH-OWENS, G.M. **TURKISH MINIATURES. Glossary, notes, bibliography, index, 55pp. BMP63, 2.10p.**
A discussion of Turkish miniature painting, accompanied by twenty-five plates, eight in color.

MEYER-BAER, KATHI. **MUSIC OF THE SPHERES AND THE DANCE OF DEATH: STUDIES IN MUSICAL ICONOLOGY. Index, 403pp. PUP70, 24.20c.**
This study, illustrated with 174 plates, is divided into two parts: *Music of the Spheres* and *Music and Death.* Ms. Meyer-Baer begins with the ancient beliefs of the Near East and Greece and continues up to the Renaissance. As she says, *It is, in part, the history of the association of the two kinds of harmony that will be traced, along paths leading from ancient theories of an orderly cosmos, through ancient and medieval concepts of multiple heavens and of celestial music and dance, to the ultimate evolution of the angel orchestras that became prevalent in Renaissance painting and sculpture.* In the second part she traces the history of the symbolic relationship music has with death.

MICHALOWSKI, KAZIMIERZ. **ART OF ANCIENT EGYPT. 75.00c.**
See the Ancient Egypt section.

MICHELL, JOHN. **THE EARTH SPIRIT: ITS WAYS, SHRINES AND MYSTERIES. 5.95p.**
See the Ancient Civilizations section.

MIZUNO, SEIICHI. **ASUKA BUDDHIST ART HORYU-JI. 15.00c.**
See the Zen Buddhism section.

MOOKERJEE, AJIT. **TANTRA ART. 37.50c.**
See the Tantra section.

MOOKERJEE, AJIT. **TANTRA ASANA. 37.50c.**
See the Tantra section.

MOOKERJEE, AJIT. **YOGA ART. 39.50c.**
See the Tantra section.

MOOKERJEE, AJIT and MADHU KHANNA. **THE TANTRIC WAY. 9.95p.**
See the Tantra section.

MORI, HISASHI. **JAPANESE PORTRAIT SCULPTURE. 12.95c.**
See the Zen Buddhism section.

MUNSTERBERG, HUGO. **SCULPTURE OF THE ORIENT. 8½"x11", 160pp. Dov72, 3.50p.**
Dr. Munsterberg, a noted authority on Oriental art, has selected the best pieces from many collections. He covers the whole range of Oriental sculpture from the twentieth century BC to the eighteenth century AD, and from every tradition. There are Shinto, Buddhist, Hindu, Jain and other religious sculptures as well as secular pieces from a wide variety of periods and locations—over 150 in all.

MURRAY, PETER and LINDA. **THE ART OF THE RENAISSANCE. Index, 286pp. Oxf63/T&H, 6.95p.**
This is a widely respected general survey which discusses both the period and the individual artists and artistic movements. Architecture, sculpture, painting, book illustration, and all aspects of the arts of design are all reviewed. 250 illustrations, some in color, illuminate the text.

MUTHERICH, FLORENTINE and JOACHIM GAEHDE. **CAROLING-IAN PAINTING. 8"x11", 127pp. Brz76, 9.95p.**
The late eighth and early ninth centuries AD marked the flowering of a new period in the history of European culture. Civilization and the arts were revived by Charlemagne and Carolingian culture and art spread throughout the Western world. This book contains an introduction and detailed descriptions of the major manuscripts of the period, together with commentaries on the forty-eight magnificent color folios reproduced in the book.

NAKATA, YUJIRO. **THE ART OF JAPANESE CALLIGRAPHY. 12.50c.**
See the Zen Buddhism section.

NARAZAKI, MUNESHIGE. **HIROSHIGE. 8.95p.**
See the Zen Buddhism section.

NARAZAKI, MUNESHIGE. **HOKUSAI. 8.95p.**
See the Zen Buddhism section.

NAYLOR, MARIA, ed. **AUTHENTIC INDIAN DESIGNS. Introduction,** 8"x11", 242pp. Dov75, 5.00p.
A collection of 2500 designs that come from all over the United States and date from prehistoric times to the end of the nineteenth century. All the reproductions are clear.

NEUMANN, ERICH. **ART AND THE CREATIVE UNCONSCIOUS.** 3.45p.
See the Jungian Psychology section.

NOMA SEIROKU. **THE ARTS OF JAPAN, ANCIENT AND MEDIEVAL, VOLUME I.** 50.00c.
See the Zen Buddhism section.

NORDENFALK, CARL. **CELTIC AND ANGLO-SAXON PAINTING.** 8"x11", 128pp. Brz76, 9.95p.
In the seventh and eighth centuries a series of illuminated manuscripts emerged from monasteries and island workshops. These include such famous manuscripts as **The Book of Kells, The Lindisfarne Gospels,** and **The Book of Durrow,** with their intricate designs as well as their extravagantly elongated and knotted representations of hounds, birds, snakes, lizards, and mythical monsters. The artists who labored on these manuscripts refused to attempt naturalistic representation, so that they could be as free with the figures in a picture as if they were calligraphic designs. This is a beautifully produced volume which includes forty-eight plates in four colors plus gold as well as many other illustrations and an excellent text.

OKAZAKI, JOJI. **PURE LAND BUDDHIST PAINTING.** 12.95c.
See the Zen Buddhism section.

OKUDAIRA, HIDEO. **NARRATIVE PICTURE SCROLLS.** 10.00c.
See the Zen Buddhism section.

OLSON, ELEANOR. **TANTRIC BUDDHIST ART.** 7.15p.
See the Tantra section.

PAL, PRATAPADITYA. **NEPAL: WHERE THE GODS ARE YOUNG.** 19.95c.
See the Tibetan Buddhism section.

PORADA, EDITH. **THE ART OF ANCIENT IRAN: PRE-ISLAMIC TIMES.** 6.95c.
See the Ancient Near East section.

PURCE, JILL. **THE MYSTIC SPIRAL.** 8"x11", 128pp. T&H74, 5.00p.
The spiral is the natural form of growth, and has become, in every culture and in every age, man's symbol of the progress of the soul towards eternal life. As the inward winding labyrinth, it constitutes the hero's journey to the still center where the secret of life is found. As the spherical vortex, spiraling through its own center, it combines the inward and outward directions of movement. In this engrossing book, Jill Purce traces its significance as one of mankind's central symbols from the double spirals of Stone Age art and the interlocking spirals of the yin-yang symbol to the whorls of Celtic crosses and the Islamic arabesque. The excellent introductory text illuminates many difficult alchemical and cosmological concepts and the illustrations, drawn from many traditions, can be studied and appreciated endlessly by those seeking an understanding of the mysteries of the cosmos. It can be looked at merely as a beautiful coffee table book or as a collection of some of the most inspiring drawings and paintings we have seen. It is one of our favorite books and we recommend it highly. 174 illustrations, 32 in full color.

RACHEWILTZ, BORIS DE. **INTRODUCTION TO AFRICAN ART.** 10.40c.
See the African Philosophies section.

RAWSON, PHILIP. **THE ART OF SOUTHEAST ASIA.** 6.95p.
See the South and Southeast Asia section.

RAWSON, PHILIP. **THE ART OF TANTRA.** 6.95p.
See the Tantra section.

RAWSON, PHILIP. **EROTIC ART OF INDIA.** 6.95p.
See the Indian Philosophy section.

RAWSON, PHILIP. **TANTRA: INDIAN CULT OF ECSTACY.** 7.95p.
See the Tantra section.

RAWSON, PHILIP and LASZLO LEGEZA. **TAO: THE EASTERN PHILOSOPHY OF TIME AND CHANGE.** 5.30p.
See the Chinese Philosophy section.

RICE, DAVID. **ISLAMIC ART. Topical annotated bibliography, index,** 288pp. Oxf65/T&H, 6.95p.
An excellent survey of Islamic art, focusing on architecture, pottery, metalwork, textiles, and miniatures. Professor Rice traces the historical development from the seventh to the early eighteenth century throughout the regions, rather than following an outline based on geographic line or materials. 249 illustrations, many in color, accompany and illuminate the text.

RICE, DAVID. **ISLAMIC PAINTING: A SURVEY.** 13.45c.
See the Islam section.

RICE, TAMARA. **ANCIENT ARTS OF CENTRAL ASIA. 252 illustrations—many in color, bibliography, index,** 288pp. Oxf65, 6.95p.
A careful regional and chronological survey of the artistic accomplishments of the Central Asian peoples. Ms. Tamara Rice examines the Central Asian artistic legacy—the exciting animal art of the Royal Scyths of southern Russia; the graceful Buddhist sculpture of Gandhara and Mathura; the exotic paintings of Khotan; and the early Christian art of Armenia, Georgia, and Caucasian Albania. In so doing, she provides a brilliant analysis of the art that evolved in that part of the world where Buddhist, Christian, and Islamic tradition converge.

ROBINSON, B.W. **PERSIAN DRAWINGS. Bibliography,** 8½"x9", 142pp. LBC65, 5.95p.
This book details the art of illuminated miniatures, which reached its peak in the medieval depictions of the adventures of the mythical hero, Rustam. In most cases Persian drawings and paintings illustrate some literary text. They are, in other words, pictures with a story, outstanding for splendid colors (real gold, true ultramarine, unmixed vermilion), subtly organized narrative elements, a wealth of detail, and a perfected draftsmanship. 100 plates, most in color, from the fourteenth through the nineteenth century, are included in the volume and the text examines the various schools and styles of Persian drawings. The plates are fully annotated.

ROLA, STANISLAS DE. **THE SECRET ART OF ALCHEMY.** 5.95p.
See the Alchemy section.

ROWLAND, BENJAMIN. **THE ART OF CENTRAL ASIA. Chronology, bibliography, index,** 232pp. Crn74, 6.95c.
A superbly illustrated explanation and critique of the ancient art forms of a variety of countries. Spanning the period from the death of Alexander the Great to the end of the classical, Mazdean, and Buddhist civilizations in Central Asia (when Islamic hordes wreaked destruction upon their culture in the seventh century), this book is a vivid chronicle of the artistic heritage of the whole area.

ROWLEY, GEORGE. **PRINCIPLES OF CHINESE PAINTING.** 4.95p.
See the Chinese Philosophy section.

SAWA, TAKAAKI. **ART IN JAPANESE ESOTERIC BUDDHISM.** 15.00c.
See the Zen Buddhism section.

SEGUY, MARIE-ROSE. **THE MIRACULOUS JOURNEY OF MAHOMET: MIRAJ NAMEH.** 35.00c.
See the Islam section.

SHARKEY, JOHN. **CELTIC MYSTERIES.** 6.15p.
See the Ancient Britain section.

SINGH, MADANJEET. **HIMALAYAN ART.** 3.95p.
See the Tibetan Buddhism section.

SIREN, OSVALD. **THE CHINESE ON THE ART OF PAINTING.** 3.95p.
See the Chinese Philosophy section.

SIVARAMURTI, C. **THE ART OF INDIA. 75.00c.**
See the Indian Philosophy section.

SMITH, BRADLEY. **JAPAN: A HISTORY IN ART. 12.95c.**
See the Zen Buddhism section.

SMITH, BRADLEY and WAN-GO WENG. **CHINA: A HISTORY IN ART. 12.95c.**
See the Chinese Philosophy section.

SNELLGROVE, DAVID, ed. **THE IMAGE OF THE BUDDHA. 45.00c.**
See the Buddhism section.

STOOKE, H.J. and K. KHANDALAVALA. **THE LAUD RAGAMALA MINIATURES. 14.25c.**
See the Indian Philosophy section.

SULLIVAN, MICHAEL. **THE ARTS OF CHINA. 7.95p.**
See the Chinese Philosophy section.

SWAAN, WIM. **THE GOTHIC CATHEDRAL. 39.95c.**
See the Sacred Geometry section.

SWARZENSKI, HANNS. **MONUMENTS OF ROMANESQUE ART. Index, 10"x12", 340pp. UCh67, 8.95p.**
This beautifully illustrated book, subtitled, *The Art of Church Treasures in North-Western Europe,* presents as an artistic whole the chief monuments in ivory, gold, bronze, enamel, and manuscript illumination of northwest Europe from AD 800-1200. Swarzenski has selected 557 illustrations which exemplify the continuity of artistic development. There are short notes on each of the plates.

SWEENEY, JAMES. **AFRICAN SCULPTURE. 5.95p.**
See the African Philosophies section.

SZE, MAI-MAI, tr. **THE MUSTARD SEED GARDEN MANUAL OF PAINTING. 8.95p.**
See the Chinese Philosophy section.

SZE, MAI-MAI. **THE WAY OF CHINESE PAINTING. 3.45p.**
See the Chinese Philosophy section.

TAMBURELLO, ADOLFO. **JAPAN. 19.95c.**
See the Zen Buddhism section.

TANSLEY, DAVID. **SUBTLE BODY. Bibliography, 8"x11", 96pp. T&H77, 7.95p.**
Down through the ages, man has held the belief that his physical form is merely a projected image and a reflection of his subtle anatomy. This volume in the **Art and Imagination** series contains 122 illustrations, fifteen in color, along with a very spiritual introductory essay. Tansley traces mentions of the spiritual body in the world's sacred literature and suggests a variety of exercises for getting in closer touch with our subtle bodies. This volume is not as well organized as some of the other books in the series and the illustrations are often not as fine. Nonetheless, Tansley is an important writer in the field, and it is interesting to have his thoughts.

TARTHANG TULKU, ed. **SACRED ART OF TIBET. 5.45p.**
See the Tibetan Buddhism section.

TERUKAZU, AKIYAMA. **JAPANESE PAINTING. 9¼"x10¾", 218pp. Riz77, 12.50p.**
Eighty-one reproductions in full color of paintings from earliest times through the nineteenth century. The quality of the reproductions is unsurpassed and an excellent text accompanies and illuminates the plates.

THOMPSON, ROBERT. **BLACK GODS AND KINGS. 18.50c.**
See the African Philosophies section.

TSUDA, NORITAKE. **HANDBOOK OF JAPANESE ART. 5.50p.**
See the Zen Buddhism section.

VAN BRIESSEN, FRITZ. **THE WAY OF THE BRUSH. Appendices, glossary, bibliography, index, 7½"x10½", 329pp. Tut62, 25.00c.**
The Way of the Brush *is an exceedingly handsome, lavishly illustrated book that is important because it opens the door on a whole new (to the western mind) world of art,*

the painting techniques and the symbolism of China and Japan. It is the most readable, the most authoritative, and the most comprehensive explanation of its kind to be published in many years. Indeed, it deservedly may be called unique.—**Chicago Sunday Tribune.** The text is topically arranged and the presentation is exceedingly thoughtful. 284 finely reproduced illustrations, many in color, accompany the text. A fine work which we recommend heartily.

YEQUAUD, YVES. **THE WOMEN PAINTERS OF MITHILA. 8.95p.**
See the Indian Philosophy section.

WADE, DAVID. **PATTERN IN ISLAMIC ART. 8½"x11", 144pp. OvP76/StV, 20.00c.**
The most complete and thorough study available on the structure of Islamic design. The book traces the evolution of this art style in which architecture and ornament were developed in accordance with the natural sciences and mathematics. By analyzing the widest possible variety of these patterns, Wade has discovered thirteen basic types—each with its own degree of complexity. By the use of cutaways, diagrams, and color overlays, the construction of even the most intricate designs is made clear. Over 106 colored illustrations follow the historical and religious development of these elaborate geometric variations that repeat the crystalline purity of atomic structure in wood, plaster, stone, tile, and metal.

WALDSCHMIDT, ERNEST and ROSE. **NEPAL: ART TREASURES FROM THE HIMALAYAS. 19.95c.**
See the Tibetan Buddhism section.

WEINER, DOUGLAS. **TIBETAN AND HIMALAYAN WOODBLOCK PRINTS. 4.00p.**
See the Tibetan Buddhism section.

WEINER, SHEILA. **AJANTA: ITS PLACE IN BUDDHIST ART. 14.75c.**
See the Buddhism section.

WEITZMANN, KURT. **LATE ANTIQUE-EARLY CHRISTIAN PAINTING. 9.95p.**
See the Christianity section.

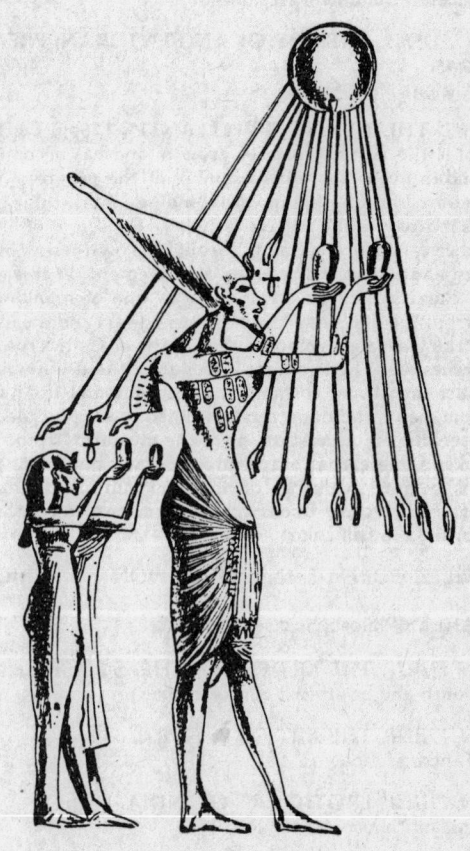

The god Aten, shown as a solar disc, receives gifts.

WELCH, STUART. **IMPERIAL MUGHAL PAINTING. Introduction, 8"x11", 119pp. Brz78, 9.95p.**
The Mughal Empire ruled in India beginning in the sixteenth century. The rulers were great patrons of the arts and the most popular technique of the period was miniature painting. The miniatures showed emperors and their courts in elaborate settings, scenes of suspense and excitement depicting hunts, demons, and elegant elephants, as well as a group of striking genre scenes. Forty paintings are reproduced in this volume—all in color, with golf leaf, and each with its own commentary.

WELCH, STUART. **A KING'S BOOK OF KINGS: THE SHAH-NAMEH OF SHAH-TAHMASP. 18.75c.**
See the Ancient Near East section.

WELCH, STUART. **PERSIAN PAINTING. 8"x11", 127pp. Brz75, 9.95p.**
The sixteenth century saw a flowering of classical miniature painting in Persia and the pages reproduced in this volume represent the most unusual and dazzling miniatures in these manuscripts. Within settings exquisitely portrayed, a world of great luxury and delicacy unfolds on every folio as palaces open onto fountains and gardens, lovers, and warriors sigh or are vanquished—all realized in shimmering, jewel-like paintings. Forty-eight miniatures are reproduced here in full color and the text traces the historical development that accompanied the art and clarifies the fine points of each miniature.

WHITFORD, CECILIA. **JAPANESE PRINTS. 8"x11", 86pp. SMP77, 5.95p.**
Forty-one full page color plates illustrate the varying styles of the Japanese print. Each print is commented on and there is also a bit of introductory information. The technical quality is excellent.

WILLET, FRANK. **AFRICAN ART. 6.95p.**
See the African Philosophies section.

WILLIAMS, C.A.S. **OUTLINES OF CHINESE SYMBOLISM AND ART MOTIVES. 5.00p.**
See the Chinese Philosophy section.

WILLIAMS, JOHN. **EARLY SPANISH MANUSCRIPT ILLUMINATION. 8"x11", 118pp. Brz77, 9.95p.**
The manuscripts in this volume were produced from the seventh through the eleventh centuries and are in the Mozarabic style (the term given to Christians who lived in the Iberian peninsula under Muslim rule). The manuscripts present a strange vision of the world with strong, deep colors that cover the picture with vibrant bands of green, red, yellow, and violet, providing the background for monsters, tempests, and human figures of every description. Forty full page color plates, introduction, commentaries.

WINNING, HASSO VON. **PRE-COLUMBIAN ART OF MEXICO AND CENTRAL AMERICA. 35.00c.**
See the Ancient Americas section.

WOSIEN, MARIA-GABRIELLE. **SACRED DANCE. 8"x11". T&H74, 5.30p.**
Creation is movement, and the sacred dance arises from the need to identify with the eternal round of the creative forces in the cosmos. Dancing intensifies awareness, so that the dancer begins to understand how the universe is made up of infinite patterns of motion around a still center. A primordial element of religious tradition, all over the world, the dance was a vital part of Early Christian worship, and survives in the whirling, orbiting movements of the dervishes of Turkey. In images ranging from Botticelli's dancing angels to the dance patterns of the South Seas, this book evokes one of man's oldest and profoundest impulses—to act out the movements of the powers that he senses within himself and within the world. An illuminating introductory text is followed by 142 illustrations, thirty in full color—all described at length.

WRAY, ELIZABETH, et al. **TEN LIVES OF THE BUDDHA. 15.00c.**
See the Jataka Tales subsection of Buddhism.

YOSHIKAWA, ITSUJI. **MAJOR THEMES IN JAPANESE ART. 15.00c.**
See the Zen Buddhism section.

ZARNECKI, GEORGE. **THE MONASTIC ACHIEVEMENT. 3.95p.**
See the Christianity section.

ZIGROSSER, CARL. **MEDICINE AND THE ARTIST. Index, 8"x11", 190pp. Dov59, 5.00p.**
Many of the greatest artists have been attracted to medical scenes. This volume reproduces 137 extraordinary works of art from the fifteenth century to the present in which some aspect of medicine or health is the subject. In addition to the prints, there is an illuminating commentary on each.

ZIMMER, HEINRICH. **THE ART OF INDIAN ASIA. 65.00c/set.**
See the Indian Philosophy section.

SACRED GEOMETRY

Geometry in ancient times was simply the culture-creating tool with which most things were made, and the importance of this particular tool to the unfolding of culture itself was vital. The system has its roots in the very beginning of time, even further back in Man's history than the ancient Egyptian dynasties, and the existence and application of the system can be shown over an incalculable length of time right up until the Middle Ages, when it finally died out still swathed in a mantle of secrecy and silence.

The system was attributed immeasurable significance as late as the period of speculation in Greece 2,500 years before our own time, and one can read of it in Plato's eighth book, in which he describes the explanation by Timaeus the philosopher on the universe and its composition. Timaeus describes, in detail, portions of the old geometric system, geometry being employed as a picture of the universe and the power of the deity, not as we use geometry today as an explanatory symbol between the speaker and the subject with the geometric pictures and vice versa, uniting these as one. The text is so cunningly composed that a thorough knowledge of the system is required in order to appreciate the full significance of the subject matter. This attempt to conceal was, of course, intentional, as both Timaeus' speech and Plato's subsequent written report were meant for the initiated and therefore to be comprehensible only to them.

The actual system and its formation have been secret from the beginning, a secret kept within certain, clearly defined circles. The holders of this knowledge, of course, made extensive use of the system and its principles in solving a number of practical and well-known projects, but merely making use of the system is not quite the same as making it public.

Ancient geometry was employed over a tremendous area, and we are able to follow its path from Egypt and her neighbouring countries out across Europe, and its effects can be noted in both Near and Far East. In those ancient times the accepted procedure was for temple brethren from one country to seek out temples in another country or region in order to receive information and teaching there. Once such a brother had spent some time—perhaps many years—in a foreign temple, he would journey back to his mother temple with his treasures: the knowledge and learning he had attained. This was the manner in which secret knowledge was transferred from one temple to another and from one country to another. This knowledge (remaining in the hands of the same groups of initiated brethren) slowly, gradually spread over wider and wider areas. And bearing in mind the many strongholds, the numerous temples within which its principles were practised, one can understand how the system has survived the decline of certain nations and the birth of others.

Seldom were the secrets of the temples entrusted to print. Communication was by word of mouth. But before a temple brother received any teaching from the inner circle he had to pledge solemnly never to reveal the secrets to any outside party. Over an endless period of time these secrets remained intact and it was not until a century before the real period of geometric reflection began in Greece that a murmur of the geometric terminology escaped from the inner temple circle, when Pythagoras returned to his homeland after many years

in Egyptian temples and started up a school in which he offered, among other studies, the teaching of a new geometric theory to non-initiated Greek students. He never revealed or taught the geometry which he had learned from the Egyptian masters since he remained true to his promises not to do so, but his new teachings were on associated lines and this was sufficient to set the ball rolling.

In fact Pythagoras had not revealed any of the mysteries: these were still sacred, and two distinct geometric schools of thought now existed in Greece. One was the ancient, traditional form of geometry whose outlines were still guarded by the temples as a part of their mystic knowledge, and this was the system of which Pythagoras and his contemporaries had full details. The second arose from the teachings of Pythagoras in his school, where he instructed the non-initiated in associated theories as a preliminary to abstract geometric thinking. These theories were not actually secret, but from this training sprang groups of scholars who tried independently to solve the riddles of ancient geometry, without success.

Through the temple society the old system had a close contact with the creative intelligentsia who were generally recruited from the temples, and it was therefore the ancient system which was employed in any practical problems facing the temple brethren or their cronies. The new geometric line of thinking was the rebel released to the public, and this was the system openly discussed by all and sundry outside temple society. There were experiments, arguments, discussions, assumptions; in short, the new thoughts were transformed into a new and developing science.

Temple society had no comment to make on the new schools of thought. For one thing, it felt a certain superiority in this direction, and for another there could be no question of joining in the discussions since this would have been impossible without revealing the temple's own system. This would have been tantamount to a breach of promise. Moreover, there was no need for a revision of thought in the temples for two thousand years were to go by before the emergent system definitely won over the ancient, traditional form. And the Middles Ages were well under way before the ancient system died out entirely, presumably with the passing of the last monastic brothers to have a knowledge of it.

Right from the earliest days the erection of churches and monasteries has been the prerogative of the temple and, later the church. When, well through the Middle Ages, this last privilege was taken from them the remains of the ancient geometrical knowledge were passed on to various guilds of craftsmen, and of the knowledge which had at one time been the bloom of all wisdom only the sad remains were left in the form of the craftsmen's guiding rules. In those periods of importance enjoyed by the system it was handed on by word of mouth, never put in writing. But if it should occasionally happen that mention was made of it in writing, the text was composed of esoteric terms and the phrasing of these was such that knowledge of the system itself was essential if the reader was to understand what the text was all about. Only the initiated could make sense from such a text, while for others it remained more or less unintelligible nonsense, and this is why students of ancient writing have been unable to trace any useful references to the old geometric system.

The ancient system of geometry is actually a related form to the one we know today, but the differences are yet so numerous and profound that it is impossible to substitute the one system for the other. Any attempt in this direction could be compared with using a measuring stick with an unknown graduation. The result finally obtained cannot be transformed straight into a form with which we are familiar. For a complete comprehension of the old system it is therefore essential that one spends the necessary time to study and reflect upon it and the thoughts which form its foundation. Any omission in this respect and a short cut to the analysis of certain buildings produces nothing but a scanty appraisal of the logic of the system's application. For although one employs—inevitably—one's knowledge of geometric principles, it is not sufficient in this instance.

Ancient geometry is not a difficult subject. It arose among people who possessed virtually no knowledge of figures, and was based on the logical consideration of primitive drawings, each drawing containing in itself the answer to the immediate problem. A square can be divided into four smaller squares by entering a cross. That is something everyone can understand, and this is the kind of observation of which the entire system is composed. Once a person has picked up this knowledge and appreciated the line of thinking which has prompted it, he is able to follow the system and its application from one region to another and from period in time to another.

Naturally experiences of this nature had to take on some written form otherwise they would be forgotten, and this form of expression was a number of geometric symbols which in their construction and development illustrate the particular geometrical aspect which they characterise. This habit of expressing an idea of a situation by means of a single symbol is a natural course of action, and we see the same type of thing used today in chemistry, mathematics, physics, and many other spheres. This procedure has furthermore the advantage that it maintains the already mentioned principle of secrecy. To the knowledgeable the symbol contained a distinct significance, while any person ignorant of the secret saw merely an undecipherable mystic sign which remained so unless he subsequently received information about its content.

—condensed from **The Secrets of Ancient Geometry**, by Tons Brunes

ADAMS, HENRY. **MONT-SAINT-MICHEL AND CHARTRES: A STUDY OF THIRTEENTH CENTURY UNITY. Index, 471pp. Dou13, 2.95p.**
This classic work grew out of the visits of Adams to northern France and it reflects the profound impression that the great cathedrals of that region had on him. The broad scope of the book, together with Adams' insight into the period, makes it one of the finest expressions of the spirit of the Middle Ages ever written. In addition, the book is an examination of the faith that brought the cathedrals into being.

ALBARN, KEITH, et al. **THE LANGUAGE OF PATTERN. Fifty-two pages of line drawings in two colors, bibliography, 8½"x11", 112pp. H&R74, 5.95p.**
Inspired by Islamic decorative pattern, the authors of this book—all designers by profession—explore pattern step-by-step, beginning with simple numerical and geometrical relationships and progressing through the dimensions, so that the reader is drawn into a visual and conceptual game of increasing complexity, as pattern and concept develop hand in hand. The authors show how even the most complex patterns are built from simple basic structures. The reader is encouraged to change scale and dimension creatively, interrelate ideas, and adopt a synthesizing approach to experience so as to counteract the analytical attitude so common in the West.

ASTEN, H. KELLER VON. **ENCOUNTERS WITH THE INFINITE. 9"x10", 364pp. KeV71, 23.80c.**
A hard to describe book which integrates geometric concepts with the

Anthroposophical philosophy developed by Rudolf Steiner and expanded by his followers. The text consists of a number of multicolored line drawings and a detailed interpretative text discussing form and linear symbolism.

BARAVALLE, HERMANN VON. **GEOMETRIC DRAWING AND THE WALDORF SCHOOL. 2.25p.**
See the Waldorf Education subsection of the Rudolf Steiner section.

BRAGDON, CLAUDE. **THE BEAUTIFUL NECESSITY. 6"x9", 111pp. TPH39, 3.75p.**
A unified collection of essays which provide an overview of the parallels between the evolution of architecture and the evolution of mankind. Ninety-one illustrations accompany and amplify the text.

BRUNES, TONS. **THE SECRETS OF ANCIENT GEOMETRY AND ITS USES. Two volumes, foldouts, 381 illustrations, 7¼"x10¼", 583pp. Rho67, 67.60c/set.**
This is an amazing set of books which graphically demonstrates Brunes' theory that the construction of the great buildings from ancient times through the Middle Ages was based on an ancient, mystical form of geometry developed in the temple at an early date and verbally transmitted among the brethren under vows of secrecy. Through an abundance of measured drawings of buildings from the Great Pyramid to Cologne Cathedral and an excellent interpretative text, Brunes reconstructs this geometry and reveals its secrets. This is a monumental work which has been acclaimed throughout the world. While it certainly will not appeal to most people, we cannot recommend it highly enough to those who are seriously interested in the ancient mystery teachings. It is one expensive set that is well worth the price. It is beautifully produced and the material is not obtainable anywhere else.

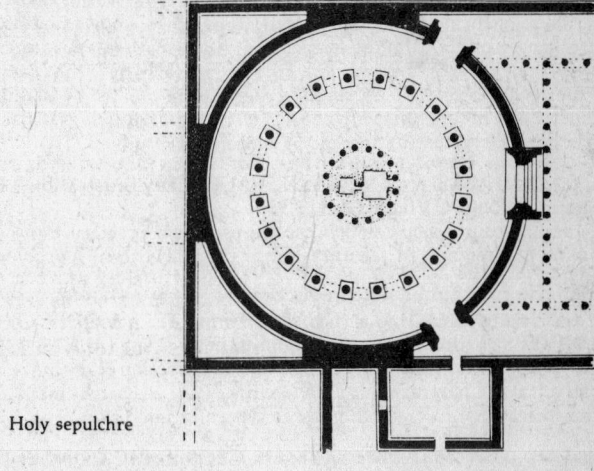

Holy sepulchre

BUSSAGLI, MARIO, ed. **ORIENTAL ARCHITECTURE. Synoptic tables, notes, bibliography, index, 10"x11½", 435pp. Abr73, 37.50c.**
A magnificent survey of the architectural traditions of the major Eastern civilizations. Bussagli is one of Europe's foremost specialists in the art of India and Central Asia. The architecture of each region is discussed by an expert in the field and 546 photographs and eighty-two diagrams, floor plans, and reconstructions accompany the texts.

CAMP, L. SPRAGUE DE. **THE ANCIENT ENGINEERS. 1.95p.**
See the Ancient Civilizations section.

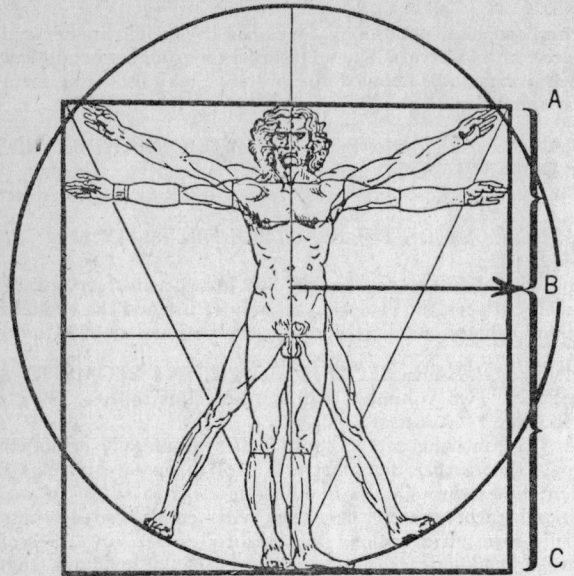

A study in proportion by Leonardo da Vinci, showing the Golden Section as a basis of measurement on the human body.

CHARPENTIER, LOUIS. THE MYSTERIES OF CHARTRES CATHEDRAL. 190pp. Avo66/RLK, 1.75p.
M. Charpentier says in effect that Chartres and other medieval cathedrals, like the great monuments of Egypt and Greece, were the manifestation of a secret communicated to mankind by occult or mystical means. This, he claims, required the services of a man equipped to receive a dedication in occult language; a man competent to translate the message into numbers and a master craftsman who knew what he was about and could express such numbers or relationships in curves, verticals and volumes. Moreover, the secret of true gothic was communicated to man with a view to a fuller realization of his own quality.—from the introduction. A fascinating, profusely illustrated study.

CRITCHLOW, KEITH. ISLAMIC PATTERNS. Bibliography, index, 8½"x10", 192pp. ScB76/T&H, 9.95p.
The geometric patterns of Islamic art yield to the sensitive observer's eye an understanding of the cosmological laws affecting all creation. Long misunderstood in the West as merely decorative, the wonderful abstractions of Islam were designed to lead the mind from the literal and mundane sphere toward the reality underlying worldly existence. Critchlow, through detailed analytical drawings, shows how Islamic art is inseparable from the science of mystical mathematics associated with the Pythagorean tradition. He shows clearly how the cosmos as experienced by man is mirrored in the patterns created by Islamic art. Illustrating his analysis with nearly 200 two color drawings, Critchlow has produced a fascinating, albeit speculative, study.

CRITCHLOW, KEITH. ORDER IN SPACE. Many illustrations, spiral bound, 12"x8¼", Vik65/T&H, 8.95p.
A design source book which can be used as a practical tool by the architect, designer, or scientist who has to deal with such problems of space.

CRITCHLOW, KEITH, et al. CHARTRES MAZE: A MODEL OF THE UNIVERSE? Illustrations throughout, notes, 24pp. RLK75, 2.75p.
An exploration of the esoteric meaning and function of the maze in the cathedral at Chartres. This is an *Occasional Paper* written by members of the Research into Lost Knowledge Organization Trust.

EL-SAID, ISSAM and AYSE PARMAN. GEOMETRIC CONCEPTS IN ISLAMIC ART. 25.00c.
See the Islam section.

FULLER, BUCKMINISTER. SYNERGETICS. Illustrations, bibliography, index, 906pp. McM78, 27.50c.
This massive volume is a distillation of Fuller's lifetime study. Here Fuller introduces the tetrahedral model as a new frame of reference to simplify understanding of the physical universe. His models are energetic relationships between events, not things. As usual with Fuller's work, the presentation is highly complex and demands careful study. Many illustrations of geometric models are included.

GHYKA, MATILA. THE GEOMETRY OF ART AND LIFE. 144 plates and drawings, notes, 191pp. Dov77, 2.75p.
Professor Ghyka believes that there is order, harmony, and proportion in human life, nature, and the finest art. Using simple formulas, most as basic as Pythagoras' theorem and requiring only a limited knowledge of mathematics, he shows the fascinating relationships among geometry, aesthetics, nature, and the human body. Beginning with ideas from Plato, Pythagoras, Archimedes, Ockham, Kepler, and others, the author explores the outlines of an abstract science of space which includes a theory of proportions, an examination of *the golden section*, a study of regular and semi-regular polyhedra, and the interlinking of these various shapes and forms. He then traces the transmission of this spatial science through the Pythagorean tradition, Greek and Gothic canons of proportion, the Qabala, masonic traditions and symbols, and modern applications.

GOODWIN, GODFREY. ISLAMIC ARCHITECTURE: OTTOMAN TURKEY. 8.40p.
See the Islam section.

GOVINDA, LAMA. THE PSYCHO-COSMIC SYMBOLISM OF THE BUDDHIST STUPA. 4.95p.
See the Buddhism section.

GRABAR, OLEG. THE FORMATION OF ISLAMIC ART. 6.95p.
See the Islam section.

HARVEY, JOHN. THE MASTER BUILDERS. Fourteen color plates, 117 line drawings, bibliography, index, 144pp. MGH71/T&H, 3.95p.
A discussion of medieval architecture focusing on the master builders. Many working plans and drawings for some of the great cathedrals are presented. Drawing on twenty-five years of research, Harvey tells how formidable problems of construction were tackled, how revolutionary building techniques were developed, how ideas traveled from country to country, and how the style known as Gothic was born. He covers the period from the twelfth century to the sixteenth. The inner meaning of the architecture is not dealt with.

HAWKINS, GERALD. BEYOND STONEHENGE. 7.25p.
See the Ancient Civilizations section.

HAWKINS, GERALD. STONEHENGE DECODED. 2.45p.
See the Ancient Britain section.

HERSEY, G.L. PYTHAGOREAN PALACES. Illustrations, bibliography, index, 7¼"x10", 216pp. Cor76, 30.00c.
An examination of Italian Renaissance domestic architecture from the viewpoint of Pythagorean geometry, which was the principal mathematical philosophy inculcated in Renaissance architectural education. *To the Pythagoreans, who were essentially number magicians,* Professor Hersey writes, *numbers were not only quantities, but qualities as well. They had fixed or predictable geometric, psychological, moral, and even personal natures.* Thus, he maintains, the distribution of elements in a building, such as columns, doors and windows, and their proportional relationships, were infused with meanings that we cannot recapture until we examine the mathematical context within which the buildings were designed. In the process of his examination he shows how theories were practically applied to several actual buildings.

HEYDEN, DORIS and PAUL GENDROP. PRE-COLUMBIAN ARCHITECTURE OF MESOAMERICA. 37.50c.
See the Ancient Americas section.

HOAG, JOHN. ISLAMIC ARCHITECTURE. 37.50c.
See the Islam section.

HORNE, ALEX. KING SOLOMON'S TEMPLE IN THE MASONIC TRADITION. 5.00p.
See the Freemasonry section.

HUNTLEY, H.E. THE DIVINE PROPORTION: A STUDY IN MATHEMATICAL BEAUTY. Illustrations, notes, index, 198pp. Dov70, 2.75p.
Using simple mathematical formulas, most requiring only a very limited knowledge of mathematics, Professor Huntley explores the relationship between geometry and aesthetics. Poetry, patterns like Pascal's triangle, philosophy, psychology, music, and dozens of mathe-

matical figures are enlisted to show that the divine proportion or golden ratio is a feature of geometry and analysis which awakens echoes in the human psyche.

HUTT, ANTHONY. ISLAMIC ARCHITECTURE: NORTH AFRICA. 8.40p.
See the Islam section.

HUTT, ANTHONY and LEONARD HARROW. ISLAMIC ARCHITECTURE: IRAN ONE. 8.40p.
See the Islam section.

KENAWELL, WILLIAM. THE QUEST AT GLASTONBURY. Notes, bibliography, 318pp. GtP65, 8.50c.
A biographical study of Frederick Bond, the man who dedicated his life to unearthing—literally and figuratively—the truth concerning England's ancient Glastonbury Abbey. Bond's observations about the abbey are also included in the text, along with photographs and line drawings.

KRAMRISCH, STELLA. THE HINDU TEMPLE. 8½"x11½", 559pp. MoB76, 75.00c.
An in depth, illustrated study which surveys both the physical conception of the temple and its philosophical underpinnings. Much of the material presented in this two volume set is derived from the early Hindu sacred scriptures. Eighty-three photographic plates and many structural line drawings accompany the text.

LETHABY, WILLIAM. ARCHITECTURE: MYSTICISM AND MYTH. Introduction, illustrations, bibliography, 304pp. Brz1882/APL, 10.00c.
This book was a milestone in the linking of mysticism and transcendental experience to the design process. The author examined folk customs, myths, and tales of many ancient civilizations in presenting his view of architecture as not just a battle of styles, nor exclusively a matter of function, but rather an expression of secret meanings that lie deeply embedded in the human psyche and are linked to ancient and universal symbolism. It is a fascinating study which has not been equaled to this day.

LLOYD, SETON, H.W. MULLER and R. MARTIN. ANCIENT ARCHITECTURE. Chronology, bibliography, index, 10"x11½", 415pp. Abr 74, 37.50c.
An in depth analysis of the architecture of Mesopotamia, Egypt, Crete, and Greece, illustrated with 346 photographs and 179 diagrams and reconstructions. The scholarship is excellent and the texts are well organized.

MACAULAY, D. CATHEDRAL. Glossary, 9½"x12", 80pp. HMC73, 8.95c.
The Gothic cathedral is one of man's most magnificent expressions as well as one of his grandest architectural achievements. This richly illustrated book shows the intricate step-by-step process of a cathedral's growth. The plan is agreed on; the site is chosen; each craftsman's contribution is presented; his tools and materials are described. The details of the construction are graphically explained, the black and white pen studies and architectural diagrams are beautifully drawn, and the brief narrative is illuminating. This is a prize winning book, designed for older children but suitable for all ages.

MACAULAY, D. PYRAMID. 8.95c.
See the Children's Books section.

MCCLAIN, ERNEST. THE MYTH OF INVARIANCE: THE ORIGIN OF THE GODS, MATHEMATICS AND MUSIC FROM THE RG VEDA TO PLATO. 5.95p.
See the Music section.

MARC, OLIVIER. THE PSYCHOLOGY OF THE HOUSE. 111 illustrations, bibliography, index, 7¼"x9½", 144pp. T&H77, 12.95c.
Is our architectural use of space the key to an understanding of our inner selves? Can the history of human collective consciousness be interpreted through buildings? Is the house a precise expression of the self? Marc, who is both an architect and an analyst, provides fascinating answers to these questions. He traces the development of human consciousness in terms of human habitations. He identifies and isolates four universal signs—circle, triangle, square, and cross—

which in one way or another form the basis of every sacred building of every historical civilization. And he shows how these signs also form the basis of the individual psyche.

MICHELL, GEORGE. THE HINDU TEMPLE. Bibliography, index, 7"x9½", 192pp. H&R77, 22.50c.
For more than 1,500 years, from the Indian subcontinent to the islands of the Indonesian archipelago, the temple has embodied and symbolized the Hindu world view at the deepest level, inspiring great achievements of art and architecture. This is an excellent introduction to the meaning and forms of the Hindu temple. Dr. Michell begins with a survey of the fundamental concepts of Hinduism and their expression in the temple, covering the symbolic processes by which meanings are identified with architectural forms. The second part explains the principles and techniques of temple building and traces the evolution of distinct temple styles. A superb collection of photographs is integrated with the text along with line drawings detailing temple plans and architectural features.

Holy sepulchre, interior.

MICHELL, JOHN. CITY OF REVELATION. 1.95p.
See the Ancient Civilizations section.

PLUMMER, GORDON. THE MATHEMATICS OF THE COSMIC MIND. Many diagrams and colored plates, 7¼"x10¾", 217pp. TPH66, 12.50c.
An unusual approach to a profound study of the universe and man. Taking as a basis the vast system of Theosophy as outlined in Blavatsky's Secret Doctrine, and applying the complexities of mathematical symbolism, Plummer leads the student toward his own discovery of some of the deeper realities of existence and of consciousness.

SIMSON, OTTO VON. THE GOTHIC CATHEDRAL. Notes, bibliography, index, 283pp. PUP56/RKP, 3.95p.
The value of The Gothic Cathedral lies in its approach to two essential problems....The first one is concerned with the appreciation of Gothic architecture....It was symbolical in its conception...mystical in its aim, and calculated in its principles....Von Simson shows that in Gothic architecture history creates its own symbols, whether political, economic, intellectual, or artistic, all of them following an independent but convergent spiritual pattern.—Yale Review.

SWAAN, WIM. THE GOTHIC CATHEDRAL. Introduction, notes, bibliography, index, 10"x12½", 328pp. Ele69, 39.95c.
The soaring lines of the Gothic cathedrals epitomize the aspirations of the medieval world. Collectively they constitute Europe's greatest architectural heritage. In this splendid book Wim Swaan, architect, art historian, and photographer, gives an illuminating account of the many and various aspects of medieval life that cathedral building involved. He covers thirty-three cathedrals in six countries and gives a detailed account of how they were built, of the styles, of the master builders, and of the political events involved. 400 photographs and diagrams, many in color, give a panoramic view of the cathedrals.

SWORDER, MARY. FULCANELLI: MASTER ALCHEMIST. 8.40c.
See the Alchemy section.

TAYLOR, THOMAS. **THE THEORETICAL ARITHMETIC OF THE PYTHAGOREANS. 15.00c.**
See the Pythagoras subsection of Ancient Greece and Rome.

TOMPKINS, PETER. **SECRETS OF THE GREAT PYRAMID. 20.00c.**
See the Ancient Egypt section.

VANDENBROECK, ANDRE. **PHILOSOPHICAL GEOMETRY. 8½"x 11", 166pp. Sad72, 7.00p.**
This is a detailed analysis of geometric forms and concepts, heavily illustrated.

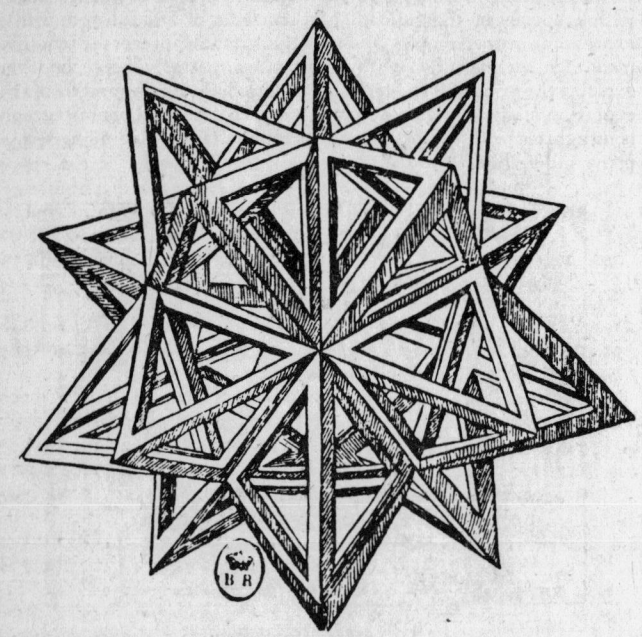

Star polyhedra, after a design by Leonardo da Vinci.

WATSON, PERCY. **BUILDING THE MEDIEVAL CATHEDRALS. 48pp. CUP76, 2.45p.**
A pictorial study, illustrated with photographs and detailed line drawings. The text is quite simplified and covers the following general topics: *Where They Built and Why; The Norman Cathedral; The Workers and Their Task; The Gothic Cathedrals; and Cathedrals Since the Middle Ages.*

WENNINGER, MAGNUS. **POLYHEDRON MODELS. Notes, 7¼"x 10", 211pp. CUP71, 6.95p.**
The author describes how to make models of all the known uniform polyhedra and some of the stellated forms. The book is fully illustrated with drawings and photographs and the instructions are clearly presented.

WHICHER, OLIVE. **PROJECTIVE GEOMETRY: CREATIVE POLARITIES IN SPACE AND TIME. Many illustrations, notes, index, 8¼"x10¼", 292pp. RPS71, 16.00c.**
The task attempted by this book is to bring to the non-mathematician fundamental truths of Projective Geometry in such a way that he might be inspired in thought and imagination to use the key they provide for the understanding of aspects of nature and of human experience to which the scientific thought otherwise remains blind.—from the foreword.

WILLIAMS, MARY, ed. **BRITAIN: A STUDY IN PATTERNS. 5.35p.**
See the Ancient Britain section.

WINSTON, RICHARD and CLARA. **NOTRE-DAME DE PARIS. Chronology, notes, bibliography, index, 9¼"x11½", 172pp. Nsw71, 12.95c.**
Notre Dame is a fine example of the Gothic cathedral and it has stood at the very center of French history since its construction. This beautiful photographic study reproduces a great deal of the important art inside and studies the architecture in detail. An interpretative text reviews the cathedral's history and some of the important events that happened in and around it. The architecture itself is analyzed in depth and the photographs are absolutely magnificent. There is also a section of excerpts from writings inspired by the grandeur of the cathedral. Short analyses of other French Gothic cathedrals are also included.

YOUNG, ARTHUR. **THE GEOMETRY OF MEANING. Index, 184pp. Del76, 4.95p.**
I would like to call this book an essay in philosophy. However, I should point out that I do not mean philosophy as it is usually practiced today, but in the older sense of the "science which investigates the facts and principles of reality." In this sense, philosophy not only encompasses the natural sciences, but explores the implications of the findings of science, and also deals with the relationship between the knower and the known. . . . Like this book, geometry came about through a quest for order. Geometry is an ordering so abstract that the role of its elements, points and lines, can be interchanged, leaving its basic propositions intact. . . . The validity of geometry is independent of the substantial nature of the elements it employs. I believe equally fundamental relationships lie at the foundation of existence itself.—from the introduction. This is a difficult, abstract book, filled with mathematical equations and analytical formulations. Young, inventor of the Bell helicopter, has devoted his life to a study of the interface between science and metaphysics.

SOUTH & SOUTHEAST ASIA

The culture of India has been one of the world's most powerful civilizing forces. Countries of the Far East, including China, Korea, Japan, Tibet and Mongolia owe much of what is best in their own cultures to the inspiration of ideas imported from India. The West, too, has its own debts. But the members of that circle of civilizations beyond Burma scattered around the Gulf of Siam and the Java Sea, virtually owe their very existence to the creative influence of Indian ideas. Among the tribal peoples of Southeast Asia these formative ideas took root, and blossomed. No conquest or invasion occurred, no forced conversion was imposed on them. They were adopted because the people saw they were good and that they could use them. The small colonies of Indian traders, who settled at points of vantage along the sea-routes into the islands and around the coast of Indochina, merely imported with them their code of living, their conceptions of law and kingship, their rich literature and highly evolved philosophy of life. They inter-married with prominent local families; and dynasties evolved capable of organizing extensive kingdoms within which their populations could live ordered and fruitful lives.

Of course the art these Indianized kingdoms produced owes its extraordinary qualities to the genius of the native peoples. For although the modes may be Indian the expression and the content are local. What the Javanese and Balinese made springs from their own genius, just as Angkor did from the genius of the Khmer. The arts of Burma and Thailand reflect the particular genius of the Burmese and Thai. The Indian modes provided themes and patterns for transformation, opening up before local peoples avenues of cultural and artistic development. Of course, there were regions where Indian colonies seem to have met little or no response, and their settlements petered out—in the Malay Peninsula, for example, in Sumatra, and perhaps in Sarawak and North Borneo. But archaeology may yet reveal more about the history of Indian colonization in the more remote parts of the Southern Seas. The best of this art combines a sensuous sweetness with a luxuriant magnificence, blending joy and delight with intense intellectual and imaginative strength. The sweetness may occasionally veer towards the febrile, the strength towards crudity. But always the virtue of each art is its own, unlike any other; each can offer us an imaginative experience which must extend our mental horizons.

—*condensed from* **The Art of Southeast Asia,** *by Philip Rawson*

BLACK, STAR *and* DAVID STUART-FOX. **BALI.** Index, 279pp. APA77, 9.00p.
A gorgeous guide to Bali, illustrated with about 200 color photographs and a lively, informative text. Maps and ordinary tourist information are appended.

BOISSELIER, JEAN, *et al.* **THE HERITAGE OF THAI SCULPTURE.** Technical appendices, notes, bibliography, index, 10"x11½", 269pp. Wea75, 60.00c.
Thai sculpture offers the viewer an intimate and direct experience of Buddhism. For the sculptors, their art transcends considerations of craft and artistry and becomes an act of devotion and piety. This book surveys the spirituality and technical originality of Thai sculpture. The text is sensitive and learned and illuminated by forty color and 129 monochrome plates. All of the individual schools are surveyed and the aesthetic principles of Thai art are fully discussed.

CADET, J.M. **THE RAMAKIEN: THE STONE RUBBINGS OF THE THAI EPIC.** Bibliography, index, 9"x11½", 256pp. Kod71, 29.50c.
The **Ramakien** is the Thai version of the most important myth in Southeast Asia—a myth that appears in varying forms in India, where it originated and is known as the **Ramayana.** The story recounts the struggle between the forces of good and evil, personified in the divine Phra Ram and the King of the Demons, Totsagan. It is the central episodes of this story that are depicted in the bas reliefs of the temple of Wat Phra Jetubon in Bangkok, the funerary temple of the ruling dynasty of Thailand. A complete set of the rubbings, 152 in number, is presented in this book. The taking of rubbings is now prohibited, so this book makes a unique contribution to our understanding of the myth. A written version of the myth, in English translation, accompanies the rubbings, and introductory material is also included.

COHEN, JOAN. **ANGKOR: MONUMENTS OF THE GOD-KINGS.** 157 illustrations, 136 in color, glossary, chronology, bibliography, index, 11½"x14", 240pp. Abr nd, 45.00c.
The great stone monuments of Angkor are among mankind's most brilliant artistic achievements. Embodying the idea of the heavenly city on Earth, they were built by a series of Khmer kings during the golden age of the empire at Angkor, from the ninth to the thirteenth century. Richly decorated in an intricate, flamboyant sculptural mode, the temples depict themes of both the Hindu and Buddhist faiths, for the unique Angkor forms of thought and imagery combined elements of each. According to Angkor religious belief, the king was divine, and his divine symbol was properly to be housed on a sacred mountain. The Khmers built pyramid temples to represent such mountains. In this volume, magnificent color plates display Angkor's glory and suggest the extraordinary experience of seeing these monuments in their jungle setting. Text and commentaries to the illustrations trace the history and development of the monuments, discuss their artistic qualities, and relate them to the context of society from which they sprang.

COOMARASWAMY, ANANDA. **THE ARTS AND CRAFTS OF INDIA AND CEYLON. 2.95p.**
See the Sacred Art section.

COOMARASWAMY, ANANDA. **HISTORY OF INDIAN AND IN-DONESIAN ART.** **Over 400 illustrations, index, 432pp. Dov27, 6.00p.**

This is an important work, focusing on architecture and sculpture though also encompassing all other art and craft forms. The work is divided into six sections, each representing a chronological cultural area. Background information on the history and geography is also provided along with philosophical, social, and religious insights.

EPTON, NINA. **MAGIC AND MYSTICS OF JAVA. 212pp. Oct74, 10.00c.**

A well written, almost travelogue-like account of Java. The author seems to have attended many ceremonies not usually accessible to the traveler and she reports her observations quite vividly. The reader gets a good feeling for the daily life of the Javanese people in addition to the magical side of the culture. Religious practices are also discussed.

COVARRUBIAS, MIGUEL. **ISLAND OF BALI. Glossary, index, 487pp. RaH37, 17.50c.**

This is universally considered a classic work on the Balinese people and their civilization. The artist in Covarrubias penetrates deeply into the spirit of the dance, theater, music, handicrafts, and sports of Bali; the anthropologist beautifully records Balinese religion, sexual customs, family life, and economic and political organization. 204 illustrations, including photographs and over ninety drawings by Covarrubias, accompany and illuminate the text.

GROSLIER, BERNARD. **THE ART OF INDOCHINA. Glossary, bibliography, index, 7"x9¼", 261+pp. Crn62, 6.95c.**

A comprehensive work which starts with prehistory and early art forms, goes on to describe the Indian and Chinese contributions, and then surveys the artistic accomplishments of the peoples of Indochina and the Khmer empire. Sixty color plates and many line drawings illuminate the text. There are also chronology tables and a foldout map.

HOEFER, H.J. **THAILAND. Glossary, index, 320pp. APA77, 9.00p.**

This is a beautiful guidebook to Thailand, with 230 color photographs of the land and people. Thirteen large maps and seventy smaller ones are included.

RAWSON, PHILIP. **THE ART OF SOUTHEAST ASIA. 251 illustrations, some in color, glossary, bibliography, index, 288pp. Oxf67, 6.95p.**

The countries of Southeast Asia are situated between two great civilizations—the Indian and the Chinese. From earliest times, they have, in their art, blended indigenous forms with those of their powerful neighbors, creating styles that are uniquely their own. This is the first authoritative study of their art in English and Rawson includes works of art in every category—from large architectural complexes to tiny bronzes. In addition, he gives the reader a great deal of information about the history, traditions, social organization, and religious beliefs of the societies of the area. He also synthesizes and clarifies the origins and evolution of artistic styles and the historic setting.

RUDOLF STEINER

Steiner thought, spoke, and wrote as a scientist. Though he challenged many of the conclusions of science, he did so as one who knew at first-hand the whole trend of scientific thought. Although his own investigations carried him into fields far beyond the range of physical science, he always carried into these investigations, and into the application of them to physical phenomena, the concepts and methods of scientific thought. Steiner made many unique contributions to twentieth century thought.

In the first place he widens the frontiers of knowledge. He declares that the phenomena, perceivable by us through our physical senses and deducible by thought from those perceptions, do not constitute the whole range of the actual realities of our universe. Behind the physical realities which we perceive—yet integrally related to them and as objectively real—there are supersensible realities. They too are directly perceptible, but only by senses other than the physical. This assertion Steiner makes, not as a hypothesis, but as a result of direct personal perception of these supersensible realities. This supersensory perception which he possessed can, he maintains, be acquired by others by the method of conscious, concentrated thinking along certain lines. At a future stage of human evolution it will be a universal faculty of mankind.

These new horizons reveal new knowledge about ourselves and the world in which we live. Perhaps the most challenging item of this new knowledge is the definite assertion that man—and the physical world—had a spiritual, and not a material, origin, and that both have a spiritual destiny. It may appear a presumption to challenge a scientific theory so well-established as that of evolution, viz. that higher forms of life and consciousness have evolved out of the lower forms of material substance, whether directly or by the *leaps* of emergent evolution. Nevertheless, Steiner, while accepting all the facts that science has discovered, does challenge the conclusions drawn from them, and his point of view involves a complete re-thinking, not only of the origin of physical and mental phenomena, but of many apparently established conclusions based upon the accepted theory of evolution. He sets out his own point of view with a wealth of description and fact. Some of it is derived from supersensible perception, and as such cannot be directly tested, but all of it is related to observable phenomena, in such a way that it is capable of just as sound confirmation from these phenomena, as that which Science can produce in favour of the generally accepted theory of evolution.

The essence of man's earthly evolution Steiner shows to have been the evolution of human consciousness, the life of the human soul. He traces this as a descent from a supersensible awareness of the beings and activities of his spirit-environment and a relatively dim apprehension of the physical world—into an increasingly conscious perception and understanding of his material environment, and a consequent dimming of his supersensible perception. Before him now lies the possibility of a re-ascent, in his achieved self-awareness, to a higher level of consciousness and existence, in which he will have spiritualised the various elements of his being—including his physical body—into a perfection of free and fully-conscious spirit-being. With such a concept of spirit-origin and exalted spirit-destiny, man is delivered from the self-contempt and

self-pity to which materialistic concepts have brought him. Moreover he is seen to hold in himself the clue to the understanding of the mysteries of cosmic life. Let man but truly know and understand himself and the nature of his being, declared Steiner, and he will find that he holds within himself the clue to the secrets of the universe—he is the microcosm within the macrocosm.

As a result of this new understanding of man, Steiner throws an entirely new light upon history. It is no longer primarily the story of man's increasing knowledge of and mastery over his material environment—although that remains a dominant fact of history. History is primarily the story of the evolution of the consciousness of Humanity towards self-conscious freedom of being, the attainment of which by man is the whole purpose of the existence of the material world. With such a clue to the understanding of history, the sequence of civilisations, the diversity of races, the emergence and variety of nationalities, and our present international problems and difficulties fall into a unity of spiritual evolution. Moreover history becomes not only an interpretation of the past, but, what it never yet has been, a clear pointer for the future.

In this new view of human history and of the origin of man and the universe, the dualism of religion and science, of secular and sacred, disappears. The whole world perceptible to the physical senses is seen to be in constant and immediate relation to the spirit world. Religion is the expression of the relation between the spirit-world and man, but later was conveyed by revelation and mystic experience through spiritual leaders, and expressed in the great world-religions. Even though no longer perceived or directly experienced by man, this spiritual relationship has always remained as an actual activity in, and concern with, the life of mankind on the part of the spirit world. The coming of Christ into human history is seen as the focal point of this relationship, the consummation of the divine approach to man of which the greatest spiritual leaders of humanity had continuously been aware. To Rudolf Steiner's spirit-perception the life and death and resurrection of Jesus Christ are seen to be the central happenings of all history, cosmic as well as earthly. On the spirit power released by that event the pattern and subsequent history of the earth and of the destiny of man depend. The earlier world-religions are seen, not as false or opposed to Christianity, nor as an equally eligible alternative, but as arising naturally out of the level of human consciousness in which they had their birth. In Christianity they are not denied, but fulfilled.

In this objective revelation of the supersensible realities working in and through human history, the individual human being holds a position of dignity and importance. His direct concern with the whole spiritual evolution of humanity is not limited to the few years of one earthly life. The individual is the warp, as his social life is the woof, of the web of human history. Rudolf Steiner sees the deed of Christ, as that which objectively delivers humanity and the earth-evolution from the inevitability of moral disintegration, and which alone offers to the individual deliverance from his past, and the possibility of final spiritual attainment.

The application of these far-reaching discoveries in regard to the nature of man and the universe, to the practical activities of human life, has had far-reaching results. In education, in agriculture, in medicine, in the treatment of the mentally abnormal, in art, and in the solution of social problems, new principles and methods have been propounded and are being widely and successfully practised.

—*condensed from* **A Scientist of the Invisible**, *by A.P. Shepherd*

waber

ASTEN, H. KELLER VON. **ENCOUNTERS WITH THE INFINITE.** **23.80c.**
See the Sacred Geometry section.

BITTLESTON, ADAM. **MEDITATIVE PRAYERS FOR TODAY.** **45pp.** **CCP75, 2.25c.**
A collection of personal prayers, written over a course of thirty years.

BITTLESTON, ADAM. **THE SPIRIT OF THE CIRCLING STARS.** **191pp. CCP75, 7.25c.**
A collection of inspirational thoughts on a variety of topics important in the experience of all of us. The material is arranged according to months and astrological signs and is designed to be dipped into from time to time. Many of the topics and discussions relate to the Christian experience as exemplified in the teaching of Rudolf Steiner.

BITTLESTON, ADAM and JOHN DAVY. **THE GOLDEN BLADE.**
This is an annual publication put together by the Anthroposophical Society in Great Britain. The quality of the articles is uniformly excellent and, in addition to essays about current developments in Anthroposophy, each issue contains translations of a few previously unpublished Steiner lectures. Book reviews are also included. Each issue is about 200 pages. The following ones are now available: 1973, $2.75p; 1974, $3.00p; 1975, $3.50p; 1976, $3.50p.

BOOS-HAMBURGER, HILDE. **CREATIVE POWER OF COLOR.** **8½"x 11", 63+pp. NKB73, 7.80p.**
A collection of exercises and affirmations based on Rudolf Steiner's approach to color in art. The sixty-six exercises are illustrated in full color. Topics include the basis for color experience, and the creative aspects of color—including an analysis of each individual color. This is the most spiritually-oriented of all the works on color and the only one with supplementary exercises. Also contains an extensive bibliography.

■ *CARLGREN, FRANS.* **RUDOLF STEINER.** **81pp. PAV72, 3.10p.**
This is a beautifully produced biographical study of Steiner. The reader can get a good feeling of all aspects of Steiner's life and work from this short, well organized volume and it is as good an introduction to Steiner as anything we can think of. Many photographs are included.

CHU, PAUL. **LIFE BEFORE BIRTH, LIFE ON EARTH, LIFE AFTER DEATH.** **194pp. API72, 2.95p.**
A topical condensed discussion of the following material, by an Anthroposophist: *the mysteries of the being of man, the works of Rudolf Steiner, man's supersensible members after death, creation, Jesus and the Christ Being, the mission of the Hebrew people, Lucifer and Ahriman, sleep, reincarnation and karma.* This is an interesting, clear digest.

DAVY, JOHN, ed. **WORK ARISING FROM THE LIFE OF RUDOLF STEINER. Illustrations, 240pp. RSP75, 5.25p.**
A collection of articles published to mark the fiftieth anniversary of Rudolf Steiner's death. Includes essays on art and architecture, education, medicine, agriculture, sociology, and religion—all of which give a clear impression of how Steiner's suggestions for working in these various fields have been put into practice and borne fruit in the world. There are additional essays on Steiner himself, the essentials of his thinking, and the society he founded.

DERRY, EVELYN. **THE CHRISTIAN YEAR. 255pp. CCP67, 6.15c.**
A meditative examination of the inner meaning of the seasons and festivals in the Christian year.

DERRY, EVELYN. **SEVEN SACRAMENTS IN THE CHRISTIAN COMMUNITY. 122pp. CCP66, 1.75p.**
In the Christian Community seven sacraments are celebrated: Baptism, Confirmation, Communion, Sacramental Consultation, Last Anointing, Marriage and the Ordinations of Priests.... The sacraments express what the grace of Christ offers to human souls. Through Him streams into us the power to become. He is the pattern of our fulfillment. He works in the unfinishedness of our selves, our life, our world. The sacraments are His words and deeds, present with us.

EASTON, STEWART. **MAN AND WORLD IN THE LIGHT OF ANTHROPOSOPHY. Notes, index, 536pp. API75, 6.95p.**
A comprehensive introduction to Steiner's work and thought, written by a man who has been active in the Anthroposophical Society for over forty years. The first part of the book discusses Anthroposophy as a body of knowledge; the second, *The Role of Anthroposophy in Practical Life,* includes chapters on education, science, and the arts.

FLETCHER, JOHN, ed. **RUSSIA: PAST, PRESENT, AND FUTURE. Index, 338pp. NKB68, 12.90c.**
A collection of articles examining the inner qualities of the Russian people written over several decades by students of Rudolf Steiner; who, in their personal lives or in their reading, have been deeply impressed by the achievements and the problems of Russia. Ninety-four illustrations (fifty-one in color) illustrate the achievements of Russian art and architecture.

FREEMAN, ARNOLD. **RUDOLF STEINER'S MESSAGE TO MANKIND. 47pp. NKB63, 1.75p.**
A topically organized short summary of Steiner's main ideas.

FRIELING, RUDOLF. **THE ESSENCE OF CHRISTIANITY. 1.00p.**
See the Christianity section.

FRIELING, RUDOLF. **HIDDEN TREASURE IN THE PSALMS. 191pp. CCP67, 6.50c.**
A study of the mystical and esoteric meaning of the sacred poetry attributed to King David. Frieling was an Old Testament scholar as well as an Anthroposophist.

FRIELING, RUDOLF. **THE METAMORPHOSIS OF THE EUCHARIST. 24pp. CCP nd, 1.00p.**

GLAS, NORBERT. **CONCEPTION, BIRTH AND EARLY CHILD-HOOD, 142pp. API72, 2.50p.**
A sensitive, intuitive account of the soul entering into a new physical vehicle and the effects the conception process has on the mother, based on Rudolf Steiner's Spiritual Science and on Dr. Glas' own experience. As the title suggests there are chapters on conception, pregnancy and birth—all oriented around the spiritual development of mother and child. The major part of the book is devoted to an analysis of the newborn's coming into the world and developing his or her senses, will, feeling, and ego. We highly recommend this volume to all who want to understand the deeper meaning and potentiality of the birth process.

GLAS, NORBERT. **THE FULFILLMENT OF OLD AGE. 131pp. API70, 5.50c.**
In this profound book Dr. Glas *tells how all of us, young or old, may grow older gracefully and continue to live a fruitful life right up to the end. The secret he reveals may be summed up in the words acceptance and metamorphosis: inward acceptance of the truth that we are no longer young, and that this truth has practical consequences, and the transformation of our declining sense faculties into their spiritual counterparts.* —**The Golden Blade, 1973.**

GOETHE, JOHANN. **AUTOBIOGRAPHY OF JOHANN WOLFGANG VON GOETHE. Two volumes, 869pp. Uch74, 10.25p/set.**
Goethe was Steiner's spiritual mentor and Goethe's philosophy and scientific approach to the study of the natural world is reflected in Steiner's work. Therefore Goethe's autobiography provides important background information for an understanding of Steiner's philosophy.

GOETHE, JOHANN. **FAUST, PART ONE. 197pp. Vik49/Pen, 2.50p.**
Faust, which Goethe began in his youth and worked on during the greater part of his lifetime, takes for its theme the universal experience of the troubled human soul. This verse translation by Philip Wayne includes a long introduction.

GOETHE, JOHANN. **FAUST, PART TWO. 288pp. Vik59/Pen, 2.50p.**
In this volume the drama, transposed to the spiritual plane, unfolds in scenes rich in mythological reference.

GOETHE, JOHANN. **THE METAMORPHOSIS OF PLANTS. 55pp. Bio74, 2.50p.**
A new edition of Goethe's major work on plants, with an introduction by Steiner.

GOETHE, JOHANN. **THEORY OF COLORS. Notes, 423pp. MIT70, 5.95p.**
Goethe, as artist and scientist, probed the phenomenon of color to its origins in the interplay of light and darkness. His investigation of the moral qualities evoked in human feeling by color laid the foundation for an aesthetic of color and the theories he presents in this volume have been very influential up to the present day—although not among the traditional scientists, Goethe felt that a knowledge of physics was an actual hindrance to understanding and he based his conclusions exclusively upon exhaustive personal observation of the phenomenon of color. Using simple equipment—vessels, prisms, lenses, and the like—the reader is led through a demonstration course not only in subjectively produced colors, but also in the observable physical phenomenon of color. The material here is fascinating, but not recommended to the casual reader. It is slow going.

GROHMANN, GERBERT. **THE PLANT. 209pp. RSP74, 8.95p.**
The observations in this volume are based on the principle of metamorphosis first described by Goethe. Grohmann's book ranges from detailed description of single plants to a relation of the plant kingdom to the whole earth—to insect and bird, to climate and altitude, as well as to man. A hundred plates and diagrams illustrate the exposition.

HECKEL, ALICE, ed. **THE PFEIFFER GARDEN BOOK. Index, 230pp. BID67, 5.55p.**
The bio-dynamic system of farming and gardening developed out of advice and instructions given to farmers by Rudolf Steiner. *Working with living plants on a soil that has life in it, we endeavor to work with the ultimate processes that shape and maintain life rather than just with a few of its material bricks.* The bio-dynamic gardeners differ from organic gardeners in their emphasis on a high humus content in the soil, their desire for balanced nutrients, and especially in their consideration of cosmic factors as they affect plant life. This book provides an adequate overview of the subject—although it is not a comprehensive discussion. The book begins with information on starting a bio-dynamic garden and goes on to a discussion of specific crops.

HEIDENREICH, ALFRED, ed. **THE CATACOMBS. 5.50c.**
See the Christianity section.

HEIDENREICH, ALFRED. **THE RISEN CHRIST AND THE ETHERIC CHRIST. 47pp. RSP69, 2.75p.**
Transcriptions of a series of lectures which discuss *the Being of Christ as it is shown in the writings of the New Testament* and refer often to Steiner's thoughts on the Christ.

HEIDENREICH, ALFRED. **THE UNKNOWN IN THE GOSPELS. 4.95c.**
See the Bibles section.

HEISLER, HERMANN. **OUR RELATIONSHIP TO THOSE WHO HAVE DIED. 32pp. SGB76, 2.50p.**
A philosophical examination based on the teachings of Steiner.

HEMLEBEN, JOHANNES. **RUDOLF STEINER. Bibliography, 176pp. Gou75, 8.50p.**
This is a well researched study of Steiner's life and work which emphasizes a true understanding of the outward events in Steiner's life. Many heretofore unpublished photographs of people and places in Steiner's life and of Steiner himself are interspersed. Hemleben also analyzes the major creative periods in Steiner's life and his main writings.

HIEBEL, FREDERICK. **TREASURES OF BIBLICAL RESEARCH. 42pp. API nd, .95p.**
Brief but detailed historical survey of the time of Christ based on the writings found in the **Dead Sea Scrolls.** Traces the identity of the Essene *Teacher of Righteousness,* and describes Jesus' life with his parents and their connection with the Essenes.

JENNY, HANS. **CYMATICS. 9"x10", about 200 pages each, ScB74, 39.50c/each.**
The term cymatics refers to the structure and dynamics of waves and vibrations. *What effects do vibrations produce in a concrete medium? What effects appear in a system and its environment when wave phenomena are inherent in that system? An answer to these questions was sought first of all in the acoustic field, where experiments revealed a characteristic phenomenology of vibrational effects and wave phenomena with typical structural patterns and dynamics (cymatics). Serial phenomena of this kind were presented in our first volume. These studies are continued in this second volume.* Each volume contains more than 150 photographs— many in color—along with a detailed written analysis of the phenomena.

KOEPF, HERBERT. **BIO-DYNAMIC AGRICULTURE. Bibliography, index, 439pp. API76, 12.00c.**
This is the most comprehensive discussion imaginable. Every aspect of agriculture is discussed from a bio-dynamic viewpoint and it is often very heavy material. We had problems getting into the book and so will most people. If you are seriously interested in the bio-dynamic methods, then this is the book for you. But beware, it takes a deep study. Many case histories and practical examples are offered.

KONIG, KARL. **THE HUMAN SOUL. 118pp. API73, 2.50p.**
A spiritual study which incorporates psychological understanding.

KYBER, MANFRED. **THE THREE CANDLES OF LITTLE VERONICA. 192pp. WaI72, 5.50p.**
A beautifully illustrated story of a child's soul in this world and the other, set in the lonely northern countryside along the Baltic coast of Germany before the age of motor transport.

LEHRS, ERNEST. **ROSICRUCIAN FOUNDATIONS OF THE AGE OF NATURAL SCIENCE AND OTHER ARTICLES. Offset, 8½"x11", 42pp. SGB76, 3.50p.**
The other articles are *The Thirty-three Years, Rhythm, The St. John's Tide Impulse and the Redemption of Science,* and *The Spirit of Science in the Anthroposophic Conception of Reincarnation.*

LEHRS, ERNEST. **SPIRITUAL SCIENCE, ELECTRICITY AND MICHAEL FARADAY. Notes, 30pp. RSP75, 2.50p.**
The first part of this essay deals with electricity as it relates to Anthroposophical concepts of man's body and soul; the second conveys a picture of Faraday—a scientist whom Steiner called *one of the greatest minds of all times.*

LINDEN, WILHELM ZUR. **A CHILD IS BORN. Bibliography, index, 199pp. API73, 4.50p.**
What do we really mean when we say: A child is born? Dr. zur Linden is concerned with a total answer to the question. Indeed he holds that it is impossible to answer any single aspect of it without facing them all. He regards the child as a threefold being of body, soul, and spirit and feels that the organism in the womb is already being prepared by the child himself as a vehicle for the expression of his soul and spirit. It must be nurtured and nourished as such a vehicle both before and after birth. Dr. zur Linden details physical treatment and environment based on Rudolf Steiner's Spiritual Science. Many practical suggestions on nutrition and childcare during pregnancy, birth, and early childhood are given.

MACBETH, NORMAN. **DARWIN RETRIED. 172pp. Del71, 2.45p.**
A carefully documented repudiation of classical Darwinism and its supporters which maintains that errors have been discovered in the reasoning behind the theory, about which the public has not been informed. Mr. Macbeth suggests the necessity of a fresh start in the study of the evolutionary mechanism.

MAYER, GLADYS. **BEHIND THE VEILS OF DEATH AND SLEEP. 44pp. NKB nd, 1.50p.**
A new approach to the subject of life after death based on Steiner's spiritual science.

MERRY, ELEANOR. **ASCENT OF MAN. 12.60c.**
See the Ancient Civilizations section.

MERRY, ELEANOR. **EASTER—THE LEGENDS AND THE FACTS. Index, 153pp. NKB67, 4.05c.**
A profound discussion of the spiritual foundations of Easter, based on the ancient mystery teachings and reviewing related material in the old Celtic legends of the Holy Grail, the story of Parsifal, and Goethe's Faust. A moving presentation which makes the true meaning of this holy day come alive.

MERRY, ELEANOR. **SPIRITUAL KNOWLEDGE. Index, notes, 115pp. NKB66, 5.05c.**
An overview of a variety of subjects including the relation of the living to the dead, life after death, the truth about spiritualism, mediumship, automatic writing, astral projection, how to distinguish between the genuine and the spurious in occult science, and much else.

MILNER, DENNIS and EDWARD SMART. **THE LOOM OF CREATION. 7½"x10", index, 319pp. H&R76, 14.95c.**
Milner and Smart believe that they have discovered experimental evidence for the forces of creation described by mystics. They have spent over ten years painstakingly researching their thesis and they have drawn on a wide spectrum of data. In advancing the thesis they begin with a review of the nature of man and his development in earlier cultures. This is followed by a survey of *the experiences and viewpoint of Expanded Awareness* in which they discuss the human experience and the processes of creation and evolution. A third section details their

experiments with etheric forces and a fourth is an extensive annotated bibliography. The presentation is highly esoteric and is largely based on the philosophical presentation of Rudolf Steiner and Guenter Wachsmuth. A great deal of fascinating material is advanced but the book is written and organized in such a way that the authors' concepts elude the reader no matter how carefully he studies the material. This is another recent work which has potential, but which very often lacks clarity. Profusely illustrated in color and black and white.

MONGES, LISA. **EURYTHMY EXERCISES. Many illustrations, spiral bound, 8½"x11", 107pp. API75, 4.95p.**
The exercises presented in this volume presuppose a knowledge of the basic principles of eurythmy.

PALMER, OTTO, ed. **RUDOLF STEINER ON HIS BOOK, THE PHILOSOPHY OF FREEDOM. Notes, bibliography, 143pp. API75, 4.50p.**
No other book Rudolf Steiner wrote was as often and exhaustively discussed by him as **The Philosophy of Freedom**. *He not only refers to it . . . to call attention to some particularly interesting matter treated in its pages; he points again and again and yet again, from every imaginable angle, to what he intended this work to accomplish—indeed to initiate.*—from the introduction.

PELIKAN, WILHELM. **THE SECRETS OF METALS. 179pp. API73, 2.95p.**
A fascinating study of the inner nature of lead, tin, iron, copper, zinc, and aluminum.

PFEIFFER, EHRENFRIED. **THE ART AND SCIENCE OF COMPOSTING. 20pp. BID59, 1.50p.**
A technical paper outlining Pfeiffer's observations and his testing methods.

PFEIFFER, EHRENFRIED. **SENSITIVE CRYSTALLIZATION PROCESSES. Notes, bibliography, 59pp. API36, 10.00p.**
A demonstration and discussion of the formative forces in the blood based on Pfeiffer's extensive research. Seventy-eight photographs are included, and each plate is extensively analyzed.

PFEIFFER, EHRENFRIED. **WEEDS AND WHAT THEY TELL. Illustrations, index, 96pp. BID nd, 2.75p.**
A biodynamic analysis which discusses how plants grow, what they reveal about their surroundings, and how their powers may be harnessed for the benefit of the human beings who appreciate and use them.

POPPELBAUM, HERMANN. **A NEW ZOOLOGY. Many illustrations, 192pp. PAV61, 11.95c.**
A deep study of the formative forces in animals based on Steiner's spiritual science and on the writings of Guenther Wachsmuth.

QUERIDO, RENE. **QUESTIONS AND ANSWERS ON REINCARNATION AND KARMA. 31pp. SGP77, 2.95p.**
Querido is one of the leading contemporary American Anthroposophists and probably the Society's leading lecturer. In this pamphlet he considers various aspects of reincarnation and karma from the Anthroposophic point of view.

RAPHAEL, ALICE. **GOETHE AND THE PHILOSOPHER'S STONE. Notes, index, 273pp. GtP65, 8.50c.**
A study of the symbolical patterns in *The Parable* and the second part of Faust.

RATH, WILHELM. **THE IMAGERY OF THE GOETHEANUM WINDOWS.** RSP76, 12.50c.
An 8¾"x13" portfolio containing two color reproductions of the Goetheanum windows along with verses expressing in rhythmical form what the windows convey to Rath.

ROSCHL-LEHRS, MARIA. **THE SECOND MAN IN US: THE FORMING OF THE INNER MAN THROUGH SPIRITUAL TRAINING.** Notes, 106pp. Gou77, 6.95p.
In 1924 Steiner appointed Dr. Roschl as leader of the *Youth Section* at the Goetheanum. She worked at developing a *young people's Anthroposophy* and the essays compiled here are the result of her work.

ROSENKRANTZ, ARILD. **A NEW IMPULSE IN ART. Many color paintings, index, 169pp.** NKB67, 7.70c.
An illustrated examination of the new impulse in art arising from Steiner's work. Rosenkrantz was one of the artists who worked with Steiner in painting the domes of the Goetheanum in Dornach. In this book he reveals many of Steiner's suggestions.

SAVITCH, MARIE. **MARIE STEINER-VON SIVERS. 238pp.** RSP67, 6.50c.
A biographical study of Rudolf Steiner's wife.

SCHINDLER, MARIA. **EUROPE, A COSMIC PICTURE. 12"x13", index, 240pp.** NKB75, 13.00c.
Looked at from an earthly standpoint, the countries of Europe appear to be separate and segregated—but Maria Schindler takes the cosmic perspective that *Europe is a whole, a Zodiac incarnate, and that the various peoples of Europe are the bearers of the twelvefold divine creative impulses of the zodiac.* Initially the book focuses on the spiritual mission of Europe which is connected with the evolution of Christianity. Ms. Schindler feels that the theme of Europe's destiny is the quest for the Holy Grail. Passing from country to country, the book gives a lucid account of the birth of each nation and its subsequent historical development. Fifty-two beautiful plates are included.

SCHURE, EDOUARD. **FROM SPHINX TO CHRIST: AN OCCULT HISTORY. 284pp.** Mul70, 2.50p.
Rudolf Steiner considered Schure to be *one of the best guides for finding the path to the spirit in our day,* stating that the ideas expressed in his writings *can awaken within every human being a premonition of the solution of the riddles of existence.* We found his work rather white-Western-Christian supremacist. This is a comprehensive presentation beginning with planetary evolution and Atlantis.

SCHURE, EDOUARD. **THE GREAT INITIATES.** Mul76, 8.95p.
A collection of essays which discuss some of the great masters throughout history and their teachings and deeds.

SCHWENK, THEODOR. **SENSITIVE CHAOS. 8½"x10", 232pp.** ScB65, 8.95p.
An examination of the nature of water and air—the fluid and streaming elements—based upon the theories and discoveries of Rudolf Steiner. Schwenk begins with a study of the archetypal forms and movements of each element and from there he traces the development of substance. He views these as *the archetypal gesture of the cosmic alphabet, the word of the universe, which uses the element of movement in order to bring forth nature and man.* The text includes many line drawings and eighty-eight remarkable photographs. Schwenk is director of a German institute devoted to the study of water.

■ *SHEPHERD, A.P.* **THE SCIENTIST OF THE INVISIBLE. 221pp.** Hod54, 9.25c.
An excellent introduction to the life and work of Steiner. It gives a clear description of the man, his times, his teachings and work in many fields. Highly recommended.

STEBBING, LIONEL. **MUSIC: IT'S OCCULT BASIS AND HEALING VALUE.** 9.10p.
See the Music section.

STEBBING, LIONEL, ed. **MUSIC THERAPY.** 7.70p.
See the Music section.

STEINER, RUDOLF. **AGRICULTURE. 175pp.** Bio74, 9.50p.
A new edition of these long out of print lectures. Fascinating material for all gardeners, including color illustrations and practical advice.

STEINER, RUDOLF. **ANCIENT MYTHS: THEIR MEANING AND CONNECTION WITH EVOLUTION. 121pp.** SBC71, 5.75c.

STEINER, RUDOLF. **ANTHROPOSOPHICAL LEADING THOUGHTS. 220pp.** RSP73, 9.60c.
This volume contains brief paragraphs written by Rudolf Steiner for members of the Anthroposophical Society, dealing with Anthroposophy as a path of knowledge. *Letters and Leading Thoughts* were formerly available as a separate volume entitled **The Michael Mystery.**

STEINER, RUDOLF. **THE APOCALYPSE OF ST. JOHN. Notes, 237pp.** RSP77, 5.50p.
A cycle of thirteen lectures on the **Book of Revelation.** Illustrations of the seven apocalyptic seals are included.

STEINER, RUDOLF. **ART IN THE LIGHT OF MYSTERY WISDOM. 169pp.** RSP70, 6.50c.

■ *STEINER, RUDOLF.* **AT THE GATES OF SPIRITUAL SCIENCE. Notes, 157pp.** RSP70, 5.50p.
The fourteen lectures in this volume serve as an excellent introduction to Rudolf Steiner's whole teaching. He covers the basic ground of his teaching on the science of the spirit and includes discussions of many other topics including the nature of man, his place in the cosmic order of things and the evolution of the earth, life after death and man's tasks in that state of being, the principle of reincarnation, and the path of meditative training.

STEINER, RUDOLF. **ATLANTIS AND LEMURIA. Spiral bound offset, 131pp.** HeR23, 3.50p.
This is Steiner's most detailed investigation of our Atlantean and Lemurian forebearers. His emphasis is on the inner conditions of life at that time.

STEINER, RUDOLF. **AN AUTOBIOGRAPHY. Photographs, bibliography, 541pp.** Mul77, 9.95p.
This is a new translation of Steiner's autobiography. It has been edited by Dr. Paul Allen and is the most comprehensive edition to date. 648 notes explain every important reference mentioned by Steiner.

STEINER, RUDOLF. **AWAKENING TO COMMUNITY. 178pp.** API75, 6.50c.
In these lectures Steiner speaks of ways in which Anthroposophical groups can become true communities through their members awakening ever more consciously to the soul-spiritual element in their fellows.

STEINER, RUDOLF. **A BACKGROUND TO THE GOSPEL OF ST. MARK. 220pp.** RSP68, 6.50c.

STEINER, RUDOLF. **THE BALANCE IN THE WORLD AND MAN, LUCIFER AND AHRIMAN. 45pp.** SBC48, 1.75p.
Three lectures given by Steiner in 1914.

STEINER, RUDOLF. **BETWEEN DEATH AND REBIRTH.** 188pp. RSP75, 10.90c.
The main concern of these lectures is with life after death, after the *Kamaloka period. They disclose some of those factors in a person's life on earth which will influence his experiences during this period as well as those in the spiritual world which will affect his future earth-life. They also make clear the great significance for spiritual progress of our connection with the earth and speak of the influence the living may have on the souls of the dead.*—from the introduction.

STEINER, RUDOLF. **THE BHAGAVAD GITA AND THE EPISTLES OF PAUL.** 102pp. API71, 5.50c.

STEINER, RUDOLF. **BUILDING STONES FOR AN UNDERSTANDING OF THE MYSTERY OF GOLGOTHA.** 239pp. RSP72, 9.60c.
The Mystery of Golgotha must be regarded as the central point in human evolution. From the Fall until the Mystery of Golgotha man experienced a progressive decline of his spiritual forces. The forces of corruption had increasingly invaded his soul and threatened to make man an automaton of the spirit. And from the Mystery of Golgotha until the end of the Earth cycle all that was lost before the Mystery of Golgotha will gradually to retrieved once more. It seems that the material in this volume would require very intensive study, as well as patient effort, to begin to grasp the importance of what Steiner would probably consider the greatest mystery.

STEINER, RUDOLF. **THE CALENDAR OF THE SOUL.** 120pp. API74, 3.95c.
A meditative verse for each week of the year, beginning at Easter, following the progress of the soul's living response to the seasons.

STEINER, RUDOLF. **CHRIST AND THE HUMAN SOUL.** 78pp. RSP72, 2.75p.

STEINER, RUDOLF. **THE CHRIST IMPULSE AND THE DEVELOPMENT OF EGO CONSCIOUSNESS.** 156pp. API76, 3.95p.
Seven lectures, delivered in 1910.

STEINER, RUDOLF. **CHRIST IN THE TWENTIETH CENTURY.** 20pp. API71, .95p.

STEINER, RUDOLF. **CHRISTIANITY AS MYSTICAL FACT.** 195pp. RSP47, 2.95p.
A revised edition of this important and basic book. Here Steiner describes the character of the ancient mystery teachings and then uses it to illumine mythology, the Greek sages, Plato and the neo-Platonists, the Gospels (especially the story of the raising of Lazarus), and post-Christian writings like those of Augustine. He also looks to the future and discusses the significance for the modern age of the ever-renewing *Christ Impulse.*

STEINER, RUDOLF. **COLOUR.** 100pp. RSP71, 4.95p.
What Rudolf Steiner gave in these lectures in 1921 was the fruit of efforts he had been engaged in for forty years toward an understanding of the nature of colour. A close connection to the world of colour can indeed be traced through the whole of his life's work, and this fact becomes particularly poignant when we realise that it was Goethe's Theory of Color that was the starting point for this life's work.—from the introduction. Extracts from Steiner's notebooks and a long series of notes are also included in this edition, along with color exercises reproduced from Boos-Hamburger's book **The Creative Power of Colour.**

STEINER, RUDOLF. **THE CONCEPTS OF ORIGINAL SIN AND GRACE.** 32pp. RSP73, 1.10p.

STEINER, RUDOLF. **COSMIC MEMORY: ATLANTIS AND LEMURIA.** 2.95p.
See the Ancient Civilizations section.

STEINER, RUDOLF. **THE DEAD ARE WITH US.** 32pp. RSP73, 1.10p.

STEINER, RUDOLF. **THE DEATH OF GOD AND IT'S FRUITS IN HUMANITY.** Offset, 8½"x11", 20pp. HeR12, 2.00p.
The title lecture is bound together with one lecture out of Steiner's series on the **Gospel of St. Mark.**

STEINER, RUDOLF. **THE DEED OF CHRIST AND THE OPPOSING SPIRITUAL POWERS LUCIFER, AHRIMAN, MEPHISTOPHELES, ASURAS.** 43pp. SBC54, 1.50p.
Two fundamental lectures, delivered in 1909.

STEINER, RUDOLF. **THE DESCENT OF THE SPIRIT: GAINING A RELATIONSHIP TO THE DEAD THROUGH THE LANGUAGE OF THE HEART.** Offset, 8¼"x11", 28pp. HeR22, 2.00p.
The title lecture bound together with *Supersensible Knowledge: Anthroposophy as a Demand of the Age.*

STEINER, RUDOLF. **THE DRIVING FORCE OF SPIRITUAL POWERS IN WORLD HISTORY.** 95pp. SBC72, 5.50c.

STEINER, RUDOLF. **EARTHLY DEATH AND COSMIC LIFE.** 160pp. RSP64, 4.95c.
The lectures in this volume *were given at a time during the First World War when many souls were passing through the gate of death. The desire for knowledge that will help to realise true links between the living and the dead is no less intense today, nor is the need of an approach in keeping with that healthy and vigilant consciousness which is proper to the modern age any less great.*—from the introduction.

STEINER, RUDOLF. **EASTER FESTIVAL IN RELATION TO THE MYSTERIES.** 78pp. RSP68, 2.75p.

STEINER, RUDOLF. **EGYPTIAN MYTHS AND MYSTERIES.** 5.95c.
See the Ancient Egypt section.

STEINER, RUDOLF. **ELEVEN EUROPEAN MYSTICS.** 251pp. Mul71, 2.50p.
Steiner relates how eleven men who lived during the period bridging Middle Ages to Renaissance resolved within themselves the conflict between their spiritual perceptions and the emerging scientific world then coming to birth.

STEINER, RUDOLF. **ESCAPE FROM TRUTH—THE LIVING RELATIONSHIP OF THE WORD WITH REALITY.** Offset, 8½"x11", 12pp. HeR16, 1.00p.

STEINER, RUDOLF. **ETHERISATION OF BLOOD.** API35, 1.10p.

STEINER, RUDOLF. **EURYTHMY AS VISIBLE MUSIC.** Illustrations, 126pp. RSP77, 8.25c.
This cycle of lectures, delivered in Dornach in 1924, contains Steiner's most advanced thoughts on eurythmy.

STEINER, RUDOLF. **THE EVENT OF THE APPEARANCE OF CHRIST IN THE ETHERIC WORLD.** Offset, 8½"x11", 36pp. HeR23, 2.50p.
The title lecture bound together with *Effects of Substance in the Cosmos and In the Human Body* and *Anthroposophy and the Ethical-Religious Conduct of Life.*

STEINER, RUDOLF. **FACING KARMA.** 20pp. API75, .95p.

STEINER, RUDOLF. **FREDERICH NIETZCHE: FIGHTER FOR FREEDOM.** 222pp. Mul60, 5.50p
Four fairly long lectures covering Nietzsche's character, path of development, philosophy, and personality.

STEINER, RUDOLF. **FROM JESUS TO CHRIST.** 9.60c.
See the Christianity section.

STEINER, RUDOLF. **FROM SYMPTOM TO REALITY IN MODERN HISTORY.** Notes, 245pp. RSP76, 12.50c.
In these lectures, Steiner surveys some of the developments in European consciousness and outlook since the fifteenth century which have gradually formed the Europe of the twentieth century. He examines the rise of nationalism and shows how a difference in religious outlook has played its part in the course of events.

STEINER, RUDOLF. **THE GOSPEL OF ST. JOHN.** 192pp. API62, 3.50p.
Steiner has a great deal to say about the Gospels. He examines each writer as a person and as a spiritual force in history. He also touches on what each Gospel conveys on material and metaphysical levels about Christ and the Christ being and how each Gospel relates to writings before and after it.

STEINER, RUDOLF. **THE GOSPEL OF ST. LUKE.** 203pp. API27, 4.95p.

STEINER, RUDOLF. **THE GOSPEL OF ST. MARK. 217pp. API50, 5.50c.**

STEINER, RUDOLF. **THE GOSPEL OF ST. MATTHEW. Offset, 8½",11", 9pp. HeR10, 1.00p.**
Lecture five of the title series.

STEINER, RUDOLF. **THE GUARDIAN OF THE THRESHOLD. 128pp. SBC73, 3.25p.**
A play.

STEINER, RUDOLF. **GUIDANCE IN ESOTERIC TRAINING. 109pp. RSP72, 6.50p.**

STEINER, RUDOLF. **THE INFLUENCES OF LUCIFER AND AHRI-MAN. 83pp. SBC54, 2.95p.**
A collection of five lectures based on Steiner's concepts of man's responsibility for the Earth.

STEINER, RUDOLF. **INITIATION AND IT'S RESULTS. Offset, spiral bound, 180pp. HeR nd, 3.00p.**

STEINER, RUDOLF. **THE INNER ASPECT OF THE SOCIAL QUES-TION. 70pp. RSP74, 2.75p.**
These lectures seek to give an understanding of the spiritual background of the social situation and indicate the moral prerequisites essential to any form of reorganization.

STEINER, RUDOLF. **INNER DEVELOPMENT OF MAN. 22pp. API70, .75p.**

STEINER, RUDOLF. **INVESTIGATIONS IN OCCULTISM. Offset, spiral bound, 206pp. HeR29, 4.50p.**

STEINER, RUDOLF. **JESUS AND CHRIST. 23pp. API76, .95p.**

STEINER, RUDOLF. **KARMIC RELATIONSHIPS.**
Steiner gave eighty-two lectures on karma in 1924 and this cycle represents his most advanced thinking on the subject. The most important of these lectures are transcribed in the volumes in this series. I, 6.50c; II, 8.25c; III, 8.25c; VI, 6.50c; VII, 6.50c; VIII, 6.50c. Each is about 200 pages.

STEINER, RUDOLF. **KNOWLEDGE AND INITIATION. Offset, 8½"x 11", 23pp. HeR22, 2.00p.**
The title lecture bound together with *Knowledge of the Christ Through Anthroposophy.*

■ *STEINER, RUDOLF.* **KNOWLEDGE OF HIGHER WORLDS AND ITS ATTAINMENT. 272pp. API47/RSP, 4.95c/2.95p.**
Steiner's famous work outlining certain spiritual practices designed as a normal and healthy path of training. It presents in detail the means whereby everyone can develop a new knowledge of the higher worlds of soul and spirit.

STEINER, RUDOLF. **THE LAST ADDRESS. 23pp. RSP67, 2.90c.**

STEINER RUDOLF. **LECTURE ON EURYTHMY. 36pp. RSP67, 2.50p.**
An introduction which Steiner gave in 1923 to the then new art of movement called eurythmy. He deals mainly with the interpretation of speech but *always regarded it as essential that in a performance there should be the interpretation of speech as well as of music.*—from the introduction.

STEINER, RUDOLF. **LIFE BETWEEN DEATH AND REBIRTH. 308pp. API68, 4.95p.**
A collection of sixteen lectures which complement those in **Between Death and Rebirth.**

STEINER, RUDOLF. **LINKS BETWEEN THE LIVING AND THE DEAD. 64pp. RSP73, 1.65p.**

STEINER, RUDOLF. **LORD'S PRAYER. 26pp. API70, .95p.**

STEINER, RUDOLF. **LOVE AND ITS MEANING IN THE WORLD. 27pp. RSP72, 1.10p.**

STEINER, RUDOLF. **MAN AS A PICTURE OF THE LIVING SPIRIT. 32pp. RSP72, 1.10p.**

STEINER, RUDOLF. **MAN—HIEROGLYPH OF THE UNIVERSE. 220pp. RSP72, 4.50p.**
Sixteen lectures which discuss man's search for concrete, realistic knowledge of his whole being and of the position he occupies in the universe.

STEINER, RUDOLF. **MAN IN THE LIGHT OF OCCULTISM, THE-OSOPHY, AND PHILOSOPHY. 214pp. RSP45, 4.75c.**
In this cycle of lectures we propose to consider man in his spiritual nature from three standpoints....I refer to the standpoints of occultism, theosophy, and philosophy.

STEINER, RUDOLF. **MANIFESTATIONS OF KARMA. 260pp. RSP36, 5.50p.**
Transcriptions of eleven lectures given in 1910.

STEINER, RUDOLF. **MAN'S BEING, HIS DESTINY AND WORLD EVOLUTION. 114pp. API52, 5.25c.**
Steiner relates man's being to the extensive spaces of the cosmos in his discussion of the period between falling asleep and waking and the path pursued by man between death and a new birth.

STEINER, RUDOLF. **MAN'S LIFE ON EARTH AND IN THE SPIRIT-UAL WORLD. Offset, 8½"x11", 86pp. HeR22, 3.00p.**
Transcriptions of the following lectures: *The Threefold Sun and the Risen Christ, The Cosmic Origin of the Human Form, Man's Life in Sleep and After Death, Life in the Spiritual Spheres and the Return to Earth, Luciferic and Ahrimanic Powers Wrestling for Man,* and *Christ and the Metamorphoses of Karma.*

STEINER, RUDOLF. **METHODS OF SPIRITUAL RESEARCH. 128pp. Mul71, 1.75p.**

STEINER, RUDOLF. **THE MISSION OF FOLK-SOULS. 189pp. RSP70, 8.00c.**
Eleven lectures which study national characteristics from the viewpoint of the psychic and spiritual elements that underlie them.

STEINER, RUDOLF. **THE MISSION OF SPIRITUAL SCIENCE AND OF ITS BUILDING AT DORNACH, SWITZERLAND. Offset, 63pp. HeR16, 1.50p.**

STEINER, RUDOLF. **MYSTERIES OF THE EAST AND OF CHRIST-IANITY. 79pp. RSP72, 2.75p.**
A discussion of the nature of the mysteries, the void, the Zarathustrian initiation, the music of the spheres, the inner relationship between the Egyptian mysteries and the Grail, and much else.

STEINER, RUDOLF. **MYSTERY KNOWLEDGE AND MYSTERY CENTERS. 207pp. RSP73, 8.00c.**
These lectures were given immediately before the refounding of the Anthroposophical Society, when Steiner wished to see the esoteric life developed more strongly. In the lecture series Steiner speaks of man's soul and of the ancient mystery teachings and what modern man can learn from these teachings. The teachings reviewed include the Ephesian, the Hibernian, the Eleusinian, and those of the Samothracian Kabiri.

STEINER, RUDOLF. **MYSTIC SEALS AND COLUMNS. Offset, stapled, 8½"x11", HeR nd, 7.50p.**

STEINER, RUDOLF. **MYSTICS OF THE RENAISSANCE AND THEIR RELATION TO MODERN THOUGHT. Spiral bound, offset, 290pp. HeR11, 5.00p.**
This is one of the few transcriptions which Steiner supervised himself. It includes lectures on Meister Eckhart, Suso, Ruysbroeck, Tauler, Agrippa, Paracelsus, Valentine Weigel, Jacob Boehme, Giordano Bruno, and Angelus Silesius. Much of the material covered here is not found in Steiner's other published lectures.

STEINER, RUDOLF. **NEWBORN MIGHT AND STRENGTH EVER-LASTING: A CHRISTMAS OFFERING. 14pp. API77, .95p.**
A lecture on the Christ being, delivered in 1913.

STEINER, RUDOLF. **NINE LECTURES ON BEES. Illustrations, 96pp.** **SGB64, 6.50p.**
A series of lectures given, on request, to workmen at the Goetheanum in 1923. The language here is simpler than that of most of Steiner's lectures.

STEINER, RUDOLF. **THE OCCULT MOVEMENT IN THE NINE-TEENTH CENTURY. 190pp. RSP73, 9.50c.**

STEINER, RUDOLF. **OCCULT MYSTERIES OF ANTIQUITY AND CHRISTIANITY. 243pp. Mul61, 2.75p.**

STEINER, RUDOLF. **OCCULT READING AND OCCULT HEARING. 80pp. RSP75, 2.25p.**
The physical world is no more than a written page before us. If we only stare at it, we can observe it without being able to read it at all. Neither do we know anything of the world if we look at it only with the faculty of physical perception, for then we do not decipher, we do not really penetrate into the world. We must read the world, learn its meaning.—Rudolf Steiner

STEINER, RUDOLF. **THE OCCULT SIGNIFICANCE OF THE BHA-GAVAD GITA. 142pp. API68, 5.50c.**

STEINER, RUDOLF. **OCCULT SIGNS AND SYMBOLS. 74pp. API72, 1.95p.**

STEINER, RUDOLF. **AN OUTLINE OF OCCULT SCIENCE. 388pp. API72, 7.50c/4.50p.**
No single book can be said to contain the whole of Anthroposophy, but this book comes the closest. It sets out in systematic fashion the fundamental facts concerning the nature and constitution of man, his history, and the history of the universe.

STEINER, RUDOLF. **OVERCOMING NERVOUSNESS. 19pp. API69, .95p.**

STEINER, RUDOLF. **THE PHILOSOPHY OF FREEDOM. 226pp. RSP64, 8.00c/3.95p.**
The central statement of Steiner's philosophy of liberation based on the mode of higher thinking. He emphasizes that an illumined use of the faculty of mind can be the means to spiritual attainment and is the factor that will lead to true inner and outer freedom.

STEINER, RUDOLF. **PRACTICAL TRAINING IN THOUGHT. 25pp. API66, .95p.**

STEINER, RUDOLF. **PRAYER. 27pp. API52, .95p.**
Transcription of a lecture given in 1910.

STEINER, RUDOLF. **PRE-EARTHLY DEEDS OF CHRIST. 16pp. SBC47, 1.25p.**
A lecture given in 1914.

STEINER, RUDOLF. **PREPARING FOR THE SIXTH EPOCH. 22pp. API57, .95p.**

STEINER, RUDOLF. **PROBLEMS OF NUTRITION. 22pp. API69, .95p.**
A brief lecture on the spiritual effects of consuming meat, alcohol, coffee, milk. *If by eating meat a person is relieved of too large a portion of his inner activities, then activities will develop inwardly that would otherwise be expressed externally. His soul will become more externally oriented, more susceptible to, and bound up with, the external world. When a person takes his nourishment from the realm of plants, however, he becomes more independent and more inclined to develop inwardly. He will become master of his whole being. The more he is inclined to vegetarianism, the more he accepts a vegetarian diet, the more he will be able also to let his inner forces predominate.*

STEINER, RUDOLF. **THE RIDDLES OF THE INNER HUMAN BEING: THE APPROACH OF THE MICHAEL FORCE. Offset, 8½"x11", 15pp. HeR23, 1.00p.**

STEINER, RUDOLF. **THE RIDDLES OF PHILOSOPHY. 479pp. API73, 6.95p.**

STEINER, RUDOLF. **A ROAD TO SELF KNOWLEDGE AND THE THRESHOLD OF THE SPIRITUAL WORLD. 174pp. RSP75, 4.50p.**
A Road to Self Knowledge consists of a graded series of eight meditations and **The Threshold of the Spiritual World** discusses man's astral and etheric bodies and his contact with other planes. Steiner felt that both of these essays completed and amplified his other writings.

STEINER, RUDOLF. **SECRETS OF THE BIBLICAL STORY OF CREATION. Offset, 8½"x11", 88pp. HeR10, 4.00p.**
Transcription of a course of seven lectures.

STEINER, RUDOLF. **SIGNS AND SYMBOLS OF THE CHRISTMAS FESTIVAL. 63pp. API69, 3.50c.**
Transcription of the title lecture and two others: *The Birth of the Light,* and *The Christmas Festival as a Symbol of the Sun Victory.*

STEINER, RUDOLF. **THE SOCIAL FUTURE. 151pp. RSP68, 2.50p.**
These lectures are designed to show that the threefold social order can bring about a healthy social organism that will overcome the polarizing tendencies of modern life and make the economy the servant of society rather than its master.

STEINER, RUDOLF. **THE SOUL'S AWAKENING. 149pp. SBC73, 3.25p.**

STEINER, RUDOLF. **THE SOUL'S PROBATION. 128pp. SBC73, 2.95p.**

STEINER, RUDOLF. **SPIRITUAL GUIDANCE OF MAN. 85pp. API50, 2.50p.**

STEINER, RUDOLF. **THE SPIRITUAL HIERARCHIES. 140pp. API70, 5.50c.**

STEINER, RUDOLF. **SPIRITUAL SCIENCE AND MEDICINE. Illustrations, index, 277pp. RSP48, 10.90c/6.50p.**
The twenty lectures in this volume were given by Steiner in response to requests by a number of physicians. Their form and content were also determined by specific questions asked by those attending the course. Basically the lectures led to a deepened understanding of man's being, without which, in Steiner's words, *it has actually become impossible to investigate the true nature of health and disease.* Many case studies included in the lectures show the importance of spiritual insights in true healing. The language is often technical.

STEINER, RUDOLF. **STAGES OF HIGHER KNOWLEDGE. 72pp. API67, 1.95p.**
A further study of the information discussed in **Knowledge of Higher Worlds**, concerned with the three stages of imagination, inspiration, and intuition.

STEINER, RUDOLF. **STRUCTURE OF THE LORD'S PRAYER. 29pp. API71, 1.10p.**

STEINER, RUDOLF. **THE STUDY OF MAN. 193pp. API66, 4.25p.**
These lectures were given as a preparation for their task to teachers of the original Waldorf School. They not only detail Steiner's educational views, but reveal his fundamental views on the psychology of man.

STEINER, RUDOLF. **SUPERSENSIBLE INFLUENCES IN THE HIS-TORY OF MANKIND. 83pp. RSP56, 2.95c.**

STEINER, RUDOLF. **SUPERSENSIBLE MAN. 101pp. RSP61, 5.50c.**
A course of five lectures given in 1923 on the occasion of the founding of the Anthroposophical Society in Holland.

■ *STEINER, RUDOLF.* **THEOSOPHY—AN INTRODUCTION TO SUPERSENSIBLE KNOWLEDGE. 195pp. API71, 5.75c/3.95p.**
As Steiner himself puts it, *The purpose of this book is to give a description of some of the regions of the supersensible world. The reader who is only willing to admit the existence of the sensible world will look upon this description as merely an unreal product of the imagination. Whoever looks for paths that lead beyond this world of the senses, however, will soon learn to understand that human life only gains worth and significance through insight into another world.* This is one of the best introductions to Steiner's thought.

STEINER, RUDOLF. **TOWARDS SOCIAL RENEWAL. Introduction, notes, 152pp. RSP77, 4.50p.**
This volume, originally entitled **The Threefold Social Order**, contains a call for liberty in human creativity, equality in the realm of human rights, and fraternity instead of competition in commerce and industry.

STEINER, RUDOLF. **TRUE AND FALSE PATHS IN SPIRITUAL INVESTIGATION.** 222pp. RSP69, 8.00c.

STEINER, RUDOLF. **THE TRUE NATURE OF THE SECOND COMING.** 81pp. RSP61, 2.25p.

STEINER, RUDOLF. **WHAT IS REVEALED WHEN ONE LOOKS BACK INTO REPEATED LIVES ON EARTH.** Offset, 8½"x11", 14pp. HeR25, 1.00p.
The title lecture bound with *Michael and the Dragon.*

STEINER, RUDOLF. **THE WISDOM OF MAN, OF THE SOUL, AND OF THE SPIRIT.** 204pp. API71, 7.50c.

STEINER, RUDOLF. **THE WORK OF THE ANGELS IN MAN'S ASTRAL BODY.** 40pp. RSP60, 1.10p.

STEINER, RUDOLF. **WORLD ECONOMY.** 188pp. RSP49, 5.50p.

UNGER, CARL. **PRINCIPLES OF SPIRITUAL SCIENCE.** 86pp. API76, 2.95p.
Anthroposophy, or spiritual science, which comprises Rudolf Steiner's researches into the supersensible nature of man and the world, is based on a carefully worked out theory of knowledge. This is developed in Steiner's earlier philosophical work....As his activities increased, however, and the significance of spiritual science for all departments of knowledge and culture became apparent, it was not possible even for Steiner, with the time at his disposal, to follow each one up in detail. Wherever possible, he found collaborators who could do this for him. Carl Unger was one of these collaborators.—from the foreword.

WACHSMUTH, GUENTHER. **REINCARNATION.** 14.00c.
See the Reincarnation and Karma section.

Waldorf Education

Rudolf Steiner has repeatedly spoken of the need for a deeper understanding of man himself and of his relationship to the world. When he called together the teachers who were to carry responsibility for the first [Waldorf] school, he gave them a new conception of the growing child and its needs. He showed how during the first seven years the little child is building its own bodily form. At birth it was given the body prepared for it by its parents and gradually this has to be replaced out of its own living forces. It is damaging to the child's health if at this stage it is approached intellectually. It needs its growth powers to build a sturdy frame. It has to explore its surroundings by finding out what its body can do, by balancing, running, and climbing. It has to acquire skills in doing up buttons and tying shoe laces. It is learning how to relate itself to the world of space, and when attempts are made to stimulate its intellect the child's forces of growth are disturbed. We have one great help in educating children under seven and that is their power of imitation. It is so important that those who look after little ones be worthy of imitation. The different stages of the child's growth are marked by physiological changes. Thus through the different stages of childhood and youth pupils are enabled to unfold their own capacities. From healthy imitation in the first years they develop strength of will. Through joy in what they learn under the guidance of a loved teacher, their feelings are enriched and give life to their thinking. During their adolescence they discover the creative quality of thought. Then they can face life with confidence in their own powers.
—*condensed from "The Normal Child," by Eileen Hutchins, from Davy's* **Work Arising**

BARAVALLE, HERMANN VON. **ASTRONOMY.** 41pp. SGP74, 3.50p.

BARAVALLE, HERMANN VON. **GEOMETRIC DRAWING AND THE WALDORF SCHOOL PLAN.** 58pp. SGP67, 3.00p.

BARAVALLE, HERMANN VON. **THE INTERNATIONAL WALDORF SCHOOL MOVEMENT.** 49pp. SGP63, 3.95p.
A history of the Waldorf school movement combined with an analysis of the main tenets of Waldorf education.

BARAVALLE, HERMANN VON. **INTRODUCTION TO PHYSICS IN THE WALDORF SCHOOL.** 44pp. SGP67, 2.25p.

BARAVALLE, HERMANN VON. **PERSPECTIVE DRAWING.** 50pp. SGP68, 2.25p.

BARAVALLE, HERMANN VON. **TEACHING OF ARITHMETIC AND THE WALDORF SCHOOL PLAN.** 90pp. SGP67, 3.00p.

CALGREN, FRANS. **EDUCATION TOWARDS FREEDOM.** 13½" x 9¾", 208pp. Lnt76, 22.65c.
This is a well illustrated documentation of Waldorf education. Examples and illustrations of children's work were collected from Waldorf schools throughout the world. The text discusses the various subjects and areas covered in the school curriculum. The bulk of the innumerable illustrations are in full color.

GLAS, WERNER. **SPEECH EDUCATION IN PRIMARY GRADES OF WALDORF SCHOOLS.** 103pp. Sun74, 5.85p.

GRUNELIUS, ELIZABETH. **EARLY CHILDHOOD EDUCATION AND WALDORF SCHOOL PLAN.** 47pp. SGP66, 2.00p.

HARWOOD, A.C. **THE WAY OF A CHILD.** 144pp. RSP40, 3.50p.
This little book is entirely based on the study of Rudolf Steiner's books and lectures on childhood and education, and many years of experience as a teacher in a school founded to carry out his ideas.—from the foreword.

HAUCK, HEDWIG. **HANDWORK AND HANDICRAFTS FROM INDICATIONS BY RUDOLF STEINER.** Many illustrations, 9"x11½", 122pp. RSP68, 8.75c.
Steiner discussed handwork in a number of his lectures on education and showed how his suggestions could be applied while he was directing the Waldorf School in Stuttgart toward the end of his life. He felt that handiwork provides the balancing element which the more intellectual activities require if the development of the child is to be harmonious.

HUTCHINS, EILEEN. **OBSERVATION, THINKING, THE SENSES.** 23pp. SGP40, 1.95p.
A series of articles relating observation, thinking, and the senses to the philosophy of Waldorf education.

JACOBS, VALERIE. **BLACK AND WHITE SHADED DRAWINGS.** Many illustrations, 64pp. RSP75, 4.95p.
An instructional course in shaded drawing, a technique which originated in a suggestion of Rudolf Steiner. Ms. Jacobs is one of the chief exponents of the technique.

MCALLEN, AUDREY. **THE EXTRA LESSON.** 76pp. RSB74, 5.50p.
Exercises in movement, drawing, and painting for helping children with difficulties in writing, reading, and arithmetic.

MCALLEN, AUDREY. **TEACHING CHILDREN TO WRITE.** Bibliography, 80pp. RSP77, 4.50p.
A practical discussion of the methods of presenting the art of handwriting from the viewpoint of Waldorf education. Ms. McAllen considers the effects of an artistic approach to the teaching of handwriting in relation to the developing soul of the child. She also covers spelling and writing difficulties and gives many examples of practical work.

METAXA, GEORGE. **MUSIC FOR CHILDREN'S EURYTHMY AND DANCE.** 26pp. SGP nd, 3.00p.

NIEDERHAUSER, HANS and MARGARET FROHLICH. **FORM DRAWING.** Oversize, 57pp. SGP74, 4.50p.
Form drawing is the term used for the exercises practiced in Waldorf schools which help train the dexterity of the children's hands in writing letters and numbers. This training goes gradually much further than writing: by learning to look at the relationships between all parts of one's drawing and the page as a whole, one develops a sense for composition and a foundation is laid for what later on will be the

study of geometry. This is a practical guide which includes many exercises and examples.

STEINER, RUDOLF. **CURATIVE EDUCATION. 222pp. RSP62, 7.50c.**
Transcription of a course of lectures for doctors and curative teachers which discusses a great variety of physical and mental disturbances and outlines suggestions for the treatment of a disturbed child.

STEINER, RUDOLF. **EDUCATION AS A SOCIAL PROBLEM. 113pp. API69, 5.50c.**
This is one of Steiner's most basic writings on Waldorf education.

STEINER, RUDOLF. **THE EDUCATION OF THE CHILD. 48pp. RSP65, 1.00p.**

STEINER, RUDOLF. **HUMAN VALUES IN EDUCATION. 189pp. RSP71, 5.50c.**
The underlying thesis of these lectures is that a true education must be founded on a knowledge of man, and that there can be no knowledge of man without love. The lectures investigate every aspect of the child's growth in his threefold aspect of body, soul, and spirit.

STEINER, RUDOLF. **THE KINGDOM OF CHILDHOOD. 162pp. API64, 4.50p.**
In these lectures Steiner shows how essential it is for a teacher to work upon himself, not merely to use his natural gifts but to transform them, to seek for unsuspected power in himself, never to become a pedant, but to make ample use of humor and keep his teaching and himself lively and imaginative. And above all, Steiner insists on the importance of doing everything in the light of the earthly world.

STEINER, RUDOLF. **PRACTICAL ADVICE TO TEACHERS. Notes, 205pp. RSP76, 10.90c/5.50p.**
Fourteen lectures given at the founding of the Waldorf School, Stuttgart, in 1919.

STEINER, RUDOLF. **STUDY OF MAN. 193pp. RSP66, 4.50p.**
These lectures were given as a preparation for their task to teachers of the original Waldorf School. They not only detail Steiner's educational views, but reveal his fundamental views on the psychology of man.

STEINER, RUDOLF. **SUPERSENSIBLE PHYSIOLOGY AND BALANCE IN TEACHING. Offset, 8½"x11", 15pp. HeR20, 2.50p.**

STEINER, RUDOLF. **THE THREE FUNDAMENTAL FORCES IN EDUCATION. Offset, 8½"x11", 15pp. HeR26, 1.00p.**
The title lecture bound together with Violet Plincke's essay *Rudolf Steiner's Gift to Education.*

STEINER, RUDOLF. **THE YOUNGER GENERATION. 179pp. API73, 3.95p.**
Subtitled, *Educational and Spiritual Impulses for Life in the Twentieth Century.*

WILKINSON, ROY. **COMMONSENSE SCHOOLING. Bibliography, 97pp. Gou75, 4.95p.**
This is an excellent treatise on Waldorf education by one of the movement's leading educators. The book is divided into the following sections: *Education Today, Purpose of Education, The Nature of the Child, School Structure and Organisation, What to Teach, The How of Various Subjects,* and *Teachers and Taught.*

WILKINSON, ROY. **LEARNING TO WRITE AND READ. 8"x10", 17pp. Wlk73, 1.00p.**

WILKINSON, ROY. **THE DEVELOPMENT OF LANGUAGE. 21pp. Wlk73, 1.20p.**
Wilkinson's books are geared toward classroom and at home use and are generally considered excellent manuals.

WILKINSON, ROY. **PLANT STUDY—GEOLOGY. 34pp. Wlk75, 3.00p.**

WILKINSON, ROY. **MAN AND ANIMAL. 22pp. Wlk75, 3.00p.**

WILKINSON, ROY. **SOCIAL ASPECTS. 8"x10", 16pp. Wlk73, 1.25p.**

WILKINSON, ROY. **STUDIES IN PRACTICAL ACTIVITIES. 26pp. Wlk75, 3.00p.**

WILKINSON, ROY. **TEACHING HISTORY I: INDIA AND PERSIA. 27pp. Wlk73, 1.60p.**

WILKINSON, ROY. **TEACHING HISTORY II: EGYPT, CHALDEA, BABYLONIA, 33pp. Wlk74, 1.60p.**

WILKINSON, ROY. **TEACHING HISTORY III: GREECE AND ROME. 37pp. Wlk74, 3.00p.**

WILKINSON, ROY. **THE TEMPERAMENTS. 25pp. Wlk73, 1.80p.**

WYATT, ISABEL and JOAN RUDEL, eds. **HAY FOR MY OX. 9"x8½", 101pp. Lnt68, 7.20c.**
A first reading book for Waldorf schools. Anthroposophic style color and black and white drawings accompany the stories.

WYATT, ISABEL and JOAN RUDEL. **THE KING AND THE GREEN ANGELICA. 9"x8½", 113pp. Lnt75, 10.55c.**
The second in a series of Waldorf readers, intended for use at the fourth class stage. The main substance of the book consists of stories of Norse heroes drawn from the collection of tales compiled by Saxo Grammaticus and other Scandinavian writers. The illustrations have been recreated from old Norse motifs, drawings, and carvings.

————**END OF WALDORF EDUCATION SUBSECTION**————

WHICHER, OLIVE. **GEORGE ADAMS: INTERPRETER OF RUDOLF STEINER, HIS LIFE AND A SELECTION OF HIS ESSAYS. Illustrations, notes, 180pp. Gou77, 7.95p.**
Among Steiner's followers, Adams was one of the ones most interested in directing scientific thinking into more spiritual channels. He wrote and worked most extensively on botany and sacred geometry. This is an excellent, detailed study of his life and work.

WHICHER, OLIVE. **PROJECTIVE GEOMETRY: CREATIVE POLARITIES IN SPACE AND TIME. 16.00c.**
See the Sacred Geometry section.

WINKLER, FRANZ. **FOR FREEDOM DESTINED. 174pp. Wal74, 6.95c.**
Subtitled, *Mysteries of Man's Evolution in the Mythology of Wagner's* **Ring Operas** *and* **Parsifal**.

WINKLER, FRANZ. **MAN: BRIDGE BETWEEN TWO WORLDS.**
Notes, bibliography, index, 268pp. Wal60, 4.50p.

EDMOND SZEKELY

Edmond B. Szekely, the eminent poet and Unitarian Bishop of Cluj, is a descendant of Csoma de Koros, Transylvanian traveler and philologist who, over a century ago, compiled the first grammar of the Tibetan language, an English-Tibetan dictionary, and wrote his unsurpassed work, **Asiatic Researches**. He also was Librarian to the Royal Asiatic Society in India. Dr. Bordeaux earned his Ph.D. degree from the University of Paris and other degrees from the Universities of Vienna and Leipzig. He also held professorships of Philosophy and Experimental Psychology at the University of Cluj. A well known philologist in Sanskrit, Aramaic, Greek, and Latin, Dr. Bordeaux speaks ten modern languages. His most important translations, in addition to selected texts from the **Dead Sea Scrolls** and the **Essene Gospel of Peace**, are selected texts from the **Zend Avesta** and from pre-Columbian codices of ancient Mexico. He is the author of sixty-eight books, on philosophy and ancient cultures, published in several countries.

SZEKELY, EDMOND. **ANCIENT AMERICA: PARADISE LOST. 4.80p.**
See the Ancient Americas section.

SZEKELY, EDMOND. **ARCHEOSOPHY: A NEW SCIENCE. Illustrations, 31pp. Aca73, 3.80p.**
Archeosophy is an application of philosophy to archaeology, through the medium of ancient symbols and pictographs.

SZEKELY, EDMOND. **THE ART OF STUDY. Aca nd, 2.50p.**
A guidebook to learning, with many practical suggestions.

SZEKELY, EDMOND. **THE BOOK OF HERBS. 46pp. Aca75, 2.25p.**
A brief compendium of diseases and remedies as well as a herbal materia medica.

SZEKELY, EDMOND. **THE BOOK OF LIVING FOODS. Aca nd, 2.95p.**
A natural foods cookbook, filled with nutritional suggestions based on Szekely's philosophy and personal experience.

SZEKELY, EDMOND. **THE BOOK OF MINERALS. 38pp. Aca71, 1.95p.**
Similar to his vitamin book, this is a brief guide to the role of each mineral in our basic biological functions, our requirements for each, mineral deficiency symptoms, best natural sources in order of importance, and a list of symptoms, with minerals to take for each. For quick reference it is hard to beat.

SZEKELY, EDMOND. **THE BOOK OF VITAMINS. 38pp. Aca71, 1.75p.**
This is a neat little summary, in outline form, of a lot of useful information. It begins with lists of vitamin deficiency symptoms in the various systems of the human body, then goes on to deal with each vitamin, listing role, positive biological functions, deficiency symptoms, and best natural sources. An easy to use quick reference.

SZEKELY, EDMOND. **BOOKS, OUR ETERNAL COMPANIONS. Illustrations, 34pp. Aca71, 1.50p.**
A general discussion of the significance of books accompanied by a listing of the great works of all times.

SZEKELY, EDMOND. **THE CHEMISTRY OF YOUTH. Aca78, 7.50p.**
Szekely's guide to the prevention of disease.

SZEKELY, EDMOND. **THE CONQUEST OF DEATH. 49pp. Aca73, 1.95p.**
Szekely's guidance on ways of prolonging life, based on his personal research and the teachings of a wide variety of cultural traditions.

SZEKELY, EDMOND. **COSMOS, MAN AND SOCIETY. 134pp. Aca73, 5.80p.**
Eleven lectures dealing with meaningful living in the twentieth century. This is his most comprehensive work on the subject, only recently reprinted.

SZEKELY, EDMOND. **COSMOTHERAPY OF THE ESSENES. 64pp. Aca75, 2.80p.**
This book outlines the methods and techniques by which we may contact the Cosmic Ocean of Life and experience within ourselves the powers which keep the universe in equilibrium and eternal evolution.—from the introduction.

SZEKELY, EDMOND. **CREATIVE EXERCISES FOR HEALTH AND BEAUTY. Aca nd, 2.95p.**
A practical, illustrated discussion of the health secrets of the ancient world.

SZEKELY, EDMOND. **DEATH OF THE NEW WORLD. Many illustrations, 9"x12", 47pp. Aca73, 4.80p.**
A narrative, taken from 200 original native drawings and pre-Columbian codices, which tells the story of the idyllic life in an Aztec paradise, the signs and portents of the coming disaster, the Conquest itself, and the story of the destruction of the native world.

SZEKELY, EDMOND. **THE DIALECTICAL METHOD OF THINKING. Aca nd, 1.95p.**
Presents the thirty-four methodical principles of the great thinkers and scientists which can be the guide to the solution of all problems.

SZEKELY, EDMOND. **THE DISCOVERY OF THE ESSENE GOSPEL OF PEACE—THE ESSENES AND THE VATICAN. 92pp. Aca76, 4.80p.**
A detailed account of the history of this text.

SZEKELY, EDMOND. **THE ECOLOGICAL HEALTH GARDEN AND THE BOOK OF SURVIVAL. Aca48, 3.95p.**
Szekely's guide to living on a creative, self sufficient homestead.

SZEKELY, EDMOND. **ESSENE BOOK OF ASHA—JOURNEY TO THE COSMIC OCEAN.** 6"x9", 146pp. Aca66, 7.50p.
A comprehensive study of the Sumerian and ancient Persian origins of the Essene traditions, and also of the esoteric key to the most ancient form of chess: an all encompassing synthesis of art, music, science, philosophy, and the basis of the most ancient system of psycho-analysis. This is a magnificent art edition with over 100 illustrations.

SZEKELY, EDMOND. **THE ESSENE BOOK OF CREATION.** 69pp. Aca75, 4.50p.
More ancient than the biblical **Genesis**, the **Essene Book of Creation** profoundly reveals man's purpose in life and the three paths to truth: the path of nature, the path of knowledge, and the path of intuition. Profusely illustrated.

SZEKELY, EDMOND. **THE ESSENE CODE OF LIFE.** 42pp. Aca75, 2.80p.
Presents the way of life followed by the Essene brotherhoods at the Dead Sea and Lake Mareotis. Szekely derived his information from an original Aramaic document found in the eighteenth century by a Frenchman which records the discourses between the Roman historian Josephus Flavius and Banus, an Essene master.

SZEKELY, EDMOND. **THE ESSENE GOSPEL OF PEACE.** 72pp. Aca75, 3.00c/1.00p.
This is a translation of a third century Aramaic manuscript, preserved in the Vatican archives, which gives Christ's views on healing and health. *For I tell you truly, except you fast, you shall never be freed from the power of Satan and form all diseases that come from Satan.... Seek the fresh air of the forest and of the fields, and there in the midst of them shall you find the angel of air to embrace all your body.... After the angel of air, seek the angel of water.... Think not that it is sufficient that the angel of water embrace you outwards only.... Seek, therefore, a large trailing gourd, having a stalk the length of a man; take out its innards and fill it with water from the river which the sun has warmed. Hang it upon the branch of a tree, and kneel upon the ground before the angel of water, and suffer the end of the stalk of the trailing gourd to enter your hinder parts, that the water may flow through all your bowels.... Then let the water run out from your bowels that it may carry away from within it all the unclean and evil-smelling things of Satan.... Renew your baptising with water on every day of your fast, till the day when you see that the water which flows out of you is as pure as the river's foam. Then betake your body to the coursing river, and there in the arms of the angel of water render thanks to the living God that he has freed you from your sins.*

SZEKELY, EDMOND. **THE ESSENE JESUS.** 71pp. 4.50p.
A reevaluation based on the **Dead Sea Scrolls.** Includes the Essene interpretation of the Sermon on the Mount and an analysis of the meaning of Christmas. Illustrated with the etchings of Dore.

SZEKELY, EDMOND. **THE ESSENE SCIENCE OF FASTING.** 48pp. Aca75, 2.80p.
A detailed guide to fasting and sobriety based both on the principles advocated by the ancient Essenes and on Mr. Szekely's own experience in his health spas. The instructions are based on classical naturopathic ideas.

SZEKELY, EDMOND. **THE ESSENE SCIENCE OF LIFE.** 54pp. Aca70, 2.80p.
A companion to the **Gospel of Peace,** this book presents the health system of the Essenes in detail.

SZEKELY, EDMOND. **THE ESSENE TEACHINGS OF ZARATHU-STRA.** 26pp. Aca74, 1.80p.
Zarathustra, the great Persian sage, profoundly inspired the Essene traditions. This volume includes ancient legends and authentic texts from the **Zend Avesta.**

SZEKELY, EDMOND. **THE ESSENE WAY.** Aca76, 2.00p.
An illustrated volume containing Dr. Szekely's lectures at the Creative Essene Workshop and Seminar held in 1975. Includes practical instructions.

SZEKELY, EDMOND. **THE ESSENES, BY JOSEPHIUS AND HIS CONTEMPORARIES.** Aca70, 1.80p.
Life in the brotherhood of the first century Essenes is described in considerable detail by noted historians and writers of the period—Josephus Flavius, Philo, Plinius, and others.

The jaguar god hit by Spanish spear.

SZEKELY, EDMOND. **THE EVOLUTION OF HUMAN THOUGHT.** 32pp. Aca71, 1.95p.
An outline of the basic ideas and teachings of eighty-seven great philosophers and thirty-eight schools of philosophy from 1000 B.C. to the present.

SZEKELY, EDMOND. **FATHER, GIVE US ANOTHER CHANCE.** 63pp. Aca69, 5.80p.
A study of the decline of our civilization and the rebirth of a new culture. This volume explains how to create the *Creative, Self-Sufficient Health Homestead.*

SZEKELY, EDMOND. **THE FIERY CHARIOTS.** 96pp. Aca71, 4.80p.
A discussion of the Essene brotherhood at the Dead Sea in Roman times covering political intrigues, the audacity of the zealots, the decadence of the rulers, and the Brothers of Light who brought peace to the age.

SZEKELY, EDMOND. **FROM ENOCH TO THE DEAD SEA SCROLLS.** 93pp. Aca75, 4.80p.
This volume distills the essence of Szekely's books on the Essenes. The recent **Dead Sea Scrolls** further corroborate his original texts. All the beauty of the Essene knowledge is contained here: the Essene communions, the sevenfold peace, the mystical Tree of Life, and how we can learn to apply the Essene teachings in our daily lives. Includes translated excerpts from the **Dead Sea Scrolls.**

SZEKELY, EDMOND. **THE GAME OF GODS.** 24pp. Aca73, 1.50p.
An archaeological reconstruction of the world picture of ancient America.

SZEKELY, EDMOND. **THE GOSPEL OF THE ESSENES.** 221pp. Dan76, 10.05c.
This volume contains the second and third books of **The Essene Gospel of Peace: The Unknown Books of the Essenes,** and **The Lost Scrolls of the Essene Brotherhood.** The Hebrew text of **The Essene Gospel of Peace** is also included.

SZEKELY, EDMOND. **GUIDE TO THE ESSENE WAY OF BIOGENIC LIVING.** Many illustrations and photographs, 178pp. Aca77, 8.80p.
This is Szekely's most complete guide to diet and health; divided into chapters on nutrition, living in the world, dwelling, meditation, sexual fulfillment, psychology and self analysis, and education. Many recipes are included along with an abundance of specific suggestions based on Szekely's more than fifty years of study, practice, and teaching.

SZEKELY, EDMOND. **HEALING WATERS.** 57pp. Aca73, 3.50p.
Guidebook to fifty European water cures.

SZEKELY, EDMOND. **HOW THE GREAT PAN DIED: THE ORIGIN OF CHRISTIANITY.** 127pp. Aca68, 7.50p.
A controversial and thorough study of the origins of Christianity, representing forty years of research.

SZEKELY, EDMOND. **THE LIVING BUDDHA.** 71pp. Aca68, 4.50p.
A comparative study of the teachings of the Buddha and of yoga. Includes a lucid explanation of the state of consciousness which the Buddha termed nirvana, the Buddha's teaching about the cause of suffering and the path of self perfection, and a discussion of the purpose and necessity of understanding the essence of the teaching Patanjali. Profusely illustrated.

SZEKELY, EDMOND. **LOST SCROLLS OF THE ESSENE BROTHERHOOD: THE ESSENE GOSPEL OF PEACE, BOOK III.** 148pp. Aca74, 5.60p.
Presents translations of the following ancient texts: *The Sevenfold Vow, The Essene Worship,* and *Texts from the Lost Essene Scrolls.* An appendix illustrates original fragments of the scrolls in Hebrew and Aramaic. Beautifully illustrated throughout.

SZEKELY, EDMOND. **LUDWIG VAN BEETHOVEN.** 1.75p.
See the Music section.

SZEKELY, EDMOND. **MAN IN THE COSMIC OCEAN.** 52pp. Aca70, 2.80p.
Presents a key to understanding the origin, structure, and function of the universe. This volume is more esoteric than Szekely's other works.

SZEKELY, EDMOND. **MESSENGERS FROM ANCIENT CIVILIZATIONS.** 2.50p.
See the Ancient Civilizations section.

SZEKELY, EDMOND. **THE NEW FIRE.** 138pp. Aca73, 4.80p.
This drama reflects the battle of the human spirit against the insecurity and futility of all things: the corruption of power, the contamination of greed, the misery and suffering of the people of every age....Ninety percent of this drama is based on fact....[In] every age, there are always a few fearless souls who, in spite of tremendous odds, persist in trying to reach the impossible goal of perfection.

SZEKELY, EDMOND. **PILGRIM OF THE HIMALAYAS.** 1.95p.
See the Tibetan Buddhism section.

SZEKELY, EDMOND. **SCIENTIFIC VEGETARIANISM.** 47pp. Aca74, 2.50p.
A good summary of the basic argument for vegetarianism which combines a scientific rationale with a spiritual focus. Szekely deals with theory, types of food to eat and not to eat, ecological considerations, and effects of thoughts on the body.

SZEKELY, EDMOND. **SEARCH FOR THE AGELESS, VOLUME I: MY UNUSUAL ADVENTURES ON THE FIVE CONTINENTS IN SEARCH FOR THE AGELESS.** 212pp. Aca77, 7.00p.
An autobiographical account of Szekely's adventures, ethnological and archaeological research, and philosophy which leads the reader throughout the world. Over 100 photographs are included.

SZEKELY, EDMOND. **SEARCH FOR THE AGELESS, VOLUME II: THE GREAT EXPERIMENT.** 170 illustrations, 328pp. Aca77, 7.00p.
The *great experiment* Szekely refers to is Rancho La Puerta, the health spa he established in Baja California. In this autobiographical account Szekely discusses how his philosophical understanding developed during his thirty-three years at Rancho La Puerta, reviews his lectures of the period, offers anecdotes about many of the guests and participants, and discusses a smattering of his pet ideas.

SZEKELY, EDMOND. **SEARCH FOR THE AGELESS, VOLUME III: THE CHEMISTRY OF YOUTH.** Illustrations, 182pp. Aca77, 7.00p.
This volume summarizes Szekely's pioneering work and theories in the fields of ecology, organic gardening, preventive medicine, and nutrition. Many specifics are offered.

SZEKELY, EDMOND. **SEXUAL HARMONY.** 58pp. Aca72, 3.50p.
A discussion of disequilibrium in sex life—both causes and cure—which takes medical, psychological and social factors into consideration.

SZEKELY, EDMOND. **THE SOUL OF ANCIENT MEXICO.** 7.50p.
See the Ancient Americas section.

SZEKELY, EDMOND. **TALKS, VOLUME II.** 36pp. Aca72, 1.95p.
Transcriptions of the following talks: *Will Power, The Future of Humanity,* and *Sleep, A Source of Harmony.*

SZEKELY, EDMOND. **TOWARD A CONQUEST OF THE INNER COSMOS.** Profuse illustrations, 63pp. Aca69, 5.80p.
A journey through different paths penetrating the innermost reality of our spiritual experience. A study of unorthodox approaches in Oriental wisdom, Western art, and mystic poetry.

SZEKELY, EDMOND. **TREASURY OF RAW FOODS.** 42pp. Aca73, 1.95p.
Szekely recommends a diet of twenty-five percent cereals and seventy-five percent raw foods. We found him a little rigid in this book, but there are a lot of interesting points in here about good foods and diet. He introduces us to the word *trophology* to describe the science of food combining. In addition to discussing body needs and the contribution of various foods, this book includes suggested menus and a number of raw food recipes.

SZEKELY, EDMOND. **UNKNOWN BOOKS OF THE ESSENES: THE ESSENE GOSPEL OF PEACE, BOOK II.** 128pp. Aca75, 5.80p.
Presents translations of the following ancient texts: *The Vision of Enoch, From the Essene Book of Moses, Communions with the Angels of the Earthly Mother, Communions with the Angels of Heavenly Father, The Sevenfold Peace from the Essene Book of Jesus, Fragments Identical with the Dead Sea Scrolls, From the Essene Book of the Teacher of Righteousness, From the Essene Gospel of John,* and *From the Essene Book of Revelations.* Beautifully illustrated.

SZEKELY, EDMOND. **THE ZEND AVESTA OF ZARATHUSTRA.** 4.80p.
See the Ancient Near East section.

TANTRA

Tantra is an Indian cult; but since it has evolved continuously from the remotest antiquity it is not limited to any of the particular Indian religions which arrived later on the historical scene. Groups of Hindus, Buddhists and Jains share Tantrik ideas and do Tantrik things; but there are symbols in the vast natural caverns of Palaeolithic Europe (c. 20,000 BC) which can be accurately matched with symbols still used today by Tantrikas. Hundreds of generations have devoted themselves to developing and refining Tantra, so that it now conveys with extraordinary purity the most essential patterns of human symbolic expression. It is widely recognized that this is what makes it so valuable for people of the present, Westerners as well as Indians.

It would be wrong to call Tantra a religion; that term has too many misleading overtones nowadays for far too many people. Tantra is not a *way of thought*, either. Thought, in the sense of ordinary logical and very useful reasoning, Tantra sees as one of the chief causes for people gradually becoming disillusioned and miserable in what they believe to be their world. So Tantra works with action. Above all, Tantra is not something meant to be read about in books, although in fact there are numerous Sanskrit books known as Tantras. The earliest, a Buddhist one, probably goes back to the sixth century AD. The most recent are nineteenth century. But what these texts consist of are prescriptions for action, including mental action, which are the whole purpose of the texts. If you don't do what your Tantra describes, then you will never get the point.

The Tantrik pictures were meant ultimately to be used, not just looked at. They are undeniably impressive; but that is not all. They are made expressly to stimulate a special kind of mental activity, and to evoke psychosomatic forces. Used in rituals which include yoga, offerings, meditation and sexual intercourse, they can change a person completely, providing him with a new basis for his life. At first, all these procedures need to be carried through in the most basic fact; for only in this way can they displace the banal everyday reality which presses so forcibly on people's lives. Later, when a Tantrika reaches a high level of achievement after many long years of effort and assimilation, the pictures may be visualized and carried out subjectively, without any risk of their collapsing into fantasy. For Tantra has no dealings with fantasy. What it describes and maps is a world of realities, a world which can only be visited by following the maps. It is there to be found; but someone who has not visited it can have no idea of what it is like. For there is no way of examining it from the outside. It is what we are—although we don't usually realize the fact—and we can never step out of it to take an analytical view.

Tantra, in fact, plunges one back into the roots of one's own identity, not just by discussing social roles and interpersonal communication, and not by offering the kind of clearcut or comforting answers given by the dogmatic theology of straight religions. Tantra says *If you do these things which Tantrikas have discovered, you will find yourself in a position to experience what the truth is about yourself and your world, as directly as you can experience the street.* Needless to say, to do those things, to get into the position from which you can experience the truth, involves a total change of personality. This takes every kind of effort— physical, sexual, mental, moral; and most are just the kinds of

effort that nothing in Western education or tradition prepares one for. Tantra calls on energies in the human body and its world which most people usually dissipate in their ultimately pointless exertions and *recreations*. But, most important of all, Tantra positively cultivates and bases itself on what most people dismiss as the pleasures of life. It does *not* say solemnly *You must abstain from all enjoyment, mortify your flesh, and obey the commands of a jealous Father-God.* Instead, it says *Raise your enjoyment to its highest power, and then use it as a spiritual rocket-fuel.* This, of course, seems a dangerous revolutionary doctrine to the orthodox in any religion. And to the orthodox the Tantrika is a scandal.

Here is an Indian description of what a Tantrik saint looks like to an outsider. He is so happy as to seem crazy; his eyes roll, reddened with wine. He sits on silk cushions surrounded by works of art, eating hot pork cooked with chillies. At his left side sits a girl skilled in the arts of love, with whom he drinks and repeatedly has ecstatic sexual intercourse; he continually makes music with his vina (a stringed instrument), and sings poems; all of which he weaves together into rituals. Everything such a man seems to be and do gives violent offence to the conventionally minded. And that, in fact, is part—but only part—of the point. For he himself has had to break any lingering attachment he may have had to even his own conventional attitudes. What he is doing fundamentally is rousing all the energies he can discover in his body, emotions and mind, and combining them into a vehicle which will carry him towards enlightenment: enlightenment being that state of knowing the truth about the origin of things and men, and their meaning, as clearly as experiencing the street. He uses every possible means, adapting every conceivable emotional stimulus and act to his purpose, on the assumption that things which you actually do repeatedly, and which have associated with them a powerful sensuous and emotive charge, change you far more effectively than anything else. And only if you combine together many different kinds of doing is the change radical.

—condensed from **Tantra,**
The Indian Cult of Ecstasy, *by Philip Rawson*

BHARATI, AGEHANANDA. **THE TANTRIC TRADITION. Notes, thirty-three page annotated bibliography, index, 348pp. Wei65/HPG, 4.50p.**
An important academic work which critically analyzes the literary, linguistic, ideological, and anthropological aspects of tantra. Professor Bharati documents his exposition with freshly translated passages from Indian and Tibetan texts. He gives special emphasis to mantra, initiation, the male-female polarity, and the history and development of tantra in India and Tibet. *Professor Bharati's survey of tantrism is an outstanding achievement. For the first time tantrism has been dealt with in relation to the total intellectual climate.*—Herbert Guenther.

BLOFELD, JOHN. **TANTRIC MYSTICISM OF TIBET: A PRACTICAL GUIDE TO THE THEORY, PURPOSE, AND TECHNIQUES OF TANTRIC MEDITATION. 4.45p.**
See the Tibetan Buddhism section.

CHAKRAVARTI, CHINTAHARAN. **TANTRAS: STUDIES ON THEIR RELIGION AND LITERATURE. Extensive textual notes in both Sanskrit and English, index, 129pp. PPu63, 14.40c.**
This is a detailed study of a little explored area of Indian thought

divided into the following chapters: *The Tantras—What They Stand For, Antiquity of Tantricism, The Age and Authorship of the Tantras, Place of the Tantras Among the Other Sastras, Ideals of Tantra Rites, How and Where the Tantras Originated, Tantra Schools, Literature of the Tantras, Tantric Authors and their Works, Tantric Form of Worship and Tantric Dieties, Kali Worship in Bengal, Cult of Durga and Durga Worship in Bengal,* and a description of the text *Paramanandamatasamgraha.*

DASGUPTA, SHASHI. AN INTRODUCTION TO TANTRIC BUDDHISM. Extensive, notes, indices, 211pp. ShP50, 3.95p.
A recent reprint of a pioneering work on tantric Buddhism. Almost all of the material is taken from unpublished manuscripts. The book was not well received when it was originally published and its flaws are apparent to the knowledgeable reader—however it does present some important material and controversial ideas. This edition is a reprint of the original one and not at all well printed. That, combined with the author's scattered writing style, makes the book hard to read.

■ **GARRISON, OMAR. TANTRA—THE YOGA OF SEX.** Many illustrations, 8½"x11", 112pp. Acd74, 7.85p.
This is one of the only serious books on tantra which was written with the general reader in mind. Garrison has thoroughly studied his subject and he includes many practical suggestions and techniques. He writes well and makes this often arcane subject understandable. The book is aimed at the reader who wants to learn the basics of tantric yoga practice.

GUENTHER, HERBERT. THE TANTRIC VIEW OF LIFE. Notes, 168pp. ShP72, 4.50p.
Guenther, a well known Tibetologist, here offers a major contribution towards the understanding of tantric Buddhism. The meaning of tantra is clearly defined and the philosophy of tantra is presented in depth. Various aspects are elucidated through original translations from important tantric texts and commentaries from Tibetan. The book concludes with a valuable discussion of the role of aesthetics and art and is illustrated with Tibetan thankas and Indian sculpture.

GUENTHER, HERBERT and CHOGYAM TRUNGPA. THE DAWN OF TANTRA. Illustrations, 92pp. ShP75, 3.50p.
In **The Dawn of Tantra** *the reader meets a Tibetan and Westerner whose grasp of Buddhist tantra is real and unquestionable....Dr. Guenther and Chogyam Trungpa met in Berkeley, California, in 1972, where together they gave a public seminar on Buddhist tanra.* **The Dawn of Tantra** *is the edited record of that seminar including part of the general discussion.*—from the introduction. Two other talks by Guenther and Trungpa are also included.

GUPTA, SANJUKTA, tr. **LAKSMI TANTRA.** Detailed notes, illustrations, index, 434pp. Bri72, 45.00c.
A translation of an important text which elucidates the Pancaratra system. Pancaratra is the oldest surviving Vishnuite sect.

JYOTIRMAYANANDA. MEDITATE THE TANTRIC YOGA WAY. Glossary, 117pp. A&U74, 4.75p.
Explains in detail ten different techniques of tantric meditation that have been practiced for centuries. They include preparatory exercises or asanas which allow the meditator to sit motionless for a period of time; and breath control, pranayama, which calms the mind. The treatment of the various techniques is unique and quite complicated. It is only recommended to those schooled in tantra, although it is quite clearly written.

MOOKERJEE, AJIT. TANTRA ART. Bibliography, 10½"x12½", 155pp. RaH72, 37.50c.
Ajit Mookerjee has probably made the most significant contribution to the field of tantra of any man in this century. Over the last three decades he has discovered an astonishing treasure of tantric manuscripts and art objects in his native India. He was the first to present these masterpieces to the West, and his books are definitive. All are magnificent and it is hard to distinguish between them. This was his first book. The ninety-seven plates—more than half in color—are well reproduced and the descriptive material is excellent. The written text contains some of the most enlightening information on tantra that we have read.

MOOKERJEE, AJIT. TANTRA ASANA. 10½"x12½", 161pp. RaH71, 37.50c.
This is the second of Mookerjee's books and it is even more beautiful

than the first. This volume includes 108 illustrations—sixty-six in color—as well as an excellent bibliography, an illuminating text, and an illustrated version of *Hymns to the Goddess.* All of Mookerjee's work is highly recommended.

MOOKERJEE, AJIT. YOGA ART. 10"x11½", 208pp. NYG75, 39.50c.
Yoga art (also known as tantric art) is formed from a number of mystical configurations that seek to clarify the viewer's perceptions and to unite him or her with the cosmic forces. The images are largely abstract and geometric and are based on a complicated system of colors, numbers, and proportions. Mookerjee is the world's foremost expert on this type of art and he contributes an authoritative text which describes the philosophical underpinnings of the art and provides an invaluable explanation of the symbolic systems that underlie the art. Richly illustrated, the book includes seventy-six color and fifty-eight black and white reproductions of meditative drawings, sculpture, pages from illuminated manuscripts, mandalas, and yantras. All have a purity of conception and design. An exceedingly beautiful book.

The monster of time.

■ **MOOKERJEE, AJIT and MADHU KHANNA. THE TANTRIC WAY: ART, SCIENCE, RITUAL.** Glossary, bibliography, index, 7½"x10¾", 208pp. NYG77, 9.95p.
This book is both an illuminating summary of tantric thought and a presentation of how tantric concepts can be incorporated into our lives. Separate sections focus on art, science, and ritual. The text is beautifully written; reading it led us to a deeper understanding of tantra than we have ever had before. The book is fully illustrated with paintings, drawings, and diagrams—eighteen color plates, 130 black and white illustrations, eighty line drawings. It is a great deal more than a coffee table picture book; we highly recommend it to all who seek to understand the life affirming philosophy of tantra.

OLSON, ELEANOR. TANTRIC BUDDHIST ART. 8"x9¼", 100pp. CIA74, 7.15p.
The illustrated catalogue of an exhibit held at the China House Gallery in New York City in 1974. The book begins with some excellent introductory material followed by fifty-four plates, some in color and all fully discussed.

PANDIT, M.P. GEMS FROM THE TANTRAS, FIRST SERIES. 106pp. Gan70, 2.95c.
Pandit has been closely associated with Sri Aurobindo and the Mother. This volume is drawn from the **Kularnava Tantra,** a presentation of practical teachings for seekers on the path. Topically arranged, including the Sanskrit text, English translation, and commentary.

PANDIT, M.P. GEMS FROM THE TANTRAS, SECOND SERIES. 114pp. Gan69, 2.95c.
Selections from various tantras emphasizing the consciousness aspect of the *Eternal Reality (Sat-Chit-Ananda)* and its special significance for the spiritual growth of man. Topically arranged, including Sanskrit texts, English translations, and commentary.

PANDIT, M.P. **KULARNAVA TANTRA.** 128pp. Gan73, 4.00c.
The Kularnava is one of the most frequently cited texts in tantric literature. The text presents all the fundamentals of the tantric school and its underlying philosophy and ethical and social implications. This edition includes an introduction by Arthur Avalon and a detailed, topically organized study by Pandit, which summarizes the text itself.

PANDIT, M.P. **KUNDALINI YOGA.** 78pp. Gan nd, 3.00c.
A brief, simple study of Woodroffe's **The Serpent Power**, summarizing the main principles of tantra yoga.

PANDIT, M.P. **LIGHTS ON THE TANTRA.** 107pp. Gan57, 2.95c.
A topically arranged discussion of the doctrines and practices of the tantras and their contribution to the spiritual and religious culture of India—in the light of Sri Aurobindo's thought. Includes extensive notes.

RAJNEESH, BHAGWAN SHREE. **THE BOOK OF THE SECRETS.** 10.95c/each.
See the Contemporary Spiritual Teachers section.

RAJNEESH, BHAGWAN SHREE. **ONLY ONE SKY.** 4.45p.
See the Contemporary Spiritual Teachers section.

RAMBACH, PIERRE. **THE SECRET MESSAGE OF TANTRIC BUD-DHISM.** 250 illustrations, twenty-four in color, 12½"x15½", 180pp. Riz78, 50.00c.
An enlightening discussion of the symbolism behind tantric forms, accompanied by an original collection of photographs of tantric art.

■ *RAWSON, PHILIP.* **THE ART OF TANTRA.** 176 plates, twenty-five in color, glossary, extensive notes, bibliography, 7½"x10", 216pp. Oxf73/T&H, 6.95c.
Rawson is the author of a number of books of Asian art and was the organizer of the recent exhibition of tantric art held in London under the auspices of the Arts Council of Great Britain. He writes this book as an interpreter, explaining with the aid of many illustrations of classic examples of tantric art, how tantra invites its followers to a personal meditative and visual exploration of self and the world. An exquisite book; we recommend it highly for those who wish a detailed study.

■ *RAWSON, PHILIP.* **TANTRA: THE INDIAN CULT OF ECSTASY.** 8"x12", 128pp. T&H74, 7.95p.
This is Rawson's second book on the subject, the better introduction for the general reader. While a large part of his first book is devoted to extensive analysis of various elements of tantra, this book has 190 illustrations, thirty-two in full color, and a good general introduction. Its aim is to turn as many people as possible on to the symbolic imagery of tantra and thereby to an understanding of the underlying philosophy. Highly recommended as both a beautiful coffee table book, and an illuminating text for the seeker.

RIVIERE, J. MARQUES. **TANTRIK YOGA.** Glossary, 126pp. Wei34, 2.95p.
The information presented in this comprehensive instruction manual is adapted from the original Sanskrit texts. It discusses the esoteric anatomy of the human body, the chakras and the kundalini, and presents methods of breath control, asanas (postures), mental and meditational exercises. Riviere also discusses Chinese, Japanese, and Tibetan techniques for the benefit of students who wish to know how they accord with the Hindu practices he presents.

SNELLGROVE, DAVID, tr. **THE HEVAJRA TANTRA.** Glossary, Sanskrit-English vocabulary, index, 363pp. Oxf59, 39.95c.
This two volume set includes an introduction discussing tantric development and the contents of the **Hevajra Tantra** and is followed by a complete translation and full explanatory notes based on the earliest commentaries. The second volume contains the Sanskrit and Tibetan texts of the **Tantra** and the Sanskrit text of one of the early commentaries, the **Yogaratnamala**.

TSUDA, SHINICHI. **THE SAMVARODAYA-TANTRA: SELECTED CHAPTERS.** Many notes, 408pp. Hok74, 37.50c.
This edition includes the Romanized Sanskrit and Tibetan texts, an English translation, and commentary. In all, nineteen chapters have been selected. Tibetan-Sanskrit and Sanskrit-Tibetan glossaries (both with English translation) are also included.

WAYMAN, ALEX. **THE BUDDHIST TANTRAS.** 12.50c.
See the Tibetan Buddhism section.

WOODROFFE, SIR JOHN. **THE GARLAND OF LETTERS.** 318pp. Gan74, 5.95c.
Sir John Woodroffe was a justice of the high court of India at Calcutta during the last part of the nineteenth century. Under the pseudonym Arthur Avalon, he devoted himself to making tantra known to the Western world as well as to the educated Hindus who learned about tantra only from his translations. Sir John was thus writing for two Puritan audiences, to whom he was trying to justify the sexual elements in tantra—and his work must be read in light of this. In any case, it remains the most substantial body of tantric scholarship extant and is still very well considered. The reader should be warned that Woodroffe uses a great number of Sanskrit terms in his exposition without defining them—so a basic knowledge of Sanskrit or a good glossary is essential. This volume is a comprehensive treatise on the power, meaning and uses of mantras.

WOODROFFE, SIR JOHN. **INTRODUCTION TO THE TANTRA SASTRA.** Gan nd, 4.95c.
Forms an introduction to the *Great Liberation* and a key to understanding tantric concepts.

WOODROFFE, SIR JOHN, tr. **ISOPANISAD/WAVE OF BLISS/THE GREATNESS OF SIVA.** 180pp. Gan71, 3.95c.
Translations of three important texts: **Isopanisad:** Isha Upanishad with tantric commentary by Satyananda; **Wave of Bliss:** a hymn in praise of Shakti, dealing with the kundalini, chakras, and tantric mantras; **The Greatness of Siva:** an ancient hymn attributed to Pushpadanta, with commentary.

WOODROFFE, SIR JOHN, tr. **THE SERPENT POWER.** 700pp. Dov19, 5.00p.
A translation of two important works on tantric yoga: **Sat-Chakra-Nirupana** and **Padhuka-Panchaka**, including descriptions of the spiritual centers of consciousness and awakening of the kundalini. This is the most extensive discussion of kundalini available, as well as Woodroffe's most popular and probably his most important translation.

WOODROFFE, SIR JOHN, tr. **TANTRA OF THE GREAT LIBERA-TION.** 405pp. Dov13, 3.95p.
Translation of **The Mahanirvana Tantra**, which is essentially a series of conversations between the God Shiva and his consort-energy, Shakti. Shiva gives instructions for meditation exercises and mental projections, yogic exercises, mantras for concentration and mind training, ceremonies of Shaktic worship, physiological information on the system of chakras, and the role of tantrism in life. Sir John has supplied extensive footnotes to explain the cryptic text, as well as a 130 page introduction explaining the anatomy of the chakras, various forms of tantra and mandalas, and the Siddhis.

WOODROFFE, SIR JOHN, tr. **TANTRARAJA TANTRA/KAMA-KALA-VILASA.** 246pp. Gan71, 5.00c.
Tantraraja Tantra is an analytical resume of the **King Among the Tantras**; **Kama-Kil-Vilasa** is the translation of an early text on Shakti tantra by Punyananda. Transliterated Sanskrit text with commentary by Natananada and Woodroffe.

WOODROFFE, SIR JOHN. **THE WORLD AS POWER.** 484pp. Gan21, 11.50c.
The author describes how the entire universe and its constituents is a spread-out, "prasara," of the Supreme Power, the Adya Sakti, the Divine Consciousness as Force. Spiritual and transcendent in its pristine station above, it bursts forth as and in the Universe, constituting or becoming the several orders of creation by a graded self formulation and modification of itself in denser and denser forms of existence. Matter, Life, Mind, are each of them different terms of the self manifestation of the One Divine Consciousness....—from the introduction.

TAROT

The origin, purpose and significance of the Tarot cards remain enshrouded in mystery, although interest in them is probably more active now than at any previous time in history. If one were to attempt to assign a reason for this popularity, an obvious first suggestion would be that it is associated with the hazardous conditions of life which have been a characteristic feature of the past half-century. We have been unwilling witnesses of social and economic upheavals which have affected countries that were formerly considered patterns of stability; we have seen the devastating results of man's inhumanity to man; and we are painfully aware of the development of weapons of aggression of such menace that they have become a potential threat to the continued existence of human life on this planet that we call earth.

All these developments have brought to the individual a feeling of insecurity, which can be diminished only by a firm conviction that we have been brought into this existence for a definite purpose, and that there is something beyond the brief span of life which has been allocated to each one of us. The normal reaction in times of stress has always been to turn to religious doctrines for support, but these also have suffered from an insidious analytical propagation of doubt which calls for *proof* before faith, and holds as suspect what cannot be appreciated and indexed by the rational mind. The result has been the creation of a void which persistently remains unsatisfied.

Many seek safety through the acquisition of the treasures of this world, or by reliance on some form of collective assurance based upon a large, powerful and impersonal group, which often is claimed to be *the State*. Other seek to *escape* by the use of psychedelic drugs, and still others turn to the ancient systems of divination.

Have we really lost direct contact with the higher powers which formerly guided and inspired humanity? Or are we so intent on searching outwards, even to the extent of embarking on a programme of interplanetary travel, that we have lost the ability to look inwards and to commune in silence with the mysterious centre and the real *Self* of each one of us? It may be that this loss is a malady which is peculiar to the peoples of the West, for many of the inhabitants of the eastern countries are still acutely conscious of the pervading influence of unseen forces. In ancient times these forces were personified as *gods*, and systems of divination were devised for the purpose of addressing queries to them.

The suggestion that the Tarot cards were originally pictorial symbols from the ancient Mystery systems is not new; it has been advanced many times, but most attempts at explanation have lacked coherence and so have failed to convince.

It may be, as one author has claimed, that the real significance of the Tarot system is concealed in the repositories of one or more secret societies, or it may be merely that we have failed to read the message that the cards have silently presented for our notice over the centuries of their existence.

There is strong probability that the Major Arcana were originally pictorial symbols which, as with all symbols, represent truth in many aspects and on many planes of thought. It is an essential characteristic of a symbol that it will convey different meanings to different people, and that each meaning will be true for each particular individual; it is most unwise for anyone to say that an interpretation by another person is *not correct*, since everything depends on the stage of development in *awareness* that has been attained by the individual. It is for this reason that there has been no attempt to give a simplified and rigid meaning to the message of the cards. The author is convinced that the use of the Major Arcana for gaming purposes, and even for questions regarding future events, are degradations from their original purpose, and he suggests that their message is just as valid today as it was many centuries ago. They are worthy of long and silent contemplation and, if they help us to discern glimpses of the wisdom of the ancient masters, they will be of immense value to us in our search for the one fundamental and indivisible truth.

—*condensed from* **The Mystical Tower of the Tarot**, *by John Blakeley*

BLAKELEY, JOHN. **THE MYSTICAL TOWER OF THE TAROT.** Notes, bibliography, index, 207pp. Wat74, 8.90p.
This is an unusual, highly esoteric interpretation of the tarot. Its most interesting feature is a translation of a Sufi allegory which bears a striking resemblance to the pictorial representation of the path as presented in the major arcana. There is also an excellent presentation of the inner meaning of the cards and a good study of the origins of tarot. Throughout the book both the ancient mystery teachings and the wisdom of the East are discussed and their relationship with the tarot is fully explored. The book includes a number of color plates.

BUESS, LYNN. **THE TAROT AND THE TRANSFORMATION.** 256pp. CSA73, 4.95p.
Buess teaches parapsychology courses at the university level. He feels that the study of the tarot provides a symbolic focus, depicting a path of growth which man travels in search of self knowledge. This is an interesting exploration of both the major and minor arcana, illustrated with the Church of Light's Egyptian deck.

■ BUTLER, BILL. **DICTIONARY OF THE TAROT.** Bibliography, 254pp. ScB75, 4.95p.
This is a handy summary of the meanings of the cards in nineteen of the most commonly used tarot decks. The comparison between the different interpretations can be useful to the student who seeks to find his own meaning rather than merely relying on one commentator. Both the major and minor arcana are discussed card-by-card, and there are also sections on the history of the tarot, methods of divination, a long glossary defining the terms used and the esoteric symbology. Both the design and the interpretation for each card and for each kind of deck are summarized separately. A useful compendium for all students of the tarot.

CALVINO, ITALO. **THE CASTLE CROSSED DESTINIES.** 129pp. HBJ77, 10.00c.
With magical dexterity, Calvino uses the device of tarot cards and their archetypal images to create a series of short fantastic narratives. In a fairytale setting—a castle and a tavern in the heart of a dense wood—a company of men and women are brought together by chance. Distraught by strange adventures, they find they have lost their voices. To communicate their fates—love affairs, battles, conquests, betrayals—they deal out, one after another, a pack of tarot cards, whose configurations reveal their plights. Calvino was inspired by the fifteenth century Visconti pack and eight cards are reproduced actual size and in full color. In addition, black and white reproductions of an eighteenth century pack run along the margins of the tales, showing the combinations out of which the stories grew.

CALVINO, ITALO. **TAROTS. Limited edition, boxed, 9"x14", 161pp. Ric75, 100.00c.**
This is an exquisitely produced volume, handlettered on beautiful blue handmade paper. The Visconti-Sforza cards are reproduced full size in color. These cards are without question the most beautiful ancient cards still extant. The background is mainly in gold leaf and the individual figures are movingly portrayed. The text of **The Castle Crossed Destinies** is included, and there is also a critical examination of the cards along with background notes and a survey of the origin of tarot cards.

CASE, PAUL. **THE BOOK OF TOKENS. 200pp. BuA34, 6.25c.**
Meditations on the occult meaning of the twenty-two Hebrew letters, as they relate to the tarot trumps. Illustrated by Case's deck.

■ *CASE, PAUL.* **HIGHLIGHTS OF THE TAROT. 64pp. BuA31, 2.00p.**
An excellent introduction to the esoteric significance of the tarot. Includes a brief analysis of each of the twenty-two major arcana cards, a history of the tarot, coloring instructions for the B.O.T.A. deck, and other background material. Very clearly presented material for the beginning student. Coloring instructions for the minor arcana are available for $1.25.

■ *CASE, PAUL.* **THE TAROT: A KEY TO THE WISDOM OF THE AGES. 214pp. Mac47, 6.95c.**
A fine, in depth analysis of each of the twenty-two major arcana cards. The presentation is designed to stimulate the reader's intuitive understanding of each card's symbolism. Case presents each card as a meditational key to self growth and awareness. The whole is related to the Qabala, the Hebrew alphabet, numbers, color, and sound. There are separate chapters on methods of study, the esoteric meaning of numbers, and tarot divination. If you have read the Case booklet and like his approach (as we do!), then move on to this material. We feel that this is the most enlightening overall book and recommend it highly.

CAVENDISH, RICHARD. **THE TAROT. Bibliography, index, 8½"x 11", 191pp. H&R75/Jos, 19.95c.**
Despite its coffee table format, this is an excellent serious study of the tarot, with explanatory diagrams and tables, illustrated with 176 color and black and white plates. Cavendish presents what is known about the tarot, its history, its uses, and its significance. He describes the earliest known packs and their development through changes in religious and political thought. Tracing the history of the arcane meanings attributed to the tarot from the eighteenth century to the present, he gives a concise but comprehensive account of the divergent interpretations of the tarot, providing a card-by-card analysis of them in relation to the Qabala, the letters of the Hebrew alphabet, symbolic animals, the elements, planets, and signs of the zodiac, human qualities, and other key ideas. He also describes the use of the tarot in magic and meditation and provides explicit instructions on laying out and reading the cards. Many of the cards illustrated are not generally available and seeing the varying symbology helps the student gain an intuitive feeling for the meaning of the cards. If it were not for the price we would recommend this book highly. Even at the price it is a good book to have.

CIRLOT, J.E. **A DICTIONARY OF SYMBOLS. 20.15c.**
See the Sacred Art section.

CROWLEY, ALEISTER. **THE BOOK OF THOTH. 6"x9", 287pp. Wei44, 12.95c/5.95p.**
An attempt to translate the mysteries of the Qabala and the tarot into pictorial form. Describes the theory of tarot including its Egyptian origins and relationship to the Qabala, the meaning of major and minor arcana cards. Includes lavishly illustrated, intensely colored pictorial interpretations of each of the cards.

D'AGOSTINO, JOSEPH. **TAROT: THE ROYAL PATH TO WISDOM. 132pp. Wei76, 2.95p.**
A meditative exploration of the symbology of the Rider deck. An adequate interpretation, but not one which pleases us. Divination instructions are included and there are brief definitions of the qualities of the minor arcana cards. The major arcana of the Rider deck is pictured.

DOANE, DORIS CHASE and KING KEYES. **HOW TO READ TAROT CARDS. 207pp. Cro67, 2.95p.**
A comprehensive how-to manual based on the Egyptian tarot. Ms. Doane is a noted astrologer and was an associate of Zain and the Church of Light for many years. She presents fourteen sample tarot readings, explaining the technique at great length. Other sections present key phrases for each of the seventy-eight cards and astrological symbolism. There is also background material and a section on how to use the cards.

■ *DOUGLAS, ALFRED.* **THE TAROT. Bibliography, index, 249pp. Vik72/Pen, 2.95p.**
We feel that this is the best overall introduction to the origin, meaning, and uses of the tarot. Long sections are devoted to the symbolism of the tarot as it has developed over the ages and to the meaning of each of the cards in the light of Jungian psychology. Material on consulting the tarot is also included and there are sections on meditation and the tarot and esoteric symbology. A well written book which we recommend highly.

THE MAGICIAN.

GARDNER, RICHARD. **EVOLUTION THROUGH THE TAROT. Illustrations, bibliography, 112pp. Wei70, 4.95p.**
A discussion of the major arcana in terms of their explanation of the meaning and purpose of human existence. Some of the exposition is based on related teachings of Jesus and parallels are made with the Gospels. A chapter is devoted to each of the trumps.

GARDNER, RICHARD. **TAROT SPEAKS. Illustrations, 105pp. Wyn71, 1.35p.**
Gardner is a psychic and here he uses his psychic abilities to let each of the major arcana cards speak through him and tell the reader its message.

KNIGHT of WANDS.

GEARHART, SALLY. **A FEMINIST TAROT: A GUIDE TO INTRA-PERSONAL COMMUNICATION. 101pp. Per77, 4.00p.**
A humanistic interpretation of the tarot, based on and illustrated with the Rider deck. The author attempts to transform the traditional masculine bias.

GRAVES, F. **THE WINDOWS OF TAROT. 95pp. M&M73, 3.95p.**
A brief presentation of the symbolism of each of the seventy-eight cards of the Aquarian tarot deck, along with an explanation of their divinatory meanings. Also includes background material, astrological correspondences, and directions for laying out spreads.

■ GRAY, EDEN. **THE COMPLETE GUIDE TO THE TAROT. 248pp. Ban70, 6.95c/1.95p.**
Eden Gray's books are the most popular introductory books on the tarot. This is her most comprehensive one. Each of her books is illustrated with all seventy-eight cards of the Waite-Rider deck, accompanied by an analysis of the symbolism of the card and its divinatory meaning. Three techniques for reading the cards are detailed at length, and additional instructional material is provided. A third of the book outlines the Qabala, astrology, and numerology—systems of thought that illuminate the tarot. There are also a glossary and a bibliography. This is the best of the books specifically keyed to the Waite-Rider deck, though the emphasis is on divination rather than self understanding.

GRAY, EDEN. **MASTERING THE TAROT. 221pp. NAL71, 1.50p.**
This is the newest of Gray's tarot books, incorporating more of her personal philosophy and tips than the others. The only reading that is outlined is the Keltic spread—and this is given at great length, accompanied by sample readings. There are interesting sections on other methods of divination using the cards and a glossary. Again, each card is analyzed in detail.

HAICH, ELISABETH. **WISDOM OF THE TAROT. 174pp. ASI75/A&U, 17.95c.**
An esoteric interpretation of the major arcana, accompanied by a pack of cards. We do not like the cards very much; they are badly drawn and not evocative, and are done with a gold foil background and in a medieval style. The commentary integrates the meditational meaning of the cards and includes references to numerology, Qabalism, esoteric Christianity, and the Eastern spiritual tradition. We cannot praise Ms.

Haich's **Initiation** highly enough, but we have difficulty relating to her other books.

HARGRAVE, CATHERINE. **A HISTORY OF PLAYING CARDS. 6½"x9¼", 462pp. Dov30, 6.95p.**
The most thorough history available of cards from the fourteenth to the twentieth century. More than 1,400 cards of all styles are illustrated and discussed.

HELINE, CORINNE. **TAROT AND THE BIBLE. 4.50p.**
See the Bibles section.

HOELLER, STEPHAN. **THE ROYAL ROAD. Illustrations, 130pp. TPH75, 2.95p.**
A handbook of Qabalistic meditations on the major arcana, expressing the quintessence of what Hoeller conceives to be the principal spiritual experiences embodied in each of the twenty-two paths. The meditations are related to the twenty-two paths connecting the ten *sephiroth* on the Tree of Life. The approach is psychological and the reader is well prepared for the journey he is to undertake by the ample background material the author supplies. A very useful work for those who seek to understand the Qabala and the tarot and their interrelations.

HOLY ORDER OF MANS. **JEWELS OF THE WISE. Illustrations, 198pp. HOM74, 3.50p.**
Just as the **Keystone of Tarot Symbolism** is quite similar to Case's **Highlights**, this volume closely resembles Case's **The Tarot**, although it is more Christian-oriented. Each of the twenty-two cards of the major arcana is analyzed in depth and the exposition includes information on the corresponding color, number, letter of the Hebrew alphabet, and astrological sign and quality. Even though the similarity to Case is great, some additional insights can be found here.

HOLY ORDER OF MANS. **KEYSTONE OF TAROT SYMBOLS. 108pp. HOM71, 3.00p.**
The Holy Order of Mans is a nonsectarian teaching order of minister-priests who have dedicated their lives to teaching and living the universal laws of creation in accordance with the teachings of Jesus Christ. Their teachings are derived from the ancient Christian mysteries. The twenty-two major arcana are discussed and a Hebrew letter is assigned to each. The exposition includes coloring instructions and meditational phrases. An interesting esoteric interpretation in light of the thirty-two Paths of Wisdom.

HOTEMA, HILTON. **THE LAND OF LIGHT. Offset, stapled, 8½"x11", 157pp. HeR nd, 5.00p.**
Includes an interpretation of the tarot based on the ancient philosophy which symbolized the Cosmic Phenomena that was presented to the Neophyte in the Sacred Drama of Initiation, and included the strangest mysteries of existence, such as reincarnation, resurrection, and eternal life.

HUSON, PAUL. **THE DEVIL'S PICTUREBOOK. Illustrations, notes, bibliography, 256pp. SBL71, 4.60p.**
This is an extremely detailed discussion of the major tarot trumps which will be illuminating for those interested in the Western esoteric tradition. Many of Huson's explanations did not resonate with us; nonetheless, he introduces material we have not seen elsewhere. The first half of the book is devoted to divination instructions and information on the history and use of tarot cards.

INNES, BRIAN. **THE TAROT—HOW TO USE AND INTERPRET THE CARDS. Bibliography, 8"x11¾", 88pp. Arc78, 10.00c.**
The finest feature of this more than adequate introductory survey is the full color reproduction of eight versions of each of the major arcana cards from eight of the best known decks. The varying images are briefly discussed and the analysis is insightful. A number of minor arcana cards are also illustrated in color. Other major chapters cover the history of the tarot and divination by the tarot.

KAPLAN, STUART. **THE ENCYCLOPEDIA OF TAROT. Index, 8¼"x11", 402pp. USG78, 14.95c.**
This is the definitive study of the tarot, based on Kaplan's years of research. The high point of the book is the illustrations—over 3,200 tarot cards are reproduced from more than 250 different tarot, tarock, and related decks dating from the fifteenth century to the present. Many are rare decks and the iconography of each is fully explored. There is also a comprehensive history of the tarot and discussion of the

evolution of the various decks. The annotated bibliography is far and away the largest we have ever seen. An important work for all who are deeply interested in the tarot.

KAPLAN, STUART. **TAROT CLASSIC. 243pp. G&D72/Hal, 2.95p.**
A good introductory book, keyed to the Tarot Classic deck. Describes the current interest in the tarot, the ancient origin of the cards and the earliest known European references to tarot, the oldest packs still in existence, the development of the tarot, the divinatory meanings of each of the major arcana and minor arcana cards, and sample card spreads and methods of divination. Includes illustrations of almost all the extant decks. The annotated bibliography is by far the most extensive we have seen.

KASDIN, SIMON. **THE ESOTERIC TAROT: THE KEY TO THE QABALA. 96pp. Wei73, 1.95p.**
An intensive discussion of the twenty-two major arcana cards using unusual symbols with specific reference to the Hebrew alphabet and **Sepher Yetzirah.** The illustrations do not resemble any deck we have seen.

KNIGHT, GARETH. **A PRACTICAL GUIDE TO QABALISTIC SYMBOLISM. 17.50c.**
See the Jewish Mysticism section.

KOPP, SHELDON. **THE HANGED MAN. 7.95c.**
See the Humanistic Psychology section.

LIND, FRANK. **HOW TO UNDERSTAND THE TAROT. 63pp. Wei69, 1.25p.**
A description of the major arcana cards, emphasizing their mythological properties, with some reference to the minor arcana cards and methods of divination.

LONG, MAX FREEDOM. **TAROT CARD SYMBOLOGY. Offset, spiral bound, 8½"x11", 83pp. HRA72, 7.55p.**
Long is best known for his pioneering studies of the psychological system of the Kahuna priests of Hawaii. He believes that the Kahunas had a hand in the investigation of the tarot and built into the cards a secret set of symbols aimed at preserving the knowledge they had developed. Long used the tarot extensively in his personal life and he felt that he had discovered a key to understanding the symbolism of the cards. This book consists of a series of articles that Long wrote on the meaning of the cards.

LOVELL, ELOIS. **WISDOM OF THE TAROT TAUGHT SIMPLY. Offset, 8½"x11", 147pp. AsA78, 7.50p.**
An esoteric, often quite disjointed analysis of the Rider tarot deck. The material is organized into lessons and extremely specific instructions are given for all aspects of the ritual of using the deck—and the author certainly does make a ritual out of it ! Astrology and numerology are incorporated into the exposition. Many of the symbological concepts introduced here cannot readily be found elsewhere.

MAXWELL, JOSEPH. **THE TAROT. 223pp. Spe75, 3.95p.**
Maxwell was a serious student of Hermetic teachings who lived from 1858-1938 and was influential in the esoteric revival of those times. He was a lawyer by profession and his writing style reflects his legalistic

bent. This volume is a resume of Maxwell's experience and wisdom. Included is a detailed study of the major arcana and a survey of the minor, with a comprehensive view of their esoteric symbolism and both their astrological and numerological significances, as well as the color symbolism. A general discussion of the tarot is also included.

MOAKLEY, GERTRUDE. **THE TAROT CARDS PAINTED BY BONIFACIO BEMBO. Bibliography, 8½"x9½", 124pp. NYP66, 10.75c.**
An iconographical and historical study of the tarot cards created for the Visconti Sforza family. Full size black and white reproductions of each of the cards are included, along with individual analyses.

OUSPENSKY, P.D. **THE SYMBOLISM OF THE TAROT: PHILOSOPHY OF OCCULTISM IN PICTURES AND NUMBERS. 63pp. Dov13, 1.75p.**
Ouspensky, Russian philosopher and mystic, is best known for his exposition of the practical psychological system of G.I. Gurdjieff. This small volume on the tarot was originally printed as a pamphlet in Russia in 1913 and it is also available as a chapter in Ouspensky's **New Model of the Universe.** Ouspensky surveys the cards of the major arcana individually and discusses them as stages along the path. An interesting approach is his pairing of the cards—as he illustrates them, each half of the pair completes the sense of the other. Ouspensky uses the Rider-Waite deck in his exposition and each of the cards is reproduced in color.

PAPUS. **THE TAROT OF THE BOHEMIANS: ABSOLUTE KEY TO OCCULT SCIENCE. 380pp. Wil nd, 6.50c/5.00p.**
Papus was the pseudonym of a learned French physician who was a Mason and a Rosicrucian. He contributed significantly to the occultism of the tarot and the assimilation of the twenty-two trump cards to the twenty-two letters of the Hebrew alphabet. This is a very complete work for the serious student, describing his tarot codices, presenting his diagrams, and summarizing his personal thesis. This is the deepest of all the tarot books and also the most fascinating. There is a long introduction by A.E. Waite as well as Papus' excellent introductory material. Keyed to the French and Marseilles deck.

ROBERTS, RICHARD. **TAROT AND YOU. 296pp. M&M71, 3.95p.**
Roberts explains the tarot as a symbolic system of self knowledge, self integration, and self transformation using a *free association* method. He gives transcripts of actual taped tarot readings using the beautiful Aquarian deck. The evocative picture on each card releases a unique meaning for each reader. Includes an introduction and eight spreads. Keyed to the Aquarian deck.

SADHU, MOUNI. **THE TAROT. 494pp. Wil62/A&U, 5.00p.**
An excellent series of 101 lessons which describe the twenty-two major arcana cards from the standpoints of symbolism, Hermetism, numerology, relationship to the Hebrew alphabet, and astrological relationships. This is a very practical exposition for the serious student, and is well illustrated.

STUART, MICHELINE. **THE TAROT: PATH TO SELF DEVELOPMENT. 57pp. ShP77, 2.95p.**
As it is truly said, the tarot is the means of living, experiencing, and not dreaming. In this short work—short because I am giving my experience, what I have lived and from this understood where to go—I deliberately omit any explanations of the symbols of the tarot.... There are many interpretations of the tarot because there are many levels of understanding. To grasp the "teaching" given in its fundamental message, we have to be directly involved with it. It is showing the way that can carry us through the dangers of straying and error to the development of our human nature, from our animal innocence to the opening of sublime life.—from the introduction. Each of the major arcana cards is discussed and illustrated. The illustrations are from the Marseilles deck.

STURZAKER, DOREEN and JAMES. **COLOUR AND THE KABBALAH. 287pp. Wei75/TPL, 9.50c.**
The authors present an intricate study of what colors mean in connection with the ten *sephiroth*, the twenty-two paths, and the twenty-two major arcana trumps, as this relates to the several worlds of Qabalistic philosophy. Most occult teachings on color are based on the seven rays of the spectrum; an innovation introduced by the Sturzakers is the concept of twelve rays, their importance in the whole of life, manifest and unmanifest, and their interaction throughout the cosmos. This is the only Qabalistic work which discusses the meaning

of the color rays in their relationship to the myriad aspects of the Tree of Life. The presentation is very esoteric, but good for those who wish to delve deeper into the rays and into how both the color rays and the Qabala relate to the tarot trumps.

STURZAKER, JAMES. **KABBALISTIC APHORISMS. 6.95c.**
See the Jewish Mysticism section.

THIERENS, A.E. **ASTROLOGY AND THE TAROT. 159pp. NPC75, 4.95p.**
Despite the title, the bulk of this volume is devoted to the tarot, with only occasional references to astrological corespondences. This is one of the only books that delves into the esoteric meaning of the individual minor arcana cards. The suits and the major arcana cards are also esoterically analyzed.

USSHER, ARLAND. **THE TWENTY-TWO KEYS OF THE TAROT. Introduction, 54pp. Duf70/Dol, 8.75c.**
The inner meaning of the major arcana cards comes to life in Ussher's narrative. Each of the cards is discussed separately and all are interrelated. Many mythological, Hebraic, and Germanic references are included in the exposition. We get a clearer picture of the meaning of each card from this short work than from any other of similar length that we can think of. The illustrations are from the Marseilles deck.

WAITE, A.E. **THE PICTORIAL KEY TO THE TAROT. 344pp. Wei10/HPG, 2.95p.**
This is the granddaddy of all the other modern tarot books and Waite is the man who designed the most popular deck. All the cards (major and minor arcana) are reproduced. A good, long introduction discusses the symbolism and the antiquity of the cards; each card is briefly analyzed; and there is a study of divination techniques and a description of several spreads as well as an annotated bibliography.

WARNER, REBECCA. **TAROT. Bibliography, oversize, 87pp. SMP74/AcE, 4.95p.**
This is the only beginning book keyed specifically to the Marseilles deck. The symbolic meanings of both the major and minor arcana are briefly analyzed. Short sections are included on the tarot and numerology and the tarot and astrology. There are also directions on reading the cards.

WILLIAMS, CHARLES. **THE GREATER TRUMPS. 230pp. Eer54/SBL, 2.95p.**
This is a novel based on the ideas expressed in the major arcana of the tarot. Williams was a writer who produced a number of little known but important books in the field of religion and theology along with a number of remarkable novels. This novel has been long out of print and has gained an underground reputation.

ZAIN, C.C. **THE SACRED TAROT. 416pp. ChL36, 6.95p.**
Thirteen comprehensive lessons on the tarot for the serious occultist. Includes information on the chronology of the tarot, reading the tarot, its scope and use, and a section on the sacred tarot as a doctrine of Qabalism. Illustrated with many charts and reproductions of the author's Egyptian tarot.

Tarot Decks

There is a traditional symbolism which is associated with the tarot. Many of the older decks bear a strong resemblance to each other. However there is no best deck, each one is a unique work and each individual has to decide which resonates with him the most.

AQUARIAN TAROT. 6.00.
This is an unusual interpretation of a medieval deck, illustrated by David Palladini. The colors are muted pastels: pinks, lavender, blues. The symbolic figures are not as evocative as in some of the other decks. Seventy-eight, 3¼"x5" cards; the minor arcana cards also have pictures on them.

BALBI TAROT DECK. 10.00.
Domenico Balbi, the designer of this 2¾"x4¼", deck, is an Italian occultist and is a painter by profession. The designs on the cards are

modern in appearance yet retain most of the usual symbology. A fifty-four page explanatory booklet is included and emphasizes an esoteric interpretation of the symbology. Seventy-eight brightly colored cards comprise this deck.

B.O.T.A. **MAJOR TAROT KEYS. 5.75.**
This 4"x7" deck contains oversize, uncolored cards, and is our favorite. The designs on the cards are often similar to the Waite-Rider deck, but there are substantial differences in the symbolism. The idea behind an uncolored deck is that as you color in each card you concentrate on every aspect of the card and its symbolism becomes a part of your being. As you color the cards in you also add your vibrations to them and they become more responsive to you. The cards bear an Arabic number in the lower left and a Hebrew letter in the lower right corner. Case's **Highlights of the Tarot** has coloring instructions.

B.O.T.A. **TAROT DECK. 2¾"x4½", 5.75.**
Small cards, including the fifty-six cards of the minor arcana. We found that it was hard to color in some parts of the large cards, so we definitely do not recommend this small deck for coloring. The minor arcana is illustrated by designs rather than by pictures.

CAGLIOSTRO TAROT. 2½"x4¼", 10.00.
A seventy-eight card color deck. The major arcana designs are an amalgam of contemporary and Egyptian figures. Astrological symbols and dates and card interpretations appear on all cards. Eighty page accompanying booklet.

QUEEN ♣ SWORDS.

THE CHURCH OF LIGHT EGYPTIAN TAROT. 5.95.
Full 2¾"x4½" deck, black and white and suitable for coloring. The cards are rich in Egyptian symbolism—all of which is fully explored in Zain's books.

CROWLEY THOTH DECK. 4½"x6¼", 12.00.
This is a variation of the Egyptian deck, designed by Aleister Crowley. The colors and designs are quite macabre. Some feel that they are the most hauntingly beautiful cards that they have seen—others recoil from them. These cards are oversize, and a complete departure from the usual tarot symbols.

DITHA MOSER TAROCK. Boxed, 2¼″x5¾″, 48.00.
A fine reproduction of a seventy-eight card deck, originally published in 1906 in Vienna. The cards contain double-ended scenes depicting a colorful variety of people, animals, houses, and objects in a black border. The court cards portray Assyrians, knights, royalty, and Egyptians. Forty page booklet in German.

EGIZIANO TAROT. 3¼″x4¾″, 12.00.
A seventy-eight card color deck which contains Spanish titles on the card along with interpretations in Italian along the card borders. The designs are based upon Eteilla. The major arcana cards contain Hebrew letters and the minor arcana are inset with traditional American and Spanish cards.

GENTILINI TAROT. 3″x4½″, 49.00.
An extremely expressive seventy-eight card modern deck, done in pastels and reflecting a blend of cubism and expressionism. The illustrations blend traditional tarot symbolism with modern scenes. The major arcana cards contain ornate borders and bear titles in both regular and reversed positions. This is our favorite of all the contemporary decks. Beautifully boxed in a sturdy velveteen case.

EL GRAN TAROT ESOTERICO. 10.00.
An unusual, very nicely colored, modern, seventy-eight, 4¾″x6¾″ card deck, which departs considerably from the traditional symbolism—and yet retains a sense of the inner meaning of the cards. The cards were designed by Maritxu, a contemporary Spanish woman who has devoted her life to a study of the tarot and to conducting tarot readings. A more than adequate seventy page explanatory booklet accompanies the deck.

GRAND ETTEILLA EGYPTIAN GYPSIES TAROT. 6.50.
This 2½″x5″ deck is the real Egyptian and Qabalistic tarot as interpreted in the seventeenth century by the famous French diviner, M. Alliette, based upon the theories of Compte de Gebelin. The Fool, instead of appearing as the first card, is placed as the last card. The designs represent a departure from the standard symbolic pictures. The designs on the cards are mostly full length figures and the titles are double ended and vary to take into account reverse meanings. A 117 page explanatory booklet is included.

GRAND TAROT BELLINE. 50.00.
These seventy-eight cards of the *Grand Format* were created by the Magus Edmond in the nineteenth century and used by him in readings for Napoleon III. Later revised and published by the Magus Belline, each card is a work of art. The cards are for professionals and are printed on fine quality card stock, and varnished for long life. The card titles and instruction booklet are in French only. This is the finest deck we have seen, 4½″x8″, in a velvet-lined boxed.

HOLY ORDER OF MANS. **TAROT TWENTY-TWO KEYS. 3.00.**
Black and white designs. The Holy Order of Mans book has explicit coloring instructions. The cards are similar in design to the B.O.T.A. deck—including the corresponding Hebrew alphabet. The cards are 4″x7″, and include the major arcana.

MAMLUK WANUWWAB. 24.00.
This is a beautifully reproduced, 3″x8¼″ version of the only Arabic playing cards extant (the Islam religion forbids gambling and card playing is considered gambling). The cards are reminiscent of many traditional minor arcanas.

THE NEW TAROT FOR THE AQUARIAN AGE. 10.00.
A new 3¼″x5″ deck whose symbols were given via the ouija board. The cards were dictated in exact detail, even to color and the placement of symbols. They were revealed at sessions that were not undertaken for the purpose of obtaining tarot symbols. The board said that the reason for their dictation at this time was both to rescue the cards from their plight as fortune telling devices and to herald the coming of a new age. We do not care for the imagery, though it is quite evocative. Ralph Metzner speaks quite highly of the deck and feels that the images seem to have a direct electrical-emotional *charge.* Includes the **Royal Maze** (a guide to the game of destiny) and three instruction booklets totaling well over 200 pages.

POINTNER TAROT DECK. 3″x5½″, 20.00.
A very unusual set of modernistic graphic designs, printed on very

heavy card stock and ornately decorated. Seventy-eight card pack. Twenty-eight page explanatory booklet.

RIDER-WAITE TAROT DECK. 2½″x4¾″, 6.50p.
The famous seventy-eight card deck designed by Pamela Coleman Smith under the direction of Arthur E. Waite. The outstanding feature of this deck is that all of the cards are presented in emblematic designs readily suitable for divination in contrast to the rigid forms of swords, batons, cups, and coins previously used in **Tarot Decks**. This is far and away the most popular and the most commonly used deck. The cards are in color. A minature deck is available for $5.00.

THE ROYAL FEZ MOROCCAN TAROT DECK. 6.50.
A very traditional deck, with simple, classical illustrations and a delicate feeling. Seventy-eight cards form the 2¾″x4¾″ deck, and an instruction booklet is included with it.

SPANISH TAROT. 2½″x4½″, 6.50.
Brightly colored classical designs, based on an original deck from 1738 which can be found in a Spanish museum. Good reproductions. The card names are in Spanish and the instruction booklet is bilingual.

SWISS TAROT CARDS. 5.50.
A small, full color seventy-eight card deck—based on classical designs.

TAROCCHINO OF MENEGAZZI. 2¼″x4¼″, 28.00.
A lovely, unusual seventy-eight color deck, just produced in Milan in 1978. Each card portrays partial or profile scenes, revealing only half the picture and leaving the balance to the interpretation of the reader. The artwork utilizes bold lines, and rich colors and gives the appearance of wood sculptures. Each card is signed and numbered by the artist.

TAROT CLASSIC. 2½″x4½″, 5.50.
This eighteenth century deck is based upon original woodcuts by Claude Burdel, with slight modifications such as the printing of the names of the cards in English. Full deck, in color, with instruction booklet.

TAROT OF MARSEILLES. 6.50.
This is one of the most ancient French decks available. Its illustrations relate the symbolic laws of the universe in a very clear manner. Full 2½″x5″ deck, in color. An instruction booklet is included.

TAROT OF THE WITCHES. 2¾"x4¼", 6.00.
A seventy-eight card color deck, with traditional symbols redone in a modern fashion. The design is extremely simple. Twenty-eight page instruction booklet by Stuart Kaplan.

VANDENBORRE TAROT DECK. 3"x5", 10.00.
A reproduction of the seventy-eight **Cartes de Suisses** deck first published in 1770. The figures are well drawn and the designs are traditional, resembling the **Marseilles** deck. Printed on heavy tan card stock.

VISCONTI SFORZA TAROCCHI DECK. 30.00.
This is far and away the most beautiful and evocative of the classical decks. It is an excellent reproduction of the original from 1430. The background of the cards is gold foil and the images are exquisitely presented. All serious students of the tarot should own this deck. Seventy-eight 3½"x7" cards, with instruction booklet.

WAITE DECK. 2¾"x4¾", 6.00.
The same symbols as the Rider-Waite deck—but the colors are a good deal more intense in this version.

WIRTH TAROT DECK. 2¾"x5¼", 8.00.
Wirth, a nineteenth century Swiss Qabalist, was a disciple of Stanislas de Guaita, an important French occultist. The designs in this deck are based on the **Tarot of Marseilles**, with a number of modifications. Eliphas Levi contributed to the design. Wirth only produced a major arcana deck and the minor arcana that appears in this deck has been created in the same style and vision. Reproductions of the cards appear in Papus' **Tarot of the Bohemians**. The cards themselves are of

excellent quality and are printed in metallic colors, including a great deal of background gold. The Hebrew letter which corresponds to each of the major arcana cards appears in the lower right hand corner. A short commentary on the cards is included. We like these cards the most of any of the classic decks.

XULTIN TAROT. 5¾"x3¾", 10.00.
Xultin is a Mayan word which means the count of the 360 holy days of the calendar. The cards in this deck depict the esoteric practices of the Mayans. They are colorful and in the style of glyphs. The designer of the deck suggests that the meanings of each card represent the relationships which we experience in life. An accompanying booklet suggests ways in which the cards can be interpreted and used for meditation.

YEAGER MEDITATION TAROT. 3"x4¾", 14.00.
A seventy-eight card color deck. Modernistic, with Egyptian overtones and based on surrealistic paintings. The cards have an eerie feeling and should appeal to those who like Crowley's deck. Each card has a black border. Instruction booklet included.

ZIGEUNER TAROT. 21.15.
This is a modernized deck which retains much of the medieval symbology. The figures look almost like cartoon characters and yet manage to convey a deep feeling. The colors are mainly pastels and there is a moire pattern in the background. This is a more interesting deck than most of the modern ones. Both major and minor arcana are included, 4¼"x6", and printed on very thick, glossy cover stock.

──────**END OF THE TAROT DECKS SUBSECTION**──────

THEOSOPHY

We often speak of Theosophy as not in itself a religion, but the truth which lies behind all religions alike. That is so; yet, from another point of view, we may surely say that it is at once a philosophy, a religion and a science. It is a philosophy, because it puts plainly before us an explanation of the scheme of evolution of both the souls and the bodies contained in our solar system. It is a religion in so far as, having shown us the course of ordinary evolution, it also puts before us and advises a method of shortening that course, so that by conscious effort we may progress more directly towards the goal. It is a science, because it treats both these subjects as matters not of theological belief but of direct knowledge obtainable by study and investigation. It asserts that man has no need to trust to blind faith, because he has within him latent powers which, when aroused, enable him to see and examine for himself, and it proceeds to prove its case by showing how those powers may be awakened. It is itself a result of the awakening of such powers by men, for the teachings which it puts before us are founded upon direct observations made in the past, and rendered possible only by such development.

As a philosophy, it explains to us that the solar system is a carefully-ordered mechanism, a manifestation of a magnificent life, of which man is but a small part. Nevertheless, it takes up that small part which immediately concerns us, and treats it exhaustively under three heads—present, past and future.

It deals with the present by describing what man really is, as seen by means of developed faculties. It is customary to speak of man as having a soul. Theosophy, as the result of direct investigation, reverses that dictum, and states that man is a soul, and has a body—in fact several bodies, which are his vehicles and instruments in various worlds. These worlds are not separate in space; they are simultaneously present with us, here and now, and can be examined; they are the divisions of the material side of Nature—different degrees of density in the aggregation of matter, as will presently be explained in detail. Man has an existence in several of these, but is normally conscious only of the lowest, though sometimes in dreams and trances he has glimpses of some of the others. What is called death is the laying aside of the vehicle belonging to this lowest world, but the soul or real man in a higher world is no more changed or affected by this than the physical man is changed or affected when he removes his overcoat. All this is a matter, not of speculation, but of observation and experiment.

Theosophy has much to tell us of the past history of man—of how in the course of evolution he has come to be what he now is. This also is a matter of observation, because of the fact that there exists an indelible record of all that has taken place—a sort of memory of Nature—by examining which the scenes of earlier evolution may be made to pass before the eyes of the investigator as though they were happening at this moment. By thus studying the past we learn that man is divine in origin and that he has a long evolution behind him—a double evolution, that of the life or soul within, and that of the outer form. We learn, too, that the life of man as a soul is of, what to us seems enormous length, and that what we have been in the habit of calling his life is in reality only one day of his real existence. He has already lived through many such days, and has many more of them yet before him; and if we wish to understand the real life and its object, we must consider it in relation not only to this one day of it, which begins with birth and ends with death, but also to the days which have gone before and those which are yet to come.

Of those that are yet to come there is also much to be said, and on this subject, too, a great deal of definite information is available. Such information is obtainable, first, from men who have already passed much further along the road of evolution than we, and have consequently direct experience of it; and, secondly, from inferences drawn from the obvious direction of the steps which we see to have been previously taken. The goal of this particular cycle is in sight, though still far above us but it would seem that, even when that has been attained, an infinity of progress still lies before everyone who is willing to undertake it.

The existence of Perfected Men, and the possibility of coming into touch with Them and being taught by Them, are prominent among the great new truths which Theosophy brings to the western world. Another of them is the stupendous fact that the world is not drifting blindly into anarchy, but that its progress is under the control of a perfectly organized hierarchy, so that final failure even for the tiniest of its units is of all impossibilities the most impossible. A glimpse of the working of that hierarchy inevitably engenders the desire to cooperate with it, to serve under it, in however humble a capacity, and some time in the far-distant future to be worthy to join the outer fringes of its ranks.

—condensed from **A Textbook of Theosophy**, *by C.W. Leadbeater*

ARUNDALE, GEORGE. **THE LOTUS FIRE: A STUDY IN SYMBOLIC YOGA. Many illustrations, index, 771pp. TPH39, 22.50c.**
A Theosophical approach to yoga and to an understanding of bodily energies based on ancient Sanskrit texts and divided into the following sections: *The Vigil of Purification, Symbols Living and Radiant, Symbols Released and Dynamic, From the Symbols to the No-Symbol,* and *Symbols at Work.* Those who are not well versed in Theosophical language and cosmology will have a hard time understanding this book. In addition to some of the more usual areas, Arundale introduces material we have not read elsewhere.

ASHISH, SRI MADHAVA. **MAN, SON OF MAN. Index, 355pp. TPH70, 5.50c.**
A companion volume to **Man, the Measure of All Things** by Ashish and Krishna Prem, taking the form of a commentary on the **Stanzas of Dzyan** which outline the processes of human evolution which have culminated in man as he is today. This is a deep book, designed to invoke a thoughtful response in the reader. The **Stanzas** were first presented to the modern world in Blavatsky's **Secret Doctrine** and are otherwise unknown to orthodox scholarship. The selections are topically organized and form an excellent presentation of the Theosophical cosmology.

Alice Bailey

Eighteen of Alice Bailey's books are the result of her collaboration with a disincarnate Tibetan sage, Djwal Khul, sometimes called D.K. or the Tibetan Master. D.K. would transmit the information to Alice Bailey telepathically. Those close to Ms. Bailey said that she was not a medium in the usual sense, but rather an alert and active participant. The books cover a wide range of information, emphasizing what Ms. Bailey calls the *science of soul contact* and the practical demonstration of spiritual principles in daily life. The aim of the teachings is said to be to lay a foundation for the esoteric truths and spiritual realities and provide the knowledge necessary to carry humanity into the New Age, once the information has been assimilated and properly utilized. Ms. Bailey has a very distinctive writing style, which takes some getting used to. Alice Bailey was also instrumental in the formation of various organizations including the Arcane School, created in 1923 as a training school for discipleship. It is a correspondence school, providing a sequential course of study and meditation.

ARCANA WORKSHOP. **FOR FULL MOON WORKERS. 16pp. ArW nd, 1.25p.**
This is an unfinished how-to manual. It is unfinished because we are always discovering more about the science of invocation and evocation with which full moon work is concerned. This how-to manual represents the discoveries, experiments and experiences of an eighteen year effort by a trained meditating group. And it is offered with the hope that it will help in the forming of full moon meditating groups all over the world.

ARCANA WORKSHOP. **FULL MOON MAGIC. .75p.**
See the Astrology section.

ARCANA WORKSHOP. **FULL MOON MEDITATIONS. 2.00p.**
See the Astrology section.

ARCANA WORKSHOP. **THE FULL MOON STORY. 65pp. ArW nd, 3.00p.**
This is the basic *full moon* study divided into the following sections: *Purpose of Full Moon Observance, New World Religion, Necessity for Groups—Inner and Outer,* and *The Immediate Task.*

BAILEY, ALICE. **THE CONSCIOUSNESS OF THE ATOM. 163pp. LPC61, 5.95c/3.00p.**
Lectures discussing evolution as it progressively affects the atomic substance of all forms, subjective and objective.

BAILEY, ALICE. **THE DESTINY OF THE NATIONS. 161pp. LPC49, 6.50c/2.75p.**
A presentation of the rudiments of national psychology through an appreciation of the astrological and seven ray rulerships and influences upon the nations.

BAILEY, ALICE. **DISCIPLESHIP IN THE NEW AGE, VOLUME I. 847pp. LPC72, 13.50c/9.00p.**
A series of personal instructions given to a small group of *chelas* (disciples) over a period of fifteen years, with related teaching on a number of subjects.

BAILEY, ALICE. **DISCIPLESHIP IN THE NEW AGE, VOLUME II. 818pp. LPC55, 13.50c/6.25p.**
Includes information about the dynamics of meditation at the time of the full moon in order to facilitate spiritual contact and the registering of divine impressions via the link from soul to mind to brain.

BAILEY, ALICE. **EDUCATION IN THE NEW AGE. 153pp. LPC nd, 6.75c/3.00p.**
This book presents a framework for the philosophy, techniques, and goals of true education as it will be understood in the new *era of the One Humanity that is dawning upon the horizon of our troubled times.* Ms. Bailey says that education is the technique of conscious evolution and the building of the bridge of consciousness that links the human personality with the divine soul.

BAILEY, ALICE. **THE EXTERNALISATION OF THE HIERARCHY. 744pp. LPC57, 13.50c/7.50p.**
A series of pamphlets, letters, and instructions to disciples during the Second World War and immediately afterward.

BAILEY, ALICE. **FROM BETHLEHEM TO CALVARY. 292pp. LPC65, 9.50c/3.75p.**
Follows the path of Christ through his six stages of initiations: birth, baptism, transfiguration, crucifixion, resurrection, and ascension.

BAILEY, ALICE. **FROM INTELLECT TO INTUITION. 275pp. LPC60, 7.50c/4.25p.**
Development of the intellect is shown as a means to an end and one step on the way to a fully awakened and active mental body.

BAILEY, ALICE. **GLAMOUR: A WORLD PROBLEM. 290pp. LPC50, 8.25c/3.25p.**

■ *BAILEY, ALICE.* **INITIATION, HUMAN AND SOLAR. 240pp. LPC51, 11.25c/4.50p.**
Recommended as a good introduction to the books, as it lays the groundwork for much of the material later presented. Includes the rules for aspirants and an explanation and description of the *occult hierarchy* of the planet.

BAILEY, ALICE. **THE LABOURS OF HERCULES. 111pp. LPC74, 2.75p.**
An esoteric interpretation of the zodiacal signs as viewed through the myths of Hercules. Each of the signs is discussed at length.

BAILEY, ALICE. **LETTERS ON OCCULT MEDITATION. 8.50c/4.00p.**
See the Meditation section.

BAILEY, ALICE. **THE LIGHT OF THE SOUL. 485pp. LPC55, 10.00c/4.75p.**
A restatement of Patanjali's *Yoga Sutras*—the classical work on raja yoga.

BAILEY, ALICE. **PROBLEMS OF HUMANITY. 181pp. LPC64, 2.75p.**
Discusses problems such as the following: continuing cleavages in consciousness, psychological evaluations and reactions to world conditions, national, religious, class, or racial prejudice, conditions of literacy, disease, and poverty.

BAILEY, ALICE. **THE REAPPEARANCE OF THE CHRIST. 191pp. LPC48, 7.00c/3.25p.**
A message concerning imminent revelations and the emergence of the *spiritual hierarchy of our planet,* led by the Christ, once humanity has prepared itself. Includes information outlining the *new world religion, the science of invocation, and the meaning and application of the great invocation.*

BAILEY, ALICE. **THE SOUL AND ITS MECHANISM. 165pp. LPC65, 6.75c/3.25p.**
Presents a method by which the soul and the personality vehicle interact and function together.

BAILEY, ALICE. **TELEPATHY AND THE ETHERIC VEHICLE. 219pp. LPC50, 7.00c/3.50p.**
Includes practical instructions.

BAILEY, ALICE. **A TREATISE ON COSMIC FIRE. 1,367pp. LPC62, 18.00c/11.75p.**
Deals with the underlying structure of occult teaching for the present era, with vast cosmic processes reproduced through all areas of life from universe to atom. The most profound and least understood of all Bailey's books.

BAILEY, ALICE. **A TREATISE ON THE SEVEN RAYS: ESOTERIC ASTROLOGY. 15.00c/7.25p.**
See the Astrology section.

BAILEY, ALICE. **A TREATISE ON THE SEVEN RAYS: ESOTERIC HEALING. 771pp. LPC53, 11.50c/7.50p.**
In this book the seven ray techniques of healing are described, the laws and rules of healing are enumerated and discussed, the requirements for healing are given in detail, and basic causes of diseases are shown. We learn, for example, that much disease can be karmic in origin, that certain diseases are inherent in the soil and the substance of the planet, and that many others are psychological arising in the mental and emotional bodies.

BAILEY, ALICE. **A TREATISE ON THE SEVEN RAYS: ESOTERIC PSYCHOLOGY, VOLUME I. 460pp. LPC36, 9.50c/4.75p.**
The sequence of books under the overall title of **A Treatise on the Seven Rays** is based on the nature and quality of the seven basic streams of energy pervading our solar system, the Earth, and all that moves within its orbit. The psychology volumes are concerned first with basic energy patterns and structures, and second with the soul and personality of man and the plan for humanity.

BAILEY, ALICE. **A TREATISE ON THE SEVEN RAYS: ESOTERIC PSYCHOLOGY, VOLUME II.** 818pp. LPC42, 12.00c/7.25p.

BAILEY, ALICE. **A TREATISE ON THE SEVEN RAYS: THE RAYS AND THE INITIATIONS.** 820pp. LPC60, 11.50c/7.25p.
The first part of this volume details rules for groups and the second part is concerned with the nine major expansions and consciousness through which the initiate becomes progressively liberated from various forms of our planetary life, ultimately proceeding upon his chosen path.

BAILEY, ALICE. **A TREATISE ON WHITE MAGIC.** 705pp. LPC51, 11.50c/5.00p.
Gives the rules for magical creation, control of the emotional body, and elevation of human consciousness into the *fifth kingdom of nature of the kingdom of souls.* Also contains many practical hints on day to day living.

BAILEY, ALICE. **THE UNFINISHED AUTOBIOGRAPHY.** 304pp. LPC51, 8.50c/4.25p.

BAILEY, FOSTER. **CHANGING ESOTERIC VALUES.** 80pp. LPC54, 2.50p.
Foster Bailey was Alice Bailey's husband and was active in her work. This is an edited and enlarged version of four lectures he gave in 1954. He shows esotericism to be a practical science of service, *responsible for the well-being of the human race in conformity with the Divine Plan.*

BAILEY, FOSTER. **RUNNING GOD'S PLAN.** 188pp. LPC72, 3.00p.
Practical essays on a variety of topics applicable to the present day.

BAILEY, FOSTER. **THE SPIRIT OF MASONRY.** 143pp. LPC57, 2.75p.
Contains five in a series of instructions D.K. intended to give to a group of Masons through the agency of Alice Bailey. The instructions were never completed and Foster was asked to publish them along with some articles on the Masons.

BAILEY, FOSTER. **THINGS TO COME.** LPC nd, 4.75p.

BANKS, NATALIE. **THE GOLDEN THREAD.** 95pp. LPC63, 2.25p.
A concise summation of the passage of the *ageless wisdom teachings* throughout the ages, periods, and epochs of Earth's history from the ancient past to modern times.

EASTCOTT, MICHAEL. **JACOB'S LADDER.** 78pp. Sdl66, 1.10p.
This small book is planned as a first step in "Approach to the Ageless Wisdom." It attempts, therefore, to cover a very wide field—our background as human beings and our "essential" nature as participants in an immense and wonderous Plan....The long series of Teachings written by the Master Djwhal Khul with Alice A. Bailey is the main source of this "approach" because, added to being the most recent, it is the most comprehensive unfoldment of the Ageless Wisdom that has ever been made.

EASTCOTT, MICHAEL. **MEDITATION AND THE RHYTHM OF THE YEAR.** 1.95p.
See the Astrology section.

EASTCOTT, MICHAEL. **THE SPIRITUAL HIERARCHY OF THE WORLD.** 108pp. Sdl73, 1.95p.
In the following pages an attempt is made to tell the story of the Spiritual Hierarchy which guides and guards our planet.

EASTCOTT, MICHAEL. **THE WORK OF THE MASTER DJWHAL KHUL WITH ALICE A. BAILEY.** 63pp. Sdl74, 1.40p.
An introduction to the writings, summarizing the message of each of the books and transcribing a number of mantrums.

EASTCOTT, MICHAEL and NANCY MAGOR. **ENTERING AQUARIUS.** 90pp. Sdl71, 1.65p.
It is not the province of this small book to search into the problems that face humanity, or dare to pose solutions; but some of the teachings of the Ageless Wisdom which throw light on these problems are presented because they uncover the meaning of much that is happening and help us to recognize mankind's destiny.

EASTCOTT, MICHAEL and NANCY MAGOR. **THE PLAN AND THE PATH.** 80pp. Sdl76, 1.95p.
Various great themes have been developed [in Bailey's books], basic unfoldments of truth that point the way to the next stage of our progress, among them that there is an unfolding Plan for our world within a great cosmic pattern, that there is a spiritual Hierarchy watching over our destiny and that the Law of Evolution guarantees our progress. Within the teaching on the Plan are found the story of life evolving through all the kingdoms of nature and the place of the individual with his trials, testings and gradual growth in the perspective of the whole.—from the foreword.

HOPKINS, JOHN. **THE MEASURE OF THE UNIVERSE.** Glossary, 151pp. Com76, 4.25p.
This volume builds on the material presented in **The Seed of Wisdom**. It is *concerned with humanity as a whole and with the relationship between humanity and those higher centres of consciousness within the body of our planet, and with even higher centres within our solar system and the universe.* The following are the main topics: *Man—the Microcosm, Man and the Macrocosm, Purpose and Perfection, The Hierarchy of Souls, Esoteric Astrology, The Measure of the Universe,* and *Evolutionary Forces.*

HOPKINS, JOHN. **THE SEED OF WISDOM.** 120pp. Com72, 4.00p.
The purpose of this volume is to serve as an introduction to the teaching expounded by Alice Bailey. All the basic material and topics are reviewed and restated here and Hopkins writes a great deal more clearly than his mentor. The following are the main topics: *The Constitution of Man, The Etheric Body, Energy Centers and the Endocrine Glands, The Soul and the Doctrine of Re-birth, Evolution, The World of Energies, The Seven Rays,* and *Meditation.*

SARAYDARIAN, TORKOM. **THE TRIANGLES OF FIRE.** 106pp. AEG77, 3.00p.
In 1937 a great Sage, called Djwhal Khul, gave to humanity the esoteric teaching on triangles. This teaching can be found in all His writings....In the past forty years the teaching on triangles has penetrated almost all countries of the world, and has created millions of triangles. A triangle is composed of three people, who daily say the Great Invocation to invoke light, love and power in order to create peace, understanding, cooperation, abundance and freedom. There are triangles that invoke light; there are triangles that spread goodwill; and there are triangles that are being prepared to be the circulatory agents of will energy. This is a comprehensive discussion of triangles—in theory and practice—accompanied by quotations from related works.

A STUDENT. **PONDER ON THIS.** 431pp. LPC74, 5.75p.
Scattered through all my writings over the years, is a mass of information which needs collating and bringing together, as a basis for the instruction of disciples....The present compilation is an attempt in this direction.—D.K. A South African student (or students) has topically arranged hundreds of extracts from the Tibetan's teachings in alphabetical order. The hope is that this selection will bring D.K.'s teaching to the attention of a wider circle of students. A massive, greatly needed effort.

A STUDENT. **SERVING HUMANITY.** 513pp. LPC72, 6.50p.
An excellent continuation of the compilations commenced in **Ponder**. There is some overlapping intentionally as some of the quotations used previously help to round out the present volume. *It is only through constant reiteration that men learn, and these things must be said again and again.* The selections seem to go into far greater depth in this volume.

A STUDENT. **THE SOUL, THE QUALITY OF LIFE.** LPC74, 10.00c.
A third compilation, again topically organized.

WILLIS, C.E. **SEED THOUGHTS FOR MEDITATION DISTILLED FROM ALICE A. BAILEY'S DISCIPLESHIP IN THE NEW AGE, VOLUME I.** Com76, 3.40p.
A pocket sized book put together by a student of the Arcane School.

───────── **END OF ALICE BAILEY SUBSECTION** ─────────

BARBORKA, GEOFFREY. **THE MAHATMAS AND THEIR LETTERS.** Index, 440pp. TPH73, 8.95c.
This is an in depth study of the letters that A.P. Sinnett received from the Mahatmas. A few of the letters are examined at length and a great deal of space is devoted to assaying the authenticity of the letters and discussing how they were received. Various proofs and testimonials are offered.

BARBORKA, GEOFFREY. THE PEOPLING OF THE EARTH. Index, 247pp. TPH75, 10.00c.
An exploration of the origins of man based on the section of **The Secret Doctrine** devoted to anthropogenesis. Taking as the basis for his exposition the mysterious stanzas from the **Book of Dzyan** as translated by H.P. Blavatsky, Barborka traces the origin and evolution of man. The reader needs to be familiar with Theosophical vocabulary and literature in order to follow the account.

BARKER, A. TREVOR, *ed.* **THE MAHATMA LETTERS TO A.P. SINNETT. 430pp. ThU23, 5.95p.**
These letters were written between the years 1880 and 1884 to A.P. Sinnett, an English civil servant in India, by two Mahatmas of Tibet whom H.P. Blavatsky had acknowledged as her teachers and the inspirers of her **Isis Unveiled** and **The Secret Doctrine**. These letters discuss the cosmology and the life and development of the human race as well as far reaching concepts of religious and scientific thought. Very important material for all readers interested in Theosophy.

BENJAMIN, HARRY. EVERYONE'S GUIDE TO THEOSOPHY. 149pp. TPH69, 4.50c.
A topically organized overview of the main features of Theosophy. The information is clearly presented and all the important concepts are included.

Annie Besant

Annie Besant was Blavatsky's chosen vehicle to head the Theosophical Society following the latter's death. In her early years with the Society Ms. Besant carried on a number of clairvoyant experiments with her close associate, C.W. Leadbeater. Later on she turned her full attentions to administration and it was she, more than anyone else, who built up the Society. In addition to her organizational skills she began a series of excellent educational institutions in India—many of which are still ongoing today, more than seventy-five years later. She also published innumerable short books (many of which were transcriptions of lectures) and a few major ones. Most are out of print; we are listing all the ones that are presently available. She wrote and talked clearly and succinctly.

BESANT, ANNIE. THE ANCIENT WISDOM. 362pp. TPH1897, 5.25c.
A basic introduction to the *ageless wisdom.*

BESANT, ANNIE. THE BIRTH AND EVOLUTION OF THE SOUL. 51pp. TPH1895, 1.50c.
Two lectures on the title theme.

BESANT, ANNIE. DEATH AND AFTER. 1.95c.
See the Reincarnation and Karma section.

BESANT, ANNIE. DHARMA. 72pp. TPH18, 1.00p.
Transcriptions of three lectures on differences, evolution, and right and wrong.

BESANT, ANNIE. DOCTRINE OF THE HEART. 107pp. TPH1899, 1.50c.
A series of extracts from letters received by the author from her Indian friends. *They are not given as being of any "authority," but merely as containing thoughts that some of us have found helpful, and that we wish to share with others.* Ms. Besant has also contributed an introduction.

BESANT, ANNIE. ESOTERIC CHRISTIANITY. 3.50p.
See the Christianity section.

BESANT, ANNIE. HINTS ON THE STUDY OF THE BHAGAVAD GITA. 127pp. TPH06, 3.00c.
A transcription of four lectures.

BESANT, ANNIE. IN THE OUTER COURT. 132pp. TPH14, 2.75c.
Transcriptions of the following five lectures: *Purification, Thought Control, The Building of Character, Spiritual Alchemy,* and *On the Threshold.*

BESANT, ANNIE. INDIAN IDEALS IN EDUCATION, RELIGION, PHILOSOPHY AND ART. 123pp. TPH25, 1.50c.
Transcription of a series of lectures on the title theme delivered at Calcutta University. Many quotations from Hindu sacred literature are included.

BESANT, ANNIE. INITIATION—THE PERFECTING OF MAN. Offset, spiral bound, 149pp. HeR23, 3.00p.
Transcriptions of a series of lectures on the Christ life and the coming *world teacher.*

BESANT, ANNIE. AN INTRODUCTION TO YOGA. 1.75p.
See the Patanjali subsection of Indian Philosophy.

BESANT, ANNIE. KARMA. 2.00c.
See the Reincarnation and Karma section.

BESANT, ANNIE. LAWS OF THE HIGHER LIFE. 68pp. TPH12, 1.50c.
Transcriptions of three lectures: *The Larger Consciousness, The Law of Duty,* and *The Law of Sacrifice.*

BESANT, ANNIE. MAN AND HIS BODIES. 117pp. TPH12, 2.75c.
Describes the occult constitution of man's personality as an aggregate of bodies or vehicles through which his immortal self or soul manifests and expresses itself. This includes his physical, etheric, astral, and mental bodies.

BESANT, ANNIE. MAN: WHENCE, HOW AND WHITHER. 7.95c.
See the Ancient Civilizations section.

BESANT, ANNIE. THE MASTERS. 54pp. TPH12, 1.95c.
An exploration of the masters *as facts and ideals:* who they are, where they live, their work, and how students can find them. There is also a section on *the perfect man* and the initiatory stages toward perfection.

BESANT, ANNIE. MEDITATIONS ON THE PATH AND ITS QUALIFICATIONS. TPH22, 2.45c.

BESANT, ANNIE. THE PATH OF DISCIPLESHIP. 153pp. TPH10, 3.75c.
An examination of the sacred path within each of us. Includes information on the qualifications for discipleship, the life of the disciple, and the future progress of humanity.

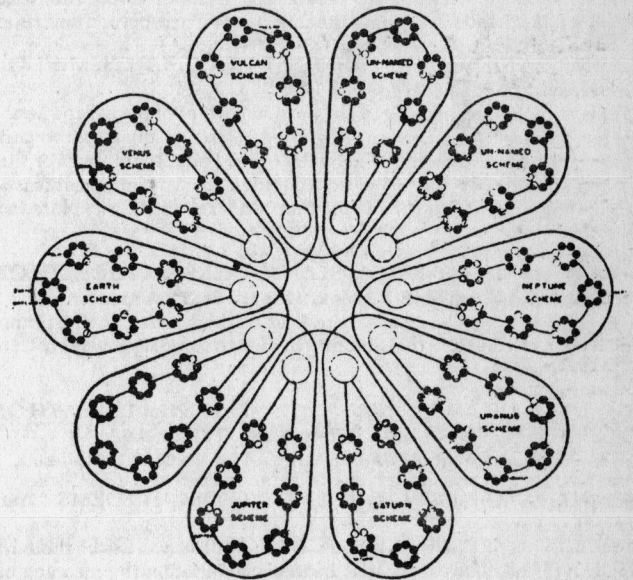

The Theosophical solar scheme.

BESANT, ANNIE. REINCARNATION. 2.25c.
See the Reincarnation and Karma section.

BESANT, ANNIE. SEVEN GREAT RELIGIONS. 3.00c.
See the Comparative Religion section.

BESANT, ANNIE. **THE SEVEN PRINCIPLES OF MAN.** 103pp. **TPH31, 1.50c.**
Describes in simple language the Theosophical concept of man as a divine being clothed in different garments or sheaths through which he is able to function at different levels of existence.

BESANT, ANNIE. **SHRI RAMACHANDRA.** 177pp. **TPH01, 2.25c.**
Selections from the **Ramayana,** designed as study lessons for Hindu students in Indian schools. The selections are topically arranged.

BESANT, ANNIE. **SOME PROBLEMS OF LIFE.** 139pp. **TPH19, 1.50c.**

BESANT, ANNIE. **A STUDY IN CONSCIOUSNESS.** Index, 382pp. **TPH04, 5.75c.**
This is one of Annie Besant's major works. As the title suggests, it is a study of consciousness in all its aspects. The book begins with a study of monads and their development and goes from there to an exploration of memory, will, desire, and emotion. As with all of the author's books, the reader needs to be well versed in Theosophy in order to comprehend the exposition.

BESANT, ANNIE. **A STUDY IN KARMA.** 2.25c.
See the Reincarnation and Karma section.

BESANT, ANNIE. **TALKS WITH A CLASS.** 206pp. **TPH22, 2.25p.**
A series of short essays on a great variety of subjects. A great deal of material is covered.

BESANT, ANNIE. **THOUGHT POWER.** 121pp. **TPH66, 1.45p.**
A discussion of the activities of the mind and the laws and principles that govern its functioning. Includes a description of the esoteric constitution of man.

BESANT, ANNIE. **WISDOM OF THE UPANISHADS.** 95pp. **TPH07, 2.50c.**
A collection of lectures.

BESANT, ANNIE and C.W. LEADBEATER. **CREATING CHARACTER.** 92pp. **TPH51, .80p.**
Two lectures on the title theme.

BESANT, ANNIE and C.W. LEADBEATER. **THE NOBLE EIGHTFOLD PATH.** 39pp. **TPH55, 1.00p.**
Transcriptions of lectures by Besant and Leadbeater on the *Noble Eightfold Path of Buddhism,* relating the concepts to Theosophical doctrine.

BESANT, ANNIE and C.W. LEADBEATER. **OCCULT CHEMISTRY.** Offset, spiral bound, 121pp. **HeR19, 5.00p.**
This is without question one of the most important of the Besant/Leadbeater works. It contains an illustrated report of their clairvoyant observations of the chemical elements of the constituent units of the cosmos. Leadbeater was an especially gifted clairvoyant and this is a fascinating presentation of an area that is still relatively unexplored to this day.

BESANT, ANNIE and C.W. LEADBEATER. **TALKS ON THE PATH OF OCCULTISM, VOLUME I.** Index, 425pp. **TPH26, 4.95c.**
A detailed commentary on **At the Feet of the Master,** the inspiring small book attributed to Krishnamurti, though some say it was written by C.W. Leadbeater.

BESANT, ANNIE and C.W. LEADBEATER. **TALKS ON THE PATH OF OCCULTISM, VOLUME II.** Index, 425pp. **TPH26, 4.95c.**
An in depth commentary on Blavatsky's **The Voice of the Silence.**

BESANT, ANNIE and C.W. LEADBEATER. **THOUGHT FORMS.** 77pp. **TPH25, 3.95c.**
Two clairvoyant Theosophists present their observations of thought and the forms which it creates. Includes material on the meaning of colors and the effects of various forms. The book includes over fifty color plates of illustrative thought forms created by emotions, music, meditation, and various kinds of feelings. An excellent presentation.

NETHERCOT, A.H. **THE FIRST FIVE LIVES OF ANNIE BESANT.** Notes, index, 422pp. **UCh60, 15.45c.**
A meticulously written biography of Annie Besant which traces Besant's *lives* in England through her conversion to Theosophy and her first departure for India. The author titles these lives as follows: *The*

Christian Wife, The Atheist Mother, The Martyr of Science, The Socialist Labor Agitator, and The Chela of the Mahatmas.

NETHERCOT, A.H. **THE LAST FOUR LIVES OF ANNIE BESANT.** Illustrations, notes, index, 483pp. **UCh63, 15.45c.**
Ms. Besant's last *lives: The Indian Educator, Propagandist and Mystic, President of the Indian National Congress, The Deserted Leader,* and *Life in Death.* Included in this volume are the stories of her role in the campaign for Indian home rule and her relationship with Krishnamurti—the young boy whom she educated to be the new Messiah and who finally repudiated the doctrines she and her associates inculcated in him. This is a fascinating tale for all those who are interested in Theosophy.

——————— END OF ANNIE BESANT SUBSECTION ———————

H.P. Blavatsky

Madame Blavatsky, or H.P.B., as she is known to Theosophists, is a mysterious figure who first came to public notice in the 1870s in the U.S. She was reputed to have spent about forty years traveling and meeting the masters of wisdom in the East and especially in Tibet. She remained in contact with these masters throughout the rest of her life. The reality of this contact was one of the most controversial aspects of her controversial life. She joined forces with Colonel Olcott in the late 1870s and together they founded the Theosophical Society. They traveled to India a few years later and settled there for a period of time. India became the headquarters of the Society and many facets of Indian philosophy were incorporated into Theosophical teachings. Some say, and with a fair amount of justice, that it was the Theosophical Society as much as anything else that reintroduced the ancient traditions to the establishment of Indian society. H.P.B.'s two major works—**Isis Unveiled** and **The Secret Doctrine**—remain the basic works and still sell well to this day.

BARBORKA, GEOFFREY. **H.P. BLAVATSKY, TIBET AND TULKU.** Notes, bibliography, index, 487pp. **TPH66, 12.00c.**
Barborka begins this study with a disclaimer which states that the book is not a biography in the usual sense of the term because so little is known of Blavatsky's life and motivations that a biographical study would be impossible. A short biographical sketch is presented in the first chapter, followed by brief surveys of Tibetan religion, language, and religious leaders, and a hypothetical analysis of Blavatsky's time in Tibet and her connections with the *Tibetans* who became her teachers. The bulk of the volume is devoted to an analysis of the ways that Blavatsky did her writing and of her role as a *tulku.* Many quotations from her writings. This is definitely not an introductory study.

BARKER, A. TREVOR, ed. **THE LETTERS OF H.P. BLAVATSKY TO A.P. SINNETT.** Notes, index, 409pp. **ThU25, 10.00c.**
A collection of revealing letters between H.P.B. and one of her closest associates. The historical references cannot always be taken at face value—the letters were written long after many of the events occurred and Blavatsky herself admits that her memory is not very exact. In any event this compilation should be fascinating reading for all students who are deeply interested in Theosophy and they form one of the only primary sources on the founder of the Theosophical Society. Most of the biographical material on Blavatsky has come from these letters.

BESANT, ANNIE. **H.P. BLAVATSKY AND THE MASTERS OF THE WISDOM.** 60pp. **TPH07, 1.75p.**
A short study which purports to trace H.P.B.'s contacts with the masters and to refute the attacks made on her character and veracity.

BLAVATSKY, H.P. **AN ABRIDGEMENT OF THE SECRET DOCTRINE.** 260pp. **TPH66, 2.25p.**

BLAVATSKY, H.P. **COLLECTED WRITINGS, VOLUMES I-X, TPH** nd, **12.00c/each.**
This massive compilation contains every word every written by H.P.B. with the exception of **Isis Unveiled** and **The Secret Doctrine.**

BLAVATSKY, H.P. **DYNAMICS OF THE PSYCHIC WORLD. 132pp. TPH72, 1.95p.**
This is a compilation from Blavatsky's writings. Topics include natural law and psychic phenomena, thought power, spiritual progress, and soul dynamics.

BLAVATSKY, H.P. **FROM THE CAVES AND JUNGLES OF HINDOSTAN. Notes, index, 759pp. TPH75, 12.50c.**
Volume XI of the **Collected Works**. This book contains H.P.B.'s impressions of India, the Indian people, and Indian religious philosophy. It can be read both as a travelogue and as a serious study of the author's impressions of a foreign, and at that time, little known civilization.

E. WIMBRIDGE. Sc 78

BLAVATSKY, H.P. **INDEX TO THE SECRET DOCTRINE. 172pp. ThC39, 5.00c.**

BLAVATSKY, H.P. **IS THEOSOPHY A RELIGION? 26pp. TPH26, .75p.**

BLAVATSKY, H.P. **ISIS UNVEILED. 1,403pp. ThU1877, 15.00c/ 10.50p (two volume set); 10.00c (one volume).**
This book, totaling more than 1,300 pages in two volumes, was H.P.B.'s first. It unites an historical review of religious and scientific ideas with the spirit of the quest for truth. Many chapters are devoted to study and explorations of manifestations of the occult from antiquity to the nineteenth century. The philosophies and sciences of the ancients are examined, not as objects of scholarly research, but in the spirit of a genuine renaissance. Of special interest to the West is an investigation of the origins of Christianity, including extensive study of the teachings of the Gnostic sects of the first centuries, and an explanation of the mysteries of Jesus. Much is said of the lore of initiates, and throughout will be found the theme of occult knowledge and its adept teachers. The first truly scientific account of the vast subject of magic is offered in this great work, which is subtitled, *A Master Key to the Mysteries of Ancient and Modern Science and Theology.* **Isis** is an exposition of the materialism of modern science and the obscurantism of modern religion.

BLAVATSKY, H.P. **KEY TO THEOSOPHY. 426pp. ThU1889, 5.00c/ 3.50p.**
Subtitled, *A clear exposition, in the form of question and answer, of the ethics, science, and philosophy for the study of which the Theosophical Society has been founded.* Includes an excellent glossary and index.

BLAVATSKY, H.P. **THE ORIGINAL PROGRAM OF THE THEOSOPHICAL SOCIETY, AND PRELIMINARY MEMORANDUM OF THE ESOTERIC SECTION. 91pp. TPH31, 2.50c.**

BLAVATSKY, H.P. **THE SECRET DOCTRINE. 1,505pp. ThU1888, 15.00c/9.00p (two volume set); 15.00c (one volume); 30.00c (six volume set).**
Completed in 1888, eleven years after **Isis**. The systematic character of this work is revealed by the subjects treated at length in its pages: *Cosmogenesis, Cosmic Evolution, Anthropogenesis, The Evolution of Symbolism, The Archaic Symbolism of the World Religions, Science and the Secret Doctrine Contrasted.* Its subtitle is, *The Synthesis of Science, Religion, and Philosophy.* It differs from **Isis** in that it deliberately unfolds a specific teaching about the nature of things. Half of its 1,500 pages are devoted to explanations of this teaching as found in an ancient scripture wholly unknown to the modern world. It is shown that the *wisdom religion* has been the inspiration of every great religion and religious teacher, and that one archaic doctrine underlies all the traditional beliefs of both East and West. The remaining portions of the volumes contain discussion and criticism of scientific conceptions. In the introduction H.P.B. wrote: **The Secret Doctrine** *is not a treatise, or a series of vague theories, but contains all that can be given out to the world in this century.* It is therefore the basic source of all Theosophical teachings in this cycle.

BLAVATSKY, H.P. **SECRET INSTRUCTIONS TO PROBATORS OF AN ESOTERIC SCHOOL. Offset, 8½"x11", 122pp. HeR69, 12.50p.**
A reproduction of an extremely rare document. Many colored illustrations are included.

BLAVATSKY, H.P. **STUDIES IN OCCULTISM. 212pp. ThU1891, 2.50p.**
Ten years after the publication of **Isis Unveiled**, foreseeing the rapid and potentially hazardous development in the twentieth century of man's latent powers, the author, in a series of articles now collected here, warned against the misuse of knowledge, lest the *psychic outrun the spiritual.*

BLAVATSKY, H.P. **THEOSOPHICAL GLOSSARY. 389pp. ThC1892, 6.00c.**
This glossary gives information on the principal Sanskrit, Pahlavi, Tibetan, Pali, Chaldean, Persian, Scandinavian, Hebrew, Greek, Latin, Qabalistic, and Gnostic words, and occult terms used in Theosophical literature.

BLAVATSKY, H.P. **TRANSACTIONS OF THE BLAVATSKY LODGE. Index, 118pp. ThU1891, 4.00c.**
Transcription of a series of discussions on the stanzas of the first volume of **The Secret Doctrine**.

BLAVATSKY, H.P. **TWO BOOKS OF THE STANZAS OF DZYAN. Notes, 325pp. TPH40, 3.00c.**
The **Stanzas of Dzyan** *are the skeleton as it were, around and attached to which the massive body of H.P. Blavatsky's great work,* **The Secret Doctrine***, is built up. . . . The aim of the present book is to lay bare the skeleton . . . so that the underlying structure of the whole may become better visible and more easily grasped.—from the introduction.* H.P.B.'s prologues and epilogues to the **Stanzas** are also included.

BLAVATSKY, H.P. **THE VOICE OF THE SILENCE. 110pp. ThU28, 3.00c/2.25p.**
English translation of portions of **The Book of the Golden Precepts**, a devotional manual.

HANSON, VIRGINIA, ed. **H.P. BLAVATSKY AND THE SECRET DOCTRINE. 227pp. TPH71, 2.25p.**
A collection of essays on the title theme which originally appeared in a special issue of **The American Theosophist**, devoted to a study of H.P.B.'s contributions to the intellectual, moral, and spiritual atmosphere of her world and to her *magnum opus.*

JINARAJADASA, C., ed. **H.P.B. SPEAKS, VOLUME I. 248pp. TPH50, 1.95c.**
Selections from letters by H.P.B. from 1875 on, her diary for 1878, and some extracts from her scrapbook.

JINARAJADASA, C., ed. **H.P.B. SPEAKS, VOLUME II. 181pp. TPH51, 2.25c.**
A continuation of the material presented in the first volume.

■ *MURPHET, HOWARD.* **WHEN DAYLIGHT COMES. Notes, bibliography, index, 292pp. TPH75, 3.50p.**
A well written biographical study which we found fascinating reading. All of the scandal and the achievements are fully revealed and the survey is as impartial as one could expect an in-house document to be. This is as good a first book to read on Theosophy as any we know of.

NEFF, MARY, ed. **PERSONAL MEMOIRS OF H.P. BLAVATSKY. 322pp. TPH37, 2.25p.**
A compilation from H.P.B.'s letters, personal journal entries, and other records.

OLCOTT, HENRY STEEL. **INSIDE THE OCCULT: THE TRUE STORY OF MADAME H.P. BLAVATSKY. Index, 491pp. RuP75, 3.95p.**
This is a recently reprinted and retitled edition of **Old Diary Leaves.** Colonel Olcott was H.P.B.'s closest associate and confidant for many years and in this volume, compiled we presume from his diaries, he details the early experience of the Theosophical Society in New York before the trip to India.

PURUCKER, GOTTFRIED DE. **H.P. BLAVATSKY: THE MYSTERY. 242pp. PoL74, 4.95p.**
The chapters of this book first appeared serially in **The Theosophical Path** (the house organ of Katherine Tingley's branch of the Society) in the 1930s. More than a simple biography of Blavatsky, the book presents an analysis of the basic Theosophical teachings as expounded in Blavatsky's written and oral teachings. The exposition is topically organized.

RYAN, CHARLES. **H.P. BLAVATSKY AND THE THEOSOPHICAL MOVEMENT. Bibliography, index, 367pp. ThU37, 4.95p.**
A newly revised edition of one of the first major studies of the title theme. Much of the volume is devoted to biography, however the emphasis is on the achievements of the Society rather than on anecdotes. There is also an analysis of H.P.B.'s major literary works. Two final chapters carry the Society and the movement up to the present time.

WACHTMEISTER, CONSTANCE, et al. **REMINISCENCES OF H.P. BLAVATSKY AND THE SECRET DOCTRINE. Illustrations, notes, 141pp. TPH76, 3.75p.**
This delightful narrative is a very colorful classic in Theosophical literature. It shares with the reader some of the insurmountable odds encountered in the production of **The Secret Doctrine** *and offers glimpses of the suprahuman dedication and sacrifice of H.P.B. in writing her magnum opus.... The special flavor of the original* **Reminiscences** *has been left untouched.*—from the publisher's note.

——————— END OF H.P. BLAVATSKY SUBSECTION ———————

BRAGDON, CLAUDE. **EPISODES FROM AN UNWRITTEN HISTORY. Offset, stapled, 109pp. HeR10, 3.00p.**
A collection of short anecdotes about the early history of the Theosophical movement and its most important personages.

CHALLONER, H.K. and ROLAND NORTHOVER. **OUT OF CHAOS. Bibliography, 216pp. TPH67, 6.00c.**
A distillation of the teachings of all the world's religions and philosophies. Topics include religion, politics, economics, and education.

COLLINS, MABEL. **LIGHT ON THE PATH AND THROUGH THE GATES OF GOLD. 114pp. ThU1888, 2.50p.**
Written down by Mabel Collins, this Theosophical classic centers its series of *occult rules* on the ancient yet ever modern theme of self knowledge and self mastery. Bound together with **Through the Gates of Gold**, this volume offers a view of those foundation principles comprising the spiritual core of all religions.

CONGER, MARGARET. **COMBINED CHRONOLOGY. 52pp. ThU73, 2.00p.**
Designed to be used with **The Mahatma Letters to A.P. Sinnett** and **The Letters of H.P. Blavatsky to A.P. Sinnett**.

COOPER, IRVING. **REINCARNATION. 115pp. TPH20, 2.95c.**
A clearly written Theosophical survey of all facets of reincarnation. Much of the book is devoted to Cooper's *proofs of reincarnation.*

EDGE, HENRY. **THE ASTRAL LIGHT. 57pp. PoL75, 1.75p.**
A Theosophical manual which begins with a study of what astral light is and goes on to a discussion of the astral light and karma and evolution. There are also sections on the denizens of the astral light and its social influence.

EDGE, HENRY. **EVOLUTION. 71pp. PoL75, 2.00p.**
A volume in the publisher's series of Theosophical manuals which briefly explores the title theme.

GARDNER, EDWARD. **THE WEB OF THE UNIVERSE. 103pp. TPH36, 3.00c.**
A good basic outline and explanation of the broad doctrines of the *ageless wisdom teaching* concerning our universe, man and consciousness, and the scheme of the solar system.

GREENWALT, EMMETT. **CALIFORNIA UTOPIA: POINT LOMA 1897-1942. Photographs, notes, bibliography, index, 261pp. PoL78, 5.95p.**
Point Loma was the headquarters of Katherine Tingley's branch of the Theosophical Society. This is an extremely complete history of the Point Loma community, the work carried on by its members, its philosophy, and its relations with outsiders including the press. Many excerpts from related writings are included.

GROVES, C.R. and CORONA TREW, eds. **MAN'S EXPANDING HORIZON. 64pp. TPH nd, 2.00p.**
A publication from the Science Group of the London Theosophical Research Centre which discusses evolution and man's role in the universe.

HAMPTON, CHARLES. **THE TRANSITION CALLED DEATH. 106pp. TPH43, 3.00c.**
A brief treatise.

HANSON, VIRGINIA. **KARMA. 2.50p.**
See the Reincarnation and Karma section.

HODSON, GEOFFREY. **AT THE SIGN OF THE SQUARE AND COMPASS. 322pp. TPH76, 8.95c.**
Next to Besant and Leadbeater, Hodson is the best known twentieth century Theosophist. He is especially noted for his clairvoyant studies of *devas* and fairies. He writes eloquently and delves into areas which none of the other Theosophists covers. This book contains a treatise on the inner meaning of masonic symbols and traditions.

HODSON, GEOFFREY. **BROTHERHOOD OF ANGELS AND OF MEN. 65pp. TPH27, 5.50c.**
This is the first of a five volume series of writings dictated to Hodson by one of the *members of the angelic hosts*. Here he explores the idea of collaboration between angels and men in the service of God and humanity and gives some guidance on how to conduct this collaboration. This is an inspiring collection of messages divided into chapters on *Patience, Peace, Education, Joy, Vision, Thoroughness, Unity,* and *Methods of Invocation.*

HODSON, GEOFFREY. **THE CALL TO THE HEIGHTS. Glossary, index, 219pp. TPH76, 3.50p.**
This book is conceived, written, and published as an offering to those who are experiencing an inward longing for spiritual light and truth, and who are seeking a way of living through which these experiences may find intelligent and useful expression. It is written in the form of a number of short essays on a variety of areas related to spiritual development.

HODSON, GEOFFREY. **FAIRIES AT WORK AND AT PLAY. 3.25p.**
See the Fairies subsection of Fairy Tales.

HODSON, GEOFFREY. **THE KINGDOM OF THE GODS. 245pp. TPH52, 15.95c.**
An extraordinary book dealing with the angelic or *deva* evolution which parallels human evolution and is concerned in part with the assistance of the evolution of nature and with the building, growing, and destroying processes of all forms. They form a hierarchical scale of existence from nature spirits, sprites, and fairies on up to the grand archangels. The book is filled with beautiful paintings done from clairvoyant perception of the angelic hosts and *deva* spirits and it contains descriptions of their activities and functions.

HODSON, GEOFFREY. **MAN'S SUPERSENSORY AND SPIRITUAL POWERS. 194pp. TPH69, 4.00c.**
The author delves into many areas of spiritual research and training. He covers a large territory of the *secret wisdom* in a clear, concise manner. The fundamental doctrine upon which the statements and teachings are based is that man is essentially divine and is in the process of becoming a god.

HODSON, GEOFFREY. **MEDITATIONS ON THE OCCULT LIFE. Index, 147pp. TPH37, 2.25c.**
Hodson shares some of his thoughts and meditations on the nature of the path of discipleship and the life of the aspirant.

HODSON, GEOFFREY. **MIRACLE OF BIRTH. 64pp. TPH29, 1.95p.**
Hodson, probably the most intuitive Theosophist of this century, presents his clairvoyant study of the formation and development of the emotional, mental, and physical bodies of a being during the prenatal period. The material is based on his observation of one individual.

HODSON, GEOFFREY. **MUSIC FORMS: SUPERPHYSICAL EFFECTS OF MUSIC CLAIRVOYANTLY OBSERVED. 12.00c.**
See the Music section.

HODSON, GEOFFREY. **OCCULT POWERS IN NATURE AND IN MAN. 179pp. TPH55, 2.50c.**
In six magnificent talks, Mr. Hodson assembled the grand perspective of the Creative Processes as generally understood by students of **The Secret Doctrine.** *The author tells us that he has three objectives in mind: to convey some comprehension of the Creative Deity itself, some understanding of the evolution of universes, and a deeper knowledge of man's place in Creation, in the Great Work.... In the opening chapter...a general view is given.... With unusual clarity there is developed a theosophical conceptualization of the unfolding Cosmos, the emanation of universes from their Divine Source. Beginning with the pre-Cosmic conditions referred to as "darkness upon the face of the waters," the author elucidates the evolution of the unfolding Divine Purpose. The remaining chapters outline a synthesis of theosophical ideas about the nature of man and his relationship with his origins.—from the foreword.*

HODSON, GEOFFREY. **AN OCCULT VIEW OF HEALTH AND DISEASE. Index, 101pp. HeR nd, 2.00p.**
In the title selection Hodson begins with an overview of health and disease and follows with discussions of the subtle bodies, mental disorders, and the ego and its vehicles. A short essay entitled, *Health and the Spiritual Life,* is also bound into the volume. This is an offset book, badly printed, underlined in places, and bound with staples.

HODSON, GEOFFREY. **THE PATHWAY TO PERFECTION. 77pp. TPH54, 2.25c.**
An excellent book dealing with the rudiments of Theosophy. Contains a fine chapter that descriptively explains the seven ray types of disciplines.

HODSON, GEOFFREY. **REINCARNATION, FACT OR FALLACY? 1.00p.**
See the Reincarnation and Karma section.

HODSON, GEOFFREY. **THE SEVEN HUMAN TEMPERAMENTS. 99pp. TPH52, 2.75c.**
An in depth discussion of the seven rays and their relation to human temperament.

HODSON, GEOFFREY. **THE SOUL'S AWAKENING. 93pp. TPH63, 3.00c.**
The author penetrates into the world of dawning soul consciousness and reveals with clarity some of the aspects of spiritual evolution. Slightly more than half the book is given to answering questions on a wide range of metaphysical and occult subjects.

HODSON, GEOFFREY. **THE SUPREME SPLENDOUR. 111pp. TPH69, 2.25c.**
This is a study of the universal creative processes, of God, of man *as a Creator In-the-Becoming,* and of the archangelic intelligences who presented the material to him and who are his teachers.

HODSON, GEOFFREY. **THUS HAVE I HEARD. Offset, stapled, 115pp. HeR29, 2.50p.**
A collection of talks on the spiritual life, cooperation with the angels, and the world teacher.

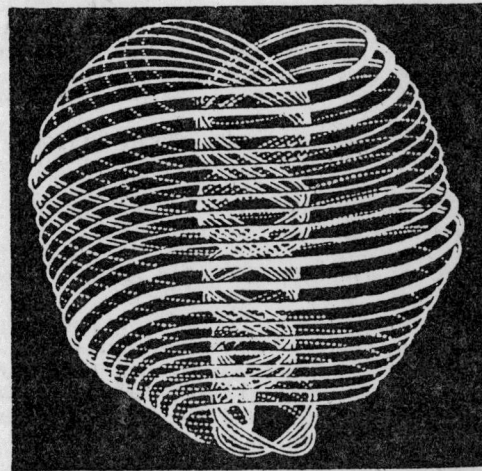

A clairvoyant's vision of an ultimate physical atom.

HUMPHREYS, CHRISTMAS. **THE FIELD OF THEOSOPHY: THE TEACHER, THE TEACHING AND THE WAY. 64pp. TPH66, 1.25p.**
Transcriptions of three lectures designed to cover three aspects of the Theosophical movement which seemed to the author inseparable— H.P. Blavatsky, **The Secret Doctrine,** and the Theosophical path. Humphreys is a leading British Buddhist and a member of the Theosophical Society.

JOHNSON, RAYNOR. **THE IMPRISONED SPLENDOUR. 5.75p.**
See the Parapsychology section.

JUDGE, WILLIAM. **ECHOES OF THE ORIENT, VOLUME I. Index, 582pp. PoL75, 7.00c.**
Judge was one of the leading figures in Theosophy in the U.S. in the early years of the Society. This is the first volume of his collected writings, and it is drawn largely from articles he wrote for **The Path** in the late nineteenth century.

JUDGE, WILLIAM. **PRACTICAL OCCULTISM. 307pp. ThU51, 6.00c.**
Judge was the founder of the Theosophical Society in the U.S. This is a selection of his letters from 1882-91 when he was beginning to actively present to America a *Western occultism* considered by him to be the foundation upon which civilization is built.

LEADBEATER, C.W. **THE ASTRAL PLANE. 2.75c.**
See the Out-of-the-Body Experiences section.

LEADBEATER, C.W. **THE CHAKRAS. Color plates, many line drawings, 132pp. TPH27, 4.75c/3.45p.**
Leadbeater was a controversial figure who worked closely with Annie Besant and was the Theosophical Society's leading clairvoyant for a long period of time. It was he who continued the contacts with the masters and he devoted much of his time to training initiates. He writes clearly and directly; next to H.P.B.'s books, his are considered the most authoritative Theosophical manuals. This book is an excellent summary of the Hindu teachings on the *chakras,* a Sanskrit term meaning wheels or discs. According to Hindu teachings, there are subtle sense organs in man's body which channel psychic energies and vital force and are related to the glandular and nervous systems. They are also said to serve as a link between physical, psychic, and superphysical states of consciousness.

LEADBEATER, C.W. **THE CHRISTIAN CREED. Spiral bound, 106pp. HeR76, 3.00p.**
It is with the elucidation of the inner sense of the Creeds...that I am concerned; and although in writing of this it will be necessary for me to make some reference to their real history, I need hardly say that I am not in any way attempting to approach the subject from the ordinary scholarly standpoint. Such information as I have to give about the Creeds is obtained neither from the comparison of ancient manuscripts nor from the study of the voluminous works of theological writers, but is simply the result of an investigation into the akashic records made by a few students of occultism.

LEADBEATER, C.W. **CLAIRVOYANCE. 3.00c.**
See the Parapsychology section.

LEADBEATER, C.W. **THE DEVACHANIC PLANE. 147pp. TPH1896, 2.25c.**
A Theosophical manual which describes Leadbeater's clairvoyant investigation of that higher level of existence called *devachan* in Eastern philosophy where bliss is said to be experienced before a new incarnation begins. This is the area commonly thought of as *heaven.*

LEADBEATER, C.W. **GLIMPSES OF MASONIC HISTORY. 8.50p.**
See the Freemasonry section.

LEADBEATER, C.W. **THE HIDDEN LIFE IN FREEMASONRY. 8.00p.**
See the Freemasonry section.

LEADBEATER, C.W. **THE HIDDEN SIDE OF THINGS. Index, 619pp. TPH13, 8.50c.**
An in depth investigation divided into the following major topics: *How We are Influenced*—by planets, by the sun, by natural surroundings, by nature spirits, by centers of magnetism, by ceremonies, by sounds, by public opinion, by occasional events, by unseen beings; *How We Influence Ourselves*—by our habits, by physical environment, by mental conditions, by our amusements; *How We Influence Others*—by what we are, by what we think, by what we do, by collective thought, by our relation to children, by our relation to lower kingdoms. Leadbeater also includes a long chapter discussing *Our Attitude Toward These Influences.*

LEADBEATER, C.W. **HOW THEOSOPHY CAME TO ME. 136pp. TPH30, 3.25c.**
A short biographical study.

LEADBEATER, C.W. **THE INNER LIFE. Introduction, index, 410pp. TPH78, 5.75p.**
This is an abridgment of Leadbeater's classic two volume work, edited and condensed by a longtime student of Theosophy, Shirley Nicholson. The material in the book arose out of a series of informal talks Leadbeater gave to residents at the Theosophical headquarters in Adyar. He later edited the talks and they were published in a Theosophical journal, and finally incorporated in **The Inner Life.** The following topics are dealt with at length: *The Great Ones and the Way to Them, Religion, The Theosophical Attitude, The Higher Planes, The Ego and His Vehicles, The After-Death Life, Astral Work, The Mental Body and the Power of Thought, Psychic Faculties, Devas and Nature Spirits, Reincarnation,* and *Karma.*

LEADBEATER, C.W. **INVISIBLE HELPERS. Index, 238pp. TPH1896, 3.75c.**
There is an ancient tradition that in times of human crisis help may come from an unseen source, that invisible servers are working to assist people in need, both in this world and in the next. In this volume Leadbeater describes several such cases.

LEADBEATER, C.W. **THE LIFE AFTER DEATH. 2.25c.**
See the Reincarnation and Karma section.

LEADBEATER, C.W. **MAN, VISIBLE AND INVISIBLE. Many beautiful color plates, 126pp. TPH02, 7.50c/4.50p.**
A very detailed analysis which records the observations of a clairvoyant investigator who described different auras as he saw them and endeavored to illustrate them with the aid of an artist. Contains material on all aspects of consciousness.

LEADBEATER, C.W. **THE MASTERS AND THE PATH. 332pp. TPH25, 8.95c.**
This is generally considered Leadbeater's major work. Drawing on his personal clairvoyant experiences and the experiences of others he writes about the personalities of the masters, their homes, work,

nature, and powers. He also describes the various stages of the path the aspirant has to tread to get into contact with the masters, from probation to acceptance as their disciples, and beyond to higher levels.

LEADBEATER, C.W. **THE MONAD. TPH20, 2.75c.**
A series of essays on higher consciousness.

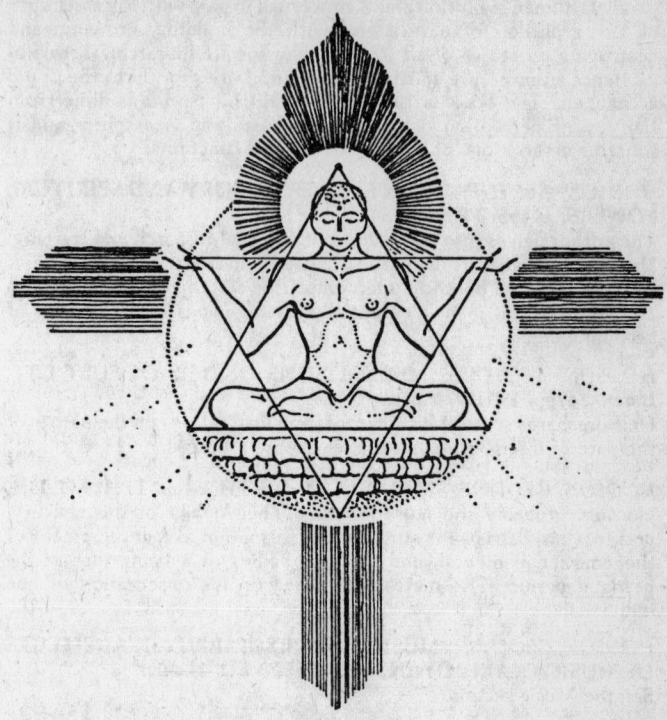

LEADBEATER, C.W. **THE PERFUME OF EGYPT (AND OTHER WEIRD STORIES). Spiral bound, 265pp. HeR nd, 6.00p.**
A collection of stories, all of which Leadbeater said were true.

LEADBEATER, C.W. **THE SCIENCE OF THE SACRAMENTS. Notes, index, 657pp. TPH20, 12.95c.**
A clairvoyant study of the occult forces at work during the Holy Eucharist and other sacraments and services of the Liberal Catholic Church. This volume is one of the most important studies available of the esoteric sacraments and is generally considered the definitive work on Liberal Catholicism.

LEADBEATER, C.W. **A TEXTBOOK OF THEOSOPHY. 163pp. TPH12, 3.45c.**
An excellent introduction to the basic concepts of Theosophy including information on the nature of the universe, the constitution of man, the meaning of death and the purpose of existence.

LEADBEATER, C.W. **THE WORLD MOTHER AS SYMBOL AND FACT. 64pp. TPH28, 2.50c.**
Transcription of a lecture on the title theme, based on Leadbeater's clairvoyant understanding.

LESLIE-SMITH, L.H., ed. **THE UNIVERSAL FLAME. 263pp. TPH75, 5.00c.**
This book was published in honor of the centenary of the Theosophical Society. *The articles, contributed by members of the Theosophical Movement in a number of countries, deal with basic principles of the Wisdom Religion....The book seeks to present in terms that are easily comprehensible the fundamental nature of the deep and stimulating ideas of this philosophy, known throughout the modern world as Theosophy—Wisdom of, and about, God.*

LINTON, GEORGE and VIRGINIA HANSON, eds. **READERS GUIDE TO THE MAHATMA LETTERS TO A.P. SINNETT. 316pp. TPH72, 4.95c.**

LUTYENS, MARY. **KRISHNAMURTI. 1.95p.**
See the Krishnamurti subsection of Contemporary Spiritual Teachers.

MEAD, G.R.S. **THE DOCTRINE OF THE SUBTLE BODY.** 109pp. TPH19, 1.45p.
The idea that the physical body of man is but the outer expression of an invisible, more dynamic embodiment of the soul is a very ancient one, and has persisted through many traditions. This work examines the *doctrine of the subtle body* as it has appeared in Western philosophical thought and early Christian teaching.

MEAD, G.R.S. **THE WORLD MYSTERY: FOUR COMPARATIVE STUDIES IN GENERAL THEOSOPHY.** Spiral bound, index, 200pp. HeR07, 4.00p.
A highly esoteric presentation consisting of the following essays: *The World-Soul, The Soul-Vestures, The Web of Destiny,* and *True Self-Reliance.* Only a dedicated Theosophist could obtain much value from these selections.

MURPHET, HOWARD. **HAMMER ON THE MOUNTAIN.** Index, 339pp. TPH72, 7.95c.
A scholarly biography of Henry Steel Olcott, one of the principal founders of the Theosophical Society and the companion of Madame Blavatsky in her travels. Includes thirty photographs.

OSBORN, ARTHUR. **THE COSMIC WOMB.** Bibliography, index, 235pp. TPH69, 2.25p.
A detailed investigation into such fundamental questions as the nature of God, ultimate reality, and the relationship of the individual to the infinite. Osborn also includes material on survival and immortality, discusses the mind-brain relationship, and has a section on God and evil and the essentials of the spiritual life.

PELT, GERTRUDE VAN. **THE DOCTRINE OF KARMA.** 1.75p.
See the Reincarnation and Karma section.

PERKINS, JAMES. **EXPERIENCING REINCARNATION.** 3.95p.
See the Reincarnation and Karma section.

PERKINS, JAMES. **A GEOMETRY OF SPACE CONSCIOUSNESS.** Illustrations, 153pp. TPH64, 5.75c.
An abstract exploration of man's physical and mental place in the cosmos.

PERKINS, JAMES. **THROUGH DEATH TO REBIRTH.** 1.95p.
See the Reincarnation and Karma section.

PLUMMER, GORDON. **THE MATHEMATICS OF THE COSMIC MIND.** 12.50c.
See the Sacred Geometry section.

POWELL, ARTHUR. **THE ASTRAL BODY AND OTHER ASTRAL PHENOMENA.** 7.95c/2.75p.
See the Out-of-the-Body Experiences section.

POWELL, ARTHUR. **THE CAUSAL BODY.** Index, 355pp. TPH28, 11.95c.
The causal body is the most subtle sheath or body which encloses man's higher ego. In it is contained the residues and cumulative essence of the entire gamut of the soul's experience while in human form through innumerable incarnations. A wealth of information is contained herein, derived from the diligent inquiry of numerous Theosophically-inclined individuals.

POWELL, ARTHUR. **THE ETHERIC DOUBLE.** 2.45p.
See the Out-of-the-Body Experiences section.

POWELL, ARTHUR. **THE MENTAL BODY.** Index, 316pp. TPH nd, 11.95c.
The third treatise by the author on important aspects of esoteric science based on well known Theosophical literature. Discusses phenomena of the mental plane such as thought transference and explains such mental activities as concentration and meditation.

POWELL, ARTHUR. **THE SOLAR SYSTEM.** Index, 356pp. TPH30, 10.50c.
An occult description of the life and evolution of our solar system with its planetary chains and hierarchy of spiritual lives.

PREM, SRI KRISHNA and SRI MADHAVA ASHISH. **MAN, THE MEASURE OF ALL THINGS.** 360pp. TPH69, 5.50c.
In this study of the symbols of cosmic origins, the authors have traced the story of the emergence of human consciousness from its divine source, seen as a symbolic, though nonetheless true, account in terms of the evolution of the concrete universe. The book throws a new light upon the **Stanzas of Dzyan,** that little known collection of verses on which Blavatsky based her monumental **Secret Doctrine.** Dzyan is analyzed stanza by stanza.

PURUCKER, GOTTFRIED DE. **THE DIALOGUES OF GOTTFRIED DE PURUCKER.** Index, 1,414pp. ThU48, 15.00c/set.
Purucker was Katherine Tingley's successor as head of her branch of the Theosophical Society. He wrote extensively on all aspects of Theosophy. This is a three volume set of transcriptions of lectures given by de Purucker between 1929 and 1933, edited by Arthur Conger. Every conceivable topic is discussed at length.

PURUCKER, GOTTFRIED DE. **THE ESOTERIC TRADITION.** Seventy page index, 1,180 pp. ThU40, 9.00p/set.
A massive two volume evaluation and explication of the ancient mystery teachings. Every aspect of the subject is covered. Dr. de Purucker was head of the Theosophical Society from 1929 to his death in 1942.

PURUCKER, GOTTFRIED DE. **FOUNTAIN-SOURCE OF OCCULTISM.** Index, 749pp. ThU74, 7.50p.
Subtitled, *A modern presentation of the ancient universal wisdom based on* **The Secret Doctrine** *by H.P. Blavatsky.*

PURUCKER, GOTTFRIED DE. **FUNDAMENTALS OF THE ESOTERIC PHILOSOPHY.** Index, 555pp. ThU32, 3.50p.
Opening with an elucidation of the three fundamental postulates on which **The Secret Doctrine** is based, the author continues his commentary on key passages selected from this masterwork. In the process he presents a comprehensive outline of the cosmic principles on which Theosophy is based. This is a good introductory study.

PURUCKER, GOTTFRIED DE. **GOLDEN PRECEPTS: A GUIDE TO ENLIGHTENED LIVING.** Glossary, 180pp. TPH71, 2.50p.
A topically arranged compilation of short passages on a wide variety of subjects related to the spiritual life.

PURUCKER, GOTTFRIED DE. **MAN IN EVOLUTION.** Bibliography, index, ThU41, 3.00p.
A philosophical discussion of Theosophical teachings on the continuing growth of human consciousness.

PURUCKER, GOTTFRIED DE. **OCCULT GLOSSARY.** 193pp. ThU33, 2.50p.
A compilation of Sanskrit, Tibetan, and occult terms used in Theosophical writings.

PURUCKER, GOTTFRIED DE. **STUDIES IN OCCULT PHILOSOPHY.** Index, 744pp. ThU45, 4.50p.
This book is largely an elucidation of meaningful passages in **The Mahatma Letters** and **The Secret Doctrine.** It gives both the mechanics and the philosophy behind the birth and evolution of man and the Earth; the processes of life, death, and rebirth; and other universal concepts.

ROSS, LYDIA. **CYCLES: IN UNIVERSE AND MAN.** 85pp. PoL75, 2.00p.
An overview of the title theme—one of the publisher's series of Theosophical manuals.

■ ROSS, LYDIA and CHARLES RYAN. **THEOSOPHIA—AN INTRODUCTION.** 57pp. PoL74, 1.75p.
This is about the best introductory survey of Theosophy that we know of. All the main tenets are concisely and clearly reviewed. The format is questions and answers.

SINNETT, A.P. **COLLECTED FRUITS OF OCCULT TEACHING.** Offset, spiral bound, 307pp. HeR19, 5.00p.
A collection of essays on various aspects of Theosophical thought.

SINNETT, A.P. **ESOTERIC BUDDHISM. 241pp. TPH1883, 11.25c.**
For untold thousands of years the system outlined here-in has been entrusted to those who were willing to pass through a lifetime of probation, to prove themselves worthy of being entrusted with nature's most subtle and profound secrets, the penalty for indiscretion being, personal disaster. An excellent introduction to the study of Eastern Hermetica and to Theosophical beliefs on the secret doctrine, by the man who received the Mahatma letters.

SINNETT, A.P. **THE OCCULT WORLD. 181pp. TPH69, 6.75c.**
Written by the president of the London Lodge of the Theosophical Society, this provocative work relates many incidents concerning Madame Blavatsky. Much of the internal life of the esoteric movement of the late nineteenth century is revealed and is of interest today since modern metaphysics has its roots in those days.

TAIMNI, I.K. **MAN, GOD, AND THE UNIVERSE. 482pp. TPH69, 3.45p.**
A thoughtful investigation of the Theosophical cosmology by one of the leading contemporary Theosophical writers. Many diagrams and charts illuminate the exposition.

TAIMNI, I.K. **SCIENCE AND OCCULTISM. 317pp. TPH74, 6.95c.**
In addition to his Theosophical activities Taimni was a professor of chemistry at an Indian university for many years. So he is eminently qualified to discuss science and occultism. He presents an in depth, conceptual investigation which is illustrated with several diagrams.

TAIMNI, I.K. **SELF-CULTURE IN THE LIGHT OF OCCULTISM. 314pp. TPH45, 5.50c.**
A fairly obtuse work which discusses ultimate reality, consciousness, and self discovery.

TINGLEY, KATHERINE. **THEOSOPHY: THE PATH OF THE MYSTIC. 171pp. ThU77, 2.50p.**
Ms. Tingley became head of the international Theosophical Society in 1896. This book *is the quintessence of the theosophical wisdom that Katherine Tingley embodied in letters, private group sessions, in talks with prisoners, students and faculty, as well as in public lectures delivered all across America and throughout the world. The book is not a text; rather, it is a mosaic of suggestions and hints for daily living, with the appeal always to the higher, altruistic side of the nature, never to the lower, personal self.*—from the foreword.

TYBERG, JUDITH. **SANSKRIT KEYS TO THE WISDOM RELIGION. Indices, 179pp. PoL68, 4.00p.**
An exposition of the philosophical and religious teachings embodied in the Sanskrit terms used in Theosophical literature.

VAN DER LEEUW, J.J. **THE CONQUEST OF ILLUSION. 234pp. TPH28, 1.95p.**
A clear exposition of the nature of illusion and the need to pierce its veil and find the reality that exists at every moment of time.

VAN DER LEEUW, J.J. **THE FIRE OF CREATION. 234pp. TPH28, 2.95p.**
An exploration of the Holy Ghost. The author was a priest in the Liberal Catholic Church.

WOOD, ERNEST. **THE SEVEN RAYS. 205pp. TPH25, 2.95p.**
It was in Blavatsky's **Secret Doctrine** that the modern world was first presented with the phrase *the seven rays.* It went along with a statement that all things and beings in the world—all forms of mind and matter— arose from combinations of seven fundamental impulses. This is a detailed presentation of the rays including a study of the source of the rays; an analysis of the characteristics of each ray; an essay on the use and danger of knowledge of the rays; and a short Sanskrit glossary.

WOOD, ERNEST. **A STUDY OF PLEASURE AND PAIN. 97pp. TPH62, 3.00c.**
The theme of this book is that pain is functional in the advancement and enrichment of life in nature and in man, and is therefore to be received with understanding. How pain arises and how it ceases, and the different kinds of pain are fully discussed and case studies are cited.

WRIGHT, LEOLINE. **MAN AND HIS SEVEN PRINCIPLES. 53pp. PoL75, 1.75p.**
Another in Point Loma's series of Theosophical manuals.

UFOs & UNEXPLAINED PHENOMENA

Very few subjects have attracted as much attention throughout the world as Unidentified Flying Objects. Nearly everyone in the civilized world has at least heard of them. Even some natives beyond the reach of modern communications have described things in the sky that fit the definition. Beyond that, however, there is little unanimity. Every individual has naturally formed his own opinion on the topic, and beliefs vary greatly. Most reasonable people would accept a full and convincing proof of the identity of these mysterious objects. UFOs remain controversial, however, because no attempt at explaining the phenomenon has been entirely successful.

The fundamental fact confronting us is the existence of a large number of UFO sighting reports. Some of these reports may be fraudulent, but most investigators have concluded that the majority are quite valid; that is, the witnesses themselves believed that they saw something real, external, artificial, and unusual.

On logical grounds it may be said that all possible explanations can be subdivided into two major categories, namely, A) physically real, manufactured objects that the witness could not relate to anything in his background, and B) something entirely different, such as obscure natural phenomena, hoaxes, or psychic projections. The possibility remains, of course, that the stimulus for a report of the first type was unique to a particular witness and could prove to be quite mundane to more knowledgable and experienced people. The heart of the whole question, therefore, is whether or not there exists a subset of experiences in Category A that are unique and puzzling to mankind as a whole, including experts in every field. The majority of witnesses think so! This conviction is shared by most of the people who have diligently studied this subject. Contrary views are more popular among those who (a) feel that examination of the data would be undignified, (b) tend to reject any new concept out of hand, and (c) suspend judgment until irrefutable evidence is presented to them. Unfortunately, little progress in this perplexing field can be achieved while the mind is preoccupied with the issue of UFO existence. The reason for this dilemma is that while mentally coursing through the arguments pro and con, one's attention is deflected from discovery of more meaningful detail. The mind is then blocked from further enlightenment. Rational progress can be achieved only by setting such unwarrranted skepticism aside, if only temporarily.

The search for truth about UFOs is severely handicapped. First of all, a sighting experience cannot be reproduced in the laboratory. Neither can a UFO be captured for detailed examination. The time and location of future sightings cannot be predicted. Spontaneous sightings are so brief and widely scattered that experts and scientific instruments can not easily be brought to the scene in time to observe the action. Is further understanding, therefore, out of the question? Probably not. But this pursuit of knowledge involves a curious irony. Although the sighting reports have been derided as *anecdotal records*, they are the only source of information on the subject. This reservoir must obviously be tapped if further insights are to be developed. The common elements threading their way through a large number of reports afford the opportunity of picking up some detail from one, more from another, and so on, until a composite picture of a typical event can be drawn.

The full magnitude of the UFO phenomenon is not commonly realized. A casual observer may have noted a dozen or so newspaper accounts in about as many years. He may have accidentally seen a few magazine articles sandwiched between sensational treatments of hunting polar bears and searching for treasure in the steaming Amazon. He may know of a few books on the subject, but not read them. Newspaper comments on the Condon Report (also unread) have assured him that there was nothing of special interest in the subject. It may be somewhat shocking for him to learn that the average number of reported sightings since 1947 is greater than 200 per year. Over 1,000 sightings were reported in 1967. As these figures apply only to the United States and UFOs are a global problem, the number of sighting reports is substantial. The total is not known, but there is every indication that it is on the order of 500,000 or larger.

—condensed from **Ufology**, *by James McCampbell*

ARNOLD, KENNETH and RAY PALMER. **THE COMING OF THE SAUCERS. Photographs, 192pp. Amh52, 3.00p.**
A documentary report of the *Tacoma Incident* (sighting) and its aftermath by two of the participants.

BERGIER, JACQUES, et al. **EXTRATERRESTRIAL INTERVENTION. 164pp. NAL74, 1.25p.**
Written by Bergier and the editors of INFO, this book provides documentation of many of the assertations of those who claim that extraterrestrial visitation is not theory but fact. Ranging widely over the world and through the scientific disciplines the authors discuss four areas of extraterrestrial activity: actual, but no longer existing civilizations, contemporary or historical cases of visitation, evidence based on animals that do not fit into accepted scientific categories, and actual cases of intervention in everyday lives.

BERLITZ, CHARLES. **THE BERMUDA TRIANGLE. Illustrations, bibliography, 203pp. Avo74/Sou, 1.95p.**
Berlitz, a noted researcher, has put together the definitive work to date on the Bermuda Triangle, reviewing many of the bizarre disappearances connected with it and proposing intriquing theories of the strange forces that may be at work there.

BERLITZ, CHARLES. **WITHOUT A TRACE. Photographs, bibliography, 190pp. Dou77, 1.95p.**
Berlitz' second book on the strange occurrences in the Bermuda Triangle area. He documents his assertions and proposes a number of theories.

BLUM, RALPH and JUDY. **BEYOND EARTH: MAN'S CONTACT WITH UFO'S.** Thirty-two pages of illustrations, bibliography, index, 248pp. Ban74, 1.75p.
A well regarded general account of recent UFO sightings by trained observers. The incidents are detailed and follow up research is discussed.

BOURRET, JEAN-CLAUDE. **THE CRACK IN THE UNIVERSE. Lengthy bibliography, 263pp. Spe77, 11.35c.**
In early 1974 one of the most far reaching and important investigations of UFOs and UFO research ever made was broadcast over French radio. This book is a resume of the most interesting parts of the series. Twenty-four highly unusual cases are related in all. A dozen French scientists and top UFO experts from the U.S., Britain, and France participated in the series.

BOWEN, CHARLES, ed. **THE HUMANOIDS. 256pp. Reg69/Fut, 3.95p.**
A collection of articles by noted scientists and astronomers such as Aime Michel, Jacques Valle, Dr. W. Buhler, and Gordon Creighton fully documenting landings and contacts (over 300 of them) between beings from outer space and people on Earth. Many previously unpublished reports are prescribed and some of the most spectacular cases are evaluated.

BUCKLE, EILEEN. **THE SCORITON MYSTERY. 303pp. Spe67, 7.00c.**
The *Scoriton* case is one of the most noted and puzzling in UFO annals. This is a full investigation of the incidents involved by Ms. Buckle and Norman Oliver—both seasoned, serious UFO investigators. Both the original incidents and subsequent telepathic communications from *Space People* are discussed and evaluated.

CATHIE, BRUCE. **HARMONIC 33. Illustrations, 207pp. Ree68, 5.95p.**
Cathie is a captain with the National Airways Corporation of New Zealand. After a close analysis of a number of confirmed UFO sightings in New Zealand, he discovered that they occurred in a regular pattern that conformed to a systematic grid pattern. Further research confirmed that the New Zealand grid was a small part of a worldwide grid and that UFO sightings are interrelated with other natural but hitherto unexplained phenomena. From these discoveries Cathie has evolved the following theory: *Even while you read this, interplanetary space-ships are rebuilding a world grid system from which, it appears, they can draw motive power, and they are also possibly using the grid for navigational purposes.* This book presents his findings and theories and discusses their implications. The study is fairly technical.

CATHIE, BRUCE and PETER TEMM. **UFO'S AND ANTI-GRAVITY. Index, 303pp. Swb71, 6.95p.**
Cathie relates how the researches described in **Harmonic 33** drew him to the conclusion that the authorities in Britain, the U.S.S.R., and the U.S. are cognizant of the grid theory and are actively using it for defensive and other purposes. He discusses the implications of this observation, and suggests a number of theories. Many diagrams and photographs are included in this technical work. Originally entitled **Harmonic 695.**

CHAPMAN, ROBERT. **UFO: FLYING SAUCERS OVER BRITAIN?** Illustrations, 189pp. May69, 1.60p.
Chapman is Science Correspondent for the **London Sunday Express.** Here he discusses some of the most noted British UFO reportings and reviews the case for and against UFOs.

CHRISTIAN, JAMES, ed. **EXTRA TERRESTRIAL INTELLIGENCE: THE FIRST ENCOUNTER. Pro76, 5.95p.**
A collection of technical articles on the title theme. The tone is serious and the authors are well known science writers.

CLARK, JEROME and LOREN COLEMAN. **THE UNIDENTIFIED.** Index, 272pp. War75, 1.50p.
An extensive general review which traces UFO sightings back to medieval times. The authors discuss the cases and present their hypothesis from the perspective of the latest UFO findings. In the process they look at stories of fairies, religious visions, *paraufological* experience, and early aircraft contacts. Many of the most noted cases are cited and firsthand reports are included. The bibliography is the most extensive we have seen.

COHANE, JOHN. **PARADOX: THE CASE FOR THE EXTRATERRESTRIAL ORIGINS OF MAN. Bibliography, index, 191pp. Crn77, 10.00c.**
In this volume Cohane refutes the Darwinian thesis that mankind evolved from the ape. He points out that Darwin had far less information about evolution than we have today and introduces his own documented theory that the only way man could have developed into his present state is if he had come to earth rather than evolved on it. His study is based on the recent works of a number of noted scientists and he carefully annotates all his assertions. He shows that there are no proven accepted fossil remains that can be directly related to our ancestry prior to 500,000 BC, and the picture since then is hardly more convincing. He also states that early man was our intellectual equal and that there is considerable evidence that we may be only now regaining knowledge lost thousands of years ago.

CONSTABLE, TREVOR. **SKY CREATURES: LIVING UFOS. Illustrations, notes, 252pp. S&S78, 1.95p.**
This is a revised edition of a book originally entitled **The Cosmic Pulse of Life.** John White describes the earlier edition as *an epochal work that explains the revolutionary biological energy behind UFOs.... With photographic evidence, the author shows that there are two main types of UFOs—intelligently constructed craft and biological organisms native to our atmosphere. He demonstrates how both types are mutually confused when they materialize to human sight.... The author synthesizes the work of Rudolf Steiner, Wilhelm Reich, and Ruth B. Drown.*

DANIKEN, ERICH VON. **MIRACLES OF THE GODS. Notes, bibliography, index, 304pp. Del75/Crg, 2.25p.**
This is the book von Daniken says he always wanted to write. In it he explores some of the miraculous events that have taken place in the world as a direct result of the visit of beings from other planets. He focuses on the present day and on the ways that these beings (whom he calls gods) are still in touch with us. He also discusses the part they play in world mythology. Many illustrations are included. As usual, von Daniken presents a variety of interesting hypotheses—few of which are factually backed up.

EBON, MARTIN, ed. **THE RIDDLE OF THE BERMUDA TRIANGLE.** 207pp. NAL75, 1.50p.
A collection of interpretative articles and first person accounts of some of the mysterious happenings in the area known as the Bermuda Triangle.

EMENEGGER, ROBERT. **UFO'S, PAST, PRESENT AND FUTURE.** 180pp. RaH74, 1.75p.
Emenegger was a skeptic until he saw the documents that form the basis of this book. Once exposed to these facts his feelings changed. He has attempted to add credibility to the subject through this carefully researched book. He has documented all his sources and often quotes directly from the U.S. government case histories. The material is presented in an easy to read fashion and is illustrated throughout.

FLAMMONDE, PARIS. **UFO'S EXIST! Notes, bibliography, index, 406pp. Put76, 1.95p.**
This is billed as being the definitive history and analysis of the UFO phenomenon, beginning with the earliest records and continuing to the present age—and it does seem to be comprehensive. Flammonde has compiled a wealth of historical data, eyewitness testimony, and scientific opinion. Extensive quotations and summaries of ancient writings are included along with an excellent survey of modern sources and incidents.

FORT, CHARLES. **THE BOOK OF THE DAMNED. 351pp. G&D19, 1.50p.**
Fort was a pioneer in the field of unexplained phenomena; he has influenced all subsequent writers and researchers. This is his most comprehensive compilation of what he terms *attested phenomena that science cannot verify and deliberately ignores.*

FORT, CHARLES. **NEW LANDS. 222pp. G&D23, .95p.**
Another compilation. Fort is not very easy to read; he uses odd language and skips around a lot.

FOWLER, RAYMOND. **UFO'S, INTERPLANETARY VISITORS. Notes, index, 365pp. ExP74, 8.50c.**
A compendium of UFO sightings. Fowler, chairman of the New

England branch of the National Investigations Committee on Aerial Phenomena, the largest civilian organization in the U.S., has been able to type the UFOs as to shape, size, and color. He also discusses the implications of the UFOs and poses questions as to the nature of the beings on the ships.

FULLER, JOHN. **INCIDENT AT EXETER.** 221pp. Ber60, 1.95p.
A detailed account of this noted UFO sighting, witnessed by five people, including two officers of the local police department.

FULLER, JOHN. **THE INTERRUPTED JOURNEY.** Illustrations, 350pp. Ber66, 1.95p.
This is the story of the time Betty and Barney Hill spent aboard alien spacecraft, being questioned and subjected to physical examinations by metallic gray humanoids. The encounter has been well documented by two of the most noted UFO research organizations. Under hypnosis, the Hills discussed and recorded the event and much of the material here is taken from these tapes.

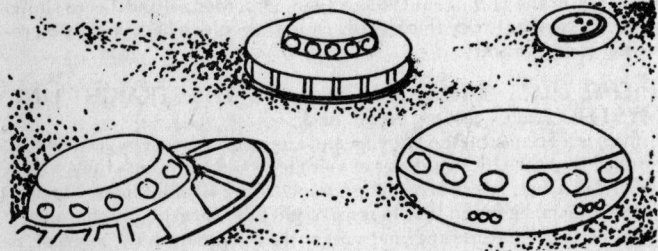

GARDNER, MARSHALL. **A JOURNEY TO THE EARTH'S INTERIOR.** Amh20, 7.50p.
A very thorough exploration of possible life in the interior of the Earth. The book is illustrated and Gardner cites all the important research and theories up to the date of publication.

HERVEY, MICHAEL. **UFO'S: THE AMERICAN SCENE.** Many photographs, index, 224pp. SMP76, 7.95c.
Hervey, Australia's leading UFO expert, has studied the subject intensively for over twenty-five years. This is a detailed study of some of the most significant American UFO sightings. Hervey concentrates on the ones that have the most evidence behind them.

HEWES, HAYDEN and BRAD STEIGER. **UFO MISSIONARIES EXTRAORDINARY,** 175pp. S&S76, 1.75p.
This is billed as *the amazing, true story of Bo and Peep—who have come from a higher level to help people on Earth ascend to the superhuman level.* These two publicly announced themselves a few years ago, and created quite a stir in some circles. Hewes and Steiger report on this phenomenon and present and comment on edited transcripts of interviews with Bo and Peep.

HOBANA, ION and JULIEN WEVERBERGH. **UFO'S FROM BEHIND THE IRON CURTAIN.** 407pp. Ban74, 1.95p.
A very complete UFO account by two European investigators and a work of good scholarship containing material unavailable in any other source. The various citings are discussed in detail and first person accounts, photographs, and line drawings complete the book. Includes an excellent annotated bibliography and a complete listing of references and sources for the illustrations.

HOLZER, HANS. **THE UFONAUTS: NEW FACTS ON EXTRATERRESTRIAL LANDINGS.** 304pp. Faw76/PnB, 1.75p.
There seems to be an unending flood of popularized books on UFOs. It is hard often to differentiate between them. If you like Hans Holzer's work, you will probably be interested in his rehash of cases and evidence. In addition, Holzer relates these well known cases to new evidence of his own and concludes with a hypothesis concerning the reality of the extraterrestrial visitations, their nature and purpose, and their likely future.

HYNEK, J. ALLEN. **THE HYNEK UFO REPORT.** Many illustrations, bibliography, 301pp. Del77, 1.95p.
Dr. Hynek was an Air Force consultant for over twenty years on **Project Blue Book.** In this book he distills over 12,000 sightings and 140,000 official **Project Blue Book** pages; separates the real from the

false; and reveals what the government suppressed, and why. This is an essential book for all who are seriously interested in UFO phenomena.

■ HYNEK, J. ALLEN. **THE UFO EXPERIENCE—A SCIENTIFIC INQUIRY.** Illustrations, index, 309pp. RaH72/Crg, 2.25p.
This is considered the best general book on UFOs—recommended to both scientist and general readers. Dr. Hynek is a noted astronomer and has been scientific consultant to the U.S. Air Force on the matter of UFOs for many years. He wrote this volume to answer the questions of anyone who is curious about the UFO phenomenon as a whole, who would like to have it appraised, and to appraise it himself.

HYNEK, J. ALLEN and JACQUES VALLEE. **THE EDGE OF REALITY.** Index, 316pp. Reg75, 5.95p.
Two of the U.S.'s most eminent researchers have collaborated on this report of what serious scientists now believe about UFOs. From the outset, Hynek and Vallee make their position clear: UFOs represent an unknown but real phenomenon. In this book they examine some specimen UFO reports—including those allegedly involving humanoids—and describe the patterns that have been perceived. They also establish a framework for the future study of the UFO phenomenon.

JENKINS, STEPHEN. **THE UNDISCOVERED COUNTRY: ADVENTURES INTO OTHER DIMENSIONS.** Photographs, 240pp. Spe77, 11.05c.
Jenkins has spent time in Mongolia and the Yucatan. He investigated recurring myths and legends and also witnessed strange phenomena. In this book he proposes various theories to explain the myths and odd happenings. This is a serious book which advances many interesting hypotheses.

JUNG, C.G. **FLYING SAUCERS: A MODERN MYTH OF THINGS SEEN IN THE SKY.** 3.95p.
See the Jungian Psychology section.

KEEL, JOHN. **THE EIGHTH TOWER.** Illustrations, notes, 218pp. Dut75, 1.75p.
This volume, subtitled, *The Cosmic Force Behind All Religious, Occult and UFO Phenomena,* is a strange amalgam of case histories from a variety of sources—most of which are directly or indirectly related to UFOs.

KEEL, JOHN. **THE MOTHMAN PROPHECIES.** 269pp. NAL75, 1.50p.
In December, 1967, a 700 foot bridge spanning the Ohio River in West Virginia suddenly collapsed, sweeping scores of people into the water and killing thirty-eight. In the months before the disaster, the area had been haunted by strange monsters and apparitions, and mysterious lights had traveled over the area on a regular schedule. Keel, a noted UFO investigator, spent a year investigating the many bizarre events and here he gives his findings, especially as they relate to the so called Mothman, a primeval monster with blazing red eyes and a pair of bat-like wings.

KEEL, JOHN. **OUR HAUNTED PLANET.** 117pp. Faw71, 1.50p.
An account of innumerable instances in man's recent history that indicate contact with an *ultra-terrestrial* source of information. This contact may be physical, psychic, or otherwise and is certainly often inexplicable by conventional means. The author sees these occurrences as a part of an extensive overhaul of the planet and an evolutionary mutation of humanity into collective *cosmic consciousness.*

KEEL, JOHN. **UFOS: OPERATION TROJAN HORSE.** Bibliography, index, 320pp. SBL70, 4.00p.
An investigation of why UFOs have cropped up so persistently throughout recorded history and why their existence has never been demonstrated beyond reasonable doubt. This is a provocative book which includes speculations about the conspiracy to discredit serious attempts to unravel the truth, about the relation between UFOs and psychic phenomena, about the existence of other space-time continua parallel to our own, and about the nature and origin of the force behind the flying saucer phenomenon. Keel has been studying and writing about UFOs for over thirty years. He is a good reporter.

KEYHOE, DONALD. **ALIENS FROM SPACE.** Index, 322pp. NAL74, 1.50p.
Major Keyhoe is a graduate of the U.S. Naval Academy and the Naval

Aviation Training Station. He has written many books and articles on UFOs, and this one is a very detailed, documented account.

KLASS, PHILLIP. **UFO'S EXPLAINED. Illustrations, notes, index, 369pp. RaH74, 2.45p.**
Klass, senior avionics editor for **Aviation Week and Space Technology** magazine, has been called the *Sherlock Holmes of UFOlogy* because of his scientific, painstaking approach that has enabled him to provide new insights into UFO cases that other investigators have pronounced to be totally inexplicable except as extraterrestrial spaceships. In this, his third book, he carefully analyzes the full spectrum of the UFO questions and provides well substantiated answers. The cases include some of the best known ones. Klass develops ten *UFOlogical Principles* which will better enable readers to understand UFO reports.

KRASPEDON, DION. **MY CONTACT WITH FLYING SAUCERS. Illustrations, 205pp. Spe59, 7.50c.**
This is considered the most outstanding book on flying saucer contact to have been published since Adamski. It recounts in detail actual conversations and gives factual descriptions of how flying saucers actually fly and are motivated, and how they overcome the forces of gravity. It also shows how those principles could be used by scientists. A serious and scholarly study.

KUSCHE, LAWRENCE. **THE BERMUDA TRIANGLE MYSTERY—SOLVED. Notes, bibliography, index, 313pp. War75/NEL, 2.25p.**
Despite the pretentious title, this does seem to be the fullest investigation of th enigma of the Bermuda Triangle available. Many of the most noted happenings are described and analyzed and what factual backing there is is cited. Kusche also reviews the major theories and advances his own.

LESLIE, DESMOND and GEORGE ADAMSKI. **FLYING SAUCERS HAVE LANDED. Bibliography, 232pp. Spe70, 8.80c.**
A well documented account which includes first person reports of actual meetings with people from other planets and photographs of UFO sightings.

LUNAN, DUNCAN. **THE MYSTERIOUS SIGNALS FROM OUTER SPACE. Notes, 412pp. Ban74, 2.25p.**
In 1973, Lunan, an eminent Scottish scientist, deciphered the mysterious radio signals that had puzzled scientists ever since they were first received in the 1920s. He identified them as a series of star maps apparently transmitted by a spaceprobe circling the earth. The messages pointed to an origin in the constellation Bootes 13,000 years ago—from a planet long considered uninhabitable. This discovery has since been supported by the January 1974 account that Russian scientists have been detecting similar signals. In this volume Lunan analyzes the meaning of these communications, and in addition he reconstructs old myths, old maps, and other early man-made records with an eye toward historical proof of contacts with other intelligences. The text is supported by notes and line drawings.

MCCAMPBELL, JAMES. **UFOLOGY. 153pp. CeA73, 4.95c.**
McCampbell is an engineer who has done pioneering research. Here he brings together his research in the following areas: certified UFOs, the vehicles, composition and luminosity, sounds, electrical interference, physiological effects, flight and propulsion, pilots and passengers, and activities on Earth. **Ufology** *is a pioneering attempt to come to grips with the physical nature of the UFO phenomenon. It points the way clearly to a scientific approach to the problem which can surely be applauded by physical scientists. The author combines logical and systematic marshalling of facts with provocative speculation to reveal an implied treasure chest of knowledge which could prove of monumental benefit to mankind.*—Dr. J. Allen Hynek.

MACVEY, JOHN. **WHISPERS FROM SPACE. Extensive illustrations, explanatory diagrams, 250pp. Grn73, 4.00p.**
Macvey is an internationally renowned expert on astronomy and astronautics. In this clearly written, well researched account he assesses the possibility that our universe is populated with intelligent beings—some of whom may belong to a culture which is vastly more technologically advanced and socially sophisticated than our own. Beginning with a discussion of the origin of the galaxies, planets, and earthly life, he considers the entire prospect of interstellar communications and travel, expertly translating complex astrophysical concepts into language comprehensible to the general reader.

MCWANE, GLENN and DAVID GRAHAM. **THE NEW UFO SIGHTINGS. 173pp. War74, 1.25p.**
A journalistic analysis of some of the most noted 1973 and 1974 sightings, with photographs.

MAGOR, JOHN. **OUR UFO VISITORS. Index, 264pp. HaH77, 8.95c.**
An investigation of UFO sightings in the Western U.S. and the Rocky Mountain Trench area in particular. The author discusses only cases which he or associates have personally investigated. Many photographs and line drawings accompany the text.

MENZEL, DONALD and ERNEST TAVES. **THE UFO ENIGMA: THE DEFINITIVE EXPLANATION OF THE UFO PHENOMENON. Illustrations, notes, index, 297pp. Dou77, 8.95c.**
The authors, an astronomer and a psychoanalyst, state that they have definitively proved that flying saucers are not extraterrestrial vehicles, but illusions produced by easily explainable meteorological and optical phenomena. Concentrating on the most widely publicized UFO sightings in the U.S. from 1963 to 1975, Drs. Menzel and Taves show in each case what they think really caused people to believe they were seeing flying saucers.

MICHEL, AIME. **FLYING SAUCERS AND THE STRAIGHT LINE MYSTERY. Index, 285pp. Plp58, 6.95c.**
Michel is a French mathematician and engineer. Almost by accident he noticed that the UFO sightings of a single day, even though they might occur far apart, fall clearly and precisely along straight lines. Making further tests, he found that these straight lines form highly characteristic patterns—webs and networks that unmistakably suggest a systematic aerial exploration. Michel carefully builds his thesis that some kind of outside intelligence must govern the movements of these UFOs in all their manifestations. This is a very careful scientific study which nonetheless should prove fascinating to those who are interested in the UFO phenomenon. Many case studies are included along with detailed notes and illustrations.

MICHEL, AIME. **THE TRUTH ABOUT FLYING SAUCERS. Index, 270pp. Jov56, 1.25p.**
It is hard to say something different about yet another UFO book—especially since it is an area which we are not very interested in. This one, however, looks a good deal more interesting than most. It seems to be well written and the cases studied are from all over the world and seem to be different than the often cited ones. Michel is a good writer and investigator and his explanations and theories are from very reputable sources. This is a clear presentation.

NADA YOLANDA. **VISITORS FROM OTHER PLANETS. Index, 334pp. MAM74, 10.00c.**
This book presents, in biographical form, many of the thousands of interdimensional communications and the experiences of Yolanda, primary Mark-Age channel or prophet. For more on Mark-Age, see their books discussed in the Revealed Teachings section. **Visitors** explains the nature and purpose of our visitors, using their own works, explanations, and suggestions. A very detailed account.

PAUWELS, LOUIS and JACQUES BERGIER. **IMPOSSIBLE POSSIBILITIES. 253pp. Avo68, 1.25p.**
A venture into the realms of human potential and the possible future of humanity when new scientific discoveries unveil the secrets of the universe. An intriguing collection of data and facts.

REHM, K. GOSTA. **UFOS—HERE AND NOW! Bibliography, 198pp. AbS74, 9.95c.**
Rehm is a Swedish lawyer and Sweden's most active UFO investigator. Here he summarizes the results of recent international investigations and presents his own observations. Eyewitness accounts from all over the world are reviewed and analyzed and photographs of the vehicles are included, along with hitherto unpublished discussions of the UFO's method of propulsion. A new theory is offered explaining the physical and psychological effects of UFO radiation.

ROULET, ALFRED. **THE SEARCH FOR INTELLIGENT LIFE IN OUTER SPACE. Bibliography, 168pp. Ber77, 1.25p.**
This is a discussion both of the possibility of intelligent life in outer space and of the ways we might communicate with that life. It is a serious presentation, citing the scientific research and speculation to

date, and includes information gleaned from radio astronomy and from space probes.

SAGAN, CARL, ed. **COMMUNICATION WITH EXTRATERRESTRIAL INTELLIGENCE. Glossary, index, 440pp. MIT73, 6.95p.**
The proceedings of an international conference on communication with extraterrestrial intelligence held in Soviet Armenia in 1971. The book includes verbatim transcripts of prepared talks and free discussions, carefully worded resolutions, excerpts from relevant articles, and several brief position papers. The material is quite technical and several of the selections are diagrammatically illustrated.

SAGAN, CARL. **THE COSMIC CONNECTION. Illustrations, index, 274pp. Del73, 1.75p.**
In nontechnical language Sagan describes the possibilities for extraterrestrial life, tells how we can go about finding it, and discusses the impact of this search and its discoveries on our lives. An important work.

SAGAN, CARL and THORNTON PAGE, eds. **UFO'S: A SCIENTIFIC DEBATE. Index, 310pp. Nor72, 3.95p.**
Fifteen distinguished scientists, from such disparate fields as astronomy, physics, meteorology, psychiatry, psychology, and sociology discuss all aspects of UFOs. They present photographs and detailed descriptions of sightings, analyze the reports of witnesses and data from equipment such as radar, and propose (or reject) hypotheses to explain the sightings. They devote special attention to the credibility of witnesses, natural phenomena that have been identified as UFOs, the unexplained cases, the connection between the UFO phenomenon and the news media, psychological factors affecting popular belief in UFOs, and the possibility that intelligent life elsewhere in the universe is trying to contact Earth.

SALISBURY, FRANK. **THE UTAH UFO DISPLAY. 299pp. DAC74, 7.95c.**
Dr. Salisbury's book is built around the carefully documented and hitherto unreported accounts of a variety of individuals who, over a period of time, have witnessed a most spectacular display of UFOs in the Uintah Basin area in Utah, and who have systematically recorded them. These sightings run into the hundreds. Only the very best and most thoroughly investigated are included here in the form of interviews, after which the author, a scientist, examines the possibilities, the various pros and cons involved, and then sums up his thoughts on these particular sightings and on sightings in general.

SANDERSON, IVAN. **INVESTIGATING THE UNEXPLAINED. Photographs, notes, index, 339pp. PrH72, 8.95c.**
A compendium of unexplained mysteries of the natural world. Sanderson is a biologist who has extensively researched this area.

SANDERSON, IVAN. **UNINVITED VISITORS. Bibliography, index, 245pp. Reg67/Spe, 6.95c.**
Sanderson looks at the possible implications of how extraterrestrials survive, where they come from, and why they come.

SHUTTLEWOOD, ARTHUR. **THE FLYING SAUCERERS. 159pp. SBL76, 1.75p.**
A collection of eyewitness accounts and personal relations of experiences with extraterrestrials who are trying to make contact with Earth. Shuttlewood also considers a number of related themes and tries to evaluate his reports.

SHUTTLEWOOD, ARTHUR. **THE WARMINSTER MYSTERY. 207pp. Tdm67, 1.35p.**
Warminster, a small English town, was the focus for a remarkable series of UFO sightings in 1965. This is the story of these sightings and it includes many eyewitness accounts.

SITCHIN, ZECHARIA. **THE TWELFTH PLANET. Bibliography, index, 384pp. S&D76/A&U, 2.50p.**
This provocative study of the origins of man on Earth is the result of thirty years of study. The author has a working knowledge of ancient Hebrew and other Semitic languages and has made a thorough study of the history and archaeology of the ancient Near East. He believes that the Nefilim, inhabitants of the *Twelfth Planet*, landed on earth 450,000 years ago, bringing with them the skills and knowledge of a highly sophisticated culture. In this book he discusses when they came and why, how they got here, and how they helped create civilization on Earth. A great deal of **Old Testament** material is incorporated into the study. Many line drawings accompany the text.

SPENCER, JOHN. **LIMBO OF THE LOST TODAY. Index, 202pp. Ban75, 1.75p.**
A collection of reports of mysterious happenings in the Bermuda Triangle area.

SPENCER, JOHN. **NO EARTHLY EXPLANATION. 178pp. Ban74, 1.75p.**
This is a not overly sensationalized account of the UFO phenomenon: its history, the major sightings, possibilities of extraterrestrial origin of life on Earth, present day extraterrestrial communications, and much else. Spencer attempts an objective presentation and it does seem fairly adequate as a mass market account. We are not sure what his credentials are, though. Includes photographs and drawings.

SPIELBERG, STEVEN. **CLOSE ENCOUNTERS OF THE THIRD KIND. 256pp. Del77, 1.95p.**
A recreation of the plot line of the movie **Close Encounters**, put together by the man who wrote and directed the movie.

STANFORD, RAY. **SOCORRO SAUCER IN A PENTAGON PANTRY.** Photographs, 211pp. BAB76, 8.95c.
In 1964 a UFO landing was reported in Socorro, New Mexico. Stanford contends that the U.S. intelligence community has managed to conceal from the public the existence of physical evidence that a technologically advanced craft of unknown origin landed at Socorro. Stanford spent over five years investigating this case and he cites many eyewitness accounts.

STEIGER, BRAD. **GODS OF AQUARIUS: UFOS AND THE TRANS-FORMATION OF MAN.** Illustrations, index, 264pp. HBJ76, 8.95c.
It is my contention that the UFO provides contemporary man with a vital, living mythological symbol, an affect image, which communicates directly to his essential self, bypassing the brain, evading acculturation, manipulating historical conditioning. I believe that the UFO will serve mankind as a transformative symbol that will unite our entire species as one spiritual organism...functioning through members, who, though separate in space, are yet one in being and belief. This is an extensive philosophical survey of the influences and effects of this consciousness. Many case studies are cited and quotations from original source documents are interspersed.

STEIGER, BRAD. **MYSTERIES OF TIME AND SPACE.** Photographs, bibliography, index, 232pp. Del74, 1.75p.
Steiger explores the underlying patterns of mysteries which challenge our most basic concepts of history, geology, and physics. He examines cases never before written about and cites eyewitness accounts (including his own). Steiger is the author of over forty books on a wide variety of topics.

STEIGER, BRAD. **PROJECT BLUE BOOK.** Photographs, 423pp. RaH76/Fut, 1.95p.
This is an edited collection of the U.S. Air Force's documents, first person reports, and case studies compiled by a special task force beginning in 1947 and continuing until recently. The inquiries were intensive and highly secret. This is the first time that their findings have been made public. The discussion is often technical and is of utmost importance to all who are interested in UFOs.

STEIGER, BRAD. **STRANGERS FROM THE SKIES.** 158pp. Tdm66, 1.05p.
A documented survey of incidents in which apparently extraterrestrial beings were reported in association with the sighting of a UFO.

STEIGER, BRAD and JOAN WHRITENOUR. **FLYING SAUCERS ARE HOSTILE.** 160pp. Tdm67, 1.05p.
An examination of those facts about flying saucers which reveal a pattern of hostility. The authors present documented cases in which UFOs have been involved in murders, kidnappings, car crashes, the destruction of airplanes, interference with space flights, and other acts of aggression.

STEIGER, BRAD and JOAN WHRITENOUR. **THE NEW UFO BREAK-THROUGH.** 155pp. Tdm68, .95p.
A general survey of UFOs and other unexplained phenomena which is well written and raises many interesting points. Numerous cases are documented.

STONELEY, JACK and A.T. LAWTON. **CETI.** Diagrams, notes, bibliography, index, 254pp. War76, 1.50p.
Stoneley is a journalist and Lawton is an authority on advanced electronics. Together they have collected an intriguing array of material on communication with extraterrestrial intelligence. Included are reports on how scientists plan to communicate across space and descriptions of the means of communication already being used.

STRINGER, E.T. **THE SECRET OF THE GODS.** Illustrations, notes, bibliography, index, 264pp. SBL74, 3.50p.
This is a discussion of tellurianism, a term coined by the author. As he says, *Every human being forms a brain cell of Tellus, the living Earth....The ultimate aim of Tellurianism is to awaken our slumbering planet....The practical work of Tellurianism involves (a) discovering for yourself the appearance, structure and movements of the real Earth, the real Sun, the real Galaxy and the real Universe; (b) determining the various cyclic influences exerted by these bodies upon your own life....What is needed is a systematization of our knowledge of these forces, drawn from many divergent sources....The framework for such a systematization I have endeavoured to provide in this book.*

STRINGFIELD, LEONARD. **SITUATION RED: THE UFO SIEGE.** Index, 240pp. Dou77, 8.95c.
Stringfield makes a valuable contribution toward ending the long Air Force censorship. Covering his twenty-six years of investigations, he presents irrefutable evidence of UFO reality and proof of cover-up....In recent years Len has concentrated on the puzzling and, at times, frightening effects caused by UFOs....Len has carefully evaluated hundreds of U.S. and foreign "scare" reports, weeding out hoaxes and dubious claims.—from the introduction by Donald Keyhoe.

TANSLEY, DAVID. **OMENS OF AWARENESS.** Many illustrations, bibliography, 318pp. Spe77, 14.25c.
A provocative study of the relationship between UFO phenomena and sacred teachings, both ancient and modern. Tansley is a healer and is acutely aware of the formative and etheric forces of the universe. He brings this understanding to his discussion of UFOs. Woven throughout the book is the theme that UFOs have something to teach us about ourselves and the world we live in.

TEMPLE, ROBERT. **THE SIRIUS MYSTERY.** Notes, bibliography, index, 301pp. SMP76, 2.50p.
This is a well documented, often mind boggling book which advances the thesis that the existence of civilization on the Earth is a result of contact from inhabitants of a planet in the system of the star Sirius prior to 3000 BC. There are traditions in present day Africa that the origins of civilization come from Sirius and these traditions are traced back by Temple to the ancient Mediterranean civilizations of Egypt and Sumer. The author shows that not only did these civilizations possess great learning and wealth but they also possessed knowledge dependent on nuclear physics and astrophysics—which they claimed was taught to them by visitors from Sirius! Temple is a scholar with impeccable credentials and he presents a mass of objective data which amply supports his thesis. We recommend this book heartily to all those interested in ancient civilizations and extraterrestrial visitations.

THOMAS, PAUL. **FLYING SAUCERS THROUGH THE AGES.** 192pp. Tdm65, .95p.
Thomas suggests that space visitors came to the Earth in ancient times and throughout history, and he cites instances of such occurrences. He quotes many biblical passages which he feels support this thesis and discusses incidents involving Church personnel.

TRENCH, BRINSLEY LE POER. **MYSTERIOUS VISITORS.** Notes, index, 192pp. PnB73, 1.85p.
Trench is the chairman of **Contact**, the world's largest UFO-watching organization. He has written many books on the subject. Here he presents a possible solution to the UFO enigma. He delves into the origin of UFOs: are they from other planets in our own galaxy or could they be from space-time continua or invisible universes intersecting our own? He offers some new explanations for the riddles of the ages, and gives the reader a glimpse of future contacts. One of the most fascinating sections offers a new, extraterrestrial explanation of the mysteries of Western religions. A very readable, well documented account.

TRENCH, BRINSLEY LE POER. **OPERATION EARTH.** Illustrations, bibliography, index, 142pp. Tdm69, .95p.
A philosophical survey of the case for UFOs. Many case studies are included.

TRENCH, BRINSLEY LE POER. **SECRET OF THE AGES.** Extensive notes, index, 192pp. Grn74, 1.60p.
Trench examines various theories about the point of origin of UFOs and presents a strong case for his theory that UFOs originate from inside the Earth. He postulates that visitors from outer space came to this planet eons ago. They became the god kings of Atlantis, erecting huge edifices around the world. They also constructed gigantic tunnel systems in which to take refuge from both the unstable seismic conditions prevailing in that era, and from attack from other extraterrestrials. When Atlantis was submerged, many of the Atlanteans took refuge in the tunnel systems, and according to Trench, their descendents are still there inside the Earth today, complete with the old Atlantean space craft and a very advanced technology. Trench also discusses evidence which indicates that the Earth is hollow, with entrances in both the polar regions.

VALENTINE, TOM. **THE LIFE AND DEATH OF PLANET EARTH: WHERE HAVE WE BEEN...WHERE ARE WE GOING. Illustrations, 175+pp. Pin77, 1.75p.**
Self-perpetuating dogma and the circular argumentation of the academic world is my target and this book marks the beginning of this reporter's campaign to expose the cracks in our historical "establishment," to reexamine erroneous scientific concepts we've all been given as absolute fact, and perhaps lead the way to a new and more accurate story of just how this planet came to be...and the realistic possibilities that loom ahead for us as time and space shrink the world we live in.

VALLEE, JACQUES. **THE INVISIBLE COLLEGE. Illustrations, bibliography, index, Dut75, 3.50p.**
In this book I propose to examine the hypothesis that UFOs may constitute a control system; that they are not necessarily caused by extraterrestrial visitors, nor the result of misidentifications and hoaxes on the part of deluded witnesses. If the hypothesis is true, then what the witnesses have seen were manifestations of a process not unlike that of a thermostat in a house. The thermostat is a mechanism that stabilizes the relationship between our body temperature requirements and the changing weather outside. Similarly, UFOs may serve to stabilize the relationship between man's consciousness needs and the evolving complexities of the world which he must understand. This book will explore this phenomenon....In this book I will not confine myself to the examination of the physical reality, but will frankly step from this into the experiential and even to the mythical.—from the introduction. Many case studies are included and the account is well organized.

VALLEE, JACQUES. **UFO'S IN SPACE: ANATOMY OF A PHENOMENON. Illustrations, notes, bibliography, index, 238pp. RaH65, 1.95p.**
An excellent scientific overview of the UFO question. Vallee begins with an overview of *The Legend of Flying Saucers* and a discussion of the probability of contact with superior galactic communities. The next two chapters are devoted to a scientific analysis of modern UFO reports. Then there is a lengthy summary of typical phases of UFO behavior. A final section contains Vallee's own theories and hypotheses. Vallee writes extremely well.

VALLEE, JACQUES and JANINE. **CHALLENGE TO SCIENCE: THE UFO ENIGMA. 268pp. RaH66/Spe, 1.95p.**
A formidable presentation by noted researchers of evidence for the global nature of UFO phenomena—with computerized classification of data, charts, graphs, photographs, and an extensive bibliography.

WALTON, TRAVIS. **THE WALTON EXPERIENCE. Photographs, 183pp. Ber78, 1.95p.**
The author of this first person account was abducted by aliens and he remained with them for five days. This is his account of the incident and its aftermath.

WILSON, CLIFFORD. **UFOS AND THEIR MISSION IMPOSSIBLE. Notes, bibliography, 235pp. NAL74/NEL, 1.50p.**
Dr. Wilson's public involvement with UFOs began with a series of radio and television appearances rebutting van Daniken's claims. Since then he has surveyed the literature and here presents his summary of the salient features of the major books and theories.

WOMEN & MEN

In childhood we are taught certain stories and myths telling of the origin of the world and of mankind and giving a general view of life and of conduct. It is as though they said: *This is the way things came into being, and this shows their essential nature and relationship.* These legends and tales which appeal so immediately to the child are for the most part as old as historical man and hark back to the infancy of the race. The views they express, insofar as they are still binding today, must represent something deeply embedded in the mind of man. Man has corrected and refined these beliefs in certain realms; in other spheres they remain powers in the background, determining his conduct. In no way are these unseen and unrecognized forces more strikingly manifested than in man's general attitude toward woman.

In the beginning—according to the record in Genesis—*God created the heaven and the earth* with all that they contained. The summit of his creation was mankind—*male and female created He them.* In this statement is expressed a belief in divine creation, but the statement is also intended to account for the simple fact that mankind is *both* male and female. The first chapter of Genesis contains, however, another and a better known version of the making of man: it is the theory of Adam's sleep and of the creation of Eve by a removal of one of his ribs. The story shows woman conceived of as a part of man, taken out of his side while he is unconscious. It is a myth which represents woman as an unconscious part of man, wholly secondary to him, without any living spirit or soul of her own. This myth, illustrates an attitude fundamental in man's view of woman. If the story had been told by women we should have had a different account of the creation. For instance, in a school examination paper the question was set: *Give an account of the creation of man.* A little girl wrote: *First God created Adam. Then He looked at him and said, "I think if I tried again I could do better." Then He created Eve.* Here we have a perfectly naive feminine version of the story.

There is a great discrepancy, I admit, between a myth hallowed by age and religious tradition and this school child's version of it. But from the psychological point of view they are nonetheless valid examples of the rift between two attitudes. This rift is illustrated, on the one hand, by man's still prevalent way of regarding woman and, on the other, by the worst exaggeration of the feminist movement.

Where does the truth lie? Is it to be found somewhere between the two points of view or is it necessary to approach the whole subject from an entirely different angle?

The first condition for an impartial investigation into the relationships between men and women is to rule out old assumptions of the superiority or the inferiority of one to the other. We must not hold the view that woman is man's inferior, nor must we take our stand on the little girl's version of the creation and assume that man is a creature who has not yet evolved to the female standard. This latter view is secretly held by many women, but they never express it directly, for to do so would be heresy. Indeed, the majority of women who hold it most firmly would deny it if challenged. But if we talk with them we can see this assumption underlying such simple comments as: *Men are so stupid, Men, poor things, they can't help it, They are all children,* and so on. The implication is that women are wiser and more adult than men, but this is kept secret. It is not

only not talked about, it is not formulated, and the women who say such things about men do not really *think* them in their heads.

Primitive woman was doubtless quite content with the role the Genesis myth assigned to her, for in primitive situations, where the biological aim is the sole guide in life, that the woman shall be attractive to the man and shall call forth and hold his interest is all that is important for life and for her. Even until today some women have remained almost as unconscious as their most remote ancestress and are still content to be only man's helpmate and counterpart. But humanity at large has moved since those days toward a greater consciousness, chiefly through the emergence of a conscious and personal ego whose aims have conflicted with the simple urges which Mother Nature first implanted in our breasts. Thus, as woman has evolved and become more aware of herself as a separate entity—an ego—a conflict has arisen within her psyche between the individual values which she has attained and the ancient, collective, feminine trends—and conflict is the beginning of consciousness.

There are three typical stages of development through which the human being passes in the gradual evolution of consciousness. These may be called the *naive*, the *sophisticated* and the *conscious*. The first, or naive, is related to nature only. It is, so to speak, the state of man before the Fall, when he was entirely innocent and at one with himself. In this stage there is hardly any differentiation between conscious and unconscious, for selfconsciousness has not arisen. The individual lives in a primitive union with nature, a state broken only by the emergence of the ego. This is a change of great importance in the development of the personality and is a definite step toward consciousness.

From this point the individual enters the period of sophistication. The natural powers within him and the resources of the world without are gradually explored and exploited, and the capacities and powers thus gained are organized under the leadership of the ego. Personal aggrandizement and the satisfaction of the ego arise and form a new life-motive. The lust for power comes to occupy an increasing place. But at this point a new factor may obtrude into the picture. The selfishness of the power attitude may obtrude itself on consciousness. Love perhaps arises which will dispute the dominant position of the ego, or some other value which transcends personal considerations may replace those formerly held. This change in emphasis inaugurates a gradual redemption of the personality from the dominance of the ego, and the third stage—the stage of consciousness—begins.

In the innocent play of domestic animals we may see certain ways of acting which we recognize as fundamentally masculine or feminine. The arts and wiles which the female uses to attract the male are so nearly akin to the ways of a pretty woman that we cannot help smiling. These things are manifestations of primitive femininity. They can be seen too in tiny children. A little girl, while still quite young, begins to act in a different way from a little boy. Where he is independent and aggressive, she is coy and winsome. She begins very early in life to gain her ends through coaxing or merely through being adorable. Her whole way of functioning is in relation to someone else from whom she may attract attention or care or love. In many grown women we see the same process at work. The woman herself is doubtless unaware of what she is doing. She may have no deeper motive than eagerness to *please*, to do what is expected of her, to fulfill another person's ideal of her. This other person is usually a man. She rarely stops to ask what she herself wants or how she feels. She is content if he is content, provided his contentment is only to be attained through her. In this way she makes of herself a sort of mirror which reflects the man's mood, his half-unrealized feelings. If he is sad, she is melancholy. If he is joyous, she bubbles with mirth. And, indeed, so subtle is her unconscious, or half-unconscious, intuition of his mood that often she will react to it while he himself is still unaware of what his mood is. So it is that he seems to discover what should be his own feeling *in her*. For men tend to be exceedingly unconscious of their own feeling moods. Even though a man may have suffered an intense personal loss he is very likely to react to it as an almost *impersonal* emergency, requiring a practical adaptation only, and to remain entirely unaware that he has also a feeling reaction to it as a *personal* experience. All he knows is that he feels out of harmony with himself. In this state he goes to see a woman such as we have been describing. She senses his mood almost before he speaks to her. Regardless of what she had been thinking or feeling before his arrival she now reflects the feeling of which he is unaware. If he has had a blow which he does not recognize as an emotional one, it is melancholy she reflects—a great vague, contentless yearning. As he does not know what there is to be sorry about, her melancholy cannot have much point or content, but this very vagueness allows his own sorrow or regret to find a place in her. He can project his unconscious feeling on to her, and no matter what it may be it can flow into her and so find its own form, undisturbed by any preconceptions on her part. He feels his personal sorrow raised to the level of a universal grief and is relieved of his own pain in contemplating the pain of mankind. By his contact with her he has gained a contact with his own feeling, and through the generalization of her mood he has found a way of adapting to his own grief which, left unrealized, might have overwhelmed him.

So it is that a man can find in such a woman an image or picture of the other part of himself, otherwise unknown to him, which indeed he does not recognize as belonging to himself. This image seems to be in her; he perceives it, but as though it were her feeling, not his own. When a subjective content is experienced in this way it is commonly spoken of as *projected*. The fact that its subjective source is not recognized means that it is in a sense *unconscious*. When projected by a man upon a woman it is like a mirage, an illusion, concealing the woman who is there; his own unconscious feeling-contents meet him in personified form. The sum of these contents make up the unrecognized part of man's psyche and when brought together into a whole constitute the man's feminine soul. This feminine soul of the man Jung has called *anima*.

These are portrayals of the anima herself, the collective soul of man, which we feel to be non-human, but many women, both in fiction and in real life, show certain anima characteristics which are more or less modified by human traits. For although it is true that a man's anima as a rule becomes apparent to him only when it is projected onto a woman, yet the anima herself is not a real woman. She represents rather a collective, or universalized, picture of woman as she has appeared through the centuries of human experience *in relation to man*. This last factor is important. All that a man sees is colored for him by his own subjective contents. And inasmuch as woman, throughout the ages, has been to man the symbol of his unknown feminine soul, his eyes have been peculiarly blinded when he has looked at her. A man

without a soul is but half a man, consequently when his soul is projected onto another human it is as though half of himself were in her. The woman becomes enormously important as well as enormously attractive to him. He longs to get into relation with her, for by so doing he will come into relation once more with his own soul, which is otherwise lost to him.
—*condensed from* **The Way of All Women**, *by M. Esther Harding*

ARGUELLES, MIRIAM and JOSE. **THE FEMININE, SPACIOUS AS THE SKY. Bibliography, 8½"x10", 152pp. ShP77, 6.95p.**
This visual study has evolved out of the authors' own experience and from their deep study of spiritual traditions. **The Feminine** transcends psychology and social theory and focuses on the relevance of the feminine principle to both men and women in their search for self understanding. The authors draw on a number of spiritual and cultural traditions, reevaluating their insights to produce a synthesis that sheds new light on the meaning of the feminine and the way it penetrates everyday life experience. The masculine principle, as it relates to the feminine, is also investigated. This is a deep, philosophical work which we recommend only to those with an interest in mythology, ancient history, comparative religion, or analytical psychology. 101 plates accompany and illuminate the text.

BARBACH, LONNIE. **FOR YOURSELF: THE FULFILLMENT OF FEMALE SEXUALITY. Bibliography, index, 236pp. Dou75, 3.95p/ 1.75p.**
This is a psychologically-oriented study of the development of sexuality in women, sympathetically written and illustrated with many case studies.

BELOTTI, ELENA. **LITTLE GIRLS. Notes, 158pp. WRP75, 2.20p.**
Ms. Belotti is the director of the Montessori Pre-Natal Center in Rome. In this book she argues that the traditional characteristics which set men and women apart in society do not originate from natural differences, but develop from social conditions which segregate children according to their sex roles from birth. Her aim is to expose the deep rooted prejudices which conspire to press female infants into the proper submissive position, first as a good little girl, and later as a good little housewife and mother. She seeks not to form little girls in the image and likeness of males, but to recognize the possibilities every individual is born with, independently of the sex to which that individual belongs.

BILLINGS, JOHN. **NATURAL FAMILY PLANNING: THE OVULATION METHOD. 8½"x11", 39pp. Ltu75, 2.50p.**
This is a well organized, useful study which includes a concise discussion of the benefits of the ovulation method, a critique of other methods, and practical information on following the ovulation method. Full information is given on how to keep an ovulation chart and pressure sensitive labels are included so you can make your own chart. The book was prepared under the auspices of the Department of

Health and Hospitals of the Catholic Welfare Bureau of the Arch-diocese of Los Angeles and it is as clearly written as any work we can imagine.

■ *BOSTON WOMEN'S HEALTH BOOK COLLECTIVE.* **OUR BODIES OURSELVES. Bibliography, 8½"x11", 276pp. S&S76, 4.95p.**
An extensively revised edition of this landmark book which presents women's views on their bodies and their health. Much of it is concerned with sexuality: its anatomy and physiology, lovemaking, relationships, lesbians, rape and self defense, VD, birth control, abortion, childbearing, menopause. The book is detailed, explicit, well illustrated, and filled with anecdotes by women as antidotes to the usual descriptions of women's sexuality written by men. There is a brief chapter on nutrition and a long one on health care. Although not everyone will agree with the feminist view which sometimes comes across heavily, every woman (or man, for that matter) will find a lot of value in this book.

CASTILLEJO, IRENE DE. **KNOWING WOMAN. 2.45p.**
See the Jungian Psychology section.

CHESLER, PHYLLIS. **ABOUT MEN. Illustrations, notes, annotated bibliography, 302pp. S&S78, 10.95c.**
Phyllis Chesler's book **About Men** *brilliantly and poetically presents the masculine experience in political, prophetic and mythological terms—and thus allows us to see it clearly for the first time.... Chesler has a unique, and startlingly truthful, view of men and the cultural prices they are forced to pay—largely by other men. Only a woman could have written this important book, the first feminist work to take men seriously, psychologically, without stereotyping them.*—Gloria Steinem.

DALY, MARY. **BEYOND GOD THE FATHER: TOWARD A PHILO-SOPHY OF WOMAN'S LIBERATION. Notes, index, 237pp. Bea73, 2.95p.**
It is truly the first philosophy of feminism, the first psychology of the feminist experience.... Daly's book goes far beyond other key works of the movement to describe a radical feminist's possible ways of being in a patriarchal world—Adrienne Rich.

DASS, RAVI and APARNA, eds. **THE MARRIAGE AND FAMILY BOOK—A SPIRITUAL GUIDE. Many photographs, 201pp. ScB78, 5.95p.**
A selection of writings from Buddhist, Hindu, Sufi, Jewish, and Christian sources on spiritual love, sex, fidelity, separation, divorce, parenthood, and ways to spiritualize the home and daily household tasks. The editors suggest exercises and meditations to help marriage partners better understand each other's expectations of their relation-ship, to overcome problems, and move beyond selfishness to mutual surrender and the cultivation of virtue. A final section contains wedding ceremonies from a variety of traditions.

DAVIS, ELIZABETH GOULD. **THE FIRST SEX. Notes, index, 382pp. Vik71, 2.95p.**
In her introduction Ms. Davis states the theme of this book: *The time has come to put woman back into the history books...to readmit her to the human race. Her contribution to civilization has been greater than man's, and man has overlooked her long enough.* Drawing on science, mythology, archaeology, and history, she comes up with some startling facts such as the following: biologically man is a mutant of woman, the Y chromosome being merely a stunted X; ancient civilizations such as the Sumerian were matriarchal societies, the collapse of these matriarchies signalized the brutalization of humanity and the increasing suppression of woman. A provocative account.

DINER, HELEN. **MOTHERS AND AMAZONS: THE FIRST FEMI-NINE HISTORY OF CULTURE. Introduction, index, 280pp. Dou73, 2.50p.**
Diner states at the beginning of this book that she *endeavors to remain as one-sided as possible [since] the other side is fairly well known.* Basing her study on the works of anthropologists and on the writings of Jung and Freud, Ms. Diner examines the idea that primitive social organiza-tions are matriarchies and that the patriarchial family is a compar-atively recent development. She begins with a lengthy mythological analysis of women, and then takes the reader on a matriarchial pilgrimage across the globe, ranging through many of the early cultures from the Sumerians and Babylonians to the ancient civiliza-tions of China and India. The book was originally published in Germany more than forty years ago. It has been translated and edited by John Lundin.

DODSON, BETTY. **LIBERATING MASTURBATION. 60pp. BsD74, 3.50p.**
Subtitled, *A Meditation on Self Love Dedicated to Women,* this pamphlet is divided into the following chapters: *The Romanticized Image of Sex, Sharing Masturbation, Going Public, Consciousness Raising, Becoming Cunt Positive, Bodysex Workshops,* and *Masturbation as Meditation.* Many case studies and individual reports are included and many pages are devoted to graphic line drawings of women's sexual organs.

EHRENREICH, BARBARA and DEIRDRE ENGLISH. **WITCHES, MID-WIVES, AND NURSES: A HISTORY OF WOMEN HEALERS. Bibliography, 64pp. WRP73, 2.40p.**
Women have always been healers. They were the unlicensed doctors of Western history. They were pharmacists, cultivating healing herbs and exchanging the secrets of their uses. They were also midwives. They learned from each other, passing their experience from neighbor to neighbor and mother to daughter. This book traces the history of women as healers and analyzes the takeover of medicine by male professionals.

EMERGENCE PUBLICATIONS. **AVOID OR ACHIEVE PREGNANCY NATURALLY. Bibliography, 51pp. Emg77, 3.00p.**
This is a careful explanation of the ovulation method developed by Dr. John Billings—a technique which teaches how to avoid or achieve pregnancy by showing how pregnancy depends not only on the sperm and egg but also upon fertile mucus secreted by the cervical mucus glands.

FALK, RUTH. **WOMEN LOVING. 550pp. RaH75, 6.95p.**
This book is a woman's experience of love. It speaks the truth of what loving is about: that it is a process, not a state that is attained; that it involves anger, confusion and pain as well as joy and peace; and that the knowing, and trusting of ourselves is the first step to touching and loving others. (Ruth Falk's) personal story, the interviews with other women, and her conceptualization of some of the issues involved are open, honest and searching. At many of the passages of the book I have sighed and said to myself, "Yes. That's how I've felt. I'm not alone." I see this book as an act of courage by a woman of great integrity, a sharing that is a gift of love.—from the preface.

FIRESTONE, ROSS. **A BOOK OF MEN: VISIONS OF THE MALE EXPERIENCE. Illustrations, 319pp. Sto75, 5.95p.**
My purpose in this book is to express the varieties of male experience, the diverse ways we come to terms with our maleness.... To get as close as possible to the tangible realities of men's lives, I have largely limited my selection to personal writings—autobiographies, journals, letters, diaries and the like. More theoretical pieces have been included only when their abstraction is infused with the urgency of self-revelation. The men brought together in this collection span the twentieth century and exemplify the range of possibilities most familiar to our time.... I have looked for writings that pinpoint the essence of a recognizable situation or attitude. Each selection resonates for me with some sort of truth about what it means to be a male.

FREMANTLE, ANNE. **WOMAN'S WAY TO GOD. Introduction, notes, 261pp. SMP77, 10.00c.**
This is an examination of the intense religious experience of nineteen women, including such well known figures as Teresa of Avila, Joan of Arc, and Mary Baker Eddy, and a host of lesser known—though often no less important—individuals. A separate chapter is devoted to each woman and pertinent biographical details and selections from her writings are offered. The style is somewhat dry and there is not enough information about any one woman to really satisfy the reader. Nonetheless, it is an interesting survey and we learned many things from it.

GARFINK, CHRISTINE and HANK PIZER. **THE NEW BIRTH CON-TROL PROGRAM. Glossary, bibliography, index, 140pp. HHP77, 4.95p.**
The new birth control program is a method for controlling fertility and pregnancy in a natural way. For this reason it has become known as Natural Family Planning. It is based on a few simple observations that when made every day, will tell a woman is she is able to conceive (fertile) or not (infertile).... Chris is a Registered Nurse [and] Hank is a Physician's Assistant.... This book is a simple how to guide for people with little medical education.—from the introduction. The book is divided into three parts: *Learning how to use the method, The basic anatomy and physiology of a*

woman of childbearing age, and *The psychology of Natural Family Planning and birth control in general*. This is the clearest presentation of natural birth control we have read.

GREER, GERMAINE. **THE FEMALE EUNUCH. Notes, 380pp. Ban70/ Grn, 2.25p.**
This is a serious and highly readable study which topically discusses the roles that women are involved in and how they came to play the roles. Virtually every aspect of female life in our contemporary society is portrayed and analyzed and positive recommendations are made. Appropriate quotations are interspersed.

GRINNELL, ROBERT. **ALCHEMY IN A MODERN WOMAN. 6.95p.**
See the Jungian Psychology section.

GUGGENBUHL-CRAIG, ADOLF. **MARRIAGE—DEAD OR ALIVE. 126pp. Spr77, 5.05p.**
A collection of analytical essays on marriage, relationship, and sexuality as these subjects relate to individuation in the Jungian sense. The author is a Jungian analyst.

HALL, MANLY P. **WOMAN: MOTHER OF ALL LIVING. 33pp. PRS55, 1.75p.**
A discourse on the role of women and worship of women in various cultures throughout history.

HALL, NOR. **MOTHERS AND DAUGHTERS. 2.75p.**
See the Jungian Psychology section.

HARDING, M. ESTHER. **THE WAY OF ALL WOMEN. 3.95p.**
See the Jungian Psychology section.

HARDING, M. ESTHER. **WOMAN'S MYSTERIES: ANCIENT AND MODERN. 3.95p.**
See the Jungian Psychology section.

HASEGAWA, SEIKAN. **ESSAYS ON MARRIAGE. 87pp. GOP77, 2.95p.**
A collection of essays on every aspect of marriage, focusing on ways in which marriage can be the relationship in which people develop their humanity and their spirituality to the fullest. Hasegawa is a Rinzai Zen monk and, while this book has nothing to say about Zen, the philosophy of Zen Buddhism permeates his writing.

JOHNSON, ROBERT. **HE. 1.95p.**
See the Jungian Psycholoy section.

JOHNSON, ROBERT. **SHE. 1.95p.**
See the Jungian Psychology section.

JONGEWARD, DOROTHY and DRU SCOTT, eds. **AFFIRMATIVE ACTION FOR WOMEN. 343pp. AdW75, 5.95p.**
A practical guide edited by the president of the Transactional Analysis Management Institute which includes information about the current status of women and presents strategies for positive change.

JONGEWARD, DOROTHY and DRU SCOTT. **WOMEN AS WINNERS. Notes, index, 318pp. AdW76, 5.95p.**
A collection of exercises, case histories, and techniques for personal change based on transactional analysis and Gestalt therapy.

KERR, GRAHAM. **SEX FOR WOMEN WHO WANT TO HAVE FUN AND LOVING RELATIONSHIPS WITH EQUALS. Bibliography, 283pp. Grv77, 3.95p.**
Ms. Kerr believes that women's sexual problems originate with sexist attitudes, imposed on us by our upbringing and reinforced by our culture. This basic attitude guides her in her approach to sexual problem solving. The information and techniques she brings to this study have come out of the feminist movement and transactional analysis. She examines the basic sexual roles, shoulds, and fears which sexism has imposed on women and which account for the vast majority of sexual problems. This is both an insightful look at sexuality today and a step-by-step manual outlining new techniques.

KIPPLEY, JOHN and SHEILA. **THE ART OF NATURAL FAMILY PLANNING. Many charts, bibliography, 247pp. CCL77, 4.95p.**
A detailed, practical workbook and reference book. This seems to be the most comprehensive text on natural family planning available.

LACEY, LOUISE. **LUNACEPTION. Notes, bibliography, index, 167pp. War75, 1.75p.**
This is an unusual story of the author's search for a new approach to contraception and the discoveries that search led to. After investigating all the generally used techniques she came upon the technique of *lunaception*, which could be used to determine when she would ovulate and also enabled her to synchronize her body cycle with the phases of the moon and thus make a connection between herself and the universe. She tells how it helps her predict, for a given day, her mood, her energy level, and even her self image—and she supplies charts and the other information needed to try the technique. We have never heard of it before, and we would not recommend relying on it without further scientific testing, but it sounds like an interesting idea.

LANSON, LUCIENNE. **FROM WOMAN TO WOMAN. Illustrations, glossary, index, 389pp. RaH75/Pen, 4.95p.**
This is a sympathetically written, useful collection of information written by a gynecologist in a question and answer format. Topics include the gynecological examination, irregular periods, menstrual cramps, fertility, menopause, and much else—all considered from a psychological as well as a physical point of view. The author's goal is to help women understand the workings of their bodies.

LAUERSEN, NIELS and STEVEN WHITNEY. **IT'S YOUR BODY: A WOMAN'S GUIDE TO GYNECOLOGY. Many illustrations, index, 571pp. G&D77, 14.95c.**
This is the most complete and comprehensive gynecological guide I have encountered. It explains in readable language not only the normal gynecological development from puberty to old age, but also the problems a woman may encounter at any stage of her life. This book should be in every woman's home for reassurance and for practical advice as to when and how to ask for professional advice.—Elisabeth Bing. The approach is not the one we favor, holistic health, nonetheless there is a tremendous amount of useful information here, including self examinations instructions.

LEDERER, WOLFGANG. **THE FEAR OF WOMEN. Illustrations, notes, bibliography, index, 368pp. HBJ68, 3.95p.**
A provocative, pioneering study. Drawing on a wide spectrum of sources—archaeology, ethnology, religion, mythology, art, literature, linguistics, psychiatry, and psychology—Dr. Lederer attempts to show not what women really are, but what men through the ages have feared them to be.

LEVINSON, DANIEL, et al. **THE SEASONS OF A MAN'S LIFE. Notes, index, 377pp. RaH78, 10.95c.**
Yale Professor Levinson and a team of psychologists, psychiatrists, and sociologists conducted a seven year study of adult development which demonstrated how human beings continue to change, throughout their lifetimes, according to an age linked timetable. Levinson's findings—based in part on intensive, longterm interviewing of forty select men—have created a stir in professional circles and received public attention as the foundation of Gail Sheehy's **Passages**. This is a well organized, detailed report of the findings, showing that whatever a man's special life experiences are, he nevertheless passes through the same strict sequence of developmental stages, and must deal with the developmental tasks appropriate to each stage. An informative work, and one which is surprisingly easy to read.

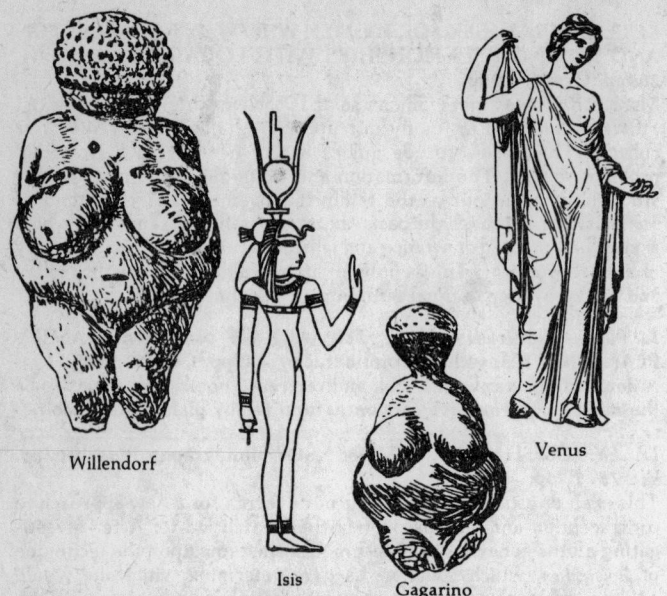

Willendorf

Venus

Isis

Gagarino

LINDBERG, ANNE. **GIFT FROM THE SEA. 143pp. RaH75, 1.95p.**
A small book that has influenced many women's lives. The setting is
the seashore; the time, a brief vacation that lifts the author from the
distractions of everyday living into the sphere of meditation. As the sea
tosses up its gifts—rare and perfect shells—so the mind, left to its
ponderings, brings up its own treasures. Each shell stands as a symbol
for various states and stages of life. Ms. Lindberg reflects on the
profound need in woman for self realization; the need for each woman
to learn and relearn the painful lesson that *woman must come of age by
herself—she must find her true center alone.*

LYON, HAROLD, JR. **TENDERNESS IS STRENGTH. 267pp. H&R77,
8.95c.**
*Hal Lyon's book can help both men and women to discover that gentleness and
forcefulness are not polar opposites, but part of the same energy. Like light, which is one
of the strongest forces in our universe and at the same time one of the softest and most
delicate, our own energy can be both tender and strong. This is a book which the
intelligent layman will find full of messages which are significant for his life.*—Carl
Rogers. This is an intensely personal book, which reads easily.

MANDER, ANICA and ANNE KENT RUSH. **FEMINISM AS THERAPY.
129pp. RaH74, 2.95p.**
The authors are active in the feminist movement in Berkeley, Ca. Here
they discuss their work and the work of others in women's consciousness raising. They also explore the use of the concepts of feminism as
the philosophical base for a new theory and practice of psychology. A
personal account.

MAYER, NANCY. **THE MALE MID-LIFE CRISIS: FRESH STARTS
AFTER FORTY. Notes, bibliography, index, 310pp. Dou78, 8.95c.**
There have been many books about the mid life crisis, most of them
critical. Ms. Mayer started out to write a book about the male
menopause; as she became immersed in the subject she began to see
the positive aspects of the changes which men go through in their
forties—a process which Carl Jung calls individuation. The result is a
book about new beginnings; about American men who are changing
their lives in remarkable and sometimes radical ways. Ms. Mayer
offers a new way to look at these changes: not as symptoms of
something wrong, but as signs of something right, normal, and
necessary. Many case histories illustrate the discussion.

MILLER, JEAN. **TOWARD A NEW PSYCHOLOGY OF WOMEN.
Index, 153pp. Bea76/Pen, 3.95p.**
Dr. Miller argues that the psychological development of both men and
women has been limited and distorted by a *framework of inequality.* She
claims that the maintenance of rigorous sexual stereotypes (dominant
males, subordinate females) has prevented men and women alike from
achieving their full human potential. Drawing on her own professional
practice as well as the clinical evidence of others, she examines
traditionally defined masculine and feminine characteristics, and

proposes a new framework in which traditional concepts take on new
meaning and values.

NEUMANN, ERICH. **THE GREAT MOTHER. 5.95p.**
See the Jungian Psychology section.

NOFZIGER, MARGARET. **A COOPERATIVE METHOD OF BIRTH
CONTROL. Notes, index, 127pp. BPC76, 2.95p.**
This is an illustrated presentation of a system of birth control
developed at the Farm in Tennessee which combines the Basal Body
Temperature Method, the Cervical Mucus Method, and the Calendar
Rhythm Method. The book is written in an understanding way and
many possible questions are answered at the end of each chapter.

OCHS, CAROL. **BEHIND THE SEX OF GOD: TOWARD A NEW
CONSCIOUSNESS TRANSCENDING MATRIARCHY AND PA-
TRIARCHY. Notes, bibliography, index, 190pp. Bea77, 3.95p.**
An original exploration of the character of religion as it evolved into a
dominant patriarchal model. Ochs concludes that the dualism is more
apparent than real, and whether the central deity is male or female is
less important than how we relate to other beings, confront death, and
find meaning in life. Ochs includes chapters on *The Frankenstein Motif,
The Eleusinian Mysteries, The Sacrifice of Isaac, The Feminization of Judaism in the
Zohar, The Cult of Mary,* and *Characteristics of Matriarchal Religion.*

PLECK, JOSEPH and JACK SAWYER, eds. **MEN AND MASCULINITY.
Notes, 184pp. PrH74, 3.45p.**
In contrast to the proliferation of volumes on women's liberation,
there is little or nothing written on the confining aspects of the
traditional man's role. This volume fills that need. It is a collection of
essays edited by two psychologists which present psychological and
sociological studies showing how suppression of emotions and anxiety
about achievement restrict men's ability to work, play, and love freely.
Most of the accounts read well and relate to a great variety of
experiences.

RAMAKRISHNA-VEDANTA CENTER. **WOMEN SAINTS OF EAST
AND WEST. 6.50c.**
See the Comparative Religion section.

RICH, ADRIENNE. **OF WOMAN BORN. Notes, index, 317pp. Ban76/
VLr, 2.95p.**
*All human life on the planet is born of woman. The one unifying, incontrovertible
experience shared by all women and men is that months' long period we spent unfolding
inside a woman's body.... Throughout this book I try to distinguish between two
meanings of motherhood, one superimposed on the other: the potential relationship of
any woman to her powers of reproduction and to children; and the institution, which
aims at ensuring that that potential—and all women—shall remain under male
control.... For most of what we know as the "mainstream" of recorded history,
motherhood as institution has ghettoized and degraded female potentialities.... This
book is not an attack on the family or on mothering, except as it is defined and restricted
under patriarchy.*—from the foreword. Ms. Rich is a well known poet.
This is a highly personal statement, based on research and on the
author's own experiences as a woman and a mother.

ROSAK, BETTY and THEODORE, eds. **MASCULINE/FEMININE: READ-
INGS IN SEXUAL MYTHOLOGY AND THE LIBERATION OF
WOMEN. Notes, annotated bibliography, 328pp. H&R69, 4.50p.**
This is an interesting collection of source readings on many aspects of
the man/woman question. The editors have divided their selections
into the following general topics: *The Man Problem, Some Male Allies,
Between the Old Feminism and the New, The New Militancy,* and *Rattling the
Invisible Chains: A Collection of Women's Liberation Manifestoes.* As might be
expected from the title, the emphasis is on the wrongs done to women
down through the ages.

ROSENBLUM, ART, ed. **THE NATURAL BIRTH CONTROL BOOK.
Annotated bibliography, 156pp. ARF76, 3.00p.**
A review and discussion of a variety of natural techniques including
mind control conception, astrological birth control, the ovulation
method, lunaception. All the necessary tables are included.

■ RUSH, ANNE KENT. **GETTING CLEAR: BODY WORK FOR
WOMEN. 8½"x11", 289pp. RaH73/Wdw, 5.95p.**
An excellent collection of body therapies, verbal therapies, and
awareness techniques in use in the Bay Area in California. *This book is
written to be experienced and not just read. You can use it by picking sections and*

subjects interesting to you and trying out some of the exercises. Any of them done over a period of time become more useful; but even done once, each will have immediate results....I am writing for women because I am a woman and can tell you what tools have been useful to me. Topically arranged, illustrated and highly recommended for all.

RUSH, ANNE KENT. **MOON, MOON. Illustrations, 8½"x11", 416pp. RaH76, 7.95p.**
This is a collectin of moon lore and thoughts on the mother goddess gleaned from a wide variety of sources, ancient and modern. The book is one to dip into from time to time rather than to read. It is a scattered book, but one that contains a bit of intriguing material. Mythological themes are interwoven throughout.

SCHOONMAKER, ANN. **ME, MYSELF, AND I: EVERY WOMAN'S JOURNEY TO HER SELF. Bibliography, 130pp. H&R77, 7.95c.**
In this book I describe four stages of growth and development for women....The four main sections present the different growth stages as a sort of psychogeography. You can think of each stage as one particular state of mind or level of consciousness. Each stage represents not only the way we behave but the way we see ourselves and relate to others. During each stage we must work through particular tasks and conflicts....When we have done fully the work of each stage and grown into it completely, then it's time to move on to the next—a major shift in our development....In order to bring each stage alive, I will use images both from mass media and from various personal experiences. —from the introduction.

SHAMBHALA PUBLICATIONS. **WOMAN: MAITREYA 4. Illustrations, notes, 8½"x9", 76pp. ShP73, 2.50p.**
Maitreya is an annual publication, each issue devoted to a particular theme. This one is a spiritual and mythological look at the higher aspects and qualities of the feminine and includes selections from the writings of Esme Wynne-Tyson, Carlo Suares, Chogyam Trungpa, Jacob Boehme, Charles Ponce, Miriam Arguelles, and Robert Louis Stevenson.

SHEEHY, GAIL. **PASSAGES: PREDICTABLE CRISES OF ADULT LIFE. Notes, bibliography, index, 574pp. Ban76/Crg, 2.50p.**
This book is so popular it scarcely needs a description. Ms. Sheehy discusses the crises that people go through as they age. Much of what she writes about is part of everyone's experience and reading the book helps us to realize that these crises are as much a part of living through the twenties, thirties, and forties as adolescence is to teenagers. Reading the book has helped countless people to understand and accept these changes. Many case histories are included along with a variety of hints for *seeing life as it is.* Ms. Sheehy writes in an informal style that carries the reader along easily.

SPINNER, STEPHANIE, ed. **MOTHERLOVE. 256pp. Del78, 1.95p.**
A collection of short stories and extracts from longer works. Sixteen female writers—from Colette and Katherine Mansfield to Joyce Carol Oates and Edna O'Brien—break through old myths of motherhood to explore the deepest feelings at the center of this uniquely female experience.

STONE, MERLIN. **WHEN GOD WAS A WOMAN. Illustrations, bibliography, index, 378pp. HBJ76, 3.95p.**
In prehistoric and early historic periods of human development, religions existed in which people revered their supreme creator as female. The Great Goddess—The Divine Ancestress—had been worshiped from the beginnings of the Neolithic periods of 7000 BC until the closing of the last Goddess temples, about AD 500....What had life been like for women who lived in a society that venerated a wise and valient female creator? Why had the members of the later male religions fought so aggressively to suppress that earlier worship—even the very memory of it? What did the legend of Adam and Eve really signify, and when and why was it written? The answers I discovered have formed the contents of this book.—from the preface. This is an unusual historical study, which appears to be well researched. The British title is **Paradise Papers.**

STUHLMAN, GUNTHER, ed. **THE DIARY OF ANAIS NIN, VOLUME I: 1931-34. Index, 378pp. HBJ66/QuB, 3.25p.**
Anais Nin's diaries have been universally acclaimed. Their heart lies in Ms. Nin's vision of life and exploration of the feminine experience. Transcending mere self revelation, the diaries examine human personality with a depth and understanding that has seldom been surpassed. The magic of the various volumes is cumulative, though each can be read and savored individually. We recommend these diaries highly to all who seek understanding of what it means to be a sensitive woman in the twentieth century.

STUHLMAN, GUNTHER, ed. **THE DIARY OF ANAIS NIN, VOLUME II: 1934-39. Index, 266pp. HBJ67/QuB, 2.95p.**

STUHLMAN GUNTHER, ed. **THE DIARY OF ANAIS NIN, VOLUME III: 1939-44. Index, 341pp. HBJ69/QuB, 2.95p.**

STUHLMAN, GUNTHER, ed. **THE DIARY OF ANAIS NIN, VOLUME IV: 1944-47. Index, 246pp. HBJ71/QuB, 2.75p.**

STUHLMAN, GUNTHER, ed. **THE DIARY OF ANAIS NIN, VOLUME V: 1947-55. Index, 284pp. HBJ74/QuB, 2.95p.**

STUHLMAN, GUNTHER, ed. **THE DIARY OF ANAIS NIN, VOLUME VI: 1955-66. Index, 430pp. HBJ76/QuB, 3.95p.**

ULANOV, ANN. **THE FEMININE IN JUNGIAN PSYCHOLOGY AND IN CHRISTIAN THEOLOGY. 16.15c.**
See the Jungian Psychology section.

WASHBOURN, PENELOPE. **BECOMING WOMAN. Bibliography, index, 192pp. H&R76, 8.95c.**
An examination of ten potential crisis points in a woman's life, such as the onset of menstruation, leaving home, marriage, and parenthood. Ms. Washbourn understands these occasions on which the issue of personal identity is raised as fundamentally spiritual crises. She defines a negative reaction as the violation of a woman's essential identity and a positive one as a discovery of self trust, renewal, and new identity. Varying reactions for each stage are fully described and there is an examination of how other cultures have dealt with the situation.

WHITEHOUSE, GEOFFREY. **EVERYWOMAN'S GUIDE TO NATURAL HEALTH. Index, 159pp. TPL74, 5.00p.**
Despite the title, this is more of a guide for mothers to be than a general study of ailments peculiar to women. Nonetheless, there is a great deal of information on specific female ailments, including woman's hormones, varicose veins, cervicitis, polyps and pruitus, ailments of the urinary system, prolapse of the uterus, breast disorders, menopause, and the pill. The material is presented in a straightforward manner and the suggestions are clearly put.

How to obtain these books

If you wish to read any of these books and they are not in your local library, show the reviews to your librarian and ask him to order them for you. In this way you will help to awaken your librarian to the importance of these books and help to make them more widely available to others.

The same thing goes for book stores. Try to get the books at the store where you bought **Inner Development.** If they don't have them in stock, ask if they will special order them for you. We have provided the publishers' addresses for the benefit of other book stores who wish to order these books. Or check your classified telephone directory for a local store that might stock these kinds of books in your community.

BUYING BY MAIL

If you cannot obtain these books locally, you can buy them from us. That's the business we are in, and we normally have about 85% of all books in this **Guide** in stock. We do a large mail order business all over the world and we try to get the books out the same day the order comes in. If you live in Great Britain or the British Commonwealth, check the publishers' listings before you order from us to see if there is a British publisher. If so, our price for the book might be higher than your local price and you would do well to try harder to purchase the book locally.

If you wish to get the books from us, please read the following ordering information carefully:

All sales are final. You can appreciate that if this were not so, we would soon become a free lending library for some people. So please read carefully the description of the book you wish to purchase. We have tried to say enough in the reviews to give you good guidance on the books. However, if you would like some additional information about a book before you buy it, write and ask us.

Of course, if a book is defective you may return it for a replacement.

Our prices are net. We sell at retail only. If you are interested in buying at wholesale, contact the publishers of the books. The only discount we offer is ten percent to recognized libraries.

Price Rises

Book prices are continuing to rise as books are reprinted. If an increase is substantial, we'll notify you before filling the order. If total increases on your order are less than $4.00, we'll send you the books and let you pay the balance later. If the price has dropped or we can substitute a paperback, we'll do so and send you a credit slip. We will automatically supply the paperback edition whenever possible, unless you specifically request hardcovers. If you wish hardcovers on books not so shown in **Inner Development,** query us and we'll tell you if we can special order them for you.

Backorders

If we are temporarily out of stock on a title, we will back order it and send it to you as soon as it is available. Most of our orders from domestic publishers take four to six weeks to arrive, but those from foreign publishers may sometimes take up to a year to reach us. If you do not wish to wait you may cancel your order at any time before the books are mailed to you. When you have already paid for a backorder, we will reserve a copy for you when the shipment comes in, so as to be sure that you get it.

Out of Print

If a book has gone out of print, we will let you know and send you a credit slip. If we have been informed that the book is being reprinted, we will back order it for you. Our experience has been that reprinting can sometimes take a month or two or as long as a couple of years.

Inquiries

Oftentimes we receive inquiries about books that are not listed in the **Guide** but that we do have in stock. These are usually new titles. Our policy in such cases is to inform you about the book and put it on hold for you. This is done as a courtesy. It takes up time and space and prevents other customers from buying the book. Therefore, we ask you to let us know within one week if you want the book.

Special Orders

Special orders must be prepaid and cannot be cancelled or returned. These are books that we do not usually stock, therefore it would be difficult for us to sell them in our shop.

Remitting Payment

You may pay us by check or money order, made payable to Yes! Inc., or by VISA or Master Charge credit cards. You can also deposit money with us and draw on it as you order. We cannot accept personal checks from foreign banks (including Canada) and all foreign bank checks and money orders must be in U.S. dollars.

POSTAGE AND HANDLING

Postage rates for books have been rising very rapidly and are likely to go on doing so. We have tried to set postage and handling charges which are fair to our customers and also reflect to some extent our costs of filling small orders. Each order is personally picked and packed by hand and we keep a separate file on each of our customers containing all of our correspondence with you. As long as you place at least one order a year, this file will be kept current and you will also receive periodic mailings of supplements or special announcements.

Domestic Charges

Our charge for domestic postage and handling is $1.00 for the first book and 30¢ for each additional book. Books and records are sent special fourth class mail or UPS. We automatically insure, at our expense, all orders over $30.00.

International Charges

Our charge for international postage and handling is $1.00 for the first book and 40¢ for each additional book. We cannot insure international parcels and we cannot take responsibility for their safe arrival. We recommend that they be sent registered. Registration costs $3.00 for each $20.00 worth of books, except to Canada where up to $140 worth of books can be registered for $3.00.

Air Mail

We normally send our books by surface mail. If you wish your order sent airmail, send us an amount for postage equal to the cost of the book. We will credit any unused money or bill you for the balance.

Supplements

We issue periodic supplements to **Inner Development** which provide reviews of new books and indicate new paperback editions. They are arranged according to the same subject headings as **Inner Development**. With these Supplements you can keep your **Yes! Bookshop Guide** constantly up-to-date.

These supplements will be sent free automatically to customers who order from us regularly.

Others, such as libraries and book stores, who wish to obtain this service may do so at a cost of $2.00 per year. If you wish to subscribe for this service, fill out the coupon below and send it in with your money.

Wellness

Our companion **Yes! Bookshop Guide** is called **Wellness**. Published in late 1977, it provides similar thoughtfully written, critical reviews on some 1500 books covering the whole range of holistic health and healing. Some comments:

"We think this book is the finest guide yet assembled to books about health and nutrition."

—**Better Nutrition**

"If there's a better, more complete guide to wholistic healing literature on the market today, we haven't seen it.!"

—**Mother Earth News**

"Wellness *is a tremendously valuable resource book, a complete guide to the literature in the field of holistic health. It is an ideal reference book; a must for every retail store.*

—**Whole Foods**

Major chapter headings in **Wellness** include: Anatomy and Physiology, Body Work, Color and Aura, Cookbooks, Death, Healing, Herbs, Homoeopathy, Life Energies, Natural Childbirth, Nutrition, Organic Gardening, and Oriental Medicine. **Wellness** has 443 pages, 5" x 8", and costs $4.95. If you don't find it at your local book store or health food store, you may obtain it from us, postpaid. Just fill in the coupon below.

- -

yes!

Bookshop, 1035 31st Street NW, Washington, DC 20007

Please send me : INNER DEVELOPMENT supplements for one year, $2.00 _____

two years, $4.00 _____

three years, $6.00 _____

WELLNESS $4.95, postpaid _____

Enclosed is $ _____

Name _____

Address _____

_____ Zip _____

Publishers' Codes & Addresses

A&P/*Aris and Phillips, Teddington Houe, Church Street, Warminster, Wilts. England*
A&R/*Angus & Robertson, 2 Fisher Street, London WC1R 4QA, England*
A&U/*Allen & Unwin, 14 Thompson Street, Winchester, MA 01890*
AAs/*The Astrological Association, 8 Stuart Close, Great Wakering, Essex, England*
Abb/*Abbey Press, Saint Meinrad, IN 47577*
Abh/*Abhinav Publications, E 37 Hauz Khas, New Delhi 110016 India*
Abi/*Abingdon Press, 201 Eighth Avenue South, Nashville, TN 37202*
Abr/*Harry N. Abrams, 110 East 59th St. NY, NY 10022*
ABS/*Aramaic Bible Society, PO Box 6406 St. Petersburg Beach, FL 33736*
Abs/*Abelard-Schuman, 666 Fifth Ave., NY, NY 10019*
ACa/*Astronomical Calendar, Dept. of Physics, Furman Univer.,Greenville, SC 29613*
Aca/*Academy Books, 3085 Reynard Way, San Diego, CA 92103*
ACB/*Anthony Clarke Books, 16 Garden Court, Wheathampstead, Hertfordshire, England*
Acd/*Academy Editions, 7 Holland St., London W8, England*
AcP/*Academic Press, Harcourt Brace Jovanovich, 757 Third Ave., NY, NY 10017*
AdA/*Advaita Ashrama, 5 Dehi Entally Rd. Calcutta 14 India*
Ada/*H. Eugene Adams, 6550 Wetherole St., Forest Hills, NY 11374*
AdV/*Ad-Ventures, 20 S. Richardson Ave., Lansdale, PA 19446*
AdW/*Addison-Wesley, Jacob Way, Reading, MA 01867*
AEG/*Aquarian Educational Group, 30188 Mulholland Hwy, Agoura, CA 91301*
Aeo/*Aeon Books, Coreki Corp. 8044 Van Nuys Blvd., Panorama City, CA 91402*
AFA/*American Federation of Astrologers, PO Box 22040, Tempe, AZ 85282*
AgY/*Agni Yoga Society, 319 West 107th St., NY, NY 10025*
AHI/*Arnold-Heinemann India, AB/9 Safdarjang Enclave, New Delhi 16, India*
AIR/*Astrological Investigation & Researchers, 2710 Laughlin Rd., Windsor, CA 95492*
All/*Allied Publishers, 15 Graham Rd., Ballard Estate, Bombay 400001 India*
Alo/*Alok Publications, A-28 East of Kaiash, New Delhi 110024 India*
Alt/*The Altai Press, Triad Reprints, PO Box 569, Cooper Station, NY, NY 10003*
Aly/*Ally Press, 1764 Gilpin St., Denver, CO 80218*
Amb/*K.H. Ambjornson, 443 Melrose Avenue, San Francisco, CA 94127*
Amh/*Amherst Press, Amherst, WI 54406*
Amo/*Amorc, Rosicrucian Park, San Jose, CA 95114*
AMS/*AMS Press, 56 E 13th St., NY, NY 10003*
Anh/*Anhinga Press, PO Box 13501, Gainesville, FL 32604*
Anj/*Anjanee Mata, Box 454, Laytonsville, CA 95454*
ANW/*Astrology Center of the Northwest, 522 N.E. 165th, Seattle, WA 98155*
AOP/*And/or Press, 3431 Rincon Annex, San Francisco, CA 94119*
APA/*Apa Productions, Killiney Box 219, Singapore 9*
Apa/*Apa Productions HK, 3210 Connaught Centre, Hong Kong*
APC/*Aquarian Publishing, Denington Estate, Wellingborough, Northants NN8 2RP England*
APH/*Asia Publishing House, 440 Park Ave. S., NY, NY 10016*
API/*Anthroposophic Press, 258 Hungry Hollow Rd., Spring Valley, NY 10977*
APL/*The Antonine Publishing Co., 440 Petershill Rd., Glasgow G21, 4PA, Scotland*
APr/*Astro-Press, 4853 Westpark Dr., North Hollywood, CA 91601*
APS/*American Philosophical Society, 104 S. 5th st., Philadelphia, PA 19106*
AqP/*Aquarian Press, 91 St. Martin's La., London WC 2, England*
ArB/*Arcane Books, US Rte. 1-A, York Harbor, ME 03911*
Arc/*Arco, 219 Park Ave. S., NY, NY 10003*
ARE/*A.R.E. Press, PO Box 595, Virginia Beach, VA 23451*
ARF/*Aquarian Research Foundation, 5620 Morton St., Philadelphia, PA 19144*
Arg/*Argus Communications, 7440 Natchez, Niles, IL 60648*
Ari/*Aries Press, 622 Grove St., Evanston, IL 60201*
ARM/*A.R.A.M., 116 E. 66th St., NY, NY 10021*
Arn/*Arno Press, 3 Park Ave., NY, NY 10016*
ARS/*Atma Ram & Sons, Kashmere Gate, Delhi-6, India*
Art/*Artibus Asiae, 6612 Ascona, Switzerland*
ArW/*Rams Dell Press, 407 N. Maple Dr. #214, Beverly Hills, CA 90214*
AsA/*Astro-Analytics Publications, 16440 Haynes St., Van Nuys, CA 91406*
ASB/*A.S. Barnes & Co., Forsgate Dr., Cranbury, NJ 08512*
AsB/*Astrological Bureau, 5 Old Quaker Hill Rd., Monroe, NY 10950*
ASI/*ASI Publishers, 127 Madison Ave., NY, NY 10016*
Ask/*Askin Publishers, #16 Ennismore Ave., Chiswick, London W41SF England*
ASL/*Arnold (E.J.) & Sons, Butterley Street, Leeds LS10 1AX, England*
ASO/*American School of Astrology, 470 Prospect St., West Orange, NJ 07052*
AsP/*Association Press, 291 Broadway, NY, NY 10007*
Ata/*Astara, 215 Mariposa Ave., Los Angeles CA 90004*
Ath/*Atheneum, Vreeland Ave., Totowa, NJ 07512*
Atp/*Anthropological Publications, Oosterhout NB, Netherlands*
ATS/*A.T.S. Press, Cambridge, MA*
AtU/*Atlantis University, Box 69990, Los Angeles, CA 90069*
AUM/*A.U.M., PO Drawer 5310, Austin, TX 78762*
Aut/*Autumn Press, 7 Littell Rd., Brookline, MA 02146*
Avo/*Avon Books, 250 W. 55th St., NY, NY 10019*
Awa/*The Awakener, Box 2299, Walnut Creek, CA 94595*

B&J/*Barrie & Jenkins, 24 Highbury Crescent, London N5 1RX England*
B&O/*Burns & Oates, 25 Ashley Pl., London SW 1 England*
B&T/*Biblio & Tannen, 63 4th Ave., NY, NY 10003*

BAB/*Blueapple Books, PO Box 5694, Austin, TX 78763*
Bag/*Dr. A. Bagchi, 55 Ramesh Mitra Rd., Calcutta, India*
BAI/*Bharat Astrology Institute, New Colony, Srikakulam, Andhra Pradesh, India*
Bak/*Douglas Baker, High Rd., Essendon, Herts., England*
Ban/*Bantam Books, 666 5th Ave., NY, NY 10019*
BaP/*Barre Publishers, South St., Barre, MA 01005*
Bat/*Batsford (B.T.) Ltd., 4 Fitzhardinge St., London W1H OAH, England*
BBB/*Bergstron & Boyle Books, 22 Maddox St., London W1 England*
BBC/*British Broadcasting Corp., 35 Marylebone High St., London W1M4AA England*
BBI/*Buddhist Books International, PO Box 665, Chatsworth, CA 91311*
BBU/*Bhavan's Book U, Chowpatly, Bombay 7, India*
BdB/*Buddhist Bookstore, 1710 Octavia St., San Francisco, CA 94109*
Bea/*Beacon Press, 25 Beacon St., Boston, MA 02108*
Bed/*Clyde Bedell, Santa Barbara, CA*
Beg/*Beguine Library, Berkeley, CA 94701*
Beh/*Behrman House, 1261 Broadway at 31st St., NY, NY 10001*
Bel/*G. Bell & Sons, 6 Portugal St., London WC2A 2HL England*
Ben/*Bench Press, PO Box 24635, Oakland, CA 94623*
Ber/*Berkley Publishing Corp., 390 Murray Hill Pkwy., E. Rutherford, NJ 07073*
BES/*Barron's Educational Series, 113 Crossways Pk Dr., Woodbury, NY 11797*
Bes/*Beshara Publications, Beshara Design Centre, Hope (Sufference) Wharf, 61 St. Marychurch St., Rotherhithe, London WC1R 4JH, England*
Bet/*Beta Books, Box 246, Chino, CA 91710*
BGr/*Bernice Grebner, 231 Montclair Ave., Peoria Hgts., IL 61614*
Bha/*M. Bhattacharyya & Co., 73 Netaji Subhas Rd., Calcutta, India*
Bih/*Bihar School of Yoga, Monghyr, Bihar, India*
Bje/*S. Banerjee, P 469, C.I.T. Keyatala, Calcutta 29, India*
Bkh/*Y. Beroukhim & Sons, Tehran, Iran*
Bla/*Blackie & Sons, Bishopsbriggs, Glasgow G64 2Nz, Scotland*
BlB/*Bellerophon Books, 133 Steuart St., San Francisco, CA 94105*
BLE/*Blaine Etheridge Books, 13977 Penrod St., Detroit, MI 48223*
Blo/*Bloch Publishing, 915 Broadway, NY, NY 10010*
BlP/*Blandford Press, Link House, West St., Poole, Dorset BH15 1LL England*
BMP/*British Museum Publications, 6 Bedford Sq., London WC1B 3RRA England*
BMS/*Buddhist Missionary Society, Jalan Berhala, Kuala Lumpur 09-06, Malaysia*
BnB/*B'nai B'rith Adult Jewish Education, 1640 Rhode Island Ave., Wash., DC 20036*
BnL/*Ernest Benn, Sovereign Way, Tonbridge, Kent England*
BnP/*Rebecca Bennet Publications, 5409 18th Ave., Brooklyn, NY 11204*
BoH/*Bodley Head, 9 Bow St., London WC2E 7AL England*
BoM/*Bobs Merrill, 4300 West 62nd St. Indianapolis, IN 46208*
Bor/*Borden Publishing, 1855 W. Main St., Alhambra, CA 91801*
BPC/*The Book Publishing Co., Rte. 1, Box 197 A, Summertown, TN 38784*
BPH/*Bhartiya Publishing House, B-9/45 Pilkhana, Sonarpura, Varanasi, India*
BPP/*Blue Pearl Press, PO Box 11071, Oakland, CA 94611*
BPS/*Buddhist Publication Society, Box 61, Kandy, Sri Lanka*
BPT/*Baha'i Publishing Trust, 415 Linden Ave., Wilmette, IL 60091*
BPu/*Buddhist Publications, Institute for Buddhist Psychology and Central Asian Stuaies, Zurich, Switzerland*
Bri/*EJ Brill, Oude Rijn 33a-35, Leiden, Netherlands*
BRP/*Berkley Research Publishing, 2490 Channing Way, Berkley, CA 94704*
BrP/*Branden Press, 221 Columbus Ave., Boston, MA 02116*
Brz/*George Braziller. 1 Park Ave., NY, NY 10016*
BsD/*Bodysex Designs, Box 1933 GPO, NY, NY 10001*
Btk/*Bhatkal Books International, 35-C Tardeo Rd., Bombay 34, India*
BTP/*Bear Tribe Publishing, PO Box 9167, Spokane, WA 99209*
BuA/*Builders of the Adytum, PO Box 42278, Dept 0, Los Angeles, CA 90042*
BUC/*Buddha's Universal Church, 720 Washington St., San Francisco, CA*
BUP/*Brown University Press, Providence, RI 02912*
BuS/*Buddhist Society, 58 Eccleston Sq., London SW1V 1PH, England*
BVB/*Bharatiya Vidya Bhavan, 1. 1, U.B., Jawaharnagar, Bungalow Rd. New Delhi, India*

C&B/*Calder & Boyars, 18 Brewer St., London W1 England*
C&H/*Chapman & Hall, 11 New Fetter La., London EC4P 4EE England*
C&S/*Chandler & Sharp Publishers, 5609 Paradise Dr., Corte Madera, CA 94925*
C&W/*Chatto, Bodley Head & Cape Services, 9 Bow St., Covent Garden, London WC2E 7AL England*
CaC/*Cassell & Co., 35 Red Lion Sq., London WC1R 4SQ England*
CaD/*Carolyn Dodson, PO Box 1233, Louisville, KY 40201*
CAp/*Colombo Apothecaries, 84 Main St., Colombo 11, Sri Lanka*
Cap/*Capra Press, 631 State St., Santa Barbara, CA 93101*
Cas/*Bruno Cassirer, 31 Portland Rd., Oxford OX2 7EZ England*
CBC/*Cosmobiology Center, 539 S. Grant St., Denver, CO 80209*
CBk/*China Books, 125 5th Ave., NY, NY 10003*
CCC/*China Cultural Corp., PO Box 3724, Hong Kong*
CCL/*Cambridge Circle, 463 Vande Hei Rd., Green Bay, WI 54301*
CCl/*Christian Classics, 205 Willis St., Westminister, MD 21157*
CCP/*Christian Community Press, 34 Glenilla Rd., London N.W. 3 England*

CeA/Celestial Arts, 231 Adrian Rd., Millbrae, CA 94030

Cer/Alfons Cers, Box 08347, Milwaukee, WI 53208

Ces/Cesara Publications, Huntington Castle, Clonegal, Enniscorthy, Eire

CGJ/C. G. Jung Institute of Los Angeles, 10349 W. Pico Blvd., Los Angeles

ChF/Churches' Fellowship for Psychical & Spiritual Studies St. Mary Abchurch, Abchurch Lane, London EC4N 7BA England

Chi/Chilton Book Co., 150 Parish Dr.,Wayne, NJ 07470

ChL/Church of Light, Box 76862, Sanford Station, Los Angeles, CA 90076

Chn/Chinmaya Books, U.S.A., PO Box 2753, Napa, CA 94558

Chs/Christananda Publishing, 977 Ashbury St., San Jose, CA 95126

CIA/China Institute in America, 125 East 65th St., NY, NY 10021

CiL/Subterranean Co., 680 East 40th Ave., Eugene, OR 97405

Cir/Circle Books, 2728 Elmwood, Ann Arbor, MI 48104

Cis/Cistercian Publications, WMU Substation, Kalamazoo, MI 49008

CIv/Creative Initiative Foundation, Palo Alto, CA

Cla/James Clarke & Co., 7 All Saints Passage, Cambridge, CB2 3LS England

Cln/Clancy Publications, 2505 N. Alvernon Way, Tucson, AZ 85712

CMG/Coward, McCann & Geoghegan, 200 Madison Ave., NY, NY 10016

CMT/Central Chimaya Mission Trust, Band Box House, 254 D, Dr. Annie Besant Rd., Prabhadevi, Bombay 400-025 India

Cnd/S. Chand & Co., Ram Nagar, New Delhi, India 110055

Cno/Canon Press, 1014 Washington Bldg., Wash., DC 20005

Col/Constellation Intl., 51 Madison Ave., NY, NY

Col/Columbia University Press, 562 W. 113th St., NY, NY 10025

Com/Compton Press, Old Brewery, Tisbury, Salisbury, Wilts SP3 6NH England

Con/Constable & Co., 10 Orange St., Leicester Sq., London WC2H 7EG England

Cop/R.C. Copriviza, 71 Oakwood St., San Francisco, CA

Cor/Cornell University Press, 124 Roberts Pl., Ithaca, NY 14850

Cos/Cosmos Books, 30 Johnson Rd., basement, Hong Kong

Cov/Coventure Books, c/o P.D.A.S. (Cowley), bldg. 18, Denham Studio Estate No. Oital Rd., Denham, Bucks, England

CPT/Chinmaya Publications Trust, 175, Rasappa Chetty St., Madras 3, India

CrA/Creative Arts & Book Co., 833 Bancroft Way, Berkeley, CA 94710

CRC/CRCS Publications, Asbill Ct. Bldg., 111 G St., Davis, CA 95616

Cre/Gordon Cremonesi Publishers, New River House, 34 Seymour Rd., London N8 OBE England

Crg/Corgi Books, Cavendish House, 57-59 Uxbridge Rd., Ealing, London, W5 England

Crn/Crown Publishers, 1 Park Ave. S., NY, NY 10016

CRs/Crane, Russak & Co., 347 Madison Ave., NY, NY 10017

CSA/CSA Press, Lakemont, GA 30552

Csm/Cosmo Publications, 24-B, Ansari Rd., Daryaganj, Delhi 110006 India

CSq/Cooper Sq. Publishers, 59 4th Ave., NY, NY 10003

CSS/Chowkhamba Sanskrit Series, PO Chowkhamba, PO Box 8, Varanasi 1, India

Css/Crossing Press, Trumansburg, NY 14886

Cst/Castle Books, 110 Enterprise Ave., Secaucus, NJ 07094

Ctr/Centaur Press Ltd, Trade Counter, 11-14 Stanhope Mews West, London SW 7 England

CUA/Catholic University of America Press, Wash., DC 20017

CUP/Cambridge University Press, 510 North Ave., NY, NY 10022

CuP/Cunningham Press, 3063 West Main, Alhambra, CA 91801

Cur/Curzon Press, 88 Gray's Inn Rd., London WC1 England

CWL/Ch'eng Wei-shih Lun Publication, 3 Fontana Gardens, Causeway Hill, Hong Kong

CWo/Collins-World, 2080 W. 117th St., Cleveland, OH 44111

CWP/Ch'eng W'en Publishing, Box 22605, Taipei, Taiwan

DAC/Devin-Adair Co., 143 Sound Beach Ave., Old Greenwich, CN 06870

DAK/Dar Al-Koran Al-Kareem, Riyad Solh Sq./Shaker & Queiny Bldg., PO Box 7492 Beirut Lebanon

DaL/Peter Davies, 15-16 Queen St., Mayfair, London W1X 8BE, England

Dar/Darr Publications, 2527 Broadway, Toledo, OH 43609

Day/Daystar Press, PO Box 1261, Ibadan, Nigeria

Del/Dell c/o Montville Warehousing Co., Change Bridge Rd., Pine Brook, NJ 07058

Den/J.M. Dent & Sons, Dunhams La., Leachworth, Herts, SG6 1LF England

Deu/Andre Deutsch, Amabel House, 14-24 Baches St., London N1 England

DeV/Devorss & Co., PO Box 550, Marina Del Rey, CA 90291

Dha/Dharma Publishing, 5856 Doyle St., Emeryville, CA 94608

DHL/Dialogue House Library, 45 W. 10th St., NY, NY 10011

DHP/Dawn Horse Press, 1530 Custer Ave.,San Francisco, CA 94124

Dia/Dial/Delacourte, 1 Dag Hammarskjold Plaza, NY, NY 10017

Dic/Dickenson Publishing Co., Belmont, CA 94002

Din/Dinosaur Publications, Beechcroft, Over Cambridge CB4 5NE England

Dip/Diploma Press, Inter'l Press Centre, 76 Shoe La., London EC4A 3JB England

Diw/Diwan Press, 1419 Polk St., San Francisco, CA 94109

DLP/Dawne-Leigh Publications, PO Box 825, San Rafael, CA 94904

DLS/Divine Life Society, PO Shivanandanagar, Dt Tehri-Garhwal, U.P. Himalyas, India

DLT/Darton Longman & Todd, 89 Lillie Rd., London SW6 1UD England

DMd/Dodd, Mead, 79 Madison Ave., NY, NY 10016

Dml/Domel Enterprises, PO Box 3829 Albuquerque, NM 87110

DoB/Dobson Books, 80 Kensington Church St., London W8 4BF England

Dol/Dolmen Press, 8 Herbert Pl., Dublin 2 Ireland

Dom/Dominie Press, 3075 Bridletowne Cir., Unit 19, Agincourt, Ontario, M1W 1S8 Canada

Don/Donning Co., 253 W. Bute St., Norfolk, VA 23510

Dou/Doubleday, 501 Franklin Ave., Garden City, NY, NY 11530

Dov/Dover Publications, 180 Varick St., NY, NY 10014

DPC/Dorene Publishing, 2809 Main St., Dallas, TX 75226

Dph/Dolphin Press, Beaulieu Ave., Christchurch, Hants, England

DRC/Digicomp Research Corp., Ithaca, NY 14850

DrF/Draco Foundation, 112 Rosedale Dr., Independence, CA 93526

Drk/Drake, 801 Second Ave., NY, NY 10017

DSP/Dharma Sara Publications, PO Box 247, Sumas, WA 98295

DTP/Doubletree Press, PO Box 1321, Walla Walla, WA 99362

Duc/Duckworth & Co., Old Piano Factory, 43 Gloucester Crescent, London NW 1, England

Duf/Dufour Editions, Chester Springs, PA 19425

Dus/Dusum-par, 1,065 11th St., Boulder, CO 80302

Dut/E.P. Dutton, 2 Park Ave., NY, NY 10016

DvP/Dove Publications, Pecos, NM 87552

DyC/John Day Co., 257 Park Ave., S., NY, NY 10010

EbV/Ebertin Verlag, D 7080 Aalen/wurtt, Federal Republic of Germany

EdE/Ediciones Euroamericanos, Perugino 35-1, Mexico 19, D.F. Mexico

EdI/Edits Publishers, PO Box 7234, San Diego, CA 92107

EEP/Este Es Press, Norlin Library, U of Colo., Boulder, CO 80302

Eer/Wm. B. Eerdmans Publishing, 255 Jefferson Ave., S.E., Grand Rapids, MI 49502

Ele/Paul Elek, 10 S. Broadway, Salem, NH 03079

Eli/Edward Elias' Modern Publishing, PO Box 954, Cairo, Egypt

Eme/Emerson Press, 28 Dean Rd., London NW2 England

Emg/Emergence, 185 Beacon Hill, Ashland, OR 97520

Eml/Emillle Museum, 206 Dungchon Dong, Yeongdungpo Ku, Seoul, Korea

EMU/Editores Mexicanos Unidos, S.A., L. Gonzalez Abregon 5-B, Apartado 45-671 Mexico 1, D.F.

Ent/Entrepreneur Press, Mission Station, Drawer 2759, Santa Clara, CA 95051

EPG/EP Group, Bradford Rd., East Ardsley, Wakefield, Yorkshire, WF3 2JN, England

EPI/Elmi Publication Institute, Nasser Khosrow Ave., Teheran, Iran

ERA/Educational Research Assoc., Box 767, Amherst, MA 01002

Erb/Erbonia Books, PO Box 396, New Paltz, NY 12561

EUP/Edinburgh U Press, 81 Adams Dr., Totowa, NJ 07512

EvB/Evans Bros Books, Montague House, Russell Sq., London WC1B 5BX England

EvC/M. Evans & Co., 216 E. 49th St., NY, NY 10017

EWC/East-West Cultural Center, 2865 W. 9th St., Los Angeles, CA 90006

EWP/East West Publications Fonds BV, PO Box 7616, The Hague, Holland

ExP/Exposition Press, 900 S. Oyster Bay Rd., Hicksville, NY 11801

Fab/Faber Books, 3 Queen Sq., London WC1N 3AU England

Faw/Fawcett Publications, Fawcett Bldg., Fawcett Pl., Greenwich, CN 06830

FFT/Food for Thought, PO Box 331, Amherst, MA 01002

FHA/Finn Hill Arts, Box 542, Silverton, CO 81433

FHP/Franciscan Herald Press, 1434 W. 51st St., Chicago, IL 60609

Fid/Fides Publishers, PO Box F, Notre Dame, IN 46556

Fin/Fine Books, 115-123 Bayham St., London NW1 OAL England

FiP/Findhorn Publications, Park, Findhorn Bay, Forres, Moray, Scotland

FLP/Foreign Language Press, Peking, China

FlP/Fleet Press, 160 5th Ave., NY, NY 10010

Fld/Philipp Feldheim, 96 E. Broadway, NY, NY 10002

Fon/Fontana Books, 14 St. James Pl., London SW1A 1PS England

For/Fortress Press, 2900 Queen La., Philadelphia, PA 19129

Fos/FOSSU, PO Box 93, Redondo Beach, CA 90277

Fou/W. Foulsham & Co., Yeovil Rd., Slough, SL1 4JH England

Fow/L.N. Fowler & Co., 1201/1203 High Rd., Chadwell Heath, Romford, Essex, England

Foy/W. & G. Foyle, 119-125 Charing Cross Rd., London, WC 2 England

FPC/Freestone Publishing, PO Box 357, Albion, CA 95410

FrC/Frank Cass & Co., 81 Adams Dr., PO Box 327, Totowa, NJ 07511

Fre/W.H. Freeman & Co., 660 Market St., San Francisco, CA 94104

FSF/Four Seasons Foundation, Bolinas, CA

FSG/Farrar, Straus, & Giroux, 19 Union Sq. W., NY, NY 10003

Fud/Fudge & Co., Sardinia House, Sardinia St., Kingsway, London, WC2A 3NW England

Fut/Futura Publications, 110 Warner Rd., London SE5 9HQ England

Fwn/Frewin & Co., Colombo, Sri Lanka

FWO/Friends of the Western Buddhist Order, Aryatara Community, 3 Plough La., Purley, Surrey, CR2 3QB, England

FWP/Four Winds Press, 908 Sylvan Ave., Englewood Cliffs, NJ 07632

G&D/Grosset & Dunlap, 51 Madison Ave., NY, NY 10010

GaB/Galahad Books, 95 Madison Ave., NY, NY 10016

Gan/Ganesh & Co., Madras-17, India

Gat/Gateway, Ferndale, Bucks County, PA 18921

GBF/Guru Bawa Fellowship, 5820 Overbrook Ave., Philadelphia, PA 19131

GCP/General Co., for Publication, PO Box 959, Tripoli, Libyan Arab Republic

GeB/Geo Books, Western Book Service, PO Box 3975, San Francisco, CA 94119

GEd/Gateway Editions, 620 W. Washington St., S. Bend, IN 46625

GeP/Genesis Press, Cupertino, CA

GFG/Gordon Fraser Gallery, Eascotts Rd., Bedford MK42 0JX England

Gif/John Gifford, 49-125 Charing Cross Rd., London WC2H 0EB England

Gir/Maurice Girodias Assoc., 220 Park Ave. S., NY, NY 10003

Git/Gita Press, Gorakhpur, India

Glz/Gollancz Services, 14 Eldon Way, Lineside Estate, Littlehampton, Sussex, England

God/David Godine, Publisher, 306 Dartmouth St., Boston, MA 02116

GOP/Great Ocean Publishers, 738 S. 22nd St., Arlington, VA 22202

Gou/Henry Goulden, 14 Hill St., Hastings, Sussex, England

GPA/George Prior Assoc. Publishers, Rugby Chambers, 2 Rugby St., London WC1N 3QN England

Gre/Greenwood Press, 51 Riverside Ave., Westport, CN 05880

Grn/Granada Publishing, 1221 Ave., of the Americas, NY, NY 10020

Grp/Aquarian World Servers, Rte. 9, Box 2370, Brooksville, FL 33512

Grv/Grove Press, 53 E. 11th St., NY, NY 10003

GSR/Golden Seal Research Hdqtrs, PO Box 27821, Hollywood, CA 90027

GtP/Garrett Publishing, 200 Park Ave., S., NY, NY 10003

Gun/M.D. Gunasena & Co., PO Box 246, 217 Olcott Mawatha Colombo 11, Sri Lanka

H&R/Harper & Row, Keystone Industrial Park, Scranton, PA 18512

HaG/George G. Harrap & Co., PO Box 70, 182-84 High Holborn, London WC1V 7AX England

HaH/Hancock House, 12008 1st Ave., S., Seattle, WA 98168

Hal/Robert Hale, Clerkenwell House, 45-47 Clerkenwell Green, London W1X 6AB England

Ham/Hamlyn Publishing Group, The Centre, Feltham, Middlesex, England

Har/Hart Publishing Co., 12 E. 12th St., NY, NY 10003

Has/Haskell House Publishers, 280 Lafayette St., NY, NY 10012

Hav/Harvester Press, 2 Stanford Terr., Hassocks, Brighton E., Sussex, England

Haw/Hawthorne Books, 260 Madison Ave., NY, NY 10016

HBJ/Harcourt Brace Jovanovich, 757 3rd Ave., NY, NY 10017

HDI/Human Dimensions Institute, 4380 Main St., Buffalo, NY 14226

HeG/Heineman Group-Windmill Press, Kingswood, Tadworth, Surrey, KT 206 TG, England

Hel/Helios Book Service, 8 Sq., Toddington, NR. Cheltenham, Glos. GL54 5DL, England

Hem/Hemisphere Press, 263 Ninth Ave., NY, NY

HeP/Hemkunt Press, 1-E/15 Patel Rd., New Delhi, 8, India

HeR/Health Research, 70 Lafayette St., Mokelumne Hill, CA 95245

Her/Heritage Store, PO Box 444-B, VA Beach, VA 23458

HFC/Hodges, Figgis & Co., 20 St. Stephens Green, Dublin 2, Ireland

HHL/Hamish Hamilton, c/o TBL Book Service, 17-23 Nelson Way, Tuscam Trading Estate Camberley, Surrey, England

HHP/Hampstead Hall Press, 38 East 57th St., NY, NY 10022

Hia/Hiawatha Publishing Co., Derry, Iowa 50220

Hic/Isabel Hickey, 35 Maple St., Watertown, MA 02172

Hie/Hieratic Publishing Co., PO Box 133, Medford, MA 02155

Him/Himalayan Institute, RD #1 Box 88, Honesdale, PA 18431

HIn/Heian International Publishing, PO Box 2402, S. San Francisco, CA 94080

Hip/Hippocrene Books, 171 Madison Ave., NY, NY 10016

HKG/Herder KG, Freiburg, West Germany

HMC/Houghton Mifflin Co., Wayside Rd., Burlington, MA 01803

Hod/Hodder & Stoughton, Mill Rd., Dunton Green, Sevenoaks, Kent TN 13 2XX England

HOH/Hohm, PO Box 75, Tabor, NJ 07078

Hoi/Hoikusha Publishing, 20, 1-chome, Uchikyuhoji-machi, Higashi-ku, Osaka, 540 Japan

Hok/Hokuseido Publishing, 3-12 Kanda Nishikicho, Chiyoda-ku Tokyo, Japan

Hol/A.J. Holman, E. Washington Sq., Philadelphia, PA 19105

HOM/Holy Order of Mans, 20 Steiner St., San Francisco, CA 94117

Hor/Horizon Press, 156 5th Ave., NY, NY 10010

HPB/Hind Pocket Books, G.T. Rd., Delhi 110032 India

HPG/Hutchinson Publishing Group, 3 Fitzroy Sq., London W1P 6JD England

HRA/Huna Research Assoc., 126 Camellia Dr., Cape Giradeau, MO 63701

Hrn/Haren & Bro., Calcutta 1, India

Hrv/Harvest Press, PO Box 1265, Santa Cruz, CA 95061

HRW/Holt, Rinehart, & Winston, 383 Madison Ave., NY, NY 10017

HSc/Human Science Press, 72 5th Ave., NY, NY 10011

HSP/Health Science Press, Hengiscote, Bradford, Holsworthy, N. Devon, EX22 7AP, England

Hub/Hubbard Press, 2855 Shermer Rd., Northbrook, IL 60062

Hug/Hughes, Dorothy, 2322 6th Ave., Seattle, WA 98121

Hul/Hulton Educational Publications, Raans Rd., Amersham, Bucks, England

HUP/Harvard University Press, 79 Garden St., Cambridge, MA 02138

HuP/Humanities Press, 171 1st Ave., Atlantic Highlands, NJ 07716

HvH/Harvest House Publishers, 17895 Sky Park Cir., Irvine, CA 92707

IAS/Institute for Astrological Studies, 60 St. Clair Ave., W., Toronto, M4V 1M7 Canada

IBC/Indian Book Co., 36 C Connaught Pl., New Delhi, 110001 India

IBH/Indological Book House, PO Box 98, Ck. 31/10 Nepali Khapra, Varansi, India

ICS/Institute of Carmelite Studies, 2131 Lincoln Rd., NE, Wash., DC 20002

IDH/Idhhb, Box 300, Mt. Tabor, NJ 07878

IET/India Book House Educational Trust, 12 Hassa Mahal, Dalamal Pk., 223 Cuffe Parade Bombay 400005 India

IIC/Institute of Islamic culture, 2 Club Rd., Lahore, Pakistan

IIS/Islamic Information Services, Radnor House, 93/97 Regent St., London W1R7TD England

Ikh/Ikwhan Press, Tucson, AZ

ImP/Images Press, 1750 Arch St., Berkeley, CA 94709

Int/International Univ. Press, 315 5th Ave., NY, NY 10016

IPB/Islamic Publications Bureau, PO Box 3881, Lagos, Nigeria

IPG/Independent Publishing Group, 14 Vanderventer Ave., Port Washington, NY 11060

IPS/Instituto Poligrafico Dello Stato, Libreria Dello Stato, Piazza G. Verdi, 10 Rome, Italy

IPy/Institute of Pyramidology, 31 Station Rd., Herpenden, Hertfordshire, England

ISU/Iowa State U Press, S. State St., Ames, Iowa 50010

ITI/Inner Traditions International, 377 Park Ave., S., NY, NY 10010

IUP/Indiana U Press, 10th & Morton Sts., Bloomington, IN 47401

IWP/Illuminated Way Press, PO Box 2449, Menlo Pk., CA 94025

IZS/Institute for Zen Studies, Hanazono College, Hanazono, Ukyo-ku, Kyoto, Japan

Jac/Ivy Jacobson, 6374 Encinita Ave., Temple City, CA 91780

J&J/Jinni & Joanne, 7560 Roosevelt Way NE, Seattle, WA 98115

Jap/Japan Publications Trading Co., 200 Clearbrook Rd., Elmsford, NY 10523

JBP/Jossey Bass, 615 Montgomery St., San Francisco, CA 94111

Jew/Jewish Publication Society, 1528 Walnut St., Phila., PA 19102

JFP/C.G. Jung Foundation for Analytical Psychology, 28 E. 39th St., NY, NY 10016

JHU/John Hopkins U Press, Balt., MD 21218

Jos/Michael Joseph, 52 Bedford Sq., London WC1B 3EF England

Jov/Jove Publications, 757 3rd Ave., NY, NY 10017

JPC/B. Jain Publishers, XV/2793, Raj Guru Rd., Chuna Mandi, Pahar Ganj, New Delhi 55, India

JPH/Jaico Publishing House, 44.45 Ezra St., Calcutta, India

JRC/Johnson Reprint, 111 5th Ave., NY, NY 10003

JTL/Japan Times, 5-4 Shibaura 4-chome, Minato-ku Tokyo, Japan

JWS/John Wiley & Sons, 605 3rd Ave., NY, NY 10016

K&A/Kahn & Averill, 25 Thurloe St., London SW7 England

K&W/Kaye & Ward, 21 New St., London EC2M 4NT England

Kae/Kaedmon Publishing Co., 150 Broadway NY, NY 10038

Kau/Wm. Kaufmann, 1 1st St., Los Altos, CA 94022

Kay/Kayhan Press, Tehran, Iran

KBS/Kokusai Bunka Shinkokai, 1-1-18, Shirokane-dai, Minato-ku, Tokyo, Japan

Ket/Keter Publishing House, Jerusalem, Israel

KeV/Verlag Walter Keller, CH-4143, Dornach, Leitmenweg 5 Switzerland

Kly/Kalyani Publishers, Delhi, India

Kno/John Knox Press, 341 Ponce De Leon Ave., NE, Atlanta, GA 30308

KNP/Khanigahi Nimatullahi, 306 West 11th St., NY, NY 10014

Kod/Kodansha Inter'l., 10 E. 53rd St., NY, NY 10022

KRI/Kundalini Research Institute, Box 1020, Claremont, CA 91711

Kro/Kronos, 400 Drummers La., Wayne, PA 19087

KTV/KTAV Publishing House, 75 Varick St., NY, NY 10013

L&W/Lawrence & Wishart, Central Books, 37 Gray's Inn Rd., London EC1 England

Lad/Ladybird Books, PO Box 12, Beeches Rd., Loughborough Leics England

LaF/Lama Foundation, Box 444,San Cristobal, NM 87564

Lan/Lang Publishing Co., Aylesbury, Bucks, England

LBC/Little Brown, & Co., 34 Beacon St., Boston, MA 02106

LDE/Lois Daton Enterprises, PO Box 106 Forest Pk Branch, Dayton, OH 45405

LdL/Librairie du Liban, Riad Solh Sq. Beirut, Lebanon

LEB/Limited Edition Books, 2121 Sheridan Rd., Evanston, IL 60201

Lem/Lemma Publishing Corp., 509 5th Ave., NY, NY 10017

Lew/Lewis Publishers, Ian Allan Group, Terminal House, Sitepperton, TW 17 8AF England

LHP/Light-house Publications, Vancouver, Canada

LiB/Libreria Britanica, Rio Ganges 64, Mexico 5 D.F. Mexico

Lip/J.B. Lippincott Co., E. Washington Sq., Phila. PA 19105

Lit/Litton Educational Publications, 7625 Empire Dr., Florence, KY 41042

LjP/Little John Publishing Co., Box 123 C., Isabella, MO 65676

LLC/Cornucopia Inst., St. Mary, KY 40063

LIP/Llewellyn Publications, PO Box 3383, St. Paul MN 55165

LnB/Links Books, 33 W. 60th St., NY, NY 10023

Lng/Ling, Dorje, PO Box 1410, San Rafael, CA 94902

Lnt/Lanthorn Press, Peredur School, East Grinstead, Sussex RH19 4NF England

LOG/Leaves of Grass Press, Germantown, PA 19144

Lon/Longman, 19 W. 44th St., NY NY 10036

Low/Peter Lowe, Eurobook, 2-4 Queens Dr., London W3 OHA England

LPC/Lucis Publishing Co., 866 United Nations Plaza, NY, NY 10017

LRP/Lamplighters Roadway Press, 44 Fairview Plaza, Los Gatos, CA 95030

Lss/Larousse & Co., 572 5th Ave., NY, NY 10036

LtA/Littlefield Adams, 8 Adams Dr., Totowa, NJ 07512

Ltu/Liturgical Press, 74 Engle Blvd., Collegeville, MN 56321

LTW/Library of Tibetan Works and Archives, Dharmsala (H.P.) India

LuH/Lund Humphries, 12 Bedford Sq., London WC1 England

Lut/Lutterworth Press, Luke House, Farnham Rd., Guildford, Surrey, England

Luz/Luzac & Co., PO Box 157 46 Great Russell St., London WC1B 3PE England

LyP/Lyrebird Press, 14 Cornwall Gardens, London SW7 4AN England

M&M/Morgan & Morgan Publishers, 145 Palisade St., Dobbs Ferry, NY 10522

Mac/Macoy Publishing Co., PO Box 9825, Lakeside Branch, Richmond, VA 23228

MAM/Mark-Age Metacenter, 327 NE 20th Terr., Miami, FL 33137

MaN/Martinus Nijhoff, PO Box 269, Lage Voorhout 9-11, The Hague, Netherlands

Man/Mandala, PO Box 796, Amherst, MA 01002

MAQ/Muhammad Abdul Quasem, Assoc. Prof. of Islamic Studies, National U of Malaysia, University Rd., Petaling Jaya, Selangor, Malaysia

Mas/Mason's Bookshop, 789 Lexington Ave., NY, NY 10021

Mat/Matagiri, Mt. Tremper, NY 12457

May/Mayflower Books, 4 Upper James St., London W1R 4BP England

MBI/Meher Baba Info., Box 1101, Berkeley, CA 94701

McD/MacDonald & Jane's Publishers, Paulton House, 8 Shepherdess Walk, London N1 7LW England

MCh/Mason Charter, 641 Lexington Ave., NY, NY 10022

McK/David McKay, 750 3rd Ave., NY, NY 10017

McM/MacMillan Co., 866 3rd Ave., NY, NY 10022

MDC/Motivation Development Centre, 115 Harvard S.E., Albuquerque, NM 87106

Meh/Meher Era Publications, Avatar Meher Baba Poona Center, 441/1
Somwar Peth, Poona 11 India
MGB/MacMillian Co., of Gt. Brit., Houndsmills, Basingstoke, Hampshire, RG21 2XS
England
MGH/McGraw-Hill Book Co., Princeton Rd., Highstown, NJ 08520
MiB/Mitchell Beazley, 14-15 Manette St., London W1V 5LB England
MiM/Mille Meditations, Tierra Del Sol CA
MiP/Mineral Perspectives, 8915 N.E. 4th Rd., Miami Shores, FL 33138
MIT/MIT Press, 28 Carleton St., Cambridge, MA 02142
Mll/Frederick Muller, Victoria Works, Edgeware Rd., London NW2 6LE England
MMA/Metropolian Museum of Art, 5th Ave., at 82nd St., NY, NY 10028
Mnj/Manjusri Publishing House, New Delhi, India
MNM/Museum of New Mexico Press, PO Box 2087, Santa Fe, NM 87501
MoB/Motilal Banarsidass, A. Ullah Marga, Jawahar Nagar, Delhi, 110007 India
Moh/Mohan Enterprises PO Box 8334, Rochester, NY 14618
Mor/Wm. Morrow & Co., Wilmor Warehouse, 6 Henderson Dr., W. Caldwell, NJ 07006
Mow/A.R. Mowbray & Co., Saint Thomas House, Becket St., Oxford OX1 1SJ England
MPC/Mayfield Publishing Co., 285 Hamilton Ave., Palo Alto, CA 94301
Mrl/Merlin Press, PO Box 12159 Santa Ana, Ca 92712
MSE/Mountain School for Esoteric Studies, 300 Kenrick St., Newton MA 02158
MTI/Merry Thoughts, 2 Bedford Hills, NY 10507
MtP/Meta Publications, Cupertino CA 95014
MuA/Muhammad Ashraf, Kashmiri Bazar, Lahore, Pakistan
Mud/Mudra, 2940 Seventh St., Berkeley, CA 94710
Muk/K.L. Mukhopadhyay, Calcutta, India
Mul/Multimedia, 100 S. Western Hwy., Blauvelt, NY 10913
MuM/Munshiram Manocharlal, PO Box 5715, 54 Rani Jhansi Rd., New Delhi, India
MUP/Manchester U Press, Oxford Rd., Manchester, M13 9PL England
Mur/John Murray, 50 Albermarle St., London, England W.1

Nag/Nagel Publications, Geneva Switzerland
NAL/New American Library, PO Box 120, Bergenfield, NJ 07621
NAP/New Age Press, 3912 Wilshire Blvd., Los Angeles, CA 90010
Nat/Naturegraph Publishers, PO Box 1075, Happy Camp, CA 96039
NDP/New Directions Publishing, 333 6th Ave., NY, NY 10014
NeH/Nelson-Hall, 325 W. Jackson Blvd., Chicago, IL 60606
NEL/New English Library, Barnards Inn, Holborn, London EC1N 2JR England
NHP/New Horizons Press, Box 1758, Chico, CA 95926
Nil/Nilgiri Press, PO Box 477, Petaluma, CA 94952
Nit/Nitty Gritty Productions, PO Box 5457, Concord CA 94524
NJM/North Jersey Metaphysical Ctr., 1032 Black Oak Ridge Rd., Wayne, NJ 07470
NKB/New Knowledge Books, PO Box 9, Horsham, Sussex RH12 2LB England
NOK/NOK Publishers, 150 5th Ave., NY, NY 10011
Nor/W.W. Norton, & Co., 500 5th Ave., NY, NY 10036
Noy/Noyes Press, Mill Rd. at Grad Ave., Park Ridge, NJ 07656
NPC/Newcastle Publishing Co., PO Box 7589, Van Nuys, CA 91409
NSP/Ninth Sign Publications, M-525, Hoboken, NJ 07030
Nsw/Newsweek Books, 444 Madison Ave., NY, NY 10022
NTE/New Thought Education Society, PO box 69, Akron, OH 44309
NUP/Northwestern U Press, 1735 Benson, Evanston, IL 60201
NUY/N.U. Yoga Trust & Ashrama, Gylling, Denmark
NWC/National War College, Taipei, Taiwan
NwM/Newark Museum, 49 Washington St., Newark, NJ 07101
NYG/New York Graphic, Greenwich, CN 06830
NYP/New York Public Library, NY, NY
NYT/New York Times Book Co., 3 Park Ave., NY, NY 10016
NYU/New York U Press, Washington Sq., NY, NY 10003

Oce/Ocean Books, 17 Shaftesbury Ave., London W1 England
Oco/Octopus Books, 59 Grosvenor St., London W1 England
Oct/Octagon Press, 14 Baker St., London W1M 1DA England
OKT/Order of the Knights Templars of Aquarius, La Maison de Leoville,
St. Ouen, Channel Island
OLL/Orient Longman, Nicol Rd., Ballard Estate, Bombay 400038 India
OmA/Omega Assoc., PO Box 801, Midlothian, IL 60445
Ona/Onaway Publications, 28 Lucky Dr., San Rafael, CA 94904
OpC/Open Court Publishing Co., PO Box 599, La Salle, IL 61301
OPL/Orbis Publishing, 20-22 Bedfordbury, London WC 2N 4BL England
OPr/Oriental Press, Amsterdam
OrB/Oriental Books Reprint Corp., 54, Ram Jhansi Rd., New Delhi, 110055 India
Orb/Orbis Books, Maryknoll, NY 10545
OrC/Orbimetrix Co., PO Box 2252, Canoga Pk., CA 91306
OrP/Oriental Publishers, 1488 Pataudi House, Daryagnj, Delhi 6 India
OSV/Our Sunday Visitor, Noll Plaza, Huntington, IN 46750
OUP/Ohio U Press, Sooth Quadrangle, Athens, OH 45701
Out/Outlet Book Co., 419 Park Ave., S., NY, NY 10016
OvP/Overlook Press, Lewis Hollow Rd., Woodstock, NY 12498
Owe/Peter Owen, 73 Kenway Rd., London SW5 ORE England
Oxf/Oxford U Press, 200 Madison Ave., NY, NY 10016

PaP/Panthean Press, Box 1122, Litchfield, CN 06759
PaR/Para Research, Rockport Whistlestop Mall, Rockport, MA 01966
PaS/Paracelsus Research Soc., PO Box 6006, Sugar House Station,
Salt Lake City, Utah 84106

Pau/Paulist Press, 545 Island Rd., Ramsey, NJ 07446
PAV/Philosophisch-Anthroposophischer Verlag, am Goetheanum
4143 Dornach/Sol., Switzerland
PBD/Popular Book Depot, Lamington Rd., Bombay 7,, India
PBR/Paragon Book Reprint, 14 E. 38th St., NY, NY 10016
Pce/Peace Press, 3828 Willat Ave., Culver City, CA 90230
Pcl/Pentacle Books, 6 Perry Rd., Bristol 1, England
Pdn/Phaidon Press, 5 Cromwell Pl., London SW7 2JL England
Pea/Peach Publishing Co., 1123-3/4 N. Sweetzer Ave., West Hollywood, CA 90069
Pel/Pelham Books, 52 Bedford Sq., London WC1 England
Per/Persephone Press, PO Box 7222, Watertown, MA 02172
PFP/Page-Ficklin Publications, 540 Emerson St., Palo Alto, CA 94301
PhH/Phoenix House, 7453 Melrose Ave., Los Angeles, CA 90046
PhL/Philosophical Library, 15 East 40th St., NY, NY 10016
PHP/Pendle Hill Publications, Wallingford, PA 19086
Php/Henry Phillips Publishing, 519 NE 83rd St., Seattle, WA 98115
Pin/Pinnacle Books, 275 Madison Ave., NY, NY 10016
PjP/Panjandrum Press, 99 Sanchez St., San Francisco, CA 94114
Plo/Philo Press, Postbus 1850, NL 1000, Amsterdam, Holland
Plp/S.G. Phillips, 305 West 86th St., NY, NY 10024
PMP/Parent's Magazine Press, 80 Newbridge Rd., Bergenfield, NJ 07621
PnB/Pan Books, 33 Tothill St., London SW 1 England
PoL/Point Loma Publications, PO Box 9966, San Diego, CA 92109
Pow/Charles T. Powner, PO Box 796, Chicago 90, IL
PPC/Pakistan Philosophical Congress, 873-875/C, Block 2, Pechs, Karachi-29 Pakistan
PPL/Pagurian Press, 10 Whitney Ave., Toronto 5, Canada
PPP/Peter Pauper Press, Mount Vernon, NY
PPr/Popular Prakasham, 35C Tardeo Rd., Bombay 34 WB India
PPu/Punthi Pustak, 34 Mohan Bagan La., Calcutta 4 India
Pra/Prajna Press, PO Box 271, Boulder, CO 80306
PrH/Prentice-Hall, Box 500, Englewood Cliffs, N.J. 07632
Prm/Promontory Press, 95 Madison Ave., NY, NY 10016
Prn/Perennial Books, Pates Manor, Bedfont, Middlesex, England
PrP/Progress Publishers, Moscow, USSR
PRS/Philosophical Research Soc., 3341 Griffith Park Blvd., Los Angeles, CA 90027
PSI/PSI Rhythms, PO Box 1838, Ormond Beach, FL 37074
PSm/Peter Smith, 6 Lexington Ave., Magnolia MA 01930
PSS/Price/Stern/Sloan, 410 North La Cienega Blvd., Los Angeles, CA 90048
PSU/Penn State U., 215 Wagner Bldg., University Park, PA 16802
PTS/Pali Text Society, Broadway House, Reading Rd., Henley-on-Thames
Oxon RG9 1EN, England
PUP/Princeton U Press, Princeton, NJ 08540
Put/G.P. Putnam's Sons, 390 Murray Hill Pkwy, E. Rutherford, NJ 07073

QPr/Quicksilver Productions, Box 702, Ashland, OR 97520
Qtb/Quartet Books, 27 Goodge St., London W1P 1FD England
Qua/Quarto Productions, 323 Castro St., San Francisco, CA 94114
Qur/Bernard Quaritch, 5-8 Lower St. John, Golden Sq., London W1R 4AU England

R&B/Rosenkilde & Bagger, 3, Kron-Prinsens-Gade, Copenhagen, Denmark
RaF/Rajneesh Foundation, Shree Rajneesh Ashram, 17, Koregaon Pk., Poona 1 India
RaH/Random House, 457 Hahn Rd., Westminister, MD 21157
RaP/Ranney Publications, PO Box 270, Mountain Ctr., CA
RaS/Radhasoami Satsang Beas, Punjab, India
RCK/Research Centre of Kabbalah, 200 Park Ave., NY, NY 10017
Rdx/Readex Books, 101 5th Ave., NY, NY 10003
Ree/A.H & A.W. Reed, 182 Wakefield St., Wellington, New Zealand
Reg/Contemporary Books, 180 N. Michigan Ave., Chicago, IL 60601
REr/Ross-Erikson, 223 Via Sevilla, Santa Barbara, CA 93109
RHI/Ram's Head, PO Box 2949, San Francisco, CA 94126
Rhi/Rhinoceros Press, Box 1186, El Cerrito, CA 94530
Rho/Rhodos, Strandgade 36, Copenhagen K, Denmark
RIC/Research Institute of Cosmobiology, PO Box 903, LaCanada, CA 91011
Ric/Franco Maria Ricci Publisher
Ric/Franco Maria Ricci Publisher, Parma, Italy
Riz/Rizzoli, 712 5th Ave., NY, NY 10019
RKP/Routledge, Kegan, Paul, Broadway House, Reading Rd., Henley-on-Thames
Oxon RG9 1EN England
RLK/Research into Lost Knowledge Organization, Common House, 6 Ravenslea Rd.
London SW12 8SB England
RMN/Rand McNally, PO Box 7600, Chicago, IL 60680
Ron/George Ronald Publisher, 46 High St., Kidlington, Oxford OX5 2DN England
ROS/R.O.S.A., 1317 Monterey, Monrovia, CA 91016
Ros/Rosicrucian Fellowship, Oceanside, CA 92054
Roy/Roy Publishing House, 197 A Kasba Rd., Calcutta 42 India
RPB/Ratna Pustak Bhandar, Kathmandu, Nepal
RPP/Real People Press, Box F, Moab, Utah 84532
RPr/Rekha Prakashan, 16 Daryaganj, Delhi 110006 India
RSP/Rudolf Steiner Press 35 Park Rd., London NW1 6XT England
Rud/Dane Rudhyar, Leyla Rael, 3635 Lupine Ave., Palo Alto, CA 94303
Rug/Dieter Ruggenberg Booksellers, Postfach 13 07 29, D-56
Wuppertal 1, Western Germany
Ruk/Ruka Publications, PO Box 1072, Santa Cruz, CA 95060
RuP/Running Press, 38 S. 19th St., Phila., PA 19103

RuS/Ruhani Satsang, Sawan Ashram, Delhi 7 India
Rus/Rusoff Books, 1302 SE 4th St , Minn., MN 55414
RVC/Ramakrishna-Vivekananda Ctr., 17 E. 94th St., NY, NY 10028
RVM/Ramakrishna Vedanta Math, 19-B Raja Rajkrishna St., Calcutta, India

S&B/Science & Behavior Books, PO Box A.J., Cupertino, CA 95014
S&D/Stein & Day, Scarborough House, Briarcliff Manor, NY 10510
S&J/Sidgwick & Jackson, 1 Tavistock Chambers, Bloomsbury Way
    London WC1A 2SG England
S&S/Simon & Schuster, 1230 Ave., of the Americas, NY, NY 10020
S&W/Sheed & Ward, 6 Blenheim St., London W1Y OSA England
SAA/Sri Aurobindo Ashram Trust, Pondicherry, India
SAB/Sino-American Buddhist Assoc., 1731 15th St., San Francisco, CA 94103
Sab/Sabian Publishing, Stanwood, WA 98292
Sad/Sadhana Press, Box 35, S. Otselic, NY, 13155
Sag/Sagar Publications, 18 Indian Oil Bhawan, New Janpath Market, New Delhi, India
SAM/Sheed, Andrews & McMeel, 6700 Squibb Rd., Mission, KS 66202
SBC/Steiner Book Centre, 151 Carisbrooke Crescent, N. Vancouver
    BC V7N 2S2 Canada
SBL/Sphere Books, 30/32 Gray's Inn Rod, London WC1X 8JL, England
ScB/Schocken Books, 200 Madison Ave., NY, NY 10016
Sch/Scherman, 68/6 Kidwai Nagar, Extension-1, Kanpur, India
SCK/Society for Promoting Christian Knowlege, Holy Trinity Church, Marylebone Rd.
    London NWI 4DU England
Scp/Scorpion Publications, PO Box 1, London WC2E England
Scr/Charles Scribners, 597 5th Ave., NY, NY 10017
Sdl/Bridging Books, PO Box 559, Ventura, CA 93001
Sea/Seabury Press, 815 2nd Ave., NY, NY 10017
See/Seed Ctr., PO Box 591, Palo Alto, CA 94302
Sem/Seema Publications, C-3/19, R.P. Bagh, Delhi 110007 India
SFB/San Francisco Book Co., San Francisco, CA
SGA/Shree Gurudev Ashram, Ganeshpuri, India
SGB/St. George Book Service, PO Box 225, Spring Valley, NY, 10977
SHP/Sepher-Hermon Press, 175 5th Ave., NY, NY
ShP/Shambhala, PO Box 271, Boulder CO 80302
Shr/Sheriar Press, PO Box 1023, N. Myrtle Beach, SC 29582
ShS/Shanti Sadan, 29 Chepstow Villas, London W11 England
ShW/Shrine of Wisdom, Fintry, Brook, Godalming, Surrey, England
SIU/Southern Illinois Press, PO Box 3697, Carbondale, IL 62901
SJU/St. John's U Press, Grand Central & Utopia Pkwys, Jamaica, NY 11432
Ski/Charles Skilton Pub. Group, 90 Broadway, London SW19 England
Sko/Skorba Publishers, 3500 Ash St., Vancouver, BC, Canada
SKP/Sawan Kirpal Publications, Rte. 1, Box 135, Afton, VA 22920
SLB/Science of Life Books, 4-12 Tattersall La., Melbourne, Victoria 3000, Australia
SIP/Sheldon Press, Marylebone Rd., London NW1 4DU England
SLS/Spoken Language Services, PO Box 783, Ithaca, NY 14850
SMP/Saint Martin's Press, 175 5th Ave., NY, NY 10010
Smy/Colin Smythe, PO Box 6, Gerrards Cross, Buckinghamshire SL9 7AE England
SnB/Sun Publishing, PO Box 4383, Albuquerque, NM 87106
Snd/Sandollar Press, 1930 De La Vina, Santa Barbara, CA 93101
SNY/State U of New York Press, 99 Washington Ave., Albany, NY 12210
Sof/Soft Press, 1050 Saint David St., Victoria BC Canada V8S 4Y8
Sol/Solunar Research Publications, PO Box 1073, Station A, Bay City, MI 48706
Som/Somaiya Publications, 172 Naigaum Cross Rd., Bombay 14 India
SOP/Sufi Order Publications, PO Box 396, New Lebanon, New York, 12125
Sou/Souvenir Press, 43 Great Russell St., London W1N 8HP England
SPC/Sufi Publishing, 53 West Ham La., London E15 4PH England
Spe/Neville Spearman, Priory Gate, 57 Friars St., Sudbury, Suffolk, England
SPL/Search Press/Burns & Oates, 2-10 Jerden Pl., London SW6 5PT England
Spr/Spring Publishers, Postfacit 190, 8024 Zurich, Switzerland
Spx/Sphinxiad, PO Box 11888, Newington, Ct. 06111
SRe/Sufism Reoriented, 1300 Boulevard Way, Walnut Creek, CA 94595
SRF/Self Realization Fellowship, 3880 San Rafael Ave., Los Angeles, CA 90065
SRM/Sri Ramakrishna Math, Mylapore, Madras, India
SrR/Sri Rama Foundation, PO Box 1569, Santa Cruz, CA 95060
SRT/Sri Ramanasramam Tiruvaunamalai, S. India
SSA/Shree Shree Anandamayee Sangha, Bhadaini, Varanasi, India
SSF/Second Society Foundation, 333 N. Michigan Ave., Chicago, IL 60601
SSk/South Sky Book Co., 107-115 Hennessy Rd., Hong Kong
SSS/Sai Baba Society, PO Box 278, Tustin, CA 92680
StA/Star Astrology, 449 McCarty, San Antonio, TX 78216
Sta/Claude Stark, PO Box 431, West Dennis, Cape Cod, MA 02670
Stk/Stackpole, Cameron & Kelker Sts., Harrisburg, PA 17105
Stl/Stelle Group, PO Box 5900, Chicago, IL 60680
Sto/Stonehill Publishing, 38 S. 57th St., NY, NY 10022
Stu/Lyle Stuart, 120 Enterprise Ave., Secaucus, NJ 07094
Stt/Seattle Book Co., PO Box 9254, Seattle, WA 98109
SUB/Scandinavian U Books, c/o Columbia U Press, 562 W., 113 St., NY, NY 10025
Suf/Sufi Order, 23 Rue de la Tuilerie, Suresnes 92/Paris, France
SUP/Stanford U Press, Stanford, CA 94305
Svt/Savitria Press, AUM, 2405 Ruscombe La.,Baltimore, Md. 21209
Swa/Swallow Press, 811 W. Junior Terr., Chicago, IL 60613
Swb/Strawberry Hill Press, 616 44th Ave., San Francisco, CA 94121
Swe/Swedenborg Foundation, 139 E. 23rd St., NY, NY 10010

SWP/Shepheard-Walwyn Publishers, 60 Fleet St., London EC4Y IJU England
SYD/S.Y.D.A. Box 11071, Oakland, CA 94611
Sym/Symbols & Signs, PO Box 4536, N. Hollywood, CA 91607

T&H/Thames & Hudson, 44 Clockhouse Rd., Farnborough, Hampshire, England
TAB/Theatre Arts Books, 333 6th Ave., NY, NY 10014
Tap/Taplinger Publishing Co., 200 Park Ave., S., NY, NY 10003
Tar/J.P. Tarcher, 9110 Sunset Blvd., Los Angeles, CA 90069
Tay/Maxine Taylor, 4 Independence Pl., NW, Atlanta, GA 30318
TBH/Book House, PO Box 734, Lahore, Pakistan
TBH/The Book House, PO Box 734, Lahore, Pakistan
TCH/Teacher's College Press, 1234 Amsterdam Ave., NY, NY 10027
TCP/Two Continents Pub. Group, 30 E. 42nd St., NY, NY 10017
Tdm/Tandem, 14 Gloucester Rd., London SW7 England
ThC/Theosophy Co., 245 W. 33rd St., Los Angeles, CA 90007
Tho/Charles C. Thomas, Publishers, 301-327 E. Lawrence Ave., Springfield, IL 62703
ThU/Theosophical U Press, PO Box Bin C, Pasadena, CA 91109
Tie/Bill Tierney, 4282 Roswell Rd., NW, Atlanta, GA 30342
TIF/Turtle Island Foundation, 2907 Bush St., San Francisco, CA. 94115
TLB/Time-Life Books, Rockefeller Plaza, NY, NY 10020
Tnt/Alec Tiranti, 72 Charlotte St., London W1 England
Tok/Tokuma Shoten Publishing, 10-1 Shimbashi 4-chome, Minato-ku, Tokyo 105 Japan
Tom/Tomorrow Publications, Denison La., 296 Vauxhall Bridge Rd., London SW1 England
Tpg/Templegate Publishers, PO Box 963, Springfield, IL 62705
TPH/Theosophical Publishing House, PO Box 270, Wheaton, IL 60187
TPL/Thorsons Publishers, Denington Estate, Wellingborough, Northants NN8 2RQ England
TrA/Transatlantic Arts, North Village Green, Levittown, NY 11756
Tre/Tree Books, PO Box 9005, Berkeley, CA 94709
Tri/Triune Books, London England
TrS/Tradional Studies Press, Box 984, Adelaide St. PO, Toronto M5C 2KA Canada
TSC/Taraporevala Sons, 210 Dr. Dadabhai Naoroji Rd., Bombay, India
TTC/T&T Clark's, 38 George St, Edinburgh EH2 2LQ Scotland
Tur/Turnstone Books, 37 Upper Addison Gardens, London W14 8AJ England
Tut/Charles E. Tuttle Co., Rutland, VT 05701

UAP/U of Alabama Press, Drawer 2877, University, AL 35486
UAr/U of Arizona, Box 3398, Tucson, AZ 85722
UCa/U of California Press, 2223 Fulton St., Berkeley, CA 94720
UCh/U of Chicago Press, 5801 S. Ellis Ave., Chicago, Illinois 60637
Ucr/Unicorn Press, PO Box 3307, Greensboro, NC 27402
UHa/U of Hawaii, 2840 Kolowalu St., Honolulu, HI 96822
UMa/U of Massachusetts Press, Amherst, MA
UMP/U of Michigan Press, 615 East University, Ann Arbor, MI 48106
UnB/University Books, New Hyde Park, NY
UNC/University of N. Carolina Press, Chapel Hill, NC 27514
UND/U of Notre Dame Press, Notre Dame, IN 46556
Ung/Frederick Ungar Publishing, 250 Park Ave., S., NY, NY 10003
Uni/Universe Books, 381 4th Ave., NY, NY 10016
UNM/U of New Mexico Press, Albuquerque, NM 87131
UNP/U of Nebraska Press, 901 N. 17th St., Lincoln, NE 68508
UnP/Unity Press, PO Box 1037, Santa Cruz, CA 95061
UOk/U of Oklahoma Press, 1005 Asp Ave., Norman, OK 73019
UPa/University of Penna. Press, 3933 Walnut St., Phila., PA 19174
UPV/University Press of Virginia, PO Box 3608, Charlottesville, VA 22903
UrB/Urantia Brotherhood, 533 Diversey Pkwy, Chicago, IL 60614
UrP/Uranian Publications, PO Box 114, Franksville, WI 53126
USC/Unity School of Christianity, Unity Village, MO 64063
USP/U of Science & Philosophy, Swannanoa, Waynesboro, VA 22980
UTk/U of Tokyo Press, Tokyo, Japan
UTo/U of Toronto Press, 33 East Tupper St., Buffalo, NY 14203
UTp/University of the Trees Press, Box 644, Boulder Creek, CA 95006
UTx/U of Texas Press, Box 7819, Austin, Texas 78712
UWa/U of Washington Press, Seattle, WA 98105

Vaj/Vajradhatu, 1345 Spruce St., Boulder, CO 80302
Val/Valhalla Paperbacks, 1331 21st St., NW, Wash., DC 20036
Van/Vanguard Press, 424 Madison Ave., NY, NY 10017
VdC/Vedanta Ctr., 130 Beechwood St., Cohasset, MA 02025
VdP/Vedanta Press, 1946 Vedanta Pl., Hollywood, CA 90068
Vik/Viking Penguin, 625 Madison Ave., NY, NY 10022
Vjr/Vajrapani Institute for Wisdom Culture, PO Box 295, Santa Monica, CA 90406
VNR/Van Nostrand Reinhold, 300 Pike St., Cincinnati, OH 45202
VPH/Vikas Publishing House, 5 Daryaganj, Ansari Rd., Delhi, 6 India
VPT/Vimal Prakashan Trust, Ahmedabad 6, India
Vul/Vulcan Books, 12722 Lake City Way, Seattle, WA 98125
VVR/Vishveshvaranand Vedic Research Institute, PO Sadhu Ashram, Hoshiarpur, India

Wad/Wadsworth Publishing, Belmont, CA 94002
Wal/Waldorf Institute/Adelphi University, Garden City, NY 11530
Wal/Walker & Co., 720 5th Ave., NY, NY 10019
WAO/We Are One, PO Box 1130, Plattsburgh, NY 12901
WAP/Neale Watson Academic Publications, 156 5th Ave., NY, NY 10010
War/Warner Paperback Library, 75 Rockefeller Plaza, NY, NY 10019
Wat/Watkins Publishing, Bridge St., Dulverton Somerset, TA22 9HJ England

WCS/William Collins & Sons, 14 St., James Pl., London SW1 A1PS England
WdF/Word Foundation, PO Box 769, Forest Hills, NY 11375
Wdf/Weidenfeld Publishers, 11 St. John's Hill, London SW11 England
Wdh/Windhorse Publications, Aryatara, 3 Plough La., Purley, Surrey CR2 3QB England
Wdw/Wildwood House, 29 King St., London WC2E 8JD England
Wea/Weatherhill, 149 Madison Ave., NY, NY 10016
Wei/Samuel Weiser, 625 Broadway, NY, NY 10012
Wes/Westminister Press, Witherspoon Bldg. Phila., PA 19107
WET/White Eagle Publishing Trust, Liss, Hampshire, England
WHA/W.H. Allen & Co., 44 Hill St., London W1X 8LB, England
WHP/Winged Heart Press, Sufi House, 6 Parkwood Rd., Wimbeldon, London SW 19 England
WIF/World of Islam Festival Publishing, 85 Cromwell Rd., London SW7 5BW England
Wil/Wilshire Book Co., 12015 Sherman Rd., N. Hollywood, CA 91605
Win/Wingbow Press, Berkeley, CA
Wiz/Wizards Bookshelf, Box 6600, San Diego, CA 92106
WkC/Work of the Chariot, PO Box 2226, Hollywood, CA 90028
WLK/Mr. R. Wilkinson, Foresters Cottage, Highgate, Forest Row, Sussex, England
Wll/Willing Publishing, PO Box 51, San Gabriel, CA
Wob/Woburn Press, Gainsborough House, 11 Gainsborough Rd., Leytonstone, London 211 1HT England
WoP/Woodbridge Press, PO Box 6189, Santa Barbara, CA 93111

WPC/Workman Publishing, 231 E. 51st St., New York, NY 10022
Wrn/Frederick Warne, 101 5th Ave., NY, NY 10003
WRP/Writers & Readers Publishing Cooperative, 9-19 Rupert St., London W1 England
WrW/Writers Workshop, 162/92 Lake Gardens, Calcutta 45, India
WSU/Washington State Univ. Press, Pullman, WA 99163
Wts/Franklin Watts, 730 5th Ave., NY, NY 10019
WUP/Wesleyan U Press, 331 East Main St., Middletown, CN 06457
WUS/World Unity & Service, PO Box 41338, Craighall, Johannesburg, 2024 Republic of South Africa
Wyd/Peter H. Wyden, 750 3rd Ave., NY, NY 10017
Wyn/Wyndham Publications, 123 King St., London W6 9JG England

YeP/Yesod Publishers, 75 Prospect Park W., Brooklyn, N.Y. 11215
YPH/Y.M.C.A Publishing House, 5 Russell St., Calcutta, India
YPS/Yoga Publication Society, PO Box 8885, Jacksonville, FL 32211
YUP/Yale U Press, 92 A Yale St., New Haven, CN 06520

ZCe/Zen Center, 300 Page St., San Francisco, CA 94102
Zen/Zen Center of Los Angeles, 927 S. Normandie Ave., Los Angeles, CA 90006
ZMS/Zen Mission Society, Shasta Abbey, Mt. Shasta, CA 96067
Zol/Zollikofer & Co., St. Gall, Switzerland

Acknowledgements

Among the many people who helped with this book, I would like particularly to thank the following: Cece Rantz and Rachel Reynolds, the typesetters; Diane Baker and Julie Upton, the proofreaders; Kathy O'Neill, Joan Stevenson, and Paulis Waber, the paste-up artists; Barbara Shear, the designer; and Wayne Hagood, the compiler of the author index. Special thanks to my husband Ollie, who contributed an endless amount of psychic, spiritual, and occasionally practical support.

I would also like to thank the authors and publishers of the following books (listed in the order in which they appear in **Inner Development**) from which I have taken excerpts and condensed material to use as introductions to chapters:

African Religions and Philosophy by John Mbiti, copyright by the author and published by Doubleday and Company; **Maps of Consciousness** by Ralph Metzner, copyright by the author and published by Macmillan Publishing Company, Inc.; **John Dee** by Peter French, copyright by the author and published by Routledge Kegan Paul, Ltd. **Teachings from the American Earth** by Dennis and Barbara Tedlock, copyright by the authors and published by W.W. Norton and Co.; **The Ancient Sun Kingdoms of the Americas** by Victor von Hagen, copyright by the author and published by Thames & Hudson, Ltd.; **The Secret Country** by Janet and Colin Bord, copyright by the authors and published by Granada Publishers, Ltd.; **Ancient Egypt** by Lionel Casson, copyright and published by Time-Life Books; **Classical Greece** by C.M. Bowra, copyright and published by Time-Life Books; **The Face of the Ancient Orient** by Sabatino Moscati, copyright by the author and published by Doubleday and Company; **A Handbook for the Humanistic Astrologer** by Michael Meyer, copyright by the author and published by Doubleday and Company; **The Cosmic Frontiers of General Relativity** by William J. Kaufmann III, copyright by the author and published by Little Brown, Inc.; **The Bible Designed to be Read as Living Literature** by Ernest Bates, copyright by the author and published by Simon & Schuster, Inc.; **Biorhythm** by Bernard Gittleson, copyright by the author and published by Arco Books; **Three Ways of Asian Wisdom** by Nancy Wilson Ross, copyright by the author and published by Simon and Schuster; **The Tantric Mysticism of Tibet** by John Blofeld, copyright by the author and published by Allen & Unwin Ltd.; **The World of Zen** by Nancy Wilson Ross, copyright by the author and published by Random House, Inc. **The Uses of Enchantement** by Bruno Bettelheim, copyright by the author and published by Random House, Inc.; **Taoist Tales** by Raymond Van Over, copyright by the author and published by New American Library, Inc.; **Sacred Traditions and Present Need** by Jacob Needleman and Dennis Lewis, copyright by the authors and published by Viking-Penguin, Inc.; **A Sense of the Cosmos** by Jacob Needleman, copyright by the author and published by Doubleday and Company; **Awakening, Ways to Psycho-Spiritual Growth** by C. William Henderson, copyright by the author and

published by Prentice-Hall, Inc.; **The Dream Game** by Ann Faraday, copyright by the author and published by Harper & Row, Inc.; **Human Values in the Classroom** by Robert and Isabel Hawley, copyright by the authors and published by Hart Publishers, Inc.; **Interpretation of Fairy Tales** by Marie-Louise von Franz, copyright by the author and published by Spring Publications; **The Pattern of the Past** by Guy Underwood, copyright by the author and published by Sphere Books, Ltd.; **The Quest of the Holy Grail** by P.M. Matarasso, copyright by the author and published by Viking-Penguin, Inc.; **The Psychology of Handwriting** by Nadya Olyanova, copyright by the author and published by Wilshire Books; **Transpersonal Psychologies** by Charles Tart, copyright and published by Harper & Row, Inc.; **Toward a Psychology of Being** by Abraham Maslow, copyright by the author and published by Litton Educational Publishers; **Hinduism** by Louis Renou, copyright by the author and published by George Braziller, Inc.; **TNT--The Power Within You** by Claude Bristol and Harold Sherman, copyright by the authors and published by Prentice-Hall, Inc.; **Islam and the Arab World** edited by Bernard Lewis, copyright and published by Thames & Hudson, Ltd.; **Kabbalah: The Way of the Jewish Mystic** by Perle Epstein, copyright by the author and published by Doubleday and Company; **C.G. Jung, His Myth in Our Time** by Marie-Louise von Franz, copyright and published by the C.G. Jung Institute; **Voluntary Controls** by Jack Schwarz, copyright by the author and published by E.P. Dutton and Co., Inc.; **Sound and Symbol** by Victor Zuckerkandl, copyright by the author and published by Princeton University Press; **Mysticism** by F.C. Happold, copyright by the author and published by Penguin Books, Ltd.; **Myths of the World** by Padraic Colum, copyright by the author and published by Grosset and Dunlap, Inc.; **It's All in Your Numbers** by Kathleen Roquemore, copyright by the author and published by Harper & Row, Inc.; **Journeys Out of the Body** by Robert Monroe, copyright by the author and published by Doubleday and Company; **The Art of Hand Analysis** by Mir Bashir, copyright by the author and published by Frederick Muller, Ltd.; **Supersenses** by Charles Panati, copyright by the author and published by The New York Times Book Company; **Reincarnation, Key to Immortality** by Marcia Moore and Mark Douglas, copyright by the author and published by Arcane Books; **The Portable Renaissance Reader** by James Bruce Ross and Mary Martin McLaughlin, copyright and published by Viking-Penguin, Inc.; **The Betty Book** by Stewart Edward White, copyright by the author and published by E.P. Dutton and Co., Inc.; **The Secret Doctrine of the Rosicrucians** by Magnus Incognito, copyright and published by the Yogi Publication Society; **Sacred Art in East and West** by Titus Burckhardt, copyright by the author and published by Perennial Books, Ltd.; **The Secrets of the Ancient Geometry** by Tons Brunes, copyright by the author and published by Rhodos Publishers; **A Scientist of the Invisible** by A.P. Shepherd, copyright by the author and published by Hodder and Stoughton, Ltd.; **Tantra, the Indian Cult of Ecstasy** by Philip Rawson, copyright by the author and published by Thames & Hudson, Ltd.; **The Mystical Tower of the Tarot** by John Blakeley, copyright by the author and published by Watkins Publishers, Ltd.; **A Textbook of Theosophy** by C.W. Leadbeater, copyright and published by Theosophical Publishing House; **Ufology** by James McCampbell, copyright by the author and published by Celestial Arts Publishing Company; and finally, **The Way of All Women** by M. Esther Harding, copyright by the author and published by Harper & Row, Inc.

The Illustrations used in **Inner Development** are from the following sources:

Page 9, **The African Genius** by Basil Davidson; 11, **The Rain God's Daughter** by Amabel Williams-Ellis; 14, **Alchemy** by Titus Burckhardt; 18, **Reason, Experiment & Mysticism** by M.L. Bonelli and William Shea; 22,27, **Authentic Indian Designs** edited by Maria Naylor; 24, **Many Smokes, Many Moons** by Jamake Highwater; 32,39,41,42, **The Soul of Ancient Mexico** by Edmond Szekely; 36, **Ancient America** by Edmond Szekely; 45, **Glastonbury** edited by Anthony Roberts; 48, **Celtic Art** by George Bain; 53, **Technology in the Ancient World** by Henry Hodges; 55, **Atlantis, Mother of Empires** by Robert Stacy-Judd; 57, **The Atlas of Early Man** by Jacquetta Hawkes; 61,63, 67, **Osiris and the Egyptian Resurrection** by E.A. Wallis Budge; 70, **Everyday Life in Ancient Egypt** by Jon M. White; 72,506,512, **The Children's Homer** by Padraic Colum; 80, **Pythagoras** by Thomas Stanley; 86,88, **The Essene Book of Asha** by Edmond Szekely; 88, **Amulets and Superstitions** by E.A. Wallis Budge; 91, **The Neolithic of the Near East** by James Mellart; 98,100,102,110,113,125,126,530,532, **The Coffee Table Book of Astrology** by John Lynch; 106, **Astrology** by Louis McNeice; 119, 134, **Atlas of the Planets** by Vincent de Callatay and Audouin Dollfus; 124, **Astrology, Sense or Nonsense** by Roy Gallant; 130,133, **Watchers of the Stars** by Patrick Moore; 169,176,178, **The Cult of Tara** by Stephen Beyer; 183, **The Seven Lucky Gods of Japan** by Reiko Chiba; 185, **Zen Keys** by Thich Nhat Hanh; 188, **Nihongi** by W.G. Ashton; 191, **The Ten Foot Square Hut** by A.L. Sadler; 193, **The Floating World in Japanese Fiction** by Howard Hibbitt; 196,199, **Mudra** by Chogyam Trungpa; 201, **The Empty Mirror** by JanWillem ven de Wetering; 206, **Jataka Tales** by Nancy De Roin and Ellen Lanyon; 208, **Jack and the Beanstalk and Cinderella** by Jan Pienkowski; 210, **Harold and the Purple Crayon** by Crockett Johnson; 212, **Little Owl** by JanWillem van de Wetering; 13, **The Juniper Tree** translated by Lore Segal; 216,237, **Outline of Chinese Symbolism and Art Motives** by C.A.S. Williams; 221,234, **The Dream of the Red Chamber** by Hyng Low Meng; 222, **The Flying Horses** by Jo Marton and Robert Gittings; 224, **Dear Monkey** by Alison Waley; 228, **The I Ching and Mankind** by Diana Hook; **Lao Tzu** by John C.H. Wu and Paul K.T. Sih; 232, **The Mind of China** by Ben-Ami Scharfstein; 233, **The Grand Titration** by Joseph Needham; 244,258, **The Dore Bible Illustrations;** 246, **St. Francis of Assisi** by Thomas of Celano; 250, **Stars of the Bible** by E.W. Matthews; 255, **What Is Contemplation** by Thomas Merton; 284,460, **Maps of Consciousness** by Ralph Metzner; 300,324, **An Encyclopedia of Fairies** by Katherine Briggs; 303,316, **Supertot** by Jean Mrazollo; 309, **Child's Play** by Lynda Madaras; 312, **Great Perpetual Learning Machine** by Jim Blake and Barbara Ernst; 316, **The Little Prince** by Antoine de St. Exupery; 322, **Hansel and Gretel** by Jan Pienkowski; 322, **Russian Fairy Tales** by Afanas'ev Aleksandr; 323, **The Touchstone**by Robert Louis Stevenson; 326, **The Story of Rama and Sita** by Joanna Troughton; 328, **The Reward Worth Having** by Jay Williams and Mercer Meyer; 329, **East of the Sun and West of the Moon** by Kay Nielsen; **Abel's Island** by William Steig; 340, **The Story of King Arthur and His Knights** by Howard Pyle; 333, **The Arthur Rackham Fairy Book;** 336, **Cathedral** by David Macauley; 341, **Parsival or a Knight's Tale** by Richard Monaco; 348, **The Enneagramma of the Man of Unity** by Irmis Popoff; 365, **A Spiritual Psychology and Alchemy** by C.G. Jung; 379,385, **The Mahabharata** by R.K. Narayan; 382,387 **In Praise of Krishna** by Edward Dimock; 392, **Quest for Sita** by Maurice Collis; 413,438, **Gulistan, Tales of Ancient Persia** by Karl Thylmann; 416,429,441, **Arabian Nights Entertainment** by Andrew Lang; 423, **The Formation of Islamic Art** by OLeg Grabar; 432, **The Last Barrier** by Reshad Field; 443, **The Arabian Nights** by E. Dixon; 448, **A Kabbalah for the Modern World** by Migene Gonzalez-Wippler; 452, **The Way of the Kabbalah** by Z'ev ben Shimon Halevi; 457, **Hebrew Alphabets** by Rueben Leaf; 467, **Gods and Heroes** by Gustav Schwab; **Psychology and Alchemy** by C.G. Jung; 479, **Mudra** by E. Dale Saunders; 486, **The Spiritual Diary** by Douglas Baker; 489, **William Blake** by Caroline Keay; 492, **The Magic of Findhorn** by Paul Hawken; **The Phoenix** by Manly P. Hall; 497, **The Gospel of Relativity** by Walter Starcke; 501, **Swedenborg's Journal of Dreams;** 509, **The Children's Odin** by Padraic Colum; 510, **Dictionary of Mythology** by Bergen Evans; 514, **Mythology** by Edith Hamilton; 517, **Tragedy of the Norse Gods** by Ruth Pitt; 519, Myths of the World by Padraic Colum; 532, **Psi Search** by Norma Bowles and Fran Hynds; 575,577, **The Dome** by Smith; 584, **The Art of the Dance** by Isadora Duncan; 585, **Henry Evans Botanical Prints;** 591, **The Soul of Ancient Mexico** by Edmond Szekely; 592, **The Death of the New World** by Edmond Szekely; 598,601,602, **A Complete Guide to the Tarot** by Eden Gray; 599,600, **The Pictorial Key to the Tarot** by A.E. Waite; 607, **The Web of the Universe** by E.L. Gardner; 612, **Through Death to Rebirth** by James Perkins; 623, **The Song of Songs** by Robert Graves.

Final thanks to Penguin Books Ltd. for supplying us with the British sources of books in **Inner Development.**

Author's Index

Diaz del Castillo, Bernal 33
Dick, William 533
Dickinson, William 323
Digby, Adrian 34
Dilard, Annie 491
Dillon, John 73
Dimock, Edward 376,381
Dimock, George 76,516
Dimont, Max 448
Diner, Helen 624
Dionysius the Areopagite 244
Ditfurth, Moimar von 132
Divina 492
Diwakar, R R 389
Dixon, E 414
Doane, Doris Chase 98-99, 125, 598
Dobbs, Betty 17
Doberer, Kurt 17
Dobson, W A C H 232
Dobyns, Zipporah 99,124
Dodds, E R 73
Dods, Marcus 240
Dodson, Betty 624
Dodson, Carolyn 99
Dodson, Fitzhugh 308
Dogen 183
Doi, A Rahman 419,422,437
Doi, Takeo 184
Dollfus, Audouin 131
Donadoni, Sergio 63,568
Donaldson, James 257
Donat, Emma 99,124
Donath, Dorothy 152
Donington, Robert 461,482
Donkin, William 431
Donnelly, Ignatius 52
Donnelly, Morwenna 373
Dore, Gustave 142,243
Doria, Charles 87,508
Dorson, Richard 189,323
Dottin, Georges 46
Doty, William 508
Douglas, Alfred 228,533,598
Douglas, Mark 110,548,551
Douglas, Mary 510
Douglas, Nik 170-171,558
Dowman, Keith 171
Downing, George 474
Dowrick, Stephanie 73,508
Dowson, John 376,508
Doyle, Arthur Conan 324
Drake, W Raymond 34,54-55,73,87
Dresner, Samuel 448
Driessens, Georges 171
Droiton, Etienne 87
Drummond, Richard 152
Drury, Allen 63
Duce, Ivy 431
Duchesne-Guillemin, J 87
Dudley, Geoffrey 299
Duff, Maggie 208
Dumezil, Georges 404,508
Dumont, Theron 410,474
Dumoulin, Heinrich 152,184
Duncan, Malcolm 336
Dunn, C J 187
Dunn, Charles 184
Dunn, Judy 308
Duran, Diego 34
Durckheim, Karlfried 184,474,491
Durdin-Robertson, Lawrence 87,508
Dutt, Nalinaksha 152
Dutt, Romesh 392
Dutt, Sukumar 152
Duus, Peter 184
Duz, M 99
Dvorkes, Joshua 446
Dwivedi, R C 376
Dyer, Colin 336

Eager, Edward 323
Earhart, H Byron 184
Eastcott, Michael 99,474,606

Eastman, Charles 23
Easton, Stewart 582
Eastwick, Edward 440
Easwaran, Eknath 376,378,400,474
    541
Eaton, Evelyn 23
Eaton, Richard 419
Eberhard, Wolfram 220,323
Eberle, Luke 244
Ebertin, Elsbeth 99
Ebertin, Reinhold 96,97
Ebon, Martin 479,616
Eckhart, Meister 244
Eddington, Arthur 132
Edge, Henry 610
Edgerton, Franklin 152,376,378,394
Edinger, Edward 461
Edmonds, Simeon 533
Edmunds, Francis 589
Edmunds, H Tudor 533
Edwards, A Hart 440
Edwards, Alexis 492
Edwards, I E S 63,69,87
Edwards, Paul 518
Edwards, Tilden 244
Eells, Charles 239
Effendi, Shoghi 139
Efros, Israel 448
Egudu, Romanus 11
Ehrenreich, Barbara 624
Ehrenwald, Jan 533
Eido Shimano Roshi 184
Einstein, Albert 132
Ekvall, Robert 171
El-Said, Issam 419,576
Elahi, Maqbool 419
Elchaninov, Alexander 245
Elder, E Rozanne 245
Elenbaas, Virginia 99
Eliade, Mircea 265-266,376,388,508-
    509
Elias, E A 415
Elias, Edward 415
Elias, J 308
Eliot, Alexander 509
Eliot, Charles 184,376
Elixir 492
Elliot, Geraldine 11,323
Elliott, Aubrey 11
Elliott, R W V 55
Ellis, A B 11
Ellmann, Richard 502
Ellwood, Robert 266
Elsnau, Mary 99
Elvin, Mark 226
Elwell-Sutton, L P 435
Embree, Ainslie 264,376
Emenbegger, Robert 616
Emerson, Ralph Waldo 491
Emery, Stewart 289
Emmerick, R E 152
Enciso, Jorge 34,568
Engel, Frederic 34
Engelbrektson, June 132
Englebert, Omer 245
English, Deirdre 624
English, Jane 224,230
Enoch 142
Enomiya-Lassalle, H M 184
Eogan, George 47
Epictetus 491
Epstein, Isidore 448
Epstein, Perle 266,445,448
Epton, Nina 580
Erb, Peter 241
Erdman, David 488
Erodes, Richard 23-24,323
Erlewine, Margaret 125
Erlewine, Michael 100,124-125
Erlewine, Stephen 100
Erman, Adolf 63
Ernst, Barbara 303
Ernst, Ken 308,368
Eschenbach, Wolfram von 340

Eshelman, James 117
Esin, Emel 419
Espenshade, Edward 125
Essick, Robert 488
Esslemont, J E 139
Esterson, A 362
Ettinghausen, Richard 419,568
Evans, Bergen 509
Evans, Colin 100
Evans, David 132
Evans, John 338
Evans, Richard 361,461
Evans, Sebastian 340
Evans-Wentz, W Y 46,171,174,324,461
Evelyn-White, H G 512
Everard, Dr. 64
Evslin, Bernard 509,513

Faber, Adele 309
Fabia, Madame 296
Fabricius, Johannes 17
Fadiman, James 287,311,356
Fagan, Brian 34,55,63
Fagan, Cyril 117
Fagan, Joen 357
Fahy, Benen 245
Fairservis, Walter 376
Fairweather, William 245
Fakhry, Ahmed 63
Falcon, Hal 344
Falk, Ruth 624
Fanning, A E 133
Fantini, Mario 309
Faraday, Ann 297,299
Farah, Caesar 419
Farb, Peter 23
Faris, Nabih Amin 420
Farmer, Penelope 509
Farrington, Ian 40
Faruqi, Burhan 419
Faruqi, Ismail 266
Farzan, Massud 419,426
Fast, Howard 184,474
Fatemi, Faramarsz 426
Fatemi, Fariborz 426
Fatemi, Nastrollah 426
Faulkner, R O 63
Fausset, Hugh 267,491
Fawdry, Marguerite 226
Feder, Norman 23,568
Fedotov, G P 245
Feibleman, James 73,267
Feild, Reshad 419
Feinberg, Gerald 133
Feldman, Herman 141
Fell, Barry 34
Fell, Christine 517
Feng, Gia-Fu 224,230
Fenn, C H 218
Fenollosa, Ernest 218,568
Fenton, J C 142
Fenwick, Sheridan 290
Ferdowsi 87
Ferguson, Everett 253
Ferguson, John 491
Ferguson, William 34
Fernando, K C 161
Fernie, William 338
Ferris, Timothy 133
Feuerstein, Georg 376,378
Fiarotta, Noel 304
Fiarotta, Phyllis 304
Ficino, Marsilio 554
Field, Claud 420
Fillmore, Charles 142
Findlay, J N 77
Finegan, Jack 87
Fingarette, Herbert 225
Finkelstein, Louis 448
Finley, M I 55,73
Fiore, Edith 549
Firebrace, Roy 117
Firestone, Ross 624
Fischer, Louis 377

Fitzgerald, Donalie 296
Fitzgerald, Edward 430
Fitzgerald, Robert 513
Flaceliere, Robert 73,509
Flammonde, Paris 616
Flannery, Mary 502
Fleer, Gedaliah 448
Fleming-Mitchell, Leslie 100
Flemming, Bonnie 304
Fletcher, John 582
Flint, Max 55
Flugelman, Andrew 277
Flynn, Elizabeth 309
Fodor, Nandor 533
Foelsch, Kuno 100
Fohrer, Georg 449
Fokker, Nicolas 568
Fong, Wen 233
Fontenay, Charles 225
Ford, Arthur 558
Ford, Patrick 515
Ford, S H 63
Forde, Daryll 11
Forde-Johnston, J 46
Fordham, Frieda 461
Fordham, Michael 461-462
Forem, Jack 479
Foreman, Michael 208,220,320,324-325
Forman, Werner 32
Forrester-Brown, James 142
Forrey, Alyse 125
Fort, Charles 616
Fortune, Dion 449,492-493
Foucher, A 153
Fouke, George 304
Fowler, Raymond 616
Fox, Anne Valley 360
Fox, Denton 517
Fox, Hugh 34
Fozdar, Jamshed 153
Frager, Robert 356
Fraiberg, Selma 309
Framer, Penelope 208
Francis de Sales, St 246
Francis of Assisi, St 245
Franck, A 449
Franck, Frederick 184,185,246
Frank, Jori 121
Frankel, Hans 220
Frankfort, Henri 63,88
Frankl, Viktor 356-357
Franz, Marie-Louise von 17,319,324,
    459,462,464,509
Frauwallner, Erich 376
Frazer, James 510
Frazier, Allie 153,267,376
Frederick, Carl 290
Frederick, Filis 431
Freeman, Arnold 582
Freire, Paulo 309
Fremantle, Anne 624
Fremantle, Francesca 171
French, Peter 16,277
French, R M 262
French, W 344
Freud, Sigmund 299
Frey-Rohn, Liliane 462
Friedenberg, Edgar 361
Friedlander, Ira 419,422
Friedlander, M 452
Friedlander, Paul 77
Friedman, Irving 455
Friedman, Maurice 447
Frieling, Rudolf 142,246,582
Frith, Henry 529
Frith, Nigel 381
Fritsch, Charles 87
Frohlich, Margaret 590
Fromm, Erich 142,185,299,357,462,510
Frost, S E 267
Frye, Northrup 488
Frye, R N 88
Frye, Richard 419

646